South America

a Lonely Planet shoestring guide

James Lyon
Wayne Bernhardson
Andrew Draffen
Krzysztof Dydyński
María Massolo
Rob Rachowiecki
Deanna Swaney

South America

6th edition

Published by
Lonely Planet Publications
Head Office: PO Box 617, Hawthorn, Vic 3122, Australia
Branches: 150 Linden St, Oakland, CA 94607, USA
                10a Spring Place, London NW5 3BH, UK
                1 rue du Dahomey, 75011 Paris, France

Printed by
Colorcraft Ltd, Hong Kong

Photographs by
Wayne Bernhardson   Krzysztof Dydyński   Richard I'Anson
James Lyon   John Maier, Jr

Front cover: Chillies and limes – the colours and flavours of South America
(Suzanne L Murphy, DDB Stock Photo)

First Published
January 1980

This Edition
January 1997

National Library of Australia Cataloguing in Publication Data

South America.

    6th ed.
    Includes index.
    ISBN 0 86442 401 9.

    1. South America – Guidebooks. I. Lyon, James. (Series:
    Lonely Planet on a shoestring).

918.0439

text & maps © Lonely Planet 1997
photos © photographers as indicated 1997
Tierra del Fuego climate chart compiled from information supplied by Patrick J Tyson, © Patrick J Tyson, 1996

James Lyon

An Australian by birth and a sceptic by nature, James studied sociology, economics and Spanish, before starting a not-very-promising career as a public bureaucrat. Travel became a major distraction, but eventually qualified him to work as an editor in Lonely Planet's Melbourne office. After a couple of years, he jumped at the chance to update LP's guide to *Bali & Lombok*, and he has since been fully occupied researching and writing guides to *Mexico* and *California & Nevada*, sometimes travelling with his wife, Pauline, and their two young sons.

Wayne Bernhardson

Wayne was born in Fargo, North Dakota, grew up in Tacoma, Washington, and earned a PhD in geography at the University of California, Berkeley. He has travelled extensively in Mexico and Central and South America, and lived for extended periods in Chile, Argentina and the Falkland Islands (Islas Malvinas). His other LP credits include the latest editions of the *Chile & Easter Island, Argentina, Uruguay & Paraguay* and *Baja California* guides. Wayne resides in Oakland, California, where his Alaskan malamute Gardel has the same charismatic smile as his legendary *porteño* namesake.

Andrew Draffen

Born in Australia, Andrew has travelled and worked his way around Australia, Asia, North America and the Caribbean, and settled just long enough in Melbourne to complete an Arts degree, majoring in history. During his first trip to South America in 1984, Andrew fell in love both with Brazil and with his future wife, Stella. They have since toured extensively in Brazil, Europe and Asia, and today travel with their young children, Gabriela and Christopher, whose great-great-grandfather introduced football to Brazil.

Krzysztof Dydyński

Krzysztof was born and raised in Warsaw, Poland. Though he became an assistant professor in electronic engineering, he soon realised that there's more to life than microchips. He took off to Afghanistan and India in the mid-1970s and has been back to Asia several times since. In the 1980s a newly discovered passion for Latin America took him to Colombia, where he lived for over four years, and all over the continent. In search of a new incarnation, he has made Australia his home and worked for LP as an artist and designer. He is the author of LP guides to *Colombia*, *Venezuela* and *Poland* and has contributed to other Lonely Planet books.

María Massolo

María was born in Olavarría, Buenos Aires province (the 'cement capital' of Argentina), studied literature at the Universidad de Buenos Aires, and holds an MA in folklore and a PhD in anthropology from the University of California at Berkeley. María lives in Oakland, California, with husband and co-author Wayne Bernhardson, their daughter Clío and their Alaskan malamute Gardel. María divides her efforts between an academic career, travel and translation.

Rob Rachowiecki

Rob was born near London, became an avid traveller while still a teenager, and has visited countries as diverse as Greenland and Thailand. He spent most of the 1980s in Latin America – travelling, mountaineering and teaching English – and now works in Peru and Ecuador part time as a leader for Wilderness Travel, an adventure travel company. He is the author of LP's *Ecuador*, *Peru*, *Costa Rica* and *Southwest USA* guides and has contributed to *Central America on a shoestring* as well as to books by other publishers. When not travelling, Rob lives in Arizona with his wife Cathy and their three children, Julia, Alison and Davy.

Deanna Swaney

A longtime travel addict, Deanna escaped a career in computer programming in Anchorage, Alaska, at the first opportunity, and made a break for South America to write LP's *Bolivia – travel survival kit*. Subsequent travels through a course of island paradises – Arctic and tropical – resulted in three more LP guides: *Tonga*, *Samoa* and *Iceland, Greenland & the Faroe Islands*. Deanna returned to dry land for *Zimbabwe, Botswana & Namibia* and has since co-authored the 2nd editions of *Brazil* and *Mauritius, Réunion & Seychelles*, authored the 2nd edition of *Madagascar & Comoros* and contributed to shoestring guides to Africa and Scandinavia. Deanna now divides her time between travel and her froggy lakeside base in the English West Country.

From the Authors

From James I had a wonderful time travelling in South America, and I am grateful to many travellers and local people for their friendliness, support and information. The tourist offices in Georgetown, Cayenne, São Luís and Salvador were especially helpful. At home, thanks to Rob van Driesum, who encouraged me to take on this project, to the editors and cartographers who put it together and, as ever, to Pauline, my research assistant, administrator, wife and muse.

From Wayne Special mention to Fito and Mary Massolo of Olavarría, Buenos Aires province, my Argentine family for so many years, to Rodolfo Massolo (hijo), and to everyone else mentioned in the *Argentina, Uruguay & Paraguay* guide. A particularly obsequious thanks to David Roberts of the *Santiago News Review* for saving me the hassle of dragging a computer to the Southern Cone, and to Deanna Swaney for help with the La Quiaca entry.

From Andrew Special thanks to my Brazilian family in São Paulo, especially Vera Miller, my favourite mother-in-law; Iara Costa da Pinto (São Paulo) for her hospitality on many Brazil trips; Ivana and Portugues (São Paulo); John and Massae (Rio); Mike and Ivandy (Rio); Frank and Helen Draffen (Australia); and Stella, Gabriela and Christopher, who make it all worthwhile. I would like to dedicate my section of the book to Stella's beloved Vovó, Heloisa Alves de Lima e Motta, who passed away earlier this year – a remarkable lady who is greatly missed.

From María I want to thank the following people for their contributions and help: in the USA, Wayne Bernhardson, Clío Bernhardson-Massolo and Peter Grace; and in Chile, Lucy Araya, Hugo Moreira, Alejandro Cruz, José A Olavarría, Claudia Blancaire, Luis B Canales, Gabriela Neira Morales, Guillermo Coronado Barría, Fernando Gomez, Marcela Benavides, Adrian Turner, Gerardo Perez C and Danila Condore Blanco, Pablo Fernández Doren, the staff at the Youth Hostel in Santiago, and Paul Bazelmans.

From Rob I thank the folks at the South American Explorers Club in Lima and Quito; Dr Richard Ryel of the ACEER Foundation; Barry Walker of Expediciones Manu; T'ai Roulston and Marsha Morrow in Puerto Maldonado; in Cuzco, Paul Cripps, Holber Tito Vizcarra, Carlos Milla Vidal, José Correa and Victor; in Trujillo, Clara Luz Bravo and Michael White; in Huancayo, Lucho Hurtado and Beverly Stuart de

Hurtado; in Tacna, Juan Carlos Godinez Ibarra; Pablo Morales and chef Alfonso of Pyramid Adventures for their company in the Cordillera Blanca; César Moreno Sánchez; and the Huarmey Tourist Authority. Thanks also to Wayne Bernhardson; to the many readers who wrote with ideas, suggestions and updates; and finally, to my family for their love and understanding.

From Deanna Thanks to Yossi Brain, Matthew Parris, Dr Hugo Berrios and the Reseguín gang – Peter Hutchison, Andy St Pierre, Ulli Schatz, Sylvie, Alix Shand, Alex downstairs, and the enormous slug. Also, thanks to Trex, Jonathon Derksen, Carmen Julia, Álvaro, Planet José, Pig & Whistle Martin and lots of other clued-in *paceños*. I'm also grateful to Guy Cox, Robin Clarke and Miriam Melgar; John Carey; Margarita van't Hoff and Pieter de Raad; Tito Ponce Lopez; Anne Meadows and Daniel Buck; Tim Killeen; Tim Bowyer; Robert Eichwald; Fabiola, Beatriz and Nicolás; Marc Steininger; Wayne Bernhardson; Louis Demers; and Norbert Schürer. And there were many more: Loreen Olufsen, Uta Lütke-Wöstmann, Eduardo Garnica, Ernst and Norbert Schürer, Evangelos Kotsopoulos, Anne Bois d'Enghien, François Laviolette, Greg and Katie Cumberford, and Todd Miner. Finally, love, thanks and lots of other positive sentiments to Earl, Dean and Jennifer Swaney; Robert Strauss; Rodney Leacock; and Keith and Holly Hawkings and Dave Dault, back home in Anchorage.

From the Publisher
This 6th edition of *South America on a shoestring* was edited and proofed at Lonely Planet's Melbourne office by Nick Tapp with assistance from Katie Cody (and Jonah kicked in, too), Anne Mulvaney, Brigitte Barta, Karin Riederer, Miriam Cannell, Lindsay Brown, Steve Womersley, Janet Austin and Adrienne Costanzo. Lou Callan helped with the language sections. Marcel Gaston led the mapping team of Paul Clifton, Dorothy Natsikas, Michael Signal, Lyndell Taylor, Anthony Phelan, Chris Lee Ack and Jane Hart in Melbourne, and Alex Guilbert &

Co in Oakland, California. Marcel also laid the book out. David Kemp and Simon Bracken designed the cover. Nick did the index. Thanks to the readers' letters team of Julie Young and Shelley Preston in Australia, Sacha Pearson in the USA, Arnaud Lebonnois in France and Simon Goldsmith in the UK. Our thanks also to the many readers and travellers who wrote in with information:

Shiela Acramen, Jadwiga Adamczuk, D Agius, Robert Ajensen, Isabel Allen, Juan Altmann, J & C Anderson, Vidar Andezsen, M Andrews, Bryony Angell, J Aragones, Dominique Argenson, Egan Arnold, Pamela Attree, Samantha Ayre, Jerry Azevedo, Nettie Bak, Irmgard Bauer, K Baxter, Patrice Belie, Frederick Belland, Anja Bendix, Jan Bennik, Michael Berry, Trevor Berryman, Helene Bianchi, M Bischer, Warren Bock, Keith Boots, C Borzutzky, Jean-Roch Bouchard, Anthony Boult, A Braghetta, A Brand, Matthew Briggs, Linda Broschofsky, Richard Browne, Philippa Budger, Christiane Buie, Alberto Cafferata, Jim & June Campbell, Katherine Campbell, Sean D Casey, Aileen Christodoulou, Andrew Cockburn, Karen Cockburn, Chris Cooper, Xavier Cortal Escarra, Janet Cotter-Howells, James Cowie, Clare Cronin, Wojciech Dabrowski, Ana de Miguel, Xavier De Patoul, N Desmaris, Martin Dillig, Mike Drollet, R Dryland, Sarah Durfie, Shaun Dwyer, Jayne Dyer, Joanne Earl, Eduard Egelie, Alex Encel, Julie Escott, Zina Etheridge, Michael Falk, Martin Fiems, Robert Folger, M Foster, John Frize, Miguel Fuertes, Christian Gaebler, Eric Gagnon, C Geanuracos, Richard Gennara, Zulfikar Ghose, Michael Giacometti, Mike Ginsburh, Jennifer Glass, John Gravley, Giorgio Grazzini, Kathy Griffiths, David Grill, Rita Gruenfelcher, Daniel Guerrero, Anna C Gustafson, I Haaijer, Michael Hailstone, Kenneth Hake, Ulrike Hallensleben, P Hamilton, Brian Handy, Eric Haskell, Paul Hatfield, Sally Hayden, Karsten Heck, Lars Heitmann, Dr Karl H Heller, Klaus Henke, Steve Herrick, Sven Herrmann, Pat Hickey, Jana Hopfinger, Armin Howald, Hisayo Izumo, Stephanie Jackson, Mandy Jacobsen, Malcolm James, Marie Jenneteg, Evan Jones, Hugo Kaelen, Jean Kahe, Arne Kasper, Oliver Kempe, Beau Kempen, VJ Kemper, K Kerschbaumer, Christine Kincart, Hugh Kirkman, Oystein Klausen, Marynia Koster, Randall Krueger, Gerald Kuhl, Kurt Kutay, Karen Kvaal, Terry Lamb, Patrick Landewe, Mark Laptin, Margrid Leben, Juan & Marianne Lecaro, P Levasier, Keith Liker, Eric Linder, Daniel Lloyd, Teresa Lloyd, Andrea Lobbecke, Jon Lurie, JM Le Feure, Ben & Blanche Maartman, Lynette Manuel, Tim & Caroline Marks, Roger Marsden, John Masters, Yvonne & David McCredie, Mike McDonald, Cheryl & Bruce

McLaren, J McLaughlin, Don McNeill, Geraldine McQuaid, Thomas Meiburg, Peter Mellas, Steve Menary, Eleanore Merrill, Ludo Mevissen, Ulrike Meyer, Shellie Michael, Patrick Miller, JJ & R Moilliet, Gavin & Anna Moore, Sandra Moore, J Muslera, Trui Naeyaert, Daniel Nebenzal, Clare Nichols, Julie Nield, Christian Nonis, Linda Norman, John & Marg Northcote, Joop Nyboek, Caoimhin O'Cuinn, Karen O'Donahoo, J O'Donoghue, Eugene & Mayumi Orwell, J Overnell, Gary Palmer, Nathaniel Parbhu, Arnold Parzer, Jeremy Paul, Roger Acram Paul, Debra Pett, Oliver Plath, Aase Popper, Nancy Porter, A Potma, Annette Powell, Julianne Power, Juan Carlos Querejazu, Choonglim Rah, R Ramroxna, Kate Raphael, Chris Read, Terry Redding, Dave Redmond, Stephane Robert, M Roberts, Neil & Shirley Roberts-Brown, Frank Rommel, Esther Romo-Oester, Laila Rosten, Hegetschweiler Rotzler, Robin Rowenhill, Deborah Rowland, Eric Rubin, Ross Runham, Salles Remi Salles, Christian Schindler, Carole Schmid, Tony Schneider, David Schnier, T Schweitzer, Kurt Shafer, A Shaler, Caroline T Shaw, Henny Slabbekoom, David Smith, Yaniv Sneor, Clayton Sparks, Garry Sprague, Jo Steele, Ben Stricks, Julie Sutherland, Richard Talbot, G Tanguay, J Tarwood, Marlies Thielpape, Michael Thomas, Robert Thomas, Nick Toll, Arnoud Troost, Stephen Ulrich, Francisco Valle, John van der Rest, Bettina van Elk, Ruud van Ginkel, Erwin Verhoeven, John Versmissen, Dre Visscher, Harald Volz, Peter Waanders, Jan Wagner, Glenn Ward, Carla Weemaes, Lina & Jens Weibull, A Wheeler, Alleta Whitely, Helen Whitford, N Whittaker, Russell Willis, Diarmuid Wilson, Gareth Wilson, Mike Wilson, Nick Wilson, Robert Wilson, Giorgina Woern, Dan Workman, C Wrenthore, Felice Wyndham, Kimberley Y Heath, Michaela Young-Mitchell

This Book

The first editions of *South America on a shoestring* were written by Geoff Crowther, but later editions have drawn increasingly on the expertise of authors of Lonely Planet guides to individual South American countries. This 6th edition has been revised and updated by a team of writers: James Lyon researched and updated northern Brazil and the Guianas and helped to bring the introductory chapters up to date; Wayne Bernhardson researched and updated the chapters on Argentina, the Falkland Islands, Paraguay and Uruguay; Andrew Draffen did the same for southern Brazil; Krzysztof Dydynski, for Colombia and Venezuela; María Massolo, for Chile; Rob Rachowiecki, for Ecuador and Peru; and Deanna Swaney, for Bolivia

Warning & Request

Things change – prices go up, schedules change, good places go bad and bad places go bankrupt – nothing stays the same. So if you find things better or worse, recently opened or long since closed, please write and tell us and help make the next edition better.

Your letters will be used to help update future editions and, where possible, important changes will also be included in an Update section in reprints.

We greatly appreciate all information that is sent to us by travellers. Back at Lonely Planet we employ a hard-working readers' letters team to sort through the many letters we receive. The best ones will be rewarded with a free copy of the next edition or another Lonely Planet guide if you prefer. We give away lots of books, but, unfortunately, not every letter/postcard receives one.

Contents

BOLIVIA 231

BRAZIL 319

COLOMBIA...613

ECUADOR 707

GLOSSARY 1149

INDEX 1155

Map Legend

BOUNDARIES

.... International Boundary

.... Regional Boundary

.... Disputed Boundary

ROUTES

Sealed Unsealed

.... Freeway

.... Major Road

.... Secondary Road

.... Minor Road or Track

.... City Road

.... City Street

.... Railway

.... Metro, Underground Railway

.... Tram

.... Walking Track

.... Walking Tour

.... Ferry Route

.... Cable Car or Chairlift

AREA FEATURES

.... Parks

.... Built-Up Area

.... Pedestrian Mall

.... Market

+ + + + + + ... Christian Cemetery

× × × × × × .... Non-Christian Cemetery

.... Reef

.... Beach or Desert

.... Rocks

HYDROGRAPHIC FEATURES

.... Coastline

.... River, Creek

.... Intermittent River or Creek

.... Rapids, Waterfalls

.... Lake, Intermittent Lake

.... Canal

SYMBOLS

✪	CAPITAL	National Capital	○	ⓟ	Embassy, Petrol Station
◉	Capital	Regional Capital	✈	✚	Airport, Airfield
⬤	CITY	Major City	🛏	✿	Swimming Pool, Gardens
●	City	City	❖	🐘	Shopping Centre, Zoo
●	Village	Village	⚲	🎍	Winery or Vineyard, Picnic Site
			🅜	A25	Metro Station, Route Number
■	▼	Place to Stay, Place to Eat	🏛	⚑	Stately Home, Monument
☕	🍺	Cafe, Pub or Bar	⛩	▣	Castle, Tomb
✉	☎	Post Office, Telephone	⌒	⌂	Cave, Hut or Chalet
❶	❸	Tourist Information, Bank	▲	☀	Mountain or Hill, Lookout
☖	🅿	Transport, Parking	🗼	⤫	Lighthouse, Shipwreck
🏛	⌂	Museum, Youth Hostel	)(	◎	Pass, Spring
⊕	🏕	Caravan Park, Camping Ground	🐾	⚑	Beach, Surf Beach
⛪	✚	Church, Cathedral	∴		Archaeological Site or Ruins
☪	✡	Mosque, Synagogue			Ancient or City Wall
卍	卐	Buddhist Temple, Hindu Temple			Cliff or Escarpment, Tunnel
✚	★	Hospital, Police Station			Railway Station

Note: not all symbols displayed above appear in this book

WAYNE BERNHARDSON

RICHARD I'ANSON

WAYNE BERNHARDSON

JOHN MAIER, JR

RICHARD I'ANSON

Top: Cuernos del Paine, PN Torres del Paine, in Chilean Patagonia
Left: Andean Indian woman on market day, Chinchero, Peru
Middle: Theatre on Isla Martín García, Buenos Aires province, Argentina
Right: Corcovado and *Cristo Redentor* at sunset, Rio de Janeiro, Brazil
Bottom: Bolivia's administrative capital, La Paz, at dusk

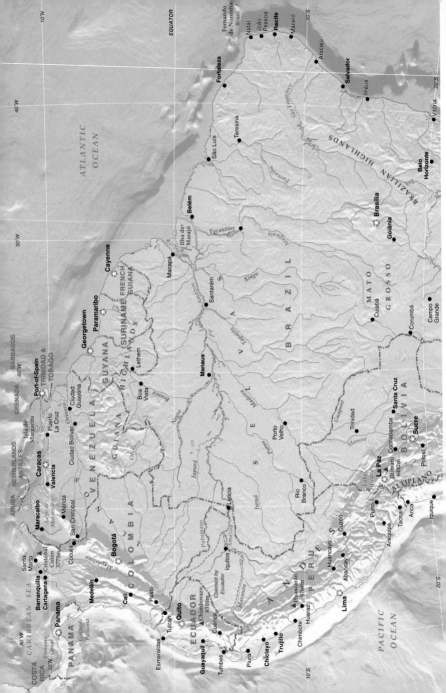

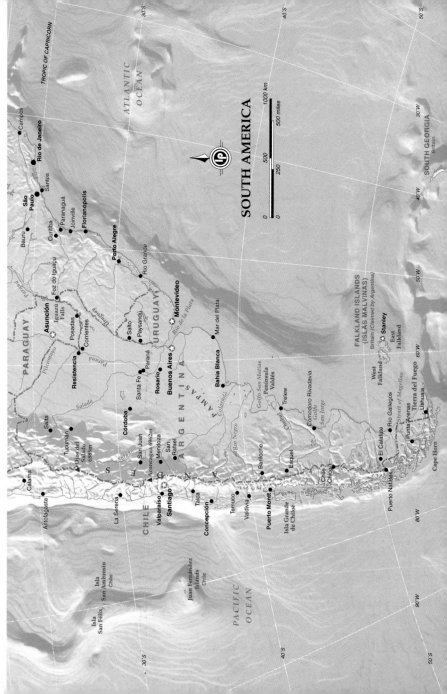

RICHARD I'ANSON

JAMES LYON

WAYNE BERNHARDSON

WAYNE BERNHARDSON

KRZYSZTOF DYDYNSKI

KRZYSZTOF DYDYNSKI

A: Boy with llama, Peru
B: Setting up for a street party in Cayenne, French Guiana
C: Iglesia de Llingua, Chiloé archipelago, Chile
D: Palacio de las Aguas Corrientes, Buenos Aires, Argentina
E: Colourful shop front, Colombia
F: Older architecture of the Venezuelan capital, Caracas

Introduction

South America is a great region for travellers. Its sheer size and diversity offer something for every interest, and lots of opportunities to get off the beaten track and into areas where visitors are a rarity. The continent extends thousands of miles, from the equatorial tropics to the sub-Antarctic, and includes 14 countries and territories with diverse Indian cultures and a rich colonial legacy. Spain and Portugal have left a huge imprint on South America, but there is a rich mix of other European, African, Caribbean, Asian and indigenous cultures.

Your interest is mountains? The Andes are a mecca for the climber or trekker. Beaches? Loll on untouched tropical islands, or hit Brazil's *barracas* for cold beer, beautiful bodies and blaring music. Jungles? Despite deforestation, vast tracts of tropical rainforest still exist. Rivers? The Amazon is the

biggest anywhere. Waterfalls? The world's highest and most voluminous waterfalls are here. Cities? Try the roaring megalopolis of São Paulo, the European style of Buenos Aires, the faded funkiness of Paramaribo, or dozens of small cities with colonial charm and character. Ancient ruins? You can see mysterious Machu Picchu or discover Ciudad Perdida, the 'Lost City' of Colombia. Contemporary culture? South American music, whether it be vibrant Latin rhythms or the haunting flutes of the Andes, is heard everywhere on the continent.

None of these sights and experiences need cost you an arm and a leg. While prices have risen over the last few years, the Andean countries are still a bargain, and careful budget travellers can enjoy even relatively expensive countries like Argentina. Economic changes have brought improved infrastructure in many countries: phones work, buses run on time and the electricity supply lasts all night, mostly. Some places are still risky because of guerrillas, drug runners and robbers, but you can avoid the first two and take precautions against the third, and you're unlikely to find trouble.

Transport options range from the roof of a train to a luxury bus, rickety riverboat, dugout canoe or your own two feet. You can sleep in a hostel, a high-rise, a love hotel or a hammock; drink sickly-sweet Inca Cola or overproof *cachaça*; and eat anything from pizza to piranha, barbecued beef to spicy sea urchin. Adventurous travellers will find South America is still an adventure.

Facts about South America

HISTORY

Pre-Columbian South America

Prehistory Well over 12,000 years ago, when the accumulated ice of the great polar glaciers of the Pleistocene epoch lowered sea levels throughout the world, the ancestors of American Indians crossed from Siberia to Alaska via a land bridge over the Bering Strait. Subsequent migrations distributed the population southward through North and Central America and down to the southern tip of South America.

The first inhabitants of South America were nomadic hunter-gatherers who lived in small bands. It's likely that agriculture developed gradually in the tropical lowlands from around 5000 BC, with the planting of wild tubers like manioc (cassava) and sweet potato, under systems of shifting cultivation. One of the continent's greatest contributions to the world is the humble potato, a root crop domesticated in the Andean highlands.

About the same time, seed crops like beans began to be farmed in the highland areas, and large deposits of animal bones are the first evidence of the domestication of animals such as the llama. From about 4000 BC, there is evidence of seed agriculture in Peru's coastal lowlands. The cultivation of maize, probably imported from Mexico before 2500 BC but perhaps much earlier, is closely correlated with the development of settled agriculture communities.

Coastal & Highland Civilisations Complex societies developed first in the valleys of coastal Peru. Some scholars believe this was because populations grew to occupy all the available cultivable land, and then turned to conquest of neighbouring valleys. Conquerors became rulers, and the conquered became their subjects, thus developing the social and economic hierarchies of these early states.

These embryonic states ultimately developed into major civilisations like the Wari

Empire of the Peruvian central highlands, the Tiwanaku (Tiahuanaco) culture of highland Bolivia, the Chimú of northern coastal Peru and, ultimately, the Inca empire of Cuzco, known more properly as Tawantinsuy (or Tahuantinsuyo). Most of these cultures are known through archaeological remains, particularly ceramics (see the Peru chapter for more details).

The Inca Empire The Inca developed the most sophisticated of South America's pre-Columbian highland civilisations. At its peak, at the time of the Spanish invasion, the Inca empire governed at least 12 million people from northern Ecuador to central Chile, traversing the Andes with over 8000 km of highways, but it was never able to penetrate deep into the Amazon lowlands. This overextended empire, racked by dissension and civil war, proved vulnerable to invasion by a very small force of Spaniards.

Tropical Rainforest Peoples The inhabitants of tropical rainforest regions such as the Amazon Basin did not develop complex civilisations like those found in the Andes. The population of rainforest areas at the time of European contact is not known for certain, but there is evidence of substantial villages of up to 5000 or more people. Archaeological remains are few because most tools and other artefacts were made of perishable materials such as wood and bone.

Southern South America Inca rule barely touched the area of central Chile or northern Argentina. The Araucanian (Picunche and Mapuche) Indians of Chile and Argentina fiercely resisted incursions from the north. The Picunche lived in permanent agricultural settlements, while the Mapuche, who practised shifting cultivation, were more mobile. Several groups closely related to the Mapuche (Pehuenches, Huilliches, and Puelches) lived in the southern lake district, while Cunco Indians fished and farmed on the island of Chiloé and along the shores of the gulfs of Reloncaví and Ancud.

In the forested delta of the upper Río Paraná, Guaraní shifting cultivators relied on maize and tuber crops like manioc and sweet potatoes. In the Pampas to the south and well into Patagonia, highly mobile people hunted the guanaco (a wild relative of the Andean llama) and the rhea (a flightless bird resembling the ostrich) with bows and arrows or *boleadoras* (heavily weighted thongs).

South of the mainland, on the islands of Tierra del Fuego, numerous small populations of Indians subsisted on hunting and fishing – the Chonos, Qawashqar (Alacalufes), Tehuelches, Yamaná (Yahgans), and Onas (Selknam). These isolated archipelagic peoples long avoided contact with Europeans, but are now extinct or nearly so.

European Contact

Christopher Columbus (known in Spanish as Cristóbal Colón) led the first recorded European 'discovery' of the Americas, though in fact he was seeking a new route to Asia's spice islands. Bankrolled by Queen Isabella of Spain, and given an exceedingly broad grant of authority over any territory he might discover, this dubiously qualified Genoese mariner sailed westward, making landfalls on several Caribbean islands which he believed to be part of Asia. In fact it was the Portuguese navigator Vasco da Gama who found the sea route to Asia, around the Cape of Good Hope and across the Indian Ocean; the Spanish discovery of the New World was second prize. These momentous discoveries raised the stakes in the rivalry between Spain and Portugal.

The Treaty of Tordesillas When Portugal protested that the Spanish voyages had encroached on its Atlantic sphere of influence, in violation of earlier agreements, the Spanish monarchs asked Pope Alexander VI to resolve the dispute. In 1494, representatives of the two countries met in the northern Spanish town of Tordesillas, where they established a line of demarcation at about 48° west of Greenwich, giving Africa and Asia to Portugal and all of the New World to Spain. Significantly, however, this agreement placed the coast of Brazil (not discovered until six years later) on the Portuguese side of the line, giving Portugal unanticipated access to the new continent. The treaty was ratified in 1506, though no other European maritime power, and certainly none of the indigenous people of the Americas, ever agreed to the arrangement.

Exploration, Conquest & Colonisation

The island of Hispaniola became the first

Inca Empire: Early 16th Century

Quito
Cajamarca
Chan Chan
Huamachuco
Recuay
Chancay
Pachacamác
Machu Picchu
Ica
Cuzco

— Royal Road of the Incas

‑‑‑‑ Modern borders shown for reference

European settlement and Columbus' base for further exploration. Between 1496 and 1518, he and other voyagers charted the Caribbean Sea and the Gulf of Mexico, the Venezuelan and Guyanese shores to the mouth of the Amazon, and the Brazilian coastline. This phase of coastal exploration effectively ended when Portuguese Ferdinand Magellan sailed down South America's east coast, through the strait which now bears his name, and across the Pacific to reach the Philippines in 1521. This demonstrated that America was no short cut to Asia, and Europeans turned their efforts to occupying, plundering and otherwise profiting from the new territories.

Jamaica, Cuba and Puerto Rico followed Hispaniola as early Spanish settlements. Cortés' conquest of Mexico led to further land expeditions, one of which returned with rumours of a golden kingdom, Birú (Peru), to the south of Panama. After Francisco Pizarro's preliminary expeditions down South America's Pacific coast (1524 and 1526) confirmed some of these rumours, he went to Spain, where he convinced authorities to finance an expedition of 200 men and grant him authority over the lands he would survey.

Spain's invasion of the Americas was accomplished by groups of adventurers, lowlifes and soldiers of fortune. Few in number, the conquerors were determined and ruthless, exploiting factionalism among Indian groups and frightening indigenous peoples with horses, vicious dogs and firearms.

The Conquest of the Inca

Pizarro's advance into Peru was rapid and dramatic. His well-armed soldiers terrorised the Indians, but his greatest ally was infectious disease to which indigenous people lacked any immunity. In about 1525, the Inca ruler Huayna Capac died, probably of smallpox contracted through messengers who had been in contact with the Spaniards.

Before he died, Huayna Capac divided his empire, giving the northern part to Atahualpa and the more southerly Cuzco area to another

son, Huáscar. Civil war followed, and after several years of fighting, Atahualpa's troops defeated and captured Huáscar outside Cuzco.

Meanwhile, Pizarro had landed in northern Ecuador and marched south in the wake of Atahualpa's conquests. On 16 November 1532, a fateful meeting between Atahualpa and Pizarro took place in Cajamarca. Atahualpa was ambushed and captured by the Spaniards, who killed thousands of unarmed Indians. In an attempt to regain his freedom, Atahualpa offered a ransom – one room full of gold and two of silver. Pizarro sent three of his soldiers to Cuzco in early 1533, and they proceeded to strip Coricancha, the Gold Courtyard, of its splendid ornamentation, melting and crushing beautiful artefacts to ensure that the room was really filled with gold. Despite the ransom, the treacherous Spanish put Atahualpa through a sham trial, and he was executed by strangulation.

When Pizarro entered Cuzco, on 8 November 1533, he was permitted into the heart of the Inca empire by a people whose sympathy lay more with the defeated Huáscar than with Atahualpa. Pizarro appointed Manco Inca, a half-brother of Huáscar, as a puppet Inca ruler. In 1536, Manco Inca fled from the Spanish and raised a huge army, estimated at well over 100,000, and laid siege to Cuzco. Only a desperate break-out from Cuzco and a violent battle saved the Spaniards from defeat. Atahualpa's nephew, Tupac Amaru, also fought valiantly against the Spanish, until his beheading in the Plaza of Cuzco in 1572.

The Spanish Empire in South America

Lima, founded in 1535 as the capital of the new Viceroyalty of Peru, was the base for most of the further exploration and conquest of the continent. Sebastián Benalcázar travelled from Lima via Quito to the highlands of Colombia in 1538, and by 1540, Pedro de Valdivia had penetrated as far as Chile's Río Biobío. Expeditions south, along and over the Andes, founded Tucumán and Mendoza.

Pedro de Mendoza formed a settlement at the mouth of the Río de la Plata in 1535,

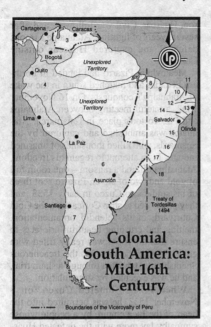

Colonial South America: Mid-16th Century

Boundaries of the Viceroyalty of Peru

1	Audiencia de Panamá
2	Audiencia de Sante Fé
3	Audiencia de Santo Domingo
4	Audiencia de Quito
5	Audiencia de Lima
6	Audiencia de Charcas
7	Audiencia de Chile
8	Capitânia do Grão-Pará
9	Capitânia do Maranhão
10	Capitânia do Ceará
11	Capitânia do Rio Grande do Norte
12	Capitânia da Paraíba
13	Capitânia de Pernambuco
14	Capitânia de Sergipe
15	Capitânia da Bahia
16	Capitânia do Espíritu Santo
17	Capitânia do Rio de Janeiro
18	Capitânia de São Vicente

which later moved upriver to Asunción, Paraguay. The coast of Venezuela was settled from Hispaniola and later became part of the Viceroyalty of Nueva Granada.

Administration The Viceroyalty of Peru was the seat of all power in Spanish America. As the monarch's representative in Lima, the viceroy headed a hierarchy of lesser officials. The main functionaries were: the presidents of *audiencias*, who held civil power in areas where no viceroy was resident; and the *corregidores*, who each governed a provincial city and its surrounding area. The corregidor was usually associated with a *cabildo* (town council), which was about the only representative institution.

Only *peninsulares* (those born in Spain) could hold senior positions. *Criollos* (creoles), born in the New World of Spanish parents, could hold a commission in a colonial army or serve on a cabildo. As the peninsulares generally spent a term in the colonies before returning to Spain, the criollos became the main land-holders, merchants and entrepreneurs. People of mixed parentage, usually of a Spanish father and an Indian mother, were known as *mestizos* and were generally excluded from higher positions, while *indígenas* (native Americans) comprised the bottom stratum of society.

Despite the highly centralised administration, there were enormous practical difficulties in imposing imperial control. These limitations led to considerable local autonomy in government and commerce, as well as to abuse, corruption and a flourishing contraband trade, which further undermined peninsular authority.

Spaniards & Indians The primary goal of the first Spaniards was the acquisition of gold and silver, and they ruthlessly appropriated precious metals, through outright robbery when possible, and by other, equally brutal means when necessary.

The Spaniards exploited indigenous populations through such mechanisms as the *encomienda* (best translated as 'entrustment'), by which the Crown granted an individual Spaniard rights to Indian labour and tribute in a particular village or area. In theory, Spanish legislation required the holder of the encomienda, the *encomendero*, to reciprocate with instruction in the Spanish language and the Catholic religion, but in practice, imperial administration could not ensure compliance or avoid serious abuses. Spanish overseers worked Indians mercilessly in the mines and extracted the maximum in agricultural produce.

In the most densely populated parts of the Americas, some encomenderos became extraordinarily wealthy, but the encomienda system itself failed when Indian populations declined rapidly because of introduced diseases, such as smallpox, influenza and typhus. In some parts of the New World, these diseases reduced the indigenous population by more than 95%.

This demographic collapse had a lasting impact on South American societies and economies. As encomiendas became worthless, encomenderos and others assembled *latifundios* (large properties) from the holdings of the depleted Indian communities. The decline of indigenous populations resulted in *mestizaje*, the creation of a mixed-race population of European and Indian descent. In the north of the continent, African slaves were introduced to make up for the lack of indigenous labour.

The Colonial Economy After the initial period of plunder, the mines were the principal source of royal revenue; one-fifth of all precious metals, the *quinto real* or 'royal fifth', went to the crown. To discourage piracy and simplify taxation, all colonial exports had to go to Spain via the officials of Lima and the ports of Veracruz (Mexico), Cartagena (Colombia) and Portobelo (Panama). Goods from Buenos Aires, for instance, went overland to Lima, by sea to Panama and overland across the isthmus before being loaded onto ships across the Atlantic, since officially they could not be shipped directly to Europe.

Under a crown monopoly, a merchant guild based in Spain controlled all trade with the colonies. With their related guilds in Lima and Mexico, Spanish merchants fixed high prices for European goods in the colonies, and taxes were levied on the imports. These taxes and restrictions on trade caused great discontent in the colonies, particularly amongst criollos, whose prosperity depended more on local development than on generating wealth for Spanish merchants and the crown.

The Church
The conversion of indigenous people to the Catholic faith was the moral rationale for the conquest, and the church was an active partner in the Iberian domination of South America, and even held encomiendas in its own right. Nevertheless, some members of the church did protest at the treatment of the Indians. The Dominican Father Bartolomé de las Casas was a one-time conquistador who later spoke out against corrupt officials and encomenderos, and even advocated restitution for all the wealth that Spain had plundered from the Americas.

Of the various Catholic orders active in South America, the Jesuits worked most closely with the Indians, especially in Brazil and the south of the continent. They recorded Indian languages, established missions in which Indians were resettled, and defended the Indians against the worst excesses of the colonial system. Their actions antagonised both the Spanish and Portuguese authorities, who eventually expelled the Jesuits from Brazil in 1759, and from the Spanish colonies in 1767. One Brazilian statesman wrote: 'Without the Jesuits, our colonial history would be little more than a chain of nameless atrocities.'

Other European Colonies
Portugal's colonisation of Brazil was far less systematic than Spain's practices in the rest of South America. Whereas Spain set up a colonial bureaucracy accountable to the crown, Portugal divided the country into parallel strips extending to the Line of Tordesillas, and established *capitânias* (donatary or hereditary captaincies), which gave individuals almost unlimited powers within their domain. When this proved unsatisfactory, the crown assumed direct control. For details, see the Brazil chapter.

Other European powers to claim territory

in South America were Britain, Holland and France, which sought to extend their influence from the Caribbean to the mainland. Though the Spanish and Portuguese always regarded the presence of these countries as an incursion, the territories on the north-east coast of the continent were, relatively, so unattractive that neither peninsular power could spare the resources to eject the rivals. See the chapter on the Guianas for more details.

Revolution & Independence
The Spanish Colonies Pressure for independence came mainly from criollos, who resented the political and social dominance of the peninsulares and the colonial administration's restrictive trade policies. Educated criollos' knowledge of the Enlightenment, the US War of Independence and the French Revolution contributed to a pro-independence attitude. But it was events in Europe which really precipitated the independence movement.

In 1796, Spain formed an alliance with France, making Spanish vessels a legitimate target for the British navy (in addition to the unofficial privateers, who had been attacking Spanish ships for years). This disrupted communication and trade with the Americas, forcing the colonies into practical, if not official, independence. The defeat of a British invasion of Buenos Aires in 1806 added to the colonists' growing sense of self-confidence and self-sufficiency.

The following year, Napoleon forced the abdication of Spanish monarch Charles IV, replacing him with Napoleon's own brother Joseph. Criollo leaders forced royal officials to hand over power to local juntas, supposedly until the restoration of a legitimate monarch. The criollos were reluctant to relinquish power when, after Napoleon's defeat in 1814, Ferdinand VII became King of Spain. The end of the European wars enabled more troops to be deployed in the Americas, but the burden was on the Spanish to reassert control, particularly in Venezuela and Argentina, which had effectively declared independence.

The two main currents of the independence movement converged on Peru from these two areas. Argentina overcame Spain's attempted reconquest, and its forces, under José de San Martín, crossed the Andes to liberate Chile (1817-18) and finally sailed up the coast to take Lima (1821). From 1819 to 1821, Simón Bolívar and his followers advanced overland to Peru from Venezuela via Colombia and Ecuador.

At their famous meeting at Guayaquil in 1822, the apolitical San Martín found himself in conflict with Bolívar, who had strong political ambitions. San Martín saw the installation of a powerful leader, even a monarch, as essential to avoid the disintegration of Peru, while Bolívar insisted on a constitutional republic. In a complicated exchange, which aroused ill-feeling in both camps, Bolívar won the day and San Martín returned to the south.

In the long run, both were disappointed. The proliferation of *caudillos* (local warlords) set a deplorable pattern for most of the 19th century. San Martín returned to an Argentina racked by internal dissension, and left almost immediately for self-imposed exile in France. Bolívar's dream of a strong republic of Gran Colombia was shattered by difficulties which led to the secession of Ecuador and the separation of Colombia and Venezuela.

Brazil Brazil became autonomous in 1807, when the Portuguese prince regent, exiled after Napoleon's occupation of Portugal, established himself in Brazil. He later returned to Europe, leaving his son Pedro as prince regent, but when the Portuguese parliament tried to reclaim the colony, Dom Pedro proclaimed himself emperor of an independent Brazil.

After Independence
South America's modern political map reflects, to a great degree, the viceroyalties, audiencias and presidencias of the Spanish Empire. After independence, the former colonies became separate countries whose borders generally followed colonial admin-

istrative divisions, modified by the ambitions of the independence leaders. The consolidations, secessions and territorial disputes which followed, and in some cases still persist, are outlined in the geography section and in individual country chapters.

The social structure of the new countries changed slowly. Criollos replaced peninsulares at the apex of the hierarchy, but mestizos and Indians continued to be their social and economic inferiors. Within the criollo elite, there emerged divisions between educated, urban liberals and conservative, rural land-holders with traditional Spanish Catholic values. The former group favoured a centralised government which looked to Enlightenment Europe for inspiration, while the latter group sought to retain the privileges it had attained under colonial rule.

Rural landowners (*hacendados* or *gamonales*) prevailed in the short run. Powerful caudillos with private armies exerted considerable influence on national politics and filled the power vacuum left by the departed colonial regime. Because this strong leadership was based on personality and personal following rather than on ideology or collective interest, it did not offer any continuity beyond that individual leader. The instability and violence which have characterised the South American republics have many roots in this period.

While each country has developed separately since independence, there have been a number of common elements, particularly the alternation between dictatorship and instability, and the contrast between the powerful elite and the powerless masses. Indian populations have fared badly in almost every country, suffering marginalisation at best, genocide at worst. Only recently have some groups been able to reassert their identity and exercise political power. Foreign economic and political intervention has also been a factor in the development of most countries in South America, though direct military involvement has been a rarity, and many of the republics have very independent foreign policies.

GEOGRAPHY

Apart from the main physical and political divisions of the continent, it's common to refer to the 'Andean countries' (Colombia, Ecuador, Peru and Bolivia) and the 'Southern Cone' (comprising Argentina, Uruguay, Paraguay, Chile, and southern Brazil).

Physical Features

The great mountain system of the Andes forms the western margin of the continent, snaking nearly 8000 km from Venezuela to southern Patagonia. From its northern extremity in Venezuela, the *cordillera* (range) extends south-west to form the eastern segment of several ranges in Colombia, which join to form a single range in the south of the country. In Ecuador, the Andes divide into two major volcanic chains, separated by a broad plateau. The Central Andes, in Peru, comprise three south-east trending ranges which meet the *altiplano* (high

South America - Physical Features

plateau) on the Bolivian border. South of Bolivia, the mountain range forms the border between Chile and Argentina, and extends to the southern tip of the continent.

The other dominant physical feature is the Amazon Basin, which drains an area of about seven million sq km, extending 3000 km from the eastern slopes of the Andes to the Atlantic and bounded by the highlands of the Guiana Shield to the north and the Brazilian Shield to the south.

Other physical features are the smaller Orinoco River Basin, which drains the Llanos (plains) of Venezuela; the barren Chaco of southern Bolivia; the extensive Paraná-Paraguay river system; the fertile Pampas of Argentina and Uruguay; and arid Patagonia, in the far south. A narrow strip of coastal plains around much of the continent, while not prominent on a map, contains some of the most densely populated areas, especially in Brazil, Argentina, Uruguay and Peru.

Political Geography & Borders

South America's colonial political boundaries were indistinct, and the creation of new states resulted in many territorial disputes, some of which still persist. The Peru-Ecuador border is especially contentious, and was the subject of armed confrontation in 1995. Others in dispute are Venezuela-Guyana, Guyana-Suriname, and Suriname-French Guiana. Argentina's claim to the Falkland Islands/Islas Malvinas led to open warfare in 1982. A long-standing dispute between Chile and Argentina over three small islands in the Beagle Channel was settled by arbitration in 1979.

Geopolitics One of the mainstays of military ideology, especially in the Southern Cone countries, is the 19th-century European notion of geopolitics. According to this view, the state is like a biological organism which must grow or die. This means a state must effectively occupy the territories which it claims as its own, even if this brings it into conflict with other states. Such thinking was clearly a major factor in Argentine General Galtieri's decision to invade the Falklands/ Malvinas in 1982. Argentine and Chilean territorial claims in Antarctica also show elements of geopolitical thinking.

CLIMATE

Because of South America's wide range of latitudes and altitudes, it has a great variety of climates. Warm and cold ocean currents, trade winds and topography also have an influence on the climate. Over two-thirds of the continent lies within the tropics. There are wet, humid tropical areas, including the Amazon Basin, northern Brazil and the Guianas, and the west coast of Colombia and Ecuador. These are areas of *selva* (natural tropical rainforest), with average daily maximum temperatures of about 30°C all year round and over 2500 mm of rain per annum. There are also drier tropical areas, such as the Brazilian Highlands and the Orinoco Basin, which are still hot but enjoy cool nights and a distinct dry season.

South of the Tropic of Capricorn, Paraguay and southern Brazil are humid subtropical zones, while most of Argentina and Chile have temperate mid-latitude climates, with mild winters and warm summers ranging from 12°C in July to 25°C in January, depending on landforms and latitude. Rainfall, occurring mostly in winter, varies from 200 mm to 2000 mm per annum, depending on winds and the rain shadow effect of the Andes.

The main arid regions are Patagonia, in the rain shadow east of the Andes, and northern Chile and Peru, between the Andes and the Pacific coast, where the cold Humboldt current creates a cloudy but dry climate. About every seven years, however, the El Niño effect, associated with changes in Pacific Ocean circulation patterns and rising sea surface temperatures, brings heavy rain and floods in these desert areas. There are two smaller arid zones, the north-eastern Brazilian *sertão*, where severe droughts wreak great hardships on peasant peoples, and along the north coast of Colombia and Venezuela.

The high Andes, above 3500 metres, and

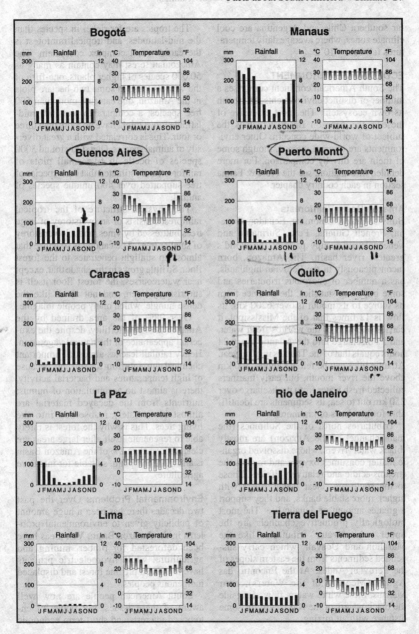

far southern Chile and Argentina are cool climate zones, where average daily temperatures fall below 10°C.

ECOLOGY & ENVIRONMENT

The South American continent comprises a number of distinct environments, each with its own ecosystem. The most extensive of these is the Amazon Basin, which is the subject of world-wide concern. Other environments are of great interest, though some of them are tiny by comparison. For more detailed information, see the Flora & Fauna section in each country chapter.

Amazon Basin Rainforests

Bolivia, Brazil, Colombia, Ecuador, Guyana, French Guiana, Peru, Suriname and Venezuela all occupy parts of the world's greatest river basin. The Amazon, born inconspicuously in the Peruvian highlands, has a number of enormous tributaries and some imposing statistics: the distance from its source to its mouth is over 6200 km, its flow is 12 times that of the Mississippi, it carries one-fifth of the world's fresh water, and its discharge into the Atlantic every 24 hours equals that of the Thames in a full year. Atlantic tides can be felt at Obidos, 500 km above the river mouth, but early mariners collected fresh water from its discharge over 250 km out to sea; its sediments are identifiable for hundreds of km more.

Tributaries north of the Solimões (the main channel of the Amazon) are mostly 'black water' rivers, whose dissolved organic matter consumes oxygen and renders the streams acidic and relatively lifeless. Those to the south are 'clear water' rivers with higher, more stable banks, and they support a greater amount of aquatic life. The most biologically productive channels are the upper 'white water' tributaries like the Marañon and Ucayali, which carry suspended sediments from the eastern slopes of the Peruvian Andes. At the Encontro das Aguas (Meeting of the Waters), near Manaus, these white waters flow alongside the black waters of the Rio Negro for some distance without mixing.

The tropics are far richer in species than the mid-latitudes, and tropical rainforest is the earth's most complex ecosystem. The Amazonian forest may contain as many as 50,000 species of higher plants, one-fifth of the world's total. In some two-hectare plots in the Amazon, one can find more than 500 tree species; a comparable plot in a mid-latitude forest might have no more than three or four. This is correlated with a great diversity of animal species. One study found 3000 species of beetle in five small plots of rainforest, and estimated that each species of tree supported over 400 unique species of animal.

The physical structure of the tropical rainforest consists of an overstorey of large trees buttressed by vines, and a lower storey of smaller trees. The canopy is so dense that almost no sunlight penetrates to the forest floor. So little grows in this shade that, except near watercourses, the forest floor itself is surprisingly open, and not at all like the dense 'jungle' which many people imagine.

Over 98% of the area drained by the Amazon is of low fertility, despite the exuberant appearance of the natural vegetation. Heavy rainfall leaches almost all important chemical nutrients from the soil and, because of high temperatures and bacterial activity, there is almost no accumulation of humus; nutrients from the decayed material are almost immediately reabsorbed into the living trees. This is why the forest is rarely able to regenerate itself after large areas are cleared. Less than 2% of the Amazon Basin is alluvial flood plain, suitable for intensive agriculture.

Environmental Problems Over the past two decades there has been a huge amount of publicity given to environmental problems in the Amazon Basin. Vast areas have been deforested for timber, mining and agriculture, while hydroelectric projects have inundated pristine forest and displaced indigenous peoples.

South American people are now well aware of these issues, but powerful entrenched interests and short-term economic considerations have often overwhelmed long-term environmental concerns. There are very different conditions in various parts of the region; in recent years the tributaries of the Amazon have suffered the worst depredations. Brazilian projects such as the Tucuruí dam on the Rio Tocantins, the Transamazon Highway, tree plantations on the Rio Jarí and gold mining in Roraima have brought deforestation, siltation, and mercury contamination of rivers.

On a global scale, the Amazon rainforest is believed to moderate climatic patterns, so its destruction will contribute to global warming. Rainforests are also vital for maintaining biodiversity: roughly half of the planet's 1.5 million known species live in tropical rainforests, and millions more species are as yet undocumented. Deforestation results in countless extinctions, and many of the species being lost may have medicinal or agricultural potential which has never been assessed. Deforestation also threatens many indigenous people who still depend on the forest to maintain their way of life.

Efforts are now under way to show that the economic value of the standing rainforest is greater than the mineral, timber and grazing wealth to be realised by deforestation. One way to make tropical rainforest economically productive, without cutting it down, is to protect it and make it accessible to visitors; ecotourism is becoming increasingly important to South American countries rich in such natural resources.

The total deforestation may be less than some alarmist estimates have suggested. According to the World Resources Institute, less than 10% of Brazil's forested Amazon has been lost – but the *rate* of deforestation (at least 1.7 million hectares per annum) is so startling that many fear it is an irreversible trend.

Traditional Shifting Agriculture The widespread practice of slash-and-burn agriculture is sometimes seen as a culprit in the deforestation of the Amazon and other rainforest regions, but it is actually a sustainable technique well suited to the rainforest ecosystem. Indigenous peoples such as the Kuikuru, of Brazil's upper Rio Xingú, have farmed nearby forest for as long as 90 years at a stretch without exhausting its resources or reducing forest cover, and major civilisations such as the Maya depended at least in part on agriculture of this kind.

Shifting agriculture certainly appears disruptive – the forest understorey is hacked away with a machete, large trees are felled, and the debris is piled up and burned. In fact, the burning liberates plant nutrients for growing crops, in an accelerated version of the natural cycle which depends on decomposition and reabsorption of plant materials.

A variety of crops is planted, in a structure resembling that of a natural rainforest, with an upper storey of fruit trees, an intermediate level of plants like maize and sugar cane, and a surface layer of tubers and ground-cover plants which protect the soil surface. A single plot might contain five varieties of bananas, three types of plantains, several tubers (including yams, sweet potatoes and cassava), tree crops (like peach palm, avocado and papaya), sugar cane, tobacco, cotton, and annuals like chiles, maize, beans, tomatoes and squash. The variety of plants discourages natural pests (which thrive in large stands of a single crop), thus helping to ensure a steady harvest.

Fertility on these small plots drops rapidly after two or three years, but the tree crops are good for several more years. A long fallow period, up to 30 years, then allows recovery of the forest.

If increased population or market pressures reduce fallow periods, the forest may not have sufficient time to recover. Innovations such as chainsaws can upset the delicate balance on which the system depends. When the system is extended into drier environments, it may fail, and when inexperienced immigrants attempt to farm the forest, results can be disastrous. Nevertheless, travellers who see a smouldering plot in the rainforest should not assume the worst; there is a strong correlation between the presence of indigenous peoples and the preservation of the selva.

The Central Andean Region

The ecology of the Central Andean region, between the coast and the cordillera from northern Chile to northern Peru, is also unique. The coastal Atacama desert, the world's driest, is almost utterly barren in the rain shadow of the high Andes. The cold Peru (Humboldt) current moderates the temperature one would expect at this tropical latitude, but produces convective fogs known as *garúa* or *camanchaca*, which support the hillside vegetation known as *lomas* in the coastal ranges. The only other vegetation occurs in the valleys of the several transverse rivers which descend from the Andes.

Precipitation and vegetation increase with altitude and distance from the coast, as well as from south to north. Traditionally, Andean peoples in different agro-pastoral 'niches' produced different, complementary products, which they exchanged with their kin in other zones. Coastal products included cotton, fish, guano (for fertiliser) and coca, while the higher *sierra* (mountain range) yielded maize and tubers, such as potatoes, on impressive agricultural terraces. On the heights of the altiplano, where cultivation was impossible, salt, wool and meat were the bases of subsistence.

This integrated economic system was disrupted by colonisation, but survives in many parts of the Andean region. The Andes are still a repository for a plant genetic diversity which parallels that of the Amazon. Some 6000 different varieties of potatoes are raised by Andean peasants, and are an important source of genetic material for improved potato varieties.

Tropical Cloud Forests

In remote valleys at higher elevations, these forests trap (and help create) clouds, which drench the forest in a fine mist, allowing some particularly delicate forms of plant life to survive. Cloud forest trees are adapted to steep rocky soils and a harsh climate. They have a characteristic low, gnarled growth, dense, small-leaved canopy, and moss-covered branches supporting orchids, ferns, bromeliads and a host of other epiphytes (aerial plants which gather moisture and nutrients without ground roots). It is the home of such rare species as the woolly tapir, the Andean spectacled bear and the puma. This habitat is particularly important as a source of fresh water and to control erosion.

High-Altitude Grassland

Even higher than the cloud forest, the *páramo* is the natural 'sponge' of the Andes: it catches and gradually releases much of the water that is eventually used by city dwellers. The páramo is characterised by a harsh climate, high levels of ultraviolet light and wet, peaty soils. It is a highly specialised highland habitat unique to tropical America, and found only from the highlands of Costa Rica to the highlands of northern Peru. Páramo flora is dominated by hard grasses, cushion plants and small herbaceous plants, which have adapted well to the harsh environment. The páramo also features dense thickets of *Polylepis* species *(queñua* in Spanish), members of the rose family. With the Himalayan pines, they share the world altitude record for trees. Once considerably more extensive, they have been pushed back into small pockets by fire and grazing. A spiky, resistant tussock grass, locally called *ichu*, is often encountered. It grows in large clumps and makes walking uncomfortable.

Tropical Dry Forest

Hot areas with well-defined wet and dry seasons support dry forests. In South America these climatic conditions are mostly found near the coast. The trees lose their leaves during the dry season and are more widely spaced than in the rainforest. Because coastal regions are the most densely populated, this is a fast-disappearing habitat: only about 1% of the continent's tropical dry forest remains undisturbed.

Mangroves

Mangrove swamps are one of the most fascinating habitats of the coastal lowlands. Mangroves are trees with the remarkable ability to grow in salt water. They have a broadly spreading system of intertwining stilt roots to support the tree in unstable sandy or silty soils. Mangrove forests trap sediments and build up a rich organic soil, which in turn supports other plants. In between the roots, a protected habitat is provided for many types of fish, mollusc and crustacean as well as other animals, while the branches provide nesting areas for sea birds.

Islands

Island groups off South America's coast are some of the most isolated spots in the world. The Galápagos Islands (off Ecuador) have been known for their wildlife since Darwin's day, but Chile's Juan Fernández archipelago, Brazil's Fernando de Noronha archipelago, and the Falklands/Malvinas also have unique island ecosystems and are havens for many plant and animal species, birds and marine life.

ECONOMY

Despite improvements in the early 1990s, South America is still widely perceived as an economic disaster zone of low living standards, hyperinflation and unsustainable levels of foreign debt. Some of these problems stem in part from a long history of foreign domination, political instability, social inequality and the failure to develop a sound domestic infrastructure. Other economic problems, like the debt crisis, are of more recent origin.

Post-Independence Economies

From about 1850 to the start of WW I, several South American countries enjoyed a period of growth and relative prosperity based on commodity exports like coffee and sugar (Brazil), guano and copper (Peru), nitrates (Chile), and grain, beef and wool (Argentina and Uruguay). Much of this development was supported by foreign capital and foreign expertise. Countries like Colombia, Bolivia and Ecuador lagged behind because of internal instability or lack of exploitable resources.

Wild fluctuations in the available foreign capital and in demand for exports during WW I and the Great Depression of the 1930s brought greater government intervention in South American economies. Initially, this took the form of regulations and controls aimed at protecting foreign investment, though there was direct government involvement in mining and transport. WW II was a time of strong demand for South America's food and raw materials, but imported, manufactured goods from Europe and North America were in short supply. Industrialisation, often identified with nationalism, became a key economic goal after the war.

Industrialisation required more capital than foreign private investment could readily provide, especially given postwar Europe's ruinous economic situation. Moreover, in projects involving natural resources and infrastructure (roads, telecommunications, electricity), locals worried that overseas capital might compromise economic autonomy and foreign investors feared nationalisation of their assets. The solution was for governments to borrow from overseas and become direct participants in economic enterprises. Argentina set up the YPF (Yacimientos Petrolíferos Fiscales) to develop oil reserves. Brazil's government entered the petroleum and steel industries, Bolivia's invested in tin, Chile's in copper, Colombia's in iron and steel, Uruguay's in meat packing, and so on.

Brazil, Argentina and Chile have been most successful in achieving industrialisation, while the Andean countries of Bolivia, Colombia, Ecuador and Peru have fallen behind. Industry, however, has been largely geared to protected local markets rather than to international trade; the traditional primary products of the mines, ranches, plantations and grain farms continue to dominate the export sector. Venezuela is the wealthiest of the South American republics, but this is based almost solely on oil revenues. In poorer countries, many rural people survive on small subsistence plots, but the lack of opportunity in the countryside has driven many to the shantytowns surrounding modern capitals and other large cities.

The Debt Crisis In the 1970s and 1980s, as dictatorships provided an appearance of stability and Western banks were awash with petrodollars, South American governments accelerated their borrowing. Much of the money went to grandiose but unproductive developments such as Brazil's new capital city, and massive hydroelectric projects like Itaipú and Yacyretá. Much was also squandered on military hardware and syphoned off by corrupt officials.

This infusion of foreign capital, supplemented by deficit spending without a corresponding increase in productivity, triggered serious inflation in most countries. In Brazil, for example, rates in mid-1993 consistently topped 30% per month. This and other economic problems decreased the ability to service foreign debt, and governments borrowed more just to pay the interest. The crisis emerged when the volume of doubtful debts reached a level which threatened the stability of Western banks. Countries became unable to pay the interest on their borrowings, but the banks could not admit that the debts were worthless. The situation led to a series of debt reschedulings and restructurings, and also forced countries to adopt economic reforms prescribed by the IMF, World Bank, and other international creditors.

Economic Restructuring Most South American countries adopted policies of reduced government spending and tight monetary restraint to prevent severe inflation. Many state-owned industries – telecommunications, railways and even highways – were privatised. The economic reforms often increased unemployment, as inefficient enterprises were closed or restructured, and income inequality worsened as the incomes of lower-paid workers and government employees were pegged back. The total debt burden remains, but economic growth

and stronger currencies have improved the capacity to service debt. Latin America's total debt is now equal to about twice the value of current annual exports – about the same debt-to-export ratio as at the start of the 1980s borrowing binge.

The Tequila Effect With an apparent improvement in economic stability, and governments effectively precluded from further borrowing, there was a boom in private portfolio investment in Latin America, with generally buoyant stock markets and solid economic growth in 1993 and 1994. In December 1994, a panic withdrawal of capital from Mexico led to a collapse in its stock market and a 40% devaluation of its currency. This was followed by a big sell-off of all South American stocks, and a dive on the markets – the so-called Tequila Effect. The effect has underscored again the problems of depending on foreign capital. The country which came out best in 1995 was Chile, notable for its strategy of boosting domestic savings with a national pension plan.

Trade Blocks In an attempt to gain more benefits from trade within the region, two major trading blocks have emerged. Argentina, Uruguay, Paraguay and Brazil make up the Mercosur group; while Colombia, Venezuela, Ecuador, Peru and Bolivia form the Andean Group. Neither of these groups, however, has yet achieved a complete elimination of internal trade barriers or a uniform policy on external trade. Chile is pressing for admission to NAFTA (the North American Free Trade Association, comprising the USA, Canada, and Mexico), but this is not likely in the near future. Guyana and Suriname are members of Caricom, the Caribbean Common Market, while French Guiana is officially a part of France and therefore of the European Union.

POPULATION & PEOPLE
While South America's population is growing at a fairly modest rate of 1.9% per

annum, that growth rate varies widely both among and within countries. The Southern Cone states of Argentina, Chile and Uruguay have relatively stable populations, while numbers in the Andean and tropical countries are increasing rapidly. Infant mortality rates are shockingly high in some countries, most notably Bolivia, Brazil and Peru.

Nearly three-quarters of all South Americans live in cities, while large areas such as the Amazon Basin and Atacama desert are almost uninhabited. Population growth and internal migration has seen the emergence of super cities, like São Paulo (19 million), Buenos Aires (11 million), Rio de Janeiro (10 million), Lima (eight million) and Bogotá (seven million). These megalopolises concentrate some of the most severe social and environmental problems on the continent.

Many countries, in particular Bolivia, Ecuador, Peru, Colombia, Brazil and Venezuela, have very young populations, with nearly 40% of the people under 15 years old. Not only does this mean that populations will continue to grow rapidly as these individuals reach child-bearing age, but it is doubtful whether local economies can provide employment for so many in such a short time.

ARTS

While it is common to refer to Latin America – of which South America is far and away the largest part – as a single cultural entity, most of the arts have a distinctly national or even regional character. Internationally, the continent is best known for its music, especially Brazilian and Andean styles, and for dances like tango and samba. Look in the individual country chapters for more information.

South American literature is also well established. Look in country chapters for more about the most famous writers, including Jorge Luis Borges (Argentina); Jorge Amado (Brazil); Pablo Neruda, Gabriela Mistral, and Isabel Allende (Chile); Gabriel García Márquez (Colombia); and Mario Vargas Llosa (Peru). All the greatest works are available in English; see the Books section in the Facts for the Visitor chapter for a few suggestions.

SOCIETY & CONDUCT
Traditional Cultures

The peasant populations of the Andean highlands are often considered to have the most 'traditional' way of life; they still raise potatoes on small plots and herd llamas and alpacas on the pastures of the altiplano. But over centuries they have adopted many European customs, sold their surpluses in local markets and shipped wool to European mills. Similarly, the indigenous peoples of the Amazon, even in very isolated areas, obtained European goods like metal axes, fish hooks, and machetes. Access is restricted to many of the areas where people retain the most 'traditional' way of life. It is essential to respect these restrictions: they help to protect the indigenous people from unwanted interference, and from diseases to which they have little immunity.

Avoiding Offence

In general, South Americans are friendly, gregarious and not easily offended, but will always expect to exchange pleasantries before getting to the point of a conversation; not to do so is the mark of an ill-bred person. Public behaviour can be very formal, especially among government officials, who expect respect and deference.

Don't photograph individuals without their permission, especially indigenous people. If someone is giving a public performance, such as a street musician or a dancer at Carnaval, or is incidental to a photograph, for example in a broad cityscape, it is not usually necessary to request permission – but if in doubt, ask or refrain.

Appearance & Conduct

Official discrimination against individuals of casual appearance has diminished in recent years, but foreign travellers should still try to be inconspicuous and not offend the local standards of grooming and behaviour. It is usually enough to be clean and neat, if not formally dressed.

Even travellers of modest means may seem extraordinarily wealthy, and flaunting things like cameras, watches, jewellery etc can only heighten that impression, and may attract thieves. Police and military officials are often poorly paid, and may resent affluent visitors who do not behave appropriately.

Prostitution

Prostitution exists in most of the continent, but is most prevalent in Brazil, where the distinction between prostitution and promiscuity can sometimes be hazy. Sexual contact between locals and visitors, male and female, straight and gay, is quite common, and some areas could be described as sex-tourism destinations. AIDS is widespread, and not just among gays. Child prostitution is not common, but unfortunately it is a reality. There are severe penalties for those convicted of involvement in child prostitution and very real risks of entrapment.

RELIGION

About 90% of South Americans are at least nominally Roman Catholic. Virtually every town and city has a central church or cathedral and a calendar loaded with Catholic holidays and celebrations. Spreading the faith was a major objective of colonisation.

Among Indian peoples, allegiance to Catholicism was often just a veneer, disguising precolonial beliefs which the Church ostensibly forbade. Similarly, black slaves in Brazil gave Christian names and forms to their African gods, whose worship was discouraged or forbidden. Cults and sects have proliferated to this day, but they do not exclude Christianity. There is no conflict between attending mass on Sunday and seeking guidance from a *brujo* (witch) the next day.

Over recent decades, in part because of a complacent Church and rapid economic change, evangelical Protestantism has made inroads among traditionally Catholic peoples. At the same time, activist elements within the Catholic Church have promoted social justice in the name of 'Liberation Theology' – despite serious threats from reactionary elements in several South American countries.

LANGUAGE
Latin American Spanish

Spanish is the first language of the vast majority of South Americans; Brazilians speak Portuguese but often understand Spanish. Without a basic knowledge of Spanish, travel in South America can be difficult. Besides its practical value in helping you find your way around, order in restaurants and get yourself out of trouble, speaking the language enables you to communicate with locals and make friends.

Before going, try to attend an evening course in Spanish or borrow a record/cassette course from the library. Buy a book on grammar and a phrasebook (such as Lonely Planet's *Latin American Spanish phrasebook*) and try to find a Latin American to practise with. Learning the basics of Spanish is not difficult for an English speaker, there are many related words, and Latin Americans are very tolerant of grammatical mistakes.

Remember that there are significant differences between European and American Spanish. Even within the Americas, accents, pronunciation and vocabulary vary considerably from one country to the next. Chilean Spanish, in particular, can be awkward for inexperienced speakers. Some words which are totally innocuous in one country can be grievous insults in another: avoid slang unless you are certain of its every meaning.

Pronunciation Most sounds in Spanish have English equivalents, and written Spanish is largely phonetic.

Vowels Spanish vowels are very consistent and have easy English equivalents.

a as in 'f**a**ther'
e as in 'm**e**t'
i as in 'h**i**t'
o as in 'h**o**t'
u as in 'f**oo**d'. After consonants other than 'q', it is more like the English 'w'. When modified by an umlaut, as in 'Güemes', it is also pronounced 'w'.
y is a consonant, except when it stands alone or appears at the end of a word, in which case its pronunciation is identical to the Spanish 'i'

ll as the 'y' in '**y**ellow', except in Argentina, where it is as the 's' in 'plea**s**ure'
ñ like 'ni' in 'o**ni**on'
r as in English, except at the beginning of a word, when it is often rolled
rr very strongly rolled
v see 'b' above
x as in 'ta**x**i', except for a very few words for which it follows Spanish or Mexican usage as 'j'
z as in '**s**un'

Diphthongs A diphthong is a combination of two vowels to form a single syllable. In Spanish, the formation of a diphthong depends on combinations of 'weak' vowels ('i' and 'u') or strong ones ('a', 'e' and 'o'). Two weak vowels or a strong and a weak vowel make a diphthong, but two strong ones are separate syllables.

A good example of two weak vowels forming a diphthong is the word *diurno* ('during the day'). The final syllable of *obligatorio* ('obligatory') is a combination of weak and strong vowels.

Consonants Spanish consonants generally resemble their English equivalents, but there are some major exceptions:

b resembles its English equivalent, but is undistinguished from 'v'. For clarification, refer to the former as 'b larga', the latter as 'b corta'
c like the 's' in '**s**ee' before 'e' and 'i'; otherwise like the English 'k'
d as in '**d**og'in an initial position; otherwise like 'th' in 'fea**th**er'
g like the 'ch' in the Scottish 'lo**ch**' before 'e' and 'i', otherwise like 'g' in '**g**o'
h invariably silent. If your name begins with this letter, listen carefully when immigration officials summon you to pick up your passport
j like the 'ch' in the Scottish 'lo**ch**'

Stress Stress is very important, since it can change the meaning of words. In general, words ending in vowels or the letters 'n' or 's' have stress on the next-to-last syllable, while those with other endings have stress on the last syllable. Thus *vaca* ('cow') and *caballos* ('horses') are both stressed on the next-to-last syllable, while *ciudad* ('city') and *infeliz* ('unhappy') both have stress on the last syllable.

Variations on these normal stress patterns are often indicated by a visible accent over a vowel, which can occur anywhere in a word, and overrides the general rules above. Thus *sótano* ('basement'), *América* and *porción* ('portion') all have stress on different syllables. When a word with a written accent appears in capital letters, the accent is often not written, but is still pronounced.

Agreement An adjective, like the definite or indefinite article, must agree in gender and number with the noun it describes.

a good boy	*un chico bueno*
the pretty house	*la casa bonita*
some pretty rooms	*unos cuartos bonitos*
the good girls	*las chicas buenas*

Greetings & Civilities In their public behaviour, South Americans are very conscious of civilities, sometimes to the point of ceremoniousness. Never, for example, approach a stranger for information without extending a greeting like *buenos días* or *buenas tardes*.

Hello.	*¡Hola!*
Good morning.	*Buenos días.*
Good afternoon.	*Buenas tardes.*
Good evening/night.	*Buenas noches.*
Goodbye.	*Adiós/Chau.*
Mr/Sir	*Señor* (formal)
Mrs/Madam	*Señora* (formal)
unmarried woman	*Señorita*
pal/friend	*compadre*

Bye, see you soon.
   Hasta luego.
I hope things go well for you.
   Que le vaya bien. (used when parting)

Basics

Yes.	*Sí.*
No.	*No.*
Please.	*Por favor.*
Thank you.	*Gracias.*
Many thanks.	*Muchas gracias.*
You're welcome.	*De nada.*
Excuse me.	*Permiso.*
Sorry.	*Perdón.*
Excuse me.	*Disculpe.*
Good luck!	*¡Buena suerte!*

Small Talk

How are you?
   ¿Cómo está? (formal)
   ¿Cómo estás? (familiar)
How are things going?
   ¿Qué tal?
Fine, thanks.
   Bien, gracias.
Very well.
   Muy bien.
Very badly.
   Muy mal.
What is your name?
   ¿Cómo se llama?(formal)
   ¿Cómo te llamas?(familiar)
My name is ...
   Me llamo ...
Where are you from?
   ¿De dónde es? (formal)
   ¿De dónde eres? (familiar)

I am from ...
   Soy de ...
How old are you?
   ¿Cuántos años tiene?
Are you married?
   ¿Es casado/a?
I am single.
   Soy soltero/a.
I am married.
   Soy casado/a.
Can I take a photo?
   ¿Puedo sacar una foto?
Of course. Why not. Sure.
   Por supuesto. Cómo no. Claro.

Curious South Americans, from officials to casual acquaintances, will often want to know what travellers do for a living. If it's something that seems unusual (many would find it difficult to believe, for example, that a gardener could earn enough money to travel the world), it may be easiest to claim to be a student or teacher.

What do you do?
   ¿Qué hace?
What's your profession?
   ¿Cuál es su profesión?

I am a ...	*Soy...*
student	*estudiante*
teacher	*profesor/a*
nurse	*enfermero/a*
lawyer	*abogado/a*
engineer	*ingeniero/a*
mechanic	*mecánico/a*

Language Difficulties

I don't speak much Spanish.
   Hablo poco castellano.
I (don't) understand.
   (No) entiendo.
Do you speak English?
   ¿Habla inglés?
Could you repeat that?
   ¿Puede repetirlo?
Could you speak more slowly please?
   ¿Puede hablar más despacio por favor?

How does one say ...?
¿Cómo se dice ...?
What does ... mean?
¿Qué quiere decir ...?

Toilets

The most common word for 'toilet' is *baño*, but *servicios sanitarios* ('services') is a frequent alternative. Men's toilets will usually bear a descriptive term such as *hombres*, *caballeros* or *varones*. Women's will be marked *señoras* or *damas*.

Getting Around

Where is ...?	*¿Dónde está ...?*
the airport	*el aeropuerto*
the train station	*la estación de ferrocarril*
the bus terminal	*el terminal de buses*
the ticket office	*la boletería*

What time does ... leave/arrive?	*¿A qué hora sale/llega ...?*
the aeroplane	*el avión*
the train	*el tren*
the bus	*el colectivo/ micro/camión/ ómnibus/ la flota*
the ship	*el barco/buque*

I'd like a ticket to ...
Quiero un boleto/pasaje a ...
What's the fare to ...?
¿Cuánto cuesta hasta ...?
Is there a student discount?
¿Hay descuento estudiantil?

1st class	*primera clase*
2nd class	*segunda clase*
single/one-way	*ida*
return/round trip	*ida y vuelta*
car	*auto/carro/coche*
taxi	*taxi*
truck	*camión*
pick-up (truck)	*camioneta*
bicycle	*bicicleta*
motorcycle	*motocicleta/moto*

hitchhike	*hacer dedo*
sleeper	*camarote*
left luggage	*guardería/equipaje*

Directions

How do I get to ...?
¿Cómo puedo llegar a ...?
Is it far?
¿Está lejos?
Go straight ahead.
Siga/Vaya derecho.
Turn left.
Voltée a la izquierda ...
Turn right.
Voltée a la derecha

north	*norte*
south	*sur*
east	*este/oriente*
west	*oeste/occidente*

Accommodation

Where is ...?	*¿Dónde hay ...?*
a hotel	*un hotel*
a boarding house	*una pensión/ residencial*
a youth hostel	*un albergue juvenil*

What does it cost per night?
¿Cuánto cuesta por noche?
Does it include breakfast?
¿Incluye el desayuno?
May I see the room?
¿Puedo ver la habitación?
I don't like it.
No me gusta.

single room	*habitación para una persona*
double room	*habitación doble*
full board	*pensión completa*
shared bath	*baño compartido*
private bath	*baño privado*
too expensive	*demasiado caro*
discount	*descuento*
cheaper	*más económico*
the bill	*la cuenta*

Around Town

I'm looking for ...	*Estoy buscando ...*
the bank	*el banco*
the ... embassy	*la embajada ...*
my hotel	*mi hotel*
the market	*el mercado*
the post office	*el correo*
the tourist information office	*la oficina de turismo*

What time does it open/close?
¿A qué hora abre/cierra?
I want to change some money/
travellers' cheques
Quiero cambiar dinero/cheques de viajero.
What is the exchange rate?
¿Cuál es el tipo de cambio?
I want to ring (Canada).
Quiero llamar a (Canadá).

letter	*carta*
airmail	*correo aéreo*
registered mail	*certificado*
stamps	*estampillas*
credit card	*tarjeta de crédito*
black market	*mercado negro/ paralelo*
exchange houses	*casas de cambio*

Food

breakfast	*desayuno*
lunch	*almuerzo*
dinner	*cena*
(cheap) restaurant	*restaurante (barato)*

Useful Signs

ENTRANCE	*ENTRADA*
EXIT	*SALIDA*
INFORMATION	*INFORMACION*
OPEN	*ABIERTO*
CLOSED	*CERRADO*
NO SMOKING	*NO FUMAR*
POLICE	*POLICIA*
TOILETS	*SERVICIOS*

I would like ...
Quisiera ...
Is service included in the bill?
¿El servicio está incluido en la cuenta?
I'm a vegetarian.
Soy vegetariano/a.

Shopping

Can I look at it?
¿Puedo mirarlo/a?
How much is it?
¿Cuánto cuesta?
That's too expensive for me.
Es demasiado caro para mí
Do you accept credit cards?
¿Aceptan tarjetas de crédito?

bookshop	*la librería*
general store/shop	*la tienda*
laundry	*la lavandería/ el lavadero*
market	*el mercado*
pharmacy/chemist	*la farmacia/ la droguería*
supermarket	*el supermercado*

Health

I need a doctor.
Necesito un médico.
Where is the hospital?
¿Dónde está el hospital?
I'm allergic to antibiotics/penicillin.
Soy alérgico/a a los antibióticos/ la penicilina.
I'm pregnant.
Estoy embarazada/encinta.
I have been vaccinated.
Estoy vacunado/a

Emergencies

Danger/Careful!	*¡Cuidado!*
Help!	*¡Socorro!*
Fire!	*¡Incendio!*
Thief!	*¡Ladrón!*
I've been robbed.	*Me robaron.*
Don't bother me!	*¡No me moleste!*
Go away!	*¡Déjeme!*
Go away! (stronger)	*¡Que se vaya!*
Get lost!	*¡Váyase!*

Time & Dates

today	*hoy*
this morning	*esta mañana*
this afternoon	*esta tarde*
tonight	*esta noche*
yesterday	*ayer*
tomorrow	*mañana*
week/month/year	*semana/mes/año*
last week	*la semana pasada*
next month	*el mes que viene*
always	*siempre*
now	*ahora*
before/after	*antes/después*

It's early/late.
  Es temprano/tarde.
What time is it?
  ¿Qué hora es?
It's one o'clock.
  Es la una.
It's seven o'clock.
  Son las siete.

Days of the Week

Monday	*lunes*
Tuesday	*martes*
Wednesday	*miércoles*
Thursday	*jueves*
Friday	*viernes*
Saturday	*sábado*
Sunday	*domingo*

Cardinal Numbers

1	*uno/una*
2	*dos*
3	*tres*
4	*cuatro*
5	*cinco*
6	*seis*
7	*siete*
8	*ocho*
9	*nueve*
10	*diez*
11	*once*
12	*doce*
13	*trece*
14	*catorce*
15	*quince*
16	*dieciseis*
17	*diecisiete*
18	*dieciocho*
19	*diecinueve*
20	*veinte*
21	*veintiuno*
30	*treinta*
40	*cuarenta*
50	*cincuenta*
60	*sesenta*
70	*setenta*
80	*ochenta*
90	*noventa*
100	*cien*
101	*ciento uno*
200	*doscientos*
1000	*mil*
5000	*cinco mil*
10,000	*diez mil*
50,000	*cincuenta mil*
100,000	*cien mil*
one million	*un millón*

Other Languages

Portuguese For information on Brazil's official language, see the Language entry in the Facts about the Country section of that chapter.

Indian Languages There are hundreds of different South American Indian languages, some of them spoken by very few people. In the Andean countries and parts of Chile and Argentina, however, millions of people speak Quechua and Aymara, and travellers may come into contact with people who speak only one of those languages.

Native English-speakers may find grammar and pronunciation of these languages quite difficult. If you're serious about learning them, or will be spending a lot of time in remote areas, look around La Paz or Cuzco for a good course. Dictionaries and phrasebooks are available through Los Amigos del Libro and larger bookshops in La Paz, but the translations are in Spanish. Lonely Planet's *Quechua phrasebook* is primarily for travellers to Peru, with grammar and vocabulary in the Cuzco dialect, but will also be useful for visitors to the Bolivian highlands.

The following list of words and phrases is obviously minimal, but it should be useful in areas where these languages are spoken. Pronounce them as you would a Spanish word. An apostrophe represents a glottal stop (the 'sound' in the middle of 'oh-oh!').

English	Aymara	Quechua
Where is...?	Kaukasa...?	Maypi...?
to the left	chchekaru	lokeman
to the right	cupiru	pañaman
How do you say...?	Cun sañasauca'ha...?	Imainata nincha chaita...?
It is called...	Ucan sutipa'h...	Chaipa'g sutin'ha...
Please repeat.	Uastata sita.	Ua'manta niway.
It's a pleasure.	Take chuima'hampi.	Tucuy sokoywan.
What does that mean?	Cuna sañasas muniucha'ha?	Imata'nita munanchai'ja?
I don't know.	Janiwa yatkti.	Mana yachanichu.
I am hungry.	Mankatawa hiu'ta.	Yarkaimanta wañusianiña.
How much?	K'gauka?	Maik'ata'g?
cheap	pisitaqui	pisillapa'g
condor	malku	cóndor
distant	haya	caru
downhill	aynacha	uray
father	auqui	tata
food	manka	mikíuy
friend	kgochu	kgochu
Hello!	Laphi!	Raphi!
house	uta	huasi
I	haya	ñoka
llama	yama-karhua	karhua
lodging	korpa	pascana
man	chacha	k'gari
miner	koyiri	koya'g
moon	pha'gsi	kiya
mother	taica	mama
near	maka	kailla
no	janiwa	mana
river	jawira	mayu
ruins	champir	champir
snowy peak	kollu	riti-orko
sun	yinti	inti
teacher	yatichiri	yachachi'g
thirst	phara	chchaqui
trail	tapu	chakiñan
very near	hakítaqui	kaillitalla
water	uma	yacu
when?	cunapacha?	haiká'g?
woman	warmi	warmi
yes	jisa	ari
you	huma	khan
young	wuayna	huayna

English	Aymara	Quechua
1	*maya*	*u'*
2	*paya*	*iskai*
3	*quimsa*	*quinsa*
4	*pusi*	*tahua*
5	*pesca*	*phiska*
6	*zo'hta*	*so'gta*
7	*pakalko*	*khanchis*
8	*quimsakalko*	*pusa'g*
9	*yatunca*	*iskon*
10	*tunca*	*chunca*
11	*tuncamayani*	*chunca u'niyo'g*
12	*tuncapayani*	*chuncaiskai'niyo'g*
13	*tuncaquimsani*	*chunca quinsa'niyo'g*
14	*tuncapusini*	*chunca tahua'yo'g*
15	*tuncapescani*	*chunca phiska'nio'g*
16	*tunca zo'htani*	*chunca so'gta'nio'g*
17	*tuncapakalkoni*	*chunca khanchisniyo'g*
18	*tunca quimsakalkoni*	*chunca pusa'gniyo'g*
19	*tunca yatuncani*	*chunca iskoniyo'g*
20	*pa tunka*	*iskai chunca*

Facts for the Visitor

PLANNING

When to Go

When you go depends on what you want to do. Hikers and trekkers should avoid the rainy season, which varies from country to country: in most of Peru, the winter months of June, July and August are the driest, while in Chile, the summer months of December, January and February are best. Visitors to the Southern Cone also find that longer summer days (around December) permit great flexibility in outdoor activities. Brazilian beaches are great in the northern winter, and you can stay on until Carnaval, around the end of February. Skiing is best from June to September. For more information, see the Climate section in the Facts about South America chapter, and the individual country chapters.

How Long?

A month is good, a year is better, a lifetime is not enough. In practice, since for most travellers South America is a remote destination and just to get there is an expensive business, budget travellers often expect to stay for some time – perhaps six months or more. Good planning, however, can make even a short trip worthwhile.

What to Bring

Travel light: overweight baggage soon becomes a nightmare, especially in hot weather and on public transport. Official prejudice against backpacks has dissipated in recent years, so most budget travellers prefer them; internal-frame packs are more suitable than those with external frames. If you travel very light, a bag with a shoulder strap is still easy to carry, and perhaps more secure: a backpack is vulnerable to a thief with a razor.

A robust convertible backpack with zip-away straps is a good compromise. For long, dusty bus trips, carry a large, strong plastic bag or even a lockable duffel for the luggage compartment or roof.

Unless you're staying exclusively in the lowland tropics, bring a sleeping bag. Above 3000 metres and in the far south, nights get very cold; not all budget hotels provide enough blankets, and buses, trains and especially trucks are often unheated. You can buy additional warm clothing at reasonable prices in the Andean countries. A sleeping-bag liner can discourage mosquitoes, but a mosquito net is better. A hammock is essential for river travel, and can be bought locally.

Some people take a small tent and portable stove, which give you greater independence in out-of-the-way places and expand your budget alternatives in the costlier Southern Cone. Hired equipment is available in popular trekking areas like Peru's Inca Trail, but if you want to camp regularly, you should bring your equipment with you.

Don't forget small essentials: a combination pocketknife such as a Swiss Army knife; a needle, cotton and a small pair of scissors; a padlock; and one or two good long novels (English-language books are usually expensive). Most toiletries (toilet paper, toothpaste, shampoo etc) are easily found in large cities and even small towns. Bring some condoms, whether you think you will need them or not. Virtually every small shop sells packets of washing powder just large enough for a pile of laundry. See the Health section for suggestions for a personal medical kit.

HIGHLIGHTS

The highlights depend on what you like most. There are specific suggestions in each country chapter, but here are some more general considerations.

If you like mountains, any part of the Andes, from Venezuela to Chile, will present opportunities for climbing and trekking, and alpine scenery. Argentina and Chile have the best ski areas.

Brazil is the best known beach destination, but there are also great beaches in Venezuela and on Colombia's Caribbean coast. Brazil has the best surf.

South America's scenic highlights include the Chilean-Argentine Lake District, the Torres del Paine and the fjords of Southern Chile, Argentina's Moreno Glacier, and some spectacular waterfalls: Angel Falls in Venezuela; Kaieteur in Guyana; and Iguazú, on the Brazil-Argentina border.

Many travellers go to Brazil to experience tropical rainforest, but there are also accessible areas of pristine Amazon rainforest in Bolivia, Ecuador, Bolivia, and Colombia, while the Guianas have possibilities for ecotourism which have scarcely been developed. Other areas to see birds and wildlife include Brazil's Pantanal, Esteros del Iberá in Argentina, and some of the offshore island groups: the Galápagos, the Juan Fernández archipelago, and the Falklands/Malvinas.

For archaeology enthusiasts, the most famous ruins are those of Peru's Machu Picchu, but other highlights include Ciudad Perdida (the Lost City) in Colombia and the mysterious statues of Easter Island. More recent ruins are the abandoned missions of Argentina and Paraguay.

Fine colonial architecture is found all over the continent, but some of the best examples are Cartagena (Colombia); Salvador da Bahia, Ouro Prêto, Olinda, and at least half a dozen more towns in Brazil; Colonia in Uruguay; Cajamarca in Peru; and Sucre and Potosí in Bolivia.

A real highlight of contemporary South America is the music, and the best places to hear it are the towns and cities of Brazil, the Caribbean coastal areas (especially if you like reggae), and Ecuador, Peru and Bolivia (for Andean music).

VISAS & DOCUMENTS

As well as a passport, you'll need visas, air tickets, and a health certificate. Make copies of all these documents, as well as details of your credit cards and travellers' cheques, and carry them separately from the originals. The copies will be invaluable if originals are lost or stolen. Certified copies will have more credibility.

Visas

A visa is an endorsement in your passport, usually a stamp, permitting you to enter a country and remain for a specified time. It is obtained from a foreign embassy or consulate of that country. You can often get them in your home country, but it's usually possible to get them en route, which may be better if your itinerary is flexible: most visas are only good for a limited period after they're issued. Ask other travellers about the best places to get them, since two consulates of the same country may enforce different requirements: the fee might vary, one might want to see your money or an onward ticket while another might not ask, or one might issue them on the spot while another might take days to do so.

If you really need a visa in a hurry, ask nicely and explain your reasons: consulates can often be very helpful if the officials sympathise and your papers are in order. Sometimes they will charge a fee for fast processing, but don't mistake this for a bribe.

Nationals of most European countries and Japan require few visas, but travellers from the USA need some and those from Australia, New Zealand and South Africa might need quite a few. Carry a handful of passport-size photographs for visa applications, though most small border towns have a photographer who can do them.

Visa requirements are given in the Facts for the Visitor section of each individual country chapter. If you know you need a visa for a certain country and arrive without one, you may have to return to the nearest consulate for a visa before being admitted. Authorities sometimes issue visas at the border, but take nothing for granted. Also, a visa in itself may not guarantee entry: you may still be turned back at the border if you don't have 'sufficient funds' or an onward or return ticket.

'Sufficient Funds' Getting visas is generally routine, but officials may ask, either verbally or on the application form, about your financial resources. If you lack 'sufficient funds' for your proposed visit, officials may limit the length of your stay, but once in the country, you can usually renew or extend your visa by showing a wad of travellers' cheques. A credit card or two is often convincing evidence of sufficient funds.

Onward/Return Tickets Several countries require you to have a ticket out of the country before they will grant you a visa, or admit you at the border. This onward (or return) ticket requirement is a major nuisance for budget travellers, especially overlanders. Peru, Colombia, Venezuela, Brazil, and French Guiana demand this at present, though enforcement is sometimes sporadic. This creates no problems if you plan to leave the country from your point of arrival, but if you want to enter at one point and leave at another, you may need an onward ticket.

It is no longer easy to evade this requirement by purchasing an MCO (Miscellaneous Charges Order), a document which looks like an airline ticket but can be refunded in cash or credited towards a specific flight with any IATA carrier. Most consular and immigration officials no longer accept an MCO as an onward ticket, so you may have to buy a refundable onward or return ticket; look for the cheapest available and be sure you can get a refund without waiting months. Don't forget to ask specifically where you can get a refund, as some airlines will only refund tickets at the office of purchase or at their head office.

Travellers from Costa Rica or Panama to Colombia or Venezuela cannot even buy a one-way ticket without also buying an onward ticket, and so must work out in advance where to go after leaving Colombia or Venezuela.

You may be able to circumvent the onward ticket requirement by showing enough money for a ticket home, as well as sufficient funds for your stay. Having a recognised, international credit card or two might help. A prosperous appearance and a sympathetic official will improve your chances.

Documents
The essential documents are a passport and an International Health Certificate. If you already have a passport, make sure it's valid for a reasonably long period of time (at least six months beyond the projected end of your trip) and has plenty of blank pages for stamp-happy officials. A government health department, your physician or the doctor who gives you your vaccinations can provide the Health Certificate.

If you're planning to drive anywhere, obtain an International Driving Permit or Inter-American Driving Permit (Uruguay theoretically recognises only the latter). For about US$10, any motoring organisation will issue one on presentation of a current state or national driving licence.

An International Student Identity Card (ISIC) is useful in some places for reductions on admission charges to archaeological sites and museums. At times, it will also entitle you to reductions on bus, train and air tickets. In some countries, such as Argentina, almost any form of university identification will suffice. It's sometimes possible to obtain a plausible-looking ISIC card if you book a flight with one of the 'bucket shop' ticket agencies. Another possibility is to buy a fake card (average price around US$10), but examine them carefully if you decide to buy one, as they vary in quality.

A Youth Hostel Association (YHA) membership card can be useful in Brazil, Chile, Argentina and Uruguay, where there are numerous hostels and accommodation costs tend to be higher. Hostels may accept non-members, but at a higher rate.

MONEY
Costs
The cost of travelling varies greatly between the different countries of South America, but there are other factors as well which make it difficult to give a precise figure. Generally speaking, it will cost less (per person) if you travel as a couple or in a small group, and you will spend less if you travel slowly with long stops. It will cost more if you want comforts like air-conditioning and a private

bathroom, if you want to eat in good restaurants, if you do expensive tours to places like the Galápagos Islands, or if you indulge in expensive activities like skiing or going to nightclubs.

To give a very rough idea of relative costs, let's assume you're travelling with another person, mostly by bus, staying in cheap but clean hotels, and eating in cheap restaurants and food stalls, with the occasional splurge on sightseeing or whatever. You could budget on the following as a safe minimum, per person per day:

Argentina – US$30 to US$40 (less if you camp out a lot; more in Buenos Aires)
Bolivia – less than US$20 (less than US$15 is feasible)
Brazil – around US$30 (this may come down somewhat if the currency depreciates)
Chile – around US$30
Colombia – US$20 to US$25
Ecuador – less than US$20 (quite a bit more with a trip to the Galápagos)
Falkland Islands – at least US$50
French Guiana – at least US$40
Guyana – US$20 to US$30
Paraguay – under US$30
Peru – around US$20, maybe less
Suriname – around US$25
Uruguay – US$25 to US$35
Venezuela – US$20 to US$25

Carrying Money

It is preferable to bring money in US dollars, though banks and *casas de cambio* (exchange houses) in capital cities will change pounds sterling, Deutschmarks, Japanese yen and other major currencies. Changing these currencies in smaller towns and on the street can be next to impossible.

Everyone has a preferred way to carry money. Some use money belts, others have hidden pockets inside their trousers, or leg pouches with elastic bands, and others hang a pouch round their neck. Leather money belts, which appear from the outside to be ordinary belts, seem to be effective but their capacity is limited. If you use a neck pouch, incorporate a length of guitar string into the strap so that it can't be cut without alerting you.

Travellers' Cheques

Travellers' cheques are the safest way to carry money. American Express, Thomas Cook, Citibank and Visa are among the best known brands and, in most cases, offer instant replacement in case of loss or theft. Cheques issued by smaller banks with limited international affiliations may be difficult to cash, especially in more remote areas. To facilitate replacement in case of theft, keep a record of cheque numbers and the original bill of sale in a safe place. Even with proper records, replacement can take time: too many travellers have been selling cheques on the black market, or simply pretending to lose them and then demanding replacement.

Have some travellers' cheques in small denominations such as US$20 and US$50. If you carry only large denominations, you might find yourself stuck with a large amount of local currency on leaving a country, which can only be reconverted at a poor rate of exchange.

In some countries, notably Argentina, travellers' cheques are increasingly difficult to cash, and banks and cambios charge commissions as high as 10%. For this reason, travellers to Argentina and rural areas of some other countries may wish to consider cash dollars.

Cash

Carry some cash, because it's easier to change in small places or when banks are closed. It's also more convenient, just before leaving a country, to change some small dollar bills than a travellers' cheque. Cash is also convenient when there's a black market, parallel market or unofficial exchange rate. On the other hand, it is riskier to carry cash than travellers' cheques: nobody will give you a refund for lost or stolen cash.

In some countries, including Chile and Uruguay, you can exchange US dollar travellers' cheques for US dollars in cash at banks and cambios, in order to top up on cash from time to time. In Argentina in particular, US dollars in cash are preferable, as travellers' cheques are difficult and expensive to negotiate, and the risk involved in carrying cash is relatively small.

Credit Cards

Credit cards can be very useful. As automatic teller machines (ATMs) become more widespread, some travellers are carrying fewer travellers' cheques and withdrawing cash from machines as they need it. The rate of exchange is usually as good as, or better than, any bank or legal moneychanger. Some banks will issue cash advances on major credit cards. The most widely accepted is Visa, followed by MasterCard (those with UK Access should insist on their affiliation to MasterCard). American Express, Diner's Club and others are also valid in many places. Many ATMs are connected to the Cirrus or Plus network.

Credit cards can also be used to pay shop, hotel and restaurant bills, but users should note two points. Firstly, in some countries (notably Argentina), businesses may add a surcharge *(recargo)* of 5% to 10% on credit-card purchases, so ask first. Alternatively, merchants may give a discount for cash purchases. Secondly, the amount you have to pay depends on the exchange rate at the time of posting the overseas charge to your account at home, which can be weeks later. If the overseas currency is depreciating, the amount on your credit-card account will be less than the dollar cost you calculated at the time of purchase; a strengthening currency in the country of the purchase will mean the cost in dollars (or other foreign currency) will be greater than you expected.

Credit-card fraud can be a problem, especially in Brazil. Never let the card out of your sight. If you rely on ATMs, take two or more cards. If you only have one, and it's lost or swallowed by an ATM, you could be in big trouble. Keep your cards separately, and note the numbers of the cards and the emergency phone numbers of the card companies.

International Transfers

If you're out of money, ask your bank at home to send a draft, specifying the city, the bank and the branch of destination. Cable transfers should arrive in a few days, but you can run into complications, even with supposedly reliable banks. Mail drafts will take at least two weeks and often longer. Some banks delay releasing transferred money because they earn interest on hard currency deposits.

Some countries will let you have your money in US dollars, while others will only release it in local currency. Be certain before you arrange the transfer; otherwise, you could lose a fair amount of money if there's a major gap between official and unofficial exchange rates. Bolivia, Ecuador, Chile and Uruguay will let you have all your money in dollars, but regulations change frequently, so ask for the latest information.

If you find yourself penniless, you'll have to find a job or go to your nearest embassy for repatriation. If you are repatriated, many embassies will confiscate your passport and hold it until you repay the debt – and they'll fly you back in full-fare tourist class. French embassies don't usually repatriate their citizens and US embassies rarely do so.

Currency Exchange

The unofficial exchange rate for the US dollar can be much higher than the bank rate, because official rates do not always reflect the market value of local currency. Official rates may be artificially high for political reasons, or may not be adjusted sufficiently for inflation, which sometimes reaches 50% per month.

The unofficial rate is often known as the *mercado negro* (black market) or *mercado paralelo* (parallel market). In some countries, including Brazil, you can obtain the current street rate at cambios or travel agencies. In other countries, you can change money at hotels or in shops which sell imported goods (electronics dealers are an obvious choice). Official exchange rates are increasingly realistic in most South American countries, so the role of the black market is declining.

If you change money on the street, observe a few precautions. Be discreet, as it's often illegal, though it may be tolerated. Have the exact amount handy, to avoid pulling out large wads of notes. Beware of sleight-of-hand tricks: insist on personally counting out the notes you are handed one by one, and don't hand over your dollars until satisfied you have the exact amount agreed upon. One common trick is to hand you the agreed amount, less a few pesos, so that, on counting it, you will complain that it's short. They take it back, recount it, discover the 'mistake', top it up and hand it back, in the process spiriting away all but one of the largest bills. For certainty, recount it yourself and don't be distracted by supposed alarms like 'police' or 'danger'.

In recent years, inflation in most of the region has subsided from previously astronomical levels, but prices can still be unpredictable. A currency devaluation means that local prices drop in relation to hard currencies like the US dollar, but normally local prices soon rise, so dollar costs soon return to previous levels (or higher). These factors make it difficult to quote prices in local currencies, but one thing is certain: if a hotel or restaurant was cheap before price increases, it's still going to be cheap afterwards relative to other hotels and restaurants. Prices tend to be more stable in terms of US dollars, so prices have been quoted in dollars throughout most of this book.

Bargaining

Probably the only things you'll have to haggle over are long-term accommodation and purchases from markets, especially craft goods whose prices are normally very negotiable. Haggling is the norm in the Andean countries, but in the Southern Cone, it's much less common. Patience, humour and an ability to speak the local language will make the process more enjoyable and productive.

USEFUL ORGANISATIONS
South American Explorers Club

This very informative, nonprofit organisa-

tion has offices in Lima (Peru) and Quito (Ecuador); for addresses, see the entries for those cities. There were plans to open an office in La Paz, Bolivia, but it hasn't happened yet. Check with the club about this. There is also a US office (☎ (607) 277-0488) at 126 Indian Creek Rd, Ithaca, NY 14850. This is where their magazine is published; if you're interested in joining, send US$4 for a sample copy and further information.

The SAEC was founded in 1977 and functions as an information centre for travellers, adventurers, scientific expeditions etc. The club's Lima office has an extensive library of books, maps and trip reports left by other travellers. Many maps and books are for sale. Useful current advice can be obtained about travel conditions, currency regulations, weather conditions and so on.

The club is an entirely member-supported, nonprofit organisation. Membership costs US$40 per individual per year (US$60 for a couple) and includes four quarterly issues of the excellent and informative *South American Explorer* magazine. In addition, members receive full use of club facilities, which include: an information service and library; introductions to other travellers and notification of expedition opportunities; storage of excess luggage (anything ranging from small valuables to a kayak); storage or forwarding of mail addressed to you at the club; a relaxing place in which to read and research, or just to have a cup of tea and a chat with the friendly staff; a book exchange; buying and selling of used equipment; discounts on the books, maps and gear sold at the club; and hotel reservations, flight confirmations and other services. Nonmembers are welcome to visit the club but are asked to limit their visit to about half an hour, and they are not eligible for membership privileges until they cough up their US$40. Paid-up members can hang out all day – a welcome relief from the madhouse bustle of a large city like Lima. The club is highly recommended.

Environmental Organisations

See the Argentina, Bolivia, Chile, Paraguay, Peru and Falkland Islands chapters for local organisations promoting environmental preservation, or contact any of the following groups;

Australia
    Friends of the Earth, 312 Smith St, Collingwood, PO Box 222, Fitzroy, Vic 3065 (☎ (03) 9419-8700)

Greenpeace Australia Ltd, 1st floor, 1 Lygon St, Carlton, Vic 3053 (☎ (03) 9662-9899)

UK

Friends of the Earth, 26/28 Underwood St, London N17JU

Survival International, 11-15 Emerald St, London WC1N 3QL (☎ (0171) 242-1441)

WWF, Panda House, Weyside Park, Godalming, Surrey GU7 1BP

USA

The Rainforest Action Network (RAN), 301 Broadway, Suite A, San Francisco, CA 94133 (☎ (415) 398-4404)

Conservation International, 1015 18th St, NW, Suite 1000, Washington, DC 20036 (☎ (202) 429-5660)

Cultural Survival, 215 First St, Cambridge, MA 02142 (☎ (617) 621-3818)

The Nature Conservancy, 1815 N Lynn St, Arlington, VA 22209 (☎ (703) 841-5300)

The Chico Mendes Fund, Environmental Defense Fund, 257 Park Ave South, New York, NY 10010

Rainforest Alliance, 270 Lafayette St, Suite 512, New York, NY 10012

The Rainforest Foundation Inc, 1776 Broadway, 14th floor, New York, NY 10019

POST & COMMUNICATIONS
Sending Mail

The quality of postal service varies between countries. Generally, important mail and parcels should be sent by registered or certified service. Sending parcels can be awkward, as often a customs officer must inspect the contents before a postal clerk can accept them. In Peru and Bolivia, the parcel must also finally be stitched up in linen before the clerk can accept it. The place for posting overseas parcels is sometimes different from the main post office. UPS or other private services are available in some countries, and provide an efficient but expensive alternative.

Receiving Mail

The simplest way of receiving mail is to have letters sent to you c/- Lista de Correos, followed by the name of the city and country where you plan to be. Mail addressed in this way will always be sent to that city's main post office. In most places, the service is free, or has a small fee. In Argentina, it's very expensive; try to use a hotel or private

address if possible. Most post offices hold mail for a month or two, then return it to the country of origin or destroy it.

American Express operates a mail service for clients, including those who use American Express travellers' cheques. Some embassies will hold mail for their citizens, among them Australia, Canada, Germany, Israel and Switzerland. British and US embassies are very poor in this regard; letters addressed to a British embassy will be sent to the main post office.

To collect mail from a post office, American Express office or embassy, you need to produce identification, preferably a passport. If expected correspondence does not arrive, ask the clerk to check under every possible combination of your initials, even 'M' (for Mr, Ms etc). There may be particular confusion if correspondents use your middle name, since Spanish Americans use both paternal and maternal surnames for identification, with the former listed first. Thus a letter to Augusto Pinochet Ugarte will be filed under 'P' rather than 'U', which is fine for a Chilean, whereas a letter to George Bernard Shaw may be found under 'B' even though 'Shaw' is the surname. Note that in Brazil the maternal surname is listed first.

Local Addresses

Many South American addresses in this book contain a post-office box number as well as a street address. A post-office box is known as an *apartado* (abbreviated to Ap or Apto) or a *casilla de correos* (Casilla, CC).

Telephone

Traditionally, governments have operated national and international communications systems and, traditionally, services have been wretched. Several countries have recently privatised their phone systems, choosing high charges over poor service, and sometimes getting both.

Direct overseas lines, accessed via special numbers and billed to an account at home, have made international calls much simpler. There are different access numbers for each telephone company in each country – get a list from your phone company before you leave home.

It is sometimes cheaper to make a reverse-charge (collect) or credit-card call to Europe or North America than to pay for the call at the source. For more detail, see individual country chapters.

E-mail

Connection to the Internet is available in some countries, including Brazil and Argentina. The shortcomings of the telephone system have limited development in other countries. As phone systems improve, expect more public access points. Contact your server before you leave home, and ask for any suggestions about accessing 'the net' from South America.

Fax & Telegraph

Offices providing these services are sometimes private, sometimes state-run. For more detail, see individual country chapters.

BOOKS

Many very fine books are readily available in general-interest bookshops or, in the case of specialised items, in university libraries.

Most books are published in different editions by different publishers in different countries. As a result, a book might be a hardcover rarity in one country while it's readily available in paperback in another. Fortunately, bookshops and libraries search by title or author, so your local bookshop or library is best placed to advise you on the availability of the following recommendations and those that appear in individual country chapters.

Lonely Planet Guides

It's impossible to cover every detail of travel in South America in this book, so if you need greater detail on specific places, you may want to supplement it with other books.

Lonely Planet produces regularly updated travel survival kits for individual South American countries, with a wealth of information, numerous maps, illustrations and colour photos. Titles to look for are:

Argentina, Uruguay & Paraguay, 2nd edition, by Wayne Bernhardson
Bolivia, 3rd edition, by Deanna Swaney & Robert Strauss
Brazil, 3rd edition, by Andrew Draffen et al
Chile & Easter Island, 4th edition, by Wayne Bernhardson
Colombia, 2nd edition, by Krzysztof Dydyński
Ecuador & the Galápagos Islands, 4th edition, by Rob Rachowiecki
Peru, 3rd edition, by Rob Rachowiecki
Venezuela, 1st edition, by Krzysztof Dydynski

For even more detailed information, there are city guides for:

Buenos Aires, 1st edition, by Wayne Bernhardson
Rio de Janeiro, 1st edition, by Andrew Draffen

Also useful are several phrasebooks:

Brazilian phrasebook, 2nd edition, by Mark Balla
Latin American Spanish phrasebook, 2nd edition, by Anna Cody
Quechua phrasebook, 1st edition, by Ronald Wright

For detailed trekking info, look for Lonely Planet's *Trekking in the Patagonian Andes*, by Clem Lindenmayer. If you're planning to visit Central as well as South America, get a copy of Lonely Planet's *Central America on a Shoestring*, 2nd edition, by Nancy Keller, Tom Brosnahan, Rob Rachowiecki et al, which covers the region from Belize to Panama.

Other Guidebooks

Lynn Meisch's *A Traveller's Guide to El Dorado & the Inca Empire* has an excellent coverage of Andean crafts, especially weaving (a subject which takes up nearly half the book), but it's thin on practical details.

For general advice read *The Tropical Traveller* by John Hatt. This is an excellent compilation of information on all aspects of travel in the tropics and is entertainingly written.

William Leitch's beautifully written *South America's National Parks* is essential background for trekkers, superb on environment and natural history but weaker on practical matters. Bradt Publications also produces guides for trekking in the mountains and off-the-beaten-track excursions. Some of them may be hard to find, but the series includes the following:

Climbing & Hiking in Ecuador, by Rob Rachowiecki & Betsy Wagenhauser

No Frills Guide to Venezuela, by Hilary Dunsterville Branch

Backpacking and Trekking in Peru & Bolivia, by Hilary Bradt

Backpacking in Chile & Argentina, edited by Clare Hargreaves

Backcountry Brazil, by Alex Bradbury

South American River Trips, by Tanis & Martin Jordan

Another useful title is *Trails of the Cordilleras Blanca & Huayhuash of Peru*, by Jim Bartle, which contains excellent trail descriptions with maps and colour photographs, but may be out of print.

For information about skiing and surfing in South America, see the publications listed in the Activities section above.

Travel

US writer Peter Matthiessen describes a journey from the rivers of Peru to the mountains of Tierra del Fuego in *The Cloud Forest*; his experiences led to his novel *At Play in the Fields of the Lord* (see below). Alex Shoumatoff's *In Southern Light* explores first-hand some of the fantastic legends of the Amazon. Chilean writer Luis Sepúlveda's gripping personal odyssey takes him to different parts of the continent, and beyond, in *Full Circle: a South American journey*, translated into English for Journeys, Lonely Planet's new travel literature series.

Many readers may feel ambivalent about anyone who drives from Tierra del Fuego to the North Slope of Alaska in 23½ days (verified in *The Guinness Book of Records*), but Tim Cahill's hilarious encounters with customs officials and other bureaucrats alone make *Road Fever* worth reading. Eric Lawlor's *In Bolivia* moves at a slower pace, but with equally good humour and a greater appreciation of Andean culture. *Driving to*

Heaven, by Derek Stansfield, describes a 10-month campervan trip in South and Central America; order from the author at Ropley, Broad Oak, Sturminster Newton, Dorset, UK.

Jonathan Hewat, who drove a Volkswagen Kombi around the world, wrote a book called *Overland and Beyond*, which is worthwhile for anyone contemplating such a trip.

Flora & Fauna Guides

Neotropical Rainforest Mammals: A Field Guide, by Louise Emmons & François Feer, provides colour illustrations for identification. Birders in the Amazon region might try *South American Birds: A Photographic Aid to Identification*, by John S Dunning; *A Guide to the Birds of Colombia*, by Stephen L Hilty & William L Brown; or *A Guide to the Birds of Venezuela*, by Rodolphe Meyer de Schauensee & William Phelps.

More inclusive is Meyer de Schauensee's *A Guide to the Birds of South America*.

Piet van Ipenburg & Rob Boschhuizen's *Ecology of Tropical Rainforests: An introduction for Eco-tourists* is a booklet packed with intriguing minutiae about sloths, bats, strangler figs and other rainforest biota. It's available in the UK from J Forrest, 64 Belsize Park, London NW3 4EH, or in the USA from M Doolittle, 32 Amy Rd, Falls Village, CT 06031; all proceeds go to the Tambopata Reserve Society, which is funding research in the south-eastern Peruvian rainforests.

Prehistory & the Incas

One key book on early South America is Edward P Lanning's *Peru Before the Incas*, but for an innovative approach to Amazonian prehistory, see Donald Lathrap's *The Upper Amazon*, which argues for the tropical lowlands as a hearth of South American cultural development.

Several indigenous and Spanish chroniclers left accounts of their times. Garcilaso de la Vega, son of an Inca princess, wrote *Royal Commentaries of the Incas*, available in many editions, but much criticised for exaggerations and misrepresentations of detail. Father Bernabé Cobo's 17th-century *History of the Inca Empire* draws on Garcilaso but also includes much original material from his own observations. Huamán Poma de Ayala's 17th-century *Letter to a King* is an eloquent letter of protest against Spanish abuses of indigenous peoples.

Conquest of the Incas, by John Hemming, is a fine interpretation of the clash between he Spaniards and the lords of Cuzco.

European Invasion & the Colonial Era

Carl O Sauer's *The Early Spanish Main* portrays Columbus as an audacious bumbler whose greed coloured his every perception of the New World. On the achievements of other early European explorers, see JH Parry's *The Discovery of South America*. To learn who the conquistadors really were, read James Lockhart's fascinating *The Men of Cajamarca*, a series of biographical studies of the first Europeans in Peru, from Pizarro to his lowliest soldier.

James Lockhart & Stuart Schwartz's *Early Latin America* makes an unusual but persuasive argument that the structures of indigenous societies were more important than Spanish domination in the cultural transitions of the colonial period. Magnus Mörner's *The Andean Past: Land, Societies and Conflicts* deals with the struggles of the Quechua and Aymara peoples in a cultural and ecological context. Charles Gibson's standard *Spain in America* focuses on the institutions of Spanish rule.

Alfred Crosby's *Ecological Imperialism: the Biological Expansion of Europe, 900-1900* chronicles the environmental transformation of southern South America under colonial rule. His earlier book *The Columbian Exchange* details the microbial invasion which changed South American demography, and evaluates the impact of European plants and animals in the Americas, and American plants and animals in Europe and worldwide.

For a regional approach to the demographic collapse, see William Denevan's edited collection *The Native Population of the Americas in 1492*.

Independence & the Republican Era

For the South American wars of independence, a standard work is John Lynch's *The Spanish-American Revolutions 1808-1826*. For an overview of social problems in Latin America, see Eric Wolf & Edward Hansen's *The Human Condition in Latin America*. For other titles, see individual country chapters.

Amazonia

A classic 19th-century account is Henry Walter Bates's *The Naturalist on the River Amazon*. Roughly contemporaneous is AR Wallace's *Travels on the Amazon and Rio Negro*. Anthony Smith's *Explorers of the Amazon* is a series of essays on explorers of various kinds, from conquerors to scientists to plant collectors to rubber barons.

Despite shortcomings, Betty J Meggers' *Amazonia: Man and Culture in a Counterfeit Paradise* is essential reading for its description of traditional rainforest cultures and the environment. Perhaps the best overall account of the plight of the global rainforests is journalist Catherine Caufield's *In the Rainforest*, which contains substantial material on Amazonia but also covers other imperilled areas. More recent is *The Fate of the Forest: Developers, Destroyers, and Defenders of the Amazon*, Susanna Hecht & Alexander Cockburn.

On the situation of indigenous peoples, see Shelton Davis' *Victims of the Miracle: Development and the Indians of Brazil*. Julie Sloan Denslow & Christine Padoch's *People of the Tropical Rainforest* is an edited and well-illustrated collection of articles on tropical ecology and development, which deals with rainforest immigrants as well as indigenous peoples. For an assessment of the impact of mining, see David Cleary's *Anatomy of the Amazon Gold Rush*.

Fiction

Mathiessen's *At Play in the Fields of the Lord*, set in Peru's Amazon rainforests, is a tale of conflict between the forces of 'development' and indigenous peoples. Another superb novel on similar themes is Raymond Sokolov's *Native Intelligence*.

Nobel Prize winner Gabriel García Márquez has been the leader of Latin America's fiction boom; his *One Hundred Years of Solitude* is perhaps South America's most famous fictional work. Another major writer is Peru's Mario Vargas Llosa, whose *The Real Life of Alejandro Mayta* offers insights into his country's current political dilemmas; also try *Aunt Julia and the Scriptwriter*.

Many books by the late Brazilian novelist Jorge Amado, most notably *Dona Flor and Her Two Husbands* and *Gabriela, Clove and Cinnamon*, are easy to find in English. Contemporary satirist Márcio Souza has written *Emperor of the Amazon* and *Mad Maria*, both of which deal with attempts to conquer the rainforest.

General History

George Pendle's *A History Of Latin America* is a readable but very general account of the region since the European invasions.

Eduardo Galeano's *Open Veins of Latin America: Five Centuries of the Pillage of a Continent* is an eloquent polemic on the continent's cultural, social and political struggles from a leftist perspective by a famous Uruguayan writer. The *Memories of Fire* trilogy, by the same author, is wonderfully readable and well recommended. John A Crow's *The Epic of Latin America*, 3rd edition, is an imposing but readable volume which covers nearly the whole of the region from Mexico to Tierra del Fuego, from prehistory to the present.

Periodicals

The best regular source of South American news is the *Miami Herald*, which publishes an overseas edition available in capital cities, and a few other centres, throughout South America. The *Economist* also has good coverage of the region.

The *Latin American Weekly Report* has about a dozen pages of the latest news from Latin America and the Caribbean. It's available by airmail subscription from Latin

American Newsletters (☎ (0171) 251-0012, fax 253-8193), 61 Old St, London EC1V 9HX, UK. They also publish a range of more specialised newsletters on specific parts of the region.

For up-to-date information on safety, political and economic conditions, health risks, costs etc, for all Latin American countries, see the *Latin American Travel Advisor*, an impartial 16-page quarterly newsletter published in Ecuador. Current issues cost US$15, back issues are US$7.50, any four issues cost US$39. They're sent by airmail from LATA, PO Box 17-17-908, Quito, Ecuador (fax (593-2) 562-566, e-mail lata@pi.pro.ec).

MAPS

ITM (International Travel Map) Productions distributes an excellent, informative three-sheet map of the continent, at a scale of 1:4,000,000. ITM is at Box 2290, Vancouver, BC, V6B 3W5, Canada. In Europe, ITM maps are distributed by Bradt Publications, 41 Nortoft Road, Chalfont St Peter, Bucks, England SL9 0LA. The maps might be a bit big for field use, but are helpful for planning a trip. They are the work of the late Kevin Healey, who was an independent Melbourne cartographer.

Bartholomew's *America, South* is a reasonable alternative, despite lack of detail and occasional inaccuracies.

FILM & PHOTOGRAPHY

The latest in consumer electronics is available throughout South America, but import duties make cameras and film very expensive, up to three times their cost in North America or Western Europe. Developing is also expensive. Bring as much film as you can; you can always sell anything you don't need to other travellers. Locally manufactured film is reasonably good, but no cheaper than imported.

A good range of film, including B&W and slide film, can now be purchased at reasonable prices in many parts of Bolivia, in Asunción (Paraguay), and in the duty-free zones at Iquique and Punta Arenas (Chile).

Paraguay's and Chile's free zones have camera equipment at prices only slightly higher than in North America, even if the selection is not so great. In Brazil, Salvador and Manaus are good places to stock up on film and equipment.

In tropical conditions some photographers prefer Fujichrome, which renders greens exceptionally well and is readily available in the cities mentioned above. Kodachrome, which is better at portraying reds and nearby colours of the spectrum, is often more suitable for deserts and urban areas, but is only available at relatively slow speeds, up to ISO (ASA) 200. It is almost impossible to get Kodachrome processed in South America. E6 processing for other types of slide film is available in larger centres, but the quality may be unreliable. Have one roll processed and check the results before you hand over your whole collection. Most professionals take their film home for processing.

For the low light conditions of the Amazonian rainforests, it's a good idea to carry a few rolls of high-speed (ISO 400) film, and a flash.

Always protect camera lenses with an ultraviolet (UV) filter. In high-altitude tropical light conditions in the Andes, the UV filter may not be sufficient to prevent washed-out photos; a polarising filter can correct this problem.

Photographic Etiquette

Ask for permission before photographing individuals, particularly indigenous people. If someone is giving a public performance (such as a street musician or a dancer at Carnaval), or is incidental to a photograph (in a broad cityscape, for example), this is not usually necessary – but if in doubt, ask or refrain.

HEALTH

Travel health depends on your predeparture preparations, your day-to-day health care and how you handle any medical problem or emergency that does develop. The list of dangers may look frightening, but with a little luck, some basic precautions and adequate information few travellers experience more than an upset stomach.

Travel Health Guides

There are a number of books on travel health:

Staying Healthy in Asia, Africa & Latin America, Dirk Schroeder; probably the best all-round guide to carry, as it's compact but very detailed and well organised

Travellers' Health, Dr Richard Dawood; comprehensive, easy to read, authoritative and also highly recommended, although it's rather large to lug around

Where There is No Doctor, David Werner; a very detailed guide intended for someone, like a Peace Corps worker, going to work in an underdeveloped country, rather than for the average traveller

Travel with Children, Maureen Wheeler; includes basic advice on travel health for younger children.

Predeparture Planning

Health Insurance A travel insurance policy to cover theft, loss and medical problems is a good idea. There is a wide variety of policies available and your travel agent will be able to make recommendations. The policies handled by STA Travel and other student travel organisations are usually good value. Some policies offer lower and higher medical-expense options but the higher ones are chiefly for countries such as the USA which have extremely high medical costs. Check the small print:

- Some policies specifically exclude 'dangerous activities' which can include scuba diving, motorcycling, even trekking. If such activities are on your agenda you don't want this sort of policy.
- You may prefer a policy which pays doctors or hospitals direct rather than you having to pay on the spot and claim later. If you have to claim later make sure you keep all documentation. Some policies ask you to call back (reverse charges) to a centre in your home country where an immediate assessment of your problem is made.
- Check that the policy covers ambulances or an emergency flight home. If you have to stretch out you will need two seats and somebody has to pay for them!

Medical Kit It's wise to carry a small, straightforward medical kit. The kit should include:

- Aspirin or paracetamol (acetaminophen in the USA) – for pain or fever
- Antihistamine (such as Benadryl) – useful as a decongestant for colds and allergies, to ease the itch from insect bites or stings, and to help prevent motion sickness. There are several on the market – discuss your requirements with a pharmacist or doctor. Antihistamines may cause sedation and interact with alcohol so care should be taken when using them.
- Antibiotics – useful if you're travelling well off the beaten track, but they must be prescribed and you should carry the prescription with you. If you are allergic to commonly prescribed antibiotics such as penicillin or sulpha drugs, carry this information when travelling.
- Loperamide (eg Imodium) or Lomotil for diarrhoea; prochlorperazine (eg Stemetil) or metaclopramide (eg Maxalon) for nausea and vomiting. Antidiarrhoea medication should not be given to children under the age of 12.
- Rehydration mixture – for treatment of severe diarrhoea. This is particularly important if travelling with children, but is recommended for everyone.
- Antiseptic such as povidone-iodine (eg Betadine), which comes as a solution, ointment, powder and impregnated swabs – for cuts and grazes
- Calamine lotion or Stingose spray – to ease irritation from bites or stings
- Bandages and Band-aids – for minor injuries
- Scissors, tweezers and a thermometer (note that airlines prohibit mercury thermometers)
- Cold and flu tablets and throat lozenges
- Insect repellent, sunscreen, chap stick and water purification tablets
- A couple of syringes, in case you need injections in a country with medical hygiene problems. Ask your doctor for a note explaining why they have been prescribed.

Antibiotics should ideally be administered only under medical supervision and should never be taken indiscriminately. Take only the recommended dose at the prescribed intervals and continue using the antibiotic for the prescribed period, even if the illness seems to be cured earlier. Antibiotics are quite specific to the infections they can treat. Stop immediately if there are any serious reactions and don't use the antibiotic at all if you are unsure that you have the correct one.

In many countries, if a medicine is available at all it will generally be available cheaply over the counter. Be careful when buying drugs – the expiry date may have passed or correct storage conditions may not have been followed. Bogus drugs are common and it's possible that drugs which are no longer recommended elsewhere are still being dispensed in parts of South America.

In very poor areas, you might donate any unwanted medicines, syringes etc to a local clinic, rather than carry them home.

Health Preparations Make sure you're healthy before you start travelling. Make sure your teeth are OK; there are lots of places where a visit to the dentist would be the last thing you'd want.

If you wear glasses take a spare pair and your prescription. In most of South America you can get new spectacles made up quickly and competently.

If you require a particular medication take an adequate supply, as it may not be available locally. Take the prescription, and part of the packaging showing the generic name. The drug may be sold locally under a different brand name.

Immunisations Vaccinations provide protection against diseases you might meet along the way. In the Southern Cone countries, no immunisations are necessary, but in tropical and Andean regions it is necessary to take precautions.

International health regulations have been dramatically reduced over the last 10 years, but it is still a requirement to have a yellow fever vaccination if you're coming from an infected area, and most of tropical South America is officially infected. Other vaccinations are recommended for travel in South America for your own protection, even though not required by law. All vaccinations should be recorded on an International Health Certificate, which is available from your physician or government health department.

Plan ahead for getting your vaccinations: some of them require an initial shot followed by a booster, while some vaccinations should not be given together. Seek medical advice at least six weeks prior to travel.

Most travellers will have been immunised against various diseases during childhood but your doctor may recommend booster shots against polio. The period of protection offered by vaccinations differs widely and some are contraindicated if you are pregnant. Vaccinations usually recommended for South America include:

Yellow Fever Protection lasts 10 years and is recommended for all of tropical South America (see map). You may have to go to a special yellow-fever vaccination centre. Vaccination is contraindicated during pregnancy but if you must travel to a high-risk area it is probably advisable.

Tetanus & Diphtheria Initial immunisation requires two shots, six weeks apart. Boosters are necessary every 10 years. Protection is highly recommended.

Poliomyelitis A booster of either the oral or injected vaccine is required every 10 years to maintain immunity. More frequent boosters may be needed in tropical areas. Polio is a very serious, easily transmitted disease which still occurs in South America.

Typhoid Available as either an injection or oral capsules. Protection lasts from one to five years depending on the vaccine and is useful if you are travelling for long periods in rural, tropical areas. You may get some side effects such as pain at the injection site, fever, headache and a general unwell feeling. A new single-dose injectable vaccine, which appears to have few side effects, is now available but is more expensive. With the oral form, side effects are unusual; occasionally stomach cramps occur.

Hepatitis A This disease is endemic in South America, but can be prevented by either gamma globulin antibody or with a new vaccine called Havrix. Havrix provides long-term immunity (possibly more than 10 years) after an initial course of three injections over nine months. It is more expensive than gamma globulin but provides longer protection. It will take at least three weeks to provide satisfactory protection, so get it well before you travel. Gamma globulin is not a vaccine but a ready-made antibody which reduces the chances of hepatitis infection. It should be given as close

as possible to departure because it is most effective in the first few weeks after administration, after which its effectiveness tapers off over three to six months.

Hepatitis B Travellers at risk of contact (see the Infectious Diseases section) are strongly advised to be vaccinated, especially if they are children or will have close contact with children. The vaccination course comprises three injections given over a six-month period, then boosters every five to five years. The initial course of injections can be given over as short a period as 28 days, then boosted after 12 months, if more rapid protection is required.

Cholera Cholera outbreaks have occurred recently in South America (see map). It's most likely in the presence of unsanitary conditions, and is usually transmitted by water. Vaccination gives poor protection, lasts only six months, and is contraindicated in pregnancy. Cholera vaccination is not required by international law, but still seems to be required at some South American border crossings.

Meninogococcal Meningitis Vaccination may be advisable if you plan to travel rough in the Amazon region. A single injection will give good protection against the A, C, W and Y groups of the bacteria for at least a year. The vaccine is not, however, recommended for children under 2 years because they do not develop satisfactory immunity from it.

Rabies Prophylactic rabies vaccination involves having three injections over 21 to 28 days and should be considered by those who will spend a month or longer in South America, especially if they are cycling, handling animals, caving, or travelling to remote areas. Children may not report a bite, and are therefore at greater risk than adults. If someone who has been vaccinated is bitten or scratched by an animal they will require two booster injections of vaccine.

Tuberculosis TB risk should be considered for people travelling more than three months in South America. As most healthy adults do not develop symptoms a skin test before and after travel to determine whether exposure has occurred is recommended. Vaccination for children who will be travelling for more than three months is recommended.

Smallpox Smallpox has now been wiped out worldwide, so immunisation is no longer necessary.

Basic Rules

Care in what you eat and drink is the most important health rule; stomach upsets are the most likely travel health problem (between 30% and 50% of travellers in a two-week stay experience this) but the majority of these

Yellow Fever Areas

Cholera Areas

upsets will be relatively minor. Don't become paranoid; trying the local food is part of the experience of travel.

Water The number-one rule is *don't drink the water*, and that includes ice. If you don't know for certain that the water is safe, always assume the worst. Reputable brands of bottled water or soft drinks are generally fine, although in some places bottles refilled with tap water are not unknown. Take care with fresh fruit juice, particularly if water may have been added. Milk should be treated with suspicion, as it is often unpasteurised. Boiled milk is fine if it is kept hygienically. Tea or coffee should also be OK, since the water should have been boiled.

Water Purification The simplest way of purifying water is to boil it thoroughly for five minutes. At high altitude water boils at a lower temperature, so germs are less likely to be killed.

Simple filtering will not remove all dangerous organisms, so if you cannot boil water it should be treated chemically. Chlorine tablets (Puritabs, Steritabs or other brand names) will kill many but not all pathogens; they won't kill *Giardia* or amoebic cysts. Iodine is very effective in purifying water and is available in tablet form (such as Potable Aqua), but follow the directions carefully and remember that too much iodine can be harmful.

Tincture of iodine (2%) or iodine crystals can also be used. Add four drops of tincture of iodine per litre or quart of clear water, and leave it to stand for 20 to 30 minutes before drinking. Flavoured powder will disguise the taste of treated water and is a good idea if you are travelling with children.

Micropur water filters remove parasites, bacteria and viruses, and, although expensive, over a long trip they may be cheaper than buying water.

Food If you can cook it, boil it or peel it you can eat it; otherwise forget it. Salads and fruit should be washed with purified water or peeled where possible. Ice cream is usually OK if it is a reputable brand name, but beware of street vendors and of ice cream that has melted and been refrozen. Thoroughly cooked food is safest, but not if it has been left to cool or if it has been reheated. Shellfish such as mussels, oysters and clams should be avoided as well as undercooked meat, particularly in the form of mince. Steaming does not make shellfish safe for eating.

If a place looks clean and well run and if the vendor also looks clean and healthy, then the food is probably safe. In general, places that are packed with travellers or locals will be fine, while empty restaurants are questionable. The food in busy restaurants is cooked and eaten quite quickly with little standing around and is probably not reheated.

Nutrition If your food is poor or limited in availability, if you're travelling hard and fast and therefore missing meals, or if you simply lose your appetite, you can soon start to lose weight and place your health at risk.

Make sure your diet is well balanced. Eggs, beans, and nuts are all safe ways to get protein. Fruit you can peel (bananas, oranges or mandarins, for example) is usually safe (melons can harbour bacteria in their flesh and are best avoided) and a good source of vitamins. Try to eat plenty of grains (including rice) and bread. Food is generally safer if it is cooked well, but overcooked food loses much of its nutritional value. If your diet isn't well balanced or if your food intake is insufficient, it's a good idea to take vitamin and iron pills.

In hot climates make sure you drink enough: don't rely on feeling thirsty to indicate when you should drink. Not needing to urinate or very dark yellow urine is a danger sign. Always carry a water bottle with you on long trips. Excessive sweating can lead to loss of salt and therefore muscle cramping. Salt tablets are not a good idea as a preventative, but in places where little salt is used, adding it to food can help.

Everyday Health Normal body temperature is 37°C or 98.6°F; more than 2°C (4°F) higher indicates a high fever. The normal adult pulse rate is 60 to 100 per minute (children 80 to 100, babies 100 to 140). You should know how to take a temperature and a pulse rate. As a general rule the pulse increases about 20 beats per minute for each °C (2°F) rise in fever.

Respiration (breathing) rate is also an indicator of illness. Count the number of breaths per minute: between 12 and 20 is normal for adults and older children (up to 30 for younger children, 40 for babies). People with a high fever or serious respiratory illness (like pneumonia) breathe more quickly than normal. More than 40 shallow breaths a minute may indicate pneumonia.

Personal Care Wash your hands before a meal and after using the toilet. Clean your teeth with purified water rather than straight from the tap. Avoid climatic extremes: keep out of the sun when it's hot; dress warmly when it's cold.

You can get worm infections through walking barefoot, or dangerous coral cuts by walking over coral without shoes. Avoid insect bites by covering bare skin when insects are around, by screening windows or beds and by using insect repellents. Seek local advice: if you're told the water is unsafe due to jellyfish, crocodiles or bilharzia, don't go in. In situations where there is no information, discretion is the better part of valour.

Medical Problems & Treatment

Potential medical problems can be broken down into several areas. Firstly there are the problems caused by extremes of temperature, altitude or motion. Then there are diseases and illnesses caused through poor environmental sanitation, insect bites or stings, and animal or human contact. Finally, there are simple cuts, bites and scratches, which can also cause problems.

Self-diagnosis and treatment can be risky, so wherever possible seek qualified help. Although we do give drug dosages in this section, they are for emergency use only.

Medical advice should be sought where possible before administering any drugs.

An embassy or consulate can usually recommend a good place to go for such advice. So can five-star hotels, although they often recommend doctors with five-star prices. (This is when that medical insurance really comes in useful!) In some places standards of medical attention are so low that for some ailments the best advice is to get on a plane and go somewhere else.

Environmental Hazards

Sunburn In the tropics, the desert or at high altitude you can get sunburnt surprisingly quickly, even through cloud. Use a sunscreen and take extra care to cover areas which don't normally see sun – eg your feet. A hat provides added protection, and you should also use zinc cream or some other barrier cream for your nose and lips. Calamine lotion is good for mild sunburn.

Too much sunlight, whether it's direct or reflected (glare), can damage your eyes. If your plans include being near water, sand or snow, then good sunglasses are doubly important. Good quality sunglasses are treated to filter out ultraviolet radiation. However, poor quality lenses cause pupil dilation, thereby adsorbing more ultraviolet light than they would if no sunglasses were worn. Excessive ultraviolet light will damage the surface structures and lens of the eye.

Prickly Heat Prickly heat is an itchy rash caused by excessive perspiration trapped under the skin. It usually strikes people who have just arrived in a hot climate and whose pores have not yet opened sufficiently to cope with greater sweating. Keeping cool but bathing often, using a mild talcum powder or even resorting to air-conditioning may help until you acclimatise.

Heat Exhaustion Dehydration or salt deficiency can cause heat exhaustion. Take time to acclimatise to high temperatures and make sure you get sufficient liquids. Wear loose

clothing and a broad-brimmed hat. Do not do anything too physically demanding.

Salt deficiency is characterised by fatigue, lethargy, headaches, giddiness and muscle cramps and in this case salt tablets may help. Vomiting or diarrhoea can deplete your liquid and salt levels. Anhydrotic heat exhaustion, caused by an inability to sweat, is quite rare. Unlike the other forms of heat exhaustion it is likely to strike people who have been in a hot climate for some time, rather than newcomers.

Heat Stroke This serious, sometimes fatal, condition can occur if the body's mechanism for regulating heat breaks down and the body temperature rises to dangerous levels. Long, continuous periods of exposure to high temperatures can leave you vulnerable to heat stroke. You should avoid excessive alcohol or strenuous activity when you first arrive in a hot climate.

The symptoms are feeling unwell, not sweating very much or at all and a high body temperature (39°C to 41°C). Where sweating has ceased the skin becomes flushed and red. Severe, throbbing headaches and lack of coordination will also occur, and the sufferer may be confused or aggressive. Eventually the victim will become delirious or convulse. Hospitalisation is essential, but meanwhile get victims out of the sun, remove their clothing, cover them with a wet sheet or towel and fan them continuously.

Fungal Infections Fungal infections, which occur with greater frequency in hot weather, are most likely to occur on the scalp, between the toes or fingers (athlete's foot), in the groin (jock itch or crotch rot) and on the body (ringworm). You get ringworm (which is a fungal infection, not a worm) from infected animals or by walking on damp areas, like shower floors.

To prevent fungal infections wear loose, comfortable clothes, avoid artificial fibres, wash frequently and dry carefully. If you do get an infection, wash the infected area daily with a disinfectant or medicated soap and water, and rinse and dry well. Apply an antifungal cream or powder like the widely available Tinaderm. Try to expose the infected area to air or sunlight as much as possible and wash all towels and underwear in hot water as well as changing them often.

Hypothermia Exposure to cold can lead to hypothermia. If you are trekking at high altitudes or simply taking a long bus trip over mountains, particularly at night, be prepared. In the Andes, you should always be prepared for cold, wet or windy conditions, especially if you're out walking or hitching.

Hypothermia occurs when the body loses heat faster than it can produce it, and the core temperature of the body falls. It is surprisingly easy to progress from very cold to dangerously cold due to a combination of wind, wet clothing, fatigue and hunger, even if the air temperature is above freezing. It is best to dress in layers; silk, wool and some of the new artificial fibres are all good insulating materials. A hat is important, as a lot of heat is lost through the head. A strong, waterproof outer layer is essential, as keeping dry is vital. Carry basic supplies, including lots of fluid to drink, and food containing simple sugars to generate heat quickly. A space blanket is a good thing to carry in cold environments.

Symptoms of hypothermia are exhaustion, numb skin (particularly toes and fingers), shivering, slurred speech, irrational or violent behaviour, lethargy, stumbling, dizzy spells, muscle cramps and violent bursts of energy. Irrationality may take the form of sufferers claiming they are warm and trying to take off their clothes.

To treat mild hypothermia, first get the person out of the wind and/or rain, remove their clothing if it's wet and replace it with dry, warm clothing. Give them hot liquids – not alcohol – and some high-kilojoule, easily digestible food. Do not rub victims; instead allow them to slowly warm themselves. This should be enough to treat the early stages of hypothermia. The early recognition and treatment of mild hypothermia is the only way to prevent severe hypothermia, which is a critical condition.

Altitude Sickness Acute Mountain Sickness or AMS can occur at high altitude and can be fatal. It's a common hazard in the Andes and the altiplano region, where AMS is called *apunamiento* or *soroche*. There is no hard-and-fast rule as to how high is too high: AMS has been fatal at altitudes of 3000 metres, although 3500 to 4500 metres is the usual range. The lack of oxygen over about 2500 metres affects most people to some extent. It may be mild (benign AMS) or severe (malignant AMS) and occurs because less oxygen reaches the muscles and the brain at high altitude, requiring the heart and lungs to compensate by working harder. Symptoms usually develop during the first 24 hours at altitude, but may be delayed up to three weeks.

Symptoms of benign AMS include headache, lethargy, dizziness, difficulty sleeping and loss of appetite. Malignant AMS may develop from benign AMS or without warning and can be fatal; symptoms include breathlessness, dry cough (which may progress to the production of pink, frothy sputum), severe headache, lack of coordination and balance, confusion, irrational behaviour, vomiting, drowsiness and unconsciousness.

In benign AMS the treatment is to remain resting at the same altitude until recovery, usually a day or two. Everyday painkillers such as aspirin or paracetamol, or *chachacoma*, a herbal tea made from a common Andean shrub, will relieve symptoms until your body adapts. If symptoms persist or become worse, descent is necessary; even 500 metres can help.

Another excellent remedy for mild symptoms is *mate de coca* (tea made from coca leaves), which you can get in most cafés in Peru and Bolivia. You can also buy leaves legally for US$4 to US$5 per kilo in *tiendas* (small general stores) throughout Peru and Bolivia, or from the herbal stalls found in every market. The practice of chewing coca leaves goes back centuries and is still common among the Indians of the Andean altiplano to dull the pangs of hunger, thirst, cold and fatigue. They chew the leaves with a little ash or bicarbonate of soda, as the alkalinity releases the mild stimulant contained in the leaves.

The treatment of malignant AMS is immediate descent to a lower altitude. There are various drug treatments available but they should never be used to avoid descent or enable further ascent by a person with AMS.

A number of measures can be adopted to prevent acute mountain sickness:

- Ascend slowly. Have frequent rest days, spending two to three nights at each rise of 1000 metres. If you reach a high altitude by trekking, acclimatisation takes place gradually and you are less likely to be affected than if you fly direct.
- The altitude at which you sleep is an important factor. It is always wise to sleep at a lower altitude than the greatest height reached during the day. Also, once above 3000 metres, care should be taken not to increase the sleeping altitude by more than 300 metres per day.
- Drink extra fluids. The mountain air is dry and cold and moisture is lost as you breathe.
- Eat light, high-carbohydrate meals for more energy.
- Avoid alcohol as it may increase the risk of dehydration.
- Avoid sedatives.
- The drugs acetazolamide (Diamox) and dexamethasone have been recommended for prevention of AMS. They can reduce the symptoms, but they also mask warning signs; severe and fatal AMS has occurred in people taking these drugs. In general they are not recommended for travellers.

Motion Sickness Eating lightly before and during a trip will reduce the chances of motion sickness. If you are prone to motion sickness try to find a place that minimises disturbance – near the wing on aircraft, close to midships on boats, near the centre on buses. Fresh air usually helps; reading and cigarette smoke don't. Commercial motion-sickness preparations, which can cause drowsiness, have to be taken before the trip commences; when you're feeling sick it's too late. Ginger (available in capsule form) and peppermint (including mint-flavoured sweets) are natural preventatives.

Jet Lag Jet lag is experienced when a person travels by air across more than three time zones (each time zone usually represents a one-hour time difference). It occurs because many of the functions of the human body (such as temperature, pulse rate and emptying of the bladder and bowels) are regulated by internal 24-hour cycles called circadian rhythms. Bodies take time to adjust to the 'new time' at the end of a flight, and travellers may experience fatigue, disorientation, insomnia, anxiety, impaired concentration and loss of appetite. These effects will usually be gone within three days of arrival, but there are ways of minimising the impact of jet lag:

- Rest for a couple of days prior to departure; try to avoid late nights and last-minute dashes for travellers' cheques, passport etc.
- Try to select flight schedules that minimise sleep deprivation; arriving late in the day means you can go to sleep soon after you arrive. For very long flights, try to organise a stopover.
- Avoid excessive eating (which bloats the stomach) and alcohol (which causes dehydration) during the flight. Instead, drink plenty of non-carbonated, non-alcoholic drinks such as fruit juice or water.
- Avoid smoking, as this reduces the amount of oxygen in the aeroplane cabin even further and causes greater fatigue.
- Make yourself comfortable by wearing loose-fitting clothes and perhaps bringing an eye mask and ear plugs to help you sleep.

Infectious Diseases

Diarrhoea A change of water, food or climate can all cause the runs; diarrhoea caused by contaminated food or water is more serious. Despite all your precautions you may still get a mild bout of travellers' diarrhoea, but a few rushed toilet trips with no other symptoms are not indicative of a serious problem. Moderate diarrhoea, involving half-a-dozen loose movements in a day, is more of a nuisance.

Dehydration is the main danger with any diarrhoea, particularly for children, who can become dehydrated quite quickly. Fluid replacement is the mainstay of treatment. Weak black tea with a little sugar, soda water, or soft drinks allowed to go flat and diluted 50% with water are all good. With severe diarrhoea a rehydrating solution is necessary to replace minerals and salts. Commercially available ORS (oral rehydration salts) are very useful; add the contents of one sachet to a litre of boiled or bottled water. In an emergency you can make up a solution of eight teaspoons of sugar to a litre of boiled water and provide salted cracker biscuits at the same time. Stick to a bland diet as you recover.

Lomotil or Imodium can be used to bring relief from the symptoms, although they do not actually cure the problem. Only use these drugs if absolutely necessary – eg if you *must* travel. For children under 12 years Lomotil and Imodium are not recommended. Under all circumstances fluid replacement is the most important thing to remember. Do not use these drugs if the person has a high fever or is severely dehydrated.

In certain situations antibiotics may be indicated:

- Watery diarrhoea with blood and mucus (gut-paralysing drugs like Imodium or Lomotil should be avoided in this situation)
- Watery diarrhoea with fever and lethargy
- Persistent diarrhoea not improving after 48 hours
- Severe diarrhoea, if it is logistically difficult to stay in one place

The recommended drugs (adults only) would be either norfloxacin 400 mg twice daily for three days or ciprofloxacin 500 mg twice daily for three days.

The drug bismuth subsalicylate has also been used successfully. The dosage for adults is two tablets or 30 ml and for children it is one tablet or 10 ml. This dose can be repeated every 30 minutes to one hour, with no more than eight doses in a 24-hour period.

For children, the best drug would be co-trimoxazole (Bactrim, Septrin, Resprim) with dosage dependent on weight. A five-day course is given.

Ampicillin has been recommended in the past and may still be an alternative.

Giardiasis The parasite causing this intestinal disorder occurs in contaminated water. The symptoms are stomach cramps, nausea, a bloated stomach, watery, foul-smelling diarrhoea and frequent gas. Giardiasis can appear several weeks after exposure to the parasite. The symptoms may disappear for a few days and then return; this can go on for several weeks. Tinidazole, known as Fasigyn, and metronidazole (Flagyl) are the recommended drugs for treatment. Either can be used in a single treatment dose. Antibiotics are of no use.

Dysentery This serious illness is caused by contaminated food or water and is characterised by severe diarrhoea, often with blood or mucus in the stool. There are two kinds of dysentery. Bacillary dysentery is characterised by a high fever and rapid onset; headache, vomiting and stomach pains are also symptoms. It generally does not last longer than a week, but it is highly contagious. Amoebic dysentery is often more gradual in the onset of symptoms, with cramping abdominal pain and vomiting less likely; fever may not be present. It will persist until treated and can recur and cause long-term health problems.

A stool test is necessary to diagnose which kind of dysentery you have, so you should seek medical help urgently. In case of an emergency the drugs norfloxacin or ciprofloxacin can be used as presumptive treatment for bacillary dysentery, and metronidazole (Flagyl) for amoebic dysentery.

For bacillary dysentery, norfloxacin 400 mg twice daily for seven days or ciprofloxacin 500 mg twice daily for seven days are the recommended dosages.

If you're unable to find either of these drugs, then a useful alternative is co-trimoxazole 160/800 mg (Bactrim, Septrin, Resprim) twice daily for seven days. This is a sulpha drug and must not be used by people with a known sulpha allergy. For children, the drug co-trimoxazole is a reasonable first-line treatment.

For amoebic dysentery, the recommended adult dosage of metronidazole (Flagyl) is one 750-mg to 800-mg capsule three times daily for five days. Children aged between eight and 12 years should have half the adult dose; the dosage for younger children is one-third the adult dose. An alternative to Flagyl is Fasigyn, taken as a two-gram daily dose for three days. Alcohol must be avoided during treatment and for 48 hours afterwards.

Cholera Cholera vaccination is not very effective. The bacteria responsible for this disease are waterborne, so attention to the rules of eating and drinking should protect the traveller. Outbreaks of cholera are generally widely reported, so you can avoid problem areas.

The disease is characterised by a sudden onset of acute diarrhoea with 'rice water' stools, vomiting, muscular cramps, and extreme weakness. Medical help is needed, but treat the patient for dehydration, which can be extreme. If there is an appreciable delay in getting to hospital then begin taking tetracycline. The adult dose is 250 mg four times daily. It is not recommended for children under nine years, nor for pregnant women. An alternative drug is Ampicillin. Remember that while antibiotics might kill the bacteria, it is a toxin produced by the bacteria which causes the massive fluid loss. Fluid replacement is by far the most important aspect of treatment.

Viral Gastroenteritis This illness is caused by a virus, and is characterised by stomach cramps, diarrhoea, and sometimes vomiting and/or a slight fever. All you can do is rest and drink lots of fluids.

Hepatitis Hepatitis is a general term for inflammation of the liver. There are many causes of this condition, including infection, drugs or alcohol.

Viral hepatitis is an infection of the liver, which can lead to jaundice (yellow skin), fever, lethargy and digestive problems. It may have no symptoms at all, with the infected person not knowing that they have the disease. The discovery of new strains has

led to a virtual alphabet soup, with hepatitis A, B, C, D, E, G and others. These letters identify specific agents that cause viral hepatitis. Travellers shouldn't be too concerned; hep C, D, E and G are fairly rare (so far), and following the same precautions as for A and B should be all that's necessary to avoid them.

Viral hepatitis can be divided into two groups on the basis of how it is spread. The first route of transmission is via contaminated food and water (leading to hepatitis A and E) and the second route is via blood and bodily fluids (resulting in hepatitis B, C and D).

Hepatitis A This is a very common disease in countries with poor standards of sanitation. Most people in developing countries are infected as children and develop lifelong immunity. Those from developed countries are less likely to have been exposed to hepatitis A, and are therefore at greater risk. The routes of transmission are via contaminated water, shellfish contaminated by sewerage, or foodstuffs sold by food handlers with poor standards of hygiene.

The symptoms are fever, chills, headache, fatigue, feelings of weakness and aches and pains, followed by loss of appetite, nausea, vomiting, abdominal pain, dark urine, light-coloured faeces, jaundiced skin, and the whites of the eyes may turn yellow. In some cases you may feel unwell, tired, have no appetite, experience aches and pains and be jaundiced. You should seek medical advice, but in general there is not much you can do other than rest, drink lots of fluids, eat lightly and avoid fatty foods. People who have had hepatitis must forgo alcohol for six months after the illness, while their liver recovers.

Taking care with what you eat and drink can go a long way towards preventing this disease. It is a very infectious virus, so if there is any risk of exposure, prophylaxis is highly recommended (see above under Immunisations).

Hepatitis E This is a very recently discovered virus, of which little is yet known. It appears to be rather common in developing countries, generally causing mild hepatitis, although it can be very serious in pregnant women. Care with water supplies is the only current prevention, as there are no specific vaccines for this type of hepatitis. At present it doesn't appear to be too great a risk for travellers.

The following strains are spread by contact with blood and bodily fluids:

Hepatitis B This disease, which used to be called serum hepatitis, is very common, with almost 300 million chronic carriers in the world. It is spread through infected blood, blood products or bodily fluids, by sexual contact, unsterilised needles, blood transfusions, or small breaks in the skin. Having tattoos, body piercing, or even a shave in a non-sterile establishment are all potentially risky. The symptoms of type B are much the same as type A, but more severe. Hep B may lead to irreparable liver damage or even liver cancer. Although there is no treatment for hepatitis B, a cheap and effective vaccine is available; for long-lasting cover you need a six-month course. Get hepatitis B vaccination if you anticipate contact with blood or body fluids, either as a health-care worker or through sexual contact with the local population, particularly if you intend to stay in the country for a long period of time.

Hepatitis C This is another recently defined virus which seems to lead to liver disease more rapidly than hepatitis B. The virus is spread by contact with blood, usually via contaminated transfusions or shared needles. Avoiding these is the only means of prevention, as there is no available vaccine.

Typhoid Typhoid fever is a gut infection acquired from contaminated water or food, and vaccination is not totally effective. It is one of the most dangerous infections, so medical help must be sought.

In its early stages typhoid resembles many other illnesses: early symptoms are a headache, a sore throat, and a fever which rises a little each day until it is around 40°C or more. The pulse is often slow relative to the degree of fever present and gets slower as the fever rises, unlike a normal fever where the pulse increases. There may also be vomiting, diarrhoea or constipation. In the second week the high fever and slow pulse continue and a few pink spots may appear on the body; trembling, delirium, weakness, weight loss and dehydration are other symptoms.

If there are no further complications, the fever and other symptoms will slowly diminish during the third week. Get medical help before this because pneumonia (acute infection of the lungs) or peritonitis (perforated bowel) are common complications, and because typhoid is very infectious. The fever should be treated by keeping the victim cool and dehydration should also be watched for.

The drug of choice is ciprofloxacin at a dose of one gram daily for 14 days. It is quite expensive and may not be available. People who are allergic to penicillin should not be given Ampicillin. The alternative, chloramphenicol, has been the mainstay of treatment for many years and it is still recommended in many countries, though it has some side affects. The adult dosage is two 250-mg capsules, four times a day. Children aged between eight and 12 years should have half the adult dose; younger children should have one-third the adult dose.

Worms These parasites are most common in rural, tropical areas. They can be present on unwashed vegetables or in undercooked meat, and can be picked up by walking in bare feet. Infestations may not show up for some time, and although they are generally not serious, they can cause severe health problems if left untreated. A stool test is necessary to pinpoint the problem and medication is often available over the counter. A stool test when you return home is not a bad idea.

Tetanus This potentially fatal disease is found worldwide, most commonly in undeveloped tropical areas. It is difficult to treat but preventable with immunisation. Tetanus occurs when a wound becomes infected by a germ which lives in soil and in the faeces of horses and other animals. Clean all cuts, punctures or animal bites. Tetanus is also known as lockjaw, and the first symptom may be discomfort in swallowing, or stiffening of the jaw and neck; this is followed by painful convulsions of the jaw and whole body.

Rabies Rabies is a fatal viral infection found in many countries and is transmitted by a bite or scratch from an infected animal. Dogs are noted carriers, as are monkeys, cats and bats. Any bite, scratch or even lick from a warm-blooded, furry animal should be cleaned immediately and thoroughly. Scrub with soap and running water, and then clean with an alcohol or iodine solution. If there is any possibility that the animal is infected, medical help should be sought immediately to prevent the onset of symptoms and death. In a person who has not been immunised against rabies this involves having five injections of vaccine and one of immunoglobulin over 28 days starting as soon as possible after the exposure. Even if the animal is not rabid, all bites should be treated seriously as they can become infected or can result in tetanus.

A rabies vaccination is now available and should be considered if you work with animals, intend to explore caves (bat bites can be dangerous), or travel in areas where medical help is more than two days away.

Meningococcal Meningitis This is a bacterial infection of the lining of the brain. It is very serious and can be fatal. There is a risk of meningitis in upper Amazon regions of Brazil, Peru, Ecuador, Colombia and Venezuela, and in Chile. A scattered, blotchy rash, fever, severe headache, sensitivity to light, and neck stiffness which prevents forward bending of the head are the first symptoms. Death can occur within a few hours, so immediate treatment is important.

Treatment is large doses of penicillin given intravenously, or, if that is not possible, intramuscularly (ie in the buttocks). Vaccination offers good protection for over a year.

Check for reports of current epidemics, and avoid those areas.

Tuberculosis (TB) Tuberculosis is a bacterial infection which is usually transmitted from person to person by coughing but may be transmitted through consumption of unpasteurised milk. Milk that has been boiled is safe to drink, and the souring of milk to make yoghurt or cheese also kills the bacilli. Typically many months of contact with the infected person are required before the disease is passed on. The usual site of the disease is the lungs, although other organs may be involved. Most infected people never develop symptoms. In those who do, especially infants, symptoms may arise within weeks of the infection occurring and may be severe. In most, however, the disease lies dormant for many years until, for some reason, the infected person becomes physically run down. Symptoms include fever, weight loss, night sweats and coughing.

Bilharzia Bilharzia is carried in water by minute worms and is present in the coastal regions of north-eastern Brazil, Suriname and north-central Venezuela. The worms enter through the skin and attach themselves to the intestines or bladder, where they produce large numbers of eggs. The first symptom may be a tingling and sometimes a light rash around the area where the worm entered. Weeks later, when the worm is busy producing eggs, a high fever may develop. A general feeling of being unwell may be the first symptom, while abdominal pain and blood in the urine are later signs. The infection often causes no symptoms until the disease is well established (several months to years after exposure) and damage to internal organs irreversible.

Avoid swimming or bathing in fresh water where bilharzia may be present, especially dams. Even deep water can be infected. If you do get wet, dry off quickly and dry your clothes as well. If you may have been exposed to bilharzia, talk to a doctor even if you don't have any symptoms: the early stages can be confused with malaria or typhoid. If you cannot get medical help immediately, praziquantel (Biltricide) is the recommended treatment. The recommended dosage is 40 mg per kg body weight in divided doses over one day. Niridazole is an alternative drug.

Diphtheria Diphtheria can be a skin infection or a more dangerous throat infection. It is spread by contaminated dust contacting the skin or by the inhalation of infected cough or sneeze droplets. Frequent washing and keeping the skin dry will help prevent skin infection. Treatment of diphtheria throat infection is by intravenous infusion of diphtheria antitoxin. The antitoxin is produced in horses so may be associated with allergic reactions in some people. Because of this it must be administered under close medical supervision. Antibiotics such as erythromycin or penicillin are then given to eradicate the diphtheria bacteria from the patient. A vaccination is available to prevent the throat infection.

Sexually Transmitted Diseases Sexual contact with an infected sexual partner spreads these diseases. While abstinence is the only 100% preventative, using condoms is also effective. Condoms (*preservativos*) are widely available in pharmacies, but bring some anyway. Gonorrhoea, herpes and syphilis are the most common of these diseases; sores, blisters or rashes around the genitals, discharges, and pain when urinating are common symptoms. Symptoms may be less marked or not observed at all in women. Syphilis symptoms eventually disappear completely but the disease continues and can cause severe problems in later years. The treatment of gonorrhoea and syphilis is with antibiotics. There is no cure for herpes, nor for AIDS.

HIV/AIDS HIV, the human immunodeficiency virus, may develop into AIDS, acquired immune deficiency syndrome (SIDA in Spanish and Portuguese). HIV is a growing problem in South America, and especially in Brazil. Any exposure to blood, blood products or bodily fluids may put an individual at risk. Transmission is predominantly through heterosexual sexual activity, though it is also prevalent amongst gays. Apart from abstinence, the most effective preventative is always to practise safe sex using condoms. It is impossible to detect the HIV-positive status of an otherwise healthy-looking person without a blood test.

HIV/AIDS can also be spread via infected blood transfusions, but blood supplies in most reputable hospitals in South America are now screened, so the risk is low. It can also be spread by dirty needles used for vaccinations, acupuncture, tattooing, or intravenous drug use. Take a needle and syringe pack with you in case you need an injection. Otherwise, ask to see the syringe unwrapped in front of you. Fear of HIV infection should never preclude treatment for serious medical conditions: the consequent risk of infection is very small indeed.

Insect-Borne Diseases

Malaria This serious disease is spread by mosquito bites, and is widespread in tropical South America, where drug-resistant strains of the disease are prevalent (see map). The main risk areas are along the coasts and in rainforest regions; areas above 2500 metres are safe. It is imperative to protect yourself against mosquito bites and to take malarial prophylactics. Antimalarial drugs do not prevent you from being infected, but kill the parasites during a stage in their development. Symptoms include headaches, fever, chills and sweating which may subside and recur. Without treatment malaria can develop more serious, potentially fatal effects.

There are a number of different types of malaria. The one of most concern is falciparum malaria, responsible for the very serious cerebral malaria.

In recent years malaria has become increasingly resistant to commonly used antimalarials like chloroquine, maloprim and proguanil. Newer drugs such as mefloquine (Lariam) and doxycycline (Vibramycin, Doryx) should be considered for South America, which has chloroquine

Malarial Areas

Limited Risk Area
Malaria Risk Area
Multidrug-Resistant Malaria Risk Area

and multidrug-resistant malaria. Expert advice should be sought: factors to consider when deciding on antimalarial medication include the area to be visited, the risk of exposure to malaria-carrying mosquitoes, your medical history, and your age and pregnancy status, and the likely side effects. It is also important to be sure of the correct dosage for prevention, and also for treatment if you will be in a high-risk area isolated from medical care. While no antimalarial is 100% effective, taking the most appropriate drug significantly reduces the risk of contracting the disease.

The primary prevention is protection from mosquito bites. The mosquitoes that transmit malaria bite from dusk to dawn and during this period travellers are advised to:

- wear light-coloured clothing
- wear long pants and long-sleeved shirts
- use mosquito repellents containing the compound DEET on exposed areas (overuse of DEET may be harmful, especially to children, but its use

is considered preferable to being bitten by disease-transmitting mosquitoes)
- avoid highly scented perfumes or aftershave
- use a mosquito net; some of the new ones are compact and impregnated with repellent

Malaria can be diagnosed by a simple blood test. Symptoms range from fever, chills and sweating, headache and abdominal pains to a vague feeling of ill-health. Seek examination immediately if there is any suggestion of malaria. Some species of the parasite may lie dormant in the liver, but they can be eradicated using a specific medication. Malaria is curable, as long as the traveller seeks medical help when symptoms occur.

Dengue Fever There is no prophylactic for this mosquito-spread disease, so the main preventative measure is to avoid mosquito bites. A sudden onset of fever, headaches and severe joint and muscle pains are the first signs, then a rash starts on the trunk of the body and spreads to the limbs and face. After a few more days, the fever will subside and recovery will begin. Serious complications are not common but full recovery can take up to a month or more.

Yellow Fever This disease is endemic in tropical South America, and is transmitted to humans by mosquitoes. Initial symptoms are fever, headache, abdominal pain and vomiting. There may appear to be a brief recovery before the disease progresses to more severe complications, including liver failure. There is no medical treatment apart from keeping the fever down and avoiding dehydration, but yellow fever vaccination gives good protection for 10 years (see above under Immunisations).

Filariasis This is a mosquito-transmitted parasitic infection found in parts of South America. Symptoms vary depending on which filarial parasite species has caused the infection. They include fever, pain and swelling of the lymph glands, inflammation of lymph drainage areas, swelling of a limb or the scrotum, skin rashes, and blindness. Treatment is available to eliminate the parasites from the body, but some of the damage they cause may not be reversible. Medical advice should be obtained promptly if the infection is suspected.

Typhus Typhus is spread by ticks, mites or lice. It begins with fever, chills, headache and muscle pains followed a few days later by a body rash. There is often a large painful sore at the site of the bite and nearby lymph nodes are swollen and painful. Treatment is with tetracycline, or chloramphenicol under medical supervision.

Check your skin carefully for ticks after walking in a danger area such as a tropical forest. A strong insect repellent can help, and serious walkers in tick areas should consider having their boots and trousers impregnated with benzyl benzoate and dibutylphthalate.

Chagas' Disease In remote rural areas of South America this parasitic disease is transmitted by the reduvid bug, locally called the *vinchuca* or *barbeiro*. It infests crevices and palm fronds, often lives in thatched roofs, and comes out to feed at night. A hard, violet-coloured swelling appears at the site of the bite in about a week. The disease is treatable in the early stages, and the body usually overcomes the disease unaided, but if it continues it can eventually be fatal. Avoid sleeping in thatched-roof huts, or use a mosquito net, insecticides and repellents, and check for hidden insects.

Cuts, Bites & Stings
Cuts & Scratches Skin punctures can easily become infected in hot climates and may be difficult to heal. Treat any cut with an antiseptic such as povidone-iodine. Where possible avoid bandages and Band-aids, which can keep wounds wet. Coral cuts are notoriously slow to heal and if they are not adequately cleaned small pieces of coral can become embedded in the wound. Avoid coral cuts by wearing shoes when walking on reefs, and clean any cut thoroughly with sodium peroxide if available.

Bites & Stings Bee and wasp stings are usually painful rather than dangerous. Calamine lotion or Stingose spray will give relief and ice packs will reduce the pain and swelling. Scorpions often shelter in shoes or clothing and their stings are notoriously painful: check your clothing before you dress.

Bichos de Pé These small parasites live on beaches and in sandy soil in North-East Brazil. They burrow into the thick skin of the foot at the heel, toes and under the toenails and appear as dark boils. They must be incised and removed completely. Do it yourself with a sterilised needle and blade. To avoid *bichos de pé* wear footwear on beaches and dirt trails, especially where animals are present.

Snakes To minimise your chances of being bitten always wear boots, socks and long trousers when walking through undergrowth where snakes may be present. Don't put your hands into holes and crevices, and be careful when collecting firewood.

Snake bites do not cause instantaneous death and antivenenes are usually available. Keep the victim calm and still, wrap the bitten limb tightly, as you would for a sprained ankle, and attach a splint to immobilise it. Then seek medical help, if possible with the dead snake for identification. Don't attempt to catch the snake if there is even a remote possibility of being bitten again. Tourniquets and sucking out the poison are now comprehensively discredited.

Bedbugs & Lice Bedbugs live in various places, but particularly in dirty mattresses and bedding. Spots of blood on bedclothes or on the wall around the bed can be read as a suggestion to find another hotel. Bedbugs leave itchy bites in neat rows. Calamine lotion or Stingose spray may help.

All lice cause itching and discomfort. They make themselves at home in hair (head lice), clothing (body lice) or in pubic hair (crabs). You catch lice through direct contact with infected people or by sharing combs, clothing and the like. Powder or shampoo treatment will kill the lice, and infected clothing should then be washed in very hot water.

Leeches & Ticks Leeches may be present in damp rainforest conditions; they attach themselves to your skin to suck your blood. Trekkers often get them on their legs or in their boots. Salt or a lighted cigarette end will make them fall off. Pulling them off increases the likelihood of infection. An insect repellent may keep them away.

Check your body for ticks, too (see under Typhus). If a tick is found attached, press down around the tick's head with tweezers, grab the head and gently pull upwards. Avoid pulling the rear of the body as this may squeeze the tick's gut contents through the attached mouth parts into the skin, increasing the risk of infection and disease. Smearing chemicals on the tick will not make it let go and is not recommended.

Women's Health
Gynaecological Problems Lowered resistance – which can be due to poor diet, the use of antibiotics for stomach upsets, and even contraceptive pills – can lead to vaginal infections when travelling in hot climates. Good personal hygiene, and wearing skirts or loose-fitting trousers and cotton underwear, will help to prevent infections.

Yeast infections, characterised by a rash, itch and discharge, can be treated with a vinegar or lemon-juice douche, or with yoghurt. Nystatin, miconazole or clotrimazole suppositories are the usual medical prescription. Trichomoniasis and gardnerella are more serious infections; symptoms are a smelly discharge and sometimes a burning sensation when urinating. Male sexual partners must also be treated, and if a vinegar-water douche is not effective, medical attention should be sought. Metronidazole (Flagyl) is the prescribed drug.

Pregnancy Most miscarriages occur during the first three months of pregnancy, so this is the most risky time to travel as far as your own health is concerned. Miscarriage is not uncommon, and can occasionally lead to severe bleeding. The last three months should also be spent within reasonable distance of good medical care. A baby born as early as 24 weeks stands a chance of survival, but only in a good modern hospital. Pregnant women should avoid all unnecessary medication, but vaccinations and malarial prophylactics should still be taken where possible. Additional care should be taken to prevent illness and particular attention should be paid to diet and nutrition. Alcohol and nicotine, for example, should be avoided.

DANGERS & ANNOYANCES
There are quite a few potential dangers, but don't be put off. Most areas are quite safe, and with sensible precautions you are unlikely to have any problems.

Theft
Theft can be a big problem in some countries, especially Colombia, Peru and parts of Brazil. Rob Rachowiecki, author of the Peru and Ecuador chapters and several other LP guides, makes the following recommendations which are appropriate wherever there is a high risk of theft:

As well as pickpockets and bag-snatchers, there are the razor-blade artists, who slit open your luggage when you're not looking. This includes a pack on your back, or even your trouser pocket. To avoid this, many travellers carry their day packs on their chests during trips to markets, etc. When walking with my large pack, I move fast and avoid stopping, which makes it difficult for anyone intent on cutting the bag. If I have to stop, at a street crossing for example, I move gently from side to side so I can feel if anyone is touching my pack, and I look around a lot. I don't feel paranoid – walking fast and looking around on my way from bus station to hotel has become second nature to me, and I never place a bag on the ground unless I have my foot on it.

One of the best solutions to the rip-off problem is to travel with a friend and to watch one another. An extra pair of eyes makes a lot of difference. I often see shifty-looking types eyeing luggage at bus stations, but they notice if you are alert and are less likely to bother you. They'd much rather steal something from the tired and unalert traveller who has put a bag on a chair whilst buying a coffee. Ten seconds later, the traveller has the coffee – but the thief has the bag!

Thieves look for easy targets. Leave your wallet at home; it's an easy mark for a pickpocket. Carrying a small roll of bills loosely wadded under a handkerchief in your front pocket is as safe a way as any of carrying your daily spending money. The rest should be hidden. Always use at least a closeable inside pocket or preferably a body pouch, money belt or leg pouch to protect your money and passport. Carry some of your money in travellers' cheques.

Pickpockets are not the only problem. Snatch theft is also common so don't wear gold necklaces and expensive wristwatches or you're liable to have them snatched from your body. Snatch theft can also occur if you carry a camera loosely over your shoulder or place a bag down on the ground for just a second!

Thieves often work in pairs or groups. Whilst your attention is being distracted by one, another is robbing you. Distractions I have seen used include a bunch of kids fighting in front of you, an old lady 'accidentally' bumping into you, someone dropping something in your path or spilling something on your clothes – the possibilities go on and on. The only thing you can do is to try, as much as possible, to avoid being in very tight crowds and to stay alert, especially when something out of the ordinary occurs.

On buses and trains, keep an eye on your baggage at all times, but especially at night. Don't fall asleep in a railway compartment unless a friend is watching you and your gear, or you'll wake up with everything gone. When a bus stops, if you can't see what's happening to your gear, get off and have a look.

Trouble Spots

Some countries and areas are more dangerous than others; see individual country chapters for details. The more dangerous places warrant extra care, but don't feel you should avoid them altogether. Peru has been regarded as the most hazardous country for travellers, but it's safer now than in the past. Peruvian authorities have improved policing of tourist areas over the last couple years, especially on trains, but be vigilant. There have been robberies, some of them armed, on the Inca Trail to Machu Picchu. It's wise not to go alone. Peru's main guerrilla groups have been largely suppressed, and most areas of the country are now much safer.

Robbery, sometimes violent, is also prevalent in Colombia, Brazil, Venezuela and Guyana, so take extra care, and don't carry valuables. In Brazil, the main trouble spots are the beaches of Rio and the North-East, where muggings occur even at midday and gangs roam the beaches watching for unattended articles. Ecuador, Bolivia and Suriname are considerably safer, but travellers should not be complacent. Argentina, Chile, Uruguay, Paraguay and French Guiana are probably the safest places on the continent.

Drugs

Marijuana and cocaine are big business in parts of South America, and are available in many places but illegal everywhere. Penalties are severe, and drugs are used to set up travellers for blackmail and bribery. Avoid any conversation with someone who offers you drugs. Any roll-your-own cigarettes or cigarette papers can arouse suspicion. If you are in an area where drug trafficking is prevalent, ignore it, and do not show any interest whatsoever.

Don't accept food, drinks, sweets or cigarettes from strangers on buses, trains or in bars. They may be laced with a powerful sedative drug, and you will be robbed while you're unconscious.

Baggage Insurance & Theft Reports

Baggage insurance is worth its price in peace of mind. Make sure that if any clauses in the policy limit the amount you can claim on any article, the amount is sufficient to cover replacement. If you have anything stolen, you must usually inform the insurance company by air mail and report the loss or theft to local police within 24 hours. At the police station, you complete a *denuncia* (statement), a copy of which is given to you for your claim on the insurer. The denuncia usually has to be made on *papel sellado* (stamped paper), which you can buy for a few cents at any stationer.

In city police stations, you might find an English-speaking interpreter, but in most cases, you'll either have to speak the local language or provide an interpreter. Prepare a list of stolen items and their value. When you make a claim, especially for a valuable item, the insurance company often demands a receipt to prove that you bought it in the first place.

It can be expensive and time-consuming to replace a lost or stolen passport. Apart from the cost of backtracking to the nearest embassy or consulate, there will be telex charges to your home country to check the details of your previous passport, plus the cost of a new passport.

If you are robbed, a photocopy (even better, a certified one) of original passports, visas and air tickets, and a careful record of credit card numbers and travellers cheques will prove invaluable.

Police & Military

Corruption is a very serious problem among Latin American police, who are generally poorly paid, poorly educated and poorly supervised. In many countries, they are not reluctant to plant drugs on unsuspecting travellers or enforce minor regulations to the letter in hopes of extracting *coimas* (bribes).

If you are stopped by 'plain clothes policemen', *never* get into a vehicle with them. Don't give them any documents or show them any money, and don't take them to your hotel. If the police appear to be the real thing, insist on going to a bona fide police station on foot.

The military retain considerable influence even under civilian government. Avoid approaching military installations, which may display warnings like 'No stopping or photographs – the sentry will shoot'. In the event of a coup or other emergency, state-of-siege regulations suspend civil rights; always carry identification and be sure someone knows your whereabouts. Contact your embassy or consulate for advice.

Natural Hazards

The Pacific coast of South America is part of the 'ring of fire' which stretches from Asia to Alaska and Tierra del Fuego, and subject to volcanic eruptions. In 1991, for example, the eruption of Volcán Hudson in Chile's Aisén Region buried parts of southern Patagonia knee-deep in ash. Volcanoes usually give some notice before blowing,

and are therefore unlikely to pose any immediate threat to travellers.

Earthquakes are common, occur without warning and can be very serious. Andean construction rarely meets seismic safety standards; adobe buildings are particularly vulnerable.

WOMEN TRAVELLERS

Women in South America rarely travel alone, and single women travellers may find themselves the object of curiosity – sometimes well-intentioned, sometimes not. In the Andean region, especially in smaller towns and rural areas, modest dress and conduct are the norm, while in Brazil and the more liberal Southern Cone countries, standards are more relaxed, especially in beach areas. A good rule is to follow local practice and take your cues from local women. For more detail, see individual country chapters.

Machista attitudes, stressing masculine pride and virility, are widespread among South American men. They are often expressed in boasting, and in exaggerated attention towards women. Snappy put-down lines are not a good way to deal with unwanted advances: they may be just the sort of response the man is hoping for, or may make him feel threatened and perhaps aggressive. It's probably better to invent a husband, and leave the guy with his pride intact, especially in front of others.

ACTIVITIES
Surfing

South America's best surfing is probably on the Brazilian coast, though Brazilian surfers can be possessive about their breaks and aggressive in the water. There are thousands of kilometres of coast, with surf from Santa Catarina to São Luís. Other areas with surfing potential include Uruguay, Mar del Plata in Argentina, and Chile's central and northern coast. There are also breaks on the coasts of Peru, Ecuador, and Venezuela. Some of the more far-flung possibilities are on the Galápagos Islands, Juan Fernández Archipelago, and Easter Island.

For detailed information, get a copy of the

Journal of International Surfing Destinations for the area that interests you. You can get a full list, and order the ones you want, from Surfer Publications (☎ (714) 496-5922, fax 496-7849), PO Box 1028, Dana Point, CA 92629, USA.

Diving

The major destinations for divers are the Caribbean coast of Colombia and Venezuela, and islands like Providencia (a Colombian-owned island which is actually nearer to Nicaragua), the Galápagos, and the Brazilian archipelago of Fernando de Noronha, out in the Atlantic.

Skiing

South America's most important downhill ski areas are in Chile and Argentina, with a rugged possibility in the high Andes of Bolivia. For more detail, see the chapters on those countries. There's also plenty of snow in the Andes of Peru, Ecuador, Colombia and Venezuela, where ski touring might be a possibility. Chris Lizza's *South America Ski Guide* is the best source of information.

Trekking

South America is an increasingly attractive destination for trekkers. In the Andean countries, many of the old Inca roads are ready-made for scenic excursions, but lesser-known mountain ranges like Colombia's Sierra de Santa Marta also have great potential. The national parks of southern South America, such as Chile's Torres del Paine and Argentina's Nahuel Huapi, are most like those of Europe and North America in their trail infrastructure and accessibility. Detailed books on trekking are listed in the Books section below and in individual country chapters.

Mountaineering

On a continent with one of the world's great mountain ranges, climbing opportunities are almost unlimited. Ecuador's volcanoes, the high peaks of Peru's Cordillera Blanca, and Argentina's Aconcagua (the continent's highest verified peak) are all suitable for mountaineering, but perhaps the most challenging technical climbs are in the FitzRoy range of Argentina's Parque Nacional Los Glaciares. Brazil lacks big mountains, but rock climbing is very popular around Rio.

River Rafting

Chile's Río Biobío features some of the world's finest Class-5 white water, though it may yet be drowned by a proposed hydroelectric project. River running is also possible in Peru on the Urubamba and other rivers near Cuzco, and in the very difficult Río Colca canyon near Arequipa; and on several rivers around Bariloche in Argentina.

Sea Kayaking

Southern Chile, particularly the island of Chiloé and the Canal Moraleda south to Laguna San Rafael, is increasingly popular with sea kayakers.

Language Courses

In most South American capitals, other major cities, and a few smaller provincial towns, there are language courses in Spanish, Portuguese and Indian languages such as Quechua and Aymara. For details, see individual country chapters.

Spectator Sport

In South America, sport means soccer. Argentina, Brazil and Uruguay have all won the World Cup, though many of the best athletes have abandoned their own countries to play for higher salaries in Europe. Other sports which enjoy widespread popularity are motor racing, basketball, cycling, tennis and volleyball (especially in Brazil). Bullfighting is popular in Venezuela and Colombia, and can also be seen in Peru and Ecuador.

WORK

Except for teaching or tutoring of English, opportunities for employment are few and poorly paid, and usually illegal as well. Even tutoring, despite good hourly rates, is rarely remunerative because it takes time to build up a clientele. The best places are probably

Buenos Aires and Santiago, where living expenses are also high. Rio and the larger cities of Brazil may also have possibilities. See individual country chapters for details.

ACCOMMODATION

The cost of accommodation varies greatly from country to country, with Andean countries being the cheapest and the Southern Cone being the most expensive. French Guiana and the Falkland Islands are exceptionally expensive. The cheapest rooms can be as little as US$4 per night, but in the most expensive areas, it may be impossible to find accommodation for less than US$35 for a double room.

The cheapest places are *hospedajes*, *casas de huéspedes*, *pensiones* or *dormitorios*. An *albergue* is a hostel, and may or may not be an official *albergue juvenil* (youth hostel). The terminology varies in each country. Basic accommodation provides a bed with clean sheets and a blanket or two, table and chair, sometimes a fan for cooling, but rarely any heating in cold climates. Showers and toilets are shared, and there may or may not be hot water. Cleanliness varies widely, but some places are remarkably good.

Hotels proper are generally dearer, but distinctions can be unclear. In some countries, especially southern Chile and Argentina, the cheapest places may be *casas familiares*, family houses whose hospitality makes them excellent value.

Many of the cheapest places have partitioned larger rooms to accommodate more guests. These hardboard (or cardboard!) partitions often fail to reach the ceiling – you can't see other occupants, but you can certainly hear them, and vice versa. If the place doubles as a brothel, you may experience several hours of sighs, cries and giggles, banging doors, flushing toilets and testy customers. If you're really tired, this may not disturb you, but light sleepers can find it trying. Since South Americans are generally gregarious and tolerant of extraneous noise, complaining rarely helps. One solution is to choose a room well away from the foyer or

TV lounge, perhaps at the end of the hall, where you'll only have neighbours on one side.

Some cheap hotels specialise in renting rooms by the hour. These 'love hotels' can be an acceptable budget accommodation alternative, though they may be reluctant to take travellers who want to use a room for the whole night. This applies especially on weekends, when the hotel can make more money from a larger number of shorter stays.

In Brazil and some other places, the room price usually includes breakfast, which can be very good. It's worth paying a little extra for a place with a quality breakfast.

Hot water supplies are often erratic, or may only be available at certain hours of the day. It's something to ask about. Some hotels charge extra for hot showers, and a few have no showers at all – but you can use public baths instead.

Beware the electric shower, a single cold-water shower head hooked up to an electric heating element which is switched on for a hot (more likely tepid) shower. Don't touch the heating unit, or anything metal, while in the shower or you may get a shock – never strong enough to throw you across the room, but unpleasant nevertheless.

Toilets can be quite easily blocked: low-grade toilet paper clogs the system and the toilet can overflow. There is usually a basket for used toilet paper, which may seem pretty unhygienic, but is a lot better than a flood on the floor. A well-run hotel, however cheap, will empty the receptacle and clean the toilet every day.

Camping

Camping is an obvious choice in parks and reserves, and a useful budget option in the more expensive countries of southern South America. In the Andean countries, there are few organised camping grounds, and accommodation is so cheap that camping is probably not worth the trouble or risk, but in Argentina, Chile, Uruguay and parts of Brazil, camping holidays have long been popular with local people. It's better to bring your own equipment from overseas than to buy locally.

FOOD

There are many national and even regional specialities – see the Food section in each country chapter. There is also plenty of gringo-style fast food: hamburgers, pizzas, and grilled chicken can be found in most large towns. Good seafood is available in coastal areas. Immigrant groups have introduced other possibilities – you can find Chinese, Korean, Japanese, Middle Eastern, or Italian food in some surprising places.

Nearly every town has a market with cheap and plentiful fruit and vegetables, some which you've never seen before. At street stalls and small local cafés you might fill yourself for a dollar or two. Lunch is the biggest meal of the day, and usually the cheapest: most cafés offer a cheap *comida corrida* or *menú del día* (set meal) for lunch, though it can get monotonous.

Even in carnivorous countries like Argentina, vegetarianism is no longer the mark of an eccentric. Most restaurants can prepare dishes without meat: plead an allergy *(alergia)*.

DRINKS

South Americans drink prodigious amounts of sugary soft drinks, including the ubiquitous Coca-Cola and 7-Up; Peru has the indigenous Inca Cola, which tastes like boiled lollipops and has a colour not found in nature. Mineral water *(agua mineral)*, both carbonated *(con gas)* and plain *(sin gas)*, is widely available.

Most cafés sell bottled lager-type beers, which are usually good, cold, and cost about twice as much as soft drink. *Chopp* (draught beer, pronounced *shop*) is cheaper and often better. Rum is a popular spirit in Venezuela, Colombia, Ecuador, Guyana and Peru. Sugar cane-alcohol, variously called *aguardiente*, *pinga* and *cachaça* is a low-cost, high-proof option for drunks on a budget. The grape brandy *pisco* is popular in Peru and Chile.

Chile and Argentina produce South America's best wines, along with those from the Tarija region of Bolivia. Wine is also made in Brazil and Peru.

Getting There & Away

AIR

The cost of flying directly to South America depends on where you're coming from, when you're travelling, your destination in South America, your access to discount travel agencies, and whether you can take advantage of advance-purchase fares and special deals. Patience and flexibility will get you the best deal. An understanding of some basics will help; see the Air Travel Glossary.

Start shopping for airfares early. Some of the cheapest tickets have to be bought months in advance, and some popular flights sell out. Airlines can supply information on standard fares, routes and timetables, but they don't usually sell the cheapest tickets.

The fares quoted in this book are a guide only; they are approximate and based on the rates advertised by travel agents at time of going to press. Quoted airfares do not imply a recommendation for the carrier.

Bucket Shops, Consolidators & Charter Flights

Some travel agencies specialise in officially or unofficially discounted air tickets. In the UK they are unbonded agencies called bucket shops. In the USA, the cheapest fares are available through 'consolidators'.

Bucket shop tickets often cost less than advance-purchase fares, without advance purchase or cancellation penalties, though some agents have their own penalties. Most bucket shops are well established and honourable, but unscrupulous agents might take your money and disappear before issuing a ticket, or issue an invalid or unusable ticket. Check carefully before handing over the money, and confirm the reservation directly with the airline.

From continental Europe, the cheapest deal may be on a charter flight, and some agencies specialise in these. The dates of charter flights are fixed, and quite inflexible.

Round-the-World Fares

From some regions, notably Australia, Asia and Africa, a Round-the-World (RTW) ticket may cost about the same as a return excursion fare. This can be a great deal if you want to visit, say, Europe as well as South America. You must travel round the world in one direction and cannot backtrack; you are usually allowed between five and seven stopovers.

Passes

There are several types of air pass available, some covering several South American countries. Usually they must be bought outside the country, in conjunction with an international ticket, so you have to consider this option before you leave. For more information, see the Getting Around chapter.

Stopovers

Flights from North America and Europe may permit stopovers on the way to the destination city. This can effectively give you a free air connection within South America, so it's worth considering when comparing international flights. International flights can also include an onward connection at a much lower cost than a separate fare.

Travellers with Special Needs

If you have special needs of any sort – you've broken a leg, you're vegetarian, travelling in a wheelchair, taking the baby, terrified of flying – you should let the airline know as soon as possible so that they can make arrangements accordingly. You should remind them when you reconfirm your booking (at least 72 hours before departure) and again when you check in at the airport. It may also be worth ringing round the airlines before you make your booking to find out how they can handle your particular needs.

Most international airports will provide

escorts from check-in desk to plane where needed, and there should be ramps, lifts, and accessible toilets and phones. Aircraft toilets, on the other hand, are likely to present a problem; travellers should discuss this with the airline at an early stage and, if necessary, with their doctor.

Guide dogs for the blind will often have to travel in a specially pressurised baggage compartment with other animals, though smaller guide dogs may be admitted to the cabin. All guide dogs will be subject to the same quarantine laws (six months in isolation etc) as any other animal when entering or returning to countries currently free of rabies, such as the United Kingdom or Australia.

Deaf travellers can ask for airport and in-flight announcements to be written down for them.

Children under two travel for 10% of the standard fare (or free, on some airlines), as long as they don't occupy a seat. They don't get a baggage allowance either. 'Skycots' should be provided by the airline if requested in advance; these will take a child weighing up to about 10 kg. Children between two and 12 can usually occupy a seat for half to two-thirds of the full fare, and do get a baggage allowance. Strollers can often be taken as hand luggage.

Courier Flights

Courier companies sometimes provide cheap tickets to solo travellers who can take urgent freight as part of their baggage. The tickets can have fairly strict requirements like a short turnaround time (some tickets are valid for only a week or so, others for a month, but few for any longer), and limits on personal luggage (you can usually take only carry-on luggage). For information on courier fares, send US$5 for the latest newsletter from Travel Unlimited, PO Box 1058, Allston, MA 02134, USA.

To/From the UK

Fares from London used to be the cheapest in Europe, but some other cities now have similar fares. The cheapest destinations in South America are generally Caracas (Venezuela) and Bogotá (Colombia).

Some London agencies specialise in South America. One very good agency is Journey Latin America (JLA; ☎ (0181) 747-3108, fax 742-1312), 14-16 Devonshire Rd, Chiswick, London W4 2HD, which will make arrangements over the phone. Ask for *Papagaio*, its useful free magazine. JLA is very well informed on South American destinations, has a good range of South American air passes, and can issue tickets from South America to London and deliver them to any of the main South American cities, which is cheaper than buying the same ticket in South America. You could also try South American Experience (☎ (0171) 976-5511, fax 976-6908), 47 Causton St, Pimlico, London SW1P 4AT.

A good, reputable general agency is Trailfinders (☎ (0171) 938-3366), 42-50 Earls Court Rd, London W8 6FT. It has cheap flights to a wide variety of destinations; ask about RTW tickets. Its useful travel newspaper, *Trailfinder*, is free. Also worth trying are STA Travel (☎ (0171) 937-9921), and Travel Bug (☎ (0161) 721-4000). There are countless bucket shops, with well-advertised services and prices. Travel agents which are 'bonded' (eg by ATOL, ABTA or AITO) give you some protection if the company goes broke.

Some of the best sources of information about cheap fares around the world are the weekend editions of the national newspapers. In London try also the *Evening Standard*, the listings magazine *Time Out*, and *TNT*, a free weekly magazine, ostensibly for antipodeans but full of relevant travel information for anyone. *TNT* comes out every Monday and is found in dispenser bins outside underground stations.

Some current low-season fares advertised from London follow. They are examples of what is possible rather than necessarily an indication of what will be available. Note that the cheapest fares may have very restrictive conditions and limited availability, and 'come-on' advertisements for cheap fares are common.

Air Travel Glossary

Apex Apex, or 'advance purchase excursion' is a discounted ticket which must be paid for in advance. There are penalties if you wish to change it.

Baggage Allowance This will be written on your ticket: usually one 20-kg item to go in the hold, plus one item of hand luggage.

Bumped Just because you have a confirmed seat doesn't mean you're going to get on the plane; see Overbooking.

Cancellation Penalties Penalties for cancelling or changing flight arrangements, commonly a condition of Apex tickets or a sanction against 'no-show' passengers. You can insure against incurring these penalties due to circumstances beyond your control.

Check-In Airlines ask you to check in a certain time ahead of the flight departure (usually 1½ hours on international flights). If you fail to check in on time, the airline can cancel your booking and give your seat to somebody else.

Confirmation Having a ticket written out with the flight and date you want doesn't mean you have a seat until the agent has checked with the airline that your status is 'OK' or confirmed. Meanwhile you could be 'on request' only.

Discounted Tickets There are two types of discounted fares, officially discounted (see Promotional Fares) and unofficially discounted. The lowest prices often impose drawbacks, such as flying with unpopular airlines, inconvenient schedules, or unpleasant routes and connections. Discounted tickets only exist where there is fierce competition.

Full Fares Airlines traditionally offer 1st-class (coded F), business-class (coded J) and economy-class (coded Y) tickets. These days there are so many promotional and discounted fares available from the regular economy class that few passengers pay full economy fare.

Lost Tickets If you lose your airline ticket an airline will usually treat it like a travellers' cheque and, after enquiries, issue you with another one. Legally, however, an airline is entitled to treat it like cash so that if you lose it, it's gone forever. Take good care of your tickets.

MCO A Miscellaneous Charges Order is a voucher for a specified dollar amount, which resembles a plane ticket and can be applied toward any flight with any IATA airline. In South America, an MCO does not usually count as an onward or return ticket where this is a condition of entry to a country; for other ways to satisfy this requirement, see individual country chapters.

No-Shows Passengers who fail to show up for their flight. Full fare passengers who fail to turn up are sometimes entitled to travel on a later flight, but others may be subject to cancellation penalties.

On Request The status of an unconfirmed booking for a flight; see Confirmation.

Open-Jaw Ticket A return ticket which lets you fly out to one place but return from another – useful if you want to do part of a trip overland.

To	One-Way	Return
Bogotá	£235-260	£404-475
Buenos Aires	£338-354	£495-616
Caracas	£194-230	£380-414
La Paz	£390-447	£600-722
Lima	£276-284	£456-495
Quito	£276-297	£440-503
Recife	£290-360	£466-603
Rio de Janeiro	£300	£429-550
Santiago	£337-351	£603-634

For courier flights, try Polo Express (☎ (0181) 759-5383) or Courier Travel Service (☎ (0171) 351-0300).

To/From Continental Europe

The best places in Europe for cheap airfares are the 'student' travel agencies in Amsterdam, Brussels, Paris, Frankfurt and possibly Athens (you don't have to be a student). If airfares are expensive where you live, try contacting a London agent, who may be able to issue a ticket by mail. It costs more to fly during high-season months, usually July, August, September and December.

The cheapest flights from Europe are typically charters, usually with fixed dates for both outward and return flights.

The cheapest destinations in South America are generally Caracas (Venezuela), Bogotá (Colombia) and possibly Recife or Rio de Janeiro (Brazil). Some options for cheap fares on scheduled flights are: Air France from Paris to Cayenne; Air Portugal

Overbooking Airlines often book more passengers than they have seats. Usually the excess passengers take the seats of those who fail to show up, but occasionally somebody gets 'bumped' – usually passengers who check in late.

Promotional Fares Officially discounted fares, such as Apex fares, which are available from travel agents or direct from the airline.

Reconfirmation About 72 hours before a flight, passengers must contact the airline and 'reconfirm' that they intend to be on the flight. If you don't do this the airline can delete your name from the passenger list and you could lose your seat. You don't have to reconfirm the first flight on your itinerary or if your stopover is less than 72 hours. It doesn't hurt to reconfirm more than once.

Restrictions Discounted tickets often have various restrictions on them; advance purchase is the most usual one (see Apex). Others are restrictions on the minimum and maximum period you must be away, such as a minimum of 14 days or a maximum of one year. See Cancellation Penalties.

Stand-By A discounted ticket where you only fly if there is a seat free at the last moment. Stand-by fares are usually only available on domestic routes.

Ticket Out An entry requirement for several South American countries is that you have an onward or return ticket, ie a ticket out of the country. If you don't want to buy an onward ticket to a neighbouring country, get a ticket from a reliable airline which can later be refunded if you don't use it. Onward/return tickets may not be required at land borders, and there may be other ways around the problem if you plan ahead; see the Facts for the Visitor sections for individual countries.

Transferred Tickets Airline tickets cannot be transferred from one person to another. Travellers sometimes try to sell the return half of their ticket, but officials can ask you to prove that you are the person named on the ticket. This is unlikely to happen on domestic flights, but an international flight ticket, and even a boarding pass, may be checked against your passport.

Travel Agencies Travel agencies vary widely and you should ensure you use one that suits your needs. Some do only cheap air tickets, others sell mainly package tours, while full-service agencies handle everything from tours and tickets to car rental and hotel bookings. Agencies specialising in discounted tickets may have the lowest prices, but can be less useful for other things, such as hotel bookings or specialised advice.

Travel Periods Some fares vary with the time of year. There are often a low (off-peak) season and a high (peak) season, and sometimes intermediate (or shoulder) seasons as well. At peak times, both officially and unofficially discounted fares will be higher, or completely unavailable. Usually the fare depends on your outward flight: if you depart in the high season and return in the low season, you pay the high-season fare. ■

from Lisbon or Oporto to Rio, São Paulo, Santo Domingo or Caracas; VASP from Brussels to Brazil; Avianca from Paris to Caracas. Another alternative might be Lapsa (Líneas Aéreas Paraguayas) flights from Frankfurt or Brussels to Asunción.

To/From the USA & Canada

The major gateways are Miami, New York and Los Angeles; Miami is usually cheapest. Inexpensive tickets from North America usually have restrictions: the fares must often be purchased two weeks in advance and usually you must stay at least a week and no more than three months (prices often double for longer periods). High season for most airlines is from early June to mid-August.

For an idea of what's available, peruse the Sunday travel sections of papers like the *New York Times*, *Los Angeles Times* and *San Francisco Examiner*. Details change frequently. Most cities in the USA also have free weekly 'alternative' newspapers which are good places to browse for travel bargains. It pays to shop around.

Travel agencies known as 'consolidators' generally have the best deals. They buy tickets in bulk, then discount them to their customers, or sell 'fill-up fares', which can be even cheaper (with additional restrictions). Look for agencies specialising in South America.

Offices of Council Travel and STA Travel sell cheap tickets in most major cities, including New York, Boston, Dallas, Los Angeles, San Diego, San Francisco, Seattle and Honolulu. Travel CUTS, Canada's national student travel agency, has offices in Vancouver, Victoria, Edmonton, Saskatoon, Toronto, Ottawa, Montreal and Halifax. Again, you needn't be a student to use their services.

Council Travel
205 East 42nd St, New York, NY 10017 (☎ (800) 223-7402, fax (212) 972-3231)

STA
Suite 2100, 5900 Wiltshire Blvd, Los Angeles, CA 90036 (☎ (800) 777-0112, fax (213) 937-2739)

Travel CUTS
171 College St, Toronto, Ontario M5T 1P7 (☎ (416) 977-3703, fax 977-4796)

New York and Miami are the only places to look for courier flights to South America. For the widest selection of destinations, try Now Voyager (☎ (212) 431-1616), Air Facility (☎ (718) 712-0630) or Travel Courier (☎ (718) 738-9000) in New York, and Linehaul Services (☎ (305) 477-0651) or Discount Travel International (☎ (305) 538-1616) in Miami.

Sample Fares The best fares to a country are often with its national airline. The following examples are official excursion fares for the low season (unless otherwise stated), but you might get better prices from a consolidator.

AeroPerú (☎ (800) 777-7717)
A 60-day advance-purchase return fare to Lima costs US$516 from Miami, US$883 from Los Angeles; in high season it's US$983 and US$913. An air pass sold in conjunction with the international ticket offers cheap connections to most main cities in South America.

Avianca (☎ (800) 284-2622)
The Colombian airline has 60/90-day excursion fares to Bogotá for US$395/499 from Miami, or US$654/762 from Los Angeles.

LanChile (☎ (800) 735-5526)
Several flights weekly depart from New York, Miami, Los Angeles and Montreal. The 90-day excursion fare from New York/Miami to Santiago is US$1209/1100, and includes a free stopover in Lima. Flights from Los Angeles cost US$1244, with no stopover. From Montreal, it's C$1249.

Lapsa (Líneas Aéreas Paraguayas; ☎ (800) 795-2772)
This airline, also called Air Paraguay, is a traditional budget carrier and has a 90-day ticket to Asunción for US$720/900/1080 from Miami/New York/Los Angeles. This includes coupons for two other flights in South America (see the Getting Around chapter for more details of this deal).

Lloyd Aéreo Boliviano (LAB; ☎ (800) 327-7407)
LAB has a 60-day excursion fare from Miami to La Paz for $744 return; its 90-day excursion fare to Santiago de Chile, for US$880, includes a stopover in Bolivia.

Varig (☎ (800) 468 2744)
A 90-day return ticket to Rio costs around US$726 from Miami, US$787 from New York, or US$886 from Los Angeles.

Viasa (☎ (800) 468-4272)
One of the cheapest fares to South America is Viasa's excursion fare from Miami to Caracas, at only US$278 in low season.

For details of air passes for travel within South America, see the Getting Around chapter.

Circle-Pacific Fares Easter Island is usually an expensive side trip from Chile, but you may be able to get there economically using a Circle-Pacific fare with LanChile plus other airlines. A possible route is from the USA to Santiago, Easter Island, Papeete, Hawaii and back to the USA.

To/From Australia & New Zealand
The most direct connection to South America from Australia or New Zealand is with Aerolíneas Argentinas from Sydney via Auckland to Buenos Aires, with connections to Santiago, Montevideo, Lima, La Paz, Santa Cruz, Rio de Janeiro, Caracas and elsewhere at little or no extra cost. From other Australian and New Zealand cities you may have to add the cost of getting to Sydney or Auckland, respectively, though some travel agents may include the connection in the overall fare. The official low-season

excursion fare ex Sydney is A$1999 for a stay of up to 21 days, A$2299 for up to 45 days, or A$2599 for six months, but you can usually get it a bit cheaper – maybe A$2030 for the 45-day fare, or A$2200 ex Melbourne. Official low-season excursion fares ex Auckland are NZ$2375 (45 days; available low season only, and must be paid in full when reservation made), NZ$2375 (two months) and NZ$3325 (six months). For high-season departures (December, January and February) only the six-month fare is available.

The other South American route is with Qantas or Air New Zealand from Sydney to Tahiti, connecting with a LanChile flight via Easter Island to Santiago, with free onward flight to either Rio or Buenos Aires. Connections can be awkward on this route, making for a long trip. The cost of an excursion fare depends on the length of stay – A$1999 for 21 days, A$2299 for 45 days, A$2399 for 90 days. You could probably get a 90-day fare for A$2255 ex Sydney at a discount travel agent. There is also a Circle-Pacific fare, which offers the same route to Santiago plus stops in Buenos Aires, Lima and Los Angeles, for A$2599.

In terms of airfares only, it may be marginally cheaper to go to South America via the USA. A Sydney-Los Angeles flight costs from about A$1250 return, valid for six months. A cheap fare from Los Angeles to say, Rio de Janeiro, could cost another US$700 (A$933) return; a total of about A$2185, compared to about A$2300 for a discount Aerolíneas Argentinas fare to Rio via Buenos Aires. In practice, even a day or so in LA would eat up all the savings in airfares, so it's not good value unless you want to visit the USA anyway. It may be worth it for travel to Colombia or Venezuela, but not for cities further south. Qantas and Varig offer good combination fares via the USA.

The best RTW options are probably those with Aerolíneas Argentinas combined with other airlines (including Air New Zealand, British Airways, Iberia, Singapore Airlines, Thai or KLM). A one-year RTW ticket with one stop in Asia, two in Europe and one in South America will cost as little as A$2250. High, low and shoulder seasons for RTW tickets depend on the season at the most popular part of the route – if you want to leave Australia in August, that's peak season for any RTW ticket that includes Europe, even if you won't arrive in Europe until three months later.

For more information, contact:

Aerolíneas Argentinas
    Level 2, 580 George St, Sydney 2000 (☎ (02) 9283-3660)
    Level 6, Nauru House, 80 Collins St, Melbourne 3000 (☎ (03) 9650-7111)
LanChile
    Level 4, 30 Clarence St, Sydney 2000 (☎ (02) 9299-5599)
Varig
    403 George St, Sydney 2000 (☎ (02) 9321-9179
    310 King St, Melbourne 3000 (☎ (03) 9679-6856)

A number of agents offer cheap air tickets out of Australia. STA Travel has offices in all capital cities and on many university campuses. Flight Centres International also specialises in cheap airfares and has offices in most capital cities, and many suburban branches. Inca Tours (☎ (1800) 024-955) is staffed by very knowledgeable people, who arrange tours to South America as well as giving advice and selling tickets to independent travellers. Destination Holidays (☎ (03) 9725-4655, (1800) 337-050) also specialises in travel to Latin America. Also, check the advertisements in Saturday editions of newspapers like Melbourne's *Age* or the *Sydney Morning Herald*.

To/From Asia

There are few direct flights from Asia to South America, and the cheapest options are via London to Caracas or Bogotá, or via Los Angeles to the rest of South America. The cheapest Asian city in which to buy tickets is Bangkok, but Hong Kong, Kuala Lumpur, and Singapore are pretty good, too. STA has offices in all these cities. Japan Airlines

(JAL) and Singapore Airlines are good prospects at the moment.

Varig flies from Tokyo to Rio and Buenos Aires, with a stop in Los Angeles. JAL flies Tokyo-Los Angeles-Rio de Janeiro-São Paulo, and often has the best fares to Rio from the west coast of the USA.

For information about cheap fares, the monthly *Business Traveller* is available at newsstands, or from 13th floor, 200 Lockhart Rd, Hong Kong.

To/From Central America

Flights from Central American countries are usually subject to high tax, and bucket shop deals are almost unobtainable. Nevertheless, most travellers fly from Central to South America, as it's still cheaper than going overland.

You must have an onward ticket to enter Colombia whether you fly, go by boat, or travel overland through the Darién Gap. Because of this requirement, no airline in Panama or Costa Rica will sell you a one-way ticket to Colombia unless you already have an onward ticket or are willing to buy one; if you're refused entry to Colombia, the airline must fly you back at its own expense. If you need a Colombian visa, you will probably have to show an onward ticket anyway. Venezuela also demands an onward ticket. Some airlines will refund the unused portion of a return ticket; check this with the airline before you buy the ticket. The only way to avoid the onward/return ticket requirement is to fly from Central America to Ecuador or Peru.

Via San Andrés Island Several airlines land at San Andrés, an island off the coast of Nicaragua which is actually Colombian territory. From San Andrés, you can continue on a domestic Colombian flight to Barranquilla for US$128, Cartagena for US$128 or Bogotá for US$180. From all Central American countries except Panama, it's cheaper to go via San Andrés than to fly directly to the Colombian mainland. For more details, see the San Andrés section of the Colombia chapter.

To/From Costa Rica Flights to South America from Costa Rica are only slightly dearer than those from Panama. The Costa Rican student organisation OTEC offers some cheap tickets.

To/From Panama Panama requires an onward or return ticket before you enter the country (a bus ticket is acceptable, but the return half is not refundable). Panama's high cost of living also means that time spent looking for a ticket can be a significant expense. Flight options from Panama to Colombia include:

Destination	Airline	One-Way Fare
Bogotá	SAM, Avianca	US$156
Cali	Avianca	US$169
Cartagena	Copa	US$123
Medellín	Copa, SAM	US$123

The Colombian airline SAM and the Panamanian carrier Copa generally offer the cheapest deals to these places and elsewhere in the region. Sahsa is also worth checking out.

Copa is not a IATA carrier, so its tickets are not transferable to other airlines. Copa offices in Cartagena, Barranquilla and Medellín should refund unused return halves of tickets, but check in advance. If possible, apply in Barranquilla, since applications in Cartagena are referred to Barranquilla anyway. Refunds, in Colombian currency only, take up to four days.

Other Options If you don't want to fly direct from Panama to Colombia, and would like to go at least part of the way through the Darién Gap, Copa and Ansa have internal flights to Puerto Obaldía (near the Colombian border), and Transportes Aéreos Interioranos flies to the San Blas Islands (off the north coast). These flights depart from Panama City's domestic airport at La Paitilla.

LAND
The Darién Gap

From North America, you can travel overland only as far south as Panama. There is no road connection on to Colombia: the Carretera Panamericana (Pan-American Highway) ends at Yaviza, in the vast rainforest wilderness called the Darién, in

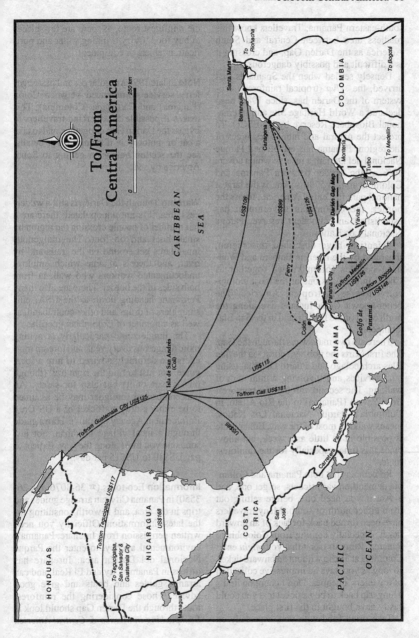

To/From
Central America

0   125   250 km

CARIBBEAN
SEA

Isla de San Andrés
(Col)

COLOMBIA

To Ríohacha
To Bogotá

Santa Marta

Barranquilla

Cartagena

Monteria

To Medellín

Turbo

See Darién Gap Map

Riosucio

To/from Medellín US$126
To/from Bogotá US$146

Panama City

Colón

Ferry

US$106

US$99

US$126

Golfo de
Panamá

PANAMA

US$115

To/from Cali US$181

US$95

HONDURAS

To/from Guatemala City US$125

To/from Tegucigalpa US$117

US$168

To Tegucigalpa,
San Salvador &
Guatemala City

NICARAGUA

Managua

Carretera Panamericana

COSTA
RICA

San
José

PACIFIC
OCEAN

south-eastern Panama. Travellers know this roadless area between Central and South America as the Darién Gap, and crossing it is a difficult and possibly dangerous trip.

Densely settled when the Spaniards first arrived, the *selva* (tropical rainforest) ecosystem of the Darién has, since 1980, been declared a World Heritage Site and International Biosphere Reserve by UNESCO. To protect the natural and human resources of the region, Panama has established Parque Nacional del Darién, a reserve which covers 90% of the border between Panama and Colombia and, at 5790 sq km, is the largest national park in Central America. Across the border, the Colombian government has established an equivalent reserve, Parque Nacional Los Katíos.

Scientists have described this region, inhabited by the riverine Emberá and Wounaan peoples (often known together as Chocó Indians), as one of the most biologically diverse in tropical America. The better-known Cuna Indians live along the north coast of the Darién, and in the San Blas archipelago.

There are two main ways through the Gap. The first skirts the northern coast via the San Blas archipelago and Puerto Obaldía, using boat services and involving a minimum of walking. The second, through the rainforest from Yaviza (Panama) to the Río Atrato, in Colombia's Parque Nacional Los Katíos, means walking most of the way. Either route is possible in as little as a week, but allow twice this time, especially for the rainforest route.

Remember that both Panama and Colombia demand onward tickets, so get one, and a visa if you need one, before setting out from either north or south. Many travellers have been turned back for lack of an onward ticket, especially coming from Colombia to Panama. Rumour has it that you *might* enter Colombia at Turbo without an onward ticket, so long as you have an impressive collection of travellers' cheques. Don't count on it: it's a long trip back to buy a ticket that you could easily have bought in the first place.

Take dried food with you, especially on the rainforest route, as there are few places to buy food. Carry drinking water and purification tablets or equipment.

Note In late 1994 a regular car and passenger ferry service commenced between Colón (Panama) and Cartagena (Colombia). This makes it possible for overland travellers to bypass the Darién Gap altogether, and to take a car or motorcycle if required. For details, see the section below on getting to South America by sea.

Warning Though the Darién is still a wilderness area, it is not unpopulated; there are a fair number of people crossing the region by small boat and on foot. The indigenous inhabitants get around on the trails and by river, and there's a mine which employs undocumented workers who walk in from both sides of the border. There are also many Peruvians heading north to the USA, plus smugglers of drugs and other contraband, as well as a number of Colombian guerillas.

The jungle route particularly is getting more dangerous every year, and foreign travellers are definitely advised to hire a local guide, not just to find the right trail (though this is part of it) but also for safety. An unaccompanied foreigner may be assumed to be either a drug trafficker or a US Drug Enforcement Agency operative. Hire a guide through a local village headman, not just someone you meet along the way. Expect to pay US$10 to US$15 per day.

Information Eco-tours (☎ 36-3076, fax 26-3550) in Panama City can arrange guides and trips in the area, and is worth consulting for the latest information. Officially you need written permission from Inrenare, Panama's environmental agency, to enter the Parque Nacional del Darién area. Inrenare has offices in Panama City and El Real, and can arrange guides and boats and give good advice. Those considering the rainforest route through the Darién Gap should look at *Backpacking in Mexico & Central America*

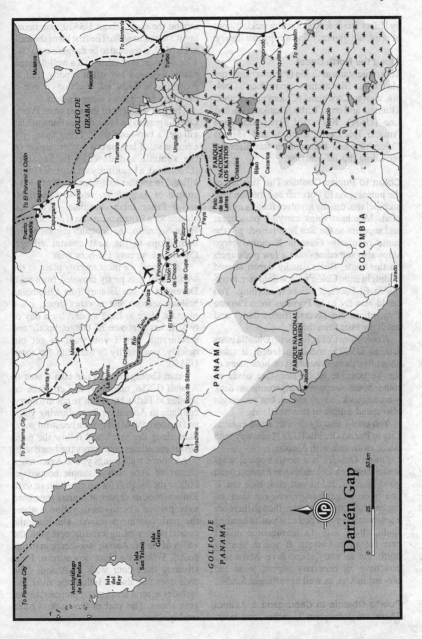

Darién Gap

by Hilary Bradt & Rob Rachowiecki. It's out of print, but you may find a copy in a library.

Along the North Coast

This route starts at Colón (Panama) and goes via the San Blas archipelago to Puerto Obaldía, then to Capurganá (Colombia), Acandí, Titumate and on to Turbo. Thanks to Carlton Lee (USA), Krzysztof Dydynski, Juan Amado Iglesias (Panama), and various Colombian and Panamanian travellers for providing this information.

Colón to Puerto Obaldía This first leg of the journey, via El Porvenir and the San Blas archipelago, usually involves finding a cargo boat. Merchant ships carrying passengers and supplies to the San Blas Islands ply the route regularly. Guardia Nacional cargo ships also sometimes take a few passengers on this route. Boats usually depart around midnight from Colón's Coco Solo pier, arriving in El Porvenir the next morning. You could also fly to El Porvenir from Panama City (there are several flights daily) and catch the boat from there.

A boat from Colón to Puerto Obaldía costs around US$25, meals included. It takes about five days, depending on how many of the 48 possible island stops are made en route. Make sleeping arrangements on deck – a hammock is very useful, but you might also spend a night or two on islands.

You could also fly directly from Panama City to Puerto Obaldía (US$21 one way with Ansa, twice that with Aerotaxi).

Puerto Obaldía is a small tropical way-station between Colombia and Panama, with good beaches, palms and clear blue sea. If you're on a tight budget, you can sleep on the beach south of the town, though there are a few hotels if you'd prefer. If you're heading south, check with the immigration officer here for an exit stamp. If you're heading north, get an entry stamp here. Make sure you have all necessary papers, visas and onward tickets, as well as sufficient funds.

Puerto Obaldía to Capurganá & Acandí There are infrequent launches and boats

around the coast (about US$20, one hour), but it's better to walk. The first bit of the trail, to La Miel, is reputed to be dangerous so take a local guide. From there it's a well-defined, easily followed but often muddy trail to Acandí; if in doubt, ask directions at one of the many farmhouses along the way.

The first segment of the trail from Puerto Obaldía goes to La Miel, the last Panamanian village, a two-hour walk. From there, you climb a small hill, pass a border marker on the summit and descend to Sapzurro (Colombia), a beautifully set bayside fishing village, in another half-hour. Sapzurro has a couple of *hospedajes*, several restaurants and a Panamanian consulate – your last chance for a Panamanian visa if northbound. From Sapzurro, the footpath climbs again, then drops to the next coastal village, Capurganá, an easy 1½-hour walk.

Capurganá, the most touristy place in the whole area, gets pretty crowded from mid-December to late January (the Colombian holiday season), but at other times, it's a pleasant place to hang around for a day or two. It has a choice of budget hotels and restaurants, but if you want to get out quickly, you can fly to Medellín for about US$50.

From Capurganá, you can take a boat to Acandí (US$6, one hour) and continue on another to Turbo, but if you're not in a hurry, continue to Acandí on foot, allowing yourself the best part of a day for a beautiful walk. Start along the beach and follow the path, which sometimes cuts across the headlands.

An hour's walk brings you to Aguacate, a cluster of huts with a simple hospedaje. Follow the footpath for another hour or so to Rufino, another cluster of houses (one used to be painted a conspicuous yellow), where the path continues inland, climbing the coastal ridge, passing it and dropping into the valley of the Río Acandí (another hour to this point). Follow the river downstream for a leisurely three-hour walk to Acandí. The path does not always follow the river and includes several fords, so be prepared to wet your shoes. This part of the track is often muddy.

Acandí is a fair-sized village with a church, two or three hotels, a few cafés, and several small shops selling mostly bottled and canned goods of limited variety and quantity. Some shops will change dollars into Colombian pesos, and will probably give a better rate than in Capurganá, or even in Turbo, the next stop.

Acandí to Turbo There's a launch from Acandí every morning to Turbo via Titumate, and there may be other boats direct to Turbo. The three to four-hour journey costs around US$10, but is only reliable during the first half of the year, when the sea is not too rough; at other times, it leaves in good weather only, but it's never a very smooth journey. Be prepared to get soaked, wrap anything you want to keep dry in plastic, and try to sit in the rear of the boat.

Turbo, a drab and dangerous port on the Golfo de Urabá, has a variety of fresh and canned foods, so northbound travellers should stock up here. Whether north or southbound, you need to obtain an exit or entry stamp at the Policía Distrito Especial, two blocks down from the harbour. It's very informal and quick as long as your papers are in order.

Turbo has no bank, but many shops and the more expensive hotels will exchange cash dollars – usually at a poor rate. Change just enough to get to Medellín or Cartagena. For accommodation and other details, see the Turbo section in the Colombia chapter.

Turbo has no Panamanian consulate, so northbound travellers should get a visa beforehand. It may be possible to get one in Sapzurro, but if the consulate there is closed for some reason, you will have to backtrack to Medellín or Barranquilla. To enter Panama, be sure you have an onward ticket as well; many travellers have been forced to backtrack to Medellín to get one.

The journey from Colón to Turbo is possible in as little as a week, but could easily take double that or longer, especially if you have to wait around for boats between Colón and Puerto Obaldía, or if you stay somewhere on the way. The San Blas archipelago,

Sapzurro and Capurganá are the most pleasant places to break the journey.

Through the Rainforest

The original information about this route comes from Lilian Wordell (Ireland), updated with more recent advice from both locals and travellers, particularly Peter Herlihy (USA).

To Boca de Cupe This trip should only be undertaken in the dry season, from December to March (perhaps in July and August, if little rain has fallen), and never without preparation. The rest of the time, the trails are almost impossibly waterlogged and the rivers are torrents full of broken trees and debris. Towards the end of the dry season, the rivers get low and it's often difficult to find boats.

Ideally, you need camping gear and decent hiking boots, but a tent is not imperative: keep baggage to a minimum. You might make it in eight days, but be prepared for a longer trek and try to do it as quickly as possible. The total cost will be no cheaper than flying from Panama to Colombia, by the time you add up the cost of buses, boats, accommodation, food and a guide.

Heading to South America, there are two possible starting points: Yaviza (reached by bus from Panama City) or El Real (a boat trip from Panama City). Both routes converge at Boca de Cupe, where you go through Panamanian exit formalities.

Via Yaviza You reach Yaviza from Panama City by bus on the Panamericana (US$14, 10 hours). It's a long, hard trip on a dirt road, dependable only in the dry season; during the rest of the year, buses may only get as far as Canglón (US$11, eight hours). Alternatively you can fly with Parsa between Panama City and Yaviza (US$40 one way, three flights a week). Yaviza has one hotel.

From Yaviza, the trek to Unión de Chocó, on the Río Tuira, takes about a day. First cross the river by canoe (US$1), then walk about 3½ hours to Pinogana. After fording the river here or crossing by dugout (US$1), walk for three to four hours along a jeep track to Aruza. Ford the river at Aruza and then walk another 45 minutes to Unión de Chocó. From there, continue on the same side of the Tuira to Yape and Capetí (also known as Capetuira) before finally crossing to Boca de Cupe. It's a very pleasant walk, which will take about five hours. Emberá Indians live in the area.

Alternatively, you may find a boat from Yaviza to Boca de Cupe by asking around.

Via El Real Banana boats to El Real depart from Panama City's Muelle Fiscal, take from 12 to 36 hours and cost about US$12 per person, including simple meals on board. There's no fixed schedule, but try to get a passage on one of the larger, more comfortable boats.

The port at El Real is some distance from the town itself, so you first have to go about five km upstream, to the Mercadero, for a boat to Boca de Cupe. The best place to inquire is the general store; most provisions arrive by boat, so the owner is generally clued-up about what's going on. Prices for the four-hour trip to Boca de Cupe are negotiable, as are all the boat trips on this route. A very rough road now runs from El Real most of the way to Boca de Cupe. If it's not closed by wet weather, you may get a lift on a truck. In El Real you can camp either at the port or at the Mercadero.

Boca de Cupe to Púcuro Boca de Cupe is the last town of any size until near the end of the trail. If you're heading south, get your exit stamp from Panamanian immigration, in a shop alongside the river. If you're heading north, you'll need an entry stamp from the same place. You can stay overnight with a local family and buy food here; try María's place, which also serves meals.

At Boca de Cupe, you may wait two or three days for a boat to the Indian village of Púcuro, a five or six-hour trip (US$15 to US$30). When the river is high, you land right at the village; otherwise, it's a half-hour walk. Ask someone where you can stay for

the night; the village chief may let you sleep in the meeting hall for a fee (but don't expect any privacy), but there are other possibilities. If you want to keep moving, ask where the trail to Paya starts.

If there is enough water in the rivers, you may be able to charter a canoe from Boca de Cupe all the way to Paya.

Púcuro to Paya The 18-km walk to Paya, the next village, can be done in a day and involves four river crossings (all rivers are fordable); after the third crossing, the trail is faint. There are good camp sites just before the third crossing and just after the last. Guides can be hired in Púcuro for this section of the trail for about US$30, but don't pay in advance. The walk should take about six hours.

At Paya, you will probably meet the chief's son, who will have you taken either to the barracks (about two km away, where you can stay for the night and buy cheap meals) or to the house of any gringo who is staying there on a study programme.

Paya was once a centre of traditional learning, with a historic mountain where Cuna *sahilas* (shamans) came to study traditional arts like magic, medicine and history. The area fell on hard times about a century ago as the Emberá pushed the Cuna out. It's still an interesting place, but be discreet with your camera, and ask permission before taking photographs. There's a foot-and-mouth disease control station where arrivals from Colombia will have their baggage inspected and anything made of leather, or vaguely resembling leather, will be dipped in a mild antiseptic to kill any pathogens.

Paya to Cristales The next part of the trail, from Paya to Cristales via Palo de las Letras (the border marker between Panama and Colombia), is the most difficult stage. It usually takes one or two days, though you can do it in 10 hours under ideal conditions. It's also the part where you're most likely to get lost. Ask the chief to arrange for guides, who prefer to work in pairs and will cost about US$70 for the 10-hour trek to Cristales.

The first part of the trail to Palo de las Letras is three hours uphill, and difficult; a 1972 British Army expedition cut a trail, which is long gone. From the border, it's downhill about 20 km (six hours) to Cristales, but there are several river crossings where the trail becomes indistinct or confusing. Quite a few travellers have had misadventures near the end of this leg of the journey.

Cristales is the next stop, but only half an hour downstream is the headquarters of Parque Natural Nacional Los Katíos, where bed and board are available at very reasonable rates. The park is across the river and the staff at the park headquarters is very friendly and helpful. They may let you sleep on the porch free of charge.

Cristales to Turbo The last part of the trip is by a combination of motorised dugouts and banana boats, which shouldn't cost more than about US$25 in total. If park staff members are going for supplies in Turbo, it can be done in one haul, but if not, you'll first have to find a motorised dugout to Bijao (US$5, two hours) and then, possibly, another to Travesía on the Río Atrato (three hours). The best person to ask about boats in Bijao is the store owner, but you may have to wait a few days before a boat turns up. There is a shop in Travesía with expensive food, soft drinks and beer.

Fast passenger motorboats come through from the town of Riosucio every morning, stop at Travesía and continue to Turbo (US$10, two hours). If you decide to take one of the cargo boats on the Atrato, allow an entire day. For information about Turbo, see the previous section, Along the North Coast.

Other Routes
Various other routes are possible through or around the Darién Gap. All of them are potentially difficult, and you should seek local information. Think about where you will get entry and exit stamps.

You can get boats along the Pacific coast between Jaqué (Panama) and Jurado

(Colombia). Both have onward connections by boat or small plane, and you can also reach Jurado overland from Riosucio.

A variant on the usual overland route is from Paya to Unguia (Colombia), which will involve about 18 hours walking and at least one night in the jungle. A guide is essential.

Another option is to leave the Carretera Panamericana north of Yaviza, and walk north-east to reach the coast at either Puerto Obaldía (on the Panama side) or Acandí (in Colombia). Again, a guide is essential.

There are also several alternative walking tracks between Yaviza and Travesía; get local advice and a good guide.

SEA
To/From Panama
For a year or so, the Colombian ferry *Crucero Express* offered travellers the opportunity to travel by ferry between Colón, in Panama, and Cartagena. Unfortunately, this ferry is no longer in operation, as the service was cancelled in late 1996. The alternative at present is to take one of the cargo boats that operate between Colón and Barranquilla, some of which will also take motorcycles and cars. Not surprisingly, though, these services are irregular and infrequent. It costs US$50 for a motorcycle and US$125 for a car.

Remember that both Panama and Colombia require an onward or return ticket as a condition of entry. The requirement may not be enforced in Colombia, but get a ticket anyway. Panama requires a visa or tourist card, onward ticket, and sufficient funds, and has been known to turn back arrivals who don't meet the requirements. The Panamanian consulate in Cartagena is reportedly helpful.

To/From North America
The best chance for a passenger berth on a cargo ship is from US ports on the Gulf of Mexico. The cheapest option is Venezuelan Lines (CAVN; ☎ (713) 461-2286), 820 Gessner, Houston, TX 77024, which has monthly sailings to several Venezuelan

ports, but passengers must disembark at the first stop, which is usually Maracaibo. These ships can take between seven and 12 passengers for about US$200 one way, but usually need a month's notice; berths are almost unobtainable in July, August and September. Remember that, for most travellers, Venezuela requires a visa and a return or onward ticket.

Lykes Lines (☎ (504) 523-6611), 300 Poydras St, New Orleans, LA 70130, sails from Pensacola, New Orleans and Houston to the Peruvian ports of Callao, Matarani and Salaverry. Fares for the 10-day trip to Callao are about US$1000. For an account of one of their voyages on the Pacific coast of South America, read John McPhee's *Looking for a Ship*.

Getting Around

AIR

Because of vast distances between population centres and geographical barriers to overland travel, South America was one of the first regions to develop air services between, and within, its countries. There is an extensive pattern of domestic flights, with surprisingly low prices, especially in the Andean countries. After several 18-hour-plus bus journeys across mountains on atrocious roads, you may decide, as many travellers do, to take an occasional flight.

There are drawbacks, however. Airports are often far from city centres, and public buses don't run all the time, so you may have to pay a lot for taxis to/from the airports. (though it's generally easier to find a cheap taxi *to* an airport than *from* one). Airport

Airfares
Approximate one-way fares in US$

taxes can add quite a bit to the cost of air travel; they are usually higher for international departures.

In some areas, planes rarely depart on time – AeroPerú and LAB (the Bolivian airline) are notorious for last-minute cancellations – so a backlog of passengers builds up, all intent on getting on the next flight, with resultant bedlam at the check-in counter. Avoid scheduling a domestic flight with a tight connection for an international flight. Reconfirm all flights 48 hours before departure, regardless of what anyone tells you, to be certain of a seat.

Internal flights in Chile, Argentina, Brazil and Venezuela tend to be considerably more expensive. You may hear stories about free flights on military aircraft from time to time, but don't count on catching one.

Flights from North America and Europe may permit stopovers on the way to the destination city. It's worth considering this when shopping for an international flight, as it can effectively give you a free air connection within South America. Onward connections in conjunction with an international flight can also be a cheap way to get to another South American city.

Air Passes

Air passes offer travel within a specified country or region, for a specified period, for a fixed total price. There are various conditions and restrictions, but tickets must usually be bought outside the countries for which they are valid.

Air passes can be good value for covering long distances, and are useful if your time is limited, but they do have shortcomings. Firstly, they are usually quite inflexible: once you start using a pass, you're locked into a schedule and you can't change it without paying a penalty. Secondly, the validity period can be restrictive: a Brazil air pass is great value for getting to remote parts of the country, but it's only good for 21 days and you may want to spend much longer in some areas. Thirdly, air passes usually require you to enter the country on an international flight; you can't travel overland to a country, then start flying around on an air pass.

Multi-Country Air Passes A few air-pass schemes cover two or more countries, and are of particular interest:

AeroPerú – has a South America fare which includes a return flight from the USA to Lima, plus four coupons for flights within the continent to cities including Caracas, Guayaquil, La Paz, Santiago, São Paulo, Rio and Buenos Aires. Valid for 60 days and available only in the USA, it costs US$1099 from Miami, and US$1299 from Los Angeles (about US$200 more in high season, from 1 July to 15 August). Additional coupons can be bought for flights within Peru (US$25) and to other South American cities (US$100). Check with AeroPerú (☎ (800) 777-7717 in the USA) for full details.

LanChile & Aerolíneas Argentinas – The new Southern Lakes Pass is good value if you want to visit the Lake District. For US$318 it allows you to fly from Santiago to Puerto Montt, travel by land through the Lake District to Bariloche, then fly to Buenos Aires and back to Santiago.

Lapsa (Líneas Aéreas Paraguayas) – offers a 90-day pass in conjunction with international tickets. For US$720/900/1080 you can fly from Miami/New York/Los Angeles to Asunción, with stopovers in a choice of two other South American cities; coupons for extra stops can be purchased for US$90 each. The fare costs US$100 more in high season. Call Lapsa (☎ (800) 795-2772 in the USA) for details.

Mercosur Pass This mileage-based pass allows travellers to fly to cities in Brazil, Paraguay, Argentina and Uruguay on virtually any major carrier in those countries. The flights must be completed over a minimum of seven days and a maximum of 30 days, and there's a maximum of two flights in any country. If it's well organised, this can be cheaper than some domestic air passes, but you may need a patient travel agent to arrange the optimum itinerary.

The cost is based on the number of standard air miles (not km!) you want to cover:

No of miles	Cost (US$)
1200-1900	225
1901-2500	285
2501-3200	345
3201-4200	420
4201-5200	530
5201-6200	645
6201-7200	755
over 7200	870

Single-Country Air Passes Most air passes are only for use within one country, and are usually purchased in combination with a return ticket to that country. The following countries offer domestic air passes; for more details, see the Getting Around section of each country chapter.

Argentina

Aerolíneas Argentinas and Austral both carry travellers using a Visit Argentina Pass, which costs US$450 for four flights in 30 days, and US$120 for additional flight coupons.

Bolivia

The Lloyd Aéreo Boliviano LABpass is a real bargain, permitting four flights to any of half a dozen Bolivian cities for only US$150.

Brazil

VASP, Transbrasil and Varig all offer a Brazil Air Pass, good for five flights in 21 days (on one airline only) for US$440; additional flights cost US$100.

Chile

LanChile offers a 21-day Visit Chile Pass, which allows flights all over the country for US$550, or to destinations either north or south of Santiago for US$300. For US$1080 you can have stops north or south of Santiago plus Easter Island; or for US$1290, the whole country plus Easter Island.

Colombia

Avianca's 21-day Descubra Colombia fare allows up to five stops for US$190, or US$280 including flights to San Andrés and Leticia, if you fly into Colombia with Avianca; it costs US$409/529 if you arrive with another carrier.

Peru

Americana has a 30-day air pass which offers one flight for US$55, up to five flights for US$215.

Venezuela

Avensa and Servivensa have an air pass for which you have to buy at least four coupons, which range from US$40 for local flights to US$200 for international flights.

BUS

Road transport, especially by bus, is well developed throughout the continent, but road conditions and the quality of the buses vary widely.

Highland Peru has some of the worst roads, and bad stretches can be found in parts of Colombia, Bolivia and the Brazilian Amazon. Much depends on the season – vast deserts of red dust in the dry season become oceans of mud in the rainy season. In Chile, Argentina, Uruguay, coastal and southern Brazil, and most of Venezuela, roads are generally better, though poor maintenance can be a problem.

In more remote areas, buses may be stripped to their bare essentials; tyres often haven't seen tread for years and they all seem to be held together by a double set of springs at the back, which makes the suspension rock-hard and ensures that each and every bump is transmitted directly to your backside. When all the seats are taken, the corridor is then packed to capacity and beyond, and the roof is loaded with cargo to at least half the height of the bus, and topped by the occasional goat. You may have serious doubts about ever arriving, and panic when the bus hits a pothole or a section of road with the wrong camber and lurches to one side. But the buses usually make it, and after a shower and a sleep, you'll wake up and start laughing about the trip.

At the other extreme, you'll find very comfortable coaches in Venezuela, Argentina, Brazil, Chile, Colombia and Uruguay. In the last four countries, there are even sleepers on long hauls, but the ordinary buses are comfy enough in comparison with those in the Andean countries.

Most major cities and towns have a *terminal de autobuses* (long-distance bus terminal); in Brazil, it's called a *rodoviária*. Often this is outside the centre of town and you'll need a local bus or taxi to reach it. The biggest and best terminals also have restaurants, shops, showers and other services, and the surrounding area is often a good place to look for cheap accommodation and food. Most bus companies will have a ticket office at the central terminal, and have information boards showing routes, departure times, fares and whether the bus is direct or otherwise. Seats are numbered and booked in advance, but, except on major routes between large cities, it's unlikely that all seats will be booked more than an hour before departure.

Some cities have several terminals, each serving a different route. Sometimes each bus company has its own terminal, which is particularly inconvenient. This is most common in Colombia, Ecuador and Peru, particularly in smaller towns but notably in Lima. A small, one-company terminal may be nothing more than a parking area and a ticket seller.

TRAIN

South American railways, covering some of the most spectacular routes on earth, are invariably cheaper than buses (even in 1st class) but they're also slower. Railway enthusiasts should note the following routes:

Puno/Juliaca-Arequipa (Peru)
   Climbing from the shores of Lake Titicaca (3812 metres), it crosses a 4600-metre pass.
La Paz-Arica (Bolivia-Chile)
   It descends from 4000 metres to sea level.
Oruro-Calama (Bolivia-Chile)
   The drop from 4000 metres to sea level takes you through spectacular lunar landscapes and extinct volcanos.
Salta-San Antonio de los Cobres (Argentina)
   The Tren a las Nubes (Train to the Clouds) runs through the arid foothills on the eastern slope of the Andes, with spectacular bridges and tunnels. It's difficult, but possible, to continue by freight train over the Andes to Chile.
Curitiba-Paranaguá (Brazil)
   Descending steeply to the coastal lowlands, this trip offers some unforgettable views.
Campo Grande-Corumbá (Brazil)
   This train crosses the Pantanal going to/from the Bolivian frontier, and is popular with travellers.

There are several types of passenger trains in South America. The *ferrobus* is a relatively fast, diesel-powered single or double car, which caters for passengers going from A to B but not to intermediate stations. Meals are often available on board. You must book

your ticket in advance (well in advance on popular routes like La Paz-Arica). These are the most expensive trains and the preferred means of transport in Bolivia; they're excellent value.

The *tren rápido* is more like an ordinary train, pulled by either a diesel or steam engine. It is relatively fast, makes only a few stops and is generally cheaper than a ferrobus. Ordinary passenger trains, sometimes called *expresos* ('express' is a relative term), are slower, cheaper and stop at most stations en route. There are generally two classes, with 2nd class being very crowded. Lastly, there are *mixtos*, mixed passenger and freight trains, which take everything and everyone, stop at every station and a lot of other places besides, take forever to reach their destination and are dirt cheap.

In several countries, most notably Argentina and Uruguay, passenger trains have nearly disappeared because the large operating deficits of these state enterprises were unsustainable. Brazil is also curtailing its passenger rail services.

Metropolitan Services

Several of the large cities have commuter rail services, usually underground in the central city area. The most extensive systems are in Buenos Aires, Rio de Janeiro, São Paulo, Caracas and Santiago.

CAR & MOTORCYCLE

In parts of South America such as Patagonia, where distances are great and buses can be infrequent, driving yourself is worth considering, despite the expense. You must have an International or Inter-American Driving Permit to supplement your home driving licence.

Advantages of driving include freedom from timetables, the ability to stay wherever you like (particularly if you have camping equipment), the opportunity to get off the beaten track and the flexibility to stop whenever you see something interesting. Disadvantages include security problems, most notably in the Andean countries and Brazil; reinforce your security system before arriving in South America, avoid leaving valuables in the vehicle whenever possible, and always lock it securely.

Road Rules

Most South American countries drive on the right; Guyana and Suriname are the exceptions. Road rules are frequently ignored and seldom enforced, road conditions can be hazardous, and many drivers, especially in Argentina and Brazil, are very reckless and even wilfully dangerous.

Rental

Major international rental agencies such as Hertz, Avis and A1 have offices in South American capitals and other major cities, but there are also local agencies. To rent a car, you must have a valid driving licence and be at least 25 years of age. It may also be necessary to present a credit card such as MasterCard or Visa, or pay a large cash deposit.

Even at smaller agencies, rental charges are very high, but if several people share expenses, it's feasible. If the vehicle enables you to camp out, the saving in accommodation may offset much of the car rental cost, especially in the Southern Cone countries.

Purchase

If you're spending several months in South America, purchasing a car is worth consideration. It's likely to be cheaper than renting, especially if you can resell it at the end of your stay. On the other hand, any used car can be a risk, especially on rugged back roads.

The best countries in which to purchase cars are Argentina, Chile and Brazil, but you must often deal with exasperating bureaucracies. By reputation, Santiago de Chile is the best place to buy a car, and Asunción (Paraguay) is the best place to sell. Be certain of the title; as a foreigner, you may find it very useful to get a notarised document authorising your use of the car, since the bureaucracy may take some time to change the title. In some instances, you may find

obstacles to taking a vehicle purchased in South America across international borders.

Officially, you'll need a *carnet de passages* or a *libreta de pasos por aduana* to cross most land borders in your own vehicle. The best source of advice is the national automobile club in the country where you buy the car.

Shipping a Vehicle

A surprising number of people take their own transport.

Documents You must submit three notarised copies of the car's title to the shipper, plus a letter of permission from the lienholder if the car is not completely paid for. In practice, most countries seem to have dispensed with the requirement for a *carnet de passages* or a *libreta de pasos por aduana*, but officially one of these documents is still usually required; check (well before shipping) with the appropriate consulates, especially for any country where your vehicle will arrive by air or sea. On arrival, make it clear to customs officials that the vehicle is only in transit; in the case of Chile, for example, the maximum stay is 90 days. Once you have entered South America, border crossings should be routine in a vehicle from your home country.

Some travellers have had horrendous experiences taking vehicles, especially motorcycles, from Panama to South America without proper documentation. Before heading south, check with the consulates of the countries you will be visiting.

To/From North America Shipping a car to South America is not cheap, but the bureaucracy is less demanding than in the recent past. Prices are variable, so call several places before committing yourself; look in the Yellow Pages under 'Automobile Transporters' for toll-free 800 numbers.

It is generally cheapest to ship from US Atlantic ports than from Pacific ports. As a destination, Valparaíso is one of the better choices, since Chile's bureaucracy is amongst the most reasonable; Barranquilla

(Colombia) and Guayaquil (Ecuador) are other possibilities. You must usually give one or two weeks' notice to the shipper, and expect it to take a month or more from the date of sailing. Approximate costs from eastern US ports start at around US$1500 to Barranquilla or Valparaíso.

To/From Central America Another alternative is to drive through Central America and ship your vehicle from Panama to Colombia. In the past, this has been expensive and difficult, but may be greatly simplified with the *Crucero Express* ferry service between Colón and Cartagena (see the Getting There & Away chapter). The cost should be around US$50 for a motorbike and US$125 for a car, plus at least US$90 for passengers. There is still a lot of paperwork, especially on the Panamanian side. You'll need all the papers for car ownership, registration and insurance, an international driving permit and (in theory anyway) a carnet.

Other options are cargo ships from Colón to Colombia's Pacific port of Buenaventura, or the Caribbean port of Barranquilla, but these will be more expensive than the ferry. Smaller cargo vessels depart from Coco Solo pier in Colón. Their service is probably the most risky and uncomfortable. Prices are very negotiable; they might start out asking US$1500 and come down to half that. More established shippers will be more expensive, but they may help you with Colombian paperwork.

You could also ship a car or, especially, a motorbike by air. You may be able to get a special rate for air cargo if you are also flying with the same airline. Ask at the cargo departments of the airlines that fly the route (like Copa), or at the cargo terminal at Tocumen international airport in Panama City. Travel agents can sometimes help.

Security
If you cannot stay with your vehicle every minute, you can expect that something will be stolen from it. Stealing from vehicles being shipped is big business. If you ship the vehicle with all your possessions in it, take every precaution, and even then, don't be surprised if thieves get your stuff. Remove everything removable (hubcaps, wipers, mirrors etc) and take everything visible out of the interior. Camper vans are a special target: seal off the living area from the driving compartment, double-lock the living area, cover the windows so no one can see inside, and double-lock your possessions *again* inside the cabinets.

BICYCLE
Bicycling is an interesting and inexpensive alternative, especially in the Southern Cone countries, where roads are better and transport costs tend to be higher. Racing bicycles are suitable for paved roads, but on the mostly gravelled or dirt roads of the Andes, a mountain bike *(todo terreno)* is a better choice. Bring your own bicycle, since locally manufactured ones are less sturdy and dependable.

There are many good cycling routes, especially in the lake districts of Chile and Argentina. Mountain bikers have even cycled the length of Brazil's Trans-Amazon Highway.

Bicycle mechanics are common even in small South American towns but will almost certainly lack the parts you need. Before coming to South America, make an effort to become a competent bicycle mechanic, and purchase spares for the pieces most likely to fail.

There are several other drawbacks to cycling. One is the weather; rain in Brazil or wind in Patagonia can slow your progress to a crawl. High altitude and poor roads are factors in the Andean countries. Brazilian and Argentine motorists, with a total disregard of anyone but themselves, are a serious hazard to cyclists.

HITCHING
Hitching is never entirely safe in any country in the world, and for safety reasons it can't be recommended. Travellers who decide to hitch should understand that they are taking a small but potentially serious risk. Hitching is less dangerous if you travel in pairs and let

someone know where you are planning to go.

Though it is possible to hitchhike all over South America, free lifts are the rule only in Argentina, Chile, Uruguay and parts of Brazil. Elsewhere, drivers expect payment for lifts, and hitching is virtually a form of public transport, especially among poor people, and in the highlands, where buses can be infrequent. There are more or less fixed fares over certain routes – just ask the other passengers what they're paying. It's usually less than the bus fare, but can be the same in some places. You get a better view from the top of a truck and people tend to be friendlier, but if you're hitching on the Andean altiplano, take warm clothing. Once the sun goes down or is obscured by clouds, it gets *very* cold.

There's no need to wait at the roadside for a lift, unless it happens to be convenient. Almost every town has its central truck park, often in or near the market. Ask around for a truck going in your direction and how much it will cost; be there about half an hour before the driver says he's going. If the driver has a full load of passengers, you'll leave more or less on time, but if not, he may spend some time driving around town hunting for more. It is often worth soliciting a ride at *servicentros* on the outskirts of large cities, where drivers refuel their vehicles. Private cars are often stuffed with families and children.

BOAT
Riverboat

Many travellers dream about cruising down big rivers like the Orinoco or Amazon, but you'll have a more idyllic time on one of the smaller rivers like the Mamoré or Beni, where boats hug the shore and you can see and hear the wildlife. An alternative is the Río Paraguay, upstream from Asunción (Paraguay) to Brazil.

The Amazon, by contrast, is densely settled, especially in its lower reaches, while economic imperatives have reduced opportunities for passenger travel in its upper reaches.

Boats vary greatly in size and standards, so it's wise to check the vessel before you buy a ticket. Fares for a given route and class vary a little, and it can be worth shopping around. When you pay the fare, get a ticket with all the details on it. Downriver travel is considerably faster than up, but the upriver trip goes closer to the shore and is consequently more scenic. The time taken between ports is unpredictable: from Manaus to Belém should be about four days, but commonly takes six or more. River travel is not for those on a tight schedule.

Food is usually included in ticket prices, and includes lots of rice, beans and some meat, but bring bottled water, fruit, and snacks as a supplement. The evening meal on the first night of a trip is not usually included. Drinks and extra food are usually sold on board, but at high prices. Bring some spare cash, and insect repellent.

Unless you have cabin space, you'll need a hammock, as well as rope to string it up. It can get windy and cool at night, so a sleeping bag is also recommended. Usually there are two classes of hammock space, with the upper deck costing slightly more; it's cooler and worth the extra money. Be on the boat at least eight hours before departure to get a good hammock space, away from engine noise and toilet odours.

Beware of theft on boats – a very common complaint. Don't entrust baggage to a boat official or allow it to be stored in a locker unless you are quite certain about the identity of the official. Bogus officials and locker thefts have been reported.

Lake Crossings

There are outstanding lake excursions in southern Chile and Argentina, and on Lake Titicaca in Bolivia (see those chapters for details).

Sea Trips

The best sea trip in South America is down the Chilean coast from Puerto Montt to Puerto Natales. Short boat rides in a number of countries take you to islands not far from the mainland, including Ilha Grande, Ilhabela and Ilha de Santa Catarina in Brazil, Isla Grande de Chiloé in Chile, and Isla Grande de Tierra del Fuego. More distant islands are usually reached by air, but ocean trips to the Galápagos and Juan Fernández islands are a possibility.

ORGANISED TOURS

A growing number of companies offer organised tours to South America. Some are comfortable 10-day excursions around the main attractions, while others offer months of overland travel in expedition vehicles. Some cater to the ecotourist with rainforests, wilderness and wildlife, while others arrange skiing, trekking, rafting or kayaking packages for the outdoor enthusiast.

The following are some companies which specialise in tours to South America:

Australia

Inca Tours, 5 Alison Rd, Wyong, NSW 2259 (☎ (1800) 024-955)

South America Travel Centre, 104 Hardware St, Melbourne, Vic 3000 (☎ (03) 9642-5353, fax 9642-5454)

World Expeditions, 377 Sussex St, Sydney, NSW 2000 (☎ (02) 9261-1974)

UK

Explore Worldwide, 1 Frederick St, Aldershot, Hants GU11 1LQ (☎ (0252) 34-4161, fax 343170)

Journey Latin America (JLA), 14-16 Devonshire Rd, Chiswick, London W4 2HD (☎ (0181) 747-3108, fax 742-1312)

South American Experience, 47 Causton St, Pimlico, London SW1P 4AT (☎ (0171) 976-5511, fax 976-6908)

USA

Forum International, 91 Gregory Lane, Pleasant Hill, CA 94523 (☎ (510) 671-2993, fax 946-1500)

Ladatco, 2220 Coral Way, Miami, FL 33145 (☎ (800) 327-6162)

Argentina

The cultural dominance of immigrants in Argentina led historian Alfred Crosby to call the River Plate (Río de la Plata) region a 'neo-Europe', where trans-Atlantic plants and animals transformed the natural environment and ensured the demise of pre-Columbian cultures. Having fed its European parent with grains and beef, made a mark in literature and exported the tango to continental salons, Argentina is a country in which foreigners feel at ease and inconspicuous, but persistent regionalisms and unexpected cultural diversity undermine the notion of uniform nationality.

Argentina has a string of alpine parks among the glaciers and blue-green lakes of its southern cordillera. The Central Andes contain some of the continent's highest peaks, the colourful northern deserts are no less impressive, and the Iguazú Falls, shared with Brazil, are legendary. Desolate southern Patagonia, with its massive concentrations of sub-Antarctic wildlife, forms a striking contrast to Buenos Aires' cosmopolitan frenzy.

Country Name República Argentina
Area 2,766,890 sq km
Population 34.3 million
Population Density 12.5 per sq km
Capital Buenos Aires
Head of State President Carlos Saúl Menem
Official Language Spanish
Other Languages English, Italian, German, Mapuche, Quechua, Toba and other Indian languages
Currency Peso ($)
Exchange Rate US$1 = Ar$1
Per Capita GNP US$7990
Inflation Rate 3.9%

Facts about the Country

HISTORY

In pre-Columbian times, sedentary Diaguita Indians cultivated maize in the Andean North-West (Noroeste Andino); to the east, in the forested Paraná delta, the Guaraní grew maize and tubers like manioc (cassava). Mostly, though, nomadic peoples hunted the guanaco (a relative of the llama) and the ostrich-like rhea on the Pampas and in Patagonia, though Fuegian Indians gathered shellfish and birds' eggs.

Indian resistance forced early Spaniards from Buenos Aires. Spanish forces established the city anew by 1580, but it languished compared to Tucumán, Córdoba and Salta, which provided mules, cloth and foodstuffs for the mines of Alto Perú (Bolivia). Spaniards from Chile settled the trans-Andean Cuyo region, which produced wine and grain.

The North-West's declining Indian population, and the Indians' relatively small numbers in the rest of the country, produced a peculiarly Argentine maldistribution of land. The hacienda was less important than in Peru or Mexico; instead, the livestock *estancia* dominated development.

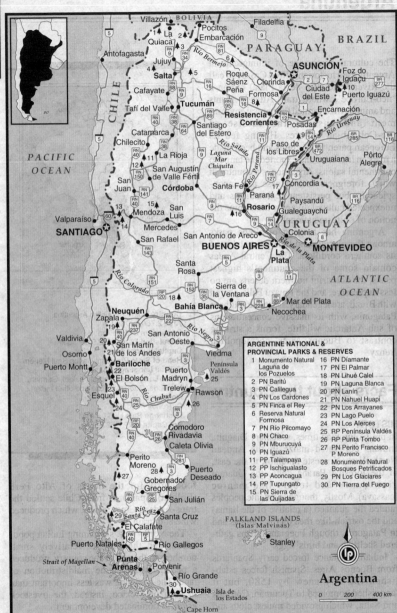

ARGENTINE NATIONAL & PROVINCIAL PARKS & RESERVES

1 Monumento Natural Laguna de los Pozuelos
2 PN Baritú
3 PN Calilegua
4 PN Los Cardones
5 PN Finca el Rey
6 Reserva Natural Formosa
7 PN Río Pilcomayo
8 PN Chaco
9 PN Mburucuyá
10 PN Iguazú
11 PP Talampaya
12 PP Ischigualasto
13 PP Aconcagua
14 PP Tupungato
15 PN Sierra de las Quijadas
16 PN Díamante
17 PN El Palmar
18 PN Lihué Calel
19 PN Laguna Blanca
20 PN Lanín
21 PN Nahuel Huapi
22 PN Los Arrayanes
23 PN Lago Puelo
24 PN Los Alerces
25 RP Península Valdés
26 RP Punta Tombo
27 PN Perito Francisco P Moreno
28 Monumento Natural Bosques Petrificados
29 PN Los Glaciares
30 PN Tierra del Fuego

Argentina

0   200   400 km

Spaniards returning to the Pampas in the late 16th century found that cattle and horses had become the agents of 'ecological imperialism' – with commerce shackled by Spanish mercantile interests, colonial Buenos Aires subsisted on livestock – though the taming of feral horses also aided indigenous resistance. Without horses and cattle, the legendary gaucho could never have existed, but their growing commercial importance brought about his demise.

Growth & Independence

Buenos Aires' designation as capital of the new Viceroyalty of Río de la Plata, in 1776, demonstrated that it had outgrown Spanish domination. After expelling British invaders in 1806 and 1807, confident *criollos* revolted against Spain in 1810, declaring independence in 1816.

Despite this unity, provincial *caudillos* (local strongmen) resisted Buenos Aires' authority. President DF Sarmiento castigated demagogic caudillos in his writings, yet they commanded great loyalty. Darwin observed that Juan Manuel de Rosas 'by conforming to the dress and habits of the Gauchos... obtained an unbounded popularity in the country'.

Provincial Federalists, allied to conservative landowners, opposed Buenos Aires' Unitarists, who looked to Europe for capital, immigrants and ideas. The two parties' bloody, vindictive conflicts nearly exhausted the country.

The Reign of Rosas

Rosas represented *estancieros*, but also helped centralise power in Buenos Aires, building a large army, creating the ruthless *mazorca* (political police), institutionalising torture and forcing overseas trade through the port city. In Sarmiento's words, Rosas 'applied the knife of the gaucho to the culture of Buenos Ayres, and destroyed the work of centuries – of civilisation, law and liberty'. The Unitarists, and some of Rosas' former allies, forced him from power in 1852.

The Roots of Modern Argentina

The 1853 Unitarist constitution even allowed the president to dissolve provincial administrations. Its liberal economic ideology opened the Pampas, Mesopotamia and Córdoba to foreign investment, trade and immigration, but barely affected interior provinces.

European immigrants filled key roles in crafts and commerce. Basque and Irish refugees tended the sheep which displaced semi-wild cattle on many estancias. After 1880, Argentina became a major exporter of cereals, as immigrant Swiss, Germans and Italians proved successful farmers in Santa Fe and Entre Ríos, but bargain sales of public lands encouraged speculation and reduced such opportunities. Many immigrants, faced with rural sharecropping or seasonal labour, remained in Buenos Aires.

British capital built the highly developed rail network that fanned out in all directions from Buenos Aires, but vulnerability to global economic fluctuations stimulated debate over foreign investment and encouraged protectionism. The only sectors to benefit from protection were producers of agricultural commodities like wheat, wine and sugar. The growth in these sectors, which encouraged land speculation, a boom in land prices, and paper money loans, whose depreciation nearly bankrupted the country.

By reducing rural opportunities, speculation also encouraged urban growth; in the 1880s, immigration nearly doubled Buenos Aires' population. Urban services like transport, power and water improved, but industry could not absorb all the immigrants. At the onset of the 1929 depression, the military took power from ineffectual civilians, but an obscure colonel, Juan Domingo Perón, was the first leader to really confront the crisis.

Perón & His Legacy

As Juan Perón (born 1895) grew to maturity, Argentina was one of the world's most prosperous countries, but many resented the *oligarquía terrateniente* (landed elite) and British interests that had built the railways and flooded local markets with cheap manufactured goods.

From a minor post in the labour ministry, Perón won the presidency in 1946, and again in 1952. His economic programme, stressing domestic industrialisation and economic independence, appealed to conservative nationalists and to working-class elements who mistrusted foreign capital and benefited from improved wages, pensions, job security and working conditions. Remarkably, Perón avoided alienating either sector, despite a virtual civil war between them.

Economic difficulties, especially a shortage of capital from war-torn Europe, undermined Perón's second presidency. A 1955 coup against him began nearly three decades of disastrous military rule.

Exile & Return

His party banned and factionalised, Perón wandered to several countries before settling in Spain to plot his return with a bizarre retinue of advisers, including spiritualist José López Rega. Their opportunity came when Peronist Héctor Cámpora won the presidency in 1973. Cámpora's early resignation brought new elections, won handily by Perón, but Perón's death in mid-1974 left the country in chaos. Manipulated by López Rega, Perón's ill-qualified wife María Estela Martínez (Isabelita) inherited the presidency. The left-wing Montoneros went underground, kidnapping and executing their enemies, robbing banks and bombing foreign companies, while the ERP (Ejército Revolucionario Popular; People's Revolutionary Army) battled in Tucumán's mountainous forests. López Rega's AAA (Alianza Argentina Anticomunista; Argentine Anti-Communist Alliance) assassinated labour leaders, academics and other 'subversives'.

The Dirty War (1976-83)

In March 1976, the military overthrew inept Isabel Perón in a bloodless coup, but General Jorge Videla's regime instituted an unparalleled reign of terror, the so-called Proceso de Reorganización Nacional (Process of National Reorganisation). In theory and rhet-oric, the Proceso was to create a basis for enduring democracy by stabilising the economy and eliminating corruption. In practice, it was an orgy of corruption in the name of development, accompanied by state-sponsored violence and anarchy.

The army quickly eliminated the ERP, but thousands of innocents died in the infamous Guerra Sucia (Dirty War) against the more intricately organised Montoneros. Paramilitary death squads such as the AAA claimed many more victims.

The 'Disappeared'

The dictatorship barely distinguished between guerrillas, those who assisted guerrillas, those who sympathised with the guerrillas without assisting them, and those who expressed reservations about the dictatorship's indiscriminate brutality. For at least 9000 people and perhaps many more, to 'disappear' meant to be detained, tortured and probably killed, without legal process.

The government rarely acknowledged detentions, though it sometimes reported deaths of individuals in 'battles with security forces'. A few courageous individuals and groups, including Nobel Peace Prize winner Adolfo Pérez Esquivel and the Madres de la Plaza de Mayo (women who kept a vigil for their disappeared children in Buenos Aires' Plaza de Mayo), kept the story in public view, but the Dirty War ended only when the forces attempted a real military objective – the Falkland Islands.

The Falklands War

During military rule, lip service to austerity attracted billions of loan dollars, which went to grandiose public works, Swiss bank accounts, and the latest weapons. Almost overnight, the import splurge and debt burden brought economic collapse, devaluation gutted the peso, inflation returned to astronomical levels and the Proceso came undone.

In early 1981, General Roberto Viola replaced Videla as de facto president, but General Leopoldo Galtieri soon replaced the ineffectual Viola. When continuing economic deterioration and popular discontent brought mass demonstrations, a desperate Galtieri invaded the British-controlled Falkland Islands (Islas Malvinas) in April 1982.

Occupation of the Malvinas, claimed by Argentina for 150 years, unleashed a wave of nationalist euphoria, but Argentina's illtrained, poorly motivated forces soon surrendered. The military withdrew from government and, in 1983, Argentines elected Raúl Alfonsín, of the Radical Civic Union, to the presidency.

Aftermath

Alfonsín's pledge to try military officers for human rights violations brought convictions of Videla, Viola and others for kidnap, torture and murder, but attempts to extend the trials to include junior officers led to military discontent and a 'Law of Due Obedience' that eliminated prosecutions of those who had been 'following orders'.

Current President Carlos Menem, himself a prisoner during the Dirty War, inexplicably pardoned Videla and other top military officers. Recent revelations from lower level officials confirmed practices like the execution of drugged prisoners by dropping them from aeroplanes into the ocean, leading to an unprecedented apology to the Argentine people from the present head of the army, but Menem's pardon and the Law of Due Obedience have precluded further legal options.

GEOGRAPHY & CLIMATE

Argentina's land area of about 2.8 million sq km, excluding South Atlantic islands and Antarctic claims, makes it the world's eighth-largest country, slightly smaller than India. The major geographic regions are:

Cuyo & the Andean North-West

The Andes are a formidable barrier in that area colonised from Peru. Perennial streams provide irrigation water, but only a few inhabitants live in scattered mining settlements or herd llamas on the high *puna*. South of Tucumán province, rainfall is inadequate for crops, but irrigation has boosted the wine-producing Cuyo region (Mendoza, San

Juan and San Luis provinces). La Rioja and Catamarca provinces are less well-to-do. In western Jujuy and Salta provinces, soaring volcanic peaks punctuate the puna and *salares* (salt lakes), while to the east, foothills give way to dissected river valleys and the lowlands of the Gran Chaco. The hot subtropical lowlands of Santiago del Estero are transitional between the Chaco and the Andes.

Mesopotamia & the North-East

East of the Andes, northern Argentina is a subtropical lowland with very hot summers. The provinces of Entre Ríos and Corrientes comprise most of the area known as Mesopotamia, between the Paraná and Uruguay rivers, where heavy rainfall supports swampy lowland forests and upland savannas. Misiones province, even more densely forested and surrounded on three sides by Brazil and Paraguay, contains part of the awesome Iguazú Falls.

The Chaco

The Argentine Chaco includes the provinces of Chaco and Formosa, eastern areas of Salta and Santiago del Estero, and the northern edges of Santa Fe and Córdoba. It is part of the much larger Gran Chaco region, which extends into Bolivia, Paraguay and Brazil. Open savanna alternates with thorn forest, but erratic precipitation makes rain-fed cultivation risky. Summers are brutally hot.

The Pampas

Argentina's agricultural heartland is a nearly level plain of wind-borne loess and riverborne sediments, once covered by native grasses and now occupied by grain farms and estancias. More properly subdivided into the Humid Pampas, along the littoral, and the Dry Pampas of the west and south, the region comprises the provinces of Buenos Aires, La Pampa and much of Santa Fe and Córdoba. The Atlantic coast features attractive sandy beaches.

Patagonia & the Lake District

Patagonia is the thinly populated region

south of the Río Colorado, consisting of Neuquén, Río Negro, Chubut and Santa Cruz provinces. It is mostly arid, but the far southern Andes have the largest southern hemisphere glaciers outside Antarctica. East of the Andes, cool arid steppes pasture huge flocks of sheep, while the Río Negro and Chubut valleys support crop and fruit farming. Patagonia is also an energy storehouse, with oil and coal deposits. The regional climate is generally temperate, but winter temperatures can drop well below freezing.

Tierra del Fuego
The 'Land of Fire' consists of one large island (Isla Grande de Tierra del Fuego), unequally divided between Chile and Argentina, and many smaller ones. Isla Grande's northern half resembles the Patagonian steppe, while dense forests and glaciers cover its mountainous southern half. The maritime climate is surprisingly mild, even in winter, but changeable.

FLORA & FAUNA
The extensive Pampas are primarily sprawling grasslands, with gallery forests along the major rivers. In the higher altitudes of the Andes, and the high latitudes of Patagonia, pasture grasses are much sparser. The main forested areas are subtropical Misiones province, and the eastward-sloping Andes from Neuquén province south, where species of southern beech predominate.

The guanaco, a wild relative of the llama, once grazed the Pampas, but overhunting and the encroachment of cattle estancias have reduced its range to Patagonia and parts of the Andean North-West. Bird life is varied along the rivers and coasts, and on low-lying Pampas wetlands. Coastal Patagonia supports dense concentrations of marine fauna, including sea lions, elephant seals, and penguins.

GOVERNMENT & POLITICS
The constitution of 1853 established a federal system, with equal executive, legislative and judicial branches. The president

and the Congreso Nacional (comprising a 254-member Cámara de Diputados and a 72-member Senado) are popularly elected, as are provincial governors and legislatures. In practice, the president often governs by decree and intervenes in provincial matters.

Administratively, the country consists of the federal district of Buenos Aires, and 23 provinces. Argentina also claims South Atlantic islands (including the British-ruled Falkland Islands/Islas Malvinas) and a slice of Antarctica, where claims are on hold by international agreement.

Political Parties
Of 18 parties in the Congreso, the most important are the Peronists (Justicialists) of current President Carlos Menem, the Radicals of ex-President Raúl Alfonsín, and the left-centre Frente Grande of ex-Peronist and recent presidential runner-up José Octavio Bordón. Until the 1940s, when Peronism absorbed labour unions and other underrepresented sectors, the middle-class Radicals opposed parties tied to conservative landowners.

Within the Peronist party there remain implacable factions which, in the mid-1970s, conducted open warfare against each other. There is still friction between the economic 'neoliberals' of Menem, and leftists who see his policies as capitulation to institutions like the World Bank. Right-wing nationalists are no happier, despite their loathing of the left.

The Military
Since overthrowing Radical President Hipólito Yrigoyen in 1930, the military has often felt 'obliged' to intervene in government because of civilian incompetence and corruption, but often undermines the civil order. In an extraordinary episode in 1995, army chief of staff Eduardo Bauza went on nationwide television to apologise to the public for his service's role in the repression of the 1970s. The navy, however, has remained unrepentant.

ECONOMY
Since colonial times, Argentina's economy

has relied on export commodities – hides, wool, beef and grains – from the Pampas. Self-sufficient in energy resources, the country has failed to capitalise on its advantages, despite superficial prosperity. Its borrowing binge of the 1970s and 1980s funded capital-intensive projects that encouraged graft and fuelled inflation.

Control of the richest agricultural lands by a handful of families relegated many rural people to marginal lands or to roles as dependent labourers. Perón demonstrated that Argentina needed to develop its industrial base to benefit the general populace, but state intervention outlived its usefulness. Corrupt, inefficient enterprises contributed to inflation often exceeding 50% per month.

The usual response to inflation was wage and price indexing, which in turn reinforced the inflationary spiral. The Menem administration has apparently managed to break the spiral by reducing the deficit, selling state enterprises and restricting unionism, but side effects have included unemployment approaching 20% annually, but several privatisation projects have gone awry.

Selling off state assets like Aerolíneas Argentinas was a one-time bonanza that reduced or eliminated short-term budget deficits, but greater productivity and a more efficient tax system will have to do so in the future. The legacy of state domination has fostered a large informal sector operating parallel to the official economy in providing goods and services.

POPULATION & PEOPLE

Over a third of Argentina's 34.3 million people reside in Gran Buenos Aires (the Capital Federal and its suburbs in Buenos Aires province). Nearly 90% live in cities; other major urban centres are Rosario, Córdoba, Tucumán, Mendoza and Bahía Blanca. Patagonia's population is small and dispersed.

Following Juan Bautista Alberdi's dictum that 'to govern is to populate', early Unitarists promoted European immigration. From the mid-19th century, Italians,

Basques, Welsh, English, Ukrainians and others streamed into Buenos Aires. Some groups have maintained a distinctive cultural identity, like Buenos Aires' Jewish community and Anglo-Argentines across the country.

Middle Easterners, though few, have been influential; President Menem is of Syrian ancestry. Escobar, a Buenos Aires suburb, has an established Japanese community, and Asian faces are becoming more common. Some groups are marginalised, like Chileans on sheep estancias in Patagonia, and Bolivian labourers (*peones golondrinas*, or 'swallow labourers') in the North-West's sugar harvests, but many Paraguayans and Uruguayans are permanent residents.

The major indigenous nations are the Quechua of the North-West and the Mapuche of northern Patagonia, but Matacos, Tobas and others inhabit the Chaco and north-eastern cities including Resistencia and Santa Fe.

ARTS

Though in many ways derivative of European precedents, Argentine arts have been influential beyond the country's borders. In the 19th and early 20th centuries Buenos Aires emulated French cultural trends in art, music and architecture. There are many important museums and galleries, especially in Buenos Aires.

Visual Arts

Public art tends towards the pompously monumental, but arbiters of official taste rarely acknowledge the thriving alternative and unconventional art scene. Buenos Aires is the focus of the art community, but there are unexpected outliers like Resistencia, capital of Chaco province.

Literature

Writers of international stature include Jorge Luis Borges, Julio Cortázar, Ernesto Sábato, Manuel Puig, Osvaldo Soriano and Adolfo Bioy Casares. For suggested reading, see the Facts for the Visitor section below.

Classical Music, Dance & Theatre

The palatial Teatro Colón, home of the Buenos Aires opera, is one of the world's finest facilities. Classical music and ballet, as well as modern dance, appear here and at similar venues. Buenos Aires has a vigorous theatre community, but even in the provinces, live theatre is an important medium of expression.

Cinema

Argentine cinema has achieved international stature, despite limited funds, through directors like Luis Puenzo (*The Official Story*), Eliseo Subiel (*Man Facing South-East*), Héctor Babenco (*Kiss of the Spider Woman*), and the late María Luisa Bemberg (*Camila, Miss Mary*). Many films are available on video.

Tango & Folk Music

Legendary figures like Carlos Gardel, Julio Sosa and Astor Piazzola popularised the tango as music and dance, while contemporaries like Susana Rinaldi, Eladia Blásquez and Osvaldo Pugliese carry on the tradition. Folk musicians like Mercedes Sosa, Tarragó Ross, Leon Gieco and Conjunto Pro Música de Rosario are popular performers.

Popular Music

Charly García, whose version of the national anthem does what Jimi Hendrix did for *The Star-Spangled Banner*, is the country's best known musician, but Buenos Aires' thriving blues/rock scene includes groups like Los Divididos and Memphis La Blusera.

Les Luthiers, who build many of their unusual instruments from scratch, satirise nationalist sectors in the middle class and the military. Many performers are more conventional and derivative – before reporting an Elvis sighting in Buenos Aires, make sure it isn't Sandro, a living Argentine clone of The King.

SOCIETY & CONDUCT

Foreign travellers are less incongruous in Argentina than in countries with large indigenous populations, and gregarious Argentines often include them in daily activities. One such activity is to *tomar un mate*, a social ritual throughout the region; *mate* ('Paraguayan tea') is drunk bitter in the south, or with added sugar and *yuyos* (herbs) in the north.

RELIGION

Roman Catholicism is the state religion, but popular beliefs diverge from official doctrine. Spiritualism and veneration of the dead, for instance, are widespread – visitors to Recoleta and Chacarita cemeteries will see endless processions of pilgrims communicating with cultural icons like Juan and Evita Perón, Carlos Gardel and psychic Madre María. Cult beliefs like the Difunta Correa of San Juan province attract hundreds of thousands of adherents, while evangelical Protestantism is also growing.

During the Dirty War, the Church generally supported the dictatorship despite persecution, kidnapping, torture and murder of religious workers among the poor and dispossessed. Social activism has resumed in today's more permissive climate.

LANGUAGE

Spanish is universal, but some immigrants retain their language as a badge of identity. Italian is widely understood, while Anglo-Argentines speak a precise, clipped English. In Chubut, Welsh has nearly disappeared, despite persistent cultural traditions. Most Quechua-speakers, numerous in the North-West, are bilingual in Spanish. At least 40,000 Mapuche-speakers live in the southern Andes, while north-eastern Argentina has about 15,000 Guaraní-speakers, as many Tobas and about 10,000 Matacos.

Argentine Spanish

Local characteristics readily identify an Argentine elsewhere in Latin America, or abroad. The most prominent are the *voseo* (usage of the pronoun *vos* in place of *tu*) and pronunciation of 'll' and 'y' as 'zh' (as in 'pleasure') rather than 'y' (as in English 'you'). The speech of Buenos Aires abounds with *lunfardo*, the city's colourful slang.

Facts for the Visitor

VISAS & EMBASSIES

Most foreigners do not need visas, but Australians and New Zealanders must pay US$30 for one. At major border crossings, officials issue a free, renewable 90-day tourist card, but at minor crossings, they often ignore this formality.

Argentine Embassies Abroad

For embassies and consulates in neighbouring countries, see entries for main cities and border towns in those chapters.

Australia
  1st floor, MLC Tower, Keltie St, Woden, ACT 2606 (☎ (06) 282-4555, fax 285-3062)
Canada
  Suite 620, 90 Sparks St, Ottawa, Ontario (☎ (613) 236-2351)
France
  6 Rue Cimarosa, Paris 75016 (☎ (1) 45 53 14 69)
Germany
  Adenauerallee 50-52, Bonn (☎ (0228) 22 20 11)
UK
  53 Hans Place, London SW1 X0LA (☎ (0171) 584-6494, Consulate: 589-3104)
USA
  1600 New Hampshire Ave NW, Washington, DC 20009 (☎ (202) 939-6411)

Visa Extensions

For a 90-day extension, visit Migraciones (☎ 312-7985), at Avenida Antártida Argentina 1365 in Buenos Aires or in provincial capitals, or provincial delegations of the Policía Federal.

Foreign Embassies in Argentina

For details of foreign embassies, see the Buenos Aires city section.

CUSTOMS

Officials usually defer to foreign visitors, but arrivals at Buenos Aires' Ezeiza airport may be asked about electronic equipment, which is much cheaper abroad. Arrivals from the central Andean countries may experience drug searches, and officials will confiscate fruits and vegetables from Chile or Brazil.

MONEY

The *peso* ($) comes in banknotes of one, two, five, 10, 20, 50 and 100 denominations. It is subdivided into 100 *centavos*, with coins of one, five, 10, 25 and 50 centavos.

Exchange Rates

Since its adoption in early 1992, the peso has remained on a par with the US dollar. Prices in this chapter are in US dollars, and will be the same in pesos unless the currency devalues. For latest trends, see *Ambito Financiero* or the *Buenos Aires Herald*.

Approximate official rates at July 1996 were as follows:

Australia	A$1 =	$0.79
Canada	C$1 =	$0.74
France	FF1 =	$0.19
Germany	DM1 =	$0.66
Japan	¥100 =	$0.93
New Zealand	NZ$1 =	$0.68
United Kingdom	UK£1 =	$1.55
USA	US$1 =	$1

Changing Money

Cash dollars can be exchanged at banks, *cambios* (exchange houses), hotels, travel agencies, in shops or on the street, but are also widely accepted in lieu of pesos. Travellers' cheques, increasingly difficult to cash, suffer large commissions. *Cajeros automáticos* (ATMs) are abundant and can also be used for cash advances on major credit cards. Many but not all ATMs dispense either pesos or US dollars.

Credit Cards

MasterCard and Visa are the main credit cards, but American Express and others are also valid in many places. MasterCard, affiliated with the local Argencard, is more widely accepted than Visa.

Many businesses add a *recargo* (surcharge) of 10% or more to credit purchases; conversely, some give cash discounts of 10%

or more. Be aware of exchange rate fluctuations, which can bring unpleasant (or pleasant) surprises when a transaction is finally posted to your overseas account.

Costs
The fixed exchange rate has driven some prices to European levels, but budget travel is not impossible. Modest lodging, food and transport are still reasonable; after the initial shock, arrivals from cheaper countries like Bolivia should adapt to local conditions, but allow at least US$30 per day for food and lodging. Prices are subject to wild fluctuations.

Tipping & Bargaining
Waiters and waitresses are poorly paid; if you can afford to eat out, you can afford the customary 10% *propina*.

Bargaining is customary in the North-West, and in artisan's markets country-wide. Even in Buenos Aires, city leather shops may listen to offers. Late in the evening, hotels may give you a break on room prices; if you stay several days, they almost certainly will. Ask for cash discounts at better hotels.

WHEN TO GO
Buenos Aires' urban attractions transcend the seasons, but Patagonian destinations like the Moreno Glacier are best in summer. Iguazú is best in the southern winter or spring, when heat and humidity are less oppressive. Skiers enjoy the Andes from June to September.

TOURIST OFFICES
Almost every province and municipality has a tourist office, often on the main plaza or at the bus terminal. Each province has a tourist office in Buenos Aires. A few municipalities have separate offices.

Overseas Representatives
Larger Argentine diplomatic missions, such as those in New York and Los Angeles, usually have a tourist representative in their delegation.

USEFUL ORGANISATIONS
ASATEJ (☎ 311-6953, fax 311-6840), Argentina's nonprofit student travel agency, is on the 3rd floor, Florida 835, 1005 Buenos Aires. The Administración de Parques Nacionales (☎ 311-0303, ext 165), Santa Fe 690 in Buenos Aires, provides information on national parks. Another useful contact for conservationists is the wildlife organisation Fundación Vida Silvestre Argentina (☎ 331-4864), Defensa 245 in Buenos Aires.

BUSINESS HOURS & HOLIDAYS
Traditionally, businesses open by 8 am, break several hours for lunch and a brief *siesta*, then reopen until 8 or 9 pm. This schedule is still common in the provinces, but government offices and many businesses in Buenos Aires have adopted an 8 am to 5 pm schedule for 'greater efficiency' and, especially in government, reduced corruption.

Government offices and businesses close on national holidays. The following list does not include provincial holidays.

1 January
   Año Nuevo (New Year's Day)
March/April (dates vary)
   Viernes Santo/Pascua (Good Friday/Easter)
1 May
   Día del Trabajador (Labour Day)
25 May
   Revolución de Mayo (May Revolution of 1810)
10 June
   Día de las Malvinas (Malvinas Day)
20 June
   Día de la Bandera (Flag Day)
9 July
   Día de la Independencia (Independence Day)
17 August
   Día de San Martín (Anniversary of San Martín's death)
12 October
   Día de la Raza (Columbus Day)
25 December
   Navidad (Christmas Day)

POST & COMMUNICATIONS
Post
Encotesa or Correo Argentino, the recently privatised postal service, has among the world's highest overseas rates; surface mail

is cheaper but less dependable. Encotesa is so frequently paralysed by strikes and corruption that many items never arrive and may be opened if they appear valuable; send essential mail *certificado* (registered). Private couriers are expensive but far more dependable.

Encotesa charges for poste restante or *lista de correos* services. Arrange for delivery to a private address, such as a friend's residence or a hotel, to avoid this costly and bureaucratic annoyance.

Telephone

French and Spanish interests control telephone services through their local affiliates Telecom and Telefónica, but there are many private *locutorios* (long-distance offices). Argentina's international country code is 54.

Reverse-charge (collect) calls to North America or Europe are possible from most (but not all) long-distance offices; be certain, or you may have to pay costs out of pocket. Rates are so high that even weekend and evening discounts are no bargain.

Most public telephones use tokens (*fichas* or *cospeles*), available from kiosks and telephone offices. Magnetic debit cards (*tarjetas*) are available in values of 25, 50, 100 and 150 fichas. It is possible to get direct access to home-country operators for cheaper reverse-charge and credit-card calls from both private and public telephones, but private locutorios rarely permit their facilities to be used for such calls, since they make no profit on them. The current alternatives are:

France	☎ 0033-800-999-111
Italy	☎ 0039-800-555-111
Spain	☎ 0034-800-444-111
USA – AT&T	☎ 001-800-200-1111
USA –MCI	☎ 001-800-333-1111
USA – Sprint	☎ 001-800-777-1111

TIME

Argentina is three hours behind GMT/UTC. The city and province of Buenos Aires observe daylight-saving time (summer time), but the provinces do not.

ELECTRICITY

Electric current operates on 220V, 50 Hz.

WEIGHTS & MEASURES

The metric system is official.

BOOKS & MAPS

Literature

Jorge Luis Borges, known for short stories and poetry, is a world literary figure whose erudite language and references sometimes make him inaccessible to readers weak in the classics. Ernesto Sábato's psychological novel *On Heroes and Tombs*, a favourite among Argentine youth in the 1960s, explores people and places in Buenos Aires.

Parisian resident Julio Cortázar emphasised Argentine characters in novels like *Hopscotch* and *62: A Model Kit*; one of his short stories inspired the 1960s film *Blow-Up*. Manuel Puig's novels *Kiss of the Spider Woman* and *Betrayed by Rita Hayworth* focus on popular culture's ambiguous role in Argentina. Adolfo Bioy Casares' *The Invention of Morel* also deals with the inability or unwillingness to distinguish between fantasy and reality. In Osvaldo Soriano's novel *Shadows*, the protagonist is lost in an Argentina where the names are the same, but all the familiar landmarks and points of reference have lost their meaning.

History

For colonial times, see the book section in the Facts about South America chapter. James Scobie's *Argentina: A City and a Nation* is a standard history. David Rock's *Argentina 1516-1987: From Spanish Colonization to the Falklands War & Alfonsín* is more comprehensive. DF Sarmiento's 19th-century classic *Life in the Argentine Republic in the Days of the Tyrants* is an eloquent, but often condescending, critique of Federalist caudillos and their followers.

Several books have compared Argentina with other commodity exporters. They include Jeremy Adelman's *Frontier Development: Land, Labour and Capital on the Wheatlands of Argentina and Canada*. On the gaucho, see Richard W Slatta's *Gauchos & the Vanishing Frontier*. A recent intellectual history of the country is Nicholas Shumway's *The Invention of Argentina*.

Perón & His Legacy

Among many books on Perón are Joseph Page's *Perón: a Biography* and Robert Crassweller's *Perón & the Enigma of Argentina*. Tomas Eloy Martínez's *The Perón Novel* is a fascinating fictionalised effort. In his grim essay *The Return of Eva Perón*, VS Naipaul argues that state violence has long permeated Argentine politics.

Politics & the Military

Robert Potash has published two books on military interference in politics: *The Army & Politics in Argentina, 1928-1945: Yrigoyen to Perón* and *The Army & Politics in Argentina, 1945-1962: Perón to Frondizi*. A more general account, also dealing with Chile, Brazil and Paraguay, is Cesar Caviedes' *The Southern Cone: Realities of the Authoritarian State*.

On the democratic transition, see Monica Peralta-Ramos & Carlos Waisman's *From Military Rule to Liberal Democracy in Argentina*. David Erro's *Resolving the Argentine Paradox: Politics and Development, 1966-1992* provides a good analysis of contemporary politics and policies through the early Menem years, though it may be overly optimistic about current trends.

The Dirty War

The classic account of 1970s state terrorism is Jacobo Timmerman's *Prisoner Without a Name, Cell Without a Number*. See also John Simpson & Jana Bennett's *The Disappeared: Voices from a Secret War*.

Travel

In *The Voyage of the Beagle*, Darwin's account of the gauchos evokes a way of life to which Argentines still pay symbolic homage. Make a special effort to locate

Lucas Bridges' *The Uttermost Part of the Earth*, about his life among the Indians of Tierra del Fuego. Bruce Chatwin's *In Patagonia* is one of the most informed syntheses of life and landscape for any part of the world. Paul Theroux's overrated and patronising bestseller *The Old Patagonian Express* does not merit attention from serious travellers.

One of the more unusual, unlikely pieces of travel literature in recent years is Ernesto Guevara's *The Motorcycle Diaries: a Journey Around South America*, an early 1950s account of two Argentine medical students who rode a dilapidated motorcycle across northern Patagonia and into Chile before abandoning it to continue their trip by stowing away on a coastal freighter. Guevara, who died in 1967 in Bolivia, is better known by the common Argentine nickname 'Che'.

Maps

The Automóvil Club Argentino (ACA) publishes excellent provincial road maps, indispensable for motorists and an excellent investment for others (members of ACA's overseas affiliates get discounts). Tourist office maps vary in quality but are usually free.

MEDIA

Newspapers & Magazines

Buenos Aires' most important dailies are *La Prensa*, *La Nación* and the middle-of-the-road tabloid *Clarín*, which has an excellent Sunday cultural section. *Página 12* provides a refreshing leftist perspective and often breaks important stories which mainstream newspapers are slow to cover. *Ambito Financiero* is the voice of the business sector, but also provides good cultural coverage.

The daily *Buenos Aires Herald* covers the world from an Anglo-Argentine perspective of business and commerce, but its perceptive weekend summaries of Argentine politics and economics are essential. It also has a well-deserved reputation for editorial boldness, having condemned military and police abuses during the Dirty War.

Radio & TV

On the AM band, nationwide Radio Rivadavia is a hybrid of top-40 and talk radio. At least a dozen FM stations in Buenos Aires specialise in styles from classical to pop to tango.

Legalisation of nonstate TV and the growth of international cable services have brought a wider variety of programming to the small screen.

FILM & PHOTOGRAPHY

Film costs at least double what it does in North America or Europe, and processing is even dearer. Print film is widely available, slide film far less so.

HEALTH

Argentina requires no vaccinations, but visitors to nearby tropical countries should consider measures against typhoid, malaria and other diseases (see Health in the Facts for the Visitor chapter); cholera is a concern in parts of Salta, Jujuy and the Chaco. Urban water supplies are usually potable, making salads safe to eat. Many prescription drugs are available over the counter.

ACTIVITIES

Skiing, though expensive, is gaining popularity, as are white-water rafting, climbing, trekking, windsurfing and hang-gliding. The major ski resorts are Las Leñas in Mendoza province, Chapelco in Neuquén province, and Cerro Catedral near Bariloche, Río Negro province. The major trekking areas are the Andean Lake District and the southern Patagonian cordillera, while white water is best around Mendoza and Bariloche.

HIGHLIGHTS

For most visitors from abroad, Argentina's principal attractions will be both cultural and natural. The following list, starting in the north and working south, includes some of the country's best known tourist attractions and some lesser, but still deserving ones.

Quebrada de Humahuaca
The scenic desert canyons of the Andean North-West, with their large Indian populations and colonial churches, are an outlier of the central Andean countries.

Iguazú Falls
Despite increasing commercialisation, the thunderous falls at Iguazú are still one of the continent's most breathtaking sights.

Buenos Aires
A self-consciously European sophistication, combined with the romantic image of the tango, is only the stereotypical trademark of a city that has much more to offer. When you tire of urban attractions, escape to the lush nearby delta of the Río Paraná.

Cuyo
Argentina's wine country also features recreational attractions like Parque Provincial Aconcagua and the offbeat Difunta Correa shrine.

Lake District
Soaring volcanoes, shimmering lakes, sprawling forests and trout-rich rivers make the eastern Andean slopes a recreational paradise. Its traditional focus is San Carlos de Bariloche, on Lago Nahuel Huapi, but many other places are more suitable for extended visits.

Península Valdés
The unique, abundant wildlife and desert scenery of the Patagonian coast draw visitors to this popular wildlife reserve in Chubut province.

Moreno Glacier
In Santa Cruz province, one of the world's few advancing glaciers is even more awesome when the lake behind it causes it to burst (about every four years).

ACCOMMODATION

Camping & Refugios

Budget travellers *must* consider camping to control expenses. Almost every major city and many smaller towns have woodsy sites where you can pitch a tent for less than US$5, with hot showers, toilets, laundry, firepits and other facilities. Most Argentines arrive by car, but camping grounds are often central and backpackers are welcome.

Organised sites in national parks resemble those in cities and towns, and more isolated, rustic alternatives exist. Some parks have *refugios*, basic shelters for trekkers and climbers.

Hostels

The Asociación Argentina de Albergues de

la Juventud (☎ 476-1001), at Talcahuano 214, 2nd floor, Buenos Aires, is open on weekdays from 11 am to 7 pm. Hostels, usually open in summer only, can be found in Buenos Aires, the Atlantic Coast, Sierra de la Ventana, Córdoba province, Puerto Iguazú, Mendoza, Salta and Jujuy provinces, and the Patagonian Lake District.

Casas de Familia
Tourist offices in small towns and some larger cities keep lists of inexpensive *casas de familia* (family houses), which usually offer access to cooking and laundry facilities, hot showers and local hospitality.

Hospedajes, Pensiones & Residenciales
Differences among these types of permanent accommodation are unclear, but all may be called hotels. An *hospedaje* is usually a large family home with extra bedrooms and shared bath. A *pensión* offers short-term accommodation in a family home, but may have permanent lodgers and serve meals. *Residenciales* are permanent businesses in buildings designed for short-stay accommodation. Rooms and furnishings are modest; a few have private bath, but toilet and shower facilities are usually shared with other guests.

Hotels
Hotels proper vary from basic one-star accommodation to five-star luxury, but many one-stars are better value than three or four-star places. Rooms generally have private bath, often telephone, sometimes *música funcional* (elevator Muzak) or TV. Most have a *confitería* or restaurant; breakfast may be included. Those in higher categories have room and laundry service, swimming pools, bars, shops and other luxuries.

FOOD
Traditionally, even ideologically, most Argentines still consider *carne* (meat) essential to any meal. Carnivores will devour the *parrillada*, a mixed grill of steak, other beef cuts, and offal.

Italian influence is apparent in dishes like spaghetti, lasagne and ravioli, but don't overlook the inexpensive staple *ñoquis* (gnocchi). Since the early 1980s, vegetarian fare has acquired a niche in Buenos Aires and a few other cities. Chinese *tenedor libre* (all you can eat) is often great value.

From Mendoza northward, Middle Eastern food is common. The Andean North-West is notable for spicy dishes like those of Bolivia or Peru, while Mesopotamian river fish is delectable. In Patagonia, lamb often replaces beef in the parrillada. Trout, boar and venison are also regional specialities.

Places to Eat
Budget travellers in the north should frequent central markets for cheap meals; *rotiserías* (delis) have quality chicken, empanadas, pies and *fiambres* (processed meats) for a fraction of restaurant prices.

For fast food, try bus terminals, train stations or the *comedor*, which usually has a limited menu with simple but filling fixed-price meals. Comedores also serve *minutas* (short orders) like steak, eggs, *milanesa* (breaded steak), salad and chips.

Confiterías usually serve sandwiches such as *lomito* (steak), *panchos* (hot dogs) and hamburgers. *Restaurantes* have larger menus, professional waiters and more elaborate decor.

Cafés & Bars
Cafés are important gathering places, the site for everything from marriage proposals to business deals and revolutions. Many Argentines dawdle for hours over a single cup of coffee, but simple meals are also available. Cafés also serve alcohol.

Bars are establishments for drinking alcohol. In small towns, they're a male domain and women usually avoid them.

Breakfast
Argentine breakfasts are scanty. Most common is coffee, tea or *mate* with *tostadas* (toast), *manteca* (butter) and *mermelada* (jam). In cafés, *medialunas* (croissants), either sweet or *saladas* (plain), accompany

café con leche (coffee with milk). A *tostado* is a thin-crust toasted sandwich with ham and cheese.

Snacks

The *empanada* is a turnover of vegetables, hard-boiled egg, olive, beef, chicken, ham and cheese or other filling. Empanadas *al horno* (baked) are lighter than *fritas* (fried).

Pizzerías sell cheap slices at the counter, but there are more options when seated for an entire pizza. Common slices include *fugazza*, a cheap and delicious cheeseless variety with sweet onions, or *fugazzeta* (mozzarella added), sometimes eaten with *fainá*, a baked chickpea (garbanzo) dough.

Main Dishes

Argentines compensate for light breakfasts with enormous lunches and dinners (the latter never before 9 pm, often much later). An important custom is the *sobremesa*, dallying at the table to discuss family matters or other events of the day.

An *asado* or parrillada is the standard main course, prepared over hot coals and accompanied by the marinade *chimichurri*, with chips or salad on the side. Carnivores will savour the tender, juicy *bife de chorizo*, but try also *bife de lomo* (short loin), *bife de costilla* or *chuleta* (T-bone steak), *asado de tira* (roast rib) or *vacío* (sirloin). *Matambre relleno* is stuffed and rolled flank steak, baked or eaten cold as an appetiser. Offal dishes include *chinchulines* (small intestines), *tripa gorda* (large intestine) and *morcilla* (blood sausage).

Most restaurants prepare beef *cocido* (well done), but serve it *jugoso* (rare) or *a punto* (medium) on request. *Bife a caballo* comes with two eggs and chips.

Carbonada is a beef stew of rice, potatoes, sweet potatoes, maize, squash, and chopped apples and peaches. *Puchero* is a casserole with beef, chicken, bacon, sausage, blood sausage, maize, peppers, tomatoes, onions, cabbage, sweet potatoes and squash. The cook may add garbanzos or other beans, accompanied by rice cooked in the broth.

Pollo (chicken) sometimes accompanies the parrillada, but usually comes separately, with chips or salad. The most common fish is *merluza* (hake), usually fried in batter and served with mashed potatoes.

Desserts

Fresh fruit is the usual *postre* at home; in restaurants, diners choose *ensalada de fruta* (fruit salad), *flan* (egg custard) or *queso y dulce* (cheese with preserved fruit, also known as *postre vigilante*). Flan comes topped with *crema* (whipped cream) or *dulce de leche* (caramelised milk).

Ice Cream

Argentina's Italian-derived *helados* may be South America's best. Smaller *heladerías* make their own in small batches – look for the words *elaboración propia* or *elaboración artesanal*.

DRINKS
Soft Drinks

Argentines drink prodigious amounts of sugary soft drinks. If carbonated *(con gas)* mineral water is unavailable, *soda* in large siphon bottles is usually the cheapest thirst-quencher.

Juices & Licuados

For fresh orange juice, ask for *jugo de naranja exprimido* to avoid tinned juice. *Pomelo* (grapefruit), *limón* (lemon) and *ananá* (pineapple) are also common. *Jugo de manzana* (apple juice) is a speciality of Patagonia's Río Negro valley.

Licuados are milk-blended fruit drinks. Common flavours are banana, *durazno* (peach) and *pera* (pear).

Coffee, Tea & Chocolate

Foreigners should not decline an invitation for *mate* ('Paraguayan tea'). Caffeine addicts may overdose; even in the smallest town, coffee will be espresso. *Café chico* is thick, dark coffee in a very small cup. *Cortado* is a small coffee with a touch of milk, usually served in a glass; *cortado doble* is a larger portion. *Café con leche* (a *latte*) is served for breakfast only; after lunch or dinner, request a cortado.

Tea usually comes with lemon slices. If you want milk, avoid *té con leche*, a tea bag immersed in tepid milk; rather, ask for *un poquito de leche*. For breakfast, try a *submarino*, a semisweet chocolate bar dissolved in steamed milk.

Alcohol
Beer, wine, whisky and gin should satisfy most drinkers, but *ginebra bols* and *caña* (cane alcohol) are specialities. Quilmes and Bieckert are popular beers; in bars or cafés, ask for *chopp* (draught or lager).

Argentine wines are less famous than Chilean, but both reds *(tintos)* and whites *(blancos)* are excellent. When prices on everything else skyrocket, wines miraculously remain reasonable. The major wine-producing areas are near Mendoza, San Juan, La Rioja and Salta. Among the best known brands are Orfila, Suter, San Felipe, Santa Ana and Etchart.

ENTERTAINMENT
Argentines are fond of music and dancing. Dance clubs in Buenos Aires and the provinces get going between about midnight and 2 am and don't close until after sunrise. Live music is best in the tango, rock and jazz clubs of Buenos Aires. Live theatre, both the well-supported official variety and low-budget alternatives, is well attended and of good quality. The video revolution has cut into attendance at cinemas and many outside Buenos Aires have closed. Still, in the capital and larger cities, major cinemas show the latest films from Europe, the USA and Latin America, and repertory houses, cultural centres and universities screen classics and less commercial releases.

SPECTATOR SPORT
Rugby, basketball, field hockey, tennis, polo, golf, motor racing, skiing, cycling and fishing are popular participant sports, but soccer is an obsession – with teams like River Plate and Boca Juniors (based in Buenos Aires' immigrant Italian barrio of La Boca) all over the country. Professional soccer is world-class, but many Argentine footballers play for higher salaries in Europe. The national team has twice won the World Cup.

THINGS TO BUY
Argentine leather goods – especially shoes – are famous, and many shops in Buenos Aires cater to the tourist trade. Shopkeepers are aggressive but sometimes open to bargaining. Bariloche is well known for woollen clothing. *Mate* paraphernalia make good souvenirs, and the variety of handicrafts found in *ferias* (artisans' markets) throughout the country is extensive. Buenos Aires has a superb selection of bookshops, but foreign-language books tend to be very expensive.

Getting There & Away

AIR
To/From Chile
Many airlines fly between Aeropuerto Internacional Ezeiza (Buenos Aires) and Santiago (Chile), but major airlines also fly to Mendoza and Córdoba. Regional carriers connect Bariloche to Puerto Montt (Chile) and Neuquén to Temuco (Chile). Several minor airlines fly between Punta Arenas, Chile, and destinations in Santa Cruz province and Argentine Tierra del Fuego.

To/From Bolivia
La Paz is the principal destination, but some flights go to Santa Cruz de la Sierra, occasionally via Córdoba and Salta.

To/From Paraguay
Asunción is the only Paraguayan city with air connections to Argentina.

To/From Brazil
From both Ezeiza and Aeroparque, Buenos Aires' second airport, Rio de Janeiro and São Paulo are the main destinations, with Porto Alegre and Florianópolis secondary. Flights

from Córdoba, Mar del Plata and Tucumán also go to Rio and São Paulo.

To/From Uruguay

There are numerous flights from Aeroparque to Montevideo; the only other Uruguayan destinations are Punta del Este and Colonia del Sacramento. Some long-distance international flights continue from Ezeiza to Montevideo.

LAND
To/From Chile

The very long border between Argentina and Chile has many border crossings. For details, see the Getting There & Away section for Chile, where there is a map showing many of the routes through the Lake District. Except in Patagonia, every land border involves crossing the Andes. The only train, from Baquedano (Chile) to Salta (Argentina), is not a regular passenger service.

To/From Bolivia

La Quiaca to Villazón Many buses go from the Argentine towns of Jujuy and Salta to La Quiaca, where you must walk or take a taxi across the Bolivian border.

Aguas Blancas to Bermejo From Orán, reached by bus from Salta or Jujuy, take a bus to Aguas Blancas and then Bermejo, where you can catch a bus to Tarija.

Pocitos to Yacuiba Buses from Jujuy or Salta go to Tartagal and on to the Bolivian border at Pocitos/Yacuiba, where there are trains to Santa Cruz de la Sierra.

To/From Paraguay

Clorinda to Asunción Frequent buses cross the Puente Internacional Ignacio de Loyola to the Paraguayan capital.

Posadas to Encarnación Buses use the Puente Internacional Beato Roque González, but launches still connect the Paraná river docks.

Puerto Iguazú to Ciudad del Este Frequent buses connect Puerto Iguazú (Misiones province) to Ciudad del Este (Paraguay) via Foz do Iguaçu (Brazil). Occasional launches cross to the Paraguayan town of Puerto Presidente Franco without passing through Brazil.

To/From Brazil

The most common crossing is from Puerto Iguazú (Argentina) to Foz do Iguaçu (Brazil), but you can also go from Paso de Los Libres (Corrientes province) to Uruguaiana (Brazil).

To/From Uruguay

Gualeguaychú to Fray Bentos Three buses daily cross the Puente Internacional Libertador General San Martín.

Colón to Paysandú The Puente Internacional General José Gervasio Artigas links these two cities.

Concordia to Salto The bridge across the Salto Grande hydroelectric complex, north of Concordia, unites these two cities.

RIVER
To/From Uruguay

Buenos Aires to Colonia Morning and evening ferries sail from Buenos Aires to Colonia in 2½ hours). Hydrofoils take only 45 minutes.

Tigre to Carmelo Launches cross the Río de la Plata estuary daily from Tigre, a Buenos Aires suburb.

TOURS

Travel agents specialising in South America (see the Getting There & Away chapter) offer tours to Argentina, usually including Buenos Aires, Iguazú Falls, and parts of Patagonia, usually the Moreno Glacier and Tierra del Fuego. Some companies specialise in outdoor activities or ecotourism.

LEAVING ARGENTINA

International passengers from Ezeiza airport pay a US$13 departure tax in either US dollars or local currency. On flights to Uruguay, the tax is US$5.

Users of Buenos Aires' new hydrofoil port at Dársena Norte pay US$6 to Colonia or US$10 to Montevideo.

Getting Around

AIR

Argentine air traffic, routes and fares have undergone a major transformation since the privatisation of Aerolíneas Argentinas (domestic as well as international routes) and Austral (domestic routes only). While these two airlines have the most extensive services, some existing secondary airlines have expanded routes, others have come into existence, and both have undercut the fare structure of the established carriers.

Líneas Aéreas Privadas Argentinas (LAPA) competes with Aerolíneas and Austral on many routes, but it has lower capacity. Dinar Líneas Aéreas, a recent starter, flies to north-western Argentina.

Líneas Aéreas del Estado (LADE), the air force's passenger service, flies mostly to Patagonian destinations, but reduced state subsidies have meant greatly diminished services. Transportes Aéreos Neuquén (TAN), a provincial airline, has fairly extensive schedules from Mendoza in the north to El Calafate in the south, while Sapse goes from Buenos Aires all the way to Esquel, but other Patagonian carriers have smaller and slower planes. In summer and around holidays, all Patagonian flights may be heavily booked; early reservations are advisable.

Air Passes

Aerolíneas Argentinas' 'Visit Argentina' fare, also valid on Austral, lets you fly anywhere served by either airline so long as you make no more than one stop in any city except for an immediate connection, but it is more expensive and less flexible than in the past.

Four flight coupons, valid for 30 days, cost US$450; additional coupons, up to a maximum of eight, cost US$120 each. One coupon must be used for each numbered flight so that a flight from Puerto Iguazú to Bariloche, for example, requires the use of two coupons because there is a stopover to change planes in Buenos Aires. Conditions permit one change of itinerary without charge, but each additional change costs US$50.

An interesting new option is the mileage-based Mercosur pass, which allows travellers to visit areas in Brazil, Paraguay, Argentina and Uruguay on virtually any major carrier in those countries, but must include at least one international flight. Properly organised, this can be cheaper than

Aerolíneas' Visit Argentina pass, but you need a patient travel agent to design the optimum itinerary.

Timetables

Aerolíneas, Austral and the other airlines publish detailed timetables, to which they adhere very closely. LADE may leave early if its flight is full or nearly full, so don't be getting to the airport late. There is a list of principal airline offices, both international and domestic, in the Buenos Aires section, and addresses of regional offices appear in each city section.

Departure Tax

Argentine domestic flights carry a departure tax of about US$3 except at Chapelco (San Martín de los Andes), where it is only US$1.50.

BUS

Most cities have central terminals, but in some, bus companies are clustered near the city centre. Fares and schedules are usually posted prominently. Long-distance buses are fast and comfortable, have toilets, and serve coffee or snacks. Some provide meals, but others stop at roadside restaurants.

Some buses have *coche cama* recliners at premium prices, but regular buses are fine even on very long trips. Local or provincial *común* services are more crowded, make frequent stops and take longer than *expreso* buses.

Reservations

During holiday periods or on routes with limited seats, buy tickets in advance. The winter holidays around Independence Day (9 July), and international services from Salta to Calama (Chile) and from Comodoro Rivadavia (Chubut province) to Coyhaique (Chile), are often fully booked.

Costs

Bus fares are about US$0.04 per kilometre, but about US$3 per hour is a good rule of thumb. University students and teachers may receive 20% discounts.

TRAIN

Most passenger rail services have ceased, but Buenos Aires province assumed Ferrocarril Roca services from Buenos Aires to Mar del Plata and the beach resorts, Río Negro province operates the same line from Bahía Blanca to Bariloche, and Tucumán province runs the Ferrocarril Mitre to Rosario, Santiago del Estero and San Miguel de Tucumán.

TAXI

In areas like Patagonia, where public transport can be scarce, try hiring a cab with driver to visit remote places. If you bargain, this can be cheaper than a rental car.

CAR & MOTORCYCLE

Especially in Patagonia, where distances are great and buses infrequent, even budget travellers may splurge on an occasional rental. The price of *nafta* (petrol) has risen to about US$0.75 per litre in much of the country, though in Patagonia (from El Bolsón southwards on Ruta Nacional (RN) 258, and south from Sierra Grande on RN 3) subsidies reduce it to about half that. Argentina requires an International or Inter-American Driving Permit in addition to your national or state driving licence. Insurance is obligatory.

Argentine highways consist of national routes (Rutas Nacionales, abbreviated RN in this book) and provincial routes (Rutas Provinciales, abbreviated RP).

Road Rules

Police rarely patrol the highways, where reckless drivers often cause high-speed, head-on crashes, but they do conduct meticulous document and equipment checks at major highway junctions and checkpoints. Minor equipment violations carry large fines but are usually opportunities for graft. If uncertain of your rights, calmly state your intention to contact your consulate. Offer a *coima* (bribe) only if certain that it is 'appropriate' and unavoidable.

Automóvil Club Argentino (ACA)

The Automóvil Club Argentino (ACA) has offices, service stations and garages throughout the country, offering free road service and towing in and around major cities. ACA also recognises members of its overseas affiliates, such as the American Automobile Association (AAA), as equivalent to its own members and grants them the same privileges, including discounts on maps, accommodation, camping, tours and other services.

ACA's headquarters (☎ 802-6061) is at Avenida del Libertador 1850, Palermo, Buenos Aires.

Rental

Major international agencies have offices in Buenos Aires, major cities and other tourist areas. To hire a car, you must have a valid driving licence, be 25 years of age, and leave a deposit or present a credit card.

Even at minor agencies, rental charges are now very high, the cheapest and smallest vehicles going for about US$27 per day plus US$0.27 per km (you can sometimes negotiate a lower rate by paying cash rather than by credit card), even higher in Patagonia. Camping rather than staying in hotels offsets some of these costs.

Purchase

For extended visits, buying a car is worth considering, though any used car is a risk, especially on rugged back roads. Argentina's automobile industry has left a reserve of decent used cars, mostly Peugeots and Ford Falcons. A usable car will cost at least US$3000, and prices will be higher for a *gasolero*, which uses cheaper diesel fuel.

Purchasers must deal with an exasperating bureaucracy. Be sure of the title *(tarjeta verde*, or 'Green Card') and that licence tax payments are up to date. Obtain a notarised document authorising use of the vehicle, since the bureaucracy moves slowly in changing vehicle titles.

Some customs officials may refuse foreigners permission to take a car out of the country, even with a notarised authorisation, but certain frontier posts (like Puerto Iguazú and Bariloche/Osorno) appear to be flexible. Contact your consulate for assistance and advice.

BICYCLE

Recreational cycling is increasingly popular among Argentines, and increasing numbers of travellers are enjoying cycling around the country. Racing bicycles are suitable for paved roads, but on gravelled roads a mountain bike (todo terreno) is advisable.

The best routes are around Bariloche and in the Andean North-West: the highway from Tucumán to Tafí del Valle, the direct road from Salta to Jujuy, and the Quebrada de Cafayate are exceptionally beautiful rides on generally good surfaces. Drawbacks include the wind (a nuisance which can slow progress to a crawl in Patagonia) and reckless motorists. Less travelled secondary roads, carrying little traffic, are excellent alternatives.

HITCHING

Private cars are often stuffed with families, but at servicentros on the outskirts of large cities, where truckers refuel their vehicles, it's worth soliciting a ride. In Patagonia, distances are great and vehicles few, so expect long waits and carry snack foods and warm, windproof clothing. Especially in the desert north, carry extra water as well.

BOAT

Opportunities for internal river travel are few. A passenger ferry runs from Rosario (Santa Fe province) across the Paraná to Victoria (Entre Ríos province). There are also launches around the Paraná delta from Tigre, a Buenos Aires suburb.

LOCAL TRANSPORT
To/From the Airport

Most cities have airport minibuses, operated by the airline or a private carrier, but regular public transport often stops at the airport. See city entries for details.

Bus

Even small towns have good bus systems.

On boarding, indicate your destination and the driver will tell you the fare and issue a ticket, which may be inspected en route. A few cities use tokens in lieu of cash, and some now have automatic ticket machines. Pay attention to placards indicating a bus' ultimate destination, since identically numbered buses may cover slightly different routes.

Train

Private operators have assumed control of commuter trains from Constitución, Retiro and Once stations to suburbs of Buenos Aires. There are also trains from Rosario to its suburbs.

Underground

Buenos Aires' aged but improving Subte is an excellent way of getting around the city centre.

Taxi

Buenos Aires' reasonably priced taxis have digital read-out meters. It is customary to leave small change as a tip. Remises are radio taxis, marginally cheaper than regular taxis, but without meters, so agree on the fare in advance. Outside Buenos Aires, taxi meters are generally less common.

ORGANISED TOURS

Companies based in Buenos Aires arrange tours within Argentina. Small operators run tours of local attractions, particularly to out-of-the-way parks and wilderness areas which can be difficult reach. These are mentioned in the entries for individual places.

Buenos Aires

Argentina's capital and largest city is not part of Buenos Aires province, but a separate federal district, the Capital Federal. Most destinations in Buenos Aires province are covered in later sections on the Atlantic Coast and the Pampas.

History

In 1536, Pedro de Mendoza's 1600 men camped on a bluff above the Río de La Plata, but within five years, Querandí resistance forced them out for nearly half a century.

Spanish mercantile restrictions slowed Buenos Aires' growth, but frustrated criollo merchants exchanged contraband with the Portuguese and British. Independence, in 1816, did not resolve conflicts between conservative provincial landowners and residents of Buenos Aires, who maintained an international orientation, both commercially and intellectually. European immigration swelled the population from 90,000 at the overthrow of caudillo Juan Manuel de Rosas (in 1852) to over a million by the turn of the century, when Buenos Aires was Latin America's largest city.

As families crowded into substandard housing, industry kept wages low, and labour became increasingly militant. In 1919, military suppression of a metalworkers' strike in La Semana Trágica (The Tragic Week) set an unfortunate precedent for coming decades. In the 1930s, a massive modernisation programme obliterated narrow colonial streets to create major avenues like Santa Fe, Córdoba and Corrientes.

After WW II, Gran (Greater) Buenos Aires absorbed many once-distant suburbs, and now faces massive pollution, noise, decaying infrastructure and declining public services, unemployment and underemployment, and spreading shantytowns. Since the restoration of democracy in 1984, however, Buenos Aires has enjoyed a freewheeling political dialogue, the publishing industry has rebounded, and arts and music flourish within economic limits. Buenos Aires may have seen better days, but survives to offer a rich urban experience.

Orientation

Buenos Aires' size is intimidating, but a brief orientation suffices for its compact centre and more accessible *barrios* (boroughs or neighbourhoods). The major thoroughfare is broad Avenida 9 de Julio, which runs from Plaza Constitución to Avenida del Libertador and exclusive northern suburbs. Except for Avenida 9 de Julio, all north-south street names change at Avenida de Mayo.

Most *porteños* (residents of Buenos Aires) 'belong' to barrios which tourists rarely see, but five main ones contain most of the capital's attractions. The *microcentro* (north of Avenida de Mayo and east of Avenida 9 de Julio) includes popular tourist areas like the Florida and Lavalle pedestrian malls, Plaza San Martín, and the commercial and entertainment areas of Corrientes, Córdoba and Santa Fe. Beyond Santa Fe are chic Recoleta/Barrio Norte and Palermo, while south of Plaza de Mayo are colourful, working-class San Telmo and La Boca.

Information

Tourist Offices All tourist offices have English-speaking staff. The Dirección Nacional de Turismo (☎ 312-2232), Avenida Santa Fe 883, is open on weekdays from 9 am to 5 pm. Municipal kiosks, on Florida between Córdoba and Paraguay, at Florida and Roque Sáenz Peña, and at Roberto M Ortiz and Avenida Quintana in Recoleta, have excellent maps; they're open on weekdays from 8.30 am to 8.30 pm, and on Saturday from 9 am to 7 pm (except for Recoleta, from 10 am to 9 pm daily except Sunday, when it's open from noon to 8 pm).

In the Centro Cultural San Martín at Sarmiento 1551, 5th floor, the municipal Dirección General de Turismo, (☎ 476-3612, 371-1496) organises free weekend guided walks of certain barrios, weather permitting, on Saturday and Sunday at 5 pm in summer, at 3 pm the rest of the year.

Money Dozens of cambios line Calle San Martín, south of Avenida Corrientes, but the only real reason to use them is to change travellers' cheques. American Express, Arenales 707, cashes its own travellers' cheques without commission. Visa and MasterCard holders can get cash advances at most banks in the city centre, and ATMs are ubiquitous.

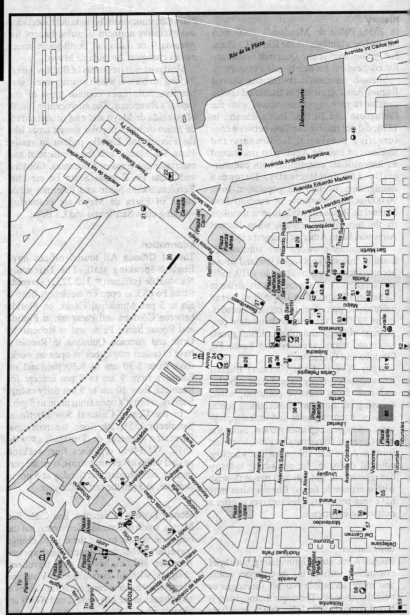

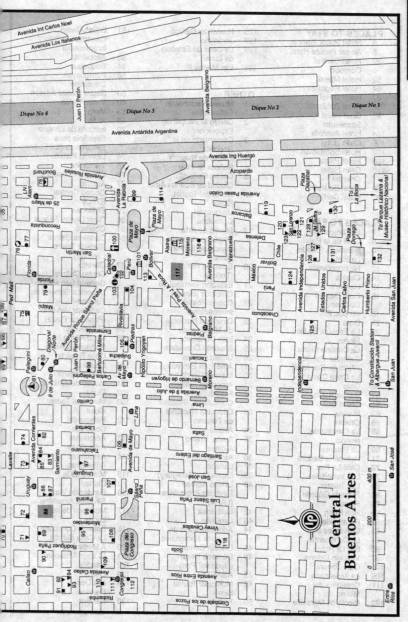

Central Buenos Aires

PLACES TO STAY

- 6 Hotel Plaza Francia
- 8 Alvear Palace Hotel
- 29 Hotel Central Córdoba
- 52 Hotel Maipú
- 64 Hotel Regidor
- 67 Hotel O'Rei
- 82 Hotel Bahía
- 91 Gran Hotel Sarmiento
- 104 Hotel Avenida
- 106 Chile Hotel
- 107 Hotel Sportsman
- 108 Hotel Plaza
- 110 Gran Hotel Oriental
- 126 Hotel Bolívar
- 132 Hotel Carly

PLACES TO EAT

- 7 El Sanjuanino
- 9 Café de la Paix
- 10 Heladería Freddo
- 12 La Biela
- 13 Hippopotamus
- 14 Clark's
- 15 Harper's
- 16 Gato Dumas Cocinero
- 18 Au Bec Fin
- 28 Dora
- 39 La Esquina de las Flores
- 41 La Cantina China
- 47 Galerías Pacífico (Patio de Comidas)
- 55 La Casa China
- 56 Coto
- 57 Bar La Robla
- 61 China Doll
- 62 Macau
- 66 Oriente
- 68 La Casona del Nonno
- 69 La Estancia
- 71 Heladería Cadore
- 72 Café La Paz
- 73 Los Inmortales
- 83 Los Teatros
- 85 Pizzería Güerrín
- 86 Pippo
- 90 Han Kung
- 92 Ratatouille
- 93 Cervantes II
- 94 La Continental
- 95 Bar La Robla
- 97 Vecchio Unione
- 105 Café Tortoni
- 109 La Americana
- 111 Confitería del Molino
- 123 Nicole de Marseille

- 125 Hostal del Canigó
- 127 Jerónimo
- 129 La Casa de Esteban de Luca
- 131 Las Marías II

OTHER

- 1 Museo Nacional de Bellas Artes
- 2 Centro Municipal de Exposiciones
- 3 Cementerio de la Recoleta
- 4 Iglesia de Nuestra Señora de Pilar
- 5 Centro Cultural Ciudad de Buenos Aires
- 11 Municipal Tourist Kiosk
- 17 Uruguayan Consulate
- 19 Museo de Arte Hispanoamericano Isaac Fernández Blanco
- 20 Estación Retiro (Trains)
- 21 Estación Terminal de Omnibus (Buses)
- 22 Correo Postal Internacional
- 23 Dirección Nacional de Migraciones
- 24 Irish Consulate
- 25 Brazilian Consulate
- 26 United Airlines
- 27 American Express
- 30 Manuel Tienda León
- 31 American Airlines
- 32 French/Swiss Consulates, Swissair
- 33 Dirección Nacional de Turismo
- 34 Alitalia
- 35 Iberia, United Airlines
- 36 Air France
- 37 Ladeco
- 38 Lapsa (Air Paraguay)
- 40 Líneas Aéreas Privadas Argentinas (LAPA)
- 42 Lufthansa
- 43 LanChile
- 44 Administración de Parques Nacionales
- 45 Lincoln Center
- 46 Dársena Norte (Hydrofoil Port)
- 48 ASATEJ
- 49 Municipal Tourist Kiosk
- 50 Ferrytur

- 51 BritishAiways, Canadian Airlines International
- 53 Aliscafos
- 54 Buquebus
- 58 Paraguayan Consulate
- 59 Sapse Líneas Aéreas
- 60 Teatro Colón
- 63 Varig
- 65 KLM
- 70 Instituto de Lengua Española para Extranjeros (ILEE)
- 74 Librería Platero
- 75 Telefónica
- 76 Chilean Consulate
- 77 Austral
- 78 Correo Central (GPO)
- 79 El Ateneo
- 80 Dinar Líneas Aéreas
- 81 Obelisco
- 84 Cartelera Baires (Galería Teatro Lorange)
- 87 Oliverio
- 88 Centro Cultural General San Martín, Dirección General de Turismo
- 89 Cartelera Vea Mas (Paseo La Plaza)
- 96 El Subsuelo
- 98 Lloyd Aéreo Boliviano (LAB)
- 99 Casa Rosada
- 100 Catedral Metropolitana
- 101 Museo del Cabildo
- 102 Pluna
- 103 Municipal Tourist Kiosk
- 112 Palacio del Congreso
- 113 Aerolíneas Argentinas
- 114 Aerolíneas Argentinas
- 115 Museo de la Ciudad
- 116 Fundación Vida Silvestre Argentina
- 117 Manzana de las Luces
- 118 Bolivian Consulate
- 119 La Casa Blanca
- 120 A Media Luz
- 121 El Viejo Almacén
- 122 Hendrix
- 124 LADE
- 128 Los Dos Pianitos
- 130 Bar Sur

Post The Correo Central, Sarmiento 189, is open on weekdays from 9 am to 7.30 pm. For international parcels weighing over one kg, go to the Correo Postal Internacional, on Antártida Argentina near Retiro station.

Telephone Public phones are numerous and much improved. For local calls, carry a pocketful of cospeles, available from kiosks, or a magnetic phonecard. Telefónica's long-distance office at Corrientes 701 is open 24 hours, but there are many private locutorios.

Buenos Aires' telephone code is 01.

Foreign Embassies Many countries maintain embassies in Buenos Aires.

Australia
    Villanueva 1400 (☎ 777-6580)
Bolivia
    Avenida Belgrano 1670 (☎ 381-0539)
Brazil
    5th floor, Carlos Pellegrini 1363 (☎ 394-5227/5260)
Canada
    Tagle 2828 (☎ 805-3032)
Chile
    9th floor, San Martín 439 (☎ 394-6582)
France
    3rd floor, Santa Fe 846 (☎ 312-2409)
Germany
    Villanueva 1055 (☎ 778-2500)
Ireland
    Suipacha 1380 (☎ 326-2612)
Paraguay
    Viamonte 1851 (☎ 812-0075)
Switzerland
    10th floor, Santa Fe 846 (☎ 311-6491)
UK
    Dr Luis Agote 2412 (☎ 803-7070)
Uruguay
    Las Heras 1907 (☎ 807-3044)
USA
    Colombia 4300 (☎ 774-4533)

Immigration The Dirección Nacional de Migraciones (☎ 312-3288) is at Antártida Argentina 1335.

Cultural Centres The high-rise Centro Cultural San Martín (☎ 374-1251), Sarmiento 1551, has free or inexpensive galleries, live theatre, lectures and films. Most visitors enter from Corrientes, between Paraná and Montevideo. At Junín 1930 in Recoleta, the Centro Cultural Ciudad de Buenos Aires (☎ 803-1041) also offers free or inexpensive events.

The United States Information Agency's Lincoln Center (☎ 311-7148), Florida 935, has an excellent library with US newspapers and magazines; it also provides satellite TV.

Travel Agencies ASATEJ (☎ 311-6953, fax 311-6840), Argentina's nonprofit student travel agency, is on the 3rd floor, Oficina 319-B, at Florida 835. Open on weekdays from 11 am to 7 pm, it seeks out the cheapest airfares, arranges bargain tours, and has a brochure of discount offers for holders of international student cards.

Bookshops Buenos Aires' landmark bookshop El Ateneo (☎ 325-6801), Florida 340, has a large selection of travel books, including Lonely Planet guides, but foreign-language books are expensive. For the most complete guidebook selection, including nearly every LP title in print, visit Librerías Turísticas (☎ 963-2855, ☎ & fax 962-5547), at Paraguay 2457 (Subte: Pueyrredón). Its prices are also the most reasonable for foreign-language guidebooks.

Visiting academics and curiosity-seekers should explore the basement stacks at Platero (☎ 382-2215), Talcahuano 485.

Maps Metrovías, the private operator of the Subte, publishes an excellent pocket-sized map of its service area, available free from most public information offices. For visitors spending some time here, Lumi Transportes' *Capital Federal* (US\$10), in compact, ring-binder format, indexes all city streets and bus routes.

Medical Services The Hospital Municipal Juan Fernández (☎ 801-5555) is at Avenida Cerviño 3356, Palermo. The highly regarded British Hospital (☎ 304-1081) is at Perdriel 74, a few blocks north-west of Constitución train station.

Avenida de Mayo & the Microcentro

In 1580, Juan de Garay laid out the Plaza del Fuerte that became **Plaza de Mayo** after 1810. Most public buildings date from the 19th century, when Avenida de Mayo first connected Plaza de Mayo to **Plaza del Congreso**. Avenida Santa Fe is the most fashionable shopping area, and Florida and Lavalle are pedestrian malls. Demolition of older buildings created the avenues of Corrientes (the theatre district), Córdoba and Santa Fe. Even wider Avenida 9 de Julio, with its famous **Obelisco** at the intersection of Corrientes, is a pedestrian's nightmare, but has a tunnel beneath it.

At the north end of the microcentro, beyond **Plaza San Martín** and its magnificent *ombú* tree, stands the **Torre de los Ingleses**, a Big Ben clone. Since the Falklands War, it stands in the renamed **Plaza Fuerza Aérea Argentina** (Air Force Plaza).

Museo del Cabildo Modern construction truncated the colonial arches that once ran the width of Plaza de Mayo, but this building itself remains still more interesting than its scanty exhibits. At Bolívar 65, it's open Thursday to Sunday from 2 to 6 pm. Admission costs US$1.

Catedral Metropolitana This religious landmark also contains the tomb of José de San Martín, Argentina's most revered historical figure.

Casa Rosada Off limits during the dictatorship of 1976-83, the presidential palace is no longer a place to avoid. The basement museum (☎ 476-9841), entered at Hipólito Yrigoyen 219, exhibits the personal effects of Argentine presidents. Opening hours are Thursday and Friday only, noon to 6 pm.

Palacio del Congreso Completed in 1906 after costing twice its allotted budget, this building set a standard for Argentine public works projects. It faces Plaza del Congreso and its **Monumento a los Dos Congresos** (Buenos Aires in 1810 and Tucumán in 1816), commemorating the events that led to

independence. Its granite steps symbolise the Andes, while the fountain represents the Atlantic Ocean.

Teatro Colón For decades, visitors have marvelled at the Teatro Colón (☎ 382-6632), a world-class facility for opera, ballet and classical music, which opened in 1908. Occupying an entire block bounded by Libertad, Tucumán, Viamonte and Cerrito (Avenida 9 de Julio), the imposing seven-storey building seats 2500 spectators and has standing room for another 1000. Worthwhile guided tours (US$5) take place hourly between 9 am and 4 pm on weekdays, and 9 am and noon on Saturdays, and are available in Spanish, English and several other languages.

San Telmo

South of Plaza de Mayo, parts of San Telmo are still an artists' quarter with low rents. The barrio saw rugged street fighting in 1806 and 1807, when a criollo militia drove British troops back to their ships. It was fashionable until a 19th-century yellow-fever epidemic drove the porteño elite to higher ground and many houses became *conventillos*, sheltering immigrants in cramped quarters with poor sanitary facilities – conditions which have not totally disappeared.

The **Manzana de las Luces** (Block of Enlightenment), bounded by Alsina, Bolívar, Perú and Moreno, includes the Jesuit **Iglesia San Ignacio**, Buenos Aires' oldest church. At Defensa and Humberto Primo, **Plaza Dorrego** hosts the Feria de San Telmo, a Sunday flea market. At Defensa and Brasil, believed to be the site of Pedro de Mendoza's first encampment, **Parque Lezama** contains the **Museo Histórico Nacional** (theoretically open Wednesday through to Sunday from 2 to 6 pm, but frequently closed for repairs).

La Boca

Literally Buenos Aires' most colourful neighbourhood, La Boca was built up by Italian immigrants along the **Riachuelo**, a narrow waterway lined by meat-packers and warehouses. Part of its colour comes from the brightly painted houses of the **Caminito**, a pedestrian walk named for a popular tango; the rest comes from the petroleum sludge and toxics that tint the waters of the Riachuelo.

Immigrants could find a foothold here, but British diplomat James Bryce described Boca houses as 'dirty and squalid...their wooden boards gaping like rents in tattered clothes'. Boca's status as an artists' colony is the legacy of painter Benito Quinquela Martín, but it's also a solidly working-class neighbourhood, whose symbol is the Boca Juniors soccer team. The No 86 bus from Plaza del Congreso is the easiest way to get there.

Once the home and studio of Quinquela Martín, the fine-arts **Museo de Bellas Artes de La Boca**, Pedro de Mendoza 1835, is open Tuesday to Saturday from 8 am to 6 pm. Admission is free.

Recoleta

Upper-class porteños relocated in now fashionable Recoleta, north of the microcentro, after the San Telmo yellow fever epidemic of the 1870s. The barrio is famous for the **Cementerio de la Recoleta**, a necropolis where, in death as in life, generations of Argentina's elite rest in ornate splendour. The colonial **Iglesia de Nuestra Señora de Pilar** (1732) is an historical monument; nearby are the **Centro Cultural Ciudad de Buenos Aires** and the **Centro Municipal de Exposiciones**, which hosts many cultural events. Attractive gardens and open spaces include **Plaza Alvear**, **Plaza Francia** and other parks toward Palermo.

The **Museo Nacional de Bellas Artes** houses works by Renoir, Rodin, Monet, Van Gogh and Argentine artists. At Avenida del Libertador 1473, it's open daily except Monday from 12.30 to 7.30 pm; on Saturday it opens at 9.30 am. Admission is free.

Palermo

Rosas' most positive legacy is the open spaces of Palermo, which became parkland after his overthrow by Entre Ríos caudillo

and former ally Justo José de Urquiza (who sits astride his horse in a massive monument at Sarmiento and Figueroa Alcorta).

Palermo contains the **Jardín Botánico Carlos Thays** (botanical gardens), **Jardín Zoológico** (zoo), **Rosedal** (rose garden), **Campo de Polo** (polo grounds), **Hipódromo** (racetrack) and **Planetarium**. Some of these uses were obviously not for the masses, but the elite no longer monopolises the area.

Language Courses

The Sunday classified section of the *Buenos Aires Herald* lists possibilities for language instruction. The Instituto de Lengua Española para Extranjeros (ILEE, ☎ 375-0730, fax 864-4942), Oficina C, 7th floor, Lavalle 1619, can help arrange accommodation with porteño families.

Places to Stay

Hostel In a rambling but charming building at Brasil 675, near Constitución station, the official *Albergue Juvenil* (☎ 394-9112) is easily reached by Subte. Prices are US$9 per person with breakfast; HI membership is obligatory.

Hotels The best located budget hotel is *Hotel O'Rei* (☎ 393-7186), Lavalle 733. Quiet, clean and very friendly, it has singles/doubles with shared bath for US$19/25. Central, attractive *Hotel Maipú* (☎ 322-5142), Maipú 735, has simple but pleasant rooms for US$19/24 with shared bath, and doubles with private bath for US$25. Another recommended place is *Hotel Bahía* (☎ 35-1780), Corrientes 1212, (US$20 single or double).

In San Telmo, amiable, well-maintained *Hotel Zavalía* (☎ 362-1990), Juan de Garay 474, has singles/doubles with shared bath for only US$8/12, but children make it noisy at times. Closer to Plaza Dorrego, run-down but passable *Hotel Carly* (☎ 361-7710), Humberto Primo 464, charges US$12/14 for a single/double with shared bath. At *Hotel Bolívar* (☎ 361-5105), the barrio's budget

ARGENTINA

favourite at Bolívar 886, several rooms have sunny balconies for US$17 per single, US$22 per double with private bath.

Near Congreso, a good budget area, *Hotel Sportsman* (☎ 381-8021) occupies a nice older building at Rivadavia 1425; rates are US$15/24 with shared bath, US$28/35 with private bath. At scruffy but passable *Hotel Plaza* (☎ 371-9747), Rivadavia 1689, small singles with shared bath cost US$18, slightly more with private bath. Greatly improved *Gran Hotel Oriental* (☎ 951-6427), Mitre 1840, has rooms with shared bath for US$16/18 and others with private bath for US$20/22. Still decent value is friendly *Gran Hotel Sarmiento* (☎ 476-2764), on a quiet block at Sarmiento 1892, where simple but very clean rooms (some a bit cramped) with private bath cost US$25/35.

Travellers able to spend a bit more can find good value. Corner rooms at *Chile Hotel* (☎ 34-5664), Avenida de Mayo 1297, have huge balconies with views of the Congreso and the Casa Rosada (US$30/45 with private bath). Correspondents offer mixed reviews of remodelled *Hotel Avenida* (☎ 331-4341), Avenida de Mayo 623, where singles/doubles for US$35/45 with private bath are much improved but the mood of the staff is less than cheerful. Cosy *Hotel Central Córdoba* (☎ 311-1175), modest but friendly and pleasant, is also very central, at San Martín 1021 (US$32/42).

For US$50/60 with breakfast, *Hotel Regidor* (☎ 314-7917), Tucumán 451, is excellent value, but can be snooty towards casually dressed visitors. Few places can match the old-world charm of *Hotel Plaza Francia* (☎ 804-9631), Eduardo Schiaffino 2189 in Recoleta (about US$135/180). At the revered, elegant *Alvear Palace Hotel* (☎ 804-4031), Alvear 1891 in Recoleta, doubles can cost US$260 or more.

Places to Eat

In ordinary restaurants, standard fare is pasta, minutas such as milanesa, and cheaper cuts of beef, plus chips, salads and desserts. For a little more, you can eat similar food of better quality, but meals at top restaurants can be very costly.

Parrillas Charles Darwin, crossing the Pampas in the 1830s, expressed astonishment at the gauchos' meat diet, which 'would only have agreed with me with hard exercise'. You can probably indulge yourself on this succulent grilled meat, so long as you don't make a lifestyle of it.

If you visit only one parrilla, make it *La Estancia*, Lavalle 941, and overlook the hired tourist gauchos to focus on the excellent, moderately priced food. *Dora*, Avenida Alem 1016, is popular in part for its massive portions; most dishes suffice for two people, and the imposing half-portion of bife de chorizo (US$9) weighs nearly half a kilo. *Cervantes II*, Perón 1883, serves enormous portions of standard Argentine fare at modest prices, but is often very crowded. One of the most popular, economical parrillas is *Pippo*, Paraná 356.

Italian *La Casona del Nonno*, Lavalle 827, has good lunch specials for US$4 and a separate, well-ventilated tobacco-free area. Also very inexpensive is *Vecchio Unione*, Perón 1372. *Fiori y Canto*, on the edge of Palermo Viejo at Córdoba 3547, is an attractive combination of pizzería, parrilla and pasta restaurant with particularly delicious home-made bread.

Pizzerías Unsung *Pizzería Güerrín*, Corrientes 1372, sells inexpensive individual slices of superb fugazza, fugazzeta and other specialities, plus excellent empanadas and cold lager beer. At Callao and Mitre, *La Americana* has very fine pizza and exceptional empanadas, but the best chicken empanadas (usually breast meat) are at *La Continental*, Callao 202.

Visit the original branch of *Los Inmortales*, at Corrientes 1369 beneath the conspicuous billboard of Carlos Gardel, to see the historic photographs of Gardel and his contemporaries on the walls. Another recommended pizzería is reader-endorsed

Las Marías II, at Bolívar 964-66 in San Telmo.

European/International Many new restaurants have opened in Plaza del Pilar, at Avenida Pueyrredón 2501 alongside the Centro Cultural Recoleta; more easily reached from the Calle Junín entrance to the Centro, they range from modest fast-food offerings to elaborate and sophisticated fare. If price is no object, out Recoleta institutions like *Gato Dumas Cocinero* at Junín 1747, *Harper's* at Junín 1763, *Clark's* at Junín 1777, and *Hippopotamus* at Junín 1787.

An inexpensive choice in San Telmo is *Jerónimo*, Estados Unidos 407, where main courses cost between US$3 and US$5 and desserts are about US$1.50. *Restaurant Ruso*, Azcuénaga 1562 in Barrio Norte, is a new restaurant specialising in Russian food at reasonable prices (by Barrio Norte standards). Also in Barrio Norte, at Santa Fe 2321, attractive *Guadalest* serves fine pasta and imposing desserts – most of them large enough for two – and has a good non-smoking section.

Spanish Spanish restaurants are usually the best alternatives for seafood, generally not a high priority for Argentines. In addition to a pleasant atmosphere, *Los Teatros*, Talcahuano 360, has outstanding seafood, chicken and pasta dishes. Part of San Telmo's Casal de Catalunya cultural centre at Chacabuco 863, *Hostal del Canigó* serves Catalonian specialties like pollo a la punxa (chicken with calamari). Prices are not cheap (the fixed-price menú ejecutivo costs US$9), but portions are large. A nice touch is the complimentary glass of sherry.

Bar La Robla, at Viamonte 1613 and Montevideo 194, has both excellent seafood and standard Argentine dishes, in a pleasant environment at moderate prices. Its US$3.50 lunch specials, with an appetiser and a small glass of clericó, are excellent value. San Telmo's *La Casa de Esteban de Luca* has very fine food at moderate prices in a restored colonial house at Defensa 1000.

French It's stretching it a bit to call *Nicole de Marseille*, Defensa 714, a French or even Franco-Argentine restaurant, but three-course weekday lunches (US$6) present a wide choice of main courses and desserts. A new addition is the appealing *French Bistro*, French 2301 in Barrio Norte.

Widely acknowledged as one of Buenos Aires' best restaurants, *Au Bec Fin*, Vicente López 1825 in Recoleta, has prices to match.

Asian Most Asian food is unremarkable Cantonese, but tenedor libre restaurants, as cheap as US$4, are a good budget option. Most also have salad bars with excellent ingredients, but also tack on a US$1 surcharge if you don't order anything to drink. Try *Macau* at Suipacha 477, *China Doll* at Suipacha 544, or *Han Kung* at Rodríguez Peña 384.

A step up from most all-you-can-eats is *Gran Fu Ia*, Las Heras 2379, a few blocks from Recoleta cemetery; the US$8 price tag reflects its higher quality. Other possibilities for better quality Chinese food include *La Cantina China* at Maipú 976, *La Casa China* at Viamonte 1476, or *Oriente* at Maipú 512.

Latin American & Regional *La Casa de Orihuela*, Alsina 2163 near Congreso, serves exceptionally well-prepared Peruvian and regional dishes; its US$6 fixed-price lunch is well worth a detour from other parts of town. *El Sanjuanino*, Posadas 1515 in Recoleta, serves regional versions of Argentine dishes like empanadas, locro and sweets. Jujuy cuisine is the rule at friendly *La Carretería*, Brasil 656 (across from the youth hostel).

Vegetarian Since the mid-1980s, the carnivorous capital has enjoyed a vegetarian boom, and nearly all of the new places have the additional appeal of being tobacco-free. Some failed because of blandness, but many have survived, like the self-service, tenedor libre *Ratatouille*, Sarmiento 1810, for US$8. One of the most enduring vegetarian places,

La Esquina de las Flores at Avenida Córdoba 1599, also has a health-food shop; its daily fixed-price meals cost US$10 (US$6 for children), but there are less expensive à-la-carte choices.

Fast Food Fast-food restaurants are generally inferior to standard inexpensive eateries, but the Patio de Comidas on the lower level of the Galerías Pacífico on the Florida *peatonal* (pedestrian mall) has a number of moderately priced fast-food versions of very good restaurants for about US$5 to US$7. The express cafeteria at supermarket *Coto*, Viamonte 1571, offers a variety of cheap (US$3 or less) meals of good quality.

Cafés & Confiterías Porteños spend hours solving their own problems, the country's and the world's over a chessboard and a cortado at places like century-old *Café Tortoni*, Avenida de Mayo 829. The almost Rococo interior at *Confitería del Molino*, Callao 20, also merits a visit.

Famous for Bohemian atmosphere is the spartan *Café La Paz*, Corrientes 1599. Some upper-class porteños dawdle for hours over caffeine from *La Biela*, Quintana 598 in Recoleta. The rest exercise their purebred dogs nearby; watch your step crossing the street to *Café de la Paix*, Quintana 595.

Ice Cream Chocoholics should not miss the exquisite chocolate amargo (semisweet chocolate) and chocolate blanco (white chocolate), at *Heladería Cadore*, Corrientes and Rodríguez Peña. In Recoleta, try *Freddo*, at Ayacucho and Quintana and several other locations. Many ice-creameries close in winter.

Entertainment
Carteleras along Avenida Corrientes sell heavily discounted tickets for entertainment events including movies, live theatre and tango shows; since the number of tickets may be limited, buy them as far in advance as possible. The most convenient are Cartelera Vea Mas (☎ 372-7285/7314, Int 219), Local 19 in the Paseo La Plaza complex at

Corrientes 1660, and Cartelera Baires (☎ 372-5058), Local 25 in the Galería Teatro Lorange at Corrientes 1372.

Cinemas The main cinema zones, along Lavalle west of Florida, and on Avenidas Corrientes and Santa Fe, feature first-run films from around the world, but there's also an audience for unconventional and classic films. Many offer half-price tickets on Wednesday. The *Sala Leopoldo Lugones* at the Teatro General San Martín, Avenida Corrientes 1530, offers thematic foreign film cycles and occasional reprises of outstanding commercial films.

Translations of English-language titles can be misleading, so check the *Buenos Aires Herald* to be sure what's playing. Foreign films usually have Spanish subtitles.

Theatre Avenida Corrientes, between 9 de Julio and Callao, is the capital's Broadway or West End. The *Teatro General San Martín* (☎ 374-8611), Corrientes 1530, has several auditoriums and frequent free events. For complete listings, see the *Buenos Aires Herald* or *Clarín*.

Live Music & Dance Clubs Buenos Aires has a thriving rock and blues scene; for the latest information, consult Friday's 'Suplemento Jóven', which also lists free events, in *Clarín*, and the weekend editions of *Página 12*.

El Subsuelo (☎ 476-2479), in the basement at the Pasaje de la Piedad alleyway just off Mitre 1571, is an intimate venue with good live music, including rock, blues and jazz. *Hendrix*, San Lorenzo 354, is worth a trip to San Telmo. For live jazz, try also *Oliverio* (☎ 371-6877), Paraná 328.

Discos tend to be exclusive and expensive (US$20 up, with pricey drinks), such as *Hippopotamus* at Junín 1787 and *Africa* in the Alvear Palace Hotel. Less expensive, with a young and lively crowd, is *Gallery*, Azcuénaga 1771 in Barrio Norte/Recoleta. The cover charge is US$6, while large drinks cost about US$5 each.

Tango Finding spontaneous tango is not easy, but plenty of places portray Argentina's most famous cultural export, for up to US$40 per show in San Telmo and La Boca. The best value is Plaza Dorrego's free city-sponsored 'Tango y Baile', on alternate Saturday nights in summer.

From its publicity, *La Casa Blanca* (☎ 331-4621), Balcarce 668 in San Telmo, appears to take pride in hosting disgraced heads of state like Brazil's Fernando Collor de Mello and Mexico's Carlos Salinas de Gortari. Other San Telmo *tanguerías* include *El Viejo Almacén* (☎ 362-3602), at Balcarce and Independencia, *Bar Sur* (☎ 362-6086), at Estados Unidos 299, *A Media Luz* (☎ 331-6146), at Chile 316, and *Los Dos Pianitos* (☎ 361-2188), at Pasaje Giuffra 305.

Things to Buy

The main shopping zones are along Florida (see the impressive recycled Galerías Pacífico shopping centre at Florida and Córdoba), Avenida Santa Fe, and Recoleta. The Feria de San Telmo flea market, on Plaza Dorrego, takes place on Sunday from 10 am to about 5 pm. Good antique shops and restaurants are nearby, with spontaneous live entertainment from buskers and mimes. Best buys are jewellery, leather, shoes and *mate* paraphernalia.

Getting There & Away

Air Many major international airlines have Buenos Aires offices.

Aerolíneas Argentinas
    Paseo Colón 185 (☎ 343-2071/89)
    Perú 2 (☎ 343-8551/59)
Air France
    Avenida Santa Fe 963 (☎ 327-0202)
Alitalia
    Suipacha 1111, 28th floor (☎ 321-8421)
American Airlines
    Avenida Santa Fe 881 (☎ 312-3640)
British Airways
    Avenida Córdoba 650 (☎ 325-1059)
Canadian Airlines International
    Avenida Córdoba 656 (☎ 322-3732)
Iberia
    Carlos Pellegrini 1163, 1st floor (☎ 327-2739/52)

KLM
    Reconquista 559, 5th floor (☎ 480-9470)
Ladeco
    Avenida Santa Fe 920 (☎ 326-9937)
LanChile
    Paraguay 609, 1st floor, (☎ 311-5334)
Lapsa (Air Paraguay)
    Cerrito 1026 (☎ 393-1527)
Lloyd Aéreo Boliviano (LAB)
    Carlos Pellegrini 141 (☎ 326-3595/6411)
Lufthansa
    Marcelo T de Alvear 636 (☎ 319-0600)
Pluna (Líneas Aéreas Uruguayas)
    Florida 1 (☎ 342-4420)
Swissair
    Avenida Santa Fe 846 (☎ 319-0000)
United Airlines
    Carlos Pellegrini 1165, 5th floor (☎ 326-9111)
Varig
    Florida 630 (☎ 329-9200/1)

The major domestic carriers are Aerolíneas and Austral, serving nearly every major city from Bolivia to the Beagle Channel, but alternatives are increasing.

Austral
    Corrientes 485 (☎ 325-0777)
Dinar Líneas Aéreas
    Diagonal Roque Sáenz Peña 933; this new airline flies to Tucumán, Salta and Jujuy, but capacity is limited (☎ 326-0135)
LADE
    Perú 710; serves only Patagonian destinations (☎ 361-0583)
LAPA
    Marcelo T de Alvear 790; has acquired many new planes and expanded routes to compete with Aerolíneas and Austral, and also provides regional services to Uruguay (☎ 314-1005)
Sapse Líneas Aéreas
    Tucumán 1920; a Patagonian carrier, with cheap fares (☎ 371-7066)

To Uruguay, Aeroparque Jorge Newbery is cheaper and more convenient than Aeropuerto Internacional Ezeiza.

Bus At the massive Retiro terminal, at Antártida Argentina and Ramos Mejía near the train station, each company has a desk like an airline ticket counter. The entries below are only a representative sample of very extensive schedules.

International General Urquiza (☎ 313-2771) has a nightly service to Montevideo (US$25, nine hours). La Internacional (☎ 313-3167), Nuestra Señora de la Asunción (☎ 313-2325) and Chevallier Paraguaya (☎ 313-2349) go to Asunción, Paraguay (US$56, 21 hours).

Pluma (☎ 313-3839) goes to Brazilian destinations, including Foz do Iguaçu (US$60, 19 hours), São Paulo (US$101, 42 hours) and Rio de Janeiro (US$117, 48 hours). Rápido Yguazú (☎ 313-4139) also serves Brazilian routes.

Several companies cross the Andes to Santiago, Chile (US$60, 21 hours): TAC (☎ 313-2627), Chevallier (☎ 313-3288), and Fénix Pullman Norte (☎ 313-0134).

Atlantic Coast & the Pampas Costera Criolla (☎ 313-2449) and El Cóndor (☎ 313-3695) both go to Mar del Plata (US$25, seven hours) and other beach resorts. La Estrella (☎ 313-3051), El Cóndor and Costera Criolla serve many destinations within Buenos Aires province, as far as Bahía Blanca (US$30, 10 hours). Chevallier (☎ 313-3288) and La Unión (☎ 313-3797) both go to Rosario (US$20, six hours) and points north.

Mesopotamia, Misiones & the Gran Chaco El Rápido (☎ 315-0804), Expreso Río Paraná (☎ 313-3143) and La Encarnaceña (☎ 313-2393) serve the littoral cities of Santa Fe (US$21, six hours), Paraná (US$26, seven hours) and Corrientes (US$32, 14 hours). El Norte Bis (☎ 313-2435) goes to Resistencia (US$43, 15 hours).

Empresa Tata (☎ 313-3836) serves Gualeguaychú (US$20, three hours) and other northerly destinations, passing Parque Nacional El Palmar. Expreso Singer (☎ 313-2355), Horiansky (☎ 97-6084) and Empresa Kurtz (☎ 313-0950) have buses to Posadas (US$35, 14 hours) and Puerto Iguazú (US$48, 21 hours).

Córdoba & the North-West Cacorba (☎ 313-2588) has buses to Córdoba (US$30,

10 hours) and Catamarca (US$50, 16 hours). Ablo (☎ 313-2835) goes to Rosario, Córdoba and its sierras, and La Rioja (US$53, 17 hours), as does Chevallier (☎ 313-3288).

La Estrella (☎ 313-3167) and El Trébol (☎ 315-0808) go to Termas de Río Hondo (US$43, 15 hours), Santiago del Estero and Tucumán (US$46, 16 hours). La Veloz del Norte (☎ 313-4309) goes to Salta (US$65, 22 hours); La Internacional (☎ 313-3167) also goes to Salta and Jujuy (US$77, 22 hours).

Cuyo Chevallier (☎ 313-3288) and Expreso Jocolí (☎ 311-8283) go to San Luis (US$45, 12 hours) and Mendoza (US$52, 13 hours), as does TAC (☎ 313-3627). Autotransportes San Juan (☎ 313-9625) has buses to San Luis and San Juan (US$54, 16 hours).

Patagonia Empresa Pehuenche (☎ 311-8283) goes to Santa Rosa (US$37, nine hours) and to Neuquén (US$45, 15 hours). El Cóndor (☎ 313-3687), La Estrella (☎ 313-3051) and Chevallier (☎ 313-3288) have buses to Neuquén and Bariloche (US$76, 23 hours). Other Bariloche carriers include El Valle (☎ 313-2441), which also serves San Martín de los Andes (US$70, 23 hours); Vía Bariloche (☎ 315-3122); and TAC (☎ 313-3627).

Costera Criolla/Don Otto (☎ 313-2503) is the major carrier to coastal Patagonia, including Puerto Madryn (US$57, 21 hours), Comodoro Rivadavia (US$82, 24 hours) and Río Gallegos (US$107, 40 hours). La Estrella and La Puntual (☎ 313-3742) run similar routes. Expreso Pingüino (☎ 311-5440) also goes to Río Gallegos.

Train Privatisation of Ferrocarriles Argentinos has greatly reduced long-distance rail services, but the Ferrocarril Mitre (☎ 312-6596) from Retiro station to Tucumán and the Ferrocarril Roca (☎ 304-0035) from Constitución station to Buenos Aires province and Bariloche continue to offer regular, though less frequent, passenger services.

Retiro is near the bus terminal in central Buenos Aires, while Constitución is south of the centre; Línea C of the Subte links them.

River Ferries and hydrofoils to Uruguay sail from Dársena Norte, near the city centre at Madero and Viamonte, or from Dársena Sur, Avenida Pedro de Mendoza 20 in La Boca. There is now a US$10 departure tax from these terminals.

Ferrytur (☎ 315-6800), Córdoba 699, sails twice daily on weekdays, daily on weekends, to Colonia (US$15, 2½ hours) and back; its hydrofoil *Sea Cat* goes to Colonia (45 minutes) three times daily from Monday to Saturday, twice on Sunday (US$25 one way, US$45 return). Aliscafos (☎ 314-2473), Córdoba 787, also runs several hydrofoils daily to Colonia.

Buquebus (☎ 313-4444), Córdoba 867, has three ferry sailings daily to Colonia. Its 'Aviones de Buquebus' are luxurious high-speed ferries that reach Montevideo in 2½ hours and cost US$37 in *turista* class, US$49 in *primera*.

Cacciola (☎ 749-0329), at Lavalle 520 in the riverside suburb of Tigre, goes twice daily to Carmelo, Uruguay (US$11). Movilán/Deltanave (☎ 749-4119) also goes to Carmelo twice daily. Línea Nueva Palmira (☎ 749-0537) goes to Nueva Palmira, Uruguay, daily at 7 am except Monday, when it leaves at 4.30 am.

Getting Around

To/From the Airport Nearly all domestic flights and some to neighbouring countries leave from Aeroparque Jorge Newbery (☎ 771-2071), only a few km north of the microcentro. Most international flights leave from Aeropuerto Internacional Ministro Pistarini (commonly known as 'Ezeiza', ☎ 480-0235), about 35 km south of the city centre.

To Aeroparque, take city bus No 37C ('Ciudad Universitaria') from Plaza Italia; No 45 northbound from Constitución, Plaza San Martín or Retiro; or No 160B from

Avenida Las Heras or Plaza Italia. The fare is about US$0.50.

To Ezeiza, the cheapest way (US$1, 1½ to two hours) is the No 86 bus (be sure it says 'Ezeiza', since not all No 86s go to the end of the line), which starts in La Boca and comes up Avenida de Mayo past the Plaza del Congreso. To be assured of a seat, take the more comfortable *servicio diferencial* (about US$5).

Manuel Tienda León (☎ 314-3636/2577/2579), Santa Fe 790, runs minibuses to Ezeiza (US$14 one way, 45 minutes). Its service to Aeroparque costs US$5.

Taxis are expensive for individuals, costing about US$30 plus a US$2 freeway toll, but may be cheaper than Manuel Tienda León for a group of three or four; negotiate with the driver.

Bus Sold at nearly all kiosks and bookshops, Lumi's *Capital Federal* street atlas details nearly 200 different bus routes. Many porteños have memorised the system and can instantly tell you which bus to take and where to get off, but always check the window placard for the final destination. Fares depend on distance; tell the driver your destination. Most buses now have automatic ticket machines, which also make small change.

Train Commuter trains serve most of Gran Buenos Aires from Retiro, Constitución, Lacroze and Once.

Underground Buenos Aires' antique Subte is fast and efficient, but reaches only certain parts of a city much larger than when the system opened in 1913. Four of the five lines (Líneas A, B, D, and E) run from the microcentro to the capital's western and northern outskirts, while Línea C links Retiro and Constitución. Tourist kiosks and ticket booths distribute a map of the system. Buy a pocketful of fichas (US$0.45) to avoid standing in line.

Trains operate from 5.30 am to 1.30 am;

they are frequent on weekdays, less so on weekends.

Taxi & Remises Black-and-yellow cabs are numerous and reasonably priced, with new digital read-out meters. Drivers customarily receive small change as a tip. Remises (radio taxis) have many offices around town.

AROUND BUENOS AIRES
Isla Martín García

Navigating the densely forested channels of the Delta, en route to historic Martín García, it's easy to imagine colonial smugglers hiding among the rushes. Just off the Uruguayan littoral, directly south of the city of Carmelo, the island is famous – or infamous – as a prison camp; four Argentine presidents have spent time in custody here, and the Servicio Penitenciario of Buenos Aires province still uses it as a halfway house for prisoners near the end of their terms. At present, though, it's more a combination of historical monument, nature reserve, and recreational retreat from the bustle of the capital.

Without your own boat, the only practical way to the island is the guided tour from Cacciola's Terminal Internacional (☎ 749-0329), at Lavalle 520 in the suburb of Tigre; tickets are also available at the company's microcentro office (☎ 322-0026), at Florida 520, 1st floor, Oficina 113.

The enclosed catamaran leaves Tigre at 8 am, returning from Martín García at 5 pm (be dockside at 4 pm, however), and costs US$28 return. For US$42, the tour includes lunch at Cacciola's La Fragata restaurant, but there are cheaper and better dining alternatives. Bus No 60 from Avenida Callao goes directly to Tigre.

Luján

Legend says that, in 1630, a wagon would not budge on a rutted cart road until gauchos removed from it an image of the Virgin brought from Brazil. The image's devoted owner built a chapel on the spot, 65 km west of Buenos Aires, where Argentina's patron saint now occupies the neo-Gothic **Basílica**

Nuestra Señora de Luján, the country's most important devotional site. Her day is 8 May. The town's other main attraction is a colonial museum complex.

Waiters at the many cheap restaurants along Avenida Nuestra Señora de Luján virtually drag pilgrims off the pavement. Quieter *Don Diego*, Colón 964, has excellent but pricier food.

From Plaza Miserere, north of Congreso but reached by Subte, Transporte Luján (Línea 52) runs buses to Luján (US$3), while the Ferrocarril Sarmiento runs commuter trains to and from Once station. Transportes Atlántida (Línea 57) runs buses from Palermo (Subte Plaza Italia).

San Antonio de Areco

Dating from the early 18th-century construction of a chapel in honour of San Antonio de Padua, this serene village is the symbolic centre of Argentina's vestigial gaucho culture and host to the country's biggest gaucho celebration, Día de la Tradición, in November. Nestled in the verdant Pampas of northern Buenos Aires province, 113 km west of Buenos Aires via RN 8, its main permanent attraction is the **Parque Criollo y Museo Gauchesco Ricardo Güiraldes**, honouring the author of the classic gauchesque novel *Don Segundo Sombra*.

San Antonio is a popular weekend excursion from Buenos Aires, but weekdays are less crowded (accommodation is very limited). The village's artisans are known throughout the country for *mate* paraphernalia, *rastras* (silver-studded belts) and *facones* (long-bladed knives), produced by skilled silversmiths.

Frequent buses from Buenos Aires to San Antonio take 1½ hours with Chevallier, Empresa Argentina and Rápido Argentino.

Atlantic Coast

In summer, millions of porteños take a holiday from friends, families and co-workers, only to meet them on the beaches

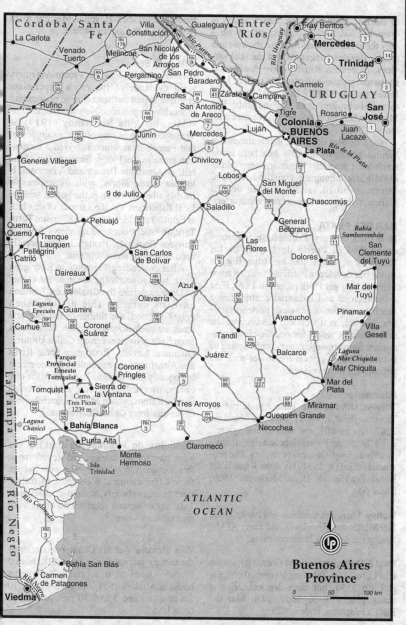

Buenos Aires Province

0   50   100 km

of Buenos Aires province. Beach access is open, but *balnearios* (resorts) are private – only those renting tents may use showers and toilets. Besides lifeguards and medical services, balnearios usually have confiterías, shops and paddle-ball courts (a current fad). Prices rise fortnightly from mid-December to mid-February, then decline until late March, when most hotels and residenciales close.

North of Mar del Plata, gentle dunes rise behind generally narrow beaches, while south-west towards Miramar, steep bluffs highlight a changing coastline. Beyond Miramar, broad sandy beaches delight bathers, fishing enthusiasts and windsurfers.

MAR DEL PLATA

Mid-19th century Portuguese investors established El Puerto de Laguna de los Padres here, about 400 km from Buenos Aires, but developer Patricio Peralta Ramos founded Mar del Plata proper in 1874. First a commercial and industrial centre, then a beach resort for upper-class porteño families, Mardel, as it's called, has become the main summer resort for middle-class vacationers. Some travellers may prefer spring or autumn, when prices are lower and the atmosphere more relaxed.

Information

Tourist Offices The Ente Municipal de Turismo (Emtur, ☎ 21777), Blvd Marítimo 2267, has an efficient information system, good maps and useful brochures; there's usually an English-speaker on duty. The provincial office (☎ 25340) is at the Rambla del Hotel Provincial, Blvd Marítimo 2500, Local 60.

Money There are cambios and banks along San Martín and Rivadavia, and many ATMs, mostly on Avenida Independencia.

Post & Communications Correo Argentino is at Luro 2460. Telefónica's central office is at Luro 2554, but there are locutorios at many places throughout town. Mar del Plata's telephone code is 023.

Medical Services Hospital Mar del Plata (☎ 22021) is at Castelli 2460.

Things to See

A stroll past Mar del Plata's mansions offers vivid evidence of the city's upper-class origins and past as the exclusive playground of wealthy Argentines. Now the Italian Consulate, the **Villa Normandy** (1919) at Viamonte 2216 is one of few examples of that French style which survived a renovation craze in the 1950s. Near the top of the hill, at Almirante Brown and Viamonte, is **Iglesia Stella Maris**, with its impressive marble altar. Its virgin is the patron saint of local fishermen. On the summit of this hill, at Falucho and Mendoza, the 88-metre **Torre Tanque** offers outstanding views from its *mirador* (lookout), though it has recently been closed for reconstruction.

After descending Viamonte to Rodríguez Peña, walk towards the ocean to the corner of Urquiza, where the **Chalet Los Troncos** gave its name to this distinguished neighbourhood; the timber of the gate and fence are *quebracho* and *lapacho* hardwoods from Salta province. Lining Calles Urquiza, Quintana, Lavalle, Rodríguez Peña, Rivas and Almafuerte are examples of more recent but equally elite design. To return to the city centre, try the longer route along Avenida Peralta Ramos, which offers beautiful views of the city from **Cabo Corrientes**.

Banquina de Pescadores Barking sea lions monitor the anglers and stevedores at this picturesque wharf in the port, where there's fine dining at a complex of restaurants or, more cheaply, at stand-up cafeterias. Take any of several southbound buses from the centre.

Villa Victoria Victoria Ocampo, founder of the literary journal *Sur* in the 1920s, hosted literary salons at this prefab Norwegian house at Matheu 1851, open daily from 10 am to 1 pm and 5 to 9.30 pm. Admission costs US$2.

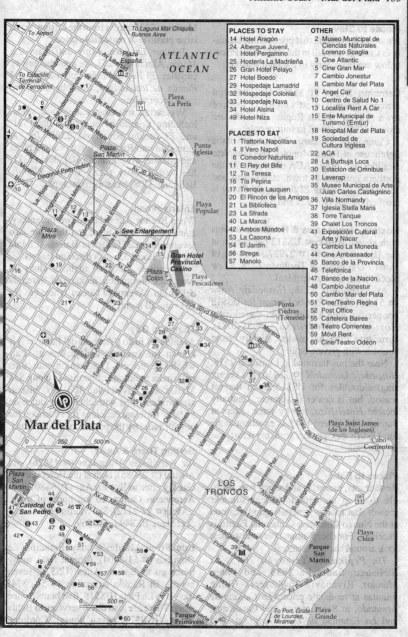

PLACES TO STAY
14 Hotel Aragón
24 Albergue Juvenil,
   Hotel Pergamino
25 Hostería La Madrileña
26 Gran Hotel Pelayo
27 Hotel Boedo
29 Hospedaje Lamadrid
32 Hospedaje Colonial
33 Hospedaje Nava
34 Hotel Alsina
49 Hotel Niza

PLACES TO EAT
1 Trattoría Napolitana
4 Il Vero Napoli
6 Comedor Naturista
11 El Rey del Bife
12 Tía Teresa
14 Tía Pepina
17 Trenque Lauquen
20 El Rincón de los Amigos
21 La Biblioteca
23 La Strada
40 La Marca
42 Ambos Mundos
54 La Casona
54 El Jardín
56 Strega
57 Manolo

OTHER
2 Museo Municipal de
   Ciencias Naturales
   Lorenzo Scaglia
3 Cine Atlantic
5 Cine Gran Mar
7 Cambio Jonestur
8 Cambio Mar del Plata
9 Angel Car
10 Centro de Salud No 1
13 Localiza Rent A Car
15 Ente Municipal de
   Turismo (Emtur)
18 Hospital Mar del Plata
19 Sociedad de
   Cultura Inglesa
22 ACA
28 La Burbuja Loca
30 Estación de Omnibus
31 Laverap
35 Museo Municipal de Arte
   Juan Carlos Castagnino
36 Villa Normandy
37 Iglesia Stella Maris
38 Torre Tanque
39 Chalet Los Troncos
41 Exposición Cultural
   Arte y Nácar
43 Cambio La Moneda
44 Cine Ambassador
45 Banco de la Provincia
46 Telefónica
47 Banco de la Nación
48 Cambio Jonestur
50 Cambio Mar del Plata
51 Cine/Teatro Regina
52 Post Office
55 Cartelera Baires
58 Teatro Corrientes
59 Móvil Rent
60 Cine/Teatro Odéon

Mar del Plata

Places to Stay

It's worth reiterating that prices climb steadily in summer and fall in the off season. Prices below are from early in the high season.

Camping Rates at Mardel's crowded camping grounds, mostly on RP 11 south of town (served by Bus Rápido del Sud), are around US$16 for up to four people.

Campamento Acuario, 7.5 km south of the lighthouse at Punta Mogotes, has complete facilities and offers ACA discounts. At the northern entrance to town, at Williams and Villalobo, *Camping El Bosque de Camet* is reached by bus Nos 221 and 541.

Hostels, Hospedajes & Hosterías Rooms with shared bath cost US$12 per person at the *Albergue Juvenil* (☎ 27927), in a wing of *Hotel Pergamino*, at Tucumán 2728, a few blocks from the bus terminal.

At Sarmiento 2258, *Hospedaje Nava* (☎ 51-7611) has four-bed rooms for US$15 per person, with a huge, clean shared bath. *Hostería La Madrileña* (☎ 51-2072), Sarmiento 2955, has modest, slightly dearer doubles with private bath.

Near the bus terminal at Lamadrid 2518, *Hospedaje Lamadrid* (☎ 25456) has decent singles/doubles for US$15/20 in the off season, but is dearer in summer. Centrally located *Hotel Niza*, run by three sisters at Santiago del Estero 1843, is excellent value for US$18 per person with breakfast and private bath.

Places to Eat

Restaurants, pizzerías and snack bars struggle to keep up with impatient summer crowds, but food is generally good; seafood at the Nuevo Complejo Comercial Puerto is excellent. For cheap minutas or sandwiches, look around the bus terminal.

Tía Pepina, H Yrigoyen 2645, *La Biblioteca*, Santa Fe 2633, and *Ambos Mundos*, Rivadavia 2644, serve filling minutas at moderate prices. *La Cantina de Armando*, at San Lorenzo and Catamarca, and *La Estancia de Don Pepito*, at Blvd

Marítimo 2235 across from the Casino, serve large portions at reasonable prices.

Trenque Lauquen, Mitre 2807, and *La Marca*, Almafuerte 253, are good but pricey parrillas. *El Rey del Bife*, Colón 2863, and *Rincón de los Amigos*, Córdoba 2588, are more economical.

Vegetarian restaurants are good value, including *Comedor Naturista*, Salta 1571, and *El Jardín*, Rivadavia 2383. *Joe*, at Lamadrid and Rawson, serves superb pizza and calzone, while *Manolo*, Rivadavia 2371, has varied, tasty pizza. *Il Vero Napoli*, Belgrano 3408, has superb lasagne.

Entertainment

When Buenos Aires shuts down in January, many shows come here, and there are also several cinemas. Cartelera Baires, at Santa Fe 1844, Local 33, sells discount tickets.

Argentines dance all night at clubs on Avenida Constitución, nicknamed 'Avenida del Ruido' (Avenue of Noise), where bus No 551 runs all night.

Things to Buy

Avenida JB Justo ('Avenida del Pullover') is known for sweaters and jackets at near-wholesale prices. The fashion-conscious will find a multitude of boutiques along San Martín and Rivadavia. *Alfajores*, biscuit sandwiches filled with chocolate, dulce de leche or fruit, are delicious for afternoon tea or with *mate*; try the popular brand Havanna.

Getting There & Away

Air Aerolíneas Argentinas (☎ 45626) and Austral (☎ 23085), both at the Hotel Provincial, fly often to Buenos Aires (US$80) from Aeropuerto Camet, 10 km north of town. LAPA (☎ 92-2112), San Martín 2648, Local 5, charges US$49 to US$69.

Bus From Mardel's busy Estación de Omnibus (☎ 51-5404), Alberdi 1602, many buses go to Buenos Aires (US$22, seven hours). El Rápido Argentino (☎ 51-0874) travels to La Plata (US$18, five hours) twice daily. There are also direct services to Bahía Blanca (US$27, seven hours), Córdoba,

Mendoza and the Mesopotamian provinces of Entre Ríos, Corrientes and Misiones.

Train The Estación Terminal de Ferrocarril (☎ 72-9553) is at Avenida Luro 4599, but Líneas Ferrocarriles (☎ 23059) also has offices in the city centre at San Martín 2300, and at the bus terminal (☎ 51-2501). The summer tourist train *El Marplatense* travels three times daily to Buenos Aires. Fares range from US$14 to US$21.

VILLA GESELL

Its perceived exclusivity keeps many visitors away from this sedate, woodsy beach resort, 100 km north of Mar del Plata via RP 11. At Avenida Buenos Aires and Circunvalación, the Dirección de Turismo (☎ 68596) has friendly staff (but very poor maps); several booths around town provide information on accommodation, places to eat, and bus schedules. Avenida 3 is the shopping and entertainment centre. Villa Gesell's telephone code is 0255.

Things to See & Do

Events like the 'Encuentros Corales' (a national choir competition) take place at the **Anfiteatro del Pinar** (amphitheatre). The **Muelle de Pesca**, at Playa and Paseo 129, offers year-round fishing. Cycling, horse riding and golf are other possible activities.

Places to Stay

Camping Camping grounds have minimum rates around US$23; most close by late March. At the north end of town, *Camping Africa* (☎ 68507), at Avenida Buenos Aires and Circunvalación, and *Camping Caravan* (☎ 68259), at Paseo 101 and Circunvalación, both have swimming pools. At the south end of Avenida 3 is *Camping Casablanca* (☎ 60771).

The youth hostel/camping ground *El Coyote* (☎ 68448) is at Alameda 212 and Calle 304 bis.

Hospedajes Most accommodation includes private bath and even telephone. Expect to pay about US$30 to US$40 per double at

Hospedaje Aguas Verdes (☎ 62040), on Avenida 5 between Paseos 104 and 105, or *Hospedaje Sarimar*, on Avenida 3 between Paseos 117 and 118. *Hospedaje Antonio* (☎ 62246), on Avenida 4 between Paseos 104 and 106, has some rooms with shared bath.

Places to Eat

La Jirafa Azul, on Avenida 3 between Avenida Buenos Aires and Paseo 102, has a good, cheap standard menu. *Cantina Arturito*, on Avenida 3 between Paseos 126 and 127, serves large portions of home-made pasta, plus shellfish and home-cured ham, at medium-plus prices. For tasty seafood, try *Marisquería El Gallego*, on Avenida 3 between Paseos 108 and 109.

For sandwiches and friendly service, try *Sangucheto*, on Paseo 104 between Avenidas 3 and 4, or *La Martona*, on Paseo 107 between Avenidas 2 and 3. *El Faro*, a rotisería at Avenida 3 and Paseo 119, has moderately priced takeaway food.

Getting There & Away

Air Aerolíneas Argentinas (☎ 68228), at Avenida Buenos Aires and Avenida 10 in town, has daily flights between Buenos Aires and Villa Gesell (US$80) in summer. Líneas Aéreas Entre Ríos (LAER; ☎ 68169), Avenida Buenos Aires between Paseos 205 and 206, and Transporte Aérea Costa Atlántica (TACA; ☎ 68585), Avenida Buenos Aires and Alameda 211, are cheaper (US$60).

Bus The Terminal de Omnibus (☎ 66058) is at Avenida 3 and Paseo 140, on the south side of town. Some long-distance buses stop at the Mini Terminal (☎ 62340), on Avenida 4 between Paseos 104 and 105.

Empresa Río de la Plata (☎ 62224), a block from the Mini Terminal, has several direct buses daily to Buenos Aires in summer, as does Antón (☎ 63215), on Paseo 108 between Avenidas 3 and 4. The seven-hour trip to Buenos Aires costs US$20.

PINAMAR

Planned by elite architect Jorge Bunge,

Pinamar is an elegant resort for Argentines who needn't work for a living, 120 km from Mar del Plata; nearby Ostende and Valeria del Mar offer more moderate prices. Visitors enjoying the usual outdoor activities must dodge dune buggies on the beach and even along nature trails.

Avenida Libertador, parallel to the beach, and the perpendicular thoroughfare Avenida Bunge are the main streets; streets on each side of Bunge form large fans, making orientation tricky. The Secretaría de Turismo (☎ 82796), Avenida Bunge 456, has a good map with useful descriptions of Pinamar, Valeria, Ostende and Cariló (an even more exclusive country-club environment).

Places to Stay

Several camping grounds, charging about US$15, line the coast between Ostende and Pinamar. Rates at Ostende's friendly *Albergue Juvenil* (☎ 82908), Nuestras Malvinas and Sarmiento in Ostende, are US$12 per person.

Prices at Pinamar's few hospedajes start around US$30 for doubles; try *Hospedaje Acacia* at Del Cangrejo 1358, *Hospedaje Rose Marie* (☎ 82522), at Las Medusas 1381, and *Hospedaje Valle Fértil* (☎ 84799), at Del Cangrejo 1110. One-star hotels, ranging from US$45 to US$65, include *Hotel Berlín* (☎ 82320), at Rivadavia 326, and *Hotel Sardegna* (☎ 82760), at Jasón 840.

Places to Eat

Con Estilo Campo, at Bunge and Marco Polo, serves fine pork and chivito a la parrilla (grilled kid goat). For good paella, cazuela and empanadas tucumanas, try *El Negro B*, at Jasón and Robinson Crusoe.

Paxapoga, at Bunge and Libertador, serves parrillada and pasta. *El Vivero*, also at Bunge and Libertador, has fine vegetarian meals. *La Reja*, at Jasón and Robinson Crusoe, offers varied pizza and great empanadas. For German desserts and baked goods, visit *Tante*, at De las Artes 35, or *Zur Tanne*, at Rivadavia and Artes.

Reservations are advisable for *Matarazzo Party*, at Bunge and Júpiter, whose spaghetti

Matarazzo offers a choice of nine different sauces. *Mamma Liberata*, at Bunge and Simbad el Marino, and *Club Italiano*, at Eneas and Cazón, also offer pasta.

Getting There & Away

Air Aerolíneas Argentinas (☎ 83299), Avenida Bunge 799, flies to Villa Gesell and Pinamar in summer, as does LAPA (☎ 84300), Avenida Shaw 600.

Bus Several companies serve Buenos Aires from the Terminal de Omnibus on Avenida Shaw, between El Pejerrey and Lenguado. Córdoba Mar del Plata (☎ 82885) goes to the interior, while Costamar connects the beaches.

NECOCHEA

The most attractive feature of this popular, family-oriented resort, 125 km south-west of Mar del Plata, is **Parque Miguel Lillo**, a huge green space along the beach whose dense pine woods are popular for cycling, riding or picnicking. The Río Quequén, rich in trout and mackerel, also allows for adventurous canoeing.

Places to Stay & Eat

The *Camping Municipal* is in Parque Lillo, but most accommodation is in the centre of town. The most reasonable are hospedajes like *Hospedaje Regis* (☎ 25870), at Diagonal San Martín 726 for US$15/20 a single/double; comparable places are *Hospedaje Bayo* (☎ 23334), at Calle 87 No 338 and *Hospedaje Colón* (☎ 24825), at Calle 62 No 3034. One-star hotels start around US$15 per person – try the simple but clean and quiet *Hotel Alvarez Palace* (☎ 23667), Avenida 79 No 304.

Tenedor libre pasta at *La Romana*, Avenida 79 between Calles 4 and 6, costs only US$4.50. *Nueva Gourmandise*, Calle 77 at Calle 6, offers a US$6 daily special. *El Palenque*, Avenida 79 and Calle 6, has good parrillada and reasonable prices.

Getting There & Away

Bus The Terminal de Omnibus (☎ 22460) is

on Avenida 58 (Sarmiento) between Calle 47 (Rondeau) and Avenida 35 (Jesuita Cardiel), near the river. Both El Cóndor and Costera Criolla have several buses daily to Buenos Aires. Empresa Córdoba Mar del Plata serves the interior.

Train The Ferrocarril Roca (☎ 22182) has three trains weekly between Necochea and Constitución, Buenos Aires.

The Pampas

Unrelentingly flat, Argentina's agricultural heartland contains a surprising number of tourist attractions in the provinces of Buenos Aires, La Pampa, and parts of Santa Fe and Córdoba. An integrated network of railways and highways connects the towns of the Pampas to the city of Buenos Aires.

Buenos Aires is Argentina's largest, richest, most populous and most important province. La Plata, the provincial capital, and the port of Bahía Blanca are key cities, while colonial Luján is a major religious centre and San Antonio de Areco is the sentimental focus of the country's gaucho culture (both Luján and San Antonio are covered in the Around Buenos Aires section, above).

Santa Fe city is the capital of its namesake province. Rosario, exporting agricultural produce, challenges Córdoba's status as the republic's 'second city'.

Settled late because of Indian resistance and erratic rainfall, La Pampa did not attain provincial status until 1951. Its varied environments include rolling hills of native *caldén* forests, extensive grasslands, and salares (salt lakes) with flamingos. Parque Nacional Lihué Calel justifies a detour from the usual routes to Patagonia.

History

In pre-Columbian times, the aboriginal Querandí hunted guanaco and rhea on the Pampas, but feral European livestock transformed the region. One 18th-century visitor estimated 48 million cattle between modern Paraguay and the Río Negro.

Having tamed wild horses, mobile Indians were formidable adversaries, but the Pampas eventually fell to cattle ranchers and farmers. Feral livestock left two enduring legacies: the culture of the gaucho, who persisted for decades as a neohunter-gatherer and then a symbol of *argentinidad* (a romantic nationalism); and environmental impoverishment, as grazing and European weeds altered the native pastures.

Only the relatively few estancieros with the luck to inherit or the foresight to grab large tracts of land benefited from hides, tallow and salt beef, which had limited overseas markets. British-built railways made beef and wool exports feasible, but improved cattle breeds required succulent feeds like alfalfa, which needed preparatory cultivation. Landowners therefore rented to *medieros* (sharecroppers who raised wheat for four or five years before moving on) and thus profited both from their share of the wheat harvest and from new alfalfa fields. Maize, wheat and linseed soon exceeded the value of animal products.

The Pampas are still famous for beef, but some struggling estancias have opened their facilities to the tourist trade – not unlike Britain's stately homes. Argentina is still a major grain exporter, while intensive cultivation of fruit and vegetables, as well as dairying, takes place near Buenos Aires and other large cities.

LA PLATA

After the city of Buenos Aires became the federal capital, Governor Dardo Rocha founded La Plata, 56 km south-east, as the new provincial capital. An important administrative, commercial and cultural centre, it has one of the country's best universities.

The superposition of diagonals on a conventional grid forms a distinctive diamond pattern linking several plazas. Most public buildings are on or near Plaza Moreno, but the commercial centre is near Plaza San Martín. The helpful Entidad Municipal de Turismo (☎ 25-8334), Calle 47 No 740, is open 8 am to 2 pm weekdays only. La Plata's telephone code is 021.

Things to See

Paseo del Bosque Plantations of eucalyptus, gingko, palm, and subtropical hardwoods cover this 60-hectare park at the north-eastern edge of town. Its facilities include the **Anfiteatro Martín Fierro**, an open-air facility which hosts summer drama festivals, the **Museo de Ciencias Naturales**, the **Observatorio Astronómico** (open on weekdays from 7 am to 1 pm), the symbolic United Nations of the **Jardín de la Paz** (Garden of Peace), a small **Jardín Zoológico** (zoo, open on weekdays from 9 am to 9 pm, and on weekends from 10 am to 9 pm) along Avenida 52, and several university departments.

La República de los Niños A steam train circles this scale reproduction of a city for children, sponsored by Eva Perón and completed shortly before her death in 1952. From Avenida 7 in La Plata, take bus No 518 or 273 to Camino General Belgrano Km 7, in the suburb of Gonnet. Admission is US$3 per person, which includes aquarium and *granja* (a small zoo of domestic animals), but the train ride and doll museum require separate admission.

Places to Stay & Eat

Friendly but run-down *Hotel Roca*, (☎ 21-4916), Calle 47 No 309, has singles/doubles for US$15/20 with shared bath, US$18/30 with private bath. Moderately priced *Hotel Saint James* (☎ 21-8089), Calle 60 No 377, charges US$25/35 without breakfast.

Among the cheaper restaurants are *Everton*, Calle 14 between Calles 63 and 64, and *Club Matheu*, on Calle 63 between Avenida 1 and Calle 2. A local recommendation is the *Colegio de Escribanos*, on Avenida 13 between Calles 47 and 48.

Pasta y Punto, Calle 47 No 787 between 10 and 11, is a very fine, pleasantly decorated Italian restaurant; another popular Italian place, at Calle 47 and Diagonal 74, is *La Trattoría*.

On warm summer nights, dawdle at the venerable *Cervecería Modelo*, on the corner of Calles 54 and 5, with cerveza tirada (lager beer), snacks and complimentary peanuts.

Getting There & Away

Bus The Terminal de Omnibus (☎ 21-0992) is at Calles 4 and 42. Río de la Plata (☎ 38537) has buses every half-hour to Once, Constitución and Retiro in Buenos Aires (US$2); there are also long-distance services.

Train Hourly trains to Constitución leave from the Estación Ferrocarril General Roca (☎ 21-9377, 21-2575), Avenida 1 and Calle 44.

BAHIA BLANCA

More a crossroads than a tourist destination, 650 km south of Buenos Aires, Bahía Blanca is South America's largest naval base, a key port for grain from Buenos Aires province and produce from the Río Negro valley, and the coastal gateway to Patagonia. Its Oficina de Información Turística (☎ 55-1110), Alsina 45, is open on weekdays from 7.45 am to 1 pm.

Correo Argentino is at Moreno 34, while Telefónica is at O'Higgins 249. The telephone code is 091.

Places to Stay & Eat

Open all year, the municipal camping ground at *Balneario Maldonado* (☎ 29511), four km south-west of the city centre, has hot water and electricity in summer only. It charges US$4 per person.

Across from the train station, several cheap but run-down hospedajes charge about US$10 per person: *Hospedaje Molinari* (☎ 22871), at Cerri 719, *Hospedaje Los Vascos* (☎ 29290), at Cerri 747, and the recommended *Hospedaje Roma* (☎ 38500), at Cerri 759. Nearer Plaza Rivadavia, at *Hotel Bayón* (☎ 22504), Chiclana 487, better but slightly dearer accommodation costs about US$12/22 for a single/double with shared bath, US$16/28 with private bath.

Around Plaza Rivadavia are several

parrillas and inexpensive pizzerías, including *Tutto Pizza* at Alsina 248, *Pizzería Roma* at Chiclana 21, and *Restaurant Víctor* at Chiclana 83, which also has seafood. *Taberna Baska*, Lavalle 284, serves appetising Spanish food at reasonable prices. *El Aljibe*, at Donado and Thompson, offers conventional Argentine fare but is pricier. For breakfast, try *Bar Lácteo La Barra*, Chiclana 155.

Getting There & Away
Air Austral (☎ 21383), Colón 59, flies twice daily to Buenos Aires except Sunday (one flight only) and daily, except Sunday, to Comodoro Rivadavia, Río Gallegos, and Río Grande. For Patagonian destinations, contact LADE (☎ 21063) and Sapse (☎ 37697), both at Darregueira 21, or TAN (☎ 55-0963) in the Galería Visión 2000 at San Martín 216.

Bus The Terminal de Omnibus San Francisco de Asís (☎ 29616) is at Estados Unidos and Brown, two km east of Plaza Rivadavia, and has frequent buses to Buenos Aires (US$30, 10 hours). Pampa goes to Mar del Plata (US$21), while El Valle serves Neuquén (US$30) via the Río Negro valley. Don Otto has buses to coastal Patagonia, as far as Río Gallegos (US$72).

Train The once-seigneurial Ferrocarril Roca (☎ 21168), Avenida Cerri 750, runs daily trains to and from Constitución (Buenos Aires), while Servicios Ferroviarios Patagónicos (Sefepa) operates a southbound rail service to Bariloche (27 hours) and intermediate points on Wednesday and Sunday evenings.

Getting Around
To/From the Airport Aeropuerto Comandante Espora (☎ 21665) is 15 km east of town, reached by city bus No 10, but Austral provides its own transport (US$3).

Bus Bus Nos 505, 512, 514, 516 and 517 go to the bus terminal. No 514 also goes to Balneario Maldonado.

SIERRA DE LA VENTANA
Granitic bedrock emerges from the deep Pampas sediments only in the ranges of Tandilia and Ventania, trending north-west to south-east. The easterly Sierras de Tandil are rounded hills of around 500 metres, but the westerly Sierra de la Ventana attracts hikers and climbers to scenic jagged peaks above 1300 metres. Its charming namesake village, 125 km north of Bahía Blanca, also offers conventional facilities including a casino, golf links and swimming pools.

Just south of the train station, the Oficina de Turismo y Delegación Municipal (☎ 91-5032), Roca 15 at Avenida San Martín, has a useful packet of maps and brochures.

Places to Stay & Eat
There are several free camp sites along the river, with access to toilets and showers at the nearby municipal swimming pool (US$2.50). If you prefer an organised camping ground, try *Autocamping* (☎ 91-5100), on Diego Meyer, which has good facilities at US$4 per adult, US$2 per child.

Sierra de la Ventana's good, moderately priced accommodation includes *Hotel Argentino*, Roca 122, and *Hospedaje La Perlita* (☎ 91-5020), Malvinas and Pasaje 3, both of which charge US$15 per person. *Residencial Carlitos* (☎ 91-5011), at Coronel Suárez and Punta Alta in nearby Villa Arcadia, has doubles for US$21 but is a bit standoffish. ACA's *Motel Maitén* (☎ 91-5073), Iguazú 93, is good value at US$18 per person for members and US$23 for non-members, with breakfast.

Restaurant Ser, on Güemes just off the main drag, has good pizza and pasta, with large portions, but drinks are expensive. *El Establo*, on San Martín between Islas Malvinas and Avenida Roca, is a passable pizzería.

Getting There & Away
Sierra de la Ventana's modest Terminal de Omnibus is at San Martín and Iguazú. La Estrella has nightly buses to Buenos Aires (US$25, 7½ hours) at 11.40 pm. There are also buses to Bahía Blanca at 6.40 am and 7.45 pm daily.

AROUND SIERRA DE LA VENTANA

Popular for ranger-guided walks and independent hiking, the 6700-hectare **Parque Provincial Ernesto Tornquist**, west of the village, is the starting point for the 1136-metre summit of **Cerro de la Ventana**. The walk takes about two hours for anyone except the wheezing porteño tobacco addicts who struggle to the crest of what is probably the country's most climbed peak.

Rangers at the trailer at the trailhead collect a US$1 entry fee and routinely deny permission to climb after 1 pm; insistent hikers can get permission by signing a waiver. The friendly *Campamento Base* has good shade, clean baths and excellent hot showers for US$4 per person.

SANTA FE

Capital of its namesake province, the city of Santa Fe is a leading agro-industrial centre. Tributaries of the Río Paraná surround Santa Fe, but the main channel flows about 10 km east; in 1983, the powerful rising river mangled the Puente Colgante (Hanging Bridge), which connected the city with Paraná, 25 km east, forcing the province to build a replacement.

Relocated in the mid-17th century because of Indians, floods and isolation, the city duplicates the original plan of Santa Fe La Vieja, but a 19th-century neo-Parisian building boom and more recent construction have left only isolated colonial buildings, mostly near Plaza 25 de Mayo. Avenida San Martín, north of the plaza, is the main commercial artery.

Information

The Dirección Municipal de Turismo (☎ 30982), at the bus terminal, Belgrano 2910, is open daily from 7 am to 1 pm and 2 to 8 pm.

Tourfe, San Martín 2500, collects 3% commission on travellers' cheques; there are several ATMs on San Martín. Correo Argentino is at Avenida 27 de Febrero 2331. Telecom is here, and upstairs at the bus terminal; the telephone code is 042.

Things to See

Some colonial buildings are museums, but the churches still serve ecclesiastical functions, like the mid-17th century **Templo de Santo Domingo**, on the corner of 3 de Febrero and 9 de Julio. The exterior simplicity of the Jesuit **Iglesia de la Compañía** (1696), on Plaza 25 de Mayo, masks an ornate interior. The **Casa de los Aldao**, Buenos Aires 2861, is a restored two-storey house from the early 18th century.

Built in 1680, the **Convento y Museo de San Francisco** at Amenábar 2257, south of Plaza 25 de Mayo, is Santa Fe's most important landmark. Its metre-thick walls support a roof of Paraguayan cedar and hardwood beams, fastened with fittings and wooden spikes rather than nails. The doors are hand-worked originals, while the Baroque pulpit is laminated in gold. Its museum covers secular and religious topics from colonial and republican eras.

In a damp 17th-century building at San Martín 1490, the **Museo Histórico Provincial Brigadier General Estanislao López** has permanent exhibits on the 19th-century civil wars, provincial governors (and caudillos), period furnishings and religious art, plus a room with displays on more contemporary themes. The most interesting display at the **Museo Etnográfico y Colonial Juan de Garay**, 25 de Mayo 1470, is a scale model of Santa Fe La Vieja on the Río San Javier. There are also colonial artefacts, Indian basketry, Spanish ceramics, and coins and other money.

Santa Fe's museums are generally open on weekdays from 8.30 am to 12.30 pm and 3 to 7 pm, and on weekends and holidays from 9.30 am to 12.30 pm and 4 to 7 pm.

Places to Stay

Santa Fe tolerates free camping in Parque General Belgrano, at the south end of San Martín.

The cheapest regular accommodation is *Residencial Las Vegas*, Irigoyen Freire 2246, where singles/doubles cost only US$10/16. At *Hotel Gran Terminal* (☎ 32395), Yrigoyen 2222, rooms with shared bath cost

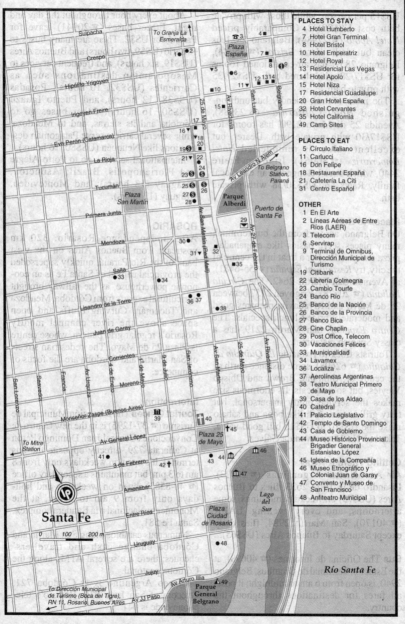

PLACES TO STAY
4 Hotel Humberto
7 Hotel Gran Terminal
8 Hotel Bristol
10 Hotel Emperatriz
12 Hotel Royal
13 Residencial Las Vegas
14 Hotel Apolo
15 Hotel Niza
17 Residencial Guadalupe
20 Gran Hotel España
32 Hotel Cervantes
35 Hotel California
49 Camp Sites

PLACES TO EAT
5 Círculo Italiano
11 Carlucci
16 Don Felipe
18 Restaurant España
21 Cafetería La Citi
31 Centro Español

OTHER
1 En El Arte
2 Líneas Aéreas de Entre Ríos (LAER)
3 Telecom
6 Servirap
9 Terminal de Omnibus, Dirección Municipal de Turismo
19 Citibank
22 Librería Colmegna
23 Cambio Tourfe
24 Banco Río
25 Banco de la Nación
26 Banco de la Provincia
27 Banco Bica
28 Cine Chaplin
29 Post Office, Telecom
30 Vacaciones Felices
33 Municipalidad
34 Lavamex
36 Localiza
37 Aerolíneas Argentinas
38 Teatro Municipal Primero de Mayo
39 Casa de los Aldao
40 Catedral
41 Palacio Legislativo
42 Templo de Santo Domingo
43 Casa de Gobierno
44 Museo Histórico Provincial Brigadier General Estanislao López
45 Iglesia de la Compañía
46 Museo Etnográfico y Colonial Juan de Garay
47 Convento y Museo de San Francisco
48 Anfiteatro Municipal

Santa Fe

0   100   200 m

US$15 per person, while those with private bath cost US$20/32. Comparably priced *Hotel Apolo* (☎ 27984), Belgrano 2821, is clean but dark. *Hotel Bristol* (☎ 35044), Belgrano 2859, has air-conditioned rooms for US$17/28 with shared bath, US$27/35 with private bath.

The more central, friendly but undistinguished *Hotel California* (☎ 23988), Avenida 25 de Mayo 2190, has rooms for US$17/30 with private bath. Dearer, but excellent value, is remodelled *Hotel Emperatriz* (☎ 30061), Irigoyen Freire 2440, which once belonged to an elite local family. Rates are US$30/38 with private bath.

Places to Eat
On Belgrano, across from the bus terminal, many places serve basics like empanadas, pizza and parrilla. For a treat in the centre of the city, try *Restaurant España* (☎ 55-6481), at Avenida San Martín 2642. The *Círculo Italiano* (☎ 20628), Yrigoyen 2457 between 25 de Mayo and Rivadavia, prepares good and moderately priced lunch specials. The *Centro Español*, San Martín 2219, has a classy Spanish restaurant.

Tourists flock to riverside *El Quincho de Chiquito* (☎ 62608), some distance north of the centre at Almirante Brown and Obispo Vieytes, but so do locals. Its enormous size makes the service pretty impersonal, but tasty grilled river fish like boga and sábalo make the US$10 to US$15 bill good value. Take bus No 16 on Avenida Gálvez.

Getting There & Away
Air Aerolíneas Argentinas (☎ 20713), Lisandro de la Torre 2633, flies to Buenos Aires (US$73) on weekday mornings, some afternoons, and every evening. LAER (☎ 40170), San Martín 2984, flies daily except Saturday to Buenos Aires (US$65).

Bus The Oficina de Informes (☎ 40698), at the Estación Terminal de Omnibus, Belgrano 2940, is open from 6 am to midnight; it posts all fares for destinations throughout the country.

About every hour throughout the day and night, Etacer buses (☎ 20941) leave for Paraná for US$2. There are many buses to Rosario (US$9, two hours) and Buenos Aires (US$19, six hours), and frequent services to Mesopotamian destinations such as Corrientes (US$32, 10 hours), Posadas (US$38, 12 hours), and Puerto Iguazú (US$50, 16 hours). Other buses go to Córdoba and its sierras, and to Mendoza, while several carriers serve Patagonian destinations like Neuquén (US$80, 16 hours).

International services go to Porto Alegre and Florianópolis, Brazil; Asunción, Paraguay (13 hours); and Montevideo, Uruguay (12 hours).

ROSARIO
After independence Rosario, 320 km upstream from Buenos Aires on the west bank of the Río Paraná, quickly superseded the provincial capital of Santa Fe as an economic powerhouse, as the railway brought agricultural exports from Córdoba, Mendoza and Tucumán. Curving bluffs and open space above the river channel modify Rosario's regular grid pattern, whose centre is Plaza 25 de Mayo. The pedestrian streets of San Martín and Córdoba are the focus of commerce.

Information
Tourist Offices The Dirección Municipal de Turismo (☎ 37-1295) is in the new Centro de Convenciones General Juan Domingo Perón at Cafferata 729, directly opposite the bus terminal. It's open on weekdays only from 8 am to 3 pm, but maintains a secondary office (☎ 40-8583), open on weekends and holidays only from 9 am to 7 pm, at the Monumento Nacional a la Bandera complex, Santa Fe 581.

Numerous cambios along San Martín and Córdoba change cash and travellers' cheques; there are several ATMs along the Córdoba peatonal.

Correo Argentino is at Córdoba 721, Telecom at San Luis 936. Rosario's telephone code is 041.

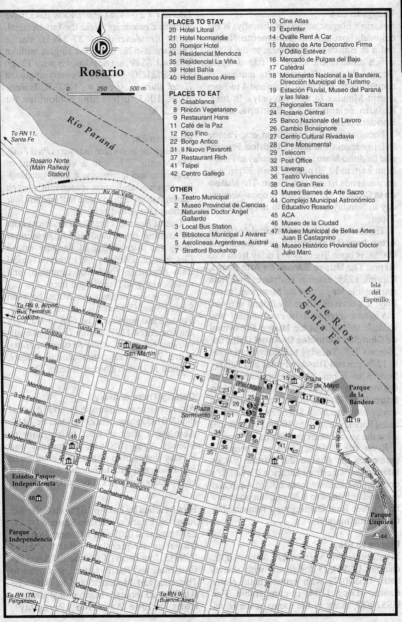

Rosario

0   250   500 m

Río Paraná

To RN 11,
Santa Fe

Rosario Norte
(Main Railway
Station)

PLACES TO STAY
20 Hotel Litoral
21 Hotel Normandie
30 Romijor Hotel
34 Residencial Mendoza
35 Residencial La Viña
39 Hotel Bahía
40 Hotel Buenos Aires

PLACES TO EAT
6 Casablanca
8 Rincón Vegetariano
9 Restaurant Hans
11 Café de la Paz
12 Pico Fino
22 Borgo Antico
31 Il Nuovo Pavarotti
37 Restaurant Rich
41 Taipei
42 Centro Gallego

OTHER
1 Teatro Municipal
2 Museo Provincial de Ciencias
   Naturales Doctor Angel
   Gallardo
3 Local Bus Station
4 Biblioteca Municipal J Alvarez
5 Aerolíneas Argentinas, Austral
7 Stratford Bookshop

10 Cine Atlas
13 Exprinter
14 Ovalle Rent A Car
15 Museo de Arte Decorativo Firma
   y Odilio Estévez
16 Mercado de Pulgas del Bajo
17 Catedral
18 Monumento Nacional a la Bandera,
   Dirección Municipal de Turismo
19 Estación Fluvial, Museo del Paraná
   y las Islas
23 Regionales Tilcara
24 Rosario Central
25 Banco Nazionale del Lavoro
26 Cambio Bonsignore
27 Centro Cultural Rivadavia
28 Cine Monumental
29 Telecom
32 Post Office
33 Laverap
36 Teatro Vivencias
38 Cine Gran Rex
43 Museo Barnes de Arte Sacro
44 Complejo Municipal Astronómico
   Educativo Rosario
45 ACA
46 Museo de la Ciudad
47 Museo Municipal de Bellas Artes
   Juan B Castagnino
48 Museo Histórico Provincial Doctor
   Julio Marc

Isla
del
Espinillo

Entre Ríos
Santa Fe

Av del Valle
Rivadavia
Güemes
Brown
Jujuy
Salta
Catamarca
Tucumán
Urquiza
San Lorenzo
Santa Fe
Córdoba
Rioja
San Luis
San Juan
Mendoza
3 de Febrero
9 de Julio
E Zeballos
Montevideo

To RN 9, Airport,
Bus Terminal,
Córdoba

Catalb
Rodriguez
Puerreedón
Santiago
Alvear
Bvld Oroño
Balcarce
Moreno
Dorrego
Italia
España
Paraguay
Corrientes
Entre Ríos
Mitre
Sarmiento
San Martín
Maipú
Laprida
Buenos Aires
1 de Mayo
9 de Diciembre
26 de Diciembre
Hyacinto
Colón
Mendoza
Necochea
Chacabuco
Esmeralda
Belatti

Plaza
San Martín

Plaza
25 de Mayo

Parque
de la
Bandera

Plaza
Sarmiento

[Ped Mall]

Av Carlos Pellegrini
Cochabamba
Pasco
Ituzaingó
Cerrito
Riobamba
La Paz
Viamonte
Ocampo

Estadio Parque
Independencia

Parque
Independencia

Parque
Urquiza

To RN 178,
Pergamino

27 de Febrero

To RN 9,
Buenos Aires

Av de la Libertad
Av de Belgrano
Av de la tradición

Things to See

Rosario's biggest attraction (literally) is the colossal, boat-shaped **Monumento Nacional a la Bandera** (Monument to the Flag), which shelters the crypt of flag designer General Manuel Belgrano. Its museum is open daily from 9 am to 1 pm and 4 to 7 pm except Monday (4 to 7 pm only). In June, Rosario celebrates **La Semana de la Bandera** (Flag Week).

Focusing on the republican era, Parque Independencia's **Museo Histórico Provincial Dr Julio Marc** is open Tuesday to Friday from 9 am to 12.30 pm and 3 to 6.30 pm, and on weekends from 3 to 6.30 pm. The **Museo de la Ciudad**, Oroño 2350, is open Wednesday to Sunday from 9 am to noon and 3 to 7 pm.

The fine-arts **Museo Municipal de Bellas Artes Juan B Castagnino**, at Pellegrini and Oroño, is open Tuesday to Friday from 4 to 10 pm. The **Museo Barnes de Arte Sacro**, Laprida 1235, exhibits sculptures by a man responsible for parts of the Monument to the Flag; it's open on Thursday from 4 to 6 pm.

Visitors interested in environment and wildlife should visit the **Museo Provincial de Ciencias Naturales Dr Angel Gallardo**, Moreno 758, Tuesday to Friday from 9 am to 12.30 pm and Tuesday, Friday and Sunday from 3 to 6 pm. The planetarium, at the **Complejo Municipal Astronómico Educativo Rosario** in Parque Urquiza, has weekend shows from 5 to 6 pm. On Tuesday and Thursday from 9 to 10 pm, visitors can view the austral skies through its telescopes.

River life – flora, fauna and people – permeates the **Museo del Paraná y Las Islas** in the waterfront Estación Fluvial. It's open on Wednesday from 2.30 to 4 pm and on Sunday from 4 to 6.30 pm, but go at any hour to see Raúl Domínguez's romantic but fascinating murals.

Places to Stay

Friendly *Hotel Normandie*, Mitre 1030, charges US$14/23 for rooms with shared bath, US$20/27 with private bath. *Hotel Bahía*, Maipú 1254, is comparable. For US$20/30, many of the rooms at the *Hotel Litoral* (☎ 21-1426), Entre Ríos 1043, have attractive balconies. Near the bus terminal, *Hotel Residencial* (☎ 37-3413), Pasaje Quintanilla 628, has good singles without TV for US$19; singles/doubles with TV go for US$21/30. Friendly, recently upgraded *Hotel Buenos Aires* (☎ 24-2034), Buenos Aires 1063, offers singles/doubles for US$25/30.

Places to Eat

Probably the best value in town is *Pico Fino*, San Martín 783, with a varied menu of Argentine and international food, outstanding service, and very reasonable – even reasonable enough to make half-pizzas (four portions) for solo diners.

One of Rosario's best Italian choices is an outstanding rotisería alongside *Restaurant Rich*, San Juan 1031. Moderately priced *Casablanca*, Córdoba 1471, serves typical Italo-Argentine food like canneloni and ravioli, along with cold lager beer.

Rincón Vegetariano, on Mitre between Santa Fe and Córdoba, is a meatless alternative to local parrillas. The *Centro Gallego*, Buenos Aires 1127, serves fixed-price all-you-can-eat meals, while *Restaurant Hans*, Mitre 775, is also economical. *Taipei*, Laprida 1121, is a Chinese tenedor libre.

Getting There & Away

Air Aerolíneas Argentinas and Austral (☎ 48-0185) share offices at Santa Fe 1410. Aerolíneas flies at least twice daily to Buenos Aires (US$61); Wednesday and Sunday flights from Aeroparque continue to São Paulo and Rio de Janeiro. Austral flies on weekdays only to Córdoba (US$63).

Bus Reached by bus No 101 from Calle San Juan, the Estación Mariano Moreno (☎ 37-2384/5/6) is at Cafferata 702, near Santa Fe. Buses go frequently to Buenos Aires (US$15, four hours), Córdoba and Santa Fe, Corrientes and Puerto Iguazú, less often to Tucumán and Mendoza, and to Bariloche (US$76, 23 hours). International destinations include Asunción (Paraguay),

Montevideo (Uruguay), and Porto Alegre and Rio de Janeiro (Brazil).

Train Passenger services on the Ferrocarril Mitre, three times weekly between Retiro (Buenos Aires) and Tucumán, use Estación Rosario Norte (☎ 39-2429), Avenida del Valle 2700. Take bus No 120 from San Juan and Mitre.

Getting Around
To/From the Airport Aerolíneas runs minibuses to Aeropuerto Fisherton, eight km west of town.

Bus The extensive local bus system is centred on Plaza Sarmiento.

SANTA ROSA
Santa Rosa de Toay, 600 km from Buenos Aires via RN 5, is a tidy, pleasant city of 80,000. Plaza San Martín is the commercial centre of the city's standard grid, north of Avenida España. The modern Centro Cívico is on Avenida Pedro Luro, seven blocks east.

Information
The enthusiastic Dirección Provincial de Turismo (☎ 24404), at Avenida Pedro Luro and Avenida San Martín directly across from the bus terminal, has English-speaking staff, maps, brochures, and selected local handicrafts in the Mercado Artesanal on the premises. Opening hours are weekdays 7 am to 8 pm, weekends 9 am to noon and 4 to 8 pm. The municipalidad maintains a Centro de Información Turística at the bus terminal, open 24 hours.

Several banks change cash but not travellers' cheques. Banco de La Pampa has an ATM alongside the provincial tourist office, and another at Pellegrini 255. Correo Argentino is at Hilario Lagos 258, with Telefónica next door. The telephone code is 0954.

Museums
At Pellegrini 190, Santa Rosa's **Museo de Ciencias Naturales y Antropológicas** contains natural science, archaeological,

historical, artisanal and fine arts collections. The **Museo de Artes**, at 9 de Julio and Villegas, contains works by Argentine and provincial artists.

Places to Stay & Eat
One of Argentina's last free camping grounds is at Laguna Don Tomás, at the west end of Avenida Uruguay. From the bus terminal, take the local Transporte El Indio bus, and take mosquito repellent. At *Hospedaje Mitre* (☎ 25432), Emilio Mitre 74, singles/doubles are US$15/27 with shared bath, US$21/34 with private bath. *Hostería Santa Rosa* (☎ 23868), Hipólito Yrigoyen 696, charges a little more.

The *Club Español* at Hilario Lagos 237 has excellent Argentine/Spanish food, outstanding service and reasonable prices. For regional specialities, try *Rancho de Pampa Cuatro* at Corrientes 69, opposite the bus terminal. At *Sr Quintana*, Urquiza 336, the US$11 parrillada includes a superb buffet so filling that it barely leaves any room for meat.

Getting There & Away
Air Austral (☎ 22388), Rivadavia 256, flies daily from Buenos Aires (US$105), continuing to Viedma and then back to Buenos Aires. LAER (☎ 25952), Pellegrini 219, flies on Monday, Wednesday and Friday to Buenos Aires (US$99).

Bus The Estación Terminal de Omnibus (☎ 22592) is at the Centro Cívico, at Luro and San Martín. Chevallier has four buses daily to Buenos Aires (US$28, six hours) and one to San Martín de los Andes and Bariloche (US$50, 21 hours). Others go to the Mesopotamian littoral, Comodoro Rivadavia and Caleta Olivia, and Mendoza.

Train The Ferrocarril Sarmiento (☎ 33451) is at Alsina and Pellegrini, but services are slower and less convenient than buses. Trains to Once station, Buenos Aires, leave on Sunday, Wednesday and Friday at 10 pm.

Car For a rental car to visit Parque Nacional Lihué Calel, try Localiza (☎ 25773), at Moreno and Hipólito Yrigoyen.

PARQUE NACIONAL LIHUE CALEL

Lihué Calel's small, remote mountain ranges, 226 km south-west of Santa Rosa via RN 152, were a stronghold of Araucanian resistance during General Roca's so-called Conquista del Desierto (Conquest of the Desert). Its salmon-coloured exfoliating granites, reaching 600 metres, offer a variety of subtle environments, changing with the season or even with the day.

In this 10,000-hectare desert, sudden storms can bring flash floods and create spectacular, temporary waterfalls. Even when there's no rain, subterranean streams nourish the *monte*, a scrub forest of surprising botanical variety.

The author saw a puma on his last visit, but the most common mammals are guanaco, *mara* (Patagonian hare) and *vizcacha*, a wild relative of the chinchilla. Bird species include the rhea or *ñandú* and birds of prey like the *carancho* (crested caracara).

Things to See & Do

From the park camping ground, a signed trail leads through a dense thorn forest of caldén (*Prosopis caldenia*, a local species of a common genus) and similar trees, to a site with petroglyphs, unfortunately vandalised. From the petroglyphs, another trail reaches the 589-metre summit of **Cerro de la Sociedad Científica Argentina**, with outstanding views of the entire sierra, surrounding marshes and salares. The boulders are slippery when wet; notice the flowering cacti between them.

Places to Stay

The free camping ground near the visitor centre has shade, picnic tables, firepits, cold showers and many birds. Bring food – the nearest supplies are at the town of Puelches, 35 km south. The *ACA Hostería*, on the highway, has rooms and a restaurant.

Getting There & Away

The only remaining regular bus service using RN 152 from Santa Rosa is Chevallier's weekly service to Neuquén at midnight on Wednesday/Thursday, which drops passengers at Lihué Calel for US$22. Rapibus (☎ 28903), Avenida Luro 1340 in Santa Rosa, has begun a minibus service to and from the town of Puelches (US$12), passing Lihué Calel, on Monday, Wednesday and Friday at 6 am.

Mesopotamia, Misiones & the Gran Chaco

Mesopotamia, the area between the Paraná and Uruguay rivers, offers a variety of recreational opportunities on the rivers and in the parks of Entre Ríos and Corrientes provinces. Subtropical Misiones province, nearly surrounded by Paraguay and Brazil, features ruined Jesuit missions and the spectacular Iguazú Falls. Across the Paraná, the Gran Chaco is Argentina's 'empty quarter'.

History

After Spaniards reached the upper Paraná, obtaining provisions from the Guaraní, settlement proceeded southward from Asunción (Paraguay). Corrientes was founded in 1588, and Santa Fe at about the same time. For more information on early Spanish activities, see the Paraguay chapter.

Jesuits established 30 Guaraní *reducciones* in the upper Paraná. These settlements resembled other Spanish municipalities, but non-Jesuits envied their political and economic autonomy – mostly because the Jesuits monopolised Indian labour in an area where the encomienda was weak. Concerned that Jesuits were creating a state within a state, Spain expelled them from the Americas in 1767. Argentina took definitive control of the territory, contested by Brazil and Paraguay, after the War of the Triple Alliance (1865-70).

Briefly an independent republic, Entre

Ríos became a Unitarist stronghold after Rosas took power. Local caudillo Justo José Urquiza brought about Rosas' defeat and the eventual adoption of Argentina's modern constitution.

In the dense thorn forests of Chaco and Formosa provinces, oppressive heat and hostile Indians discouraged early exploration. After 1850, woodcutters from Corrientes, exploiting the *quebracho* (axebreaker) tree for tannin, literally cleared the way for cotton and cattle.

PARANA

Capital of the Argentine confederation from 1853 to 1861, now capital of Entre Ríos province, Paraná takes pride in having cooperated with Santa Fe to build the Hernandarias tunnel under the main channel of the Río Paraná, despite active opposition from the federal government.

On the east bank of the Río Paraná, the city's rather irregular plan has several diagonals, curving boulevards and complex intersections. From Plaza Primero de Mayo, the town centre, Calle San Martín is a peatonal for six blocks. At the west end of San Martín, Parque Urquiza extends more than a km along the riverfront.

Information

The Secretaría de Turismo Municipal (☎ 22-1632) is at 25 de Mayo 44, on Plaza Primero de Mayo; hours are daily from 8 am to 8 pm.

Tourfe, the local cambio, is on the San Martín peatonal, but there are several ATMs. Correo is at Avenida 25 de Mayo and Monte Caseros, while Telecom is at San Martín 735. Paraná's telephone code is 043.

Things to See

The **Iglesia Catedral** has been on Plaza Primero de Mayo since 1730, but the current building dates from 1885. When Paraná was capital of the confederation, the Senate deliberated at the **Colegio del Huerto**, at 9 de Julio and 25 de Mayo.

A block west, at Corrientes and Urquiza, are the **Palacio Municipal** (1889) and the **Escuela Normal Paraná**, a school founded

by noted educator and President DF Sarmiento. Across San Martín, at Avenida 25 de Mayo 60, is the **Teatro Municipal Tres de Febrero** (1908). At the west end of the San Martín peatonal, on Plaza Alvear, the **Museo Histórico de Entre Ríos Martín Leguizamón** flaunts provincial pride, as knowledgeable but patronising guides go to rhetorical extremes describing the role of local caudillos in Argentine history. Hours are Tuesday to Friday from 8.30 am to noon and 2 to 8 pm, Saturday 9 am to noon and 3 to 6 pm, and Sunday 9 am to noon.

The adjacent subterranean **Museo de Bellas Artes Pedro E Martínez** shows works by provincial artists. Morning hours are Tuesday to Sunday from 9 am to noon, all year round. Winter afternoon hours are Tuesday to Saturday from 3 to 6 pm; summer afternoon hours are 5 to 8 pm.

Only very recently inaugurated, the **Museo de la Ciudad** (☎ 23-4454) focuses on Paraná's urban past and surroundings. On the *costanera* (riverfront road) Avenida Laurencena in Parque Urquiza, it's open on Monday from 3 to 7 pm, on Tuesday to Saturday from 9 am to noon and 3 to 6 pm, and on Sunday from 5 to 9 pm.

River Excursions

Hour-long excursions on the motor vessel *Realidad II* (US$7) leave from the Puerto Nuevo at Costanera and Vélez Sarsfield daily at 5.20 pm; make reservations at Turismo Fluvial (☎ 22-5104), San Martín 960. The *Realidad II* also carries passengers to nearby Isla Puente for picnics and the like, for US$2.50 return; departures are more or less hourly between 10.30 am and 8 pm.

Places to Stay

Bus Nos 1 and 6 ('Thompson') link *Camping Balneario Thompson* (☎ 22-1998), the most convenient camping ground, to the centre. Sites cost US$8 for two people.

Hotel City (☎ 21-0086), Racedo 231, has cool rooms with high ceilings for US$19/30 with private bath, slightly less with shared bath. Rates are similar at *Hotel 9 de Julio*

(☎ 21-3047), Avenida 9 de Julio 674. Clean, attractive *Hotel Bristol* (☎ 21-3961), Alsina 221, costs US$24/35 with private bath.

Places to Eat

River fish is the local speciality; for a bargain on tasty grilled boga, try the takeaway *Pollolandia*, Tucumán 418, which also grills chicken over the coals. Traditionally, one of Paraná's best restaurants is *Luisito*, 9 de Julio 140.

Other recommended restaurants include *El Moncholo* at Antonio Crespo and Scalabrini, *Quinchos de Paja* (☎ 23-1845), at Avenida Laurencena and Juan de San Martín, the *Club Atlético Echagüe* at 25 de Mayo 555, and the *Club Atlético Estudiantes* at the west end of Avenida Laurencena. *Don Charras* is a highly regarded parrilla at Avenida Raúl Uranga 1127.

Getting There & Away

Air Aerolíneas Argentinas (☎ 21-0003) has offices at Corrientes 563, but all flights leave from Santa Fe's Aeropuerto Sauce Viejo. LAER (☎ 21-6375), 25 de Mayo 119, flies from Paraná to Aeroparque (US$65) four times daily on weekdays, but only once daily on weekends. It runs its own minibus to Aeropuerto Ciudad de Paraná, just outside the city limits.

Bus The new Terminal de Omnibus (☎ 22-1282) is on Avenida Ramírez between Posadas and Moreno, opposite Plaza Martín Fierro. About every hour throughout the day and night, Etacer buses (☎ 21-6809) leave for Santa Fe (US$2). There are numerous buses to Rosario (US$11, three hours) and Buenos Aires (US$26, eight hours), and additional services to northern littoral destinations like Corrientes, Posadas, and Puerto Iguazú. Other long-distance services go to Córdoba, Mar del Plata, Mendoza, Neuquén and Bariloche, but Santa Fe has better long-distance connections.

International carriers include Cora (to Montevideo, Uruguay) and Singer (to Porto Alegre, Brazil).

GUALEGUAYCHU

In the first sizeable city north of Buenos Aires, on a tributary of the Río Uruguay, Gualeguaychú's Carnaval has an international reputation, so stop here if you can't make Rio or Bahia. RN 14 passes west of Gualeguaychú, while RN 136, a side road, bypasses the city centre en route to Fray Bentos, Uruguay.

Plaza San Martín marks the city centre. The Dirección Municipal de Turismo (☎ 23668), on Avenida Costanera near the bridge across the Río Gualeguaychú, keeps long hours. Casa Goyo, on Ayacucho near San Martín, changes cash dollars but not travellers' cheques; several banks have ATMs. Uruguay has a consulate (☎ 26168), at Rivadavia 510. The telephone code is 0446.

There is a good selection of handicrafts at the Centro Artesanal San José, housed in the colonial **Casa de Andrade** at Andrade and Borques. José Alvarez, founder of the satirical turn-of-the-century magazine *Caras y Caretas*, was born in the **Casa de Fray Mocho**, Fray Mocho 135 (Fray Mocho was his pen name).

Places to Stay & Eat

Camping La Delfina (☎ 23984), across the Río Gualeguaychú in Parque Unzué, has good facilities (US$8 for two people). Clean, friendly *Pensión Gualeguaychú*, Avenida 25 de Mayo 456, has singles for US$10 with shared bath. At *Hospedaje Mayo* (☎ 27661), Bolívar 550, singles/doubles with private bath cost US$12/20. *Residencial Marina* (☎ 27159), 25 de Mayo 1031, has quiet, spacious rooms with good beds for US$15/25.

Most restaurants line the Costanera, but try also the *Círculo Italiano* at San Martín 647 or *París* at Pellegrini 180. *Pizzería Don Julián* is at Urquiza 607, while *Pizza San Remo* is at 25 de Mayo 634.

Getting There & Away

From the Terminal de Omnibus (☎ 27987), at Bolívar and Monseñor Chalup (formerly Chile), several companies go to Buenos

Aires (US$20, three hours). Ciudad de Gualeguay has five buses daily to Paraná (US$16, six hours). Ciudad de Gualeguaychú goes daily to Corrientes.

ETA runs three buses daily (except Sunday) to Fray Bentos, Uruguay (US$4), two of which continue to Mercedes (US$5), with connections to Montevideo.

PARQUE NACIONAL EL PALMAR

The yatay palm (*Syagrus yatay*) covered much of the littoral until 19th-century agriculture, ranching and forestry destroyed palm savannas and inhibited their reproduction. On the west bank of the Río Uruguay, 360 km north-west of Buenos Aires, the relict yatays of 8500-hectare El Palmar have again begun to thrive, under protection from fire and grazing. Reaching 18 metres in height, the larger specimens accentuate a soothing subtropical landscape.

To see wildlife, walk along the watercourses or through the palm savannas early in the morning or just before sunset. The most conspicuous bird is the ñandú, or rhea (*Rhea americana*), but look for parakeets, cormorants, egrets, herons, storks, caracaras, woodpeckers and kingfishers. The carpincho (capybara), a semiaquatic rodent weighing up to 60 kg, and the vizcacha, a relative of the chinchilla, are the most conspicuous mammals.

At night, squeaking vizcachas infest the camping ground at Arroyo Los Loros and gigantic toads invade the showers and toilets, but both are harmless. The yarará, a highly poisonous pit viper, is not; bites are uncommon, but watch your step and wear high boots and long trousers when hiking.

Things to See & Do

Across from the camping ground, the **Centro de Interpretación** offers evening slide shows and contains a small reptile house. At Los Loros camping ground, rental canoes are available for exploring the placid river. A short hike from the camping ground, **Arroyo Los Loros** is a good place to observe wildlife.

Five km from the camping ground,

Arroyo El Palmar is a pleasant stream with a beautiful swimming hole, and a good site for bird-watching. Crossing the ruined bridge, you can walk several km along a palm-lined road being reclaimed by savanna grasses.

Places to Stay & Eat

Los Loros camping ground (☎ (0447) 93031) has good sites (US$4 per tent and US$4 per person), hot showers, a shop and a confitería.

Getting There & Away

Any northbound bus from Buenos Aires to Concordia can drop you at the entrance (admission US$2.50). No public transport serves the visitor centre and camping ground, but hitching is feasible.

CORRIENTES

Just below the confluence of the Paraná and Paraguay rivers, one of Argentina's oldest cities and capital of its namesake province, Corrientes is 1025 km from Buenos Aires. Its once-moribund **Carnaval Correntino** has recently experienced a revival, attracting crowds up to 80,000. Across the Paraná is Resistencia, capital of Chaco province.

Plaza 25 de Mayo is the centre of Corrientes' extremely regular grid plan, but public buildings are more dispersed than in most Argentine cities. The commercial centre is the Junín peatonal, between Salta and Catamarca, but the most attractive area is the shady riverside Parque Mitre.

Information

Much improved over recent years, the Dirección Provincial de Turismo (☎ 27200), 25 de Mayo 1330, is open on weekdays from 7 am to 1 pm and 3 to 9 pm, and on Saturday from 9 am to noon and 5 to 8 pm. Cambio El Dorado is on 9 de Julio between Córdoba and Catamarca, and several banks on Córdoba and 9 de Julio have ATMs. Correo Argentino is at San Juan and San Martín, while Telecom is at Pellegrini 1175 and on Catamarca between Belgrano and Moreno. The telephone code is 0783.

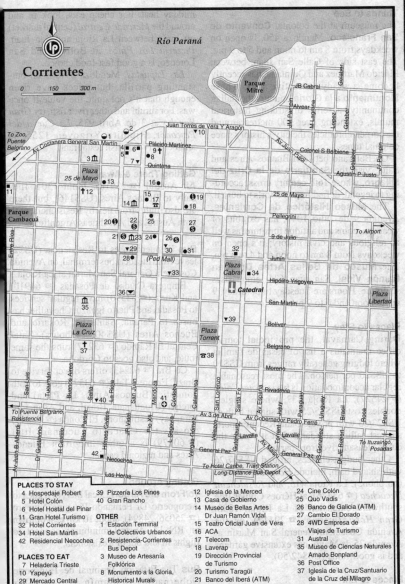

Corrientes

Río Paraná

0   150   300 m

Parque Mitre

Things to See

The museum at the colonial **Convento de San Francisco**, Mendoza 450, is open on weekdays from 8 am to noon and 5 to 9 pm. The east side of Calle San Juan, between Plácido Martínez and Quintana, has recently become a shady, attractive park whose **Monumento a la Gloria** honours the Italian community; a series of striking historical murals, extending over 100 metres around the corner, chronicles the city's history since colonial times.

On Belgrano between Buenos Aires and Salta, visit the **Santuario de la Cruz del Milagro**, whose 16th-century cross, according to legend, defied Indian efforts to burn it.

The **Museo Histórico de Corrientes**, Avenida 9 de Julio 1044, has exhibits of weapons, coins and antique furniture, as well as religious and civil history; it's open on weekdays from 8 am to noon and 4 to 8 pm. The **Museo de Bellas Artes Dr Juan Ramón Vidal**, San Juan 634, emphasises sculpture. Hours are Tuesday to Saturday, 9 am to noon and 6 to 9 pm.

Places to Stay

During Carnaval, the provincial tourist office maintains a list of casas de familia where lodging generally ranges from US$10 to US$20 per person. The most reasonable regular accommodation is basic *Hotel Colón* (☎ 24527), La Rioja 437, where singles/doubles cost US$15/25 with shared bath or US$23/33 with private bath. Recent reports suggest falling standards, but it's near the city's pleasant riverfront parks.

Other budget choices, around US$17/26 with shared bath, include *Hospedaje Robert* (no phone), La Rioja 415, and *Residencial Necochea* (☎ 65476), at Héroes Civiles (the southward extension of La Rioja) 1898. *Gran Hotel Turismo* (☎ 29112), on the Avenida Costanera General San Martín at Avenida 25 de Mayo, has extensive gardens and is good value (US$42/50).

Places to Eat

The Junín peatonal has many cafés and confiterías, but shuts down during the midday heat. For cheap eats, look in and around the *Mercado Central* (central market) on Junín between La Rioja and San Juan. *Pizzería Los Pinos*, at Bolívar and San Lorenzo, is a good fast-food choice.

Las Espuelas, Mendoza 847, is an outstanding parrilla, but prices have risen enough that it's not quite the value it once was. For surubí and other river fish, try *Gran Rancho* at 3 de Abril 935. *La Cueva del Pescador*, Hipólito Yrigoyen 1255, is another very fine fish restaurant.

Getting There & Away

Air Austral (☎ 23918), Junín 1301, flies daily to Buenos Aires (US$146), but there are also flights from nearby Resistencia, with both Austral and Aerolíneas Argentinas.

Bus Frequent buses to Resistencia (US$2) leave from the local bus terminal, on Avenida Costanera General San Martín at La Rioja.

Empresa Ciudad de Posadas (☎ 64910) and Kurtz (☎ 63590) have regular services to Posadas and Puerto Iguazú. Chevallier has buses to Paraná, Santa Fe, Rosario and Buenos Aires (US$40, 14 hours). Tata/Central El Rápido (☎ 63227) runs the same route, and also goes to Córdoba.

Co-Bra (☎ 62243) offers direct service to Brazil. Empresa Tala (☎ 63577) goes to both domestic (Buenos Aires, La Plata) and foreign (Uruguaiana, Brazil, and Asunción, Paraguay) destinations. El Zonda (☎ 63842) crosses the Chaco to Tucumán. Itatí (☎ 60279) is another important Buenos Aires and regional carrier.

Getting Around

To/From the Airport Local bus No 8 goes to Aeropuerto Dr Fernando Piragine Niveyro (☎ 25056, 24894), about 10 km east of town on RN 12. Austral minibuses connect to flights in and out of Resistencia.

Bus The Estación Terminal de Transporte Gobernador Benjamín S González (☎ 62243, 60137) is the long-distance bus terminal, out Avenida Maipú. From the local bus station on Avenida Costanera, take bus No 6.

ESTEROS DEL IBERÁ

The Esteros del Iberá, a 13,000-sq-km marshland in north-central Corrientes province, compares favourably to the Brazilian Pantanal for its fauna and flora, though plans for a national park are on hold. The most notable animal species are reptiles like the cayman, mammals like capybara and Pampas and swamp deer, and 280 species of birds. Canoe trips are possible from Colonia Pellegrini, on Laguna Iberá. No hotels yet exist, but camping is possible.

Buses from Corrientes to Paso de Los Libres stop at Mercedes, where RP 40 leads north-east to Colonia Pellegrini; occasional trucks from Mercedes go to Colonia Pellegrini, or try hitching. For tours, contact Turismo Operativo Misionero (☎ (0752) 27591), at Urquiza and Zapiola, Posadas; at Mariano Moreno 58 (☎ (0757) 21240 in Puerto Iguazú; or at Avenida Corrientes 753, Buenos Aires (☎ (01) 393-3476).

PASO DE LOS LIBRES

Paso de Los Libres, 700 km north of Buenos Aires, is directly across the Río Uruguay from Uruguaiana (Brazil), by a bridge about 10 blocks south-west of central Plaza Independencia. The main commercial street is Avenida Colón.

Alhec Tours, Colón 901, changes cash but not travellers' cheques. Correo Argentino is at General Madariaga and Juan Sitja Min. Telecom is at General Madariaga 854, half a block north of the Plaza; the telephone code is 0772.

The **Cementerio de la Santa Cruz**, just beyond the bus station, holds the tomb of Amado (Aimé) Bonpland, a naturalist and travel companion of Alexander von Humboldt. Ask for directions to 'El sabio Bonpland'. Paso de los Libres has a lively **Carnaval**.

Places to Stay & Eat

The *Camping Municipal*, north of the train station, charges US$10 per site. *Residencial*

Colón Hotel, Avenida Colón 1065, costs US$15 per person with private bath. Shabby but comfortable *Hotel Buen Comfort* (☎ 21848), Coronel López 1091, has rooms with bath and air-con for US$20/30.

ACA has a restaurant near the border complex, but try also *La Victoria*, Colón 585.

Getting There & Away

Air LAER (☎ 22395), Colón 1007, flies to Concordia and Buenos Aires (US$84) several times weekly.

Bus The Terminal de Omnibus (☎ 21608) is at Avenida San Martín and Santiago del Estero. Singer and Crucero del Norte stop here three times daily en route between Buenos Aires and Posadas (six hours). There are also daily buses to La Plata, Paraná and Santa Fe, and a daily service to Rosario except for Thursday. Daily, except Thursday, Paso de Los Libres is a stopover between Córdoba and Puerto Iguazú. Provincial services run three times daily to Corrientes.

YAPEYÚ

Birthplace of General José de San Martín, Yapeyú is a charming village, 55 km north of Paso de Los Libres. Founded in 1626, it once had a population of 8000 Guaraní Indians, who tended up to 80,000 cattle; after expulsion of the Jesuits, the Indians dispersed and the mission fell into ruins, but villagers built many houses of salvaged red sandstone blocks.

Things to See

The **Museo de Cultura Jesuítica**, consisting of several modern kiosks on the foundations of mission buildings, has a sundial, a few other mission relics and interesting photographs.

Plaques in the pretentious temple sheltering the **Casa de San Martín**, the modest birthplace of Argentina's greatest hero, include one from pardoned Dirty War lifer General Videla, asserting his 'most profound faith' in San Martín's ideals. Next door is the **Museo Sanmartiniano**.

Places to Stay & Eat

At the *Camping Municipal* near the river, sites cost US$5, with hot showers. Insects can be abundant, and the most low-lying sites can flood in heavy rain.

Hotel San Martín, Sargento Cabral 712, is bright and cheerful for US$15/20 a single/double. *El Parador Yapeyú* (☎ (0772) 93-056), at the entrance to town, has bungalows for US$30/40.

Restaurant Bicentenario has good food, reasonable prices and friendly, attentive service. There is an another passable restaurant alongside Hotel San Martín.

Getting There & Away

Services from the bus station, two blocks south of the plaza, resemble those from Paso de Los Libres.

POSADAS

Posadas (population 200,000), on the south bank of the upper Río Paraná, became capital of the new territory of Misiones in the 1880s. Travellers stopping here en route to Iguazú should not miss Jesuit ruins at San Ignacio Miní, about 50 km east, or at Trinidad (Paraguay), across the river.

Orientation

Plaza 9 de Julio is the centre of Posadas' standard grid. Streets have recently been renumbered, but local preference for the old system has created confusion. Wherever possible, information below refers to locations instead of street numbers (which, if given, list the new number first and the old number in parentheses).

Information

The Secretaría de Estado de Turismo (☎ 33185), Colón 1985 (formerly 393) between Córdoba and La Rioja, has numerous maps and brochures; weekday hours are 6.30 am to 12.30 pm and 2 to 8 pm. Holiday and weekend hours are from 8 am to noon and 4 to 8 pm.

Money Cambio Mazza, on Bolívar between San Lorenzo and Colón, changes travellers' cheques. There are several ATMs in the city centre.

Post & Communications Correo Argentino is at Bolívar and Ayacucho. Telecom is at Colón and Santa Fe, but there are other locutorios on Junín between Bolívar and Córdoba. Posadas' telephone code is 0752.

Foreign Consulates Paraguay's consulate (☎ 23850), on San Lorenzo between Santa Fe and Sarmiento, is open on weekdays from 8 am to noon. Brazil's consulate (☎ 24830), at Mitre 1242 (631) near the entrance to the Encarnación bridge, offers same-day visa service and does not insist on a photograph. Hours are weekdays 9 am to 1 pm and 4 to 6.30 pm.

Travel Agencies Turismo Operativo Misionero (☎ 27951), at Urquiza (the westward extension of Guacurarí) and Zapiola, runs trips to less accessible natural attractions like the Esteros del Iberá and parts of Parque Nacional Iguazú.

Museo de Ciencias Naturales e Históricas

The natural history section of this worthwhile museum, on San Luis between Córdoba and La Rioja, focuses on invertebrates, vertebrates, and provincial geology and mineralogy; it also has an excellent serpentarium, an aviary and an aquarium. The historical section stresses prehistory, the Jesuit missions and modern colonisation.

Regular hours are Tuesday to Friday 8 am to noon and 3 to 7 pm, weekends 9 am to noon. Winter holiday hours are 9 am to noon and 3 to 8 pm, daily except Monday.

Places to Stay

Budget travellers should consider Encarnación (Paraguay), for lower prices and better value.

Hostel For US$8 per night, there's hostel accommodation at the *Albergue Juvenil* (☎ 23700), at the Anfiteatro MA Ramírez, on the riverfront at the north end of Alberdi.

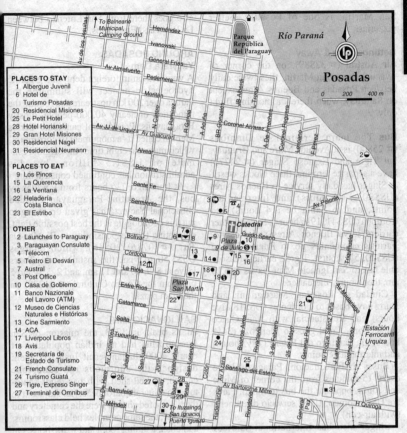

PLACES TO STAY
1 Albergue Juvenil
6 Hotel de
   Turismo Posadas
20 Residencial Misiones
25 Le Petit Hotel
28 Hotel Horianski
29 Gran Hotel Misiones
30 Residencial Nagel
31 Residencial Neumann

PLACES TO EAT
9 Los Pinos
15 La Querencia
16 La Ventana
22 Heladería
   Costa Blanca
23 El Estribo

OTHER
2 Launches to Paraguay
3 Paraguayan Consulate
4 Telecom
5 Teatro El Desván
7 Austral
8 Post Office
10 Casa de Gobierno
11 Banco Nazionale
   del Lavoro (ATM)
12 Museo de Ciencias
   Naturales e Históricas
13 Cine Sarmiento
14 ACA
17 Liverpool Libros
18 Avis
19 Secretaría de
   Estado de Turismo
21 French Consulate
24 Turismo Guatá
26 Tigre, Expreso Singer
27 Terminal de Omnibus

Posadas

Residenciales & Hotels Recent visitors
have questioned standards at popular *Residencial Misiones* (☎ 30133), on Avenida
Azara between La Rioja and Córdoba, where
singles/doubles with private bath are
US$15/25. A good, comparably priced
choice is *Residencial Neumann* (☎ 24675),
on Roque Sáenz Peña between Mitre and
Santiago del Estero. A reader recommendation, seconded by locals, is *Le Petit Hotel*
(☎ 36031), on Santiago del Estero between
Rivadavia and Buenos Aires, for US$20/30
with private bath. Despite its impersonal
appearance, the high-rise *Hotel de Turismo*

Posadas (☎ 37401), at Bolívar and Junín, is
friendly and its balconies have excellent
river views; rates are US$25/38.

Places to Eat
There are many interchangeable, inexpensive eating places along San Lorenzo west of
the plaza. The spiffiest parrilla is *La
Querencia* on Bolívar, across from Plaza 9
de Julio. *La Ventana*, Bolívar 1725 (580)
between Avenida Azara and Calle Buenos
Aires, has a varied menu with large portions
and reasonable prices (for some items). *Los
Pinos*, on San Lorenzo between Bolívar and

San Martín, is one of Posadas' better pizzerías.

Getting There & Away
Air Austral (☎ 32889), on the corner of Ayacucho and San Martín, flies twice daily between Posadas and Buenos Aires except on Saturday, when there's a morning flight only.

Bus The main Terminal de Omnibus (☎ 25800) is at Avenida Mitre and Uruguay, but Tigre and Expreso Singer (☎ 24771) have a separate terminal three blocks west.

Singer has daily service to Buenos Aires (US$30, 13½ hours) and intermediate points, and to Santa Fe (14 hours) and Córdoba (US$41, 19½ hours). Several other carriers serve Buenos Aires and Rosario. Various companies go to Puerto Iguazú (US$20, 5½ hours). Tigre's earliest reasonable bus to San Ignacio Miní leaves at 6.10 am, then hourly thereafter.

Ciudad de Posadas, Martignoni, and Kurtz have buses to Corrientes (US$18, five hours) and Resistencia, with trans-Chaco connections. Cotal goes to Mendoza (34½ hours) via Santiago del Estero (18½ hours) and intermediate points.

Buses to Encarnación, Paraguay, leave every 15 minutes from the corner of Mitre and Junín, opposite the bus terminal. Fares are US$1 común, US$2 servicio diferencial (with air-con).

Singer also has international services daily to Asunción (5½ hours) all year and to Brazil in summer. Nuestra Señora de la Asunción also does the Asunción route.

Boat Launches across the Paraná to Encarnación (US$1) continue to operate despite the new bridge, but may cease as the reservoir behind Yacyretá dam floods low-lying parts of the two cities. They leave from the dock at the east end of Avenida Guacurarí.

Getting Around
To/From the Airport Austral runs minibuses to Aeropuerto Internacional Posadas, 12 km south-west of town via RN 12; the No 8 bus

also goes there from San Lorenzo between La Rioja and Entre Ríos.

AROUND POSADAS
Yacyretá Dam
A vivid lesson in foreign debt, this gigantic hydroelectric project will submerge the Paraná over 200 km upstream and require the relocation of nearly 40,000 people, mostly Paraguayans. Presidential candidate Carlos Menem called it 'a monument to corruption' which may cost eight times the original estimate of US$1.5 billion, but his administration has continued construction.

At Ituzaingó, 1½ hours from Posadas by bus, the Argentine-Paraguayan Entidad Binacional Yacyretá has given up trying to put this boondoggle in the best possible light, delegating that responsibility to Ri-Mar-Os Tur (☎ (0786) 20546), which charges US$3.50 to visit the installations. Tours leave at 8, 9, 10 and 11 am, and 2, 3, 4 and 5 pm from the Centro Cultural (☎ 21278) on the main plaza.

SAN IGNACIO MINI
At its peak, in 1733, the mission of San Ignacio Miní had an Indian population of nearly 4000. Italian Jesuit Juan Brasanelli designed the enormous red sandstone church, embellished with bas-relief sculptures in 'Guaraní baroque' style. Adjacent to the tile-roofed church were the cemetery and cloisters; the same complex held classrooms, a kitchen, a dining room and workshops. On all sides of the Plaza de Armas were the living quarters.

San Ignacio Miní, 56 km east of Posadas via RN 12, is an easy day trip from Posadas, but staying overnight allows more time to explore the mission ruins.

Places to Stay
The cheapest accommodation is German-run *Hospedaje Los Salpeterer* at Sarmiento and Centenario, where rooms with shared bath cost US$7 per person with access to kitchen facilities, while those with private bath cost US$10. Another possibility is *Hospedaje El Descanso*, a bit farther from the ruins at

Pellegrini 270. Highly recommended *Hotel San Ignacio* (☎ 70047), Sarmiento 823, has singles/doubles with bath for about US$20/30.

There are several decent restaurants across from the entrance to the ruins, where *El Jardín* has good, filling dinners starting at US$4.

Getting There & Away

The bus terminal is at the north end of Sarmiento. Empresa Tigre and other companies have 26 daily buses to Posadas (US$3.50), the last at 10.40 pm. Tigre has three buses daily to Puerto Iguazú (US$17), but other buses along RN 12 stop for roadside passengers.

PUERTO IGUAZÚ

Puerto Iguazú hosts most visitors to the Argentine side of the Iguazú Falls (for details of the Brazilian side, see Foz do Iguaçu in the Brazil chapter). The town's very irregular city plan is at least compact enough for relatively easy orientation. The main drag is the diagonal Avenida Victoria Aguirre.

Information

The Secretaría de Turismo (☎ 20800), Avenida Victoria Aguirre 311, is open on weekdays from 8 am to 8 pm, and on weekends from 8 am to noon and 4.30 to 8 pm.

Change cash or travellers' cheques at Cambio Dick, Avenida Aguirre 471, but note some reports of very high commissions on cheques. Before buying Brazilian currency, ask other travellers about trends in Foz do Iguaçu.

Correo Argentino is at Avenida San Martín 780. Telecom is at Victoria Aguirre 146 Sur, but Cabina Hola, on Aguirre near Bonpland, is more central. Puerto Iguazú's telephone code is 0757.

Brazil's efficient consulate, on Avenida Victoria Aguirre between Avenida Córdoba and Curupy, turns around visa applications quickly. It's open on weekdays from 8 am to noon.

Places to Stay

Foz do Iguaçu, on the Brazilian side of the falls, is usually cheaper than Puerto Iguazú, but the overvalued Brazilian *real* has made Puerto Iguazú more competitive.

Camping *Camping El Pindó*, at Km 3.5 of RN 12 on the edge of town, charges US$3 per person and US$3 per vehicle.

Hostel Puerto Iguazú's *Albergue Juvenil* (☎ 20529), in the Residencial Uno at Fray Luis Beltrán 116, charges US$6 with breakfast.

Residenciales & Hotels *Residencial Arco Iris* (☎ 20636), Curupy 152, is very popular with travellers for US$15/20 a single/double with private bath. Shady *Hostería Los Helechos* (☎ 20338), at Paulina Amarante 76 near Beltrán, is superb value for US$15/25, a bit more in the high season. At Victoria Aguirre 915, for about the same price, *Residencial King* (☎ 20360) has attractive grounds and a swimming pool.

Places to Eat

The *Fechoría Bar* (☎ 20182), Eppens 30, is a good breakfast choice. *La Plaza* is a lively confitería on Aguirre near Brasil. Two recommended parrillas are *Tomás* at the bus terminal, and *Charo* at Córdoba 106; the former's owner is an accomplished harpist. Increasingly pricey *Restaurant Saint George*, Córdoba 148, has superb food and service.

Getting There & Away

Air Aerolíneas Argentinas (☎ 20168), Aguirre 295, flies to Aeroparque (US$184), and on Tuesday and Saturday has an international service to and from São Paulo and Rio de Janeiro. Aerolíneas 'Conozca Cataratas' fare offers a 35% discount on return trips from Buenos Aires, valid for three to five days only.

Dinar Líneas Aéreas (☎ 20566), Córdoba 236, flies to Aeroparque (US$130) on Thursday and Sunday afternoons. LAPA

ARGENTINA

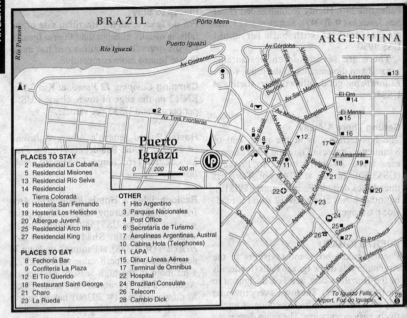

PLACES TO STAY
2 Residencial La Cabaña
5 Residencial Misiones
13 Residencial Río Selva
14 Residencial
   Tierra Colorada
16 Hostería San Fernando
19 Hostería Los Helechos
20 Albergue Juvenil
25 Residencial Arco Iris
27 Residencial King

PLACES TO EAT
8 Fechoría Bar
9 Confitería La Plaza
12 El Tío Querido
18 Restaurant Saint George
21 Charo
23 La Rueda

OTHER
1 Hito Argentino
3 Parques Nacionales
4 Post Office
6 Secretaría de Turismo
7 Aerolíneas Argentinas, Austral
10 Cabina Hola (Telephones)
11 LAPA
15 Dinar Líneas Aéreas
22 Hospital
24 Brazilian Consulate
26 Telecom
28 Cambio Dick

(☎ 20214), Bonpland 110, Local 7, has a similar schedule, but charges only US$99.

Bus The Terminal de Omnibus is at Avenidas Córdoba and Misiones. Many companies have services to Posadas, Buenos Aires (US$45, 22 hours) and intermediate points. Cotal's direct service to Mendoza is a 40-hour marathon via Santiago del Estero and San Juan.

Getting Around

To/From the Airport Expreso Aristóbulo del Valle (☎ 20348), Entre Ríos 239, charges US$3 to the airport. Taxis cost around US$18.

Bus Frequent buses to Parque Nacional Iguazú (US$2) leave from the bus terminal, as do international buses to Foz do Iguaçu (US$2) and Ciudad del Este, Paraguay.

Taxi Groups of three people or more hoping

to see both sides of the falls, as well as Ciudad del Este and the Itaipú hydroelectric project, may find a shared cab or remise cheaper than a tour; expect to pay about US$60 to US$70 for a full day's sightseeing. Contact the Asociación de Trabajadores de Taxis (☎ 20282), at Aguirre and Brasil, or simply approach a driver.

PARQUE NACIONAL IGUAZU

Guaraní legend says that Iguazú Falls originated when a jealous forest god, enraged by a warrior escaping downriver by canoe with a young girl, caused the riverbed to collapse in front of the lovers, producing a precipitous falls over which the girl fell and, at their base, turned into a rock. The warrior survived as a tree overlooking his fallen lover.

The falls' geological origins are more prosaic. In southern Brazil, the Río Iguazú passes over a basalt plateau which ends just above its confluence with the Paraná. Where the lava stopped, at least 5000 cubic metres of water per second plunge 70 metres into the sedimentary terrain below. Before reaching the edge, the river divides into many channels to form several distinctive *cataratas*.

The most awesome is the semicircular Garganta del Diablo (Devil's Throat), a deafening and dampening part of the experience, approached by launch and via a system of *pasarelas* (catwalks). Despite pressures for development, the 55,000-hectare park is a natural wonderland of subtropical rainforest, with over 2000 identified plant species, countless insects, 400 bird species, and many mammals and reptiles.

Iguazú Falls
Before seeing the falls themselves, look around the museum, and climb the nearby tower for a good overall view, but plan hikes before the midmorning tour-bus invasion. Descending from the visitor centre, you can cross by free launch to **Isla Grande San Martín**, which offers unique views and a refuge from the masses on the mainland.

Flood damage has isolated the catwalks to **Garganta del Diablo**, but you can still reach the lookout by a road to Ñandú and a launch (US$5). Of all sights on earth, this must come closest to the experience of sailing off the edge of the earth imagined by early European sailors, as the deafening cascade plunges to a murky destination, blurred by the rising vapour soaking the viewer.

Hiking, Cycling & Rafting
Best in the early morning, the **Sendero Macuco** nature trail leads through dense forest, where a steep sidetrack goes to the base of a hidden waterfall. Another trail goes to the *bañado*, a marsh abounding in bird life.

To get elsewhere in the forest, explored by few visitors, hitch or hire a car to go out on RP 101 towards Bernardo de Irigoyen. Floating Iguazú, at the visitor centre, arranges 4WD trips to the Yacaratia forest trail, organises rafting excursions, and also rents mountain bikes. La Gran Aventura also

arranges recommended raft/boat trips on the river for US$25.

Getting There & Away
For bus information, see the Puerto Iguazú section. Park admission costs US$3 per person and includes the launch to Isla Grande San Martín. If you miss the last regular bus, enquire at the front desk of the Hotel Internacional for the employees' bus, which returns to Puerto Iguazú around 8 pm.

RESISTENCIA
Resistencia, across the Paraná from Corrientes, is capital of Chaco province and a major crossroads for Paraguay, Santa Fe, and trans-Chaco routes to the North-West. Despite a frontier past, it prides itself on a reputation as the 'city of sculptures', for the statues in almost every public space.

Plaza 25 de Mayo occupies four square blocks in the city centre. The Dirección Provincial de Turismo (☎ 23547), upstairs at Juan B Justo 135, is friendly, well-informed and occasionally has an English-speaker. It's open on weekdays from 7.30 am to 1 pm and 3 to 7.30 pm.

Cambio El Dorado, on the corner of Yrigoyen and Pellegrini, changes travellers' cheques at reasonable rates, while there are ATMs at several banks near Plaza 25 de Mayo. Correo Argentino faces the plaza, at Sarmiento and Yrigoyen, while Telecom is at J M Paz and J B Justo. The telephone code is 0722.

Things to See
The tourist office map, pinpointing 75 **outdoor sculptures**, is a good introduction to the city. The sculpture-oriented **Museo Provincial de Bellas Artes**, at Avenida 9 de Julio 254, is open Tuesday to Friday from 8 am to noon and 6 to 8.30 pm. A new **Museo de la Escultura en Madera** (Museum of Wood Sculptures) is due to open near the Domo del Centenario, a performing arts amphitheatre in Parque 2 de Febrero, north of the city centre.

The unexpectedly good **Museo Policial**, Roca 223, features exhibits – some of them remarkably sympathetic to outlaws – on *cuatrerismo* (cattle rustling, still common in the province today) and social banditry. Hours are Tuesday to Friday, 9 am to noon and 6 to 8 pm, Sunday and holidays 6 to 9 pm.

El Fogón de los Arrieros, Brown 350, is famous for its eclectic assemblage of art objects from around the Chaco, Argentina and the world. It's open Monday to Saturday from 8 am to noon, with a bar open in the evenings. Admission is US$2.

Places to Stay

Camping *Camping Parque 2 de Febrero*, Avenida Avalos 1100, has excellent facilities for US$4 per person.

Hostel The *Casa del Docente* (☎ 24564), French 555, offers beds for US$7 per night.

Hospedajes & Residenciales Despite a run-down exterior, *Residencial Alberdi*, Alberdi 317 between Ameghino and Obligado, has decent rooms with shared bath for US$18 per person, but is often full. Comparably priced *Residencial San José* (☎ 26062), Rawson 304, is scruffy but clean, with one truly enormous room.

Places to Eat

An old mainstay is *El Círculo*, Güemes 350, with decent fixed-price meals and huge portions. Most restaurants are parrillas, like recommended *La Estaca* at Güemes 202, but for variety try *Por la Vuelta* at Obligado 33 for international food or *Trattoria Italiana* at H Yrigoyen 236. *Cueva del Pescador*, Avenida Paraguay 24, is a very fine fish and seafood restaurant which also has a branch across the river in Corrientes.

The very attractive *Café de la Ciudad*, on the corner of Yrigoyen and Pellegrini, was once a sleazy bar; alongside it on Yrigoyen, equally new *Heladería New York* has outstanding ice cream. Pricey *La Bohemia* (☎ 42251), in an old house at Corrientes 366, has tango shows on Friday night; reservations are advisable.

Getting There & Away

Air Aerolíneas Argentinas (☎ 22854) and Austral (☎ 27389) are both at Rawson 99. Aerolíneas flies to Buenos Aires on Wednesday, Friday and Sunday nights, while Austral flies there on Monday, Tuesday, Thursday and Saturday afternoons. See also the schedule for nearby Corrientes.

Bus Resistencia's new Estación Terminal de Omnibus (☎ 46986/7), at Avenida MacLean and Islas Malvinas, replaces the dilapidated city terminal. Godoy Resistencia buses make the rounds between Corrientes and Resistencia at frequent intervals throughout the day.

Several companies go south to Reconquista, Santa Fe, Rosario and Buenos Aires (US$43, 15 hours), north to Formosa and Asunción, Paraguay, and east to Posadas and Puerto Iguazú. La Estrella (☎ 25221) goes to the village of Capitán Solari, near Parque Nacional Chaco, four times daily. La Estrella and Cacorba (☎ 21521) alternate daily service to Córdoba.

Central Sáenz Peña (☎ 21521) alternates with La Veloz del Norte in crossing the Chaco to Salta (US$40, 16 hours) daily, while El Rayo (☎ 21123) takes a more southerly route to Santiago del Estero and Tucumán. Cotal (☎ 21521) serves Mendoza and San Juan on Tuesday, Thursday and Saturday via Catamarca and La Rioja. Godoy SRL (☎ 20730, 23824) heads north to Formosa, and also goes to Naick-Neck and Laguna Blanca, near Parque Nacional Pilcomayo.

Getting Around

To/From the Airport Aeropuerto San Martín is six km south of town on RN 11; take bus No 3 (black letters) from the post office.

To/From the Bus Station Take bus No 3 or No 10 from the Casa de Gobierno on Plaza 25 de Mayo.

PARQUE NACIONAL CHACO

This little-visited park, 115 km north-west of Resistencia, preserves 15,000 hectares of swamps, grasslands, palm savannas, scrub and dense gallery forests in the humid eastern Chaco. Mammals are few, but birds include rheas, jabirú storks, roseate spoonbills, cormorants, and caracaras. The most abundant species is the mosquito, so visit in the relatively dry, cool winter and bring insect repellent.

Hiking and bird-watching are best in the early morning or around sunset; park personnel accompany visitors if their duties permit. Some marshy areas are accessible only on horseback – enquire in Capitán Solari for horses and guides.

Places to Stay & Eat

Camping is the only accommodation option at the park. The shaded area has clean toilets and (cold water) showers, but a tent is essential. Sometimes on weekends, a snack bar sells meals, but bring supplies from Resistencia.

Getting There & Away

La Estrella runs four buses daily from Resistencia to Capitán Solari (2½ hours), and from there you must walk or catch a lift to the park entrance.

FORMOSA

From Formosa city, capital of Formosa province, it's possible to cross the northern Chaco to Jujuy, Salta or Bolivia, or continue to Paraguay. November's week-long **Fiesta del Río** features an impressive nocturnal religious procession in which 150 boats from Corrientes sail up the Río Paraguay.

Formosa has no real bargain accommodation, but *Residencial Rivas* (☎ 20499), at Belgrano 1399 near the old bus terminal, has clean, comfortable singles/doubles for about US$20/25. Navarro (☎ 23598), at Alberdi and Corrientes, has buses to Clorinda and Laguna Naick-Neck (Parque Nacional Río Pilcomayo) daily at 5.30 am and 2 and 8 pm.

PARQUE NACIONAL RIO PILCOMAYO

West of Clorinda, the wildlife-rich marshlands of 60,000-hectare Parque Nacional Río Pilcomayo hug the Paraguayan border. Its

outstanding feature is shimmering **Laguna Blanca** where, at sunset, yacarés lurk on the lake surface. Other wildlife, except for birds, is likelier to be heard than seen among the dense aquatic vegetation.

Parque Nacional Río Pilcomayo's free camping facilities are little used except on weekends; just outside the park entrance, a small shop sells basic food and cold drinks, including beer. There is bus service with Navarro from Formosa and Clorinda along RN 86 to Laguna Naick-Neck, where a well-marked turn-off leads to the Laguna Blanca ranger station. From the turn-off, intending visitors have to hike or hitch the last five km.

Córdoba Province

Córdoba province is bounded by the Andean provinces to the north-west, Cuyo to the south-west, the Chaco to the north-east and the Pampas to the south-east. Popular with Argentine tourists, its key attractions are the city of Córdoba and its scenic mountain hinterland, the Sierras de Córdoba.

History

Comechingones Indians briefly resisted the Spaniards, but by 1573, Jerónimo Luis de Cabrera founded the city of Córdoba. In colonial times, Córdoba's ecclesiastical importance made it a centre for education, arts and architecture, but after independence, the city had to reorient itself to the political and economic whims of Buenos Aires as immigrants flooded the province, thanks to the railway. From 1882 to 1896, the number of agricultural colonies increased from just five to 176, but Córdoba's national role actually declined because of phenomenal growth on the Pampas.

Eventually the local establishment's exaggerated conservatism aroused an aggressive reform movement that had a lasting impact locally and nationally. In the late 1960s, a coalition of students and auto workers nearly unseated a de facto military government in an uprising known as the *cordobazo*. After the chaos of the 1970s and early 1980s, the region's economy has declined as a result of the automobile industry's obsolete equipment and the country's economic stagnation.

CORDOBA

Sited on the south bank of the Río Primero (or Suquía), 400 metres above sea level at the foot of the Sierra Chica, the city of Córdoba has sprawled north of the river and into the countryside, but its compact centre is easily explored on foot.

Plaza San Martín is the nucleus for Córdoba's one million inhabitants, but the commercial centre is north-west of the plaza, where the Avenida 25 de Mayo and Indarte pedestrian malls cross. Calle Obispo Trejos, south of the plaza, has the finest concentration of colonial buildings.

Information

The municipal Dirección de Turismo (☎ 22-5761), downstairs at Calle Rosario de Santa Fe 39, on Plaza San Martín, is open on weekdays from 8 am to 9 pm, and on weekends from 9 am to noon and 5 to 8 pm. There is also a branch of the provincial Subsecretaría de Turismo (☎ 23-4169), at the bus terminal, open on weekdays from 7.30 am to 8.30 pm, and on weekends from 8 am to 8 pm.

For changing cash or travellers' cheques (beware hefty commissions), try Exprinter at Rivadavia 39. There are ATMs in the city centre and at the bus station. Correo Argentino is at Avenida General Paz 201, Telecom at Avenida General Paz 36. Córdoba's telephone code is 051.

Things to See

To see Córdoba's colonial buildings and monuments, start at the **Cabildo**, on Plaza San Martín, and the **Casa del Obispo Mercadillo**, Rosario de Santa Fe 39. At the plaza's south-west corner, crowned by a Romanesque dome, the **Iglesia Catedral** (begun in 1577) shows a mixture of styles.

The Jesuit **Iglesia de La Compañía** (1645), at Obispo Trejos and Caseros, has a modest exterior, but its unique interior features a timber roof shaped like an inverted ship's hull. The **Universidad Nacional de Córdoba** (1613) is at Obispo Trejos 242, but see also the nearby **Colegio Nacional de Monserrat** (1782). At Rosario de Santa Fe 218, the **Museo Histórico Provincial Marqués de Sobremonte** is open Tuesday to Friday from 8.30 am to 1.30 pm.

Places to Stay

Parque General San Martín, 13 km from the city centre, has a spacious but basic *camping ground* (US$4 per site). Bus No 31 from Plaza San Martín goes to the Complejo Ferial, an exhibition and entertainment complex about one km from the park.

Quiet, friendly and very basic but not really bad, *Residencial Thanoa*, San Jerónimo 479, costs just US$10 per person with shared bath. The spotlessly clean *Hospedaje Suzy*, Entre Ríos 528, has singles only for just US$8 with shared bath. *Hospedaje Vásquez* (☎ 23-8268), Santiago del Estero 188, has 15 plain rooms with private bath and ceiling fans for US$10 per person.

Not quite equal to its Buenos Aires namesake, *Hotel Claridge* (☎ 21-5741), 25 de Mayo 218, has rooms with balcony and balky air-con on a quiet pedestrian street for US$18/34. The attractive, well-maintained *Hotel Garden* (☎ 21-4729), 25 de Mayo 35, is good value for about US$26/46. The reader-recommended *Hotel Felipe II* (☎ 21-4752), San Jerónimo 279, has quiet singles/doubles for US$30/50.

Places to Eat

The municipal *Mercado Norte* at Calle Rivadavia and Oncativo has excellent inexpensive eats – pizza, empanadas and lager beer. Many other inexpensive places line Blvd Perón, near the train and bus terminals, and side streets like San Jerónimo. *Pizzería Italiana*, San Jerónimo 610, is a decent choice despite its unimpressive appearance. *Pizzería San Merino*, on the corner of Chacabuco and Entre Ríos, is also worth a try.

For lunch, *La Cabaña de Rubén*, Obispo

Trejos 169, has a good selection of reasonable, fixed-price meals and other more elegant dishes. *Estancia La María*, 9 de Julio 364, is a parrilla. Recommended cafés include *Café Jameo* at Chacabuco 294 and *Café Pause* at Chacabuco 216.

Getting There & Away

Air Aerolíneas Argentinas (☎ 21-5003), Avenida Colón 520, has at least two flights daily to Buenos Aires (US$49 with 24-hour advance purchase), while Austral (☎ 34883), Buenos Aires 59, has nearly as many to Buenos Aires as well as 17 weekly to Mendoza, and others to the north-west.

Aerolíneas' Monday 12.15 pm flight from Aeroparque (US$134) continues to Salta and to Santa Cruz, Bolivia, while its midday flight on Monday, Thursday and Friday goes to São Paulo and Rio de Janeiro. There's also a Sunday morning flight to Tucumán and Rio.

LAPA (☎ 22-0188), Caseros 355, flies twice or three times daily to Buenos Aires (US$59), and three times weekly to Tucumán and Salta. TAN (☎ 22-4634), 25 de Mayo 49, flies three times weekly to Neuquén (US$129).

Bus More than just a bus station, the Nueva Estación Terminal de Omnibus de Córdoba (NETOC, ☎ 34169) at Blvd Perón 380 includes two banks and an ATM, a pharmacy, a travel agency, telephones, a post office, a day-care centre, first aid, a photo lab, and 40 shops and restaurants. By the way, 42 bus companies serve local, provincial, national and international destinations.

Many companies go to Buenos Aires (US$30, 10 hours). Socasa goes to San Juan twice weekly. Expreso Uspallata and TAC go to Mendoza (US$35, eight hours), with connections to Santiago, Chile. Tas Choapa also has Chilean connections via Mendoza.

TUS/TUP serve Bahía Blanca, Santa Rosa (La Pampa) and Bariloche five times weekly (US$105, but ask about student/retired discounts; 22 hours). Empresa Córdoba Mar del Plata and others go to Atlantic coastal resorts.

Veloz del Norte goes to Salta (US$54, 12 hours), while Panamericano goes to Tucumán, continuing to Bolivian border crossings at La Quiaca and Pocitos. El Tucumano has similar regional services; Balut serves Salta and Jujuy. Expreso Singer offers through buses to Posadas (US$41, 19½ hours) and Puerto Iguazú. Cora (☎ 25-4765) serves Montevideo (US$47) four times weekly, with connections to Brazil.

Getting Around

To/From the Airport From the bus terminal, take the Empresa Ciudad de Córdoba (☎ 24-0048) bus marked 'Salsipuedes' to Aeropuerto Pajas Blancas, 15 km north of town. Airport Kombis (☎ 92-2361) leave from Hotel Sussex, San Jerónimo 125.

AROUND CORDOBA

Cosquín

Cosquín's Festival Nacional del Folklore (national folklore festival), held every January for more than 30 years, has declined by most accounts, but the surrounding countryside still makes the town one of the more appealing destinations near the provincial capital, which is 63 km away by RN 38.

Cerro Pan de Azúcar, east of town, offers good views of the Sierras and the city of Córdoba. Hitch or walk (buses are few) five km to a saddle, where an *aerosilla* (chair lift) climbs to the top, but a steep 25-minute walk to the 1260-metre summit saves US$5. Also at the saddle is a confitería whose owner, a devotee of Carlos Gardel, has decorated his business with Gardel memorabilia and built a mammoth statue of the great man.

Owner-operated *Rincón Serrano* (☎ (0541) 51311), A Sabattini 739, is very friendly and quiet. Summer prices are about US$27/37 for a single/double, but out of season may be barely half that. Santa María de la Punilla, just south of Cosquín, has a good camping ground. La Capillense and La Capilla run buses from Córdoba.

La Falda

This pleasant woodsy resort 78 km from Córdoba, at the western base of the Sierra

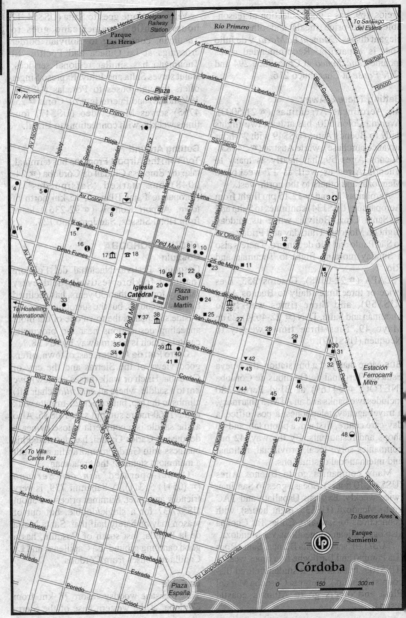

Córdoba

To Belgrano Railway Station
Río Primero
To Santiago del Estero
Parque Las Heras
Av Las Heras
12 de Octubre
Rincón
Iberbau
Rincón
Av Alcorta
Iberbau
To Airport
Igualdad
Libertad
Blvd Guzmán
Humberto Primo
Plaza General Paz
Tablada
Rioja
1
Sarmiento
2
Oncativo
Jujuy
Sucre
Tucumán
Av General Paz
San Martín
Catamarca
Lima
Santa Rosa
Rivera Indarte
Av Colón
7
Av Olmos
3
4
5
6
9 de Julio
15
16
Dean Funes
17
18
Ped Mall
8 9 10
12
Salta
Santiago del Estero
Blvd Orlando
13
27 de Abril
19
21
22
25 de Mayo
23
11
Iglesia Catedral
20
Plaza San Martín
24
Rosario de Santa Fe
Av Marcelo T de Alvear
33
Caseros
37
38
San Jerónimo
26
27
To Hostelling International
Duarte Quirós
Belgrano
36
35
34
39
40
41
Entre Ríos
28
29
30
31
32
Blvd Perón
Estación Ferrocarril Mitre
Blvd San Juan
Corrientes
42
43
44
Avellaneda
Suárez
Obispo Trejo
Av Vélez Sarsfield
49
Montevideo
Blvd Junín
45
46
Buenos Aires
47
San Luis
Ituzaingó
Independencia
Rondeau
Av Chacabuco
Salguero
Paraná
Balcarce
Derqui
48
To Villa Carlos Paz
Laprida
50
San Lorenzo
Av H Yrigoyen
Obispo Oro
Av Rodríguez
Rivera
Derqui
To Buenos Aires
Peredo
La Brañaga
Parque Sarmiento
Peredo
Estrada
Av Leopoldo Lugones
Plaza España
Córdoba
Crisol
0   150   300 m
To Santiago del Estero
Sabattini

PLACES TO STAY		4	Córdoba Open Plaza	34	Colegio Nacional de
8	Hotel Garden	5	Aerolíneas		Monserrat
11	Hotel Claridge		Argentinas	35	Seminario
13	Hospedaje Vásquez	6	Córdoba Rent a Car		Convictorio de San
25	Hotel Sussex		(Hotel Astoria)		Javier, Universidad
27	Hotel Felipe II	7	Post Office		Nacional de
28	Hospedaje Dory's	9	TAN		Córdoba
29	Residencial Thanoa	10	Mundo Aborigen	36	Iglesia de la
30	Residencial Mallorca	12	Viajes Aeroturis		Compañía
31	Residencial Central	14	Simonelli Viajes	38	Iglesia de Santa
41	Residencial San		(Amex)		Teresa y Convento
	Francisco	16	Subsecretaría de		de Carmelitas
46	Hospedaje Suzy		Turismo		Descalzas de San
47	Residencial El Cielo	17	Museo Doctor		José, Museo de
			Genaro Pérez		Arte Religioso
PLACES TO EAT		18	Telecom		Juan de Tejeda
2	Mercado Norte	19	Cambio Barujel	39	Museo de la
15	Estancia la María	20	Cabildo		Ciudad
32	Pizzería Italiana	21	Dirección de Turismo,	40	Al Rent A Car (Hotel
37	La Cabaña de Rubén		Casa del		Dorá)
42	Pizzería San Merino		Obispo Mercadillo	45	Avis
43	Café Pause	22	Cambio Exprinter	48	Nueva Estación
44	Café Jameo	23	Viajes Oceania		Terminal de
		24	Austral		Omnibus de
OTHER		26	Museo Histórico		Córdoba (NETOC)
1	ACA		Provincial Marqués	49	Swept
3	Hospital de Urgencias		de Sobremonte	50	Club Andino de
		33	LAPA		Córdoba

Chica, features a **Museo de Trenes en Miniatura** (Miniature Train Museum) and the **Museo Arqueológico Ambato**. The scenic zigzag road over the Sierra Chica to Salsipuedes, Río Ceballos and back to Córdoba climbs to 1500 metres, but there are no buses.

Nearby Villa Hermosa's *Camping Municipal* charges US$3 per person. Quiet, clean and friendly *Hotel El Piccolo* (☎ 23343), Uruguay 51 near Avenida Edén, charges US$14 per person with private bath; it does a great deal of repeat business. *Old Garden Residencial* (☎ 22842), Capital Federal 28, has a pool and beautiful gardens but is notably more expensive at US$44 double. Among several decent restaurants on Avenida Edén is *Confitería Kattak*, Edén 444.

La Capillense and El Cóndor have buses from Córdoba.

Candonga

Candonga's 18th-century chapel was once part of the Jesuit Estancia Santa Gertrudis,

whose overgrown ruins are still visible in this placid canyon. Lacking direct public transport, try hitching from El Manzano, 40 km north of Córdoba (reached by Empresa Ciudad de Córdoba or Sierras de Córdoba).

A day trip is worthwhile, but there is good accommodation at *Hostería Candonga* (☎ 71-0683 in Córdoba for reservations), where US$35 per person buys room plus all meals, including regional specialities like asado con cuero, locro, empanadas and home-made desserts.

Jesús María

After losing their operating funds to pirates off the coast of Brazil, the Jesuits produced and sold wine from Jesús María to support their university in colonial Córdoba. These days the town of Jesús María, 51 km north of Córdoba via RN 9, hosts the annual **Fiesta Nacional de Doma y Folklore**, a celebration of gaucho horsemanship and customs.

Set among very attractive grounds, the church and convent now constitute the **Museo Jesuítico Nacional de Jesús**

María, open on weekdays from 8 am to noon and 2 to 7 pm (3 to 7 pm in summer), and on weekends from 2 to 6 pm (3 to 7 pm in summer) only. Five km away is the colonial posthouse of **Sinsacate**, site of a wake for the murdered La Rioja caudillo Facundo Quiroga in 1835. It's open from mid-November to mid-March daily from 3 to 7 pm, and the rest of the year daily from 2 to 6 pm, but the caretaker is notoriously unpunctual. Admission costs US$1 to each site.

Ciudad de Córdoba and Cadol run buses to and from the town of Jesús María.

Alta Gracia

Only 35 km south-west of Córdoba, Alta Gracia's estancia supplied food and other provisions for Jesuits in the city until 1767. The house of Santiago Liniers, one of the last Spanish viceroys and a hero in the British invasion of 1806, is now a museum; Liniers was executed for resisting Argentine independence, and is buried in his native France. The late Spanish composer Manuel de Falla's house is also a museum.

Satag has regular bus services to and from Córdoba.

Cuyo

Cuyo consists of the Andean provinces of Mendoza and San Juan, and adjacent San Luis. Once part of Chile, Cuyo retains a strong regional identity. Despite the rain-shadow effect of Aconcagua (6962 metres) and other formidable peaks, enough snow accumulates to sustain rivers that irrigate extensive vineyards.

With its varied terrain and climate, Cuyo offers outdoor activities all year round. Summer activities include climbing, trekking, riding, hang-gliding, canoeing, fishing, water-skiing, windsurfing and sailing. Skiing is increasingly popular in winter. Many travellers visit Mendoza, but the other provinces, especially San Juan, provide off-the-beaten-track experiences.

History

Spaniards from Chile crossed 3850-metre Uspallata pass to establish encomiendas among the indigenous Huarpe, but Mendoza's winter isolation stimulated economic independence and political initiative. Still, for many decades, links to the viceregal capital in Lima were via Santiago and the Pacific, rather than overland via Tucumán and Bolivia.

Colonial vineyards were important, but independence eliminated traditional outlets for their produce. Arrival of the railway, in 1884, and improved irrigation brought expansion of grape and olive cultivation, plus alfalfa for livestock. Modern Cuyo is one of Argentina's most important agricultural regions.

MENDOZA

Founded in 1561, at an altitude of 761 metres, the capital of Mendoza province is a lively city of 500,000, with an important university and, thanks to nearby oilfields, a growing industrial base. Modern quake-proof construction has replaced fallen historic buildings, but Mendoza's *acequias* (irrigation canals) and tree-lined streets create a pleasing environment.

Orientation

Plaza Independencia fills four square blocks in the town centre. Two blocks from each of its corners are smaller satellite plazas; Plaza España deserves special attention for its Saturday artisans' market.

Pavement cafés on Avenida San Martín, which crosses the city from north to south, are good places to meet locals. The poplar-lined Alameda, beginning at the 1700 block of San Martín, was a traditional site for 19th-century promenades.

Information

The municipal Centro de Información y Asistencia al Turismo (☎ 24-5333) on the Garibaldi peatonal near Avenida San Martín, is open from 9 am to 9 pm, has good maps and detailed informational hand-outs, and there's usually an English-speaker on hand.

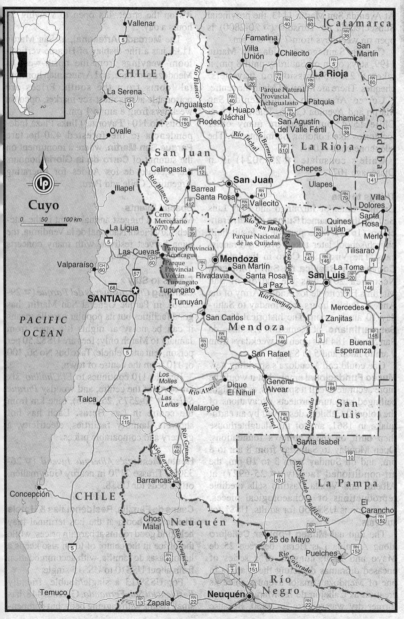

Cuyo

0   50   100 km

PACIFIC OCEAN

At Avenida San Martín 1143, the provincial Subsecretaría de Turismo (☎ 20-2800) is open on weekdays from 7 am to 9 pm.

Cambio Santiago, Avenida San Martín 1199, stays open on Saturday until 8 pm; it takes a 2% commission on travellers' cheques. There are many ATMs in the centre.

Correo Argentino is at Avenida San Martín and Avenida Colón. Telefónica is at Chile 1574, but there are many other locutorios like Fonobar, Sarmiento 23. The telephone code is 061.

Chile's consulate (☎ 25-5024) is at Olascoaga 1071.

Things to See

On the corner of Ituzaingó and Fray Luis Beltrán, the misnamed **Ruinas de San Francisco** (1638) were part of a Jesuit-built church/school later taken over by Franciscans. The Virgen de Cuyo in the **Iglesia, Convento y Basílica de San Francisco**, Necochea 201, was the patron of San Martín's Ejército de los Andes (Army of the Andes). Public hours are Monday to Saturday 10 am to noon. The historical **Museo Sanmartiniano**, at Remedios Escalada de San Martín 1843, is open on weekdays from 9 am to noon and 5 to 8 pm.

One could call Mendoza's sparkling new **Museo Fundacional** empty, but it would be more accurate to call it spacious, as the high-ceilinged structure protects excavations of the colonial Cabildo, destroyed by an earthquake in 1861, and of the slaughterhouse then built on the Cabildo's foundations. Open Monday to Saturday from 8 am to 8 pm, and on Sunday from 3 to 10 pm, the air-conditioned facility (☎ 25-6927) at Alberdi and Videla Castillo sells credible reproductions of archaeological pieces. Admission is US$1.50 for adults, US$1 for students.

The unusual **Museo Popular Callejero** along Avenida Las Heras, between 25 de Mayo and Perú, consists of a series of encased dioramas depicting the changes in one of Mendoza's major avenues since its creation as Callejón de las Maruleilas, in a former dry watercourse, in 1830. Because it's on the street, it's open to viewing 24 hours a day.

The **Mercado Artesanal**, at San Martín 1133, has a fine display of Huarpe vertical-loom weavings from the north-west of Mendoza province, and Araucanian horizontal looms from the south. Prices are reasonable at this must-see market, open on weekdays from 8 am to 1 pm.

Bus No 110 ('Favorita') links Plaza Independencia to the forested 420-hectare **Parque San Martín**, where a monument on the summit of **Cerro de la Gloria** honours the Ejército de los Andes for liberating Argentina, Chile and Peru.

Special Events

Mendoza's biggest annual event is the late-February Fiesta Nacional de la Vendimia, the wine harvest festival, with many concerts and folkloric events.

Places to Stay

Camping *Churrasqueras del Parque* (☎ 29-6656), in Parque General San Martín, has good facilities but its popular parrilla means it can be noisy at night. It's open from January to March only; fees are US$2.50 per person, tent and vehicle. Take bus No 50, 100 or 110 from the centre of town.

Bus No 110 continues to *El Challao*, six km north of the centre, and woodsy *Parque Suizo* (☎ 30-2575, 25-2995), nine km from the centre in Las Heras. Each has hot showers, laundry facilities, electricity, a grocery and comparable prices.

Hostel Mendoza's *Albergue Juvenil* (☎ 26-3300), Tirasso 2170 in nearby Guaymallén, offers beds for US$8.

Casas de Familia, Residenciales & Hotels
The tourist booth at the bus terminal may help find good rooms at bargain prices, while the office in the centre of town also keeps a list of casas de familia, with accommodation from about US$10 to US$15 single.

For US$9/13 a single/double, friendly *Residencial San Fernando*, Güemes 448, has small rooms with sagging beds, but compensates partly with a pleasant patio. There are several other marginal cheapies here, barely a block from the bus terminal, but look for the pavement greenery at appropriately named *Residencial El Jardín*, at Güemes and Yapeyú, which is excellent value for US$25 a double.

Central *Hotel Montecarlo* (☎ 25-9285), General Paz 360, is very reasonably priced at US$10 per person. Recommended *Hotel Galicia* (☎ 20-2619), San Juan 881, is central, clean and friendly for US$15/20 a single/double with shared bath, US$30 private bath. Equally central *Hotel Vigo* (☎ 25-0208), Necochea 749, is perhaps one of the best inexpensive hotels in town, a bit run-down but with a nice garden; rates are US$15/26 for singles/doubles.

Modest, friendly *Hotel Lucense* (☎ 24-5937), Chile 759, has rooms with shared bath for about US$15/24. Due to its good value and excellent location, *Hotel Rincón Vasco* (☎ 23-3033), Las Heras 590, is becoming a travellers' favourite; rates are US$30/40, but try negotiating cheaper rates.

Places to Eat

Mendoza's best value is the *Mercado Central*, at Avenida Las Heras and Patricias Mendocinas, where a variety of stalls offer inexpensive pizza, empanadas, and the like.

Boccadoro, Mitre 1976, and *Trattoría Aveni*, 25 de Mayo 1163, are parrillas, the latter with some interesting fish dishes. Several places specialise in pasta, including recommended *Montecatini* at General Paz 370 and *Trevi* at Las Heras 70. For pizza, try *Rincón de La Boca*, with good fugazzeta and chopp, plus friendly service and pavement seating at Las Heras 485.

Middle Eastern cuisine is the rule at the *Sociedad Libanesa*, Necochea 538. The popular *Asia*, San Martín 821, is one of Mendoza's few tenedor libre Chinese restaurants, while a good vegetarian choice is *El Vergel*, Catamarca 76.

Longtime Mendoza residents recommend *La Selecta*, near the corner of Primitivo de la Reta and Garibaldi; *Trattoría La Veneciana* at Avenida San Martín 739 for pasta; and *El Retortuño*, on Dorrego near Adolfo Calles in Guaymallén, for regional specialties and live music on weekend evenings; take the 'Dorrego' trolleybus.

Getting There & Away

Air Aerolíneas Argentinas (☎ 20-4185), Sarmiento 82, flies daily to Santiago, Chile, and several times daily to Buenos Aires (US$178; US$59 with 24-hour advance purchase). Ladeco (☎ 29-9336), Sarmiento 144, has 14 flights weekly to Santiago.

Austral (☎ 20-2200), Avenida San Martín 921, has three flights every weekday to Buenos Aires, but fewer on weekends; schedules to Córdoba (US$77) are similar.

LAPA (☎ 29-1061), España 1012, flies weekday mornings and every afternoon except Sunday to Buenos Aires (US$79), but early reservations are essential on these very crowded flights. TAN (☎ 34-0240), also at España 1012, has nine flights weekly to Neuquén (US$121).

Bus Mendoza's Terminal de Omnibus (☎ 26-0980, 25-6870) is at Avenida Gobernador Videla and Avenida Acceso Este, in nearby Guaymallén. Hot showers are available for US$2.

TAC goes daily to Buenos Aires (US$54, 14 hours) and also to Mar del Plata, Bariloche (20 hours), Córdoba (US$35, eight hours) and points north, and to Santiago (US$25, seven hours). La Estrella and Libertador go to Tucumán (US$46, 14 hours) and intermediates, while La Veloz del Norte goes to Salta (US$61, 19 hours). Cotal runs buses to Posadas, Puerto Iguazú (US$98, 36 hours) and intermediates three times weekly.

Colta and La Cumbre have a daily service to Córdoba via the Altas Cumbres route. Expreso Uspallata goes frequently to Uspallata, twice daily to Las Cuevas, on weekends and holidays to Puente del Inca, and twice daily to Malargüe and San Rafael. El Rápido and Alto Valle have daily buses to Neuquén.

Andesmar's southbound services go to Comodoro Rivadavia (29 hours) via

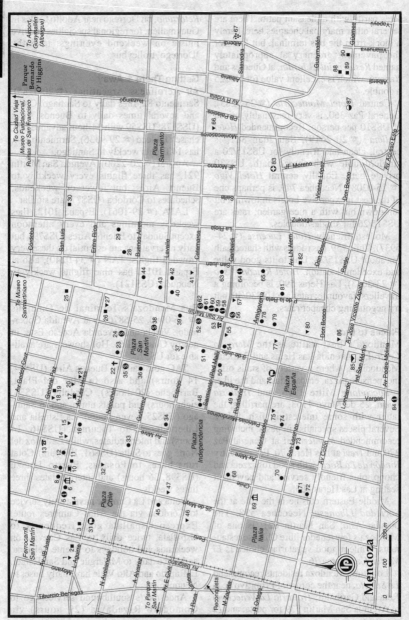

Mendoza

PLACES TO STAY
2   Hotel Laerte
3   Hotel Vigo
4   Hotel Petit
11 Hotel Rincón
    Vasco
19 Hotel Montecarlo
25 Hotel City
26 Imperial Hotel
30 Hotel Escorial
71 Hotel Lucense
82 Hotel Galicia
88 Hotel Terminal
89 Residencial
    Evelyn
90 Residenciales 402,
    San Fernando,
    Betty

PLACES TO EAT
1   Centro Andaluz
10 Café Mediterráneo
14 Rincón de La Boca
15 La Estancia
17 Café La Avenida
18 Montecatini
20 La Marchigiana
21 Mercado
    Central
27 Trevi
32 Sociedad
    Libanesa
37 Dalí
41 El Vergel
46 La Casa de Tristán
    Barraza
47 Trattoria Aveni
55 Il Tucco
57 La Selecta
66 Línea Verde
75 Club Español
77 Vieja Recova
80 Asia

86 Trattoria La
    Veneciana

OTHER
5   Centro de
    Información y
    Asistencia al
    Turismo
6   Canadian Bicicletas
7   Museo Popular
    Callejero
8   Empresa Jocolí
9   Esquí Mendoza
    Competición
12 Turismo Mendoza
13 Telefónica
16 Operadores Mendoza
22 Iglesia, Convento y
    Basílica de San
    Francisco
23 Migraciones
24 Banco de la Nación
28 Cine Mendoza
29 Avis
31 Italian Consulate
33 Localiza Rent A Car
34 Turismo Mamb
35 Banco de Galicia
    (ATM)
36 Hunuc Huar
    Expeditions/Vida y
    Aventuras
38 Banco de Mendoza
39 Y Libros
40 Cine Lavalle
42 Cine Emperador
43 Cine Opera
44 Cine Gran Rex
45 Instituto Dante
    Alighieri
48 Cámara de Diputados
49 LAPA/TAN
50 Ladeco

51 LanChile
52 Cambio Exprinter
53 Fonobar
54 Aerolíneas Argentinas
56 Citibank (ATM)
58 Centro de
    Información y
    Asistencia al
    Turismo
59 Mercado Artesanal
60 Subsecretaría de
    Turismo
61 Aymará Turismo
62 Cambio Santiago
63 Rubén Simoncini
    Libros
64 Turismo Sepean
65 Al Rent A Car
67 Bodega Toso
68 Instituto Cultural
    Argentino
    Norteamericano
69 Museo del Pasado
    Cuyano
70 Los Penitentes (Ski
    Resort)
72 Laverap
73 La Lavandería
74 Club Andino
    Italiano/Centro
    Italiano
76 German Consulate
78 ACA
79 Austral
81 Dollar Rent A Car
83 Hospital Central
84 Terraza
    Mirador/Dirección
    Municipal de
    Turismo
85 Post Office
87 Terminal de
    Omnibus

Neuquén (US$46, 13 hours) and Puerto Madryn (24 hours), connecting to Río Gallegos (41 hours); it also provides direct service to Bariloche and Esquel (25 hours). In summer Andesmar buses reach the southern coast of Buenos Aires province, and they also travel north to Jujuy (20 hours). El Rápido runs international services to Lima and Montevideo.

Getting Around
To/From the Airport Bus No 60 ('Aeropuerto') from Calle Salta goes straight to Aeropuerto Internacional Plumerillo (☎ 30-

7837, 30-6484), six km from the city centre on RN 40.

Bus Take local trolleybus 'Villa Nueva' from Lavalle, between San Martín and San Juan, to the terminal, just beyond the city limits, at Avenida Gobernador Ricardo Videla and Acceso Este.

AROUND MENDOZA
Wineries
Most wineries near Mendoza offer tours and tasting. The most convenient is **Bodega Toso** (☎ 38-0244), Alberdi 808 in

Guaymallén; friendly and informative, it's open on weekdays from 7.30 am to 6 pm, and on Saturday from 8.30 to 11.30 am. From the corner of San Martín and Lavalle in central Mendoza, walk seven blocks east to Alberdi, then turn right and go one block south to the vineyard.

Bus Nos 170, 172, and 173 go to Coquimbito, Maipú, where **Bodega La Rural** (☎ 97-2013), on Montecaseros, opens on weekdays from 9 to 11 am and 3 to 6.30 pm, and on Saturday from 9 am to 11 am only. The Museo Francisco Rutini there displays wine-making tools used by 19th-century pioneers, as well as colonial religious sculptures from the Cuyo region.

Los Penitentes

Both scenery and snow cover are excellent at Los Penitentes, 165 km from Mendoza, which offers downhill and nordic skiing at an altitude of 2580 metres. Lifts and accommodation are very modern; the maximum vertical drop on its 21 runs exceeds 700 metres. For detailed information, contact the Los Penitentes office (☎ 29-4868, 29-5500), at San Lorenzo 433, Mendoza.

USPALLATA

In an exceptionally beautiful valley surrounded by polychrome mountains, 105 km west of Mendoza at an altitude of 1751 metres, this crossroads village along RN 7 is a good base for exploring the surrounding area.

One km north of the highway junction towards Villavicencio, a signed side road leads to ruins and a museum at the **Bóvedas Históricas Uspallata**, a metallurgical site since pre-Columbian times. About four km north of Uspallata, in a volcanic outcrop near a small monument to San Ceferino Namuncurá, is a faded but still visible set of **petroglyphs**.

Places to Stay & Eat

Uspallata's poplar-shaded *Camping Municipal* (☎ 20009), 500 metres north of the Villavicencio junction, charges only US$3 per site. The north end of the facilities, near

the wood-stoked hot showers, is much quieter and the best place to pitch a tent.

Union-built *Hotel Uspallata* (☎ 20003) is a bit shopsoiled since its Peronist glory days but still offers expansive grounds, tennis courts, a huge swimming pool, a bar, a bowling alley, pool tables and a restaurant. At just US$20/37 for a single/double, it's one of the best value places in the country.

Behind the YPF station, *Dónde Pato* and *Parrilla San Cayetano* are both convenient stops, with decent food, for travellers en route to and from Chile.

Getting There & Away

Expreso Uspallata provides bus services between Mendoza and Uspallata, as far as Puente del Inca.

PARQUE PROVINCIAL ACONCAGUA

North of RN 7, nearly hugging the Chilean border, Parque Provincial Aconcagua protects 71,000 hectares of the wild high country surrounding South America's highest summit, 6962-metre Cerro Aconcagua. Passing motorists can stop to enjoy the view of the peak from **Laguna Horcones**, a two-km walk from the parking lot just north of the highway, where a ranger is available on weekdays from 8 am to 9 pm, and on Saturday from 8 am to 8 pm.

Cerro Aconcagua

Reaching Aconcagua's summit requires a commitment of at least 13 to 15 days, including time for acclimatisation. Potential climbers should acquire RJ Secor's new climbing guide *Aconcagua*. Non-climbers can trek to base camps and refugios beneath the permanent snow line.

Permits are obligatory both for trekking and climbing; rangers will not permit visitors to proceed without one. These permits, which cost US$40 for trekkers and US$80 for climbers, are valid for three weeks and available in Mendoza only, at the provincial Subsecretaría de Turismo (☎ 20-2800), Avenida San Martín 1143.

Many adventure travel agencies in and around Mendoza arrange excursions into the high mountains. The most established local operators are Fernando Grajales (☎ & fax 29-3830), José Francisco Mendoza 898, 5500 Mendoza, and Rudy Parra's Aconcagua Trek (☎ & fax 24-2003), Güiraldes 246, 5519 Dorrego, Mendoza. A reliable North American operator is OTT Expeditions (☎ (510) 865-9956), PO Box 5431, Berkeley, CA 94705.

Puente del Inca

This natural stone bridge over the Río Mendoza, 2720 metres above sea level and 177 km from Mendoza, is one of Argentina's most striking natural wonders. *Hostería Puente del Inca* (☎ (061) 29-4124 in Mendoza) charges US$40/50 for a single/double with breakfast, but multi-bed rooms cost US$25 per person with breakfast. Climbers and trekkers can pitch tents by the church.

Cristo Redentor

Pounded by chilly winds, nearly 4000 metres above sea level on the rugged Argentina-Chile border, the high Andes make a fitting backdrop for this famous monument, erected after settlement of a territorial dispute in 1902. The view is a must-see either by tour or private car, but the first autumn snowfall closes the hairpin road. At Las Cuevas, 10 km before the border, travellers can stay at *Hostería Las Cuevas*.

MALARGÜE

From precolonial times, Pehuenche Indians hunted and gathered in the valley of Malargüe, 189 km south-west of San Rafael via paved RN 40, but the advance of European agricultural colonists dispossessed the aboriginal inhabitants. Today petroleum is the principal industry, followed by uranium processing, but Malargüe is also a year-round outdoor activity centre: nearby Las Leñas offers excellent skiing.

The Dirección de Turismo (☎ 71060) is in the Municipalidad at Fray Inalicán and N Uriburu. Malargüe's telephone code is 0627.

Places to Stay & Eat

Malargüe has abundant, reasonably priced accommodation, but prices can rise during the ski season. Both *Camping Municipal Malargüe* (☎ 71059) and *Camping Polideportivo* are on Alfonso Capdeville, at the north end of town.

The cheapest regular accommodations are *Hospedaje Sheril* (☎ 71337), which charges US$10 per person, and *Hospedaje Eben-Ezer* (☎ 71224), where singles/doubles with shared bath cost only US$11/20. In the US$15/25 range are *Hotel Theis* (☎ 71429), at Avenida San Martín 938 and *Hotel Rioma* (☎ 71065), at Fray Inalicán 68. *Hotel Bambi* (☎ 71237), Avenida San Martín 410, charges US$20/35 with private bath.

Getting There & Away

TAC and Expreso Uspallata run at least five buses daily to San Rafael and Mendoza. Transportes Diego Berbel, at Emilio Civit and Comandante Salas, runs buses to Las Leñas and other recreation areas.

AROUND MALARGÜE
Las Leñas

Designed primarily to attract wealthy foreigners, Las Leñas is Argentina's most self-consciously prestigious ski resort, but despite the glitter it's not totally out of the question for budget travellers. Since opening in 1983, it has attracted an international clientele which spends the days on the slopes and the nights partying until the sun comes up.

Open from mid-June to early October, with international competitions every year, Las Leñas is 445 km south of Mendoza and 200 km south-west of San Rafael via RN 40 and RP 222; it is only 70 km from Malargüe via RN 40 and RP 222. Its 33 runs cover 3300 hectares, with a base altitude of 2200 metres, but the slopes reach 3430 metres for a maximum drop of 1230 metres. Arrange winter holidays through Badino Turismo (☎ 326-1351, fax 393-2568), Perón 725, 6th floor, in Buenos Aires.

Lift Tickets Prices vary from early to mid and late season, but the following 1995 figures (in US dollars) should provide some idea what to expect in different periods. The 'value' period runs from 17 June to 1 July and 17 to 30 September; 'special', from 2 to 8 July and 27 August to 16 September; 'peak', from 9 to 22 July and 6 to 26 August; and 'holiday', from 23 July to 5 August.

Ticket Type	Holiday	Peak	Special	Value
3-day Adult	115	95	85	75
4-day Adult	155	125	115	100
7-day Adult	250	200	170	150
14-day Adult	450	340	305	270

SAN JUAN

Though a provincial capital, San Juan de la Frontera, 170 km north of Mendoza, has kept the rhythm and cordiality of a small town. Juan Perón's relief efforts after San Juan's massive 1944 earthquake first made him a public figure; since then, modern construction, wide tree-lined streets and exceptional tidiness characterise the city centre.

Orientation & Information

San Juan's grid makes orientation easy, but the addition of cardinal points to street addresses helps even more. East-west Avenida San Martín and north-south Calle Mendoza divide the city into quadrants; the functional centre is south of San Martín.

Open daily from 8 am to noon and 4 to 8 pm, the Subsecretaría de Turismo (☎ 22-7219), Sarmiento 24 Sur, has a good map of the city and its surroundings, plus useful brochures on the rest of the province. Cambio Cash, Tucumán 210 Sur, and travel agencies change money, and Banco de San Juan has an ATM at Rivadavia 44 Este. Correo Argentino is at Avenida José Ignacio de la Roza 259 Este, Telefónica is at Laprida 180 Oeste. The telephone code is 064.

Things to See

At Avenida San Martín and Entre Ríos, the only surviving part of the earthquake-ravaged 17th-century **Convento de Santo Domingo** is the cell occupied by San Martín

in 1815, with a small museum entered at Laprida 96 Oeste. The Italian-designed **Iglesia Catedral**, at Mendoza and Rivadavia, on the plaza, was inaugurated in 1979.

At San Martín and Catamarca, the **Museo de Ciencias Naturales** has a fine collection of provincial plants, animals and minerals, plus fossils from Ischigualasto and Ullum. In the Parque de Mayo, at Avenida 25 de Mayo and Urquiza, the **Mercado Artesanal Tradicional** has brightly coloured *mantas* (shawls) from Jáchal, pottery, horse gear, basketry, traditional silver knife handles and *mate* gourds.

Educator and provincial governor Domingo Faustino Sarmiento, also President of Argentina (1868-74), was born in the colonial **Casa de Sarmiento**, Sarmiento 21 Sur. Exiled in Chile during the time of Rosas, he wrote the polemic *Life in the Argentine Republic in the Days of the Tyrants*, arguing that Unitarism embodied European 'civilisation', while Federalism represented unprincipled 'barbarism'. The nostalgic *Recuerdos de Provincia* recounted his childhood in this house, which is open daily except Monday.

Places to Stay

Empresa de la Marina buses go to *Camping El Pinar*, the municipal site on Avenida Benavídez Oeste, six km from the centre of town. Charges are US$3 per person, US$2 per tent.

At España 248 Sur, *Residencial San Francisco* (☎ 22-3760) has modest but clean singles/doubles for US$15/20. Similar in standard are *Residencial El Mendocino* (☎ 22-5930), at España 234 Norte for US$25 a double, and *Residencial Sussex* at España 402 Sur.

Small rooms at friendly *Residencial Hispano Argentino*, Estados Unidos 381 Sur, cost US$12 per person with shared bath. *Residencial Embajador* (☎ 22-5520), Avenida Rawson 25 Sur, has nice, clean rooms at US$18/30 for a single/double. Tidy *Hotel Central* (☎ 22-3174), Mitre 131 Este, is central but quiet, with firm beds, for US$18 per person with private bath.

Places to Eat

Club Sirio Libanés, Entre Ríos 33 Sur, serves moderately priced Middle Eastern food. *La Nona María*, west of the centre at Avenida San Martín and Perito Moreno, has excellent pasta. *El Rincón Cuyano*, Sarmiento 394 Norte, has a standard Argentine menu, but the food is good, the service friendly and prices reasonable. The vegetarian *Soychu*, Ignacio de la Roza 223 Oeste, serves an outstanding tenedor libre lunch. *El Supermercado*, on General Acha between Santa Fe and Córdoba, is a traditional market with good paella.

Bigotes, Las Heras between 9 de Julio and General Paz, has tenedor libre beef, chicken and salads for a reasonable price. Pizzería *Un Rincón de Napoli*, Rivadavia 175 Sur, has a wide selection of toppings and good beer. For sandwiches, try *Lomos al Tiro*, at Mendoza and Avenida San Martín.

Getting There & Away

Air Aeropuerto Las Chacritas (☎ 25-0486) is on RN 20, 13 km south-east of town. Aerolíneas Argentinas (☎ 22-0205), Mendoza 468 Sur, flies nightly to Buenos Aires (US$178). Austral (☎ 21-4038), Aberastain 2 Norte, flies daily (except Sunday) to Córdoba (US$71).

Bus The Terminal de Omnibus (☎ 22-1604) is at Estados Unidos 492 Sur. Empresa Del Sur y Media Agua has frequent buses to Mendoza (US$11, two hours) and daily service to Rosario and Neuquén (US$54). Autotransportes San Juan runs frequent buses to Buenos Aires (US$40, 16 hours) and goes daily to Mar del Plata (US$56) at noon.

Socasa has two buses daily to Córdoba (US$25). La Estrella and Libertador run direct buses to Mendoza, La Rioja (six hours), Catamarca (eight hours) and Tucumán (13 hours). Ticsa buses travel daily to Bahía Blanca, three times weekly to Neuquén, on Wednesday to San Martín de

los Andes, and on Friday and Sunday to Bariloche. On Tuesday and Friday it goes to Santiago de Chile (US$30, nine hours).

TAC has frequent buses to Mendoza and daily service to Chile (Santiago, Valparaíso and Viña del Mar). It also serves northern San Juan, (Jáchal and Pismanta), Bariloche (US$72), and San Luis and Paraná.

Empresa Iglesia serves provincial destinations only. Empresa Vallecito has a daily bus to Caucete, the Difunta Correa shrine (US$3), and San Agustín del Valle Fértil.

AROUND SAN JUAN
Museo Arqueológico La Laja

Emphasising regional prehistory, this Moorish-style building 25 km north of San Juan displays mummies, artefacts, petroglyphs and plant remains in seven separate showrooms. Outside are reproductions of natural environments, farming systems, petroglyphs and built-to-scale house types.

This former hotel's thermal baths are still in use. From Avenida Córdoba in San Juan, take bus No 20 ('Albardón') at 8 am or 1 or 4 pm. At other times, take any No 20 'Albardón' bus to Las Piedritas and hitch or walk the last five km.

Vallecito

According to legend, Deolinda Correa trailed her conscript husband on foot through the desert during the civil wars of the 1840s before dying of thirst, hunger and exhaustion, but passing muleteers found her infant son alive at her breast. Vallecito, 60 km south-east of San Juan, is widely believed to be the site of her death.

Since the 1940s, the once simple **Difunta Correa shrine** has become a small town, with its own petrol station, school, post office, police station and church, plus 17 chapels or exhibit rooms where devotees leave elaborate ex-votos in exchange for supernatural favours. Her cult may be the strongest popular belief system in a country with a variety of unusual religious practices tenuously related to Roman Catholicism, the official state religion.

Truckers are especially devoted believers

from La Quiaca to Ushuaia, roadside shrines display her image, surrounded by candles, small banknotes, and bottles of water left to quench her thirst. Despite official Church antagonism, the shrine has grown rapidly; at Easter, 1 May and Christmas, up to 200,000 pilgrims visit the site.

Vallecito has one inexpensive hostería and a decent restaurant, but accommodation is better in San Juan. Like the pilgrims, you can camp almost anywhere. Empresa Vallecito buses arrive regularly from San Juan, but any other eastbound bus will drop you at the site.

PARQUE PROVINCIAL ISCHIGUALASTO

At every meander in the canyon of Parque Provincial Ischigualasto, a desert valley between sedimentary mountain ranges, the intermittent waters of the Río Ischigualasto have exposed a wealth of Triassic fossils, up to 180 million years old, and carved distinctive shapes in the monochrome clays, red sandstones and volcanic ash. The desert flora of algarrobo trees, shrubs and cacti complement the eerie landforms.

Camping is permitted at the visitor centre, which also has a confitería with simple meals, cold drinks, and limited supplies. There are toilets and showers, but water shortages are common.

Getting There & Away

Ischigualasto is about 80 km north of San Agustín del Valle Fértil via RP 510 and a paved side road to the north-west. Given its size and isolation, the only practical way to visit the park is by vehicle. After you arrive at the visitor centre and pay the US$3 entrance fee, a ranger accompanies your vehicle on a two-hour, 45-km circuit, but some roads may be impassable after rain, necessitating a shorter trip.

If you have no vehicle, ask the tourist office in San Agustín about hiring a car and driver there or contact the park in advance so that the off-duty ranger can pick you up at Los Baldecitos police checkpoint on RP 510, reached by the Empresa Vallecito bus to La Rioja. Write to Dante Herrera at Parque Provincial Ischigualasto, (5449) San Agustín del Valle Fértil, Provincia de San Juan.

SAN LUIS

Capital of its province, San Luis (population 110,000) is 260 km east of Mendoza. Its commercial centre is along the parallel streets of San Martín and Rivadavia, between Plaza Pringles on the north and Plaza Independencia to the south.

The Dirección Provincial de Turismo (☎ 23957), open on weekdays from 8 am to 1 pm and 4 to 8 pm, is at the triangular junction of Junín, San Martín and Avenida Illia. Alituris, Junín 868, changes US dollars and Chilean pesos, while Banco de Galicia has an ATM at Belgrano and Rivadavia. Correo Argentino is at Arturo Illia and San Martín, Telefónica at Colón and Lavalle. The telephone code is 0652.

Things to See

The 1930s **Iglesia de Santo Domingo**, on Plaza Independencia, replaced a 17th-century predecessor but kept its Moorish style; note the algarrobo doors on remaining parts of the old church next door. Next to the church, on Avenida 25 de Mayo, the **Mercado Artesanal** sells fine hand-made wool rugs, as well as ceramics, onyx carvings, and weavings. It's open on weekdays from 7 am to 1 pm.

Places to Stay & Eat

Residencial San Antonio (☎ 22717), at Avenida Lafinur and Avenida España, is the cheapest in town at US$12/20 with breakfast, while *Hotel César* (☎ 20483), Falucho 163, costs US$14 per person. *Residencial Buenos Aires* (☎ 24062), Buenos Aires 834, has modest but adequate rooms for US$14/25. *Residencial María Eugenia* (☎ 30361), 25 de Mayo 741, has large, very clean rooms with shared bath for US$15/25.

A good breakfast choice is the bus station's *Confitería La Terminal*, which serves terrific café con leche with croissants. *El Abuelo*, at J Roca and General Paz, has good lunches at moderate prices. *Restaurant*

Argentino, Illia 352, serves large portions of pasta.

Sofia (formerly Taberna Vasca), at Colón and Bolívar, has mostly Spanish cuisine; try the seafood dishes. *El Triángulo*, at Caseros 866 and Illia, has a varied menu and reasonable prices.

Getting There & Away

Air Austral (☎ 23407), Colón 733, flies daily except Sunday to Buenos Aires (US$172). LAPA (☎ 22499), Illia 331, flies on weekday mornings and some evenings to the capital (US$69).

Bus San Luis' Terminal de Omnibus is on España between San Martín and Rivadavia.

Autotransportes San Juan (☎ 24998) travels daily to San Juan, four times daily to Buenos Aires (US$45, 12 hours), and to Mar del Plata (US$50). Chevallier (☎ 24937) has three buses nightly to Buenos Aires. Empresa del Sur y Media Agua goes to Rosario and San Juan, while Ticsa heads south to Bariloche (via the Río Negro valley and Neuquén) four times weekly.

TAC (☎ 23110) has hourly buses to Mendoza, three daily to Córdoba and one to Rosario. Colta (☎ 25248) has buses to Córdoba and its sierras, Mendoza and Santiago de Chile. Jocolí (☎ 20716) goes to Mendoza, Buenos Aires, Mar del Plata and Santa Rosa, and to provincial destinations.

The Andean North-West

The North-West (Noroeste) comprises the provinces of Jujuy, Salta, Tucumán, La Rioja, Catamarca and Santiago del Estero. Its pre-Columbian and colonial past makes the trip to the Argentine heartland a journey through time as well as space.

History

In pre-Columbian times, two-thirds of the population of what is now Argentina inhabited the North-West. The widespread Diaguita, the Lule south and west of modern Salta, the Tonocote of Santiago del Estero, and the Omahuaca of Jujuy were all, in some ways, cultural outliers of the agricultural civilisations of the Central Andean highlands. Even today, the northern provinces resemble the Andean countries and Quechua communities reach as far south as Santiago del Estero.

Diego de Almagro's expedition from Cuzco to Chile passed through Jujuy and Salta, but the earliest city was Santiago del Estero (1553). Indians destroyed several others before the founding of San Miguel de Tucumán (1565), Córdoba (1573), Salta (1582), La Rioja (1591) and San Salvador de Jujuy (1593). Catamarca was founded more than a century later. Unimpressive in their infancy, these settlements still established the basic elements of colonial rule: the *cabildo* (town council), the church, and the rectangular plaza with its clustered public buildings.

As Indians fell to disease and exploitation, encomiendas lost their economic value, but colonial Tucumán provided mules, cotton and textiles for the mines of Potosí. Opening the Atlantic to legal shipping in late colonial times relegated Jujuy and Salta to marginality, but the sugar industry increased Tucumán's economic importance.

SAN SALVADOR DE JUJUY

San Salvador de Jujuy was a key stopover for colonial mule traders en route to Potosí, but sugar cane became a major commodity at Jesuit missions and, later, British plantations. During the wars of independence, General Manuel Belgrano directed the evacuation of the city to avoid royalist capture; every August Jujuy's biggest event, the week-long **Semana de Jujuy**, celebrates the *éxodo jujeño* (Jujuy exodus).

Orientation & Information

At the mouth of the Quebrada de Humahuaca, the colonial centre of the city (population 200,000) is Plaza Belgrano. Between Necochea and Lavalle, the 700 block of Belgrano (the main commercial street) is a peatonal. RN 9 leads north up the

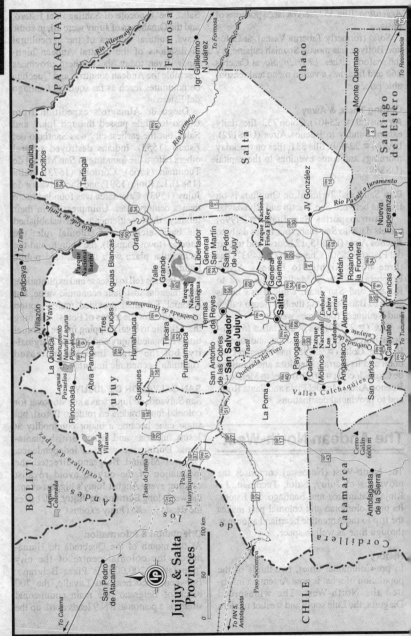

Jujuy & Salta Provinces

0   50   100 km

0   50 miles

Quebrada, while RN 66 leads south-east to RN 34, the main route to Salta.

The Dirección Provincial de Turismo (☎ 28153), Belgrano 690, has abundant maps, brochures and other materials. Hours are 7 am to 1 pm and 3 to 8 pm daily. The office at the bus terminal is open from 8 am to noon and 3 to 8 pm.

Cambio Dinar, Belgrano 731, and Noroeste Cambio, Belgrano 711, change cash and travellers' cheques. Correo Argentino is at Lamadrid and Independencia, Telecom at Senador Pérez 141. Jujuy's telephone code is 0882.

Bolivia's consulate (☎ 22010), Arenales 641, is open on weekdays from 8 am to 1 pm.

Things to See

On Plaza Belgrano, Jujuy's **Iglesia Catedral** (1763) features a Spanish Baroque pulpit, laminated in gold and built by local artisans under a European master. The colonnade along the Belgrano side has an artisans' market.

Also on Plaza Belgrano, the colonial **Cabildo** deserves more attention than the **Museo Policial** within. The **Museo Histórico Provincial**, Lavalle 256, has rooms dedicated to distinct themes in provincial history. The **Iglesia Santa Barbara**, at Lamadrid and San Martín, contains several paintings from the Cuzco school.

Jujuy's **Mercado del Sur**, opposite the bus terminal, is an Indian market where Quechua men and women swig *mazamorra* (a cold maize soup) and surreptitiously peddle coca leaves (unofficially tolerated for indigenous people).

Places to Stay

Bus No 4 goes to the clean, friendly *Camping Municipal*, three km north of Parque San Martín on Avenida Bolivia. Charges are US$5 for vehicle, tent and up to four people, plus occasional hot water.

Residencial Río de Janeiro (☎ 23700), José de la Iglesia 1356, has doubles with shared bath for US$13. Declining *Residencial Los Andes* (☎ 24315), República de Siria 456, will do in a pinch for US$11/16 a

single/double with shared bath, US$13/19 with private bath.

Residencial Norte (☎ 22721), Alvear 444, has US$12 doubles and a decent restaurant. Friendly and central *Hotel Belgrano* (☎ 30393), at Belgrano 627 across from the tourist office, charges US$12/15 single with shared bath, US$15/18 with private bath. Other reasonable alternatives include *Residencial Chung King* (☎ 28142) at Alvear 627 for US$12/14 with shared bath, US$15/20 with private bath.

Places to Eat

Restaurant Club Teléfono, Alvear 1050, also has cheap, basic but nourishing four-course meals. *El Pan Casero*, Belgrano 619, is a natural-foods bakery.

Upstairs at the *Mercado Central*, at Alvear and Balcarce, several restaurants serve regional specialities which are generally spicier than in the rest of Argentina – try chicharrón con mote (stir-fried pork with boiled maize). Another local favourite is the modest-looking *La Sucreña*, on Leandro Alem east of the bus terminal. *La Pizzería*, Alvear 921, is a good choice for pizza.

For standard Argentine fare, try parrillas like *La Rueda*, Lavalle 329, and moderately priced *Krysys*, Balcarce 272. Misleadingly named *Chung King*, Alvear 627, has an extensive Argentine menu and fine service.

Getting There & Away

Air Austral (☎ 27198), San Martín 735, flies on weekday mornings and evenings to Aeroparque (US$230), and on Monday, Wednesday and Saturday to Tucumán (US$55) and Córdoba (US$133).

Dinar Líneas Aéreas (☎ 37100), Senador Pérez 308, Local 3, flies to Tucumán (US$45) and Aeroparque (US$184) once every weekday afternoon except Friday, when it has two flights.

Bus The Terminal de Omnibus (☎ 26229), at Dorrego and Iguazú, has both provincial and long-distance services. Several companies go to Buenos Aires (US$64, 22 hours). Panamericano goes south to Tucumán

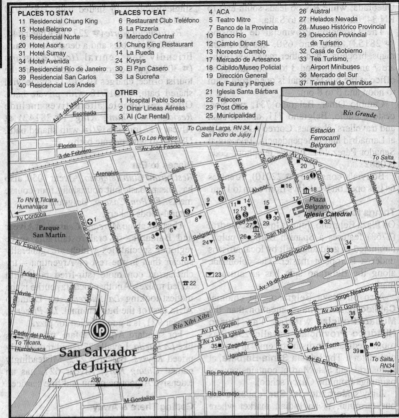

PLACES TO STAY	PLACES TO EAT	4 ACA	26 Austral
11 Residencial Chung King	6 Restaurant Club Teléfono	5 Teatro Mitre	27 Helados Nevada
15 Hotel Belgrano	8 La Pizzería	7 Banco de la Provincia	28 Museo Histórico Provincial
16 Residencial Norte	9 Mercado Central	10 Banco Río	29 Dirección Provincial
20 Hotel Asor's	11 Chung King Restaurant	12 Cambio Dinar SRL	de Turismo
31 Hotel Sumay	14 La Rueda	13 Noroeste Cambio	32 Casa de Gobierno
34 Hotel Avenida	24 Krysys	17 Mercado de Artesanos	33 Tea Turismo,
35 Residencial Río de Janeiro	30 El Pan Casero	18 Cabildo/Museo Policial	Airport Minibuses
39 Residencial San Carlos	38 La Sucreña	19 Dirección General	36 Mercado del Sur
40 Residencial Los Andes		de Fauna y Parques	37 Terminal de Omnibus
	OTHER	21 Iglesia Santa Bárbara	
	1 Hospital Pablo Soria	22 Telecom	
	2 Dinar Líneas Aéreas	23 Post Office	
	3 AI (Car Rental)	25 Municipalidad	

(US$15, five hours) and Córdoba and north to destinations in the Quebrada de Humahuaca as far as La Quiaca (US$20, seven hours). Cooperativa Norte and Atahualpa both stop in Jujuy en route north.

Itatí crosses the Chaco weekly to Corrientes and Iguazú. Andesmar runs southbound buses to Salta, Tucumán, Catamarca (9½ hours), La Rioja (12 hours), San Juan (18 hours) and Mendoza (20 hours). Chile-bound buses from Salta stop in Jujuy before crossing the Paso de Jama to Calama and Iquique (US$60), but make reservations far in advance.

Getting Around

To/From the Airport Tea Turismo, 19 de Abril 485, runs minibuses to Aeropuerto El Cadillal, 27 km south-east of town, for US$5.

AROUND JUJUY

Termas de Reyes

Don't leave Jujuy without wallowing in the thermal baths (US$6) at *Hostería Termas de Reyes* (☎ 35500), overlooking the scenic canyon of the Río Reyes, easily reached from Jujuy. Bring food, since the hostería's restaurant is expensive.

QUEBRADA DE HUMAHUACA
North of Jujuy, the Quebrada de Humahuaca is a painter's palette of colour on barren hillsides, dwarfing hamlets where Quechua peasants scratch a living from maize and scrawny livestock. On this colonial post-route to Potosí, the architecture and other cultural features recall Peru and Bolivia.

Earthquakes levelled many adobe churches, but they were often rebuilt in the 17th and 18th centuries with thick walls, simple bell towers, and striking doors and wood panelling from the *cardón* cactus. Points of interest are so numerous that a car would be useful, but buses are frequent enough that you should be able to flag one down when you need it.

The Lower Quebrada
A few km west of RN 9, the polychrome Cerro de los Siete Colores (Hill of Seven Colours) is a backdrop for **Purmamarca's 17th-century church**. Part of a chain of way stations that ran from Lima to Buenos Aires, **La Posta de Hornillos** is 11 km north of the Purmamarca turn-off. Informal but informative guided tours are available.

Only a few km south of Tilcara, the hillside cemetery of **Maimará** is a can't-miss photo opportunity. In the roadside village of **Uquía**, the 17th-century **Iglesia de San Francisco de Paula** displays a restored collection of paintings from the Cuzco school, featuring the famous *Angeles arcabuceros*, angels armed with Spanish colonial weapons.

Tilcara
Tilcara's hill top *pucará*, a pre-Hispanic fortress with unobstructed views, is its most conspicuous attraction, but the village's museums and artists' colony reputation help make an appealing stopover. At 2461 metres above sea level, it has an irregular street plan beyond the central Plaza Prado; people generally ignore street names and numbers, but the hotel/restaurant El Antigal distributes a useful brochure. The telephone co-op is at the Hotel de Turismo, Belgrano 590; the telephone code is 0882.

Things to See In a beautiful colonial house, open daily from 9 am to 9 pm, the well-organised **Museo Arqueológico Dr Eduardo Casanova** displays regional artefacts. Admission is US$2 (free on Tuesday).

The **Museo Ernesto Soto Avendaño**, open Tuesday to Saturday from 9 am to noon and 3 to 6 pm, displays the work of a sculptor who spent most of his life here. The **Museo José Antonio Terry** honours a Buenos Aires-born painter whose themes were largely rural and indigenous. It's open daily, except Monday, from 9 am to 5 pm. Admission costs US$2 (free on Thursday).

Rising above the sediments of the Río Grande valley, an isolated hill is the site of **El Pucará** (admission US$2), one km south of Tilcara's centre.

Places to Stay & Eat *Autocamping El Jardín*, near the river, has hot showers and attractive vegetable and flower gardens, all for US$4 per person. The free site near the YPF petrol station has picnic tables, but lacks potable water and sanitary facilities.

Residencial El Edén, on Rivadavia 1½ blocks from Plaza Prado, charges US$7/10 for a single/double for rooms with sagging beds and shared bath (cold showers only), but it's clean and friendly. Juan Brambati offers lodging for US$10 per person, with breakfast and dinner extra; write to Juan Brambati, 4624 Tilcara, Provincia de Jujuy, for more information or booking.

Residencial El Antigal (☎ 95020), on Rivadavia half a block from Plaza Prado, is probably the best choice in town at US$20/30 with private bath, hot water, and an outstanding restaurant emphasising regional cuisine.

Getting There & Away Both north and southbound buses stop on Plaza Prado.

Humahuaca
Straddling the Río Grande, nearly 3000 metres above sea level, Humahuaca is a mostly Quechua village of cobbled streets lined with adobe houses. The tourist office, in the Cabildo at Tucumán and Jujuy, is open

on weekdays only. Correo Argentino is across from the plaza, while there's also a locutorio on the corner of Tucumán and Jujuy. Humahuaca's telephone code is 0887.

Things to See From the clock tower in the **Cabildo**, a life-size figure of San Francisco Solano emerges daily at noon. Arrive early, since the clock is erratic and the figure appears only very briefly.

Humahuaca's patron saint resides in the colonial **Iglesia de la Candelaria**, which contains 18th-century oils by Cuzco painter Marcos Sapaca. Overlooking the town, Tilcara sculptor Ernesto Soto Avendaño's **Monumento a la Independencia** is a textbook example of *indigenismo*, a distorted, romantic nationalist tendency in Latin American art and literature.

The **Museo Folklórico Regional**, Buenos Aires 435/447, is open daily from 8 am to 8 pm for formal tours only (US$5 per person for a minimum group of three or four); local writer Sixto Vázquez Zuleta (who goes by his Quechua name 'Toqo'), is a mine of information on local history and culture.

Ten km north of Humahuaca by a dirt road on the east side of the bridge over the Río Grande, north-western Argentina's most extensive pre-Columbian ruins cover 40 hectares at **Coctaca**. Many appear to be broad agricultural terraces on an alluvial fan, but there are also obvious outlines of clusters of buildings.

Places to Stay & Eat The municipal camp site across the bridge remains closed, but it's possible to park or pitch a tent there for free. Open all year round, the *Albergue Juvenil*, Buenos Aires 435, does not require a hostel card; for US$5 per person, it offers hot showers and kitchen facilities.

Residencial Humahuaca, at Córdoba 401 near Corrientes half a block from the bus terminal, charges US$10/15 a single/double for rooms with shared bath, US$13/18 with private bath. *Residencial Colonial* (☎ 21007), Entre Ríos 110, costs about the same.

Near the bus terminal, *Restaurant El Rancho* doesn't look like much, but has outstanding spicy empanadas and humitas (corn tamales). Recent readers' recommendations include *Cacharpaya* on Jujuy between Santiago del Estero and Tucumán (for tamales, empanadas and chicken), up-market *Humahuaca* at Tucumán 22, and *Peña de Fortunato* on the corner of San Luis and Jujuy (regional cuisine and live folkloric music).

Getting There & Away The Terminal de Omnibus is very central at Belgrano and Entre Ríos, with frequent services to Jujuy and La Quiaca (US$25, 2½ hours).

LA QUIACA

North of Humahuaca, gravelled RN 9 climbs steeply to the altiplano, where agriculture is precarious and peasants subsist on llamas, sheep, goats and the few cattle that can graze the sparse *ichu* grass. At the end of the road are La Quiaca and its Bolivian twin, Villazón. For more details on the border crossing, and a map of the two towns, see the Villazón section in the Bolivia chapter.

La Quiaca has no tourist office, but the ACA station on RN 9 has maps. If Banco Nación will not cash travellers' cheques, try Universo Tours in Villazón. La Quiaca's Bolivian Consulate, on the corner of San Juan and Arabe Siria, charges a hefty US$15 for visas.

Places to Stay

Accommodation is cheaper on the Bolivian side, but try very basic *Alojamiento Pequeño* at Bolívar and Balcarce, or *Hotel Frontera* on 25 de Mayo, for about US$7 per person. Recommended by several LP correspondents, *Hotel Cristal* (☎ (0885) 2255), Sarmiento 543, charges about US$17/28 for singles/doubles.

Getting There & Away

Panamericano and Atahualpa have frequent buses to Jujuy and Salta.

AROUND LA QUIACA

Take Flota La Quiaqueña or a shared cab to the village of **Yavi**, 16 km east of La Quiaca, where the 17th-century **Iglesia de San Francisco** is renowned for its altar, paintings, and carved statues. A nearby **colonial house** belonged to the Marqués Campero, whose marriage to the holder of the original encomienda created a family which dominated the region's economy in the 18th century.

SALTA

In a basin surrounded by verdant peaks, 1200 metres above sea level, Salta's agreeable climate attracted early Spaniards, who could pasture animals nearby and raise crops that could not grow in Bolivia's frigid highlands. When the railway made it feasible to haul sugar to the Pampas, the city partly recovered from its 19th-century decline.

South-west of the central Plaza 9 de Julio is Salta's commercial centre. Alberdi and Florida are pedestrian malls between Caseros and Avenida San Martín.

Information

The Empresa Salteña de Turismo (Emsatur, ☎ 21-5927), at Buenos Aires 93 near Alvarado, has some brochures and maps, but is most helpful in locating private accommodation. Hours are 8 am to 9 pm daily. The smaller office at the bus terminal closes for siesta.

Cambio Dinar, Mitre 101, changes cash and travellers' cheques. Correo Argentino is at Dean Funes 140, Telecom at Vicente López 146 and at Belgrano 824. The telephone code is 087.

Bolivia's consulate (☎ 21-1927) is at Santiago del Estero 179.

Things to See

Museums The 18th-century **Cabildo**, Caseros 549, houses the **Museo Histórico del Norte** (admission US$1), with religious and modern art, period furniture, historic coins, paper money, and horse-drawn vehicles. Hours are Tuesday to Saturday, 10 am to 2 pm and 3.30 to 7.30 pm, and Sunday 10 am to 2 pm.

In the Casa Arias Rengel, a colonial mansion at Florida 18, the **Museo de Bellas Artes** (admission US$1) displays modern painting and sculpture. It's open daily, except Monday, from 9 am to 1 pm and 3 to 9 pm.

Churches The 19th-century **Iglesia Catedral**, España 596, guards the ashes of General Martín Miguel de Güemes, a hero of the wars of independence. Ornate almost to the point of gaudiness, the **Iglesia San Francisco**, at Caseros and Córdoba, is a local landmark. Only Carmelite nuns can enter the 16th-century adobe **Convento de San Bernardo**, at Caseros and Santa Fe, but anyone can admire its carved algarrobo door.

Cerro San Bernardo For views of Salta and the Lerma valley, take the *teleférico* (gondola) from Parque San Martín to the top and back (US$6), or climb the trail from the top of Avenida General Güemes.

Places to Stay

Camping Salta's excellent *Camping Municipal Carlos Xamena* (☎ 23-1341) features a gigantic swimming pool. Fees are US$2 per car, US$3 per tent and US$2 per adult. From the centre of town, take bus No 13 ('Balneario').

Hostels Salta's official *Albergue Juvenil* (☎ 31-2891), Buenos Aires 930, is so popular that reservations are desirable; rates are US$8 per person. Take bus No 12 from the bus terminal. *Residencial San Jorge* (☎ 21-0443), Esteco 244, also offers hostel accommodation for US$8 (shared bath) or US$12 (private bath). Take local bus No 3 or No 10 from the terminal.

Casas de Familia, Residenciales & Hotels Emsatur keeps a list of private house alternatives to bottom-end hotels. At Mendoza 915, María de Toffoli offers rooms with kitchen facilities, spotless baths and patio access for

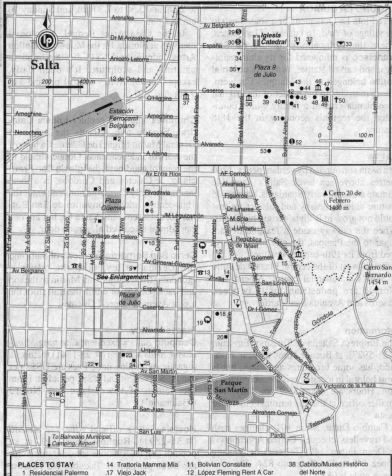

Salta

US$10 per person (her two sisters let rooms in their own adjacent houses).

Between the bus terminal and the city centre, reasonably quiet *Residencial Royal*, Alvarado 107, has singles/doubles with shared bath for US$10/14. Neocolonial *Residencial Elena* (☎ 21-1529), Buenos Aires 256, costs US$15/22 for a single/double but seems reluctant to accept single travellers. A recent discovery is *Residencial Palermo* (☎ 22-0426), Balcarce 980, with good facilities for US$12 single.

Italian-run *Hotel Italia* (☎ 21-4050), Alberdi 231, charges about US$17/22 for plain but spacious and sunny rooms.

Places to Eat
At Salta's large and lively *Mercado Central*, Florida and San Martín, you can supplement cheap pizza, empanadas and humitas with fresh fruit and vegetables. Despite its unappealing moniker, *Snack Bar Whympy* at Zuviría 223 is good, inexpensive and filling. The *Sociedad Italiana*, Zuviría and Santiago del Estero, has quality four-course meals for about US$6.

La Posta, España 476, is a highly recommended but pricey parrilla. *Viejo Jack* at Avenida Virrey Toledo 145 and *Viejo Jack II* at Avenida Reyes Católicos 1465, are separate branches of a popular parrilla that has drawn enthusiastic reviews from readers. For Italian food, check *Trattoría Mamma Mia*, Virrey Toledo 200.

Getting There & Away
Air Aerolíneas Argentinas (☎ 31-5738) and Austral (☎ 31-0258) share offices at Caseros 475. Monday's Aerolíneas flights between Aeroparque and Santa Cruz, Bolivia (US$127) also stop in Córdoba (US$128). Austral flies at least daily to Buenos Aires (US$225).

Dinar Líneas Aéreas (☎ 31-0606), Buenos Aires 46, Local 2, flies most days to Tucumán (US$30) and Buenos Aires (US$180). LAPA (☎ 21-0386), Caseros 492, flies on Tuesday, Thursday and Saturday

afternoons to Aeroparque (US$129) via Tucumán (US$29).

Bus Salta's Terminal de Omnibus (☎ 21-4716), on Avenida Hipólito Yrigoyen south-east of the city centre, has frequent long-distance services. A few companies have offices nearby or elsewhere in town.

La Veloz del Norte serves Mar del Plata (US$85, 29 hours), Buenos Aires (US$64, 22 hours), Santa Fe (US$50, 15 hours), Mendoza (US$61, 19 hours), San Juan (US$50, 17 hours), Córdoba (US$45), Resistencia (US$40, 16 hours), La Rioja (US$35), Catamarca (US$26) and Santiago del Estero (US$20). Panamericano goes to Tucumán (US$17), Santiago del Estero and Córdoba. Andesmar goes to Cuyo and Patagonia.

Atahualpa goes to Jujuy and up the Quebrada de Humahuaca to La Quiaca (nine hours), across the Chaco to Formosa, and to Antofagasta, Chile (Wednesday, summer only). Géminis (☎ 21-2758), opposite the terminal at Dionisio Puch 117, has summer crossings on Saturday to Antofagasta (US$40), Calama, Iquique (US$50) and Arica (US$55). Buses to Chile are always full, so make early reservations.

El Indio goes three times daily to Cafayate (US$15, four hours). Daily buses climb the Quebrada del Toro to San Antonio de los Cobres (US$14). Empresa Marco Ruedas (☎ 21-4447), Islas Malvinas 393, serves the altiplano village of Cachi.

Train The Ferrocarril Belgrano (☎ 21-3161), Ameghino 690, no longer offers regular passenger services, but contact Turismo Tren a las Nubes (☎ 21-6394, fax 31-1264), Caseros 443, for the scenic ride to and beyond the mining town of San Antonio de los Cobres on the famous Tren a las Nubes (Train to the Clouds). Getting on the cheaper local freight, which leaves on Wednesday at about 7 am, is difficult but not impossible.

Getting Around
To/From the Airport Buses to Aeropuerto

Internacional El Aybal (☎ 23-1648), south-west of town on RP 51, cost US$3.

To/From the Bus & Train Stations Local bus No 5 connects the train station and the city centre with the bus terminal.

PARQUE NACIONAL CALILEGUA

On Jujuy's eastern border, the arid altiplano surrenders to dense subtropical cloud forest in the Serranía de Calilegua, where 3600-metre Cerro Hermoso offers limitless views of the Gran Chaco. Bird life is abundant, and there is a wide variety of flora, changing with the increasing altitude.

The park headquarters and visitor centre (☎ 22046) is in the village of Calilegua, just north of Libertador General San Martín. Donated by the Ledesma sugar mill, the visitor centre has exhibits on all the region's national parks.

Beware mosquitoes at the developed camp site at Aguas Negras, on a short side road near the entrance station. Camping is also possible on a level area near the ranger station at Mesada de las Colmenas.

Getting There & Away

Veloz del Norte's Salta-Orán service stops at the excellent Club Social San Lorenzo restaurant, next door to park headquarters. From the bus terminal at Libertador General San Martín, a 4WD pick-up climbs to Parque Calilegua and Valle Grande (US$13) on Tuesday and Saturday at 7.30 am; return trips are on Sunday and Thursday at 9 am. You could also try hitching with logging trucks to Valle Grande.

QUEBRADA DE CAFAYATE

Beyond the village of Alemanía, 100 km south of Salta, verdant forest becomes barren sandstone in the Quebrada de Cafayate. The eastern Sierra de Carahuasi is the backdrop for distinctive landforms like Garganta del Diablo (Devil's Throat), El Anfiteatro (The Amphitheatre), El Sapo (The Toad), El Fraile (The Friar), El Obelisco (The Obelisk) and Los Castillos (The Castles). Nearer Cafayate is an extensive dunefield at Los Médanos.

Getting There & Away

Other than car rental or brief, regimented tours, the only ways to see the Quebrada are by bus, thumb or foot. To walk the canyon at your own pace (carry food and water), disembark from any El Indio bus and catch a later one; a good starting point is the impressive box canyon of Garganta del Diablo. The most interesting portion is too far to walk in a single day, but you can double back from Cafayate.

CAFAYATE

Many tourists and major vineyards enjoy the warm, dry and sunny climate of Cafayate (1600 metres), at the mouth of the Valles Calchaquíes. It's not overrun with visitors, but there are many young artists and artisans. RN 40 (Avenida Güemes) goes north-west to Molinos and Cachi, while RP 68 goes to Salta.

The information kiosk on Güemes, opposite the plaza, keeps erratic hours. Change money in Salta, if possible, or try Banco de la Nación here. Make long-distance calls at the Cooperativa Telefónica on the south side of the plaza. Cafayate's telephone code is 0868.

Things to See

Drop by Rodolfo Bravo's house, on Calle Colón, at any reasonable hour to see his personal **Museo Arqueológico** (admission US$1) of Calchaquí (Diaguita) ceramics. Colonial and other artefacts include elaborate horse gear and wine casks.

On Güemes near Colón, the **Museo de Vitivinicultura** details the history of local wines. Ask at the bodegas for tours and tasting; try the sweet white *torrontés*.

Places to Stay & Eat

Camping Lorahuasi (US$2 per car, person and tent) has hot showers, a swimming pool and a grocery. *Hotel Gran Real* (☎ 21231) Güemes 128, has limited hostel accommodation with kitchen facilities for US$12. *Residencial Colonial* (☎ 21223), Diego de Almagro 134, charges US$12 per person with shared bath, but lacks hot water at times

Hospedaje Arroyo, Quintana de Niño s/n, may be even a bit cheaper. For US$25/32 a single/double, *Hotel Briones* (☎ 21270), on the plaza, is not such good value as it once was, but still has a decent confitería.

Local cuisine emphasises parrillada, as at *La López Pereyra*. Try also *La Carreta de Don Olegario*, opposite the plaza; there are several cheaper places.

Getting There & Away

El Indio has three buses daily to Salta (US$15, four hours), except Thursday (four buses). There are also four daily to San Carlos, up the Valles Calchaquíes, and one to Angastaco (US$7).

Daily buses to Santa María pass the important ruins at Quilmes (see below), in Tucumán province. Several buses weekly connect Cafayate with the city of Tucumán via the scenic route through Tafí del Valle.

AROUND CAFAYATE

Valles Calchaquíes

In this valley north and south of Cafayate, once a principal route across the Andes, Calchaquí Indians resisted Spanish attempts to impose forced labour obligations. Tired of having to protect their pack trains, the Spaniards relocated many Indians to Buenos Aires, and the land fell to Spaniards, who formed large rural estates.

Cachi North-west of Cafayate, Cachi's scenic surroundings, 18th-century church and archaeological museum make it the most worthwhile stopover in the Valles Calchaquíes. For accommodation, try the municipal camping ground and hostel, or *Hotel Nevado de Cachi* (US$8 per person).

You can reach Cachi either from Cafayate or, more easily, by Marcos Rueda bus from Salta (US$13), which uses the scenic Cuesta del Obispo route past Parque Nacional Los Cardones.

Quilmes This pre-Hispanic pucará, in Tucumán province only 50 km south of Cafayate, is probably Argentina's most extensive preserved ruins. Dating from about 1000 AD, this complex urban settlement covered about 30 hectares, housing perhaps 5000 people. The Quilmes Indians abided contact with the Incas but could not outlast the Spaniards, who, in 1667, deported the last 2000 to Buenos Aires.

Quilmes' thick walls underscore its defensive functions, but evidence of dense occupation sprawls north and south of the nucleus. Camping is possible near the small museum, where US$2 admits you to the ruins. Buses from Cafayate to Santa María pass the junction, but from there, it's five km to the ruins by foot or thumb.

SAN ANTONIO DE LOS COBRES

Colonial pack trains to Peru usually took the Quebrada de Humahuaca, but an alternative crossed the Puna de Atacama to the Pacific and thence to Lima. For travellers on this route, bleak San Antonio (3700 metres) must have seemed an oasis. Well into this century, it was a stopover for drovers moving stock to Chile's nitrate mines, but railways and roads have supplanted mules.

San Antonio, a largely Indian town with posters and political graffiti that tell you it's still part of Argentina, has basic lodging at *Hospedaje Belgrano* or *Hospedaje Los Andes* (about US$8 per person with shared bath). Hospedaje Los Andes has a restaurant.

Hostería de las Nubes has 12 rooms with private baths, double-glazed windows and a restaurant, for US$40/50 a single/double, including breakfast. Make reservations at Turismo Tren a las Nubes (☎ (087) 31-4984, fax 31-1264), Caseros 443 in Salta.

El Tren a las Nubes

From Salta, the Tren a las Nubes (Train to the Clouds) makes countless switchbacks and spirals to ascend the Quebrada del Toro and reach the high puna. Its La Polvorilla viaduct, crossing a broad desert canyon, is a magnificent engineering achievement unjustified on any economic grounds.

Movitren (☎ (087) 31-4984, fax 31-1264), Caseros 443 in Salta, operates full-day excursions as far as La Polvorilla; most trips take place on weekends only from

April to October, but can be more frequent during July holidays. The US$95 fare does not include meals, which cost around US$11. Some travellers have purchased slightly less comfortable 'discount carriage' tickets for US$50.

Freight Trains From Salta, Rosario de Lerma or San Antonio, a more economical alternative is one of the weekly freight trains that reach the border at Socompa, where a Chilean freight train goes to Baquedano, about 100 km from Antofagasta on the Ruta Panamericana. This segment is not for the squeamish: the Chilean crew is unfriendly and the train truly filthy. Purchase Chilean pesos before leaving Salta to pay for the ticket, which is not guaranteed.

At Socompa, clear Argentine and Chilean immigration before asking permission to ride the train – and expect to wait several days. It descends through vast deserts to the abandoned station of Augusta Victoria, where you may disembark to try hitching to Antofagasta; mining trucks are almost certain to stop.

Getting There & Away
El Quebradeño runs five weekly buses from Salta (US$15, four hours). See the Tren a las Nubes section for details of the train from Salta to San Antonio and beyond.

TUCUMAN
Independence Day (9 July) celebrations are especially vigorous in San Miguel de Tucumán, which hosted the congress that declared Argentine independence in 1816. Unlike Salta and Jujuy, it successfully reoriented its post-independence economy, as the railway brought it just close enough to Buenos Aires to take advantage of the federal capital's growing market for sugar. The city still preserves notable colonial remnants near Plaza de la Independencia.

Information
Tucumán's provincial Secretaría de Estado de Turismo y Deportes (☎ 22-2199), 24 de Setiembre 484, is open on weekdays from 7 am to 1 pm and 4 to 9 pm, and on weekends from 9 am to 1 pm and 5 to 9 pm. The municipal Dirección de Producción y Turismo (☎ 22-9696), Avenida Avellaneda 190, is open on weekdays from 8.30 am to 4.30 pm. It has decent maps and brochures, and a useful 35-page *Guía de Servicios*.

Maguitur, San Martín 765, cashes travellers' cheques (2% commission), but ATMs are numerous. Correo Argentino is at Avenida 25 de Mayo and Córdoba. Telecom is at Maipú 480; Tucumán's telephone code is 081.

Things to See
The most imposing landmark in the city centre is the turn-of-the-century **Casa de Gobierno**, which replaced the colonial cabildo on Plaza Independencia. The **Museo Iramain**, Entre Ríos 27, stresses Argentine art and sculpture; it's open on weekdays from 8 am to noon and 2 to 7 pm, and on Saturday from 8 am to noon only. The fine-arts **Museo de Bellas Artes Timoteo Navarro** (1905), 9 de Julio 44, is open on weekdays from 9.30 am to 12.30 pm and 5 to 8.30 pm, and on weekends from 5.30 to 8.30 pm only.

Other noteworthy museums include the **Museo Histórico de la Provincia** at Congreso 56, open on weekdays only from 9 am to 12.30 pm as well as daily from 5 to 8 pm; and the **Museo Arqueológico**, which focuses on north-western Argentine prehistory, at 25 de Mayo 265, open on weekdays from 8 am to noon and 5 to 9 pm.

Casa de la Independencia On 9 July 1816, Unitarist lawyers and clerics declared independence (Federalists boycotted the meeting) at this dazzlingly white colonial house (admission US$1) at Congreso 151. Hours are Tuesday to Friday 8.30 am to 1 pm and 3 to 7.30 pm, and on weekends from 9 am to 1 pm.

Museo Folklórico Manuel Belgrano This pleasant facility displays horse gear, indigenous musical instruments, weavings, and woodcarvings, Quilmes pottery and samples of *randa* lace. The museum shop sells some items. At 24 de Setiembre 565, it's open on weekdays from 7 am to 1 pm and 3 to 9 pm, and on weekends from 9 am to 1 pm and 4 to 9 pm. Admission is free.

Casa del Obispo Colombres In Parque 9 de Julio (once a plantation), this 18th-century house preserves the first ox-powered *trapiche* (sugar mill) of Tucumán's post-independence industry. Guided tours in Spanish explain the mill's operations. Hours are weekdays 8 am to noon and 2 to 6 pm, weekends 9 am to 7 pm. Admission is US$1.

Mercado de Abasto Brightly painted horse-drawn carts from the countryside haul their goods to this lively market at San Lorenzo and Miguel Lillo, 10 blocks west and three blocks south of Plaza Independencia. Unlike most markets, it is liveliest in mid to late afternoon.

Places to Stay
Camping Unfortunately, Tucumán's mayor closed conveniently central *Las Lomitas* in Parque 9 de Julio in late 1994, but information is included here on the chance it may reopen. To reach it, either walk down Avenida Benjamín Aráoz past the university – it's about 20 minutes from the new bus terminal – or take bus No 1 from Crisóstomo Alvarez.

Hostel Tucumán's *Albergue Juvenil* (☎ 31-0265), Junín 580, charges US$15 with breakfast. It occupies part of the mid-range Hotel Miami.

Hospedajes, Residenciales & Hotels
Rock-bottom but marginal, for about US$10/15, are *Hospedaje Charcas*, on Charcas near the new bus terminal, and *Hospedaje Autopista* on the corner of Avenida Benjamín Aráoz and Sargento Gómez. Near the Mitre station, try the improving *Hotel Tucumán* (☎ 22-1809), at Catamarca 563, where singles/doubles with shared bath cost US$10/14, with private bath US$14/21. Friendly and central *24 Palace*

Hotel (☎ 22-3855), 24 de Setiembre 233, is perhaps the best value in the city centre, with singles/doubles for US$18/28.

Places to Eat
One of the best choices for inexpensive food is the *Mercado de Abasto* (see above), but the more central *Mercado del Norte*, at Mendoza and Maipú, is another possibility.

In the centre, try the *Feria de Artesanos Tucumanos*, on 24 de Setiembre half a block from Plaza Independencia, where a variety of small stands prepare tasty regional specialties; the first one on your left as you enter has exceptional humitas and chicken empanadas. For breakfast, try inexpensive *Café de la Fuente*, 25 de Mayo 183.

Middle Eastern food is the speciality at *Adela*, 24 de Setiembre 358, and at *Restaurant Sirio Libanés* on Maipú between Corrientes and Santiago del Estero. *La Mesa*, San Martín 437, is a very good and reasonably priced parrilla.

Getting There & Away
Air Aerolíneas Argentinas (☎ 31-1030), 9 de Julio 112, flies at least twice daily to Aeroparque (US$207), stopping on Sunday evenings in Córdoba. Austral (☎ 31-0427, 31-0889), 24 de Setiembre 546, has daily flights to and from Córdoba (US$82); northbound flights continue to Salta and/or Jujuy (US$55).

LAPA (☎ 30-2630) is at Crisóstomo Alvarez 620, 1st floor, Oficina 3; it flies on Tuesday, Thursday and Saturday to and from Buenos Aires (US$99); northbound flights continue to Salta (US$29). Dinar Líneas Aéreas (☎ 22-2974), at 9 de Julio and 24 de Noviembre, has five flights weekly to Aeroparque (US$166), five to Salta (US$30) and six to Jujuy (US$45).

Bus At Brígido Terán 350, Tucumán's sparkling new Estación de Omnibus opened in December 1994. Shopping del Jardín's information booth (☎ 30-6400, 30-2060) is open daily from 6.30 am to 11.30 pm and

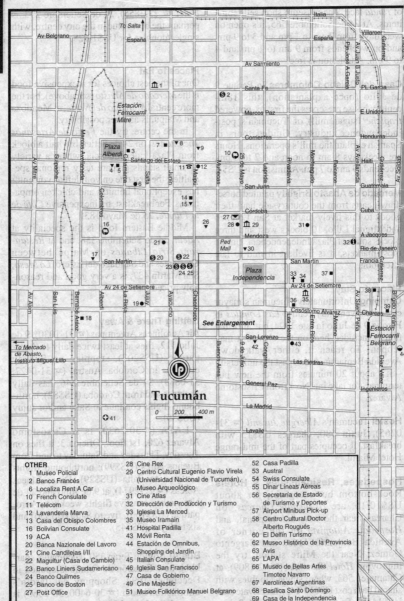

Tucumán

0   200   400 m

OTHER
1 Museo Policial
2 Banco Francés
6 Localiza Rent A Car
10 French Consulate
11 Telecom
12 Lavandería Marva
16 Bolivian Consulate
19 ACA
20 Banca Nazionale del Lavoro
21 Cine Candilejas I/II
22 Maguitur (Casa de Cambio)
23 Banco Liniers Sudamericano
24 Banco Quilmes
25 Banco de Boston
27 Post Office

28 Cine Rex
29 Centro Cultural Eugenio Flavio Virela
    (Universidad Nacional de Tucumán),
    Museo Arqueológico
31 Cine Atlas
32 Dirección de Producción y Turismo
33 Iglesia La Merced
35 Museo Iramain
41 Hospital Padilla
43 Móvil Renta
44 Estación de Omnibus,
    Shopping del Jardín
45 Italian Consulate
46 Iglesia San Francisco
47 Casa de Gobierno
49 Cine Majestic
51 Museo Folklórico Manuel Belgrano

52 Casa Padilla
53 Austral
54 Swiss Consulate
55 Dinar Líneas Aéreas
56 Secretaría de Estado
    de Turismo y Deportes
57 Airport Minibus Pick-up
58 Centro Cultural Doctor
    Alberto Rougués
60 El Delfín Turismo
62 Museo Histórico de la Provincia
63 Avis
65 LAPA
66 Museo de Bellas Artes
    Timoteo Navarro
67 Aerolíneas Argentinas
68 Basílica Santo Domingo
69 Casa de la Independencia

provides information on the Estación and the shopping centre only.

Aconquija goes to Tafí del Valle (US$9, three hours) three times daily, and to Cafayate (US$20, seven hours) twice daily. El Tucumano goes to Córdoba (8½ hours), Rosario, Buenos Aires, Termas de Río Hondo, Santiago del Estero, Salta (4½ hours) and Jujuy (5½ hours); Veloz del Norte crosses the Chaco to Resistencia.

Panamericano heads north to Salta and Jujuy, south to Córdoba. Bosio has similar routes and also goes to Mendoza. La Estrella goes daily to Mendoza via Catamarca and La Rioja, and also to Santa Fe, Rosario, Buenos Aires, Mar del Plata, Salta, Jujuy, Santa Rosa and Neuquén. TAC goes to Catamarca, La Rioja, San Juan, Mendoza (US$48, 15 hours), Buenos Aires (US$57, 16 hours), and Patagonian destinations. It also has international services to Santiago de Chile. Andesmar stops here en route between Mendoza and Jujuy.

El Rayo crosses the Chaco to Resistencia and Corrientes (US$34, 13 hours). Empresa Itatí goes to Posadas, Puerto Iguazú, and Buenos Aires (US$60, 20 hours). Atahualpa goes to Pocitos, on the Bolivian border, for US$30, and to Jujuy, Córdoba, Rosario and Buenos Aires. Chevallier serves Rosario, Córdoba and Buenos Aires, more cheaply than Itatí. There are frequent buses to Termas de Río Hondo and Santiago del Estero.

Train From the Ferrocarril Mitre station (☎ 31-0725), at Catamarca and Corrientes, opposite Plaza Alberdi, *El Tucumano* goes to Buenos Aires via Santiago del Estero (La Banda) and Rosario on Tuesday, Thursday and Saturday.

Getting Around

To/From the Airport Empresa Sáenz Alderete minibuses to Aeropuerto Internacional Benjamín Matienzo (US$2.50) leave 1¼ hours before flight time from a space opposite the entrance to Gran Hotel Corona on 9 de Julio, half a block south of Plaza Independencia.

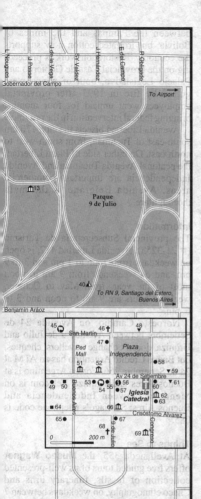

Bus City buses do not accept cash; buy cospeles (US$0.50 each) at kiosks in the centre of town.

TAFI DEL VALLE

South-west of Tucumán, RP 307 snakes up a narrow gorge, opening onto a misty valley where, in summer, *tucumanos* seek relief in the cool heights around Tafí del Valle. Beyond Tafí, about 100 km from the provincial capital, the road zigzags over the 3050-metre Abra del Infiernillo, an alternative route to Cafayate and Salta.

At 2000 metres, a temperate island in a subtropical sea, Tafí grows seed potatoes, sends fruits (apples, pears and peaches) to Tucumán, and pastures cattle, sheep and, at higher altitudes, llamas. At Tafí's Centro Cívico, the helpful Casa del Turista (☎ 21020) is open on weekdays from 7.30 am to 7.30 pm, and on weekends from 10 am to 4 pm. Long-distance telephones are also here; Tafí's telephone code is 0867.

Tafí's 18th-century Jesuit **Capilla La Banda** contains a worthwhile museum. At **Parque Los Menhires**, at the south end of La Angostura reservoir, over 80 aboriginal granite monuments, collected from nearby archaeological sites, resemble the standing stones of the Scottish Hebrides.

Tafí's recently reopened *Autocamping del Sauce* (☎ 21084) is acceptable for US$2.50 per person; tiny cabañas, with bunks for US$5 per person, would be very cramped at their maximum capacity of four people.

Hospedaje La Cumbre, Diego de Rojas 311, charges US$10 per person for rooms with shared bath, with meals for US$4. *El Rancho de Félix* serves regional food and is probably the best choice in town, but *La Rueda* is also worth a look.

Getting There & Away

From the bus station on the north side of the plaza, Empresa Aconquija has five buses daily to Tucumán.

SANTIAGO DEL ESTERO

Founded in 1553, Argentina's oldest city (population 150,000) was a stopover between the Pampas and the mines of Bolivia, but irrigated cotton now supports the economy. Restoration work is proceeding on the provincial Casa de Gobierno and Palacio Legislativo, both of which were gutted by fire in 1993 after provincial employees went unpaid for four months, bringing federal intervention in the province.

Avenida Libertad bisects the city, 170 km south-east of Tucumán, from south-west to north-east. On either side of Plaza Libertad, the peatonal Avenida Tucumán and Avenida Independencia are important commercial areas. Avenida Belgrano is the main thoroughfare.

Information

The provincial Subsecretaría de Turismo (☎ 21-3253), Avenida Libertad 417, is open on weekdays from 7 am to 1 pm and 3 to 9 pm, and on weekends from 9 am to noon most of the year; from May to October, weekend hours are 9 am to noon and 3 to 6 pm.

Noroeste Cambio, on Avenida 24 de Setiembre between Avenida 9 de Julio and Urquiza, doesn't change travellers' cheques, but Banco Crédito Argentino has an ATM at 24 de Setiembre 256. Correo Argentino is at Buenos Aires and Urquiza. Telecom is on Mendoza between Independencia and Buenos Aires; Santiago's telephone code is 085.

Things to See

At Avellaneda 355, the **Museo Wagner** offers free guided tours of its well-presented collection of fossils, funerary urns and Chaco ethnography, on weekdays between 7 am and 1 pm. Exhibits at the **Museo Histórico Provincial**, Urquiza 354, emphasise postcolonial history; it's open on weekdays from 8 am to noon.

Places to Stay & Eat

At shady *Campamento Las Casuarinas*, in Parque Aguirre less than one km from Plaza Libertad, fees are about US$5 per site.

Residencial Santa Rita, Santa Fe 273, has singles/doubles with shared bath for

US$12/20, with private bath for US$14/25. Tiny *Residencial Emaus*, Moreno Sur 673, is friendly and spotlessly clean (US$15/19); comparably priced *Residencial Petit Colonial* (☎ 21-1261) is in the centre of town at La Plata 65.

The student-oriented *Comedor Universitario*, Avellaneda 364, has uninspiring cheap food. Better but still reasonably priced meals are available at the *Comedor Centro de Viajantes*, Buenos Aires 37. Moderately priced *Mía Mamma*, 24 de Setiembre 15, has an extensive Italian menu, plus a good, inexpensive salad bar. *Taffik*, at Jujuy and Tucumán, serves Middle Eastern food.

Getting There & Away

Air Austral (☎ 22-4335), Buenos Aires 60, flies on weekdays only to Aeroparque (US$176) and to Jujuy (US$83).

Bus Santiago's ageing Estación Terminal de Omnibus (☎ 21-3746) is at Pedro León Gallo and Saavedra, eight blocks south of Plaza Libertad.

Many companies go to Termas de Río Hondo (US$3, one hour) and Tucumán (US$7). Panamericano goes north to Salta (US$25, six hours) and Jujuy (US$28, seven hours), and eight times daily to Córdoba (US$19). La Veloz del Norte goes to Buenos Aires and intermediates, and to north-western destinations. Central Argentino goes to Buenos Aires (US$45, 13 hours) and La Plata.

Cotal goes to Mendoza (US$36), San Juan (US$32), Catamarca, Corrientes, and Posadas. TAC and Gutiérrez both go to Buenos Aires, while TAC, Libertador and Bosio have additional services to Cuyo.

El Santiagueño goes to Córdoba (US$19, six hours). Cacorba has five buses daily to Córdoba and one to Buenos Aires. Chevallier and Empresa Tata both run buses to Rosario (US$25) and Buenos Aires. La Estrella serves Santa Fe (US$30), Paraná (US$32), and Mar del Plata (US$52).

El Rayo and Empresa Martín cross the Chaco to Resistencia (US$25), and Corrientes (US$27, nine hours), connecting

to Posadas and Puerto Iguazú. Patagonian carrier Ute Comahue goes to Neuquén, Bariloche, Río Gallegos and intermediates. TUS and TUP go to Santa Rosa (La Pampa) and Patagonian destinations.

Train The Ferrocarril Mitre's *El Tucumano*, linking Buenos Aires and Tucumán, stops at the suburban La Banda station on Monday, Wednesday and Friday northbound, and on Tuesday, Thursday and Sunday southbound.

Getting Around

To/From the Airport Bus No 19 goes to Aeropuerto Mal Paso, six km south-west of the city centre.

To/From the Train Station From Moreno and Libertad in central Santiago, bus Nos 10, 14, 18 and 21 all go to the Mitre station in La Banda.

LA RIOJA

In 1591, Juan Ramírez de Velasco founded Todos los Santos de la Nueva Rioja, 154 km south of Catamarca at the base of the Sierra del Velasco, and missionary pacification of the Diaguita also aided Spanish colonisation. An 1894 earthquake destroyed many buildings, but the restored commercial centre, near Plaza 25 de Mayo, replicates colonial style.

The province's memorable historical figures include caudillos like Facundo Quiroga – objects of Sarmiento's tirades against provincial strongmen – but the province also nurtured intellectuals like Joaquín V González, founder of La Plata university. Facundo's modern counterparts, including President Carlos Menem's *riojano* family, are politically influential. Corruption and nepotism are widespread.

Information

The Dirección Municipal de Turismo (☎ 28834), Avenida Perón 715, is open on weekdays from 8 am to 1 pm and 4 to 9 pm, and on Saturday from 8 am to noon. Banks keep limited hours, but Banco de Galicia has an ATM at San Nicolás de Bari and Buenos

Aires. Correo Argentino is at Avenida Perón 764. Telecom is at Pelagio Luna and Joaquín V González; La Rioja's telephone code is 0822.

Things to See

The **Museo Folklórico**, in a re-created 19th-century house at Pelagio Luna 811, displays ceramic reproductions of mythological figures from local folklore. It's open Tuesday to Sunday from 8 am to noon and 4 to 8 pm. Over 12,000 pieces, from tools and artefacts to Diaguita ceramics and weavings, fill the **Museo Inca Huasi**, Alberdi 650. The **Museo Histórico**, Adolfo Dávila 79, contains memorabilia of Facundo Quiroga.

Built by the Diaguita under Dominican overseers, the **Convento de Santo Domingo** (1623), at Pelagio Luna and Lamadrid, is the country's oldest. The **Convento de San Francisco**, at Avenida 25 de Mayo and Bazán y Bustos, houses the Niño Alcalde, an important religious icon. The **Iglesia Catedral**, at San Nicolás and Avenida 25 de Mayo, contains the image of patron saint Nicolás de Bari, another devotional object.

Special Events

The 31 December ceremony El Tinkunako re-enacts San Francisco Solano's mediation between the Diaguitas and the Spaniards in 1593. For accepting peace, the Diaguitas imposed two conditions: resignation of the Spanish mayor and his replacement by the Niño Alcalde (see previous section).

Places to Stay

Camping *Country Las Vegas*, at Km 7 on RP 1 west of town, charges around US$5 per tent and US$4 per person; to get there, catch city bus No 1 southbound on Perón.

Casas de Familia, Residenciales & Hotels

The tourist office maintains a list of casas de familia offering accommodation for about US$12 per person. *Residencial Sumaj Kanki*, at Avenida Castro Barros and Coronel Lagos, provides modest but clean accommodation for about US$10 per person with shared bath. Around the corner at friendly *Residencial Petit*, Lagos 427, singles with shared bath go for US$13, while singles/doubles with private bath cost US$20/35. Once a grand place, the building still conserves some of its past splendour.

Hotel Savoy (☎ 26894), Avenida Roque A Luna 14, has comfortable rooms with bath, air-con and telephone for US$25/30, and has a bar and confitería for breakfast.

Places to Eat

For spicy regional specialities, try *La Cantina de Juan*, Hipólito Yrigoyen 190; *La Vieja Casona*, Rivadavia 427; *El Milagro*, Avenida Perón and Remedios de Escalada; and *La Lala*, Avenida Quiroga and Güemes. All serve standard Argentine dishes like parrillada as well.

For Middle Eastern food, another regional speciality, try *El Nuevo Candil*, Rivadavia 461. A good-value place is the *Comedor de la Sociedad Española*, 9 de Julio 237, with tasty Spanish food. *Il Gatto*, Pelagio Luna 555, is part of a chain but still has very decent pizza and pasta at moderate prices.

Getting There & Away

Air Aerolíneas Argentinas (☎ 27355), Belgrano 63, flies every morning except Sunday to Catamarca and Buenos Aires, with additional flights on Wednesday and Friday afternoons.

Bus La Rioja's Estación Terminal de Omnibus (☎ 25453) is at Artigas and España.

El Cóndor travels frequently to Córdoba; Cacorba, Riojacor and El Rápido also serve Córdoba. Cotal goes to Mendoza, Catamarca, Santiago del Estero, Reconquista, Resistencia, Corrientes and Puerto Iguazú.

Libertador has daily buses to Mendoza (US$29, 9½ hours), San Juan (US$22, 7½ hours), Catamarca (US$11, two hours) and Tucumán (US$26, 4½ hours). Autotransporte Mendoza and Bosio also go to Cuyo.

Ablo serves Córdoba (US$12), Santa Fe, San Luis, Buenos Aires (US$45, 17 hours) and Mar del Plata. La Estrella goes to destinations throughout Cuyo and the

North-West. Empresa General Urquiza goes to Santa Fe and Buenos Aires. Andesmar serves Catamarca, Tucumán, Salta and Mendoza, connecting to Patagonian destinations like Bariloche, Esquel and Río Gallegos.

CATAMARCA

Settled only in 1683, San Fernando del Valle de Catamarca has remained an economic backwater, but on major holidays attracts many visitors. Flanked by the Sierra del Colorado in the west and the Sierra Graciana in the east, it is 156 km north-east of La Rioja. Shady Plaza 25 de Mayo offers refuge from summer heat in an otherwise treeless city.

Information

The helpful Dirección Municipal de Turismo (☎ 32647), Virgen del Valle 951, is open on weekdays from 7 am to 1 pm and 2 to 8 pm, and on weekends from 8 am to noon and 3 to 8 pm. Around the corner on General Roca is the Dirección Provincial de Turismo.

Banco de la Nación is at San Martín 626, while Banco de Galicia has an ATM on Rivadavia between República and Esquiú. Correo Argentino is at San Martín 753. Telecom, Rivadavia 758, is slow at arranging international calls. Catamarca's telephone code is 0833.

Things to See

The neocolonial **Iglesia y Convento de San Francisco**, at Esquiú and Rivadavia, contains the cell of Fray Mamerto Esquiú, famous for vocal defence of the 1853 constitution. After being stolen and left on the roof years ago, a crystal box containing his heart now sits in a locked room.

Tedious presentation undermines outstanding materials in the **Museo Arqueológico Adán Quiroga**, on Sarmiento between Esquiú and Prado. Hours are weekdays 8 am to 1 pm and 2.30 to 8 pm, and weekends 8 am to noon. Opposite the plaza, the **Catedral** contains the Virgen del Valle, one of northern Argentina's most venerated images.

Special Events

On the Sunday after Easter, thousands of pilgrims honour the Virgen del Valle in the Fiesta de Nuestra Señora del Valle.

Places to Stay

Camping Catamarca's normally pleasant *Autocamping Municipal*, about four km from the city centre, gets heavy weekend and holiday use, and also has ferocious mosquitoes. Rates are US$6 per tent per day; take bus No 10 from Convento de San Francisco, on Esquiú, or from the bus terminal.

Casas de Familia, Residenciales and Hotels The tourist office keeps a list of casas de familia. Drab *Residencial Yunka Suma*, Vicario Segura 1255, is suitable for one night only at US$7 per person with shared bath. Friendly *Residencial Avenida* (☎ 22139), Avenida Güemes 754, is acceptable but not great value at US$15/23 with shared bath, US$19/27 with private bath. The architecturally drab but congenial *Sol Hotel* (☎ 30803), Salta 1142, is good value at US$20/28 with shared baths and kitchenettes, slightly more with private bath.

Places to Eat

In the gallery behind the Catedral, *Comedor El Peregrino* offers two courses (empanadas and pasta) for about US$4. At *Rancho Grande*, República 750, a plentiful parrillada for two with salad and wine costs US$15; at night there is folk music. *La Colonial*, República 574, is a good, moderately priced pizza and pasta place.

Logically enough, the *Sociedad Italiana* at Moreno 152 also specialises in pasta, as does *Trattoría Montecarlo*, on República opposite Plaza 25 de Mayo. The *Sociedad Española*, close to the tourist office at Virgen del Valle 725, has good seafood and traditional Spanish dishes.

Things to Buy

For hand-tied rugs, visit the Mercado Artesanal Permanente y Fábrica de Alfombras, Virgen del Valle 945, which also sells ponchos, blankets, jewellery, red onyx sculptures, musical instruments, hand-spun wool, and baskets.

Getting There & Away

Air Aerolíneas Argentinas (☎ 24460), Sarmiento 589, has morning flights to Aeroparque daily, except Sunday, with afternoon flights on Wednesday and Friday only.

Bus Catamarca's once-depressing Terminal de Omnibus (☎ 23415), Avenida Güemes 856, is undergoing a much-needed face-lift. Chevallier (☎ 30921) has two buses each evening to Buenos Aires (US$45, 16 hours), via Córdoba (US$16) and Rosario. Cacorba serves the same route.

La Estrella goes to Tucumán (4½ hours), Jujuy (9½ hours), Mendoza, and San Juan, while TAC goes to Córdoba, Tucumán and Buenos Aires. Libertador stops at Catamarca en route between Mendoza (nine hours), San Juan (seven hours), La Rioja (US$6.50, 2½ hours) and Tucumán. Andesmar has routes from the Bolivian border to Patagonia via Mendoza.

Cotil runs buses to the Sierras de Córdoba via La Rioja (US$6.50). Bosio serves Tucumán (US$10, six daily), Salta, La Rioja, San Juan, Mendoza and Santiago del Estero. Cotal goes to Santiago del Estero (US$12, five hours), Reconquista (US$35, 16 hours), Corrientes (US$45, 17 hours), Posadas (US$58, 22 hours), San Juan (US$18, nine hours), and Mendoza (US$22, 11 hours). Robledo goes on Tuesday and Friday to Patagonian destinations including Trelew (US$80) and Comodoro Rivadavia (US$122).

Patagonia

Patagonia is the enormous region beyond Buenos Aires province, south of the Río Colorado to the Straits of Magellan. Glaciers dot the mountainous interior of Río Negro and Neuquén provinces, which stretch all the way to the Atlantic. Santa Cruz province features the Moreno Glacier and the pinna-

cles of the FitzRoy range. Near the Andean divide, forests of southern beech, alerce and the distinctive pehuén (monkey puzzle tree) cover the slopes.

Patagonia's major economic institution is the sprawling sheep estancia, but large oilfields in Chubut, Neuquén and Tierra del Fuego keep Argentina self-sufficient in petroleum. The Andean national parks have encouraged a major tourism industry.

History

One theory credits Magellan's crew with the toponym Patagonia, after they encountered Tehuelche Indians whose large moccasins made their feet seem exceptionally large – in Spanish, *pata* means paw or foot. Bruce Chatwin, however, speculated that Magellan applied the term 'Patagon', from a fictional monster in a Spanish romance, to the Tehuelches.

Darwin dispelled some of the mystery surrounding the Tehuelches, but recognised that the arrival of whites meant the disappearance or subjugation of the Indian. Recording a massacre by Argentine soldiers, he observed that 'Great as it is, in another half century I think there will not be a wild Indian in the Pampas north of Río Negro'.

In 1865 Welsh colonists settled peaceably in eastern Chubut, but from 1879 General Julio A Roca carried out the Conquista del Desierto, a ruthless war of extermination against the indigenes. Soon more than half a million cattle and sheep grazed large estancias on former Indian lands in northern Patagonia. In a few favoured zones, like the Río Negro valley near Neuquén, irrigated agriculture and the arrival of the railway brought colonisation and prosperity.

CARMEN DE PATAGONES

Founded in 1799, Carmen is really the southernmost city in Buenos Aires province and an economic satellite of the larger city of Viedma, capital of Río Negro province. The municipal Oficina de Turismo, across from Plaza 7 de Marzo, provides a good town map. Carmen's telephone code is 0920, the same as Viedma's.

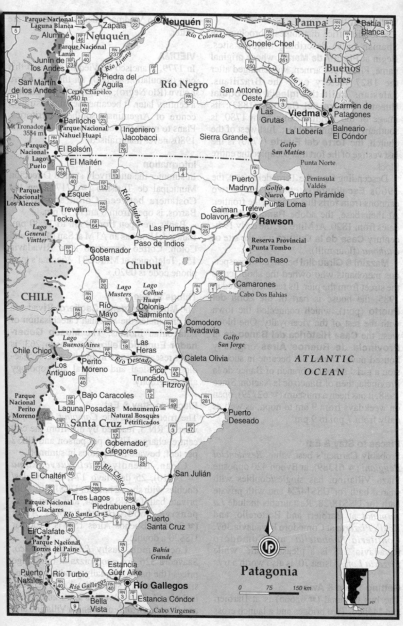

Patagonia

0   75   150 km

Walking Tour

The tourist office distributes a brochure (in Spanish only) describing historic sites. Begin at **Plaza 7 de Marzo**, whose original name, Plaza del Carmen, was changed after the 1827 victory over the Brazilians. Salesians built the **Iglesia Parroquial Nuestra Señora del Carmen** (1883); its image of the Virgin, dating from 1780, is southern Argentina's oldest. Just west of the church, the **Torre del Fuerte** (1780) is the last vestige of the fort that occupied the entire block.

Descending from the Torre del Fuerte, the 1960s **Escalinata** (steps) displays two cannons from forts that guarded the frontier. At their base, the adobe **Rancho de Rial** dates from 1820. At Mitre 27, the early 19th-century **Casa de la Cultura** was the site of a *tahona* (flour mill).

Mazzini & Giraudini belonged to prosperous merchants who owned the shop across the street from the pier. Its façade restored in 1985, the house is part of the **Zona del Puerto** (port), which connected the town with the rest of the viceroyalty. One block west, the **Casa Histórica del Banco de la Provincia de Buenos Aires** originally housed naval stores, but became in succession a girls' school, a branch of Banco de la Provincia, then of Banco de la Nación. Since 1988, it has been a museum (☎ 62729), open on weekdays from 9 am to noon, as well as daily from 7 pm to 9 pm.

Places to Stay & Eat

Probably Carmen's best value, *Residencial Reggiani* (☎ 61389), at Bynon 420 opposite Plaza Villarino, has singles/doubles with shared bath for US$14/24 and with private bath for US$18/28. Restaurants include *La Terminal* at Barbieri and Bertorello, and *Koki's Pizzería* at Comodoro Rivadavia 367. *Confitería Sabbatella* at Comodoro Rivadavia 218 is a pleasant café, while *Pizzería Loft*, Alsina 70, is also worth a try.

Getting There & Away

The bus terminal (☎ 62666) is at Barbieri and Méjico. Two bridges and a launch cross the river to Viedma, where connections are better.

VIEDMA

In 1779, Francisco de Viedma founded this city (population 40,000) on the Río Curru Leuvu (Río Negro), 30 km from the Atlantic; a century later, it became the administrative centre of Argentina's southern territories. Plans to move the federal capital here in the 1980s never materialised.

Information

In summer the attentively staffed Dirección Municipal de Turismo (☎ 27171), on the Costanera between Colón and Alvaro Barros, is open from 8 am to 10 pm.

Banks are open from 8 am to 12.30 pm. Banco del Sud has an ATM at San Martín and Colón. Correo Argentino is at Rivadavia 151, Telefónica at Mitre 531. Viedma's telephone code is 0920.

Things to See

The **Museo Cardenal Cagliero**, Rivadavia 34, chronicles the Salesian catechisation of Patagonian Indians. The **Museo Gobernador Eugenio Tello**, San Martín 263, is also a research centre in architecture, archaeology, physical and cultural anthropology and geography.

Places to Stay & Eat

The friendly riverside *Camping Municipal* west of RN 3, reached by bus from the city centre, charges US$4 per person and US$2 per tent; beware mosquitoes in summer.

Clean, friendly *Hotel Nuevo Roma* (☎ 24510), 25 de Mayo 174, has singles/doubles with shared bath for US$12/15, with private bath for US$17/24, and good, inexpensive food. *Hotel Buenos Aires* (☎ 24351), Buenos Aires 153, is basic for US$20 a double.

Locals mob flashy *Pizzería Acrílico*, Saavedra 326, for good pizza at mid-range prices (the pasta is equally good but expensive by Argentine standards). Local parrillas include *El Tío* at Avenida Zatti and Colón and *Rancho Grande* at Avenida Villarino and

Colón. *Simbiosis* at Mitre 573 and *Munich* at Buenos Aires 169 have more varied menus.

Getting There & Away

Air Austral (☎ 22018), Yrigoyen 211, flies daily except Saturday to Buenos Aires (US$151) at 7 pm. LADE (☎ 24420), Saavedra 403, and Sapse (☎ 21330), San Martín 57, fly to Buenos Aires and Patagonian destinations.

Bus Viedma's new Terminal de Omnibus is south of the centre, at Guido 1580. La Puntual/El Cóndor (☎ 22748) has daily service north to Buenos Aires (US$62, 14 hours) and south along RN 3, and to Bariloche (US$52, 19 hours). Don Otto (☎ 25952) reaches Patagonian destinations along RN 3 as far south as Río Gallegos.

Central Argentino stops in Viedma en route between Rosario and Comodoro Rivadavia, while TUS/TUP (☎ 22748) links Viedma with Santa Fe and Córdoba. El Valle (☎ 22748) ascends the Río Negro valley to Neuquén and Bariloche, while Ticsa (☎ 21385) goes to Santa Rosa (La Pampa), San Luis and San Juan.

Train Sefepa runs northbound passenger trains on the Ferrocarril Roca (☎ 22130): on Tuesday night they go to Bahía Blanca only (eight hours); and on Friday and Monday evenings, to Buenos Aires (20 hours). Southbound trains to Bariloche (10 hours) leave on Sunday and Wednesday evenings, and Thursday and Saturday afternoons.

BARILOCHE

In San Carlos de Bariloche, 460 km southwest of Neuquén on Lago Nahuel Huapi, architect Ezequiel Bustillo adapted Middle European styles into an attractive urban plan, but the past decade's deplorable orgy of construction has overwhelmed Bustillo's efforts and, consequently, destroyed Bariloche's perceived exclusivity. The silver lining is that prices have remained reasonable and have even fallen in recent years. The influx of visitors from South America's largest

country has led to the ironic nickname 'Brasiloche'.

At an altitude of 770 metres, the city has a regular grid between the Río Ñireco and Bustillo's Centro Cívico; north-south streets rise steeply from the lake. The major commercial zone is Avenida Bartolomé Mitre.

Information

The Secretaría Municipal de Turismo (☎ 23022) is on the south side of the Centro Cívico, at the west end of Avenida Bartolomé Mitre. It opens from 8.30 am to 9 pm daily. The Intendencia de Parques Nacionales (☎ 23111), San Martín 24, and the Club Andino Bariloche (☎ 22266), 20 de Febrero 30, are good sources of information on Parque Nacional Nahuel Huapi.

Money Cambio Olano, Quaglia 238, changes travellers' cheques (beware the 15% commission). ATMs are abundant.

Post & Communications Correo Argentino is at the Centro Cívico. Just outside the tourist office are direct lines to the USA, France and several other countries for reverse-charge and credit-card calls. The largest of several locutorios is at Bariloche Center, San Martín and Panozzi. Bariloche's telephone code is 0944.

Chilean Consulate Open on weekdays from 9 am to 2 pm, the Chilean Consulate (☎ 23050) is at Juan Manuel de Rosas 187.

Centro Cívico

Recent construction has erased much of Bariloche's charm, but Bustillo's log-and-stone public buildings still merit a visit. Lifelike stuffed animals, well-prepared archaeological and ethnographic materials, and critically enlightening historical evaluations on topics like Mapuche resistance to the Conquista del Desierto and Bariloche's urban development make the diverse, recently remodelled **Museo de la Patagonia** one of the country's best. It has a specialised library and a bookshop.

Admission costs US$2.50. Opening hours

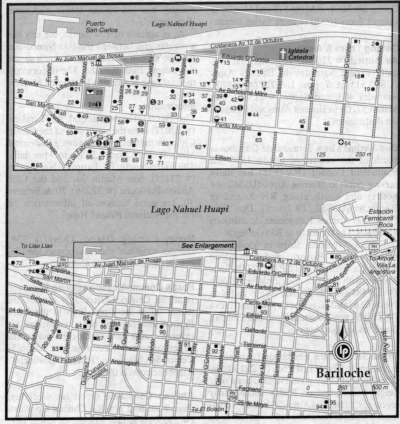

are Monday 10 am to 1 pm, Tuesday to Friday 10 am to 12.30 pm and 2 to 7 pm, and Saturday 10 am to 1 pm.

Skiing

Gran Catedral, the largest and most popular area, amalgamates two formerly separate areas, Cerro Catedral and Lado Bueno, so skiers can buy one ticket valid for lifts in both areas. Lift passes start at US$32 per day for adults, but one-week passes entail substantial savings. Rental equipment is available both at Gran Catedral and in Bariloche, but good equipment is costly.

Places to Stay

The municipal tourist office's computer tracks current prices of everything from camping grounds and private houses to five-star hotels. Reasonable lodging is available even in the high season.

Camping The nearest organised camping area is *La Selva Negra* (☎ 41013), three km west of town on the Llao Llao road. Fees are US$8 per site.

Hostels Bus Nos 10, 20 and 21 reach popular *Albergue Alaska* (☎ 61564), 7.5 km outside town on the Llao Llao road, which

PLACES TO STAY		
1	Hotel Pilmayquén	
11	Hostería Posada del Sol	
18	Residencial Tito	
45	Albergue Los Andes	
46	Hospedaje El Mirador	
57	Residencial Nogaré	
65	Hotel Campana	
68	Residencial Lo de Gianni	
70	Casa de Familia Ferreyra	
80	Casa de Familia Heydée	
82	Casa de Familia Pirker	
83	Casa de Familia Arko	
84	Casa de Familia Lamuniére	
85	Residencial Martín	
87	Residencial San Fernando	
89	Hostería del Inca	
91	Casa de Familia Vallejo	
92	Residencial Torres	
94	Hospedaje Monte Grande	

PLACES TO EAT		
3	Helados Bari	
7	El Viejo Munich	
12	Dino's	
13	Pin 9	
14	Familia Weiss	
15	Confitería Copos	
16	Pizzería Vogue	
17	El Mundo de la Pizza	
26	Cocodrilos	
27	Restaurant Lennon	
28	La Andinita	
29	Abuela Goye	
30	La Alpina	
34	El Rincón	

36	Restaurant Jauja
51	La Esquina de las Flores
60	Rigoletto, El Boliche de Alberto 2
62	La Vizcacha
69	Ła Andina
71	Parrilla 1810
79	Bagdad Café

OTHER	
2	ACA
4	Migraciones
5	Museo de la Patagonia
6	Carro's
8	Italian Consulate
9	LAPA
10	TAN
19	Honda Diéguez
20	AI
21	Avis
22	Bariloche Center
23	Post Office
24	Secretaría Municipal de Turismo
25	Baruzzi
31	Cambio Olano
32	Aerolíneas Argentinas, LADE
33	Paseo de los Artesanos
35	Cumbres Patagonia, Argentoura Travel
37	Expediciones Náuticas
38	Laverap
39	Hiver Turismo (Amex)
40	Spanish Consulate
41	Local Bus Station
42	Airport Minibuses, Catedral Turismo
43	Ente Provincial del Turismo

44	Sapse
47	Catedral
48	Tanguería, Gallery
49	Mochilas Guarderías, Rafting Adventure
50	Lavadero Huemul
52	Intendencia de Parques Nacionales
53	Centro de Información Turística (Datos Andinos Patagónicos)
54	Club Andino Bariloche
55	Museo Arquitectónico
56	Cine Arrayanes
58	Banco de Galicia
59	Dollar Rent-A-Car
61	SCUM
63	Budget
64	Hospital Zonal
66	Asociación Argentina de Guías de Montaña
67	Solo Bici
72	Grisú
73	Cerebro
74	Rockett
75	Mercado Artesanal
76	Museo Ictícola, Club de Caza y Pesca
77	Bikeway
78	German Consulate
81	Pub Moritz
82	Austrian Consulate
86	Baratta e Hijos
88	Safaris Acuáicos
90	Bariloche Mountain Bike
93	Pochi
95	Ramírez (Mountain Bikes)

costs US$10 per person with kitchen and laundry facilities, rents mountain bikes, and arranges tours and ski transfers. The more central *Albergue Los Andes* (☎ 22222), Moreno 594, charges US$13 but lacks a kitchen.

Casas de Familia Bariloche's best value places start around US$10 per person and include that of the Vallejos at Emilio Frey 635, which has hot showers and cooking facilities. The Ferreyra family (☎ 22556),

Elflein 163, is a more central possibility. Woodsy Barrio Belgrano has several slightly dearer choices, including Señora Marianne Pirker (☎ 24873), at 24 de Septiembre 230, and Señora Rosa Arko (☎ 23109), at Güemes 691.

Residenciales, Hosterías & Hotels Recommended *Hostería del Inca* (☎ 22644), Gallardo 252, has singles/doubles for US$10/20. For around US$12 per person, among the better value options in regular accommodation are *Residencial Lo de Gianni* (☎ 33059), at Elflein 49 and *Residencial San Fernando* (☎ 25150), at 20 de Febrero 664. Convenient *Hostería Posada del Sol* (☎ 23011), Villegas 148, costs US$14 with breakfast. Friendly *Hotel Campana* (☎ 22162), Belgrano 165, is comparably priced.

Places to Eat

Some places, like *Familia Weiss* at Palacios 167, specialise in regional specialities like smoked game and fish. Buenos Aires' landmark vegetarian restaurant *La Esquina de Las Flores* recently opened a branch at 20 de Febrero and Juramento.

French-Italian *Rigoletto*, Villegas 363, emphasises pasta, lomo and trout. *La Vizcacha*, Rolando 279, is one of the country's best and most reasonable parrillas. *La Andina*, Elflein 95, has drawn praise for good food, large portions and moderate prices. Recommended *El Rincón*, Villegas 216, features parrillada, trout and wild game, but is not cheap.

Cocodrilos, Mitre 5, serves a very fine, reasonably priced fugazzeta, but their other pizza is dearer. Try also *La Andinita*, Mitre 56 (excellent fugazzeta), or *El Mundo de la Pizza* at Mitre 370.

La Alpina, Moreno 98, is a good and popular confitería. *Copos*, Mitre 392, has excellent coffee and hot chocolate, and fresh croissants at reasonable prices. Befitting its name, *El Viejo Munich*, Mitre 102, has excellent draught beer with complimentary peanuts.

Things to Buy

Del Turista and Fenoglio, facing each other on Mitre, are chocolate supermarkets and are also good places for a stand-up cup of coffee, hot chocolate or dessert. Local artisans display their wares in wool, wood, leather and other media at the Paseo de los Artesanos, at Villegas and Perito Moreno.

Getting There & Away

Air Aerolíneas Argentinas (☎ 23091, 22425) and LADE (☎ 23562) are both at Mitre 199.

Aerolíneas has 10 flights weekly to Buenos Aires (US$244), while LADE flies sporadically to various Patagonian destinations. TAN (☎ 27889), Villegas 144, and Sapse (☎ 28257), Palacios 266, also fly to Patagonian destinations, while LAPA (☎ 23714), Villegas 137, flies daily except Thursday and Saturday to Buenos Aires (US$149).

Bus Bariloche now uses the old train station, Estación Ferrocarril Roca, as its Terminal Ferroviario (☎ 26999), but some companies continue to have offices in the city centre. Many companies go to Buenos Aires (22 hours) for prices ranging from US$55 to US$72.

Tirsa goes on Tuesday and Sunday to Rosario (US$83, 24 hours), while TUS serves Córdoba five times weekly (US$105, 22 hours). Don Otto goes daily to El Bolsón (US$10), Esquel (US$21) and Comodoro Rivadavia (US$68, 14 hours), with connections to Río Gallegos (US$108; one correspondent calls the 28-hour plus voyage 'agonising'). Don Otto also has service to Trelew (US$51) and Puerto Madryn (US$55). Several other companies go to El Bolsón.

Mercedes runs daily buses to Neuquén (US$30, seven hours) and, along with El Rápido, to Necochea (US$73), Miramar (US$80) and Mar del Plata (US$83). Vía Bariloche has additional daily long-distance services to Buenos Aires (US$95), connecting to Posadas (US$135) and Puerto Iguazú (US$150). Andesmar runs extensive services north towards the Bolivian border, including Mendoza (US$61), San Juan (US$69), La Rioja (US$80), Catamarca (US$86), Tucumán (US$96), Salta (US$109), and Jujuy (US$110). TAC runs three buses weekly to Mendoza (US$68, 22 hours), with connections to Córdoba (US$88).

Turismo Algarrobal serves Villa La Angostura, on the north side of Lago Nahuel Huapi (US$6.50, two hours). La Puntual connects Bariloche with Viedma (US$52, 16 hours), stopping en route at Ingeniero Jacobacci (US$14) for connections with the narrow gauge railway to Esquel. Ko-Ko has buses to Junín de los Andes (US$19) and San Martín de los Andes (US$22), some via the longer, paved La Rinconada (RN 40) route rather than the more scenic Siete Lagos route.

Several companies connect Bariloche with Osorno and Puerto Montt, Chile, including Mercedes, Bus Norte, TAS Choapa, and Cruz del Sur. Fares vary between US$18 and US$25.

Bus & Boat Catedral Turismo (☎ 25443), Bartolomé Mitre 399, arranges the bus-boat combination over the Andes to Puerto Montt for US$90; it leaves on weekdays at 9 am.

Train Sefepa (Servicio Ferrocarril Patagónico, ☎ 23172) leaves from the Estación Ferrocarril Roca across the Río Ñireco along RN 237. On Monday afternoon, the *tren tradicional* (no sleepers) does the 36-hour trip to Constitución, Buenos Aires; On Friday evening it goes only as far as Viedma. The more comfortable *tren español* leaves on Friday afternoon for Constitución, while its Tuesday evening service goes only to Bahía Blanca. Fares to Constitución range from US$53 (primera) to US$98 (dormitorio).

Getting Around

To/From the Airport Sapse and TAN run their own airport minibuses, while LADE, LAPA and Aerolíneas use Transporte Alí, which leaves Aerolíneas' offices in the city centre 1½ hours before each flight. Fares are US$3.

Bus From the corner of Moreno and Rolando, Codao and Micro Omnibus 3 de Mayo run hourly buses to Cerro Catedral (US$2.40 one way). In summer 3 de Mayo goes four times daily to Lago Mascardi; its No 50 bus goes to Lago Gutiérrez every 30 minutes, while in summer its Línea Mascardi goes to Villa Mascardi and Los Rápidos/Lago Los Moscos four times daily. Its Línea El Manso goes twice daily to Río Villegas and El Manso, on the south-western

border of the Parque Nacional Nahuel Huapi.

From 6 am to midnight, bus No 20 leaves every 20 minutes to Llao Llao and Puerto Pañuelo. No 10 also goes to Llao Llao via Colonia Suiza, seven times daily, allowing you to do the Circuito Chico (see Parque Nacional Nahuel Huapi, below) on public transport.

Car Rental agencies include Avis (☎ 25371), at Libertad 124, AI (☎ 26420), at San Martín 235, and Budget (☎ 22482), at Moreno 461.

Bicycle A number of places rent mountain bikes, usually including gloves and helmet, for about US$20 per day. Try Bariloche Mountain Bike at Gallardo 375, Solo Bici (☎ 23574), at Neumeyer 40, or Honda Diéguez (☎ 28614), at Otto Goedecke 169.

PARQUE NACIONAL NAHUEL HUAPI

Lago Nahuel Huapi, a glacial relic over 100 km long, attracts so many visitors that its natural attributes are at risk, though native and introduced fish species still offer excellent sport. To the west, 3554-metre Tronador marks the Andean crest and the Chilean border. Humid Valdivian forest covers the lower slopes, while summer wild flowers blanket alpine meadows.

Things to See & Do

Travel agencies offer tours of the **Circuito Chico** loop between Bariloche and Llao Llao, but public transport is cheaper and more flexible. En route, **Cerro Campanario's** chair lift (US$7) offers panoramic views, while Llao Llao's **Puerto Pañuelo** is the departure point for the boat-bus excursion to Chile.

From Llao Llao, continue to **Colonia Suiza**, whose modest confitería has excellent pastries. The road passes the trailhead to 2075-metre **Cerro López** (a four-hour climb) while returning to Bariloche. **Cerro Otto** (1405 metres) is an eight-km walk on a gravel road west from Bariloche, but a gondola (US$15) also goes to the summit.

At **Cerro Catedral** (2400 metres), a ski

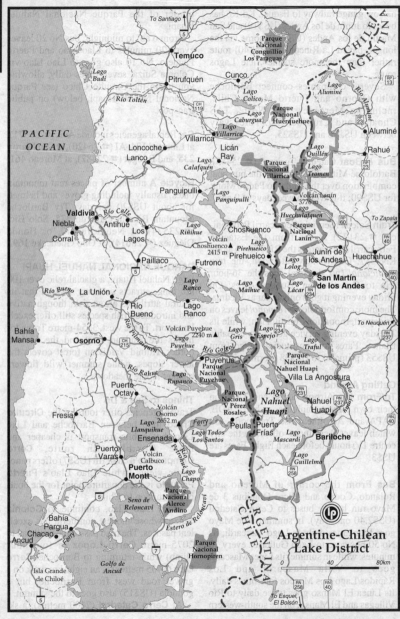

PACIFIC
OCEAN

Temuco

Pitrufquén

Cunco

Parque
Nacional
Conguillio
Los Paraguas

Lago
Budi

Río Toltén

CH
119

Lago
Colico

Lago
Caburgua

Lago
Villarrica

Parque
Nacional
Huerquehue

Loncoche

Villarrica

Lican
Ray

Lanco

Parque
Nacional
Villarrica

Lago
Calafquén

Lago
Quillén

Lago
Alumine

RP
13

Aluminé

Rahué

RP
23

Panguipulli

Lago
Panguipulli

Parque
Nacional
Lanin

Volcán Lanín
3776 m

Lago
Tromen

Lago
Huechulafquen

RP
60

To Zapala

Valdivia

Niebla

Antihue

Los
Lagos

Río Calle

Lago
Riñihue

Choshuenco

Lago
Pirehueico

Pirehueico

Parque
Nacional
Lanin

RN
40

Corral

Volcán
Choshuenco
2415 m

Junin de
los Andes

Huechahue

Paillaco

Futrono

Lago
Ranco

Lago
Maihue

Lago
Lolog

Lago
Lácar

**San Martin
de los Andes**

RN
234

To Neuquén

La Unión

Río Bueno

Río
Bueno

Lago
Ranco

Volcán Puyehue
2240 m

Lago
Gris

Lago
Puyehue

Río Golgol

Lago
Espejo

RN
234

Lago
Traful

RN
237

Osorno

CH
215

Río Pilmaiquén

Lago
Rupanco

Puyehue
Parque
Nacional
Puyehue

Parque
Nacional
Nahuel Huapi

Villa La Angostura

Bahía
Mansa

Río Rahue

Puerto
Octay

Volcán
Osorno
2652 m

Parque
Nacional
V Pérez
Rosales

**Lago
Nahuel
Huapi**

RN
231

Nahuel
Huapi

RN
237

Fresia

Lago
Llanquihue

Ensenada

Ferry

Peulla

Puerto
Frías

Lago
Mascardi

Bariloche

RN
40

Puerto
Varas

Volcán
Calbuco

Lago Todos
Los Santos

Lago
Guillelma

Río Petrohué

Lago
Chapo

Parque
Nacional
Alerce
Andino

RN
258

**Puerto
Montt**

Bahía
Pargua

Chacao

Ancud

Seno de
Reloncaví

Estero de Reloncaví

Ferry

Golfo de
Ancud

Parque
Nacional
Hornopiren

**Argentine-Chilean
Lake District**

0   40   80km

Isla Grande
de Chiloé

5

ARGENTINA
CHILE

To Esquel,
El Bolsón

RN
258

RN
40

centre 20 km west of Bariloche, chair lifts and a large cable car climb to a restaurant/confitería with excellent panoramas (US$8). Several trails begin here, including one to the Club Andino's Refugio Frey.

For US$12 per person, the Club Andino Bariloche organises transport to Pampa Linda and **Monte Tronador** daily at 9 am, returning at 5 pm; some have found the trip dusty and unpleasant.

Activities

Fishing For details on licences, regulations and rental equipment, contact the Club de Caza y Pesca (☎ 22403), at Costanera 12 de Octubre and Onelli, Bariloche.

White-Water Rafting Several Bariloche companies arrange rafting on the Río Manso, a Class 3 descent with enough rapids to be interesting, for about US$65. Among them are Expediciones Náuticas (☎ 27502), at Rolando 268, Local 4; Safaris Acuáticos (☎ 32799), at Morales 564 and Rafting Adventure (☎ 32928), Avenida San Martín 82, 2nd floor.

Places to Stay

Besides camping grounds near Bariloche, there are sites at Lago Mascardi, Lago Los Moscos, Lago Roca, Lago Guillelmo and Pampa Linda. With permission from rangers, free camping is possible in certain areas. Alpine *refugios* charge US$7 per night, US$2 for day use, and US$2 extra for kitchen privileges.

EL BOLSON

In south-western Río Negro, 130 km from Bariloche, rows of poplars shelter chacras devoted to hops, soft fruits like raspberries, and orchard crops like cherries and apples. El Bolsón's self-proclaimed status as a 'non-nuclear zone' and 'ecological municipality' is a pleasant relief from Bariloche's commercialism. Most services are on Avenida San Martín, which runs along the landmark, semi-oval Plaza Pagano.

Information

The Dirección Municipal de Turismo (☎ & fax 92604), at the north end of Plaza Pagano, is open in summer daily from 9 am to 9.30 am, and the rest of the year from 9 am to 6 pm.

Neither Banco Nación nor Banco de la Provincia, both near Plaza Pagano, has an ATM. Correo Argentino is at Avenida San Martín 2608. The Cooperativa Telefónica is at the south end of Plaza Pagano; El Bolsón's telephone code is 0944, the same as Bariloche's.

Feria Artesanal

On Thursday and Saturday in summer, and on Saturday only the rest of the year, local artisans offer their wares at the south end of the Plaza Pagano from 10 am to 2 pm. Food stalls sell delicacies like home-made empanadas and sausages, Belgian waffles with fresh raspberries, and locally brewed beer.

Places to Stay

For US$4 per person, riverside *Camping del Sol*, at the west end of Avenida Castelli, has hot showers and a small confitería. Hourly buses go to *Albergue El Pueblito*, an excellent facility in Barrio Luján, about four km north of town. Rates are US$8 with hostel card, US$9 without.

The tourist office doesn't approve of informal *Hospedaje Los Amigos*, on Islas Malvinas at the east end of Balcarce, which charges about US$6 per person; with a tent you can camp in the garden for a bit less. For US$10 per person with shared bath, try *Hospedaje Piltriquitrón* at Saavedra 2729 or *Hospedaje Unelén* (☎ 92729), at Azcuénaga 350. A recent reader's recommendation is *Residencial Salinas*, Roca 641, where US$10 rooms include a private log fire.

Places to Eat

The periodic *Feria Artesanal* (see separate entry above) is the best value. *Huilén*, San Martín 2524, has superb breakfasts for just US$2.50. *Cerro Lindo*, Avenida San Martín 2526, has large, tasty pizzas, good music, and excellent, friendly service.

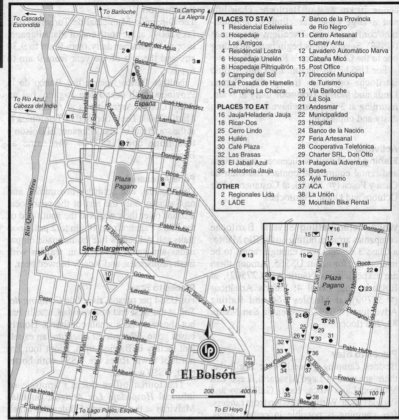

For a splurge, the varied menu at *Jauja*, Avenida San Martín 2867, is among the best value places in Argentina; save room for the astoundingly good home-made, fruit-flavoured ice cream next door at *Heladería Jauja*. *Las Brasas*, at Sarmiento and Hube, is a superb choice for beef.

Getting There & Away
Air LADE (☎ 92206), Castello 3253, flies infrequently to Chapelco (US$25), Comodoro Rivadavia (US$64) and other Patagonian destinations. Aylé Turismo (☎ 92329), in the Galería del Cerro opposite the ACA station on San Martín, is the agent for Sapse, which flies occasionally to Bariloche (US$23), Viedma (US$123) and Buenos Aires (US$150).

Bus Several companies go to Bariloche (US$10, three hours), including Andesmar at Sarmiento 2678, Vía Bariloche at Roca 357, La Unión at San Martín and Berutti, Don Otto and Charter SRL at San Martín 2536, and Mercedes on Castelli near San Martín. Andesmar, Mercedes and Don Otto go to Esquel (US$16, three hours), with Don Otto continuing to Comodoro Rivadavia. Mercedes also serves El Maitén, Neuquén and Buenos Aires, but Andesmar has the most extensive northbound connections. El Sureño, Sarmiento 2678, goes to Buenos Aires nightly (US$75, 26 hours).

Zabala Daniel, Perito Moreno 2377, has the only service to Esquel via Parque Nacional Los Alerces, daily at 11 am and 5 pm in summer (some have complained about seat availability on open tickets to continue to Esquel).

AROUND EL BOLSON

On a ridge eight km west of town, the metamorphic **Cabeza del Indio** formation resembles a profile of the 'noble savage'. The trail, traversing a narrow ledge, gives superb views of the Río Azul and Lago Puelo. Walk, hitch or take a taxi from El Bolsón to the trailhead.

The granitic ridge of 2260-metre **Cerro Piltriquitrón** dominates the landscape east of Bolsón. From the 1000-metre level, reached by road (about US$15 by taxi, or an 11-km walk), an hour's walk leads to *Refugio Piltriquitrón* (☎ 92024; US$7 per person, meals extra; sleeping bag essential). Another tiring two hours walk earns the summit.

Only 15 km south of El Bolsón, the windy azure waters of **Parque Nacional Lago Puelo** are suitable for water sports and camping (some sites are free). There are regular buses, but reduced Sunday services.

NEUQUEN

At the confluence of the Limay and Neuquén rivers, 265 metres above sea level, this provincial capital (population 300,000) is an agricultural service centre for the Río Negro valley. East-west RN 22 is the main highway through town, while the main north-south thoroughfare is Avenida Argentina (Avenida Olascoaga beyond the train station).

Information

The provincial Subsecretaría de Turismo (☎ 24089) is at Félix San Martín 182, three blocks south of the train station. Open on weekdays from 7 am to 9 pm, and on weekends from 8 am to 9 pm, it has excellent data on the entire province.

Neuquén has two cambios: Olano at JB Justo and Yrigoyen, and Pullman at Ministro Alcorta 144, but several banks have ATMs. Correo Argentino is at Rivadavia and Santa Fe. Telefónica is on Alberdi, between Santa Fe and Córdoba; the telephone code is 099.

Things to See

The **Sala de Arte Emilio Saraco**, in the old cargo terminal at the railway station, has current art exhibits and is well worth a look if you're killing time waiting for a bus connection. **Juntarte en el Andén**, an outdoors art space across the tracks at the former passenger terminal, is also the site of the **Sala Teatral Alicia F Reyes**, a performing arts venue.

Places to Stay & Eat

Dingy *Residencial Imperio* (☎ 22488), Yrigoyen 65, charges US$12/18 for a single/double, while basic *Hotel Continental* (☎ 23757), Perito Moreno 90, has rooms with private bath for US$15/20. *Residencial Inglés* (☎ 22252), Félix San Martín 534 costs US$15/25. Mid-range accommodation starts around US$22/32 at *Residencial Neuquén* (☎ 22403), Roca 109.

Confiterías along Avenida Argentina are pleasant for breakfast and morning coffee. *El Plato*, Alberdi 158, has good US$5 lunch specials. *Franz y Peppone*, at 9 de Julio and Belgrano, is an unusual combination of Italian and German cuisine. *Las Tres Marías*, Alberdi 126, deserves special mention for its exceptionally diverse menu at moderate prices, in addition to cheap daily specials. *La Nonna Franchesca*, 9 de Julio 56, has attractive decor in addition to outstanding pasta and French cuisine.

Getting There & Away

Air Austral (☎ 22409), Avenida Argentina 363, flies to Buenos Aires (US$178) three times daily except on Saturday, when it goes twice. LAPA (☎ 24540), Diagonal Alvear 135, flies on weekday afternoons to Aeroparque (US$99). Chilean carrier Ladeco

(☎ 73954), Miguel Muñoz 344, 1st floor, flies on Monday and Friday to Temuco and Santiago.

LADE (☎ 22453), Almirante Brown 163, TAN (☎ 23076), 25 de Mayo 180, and Kaikén Líneas Aéreas (☎ 47-1333), Avenida Argentina 327, fly to mostly Patagonian destinations but also serve Mendoza and Córdoba.

Bus Neuquén's Terminal de Omnibus (☎ 24903) is at Bartolomé Mitre 147. El Petróleo and El Valle are the major provincial carriers, with regular services to Zapala (US$9, three hours), Junín de los Andes (US$28, six hours), and San Martín de los Andes (US$30, seven hours).

El Valle, Mercedes and Vía Bariloche all serve Bariloche (US$30, seven hours). Many companies go to Buenos Aires (US$45, 15 hours), while TUS/TUP go daily to Córdoba (US$72, 17 hours) and also to San Martín de los Andes and Bariloche.

Alto Valle and TAC both go to Mendoza (US$45, 12 hours); Alto Valle also goes to Esquel (US$51, 12 hours), Córdoba and Paraná. Empresa del Sur y Media Agua also goes to the Cuyo provinces.

Andesmar has the most extensive nationwide routes, from Jujuy (US$96) in the north to the Patagonian coastal destinations of Puerto Madryn (US$39, 10 hours), Trelew (US$42, 11 hours), and Río Gallegos (US$111, 28 hours). Don Otto also serves the far south.

Andesmar also crosses the Andes to the Chilean cities of Osorno (US$45), Valdivia (US$46), Temuco (US$49) and Santiago (US$58). La Unión del Sud and Empresa San Martín use the scenic Tromen pass route to Villarica and Temuco. Igi-Llaima also has Chilean services.

JUNIN DE LOS ANDES

Neuquén's 'trout capital', a modest livestock centre (population 8000) on the Río Chimehuín, is 41 km north of San Martín de los Andes, and has better access to many parts of Parque Nacional Lanín. The enthusiastic Secretaría Municipal de Turismo

(☎ 91160) is at Padre Milanesio 596, opposite Plaza San Martín. Opening hours are 7 am to 9.40 pm daily; fishing permits are available here.

Places to Stay & Eat

The riverside *Camping Club Caza y Pesca* (☎ 91296), three blocks east of the plaza, has all facilities for US$5 per person per day, plus a one-time US$5 tent charge. *Residencial Marisa* (☎ 91175), Blvd Rosas 360, charges US$20/25 for a single/double with private bath. At *Residencial El Ceubo* (☎ 91182), Lamadrid 409, a double costs US$30.

The varied main courses at *Ruca Hueney*, Padre Milanesio 641, range from US$6 to US$12. *Roble Bar*, Ginés Ponte 331, is Junín's main pizzería, with baked empanadas and sandwiches in addition. *Rotisería Tandil*, Coronel Suárez 431, has superb takeaway empanadas.

Getting There & Away

Air Aeropuerto Chapelco is midway between Junín and San Martín de los Andes; for flight details, see the San Martín section.

Bus Bus services from the terminal, at Olavarría and Félix San Martín, closely resemble those from San Martín de los Andes (see below).

SAN MARTIN DE LOS ANDES

San Martín (altitude 642 metres), on Lago Lácar, retains some of the charm that once attracted people to Bariloche, but burgeoning hotels, spreading restaurants and insidious timeshares are transforming it into a costly tourist trap. At the Centro Cívico, San Martín and Rosas, the well-organised Secretaría Municipal de Turismo (☎ 27347) is open daily from 7 am to 10 pm.

The only official cambio is Andina Internacional at Capitán Drury 876, but Banco de la Provincia has an ATM at Avenida San Martín 899. Correo Argentino is at the Centro Cívico. The Cooperativa Telefónica is at Capitán Drury 761; San Martín's telephone code is 0972.

Skiing

Cerro Chapelco's Centro de Deportes Invernales (☎ 27460), 20 km south-east of San Martín, is one of Argentina's principal winter sports centres. Rental equipment is available on site as well as in town.

Places to Stay & Eat

On the eastern outskirts of town, the spacious *Camping ACA* (☎ 27332) charges US$5 per person. San Martín's *Albergue Juvenil*, 3 de Caballería 1164, charges US$10 per person but lacks kitchen facilities.

Conventional bottom-end accommodation starts around US$20/30 for a single/ double with private bath at *Residencial Los Pinos* (☎ 27207), Almirante Brown 420, just outside the busy centre. Since its remodelling, *Residencial Villalago* (☎ 27454), Villegas 717, has risen to US$35 for a double without breakfast.

Stick with basics like ham and cheese at the friendly, informal *La Creperie*, San Martín 820, which fills dessert crêpes with sugary preserves rather than fresh fruit. *Rotisería Alemana*, San Martín 985, has a US$4 lunch menu, while *Rotisería Viviana*, San Martín 489, has cheap but excellent baked empanadas; both are excellent choices for takeaway food.

Locals mob *Piscis*, an outstanding mid-price parrilla at Villegas and Mariano Moreno, and the comparable *Sayhueque*, Rivadavia 825.

Getting There & Away

Air Austral (☎ 27003), Avenida San Martín 890, flies four times weekly to Esquel (US$71) and Buenos Aires (US$236). LADE (☎ 27672), Avenida San Martín 915, and TAN (☎ 27872), Belgrano 760, fly to Patagonian destinations.

Bus The Terminal de Omnibus (☎ 27044) is at Villegas and Juez del Valle. Regional carrier El Petróleo goes to Junín de los Andes and the Río Negro valley and Neuquén (US$22), and to the Chilean border at Pirehueico (US$5.50). Transportes Ko Ko goes to Villa la Angostura (US$13, three

hours) and to Bariloche (US$22, 5½ hours). El Valle, La Estrella and Chevallier go to Buenos Aires (US$70, 23 hours). TAC goes to Mendoza on Sunday. TUS goes to Córdoba on Monday and Thursday mornings (US$94).

Buses JAC has four weekly departures for the Chilean destinations of Pucón, Villarica, Temuco and Santiago, while Igi-Llaima and Empresa San Martín both go three times weekly to Temuco (US$25).

Lake Navegación Lago Lácar (☎ 27750), located in the Terminal de Omnibus, sails from the Muelle de Pasajeros (passenger pier) on the Avenida Costanera to Paso Hua Hum on the Chilean border, daily except Sunday at 9 am. The fare is US$20, plus a US$3.50 national park fee.

PARQUE NACIONAL LANIN

Tranquil Lanín, extending about 150 km north from Nahuel Huapi to Lago Ñorquinco, has escaped the frantic commercialism which has blemished the Bariloche area. Extensive stands of the broadleaved deciduous southern beech *raulí* and the curious pehuén (monkey puzzle tree) flourish on the lower slopes of snowcapped, 3776-metre Volcán Lanín, in addition to the *lenga*, *ñire*, and *coihue* that characterise more southerly Patagonian forests. Pleistocene glaciers left behind numerous finger-shaped lakes with excellent camp sites.

For detailed information, contact the Intendencia of Parque Nacional Lanín (☎ 27233), Emilio Frey 749, San Martín de los Andes.

Things to See & Do

From San Martín, you can sail west on **Lago Lácar** to Paso Hua Hum and cross by road to Pirehueico, Chile, but there is also bus service. Hua Hum has both free and organised camping, plus hiking trails. Fifteen km north of San Martín, almost undeveloped **Lago Lolog** has good camping and fishing.

Source of the Río Chimehuín, **Lago Huechulafquen** is easily accessible from

Junín, despite limited public transport. There are outstanding views of Volcán Lanín, and several excellent hikes. Campers at the free sites in the narrow area between the lakes and the road should dig a latrine and remove their rubbish; Mapuche-operated camping grounds at *Raquithue* and *Piedra Mala* are more hygienic alternatives at about US$3 per person, while *Bahía Cañicul* is dearer at US$7 but grants ACA discounts. Bring supplies from Junín de los Andes.

The forested **Lago Tromen** area, the northern approach to Volcán Lanín, opens earlier in the season for hikers and climbers than the route from Huechulafquen.

Getting There & Away

Public transport is limited, but hitching is feasible in the high season. Buses to Chile over the Hua Hum and Tromen passes may drop passengers at intermediate points, but are often crowded. Pick-up trucks from Junín carry six or seven backpackers to Huechulafquen for US$7 each.

VILLA LA ANGOSTURA

On the north shore of Lago Nacional Nahuel Huapi, this placid resort takes its name from the 91-metre isthmus which connects it to the Quetrihué peninsula, whose most striking natural asset is Parque Nacional Los Arrayanes. The commercial centre of El Cruce straddles the highway, while residential La Villa (which still has hotels, shops and services) is closer to the lake.

The Dirección Municipal de Turismo (☎ 94124), at El Cruce, has a good selection of maps and brochures. Correo Argentino and the Parques Nacionales office are in La Villa, while there's a locutorio in the Galería Inacayal at El Cruce. The telephone code is 0944.

Things to See & Do

Parque Nacional Los Arrayanes On the Quetrihué peninsula, this overlooked park protects the cinnamon-barked arrayán, a myrtle relative. At the south end of the peninsula, park headquarters is a three-hour hike from La Villa, but start early in the morning:

hikers must leave the park by 4 pm (ask the El Cruce tourist office for brochures). Mountain bikes are available at El Cruce (US$5 per hour, cheaper for a full day).

At the La Villa entrance, a very steep, 20-minute hike goes to two panoramic viewpoints over Nahuel Huapi.

Siete Lagos RP 234 follows this exceptionally scenic route to San Martín de los Andes. For transport details, see the Getting There & Away section for La Villa (below).

Places to Stay & Eat

Camping El Cruce (☎ 94145), on Avenida Los Lagos 500 metres beyond the tourist office, charges US$5 per person, but toilets may be dirty. *Residencial La Granja* (☎ 94193), on Calle Nahuel Huapi in La Villa, is the most reasonable at US$20/35 for singles/doubles.

In El Cruce, *Parrilla Las Varas* alongside Turismo Angostura is a favourite, but *Cantina Los Amigos* on Los Taiques is also well established. For regional specialities in La Villa, try highly regarded but relatively expensive *Cuernavaca* on Calle Nahuel Huapi.

Getting There & Away

All buses stop near the tourist office in El Cruce. Transporte Algarrobal on Los Arrayanes has two buses daily to Bariloche (US$6.50). Transporte Unión del Sud goes to Neuquén (US$30) via San Martín de los Andes (US$10) and Junín de los Andes (US$12) three times weekly; for information and tickets, go to Cantina Los Amigos on Los Taiques. Andesmar, on Avenida Los Lagos, also goes to San Martín and Neuquén.

International services between Bariloche and Chile pass through El Cruce, but are often full. Enquire at Cantina Los Amigos.

PUERTO MADRYN

Founded by Welsh settlers in 1886, this sheltered desert port on the Golfo Nuevo, 1371 km south of Buenos Aires, has taken off as a tourist destination because its proximity to the provincial wildlife sanctuary of Península Valdés attracts foreigners, and the good beaches bring domestic tourists. Street names alone remain of its Welsh past.

Information

From mid-December to mid-March, the Secretaría de Turismo y Medio Ambiente (☎ 70100), Avenida Roca 223, is open daily from 7 am to 1 am, but the rest of the year hours are 8 am to 2 pm and 3 to 9 pm.

There are several cambios on Avenida Roca and 28 de Julio. Banco Almafuerte, at Roque Sáenz Peña and 25 de Mayo, cashes travellers' cheques and has an ATM.

Correo Argentino is at Belgrano and Gobernador Maíz. Telefónica Patagónica, MA Zar 289, permits overseas reverse-charge and credit-card calls. Puerto Madryn's telephone code is 0965.

Nearly all the guides speak English at Sur Turismo (☎ 73585), Avenida Roca 175, which organises tours of the Madryn area and Península Valdés, but there are many similar agencies.

Places to Stay

Camping Towards Punta Cuevas, *Camping Municipal Sud* (☎ 79124) has comfy 'A' and 'B' areas (US$14 daily for four), but perfectly acceptable 'C' and 'D' areas cost less than half that.

Hostel *Hotel Yanco* (☎ 71581), Avenida Roca 626, has hostel accommodation for US$12, breakfast included.

Hotels & Residenciales Despite reports of considerable night activity, *Antiguo Hotel* (☎ 73742), 28 de Julio 149, is friendly and pleasant for US$10 per person with bath. *Hotel Tandil* (☎ 71017), JB Justo 770, likewise charges just US$10 per person.

Residencial Jo's (☎ 71433), Bolívar 75, has good value singles/doubles for US$15/25, while *Residencial Petit* (☎ 71460) at MT de Alvear 845 has rooms with private bath at US$15 per person. Comparably priced *Residencial Vaskonia* (☎ 72581), 25 de Mayo 43, is probably the best budget hotel.

Places to Eat

La Estancia de Madryn, on Avenida Gales between Marcos A Zar and San Martín, has excellent parrillada, reasonable prices, and great atmosphere. *La Esquina*, at Avenidas Roca and Gales, specialises in seafood and pasta, while *Mi Pequeño Restaurant*, Avenida Roca 822, has seafood, pasta and parrillada.

Pizzería Roselli, at Avenida Roca and Roque Sáenz Peña, is extremely popular, but the best pizzas are at *Cabil-Dos*, H Yrigoyen and Avenida Roca, which also serves great baked empanadas.

Ancora, at 25 de Mayo and 9 de Julio, is an outstanding pizza and pasta restaurant with unpretentious decor, but the very low pasta prices are a bit misleading because the choice of sauce is additional. *Las Pastas de la Nonna*, 9 de Julio 345, is a bit more expensive.

Getting There & Away

Air Puerto Madryn has its own airport, but most flights arrive at Trelew, 65 km south.

Bus Puerto Madryn's Terminal de Omnibus is on H Yrigoyen between MA Zar and San Martín. Línea 28 de Julio runs frequent buses to Trelew (US$3) and back.

Andesmar has daily buses to Mendoza (23 hours) and goes to Río Gallegos three times weekly. TAC, opposite the terminal, goes to Buenos Aires, Córdoba (US$72, 18 hours), Cuyo and the North-West, and to Río Gallegos (US$73, 20 hours). Que Bus, Avenida Roca 187, goes to La Plata and Buenos Aires (US$100 return with meals).

Don Otto has one daily bus to Buenos Aires, one to Río Gallegos and intermediates, goes to Neuquén (US$39, 12 hours) five times weekly, and to Esquel (US$39, eight hours) four times weekly. El Condor/La Puntual also has daily buses to Buenos Aires (US$57, 18 hours). TUP travels three times weekly to Córdoba, while Mar y Valle has three buses weekly to Esquel.

Getting Around

To/From the Airport From the Trelew

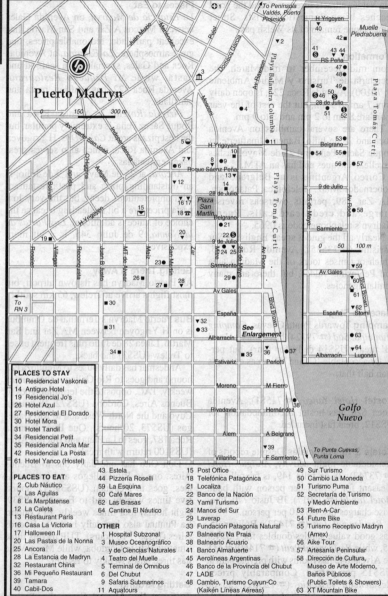

Puerto Madryn

To Península
Valdés, Puerto
Pirámide

Muelle
Piedrabuena

RS Peña

H Yrigoyen

28 de Julio

Belgrano

9 de Julio

Sarmiento

Av Gales

España

Albarracín

Golfo
Nuevo

To Punta Cuevas,
Punta Loma

Playa Tomás Curti

Playa Balandra Columba

Playa Tomás Curti

Plaza
San
Martín

H Yrigoyen

Roque Sáenz Peña

28 de Julio

Belgrano

9 de Julio

Sarmiento

Av Gales

España

Albarracín

Estivariz

Moreno

Rivadavia

Alem

Villariño

Perlotti

M Fierro

Hernández

A Belgrano

F Sarmiento

See
Enlargement

To
RN 3

PLACES TO STAY
10 Residencial Vaskonia
14 Antiguo Hotel
19 Residencial Jo's
26 Hotel Azul
27 Residencial El Dorado
30 Hotel Mora
31 Hotel Tandil
34 Residencial Petit
35 Residencial Ancla Mar
42 Residencial La Posta
61 Hotel Yanco (Hostel)

PLACES TO EAT
2 Club Náutico
7 Las Aguilas
8 La Marplatense
12 La Caleta
13 Restaurant París
16 Casa La Victoria
17 Halloween II
20 Las Pastas de la Nonna
28 La Estancia de Madryn
36 Mi Pequeño Restaurant
39 Tamara
40 Cabil-Dos

43 Estela
44 Pizzería Roselli
59 La Esquina
60 Las Brasas
62 Las Brasas
64 Cantina El Náutico

OTHER
1 Hospital Subzonal
3 Museo Oceanográfico
   y de Ciencias Naturales
4 Teatro del Muelle
5 Terminal de Omnibus
6 Del Chubut
9 Safaris Submarinos
11 Aquatours

15 Post Office
18 Telefónica Patagónica
21 Localiza
22 Banco de la Nación
23 Yamil Turismo
24 Manos del Sur
29 Laverap
33 Fundación Patagonia Natural
37 Balneario Na Praia
38 Balneario Acuario
41 Banco Almafuerte
45 Aerolíneas Argentinas
46 Banco de la Provincia del Chubut
47 LADE
48 Cambio, Turismo Cuyun-Co
   (Kaikén Líneas Aéreas)

49 Sur Turismo
50 Cambio La Moneda
51 Turismo Puma
52 Secretaría de Turismo
   y Medio Ambiente
53 Rent-A-Car
54 Future Bike
55 Turismo Receptivo Madryn
   (Amex)
56 Aike Tour
57 Artesanía Peninsular
58 Dirección de Cultura,
   Museo de Arte Moderno,
   Baños Públicos
   (Public Toilets & Showers)
63 XT Mountain Bike

airport, Madryn-bound passengers must walk to the airport entrance on RN 3 and wait for the hourly intercity bus, which does not enter the airport.

Car Useful on Península Valdés, rental cars can cost upwards of US$100 per day at Rent-A-Car (☎ 71797), Avenida Roca 277; Localiza (☎ 71660), Belgrano 196, and Cuyun-Co (☎ 51845), Avenida Roca 171.

RESERVA FAUNISTICA PENINSULA VALDES

On Ruta 3 about 18 km north of Puerto Madryn, RP 2 branches off to Península Valdés, where large numbers of sea lions, elephant seals, guanacos, rheas, Magellanic penguins and many other sea birds frequent the beaches and headlands. August is the best month for whales, but there are sightings as late as December.

Provincial officials collect US$5 per person, US$3 per child at the entrance on the Istmo Carlos Ameghino. In the Golfo San José, just to the north, gulls, cormorants, flamingos, oystercatchers and egrets nest on **Isla de los Pájaros**, a sanctuary visible through a powerful telescope.

From July to December at the village of Puerto Pirámide, launches can approach right whales in the harbour, whose warm, clear waters lap at the sandy beach. Carless visitors can walk four km to a sea-lion colony, with good views (and sunsets) across the Golfo Nuevo; for other sites, rent a car or take an organised tour.

Just north of **Punta Delgada**, a large sea-lion colony is visible from the cliffs, but better sites are farther north, where **Caleta Valdés** is a sheltered bay with a long gravel spit, where elephant seals (easily photographed, but do not approach too closely) come ashore in spring and guanaco stroll the beach. Between Caleta Valdés and Punta Norte is a substantial colony of burrowing Magellanic penguins. At **Punta Norte** proper is a huge mixed colony of sea lions and elephant seals; clearly marked trails and fences discourage visitors (and sea lions) from too close an encounter.

Places to Stay & Eat

Puerto Pirámide's municipal *camping ground*, sheltered from the wind by dunes and trees, charges US$4 per person. It has clean toilets, hot showers (carefully timed because of water shortages) and a shop with basic provisions.

At *Hospedaje El Español* (☎ 95031) basic accommodation means simple but clean rooms and toilets, plus hot showers, for US$10 per person. *El Libanés* (☎ 95007) has modest rooms for US$20 per person with bath in summer, slightly cheaper out of season, and a small confitería. *Pub Paradise* (☎ 95030) serves sandwiches and pizza, and offers B&B for US$20 per person. The *Hostería ACA* (☎ 95004), has singles/doubles for US$39/52 and a restaurant.

Highly recommended *Faro Punta Delgada* (☎ (0965) 71910, fax 51218), Avenida Julio Roca 141 in Puerto Madryn, has 30 doubles with private bath on the site of the old lighthouse, a good base for exploring the peninsula. Rates are US$40 for a double, US$100 with full board.

Getting There & Away

On Tuesday, Thursday, Saturday and Sunday at 8.55 am, the Mar y Valle bus goes from Puerto Madryn to Puerto Pirámide (US$6.50), returning at 7 pm. Tours from Puerto Madryn may drop off visitors at Puerto Pirámide and permit them to return another day for no additional charge, but verify this before doing so.

Getting Around

For sites any distance from Pirámide, the alternatives are renting a car or taking an organised tour. Most Puerto Madryn travel agencies organise day trips for about US$30, not including admission. Some frustrated travellers have complained of too much time at confiterías and too little at wildlife sites, so speak to other travellers about their experiences, discuss the tour with the operator to be sure that their expectations are the same as yours, and do not hesitate to relay complaints to Puerto Madryn's Secretaría de Turismo y Medio Ambiente.

TRELEW

Actively courting the tourist trade, the Chubut valley town of Trelew is a convenient staging point for the nearby Welsh villages of Gaiman and Dolavon, as well as the massive Punta Tombo penguin reserve. Trelew's centre is Plaza Independencia, while most of the sights are on Calles 25 de Mayo and San Martín, and along Avenida Fontana. Named for early settler Lewis Jones, it is 65 km south of Puerto Madryn. The major cultural event is early September's **Eistedvod de Chubut**, celebrating Welsh traditions.

Information

The cheerful Dirección Municipal de Turismo (☎ 20139), San Martín 171, is open on weekdays from 7 am to 1 pm and 5 to 8 pm. The bus terminal branch (☎ 20121) is open from 8 am to 1 pm and 4.30 to 9.30 pm. The information kiosk (☎ 33746) at the airport opens for arriving flights.

Sur Turismo, Belgrano 326, changes cash and travellers' cheques, and several banks have ATMs. Correo Argentino is at Avenida 25 de Mayo and Mitre. Telefónica is on the corner of Julio Roca and Fontana; the telephone code is 0965.

Travel agencies organising tours to Península Valdés (US$35) and Punta Tombo (US$45) include Sur Turismo; Punta Tombo Turismo at San Martín 150; and Estrella del Sur Turismo at San Martín 129.

Things to See

The Dirección Municipal de Turismo distributes an informative brochure, in Spanish and English, describing historic buildings like the **Banco de la Nación** (the first bank); **Salón San David** (a community centre where the Eisteddfod takes place); the **Capilla Tabernacl** (1889); the **Teatro Verdi** (1914); **Plaza Independencia** (with its Victorian kiosk); the **Distrito Militar** (which housed Trelew's first school); and the **Teatro Español**.

In the former railway station, at Avenida Fontana and 9 de Julio, the **Museo Regional** has good artefacts, but lacks any explanatory or interpretive material on the Welsh settlements. It's open 7 am to 1 pm and 3 to 8 pm weekdays; admission costs US$2 for adults, US$1 for children.

Fossils, especially dinosaurs, are superb at the new **Museo Paleontológico Egidio Feruglio**, Avenida 9 de Julio 631, open on weekdays from 8.30 am to 12.30 pm and 1.30 to 8 pm, on Saturday from 9 am to noon and 2 to 9 pm, and on Sunday and holidays from 2 to 9 pm only. Admission is US$4 for adults, US$2 for students, the retired, and children under 12.

Places to Stay & Eat

Trelew's *Albergue Municipal* (☎ 20160), Mitre 37, has 40 dormitory-style beds available for US$5 per person. *Hotel Argentino* (☎ 36134), Mathews 186, is clean and comfy for US$12 per person. Popular with travellers, the modest rooms at *Residencial Rivadavia* (☎ 34472), Rivadavia 55, are good value for US$15 per person with private bath.

The *Comedor Universitario*, at Fontana and 9 de Julio, offers wholesome meals at bargain prices. *Delikatesse*, west of the city centre at AP Bell 434, offers wild game and other unusual foods as well as Italian cuisine and pizza. *La Cantina*, at 25 de Mayo and A P Bell, specialises in pasta and seafood, as do *La Posada del Cabezón*, Don Bosco 23, and the recommended *El Galeón*, San Martín 118.

Getting There & Away

Air At 25 de Mayo 33, Aerolíneas Argentinas (☎ 35297) flies twice daily to Aeroparque (US$183), and daily to Río Gallegos (US$138) and Ushuaia (US$157). LAPA (☎ 23440), Avenida Fontana 285, flies on Monday, Wednesday and Saturday to Aeroparque (US$99), and on Monday and Friday to Río Gallegos (US$89).

LADE (☎ 35740), Avenida Fontana 227, and TAN (☎ 34550), Belgrano 326, serve Patagonian destinations.

Bus Trelew's Terminal de Omnibus (☎ 20121) is at Urquiza and Lewis Jones, six blocks north-east of the centre. Empresa 28 de Julio goes frequently to Puerto Madryn (US$4), Gaiman (US$1.40) and Dolavon (US$2.60). Mar y Valle runs buses to Puerto Pirámide on Tuesday, Thursday, Saturday and Sunday, leaving Trelew at 7.45 am and returning from Puerto Pirámide at 6.30 pm.

Several companies go to Buenos Aires (US$76, 22 hours). Don Otto goes to Comodoro Rivadavia (US$22, five hours), Puerto Deseado, Río Gallegos (US$71, 18 hours), Esquel and Neuquén. Andesmar goes daily to Neuquén (US$38, 10 hours) and Mendoza (US$76, 24 hours), three times weekly to Río Gallegos (US$68, 17 hours). Central Argentino goes to Viedma/Carmen de Patagones (US$28, seven hours), Bahía Blanca (US$45, 12 hours) and Rosario (US$100). TAC has extensive coastal routes from Buenos Aires to Río Gallegos, plus interior routes to Cuyo and the North-West. TUP (☎ 21343) travels to Santa Rosa (US$46) and Córdoba (US$78) three afternoons weekly. Transportadora Patagónica goes to Bariloche (US$66) and Mar del Plata (US$72).

Getting Around

Car rental agencies include Dollar at San Martín 148, Alquilauto Fiorasi at España 344, and Avis at Paraguay 105.

AROUND TRELEW
Gaiman

Chubut's oldest municipality and one of the few demonstrably Welsh towns remaining in Patagonia, Gaiman is 17 km west of Trelew. Attended by Welsh and English-speaking volunteers, the **Museo Histórico Regional de Gaiman** occupies the old railway station, at Sarmiento and 28 de Julio. One of Patagonia's oddest sights is eclectic **Parque El Desafío**, built by local political protester and conservationist Joaquín Alonso, but the admission price has risen to US$5.

From about 3 pm, several teahouses offer a filling *té galés* of home-made cakes and sweets for about US$10; all of them are good, so for better service choose one without a tour bus outside. There is a small, inexpensive camping ground on the river.

Empresa 28 de Julio has several buses a day from Trelew via Gaiman to Dolavon. The return fare to Gaiman is US$2.50.

Dolavon

RP 7 leads 35 km west from Trelew to historic Dolavon, whose old flour mill, now a museum, still has a functioning water wheel. Empresa 28 de Julio runs 10 buses daily from Trelew.

Reserva Provincial Punta Tombo

From September to April, half a million Magellanic penguins breed at Punta Tombo, 110 km south of Trelew. Other sea and shore birds include cormorants, giant petrels, kelp gulls, flightless steamer ducks and oyster-catchers.

Early morning visits beat tourist buses from Trelew, but camping is forbidden. Most of the nesting area is fenced off; this does not prevent approaching the birds for photos, but remember that penguin bites can require stitches. To get there, arrange a tour in Trelew (about US$45), hire a taxi, or rent a car. There is a US$5 entry fee.

COMODORO RIVADAVIA

Founded in 1901, Comodoro Rivadavia boomed a few years later, when well-diggers made a fortuitous petroleum strike. The state soon dominated the sector through recently privatised Yacimientos Petrolíferos Fiscales (YPF). Argentina is self-sufficient in petroleum, about one-third of it coming from this area.

Comodoro is a frequent stopover for southbound travellers. The main commercial street is Avenida San Martín, which trends east-west below 212-metre Cerro Chenque. With Avenida Alsina and the Atlantic shoreline, San Martín forms a triangle that defines the city centre.

Comodoro's helpful Dirección de Turismo (☎ 22376), at Pellegrini and Rivadavia, is open on weekdays from 7 am to 8 pm, and on weekends from 1 to 8 pm; it also has space at the bus terminal but depends on volunteer help there. Most of Comodoro's banks and ATMs are along Avenida San Martín, where travel agencies will also change cash. Correo Argentino is at San Martín and Moreno. City centre locutorios include one at the bus terminal; Comodoro's telephone code is 0967.

Museo del Petróleo

Vivid exhibits on the region's natural and cultural history, early and modern oil technology, and social and historical aspects of petroleum development distinguish this museum, a legacy of YPF and now managed by the Universidad Nacional de Patagonia. There are also fascinating, detailed models of tankers, refineries, and the entire zone of exploitation.

Actually located in the suburb of General Mosconi, just north of Comodoro, the museum is on Lavalle between Viedma and Carlos Calvo, reached by either the No 7 Laprida or No 8 Palazzo bus from central Comodoro. Admission is free. It's open on weekdays from 10 am to 8 pm, and on weekends from 2.30 to 8.30 pm.

Places to Stay & Eat

Comodoro has official hostel accommodation at the *Residencial Atlántico* (☎ 23145), at Alem 30; rates are US$12 with breakfast, but there are no kitchen facilities. The most popular budget hotel is *Hotel Comercio* (☎ 32341), Rivadavia 341, whose vintage bar and restaurant alone justify a visit. Singles/doubles with shared bath cost US$10/12, but rooms with private bath cost US$30 for a double.

Dino, upstairs on the corner of San Martín and Mitre, is a cheap confitería which is good for breakfast. On the corner of Rivadavia and Alvear, *Rotisería Andafama* prepares a wide variety of exquisite empanadas for takeaway.

Jammed with locals at lunch time, *La Esquina de Lomo*, Rivadavia at Güemes, prepares superb bife de chorizo and lasagne. *Gran Pizzería Romanella*, 25 de Mayo 866, serves the obvious.

Getting There & Away

Air Austral (☎ 22191), 9 de Julio 870, flies frequently to Buenos Aires (US$199), while southbound flights are daily except Sunday

to Río Gallegos (US$103) and Río Grande (US$126). Roqueta Travel (☎ 32400), Rivadavia 396, is the representative of LAPA, which flies less frequently to Río Gallegos (US$69) and Buenos Aires (US$99). For Patagonian services, contact LADE (☎ 36181), Rivadavia 360; TAN representative Agencia Atlas (☎ 35228), Rivadavia 439; or Kaikén Líneas Aéreas (☎ 21405), Sarmiento 733.

Bus Comodoro's Terminal de Omnibus (☎ 27305) is at Ameghino and 25 de Mayo. Many companies have buses to Buenos Aires (US$82, 24 hours) and intermediates, southbound to Río Gallegos (US$49, 11 hours), and to Esquel (US$33, eight hours), El Bolsón, Bariloche (US$47, 14 hours) and Neuquén.

TAC has extensive routes southbound to Río Gallegos and northbound to Buenos Aires, but also serves Cuyo and north-western destinations as far as Jujuy. Andesmar also goes to Cuyo, Chile and north-western Argentina. La Unión goes hourly to Caleta Olivia, with connections to Puerto Deseado (US$17, four hours), and twice daily to Perito Moreno and Los Antiguos (US$20, six hours). Angel Giobbi (☎ 34841) departs at 1 am on Monday and Thursday for Coyhaique, Chile (US$40) via Río Mayo, but these buses are often very full. Turistas provides additional services to Coyhaique.

Getting Around

To/From the Airport The No 8 Patagonia Argentina (Directo Palazzo) bus goes to Aeropuerto General Mosconi (☎ 33355 ext 163) from the central bus terminal.

MONUMENTO NATURAL BOSQUES PETRIFICADOS

In Jurassic times, 150 million years ago, vulcanism levelled this southern Patagonian area's extensive *Proaraucaria* forests and buried them in ash; later erosion exposed mineralised trees three metres in diameter and 35 metres long. Until legal protection, souvenir hunters regularly plundered the area; do not perpetuate this tradition for even the smallest specimen.

From RN 3, 157 km south of Caleta Olivia, a gravel road leads 50 km west to the park's modest headquarters. Camping is free at the dry creek nearby, but bring water if you have a vehicle; otherwise, the ranger *may* be able to spare some. Buses from Comodoro Rivadavia or Caleta Olivia will drop you at the junction, but you may wait several hours or more for a lift.

LOS ANTIGUOS

Aged Tehuelche Indians frequented this 'banana belt' on the south shore of Lago Buenos Aires, where rows of poplars now shelter irrigated chacras whose abundant fruit, for lack of markets, is absurdly cheap. Los Antiguos' Fiesta de la Cereza (cherry festival) runs for three days in mid-January. The nearby countryside has good fishing and hiking.

Both the tourist office and bank are on Avenida 11 de Julio, the main street, which runs the length of town. Local fruits (cherries, raspberries, strawberries, apples, apricots, pears, peaches, plums and prunes) are delectable. Purchase these, and homemade preserves, directly from producers – Chacra El Porvenir is within easy walking distance of Avenida 11 de Julio.

Places to Stay & Eat

The cypress-sheltered *Camping Municipal*, at the east end of Avenida 11 de Julio, charges US$2.25 per person, plus US$1.30 per tent and per vehicle. Hot showers are available from 5.30 to 10 pm. A handful of cabins sleep up to six people, for US$8.50 per cabin.

Hotel Argentino, which charges US$18/32 for a single/double with private bath, also has excellent meals, with desserts of local produce, and outstanding breakfasts, but prices have risen to US$14 for lunch or dinner. *El Disco*, a parrilla, is a bit cheaper.

Getting There & Away

LADE and Pingüino serve the nearest airport, at Perito Moreno 64 km east. Buses El Pingüino and La Unión run between

Caleta Olivia and Los Antiguos (US$20, six hours). Transportes VH crosses the border to Chile Chico (US$3 return) three times daily from Monday to Thursday, once on Friday and Saturday.

ESQUEL

In the foothills of western Chubut, sunny Esquel is the gateway to Parque Nacional Los Alerces and other Andean recreation areas, and the terminus for the picturesque narrow-gauge railway from Ingeniero Jacobacci in Río Negro province. Founded at the turn of the century, the town of 23,000 is also the area's main commercial and livestock centre.

Information

Esquel's well-organised Dirección Municipal de Turismo (☎ 2369), at Sarmiento and Alvear, maintains a thorough list of lodging and recreation options, and also sells fishing licences.

Banco Nación, at Alvear and Roca, changes American Express travellers' cheques; Banco de la Provincia del Chubut has an ATM at Alvear 1131. Correo Argentino is at Alvear 1192. There are numerous locutorios; Esquel's telephone code is 0945.

Things to See

The **Museo Indigenista**, part of the Dirección Municipal de Cultura, is at Belgrano 330. The **Estación Ferrocarril Roca**, at Brown and Roggero, is now also a museum, but travellers arriving by air or bus should still not miss the arrival of **La Trochita**, the narrow-gauge steam train (serious railway fanatics will find the town of El Maitén, on the border of Río Negro province, even more interesting because of the extraordinary concentration of antique rail equipment in its workshops).

Places to Stay

Autocamping La Colina (☎ 4962), Humphreys 554 near Darwin, costs US$3.50 per person and also has hostel accommodation at US$8/15 for a single/double. Check the tourist office for the latest private house listings, but try Raquel Alemán de Abraham (☎ 2696) at Alberdi 529 for US$10 with shared bath; or Isabel Barutta's highly recommended *Parador Lago Verde* (☎ 2251), Volta 1081, for US$13/24 a single/double with private bath.

Hospedaje Argentino (☎ 2237), 25 de Mayo 862, is the cheapest formal accommodation at US$18/28 for a single/double. *Hospedaje Zacarías* (☎ 2270), General Roca 634, is slightly more expensive at US$20/30 with private bath. Highly regarded *Hotel Ski* (☎ 2254), San Martín 961, charges US$20/35.

Places to Eat

Confitería Atelier, open 24 hours at 25 de Mayo and San Martín, has excellent coffee and chocolate. *Confitería Exedra*, at 25 de Mayo and Alvear, is also worth a visit, as is lively *Confitería Maika* at 25 de Mayo and San Martín.

El Rancho, Rivadavia 726, is a reasonable parrilla with a salad bar. *Restaurant Jockey Club*, Alvear 949, is comparable. *Vascongada* (☎ 4609), 9 de Julio and Mitre, has good food in generous portions, with friendly and attentive service. *Alha Washala*, at 9 de Julio and Sarmiento, is also highly regarded, along with *Don Chiquino*, 9 de Julio 964, which specialises in pasta.

Getting There & Away

Air Austral (☎ 3413, 3614), Fontana 406, flies on Monday, Wednesday, Friday and Sunday to Aeroparque (US$256). For Patagonian services, contact LADE (☎ 2124), Alvear 1085; TAN and Sapse representative Fairways (☎ 3380), at Roca 689; and Kaikén Líneas Aéreas (ask travel agents for details).

Bus Esquel's congested Terminal de Omnibus is at the junction of Avenidas Fontana and Alvear, but local authorities have projected a new terminal six blocks north. There are frequent buses to El Bolsón (US$12, 2½ hours) and Bariloche (US$21, six hours), Comodoro Rivadavia (US$38,

eight hours), connecting to Río Gallegos (US$81), and Buenos Aires (US$95, 28 hours). Mercedes, Don Otto La Unión and El Sureño are the main carriers.

Empresa Chubut has daily service to Trelew (nine hours) and Puerto Madryn (US$39, 10 hours). Mar y Valle runs similar routes. Andesmar goes daily to Bariloche and Mendoza (US$85), with connections to the North-West.

Travellers unable to get a train ticket can take Transportes Jacobsen to El Maitén and Ingeniero Jacobacci (US$10, five hours) on Friday at 8 am. Codao serves provincial destinations like Trevelin and Corcovado. Transportes Esquel goes to Parque Nacional Los Alerces three times daily, combining with lake excursions. Zabala Daniel runs the only service to El Bolsón (US$18) via Los Alerces, at noon and 6 pm, but there have been complaints about seat availability for travellers with open tickets to continue to El Bolsón.

Train The Ferrocarril General Roca (☎ 2734) is on the corner of Brown and Roggero. Its narrow-gauge steam train *El Trencito* or *La Trochita* connects Esquel with Ingeniero Jacobacci (☎ (0971) 2089), on the main line between Bariloche and Constitución (Buenos Aires). It leaves Jacobacci on Tuesday at 6 am, arriving in Esquel at 7 pm; the return service leaves Esquel on Wednesday at 10 am, arriving at Jacobacci at midnight. Fares range from US$26.50 to US$32.50.

Getting Around

To/From the Airport Esquel Tours, Fontana 754, runs airport minibuses.

AROUND ESQUEL
Trevelin

Only 24 km south of Esquel, Trevelin is interior Chubut's only notable Welsh community. The Dirección de Turismo, Deportes y Actividades Recreativas (☎ 80120) on octagonal Plaza Fontana occasionally has discount coupons for local teahouses, the town's major attraction. The **Museo Molino**

Viejo, a restored flour mill, and the **Capilla Bethel** (1910), a Welsh chapel, are landmarks.

Trevelin has a good camping ground, but lodging is otherwise limited. *Nain Maggie*, Perito Moreno 179, is the oldest teahouse, but *El Adobe*, *Las Mutisias* and *Te Cymreig Yng Nghwm Hyfryd* are all worth a visit. There are six buses on weekdays from Esquel (US$1.50), four on weekends.

PARQUE NACIONAL LOS ALERCES

West of Esquel, this spacious Andean park protects extensive stands of alerce *(Fitzroya cupressoides)*, a large (up to 60 metres tall and four metres in diameter) and long-lived (400 years or more) conifer of the humid Valdivian forests. Other common trees include cypress, incense cedar, southern beeches, and arrayán. The *chusquea* (solid bamboo) undergrowth is almost impenetrable.

The receding glaciers of Los Alerces' peaks, which barely reach 2300 metres, have left nearly pristine lakes and streams, with charming vistas and excellent fishing. Westerly storms drop nearly three metres of rain annually, but summers are mild and the park's eastern zone is much drier.

Information
For an introduction to the park's cultural and natural history, visit the **Museo y Centro de Interpretación** at Villa Futalaufquen, where rangers provide information from 8 am to 9 pm daily in summer.

Things to See & Do
Traditionally, the most popular excursion sails from Puerto Limonao on Lago Futalaufquen up the Río Arrayanes to Lago Verde, but dry years and low water have eliminated part of this segment. Launches from Puerto Chucao, on Lago Menéndez, cover the second segment of the trip to **El Alerzal**, an accessible stand of alerces, which, except in parks, are under logging pressure. Buy advance tickets for the voyage (US$53 from Limonao, US$33 from Chucao) in Esquel.

A one-hour stopover permits a hike around a loop trail which passes Lago Cisne and an attractive waterfall to end up at **El Abuelo** (The Grandfather), the finest single alerce in the area. Guides are knowledgeable, but the group can be uncomfortably large.

Places to Stay
At organised camping grounds at Los Maitenes, Lago Futalaufquen, Bahía Rosales, Lago Verde and Lago Rivadavia, charges are US$5 per person per day, plus a one-time charge of US$3 per car or tent. There are free sites near some of these locations. Lago Krüger, reached by foot from Villa Futalaufquen, has a camping ground (US$6 plus US$4 per tent) and a refugio (US$12 per person).

Cabañas Los Tepues, on Lago Futalaufquen, rents five-person cabins for US$100 per day (up to eight people). *Motel Pucón Pai* has doubles with private bath and breakfast for US$90, with half-board for US$118.

Getting There & Away
For details, see the Esquel section above.

RIO GALLEGOS
In addition to servicing the wool industry, this port (population 65,000) ships coal and refines oil. Many travellers only pass through en route to El Calafate and the Moreno Glacier, Punta Arenas or Tierra del Fuego, but a day here need not be a wasted one.

Río Gallegos' two main streets, Avenida Julio Roca and Avenida San Martín, run at right angles to each other. Most sights and services are in the south-western quadrant formed by these avenues.

Information
The energetic Subsecretaría de Turismo de la Provincia (☎ 22702), Avenida Roca 1551, is open on weekdays from 9 am to 8 pm. The Dirección Municipal de Turismo maintains a Centro de Informes (☎ 24999) at the bus

terminal and another at Avenida San Martín and Avenida Roca.

El Pingüino, Zapiola 469, changes cash and travellers' cheques (with commission). Most banks are on or near Avenida Roca; Banco del Sud has an ATM at Alcorta 32. Correo Argentino is at Roca and San Martín. The most central of numerous locutorios is at Avenida Roca 1328; Río Gallegos' telephone code is 0966. The Chilean Consulate, Mariano Moreno 136, is open on weekdays from 9 am to 2 pm.

Things to See

At Perito Moreno 45, the **Museo Provincial Padre Jesús Molina** has good exhibits on geology, Tehuelche ethnology (superb photographs), and local history; it's open daily on weekdays from 10 am to 5 pm, and on weekends from 3 to 8 pm. In a metal-clad house typical of southern Patagonia, the **Museo de los Pioneros** at Elcano and Alberdi documents early immigrant life; it's open daily from 3 to 8 pm.

Places to Stay

The best cheap accommodation may be the dormitories in the *Gimnasio Juan B Rocha*, on Avenida Eva Perón just north of the bus terminal, for around US$5 per person; ask the tourist information staff there if it's open. For US$15, shared-bath singles at *Hotel Colonial* (☎ 22329), Bernardino Rivadavia and Urquiza, are reasonable value. Boxy but friendly *Hotel Ampuero* (☎ 22189), Federico Sphur 38, charges US$17/30.

Rooms with washbasin and mirror (shared bath) cost only US$17/22 at simple but spotless *Hotel Covadonga* (☎ 20190), Avenida Roca 1244; rooms with private bath are dearer. *Hotel Nevada* (☎ 22155), Zapiola 486, is good value for US$22/38.

Places to Eat

Improving *Restaurant Díaz*, Avenida Roca 1143, has reasonable minutas, as does *Snack Bar Jardín*, Avenida Roca 1311. In the historic Sociedad Española building at Avenida Roca 862 is the highly regarded *El Horreo*; directly alongside it is equally appealing

Pizzería Bertolo (indifferent service, however). *Pietro*, Avenida Roca 1148, is another good pizza choice.

Le Croissant, at Zapiola and Estrada, has a wide variety of attractive baked goods, prepared on the premises. *Heladería Tito*, Zapiola and Corrientes, has very imaginative ice-cream flavours.

Getting There & Away

Air Aerolíneas Argentinas (☎ 22495), Avenida San Martín 545, flies twice daily to Buenos Aires (US$236), and frequently to Río Grande and Ushuaia. Austral, at the same address, flies daily except Sunday to Buenos Aires and intermediates, and to Río Grande. LAPA (☎ 28382), Estrada 71, flies on Monday and Friday to Comodoro Rivadavia (US$69), Trelew (US$89) and Buenos Aires (US$149, at 1.30 am).

For Patagonian services, consult LADE (☎ 22316), Fagnano 53; TAN (☎ 25259), at the airport only; Kaikén Líneas Aéreas agent Tur Aike (☎ 24503), Zapiola 63; or El Pingüino (☎ 27326), at Roca and San Martín. Check travel agencies for Aerovías DAP's new service to Punta Arenas, Chile (US$49).

Bus Río Gallegos' Terminal de Omnibus is on the corner of RN 3 and Avenida Eva Perón, but some companies have convenient offices in the centre of town.

El Pingüino (☎ 27326), in the centre at Roca and San Martín, goes to Río Turbio (US$15), to Puerto Natales, Chile (US$18, six hours), daily to Punta Arenas (US$20, six hours) and to El Calafate (US$24). Transporte Mansilla (☎ 22701), San Martín 565, Transporte Vera and Buses Ghisoni also do the six-hour trip to Punta Arenas.

Several companies go to Buenos Aires (US$107, 40 hours), while Andesmar (☎ 25879) links Gallegos with coastal destinations, interior Patagonia, Cuyo, and the North-West. TAC goes to interior Patagonian destinations as well as Buenos Aires.

Interlagos Turismo (☎ 22466) at Roca 998 goes to El Calafate (US$25) and the Moreno Glacier. Pingüino and Interlagos

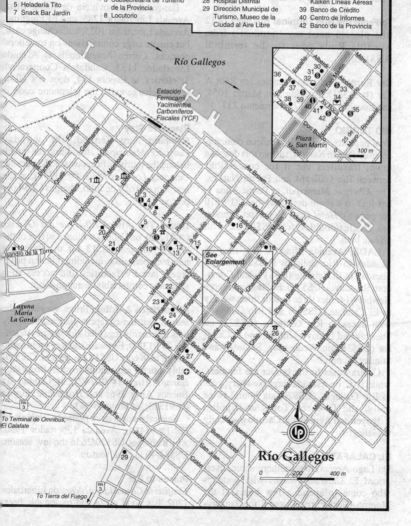

PLACES TO STAY
4 Hotel Ampuero
6 Hotel Punta Arenas
10 Hotel Nevada
12 Hotel Covadonga
19 Hotel Liporace
20 Hotel Oviedo
22 Hotel Cabo Virgenes
23 Hotel Colonial

PLACES TO EAT
5 Heladería Tito
7 Snack Bar Jardín

11 Le Croissant
14 Pietro
15 Restaurant Díaz
41 El Horreo,
   Pizzería Bertolo

OTHER
1 Museo Provincial Padre
   Jesús Molina
2 Museo de los Pioneros
3 Subsecretaría de Turismo
   de la Provincia
8 Locutorio

9 Cambio El Pingüino
13 LAPA
16 Localiza
17 ACA
18 Artesanías Keokén
21 Aike Lavar
24 Migraciones
25 Chilean Consulate
26 Telefónica
27 Rent A Car
28 Hospital Distrital
29 Dirección Municipal de
   Turismo, Museo de la
   Ciudad al Aire Libre

30 Aerolíneas Argentinas,
   Austral
31 Cambio Sur
32 El Pingüino
33 Banco del Sud
34 Post Office
35 Banco de la Nación
36 LADE
37 Interlagos Turismo
38 Tur Aike,
   Kaikén Líneas Aéreas
39 Banco de Crédito
40 Centro de Informes
42 Banco de la Provincia

Río Gallegos

Estación
Ferrocarril
Yacimientos
Carboníferos
Fiscales (YCF)

Plaza
San Martín

0   100 m

Laguna
María
La Gorda

See
Enlargement

To Terminal de Omnibus,
El Calafate

To Tierra del Fuego

Río Gallegos

0   200   400 m

buses to Calafate leave from the airport 30 minutes after flight arrivals, but seats may be few.

Getting Around
To/From the Airport Cabs to or from Aeropuerto Internacional Río Gallegos cost about US$6; to save money, share.

To/From the Bus Terminal Bus No 1 or 12 (the placard must say 'terminal') from Avenida Roca goes to the terminal (US$1.20).

Car Rental The main agencies are Rent A Car (☎ 21321), Avenida San Martín 1054, and Localiza (☎ 24417), Sarmiento 237.

RIO TURBIO
Coal deposits, worked by Chilean commuters from Puerto Natales, sustain this desolate town; travellers use it for connections between Río Gallegos and Puerto Natales. The *Albergue Municipal*, at Paraje Mina 1, has four-to-a-room dormitory beds (US$10 per person); *Hotel Gato Negro*, on Laprida, has singles/doubles for US$23/32 with private bath.

LADE, Avenida Mineros 375, flies on Monday to Río Gallegos (US$24) and on Tuesday to El Calafate (US$17) and Comodoro Rivadavia (US$79). El Pingüino, Jorge Newbery 14, flies three or four times weekly to El Calafate (US$30) and Río Gallegos, with buses to Río Gallegos (US$23) on Tuesday and Friday evenings, and to Calafate (US$38) on Wednesday, Saturday and Sunday evenings.

Cootra buses to the border are frequent, while TAC, on Avenida Jorge Newbery, goes to Río Gallegos (US$20, six hours) twice daily, and Quebeck Tours at Hipólito Yrigoyen and Agustín del Castillo goes daily to Gallegos.

EL CALAFATE
On Lago Argentino's southern shore, overpriced El Calafate swarms with porteños who come to spend a few hours at the Moreno Glacier: try to avoid the January-

February peak season. From May to September, prices are more reasonable but the main attractions are less accessible.

Calafate's much improved Ente Municipal Calafate Turismo (Emcatur, ☎ 91090), near the bridge at the eastern approach to town, is open daily from 8 am to 10 pm; there's usually an English-speaker on hand.

Banco de la Provincia de Santa Cruz, Avenida Libertador 1285, and El Pingüino, Avenida Libertador 1025, both change cash, but charge large commissions on travellers' cheques. Correo Argentino is at Avenida Libertador 1133. Calafate's Cooperativa Telefónica, at Espora 194, does not allow reverse-charge calls; the telephone code is 0902.

Places to Stay
Camping Now fenced, the woodsy *Camping Municipal*, straddling the creek behind the tourist office, costs US$8 per site. *Camping Los Dos Pinos* (☎ 91271), at the northern end of 9 de Julio, charges US$4 per person.

Hostel The official *Albergue del Glaciar* (☎ 91243), on Calle Los Pioneros, east of the arroyo, charges US$13 for members and non-members alike, including kitchen privileges, laundry facilities and access to a spacious, comfortable common room.

Hospedajes & Hotels Prices vary with the season, but the cheapest places are family inns like highly regarded *Hospedaje Alejandra* (☎ 91328), Espora 60, where rooms with shared bath cost US$10 per person. Comparably priced are recommended *Hospedaje Buenos Aires* (☎ 91147), at Ciudad de Buenos Aires 296, and *Hospedaje Jorgito* (☎ 91323), at Moyano 943.

Several readers have praised *Cabañas del Sol* (☎ 91439), Avenida Libertador 1956, which charges US$20/26 in the low season, US$31/40 in peak season.

Places to Eat
Confitería Casa Blanca, Avenida Libertador 1202, has good pizza and reasonable beer;

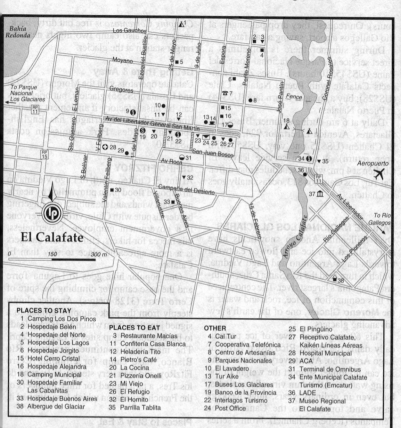

El Calafate

0   150   300 m

PLACES TO STAY
1 Camping Los Dos Pinos
2 Hospedaje Belén
4 Hospedaje del Norte
5 Hospedaje Los Lagos
6 Hospedaje Jorgito
15 Hotel Cerro Cristal
16 Hospedaje Alejandra
18 Camping Municipal
30 Hospedaje Familiar
   Las Cabañitas
33 Hospedaje Buenos Aires
38 Albergue del Glaciar

PLACES TO EAT
3 Restaurante Macías
11 Confitería Casa Blanca
12 Heladería Tito
14 Pietro's Café
20 La Cocina
21 Pizzería Onelli
23 Mi Viejo
26 El Refugio
32 El Hornito
35 Parrilla Tablita

OTHER
4 Cal Tur
7 Cooperativa Telefónica
8 Centro de Artesanías
9 Parques Nacionales
10 El Lavadero
13 Tur Aike
17 Buses Los Glaciares
19 Banco de la Provincia
22 Interlagos Turismo
24 Post Office

25 El Pingüino
27 Receptivo Calafate,
   Kaikén Líneas Aéreas
28 Hospital Municipal
29 ACA
31 Terminal de Omnibus
34 Ente Municipal Calafate
   Turismo (Emcatur)
36 LADE
37 Museo Regional
   El Calafate

Pizzería Onelli, across the street, also has adherents. *Paso Verlika*, Avenida Libertador 1108, is popular and reasonably priced, especially the pizza. *Mi Viejo*, Avenida Libertador 1111, is a popular but pricey parrilla, while *El Refugio*, Avenida Libertador 963, is a good choice for a splurge.

Otherwise appealing *La Cocina*, a new restaurant on Avenida Libertador with an innovative Italian menu, stubbornly charged the author for two beers even though the second replaced one that had a fly in it.

Getting There & Away
Air For air services elsewhere in Patagonia

and Tierra del Fuego, consult LADE (☎ 91262), Avenida Libertador 699; El Pingüino (☎ 91273), Avenida Libertador 1025; or Líneas Aéreas Kaikén agent Receptivo Calafate (☎ 91116), Avenida Libertador 945.

Bus El Calafate's new Terminal de Omnibus is on Avenida Roca, easily reached by a staircase from Avenida Libertador. Buses Pingüino, Avenida Libertador 1025, and Interlagos, Avenida Libertador 1175, both cover the 320 km of RP 5 and RP 11 between Calafate and Río Gallegos (US$25, six hours). On request, they drop passengers at Río Gallegos airport, saving a cab fare.

During summer there is sometimes a direct service to Parque Nacional Torres del Paine (US$45, 10 hours). Buses Zaahj connects Calafate with Puerto Natales, Chile (US$28); buy a cheaper return fare (US$44) in Puerto Natales.

Daily at 6 am during summer, Buses Los Glaciares, Avenida Libertador 924, goes to El Chaltén (US$25 one way, US$50 with open return). A return service leaves El Chaltén at 4 pm; winter schedules may differ. Cal Tur, Los Gauchos 813, occasionally goes to Chaltén.

PARQUE NACIONAL LOS GLACIARES

Over millennia, Andean snowfields have recrystallised into ice and flowed eastward towards Lago Argentino and Lago Viedma, which in turn feed the Río Santa Cruz, southern Patagonia's largest river. The centrepiece of this conjunction of ice, rock and water is the **Moreno Glacier**, one of the earth's few advancing glaciers.

This 60-metre-high river of ice periodically dams the Brazo Rico (Rico Arm) of Lago Argentino. About every four years, the ice can no longer support the weight of the rising water and the dam virtually explodes, but even in ordinary years, huge icebergs calve and topple into the Canal de los Témpanos (Iceberg Channel). From a series of catwalks and platforms, you can see, hear and photograph the glacier safely, but descending to the shores of the canal is now prohibited.

Launches from Puerto Bandera, 45 km west of El Calafate, visit the massive **Upsala Glacier**; many recommend this trip for the hike to iceberg-choked Lago Onelli. It is possible to camp and return to Puerto Bandera another day.

Places to Stay

On Península Magallanes, en route to the Moreno Glacier, *Camping Río Mitre* and *Camping Bahía Escondida* charge US$5 per person. About midway between the two,

Camping Correntoso is free but dirty; backpackers can also camp two nights near the ranger station at the glacier.

Getting There & Away

Calafate operators visit the Moreno (US$25) and Upsala (US$55) glaciers, but brief tours can be unsatisfactory if inclement weather limits visibility. Interlagos has English-speaking guides. Park admission costs US$3.50.

CERRO FITZROY

At tiny El Chaltén, north of Lago Viedma on an exposed flood plain pummelled by nearly incessant winds and the subject of a lingering border dispute with Chile, virtually everyone is a government employee. Nevertheless, this mecca for hikers, climbers and campers is a more agreeable place to stay than El Calafate.

One popular hike goes to Laguna Torre and the base camp for climbing the spire of Cerro Torre (3128 metres). Another climbs steeply from the park camping ground to a signed junction, from which a sidetrack leads to backcountry camp sites at Laguna Capri. The main trail continues gently to Río Blanco, base camp for climbing Cerro FitzRoy, and then very steeply to Laguna de los Tres, a tarn named for three members of the French expedition which first climbed it.

Places to Stay & Eat

Parques Nacionales' free *Camping Madsen* has running water and abundant firewood, but no toilets – you must dig a latrine. If you don't mind walking about 10 minutes, shower at friendly *Confitería La Senyera* for about US$1; after drying off, try their enormous portions of chocolate cake and other snacks. Other camping grounds charge from US$6 to US$8 per person. *Albergue Los Ñires* is a small (eight-bed) hostel that charges US$10 per person or US$4 per person for camping; its pub-restaurant is called *The Wall*.

For cheap eats, try Juan Borrego's converted bus, which is also a climbers' hang-out. *Chocolatería Josh Aike* has been recommended for meals, while supplies (including fresh bread) are available at *Kiosko Charito* and *El Chaltén*.

Getting There & Away
See the El Calafate section for transport details.

Tierra del Fuego

Over half of Isla Grande de Tierra del Fuego, and much of the surrounding archipelago, belongs to Chile. For details of Chilean towns, see the Chile chapter.

History
Early European navigators feared and detested the stiff westerlies, hazardous currents and violent seas which impeded their progress towards Asia. None had any serious interest in this remote area, whose indigenous peoples were mobile hunter-gatherers.

The Ona (Selknam) and Haush subsisted on terrestrial animals like the guanaco, while Yahgans and Alacalufes ('Canoe Indians') lived on fish, shellfish and marine mammals. Despite inclement weather, they used little or no clothing, but constant fires kept them warm and gave the region its name.

Spain's withdrawal from the continent opened the area to European settlement, and the demise of the indigenous Fuegians began. Thomas Bridges, a young missionary from Keppel Island in the Falklands, learned to speak Yahgan and settled at Ushuaia, in what is now Argentine Tierra del Fuego. Despite honest motives, the Bridges family and others exposed the Fuegians to diseases to which they had little resistance. Estancieros made things worse by persecuting Indians who preyed on domestic flocks as the guanaco declined.

Despite minor gold and lumber booms, Ushuaia was at first a penal colony for political prisoners and common criminals. Wool is the island's economic backbone, but the area near San Sebastián has oil and natural gas. Tourism has become so important that

flights and hotels are heavily booked in summer.

Geography & Climate
Surrounded by the stormy South Atlantic, the Strait of Magellan and the easternmost part of the Pacific Ocean, Tierra del Fuego is an archipelago of 76,000 sq km. Though most of the main island belongs to Chile, the Argentine cities of Ushuaia and Río Grande have the bulk of the population.

Northern Isla Grande is a steppe of unrelenting wind, oil derricks and enormous flocks of Corriedales, while the wetter, mountainous south offers scenic glaciers, forests, lakes, rivers and sea coasts. The maritime climate is surprisingly mild, but changeable enough that warm, dry clothing is essential even in summer.

Getting There & Away
Since no public transport goes to the ferry at Punta Delgada, the simplest overland route to Argentine Tierra del Fuego is via Porvenir (Chile) across the Strait of Magellan from Punta Arenas. The only border crossing is San Sebastián, midway between Porvenir and Río Grande.

RIO GRANDE
Río Grande, a windswept wool and petroleum service centre facing the open South Atlantic, is making a genuine effort to beautify and improve itself, but still has a long way to go. Most visitors pass through quickly en route to Ushuaia, but the surrounding countryside can be appealing.

The Instituto Fueguino de Turismo (Infuetur, ☎ 21373), in the lobby of the Hotel Yaganes at Belgrano 319, is open on weekdays from 10 am to 5 pm. For money exchange try Banco Nación, on San Martín at Avenida 9 de Julio. Correo Argentino is at Ameghino 712. Locutorio Cabo Domingo is at San Martín 458; the telephone code is 0964.

Places to Stay & Eat
Hospedaje Irmary (☎ 23608), Estrada 743, has beds for US$8 per person with shared

ARGENTINA

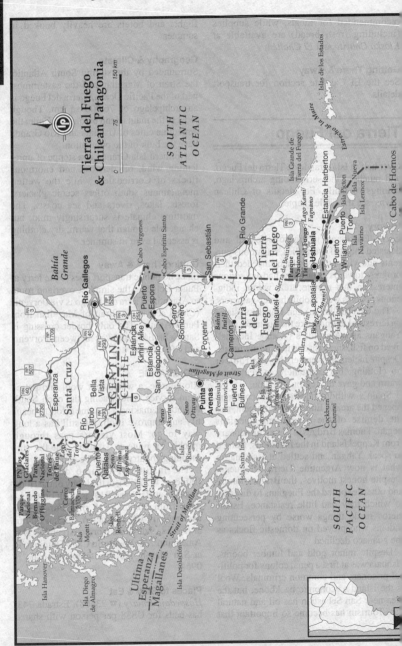

Tierra del Fuego
& Chilean Patagonia

SOUTH
ATLANTIC
OCEAN

0   75   150 km

SOUTH
PACIFIC
OCEAN

Cabo de Hornos

bath, while *Hospedaje Noal* (☎ 22857), Rafael Obligado 557, charges US$13 per person with shared bath, US$15/35 for a single/double with private bath and breakfast. Recommended *Hospedaje Miramar* (☎ 22462), Mackinlay 595, has clean, well-heated rooms at US$16 per person with shared bath, US$18 with private bath.

Hospedaje Villa, at San Martín 277, *Hotel Ibarra*, on Rosales near Fagnano, and *Hotel Los Yaganes*, at Belgrano 319, all have restaurants, but try also *El Porteñito*, Lasserre 566, near Belgrano. *La Nueva Piamontesa*, Belgrano 464, is an outstanding rotisería with reasonable takeaway food.

Getting There & Away
Air Aerolíneas Argentinas and Austral share offices (☎ 22748), at San Martín 607. Frequent flights go to Ushuaia (US$26), Buenos Aires (US$236) and intermediates. For Patagonian services, try LADE (☎ 21651), Lasserre 447; Kaikén Líneas Aéreas (☎ 30665), Perito Moreno 937; and Aerovías DAP (☎ 30249), 9 de Julio 597, which flies daily except Sunday to Punta Arenas, Chile (US$50).

Bus Río Grande's Terminal de Omnibus is at the foot of Avenida Belgrano, but some companies have offices elsewhere as well. Transportes Los Carlos, Estrada 568, goes daily to Ushuaia (US$20, four hours) in summer, less often in winter, and to Punta Arenas (US$30, 10 hours) on Monday and Friday at 7 am, and on Tuesday, Thursday and Saturday at 7.30 am. Tecni-Austral, Rivadavia 996, goes to Ushuaia daily at 7.30 am.

Transporte Pacheco goes to Punta Arenas on Tuesday, Thursday and Saturday at 7.30 am. Transporte Senkovic goes on Wednesday and Saturday at 6.30 am to Porvenir (US$20 one way, seven hours; US$36 return) in Chilean Tierra del Fuego, meeting the Punta Arenas ferry.

AROUND RIO GRANDE
The missionary order which proselytised local Indians established the **Museo Salesiano**, 11 km north of town on Ruta 3, which has exhibits on geology, natural history and ethnography. **Lago Fagnano** (also known by its Oma/Yahgan name, Kami), the huge glacial trough on RN 3 between Río Grande and Ushuaia, merits a visit; stay at *Hostería Kaikén* (US$15 a single).

USHUAIA
Over the past two decades, fast-growing Ushuaia has evolved from a village into a city of 42,000, sprawling and spreading from its original site, but the setting is still one of the most dramatic in the world, with jagged glacial peaks rising from sea level to nearly 1500 metres. The surrounding area offers hiking, fishing and skiing, and the chance to go as far south as roads go: RN 3 ends at Bahía Lapataia, 3242 km from Buenos Aires.

In 1870 the British-based South American Missionary Society based itself here, but only artefacts, middens and memories remain of its Yahgan neophytes. Argentina incarcerated notorious criminals and political prisoners at Ushuaia until 1947, after which it became a key naval base and, gradually, a tourist destination. Forestry, fishing and electronics assembly have become significant.

Shoreline Avenida Maipú leads west to Parque Nacional Tierra del Fuego. One block north is parallel Avenida San Martín, the main commercial street.

Information
Tourist Office The municipal Dirección de Turismo (☎ 32000), at Avenida San Martín 660, keeps a complete list of accommodation and current prices, assists in finding a room with private families, and posts a list of available accommodation after closing time. The friendly, patient and helpful staff usually includes an English-speaker, less frequently a German, French or Italian-speaker. Hours are weekdays 8.30 am to 8.30 pm, Sunday and holidays 9 am to 8 pm.

Money Banco del Territorio, San Martín 396, cashes travellers' cheques for a 3%

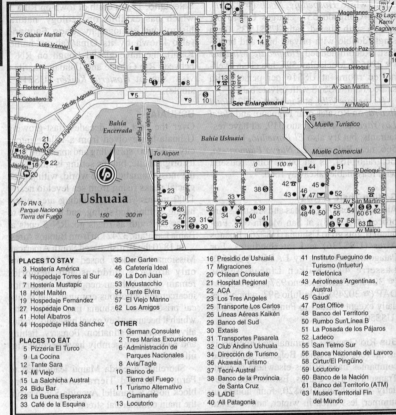

Ushuaia

To Glaciar Martial
To Lago Kami/Fagnano

Bahía Encerrada

Bahía Ushuaia

To Airport

Muelle Turístico

Muelle Comercial

See Enlargement

To RN 3,
Parque Nacional
Tierra del Fuego

PLACES TO STAY
3 Hostería América
4 Hospedaje Torres al Sur
7 Hostería Mustapic
18 Hotel Maitén
19 Hospedaje Fernández
27 Hospedaje Ona
41 Hotel Albatros
44 Hospedaje Hilda Sánchez

PLACES TO EAT
5 Pizzería El Turco
9 La Cocina
12 Tante Sara
14 Mi Viejo
15 La Salchicha Austral
24 Bidu Bar
28 La Buena Esperanza
33 Café de la Esquina

35 Der Garten
46 Cafetería Ideal
49 La Don Juan
53 Moustacchio
54 Tante Elvira
57 El Viejo Marino
62 Los Amigos

OTHER
1 German Consulate
2 Tres Marías Excursiones
6 Administración de
   Parques Nacionales
8 Avis/Tagle
10 Banco de
   Tierra del Fuego
11 Turismo Alternativo
   Caminante
13 Locutorio

16 Presidio de Ushuaia
17 Migraciones
20 Chilean Consulate
21 Hospital Regional
22 ACA
23 Los Tres Angeles
25 Transporte Los Carlos
26 Líneas Aéreas Kaikén
29 Banco del Sud
30 Extasis
31 Transportes Pasarela
32 Club Andino Ushuaia
34 Dirección de Turismo
36 Akawaia Turismo
37 Tecni-Austral
38 Banco de la Provincia
   de Santa Cruz
39 LADE
40 All Patagonia

41 Instituto Fueguino de
   Turismo (Infuetur)
42 Telefónica
43 Aerolíneas Argentinas,
   Austral
45 Gaudí
47 Post Office
48 Banco del Territorio
50 Rumbo Sur/Línea B
51 La Posada de los Pájaros
52 Ladeco
55 San Telmo Sur
56 Banca Nazionale del Lavoro
58 Cirtur/El Pingüino
59 Locutorio
60 Banco de la Nación
61 Banco del Territorio (ATM)
63 Museo Territorial Fin
   del Mundo

commission, and has an ATM at San Martín 152. Banca Nazionale del Lavoro, Maipú 297, and Banco de Tierra del Fuego, San Martín 1052, also have ATMs.

Post & Communications Correo Argentino is at Avenida San Martín and Godoy. Besides convenient locutorios at San Martín 133 and San Martín 957, the Dirección de Turismo has a very convenient international line for reverse-charge and credit-card calls to several foreign countries. Ushuaia's telephone code is 0901.

Foreign Consulate Chile's consulate (☎ 22177), Malvinas Argentinas 236, is open on weekdays from 9 am to 1 pm.

Things to See & Do
At Maipú and Rivadavia, the **Museo Territorial Fin del Mundo** has exhibits on natural history, Indian life and early penal colonies, and re-creations of an early general shop and bank. Well worth its US$2 admission, the museum is open Monday to Saturday from 4 to 8 pm.

Closed as a penal institution since 1947, the **Presidio de Ushuaia** held as many a

600 inmates in 380 cells designed for one prisoner each. Now a museum, it's open to the public daily from 5.30 to 9 pm. Admission costs US$2; use the entrance at Yaganes and Gobernador Paz rather than the military entrance at Yaganes and San Martín.

A magnificent walk to **Martial Glacier** starts at the west end of San Martín, climbing the zigzag road (with hiker short cuts) to a ski run seven km north-west of town. About two hours from the base of the lift, the glacier yields awesome views of Ushuaia and the Beagle Channel. Transportes Pasarela, Fadul 40, runs a shuttle to the lift (US$5 return) four times daily.

Places to Stay
Camping Ushuaia's free *Camping Municipal*, eight km west of town on RN 3, has minimal facilities. The *Camping del Rugby Club Ushuaia*, four km west of town, charges an extortionate US$15 per tent, but at least has reasonable facilities.

Casas de Familia The Dirección de Turismo arranges accommodation in private homes, but usually only in peak season. Prices are in the US$20 per person range, sometimes slightly cheaper.

Hospedajes, Pensiones & Residenciales *Hospedaje Torres al Sur*, Gobernador Paz 1437, costs US$15 for a single. The Dirección de Turismo discourages visitors from staying at *Hospedaje Hilda Sánchez* (☎ 23622), Deloquí 391, but many travellers have found her place congenial, if crowded and a bit noisy at times. Rates are US$15 per person, and it's open all year.

Hostería Mustapic (☎ 21718), Piedrabuena 230, charges US$25/35 with shared bath, US$30/40 with private bath. Enthusiastically recommended *Hospedaje Fernández* (☎ 21192), Onachaga 68 at Fitzroy, has doubles at US$49.

Places to Eat
Near the Muelle Turístico, *La Salchicha Austral* is among the most economical eateries, and *La Cocina*, on Avenida Maipú

between Belgrano and Piedrabuena, serves excellent three-course meals for US$6.50. *Der Garten*, in the galería alongside the Dirección de Turismo, has similar weekday specials.

At San Martín and Rosas, the *Bidu Bar* is a popular place to wait for the 3 am Punta Arenas bus; it has decent but not cheap meals. The US$12 tenedor libre at *Cafetería Ideal*, Avenida San Martín 393, isn't really a bargain, but some travellers make it their only meal of the day. *Mi Viejo*, Gobernador Campos 758, also has a tenedor libre special.

Reservations are essential for groups of any size at more elaborate restaurants like *Moustacchio*, San Martín 298; *Tante Elvira*, San Martín 234; and *El Viejo Marino*, Maipú 297, a seafood restaurant.

Getting There & Away
Air A new 2700-metre runway will permit planes larger than 737s to land safely, and Aerolíneas Argentinas' loss of a landing monopoly may soon permit long-distance competition from foreign airlines. LAPA was due to begin flights into Ushuaia in August 1995.

Aerolíneas Argentinas and Austral, sharing offices (☎ 21091), at Roca 126, fly often to Río Gallegos (US$56), Trelew (US$157) and Buenos Aires (US$252). For Patagonian services, including Punta Arenas, Chile, consult LADE (☎ 21123), in the Galería Albatros at Avenida San Martín 564; Líneas Aéreas Kaikén (☎ 23663), at San Martín 857; and El Pingüino agent Cirtur (☎ 21004), Maipú 237.

Ladeco (☎ 31110), Gobernador Godoy 115, flies on Tuesday and Saturday to Punta Arenas (US$110), Puerto Montt and Santiago. Consult travel agencies for Aerovías DAP, which flies on Tuesday, Thursday and Saturday to Punta Arenas (US$60), and on Monday, Wednesday and Friday to Puerto Williams, on Isla Navarino (US$37).

Bus Transporte Los Carlos (☎ 22337), Rosas 85, crosses Paso Garibaldi to Río Grande at least daily (US$20, four hours); on Monday and Friday at 3 am it goes directly to Punta Arenas, Chile (US$48). Tecni-Austral (☎ 23396), in the Galería del Jardín at 25 de Mayo 50, goes to Río Grande, daily at 6 pm.

Getting Around
Rates for a Fiat Spazio start around US$30 per day plus US$0.30 per km, plus at least US$15 insurance daily, at Avis/Tagle (☎ 22744), San Martín and Belgrano, and Localiza (☎ 30663), at Hotel Albatros, and reach up to US$120 per day plus mileage for a Toyota 4WD.

PARQUE NACIONAL TIERRA DEL FUEGO
Argentina's only coastal national park, 18 km west of Ushuaia, extends north from the Beagle Channel to comprise rivers, lakes, forests and glaciers beyond Lago Fagnano. Southern beeches like the evergreen coihue and deciduous lenga thrive on heavy coastal rainfall, and the deciduous ñire tints the hillsides in autumn. Sphagnum peat bogs on the self-guided nature trail at Laguna Negra support ferns, wild flowers, and insectivorous plants. Marine mammals are most common on offshore islands.

Inland, there are guanacos and foxes, but visitors are most likely to see two unfortunate introductions: the European rabbit and the North American beaver. The Andean condor and the maritime black-browed albatross overlap ranges on the coast, but neither is common. Shore birds like cormorants, gulls, terns, oystercatchers, grebes, steamer ducks and kelp geese are common. The large, striking upland goose (cauquén) is common inland. Claudio Venegas Canelo's Aves de Patagonia y Tierra del Fuego Chileno-Argentina (Punta Arenas, 1986) is an outstanding guide to the area's bird life.

Trekking
It's possible to hike from Lapataia along the north shore of Lago Roca to the Chilean border, but authorities have inexplicably closed the upper Río Pipo towards Lago Kami/Fagnano, the best trekking area in the park.

Places to Stay
The only organised camp site, Camping Lago Roca, has a confitería and hot showers for US$4 per person. Camping Ensenada, Camping Las Bandurrias, Camping Laguna Verde, Camping Los Cauquenes and Camping Río Pipo are free sites which, unfortunately, are disgracefully filthy, with scattered toilet paper (and worse) everywhere.

Getting There & Away
During summer, Transportes Pasarela (☎ 21735), Fadul 40 in Ushuaia, makes five trips daily to the park (US$10), and you need not return the same day. Park admission, payable at the ranger station on RN 3, is US$3.50 per person.

Bolivia

Bolivia is the Tibet of the Americas – the highest and most isolated of the Latin American republics. A landlocked country lying astride the widest stretch of the Andean Cordillera, Bolivia spills through a maze of tortured hills and valleys into the vast forests and savannas of the Amazon and Paraná basins, its geographical and climatic zones ranging from snowcapped Andean peaks to vast, low-lying savannas and jungles. With two major indigenous groups and several smaller ones, Bolivia is also the most Indian country on the South American continent. Over 50% of the population are of pure Amerindian blood and many people maintain traditional cultural values and belief systems.

Bolivia has certainly had a turbulent and explosive history, but nowadays its image as a haunt of revolutionaries and drug barons is greatly overstated. The country combines unimaginable landscapes, colonial treasures, colourful indigenous cultures and remnants of mysterious ancient civilisations, and despite its former political strife and problematic drug trade, it remains one of South America's most peaceful, secure and inviting countries. This, together with its natural beauty and cultural wealth, makes Bolivia ideal for independent adventuring.

Country Name República de Bolivia
Area 1,098,580 sq km
Population 7,880,000
Population Density 7.17 per sq km
Capitals La Paz & Sucre
Head of State President Gonzalo Sánchez de Lozada
Official Language Spanish
Other Languages Quechua, Aymara
Currency Boliviano (B$)
Exchange Rate US$1 = B$5.12
Per capita GNP US$650
Inflation Rate 10%

Facts about the Country

HISTORY
Pre-Columbian Times

There's much speculation about humanity's earliest history in Bolivia. It's certain that early advances towards agricultural civilisation took place on the altiplano.

From about 1500 BC, Aymara-speaking Indians, possibly from the mountains of what is now central Peru, swept across into the Bolivian Andes to occupy the altiplano. The years between about 500 and 900 AD were marked by the imperial expansion and increasing power and influence of the new Tiahuanaco (or Tiwanaku) culture. Their ceremonial centre (also known as Tiahuanaco), on the shores of Lake Titicaca, grew and prospered, developing into the religious and political centre of the altiplano.

After about the 9th century AD, however, Tiahuanaco's power waned and its civilisation declined. One theory attributes this decline to a drop in the level of Lake Titicaca,

BOLIVIA

Bolivia

which left the lakeside settlement far from shore. Another theory postulates that Tiahuanaco was attacked and its population massacred by the warlike Kollas (or Collas), also known as the Aymara, from the west. Relics of the Tiahuanaco culture, which are displayed in museums around the country, reflect a high level of technical precision.

Before the Spanish conquest, the Bolivian altiplano had been incorporated into the Inca empire as the southern province of Kollasuyo. The Quechua-speaking Indians who now live around Lake Titicaca first immigrated under the Inca policies of resettling groups of their tribes in the newly conquered colonies and imposing Quechua as the lingua franca of the Central Andes.

The Spanish Conquest

By the late 1520s internal rivalries had begun to take their toll on the Inca empire, but it was the arrival of the Spaniards, first thought to be emissaries of the Inca sun god, that dealt the final blow. The Inca emperor Atahualpa was captured in 1532, and by 1537, the Spanish had consolidated their forces in Peru and securely held Cuzco (the seat of Inca power).

After the fall of the Inca empire, Alto Perú, as the Spaniards called Bolivia, fell briefly into the possession of the *conquistador* Diego de Almagro. Francisco Pizarro dispatched his brother, Gonzalo, to head an expedition to subdue the southern province of Kollasuyo. The Pizarros were, no doubt, attracted by the prospect of silver mines which had been worked in Inca times. Gonzalo Pizarro organised the Charcas administrative unit in what is now central Bolivia and there, in 1538, Pedro de Anzures founded the township of La Plata. La Plata later changed its name to Chuquisaca, and then to its present name, Sucre. It soon grew into the administrative, religious and educational centre of the eastern Spanish territories.

In 1545, vast deposits of silver were discovered at Potosí, and quickly gained prominence due to their abundant, high-quality ores. Before long, the settlement had grown into the largest city on the continent – but not without cost. The atrocious conditions in the Potosí mines led to the deaths of innumerable Indians and African slaves.

In 1548 Alonso de Mendoza founded the city of La Paz on the main silver route from Potosí to the Pacific coast, where it served as a staging post and administrative centre. In 1574, the Spaniards founded Cochabamba, which soon became the granary of Bolivia, and Tarija, which served to contain the uncooperative Chiriguano Indians. Thus, at the close of the 16th century, Bolivia's settlement patterns had been established, within the realm of Spain's South American empire.

Independence

In 1781 a futile attempt was made to expel the Spaniards and re-establish the Inca empire. Some 30 years later, in May 1809, Chuquisaca (Sucre) became the scene of an overt call for independence, and a local government was established. From Chuquisaca, one of the most fertile centres of liberal thinking on the continent, advanced political doctrines radiated throughout Spanish America.

In 1824, after 15 years of war, the liberation of Peru from Spanish domination was finally won in the battles of Junín and Ayacucho. However, in Alto Perú (Bolivia), the royalist General Pedro Antonio de Olañeta still opposed the liberating forces. In 1825, when offers of negotiation failed, Simón Bolívar dispatched an expeditionary force to Alto Perú under General Antonio José de Sucre. With the defeat of Olañeta at the battle of Tumusla, resistance came to an end. On 6 August 1825, independence was proclaimed and Alto Perú became the Republic of Bolivia. Bolívar and Sucre, incidentally, became the first and second presidents of the new republic.

In 1828, Andrés de Santa Cruz (who had a Spanish father and an Indian mother) took power and in 1836, influenced by romantic attachments to Inca ideals, formed a confederacy with Peru. This triggered a protest by Chile, whose army defeated Santa Cruz in 1839, breaking the confederation and submerging Bolivia in political chaos. The confusion peaked in 1841, at which time three different governments claimed power simultaneously.

The pattern of spontaneous and unsanctioned changes of government took root at this time, and continued through the 1980s in a series of coups and military interventions. One military junta after another usurped power from its predecessor; as of 1992, Bolivia had endured 188 changes of government in its 167 years as a republic. With such internal strife, it is not surprising that external affairs haven't always run smoothly either.

Loss of Territory

By the mid-19th century, the discovery of rich deposits of guano and nitrates in the Atacama region changed a desolate and sparsely populated desert into an economically strategic area. As Bolivia lacked the population and resources to settle, develop and exploit its coastal area, it contracted Chilean companies to carry out development projects. In 1879, when the Bolivian government proposed a tax on the minerals, Chile occupied Bolivia's Litoral department,

BOLIVIA

prompting Bolivia and Peru to declare war on Chile.

Between 1879 and 1883, in the War of the Pacific, Chile took 350 km of coastline, leaving Bolivia with no outlet to the sea. Though Chile tried to compensate Bolivia with a railway from Antofagasta to Oruro, and duty-free facilities for the export of Bolivian commodities, Bolivians refused to accept their *enclaustramiento* (landlocked status) and have taken every opportunity to voice their demand for access to the sea. Even now, the government uses the issue as a rallying cry whenever it wants to unite the people in a common cause.

Bolivia's next loss was in 1903, when Brazil annexed some 100,000 sq km of the Acre region, which stretched from Bolivia's present Amazonian border to about halfway up Peru's eastern border. The reason this time was rubber. Centred in Manaus (Brazil), the rubber boom took off in the second half of the 19th century and by 1890 accounted for one-tenth of Brazil's export earnings. Bolivia participated in the boom by plundering the forests of the Acre, until Brazil eventually engineered a dispute over sovereignty, and the Brazilian army was sent in.

Between 1932 and 1935, Bolivia fought a third devastating war, this time against Paraguay for control of the Chaco region. This area had previously been of little interest to either country, as it had very limited agricultural potential and was inhabited only by a few tribes of Indians.

The trouble started when various North American and European oil companies began to speculate about potential oil deposits in the area. In a bid to secure favourable franchises, a quarrel was engineered, with Standard Oil supporting Bolivia and Shell siding with Paraguay. Although Bolivia had more soldiers, fighting conditions in the Chaco favoured the Paraguayans. The climate took a heavy toll on the highland Indian troops of Bolivia, and Bolivia was gradually beaten. By the terms of the peace settlement, negotiated in 1938, the greater part of the disputed areas of the Chaco went to Paraguay, costing Bolivia another 225,000 sq km of its territory. The anticipated oil reserves were never actually found in the Chaco.

The conflict with Paraguay disrupted the economy, discredited the army, spread new ideas among the urban workers and miners and sowed discontent among intellectuals, resulting in a process of social ferment.

Modern Times

After the Chaco War, friction between poor miners and their absentee bosses began to escalate. Radicals, especially in Oruro, gathered beneath the banner of Victor Paz Estenssoro's Movimiento Nacional Revolucionario (MNR). The presidential elections of 1951 took place in an atmosphere of general unrest and finally brought victory to Paz Estenssoro, but a military coup that prevented him from taking power provoked an armed revolt by the miners. After heavy fighting in the April Revolution of 1952, military forces were dispersed and forced to capitulate, and Paz Estenssoro and the MNR took the helm for the first time.

The new government announced social and economic reforms aimed at ensuring the participation of all social sectors. The mining properties were nationalised and the sole right to export mineral products was vested in the state; universal suffrage and an unprecedented policy of agrarian and educational reform, including the redistribution of estates among the peasants and the restructuring of the educational system to provide schooling for everyone, were introduced.

For the first time since the invasion of the Spaniards, indigenous people felt that they had a voice in the Bolivian government. The MNR government lasted 12 years under various presidents; Paz Estenssoro himself returned to power in 1960 for another four-year term, and was elected again in 1964.

The party, however, was unable to raise the standard of living substantially or increase food production, and Paz Estenssoro was forced to become more and more autocratic as dissension in his own ranks increased. Shortly after Paz Estenssoro's re-election in 1964, he was overthrown by

General René Barrientos, thereby initiating another period of dictatorship and plunging Bolivia into renewed political instability.

A series of military regimes ensued until 1982, when the civilian left-wing leader of the Movimiento de la Izquierda Revolucionaria (MIR), Hernán Siles Zuazo, came to power. His term was fraught with labour disputes, high levels of government spending, monetary devaluation and a staggering inflation rate.

When Siles Zuazo gave up after three years and called general elections, Victor Paz Estenssoro returned to politics to become president for the third time. During his four-year term (1985-89), the shattered economy was revived but social problems remained unsolved.

According to the Bolivian constitution, 50% of the popular vote is required for a candidate to become president in direct elections – otherwise, the congress must make the decision. In the 1989 elections, none of the candidates obtained the necessary majority. Subsequently, the right-wing Acción Democrática Nacionalista (ADN) made a deal with the MIR, and the MIR leader, Jaime Paz Zamora, was elected president in exchange for leaving the most important ministries to the opposition.

Bolivia's current president, MNR leader Gonzalo Sánchez de Lozada ('Goni'), defeated former military dictator Hugo Banzer Suárez in elections on 6 June 1993. Sánchez de Lozada and his Aymara running mate, Victor Hugo Cárdenas, appealed to Indian peoples, while urbanites in general embraced his free-market economic policies. So far, his main emphasis has been on privatisation; his policy has initially included the sale of six large state-owned companies (with an eye toward eventually privatising up to 150 companies) and the privatisation of the mining industry through joint ventures in which overseas investors are automatically granted up to 50% ownership.

On 19 April 1995, however, violent labour protests and strikes over the economic policies resulted in the declaration of a 90-day state of siege and the arrest of 374 labour leaders, who were taken to remote parts of the country and detained for several weeks. Initially, travel was restricted and curfews were in place, but gradually, the measures were relaxed. By late 1995, labour grievances still hadn't been resolved, but apart from protests by university students over funding shortages, the social unrest had taken a back seat to cocaine-related problems in the Chapare. On 19 July, the state of siege was renewed in the face of labour unrest in Oruro and Potosí and violence over coca eradication in the Chapare region.

Coca, Cocaine & the Drug War

From time immemorial, coca has played a role in Bolivian culture and history. The Inca love goddess was represented with coca leaves in her hands. Legend has it that Manco Capac, the son of the sun god, who mystically appeared on Isla del Sol in Lake Titicaca, also brought the divine coca leaf, which alleviates hunger and strengthens the feeble.

By the time of the Spanish conquest, the use of coca, which had previously been restricted to privileged families and religious ceremonies, was widespread among Indians, sustaining them through prolonged periods of exhausting labour under severe conditions.

Coca leaves are still chewed. When combined with ashes of other plants, mainly *quinoa*, they yield their alkaloid drug, the basis of cocaine. The juices extracted produce a feeling of wellbeing, giving a high degree of insensitivity to hunger, cold, fatigue and pain, and indifference toward hardship and anxiety. The Spaniards rapidly learnt that coca was a perfect stimulant to increase the efficiency of Indian labour, and promoted its use. Consequently, they introduced commercial plantations, first in the Yungas, still the country's leading producer of coca leaves. The success of La Paz as a city was partially due to the traffic of coca from the Yungas to the Potosí mines. Today, much of this leaf is refined into cocaine or taken to other Latin American countries to be processed. At least 60,000 hectares of coca are currently under cultivation.

In 1989, one-third of the Bolivian workforce was dependent on the illicit production and trafficking of cocaine. By far the most lucrative of Bolivia's economic products, it was generating an annual income of US$1.5 billion, of which just under half remained in Bolivia. Many miners laid off during Paz Estenssoro's austerity measures turned to cocaine as a source of income. Ensuing corruption, acts of terrorism and social problems threatened government control over the country which, in the international perspective, became synonymous with cocaine production.

US threats to cease foreign aid unless efforts were made to stop cocaine production forced Paz Estenssoro to comply with their proposed coca eradication programme. Instead of eliminating the trade, however, the US eradication directive brought about the organisation of increasingly powerful and vociferous peasant unions and interest groups. This, combined with lax enforcement, corruption and skyrocketing profit potential, actually resulted in an increase in cocaine production.

Peasants were offered US$2000 each by the government to destroy their coca plantations and plant alternative crops, such as coffee, bananas and cacao. In early 1990, a drop in the price of coca paste brought about a temporary lull in production, and some coca farmers sold out to the government's proposed crop substitution programme. Many, however, simply collected the money and moved further north to replant.

As early as 1987, the USA had been sending Drug Enforcement Agency (DEA) squadrons into the Beni and Chapare regions of northern Bolivia to assist in the programme. In May 1990, Paz Zamora appealed for increased US aid to support the weakened Bolivian economy. In response, US President George Bush sent US$78 million in aid and stepped up US 'Operation Support Justice' activities. In June 1991, Bolivian police and DEA agents staged a daylight helicopter raid on Santa Ana del Yacuma, north of Trinidad, and seized 15 cocaine laboratories, nine estates, numerous private aircraft and 110 kg of cocaine base; however, no traffickers were captured, having been given sufficient warning to escape. Several later surrendered under Bolivia's lenient 'repentance law'. In mid-1992, Bolivia's Senate voted to expel US troops participating in antinarcotics activities, but it didn't hold.

In early 1995, the USA had grown impatient with what it considered to be Bolivia's failure to destroy its coca crop in a timely manner, and set a deadline of 30 June 1995 for the eradication of nearly 2000 hectares of coca in the Chapare and an additional 3500 hectares by the end of the year. It also demanded Bolivia's signature on an extradition treaty which would send drug traffickers to trial in the USA. If Bolivia refused or failed, US loans, aid and funding would be cut off.

In April, a geographically challenged US Congressman, Dan Burton, suggested the USA spray the Bolivian coca crop with herbicides dropped by planes based on ships 'off the Bolivian coast'. After the laughter had subsided, protests were launched against the US and Bolivian governments for ever suggesting such a thing and the Coca Leaf Growers Association again pointed out that the problem lay not with Bolivian coca growers, but with a burgeoning US market for cocaine.

In any case, Bolivia met the 30 June deadline by paying farmers US$2500 for each hectare destroyed,

which placed a heavy strain on government resources. Problems arose, however, during eradication attempts inside Isiboro-Sécure National Park, which is public land and not eligible for compensation payments. When the 90-day state of siege imposed on 19 April expired (see under Modern Times in the History section earlier in this chapter), violence ensued, resulting in the deaths of five farmers, 287 arrests and the renewal of the state of siege. At this point, the USA started moaning about human rights abuses surrounding the eradication programme – although they themselves had ordered it – while DEA officers openly admitted they'd done nothing to prevent the violence. Over the following weeks, things calmed down, but nothing was settled, and the 31 December 1995 eradication deadline threatened to result in a resumption of unrest.

In August 1995, the Bolivian government rejected a US proposal for militarisation of the anti-drug war, on the grounds that it would compromise its self-determination and obfuscate the real problem, which lay in the profitability of cocaine, thanks mainly to the US market. 'The US washes its hands, evading its internal responsibilities, to take the anti-drug struggle to other countries.' said Senator Carlos García of CONDEPA (Conciencia de Patria). Given the circumstances, it's hard to argue with him.

GEOGRAPHY

Despite the loss of huge chunks of territory in wars and cessions, Bolivia remains South America's fifth-largest country. It encompasses 1,098,000 sq km (the area of France and Spain combined) and is bounded by Peru, Brazil, Paraguay, Argentina and Chile. There are five geographical regions: the altiplano (or 'high plain'), the highland valleys, the Yungas, the Gran Chaco and the Amazon Basin.

Through the western region of Bolivia run two chains of the Andes which extend from the Peruvian border to Chile and Argentina, with many peaks rising above 6000 metres. The western chain, the Cordillera Occidental, stands as a barrier between Bolivia and the Pacific coast. The eastern chain, the Cordillera Real, runs first in a south-eastern direction, then turns south across central Bolivia, and becomes the Cordillera Central.

The altiplano, whose altitude ranges from 3500 to 4000 metres, is bounded by these two great cordilleras. The altiplano itself is a haunting place – an immense, nearly treeless plain stretching to the horizon, punctuated by mountain barriers and solitary volcanic peaks. Near the northern end of the Bolivian altiplano, along the Peruvian border, lies Lake Titicaca, which is generally considered to be the world's highest navigable lake.

At its southern end, the land becomes drier and less populated. Here one finds the remnants of two other great lakes, the Salar de Uyuni and the Salar de Coipasa. These two salt deserts and the surrounding salty plains form an eerie, empty expanse.

East of the Cordillera Central are the highland valleys, a region of scrambled hills and valleys and fertile basins with a Mediterranean climate, where olives, nuts, wheat, maize and grapes are cultivated.

North of the Cordillera Real, where the Andes fall away into the Amazon Basin, the Yungas form a transition zone between dry, arid highlands and humid lowlands.

The northern and eastern areas include flat and sparsely populated lowlands composed of swamps, savannas, scrub and rainforest. These encompass about half of Bolivia's total area.

In the south-eastern corner of Bolivia lies the flat, nearly impenetrable scrubland of the Gran Chaco. The level terrain is covered by a tangled thicket of small thorny trees and cactus. As the region is almost completely uninhabited, native flora and fauna thrive undisturbed.

CLIMATE

Because of its topography, Bolivia has a wide range of altitude-affected climatic patterns. Within its frontiers, every climatic zone can be found, from steaming rainforest heat to Arctic cold.

The rainy period lasts from November to March (the southern summer) through most of the country. Of the major cities, only Potosí normally receives snow (between February and April), but in Oruro and La Paz snow is also possible at the end of the rainy season. On the altiplano and in the highlands, subzero temperatures are frequent, especially at night. Winter in Cochabamba, Sucre and Tarija is a time of clear skies and optimum temperatures. The Amazon Basin

is always hot and wet, with the drier period falling between May and October. The Yungas region is cooler but fairly wet year round.

FLORA & FAUNA

Bolivia's several national parks and reserves are home to a myriad of animal and bird species. Some parks which are accessible to visitors – albeit often with difficulty – include:

Parque Nacional Alto Madidi
This new park protects a wide range of wildlife habitats, and is thought to be home to more than 1000 species of birds. Populated portions of the park along the Río Tuichi have been given a special distinction under UNESCO's Biosphere statutes, which will allow the indigenous Chimane and Tacanas people to continue with their traditional lifestyles. If plans for a simple tourist complex at Laguna Chalalan go ahead, Alto Madidi will rival Peru's Parque Nacional Manu as one of the world's best places to observe rainforest species.

Parque Nacional Amboró
Amboró, near Santa Cruz, was expanded and classified as a national park in 1990. It is home to the rare spectacled bear, jaguars, capybaras, peccaries and an astonishing variety of bird life. Access is via Buena Vista or Samaipata. Further information is available from Fundación Amigos de la Naturaleza (FAN) (☎ (03) 524 921, fax 533 389), Casilla 4200, Santa Cruz. The office is behind a prominent white wall in La Nueve, eight km west of Santa Cruz.

Parque Nacional Carrasco
This remote extension to Amboró attempts to protect some remaining stands of rainforest in the volatile Chapare region. The most accessible site is the Cuevas de los Pájaros Nocturnos, which is most easily reached with Fremen Tours (☎ (042) 47126, fax 48500), Casilla 1040, Calle Tumusla O-245, Cochabamba.

Parque Nacional Isiboro-Sécure
Unfortunately, due to a 1905 policy to colonise this area of the Chapare (northern Cochabamba Department), the Indian population has been either displaced or exterminated, and most of the wildlife has vanished, except in the more remote areas. Access is difficult, and because this park lies along a major coca and cocaine-trafficking route, extreme caution is required if you plan to visit the area. Fremen Tours (☎ (042) 47126), Casilla 1040, Calle Tumusla O-245, Cochabamba, runs river trips into the park's best known site, Laguna Bolivia.

Parque Nacional Noel Kempff Mercado
This remote park near the Brazilian border is named in honour of the distinguished Bolivian biologist who was murdered by renegades in 1986. It contains a variety of Amazon wildlife and some of the most inspiring natural scenery in Bolivia. Overland access is possible from either Bolivia or Brazil, but requires fortitude; most visitors fly from Santa Cruz. See under Parque Nacional Amboró for the FAN information address.

Parque Nacional Sajama
This national park, which adjoins Chile's magnificent Parque Nacional Lauca, contains Volcán Sajama (6542 metres), one of Bolivia's highest peaks. It lies on the main route between La Paz and Arica, Chile, but apart from a couple of private alojamientos, no tourist facilities are available on the Bolivian side.

Parque Nacional Torotoro
Palaeontologists will be interested in the biped and quadruped dinosaur tracks from the Cretaceous period, which can be found in the enormous rock formations near the village of Torotoro. The park also boasts caves, ancient ruins and lovely landscapes. The Asociación Experimental Torotoro (☎ (042 25843) in Cochabamba, can supply visitor information.

Parque Nacional Tunari
This park, right in Cochabamba's back yard, features the Lagunas de Huarahuara, small lakes containing trout, and pleasant mountain scenery. Picnic areas and camp sites are available. The entrance lies within hiking distance of the city centre.

Parque Nacional Ulla-Ulla
Excellent hiking is possible in this remote park abutting the Peruvian border beneath the Cordillera Apolobamba. It was established in 1972 as a vicuña reserve and presently contains 2500 vicuñas and a large population of condors. For information see Instituto de Fomento Lanero (INFOL) (☎ (02) 379 048), Casilla 732, Calle Bueno 444, La Paz.

Reserva Biosférica del Beni
The 334,200-hectare Beni Biosphere Reserve, near San Borja in the Amazon Basin, exists in conjunction with the adjacent Reserva Forestal Chimane. It is home to at least 500 species of tropical birds and more than 100 species of mammals. The entry station, at Porvenir, is on the main La Paz-Trinidad road.

Reserva de Vida Silvestre Ríos Blanco y Negro
This remote 1.4 million-hectare wildlife reserve takes in vast tracts of rainforest, but there has recently been logging encroachment along the eastern boundaries. Wildlife includes anteaters, peccaries and tapirs, and over 300 bird species. Accommodation and access are expensive, but a visit is highly worthwhile. For information, contact Amazonas Adventure Tours (☎ (03) 422 760, fax 422 748), Avenida San Martín 756, 3° Anillo Interno, Barrio Equipetrol, Casilla 2527, Santa Cruz.

GOVERNMENT

In theory, Bolivia is a republic with legislative, executive and judicial branches of government. The first two convene in La Paz and the Supreme Court sits in Sucre, the legal capital. The president is elected to a four-year term, but cannot hold more than one consecutive term. The legislature consists of a Senate and a Chamber of Deputies. Politically, Bolivia currently has one of Latin America's most stable governments.

ECONOMY

Major Bolivian mineral resources include tin, tungsten, antimony, sulphur, copper, silver and gold, but despite this unquestionable wealth of natural resources, Bolivia remains among the poorest Latin American nations. It has been described as 'a donkey burdened with silver' and 'a beggar sitting on a golden chair.'

Thanks to the remoteness of many mines and the distances over which raw metals must be freighted, Bolivia is a high-cost mineral producer. This, together with lack of skill and capital, corruption, disorganisation, and internal strife between the miners' union, cooperatives and the state (which promotes privatisation) makes the mining industry uncertain. Investors are currently looking towards the eastern lowlands, where deposits of natural gas, iron, manganese and petroleum have been discovered.

Bolivia satisfies most of its own agricultural requirements, and exports cotton and soya from the eastern lowlands, as well as some sugar and Yungas coffee. However, illicit exports of coca products exceed all legal agricultural exports combined.

POPULATION & PEOPLE

With just 7.9 million people, Bolivia is thinly populated. Despite its cold, arid climate, the altiplano has long been the country's most densely populated region, with 70% of the people.

Between 50 and 60% of the total population is of pure Indian descent, and most people speak either Quechua or Aymara as a first language. They are traditionally oriented and strongly resist cultural change. About 35% of the population is made up of *mestizos* (of Spanish and Indian blood) and nearly 1% is of African heritage, mostly descended from the slaves conscripted to work the Potosí mines. The remainder of the population is primarily of European descent, with a small Asian minority. The sparsely populated northern and eastern lowlands are currently in the relatively early stages of settlement. In the eastern lowlands, Mennonite farmers have established dairy industries, and Santa Cruz has become a cosmopolitan city, with immigrants from many countries.

The standard of living of most Bolivians is low and in places, such as the El Alto suburb of La Paz (which is becoming a city in its own right), housing, nutrition, education, sanitation and hygiene are appalling. About 8% of infants die before their first birthday and the average life expectancy is only 60 years for men and 65 years for women.

ARTS
Dance

The pre-Hispanic dances of the altiplano were celebrations of war, fertility, hunting prowess, marriage or work. After the Spanish arrived, traditional European dances and those of the African slaves brought to work in the mines were introduced and developed into the hybrid dances that characterise Bolivian festivities today.

If Bolivia has a national dance, it is the *cueca*, danced by handkerchief-waving couples to 3/4 time. It is derived from the Chilean cueca, which in turn is a Creole adaptation of the Spanish fandango. Its liberally interpreted choreography is danced primarily during fiestas by whirling couples, called *pandillas*. The dance is intended to convey a story of courtship, love, loss of love and reconciliation. Another popular dance is the *huayno*, which originated on the altiplano.

The *auqui-auqui* (old man dance) parodies high-born colonial gentlemen by portraying them ludicrously with a top hat, gnarled cane and exaggerated elderly posture.

Another tradition is the *tinku*, which is actually a ritual fight that loosely resembles a dance. It's most practiced during festivals in northern Potosí Department. Tinkus may begin innocently enough but, near the end of the celebrations, they can often erupt into drunken mayhem.

The unique traditions of Tarija, in the south, have developed the *chapaqueada*. It's associated with religious celebrations, particularly San Roque, and is performed to the strains of Tarija's unusual musical instruments. Also popular in Tarija is *la rueda* (the wheel), which is danced throughout the year.

In San Ignacio de Moxos and around the Beni lowlands, festivities are highlighted by the *machetero*, a commemorative folkloric dance accompanied by drums, violins and *bajones* (pan flutes). Dancers carry wooden machetes and wear crowns of brilliant macaw feathers, wooden masks, and costumes of cotton, bark and feathers.

Other popular dances in the northern lowlands include the *carnaval* and the *taquirari beniano*, both adapted from the altiplano, and the *chovena*, from north-eastern Bolivia.

The most unusual and colourful dances are performed at festivals on the high altiplano, particularly during Carnaval. *La Diablada* (the Dance of the Devils) fiesta at Oruro draws crowds from all over. The most famous and recognisable of the Diablada dances is *la morenada*, which re-enacts the dance of black slaves brought to the courts of Viceroy Felipe III. Costumes consist of hooped skirts, shoulder mantles, and dark-faced masks adorned with plumes. Another dance with African origins is *los negritos*. Performers beat on drums, the rhythm reminiscent of the music of the Caribbean.

The *los llameros* represent Andean llama herders, *waca takoris* satirise Spanish bullfighters and *waca tintis* represent the bullfighting *picadores*. The *los Incas* commemorates the original contact between the Incan and southern European cultures, while *las tobas* is performed in honour of the lowland Indians who were forcefully absorbed into the Inca empire.

Music

Although the musical traditions of the Andes have evolved from a series of pre-Inca, Inca, Spanish, Amazonian and even African influences, each region of Bolivia has developed distinctive musical traditions, dances and instruments. The strains of Andean music from the cold, bleak altiplano are suitably haunting and mournful, while those of warmer Tarija, with its bizarre musical

BOLIVIA

instruments, take on more vibrant and colourful tones.

Although the original Andean music was exclusively instrumental, recent trends toward popularisation of the magnificent melodies have inspired the addition of appropriately tragic, bittersweet or morose lyrics.

In the far eastern and northern lowland regions of Bolivia, Jesuit influences upon Chiquitano, Moxos and Guaraní musical talent left a unique legacy which is still in evidence and which remains particularly strong in the musical traditions of neighbouring Paraguay. In addition to economic ventures, the Jesuits encouraged education and European culture among the tribes. Extremely able artists and musicians, the Indians handcrafted musical instruments – the renowned violins and harps featured in Chaco music today – and learned and performed Italian Baroque music, including opera! In the remotest of settings, they gave concerts, dances and theatre performances which could have competed on a European scale.

In Bolivia, folk music shows are called *peñas* and operate, for locals and tourists, in most larger cities.

Musical Instruments Although the martial honking of tinny and poorly practised brass bands seems an integral part of most South American celebrations, the Andean musical traditions employ a variety of instruments which date back to precolonial days.

Only the popular ukulele-like *charango* (based on the Spanish *vihuela* and *bandurria*, early forms of the guitar and mandolin) has European roots. By the early 17th century, Andean Indians had blended and adapted the Spanish designs into one which would better reproduce their pentatonic scale: a 10-stringed instrument with llama-gut strings (arranged in five pairs) and a *quirquincho* (armadillo carapace) soundbox. Modern charangos are scarcely different from the earliest models, but due to the scarcity and fragility of quirquinchos, and to efforts to improve sound quality, wood is now the material of choice for charango soundboxes. Another stringed instrument, the *violín chapaco* originated in Tarija and is a variation on the European violin. Between Easter and the Fiesta de San Roque (held in early September), it is the favoured instrument.

Prior to the advent of the charango, melody lines were carried exclusively by woodwind instruments. Best recognised are the *quena* and the *zampoña* (pan flute), which feature in the majority of traditional musical performances. Quenas are simple reed flutes played by blowing into a notch at one end. The more complex zampoñas are played by forcing air across the open ends of reeds lashed together in order of their size, often in double rows. Both quenas and zampoñas come in a variety of sizes and tonal ranges. Although the quena was originally intended for solo interpretation of musical pieces known as *yaravíes*, the two flutes are now played as part of a musical ensemble. The *bajón*, an enormous pan flute with separate mouthpieces in each reed, accompanies festivities in the Moxos communities of the Beni lowlands. While being played, it must be rested on the ground or carried by two people.

Other prominent wind instruments include the *tarka* and the *sikuri*, lead instruments in the breathy *tarkeadas* and *sikureadas* of the rural altiplano, and the *pinquillo*, a Carnaval flute which comes in various pitches.

Woodwinds unique to the Tarija area are the *erke*, the *caña* and the *camacheña*. The erke, also known as the *phututu*, is made from a cow's horn and is played exclusively between New Year and Carnaval. From San Roque (in early September) to the end of the year, the camacheña, a type of flute, is used. The caña, a three-metre cane pole with a cow's horn on the end, is similar in appearance and tone to an alphorn. It's featured all year round in Tarija.

Percussion also figures in most festivals and other folk musical performances as a backdrop for the typically lilting strains of the woodwind melodies. In highland areas, the most popular drum is the largish *huankara*. The *caja*, a tambourine-like drum played with one hand, is used exclusively in Tarija.

Artists & Recordings Although there is a wealth of yet-to-be-discovered musical talent in Bolivia, key players are influencing musical trends and tastes worldwide with their recordings and occasional performances abroad.

Many visitors, especially those who've attended peñas or fiestas, are captivated by the music and set out in search of recordings to take home. Compact discs haven't yet made their debut in Bolivia, so unless you have space to carry bulky and fragile record albums in your luggage, you'll have to resort to cassette tapes. Unfortunately, original recordings are hard to come by and those sold in music shops and markets are typically low-quality bootlegged copies which are prone to rapid self-destruction, so copy them onto a better tape before giving them much play time. They are cheap, however – around US$3 each.

Major artists you may want to look for include charango masters Ernesto Cavour, Celestino Campos and Mauro Núñez. Look out for the recording *Charangos Famosos*, a selection of well-known charango pieces.

The Bolivian group that's been the most successful abroad is Los Kjarkas. They've recorded at least a dozen albums, including the superb *Canto a la Mujer de Mi Pueblo*. The track entitled 'Llorando se Fue', by the late Bolivian composer Ulises Hermosa and his brother Gonzalo, was recorded by the French group Kaoma in 1989 and became a worldwide hit as 'The Lambada'. In 1990 the Hermosa brothers finally received official recognition for their authorship of the song. Other groups worth noting are Savia Andina, Chullpa Ñan, Rumillajta, Los Quipus, Grupo Cultural Wara, Los Masis and Yanapakuna.

In the USA, tapes of Bolivian music are available through the South American Explorers Club.

Weaving

Spinning and weaving methods have changed little in Bolivia for centuries. In rural areas, girls learn to weave before they reach puberty and women spend nearly all their spare time spinning with a drop spindle or weaving on heddle looms. Prior to Spanish colonisation, llama and alpaca wool were the materials of choice, but sheep's wool has now emerged as the most readily available and least expensive medium.

Bolivian textiles come in diverse patterns, and the majority display a degree of skill that results from millennia of tradition. The beautiful and practical creations are true works of art, and motivated visitors who avoid such over-touristy haunts as Tarabuco and Calle Sagárnaga in La Paz may find real quality at good prices.

Regional differences are manifest in weaving style, motif and use. Weavings from Tarabuco, near Sucre, are made into the colourful costumes (men wear a *chuspa*, or coca pouch, and a trademark red-striped poncho) and intricate zoomorphic patterns seen around the popular and touristy Sunday market in Tarabuco.

The most famous and celebrated of Bolivian weavings are the red-and-black zoomorphic designs from Potolo, north-west of Sucre. Themes range from faithful representations of animals to creative and mythical combinations of animal forms: horses figure prominently, as do avian aberrations. The patterns are not necessarily symmetrical, and the relative size of figures represented often does not conform to reality – it is not unusual for a gigantic horse to be depicted alongside a tiny house. Potolo pieces are prized by weaving buffs and command relatively high prices.

Zoomorphic patterns are also prominent in the wild Charazani country north of Lake Titicaca and in several areas in the vicinity of La Paz, including Lique and Calamarka. Some extremely fine weavings originate in Sica Sica, one of the many dusty and nondescript villages between La Paz and Oruro, while in Calcha, south-east of Potosí near the boundary of Chuquisaca, expert spinning and an extremely tight weave – over 150 threads per inch – combine in some of Bolivia's best clothing textiles.

Those interested in Bolivian textiles may want to look at the books *A Travellers' Guide to Eldorado and the Inca Empire*, by weaving expert Lynn Meisch, or the hard-to-find *Weaving Traditions of Highland Bolivia*, by Laurie Adelson & Bruce Takami, published by the Los Angeles Craft & Folk Art Museum. Another excellent booklet on Bolivian textile arts is *Bolivian Indian Textiles*, by Tamara E Wasserman & Jonathon S Hill, available through the South American Explorers Club.

Architecture

The pre-Columbian architecture of Bolivia is seen in the largely ruined walls and structures of Tiahuanaco, and the numerous Inca

BOLIVIA

remains scattered about the country. Restoration of these sites has been based on architectural interpretation by archaeologists, without revealing much about their artistic values. The classic polygonal cut stones which dominate many Peruvian Inca sites are, in Bolivia, found only on Isla del Sol and Isla de la Luna, in Lake Titicaca.

Surviving colonial architecture, the vast majority of which is religious, is divided into four major overlapping periods: Renaissance (1550-1650); Baroque (1630-1770); mestizo (1690-1790), which was actually a variation on Baroque; and the modern period (post-1790). Around 1790, the beginnings of the modern period were marked by a brief experimentation with the neoclassical style, which was then followed by a return to the neo-Gothic.

Renaissance churches are simple in design. They were constructed primarily of adobe, with courtyards, massive buttresses and naves without aisles. One of the best examples may be seen at the village of Tiahuanaco. Some Andean Renaissance churches indicate Moorish Mudejar influences. The three classic examples of Mudejar Renaissance design are found at San Miguel and San Francisco (in Sucre) and at Copacabana, on the shores of Lake Titicaca.

Baroque churches were constructed in the form of a cross, with an elaborate dome and walls made of either stone or reinforced adobe. The best examples of pure Baroque are the churches of the Compañía in Oruro, San Agustín in Potosí and Santa Bárbara in Sucre.

Mestizo elements in the form of whimsical decorative carvings were introduced late in the Baroque period, and were applied with what appears to be wild abandon. Prominent themes included densely packed tropical flora and fauna, Inca deities and designs, and bizarre masks, sirens and gargoyles. The interesting results are best seen at the churches of San Francisco (in La Paz), San Lorenzo, Santa Teresa and the Compañía (in Potosí) and the rural churches of Sica Sica and Guaqui (in La Paz Department).

Neoclassical design, which dominated between 1790 and the early 20th century, is observed in the church of San Felipe Neri in Sucre, and the cathedrals in Potosí and La Paz.

Paralleling the mainstream church construction in the mid-18th century, the Jesuits in the Beni and Santa Cruz lowlands were designing churches showing evidence of Bavarian Rococo and Gothic influences. Their most unusual effort, however, was the bizarre mission church at San José de Chiquitos, the design of which is unique in Latin America. Its European origins aren't clear, but it bears superficial resemblance to churches in Poland and Belgium.

RELIGION

Bolivians enjoy complete religious freedom. Due to their Spanish colonial past, 95% of Bolivians profess Roman Catholicism. There is, however, a blending of ancient traditions and beliefs and cults with the Christian faith, which has resulted in a peculiar syncretism. This is particularly evident among Indian communities.

LANGUAGE

Spanish is the official language of Bolivia, and most people speak and understand it to some extent. However, more than half of Bolivia's people speak Quechua or Aymara as a first language.

Facts for the Visitor

VISAS & EMBASSIES

Bolivian visa requirements change with astonishing frequency and may at times seem arbitrary; each Bolivian consulate and border crossing has its own requirements and associated prices.

Currently, citizens of Argentina, Austria, Chile, Colombia, Ecuador, Israel, Paraguay, Switzerland, Uruguay, Scandinavian countries (including Finland and Iceland), the UK, Germany, Ireland, Italy and Spain – do not require visas for stays of up to 90 days.

Citizens of the USA, Canada, Australia, New Zealand, France, Belgium, Luxembourg, Portugal and most other noncommunist countries outside the Middle East, south Asia, South-East Asia, the former Soviet Union or North Africa are granted stays of 30 days without a visa.

South Africans, Dutch and Brazilians require visas, which are issued by Bolivian consular representatives in their home countries or in neighbouring South American countries. The cost varies according to the consulate and the nationality of the applicant, and may be up to US$50 for a one-year multiple-entry visa.

Officially, everyone entering Bolivia requires proof of onward transport and sufficient funds for their intended stay; in practice officials rarely scrutinise these items. Passports must be valid for one year beyond the date of entering the country. Entry or exit stamps are free of charge and attempts at charging should be met with polite refusal; in hopes of stamping out corruption, immigration offices now display notices to this effect.

Visas and lengths of stay may be extended with little ado at immigration offices in major cities. (If you only want to extend your stay, don't inadvertently ask for a visa extension, or that's what you'll get – as one reader learned – and you could have problems when leaving the country.) Length-of-stay extensions are free to most nationalities, but US passport holders must pay US$20 for each month over their original 30 days. Overstayers are fined US$1.10 per day, and may face a measure of red tape at the border or airport when leaving the country.

Bolivian Embassies Abroad
Bolivia is represented in the following countries:

Australia/New Zealand
Consulate: Suite 512, 5th floor, Pennys Building, 210 Queen St, GPO Box 53, Brisbane, Qld 4001 (☎ (07) 3221 1606)
Canada
Embassy: 17 Metcalfe St, Suite 608, Ottawa, Ontario K1P 426 (☎ (613) 236-5730)

France
Consulate General: 12 Avenue du Presidente Kennedy, 75016 Paris 16 (☎ 01 42 88 34 32)
Germany
Embassy: Konstantinstrasse 16, D-5300 Bonn 2 (☎ (0228) 36 20 38)
UK
Embassy: 106 Eaton Square, SW12W London (☎ (0171) 235-4248)
USA
Consulate General: 211 E 43rd St, Room 802, New York, NY 10017 (☎ (212) 687-0530)
Embassy: 3014 Massachusetts Ave NW, Washington, DC 20008 (☎ (202) 483 -4410)
Consulate: 870 Market St, San Francisco, CA

Foreign Embassies in Bolivia
See the La Paz section later in this chapter for details of foreign legations in Bolivia.

DOCUMENTS
Personal documents – passports, visas, *cédulas* (identification cards) etc, or photocopies of these items – must be carried at all times to avoid fines during police checks and lost time at the police station while paperwork is shuffled. This is most strictly enforced in lowland regions.

Anyone coming from a yellow-fever infected area needs a certificate of yellow-fever vaccination. Travellers entering Brazil from Bolivia are also required to have proof of yellow fever vaccination.

CUSTOMS
Visitors are permitted to import duty-free two bottles of alcohol, up to 500 grams of tobacco, 50 cigars and 200 cigarettes. Drugs and firearms are prohibited.

MONEY
Currency
Bolivia's unit of currency is the *boliviano* (B$), which is divided into 100 *centavos*. Bolivianos come in five, 10, 20, 50, 100 and 200 denomination notes, with coins worth five, 10, 20 and 50 centavos, and one and two bolivianos. Bolivian currency is extremely difficult to change outside Bolivia, so don't wind up with more than you'll need.

The official rate represents the currency's actual value, and there's no black market.

BOLIVIA

BOLIVIA

Exchange Rates

Approximate official rates are:

Australia	A$1	=	B$4.01
Canada	C$1	=	B$3.75
France	FF1	=	B$0.99
Germany	DM1	=	B$3.34
Japan	¥100	=	B$4.71
New Zealand	NZ$1	=	B$3.47
United Kingdom	UK£1	=	B$7.88
USA	US$1	=	B$5.12

As a rule, visitors fare best with US dollars, which are the only foreign currency accepted throughout Bolivia. Currencies of neighbouring countries may be exchanged in border areas and at certain La Paz casas de cambio. American Express travellers' cheques seem to be the most widely accepted brand, though you shouldn't have problems with other major brands.

Currency may be exchanged at casas de cambio and at some banks in larger cities. All casas de cambio change cash dollars and some also change travellers' cheques. You can often change money in travel agencies, jewellery or appliance stores, pharmacies etc. These establishments deal mainly with cash, though a few also accept travellers' cheques. Street moneychangers operate virtually around the clock in most cities and towns but they only change cash dollars, paying roughly the same as casas de cambio and other establishments. They're convenient after hours, but you must guard against rip-offs.

The rate for cash doesn't vary much from place to place, although rates may be slightly lower in border areas. The rate for travellers' cheques is best in La Paz, where it nearly equals the cash rate; in other large cities it's 3 to 5% lower, and in smaller towns it may be impossible to change travellers' cheques at all. Some La Paz casas de cambio exchange travellers' cheques for cash dollars for a 1 to 3% commission. It's a good idea to have some cash dollars if you are heading into the interior, especially off the La Paz-Cochabamba-Santa Cruz axis.

When exchanging money, ask for the cash in small denominations, as there are chronic problems with change. Another problem concerns mangled notes; unless both halves of torn and repaired notes bear identical serial numbers, the note is worthless. Also, don't accept any old B$2 notes; they're worthless and merchants often try to pawn them off on foreigners.

Credit Cards

Major cards, such as Visa, MasterCard and American Express, may be used in larger cities at first-rate hotels, restaurants and tour agencies.

Because travellers' cheques may be difficult to change in some places, there's a good case for carrying a Visa or MasterCard credit card. Visa, and often MasterCard, cash withdrawals of up to US$300 per day are available with no commission and a minimum of hassle, from branches of the Banco de Santa Cruz, Banco Mercantil and the Banco Nacional de Bolivia in La Paz, Sucre, Cochabamba and Santa Cruz. Banco de La Paz charges 1.75% commission on cash withdrawals.

WHEN TO GO

Bolivia lies in the southern hemisphere; winter runs from May to October and summer from November to April. The most important climatic factor to remember is that it's generally wet in the summer and dry in the winter.

While the highlands and altiplano can be cold in the winter and wet in the summer, the only serious barrier to travel will be the odd road washout. In the tropical lowlands, however, summer can be miserable with mud, steamy heat, bugs and relentless downpours. Travel is difficult, and services may be stifled by mud and flooding. On the other hand, these conditions necessitate an increase in river transport, so it can be the best season to look for cargo boats in northern Bolivia.

Also consider that the high tourist season falls in the winter (late June to early September), due not only to climatic factors, but also to the timing of European and North American summer holidays and the fact that it's also Bolivia's major fiesta season. This means that both overseas visitors and lots of South Americans are travelling during this period. This can be an advantage if you're looking for people to form a tour group for the South-Western Circuit or the Cordillera Apolobamba, but average prices for food, accommodation, transport, tours and artesanía are a bit higher than in other seasons.

TOURIST OFFICES

The government tourist information body, the Secretaria Nacional de Turismo (Senatur), has offices in La Paz and several other cities. There is still little printed tourist information, but the typically enthusiastic staff members do their best to help.

USEFUL ORGANISATIONS

The following groups in Bolivia promote environmental preservation:

Armonía, Casilla 3045, La Paz (☎ (02) 792 337) or Casilla 3081, Santa Cruz (☎ (03) 522 919, fax 324 971)

Asociación Boliviana para la Protección de las Aves, Calle Jordán O-151, Casilla 3257, Cochabamba (☎ (042) 26322, fax 24837)

Asociación para la Protección del Medio Ambiente de Tarija, Calle O'Connor 449, Casilla 59, Tarija (☎ (066) 33873, fax 45865)

Asociación Sucrense Ecológica, Calle Avaroa 326, Sucre (☎ (064) 32079, fax 22091)

Conservación Internacional, Casilla 5633, Avenida Villazón 1958-10A, La Paz (☎ (02) 341 230)

Fundación Amigos de la Naturaleza (FAN), Casilla 4200, Santa Cruz (☎ (0944) 524 921, fax 533 389)

Instituto de Ecología, Casilla 10077, Calle 27, Cotacota, La Paz (☎ (02) 792 582, fax 391 176)

BUSINESS HOURS & HOLIDAYS

Very little opens before 9 or 9.30 am, although markets may see dribbles of activity as early as 6 am. In the cities, an increasing number of restaurants are opening at 8 am to serve breakfast. Shops, travel agencies and banks open around 9 am.

At noon, cities virtually close down, with the exception of markets and restaurants serving lunch-hour crowds. The afternoon resurrection begins at between 2 and 4 pm, and most businesses remain open until at least 8 or 9 pm. Bars and restaurants generally close at around 10 pm. On Saturday, shops, services and some eateries close down at 1 pm but street markets run until at least mid-afternoon and often into the evening. Sundays are generally dead, but ice-cream parlours, street vendors and some markets operate during the day.

Public Holidays

Bolivian public holidays include:

1 January
　　Año Nuevo (New Year's Day)
February/March (dates vary)
　　Carnaval
March/April (dates vary)
　　Semana Santa (Easter Week)
1 May
　　Día del Trabajador (Labour Day)
May
　　Corpus Christi
5-7 August
　　Días de la Independencia (Independence Days)
12 October
　　Día de la Raza (Columbus Day)
2 November
　　Día de los Muertos (All Souls' Day)
25 December
　　Navidad (Christmas Day)

In addition, each department has its own holiday: 22 February in Oruro, 15 April in Tarija, 25 May in Chuquisaca, 16 July in La Paz, 14 September in Cochabamba, 24 September in Santa Cruz and Pando, and 18 November in Beni.

SPECIAL EVENTS

Bolivian fiestas are invariably of religious or political origin, normally commemorating a Christian or Indian saint or god, or a political event such as a battle or revolution. They typically include lots of folk music, dancing, processions, food, alcohol, ritual and general unrestrained behaviour. Water balloons (tourists are especially vulnerable!), fireworks and brass bands figure prominently.

The following is a list of major events:

BOLIVIA

24 January
  Alasitas, La Paz
First week in February
  Virgen de Candelaria, Copacabana
February/March (the week before Lent; dates vary)
  La Diablada, Oruro
Second Sunday in March
  Phujllay, Tarabuco
Late May or early June
  El Gran Poder, La Paz
31 July
  Santo Patrono de Moxos, San Ignacio de Moxos
10-13 August
  San Lorenzo, San Lorenzo
15-18 August
  Virgen de Urcupiña, Quillacollo
Late August
  Chu'tillos, Potosí
First week in September
  San Roque, Tarija

POST & COMMUNICATIONS

All major and minor cities have both Empresa Nacional de Telecomunicaciones (ENTEL) and post offices (Correos de Bolivia). From major towns, the post is generally reliable, but when posting anything important, it's still wise to pay an additional US$0.20 to send it certified mail. Poste restante (occasionally called *lista de correos*) is available in larger cities and towns. The only posting boxes are inside post offices.

Local telephone calls can be made from ENTEL offices for just a few centavos. In La Paz and in some tiny villages, you'll find pay telephone boxes. Alternatively, small street kiosks are often equipped with telephones which may be used for brief local calls. These cost around US$0.20. Card phones and telephone cards have been introduced, but as yet are available only at larger ENTEL offices and major airports.

Codes for making long-distance telephone calls within Bolivia are given in individual city and town sections; when phoning from outside Bolivia, drop the initial zero from the code. Bolivia's country code is 591. The international direct-dialling access code is 00. For reverse-charge (collect) calls from a private line, dial the international operator (☎ 356 700, La Paz) and explain that the call is *por cobrar*.

ENTEL offices will not accept reverse-charge calls.

TIME

Bolivian time is four hours behind Greenwich Mean Time. When it's noon in La Paz, it's 4 pm in London, 11 am in New York, 8 am in San Francisco, 4 am the following day in Auckland and 2 am the following day in Sydney and Melbourne.

ELECTRICITY

Bolivia uses a standard current of 220V at 50 Hz except in La Paz and a few selected locations in Potosí which use 110V at 50 Hz. Ask before you plug in. In some areas, the water and power are routinely turned off at certain times of day and/or at night. If you're a night owl, have a torch on hand.

WEIGHTS & MEASURES

Like the rest of South America, Bolivia uses the metric system. For converting between metric and imperial units, refer to the table at the back of the book.

Uniquely South American measurements which are used occasionally in Bolivia include the *arroba*, which is equal to 11.25 kg, and the *quintal*, which is equal to four arrobas, or 45 kg.

BOOKS

There is a general reading list in the introductory Facts for the Visitor chapter. For further travel information on Bolivia, pick up Lonely Planet's *Bolivia – a travel survival kit*, which gives a complete rundown on the country. If you intend to go hiking or trekking, look for *Backpacking and Trekking in Peru & Bolivia*, by Hilary Bradt, which covers major hikes in the Cordillera Real and the Yungas.

A Traveller's Guide to El Dorado & the Inca Empire by Lynn Meisch is an excellent book providing timeless information about Colombia, Ecuador, Peru and Bolivia, especially their weaving and textiles.

English, German and French language publications are available from Los Amigos del Libro, with outlets in La Paz and Cochabamba. They're quite pricey (due mainly to a weighty import duty), but they do offer a good selection of popular paperbacks, Latin American literature, magazines, dictionaries and histories, as well as glossy coffee-table books dealing with the anthropology, archaeology and scenery of Bolivia. The Librería del Turista on Plaza San Francisco in La Paz sells a limited range of books and maps on Bolivia and its history. *Newsweek*, *Time* and *The Economist* are sold at kiosks and bookshops in La Paz, Santa Cruz and Cochabamba.

Spanish-language books, including novels and classic literature, are found at Los Amigos del Libro and similar shops. Most *librerías* (bookshops) and street sellers, however, sell only stationery, pulpy local publications, comics and school texts.

MAPS

Government mapping topo sheets and speciality maps are available from the Instituto Geográfico Militar (IGM), whose head office is on Avenida Bautista Saavedra in Miraflores, La Paz. It's in a military compound, and visitors must present their passport at the entrance. There's also a smaller outlet at Oficina 5, Calle Juan XXIII 100, off Calle Rodríguez between Calles Linares and Murillo, also in La Paz. Here, you select and pay for maps, and they'll be ready for collection the following day.

Both offices sell topo sheets and thematic national maps at a scale of 1:50,000 and 1:250,000, covering some 70% of Bolivia, and if the sheet you want is sold out, they'll provide photocopies at discounted prices. Notable areas which are unavailable, for security reasons, include the Tipuani Valley, the Cordillera Apolobamba and Noel Kempff Mercado National Park.

Bolivian geologic maps are sold at Geobol, on the corner of Ortiz and Federico Zuazo in La Paz; take your passport. For trekking maps of the Cordillera Real and Sajama, the colourful contour maps produced by Walter Guzmán (US$5 to US$8.25) are good. Try the Librería Don Bosco and the Librería del Turista, both in

La Paz. Climbing maps of Illimani and Illampu at a scale of 1:50,000 are published in Munich by the Deutscher Alpenverein and are distributed internationally.

MEDIA

Cochabamba, La Paz, Potosí, Oruro and Santa Cruz all have daily newspapers. There's also an English-language weekly, *The Bolivian Times*, which is sold at newsstands and bookshops in major cities. *Newsweek*, the *International Herald Tribune*, *Time* and the *Miami Herald* are sold at some street kiosks in larger cities and at Los Amigos del Libro in La Paz, Cochabamba and Santa Cruz.

Bolivia has two government-run and five private TV stations and 125 radio stations broadcasting in Spanish, Quechua and Aymara. Recommended listening includes FM-96.7 in La Paz, which plays classic rock and pop music, and Radio Latina in Cochabamba, at the upper end of the FM band, which plays a mix of Andean folk music, salsa and local rock.

HEALTH

Bolivia is not a particularly unhealthy country, but sanitation and hygiene are poor, and you should pay attention to what you eat. If an inexpensive restaurant or market stall is popular with locals, chances are it's a good choice. Some tap water is safe to drink, but if you'd rather not chance it and can't boil it, opt for bottled mineral water. The most widely available brand is Viscachani, but unfortunately, the mineral in question here appears to be salt. If you can find them, Salvietti from Sucre and Vertiente from Cochabamba are better choices.

Most Bolivians live between 3000 and 4000 metres, and altitude sickness can occur. Read carefully the information on altitude-related health problems in the Health section of the Facts for the Visitor chapter.

A yellow-fever vaccination certificate is required for overland travel from Bolivia into Brazil.

WORK

There is a great number of voluntary and nongovernment organisations at work in Bolivia, and quite a few international companies have offices there, but travellers looking for paid work on the spot probably won't have much luck.

Qualified English teachers wishing to work in La Paz or other cities may want to try the professionally run Centro Boliviano Americano (☎ 351 627), Avenida Aniceto Arce at Parque Zenón Iturralde, La Paz. However, new teachers there must forfeit two months salary in order to pay for their training.

Alternatively, phone Señor Emo Alandia at the Pan American English Language Institute (☎ 379 654), Pasaje Bernardo Trigues, to arrange an interview. This friendly institution is almost always looking for qualified staff.

If you prefer voluntary work with an emphasis on environmental protection, contact Earthwatch (☎ (617) 926 8200), 680 Mt Auburn St, Box 403, Watertown, MA 02272, USA.

ACTIVITIES

Hiking, trekking and mountaineering are among the most rewarding ways to gain an appreciation of the Andes. Like the Himalaya, the mountain backbone of South America is not a wilderness area and has been inhabited for thousands of years by farmers and herders. While most of the popular hikes and treks in Bolivia begin near La Paz, traverse the Cordillera Real along ancient Inca routes, and end in the Yungas, many areas of the country are suitable for hiking.

An increasing number of La Paz agencies organise technical climbs and expeditions into the Cordillera Real and to Volcán Sajama near the Chilean border, Bolivia's highest peak. For a list of recommended agencies, see under La Paz.

For an alternative perspective on downhill skiing, you may want to check out Chacaltaya, near La Paz, which is the world's highest developed ski resort. The words 'developed' and 'resort' are used rather loosely: facilities are limited to a draughty warm-up hut and a challenging makeshift ski-tow, and snow conditions range from icy to icier, but if you're up for a high-altitude challenge, you can still have a lot of fun. For more information, see Around La Paz later in this chapter.

HIGHLIGHTS

Although much of Bolivia has been ignored by tourism, there's a fairly rutted trail connecting Lake Titicaca and La Paz, which are often visited on a side trip from Peru. Beyond La Paz, however, is a wealth of cultural, historical and natural wonders. Don't miss the fabulous colonial architecture of Sucre and Potosí; the brilliant canyon country around Tupiza; a religious or indigenous fiesta or a folk music programme; the misty valleys of the Yungas; a trek through the Cordillera Real; a journey to the lakes and volcanoes of the far south-west; or a stay in one of the country's charming small towns and villages, particularly Coroico, Copacabana, Rurrenabaque, Sorata or San Ignacio de Moxos.

ACCOMMODATION

Throughout Bolivia, the prices and value of accommodation are not uniform. The cheapest accommodation is found in Copacabana, while the Amazon region is generally the most expensive. All accommodation rates are negotiable, especially during slow periods; prices given in this chapter are applicable in the high season (late June to early September).

Room availability in Bolivia is rarely a problem. The main exception is during major fiestas, when prices double and rooms are occupied by visiting nationals. On weekends you may have problems finding a room in Coroico, and during the winter months Uyuni also experiences accommodation shortages.

The Bolivian hotel rating system divides accommodation into categories which, from bottom to top, include *posadas*, *aloja-*

mientos, residenciales, casas de huéspedes, hostales and *hoteles.* This rating system reflects the price scale and, to some extent, the quality.

Posadas are the bottom end – the cheapest basic roof and bed available; they're frequented mainly by *campesinos* (peasants) visiting the city. They cost between US$1 and US$2.50 per person and vary in quality, normally from bad to worse. Hot water is unknown, and some even lack showers.

A step up are the alojamientos, which are also generally quite basic, but are considerably better and cost a bit more. Bath facilities are almost always communal, but some do offer hot showers. The value varies widely – some are clean and tidy, while others are disgustingly seedy. Prices range from US$1.20 per person in Copacabana to around US$6 in some Amazon Basin towns.

Residenciales, casas de huéspedes and hostales all serve as finer budget hotels, but their quality also varies and some alojamientos have taken to calling themselves 'residenciales' to improve their image. Still, most are acceptable and you'll often have a choice between shared or private baths. Plan on US$8 to US$20 for a double with private bath, and about 30% less without.

Moving up-market, there's a whole constellation of hotels, which vary in standard from literal dumps to five-star luxury. The lower range hotels can be amazingly cheap while the most expensive hotels top US$100 per person.

Most Bolivian hotel owners are friendly, honest people who demand the same standards of their staff. Still, use common sense and don't leave valuables in hotel rooms unless you're certain they're secure. If you'll be away for a few days, most hotels will watch luggage free of charge.

Bolivia offers excellent camping, especially along trekking routes and in remote mountain areas. There are very few organised camp sites, but if you have camping gear, you can pitch a tent almost anywhere outside population centres. Remember, however, that highland nights can be freezing.

FOOD

Thanks to its many climatic zones, Bolivia offers diverse traditional cuisines. Altiplano fare tends to be starchy and loaded with carbohydrates. Potatoes come in dozens of varieties, most of them small and colourful. Freeze-dried potatoes, called *chuño* or *tunta,* often accompany meals. In the lowlands, the potato and its relatives are replaced by *yuca* (cassava), and other vegetables figure more prominently.

The predominant meats are beef, chicken and fish. The poorer campesinos eat *cordero* (mutton), *cabrito* (goat), llama and, on special occasions, *carne de chancho* (pork). The most popular fish on the altiplano is *trucha* (trout) from Lake Titicaca. The lowlands have a great variety of freshwater fish, including *sábalo, dorado* and the delicious *surubí.*

Some popular Bolivian dishes include *chairo* (a kind of lamb or mutton broth with potatoes, chuños and other vegetables), *sajta* (chicken served in hot pepper sauce), *saice* (a spicy meat broth), *pacumutu* (filleted beef chunks), *silpancho* (pounded beef schnitzel) and *pique a lo macho* (chopped beef served with onions and other vegetables).

For a mid-morning snack, many Bolivians eat *salteñas,* delicious rugby ball-shaped meat and vegetable pasties which originated in Salta, Argentina. They're stuffed with beef or chicken, olives, egg, potato, onion, peas, carrots and other items. A similar concoction is the *tucumana,* which is square-shaped and generally contains more juice.

Standard meals are *desayuno* (breakfast), *almuerzo* (lunch, although the word normally refers to a set lunch served at midday) and *cena* (dinner). For almuerzo, many restaurants, from backstreet cubbyholes to classy establishments, offer bargain set meals consisting of soup, a main course, and tea or coffee. In some places, a salad starter and a simple dessert are included. Almuerzos cost roughly half the price of à la carte dishes – from US$1 to US$3, depending on the class of restaurant. Market *comedores* almost always offer the cheapest options, and they're normally not too bad.

BOLIVIA

DRINKS

Beyond the usual black tea, coffee and chocolate, typical local hot drinks include *mate de coca* (coca leaf tea) and *api*. Api, a sweet breakfast drink made of maize, lemon and cinnamon, is served mainly in markets. Coke, Sprite, Pepsi, Fanta etc are available, as well as locally produced soft drinks of varying palatability. Many markets and restaurants serve up *licuados*, which are delicious fruit shakes made with either milk or water.

Most of Bolivia's wine is produced around Tarija with varying degrees of success. The best – and most expensive – is Concepción San Bernardo de la Frontera, which sells for around US$5 per bottle. The same wineries also produce *singani*, a spirit obtained by distilling poor-quality grape products. The most popular cocktail is *chuflay*, a pleasant blend of singani, 7-Up, ice and lemon. Bolivian beers aren't bad either; popular brands include Huari, Paceña, Tropical Extra, Sureña and Potosina.

The favourite alcoholic drink of the Bolivian masses is *chicha cochabambina*, which is obtained by fermenting maize. It is made all over Bolivia, especially in the Cochabamba region. Other versions of chicha, often nonalcoholic, are made from maize, sweet potato, peanuts, cassava and other fruits and vegetables.

Getting There & Away

Only a few airlines offer direct services to Bolivia and fares are typically high; those from Peru and Chile are the most economical. It often works out cheaper to fly into a neighbouring country (such as Peru, Chile, Brazil or Argentina), and then travel overland to Bolivia. The same goes with departure; it's very difficult to find a discounted fare out of the country.

AIR

The national airline is Lloyd Aéreo Boliviano (☎ (02) 367 710, La Paz), commonly known as LAB, which offers both domestic and international flights.

To/From Argentina

LAB has a service from Buenos Aires to La Paz via Santa Cruz on Tuesday, Friday and Sunday. Fares are US$310 to La Paz and US$256 to Santa Cruz. On Sunday, this flight also serves Salta, Argentina. On Monday, Aerolíneas Argentinas (☎ (02) 375 711, fax 391 059, La Paz) flies between Buenos Aires and Santa Cruz via Salta and Córdoba, and on Thursday and Saturday, between Buenos Aires and La Paz.

To/From Brazil

LAB has flights between Rio de Janeiro, São Paulo and La Paz, via Santa Cruz four times weekly. One-way fares from Rio/São Paulo are US$341/317 to La Paz and US$273/262 to Santa Cruz. Varig (☎ (02) 811 925, La Paz) flies the same route on Tuesday, Thursday, Friday and Saturday. On Friday, AeroPerú (☎ (02) 370 002, La Paz) flies between La Paz, Santa Cruz, Rio de Janeiro and São Paulo. In addition, LAB does a Thursday run between Manaus and Santa Cruz for US$207 one way.

To/From Chile

LanChile (☎ (02) 358 377, La Paz) and LAB both fly daily between La Paz, Arica, Iquique and Santiago. The fare to Arica is US$92 and to Santiago, US$215.

To/From Paraguay

LAB flies between Asunción, Santa Cruz and La Paz on Tuesday and Friday. One-way fares from La Paz to Asunción are US$168 from Santa Cruz, US$215 from La Paz.

To/From Peru

LAB, KLM (☎ (02) 323 965, La Paz), AeroPerú and Lufthansa (☎ (02) 372 170, La Paz) all fly between Lima and La Paz. LAB has a service on Tuesday, Thursday, Saturday and Sunday for US$180 one way. From Cuzco to La Paz, AeroPerú flies daily except Sunday and KLM flies twice weekly. Peru levies an air ticket tax of 21% for Peruvian residents and 7% for nonresident tourists.

BUS, TRAIN & BOAT
To/From Argentina
From Salta or Jujuy in north-western Argentina, buses leave every couple of hours during the day for La Quiaca, which lies opposite the Bolivian town of Villazón. It takes about 20 minutes to walk between the Argentine and Bolivian bus terminals, excluding immigration procedures, but taxis are available.

From Villazón, buses run to Tupiza and Potosí, and trains leave for Tupiza, Uyuni, Oruro and La Paz on Monday, Tuesday, Thursday and Friday; an express train runs on Saturday.

The border crossing at tiny Pocitos is just a short distance south of Yacuiba, Bolivia and north of Tartagal, Argentina. The walk across the border between Pocitos, Argentina and Pocitos, Bolivia takes about 10 minutes. There are taxis between Pocitos and Yacuiba and buses to and from Tartagal.

From Tucumán in north-central Argentina, take a bus to Embarcación and Tartagal, and from there to Pocitos on the frontier. From Yacuiba, buses run to Santa Cruz, Tarija and the rest of Bolivia. Trains leave Yacuiba for Santa Cruz daily except Wednesday and Sunday.

The third Bolivia-Argentina border crossing is at Bermejo/Aguas Blancas, which is sometimes used by travellers. It's accessed via Tarija in Bolivia and Oran in Argentina.

To/From Brazil
Corumbá, opposite the Bolivian border town of Quijarro, is the busiest port of entry between Bolivia and Brazil, with both rail and bus connections from São Paulo, Rio de Janeiro, Cuiabá and southern Brazil.

Once in Corumbá, take a bus to the border, and from there go by taxi to the Quijarro railhead (US$1 per person). From Quijarro, passenger trains leave for Santa Cruz on Monday, Tuesday, Thursday and Saturday. The more frequent freight trains will also accept passengers in the *bodegas* (boxcars),

but they may be less comfortable. During the wet, you may wait several days.

From Cáceres, south-west of Cuiabá, you can cross to San Matías in Bolivia, and from there either take a bus to San Ignacio de Velasco or fly to Santa Cruz (via Roboré).

From Brasiléia, in the state of Acre, you can cross into Cobija, Bolivia, where you'll find buses to Riberalta. From there, dry-weather roads run to La Paz and Guayaramerín.

A more popular crossing is by ferry from Guajará-Mirim in Brazil across the Río Mamoré to Guayaramerín, Bolivia. From there, you can travel by bus to Riberalta and on to Cobija, Rurrenabaque or La Paz.

To/From Chile
Ferrobuses run between La Paz and Arica, with immigration formalities at the Visviri/Charaña border crossing. They leave Arica on Tuesday and Saturday mornings, as well as on Thursday in the summer. This trip can get extremely cold, especially in the border area, so bring warm clothing.

Twice weekly, Flota Litoral buses cover the route between their Calle Chacabuco office in Arica and the main La Paz terminal, via the Chungará/Tambo Quemado border crossing. The very rough route is currently being paved; when finished, the 18-hour trip will be shortened to just seven hours. Trans-Sabaya also has a twice-weekly service between Oruro and Chungará (Lauca National Park), with direct connections to Arica.

Agencia Martínez, also in Arica, runs a Wednesday bus service from Arica to Visviri, to meet the Bolivian train which connects Viacha (south of La Paz) with the border town of Charaña.

Coming from Antofagasta, you must first take a bus to Calama (US$3, two hours). From there, a Wednesday evening train goes to Ollagüe on the Bolivian border, eight hours uphill from Calama. In Ollagüe, passengers cross the border to Avaroa on foot to connect with the Bolivian train to Uyuni and Oruro. At the Tramaca bus terminal in Antofagasta, you can buy a combination bus and train ticket all the way to La Paz. As on all routes between Chile and Bolivia, warm clothes are vital.

To/From Paraguay

The three-day overland route between Bolivia and Paraguay is extremely rough and sandy, but the trip is now negotiated by hardy *camiones* (trucks) and buses during the winter dry season. From Asunción to Santa Cruz, Flota Santa Ana at the main bus terminal leaves on Monday, Wednesday and Friday, and STEL Turismo (☎ 26059, Asunción) leaves Tuesday at 4 pm from Asunción and on Friday from Santa Cruz. The fare is US$72. Trucks run every few days between Filadelfia (Paraguay) and Boyuibe (Bolivia), charging US$10 to US$15 per person.

Alternatively, you can travel up the Río Paraguay from Asunción to Corumbá on the Brazil-Bolivia border. The regular riverboats are currently in mothballs, but if you have time, you can still do the trip in stages (for more information, see Getting There & Away under Corumbá in the Brazil chapter).

To/From Peru

There are two routes from Puno, which is Peru's main access point for Bolivia. The quicker but less interesting is by *micro* (small bus) from Puno to the frontier at Desaguadero, where you can connect with Bolivian transport to La Paz.

The more scenic and interesting route is via Copacabana and the Estrecho de Tiquina (Straits of Tiquina). Minibuses leave from Puno and enter Bolivia at Yunguyo, 11 km from Copacabana. There you connect with another minibus, or with a bus company, for the four to five-hour trip to La Paz, including the boat across the straits. The entire run from Puno to La Paz can be done in a day, but the Copacabana area merits a couple of days exploration.

There are other obscure border crossings, such as the one from Puerto Acosta north of Lake Titicaca and a couple of ports of entry along the rivers of the north, but they require some effort and there's no public transport available.

LEAVING BOLIVIA

Airports charge a US$20 departure tax on international flights for those who have spent less than 90 days in Bolivia. Those staying longer than 90 days must pay an additional US$30. The tax is payable to the aviation authority, AASANA, after check-in.

Getting Around

AIR

Domestic air services are provided by Lloyd Aéreo Boliviano (LAB), the national airline, and AeroSur. Both have a wide network with frequent flights, and services to virtually everywhere you might wish to go. Service on LAB has improved considerably over the past several years, but delays and cancellations are still frequent in the Amazon lowlands. AeroSur offers generally better service, but fares are slightly higher, especially in the Amazon region.

The military airline, Transportes Aéreos Militares (TAM), is not usually recommended for the general public. Fares are cheaper than LAB's, but you can't book a seat unless you buy a ticket, and flights are often late or cancelled.

The following are sample one-way LAB fares from La Paz:

Cochabamba	US$41
Puerto Suárez	US$145
Riberalta	US$128
Santa Cruz	US$91
Sucre	US$56
Tarija	US$88
Trinidad	US$57

LAB offers a special deal known as LABpass, an air pass which allows four flights between any of the main cities served by LAB: La Paz, Cochabamba, Sucre, Santa Cruz, Tarija and Trinidad. It costs US$150 and is available from LAB offices and travel agencies.

The domestic airport departure tax *(dere-*

cho del aeropuerto) ranges from US$1.20 to US$2 and is paid at the airport after check-in.

BUS & CAMION

The Bolivian road network isn't great, but it's improving all the time as more and more km are paved. Unpaved roads range from good-grade dirt to mud, sand or potholed gravel. Modern coaches use the best roads, while older vehicles cover minor secondary routes.

Long-distance bus lines are called *flotas*. Large buses are called *buses* and small ones are called *micros*. A bus terminal is a *terminal terrestre*.

To be safe, reserve bus tickets at least several hours in advance. Most buses depart in the afternoon or evening, to arrive at their destination in the wee hours of the morning. However, on major routes, such as La Paz-Cochabamba, there are also daytime departures.

An alternative to night bus travel is the *camión* (truck). This is a very popular mode of transport among campesinos, as the camiones normally charge around half to two-thirds the bus fare. Camión rides can be excruciatingly slow and rough, depending on the cargo and the number of passengers being carried, but they do offer the best views of the typically spectacular countryside. Each town has one or two places where camiones gather to wait for passengers; some even have scheduled departures. Otherwise, the best place to hitch lifts will be the appropriate *tranca*, a police checkpoint at every town exit.

On any bus or camión trip in the highlands, day or night, take plenty of warm clothing. At night on the altiplano, temperatures can drop to well below freezing. Even in the lowlands, nights can be surprisingly chilly.

TRAIN

The Bolivian national railroad, ENFE, has 4300 km of rail lines in two networks. The Red Occidental (Western Network) has its nerve centre in Oruro with service to La Paz, Cochabamba, Sucre, Potosí, Villazón (on the Argentine border), Avaroa and Charaña (both on the Chilean border); the Red Oriental (Eastern Network) has its focus on Santa Cruz, with lines to Quijarro on the Brazilian border and Yacuiba on the Argentine border.

There are four sorts of trains. The best is usually the *ferrobus*, which is available on limited runs. It's fairly quick and comfortable and usually runs on time. Another is the *tren expreso* (also known as the *tren bala* – the bullet train – or *tren especial*), which is slower and less expensive than the ferrobus. These trains carry relatively comfortable coaches with 1st-class (Pullman) seats, as well as crowded 2nd-class (*especial*) coaches, a dining car and normally at least one passenger bodega (boxcar). (In some cases, travel in the bodegas is more comfortable than in the 2nd-class coaches.) On the Red Oriental, they also carry *Bracha* coaches, with air-con, videos and meal service.

Next comes the *tren rápido* (literally 'fast train', though it is actually very, very slow and normally stops at every station) and, finally, the *tren mixto*, an excruciatingly slow mixed goods train which has no delusions about its velocity and carries most of its passengers in bodegas. Only 2nd class is available.

Because of their low fares, these last two types are used mainly by the campesinos, their children, their luggage and their animals – you'll have lots of company. The trenes mixtos rarely run to a real schedule and may well hold the slow speed record for the continent.

Overall, rail travel in Bolivia (especially on the tren mixto or tren rápido) requires some determination, a strong constitution and vast reserves of patience. Few stations have printed timetables; instead, departure times are scrawled on a blackboard. When buying tickets, take your passport. For the ferrobus, you can purchase tickets up to a week in advance, but for other trains, tickets are available only on the day of departure. Unfortunately, ticket windows open erratically, so procuring tickets isn't entirely

BOLIVIA

BOLIVIA

straightforward. The best information will normally come from the *jefe de la estación* (stationmaster).

BOAT

Half of Bolivia's territory lies in the Amazon Basin, where rivers are the main transport arteries and transport is by cargo boats, which carry passengers, vehicles and livestock. The main highways of the region are the Ichilo, Mamoré, Beni, Madre de Dios and Guaporé rivers – all Amazon tributaries. For more information about boats, refer to the Amazon Basin section.

ORGANISED TOURS

Organised tours, based mainly in La Paz, are rapidly becoming more popular. Shorter tours are normally arranged through hotels, agencies and tourist offices, and if you're in a hurry, they're a convenient way to quickly visit an attraction you'd otherwise miss. They're also relatively inexpensive, averaging US$20 for a day trip and less for a half-day trip.

Tours are excellent for visiting Tiahuanaco, for example. An English-speaking guide is normally included, and the ruins can become more than an impressive 'heap of rocks'. A short tour is also useful for visiting the Chacaltaya ski slopes, which are difficult to reach on your own. Similarly, longer excursions to such remote attractions as Laguna Colorada or the Cordillera Apolobamba are most conveniently done through tour agencies.

For the more adventurous, who nevertheless don't want to strike out into the wilderness alone, there are a number of outfits which offer trekking, mountain climbing, river running and rainforest exploration packages. For mountain trekking or climbing in the Cordilleras, tour operators offer customised expeditions. They can arrange anything from just a guide and transport right up to equipment, porters and even a cook. Some also hire trekking equipment.

Recommended adventure tour companies include:

Amazonas Adventure Tours, 756 Avenida San Martín, 3rd Anillo Interno, Barrio Equipetrol, Casilla 2527, Santa Cruz (☎ (03) 422 760, fax 422 748). This company specialises in visits to the remote Reserva de Vida Silvestre Ríos Blanco y Negro and the jungle resort at Perseverancia.

America Tours, Avenida 16 de Julio 1490, ground floor, Casilla 2568, La Paz (☎ (02) 328 584, fax 374 204). This agency specialises in cultural and ecotourism trips to the Sajama and the far southwest, Rurrenabaque and the Beni, and the Jesuit missions.

Andean Summits, Calle Sagárnaga 189, 1st floor, Casilla 6976, La Paz (☎ & fax (02) 317 497). Andean Summits offers mountaineering and trekking all over Bolivia, plus other adventure tours and archaeology trips.

Colibri, Calle Sagárnaga 309, Casilla 7456, La Paz (☎ (02) 371 936, fax 355 043). Colibri offers comprehensive adventure travel services: trekking, mountaineering, mountain biking, jungle trips and 4WD tours and hires climbing and trekking gear.

Colonial Tours, Expediciones Bolivia, Calle México 1733, Casilla 5108, La Paz (☎ & fax (02) 316 073). This friendly agency offers customised mountaineering and trekking plus classical and cultural tours. Walk-in clients are welcome. The Curva to Pelechuco trek in the Cordillera Apolobamba is an especially good deal at US$280 per person, including transport, equipment, meals, a guide and porters.

Diana Tours, Calle Sagárnaga 328, Hotel Sagárnaga, La Paz (☎ (02) 358 757). This company does good-value city tours as well as day trips to Tiahuanaco, Valle de la Luna, Chacaltaya, the Yungas and cheap tours to Copacabana and Puno.

Fremen Tours, Calle Belisario Salinas 429, La Paz (☎ (02) 327 073); Casilla 1040, Calle Tumusla 0-245, Cochabamba (☎ (042) 47126, fax 48500). This up-market company specialises in the Amazon area, including the Chapare region, Parque Nacional Isiboro-Sécure, La Puente – a wilderness resort near Villa Tunari – and the *Reina de Enin* riverboat based in Trinidad.

Huayna Potosí Tours, Hotel Continental, Calle Illampu 626, Casilla 731, La Paz (☎ (02) 323 584, fax 378 226). The owner of this agency, Dr Hugo Berrios, built and operates the rather luxurious mountain hut, Refugio Huayna Potosí (US$7 per night), which serves as a base camp for Huayna Potosí expeditions. Dr Berrios, who is an A-1 character and speaks both English and French, also organises good-value treks and climbs in the Cordillera Real and Cordillera Apolobamba, as well as other areas of Bolivia.

Ozono, Office 101, 1st floor, Edificio Guanabara, Avenida Arce esquina Cordero, Casilla 7243, La Paz (☎ & fax (02) 722 240; e-mail ozono@bolivia.com). This innovative adventure travel company specialises in mountaineering, trekking, rock climbing, extreme skiing, 4WD trips and lowland expeditions, with emphasis on activities and destinations well off the beaten path. It's run by two British mountain and trekking guides and a *paceño* (an inhabitant of La Paz) who has worked in Canada as a ski instructor.

TAWA Tours, Calle Sagárnaga 161, 1st floor, Casilla 8662, La Paz (☎ (02) 325 796, fax 391 175). TAWA offers a wide selection of adventure tourism options, including mountaineering, cross-country skiing, jungle trips, trekking, horse riding and mountain biking in all parts of Bolivia.

La Paz

The home of more than a million Bolivians, over half of Indian heritage, La Paz is the country's largest city and its centre of commerce, finance and industry. Although Sucre remains the judiciary capital, La Paz has usurped most government power and is now the de facto capital.

La Paz was founded by Alonso de Mendoza in 1548, following the discovery of gold in the Río Choqueyapu. Although gold fever didn't last long, the town's location on the main silver route from Potosí to the Pacific assured stable progress. It wasn't until the middle of the present century that peasant migration from the countryside caused the city to expand rapidly.

A visitor's first view of La Paz will be unforgettable. The city's bleak approaches are flanked by the grey, littered and poverty-plagued sprawl of El Alto, which was once merely a La Paz suburb, but has now burgeoned into a separate entity. At its edge, however, the earth drops away as if all the poverty and ugliness has been obliterated, and there, 400 metres below, is La Paz, filling the bowl and climbing the walls of a gaping canyon nearly five km from rim to rim. On a clear day, the snowcapped triple peak of Illimani (6402 metres) towers in the background.

Since La Paz is nearly four km above sea level, warm clothing is needed through much of the year. In the summer, the climate can be harsh; rain falls on most afternoons; the canyon may fill with clouds or the steep streets may become torrents of run-off. Daytime temperatures hover around 18°C, though dampness can make it seem colder. In the winter, days are slightly cooler, but the crisp, clear air is invigorating. While the sun shines, the temperature may reach the mid to high teens, while at night, it often dips below freezing.

La Paz offers a range of hotels, restaurants, entertainment venues and activities, and the longer you stay, the more apparent this will become. You can spend hours exploring the city's colourful backstreets and markets, or just sit back and watch urban Bolivians circulating through their daily tasks and routines: the *cholas* (city-dwelling Quechua or Aymara women) with their obligatory bowler hats and voluminous skirts, the police and military types, the beggars, and the well-dressed business-people and politicians.

Orientation

It's almost impossible to get lost in La Paz. There's only one major thoroughfare which follows the canyon of the Río Choqueyapu (which flows mostly underground these days). It changes names several times from top to bottom: Avenidas Ismael Montes, Mariscal Santa Cruz, 16 de Julio (the Prado) and Villazón. At the lower end, it splits into Avenida 6 de Agosto and Avenida Aniceto Arce. If you become disoriented and want to return to this main street, just head downhill. Away from this thoroughfare, streets climb steeply uphill, and many are cobbled or unpaved. Above the downtown skyscrapers, the adobe neighbourhoods and the informal commercial areas climb toward the canyon's rim.

Information

Tourist Office Senatur has its La Paz office at Plaza del Estudiante, on the corner of México and 16 de Julio. It's open Monday to Friday from 8.30 am to 8 pm and on Saturday from 8.30 am to 1 pm. It has a book of visitor

BOLIVIA

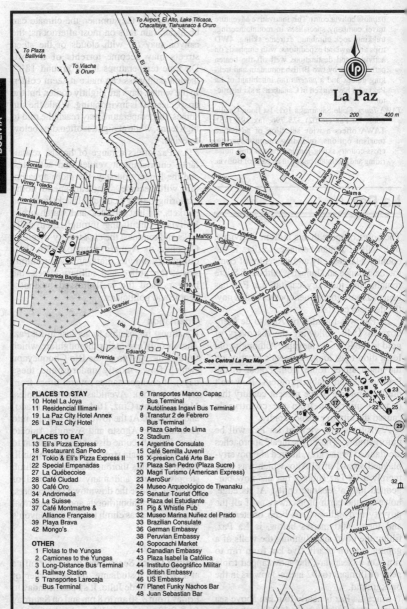

To Airport, El Alto, Lake Titicaca,
Chacaltaya, Tiahuanaco & Oruro

To Plaza
Ballivián

To Viacha
& Oruro

La Paz

0   200   400 m

See Central La Paz Map

PLACES TO STAY
10 Hotel La Joya
11 Residencial Illimani
19 La Paz City Hotel Annex
26 La Paz City Hotel

PLACES TO EAT
13 Eli's Pizza Express
18 Restaurant San Pedro
21 Tokio & Eli's Pizza Express II
22 Special Empanadas
27 La Québecoise
28 Café Ciudad
30 Café Oro
34 Andromeda
35 La Suisse
37 Café Montmartre &
   Alliance Française
39 Playa Brava
42 Mongo's

OTHER
1 Flotas to the Yungas
2 Camiones to the Yungas
3 Long-Distance Bus Terminal
4 Railway Station
5 Transportes Larecaja
   Bus Terminal

6 Transportes Manco Capac
   Bus Terminal
7 Autolíneas Ingavi Bus Terminal
8 Transtur 2 de Febrero
   Bus Terminal
9 Plaza Garita de Lima
12 Stadium
14 Argentine Consulate
15 Café Semilla Juvenil
16 X-presion Café Arte Bar
17 Plaza San Pedro (Plaza Sucre)
20 Magri Turismo (American Express)
23 AeroSur
24 Museo Arqueológico de Tiwanaku
25 Senatur Tourist Office
29 Plaza del Estudiante
31 Pig & Whistle Pub
32 Museo Marina Nuñez del Prado
36 German Embassy
38 Peruvian Embassy
40 Sopocachi Market
42 Canadian Embassy
43 Plaza Isabel la Católica
44 Instituto Geográfico Militar
45 British Embassy
46 US Embassy
47 Planet Funky Nachos Bar
48 Juan Sebastian Bar

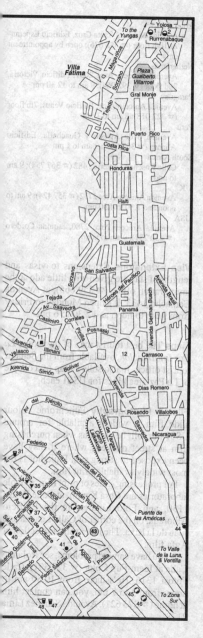

recommendations, and distributes a host of other brochures dealing with La Paz and the entire country, some in English, French and German (however, if you speak even a little Spanish, the original Spanish versions may make more sense than the often amusing translations).

Money Most of the casas de cambio are found in the central area of the city. Casa de Cambio Sudamer, on Calle Colón, changes travellers' cheques and is open from 8.30 am to noon and 2 to 6 pm on weekdays and from 9 am to noon on Saturday. It also sells currency from neighbouring countries (when it's available). Some casas de cambio also change travellers' cheques into cash for a 1% commission, which is worth considering, as outside La Paz you'll get 3 to 10% less for cheques than for cash. Both Sudamer and Casa de Cambio Silver, at Calle Mercado 979, have been recommended. Remember to check carefully for counterfeit US dollar notes, which have been surfacing with increasing frequency.

On Saturday, you can change cash or travellers' cheques at most casas de cambio in the morning only. On Sunday or after hours, go to the Hotel Gloria, the Residencial Rosario or the El Lobo restaurant. Around the intersections of Calle Colón, Avenida Camacho and Mariscal Santa Cruz, *cambistas* (street moneychangers) will change cash for slightly lower rates than casas de cambio, but stay attentive during the transaction.

Visa and MasterCard cash withdrawals of up to US$300 daily are available with no commission and a minimum of hassle from the Banco de Santa Cruz, at Calle Mercado 1077; Banco Mercantil, on the corner of Calles Mercado and Ayacucho; and Banco Nacional de Bolivia, on the corner of Calle Colón and Avenida Camacho. Banco de La Paz charges 1.75% commission on cash withdrawals. Cash withdrawals on Visa cards are also available at Enlace automatic cash machines dotted around the city.

The American Express representative is Magri Turismo (see Travel Agencies).

Post & Communications The main post office, on the corner of Avenida Mariscal Santa Cruz and Calle Oruro, is open Monday to Friday from 8.30 am to 8 pm, Saturday from 9 am to 7 pm and Sunday from 9 am to noon. Post sent to poste restante should be addressed as follows: your name (with surname underlined and capitalised), Poste Restante, Correo Central, La Paz, Bolivia. Mail is held for three months. The service is free, but you must present your passport when collecting post. Poste restante is sorted into foreign and Bolivian stacks, so those with Latin surnames should check the Bolivian stacks as well.

The ENTEL office, at Calle Ayacucho 267, is open daily from 7.30 am to 10.30 pm for national and international telephone calls. ENTEL also has telegram and telex services, as well as a rather inefficient fax office. The public fax numbers in La Paz are 391784 and 367625. There is also an increasing number of convenient *entelitos* or 'little ENTELs' scattered around the city.

La Paz's telephone code is 02.

Foreign Embassies & Consulates The following countries are among those with representation in La Paz. All opening hours are Monday to Friday only:

Argentina
  Edificio Banco de la Nación Argentina, 2nd floor (☎ 353 089); 8.30 am to 1.30 pm
Brazil
  Avenida 20 de Octubre 2038, Edificio Foncomin, 9th to 11th floors (☎ 350 769); 9 am to 1 pm
Canada
  Plaza Avaroa, Avenida 20 de Octubre 2475 (☎ 375 224); 9 am to noon
Chile
  Avenida Hernando Siles 5843, Calle 13, Obrajes (☎ 785 046); 8.30 am to 1 pm and 3 to 6 pm
Colombia
  Plaza Avaroa, Avenida 20 de Octubre 2427, 2nd floor (☎ 359 658); 9 am to 2 pm
France
  Avenida Hernando Siles 5390, Calle 8, Obrajes (☎ 786 189); 9 am to noon
Germany
  Avenida Aniceto Arce 2395 (☎ 390 850); 9 am to noon

Israel
  Avenida Mariscal Santa Cruz, Edificio Esperanza 10th floor (☎ 358 676); open by appointment only
Netherlands
  Avenida Aniceto Arce 2031, Edificio Victoria, 2nd floor (☎ 392 064); 9 am to 12.30 pm
Paraguay
  Avenida Aniceto Arce, Edificio Venus, 7th floor (☎ 322 018); 8 am to 1 pm
Peru
  Avenida 6 de Agosto y Guachalla, Edificio Alianza (☎ 367 640); 9 am to 1 pm
South Africa
  Calle Rosendo Gutiérrez 482 (☎ 367 754); 9 am to noon
UK
  Avenida Aniceto Arce 2732 (☎ 357 424); 9 am to noon and 1.30 to 4.30 pm
USA
  Avenida Aniceto Arce 2780, esquina Cordero (☎ 430 251); 9 am to noon

Visa Extensions Extensions to visas and lengths of stay are given with little ado at the immigration office (☎ 359 665), at Avenida Camacho 1433. It's open Monday to Friday from 9 am to noon and 2.30 to 6 pm.

Maps The best tourist map of the city is *La Paz Información*, available from the Senatur tourist office. It also sells a map of a couple of La Paz area hikes for US$1 each.

Film & Photography Fujichrome colour slide film is widely available for around US$7 per roll; be cautious when purchasing film at street markets, where it may have been exposed to strong sun. Fujicolor is the most widely available print film.

For processing slides or print film, reliable laboratories are Casa Kavlin, at Calle Potosí 1130, and Foto Linares, in the Edificio Alborada, on the corner of Calle Loayza and Juan de la Riva. The latter sells a selection of Agfa film.

If you have camera problems, see Rolando Calla at Idem-Fuji Color (☎ 327 391), Calle Potosí 1316. He's there from 10.30 am to noon; from 3 to 7 pm, you can contact him at home (☎ 373 621), Avenida Sánchez Lima 2178.

Medical Services The Unidad Sanitario Centro Piloto, near the brewery just off upper Avenida Ismael Montes, is open from 8.30 am to noon and 2.30 to 6.30 pm. Anyone heading for the lowlands can pick up yellow fever vaccinations, and free chloroquine to be used as a malaria prophylaxis. Avoid chloroquine, however, if you've previously been taking mefloquine (Lariam), as the combination is potentially harmful.

Rabies vaccinations are available for US$1. Anyone bitten or scratched by a suspect animal must take daily vaccinations for seven subsequent days, and three more over the next two months.

If you're in need of an English-speaking doctor, try Clínica Americana (☎ 783 509), at 5809 Avenida 14 de Septiembre, Calle 9, in Obrajes. The sign outside says 'Hospital Metodista'. The German clinic, Clínica Alemana (☎ 329 155), is at Avenida 6 de Agosto 2821.

Things to See

La Paz has conventional tourist attractions such as churches and museums. For those seeking something different, it's a city that invites leisurely exploration, to appreciate the architectural mishmash, colourful street scenes, busy market life, and the strong flavour of the country's Indian cultures, which is more in evidence here than in other Latin American capitals.

The most unusual market is the **Mercado de Hechicería** or **Mercado de los Brujos** (Witches' Market), near the corner of Calles Santa Cruz and Linares. Here, merchants sell a variety of herbs, seeds, figurines, magical ingredients and other strange things – such as dried llama foetuses – intended as remedies for any combination of ills or as protection from the malevolent spirits which populate the Aymara world. In the same area, mainly along Sagárnaga and Linares, are plenty of handicraft shops and street stalls selling beautiful Indian weavings (ponchos, *mantas* (shawls), coca pouches), musical instruments, silver antiques, 'original' Tiahuanaco artefacts and a wealth of other tourist-oriented stuff. Higher up, around

Buenos Aires, Graneros and Max Paredes, you'll find the **Mercado Negro**. The name means 'black market' but it's mainly above board and is a good place to bargain for clothing and ordinary household goods. It is, however, notorious for pickpockets and skilful rip-offs; don't let yourself become distracted and avoid carrying anything of value.

Construction of the **Iglesia de San Francisco**, on the plaza of the same name, started in 1549 but was not finished until the mid-18th century. The architecture of this imposing church reflects the mestizo style, with emphasis on nature and natural forms. On Saturday mornings, you may see colourful Indian wedding processions. Other churches are of limited interest, though you might enjoy the impressive façade of **Iglesia de Santo Domingo**, on the corner of Yanacocha and Ingavi.

Museums La Paz has several worthwhile museums, some housed in beautifully restored colonial mansions. The **Museo de Etnografía y Folklore** is in the former Casa del Marquez de Villaverde, on the corner of Ingavi and Sanjinés. It has a fine collection of weavings and other crafts from several ethnic groups throughout the country. It's open Monday to Friday from 8.30 am to noon and 2.30 to 6.30 pm. Admission is free.

The **Museo Nacional del Arte** is in the Palacio de los Condes de Arana, an impressive 18th-century mansion at the corner of Comercio and Socabaya. It displays colonial and contemporary painting and is open Tuesday to Friday from 9.30 am to 12.30 pm and 3 to 7 pm and on Saturday from 9.30 am to 1.30 pm. Admission costs US$0.70.

You can also visit the **Museo Marina Núñez del Prado**, dedicated to Bolivia's most renowned sculptor, at Calle Ecuador 2034. It's open Monday to Friday from 9 am to noon and 2 to 6 pm.

The **Museo Arqueológico de Tiwanaku**, on the corner of Calles Federico Suazo and Tiwanaku, holds a collection of pottery, small stone sculptures, textiles and other artefacts, and utensils from different stages

BOLIVIA

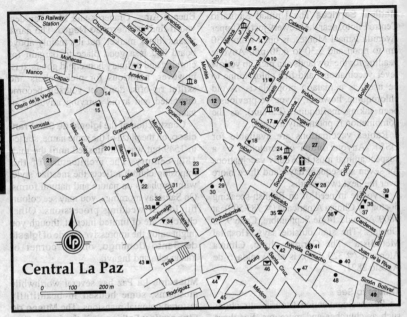

Central La Paz

0   100   200 m

of the Tiahuanaco (Tiwanaku) culture. It's open Tuesday to Friday from 9 am to noon and 2.30 to 6.45 pm, and on Saturday from 10 am to 12.30 pm and 2.30 to 6.30 pm. Admission for foreigners is US$1.

If you're interested in the city's past traditions, visit the **Museo Tambo Quirquincho**, a former *tambo* (wayside market and inn) on Calle Evaristo Valle, just off the Plaza Alonso de Mendoza. It displays old-time dresses, silverware, photos, artwork and a collection of Carnaval masks. It's open Tuesday to Friday from 9.30 am to 12.30 pm and 3.30 to 7 pm, and on weekends from 10 am to 12.30 pm. Admission is US$.50 on weekdays and free on Saturday.

Four interesting museums – the **Museo de Metales Preciosos Precolombinos**, the **Museo del Litoral Boliviano**, the **Museo Casa Murillo** and the **Museo Costumbrista Juan de Vargas** – are clustered together along Calle Jaén, a beautifully restored colonial street, and can easily be bundled into one

visit. The museums are open Tuesday to Friday from 9.30 am to noon and 2.30 to 6.30 pm, and on weekends from 10 am to 12.30 pm. Foreigners pay US$2 for a combination ticket which covers admission to all four. On Saturday, admission is free for everyone.

Special Events

La Paz enjoys several local festivals and holidays during the year, but El Gran Poder (late May/early June) and Alasitas, the festival of abundance (24 January), will be of particular interest to visitors. The Fiestas Universitarias take place during the first week in December, accompanied by riotous merrymaking.

Places to Stay

Most bottom-end hotels lock up at midnight; all places listed here have hot water at least part of the day.

A cheap, clean, secure and friendly place,

PLACES TO STAY		34	El Montañés	12	Plaza Pérez Velasco
1	Hostería Florida	36	Boutique del Pan	13	Mercado Lanza
2	Alojamiento	38	El Vegetariano	14	Plaza Vicenta
	Universo	42	Confitería Club de La		Juariste Eguino
9	Hostal Ingavi		Paz	16	Museo de Etnografía
15	Hotel Continental	44	Acuario II		y Folklore
17	Hostal Austria	47	Café Verona	21	Mercado Negro
20	Residencial Rosario			23	Iglesia de San
25	Hotel Torino	**OTHER**			Francisco
32	Hotel Sagárnaga	3	Museo de Metales	24	Museo Nacional del
33	Hotel Alem		Preciosos		Arte
37	Hotel Viena		Precolombinos,	26	Catedral
39	Hostal República		Museo del Litoral,	27	Plaza Murillo
43	Hotel Milton		iMuseo Cos-	30	Peña Naira
			tumbrista Juan de	31	Mercado de
PLACES TO EAT			Vargas & Museo		Hechicería
4	Casa de los Paceños		Casa Murillo	35	ENTEL (Main Office)
7	El Palacio de Pescado	5	Peña Marka Tambo	40	Immigration
18	Café Pierrot	6	Plaza Alonzo de	41	Casa de Cambio
19	La Hacienda		Mendoza		Sudamer
22	El Lobo	8	Museo Tambo	45	Plaza Belzu
28	Pollo Copacabana		Quirquincho	46	Main Post Office
29	Restaurant Veg-	10	Cinemateca Boliviana	48	LAB Office
	etarianista Lila Vaty	11	Teatro Municipal	49	Mercado Camacho

with hot showers, is *Alojamiento Universo* (☎ 340 341), at Calle Inca Mayta Capac 175, which charges just US$2.25 per person. Ground-floor rooms are nicer than those upstairs.

A favourite with Peace Corp volunteers – and a very friendly option – is the *La Paz City Hotel* (☎ 322 177), near Plaza San Pedro. Singles are US$5.50; larger rooms cost US$4 per person. It also has an annex on Calle México.

If being central is a concern, the convenient *Hotel Torino* (☎ 341 487), at Calle Socabaya 457 is a good bet. Its demeanour has grown a bit surly – an unfortunate by-product of its former reputation as *the* travellers' crash pad – but it's still quite popular with mountaineers. Services for guests include a book exchange and a free left-luggage service. The attached bar-restaurant serves good almuerzos for under US$2 and offers live music on weekends. In the evening, however, the din often spills over into the hotel. Singles/doubles cost US$8/11 without bath or US$16/21 with bath.

The current backpackers' favourite – and

rightfully so – is the friendly and centrally located *Hostal Austria* (☎ 351 140), at 531 Yanacocha. It has safe gas-heated showers and cooking facilities. One to four-bed rooms with shared bath cost US$5 per person. Although several basic rooms lack windows, it's always full. When booking, make it clear when you expect to arrive, and don't be late; otherwise, your booking may disappear.

In the same area is *Hostal Ingavi* (☎ 323 645), Calle Ingavi 727, which charges a negotiable US$6.50 per person with shared bath. Although it's a bit noisy and less than sparkling-clean, it is acceptable.

A new option is the relatively elegant *Hotel La Joya* (☎ 324 346, fax 350 959), near Plaza Garita de Lima in the Mercado Negro. The official rates of US$13/17 without bath and US$21/28 with bath place it in the mid-range, but when space is available, backpackers can stay for US$6.50 per person.

A pleasant, inexpensive place is *Residencial Illimani* (☎ 325 948), at Avenida Illimani 1817, not far from the stadium. It's away from the action but it's quiet and friendly and singles/doubles without bath cost US$5/7.50.

Also recommended is *Hostería Florida* (☎ 363 298), Calle Viacha 489. The street unfortunately serves as a public toilet, but it's friendly and rooms are clean and comfortable and cost just US$6 per person with private bath. Upper-floor rooms may offer excellent views of the city and proximity to the TV lounge, but the lift is (apparently permanently) broken.

Overlooking 'artesanía alley' on steep and bustling Calle Sagárnaga is the recommended *Hotel Sagárnaga* (☎ 350 252). Rooms cost US$21/28 with bath, and US$13/17 without (including continental breakfast). Next door is the pleasant *Hotel Alem* (☎ 367 400), with singles/doubles for US$7/11 without bath and US$13.50/18.50 with bath and breakfast.

It seems the much-lauded *Residencial Rosario* (☎ 325 348), at Calle Illampu 704, has let success go to its top floor. The staff have become a bit blasé, prices have risen and all available space has been converted into a rabbit warren of stairways and passages to accommodate its enormous popularity. Still, it remains ultraclean and pleasantly quiet: a sort of travellers' capsule with Bolivia just outside the door. Singles/doubles/triples without bath cost US$14/18/25. Rooms with private bath cost US$24/30/38 and are reserved primarily for tour groups.

At Calle Illampu 626, on Plaza Eguino, is the two-star *Hotel Continental* (☎ & fax 378 226). Prices aren't bad at US$13.50/17.50 for singles/doubles without bath and US$21/28 with bath. *Hotel Milton* (☎ 368 003), at Calle Illampu 1224, is clean, has good hot showers and costs US$18/24 for singles/doubles with bath.

The sparkling *Hostal República* (☎ 357 966), at Calle Comercio 1455, is in a lovely historic building which was once the home of a Bolivian president. Rooms cost US$16/21 with private bath, US$9.50/13 without.

An interesting mid-range place is *Hotel Viena* (☎ 326 090), at Calle Loayza 420, a Baroque-style building with immense high-ceilinged rooms; room No 113 is especially nice. Singles/doubles with shared bath cost US$9/13.50.

Places to Eat

La Paz's wealth and quality of restaurants is generally very good, but many are relatively expensive. Most budget options offer set meals (mainly almuerzo but sometimes also cena) and a short list of the most common dishes such as lomo, churrasco, milanesa and silpancho (all meat dishes). Some also include such regional specialities as sajta and chairo (see the Food section in this chapter) and ranga (tripe with yellow pepper, potato, and tomato and onion sauce). Most of La Paz's up-market restaurants are concentrated at the lower end of town: around Avenidas 20 de Octubre, 6 de Agosto and 16 de Julio (it must be easy to remember historical dates in La Paz!), and the Zona Sur.

Breakfast Because most breakfast venues don't open until 8.30 or 9 am, early risers desperate for a caffeine jolt before they can face the day will find bread rolls and riveting coffee concentrate at the markets for around US$0.40.

One exception to the late-opening rule is *La Fuente* at the Residencial Rosario, which serves fresh fruit, juices, delicious bread and all the other elements of continental and American breakfasts. Another is *Café Torino*, beside the Hotel Torino, which opens at 7.30 am.

For healthy vegetarian breakfasts of porridge, yoghurt, juice, granola and crêpes, try *El Vegetariano*, on Calle Loayza between Calles Potosí and Comercio, which opens at 9.15 am. If you prefer a quick coffee and a roll or salteña, go to *Confitería Club de La Paz*, a literary café and haunt of politicians and other interesting people, at the sharp corner of Avenidas Camacho and Mariscal Santa Cruz. Those hankering after sticky doughnuts and rich hot cocoa can resort to *California Donuts* on Avenida Camacho.

Snacks If you don't mind its hectic setting, the cheapest end of the scale is the markets;

of which there are several. Unfortunately, the most central, *Mercado Lanza*, off Plaza Pérez Velasco, has a rather dirty, unpleasant comedor. Better is the *Mercado Camacho*, on the corner of Camacho and Bueno, where you'll find takeaway snack stands selling empanadas and chicken sandwiches, and comedores with covered sitting areas. A filling meal of soup, a meat dish, rice, lettuce and oca or potato is less than US$1. Other places for cheap informal market meals include the Buenos Aires and cemetery areas.

A good place for salteñas is the *Tokio* (not to be confused with the New Tokyo), on the Prado. It's pricey, however, and the salteñas available in the markets for a third of the price are also excellent; try the street stalls opposite the cemetery. For excellent empanadas, go to the first landing on the steps between the Prado and Calle México. For US$0.40, you'll get an enormous beef or chicken empanada especial and your choice of sauces.

The *Boutique del Pan* on Calle Potosí near Loayza is a bakery selling any imaginable bread concoction: brilliant fruit bread, rolls, brown bread and so on. The oddly named *Industria Alimentar El Luis* on Calle Socabaya is actually a bakery selling good bread and pastries. If you're a fan of sweet biscuits (cookies), make a pilgrimage to *The Hutch* near Calle 21 in San Miguel (Zona Sur). It's just below the Ketal supermarket. One could wax poetic about the chocolate chips.

A favourite for sweet snacks is *Kuchen Stube*, at Calle Rosendo Gutiérrez 461, where you can stuff yourself with decadent European coffee, pastries, biscuits and other sweets. Some of the best coffee in town is served up at *Café Oro* on Avenida Villazón below Plaza del Estudiante. Another friendly coffee shop is the *Pierrot*, on the ground floor of the Hotel Gloria.

For a reasonable burger, *California Burgers* on Avenida Camacho or *Denny's* on Mariscal Santa Cruz are two possibilities. Alternatively, there's the unfortunately named *Clap*, with two locations – Avenida Aniceto Arce and Belisario Salinas. For quick chicken, try *Pollo Copacabana*, where you'll get roast chicken, chips and fried plantain smothered in ketchup, mustard and ají (chilli sauce) for US$2. There are locations on Calle Potosí and on Calle Comercio. Beside the former is a wonderful sweets shop selling Bolivia's own Breick chocolate – some of the best!

Lunch Lunch options are numerous and limited only by what you're prepared to pay. For the strictest budgets, the markets are naturally the cheapest options at around US$1 for a filling plateful. In addition, there are plenty of 'mom and pop' cubbyhole restaurants displaying chalkboard menus at their doors; you can assume that these places are really cheap. As a general rule, the higher you climb from the Prado, the cheaper the meals will be.

There are lots of acceptable budget restaurants on Evaristo Valle, where almuerzo or cena can cost as little as US$1. Try the *Pensión Yungueña*, at Evaristo Valle 155 or the recommended *Snack El Diamante*, at Calle Manco Capac 315. *La Hacienda*, diagonally opposite the Residencial Rosario on Calle Illampu, is known for its homemade chicken soup. *Snack El Montañés*, directly opposite Hotel Sagárnaga, has good light meals and desserts.

Along Calle Rodríguez, several places serve almuerzos for US$0.50. The same street also boasts several excellent ceviche restaurants, where Peruvian-style ceviche costs around US$1.50. The best is *Acuario II* (no sign), which is opposite the Acuario I. Another great ceviche option is the *Playa Brava Cevichería* on Fernando Guachalla, opposite Sopocachi market.

Such Bolivian specialities as charque kan (mashed hominy with strips of dried llama meat), chorizo (spicy sausage), anticuchos (beef heart kebabs) and chicharrón (grilled chicken or beef) are available at *Típicos*, on the 6th level of the Shopping Norte arcade, at Potosí and Socabaya. On weekdays, *Restaurant San Pedro*, near Plaza San Pedro, serves good-value four-course almuerzos for

US$1. On Sunday, it does an elaborate 'executive lunch', with wine, for US$1.75.

A favourite fast-food venue is *Eli's Pizza Express*, with locations at 1491 and 1800 Ave 16 de Julio. You can choose between pizza, pasta, pastries and rather unusual tacos. The food is only mediocre, but there's no waiting. Perhaps the best pizza in town is available at *Sergio's*, a hole-in-the-wall place on Avenida Villazón near the Aspiazu steps.

Café Montmartre, at Alliance Française on Calle Fernando Guachalla, has lunch specials, with some vegetarian choices, for US$3.

Also recommended is *Andromeda*, at the bottom of the Aspiazu steps on Avenida Arce. It serves vegetarian almuerzos on Monday and Wednesday, with meat dishes and vegetarian options on other days. On Friday, it's always a fish dish.

At *Café Ciudad*, on Plaza del Estudiante, service is slow and the food is ordinary, but the full menu is available 24 hours a day, seven days a week, and they don't mind travellers lingering over coffee and snacks. Try the apple pie. *Café Verona*, on Calle Colón near Avenida Mariscal Santa Cruz, is recommended for its US$1.50 sandwiches, US$3 pizzas and US$3.50 almuerzos. Also very popular is *La Fiesta*, which is on Mariscal Santa Cruz opposite the bottom of Calle Socabaya. Lunches cost US$1.75, but the breakfasts are slightly overpriced.

The tiny *El Vegetariano* (see under Breakfast) serves great-value vegetarian almuerzos. You can also pick up excellent vegetarian salteñas for US$0.40. Another recommended vegetarian restaurant is at *Hotel Gloria*, Calle Potosí 909, which serves set lunches for US$2.50. It's popular, so arrive before 12.30 pm.

On Calle Sagárnaga near Plaza San Francisco and at Calle Illampu 868 are the two branches of the *Restaurant Vegetarianista Lila Vaty*, which does vegetarian and macrobiotic meals. It's open Monday to Saturday from 10 am to 10 pm. It also sells health foods and runs courses in yoga and vegetarian cuisine. Nearby, on Sagárnaga between Linares and Murillo, is the equally recommended *Imperial*, which emphasises Indian vegetarian cuisine. It's off the street in an arcade.

Dinner Many of the suggested lunch places also serve dinner. *La Fuente* and *Tambo Colonial* at the Residencial Rosario are recommended, especially for their cream of asparagus and French onion soup, crumbed chicken and pasta dishes. An excellent option for Italian food is the good-value *Pronto Ristorante*, at Calle Jáuregui 2248, half a block from Avenida 6 de Agosto. The pasta is home-made.

Fish fans will find good deals at *El Palacio de Pescado*, on Avenida América. You'll pay an average of US$2 for surubí, pacu, trucha, pejerrey, sábalo etc.

Inexpensive lunches or dinners are also available at the popular but rather aloof *El Lobo*, on the corner of Calles Santa Cruz and Illampu. The curry and chicken dishes are particularly good. You may want to look at their books of travellers' recommendations in both English and Hebrew.

A good choice for fondue and other European dishes is *La Suisse* (☎ 353 150), but it's rather expensive and you need at least two diners. *La Québecoise* at Calle 20 de Octubre 2355 is also not cheap, but it's recommended for its excellent food and atmosphere. Another exceptional choice is *La Casa de los Paceños*, at Calle Sucre 856, near Pichincha. In addition to set almuerzos for US$1.50, this friendly family-run place serves typical La Paz dishes, including saice, sajta, fricasé (stew with ground maize), chairo paceño (mutton or beef soup with chuño and hominy) and fritanga (fried pork). It's open for lunch daily except Monday, and for dinner from Tuesday to Friday.

Sunday dinners may be difficult because few places are open. *Café Verona* is especially popular on Sunday evenings, when it's the only light on in this part of town. Other Sunday alternatives include *Mongo's Rock Bottom Café*, an American-style bar/restaurant at Hermanos Manchego 2444 above Plaza Isabel la Católica. Specialities include onion rings, nachos, enormous burgers, Budweiser beer and American football on a big-screen TV. In Calacoto, between Calles 15 and 16 in the Zona Sur (accessible by radio taxi, micro or minibus), is *Abracadabra*, which serves trendy American-style meals: steaks, ribs, pizza and salads. However, check your bill carefully, especially if you're in a large group.

Entertainment

Typical of La Paz (and all Bolivia) are folk music venues known as peñas. Most present traditional Andean music, rendered on zampoñas, quenas and charangos, but also often include guitar shows and song recitals. The best known is probably *Peña Naira*, at Sagárnaga 161, just above Plaza San Francisco, but it's geared toward foreign tourists. The *Casa del Corregidor* (a very nice place in itself), at Murillo 1040, and *Marka Tambo*, at Jaén 710, are better. The Naira is open nightly, except Sunday; other peñas have shows only on Friday and Saturday nights. They all start at around 10 pm and last until 1 or 2 am. Admission is around US$5 to US$6 and normally includes the first drink.

There are scores of inexpensive local drinking dens scattered around the city, but unaccompanied women should steer clear and no-one should sit down to drink with Bolivians in one of these unless they intend to pass out later in the evening. A tame local option is the informal *Café Semilla Juvenil*, Almirante Grau 443, with weekend talks and music events.

There are also a few more elegant bars, which are frequented by foreigners and middle-class Bolivians. Highly recommended are the British-style pubs, *The Pig & Whistle* on Calle Goitia, near Avenida Arce, and the *Britannia* between Calles 15 and 16 in Calacoto. During the Friday happy hour (7 to 8 pm), the latter serves free pub snacks and half-price drinks. *Mongo's*, at Calle Hermanos Manchego 2444, offers American beer and is open seven nights a week. Side by side on Calle Montículo, near Calle Ecuador, are the pleasant but tame

Juan Sebastian Bar and the pleasantly spacey *Planet Funky Nachos Bar*, which does indeed serve nachos. The *X-presión Café Arte Bar*, at Calle Zoilo Flores 1334 in San Pedro, offers live music on Friday and Saturday, and a Brazilian night on Wednesday. Resolana, upstairs at Calle Sagárnaga 161, has live jazz performances on weekends.

Your best chances of seeing a quality film are at the Cinemateca Boliviana, on the corner of Pichincha and Indaburo. Other La Paz cinemas show first-run films (many of which deserve to be last-run). The Teatro Municipal, on the corner of Sanjinés and Indaburo, has an ambitious programme of folklore shows, folk music concerts and foreign theatrical presentations.

Getting There & Away

Air El Alto airport sits on the altiplano at 4018 metres, 10 km from the centre of La Paz. Micro 212 runs between Plaza Isabel la Católica and the airport and costs US$0.75; the radio taxi fare is US$5. Heading into town from the airport, catch micro 212 outside the terminal. It will drop you anywhere along the Prado.

The following is a list of some airline offices in La Paz:

Aerolíneas Argentinas
 Avenida 16 de Julio 1486, Banco de la Nación Argentina, ground floor (☎ 351 711, fax 391 316)
AeroPerú
 SKORPIOS, Avenida 16 de Julio 1490, Edificio Avenida (☎ 370 002, fax 291 313)
AeroSur
 Avenida 16 de Julio 1607 (☎ 371 833, fax 390 457)
American Airlines
 Plaza Venezuela 1440, Edificio Herrmann P Busch (☎ 351 360, fax 391 080)
British Airways
 Edificio Mariscal Ballivián, 12th floor (☎ 373 857, fax 391 072)
Faucett Peruvian Airlines
 Edificio Cámara de Comercio Office 4, ground floor (☎ 325 764, fax 350 118)
Iberia
 Avenida 16 de Julio 1616, Edificio Petrolero, 2nd floor (☎ 358 605, fax 391 192)

KLM
Plaza del Estudiante 1931 (☎ 323 965, fax 362 697)

LanChile
Avenida 16 de Julio, Edificio Mariscal de Ayacucho, Suite 104 ground floor (☎ 358 377, fax 392 051)

LAB
Avenida Camacho 1460 (☎ 367 710)

Lufthansa
Avenida Mariscal Santa Cruz, Edificio Hansa 7th floor (☎ 372 170, fax 391 026)

TAM
Avenida Ismael Montes 728 (☎ 379 285, fax 390 705)

United Airlines
Calle Mercado 1328, Edificio Ballivián 1606 (☎ 328 397, fax 391 505)

Varig
Edificio Cámara de Comercio, Avenida Mariscal Santa Cruz 1392 (☎ 314 040, fax 391 131)

Bus The main bus terminal (☎ 367 275) is at Plaza Antofagasta, a 15-minute walk from the city centre. Bus fares are relatively uniform between companies, but competition on most routes is such that discounts are available for the asking.

Buses to Oruro run about every half an hour (US$2.20, three hours). To Uyuni, Panasur departs on Tuesday and Friday at 5.30 pm for US$10. Plenty of flotas go to Cochabamba, leaving either in the morning or between 8 and 9 pm (from US$4, six hours). Many of these continue on to Santa Cruz or connect with a Santa Cruz bus in Cochabamba.

Buses to Sucre (US$12) normally pass through Cochabamba, and some require an eight to 10-hour stopover there. Numerous flotas run daily to Potosí, departing between 6 and 6.30 pm (US$8, 10-12 hours). Have warm clothes handy for this typically chilly trip. Some Potosí buses continue on to Tarija, Tupiza, Yacuiba or Villazón.

Manco Capac and Transtur 2 de Febrero run to Copacabana (US$3, five hours) several times daily from Calle José María Aliaga, near the cemetery. Fares are US$2. Alternatively, for US$6, there are more comfortable tourist minibuses (see Tours), which normally do hotel pick-ups. From Copaca-

bana, numerous minibuses and micros run to Puno (Peru).

Autolíneas Ingavi has four buses daily to Desaguadero via Tiahuanaco, leaving from Calle José María Asín near the cemetery. Nearby are Transportes Larecaja and Flota Unificado Sorata, both on Calle Angel Babia, which operate daily morning and early afternoon buses to Sorata. Seats are in short supply, so book your ticket at least the day before.

A number of flotas in Barrio Villa Fátima, which you can reach by micro or minibus *trufi* (see the following Getting Around section) from the Prado or Calle Camacho, offer daily services to the Yungas and beyond: Coroico, Chulumani, Rurrenabaque, San Borja, Riberalta and Guayaramerín. Camiones to the Yungas leave from near the petrol station in Villa Fátima.

To Arica (Chile), Flota Litoral (☎ 358 603) officially leaves on Tuesday and Friday (US$22), travelling via Tambo Quemado and Lauca National Park. It also has a Tuesday, Saturday and Sunday service to Iquique (Chile) at 5 pm for US$25. Géminis, which goes to Iquique on Tuesday and Saturday, is more expensive. Warm clothing is essential for either option.

Train The Estación Central (☎ 373 068) is on upper Manco Capac, steeply uphill from the city centre. Note that arranging rail tickets from La Paz is somewhat less than straightforward, and may involve lots of wasted time. If you're interested in a rail journey, in most cases, you're better off taking a bus to Oruro to arrange onward rail transport there.

Ferrobuses leave for Potosí and Sucre on Tuesday and Saturday at 5 pm. The 1st-class fares are US$11/13 to Potosí/Sucre.

The ferrobus to Arica (Chile) departs on Monday and Friday at 7.15 am and costs US$52. In the summer, there's an additional departure on Wednesday at 8 am. The train to Charaña, on the border, departs from Viacha, south-east of La Paz, on Wednesday at 3 pm. It costs US$3 in 2nd (especial).

To Villazón, the *Expreso del Sur* runs on

Friday at 1 pm (US$19/17 1st/2nd, 18 hours). The 1st/2nd-class fares to Uyuni and Tupiza, which are intermediate stops, are US$13/11.50 and US$17/15, respectively. Other trains to Uyuni, Tupiza and Villazón run only from Oruro. This train formerly continued to Buenos Aires, but passenger services within Argentina have been suspended and are unlikely to resume.

Getting Around

La Paz is well served by its public transport system. Basically, you can choose between micros, which charge US$0.18 (B$0.90); trufis – either cars or minibuses – which charge US$0.20 (B$1) around town, US$0.60 (B$3) to the airport and US$0.40 (B$1.70) to the Zona Sur; shared taxis, which charge US$0.40 (B$2) per person around the centre, although this may be a bit more for long uphill routes; and radio taxis, charging US$1.20 (B$6) around the centre, US$1.60 (B$8) to the cemetery district, US$2.20 (B$11) to Zona Sur and US$7.20 (B$35) to the airport. Radio taxi charges are for up to four passengers and include pick-up, if necessary.

Any of these vehicles can be waved down anywhere, except near intersections or in areas cordoned off by the police. In the case of micros and trufis, destinations are identified on placards on the roof or windscreen.

AROUND LA PAZ
Valle de la Luna

The Valle de la Luna (Valley of the Moon) is a pleasant and quiet half-day break from urban La Paz. It isn't a valley at all, but a bizarre eroded hillside maze of canyons and pinnacles technically known as badlands. It lies about 10 km down the canyon of the Río Choqueyapu from the city centre.

To get there, catch a Mallasa-bound micro or trufi from the Prado. Continue past Calacoto and Barrio Aranjuez and up the hill to the fork in the road; the right fork goes to Malasilla Golf Course. Get off the bus and walk for a few minutes toward Mallasa village. When you see a football pitch, you're at the top of Valle de la Luna. If you're

walking through the valley, use extreme caution; the route is badly eroded and unconsolidated silt makes it slippery and dangerous.

Afterwards, you can also visit the blossoming resort village of Mallasa and La Paz's spacious new **zoo**. From the top of Valle de la Luna, catch a micro marked 'Mallasa' or 'Zoológico', or continue on foot; it's just a couple of km. The zoo is open daily from 9 am to noon and 2.30 to 6 pm. Admission is US$0.70.

Chacaltaya

The world's highest downhill ski area lies on the slopes of Chacaltaya, at an altitude of 5200 metres. It's accessed by a rough 35-km road from La Paz, but at present, the only public access is by organised tour. A walk to the top of the ski tow and on to the summit (5395 metres) affords superb views of surrounding peaks.

On weekends during the season (normally February to early May), Club Andino Boliviano (☎ 365 065), Calle México 1638, offers weekend ski trips. There are no lifts; you'll have to battle with a primitive cable tow. Club Andino has a dilapidated ski lodge where you can buy snacks and hot drinks, hire ski gear and even stay the night (US$3). It's better, however, to stay in the weather laboratory just downhill, which has accommodation for a few guests. A number of La Paz tour agencies offer daily tours to Chacaltaya (US$12), but they don't include skiing.

Tiahuanaco

Tiahuanaco, also spelled Tiwanaku, is Bolivia's most significant archaeological site, 72 km from La Paz on the road toward Desaguadero, on the Peruvian border.

Little is known of the Tiahuanaco people who constructed this great ceremonial centre on the southern shore of Lake Titicaca. Archaeologists generally agree that the civilisation that spawned Tiahuanaco rose about 600 BC. The ceremonial site was under construction around 700 AD, but after

BOLIVIA

1200 AD the group had melted into obscurity. However, evidence of its influence, particularly in the area of religion, has been found throughout the vast area that later became the Inca empire.

There are a number of large stone slabs (up to 175 tonnes in weight) strewn around the site, a ruined pyramid, the remains of a ritual platform and many other ruins. Across the railway line from Tiahuanaco is the excavation of **Puma Punku** (Gateway of the Puma), and a site museum which is open sporadically.

Foreigners pay US$2 admission. If you're not in a tour group, you can hire a guide who will provide a greater appreciation of Tiahuanaco's history. They're available outside the fence for around US$2.50, but you'll have to bargain for that price.

Getting There & Away One way to see Tiahuanaco is en route from La Paz to Puno, Peru. From La Paz, Autolíneas Ingavi has four daily buses to Tiahuanaco (US$0.50, 2½ hours), some of which continue to Desaguadero. To return to La Paz after a day trip to Tiahuanaco, flag down a bus, almost always a crowded option, or walk into the village of the same name, about one km west of the site, and catch one along the main street.

A dozen or more La Paz tour agencies offer guided tours to Tiahuanaco for around US$12.

The Yungas

The dramatic Yungas, which lie north-east of La Paz, beyond the Cordillera Real, are characterised by steep forested cliffs which loom above humid, cloud-filled gorges. They form a natural division between the cold, barren altiplano and the Amazonian rainforests of northern Bolivia. The relatively short trip from 4600-metre La Cumbre pass into the Alto Beni entails a loss of 4343 metres elevation. Tropical fruits, coffee, sugar cane, cacao and coca all grow in the

Yungas with minimal tending and the climate is moderate, with rain or mist possible at any time of year.

COROICO

Most popular among travellers is the small village of Coroico, perched on the shoulder of Cerro Uchumachi at an altitude of 1500 metres. The village serves mostly as a holiday resort for middle-class paceños and a retreat for an increasing number of European immigrants.

Coroico is also a perfect place for relaxation or short hiking trips into the countryside. Riders can hire horses from Rancho Beni for US$5 per hour, with a guide, but don't accept horses that appear to be less than fit and healthy.

Coroico's telephone code is 0811.

Places to Stay

One of Bolivia's nicest backpackers' haunts is the friendly and comfortable *Hotel Esmeralda* (☎ 6017), 300 metres up the hillside from the centre. The restaurant and the views defy description and for relaxation, there's a pool and a sunny patio. Rooms cost US$7/10 per person, without/with bath. Phone for free pick-up from the plaza. Be warned, however, that bookings won't necessarily guarantee a room.

The cheapest place is the *Alojamiento de la Torre* which charges US$2 per person. The nicer *Hostal Kory* is also a good bet. For US$5 per person you get a restaurant, swimming pool and excellent views. The new *Hostal La Casa*, down the stairs from the Kory, has rooms with shared bath for US$3 per person. Another favourite is the German-run *Hostal Sol y Luna*, half an hour's walk from town. Double *cabañas* (cabins) cost US$4 per person, rooms are US$3 per person, and camp sites cost US$2 per person.

The exceptionally friendly and good value *Hotel Don Quixote*, 800 metres from the plaza, is popular with Bolivians and makes an excellent alternative. Rooms with all the amenities of a solid mid-range option cost just US$7.50 per person.

Places to Eat

For its size, Coroico offers a boggling variety of excellent eateries. Try *Bamboo's* for tasty Mexican dishes and the *Back-Stube Konditorei*, near Hostal Kory, for great breakfasts (with Yungas coffee), unbeatable pizza, pasta, soups, omelettes and German-style cakes and pastries. European cuisine is available at the German-run *La Casa* (closed Monday); book in advance for fondue or raclette (US$5 per person, minimum two people). Two notable pizzerias are *Reddy's* and the *Daedalus Pub*. The funky *Taurus Pub* is fun for a drink or snack.

Hotel Esmeralda and Hostal Kory also have recommended restaurants. The former offers a good vegetarian selection.

Getting There & Away

The frightening road between La Paz and Coroico drops over 3000 metres in 80 km, flanked by stunning vertical scenery. Buses and minibuses leave from the Villa Fátima neighbourhood of La Paz, and camiones leave regularly from the Villa Fátima petrol station, but for peace of mind, the minibuses are probably the best way to go. There's now a lot of competition on the route, so you'll have no problem finding transport, but most departures are in the mornings and on weekends.

For Yolosa, seven km downhill from Coroico, you can catch buses and camiones heading for Guanay and Rurrenabaque, and further into Bolivian Amazonia.

TREKS IN THE CORDILLERA REAL

There are several interesting treks between the altiplano and the Yungas, all of which cross the Cordillera Real on relatively low passes. The most popular are the Choro (La Cumbre to Coroico), Taquesi and Yunga Cruz. These two to four-day walks all begin in the Cordillera Real and end in the Yungas. Each begins with a brief ascent, then trends downhill, offering spectacular scenery, varying from the high-mountain landscapes to the exuberant vegetation of the Yungas. Hikers should carry food and camping equipment, including a tent, sleeping bag, rainproof

gear, torch etc. Security should be a concern, especially on the Choro trek, where there have been several nasty incidents.

Serious hikers should consult Lonely Planet's *Bolivia – a travel survival kit* or Bradt Publications' *Backpacking and Trekking in Peru & Bolivia*. They include maps and detailed descriptions of these treks, as well as other routes.

SORATA

Sorata is often described as having the most beautiful setting in Bolivia, and this is no exaggeration. It sits at an altitude of 2695 metres in a valley beneath the towering snowcapped peaks of Illampu (6362 metres) and Ancohuma (6427 metres) and is popular with mountaineers.

Most visitors make a day trip of the 10-km hike to the Gruta de San Pedro (San Pedro Cave), a 2½-hour walk from Sorata, but a number of other hiking options are available. One ambitious undertaking is the six or seven-day trek along El Camino del Oro, an ancient route used as a commerce and trade link between the altiplano and the Río Tipuani goldfields (enquire locally about security before attempting this trek). Alternatively, there's the challenging Mapiri Trail (five days) or the steep climbs up to Laguna Challata (a long day hike), Comunidad Lakathiya (a long day hike) or Laguna Glacial (three days).

Information

For trekking information, go to the Residencial Sorata, where independent hikers will find suggestions, directions, and guides for hire. If you prefer an organised trek, see Hotel Copacabana, which hires out guides as well as camping and climbing equipment.

Sorata's telephone code is 0811.

Places to Stay

For its friendly antique atmosphere and brilliant flower garden, the Canadian-run *Residencial Sorata* (☎ 5044), on the main plaza, is an accommodation highlight. Grand and spacious rooms cost US$4/6 per person without/with bath. Smaller rooms are US$3 per person. There's a restaurant, lounge area, table tennis and a book exchange, and videos are shown nightly.

Another popular spot is the German-run *Hotel Copacabana* (☎ 5042), seven minutes from the plaza toward San Pedro. Rooms cost US$4 per person with shared bath, and doubles with bath cost US$18.50. Owners Eduard and Diana are video fiends, and their growing collection is available to guests.

The cheapest place is the *Perla Andina*, just below the main plaza, where very basic rooms cost just US$1 per person. The *Hotel San Cristóbal* charges US$2.50 per person, with cold water only.

Places to Eat

The best place to eat is the *Casa de Papaco*, signposted as 'Ristorante Pizzeria Italiano'. Run by a gentleman from Bologna, it offers genuine Italian cuisine – and even a good espresso – in a garden setting. Plan on US$5 per person.

If your budget doesn't stretch that far, go for the small, inexpensive restaurants around the plaza; filling almuerzos cost only US$1. The *Residencial Sorata* and *Hotel Copacabana* also have decent restaurants.

Getting There & Away

Sorata is a long way from the other Yungas towns and there's no road connecting it directly with Coroico; you must go through La Paz. From La Paz, Transportes Larecaja and Flota Unificado Sorata leave two to six times daily (from 6 am to 2 pm) from Calle Angel Babia, near the cemetery. Buses get crowded, so book tickets the previous day to be assured of a seat. The trip costs US$2 and takes 4½ hours; foreigners must register at the military post near Achacachi, so have your passport handy.

To travel between Copacabana and Sorata, you must alight at Huarina and wait for another bus.

GUANAY

Isolated Guanay makes a good base for visits to the gold-mining operations along the Río Mapiri and Río Tipuani. It's also at the end

of the El Camino del Oro trek, which descends from Sorata. The miners and panners are down-to-earth, and if you can excuse the utter rape of the landscape they've perpetrated for the sake of gold, a visit will prove interesting. Access to the mining areas is by jeep along the Llipi road, or by motorised dugout canoes up the Río Mapiri. These can be hired in Guanay.

Places to Stay & Eat

The *Hotel Pahuichi*, one block downhill from the plaza, is far and away the best value in town, and also has Guanay's best and most popular restaurant. A good, friendly alternative is the *Hotel Minero* next door. Both these places charge US$2 per person. *Alojamiento Plaza* and *Alojamiento Santos*, both on the plaza, are also fine and charge just US$1.60 per person.

For large steaks and fresh juices try *Las Parrilladas* on the road leading down to the port. The *Fuente de Soda Mariel*, on the plaza, does empanadas, cakes, ice cream, licuados and other snacks.

Getting There & Away

The bus offices are all around the plaza, but buses leave from a block away. Four companies offer daily runs both to and from La Paz, via Caranavi and Yolosa. Most leave Guanay between 4.30 and 5 pm. Only Trans Totaí has a morning departure, at 8 am. From Guanay to Caranavi takes four hours; then it's seven more to La Paz. Camiones are also plentiful and cheaper, but the trip takes longer. To get to Coroico, alight at Yolosa (most buses pass Yolosa in the wee hours of the morning) and catch a pick-up truck up the hill. To reach Rurrenabaque, Trinidad or Riberalta, get off in Caranavi to connect with a northbound bus.

Alternatively, you can travel by canoe along the Río Beni to or from Rurrenabaque. Make arrangements at the Agencia Fluvial in either Guanay or Rurrenabaque. The canoes comfortably hold 10 people and their luggage. The normal rate charged to foreigners is US$20 per person, but if you find someone going anyway, you may be able to negotiate a better rate.

BOLIVIA

Lake Titicaca

Lake Titicaca, over 230 km long and 97 km wide, is one of the world's highest navigable lakes. Straddling the Peru-Bolivia border, it lies in a depression of the altiplano at an elevation of 3820 metres, and covers an area of over 8000 sq km. It's a remnant of the ancient inland sea known as Lago Ballivián, which covered much of the altiplano before geological faults and evaporation caused the water level to drop.

The lake offers an incongruous splash of blue amidst the parched dreariness of the altiplano, and clear waters reminiscent of the Greek islands. According to ancient cosmological myths, this was the birthplace of the sun, and the Incas believed that their first emperor rose from the rock called Titicaca, or 'rock of the puma', on the northern tip of Isla del Sol. The lake is still revered by the Aymara people who live on its shores.

COPACABANA

Copacabana is a sunny town on the southern

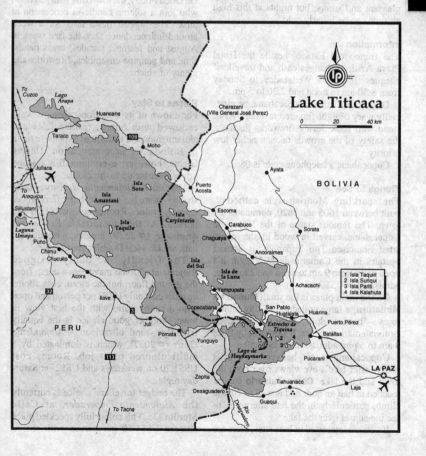

Lake Titicaca

0   20   40 km

shore of Lake Titicaca, near the Peruvian border. In the 16th century, after Copacabana was presented with an image of the Virgin of Candelaria, there was a rash of miracles in the town. Since then Copacabana has been a pilgrimage site, and today, the Virgin is the patron saint of Bolivia.

Copacabana is well known for its fiestas, which bring the town to life. At other times, it's a sleepy little place visited mainly as a pleasant stopover between La Paz and Puno, Peru. It's also a convenient base for visits to Isla del Sol (Island of the Sun). From February to November, the climate is mostly pleasant and sunny, but nights at this high altitude can be bitterly cold.

Information

The Banco del Estado, beside the Hotel Playa Azul, exchanges cash and travellers' cheques. It's open Wednesday to Sunday from 8.30 am to noon and 2.30 to 5 pm.

During festivals in Copacabana, be especially wary of light-fingered revellers. Also, stand well back during fireworks displays; the safety of the crowds takes a rather low priority.

Copacabana's telephone code is 0862.

Things to See

The sparkling Moorish-style **cathedral**, built between 1605 and 1820, dominates the town. The famous statue of the Virgen de Copacabana, carved in wood by the Indian artist Francisco Tito Yupanqui, is housed upstairs in the Camarín de la Virgen. It's open daily from 9 am to noon and 2 to 6 pm; admission is US$0.40.

On the main plaza is the small **Museo en Miniatura**, a large collection of tiny miniatures – bottles, dolls, furniture and even Bolivian market scenes. It's open daily from 9 am to 5 pm; admission is US$0.50.

Copacabana is set between two hills which offer bird's-eye views over both the town and the lake. **Cerro Calvario** can be reached in half an hour and is well worth the climb, particularly in the late afternoon, to see the sunset over the lake.

If you are interested in Inca sites, there are a couple of unimpressive rocks around the town: the **Tribunal del Inca**, near the cemetery, **Horca del Inca**, on the hill Niño Calvario, and **Baño del Inca**, north of the village.

Special Events

Copacabana hosts three major annual fiestas. On the first two days of February, the Fiesta de la Virgen de Copacabana is celebrated. Indians and dancers from both Peru and Bolivia perform traditional Aymara dances; there's much music, drinking and feasting. On Good Friday, the town fills with pilgrims, who join a solemn candle-lit procession at dusk. The biggest fiesta lasts for a week around Independence Day, the first week in August and features parades, brass bands, flute and panpipe ensembles, fireworks and plenty of chicha.

Places to Stay

For a town of its size, Copacabana is well-endowed with hotels, residenciales and alojamientos and is the least expensive town in Bolivia for accommodation. During fiestas, however, everything fills up and prices increase up to threefold.

The small *Alojamiento Urinsaya* looks shabby from the outside but offers good, friendly value. Rooms cost US$1.50 per person. At the comfortable *Residencial Aransaya* (☎ 2229) singles without/with bath are US$4/5. Doubles are US$6/8.

The friendly and oddly designed *Alojamiento Aroma* may seem a dump from the ground floor, but the clean, cosy rooms upstairs cost only US$2 per person and open onto a sunny patio with the best view in town. Another good choice is the equally friendly – and ultraclean – *Alojamiento Oasis* (☎ 2037), which is dominated by a multicoloured paint job. Rooms cost US$1.20 on weekdays and US$2 on Saturday nights.

The budget travellers' choice is currently the *Alojamiento Emperador*, at Calle Murillo 235. This colourfully speckled place charges US$1.50 per person with shared bath, and there's a sunny mezzanine that's ideal for lounging. Nearer the lake is the basic but fine *Alojamiento Kota Kahuaña*, which charges US$1.20/2 without/with bath. Guests have access to kitchen facilities.

The newly refurbished *Hotel Ambassador*, a good mid-range option, has rooms with bath for US$6.20. Most tour groups wind up at *Hotel Playa Azul* (☎ 2227), where singles/doubles cost US$22/31 with bath and an obligatory three-meal plan. The bland *Hotel Prefectural* (☎ 2002), near the beach, affords a lovely view of the lake and surrounding mountains. Clean, stark rooms

are US$12. A nicer alternative is the new colonial-style *Residencial Rosario del Lago*, which is owned by the folks who run the Residencial Rosario in La Paz. It has a good view of the lake; singles/doubles cost US$14/18 without bath, or US$24/30 with. All rates include breakfast.

Places to Eat

The local speciality is trucha criolla from Lake Titicaca, which may be the world's largest trout. Otherwise, there's little gastronomic originality in Copacabana; everything

PLACES TO STAY
1 Residencial Rosario del Lago
2 Hotel Prefectural
3 Alojamiento Kota Kahuaña
4 Alojamiento Aroma
8 Alojamiento Urinsaya
9 Hotel Ambassador
10 Residencial & Pensión Aransaya
12 Hotel Playa Azul
14 Alojamiento Oasis
15 Alojamiento Emperador

PLACES TO EAT
5 El Rey
11 Snack 6 de Agosto
13 Puerta del Sol

OTHER
4 Bicycle Rental
7 Cerro Calvario
16 ENTEL Office
17 Catedral
18 Transportes Manco Capac Bus Terminal
19 Plaza 2 de Febrero
20 Market
21 Transtur 2 de Febrero Bus Terminal
22 Post Office
23 Museo en Miniatura
24 Tribunal del Inca

Copacabana

0   100   200 m

Lake Titicaca

BOLIVIA

is served up with greasy rice, fried potatoes and lettuce.

The recommended *Pensión Aransaya*, which is accessible to tight budgets, serves great trout dishes. *Snack 6 de Agosto*, just up the street, is also very good value, serving breakfast, chicken dishes, pejerrey, milanesa and their speciality, suckling pig. Trout dishes cost US$3.50. Service may be crusty, but the food is exceptionally well prepared.

From the outside, the *Puerta del Sol* appears inviting, but at the time of research, the food didn't measure up; especially avoid the spaghetti. Don't be fooled by the name of the *Restaurant Nápoles*; the original chef left so they no longer serve Italian cuisine. On sunny days, *El Rey* and other beach restaurants have tables outside, where you can have a drink and observe Bolivian beach life, such as it is.

As usual, the cheapest meals are in the market food hall. If you need a sugar rush in the morning, go down there and treat yourself to a breakfast of hot api morado (a purple maize drink) and syrupy buñuelos (doughnuts).

Getting There & Away

Both Transportes Manco Capac and Transtur 2 de Febrero have daily connections to La Paz, with extra departures on Sunday. The spectacular trip costs US$2 and takes four hours.

The cheapest way to reach Puno (Peru) is to catch a bus or minibus from Plaza Sucre to the border at Yunguyo (US$0.40), where you'll find onward transport to Puno (two hours).

Tours between Puno and La Paz are extremely popular, and all of them pass through Copacabana. When buying a ticket, you can arrange with the agent to break the journey in Copacabana, then continue to La Paz or Puno with the same agency. If there's space available, anyone can use these tour buses. They gather in front of the Pensión Aransaya and Hotel Ambassador between noon and 2 pm. The fare to either destination is US$5. Although there are plenty of them, many arrive full, so if you want to be sure of

a seat, book in advance at one of the tour agencies in Copacabana.

Getting Around

Bicycles are available for rent at Calle 6 de Agosto 125 or on the beach, but foreigners are charged several times the local rate: US$1.25 per hour, US$5 for six hours and US$8 for 12 hours (6 am to 6 pm). Negotiate!

COPACABANA TO YAMPUPATA WALK

The walk from Copacabana to Yampupata (just across the strait from the Isla del Sol) is recommended for its scenery and, combined with a couple of days on the island, makes a fabulous trip.

From Copacabana, head north-east along the road across the flat plain. After an hour, you'll reach the isolated Hinchaca fish hatchery and reforestation project on your left. Just beyond the hatchery, cross the stream on your left and follow the obvious Inca road up the steep hill. This stretch shows some good Inca paving and makes a short cut, rejoining the track at the crest of the hill. At the fork in the road here, take the left turning, which leads down to the village of Titicachi.

At the next village, Sicuani, José Quispe Mamani and his wife, Margarita Arias, have started the *Hostal Yampu*. Basic accommodation costs US$1 per person; breakfast and lunch cost US$1 each and dinner is US$0.50. For US$0.75, you can do a spin around the bay in a *totora*-reed boat (see the Floating Islands section in the Peru chapter).

After about four hours walking from Copacabana, you'll reach Yampupata, where you can hire a rowboat to Pilko Kaina on the Isla del Sol for US$1 per person and to the Escalera del Inca for US$1.50.

The easiest way to return from Yampupata to Copacabana is on the daily minibus which leaves from Yampupata at 9.30 am, and from Copacabana at around 8 am. There are also boats leaving between 8 and 9 am every Thursday, Saturday and Sunday (US$2 per person), and a Saturday camión, which costs US$0.75 per person and leaves in the early to mid-afternoon (the trip may be slow, since it stops to sell produce). Or you can walk, of course.

ISLA DEL SOL & ISLA DE LA LUNA

Isla del Sol is the legendary site of the Incas' creation, and has been credited as the birthplace of all sorts of important entities, including the sun itself. It was there that the bearded white god Viracocha and the first Incas, Manco Capac and his sister/wife Mama Huaca (or Mama Ocllo), all made their mystical appearances. The Aymara and

Quechua people accept these legends as history, and Isla del Sol remains sacred.

Isla de la Luna (the Island of the Moon) is smaller and less visited by tourists. Isla de la Luna was the site of the convent housing the virgins of the sun. Foreigners are charged US$1 per person to land on the island.

Isla del Sol is the larger of the two islands. There are a couple of small villages, of which Cha'lla is the largest. Scattered about the island are ancient Inca ruins, including the Pilko Kaina ruins at the southern end and, in the north, the Chincana complex, which is

BOLIVIA

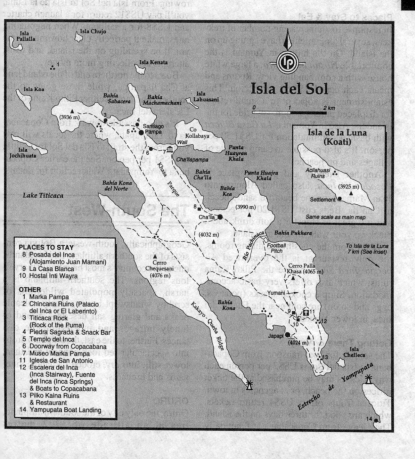

Isla del Sol

0   1   2 km

Isla de la Luna (Koati)

Same scale as main map

PLACES TO STAY
8 Posada del Inca
   (Alojamiento Juan Mamani)
9 La Casa Blanca
10 Hostal Inti Wayra

OTHER
1 Marka Pampa
2 Chincana Ruins (Palacio
   del Inca or El Laberinto)
3 Titicaca Rock
   (Rock of the Puma)
4 Piedra Sagrada & Snack Bar
5 Templo del Inca
6 Doorway from Copacabana
7 Museo Marka Pampa
11 Iglesia de San Antonio
12 Escalera del Inca
   (Inca Stairway), Fuente
   del Inca (Inca Springs)
   & Boats to Copacabana
13 Pilko Kaina Ruins
   & Restaurant
14 Yampupata Boat Landing

the site of the sacred rock where the Inca creation legend began. Foreigners pay US$1 admission to each complex. At Cha'llapampa, there's a museum of artefacts, some made of gold, from the underwater excavations near Koa Island, which may be visited on the same ticket as Chincana.

Networks of walking tracks make exploration easy, but the altitude may take a toll. The island's sites are too numerous to mention every one here; you can do a walking circuit of them in a long day, but it would be easier devoting a day each to the northern and southern ends.

Places to Stay & Eat

In response to an increasing number of trekkers, several alojamientos have sprung up on the island. On the hilltop in Yumani is the comfortable *Hostal Inti Wayra*, a large white house with a commanding view. Rooms and meals each cost US$1.50 per person. This establishment is adjacent to a small refuge for displaced pumas, a source of pride for the islanders. Also in Yumani is *La Casa Blanca* with basic accommodation for US$1.50 per person. It's also possible to camp outside of villages and on beaches.

Another friendly and popular place is *Posada del Inca*, also called Alojamiento Juan Mamani, on the beautiful sandy beach in Cha'lla. Beds cost US$1.20 per person, and it's great to stop for a soft drink and a break on your walk around the island.

Apart from the guesthouse dining rooms, the only restaurant is the overpriced *Albergue Inca Sama* beside the Pilko Kaina ruins, which also offers very basic accommodation. Simple cooked snacks (potatoes, eggs and so on) are sold near the Fuente del Inca, in lower Yumani.

Getting There & Away

The set rate for boat transport from Copacabana to Isla del Sol is US$2 per person each way. Tickets may be purchased at the ticket offices on the beach, or at agencies in town. Titicaca Tours offers US$4 return tickets, which are good for three days on the island. They leave from Copacabana at 8 am daily

and return from the Escalera del Inca at 10.30 am and from Cha'llapampa at 2.30 pm. Buy tickets at the beach office in Copacabana or Hostal Inti Wayra on the island.

The standard rate for day tours, including return transport from Copacabana and stops at the northern or southern ruins complexes, is US$5 per person, excluding admission to the ruins.

Individual charter is also available. To hire a launch, you'll pay around US$30 per day for up to 12 passengers. Sailboats cost around US$15, but the journey takes up to four hours each way, and you may end up rowing. From Isla del Sol to Isla de la Luna, you'll pay US$12 return for a launch charter and US$8 for a sailboat. When negotiating rates, make it perfectly clear how much time you'll be spending on the island, and resist attempts at collecting more money.

Boats to the northern end of the island land at Cha'llapampa, while those going to the southern end land at either Pilko Kaina or the Escalera del Inca.

It's also possible to walk from Copacabana to Yampupata, where the locals will row you across the strait to Isla del Sol for as little as US$1 per person. See the earlier Copacabana to Yampupata Walk section for details.

The South-West

Geographically, south-western Bolivia consists of the southern altiplano and highlands, one of the country's most hauntingly marvellous regions. The southern altiplano is a harsh, sparsely populated wilderness of scrubby windswept basins, lonely volcanic peaks and glaring salt deserts – a land of lonely mirages and indeterminable distances. Further to the east, the altiplano drops into spectacular red rock country and then, lower still, into dry, eroded badlands, vineyards and orchards.

ORURO

Oruro, the only city of the southern altiplano, lies at an altitude of 3702 metres

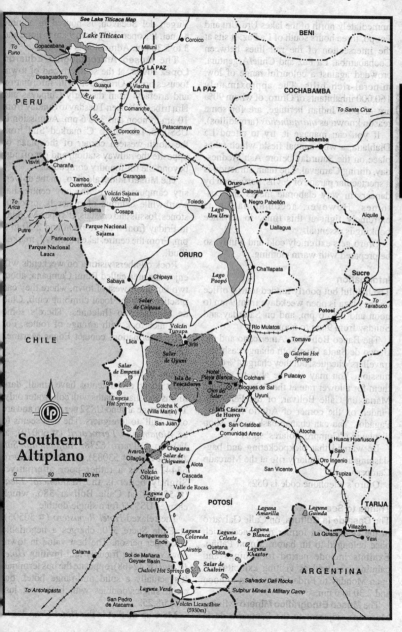

BOLIVIA

Southern Altiplano

0   50   100 km

immediately north of the lakes Uru Uru and Poopó, three hours south of La Paz. It sits at the intersection of the rail lines between Cochabamba, La Paz and Chile/Argentina, crowded against a colourful range of low, mineral-rich hills. The approximately 160,000 inhabitants of Oruro, of whom 90% are of pure Indian heritage, are for some reason known as *quirquinchos* (armadillos).

If you can manage it, try to attend La Diablada, a wild annual fiesta which takes place on the Saturday before Ash Wednesday, during Carnaval. The main attraction is a spectacular parade of devils, performed by dancers in very elaborate masks and costumes. However, accommodation is extremely tight at this time, so advance booking is essential.

Oruro gets extremely cold and windy, so be prepared with warm clothing.

Information

The helpful but poorly funded tourist office on the plaza is open weekdays from 9 am to noon and 2 to 6 pm, and on Saturday and Sunday from 9 am to noon.

The Banco Boliviano Americano and the Banco de Santa Cruz both change cash and travellers' cheques, but they charge 4% commission. You may also be able to change them for a lower rate at the Farmacia Santa Marta, on Calle Bolívar, or the Ferretería Findel, on the corner of Adolfo Mier and Pagador. You can change cash at any shop displaying 'Compro Dólares' signs.

Be warned that pickpocketing and bag-slashing are particularly rife at the Mercado Campero.

Oruro's telephone code is 052.

Things to See

The **Casa de la Cultura**, on Calle Galvarro in the centre, is a former residence which once belonged to tin baron, Simon Patiño. Exhibits include period furnishings and paintings, as well as visiting exhibits. It's open Monday to Friday from 9 am to noon and 2.30 to 6 pm.

The **Museo Etnográfico Minero** (Mining Museum), adjacent to the Santuario de la Virgen del Socavón, is housed in a mine tunnel. It's open daily from 9 am to noon and 3 to 5.30 pm. Admission is US$0.75.

The **Museo Antropológico Eduardo López Rivas**, at the southern end of town, focuses on the Oruro area, with information and artefacts from the early Chipayas and Uru tribes. It's open Tuesday to Sunday from 10 am to noon and 3 to 6 pm. Admission is US$0.75. Take micro 'C' marked 'Sud' from the north-western corner of the plaza or opposite the railway station, and get off just beyond the tin-foundry compound.

The **Museo Mineralógico**, on the university campus south of the city centre, has worthwhile exhibits of minerals, precious stones, fossils and crystals. It's open Monday to Friday from 8 am to noon and 2.30 to 5 pm. From the centre, take micro 'A', marked 'Sud'.

Rock climbers visiting on weekends will enjoy the area called Rumi Campana, about two km north-west of town, where they can practice with the local climbing club, Club de Montañismo Halcones. There's some very nice rock with a range of routes. For more information, contact Edgar Martínez (☎ 50793).

Places to Stay

Most cheap alojamientos have small, dark rooms and shared baths with cold water only. They charge around US$2 per person and are often 'full' to foreigners. The best seems to be *Alojamiento Ferrocarril* (☎ 60079), at Velasco Galvarro 6278. *Alojamiento San Juan de Dios* (☎ 53083), at Velasco Galvarro 6344, makes a rather poor alternative. Slightly better is the *Residencial Ideal* (☎ 52863), at Calle Bolívar 386, which charges US$5/7 for a single/double.

The relaxed *Hotel Repostero* (☎ 50505), at Calle Sucre 370, charges a negotiable US$5 per person. The best value in town, however, is the friendly and inviting *Hotel Bernal* (☎ 42468), opposite the bus terminal. It's actually a solid mid-range hotel, but clean singles/doubles with bath cost just US$5/8.25.

More up-market is the *Hotel Gran Sucre*

BOLIVIA

PLACES TO STAY
2 Hotel Bernal
22 Hotel Gran Sucre
25 Residencial Ideal
27 Hotel Repostero
28 Alojamiento Ferrocarril
29 Alojamiento San Juan de Dios

PLACES TO EAT
5 Restaurant La Plata
7 Rabitos
8 Coral
9 Super Salteñas
10 Gaviota
11 La Cabaña
13 Unicornio
14 La Casona
19 Le Grill
26 El Huerto
30 Nayjama

OTHER
1 Bus Terminal
3 La Diablada Masks & Costumes
4 Mercado Fermín Lopez
6 Casa de la Cultura
12 Catedral
15 Post Office
16 Museo Etnográfico Minero
    & Santuario del Socavón
17 Immigration
18 Tourist Office
20 Farmacia Santa Marta
21 Banco Boliviano Americano
23 Ferretería Findel
24 Mercado Campero
31 Railway Station

Oruro

0   100   200 m

To Museo Mineralógico,
Museo Nacional Antropológico
Eduardo López Rivas & Zoo

(☎ 53838), at Calle Sucre 510. Rooms are US$12.50/21 with bath and hot shower.

Places to Eat

Unless you're fond of market breakfasts, your Oruro mornings may be disappointing. Most places don't open until 11 am or later. The best salteñas are found at *La Casona*, on Avenida Presidente Montes, just off the Plaza 10 de Febrero, and *Super Salteñas*, on Soria Galvarro. Both these places serve sandwiches at lunch time and pizza in the evening.

For bargain lunch specials, check out the small eateries around the railway station or at *Coral* on Calle 6 de Octubre, *Rabitos* on Ayacucho, *Le Grill* on Calle Bolívar and *Gaviota* on Calle Junín. *Unicornio* is good for snacks and lunches, and it's even open Sunday afternoons.

Nayjama, on the corner of Pagador and Aldina, has good lunches and typical dishes for under US$4. Vegetarian dishes are available at *El Huerto*, on Calle Bolívar; almuerzos cost from US$1 to US$1.50. *El Fondito*, on Avenida Villarroel near the bus terminal, specialises in pork dishes, including quintas (pork fricassee). For typical Bolivian dishes, there's *La Cabaña* on Calle Junín and *Restaurant La Plata* on Calle La Plata.

Market food stalls in both the *Mercado Campero* and *Mercado Fermín López* feature noodles, falso conejo ('false rabbit', a rubbery meat-based concoction), mutton soup, beef and thimpu de cordero (boiled potatoes, oca, rice and carrots over mutton, smothered with hot llajhua sauce).

If you're after something totally unexpected in Oruro, check out *Pub the Alpaca* at Calle La Paz 690, near Plaza de Ranchería. It's actually quite a lot like an English pub and owners Eva and Willy speak a range of European languages.

Things to Buy

The design, creation and production of Diablada costumes and masks has become an art and a small industry. On Avenida La Paz, between León and Villarroel, you can find shops selling these devilish things.

Getting There & Away

Bus All buses leave from and arrive at the Terminal de Omnibuses Hernando Siles, north of the centre. Buses to La Paz run every half an hour or so (US$2.20, three hours). There are also several daily buses to Cochabamba (US$4.50, six hours) and Potosí (US$4, seven hours) and Santa Cruz (US$12, 20 hours). To Sucre, you must go via either Cochabamba or Potosí.

For Tambo Quemado and Chungará (Chile), with connections to Arica (Chile), Trans-Sabaya leaves Tuesday and Saturday at 9.30 am. The fare to Chungará is US$8.50; to Arica, it's US$17.

Train Thanks to its mines, Oruro is a railway centre and has one of the most organised and efficient stations in Bolivia. Because rail service between La Paz and Oruro is slow and difficult to arrange, most people travel by bus from La Paz to Oruro and begin their rail journey there.

From Oruro, you can travel to Uyuni, where the rail line splits; one line goes to Tupiza and Villazón (Argentine border) and the other to Chile. Going east, there are lines to Cochabamba, and to Potosí and Sucre via Río Mulatos.

Some updated schedules and fares from Oruro follow:

Avaroa
   tren rápido – Sunday at 7.35 pm (US$6.50 2nd 12 hours); for Calama (US$15 2nd, 22 hours) change at Avaroa/Ollagüe border post to Chilean train
Cochabamba
   ferrobus – Wednesday and Friday at 2 pm (US$3.60/2.80 1st/2nd, five hours)
   tren rápido – Thursday at 8.20 am (US$3.20/2.50 1st/2nd, 11 hours)
Potosí/Sucre
   ferrobus – Tuesday and Saturday at 9.10 pm (to Potosí US$8.60 1st, seven hours; to Sucre US$10.20, 12 hours)
Villazón, via Uyuni and Tupiza
   tren expreso – Friday at 5.30 pm (US$17/15 1st/2nd class, 12 hours)

tren rápido – Monday and Thursday at 7 pm (US$7.50 1st, 15 hours)
tren mixto – Wednesday and Sunday at 7 pm (US$5.50 2nd, 17 hours)

UYUNI

The largest and the most important town in south-western Bolivia is Uyuni, a normally cold, windy and otherworldly desert community. The most interesting site in town is a yard of decaying steam locomotives, which appear to have chugged into the desert and expired.

Bring your winter woollies. The area can get very chilly indeed, and it's often impossible to escape the elements.

Information

The new Uyuni tourist information office (☎ 2098, fax 2060) is already one of Bolivia's best, thanks to the committed efforts of director Señor Tito Ponce López. It's worth a visit.

If you're travelling on to Chile from Uyuni, you must pick up your Bolivian exit stamp at the immigration office in Uyuni.

Uyuni's telephone code is 0693.

Organised Tours

A growing number of Uyuni agencies arrange tours of the Salar de Uyuni, Laguna Colorada, Sol de Mañana, Laguna Verde, and beyond, and the increased competition has meant lower priced tours. You can choose between tour buses holding up to 30 people or small jeeps holding six or seven.

During the high season (July to early September), for the popular four-day circuit around the Salar de Uyuni, Laguna Colorada, Sol de Mañana and Laguna Verde, you'll pay as much as US$450 for a jeep tour, without food. During slower periods, the same trip can cost as little as US$300. Bus tours often work out cheaper per person, but the atmosphere is different than with a small group. If you have any appetite at all, you're advised to organise your own food, as most companies cut corners wherever possible. Accommodation is in private homes and campamentos (scientific or military camps).

If you have more time, you can add Llica and the 5432-metre Volcán Tunupa (both across the Salar de Uyuni) or Laguna Celeste, a chlorine-blue lake a day's drive north-east of Laguna Verde. If you're heading for San Pedro de Atacama in Chile, you can arrange to be dropped off at Laguna Verde, where groups will be picked up by a Chilean agency for around US$50. Before leaving Uyuni, stop at immigration to check out of Bolivia.

For further information, see the following sections on the Salar de Uyuni and Salar de Coipasa, and the South-Western Circuit.

Recommended companies include:

Brisa Tours, Avenida Ferroviaria 320 (☎ 2096)
Cisne Tours, Avenida Arce (☎ 2121)
Olivos Tours, Avenida Ferroviaria (☎ 2173)
Toñito Tours, Avenida Ferroviaria 152 (☎ & fax 2094)
Trans-Andino Tours, Avenida Arce 2 esquina Ferroviaria (☎ 2132)
Tunupa Tours, Avenida Ferroviaria (☎ 2099)

Places to Stay

Uyuni's recent tourism boom has meant that hotels fill up quickly, so a booking may offer some peace of mind. The most popular place is *Hotel Avenida* (☎ 2078), opposite the railway station. Singles/doubles without bath cost US$2.40/4.40. Showers are available until noon and cost US$1. Doubles with private bath are US$12.50.

Alternatively, there's *Residencial Sucre* (☎ 2047), which charges US$2.50 per person with shared bath. Nicer is the friendly *Hostal Tunupa* (☎ 2023), in a green building a block south of the railway station; the sign says 'Agencia de Aduanas'. Rooms cost US$2.50 per person including hot showers.

If you're desperate, there is a trio of cheap places on Plaza Arce: *Residencial Copacabana*, the filthy *Residencial Uyuni* (no shower or sink) and *Residencial Urcupiña*, which is the best of the lot. All of them charge US$1.60 per person.

Places to Eat

A favourite food haunt is the *16 de Julio*, with warming high-carbohydrate fare. It's

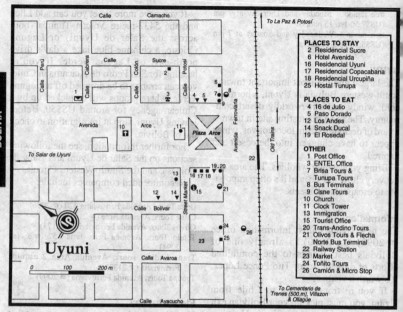

PLACES TO STAY
2 Residencial Sucre
6 Hotel Avenida
16 Residencial Uyuni
17 Residencial Copacabana
18 Residencial Urcupiña
25 Hostal Tunupa

PLACES TO EAT
4 16 de Julio
5 Paso Dorado
12 Los Andes
14 Snack Ducal
19 El Rosedal

OTHER
1 Post Office
3 ENTEL Office
7 Brisa Tours & Tunupa Tours
8 Bus Terminals
9 Cisne Tours
10 Church
11 Clock Tower
13 Immigration
15 Tourist Office
20 Trans-Andino Tours
21 Olivos Tours & Flecha Norte Bus Terminal
22 Railway Station
23 Market
24 Toñito Tours
26 Camión & Micro Stop

To La Paz & Potosí

Old Trains

To Salar de Uyuni

To Cementerio de Trenes (500 m), Villazon & Ollagüe

Uyuni

0   100   200 m

the first place open for breakfast, but don't arrive much before 8 am. Almuerzos cost US$1.20. The *Paso Dorado* next door has all the standards plus pizza, pancakes and burgers. *El Rosedal*, across the plaza, also offers a Bolivian menu; check out the unique kerosene drip heater in the middle of the room. A good choice for standard Bolivian fare is *Los Andes*. For a dose of charque kan (mashed hominy with strips of dried llama meat, an Uyuni speciality) or chicken and chips, try the basic *Snack Ducal*, two blocks away.

Getting There & Away

There are several daily buses to Potosí (US$3.75) and Sucre (US$7.50) between 10.30 am and 1 pm. All leave from Avenida Ferroviaria. Flota 11 de Julio goes to Tupiza (US$3) on Wednesday and Sunday at 3 pm. Panasur buses to Oruro (US$8) and La Paz (US$10) leave on Wednesday and Sunday at

6 pm from just south of the plaza. Flecha Norte goes to Oruro at 8 am daily.

Uyuni's railway connections grow more efficient every year, and the town now boasts a sparkling new railway station. The railway links Uyuni with Oruro, Tupiza and Avaroa. Trains run to Oruro daily except Wednesday and Sunday. The Friday express train continues on to La Paz. To Tupiza and Villazón, trains leave on Monday, Tuesday, Thursday and Friday, normally in the middle of the night. Trains run to Avaroa on Monday and Thursday at 5 am.

THE SOUTH-WESTERN CIRCUIT
Salar de Uyuni

The Salar de Uyuni, an immense saltpan at an altitude of 3653 metres, stretches over an area of about 12,000 sq km. It was part of a prehistoric salt lake, Lago Minchín, which covered most of south-western Bolivia. When it dried up, it left a couple of puddles, Lago Poopó and Lago Uru Uru, and several saltpans, including the Salar de Uyuni and Salar de Coipasa.

Apart from Uyuni, the most important villages are Colchani on the eastern shore and Llica on the west, where there's a basic alojamiento and accommodation in the *alcaldía* (town hall) for US$1. A maze of tracks crisscrosses the Salar and connects settlements around it. Several islands are scattered over this salt desert. Isla de Pescadores, in the heart of the Salar, bears amazing stands of cactus and a stranded colony of vizcachas (long-tailed rabbit-like rodents related to chinchillas). Isla Cáscara de Huevo is known for its rose-like salt formations.

New attractions include a factory making outdoor furniture and sculpture from salt, and the Hotel Playa Blanca, which is constructed entirely of salt. Beds cost US$20 per person and may be booked through Hidalgo Tours in Potosí.

Uyuni agencies run day trips which take in the Salar de Uyuni highlights and cost US$120 for groups of seven people.

The Far South-West
The spectacular Laguna Colorada and Laguna Verde, among other attractions, lie in the far south-west, the most remote highland area of Bolivia, in a surreal and nearly tree-less landscape interrupted by gentle hills and by high volcanoes that rise abruptly near the Chilean border.

Laguna Colorada, a fiery red lake about 25 km from the Chilean border, is inhabited by rare James' flamingos. On its western shore is Campamento Ende, and beside it, there's a squalid meteorological station, where visitors without tents will find a place to crash. A marginal bed in a draughty, unheated room costs US$2 per person. If you're relegated to the adobe floor, you'll pay only US$1.

The clear air is bitterly cold, and at night the temperature drops below -20°C. The air is perfumed with the scent of the *llareta* – a dense-growing, moss-like shrub which is almost as hard as rock and must be broken apart to be burned for fuel.

Most transport to and around Laguna Colorada will be supplying or servicing mining and military camps or the developing geothermal project 50 km south at Sol de Mañana. The real interest here is the 4800-metre high geyser basin, with its bubbling mud pots, hellish fumaroles and thick aroma of sulphur fumes. Be extremely careful when approaching the site; any damp or cracked earth is potentially dangerous, and cave-ins do occur, sometimes causing serious injury.

Laguna Verde, a stunning blue-green lake at 5000 metres, is tucked into the south-western corner of Bolivia. Behind the lake rises the dramatic cone of 5930-metre Volcán Licancábur.

Getting There & Around
The easiest way to visit far south-western Bolivia is with an organised tour from Uyuni. See Organised Tours under the earlier Uyuni section. Tours can also be arranged in La Paz and Potosí.

Alternatively, you can attempt a trip on your own, but this is not to be taken lightly. Transport is basically by cargo or petrol trucks that serve the mines, so prepare for lengthy waits, as days often pass without a sign of activity. The best time to explore the region is between April and September, when the days are cold but dry. During the rest of the year, the roads can turn into quagmires and transport is scarce.

This sparsely populated region is even more remote than the *salares* (salt lakes), but there are several mining and military camps and weather stations which will often provide a place to crash. You must nevertheless be self-sufficient; bring camping gear, warm clothing, food, water, compass, maps and so on.

TUPIZA
Tranquil and friendly Tupiza, with a population of around 20,000, is set in the valley of the Río Tupiza, surrounded by the rugged Cordillera de Chichas.

The charm of Tupiza lies in the surrounding countryside – an amazing landscape of rainbow-coloured rocks, hills, mountains and canyons. A reddish colour predominates,

BOLIVIA

but brown, sepia, cream, green, blue, yellow and violet can all be found in the landscape. Hiking opportunities are numerous and, whichever route you take, you'll be amazed by the variety of strange rock formations, deep gorges and canyons, chasms of rugged spires and pinnacles, dry washes and cactus forests.

The landscape is a vision from the Old West, and appropriately so. Tupiza lies in the heart of Butch Cassidy and the Sundance Kid country. After robbing an Aramayo payroll at Huaca Huañusca, about 40 km north of Tupiza, the pair reputedly met their untimely demise in the mining village of San Vicente.

Information

You'll see lots of 'Compro Dólares' signs around town. Try the Cooperativa El Chorolque, on Plaza Independencia, or the two hardware stores, Ferretería Cruz (on Avenida Santa Cruz) and Ferretería Marco Hermanos (on the corner of Avenida Santa Cruz and Florida). There's nowhere to change travellers' cheques, but in an emergency, ask around for Señor Umberto Bernal, who may be able to help.

Tupiza's telephone code is 0694.

Things to See & Do

Tupiza's surroundings are best seen on foot, and there are some incredible landscapes within easy walking distance of town. Recommended destinations include the Quebrada de Palala (five km each way), El Sillar (16 km each way), Quebrada Seca (five to 10 km each way), the Quebrada de Palmira (five km each way) and El Cañon (five km each way). The Instituto Geográfico Militar on the plaza sometimes has topographic maps to sell.

The short walk up **Cerro Corazón de Jesús** will provide lovely views over the town, particularly at sunrise or sunset.

Organised Tours

Tupiza Tours (☎ & fax 3001) at Hotel Mitru offers good-value day trips exploring Tupiza's wild quebradas. It also runs tours (US$60 per person) along the trail of Butch and Sundance to Huaca Huañusca (worthwhile for the scenery alone!) and the bleak and lonely mining village of San Vicente where, in 1908, the outlaws' careers abruptly ended.

To learn more about the story, see the very readable *Digging Up Butch & Sundance* by Anne Meadows (Bison Books, University of Nebraska Press, 1996). If you want to reach San Vicente on your own, ask Hotel Mitru about arranging a taxi; you'll pay US$80 to US$100 for the 10-hour return trip.

Places to Stay

The friendly, bright and airy *Hotel Mitru* (☎ & fax 3001) and the affiliated *Hotel Mitru Anexo* are both good choices. Rooms without/with bath cost US$4.20/6.20 per person; dormitory rooms with four beds cost just US$2 per person.

The *Residencial Centro*, on Avenida Santa Cruz, costs US$4/6 for a single/double with private bath. The popular and cosy-sounding *Residencial My Home*, at Avaroa 288, charges US$4.20 per person with private bath, US$2.75 without.

Another decent place is the *Residencial Valle Hermoso* (☎ 2592), which charges US$2 per person; showers are an additional US$0.75.

Places to Eat

The dining rooms at *Residencial My Home* and the *Hotel Mitru* each serve good set meals. *Confitería Los Helechos* is the only restaurant that keeps reliable hours. Breakfasts are especially nice, served with quince jam and real coffee. Later in the day, they do good burgers, milanesa, chicken, licuados, and a variety of cocktails. The associated restaurant next door serves well-prepared and filling local dishes. You'll find Tupiza's best salteñas at the friendly *Il Bambino*, which also has almuerzos for US$1.20.

Inexpensive almuerzos and cenas are served in the small restaurants around the bus terminals; the *Pensión Familiar* is recommended. In the afternoon, you'll find filling meals of rice, salad, potatoes and the main dish for US$1 at the food stalls near the

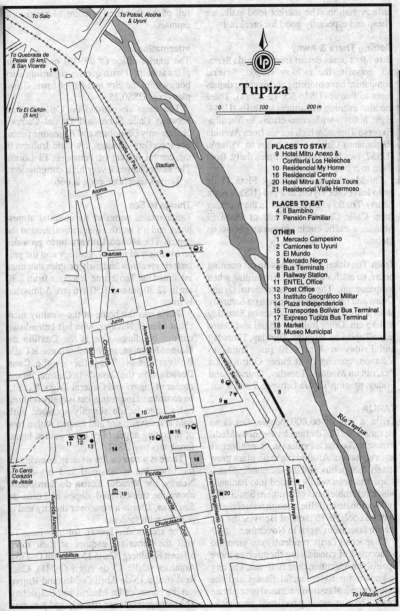

Tupiza

0   100   200 m

PLACES TO STAY
9 Hotel Mitru Anexo &
   Confitería Los Helechos
10 Residencial My Home
16 Residencial Centro
20 Hotel Mitru & Tupiza Tours
21 Residencial Valle Hermoso

PLACES TO EAT
4 Il Bambino
7 Pensión Familiar

OTHER
1 Mercado Campesino
2 Camiones to Uyuni
3 El Mundo
5 Mercado Negro
6 Bus Terminals
8 Railway Station
11 ENTEL Office
12 Post Office
13 Instituto Geográfico Militar
14 Plaza Independencia
15 Transportes Bolívar Bus Terminal
17 Expreso Tupiza Bus Terminal
18 Market
19 Museo Municipal

railway station. The market food stalls are cheap and especially good for breakfast.

Getting There & Away

Bus Most buses depart from Avenida Serrano, opposite the railway station. Several companies have morning and evening departures to Potosí (US$6.50, 12 hours). There are also evening departures to Tarija (US$4, eight hours), with connections to Yacuiba. Expreso Tupiza, which leaves from Avenida Regimiento Chichas, has buses to Villazón (US$2, two hours) several times daily, from 7 am to 5 pm.

On Monday and Thursday, Flota 11 de Julio leaves for Uyuni at 2 pm (US$3, eight hours). Trucks to Uyuni leave in the morning from Calle Charcas just east of Plaza El Mundo, a traffic circle around an enormous globe.

Train The ticket window has no set opening hours, so ask for local advice regarding when to queue up. The express train to Uyuni, Oruro and La Paz passes Tupiza on Saturday at 4.15 am; to Villazón, it passes on Saturday at 4.15 am. Other trains to Uyuni and Oruro leave Tupiza on Monday, Tuesday, Thursday and Friday at 4 or 4.30 pm. Trains to Villazón, coming from either Oruro or La Paz, run on Monday, Tuesday, Thursday and Friday, passing Tupiza between 7 and 9 am.

TARIJA

Tarija, a city of 60,000 people, lies at an elevation of 1924 metres. Its distinctly Mediterranean flavour is evident in its architecture and vegetation. Around the main plaza grow stately date palms, and the surrounding landscape has been wildly eroded into badlands which resemble parts of southern Spain. The valley climate is idyllic, though winter nights may be cool. As in most of Bolivia, the dry season lasts from April to November.

Chapacos (Tarija residents) are proud to be accused of considering themselves more Spanish or Argentine than Bolivian. The city is known for its colourful fiestas and the unique musical instruments used to celebrate them. The surrounding badlands are chock-full of the fossilised remains of prehistoric animals.

Information

The tourist office (☎ 25948) on the main plaza is helpful with queries regarding sites both within the city and out of town. Town plans cost US$0.25.

The casas de cambio on Calle Bolívar between Calle Sucre and Daniel Campos change only US dollars and Argentine pesos. For travellers' cheques, try Café Irubana in the central market or Ferretería El Lorito. The latter charges a very high commission.

Tarija's telephone code is 066.

Things to See

Tarija retains some of its colonial atmosphere and it's worth a quick stroll around the centre. The **Museo Universitario** provides an overview of history, geology and the prehistoric creatures and early peoples that once inhabited the Tarija area. It's open from 8.30 am to 12.30 pm and 2.30 to 6 pm. Admission is free.

Tarija was the home of the wealthy merchant Moisés Navajas, who left behind two curious buildings. One is the **Castillo de Moisés Navajas**, an obtrusive home at Calle Bolívar E-644. The other is the **Casa Dorada**, now the Casa de la Cultura, on the corner of Ingavi and General Trigo. It could be considered imposing, but is really nothing but a large façade sloppily splashed with gold and silver paint and topped with a row of liberating angels! For brief guided tours, foreigners pay US$1.

There is a **zoo** on the western outskirts of the town but it is small and run-down. Nearby, the **Mirador Loma de San Juan**, above the tree-covered slopes of Loma de San Juan, affords a view over the city and is popular with students.

The area is also known for its wines. To visit the **wineries**, enquire at their town offices: Kohlberg (Calle 15 de Abril O-275), Aranjuez (Calle 15 de Abril O-241), Casa Real (Calle 15 de Abril O-246) and Rujero (on the corner of La Madrid and Suipacha). The managements are friendly and you may

BOLIVIA

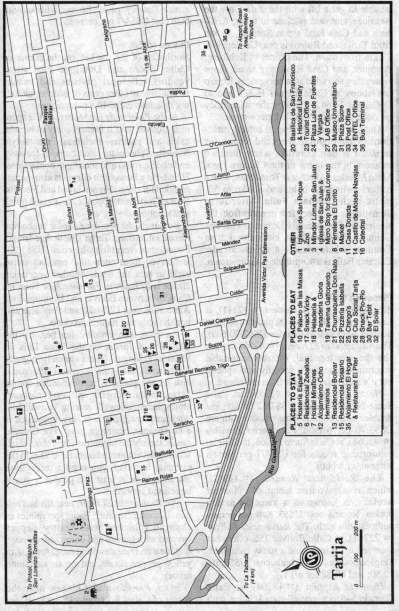

Tarija

0   100   200 m

To Potosí, Villazón &
San Lorenzo Tomatitas

To Airport, Fossil
Area, Bermejo &
Yacuiba

To La Tablada
(4 km)

Río Guadalquivir

PLACES TO STAY

5 Hostería España
6 Residencial Zeballos
7 Hostal Miraflores
12 Alojamiento Ocho
   Hermanos
13 Residencial Rosario
15 Alojamiento El Hogar
35 & Restaurant El Pifer

PLACES TO EAT

10 Palacio de las Masas
17 Snack Vicky
18 Panadería Gloria
19 Taverna Gattopardo
21 Chirrasquería Don Ñato
22 Pizzería Isabella
25 Chingo's
26 Club Social Tarija
28 Snack Pío-Pío
30 Bar Tebit
32 El Solar

OTHER

1 Iglesia de San Roque
2 Mirador Loma de San Juan
3 Zoo
4 Iglesia de San Juan &
   Ferro Stop Tor San Lorenzo
8 Feletería El Lotito
9 Market
11 Casa Dorada
14 Castillo de Moisés Navajas
16 Catedral
20 Basílica de San Francisco
   & Historical Library
23 Telefónica Office
24 Plaza Luis de Fuentes
   y Vargas
27 LAB Office
29 Museo Universitario
31 Plaza Sucre
33 Post Office
34 ENTEL Office
36 Bus Terminal

be able to get a lift with the staff. Only the Aranjuez vineyard is close to town; Kohlberg and Casa Real are in Santana, 15 km from Tarija, and Rujero is near Concepción, 27 km from town. The offices of Kohlberg, Aranjuez and Casa Real have small shops where they sell wine at factory prices. Rujero has shops at Calle Ingavi E-311 and at O'Connor N-642. Besides the wine, they produce singani, a distilled grape spirit.

Outside the city are several natural attractions. One popular weekend venue for *tarijeños* is **San Lorenzo**, where there's a museum in the home of the Chapaco hero, Moto Méndez. Another is **Tomatitas**, with a natural swimming hole, and a hike to 50-metre-high **Coimata Falls**. Micros to Tomatitas leave every few minutes from the western end of Avenida Domingo Paz. For Coimata Falls, walk or hitch five km to Coimata, where there's a small cascade. Coimata Falls is a 40-minute walk upstream.

Places to Stay

Alojamiento Ocho Hermanos (☎ 42111), at Calle Sucre N-782, has tidy, pleasant singles/doubles with shared bath for US$3.70/6.20. The *Alojamiento El Hogar* (☎ 43964), opposite the bus terminal, offers comfortable accommodation and a friendly atmosphere, but it's a 20-minute walk from the centre.

Hostal Miraflores (☎ 43355), at Calle Sucre N-920, charges US$7/12 for singles/doubles with bath. Rooms without bath are US$3.70 per person. *Residencial Zeballos* (☎ 42068), at Calle Sucre N-966, has bright, comfortable rooms for US$4/7 per person without/with bath.

The *Residencial Rosario* (☎ 43942), which is a favourite haunt of volunteer workers, is known as a value-for-money option. Rooms cost US$3.70/6 per person without/with bath. The *Residencial Bolívar* (☎ 22741), at Calle Bolívar 256, offers hot showers, a TV room and a sunny courtyard. Singles/doubles with bath cost US$7.50/12.50; add US$2 for a TV.

Hostería España (☎ 43304), at Calle Corrado 546, is a good all-round choice, with a nice flowery patio. Rooms without/with bath cost US$4/7 per person.

Places to Eat

North-east of the market, on the corner of Calles Sucre and Domingo Paz, street vendors sell local pastries and snacks unavailable in other parts of Bolivia, including delicious crêpe-like panqueques.

At the *Palacio de las Masas*, on Campero near Bolívar, you'll find a variety of breads, cakes and pastries, including French-style baguettes, chocolate cake, cuñapes (cassava and cheese rolls) and meringue confections. *Heladería y Panadería Gloria* is also recommended for cakes, French bread and biscuits. *Snack Vicky*, just opposite, is a good quick snack option.

For lunch, the popular *El Solar* vegetarian restaurant, attracts Tarija's New Age fringe. Four-course vegetarian lunches (US$1.20) are served from noon to 2 pm, but arrive early to beat the herd. Another vegetarian choice is *Restaurant Familiar Aloe Vera*, on Campos between Bolívar and Domingo Paz. Almuerzos cost US$1.20 and they also sell health foods and natural products.

For more conservative lunches, try the *Club Social Tarija*, on the Plaza Luis de Fuentes y Vargas. The extremely popular Swiss and Czech-run *Taverna Gattopardo*, also on the plaza, is recommended for its pizza, pasta, burgers and very pleasant atmosphere. Sidewalk seating is available. Another plaza pizzeria is *Isabella*, which is a bit cheaper, but more basic. For Chinese meals, there's the highbrow *Bar Tebit*, which serves a decent lunch buffet for US$2. In the evening, however, you need a reservation and must have at least two people or you'll be refused service.

The *Restaurant El Piter*, near the bus terminal, emphasises such Tarija specialities as chancao (chicken with yellow pepper covered with tomato and onion sauce), saice (hot meat and rice stew) and ranga (tripe with yellow pepper, potato, and tomato and onion sauce).

Snack Pio-Pio and *Chingos*, near the corner of Calles Sucre and 15 de Abril, are local youth hang-outs serving chicken and chips. *Heladería La Fontana* is good for ice-cream confections. For rather greasy meat dishes, try *Churrasquería Don Nato*, at Calle 15 de Abril 842.

Getting There & Away

Air The Oriel Lea Plaza airport lies three km east of town along Avenida Victor Paz Estenssoro. LAB (☎ 45706), on the main plaza, has connections daily except Sunday between Tarija, La Paz and Cochabamba. LAB also connects Tarija with Santa Cruz, Yacuiba and Sucre. For taxis from the airport into town, step just outside the airport gate and you'll pay just US$0.40 per person, less than half the price charged inside the airport.

Bus The bus terminal is at the east end of town, on Avenida Victor Paz Estenssoro. It's a 20-minute walk from the city centre.

Buses to Potosí, with connections to Oruro, Cochabamba and Sucre, run daily in the afternoon (US$7, 12 hours). Buses to Villazón, which follow a spectacular route, depart daily in the evening (US$3, 10 hours). For Tupiza, there are daily departures in the evening (US$4, eight hours). To Yacuiba, buses leave between 6 and 7 pm daily (12 hours, US$8). Unfortunately, this incredibly beautiful journey is all done at night. To hitch to Villa Montes or Yacuiba, wait at the tranca (police checkpoint) east of town.

VILLAZON

Villazón is the main border crossing between Bolivia and Argentina. It's a dusty, haphazard settlement which contrasts sharply with tidy La Quiaca, just over the border (see the Argentina chapter for details). In addition to being a point of entry, Villazón serves as a warehouse and marketing centre for contraband (food products, electronic goods and alcohol) being smuggled into Bolivia on the backs of peasants, who form a human cargo train across the frontier.

Information

Money To change cash dollars or Argentine pesos into bolivianos, you'll get reasonable rates from the casas de cambio along Avenida República Argentina. However, not all places offer the same rates, so shop around. If dollars are currently in demand, Universo Tours will change travellers' cheques.

On the Argentine side, dollars and Argentine pesos are exchanged at a par, but be warned that dollar notes with even the slightest flaw aren't accepted anywhere.

Time From October to April, there's a one-hour time difference between Bolivia and Argentina (noon in Villazón is 1 pm in La Quiaca). From May to September, the Argentine province of Jujuy, where La Quiaca is located, operates on Bolivian time (only a bit more efficiently).

Dangers & Annoyances For some reason, you'll need to be more on your guard in Villazón than other parts of Bolivia. I've encountered several 'fake police' scams there and on my most recent trip, a bus station baggage handler attempted to disappear with my pack. Readers have also reported problems, mainly pickpockets and other sneak thieves. Counterfeit US banknotes are also making appearances.

Places to Stay & Eat

A nice place to crash is the *Residencial Martínez* (☎ 562), near the bus terminal. Singles/doubles with shared bath cost US$4/6. The *Grand Palace Hotel* (☎ 333) across the street isn't quite as nice, and definitely not as friendly, but it costs only US$3 per person without bath. A travellers' favourite is the *Residencial El Cortijo* (☎ 209), two blocks from the bus terminal. Singles/doubles with shared bath cost US$4/7.

For meals, there isn't much choice. Try the *Charke Kan Restaurant*, opposite the bus terminal, which is good, but rather grimy. Alternatively, pop over to La Quiaca for an immense steak at the *Hotel de Turismo* or a pasta al pesto at the *Confitería La Frontera* in the hotel of the same name.

BOLIVIA

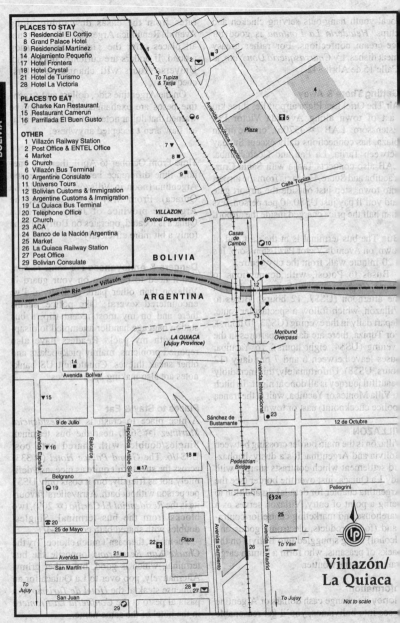

PLACES TO STAY
3 Residencial El Cortijo
8 Grand Palace Hotel
9 Residencial Martínez
14 Alojamiento Pequeño
17 Hotel Frontera
18 Hotel Crystal
21 Hotel de Turismo
28 Hotel La Victoria

PLACES TO EAT
7 Charke Kan Restaurant
15 Restaurant Camerun
16 Parrillada El Buen Gusto

OTHER
1 Villazón Railway Station
2 Post Office & ENTEL Office
4 Market
5 Church
6 Villazón Bus Terminal
10 Argentine Consulate
11 Universo Tours
12 Bolivian Customs & Immigration
13 Argentine Customs & Immigration
19 La Quiaca Bus Terminal
20 Telephone Office
22 Church
23 ACA
24 Banco de la Nación Argentina
25 Market
26 La Quiaca Railway Station
27 Post Office
29 Bolivian Consulate

To Tupiza
& Tarija

Avenida República Argentina

Plaza

Calle Tupiza

VILLAZON
(Potosí Department)

Casas
de
Cambio

BOLIVIA

Río Villazón

ARGENTINA

Moribund
Overpass

LA QUIACA
(Jujuy Province)

Avenida Bolívar

9 de Julio

Sánchez de
Bustamante

Avenida Internacional

12 de Octubre

Avenida España

Balcarce

República Árabe Siria

Pedestrian
Bridge

Pellegrini

Belgrano

Avenida Sarmiento

Avenida La Madrid

25 de Mayo

To Yavi

Avenida

San Martín

Plaza

To
Jujuy

San Juan

To Jujuy

**Villazón/
La Quiaca**

Not to scale

Getting There & Away

Bus All northbound buses depart from the central terminal in Villazón. Buses leave for Tupiza in both the morning and afternoon (US$2, 2½ hours). Several daily afternoon buses leave for Potosí (US$8, 13 hours) via Tupiza, with connections to Sucre, Cochabamba and La Paz. Buses to Tarija leave between 7 and 8 pm daily (US$3, eight hours).

Train Trains to Tupiza, Uyuni and Oruro depart on Monday, Tuesday, Thursday and Friday at 4 or 4.30 pm. There's no longer onward rail service into Argentina.

To/From Argentina Crossing the border is normally no problem. Immigration offices lie on either side of the international bridge. Formalities are normally minimal and friendly, but those entering Argentina can count on an exhaustive customs search about 20 km south of the border. Villazón has an Argentine consulate, and there's a Bolivian consulate in La Quiaca.

Cochabamba

After its founding in 1574, Cochabamba quickly developed into the country's foremost granary, thanks mainly to its fertile soil and mild climate. It long held the title of Bolivia's second city, but has recently been knocked into third place by booming Santa Cruz. Nonetheless, Cochabamba remains a progressive and economically active city, with a growing population of over 400,000.

The city has a warm, dry and sunny climate, offering pleasant relief after the chilly altiplano, but apart from that, there's little for tourists. Once you've seen the museums and done some shopping, it's time to head for the hinterlands. At some point, try to sample *chicha cochabambina*, an alcoholic maize brew typical of the region.

Information

Tourist Office The tourist office on the plaza

is open Monday to Friday from 9 am to noon and 2 to 6 pm. It sells photocopied town plans for US$1.20.

Cochabamba's telephone code is 042.

Money For American Express travellers' cheques, the Banco BISA gives the best rate in town; unfortunately, it doesn't change any other brand. Cambios Universo, just off the plaza, American Exchange and Exprint-Bol also change travellers' cheques; the latter two normally give better rates. Street moneychangers gather around the ENTEL office and along Avenida Heroínas.

Visa and MasterCard cash advances are available at major banks and at Enlace machines around the city.

Things to See

The **Museo Arqueológico**, on 25 de Mayo between Avenida Heroínas and Colombia, is one of Bolivia's finest. Exhibits include thousands of artefacts, dating from as early as 15,000 BC and as late as the colonial period. Admission is US$1, and the tour takes about 1½ hours. It's open Monday to Friday from 9 am to noon and 2 to 6 pm, and on Saturday from 9 am to 1 pm.

The **Palacio de Portales**, in the barrio of Queru Queru, is more evidence of the extravagance of tin baron Simón Patiño. It was built between 1915 and 1925 and, except perhaps for the brick, everything was brought from Europe – the floors, fireplaces, furniture, tapestry etc. It's open Monday to Friday from 5 to 6 pm, Saturday from 10 to 11 am and Sunday from 11 am to noon. The attached art museum is open Monday to Saturday from 2.30 to 6.30 pm. Foreigners pay US$1 for guided tours. Take micro 'G' from the corner of Avenida Heroínas and Calle San Martín.

Two to three hours walk from the village of Sipe-Sipe, 27 km from Cochabamba, are the worthwhile ruins of **Inca-Rakay**. Sipe-Sipe is accessible by micro via Quillacollo.

Language Courses

Cochabamba is probably the best place in Bolivia to hole up for a few weeks of Spanish

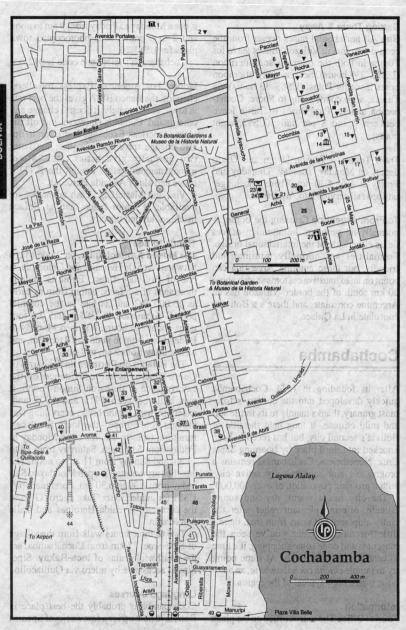

BOLIVIA

Avenida Portales
Avenida Santa Cruz
Potosí
Pando

Avenida Uyuni

Stadium

Río Rocha

To Botanical Gardens & Museo de la Historia Natural

Avenida Ramón Rivero

Oruro
Lanza
Antezana
Avenida Oquendo

Avenida Villazón
Avenida Ballivián
La Paz
Chuquisaca
Salamanca
Paccieri

16 de Julio
Venezuela

Junín

José de la Reza
México
Rocha
Mayor
Hamiraya

Baptista
España
Ecuador
Colombia

La Paz

Celia Tumusla

To Botanical Garden & Museo de la Historia Natural

Avenida de las Heroínas
Libertador
Bolívar

Avenida Ayacucho
Avenida
Sucre
Lanza
Antezana

General
Acha

Santivañez

Jordán

Calama

Cabrera

Avenida Aroma

To Sipe-Sipe & Quillacollo

Avenida Aroma

Avenida Aguirre

Avenida 9 de Abril
Brasil

Avenida Sucre

Avenida Ayacucho

Totora

To Airport

Tapacari
Uiza
Arani

Angostura

Avenida Barrientos
Chipri
Riberalta

Punata
Tarata

Pulagayo

Avenida República

Avenida de la Independencia

Guayaramerín
Mocos
Manuripi

Laguna Alalay

Cochabamba

0   200   400 m

Plaza Villa Bella

Enlargement:

Paccieri
España
Rocha
Venezuela
Lanza

Baptista
Mayor

Avenida San Martín

Ecuador

Colombia

Avenida Ayacucho

Avenida de las Heroínas

Achá

Avenida Libertador
Bolívar

General

Sucre
25 de Mayo

Jordán
Esteban Arce

0   100   200 m

PLACES TO STAY		12	Rondevu	27	Catedral
11	Residencial Familiar Anexo	13	Confitería Bambi	29	'The Big Screw'
		15	Tea Room Zürich	34	Banco BISA
28	Residencial Colonial	16	Snack Uno	37	Mercado Cancha
30	Hostal Central	17	Confitería Cecy		Calatayud
31	Residencial Familiar	18	California Burgers &	38	Flota 7 de Junio
32	Residencial Florida		Donuts	39	Micros & Buses to
33	Alojamiento	19	Heladería Dumbo		Chapare
	Cochabamba	21	Pizza Llauchas	41	Micros to Quillacollo,
35	Alojamiento Escobar	26	Restaurant Lose		Payrumani,
36	Residencial Escobar	40	Bar Pensión Familiar		Sipe-Sipe etc
42	Residencial Elisa			43	Bus Terminal
		OTHER		44	Heroínas de la
PLACES TO EAT		1	Palacio de Portales		Coronilla
2	IC Norte	4	Plaza Colón		Monument
3	Bibossy	14	Museo Arqueológico	45	Railway Station
5	El Rincón Salon de Té	20	Tourist Information	46	Mercado de
6	La Cantonata	22	Post Office		Ferias
7	Café Bistro El Carajillo	23	LAB Office	47	Micros to Tarata
8	Metrópolis	24	ENTEL Office	48	Micros to Cliza
9	Gopal	25	Plaza 14 de	49	Micros to Punata &
10	La Salsa Café		Septiembre		Arani

or Quechua lessons. There are plenty of private teachers charging around US$5 per hour, but not all are experienced. One of the best is Señor Reginaldo Rojos (☎ 42322), who offers intensive instruction in both Spanish and Quechua. Also recommended are Marycruz Almanza Bedoya (☎ 27923 or 87201) and Ms Haydee Lobo (☎ 41447), who has many years experience teaching both Spanish and Quechua. Alternatively, you could ask for recommendations at the Centro Boliviano-Americano (☎ 21288), on Calle 25 de Mayo.

Special Events

If you're visiting the area around 15 to 18 August, try to catch the Fiesta de la Virgen de Urcupiña at Quillacollo, 13 km from Cochabamba, the biggest annual event in Cochabamba department.

Places to Stay

The cheapest decent accommodation is *Alojamiento Cochabamba* (☎ 25067), at Calle Nataniel Aguirre S-591. Although basically a flophouse, it's popular with budget travellers. Rooms with common bath cost US$2.20 per person, without breakfast.

Near nerve-racking Avenida Aroma are the *Residencial Escobar* (☎ 29275), at Uruguay E-0213, which charges US$3 per person with common bath, and *Alojamiento Escobar* (☎ 25812), at Calle Aguirre S-0749, which charges US$2 per person. They're nothing to write home about, but they are cheap.

One of Bolivia's nicest inexpensive digs is *Residencial Elisa* (☎ 27846), at Calle Agustín López 834 near Avenida Aroma. Although the location is rather dodgy, just inside the door of the Elisa is a different world, with a grassy courtyard and clean, sunny garden tables. The friendly owner can help with tourist information. Rooms with/without bath cost US$7/4.

Another excellent choice is *Residencial Florida* (☎ 57911), at Calle 25 de Mayo S-0583. There's hot water until 1 pm, and the friendly owner cooks a mean breakfast for her guests. For single/double rooms, you'll pay US$6/11.50 with bath and US$4/7.75 without.

Residencial Familiar (☎ 27988), Calle Sucre E-554, and *Residencial Familiar Anexo* (☎ 27986), Calle 25 de Mayo N-0234, are popular with both Bolivian and foreign travellers. Slightly overpriced rooms without bath are US$4 per person; note that the door locks aren't always secure.

The friendly, clean and secure *Hostal Colonial* is rapidly becoming a travellers' favourite. Try to get a room upstairs overlooking the lovely courtyard gardens. Singles/doubles with bath cost US$6/9. *Hostal Central* (☎ 23622, fax 49397), on Calle General Achá, is excellent value at US$7 per person with private bath, TV and continental breakfast.

Places to Eat

For breakfast or lunch, the market is cheap for simple but varied and tasty meals, and you'll find a variety of fruits grown in the mild Cochabamba Valley. The most central market is on Calle 25 de Mayo between Sucre and Jordán. Other markets include the *Mercado de Ferias*, at the railway station, and *La Cancha Calatayud*, along Avenida Aroma between San Martín and Lanza. It claims to be – and probably is – Bolivia's largest. If you're into processing and packaging, don't miss the trendy and amazing North American-style supermarket *IC Norte*.

For breakfast, *Kivón Helados*, at Avenida Heroínas E-352, serves great juice, eggs, toast and chocolate, as well as Irish coffee and salteñas. They'll also pile on the pancakes, French toast, eggs, ham and so on. *Pizza Llauchas*, half a block from the plaza, serves nice salteñas and llauchas (cheese rolls). On the corner of General Achá and Avenida Villazón, street vendors sell delicious papas rellenas (potatoes filled with meat or cheese).

Economical almuerzos are everywhere. Try *Bar Pensión Familiar*, Avenida Aroma O-176, where you'll get a meal of salad, soup, a main course and a dessert for US$1.50, and the beer is inexpensive, too. Other good bets are *Anexo El Negro*, at Calle Esteban Arce between Jordán and Calama, *Rellenos Calama*, at Calama between 16 de Julio and Antezana, and *El Caminante*, at Calle Esteban Arce near Cabrera. *Café Express Bolívar*, at Avenida Libertador Bolívar 485, offers what may be Cochabamba's best espresso and cappuccino.

Avenida Heroínas is fast-food row, and the *Confitería Cecy* is good for burgers, chips, chicken, pizza and other snacks. The friendly owner bakes award-winning salteñas, which are available mid-morning. Other similar places include *California Burgers & Donuts*, with good strong Irish coffee and the bizarrely decorated *Unicornio*.

Heladería Dumbo, with its landmark flying elephant, and *Confitería Bambi*, at Colombia and 25 de Mayo, may infringe Disney copyright, but both serve good light meals and ice cream. For excellent Venezuelan arepas, go to *Restaurante la Caraqueña* on the Plaza de Calacala, north of the centre; take micro 'A'.

El Rincón Salón de Té, at Mayor Rocha 355, offers coffee, cheesecake and lemon meringue pie; it's recommended for afternoon tea. Alternatively, try the coffee, doughnuts and eclairs at the *Tea Room Zürich*, at Avenida San Martín 143. It's open daily except Tuesday from 9.30 to 11.30 am and 2 to 7.30 pm.

Moving up in price, there's a string of sidewalk cafés along Avenida Ballivián, offering European, Bolivian and North American fare in a pleasant environment. If you're really hungry, try *Bibossy*, at Avenida Ballivián N-539, where the lunch portions bury the plate! A good spot for lunch or dinner is the Korean-run *Restaurant Lose* on the plaza; it's especially good for Chinese meals.

What may be Bolivia's finest Mexican food – including tacos, enchiladas, burritos, quesadillas and other treats – is available at *La Salsa Café*, at Calle 25 de Mayo 217. It also offers a variety of international sandwiches, breakfasts, chilli dogs, burgers, chicken and chips, ice cream and Bolivian specialities.

Cochabamba's best vegetarian food is found at *Snack Uno* on Avenida Heroínas. Almuerzos cost US$1.20; pizza and pasta dishes are also available. The salteñería next door is also recommended. An alternative is *Chifal* on Jordan near 25 de Mayo, which serves buffet lunches for US$1.75. The *Gopal* vegetarian restaurant has recently gone downhill, but is still an option if you stick with simple dishes.

For pizzas, you'll enjoy *Rondevu* (☎ 53937), on the corner of Calle 25 de Mayo and Colombia. At España and Mayor Rocha, concealed behind rose-coloured stucco, is one of the city's best restaurants, *La Cantonata*, which makes an exceptionally good splurge. Diagonally across the street is *Café Bistro El Carajillo*, a lively place for a drink and bar snacks.

A popular eating, drinking and socialising spot, especially with expats and overseas volunteer organisations, is the *Metropolis*. Specialities include soup, salad, pasta, pancakes and occasionally even ceviche and goulash.

Things to Buy
The health food shop, Coincoca, at Calle Ayacucho S-259, specialises in products made from the coca leaf. However, the grape-flavoured coca chewing gum (an appetite suppressant for dieters) may not deceive sniffer dogs at airports.

Getting There & Away
Air Cochabamba is served by both LAB (☎ 50760) and AeroSur (☎ 28385). LAB charges US$41 to La Paz, US$53 to Santa Cruz and US$35 to Sucre. The airport is accessible on micro 'B' from the main plaza. Taxis from the centre cost about US$1 per person.

Bus Cochabamba's central bus terminal is on Avenida Ayacucho just south of Avenida Aroma. Most buses to La Paz – there are at least 20 buses per day – leave between 7 and 9 pm, though there are also several morning departures (US$8, eight to 10 hours). Most buses to Santa Cruz leave between 4 and 6 pm (US$7, 10 to 12 hours), but there is an increasing number of morning departures. Santa Cruz buses now follow the new road via Chapare rather then the former, more scenic, route over Siberia Pass.

Five to 10 buses leave for Sucre daily between 4.30 and 6.30 pm (US$7, 12 hours). Some then continue to Potosí (at least US$2

more). To Villa Tunari (US$2, five to six hours) and Puerto Villarroel in the Chapare region, micros leave in the morning from the corner of 9 de Abril and Oquendo. Flota 7 de Julio buses leave for Villa Tunari several times each morning.

Trufis and micros to eastern Cochabamba villages leave from along Calle Manuripi; to the western part of the valley, they leave from the corner of Avenidas Ayacucho and Aroma.

Train Ferrobuses to Oruro run on Wednesday and Friday at 2 pm (US$3.60/2.80 1st/2nd class, five hours). The tren rápido leaves on Sunday at 8 am (US$3.20/2.50 1st/2nd class, 11 hours).

Camión Camiones to Sucre and Santa Cruz leave from Avenida de la Independencia, 1½ km south of the railway station. Expect to pay roughly half the bus fare.

Potosí

The renown of Potosí – its fame and splendour but also its tragedy and horror – is inextricably tied to silver. The city was founded in 1545, following the discovery of ore in silver-rich Cerro Rico, the hill which overlooks the town. The veins proved to be so rich that the mines quickly became the world's most prolific. Despite its setting at an altitude of 4070 metres, Potosí blossomed, and towards the end of the 18th century, grew into the largest and wealthiest city in Latin America. Silver from Potosí underwrote the Spanish economy, and its monarch's extravagance, for over two centuries. Millions of conscripted labourers were put to work in the mines, where conditions were so appalling that miners died in considerable numbers, either from accidents or diseases such as silicosis pneumonia.

The boom, however, was not to last. At the turn of the 19th century, the silver production waned and decline set in. During the present century, it was only a demand for tin that rescued Potosí from obscurity and brought a

BOLIVIA

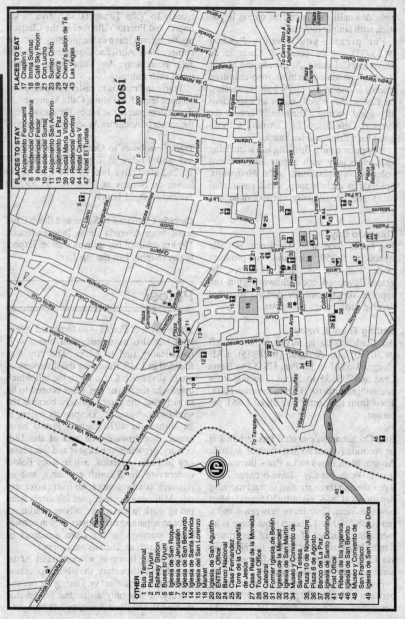

Potosí

PLACES TO STAY
4 Alojamiento Ferrocarril
8 Residencial Copacabana
10 Residencial Felcar
11 Residencial Sumaj
13 Alojamiento San Antonio
16 Alojamiento La Paz
39 Hostal María Victoria
40 Residencial Central
44 Hotel Carlos V
47 Hotel El Turista

PLACES TO EAT
17 Chaplin's
18 Imma Sumac
19 Café Sky Room
21 Don Lucho
23 Sumac Orko
29 Kivo's
42 Cherry's Salón de Té
43 Las Vegas

OTHER
1 Bus Terminal
2 Plaza Uyuni
3 Railway Station
5 Buses to Uyuni
6 Iglesia de San Roque
7 Iglesia de Jerusalén
9 Iglesia de San Bernardo
12 Iglesia de Santa Mónica
14 Iglesia del San Lorenzo
15 Mercado
20 Iglesia de San Agustín
22 ENTEL Office
24 Banco Nacional
25 Casa Fernandez
26 Torre de la Compañía
     de Jesús
27 Casa Real de la Moneda
28 Catedral
30 Tourist Office
31 Former Iglesia de Belén
32 Iglesia de la Merced
33 Iglesia de San Martín
34 Museo y Convento de
     Santa Teresa
35 Plaza 10 de Noviembre
36 Plaza 6 de Agosto
37 Banco de La Paz
38 Iglesia de Santo Domingo
41 Post Office
45 Ribera de los Ingenios
46 Iglesia de San Benito
48 Museo y Convento de
     San Francisco
49 Iglesia de San Juan de Dios

slow but steady recovery. Silver extraction continues on only a small scale, but reminders of the grand colonial city are still evident in the narrow streets, formal balconied mansions and ornate churches.

Superlatives buffs will be happy to learn that Potosí is the world's highest city, and the fact will be driven home when you're climbing the streets or shivering with cold at night. Warm clothing is essential!

Information
Tourist Office The Senatur tourist office (☎ 25288), upstairs on the corner of Matos and Calle Quijarro, is theoretically open from 9 am to noon and 3 to 6 pm, Monday to Friday, but going there is a waste of time in a city where there are a number of better things to do.

Potosí's telephone code is 062.

Money Lots of businesses along Calle Bolívar and Calle Sucre change cash US dollars at a reasonable rate – look for the 'Compro Dólares' signs. Travellers' cheques fetch a poor rate in Potosí – up to 10% less than the official rate. The Banco Nacional on Calle Junín changes travellers' cheques; on weekends and evenings, change them at Casa Fernández, on Calle Sucre. Visa cash advances are available at Banco de La Paz, on the plaza; you can receive the cash in bolivianos or US dollars.

Things to See
The entire central area of Potosí contains a wealth of colonial architecture, and it's worth allowing a couple of hours to stroll around. Unfortunately, many worthwhile churches are closed to the public or open only rarely. The **cathedral** (which is open regularly) has a particularly fine interior, while the **Iglesia de San Lorenzo** is famous for its classic mestizo façade.

The city has two convent museums open to the public, both with examples of religious art. The **Convento de San Francisco** is open Monday to Friday from 10 am to noon and 2.30 to 5 pm, and on Saturday from 10 am to noon. Foreigners pay US$1.50. The

highlight is the view from the roof. The **Convento de Santa Teresa** is open Monday to Saturday from 8.30 am to noon and 2.30 to 6 pm. Admission to either, including a one-hour guided tour, is US$2. Photography permits in either place cost an extra US$2 for cameras and US$3 for videos.

The **Casa Real de la Moneda**, the Royal Mint, is the city's star attraction and one of Bolivia's best museums. The current building, which occupies an entire block near the cathedral, was built between 1753 and 1773 to control the minting of colonial coins right where the metal was mined. It's now a museum housing wooden colonial-era minting machines, religious art, Bolivian war relics, Tiahuanaco artefacts and even the country's first locomotive – all worth seeing. The building itself, which has been carefully restored, is exceptionally impressive. For three-hour tours, foreigners pay US$1.75. Tours are conducted at 9 am and 2 pm, Monday to Saturday. Photography permits cost an extra US$2.

A good day hike is to the **Lagunas del Kari Kari**, east of town. These artificial lakes were constructed in the late 16th and early 17th centuries by Indian slaves, to provide water for the city and hydro power to run its 132 *ingenios* (smelters). Travel agencies offer full and half-day tours to the Lagunas. Alternatively, you can head off on your own. Pick up the 1:50,000 topo sheet 6435-II, *Potosí (Este)*, at the Instituto Geográfico Militar on Calle Sucre.

Outside Potosí are several hot spring resorts; the most popular is at **Tarapaya**, 25 km from the city. To get there, find a camión at Plaza Chuquimia, uphill from the bus terminal. Micros also run until mid-afternoon and cost US$0.50.

Cooperative Mines Visiting the cooperative mines may be the most memorable experience you'll have in Bolivia and you'll probably be left in a state of shock. The working conditions, which remain unchanged from colonial times, can only be called medieval. All work is done by hand with primitive tools and the temperatures underground vary from below freezing – the altitude is over 4200 metres – to a stifling 45°C in the mountain's depths. Miners, exposed to all sorts of noxious chemicals and gases, normally die of silicosis pneumonia within 10 years of entering the mines.

Quite a few young Potosí men offer guided tours through the mines, and each tour agency has its own pool of guides. Some guides are well known and very experienced but you may also want to try our new and enthusiastic guides. Tours cost around US$5 per person, but prices can double during periods of high demand.

Wear the worst clothes you have; walking in the mine is difficult, ceilings are low and passageways are steep and muddy. Visitors are able to speak with the miners about their work, and it's friendly – but not required or even expected – to offer cigarettes, coca leaves, or some other small token as a tip. Photography is permitted, but you'll need a flash.

Special Events

Although Potosí has a number of annual fiestas, a new and popular addition is the Fiesta de Chu'tillos, which takes place around the end of August. It features traditional dancing from all over South America, as well as special performances from other continents. Accommodation bookings are essential for this period. Alternatively, turn up a week early; the week preceding the festival is given over to practicing for the big event and can be nearly as exciting as the real thing!

Places to Stay

Only top-end hotels have heating and there may be blanket shortages in cheaper accommodation, so you may want to bring a sleeping bag. Cheaper places charge US$0.50 extra for hot showers.

The favourite budget hotel seems to be the *Residencial Sumaj* (☎ 23336), near the Plaza del Estudiante. It's close to both the bus terminal and the railway station and although its appeal escapes many people, it somehow

keeps plugging along. Small, dark rooms without private bath cost US$3 per person, and for an additional US$1, you'll get a basic breakfast. The hot water availability is hit or miss. Beware of thieves posing as mine guides.

Another favourite is the friendly *Hostal Carlos V* (☎ 25121). It's in a cosy old colonial building with a covered patio. Rooms cost US$3.50 per person. Even nicer is the *Hostal María Victoria*, located in a colonial home surrounding a classic sunny courtyard. Rooms cost a negotiable US$3 per person. Breakfast and snacks are available and the friendly and helpful staff really make travellers feel welcome.

The adequate *Residencial Central* (☎ 22207), in a quiet old part of town, has a traditional *potosino* overhanging balcony. Rooms cost US$3.50 per person. *Hotel El Turista* (☎ 22492), at Calle Lanza 19, is a long-standing Potosí favourite, and offers good value for money. The friendly owner, Señor Luksic provides good, reliable tourist information and some of Bolivia's best hot showers between 6.30 and 11 am. Rooms cost US$7/11. For a room with a view, request a room on the top floor.

Also recommended is *Residencial Felcar* (☎ 24966), at Serrudo 345, which offers free hot showers, clean rooms and a sunny patio. Rooms cost US$3 per person. *Alojamiento San Antonio* (☎ 23566), at Calle Oruro 136, costs US$2.75 per person with warmish common showers; singles/doubles with bath are US$7/11. It serves as a youth hostel, but isn't the best value around. *Residencial Copacabana* (☎ 22712), at Avenida Serrudo 319, costs US$3 per person without private bath. There's an attached restaurant.

As its name would imply, *Alojamiento Ferrocarril* (☎ 24294) is near the railway station. It's among the friendliest of the bargain basement options, and has hot showers. Singles/doubles cost US$2.75/4. An old travellers' standard is *Alojamiento La Paz* (☎ 22632), at Calle Oruro 262, but people often have shocking tales to tell about the showers! Rooms cost US$2.50 per person; the dodgy showers are extra.

Places to Eat

The market *comedor* offers inexpensive breakfasts, and the *ice-cream shop* beside the cathedral and a couple of small *bakeries* along Calle Padilla do American and continental breakfasts. In any case, nearly everything else is locked up tight until midmorning, but most hotels and residencials also offer some sort of breakfast option. Pizza and pasta are the emphasis at *Kivo's*, beside the tourist office. You'll also find pizzas at *Pizzería Argentina*, on Calle Linares just above the plaza.

For great salteñas, go to *Café Imma Sumac*, at Calle Bustillos 987. In the morning, meatless salteñas potosinas are sold on the street near Iglesia de San Lorenzo for US$0.20. Meat empanadas are sold around the market until early afternoon, and in the evening, street vendors sell cornmeal humitas.

Some of Potosí's best and most innovative meals are served at *Don Lucho*, which does pretty good almuerzos for US$3, including soup, salad, a main course and dessert. Dinners are even better, ranging from pasta to filet mignon with béchamel sauce. Almost as good, but a bit expensive, the *Las Vegas* is near the corner of Calles Padilla and Linares. Its exhaustive four-course lunch specials run at about US$4; the house speciality is pique a lo macho (chopped beef served with onions and other vegetables).

The *Sumac Orko*, at Calle Quijarro 46, offers filling almuerzos with salad, soup, a meat dish and dessert for just US$1.50. In the evening, à la carte options include trucha al limón (lemon trout) and picante de perdiz (spicy partridge). The *Sky Room* restaurant near the market on Calle Bolívar does excellent mid-range beef and chicken specialities.

An especially friendly choice is *Chaplin's*, on Bustillos near the market. It serves delicious vegetarian lunches of vegetable noodle soup, spicy lentils, potatoes, rice, fruit juice and papaya for US$1.20. It's also popular for dinners and on Friday and Saturday evenings, it does excellent Mexican tacos.

For delicious, good-value apple strudel, chocolate cake, lemon meringue pie or other cakes and pastries, or just a cup of coffee or tea, try the popular *Cherry's Salon de Té*, on Calle Padilla. It's open all afternoon and makes a good pit stop while you're out exploring the town.

Entertainment

Don't miss the Friday night peña at *Don Lucho*, which is perhaps the best in Bolivia. If you're lucky, you may even hear the lively and driving music of the local group, Arpegio Cinco, as well as examples of the unique nasal accompaniment to Potosí department's own ritual martial art, the *tinku*.

Getting There & Away

Air Potosí boasts the world's highest commercial airport, but although the runway has recently been extended to 4000 metres to accommodate larger planes, the city isn't yet on the LAB or AeroSur timetables. That will probably change soon, but currently, your best option is to take a bus to Sucre and fly from there.

Bus The bus terminal is a long way from the centre, but micros and minibuses run frequently from the centre and taxis are just US$0.40. There are numerous buses to La Paz every day (US$8, 10 to 12 hours), but all leave in the evening. If you prefer to travel by day, Trans Bustillo has a 6.45 am bus to Oruro (US$4, seven hours), from where you'll easily find a bus to La Paz.

Buses leave for Tupiza (US$6.50, 12 hours) and Villazón (US$8, 13 hours) daily at 8.30 am and 6 pm. Buses to Tarija run at 9.30 am, and at 2 and 4 pm (US$7, 12 hours).

Buses to Sucre (US$3, 3½ hours) leave daily at 7 or 7.30 am and 5 pm. The cheapest way between Potosí and Sucre is by camión or micro. They leave from Plaza Uyuni when full, normally every half an hour or so.

Buses to Uyuni (US$3.50, eight hours) depart between 9.30 am and noon from higher up on Avenida Antofagasta, near the railway line. Camiones to Uyuni leave from the same place.

Train The ferrobus to Oruro (US$8.60/5.50, seven hours) and La Paz (US$11/8, 12 hours) leaves on Wednesday and Sunday at 7.30 pm. The ferrobus to Sucre (US$4.10/3.30, four hours) departs on Wednesday and Sunday at 4.25 am. Prices given are for 1st/2nd (Pullman/especial) class.

Sucre

Set in a valley surrounded by low mountains, Sucre is a small, pleasant city of 100,000 people, and retains the colonial flavour of its heritage in its numerous churches, museums and ancient mansions and in its atmosphere. Although La Paz has usurped most of the governmental power, the Supreme Court still convenes in Sucre and with a sort of wistful pride, *sureños* (as the city's inhabitants are known) maintain that their city remains the real heart of Bolivian government.

Sucre was founded in 1538 (under the name of La Plata) as the Spanish capital of the Charcas, a vast region stretching from southern Peru to Río de la Plata in present-day Argentina. In 1776, when the new territorial division was created by the Spaniards, the city's name was changed to Chuquisaca.

During the long colonial period, La Plata/Chuquisaca was the most important centre in the eastern Spanish territories, and influenced much of Bolivia's history. It was here that independence was declared on 6 August 1825 and the new republic was created and named after its liberator, Simón Bolívar. Several years later, the name of the city was changed again, to Sucre, in honour of the general who promoted the independence movement.

Information
Tourist Office The tourist office (☎ 35994), in the Caserón de la Capellanía, isn't terribly helpful, but the staff can answer specific questions. It's open from 8.30 am to noon and 2.30 to 6.30 pm. There's also a helpful university tourist office (☎ 23763) at Calle

Nicolás Ortiz 182, which will provide expert guides for city sightseeing.

Sucre's telephone code is 064.

Money There are a couple of casas de cambio around the main market. Casa de Cambio Ambar changes travellers' cheques, as does Banco Nacional (and at a better rate). Street moneychangers operate along Avenida Hernando Siles, behind the main market. There are also quite a few businesses around town displaying 'Compro Dólares' signs, but they only change cash. Visa cash advances are available at the Banco de Santa Cruz.

Things to See
Sucre boasts a host of lovely colonial churches. The **cathedral**, on the plaza, dates from the 16th century, though there were major additions in the early 17th century. It's normally open in the morning. Just down the block is the entrance to the **Museo de la Catedral**, which holds a remarkable collection of religious relics. It's open Monday to Friday from 10 am to noon and 3 to 5 pm, and on Saturday from 10 am to noon. Admission is US$0.75.

The **Iglesia de la Merced** has the finest interior of any Sucre church, but it's rarely open. Both the **Iglesia de San Miguel** and the **Iglesia de San Francisco** reflect Mudejar influences, particularly in their ceiling designs. The beautiful **Convento de San Felipe Neri** is open from 4 to 6 pm, Monday to Friday, when school is in session. Visitors must have a guide (free) from the university tourist office.

It's worth trekking up the hillside to the **Iglesia de la Recoleta**, which affords superb views over the city. The **Museo de la Recoleta**, inside the church, contains quite a few anonymous paintings and sculptures, and is open Monday to Friday from 9 to 11 am and 3 to 5 pm. Admission, including a guided tour, costs US$1. If you're interested in sacred art, there's the **Museo de Santa Clara**, at Calvo 212, open Monday to Friday from 9 to 11 am and 3 to 5 pm. If it's closed, knock on the door on Calle Avaroa. Admission is US$1.

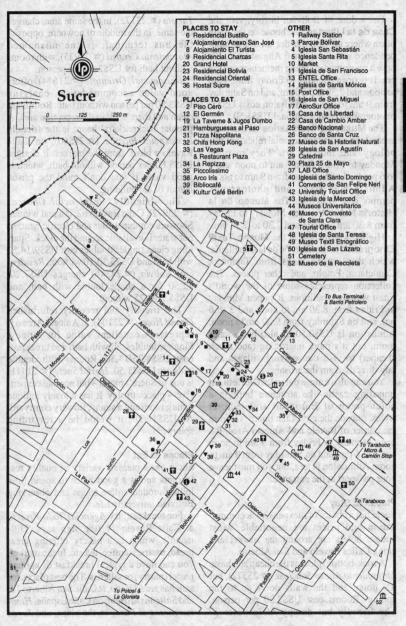

Sucre

BOLIVIA

0   125   250 m

PLACES TO STAY
6   Residencial Bustillo
7   Alojamiento Anexo San José
8   Alojamiento El Turista
9   Residencial Charcas
20 Grand Hotel
23 Residencial Bolivia
24 Residencial Oriental
36 Hostal Sucre

PLACES TO EAT
2   Piso Cero
12 El Germén
19 La Taverne & Jugos Dumbo
21 Hamburguesas al Paso
32 Pizza Napolitana
32 Chifa Hong Kong
33 Las Vegas
    & Restaurant Plaza
34 La Repizza
35 Piccolissimo
39 Arco Irís
39 Bibliocafé
45 Kultur Café Berlin

OTHER
1   Railway Station
3   Parque Bolívar
4   Iglesia San Sebastián
5   Iglesia Santa Rita
10 Market
11 Iglesia de San Francisco
13 ENTEL Office
14 Iglesia de Santa Mónica
15 Post Office
16 Iglesia de San Miguel
17 AeroSur Office
18 Casa de la Libertad
22 Casa de Cambio Ambar
25 Banco Nacional
26 Banco de Santa Cruz
27 Museo de la Historia Natural
28 Iglesia de San Agustín
29 Catedral
30 Plaza 25 de Mayo
37 LAB Office
40 Iglesia de Santo Domingo
41 Convento de San Felipe Neri
42 University Tourist Office
43 Iglesia de la Merced
44 Museos Universitarios
46 Museo y Convento
    de Santa Clara
47 Tourist Office
48 Iglesia de Santa Teresa
49 Museo Textil Etnográfico
50 Iglesia de San Lázaro
51 Cemetery
52 Museo de la Recoleta

To Bus Terminal
& Barrio Petrolero

To Tarabuco
Micro &
Camión Stop

To Tarabuco

To Potosí &
La Glorieta

For a dose of Bolivian history, visit the **Casa de la Libertad**, the house on the main plaza where the Bolivian declaration of independence was signed on 6 August 1825. It's now a museum displaying mementos of the era. It is open Monday to Friday from 9 am to noon and 2.30 to 5.30 pm, and on Saturday from 9 am to noon. Admission costs US$1; photography is an additional US$1.50.

The **Museos Universitarios** take in three separate museums for colonial relics, anthropology and modern art. They're open Monday to Friday from 9 am to noon and 2 to 6 pm, and on Saturday from 9 am to noon. Admission is US$1.50. The **Museo de la Historia Natural** is open Monday to Friday from 8.30 am to noon and 2.30 to 5.30 pm.

Highly worthwhile is the **Museo Textil Etnográfico** in the Caserón de la Capellanía, which displays weavings from Tarabuco, Candelaria, Potolo, and other places. The collection represents some of the world's finest weaving traditions. It's open Monday to Friday from 8.30 am to noon and 3 to 6 pm, and on Saturday from 9.30 am to noon. Admission is US$0.50. It also has a sales room, but it's more interesting (and much cheaper) to visit the weaving villages and buy directly from the artisans.

You can also traipse out to **La Glorieta**, an imposing castle-like structure built in a hotch-potch of European architectural styles, outside the city. Take micro 'G' from the corner of Ravelo and Aniceto Arce. It's open Monday to Friday from 9 am to noon and 2 to 6 pm, and on Saturday from 9 am to noon. Admission is free, but you must leave your passport at the entrance.

Places to Stay

Sucre has a choice of inexpensive accommodation and prices are negotiable. Most budget hotels are around the market and along Calles Ravelo and San Alberto.

A rock-bottom place is the cheap and basic *Alojamiento Anexo San José* (☎ 25572), but it's noisy and the walls don't go to the ceiling. Rooms cost US$2.30 per person. The friendly but dumpy *Alojamiento El*

Turista (☎ 23172), in the same area, charges the same. In the middle of nowhere, opposite the bus terminal, is the misnamed *Alojamiento Central* (☎ 23935), with rooms without bath for US$2.50 per person.

Residencial Oriental (☎ 21644) offers good-value accommodation, charging US$3.80 per person without bath. Rooms are clean and there's TV in the reception area. A popular backpackers' haunt is the friendly *Residencial Bustillo* (☎ 21560), on Calle Ravelo a block from the market. It charges US$3.80 per person without bath, which is good value if you don't mind the prison layout of the building.

The friendly *Residencial Charcas* (☎ 23972), Calle Ravelo 62, is a real winner. Showers combine solar and electric heat, so hot water is available around the clock. Sparkling clean singles/doubles cost US$9/14.50 with bath and US$5.20/10 without. *Residencial Bolivia* (☎ 24346) charges US$7.20/12.50 for a single/double with bath and US$5.20/8.25 without.

The friendly and recently refurbished *Grand Hotel* (☎ 22104), at Aniceto Arce 61, represents excellent value for money. Singles/doubles, all with bath and breakfast, cost US$8.25/14.50. Rooms with double beds are US$11.50. *Hostal Sucre* (☎ 21411) is one of Sucre's nicest – but not most expensive – places to stay. It has a lovely antique dining room and a sunny, flowery courtyard. At US$16/20, it would be a rewarding splurge.

Places to Eat

Sucre has a pleasant variety of quality restaurants and is a good place to spend time lolling around coffee shops and observing Bolivian university life.

For breakfast, try *Agencias Todo Fresco*, at Calle Ravelo 74 (the sign says 'Dillmann'), which is a bakery offering great bread, pastries, coffee, tea etc. In the market, you can have a typical breakfast of api and pastel (pastry) or salteñas. The best places for salteñas are *El Patio*, at Calle San Alberto 18, and *Salteñas Miriam*, on Calle España. *Hamburguesas al Paso*, on the plaza, and *Jugos*

Dumbo, around the corner, open early to serve salteñas, coffee, tea, juice and licuados. The highly recommended *Arco's Coffee Shop* on Aniceto Arce near Ravelo also serves breakfasts (from 8 am) and healthy sandwiches.

Pizza Napolitana, on the plaza, does well as a hang-out for the under-21 university crowd, with ice cream and pizzas leading the menu selections. Also excellent for pizza – as well as pasta, chicken and even ribs – is *Kactus*, just off the plaza on Calle España. Chicken-and-chips shops are found along Avenida Hernando Siles between Tarapaca and Junín. *La Repizza* does meat or vegetarian pizzas and pasta dishes. The four-course almuerzos cost just US$1.20 and are very popular with students.

The long-running *Las Vegas*, on the plaza, is good if you want to hang out in the centre of things, but it's nothing out of the ordinary. The *Restaurant Plaza* next door offers a similar menu and the outdoor balconies upstairs are also a great place to drink a beer on Sunday afternoons. Plusher restaurants with fine fare are *El Solar*, on the corner of Calles Bolívar and Azurduy, and better still, *Piso Cero*, at Avenida Venezuela 1241.

An expensive but very good Chinese place is the *Chifa Hong Kong*, on the plaza. For fair Italian food, there's *Piccolissimo*, which is about as elegant as Sucre gets. Plan on US$5 to US$7 per person, or more if you splurge on a bottle of Chilean wine. Afterward, enjoy a really good cup of espresso or cappuccino. The excellent Alliance Française restaurant, *La Taverne*, serves a mean ratatouille for US$1.50, as well as coq au vin, quiche Lorraine and other continental favourites. Films (mostly French) are shown nightly.

There's also a quartet of German-run options. The best is *Bibliocafé*, with a dark but cosy atmosphere, good music and stacks of *Geo* and *Der Spiegel* on the shelves. The pasta dishes are recommended, as is the banana, chocolate and cream crêpe. It's only open in the evening and gets crowded, so come early. Another is the German coffee shop and restaurant, *Kultur Café Berlin*, at

Calle Avaroa 326. It's open for lunch from 12.30 to 3 pm. Don't miss their papas rellenas (potatoes with spicy fillings) which cost just US$0.30. The third is *Arco Iris*, where the menu includes such delights as roeschti, fondue bourguignonne, mousse au chocolat and head-buzzing cappuccino. Vegetarian meals are available, and they occasionally show videos and arrange peñas featuring local bands. Finally, there's the bright and airy *Restaurant El Germén* at the Hostal San Francisco, which does excellent vegetarian dishes and German-style pastries; it also has a book-exchange service.

The market also provides some highlights; don't miss the fruit salads and juices, which are among the best in the country. Try *jugo de tumbo* (juice of unripe yellow passion fruit) or any combination of melon, guava, pomelo, strawberry, papaya, banana, orange, lime etc. The vendors and their blenders always come up with something indescribably delicious.

Getting There & Away

Air LAB (☎ 22666) and AeroSur (☎ 24895) both have flights to and from La Paz, Cochabamba, Santa Cruz, Tarija, Camiri and other towns. You can reach the airport on micro 'F' for US$0.10 (B$0.50), or by taxi for US$1.50.

Bus The bus terminal is accessed by micro 'A' from the centre, but the micros are tiny and could be a nightmare with luggage. There are numerous daily buses to Cochabamba (US$7, 12 hours), all of which leave around 6 or 7 pm; many of these continue on to Santa Cruz (US$10, 24 hours). Direct buses to Santa Cruz – that is, they don't pass through Cochabamba – leave on Tuesday, Friday and Sunday (US$8, 18 hours). Several companies leave daily for Potosí (US$3, 3½ hours) at 7 or 7.30 am and at 5 pm.

A number of flotas also connect Sucre with La Paz. Morning departures travel via Oruro (US$8, 20 hours) and arrive the following morning; most evening departures travel via Cochabamba and don't arrive until the following afternoon.

Train The ferrobus to Potosí (US$4, 4½ hours), Oruro (US$10.20, 12 hours) and La Paz (US$10.50, 12 hours) leaves on Wednesday and Sunday at 3 pm.

Camión Camiones for Punilla, Chataquila, Potolo, Ravelo, and points north and west leave in the morning from the Río Quirpinchaca bridge, en route to the airport. Camiones to Tarabuco, Candelaria and points south depart from the stop on Avenida de las Américas.

AROUND SUCRE
Tarabuco

This small, predominantly Indian village, 65 km south-east of Sucre, is widely known for its beautiful handmade weavings and for the colourful Sunday market which spreads over the length and breadth of the town. You can buy amazing ponchos and mantas, as well as charangos (please have mercy on endangered armadillos and purchase only wooden ones), but prices are high and the scene is extremely touristy.

If you'd rather not join a tour group, camiones leave from Avenida de las Américas in Sucre between 6.30 and 9.30 am on Sunday. The charge is US$1 per person and the trip takes two to three hours, with beautiful scenery en route. Camiones returning to Sucre park at the top of the main plaza in Tarabuco. They're meant to leave between 2 and 3.30 pm on Sunday but will wait until they are 'full'.

Cordillera de los Frailes

This imposing range runs through much of western Chuquisaca and northern Potosí departments, and offers some wonderful trekking opportunities. Sites in the Sucre area worth visiting include the Capilla de Chataquila, the six-km Camino del Inca, the rock paintings of Pumamachay, the weaving village of Potolo, the pastoral village of Chaunaca, dramatic Maragua Crater and the hot springs at Talula. There are plenty of trekking routes, but they traverse little-visited areas; to minimise cultural impact – and avoid getting hopelessly lost – a guide will be essential.

A couple of Sucre travel agencies offer brief jaunts around Pumamachay, but a private guide will allow you to explore further. Highly recommended are Lucho and Dely Loredo, who know the area well and offer a variety of itineraries. For one person, they charge US$25 per day; larger groups pay considerably less per person. Contact the Loredos by taking a US$0.40 taxi ride to their home at Barrio Petrolero, Calle Panamá final esquina Calle Comarapa, 127.

Santa Cruz

Santa Cruz de la Sierra was founded in 1561 by the Spaniard Ñuflo de Chaves; the town originally lay 220 km east of its current location. Around the end of the 16th century, however, it proved vulnerable to Indian attack and was moved to its present position, 50 km east of the Cordillera Oriental foothills.

Over the past four decades, Santa Cruz has mushroomed from a backwater cow town of 30,000 to its present position as Bolivia's second largest city, with 800,000 people.

Santa Cruz today is a big city near the edge of the wilderness, and although its growth continues at a phenomenal rate, this cosmopolitan city retains traces of its dusty past, evident in its wide streets, frontier architecture and small-town atmosphere. Once an isolated agricultural outpost, it has developed into a hub of transport and trade, with direct flights to Miami and Europe, but forest-dwelling sloths still hang in the trees of the main plaza. The city's reputation as a drug-trafficking mecca has recently been eclipsed by a boom in tropical agriculture, and large corporate plantations of sugar, rice, cotton, soybeans and other warm-weather crops now dominate the vast and once forested lowlands east of the city.

BOLIVIA

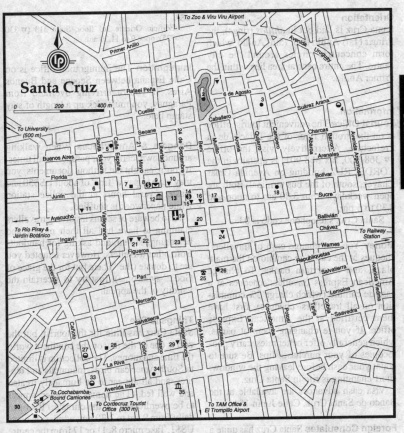

Santa Cruz

To Zoo & Viru Viru Airport

0   200   400 m

To University (500 m)

To Río Piray & Jardín Botánico

To Cochabamba-Bound Camiones

To Cordecruz Tourist Office (300 m)

To Railway Station

To TAM Office & El Trompillo Airport

Primer Anillo

Rafael Peña

Cuellar

Seoane

Buenos Aires

Florida

Junín

Ayacucho

Ingavi

Figueroa

Pari

Mercado

Salvatierra

La Riva

Avenida Irala

Caballero

6 de Agosto

Suárez Arana

Charcas

Arenales

Bolívar

Sucre

Ballivián

Chávez

Warnes

Republiquetas

Salvatierra

Lemoine

Saavedra

PLACES TO STAY	15 La Pascana	12 Casa de la Cultura
6 Alojamiento Santa	16 Bar Hawai	Raúl Otero Reiche
Bárbara	21 Galeón Peruano	& Tourist Office
7 Hotel Bibosi	22 La Olla Que Canta	13 Plaza 24 de
17 Residencial Bolívar	24 Bar El Tapekuá	Septiembre
20 Residencial Ballivián	29 La Bella Napoli	14 Cambios Alemán &
23 Hotel Italia		Mendicambio
28 Alojamiento Lemoine	**OTHER**	18 Lavandería
31 Residencial Grigotá	2 Parque El Arenal &	19 Catedral
32 Residencial 15 de	Museo	25 ENTEL Office
Octubre	Antropológico	26 LAB Office
	3 Mercado Los Pozos	27 Taxis to Samaipata
PLACES TO EAT	4 Micros to Cotoca &	30 Mercado La Ramada
1 Las Tres BBB	Puerto Pailas	33 Bus Terminal
10 Mama Rosa's Pizzería	5 Immigration	34 AeroSur Office
11 Restaurante	8 Banco de Santa Cruz	35 Museo de la Historia
Vegetarianista	9 Post Office	Natural

Orientation

Santa Cruz is laid out in *anillos* (rings), the Primer (1st) Anillo to 5° (5th) Anillo, which form concentric circles around the city centre. The entire central area lies within the Primer Anillo.

Information

Tourist Office The convenient tourist office is on the ground floor of the Palacio de la Prefectura. Alternatively, visit the office (☎ 368 900, fax 368 901) is upstairs in the CORDECRUZ building on Avenida Omar Chávez, south of the bus terminal. Both are open weekdays from 8.30 am to noon and 2.30 to 6 pm.

Santa Cruz's telephone code is 03.

Money You can change cash or travellers' cheques at the casas de cambio on the main plaza, and at certain banks. To change American Express travellers' cheques at a casa de cambio (which charge 3% commission on all travellers' cheques), first have them certified at the American Express office. If you're changing them at banks, which generally offer better rates, carry photocopies of your purchase slips. Be sure to count your cash before leaving the window: short-changing is rife in Santa Cruz.

Visa cash advances are available at the Banco de Santa Cruz, Calle Junín 154.

Foreign Consulates Santa Cruz has quite a few consulates. Opening hours refer to weekdays only:

Argentina
Banco de la Nación Argentina, Plaza 24 de Septiembre (☎ 324 153); open 9 am to noon.
Brazil
Avenida Busch 330 (☎ 344 400); open 9.30 am to 12.30 pm and 3.30 to 6.30 pm
France
Calle Avaroa 70 (☎ 334 818); open 3 to 6.30 pm
Germany
Avenida de las Américas 241 (☎ 324 825); open 8.30 am to 1 pm
Netherlands
Calle Buenos Aires 172 (☎ 340 331); open 8.30 am to noon

USA
Edificio Oriente 3rd floor, Suite 313 (☎ 330 725); open 9 to 11.30 am

Immigration The immigration office is on Calle España between Seoane and Buenos Aires. If you're arriving overland from Paraguay, you must pick up a length of stay stamp here.

Dangers & Annoyances When walking around town, carry your passport at all times. If you're caught out without documents, you may have to pay a 'fine' of about US$50 and waste several hours at the police station while paperwork is shuffled.

Also beware of scams involving travellers claiming to have had all their money and belongings stolen, and asking for handouts from other travellers. However tempted you are to donate (the 'There but for the grace of God...' syndrome), first try to ascertain the validity of the appeal.

Things to See

Santa Cruz has little for the tourist, but the **zoo** is one of the few on the continent worth the time and money. The collection is limited to South American birds, mammals and reptiles, and all appear to be humanely treated and well fed. (The llamas, however, appear to be overdressed for the climate.) It's open daily from 9 am to 7.30 pm; admission costs US$1. Take micro 8, 11 or 17 from the centre or from El Arenal, or catch a taxi (US$1.50).

Locals relax around the lagoon at **Parque El Arenal**. On an island in the lagoon, a bas-relief mural depicts historical and modern-day aspects of Santa Cruz. This building also contains a small anthropological museum.

The **Casa de la Cultura Raúl Otero Reiche** on the plaza is a rather informal museum of Bolivian art. Although the paintings are poorly lit and haphazardly arranged around the building and its offices, originality runs high. Look especially for the works of such contemporary Bolivian artists as Lorgio Vaca, Herminio Pedraza and Tito

Kurasotto. It's open weekdays from 8.30 am to noon and 2.30 to 6 pm; admission is free.

A new item of interest is the **Museo de la Historia Natural** on Avenida Irala, which will give you the lowdown on the flora, fauna and geology of eastern Bolivia. It's open daily from 9 am to noon and 3 to 6 pm.

Places to Stay

If you've just arrived at the bus terminal and don't feel like walking too far, there is a selection of cheap places near the bus terminal. Two blocks away on a crowded market street is the friendly *Residencial Grigotá* (☎ 337 699), where fairly clean rooms cost US$4 per person without bath. For a double bed with private bath, you'll pay US$10.50.

Another nearby option is *Residencial 15 de Octubre* (☎ 342 591), Calle Guaraní 33. It's more spartan than the Grigotá, but costs just US$3.50 per person without bath. An even more basic place in the bus terminal area is the *Alojamiento Lemoine* (☎ 346 670), at Calle Lemoine 469. Rooms without bath cost US$3 per person, but it's rather noisy.

If you prefer something more central, *Alojamiento Santa Bárbara* (☎ 321 817), Calle Santa Bárbara 151, offers simple but comfortable accommodation for US$4 per person.

A long-time travellers' favourite is the clean and bright *Residencial Bolívar* (☎ 342 500), at Calle Sucre 131. With good breakfasts, inviting courtyard hammocks, excellent hot showers and a couple of charming toucans (which have the run of the place), it's still a good choice. Rooms without private bath cost US$5 per person. If the Bolívar is full, a good alternative is *Residencial Ballivián* (☎ 321 960), which has a lovely courtyard and comfortable rooms for US$4 per person without bath.

The more up-market *Hotel Bibosi* (☎ 348 548), Calle Junín 218, is quite friendly, with clean, spacious rooms and a great rooftop view. Rooms with fan, telephone, bath and breakfast cost US$15.50/25. The ultraclean *Hotel Copacabana* (☎ 321 845), at Junín 217, is good value at US$6.20/10 for

singles/doubles without bath. With a private bath, they're US$15.50/23, and with air-con the cost is US$21/30. The central *Hotel Italia* (☎ 323 119), at Calle René Moreno 167, charges US$20/30 for singles/doubles with air-con, TV, phones and hot showers.

Places to Eat

For a simple and inexpensive breakfast, try the *mercados La Ramada* and *Los Pozos*. You'll also find meals during the day, but you may be put off by the heat around the cooking areas. Mercado Los Pozos is especially good for a variety of unusual tropical fruits. For inexpensive roast chicken, churrasco, chips and fried plantains, stroll down Pollo Alley (also known as Avenida Cañoto), where there are dozens of nearly identical grill restaurants. *Restaurante 30 de Marzo* is recommended.

Inexpensive vegetarian almuerzos and dinners are served at *Restaurant Familiar Vegetariano*, at Calle Velasco 225, and *Restaurant Vegetarianista* near the corner of Ayacucho and Sara. The popular *La Pascana*, on the plaza, serves huge four-course meals *(platos fuertes)* for US$4. The equally popular *Mama Rosa's Pizzeria*, diagonally across the plaza, offers nice pizza, chicken and fast food. It's open daily from noon to midnight. Another plaza option, the quiet *Restaurant Plaza*, at Calle Libertad 116, is recommended for its soup and US$1.50 almuerzos. Other favourite local lunch spots include the *Galeón Peruano* and *La Olla Que Canta*, both of which offer good food for very good prices.

The cosy Swiss/Bolivian-owned *Bar El Tapekuá* (☎ 343 390), on the corner of Calles Ballivián and La Paz, serves pub meals from Wednesday to Saturday evenings. The musician owner appreciates good music – from Thursday to Saturday there are live performances for a US$1 cover charge.

La Bella Napoli, in a rustic barn six blocks south of the plaza, serves fine pasta dishes on chunky hardwood tables, but it's not cheap and is a dark walk back to the centre at night. A great splurge is *Crêperie El Boliche*, on Calle Arenales between Murillo

BOLIVIA

and Beni. You can choose from crêpe dishes, salads, ice-cream confections, cakes and cocktails for around US$11 per person.

A recommended fish restaurant is *El Pez Gordo* (☎ 361 921) at Avenida Uruguay 783 (northern end of the Primer Anillo), near Suárez Arana. Opposite Parque El Arenal is the oddly named *Las Tres BBB*, which serves ceviche and other fish dishes.

If you're craving Mexican food, try *Tequila's Bar Restaurant* (☎ 432 186), a mid-range restaurant at Avenida Cristóbal de Mendoza 605 (northern end of the 2° Anillo). If you prefer something within walking distance from the centre, there's *Cactus* at Avenida Uruguay 642. An expensive but excellent Japanese option – serving sushi, sashimi, tempura and a vast range of other Japanese specialities – is *Yorimichi* (☎ 347 717), at Avenida Busch 548. Bookings are recommended.

Popular spots for ice cream, sundaes, cakes, light meals or just speciality coffee drinks include *Hawai*, a block east of the plaza, and *Kivón*, at Ayacucho 267.

Entertainment

Santa Cruz has a disproportionate number of discos and karaoke bars, a fact which reflects the city's liberal, cosmopolitan character. They're almost all outside the central area, so you'll need a taxi (US$1 to US$2). Cover charges start at around US$2; if you want to conserve funds, avoid the bar. Most places open at 9 pm but don't warm up until 11 pm, then continue until 3 am. The city also has a number of cinemas, and generally, the films are of better quality than those shown elsewhere in Bolivia.

Getting There & Away

Air Both LAB (☎ 344 411) and AeroSur (☎ 364 446) have several daily flights to Cochabamba, La Paz and Sucre, as well as daily service to most other Bolivian cities. The modern Viru Viru international airport, 15 km from the centre, handles both domestic and international flights. The frequent minibus service from the terminal costs US$0.75 and takes half an hour.

Bus The long-distance bus terminal is on the corner of Avenidas Cañoto and Irala. There are plenty of daily services to Cochabamba (US$7, 12 hours), from where you'll find connections to La Paz, Oruro, Sucre, Potosí and Tarija. Most flotas offer both morning and evening services. For a camión to Cochabamba (US$4 to US$6, about 16 hours), go to Avenida Grigotá near the 3rd Anillo; most cargo traffic still uses the old road via Samaipata and Siberia, so carry warm clothing.

Several companies offer direct service to Sucre (that is, they don't pass through Cochabamba) in the afternoon on Monday, Wednesday and Saturday (US$8). From Sucre, buses continue to Potosí. Most services to Camiri and Yacuiba depart around mid-afternoon. Buses to Comarapa and Vallegrande leave both in the morning and afternoon. Flota Chiquitano leaves nightly at 7 pm for Concepción and San Ignacio.

To Trinidad and beyond, a number of buses leave between 5.30 and 7 pm nightly (US$7, 12 hours). Although the road is theoretically open year round, the trip gets rough in the rainy season.

Train The railway station, on Avenida Brasil, is beyond easy walking distance from the centre, but it's easily accessed via micro 12 in 10 minutes or so. There are two railway lines: one to Quijarro on the Brazilian border, and another to Yacuiba on the Argentine border.

Schedules are flexible and securing tickets may involve a bit of pushing and shoving at the ticket window. During times of high demand, tickets are hard to come by and carriages become so crowded with people and luggage that there's no room to sit. The alternative is to stake out a place in the bodegas (boxcars) and purchase a 2nd-class ticket from the acrobatic conductor (for 20% more than the ticket window price).

To/From Argentina The ferrobus to Yacuiba (US$18.50/15.50) leaves Santa Cruz on Wednesday at 7 pm, and returns from Yacuiba on Friday at 5 pm. The tren rápido

(US$12.80/10.70 in 1st/2nd) runs on Monday and Friday at 3.40 pm and the tren mixto (US$14.60/12.40) on Wednesday and Sunday at 8.30 am. From Santa Cruz to Yacuiba, the bodegas are empty, but on the return they're brimming with Argentine goods and aren't as comfortable.

From Yacuiba, shared taxis go to immigration at Pocitos (US$1 per person), five km away on the border. From the Argentine side, buses leave for Tartagal every two hours or so. Reserve Argentine bus tickets in Yacuiba at the TVO Expreso Café. Remember that Bolivian time is one hour behind Argentine time.

To/From Brazil The railway line between Santa Cruz and Quijarro passes through soya plantations, forest, scrub and oddly shaped mountains to the steamy, sticky Pantanal on the frontier. Carry enough mosquito repellent to help you cope with long and unexplained stops in low-lying, swampy areas.

The optimistically named *Expreso del Oriente* (yes, the Orient Express!) leaves on Monday, Wednesday and Friday at 1.50 pm eastbound and on Tuesday, Thursday and Saturday at 1.45 pm westbound (US$20.50/17 in 1st/2nd class). It also carries the Bracha carriage (US$25), which may be booked through Santa Cruz travel agencies. The tren rápido (US$14.50/12.20) runs on Tuesday and Sunday at 1.50 pm eastbound and Monday and Thursday at 1.45 pm westbound. The tren mixto (US$14 2nd class) runs at 9.15 am on Monday and Friday eastbound and on Tuesday and Saturday at 6.30 pm westbound. Freight trains with open bodegas may run at any time and cost US$14 per person.

Taxis from Quijarro to the Brazilian border (US$1 per person), two km away, meet arriving trains. You can change dollars or bolivianos into *reais* (pronounced *HAY-ice*) on the Bolivian side, but the boliviano rate is poor. Note that there's no Brazilian consulate in Quijarro, so if you need a visa, get it in Santa Cruz. Yellow-fever certificates are required to enter Brazil from Bolivia.

We've had reports of officials demanding US$10 bribes for exit stamps at Quijarro. If you're heading straight to Brazil, it may be easier to pick up the stamp from immigration at the Santa Cruz railway station.

AROUND SANTA CRUZ
Samaipata

The village of Samaipata, at 1660 metres in the foothills of the Cordillera Oriental, is a popular weekend destination for *cruceños* and a great place to hole up for a couple of days. This quiet village has also attracted a few foreign settlers and lowland Bolivians, and a cosmopolitan society is developing.

The main attraction is El Fuerte, a pre-Inca ceremonial site on a hilltop 10 km from the village. The view from the ruins takes in the characteristic hills and valleys of the transitional zone between the Andes and low-lying areas further east. Hitching from the village is easiest on weekends, but it also makes a fine day walk. It's open daily from 9 am to 5 pm and foreigners pay US$2 admission. Taxis for the return trip, including a 1½ hour stop at the ruins, cost US$8 for up to four people. In the village is a small archaeological museum which is open from 9 am to noon and 2.30 to 6.30 pm. Admission for foreigners is US$1.

Samaipata's telephone code is 0944.

Places to Stay The basic but friendly *Hotel Fuerte City* (☎ 6118) is a good choice for budget travellers. Rooms without bath cost US$5 per person, including a continental breakfast. *Residencial Don Jorge* (☎ 6086) charges US$3 per person, plus US$1 for a continental breakfast. Other inexpensive options include *Hotel Pascana* and *Hotel Mily*.

A quiet and relaxing choice is the *Hospedaje La Víspera*, on an experimental biological farm 800 metres from the plaza. There's a great view over the valley, and owners Margarita and Pieter hire horses and organise trekking trips. On weekdays/weekends, the self-catering guesthouse, which accommodates up to 15 people, costs US$26/37 for up to six people, plus US$4 for each extra person. Book through Tropical

Tours (☎ 361 428) in Santa Cruz. When there's space, they'll accept backpackers for US$6 per person. Bring a torch, as there's no street lighting between the village and the guesthouse.

Bolivia's leap into European-style camping begins at *Achira Kamping* at Km 112, eight km east of Samaipata. It has cabañas, camp sites, baths, showers and washing sinks as well as a social hall with a restaurant and games room. Contact the Urbarí Racquet Club (☎ 343 836), Barrio Urbarí, Calle Igmirí 590, Santa Cruz. More basic is the secluded *Mama Pasquala's*, 500 metres upstream from the river ford en route to El Fuerte. Camp sites/cabañas cost US$1/2 per person.

Places to Eat For snacks, try the hamburgers, chicken and delicious jugo de mandarina at *Hamburguesa Tobby*. You'll find great pizza and home-baked goodies at the *Churrasquería-Pizzería El Chancho Rengo*. For excellent European gourmet meals, try the good-value *Landhaus*, below the aeroplane near the northern end of the village. It's open evenings, Thursday to Sunday.

Getting There & Away Taxis to Samaipata leave when full from near the bus terminal in Santa Cruz. They carry up to four passengers and cost US$3 per person. Alternatively, micros depart approximately twice daily and cost US$2.30. The trip takes about 2½ hours each way.

Parque Nacional Amboró

The village of Buena Vista, two hours northwest of Santa Cruz, is the staging point for trips into the forested lowland section of Parque Nacional Amboró, but the administrators at the FAN office in Santa Cruz may try to discourage visits. For information, visit the BID office just south of the plaza in Buena Vista. Alternatively, speak to the people at Hotel Amboró (☎ (0932) 2054), one km south-west of Buena Vista.

Rooms at *Hotel Amboró* cost US$30 per person, with full board. Camping is also permitted. More basic accommodation is available for US$2.70 per person at *Residencial Nadia* (☎ 2049) in the village. The owner is a former park ranger and is a good source of information on Amboró. In the park itself are four basic cabañas which cost US$2 per person; reserve through BID in Buena Vista.

San José de Chiquitos

A pleasant place to break the rail journey from Santa Cruz to Brazil, this former Jesuit mission has a unique and beautiful church. The recommended *Hotel Raquelita* charges US$4/5 per person without/with bath.

The Amazon Basin

The Amazon Basin, which takes in half of Bolivia's total territory, is an excellent place to observe the rainforest. While much of the accessible portion of the better known Brazilian Amazon is degraded and heavily populated, northern Bolivia remains relatively undeveloped. The waterways are also narrower, so river travellers will see more of the wildlife.

There are no scheduled passenger services; boats that ply the northern rivers are mainly cargo vessels, and passenger comfort was the last thing their builders had in mind. Cabins are reserved for the crew and are rarely available to passengers. Most passages include meals, but the menu is typically monotonous and the water comes straight from the river. Prospective river travellers should bring a hammock, a sleeping bag (nights can be chilly), a water container, water purification tablets, antimalarials, mosquito protection and some snacks. The most popular river routes are Puerto Villarroel to Trinidad on the Río Ichilo and Trinidad to Guayaramerín on the Río Mamoré.

Towns with air services include Cobija, Guayaramerín, Riberalta, Trinidad, Rurrenabaque, Reyes, San Borja, Santa Ana, San Joaquín and Magdalena. Remember that timetables are 'flexible' and flights are often

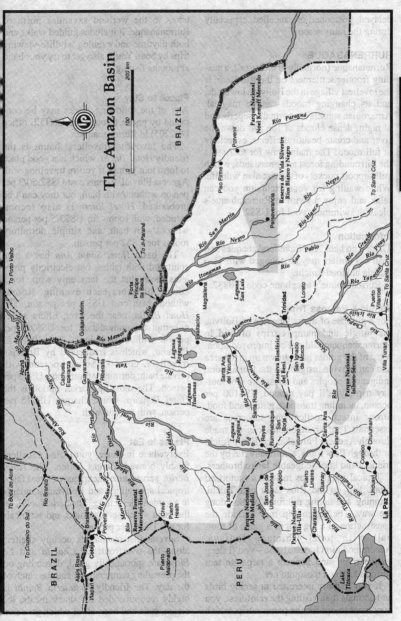

The Amazon Basin

0   100   200 km

BRAZIL

PERU

BOLIVIA

Lake Titicaca

La Paz

delayed, postponed or cancelled, especially during the rainy season.

RURRENABAQUE

Rurrenabaque (normally just 'Rurre'), a bustling frontier settlement on the Río Beni, is the loveliest village in the Bolivian lowlands, and its changing moods can be magical. Amazonian sunsets are normally superb, and at night, dense clouds of fog roll down the river and create beautiful effects, especially at full moon. The main draw for tourists is the surrounding forest and grasslands, which still support pockets of Amazonian wildlife. While waiting for your excursion you can relax and enjoy a swim in Rurrenabaque's pleasant swimming pool for US$2.

Information

There's no bank, but travellers' cheques and cash US dollars may be changed with Tico Tudela at Hotel Tuichi.

Rurrenabaque's telephone code is 0832.

Jungle & Pampas Trips

For a glimpse of the wilder side of Bolivia, the jungle and pampas trips offered in Rurrenabaque could not be improved upon. Most of the guides have grown up in the area and can provide insights on the fauna, flora, indigenous peoples and forest lore. For four-day trips, you'll pay around US$100 per person, including transport, guides and food. Strong insect repellent and sunscreen are essential. Tour arrangements can be made through Agencia Fluvial at the Hotel Tuichi or through Eco-Tours, a company run by the friendly and knowledgeable Janko brothers.

Typical jungle trips include a motorised canoe trip up the Ríos Beni and Tuichi, camping and taking rainforest walks along the way. The return trip may include the construction of a log raft or a game of football with local Chimane Indians. Accommodation is quite basic – you'll sleep on the river sand beneath a tarpaulin tent surrounded by a mosquito net.

If you're more interested in seeing birds and animals than visiting the rainforest, you may want to opt for the pampas trip, which takes in the wetland savannas north of Rurrenabaque. It includes guided walks and both daytime and evening wildlife-viewing trips by boat. You'll also get to try your hand at piranha fishing.

Places to Stay

Any of the following places may be contacted by phone through the ENTEL office (☎ 2205) in Rurrenabaque.

The favourite travellers' haunt is the friendly *Hotel Tuichi*, which is a good place to form tour groups if you're travelling with Agencia Fluvial. Rooms cost US$2.50/3 per person without/with bath, but they can't be prebooked. *Hotel Rurre* is also recommended, with rooms for US$3/5 per person without/with bath, and simple dormitory rooms for US$2 per person.

The basic *Hotel Santa Ana* has a nice courtyard with tables, but electricity problems mean that the fans only work for a couple of hours each evening. Rooms without bath cost US$3 per person. The *Hotel Berlin*, near the river, offers rather unkempt accommodation for US$2/3 per person without/with bath. The *Hotel El Porteño*, which is frequented by Bolivian travellers, costs US$6 per person with private bath; dormitory rooms cost US$2 per person. The most up-market option is the *Hotel Taquara*, which charges US$15 per person, with fan and bath.

Places to Eat

Everywhere in Rurre, you'll find excellent freshly brewed Yungas coffee. The *Hotel Berlin* serves nice inexpensive breakfasts, tropical specialities and Bolivian standards in a garden-like setting. The *Sede Social*, on the main street, serves drinks and set meals for just US$1 per person.

Several fish restaurants occupy shelters along the riverfront: *La Chocita* and *La Playa* are sporadically good, depending on the prevailing temperament and the catch of the day. The friendly *Heladería Bambi* is highly recommended for snack meals, ice cream, soda and beer, all of which go down well on a typically hot and sticky Rurre afternoon.

Getting There & Away

Air In theory, TAM has US$45 flights to and from La Paz on Monday mornings. In reality, they're often cancelled.

Bus When the roads are dry, buses run daily between Rurrenabaque and La Paz (US$12.50, 18 hours). There are also daily runs to Trinidad (US$9, eight hours) via Yucumo, San Borja and San Ignacio de Moxos. Buses leave for Riberalta (US$14.50, 13 hours) and Guayaramerín (US$16.50, 15 hours) on Wednesday, Friday and Sunday.

Boat Thanks to the Guayaramerín road, river-cargo transport down the Beni to Riberalta is now limited (see under Riberalta), but you can find motorised canoe transport upriver to Guanay for around US$20 per person. Ask at the Hotel Tuichi for information. Taxi ferries to San Buenaventura, on the opposite shore of the Río Beni, cost US$0.20.

AROUND RURRENABAQUE
Parque Nacional Alto Madidi

The Río Madidi watershed, which has been slated for oil exploration, still contains one of the most intact ecosystems in all of South America. The most ecologically sound section of it is now protected by the new Parque Nacional Alto Madidi, which takes in a range of wildlife habitats from steaming lowland rainforests to 5500-metre Andean peaks. It's thought that the park is home to more than 1000 species of birds – over 10% of all known species in the world.

The populated portions of the park along the Río Tuichi have been given a special distinction under UNESCO's Biosphere statutes, which will allow indigenous people to continue with their traditional lifestyles – hunting, fishing and using other forest resources. Hence, for the Chimane and Tacanas tribes, the national park has very little effect on their lifestyle.

The greatest threat to the park is from logging activity, both around the Tuichi and at the northern end of the park, near Ixiamas. Currently, 200 independent loggers are cutting mahogany, cedar and other valuable trees, as well as hunting both for food and for profit. As a result, areas which were rich in wildlife just five years ago are now hunted out. It's hoped that such activities can be controlled and that ecotourism will generate enough money to prevent further forest destruction.

There are plans to establish a simple tourist complex at Laguna Chalalan, a lovely ox-bow lake by the Tuichi near San José de Uchupiamonas. If this happens, it will rival Peru's Parque Nacional Manu as one of the world's best places to observe rainforest species.

Getting There & Away Most of the national park is, for practical purposes, inaccessible, which is why it remains a treasure. Agencia Fluvial in Rurrenabaque can arrange guides to take you up the Tuichi and over the hills into the Madidi headwaters. Plan on at least seven days for this spectacular trip. The more adventurous can hire a guide in Apolo and hike down into the park, but this is an arduous trip (getting to Apolo is an adventure in itself) which is only for the fit and well-prepared.

TRINIDAD

The city of La Santísima Trinidad (the Most Holy Trinity), at an altitude of 237 metres, was founded on 13 June 1686 by Padre Cipriano Barace, as the second Jesuit mission in the flatlands of the southern Beni. Trinidad, which looks like Santa Cruz did 20 years ago, is now the Beni capital and the nerve centre of the Bolivian Amazon. Although it's not Bolivia's most prepossessing city – the open sewers are enough to put anyone off – the population has now passed 40,000 and is likely to keep growing.

Information

You'll find street moneychangers on Avenida 6 de Agosto between Calle Nicolás Suárez

BOLIVIA

and Avenida 18 de Noviembre, but they only deal in cash US dollars. You can change travellers' cheques without hassles at Banco Sur half a block from the plaza.

Don't rely too heavily on street names in Trinidad. They've been changed several times over the past decade, and it seems that no two maps can agree on what the current names are.

Trinidad's telephone code is 046.

Things to See
Trinidad's most interesting sights are outside town. In the **Llanos de Moxos**, over 100 km of canals and causeways, and hundreds of *lomas* (artificial mounds), built to permit cultivation in a seasonally flooded area, are evidence of much larger aboriginal populations in pre-Columbian times. At **Chuchini**, 17 km from Trinidad, there's a small archaeological museum, a restaurant, a camping ground and expensive bungalows (US$35 per person). However, they're now charging day visitors US$10 per person, which is well over the top for what's on offer. If you're undaunted, hitching is best on Sunday, though you may have to walk the last five km from Loma Suárez.

Laguna Suárez (not to be confused with Loma Suárez), a large, artificial lake five km from Trinidad, was probably constructed by the ancient Paititis. It's a relaxing spot and is popular on Sunday when local families turn out to picnic, drink in the bar and eat lunch at the lakeside Restaurant Tapacaré. There's no public transport; you'll have to walk, take a taxi, hire a motorbike or hitch. Admission is US$0.50.

Further afield is the lovely Ignaciano Indian village of **San Ignacio de Moxos**, 89 km west of Trinidad. The highlight is the annual Fiesta del Santo Patrono de Moxos, held on 31 July.

Places to Stay
The best budget hotel is probably *Hotel Yucuma* (☎ 20690), where basic rooms without/with bath cost US$4/5 per person. Another good choice is *Hotel Paulista* (☎ 20018), which charges US$5/9.50 for singles/doubles without bath, or US$8.25/13.50 with bath. The cheapest place is *Alojamiento Ortiz*, which costs US$3 per person.

Trinidad also has a crop of budget hotels strung along Avenida 6 de Agosto. The best seems to be *Residencial Palermo* (☎ 20472), which costs US$2.40/4.10 per person without/with bath. The slightly nicer *Hotel Beni* (☎ 20522) charges US$8/12 for singles/doubles with bath, and US$5/8 without. A recommended mid-range place is *Hotel Monte Verde* (☎ 22044). With a bit of friendly bargaining, you can get singles/doubles with bath and fan for US$15.50/21.

Places to Eat
If your budget is a major concern, there's always the *Mercado Municipal*. For a pittance, you can try the local speciality, arroz con queso (rice with cheese), plus kebab, yuca, plantain and salad.

Snacks, light meals and full breakfasts are served at *Heladería Kivón*, on the plaza, and it's open when everything else is closed, including mornings and Saturday afternoons. Also on the plaza are *La Casona* pizzería and *Carlitos*, which specialises in that Beni forte, parrillada (barbecued meat). Nearby *Snack Brasilia* does a standard menu of good, inexpensive lunch options. Another snack option, *Heladería Iglu*, is worth visiting for its amazing jungle courtyard setting alone.

Trinidad is cattle country, so beef is plentiful. Recommended for its food and atmosphere is *El Pacumutu*. Pacumutus are chopped chunks of beef. Get a *medio* (half) for two people, and it'll still be too much, especially with the trimmings. Also recommended is the Chinese *El Dragón Chino* opposite the market. For fish, try *El Moro*, on the corner of Avenidas Simón Bolívar and José Natusch Velasco or better still, head out to Puerto Barador, where makeshift restaurants serve up the catch of the day.

Getting There & Away
Air Both LAB (☎ 20595) and AeroSur (☎ 20765) operate flights between Trinidad

BOLIVIA

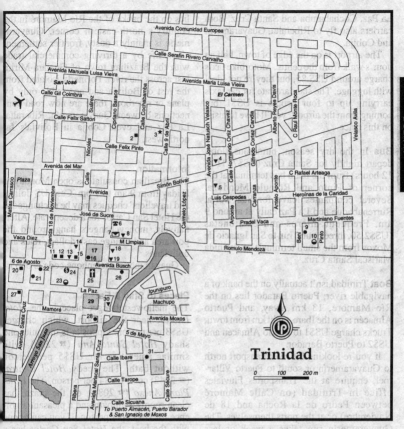

Trinidad

0   100   200 m

PLACES TO STAY
2 Alojamiento Ortiz
11 Hotel Monte Verde
12 Hotel Beni
15 Residencial Paulista
20 Residencial Palermo
27 Hotel Yacuma

PLACES TO EAT
4 El Moro
5 El Pacumutu
8 Heladería Iglu
13 Snack Brasilia
14 Carlitos
18 La Casona
19 Heladería Kivón
30 El Dragón Chino

OTHER
1 Airport
3 Police
6 ENTEL Office
7 Post Office
9 Mercado Fátima
10 Bus Terminal
16 Motorbike Rental
17 Plaza General José Ballivián
21 LAB Office
22 Motos de Alquiler (Motorbike Rental)
23 Micros to San Ignacio de Moxos
24 Banco Sur
25 Catedral
26 Immigration
28 Transportes Fluviales (River Transport Office)
29 Market
31 Mercado Pompeya

La Paz, Cochabamba and Santa Cruz. Both carriers also fly to Riberalta, Guayaramerín and Cobija.

The airport is on the edge of town, half an hour's walk from the centre. Motorbike taxis charge around US$.85, but they're not ideal with luggage. The standard rate for car taxis carrying up to four people is US$1, but coming from the airport, you'll have to insist on this price.

Bus In the dry season, numerous flotas depart nightly for Santa Cruz (US$7, 11 to 12 hours) from the main bus terminal, at the corner of Pinto and Rómulo Mendoza. Several companies leave for San Borja, Rurrenabaque and La Paz daily at around 9 am. Frequent micros and camionetas (US$2.50, three hours) run to San Ignacio de Moxos from the small terminals on Avenida Mariscal Santa Cruz.

Boat Trinidad isn't actually on the bank of a navigable river; Puerto Barador lies on the Río Mamoré, 13 km away, and Puerto Almacén is on the Ibare, eight km from town. Trucks charge US$1 to Puerto Almacén and US$2 to Puerto Barador.

If you're looking for river transport north to Guayaramerín or south to Puerto Villarroel, enquire at the Transportes Fluviales office in Trinidad (on Calle Mamoré between Pedro de la Rocha and 18 de Noviembre) or at the ports themselves. The Guayaramerín run takes a week or less (larger boats do it in three to four days) and costs around US$25, including food. To Puerto Villarroel in the Chapare, smaller boats take eight to 10 days.

Getting Around

Motorbikes can be hired on the plaza or at Motos de Alquiler for around US$20 per 24-hour day. You'll need a driving licence (car or motorcycle) from home. Motorbike taxis around town cost US$0.30 (B$1.50) while auto taxis charge US$0.40 (B$2).

GUAYARAMERIN

Guayaramerín, Bolivia's back door to Brazil, lies on the banks of the Río Mamoré in the country's north-eastern corner. Guayaramerín is mainly a dusty, frontier settlement given life by a thriving commercial trade with the Brazilian town of Guajará-Mirim just across the river. Formerly isolated from the rest of Bolivia and accessible only by plane or riverboat, there are now road connections between Guayaramerín, Riberalta, La Paz and even Cobija in Bolivia's far north-west.

Information

The Brazilian consulate is open Monday to Friday from 9 am to 1 pm. Cash US dollars and travellers' cheques may be exchanged at the Hotel San Carlos for a decent rate. Alternatively, moneychangers hang around the port area and change cash dollars, reais and bolivianos.

Guayaremerín's telephone code is 0855.

Places to Stay & Eat

The mellowest budget place is the *Hotel Litoral*, near the airport, which charges US$3 per person. Opposite is the quiet and shady *Hotel Santa Ana* (☎ 2206), with similar amenities for US$5 per person without bath. The seedy *Hotel Central* (☎ 2042) costs US$4 per person. The *Hotel Plaza Anexo* (☎ 2086), on the plaza, has clean rooms with bath and a pleasant ambience for US$5 per person. If you can't cope with the heat, the *Hotel San Carlos* has a swimming pool and singles/doubles with bath and air-con for US$21/31.

Guayaramerín is fortunate enough to have the Beni's best restaurant, which is, in fact, called the *Only Restaurant* (☎ 2397). With an extensive international menu and a cool outdoor garden, it's very popular. Paradoxically, there's a second *Only Restaurant* which specialises is pseudo-Chinese dishes. A recommended lunch and dinner place near the plaza is *Made in Brasil*, which provides home cooking for the town's many Brazilian expats. Prices, which are quoted in reais, are generally higher than in Bolivian establishments. *Los Bibosis*, on the plaza, serves meals and snacks but is mostly a drinking joint.

Getting There & Away
Air LAB (☎ 2140) and AeroSur (☎ 2201) both fly between Trinidad and Guayaramerín, with connections to and from La Paz. With LAB, you can fly to or from Cobija on Monday and Friday.

Bus Most bus terminals are at the western end of town, beyond the market. Several companies have services to Riberalta (US$2, three hours); each has two to four departures daily. Cars and camiones to Riberalta leave from opposite the 8 de Diciembre bus terminal. In the dry season, several flotas leave daily for Rurrenabaque (US$16.50, 15 hours) and La Paz (US$27, 35 hours), and there are departures to Cobija (US$15.50, 14 hours) on Monday, Wednesday and Friday at 7 am. Trans-Amazonas goes to Trinidad (US$21, 17 hours) on Thursday at 8.30 am.

Boat Boats up the Río Mamoré to Trinidad leave almost daily (US$35 with food, five to seven days). A notice board outside the port captain's office lists departures.

To/From Brazil Frequent motorboat ferries cross the river between the two ports; they cost US$0.80 from Bolivia and US$1.50 from Brazil. There are no restrictions on crossing between Guayaramerín and Guajará-Mirim, but if you intend to travel further into Brazil, or are entering Bolivia here, you must pick up entry/exit stamps. The Bolivian immigration office is in the port area; on the Brazilian side, have your passport stamped at the Polícia Federal. A yellow fever vaccination certificate is required to enter Brazil from Bolivia.

RIBERALTA
On the banks of the Río Beni, Riberalta is the major town in Bolivia's northern frontier region. It was once a thriving centre of rubber production, but with increased international competition and the development of synthetics, that industry declined. The town has now fallen back on its current mainstay industry: the cultivation, production and export of brazil nuts and their oil. Since the opening of the road link with La Paz, Riberalta's importance as a river port has declined.

There isn't a lot for visitors, but Riberalta is a pleasant enough town. In the heat of the day, strenuous activity is suspended and the locals search out the nearest hammock; visitors would be advised to follow their example – the heat can be paralysing. On clear nights, however, the place comes to life with cruising motorbikes. Amid the buzz of activity, don't fail to notice the technicolour Amazonian sunsets, which will always provide an impressive show.

Riberalta's telephone code is 0852.

Places to Stay
Very nice is the spotless *Residencial Los Reyes* (☎ 615) near the airport. It costs US$3/5 per person for a room without/with bath. The cheapest place is *Alojamiento Navarro*, where dormitory accommodation costs US$1.50 per person (don't leave your things in the rooms!). Double rooms are US$3.

Alojamiento Comercial Lazo (☎ 380) has basic singles/doubles for US$5.50/6.20 with bath, and US$2/3 without. *Residencial Katita* (☎ 386), a friendly new place with a public restaurant, charges just US$3 per person. A good lower mid-range choice is *Hotel Amazonas* (☎ 2339), which charges US$6.20/11 with bath.

Places to Eat
La Cabaña de Tío Tom, on the plaza, serves good coffee, ice cream, juices, shakes, flan and sandwiches, as well as Beni beef. What's more, the pavement seating provides a front-row seat for the nightly Kawasaki derby on the plaza. An alternative, also on the plaza, is *Don Tabe*. Both these places serve breakfast from 8.30 am. If you're up earlier, either go to the market or the Hotel Colonial, which serves breakfast from 7 am.

The *Club Social* on the plaza serves inexpensive set lunches, superb filtered coffee, drinks and fine desserts; determine prices in advance. The *Club Social Japonés*, near the market, doesn't serve anything Japanese, but it does do Bolivian and Amazonian dishes. Opposite the market is *Churrasquería El Pahuichi*, which is big on Beni beef. The outdoor seating is particularly pleasant.

Getting There & Away

Air LAB (☎ 239) and AeroSur (☎ 2798) serve Riberalta, with several weekly flights to Trinidad and connections to La Paz, Santa Cruz and Cochabamba. LAB also flies to and from Cobija on Monday and Friday. The airport is a 15-minute walk from the main plaza.

Bus Several flotas do daily runs between Riberalta and Guayaramerín (US$2, three hours). Alternatively, wait for a car or camión along Avenida Héroes del Chaco. All flotas travelling between Guayaramerín and Cobija, Rurrenabaque and La Paz also stop en route at their Riberalta offices. Tickets cost US$2 less than from Guayaramerín, and the trips are three hours shorter.

Boat Boats up the Río Beni to Rurrenabaque are now rare, and in any case, they normally only run when the road becomes impassable (October to May). If you do find something, plan on US$20 to US$35 for the five to eight-day trip. For departure information, check the board in the port captain's office.

Brazil

Facts about the Country

HISTORY
Pre-Columbian Times

The Brazilian Indians did not develop a bureaucratic, centralised civilisation like those of the Andes, and left little for archaeologists to discover because the artefacts of their society were largely made of perishable materials. Some scholars believe that when the Portuguese arrived, at least seven million Indians were living in the territory that is now Brazil. Today, there are less than 200,000, most in the jungles of the interior.

Some Indians lived in small groups and were primarily hunter-gatherers, but most were shifting agriculturalists who lived in villages, some of which may have had as many as 5000 inhabitants. They lived in long communal huts, and music, dance and games played a very important role in their culture. Little surplus was produced and they had very few possessions. Every couple of years, the village would pack up and move on. This life was punctuated by frequent tribal warfare and ritual cannibalism.

The Colonial Period

In 1500 Pedro Cabral sailed from Lisbon down the coast of Africa, bound for India. Nobody knows quite why he wandered so far off course, but he veered west across the Atlantic and discovered Brazil, landing at present-day Porto Seguro. Cabral and his crew stayed only nine days in the land they dubbed Terra da Vera Cruz (Land of the True Cross), then sailed on.

Subsequent Portuguese expeditions were disappointed by what they found. The Indians' stone-age culture produced nothing for the European market, though a few Portuguese merchants sent ships to harvest the *pau do brasil* (brazil wood tree), which pro-

Country Name República Federativa do Brasil
Area 8,547,403 sq km
Population 155 million
Population Density 18 per sq km
Capital Brasília
Head of State President Fernando Henrique Cardoso
Official Language Portuguese
Other Languages many Indian languages
Currency real
Exchange Rate US$1 = 1.02 real (Feb 1996)
Per Capita GNP US$3542
Inflation Rate 23% (late 1995)

duced a red dye. Brazil wood remained the only exportable commodity for the first half of the 16th century – long enough for the colony to change its name from Terra de Vera Cruz to Brazil.

In 1531 King João III of Portugal sent the first settlers to Brazil, under the direction of Martim Afonso de Sousa. They founded São Vicente, near the modern-day port of Santos. In 1534, fearing the ambitions of other European countries, the king divided the coast into 12 hereditary captaincies, which were given to friends of the crown. Four of these captaincies were never settled and four were destroyed by Indians. Only Pernambuco and São Vicente were profitable. In 1549, the king sent Tomé de Sousa to be the first governor of Brazil, to centralise authority and to save the remaining captaincies. The new capital of Portuguese Brazil was established at Bahia.

The colonists soon discovered that the land and climate were ideal for growing sugar cane, but they needed labour, so they enslaved the Indians. The capture and sale of Indian slaves became Brazil's second commerce, dominated by the *bandeirantes*, men from São Paulo who were mostly sons of Portuguese fathers and Indian mothers. They hunted the Indians into the interior, and by the mid-1600s they had reached the peaks of the Peruvian Andes. Their exploits, more than any treaty, secured the huge interior of South America for Portuguese Brazil.

The Jesuits, seeking to protect Indians fleeing from bandeirante attacks, built missions in the remote interior, near the present-day borders with Paraguay and Argentina. But these were not, as they had hoped, beyond the grasp of the bandeirantes. The Jesuits armed the Indians and desperate battles took place. Eventually, with the collusion of the Portuguese and Spanish crowns, the missions fell, and the Jesuits were expelled from Brazil in 1759.

During the 17th century African slaves largely replaced Indians on the plantations. They were better workers and less vulnerable to European diseases, but they resisted slavery strongly. *Quilombos*, communities of runaway slaves, were common throughout the colonial period. They ranged from *mocambos*, small groups hidden in the forests, to the great republic of Palmares in northern Alagoas and southern Pernambuco states, which survived for much of the 17th century.

In the 1690s gold was discovered in south-central Minas Gerais, and soon the rush was on. Brazilians and Portuguese immigrants flooded into this territory, and countless

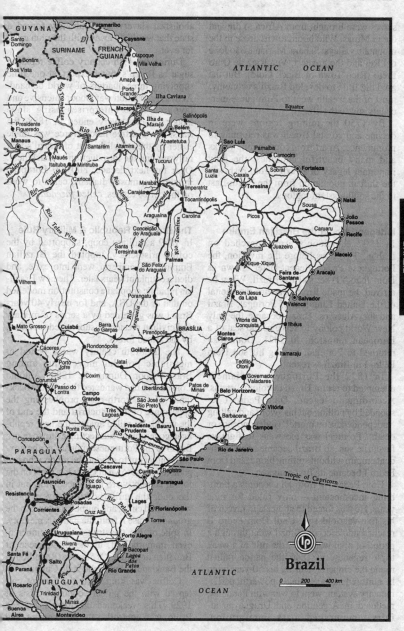

Brazil

0   200   400 km

slaves were brought from Africa to dig and die in Minas. Wild boom towns arose in the mountain valleys: Sabara, Mariana, São João del Rei and the greatest, Vila Rica de Ouro Prêto (Rich Town of Black Gold). But the gold did little to develop Brazil's economy: most of the wealth went to Portuguese merchants and to the king.

By 1750 the mining regions were in decline and coastal Brazil was returning to prominence. Apart from some public works and many beautiful churches, the only important legacy of Brazil's gold rush was the shift in population from the North-East to the south-eastern regions.

Independence & the Brazilian Empire

In 1807 Napoleon's army marched on Lisbon. Two days before the invasion, the Portuguese Prince Regent (later known as Dom João VI) set sail for Brazil. When he arrived, he made Rio de Janeiro the capital of the United Kingdom of Portugal, Brazil and the Algarves. Brazil became the only New World colony to serve as the seat of a European monarch. In 1821, Dom João returned to Portugal, leaving his son Dom Pedro I in Brazil as regent.

In 1822 the Portuguese parliament attempted to return Brazil to colonial status. According to legend, Dom Pedro I responded by pulling out his sword and yelling 'Independência ou morte!' (independence or death). Portugal was too weak to fight its favourite son, so Brazil became an independent empire without spilling blood, and Dom Pedro I became its first emperor.

Dom Pedro I – from all accounts a bumbling incompetent – only ruled for nine years. He was forced to abdicate in favour of his five-year-old son. Until Dom Pedro II reached adolescence, Brazil went through a period of civil war under the rule of a weak triple regency. In 1840 the nation rallied round the emperor. During his 50-year reign he nurtured an increasingly powerful parliamentary system, went to war with Paraguay, meddled in Argentine and Uruguayan affairs, encouraged mass immigration,

abolished slavery and ultimately forged a state that would do away with the monarchy for ever.

During the 19th century coffee replaced sugar as Brazil's major export, at one time supplying three-quarters of world demand. At first, production was labour-intensive and favoured large enterprises using slave labour. When slavery ended in 1888, the transition to a free labour force was made easier by the establishment of Brazil's first railways and the introduction of machinery. Over the next decade, 800,000 European immigrants, mostly Italians, came to work on the coffee estates, called *fazendas*.

The Brazilian Republic & Military Rule

In 1889 a military coup, supported by the coffee aristocracy, toppled the Brazilian Empire. The emperor went into exile, and died a couple of years later. The new Brazilian republic adopted a constitution modelled on that of the USA, and for nearly 40 years Brazil was governed by a series of military and civilian presidents supervised, in effect, by the armed forces.

The late 19th century was a period of messianic popular movements among Brazil's poor. During the 1880s Antônio Conselheiro had wandered through the backlands of the north-east, prophesying the appearance of the Antichrist and the end of the world. He railed against the new republican government. Suspecting a plot to return Brazil to the Portuguese monarchy, the government set out to subdue the rebels who had gathered in the town of Canudos. Only on the fourth attempt were they successful, but in the end, the military killed every man, woman and child, and burned the town to the ground to erase it from the nation's memory. In spite of this, the struggle is remembered, even immortalised, in the masterpiece of Brazilian literature, *Os Sertões* (Rebellion in the Backlands), by Euclides de Cunha.

Coffee was king until the market collapsed with the global economic crisis of 1929. This weakened the planters of São Paulo, who controlled the government, and an opposition Liberal Alliance was formed with the support of nationalist military officers. When their presidential candidate, Getúlio Vargas, lost the 1930 elections, the military seized power and installed him as provisional president.

Vargas proved to be a skilled strategist, and was to dominate the political scene for the next 20 years. In 1937, on the eve of a new election, Vargas sent in the military to shut down Congress and took complete control of the country. His regime was inspired by the Italian and Portuguese fascist states of Benito Mussolini and Antonio de Oliveira Salazar, but during WW II he sided with the Allies. At the end of the war Vargas was forced to step down, but he had another term as president, from 1951 to 1954, before finally being forced out of office.

Juscelino Kubitschek was elected president in 1956. The first of Brazil's big spenders, he built Brasília, the new capital, which was supposed to catalyse the development of the interior. By the early 1960s, the economy was battered by inflation, and fears of communism were fuelled by Castro's victory in Cuba. Again, Brazil's fragile democracy was crushed and the military overthrew the government.

Borrowing heavily from the international banks, the generals benefited from the Brazilian 'economic miracle' of steady growth in the late 1960s and early 1970s. But in the 1980s, with the miracle petering out and popular opposition growing, the military announced the *abertura* (opening) and began a cautious return to civilian government. A presidential election was held in 1985, under an electoral college system designed to ensure the victory of the military's candidate. Surprisingly, the opposition candidate, Tancredo Neves, was elected, but he died before he could take office, and José Sarney, the vice president elect, took office as president.

In 1987, with Sarney at the helm, the politicians were working on a new constitution. The military remained powerfully in the background, and little had changed in the day-to-day lives of most Brazilians.

Modern Times

November 1989 saw the first presidential election by popular vote in nearly 30 years. Voters elected Fernando Collor de Mello over the socialist Luiz da Silva (known as Lula), by a narrow but secure majority.

Collor gained office promising to fight corruption and reduce inflation, but by the end of 1992 he had been removed from office and indicted by Federal Police on charges of corruption – accused of being the leader of a gang which used extortion and bribery to suck more than US$1 billion from the economy. Collor joined the long list (11 out of 24) of Brazilian presidents who have left office before the end of their mandate.

Vice President Itamar Franco became president in December 1992 after Collor's forced resignation. Considered provincial and unprepared to take office, Itamar surprised his critics with a competent and honest administration. His greatest achievement was to begin the long-awaited stabilisation of the economy with the introduction in July 1994 of the Plano Real, the most successful economic plan in a decade.

The election year 1994 was an emotional one for Brazilians. Grief gripped the country with the death of Formula One hero Ayrton Senna, turning him from living legend into a Brazilian sporting god. Two months later, sorrow turned to joy as the Brazilian football team became *tetracampeão*, with Brazil becoming the first country to win the World Cup four times.

Early election favourite was the Worker's Party candidate, Lula, back for a second attempt after losing to Collor in 1989. His downfall was the government's Plano Real, introduced in July 1994, which he criticised early. The architect of the plan, Itamar's finance minister Fernando Henrique Cardoso, became known as 'Father of the Real' and rode its success all the way to a landslide victory in the presidential elections in October. After more than a year in office, Cardoso is still popular. The Plano Real continues to hold inflation in check, but unemployment is rising in the industrial heartland.

BRAZIL

An ex-sociology professor from São Paulo, Cardoso is a social democrat committed to economic progress and growth, as well as tackling Brazil's social problems. But as he tries to push through important constitutional reforms in the areas of taxation, social security and public administration, it's clear that social justice and economic growth don't always coincide, especially in a country as volatile as Brazil. As the 21st century approaches, many problems remain: corruption, violence, urban overcrowding, lack of essential health and education facilities, environmental abuse and dramatic extremes of wealth and poverty.

Brazil has long been known as a land of the future, but the future never seems to arrive.

GEOGRAPHY
The world's fifth-largest country, after Russia, Canada, China and the USA, Brazil borders every country in South America, except Chile and Ecuador. Its 8.5 million sq km cover almost half the continent.

Geographic Regions
Brazil can be divided into several major geographic regions: the south-eastern coastal area of São Paulo and its hinterland; the Paraná Basin of the far south; the 'drought polygon' of the north-east; the central west of the Brazilian Shield; and the tropical north of the Amazon Basin and the southward-draining Guiana Shield.

The south-eastern coastal area is bordered by the mountain ranges that lie between it and the central plateau. From Rio Grande do Sul to Bahia, the mountains come right to the coast, but beyond Bahia, in the drought-prone north-east, the coastal lands are flatter.

South of the Amazon, the Brazilian Shield is an extensive area of weathered bedrock whose key feature is the Planalto, a plateau with an average altitude of only 500 metres. Several minor mountain ranges rise out of it, the highest of them in Minas Gerais. The western Planalto is a huge expanse of savanna grassland known as the Mato Grosso.

Many rivers drain into the Amazon Basin

from the Brazilian Shield to the south, the Andes to the west and the Guiana Shield to the north. The 6275-km Amazon is the world's largest river, and with its tributaries carries about 20% of the world's fresh water. The basin contains some 30% of the world's remaining forest.

The Paraná Basin is characterised by open forest, low woods and scrub land. Its two principal rivers, the Paraná and the Paraguay, run south through Paraguay and Argentina. The swampy area of the basin, towards the Paraguayan border, is known as the Pantanal.

CLIMATE
The Brazilian winter is from June to August, but it is cold only south of Rio de Janeiro, where the average temperature during the winter months is between 13°C and 18°C.

In most of Brazil, short tropical rains are frequent all year round but rarely interfere with travel plans. The *sertão* (the dry interior of the North-East) is an exception: here, there are heavy rains for a few months of the year, and periodic droughts devastate the region.

The Amazon Basin receives the most rain in Brazil. It is not nearly as hot as most people presume – the average temperature is 27°C – but it *is* humid.

FLORA & FAUNA
The richness and diversity of Brazilian flora and fauna are astounding, and the country ranks first in the world for its variety of primate, amphibian and plant species; third for bird species; and fourth for butterfly and reptile species. See the Pantanal and Amazon sections for further information.

GOVERNMENT
Brazil slowly returned to democracy in the 1980s, with a new constitution in 1988. In 1994 Fernando Henrique Cardoso became only the second president elected by popular vote in 33 years.

The 1988 constitution allows the president to choose ministers of state, initiate pieces of legislation and maintain foreign relations, and gives him or her the right of total veto in

NUMBERED STATES

1 Rio Grande do Norte
2 Paraíba
3 Pernambuco
4 Alagoas
5 Sergipe
6 Distrito Federal

The States of Brazil

congress. The president is also commander-in-chief of the armed forces.

These presidential powers are balanced by a bicameral legislature, which consists of a 72-seat Senate and a 487-seat Chamber of Deputies. Presidential, state and congressional elections are held every four years. Municipal elections are held every three years.

Elections are colourful affairs, regarded by the democracy-starved Brazilians as yet another excuse for a party, but politics itself remains largely the preserve of the wealthy. Corruption is rife, especially at the state and local government levels.

ECONOMY

Before 1994 the only certainty in the Brazilian economy was its uncertainty. Wild boom-and-bust cycles had decimated the economy in the previous decade. Then came the Plano Real, stabilising the currency, ending the inflation that had corroded the salaries of the lowest wage earners, and provoking a rise in consumption. Of the seven economic plans introduced in the eight years up to 1994, the Real was the first without shocks or broken contracts. Backed by the record volume of international reserves (achieved after a healthy 4.2% increase in the gross national product in 1993), the real began on a one-for-one parity with the US dollar. Then the unthinkable happened: the real became worth more than the dollar.

But economists predict that without constitutional changes, the government deficit will soon blow out. There's no law to prevent the government from printing reais to pay for large budget deficits. If that happens, inflation will be back.

At least the Plano Real has shown the great potential of the Brazilian economy. All the ingredients for progress are there: a large labour force, the means of production, transport systems and markets for the products. The question is whether or not they can be coordinated efficiently.

The harsh reality is that the richest 10% of Brazilians control 54% of the nation's wealth; the poorest 10% have just 0.6% – and the gap is widening. Unemployment is rampant and seven out of 10 Brazilians still live in poverty.

POPULATION & PEOPLE
Brazil's population is around 155 million, making it the world's sixth most populous country. Still, Brazil is one of the least densely populated countries in the world, averaging only 15 people per sq km. The population is concentrated along the coastal strip and in the cities, where two out of every three Brazilians now live. Greater São Paulo has over 19 million residents, and greater Rio has over 10 million.

In this developing country, 40 million people are malnourished, 25 million live in *favelas* (shantytowns), 12 million children are abandoned and more than seven million children between the ages of seven and 14 don't attend school. Sixty million people live in squalor, without proper sanitation, clean water or decent housing. Brazil, with its dreams of greatness, has misery that compares with the poorest countries in Africa and Asia.

The Portuguese colonised Brazil largely through miscegenation with both the Indian population and with African slaves. The blacks and the Indians also intermarried, and the three races became thoroughly mixed.

This intermarriage continued, almost as a semiofficial colonial policy, for hundreds of years, and has led to a greater mixing of the races than in any other country on the continent.

At present, the number of Indians in Brazil is estimated at less than 200,000. Of the several hundred tribes already identified, most are concentrated in the Amazon region, and virtually all Brazilian Indians face a host of problems which threaten to destroy their environment and way of life.

ARTS & CULTURE
Brazilian culture has been shaped not only by the Portuguese, who gave the country its language and religion, but also by Amerindians, black Africans and settlers from Europe, the Middle East and Asia.

Although often ignored, denigrated or feared by urban Brazilians, Indian culture has helped shape modern Brazil and its legends, dance and music. Many indigenous foods and beverages, such as tapioca, manioc, potatoes, *mate* and *guaraná*, have become Brazilian staples. The Indians also gave the colonisers numerous objects and skills which are now in daily use in Brazil, such as hammocks, dugout canoes, thatched roofing, and weaving techniques.

The influence of African culture is also very powerful, especially in the North-East. The slaves imported by the Portuguese brought with them their religion, music and cuisine, all of which have profoundly influenced Brazilian identity. *Capoeira*, an African martial art developed by slaves to fight their oppressors, has become very popular in recent years, and throughout Brazil, you will see *rodas de capoeiras*, semicircles of spectator-musicians who sing the initial *chula* before the fight and provide the percussion during the fight.

Foreigners planning a trip to Brazil can learn a great deal about the country through viewing some of the outstanding Brazilian films of the past several decades, many of which are available on video. One of the best known is *Black Orpheus*, an adaptation of the classical myth, set in Rio during Carnaval. More recent successes include *Dona Flor and Her Two Husbands* (an adaptation of Jorge Amado's novel starring Sonia Braga), *Pixote*, a naturalistic tale of street children in southern Brazil, and *Bye Bye Brasil*, an entertaining but poignant road movie showing recent changes in Brazilian society (including the development of the Amazon) through the eyes of a travelling circus.

RELIGION
It's usually said that Brazil is a Catholic country, and that it has the largest Catholic population of any country in the world. However, religion in Brazil is notable for its diversity and syncretism. There are dozens of sects and religions, though the differences are often ill-defined.

The religion of the African slaves was prohibited, for fear that it would serve to reinforce group identity. To avoid persecution, the slaves assimilated their African gods *(orixás)* with the Catholic saints, developing cults such as Macumba and Candomblé that also included aspects of Indian religions and European spiritualism. Today, these cults are thriving in Brazil, along with less orthodox ones, some involving animal sacrifice, black magic and hallucinogens. Much of Candomblé is still secret; it was prohibited in Bahia until 1970.

Candomblé is also a medium for cultivating African traditions (music, dance and language) into a system that aims to worship and enjoy life in peace and harmony.

In Candomblé, each person has a particular orixá to protect them and their spirit, and relies on Exú, a mediator between the material and spiritual worlds. To keep them strong, the orixás and Exú must be given food. Exú likes alcoholic drinks, cigarettes, cigars, strong perfumes and meats. The orixás, like the Greek gods, are often involved in struggles for power.

The Afro-Brazilian rituals are practised in a *casa de santo* or *terreiro*, directed by a *pai* or *mãe de santo* (literally father or mother of the saint – the Candomblé priest or priest-ess). In Bahia and Rio, millions of Brazilians go to the beach during the festivals at the year's end to pay homage to Iemanjá, the queen of the sea. Flowers, perfumes, fruits and even jewellery are tossed into the sea to please the mother of the waters and to gain her protection in the new year.

LANGUAGE
When they settled Brazil in the 16th century, the Portuguese encountered the diverse languages of the Indians. These, together with the various idioms and dialects spoken by the Africans brought in as slaves, extensively changed the Portuguese spoken by the early settlers. Along with Portuguese, Tupi-Guaraní, written down and simplified by the Jesuits, became a common language, understood by the majority of the population. It even became the main language spoken until the middle of the 18th century, but its usage diminished with the great number of Portuguese gold-rush immigrants and a royal proclamation in 1757 prohibiting its use. With the expulsion of the Jesuits in 1759, Portuguese was well and truly established as the national language.

Still, many words remain from the Indian and African languages. From Tupi-Guaraní come lots of place names (eg Guanabara, Tijuca and Niterói), animal names (eg *capivara*, *piranha* and *urubu*) and plant names (eg *mandioca*, *abacaxí*, *caju* and *jacarandá*). Words from the African dialects, mainly those from Nigeria and Angola, are used in Afro-Brazilian religious ceremonies (eg Orixá, Exú and Iansã), cooking (eg *vatapá*, *acarajé* and *abará*) and general conversation (eg *samba*, *moleque* and *mocambo*).

Within Brazil, accents, dialects and slang *(gíria)* vary regionally. The *carioca*, or inhabitant of Rio de Janeiro, inserts the 'sh' sound in place of 's'. The *gaúcho* speaks a Spanish-sounding Portuguese, the *baiano* (from Bahia) speaks slowly, and the accents of the *cearense* (from Ceará) are often incomprehensible to outsiders.

Portuguese is similar to Spanish on paper, but sounds completely different. You will do quite well if you speak Spanish in Brazil, although in general, Brazilians will understand you better than you understand them. Try to develop an ear for Portuguese – it's a beautiful language. Brazilians are easy to befriend, but the vast majority speak little or no English. This is changing, as practically all Brazilians in school are learning English.

Most phrasebooks are not very helpful; their vocabulary is often dated and contains the Portuguese spoken in Portugal, not Brazil. Notable exceptions are Lonely Planet's *Brazilian phrasebook*, and a Berlitz phrasebook for travel in Brazil. Make sure any English-Portuguese dictionary is a Brazilian Portuguese one. It's easy to arrange tutorial instruction through any of the Brazilian-American institutes where Brazilians go to learn English, or at the IBEU (Instituto Brasil Estados Unidos) in Rio.

Basics

Hello.	*Oi.*
Goodbye.	*Tchau.*
Good morning.	*Bom dia.*
Good afternoon.	*Boa tarde.*
Good evening.	*Boa noite.*
Please.	*Por favor.*
Thank you (very much).	*(Muito) obrigado.* (males)
	(Muita) obrigada. (females)
Yes.	*Sim.*
No.	*Não.*
Maybe.	*Talvez.*
Excuse me.	*Com licença.*
I'm sorry.	*Desculpe (meperdoe).* (lit: forgive me)

I (don't) understand.
  Eu (não) entendo.
Please write it down.
  Escreva por favor.
Do you speak English?
  Você fala inglês?

Small Talk

What is your name?
  Qual é seu nome?

My name is ...
  Meu nome é ...
How are you?
  Como vai você/Tudo bem?
I'm fine, thanks.
  Vou bem/Tudo bem, obrigado/a.
I'm a tourist/student.
  Eu sou um turista/estudante.
Where/What country are you from?
  Aonde/Da onde você é?
I am from ...
  Eu sou ...
How old are you?
  Quantos anos você tem?
I am ... years old.
  Eu tenho ... anos.

Getting Around

I want to go to ...
  Eu quero ir para ...
I want to book a seat for ...
  Eu quero reservar um assento para ...

What time does the ... leave/arrive?	*A que horas ... sai/chega?*
bus	*onibus*
tram	*bonde*
train	*trem*
boat	*barco*

one-way/return ticket	*passagem de ida/volta*
station	*estação*
ticket office	*bilheteria*
timetable	*horário*

I would like to hire a ...	*Eu gostaria de alugar um/uma ...*
bicycle	*bicicleta*
motorcycle	*moto*
car	*carro*
guide	*guia*
horse	*cavalo*

Where is ...?	*Aonde é ...?*
Is it near/far?	*É perto/longe?*
Go straight ahead.	*Vá em frente.*
Turn left.	*Vire a esquerda.*
Turn right.	*Vire a direita.*

Accommodation

youth hostel	*albergue da juventude*
camping ground	*camping*
hotel	*hotel*
guesthouse	*pousada*

Do you have a room available?
Você tem um/uma quarto para alugar?
How much is it per night/per person?
Quanto é por noite/por pessoa?
Is service/breakfast included?
O serviço/café de manha está incluído?
Can I see the room?
Posso ver o quarto?
Where is the toilet?
Aonde é o banheiro?

Around Town

Where is the/a ...? *Aonde é o/a ...?*

bank	*banco*
exchange office	*casa de câmbio*
city centre	*centro da cidade*
embassy	*embaixada*
post office	*correio*
telephone centre	*telefônica*
tourist office	*posto de informações turísticas*

I'd like to change some money/travellers' cheques.
Eu gostaria de trocar um pouco de dineiro/cheques de viagem.

Food & Shopping

I would like the set lunch please.
Eu gostaria do prato feito por favor.
Is service included in the bill?
O serviço está incluído na conta?
I am a vegetarian.
Eu sou vegetariano/a.
How much does it cost?
Quanto custa?
It's too expensive for me.
É muito caro para mim.
Can I look at it?
Posso ver?

Do you take travellers' cheques/credit cards?
Você aceita cheques de viagem/cartões de crédito?

Times & Dates

What time is it?	*Que horas são?*

It's ...	*São ...*
1.15	*uma e quinze*
1.30	*uma e meia*
1.45	*uma e quarenta e cinco*

When?	*Quando?*
o'clock	*horas*
yesterday	*ontem*
today	*hoje*
tonight	*hoje de noite*
tomorrow	*amanhã*
morning	*a manhã*
afternoon	*a tarde*

Sunday	*domingo*
Monday	*segunda-feira*
Tuesday	*terça-feira*
Wednesday	*quarta-feira*
Thursday	*quinta-feira*
Friday	*sexta-feira*
Saturday	*sábado*

Numbers

0	*zero*
1	*um/uma*
2	*dois/duas*
3	*três*
4	*quatro*
5	*cinco*
6	*seis* (when quoting telephone or house numbers, you'll hear *meia*)
7	*sete*
8	*oito*
9	*nove*
10	*dez*
11	*onze*
12	*doze*
13	*treze*
14	*catorze*
15	*quinze*
16	*dezesseis*

BRAZIL

17	dezessete
18	dezoito
19	dezenove
20	vinte
30	trinta
40	quarenta
50	cinqüenta
60	sessenta
70	setenta
80	oitenta
90	noventa
100	cem
1000	mil
one million	um milhão

Health & Emergencies

I'm allergic to penicillin/antibiotics.
Eu sou allergico/a a penicilina/antibióticos

I'm ...	Eu sou ...
diabetic	diabético/a
epileptic	epilético/a
asthmatic	asmático/a

antiseptic	antiséptico
aspirin	aspirina
condoms	camisinhas
contraceptive	contraceptivo
sunblock cream	creme de proteção solar
tampons	absorventes internos

Help!	Socorro!
Go away!	Va embora!
Call a doctor!	Chame o médico!
Call the police!	Chame a polícia!

Slang

Brazilians pepper their language with strange oaths and odd expressions. Literal translations are in brackets:

Hello!	Oi!
Everything OK?	Tudo bem?
Everything's OK	Tudo bom.
That's great/Cool!	Chocante!
That's bad/Shit!	Merda!

Great/Cool/OK!	'ta lógico/'ta ótimo/'ta legal!
My God!	Meu deus!
It's/You're crazy!	'ta louco!
Gosh!	Nossa! (Our Lady!)
Whoops!	Opa!
Wow!	Oba!
You said it!	Falou!
I'm mad at ...	Eu estou chateado com ...
Is there a way?	Tem jeito?
There's always a way.	Sempre tem jeito.
(curse word)	Palavrão!
shooting the breeze	batendo um papo
marijuana	fumo (smoke)
guy	cara
girl	garota
money	grana
bum	bum-bum/bunda
bald	careca
a mess	bagunça
a fix/problem	abacaxí
the famous 'Brazilian bikini'	fio dental (dental floss)

Body Language

Brazilians accompany their oral communication with a rich body language, a sort of parallel dialogue. The thumbs up of *tudo bem* is used as a greeting, or to signify OK or thank you. The authoritative *não, não* finger-wagging is most intimidating when done right under a victim's nose, but it's not a threat. To indicate *rápido!* (speed and haste), thumb and middle finger touch loosely while rapidly shaking the wrist. If you don't want something (*não quero*), slap the back of your hands as if ridding yourself of the entire affair.

Facts for the Visitor

VISAS & EMBASSIES

American, Canadian, Australian and NZ citizens require visas, but UK citizens do not. Tourist visas are issued by Brazilian diplomatic offices. They are valid for arrival in Brazil within 90 days of issue and then for a

90-day stay in Brazil. Visas can be renewed in Brazil for an additional 90 days.

It should only take about three hours to issue a visa, though this can vary; you will need a passport (valid for at least six months), a single passport photograph (either B&W or colour) and either a return ticket or a statement from a travel agent, addressed to the Brazilian diplomatic office, stating that you have the required ticketing. If you only have a one-way ticket, they may accept a document from a bank or similar organisation proving that you have sufficient funds to stay and buy a return ticket.

Intending visitors under 18 years of age must submit a notarised letter of authorisation from their parents or legal guardian.

Tourist Card

When you enter Brazil, you will be asked to fill out a tourist card, which has two parts. Immigration officials will keep one part. The other part will be attached to your passport, to be detached by immigration officials when you leave. Make sure you don't lose it; otherwise, your departure could be delayed while officials check your story.

Visa Extensions

The Polícia Federal handles visa extensions, but you must go to them before your visa lapses, preferably 15 days in advance. They have offices in major cities. An extension costs about US$12, and in most cases it is granted automatically. However, the police may require you to have a ticket out of the country and proof of sufficient funds. You are not obliged to extend your visa for the full 90 days, and if you leave Brazil, you cannot return until your current visa expires.

Brazilian Embassies Abroad

Brazil has embassies and consulates in neighbouring countries and the following countries:

Australia
    19 Forster Crescent, Yarralumla, ACT 2600 (☎ (06) 273-2372)

Canada
    255 Albert St, Suite 900, Ottawa, Ontario K1P6A9 (☎ (613) 237-1090)
France
    34 Cours Albert, 1er, 75008 Paris (☎ 01 42 25 92 50)
Germany
    Kurfürstendamm 11, 1 Stock, 1 Berlin 15 (☎ (030) 8 83 12 08)
UK
    32 Green St, London W1Y 4AT (☎ (0171) 499-0877)
USA
    Embassy: 3006 Massachusetts Ave, Washington, DC (☎ (202) 745-2700)
    Consulate General: 630 Fifth Ave, Suite 2720, New York, NY (☎ (212) 757-3080)

New Zealanders must apply to the Brazilian Embassy in Australia for their visas; this can be done easily through a travel agent.

For addresses of foreign representatives in Brazil, see under individual cities. Embassies are in Brasília, the national capital, but there are consulates in many cities, which are more convenient for most travellers.

CUSTOMS

Travellers entering Brazil are allowed to bring in one radio, tape player, typewriter, video and still camera. Personal computers are allowed.

At airport customs, they use the random check system. After collecting your luggage you pass a post with two buttons; if you have nothing to declare, you push the appropriate button. A green light means walk straight out; a red light means you've been selected for a baggage search.

Customs searches at land borders are more thorough, especially if you're coming from Bolivia.

MONEY
Currency

At the moment, the monetary unit of Brazil is the *real* (pronounced *HAY-ow*); the plural is *reais* (pronounced *HAY-ice*). It's made up of 100 *centavos*. The frustratingly similar coins are: one, five, 10, 25 and 50 centavos. There's also a one-real coin as well as a one-real note. The notes are different colours, so there's no mistaking them. As well as the green one-real note there's a blue/purple five, a red 10, a brown 50 and a blue 100.

Exchange Rates

There are currently three types of exchange rate in Brazil: official (also known as *comercial* or *câmbio livre*), *turismo* and *paralelo*. Exchange rates are written up every day on the front page and in the business sections of the major daily papers, and announced on the evening TV news.

Approximate bank rates in July 1996 were as follows:

Australia	A$1	=	R$0.79
Canada	C$1	=	R$0.74
France	FF1	=	R$0.20
Germany	DM1	=	R$0.66
Japan	¥100	=	R$0.93
New Zealand	NZ$1	=	R$0.69
United Kingdom	UK£1	=	R$1.56
USA	US$1	=	R$1.01

Cash & Travellers' Cheques

US dollars cash are easier to trade and are worth a bit more when you exchange, but travellers' cheques are an insurance against loss. They can be hard to change sometimes, and that's why you might prefer to carry a Visa card (see Credit Cards).

American Express is the most recognised brand, but Thomas Cook, Barclays and First National City Bank travellers' cheques are also good. Get travellers' cheques in US dollars and carry some small denominations for convenience. Have some emergency US cash to use when the banks are closed.

Credit Cards

International credit cards like Visa, American Express and MasterCard are accepted by many expensive hotels, restaurants and shops. But it's surprising how many don't accept credit cards. Make sure you ask first if you plan to use one. At present, you get billed at the turismo rate in reais.

Visa is the most versatile credit card in Brazil, and getting cash advances with a Visa card is becoming easier. International Visa card holders can use the Bradesco bank's automatic teller machines; get hold of a list of ATM locations from one of their branches. Banco do Brasil also gives cash advances on Visa, even in some small towns with no other exchange facilities.

American Express card-holders can purchase US-dollar travellers' cheques from American Express offices in the large cities. MasterCard holders can pay for many goods and services with their card, but cash advances are difficult.

Credit-card fraud is rife in Brazil: never let your card out of your sight, especially in restaurants.

Changing Money

Changing money in the large cities in Brazil is easy. Almost anyone can direct you to a *casa de câmbio* (money exchange house), where Brazilians and foreigners can buy and sell dollars with no restriction. In small towns without a bank, you'll have to ask around. Someone will usually be able to direct you to someone who buys cash dollars.

Change, variously referred to as *troco* or *miúdo*, is often unobtainable. When you change money, ask for lots of small bills.

Changing money at weekends, even in the big cities, can be extremely difficult, so make sure you have enough to last until Monday. If you do get stuck, the best places to try are the large hotels, expensive restaurants, travel agents, jewellery shops and souvenir shops.

Don't change money on the streets, follow moneychangers into unfamiliar areas or give money or unsigned cheques up front.

Costs

Because of wild fluctuations in the economy, it's difficult to make any solid predictions about how much you'll spend. Since the introduction of the real, inflation has fallen to less than 2% per month, and although this inflation rate is still well above the US level, the real has appreciated by about 15% against the US dollar because of increased US-dollar flow into Brazil. As a result, Brazil as become a somewhat expensive destination for foreign travellers.

Since our last edition, prices have risen anywhere from 30 to 100%. How long it will stay this way is uncertain, though prices should drop off a bit from their current levels.

If you're travelling on buses every couple of days, staying in hotels for US$15 or US$20 a night, and eating in restaurants and/or drinking in bars every night, US$40 to US$50 a day is a rough estimate of what you would need. It's possible to do it for less, of course. If you plan to lie on a beach for a month, eating rice, beans and fish every day, US$20 to US$30 would be enough.

Bargaining

Bargaining for hotel rooms should become second nature. Before you agree to take a room, ask for a better price. *'Tem desconto?'* ('Is there a discount?') and *'Pode fazer um melhor preço?'* ('Can you give a better price?') are the phrases to use. There's often a discount for paying *ávista* (cash) or for taying during the *baixa estaço* or *época baixa* (low season) when hotels need guests to cover running costs. It's also possible to reduce the price if you state that you don't want a TV, private bath, or air-con. If you're staying longer than a couple of days, ask for a discount. Once a discount has been quoted, make sure it is noted on your bill at the same time: this avoids misunderstandings at a later date. Bargain also in markets and in unmetered taxis.

WHEN TO GO

See the information under Climate in the Facts about the Country section for details of seasonal factors that may influence your decision on when to visit the country. There are few regions that can't be comfortably visited all year round. During summer (December to February), when many Brazilians are on vacation, travel is difficult and expensive. School holidays begin in mid-December and continue until Carnaval, which is usually in late February.

WHAT TO BRING

The happiest travellers are those who can slip all their luggage under their plane seats. Pack light.

What you bring will depend on what you want to do. If you're planning a river or jungle trip, read the Amazon section in advance. If you're travelling cheap, a cotton sheet sleeping-sack will come in handy.

With its warm climate and informal dress standards, you don't need to bring many clothes to Brazil. Except for the South and Minas Gerais, where it gets cold in the winter, the only weather you need to contend with is heat and rain, and whatever you're lacking you can purchase while travelling. Buying clothes in Brazil is easy and has the added advantage of helping you appear less like a tourist.

You don't need to pack more than a pair of shorts, trousers, a couple of T-shirts, a long-sleeved shirt, bathing suit, towel, underwear, walking shoes, thongs and a light rain jacket. Quick-drying, light cotton clothes are the most convenient. Suntan lotion and sun-protection cream are readily available in Brazil. Most other toiletries are also easy to get.

Usually, one set of clothes to wear and one to wash is adequate. It's probably a good idea if one set of clothes is somewhat presentable for a visit to a good restaurant or club (or to renew your visa at the federal police station). While dress is informal, many Brazilians are very fashion conscious and pay close attention to both their own appearance and yours.

TOURIST OFFICES

The headquarters of Embratur, the Brazilian Tourist Board (☎ 224-2872), is at Setor Comercial Norte, Quadra 2, Bloco G, Brasília, DF, CEP 70710. There is also an Embratur office (☎ 273-2212, fax 273-9290) in Rio de Janeiro, at Rua Mariz e Barros 13, 4th floor.

Tourist offices elsewhere in Brazil are generally sponsored by individual states and municipalities. In many places, these offices rely on shoestring budgets, which are chopped or maintained according to the whims (or feuds) of regional and local politicians. Keep your sense of humour, prepare for pot luck and don't expect too much!

USEFUL ORGANISATIONS

The Brazilian American Cultural Center (☎ (212) 730-1010, or toll-free (1-800) 222-2746), at 16 West 46th St, New York, NY 10036, is a tourism organisation which offers its members discounted flights and tours. Members can send money to South America using BACC's remittance service. The organisation can also secure tourist visas for members, through the Brazilian Consulate in New York.

For information about the network of Brazilian youth hostels, contact the Federação Brasileira dos Albergues de Juventude (☎ & fax (021) 531-1753), Rua da Assembléia 10, sala 1211, Centro, Rio de Janeiro, CEP 20011, RJ. Include an envelope and postage.

BUSINESS HOURS

Most shops and government services are open Monday to Friday from 9 am to 6 pm, and Saturday from 9 am to 1 pm. Some shops stay open later than 6 pm in the cities, and the huge shopping malls often stay open until 10 pm and open on Sunday as well. Banks generally open from 10 am to 4.30 pm. Business hours vary by region, and are taken less seriously in remote locations.

HOLIDAYS

National holidays fall on the following dates:

1 January
   New Year's Day
6 January
   Epiphany
February/March (four days before Ash Wednesday)
   Carnaval
March/April (dates vary)
   Easter
21 April
   Tiradentes Day
1 May
   May Day
June
   Corpus Christi
7 September
   Independence Day

1 October
   Our Lady of Aparecida Day
2 November
   All Souls' Day
15 November
   Proclamation Day
25 December
   Christmas Day

SPECIAL EVENTS

Major cultural events and festivals include:

1 January
   New Year & Festa de Iemanjá (Rio de Janeiro)
   Procissão do Senhor Bom Jesus dos Navegantes (Salvador, Bahia)
1-20 January
   Folia de Reis (Parati, Rio de Janeiro)
Second Sunday in January
   Bom Jesus dos Navegantes (Penedo, Alagoas)
Second Thursday in January
   Lavagem do Bonfim (Salvador, Bahia)
24 January to 2 February
   NS de Nazaré (Nazaré, Bahia)
February
   Grande Vaquejada do Nordeste (Natal, Rio Grande do Norte)
2 February
   Festa de Iemanjá (Salvador, Bahia)
February
   Carnaval (All over Brazil)
February/March (dates vary)
   Lavagem da Igreja de Itapoã (Itapoã, Bahia)
   Shrove Tuesday (and the preceding three days to two weeks, depending on the place)
Mid-April
   Drama da Paixão de Cristo (Brejo da Madre de Deus, Pernambuco)
April/May (15 days after Easter)
   Cavalhadas (Pirenópolis, Goiás)
Late May/early June
   Festa do Divino Espírito Santo (Parati, Rio de Janeiro)
June
   Festas Juninas & Bumba Meu Boi (celebrated throughout June in much of the country, particularly São Luis, Belém and throughout Pernambuco and Rio states)
   Festival Folclórico do Amazonas (Manaus, Amazonas)
22 -24 June
   São João (Cachoeira, Bahia & Campina Grande, Paraíba)
July
   Festa do Divino (Diamantina, Minas Gerais)
   Regata de Jangadas Dragão do Mar (Fortaleza, Ceará)

15 August
  Festa de Iemanjá (Fortaleza, Ceará)
Mid-August
  Festa da NS de Boa Morte (Cachoeira, Bahia)
September
  Festival de Cirandas (Itamaracá, Pernambuco)
  Cavalhada (Caeté, Minas Gerais)
12 October
  Festa de NS Aparecida (Aparecida, São Paulo)
October (starting second Sunday)
  Círio de Nazaré (Belém, Pará)
October (second half)
  NS do Rosário (Cachoeira, Bahia)
November
  NS da Ajuda (Cachoeira, Bahia)
1-2 November
  Festa do Padre Cícero (Juazeiro do Norte, Ceará)
8 December
  Festa de NS da Conceição (Salvador, Bahia)
  Festa de Iemanjá (Belém, Pará & João Pessoa, Paraíba)
31 December
  Celebração de Fim de Ano & Festa do Iemanjá (Rio de Janeiro)

POST & COMMUNICATIONS
Post
Postal services are usually pretty good in Brazil although we do hear plenty of complaints from readers. Most mail seems to get through, and air-mail letters to the USA and Europe usually arrive in a week or so. For Australia, allow two weeks. Rates for mail leaving Brazil are amongst the highest in the world – almost US$1 for an international letter or postcard! Most *correios* (post offices) are open Monday to Friday from 9 am to 6 pm and Saturday morning.

The *posta restante* system seems to function reasonably well and will hold mail for 30 days. A reliable alternative for American Express customers is to have mail sent to an American Express office.

Telephone
International Calls Brazil's international telephone code is 55. Phoning abroad from Brazil is very expensive. To the USA and Canada, it costs approximately US$2.50 a minute. To the UK and France, the charge is US$3 a minute. Prices are 25% lower from 8 pm to 6 am daily and all day Sunday. To Australia and New Zealand, calls cost US$4

a minute (there are no cheaper times to these two countries).

Every town has a *posto telefônico* (phone company office) for long-distance calls, which require a large deposit. If you're calling direct from a private phone, dial 00, then the country code number, then the area code, then the phone number. For information on international calls, dial ☎ 00-0333.

International reverse-charge (collect) calls *(a cobrar)* can be made from any phone. To get the international operator, dial ☎ 00-0111 or 107 and ask for the *telefônista internacional*. Embratel, the Brazilian telephone monopoly, now offers home-country direct services for the following countries:

Australia	☎ 000-8061
Canada	☎ 000-8014
France	☎ 000-8033
Germany	☎ 000-8049
Israel	☎ 000-8097
Italy	☎ 000-8039
Japan	☎ 000-8081
Netherlands	☎ 000-8031
UK	☎ 000-8044
USA – AT&T	☎ 000-8010
USA – MCI	☎ 000-8012
USA – Sprint	☎ 000-8016

National Calls National long-distance calls can also be made at the local phone company office, unless you're calling collect. For reverse-charge calls within Brazil, dial 9, then area code, then phone number. A recorded message in Portuguese will ask you to say your name and where you're calling from, after the beep. The person at the other end then decides if they will accept the call.

Local Calls Brazilian public phones are nicknamed *orelhões* (big ears). They use *fichas* (coin-like tokens) or *cartão telefônicos* (phonecards). Both can be bought at newsstands, pharmacies etc. Phonecards range in value from 30 centavos (good for 10 local calls) to three reais. When your time is up, you will be disconnected without warning. To call the operator, dial ☎ 100; for information, call ☎ 102.

Fax, Telex & Telegraph

Post offices send and receive telegrams, and the larger branches also have fax services. Fax transmission costs US$10 per page to the USA and Canada, US$18 to Australia and New Zealand, and US$12 to the UK.

TIME

Brazil has four official time zones, generally depicted on maps as a neat series of lines. The standard time zone covers the eastern, north-eastern, southern and south-eastern parts of Brazil. This zone is three hours behind GMT/UTC. Brazil uses daylight-saving time, which requires clocks to be set one hour ahead in October and back one hour in March or April.

ELECTRICITY

Electrical current is not standardised in Brazil, so it's a good idea to carry an adapter if you can't travel without your hair dryer. In Rio de Janeiro and São Paulo, the current is almost exclusively 110 or 120V, 60 Hz AC. Salvador and Manaus have 127V service. Recife, Brasília and various other cities have 220V service. Check before you plug in. The most common power points have two round sockets.

WEIGHTS & MEASURES

Brazil uses the metric system. There is a metric conversion table at the back of this book.

BOOKS

History

John Hemming's *Red Gold: The Conquest of the Brazilian Indians* follows the colonists and Indians from 1500 to 1760, when the great majority of Indians were effectively either eliminated or pacified. Hemming, a founder of Survival International and an eloquent campaigner for Indian rights, has extended his analysis of Indian history in *Amazon Frontier: The Defeat of the Brazilian Indians*.

The most famous book on Brazil's colonial period is Gilberto Freyre's *The Masters & the Slaves: A Study in the Development of Brazilian Civilization*.

The not-to-be-believed rebellion in Canudos by the followers of the mystic Antônio Conselheiro has been immortalised in *Rebellion in the Backlands* by Euclides da Cunha. Mixing history, geography and philosophy, *Os Sertões* (in Portuguese) is considered the masterpiece of Brazilian literature. An eloquent and engrossing fictionalised account of Canudos is given by Mario Vargas Llosa in his novel *The War of the End of the World*.

For readers who like their history with a dose of fiction, *Brazil* by Errol Lincoln Uys is an interesting novel that traces the history of two Brazilian families.

Travel

Highly recommended for its style and humour, Peter Fleming's *Brazilian Adventure* is about the young journalist's expedition into Mato Grosso in search of the missing Colonel Fawcett. Moritz Thomsen's *The Saddest Pleasure: A Journey on Two Rivers* is a highly recommended book (skip the sickly introduction) about the author's experiences in South America, including journeys through Brazil and along the Amazon.

The Amazon & Indians

Both of John Hemming's works, described in the History category, detail the history of the Portuguese colonisation, subjugation and enslavement of the Indian.

Amazonia, by the renowned explorer and photographer Loren McIntyre, records in magnificent photographs the gradual demise of the region and its original inhabitants.

Alex Shoumatoff has written some excellent Amazon books, all of them entertaining combinations of history, myth and travelogue. His *The World is Burning* recounts the Chico Mendes story.

The Fate of the Forest: Developers, Destroyers, and Defenders of the Amazon by Susanna Hecht & Alexander Cockburn is one of the best analyses of the complex web of destruction, and provides ideas on ways to mend the damage.

Travel Guides

A Brazilian travel guide is published annually by Quatro Rodas. Called *Quatro Rodas: Guia Brasil*, it's readily available at most newsagents and contains a wealth of information (in Portuguese) about accommodation, restaurants, transport, sights etc. If you buy it in Brazil, it also comes with an excellent fold-out map of the country. Budget travellers should check out *Viajar Bem e Barato*, Quatro Rodas' guide to cheap travelling (in Portuguese).

MAPS

Within Brazil, most maps are produced by Quatro Rodas, which also publishes the *Quatro Rodas: Guia Brasil*. This guide is complemented by *Guia Rodoviário*, a compact book of maps in a handy plastic case, which covers individual states. The city maps in *Quatro Rodas: Guia Brasil* help with orientation.

MEDIA

Newspapers & Magazines

English By far the best English-language newspaper is the Latin American edition of the *Miami Herald*, which costs about US$5. *Time* and *Newsweek* magazines are available throughout Brazil. In the big cities, you can find all sorts of imported newspapers and magazines at some newsstands, but they are very expensive.

Portuguese The *Folha de São Paulo* is Brazil's finest newspaper. It has excellent coverage of national and international events and is a good source for entertainment in São Paulo. The *Jornal do Brasil* and *O Globo* are Rio's main daily papers. Among weekly magazines, *Veja*, the Brazilian *Time* clone, is the country's best selling magazine.

The latest environmental and ecological issues (both national and international) are covered in the monthly magazine *Ecología e Desenvolvimento*, published by Editora Terceiro Mundo (☎ 221-7511) in Rio de Janeiro.

TV

English Cable TV is a recent addition with ESPN (the sports network), CNN (Cable News Network), RAI (Radio Televisione Italia) and, of course, MTV (music television) available to those few who can afford them.

Portuguese Many of the worst American movies and TV shows are dubbed into Portuguese and shown on Brazilian TV. The most popular programmes on Brazilian TV are the *novelas* (soap operas), which go on the air at various times from 7 to 9 pm. The news is on several times a night, but broadcast times vary from place to place.

FILM & PHOTOGRAPHY

Kodak and Fuji print film are sold and processed almost everywhere, but you can only get slide film developed (expensively) in the big cities. If you're shooting slides, it's best to bring film with you and have it processed back home.

HEALTH

Your chances of contracting a serious illness in Brazil are slight. You will be exposed to environmental factors, foods and sanitation standards that are probably quite different from what you're used to, but if you take the recommended jabs, faithfully pop your anti-malarials and use common sense, there shouldn't be any problems.

While there's no worry of any strange tropical diseases in Rio and points farther south, remember that Amazonas, Pará, Mato Grosso, Amapá, Rondônia, Goiás, Espírito Santo and the North-East have some combination of the following: malaria, yellow fever, dengue fever, leprosy and leishmaniasis. Health officials periodically announce high rates of tuberculosis, polio, sexually transmitted diseases, hepatitis and other endemic diseases.

Bichos de pé are small parasites that live on Bahian beaches and in sandy soil. They burrow into the thick skin of the heel, toes and under toenails, appearing as dark boils.

BRAZIL

Bichos de pé must be incised and removed completely; if you do it yourself, use a sterilised needle and blade. Better still, avoid them by wearing footwear on beaches and dirt trails.

For more information on Health see the Facts for the Visitor chapter.

WOMEN TRAVELLERS

In São Paulo, where there are many people of European ancestry, white women without travelling companions will scarcely be given a sideways glance, but in the more traditional rural areas of the North-East, where a large percentage of the population is of mixed European, African and Indian origin, blonde-haired and light-skinned women – especially those without male escorts – may arouse curiosity. It's best to dress conservatively. What works in Rio will not necessarily be appropriate in a North-Eastern city or a Piauí backwater.

Flirtation (often exaggerated) is a prominent element in Brazilian male-female relations. It goes both ways, and is nearly always regarded as amusingly innocent banter. If unwelcome attention is forthcoming, you should be able to stop it by merely expressing distaste or displeasure.

It's a good idea to keep a low profile in the cities at night, and avoid going alone to bars and nightclubs. Similarly, women should not hitch, either alone or in groups, and even men or couples should exercise discretion when hitching. Most importantly, the remote, rough-and-ready areas of the north and west, where there are lots of men but few local women, should be considered off limits to lone female travellers.

DANGERS & ANNOYANCES

Robberies on buses, on city beaches and in areas visited by many tourists are extremely common. Thieves tend to work in gangs, are armed with knives and guns, and are capable of killing those who resist them. Much of the petty street crime in Rio, São Paulo, Salvador and Manaus is directed against tourists – Rio's thieves refer to them as *filet mignon*. Be especially careful on the city beaches;

take enough money for lunch and drinks, and nothing else. Don't hang out on the beaches at night. When reporting a theft, be wary of the police. They have been known to plant drugs and to sting gringos for bribes. For advice on security precautions, see the Dangers & Annoyances information in the introductory Facts for the Visitor chapter.

ACTIVITIES

Surfing

Surfing is popular all along the coast and there are some excellent waves to be had, especially in the south. Santa Catarina has the best surfing beaches and holds the Brazilian championships at Joaquina beach near Florianópolis. In Rio state, Saquarema has the best surf. Búzios and Itacoatiara beach in Niterói are also popular breaks. There's also plenty of surf close to the city of Rio; see the Rio de Janeiro section for details. The waves are best in winter.

Hiking & Climbing

Hiking and climbing in Brazil are best during the cooler months of the year – April to October. During the summer, the tropical sun heats the rock up to oven temperatures and turns the jungles into steamy saunas. People still climb during the summer, although usually in the early morning or late afternoon when the sun's rays are not so harsh.

Brazil has lots of fantastic rock climbs, ranging from the beginner level to routes still unconquered. Rio de Janeiro is the centre of rock climbing in Brazil: there are 350 documented climbs that can all be reached within 40 minutes from the city centre.

There are lots of great places to hike in Brazil, both in the national and state parks and along the coastline. Lots of good hikes are mentioned in the appropriate sections. It's also a good idea to contact some of the climbing clubs (see the Rio city section for addresses), which have details of trekking options.

HIGHLIGHTS

The city of Rio de Janeiro, despite a full set of urban problems, is still a marvellous place.

Rio's Carnaval is the most famous festival, but the Brazilian passion for music and dance is a highlight seen everywhere and every day, as well as in thousands of annual celebrations all over the country. There are many miles of quiet coastline, but the real Brazilian beach scene features *barracas* (stalls or huts) with loud music, wild dancing, cold beer and beautiful bodies; check it out anywhere from Ilha da Santa Catarina to the North-East.

Many of the historic colonial cities have been restored, and are truly gorgeous; some of the best are Ouro Prêto, Congonhas, Diamantina, Parati, Salvador da Bahia, Olinda and São Luís. Ecotourists and wildlife buffs will want to do a trip into the Amazon rainforest, but the Pantanal and the Atlantic rainforest also have a fantastic biodiversity, and are well worth a visit. And for a scenic highlight, it's hard to top the Iguaçu Falls.

ACCOMMODATION

Camping is becoming increasingly popular in Brazil, and is a viable alternative for travellers on limited budgets or those who want to explore some of the country's national or state parks. For detailed information on camping grounds, buy the *Guia Quatro Rodas Camping Guide* from any newsstand. You may also want to contact the Camping Club of Brazil, Rua Senador Dantas 75, 25th floor, Rio de Janeiro. The club has 52 sites in 14 states.

There are now more than 90 *albergues de juventude* (youth hostels) in Brazil, and more are planned. Most state capitals and popular tourist areas have at least one. A night in a hostel will cost around US$12 per person, if you're a member. It's not always necessary to be a member to stay in one, but it'll cost more if you're not. International Youth Hostel cards are accepted, but if you arrive in Brazil without one, you can buy guest membership cards. For the address of the Brazilian Youth Hostel Federation (FBAJ), see the Useful Organisations section earlier in this chapter. The FBAJ publishes a useful directory of Brazilian hostels, and it's available from most newsstands for US$15.

The cheapest places to stay are *dormitórios*. These have several beds to a room, and may cost as little as US$5 per night. Most budget travellers stay at a cheaper *pousada* (small guesthouse) or *hotel*, where a *quarto* (room without a bathroom) costs as little as US$8 to US$10. Rooms with a private bathroom are called *apartamentos*.

Most hotels in Brazil are regulated by Embratur, the Brazilian tourism authority, which rates the quality of hotels from one to five stars. Regulated hotels must have a price list with an Embratur label, a copy of which is usually posted on the wall in each room. Even so, it still pays to bargain.

If you're travelling in the Amazon or the North-East, where there are no hotels, a hammock and a mosquito net are essential. With these basics, and help from friendly locals, you can get a good night's rest anywhere. Most fishing villages along the coast have seen an outsider or two and will put you up for the night. If they've seen a few more outsiders, they'll probably charge you a couple of dollars.

FOOD

The staples of the Brazilian diet are *arroz* (white rice), *feijão* (black beans) and *farofel* (manioc flour), also called *farinha*. These are usually combined with *carne* (steak), *frango* (chicken) or *peixe* (fish) to make up the *prato feito* (set meal) or *prato do dia* (plate of the day). These set meals are typically enormous and cheap, but after a while, they can become monotonous. Lunch is the big meal of the day, and *lanchonetes* (snack bars) throughout the country will have a prato do dia on offer. In the cities, there is more variety. Many restaurants and lanchonetes also offer pay-by-weight *(comida por kilo)* buffets.

A *churrascaria* is a restaurant serving barbecued meat and many offer *rodízio* (a meat smorgasbord). They are especially good in the south.

Brazilian Dishes
The following are some common dishes:

BRAZIL

Acarajé – this is what the baianas, Bahian women in flowing white dresses, traditionally sell on street corners throughout Bahia. Acarajé is made from peeled brown beans, mashed in salt and onions and then fried in *dendê* oil. Inside these delicious fried balls is *vatapá* (see this list), dried shrimp, pepper and tomato sauce. Dendê oil is strong stuff; many stomachs can't handle it.

Carne de sol – this tasty salted meat is grilled, then served with beans, rice and vegetables.

Caruru – one of the most popular Brazilian dishes brought here from Africa, this is made with okra or other vegetables cooked in water. The water is then drained, and onions, salt, shrimps and malagueta peppers are added, mixed and grated together with the okra paste and dendê oil. Traditionally, a sea fish such as garoupa is then added.

Cozido – the term refers to any kind of stew, usually with more vegetables (eg potatoes, sweet potatoes, carrots and manioc) than other stew-like Brazilian dishes.

Feijoada – the national dish of Brazil, feijoada is a meat stew served with rice and a bowl of beans. It's served throughout the country, and there are many variations.

Moqueca – this is both a kind of sauce or stew and a style of cooking from Bahia. There are many kinds of moqueca: fish, shrimp, oyster, crab or a combination. The moqueca sauce is defined by its heavy use of dendê oil and coconut milk, often with peppers and onions. A moqueca must be cooked in a covered clay pot.

Pato no tucupi – roast duck, flavoured with garlic and cooked in the *tucupi* sauce made from the juice of the manioc plant and *jambu*, a local vegetable, is a very popular dish in Pará.

Peixe a delícia – this dish of broiled or grilled fish is usually made with bananas and coconut milk. It's delicious in Fortaleza.

Pirarucu ao forno – pirarucu is the most famous fish from the rivers of Amazônia. It's oven-cooked with lemon and other seasonings.

Tutu á mineira – this bean paste with toasted bacon and manioc flour, often served with cooked cabbage, is typical of Minas Gerais.

Vatapá – a seafood dish with a thick sauce made from manioc paste, coconut and dendê oil, vatapá is perhaps the most famous Brazilian dish of African origin.

Fruit

From the savoury nirvana of *graviola* to the confusingly clinical taste of *cupuaçú*, fruits and juices are a major Brazilian highlight. Many of the fruits of the North-East and Amazon have no English-name equivalent; you'll just have to try their exotic tastes.

DRINKS

Fruit juices, called *sucos*, are divine in Brazil. If you don't want sugar and ice, ask for them *sem açúcar e gelo* or *natural*. To avoid getting water mixed with them, ask for a *suco com leite*, also called a *vitamina*, which is juice mixed with milk. Orange juice is rarely diluted. The Brazilian soft drink *guaraná* is made from the berry of an Amazonian plant, and has a delicious, distinctive taste.

A *cerveja* is a 600-ml bottled beer. A *cervejinha* is 300 ml of bottled or canned beer. *Chopp* (pronounced *shoppee*) is a pale blond Pilsner draught, lighter than and far superior to canned or bottled beer.

Cachaça, pinga or *aguardente* is a high-proof, dirt-cheap sugar-cane alcohol, produced and drunk throughout the country. Cachaça literally means 'booze'. Pinga (literally, 'drop') is considered more polite, but by any name, it's cheap and toxic. A cheap cachaça can cut a hole in the strongest stomach lining. Velho Barreiro, Ypioca, Pitú, Carangueijo and São Francisco are some of the better labels.

Caipirinha is the Brazilian national drink. The ingredients are simple (cachaça, lime, sugar and crushed ice), but a well-made caipirinha is a work of art. *Caipirosca* is a caipirinha made with vodka instead of cachaça. *Caipirissima* is still another variation, using Bacardi rum instead of cachaça. *Batidas* are wonderful mixes of cachaça, sugar and fruit juice.

Getting There & Away

For information on getting to South America see the introductory Getting There & Away chapter.

AIR
To/From Argentina
There are several flights every day between

Buenos Aires and Rio de Janeiro, and good air connections to other main Brazilian cities.

To/From Bolivia

There are five Varig flights per week between La Paz and Rio, all of which stop over at São Paulo. Transportes Aéreos Militares (TAM) operates flights each way between Cáceres and San Matías and Santa Cruz (via Roboré) on Saturday.

To/From Colombia

Varig has two flights a week between Bogotá and Rio.

To/From the Guianas

Suriname Airways (SLM) and TABA fly between Belém (Brazil), Cayenne (French Guiana) and Paramaribo (Suriname). There are also flights from Macapá. There are no direct flights to Guyana from any Brazilian city.

To/From Paraguay

Varig has daily flights from Asunción to Rio, and other airlines also cover the route.

To/From Peru

AeroPerú and Varig fly between Lima (Peru) and Rio several times a week. Cruzeiro do Sul flies twice a week from Iquitos (Peru) to Manaus (Brazil).

To/From Uruguay

There are flights every day between Montevideo and Rio.

To/From Venezuela

Varig has two flights per week between Caracas and Rio.

LAND

To/From Argentina

Most travellers pass through Foz do Iguaçu (see the Foz do Iguaçu entry in the Paraná section for more information).

To/From Bolivia

Corumbá Opposite the Bolivian border town of Quijarro, Corumbá is the busiest port of entry along the Bolivia-Brazil border. It has both train and bus connections from São Paulo, Rio de Janeiro, Cuiabá and southern Brazil. During the dry season there's a daily train between Quijarro and Santa Cruz, but during the wet season there may be waits of several days. For further information, see Corumbá in the Central West section.

Cáceres From Cáceres, west of Cuiabá, you can cross to San Matías in Bolivia. Daily buses do the 4½-hour trip for US$10. During the dry season, there's also a daily bus between the border town of San Matías and San Ignacio de Velasco (see the Jesuit Missions section in both this and the Bolivia chapters), where you'll find flights and bus connections to Santa Cruz.

Coming from Bolivia, there are daily *micros* (again, only during the dry season) from San Ignacio de Velasco to the border at San Matías, from where you'll find onward transport to Cáceres and Cuiabá.

Guajará-Mirim Another popular crossing is between Guajará-Mirim in Brazil and Guayaramerín, Bolivia, via motorboat ferry across the Rio Mamoré. Guayaramerín is connected with Riberalta by a road, which should be extended to Cobija/Brasiléia in the near future. Another route runs south to Rurrenabaque and La Paz, with a spur to Trinidad. For further information see Guajará-Mirim and Guayaramerín in the Rondônia and Acre sections of this chapter.

Brasiléia In Acre state, there's a border crossing between Brasiléia and Cobija, Bolivia. For more details, see Brasiléia in the Acre section of this chapter.

To/From Colombia

The Colombian border crossing is at Leticia/Tabatinga. For further information on the Triple Frontier region, refer to Benjamin Constant and Tabatinga in the Amazonas section of this chapter.

To/From French Guiana

You can cross the Oiapoque River between Oiapoque (Brazil) and St Georges (French Guiana), from where there are heavily booked flights to Cayenne, but no road connections as yet. For further information, see Oiapoque, in the Amapá section of this chapter.

BRAZIL

To/From Guyana

The border crossing is from Bonfim (reached via Boa Vista), in Roraima state, to Lethem, which is connected to Georgetown by a very rough road, or an often-full flight. See the Roraima section for more details.

To/From Paraguay

Foz do Iguaçu/Ciudad del Este and Ponta Porã/Pedro Juan Caballero are the two major border crossings. See Foz do Iguaçu in the Paraná section and Ponta Porã in the Mato Grosso section for details.

To/From Peru

There is a border crossing to Iñapari (Peru) at Assis Brasil. For more details, see Brasiléia and Assis Brasil in the Acre section.

To/From Uruguay

Coming from Uruguay, travellers usually pass through the border towns of Chuy, Uruguay and Chuí, Brazil; the international border is the main street. There are four other border crossings: at Aceguá; from Rivera to Santana do Livramento; from Artigas to Quaraí; and at Barra do Quaraí, near the border with Argentina.

If you're driving from Brazil, you'll need to stop at the Brazilian checkpoint to get an exit stamp, and at the Uruguayan checkpoint for the Uruguayans to check that you have a Brazilian exit stamp and a Uruguayan visa (if you need one). Buses will stop at the checkpoints.

To/From Venezuela

From Boa Vista (Roraima state), you can cross into Venezuela via the border town of Santa Elena.

RIVER
To/From Paraguay

There are boats sailing along the Río Paraguay between Asunción and Corumbá (Mato Grosso do Sul). For further details, see the Getting There & Away information under Corumbá and Asunción in this and the Paraguay chapters, respectively.

To/From Peru

The main route between Brazil and Peru is along the Amazon between Iquitos and Islandia (the Peruvian port village on an island at the junction of the Rio Yauari and the Amazon, opposite Benjamin Constant). Some boats leave from Ramón Castilla, a few km farther upstream in Peru. For further information see the Amazonas section.

ORGANISED TOURS

Most tour operators include Brazil as part of a South American tour; see the introductory Getting There & Away chapter for details.

LEAVING BRAZIL

The airport tax for international flights, around US$18, is usually paid on departure.

Getting Around

AIR

Flying in Brazil is very expensive (eg Rio-Manaus return costs around US$1000), but as distances are enormous, the occasional flight may be worth it. Brazil has three major national carriers and several smaller regional airlines. The biggies are VASP, Transbrasil and Varig. Every major city can be reached by at least one of these airlines. It's usually not difficult to get on a flight, except between December and Carnaval (late February) and in July. The smaller domestic airlines include Nordeste, Rio Sul, TABA, Votec and TAM. There are also many air-taxi companies, which mostly fly in the Amazon region.

Aeronautica, the military air-transport service, has been known to give free flights when there is extra space, but you might have to wait a while. First the officers get a seat, then the soldiers, then the civilians. Go to the desk marked 'CAN' in the airport and ask about the next military flight, then show up again two days before scheduled departure time and sign up. It helps to have a letter of introduction from a consulate.

Air Pass

The Brazil Air Pass is the cheapest way to fly in Brazil. The air pass costs US$440 and buys you five flight coupons for five flights. For US$100 each, you can buy an additional four flight coupons. All travel must be completed within 21 days. The pass must be purchased outside Brazil. You'll get a Miscellaneous Charges Order (MCO), refundable if not used, in your name with 'Brazil Air Pass' stamped on it; you exchange this for an air pass from one of the three airlines in Brazil. Alternatively, you can decide your itinerary in advance.

All three airlines offer the same deal, and all three fly to most major cities, though Varig flies to more cities than the other two. If you are buying an air pass and have specific plans to go to a smaller city, check with a travel agent to see which airline goes there.

The air pass cannot be used to fly on the Rio-São Paulo shuttle, which lands at the downtown airports of both cities, but it can be used to fly between the international airports of both cities.

Warning Air-pass holders who get bumped from a flight for any reason should reconfirm *all* their other flight reservations.

Airport Tax

Passengers on domestic flights pay an airport tax. This tax varies, depending on the classification of the airport, but is usually about US$6 for domestic flights.

BUS

Except in the Amazon Basin, buses are the primary form of long-distance transportation for the vast majority of Brazilians. Bus services are generally excellent: departure times are usually strictly adhered to, and the buses are clean, comfortable, well-serviced Mercedes, Volvos and Scanias. Bus travel is very cheap with fares that work out to just over US$2 per hour.

All major cities are linked by frequent buses, and there is a surprising number of scheduled long-distance buses. It's rare that you will have to change buses between two

major cities, no matter what the distance. For tips on security and bus travel see the Dangers & Annoyances information in the introductory Facts for the Visitor chapter.

There are two types, or classes, of long-distance buses. The *comum* (common) is comfortable and usually has air-con and a toilet. The *leito* or *executivo* is Brazil's version of the couchette or sleeper. Leitos, which often depart late at night, usually take as long to reach their destination as a comum and cost twice as much, but they are exceptionally comfortable. If you don't mind missing the scenery, a leito bus can get you there in comfort and save you the cost of a hotel room. Long-distance buses generally make pit-stops every three or four hours.

In every big city, and most small ones, there is a central bus terminal (*rodoviária*). The rodoviárias are most frequently on the outskirts of the city. Some are modern, comfortable stations. All have restaurants, newsstands, toilets etc, and some even have post offices and long-distance telephone facilities. Most importantly, all the long-distance bus companies operate out of the same place, making it easy to find your bus. A combined train and bus station is a *ferro-rodoviária*.

In general, it's advisable to buy a ticket at least a few hours in advance or, if it's convenient, the day before departure. On weekends and holidays, and from December to February, this is always a good idea.

You don't always have to go to the rodoviária to buy your bus ticket. Selected travel agents in major cities sell long-distance bus tickets. This incurs no extra charges and can save you a long trip out to an often chaotic rodoviária.

TRAIN

There are very few railway passenger services in Brazil, and the trend to scale down or cut more and more services continues.

Enthusiasts should not despair, however, as there are still some interesting train rides. The Curitiba-Paranaguá train offers some unforgettable views, and the 13-km run from São João del Rei to Tiradentes, in Minas

BRAZIL

Gerais, is great fun. The trip from Campo Grande to Corumbá, which crosses the Pantanal, is popular with travellers.

TAXI

Taxis are reasonably priced, if not cheap, but you should be aware of various tricks used by some drivers to increase the charges.

Taxis in the large cities usually have meters, with prices subject to frequent updates. A *tabela* (price sheet) is used to convert the price on the meter to a new price. This is OK as long as the meter works and the tabela is legal and current (don't accept photocopies). Unless you are certain about a standard price for a standard trip (and have verified this with the driver), or you have purchased a ticket from a taxi ticket office (described later in this section), you must *insist* that drivers turn on their meters (no excuses) at the beginning of the ride and show you a valid tabela at the end.

What you see is what you pay – no extras if you've only loaded a couple of pieces of baggage per person, even if the driver thinks the trip to the town centre has required 'extra' fuel. If the meter doesn't work or the driver won't engage it, negotiate a fare before getting on board or find another cab. If you want to get a rough idea about the 'going rate' prior to taking a taxi ride into town, ask a newsagent or an official at the rodoviária, train station, airport etc.

As a general rule, Tarifa I (standard tariff) applies from approximately 6 am to 10 pm Monday to Saturday; Tarifa II (higher tariff) applies outside these hours, on holidays and outside city limits. Sometimes there is a standard charge, typically for the trip between the airport and the city centre. Many airports and rodoviárias now have a system that allows you to purchase a taxi ticket from a *bilheteria* (taxi ticket office). In many cases this ticketed fare is much more than you'd pay if you walked out onto the street and hailed a taxi at the regular metered rate. If you need an early morning taxi to the airport, ask drivers the day before about the going rate, and maybe arrange to be picked up.

The same general advice applies to taxis without meters. You *must* agree on the price beforehand, and make sure there is no doubt about it. Learn the numbers in Portuguese.

If the driver claims to have no change, hold firm and see if this is just a ploy to extract more from you. You can avoid this scenario by carrying change.

If possible, orient yourself before taking a taxi, and keep a map handy in case you find yourself being taken for a blatant detour. Never use taxi touts – an almost certain rip-off. The worst place to get a cab is wherever the tourists are, so don't hire a cab near one of the expensive hotels. In Rio, for example, walk a block away from the beach at Copacabana to flag down a cab. Many airports have special airport taxis, which are about 50% more expensive than a regular taxi. If you are carrying valuables, however, the special airport taxi or a radio-taxi can be a worthwhile investment. These are probably the safest taxis on the road.

For more tips on security see the Dangers & Annoyances information in the Facts for the Visitor chapter.

CAR & MOTORCYCLE

Driving in Brazil is hazardous – because it is not policed, because of the national cult of speed and because of the poor quality of the roads in many areas.

Car Rental

Renting a car is expensive, with prices similar to those in Europe. Familiar multinationals dominate the car rental business. Hiring a car is safe and easy if you have a driving licence, a credit card and a passport.

Shop around, as companies often have promotional deals and, in times of high inflation, some are slower to put up their prices than others.

Volkswagen Golfs and Fiat Unos are the cheapest cars to rent. If the rental companies claim to be out of these, shop around. Also, when you get prices quoted on the phone, make sure they include insurance, which is legally required.

The big companies have offices at the

airport in most cities, and often in the city centre as well.

Motorcycle

Hiring a bike is almost as expensive as hiring a car. If you want to buy a bike, Brazil manufactures its own, but they are also expensive.

Motorcycles are popular in Brazil, especially in and around the cities. Theft is a big problem, and as a result you can't even insure them. Most people keep their bike in a guarded place, at least overnight. For the traveller, this can be difficult to organise, but if you can manoeuvre around the practical problems Brazil is a great place to have a motorcycle.

HITCHING

Hitching in Brazil, with the possible exception of the Amazon and Pantanal areas, is difficult. The word for hitching in Portuguese is *carona*, so *'Pode dar carona?'* is 'Can you give me/us a lift?'. The best way to hitch is to wait at a petrol station or truck stop and talk to the drivers, but even this can be difficult. A few years back, there were several assaults on drivers by hitchhikers, and the government started making public announcements to discourage the giving of rides.

BOAT

Many travellers take a boat trip on the Amazon or one of Brazil's other rivers. The government-operated Empresa de Navegação da Amazônia (ENASA) has reduced its passenger-boat services, but private companies have improved their standards and virtually superseded ENASA for passenger transportation. For more suggestions about river travel see the Getting Around chapter.

LOCAL TRANSPORT

Local bus services tend to be pretty good, with a comprehensive network of routes. Municipal buses are usually frequent, and are always cheap and crowded. In most city buses, you enter at the back and exit from the front. Crime can be a problem on buses; for

tips about security and travel on local buses, see the Dangers & Annoyances section in the Facts for the Visitor chapter.

ORGANISED TOURS

Focus Tours (☎ (612) 892-7830, fax 892-0900), 14821 Hillside Lane, Burnsville, MN 55306, USA, is rated highly for its dedication to conservation and use of naturalists as guides. Tour destinations include the Pantanal (and Chapada das Guimarães); Minas Gerais; Amazon; Parque Nacional do Itatiaia; and Serra da Canastra.

Brazil Nuts (☎ toll-free (800) 553-9959), 79 Stanford St, Fairfield, CT 06430, USA, offers various packages to Brazil, including a 'Rio like a Native' programme that's been recommended by readers.

Rio de Janeiro State

The west coast, or Costa Verde, of Rio de Janeiro State is lined with hundreds of islands, which shelter the coast and make for easy swimming and boating.

Due north of Rio city, in the Serra dos Órgãos, are the mountain resort cities of Petrópolis and Teresópolis, and superb hiking and climbing in the Parque Nacional da Serra dos Órgãos.

The quiet and clean beaches east of Rio city are a welcome change from the famous beaches of Rio and Guanabara Bay, with their high-rise hotels and bars spilling out onto the sands.

RIO DE JANEIRO

The city of Rio de Janeiro is known as *'a cidade maravilhosa'* (the marvellous city). Jammed between ocean and escarpment are nine million *cariocas*, as the inhabitants are called. This makes Rio one of the most densely populated places on earth. Despite the city's enormous problems, the cariocas pursue pleasure like no other people. Carnaval is the best known expression of their dionysian spirit, but there are many others.

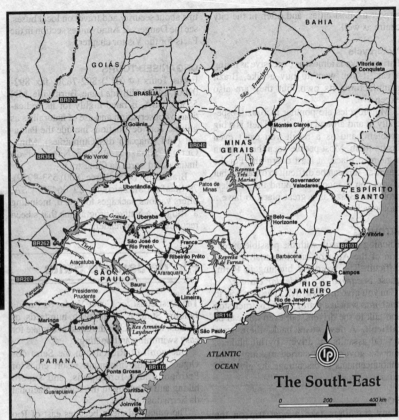

The South-East

History

A Portuguese navigator, Gaspar de Lemos, discovered Guanabara Bay in January 1502. He mistook the bay for a river, and named it Rio de Janeiro. The first settlement in the bay was established by the French under Nicolas de Villegagnon in 1555. Antarctic France, as it was called, was not a success, and despite the French alliance with the formidable Tamoio Indians, it fell to the Portuguese in 1560.

During the 17th century, Rio became an important sugar town and port. The city flourished with the gold rush in Minas Gerais at the beginning of the 18th century, and in 1763 it replaced Salvador as the colonial capital. Rio was the capital of independent Brazil until Brasília took over in 1960, but it remains the tourist capital of Brazil.

Orientation

Rio is divided into a *zona norte* (north zone) and a *zona sul* (south zone) by the Serra da Carioca, a steep mountain range in the Parque Nacional da Tijuca. Favelas cover steep hillsides on both sides of town.

Centro (the city centre) is all business

Rio de Janeiro

Linha Vermelha

Rod Washington

Avenida Brasil

Ilha do Raimundo

Aeroporto Galeão (International)

Est do Galeão

Ilha do Governador

Ilha d'Água

Ilha Seca

Penha

Olaria

Serra da Misericórdia

Bonsucesso

Av Uranos

Manguinhos

Ilha do Fundão

Ponte Presidente Arthur da Costa e Silva

Suburbana

Caju

São Christóvão

Baía de Guanabara

Avenida Brasil

Serra dos Pretos Forros

Vinte e Quatro de Mayo

Quinta da Boa Vista

Vila Isabel

Maracanã Soccer Stadium

Gamboa

Av Presidente Vargas

Av Rio Branco

Centro

Santa Teresa

See Central Rio Map

Aeroporto Santos Dumont

Serra dos Três Rios

Parque National da Tijuca

Andaraí

Rua Conde de Bonfim

Túnel Rebouças

See Glória, Catete & Flamengo Map

Glória

Catete

Praia do Flamengo

Flamengo

Rua Cosme Velho

Laranjeiras

Morro Dona Marta

Monumento do Cristo Redentor (709 m)

Estrada do Redentor

Estrada da Vista Chinesa

Estrada Dona Castorina

Botafogo

Sugar Loaf (396 m)

Copacabana

Est das Furnas

Estrada da Canoa

Jóquei Clube

Lagoa Rodrigo de Freitas

Praia de Copacabana

Est Velha

Leblon

Ipanema

Dois Irmãos

Av Niemeyer

Est da Gávea

São Conrado

Praia do Leblon

Praia de Ipanema

See Copacabana, Ipanema & Leblon Map

Praia do Vidigal

0   1.5   3 km

Minor Roads Not Shown

BRAZIL

during the day and absolutely deserted at night. The main airline offices are here, as are foreign consulates, Brazilian government agencies, money exchange houses, banks and travel agencies. The centre is also the site of the original settlement of Rio, and most of the city's important museums and colonial buildings are here.

Two wide avenues cross the centre: Avenida Rio Branco, where buses leave for the zona sul, and Avenida Presidente Vargas, which heads out to Maracaná football stadium and the zona norte. Rio's modern subway follows the route of these two avenues.

Information

Tourist Offices Riotur, the Rio city tourism agency, has a tourist information hotline called Âlo Riotur (☎ 542-8080 or 542-8004). Call it Monday to Friday, from 8 am to 6 pm, with any questions. The receptionists speak English and more often than not they'll be able to help you.

At Riotur's special 'tourist room' (☎ 541-7522), Avenida Princesa Isabel 183, Copacabana, you'll find free brochures (in Portuguese and English) which include maps. It's open Monday to Saturday from 9 am to 6 pm.

The Riotur booths at the airport and rodoviária can save you time and money: staff will phone around town and make your hotel reservation.

Money At the international airport, there are three exchange houses. In the centre of the city, on Avenida Rio Branco, there are several travel agencies/casas de câmbio (be cautious carrying money in the city centre). Most of the banks in the city have currency exchange facilities. There are also plenty of casas de câmbio in Copacabana and Ipanema.

You can get Visa cash advances at any large branch of the Banco do Brasil.

The American Express agent in Rio is Kontik-Franstur SA. It has two offices:

Botafogo
    Praia do Botafogo 228, Bloco A, sala 514 (☎ 552-7299)
Copacabana
    Avenida Atlântica 2316-A, CEP 20040 (☎ 235-1396); open for mail pick-up on weekdays from 9 am to 6 pm

Post & Communications Mail addressed to Posta Restante, Rio de Janeiro, Brazil, ends up at the post office at Rua 1 de Março 64, in the city. They hold mail for 30 days and are reasonably efficient.

Faxes and telexes can be sent from any large post office. Post offices usually open from 8 am to 6 pm weekdays and until noon on Saturday. The branch at the international airport is open 24 hours a day.

The telephone code for Rio de Janeiro is 021. International phone calls can be made from your hotel, direct or with operator assistance (☎ 00011), or from the following locations in Rio:

Aeroporto Santos Dumont
    open from 6 am to 11 pm
Centro
    Praça Tiradentes 41, open 24 hours
Copacabana
    Avenida NS de Copacabana 540 (upstairs), open 24 hours
Ipanema
    Rua Visconde de Pirajá111, open from 6 am to 11 pm
Rodoviária Novo Rio
    open 24 hours

Foreign Consulates The following countries have consulates in Rio:

Argentina
    Praia de Botafogo 228, 2nd floor, Botafogo (☎ 551-5198, fax 552-4191); Monday to Friday noon to 5 pm
Bolivia
    Avenida Rui Barbosa 664, No 101, Botafogo (☎ 551-1796, fax 551-3047); Monday to Friday 9 am to 1 pm
Canada
    Rua Lauro Muller 116, 1104 Botafogo (☎ 275-2137, fax 541-3898); Monday to Friday 9 am to 1 pm

Chile
Praia do Flamengo 344, 7th floor, Flamengo (☎ 552-5349, fax 553-0677); Monday to Friday 8.30 am to 12.30 pm

Colombia
Praia do Flamengo 284, No 101, Flamengo (☎ 552-5048; 552-5449); Monday to Friday 9 am to 1 pm

Ecuador
Avenida NS de Copacabana 788, 8th floor, Copacabana (☎ 235-6695, fax 255-2245); Monday to Friday 8.30 am to 1 pm

France
Avenida Presidente Antônio Carlos 58, 6th floor, Centro (☎ 210-1272, fax 240-8192); Monday to Friday 9 am to 12.30 pm

Germany
Rua Presidente Carlos de Campos 417, Laranjeiras (☎ 553-6777, fax 553-0184); Monday to Friday 8.30 to 11.20 am

Paraguay
Praia de Botafogo 242, 2nd floor, Botafogo (☎ 553-2294, fax 553-2512); Monday to Friday 9 am to 1 pm

Peru
Avenida Rui Barbosa 314, 2nd floor, Flamengo (☎ 551-9596, fax 551-9796); Monday to Friday 9 am to 1 pm

UK
Praia do Flamengo 284, 2nd floor, Flamengo (☎ 552-1422, fax 552-5796); Monday to Thursday 9 to 11.30 am and 1.30 to 3.30 pm, Friday 9 to 11.30 am

Uruguay
Praia de Botafogo 242, 6th floor, (☎ 553-6030, fax 551-5248); Monday to Friday 9 am to 1 pm

USA
Avenida Presidente Wilson 147, Centro (☎ 292-7117, fax 220-0439); Monday to Friday 8 am to 4.30 pm

Visa Extensions You can obtain visa extensions at the Polícia Marítima building (☎ 291-2142 ext 136), Avenida Venezuela 2, Centro (near the far end of Avenida Rio Branco), between 10 am and 3 pm. Bring a passport, money and airline ticket (if you have one). The fee is around US$12.

Bookshops Nova Livraria Leonardo da Vinci, Rio's best bookshop, is at Avenida Rio Branco 185 (one floor down, on the *sobreloja* level). A crowded shop, with knowledgeable staff and Rio's largest collection of foreign books, it's open from 9 am to 7 pm Monday to Friday, and from 10 am to 10 pm on weekends. Many newsstands in Centro, Copacabana and Ipanema carry foreign newspapers and magazines.

Emergency There are certain emergency phone numbers for which you don't need fichas to call from public phones: police (☎ 190), ambulance (☎ 192) and fire (☎ 193). There is a special police department for tourists called Rio Tourist Police (☎ 511-5112), open 24 hours at Avenida Afrânio de Melo Franco, Leblon, across the street from Scala.

Dangers & Annoyances Rio has a reputation for crime. Refer to Dangers & Annoyances in the Facts for the Visitor section earlier in this chapter.

Walking Tour
There's more to Rio than beaches. Take a bus or the metro to Cinelândia and **Praça Floriano**, the main square along Avenida Rio Branco, and the heart of Rio today. Praça Floriano comes to life at lunch time and after work, when the outdoor cafés are filled with beer drinkers, samba musicians and political debate.

Behind Praça Mahatma Gandhi, in the direction of the bay, the large aeroplane hangar is the **Museu de Arte Moderna** (Modern Art Museum). It's open Tuesday to Sunday from 1 to 7 pm. The museum grounds were designed by Brazil's most famous landscape architect, Burle Marx (who landscaped Brasília).

The most impressive building on Praça Floriano is the **Teatro Municipal**, home of Rio's opera, orchestra and gargoyles. The theatre was built in 1905, and renovated in 1934 under the influence of the Paris Opéra. The front doors are rarely open, but you can visit the ostentatious Assyrian Room Restaurant & Bar downstairs (entrance on Avenida Rio Branco). Built in the 1930s, it's completely covered in tiles, with beautiful mosaics.

On Avenida Rio Branco, you'll also find the **Museu Nacional de Belas Artes**, housing some of Brazil's best paintings. The

BRAZIL

BRAZIL

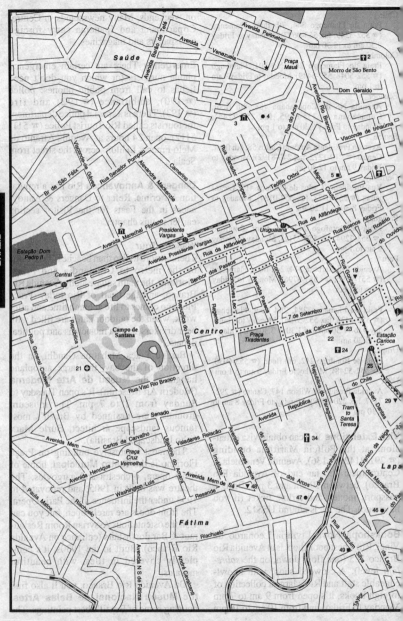

Saúde

Avenida Perimetral

Avenida Venezuela

Praça Mauá

1

2

Morro de São Bento

Dom Geraldo

Visconde de Inhaúma

Avenida Barão de Tefé

Avenida Rio Branco

Rua do Acre

3

4

Rua Senador Pompeu

Teófilo Otôni

Miguel Couto

5

6

Rua Buenos Aires

do Rosário

do Ouvidor

Rua da Alfândega

Uruguaiana

7

Presidente Vargas

Avenida Marechal Floriano

Estação Dom Pedro II

Central

Avenida Presidente Vargas

Rua da Alfândega

Senhor dos Passos

Regente

Rua Visconde Gávea

Br de São Félix

Rua Senador Pompeu

Alexandre Mackenzie

Camerino

Rua General Caldwell

República

República do Líbano

Campo de Santana

Centro

Praça Tiradentes

22

23

24

25

Estação Carioca

19

i

7 de Setembro

Rua da Carioca

Avenida Passos

Gonçalves Ledo

da Conceição

Avenida Passos

Rua Gonçalves Dias

Rua da Carioca

do Chile

Tram to Santa Teresa

Museu de Arte Moderna

Rua Visc Rio Branco

Senado

Avenida

República

República do Paraguai

29

33

Avenida Mem

Carlos de Carvalho

Ubaldino do Amaral

Praça Cruz Vermelha

Avenida Henrique

Paula Matos

Washington Luís

Valadares Relação

dos Inválidos

Avenida Gomes Freire

34

Evaristo da Veiga

Lapa

das Marrecas

do Lavradio

dos Arcos

dos Prainhas

46

Avenida Mem de Sá

Resende

48

47

Rua Joaquim Silva

Teotonio

da Lapa

49

Avenida André Cavalcanti

Avenida N S de Fátima

Fátima

Riachuelo

Riachuelo

Central Rio

Ilha das Cobras

Ilha Fiscal

0   250   500 m

Baía de Guanabara

Ferry to Niterói & Ilha de Paquetá

16 ▼

(Perimetral)

da Misericórdia

26 🏛

Castelo

Avenida Presidente Antônio Carlos

Avenida General Justo

Aeroporto Santos Dumont

Avenida Churchill

Ave Franklin Roosevelt

36 ■

30

Trevo dos Estudantes

Avenida Alm Silvio de Noronha

Parque do Flamengo

50

51

PLACES TO STAY
5 Guanabara Palace Hotel
36 Aeroporto Othon Hotel
38 Itajuba Hotel
39 Nelba Hotel
49 Hotel Marajó

PLACES TO EAT
16 Restaurante Alba Mar
19 Confeitaria Colombo
22 Bar Luis
29 Suco (Juice) Bars
32 Cheio de Vida
33 Macrobiótica
35 Outdoor Cafés & Political Debating
40 Churrascolndia Restaurante
41 Lanchonete Bariloche
48 Bar Brasil

OTHER
1 Polícia Marítima (Visa Extensions)
2 Igreja São Bento
3 Palcio da Conceicao
4 Fortaleza da Conceicao
6 Igreja NS da Candelaria
7 Palcio Itamaraty
8 Post Office
9 Igreja e Museu da Santa Cruz dos Militares
10 Igreja da Lapa
11 Chafariz da Piramide
12 Praa Quinze de Novembro
13 Igreja e Museu do Carmo
14 Paço Imperial
15 Museu Naval e Oceanogrfico
17 Igreja de São Jos
18 TurisRio & Riotur Tourist Offices
20 Riotur Booth
21 Hospital Estadual Souza Aguiar
23 Casa Oliveira
24 Convento de Santo Antnio
25 Crafts Market
26 Museu Histórico Nacional
27 Museu Nacional de Belas Artes
28 Teatro Municipal
30 Praa Ana Amelía
31 Suburban Dreams
34 Catedral de San Sebastiãn
37 Buses to Southern Suburbs: Flamengo, Copacabana etc
42 Praa Floriano
43 US Consulate
44 Varig/Cruzeiro Airlines Main Office
45 Praa Mahatma Gandhi
46 Escola da Música
47 Circo Voador
50 Museu de Arte Moderna
51 Museu dos Mortos da Segunda Guerra Mundial

most important gallery is the Galeria de Arte Brasileira, with 20th-century classics such as Cândido Portinari's *Café*. The museum is open Tuesday to Friday from 10 am to 5.30 pm, and on weekends and holidays from 3 to 6 pm. Photography is prohibited.

Head back to the other side of the Teatro Municipal and walk down the pedestrian-only Avenida 13 de Maio (on your left are some of Rio's best suco bars). Cross a street and you're in the Largo da Carioca. Up on the hill is the recently restored **Convento de Santo Antônio**. The church's sacristy, which dates from 1745, has some beautiful jacaranda-wood carving and *azulejos* (Portuguese ceramic tiles with a distinctive blue glaze). The original church here was started in 1608, making it Rio's oldest.

If you have time for a side trip, consider heading over to the nearby *bondinho* (little tram) that goes up to **Santa Teresa**, a beautiful neighbourhood of cobblestone streets and old homes. The tram goes from the corner of Avenida República do Chile and Senador Dantas, over the old aqueduct, to Santa Teresa. The Museu Chácara do Céu, Rua Murtinho Nobre 93, has a good collection of art and antiques. Favelas down the hillsides have made this a high-crime area; don't take valuables.

Returning to the centre, find the shops along 19th-century **Rua da Carioca**. The old wine and cheese shop has some of Brazil's best cheese, and bargains in Portuguese and Spanish wines. Two shops sell fine instruments made in Brazil, including all the Carnaval rhythm-makers, which make great gifts: try Casa Oliveira, at Rua da Carioca 70. There are several good jewellery shops off Rua da Carioca, on Rua Ramalho Ortigão.

When you get to Rua da Carioca 39, stop at the **Bar Luis** for a draught beer and lunch or snack. Rio's longest running restaurant (opened in 1887), Bar Luis was called Bar Adolf until WW II. For decades, many of Rio's intellectuals have chewed the fat here while drinking the best chopp in Centro.

At the end of the block, you'll pass the **Cinema Iris**, once Rio's most elegant theatre, and emerge into the hustle of Praça

Tiradentes. It's easy to see that this used to be a fabulous part of the city. On opposite sides of the square are the **Teatro João Caetano** and the **Teatro Carlos Gomez**, which present plays and dance performances. The narrow streets in this part of town house many old, mostly dilapidated, small buildings. It's worth exploring along Rua Buenos Aires as far as **Campo de Santana**, then returning along Rua da Alfândega to Avenida Rio Branco. Campo de Santana is a pleasant park, once the scene – re-enacted in every Brazilian classroom – of Emperor Dom Pedro I, King of Portugal, proclaiming Brazil's independence from Portugal.

Back near Avenida Rio Branco, at Rua Gonalves Dias 30, hit the ornate **Confeitaria Colombo** for coffee and turn-of-the-century Vienna. Offering succour to shopping-weary matrons since 1894, the Colombo is best for coffee (very strong) and desserts.

From here, cross Avenida Rio Branco, go down Rua da Assembléia to **Praça Quinze de Novembro**. In the square is the **Pyramid Fountain**, built in 1789, and a **crafts market**. Facing the bay, on your right is the **Paço Imperial**, which was the imperial palace. With independence it was ingloriously relegated to the Department of Telegraphs, but it has recently been restored. It's now a popular cultural centre.

On the opposite side of the square is the historic **Arco de Teles**, running between two buildings. The shops along the stone streets here have a waterfront character. There are several seafood restaurants, fishing supply shops and a couple of simple colonial churches. It's a colourful area.

Back at Praça Quinze de Novembro, take the overpass to the **waterfront**, where ferries and hydrofoils leave to **Niterói** and **Ilha da Paquetá**. The ferry to Niterói takes only 15 minutes and you never have to wait long. Consider crossing the bay and walking around central Niterói if you have some time (the feel is different from Rio – much more like the rest of Brazil). Even if you return immediately, the trip is worth it just for the view.

When you're facing the bay, **Restaurant Alba Mar** is a few hundred metres to your right. It's in a green gazebo overlooking the bay. The food is good and the atmosphere just right. On Saturday the building is surrounded by the tents of the **Feira de Antiguidades**, a strange and fun hodgepodge of antiques, clothes, foods and other odds and ends.

If you want to extend your walking tour, go back through Arco de Teles and follow the street around toward Rua 1 de Março. Walk up along the right-hand side and you'll come to the **Centro Cultural do Banco do Brasil** (CCBB). Go in and have a look at the building and any of the current exhibitions. Most are free. Then have a look behind the CCBB at the **Casa França-Brasil**, another cultural centre with temporary exhibitions. From there, you'll be able to see the **Igreja NS de Candelária**. Have a look inside and then keep going up Rua 1 de Março, through the naval area, to Rua Dom Geraldo, the last street before the hill. **Mosteiro de São Bento** is on top of the hill. To get there, go to Rua Dom Geraldo 40 and take the lift to the 5th floor. From Rua Dom Geraldo, head back toward Avenida Rio Branco, and try to imagine that in 1910 it was the Champs-Élysées of Rio – a tree-lined boulevard, with pavement cafes.

Sugar Loaf

Pão de Açúcar (Sugar Loaf), God's gift to the picture postcard industry, is dazzling. Two cable cars lift you 396 metres above Rio and the Baía de Guanabara. Sunset on a clear day provides the most spectacular ascent. Avoid going between 10 and 11 am or between 2 and 3 pm, when most tourist buses arrive.

The two-stage cable cars (☎ 295-8244) leave about every half-hour from Praça General Tibúrcio, at Praia Vermelha in Urca. They operate daily from 8 am to 10 pm and cost US$11.50. On top of the lower hill, there's a restaurant/theatre with some excellent musicians; check the local papers for listings.

To get to Sugar Loaf, take an Urca bus (No 107) from Centro and Flamengo or bus No

500, 511 or 512 from the zona sul. The open-air bus that runs along the Ipanema and Copacabana beaches also goes to Sugar Loaf.

Corcovado & Cristo Redentor

Corcovado (Hunchback) is the mountain (709 metres), and *Cristo Redentor* (Christ the Redeemer) is the statue on the peak; the views from here are spectacular. The statue, with its welcoming outstretched arms, stands 30 metres high and weighs over 1000 tonnes.

Corcovado lies within the Parque Nacional da Tijuca. You are strongly advised to resist the temptation to walk to the top, as there's a good chance you will be robbed. You can get there by car or by taxi, but the best way is to go up in the cog train; sit on the right-hand side going up, for the view. The round trip costs US$16.50 and leaves from Rua Cosme Velho 513 (Cosme Velho). You can get a taxi there (ask to go to the *estrada de ferro Corcovado)*; a Rua Cosme Velho bus (No 184 or 180) from Centro; a bus No 583 from Largo Machado, Copacabana and Ipanema; or a bus No 584 from Leblon.

During the high season, the trains, which only leave every half-hour, can be slow going. Corcovado, and the train, are open from 8.30 am to 6.30 pm.

Parque Nacional da Tijuca

In 15 minutes you can go from the concrete jungle of Copacabana to the exuberant green tropical jungle of Parque Nacional da Tijuca (120 sq km), a good place for picnics, walking and climbing.

The entire park closes at sunset and is heavily policed. Several readers have reported being robbed here: don't go alone. It's best to go by car, but if you can't, catch a No 221, 233 or 234 bus from Centro to Alto da Boa Vista, at the heart of the forest. An alternative route is to take the metro to Saens Peña and then any Barra da Tijuca bus; these pass the main entrance to the park.

Jardim Botânico

At Rua Jardim Botânico 920, the botanical garden was planted by order of Prince Regent Dom João in 1808. Quiet and serene on weekdays, the botanical garden blossoms with families and music on weekends. The Amazonas section, with a lake containing huge *Victoria regia* water lilies, is a highlight. The garden is open daily from 8 am to 5 pm. Entry costs US$1.50. Take insect repellent.

To get there catch a Jardim Botânico bus: No 170 from Centro; or No 571, 572 or 594 from the zona sul.

Museums

Museu Nacional This museum, at Quinta da Boa Vista, São Cristóvão, was once the palace of the emperors of Brazil. It's now a natural history museum, and has some interesting exhibits: dinosaur fossils, sabre-tooth tiger skeletons, beautiful pieces of pre-Columbian ceramics from Peru, a huge meteorite, stuffed wildlife, gory displays of tropical diseases and exhibits on the peoples of Brazil. The museum is open Tuesday to Sunday from 10 am to 5 pm; admission is about US$1 (free on Thursday). Rio's **zoo** is just behind the museum, and worth a visit. To get there, take the metro from Centro to São Cristóvão, or catch bus No 472 or 474 either from Centro or from the zona sul.

Museu do Folclore Edson Carneiro At Rua do Catete 181, Catete, is a small gem of a museum with excellent displays of folk art, a folklore library and a small bookshop which sells folk music records. It's open Tuesday to Friday from 11 am to 6 pm, and on weekends and holidays from 3 to 6 pm.

Museu da República & Palácio do Catete The Museu da República and the Palácio do Catete have been wonderfully restored. Built between 1858 and 1866, and easily distinguished by the bronze eagles on the eaves, the palace was occupied by the president of Brazil from 1896 until 1954, when Getúlio Vargas killed himself here. The museum, which occupies the palace, has a good collection of art and artefacts from the republican period. It's open Tuesday to

Friday from noon to 5 pm. Admission costs US$0.50.

Beaches

Rio is, of course, famous for its beaches. The beach is a ritual and a way of life for the carioca, and every 20 metres of coastline is populated by a different group of regulars. Some beaches, like Copacabana, are more notorious for theft than others, but wherever you go, don't take valuables. It's also not a good idea to walk down by the water at night.

Sweeping round south-east from the centre, the beaches are Flamengo, Botafogo, Leme, Copacabana, Arpoador, Ipanema, Leblon, Vidigal, Pepino and Barra da Tijuca. The last two are less crowded, and cleaner.

Copacabana Perhaps the world's most famous beach, it runs for 4.5 km in front of one of the world's most densely populated residential areas. There's always something happening on the beach during the day and on the footpaths at night: drinking, singing, eating and all kinds of people checking out the scene.

Ipanema This is Rio's richest and most chic beach. There isn't quite the frenzy of Copacabana. Ipanema is an Indian word for dangerous, bad waters: the waves can get big and the undertow is often strong, so be careful, and swim only where the locals are swimming.

Different parts of the beach attract different crowds. Posto nine is 'Girl from Ipanema' beach, right off Rua Vinícius de Morais. Today it's also known as the Cemetério dos Elefantes, because of the old leftists, hippies and artists who hang out there. The Farme de Armoedo, also called Land of Marlboro, at Rua Farme de Armoedo, is the gay section. In front of the Caesar Park Hotel there's a very young crowd.

Carnaval

Rio's glitzy Carnaval has become a big tourist attraction. More than anywhere else in Brazil, it is a spectator event, but it's a fantastic spectacle nonetheless. Every year, wealthy and spaced-out foreigners descend on Rio en masse, get drunk, get high, bag some sunrays and exchange exotic diseases. Everyone gets a bit unstuck and there are lots of car accidents. Apartment rates and taxi fares triple and quadruple, and some thieves, in keeping with the spirit of the season, rob in costume.

A couple of months before Carnaval starts, rehearsals at the *escolas de samba* (samba clubs) are open to visitors on Saturdays. These are usually in the favelas. They're fun to watch, but for your safety, go with a carioca.

The escolas de samba are, in fact, pre-dated by *bandas* (nonprofessional equivalents of the escolas de samba), which are now returning to the Carnaval scene as part of the movement to bring Rio's Carnaval back to the streets. The bandas are great fun, a good place to loosen up your hip joints for samba, and excellent photo opportunities; transvestites always keep the festivities entertaining.

Riotur has information on the scheduled bandas, or you could just show up in Ipanema (many of them are in Ipanema), at Praça General Osório or at Praça Paz around 5 pm or so, a couple of weekends before official Carnaval. Other street festivities are held in Centro, on Avenida Rio Branco.

Carnaval balls are surreal and erotic events. Tickets go on sale about two weeks before Carnaval starts, and the balls are held nightly for the week preceding Carnaval and through Carnaval. Scala (☎ 239-4448, US$40) in Leblon, Canecão (☎ 295-3055, US$40) in Botafogo, and Help disco in Copacabana (US$20), host some of the cheaper, wilder balls. If you go, don't take more money than you're willing to lose.

Tickets go on sale about two weeks before Carnaval starts and the balls are held nightly for the week preceding Carnaval and through Carnaval. Buy a copy of the *Veja* magazine with the Veja Rio insert. It has details of all the balls and bandas.

The 16 top-level samba schools prepare all year for an hour of glory in the Sambódromo, a stadium on Rua Maquis Sapucaí.

BRAZIL

The extravaganza starts around 7 pm and goes until 9 am the next day. Many tickets are sold a month in advance of the event. Getting tickets at the legitimate prices can be tough; people queue up for hours, and travel agents and scalpers snap up the best seats. But if you show up at the Sambódromo at about midnight, three or four hours into the show, you can get tickets at the grandstand for about US$10. It's safer to take the metro than the bus, and it's fun to check out the paraders in their costumes. The metro runs 24 hours a day during Carnaval.

By the way, there's nothing to stop you taking part in the parade. Most samba schools are happy to include foreigners. All you need is between US$200 and US$300 for your costume and you're in. It helps to arrive in Rio a week or two in advance to get this organised. Ask at the hotel how to go about it. It usually takes just a few phone calls.

The starting dates for the Carnaval parade in coming years are: 9 February 1997, 22 February 1998, 14 February 1999 and 5 March 2000.

Places to Stay

Reservations are a good idea, especially if you plan to stay in a mid-range or top-end hotel. Not only does it ensure you a room, you can save up to 30% by booking in advance. During the off season, you can also get good discounts on hotels in Copacabana and Ipanema by booking through a travel agent in Rio after you arrive. Andesol Turismo (☎ 541-0748), run by English-speaking Gustav Kirby, is recommended. It's at Avenida NS de Copacabana 209.

Hostels *Chave do Rio de Janeiro* (☎ 286-0303, fax 246-5553), in Botafogo, is Rio's only official YHA hostel. You'll meet lots of young Brazilians here from all over the country. It gets busy, so you need to make reservations during peak holiday times. The only problem with this place is its location, but if you get the hang of the buses quickly, it shouldn't hamper you too much. From the rodoviária catch bus No 170, 171 or 172 and

get off after the Largo dos Leões. Go up Rua Voluntários da Pátria until Rua General Dionísio, then turn left. The hostel is at No 63.

Unofficial hostels include the *Copacabana Praia Youth Hostel* (☎ 237-5422), at Rua Tenente Marones de Gusmão 85. Although a few blocks from the beach, it's still good value. A relaxed and friendly place, it charges US$12 per person, and US$30 for double apartments with a stove and a refrigerator. There's no sign, but it's easy to find. Another hostel in Copacabana is the *Copacabana Chalé* (☎ 236-0047), at Rua Pompeu Loureira 99. It's closer to the beach.

Hotels The best area for budget hotels is the Glória, Catete and Flamengo district. Hotels here are often full from December to February, so reservations are not a bad idea.

From Glória to Lapa, on the edge of the business district, near the aqueduct, there are several more budget hotels. In general, these are more run-down but hardly any cheaper, and the area is less safe at night. If, however, everything else is booked up, you'll see several hotels if you walk along Rua Joaquim Silva (near the Passeio Público), then over to Avenida Mem de Sá, turn up Avenida Gomes Freire, then right to Praça Tiradentes. The *Hotel Marajó*, Avenida Joaquim Silva 99, is recommended. It has single quartos for US$12 and double apartamentos for US$18.

Glória The *Hotel Turístico* (☎ 225-9388), Ladeira da Glória 30, is one of Rio's most popular budget hotels, and there are always plenty of gringos staying here. It's across from the Glória metro station, 30 metres up the street that emerges between two pavement restaurants. The rooms are clean and safe, with small balconies. The hotel is often full but does take reservations. Singles/doubles start at US$20/25 for quartos, US$25/30 for apartamentos.

Right near the Glória metro station, the *Hotel Benjamin Constant*, Rua Benjamin Constant 10, is one of the cheapest places around. The rooms are small and dingy but cost only US$5 per person.

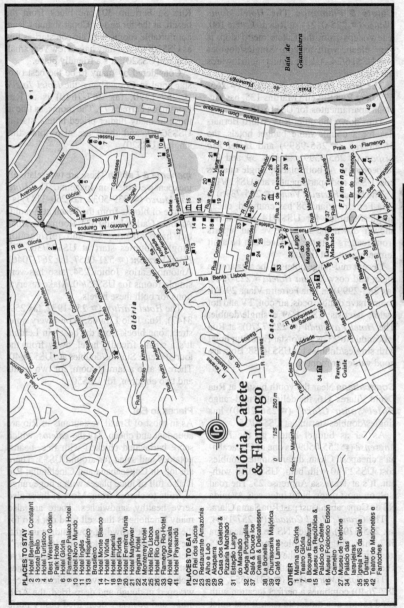

Glória, Catete & Flamengo

PLACES TO STAY
2 Hotel Benjamin Constant
3 Hostel Bello
4 Hotel Turístico
5 Best Western Golden Park Hotel
6 Hotel Glória
9 Flamengo Palace Hotel
10 Hotel Novo Mundo
11 Hotel Inglês
13 Hotel Hispânico
14 Brasileiro
17 Hotel Monte Blanco
18 Hotel Vitória
19 Hotel Imperial
20 Hotel Flórida
21 Hotel Ferreira Viana
22 Regina Hotel
24 Monterrey Hotel
25 Hotel Rio Lisboa
26 Hotel Rio Claro
33 Flamengo Rio Hotel
40 Hotel Venezuela
41 Hotel Paysandú

PLACES TO EAT
12 O Rei dos Sucos
23 Restaurante Amazônia
28 Alho e Leo
29 Alcaparra
30 Casa dos Galetos & Pizzaria Machado
31 Estação Largo do Machado
32 Adega Portuguesa
37 Salé & Douce Ice Cream & Delicatessen
38 La Bonelle
39 Churrascaria Majórica
43 Café Lamas

OTHER
1 Marina da Glória
7 Teatro Glória
8 Bosque Escultura
15 Museu da República & Palácio do Catete
16 Museu Folclórico Edson Carneiro
27 Museu de Telefone
34 Palácio das Laranjeiras
35 Igreja NS da Glória
36 Glória NS da Glória
42 Teatro de Marionetes e Fantoches

Baía de Guanabara

Praia do Flamengo

Flamengo

BRAZIL

0   125   250 m

BRAZIL

Catete & Flamengo The *Hotel Monte Blanco* (☎ 225-0121), at Rua do Catete 160, a few steps from the Catete metro stop, is very clean, with air-con. Singles/doubles cost US$16/24. Ask for a quiet room towards the back.

The *Hotel Hispánico Brasileiro* (☎ 265-5990), at Rua Silveira Martins 135, has big, clean apartamentos for US$16/18.

Turn down the quiet Rua Arturo Bernardes for a couple more budget hotels, the *Monterrey* (☎ 265-9899) and *Hotel Rio Lisboa* (☎ 265-9599), at Nos 39 and 29, respectively. At both places, single quartos cost US$8 and apartamentos are US$13/17.

The *Hotel Ferreira Viana* (☎ 205-7396) at Rua Ferreira Viana 58 has cramped, cheap singles/doubles for US$9/14 with a hot shower down the hall. We've had reports from readers that the manager can be a bit temperamental at times.

Decent mid-range hotels in the area are the clean and cosy *Regina Hotel* (☎ 225-7280, fax 285-2999), at Rua Ferreira Viana 29. All rooms have double beds, air-con, TV and hot water; it costs US$31/39 a single/double. The *Hotel Paysandú* (☎ 225-7270), at Rua Paiçandú No 23, is a two-star Embratur hotel with singles/doubles for US$34/38. Both are good value for money.

Copacabana Near the youth hostel, at Rua Décio Vilares 316, the delightful mid-range *Hotel Santa Clara* (☎ 256-2650) has singles/doubles starting at US$30/35.

As far as budget hotels go the *Hotel Angrense* (☎ 255-0509) is one of Copacabana's cheapest. Clean, dreary singles/doubles cost US$25/40 with bath, US$20/30 without. It's at Travessa Angrense 25. The road isn't on most maps, but it intersects Avenida NS de Copacabana just past Rua Santa Clara.

The *Grande Hotel Canada* (☎ 257-1864, fax 255-3705), Avenida NS de Copacabana 687, has singles/doubles for US$33/45 (there is no elevator for the cheapest rooms). The rooms are modern, with air-con and TV.

The *Hotel Martinique* (☎ 521-4552, fax 287-7640) combines a perfect location with good rooms at a moderate cost. It's at quiet Rua Sá Ferreira 30, one block from the beach, at the far end of Copacabana. Clean, comfortable rooms with air-con start as low as US$30/40, and they have a few very small singles (US$20). It's a friendly place.

Considered by many to be the best two-star hotel in Copacabana, the *Hotel Toledo* (☎ 257-1990, fax 287-7640) is at Rua Domingos Ferreira 71. The rooms, as fine as those in many higher priced hotels, start at US$36/40, and there are also some tiny singles (US$20).

Ipanema & Leblon There are two relatively inexpensive hotels in Ipanema. The *Hotel São Marco* (☎ 239-5032, fax 259-3147) is a couple of blocks from the beach at Avenida Antônio Carlos Jobim 524. Rooms are small but have air-con, TV and refrigerator. Singles/doubles start at US$25/30. The *Hotel Vermont* (☎ 521-0057, fax 267-7046), Antônio Carlos Jobim 254, also has very simple rooms for US$35/40. Make reservations for both these hotels.

The *Hotel Carlton* (☎ 259-1932, fax 259-3147), Rua João Lira 68, is on a very quiet street, one block from the beach in Leblon. It's a small, friendly hotel, away from the tourist scene. Singles/doubles are US$35/40. There is also a family room, for two adults and two children, for US$50.

Places to Eat

As in most of Brazil, restaurants in Rio are abundant and cheap. Try the *galetos*, which serve barbecued chicken with rice, beans, potatoes and salad for around US$5. There are lots in Copacabana and Cinelândia. Rio is also full of juice places with a huge range of fruits to choose from. Most of these also serve healthy sandwiches. There are also many lanchonetes that sell food por kilo for the lunchtime crowd. If your budget is tight, these are the places to look for. If you don't feel like a big lunch, lanchonetes also serve tasty snacks called *salgados*. Popular ones include the *coxinha*, savoury chicken pieces wrapped in dough and deep-fried, the Arab *quibe* and *pasteis* – deep-fried pastry puffs with cheese, mincemeat or *palmitos* (palm hearts) inside.

If you want a little more atmosphere without paying too much, try one of Rio's traditional places mentioned below.

Make a habit of asking for an *embalagem* (doggie bag) when you don't finish your food. Wrap it and hand it to a street person.

Centro *Bar Luis*, Rua da Carioca 39, is a Rio institution that opened in 1887. The city's oldest *cervejaria* (public house), on Rio's oldest street, is a bar-less old dining room serving good German food and dark draught beer at moderate prices. It's open Monday to Saturday for lunch and dinner until 11 pm.

Confeiteria Colombo is at Rua Gonçalves Dias 34, one block from and parallel to Rio Branco. It's an ornate Viennese coffee house/ restaurant where you can sit down for a meal, or stand if you're just having a dessert or cake. The Colombo is best for coffee and cake or a snack. During the week it has a reasonably priced lunch buffet.

The green gazebo structure near the Niterói ferry is *Restaurante Alba Mar* (☎ 240-8378) at Praça Marechal Âncora 184. It looks out on the Baía de Guanabara and Niterói. Go for the view and the seafood. It stays open from 11.30 am to 10 pm Monday to Saturday. Dishes start at US$10 and the peixe brasileira is recommended.

Cheio de Vida is a reasonably priced place in the centre at Avenida 13 de Maio 33, 403. It's not the easiest place to find, but it's worth the effort. The food there has a 'natural' touch. Try the zucchini pizza.

Cinelândia *Macrobiótica* (☎ 220-7585) is one floor up at Rua Embaixador Regis de Oliveira 7. Macrobiotic food is pretty popular in Brazil's cities and the dishes here are inexpensive and simple. Try the soup and rice dishes. It's open Monday to Friday from 11 am to 5.45 pm.

Lanchonete Bariloche is at Rua Alcindo Guanabara 24-D, across from Rua Senador Dantas. This cheap little counter joint has wood-grilled steaks for US$7 and is open until 2 am.

Lapa & Santa Teresa *Bar Brasil* at Rua Mem de Sá 90 in Lapa, is similar to Bar Luis in Centro. It's a traditional bar/restaurant with decent German food. It's open weekdays from 11.30 am to 11 pm and Saturday from 11.30 am to 3 pm. In Santa Teresa at Rua Almirante Alexandrino 316-B, *Bar do Arnaudo* serves Rio's best North-Eastern food. The carne do sol is excellent and cheap. It's closed on Monday.

Catete & Largo do Machado There are lots of options in the Largo do Machado area. Some cariocas feel that this is the best part of Rio for food fans. On Largo do Machado, *Estação Largo do Machado* has good fish, while *Casa dos Galetos*, on Rua Catete, is good for chicken and steak, and has reasonable salad. Also on Catete, *Pizzaria Machado* has a pasta rodízio for lunch on weekdays. *Adega Portugália*, Largo do Machado 30-A, is an Iberian-style bar and restaurant, with garlic and meat hanging from the ceiling and wine bulging off the shelves. It serves various fish and meat dishes that vary from the usual Rio fare. Try the bolinhos de bacalhau (cod-fish balls) for US$0.50 each with a Portuguese wine. *Restaurant Amazónia* (☎ 225-4622) at Rua do Catete 234 has good steak and a tasty broiled chicken with creamed-corn sauce, both for about US$10.

For an early morning (or late afternoon) juice in Catete, you can't go past *O Rei dos Sucos* (The King of Juices) on the corner of Rua Catete and Rua Silveira Martins. It has a top range of fruits, including a lot of Amazonian ones with hard-to-pronounce names.

Botafogo & Flamengo David, the owner of *Rajmahal* (☎ 541-6999) at General Polidoro 29, Botafogo, is British, but the food is all Indian and quite good. Meals cost about US$10 and the place is a bit off the beaten path. The restaurant is spacious and refreshingly calm for Rio. It's open in the evening from Tuesday to Sunday.

Café Lamas at Rua Marques de Abrantes 18-A, Flamengo, has been operating since 1874 and is one of Rio's most renowned

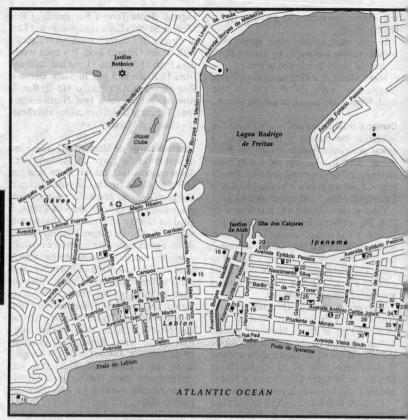

eateries. It has a lively and loyal clientele and is open for lunch and dinner with a typical meaty menu and standard prices; try the grilled linguiça, or filet mignon.

Copacabana *Lope's Confeiteria* at Avenida NS de Copacabana 1334, off Júlio de Castilhos, is an excellent lanchonete with big portions and little prices for typical Brazilian food.

Restaurante Lucas at Avenida Atlântica 3744 is across from Rua Sousa Lima and has reasonably priced German dishes starting at US$6.

Mab's, on Avenida Atlântica (the Copaca-bana side of Princesa Isabel, across from the Meridien), has excellent seafood soup in a crock, chock-full of piping hot creepy-crawlies, for US$8.

Cervantes is Rio's best sandwich joint and is also a late-night hang-out for a strange and colourful crew. It's on the infamous Avenida Prado Junior, where everyone and every-thing goes at night. Meat sandwiches come with pineapple (US$5). The steaks and fries are excellent too.

Ipanema *Via Farme* (☎ 227-0743) at Rua Farme de Amoedo 47 offers a good plate of pasta at a reasonable price, something which

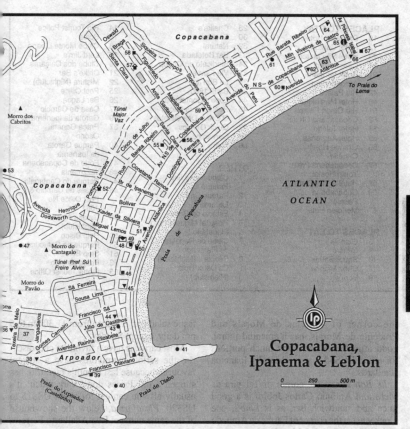

ATLANTIC
OCEAN

Copacabana, Ipanema & Leblon

0   250   500 m

is usually hard to find. The four-cheese pasta and the seafood pasta are excellent and portions are large enough for two to share. Most dishes are less than US$10. It's open from noon to 2 am.

After a day at Ipanema beach, you can stroll over to *Barril 1800*, on the beachfront at the corner of Avenida Vieira Souto and Avenida Rainha Elizabete. It's open late into the night and is for people-meeting and watching. The *Shell Station* across the street from Barril has Babushka's terrific ice cream.

Boni's, Antônio Carlos Jobim 595, is a favourite for fast food. Excellent pastries and

fresh coffee that's strong enough to turn Bambi into Godzilla. *Chaika's*, Antônio Carlos Jobim 321, is open from 8 am to 2 pm. This is where the girl from Ipanema really eats. There's a stand-up fast-food bar, and a restaurant at the back with good hamburgers, pastries and cappuccinos (a rarity in Rio). Chaika's stays busy late into the night.

Natural (☎ 267-7799) at Rua Barão da Torre 171 is a very natural health-food restaurant which has an inexpensive lunch special with soup, rice, vegies and beans, for less than US$5. Other good dishes are pancakes with chicken or vegetables.

Esquina, a 24-hour bar and restaurant at

BRAZIL

the corner of Vinícius de Morais and Prudente de Morais, has a splendid mural, good atmosphere and huge lunch portions for around US$5 – very cheap by Ipanema standards.

Le Bon Jus at the corner of Teixeira de Melo and Antônio Carlos Jobim is a good juice and sandwich bar, as is *Lino's*, one block west at the corner of Farme de Amoedo and Antônio Carlos Jobim. Readers recommend the 'heavenly' sucos.

Chez Michou, Rua Paul Redfern 44, is a popular crêperie with a young crowd. It stays open till 4 am, but is closed on Tuesday.

Leblon *Sabor Saúde*, Avenida Ataulfo de Paiva 630, is Rio's best health-food emporium and is open daily from 8.30 am to 10.30 pm. It has two restaurants: downstairs has good meals for US$6, while upstairs is more expensive (there are great buffet feasts for US$8). There's also a small grocery store and takeaway counter.

Celeiro, Rua Dias Ferreira 199, has a fantastic salad bar. It's open from 11.30 am to 5 pm daily, except Sunday.

Most cariocas have a favourite churrascaria; the serious carnivores have a current favourite because last month's favourite has slipped a bit. Prices don't vary much: it's usually all you can eat for about US$15 to US$20. *Plataforma*, below the showhouse of the same name at Rua Adalberto Ferreira 32, is one of the best. It's always busy late at night and is a big hang-out for actors and musicians. The restaurant is open from 11 am to 1 am daily.

Gávea *Guimas* (☎ 259-7996), José Roberto Macedo Soares 5, is a favourite. It's not cheap, but the prices (US$20 to US$30 per person) are fair for the outstanding cuisine you're served. Guimas offers what most restaurants in Rio lack: creative cooking. Try the pernil de carneiro (lamb with onions) or the Oriental shrimp curry and a Rio salad. The small but comfortable open-air restaurant opens at 8 pm and gets very crowded later in the evening. If you order one of the boa lembrança specials, you'll receive an attractive ceramic plate. Guimas doesn't accept credit cards.

Entertainment

To find out what's going on at night, pick up the *Jornal do Brasil* at any newsstand and turn to the entertainment section. On Friday it contains an entertainment magazine called *Programa*, which lists the week's events. Other good sources of information are the *Rio Show* insert in Friday's edition of the *O Globo* newspaper, the *Veja Rio* insert that comes out every Sunday in the *Veja* magazine, and the current Riotur guide.

Nightlife varies widely by the neighbourhood. Leblon and Ipanema have up-market trendy clubs with excellent jazz. Botafogo has cheaper, popular clubs with more dancing and samba. Cinelândia and Lapa, in the centre, have a lot of samba and pagode and are also the heart of gay Rio. Try some of the bars around Sala Cecília Mendez. Copacabana is a mixed bag: it has some good local hang-outs but also a strong tourist influence, with a lot of sex for sale.

Things to Buy

Most shops are open Monday to Friday from 9 am to 7 pm (some stay open even later) and Saturday from 9 am to 1 pm. The malls usually open from 10 am to 10 pm Monday to Friday, and from 10 am to 8 pm on weekends.

Pé de Boi Pé de Boi is in Botafogo, on Rua Ipiranga 53. It is open Monday to Friday until 7 pm, and on Saturday from 10 am to 1 pm. This shop sells the traditional artisan handicrafts of Brazil's North-East and Minas Gerais. Although the items are not cheap, it's all fine work.

FUNAI Craft Shop Brazil's Indian agency has a tiny craft shop at the Museu do Índio, Rua das Palmeiras 55, Botafogo. Open Monday to Friday from 9 am to noon and 1 to 6 pm, the shop has woven papoose slings, jewellery and musical instruments.

Casa Oliveira This beautiful music shop is in Centro, at Rua da Carioca 70 – on Rio's oldest street. It sells a wide variety of instruments, including all the noisemakers that fuel the Carnaval *baterias* (rhythm sections).

Bum Bum This place is the trendsetter of the bikini world, and it knows it. It's not cheap, but you're paying for style, not fabric. Bum Bum is in Ipanema, at Rua Vinícius de Morais 130.

Hippie Fair This is an arts and crafts fair, with many booths selling jewellery, leather goods, paintings, samba instruments and clothes. There is some awful stuff here and some that's OK. The fair takes place every Sunday at the Praça General Osório in Ipanema.

Nordeste or São Cristóvão Fair The Nordeste (North-East) fair is held at the Pavilhão de São Cristóvão, on the north side of town, every Sunday, starting early and going until about 3 pm. The fair is very North-Eastern in character. Besides food, stallholders sell cheap clothes, hammocks at bargain prices, and a few good Nordeste gifts like leather *vaqueiro* (cowboy) hats. It's great fun, as long as you're careful.

Getting There & Away

Air From Rio, flights go to all parts of Brazil and Latin America. Shuttle flights to São Paulo leave from the conveniently located Aeroporto Santos Dumont, in the city centre, along the bay. Almost all other flights – domestic and international – leave from Aeroporto Galeão.

All three major Brazilian airlines have their main offices in the centre (metro stop Cinelândia). You can also walk over to Aeroporto Santos Dumont, where they have ticket counters, and make reservations there.

Varig (☎ 292-6600 for reservations, 282-1319 for information) has its main office in Centro, at Avenida Rio Branco 277G. VASP (☎ 292-2122) has a city office at Rua Santa Luzia 735. Transbrasil (☎ 297-4422) is in the centre, at Rua Santa Luzia 651. Nordeste

Linhas Aéreas (☎ 220-4366) is at Aeroporto Santos Dumont. It goes to Porto Seguro, Ilhéus and other smaller cities in the North-East. Rio Sul (☎ 262-6911) does the same for the south, and is also at Aeroporto Santos Dumont.

International airlines include:

Aerolíneas Argentinas
Rua da Assembléia 100, 29th floor, Centro (☎ 292-4131, fax 224-4931)

AeroPerú
Praça Mahatma Gandhi 2, Centro (☎ 210-3124, fax 262-5065)

Air France
Avenida Presidente Antônio Carlos 58, 9th floor, Centro (☎ 220-8661, fax 532-1284)

Alitalia
Avenida Presidente Wilson 231, 21st floor, Centro (☎ 240-7822, fax 240-7493)

American Airlines
Avenida Presidente Wilson 165, 5th floor, Centro (☎ 210-3126, fax 220-1022)

Avianca
Avenida Presidente Wilson 165, No 801 (☎ 220-7697, fax 240-4413)

British Airways
Avenida Rio Branco 108, 21st floor, Centro (☎ 221-0922, fax 242-2889)

Iberia
Avenida Presidente Antônio Carlos 51, 8th floor, Centro (☎ 282-1336, fax 240-9842)

Japan Air Lines
Avenida Rio Branco 156, No 2014, Centro (☎ 220-6414, fax 220-6091)

KLM
Avenida Rio Branco 311A, Centro (☎ 292-7747, fax 240-1595)

LanChile
Avenida Nilo Peçanha 50, 13th floor, Centro (☎ 220-9722, fax 532-1420)

Lapsa (Líneas Aéreas Paraguayas)
Avenida Rio Branco 245, 7th floor, Centro (☎ 220-4148, fax 240-9577)

Lloyd Aero Boliviano (LAB)
Avenida Calógeras 30, Centro (☎ 220-9548, fax 533-2835)

Lufthansa
Avenida Rio Branco 156 D, Centro (☎ 282-1253, fax 262-8845)

South African
Avenida Rio Branco 245, 4th floor, Centro (☎ 262-6252, fax 262-6120)

United Airlines
Avenida Presidente Antônio Carlos 51, 5th floor, Centro (☎ 532-1212, fax 262-7786)

Bus All long-distance buses leave from the Novo Rio Rodoviária (☎ 291-5151 for information), Avenida Francisco Bicalho in Santo Christo, about five minutes north of the centre. Many travel agents in the city and zona sul sell bus tickets; it's best to purchase these a couple of days in advance.

Getting Around
To/From the Airport There are three options: air-conditioned buses, local buses and taxis. If you have any valuables, an air-con bus or a taxi is safer than a local bus.

Empresa Real air-con buses run on two routes to and from Aeroporto Galeão. The buses operate from 5.20 am to 11 pm, leave every 40 minutes to one hour and cost US$5. One route goes to the centre and to the Santos Dumont airport; the other route goes to the city centre and along the beaches of Copacabana, Ipanema, Leblon, Vidigal and São Conrado.

You can catch the bus on the 1st floor (arrivals) of the main terminal, at the Galeão sign. If you ask the driver, the buses will stop anywhere along the route. Both stop at the rodoviária, if you want to catch a bus out of Rio immediately.

If you're heading to the airport, you can catch the Empresa Real bus in front of the major hotels along the beach, but you have to flag it down. 'Galeão' should be written on the direction sign.

If you decide to travel by local bus, there is a small terminal for city buses, on Rua Ecuador (on the far corner, to your right as you leave the main terminal at Galeão).

A taxi is a good option if you have valuables, though many taxis from the airport will try to rip you off. The safest and most expensive course is to take a white radio-taxi, where you pay a set fare at the airport. A yellow-and-blue *comum* taxi is about 25% cheaper if the meter is working and if you pay what is on the fare schedule. A trip from the airport to Copacabana costs about US$30 in a comum taxi, US$40 in a radio-taxi. If you're entering Brazil for the first time, on a budget, a good compromise is to take a bus to somewhere near your destination, then take a short taxi ride to your hotel. Sharing a taxi from the airport is a good idea. Taxis will take up to four people. To ensure a bit of security, before entering the taxi at the airport you can usually get a receipt with the licence plate of your taxi and a phone number to register losses or complaints.

Bus The buses are a mixture of the good, the bad and the ugly. The good: Rio's buses are fast, frequent, cheap (US$0.50) and, because Rio is long and narrow, it's easy to get the right bus and usually no big deal if you're on the wrong one. The bad: Rio's buses are often crowded, slowed down by traffic and driven by raving maniacs who drive the buses as if they were motorbikes. The ugly: Rio's buses are the scene of many of the city's robberies, so don't carry any valuables. In addition to their number, buses have their destinations, including the areas they go through, written on the side. Nine out of 10 buses going south from the centre will go to Copacabana, and vice versa. All buses have the price displayed above the head of the money collector. The buses you need to catch for specific destinations are listed under individual sights.

Bus numbers and routes are posted, so it's pretty easy to work out which bus to catch from the rodoviária. For Copacabana, the best are bus Nos 126, 127 and 128. The best bus to Ipanema and Leblon is No 128, but you can also take No 126 or 127 to Copacabana and then catch another bus to Ipanema and Leblon. For the budget hotels in Catete and Glória, take the Gávea via Jóquei bus (No 170), which goes down Rua do Catete and then turns up Rua Pedro Américo and along Rua Bento Lisboa. If you want the Catete budget hotels, get off at the stop near the corner of Bento Lisboa and Rua Silveira Martins, then walk a block down to Rua Catete.

An alternative is to take any bus that goes to the centre on Avenida Rio Branco. Get off near the end of Avenida Rio Branco and hop on the metro. Get off the metro at Catete station, which is in the heart of the budget hotel area.

If you're staying in the Catete/Flamengo area and want to get to the beaches by bus, you can either walk to the main roadway along Parque Flamengo and take any Copacabana bus, or you can walk to Largo do Machado and take bus No 570.

Metro Rio's excellent subway system is limited to points north of Botafogo. It is open from 6 am to 11 pm daily, except Sunday. The two air-con lines are cleaner, faster and cheaper than the buses; discounts are offered on purchase of multiple tickets. The main stops for Centro are Cinelândia and Carioca.

Taxi Rio taxis are quite reasonably priced if you're dividing the fare with a friend or two. Taxis are particularly useful late at night and when carrying valuables, but they are not a completely safe and hassle-free ride. First, there have been a few cases of people being assaulted and robbed by taxi drivers. Second, and much more common, the drivers have a marked tendency to exaggerate fares. For more hints on dealing with taxis, see the information on taxis in the Getting Around section. The radio-taxis (☎ 260-2022) are 25% more expensive than the comums, but they will come to you and they are safer.

Car Car rental agencies can be found at the airport, or clustered together on Avenida Princesa Isabel in Copacabana. Rental is not cheap (about US$70 a day), but rates go down a bit in the off season. It's worth shopping around. When agencies quote prices on the phone, they usually leave out the cost of insurance, which is mandatory. Most agencies will let you drop off their cars in another city without extra charge.

ANGRA DOS REIS

Angra dos Reis is a transit point for nearby islands and beaches, not a tourist attraction in itself. The closest beaches are at Praia Grande and Vila Velha. Take the Vila Velha municipal bus.

Angra dos Reis is almost three hours (US$8) by bus from Rio de Janeiro's Novo

Rio Rodoviária. To Parati, it's a two-hour trip (US$5).

ILHA GRANDE

Ilha Grande is all beach and tropical jungle, with only three towns on the island: Freguesia de Santana (a small hamlet without accommodation), Parnaioca (a collection of homes beside a lovely strip of beach near the old prison) and Abraão (which has plenty of pousadas, camping grounds and ferry connections to Mangaratiba and Angra dos Reis). If you really want to get away from it all, Ilha Grande may well be the place to go. You can rent a boat for US$8 per hour, and buzz around to Freguesia or Parnaioca.

There are trails through the jungle to Praia Lopes Mendes (said by some to be the most beautiful beach in Brazil) and the island's other 102 beaches.

Places to Stay & Eat

The cheapest option is to camp in Abraão. If you head inland away from the dock for a block and go left, you'll find *Camping Renato* up a small path on the right 10 metres or so after you cross a creek. It has well-drained, secure sites and basic facilities, as well as a café/bar on site, and charges US$3 per person. Other camping grounds include *Das Palmeiras*, nearby on Rua Getúlio Vargas, and *Cerca Viva*, a camping ground and pousada combined. Off-site camping is forbidden.

The youth hostel, *Ilha Grande* (☎ (021) 264-6147), at Getúlio Vargas 13, is a good option. It's well located, with friendly staff. Reservations are a good idea, especially on weekends and holidays. Most of the pousadas in Abraão cost between US$30 and US$40 a double.

Restaurante de Janeth is a decent place which serves prato feitos with abundant portions of fresh fish (US$4). It's just around the corner from the church. *Casa da Mulata*, on the way to the old prison, also has good prato feitos (US$3). There are also lots of places along the beachfront.

Getting There & Away

Take a Conerj ferry from either Mangaratiba or Angra dos Reis. If you take the 5.30 am bus from Rio to Mangaratiba, you can catch the daily 8.30 am ferry from there to Abraão. The boat returns from Abraão to Mangaratiba on Monday, Wednesday and Friday at 4.30 pm, on Tuesday and Thursday at 11 am, and on Saturday and Sunday at 4 pm.

The ferry (US$5, 1½ hours) from Angra dos Reis to Abraão departs Monday, Wednesday and Friday at 4 pm, returning from Abraão at 10.15 am on the same days.

PARATI

Parati, one of Brazil's most enchanting colonial towns, is a good place from which to explore a dazzling section of the coast. It is now one of the most popular holiday spots between Rio and São Paulo, and prices are high.

Information

Tourist Offices The Centro de Informações Turísticas (☎ 71-1266 ext 20), on Avenida Roberto Silveira, is open daily from 7 am to 7 pm. Next door, Parati Tours (☎ & fax 71-1327) is useful for information and rents bicycles for US$10 per day. The Secretaria de Turismo e Cultura (☎ 71-1256), in the Antigo Quartel do Forte, near the port, is open daily from 8 am to 7 pm.

Things to See

Parati's 18th-century prosperity is reflected in its beautiful old homes and churches. In the 18th century, the population was divided amongst the three main churches: **NS do Rosário** (1725) for slaves, **Santa Rita dos Pardos Libertos** (1722) for freed mulattos and **NS das Dores** (1800) for the white elite.

The **Forte Defensor Perpétuo** was built in 1703 to protect the gold being exported from Minas Gerais, which was subject to attack by pirates. It's a 20-minute walk north from town. The fort houses the **Casa de Artista e Centro de Artes e Tradições Populares de Parati**.

To see the **beaches** and **islands**, many tourists take one of the schooners that leave from the docks around noon. A five-hour cruise costs US$18 (US$30 with lunch) The boats normally make three beach stops of about 45 minutes each.

A better alternative is to rent a small motorboat at the port. For US$10 per hour (somewhat more in summer) the skipper will take you where you want to go. Bargaining may be difficult.

The mainland beaches tend to be better than the ones on the islands. The closest fine beaches on the coast – Vermelha, Lula and Saco – are about an hour away by boat; camping is allowed. The most accessible beaches, just north of town, are Praia do Pontal, Praia do Forte and Praia do Jabaquara.

Places to Stay

From about October to February, hotels get booked up and room prices double, so reservations are a good idea. The prices quoted here are off-season rates.

There are several camping grounds on the edge of town, just over the bridge. Cheap accommodation is not hard to find. *Pousada Familiar* (☎ 71-1475), at Rua José Vieira Ramos 262, is close to the bus station and charges US$15 per person, including a good breakfast. It's a friendly place, run by a Brazilian/Belgian couple. Also recommended is the *Pousada Marendaz* (☎ 71-1369) at Rua Dr Derly Ellena 9. Run by Rachel and her four sisters, it's more of a family home than a hotel. They also charge US$15 per person.

Hotel Solar dos Gerânios (☎ 71-1550), on Praça da Matriz (also known as Praça Monsenhor Hélio Pires), is a beautiful old hotel. Singles/doubles start as low as US$15/25.

The *Hotel Coxixo* (☎ 71-1460, fax 71-1568), Rua do Comercio 362, is cosy and colonial, with beautiful gardens and a pool. Most doubles go for US$80, but if you make reservations early there are some standard doubles for US$40.

Places to Eat

Parati has many pretty restaurants, but once your feet touch the cobblestones, prices go up. To beat the inflated prices in the old part

of town, try the buffet at *Sabor da Terra*, Rua Roberto Silveira 80. Also popular is *Bar da Terra*, across the bridge and up the hill on the left-hand side. They also have live music from Thursday to Sunday nights. The best restaurants in the old town include the *Galeria do Engenho*, Rua da Lapa, which serves large and juicy steaks for US$10, and *Vagalume*, Rua da Ferraria. *Pizzaria Bucaneiros*, Rua Dr Samuel Costa, has tasty pizzas.

Getting There & Away

The rodoviária is on the main road into town, Rua Roberto Silveira, half a km up from the old town. There are six daily buses (US$12, four hours) from Parati to Rio.

Buses go from Parati to Angra dos Reis (US$5, two hours) almost every hour from 5 am to 7 pm. There are also daily buses to Ubatuba, Cunha and São Paulo.

PETRÓPOLIS

Petrópolis is a lovely mountain retreat with a decidedly European flavour, only 60 km from Rio de Janeiro – an ideal day trip. The main attraction is the **Museu Imperial**, the perfectly preserved and impeccably appointed palace of Dom Pedro II.

Places to Stay

The *Hotel Comércio* (☎ 42-3500), at Rua Dr Porciúncula 56, is directly across from the rodoviária. Quartos are clean and cheap, at US$10/20 for singles/doubles. Apartamentos cost US$25. If you want to spend a bit more, both the *Hotel York* (☎ 43-2662), at Rua do Imperador 78, and the *Casablanca Palace* (☎ 42-0162), Rua 16 de Março 123, have singles/doubles for US$45/55.

Getting There & Away

From Rio, buses to Petrópolis leave every half-hour from 5 am onwards (US$4, 1½ hours).

TERESÓPOLIS

Teresópolis is the climbing and trekking centre of Brazil. The city itself is modern, prosperous and dull; the principal attraction is the surrounding landscape of the Serra dos Orgãos.

There are extensive hiking trails, and it's possible to trek to Petrópolis. The trails aren't marked, but guides are inexpensive.

The main entrance to the **Parque Nacional Serra dos Orgãos** is open daily from 8 am to 5 pm. There's a 3.5-km walking trail, and there are waterfalls, swimming pools, tended lawns and camp sites. It's a very pretty park for a picnic. There are also some camp sites and chalets for rent at the park substation, 12 km towards Rio.

Places to Stay

The *Várzea Palace Hotel* (☎ 742-0878), at Rua Prefeito Sebastião Teixeira 41/55, behind the Igreja Matriz, is a grand old white building with red trim which has been a Teresópolis institution since 1916. Classy singles/doubles are US$20/28 without bath, US$28/35 with a bath. The *Hotel Avenida* (☎ 742-2751) is in front of the Igreja Matriz, at Rua Delfim Moreira 439. Rooms cost US$30/45.

Places to Eat

Restaurante do Armazem, Rua Delfim Moreira 410, is a comfy, inexpensive little place that serves trout with almonds and bananas, and a great home-made fruit crêpe with a choice of sauces (US$6). *Cheiro de Mato*, Rua Delfim Moreira 140, is a decent vegetarian restaurant. *O Tigre de Papel* is a good Chinese restaurant in the centre, at the end of Rua Francisco Sá.

Getting There & Away

The rodoviária is on Rua 1 do Maio, off Avenida Tenente Luiz. Buses to Rio (US$5, 1½ hours) leave every half-hour between 5 am and 10 pm. There are seven buses to Petrópolis (from 6 am to 9 pm) and plenty to Nova Friburgo.

NOVA FRIBURGO

This mountain town was established by Swiss immigrants in 1818. The Cónego neighbourhood is interesting for its German-style architecture, and for its flowers, which seem to bloom perpetually.

You can survey the surrounding area from **Morro da Cruz** (1800 metres). The cable-car station is in the centre, at Praça do Suspiro, and gondolas run up to the top from 10 am to 6 pm on holidays and weekends. **Pico da Caledônia** (2310 metres) also offers fantastic views.

The more energetic can hike to **Pedra do Cão Sentado** or explore the **Furnas do Catete** rock formations. Interesting nearby villages include the mountain towns of **Bom Jardim** (23 km north on BR-492) and **Lumiar** (25 km from Mury, just before the entrance to Friburgo). Hippies, cheap pensions, waterfalls, walking trails and white-water canoe trips abound in Lumiar.

Places to Stay

Hotel Montanus (☎ 22-1235), at Rua Fernando Bizzotto 26, has simple singles/doubles for the US$27/29, but you can bargain them down. *Fabris Hotel* (☎ 22-2852), at Avenida Alberto Braune 148, asks US$35/40 for clean singles/doubles.

In Lumiar, try the *Pousada dos Gnomos* (☎ (021) 256-3926 in Rio), with a nice waterfall close by, a good breakfast and rooms for US$40 a double.

Places to Eat

To eat very well, try one of the two Swiss/German delis on Rua Fernando Bizzotto for a hefty cold-cut sandwich on black bread with dark mustard. *Oberland*, at No 12, doubles as a restaurant, with great food: try the weisswurst (veal sausage) with sauerkraut (US$4) and chocolate cake for dessert. The *Churrascaría Majórica*, in the centre at Praça Getúlio Vargas 74, serves good filet mignon for US$15; it's enough for two.

Getting There & Away

Nova Friburgo is a little over two hours (US$6) by bus from Rio, via Niterói, on 1001 Lines. To Teresópolis, there are four daily buses (US$4, two hours).

ITATIAIA

The Itatiaia region, in the Serra da Mantiqueira, is a curious mix of old-world charm and new-world jungle. Food and lodging are expensive. Access to this region is via Resende.

Parque Nacional do Itatiaia

This 120-sq-km national park contains alpine meadows and Atlantic rainforests, lakes, rivers and waterfalls. It is the home of jaguars, monkeys and sloths.

The park headquarters, museum and Lago Azul (Blue Lake) are 10 km in from the Via Dutra highway. The museum, open Tuesday to Sunday from 8 am to 4 pm, has glass cases full of stuffed animals and pinned moths and snakes in jars.

Every two weeks, a group guided by Senhor Carlos Zikan (☎ 54-2639) scales the Agulhas Negras peak, at 2787 metres the highest in the area. Lúcia Teireira (☎ 58-2324) is another excellent guide.

It's a 26-km, eight-hour trek from the park entrance to the Abroucas refuge, at the base of Agulhas Negras. The refuge can sleep 24 people. Reservations are required. Call IBAMA (the national parks service; ☎ 52-1461) in Resende, and get maps and advice from the park IBAMA office before setting off.

Simpler hikes include the walk between Hotel Simon and Hotel Repouso, and the 20-minute walk from the Sítio Jangada to the Poronga waterfalls.

Places to Stay

Camping is the cheapest option inside the park. There's the camping ground *Aporaoca* (☎ 52-1392), four km from the main entrance. (When you get to the Gula & Artes store and the ice-cream shop, there's a signpost to the camping ground 200 metres away.) Sites are US$6 per person.

There is a youth hostel: *Ipé Amarelo* (☎ 52-1232), at Rua João Mauricio de Macedo Costa 352, in Campo Alegre, a suburb of Itatiaia. It has bicycles for rent.

Pousada do Elefante, close to the Hotel Simon, is the cheapest hotel in the park. It's basic but well located. Singles/doubles with full board cost US$40/70.

Getting There & Away

Buses from Resende to Itatiaia run every 20 minutes on weekdays, every 40 minutes on weekends, from 7 am to 11.20 pm. From Praça São José in Itatiaia, take the Hotel Simon's Kombi up to the park. It leaves at 8 and 10 am, noon, and 2, 5 and 7 pm. The ride costs US$2, and you'll also have to pay the park entry fee (US$1) as you go through the main gate. A taxi costs US$15.

SAQUAREMA

Saquarema, 100 km from Rio de Janeiro, is a horse-breeding and fruit-growing centre. You can visit the orchards and pick fruit, or hire horses and take to the hills. The beaches are a major attraction: Bambui, Ponta Negra and Jaconé, south of town, are long and empty except for a couple of fishing villages. The waves are big, particularly in Ponta Negra, and three km north of Saquarema in Praia Itaúna, where an annual surfing contest is held during the last two weeks of May.

Places to Stay

The youth hostel, *Ilhas Gregas* (☎ 51-1008), is excellent. Only 100 metres from the beach, at Rua do Prado 671 in Itaúna, it has bicycles, a swimming pool, a sauna and a bar/restaurant. It's easy to catch a taxi here from the bus station in Saquarema, but if you feel like a hike, get off the bus at the Sudoeste petrol station and walk for half an hour along Avenida Oceânica, until you get to the centre of Itaúna (where there are lots of beachfront bars and kiosks). Go along Avenida NS de Nazareth and take the second street on the left (Rua das Caravelas), then the first street on your right (Rua do Prado). *Pousada da Mansão*, Avenida Oceanica 353, is a good option. Rooms in the old mansion cost US$10/20, and you can also camp for US$5. For reservations call (☎ (021) 259-2100) in Rio. *Pousada da Titia* (☎ 51-2058), at Avenida Salgado Filho 774, is a good alternative with double apartamentos for US$20.

BRAZIL

Getting There & Away

Saquarema is serviced by frequent buses from Rio (US$4.50, two hours). To get to Cabo Frio, take a local bus to Bacaxá. From there buses depart every half-hour to Cabo Frio.

ARRAIAL DO CABO

Arraial do Cabo, 10 km south of Cabo Frio, has beaches that compare with the finest in Búzios. Praia dos Anjos has beautiful turquoise water, but there's a little too much boat traffic for comfortable swimming.

Things to See

The **Oceanographic Museum**, on the beach, is open Tuesday to Sunday from 9 am to 4.30 pm.

To see the **Gruta Azul** (Blue Cavern), on the far side of Ilha de Cabo Frio, ask the fisherfolk at Praia dos Anjos for a tour, or enquire at the Pousada Restaurante dos Navegantes, on Praia Grande. The tour should cost around US$25. The favourite beaches in town are Praia do Forno, Praia Brava and Praia Grande.

Places to Stay & Eat

Camping Praia Grande, Avenida Getúlio Vargas 103, is a walled-in grassy area reasonably close to the beach. Sites cost US$4 per person. In the centre of town, the *Hotel Praia Grande* (☎ 22-1369), at Rua Dom Pedro 41, has apartamentos for US$25/30. At Praia dos Anjos, the *Porto dos Anjos* (☎ 22-1629), Avenida Luis Correa 8, is a house that's been converted into a pousada; the double rooms (US$30) have sea views.

Garrafa de Nansen Restaurante is a classy seafood place where you can eat very well for about US$10 each. Cheaper eats are available in the centre at *Meu Cantinho*, Rua Dom Pedro I, No 18, where the US$9 fish dinners will easily feed two. At Praia Grande, the *Canoa Quebrada* restaurant is a good choice, especially if you fancy seafood moqueca. It's at Rua Epitácio Pessoa 26.

Getting There & Away

The municipal bus from Cabo Frio loops around Arraial and returns to Cabo Frio every 20 minutes.

BÚZIOS

Búzios is on a peninsula scalloped by 17 beaches. It was a simple fishing village until Brigitte Bardot and her Brazilian boyfriend discovered it. Now it is a highly developed, expensive resort.

Búzios is actually three settlements on the peninsula (Ossos, Manguinhos and Armação) and one farther north, on the mainland (Rasa). Ossos (which means bones), at the northernmost tip of the peninsula, is the oldest and most attractive.

Information

The Ekoda Tourist Agency (☎ 23-1490) in Armação, Rua das Pedras 13, is open every day from 10 am to 8 pm. It is the agent for American Express and you can also change money, and arrange accommodation (though not at the cheaper places) and tours.

Things to See & Do

In general, the southern beaches are trickier to get to, but they're prettier and have better surf. The northern beaches are more sheltered and are closer to the settlements.

The schooner *Queen Lory* makes daily trips to Ilha Feia, Tartaruga and João Fernandinho. There are a 2½-hour trip (US$15) and a four-hour trip (US$20). These trips are excellent value, especially since caipirinhas, soft drinks, fruit salad and snorkelling gear are included in the price. To make a reservation, ask at your pousada or visit Queen Lory Tours, Rua Angela Diniz 35.

Places to Stay

Campers should try *Geribá*, Praia de Geribá, which also has a few chalets for US$16 per person.

Accommodation is expensive, especially in summer, so consider looking in Saquarema or Cabo Frio, or rent a house and stay a while. In the low season, however, you should be able to find a room as cheap as those in Cabo Frio or Arraial. The *Zen-Do* (☎ 23-1542), at Rua João Fernandes 60, is a private home with rooms to let. Yesha Vanicore runs a progressive household and has doubles for US$25 in the low season. She is friendly woman, speaks English and is an excellent vegetarian cook. *Pousada Mediterrânea* (☎ 23-2353), across the road, is a little whitewashed and tiled hotel. Low-season doubles with a lovely inland view are US$30. Close to the bus station, the *Don Quixote* (☎ & fax 23-1487), Estrada da Usina Velha 300, is good value, charging US$30 a double in low season.

Places to Eat

For good, cheap food, have grilled fish and a beer right on the beach. Brava, Ferradura and João Fernandes beaches have fish restaurants. *Buzios Kilo*, Rua Manoel Touribio de Farias 351, right on Praça Santos Dumont, has a great buffet. *Chez Michou Crêperie*, on Rua das Pedras, makes almost any kind of crêpe you want.

Getting There & Away

Buses to Rio depart daily from the bus stop on Rua Turibe de Faria in Armação (US$8, three hours). From Cabo Frio to Búzios (Ossos), it's a 50-minute trip on the municipal bus.

Espírito Santo

Espírito Santo is a small state which has little to interest the traveller. Some of the fishing villages and beaches on the southern coast are attractive, but they are no match for those in Rio or Bahia.

Minas Gerais State

The main attractions for visitors to this state are the national parks, and the historic gold cities nestled in the Serra do Espinhaço, with their Baroque churches and sacred art.

BELO HORIZONTE

Belo Horizonte has nothing of special interest to the traveller. Mostly, those who stop here are on their way to Ouro Prêto or Diamantina. Belotur (☎ 222-5500), puts out a comprehensive monthly guide in Portuguese, English and French. It lists the main tourist attractions and how to get there using local buses. It also includes flight times and detailed long-distance bus schedules.

Belotur has booths at Confins airport (open daily from 8 am to 6 pm), in front of the Parque Municipal (open weekdays from 8 am to 8 pm and weekends from 8 am to 4 pm) and at the rodoviária (open the same hours as the park booth). Staff speak a bit of English and can also supply you with state tourist information. The telephone code for Belo Horizonte is 031.

Places to Stay

There are two youth hostels in town. They're your cheapest option, though both are a bit of a hike from the bus station. *Pousada Beagá* (☎ 337-1845, fax 275-3592), at Rua Santa Catarina 597, is in the suburb of Lourdes. (From the rodoviária, follow Avenida Paran up to Rua Santa Catarina.) It's open from 7 am to 11 pm. The *Pousadinha Mineira* (☎ 446-2911, fax 442-4448) is at Rua Araxá 514. From the rodoviária, follow Avenida Santos Dumont up to Rua Rio de Janeiro, then turn left and go up a couple of blocks to Avenida do Contorno. Cross the avenue and, going straight ahead, follow Rua Varginha up a few blocks to Rua Araxá.

You'll see lots of hotels right next to the rodoviária, but most are pretty dingy, and the area is a sleazy red-light district after dark. If that doesn't bother you, try the *Hotel Madrid* (☎ 201-1088), just in front of the bus station, at Rua dos Guaranis 12. Quartos here are US$12/18 a single/double; apartamentos cost US$15/20. One block farther at Rua dos Guaranis, No 124, the *Hotel Magnata* (☎ 201-5368) has simple, well-kept apartamentos for US$14/20 a single/double. Both these hotels are strictly *familiar*, meaning they don't rent rooms by the hour.

BRAZIL

Places to Eat

For lunch, *Vida Campestre Natural*, Rua Afonso Pena 774, has good, cheap, natural food. The *Dragon Centre* is a reasonable Chinese restaurant close to Praça Sete, at Afonso Pena 549. *Torino*, Rua dos Guajajaras 460, is a small place with a wood-fired oven, a varied menu and a por-kilo buffet lunch.

Getting There & Away

Air Belo Horizonte is connected to Rio and São Paulo by frequent VASP/Varig/Transbrasil *ponte aerea* (air bridge) flights. There are also daily flights to most other major cities in Brazil.

Bus Buses will take you to Rio (US$16, seven hours), São Paulo (US$18, 9½ hours), Brasília (US$26, 12 hours) and Salvador (US$48, about 22 hours). There are hourly departures for Ouro Prêto (US$4, 1¾ hours), and daily buses to Mariana (US$5, two hours), Diamantina (US$12, 5½ hours) and São João del Rei (US$7, 3½ hours).

CONGONHAS

Little is left of Congonhas' colonial past, except for Aleijadinho's extraordinary statues, the *Prophets*. For these alone, the town warrants a visit, but it's not worth staying here. With an early start, you can go by bus from São João del Rei to Congonhas, spend a few hours at the 12 *Prophets*, then go on to Conselheiro Lafaiete and Ouro Prêto (or vice versa), all in one day.

The 12 Prophets

Aleijadinho, the son of a Portuguese architect and a black slave, lived from 1730 to 1814. He lost the use of his hands and legs at the age of 30, but with hammer and chisel strapped to his arms, he advanced Brazilian sculpture from the excesses of the Baroque to a finer, more graceful Rococo. The *Prophets*, in front of the Basílica do Bom Jesus do Matosinhos, are his masterwork.

Getting There & Away

There are six buses daily from Belo Horizonte to Congonhas (US$4, 1¾ hours). The last return bus to Belo Horizonte leaves Congonhas at 8.20 pm. Buses leave every half-hour for Conselheiro Lafaiete. From there, you can catch the midnight bus to Rio. To get from Congonhas to Ouro Prêto, you can go to Belo Horizonte or make a connection in Conselheiro Lafaiete.

To get from Congonhas to São João del Rei, catch one of the Belo Horizonte to São João del Rei buses that stop off at Congonhas. There are seven a day, between 7.30 am and 8.20 pm.

OURO PRÊTO

Vila Rica, the predecessor of Ouro Prêto, was founded in 1711, in the early days of the gold rush, and became the capital of Minas Gerais in 1721. At the height of the boom, in the mid-18th century, the city had a population of 110,000 and was the richest in the New World.

As the boom declined, the miners found it more and more difficult to pay the ever-increasing gold taxes exacted by the Portuguese crown. In 1789 the Inconfidência Mineira, an attempt to overthrow the Portuguese, was crushed in its early stages.

By decree of Emperor Dom Pedro I, Vila Rica became the Imperial City of Ouro Prêto. In 1897, the state capital moved from Ouro Prêto to Belo Horizonte, thus preserving Ouro Prêto's colonial flavour. It's now a university town.

Orientation

Praça Tiradentes, a few blocks down from the rodoviária on the main road, is the town centre. The town is very hilly and the rain-slicked, cobblestone streets are steep: bring good walking shoes.

Information

The tourist office, Praça Tiradentes 41, is open from 8 am to 6 pm on weekdays, and from 8 am to 5 pm on weekends. The friendly staff speak English, provide leaflets, sell maps and arrange guides. They also have a complete list of places to stay, including the

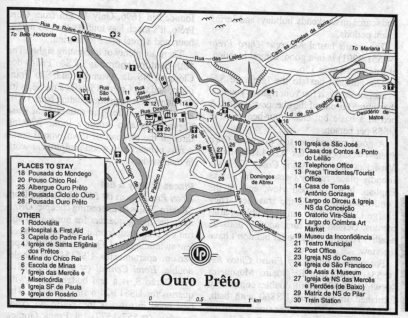

PLACES TO STAY
18 Pousada do Mondego
20 Pouso Chico Rei
25 Albergue Ouro Prêto
26 Pousada Ciclo do Ouro
28 Pousada Ouro Prêto

OTHER
1 Rodoviária
2 Hospital & First Aid
3 Capela do Padre Faria
4 Igreja de Santa Efigênia dos Prêtos
5 Mina do Chico Rei
6 Escola de Minas
7 Igreja das Mercês e Misericórdia
8 Igreja SF de Paula
9 Igreja do Rosário
10 Igreja de São José
11 Casa dos Contos & Ponto do Leilão
12 Telephone Office
13 Praça Tiradentes/Tourist Office
14 Casa de Tomás Antônio Gonzaga
15 Largo do Dirceu & Igreja NS da Conceição
16 Oratorio Vira-Saia
17 Largo do Coimbra Art Market
20 Museu da Inconfidência
21 Teatro Municipal
22 Post Office
23 Igreja NS do Carmo
24 Igreja de São Francisco de Assis & Museum
27 Igreja de NS das Mercês e Perdões (de Baixo)
29 Matriz de NS do Pilar
30 Train Station

Ouro Prêto

0   0.5   1 km

BRAZIL

cheapest, and they'll ring around to find a vacancy for you.

To pack in a lot of sightseeing with little effort, hire an official guide (US$30 for a full-day tour) at the tourist office. Cássio is one who speaks excellent English and really knows his Baroque. The tourist office also organises treks into the surrounding hills and horseback rides to Itacolomy. The cost is around US$40 for the day. Speak to João or Renaldo a day before you go, to give them enough time to get the horses ready.

If you plan to spend only one day in Ouro Prêto, make sure it's not a Monday, when virtually everything is closed!

Things to See
To see the town properly, you'll need a couple of days. Keep quirky opening times in mind when planning your itinerary.

The **Museu da Inconfidência**, on Praça Tiradentes, was formerly the municipal building and jail. It contains Tiradentes' tomb, documents of the Inconfidência Mineira, torture instruments and important works by Ataíde and Aleijadinho. The **Escola de Minas**, in the old governor's palace, also on Praça Tiradentes, has a very fine museum of mineralogy.

There are many magnificent churches in Ouro Prêto. **Matriz NS da Conceição de António Dias** and **Matriz de NS do Pilar** are the cathedrals of the two parishes. The **Igreja de Santa Efigênia dos Prêtos** was built by and for the black slave community. The **Igreja de São Francisco de Assis** also has exterior carvings by Aleijadinho and is particularly interesting.

Places to Stay
Student lodgings, known as *repúblicas*, are the cheapest places, but they are usually closed from Christmas to Carnaval. Another problem with repúblicas is their lack of security. Regular lodging tends to be expensive

and scarce on weekends, holidays and during exam periods.

The youth hostel *Albergue Ouro Prêto* (☎ 551-3201) is in a good, central location, at Rua das Mercês 136.

The pousada next to the Igreja de São Francisco de Assis (on your right as you face the church) is one of the cheapest around. A bed in a basic but clean four-bed room is US$8 per person.

A good pousada is the *Pousada Ouro Prêto* (☎ 551-3081, fax 551-4314), Largo Musicista José das Anjos Costa 72. It's a friendly place, run by Gerson, who speaks English. It has a good view, and all the comforts that delight the traveller. They charge US$15/30 for single/double apartamentos. Gerson also runs another pousada nearby. The rooms are better but don't have the view.

For more comfort, try *Pouso Chico Rei* (☎ 551-1274), Rua Brigideiro Mosqueira 90, which has wonderful doubles completely furnished in antiques (US$60 with bath, US$40 without). There's one single room for US$20. For a splurge, try *Pousada do Mondego* (☎ 551-2040, fax 551-3094), Largo do Coimbra 38, close to Igreja São Francisco. It's in an 18th-century colonial mansion. Singles/doubles cost US$80/100, or a bit more if you want the view.

Places to Eat

The typical dish of Minas is tutu a mineira, a black-bean feijoada. *Restaurante Casa Do Ouvidor*, on Rua Direita, is the place to try it. If the mineiro food is a bit heavy for you, *Café e Cia*, Rua São José 187, has good sandwiches and a great view of the town. It also has a por-kilo buffet lunch.

Getting There & Away

There are frequent bus connections between Belo Horizonte and Ouro Prêto (US$4, 1¾ hours). During the peak tourist period, buy bus tickets at least a day in advance. Buses depart daily to Rio (US$16, seven hours).

MARIANA

Mariana is a beautiful old mining town founded in 1696. Only 12 km from Ouro Prêto, it's much less touristy than its neighbour, and a great place to unwind.

There are plenty of interesting sights. The **18th-century churches** of São Pedro dos Clérigos, NS da Assunção and São Francisco, and the Catedral Basílica da Sé, with its fantastic German organ dating from 1701, are all worthwhile. The **museum** at Casa Capitular is also worth a look. Walking through the old part of town, you'll come across painters and wood sculptors at work in their studios.

Places to Stay & Eat

Hotel Providência (☎ 557-1444), Rua Dom Silveiro 233, is an interesting cheapie. Originally the living quarters for nuns, who still run a school next door, it also has an excellent swimming pool. Quartos are US$10 per person, apartamentos US$15/20 a single/double. *Hotel Central* (☎ 557-1630), Rua Frei Durão 8, is a real budget hotel, with quartos for US$13/24 a single/double. The best hotel in town is the *Pouso da Typographia* (☎ 557-1577), at Praça Gomes Freire 220. Singles/doubles cost US$45/70, but discounts are available during the week.

Portão da Praça, Praça Gomes Freire 108, serves excellent regional food. *Papinna della Nonna*, Rua Dom Viçoso 27, is an Italian restaurant.

Getting There & Away

A bus leaves Ouro Prêto for Mariana every half-hour from the far side of the School of Mineralogy. The trip takes 15 minutes. There are direct buses from Mariana to Belo Horizonte.

SÃO JOÃO DEL REI

Unlike many of the other historic cities in Minas Gerais, São João del Rei has not been frozen in time. The old central section, with its fine churches and colonial mansions, is surrounded by a small but thriving modern city.

The city is sandwiched between two hills, both of which provide excellent views, particularly at sunset. The tourist office is in the

Terminal Turistico, Praça Antonio Vargas. It's open from 6 am to 6 pm.

Things to See

The exquisite Baroque **Igreja de São Francisco de Assis** looks out on a lyre-shaped plaza lined with palm trees. This church was Aleijadinho's first complete project, though much of his plan was not realised. It is open from 8.30 am to noon and 1.30 to 9 pm. The **Igreja de NS do Carmo** was also designed by Aleijadinho. In the second sacristy is a famous unfinished sculpture of Christ. The church is open from 4 to 7 pm. The **Catedral de NS do Pilar** has exuberant gold altars and fine azulejos. It's open from 7 to 11 am and 2 to 4 pm. Make sure to take a walk at night, when floodlights illuminate the churches.

One of the best museums in Minas Gerais is the **Museu Regional do SPHAN**, a well-restored colonial mansion (1859) which has good sacred art on the first two floors and an industrial section on the 3rd floor. It's open from noon to 5.30 pm daily, except Monday.

A must for train freaks is the **Museu Ferroviário**, in the train station. This expertly renovated railway museum houses a wealth of artefacts and information about the old train days of the late 19th century. Don't forget to walk down the track to the large roundhouse; it houses the trains and is the best part of the museum. The museum is open Tuesday to Sunday from 8 am to 5 pm, though it's closed for lunch between 11 am and 1 pm. Entry costs US$0.50. See also the discussion of the 'Maria Fumaça' (Smoking Mary) train in the Getting There & Away section below.

Special Events

The Semana da Inconfidência, from 15 to 21 April, celebrates Brazil's first independence movement and the local boys who led it. São João also has a very lively Carnaval.

Places to Stay & Eat

The *Hotel Brasil* (☎ 371-2804), Avenida Presidente Tancredo Neves 395, is a former grand hotel, and a good deal at US$10 a single without breakfast.

The historic *Hotel Colonial* (☎ 371-7327) is clean and very colonial. Rooms without bath go for US$15/24 a single/double, and most have a view of the river.

For a splurge, try the *Pousada Casarão* (☎ 371-7447) at Rua Ribeiro Bastos 94. It's an elegant Minas mansion converted into an exquisite pousada, complete with swimming pool. Singles/doubles cost US$40/60.

Pizzeria Primus, Rua Arthur Bernardes 97, has good pizza (try the primus special) and is open late. For regional cooking, try *Restaurante Rex*, Rua Arthur Bernardes 137, or *Quinto do Ouro*, Praça Severiano de Resende 4. For a vegetarian lunch and a good juice, *Opção Saudavel*, Avenida Tiradentes 792, has a set menu, but order at least an hour in advance because they bring the food from home. On the same street, *Zoti* is a lively late-night place for beer and light meals.

Getting There & Away

Bus Buses leave Rio direct for São João three times daily (US$12, five hours). There are eight buses a day from São João to Belo Horizonte via Lagoa Dourada. For services to Belo Horizonte and Congonhas, see the respective Getting There & Away sections.

Train Chugging along at 25 km/h on the steam-powered Maria Fumaça down a picturesque stretch of track from São João to Tiradentes makes a great half-hour train ride. The line has operated nonstop since 1881 with the same Baldwin locomotives and is in perfect condition, after being restored. The train runs only on Friday, Saturday, Sunday and holidays, leaving São João at 10 am and 2.15 pm and returning from Tiradentes at 1 and 5 pm. Arrive early to buy your ticket (US$4). Going to Tiradentes, sit on the left-hand side for a better view.

Getting Around

From the small bus stop in front of the train station, catch the yellow local bus for the 10-minute ride to the rodoviária. You can also take a taxi for US$5. To catch a bus to the Terminal Turistico from the rodoviária, go to the bus stop on your left as you leave the rodoviária – don't go to the more obvious one directly in front of the exit.

TIRADENTES

This very pretty town, 10 km down the valley from São João del Rei, has changed little over the last two centuries. The Secretaria de Turismo, Rua Resende Costa 71, provides maps and gives information about guides and walks in the mountains of Serra de São José. Ask to see Luiz Cruz, who speaks English and is very helpful.

Things to See & Do

Named after the town's patron saint, the **Igreja Matriz de Santo António** stands on top of the hill. There are two bell towers, and a frontispiece by Aleijadinho, who also made the sundial in front of the church. The church is open from 8 am to 5 pm but usually closes from noon to 1 pm for lunch.

The **Museu do Padre Toledo** is dedicated to another hero of the Inconfidência, Padre Toledo, who lived in this 18-room house where the *inconfidêntes* used to meet. The museum features regional antiques and documents from the 18th century.

From Tiradentes, it's a three-km walk (25 minutes) to Mãe d'Agua, at the base of the **Serra de São José**, a range renowned for its untouched segments of Atlantic rainforest. Other walks include A Calçada (a stretch of the old road that linked Ouro Prêto with Rio de Janeiro), Cachoeiras do Mangue (the falls where you can see an old gold mine on the road made by slaves) and Cachoeira do Bom Despacho (a waterfall on the road from Tiradentes to Santa Cruz). Each of these walks takes about four or five hours. A seven-hour walk will allow you to cross the range. For guides, and information about walks into the mountains, ask at the tourist office.

Places to Stay

Tiradentes has lots of good but expensive pousadas and only a few cheap places. If you can't find anything within your budget, ask around for homes to stay in, or commute from São João del Rei. Try to avoid staying

here on the weekend as it gets crowded and prices double.

Pousada do Laurito is the best cheapie in town, with a good central location and singles/doubles for US$14/25. Next to the bus station, *Pousada Tiradentes* (☎ 355-1232) has charm and costs US$18/28. *Quatro Encantos* (☎ 355-1202), near the Santo Antônio church, has a great little garden and charges around US$25/45. The *Porão Colonial* (☎ 355-1251) is near the train station, has a pool and charges US$22 per person.

Getting There & Away

The best approach to Tiradentes is by train from São João del Rei (see the section on that city for details). Buses come and go between São João and Tiradentes every 40 minutes (slightly less frequently on weekend afternoons).

SÃO TOMÉ DAS LETRAS

São Tomé das Letras is a small village in a beautiful mountainous region in southern Minas, 310 km from Belo Horizonte. The name refers to inscriptions in some of the local caverns. These have inspired strange stories of flying saucers, extraterrestrials, a subterranean passageway to Machu Picchu, and so on. This is also a beautiful mountain region, with great walks and several waterfalls.

Places to Stay & Eat

São Tomé has grown a lot in the last few years, so there are lots of pousadas. Spotlessly clean is *Pensão Dona Célia* (☎ 237-1244), Rua Joaquim José Mendes Peixoto 11, for US$18 per person. *Pousada Serra Negro* (☎ 237-1200) at Rua Capitão João de Deus costs US$25/45 a single/double, which includes breakfast and lunch. There's a youth hostel 20 metres up behind the stone church to the right, and you can camp at Gruta do Leão, which supposedly has enchanted water.

Bar das Letras serves a good prato feito and *Bar do Gê* is a surprisingly good restaurant.

Getting There & Away

The town is best reached from Três Corações, 38 km to the west. Buses leave at 3.30 pm Monday to Saturday. São Tomé das Letras can also be reached from Caxambu, 60 km to the south, but not by local bus.

DIAMANTINA

Diamantina boomed when diamonds were discovered in the 1720s, after the gold finds in Minas. The diamonds are gone, but fine colonial mansions and excellent hiking in the surrounding mountains still draw visitors.

The house of Padre Rolim, one of the Inconfidêntes, is now the **Museu do Diamante** (Diamond Museum) and houses furniture, coins, instruments of torture and other relics of the diamond days. It's open from noon to 6 pm (closed Monday). The **Igreja NS do Carmo**, built in 1758, is the most opulent church in the town.

Places to Stay & Eat

The *Hotel Nosson* (☎ 531-1565), opposite the bus station, is friendly and cheap (US$8 per person), but when returning from the centre, it's a long uphill walk back. For a bit extra, the *Hotel Dália* (☎ 531-1477), at Praça Juscelino Kubitschek 25, is much better. It's in a nice old building in a good location, almost next door to the diamond museum. Quartos cost US$20/30 for singles/doubles and apartamentos go for US$25/40.

Popular pick of Diamantina's eateries is the *Cantinha do Marinho*, Beco do Motta 27, which has good mineiro dishes and a cheap buffet lunch. *Restaurante Grupiara*, Rua Campos Carvalho 12, is also recommended.

Getting There & Away

There are five buses running daily between Diamantina and Belo Horizonte (US$11, five hours).

São Paulo State

São Paulo is the industrial engine that powers Brazil's economy: 30 of Brazil's 50 largest companies are in São Paulo, as is 50% of the nation's industry. Unfortunately, government mismanagement in recent years has left the state almost bankrupt; unable to finance vital infrastructure projects.

SÃO PAULO

With over 19 million inhabitants, the city of São Paulo is South America's biggest. Its extraordinary growth over the past century has been boosted by migration from inside and outside Brazil, encouraged by the area's industrial development. Rapid growth has created massive problems, including traffic congestion, pollution and shortage of housing.

Orientation

São Paulo is a difficult city in which to orient yourself. The solution is to go underground: São Paulo's subway system (metro) is one of the best in the world.

If you are staying for a while, buy the *Guia Caroplan*, a street guide with an extensive English section, or *Guia São Paulo*, by Quatro Rodas, which has street maps and hotel and restaurant listings.

Information

Tourist Offices The city's tourist information booths have excellent city and state maps. They are also good for bus and metro information. The tourist information booth on Praça da República (along Avenida Ipiranga) is helpful; staff speak English, French, Italian and Spanish. It's open daily from 9 am to 6 pm. The phone number for the main tourist office is ☎ 267-2122 ext 627 or 640.

Other tourist offices are found at: Avenida Paulista, near MASP (open from 9 am to 6 pm); Avenida São Luís, on the corner of Praça Dom José Gaspar (open from 9 am to 6 pm daily); and Aeroporto de Congonhas (open 24 hours a day). There is also a tourist information booth in front of the shopping centre Iguatemi.

Money There are several travel agencies and casas de câmbio across from the airline

BRAZIL

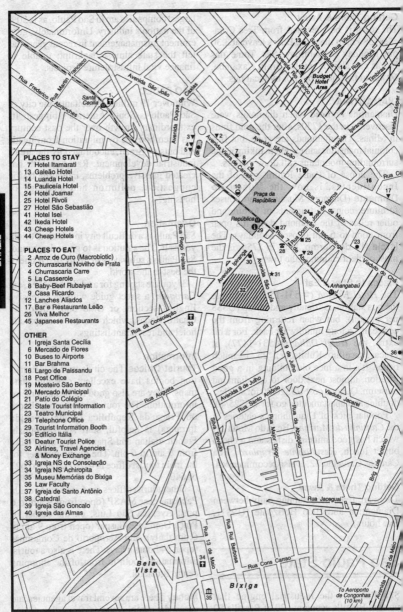

PLACES TO STAY
7 Hotel Itamarati
13 Galeão Hotel
14 Luanda Hotel
15 Paulicéia Hotel
24 Hotel Joamar
25 Hotel Rivoli
27 Hotel São Sebastião
41 Hotel Isei
42 Ikeda Hotel
43 Cheap Hotels
44 Cheap Hotels

PLACES TO EAT
2 Arroz de Ouro (Macrobiotic)
3 Churrascaria Novilho de Prata
4 Churrascaria Carre
5 La Casserole
8 Baby-Beef Rubaiyat
9 Casa Ricardo
12 Lanches Aliados
17 Bar e Restaurante Leão
26 Viva Melhor
45 Japanese Restaurants

OTHER
1 Igreja Santa Cecília
6 Mercado de Flores
10 Buses to Airports
11 Bar Brahma
16 Largo de Paissandu
18 Post Office
19 Mosteiro São Bento
20 Mercado Municipal
21 Patío do Colégio
22 State Tourist Information
23 Teatro Municipal
28 Telephone Office
29 Tourist Information Booth
30 Edifício Itália
31 Deatur Tourist Police
32 Airlines, Travel Agencies
   & Money Exchange
33 Igreja NS de Consolação
34 Igreja NS Achiropita
35 Museu Memórias do Bixiga
36 Law Faculty
37 Igreja de Santo Antônio
38 Catedral
39 Igreja São Goncalo
40 Igreja das Almas

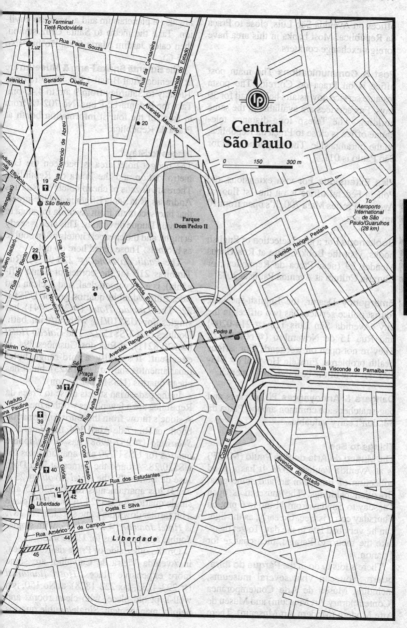

offices on Avenida São Luis, close to Praça da República. Most banks in this area have foreign-exchange counters.

Post & Communications The main post office is on Praça do Correio. The posta restante service downstairs holds mail for 30 days. Fax services are available in the same building. The Telesp long-distance telephone office is close to Praça da República, on the Ipiranga side. The telephone code for São Paulo is 011.

Visa Extensions For visa extensions, the Polícia Federal office is on the 1st floor at Avenida Prestes Maia 700. It's open from 10 am to 4 pm.

Bookshops For a good selection of English books, visit the Book Centre at Rua Gabus Mendes 29 (near Praça da República), or Livraria Cultura at Avenida Paulista 2073.

Emergency Deatur, the English-speaking tourist police service, has two offices in the city: Avenida São Luis 115 (☎ 214-0209) and Rua 15 de Novembro (☎ 607-8332). They're not open on weekends. For serious health problems, Einstein Hospital (☎ 845-1233) is one of the best in Latin America.

Dangers & Annoyances Pickpockets and bag-snatchers are common around Praça da Sé: don't carry valuables.

Things to See
The **Museu de Arte de São Paulo** (MASP) is at Avenida Paulista 1578. It has a good collection of European art and some great Brazilian paintings. The museum is open Tuesday to Sunday from 11 am to 6 pm; on Thursday entry is free. Go early, as the light can be very bad late in the day. To get there, take the metro to Paraiso, then change for Trianon.

There's lots to do in the **Parque do Ibirapuera**. You can visit several museums, including Museu de Arte Contemporânea (Contemporary Art Museum) and Museu de Arte Modern (Modern Art Museum). There

are also a planetarium and a Japanese pavilion. Take the metro to Santa Cruz station, then catch Jardim Maria Sampião bus (No 775-C).

The **Butantã Snake Farm & Museum** are at Avenida Vital Brasil 1500. They're open Tuesday to Saturday from 9 am to 4.45 pm. Take the Butantã-USP bus (No 702-U) from in front of the tourist information booth at Praça da República.

Places to Stay
The budget hotel area is between the Luz metro station and the Praça da República. There are dozens of cheap hotels on Rua dos Andradas, Rua Santa Efigênia and the streets that intersect them from Avenida Ipiranga to Avenida Duque de Caxias. This area is seedy at night, and the cheapest hotels often double as brothels. Those listed here do not.

The *Pauliceía Hotel* (☎ 220-9733), Rua Timbiras 216 (at the corner of Santa Efigênia), is a very good deal, and is clean and safe. Single/double quartos go for US$13/22. The *Luanda Hotel* (☎ 222-2441) has singles for US$10/16 without/with bath. Doubles cost US$15/22. The *Galeão Hotel* (☎ 220-8211), at Rua dos Gusmões 394, is excellent. It's really a mid-range hotel (apartamentos start at US$18/25), but it has cheap quartos (US$14 per person).

In the pedestrian streets close to Praça da República are a few places worth a mention. A stone's throw from the tourist information booth, at Rua 7 de Abril 364, the *Hotel São Sebastião* (☎ 257-4988) has single/double quartos for US$17/20 and apartamentos for US$20/28. Around the corner, at Rua Dom José de Barros 28, the *Hotel Rivoli* (☎ 231-5633) has apartamentos for US$28/35 and single quartos for US$24. A nice little place a bit farther down the same street, at No 187, is *Hotel Joamar* (☎ 221-3611), with single/double apartamentos for US$23/28.

On the other side of Praça da República, in Avenida Vieira de Carvalho, are some more expensive places. *Hotel Itamarati* (☎ 222-4133, fax 222-1878), at No 150, is a well-kept old place, with clean rooms and helpful management. Single/double quartos are US$26/30 and apartamentos US$30/36. It's quite close to the airport bus stop.

Places to Eat

São Paulo is a great place to eat. Because of the city's ethnic diversity, you can find every kind of cuisine, and there are thousands of cheap lanchonetes, pizzerias and churrascarias.

Lanches Aliados, on the corner of Avenida Rio Branco and Rua Vitória, is a cheap lanchonete with good food. *Viva Melhor*, Rua 7 de Abril 264, Centro, has some excellent, cheap natural and vegetarian lunches. It's open Monday to Friday from 11 am to 3 pm. The *Bar e Restaurante Leão*, Avenida São João 320, has all-you-can-eat Italian meals with salad bar, at reasonable prices.

Nearby, in Bela Vista district, there are two good Italian restaurants on Rua Avanhandava: *Gigetto* and *Famiglia Mancini*. The prices are moderate – US$6 for a large plate of pasta. In the Liberdade district there are lots of inexpensive Oriental restaurants.

Entertainment

The best list of events is in the weekly *Veja* magazine, which has a special São Paulo insert. Rua 13 de Maio in Bixiga hums at night. There are several clubs, many restaurants and even a revival movie theatre. It attracts a young crowd, so prices are reasonable. You can go there, look around and plan out a full evening in the one neighbourhood. The biggest club is the Café Piu-Piu, at No 134. It has music every night except Monday: jazz, rock, and a sequin-shirted, 20-gallon-hatted band that plays American country music. Café do Bixiga, at No 76, is a traditional bar that stays open late. Try the *pinga com mel*.

The Bar Brahma is the city's oldest; it's at the corner of Avenida São João and Avenida Ipiranga, in the heart of the central hotel district. From 7 pm to midnight, the antique surroundings provide ambience for equally dated live music. The best tables are upstairs. The bar is friendly and relaxing, and a popular after-work hang-out for many *paulistano* professionals (paulistanos are

residents of the city; *paulistas*, of São Paulo state). Bar Leo, at Rua Aurora 100, is open weekdays from 10 am to 8.30 pm and Saturday until 3 pm. It serves the city's best chopp.

Things to Buy

Shopping is almost as important to paulistanos as eating out. Much more interesting than the endless shopping malls are the many markets and fairs that take place around town, especially on weekends. One of the most popular is held in the Praça da República, on Sunday from 8 am to 2 pm. Liberdade, the Oriental district (only five minutes from the centre by metro), also has a big street fair all day on Sunday. Another excellent handicraft market takes place every weekend in Embu, 28 km from São Paulo.

Getting There & Away

Air From São Paulo, there are flights to everywhere in Brazil and to many of the world's major cities. Before buying your ticket, check which airport the flight departs from; see the Getting Around section for details. The São Paulo to Rio shuttle flies at least every half-hour from Congonhas airport to Santos Dumont airport, in central Rio. The flight takes less than an hour, and you can usually go to the airport, buy a ticket (US$300) and be on a plane within the hour.

Most of the major airlines have offices on Avenida São Luis, near the Praça da República. Varig (☎ 530-3922) is at Rua da Consolação 362, Transbrasil (☎ 228-2022) is at Avenida São Luis 250 and VASP (☎ 220-3622) is at Avenida São Luis 9∫.

Bus Terminal Tietê is easy to reach – it's connected to the Tietê metro station – but it can be hard to find your way around. There's an information desk in the middle of the main concourse on the 1st floor, but only Portuguese is spoken. Bus tickets are sold on the 1st floor.

Buses leave for destinations throughout Brazil, and there are also buses to major cities in Argentina, Paraguay, Chile and Uruguay.

All the following buses leave from the

Terminal Tietê. Frequent buses traverse the Via Dutra highway to Rio (429 km, six hours). The cost is US$15 for the regular bus, US$30 for the leito. There are also buses to Brasília (US$35, 16 hours), Foz do Iguaçu (US$34, 15 hours), Cuiabá (US$51, 24 hours), Campo Grande (US$34, 15 hours), Salvador (US$61, 33½ hours), Curitiba (US$14, six hours) and Florianópolis (US$23, 12 hours).

Buses to Santos, Guarujá and São Vicente leave every five minutes from a separate bus station at the end of the southern metro line (Jabaquara station). Buses to Minas Gerais (Belo Horizonte, US$18, 9½ hours) leave from Rodoviária Bresser; take the metro to Bresser.

Train Long-distance trains leave for Bauru (connections to Campo Grande and Corumbá) from Estação da Luz train station. To get there, take the metro to the Luz station. Cuts in long-distance routes continue, so check details at the information booth (☎ 991-3062) at Luz station. You can't get a direct train to Campo Grande or Corumbá from São Paulo; you have to take the train or bus from São Paulo to Bauru, catch a bus to Campo Grande and then get another train to Corumbá. Trains go to Bauru every day at 8 am, noon, and 4 and 11 pm. Buses from Bauru to Campo Grande leave at 4.30 pm. For connections from Campo Grande to Corumbá and Bolivia, see the Campo Grande Getting There & Away information in the Mato Grosso & Mato Grosso do Sul section.

Getting Around
To/From the Airport Three airports serve São Paulo: Aeroporto de Congonhas (14 km south of the centre), Aeroporto Internacional de São Paulo/Guarulhos (30 km east of the centre) and Aeroporto Viracopos (100 km from the centre, near Campinas).

At Congonhas, avoid the radio-taxis at the front of the terminal and ask for the comums; there's a small sign marking the place. The ride into town is about US$12. To catch a bus into the city, walk out of the terminal and to your right, where you'll see a busy street

with a pedestrian overpass. Head to the overpass, but don't cross; you should see a crowd of people waiting for the buses along the street, or ask for the Banderas bus. The trip takes about an hour, and the last bus leaves around 1 am.

From Aeroporto Internacional de São Paulo/Guarulhos, there's a bus that goes to Praça da República, Terminal Tietê rodoviária and Congonhas airport. It costs US$7. For the same price, another bus does a circuit of up-market hotels in the Jardims area and the centre. Another alternative is to catch the local bus to the Bresser bus terminal for US$2 and then catch the metro to your destination. From Guarulhos to the centre, a comum taxi will cost US$30, a radio-taxi US$40.

Avoid Aeroporto Viracopos if possible. A taxi from here into town will cost about US$80.

Bus Buses are slow, crowded during rush hours and not too safe. When you can, use the metro.

Metro If you're on a limited budget, a combination of metro and foot is the best way to see the city. The metro, open from 5 am to midnight, is new, cheap, safe and fast. There are currently three lines. Two intersect at Praça da Sé; the other, newer line gives access to Avenida Paulista. Tickets cost US$0.80 for a single ride, or buy a *multiplo 10*, which gives you 10 rides for US$7.50.

Taxi Both the comum and radio-taxi services are metered. Radio-taxis (☎ 251-1733) cost 50% more than the comums but will pick you up anywhere in the city.

ILHABELA
Ilhabela is the biggest island along the Brazilian coast, and is known for its excellent jungle hiking and fine cachaça.

During the summer, Ilhabela is besieged by holiday-makers from São Paulo. Weekdays in the off season are the time to go. Once you arrive, try to get away from the west coast, either by catching a boat or hiking. Of the sheltered beaches on the island's north side, Praia Pedra do Sino and Praia Jabaquara are recommended. On the east side, where the surf is stronger, try Praia dos Castelhanos, Praia do Gato or Praia da Figueira.

Places to Stay

There's a lack of cheap lodging on Ilhabela, which is why many people choose to stay in São Sebastião, where the hotels are cheaper. Near the beach, the *Pousada dos Hibiscos* (☎ 72-1375), at Avenida Pedro Paula de Morais 714, has doubles for US$60. It's 800 metres from town. If you plan on staying for a few days, self-contained chalets are a reasonably priced option. *Chalés Praia Grande* (☎ 72-1017), in the southern part of the island, is the cheapest, at US$18 per day. There are lots of camping grounds near Barra Velha, where the ferry stops, and just a bit farther south, at Praia do Curral.

Getting There & Away

The ferry from São Sebastião runs frequently. The service operates from 5.30 am until midnight. The ride lasts 15 minutes and is free for pedestrians.

Paraná

CURITIBA

Curitiba, the capital of Paraná, is one of Brazil's urban success stories. There's not much for the traveller, but it's possible to spend a pleasant day there waiting for your bus or train to leave.

Information

The Departamento de Turismo (☎ 223-3535, fax 252-3266), on the 5th floor at Rua Ébano Pereira 187, has a useful map and some brochures about the city's attractions. English and French are spoken. The telephone code for Curitiba is 041.

Largo da Ordem

Close to Praça Tiradentes and the Catedral Metropolitana, take the pedestrian tunnel and you'll be in the cobblestoned historical quarter, Largo da Ordem, a good place for a drink and some music at night.

Train Ride to Paranaguá

The railway journey from Curitiba to the port of Paranaguá, descending a steep mountainside to the coastal lowlands, is the most exciting and spectacular in Brazil.

There are two types of train: a regular train *(trem)* and a tourist train *(litorina)*. The trem runs every day in January and February. From March to September (excluding July) it runs on weekends. In July, and from October to December, it runs on Wednesday, Friday and weekends. But the trip on Wednesday and Friday is one way to Morrettes.

The trem departs at 7.30 am and leaves Paranaguá for the return trip at 4.30 pm, stopping at every station along the way. The air-con litorina runs to almost the same timetable. The difference is that in July and from October to December, it runs one way to Morrettes on Tuesday and Thursday. The litorina leaves Curitiba at 9 am and starts back at 3.30 pm. Both trains take about three hours each way. For the best view on the way down to the coast, sit on the left-hand side.

Tickets for the trem (US$7) and the litorina (US$12) are sold at the train station behind the rodoviária. They can be bought up to two days in advance, and often sell out the day before. For information, call ☎ 234-8441 in Curitiba.

Places to Stay

Across from the rodoferroviária, there are lots of inexpensive hotels. *Hotel Imperio* (☎ 264-3373), Avenida Presidente Afonso Camargo 367, is very clean and friendly, and charges US$15/20 for single/double quartos. Another good one to head for is the *Hotel Itamarati* (☎ 222-9063), Rua Tibagi 950, with single/double apartamentos for US$22/32.

A good mid-range alternative in the centre is the *Hotel O'Hara* (☎ 232-6044), in a colonial building at Rua 15 de Novembro 770,

BRAZIL

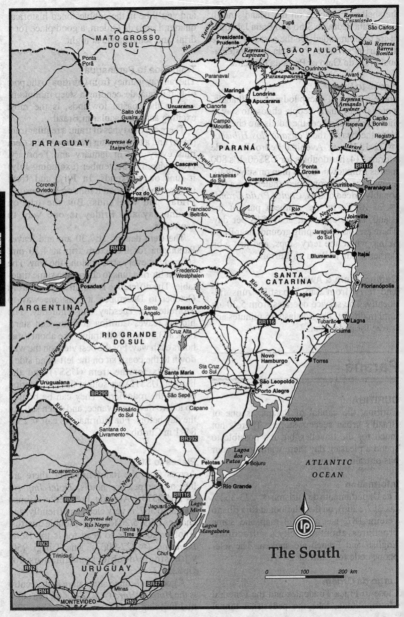

The South

opposite Praça Santos Andrade. Singles/doubles are US$40/60.

Places to Eat

The *Vherdejante* vegetarian restaurant, at Rua Presidente Faria 481, has excellent fixed-price buffet lunches and is open daily, except Sunday. In Rua 24 Horas, there are several places: *Le Lasagne* serves five types of lasagne in individual portions for US$6, while *Le Mignon* serves a varied menu, with cheap 'chef's suggestions'. The *Kabuki*, Avenida 7 de Setembro 1927, has inexpensive Japanese meals; it's closed on Monday.

Getting There & Away

Air There are flights from Curitiba to all major cities in Brazil.

Bus The entrance to the rodoferroviária is on Avenida Presidente Afonso Camargo. There are many daily buses to São Paulo (six hours), Rio (11 hours) and all major cities to the south. There are 12 buses a day to Foz do Iguaçu. From Curitiba, you can also get direct buses to Asunción (US$26), Buenos Aires (US$78) and Santiago (US$92).

Train For details of the train ride between Curitiba and Paranaguá, see the earlier Train Ride to Paranaguá section.

Getting Around

To/From the Airport Alfonso Pena airport is a 20 to 30-minute drive from the city. Cheap public Aeroporto buses leave every hour or so from the bus terminal on Rua João Negrão. A taxi costs about US$25.

PARANAGUÁ

The train ride isn't the only reason to go to Paranaguá. It's a colourful city, with an old section near the waterfront that has a feeling of tropical decadence. Paranaguá also provides access to Ilha do Mel. There's a tourist office in front of the train station. The telephone code is 041.

Museu de Arqueologia e Etnologia

Don't miss this museum at Rua 15 de Novembro 567, in the old section near the waterfront. Housed in a beautifully restored Jesuit school, the museum has many Indian artefacts, primitive and folk art, and some fascinating old tools and machines. It's open Tuesday to Sunday from noon to 5 pm.

Places to Stay & Eat

The cheapest places are along the waterfront, on Rua General Carneiro, but this area is dark and nearly deserted at night, so you need to be careful. Both the *Pensão Bela Vista* and the *Hotel Santiago*, a couple of doors away, have very beat-up, basic rooms for US$4 per person. The *Hotel Litoral* (☎ 423-1734), Rua Correia de Freitas 66, offers the best deal in town. Its rooms are large and open onto a sunny courtyard. Singles/doubles are US$10/15.

Restaurante Bobby, Rua Faria Sobrinho 750, has the best seafood. You can have a delicious meal there for US$7. The *Mercado Municipal do Café* is a good place to have lunch. It's been restored and contains five small restaurants, all serving cheap seafood.

Getting There & Away

All long-distance buses leave from the rodoviária on the waterfront. There are frequent buses to Curitiba (US$4, 1¾ hours). If you're going south, eight buses a day go to Guaratuba, where you can get another bus to Joinville.

For details of the train ride between Paranaguá and Curitiba, see the Curitiba section.

ILHA DO MEL

Ilha do Mel is an oddly shaped island at the mouth of the Baía de Paranaguá. It is popular in the summer because of its excellent beaches, scenic walks and relative isolation.

Ilha do Mel consists of two parts, connected by the beach at Nova Brasília. The bigger part is an ecological station, little visited except for Praia da Fortaleza. The main attractions of the island are close to

BRAZIL

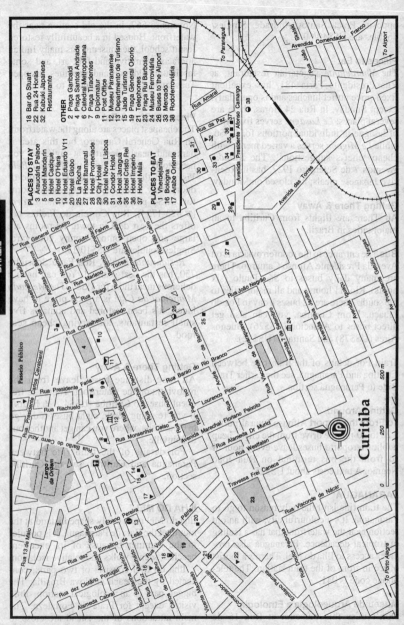

PLACES TO STAY

3 Araucária Palace
5 Hotel Mandarin
8 Hotel Cacique
10 Hotel O'Hara
14 Hotel Eduardo V11
20 Hotel Globo
21 La Rota
25 Hotel Ittararati
28 Hotel Promenade
29 City Hotel
30 Hotel Nova Lisboa
31 Condor Hotel
34 Hotel Jaragua
35 Hotel Cristo Rei
36 Hotel Imperio
37 Hotel Maia

PLACES TO EAT

1 Vherdejante
16 Bologna
17 Arabe Oriente

18 Bar do Stuart
22 Rua 24 Horás
32 Kabuki Japanese Restaurante

OTHER

2 Praça Garibaldi
4 Praça Santos Andrade
6 Catedral Metropolitana
7 Praça Tiradentes
9 Diplomatur
11 Post Office
12 Museu Paranaense
13 Departmento de Turismo
15 Jade Turismo
19 Praça General Osorio
21 Telephones
23 Praça Rui Barbosa
24 Museu Ferroviária
26 Buses to the Airport
33 Mercado
38 Rodoferroviária

Curitiba

Nova Brasília. Nearby, on the ocean side, are the best beaches – Praia Grande, Praia do Miguel and Praia de Fora. The best walks are along the ocean side (east), from the southern tip of the island up to Praia da Fortaleza. There are *bichos de pé*, so keep your shoes on when you're off the beach.

Places to Stay & Eat

If you arrive on the island on a holiday weekend or during peak season, rooms may be in short supply, but it's easy to rent some space to sling a hammock. There's also

plenty of room to camp. If you decide to sleep on the beach, watch out for the tides.

There are 10 designated camping areas on the island: seven in Praia dos Encantadas, two in Nova Brasília and one at Praia Farol das Conchas. All have electricity and water and cost US$2 per person. You're not supposed to camp outside these areas. Watch out for the tides if you decide to crash out on the beach.

There are pousadas at Nova Brasília, Praia da Fortaleza, Praia Farol das Conchas and Praia dos Encantadas. Prices range from US$10 per person in the simple places up to

PLACES TO STAY
4 Monte Líbano
5 Hotel Litoral
6 Hotel Palácio
18 Dantas Palace
19 Hotel Karibe
26 Hotel Santiago
27 Pensão Bela Vista

PLACES TO EAT
10 Restaurante Bobby
11 Vegetariano Natural
12 Café Itibere
22 Mercado Municipal do Café
28 Restaurante Danúbio Azul Panorâmico

OTHER
1 Igreja de NS do Rocio
2 Post Office
3 Local Bus Station
7 Telephones
8 Train Station
9 Tourist Office
13 Igreja NS do Rosário
14 Igreja de São Benedito
15 Tassi Turismo (Cambios)
16 Maritur Turismo (Cambios)
17 Palácio Visconde de Nácar
20 Câmbio
21 Igreja São Francisco das Chagas
23 Museu de Arqueológico e Etnologia
24 Rodoviária
25 Handicraft Market

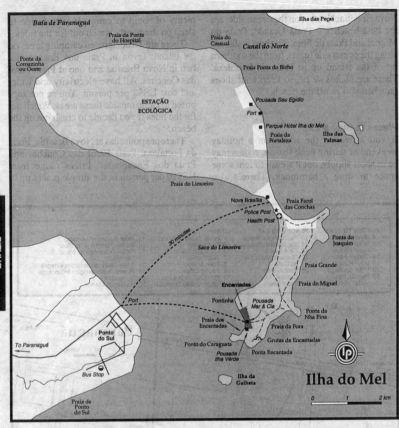

Ilha do Mel

US$40 a double. During high season, they go up by 20% to 50%. *Pousadinha* (☎ 978-3662), well signposted from Nova Brasília, is highly recommended. The staff speak French, English and Italian. Low-season prices are US$20 for a double quarto and US$25 for a double apartamento.

At Praia da Fortaleza, 200 metres past the fort, there are a couple of places. Try the *Pousada Seu Egídio*. Just before the fort is the island's only hotel, the aptly named *Parque Hotel Ilha do Mel* (☎ 223-2585, fax 232-5723), with rooms for US$40 a double.

At Praia dos Encantadas, there are two beachfront places. *Pousada Mar & Cia* (☎ 335-2611) has double quartos for US$20. Next door, the *Pousada Ilha Verde* (☎ 978-2829). Prices range from US$10 for a dorm bed to US$30 or US$40 for an apartamento.

You will find barracas with food and drink at Encantadas, Brasília and Fortaleza. On Friday and Saturday nights there is music and dancing.

Getting There & Away

Take the Pontal do Sul bus from Paranaguá. The bus stops three km from the canal where the boats leave for Ilha do Mel. There's usually a taxi, which charges an extortionate US$5 for the five-minute ride, or you can walk.

If you decide to walk when you get off the bus, go back 20 metres to the paved main road and turn right. Follow this road for a little more than one km, until it veers right and approaches the sea. Then turn left on a sandy but well-travelled road and continue for about two km, until the end, where you'll find barracas and a couple of boats. That's it.

From December to March, boats (US$3, half an hour) make the trip to the island every hour or so between 8 am and 5 pm. The rest of the year, boats aren't as frequent, but you should have no problems finding one.

FOZ DO IGUAÇU

Obviously, people visit Foz do Iguaçu to see Iguaçu Falls. It's a frenzied, unfinished-looking town that can be dangerous, particularly at night. On the Paraguayan side of the river, Ciudad del Este is a bit better. Puerto Iguazú, in Argentina, is much more mellow. Nevertheless, most budget travellers stay in Foz because there are more places to stay and it's cheaper. For information about Puerto Iguazú and the falls see the Argentina chapter.

Information

Tourist Office Foztur maintains six tourist information booths, all with the same information: maps, lists of hotels with a one-star and up rating, and tourist newspapers with English-language descriptions of the attractions. All the staff are very helpful and most speak English. Some also speak Italian, Spanish and German. There are booths at Rua Barão do Rio Branco, in the city (open from 6.30 am to 10 pm); at the rodoviária (6 am to 6 pm); at the airport (9 am until the last plane); at Ponte Presidente Tancredo Neves, on the Argentine border (8 am to 6 pm); just before the Ponte da Amizade, on the Paraguayan border (8 am to 8 pm); and at the entrance to the city, on highway BR-27 (7 am to 6 pm).

Teletur (☎ 1516) maintains a 24-hour information service with English-speaking operators.

Money Câmbio Dick, Avenida Brasil 40, or Frontur, Avenida Brasil 75, both change cash and travellers' cheques.

Visas Visitors who spend the day outside Brazil will not require visas, but those who intend to stay longer must go through all the formalities. In Foz do Iguaçu, the Argentine Consulate (☎ (045) 574-2969) is at Travessa Eduardo Branchi 26 and the Paraguayan Consulate (☎ (045) 523-2898) is at Rua Bartolomeu de Gusmão 738.

The Falls

Argentina has more of the falls than Brazil, but to see them properly, which takes at least two full days, you must visit both sides – the Brazilian park for the grand overview and the Argentine park for a closer look. The best season to see them is from August to November. From May to July, you may not be able to approach the falls on the catwalks, but the volume of water can make them even more impressive.

Places to Stay

There are three camping grounds on the Brazilian side. *Camping Club do Brasil* (☎ 574-1310) is the closest to the falls, at Rodovia das Cataratas (eight km from Foz).

The best place for budget travellers is the *Pousada da Laura* (☎ 574-3628) at Rua Naipi 629 (the sign is quite small, so look carefully). Laura speaks English, French and Spanish and her pousada is clean, safe and friendly. It's in a quieter, tree-lined street close to the local bus station, and it costs US$8 per person. The town's cheapest hotel with a pool is the *Ilha de Capri* (☎ 523-2300) at Rua Barão Rio do Branco 409. Singles/doubles go for US$30/40.

Places to Eat

A good buffet in town is *Restaurante Calamares*, Rua Rebouças 476. At US$4 for all you can eat, it's a good energy boost after a

BRAZIL

Rua Duarte da Costa

To Paraguay & Itaipu Dam

To Curitiba & São Paulo

To Rodoviária

Rua Mem de Sá

Avenida República   Argentina

Rua Rebouças

Kubitschek

Rua Xavier da Silva

Rua Rui Barbosa

Juscelino

Brasil

de

Gusmão

Rua Bartolomeu

Taroba

Avenida

Rua

Rio   Naipi

Avenida Beira

Paraná

Rio

Rua Quintino   Bocaiuva

Rua Almirante Barroso

Rua Edmundo de Barros

Rua Barão do Rio Branco

Avenida Jorge Schimmelpfeng

Rua Antônio Raposo

To Iguaçu Falls & Airport

To Argentina & Pôrto Meira

Rua Pres.   Rua Petinheiro   Avenida   Paraná

Rua   Castelo   Branco   Vermum

da Fonseca   Palxoto   Dumont

Floriano   Deodoro   Santos   Sanways

Rua   Marechal   Marechal

Jorge

Foz do Iguaçu

0   250   500 m

---

hard day at the falls. *Maria & Maria's Confeitaria* has good cakes, sandwiches and hot chocolate. There are two locations: at No 495 and No 1285 Avenida Brasil. A good churrascaria is *Búfalo Branco*, Rua Rebouças 530. Vegetarians can lunch at *Ver o Verde*, Rua Edmundo do Barros 111, between 11 am and 3 pm. It has a cheap buffet for US$5.

Getting There & Away

Air There are frequent flights from Foz do Iguaçu to Asunción, Buenos Aires, Rio and São Paulo. VASP (☎ 523-2212), Transbrasil

(☎ 574-1734), and Varig (☎ 523-2111) are all on Avenida Brasil.

Bus Foz's bus terminal (☎ 522-2680) is on Avenida Costa e Silva, several km outside town, but buses from Argentina go directly there after stopping at the local bus terminal in the town centre. The Anel Viario bus also goes there (US$0.40).

From Foz do Iguaçu, there are seven buses a day to Curitiba (US$26, 12 hours), eight to São Paulo (US$34, 15 hours) and six to Rio (US$50, 22 hours). There are several buses

PLACES TO STAY

2	Hotel Del Rey
3	Hotel Tarobá
4	Vale Verde
6	Imperial Hotel
8	Minas Foz Hotel
11	Hotel Senhor do Bonfim
12	Pousada da Laura
14	Hotel Internacional Foz
16	Hotel Diplomata
21	Hotel Luz
26	Ilha de Capri
32	Rouver Hotel

PLACES TO EAT

7	Rafain Centro Gastronmico
9	Churrascaria Búfalo Branco
10	Restaurante Calamares
15	Maria & Maria's Confeitaria #1
18	4 Sorelle
19	Restaurante Du Cheff
20	Restaurante Pei-kin
22	Bebs
23	Barbarela
25	Ver o Verde
29	Maria & Maria's Confeitaria #2
31	Bier Garten Chopparia

OTHER

1	Urban Bus Terminal (Buses to Iguaçu Falls, Argentina & Paraguay)
5	Câmbio Dick
13	Telephones
17	Paraguayan Consulate
21	Varig
24	Coart Artists' Co-operative
27	Tourist Information (Foztur)
28	Post Office
30	Telephones
33	Argentine Consulate

a day from Ciudad del Este to Asunción (US$12, seven hours).

Getting Around

To/From the Airport Catch a P Nacional bus for the half-hour trip (US$0.50). The buses depart every 22 minutes from 5.30 am to 7 pm, then every hour until 12.40 pm. A taxi costs US$25.

Bus All local buses leave from the urban bus terminal on Avenida Juscelino Kubitschek.

To/From the Brazilian Falls Catch a Cataratas bus to get to the Brazilian side of the falls. At the park entrance, the bus waits while you get out and pay

the US$1.50 entry fee. On weekdays buses depart every two hours from 8 am until 6 pm. On weekends and public holidays, the first bus departs at 8 am and the second at 10 am; thereafter, buses leave every 40 minutes until 6 pm. The last bus leaves the falls at 7 pm.

To/From the Argentine Falls In Foz, catch a Puerto Iguazú bus to get to the Argentine side of the falls. Buses leave every 13 minutes (every 50 minutes on Sunday) from 7 am until 8.50 pm. The fare is US$1.30. In Puerto Iguazú, transfer to an El Pratico bus.

At the bus station in Puerto Iguazú, you can pay for everything in one go: the bus fares to and from the park, the bus to and from Puerto Canoas, and entry to the park. The entrance fee for the park can be paid in Argentine pesos or in US dollars. If you only have reais, the ticket seller at the bus station will change into pesos the amount required for the park entrance fee; this can then be paid on arrival at the park. All up, the bus costs US$4, plus US$3 for park entry and US$4 for the boat at Puerto Canoas out to the Garganta do Diablo.

The bus leaves every hour from 6.40 am to 8.15 pm, but not at 1 pm (which is siesta time).

To/From Ciudad del Este Buses for Ciudad del Este depart from the urban terminal in Foz every 10 minutes from 7am.

Santa Catarina

Santa Catarina is one of Brazil's most prosperous states. Most travellers come for the beaches, many of which have become 'in' vacation spots for well-to-do Brazilians and Argentines. Rapid growth is changing the coastline at an unbelievable pace, often with ugly results.

FLORIANÓPOLIS

Florianópolis, the state capital, is a modern city. It spreads across the mainland and the Ilha de Santa Catarina, which are linked by a causeway. The central section is on the island, facing the Baía Sul. The island side of the city is easy to get around on foot, and there are regular public buses to the island's beautiful beaches.

Information

The information desks at the rodoviária and

BRAZIL

BRAZIL

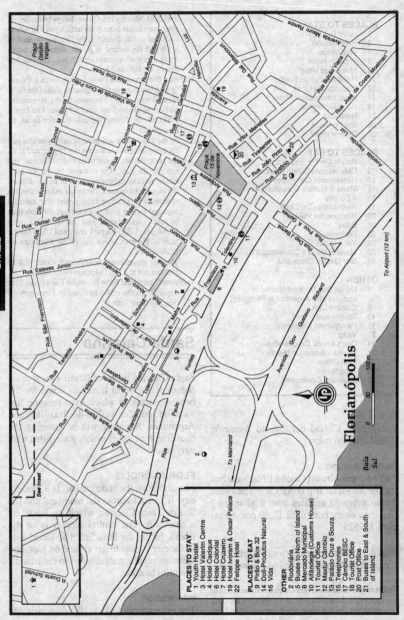

Florianópolis

PLACES TO STAY
1 Youth Hostel
3 Hotel Valerim Centre
4 Hotel Cacique
6 Hotel Colonial
7 Hotel Cruzeiro
19 Hotel Ivoram & Oscar Palace
22 Felippe Hotel

PLACES TO EAT
9 Pirão & Box 32
14 Doll-Produtos Natural
16 Vida

OTHER
2 Rodoviária
5 Buses to North of Island
8 Mercado Municipal
10 Alfândega (Customs House)
11 Tourist Office
12 Maxtur Câmbio
13 Palácio Cruz e Souza
15 Telephones
17 Câmbio BESC
18 Tourist Office
20 Post Office
21 Buses to East & South of Island

Baía
Sul

To Mainland

To Airport (12 km)

0   50   100 m

See Inset

at the airport are good for maps. The tourist office in Praça 15 de Novembre is also useful. Ask there for detailed maps of the walks you can do around Lagoa de Conceição at the centre of the island. The telephone code for Florianópolis is 0482.

Places to Stay
There's a good youth hostel (☎ 222-3781) at Rua Duarte Schutell, a 10-minute walk from the rodoviária. All the cheap hotels are in the centre of town. On Rua Conselheiro Mafra at No 399, the *Hotel Colonial* is seedy but friendly, with good-sized rooms. Quartos cost US$10/15 a single/double. The *Felippe Hotel* (☎ 222-4122) is a couple of blocks past Praça 15 de Novembro, at Rua João Pinto 26. It charges US$10 per person with breakfast. Luciano, the receptionist, speaks English.

Places to Eat
There are plenty of cheap lanchonetes in the market: *Box 32* there has some great seafood snacks. Vegetarians can get a healthy lunch at *Vida*, Rua Visconde de Ouro Prêto, next door to the blue Alliance Française building.

Getting There & Away
Air There are daily direct flights to São Paulo and Porto Alegre, as well as connections to most other cities.

The airlines all have offices in the centre, including Varig (☎ 236-1121), Transbrasil (☎ 236-1229) and VASP (☎ 224-1122).

Bus Long-distance buses travel to Porto Alegre (US$16, 7½ hours), Curitiba (US$10, five hours), São Paulo (US$23, 12 hours), Rio (US$40, 20 hours), Foz do Iguaçu (US$32, 16 hours), Buenos Aires, Argentina (US$65, 27 hours) and Montevideo, Uruguay (US$48, 21 hours).

Getting Around
To/From the Airport The airport is 12 km south of the city. A taxi costs US$10. Aeroporto buses shuttle regularly to the airport until 10 pm, departing from the first platform at the central rodoviária. It's a half-hour ride.

ILHA DE SANTA CATARINA
The east coast beaches are the prettiest and emptiest, and have the biggest waves. Most do not have hotels. The north coast beaches are calm, baylike and have resorts, while the west coast, facing the mainland, has great views and a quiet Mediterranean feel.

In the interior, the beautiful Lagoa da Conceição, surrounded by mountains and sand dunes, is a great place for walks or boat rides.

Getting Around
Local buses serve all of the island's beach towns, but they are infrequent and the schedule changes with the season, so it's best to get the times at the tourist office or the central rodoviária in Florianópolis. During the tourist season, additional micro buses leave from the centre and go directly to the beaches. Unfortunately, surfboards aren't allowed on buses.

The island is one of those places where a one-day car rental is a good way (though fairly expensive) to see most of the island and pick a beach to settle on. Alternatively, take one of the bus tours offered by the Florianópolis travel agencies. Ponto Sul (☎ 235-1399) has a good eight-hour bus tour that costs US$16.

Scuna-Sul (☎ 224-1806) operates three-hour sailboat cruises of Baía Norte for a reasonable US$15.

Rio Grande do Sul

PORTO ALEGRE
Porto Alegre, capital of Rio Grande do Sul and Brazil's sixth-biggest city, lies on the eastern bank of Rio Guaíba. Although most travellers just pass through Porto Alegre, it's a modern city and an easy place in which to spend a few days.

Information
Tourist Offices CRTur at Rua dos Andradas 736, on the ground floor of the Casa de Cultura Mario Quintana, is the state tourism

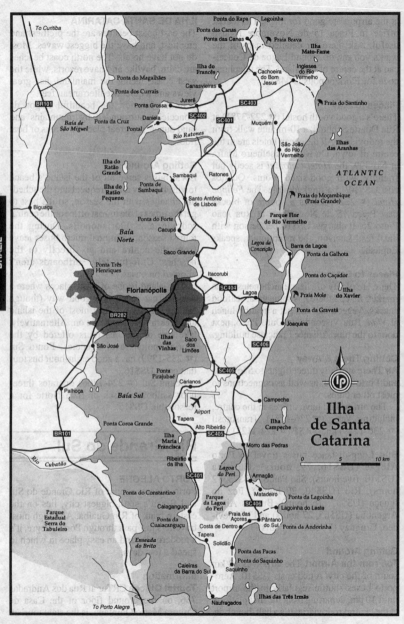

Ilha de Santa Catarina

authority. It also has branches at the airport and the bus station. The telephone code for Porto Alegre is 0512.

Foreign Consulates The following South American countries are represented by consulates in Porto Alegre:

Argentina
    Rua Prof Annes Dias 112, 1st floor (☎ 224-6810)
Paraguay
    Quintino Bocaiuva 554, sala 302 (☎ 346-1314)
Uruguay
    Rua Siqueira Campos 1171, 6th floor (☎ 224-3499)

Things to See

A good place to see gaúchos at play is the big, central **Parque Farroupilha**. On Sunday morning a market/fair, the **Brique da Redencão**, fills a corner of the park with music and antiques and leather goods for sale.

Places to Stay

Youth hostel *Tchê*, Rua Coronel Fernando Machado 681, is a friendly place to stay, but it's a bit of a hike from the metro station.

The *Hotel Uruguai* (☎ 228-7864), Rua Dr Flores 371, is clean, secure and cheap. They have single/double quartos for US$7/14 and double apartamentos for US$16. Nearby, at Avenida Vigarió José Inácio 644, the *Hotel Palácio* (☎ 225-3467) is popular with travellers and very friendly. Quartos cost US$18/26 and apartamentos go for US$25/32. Rua Andrade Neves also has a good selection of hotels and places to eat.

Places to Eat

Wherever you are, a juicy steak will be nearby. For sucos and sandwiches in the city, try *Caseiro Natural* in the *subsolo* (underground arcade) Malcom. With an excellent US$5 buffet lunch, *Ilha Natural Restaurante Vegetariano*, Rua General Vitorino 35, packs the locals in. *Chalé da Praça XV*, on Praça 15 de Novembre in front of the Mercado Público, is the most traditional bar/restaurant in the city. *Banca 40*, the Mercado Público, has excellent ice cream.

Getting There & Away

There are international buses to Montevideo, Uruguay (US$29, 13 hours), Buenos Aires, Argentina (US$53, 24 hours) and Asunción, Paraguay (US$37, 16 hours). Other buses run to Foz do Iguaçu (US$35, 18 hours), Florianópolis (US$16, 7½ hours), Curitiba (US$24, 11 hours), São Paulo (US$38, 18 hours) and Rio de Janeiro (US$55, 27 hours).

Getting Around

Porto Alegre has a one-line metro that goes from the city centre to the rodoviária and the airport. The central station, Estação Mercado Modelo, is by the port. The rodoviária is the next stop, and the airport is three stations farther. The metro runs from 5 am to 11 pm.

CHUÍ

The small border town of Chuí is about 225 km south of Rio Grande on a good paved road. One side of Avenida Brasil, the main street, is Brazilian; the other side is the Uruguayan town of Chuy. The Uruguayan side is a good place to change some money, buy cheap, duty-free Scotch whisky and post letters.

Visas

It's much better to get your Uruguayan visa in Porto Alegre than at Chuí. You will have to wait overnight. The Uruguayan Consulate (☎ 65-1151) is at Rua Venezuela 311 and is open from 9 am to 3 pm. Visas cost US$20.

Places to Stay & Eat

If you have to stay overnight in Chuí, there are a few simple hotels. Try the *Hotel e Restaurante São Francisco* (☎ 65-1096) at Rua Columbia 741. It charges US$10 per person. In Uruguay, the *Plaza Hotel*, Rua General Artigas 553, has singles/doubles for US$25/35. The restaurant in the São Francisco is as good as any around town.

Getting There & Away

The rodoviária is at Rua Venezuela 247, and buses leave frequently for most cities in southern Brazil. You can buy tickets to Montevideo on the Uruguayan side of Avenida

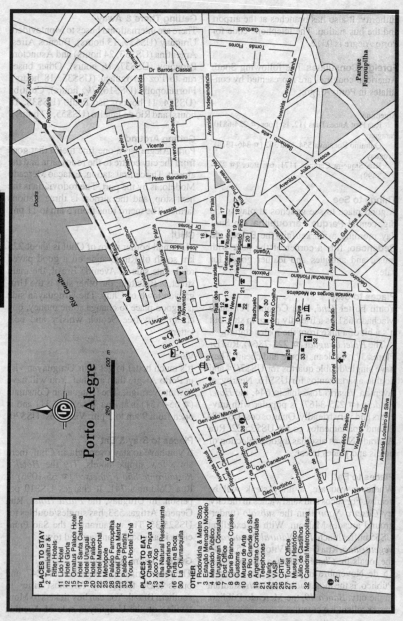

Porto Alegre

Brasil. Seven buses leave daily for Punta del Este and Montevideo. The first leaves at 4 am and the last at midnight.

To/From Uruguay All buses to Uruguay stop at the Polícia Federal on Avenida Argentina, a couple of km from town. You must get out to get your Brazilian exit stamp. In Uruguay, the bus will stop again for the Uruguayan officials to check that you have a Brazilian exit stamp and Uruguayan visa (if you need one).

SERRA GAÚCHA

North of Porto Alegre is the beautiful Serra Gaúcha, which is popular with hikers. The mountain towns of Gramado and Canela are popular resorts.

Canela

While not as up-market as Gramado, Canela is the best jumping-off point for some great hikes and bike rides in the area. There are cheaper hotels here than in Gramado, so budget travellers should make this their base. The tourist office (☎ 282-1287) in Praça João Correa is helpful.

Places to Stay & Eat The youth hostel *Pousada do Viajante* (☎ 282-2017), at Rua Ernesto Urbani 132, is the best cheapie in Canela. It's clean and friendly. The *Hotel Turis* (☎ 282-2774), at Avenida Osvaldo Aranha 223, is reasonable value (US$15 per person, including a bit of breakfast). Camping is available at *Camping Club do Brasil*, eight km from town on the park road.

Highly recommended is *Cantina de Nono*, Avenida Osvaldo Aranha 161. It has excellent pizza and reasonable Italian food. For lunch, the restaurant in the *Parque do Caracol* has a varied menu, with prato feitos for US$6.

Getting There & Away The rodoviária is in the centre of town. There are frequent buses to Porto Alegre, all travelling via Gramado 15 minutes away.

Parque Estadual do Caracol

Eight km from Canela, the major attraction of this park is a spectacular waterfall, 130 metres high. You don't have to do any hiking to see it, as it's very close to the park entrance. The park is open daily from 7.30 am to 6 pm. Entry is US$1. Take the Caracol Circular public bus from the rodoviária at 8.15 am, noon or 5.30 pm.

Parque Nacional de Aparados da Serra

This park, 70 km north of the town of São Francisco de Paula, is Rio Grande do Sul's most magnificent area and one of Brazil's great natural wonders. It preserves one of the country's last forests of *araucária* (a pine-like tree that stands up to 50 metres tall), and contains the Itaimbézinho, a fantastic narrow canyon 120 metres deep, and the Canyon da Fortaleza.

Places to Stay The closest town to the park is Cambará do Sul, where you can find simple accommodation in the *Pousada Fortaleza* (☎ 251-1224) for US$10 per person. The best place to stay is in the park itself. There are good camping spots near the now-defunct Paradouro hotel.

Getting There & Away If you can't afford to take a US$50, four-hour taxi ride from Cambarádo Sul, or to hire a car (or plane) for a day, put on your walking shoes if you expect to see both Itaimbézinho and Fortaleza. No public buses go to either, and the hitching is lousy. The closest you can get is three km from Itaimbézinho, by taking the bus to Praia Grande and asking to be dropped at the park entrance. From the other entrance, on the road between Cambará and Tainhas, it's a 15-km walk to the canyon. To get to Fortaleza, you'll either have to walk 23 km or make a deal with Borges, the taxi driver, to take you out there. There and back costs around US$25, but it's worth it.

There are various ways to get to the park itself. The best option is to come up from the coast via Praia Grande and get off the Cambar do Sul bus at the park entrance. Another possible route is to come up from

BRAZIL

São Francisco de Paula and get off at the other entrance to the park.

There's also the possibility of hiking 20 km from Praia Grande into the canyon itself, but it's dangerous without a guide. People have been trapped in the canyon by flash flooding.

JESUIT MISSIONS

Thirty ruined Jesuit missions remain of what was, in effect, a nation within the colonies during the 17th and 18th centuries. Seven lie in the western part of Rio Grande do Sul, Brazil, eight in the southern region of Itapúa, Paraguay, and the remaining 15 in Argentina.

Use Santo Angelo as a base for the Brazilian missions. São Miguel das Missões (58 km from Santo Angelo) is the most interesting of these. Every evening at 8 pm, there's a sound and light show. Nearby are the missions of São João Batista, on the way to São Miguel, and São Lourenço das Missões, 10 km from São João Batista by dirt road.

Santo Angelo has several modest hotels, but it's great to stay out at São Miguel to see the sound and light show and enjoy the view. The *Hotel Barichello* is the only place to stay and eat. It's very clean, and run by a friendly family. Singles cost US$10 and doubles with a shower are US$20.

Brasília

Brasília is in a federal district, Distrito Federal, and does not belong to any of the states. It must have looked good on paper and still looks good in photos, but the city was built for cars and air-conditioners, not people. It's a lousy place to visit and no-one wanted to live there. It's probably better to read about it instead: try Alex Shoumatoff's *The Capital of Hope*.

Orientation

The city is divided into two halves: Asa Sul and Asa Norte. Avenida W3, the main commercial street, and Avenida L2 run the length of the city and are also divided into north and south.

Information

Tourist Office Setur is the government tourist information service. Its office, inconveniently located on the 3rd floor of the Centro de Convenções, is open Monday to Friday from 1 to 6 pm. The Setur tourist information desk at the airport is open Monday to Friday from 8 am to 1 pm and 2 to 6 pm (from 10 am to 1 pm and 4.30 to 7.30 pm on weekends). The best map is in the phone book *Achei! (Found it!) O Guia de Brasília*. Brasília's telephone code is 061.

Money Banks with moneychanging facilities are in SBS (the Setor Bancário Sul, Banking Sector South) and SBN (Setor Bancário Norte, Banking Sector North). Both are close to the rodoviária. Travel agencies will also change cash dollars.

Foreign Embassies In the following addresses, SES stands for Setor de Embaixadas Sul:

Australia
  Setor de Habitações Individuais Sul, Q I-9, cj 16, casa 1 (☎ 248-1066)
Canada
  SES, Avenida das Nações Q 803, lote 16 sl 130 (☎ 321-2171)
France
  SES, Avenida das Nações, lote 4 (☎ 312-9100)
Guyana
  SES Q5, bl N, salas 601/611 (☎ 224-9229, fax 226-3022)
Germany
  SES, Avenida das Nações 25 (☎ 224-7273, fax 244-6063)
Peru
  SES, Avenida das Nações, lote 43, 70428-900 (☎ 242-9435, fax 243-5677)
Suriname
  QL-12, cj 2, casa 6, Península dos Ministros (☎ 284-5448, fax 284-3791)
UK
  SES, Avenida das Nações, Q 801, cj K lote 8 (☎ 225-2710, fax 225-1777)
USA
  SES, Avenida das Nações, Q 801, lote 3 (☎ 321-7272, fax 225-9136)

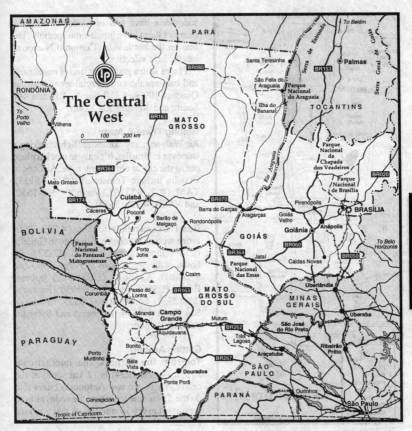

The Central West

Things to See

You can rent a car, take a bus tour or combine a city bus with some long walks to see the bulk of Brasília's edifices. Start at the **Memorial JK**, open from 9 am to 6 pm, then head to the observation deck of the **TV tower**. It's open from 9 am to 8 pm. The **Catedral Metropolitana**, open from 7.45 am to 6 pm, is worth seeing too. The most interesting **government buildings** are the Palácio do Itamaraty (open Monday to Friday until 4 pm), the Palácio da Justiça (open Monday to Friday from noon to 6 pm) and the Palácio do Congresso (open Monday to Friday from 10 to noon and 2 to 5 pm).

The **Parque Nacional de Brasília**, an ecological reserve, is a good place to relax if you're stuck in the city. The Agua Mineral bus from the city rodoviária goes past the front gate.

To get a bus tour, visit the Hotel Garvey-Park (full of travel agencies offering sightseeing tours) or book at the airport or rodoviária.

Places to Stay

Camping is possible not far from the city in the Setor de Garagens Oficiais. To get there, take the Buriti bus (No 109 or No 143) from the rodoviária. Camp sites cost US$4.

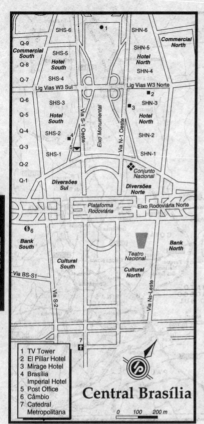

1 TV Tower
2 El Pillar Hotel
3 Mirage Hotel
4 Brasília
  Imperial Hotel
5 Post Office
6 Câmbio
7 Catedral
  Metropolitana

Central Brasília

0   100   200 m

There aren't any cheap hotels in Brasília, but there are a few cheap pensions, mostly located on W3 Sul. All charge around US$15 per person. *Pousada 47* (☎ 224-4894) is a clean, well-kept place at Quadra 703, Bloco A, Casa 41/47. Next door, at Casa 54, *Pousada da Nilza* (☎ 226-5786) is the same price, but it's much more dilapidated.

A good mid-range hotel is the *Mirage Hotel* (☎ 225-7150) in the Hotel Sector North (SHN Q 02 Bloco N). They charge US$33/54 for singles/doubles.

Places to Eat

Both of the shopping complexes near the

rodoviária have lots of places to eat, and many of them have lunch-time specials. The one on the north side (Conjunto Nacional) has the best selection.

Places with a good selection of restaurants and bars are the commercial areas between Quadras 109 and 110 South, 405 and 406 South, and 303 and 304 North.

Getting There & Away

Air With so many domestic flights making a stopover in Brasília, it's easy to catch a plane out of the city at almost any time. Airlines in Brasília include Transbrasil (☎ 243-6133), TAM (☎ 223-5179), Varig (☎ 365-1550) and VASP (☎ 321-3636).

Bus The giant rodoferroviária (☎ 233-7200) is due west of the centre. Buses go to Goiânia (US$7, three hours), Cuiabá (US$38, 20 hours, with connections to Porto Velho and Manaus), Anápolis (US$5, 2½ hours), Belém (US$65, 36 hours), Belo Horizonte (US$23, 11 hours), Rio (US$35, 18 hours), São Paulo (US$34, 16 hours) and Salvador (US$50, 25 hours).

Getting Around

To/From the Airport The international airport (☎ 365-1224) is 12 km south of the centre. There are two Aeroporto buses that do the 35-minute trip from the rodoviária to the airport every 15 minutes. A taxi will cost US$20.

Bus To get from the city rodoviária to the rodoferroviária (for long-distance buses), take bus No 131 (you can also flag it down along the main drag).

Car There are car rental agencies at the airport, the Hotel Nacional and the Hotel Garvey-Park.

Goiás

GOIÂNIA

The capital of the state of Goiás, Goiânia is

200 km south-west of Brasília. It's a fairly pleasant place, with lots of open spaces laid out around circular streets in the centre. The telephone code for Goiânia is 062.

Places to Stay & Eat

The *Hotel Del Rey* is centrally located in the Rua 8 pedestrian mall at No 321. Apartamentos cost US$15/30 a single/double. Another cheapie is the *Hotel Paissandú* (☎ 224-4925) at Avenida Goiás 1290. All rooms have fans. Apartamentos are US$17/30.

For typical Goiânian dishes, go to the *Centro de Tradições Goiánas*, No 515 Rua 4, above the Parthenon Centre, or *Dona Beija* on Avenida Tocantins between Rua 4 and Avenida Anhanguera. *Reserva Natural*, No 475 Rua 7, close to the Parthenon Centre, serves a good vegetarian lunch Monday to Friday from 11 am to 2.30 pm.

Getting There & Away

Air For major airlines, call Varig (☎ 224-5049) or VASP (☎ 223-4266). If you're interested in an air taxi call Sete Taxi Aereo (☎ 207-1519) or União (☎ 207-1600).

Bus The rodoviária (☎ 224-8466) is at No 399 Rua 44. There are buses to Brasília (US$6, three hours), Goiás Velho (US$6, 2½ hours, every hour from 5 am to 8 pm), Cuiabá (US$32, 16 hours), Pirenópolis (US$6, two hours, 7 am and 5 pm) and Caldas Novas (US$7, three hours).

Getting Around

Aeroporto Santo Genoveva (☎ 207-1288) is six km from the city. A taxi there will cost US$10. To get from the rodoviária to the corner of Avenida Anhanguera and Avenida Goiás is a 15-minute walk. Local buses can be caught from the bus stop 50 metres from the main terminal as you walk towards town.

GOIÁS VELHO

The historic city of Goiás Velho, formerly known as Vila Boa, enjoyed a brief gold rush in the 18th century and was once the state capital.

Information

Serra Dourada Turismo(☎ 371-1528), next to the river, at Avenida Sebastião Fleury Curado 2, organises treks, mountain-bike rides, horse rides and ox-cart rides into the surrounding hills. It's open from 8 am to 6 pm daily.

Things to See

Walking through Goiás Velho you quickly notice the main legacies of the gold rush: 18th-century architecture and a large mulatto and mestizo population. Of the seven churches the most impressive is the oldest, the **Igreja de Paula** (1761), on Praça Zaqueu Alves de Castro. The **Museu das Bandeiras**, in the old town council building (1766) on Praça Brasil Caiado, is also worth a visit.

Special Events

The big occasion here is Semana Santa (Holy Week). The main streets of town are lit by hundreds of torches, carried by the townsfolk and dozens of hooded figures in a procession which re-enacts the removal of Christ from the cross and his burial.

Places to Stay

The best low-budget place is the *Pousada do Ipê* (☎ 371-2065), a colonial house on Praça da Boa Vista. It offers a good breakfast and nice views, and the owners organise treks and horse rides. Quartos are US$15/27. Cheaper, but not nearly as pleasant, is the *Hotel Araguai* (☎ 371-1462), at Avenida Dr Deusdete Ferreira de Moura. It has very comfortable apartamentos for US$9/15 a single/double, and quartos for US$8/12.

Getting There & Away

There are frequent buses to Goiânia, 144 km away.

PIRENÓPOLIS

Another historic gold city, Pirenópolis is 70 km from Anápolis and 128 km from Goiânia on the Rio das Almas.

Information

Cerrado Ecoturismo (☎ 331-1374), Rua

Santana 13, organises treks, mountain-bike rides and tours at reasonable prices.

Special Events
The city is famous for the Festa do Divino Espírito Santo, 45 days after Easter. If you're in the area, don't miss this curious spectacle, which is more folkloric than religious. There is a series of medieval tournaments, dances and festivities, including a mock battle between Moors and Christians in Iberia.

Places to Stay & Eat
There are lots of pousadas in town. *Pousada Dona Geny*, Rua dos Pirineus 29, charges US$10 a head. The *Rex Hotel* (☎ 331-1121) is a step up but still pretty basic, with quartos for US$10 per person. *Pousada das Cavalhadas* (☎ 331-1261), Praça da Matriz 1, has apartamentos for US$40 a double.

All these places fill up during the festival, so most visitors camp out near the Rio das Almas or rent a room.

The *Restaurante As Flor*, in Avenida São Jayme, serves huge plates of good regional cuisine. There are 18 different desserts, each sweeter than the last. *Nena*, Rua Aurora 4, has an excellent buffet lunch of regional dishes for US$6.

Getting There & Away
There are bus services from Anápolis and Goiânia as well as from Brasília.

PARQUE NACIONAL DA CHAPADA DOS VEADEIROS
Just over 200 km north of Brasília, this scenic park located in the highest area of the Central West has become a popular destination for Brazilian ecotourists. The best time to visit the park is between May and October. The entry fee is US$1. Camping is the best option here (about US$1 a night), but basic accommodation can be found in the small nearby town of São Jorge.

Getting There & Away
From Brasília, take a bus to Alto Paraiso de Goias, where you can either catch a local bus

to São Jorge, or walk to the park, a couple of hours away.

Mato Grosso & Mato Grosso do Sul

Mato Grosso and Mato Grosso do Sul are separate states, although until the late 1970s this region was all Mato Grosso state. The vast wetlands of the Pantanal extend across parts of both states.

The Mato Grosso is home to many of Brazil's remaining Indians, whose lands are threatened by rapid agricultural development following construction of the roads from Belém to Brasília and from Cuiabá to Santarém.

CUIABÁ
Cuiabá is a lively place and a good base for excursions into the Pantanal and Chapada dos Guimarães.

Orientation & Information
The city is actually two sister cities separated by the Rio Cuiabá: old Cuiabá, where the modern town's centre is located; and Várzea Grande, to the south-west where the airport is. The tourist office (☎ 322-5363) is in the centre on Praça da República, near the post office. It's open Monday to Friday from 8 am to 6 pm. Cuiabá's telephone code is 065.

Things to See
The **Museu do Indio** (Rondon) has exhibits on the Xavantes, Bororos and Karajas tribes, and is worth a visit. It is at the university, on Avenida Fernando Correia da Costa, and opens Monday to Friday from 8 to 11.30 am and 1.30 to 5.30 pm. The university also contains a small zoo, which is worth a look. Entry is free. The **market** by the Rio Cuiabá bridge is interesting.

Organised Tours
Travel agencies in town arrange reserva-

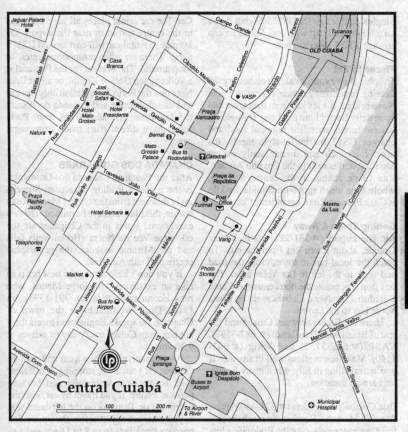

Central Cuiabá

0   100   200 m

tions, guides and transport for photo-safaris into the Pantanal and weekend trips to Chapada dos Guimarães, and can help with the logistics of more ambitious trips to Emas. Ametur (☎ 624-1000), Rua Joaquim Murtinho 242, close to Turimat, has been recommended. Their tours are expensive (around US$80 a day) but well organised. An alternative and relatively cheap excursion is with Joel Souza, a very enthusiastic guide (fluent in English, Italian and German), whose two-day Pantanal trips cost around US$130 including food, accommodation, transport and boat ride. He often meets incoming flights, and has an office (☎ 624-1386) at Avenida Getúlio Vargas 155A.

Places to Stay

A cheapie in the town centre is *Hotel Samara* (☎ 322-6001) at Rua Joaquim Murtinho 270. Their single quartos go for US$10 and double apartamentos cost US$25. A travellers' favourite is the *Hotel Mato Grosso* (☎ 321-9121), at Rua Comandante Costa 2522. It has US$25/30 apartamentos and a good breakfast. The *Jaguar Palace* (☎ 322-9044, fax 322-6698), at Avenida Getúlio Vargas 600, is a three-star hotel with a pool.

BRAZIL

Singles/doubles go for US$55/67, but if you take a Pantanal trip with Joel Souza he can arrange a 50% discount here.

Places to Eat

To splurge on exotic local fish dishes, try the floating restaurant *Flutuante*, next to Ponte Nova bridge. It's six km from the centre and open daily from 11 am to 11 pm. *O Regionalissimo* serves excellent regional food and charges US$5 for buffet-style meals. It's open for lunch and dinner, daily except Monday, and is next to the Casa do Artesão, Rua 13 de Junho. In the centre, a cheap, wholesome lunch spot with comida por kilo is *Casa Branca*, Rua Comandante Costa 565.

Getting There & Away

Air The airport (☎ 381-2211) is in Várzea Grande, about seven km from the city. To catch the local bus to town, cross the road and walk to the left to Las Velas hotel. The bus stop is opposite the hotel entrance. Catch a Jardim Primavera, Cohabcanela or Costa Verde bus to the centre.

There are flights between Cuiabá and the rest of Brazil with Transbrasil (☎ 682-3597), VASP (☎ 682-3737) and Varig (☎ 682-1140). Make reservations well in advance if you're travelling in July, when many Brazilians are on vacation.

Bus Cuiabá's rodoviária (☎ 321-4803) is on Avenida Marechal Rondon. To reach the city from the rodoviária, take the Rodoviária bus (No 202) to its final stop. Six buses a day make the trip to Poconé (US$5, two hours); the first leaves at 6 am. To Barão de Melgaço there are two buses daily at 7.30 am and 3 pm (US$11, three hours). For Chapada dos Guimarães there are six buses daily (US$4, 1½ hours), but take the 8 am bus if you've only got a day to spend there.

There are three buses daily to Cáceres (US$12, three hours); three buses daily to Porto Velho (US$38, 24 hours); and five to Goiânia (US$30, 16 hours). There are six buses daily on the route to Rondonópolis (three hours), Coxim (seven hours) and Campo Grande (10 hours).

Car The car rental places all have branches in the centre and in or near the airport. On average, a rental car will cost around US$80 a day. There are often promotional rates, so shop around. The best car for the Pantanal is a Volkswagen Golf or Kombi, or a Fiat Uno. Note that the Porto Jofre station only has gas and diesel; Poconé and Pousada do Pixaim (55 km from Poconé, 85 km from Porto Jofre) have *álcool* (fuel made from sugar cane).

CHAPADA DOS GUIMARÃES

After the Pantanal, Chapada dos Guimarães is the region's leading attraction. Surprisingly different from the typical Mato Grosso terrain, this place is not to be missed. The two exceptional sights in the Chapadas are the 60-metre Véu de Noiva (Bridal Veil) falls and the Mirante lookout, the geographic centre of South America.

If you don't have a car your best bet is to take an excursion with Jorge Mattos, who runs Ecoturismo (☎ & fax 791-1393), on Praça Dom Wunibaldo in the town of Chapada. He speaks English and meets the 8 am bus from Cuiabá every day (it arrives at 9.30 am).

An alternative is to hire a car and explore the area on your own, stopping at different rock formations, waterfalls and bathing pools at leisure. If you travel by car, visit the Secretaria de Turismo, on the left-hand side as you enter town, just before the square. It's open on weekdays from 8 to 11 am and 1 to 4 pm, and a useful map is available. You'll need it.

Places to Stay & Eat

There is good camping at Salgadeira, just before the climb into Chapada, but if you want to rough it, you could basically camp anywhere.

Accommodation in the area ranges from the very basic but friendly *Hotel São José* (☎ 791-1152), Rua Vereador José de Souza 50, which charges US$8 per person, to the *Hotel Pousada da Chapada* (☎ 791-1330), a couple of km from town on the road to Cuiabá. It charges US$60 a double.

In between are a couple of good alternatives. The very popular *Turismo Hotel* (☎ 791-1176, fax 791-1383), Rua Fernando Correo Costa 1065, offers apartamentos from US$23 per person, and also has a restaurant. *Quinco* (☎ 791-1404), Praça Dom Wunibaldo 464 (next to Ecoturismo), has simple, clean apartamentos for US$12/14 a single/double. On the main square, *Nivios* has excellent regional food – all you can eat for US$8.

Getting There & Away
Buses leave for Chapada dos Guimarães from Cuiabá's rodoviária every 1½ hours from 8 am to 6 pm (US$4).

THE PANTANAL
The Amazon may have all the fame and glory, but the Pantanal is a far better place to see wildlife. This vast area of wetlands, about half the size of France, lies mostly within the states of Mato Grosso and Mato Grosso do Sul, but also extends into the border regions of Bolivia and Paraguay.

The Pantanal is a vast alluvial plain, much of which is flooded by the Rio Paraguai and its tributaries during the wet season (October to March). It is what remains of an ancient inland sea called the Xaraés, which began to dry out at the same time as the Amazon Sea, 65 million years ago.

Birds are the most frequently seen wildlife, but the Pantanal is also a sanctuary for giant river otters, anacondas, iguanas, jaguars, cougars, crocodiles, deer, anteaters, black howler monkeys and capybaras.

The area has few people and no towns. The only road that plunges deep into the Pantanal is the Transpantaneira, which ends 145 km south of Poconé, at Porto Jofre. Only a third of the intended route from Poconé to Corumbá has been completed, because of ecological concerns and lack of funds. The best way for the budget traveller to see the wildlife of the Pantanal is to drive or hitch down the Transpantaneira, preferably all the way to Porto Jofre.

The best time to visit is during the dry season (April to September or October). The best time to see birds is July to September. Flooding, incessant rains and extreme heat make travel difficult from November to March.

If language or time is a problem and money isn't, you can write to Douglas Trent of Focus Tours (☎ & fax (612) 892-7830), 14821 Hillside Lane, Burnsville, MN 55306, USA; in Brazil, contact Focus (☎ (031) 373-3734) in Belo Horizonte, Minas Gerais. Focus specialises in nature tours and Doug is active in trying to preserve the Pantanal.

Places to Stay
Pantanal accommodation is divided into four general categories: *fazendas, pousadas, pesqueiros* and *botels*. Fazendas are ranch-style hotels which usually have horses, and often boats, for hire. Pousadas range from simple accommodation to top-end standard. Pesqueiros are hang-outs for anglers; they usually rent boats and fishing gear. A botel, a contraction of boat and hotel, is a floating lodge (usually very expensive). Reservations are needed for all accommodation, especially in July, when lots of Brazilian tourists holiday there.

Unfortunately, nearly all accommodation is expensive. It usually includes good food, modest lodging and transport by plane, boat or 4WD from Corumbá or Cuiabá. More often than not, reservations are handled through a travel agent, and you must pay in advance. It's also a good idea to call ahead for weather conditions.

Along the Transpantaneira
At Km 30, *Pousada do Araras* charges US$50 a day. It has a pool and also shows films about the Pantanal. At the Rio Pixaim, Km 65, you'll find two places; our advice is to check both before deciding where to stay, as their prices are similar. *Pousada do Pixaim* (☎ (065) 322-8961) is the more rustic of the two – a classic Pantanal building (wooden, on stilts). It has air-con, tasty meals (included in the price), clean rooms with electric showers, and the last álcool and gas pump until you return to Poconé – so fill up! Prices are US$40/48 a single/double.

Across the bridge, the much more modern *Fazenda-Hotel Beira Rio* (☎ (065) 321-9445) is just a little more expensive at US$50/60 a single/double. It's popular with package tourists from São Paulo. Boats can be rented for US$20 an hour and horses for US$12 an hour.

Forty km farther down the road is the newest and cheapest pousada on the Transpantaneira, the *Pousada O Pantaneiro* (☎ (065) 721-1545), run by Lerinho and his son Eduardo. It's a simple place, charging US$25 per person for room and board.

Porto Jofre is a one-hotel hamlet. Campers can stay at Senhor Nicolino's *fishing camp*, near the river, for US$5 per person. He provides clean bathrooms and cooking facilities, and also rents boats. Alternatively, take the turn-off (it's the only one) a couple of km to the *Hotel Santa Rosa Pantanal* (☎ 322-0948). For US$100/130 a single/double, the Santa Rosa will put you up in a bungalow that sleeps four, and feed you three fish meals a day.

Mato Grosso There are several fazendas in the northern Pantanal that are off the Transpantaneira. The *Hotel Porto Cercado* (☎ 322-0178 in Cuiabá) is easily reached by car; singles/doubles cost US$60/80, meals included. It's along the Rio Cuiabá 42 km from Poconé. The expensive *Hotel Cabanas do Pantanal* (☎ 322-4142 in Cuiabá) is 52 km from Poconé. A three-day package costs US$300.

Sapé Pantanal Lodge (☎ (065) 322-3426) is on the margins of the Rio Cuiabá, one hour by boat from the Porto Cercado. Four-day packages with full board cost US$480. This one has been highly recommended by several readers, so if money is no object, check it out.

Mato Grosso do Sul One of the cheapest places to stay in the Pantanal is the *Pesqueiro Clube do Pantanal* (☎ 242-1464 in Miranda), 168 km from Corumbá in the direction of Campo Grande. It charges about US$30 per person with full board, and fishing trips by boats can be arranged. Eight km from

Miranda is the *Hotel Beira Rio* (☎ 242-1262 in Miranda). It charges US$46 per person (full board) for rooms with air-con and hot showers.

There are a few places deeper into the Pantanal, at Passo do Lontra, 120 km and two hours (in the dry season) from Corumbá. *Cabana do Lontra* (☎ (067) 383-4532 in Campo Grande) is an excellent place, another classic Pantanal structure, with lots of wildlife around. It costs US$40 per person, including full board, but they are quite willing to bargain, especially out of season. To get there, take the dirt road leading off the road to Campo Grande. Alternatively, you can take the train to Campo Grande and have the lodge pick you up at the Carandazal station.

The top-end place in the southern Pantanal is the *Refúgio Ecológico Caiman* (☎ (067) 725-5267 in Campo Grande, (067) 242-1102 in Corumbá, (011) 246-9934 in São Paulo), 36 km from Miranda. Caiman offers 25 different programmes that can be done on foot, on horseback or by truck. All are led by one of the multilingual guides who live on the fazenda. This is real ecotourism. It isn't cheap (four-day packages start at US$500), but it's highly recommended.

Getting There & Away

There are two main approach routes to the Pantanal: via Cuiabá in the north and via Corumbá in the south. From Cuiabá there are three gateways to the Pantanal – Cáceres, Barão de Melgaço and Poconé – all of which lead to Porto Jofre on the Transpantaneira. Corumbá is best accessed by bus from Campo Grande; the route runs via Aquidauana and Miranda. Coxim, a small town on the east of the Pantanal, is a third point of entry to the Pantanal, but has a very limited tourist infrastructure.

Getting Around

Since the lodges are the only places to sleep, drink and eat, and public transportation doesn't exist, independent travel is difficult in the Pantanal. Driving is an option, but not easy. Only a few roads reach the periphery

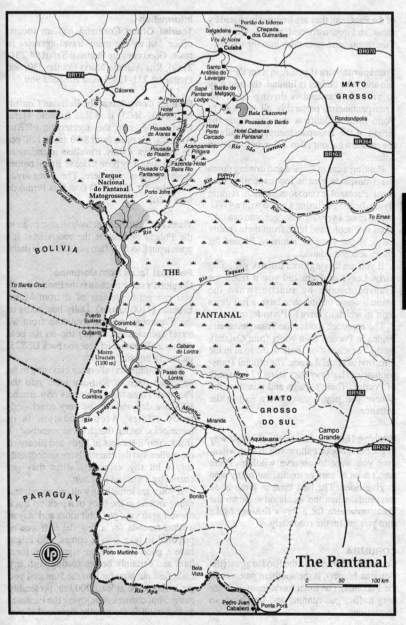

BRAZIL

The Pantanal

Portão do Inferno
Salgadeira
Chapada
dos Guimarães
Véu de Noiva
Cuiabá
BR070

BR174
Cáceres

Santo
Antônio do
Leverger

MATO
GROSSO

Poconé
Sapé de
Pantanal
Lodge
Barão de
Melgaço

Hotel
Aurora
Baía Chacororé
Rondonópolis
Pousada do Barão
Pousada
do Araras
Hotel
Porto
Cercado
Hotel Cabanas
do Pantanal
BR364
Pousada
do Pixaim
Acampamento
Pirigara
Rio São Lourenço
BR163
Fazenda-Hotel
Beira Rio
Parque
Nacional
do Pantanal
Matogrossense
Pousada Os
Pantaneiro
Rio Piquiri
Porto Jofre
Rio Cuiabá
Rio Piguiri
To Emas
Rio Correntes

BOLIVIA

THE
Rio Taquari

To Santa Cruz
Coxim

PANTANAL

Puerto
Suárez
Corumbá
Cabana
do Lontra

Quijarro
Rio Negro

Morro
Urucum
(1100 m)
Passo do
Lontra

Forte
Coimbra
BR163

Rio Paraguai
MATO
GROSSO
DO SUL

Miranda
Rio Miranda
Campo
Grande

PARAGUAY
Aquidauana
BR262

Bonito

CORUMBÁ

Porto Murtinho

Bela
Vista
0   50   100 km

Rio Apa
Pedro Juan
Caballero
Ponta Porã

of the Pantanal; they are frequently closed by rains and reconstructed yearly. Only the Transpantaneira goes deep into the region.

Transpantaneira If you're in it for the wildlife and your budget is limited, the best way to visit the Pantanal is driving down the Transpantaneira, preferably all the way to Porto Jofre. Wildlife is abundant along the length of the Transpantaneira, especially in the meadows about 10 to 20 km before Porto Jofre.

Renting a car in Cuiabá and driving down the Transpantaneira is less expensive than most Pantanal excursions, which require flying, boating or hiring a guide with a 4WD. If you're on a very tight budget, you can take a bus to Poconé and hitch from there (pretty easy); if you have to, return to Poconé for cheap accommodation.

If you are driving from Cuiabá, get going early. Leave at 4 am and you'll reach the Transpantaneira by sunrise, when the animals come to life, then have a full day's light in which to drive to Porto Jofre.

The approach road to the Transpantaneira begins in Poconé (two hours from Cuiabá), by the Texaco station. Follow the road in the direction of Hotel Aurora. The official Transpantaneira Highway Park starts 17 km south of Poconé. There's a sign and guard station (where you pay a small entry fee) at the entrance.

Hitching Hitching may be the cheapest way to go, but it doesn't allow you to stop whenever you want to observe wildlife. There aren't a lot of cars or trucks, but many stop to give rides. The best time to hitch is on weekends, when the locals drive down the Transpantaneira for a day's fishing. Make sure you get on the road early.

CORUMBÁ

Corumbá, a port city on the Rio Paraguai (the Bolivian border), is the southern gateway to the Pantanal. The town has a reputation for drug traffic, gun-running and poaching, so be cautious.

Information
Tourist Office Corumbá has no tourist office, but try the many travel agencies in town. Good ones are Pantanal Safari (☎ 231-2112), Rua Antônio Maria Coelho 330, and Pantur (☎ 231-4343), Rua América 969.

Foreign Consulates The Bolivian Consulate (☎ 231-5605) is at Rua Antônio Maria Coelho 852, near the intersection of Rua América. It's open from 8.30 am to 1.30 pm on weekdays. Oddly, travellers intending to visit Bolivia may have to leave Brazil before applying for a visa here. The Paraguayan Consulate (☎ 231-1691) is at Rua Firmo de Matos 508.

Visas For a Brazilian entry/exit stamp, go to the Polícia Federal at the rodoviária. It's open from 8 to 11.30 am and 2 to 5 pm daily.

Pantanal Tours from Corumbá
Corumbá's star attraction is the Pantanal, and you can get a preview of it from Morro Urucum (1100 metres). Daily boat tours of the Corumbá area are available from all travel agencies. An all-day trip on the boat *Pérola do Pantanal* will set you back US$25, including lunch.

Many budget travellers are choosing to go on cheap three or four-day tours into the Pantanal. These tours, generally cost around US$25 a day and can be very rough-and-ready affairs. Accommodation is in hammocks, under thatch or in somebody's shack. You'll see lots of birds and plenty of crocodiles, but the mammals are understandably a bit shy, especially when they get chased by a truck at 80 km/h.

If you want something well organised, and riding around in the back of a pick-up truck doesn't grab you, pay a bit more and stay at a hotel-fazenda for a few days. If you're prepared to take it as it comes, you might have a good time. Before signing on for a tour, and certainly before parting with any cash, find out how far into the Pantanal you go: it should be at least 200 km, preferably more. Your chances of enjoying the Pantanal and its wildlife are greatly increased if you go with a reputable guide who forsakes the 'mechanical chase' approach, and instead accompanies small groups (preferably less than five people) on an extensive walking trip through the area for several days, camping out at night (away from drinking dens!) with walks at the optimum times to observe wildlife – before sunrise, at dusk and during the night. A trip along these lines will need at least four days (preferably five).

In Corumbá, disreputable guides, known as *guias piratas* (pirate guides), are plentiful; there is a lot of cachaça-drinking to convince tourists that they're having a good time. Tales of woe with pirate guides include abandonment in the marshes, assorted drunken mayhem and even attempted rape.

Places to Stay & Eat

Close to the bus and train stations, the *Hotel Londres* (☎ 231-6717) has single/double apartamentos with fans for US$10/15. *Pousada Pantaneira* (☎ & fax 231-3934), Rua Frei Mariano 1335, near the defunct Hotel Schabib, is basic, but cheaper at US$4 per person. A Swiss woman, Claudine, organises cheap Pantanal tours from the hotel. At the *Condor*, in the town centre, quartos with fan are good value, at US$6 per person. The *Hotel Santa Rita* (☎ 231-5453), at Rua Aquino Correá 860, has good, big apartamentos for US$15/26. The ones at the front have small balconies. There's a *youth hostel* (☎ 231-2305) at Rua Antônio Maria Coelho 677.

Bar El Pacu, on Rua Cabral, is a good fish restaurant. *Churrascaria Rodeio*, 13 de Junho 760, has live music as well as tasty meat dishes. The *Restaurante Paladar*, Rua Antônio Maria Coelho, has comida por kilo.

Getting There & Away

Like Campo Grande, Corumbá is a transit point for travel to/from Bolivia and Paraguay. See the Chuí Crossing the Border section for more details.

Air The airport is three km from the town centre. VASP (☎ 231-4441, 231-4308 at the airport), Rua 15 de Novembro 392, is the only large company flying into Corumbá.

For Bolivian air connections – Lloyd Aéreo Boliviano (LAB) and Transportes Aéreos Militares (TAM) – contact Pantur (☎ 231-4343), Rua América 969.

Bus From the rodoviária, buses run to Campo Grande eight times a day (US$14, seven hours). The bus is much quicker than the train.

Train There are trains to Campo Grande every Monday and Friday at 8 am (US$12/8 in 1st/2nd class).

Once across the Bolivian border, most people will be heading towards Santa Cruz. For more details, see the requisite section of the Bolivia chapter. In Corumbá, seats on the *expreso especial Bracha*, a special 'luxury' service between the Bolivian border town of Quijarro and Santa Cruz, should be reserved three or four days in advance through Receptivo Pantanal at Rua Frei Mariano 502. Tickets cost US$25 per person.

Boat The Paraguayan government's Flota Mercante del Estado boat service between Asunción (Paraguay) and Corumbá on the Río Paraguay has been taken over by a private company, Cruceros SRL, but remains erratic. See Getting There & Away information under Asunción in the Paraguay chapter for more details.

It may be possible to arrange river transport as far as Bahía Negra (Paraguay), from where a regular boat runs to Asunción.

To/From Bolivia Brazilian immigration is at the federal police post at the Corumbá rodoviária. Anyone entering or exiting Brazil must check in here and complete immigration formalities. For about US$0.40, a city bus will take you into Corumbá, five km from the border. Everyone entering Brazil from Bolivia is required to have a yellow fever vaccination certificate.

Getting Around

A taxi to the centre of Corumbá from either

the bus or the train station costs US$2.50. For a taxi from the centre to the Bolivian border, expect to pay US$8. The city bus between the centre and the Brazilian border departs about twice an hour (US$0.80). The Brazilian border post is open daily from 8 to 11 am and 2 to 5 pm.

Bahia

Bahia is Brazil's most African state. Its capital, Salvador da Bahia, is a fascinating city, and a major tourist attraction. The Bahian coast has many fine beaches, while the inland regions, though less known, are well worth a visit. Lençois provides a handy base for hiking trips inside the spectacular Parque Nacional da Chapada Diamantina.

Bahia has some of Brazil's best artisans, who usually have small shops or sell their folk art in the local market. You can buy this in Salvador, but the best place to see or purchase the real stuff is in the town of origin.

SALVADOR DA BAHIA

Salvador da Bahia, often abbreviated to Bahia by Brazilians but also commonly called Salvador, is the capital of Bahia state and is one of Brazil's highlights.

On 1 November 1501, All Saints' Day, Amerigo Vespucci sailed into the bay, which was accordingly named Baía de Todos os Santos. In 1549, on the shores of the bay, Tomé de Souza founded what was to be Brazil's most important city for 300 years.

Thriving on the sugar trade until the mid-18th century, Salvador was the Portuguese empire's second city, after Lisbon. It was famous for gold-filled churches, beautiful mansions and many festivals. It was also famous for its sensuality and decadence. The historic centre has been attractively renovated, though the redevelopment displaced many of the former residents, and purists will say that it's not a totally authentic restoration. While visitors throng the central areas, and new industries have transformed the suburbs, many of the city's 2.1 million people are still jobless, homeless and hungry.

Orientation

Salvador sits on a peninsula at the mouth of Baía de Todos os Santos. A steep bluff divides central Salvador into two parts: Cidade Alta (Upper City), the historic section, and Cidade Baixa (Lower City), the commercial and financial centre. These are linked by the Plano Inclinado Gonçalves (funicular railway), the Lacerda Elevator and some very steep roads *(ladeiras)*. The heart of the historic centre, with most of the tourists and nightlife, is called Pelourinho; this refers, very roughly, to the area between and around Largo do Pelourinho and Terreiro de Jesus. Further south, at the tip of the peninsula, the area known as Barra has a pretty beach and is also popular. Many other beaches are found along the coast to the east.

Information

Tourist Offices Bahiatursa is the state tourism authority. The main tourist office (☎ 241-4333), with excellent staff, is in Palácio Rio Branco, Rua Chile 2. It is open daily from 8 am to 6 pm. There are also Bahiatursa tourist offices at the Mercado Modelo (☎ 241-0242), the rodoviária (☎ 358-0871), and the airport (☎ 204-1244).

Emtursa, the city of Salvador's tourism authority, has its main office (☎ 243-6555) at Largo do Pelourinho 12, and an information booth inside the Museu da Cidade across the street. They both open Tuesday to Saturday from 10 am to 6 pm.

Consulates Most Western European countries and the USA have consulates in the city. Bahiatursa has all the addresses.

Money In Cidade Alta, two good places to change money are Banep and Vent Tour, both near Terreiro de Jesus. Ignore street moneychangers: they are probably rip-off artists. There's an American Express/Kontik-Franstur SA office (☎ 242-0433) in Cidade Baixa, at Praça da Inglaterra 2, which holds mail for travellers. The main branch of

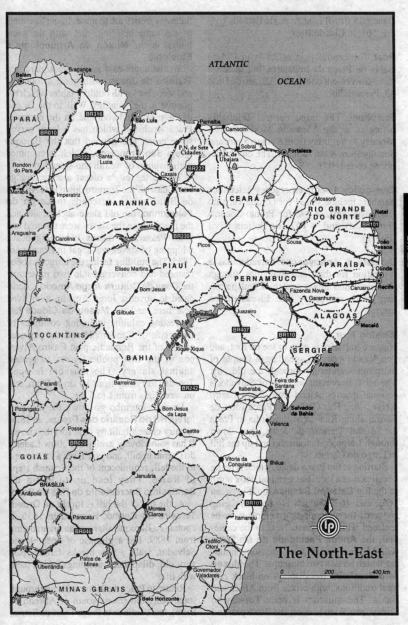

The North-East

0   200   400 km

Banco do Brasil is at Avenida Estados Unidos 561, in Cidade Baixa.

Post The central post office is in Cidade Baixa on Praça da Inglaterra, but there's a more convenient one at Rua Alfredo de Brito 43, Pelourinho.

Telephone The most central Telebahia office is at the Mercado Modêlo, open Monday to Saturday from 8 am to 5 pm, and Sunday from 8 am to noon. The city's telephone code is 071.

Emergency Useful emergency telephone numbers include ☎ 131 for Disque Turismo (Dial Tourism), ☎ 192 for Pronto Socorro (First Aid) and ☎ 197 for Polícia Civil (Police).

Dangers & Annoyances Salvador has a reputation for theft and muggings, though the Pelourinho area is now thick with patrolling police and pretty safe. Elsewhere, be careful.

Walking Tour
Historic Salvador is easy to see on foot, and you should plan on spending a couple of mornings wandering through the old city. The most important sections of Salvador's colonial quarter extend from Praça Castro Alves, along Rua Chile, past Praça Tomé de Souza, along Rua da Misericórdia to Praça da Sé and Terreiro de Jesus, then down through Largo do Pelourinho and up the hill to Largo do Carmo.

Starting at the Praça da Sé, which is being developed as a local bus terminal, look north to the big **Catedral Basílica**, built between 1657 and 1672, which is currently being restored; the deteriorating ceiling is to be replaced with fibreglass. Next to the cathedral, the **Antiga Faculdade de Medicina** (Old Medical Faculty) is a handsome building which houses two museums. The **Museu Afro-Brasileira** has displays on black cultural traditions, with orixás from Africa and Bahia. The museum is open Tuesday to Friday from 9 am to noon and 2 to 5 pm, and

Saturday from 9 am to noon. In the basement of the same building, and with the same hours, is the **Museu de Arqueologia e Etnologia**.

To the south-east is a large square, the **Terreiro de Jesus**, with trees, a fountain, and some bars with outdoor tables which are popular in the evenings. Walk to the far end of the plaza, and continue on the narrower Praça Anchieta, which has a large carved stone cross, and beyond that the Baroque **Igreja São Francisco**, which is crammed with displays of wealth and splendour.

To see the city's oldest architecture go north-east off the Terreiro down Rua Alfredo de Brito, which descends to **Largo do Pelourinho**, the old slave auction site and the place where the slaves were tortured and sold. *Pelourinho* means 'whipping post'; whipping of slaves was legal in Brazil until 1835. The building facing the Largo has been restored and converted into two museums: the **Casa da Cultura Jorge Amado** is dedicated to novelist Jorge Amado, who lived near here; and the **Museu da Cidade** has interesting exhibits including costumes of the orixás of Candomblé and the personal effects of the Romantic poet Castro Alves, one of the first public figures to protest against slavery. The museum is open Tuesday to Friday from 10 am to 6 pm, and on weekends from 1 to 5 pm.

From Pelourinho go down the hill past **Igreja NS do Rosário dos Pretos**, an 18th-century church built by (and for) the slaves. It has some lovely azulejos. Follow Ladeira do Carmo uphill, and you'll see a set of steps to the left, reminiscent of the Spanish steps of Rome. They lead up to **Igreja do Santíssimo Sacramento da Rua do Paço**.

At the top of the hill is **Igreja da Ordem Terceira do Carmo**. Founded in 1636, it contains a Baroque altar and an organ dating from 1889. For a glimpse of unspoilt old Salvador, walk a few blocks farther, past very old, dilapidated buildings which teem with life.

Return to Praça da Sé (try a detour through some other old streets south of Alfredo de Brito), and continue to Praça Tomé de Souza, with the beautiful **Palácio Rio Branco** on one side and the ugly, modern office of the mayor on the other. There's a great view over the harbour from here, near the top station of the **Lacerda Elevator**, which carries up to 50,000 passengers a day (including quite a few pickpockets). The elevator will take you down to the Cidade Baixa (lower city), close to the **Mercado Modelo**, which is a touristy market but often has live music and entertainment. The blocks to the north-east are the main commercial district.

Back at the top of the elevator, walk south-west along Rua Chile to **Praça Castro Alves**, with an imposing statue and good sea views. From there it's a short walk to the **Museu de Arte Sacra da Bahia**, at Rua do Sodré 276. The sacred art is displayed in a beautifully restored 17th-century convent. Opening hours are Monday to Friday from 9.30 to 11.30 am and 2 to 5.30 pm.

Solar do Unhão

On the bay, south-west from the centre toward Campo Grande, this old sugar estate now houses the small Museu de Arte Moderna, a good restaurant, a ceramic workshop and the ghosts of tortured slaves. This area has a reputation for crime (especially mugging of tourists), so take a taxi there and back. Opening hours are Tuesday to Sunday from 1 to 5 pm.

Barra

Five km south-west of the centre, the Forte de Santo Antonio da Barra (1598) is at the very tip of the peninsula, with nearby beaches on the bay and the Atlantic Ocean. The first Atlantic beach has a lively beach scene, but heavy pollution makes swimming inadvisable. The bay beach, Praia do Porto, is also popular and looks much cleaner. There are plenty of bars and restaurants.

Monte Serrat & Itapagipe

North of the centre, Baía de Todos os Santos curves around to the Itapagipe peninsula, with the old Monte Serrat lighthouse and the Igreja de Monte Serrat at its tip. Nearby Igreja NS do Bonfim was built in 1745, and

is famous for its miraculous power to effect cures. It's an important church for Candomblistas. Nearby is **Praia da Boa Viagem**, a popular beach lined with barracas and lively on weekends. Buses from the Lacerda Elevator base station go to Boa Viagem.

Beaches

Beautiful beaches dot the Atlantic coast east of Barra, but those close to the city are polluted. If you want to swim it's advisable to head out to Placaford, Itapoã or beyond.

Candomblé

Much of Bahian life revolves around the Afro-Brazilian cults known as Candomblé (see under Religion in the Facts about the Country section). Don't miss a night in a terreiro; Bahiatursa can provide a complete list and advise you on the schedule for the month. The centre for Candomblé in Salvador is Casa Branca, Avenida Vasco da Gama 463, in the Engenho Velho neighbourhood.

Capoeira

To visit a capoeira school, it's best to get the up-to-date schedule from Bahiatursa. The Associação de Capoeira Mestre Bimba is an excellent school.

Special Events

Although Carnaval in Salvador is justly world-famous, it is by no means the only festival worth attending. Combining elements of the sacred and profane, Candomblé and Catholicism, many of Salvador's festivals are as wild as Carnaval, and possibly more colourful.

Carnaval Carnaval, usually held in late February or early March, starts on a Thursday night and continues until the following Monday. Everything, but everything, goes during these four days, especially the trios elétricos (fast frevo-style electric music, frequently played from a truck). Carnaval here is becoming more commercialised, but this trend is still light years behind Rio.

Many clubs have balls just before and during Carnaval. If you're in the city before

BRAZIL

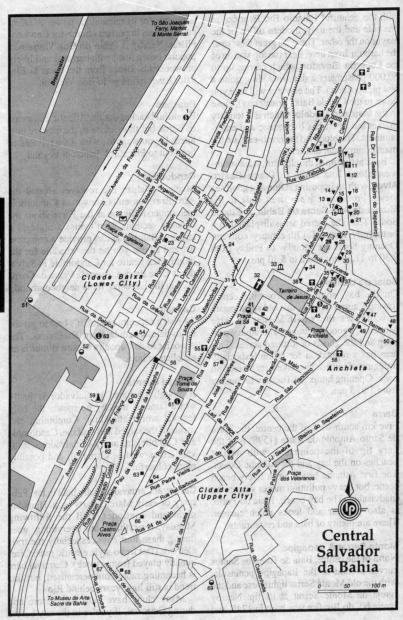

BRAZIL

Central Salvador da Bahia

0   50   100 m

PLACES TO STAY		OTHER		39	Igreja São Pedro dos
5	Albergue do Solar	1	Banco do Brasil		Clérigos
7	Albergue de	2	Igreja Convento de	40	Largo de Tereza
	Juentude do Pelô		NS do Carmo/		Batista
8	Albergue do Passo		Museu do	41	Praça da Sé Bus
12	Hotel Solara		Carmo		Terminal
13	Hotel Pelourinho	3	Igreja da Ordem	45	Igreja de Ordem
42	Hotel Ibiza		Terceira do Carmo		Terceira de São
43	Hotel America	4	Igreja do		Domingus
44	Hotel Gloria		Santíssimo	46	Vent Tour
49	Albergue de		Sacramento	50	Coração de Mangue
	Juentudedas		da Rua do Pao	51	Terminal Turístico
	Laranjeiras	11	Igreja NS do Rosário		Marítimo
57	Hotel Themis	15	Largo do Pelourinho;		(Boat to Itaparica)
63	Hotel Chile		Emtursa	52	Small Boats to
64	Palace Hotel	17	Fundação Casa de		Itaparica
66	Hotel Pousada da		Jorge Amado	53	Mercado Modelo &
	Praça	18	Museu da Cidade		Bahiatursa
68	Hotel Maridina	19	Olodum		Tourist Office
		21	Filhos do Ghandi	54	Casa dos Azulejos
PLACES TO EAT		22	Post Office	55	Igreja da Misericórdia
6	Casa da Roca	23	VASP	56	Lacerda Elevator
9	Encontro dos	24	Plano Inclinado	58	Igreja São Francisco
	Artiçtas		Gonçalves	59	Bunda Statue
10	Casa do Benin		(Funicular Railway)	60	França Bus Terminal,
14	Banzo	26	Praça Quincas Berro		Buses to São
16	Senac		D'gua		Joaquim, Ferry &
20	Restaurante da		(Praça Dois M)		Igreja NS do
	Dinha	27	Bar do Reggae		Bonfim
25	Micheluccio	30	Didá Music & Dance	61	Palácio Rio Branco &
28	Uauá		School		Bahiatursa
29	Senzala	31	Police Post		Tourist Office
34	Salada das Frutas	32	Catedral Basílica	62	Igreja NS de
35	Temporo da Dada	33	Museu Afro-		Conceicão
36	Yamoto		Brasileiro/Museu	65	Casa de Ruy Barbosa
38	Cantinho da Lua		de Arqueologia e	67	Varig
47	Bargaço		Etnologia	69	Terminal da
48	Glojú	37	Baneb		Barroquinha

the festivities start, you can also see the *blocos* (musical street groups) practising; don't miss the *afoxés* (Afro blocos). The best place to see them is Liberdade, Salvador's largest black district.

Violence can be a problem during Carnaval, and some women travellers have reported violent approaches from locals, but wild dancing behind a trio elétrico is a more common danger!

Places to Stay

Salvador has many hotels, but they can all fill up in summer holidays, big festivals and Carnaval. Bahiatursa can help you find lodging if you don't look too burnt-out or broke.

Camping On the outskirts of Itapoã, there are several camping grounds, such as *Camping Ecológico* (☎ 249-5900), Alameda da Praia s/n (*sin numero*, no number), and *Camping Clube do Brasil* (☎ 242-0482) also at Alameda da Praia s/n. At Pituaçu, about 14 km from the centre, there's *Camping Pituaçu* (☎ 231-7413) on Avenida Pinto d'Aguiar.

Hostels – city centre There are some excellent youth hostels close to the city centre. They all charge around US$10 for members, a little more for nonmembers, and sometimes a couple of dollars extra for breakfast. The *Albergue de Juventude das Laranjeiras* (☎ 321-1366) is a very flash new hostel located in the heart of Pelourinho, at Rua Inácio Acciolli 13. The *Albergue de*

Juventude do Pelô (☎ 242-8061) is also popular and conveniently located, at Rua Ribeiro dos Santos 5. Almost next door is *Albergue do Passo* (☎ 321-3656), at Rua Ribeiro dos Santos 3, while *Albergue de Juventude Solar* (☎ 241-0055) is around the corner at Rua Ribeiro dos Santos 45, and a little cheaper than the others.

Hostels – beaches The following beach hostels are listed in sequence, from Barra district along the Atlantic coast towards Itapoã. The *Albergue de Juventude Senzala* (☎ 235-4177) is at Rua Greenfeld 128, Barra, Avenida, close to the lighthouse. Also in Barra district, just a couple of blocks west of Shopping Barra, you'll find the *Albergue de Juventude da Barra* (☎ 247-5678), Rua Florianópolis 134, Jardim Brasil. Close to Ondina is the *Albergue de Juventude Solar* (☎ 235-2235), Rua Macapá 461. *Albergue de Juventude Lagash* (☎ 248-7399), Rua Visconde de Itaboraí 514, is a short walk from Amaralina beach, while *Albergue de Juventude Casa Grande* (☎ 248-0527), Rua Minas Gerais 122, is next to Pituba beach.

Hotels Cheap, good-value hotels are hard to find near the historic centre. One of the cheapest is the *Hotel Solara* (☎ 321-0202), on the downhill side of Largo do Pelourinho, which has apartamentos starting at US$18/25/35 for a single/double/triple including breakfast.

Another cheapie is *Hotel Themis* (☎ 243-1668), up on the 7th floor of the ugly Edifício Themis, Praça da Sé 57. It has a bar and restaurant with great views, but rooms are pretty run-down. Apartamentos without a view cost US$17/24/30 for a single/double/triple, apartamentos with a view cost US$20/28/35. Rua do Bispo runs off Praça da Sé, and has three of the cheapest and least attractive hotels, *Ibiza*, *America* and *Gloria*. Rooms cost from US$12 to US$15, and are strictly bottom end.

Slightly better is the *Hotel Chile* (☎ 321-0245), at Rua Chile 7 (1st floor), a short walk from Bahiatursa. Quartos start at US$11/17

for a single/double. Apartamentos cost US$27 for a double with air-con. A little farther away, *Hotel Pousada da Praça* (☎ 321-0642), at Rua Rui Barbosa 5, offers basic but clean quartos at US$14/20, and apartamentos at US$20. It's very pleasant and excellent value. Just down from Praça Castro Alves, *Hotel Maridina* (☎ 242-7176), at Avenida 7 de Setembro, Ladeira de São Bento 6 (1st floor), is a friendly, family-run hotel which also offers good value for money. Quartos with fan cost US$15/25, and apartamentos with air-con cost US$20/30.

The *Hotel Pelourinho* (☎ 321-9022), in an old converted mansion at Rua Alfredo de Brito 20 in the heart of Pelourinho, has long been a favourite with travellers, but is getting pricey. Small apartamentos with fan cost US$25/35/45 for singles/doubles/triples. The modern *Palace Hotel* (☎ 322-1155, fax 243-1109), at Rua Chile 20, is a reasonable mid-range option with comfortable quartos with fan at US$27/33, though the air-con apartamentos are much pricier, from US$58/66.

The pleasant *Hotel Caramuru* (☎ 336-9951), at Avenida 7 de Setembro 2125, is in a quiet location halfway between the centre and Barra. It's in a large colonial mansion and has spotless double quartos for US$20 and big double apartamentos for US$25. The hotel also organises Candomblé excursions and other trips.

In the Barra district, opposite the beach at Avenida 7 de Setembro 3801, the *Pousada Malu* (☎ 237-4461) is a relaxed place offering clean quartos with fan from US$18/20. Slightly more up-market options include the *Hotel Villa da Barra* (☎ 247-7908), Avenida 7 de Setembro 3959, a colourful place with a courtyard, café, and spacious apartamentos from US$35/45. Close by at Avenida 7 de Setembro 3783, the *Hotel Porto da Barra* (☎ 247-7711) has single/double apartamentos with fan at US$30/36, and double apartamentos with air-con at US$56, but substantial discounts are sometimes offered.

Out near the beach at Itapoã, the *Hotel Europa* (☎ 249-9344) has clean apartamento doubles for US$20 to US$25. Across the street there are barracas for food and drink, and buses to the centre of Salvador, 45 minutes away. *Pousada Bayona* (☎ 375-6762), Avenida Dorival Caymmi 46, is also good. This is a good area to stay if you're flying out the next day.

Places to Eat

Bahian cuisine is an intriguing blend of African and Brazilian recipes based on characteristic ingredients such as coconut cream, ginger, hot peppers, coriander, shrimp and dendê oil. For names and short descriptions of typical Bahian dishes, see Food in the Facts for the Visitor section of this chapter.

The Pelourinho area is packed with restaurants, though many of them cater for tourists and are expensive, especially at lunch time. Try *Senzala*, a por-kilo place at Rua João de Deus 9 (1st floor). Another good, cheap local lunch place is *Glojú*, at the bottom end of Rua Francisco M Barreto. *Salada das Frutas*, Rua Alfredo Brito 5, has cheap, healthy snacks, juices, refeicões and friendly atmosphere. The lower city is a better area for lunch, with many inexpensive places catering to office workers.

A long-time favourite on Terreiro de Jesus is *Cantina da Lua*. It serves good-value refeicões and is a popular hang-out in the evening, when there is often live music. Other places popular in the evening are in the block around Praça Quincas Berro D'gua. *Micheluccio*, at Rua Alfredo Brito 33, has excellent pizza. *Temporo da Dada*, at Rua Frei Vicente 5, is a lively, casual restaurant with tasty seafood – the moqueca de peixe is good. Two people can eat for around US$14. *Yamoto*, on Rua Frei Vicente, is an elegant Japanese restaurant with superb sushi; expect to pay around US$18 per person.

The restaurant at *Hotel Pelourinho* has a great view of the bay and OK food, but it's a bit overpriced. Next door to the hotel, *Banzo* is bright, animated and good value with a selection of Bahian and European dishes plus all sorts of exotic drinks – around US$10 for a main course and a drink. The balcony provides a good view of the action in Largo do Pelourinho. Across the street,

Restaurante da Dinha is good for a cheap feed and to meet locals. *Novo Tempo* is in the downstairs section of Olodum (about the biggest and best known of the blocos), with a lovely back courtyard, good music and seafood dishes from around US$12.

Also on Largo do Pelourinho is *Senac* (☎ 321-5502), a cooking school which offers a huge buffet spread of 40 regional dishes. It's not the best Bahian cooking, but for US$14 you can discover which Bahian dishes you like – and eat till you explode! Senac is open daily except Sunday from 6 to 9 pm.

Downhill from Largo do Pelourinho is *Casa do Benin* (☎ 243-7629), a superb restaurant serving excellent African food in a small, attractive courtyard. The main dishes start around US$10; try the delicious frango ao gengibre (ginger chicken). Another terrific restaurant for African-influenced cuisine is the colourful *Uau*, at Rua Gregório de Matos 36.

For a gourmet splurge (around US$15), try the excellent Bahian cuisine at *Bargaço*, in Pelourinho, on the corner of Rua Francisco M Barreto and Rua Inácio Accioli. *Encontro dos Artistas*, on Rua Ribeiro dos Santos, has a good selection of vegetarian dishes, while *Casa da Roça*, farther up the same street, is another enjoyable place with good, reasonably priced food.

Entertainment

Salvador is justly renowned for its music. The blending of African and Brazilian traditions produces popular styles, such as trio elétrico (which dominates Carnaval), tropicalismo, afoxé, caribé, reggae and lambada. Bars and clubs go in and out of fashion, so ask around. The weekly magazine *Veja* contains a supplement with the hottest nightspots.

Pelourinho is the nightlife capital of Salvador; its cobbled streets are lined with bars, and blocos practise almost every night, especially Tuesday, when bands set up on Terreiro de Jesus, Largo do Pelourinho and anywhere else they can find space. Crowds pour in to eat, drink, dance and party until the early hours. There are lots of locals and tourists, including quite a few professional and semiprofessional party girls.

Other music venues around Pelourinho include *Coracão do Mangue*, a small bar at Rua Francisco M Barreto 27 with a street stage and live music on Tuesday and Friday; and *Bar do Reggae*, at Rua Gregório de Matos 36, where dancers spill out onto the street just about every night.

Barra is full of bars, discos and music, especially on Saturday night, though it can be a bit touristy and has a slightly sleazy reputation. Pituba beach has several upmarket bars with music. Those in search of *danceterias* (dance halls) could try *Bell's Beach*, a slick place at Avenida Octávio Mangabeira, Praia do Corsário, Boca do Rio. Around the beaches, Rio Vermelho has some good nightspots, and many of the better hotels, such as the *Salvador Praia*, have fancy nightclubs.

Folklore shows, usually consisting of mini-displays of Candomblé, capoeira, samba, lambada etc, are presented in the evening at *Senac* in Pelourinho, *Solar do Unhão*, south of the city centre, and *Moenda* (☎ 231-7915), at Jardim Armação, next to the Centro de Convenções. The monthly *Agenda Cultural* gives a comprehensive rundown of music events, theatre, dance and art exhibitions.

Getting There & Away
Air There are regular international flights between Salvador and Miami, New York, Frankfurt, Paris, Rome and Buenos Aires. There are good connections to other main Brazilian cities with the major domestic airlines. Nordeste flies to smaller cities in the region, like Ilhéus and Porto Seguro. Brazilian airlines include Nordeste (☎ 381-7880), Transbrasil (☎ 241-1211), Varig (☎ 243-9311) and VASP (☎ (0800) 99-6277).

Bus There are numerous departures daily to Rio (US$67, 28 hours), four daily to Brasília (US$43, US$85 leito, 22 hours) and four to Belo Horizonte (US$44, US$67 for leito, 22 hours).

There are six departures daily to Aracaju (US$11), four to Recife (US$27, US$45 leito, 13 hours), two to Fortaleza (US$44, 20 hours), and one to Belém (US$50, 34 hours). Two buses daily go to Lençois (US$15, seven hours), Ilhéus (US$11, seven hours), and Porto Seguro (US$32, 12 hours), as well as frequent departures to Valença (US$10, five hours) and Cachoeira (US$5, two hours) – take the São Felix bus.

Getting Around
The Lacerda Elevator runs daily from 5 am to midnight, linking the lower and upper cities. The Plano Inclinado funicular finishes at 10 pm.

To/From the Airport Aeroporto Dois de Julho (☎ 204-1010) is over 30 km from the city centre, inland from Itapoã. At the airport, there's a bilheteria for overpriced taxis: it costs US$37 to Praça da Sé during the day, and US$54 at night. It's best to take the executivo Praça da Sé/Aeroporto bus (US$1.30) from the stop at Praça da Sé. You can flag it down along the coastal road. Allow at least an hour for the ride, 1¾ hours if there's traffic. If you have an early flight, stay the night at Itapoã.

To/From the Rodoviária The rodoviária (☎ 231-5711) is five km from the city centre. The best way there is the executivo bus from Praça da Sé to Iguatemi shopping centre, then walk over the pedestrian footbridge to the rodoviária. A taxi from Praça da Sé will cost about US$4.50, but the fixed-price taxi tickets from the bilheteria at the rodoviária may cost more.

Bus There are two types of local buses. Municipal buses are very cheap (around US$0.50) but crowded, very slow, and not recommended if you have any baggage. Executivo buses cost two or three times as much, but everyone gets a seat and enjoys air-con comfort; they are available on an increasing number of routes. Both types will operate from a new local bus terminal, being developed on Praça da Sé. Praça da Sé/Aeroporto executivo buses go along the beaches from Barra to Itapoã.

The Avenida da França bus terminal is in Cidade Baixa, beside the Lacerda Elevator (base station). From here, Ribeira or Bonfim buses go to the Itaparica ferry, Mercado São Joaquim market, and the Itapagipe peninsula.

ITAPARICA

This is the largest island in Baía de Todos os Santos. It is quite pretty and very popular with Salvadoreans on weekends, but is not really a must-see destination. The best part of the island is owned by Club Med, but there are still a few clean beaches, like Barra Grande, with good views of the city. At the northern tip of the island is the city of Itaparica and the São Lourenço Fort. South of the city is Ponte da Areia, a thin strip of sand with barracas serving excellent food.

You can stay at the *Albergue de Juventude Enseada de Aratuba* (☎ 971-0060), at Quadra H, lotes 12/1, or at camping grounds at Praia de Berlinque, Praia de Barra Grande, and Praia de Cacha Pregos. In Mar Grande, a good cheap option is the *Pousada Koisa Nossa* (☎ 833-1028), at Rua da Rodagam 173.

Getting There & Away

From Salvador, a small boat leaves the Terminal Turístico Maritimo behind the Mercado Modelo every half-hour and goes directly to Mar Grande (US$1, 50 minutes). A giant car-and-passenger ferry goes to the island from São Joaquim, reached by bus from the Avenida da França bus terminal (see above). Ferries operate every 45 minutes from 5 am to midnight during summer. Expect a long wait on summer weekends.

CACHOEIRA

Cachoeira – the jewel of the recôncavo (a fertile region around the Baía de Todos os Santos) – is a small city in the centre of Brazil's best tobacco-growing region. It is full of beautiful colonial architecture, uncompromised by modern buildings. It sits on the Rio Paraguaçu, with the town of São

Felix on the other side. Cachoeira is 120 km from Salvador de Bahia, so plan to stay overnight.

Information

The tourist office, in a renovated building on Rua 13 de Maio, should be able to help with accommodation and general information.

Things to See

Cachoeira is an important centre for **Candomblé**. The ceremonies are held in small homes and shacks up in the hills, usually at 8 pm on Friday and Saturday nights. Visitors are not as common here as in Salvador, and the tourist office is sometimes reluctant to give out information, but may help if you show an interest in Candomblé and respect for its traditions.

Cachoeira and São Felix are best seen on foot. The restored **Igreja da Ordem Terceira do Carmo** features a gallery of suffering polychrome Christs imported from the Portuguese colonies in Macau. You can visit Tuesday to Saturday from 2 to 5 pm and on Sunday morning.

The **Museu Hansen Bahia** displays the work of German (naturalised Brazilian) artist Hansen Bahia (closed on Tuesday and on Sunday afternoons).

The tiny **NS d'Ajuda**, on Largo da Ajuda, is Cachoeira's oldest church. Phone ☎ 1396 to arrange a visit to the church and the **Museu da Boa Morte**, an interesting museum with displays of photos and ceremonial apparel of the exclusively female Boa Morte (Good Death) cult.

Special Events

One of Cachoeira's many festivals is the fascinating Festa da NS de Boa Morte, organised by the Sisterhood of the Good Death, a secret black religious society. The festival falls on the Friday closest to 15 August and lasts three days. The Festa de São João (22-24 June) is the big popular festival of Bahia's interior.

Places to Stay

The *Pousada do Pai Thomáz* (☎ 725-1288),

BRAZIL

Rua 25 de Junho 12, has comfortable single/double apartamentos for US$9/18. The *Pensão Tia Rosa* (☎ 725-1792), opposite Museu Hansen Bahia, has basic single/double quartos for US$8/16, including a good breakfast. The *Pousada do Guerreiro*, Rua 13 de Maio 14, has ragged but clean single/double quartos for US$10/15.

Pousada do Convento de Cachoeira (☎ 725-1716) is a lovely old hotel with a courtyard and swimming pool. The dark-wood rooms of the old convent now have air-con and hot showers, and cost US$34/40 for a single/double.

Places to Eat

The *Gruta Azul* (☎ 725-1295), Praça Manoel Vitorino 2, is Cachoeira's best restaurant; ask for the boa morte drink. It opens for lunch and dinner.

Nair restaurant (often called Rian) provides excellent moqueca dishes and local specialities: try maniçoba, a typical Cachoeira dish. There's more good food at *Cabana do Pai Thomáz*, across the road from the pousada, and *Pizzaria Massapé*.

Getting There & Away

Buses depart hourly from 5.30 am to 7 pm for Salvador (US$3.50, two hours).

PRAIA DO FORTE

Praia do Forte is 80 km north of Salvador on the Rodovia do Coco (the Coconut Highway). Praia do Forte has fine beaches, a beautiful ruined castle fortress, a sea-turtle reserve and, unfortunately, no cheap hotels. Until recently a fishing village, it is being developed as an ecologically minded, upmarket beach resort.

TAMAR Turtle Reserve

The reserve is on the beach, right next to the lighthouse. Tartaruga Marinha (TAMAR) is a project started in 1982 to protect several species of marine turtle.

Places to Stay & Eat

The only cheap place to stay is the camping ground, 10 minutes walk from the beach.

The cheapest hotels, like *João Sol* (☎ 876-1054), Rua da Corvina, cost from US$30 to US$40. *Pousada Praia do Forte* (☎ 835-1410) has bungalows on the beach at US$75 for two, including full board.

Getting There & Away

The Catuense company runs buses from Salvador to Praia do Forte. The trip takes two hours, and the service operates daily between 7.30 am and 6 pm.

MORRO DE SÃO PAULO

Morro de São Paulo, at the northern tip of Ilha do Tinharé, is a tranquil, isolated fishing village with incredible beaches. Since its discovery by hip Brazilians and international travellers, it has rapidly acquired fame and a place on the best-beach lists of several Brazilian magazines. Beware of bichos de pé: don't walk barefoot through town.

Places to Stay & Eat

Morro is changing quickly with many new places, but accommodation can be tight during summer. There are nearly 70 pousadas and it's definitely worth hunting around. Close to the action, *Pousada Toucano* and *Pousada Giras Sol*, on Caminho da Praia, are two good, cheap options, with quartos for around US$12 per person. In the quieter wooded hills behind the village, look for *Pousada Macondo*, a very friendly, relaxed place with clean quartos at US$13 per person with breakfast, or *Pousada Bugainville*, with double apartamentos for US$30 (breakfast included). There are a few camping grounds, but for longer stays the best deal is to rent a house.

The main street, Caminho da Praia, is a regular restaurant strip. *Ponte de Econtro* offers a wide range of excellent, tasty vegetarian food por kilo. *Canto do Mar* and *Sabor da Terra* both have good-value seafood prato feito for around US$6. Other places serve pasta, pizza, prato feito and whatever.

Getting There & Away

To get to the island take a relaxed 1½-hour

ride (US$2) on the *Brisa Biônica* or *Brisa Triônica* from Valença to Morro de São Paulo. It's a beautiful trip.

During the summer seven boats per day depart Valença for Morro de São Paulo between 7.30 am and 5 pm. After 5 pm, someone at the port in Valença may offer to take you for double the price. There may also be direct boats to and from Salvador. During the rest of the year boats are less frequent, except on weekends; Bahiatursa should know the schedule. At any time of year, try to arrive early.

ILHÉUS

Ilhéus, the town which Jorge Amado lived in and wrote about in *Gabriela, Clove & Cinnamon*, retains some of the charm and lunacy that Amado fans know well. The colonial centre is interesting and the beaches are superb, yet the area has remained largely unaffected by tourism.

Things to See

The best thing to do in Ilhéus is just wander. If you walk up the hill to the **Convento NS da Piedade**, there's a good view of the city and littoral. The **Igreja de São Jorge** (1534), the city's oldest church, houses a small sacred art museum. It's on Praça Rui Barbosa and is open Tuesday to Sunday from 8 to 11 am and 2 to 5.30 pm.

The recently improved **Museu Regional do Cacao** displays cacao artefacts and contemporary painting by local artists. It's at Rua AL Lemos 126, and opens most afternoons, and also mornings from December to March.

Places to Stay

There is now a good range of accommodation in Ilhéus. Outside summer you can get substantial discounts off the prices quoted here. For camping grounds, try places along the road to Olivença, like *Camping Colónia*

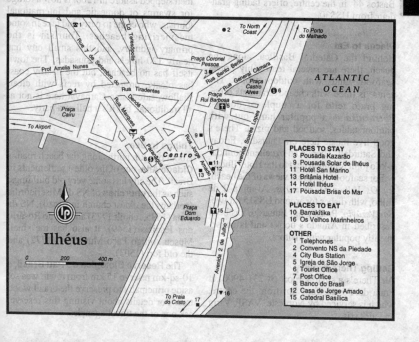

Ilhéus

0   200   400 m

To North Coast
To Porto do Malhado

ATLANTIC OCEAN

Praça Coronel Pessoa
Prof Amelia Nunes
Rua Tiradentes
Praça Rui Barbosa
Praça Castro Alves
Praça Cairu
To Airport
Centro
Praça Dom Eduardo
To Praia do Cristo

Rua 7 de Setembro do
La Teresópolis
Rua Marques
de Paranágua
Rua Jorge Amado
Avenida Soares Lopes
Rua General Câmara
Rua Bento Berito
Avenida 2 de Julho

PLACES TO STAY
3 Pousada Kazarão
9 Pousada Solar de Ilhéus
11 Hotel San Marino
13 Britânia Hotel
14 Hotel Ilhéus
17 Pousada Brisa do Mar

PLACES TO EAT
10 Barrakítika
16 Os Velhos Marinheiros

OTHER
1 Telephones
2 Convento NS da Piedade
4 City Bus Station
5 Igreja de São Jorge
7 Post Office
8 Banco do Brasil
12 Casa de Jorge Amado
15 Catedral Basílica

BRAZIL

da Stac (☎ 231-7015), 13 km from Ilhéus, or *Camping Estância das Fontes* (☎ 212-2505), 18 km away. *Pousada Solar de Ilhéus* (☎ 231-5125), at Rua General Câmara 50, is a friendly, secure, family-run place with spotless quartos from around US$20/27, including a superb breakfast; get a room with windows. The central *Hotel San Marino* (☎ 231-6511), Rua Jorge Amado 29, has four-bed quartos for US$12 per person, and double apartamentos from US$35.

Pousada Kazarão (☎ 231-5031), Praça Coronel Pessoa 38, has double quartos for US$25. The *Britânia Hotel* (☎ 231-1722), Rua Jorge Amado 16, is a pleasant old-style hotel with quartos from US$20 and apartamentos from US$25.

Even better places include *Pousada Brisa do Mar* (☎ 231-2644), on the beachfront at Avenida 2 de Julho 136, in a deco-style building with large, comfortable single/double apartamentos starting at US$35/45. *Hotel Ilhéus* (☎ 231-4242), Rua Eustáquio Bastos 44, in the centre, offers fading grandeur from US$30.

Places to Eat

Behind the Catedral Basílica, along the beach, there are several reasonably priced seafood stands with outdoor tables. The centre is filled with cheap restaurants offering prato feito for a couple of dollars. *Barrakítika* is a popular hang-out with outdoor tables, seafood and pizza. There's good live music here on Thursday, Friday and Saturday. There's an excellent comida-a-kilo joint for lunch next to the Hotel Ilhéus.

For seafood with great views of the beach, try *Os Velhos Marinheiros*, Avenida 2 de Julho, with dishes for around US$15 for two. *Bar Vezúvio*, Praça Dom Eduardo, has been described in Amado's books and is consequently popular with visitors.

Getting There & Away

Air There's a small airport (☎ 231-4900) at Praia do Pontal, four km from the centre, which is serviced by Nordeste, VASP, Varig and air taxis.

Bus For most major destinations, buses leave more frequently from Itabuna than from Ilhéus, so it's usually quicker to go to Itabuna first, then shuttle down to Ilhéus. The rodoviária in Ilhéus is a 15-minute bus ride from the centre. Buses to Salvador go through the recôncavo via Cachoeira or via Nazaré and connect with the ferry from Itaparica Island to Salvador. Ilhéus has several buses daily to Salvador (US$21, seven hours); two a day to Valença at 6.30 am and 3.15 pm (US$7.50, five hours); three daily to Porto Seguro (US$13, five hours); and buses to Itacaré via Uruçuca at 7 am and 3.30 pm (US$7, four hours).

From the city bus station, on Praça Cairu, there are buses to Olivença, the rodoviária and the airport.

PORTO SEGURO

The one-time pioneering settlement of Porto Seguro, just south of where Cabral and his men stepped ashore in 1500, is now a refuge for swarms of domestic and international tourists, who come to party and take in some mesmerising beaches. Tourism is the primary industry, and this small city has nearly 120 hotels and pousadas. The town itself has no beaches, but the nearby coast has plenty, protected by reefs with clear, shallow, safe water. Carnaval here is not at all traditional, but it's a hell of a party.

Things to See

About one km north along the beach road is **Cidade Alta**, one of the oldest settlements in Brazil. The city has some very old buildings, such as the **churches** of NS da Misericórdia (perhaps the oldest church in Brazil), NS da Pena (1535, rebuilt 1773) and NS do Rosário dos Jesuitas (1549). It also has the small Museu Antigo Paço Municipal (1772) and the old fort (1503).

The **Reserva Biológica do Pau Brasil**, a 10-sq-km reserve 15 km from town, was set aside principally to preserve the brazil wood tree. For details about visiting this reserve, ask one of the travel agencies.

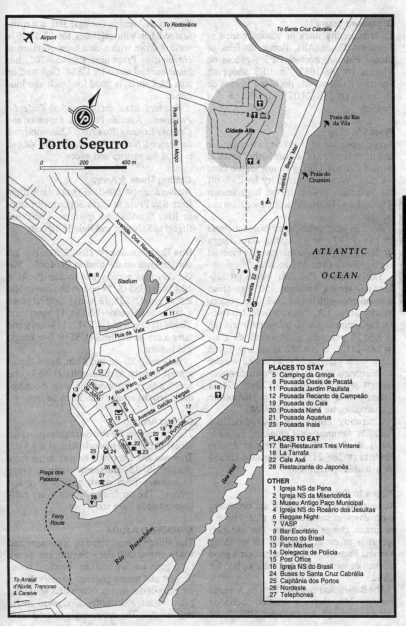

Porto Seguro

0   200   400 m

To Rodoviária

To Santa Cruz Cabrália

Airport

Rua Guava do Moço

Cidade Alta

Praia do Rio da Vila

Praia do Cruzeiro

Avenida Dos Navegantes

Avenida Beira Mar

Avenida 22 de Abril

Stadium

Rua da Vala

ATLANTIC

OCEAN

Avenida Pero Vaz de Caminha

Avenida Getúlio Vargas

Rua de Julho

Rua Oscar Oliveira

Rua P Cabral

Avenida Portugal

Sea Wall

Praça dos Pataxos

Ferry Route

Rio Buranhém

To Arraial d'Ajuda, Trancoso & Caraiva

BRAZIL

PLACES TO STAY
5   Camping da Gringa
8   Pousada Oasis de Pacatá
11 Pousada Jardim Paulista
12 Pousada Recanto de Campeão
19 Pousada do Cais
20 Pousada Naná
21 Pousada Aquarius
23 Pousada Inaia

PLACES TO EAT
17 Bar-Restaurant Tres Vintens
18 La Tarrafa
22 Cafe Axé
28 Restaurante do Japonês

OTHER
1   Igreja NS da Pena
2   Igreja NS da Misericórdia
3   Museu Antigo Paço Municipal
4   Igreja NS do Rosário dos Jesuitas
6   Reggae Night
7   VASP
9   Bar Escritório
10 Banco do Brasil
13 Fish Market
14 Delegacia de Polícia
15 Post Office
16 Igreja NS do Brasil
24 Buses to Santa Cruz Cabrália
25 Capitânia dos Portos
26 Nordeste
27 Telephones

Organised Tours

To arrange city tours or schooner trips to Trancoso, Coroa Alta, Recife da Fora or Monte Pascoal, contact BPS Agência de Viagem (☎ 288-1033), in BPS Shopping Centre, or Companhia do Mar Passeios de Escunas (☎ 288-2107), on Praça dos Pataxos.

Places to Stay

Accommodation in Porto Seguro is fancier and there is more of it than farther south at Arraial d'Ajuda. During the low season there are many vacant rooms, so try for 25% off the following prices. In the high season (December to February) accommodation can be tight.

For camping grounds, try *Mundaí Praia* (☎ 288-2287) or *Camping da Gringa* (☎ 288-2076), both outside town on the road north to Santa Cruz da Cabrália.

The well-run *Pousada Naná* (☎ 288-2265), Avenida Portugal 450, has clean apartamentos with fan for US$20 per person. Nearby, at No 524, *Pousada Inaia* has standard apartamentos with refrigerator and fan at US$20 per person. *Pousada do Cais* (☎ 288-2112), at No 382 is an arty, rustic place with individually decorated single/double rooms for US$22/44. *Pousada Aquarius* (☎ 288-2738), Rua PA Cabral 174, is friendly and quiet, with single/double apartamentos for around US$35/40.

Charming mid-range pousadas, like *Pousada Recanto de Campeão*, *Pousada Oasis de Pacatá*, and *Pousada Jardim Paulista* (☎ 288-2115), cost around US$50 for a double apartamento.

Places to Eat

Restaurants in Porto Seguro are becoming expensive – in summer many places have a minimum charge per table. The cheapest option is to eat at the stalls set up along Avenida Portugal, where you can get a good chicken or meat, salad and farofa plate for US$2.

The *Bar-Restaurant Tres Vintens*, Avenida Portugal 246, serves a delicious bobó de camarão (enough for two) for US$12. *La Tarrafa*, at Avenida Portugal 360, is a rustic seafood bar with refeições for US$7.50 – wash it down with a cold brew. *Restaurant Havana*, at Praça dos Pataxos 202, has home-cooked meals for US$4. *Cafe Axé*, on Rua PA Cabral, is good for lunch and loud music.

Readers have recommended *Cafe La Passarella*, Avenida Portugal, for pasta, and *Casa da Esquina*, Rua Assis Chateaubriand, for seafood. *Nativo*, Avenida Getúlio Vargas, is good for pastries and juices.

Getting There & Away

Air Nordeste (☎ 288-1888) has a daily flight from São Paulo to Porto Seguro with stops in Rio, Brasília and Ipatinga. VASP has flights to Salvador and Belo Horizonte.

Bus The rodoviária (☎ 288-2239) is two km outside town on the road to Eunápolis. São Geraldo runs a daily bus to São Paulo at 10.45 am (US$48, 24 hours) and one to Rio at 5.45 pm (US$35, 18 hours). Several buses a day go to Salvador (US$34, 12 hours) and Vitória da Conquista (US$17, 11 hours), and three a day go to Ilhéus (US$10, five hours) and Itabuna.

Between 5.20 am and 8 pm, buses depart almost hourly to Eunápolis (US$3, one hour), a large transport hub with more frequent bus departures than Porto Seguro.

Getting Around

The ferry across the Rio Buranhém provides access to the road towards Arraial d'Ajuda, Trancoso and Caraiva. The pedestrian ferry charges US$0.50 and seems to operate every 15 minutes from dawn until late in the evening. The car ferry operates every half-hour between 7 am and 9 pm.

ARRAIAL D'AJUDA

This village is frequented by a younger and wilder crowd than Porto Seguro, but it may have gone too hip too fast: barefoot backpackers and trendy package tourists throng the maze of dirt streets, where slick shopping galleries sit awkwardly alongside rustic reggae cafés. The increasingly littered main beach is lined with barracas, while farther south, hippies let it all hang out at Pitinga beach.

Warning There's now a police post in Arraial d'Ajuda and their attitude to drug-taking is less tolerant than in the past.

Places to Stay

For camping, try *Camping do Gordo*, which has very basic facilities and is close to the ferry landing point; or *Camping Arraial d'Ajuda*, which is closer to town, on the beach at Praia de Mucugê, and has better facilities.

New pousadas pop up every day, old pousadas change their names, and prices also change rapidly. Out of season try to negotiate discounts of 50% or more on these prices. Make sure your room has either a properly fitting mosquito net over the bed or, preferably, a fan.

For cheap deals check out Rua Jotobá, which runs parallel to Broadway one block closer to the beach. At the end of the street, *Pousada Mir a Mar* has clean single/double apartamentos with hammocks slung outside for US$15/20. Next door, *Pousada Jatoba* is more basic, and has small apartamentos for US$15 per person. In a small lane running off Rua Jotobá, *Pousada do Jasmin* is a friendly place with rustic apartamentos for US$10 per person. Just off the main square, on Broadway, *Pousada Lua Cheia* (☎ 875-1059) is a shady, relaxed place with apartamentos at US$15 per person.

Better places include *Pousada do Brigette* (☎ 875-1085) and *Pousada Buganville* (☎ 875-1007), both on Rua Almeda dos Flamboyants 170. Both pousadas are very attractive, with double rooms from US$35 to US$50. Off Caminho do Mar, *Pousada Vila do Beco* and *Pousada Le Grande Bleu* (☎ 875-1272), have large, comfortable single/double apartamentos for around US$25/40. *Pousada O Sole Mio*, about one km from the *balsa* (ferry) on the road to Arraial, has been recommended by readers for its spacious, shady gardens and good Italian food.

Places to Eat

If you like comida a kilo, *Restaurant Nóna Madeira*, on Caminho do Mar, is the best by far. A doorway on Broadway near the church leads through the family home to the friendly *Restaurant São João*, which has good-value seafood prato feito for US$5, and an extensive menu of more expensive seafood dishes.

Behind the church, *Josefina Grill Bar* is a colourful restaurant with smooth music and grilled seafood and salad dishes for US$10. Farther along the road, *Restaurant Tubarão* has tasty, wood-fired pizzas. The beach barracas have excellent fried shrimp and other seafood.

Getting There & Away

Take a ferry from Porto Seguro, then one of four approaches to Arraial d'Ajuda: a lovely four-km hike along the beach, a taxi to town, a bus to town, or a VW Kombi to Praia de Mucugê.

TRANCOSO

This village, 12 km south-west of Porto Seguro, is on a grassy bluff overlooking fantastic beaches. The central square is lined with small, colourful colonial buildings and casual bars and restaurants nestling under shady trees.

Places to Stay & Eat

If you're planning a long stay, rent a house on the beach. There are many pousadas, which can be reserved by calling the Telebahia office (☎ 867-1115). Typically, single/double quartos start at US$15/25 and apartamentos at around US$20/35, but try for discounts in the off season. *Pousada Quarto Cresente* is highly recommended. The colourful *Pousada Soloamanha*, on the main square, has dorm beds for US$10. Other places include *Pousada Toca do Sabia*, *Pousada Gulab Mahal*, and the more up-market *Pousada Hibisco* (☎ 868-1129), with double apartamentos from US$50.

For good natural food and music, head for *Restaurant Ânima* or *Bar do Tio Estragio*. *Restaurant Amadoeira* has seafood and meat refeições for US$5.

BRAZIL

Getting There & Away

The bus to Trancoso leaves every two hours from 9 am until 5 pm (less frequently during low season). It starts at the ferry landing opposite Porto Seguro and stops at the bus depot in Arraial d'Ajuda, behind the main square. The bus stops at the beach first, then continues to Trancoso village, where the accommodation is. It's a beautiful 13-km walk along the beach between Trancoso and Arraial d'Ajuda.

CARAIVA

Without running water, electricity or throngs of tourists, the hamlet of Caraiva is primitive and beautiful. Rustic pousadas will put you up for US$15 to US$20 per person.

Two buses a day make the 42-km trip along a rough dirt road from Trancoso to Caraiva. There are also two buses daily to Itabela, on BR-101, for connections north and south. Buses stop on the far side of the river, and small dugout canoes ferry passengers across to the village for US$0.50.

LENÇÓIS

Lençóis lies in a wooded, mountainous region – the Chapada Diamantina, an oasis in the dusty sertão. You'll find old mining towns, and there's great hiking nearby in the Parque Nacional da Chapada Diamantina (see the next section). If you have time for only one excursion into Brazil's northeastern interior, this is the one.

There's a helpful tourist office, but nowhere to change travellers' cheques.

Things to See & Do

The city is pretty and easily seen on foot though, unfortunately, most of the buildings are closed to the public. See the old **French vice-consulate**, a blue 19th-century building where diamond commerce was negotiated, and **Casa de Afrânio Peixoto**, a museum in the former home of the writer Afrânio Peixoto. Also worth a visit is the **Lanchonete Zacão**, run by a local historian, which displays mining relics.

Places to Stay

Reserve accommodation in advance on weekends and throughout January and February.

Cheaper places have collective rooms and charge on a per-person basis. *Camping Lumiar*, Praça do Rosário, has shady camp sites (US$2 per person), passable bathrooms, a bar and a restaurant.

Pousalegre (☎ 334-1124), a travellers' favourite, has basic quartos at US$9 per person, friendly staff and good meals. Close by, *Pousada Re* (☎ 334-1127) is another good option, with similar prices. *Pousada Sincora*, in a large colonial building, is a relaxed place with collective rooms for US$6 per person. *Pousada Diangela* (☎ 334-1192) is large, bright and pleasant with quartos for US$9 per person and apartamentos for US$13. *Casa de Helia*, Rua das Pedras 102, at US$9 per person, has been recommended.

Slightly dearer places include *Pousada Alcino* (☎ 334-1171), in a beautifully converted colonial building, and *Pousada Bicho de Mato*, a short walk from the centre. *Hotel Colonial* (☎ 334-1114) has pleasant single/double/triple apartamentos for around US$20/26/38.

Pousada Canto das Águas (☎ 334-1154), in a landscaped garden beside the river, has a restaurant, bar, pool, and apartamentos overlooking the cascades for around US$50/55/72. Also attractive is *Pousada de Lençóis* (☎ 334-1102), with air-con apartamentos from US$50/55/70.

Places to Eat

Casa Redonda is a relaxed, friendly place with great-value, tasty cooking. *Brilhante* is a colourful natural-food shop and café with healthy sandwiches, snacks and juices. The *Pousalegre* and the *Pousada Diangela* both serve inexpensive meals; try *Restaurant Diamente Brito* for comida a kilo. *Restaurant Os Artistas Damassa* has good, cheap Italian food, and for a real taste of Europe, visit *Salon Mistura Fina*, where you can sip tea while listening to classical music. Other popular restaurants in town worth visiting are *Restaurant Ynave* and *Restaurant Amigo da Onça*.

Bar Canto Verde is an ambient outdoor bar with live music in the evenings. The *Lajedo Bar & Restaurant* (across the bridge, on the other side of town), *Arte Bar* and *Zion Bar* are evening hang-outs.

Getting There & Away

Bus The rodoviária is on the edge of town, beside the river. There are three buses daily to/from Salvador (US$15, seven hours).

AROUND LENÇÓIS

For day trips around Lençóis, walk or hire a horse. Ask around town for Senhor Dazim, who hires horses for about US$3 an hour or US$26 per day. Agents in Lençóis run trips to Chapada Diamantina. Try Lentur (334-11430), which does day trips by car for US$20 per person, including guide, admission fees and torches. Protur (☎ 334-1126), Pousada Diangela and Pousada Bicho do Mato offer similar deals.

Parque Nacional da Chapada Diamantina

This park, 1520 sq km of the Sincora range of the Diamantina plateau, has several species of monkeys, beautiful views, clean waterfalls, rivers and streams, and an endless network of trails. Rock hounds appreciate the curious geomorphology of the region. Foreigners and Brazilians living in Lençóis have joined a strong ecological movement which is in direct opposition to the extractive mentality of the *garimpeiros* (prospectors), who have caused much damage.

Information The park has minimal infrastructure for visitors. Knowledgeable guides can greatly enhance enjoyment of trips into the park. Contact Roy Funch, at Funkart Artesanato, in Lençóis, or Luís Krug at Pousada Canto das Águas, in Lençóis. Claude Samuel runs trips into the park from the Pousada Candombá (☎ 332-2176) in Palmeiras.

Short Hikes A pleasant 1½-hour hike can be taken upstream along the Rio Lençóis to Salão de Areias Coloridas (Room of Coloured Sands), where artisans gather material for bottled sand paintings, then on to Cachoeira da Primavera waterfall.

Another relaxing hike (45 minutes) can be made to Ribeirão do Meio, a series of swimming holes with a natural waterslide (bring old clothes or borrow a burlap sack). Bathers have had nasty accidents walking up the slide: swim across to the far side of the pool and climb the dry rocks.

Lapa Doce About 70 km north-west of Lençóis, followed by a 25-minute hike, is a huge cave formed by a now-dry subterranean river. You will need a guide (Luís is an expert on the place) and you should bring a torch.

Rio Mucugêzinho This river, 30 km from Lençóis, is a super day trip. Take the 8 am Palmeiras/Seabra bus and ask the driver to let you off at Barraca do Pelé; the bus passes again at around 4 pm on its return trip to Lençóis. From Barraca do Pelé, pick your way about two km downstream to Poço do Diabo (Devil's Well), a swimming hole with a 30-metre waterfall.

Morro do Pai Inácio At 1120 metres, this is the most prominent peak in the immediate area. It's 27 km from Lençóis and easily accessible from the highway. An easy but steep trail goes 200 metres up to the summit for a beautiful view. The trail along **Barro Branco** between Lençóis and Morro do Pai Inácio is a good four or five-hour hike.

Palmeiras, Capão & Cachoeira da Fumaça

Palmeiras is a drowsy little town 56 km west of Lençóis, with a scenic riverside position and streets lined with colourful houses. There are several cheap pensões.

The hamlet of Capão is 20 km from Palmeiras by road (or use the hiking trail connecting Capão with Lençóis). From here, there's a six-km trail (two hours on foot) to the top of Cachoeira da Fumaça, also known

BRAZIL

as the Glass waterfall (after missionary George Glass), which plummets 420 metres – the longest waterfall in Brazil. The route to the bottom of the waterfall is very difficult and not recommended.

For a much longer trip, there's the **Grand Circuit Route**, a 100-km walk, best done in a clockwise direction. It takes about five days, but allow eight days if you include highly recommended side trips such as Igatú and Cachoeira da Fumaça.

Sergipe

Sergipe, north of Bahia, is Brazil's smallest state. There are a couple of interesting historic towns, but the beaches are not much good and the capital, Aracaju, is not overwhelmingly attractive.

ARACAJU
Aracaju has little to offer the visitor, but it's pleasant enough and a good base for trips to the colonial villages of Laranjeiras and São Cristóvão. The Centro do Turismo houses the Emsetur tourist office (☎ 224-5168; open 8 am to 10 pm daily) and an *artesanato* market. Praia Atalaia Velha, on Avenida Atlântica, is an overdeveloped and mediocre beach. The telephone code is 079.

Places to Stay
There are many hotels out at Praia Atalaia Velha, but the ones in the centre are more convenient and better value. Ask for low-season discounts between March and June and during August and September. For camping, try *Camping Clube do Brasil* (☎ 243-1413) on Atalaia Velha.

The best budget option is the central *Hotel Amado* (☎ 222-8932), with clean single/double apartamentos for US$14/20, or US$20/25 with air-con. For rock-bottom accommodation, *Hotel Sergipe* (☎ 222-7898) charges US$9/11 for apartamentos, and is the choice of locals wanting a quickie. For much better value try the *Hotel Oasis* (☎ 224-1181), which has bright apartamen-

tos starting at around US$20, or *Hotel Brasília* (☎ 222-8020), with apartamentos for US$19/29. A popular mid-range hotel is the *Jangadeiro* (☎ 211-1350), in the city centre, for US$26/30.

Places to Eat
Cacique Chá (closed on Sunday), a good garden restaurant, is on Praça Olímpio Campos. *Artnatus* serves plain vegetarian food and is only open for lunch. The cafés in the Casa do Turismo are good for a snack and drinks. Good seafood restaurants at Atalaia Velha include *Taberna do Tropeiro* (live music in the evening), Avenida Oceânica 6, and the highly recommended *O Miguel* (closed Monday), at Rua Antônio Alves 340.

Getting There & Away
Air Major airlines fly to Rio, São Paulo, Salvador, Recife, Maceió, Brasília, Goiânia and Curitiba.

Bus Long-distance buses leave from the rodoviária nova (new bus terminal), about four km from the centre. There are nine buses a day to Salvador (US$11). Some take the new Linha Verde route along the coast (4½ hours), and the rest go inland via Entre Rios (six hours). There are four departures daily to Maceió (US$10, five hours), and two to Recife (US$15, nine hours).

Buses to São Cristóvão and Laranjeiras (see the following sections) operate from the rodoviária velha (old bus terminal). The shuttle service between the bus terminals costs US$0.30 and takes 25 minutes.

SÃO CRISTÓVÃO
Founded in 1590, São Cristóvão was the capital of Sergipe until 1855. The old part of town, up a steep hill, has a surprising number of 17th and 18th-century buildings along its narrow stone roads. Of particular distinction are the **Igreja e Convento de São Francisco**, on Praça São Francisco, and the **Igreja de Senhor dos Passos**, on Praça Senhor dos Passos.

São Cristóvão is 25 km south of Aracaju and seven km off BR-101. The rodoviária is down the hill, below the historical district on Praça Dr Lauro de Freitas. There are frequent buses to Aracaju, but no direct buses south to Estância. On weekends, a tourist train goes from Aracaju to São Cristóvão; contact Emsetur in Aracaju for details.

LARANJEIRAS

Nestled between three lush, church-topped hills, Laranjeiras is the colonial gem of Sergipe. It has several churches and museums worth visiting, and the surrounding hills offer picturesque walks with good views.

The city tourist office is in the Trapiche building in the Centro de Tradições, on Praça Samuel de Oliveira. The only pousada in town is the *Pousada Vale dos Outeiros* (☎ 281-1027), Rua José do Prado Franco 124. It's a friendly place with single/double quartos for US$15/20 and double apartamentos with air-con for US$30.

Buses (US$1, 35 minutes) run between Laranjeiras and Aracaju's rodoviária velha every half-hour from 5 am to 9 pm, but any bus travelling the BR-101 can let you off at the turn-off for Laranjeiras.

Alagoas

The small state of Alagoas is one of the pleasant surprises of the North-East. Its beaches are enchanting, and inland there is a fabulous stretch of lush sugar-cane country.

MACEIÓ

Maceió, the capital of Alagoas, has a small historical area but is mostly modern. A recent boom in tourism has seen rapid development of the city beaches, particularly between Ponta Verde and Praia de Jatiúca.

Information

Ematur (☎ 221-9393), the state tourism organisation, is at Avenida Duque de Caxais 2014. Emturma (☎ 223-4016), the municipal tourism body, is at Rua Saldanha da Gama 71. There are tourist information booths at Praia Pajuçara, Ponte Verde, Praia Jatiúca and the airport. The telephone code for Maceió is 082.

Things to See & Do

The **Museu do Instituto Histórico**, Rua João Pessoa, has exhibits about regional history.

Beaches close to Centro are polluted, and Praia Pajuçara and Praia dos Sete Coqueiros (three to four km away) are becoming dirtier. The best **beaches** are farther north, including Ponta Verde (five km), Jatiúca (six km), Jacarecica (nine km), Guaxuma (12 km), Garça Torta (14 km), Riacho Doce (16 km) and Pratagi (17 km).

These tropical paradises get busy on weekends and throughout the summer. On Pajuçara, *jangadas* (traditional sailboats) will take you out to the reef for US$4; the marine life there is best seen at low tide.

The schooner *Lady Elvira* departs daily from Pontal da Barra for a five-hour cruise to islands and beaches (US$30 with lunch, US$20 without); contact Ematur. Small motorboats make similar cruises from Pontal da Barra (US$10).

Locals reckon Barra de São Miguel has the best Carnaval in the area. Festa do Mar takes place in December.

Places to Stay

For camping try *Camping Jatiúca* (☎ 235-1251), Praia Cruz das Almas, around six km from the centre. Hostels close to Maceió include: *Albergue de Juventude Pajuçara* (☎ 231-0631), Rua Quintino Bocaiuva 63, Pajuçara, which is safe, clean and friendly; *Albergue de Juventude Nossa Casa* (☎ 231-2246), at Rua Prefeito Abdon Arroxelas 177, Praia de Ponta Verde; and *Albergue de Juventude Stella Maris* (☎ 325-2217), Avenida Engenheiro Paulo Brandão Nogueira 336, on Praia Jatiúca.

In the city, try *Hotel dos Palmares* (☎ 223-7024), Praça dos Palmares 253, with quartos for US$18/28 including breakfast. Nearby, the *Hotel Maceió* (☎ 223-1883), Rua Dr Pontas de Miranda 146, offers cell-like but clean apartamentos at US$12/24 for singles/

BRAZIL

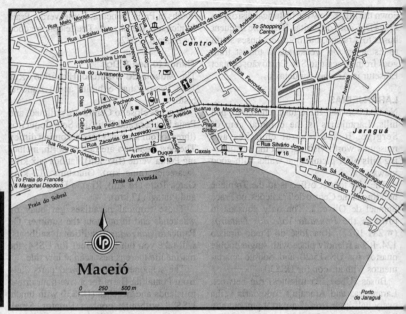

doubles. *Hotel Ney* (☎ 221-6500), midway between the city centre and Praia de Pajuçara, has apartamentos with air-con from US$25/32; some rooms are better than others. A mid-range option is *Hotel Beiriz* (☎ 221-1080), at Rua João Pessoa 290, a three-star hotel with pool, restaurant and air-con rooms from US$42.

Praia de Pajuçara, between the city centre and the better beaches, has plenty of budget accommodation. Try *Pousada Piscina do Mar* (231-6971), on the beachfront, at Avenida Dr Antônio Gouveia 123. Clean apartamentos cost US$15/25. Places on Rua Jangadeiros Alagoanos include *Pousada da Praia* (☎ 231-6843), at No 545, with basic quartos for US$15/20; *Pousada Saveiro* (☎ 231-9831), up the road at No 905, which is friendly and good value; and *Pousada Amazonia*, at No 1089, with bright, clean quartos from US$9 per person.

For better beachside places, try the older hotels along Praia de Pajuçara. *Hotel Praia Bonita* (☎ 231-2565), at Avenida Antônio Gouveia 943, Praia de Pajuçara, has clean double apartamentos with air-con for US$35. *Pousada Cavalo Marinho* (☎ 235-1247, fax 235-3265), about 15 km from the centre at Rua da Praia 55, Praia Riacho Doce, has been recommended, and has doubles from around US$25.

Places to Eat

For a seafood splurge in the city centre, visit *Lagostão* (☎ 221-6211) at Avenida Duque de Caxias 1384. A cheaper option, just one block east on the same road, is *Como Anti-gamente*, which does prato feito for US$5.

Most of the beaches offer a wide choice of food, with barracas and snack bars serving seafood and local dishes. At Praia Pajuçara, *Paraíso* is a casual little café with a great range of juices and snack foods. *O Komilão* is friendly with reasonably priced seafood, and *Pizzaria Paju* has good pizza and pasta.

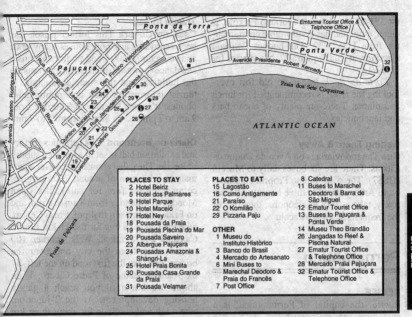

PLACES TO STAY
2 Hotel Beiriz
5 Hotel dos Palmares
9 Hotel Parque
10 Hotel Maceió
17 Hotel Ney
18 Pousada da Praia
19 Pousada Piscina do Mar
20 Pousada Saveiro
23 Albergue Pajuçara
24 Pousadas Amazonia & Shangri-La
25 Hotel Praia Bonita
30 Pousada Casa Grande da Praia
31 Pousada Velamar

PLACES TO EAT
15 Lagostão
16 Como Antigamente
21 Paraíso
22 O Komilão
29 Pizzaria Paju

OTHER
1 Museu do Instituto Histórico
3 Banco do Brasil
4 Mercado do Artesanato
6 Mini Buses to Marechal Deodoro & Praia do Francês
7 Post Office
8 Catedral
11 Buses to Marachel Deodoro & Barra de São Miguel
12 Ematur Tourist Office
13 Buses to Pajuçara & Ponta Verde
14 Museu Theo Brandão
26 Jangadas to Reef & Piscina Natural
27 Ematur Tourist Office & Telephone Office
28 Mercado Praia Pajuçara
32 Ematur Tourist Office & Telephone Office

BRAZIL

Getting There & Away

Air Maceió is connected by air with Rio, São Paulo, Brasília and all the major centres of the North-East. Airlines include Varig (☎ (0800) 99-7000), VASP (☎ (0800) 99-8227) and Transbrasil (☎ 221-8344). Aeroporto dos Palmares (☎ 322-1300) is 20 km from the centre; get a bus at Praça Sinibu, or a taxi for around US$15.

Bus There are frequent departures daily to Recife (US$8, four hours), Aracaju (US$10, five hours), and Salvador (US$28, 10 hours).

PENEDO

Penedo, known as the capital of the lower São Francisco, is a fascinating colonial city almost untouched by tourism. Attractions include many Baroque churches and colonial buildings, and the opportunity to travel on the Rio São Francisco. Penedo bustles with people from the smaller villages up and down the river who come to buy and sell goods.

Saturday is the major market day and the easiest day to find a boat up or down the São Francisco. For a short excursion take one of the motorboats that depart every half-hour to Neópolis, a few km downriver, or one of the frequent boats to Carrapicho, a small town noted for its ceramics.

The tourist office (open daily from 8 am to noon and 2 to 5 pm) and a small city museum are in the Casa da Aposentadoria, just up from the fort on Praça Barão de Penedo.

Places to Stay & Eat

Penedo has some lovely old hotels down by the waterfront and around Avenida Floriano Peixoto. *Pousada Colonial* (☎ 551-2677), Praça 12 de Abril, is a beautiful converted colonial home on the waterfront with spacious apartamentos from US$18/25 for singles/doubles. *Hotel São Francisco*

(☎ 551-2273), Avenida Floriano Peixoto, is clean, quiet and has comfortable apartamentos from US$24/32. The budget *Pousada Familiar*, at Rua Siqueira 77, has quartos for US$7/14.

Forte da Rocheira, in an old fort overlooking the river, is recommended for lunch and dinner. There are plenty of cheap bars and lanchonetes.

Getting There & Away
Bus The rodoviária is on Avenida Duque de Caxias. There are six buses daily to Maceió (US$7). The 6 am bus to Propriá continues on to Aracaju (US$5, three hours). Alternatively, take a ferry to Neópolis, then one of the frequent buses to Aracaju.

Pernambuco

RECIFE
Recife, the capital of Pernambuco, is a sprawling, modern conurbation with some interest in the old central area. The upmarket beach suburb of Boa Viagem is OK, but the main attraction is nearby Olinda.

Information
Tourist Office Empetur (☎ 241-2111), the state tourism bureau, has a tourist information desk at the Casa de Cultura, and at the Terminal Integrado de Passageiros (TIP), a combined metro terminal and rodoviária.

Post & Communications The main post office is at Avenida Guararapes 250. There are also post offices at the airport and TIP. TELPE (the state telephone company) has 24-hour telephone stations at TIP and the airport; there are also telephones in the Casa de Cultura. The telephone code is 081.

Travel Agencies Andratur (☎ 326-4388), at Avenida Conselheiro Aguiar 3150, Loja 6 (Boa Viagem), sells discounted international air tickets and expensive package tours to the paradise isles of Fernando de Noronha.

Things to See
Casa da Cultura This former prison has been renovated and now houses many craft and souvenir shops. Good traditional music and dance shows are often performed outside the building, and the complex contains a tourist information desk and public telephones. It's open Monday to Saturday from 9 am to 7 pm and on Sunday from 2 to 7 pm.

Olaria de Brennand This ceramics factory and exhibition hall is set in a forested suburb of Recife. The gallery/museum houses a permanent exhibition of around 2000 original ceramic pieces *(not* for sale). It's open Monday to Thursday from 8 am to 5 pm, and on Friday from 8 am to 4 pm. From Centro, take the Caxangá bus for the 11-km ride to Caxangá bus terminal. Walk another 100 metres away from the city and over the bridge, then take the first road on the left, by the roadside statue of Padre Cicero. Walk about two km until you reach a gaudy housing development. At the T-junction, take a left and continue for about three km through forest to the office. The walk takes about 1¼ hours. You could also take a taxi or a tour. A small sample of Brennand ceramics can be seen in the shop (☎ 325-0025) at Avenida Conselheiro Aguiar 2966, Loja 4, Galeria Vila Real, in Boa Viagem.

Museu do Homem do Nordeste The Museum of the North-East is Recife's best museum, with anthropology and popular art sections and an exhibit on local herbal medicine (open daily till 5 pm). It's east of the city centre, along Avenida 17 de Agosto. Catch the Dois Irmãos bus from Parque 13 de Maio, Centro.

Museu do Trem Train buffs may enjoy this museum, adjacent to the metro station.

Special Events
Recife and Olinda may hold the best Carnaval in Brazil. Two months before the start of Carnaval, there are *bailes* (dances) in the clubs and Carnaval blocos practising on the streets. Galo da Madrugada, Recife's largest

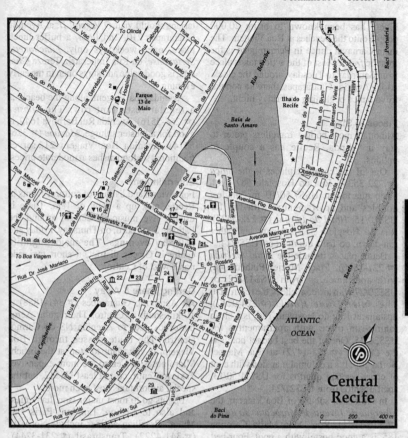

Central Recife

BRAZIL

PLACES TO STAY	OTHER	21	Praça da Independência
2 Hotel Suíça	1 Fortaleza de São João Batista do Brum	22	Casa da Cultura (Tourist Office & Telephones)
8 Hotel Central	3 Buses to Olinda		
9 Hotel América	5 Teatro Santa Isabel	24	Nossa Senhora do Carmo
10 Hotel do Parque	6 Praça da República		
12 Inter Laine Hotel	7 Polícia Federal	25	Praça 17
	11 Museu Archeológico	26	Recife Metro Station & Museu do Trem
23 Hotel 4 de Outubro	13 Galeria de Arte Metropolitana		
	14 Capela Dourada da Ordem Terceira de São Francisco	27	Patio de São Pedro
PLACES TO EAT		28	Mercado do São José
4 Livro 7 Bookshop & China Brazil Restaurant	15 Matriz da Boa Vista		
	17 Post Office	29	Forte das Cinco Pontas (Museu da Cidade)
16 Lanchonette Sertanense	19 Matriz de Santo Antônio		
18 O Vegetal II	20 Igreja de Santo Antonio		

bloco, has been known to bring 20,000 people onto the beaches at Boa Viagem. The main Carnaval dance in Pernambuco is the frenetic *frevo*. Most of the action takes place from Saturday to Tuesday, around the clock. Along Avenida Guararapes, there's a popular frevo dance beginning on Friday night.

Places to Stay

Although most budget travellers prefer to stay in Olinda, Recife has a couple of options.

One of the cheapest places is the *Suiça* (☎ 222-3534), Rua do Hospício 687, with basic quartos at US$7.50/10 for singles/doubles and apartamentos with fan for US$10/15. *Hotel do Parque* (☎ 222-5427), Rua do Hospício 51, is quaint but rather run-down; no-frills quartos cost US$9/14.

Better places include the *Hotel América* (☎ 221-1300), Praça Maciel Pinheiro 48, with apartamentos from US$15/22, or US$20/27 with air-con; check the room first. The *Inter Laine Hotel* (☎ 224-9217), upstairs at Rua do Hospício 186, is a clean family-run place with apartamentos for US$20/25. One of the best budget hotels is the *Central* (☎ 221-1472) at Rua Manoel Borba 209. It's a colonial mansion with a lot of character and quartos for US$11.50/13, apartamentos from US$21/24.

In the beach suburb of Boa Viagem, the *Albergue de Juventude Maracatus do Recife* (☎ 326-1221), Rua Dona Maria Carolina 185, is a good hostel with a pool. Four-bed dorm rooms cost US$12 for members, US$15 for nonmembers. Mid-range hotels are on and around Rua Felix de Brito Melo. The *Hotel Pousada Aconchego* (☎ 326-2989, fax 326-8059), at No 382, has a swimming pool, restaurant and apartamentos for US$38/48. The *Hotel Pedro do Mar* (☎ 325-5340), at No 604, is a friendly place with apartamentos for US$37/43, or US$28/32 for longer stays.

Places to Eat

Centro is loaded with lunch places, and at night it's easy to find something to your liking around the Pátio de São Pedro. Vege-tarians should visit *O Vegetal II*, at Avenida Guararapes 210, 2nd floor, a buffet lunch place, open weekdays only. *Lanchonette Sertananse*, on Rua Imperatriz Teraza Cristina, is good value and stays open in the early evening.

Avenida Boa Viagem, along the beach, is a regular restaurant row. The *Lobster* (☎ 268-5516), Avenida Rui Barbosa 1649, is good for a lobster splurge. *Maxime* (☎ 326-5314), Avenida Boa Viagem 21, serves traditional seafood dishes at moderate prices.

Entertainment

For reviews and listings of cultural events in Recife, pick up a copy of *Veja*. There is usually live music in Centro, around the Pátio de São Pedro, on Thursday, Friday and Saturday evenings. The major nightlife centre is Graças district, a short taxi ride north-west of Centro.

Getting There & Away

Air Aeroporto Guararapes (☎ 341-1888) is 10 km south of Centro. The regular Aeroporto bus goes to Avenida NS do Carmo, Centro. The route passes through Boa Viagem, if you want to stop at the beach. Micro buses to Centro are more expensive. Taxis to Centro cost at least US$12, but the special airport taxis cost even more.

Flights go to most major Brazilian cities, and also to Lisbon, London, Paris and Miami. Brazilian airlines include Nordeste (☎ 341-4222), Transbrasil (☎ 231-3244), Varig (☎ 424-2155) and VASP (☎ 421-3611).

Bus TIP (☎ 455-1999) is 14 km south-west of Centro. TIP handles all interstate departures and many connections for local destinations.

There are frequent daily departures to Maceió (US$8, four hours), at least five to Salvador (US$28, 12 to 14 hours) and one to Rio (US$78, about 36 hours). Heading north, there are buses to João Pessoa (US$5, two hours), Natal (US$10, five hours), Fortaleza (US$26, 12 hours), São Luis (US$50, 23 hours) and Belém (US$64, 34 hours). There are frequent services to Caruaru, Garanhuns and Triunfo.

Getting Around

Bus The local bus system is confusing. Any Rio Doce bus should get you to Olinda from the city centre, but the most straightforward place to catch one is on the north side of Parque 13 de Maio. Taxis from Centro to Olinda cost about US$7 and take 20 minutes.

From Centro to Boa Viagem, take any CDU/Boa Viagem bus. To return to Centro, take any Dantas Barreto bus. The Piedade/Rio Doce bus runs between Boa Viagem and Olinda.

Metro The metro system is very useful for the 25-minute trip (US$0.50) between TIP and the metro station in Centro.

OLINDA

Olinda, Brazil's first capital, sits on a hill overlooking Recife and the Atlantic. It's a gorgeous little town with one of the best collections of colonial buildings in Brazil.

Information

The main tourist office (☎ 429 1039), at Rua do Sol 127 (in the grounds of the Hotel Pousada São Francisco), has maps, walking-tour brochures and information about art exhibitions and music performances. It's open Monday to Friday from 8 am to 1.30 pm. Banks up near the beaches change money.

Walking Tour

Starting at Praça do Carmo, visit the recently restored **Igreja NS do Carmo**. Then follow Rua de São Francisco to **Convento São Francisco** (1585), which also encloses the **Capela de São Roque** and the **Igreja de NS das Neves**: approximate daily opening hours for this group are 8 to 11.30 am and 2 to 4.30 pm.

At the end of the street, turn left onto Rua Frei Afonso Maria and you'll see the **Seminário de Olinda** and **Igreja NS da Graça** (1549) on the hill above. Daily visiting hours are 8 to 11.30 am and 3 to 5 pm.

Continue up the street, then turn left at Rua Bispo Coutinho and climb up to **Alto da Sé**, (Cathedral Heights), which is a good spot to enjoy superb views of Olinda and Recife. There are outdoor restaurants and a small craft market. It's a big hang-out at night, with people, food, drinking and music. The imposing **Igreja da Sé** (1537) is open on weekends from 8 am to noon.

Continue a short distance along Rua Bispo Coutinho until you see the **Museu de Arte Sacra de Pernambuco** (MASPE) on your right. MASPE is housed in a beautiful building (1696) that was once Olinda's Episcopal Palace and Camara (Government Council). The museum contains a good collection of sacred art. It's open Tuesday to Saturday from 8 am to 2 pm.

About 75 metres farther down the street, turn right into a patio to visit **Igreja NS da Conceição** (1585).

Retrace your steps and continue down the street, now named Ladeira da Misericórdia, to **Igreja da Misericórdia** (1540), which has fine azulejos and gilded carvings inside. It's open daily from 8 to 11.30 am and 2 to 5 pm.

Turn right onto Rua Saldanha Marinho to see **Igreja NS do Amparo** (1581), which is currently under renovation.

Descend Rua do Amparo until you see the **Museu do Mamulengo**, on your right, which has a colourful collection of antique wooden puppets. A few doors down, at Rua do Amparo 45, is the house of Silvio Botelho, the creator of the *Bonecos Gigantes de Olinda*, giant papier-mâché puppets which are used in Carnaval festivities.

Continue along Rua do Amparo to join Rua 13 de Maio to see the **Museu de Arte Contemporânea** (MAC). This contemporary art museum is recommended for its permanent and temporary exhibits. The museum is housed in an 18th-century *ajube*, a jail used by the Catholic church during the Inquisition. With its new paint job it's hard to imagine its grim past. It's open Tuesday to Friday from 9 am to noon and 2 to 5 pm, and on Saturday and Sunday from 2 to 5 pm.

Rua 13 de Maio continues in a tight curve to a junction with Rua Bernardo de Melo and

Olinda

0   50   100 m

ATLANTIC OCEAN

Rua São Bento. If you walk up Rua Bernardo de Melo, you'll come to **Mercado da Ribeira**, an 18th-century structure that is now home to art and artisan galleries.

Go down Rua São Bento to the huge **Mosteiro de São Bento** (1582), which has some exceptional woodcarving in the chapel. The monastery is open daily from 8 to 11 am and 2 to 5 pm.

Special Events

Olinda's Carnaval, which lasts a full 11 days, has been very popular with Brazilians and travellers for years. Because so many resi-

dents know each other, it has an intimacy and security that you don't get in big city carnavals. It's a participatory event here – you'll need a costume!

The Folclore Nordestino festival at the end of August features dance, music and folklore from many parts of the North-East.

Places to Stay

Reserve accommodation several months in advance and be prepared for massive price hikes during Carnaval.

Camping Olinda (☎ 429-1365), Rua do Bom Sucesso 262, is within easy reach of the

PLACES TO STAY
15 Pousada dos Quatro Cantos
20 Pousada Saude
21 Pousada d'Olinda
22 Albergue Pousada do Bonfim
25 Hotel Pousada São Francisco & Tourist Office
26 Pousada Flor da Manhã
27 Albergue de Olinda
42 Albergue do Sol

PLACES TO EAT
4 Oficina do Sabor
14 Restaurante L'Atelier
24 John's Café
28 Donana
33 Mourisco
34 Ponto 274

35 Creperie
37 Viva Zapata
39 Pizzaria Leque Moleque

OTHER
1 Farol de Olinda (Lighthouse)
2 Igreja NS da Conceicao
3 Igreja NS do Amparo
5 Igreja da Misericórdia
6 Observatorio Astronômico
7 Museu de Arte Sacra de Pernambuco (MASPE)
8 Seminário de Olinda/Igreja NS da Graça
9 Praça Dantas Barrêto
10 Convento São Francisco

11 Igreja da Sé
12 Igreja NS do Bonfim
13 Museu do Mamulenco
16 Igreja da Boa Hora
17 Museu de Arte Comtemporânea
18 Senado Ruins
19 Mercado da Ribeira
23 Telephone Office
29 Post Office
30 Atlântico Nightclub
31 Praça do Carmo & Buses to Recife
32 Igreja NS do Carmo
36 Igreja São Pedro
38 Palácio dos Governadores
40 Itapema Office
41 Mosteiro de São Bento
43 Mercado Popular

historical district. *Pousada Flor da Manhã* (☎ 429-2266), Rua de São Francisco 162, in an old villa, has a range of accommodation. Dorm beds are US$12, simple rooms US$18, and the best rooms, with a great view, from US$25. They may give you a better price for a longer stay. *Albergue do Sol* (☎ 439-1134), right on the waterfront at Avenida Manoel Borba 300, has dorm beds at similar prices. It's not fancy, but the ocean outlook and the small swimming pool make up for it. *Albergue de Olinda* (☎ 429-1592), Rua do Sol 233, is an official youth hostel, nice and friendly, with dorm beds at US$13/15 for members/nonmembers. Apartamentos are also available from around US$20.

Albergue Pousada do Bonfim (☎ 429-1674), Rua do Bonfim 115-B, is popular with budget travellers, with dorm beds for US$12, good meals and a friendly atmosphere. *Pousada Saude*, at Rua 7 de Setembro 8, is very much a family place, offering basic quartos from US$8 per person. Nearer the beaches, *Albergue de Juventude Cheiro do Mar* (☎ 429-0101), Avenida Marcos Freire 95, has dormitory beds for around US$12.

In the medium-price range, the *Pousada dos Quatro Cantos* (☎ 429-0220, fax 429-1845), at Rua Prudente de Morais 441, is a beautiful colonial building with a leafy courtyard and a range of single/double rooms from US$29/34, apartamentos for US$42 and a suite for US$68. The *Pousada d'Olinda* (☎ 439-1163), Praça João Alfredo 178, is an up-market place with a swimming pool and garden. Quartos go for US$18/24, and apartamentos start at US$25/32.

The *Hotel Pousada São Francisco* (☎ 429-2109, fax 429-4057), Rua do Sol 127, is a modern hotel with apartamentos from US$38/43. Most up-market hotels are new places along the beaches north of town. *Hotel Sofitel Olinda* (☎ 431-2955) is the fanciest, from around US$100.

Places to Eat
Lots of restaurants are tucked away in the cobbled streets of the old city; some are pricey, but most have a few inexpensive dishes on the menu. Cheaper places include *John's Café*, on Praça do Carmo, a friendly café serving home-made pies, pastries and delicious ice cream. Nearby, *Pizzaria Leque Moleque*, on Rua Manoel Ribeiro, has great-value pizzas in a nice outdoor setting. The restaurant at *Pousada Flor de Manhã* can also be good value, with seafood and salads for around US$6.

Viva Zapata, Rua 27 de Janeiro 65, is a stylish Mexican restaurant open Thursday to Sunday from 7 pm to midnight. For regional food try *Ponto 274*, a garden restaurant at Rua São Bento 274, with tasty, home-cooked fish, chicken and beef dishes for US$7 to US$10; or *Oficina do Sabor*, Rua do Amparo 329, an elegant place which could be worth a splurge.

Top-end options include *Mourisco*, one of Olinda's best fish restaurants, and *Restaurante L'Atelier* (☎ 429-3099), a French restaurant at Rua Bernando de Melo 91.

Getting There & Away

The main bus stop in Olinda is on Praça do Carmo. Rio Doce/Conde da Boa Vista buses go to central Recife. Taxis cost about US$5. Long-distance buses depart from TIP in Recife, but you can book tickets at the Itapema office in Olinda.

Getting Around

Chartering a minibus between a few people is a good way to see surrounding attractions like Porto de Galinhas, Itamaracá, Caruaru, Fazenda Nova (Nova Jerusalém), and Olaria Brennand. There are a few small operators around; ask for a recommendation at the place where you are staying.

CARUARU

On Wednesday and Saturday, Caruaru has a folk-art fair featuring the town's famous ceramic artwork. Singers and poets perform the *literatura de cordel* (literally, string literature) – folk poetry, sold in little booklets which hang by string from the vendors' stands. Caruaru is an easy day-trip from Recife on shuttle buses (US$7, two hours), which depart half-hourly.

FAZENDA NOVA & NOVA JERUSALÉM

The small town of Fazenda Nova, 50 km from Caruaru, is famous for its theatre-city reconstruction of Jerusalem, known as Nova Jerusalém. The time to visit is during Semana Santa, when several hundred of the inhabitants of Fazenda Nova perform the Paixão de Cristo (Passion Play).

Places to Stay

There's a camping ground, *Camping Fazenda Nova*, or you can stay in the centre of town, at the *Grande Hotel* (☎ 732-1137), Avenida Poeta Carlos Pena Filho s/n, which has apartamentos for around US$24.

Getting There & Away

During Semana Santa there are frequent buses from Recife and special package tours are offered by travel agencies. At other times there are daily buses between Fazenda Nova and Caruaru.

Paraíba

JOÃO PESSOA

João Pessoa, the capital of Paraíba, is a noisy, bustling place, worth a quick look before you head to the beaches.

Information

PBTUR (☎ 226-7078), Avenida Almirante Tamandaré 100, in Praia Tambaú, east of town, provides maps and leaflets.

Igreja São Francisco

This is the town's principal tourist attraction and one of Brazil's finest churches. Its construction was interrupted by battles with the Dutch and the French, so the result is a beautiful but architecturally confused complex built over three centuries. The church is open Tuesday to Saturday from 8 to 11 am and 2 to 5 pm, and Sunday from 2 to 5 pm.

Beaches

Praia Tambaú, seven km directly east of the city centre, is rather built-up, but clean and nice. South of Tambaú is Praia Cabo Branco. From there, it's a glorious 15-km walk along Praia da Penha to Ponta de Seixas, the easternmost tip of South America. There are good beaches north of Tambaú, too.

Places to Stay

At the easternmost tip of Brazil is *Camping-*

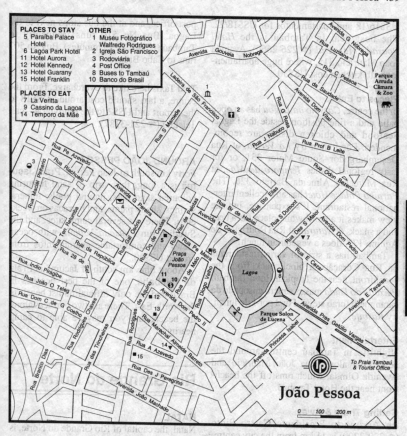

PLACES TO STAY
5 Paraíba Palace Hotel
6 Lagoa Park Hotel
11 Hotel Aurora
12 Hotel Kennedy
13 Hotel Guarany
15 Hotel Franklin

PLACES TO EAT
7 La Veritta
9 Cassino da Lagoa
14 Tempero da Mãe

OTHER
1 Museu Fotográfico Walfredo Rodrigues
2 Igreja São Francisco
3 Rodoviária
4 Post Office
8 Buses to Tambaú
10 Banco do Brasil

João Pessoa

0   100   200 m

BRAZIL

PB-01, run by Camping Clube do Brasil at Praia de Seixas, 16 km from João Pessoa.

In the city centre, *Hotel Aurora* (☎ 241-3238), Praça João Pessoa 51, has adequate quartos for US$8/12, and apartamentos with fan for US$15/20. Rooms overlooking the street can be noisy. *Hotel Franklin* (☎ 222-3001), Rua Rodrigues de Aquino 293, is a basic, family-run place with quartos for US$8/14. *Hotel Kennedy* (☎ 221-4924), Rua Rodrigues de Aquino 17, has air-con apartamentos for US$25/30 with sumptuous breakfast included; with fan and no breakfast, the price drops to US$7/10.

The *Paraíba Palace Hotel* (☎ 221-3107, fax 241-2007), at Praça Vidal de Negreiros s/n, is an impressive colonial palace with a swimming pool and restaurant. It currently costs from US$35/45 for standard apartamentos, but the bargain prices can't last.

Out at Praia Tambaú there's the friendly *Albergue de Juventude Tambaú* (☎ 226-5460), at Rua Bezerra Reis 82. Another hostel, *Albergue de Juventude Cabo Branco* (☎ 226-3628), is a little farther south at Avenida Padre José Trigueiro 104 in Cabo Branco. *Hotel Gameleira* (☎ 226-1576), at Avenida João Maurício 157, has quartos for

US$16/18 and apartamentos for US$18/22. The best deal in Tambaú is the *Hotel Pousada Mar Azul* (☎ 226-2660), Avenida João Maurício 315, where huge apartamentos with kitchen cost US$30.

Places to Eat
In the centre, *Cassino da Lagoa* has an open patio and a fine position beside the Lagoa. Seafood and chicken dishes are recommended. For Italian try *La Veritta*, at Rua Desembargador Souto Maior 331, or for tasty regional dishes *Temporo da Mãe*, at Rua Marechal Almeida Barreto 326. The *Paraíba Palace Hotel* has an excellent international restaurant. It's expensive, but the view makes it a worthwhile place for a beer and a snack. *O Natural*, at Rua Rodrigues de Aquino 177, does a vegetarian lunch.

Tambaú has a strip of varied restaurants on Rua Coração, a block back from the beachfront, near the Tropical Hotel Tambaú. *Peixada do Duda* makes superb ensopado de caranguejo (crab stew). For a por-kilo lunch, try *Rosbife*.

Entertainment
Nightlife in Tambaú centres around the beachfront along Rua João Maurício and Avenida Olinda, which runs off the beachfront near the Hotel Tambaú.

Getting There & Away
Air Aeroporto Presidente Castro Pinto (☎ 229-3200) is 11 km from the city centre. Flights operate to Rio, São Paulo and the major cities of the North-East and the North. Airlines include Transbrasil (☎ 241-2822), Varig (☎ 221-1140) and VASP (☎ 221-3434).

Bus The rodoviária (☎ 221-9611) is on Avenida Francisco Londres. There are frequent buses to Recife (US$6, two hours), Natal (US$6.50, 2½ hours) and Fortaleza (US$23, 10 hours).

Getting Around
Bus Local buses can be boarded at the rodoviária, at the bus stop next to the main post office, and at the bus stops next to the Lagoa. Bus No 510 runs frequently to Tambaú (US$0.30, 25 minutes). Bus No 507 runs to Cabo Branco.

Taxi Taxis here like to overcharge. From the centre, a taxi should cost around US$18 to the airport and US$2 to the rodoviária – call Teletaxi (☎ 221-3187).

AROUND JOÃO PESSOA
Forty km south of João Pessoa, **Praia Jacumã** is a long, thin strip of sand featuring coloured sand bars, natural pools, mineral springs, shady palms, and barracas on weekends. There are several camp sites, and the Swedish run *Pousada Valhall*, with ocean views and comfortable apartamentos from around US$20.

About nine km south of Jacumã is **Praia de Tambaba**, one of the best beaches in Brazil and the only official nudist beach in the North-East. There are two barracas along the beach, and you may be able to camp nearby.

Rio Grande do Norte

NATAL
Natal, the capital of Rio Grande do Norte, is a clean, bright city which is being developed at top speed into the beach capital of the North-East.

Information
The best source of tourist information may be at the rodoviária nova (☎ 231-1170), which has a tourist information booth open daily from 8 am to 6 pm. It has maps and brochures and can book hotels. The Centro de Turismo (☎ 212-2267) in the Casa de Detenção on Rua Aderbal Figueiredo is not as useful. There's also SECTUR (☎ 221-5729), the municipal tourism authority, and EMPROTURN (☎ 219-3400), the state

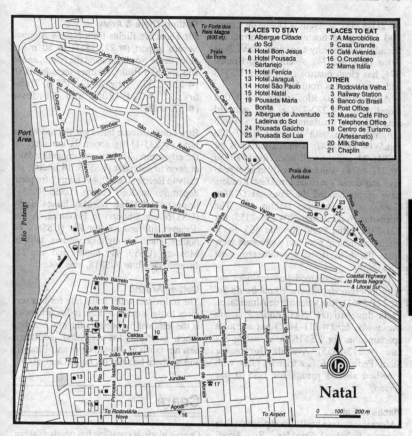

PLACES TO STAY
1 Albergue Cidade do Sol
4 Hotel Bom Jesus
8 Hotel Pousada Sertanejo
11 Hotel Fenícia
13 Hotel Jaraguá
14 Hotel São Paulo
15 Hotel Natal
19 Pousada Maria Bonita
23 Albergue de Juventude Ladeina do Sol
24 Pousada Gaúcho
25 Pousada Sol Lua

PLACES TO EAT
7 A Macrobiótica
9 Casa Grande
10 Café Avenida
16 O Crustáceo
22 Mama Itália

OTHER
2 Rodoviária Velha
3 Railway Station
5 Banco do Brasil
6 Post Office
12 Museu Café Filho
17 Telephone Office
18 Centro de Turismo (Artesanato)
20 Milk Shake
21 Chaplin

BRAZIL

Natal

0   100   200 m

tourism authority, neither conveniently located.

Natal's telephone code is 084.

Things to See & Do

The pentagonal **Forte dos Reis Magos** and the **Museu da Câmara Cascudo**, at Avenida Hermes da Fonseca 1398, are the principal sights of Natal. The museum features a collection of Amazon Indian artefacts. It's open Tuesday to Friday from 8 to 11.30 am and 2 to 5 pm, and on Saturday from 8 to 11.30 am.

Natal's **city beaches**, Praia do Meio,

Praia dos Artistas, Praia da Areia Preta, Praia do Pinto and Praia Mãe Luiza, stretch well over nine km, from the fort to the lighthouse. Most have bars, nightlife, big surf and petty crime.

Beach-buggy excursions are offered by a host of *bugeiros* (buggy drivers), for about US$70 per buggy per day. Encourage the driver to stay in established buggy areas and not to damage the more remote and pristine beaches.

Places to Stay

In the city centre, *Albergue Cidade do Sol*

(☎ 211-3233), at Avenida Duque de Caxais 190 is a good hostel. Also central, the friendly and security-conscious *Hotel Bom Jesus* (☎ 212-2374), Avenida Rio Branco 374, has clean quartos from about US$18 and apartamentos from US$24.

Along Avenida Rio Branco you'll find *Hotel Natal* (☎ 222-2792), with standard single/double apartamentos at US$18/25 (slightly more with air-con); *Hotel São Paulo* (☎ 211-4130), with apartamentos for US$16/24; and the well-worn *Hotel Fenícia* (☎ 211-4378), which is actually more expensive and doesn't include breakfast. Readers have recommended the *Pousada O Meu Canto*, at Rua Manoel Dantas 424. The three-star *Hotel Jaraguá* (☎ 221-2355, fax 221-2351), Rua Santo Antônio 665, has a sauna, swimming pool and panoramic view from the 17th floor; apartamentos cost US$46/53.

Beachside accommodation includes the nifty *Albergue de Juventude Ladeira do Sol* (☎ 221-5361), Rua Valentim de Almeida, on Praia dos Artistas. Next door, *Pousada Ondas do Mar* (☎ 211-3481) has adequate apartamentos for US$16/24. *Pousada Sol Lua* (☎ 212-2855), Avenida Governador Silvio Pedrosa 146, is a friendly place with four-bed shared rooms for US$10 per person.

Places to Eat

A Macrobiótica is a health-food place on Rua Princesa Isabel. *O Crustáceo*, Rua Apodi 414, specialises in seafood and has a large tree poking through the roof. For regional food, try *Casa Grande*, Rua Princesa Isabel 529. *Mama Itália*, Rua Silvio Pedrosa 43, has a wide range of excellent pastas and pizzas. For coffee, go to *Café Avenida*, on Avenida Deodoro, which also serves a delicious selection of pastries and cakes.

Entertainment

Chaplin is a pricey and popular bar on Praia dos Artistas. Across the road, *Milk Shake* has good live music and dancing most nights. For folkloric shows and dancing, try *Zás-Trás*, Rua Apodi 500, in the Tirol district.

Getting There & Away

Air There are flights from Natal's Augusto Severo airport (☎ 272-2811) to all major cities in the North-East and the North, and to Rio and São Paulo. Airlines include VASP (☎ 222-2290), Varig (☎ 221-1537), Transbrasil (☎ 221-1805) and Nordeste (☎ 272-3131).

Bus Long-distance buses use the rodoviária nova (☎ 231-1170), about six km south of the city centre. There is one departure daily at noon to Salvador (US$33, 18 hours); six daily to Recife (US$10, 4½ hours); frequent departures to João Pessoa (US$6.50, 2½ hours); and three regular buses daily (US$16, eight hours) to Fortaleza. A bus departs daily at noon for Rio (US$80, 44 hours). There are eight departures daily to Mossoró (US$9, 4½ hours) and one for Juazeiro do Norte (US$18, nine hours).

Getting Around

The rodoviária velha is the hub for bus services to the airport, and the rodoviária nova is the terminal for buses to the city beaches (such as Praia dos Artistas), southern beaches (such as Ponta Negra and Pirangi) and northern beaches (as far as Genipabu).

Ceará

Ceará's glorious coastline has nearly 600 km of magnificent beaches. The state also has a rich cultural and craft tradition, but economically it is largely poor and undeveloped. Poverty and disease are rampant with dengue and yellow fever prevalent.

FORTALEZA

Fortaleza, the capital of Ceará, is now a major fishing port and commercial centre, and it's sprouting a dense crop of modern tourist hotels.

Orientation & Information

The city centre forms a grid above the old historical section and includes the Mercado

Central (Central Market), the cathedral, and major shopping streets and government buildings.

East of the centre are the beaches of Praia de Iracema and Praia do Ideal. Continuing eastwards, Avenida Beira Mar (also called Avenida Presidente John Kennedy in places) links Praia do Diário and Praia do Meireles, which are lined with big hotels.

Coditur, the state tourism organisation, runs the helpful Centro de Turismo (☎ 231-3566), Rua Senador Pompeu 350, inside a renovated prison, open Monday to Saturday from 8 am to 6 pm.

The telephone code for Fortaleza is 085.

Beaches

Nightlife is hot round Praia de Iracema and the Ponte dos Ingleses jetty. Further east, the foreshore at Praia do Meireles has lots of craft stalls and outdoor entertainment. These beaches may be polluted, but locals do swim at them. Praia do Futuro, several km east of the city, is much cleaner, and the barracas are popular party places, but don't hang around when the beach is deserted.

Special Events

The Regata de Jangadas, a regatta of traditional balsa-log sailing craft between Praia do Meireles and Praia Mucuripe, is held in the second half of July. The Iemanjá festival is held on 15 August at Praia do Futuro. The Semana do Folclore, the town's folklore week, takes place in the Centro do Turismo from 22 to 29 August.

Places to Stay

There are some cheap dives around the city centre, but no real reason to stay there. *Hotel Passeio* (☎ 252-2104), Rua Dr João Moreira 221, is a nice old place, with reasonable single/double apartamentos for US$23/29; air-con is US$7 more. Between the centre and the beaches, the friendly and clean *Pousada do Tourista* (☎ 231-8481), Rua Dom Joaquim 351, has quartos for US$15/25. Nearby, *Pousada Savoy* (☎ 226-8426) has apartamentos (with fan) for US$18/25, but may offer a special price of US$12.

Praia de Iracema is a more interesting area to stay. The *Albergue de Juventude Praia de Iracema* (☎ 252-3267), Avenida Almeida Barroso 998, charges US$10/18 for members/nonmembers. Right next door, *Abril em Portugal* (☎ 231-9508), is a friendly family pousada with single/double apartamentos for US$15/20. Around the corner, the colourful *Pousada Portal de Iracema* (☎ 231-0066) has clean quartos for US$20/35 and comfortable apartamentos with air-con and refrigerator for US$45/60.

Hotel Pousada Ondas Verdes (☎ 226-0871), Avenida Beira Mar 934, has quite ordinary apartamentos for US$30/35, some with a sea view. Nearby, the *Turismo Praia Hotel* (☎ 231-6133) asks US$40/55 and up.

Praia do Meireles is mostly high-rise hotels, but a few smaller places on the blocks behind are good value. *Pousada Portal do Sol* (☎ 261-5767), at Rua Nunes Valente 275, is a converted residence with a pool, meals available, and apartamentos from around US$25/40. Close by, at Rua Nunes Valente 245, the *Pousada Terra do Sol* (☎ 261-9509) has clean apartamentos with fan for US$15/25. There are several others in the area.

The *Albergue de Juventude da Fortaleza* (☎ 244-1850), at Rua Rocha Lima 1186, is good, but it's in Aldeota district, a long way from the centre and the beaches.

Places to Eat

Fortaleza features fantastic fruit and fish. The centre is OK for snacks and prato feito at lunch time. *Restaurante Alivita*, Rua Barão do Rio Branco 1486, does vegetarian lunches on weekdays. The courtyard of the *Centro de Turismo* has a nice restaurant with shaded outdoor tables.

In the evening, look around the city beaches. Along Praia de Iracema, near the Ponte dos Ingleses, there are some excellent restaurants, including *La Boheme*, a sophisticated, arty place where the chairs are individually painted. For Italian food, stop at *La Trattoria*.

Lots of eateries line the beachfront at Praia do Meireles, from snack bars to barracas, but

BRAZIL

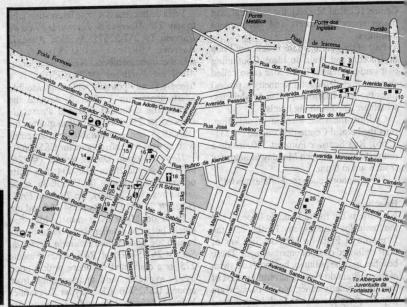

you might get better value a few blocks inland. A cheap fast-food place is *Zelmo*, on Avenida Barão de Studart. Farther up the same street is the *Mikado*, a Japanese restaurant specialising in teppanyaki.

Entertainment

Pirata Bar, near Praia de Iracema, has live music for avid forró or lambada fans, who can dance until they drop (US$5 cover charge). *Bar d'Italia* is a lively bar right next to the Ponte dos Ingleses, and there's plenty more action in the area. During holiday season the hotel strip on Praia do Meireles is full of outdoor bars, and merchants and artists hawking their goods.

Getting There & Away

Air Aeroporto Pinto Martins (☎ 272-6166) is six km south of the city centre. Flights operate to Rio, São Paulo and major cities in the North-East and the North, with Trans-

brasil (☎ 272-4669), Varig (☎ 244-5101) and VASP.

Bus The rodoviária (☎ 272-1566) is about six km south of the centre. Take any local Alencar, Ferroviária or Aguanambi bus. Bus services run daily to Salvador (US$43, 20 hours), three times daily to Natal (US$16, eight hours), at least twice daily to Teresina (US$20, nine hours), three times daily to São Luis (US$36, 16 hours), once daily to Recife (US$26, 12 hours), and six times daily to Belém (US$46, 25 hours).

The Redencão bus company runs buses at 9 am and 9 pm daily to Jericoacoara (US$10, 7½ hours). Empresa São Benedito runs four buses daily to Canoa Quebrada (US$6, 3½ hours). Ipu Brasileira has buses to Ubajara six times a day (US$10, six hours).

Getting Around

From the airport, take an Escolar Tecnica bus, then change to a Circular bus to reach

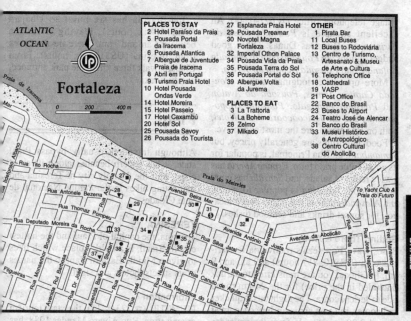

ATLANTIC
OCEAN

Praia de Iracema

Mar

Fortaleza

0   200   400 m

PLACES TO STAY
2 Hotel Paraíso da Praia
5 Pousada Portal da Iracema
6 Pousada Atlantica
7 Albergue de Juventude Praia de Iracema
8 Abril em Portugal
9 Turismo Praia Hotel
10 Hotel Pousada Ondas Verde
14 Hotel Moreira
15 Hotel Passeio
17 Hotel Caxambú
20 Hotel Sol
25 Pousada Savoy
26 Pousada do Tourísta

27 Esplanada Praia Hotel
29 Pousada Preamar
30 Novotel Magna Fortaleza
32 Imperial Othon Palace
34 Pousada Vida da Praia
35 Pousada Terra do Sol
36 Pousada Portal do Sol
39 Albergue Volta da Jurema

PLACES TO EAT
3 La Trattoria
4 La Boheme
28 Zelmo
37 Mikado

OTHER
1 Pirata Bar
11 Local Buses
12 Buses to Rodoviária
13 Centro de Turismo, Artesanato & Museu de Arte e Cultura
16 Telephone Office
18 Cathedral
19 VASP
21 Post Office
22 Banco do Brasil
23 Buses to Airport
24 Teatro José de Alencar
31 Banco do Brasil
33 Museu Histórico e Antropológico
38 Centro Cultural do Abolicão

Praia do Meireles

To Yacht Club & Praia do Futuro

BRAZIL

the city beaches. A taxi to the centre costs US$16 with a ticket from the airport, or about half that from the road outside.

CANOA QUEBRADA

Once a tiny fishing village cut off from the world by its huge, pink sand dunes, Canoa Quebrada, about 160 km south-east of Fortaleza, is still small and pretty, but now attracts lots of hip international types and bus loads of weekend tourists. The main attractions are the beach, the sunset, riding horses bareback (four hours for US$8 after bargaining) and dancing forró or reggae by the light of gas lanterns.

Don't go barefoot: bichos de pé are prevalent here.

Albergue Lua Estrela (☎ 421-1401) is a youth hostel which looks more like a resort hotel; there are great views from the restaurant. *Pousada Alternativa* (☎ 421-1401) is friendly and good value, from US$8/10. Other budget options are *Pousada Lua*

Morena, *Duna's Pousada*, and *Pousada Ma Alice* (☎ 421-1401).

There are three buses daily to Canoa Quebrada from Fortaleza's rodoviária, at 8.30 am and 1.40 and 2.40 pm (US$6, 3½ hours).

JERICOACOARA

This remote beach and small fishing village, 290 km north-west of Fortaleza, is now popular with backpackers and hip Brazilians. Avoid bichos de pé by not walking barefoot. Forró is featured every Wednesday and Saturday – just follow the music. You can also play in the sand dunes, hire horses, ride on a jangada, or walk to Pedra Furada, three km east along the beach.

Places to Stay & Eat

There is plenty of cheap accommodation, but it's not necessarily clean or with electricity or running water. For longer stays, ask about renting a house. Bring a hammock or bed roll. Reservations can be made by calling the village telephone office (☎ 621-0544). An excellent cheapie is *Pousada Casa do Turismo*, on Rua Das Dunas. Other good budget options are *Pousada Islana*, *Pousada Calanda*, and *Pousada Acoara do Jerico*.

More up-market lodgings include *Pousada Capitão Tomás*, *Pousada do Avalon* and *Pousada Papagaio*. *Pousada Hippopotamus* and the *Jericoacoara Praia Hotel*, both on Rua Forró, are the most expensive.

Food and drinks are generally pricey, but *Samambaia*, on Rua Principal, is popular for its good-value prato feito. *Espaco Aberta* has a wide range of salads; and *Senzala* has good Italian food. *Jerizelba* is popular for pizza, and *Alexandre Bar* is the prime beach location for sunset drinks and seafood dishes.

Getting There & Away
Buses leave Fortaleza's rodoviária for Jericoacoara (US$10, 7½ hours) at 9 am and 9 pm. In Gijoca, you are transferred to a truck (included in the price) for the 24-km rodeo ride to Jericoacoara. The night bus is quicker and cooler, but you arrive in Jericoacoara at around 3.30 am; people from the pousadas meet the bus. Operators in Fortaleza offer tour packages.

PARQUE NACIONAL DE UBAJARA
The main attractions of this park, near the small town of Ubajara about 290 km west of Fortaleza, are the caves and the cable-car ride down to them. There are also beautiful vistas, forests, waterfalls, and cooler temperatures – it's 750 metres above sea level.

The *teleférico* operates daily from 8.30 am to noon and 1 to 4 pm. It costs US$3 including a guided tour through the caves.

Sítio do Alemão, about 1.5 km from the park entrance, has spotless chalets for US$10 per person, and provides useful information about local attractions. Near the park entrance, *Pousada da Neblina* (☎ 634-1297) has a swimming pool and apartamentos from US$30, while *Pousada Gruta de Ubajaras* (☎ 634-1375) is much cheaper. Both have restaurants. In Ubajara, *Churrascaria Hotel Ubajara* (☎ 634-1261) has single/double quartos for US$9/18.

Ipu-Brasília has six buses to Ubajara (US$10, six hours), leaving Fortaleza between 4 am and 9 pm. There are also buses from Teresina (US$10, six hours). From Ubajara, walk three km to the park entrance, or take a taxi.

Piauí

Although travellers usually bypass Piauí state, it has superb beaches along its short coast, plus the friendly city of Teresina and interesting hikes in the Parque Nacional de Sete Cidades.

TERESINA
Teresina, the capital of Piauí and the hottest city in Brazil, is a quirky place which likes to give a Middle Eastern slant to the names of its streets, hotels and sights.

Information
PIEMTUR (☎ 223-4417), the state tourism organisation, Rua Alvaro Mendes 1988, has helpful staff who happily dole out literature and advice. It's open weekdays from 9 am to 6 pm. The busy IBAMA office (☎ 232-1652), Avenida Homero Castelo Branco 2240 (Jockey Club district), provides information about national parks in Piauí. It's open weekdays from 8 am to 5.45 pm. Servitur Turismo (☎ 223-2065), Rua Eliseu Martins 1136, arranges tours of Piauí's attractions.

The telephone code for Teresina is 086.

Things to See
The **Museu Histórico do Piauí** displays an eclectic assortment of fauna, flora, antique radios and other ancient wonders. It's open Tuesday to Sunday; entry is nominal and a guide is provided. For something different, visit **Museu de Arte Didática**, which houses artworks from the ancient civilisations of Assyria, Babylon and Egypt (open Tuesday to Friday from 7 to 11 am and 1 to 6 pm).

The **Centro Artesanal** is a centre for artesanato from Piauí and a pleasant spot to browse among shops which sell leatherwork, fibre furniture, intricate lacework, colourful hammocks, opals and soapstone.

Places to Stay

PIEMTUR Camping (☎ 222-6202) is 12 km out of the city on Estrada da Socopo, the road running east towards União.

Rua São Pedro is the street for rock-bottom options. For more comfort, try *Hotel São Benedito* (☎ 223-7382), Rua Senador Teodoro Pachêco 1199, a friendly place with quartos for US$7/12 for singles/doubles and apartamentos for US$10/15. *Hotel Fortaleza* (☎ 222-2984), on Praça Saraiva, has quartos (with fan) for US$9/18, and air-con apartamentos for US$25/35. The two-star *Hotel Sambaiba* (☎ 222-6711), Rua Gabriel Ferreira 340, gives a good deal, with apartamentos for US$38/42.

Places to Eat

Restaurante Típico do Piauí, inside the Centro Artesanal, serves regional dishes. For seafood, try *Camarão do Elias*, Avenida Pedro Almeida 457. For a splurge, visit the *Forno e Fogão*, inside the Hotel Luxor, for a gigantic buffet lunch. *Chez Matrinchan*, at Avenida NS de Fatima 671 (Jockey Club district), is divided into three sections: a restaurant serving French cuisine, a pizzeria and a nightclub with live music on Friday and Saturday nights.

Getting There & Away

The airport, six km north of the centre, has flights to Rio, São Paulo and the major cities in the North-East and North, with Varig (☎ 223-4427) or VASP (☎ 223-3222).

Teresina has regular bus connections with Sobral (US$13.50, seven hours), Fortaleza (US$20, nine hours), São Luís (US$13, seven hours) and Belém (US$28, 15 hours, five times a day).

To Parnaíba there are two executivo buses (US$12, four hours) and several standard buses (US$10, six hours) daily. There are bus connections twice daily to São Raimundo Nonato (US$20, 10 hours) and hourly to Piripiri (US$6, three hours).

Getting Around

From the rodoviária to the centre, the cheapest, slowest and hottest option is to take the bus from the stop outside the rodoviária. A taxi costs US$9 at the bilheteria, but much less if you flag it down outside.

LITORAL PIAUIENSE

Parnaíba, once a major port at the mouth of the Rio Parnaíba, is being developed as a beach resort, along with the town of Luís Correia, 18 km away. Porto das Barcas, the old warehouse section along the riverfront, has been carefully restored and contains a PIEMTUR tourist office, a maritime museum, an artesanato centre, art galleries, bars and restaurants.

Praia Pedra do Sal, 15 km north-east of town, on Ilha Grande Santa Isabel, is a good beach. Lagoa do Portinho, a lagoon surrounded by dunes, is about 14 km east on the road to Luís Correia.

Places to Stay

There's a *youth hostel* in Porto das Barcas (Parnaíba) and a camping ground at Lagoa do Portinho, where the *Centro Recreativa Lagoa do Portinho* (☎ 322-2165) provides apartamentos and chalets, at US$10 and US$14 per person. The *Hotel Cívico* (☎ 322-2470), Avenida Governor Chagas Rodrigues 474, in the centre of town, has a swimming pool and apartamentos for US$18/25.

Getting There & Away

There are daily buses to/from Teresina.

PARQUE NACIONAL DE SETE CIDADES

Sete Cidades is a small national park. Its interesting rock formations, estimated to be at least 190 million years old, resemble *sete cidades* (seven cities). The appeal for visitors lies in the walking opportunities; the loop through the seven cities is a couple of hours leisurely stroll. The park is open from 6 am to 6 pm.

Abrigo do IBAMA is the most popular place to stay, with an inexpensive hostel and designated camp sites at the park entrance. More up-market is the *Hotel Fazenda Sete*

BRAZIL

Cidades (☎ 276-1664), a two-star resort hotel with attractive apartamentos for US$24/38. It's a cool and shady spot, six km from the park entrance, and there's a restaurant and a pool.

The park is 180 km from Teresina and 141 km from Ubajara (Ceará state) on a fine paved road. Take any bus between Fortaleza and Teresina and get off at Piripiri. From there, an IBAMA courtesy bus for the 26-km trip to the park leaves from Piripiri at 7 am and returns from Abrigo do IBAMA at 4 pm.

Maranhão

Maranhão is the North-East's second-largest state (after Bahia) but has a population of only five million.

SÃO LUÍS

São Luís, the capital of Maranhão, is a city with unpretentious colonial charm and a rich folkloric tradition – definitely a highlight for travellers in the North-East. In the historic centre of São Luís, Projeto Reviver (Project Renovation) has created a charming and beautifully restored colonial precinct.

Information

Tourist Office Maratur, the state tourism organisation, has its head office on Rua da Estrêla, in the historical district, and information booths at the rodoviária and several other points.

Telephone The code for São Luís is 098.

Travel Agencies In the shopping gallery at Rua do Sol 141 are several travel agencies offering organised tours to Alcântara, Parque Nacional dos Lençóis and other Maranhão destinations. Good agencies include Taguatur (☎ 232-0906), Loja 14, and Delmundo Turismo (☎ 222-8719), close by on Rua da Riberão.

Things to See

The whole historical district is a must-see, with its cobbled streets and azulejo facades. Some worthwhile museums are housed in various historic buildings, and there are frequent outdoor cultural performances-cum-parties. **Museu de Artes Visuais** has good examples of traditional arts (open weekdays from 8 am to 1 pm and 4 to 6 pm). Nearby is the interesting old circular marketplace. The **Museu do Negro** records the history of slavery in Maranhão (open Monday to Saturday in the afternoon). On the hill north of the historical district is **Catedral da Sé**, constructed by Jesuits in 1726, and the **Palácio dos Leões**, a French fortress built in 1612, now the state governor's pad.

The **Museu Histórico e Artístico**, on Rua do Sol, is a restored 1836 mansion with attractive displays of artefacts from wealthy Maranhão families.

Across the river north of town are the modern suburb of São Francisco and a number of good **beaches**, which are a total party scene on weekends and holidays.

Special Events

Distinctive local dances and music are performed all year round, with active samba clubs turning it on especially for Carnaval. The Tambor de Mina festivals, in July, are important Afro-Brazilian religious occasions. The famous Bumba Meu Boi festival runs from late June to mid-August.

Places to Stay

Unicamping (☎ 222-2552) is near Calhau beach, eight km from town.

The nicest budget option in the city is *Hotel Casa Grande* (☎ 232-2432), an old building on Rua Isaac Martins. Large, clean apartamentos cost US$14/16/20 for singles/doubles/triples, with breakfast. *Hotel Estrêla* (☎ 222-7172), at Rua da Estrêla 370 in the heart of the historical district, is basic but clean, with quartos for US$15/20/30. *Hotel Casa Praia* (☎ 221-4144), close by at Rua 14 de Julho 20, is even less fancy, with quartos for US$15/20 and overpriced apartamentos for US$30. *Hotel Lord* (☎ 222-

5544), Rua de Nazaré 258, is a large, time-worn hotel with comfortable quartos for US$18/24 for singles/doubles, and also air-con apartamentos. Check the room and discuss the price.

Pousada Colonial (☎ 232-2834), Rua Afonso Pena 112, in a restored colonial mansion, has comfortable little aparta-mentos for US$42/50, maybe less for cash. *Pousada do Francês* (☎ 221-4866), Rua 7 de Setembro 121, is even nicer, with well-equipped air-con apartamentos for US$38/55. The five-star *Vila Rica* (☎ 232-3535) is the best in town, with rooms from US$274!

Out at Ponta d'Areia beach, *Pousada Tia Maria* (☎ 227-1534) at QO 1, lote 12, has apartamentos for around US$20/27.

Places to Eat

It's delightful but expensive eating in the historical district at places like *Restaurant Antigamente* with outdoor tables. *Ficcus*, a little farther south on Rua da Estrêla, is quite good and very reasonably priced. *Pizzaria Alcântara*, on Rua Portugal, has pizzas and refeicões and is quite good value for this area.

On Praça João Lisboa, *Restaurant Pala-dar* serves economical por-kilo lunches, and stalls provide cheap food in the evening. The *Base da Lenoca*, Praça Dom Pedro II, is popular but pricey (main courses from US$12 to US$15), with cool breezes and great views. *Restaurant Senac* is another up-market option, in a fine old colonial building. *Naturista Alimentos*, at Rua do Sol 517, has the best vegetarian food in the city.

Entertainment

São Luís is the top reggae centre of the North-East, and several places have ear-splitting sound systems and hordes of *reggeiros*. The action is at a different place every night; ask the tourist office for sugges-tions, and don't bring valuables. For pagode music and dancing, barracas and *boates* (nightclubs) blast it out by day and night.

Getting There & Away

Air Aeroporto do Tirirical (☎ 225-0044) has flights to/from Rio, São Paulo and major northern cities with Transbrasil (☎ 223-1414), Varig (☎ 231-5066) or VASP (☎ 222-4604).

Bus The rodoviária (☎ 223-0253) is about eight km south-east of the city centre. There are frequent buses daily to Teresina (US$13, seven hours), two daily to Belém (US$21, 12 hours), three daily to Fortaleza (US$34, 18 hours) and two to Recife (US$50, 24 hours).

Boat From the *hidroviária* (boat terminal) west of the centre, there are regular ferries to Alcântara; sailing times depend on the tides. The tourist boat leaves at about 9 am, returns at about 4 pm, and takes about 50 minutes (US$6 one way). More crowded public boats leave at 7 am (US$3). Two antiquated sail-boats also ply the route, leaving the hidroviária at around 7 am and 4 pm. This pirates-of-the-Caribbean experience takes about 1½ hours and costs about US$2.

Getting Around

São Cristóvão buses run to the airport from the bus stop on Rua da Paz in about 45 minutes. To get to the rodoviária, catch a Rodoviária bus from the same place. Bilhete-ria taxi tickets from the airport cost a rip-off US$15. Buses to the beaches leave from the Praia Grande terminal west of the centre.

ALCÂNTARA

Across the Baía de São Marcos from São Luís is the old colonial town of Alcântara. Founded in the early 1600s with extensive slave labour, the town was the hub of the region's sugar and cotton economy, and the residential area of Maranhão's rich land-owners. The new rocket-launching facility, Centro do Lançamento de Alcântara, pro-vides a modern contrast.

As you walk round the picturesquely decrepit town, look in particular for the beau-tiful row of two-storey houses on Rua Grande, the **Igreja de NS do Carmo** (1665), Rua Amargura, and the **pelourinho** (whip-ping post) on Praça da Matriz. The **Museu Histórico** displays a collection of sacred art,

To São Francisco District

Ponte José Sarney

Rio Anil

Avenida Beira Mar

Rua 15 de Novembro

Rua do Machado

Rua Jonsem

Miller

Rua Riacho

Rua da Savedro

Rua do Ribeiro

Rua Santo Antônio

Praça Antônio Lobo

Rua Graça Aranha

Beco da Silva

Rua do Alecrim

Rua Isaac Martins

Rua do Egito

Praça Dom Pedro II

Rua dos Afogados

Rua de Nazaré

Rua São João

Rua do Sol

Rua Flores

Rua 7 de Setembro

Trav da Passagem

Rua Portugal

Rua

Humberto de Campos

Praça João Lisboa

Rua da Paz

Rua dos Craveiros

Rua dos Mangueiras

Rua do Comercio

Rua da Alfândega

Rua Godofredo Viana

Rua Grande

Rua João Vital

Rua da Palma

Rua de Santana

Tr Boaventura

Rua 28 de Julho

Rua do Mocambo

Beco da Prensa

Rua Direita

Rua Afonso Pena

Rua do Inveja

Avenida Magalhães de Almeida

Rua Regente Braulio

Rua do Deserto

Rua do Saúde

Beco Escuro

Rua de Manga

Beco do Monte

Rua Jacinto Maia

Praça do Mercado

Ribeira

Rua Luciano Reis

Rua de Santa Rita

Historic Centre

Portinho

Guaxenduba

T do M Central

Rua Candido

Rua de Pelho

Rua de São Pantaleão

Travessa da Lapa

Avenida Senador Vitorino Feira

T do Gasometro

Rua Antônio Rayol

Rua da Cotovia

Rua do Santiago

Rua Ivar Saldanha

Beco das Minas

Central São Luís

0   250   500 m

festival regalia and furniture (closed Monday).

On the first Sunday after Ascension Day, Alcântara celebrates the **Festa do Divino**, one of the most colourful annual festivals in Maranhão.

Places to Stay & Eat

Alcântara has simple *camp sites* close to Praça da Matriz and near the lighthouse. Inexpensive hotels include *Pousada do Imperador*, on Rua Grande, *Pousada Pelourinho*, beside Praça da Matriz, and the recommended *Pousada do Mordomo Régio* (☎ 101). *Chale da Baronesa*, on the beachfront at Praia da Baronesa, is particularly quiet and relaxing.

The hotels all have restaurants, and there are others along Rua Neto Guterrez.

Getting There & Away

The only access is by ferry from São Luís.

PARQUE NACIONAL DOS LENÇÓIS MARANHENSES

Natural attractions here include 1550 sq km of beaches, mangroves, lagoons, dunes and local fauna (turtles and migratory birds). The sand dunes are thought to resemble *lençóis* (bedsheets) strewn across the landscape. Tourism infrastructure is minimal.

Information is available in São Luís from the tourist office, IBAMA (☎ 222-3006), Avenida Jaime Tavares 25, or one of the travel agencies. Three-day tours cost from around US$175, including transport, accommodation and a guide.

It's also possible to arrange a visit from the pretty little town of **Barreirinhas**, two hours away by boat. *Pousada Lins* (☎ 349-1203), Avenida Joaquim Soeiro de Cavalho 550, is a nice, inexpensive place to stay. They organise day trips upriver to the park, which cost US$90 for up to five people.

Buses to Barreirinhas leave at 7 am daily from the rodoviária in São Luís (US$16, around eight hours). Book tickets well in advance if possible, at Taguatur.

Pará

The state of Pará covers over one million sq km. It includes a major stretch of the Amazon and huge tributaries such as the Rio Trombetas, Rio Tapajós and Rio Xingu. Much of the southern part of the state has been deforested, and there are serious ecological problems as a result of uncontrolled mining, land disputes and ranching.

BELÉM

Belém is the economic centre of the north and the capital of the state of Pará. Parts of the city are almost decrepit, but the central area is pleasant. Belém is one of the rainiest cities in the world, but the rain often brings brief, welcome relief from the oppressive heat.

Information

Tourist Office Paratur (☎ 224-7184), the state tourism agency, has its main office at the Feira de Artesanato do Estado, Praça Kennedy. It's open weekdays from 8 am to 6 pm.

Money The main branch of Banco do Brasil is at Avenida Presidente Vargas 248, and there are several câmbios which change travellers' cheques, like Casa Francesa, on Padre Prudencio.

Telephone Belém's telephone code is 091.

Consulates The French Consulate (☎ 224-6818) is at Avenida Presidente Pernambuco 269, and is open weekdays from 7.30 am to noon. It issues visas for French Guiana, but this may take some days: it's better to get one at home or at a French embassy.

Travel Agencies Several agencies offer city tours, river tours and excursions to Ilha de Marajó, and it's worth shopping around. Try the following:

Amazon Star Turismo, Rua Carlos Gomes 14 (☎ 224-6244)

Amazon Travel Service, Rua dos Mundurucus 1826 (☎ 241-1099)

Ciatour, Avenida Serzedelo Correia 163 (☎ 223-0787)

Lusotour, Avenida Braz de Aguiar 471 (☎ 241-1011)

Mururé Turismo, Avenida Presidente Vargas 134 (☎ 241-0891)

Neytur Turismo, Rua Carlos Gomes 300 (☎ 241-0777)

Dangers & Annoyances Pickpockets are a problem at Mercado Ver-o-Peso. Theft is common on riverboats and from rooms in cheap hotels.

Things to See

The main street is Avenida Presidente Vargas, and it's an interesting walk from the waterfront to the **Praça da República**, where people relax and socialise in the early evening. Facing the praça, the neo-classical **Teatro da Paz** (1874) is richly decorated inside and is open for visits on weekdays (US$2).

South-west of Vargas are some narrow shopping streets and the **Cidade Velho** (Old Town). There is some colonial architecture, but it is mostly run-down or unsympathetically modernised. Down on the waterfront, **Mercado Ver-o-Peso** covers several blocks and goes all day, every day. There's not much for tourists to buy, but there's an amazing variety of produce and people. Get there early, when the boats are unloading their catches at the south end of the market.

Behind the fishing port is **Praça do Relógio**, with a Big Ben replica. The next block is Praça Dom Pedro II, with two museums on its east side, both grand and beautifully restored buildings. **Palácio Antônio Lemos** houses the Museu da Cidade (☎ 242-3344), and the mayor's offices. Also called the Palácio Azul (blue palace), it's a late 19th-century building in Brazilian imperial style, with vast rooms and opulent imported furniture. Entry is free, and opening hours are Tuesday to Friday from 9 am to noon and 1 to 6 pm plus weekend mornings. **Palácio Lauro Sodré**, built in

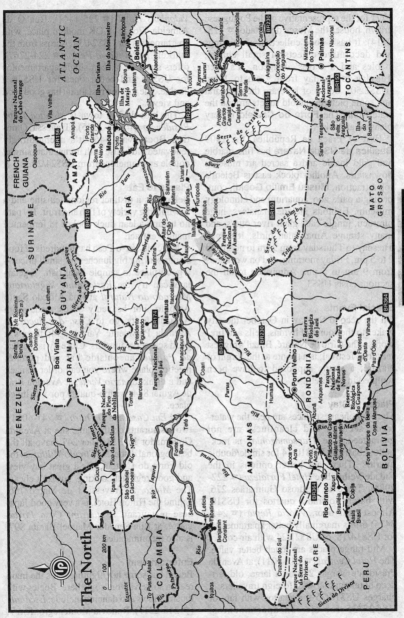

1771 for the representative of the Portuguese crown, houses the Museu do Estado (☎ 225-2414). It has a good collection of paintings and decorative objects, a small chapel, stables and a slaves' dungeon. It's open Tuesday to Sunday from 9 am to 1 pm (US$2.50). South of here are the cathedral and some picturesque old streets around the waterfront. The **Forte do Castelo** is very pleasant at dusk.

East of Praça da República, the 1909 **Basílica de NS de Nazaré** has fine marble and gold inside and a sacred art museum downstairs. Another block east is Belém's top attraction, **Museu Emílio Goeldi**, comprising a park, zoo, aquarium and ethnology museum. Exhibits include manatees, huge pirarucu, jungle cats, giant river otters, and many strange Amazonian birds. It's open Tuesday to Thursday from 9 am to noon and 2 to 5 pm, Friday morning, and on weekends from 9 am to 5 pm. Admission to all the sections costs US$3.

Special Events
On the second Sunday in October the city wakes to the sound of hymns, bells and fireworks. The Círio de Nazaré, Brazil's biggest religious festival, is a tribute to the Virgin of Nazaré, a statue supposed to have been sculpted in Nazareth.

Places to Stay
The very cheapest places are near the waterfront; security and cleanliness are not guaranteed. The *Transamazonias* is rockbottom basic, at US$10/14 for single/double quartos. There are better options in the Cidade Velho, like *Hotel Fortaleza* (☎ 222-2984), Travessa Frutuoso Guimarães 276, with barely tolerable quartos for US$10. Almost next door, *Vitória Régia* (☎ 241-3475) offers marginally better apartamentos for US$14/18, or US$21/24 with air-con.

Mid-range places are much better value. The *Hotel Central* (☎ 242-3011), at Avenida Presidente Vargas 290, is a large, old, art-deco hotel popular with foreign travellers. It charges US$18/25 for quartos with fan, or US$28/35 for air-con apartamentos.

Vidonho's Hotel (☎ 225-1444), Rua Ó de Almeida 476, is an OK modern place, with apartamentos for US$24/34. Across from the market, *Hotel Ver-o-Peso* (☎ 224-2267), offers standard air-con single apartamentos for US$25 and better ones for US$28 a double. The rooftop restaurant has good food and views.

The best deal in town is *Manacá Hotel Residência* (☎ 223-3335), Travessa Quintino Bocaiúva 1645. It's a charmingly renovated old house with immaculate single/double apartamentos from US$24/29.

Places to Eat
Belém has a distinct regional cuisine and a bewildering variety of fish and fruit. Try pato no tucupi, a lean duck cooked in fermented manioc extract.

Mercado Ver-o-Peso has hundreds of food stands serving big lunches for small prices – a good place to sample local fish. Vegetarians can try the *Restaurante Vegetariano Mercado do Natural* at Rua Alfredo Santo Antônio. For heavenly sucos made from Amazon fruits, go to *Casa dos Sucos*, at Avenida Presidente Vargas 794; there's a good self-serve upstairs. Close by is the *Bar do Parque*, an outside bar and popular meeting place where you can order a snack and a drink. *Spazzio Verde*, at Avenida Brás de Aguiar 824, is a top-quality por-kilo lunch place.

Lá Em Casa and *O Outro* (☎ 241-4064), two restaurants on the same site at Avenida Governador José Malcher 247, have all the best regional dishes. *O Círculo Militar*, at the old Forte do Castelo, has a great bay view and good regional cooking, but isn't cheap. The *Miako*, at Travessa 1 de Março 766, behind the Hilton Hotel, is a very good Japanese restaurant. *Restaurant Casa Portuguesa*, at Rua Senador Manoel Barata 897, is also recommended.

Entertainment
Belém has some hot nightlife – it's the main reason some visitors come here. Boates with music, shows and dancing include: *Escápole* (☎ 248-2217), Rodovia Montenegro, Km 7,

No 400; *Vallery* (☎ 225-2259), Avenida Pedro Alvares Cabral 33; *Boite Olé-Olá* (☎ 243-0129), Avenida Tavares Bastos 1234; and *Lapinha* (☎ 229-3290), Travessa Padre Eutíquio 3901. Most are away from the centre, so you'll need a taxi there and back.

There's great traditional music and dance, such as *carimbó*, but performances are hard to find – ask at the tourist office. *Sabor da Terra* (☎ 223-6820), Avenida Visconde de Souza Franco 685, is a restaurant and club with regular folkloric shows.

Samba clubs include *Rancho Não Posso me Amofiná* (☎ 225-0918), at Travessa Honório José dos Santos 764, in the Jurunas district, and *Quem São Eles* (☎ 225-1133), at Avenida Almirante Wandenkolk 680, in the Umarizal district (the closest one to the city centre). The clubs operate every weekend but are best around Carnaval.

Getting There & Away

Air Flights go to Macapá, Santarém, Manaus and major Brazilian cities, as well as Cayenne (French Guiana), Paramaribo (Suriname) and Miami. Airlines include Surinam Airways (☎ 212-7144), TABA (☎ 223-6300), Transbrasil (☎ 224-6977), Varig (☎ 225-4222), and VASP (☎ 224-5588).

Bus There are regular bus services to São Luís (US$26, 12 hours), Fortaleza (US$47, 25 hours), Recife (US$61, 34 hours) and Rio de Janeiro (US$106, 52 hours). There also direct buses to Belo Horizonte (US$92, 30 hours), São Paulo (US$97, 46 hours) and Brasília (US$69, 36 hours). There are no direct buses to Santarém; you might get there via Marabá, but boats are a better option.

Boat Private companies provide most of the river transport. You can book a ticket with an agency, or go to the docks and find a boat yourself. ENASA, the government line, still operates some services. Its office (☎ 223-3834) is at Avenida Presidente Vargas 41. Agencia de Navegação a Serviço da Amazonia, or AGENASA (☎ 246-1085), is the largest agency. It has a booth at the rodo-viária for ticket sales and provides transport to the port. Numar Agency (☎ 223-8296) sells tickets at similar prices. Other agencies are along Rua Castilho França and the praça opposite the ENASA building.

The best place to look yourself is Portão 17 (Armazém 9), about where Avenida Visconde de Souza Franco meets Avenida Marechal Hermes. Boats also depart from the Porto do Sal (in Cidade Velho) and the Porto das Lanchas (between Mercado Ver-o-Peso and the Forte do Castelo).

Boats depart on most days for the upriver trip to Manaus via Santarém and numerous other ports. A ticket to Manaus is around US$91 for hammock space, or US$140 per person in a four-berth cabin; tickets to Santarém cost US$51/81. It takes at least five days to reach Manaus, or two days to Santarém, but frequently much longer. The regular ENASA service leaves Belém every Wednesday at 8 pm, arriving in Santarém at noon on Saturday and in Manaus on Tuesday morning. It's cheaper than the private companies, but boats are apparently very crowded, prone to theft, and serve poor food. Arrive early on the day of departure, and take your own snacks and water. ENASA does a monthly Amazon Cruise luxury service to Manaus from US$430 per person.

To Macapá, on the north side of the Amazon, there are boats leaving most days, which take 24 hours for the trip. SENAVA (☎ 222-8710), at Rua Castilho França 234, AGENASA and Numar all sell tickets for this trip, from US$17 in hammock space and US$90 in a cabin.

For Ilha de Marajó, the Arapari boat service to Câmara leaves Escadinha port Monday to Saturday at 7 am (US$17, three hours). The ENASA ferry to Soure departs on Friday at 8 pm and Saturday at 2 pm (US$26/ 14 in 1st/economy class, five hours).

Boats to Ilha do Mosqueiro leave Porto Rodomar daily at 9 am, and cost US$0.30 on weekdays and US$1.80 on weekends.

Getting Around

To/From the Airports The main airport,

BRAZIL

BRAZIL

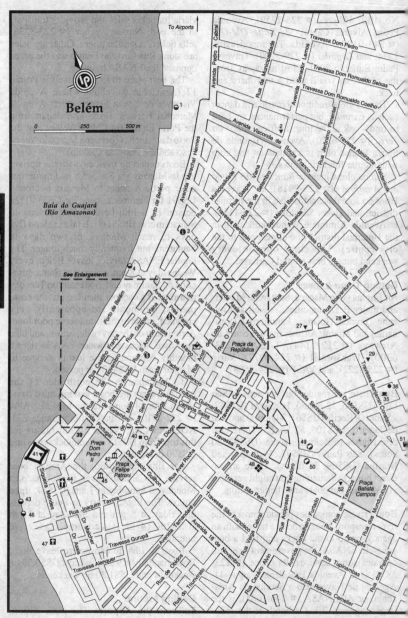

To Airports

Belém

0   250   500 m

Baía do Guajará
(Rio Amazonas)

See Enlargement

Porto de Belém

Travessa Dom Pedro

Travessa Dom Romualdo Seixas

Travessa Dom Romualdo Coelho

Avenida Pedro A Cabral

Rua da Municipalidade

Rua Senador Lemos

Avenida Senador Lemos

Travessa Almirante

Rua Jerônimo Pimentel

Travessa Quintino Bocaiúva

Rua Boaventura da Silva

Travessa Benjamin Constant

Avenida Visconde de Souza Franco

Avenida Marechal Hermes

Rua da Municipalidade

Rua de Municipalidade

Rua Gaspar Viana

Rua 28 de Setembro

Rua Sen Manoel Barata

Rua 15 de Novembro

Rua de Almeida

Travessa Rui Barbosa

Rua Tiradentes

Travessa da Piedade

Frei Gil de Vilanova

Avenida Pres Vargas

Travessa de Março

Avenida Assis de Vasconcelos

Rua O Cruz

Rua Aristides Lobo

Praça da República

Rua Arcipreste Correa

Rua Carlos Correa

Avenida Serzedelo Correia

Avenida D. Morais

Travessa Benjamin Constant

Rua Costinho França

Rua Gaspar Viana

Rua O Antônio

Rua João Alfredo

Rua 28 de Setembro

Rua 13 de Maio

Padre Prudêncio

Travessa Frutuoso Guimarães

Travessa Campos Sales

Rua Sen Manoel Barata

Travessa Padre Eutíquio

Avenida Portugal

Praça Dom Pedro II

Praça Felipe Patroni

Des Inácio Guilhon

Rua João Diogo

Rua Aver Rocha

Travessa São Pedro

Travessa São Francisco

Rua Siqueira Mendes

Rua Joaquim Távora

Dr Malcher

Dr Assis

Avenida Tamandaré

Avenida 16 de Novembro

Rua Veiga Cabral

Travessa Gurupá

Travessa Alenquer

Rua de Óbidos

Rua do Triunvirato

Rua Cezário Alvin

Avenida Roberto Camelier

Rua Arcipreste M Teodoro

Rua Conselheiro Furtado

Praça Batista Campos

Rua dos Mundurucus

Rua dos Tamoios

Rua dos Apinagés

Rua dos Tupinambás

Rua dos Pariquis

BRAZIL

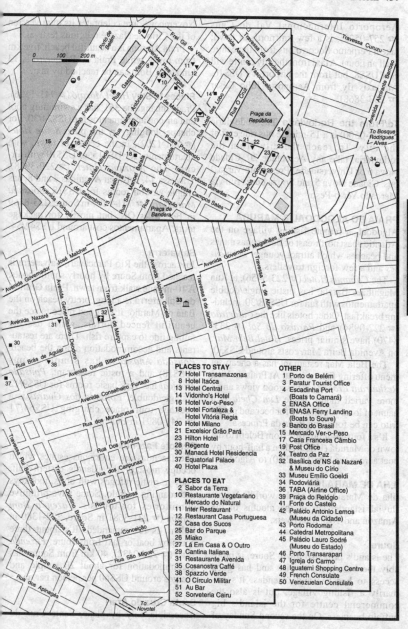

PLACES TO STAY
7 Hotel Transamazonas
8 Hotel Itaóca
13 Hotel Central
14 Vidonho's Hotel
16 Hotel Ver-o-Peso
18 Hotel Fortaleza &
   Hotel Vitória Regia
20 Hotel Milano
21 Excelsior Grão Pará
23 Hilton Hotel
28 Regente
30 Manacá Hotel Residencia
37 Equatorial Palace
40 Hotel Plaza

PLACES TO EAT
2 Sabor da Terra
10 Restaurante Vegetariano
   Mercado do Natural
11 Inter Restaurant
12 Restaurant Casa Portuguesa
22 Casa dos Sucos
25 Bar do Parque
26 Miako
27 Lá Em Casa & O Outro
29 Cantina Italiana
31 Restaurante Avenida
35 Cosanostra Caffé
38 Spazzio Verde
41 O Círculo Militar
51 Au Bar
52 Sorveteria Cairu

OTHER
1 Porto de Belém
3 Paratur Tourist Office
4 Escadinha Port
   (Boats to Camará)
5 ENASA Office
6 ENASA Ferry Landing
   (Boats to Soure)
9 Banco do Brasil
15 Mercado Ver-o-Peso
17 Casa Francesa Câmbio
19 Post Office
24 Teatro da Paz
32 Basílica de NS de Nazaré
   & Museu do Círio
33 Museu Emílio Goeldi
34 Rodoviária
36 TABA (Airline Office)
39 Praça do Relógio
41 Forte do Castelo
42 Palácio Antonio Lemos
   (Museu da Cidade)
43 Porto Rodomar
44 Catedral Metropolitana
45 Palácio Lauro Sodré
   (Museu do Estado)
46 Porto Transarapari
47 Igreja do Carmo
48 Iguatemi Shopping Centre
49 French Consulate
50 Venezuelan Consulate

Aeroporto Internacional Val de Cans (☎ 257-0522), is a few km north of town; take a Perpétuo Socorro bus from the centre (half an hour). A taxi from the city centre will cost US$8, but from the airport it's US$16. Air taxis fly from Aeroporto Júlio César (☎ 233-3868).

To/From the Rodoviária The rodoviária (☎ 228-0500) is a 15-minute bus ride east of the city. To reach the city from the rodoviária, take any Aeroclube 20, Cidade Nova 6 or Universidade (Presidente Vargas) bus. Cidade Nova 5 and Souza buses run via Mercado Ver-o-Peso.

PRAIA DO ALGODOAL & MARUDÁ

Algodoal, a remote fishing village on the Atlantic coast north-east of Belém, has dunes and beaches which attract younger *belenenses* and a few foreign travellers.

The *Cabanas Hotel* (☎ 223-5456), at Rua Magalhães Barata, has rustic single/double apartamentos with fan for US$18/30, including breakfast. Other hotels like the *Caldeirão* (☎ 227-0984) and *Paraiso do Sol* (☎ 233-8470) have similar prices. *Hotel Bela Mar*, on Avenida Beira Mar, costs around US$30.

The Bela Mar restaurant has a cheap set menu offering fish or meat. At Praia da Vila, *Restaurant Praia Mar* has good views and a more varied menu, while *Lua Cheia* is a haunt of local youth. Bars for beer and peixe-frito can be found on Praia da Princesa.

It's a four-hour bus ride from Belém to the town of Marudá (US$5), then a half-hour by boat across the bay (US$2.50) to Algodoal.

ILHA DE MARAJÓ

Ilha de Marajó, one of the world's largest fluvial islands, lies at the mouths of the Amazon and Tocantins rivers.

Soure

The island's principal town, Soure, is probably the best place to visit and has good access to beaches and fazendas. It's primarily a fishing village, but is also the commercial centre for the island's big buffalo business. On the second Sunday of November Soure celebrates its own version of the Círio de Nazaré religious festival.

Praia Araruna is a beautiful beach, five km from town, while Praia do Pesqueiro is 13 km away. Both can be reached by taxi.

Places to Stay *Hotel Marajó* (☎ 741-1396), Praça Inhangaíba 351, has a swimming pool and air-con apartamentos for US$24/30. For cheaper lodging, try the plain *Soure Hotel* (☎ 741-1202), in the centre of town, with apartamentos for US$15, or US$19 with air-con. The *Araruna Hotel* (☎ 229-3928), Travessa 14, between Avenidas 7 and 8, has simple air-con rooms for US$18. *Pousada Marajoara* (☎ 741-1287 in Soure; 223-8369 in Belém) is OK, but mostly for package tours. Apartamentos cost around US$42/54.

Salvaterra

Just across the Rio Paracauari, Salvaterra is reached from Soure by hourly shuttle boats. A 10-minute walk from town, **Praia Grande de Salvaterra** is a long, pretty beach on the Baía de Marajó. It's a good place to see the beautiful fenced corrals, which use the falling tide to capture fish. There are restaurants and accommodation along the beach. *Pousada Anastácia* has simple rooms (US$18) and a rustic restaurant. *Pousada Tropical* has very basic rooms for US$9/12 a single/double. *Pousada dos Guarás* is a package tour place charging US$64/71 (☎ 241-0891 in Belém).

Remote Fazendas

The fazendas are enormous estates which occupy most of the island's eastern half. They're rustic refuges with birds, monkeys and roaming buffalo. Some have primitive dormitories for tourists. *Fazenda Bom Jardim* (☎ 231-3681 in Soure, 222-1380 in Belém) is recommended. It's about three hours by boat or taxi from Soure. *Fazenda Jilva* (☎ 225-0432), 40 km from Soure, has accommodation for about 20 people and charges around US$60 per person per day.

Santa Cruz do Arari

Accessible only by plane, Santa Cruz do

Arari, beside Lagoa Arari, is completely submerged during the rainy season, and is famous for its fishing. The western half of the island is less populated and less interesting for travellers.

Getting There & Away
Air Air taxis fly regularly between Belém, Soure and other towns on the island. It's a beautiful 25-minute flight. The standard price is US$50, but it's cheaper if you form a group: a five-seater plane costs US$175.

Boat See the Belém section for details of the daily services to Soure and Câmara. To Afuá, on the other side of the island, there are boats from Macapá.

Tours Several agencies in Belém offer tours to Ilha de Marajó, but it's easy enough to do it independently.

SANTARÉM
Santarém, about halfway between Manaus and Belém, is the third-largest city of the Amazon (population 265,000), but it feels like a quiet backwater. The area has some pretty beaches and unspoilt rainforest. There's no tourist office, but you may be able to get some information from the following agencies, which organise jungle tours and excursions around Santarém:

Amazon Tours, Travessa Turiano Meira 1084 (☎ 522-1098, fax 522-2620)
Amazônia Turismo, Rua Adriano Pimentel 44 (☎ 522-5820)
Jatão Turismo, Avenida Rui Barbosa opposite Banco do Brasil (☎ 523-7766)
Santarém Tur, at the Tropical Hotel (☎ 522-1533, fax 523-2037)

Amazon Tours is run by Steve Alexander, author of *Alexander's Guide to Santarém*, a helpful and knowledgeable guy. He offers a variety of tours, from half-day trips (US$30) to full-day river excursions (US$55) and three-day combination tours (US$350 per person fully inclusive). There's usually a minimum of six people, and advance booking is highly desirable.

Things to See
Walk along the waterfront on Avenida Tapajós from the Docas do Pará to Rua Adriano Pimentel, and continue to the Praça Barão, where the **Centro Cultural João Fona** has a collection of pre-Columbian pottery.

Places to Stay
Hotel Alvorada (☎ 522-5340), opposite the Restaurante O Mascote, is a friendly, old-fashioned place with quartos at US$10/16 for singles/doubles with fan, or US$15/26 with air-con. *Hotel Brasil* (☎ 522-4719), at Travessa dos Martires 30 in the commercial area, has basic quartos with minimal privacy for US$10/15. Slightly more expensive, and not particularly good value, is *Hotel Central Plaza* (☎ 522-3814), near the market, with apartamentos for US$15/20, or US$20/25 with air-con.

Better hotels include the *Santarém Palace* (☎ 523-2820), Avenida Rui Barbosa 726, with apartamentos for US$36/42, but it's nothing special. The *New City Hotel* (☎ & fax 523-2351), Travessa Francisco Correia 200, has standard apartamentos for US$35/46; try for an upstairs room.

Hotel Tropical (☎ 522-1533), Avenida Mendonça Furtado 4120, is the only luxury hotel in Santarém. Despite the air-con, swimming pool, restaurant and bar, it's definitely a bit worn. Regular room rates are around US$83/95, but budget rooms are only US$36/43 and are identical except for the frigobar.

Places to Eat
Restaurante O Mascote, on Praça do Pescador, is Santarém's best restaurant and music hang-out. Its sibling, *Mascotinho*, is good for pizza and beer overlooking the river. *Mistura Brasileira*, also on the waterfront, has buffet lunches for under US$5. *Delicia Natural*, on Rua Siquiera Campos, is good for a suco.

Getting There & Away
Air TABA (☎ 522-1939) serves the small towns of the Amazon interior, while Varig (☎ 522-2084) and VASP (☎ 522-1680)

BRAZIL

provide connections to major Brazilian cities via Manaus and Belém.

Bus The rodoviária (☎ 522-1342) is about six km from the centre. There are regular buses to Itaituba (370 km), and during the dry season there are buses on the Transamazônica highway (BR-230) to Marabá (1087 km), from where you can continue to Belém (1369 km) via Imperatriz. Bus services to Cuiabá have been discontinued due to poor conditions on highway BR-163. Bus travel can be miserable or impossible during the wet season. Most travellers still rely on river transport.

Boat Larger boats go from Docas do Pará, west of the old part of town, where there are ticket agents. Cabins will usually be fully booked when boats stop at Santarém. Hammock class costs about US$51 to Belém or Manaus, which should take two or three days, respectively, but don't count on it. There are also boats to Porto Santana, near Macapá, and up the Rio Tapajós to Itaituba (12 to 24 hours).

Getting Around

The airport is 15 km from the centre; a bus operates from 6 am to 7 pm. Taxis ask for US$20 from the airport, but may settle for US$10. The New City Hotel offers free transport from the airport.

AROUND SANTARÉM
Alter do Chão

Becoming popular for its lovely lagoon, beaches and fishing, Alter do Chão is 35 km west of Santarém, and is easily reached by bus from the market. The last bus back is at 6 pm, so it's worth staying a night.

Pousada Alter-do-Chão (☎ 522-3410), at Rua Lauro Sodré 74, has simple apartamentos with fan for US$24, and a great view of the beach from the verandah. *Pousada Tupaiulândia* (☎ 523-2157) is about the same price, while *Tia Marilda* is slightly cheaper. There are good restaurants on the square.

The **Centro de Preservação da Arte**

Indígena Cultura e Ciências is an excellent and comprehensive exhibit of Indian art and artefacts, with a large variety of items for sale. Entry is US$3.

Fordlândia & Belterra

In the 1920s Henry Ford built an American town here to service these two plantations, but failed to cultivate rubber efficiently. It's now a Ministry of Agriculture research station.

During the dry season a bus leaves Santarém at 11.30 am for the 67-km trip, returning at 2.30 pm. Amazon Tours does excursions which allow more time to look around (US$90 for two or three people).

Amapá

Amapá is Brazil's second-largest state, with only about 290,000 people, two thirds of whom live in Macapá. Most of the state is inaccessible.

MACAPÁ

Macapá, the state capital, was officially founded in 1815 in a strategic position on the Amazon estuary. An old Portuguese fort and the pleasant riverfront are the town's main attractions.

Information

The DETUR/AP tourist office (☎ 222-4135, fax 222-3071) is at Avenida Raimundo Alvares da Costa 18, Centro. There's no French consulate here, so if you need a visa for French Guiana, get it in Belém or, preferably, at a French embassy or before you leave home.

The telephone code for Macapá is 096.

Things to See

The **Forte São José de Macapá** was built in 1782 by the Portuguese for defence against French invasions. The African village of **Curiaú**, eight km from Macapá, was founded by escaped slaves. You can catch a bus at Praça São José which goes to

Marco Zero do Equador (the equator) via Porto Santana and Fazendinha and then returns to Macapá. **Bonito** and the **Igarapé do Lago**, 72 km and 85 km from Macapá, are good places for swimming, fishing and jungle walks.

Places to Stay & Eat

Hotel Santo Antonio (☎ 222-0226), Rua Coriolando Jucá 485, opposite Cine Ouro, has dorm beds for about US$8 and single/double apartamentos for US$15/20, US$20/25 with air-con. The *Emerick Hotel* (☎ 223-2819), Avenida Coaraci Nunes 333, has a good atmosphere, quartos from US$10, and air-con apartamentos for US$24/30. *Kamila Hotel* (☎ 222-0250), at Júlio Maria Lombaerd 48, is small and well located, with apartamentos for US$14/16, or US$20/25 with air-con.

The two-star *Amapaense Palace* (☎ 222-3367), on Rua Tiradentes, has large, well-equipped apartamentos for US$36/48, and cheaper, windowless rooms. The *Novotel Amazonas* (☎ 223-1144) charges US$126/152.

Comida-a-kilo restaurants include *Tom Marrom* on the corner of Rua Tiradentes and Avenida Vargas and *Só Assados* at Avenida Henrique Galúcio 290. *A Peixaria*, Avenida Mãe Luzia 84, is one of the few places for good seafood.

Getting There & Away

Air TABA (☎ 223-1551) flies to Cayenne (French Guiana) on Monday, Wednesday and Friday (US$146/172 one way/return), and also to Oiapoque, at the border (US$199). Both TABA and Varig (☎ 223-1743) have regular flights to Belém.

Bus BR-156, the road to Oiapoque (on the border with French Guiana), is paved for only the first 170 km. The remaining 450 km is unpaved, but passable year round, though it may be slow going in the wet season, and there are almost no services on the way. The few towns en route are well off the highway, so it's hard to break the journey. Buses (US$44) leave daily from a stop at Policia Técnica, outside Macapá, and take at least 12 hours (16 or even 24 hours in the wet season). Go to Lanche no Ponto, at the local bus terminal, for details. Pick-up trucks also take paying passengers on this route and are slightly faster.

Boat For information about boat schedules and fares, contact SENAVA (☎ 222-3648), Avenida Engenheiro Azarias Neto 20, or Capitânia dos Portos (☎ 222-0415), Avenida FAB 427. Several boats per week go to Santarém (at least two days, around US$55 for hammock space) and Belém (24 hours; from US$17 for hammock space), departing from Porto Santana, 20 km south-west of Macapá – there are frequent buses. If you need to stay in Porto Santana, try *Hotel Muller* (☎ 632-6881).

OIAPOQUE

This remote border town is the only legal border crossing between Brazil and French Guiana, and also a gateway to backcountry mining camps. Smuggling and illegal immigration are rife, and it's not a safe town. There are some cheap and nasty hotels; the *Government Hotel* and *Kayama* are probably the best. Oiapoque is reached by rough road or plane from Macapá.

To/From French Guiana

Get your Brazilian exit stamp from the Polícia Federal in Oiapoque, cross the Oiapoque River by motorboat (US$4 or FF20, 20 minutes), and get your French Guianese entry stamp at the *gendarmerie* in St Georges. The casa de câmbio at the harbour in Oiapoque has poor rates, and there's nowhere to change money in St Georges, so bring francs from Macapá, Belém or home. From St Georges you'll have to fly to Cayenne, or perhaps catch one of the coastal freight boats. A trail has been cut, but there's no road yet.

Given the difficulty of getting to Oiapoque and the absence of overland connections from St Georges, it's much easier to fly directly to Cayenne from Macapá or Belém. Travelling overland to/from French Guiana

BRAZIL

is also problematic because of the official requirement for an onward or return ticket from the territory.

Tocantins

The state of Tocantins was created by a constitutional amendment in 1989, encompassing what was the northern half of Goiás state. The small town of Palmas became the state capital and the site of grandiose developments. Its population has grown from 2000 to 25,000, but there's no reason to visit.

ILHA DO BANANAL

The Rio Araguaia begins in the Serra dos Caiapós and flows 2600 km northwards to join the Rio Tocantins near Marabá in Pará. At the south-west corner of Tocantins state, the Rio Araguaia bifurcates into the greater and lesser Araguaia rivers, which then rejoin, having formed the largest river island in the world, Ilha do Bananal, covering some 20,000 sq km. Much of the island is covered with forest, and a big chunk is an Indian reserve, the **Parque Nacional do Araguaia**, inhabited by Carajás and Javaés Indians. The island is rich in wildlife, but difficult to access.

You can obtain permission to visit the park from IBAMA (the national parks service) in Brasília or Palmas (☎ 215-1873, 215-1865), or from the park director (☎ 224-2457, 224-4809), who lives in Goiânia (Goiás state). Of course, if you just show up, you may save a lot of time and hassle and get in just the same. There is simple accommodation available on the island but no food other than what you bring. The ranger may be able to arrange 4WDs or boats.

Getting There & Away

It's probably easiest to reach the Araguaia from Goiânia, in Goiás state. The town of Aruanã, accessible by bus from Goiânia (310 km via the town of Goiás), is the gateway to the Araguaia. There is a camping ground

(open in July) at Aruanã. Hire a *voadeira* (a small aluminium motorboat) and guide for a river trip to Ilha do Bananal.

From Barra do Garças, in Mato Grosso, there's a bus to São Felix do Araguaia, which also has access to Bananal.

Another way to reach Parque Nacional da Araguaia is from the small fishing village of Barreira da Cruz, on the margin of Rio Javaés, 52 km from Lagoa da Confusão, in Tocantins state. There are buses between Lagoa da Confusão and Barreira da Cruz.

Amazonas

Amazonas, covering an area of over 1.5 million sq km, is Brazil's largest state, and with only about two million people, it's quite sparsely populated.

MANAUS

Manaus is on the Rio Negro, 10 km upstream from the confluence of the Solimões and Negro rivers, which join to form the Amazon. A fort was built here in 1669, but the town really grew with the boom in the rubber industry in the late 19th century. At its peak, Manaus had a rich elite of plantation owners, rubber traders and bankers, with ocean-going steamships bringing every luxury up the Amazon and returning to Europe and America laden with latex. When the rubber boom ended, around 1914, Manaus fell into decline. It has revived since the 1960s, when it was declared a Free Trade Zone. Road connections to the north and south, the establishment of new factories and growth in tourism have led to rapid population increase – from 250,000 to well over a million in the last 30 years.

The city had become dirty and run-down but is now improving, though you still need to be careful of theft. Much of the central shopping area (the Zona Franca) has been renovated, with many pedestrian precincts, while the older streets to the south-east retain a certain sleazy charm. There's also some raunchy nightlife. Some opulent buildings remain from the boom days, but it's no architectural treasure house. Manaus is interesting, but it's not pretty. Most visitors come to arrange a rainforest excursion with one of the many tour operators, but there is no natural rainforest close to Manaus; you need at least three days to reach an area that is reasonably untouched.

Orientation
The most interesting parts of Manaus are close to the waterfront. Avenida Eduardo Ribeiro is lined with airline offices, banks and Manaus' fancier shops.

Information
Tourist Office Emamtur (☎ 633-2850), the state tourism organisation, has its headquarters at Avenida Paés de Andrade 379 (previously called Avenida Tarumã), open weekdays from 8 am to 1 pm. It's a bit of a hike from the city centre, but worth a visit. You may also be able to get some information at the opera house.

For details about national parks in Amazonas, contact IBAMA (☎ 237-3710), Rua Ministro João Gonçalves de Souza, BR-319, Km 01, Distrito Industrial.

Money There are plenty of banks, but Casa de Câmbio Cortéz, on Avenida 7 de Setembro, is quicker and opens longer hours and on Saturday.

Post & Communications Manaus' post office, on Rua Marechal Deodoro, opens weekdays from 8 am to 5 pm, and on Saturday from 8 am to noon. The postal system has a poor reputation for reliability.

There's a TeleAmazon telephone office on Rua Guilherme Moreira, open daily from 8 am to 11 pm. The telephone code is 092.

Foreign Consulates Visas to neighbouring countries can be issued in Manaus, but those for French Guiana will take weeks as applications are referred to Brasília.

Foreign consulates include:

Bolivia
    Avenida Eduardo Ribeiro 520, sala 1410, Centro (☎ 234-6661)
Colombia
    Rua Dona Libânia 262 (☎ 234-6777)
France
    Conjunto Jardin Espanha III, Q 02, 19 Parque Dez (☎ 236-3513)
Germany
    Rua Barroso 355, 1 Andar, sala A, Centro (☎ 232-0890)
Peru
    Rua Ramos Ferreira 664, Centro (☎ 633-1954)
UK
    Rua Puraqué 240, Distrito Industrial (☎ 237-7038)
USA
    Rua Recife 1010, Adrianópolis (☎ 234-4546)
Venezuela
    Rua Ferreira Pena 179, Centro (☎ 233-6004)

Things to See
The **Porto Escadaria dos Remédios** is a good place to watch the locals at work. Looming above the dock is the imposing cast-iron structure of the **Mercado Municipal**, designed in 1882 by Adolfo Lisboa after Les Halles in Paris. In the market area, you can buy provisions for jungle trips.

The famous opera house, **Teatro Amazonas**, was built in Italian Renaissance style at the height of the rubber boom. Completed in 1896, it was most recently renovated in 1990, and is open daily from 10 am to 5 pm. Admission is US$5, and includes a compulsory guided tour.

The **Museu do Homem do Norte**, at Avenida 7 de Setembro 1385, is an ethnology and anthropology museum dedicated to the river-dwelling *caboclos* (people of white and Indian mix). It's open Monday to Thursday from 9 am to noon and 1 to 5 pm, and Friday from 1 to 5 pm (US$1). To reach the museum from the city centre, take the Coroado bus.

The **Museu do Indio**, near the intersection of Avenidas Duque de Caxias and 7 de Setembro, has good exhibits on tribes of the upper Rio Negro. It's open weekdays from 8.30 to 11 am and 2.30 to 5 pm, and on Saturday morning.

The **Encontro das Águas** (Meeting of the Waters), where the inky-black waters of the Rio Negro meet the lemon-yellow waters

BRAZIL

BRAZIL

Manaus

PLACES TO STAY

4	Hospedaria de Turismo 10 de Julho
6	Taj Mahal Continental Hotel
17	Hotel Krystal
30	Hotel Lord
34	Central Hotel Manaus
35	Hotel Rei Salomão
36	Hotel Nacional
39	Hotel Amazonas
43	Hotel Sol
47	Hotel Jangada & Hotel Ideal
48	Pensão Sulista
49	Ana Cassia Palace Hotel
50	Hotel Continental
51	Hotel Rio Branco
52	Hotel Dona Joana

PLACES TO EAT

8	Mandarim
9	Skina dos Sucos
11	Restaurant Araujos
12	Restaurante La Veneza
13	Sorveteria Glacial
14	Chapety Health Foods
22	Restaurante Fiorentina
31	Mister Pizza
33	Churrascaria Búfalo
41	Big Frango
42	Ornock Restaurant
44	Calçada do Rogério
53	Galo Carijó

OTHER

1	Emamtur Tourist Office
2	Bairro de São Raimundo (Low-Water Port)
3	Bar do Armando
5	Teatro Amazonas (Opera House)
7	Colombian Consulate
10	Moneychanger
15	Museu do Instituto Geográfico e Histórico do Amazonas
16	Biblioteca
18	Casa de Câmbio Cortez
19	Museu do Homem do Norte
20	Palácio Rio Negro
21	Praça da Policia
23	Banco do Brasil
24	Praça da Matriz & Catedral
25	Museu do Porto
26	Local Bus Terminus
27	Relógio Municipal (Town Clock)
28	Post Office
29	Telephone Office
32	Bus to Hotel Tropical
37	Rodomar, Museu do Porto & Porto Flutuante
38	British Customs House (Alfndega)
40	Bar São Marcos
45	Arts Centre Chaminé
46	Bar Você Decidé
54	Mercado Municipal & Porto Escadaria dos Remédios
55	Bairro de Educandos

of the Rio Solimões, is well worth seeing, but it's not absolutely necessary to take a tour. It can be seen just as well from the ferry which shuttles between Careiro and the Porto Velho highway (BR-319). If you do include the meeting of the waters in your tour, you may lose time that could be spent exploring the more interesting sights farther along the river.

Jungle Tours

The top priority for most visitors is a jungle tour to see the wildlife and experience the rainforest at close quarters. It's possible to arrange anything from standard day trips to month-long expeditions in the hinterland. Tour-agency representatives (or touts) meet new arrivals at the airport, and can offer useful information, and maybe transport to the centre, but hold off booking a tour until you've had time to shop around. There are dozens of agencies with trendy names ('Eco' and 'Green' are standard prefixes) and glossy brochures. Many of the small agencies are working together, and competing agencies actually book people on the same trips.

A standard one-day boat tour goes downstream to the Encontro das Águas, returns to the Lago Januaário reserve for a short guided jungle walk, stops at a shop selling Indian souvenirs, spends some time fishing for piranha and looking for jacaré by torchlight, and includes lunch, dinner, and cachaça on the boat. In the wet season, trips should include a canoe trip on the *igarapés* (small jungle streams), but this isn't possible in the dry season. It's a long day, and much of it is spent just sitting in a boat. As a rainforest experience it's better than nothing, especially if you can cruise the igarapés, but it's not as satisfying as a longer trip into a more pristine area. Agencies charge from US$50 to US$80 and up for these trips, and they're not great value if you pay the higher price.

On a three or four-day boat trip, you can expect a close-up experience of jungle flora, with abundant bird life and a few jacaré. It's also a chance to see what life is like for the caboclos in the vicinity of Manaus. You *cannot* expect to meet remote Indian tribes or see lots of free-ranging wildlife. Most of the longer trips go up the Rio Negro.

Ignore the flowery propaganda and ask the tour operator or agent for exact details. Who will be the guide, and do they speak English? Does the tour include extended travel in small boats (without use of motor) along igarapés? How much time is spent getting to and from your destination? What is the breakdown of the costs for food, lodging, fuel and guides? You may want to pay some of these expenses en route, thereby avoiding fanciful mark-ups. Insist on paying a portion of the costs at the beginning of the trip and the rest at the end. This encourages operators and guides to define and stick to a schedule, and gives you some leverage if promises are not kept.

If you want to do an extended trip in the Amazon region, try a short trip from Manaus first. This will help you plan longer trips, either from Manaus or from other parts of the Amazon. The latter option is becoming increasingly popular among travellers disenchanted with Manaus. Jungle trips are probably cheaper in Peru, Ecuador and Bolivia.

Tour Operators The bigger tour operators are pricey (US$100 to US$200 per person per day), but they should be relatively hassle-free and have English-speaking guides. Most of them operate 'jungle lodges' which provide a comfortable base well outside Manaus and with access to relatively unspoilt rainforest. They are often booked by overseas travel agents as part of an international package. Reputable larger firms include:

Amazon Explorers, Rua Nhamundá 21, Praça Auxiliadora – expensive, with good English speaking guides (☎ 232-3052, fax 234-5759)
Anavilhanas Turismo, Rua Coração de Jesus 11, Barrio São Raimundo (☎ 671-1411)
Ecotéis, Rua Doutor Alminio 30 (☎ & fax 233-7642)
Fontur, Estrada da Ponta Negra at the Hotel Tropical (☎ 656-2807, fax 656-2167)
Guanavenas Turismo, Rua Constantino Nery 2486 (☎ 656 3656, fax 656-5027)

Iaratour, Rua Mundurucus 90, sala 207 (☎ & fax 633-2330)
Nature Safaris, Rua Leonardo Malcher 734 (☎ 622-4144, fax 622-1420)
Rio Amazonas Turismo, Rua Silva Ramos 41 (☎ 234-7308, fax 233-5615)
Selvatur, Hotel Amazonas, Praça Adalberto Valle – accommodates large tour groups on huge catamaran boats, has a 'Meeting of the Waters' day tour (US$60) (☎ 622-2088, fax 622-2177)
Swallows & Amazons, Rua Quintino Bocaiuva 189, Centro (☎ & fax 622-1246)

If you speak a little Portuguese and don't mind travelling a bit rough, there are plenty of smaller operators and independent guides offering tours. Allow at least a day to hammer out a deal, change money, arrange supplies and buy provisions. When serious haggling is called for, ask the tour operator to itemise expenses. If the food budget seems unreasonable, buy provisions yourself; if the fuel budget seems too high, offer to pay separately for that. Then subtract those items from the original quote. As a rough rule of thumb, expect prices to start around US$45 per person per day, including boat transport, guide, food, and hammock lodging (minimum two people on a three-day, two-night trip).

Independent guides sometimes work for the big operators, and often also work together, so be quite sure you know who will be running the trip. The guide should be registered with Embratur and have an identity card. Two smaller agencies/operators are Amazonas Indian Turismo (☎ 233-3140), Rua dos Andrades 335, and Queiroz Tour (☎ 233-3354), Avenida Joaquim Nabuco 337.

A good person to talk to is Chris at the Hotel Rio Branco (☎ 233-4019). He books trips with two guides, Gerry Hardy and Elmo de Morais Lopes, operating from Manacapuru, and can give advice on other small operators.

Moaçir Fortes of Amazon Expeditions (☎ 232-7492) speaks English, and operates his own boat from the Porto Flutuante. He runs a small, 1st-class operation, charging US$80 to US$100 per person per day.

Special Events

Carnaval is big here, with spectacular parades which climax in the huge sambódromo. A folklore festival held during the second half of June coincides with a number of saints' days and culminates in the Procissão Fluvial de São Pedro, when hundreds of boats parade on the river.

Places to Stay

There's plenty of cheap lodging, ranging from grungy to decent.

Hotel Rio Branco (☎ 233-4019), at Rua dos Andradas 484, is a popular budget place. Apartamentos with fan cost around US$10, while air-con apartamentos are US$15/19 for singles/doubles. *Hotel Ideal* (☎ 233-9423), across the street, is good and only slightly dearer; some rooms lack windows. A little farther up, the basic *Hotel Jangada* (☎ 232-2248) offers dorm beds with fan for US$7 and double rooms for US$13. There are other cheapies on Rua José Paranaguá, two streets to the north. Some are short-stay places, but the *Hotel Sol* and *Hotel Floresta* should be OK.

Pensão Sulista (☎ 234-5814), Avenida Joaquim Nabuco 347, has clean quartos with fan for US$8/14, while air-con doubles are US$20. *Hotel Continental* (☎ 233-3342), at Rua Coronel Sergio Pessoa 198 near Praça dos Remedios, has comfortable air-con apartamentos for US$20/26, some with good views.

Hospedaria de Turismo 10 de Julho (☎ & fax 232-6280), at Rua 10 de Julho 679, is in a nice area near the opera house. It has clean, secure, good-value air-con apartamentos for US$15/20, and fresh juice for breakfast.

Modern, mid-range hotels are mostly in the Zona Franca. Discounts are common, but check the room and ensure that the facilities work. *Hotel Rei Salomão* (☎ 234-7344), Rua Dr Moreira 119, is a spiffy three-star place with apartamentos for US$43/53. *Central Hotel Manaus* (☎ 622-2600), Rua Dr Moreira 202, is OK and similarly priced. *Ana Cassia Palace Hotel* (☎ 622-3637), Rua dos Andradas 14, has apartamentos for US$65/82 but offers a 20% cash discount.

Manaus' premier luxury hotel is the 600-room *Tropical Hotel* (☎ 658-5000, fax 658-5026), a self-contained resort 16 km out of Manaus, at Ponta Negra. Rooms start around US$175, but you can come and use the superb giant pool and the great beach. The hotel provides a shuttle service (US$5) to and from Rua Dr Moreira.

Places to Eat

Avenida Joaquim Nabuco, near the cheap hotel area, has several eateries (and quite a few prostitutes in the evening). Try *Big Frango* for cheap chicken or the *Ornock Restaurant*, opposite, for local food and fresh fish. A more expensive option is *Churrascaria Búfalo*, Avenida Joaquim Nabuco 628, which serves massive steaks and a meaty a-kilo buffet.

Nearby places include *Galo Carijó*, on Rua dos Andradas, favoured by locals for fresh fish, and *Calçada do Rogério*, at Rua José Paranaguá 590.

There are some good places around the centre, like *Mandarim* at Avenida Eduardo Ribeiro 650, which serves inexpensive Chinese food and a US$8 buffet lunch. Diagonally opposite, *Skina dos Sucos* has tasty snacks and great juices of strange fruits like guaraná, acerola, cupuaçu or graviola. *Street stalls* serve hamburgers, sandwiches, and more local specials like tacacá, a gummy soup made from manioc root, lip-numbing jambu leaves and relatively innocuous dried shrimp.

For pizza and pasta, there's *Mister Pizza*, opposite Praça da Policia, or the more up-market *Restaurante Fiorentina* (☎ 232-1295). And to finish off, *Sorveteria Glacial* is the most popular ice-cream parlour in town.

Entertainment

Você Decidé, an open-air bar on Avenida Joaquim Nabuco, is something of a hang-out for travellers, with beer, snacks, music and not entirely respectable local girls and guys. *Bar do Armando*, near the Teatro Amazonas, is a traditional rendezvous open from noon

BRAZIL

to midnight. The dancing establishments are all clustered in the Cachoeirinha district, north-east of the centre. *Nostalgia*, at Avenida Ajuricaba 800, is a hot spot for forró.

Things to Buy

Indian crafts are sold at the Museu do Indio, where FUNAI has a shop selling articles produced by the Wai Wai and Tikuna peoples. Art-Com Souvenir near the Teatro Amazonas, has a good selection of crafts, old postcards and guaraná products.

Getting There & Away

Air The Aeroporto Internacional Eduardo Gomes (☎ 621-1431) is on Avenida Santos Dumont, 14 km north of the city centre. There are international flights to Caracas, Iquitos, Bogotá, La Paz and Miami with LAB (☎ 232-7701). Manaus is not a good place to buy cheap tickets.

VASP (☎ 622-3470), Transbrasil (☎ 622-3738) and Varig (☎ 622-3090) serve all major cities in Brazil. Air taxis and TABA (☎ 633-3838) fly to smaller Amazonian settlements.

Bus The rodoviária (☎ 236-2732) is six km north of the centre. Phone for information on road conditions. The BR319 road south of Manaus is in disrepair, and no buses serve the route. The 770-km BR-174 road north to Boa Vista is improving, but still has some unpaved sections. There are two buses a day (US$46, 15 hours).

Boat Three major ports in Manaus function according to high and low water levels. Bairro Educandos is the port for sailings to Porto Velho. For sailings on the Rio Negro as far as Caracaraí, the requisite high-water port is Ponte de São Raimundo; the low-water port is Bairro de São Raimundo, about 2.5 km away. The Porto Flutuante serves mainstream Amazon destinations – Belém, Santarém, Tefé and Benjamin Constant – and is the port used by ENASA.

For information, visit the Rodomar at the Porto Flutuante. The Rodomar has a com-

plex of counters arranged like those at a bus terminal, with fares and destinations prominently posted. The ENASA ticket office (☎ 633-3280) is at Rua Marechal Deodoro 61. The Superintendência Nacional de Marinha Mercante, or SUNAMAM (☎ 633-1224), at the Merchant Marine Headquarters, also has information about sailing times, fares, distances and ports of call.

Ports of call are marked on the boats, and fares are pretty much standardised according to distance. The boats usually pull out at 6 pm regardless of the destination. Bring bottled water, extra food, a hammock, and rope to string it up. A sleeping bag is good for cool nights.

Various companies operate passenger boats between Manaus, Santarém and Belém. Prices for hammock space average US$43 to Santarém and US$90 to Belém. Luxury ENASA ferry-catamarans take two days to Santarém and four days to Belém (from US$430). ENASA also has a weekly boat to Belém on Thursday, which costs US$65 and gets crowded.

It's a seven-day trip (if all goes well) to Tabatinga, or longer if the boat makes many stops (about US$85/250 for hammock/cabin). There are onward services from Tabatinga to Iquitos (Peru).

Another long river journey is from Manaus up the Rio Madeira to Porto Velho. The one-week trip costs about US$75/105 in a hammock/cabin.

In the wet season, you may be able to find a cargo boat to Caracaraí on the Rio Branco, which will take around four days. From Caracaraí there's a bus to Boa Vista (about four hours). Another remote river destination is São Gabriel da Cachoeira, about five or six days up the Rio Negro.

Getting Around

To/From the Airport The Aeroporto Internacional bus runs between the local bus terminus and the airport from 6 am to midnight (US$0.35, 40 minutes). A bilheteria taxi ticket from the airport to the centre is US$20.

To/From the Rodoviária Ileia, Santos Dumont and Aeroporto Internacional buses run from the centre via the rodoviária.

Bus The local bus terminus is on Praça da Matriz, near the cathedral. From here you can catch buses to Ponta Negra. Alternatively, take the Tropical Hotel shuttle bus (US$5) from Rua Dr Moreira.

TABATINGA & BENJAMIN CONSTANT

These two Brazilian ports are on the border between Brazil, Colombia and Peru, known as the Triple Frontier. Neither is particularly attractive, and most travellers view them as transit points. If you have to wait a few days for a boat, the Colombian border town of Leticia is a much more salubrious place to hang out.

Getting There & Away

Air From Tabatinga there are three flights weekly to Manaus (US$140) and two to Iquitos in Peru (US$121 one way, US$156 return). Apart from these commercial passenger flights, cargo planes operate irregularly from Tabatinga to Manaus, and military planes from Ramón Castilla (Peru) to Iquitos.

Boat Boats down the Amazon to Manaus leave from Benjamin Constant, but usually call at Tabatinga, too. Regular boats depart from Tabatinga (theoretically) Wednesday and Saturday mornings, and from Benjamin Constant Wednesday and Saturday nights. The trip takes four days and costs US$85 in your own hammock. Many other irregular cargo boats take passengers on deck, and some have cabins. Prices and journey times are similar. In the opposite direction, upstream from Manaus to Benjamin Constant, the trip takes between six and 10 days. Food is included but it is of poor quality.

There are frequent colectivos between the Leticia and Tabatinga ports (US$0.40); it's a 20-minute walk. Entering Brazil, get an entry stamp from officials in Tabatinga (who

like prospective visitors to dress neatly). There is a ferry service, with two boats sailing daily between Tabatinga and Benjamin Constant (US$2.50, 1½ hours).

Upstream to Iquitos (Peru) from Leticia (Colombia), there is now an Expresso Loreto rápido (fast-boat) passenger service twice weekly. It takes 10 to 12 hours and costs US$50. Alternatively, irregular cargo boats depart from Santa Rosa (Peru), which has replaced the Ramón Castilla port (across the river from Tabatinga), and from Islandia (Peru), on an island opposite Benjamin Constant. The journey takes about three days and costs US$40, food included. Coming downstream from Iquitos to Santa Rosa takes only about 36 hours. You can obtain your entry stamp from Peruvian officials in Puerto Alegría.

Roraima

North of Roraima is perhaps the ultimate Amazon frontier, a rugged land which is home to the Yanomami, who represent about one-third of the remaining tribal Indians of the Amazon. Although the Brazilian government has declared their lands a special Indian reserve, miners, timber cutters and new roads encroach on the area.

BOA VISTA

This new, planned city, shaped like an archway, is pretty unattractive, and most travellers just pass through going to/from Venezuela or Guyana. There are some attractions in the surrounding area, which is becoming more accessible.

Information

The friendly and helpful information office at the rodoviária (☎ 623-1238) has maps, tour information, and accommodation listings (open weekdays from 8 am to 6 pm). CODETUR (☎ 623-1230), the state tourism

BRAZIL

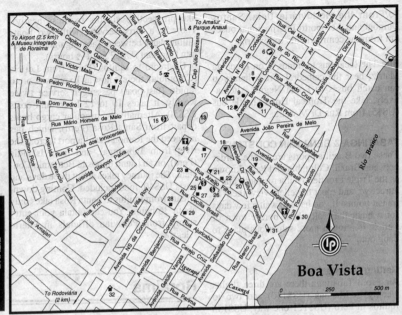

Boa Vista

administration, at Rua Coronel Pinto 241, is not so useful.

The telephone code for Boa Vista is 095.

Casa de Câmbio Pedro José, on Rua Araújo Filho, keeps longer hours than Banco do Brasil.

The Venezuelan Consulate, Avenida Benjamin Constant 525E, opens weekdays from 8 am to noon. Arrive early and they may process your visa by noon. Bring one photo, an outbound ticket from Venezuela, and some US dollars cash for the visa fee (a minimum of US$10 for British applicants, US$2 for US nationals). Get your visa beforehand to avoid being delayed in Boa Vista.

Things to See & Do

About 1.5 km north-west of the centre is **Parque Anauá**. It has gardens, a lake, a museum, an amphitheatre and an aquatic park, and you might catch a concert in the *forródromo*. The main beach is **Praia Grande**, opposite Boa Vista on the Rio Branco.

Places to Stay & Eat

Pousada Beija-Flor (☎ 224-8241), Avenida NS da Consolata, has dorm beds for US$7, arranges trips into the surrounding countryside, and generally knows what travellers want. *Hotel Brasil* (☎ 224-9421), Avenida Benjamin Constant 331, is a rock-bottom cheapie with quartos for around US$10. *Hotel Colonial* (☎ 224-5190), Rua Ajuricaba 532, has simple, comfortable, air-con apartamentos for US$16, while the nearby *Hotel Imperial* (☎ 224-5592), Avenida Benjamin Constant 433, is tolerable for US$15. For more comfort, try *Hotel Euzebio's* (☎ 224-0300), Rua Cecília Brasil 1107, with apartamentos from around US$30/35, or *Aipana Plaza* (☎ 224-4800), Joaquim Nabuco 53, about the best in town, with a pool and rooms from US$75/96.

Mister Kilo, Rua Inácio Magalhães 346,

PLACES TO STAY
1 Uiramutan Palace
4 Hotel Euzebio's
17 Aipana Plaza
22 Hotel Barrudada
23 Hotel Ideal
25 Hotel Monte Libano
27 Hotel Brasil
28 Hotel Colonial
29 Hotel Imperial
32 Pousada Beija Flor

PLACES TO EAT
2 Pigalle
3 La Carreta
8 Coisas da Terra
18 La Gondola
19 Mister Kilo
21 Margô Pizzaria
31 Black & White

OTHER
5 Telephone Office
6 Venezuelan Consulate
7 Porto do Babá
9 Prefeitura
10 Post Office
11 CODETUR Tourist Office
12 Biblioteca e Palácio da Cultura
13 Praça do Centro Cívico
14 Palácio do Governo
15 Banco do Brasil
16 Catedral
20 Central Bus Terminal
24 Casa de Câmbio Ke
26 Casa de Câmbio Pedro José
30 Centro do Artesanato

has good-value self-service meals, and *La Gondola*, at Avenida Benjamin Constant 35W, does inexpensive prato feito. *La Carreta*, next to Hotel Euzebio's, may be the best restaurant in town. For local fish dishes, try *Black & White*, at Praça Barreto Leite 11, or for pizza and pasta, *Margô Pizzaria*.

Getting There & Away
Air There are daily flights to/from Manaus with Varig (☎ 224-2226), and three per week with META air taxis (☎ 224-7300) for US$135.

Bus Buses to Manaus depart at 8.30 am and 1 pm (US$46, 15 to 20 hours depending on road conditions). Another option is a bus to Caracaraí (US$8, two hours), then a boat to

Manaus (seven to 10 days). The rodoviária (☎ 623-1238) is three km west of the centre; get a Joquey Clube bus along Avenida Villa Roy or a taxi.

AROUND BOA VISTA
Pedra Pintada, 140 km north of Boa Vista, is a mushroom-shaped boulder about 60 metres across and 35 metres high, with ancient painted inscriptions on its external face and caves at its base. Estação Ecológica da Ilha de Maracá, an ecological reserve 120 km away, can be visited with permission from IBAMA (☎ 224-4011). Mt Roraima (2875 metres) straddles the Brazil-Venezuela-Guyana border, but the easiest access is from Venezuela (see that chapter).

The easiest way to visit these places is with a local tour operator such as Iguana Tours (☎ 224-6576), Amatur (☎ 224-0004), or Jean-Luc Félix (☎ 224-6536).

To/From Venezuela
There's beautiful scenery on the three-hour ride to Santa Elena, just across the Venezuelan border. There are five departures daily, between 7 am and 5.30 pm, from the rodoviária in Boa Vista (US$11.50). Several buses a week go direct to Ciudad Bolívar (US$26, 16 hours). Reserve a seat the day before.

To/From Guyana
Buses leave Boa Vista for Bonfim daily at 7.30 am, 3 pm and 5 pm (US$6, 125 km, two hours). Take the earliest bus to avoid being stuck in Bonfim for the night. Tell the driver you're heading for Guyana, and ask where to get off. Sometimes buses stop at a checkpoint before Bonfim, where you may be able to get an exit stamp from the Polícia Federal and a jeep for the five km to the border post (US$3). Otherwise, stay on the bus until the stop after the bus station, then walk two km to the border crossing. The border is open until 6 pm, and you should be able to get an exit stamp from the Brazilian immigration post. Then hire a boat across the Rio Tacutu to Lethem, in Guyana. Guyanese officials

tend to scrutinise travellers carefully, so be sure your papers are in order.

Overland travel from Lethem to Georgetown is feasible but difficult. There are heavily booked flights to Georgetown on Tuesday, Wednesday, Friday and Saturday at 7 am; see under Lethem in the Guianas chapter for more information.

Rondônia

Previously an undeveloped frontier region, Rondônia has undergone rapid change with the construction of BR-364. Massive deforestation has left vast tracts of land looking like the aftermath of a holocaust. Most travellers only pass through on the way to or from Peru or Bolivia. Rondônia is a route for the distribution of cocaine from those two

countries, which should not affect travellers provided they mind their own business.

PORTO VELHO

Porto Velho, capital of Rondônia, is on the south bank of the Rio Madeira, near the border with the state of Amazonas. There's not much of interest for visitors, but it gives access to Rio Branco, Guajará-Mirim and the Bolivian border.

Information

The Departamento de Turismo de Rondônia (DETUR) office (☎ 223-2276), at Avenida Padre Chiquinho 670, Esplanada das Secretarias, is difficult to find and not very useful. It's open weekdays from 8 am to noon and 2 to 6 pm.

IBAMA (☎ 223-33607), Avenida Jorge Teixeira 3477, Bairro CE Silva, gives infor-

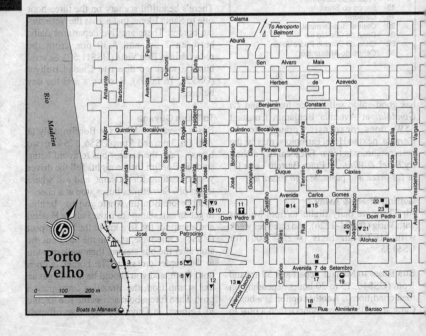

Porto Velho

mation and permits for national parks and ecological reserves in Rondônia.

The telephone code for Porto Velho is 069.

Estação Madeira-Mamoré & Museu Ferroviário

The Madeira-Mamoré railway was completed in 1912, costing many years and many lives, but it quickly fell into disuse. The Maria Fumaça steam locomotive now does tourist excursions to Santo Antônio (seven km away) on Sunday and holidays (US$1.50 return). A free museum displays train relics, memorabilia, photographs, and the 1872 Colonel Church steam locomotive; it's open weekdays from 8 am to 5 pm.

Tours

One of the few people doing jungle tours here is Carlos Grandes Perez, contactable through the Hotel Nunes. His trips have been recommended.

PLACES TO STAY
13 Hotel Yara
14 Hotel Central
16 Hotels Nunes & Solara
17 Hotel Cuiabano
18 Hotel Regina
22 Hotel Vila Rica
23 Hotel Seltom
24 Hotels Ouro Fino & Amazonas

PLACES TO EAT
1 Mirante II Restaurant
6 Night Food Stalls
8 Divina Gula
9 Genghis Khan
12 Restaurant Almanara
20 Pizza Restaurant & Bar
21 Restaurant Ling

OTHER
2 Museu Ferroviário
3 Estação Madeira-Mamoré
4 Booze Cruises
5 Post Office
7 Telephone Office
10 Banco do Brasil
11 Cathedral
14 Varig
19 Buses to Airport & Rodoviária
25 Rodoviária

To Guajará-Mirim

Places to Stay

The friendly *Hotel Cuiabano* (☎ 221-4084), Avenida 7 de Setembro 1180, has basic singles/double quartos for US$8/10 and apartamentos with fan for US$12. Just across the street, *Hotel Nunes* (☎ 221-1389) has clean double apartamentos for US$15. A few metres away, the grungy *Hotel Sonora* is a third-best choice.

Near the rodoviária, *Hotel Ouro Fino* (☎ 223-1101) has clean but musty quartos (with fan) for US$10/14. The *Hotel Amazonas*, next door, is even cheaper.

Better places include the *Hotel Regina* (☎ 224-3411), Rua Almirante Baroso 1127, where spotless apartamentos with air-con, fridge and TV cost US$24/40.

The five-star *Hotel Vila Rica* (☎ 224-3433) is Porto Velho's best, for US$94, but its nearby sibling, the three-star *Hotel Seltom* (☎ 224-3358), is better value for US$55/73.

Places to Eat

Avenida Rogério Weber, near the corner of Avenida 7 de Setembro, has a good selection of night *food stalls* with excellent, fresh chicken, meat and salad dishes.

Restaurante Mirante II, nearby on Avenida Major Amarante, serves fish and other dishes and has a great view over the river.

Divina Gula, on Avenida Carlos Gomes, does a good por-kilo lunch, while *Genghis Khan*, across the road, specialises in Japanese food such as sukiyaki and noodle dishes.

The best place for fish is *Remanso do Tucunaré*, at Avenida Brasília 1506. For Chinese food, try *Restaurant Ling*, on Avenida Joaquim Nabuco. There's a *Pizza Restaurant & Bar* just around the corner. Lebanese-Brazilian food is on offer at *Restaurant Almanara*, on Avenida José de Alencar just south of Avenida 7 de Setembro.

Entertainment

Baretur and Plaktur, the tour agencies at the train-station docks, run daily one-hour booze cruises between 2 and 11 pm (US$2.50, excluding drinks).

Getting There & Away

Air Aeroporto Belmont (☎ 221-3935) is seven km out of town; catch a Hospital de Base via Aeroporto bus on Avenida 7 de Setembro. There are flights from Porto Velho to all major Brazilian cities with VASP (☎ 223-3755), Varig (☎ 221-8555) and TABA (☎ 221-5172).

Bus The rodoviária (☎ 221-2141) is about two km from the centre, reached by local bus from the stop on Avenida 7 de Setembro. Porto Velho has bus connections to Rio Branco (US$18.50, about 10 hours; five daily), Guajará-Mirim (US$17, five hours; eight daily), and also to Cuiabá, Humaitá and Costa Marques. Road conditions are generally poor, especially during the wet season, so schedules can be approximate.

Boat Boats between Porto Velho and Manaus cost about US$75/105 for hammock/cabin accommodation, including three meals a day; take bottled water. The boats are small and the ride is long, so check out your fellow passengers before committing yourself. Some boats go directly to Manaus, while others require transfer halfway down the Madeira, at Manicoré. The trip takes anywhere from three days to a week, depending on breakdowns, the water level and whatever. Taking a bus to Humaitá (203 km) to catch a boat might save about 24 hours.

GUAJARÁ-MIRIM

Guajará-Mirim is on the Brazilian side of the border, with Guayaramerín on the Bolivian side. The Bolivian town is experiencing a boom since the upgrading of roads on both sides, and has crowds of Brazilians popping over to shop.

The Bolivian Consulate, at Avenida Costa Marques 495, opens on weekday mornings. You'll need two photographs for a visa.

Places to Stay

It's worth ringing ahead to book a hotel if you'll arrive on a weekend. The cheapest place in town is the *Hotel Chile* (☎ 541-

3846), with single/double quartos for US$10/17 and musty air-con apartamentos for US$18/24. The *Fenix Palace Hotel* (☎ 541-2326), centrally located at Avenida 15 de Novembre 459, has quartos for US$10/18 and apartamentos with fan for US$18/30. Across the road, the popular *Hotel Mini-Estrela Palace* (☎ 541-2399) charges US$17/30 for apartamentos.

Comfortable *Hotel Pousada Tropical* (☎ 541-3308) has apartamentos for US$12/24, or US$28 with air-con. The more up-market *Alfa Hotel* (☎ 541-3121) charges US$25/38 for single/double apartamentos, breakfast included.

Places to Eat

Guajará-Mirim's best restaurant, the *Oasis*, is next door to the Hotel Mini-Estrela Palace. Across the road, *Pizzaria Stop Drink's* has a wide range of pizzas, and is popular at night – sometimes *all* night.

Getting There & Away

Bus There are eight bus connections daily to Porto Velho (US$17, around 5 hours) Express buses at 2 pm and midnight take only about four hours.

Boat It's possible to travel by boat up the Mamoré and Guaporé rivers to Costa Marques via Forte Príncipe da Beira. Ask about schedules at the not-terribly-helpful Capitânia dos Portos (☎ 541-2208).

To/From Bolivia It's easy to pop across the Rio Mamoré to visit Guayaramerín, which has cheaper accommodation than Guajará-Mirim. Between early morning and 6.30 pm, small motorised canoes and larger motor ferries cross every few minutes (US$1.50). After hours, there are only express motorboats (US$4 to US$5.50 per boat). Those travelling beyond the frontier area will have to complete border formalities.

Leaving Brazil, you may need to have your passport stamped at the Bolivian Consulate in Guajará-Mirim before getting a Brazilian exit stamp at the Polícia Federal (☎ 541-2437) on Avenida Presidente Dutra.

Once across the river, get an entrance stamp from Bolivian immigration at the ferry terminal.

Leaving Bolivia, have your passport stamped by Bolivian immigration, then get a Brazilian entry stamp at the Polícia Federal in Guajará-Mirim. Officials don't always check, but technically everyone needs a yellow-fever vaccination certificate to enter Brazil here. If you don't have one, the convenient clinic at the Brazilian port can do it hygienically.

Acre

The state of Acre has become a favoured destination for developers and settlers, who have followed BR-364 through Rondônia and started claiming lands, clearing forest and setting up ranches. The resulting conflict over land ownership and sustainable use of the forest received massive national and international attention when Chico Mendes, a rubber-tapper and opponent of rainforest destruction, was assassinated in 1988.

RIO BRANCO

Rio Branco, capital of Acre state, was founded in 1882 on the banks of the Rio Acre.

Information

The Departamento de Turismo (☎ 223-1900), Avenida Getúlio Vargas 659, is helpful. It's open weekdays from 8 am to 1 pm.

The telephone code for Rio Branco is 068.

Things to See

The **Casa do Seringueiro** has exhibits on the life of a typical *seringueiro* (rubber-tapper), and a small area devoted to Chico Mendes. It is open Tuesday to Friday from 7 am to noon, and sporadically on weekends from 4 to 7 pm.

The **Museu da Borracha**, with interesting ethnological, archaeological and

historical exhibits, opens Tuesday to Friday from 9 am to noon and 2 to 5 pm, and weekends from 4 to 7 pm.

The **Colônia Cinco Mil** (literally, Colony of the 5000) is a religious community which follows the doctrine of Santo Daime. Visits can be arranged by contacting the Daimista Kaxinawá Restaurant in Rio Branco. The best day to visit is Wednesday, when the main weekly festival is celebrated. If you stay overnight, no fee will be charged, but you will be expected to share the costs of transport and food.

In 1991 the **Parque Ecológico Plácido de Castro** was opened 94 km east of Rio Branco, on the Brazil-Bolivia border. The park offers good swimming at river beaches, and walks through the forests along the paths originally used by rubber-tappers. There are five bus departures daily from Rio Branco to Plácido de Castro. There's accommodation at *Hotel Carioca* (☎ 237-1064) and several inexpensive pensões, as well as restaurants and even a danceteria.

Places to Stay

Albergue de Juventude Fronteira Verde (☎ 225-7128), on Travessa Natanael de Albuquerque, is a cheap, friendly place to stay. It's a short walk across the bridge at the southern end of Avenida Getúlio Vargas. *Albemar Hotel* (☎ 224-1938), Rua Franco Ribeiro 99, has single/double apartamentos for US$14/24, and a bar and restaurant. The *Loureiro Hotel* (☎ 223-1560), Rua Marechal Deodoro 196, has apartamentos from US$12/18.

The *Inácio Palace Hotel* (☎ 224-6397), Rua Rui Barbosa 72, is an ugly building with comfortable air-con apartamentos from US$15 to US$30. *Hotel Rio Branco* (☎ 224-1785), Rua Rui Barbosa 193, has efficient service, bright decor and neat apartamentos for US$49/65, with an excellent breakfast. *Hotel Rodoviária*, opposite the rodoviária, has clean quartos for US$6/8.

Places to Eat

Pizzaria Boloto, next to the Inácio Palace Hotel, and the *Anexo Bar & Restaurant* both do tasty Italian food and regional dishes. *Casarão*, Avenida Brasil 310, is popular with locals. *Cafe do Ponte*, on Avenida Getúlio Vargas, is a cute little place with good coffee, pastries and ice cream. Vegetarians can browse in the well-stocked health-food shop next to the Hotel Rio Branco.

Just over the bridge, on the riverfront, the *Café Crystal*, Rua 24 de Janeiro, has pizzas, rodízio and a wide range of juices. There's live music here on Thursday, Friday and Saturday. There's live music on Tuesday at the *Kaxinawá Restaurant*, and also in the outdoor bars at the small square nearby.

Getting There & Away
In the wet season roads may be closed so you'll have to take a plane or boat. In the dry season river levels fall and the boats may stop running.

Air Aeroporto Internacional Presidente Medici (☎ 224-6833) is about two km out of town on AC-40, at Km 1; take the Norte/Sul bus to the city centre. Flights go to/from Cruzeiro do Sul, Manaus, Porto Velho, Cuiabá, Rio and São Paulo with VASP (☎ 224-6585) or Varig (☎ 224-2559). Aero-Sur (☎ 223-1350) flies to Puerto Maldonado (in Peru) a couple of times a week. There are also various air-taxi companies at the airport, such as TACEZUL (☎ 224-3242) and TAVAJ (☎ 224-5981).

Bus The rodoviária (☎ 224-1182) is a couple of km out of town on the Norte/Sul bus route. There are buses to/from Porto Velho (US$18.50, about 10 hours; five daily), Brasiléia (US$16, six hours; five daily), Xapuri, Plácido de Castro and Boca do Acre (in Amazonas state).

Boat To enquire about boats, either go direct to the port at the eastern end of Avenida Epaminondas Jácome or contact Paulo (☎ 223-1050). You might score a ride at the port; if there's a group of you, prices quoted for a 1½-day trip to Boca do Acre (Amazonas) are around US$65. From Boca do Acre,

there is river traffic along the Rio Purus as far as the Amazon, and even to Manaus.

XAPURI
Xapuri, 188 km south-west of Rio Branco, is where Chico Mendes was assassinated in 1988. There are two cheap hotels, and three buses a day to/from Rio Branco (US$8, 3½ hours).

BRASILÉIA
The small town of Brasiléia lies on Brazil's border with Bolivia, separated from Cobija (its Bolivian counterpart) by the Rio Abunã and the Rio Acre. Brasiléia has nothing to interest travellers except an immigration stamp into or out of Brazil.

The Bolivian Consulate, at Rua Major Salinas 205, opens weekdays from 8 to 11 am. For a Brazilian entry or exit stamp, dress up nicely and visit the Polícia Federal, two km from the centre. It's open daily from 8 am to noon and 2 to 5 pm.

If you're stuck in Brasiléia, try the *Hotel Fronteiras* (☎ 546-3045), near the church in the centre, with apartamentos for US$12/15; or the similarly priced *Hotel Kador* (☎ 546-3283), on the road between the international bridge and the Polícia Federal.

From the rodoviária, buses go to Rio Branco (five daily, six hours; US$16), and Assis Brasil in the dry season (roughly, from June to October). During the rainy season you may be able to organise a ride in a truck; contact Transport Acreana in Brasiléia.

To/From Bolivia
You'll have to get stamps from Bolivian Migración in Cobija, and from the Brazilian Polícia Federal just outside Brasiléia. A yellow-fever vaccination certificate is technically required to enter Brazil from Cobija. They don't usually check, but if you need a vaccination you'll have to find a local doctor. There's no vaccination clinic in Brasiléia.

It's a long slog across the bridge from Cobija to Brasiléia, but taxis will take you from Cobija to the Polícia Federal in Brasiléia, wait while you complete immigration formalities, then take you to the city centre or to the rodoviária. It's about US$3.50 if you negotiate the route and the fare in advance. Going the other way, taxis try to charge double this price.

Alternatively, take a rowboat ferry (US$0.50 per person) across the Rio Acre to the landing in the centre of Brasiléia. From here it's about one km to the rodoviária and another 1.5 km to the Polícia Federal.

Chile

Chile stretches 4300 km from Peru to the Strait of Magellan. Its contrasts include the scenic but nearly sterile Atacama Desert in the north, the metropolis of Santiago and its Valle Central (central valley), a verdant lake district, and the glacial landscapes of Patagonia in the south. Within just hours of each other are world-class Andean skiing and scores of Pacific beach resorts.

Many Chileans are of European descent, but indigenous traditions persist. In the north, Aymara Indians farm the Andean foothills and tend llamas and alpacas on the *altiplano*. Mapuche Indians still inhabit the south, where they earned respect for their resistance to Chilean expansion in the 19th century.

Adventurous visitors will appreciate Polynesian Easter Island (Rapa Nui), with its giant stylised statues, and the Juan Fernández Islands, a botanical wonderland best known for the marooned Scotsman Alexander Selkirk, who inspired the novel *Robinson Crusoe*.

Country Name República de Chile
Area 756,950 sq km
Population 14,161,216
Population Density 18.7 per sq km
Capital Santiago
Head of State President Eduardo Frei Ruiz-Tagle
Official Language Spanish
Other Languages Aymara, Mapuche, Rapa Nui
Currency Peso ($)
Exchange Rate US$1 = Ch$411
Per Capita GNP US$7,010
Inflation Rate 8.7%

Facts about the Country

HISTORY
Pre-Columbian Times
Inca rule touched Chile, but northern Aymara and Atacameño farmers and herders predated the Inca lords of Cuzco, while Changos fished coastal areas and Diaguitas farmed the interior of Coquimbo. Beyond the central valley, Araucanian (Mapuche) Indians resisted Inca aggression. Cunco Indians fished and farmed on the island of Chiloé. Smaller groups long avoided European contact in the far south, but are now nearly extinct.

The Colonial Period
A year after leaving Peru in 1540, Pedro de Valdivia reached the Mapocho valley to found the city of Santiago. Mapuche assaults threatened the fledgling capital, but the determined Spaniards held out and their situation improved. Valdivia also worked southward, founding Concepción, Valdivia and Villarrica. Before his death in 1553 at the hands of the Mapuche, he had laid the foundation for a new society.

Failing to find much gold and silver, the Spanish invaders set up *encomiendas* (forced labour systems) to exploit the north's relatively large, sedentary population. The

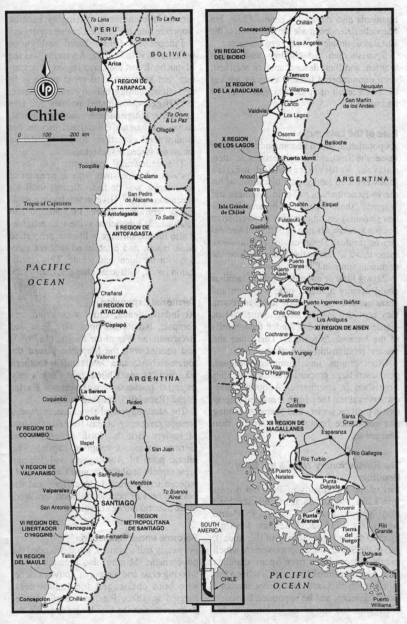

Spaniards also dominated central Chile, but Mapuche defenders made the area south of the Río Biobío unsafe for over three centuries.

Spanish men had children with Indian women, and their descendants, or *mestizos*, soon outnumbered Indians as many natives died as a result of epidemics, forced labour and warfare.

Rise of the Latifundio

As population-based encomiendas lost their value, the Spaniards sought economic alternatives. Valdivia rewarded mestizo followers with land grants like those of his native Extremadura, in Spain. Landless and 'vagrant', these 'Spaniards' became *inquilinos* (tenants) on units which evolved from livestock *estancias* into agricultural *haciendas* or *fundos*. These estates *(latifundios)*, many intact as late as the 1960s, became the dominant force in Chilean society.

Paying little or no rent, inquilino families could occupy a shack, raise a garden and graze animals on hacienda land. In return, they provided labour during annual rodeos (cattle roundups) and defended the interests of the *hacendado* (owner). This 'man and master' relationship permeated society.

Other groups, like immigrant Basques, purchased large properties as their families flourished in commerce. Adopting landowners' values, they have remained important in politics, society and business. Mining and commerce brought more wealth than land per se.

The Revolutionary Wars & the Early Republic

Part of the Viceroyalty of Peru but distant from Lima, the Audiencia of Chile stretched roughly from modern Chañaral to Puerto Aisén. By 1818, José de San Martín's Ejército de los Andes (Army of the Andes), part of the South American movement which sought independence from Spain, marched from Argentina into Chile, took Santiago and sailed north to Lima. His forces included many Chileans, and he appointed Bernardo O'Higgins, the son of an Irishman, as his second-in-command. O'Higgins became 'supreme director' of the Chilean republic.

Independent Chile shared ambiguous boundaries with Bolivia, Argentina and the Mapuche. It lost the Cuyo region to Argentina, but soon achieved rapid progress in agriculture, mining, industry and commerce.

O'Higgins dominated politics for five years after independence, enacting political, social, religious and educational reforms, but landowners' objections to his egalitarian measures forced his resignation.

The landowners' spokesman was Diego Portales, a businessman who, as minister of the interior, was de facto dictator until his execution in 1837. His custom-drawn constitution centralised power in Santiago and established Catholicism as the state religion. It also limited suffrage to literate, propertied adult males, and established indirect elections for president and senate. This constitution lasted, with some changes, until 1925.

Territorial Expansion

At independence, Chile was small and compact, but its triumphs over Peru and Bolivia in the War of the Pacific (1879-83) and treaties with the Mapuche placed the nitrate-rich Atacama Desert and the southern lake district under Chilean rule. Chile's only imperial possession was remote Easter Island (Rapa Nui), annexed in 1888.

The Atacama proved a bonanza, as nitrates brought prosperity, at least to certain sectors of society. British, North American and German investors supplied capital. The nitrate ports of Antofagasta and Iquique grew rapidly until the Panama Canal (1914) reduced traffic around Cape Horn and the development of petroleum-based fertilisers made mineral nitrates obsolete.

Reforms under Balmaceda

For nearly half a century, nitrates funded the government. Mining also created a new working class and a class of nouveau riche, who both challenged the landowners. Elected in 1886, President José Manuel Balmaceda was the first leader to tackle the dilemma of unequally distributed wealth and power.

Balmaceda promoted government services and public works, but an attempt by the Congress to depose him in 1890 triggered a civil war which resulted in 10,000 deaths. After taking asylum in the Argentine embassy, Balmaceda committed suicide. His successors continued many of his projects and also opened the Congress to popular elections, but major reform lagged until after WW II.

The Postwar Period
Despite hard times due to declining sales of nitrates, President Arturo Alessandri Palma instituted land and income taxes to fund health, education and welfare reforms, but conservative obstruction and army opposition forced his resignation in 1924. For several years the dictatorial General Carlos Ibáñez del Campo held the presidency and other positions of power, but opposition to his policies (exacerbated by global depression) forced him into exile.

Stalinists, Trotskyites and other radicals and reformists created a bewildering mix of new political entities, but the democratic left dominated the 1930s and 1940s. CORFO, the state development corporation, played a major economic role. The USA's economic role also grew as North American companies gained control of copper mines, now the cornerstone of the economy.

Rural Developments
In the 1920s, up to 75% of Chile's rural population still lived on latifundios holding 80% of prime agricultural land. Inquilinos' subsistence depended on haciendas and their votes belonged to landowners. As industry expanded and public works advanced, urban workers' welfare improved, but that of rural workers declined, forcing day labourers to the cities. Inquilinos suffered reduced privileges, while their labour obligations became more burdensome. An abundant labour force gave haciendas little incentive to modernise, and production stagnated until the crisis of the 1960s.

The Christian Democratic Ascendancy
In 1952, Ibáñez del Campo again won the presidency, because of widespread disenchantment with his predecessor Gabriel González Videla, but his surprising attempts to curtail landowners' power faltered. In the 1958 presidential elections, Arturo Alessandri's popular son, Jorge, representing a coalition of conservative and liberal parties, won a close race, defeating Salvador Allende, who led the leftist Popular Action Front (FRAP), and Eduardo Frei, standing for the reformist Christian Democrats (DC). In the 1961 congressional races, opposition parties improved their showing and forced Alessandri to accept modest land reform which began a decade's battle with the fundos.

In the 1964 presidential election Frei, supported by both the DC and conservative groups, won a landslide over Allende, who was undermined by party factionalism. The DC's genuinely reformist policies threatened both the elite's privileges and the left's working-class base, but the government soon encountered serious problems as economic decline drove displaced rural workers to urban squatter settlements (*callampas*, or mushrooms, since they seemed to spring up overnight). One common response to these problems was to attack the US-dominated export sector; Frei advocated the Chileanisation of the copper industry, while Allende and his backers supported nationalisation.

The Christian Democrats also faced challenges from violent groups like MIR (the Leftist Revolutionary Movement), who found support among coal miners, textile workers and other urban labourers, and also agitated for land reform. Too slow for leftists, Frei's reforms were too rapid for obstructionist conservatives – and, in this increasingly polarised society, there was even dissension among Christian Democrats.

Allende Comes to Power
In 1970, Allende's Unidad Popular (Popular Unity or UP) coalition offered a radical programme advocating nationalisation of industry and expropriation of latifundios. After he won a relative majority and agreed

to constitutional guarantees, Allende took office with congressional approval, but the coalition quarrelled over the administration's objectives.

Allende's programme, evading rather than confronting Congress, included state control of many private enterprises and massive income redistribution. Increased public spending briefly stimulated growth, but falling production brought shortages, soaring inflation and black marketeering.

Politics grew more confrontational as peasants, frustrated with agrarian reforms which favoured inquilinos over sharecroppers and *afuerinos* (day labourers), seized land, and harvests declined. Expropriation of copper mines and other enterprises, plus conspicuously friendly relations with Cuba, provoked hostility from the USA. Compromise was impossible between extreme leftists, who believed that only force could achieve socialism, and their rightist counterparts, who believed that only force could prevent it.

Golpe de Estado

On 11 September 1973, General Augusto Pinochet led a brutal *golpe de estado* (coup d'état) that resulted in the death of Allende (an apparent suicide) and thousands of his supporters. The military argued that force was necessary because Allende fomented chaos and was planning to overthrow the constitutional order.

Inept policies had brought about economic chaos, but reactionary sectors also undercut Allende's government by manipulating scarcities of commodities and food. Allende's pledges to the opposition were credible, but his inability or unwillingness to control groups to his left terrified the middle classes and outraged the oligarchy, underlining his failure.

Military Dictatorship

Most politicians expected a quick return to civilian rule, but Pinochet took 16 years to remake Chile's political and economic culture, largely by terror. International assassinations were not unusual; most notorious

was that of ex-Foreign Minister Orlando Letelier by a car bomb in Washington, DC, in 1976. In 1980, Pinochet submitted a new constitution to the voters; about two-thirds approved it and ratified his presidency until 1989, despite many abstentions.

Current Politics

In October 1988, voters rejected Pinochet's bid to extend his presidency until 1997. In 1989, 17 parties formed the coalition known as Concertación para la Democracia (Consensus for Democracy). Patricio Aylwin, who was chosen as a compromise presidential candidate, defeated both Pinochet's reluctant protégé, Hernán Büchi, standing for the Renovación Nacional party, and a right-wing independent candidate, Francisco Errázuriz. In late 1993 Chileans chose Eduardo Frei Ruiz-Tagle, son of former president Eduardo Frei Montalva, to succeed Aylwin. Frei has continued Aylwin's economic policies, and has proposed legislation on divorce and the environment.

The Military

All the services enjoy autonomy, despite a proposed constitutional amendment to strengthen presidential authority. Of Chile's 123,000 uniformed personnel, more than half are in the army; nearly half of those are officers and noncommissioned officers. The services are highly disciplined, cohesive and more loyal to their commanders than to civilian authority. Thanks to provisions assuring them 10% of profits from state copper sales, Chile's military budget is larger than any of its neighbours.

GEOGRAPHY & CLIMATE

Chile's 800,000 sq km contains stony Andean peaks, snowcapped volcanoes, broad river valleys and deep canyons, sterile deserts, icy fjords, deep blue glaciers, turquoise lakes, sandy beaches and rocky headlands. Continental Chile extends from tropical Arica to sub-Antarctic Punta Arenas; on average less than 200 km wide, Chile rises from sea level to above 6000 metres. Its Antarctic claims overlap those of Britain and Argentina.

Chile's 13 administrative regions are numbered ordinally from north to south, except for the Metropolitan Region of Santiago. The regions of Tarapacá and Antofagasta comprise the Norte Grande (Great North), dominated by the barren Atacama Desert.

The regions of Atacama and Coquimbo form the mineral-rich Norte Chico (Little North), an area of scrub and occasional forest. Beyond the Río Aconcagua begins the fertile heartland of Middle Chile, where the Valle Central contains the capital, Santiago, the port of Valparaíso, and most of the country's industry and employment.

South of Concepción, the Río Biobío marks Chile's 19th-century frontier and the Mapuche Indian homeland. South of Temuco, the scenic Lake District has snow-capped volcanoes, many still active, framing its numerous foothill lakes. South of Puerto Montt, Chiloé is the largest island wholly within Chile, with a lengthy coastline, dense forests and many small farms.

Chilean Patagonia, comprising the regions of Aisén and Magallanes, experiences cool summers but relatively mild winters, as does the island of Tierra del Fuego, divided between Chile and Argentina.

The Andes run the length of the country. In the far north volcanoes reach above 6000 metres, as does the imposing wall of sedimentary and volcanic peaks east of Santiago. South of the Biobío, the Andes are a less formidable barrier.

FLORA & FAUNA

Chile's northern deserts and high-altitude steppes, soaring mountains, alpine and sub-Antarctic forests, and extensive coastline all support distinctive flora and fauna. To protect these environments Chile's Corporación Nacional Forestal (CONAF) administers an extensive system of national parks.

The northern highlands support large populations of the endangered vicuña and huge nesting colonies of flamingos. The coastal areas of the desert regions offer pelicans, penguins, otters and sea lions. The Andean portion of La Araucanía houses

large forests of araucaria (monkey-puzzle tree), cypress and southern beech. In the extreme south, Parque Nacional Torres del Paine is a UNESCO Biosphere Reserve with a wealth of wildlife, including the Patagonian guanaco.

GOVERNMENT

The constitution allows a popularly elected president and the establishment of a Congress with a 46-member Senate and a 120-member Chamber of Deputies, but eight institutional senators are Pinochet appointees. The president resides in Santiago but the Congress meets in Valparaíso. Despite regionalisation, administration is highly centralised.

ECONOMY

One Latin American economist has called Chile a fruit fly because every economic experiment happens so much faster there. In an early experiment in neoliberal economics, Pinochet's government enlisted economists from the University of Chicago to reduce expenditures and to encourage foreign investment through the adoption of laissez-faire practices.

For some years, inflation remained high, industrial production declined and some inefficient industries disappeared, but 'non-traditional' exports like off-season temperate fruits helped compensate for falling copper prices. The new policies had great social costs; only soup kitchens prevented starvation in some callampas.

Chile is often cited as a success story because of 10 consecutive years of economic growth at 6% per annum. Exports are now more diverse and less vulnerable to international market fluctuations, Chile has repaid some of its foreign debt, and inflation has fallen to a modest 8%. However, the growth of national income has benefited the poor only incidentally, and countless city dwellers still earn a precarious livelihood as street vendors.

Much of the growth has been in exports of natural resources, which may not be sustainable. Chile is the world's largest producer and exporter of copper, but it also exports

CHILE

other metals and minerals, wood and wood products, fish, fishmeal and fruits to the EU, Japan, the USA, Argentina and Brazil. When a recent forestry study concluded that in 25 to 30 years the country might have no more trees worth cutting down, the industry's strong reaction forced the dismissal of the study's director.

While Chile is keen to join NAFTA, the North American free-trade bloc which includes the USA, Canada and Mexico, Republican conservatives in the USA oppose its entry on the pretext of fearing another Mexican-style crash. In reality, the opposition relates more to US domestic politics than to international trade partners. Meanwhile, with NAFTA on the back burner, Chile has managed to reduce trade barriers with Mercosur countries.

POPULATION & PEOPLE

Over a third of Chile's 14 million people reside in Gran Santiago (the capital and its suburbs). About 75% live in Middle Chile, only 20% of the country's total area. More than 80% live in cities, but south of the Biobío, the peasant population is still dense.

As most Chileans are mestizos, class is a greater issue than race. La Araucanía has a large Mapuche population. In the north, Aymara and Atacameño peoples farm terraces in the *precordillera*, and pasture llamas and alpacas in the altiplano.

After 1848, many Germans settled in the Lake District. Other immigrants came from France, Italy, Yugoslavia (especially to Magallanes and Tierra del Fuego) and Palestine.

ARTS

Famous Chilean writers include Nobel Prize poets Gabriela Mistral and Pablo Neruda (who was also an important political activist). Much of their work is available in English translation – see the Facts for the Visitor section.

Until 1973, Chilean cinema was among Latin America's most experimental. Director Alejandro Jodorowsky's surrealistic *El Topo* (The Mole) was an underground success overseas, while exiled Miguel Littín's *Alsino*

and the Condor, nominated for an Academy Award in 1983, is readily available on video.

La Nueva Canción Chilena (the New Chilean Song Movement) wedded Chile's folkloric heritage to the political passions of the late 1960s and early 1970s. Its most legendary figure is the late Violeta Parra, but her performing children, Isabel and Angel, established the first of many *peñas* (musical and cultural centres) in the mid-1960s. Individuals like Victor Jara (executed in 1973) and groups like Quilapayún and Inti-Illimani have acquired international reputations.

SOCIETY & CONDUCT

Because of the European influence, English-speaking visitors will find Chile more accessible than some other Latin American countries. Chileans are exceptionally hospitable and frequently invite foreigners to their homes.

RELIGION

About 90% of Chileans are Roman Catholic; the Church has many factions, but its Vicaria de la Solidaridad staunchly defended human rights during the dictatorship. Evangelical Protestantism is growing, but Mormon proselytising has made their churches targets of leftist bombings.

LANGUAGE

Spanish is the official language, but a handful of Indian languages are still spoken. In the north, over 20,000 speak Aymara; in the south there are perhaps half a million Mapuche speakers. About 2000 people speak Rapa Nui, the Polynesian language of Easter Island.

Chilean Spanish

Chileans relax terminal and even some internal consonants, making it difficult to distinguish plural from singular: *las islas* (the islands) may sound more like *la ila*. They also speak more rapidly than other South Americans, and rather less clearly: the conventional *¿Quieres..?* (Do you want..?) sounds like *¿Querí..?* on the tongue of a Chilean.

Facts for the Visitor

VISAS & EMBASSIES

Most nationalities don't need to get a visa in advance. Arriving visitors receive a 90-day tourist card, renewable for another 90 days at the Departamento de Extranjería (☎ 672-5320), Moneda 1342 in Santiago. A few nationalities, including New Zealanders, do need a visa, but the requirements change, and Chilean embassies recommend that people check before their visit for the latest information. Request a multiple-entry visa if you want to travel in the Lake District. If staying more than six months, make a brief visit to a neighbouring country, then return.

Chilean authorities take the tourist card very seriously; for a replacement, go to the Policía Internacional (☎ 737-1292), General Borgoño 1052, Santiago.

Chilean Embassies Abroad

Chilean representations abroad include:

Australia
  10 Culgoa Circuit, O'Malley, ACT 2606 (☎ (06) 286-2430)
Canada
  Suite 605, 151 Slater St, Ottawa, Ontario (☎ (613) 235-4402)
  Consulate: Suite 800, 170 Bloor Street W, Toronto, Ontario (☎ (416) 924-0106)
Germany
  Kronprinzenstrasse 20, Bonn (☎ (0228) 36 30 80)
UK
  12 Devonshire Rd, London (☎ (0171) 580-6393)
USA
  1736 Massachusetts Avenue NW, Washington, DC (☎ (202) 785-3159)
  Consulates: 1732 Massachusetts Avenue NW, Washington, DC (☎ (202) 785-1746)
  Room 302, 866 United Nations Plaza, New York, NY (☎ (212) 980-3366)
  Suite 2450, 1900 Avenue of the Stars, Los Angeles, CA (☎ (310) 785-0047)
  Suite 1062, 870 Market St, San Francisco, CA (☎ (415) 982-7662)

Foreign Embassies in Chile

For details of foreign representation in Chile, see the Santiago section.

DOCUMENTS

Passports are essential for cashing travellers' cheques, checking into hotels and other routine activities. Motorists need an International Driving Permit as well as a state or national licence. International Health Certificates are optional.

CUSTOMS

There are no currency restrictions. Duty-free allowances include 400 cigarettes or 50 cigars or 500 grams of tobacco, 2.5 litres of alcoholic beverages, and perfume for personal use.

Inspections are usually routine, but some travellers have undergone more thorough examinations because of drug smuggling from Peru and Bolivia. Arrivals from free zones in the First Region (Tarapacá) and the 12th Region (Magallanes) are subject to internal customs inspections. The Servicio Agrícola-Ganadero (SAG) inspects luggage for fresh produce at international borders and domestic checkpoints.

MONEY

The unit of currency is the *peso* (Ch$). There are banknotes for 500, 1000, 5000 and 10,000 pesos; and coins for one, five, 10, 50 and 100 pesos.

US dollars are the preferred currency, but Argentine pesos can be readily exchanged in Santiago, at border crossings and in tourist areas like Viña del Mar and the Lake District.

Exchange Rates

Approximate official rates at July 1996 were as follows:

Australia	A$1	= Ch$323
Canada	C$1	= Ch$302
France	FF1	= Ch$80
Germany	DM1	= Ch$269
Japan	¥100	= Ch$379
New Zealand	NZ$1	= Ch$280
United Kingdom	UK£1	= Ch$635
USA	US$1	= Ch$411

Cambios pay a parallel rate, slightly higher than the official rate. Cash earns a better rate

CHILE

than travellers' cheques and avoids commissions (though these are usually modest). Hotels, travel agencies, street moneychangers and some shops also change cash. For the latest information, see the financial daily *Estrategia*.

Costs

Chile is no longer a bargain, but modest lodgings, food and transport are still cheaper than in Europe, North America or Argentina. Allow at least US$25 per day for food and accommodation; by purchasing market food or eating at modest restaurants, you may get by for US$20.

Credit Cards

Usually purchases and cash advances on credit card will be charged at the disadvantageous bank rate. Automatic teller machines (called Redbanc) exist in most cities, but some only take Visa, the most widely accepted card.

Tipping

In restaurants, it is customary to leave a 10% *propina* (tip).

Bargaining

Bargaining is customary only in markets. Hotel prices are generally fixed and prominently displayed, but try haggling in a slow summer or during the off season.

WHEN TO GO & WHAT TO BRING

Santiago and Middle Chile are best in spring or during the autumn harvest, but skiers will prefer the northern-hemisphere summer. Natural attractions like Torres del Paine and the Lake District are best in summer, but rain is always possible and a compact umbrella is useful. Even non-campers may consider a warm sleeping bag for budget hotels in Patagonia.

At high altitudes, carry warm clothing even in summer. The altiplano's summer rainy season usually means only a brief afternoon thunderstorm.

Rapa Nui is cooler, slightly cheaper and far less crowded outside the summer. Likewise, March is an excellent time to visit the Juan Fernández Islands.

TOURIST OFFICES
Local Offices

Sernatur, the national tourist service, has offices in regional capitals and several other cities. Many cities have their own tourist offices, usually on the main plaza or at the bus terminal, sometimes only open in summer.

Foreign Reps

Chilean consulates abroad often provide tourist information. Try also LanChile or Ladeco, the two major international airlines, for information.

USEFUL ORGANISATIONS

Corporación Nacional Forestal, or CONAF (☎ 696-6677), administers national parks from Avenida Bulnes 285, Departamento 303, Santiago; its regional offices are also very helpful.

Conservationists may also contact Comité Pro Defensa de la Fauna y Flora, or CODEFF (☎ 696-1268), Sazie 1885, Santiago. Climbers should call the Federación de Andinismo (☎ 222-0888), Almirante Simpson 77, Santiago. The Sociedad Lonko Kilapán (☎ 21-3134), Aldunate 12, Temuco, promotes sustainable development among indigenous peoples.

BUSINESS HOURS & HOLIDAYS

Most businesses open by 8 am, but shops close at midday for three or four hours, then reopen until closing at 8 or 9 pm. In Santiago, government offices and many businesses have adopted a 9 am to 6 pm schedule. Banks and some government offices are open to the public only in the mornings. Government offices and businesses close on the following national holidays:

1 January
    Año Nuevo (New Year's Day)
March/April (dates vary)
    Semana Santa (Holy Week)

1 May
  Día del Trabajo (Labour Day)
21 May
  Glorias Navales (Naval Battle of Iquique)
30 May
  Corpus Christi
29 June
  San Pedro y San Pablo (St Peter's & St Paul's Day)
15 August
  Asunción de la Virgen (Assumption)
11 September
  Pronunciamiento Militar de 1973 (Military Coup of 1973)
18 September
  Día de la Independencia Nacional (Independence Day)
19 September
  Día del Ejército (Armed Forces Day)
12 October
  Día de la Raza (Columbus Day)
1 November
  Todos los Santos (All Saints' Day)
8 December
  Inmaculada Concepción (Immaculate Conception)
25 December
  Navidad (Christmas Day)

SPECIAL EVENTS

Throughout the year, Chileans celebrate a variety of local and national cultural festivals. Other than religious holidays, the most significant are the mid-September *fiestas patrias*.

POST & COMMUNICATIONS

Postal services are sometimes slow, but telephone services have improved greatly over the past decade. Telegraph, telex and fax services are also good.

Postal Services

Post offices are open weekdays from 8 am to 7 pm, and Saturday from 8 am to 2 pm. Send essential overseas mail *certificado* to ensure its arrival. Parcel post is efficient, though a customs official may inspect your package before a clerk will accept it. Vendors near the post office wrap parcels for a small charge.

Poste restante and *lista de correos* are equivalent to general delivery. Lista de correos charges a nominal fee (about US$0.20 per letter). Santiago's American

Express office holds client mail, as do some embassies for their citizens. Instruct correspondents to address letters clearly and to indicate a pick-up date (*'Guardar hasta...'* means 'Keep until...'). International Federal Express services are available in Santiago.

Telephone

Entel, the former state monopoly, Compañía de Teléfonos de Chile (CTC) and several other companies offer domestic and international long-distance services throughout the country.

Domestic long-distance calls from Santiago are generally less than US$1 for three minutes. Approximate charges to North America are US$1.30 per minute, to England or Australia US$2.25 per minute, and to other Latin American countries US$2 per minute. Late-evening discounts make calls to the USA less than US$1 per minute.

Calls from public phones cost Ch$100 (about US$0.25) for three minutes. When the liquid-crystal readout reaches zero, insert another coin. Phone boxes do not provide change, but if there is at least Ch$50 credit remaining, you may make another call by pressing a button. Magnetic telephone cards are more convenient than coins.

Long-distance domestic and overseas calls are possible from phone boxes, which accept coins and cards. Reverse-charge overseas calls are simple to make but credit-card calls are possible only from private phones or from the grey-blue *teléfonos inteligentes*. Dial ☎ 800-800-288 (☎ 12300311 from Entel phones) for an AT&T operator. Phone offices are ubiquitous, and private ones are often cheaper than Entel or CTC.

Chile's country code is 56.

TIME

For most of the year Chile is four hours behind GMT/UTC, but from mid-December to mid-March (summer), the country observes daylight-saving time. Easter Island is two hours behind the mainland.

ELECTRICITY

The electricity supply is 220V. Sockets take

CHILE

two round prongs, and adapters are readily available.

LAUNDRY

In recent years, self-service laundrettes have become more common, but it is only slightly dearer to leave your load and pick it up later. Most budget hotels have a place to wash clothes; maid service is usually reasonable, but agree on charges beforehand.

BOOKS

Literature & Fiction

Poets Pablo Neruda and Gabriela Mistral are major literary figures. Available in translation are Neruda's *The Heights of Machu Picchu, Canto General, Passions and Impressions* and his rambling *Memoirs*. US poet Langston Hughes has translated *Selected Poems of Gabriela Mistral*; the Library of Congress and Johns Hopkins Press published a different book with the same title in 1971.

Isabel Allende's magical realist novels have made her popular overseas and in Chile; *House of Spirits, Of Love and Shadows, Eva Luna* and *Paula* are available in paperback. José Donoso's novel *Curfew* offers a view of life under dictatorship through the eyes of a returned exile.

History

For general history, read Arnold Bauer's *Chilean Rural Society from the Spanish Conquest to 1930*.

Edy Kaufman's *Crisis in Allende's Chile: New Perspectives* is a wide-ranging attempt to explain Allende's failure.

James Petras & Morris Morley's *The United States & Chile: Imperialism & the Overthrow of the Allende Government* stresses US subversion of the Unidad Popular. For a more neutral perspective, read Robert J Alexander's *The Tragedy of Chile*.

Thomas Hauser's *The Execution of Charles Horman: An American Sacrifice*, which implicated US officials in the death of a US activist in the 1973 coup, was the basis of the 1982 film *Missing*.

Chile: The Pinochet Decade, by Phil O'Brien & Jackie Roddick, covers the Pinochet government's early years and its radical economic measures. Genaro Arriagada's *Pinochet: the Politics of Power* details the regime's evolution from a collegial junta to a personalistic, but institutionalised, dictatorship.

Pamela Constable & Arturo Valenzuela's *A Nation of Enemies* eschews partisan rhetoric to focus on the intricacies and implications of events since 1973.

Easter Island (Rapa Nui)

See the Easter Island section for details on the voluminous amount of literature about this island.

Travel Guides

For more detailed travel information, there is Lonely Planet's *Chile & Easter Island – travel survival kit*, 4th edition. Illustrated with exceptional photographs, the *APA Insight Guides* volume on Chile is excellent at cultural and historical analysis but weak on practical matters. The annually updated and reasonably priced Turistel series, published by the Compañía de Teléfonos, has separate volumes on northern, central and southern regions, plus an additional one on camping. A new English version combines the three main guides in a single volume. Oriented toward motorists, Turistel provides excellent maps and thorough background, but ignores budget alternatives.

MAPS

Turistel's maps are great value, but several others are available from shops and street vendors. Esso's inexpensive series includes indexed street maps of Santiago, Antofagasta, Valparaíso, Viña del Mar, Concepción and Talcahuano.

The Instituto Geográfico Militar's *Plano Guía del Gran Santiago* (1989) is the equivalent of *London A-Z*, while its *Guía Caminera* (1991) is an up-to-date highway map. Their 1:50,000 topographic series (about US$8 per sheet) is valuable for trekkers.

MEDIA

The press is still recovering from the dictatorship but the end of state monopoly on the electronic media has opened the airwaves to a greater variety of programming.

Newspapers & Magazines

Santiago's oldest daily, *El Mercurio*, follows a conservative editorial policy. *La Epoca*, born during the 'No' campaign against Pinochet's continuance in office, is a serious Christian Democratic tabloid, while *La Nación* is the official government daily. Sleazy tabloids like *La Segunda* sensationalise crime and radical political dissent (which they seem to consider synonymous).

Estrategia, the voice of the financial sector, is the best source of information on exchange rates. The twice-weekly *News Review* serves the English-speaking population; its Saturday edition includes Britain's *Guardian Weekly*.

Radio & TV

Radio broadcasting is less regulated than before, with many stations on both AM and FM bands. TV stations include state-owned TVN (Televisión Nacional), the Universidad Católica's Channel 13, and several private stations. International cable services are widely available.

HEALTH

After localised cholera outbreaks in 1992, the Ministry of Health prohibited restaurants from serving raw vegetables, although the ban was recently lifted for lettuce, cabbage, celery, cauliflower, beets and carrots. *Ceviche* (raw seafood) is also suspect. Santiago's drinking water is adequately treated, and the author has drunk tap water in most areas without problems, but bottled mineral water is a good alternative.

Basic Rules & Precautions

Most Chilean food is relatively bland and shouldn't cause problems but be careful about some varieties of shellfish, such as mussels and scallops, served raw. Take precautions with rural drinking water, as latrines may be close to wells or local people may take untreated water from streams or ditches. Water in the Atacama has a strong taste, often salty, due to its high mineral content; Easter Island's water has a similar reputation, but the author found it both safe and tasty.

WOMEN TRAVELLERS

Chile is a very safe country for women travelling in groups or alone although it is important to take certain precautions. Avoid hitching a ride in a vehicle in which you are outnumbered by males, and remember that in certain areas population centres are few and widely separated so the rides are long. A Swedish reader complained that the prejudice Chilean men have toward Scandinavian women accompanied her wherever she went. Although the fantasy of sexual liberalism is extended to European and North American women as well, it does not seem to translate into aggressive behaviour toward them beyond the occasional *piropo* (a comment made out loud to a woman passing in the street), which is best ignored.

Chilean women are very gregarious so it is rare to see them alone in public places. I (María) noticed that in restaurants waiters took longer than usual to come to my table. After a while it dawned on me that when they did they invariably asked, 'Are you waiting for someone?'. Since it is so unusual to see a woman eating alone, they were allowing time for my potential companion to arrive!

DANGERS & ANNOYANCES

Personal Security & Theft

Truly violent crime is rare in Santiago, but purse snatchings are not unusual; Valparaíso has a reputation for robberies in some neighbourhoods. Summer is the crime season in beach resorts – be alert for pickpockets and be careful with valuables.

Despite the return to democracy, armed opposition groups sometimes commandeer taxis or private cars and are pursued by the police, but the odds of being caught in the crossfire are small.

Unauthorised political demonstrations can be very contentious; the police may use tear gas or water cannons – known as *guanacos*, after the spitting wild camelids – to break them up. US institutions, such as banks, churches and even Mormon chapels, have in the past been targets of protest.

For emergencies call ☎ 133, the number for the *carabineros* (police) throughout the country; updated information on border crossings is also available.

Police & the Military

In routine circumstances, police behave professionally and politely; *never* attempt to bribe them. Avoid photographing military installations. In the event of a coup or other emergency, carry identification and contact your embassy or consulate for advice.

Natural Hazards

Volcanic eruptions are not rare: most recently, in 1991, Volcán Hudson, in the Aisén Region, buried Chile Chico and Los Antiguos, Argentina, knee-deep in ash. Earthquakes are very common and can be very serious.

Volcanoes usually give notice before blowing big, but a few resorts are especially vulnerable, notably Pucón, at the base of Volcán Villarrica. Earthquakes strike without warning and local buildings, especially those built from adobe, are often unsafe; travellers in budget hotels should make contingency plans for safety or evacuation before going to sleep.

Recreational Hazards

Many of the finest beach areas have dangerous offshore currents. While some beaches are polluted, there are usually warning signs. Because of accidents, authorities no longer permit solo trekking in wilderness areas like Torres del Paine.

WORK

Many travellers work as English-language instructors in Santiago, but wages are fairly low and full-time employment is rare. Reputable employers insist on work or residence permits from the Departamento de Extranje-

ría (☎ 672-5320), Moneda 1342 in Santiago, open from 9 am to 1.30 pm weekdays.

ACTIVITIES

Of the many participant and spectator sports, soccer is the most widespread. Others include tennis, basketball, volleyball and cycling, while outdoor activities like canoeing, climbing, kayaking, trekking, windsurfing and hang-gliding are gaining popularity. Rivers like the Maipo, Claro and Biobío are popular for white-water rafting, but hydroelectric development threatens the Biobío.

In summer, most Chileans head to the beach. In winter, skiing, although expensive, can be world-class. Chile's best downhill skiing is found in the high cordillera of Middle Chile.

HIGHLIGHTS

Chile has a huge variety of natural attractions, from the northern deserts to the southern Lake District and Patagonia. For outdoor enthusiasts, highlights include trekking, climbing and skiing in the Andes. The traditional architecture of Chiloé and of the houses and churches in the remote, high Andean villages of the north are very picturesque, while Mapuche textiles and silver jewellery will appeal to shoppers. Fabulous seafood, superb wines, and the friendliness of Chilean people also make for a memorable visit.

ACCOMMODATION

Accommodation, ranging from hostels and camping grounds to five-star hotels, is usually reasonable by North American or European standards. Summer prices may be 10 to 20% higher than those in the off season.

Camping & Refugios

Sernatur has a free brochure listing camping grounds nationwide. The usually woodsy sites generally have hot showers, toilets and laundry, firepits, a restaurant or snack bar, and a grocery; some have swimming pools or lake access. The Turistel camping guide has more detail and superb maps.

Camping grounds discriminate against

backpackers by imposing a five-person minimum, so for singles or couples they are often dearer than basic hotels. Free camping is possible in some remote areas, but often without any facilities.

Refugios are rustic shelters, either free or very cheap, in national parks.

Hostels

Inexpensive hostels occupy temporary sites at stadiums, camping grounds, schools and churches, and are generally open in January and February only. For the latest information, contact the Asociación Chilena de Albergues Turísticos Juveniles (☎ 233-3220), Avenida Providencia 2594, Oficina 420, Santiago. There is a growing number of permanent hostels, mostly in larger cities.

Casas de Familia & Hospedajes

In summer, especially in the Lake District, families offer inexpensive rooms with kitchen and laundry privileges, hot showers, breakfast and local hospitality. Longer established and more permanent places tend to adopt the name *hospedaje*. Ask at tourist offices.

Pensiones & Residenciales

Differences between these inexpensive permanent forms of accommodation are vague – both may be called hotels.

FOOD

The cool waters of the Humboldt Current provide superb fish and shellfish, while the fields, orchards and pastures of Middle Chile fill the table with excellent produce and meat. The best Chilean cuisine, however, may be priced beyond the reach of budget travellers.

Places to Eat

Distinctions among 'restaurants', ranging from simple snack bars to sumptuous international venues, are ambiguous. The central market in most cities has many small, cheap restaurants of surprisingly high quality.

Bars serve snacks and drinks (alcoholic and nonalcoholic), while *fuentes de soda* offer tea, coffee and sandwiches. *Cafeterías* serve modest meals. A *salón de té* is not literally a teahouse, but a bit more up-market than a cafetería. A *picada* or *picá* is a modest informal restaurant in a family home, usually serving seafood, frequented by locals, with a limited menu and large portions; some are excellent value.

Quality and service distinguish fully fledged *restaurantes*. Many places offer a cheap set meal (*comida corrida* or *colación*) for lunch and, less often, for dinner. Some common dishes are listed below.

Breakfast

Toast, marmalade, eggs *paila* (named after the pan in which they are fried and served), coffee and tea are usual breakfast fare. Sandwiches are common throughout the day; among the fillings are *churrasco* (steak), *jamón* (ham) and *queso* (cheese). Cold ham and cheese make an *aliado* which, when heated to melt the cheese, is a Barros Jarpa, after a Chilean painter. Steak with melted cheese is a Barros Luco, after former president Ramón Barros Luco (1910-15). Beefsteak with tomato and other vegetables is a *chacarero*.

Snacks

The cheapest fast food is a *completo*, a hot dog with absolutely everything. Arrivals from Argentina will find the individual Chilean *empanada* much larger than its trans-Andean counterpart, so don't order a dozen for lunch or your bus trip. Empanadas in Chile are *de pino* (ground beef) or *de queso* (cheese), fried or baked. *Humitas* are corn tamales.

Main Meals

Lunch is the biggest meal of the day. Set menus, almost identical at cheaper restaurants, usually consist of *cazuela* (a broth with potato or maize and beef or chicken), a main course of rice with beef or chicken, and a simple dessert. *Porotos* (beans) are a common budget dish. *Pastel de choclo*, a maize casserole filled with vegetables, chicken and beef, is delicious and filling.

CHILE

The biggest standard meal is *lomo a lo pobre*, an enormous slab of beef topped with two fried eggs and buried in chips – monitor your cholesterol count. Beef, in a variety of cuts and styles of preparation, is the most popular main course at *parrillas* like those in Argentina. *Pollo con arroz* (chicken with rice) is another common offering.

Seafood

Chilean seafood is among the world's best. *Curanto*, a hearty stew of fish, shellfish, chicken, pork, lamb, beef and potato, is a speciality of Chiloé and Patagonia.

Popular soups are *sopa de mariscos*, a delicious seafood soup, or *cazuela de mariscos*, more like a stew. Fish soup is *sopa de pescado*, while *paila marina* is a fish chowder. Try *chupe de congrio* (conger eel stew) or, if available, *chupe de locos* (abalone stew), both cooked in a thick sauce of butter, breadcrumbs, cheese and spices. Locos may be in *veda* (quarantine) because of over-exploitation. Some dishes, like *erizos* (sea urchins), are acquired tastes.

Do not miss market restaurants in cities like Iquique, Concepción, Temuco and Puerto Montt, but insist on thorough cooking of all shellfish. A few seafood terms worth knowing are:

crab	*cangrejo* or *jaiva*
king crab	*centolla*
mussels	*cholgas*
oysters	*ostras*
prawns	*camarones grandes*
scallops	*ostiones*
shellfish	*mariscos*
shrimp	*camarones*
squid	*calamares*

Desserts

Dessert is commonly fresh fruit or ice cream. Also try *arroz con leche* (rice pudding), *flan* (egg custard) and *tortas* (cakes). Lake District bakers of German descent prepare exquisite *kuchen* (pastries) filled with local fruit – especially raspberries.

Ethnic Food

Santiago's ethnic restaurants fill eight pages in the phone book. French, Italian, Spanish, German and Chinese are the most common, but Brazilian, Arab, Mexican and others are also available.

Northern Chilean cities have many *chifas* (Chinese restaurants), which offer a pleasant change of pace.

Vegetarian Food

Most Chileans are very fond of meat, but vegetarianism is no longer the mark of an eccentric. Santiago has excellent vegetarian fare and every town has a market with fresh produce.

DRINKS
Nonalcoholic Drinks

Chileans guzzle all the usual soft drinks and some local varieties, plus mineral water.

Mote con huesillo, sold by street vendors but closely monitored for hygiene, is a peach nectar with barley kernels. *Licuados* are milk-blended fruit drinks, sometimes made with water and often with too much sugar. Common flavours are banana, peach (*durazno*) and pear (*pera*).

In the past semisoluble instant coffee was the norm, but espresso is becoming more common. Normally, tea is served black, usually with lemon. Try herbal teas (*aguas*) such as camomile (*manzanilla*) and the digestive *boldo*.

Alcohol

Chilean wines should satisfy most alcoholic thirsts, but don't miss the powerful grape brandy (*pisco*), often served in the form of a *pisco sour* (with lemon juice, egg white and powdered sugar). It may also be served with ginger ale (*chilcano*) or vermouth (*capitán*).

Escudo is the best bottled beer, but draught beer (*chopp*, pronounced *shop*) is cheaper and often better. A cherry-like fruit, (*guinda*) is the basis of *guindado*, a fermented alcoholic drink with brandy, cinnamon and cloves.

Wines & Wine Regions Wine-growing districts stretch from the Copiapó valley of the Norte Chico as far as the Biobío. The number of regions and the abrupt topography produce a great variety. Atacama wineries specialise in pisco, but also produce small quantities of white and sparkling wines. Middle Chile's *zona de regadío* produces mostly cabernets and other reds, but acreages planted for whites are increasing. Reds give way to whites in the transitional zone of the Maule, while the Biobío drainage is an area relatively recently converted to grape growing. Farther south, commercial production is precarious.

Wine-lovers should read Harm de Blij's *Wine Regions of the Southern Hemisphere*.

ENTERTAINMENT
Cinemas
In the capital and in larger cities like Valparaíso and Viña del Mar, theatres screen the latest films from Europe, Hollywood and Latin America. Repertory houses, cultural centres and universities offer the classics or less commercial films. Prices have risen in recent years, but are still reasonable; midweek, many cinemas offer discounts.

Theatre
Throughout the country, live theatre is well attended and of high quality; it ranges from the classics and serious drama to burlesque. In the Lake District, many towns offer seasonal productions at cultural festivals.

Peñas
Peñas are nightclubs where the performers offer unapologetically political, folk-based material. The New Chilean Song Movement had its origins in the peñas of the 1960s.

Nightclubs
In cities like Santiago and Viña, nightclubs can be tacky affairs where traditional music and dances are sanitised and presented in glitzy settings for foreigners. In port cities, they can be disreputable joints.

SPECTATOR SPORT
The most popular spectator sport is soccer, whose British origins are obvious in team names like Santiago Morning and Everton, but the main teams are Colo Colo, Universidad de Chile and Universidad Católica. Other popular spectator sports include tennis, boxing and, increasingly, basketball.

THINGS TO BUY
Artisans' *ferias* (markets) display a variety of quality crafts, especially in the suburb of Bellavista in Santiago, Viña del Mar, Valdivia, the Puerto Montt suburb of Angelmó, and the village of Dalcahue (on the island of Chiloé). Copper and leather goods are excellent, and northern woollens resemble those of Peru or Bolivia. Mapuche artisans produce ceramics, basketry, silverware, woven goods and carvings.

Getting There & Away

AIR
Paying for fares in local currency takes advantage of the parallel exchange rate, but the difference is relatively small.

As of November 1995, US citizens pay an entrance fee of US$20, valid for the life of the passport; this is a Chilean response to US visa-processing charges for Chileans.

To/From Peru
AeroPerú flies daily from Lima to Santiago (US$357).

To/From Bolivia
LAB flies five times a week from Santiago to La Paz (US$345) and also connects La Paz to Arica (US$92). LanChile also flies to La Paz.

To/From Argentina
Many airlines fly from Santiago to Buenos Aires (US$240, but much lower discount fares are available), and there are also flights to Mendoza and Córdoba. The Argentine

carrier TAN links Puerto Montt to Bariloche (US$56), and Temuco to Neuquén.

To/From the Falkland Islands

Aerovías DAP flies once a week from Santiago to Stanley via Punta Arenas (US$594 from Santiago, US$237 from Punta Arenas). Flights connect with British Airways services between Santiago and London.

BUS, TRAIN & BOAT
To/From Peru

Tacna to Arica is the only land crossing from Peru; for details, see the Arica section.

To/From Bolivia

Road and rail connections between Bolivia and Chile are slow and rough. Buses from La Paz to Arica are cheaper and more frequent than the weekly passenger train, but there is a faster *ferrobus* (bus on rails). There are also buses from Colchane (Bolivia) to Iquique.

A weekly train and occasional buses link Calama to Ollagüe, connecting to Oruro and La Paz. For details, see the Calama section.

To/From Argentina

Except in far southern Patagonia and Tierra del Fuego, travel to Argentina involves crossing the Andes; some passes close in winter. The Salta-Baquedano rail crossing is not a regular passenger service. For information on passes call the carabineros on ☎ 133.

Lake District crossings, involving busboat shuttles, are very popular in summer, so make advance bookings. Since the opening of the Camino Austral south of Puerto Montt, it has become more common to cross the border there. The most common routes to Argentina are:

Calama to Salta Buses on this route now use the Paso de Jama via Jujuy, but bookings are heavy. A weekly Argentine freight train also carries passengers from Salta to Socompa, but it is difficult to catch the very uncomfortable Chilean freight to the abandoned station of Augusta Victoria.

La Serena to San Juan The 4779-metre Agua Negra pass has reopened for automobile traffic, but the bus service has not yet commenced.

Santiago to Mendoza Many buses and *taxi colectivos* serve this most popular crossing.

Temuco to Zapala & Neuquén Occasional buses use the 1884-metre Pino Hachado pass along the upper Biobío in summer. An alternative is the 1298-metre Icalma pass.

Temuco to San Martín de los Andes On this popular route, regular summer buses use the Mamuil Malal pass (Paso Tromen to Argentines).

Valdivia to San Martín de los Andes This is a bus-ferry combination over Paso Hua Hum.

Osorno to Bariloche via Paso Puyehue Very frequent buses use this quick crossing in the Lake District.

Puerto Montt to Bariloche via Parque Nacional Vicente Pérez Rosales This bus-ferry combination crosses scenic Lago Todos los Santos.

Puerto Ramírez to Esquel There are two options here, via Futaleufú or Carrenleufú.

Coyhaique to Comodoro Rivadavia The two bus services per week are usually heavily booked.

Chile Chico to Los Antiguos From Puerto Ibáñez take the ferry to Chile Chico, on the south shore of Lago Carrera, and a bus over the border.

Puerto Natales & Parque Nacional Torres del Paine to Río Turbio & Calafate Frequent buses connect Puerto Natales to Río Turbio, with connections to Río Gallegos and Calafate. At least twice weekly in summer, buses go from Torres del Paine and Puerto Natales to Calafate, the gateway to Argentina's Parque Nacional Los Glaciares.

Punta Arenas to Río Gallegos There are many buses daily on this route (six hours).

Punta Arenas to Tierra del Fuego From Punta Arenas, it's a three-hour ferry ride or a 10-minute flight to Porvenir, on Chilean Tierra del Fuego, with two buses weekly going to Río Grande (Argentina), connecting to Ushuaia. Some buses go straight to Ushuaia from Punta Arenas.

Puerto Williams to Ushuaia There is a ferry on Saturday from Isla Navarino to Ushuaia, but this service is often cancelled.

LEAVING CHILE

There is an international departure tax of US$18, payable in US dollars or pesos.

Getting Around

AIR

LanChile, Ladeco and a slightly cheaper competitor, National Airlines, offer domestic services. On most flights, a small number of half-price seats are available.

Regional airlines include DAP (from Punta Arenas to Tierra del Fuego, the Falkland Islands and Antarctica), and Lassa and Líneas Aéreas Robinson Crusoe (to the Juan Fernández Islands). Recently opened ALTA Airlines provides connections between smaller cities. Air taxis connect settlements in the Aisén region. A new airline, Aerochile, offers cheap flights between Santiago and Antofagasta, Iquique and Arica.

Air Passes
For US$300, LanChile's 21-day Visit Chile Pass allows flights to and from selected airports either north or south of Santiago (or, for an additional fee, both). To include Easter Island, the pass costs US$1080. Available only to foreigners and nonresidents, passes must be purchased outside Chile. Ladeco's more flexible pass allows stopovers at Balmaceda/Coyhaique, but it does not fly to Easter Island.

Reservations & Timetables
Both Ladeco and LanChile have computerised booking services, accept phone reservations and publish detailed timetables.

Departure Tax
The domestic airport departure tax, about US$7, is usually included in the fare.

BUS
Long-distance buses are comfortable (sometimes luxurious), fast and punctual. They usually have toilets and either serve meals or make regular food stops. By European or North American standards, fares are a bargain, but they differ among companies. Promotions (ofertas) can reduce normal fares by half; ask for student discounts.

Most cities have a central terminal, but in a few towns, companies have separate offices. Except near holidays, advance booking is unnecessary.

Types of Buses
Long-distance buses are either *pullman* or sleepers, with extra leg room and reclining seats (salón cama). The latter cost about twice as much as ordinary buses, but merit consideration on long hauls.

On back roads, transport is slower and less frequent and the buses are older and more basic. They often lack reclining seats and may be packed with the local people and their produce. *Micros* are city buses.

TRAIN
Southbound trains connect Santiago with Temuco, continuing to Puerto Montt in summer only. Classes of service are *economía*, *salón* and *cama* (sleeper). Hardbacked economy seats, though very cheap, are uncomfortable; most travellers will prefer salón. The costlier cama class has upper and lower bunks.

Schedules change, so check an official timetable. Major destinations (with salón fares) include Concepción (US$13, nine hours), Temuco (US$17, 13 hours) and Puerto Montt (US$24, 20-plus hours).

Commuter trains run from Rancagua to Santiago, and from Los Andes and San Felipe to Viña del Mar and Valparaíso.

CAR & MOTORCYCLE
Operating a car is cheaper than in Europe but dearer than in the USA; the price of petrol (bencina) is about US$0.50 per litre, that of diesel fuel (gas-oil) rather less. There is little price difference between 93-octane (super) and 81-octane (común); unleaded petrol is available everywhere. Foreign drivers need an International or Inter-American Driving Permit.

The Automóvil Club Chileno, or ACCHI (☎ 212-5702), Avenida Vitacura 8620, Santiago, offers members of affiliated overseas clubs low-cost road service and towing, plus discounts on accommodation, camping, rental cars, tours and other services. ACCHI also has a tourist information service (☎ 225-3790) at Fidel Oteíza 1960.

Rental
To rent a car you must have a valid driver's licence, be at least 25 years of age and

present either a credit card or a large cash deposit.

The cheapest vehicles can be hired for about US\$27 per day plus US\$0.20 per km, plus insurance, petrol and tax. Weekend rates (about US\$113) or unlimited mileage weekly rates (US\$394) are better value.

BICYCLE

Racing bicycles are suitable for paved routes, but on gravelled roads, a mountain bike *(todo terreno)* is a better choice. Southwards from Temuco, be prepared for rain; north of Santiago, water is scarce. In some areas, the wind can slow your progress; north to south is generally easier than south to north. Motorists are usually courteous, but on narrow roads they can be a hazard.

HITCHING

Chile is one of the best countries on the continent for hitching. Vehicles are often packed with families but truck drivers can be helpful – try asking for rides at *servicentros* on the Panamericana. In Patagonia, where distances are great and vehicles few, expect long waits and carry warm, windproof, waterproof clothing. Also carry snacks and water, especially in the desert.

Along the Panamericana, hitching is fairly easy as far as Puerto Montt, but competition is heavy in summer. In the Atacama, you may wait for some time, but almost every lift will be a long one. Along the Camino Austral, vehicles are few, except from Coyhaique to Puerto Aisén.

Bear in mind, however, that although many travellers hitchhike, it is not a totally safe way of getting around. Just because hitching tips are included in this book doesn't mean hitching is recommended.

BOAT

Although buses cover parts of the Camino Austral between Puerto Montt and Coyhaique, it's easier to take a ferry from Puerto Montt or Chiloé to Chaitén or Puerto Chacabuco. For detailed information, see the individual sections.

Puerto Montt to Puerto Chacabuco

Navimag and Transmarchilay boat services sail from Puerto Montt, or nearby Pargua, to Puerto Chacabuco (the port of Coyhaique). Transmarchilay runs the tourist ship *Skorpios* and Navimag runs the ferry *Evangelistas* to Laguna San Rafael.

Puerto Montt to Puerto Natales

Navimag's *Puerto Edén* covers this route weekly in four days and three nights.

Chiloé to the Mainland

The most frequent connection is with Transmarchilay or Cruz del Sur ferries from Chacao, at the northern tip of the island, to Pargua, across the Canal de Chacao. There are other services with Transmarchilay from Quellón (on Chiloé) to Chaitén or Puerto Chacabuco (on the mainland).

Punta Arenas to Tierra del Fuego

There are frequent ferries from Punta Arenas to Porvenir.

LOCAL TRANSPORT
To/From the Airport

LanChile and Ladeco often provide an airport shuttle. In a few places, you will have to use public transport or a taxi.

Bus

Even small towns have extensive bus systems; buses are clearly numbered and usually carry a sign indicating their destination. Pay your fare and the driver will give you a ticket, which may be checked by an inspector.

Taxi

Most cabs are metered but fares vary. In some towns, such as Viña del Mar, cabs may cost twice as much as in Santiago. In others, such as Coquimbo, meters are infrequent, so it's wise to agree upon the fare in advance. Tipping is unnecessary, but round off the fare for convenience.

CHILE

Santiago & Middle Chile

Middle Chile comprises the Metropolitan Region, plus the regions of Valparaíso, O'Higgins, Maule and Biobío. Its fertile central valley, endowed with rich soils, a pleasant climate and snowmelt for irrigation, is ideal for cereals, fruit and vineyards.

SANTIAGO

Since the 1970s, Chile's capital has grown out and up. It continues to sprawl, while high-rises have sprouted in the downtown area and in Providencia, a suburb which may become the city's commercial and financial centre. With over four million inhabitants, Santiago is one of South America's largest cities.

History

Indians nearly obliterated Santiago six months after Pedro de Valdivia founded it in 1541. Even in the late 16th century, only 700 Spaniards and mestizos, plus Indian labourers and servants, inhabited its 200 adobe houses. Occasionally flooded by the Río Mapocho, it still lacked a safe water supply and communications between town and country were hazardous.

By the late 18th century, new dykes (tajamares) restrained the Mapocho, and improved roads carried increased commerce. By the 19th century, a railway linked the capital, with more than 100,000 inhabitants, to the port of Valparaíso.

Poverty and paternalistic fundos drove farm labourers and tenants north to the nitrate mines and then into the cities; from 1865 to 1875, Santiago's population rose from 115,000 to more than 150,000.

Industrialisation created jobs, but never enough to satisfy demand. In the 1960s, continued rural turmoil resulted in squatter settlements around Santiago. Planned decentralisation has eased the pressure, and regularisation, including granting of titles, has transformed many callampas, but they still contrast with affluent eastern suburbs like El Golf, Vitacura, La Reina, Las Condes and Lo Curro.

Orientation

Santiago's core is in a compact, triangular area bounded by the Río Mapocho in the north, the Vía Norte Sur in the west, and Avenida General O'Higgins (the Alameda) in the south. Key public buildings line the Plaza de Armas, from which the pedestrian Paseo Ahumada leads south. Paseo Huérfanos is a block south of the plaza.

The attractive Cerro Santa Lucía overlooks the Alameda near Plaza Baquedano. The other main park is Cerro San Cristóbal, north of Avenida Providencia. Between the park and the Río Mapocho, on either side of Avenida Pío Nono, is the lively and fashionable area of Bellavista. Parque Forestal is a verdant buffer between the city centre and residential areas.

Information

Tourist Offices Sernatur (☎ 236-1416), at Avenida Providencia 1550 (Metro: Manuel Montt), is open on weekdays from 9 am to 5 pm, and on Saturday from 9 am to 1 pm. English is spoken, and the office has maps and abundant leaflets on the entire country. There's another office at the airport.

The *kiosco de turismo* (municipal tourist kiosk; open from 9 am to 9 pm daily) at the intersection of Ahumada and Huérfanos is also very helpful. It distributes the monthly English-language publication *Santiago Tour* (US$1.50). On Tuesday and Wednesday it offers a worthwhile free walking tour that leaves from the kiosk; the time varies, so check in advance.

Both Sernatur offices and the kiosco de turismo provide a free pocket-size *Plano del Centro de Santiago*, a map of the city centre, Providencia and other inner suburbs, with a useful Metro diagram.

Golden Rule is a new bimonthly, professionally produced English-language entertainment and tourism guide available around town for about US$2. Another useful publication, often free despite its US$2 cover price, is the bilingual *Guiamérica*, which

CHILE

To La Serena &
Mendoza (Argentina)

Santiago

0   250   500 m

Río Mapocho

Carretera Panamericana Norte

Avenida Balmaceda

Av. Fermín Vivaceta

Rivera

Lastra

Avenida Mapocho

*Low Budget
Hotel Area*

General Mackenna

Avenida

10

11 ■ 12

Martínez de Rozas

Matucana

Riquelme

Norte-Sur

Rosas

San Pablo

San Martín

Rosas

Chacabuco

Cueto

General Bulnes

Ricardo Cumming

Maturana

Catedral

Plaza
Brasil

Almirante Barroso

Santa
Ana

39

Paseo

Huérfa

Parque
Quinta
Normal

40

Huérfanos

García Reyes

75

74   73

Cienfuegos

Avenida Portales

76

Prieto

78

77

Erasmo Escala

Brasil

Los
Héroes

Avenida General O'Higgins (Alameda)

República

Cumming

Vergara

San Ignacio

To Airport

Estación
Central

ULA

Avenida República

Carrera

Latorre

Dieciocho

Ejército Libertador

Avenida Norte-Sur

Toesca

U de
Santiago

97

Sazle

Molina

Avenida España

96

101

Gorbea

98

99

100

Avenida Exposición

Avenida Grajales

Toesca

Gay

Av. 5 de Abril

To Parque
O'Higgins

CHILE

To Casa de la Cultura,
Tupahue, Enoteca &
Pedro de Valdivia

Cerro San
Cristóbal

Parque
Metropolitano

To Hotel Sheraton
San Cristóbal

Los Olivos

Echeverría

Juárez

Dominica

Manzano

Río de Janeiro

Dávila Baeza

Santa Filomena

Lillo

Andrés Bello

Dardignac

Avenida Perú

Loreto

Bombero Núñez

Purísima

Pío Nono

Constitución

Lagarrigue

Mallinkrodt

Concha

Bellavista

Santa María

Avenida Andrés Bello

Parque
Gran
Bretaña

Calicanto

Avenida Balmaceda

Esmeralda

21 de Mayo

San Antonio

Maciver

Miraflores

Mosqueto

Avenida Providencia

Avenida Condell

Rancagua

JM Caro

Parque
Forestal

J M de la Barra

Merced

Rosal

Lastarria

Villavicencio

Baquedano

Plaza
Baquedano

Cerro
Santa Lucía

Purísima

U Católica

Marcoleta

Moneda

Agustinas

Santa Lucía

Diagonal

Paraguay

Rancagua

Avenida Francisco Bilbao

Avenida General O'Higgins (Alameda)

U de
Chile

Calle París

Curicó

General Jofre

Marín

Encalada

Avenida Seminario

Ovalle

Tarapacá

San Diego

Avenida Bulnes

Arturo Prat

Ramírez

Santa Rosa

Carmen

Santa Victoria

Santa Isabel

Argomedo

Avenida Vicuña Mackenna

Avenida General Bustamente

Lord Cochrane

Nataniel Cox

San Francisco

Cóndor

Eyzaguirre

Serrano

Lira

Tocornal

Avenida Portugal

Avenida 10 de Julio

Coquimbo

CHILE

PLACES TO STAY
10 Hotel Souvenir
11 Hotel Caribe
12 Hotel Pudahuel
13 Hotels Retiro, Colonial, Florida & San Felipe
15 Nuevo Hotel
16 Hotel Cervantes
21 Residencial Santo Domingo
26 Hotel Principado
29 Holiday Inn Crowne Plaza
30 Hostal del Parque
38 Hotel España
39 Casa Familiar Señora Marta
41 Hotel Panamericano
42 Hotel Metrópoli
53 Hotel Tupahue
54 Hotel São Paulo
56 Hotel Monte Carlo
58 Hotel Riviera
60 Hotel Santa Lucía
65 Hotel Ritz
66 Hotel Gran Palace
71 Hotel Carrera
75 Hotel Tokio
76 Youth Hostel
82 Hotel Conquistador
84 Hotel El Libertador
85 Hotel Galerías
91 Hotel París
92 Residencial Londres
96 Residencial Eliana
101 Residencial Gloria

PLACES TO EAT
6 El Caramaño
7 La Venezia
8 Restaurant Arabe Karim
17 Bar Central
18 Mercado Central
31 Bontón Oriental
32 Da Carla
33 Kan-Thu
50 Chez Henry
62 Pizza Napoli
63 Pastelería Tout Paris
64 Le Due Torri
69 El Novillero
83 El Naturista

OTHER
1 Estación Cumbre
2 Santuario de la Inmaculada Concepción
3 Jardín Zoológico
4 Teatro La Feria
5 La Chascona (Museo Neruda)
9 Estación Mapocho
14 Sala Agustín Sire
19 Templo de Santo Domingo
20 Posada del Corregidor
22 Casa Manso de Velasco
23 Instituto Goethe
24 Palacio de Bellas Artes
25 Teatro Universidad de Chile
27 Parque Manuel Rodríguez
28 Argentine Consulate
30 Instituto Chileno-Francés
31 Teatro La Comedia
34 Museo Histórico Nacional
35 Main Post Office
36 CTC (Telephone)
37 Palacio Edwards
39 National Airlines
40 Museo Nacional de Historia Natural
43 Ladeco
44 Entel (Telephone)
45 Catedral
46 Municipalidad (Town Hall)
47 Museo Chileno de Arte Precolombino
48 Kiosco de Turismo
49 Plaza de Armas
51 Museo de Santiago, Casa Colorada
52 CTC (Telephone)
55 Feria Chilena del Libro
57 Bar Berry
59 LanChile
61 Teatro Municipal
67 Telex Chile (Telegraph & Telex)
68 Post Office & CTC (Telephone)
70 Plaza de la Constitución
72 American Express
73 Instituto Chileno-Norteamericano de Cultura
74 Airport Buses
77 Artequín
78 Terminal de Buses Los Héroes
79 Palacio de la Moneda
80 Bolsa de Comercio
81 Club de la Unión
86 Biblioteca Nacional
87 Universidad Católica
88 Posta Central (Medical)
89 Feria Artesanal Santa Lucía
90 Iglesia de San Francisco
93 Universidad de Chile
94 Librería Rivano
95 CONAF
97 Estación Central (Central Railway Station)
98 Terminal de Buses Alameda
99 Terminal de Buses Sur
100 Terminal Borja

CHILE

lists up-market hotels and travel agencies but also has articles on out-of-the-way places and unusual topics.

Money Many cambios on Agustinas between Bandera and Ahumada change cash and travellers' cheques. Some open on Saturday morning.

American Express (☎ 672-2156), Agusti-

nas 1360, will exchange travellers' cheques for US dollars cash. Visa (☎ 672-8518) and MasterCard (☎ 695-2023) are both at Morandé 315. With Visa or MasterCard you can get cash advances from Redbanc ATMs.

Post & Communications The main post office, on the Plaza de Armas, handles poste restante and also has a philatelic desk. For long-distance calls, go to Entel, Paseo Huérfanos 1133, or CTC's central office, Moneda 1151. Santiago's telephone code is 2.

Foreign Embassies The following countries maintain embassies in Santiago:

Argentina
Vicuña Mackenna 41 (☎ 222-8977)
Australia
Gertrudis Echeñique 420 (☎ 228-5065)
Bolivia
Avenida Santa María 2796 (☎ 232-8180)
Canada
10th floor, Ahumada 11 (☎ 696-2256)
France
Avenida Condell 65 (☎ 225-1030)
Germany
7th floor, Agustinas 785 (☎ 633-5031)
New Zealand
Isidora Goyenechea 3516 (☎ 231-4204)
Peru
Andrés Bello 1751 (☎ 235-2356, fax 235-8139)
UK
3rd floor, Avenida El Bosque Norte 0125 (☎ 231-3737)
USA
Andrés Bello 2800 (☎ 232-2600)

Cultural Centres The restored Estación Mapocho (☎ 697-2990), on the south bank of the river, has art exhibits, a theatre, a crafts shop and a café. The Centro de Extensión de la Universidad Católica, Alameda 390, regularly presents artistic and photographic exhibits.

The Instituto Chileno-Norteamericano de Cultura (☎ 696-3215), Moneda 1467, also has frequent exhibits on various topics. Its library carries North American newspapers and magazines, and shows free films (usually in video format). The Instituto Goethe (☎ 638-3185), Esmeralda 650, often offers free events, exhibits and very inexpensive intensive courses in Spanish.

Travel Agencies For good prices on air tickets, try Miguel Gallegos at Latour (☎ 225-2883), Fidel Oteiza 1933. Several agencies operate adventure or nature excursions; ask the Sernatur office for the list of agencies that belong to CATA (the associa-tion of adventure-tourism agencies), since they are the most dependable.

Bookshops The best-stocked bookshop is Feria Chilena del Libro, Huérfanos 623. Librería Albers, Merced 820, carries books and magazines in German and English, including Lonely Planet guides.

Librería Rivano, San Diego 119, Local 7, has a fine selection on Chilean history (not all displayed to the public). Chile Ilustrado (☎ 235-8145), Avenida Providencia 1652, Local 6, specialises in rare books on history, anthropology and folklore. In the same complex, a smaller shop, known simply as Books, sells used English paperbacks.

Two kiosks at the junction of Paseos Ahumada and Huérfanos carry North American and European newspapers and magazines. If a paper is more than a few days old, haggle over the price.

Emergency For medical emergencies, contact the Posta Central (☎ 634-1650), at Portugal 125 (Metro: Universidad Católica). The national emergency number is ☎ 133.

Things to See

Walking Tour Santiago's **Mercado Central**, a wrought-iron structure built in 1872 at Balmaceda and Puente, is a great place for lunch or an early dinner. The **Posada del Corregidor** (1780), Esmeralda 732, is a whitewashed adobe with an attractive wooden balcony; the **Casa Manso de Velasco**, Santo Domingo 899, is similar. To the west, at Santo Domingo 961, is the massive **Templo de Santo Domingo** (1808).

Santiago's historical centre is the Plaza de Armas, flanked by the main post office, the **Museo Histórico Nacional** and the colonial **Catedral**. At its south-west corner is Paseo Ahumada, where hawkers peddle everything from shampoo to seat belts. Buskers of diverse style and quality congregate here in the evening.

At Morandé 441 stands the former **Congreso Nacional**, now the Foreign Ministry. The nearby **Palacio Edwards**, Catedral 1187, belonged to one of Chile's elite fami-

CHILE

lies. The **Museo Chileno de Arte Pre- colombino**, at Bandera 361, was formerly the colonial customs house, built in 1805. This museum chronicles 4500 years of pre-Columbian civilisations. It's open Tuesday to Saturday from 10 am to 6 pm, and on Sunday from 10 am to 1 pm. Admission, usually US$0.85, is free on Sunday.

The late-colonial **Palacio de La Moneda** fills a block between Plaza de la Constitución and Plaza de la Libertad. Construction of this neoclassical mint began in 1788 in a flood-prone site near the Mapocho, but was completed at its present location in 1805; it later became the presidential palace. After the coup of 1973, it required extensive restoration. Other notable buildings near La Moneda are the **Bolsa de Comercio** (stock exchange), at La Bolsa 64, and the **Club de la Unión**, at Alameda 1091.

Just across the Alameda are the **Universidad de Chile** and the colonial **Iglesia de San Francisco**. Farther up the Alameda is the monolithic **Biblioteca Nacional**, at the corner of MacIver. Also of interest is the **Teatro Municipal**, Agustinas 794.

Museo de Santiago This intriguing museum in the historic Casa Colorada documents the capital's history with maps, paintings, dioramas and colonial dress. At Merced 860, it's open Tuesday to Saturday from 10 am to 4 pm, and on Sunday and holidays from 10 am to 3 pm. Admission is US$0.85.

Salvador Allende's Grave Many pilgrims visit Allende's grave, at the Cementerio General, as well as the wall commemorating those who disappeared during the dictatorship of the 1970s and 1980s.

Cerro Santa Lucía Covered with gardens, footpaths and fountains, Santa Lucía (Huelén to the Mapuche Indians) is a hilltop sanctuary from the congested city centre. An easy walk from the centre, it has a reputation for muggings at night and is much safer during the day.

La Chascona (Museo Neruda) The Fundación Neruda (☎ 777-8741) maintains this eclectic Bellavista house in a shady cul-de-sac at Márquez de la Plata 0195. Call for reservations for very thorough, hour-long tours (US$2.50) or drop by if you're in the neighbourhood. It opens Tuesday to Sunday from 10 am to 1 pm and from 2 to 6 pm. The *fundación* also arranges tours of Neruda's houses at Isla Negra and Valparaíso.

Cerro San Cristóbal North of the Mapocho, 860-metre San Cristóbal towers above Santiago. Reached by funicular railway, *teleférico* (cable car), bus or foot, it's part of **Parque Metropolitano**, the capital's largest open space.

The funicular from Plaza Caupolicán, at the north end of Pío Nono, operates daily from 10 am to 8.30 pm. A short walk from the Terraza Bellavista, the 2000-metre teleférico departs from the Estación Cumbre and connects San Cristóbal to Avenida Pedro de Valdivia Norte (a short hike from Metro Pedro de Valdivia). For about US$4, the funicular-teleférico combination is a good way to orientate yourself to Santiago's complex geography.

Places to Stay – bottom end

Hostels Ten minutes from the city centre, the newly opened and highly recommended *youth hostel* (☎ 671-8532), Cienfuegos 151, is just two blocks from the Los Héroes Metro station. The basic but comfortable rooms have lockers, and are well heated. There is hot water all day. The whole place is immaculately clean, with a very pleasant common room. They offer an inexpensive breakfast and lunch, a laundry service and will look after your luggage. It is a great place to meet Chileans and foreigners. Charges are US$12 for nonmembers (after six days you automatically become a member) and US$10 for members.

Hotels, Hospedajes & Residenciales Budget accommodation is abundant, but be selective: lodgings differ much more in quality than in price. The small and cosy

Residencial Eliana (☎ 672-6100), Grajales 2013, and Residencial Gloria (☎ 698-8315), Avenida Latorre 449, both charge US$8.

In the main budget hotel zone, a seedy area near the Terminal de Buses Norte (now closed), accommodation ranges from squalid to acceptable. Single women may wish to avoid General Mackenna, a hang-out for prostitutes. The labyrinthine Hotel Caribe (☎ 696-6681), San Martín 851, is good value at US$7 per person with shared bath and hot showers. Though popular, it's large and there's usually a room, though not always a single. Rivalling the Caribe is the more central and slightly cheaper Nuevo Hotel (☎ 671-5698), on the corner of San Pablo and Morandé. Various readers liked Hotel Pudahuel, San Pablo 1417-19; it's an old, beautiful European-style building with large, bright rooms.

Around the Alameda A better area is the Barrio París Londres, south of the Alameda, near Iglesia San Francisco. Residencial Londres (☎ 638-2215), at Londres 54, is great value at US$11/25 for a single/double with hot water; it has clean, secure rooms and pleasant staff, but it fills up quickly and singles are few.

At Hotel Paris (☎ 639-4037), around the corner at Calle París 813, doubles cost US$23. Readers have recommended the Residencial Tabita Gutiérrez (☎ 671-5700) at Príncipe de Gales 83-85, a quiet lane near Moneda and Amunátegui. This clean place is run by a friendly family who store your luggage at no charge while you are away, and include breakfast in the price for those staying more than two days. It charges US$15/22 a single/double with shared bath.

Near the Plaza Residencial Santo Domingo (☎ 639-6733), Santo Domingo 735, is very central and has singles for US$9. Also convenient is Hotel España (☎ 696-6066), at Morandé 510, with clean but stark singles/doubles for US$19/25. West of the plaza is the family-run Residencial del Norte (☎ 695-1876), Catedral 2207, charging US$10 per person.

Places to Stay – middle
Mid-range hotels are generally better value. The central Hotel Cervantes (☎ 696-5318), Morandé 631, has rooms with private bath at US$34/37 for a single/double. Some rooms are a bit cramped but others are spacious and bright. Hotel Tokio (☎ 698-4500), at Almirante Barroso 160, is good value at US$30/40.50. It has pleasant gardens and an English-speaking owner who exchanges books with guests.

One highly recommended place is the centrally located Hotel Metropoli (☎ 672-3987), Sótero del Río 465, which has rooms for US$36/44 with private bath. At the friendly Hotel Monte Carlo (☎ 639-2945), Victoria Subercaseaux 209, rooms are small but cheery, all with private baths, but beware of street noise. Rather quieter is Hotel Principado (☎ 222-8142), at Arturo Buhrle 015, just off Vicuña Mackenna (Metro: Baquedano), at US$57/73.

One reader thought Hotel Santa Lucía (☎ 639-8201), at Huérfanos 779, 4th floor, far better value than the prestigious Hotel Carrera (see below). Attractive rooms are US$55/66 with TV, telephone, safety deposit box, fridge and private bath. It is possible to reserve the quieter interior rooms that face the garden on short notice.

Places to Stay – top end
Hotel Aloha (☎ 233-2230), Francisco Noguera 146 in Providencia (Metro: Pedro de Valdivia), with doubles for US$146, has been praised. At the venerable Hotel Carrera (☎ 698-2011), Teatinos 180, rates start at US$236/248 for singles/doubles. One reader complained of an erratic hot-water supply, but affluent activists might relish the room in which, in 1985, deadly serious opponents of the dictatorship aimed a time-delay bazooka at General Pinochet's office. The recoil was too strong for the photo tripod and the shell destroyed the room's interior.

Places to Eat
Restaurants range from basic (around the bus terminals) and better (around Huérfanos and Ahumada, the Plaza de Armas and the

CHILE

Alameda) to elegant (in Providencia, Las Condes and Bellavista). Turistel's brochure *A la Carta*, sold in kiosks, lists restaurants by type of cuisine and has fine location maps.

There's a string of cheap stand-up places in the south arcade of the Plaza de Armas, where the highly regarded *Chez Henry* is no longer cheap, but neither is it outrageous – their pastel de choclo (about US$10) is the only meal you'll need all day. They also offer takeaway food.

For a wholesome but inexpensive breakfast, try *Savory Centre*, Huérfanos 840. The modest exterior at *Bontón Oriental*, Merced 345, camouflages delicacies like a very fine apple strudel. For good, cheap espresso coffee and cocoa, go to stand-up bars like *Café Haití* and *Café Caribe*, on Paseo Ahumada.

Many readers have recommended *Bar Central*, San Pablo 1063, for seafood. *El Caramaño* at Purísima 257, serves excellent Chilean food in a non-conformist setting. Carnivores can try *El Novillero*, Moneda 1145, while vegetarians can munch at the moderately priced *El Naturista*, Moneda 846, or *El Vegetariano*, Huérfanos 827, Local 18. There are fine lunch specials at *Silvestre*, Huérfanos 965.

For seafood, visit the historic *Mercado Central*, a few blocks north of the plaza. The tables among the fruit and vegetable stands have a great atmosphere, but the smaller, cheaper places on the periphery are just as good. *Donde Augusto* is a classic at the market.

Bellavista, north of the Mapocho, is a great dining area. Eateries in Pablo Neruda's old haunt include *La Venezia*, Pío Nono 200; and *Restaurant Arabe Karim*. South of the Mapocho, try *Pérgola de la Plaza*, at Lastarria 305-321, behind the Hostal del Parque, for wine and pastries.

For pasta, try *Da Carla*, at MacIver 577, or *San Marco*, at Huérfanos 618. More than one reader found *Le Due Torri*, San Antonio 258, to be among the best value in town. French cuisine is the rule at *Les Assassins*, Merced 297.

For ice cream, go to *Sebastián*, Andrés de Fuenzalida 26, in Providencia (Metro: Pedro de Valdivia), or *Coppelic*, on Avenida Providencia. One reader voted for *Dolce Bravissimo* on Paseo Ahumada 315, with its 48 natural flavours. *Bravissimo*, Providencia 1406, is a good place for tea and pastries.

Entertainment

For music and drinks Santiago has several pubs in the Bellavista area and in Providencia and Las Condes. *Berry*, at Rosas and Lastarria, is a reasonably priced place to meet local people, as is *Geopub* at Encomenderos 83 (Metro: Tobalaba).

The cinema district is along Paseo Huérfanos and nearby streets. Many cinemas have half-price discounts on Wednesday. The Universidad Católica's *Centro de Extensión*, Alameda 390, shows low-priced international films on a regular basis, as does *Cine Arte Normandie*, Tarapacá 1181.

Things to Buy

Crafts and gemstones on sale in Santiago include lapis lazuli, pottery and copperware, plus carved wooden *moai* (statues) from Easter Island. The Feria Artesanal La Merced, on the corner of Merced and MacIver, is a good place for an overview, but there are two well-stocked shops in the gallery at Moneda 1025. Also try Claustro del 900, in an old convent, at Portugal 351. One reader recommended Cooperativa Almacén Campesino, at Purísima 303 in Bellavista, for Indian ceramics, weaving and baskets. On weekends there is a good crafts market on Pío Nono in Bellavista.

Several readers enjoyed the market at Los Graneros del Alba, Avenida Apoquindo 8600; take the Metro to Escuela Militar and catch a bus out to Avenida Apoquindo. For Latin American and Andean music try Cassetería Altiplano in the Artefería Santa Lucía, Alameda 510.

Getting There & Away

Air Nearly every visitor to Chile arrives in Santiago or passes through the capital at some time. The international airport (Aeropuerto Internacional Arturo Merino Benítez;

☎ 601-9001) is 26 km from Santiago, at Pudahuel. Some domestic flights (including those to the Juan Fernández Islands) leave from suburban Aeropuerto Nacional Cerrillos (☎ 557-2640).

International airlines with offices in Santiago include:

Aerolíneas Argentinas
    Moneda 765 (☎ 639-3922)
AeroPerú
    Fidel Oteíza 1953, 5th floor (☎ 274-3434)
Aerovías DAP
    Luis Thayer Ojeda 0180, Oficina 1304 (☎ 334-9672, fax 334-5843)
American Airlines
    Huérfanos 1199 (☎ 671-3553)
British Airways
    I Goyenechea 2934, suite 302 (☎ 232-9560)
Canadian Airlines International
    Huérfanos 669, suite 311 (☎ 639-3058)
Ladeco
    Huérfanos 1157 (☎ 639-5053)
    Pedro de Valdivia 0210, Providencia (☎ 639-5053)
LanChile
    Agustinas 640 (☎ 632-3442)
    Pedro de Valdivia 0139, Providencia (☎ 232-3448)
LAB (Lloyd Aéreo Boliviano)
    Moneda 1170 (☎ 695-1290)
National
    Huérfanos 725, suite 3B (☎ 632-8040)
    Pedro de Valdivia 041, Providencia (☎ 252-0300)
Transportes Aéreos Robinson Crusoe
    Monumento 2570, Maipú (☎ 531-4343)

LanChile and Ladeco are the main domestic carriers, but there are also two budget airlines (National and Aerochile).

Bus – domestic The Terminal de Buses Norte has closed and all northbound buses leave from the Terminal Borja, at Alameda 3250 (Metro: Estación Central). It's reached by walking through the Feria Persa on the west side of the train station, and is not obvious from the Alameda itself. Most southbound buses depart from the Terminal de Buses Sur (☎ 779-1385), Alameda 3800, one block west of Metro station Universidad de Santiago, but some leave from the Terminal de Buses Los Héroes, on Pretot near the Alameda. The Terminal de Buses Alameda, on the corner of Alameda and Jotabeche, mainly serves Valparaíso and Viña del Mar.

Sample fares (in US dollars) and journey times from Santiago are:

Antofagasta	$30	18 hours
Arica	$40	28 hours
Chillán	$8	6 hours
Concepción	$9	8 hours
Copiapó	$23	11 hours
La Serena	$16	7 hours
Puerto Montt	$19	16 hours
Punta Arenas	$51	60 hours
Temuco	$15	11 hours
Valparaíso	$3	2 hours

Bus – international Most international buses use the Terminal Sur. Argentina is the most frequent destination from here; Mendoza (US$25) is about seven hours by bus. Other typical fares include Bariloche (US$40), Córdoba (US$60) and Buenos Aires (US$70).

Taxi colectivos to Mendoza are much quicker and only slightly more expensive than buses, and drivers may stop on request for photo opportunities. Outside the peak season, try haggling for discounts on tickets.

Train Southbound trains leave from the Estación Central (☎ 689-5199), Alameda 3322 (Metro: Estación Central). Only in summer is there a service south of Temuco. The station is open daily from 7 am to 11 pm. If the Estación Central is inconvenient, book at the Venta de Pasajes (☎ 639-8247), in the Galería Libertador, Alameda 853, Local 21; it's open weekdays from 8.30 am to 7 pm, and on Saturday from 9 am to 1 pm. For sample fares to some destinations, see this chapter's Getting Around section.

Getting Around
To/From the Airport The Aeropuerto Internacional Arturo Merino Benítez is in Pudahuel, 26 km west of central Santiago. Tour Express (☎ 671-7380), Moneda 1529, has about 30 buses to the airport daily (US$2, half an hour), running from 6.30 am to 9 pm.

Metropuerto provides a similar and slightly cheaper service from Los Héroes Metro station. Navett (☎ 695-6868) offers door-to-door service between Pudahuel and any part of Santiago for US$6; call a day ahead. Negotiated cab fares are about US$10 (if your Spanish is good).

The Aeropuerto Nacional Cerrillos, for domestic flights, can be reached by bus or taxi colectivo from the Alameda.

Bus Buses go to all parts of Santiago, but it takes a while to learn the system – check destination signs or ask waiting passengers. Fares are usually a flat rate of around US$0.35.

Metro The Metro operates Monday to Saturday from 6.30 am to 10.30 pm, and on Sunday and public holidays from 8 am to 10.30 pm. On Línea 1, Dirección Las Condes heads toward Escuela Militar in the eastern suburbs, while Dirección Pudahuel goes to San Pablo. (It does *not* reach the international airport.) On the north-south Línea 2, Dirección Centro goes to Puente Cal y Canto near the Mapocho, while Dirección La Cisterna heads towards the southern suburb of Lo Ovalle. Los Héroes, on the Alameda, is the only transfer station. The new Línea 5 is due to open between Baquedano, on Línea 1, and La Florida, in early 1997.

Standard fares are US$0.35 on all lines, but they change at off-peak hours. A multi-ride *boleto valor*, available at a small discount, saves time.

Taxi Colectivo Taxi colectivos carry up to five passengers on fixed routes and are quicker than buses. The fare is about US$0.70 within the city limits; to outlying suburbs, it is dearer.

Taxi Santiago has abundant metered taxis; fares vary but may soon be standardised. Most drivers are honest, courteous and helpful but a few take roundabout routes and a handful have 'funny' meters. Flagfall costs about US$0.40.

Car For details of car-rental rates, see this chapter's Getting Around section. Less well-known companies tend to be cheapest. Several well-known companies have offices in the international airport terminal. Offices in the city include:

Automóvil Club de Chile (ACCHI)
  Vitacura 8620 (☎ 274-6261)
Avis
  San Pablo 9900 (☎ 331-0121)
Budget
  Bilbao 3028 (☎ 204-9091)
Hertz
  Costanera 1469 (☎ 235-9666)

AROUND SANTIAGO
Wineries
The nearest winery is **Viña Santa Carolina** (☎ 238-2855), Rodrigo de Araya 1341, in Ñuñoa. The sprawling capital has displaced the vineyards, but the historic *casco* (big house) and *bodegas* (cellars) are open on weekends. Also within city limits is **Viña Cousiño Macul**; tours of the bodegas take place daily at 11 am. Take any bus or taxi colectivo out along Américo Vespucio Sur to Avenida Quilín.

At Pirque, south-east of Santiago, **Viña Concha y Toro** (☎ 850-3123) is Chile's largest winery. Tours take place daily, except Sunday, at 10 am to 1 pm, and 3 to 6 pm. From Plaza Italia, on the corner of Tarapacá and San Francisco, taxi colectivos cost about US$1.

Viña Undurraga (☎ 817-2308), 34 km south-west of Santiago on the old road to Melipilla, is open on weekdays from 9.30 am to noon and from 2 to 4 pm. Take Buses Peñaflor (☎ 776-1025) from the Terminal de Buses Borja, Alameda 3250.

Pomaire
In this small, dusty village near Melipilla, master potters produce fine and remarkably inexpensive ceramics. Take Buses Melipilla from the Terminal Borja, Alameda 3250.

Reserva Nacional Río Clarillo
Río Clarillo is a scenic tributary canyon of the Cajón del Maipo, south-east of Santiago.

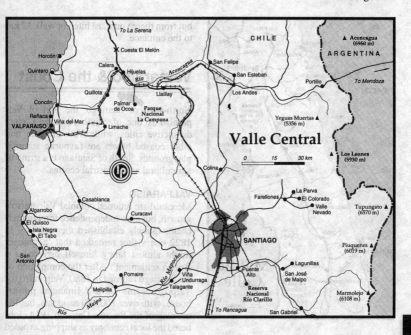

Take a taxi colectivo to Puente Alto's Plaza de Armas, where Buses LAC leave every hour to within about two km of the reserve. Entrance fees from January to March are US$4.

Ski Resorts

Chilean ski resorts are open from June to October. Rates are lower early and late in the season. The closest sites are **Farellones-El Colorado**, 40 km east of the capital, with 18 lifts (mostly drag, four chairs); and **La Parva**, 55 km from Santiago, with 13 lifts (10 drag, three chairs) and good powder snow. Centro de Ski El Colorado (☎ 246-3344, fax 206-4078), Avenida Apoquindo 4900, Local 48 in the Santiago suburb of Las Condes, offers day excursions with return transport, rental equipment and lift tickets for US$65.

The site of several downhill speed records, **Portillo** (☎ 231-3411, fax 231-7164), Roger de Flor 2911, Santiago, is 145 km north-east

of Santiago. *Hotel Portillo* is not cheap but the price includes all meals, eight days of lift tickets, and taxes. The hotel's cheaper packages involve bunks and shared bath and run at US$695 per person per week.

Would-be skiers on modest budgets could try getting there on the buses run by Manzur Expediciones (☎ 777-4284), Sótero del Río 475, suite 507, Santiago, renting equipment in Santiago rather than at the ski resorts. **Valle Nevado**, 60 km east of Santiago, has 26 runs with more challenging slopes (nine lifts). Skitotal (☎ 246-6881, fax 246-0156), Apoquindo 4900, Local 39, has daily shuttle buses to Farellones and Valle Nevado, and also rents equipment at reasonable prices.

Parque Nacional La Campana

Darwin's ascent of 1840-metre Cerro La Campana was one of his most memorable experiences. In the coast range, this park occupies 8000 hectares of jagged scrubland which shelters the rare Chilean palm (with

but from there you must hitch or walk 12 km to the entrance.

Valparaíso & the Coast

North-west of Santiago, the port of Valparaíso is one of South America's most distinctive cities, while Viña del Mar and other coastal towns are favourite summer playgrounds. South of Santiago is a string of agricultural and industrial centres.

VALPARAISO

Mercantilism retarded colonial Valparaíso's growth, but after independence foreign merchants quickly established themselves – in 1822 one visitor remarked that 'a stranger might almost fancy himself arrived at a British settlement'. After the completion of the Santiago railroad in 1880, Valparaíso (or Valpo) became Chile's financial powerhouse, with over 100,000 residents, but the opening of the Panama Canal in 1914 clobbered the local economy as shipping avoided the Cape Horn route. The Great Depression was a further calamity as it reduced the demand for minerals until after WW II.

The capital of the Fifth Region and site of the National Congress, Valparaíso (population 300,000) is 120 km north-west of Santiago and is the second-biggest city in Chile. It is an administrative centre and its key industries are food processing, and mining and fruit exports. It depends less on tourism than neighbouring Viña del Mar, but many vacationers arrive from nearby beach towns. The navy also plays an important economic role here.

Orientation

Probably only a lifetime resident can fathom Valparaíso's complex geography. In its congested centre of sinuous cobbled streets and irregular intersections, most major streets parallel the shoreline, which curves north toward Viña del Mar. Avenida Errázuriz runs the length of the waterfront, alongside the railway. Behind and above the city centre,

edible fruit) and the northernmost remaining stands of southern beech.

Palmar de Ocoa is the northern entrance to the park. The saddle of the **Portezuelo de Granizo**, a two-hour climb through a palm-studded canyon, offers some of the views which impressed Darwin. Camping is possible (US$6) but water is limited and there is a risk of bushfires, especially in summer and autumn.

Getting There & Away Sectors Granizo and Cajón Grande can be reached by Línea Ciferal from Valparaíso and Viña del Mar, every half-hour in summer. AGDABUS leaves every 20 minutes from Limache and Olmué. Both involve a one-km walk to the entrance.

For Sector Ocoa, any northbound bus from Santiago will drop you at Hijuelas (watch for the poorly marked turn-off just before the bridge over the Río Aconcagua), the hills are a warren of steep footpaths, zigzag roads and blind alleys where even the best map often fails.

Information

Tourist Offices The Municipalidad (town hall), Condell 1490, is open weekdays from 8.30 am to 2 pm and 3 to 5 pm. The well-informed staff at the kiosco de turismo on Muelle Prat have limited brochures but are helpful. The kiosk is open on Friday from 4 to 8 pm and on weekends from 10.30 am to 2.30 pm and 4 to 8 pm. Another office at the bus terminal (☎ 21-3246) is open in summer only.

Money To exchange money try Inter Cambio on Plaza Sotomayor, or Exprinter at Prat 895.

Post & Communications The main post office is on Prat at Plaza Sotomayor. CTC has offices at Esmeralda 1054, Pedro Montt 2023 and the bus terminal. Valparaíso's telephone code is 32.

Consulates The Argentine Consulate (☎ 21-3691) is at Blanco 890, Oficina 204, the Peruvian Consulate (☎ 25-3403) is at Blanco 1215 and the British Consulate (☎ 25-6117) is at Blanco 725, Oficina 26.

Medical Services The Hospital Carlos van Buren (☎ 25-4074) is at Avenida Colón 2454.

Dangers & Annoyances The hillside neighbourhoods have a reputation for harbouring thieves and robbers. Also watch for suspicious characters and diversions in the area west of Plaza Sotomayor and even in the city centre. Avoid poorly lit areas at night, and if possible, walk with a companion.

Valparaíso has the highest rate of AIDS in Chile, associated with the sex industry in this major port.

Hills of Valparaíso

On a sunny Sunday, you can spend hours riding Valparaíso's 16 *ascensores* (funiculars) and strolling the back alleys of its picturesque hillside neighbourhoods. Some ascensores, built from 1883 to 1916, are remarkable feats of engineering – **Ascensor Polanco**, on Avenida Argentina, is more like an elevator than a funicular.

One of the best areas for urban explorers is Cerro Concepción, reached by **Ascensor Concepción** on the corner of Esmeralda and Gómez Carreño, across from the **Reloj Turri**, a landmark clock tower. Cerro Alegre, behind Plaza Sotomayor, is reached by **Ascensor El Peral**, near the **Tribunales** (law courts), just off the plaza.

Things to See

The **Museo Municipal de Bellas Artes** (fine arts museum, also known as the Palacio Baburizza) is on the Paseo Yugoeslavo (take Ascensor El Peral). It is open daily, except Monday.

The **Museo del Mar Lord Cochrane** (1842), overlooking the harbour on Calle Merlet near Plaza Sotomayor (take Ascensor Cordillera), housed Chile's first observatory and now displays a good collection of model ships; it's open daily (except Monday) from 10 am to 6 pm. The **Museo Naval y Marítimo**, at a hilltop location on Paseo 21 de Mayo (take Ascensor Artillería from Plaza Aduana), focuses on the War of the Pacific. It's open daily from 10 am to 12.30 pm and from 3 to 6 pm.

Muelle Prat, at the foot of Plaza Sotomayor, is lively on weekends, with a good crafts market. Do not photograph naval vessels on harbour tours (US$1.50).

Chile's imposing new **Congreso Nacional** (National Congress) is at the junction of Avenidas Pedro Montt and Argentina, opposite the bus terminal.

La Sebastiana (☎ 25-6606), Neruda's least well-known house, at Pasaje Collado 1, Cerro Florida, reflects the poet's eclectic taste, his sense of humour, and his passion for ships. It is open daily (except Monday) from 10.30 am to 2.30 pm and from 3.30 to 6 pm. Admission is US$2.50. Take the bus Línea O Verde Mar on Avenida Argentina to the 6900 block of Avenida Alemania.

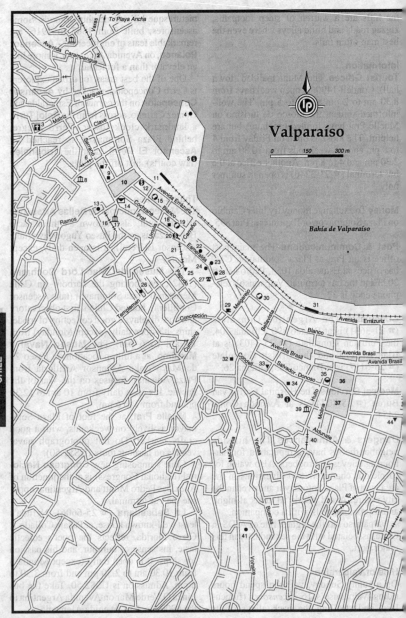

Valparaíso

0   150   300 m

Bahía de Valparaíso

To Playa Ancha

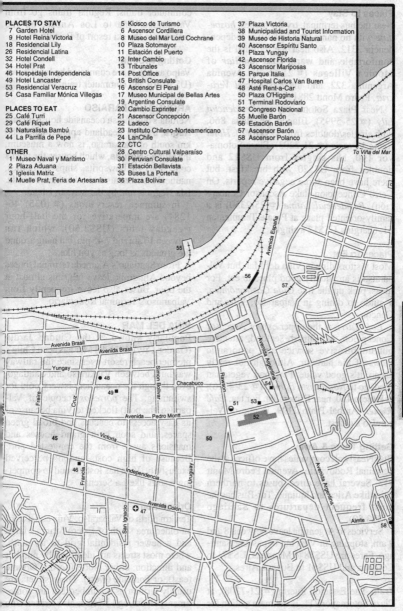

PLACES TO STAY
7 Garden Hotel
9 Hotel Reina Victoria
18 Residencial Lily
26 Residencial Latina
32 Hotel Condell
34 Hotel Prat
46 Hospedaje Independencia
49 Hotel Lancaster
53 Residencial Veracruz
54 Casa Familiar Mónica Villegas

PLACES TO EAT
25 Café Turri
29 Café Riquet
33 Naturalista Bambú
44 La Parrilla de Pepe

OTHER
1 Museo Naval y Marítimo
2 Plaza Aduana
3 Iglesia Matriz
4 Muelle Prat, Feria de Artesanías

5 Kiosco de Turismo
6 Ascensor Cordillera
8 Museo del Mar Lord Cochrane
10 Plaza Sotomayor
11 Estación del Puerto
12 Inter Cambio
13 Tribunales
14 Post Office
15 British Consulate
16 Ascensor El Peral
17 Museo Municipal de Bellas Artes
19 Argentine Consulate
20 Cambio Exprinter
21 Ascensor Concepción
22 Ladeco
23 Instituto Chileno-Norteamericano
24 LanChile
27 CTC
28 Centro Cultural Valparaíso
30 Peruvian Consulate
31 Estación Bellavista
35 Buses La Porteña
36 Plaza Bolívar

37 Plaza Victoria
38 Municipalidad and Tourist Information
39 Museo de Historia Natural
40 Ascensor Espíritu Santo
41 Plaza Yungay
42 Ascensor Florida
43 Ascensor Mariposas
45 Parque Italia
47 Hospital Carlos Van Buren
48 Asté Rent-a-Car
50 Plaza O'Higgins
51 Terminal Rodoviario
52 Congreso Nacional
55 Muelle Barón
56 Estación Barón
57 Ascensor Barón
58 Ascensor Polanco

To Viña del Mar

CHILE

Places to Stay

Near the bus terminal, try the modest *hospedaje* with no name (☎ 23-5840) at Independencia 2312. Also near the terminal is the comfortable and warm *casa familiar* of Mónica Villegas (☎ 21-5673), Avenida Argentina 322, and the *Residencial Veracruz*, Pedro Montt 2881.

Near Plaza Sotomayor, try *Residencial Lily* (☎ 25-5995), Blanco Encalada 866, with singles/doubles from US$10/20. *Hotel Reina Victoria* (☎ 21-2203), Plaza Sotomayor 190, has singles from US$12 and doubles from US$20 with breakfast, but there have been some negative reports. On Cerro Concepción (take Ascensor Concepción), *Residencial Latina* (☎ 25-2350) is a family-oriented place at Pasaje Templeman 51, charging US$12 a single.

Places to Eat

Most visitors dine in Viña del Mar, but Valparaíso is an equally good place to eat. For ideas, pick up the free *Guía Gastronómica*, a guide to dining in Valparaíso, Viña and Concón.

Café Turri, at the upper exit of Ascensor Concepción, has superb seafood, attentive but unobtrusive service and panoramic views of the harbour. Although not really cheap, it's good value. For good vegetarian food, go to *Naturalista Bambú* (☎ 23-4216), at Pudeto 450, near Esmeralda. For tea, *Café Riquet*, Aníbal Pinto 1199, is one of Valparaíso's oldest.

Getting There & Away

Bus Nearly all companies have offices at the Terminal Rodoviario, Avenida Pedro Montt 913. Several have direct buses to northern cities like Arica and Iquique. Tur-Bus has the most frequent departures to Santiago (US$3.50).

Services to Argentina leave between 8 and 9 am, stopping in Viña but bypassing Santiago. Fares are US$28 to Mendoza, US$71 to Córdoba and US$61 to Buenos Aires.

Train The Estación Puerto (☎ 21-7108), at Plaza Sotomayor 711, is the main station for commuter trains. Regular trains go from Valparaíso/Viña to Los Andes, on the highway to the ski resort of Portillo.

Getting Around

Valpo and Viña are connected by local buses (US$0.30) and commuter train.

AROUND VALPARAISO

Neruda's outlandish oceanside house on **Isla Negra**, a rocky headland approximately 80 km south of Valparaíso, is now a museum, the **Museo Neruda**, which houses the poet's collections of bowsprits, ships in bottles, nautical instruments and other memorabilia. Isla Negra is *not*, by the way, an island.

In summer, reservations (☎ (035) 46-1284) are imperative for the half-hour weekday tours (US$2.50), which run between 10 am and 7.45 pm, but hang around the grounds as long as you like.

From Santiago's Alameda terminal, buses beyond Algarrobo leave pilgrims almost at the door. Buses also leave frequently from Valparaíso's Terminal Rodoviario.

VIÑA DEL MAR

Popularly known as the Ciudad Jardín (Garden City), Viña del Mar has been Chile's premier beach resort ever since the railway was built between Valparaíso and Santiago, even though the ocean here is very cold for swimming. The *porteños* (people of Valparaíso, the port) flocked to Viña because of its easy access to beaches and broad green spaces, and soon built grand houses and mansions away from the congested port. Because of high costs and its perceived exclusivity, Viña has lost ground to competing resorts like La Serena.

Orientation

Ten km north of Valparaíso, Viña consists of an older area south of Estero Marga Marga and a newer residential grid to its north, where most streets are identified by number and direction, either Norte (north), Oriente (east), or Poniente (west). These streets are usually written as a number, but are sometimes spelt out, eg 1 Norte is also written Uno

Norte. Avenida Libertad separates the Ponientes and the Orientes. The main activity centres are south of the Marga Marga, on Plaza Vergara and Avenidas Arlegui and Valparaíso.

Information

Tourist Offices The Central de Turismo e Informaciones (☎ 88-3154), north of Plaza Vergara, is open weekdays from 9 am to 7 pm. It provides an adequate map and a useful calendar of events.

Money To exchange money try Cambios Andino at Arlegui 646, Afex at Arlegui 641 or Inter Cambio at 1 Norte 655-B.

Post & Communications The main post office is at Latorre 32, across the street from Sernatur. CTC has offices at Avenida Libertad 586 and at Valparaíso and Villanelo. Viña's telephone code is 32.

Medical Services Hospital Gustavo Fricke (☎ 67-5067) is east of the town centre, at Alvarez 1532.

Things to See

Specialising in Mapuche silver and Easter Island, the **Museo Arqueológico Sociedad Fonck**, at 4 Norte 784, is open Tuesday to Friday from 10 am to 6 pm, and on weekends from 10 am to 2 pm. Two blocks east at Quillota 214, the **Museo Palacio Rioja** is now a municipal museum, open daily except Monday.

The magnificently landscaped **Quinta Vergara** contains the Venetian-style **Palacio Vergara** (1908), which in turn contains the **Museo de Bellas Artes** (admission US$1). It's open daily, except Monday, from 10 am to 6 pm (7 pm in summer).

Frequent summer concerts complement the song festival (see below). The grounds are open daily from 7.30 am to 6 pm (8 pm in summer).

Beaches Northern suburbs like Reñaca and Concón have the best beaches, where surfing is becoming increasingly popular – take Bus

No 1 from Libertad. For more details, see the Around Viña del Mar section.

Special Events

For a week every February the ostentatious Festival Internacional de la Canción is held in the Quinta Vergara. It features the kitschiest singers from the Spanish-speaking world (for balance, there's usually at least one really insipid Anglo performer) and paralyses the country, as ticketless Chileans gaze at TV sets in homes, cafés, restaurants and bars. Patient, selective listeners may hear worthwhile folk performers.

Places to Stay

This is only a sample of the accommodation available. After Chileans finish their holidays in February, supply exceeds demand and prices drop but the weather is still ideal.

Hostel *Hotel Capric* (☎ 97-8295), Von Schroeders 39, offers very good hostel accommodation at US$8.50 for a single, and dorms in summer, with a comfortable bed, private bath and breakfast. Ask for hostel accommodation, since hotel prices are higher.

Hotels, Hospedajes & Residenciales For budget alternatives, look on or near Agua Santa and Von Schroeders, or near the bus station. Off-season prices run at about US$9 per person, but in the high season they are twice that or more. One reader loved *Residencial Verónica*, Von Schroeders 150, which has singles for about US$9. *Residencial Agua Santa* (☎ 90-1531), Agua Santa 36, is an attractive, blue Victorian building and charges US$9 in the off season; almost next door, at Agua Santa 48, is *Residencial Patricia* (☎ 66-3825), where singles are US$13.

Near the Quinta Vergara is *Residencial La Gaviota* (☎ 97-4439), Alcalde Prieto Nieto 0332, a bargain at US$15 a double with shared bath, or US$25 with private bath. Also recommended is *Residencial Oxaram* (☎ 88-2360), at Villanelo 136, in a quiet

Viña del Mar

0   200   400 m

location between Arlegui and Valparaíso; it charges US$13 for a single with breakfast.

Hotel Quinta Vergara (☎ 68-5073, fax 69-1978), Errázuriz 690, has an English-speaking manager and charges US$35/40 for a single/double with breakfast. If you have lots of cash, the best choice would be the venerable *Hotel O'Higgins* (☎ 88-2016), on Plaza Latorre. Rates start at US$86/116.

Places to Eat

For good, moderately priced Italian and Middle Eastern food, choose *Panzoni*, Pasaje Cousiño 12-B, which is small and

very popular for lunch (Cousiño is a small passageway off Valparaíso, near Plaza Sucre).

On the same block, the vegetarian restaurant *Madroño* offers bargain lunches. For coffee and dessert, try *Anayak*, at Quinta 134, or especially, *Confitería Samoiedo*, at Valparaíso 637. You may want to substitute dinner for a satisfying late tea at *Alster Pastelería Alemana* at Valparaíso 226; their kuchen de quesillo is memorable.

Entertainment

For first-run movies, try *Cine Arte* at Plaza

PLACES TO STAY		
6	Hotel San Martín	
7	Residencial 555	
12	Residencial Helen Misch	
18	Hotel Cap Ducal	
22	Residencial Victoria	
23	Residencial Caribe	
24	Residencial Marbella	
25	Residencial Blanchait	
26	Residencial Verónica	
27	Hotel Capric	
28	Residencial Villarrica	
32	Residencial Oxaram	
34	Residencial Magallanes	
43	Residencial Ona Berri	
48	Hotel O'Higgins	
52	Residencial La Gaviota	
53	Residencial France	
55	Hotel Quinta Vergara	
58	Residencial Palace	
59	Residencial Casino	
60	Residencial Lausanne	
61	Residencial La Montaña	

62	Residencial Agua Santa &	
	Residencial Patricia	

PLACES TO EAT		
29	Alster Pastelería Alemana	
35	Anayak	
40	Confitería Samoiedo	
44	Panzoni & El Naturista	
57	Centro Español	

OTHER		
1	Reloj de Sol	
2	Rent-a-Car Mach	
3	Muelle Vergara	
4	Instituto Chileno-Británico	
5	CTC (Telephone)	
8	Museo Palacio Rioja	
9	Instituto Chileno-Británico	
10	Museo Arqueológico Sociedad Fonck	
11	Centro Cultural Viña del Mar	
13	CONAF	
14	Instituto Chileno-Norteamericano	
15	Rentauto	

16	Automóvil Club de Chile	
17	Casino Municipal	
19	Museo de la Cultura	
20	Reloj de Flores del Mar	
21	Disco Scala	
30	CTC	
31	Disco Manhattan	
33	Sernatur	
36	Cambios Afex	
37	Sala Viña del Mar	
38	Post Office	
39	Central de Turismo e Informaciones, Municipalidad	
41	Plaza Vergara	
42	CTC	
45	Railway Station	
46	Teatro Municipal	
47	Sala Municipal de Exposiciones	
49	Terminal Rodoviario	
50	Mercado Municipal	
51	Hospital Gustavo Fricke	
54	Bert Rent-a-Car	
56	Palacio Vergara, Museo de Bellas Artes	

CHILE

Vergara 42, *Cine Olimpo* at Quinta 294, *Cine Premier* at Quillota 898 or *Cine Rex* at Valparaíso 758.

For dancing, Viña has *Cocodrilo* (Avenida Borgoño 13101, on the road to Reñaca), *Scratch* (at Bohn 970) and one of the biggest and cheapest, *Manhattan* (Arlegui 302, 2nd floor).

Getting There & Away

The Terminal de Buses is on the corner of Valparaíso and Quilpué, two blocks from Plaza Vergara. Most buses from Valparaíso pick up passengers here, though a few lines start in Viña. There are frequent buses to San Felipe, Los Andes and Santiago.

Getting Around

Buses marked Puerto or Aduana go to Valparaíso from Avenida Arlegui.

Taxis are twice as expensive as those in Santiago.

For the cheapest rental-car rates, try Bert Rent-a-Car (☎ 68-5515), at Alvarez 750.

AROUND VIÑA DEL MAR

North of Viña are less celebrated but very attractive beach towns. **Reñaca** has its own tourist office (☎ 90-0499) at Avenida Borgoño 14100, plus the area's most extensive beach, but little budget accommodation.

Concón, 15 km from Viña, is another popular and exclusive *balneario* (bathing resort), very famous for its seafood restaurants. For a fabulous meal try the congrio margarita (conger eel) at *La Picá Horizonte* (San Pedro 120, Concón). To get there take the bus to Caleta Higuerilla and walk up the stairs (behind Restaurant El Tiburón) across the street from the fisherman's wharf. At the top of the stairs walk one short block along the dirt road and turn right into San Pedro. The view from the restaurant is superb.

Another 23 km beyond Concón is **Quintero**, a peninsula community once part of

Lord Cochrane's hacienda. For reasonable accommodation, try *Residencial María Alejandra* (☎ 93-0266), Cochrane 157, where singles with shared bath cost about US$9.

Farther north, the port of **Horcón** is an artists' colony with a bohemian flavour and outstanding seafood restaurants like *Restaurant Santa Clara*, whose exquisite paila marina (shellfish soup) is worth the wait. Horcón is reached by Sol del Pacífico bus from Avenida Libertad in Viña.

The Southern Heartland

RANCAGUA

Capital of the Sixth Region and 86 km south of Santiago, the agricultural service centre of Rancagua (population 160,000) also depends on the copper of El Teniente, the world's largest subsurface mine. In 1814, the Desastre de Rancagua (Disaster of Rancagua) was a temporary setback for Chilean self-determination, at the hands of the Spanish Royalist troops.

For information, visit Sernatur, Germán Riesco 277. To change money, try Fincard, at Astorga 485. CONAF (☎ 23-3769), Cuevas 480, has information on Reserva Nacional Río de los Cipreses. The telephone code is 72.

Rancagua's late colonial buildings include the **Iglesia de la Merced** (O'Higgins' headquarters during the battle of Rancagua), the **Casa del Pilar de Piedra** and the **Museo Histórico Regional**.

Places to Stay & Eat

Several travellers have recommended *Hotel España* (☎ 23-0141), San Martín 367, which has singles/doubles for US$19/25 but may have cheaper rooms with shared bath. *Hotel Rancagua* (☎ 23-2663), San Martín 85, is slightly dearer. *Restaurant Casas Viejas*, Rubio 216, is recommended.

Getting There & Away

The terminal, on Ocarrol, has frequent buses to Santiago (US$2). Many southbound buses also stop in Rancagua.

Long-distance trains stop at the station on Viña del Mar between Ocarrol and Carrera Pinto, and there are also commuter services to Santiago.

AROUND RANCAGUA

Termas de Cauquenes

Only 28 km east of Rancagua, these hot springs were visited by both O'Higgins and Darwin (who called the facilities 'a square of miserable little hovels, each with a single table and bench', but also said it was 'a quiet solitary spot with a good deal of quiet beauty'). Improvements since then have placed accommodation beyond the budgets of shoestring travellers, but you can still spend the afternoon here by taking a bus from Rancagua's Mercado Municipal.

Reserva Nacional Río de los Cipreses

Fifty km south-east of Rancagua, 37,000-hectare Los Cipreses has varied volcanic landforms, hanging glacial valleys, and riverscapes. Its extensive forests shelter wildlife like guanacos, foxes, vizcachas and condors. There are many petroglyphs to see and places to camp, hike and horse ride.

No direct public transport to the park exists, but you can try to arrange transport with CONAF in Rancagua.

CURICO

An attractive city surrounded by orchards and vineyards, 195 km south of Santiago, Curicó is a good base for trips into the countryside, coastal areas and parts of the Andes. Its palm-lined Plaza de Armas, one of Chile's prettiest, has a wrought-iron bandstand and cool fountains with black-necked swans.

For information, visit the private Cámara de Turismo, in the Gobernación, on the east side of the plaza. Curi Cambio, Merced 255, changes money on weekdays only. The post office is at Carmen 556, while CTC has long-distance offices at Peña 650 and Camilo Henríquez 414. Entel, Prat 373, is open until midnight. Curicó's telephone code is 75.

Wineries
Bodega Miguel Torres (☎ 31-0455) is south of Curicó on the Panamericana. Phone ahead and take a taxi colectivo toward the village of Molina. On the same route, near the village of Lontué, is **Viña San Pedro** (☎ 49-1517).

Places to Stay & Eat
Friendly *Hotel Prat*, Peña 427, is a bargain at US$6 per person with shared bath and hot showers, but some rooms are dark and a bit drab. *Residencial Rahue*, across the street, is equally satisfactory.

Restaurant Villota, Merced 487, serves fine lunches in pleasant surroundings. For parrillada, try *El Fogón Chileno*, at Yungay 802. Pizzas, sandwiches and a variety of snacks are available at *Luzzi*, Yungay 720.

Getting There & Away
Bus The long-distance bus terminal is on Camilo Henríquez, three blocks north of the plaza. Buses to Santiago (US$4) leave every half-hour. For local and regional services, the Terminal de Buses Rurales is at the west end of Calle Prat.

Train Trains from Santiago and Temuco stop at the railway station, which is five blocks from the plaza, at the west end of Calle Prat.

AROUND CURICO
The major attraction of **Radal Siete Tazas**, east of Molina, is a series of falls and pools in the upper Río Claro. There are scenic trails up Cerro El Fraile and at Valle del Indio, with camping at the Radal and Parque Inglés sectors. CONAF's visitor centre, 50 km from Molina, can be reached from Curicó and Molina by buses (marked to Los Niches) which run daily in summer, but less often in other seasons.

TALCA
Founded in 1690 but refounded in 1742 after shaky beginnings (a major earthquake),

Talca is capital of the Seventh Region of Maule, 257 km south of Santiago. Long the residence of landowners, it's also an important commercial centre. For information, visit Sernatur, at 1 Poniente 1234. CONAF is at 2 Poniente 1180. Talca's telephone code is 71.

The **Museo O'Higginiano y de Bellas Artes** is in the house where Bernardo O'Higgins signed the declaration of independence in 1818.

Places to Stay & Eat
Near the train station, *Hotel Alcázar*, 2 Sur 1359, is clean and has rooms for US$6 per person with shared bath. Across the street, *Hotel Cordillera* (☎ 22-1817) has singles with shared bath for US$12, or with private bath for US$20.

Restaurants include the *Centro Español*, at 3 Oriente 1109, *Ibiza* (with takeaway service), at 1 Sur 1168; *El Gallo Marino*, at 1 Norte 1718; and *Mykonos*, at 1 Sur 942.

Getting There & Away
Many north-south buses stop at the Rodoviario Municipal (☎ 24-3270) at 2 Sur 1920, behind the train station.

All trains from Santiago stop at the station (☎ 22-6116), 11 Oriente 1000, at the east end of 2 Sur.

AROUND TALCA
In the Andean foothills 65 km east of Talca is **Vilches**, a CONAF reserve . It's possible to camp in the upper Río Lircay basin and hike to Laguna El Alto, Laguna Tomate and up the canyon of the Valle del Venado. Buses to Vilches go daily, except Sunday, at 1 and 5 pm from Talca.

CHILLAN
Birthplace of O'Higgins, Chillán marks the approximate northern border of La Frontera, an area controlled by the Mapuche until the late 19th century. Of all the towns on the Panamericana from Santiago to Temuco, Chillán most deserves a stopover.

Orientation & Information
Chillán (population 125,000), 400 km south

CHILE

Chillán

0   100   200 m

of Santiago, sits on an alluvial plain between the Río Ñuble and the Río Chillán. Sernatur (☎ 22-3272), in the Edificios Públicos 422 on the Plaza de Armas, is open weekdays from 9 am to 1 pm and from 3 to 7 pm, and on Saturday from 9 am to 1 pm only.

Biotour, at Constitución 550, Local 9, changes US dollars cash and travellers' cheques. The post office is at Libertad 505, while CTC is at Arauco 625. The telephone code is 42.

Things to See
Murales de la Escuela México After a 1939

earthquake, Mexican president Lázaro Cárdenas donated a new school to Chillán. At Pablo Neruda's urging, Mexican artist David Alfaro Siqueiros decorated the library with murals honouring indigenous and post-Columbian figures in each country's history – the northern wall is devoted to Mexico and the southern wall to Chile. *Hermanos Mexicanos*, a simple but powerful mural by Siqueiros' countryman Xavier Guerrero, flanks the library stairs.

The school is at O'Higgins 250. It does still function as a school but the staff welcome visitors.

PLACES TO STAY
1 Hospedaje Sonia Segui
3 Hotel Floresta
4 Claris Hotel
10 Hotel Martín Ruiz de
    Gamboa
11 Hotel Real
14 Hotel Americano
17 Hotel Rucamanqui
24 Gran Hotel Isabel
    Riquelme
25 Hotel Cordillera
27 Hotel Quinchamalí
31 Hospedaje Su Casa
33 Hospedaje Tino Rodríguez
    Sepúlveda

PLACES TO EAT
5 Planka
9 Kuranepe
12 Taipe
13 Jai Yang
20 Centro Español
32 Cocinerías del Mercado

OTHER
2 Escuela México
6 Museo Franciscano
7 Railway Station
8 Terminal de Buses
   Inter-regionales
15 Entel
16 Automóvil Club de Chile
18 Sernatur & Post Office
19 Catedral
21 Hospital
22 Centrotur
23 Biotour
26 CTC
28 Hispanotur
29 Feria
30 Terminal de Buses Rurales
34 Museo Naval Arturo Prat

Feria de Chillán Especially lively on Saturday, this is one of Chile's most colourful markets, with a great selection of crafts (leather, basketry and weaving) and mountains of fresh produce. The feria occupies the entire Plaza de la Merced and spills over into adjacent streets.

Places to Stay & Eat
Budget accommodation in Chillán starts from about US$7 at places such as *Hospedaje Sonia Segui*, Itata 288, which includes breakfast, and *Su Casa* (☎ 22-3931), at Cocharcas 555. Also try *Hospedaje Tino Rodríguez Sepúlveda*, Purén 443, which charges US$9.

Hotel Americano, Carrera 481, has singles with shared bath for US$8, while the comparable *Claris Hotel*, 18 de Septiembre 357, is dearer with private bath. *Hotel Real*, Libertad 219, charges US$10/15 for a single/double with shared bath.

The *Cocinerías del Mercado*, at Prat 826, 2nd floor, has several simple but excellent restaurants, which may move when the central market is remodelled. The *Centro Español* is at Arauco 555. Also worth a try are *Planka*, at Arauco 103, and *Kuranepe*, at O'Higgins 420.

Getting There & Away
The Terminal de Buses Inter-regionales (☎ 22-1014) is at Constitución 01, on the corner of Avenida Brasil. It has frequent north-south services, plus daily buses to Bariloche, Argentina (US$32), and to Neuquén via San Martín de Los Andes and Zapala.

For local buses, the terminal (☎ 22-3606) is at Maipón and Sargento Aldea.

The railway station (☎ 22-2424) is on Avenida Brasil at Libertad.

AROUND CHILLAN
Renowned for hot springs and skiing, **Termas de Chillán** is 80 km east, at 1800 metres, on the slopes of Volcán Chillán. Accommodation is costly, but check travel agencies for day trips.

CONCEPCION
Menaced by Indians and devastated by earthquakes, Concepción moved several times in the colonial era, but maintained seaborne communications with Santiago. After independence, coal on the Península de Lebú encouraged an autonomous industrial tradition, and glass-blowing, timber and textile industries emerged. The railway arrived in 1872, and when the Mapuche threat receded, a bridge over the Biobío gave the city a strategic role in further colonisation.

Since WW II, the major industrial project

CHILE

Concepción

0   150   300 m

To Museo de
Concepción

To Terminal Rodoviario
Chillán & Santiago

Avenida Roosevelt

Larenas

Paicaví

Ongolmo

Orompello

Tucapel

Castellón

Colo Colo

Aníbal Pinto

Caupolicán

Rengo

Lincoyán

Angol

Salas

Serrano

Avenida Arturo Prat

PA Cerda

M Rodríguez

Cruz

Bulnes

M de Rozas

Las Heras

Los Carrera

Salas

Malipú

Freire

Barros Arana

O'Higgins

San Martín

Cochrane

Chacabuco

Avenida Lamas

Esmeralda

San Pedro

Puente
Viejo

Río Biobío

Railway
Bridge

To Coronel
& Lota

PLACES TO STAY		PLACES TO EAT			
1	Hospedaje María Inés Jara	6	China Town	29	Teatro Concepción
5	Residencial	22	Pastelería Suiza & Salón Inglés	30	Instituto Chileno-Español
12	Hotel Cruz del Sur	26	Centro Español	31	Parque Ecuador
13	Residencial Colo Colo	46	El Naturista	32	Mercado Central
14	Residencial Antuco & Residencial San Sebastián	50	Chungwa	33	Inter-Santiago
				34	Entel
15	Hotel Ritz		**OTHER**	37	Instituto Chileno-Norteamericano
16	Hotel Tabancura	2	Hospital	38	Automóvil Club de Chile
20	Hotel Alonso de Ercilla	3	Casa del Arte		
23	Hotel de la Cruz	4	Barrio Universitario	41	Ladeco
35	Residencial Concepción	7	Tur-Bus & Chevalier	42	LanChile
		8	Buses Tas Choapa	44	German Consulate
36	Hotel Araucano	9	Buses Igi Llaima	45	Argentine Consulate
39	Casa Familiar González	10	Buses Cruz del Sur		
40	Casa de Huéspedes	11	Centro Italiano	46	Peruvian Consulate
42	Hotel Alborada	17	CTC	48	Galería de Historia de Concepción
43	Residencial Metro	18	Sernatur		
47	Hotel El Dorado	19	Post Office	49	Cerro Caracol
51	Apart Hotel Concepción	21	UK Consulate	52	CONAF
		24	Instituto Chileno-Alemán	54	Buses Biobío
53	Hotel Cecil	25	Instituto Chileno-Francés	55	Buses Los Alces
		27	Plaza Independencia	56	Buses J Ewert
		28	Pawulska Tour	57	Railway Station

has been the steel plant at Huachipato, but wages and living standards are low. Coupled with activism at the Universidad de Concepción, these conditions fostered a highly politicised labour movement which strongly supported Salvador Allende.

Orientation & Information

On the north bank of the Biobío, Concepción is capital of the Eighth Region. Few old buildings have survived around the pleasantly landscaped Plaza Independencia – the utilitarian buildings are a response to earthquake risk. Near the plaza the main commercial streets, Barros Arana and Aníbal Pinto, are pedestrian malls. With the port of Talcahuano, the urban area has nearly half a million people.

Well-stocked Sernatur (☎ 22-7976), Aníbal Pinto 460, is open daily from 8.30 am to 8 pm in summer; the rest of the year, it's open weekdays only from 8.30 am to 1 pm and 3 to 6.30 pm. To exchange money, try Inter-Santiago at Caupolicán 521, Local 58.

The post office is at O'Higgins 799. CTC has offices at Colo Colo 487 and Barros Arana 673, Local 5, while Entel is at Caupolicán 567, Local A. The telephone code is 41.

Things to See

On the grounds of the **Barrio Universitario**, at the corner of Chacabuco and Larenas, the highlight of the **Casa del Arte** (art museum) is *La Presencia de América Latina*, a mural by Mexican artist Jorge González Camarena.

On the edge of Parque Ecuador, the very fine **Galería de Historia de Concepción** features vivid dioramas of local and regional history. Subjects include Mapuche subsistence activities, battles with the Spaniards (note Mapuche tactics), literary figure Alonso de Ercilla, the 1939 earthquake and a finely detailed model of a local factory. It's open daily, except Monday, from 10 am to 1 pm and from 2 to 7 pm; admission is free.

Places to Stay

North of the centre, *Hospedaje María Inés Jarpa*, Maipú 1757, is a bargain at US$6 for a single (or US$13 with three meals); it has limited space and is popular with students. The basic *Casa de Huéspedes*, Rengo 855,

CHILE

charges US$7, including hot water, laundry and kitchen.

Residencial Metro (☎ 22-5305), Barros Arana 464, has rooms for US$11 per person; *Residencial O'Higgins*, (☎ 22-8303) O'Higgins 457, includes breakfast for the same price. *Residencial Colo Colo* (☎ 23-4790), Colo Colo 743, is very fine and friendly; it charges US$11 per person.

Places to Eat

Filling the entire block bounded by Caupolicán, Maipú, Rengo and Freire, the *Mercado Central* has many excellent eateries, though aggressive waiters literally try to drag customers into some venues. Try pastel de choclo, a meal in itself.

Pastelería Suiza, O'Higgins 780, has a fixed-price lunch for about US$3. The *Salón Inglés*, next door, is equally appealing. *El Naturista*, Barros Arana 342, serves vegetarian food; while *El Novillo Loco*, Pasaje Portales 539, is for carnivores. The *Centro Español*, at Barros Arana 675, and the *Centro Italiano*, at Barros Arana 935, add a European flavour. For a cheap cappuccino, try *Café Haití* at Caupolicán 511, or *Café Caribe* at Caupolicán 521.

Things to Buy

Look for woollens, basketry, ceramics, carvings and leather at the mercado central; La Gruta (Caupolicán 521, Local 64); Antumalal (Aníbal Pinto 450, Local 10); and Minga del Biobío (Barros Arana 1112).

Getting There & Away

Air Aeropuerto Carriel Sur is five km northwest of town. LanChile (☎ 24-0025), Barros Arana 451, has at least two flights daily to Santiago (US$72), except on weekends (one flight daily). On Friday evenings, it also has a flight to Punta Arenas (US$191). Ladeco (☎ 24-8824), Barros Arana 402, flies to Santiago twice daily, except on Sunday.

Bus Concepción's Terminal Rodoviario (☎ 31-0896) is at Tegualda 860, on the outskirts of town. Many bus companies have downtown offices.

Tur-Bus (☎ 23-7409), Tucapel 530, and Buses Lit (☎ 23-0726) have frequent buses to Santiago. Tas Choapa (☎ 24-0372), Barros Arana 1081, has excellent connections to northern Chile and to Argentina, along with Chevalier (☎ 31-0896), Tucapel 516. Sol del Pacífico also has frequent services to Santiago and Valparaíso.

Buses to Temuco and Puerto Montt include Varmontt (☎ 31-4010), Los Carrera 2017; Igi Llaima (☎ 31-2498), Tegualda 860, Oficina 7; Cruz del Sur (☎ 31-4372), Tegualda 860, Local 9; and Biobío (☎ 23-0672), A Prat 416; as well as Tur-Bus and Lit. Igi Llaima has buses to Los Ángeles. For services to Coronel and the Costa del Carbón, try Los Alces (☎ 24-0855), Prat 699.

Typical fares include Chillán or Los Ángeles US$2, Angol US$3, Talca US$4, Temuco US$5, Santiago US$10, Valparaíso US$12 and Puerto Montt US$12.

Train The station (☎ 22-6925) is on Avenida Prat, at the foot of Barros Arana, but there's a ticket office (☎ 22-5286) at Pinto 450, Local 16. There are four trains daily to Santiago (US$11, nine hours).

AROUND CONCEPCION
La Costa del Carbón

The 'Coast of Coal', south of Biobío, draws crowds to beaches near Coronel (which reeks of fishmeal), Lota, Arauco and the Península de Lebú. The best day trip is to Lota's **Parque Isidora Cousiño**, designed by an English landscape architect.

At ENACAR's undersea mine, you can put on a hard hat, ride in a mine cart, and chip off a hunk of coal with a pneumatic drill. These tours (US$17) take place at 10.50 am and 3 pm every day, all year. Contact the Parque Isidora Cousiño (☎ 24-9039), Carlos Cousiño 199 in Lota Alto, 8 am to 6 pm on weekdays.

Ruta de la Araucana

Local and regional authorities have begun to erect historical markers honouring soldier-poet Alonso de Ercilla y Zúñiga's epic tale

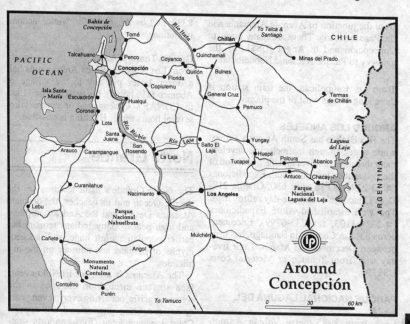

Around Concepción

0   30   60 km

La Araucana, which honoured the Mapuche resistance. At Escuadrón, 22 km south of Concepción, the **Hito Histórico Galvarino** marks the battle of Lagunillas (1557), where the Mapuche *toqui* (chief) Galvarino submitted to the Spaniards who severed both his hands. After Galvarino stoically placed his own head on the block, they refrained from executing him but he swore revenge. On being recaptured years later, he may have been executed, but some historians believe he killed himself.

Near Arauco, about two km west of Carampangue, the **Hito Histórico Prueba y Elección de Caupolicán** commemorates the site where Mapuche leader Colo Colo chose Caupolicán to lead the resistance against the Spaniards. The Mapuche defeated the Spanish at Tucapel (1553) and executed Pedro de Valdivia.

If continuing south to Angol and Los Angeles, visit **Monumento Natural Contulmo**, an 84-hectare forest reserve with trails, but without camping or picnic facilities.

LOS ANGELES

Santa María de Los Angeles (population 115,000) is not Hollywood, and the two-lane Panamericana is not a freeway. Some 110 km south of Chillán, it provides good access to the upper Biobío and to Parque Nacional Laguna del Laja. The Plaza de Armas has a kiosco de turismo. The telephone code is 43.

True budget accommodation is scarce, but the very central *Hotel y Restaurante Mazzola* (☎ 32-1643), Lautaro 579, has singles/doubles for US$22/28. For parrilla, the best option is *El Arriero*, Colo Colo 235, but the *Centro Español*, at Colón 482, has more varied fare. One reader praised the Italian food at *Di Leone*, Colón 285.

Getting There & Away

Bus The bus terminal is at Caupolicán and Valdivia, but most north-south buses leave from the junction of Avenida Alemania and the Panamericana. There are many buses to Concepción and to Angol (US$1.50), the gateway to Parque Nacional Nahuelbuta.

Train On Caupolicán, the train station is three long blocks west of the plaza.

AROUND LOS ANGELES

The **Río Biobío** has South America's finest white water, though hydroelectric development threatens the river and the livelihood of the Pehuenche Indians. South Expediciones (☎ 23-2290), O'Higgins 680, Oficina 218-D, in Concepción, has one-day rafting trips. The well established Altué Expediciones (☎ 232- 1103, fax 233-6799), Encomenderos 83, Las Condes, in Santiago, has trips between December and March. Their five-day trip (from Temuco or Victoria) costs US$790.

PARQUE NACIONAL LAGUNA DEL LAJA

Lava from 2985-metre Volcán Antuco dammed the Río Laja to form this reserve's centrepiece lake, 95 km east of Los Angeles, with forests of mountain cypress and pehuén (monkey puzzle tree). Nearly 50 bird species, including the condor, frequent the area.

The best of several hikes circles Antuco, but the higher Sierra Velluda to the southwest offers a series of impressive glaciers. Summer is fairly dry but rain and snow are common during the rest of the year. The ski season lasts from June to October.

Places to Stay & Eat

Near the park entrance, at Km 90, *Cabañas y Camping Lagunillas* (☎ 32-3606), Caupolicán 332 in Los Angeles, charges US$10 per site plus US$1 per person.

In winter, the Antuco Lodge has bunks (US$13) for 50 skiers and a restaurant; it also rents out ski equipment. For reservations, contact DIGEDER (☎ 22-9054), at O'Higgins 740, Oficina 23, in Concepción. Try also Los Angeles' *Refugio Municipal* (☎ 32-

2333 in Los Angeles) for winter accommodation.

Getting There & Away

From Los Angeles, Buses Antuco runs half a dozen buses per day to the village of Abanico (1½ hours), but walking the 11 km to CONAF's Chacay visitor centre takes several hours more. Hitching is possible.

Norte Grande

The Norte Grande's main features are the Pacific Ocean and its beaches, the desolate Atacama Desert, and the Andean altiplano and high peaks. Many Indians remain, but earlier populations left huge, stylised geoglyphs of humans and animals on the dry hillsides.

The Atacama is arid, but El Niño events (sea surface circulation changes in the western Pacific, occurring every seven years or so) can bring phenomenal downpours. Coastal *camanchaca* (fog) supports scattered semidesert *lomas* vegetation, and rainfall and vegetation increase with elevation and distance from the sea. In the precordillera (foothills), Aymara farmers cultivate potatoes up to altitudes of 4000 metres, while herders pasture llamas and alpacas on the higher *puna* (highlands).

After the War of the Pacific, Chile annexed these copper and nitrate-rich lands from Peru and Bolivia; most Atacama cities owe their existence to minerals. Nitrate *oficinas* like Humberstone flourished in the early 20th century, then withered or died when artificial fertilisers superseded mineral nitrates, and they are now ghost towns. Copper is still mined at open-pit mines like Chuquicamata, the world's largest.

Militant trade unions first developed in this area, introducing a new force into Chilean politics. Nitrates, which drew this region into the modern world, have been supplanted by copper. Chuquicamata dominates the mining sector, but fishing and tourism are growing in importance.

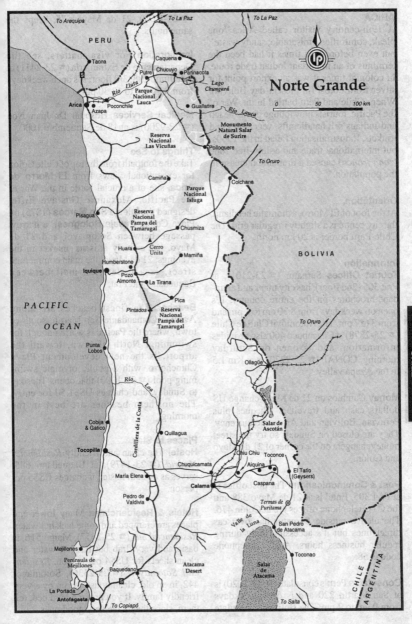

Norte Grande

0   50   100 km

PERU

To Arequipa

To La Paz

To La Paz

Tacna

Caquena

Chucuyo

Parinacota

Putre

Lago
Chungará

Río Lluta

Poconchile

Parque
Nacional
Lauca

Arica

Azapa

Guallatire

Río Lauca

Reserva
Nacional
Las Vicuñas

Monumento
Natural Salar
de Surire

Polloquere

To Oruro

Camiña

Colchane

Parque
Nacional
Isluga

Pisagua

Reserva
Nacional
Pampa del
Tamarugal

Chusmiza

BOLIVIA

Huara

Cerro
Unita

Mamiña

Humberstone

Iquique

Pozo
Almonte

La Tirana

Pica

PACIFIC

OCEAN

Pintados

Reserva
Nacional
Pampa del
Tamarugal

To Oruro

Punta
Lobos

Ollagüe

Río Loa

Cobija
& Gatico

Quillagua

Salar de
Ascotán

CHILE

Tocopilla

Cordillera de la Costa

Chuquicamata

Chiu Chiu

Toconce

María Elena

Aiquina

Caspana

El Tatio
(Geysers)

Pedro de
Valdivia

Calama

Termas de
Puritama

San Pedro
de Atacama

Valle de
la Luna

Mejillones

Península de
Mejillones

Baquedano

Atacama
Desert

Salar
de
Atacama

Toconao

La Portada

Antofagasta

To Copiapó

To Salta

CHILE
ARGENTINA

ARICA

A 19th-century visitor called Arica 'one bleak, comfortless, miserable, sandy waste', but even before Inca times it had been the terminus of an important Indian trade route. In colonial times it was an export point for silver from Potosí (in present-day Bolivia). Where Chile and Peru battled in the War of the Pacific, tourists now lounge on the beach and Indians sell handicrafts, vegetables and trinkets. Industrialisation failed in the 1960s, but international trade and a duty-free zone *(zona franca)* caused a dramatic increase in the population.

Orientation

At the foot of El Morro, a dramatic headland, the city centre is a slightly irregular grid. The Chile-Peru border is 20 km north.

Information

Tourist Offices Sernatur (☎ 23-2101), at Prat 305 (2nd floor), has city maps and abundant brochures on the entire country. It's open on weekdays from 8.30 am to 1 pm and from 3 to 7 pm. The Automóvil Club de Chile (☎ 25-2878) at Chacabuco 460 also provides information, and is open on Saturday morning. CONAF (☎ 22-2270) is at Km 1.5 in the Azapa valley.

Money Cambios on 21 de Mayo change US dollars cash and travellers' cheques plus Peruvian, Bolivian and Argentine currency. They are closed on Sunday, so try the street moneychangers on the corner of 21 de Mayo and Colón.

Post & Communications The post office is at Prat 305. Entel is at 21 de Mayo 388 and the CTC telephone offices are at Colón 476. The alcove outside Sernatur has overseas direct lines but it's accessible only during regular business hours. Arica's telephone code is 58.

Consulates Peru's consulate (☎ 23-1020) is at San Martín 220 and is open weekdays from 9 am to 2 pm. The Bolivian Consulate

(☎ 23-1030), 21 de Mayo 575, keeps the same hours.

Immigration For visa matters, see the Departamento de Extranjería (☎ 23-2411) at 7 de Junio 188, 3rd floor; it's open weekdays from 8.30 am to 12.30 pm.

Medical Services Hospital Dr Juan Noé (☎ 22-9200) is at 18 de Septiembre 1000.

Things to See

Take the footpath from the top of Calle Colón for exceptional views from **El Morro de Arica**, site of a crucial battle in the War of the Pacific. Alexandre Gustave Eiffel designed the **Iglesia San Marcos** (1875) on Plaza Colón. **Pasaje Bolognesi**, a narrow passage between Sotomayor and 21 de Mayo, has a lively artisans' market in the evenings. 21 de Mayo, the main commercial street, is a pedestrian mall between Baquedano and Prat.

Beaches The finest beaches are along Avenida Comandante San Martín, south of town, where the Pacific is warm enough for swimming. North of town, toward the airport, is the new development Playa Chinchorro, with a public olympic swimming pool (☎ 21-1000) that opens Tuesday to Sunday, and charges US$1.50 for entry. The northern beaches are best in the morning.

Places to Stay

Hostel The clean and friendly *Residencial Madrid* (☎ 23-1479), at Baquedano 685, serves as a youth hostel; it charges US$5 per person.

Hotels & Residenciales Many lower-end places are cramped and some lack hot water. *Residencial Sur* (☎ 25-2457), Maipú 516, is basic and very drab but has hot water and clean sheets for US$4 per person. *Residencial Sotomayor* (☎ 25-2336), Sotomayor 442, in an old, clean house, is run by a very friendly family. If you prefer a hard bed, tell them, since they have very good ones.

Residencial Chungará (☎ 23-1677), Patricio Lynch 675, is probably the pick of the category – bright, friendly and quiet (except for rooms nearest the TV), for US$7 per person.

Excellent value is offered by *Hotel Lynch* (☎ 23-1581), Patricio Lynch 589, where simple and clean singles/doubles with shared bath start at US$28/42.

Places to Eat

Numerous eateries line 21 de Mayo, 18 de Septiembre, Maipú, Bolognesi and Colón. Foreign travellers congregate at *Café 21*, 21 de Mayo 201, which serves snacks, coffee and excellent lager beer. Other coffee places include *Di Mango*, at 21 de Mayo 244 with tables inside and outside, and *El Altillo*, at 21 de Mayo 260, 2nd floor. For breakfast, try sandwiches and licuados at *Buen Gusto No 2*, Baquedano 559. *Restaurant Casino La Bomba*, inside the fire station at Colón 357, is an Arica institution with inexpensive midday meals and attentive service.

For seafood, there's *El Rey del Marisco*, at Colón and Maipú, 2nd floor. *El Arriero*, 21 de Mayo 385, is a fine parrilla with a pleasant atmosphere and friendly service.

Getting There & Away

Air Aeropuerto Chacalluta (☎ 22-2831) is 18 km north of Arica.

Ladeco (☎ 25-2021), 21 de Mayo 443, LanChile (☎ 25-1641), 21 de Mayo 345, and National (☎ 25-0001), 21 de Mayo 417, have daily flights to Santiago (US$130 with National, the others are more expensive; ask about discounts) and intermediate points. Sit on the left side southbound or the right side northbound for awesome views of the desert and the Andes. Aerochile (☎ 25-1010), Baquedano 277, has one flight per day to Santiago via Iquique and Antofagasta. ALTA is at 21 de Mayo 804.

LAB (☎ 25-1919), Patricio Lynch 298, has three flights weekly to La Paz. Faucett (☎ 23-1025), 7 de Junio 264, has cheap flights from Tacna to Cuzco via Arequipa or Lima. AeroPerú (☎ 23-2852) is at 7 de Junio 148, Oficina 2.

Bus & Colectivo – domestic All major companies have offices at the bus terminal (☎ 24-1390), Diego Portales 948. Frequent buses go to Iquique (US$5, four hours); taxi colectivos charge about US$11. Other typical southbound fares are Calama US$20, Viña del Mar or Valparaíso about US$38, and Santiago US$51.

For altiplano destinations, including Parinacota (US$6), Visviri (US$7.50) and Charaña, contact Buses Martínez (☎ 23-2265), Pedro Montt 620, or Transporte Humire (☎ 25-3497), Pedro Montt 662.

Buses La Paloma (☎ 22-2710), Germán Riesco 2071, goes to Socoroma (US$2), Putre (US$4, daily) and Belén.

Bus Lluta serves Poconchile from the corner of Chacabuco and Vicuña Mackenna six times daily; if hitching to Parque Nacional Lauca, take this bus and proceed from the carabineros checkpoint. Alternatively, you can take the bus to Parinacota and return with tour agencies (arrange beforehand) or hitch Bolivian trucks.

Bus & Colectivo – international Adsubliata (☎ 24-1972) goes often to Tacna in Peru (US$2). Taxi colectivos to Tacna (US$4, one hour) leave from Chacabuco between Baquedano and Colón.

Buses Litoral (☎ 25-1267), Chacabuco 454, run buses from Arica to La Paz (US$20, 18 hours, weather permitting) on Tuesday and Friday at 1 am.

Comfortable, heavily booked Géminis buses (☎ 24-1647) go to La Paz (US$35) on Wednesday and to Salta (US$50, 28 hours) weekly, via Calama (they attempt to go year round, so sometimes the passengers have to push the bus out of the mud).

Train Trains to Tacna (US$1.75, 1½ hours) depart from the Ferrocarril Arica-Tacna (☎ 23-1115), Máximo Lira 889, on Monday, Wednesday and Friday around noon and 6 pm.

The Ferrobus Arica-La Paz (☎ 23-2844) departs from opposite the Plazoleta Estación, at 21 de Mayo 51 (US$52 in US currency only including food, 12 hours).

CHILE

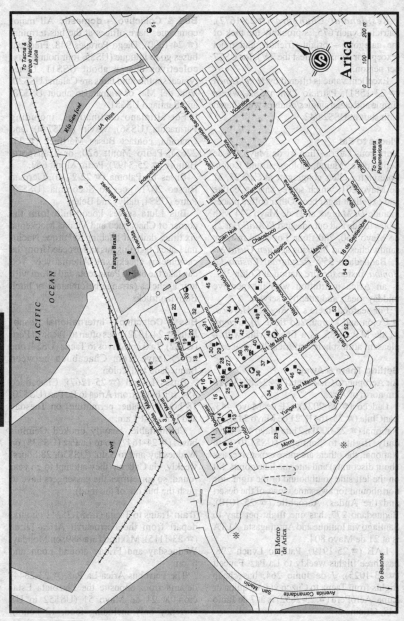

Arica

To Tacna &
Parque Nacional
Lauca

Río San José

PACIFIC OCEAN

Port

El Morro
de Arica

To Beaches

To Carretera
Panamericana

0   100   200 m

With only 42 seats, it is hard to get on in summer, and they only take reservations one week ahead. It leaves Arica on Tuesday and Saturday at 9.30 am (10.30 am in summer).

Getting Around
To/From the Airport Radio Taxis Chacalluta (☎ 25-4812), on the corner of Patricio Lynch and 21 de Mayo, has taxis (US$10) and colectivos (US$4) to Aeropuerto Chacalluta.

Bus The bus terminal can be quickly reached by taxi colectivo No 8 from 18 de Septiembre. Slow local buses and faster taxi colectivos connect the town centre and the bus terminal. Only taxi colectivos serve the Azapa valley (US$1); departing 7 am to 10 pm daily from the corner of Chacabuco and Patricio Lynch.

Car The main rental-car agencies are Hertz (☎ 23-1487), at General Velásquez 1109; Budget (☎ 25-2978); Avis (☎ 23-2210), at Chacabuco 180; and Viva (☎ 25-1121), at Baquedano 9.

AROUND ARICA
Museo Arqueológico San Miguel de Azapa
Twelve km from Arica, this archaeological museum has elaborate displays on regional cultures from the 7th century BC to the Spanish invasion. The visit is self-paced, with an informative booklet in Spanish or English. Ask about the nearby geoglyphs. The museum opens on weekdays from 10 am to 6 pm and on weekends from 1 to 6 pm. It can be reached by taxi colectivo Azapa from the corner of Chacabuco and Lynch.

Lluta Geoglyphs
Fourteen km north of Arica, paved Ruta 11 leads up the Lluta valley to Poconchile. A short distance inland, a series of hillside geoglyphs depicting llamas recalls pre-Columbian pack trains to Tiahuanaco. Bus Lluta takes you there from the corner of Chacabuco and Vicuña Mackenna.

CHILE

Poconchile

Poconchile's 17th-century **Iglesia de San Gerónimo**, restored earlier this century, is one of Chile's oldest churches. Ask for the church key at the restaurant.

Pukará de Copaquilla

As Ruta 11 zigzags up the desolate mountainside above the Lluta valley, it passes many 'candle-holder' cacti, which absorb moisture from the camanchaca. Tours to Parque Nacional Lauca stop briefly at the 12th-century Pukará de Copaquilla, a fortress built to protect farmlands in the canyon below – notice the abandoned terraces, evidence of a much larger pre-Columbian population. You can get coffee, sandwiches and *mate de coca*, and even pitch a tent, at the home of Alexis Troncoso and Andrea Chellen. Buses to Putre take you there from Calle Germán Riesco 2071 in Arica.

PUTRE

Putre, at an altitude of 3500 metres and 150 km from Arica, was a 16th-century *reducción* (a Spanish settlement established to control the Indians). Many buildings retain colonial features, most notably the restored adobe **iglesia** (1670). Local farmers raise alfalfa for llamas, sheep and cattle on ancient stone-faced terraces.

Restaurant Oasis, at Cochrane and O'Higgins, offers basic lodgings for US$5 and good plain meals. Opposite the army camp, CONAF's comfortable *refugio* charges US$14.

Buses La Paloma serves Putre daily from Arica (leaving at 6.45 am) but buses to Lauca pass by the turn-off to Putre. Mining trucks from *Hostería Las Vicuñas* (☎ 22-4466), which charges US$50/70 for a single/double with bath and breakfast, may take you to the park's Las Cuevas entrance.

PARQUE NACIONAL LAUCA

Parque Nacional Lauca is a 138,000-hectare altiplano biosphere reserve with vicuña, vizcacha and 150 species of bird, plus cultural and archaeological landmarks. The Pallachata volcanoes behind sprawling Lago Chungará are dormant, but nearby Guallatire smokes ominously.

Lauca is 160 km north-east of Arica, between 3000 and 6300 metres above sea level. Visitors should adapt to the altitude gradually; do not exert yourself at first and eat and drink moderately. If you suffer from altitude sickness try the herbal tea remedy *chachacoma*. You'll need to wear sunblock against the brutal tropical rays, but be aware that it can also snow during *invierno boliviano* (Bolivian winter, the summer rainy season).

Flocks of vicuña graze the verdant *bofedales* (boglands) and lower mountain slopes, along with domestic llamas and alpacas. Note the ground-hugging llareta, a bright green shrub with a deceptive cushion-like appearance; the Aymara use a pick or mattock to crack open dead plants for fuel.

Things to See & Do

The **Las Cuevas** entrance is an excellent place to photograph vicuñas, whose numbers have increased from barely 1000 in the early 1970s to over 27,000 today. Also have a soak in the rustic thermal baths.

Domestic stock graze the **Ciénegas de Parinacota** between the villages of Chucuyo and Parinacota, and wildlife and cultural relics are abundant; have a look at Chucuyo's colonial chapel. *Guallatas* (Andean geese) and ducks drift on the Río Lauca and nest on the banks, and chinchilla-like vizcachas peek out from rockeries. **Parinacota**, an Aymara village five km off the highway, has a fascinating 17th-century church, with Dantesque interior murals. Alpaca woollens are available here.

Over 4500 metres above sea level and 28 km from Las Cuevas, shallow **Lago Chungará** was formed when lava from 6350-metre Volcán Parinacota dammed the snowmelt stream. Birds here include flamingos, giant coots and Andean gulls. Arica's demand for hydroelectricity and the Azapa valley's thirst have created an intricate system of pumps and canals that may compromise Chungará's ecological integrity.

Places to Stay & Eat

In a pinch, the *refugio* at Las Cuevas may offer a bed. In Chucuyo, Matilde & Máximo Morales usually have a spare bed at a very reasonable price, and Matilde will prepare alpaca steaks and other simple meals for about US$3; there are two other cheap restaurants. Buy most supplies in Arica.

In Parinacota, CONAF charges US$11 for beds in a large but sparsely furnished *refugio* with solar-heated hot water; bring a sleeping bag. Tent sites cost US$6 here and at Chungará, which has picnic tables, some shelter and *very* cold nights. Chungará also has eight beds for tourists at US$11 per person.

Getting There & Away

The park straddles the Arica-La Paz highway, which is paved to the Chile-Bolivia border. For buses, see the Arica section.

Many Arica travel agencies offer tours (about US$20), leaving around 7.30 am and returning about 8.30 pm. Several agencies are located along Bolognesi, so shop around. The Aymara-run Vicuña Tour (☎ 25-3773), at Prat 430, Oficina 14, offers special trips through fascinating villages and including some hiking; the owners, a historian/geographer from Putre and a tour guide who lived for many years in the area, have extensive first-hand knowledge of the place. Birding Alto Andino (☎ 24-1322) at Baquedano 299 in Putre, runs guided bird-watching trips in the precordillera and the altiplano.

Tours are a good introduction, but try to arrange a longer stay – a rental car lets you visit more remote areas like Guallatire, Caquena and Salar de Surire (only with a high-clearance vehicle, since it involves fording the river). Carry extra fuel.

IQUIQUE

Iquique was a collection of shanties until the 19th-century mining boom, when nitrate barons built mansions and authorities piped in water from the Andes. Its Plaza de Armas, with a Victorian clock tower and a theatre with Corinthian columns, reflects this boom.

Iquique's port now ships more fishmeal than any other in the world, while the modern duty-free shopping centre (zona franca), has added to prosperity. The centre's ramshackle wooden houses, sailors' bars and street life preserve a 19th-century atmosphere.

Orientation

Iquique (population 140,000) sits at the base of the coast range, 1853 km north of Santiago and 315 km south of Arica. Avenida Baquedano, which runs north-south, is the main thoroughfare. Calle Tarapacá, which runs from Plaza Prat and east past Plaza Condell, is the secondary centre of activity.

Information

Tourist Offices Sernatur (☎ 41-1523) is at Serrano 145, 3rd floor, Oficina 303, with a branch at the zona franca in the Sector Antiguo, 1st floor. Open weekdays from 8.30 am to 1 pm and from 3 to 6 pm, it provides a free leaflet with information about what's on in Iquique.

Money Carpillo Money Exchange is at Tarapacá 376 and Casa Sciaraffia is at Tarapacá 399; there are two more cambios in the Galería Lynch, on Lynch between Serrano and Tarapacá, and there are several cambios in the zona franca.

Post & Communications The post office is at Bolívar 485. There are CTC offices at San Martín and Obispo Labbé, on Ramírez near the corner of Tarapacá, and in the zona franca. Entel is at Gorostiaga 287. Iquique's telephone code is 57.

Consulates The Bolivian Consulate (☎ 42-1777) is at Pasaje Alessandri 429, 3rd floor, Oficina 300. The Peruvian Consulate (☎ 41-1466) is at San Martín 385.

Medical Services The Hospital Regional Doctor Torres (☎ 42-2370) is on the corner of Tarapacá and Avenida Héroes de la Concepción.

Things to See

Architectural landmarks on or near Plaza Prat include the 1877 **torre reloj** (clock tower), the neoclassical **Teatro Municipal** (1890) and the Moorish **Centro Español** (1904). Calle Baquedano has several buildings in Georgian style.

The **Museo Naval** occupies the 1871 **Edificio de Aduana** (customs house), on Esmeralda between Aníbal Pinto and Baquedano. Just west of the Aduana, harbour tours leave from the **Muelle de Pasajeros** (passenger jetty), built in 1901. At Sotomayor and Vivar, the **Estación del Ferrocarril** (train station) once served the nitrate oficinas.

Once a courthouse, the **Museo Regional** features many pre-Columbian artefacts, a mock altiplano village, Aymara crafts, photos of Iquique's early days and a detailed model of Oficina Peña Chica, near Humberstone. At Baquedano 951, it's open on weekdays from 9 am to 1 pm and 3 to 6 pm. Admission is US$1.

Zona Franca Most Chileans visit Iquique, and many have moved here because of this sprawling shopping centre with imported goods. All of the Tarapacá region is a duty-free zone, and the *zofri* (as it is commonly known) has given Iquique the country's lowest unemployment rate.

To see or join in the feeding frenzy, take any northbound taxi colectivo from the centre on weekdays from 9.30 am to 1 pm and 4.30 to 9 pm, or on Saturday from 9.30 am to 1 pm only.

Beaches Playa Cavancha, at Balmaceda and Amunátegui, is Iquique's most popular beach; farther south, along Avenida 11 de Septiembre, the Playa Brava is a bit rough for swimming but fine for sunbathing. South of Iquique, public transport to the many fine and less crowded beaches is infrequent despite a superb paved highway, so renting a car is worth considering.

Places to Stay

There's a cluster of seedy residenciales on Amunátegui between Sargento Aldea and Thompson, all charging about US$5 per person. *Hostal Sol del Norte* (☎ 42-1546), Juan Martínez 852, charges US$6 per person but lacks hot water. One reader enjoyed a nameless *hospedaje* at Gorostiaga 451 (also without hot water). A step up is the very clean and friendly *Residencial José Luis* (☎ 42-2844), San Martín 601, which gets short-stay trade. Singles are US$9 with shared bath, and doubles are US$14 with private bath; all downstairs rooms have large, comfortable double beds. Interior rooms are quieter.

Probably the best value is *Residencial Catedral* (☎ 42-2184), Obispo Labbé 235, which has singles/doubles for US$13/25 with shared bath. Charging US$10 a single, the rambling *Residencial Bolívar*, around the corner at Bolívar 478, is less obviously appealing but perhaps friendlier. One reader found *Residencial Condell* (☎ 41-3948), Thompson 684, most hospitable.

Places to Eat

At the *Mercado Centenario* (central market), on Barros Arana between Sargento Aldea and Latorre, several upstairs restaurants have excellent seafood at fair prices. Other good options are *Restaurant Grecia*, at Thompson 865, *Club Croata*, at Plaza Prat 310, and a good Mexican restaurant, *Taco Taquilla*, at Thompson 123. One reader praised *Restaurant Samoa*, Bolívar 396, for its fine fixed-price lunch. The restaurant at the fire station, Serrano 520, is another excellent place for lunch.

For a splurge, try the ornate *Club Español*, on Plaza Prat, with its Moorish interior and artwork.

Getting There & Away

Air Aeropuerto Diego Aracena is 41 km south of the city centre. Ladeco has daily flights to Antofagasta and Santiago. Lan-Chile has eight flights weekly to Santiago, with four stopping in Antofagasta. Ladeco (☎ 41-3038) is at San Martín 428, Oficina 2; LanChile (☎ 41-2540) is at Aníbal Pinto 641. Aerochile (☎ 42-5295), O'Higgins 169, flies once a day to Santiago. National

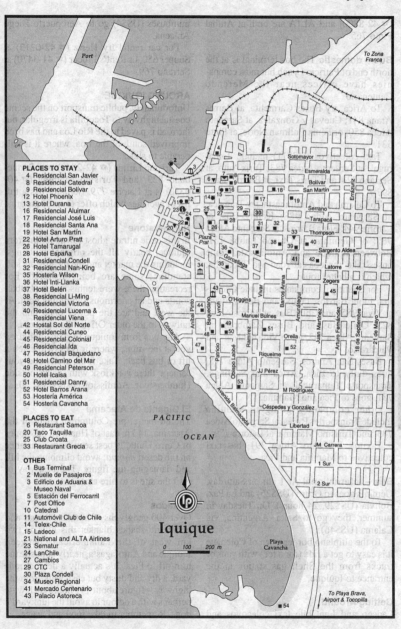

PLACES TO STAY
4 Residencial San Javier
8 Residencial Catedral
9 Residencial Bolívar
12 Hotel Phoenix
13 Hotel Durana
16 Residencial Aluimar
17 Residencial José Luis
18 Residencial Santa Ana
19 Hotel San Martín
22 Hotel Arturo Pratt
26 Hotel Tamarugal
28 Hotel España
31 Residencial Condell
32 Residencial Nan-King
35 Hostería Wilson
36 Hotel Inti-Llanka
37 Hotel Belén
38 Residencial Li-Ming
39 Residencial Victoria
40 Residencial Lucerna &
    Residencial Viena
42 Hostal Sol del Norte
44 Residencial Cuneo
45 Residencial Colonial
46 Residencial Ida
47 Residencial Baquedano
48 Hotel Camino del Mar
49 Residencial Peterson
50 Hotel Icaisa
51 Residencial Danny
52 Hotel Barros Arana
53 Hostería América
54 Hostería Cavancha

PLACES TO EAT
6 Restaurant Samoa
20 Taco Taquilla
25 Club Croata
33 Restaurant Grecia

OTHER
1 Bus Terminal
2 Muelle de Pasajeros
3 Edificio de Aduana &
    Museo Naval
5 Estación del Ferrocarril
7 Post Office
10 Catedral
11 Automóvil Club de Chile
14 Telex-Chile
15 Ladeco
21 National and ALTA Airlines
23 Sernatur
24 LanChile
27 Cambios
29 CTC
30 Plaza Condell
34 Museo Regional
41 Mercado Centenario
43 Palacio Astoreca

To Zona Franca

Port

PACIFIC

OCEAN

Iquique

0   100   200 m

Playa Cavancha

To Playa Brava,
Airport & Tocopilla

CHILE

(☎ 42-8800) and ALTA are both at Aníbal Pinto 765.

Bus – domestic The bus terminal is at the north end of Patricio Lynch but most companies have offices near the Mercado Centenario.

To Arica, try Buses Carmelita, at Barros Arana 841; Cuevas y González, at Sargento Aldea 850; or Fénix Pullman Norte, at Pinto 531.

Taxi colectivos (US$11) include Tamarugal, at Sargento Aldea 783; Turis Auto, at Serrano 724; and Turis Taxi, at Barros Arana 897-A.

To Calama and Antofagasta, try Tramaca, at Sargento Aldea 988; Kenny Bus, at Latorre 944; Flota Barrios, at Sargento Aldea 987; or Géminis, at Obispo Labbé 151. Between Iquique and Antofagasta, some buses take the coastal road via Tocopilla, which is a better route.

For Santiago, companies include Carmelita, Flota Barrios, Fénix, and Buses Evans at Vivar 955; and Chile Bus, at Barros Arana 825. Chile Bus, and Buses Zambrano at Sargento Aldea 742, go to Viña del Mar and Valparaíso.

Buses San Andrés, Sargento Aldea 798, goes daily to Pica, Arica and Santiago. Transporte Tamarugal, at Sargento Aldea 781, goes to Pica and Mamiña.

Other companies going to Mamiña include Transportes Rojas, at Sargento Aldea 783, and Turismo Mamiña, at Latorre 779.

Taxitur, Sargento Aldea 791, has taxi colectivos to Mamiña and Pica.

Bus – international At 1 am on Saturday, Géminis goes to Oruro (US$26) and La Paz, Bolivia (US$29, 24 hours). On Tuesday in summer, they go to Salta, Argentina, via Calama (US$46).

To the altiplano border town of Colchane it is easy to get a ride (for a fee) with vans or trucks from the Shell gas station at the entrance to Iquique.

Getting Around
Ladeco and LanChile taxi colectivos and minibuses (US$4) go to Aeropuerto Diego Aracena.

For car rental try Hertz (☎ 42-0213) at Souper 650, or Rent's Procar (☎ 41-3470) at Serrano 769.

AROUND IQUIQUE

Unfortunately, public transport on the scenic coastal highway to Tocopilla is irregular, but the road is paved to the Río Loa and has been improved south of the Loa, where it is vulnerable to slides.

Turismo Lirima (☎ 42-2049) is at Baquedano 823, and Turismo Mamiña (☎ 40-0330) is at Latorre 779. Sernatur has a full list of agencies which offer tours of the area.

Humberstone

In this eerie nitrate ghost town, 45 km from Iquique, nearly all the original buildings, including the market and the theatre, are still standing; some are being restored. For recreation there were tennis and basketball courts and an enormous swimming pool. At the west end are the power plant and the railway to the older Oficina Santa Laura.

Any bus from Iquique to Arica will drop you at the ruins, where it is easy to catch a lift or bus back. Take food, water and your camera; there is a kiosk with snacks outside Humberstone. Admission costs US$2.50.

El Gigante de Atacama

The 86-metre, pre-Columbian Giant of the Atacama, 14 km east of Huara on the slopes of Cerro Unita, is best seen from a distance on the desert *pampa*; avoid climbing the hill and damaging the figure. The best way to visit the site is to hire a car or taxi.

Pintados

Over 400 geoglyphs of humans, llamas and geometric shapes blanket this hillside two km west of the Panamericana between Iquique and Antofagasta, nearly opposite the turn-off to Pica. It's actually a derelict railyard, a dry and dusty but easy walk from the highway – figure about 1½ hours each way, perhaps with a detour to avoid the junkyard's dogs. Remember to take food and water.

La Tirana

In mid-July, up to 30,000 dancing pilgrims invade La Tirana (population 250), 72 km from Iquique, to worship the Virgin of Carmen. The **Santuario de La Tirana** is a broad plaza with one of Chile's oddest churches, but despite several restaurants, there are no hotels or residenciales – pilgrims camp in the open spaces to the east. The **Museo del Salitre** exhibits a haphazard assortment of artefacts from nitrate oficinas.

RESERVA NACIONAL PAMPA DEL TAMARUGAL

The dense groves lining the Panamericana south of Pozo Almonte are not a natural forest, but they are a native species; the tamarugo covered thousands of sq km until woodcutting for the mines nearly destroyed it.

CONAF's 108,000-hectare reserve has restored much of this forest, which flourishes in highly saline soils by reaching deep for ground water. The visitor centre, 24 km south of Pozo Almonte, has fine displays on local ecology. The guesthouse charges US$13 for a single; across the road is a camping ground (US$6 for shaded sites with tables and benches).

MAMIÑA

Mamiña, 73 km east of Pozo Almonte, has been a popular hot-springs resort since the nitrate era, but is much older – the **Pukará del Cerro Inca** is a pre-Columbian fortress, while the **Iglesia de Nuestra Señora del Rosario** dates from 1632.

Residencial Sol de Ipla, on Calle Ipla, charges US$16 per person with shared bath, but there are several others – the historic nitrate-era *Hotel Refugio del Salitre* (☎ 43-0330) is worth a splurge at US$51 a single. For transport, see the Iquique entry.

PICA

Diego de Almagro skirmished with Indians at Pica, another popular hot-springs resort, 119 km south-east of Iquique on the road from La Tirana. In late colonial times, it was famous for wines and fruits, while in the 19th century, it supplied wheat, wine, figs, raisins and alfalfa to the oficinas.

Pica was so dependent on outside water that the Spaniards developed an elaborate delivery system of more than 15 km of tunnels. When Iquique boomed, the Tarapacá Water Company piped water from Pica to the coast, and Pica became a 'hill station' for the nitrate barons.

Places to Stay & Eat

Camping Miraflores, charging about US$4 per person, is reportedly in disrepair. *Hostería O'Higgins* and *Hotel San Andrés* charge about US$9 per person. There are several cheap restaurants. For transport, see the previous Iquique section.

ANTOFAGASTA

Antofagasta (population 221,000), 1350 km north of Santiago and 700 km south of Arica, exports most of the Atacama's minerals, especially copper. Founded in 1870, it offered the easiest route to the interior and soon handled the highest tonnage of any South American Pacific port.

Freak floods in 1991 obliterated the southern access road to the Panamericana, but in general the climate is always clear and dry, neither too hot nor too cold.

Orientation

The city centre's western boundary is the north-south Avenida Balmaceda, which eventually becomes Aníbal Pinto; to the south, it becomes Avenida Grecia. Within this central grid, bounded also by Bolívar and Ossa, streets run south-west to north-east. Plaza Colón is at the centre.

Information

Tourist Offices Sernatur (☎ 26-4044), Maipú 240, is open weekdays from 8.30 am to 1 pm and 3 to 7.30 pm. In summer, a kiosco de turismo near Hotel Antofagasta is open daily from 9.30 am to 1.30 pm and from 4.30 to 7.30 pm. On Sunday its hours are 10.30 am to 2 pm.

Antofagasta

0   150   300 m

To Calama & Arica

Old Port

To Beaches

PLACES TO STAY				
4	Hotel Antofagasta	30	Pizzería D'Alfredo	15	ALTA Airlines
9	Residencial	32	Restaurant	16	Ladeco
	Libertad		Apoquindo	17	National Airlines
12	Hotel San Marcos	33	Restaurant	18	Plaza Colón
14	Hotel San Martín		El Arriero	19	Buses Fénix Pullman
23	Hotel Plaza	35	Casino de Bomberos		Norte
26	Residencial	38	Restaurant Shanghai	20	Buses Tur-Bus
	Riojanita	43	Rincón Don Quijote	21	LanChile
31	Hotel Diego de	47	Restaurant Bavaria	24	Buses Flota
	Almagro	54	Restaurant Un Dragón		Barrios
34	Hotel Rawaye	58	Chifa Chong Hua (1)	25	Sernatur
39	Hotel Astore	59	Chifa Chong Hua (2)	28	Cambio Inter-Santiago
40	Residencial Paola			29	CTC
41	Residencial		OTHER	36	Banco del Estado
	El Cobre	1	Muelle Salitrero	37	Teatro Pedro de la
44	Hotel San Antonio	3	SOQUIMICH		Barra
48	Hotel Rinconada	5	Kiosco de	42	Entel
53	Hotel Brasil		Turismo	45	Automóvil Club
55	Hotel América	6	Museo Regional	46	Mercado Central
		7	Railway Station	49	CTC
PLACES TO EAT		8	Buses Géminis	50	CONAF
2	Terminal Pesquero	10	Terminal de Buses	51	Bolivian Consulate
22	Café Caribe & Café		Rurales	52	Buses Tramaca &
	Haiti	11	Buses Fichtur		Buses Atahualpa
27	Fiori di Gelatto	13	Post Office & Telex	56	Hospital Regional
			Chile	57	Argentine Consulate

Money Cambios include Inter-Santiago, Latorre 2528, No 12, and Cambio San Marcos, at Latorre 2489, where they change both cash and American Express travellers' cheques. Several banks on Prat use the Redbanc ATM system, such as BCI at Washington 2683.

Post & Communications The post office is at Washington 2613. CTC is at Uribe 746, while Entel is at Baquedano 751-A. The telephone code for Antofagasta is 55.

Consulates The Argentine Consulate (☎ 22-2854), Manuel Verbal 1640, is open from 9 am to 2 pm on weekdays. The Bolivian Consulate (☎ 22-1403), Grecia 563, Oficina 23, keeps the same hours.

Medical Services The Hospital Regional (☎ 26-9009) is at Avenida Argentina 1962.

Things to See

Like Iquique, Antofagasta is an architectural curiosity. The British community left a visible imprint in the **Torre Reloj**, a replica of Big Ben on Plaza Colón; the **Barrio Histó-**

rico, between the plaza and the old port; and the **Muelle Salitrero** (nitrate pier), at the foot of Bolívar.

On the corner of Balmaceda and Bolívar, the former **Gobernación Marítima** (port authority) houses the **Museo Regional**. Across the street is the former **Aduana** (customs house), moved from the town of Mejillones in 1888. Across Bolívar is the **Estación Ferrocarril** (1887), terminus of the La Paz railway.

Places to Stay

Residencial Paola (☎ 22-2208), Prat 755, is friendly, clean and quiet at US$8 a single. *Hotel Rawaye* (22-5399), Sucre 762, is excellent value at US$8/12 for a single/double with a shared bath. Similarly priced is *Residencial Riojanita* (☎ 26-8652) at Baquedano 464.

Places to Eat

The best value is the unpretentious *terminal pesquero*, at the old port, where simple stands peddle tasty fresh shellfish and masses of pelicans jam the pier waiting for scraps. Carnivores will enjoy *El Arriero*, at

Condell 2644, a fine parrilla with excellent service. The *Casino de Bomberos*, Sucre 763, has good set lunches.

Popular *Apoquindo*, Prat 616, serves drinks, sweets and snacks. For snacks, coffee, superb ice cream and desserts, try *Fiori di Gelatto*, Latorre 250. *Café Caribe*, at Prat 486, and *Café Haiti*, at Prat 482, have quality caffeine.

Other recommended places include *Rincón Don Quijote*, at Maipú 642; *Casa Vecchia*, at O'Higgins 1456; and *La Papa Nostra*, at Medina 052, at the southern end of town near the municipal beach. *Pizzería D'Alfredo*, Condell 2539, has a large range of pizzas.

Getting There & Away

Air Aeropuerto Cerro Moreno is 25 km north of the Península de Mejillones.

Flight schedules from Santiago resemble those to Iquique and Arica. LanChile (☎ 26-5151) is at Washington 2552 and Ladeco (☎ 26-9170) is nearby at Washington 2589. National (☎ 26-4050) is at Prat 264 and ALTA (☎ 22-6089) is at Balmaceda 2584.

Bus Most bus companies operate from their terminals in the centre of town.

Tramaca (☎ 25-1770), Uribe 936, has frequent buses to Calama, plus daily service to Arica, Iquique, Santiago and intermediate destinations; it also handles tickets for the Calama-Oruro (Bolivia) railway.

Atahualpa, Uribe 936, crosses the Andes to Salta, Argentina on Saturday at 4 pm in summer (US$33). Géminis (☎ 26-3968), Latorre 3055, also goes to Salta.

Flota Barrios, Condell 2764, has daily buses to most of the same destinations as Tramaca. Tur-Bus (☎ 26-4487), Latorre 2751, serves Calama, Santiago and Arica. Fénix Pullman Norte (☎ 22-5293), San Martín 2717, runs along similar routes.

From the Terminal de Buses Rurales, Riquelme 513, Fepstur and Chadday both go to Mejillones, while Chile Bus covers major stops between Arica and Santiago. Libac, at the main terminal, connects Antofagasta with Calama and Santiago.

Typical fares are Calama US$5, Iquique US$19, Arica US$23 and Santiago US$38. Between Antofagasta and Iquique, some buses take the coastal road via Tocopilla, which is a better route.

Getting Around

Ladeco's airport bus goes to Aeropuerto Cerro Moreno; for door-to-door service, call Aerobus on ☎ 26-2727.

AROUND ANTOFAGASTA
La Portada

The Pacific has eroded a photogenic natural arch in La Portada, an offshore stack 16 km north of Antofagasta. Take bus No 15 from Sucre to the *cruce* (junction) at La Portada, then walk three km to the arch. Since the 1995 earthquake the area has been closed off, so ask at Sernatur before going.

Mejillones

Mejillones, a small beach resort 60 km north of Antofagasta, has reasonable accommodation at *Residencial Elizabeth*, Almirante Latorre 440. Fepstur and Chadday buses leave from the Terminal de Buses Rurales at Riquelme 513, Antofagasta.

Cobija & Gatico

Only a few km apart, 130 km north of Antofagasta, Cobija and Gatico are ghost towns where a few families eke out a living by fishing and collecting seaweed. In the early 19th century, despite a precarious water supply, Cobija was a flourishing port which served Bolivia's altiplano mines. After an earthquake and tsunami in 1877, it declined rapidly; by 1907, it had only 35 inhabitants.

Fresh fish may be available, but everything else is scarce; you can camp among the atmospheric adobe walls.

Tocopilla

Tocopilla (population 22,000), 190 km north of Antofagasta, is an important port for the remaining nitrate oficinas of Pedro de Valdivia and María Elena, and the site of Codelco's thermoelectric plant supplying Chuquicamata.

Cheap hotels include *Residencial Royal* (☎ 81-1448), at 21 de Mayo 1988, and *Residencial Sonia*, at Washington 1329, each charging about US$5 per person. The best restaurant is the *Club de la Unión* at Prat 1354.

Tramaca, 21 de Mayo 2196, runs buses to Antofagasta and sometimes to Iquique. Hitching, if not utterly impossible, is difficult.

María Elena, Pedro de Valdivia & the Nitrate Ghost Towns

Near the junction of the Panamericana and the Tocopilla-Chuquicamata road, María Elena is one of the last functioning oficinas. Its street plan, patterned after the Union Jack, looks better on paper than in reality. For tours, contact the SOQUIMICH public relations office (☎ 63-2731).

There's no accommodation, but decent food is available at *Restaurante Yerco* and *Restaurante Club Social*. Some Tramaca and Flota Barrios buses from Antofagasta to Calama stop here.

Pedro de Valdivia, 40 km south, is also open to the public. Meals are available at the *Club Pedro de Valdivia*. Tramaca and Flota Barrios buses go directly to Antofagasta.

Dozens of ghost towns line both sides of the Baquedano-Calama road and the Panamericana north of the Tocopilla-Chuquicamata highway.

Baquedano

Between Antofagasta and Calama, Baquedano used to be a major rail junction where the Longino (longitudinal railway) met the Antofagasta-La Paz line. The **Museo Ferroviario** is an open-air rail museum, but an infrequent, agonisingly slow and indescribably filthy freight train still runs from here to the Argentine border at Socompa – for truly intrepid travellers only.

CALAMA

Calama (population 120,000), 220 km from Antofagasta and 2700 metres above sea level, is the gateway to Chuquicamata, the oases of San Pedro de Atacama and Toconao,

and the eerie El Tatio geysers. It's also the western terminus of the Calama-Oruro (Bolivia) railway.

Orientation

Plaza 23 de Marzo is the centre of Calama. Though the town has sprawled on the north bank of the Río Loa because labourers prefer it to higher, colder Chuquicamata, its core is pedestrian-friendly.

Information

Tourist Offices The municipal tourist office (☎ 21-2654, Interno 60), Latorre 1689, is open weekdays from 8.30 am to 1 pm and from 3 to 6 pm.

Money There is a cambio at Sotomayor 1818, and others in the vicinity. BCI at Sotomayor 2002 has Redbanc.

Post & Communications The post office is on Granaderos. CTC is at Vargas 1927, while Entel is at Sotomayor 2025. Calama's telephone code is 56.

Consulates The Bolivian Consulate (☎ 21-1976), Vicuña Mackenna 2020, is open weekdays from 9.30 am to 12.30 pm and from 4.30 to 6.30 pm.

Medical Services Calama's hospital (☎ 34-2347) is on the corner of Avenida Granaderos and Cisterna, north of the plaza.

Organised Tours

Limited public transport makes tours a reasonable alternative. Itineraries vary, but the most complete one (for about US$25) goes from Calama to the El Tatio geysers and returns via villages with traditional Andean churches.

Other tours involve staying overnight in San Pedro de Atacama, stopping at Valle de La Luna (Valley of the Moon) before visiting El Tatio. Another visits the Salar de Atacama, including the village of Toconao (US$15 from San Pedro). In general, it's more convenient to make arrangements for El Tatio in San Pedro, because it's cheaper and the trip is shorter and less tiring. Tours to El Tatio leave as early as 3 am.

Tour agencies in Calama include Nativa Expediciones (☎ 21-0152), at Abaroa 1796; Turismo El Sol (☎ 34-0152), at Abaroa 1614; Loa Desert Adventure (☎ 21-2200), at Bañados Espinoza 2191; Atacama Desert Expeditions (☎ 31-2019), at Latorre 1760; and Turismo Quitor (☎ 31-4159), at Ramírez 2116, 2nd floor.

Places to Stay

Hostel The beautifully restored old *Hotel El Mirador* (☎ 34-0329) at Sotomayor 2064 has excellent hostel-style accommodation for US$11 with breakfast. The owners, descendants of War of the Pacific hero Abaroa (who lived in the house) will happily share family history with those interested. The hotel has most of the original furniture, and the owners are in the process of restoring its tower.

Hotels & Residenciales *Residencial Capri* (☎ 34-2870), Vivar 1639, is tolerable by budget standards at US$5 per person. *Residencial Toño* (☎ 34-1185), Vivar 1970, is popular with foreign visitors. It charges US$6, has clean sheets, offers many blankets and is reasonably quiet.

The clean *Residencial Splendid* (☎ 34-1841), Ramírez 1960, has singles/doubles with shared bath for US$8/13. Rates are similar at *Residencial Internacional* (☎ 34-2927), General Velásquez 1976. *Hotel Atenas* (☎ 34-2666), Ramírez 1961, has small, neat rooms for US$11/16.

Places to Eat

Restaurant Victoria, Vargas 2102, and *Restaurant Osorno*, upstairs at Granaderos 2013-B, are ordinary budget eateries. *Club Yugoslavo*, Abaroa 1869, has a good fixed-price lunch. *Bavaria Restaurant*, Sotomayor 2035, is part of an uninspiring chain. *Restaurant Sándolo*, Vivar 1982, is a parrilla that also offers fish and other seafood. For ice cream, desserts, sandwiches and coffee, visit *Fiori di Gelatto*, Ramírez 2099. *Pizzería D'Alfredo*, next door to the Club Yugoslavo

on Abaroa, across from the plaza, is very popular among locals for lunch.

Getting There & Away

Air Aeropuerto El Loa (☎ 31-1331) is a short distance south of town. Ladeco (☎ 31-2626), Ramírez 1858, has four flights weekly to Antofagasta and Santiago. LanChile (☎ 34-1477), Latorre 1499, has a similar schedule. ALTA is at Ramírez 1862.

Bus – domestic Calama has no central terminal, but most companies are fairly central and within a few blocks of each other.

Tramaca, Granaderos 3048 on the northern edge of town, has frequent buses to Antofagasta, Santiago, Arica and Iquique; buy tickets from their downtown office (☎ 34-0404) at Sotomayor 1961. Tur-Bus, Ramírez 1802, has daily buses to Santiago and Arica. Flota Barrios (☎ 34-1497), Ramírez 2298, also serves Panamericana destinations. Kenny Bus, Vivar 1954, serves Iquique via María Elena and Pozo Almonte.

Géminis (☎ 34-1993), Antofagasta 2239, has daily buses to Santiago and Arica, and goes to San Pedro de Atacama on Sunday. Morales y Moralito (☎ 34-2671), Sotomayor 1802, goes to San Pedro three times a day, and twice to Toconao. Yusmar (☎ 31-8543), Antofagasta 2041, goes four times daily to San Pedro, and twice daily to Toconao (US$4).

Typical fares are San Pedro US$2.50, Antofagasta US$5, Iquique US$9, Arica US$10 and Santiago US$35.

Bus – international Make reservations to cross the Andes to Salta, Argentina (US$45 to US$50), with Géminis or Tramaca. Buses leave on Wednesday early in the morning. To Oruro, Bolivia (US$23), Tramaca departs on Tuesday and Friday at 6 am.

Train On Wednesday at 11 pm, there is a train to Ollagüe, on the Chile-Bolivia border, with connections to Uyuni (US$16). Get tickets at the Tramaca office at Sotomayor 1961 or at Calama railway station (☎ 21-2004), Balmaceda 1777.

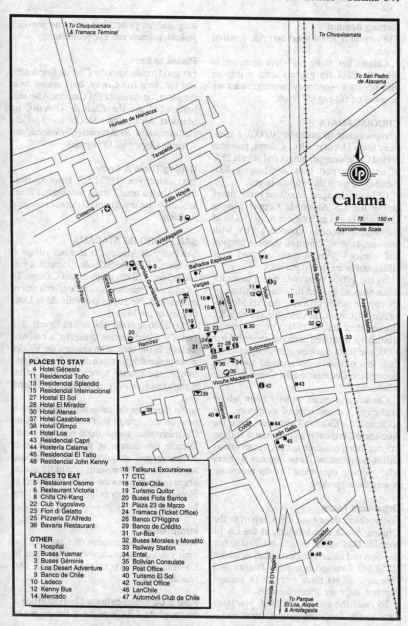

Calama

0   75   150 m

Approximate Scale

To Chuquicamata
& Tramaca Terminal

To Chuquicamata

Hurtado de Mendoza

Tarapacá

Félix Hoyos

Cisterna

Antofagasta

Bañados Espinoza

Vargas

Latorre

Ramírez

Sotomayor

Vicuña Mackenna

Balmaceda

Matta

Abaroa

Cobija

León Gallo

Ecuador

Avenida B O'Higgins

To Parque
El Loa, Airport
& Antofagasta

CHILE

PLACES TO STAY
4   Hotel Génesis
11 Residencial Toño
13 Residencial Splendid
15 Residencial Internacional
27 Hostal El Sol
28 Hotel El Mirador
30 Hotel Atenas
37 Hotel Casablanca
38 Hotel Olimpo
41 Hotel Loa
43 Residencial Capri
44 Hostería Calama
45 Residencial El Tatio
48 Residencial John Kenny

PLACES TO EAT
5   Restaurant Osorno
6   Restaurant Victoria
8   Chifa Chi-Kang
22 Club Yugoslavo
23 Fiori di Gelatto
25 Pizzería D'Alfredo
36 Bavaria Restaurant

OTHER
1   Hospital
2   Buses Yusmar
3   Buses Géminis
7   Loa Desert Adventure
9   Banco de Chile
10 Ladeco
12 Kenny Bus
14 Mercado
16 Talikuna Excursiones
17 CTC
18 Telex-Chile
19 Turismo Quitor
20 Buses Flota Barrios
21 Plaza 23 de Marzo
24 Tramaca (Ticket Office)
26 Banco O'Higgins
29 Banco de Crédito
31 Tur-Bus
32 Buses Morales y Moralito
33 Railway Station
34 Entel
35 Bolivian Consulate
39 Post Office
40 Turismo El Sol
42 Tourist Office
46 LanChile
47 Automóvil Club de Chile

Getting Around

The airport is just a short taxi ride south of town.

Calama has many car-rental agencies; to visit the El Tatio geysers, rent a jeep or pick-up truck – ordinary passenger cars are no good on the rugged roads.

CHUQUICAMATA

Chuquicamata (population 30,000), a company town 16 km north of Calama, provides half of Chile's copper output and at least 25% of its total export income. Chuqui's 400-metre-deep pit is the world's largest.

Chuqui changed hands several times before the US Anaconda Copper Mining Company began excavations in 1915. Out of nothing, Anaconda created a city with housing, schools, cinemas, shops, a hospital and clinics – though many accused it of taking out more than it put back.

By the 1960s, Anaconda was a target for those who advocated the nationalisation of the copper industry. During the Frei Montalva administration, the state gained a majority shareholding and, in 1971, Congress enthusiastically approved nationalisation. After 1973, the junta compensated companies for their loss of assets, but retained ownership through the Corporación del Cobre de Chile (Codelco).

Chuqui is a clean, orderly town whose landscape is a reminder of its history. The stadium is the **Estadio Anaconda**, while the **Auditorio Sindical** is a huge theatre with an interior mural commemorating a contentious strike. A prominent statue honours workers who operated equipment like the behemoth power shovel nearby.

Organised Tours

For weekday three-hour tours, report to the Oficina Ayuda a la Infancia, at the top of Avenida JM Carrera, by 9.45 am. Bring your passport and make a modest donation (about US$0.50). Demand is high in January and February, so get there early; with enough demand, there are afternoon tours.

To enter the smelter building, you must wear sturdy footwear, long trousers and a long-sleeved jacket, but the mine provides jackets, helmets and eye protection.

Places to Eat

For good meals, visit the *Club de Empleados* and the *Arco Iris Center*, both across from the plaza, on Avenida JM Carrera. Also recommended are the *Club de Obreros*, on Mariscal Alcázar two blocks south of the stadium, and *Restaurant Carloncho*, on Avenida Comercial O'Higgins.

Getting There & Away

Taxi colectivos (US$1.50) leave Calama from Abaroa near Vicuña Mackenna. There are also buses from Granaderos and Ramírez.

SAN PEDRO DE ATACAMA

San Pedro de Atacama is an oasis village at the north end of the Salar de Atacama, a vast saline lake, 120 km south-east of Calama. To its east rise immense volcanoes, both active and extinct. Nearby is the Valle de la Luna (Valley of the Moon).

At 2440 metres above sea level, San Pedro's adobe houses preserve a colonial feeling. In the early 20th century, the village was a major stop on cattle drives from Argentina to the nitrate mines, but the Salta-Antofagasta railway ended this colourful era.

No longer on the cattle trail, San Pedro is now on the 'gringo trail', but many young Chileans also spend their holidays here. Despite the increasing tourist trade, it is attractive and affordable. The municipal tourist office, on the north side of the plaza, keeps irregular weekday hours, but Mabel at Florida Tours is very helpful and keeps long hours.

Information

Money There is a cambio on Caracoles but their rates are considerably lower than in Calama. Also try travel agencies and residenciales.

Post & Communications The post office is on the plaza. CTC's office at the corner of

Caracoles and Pasaje Vilema, has cabins and a blue-grey teléfono inteligente where you can make credit-card calls abroad. They are open every day from 8.30 am to 8 pm. Entel is on the plaza. The telephone code is 56.

Bookshops There are two book exchanges in town. The first is on O'Higgins next to the cambio, and the other is in a corner of the grocery shop next to Residencial La Florida. Both give you one book in exchange for two.

Things to See

Museo Gustavo Le Paige In 1955, Belgian priest/archaeologist Gustavo Le Paige, assisted by villagers and the Universidad del Norte, began to assemble artefacts on the area's cultural evolution for this well-organised museum. It also includes exhibits on the Inca conquest, the Spanish invasion and modern cultural anthropology.

The museum is half a block from the plaza and charges US$2.50 admission; show student ID for a discount.

Around the Plaza Over 450 years ago, Pedro de Valdivia's entourage passed through here with seeds, pigs and chickens, and farming tools. On the east side of the plaza stands the **Casa de Pedro de Valdivia**, a restored adobe reportedly built around 1540. On the west side, the modified 17th-century **Iglesia San Pedro** was built with local materials – adobe, wood from the *cardón* cactus, and leather straps in lieu of nails.

Organised Tours

San Pedro has more than 10 travel agencies that compete fiercely, and not always ethically, to provide tours to nearby attractions, which are some distance from town. Three locally owned and operated agencies, which often combine efforts are Expediciones Florida (☎ 85-1087), next to the residencial with the same name; Solor Expediciones (☎ 85-1008), next to Residencial Rayco; and Atacama Inka Tour (☎ 85-1062), on the plaza.

Horse-riding tours provide an alternative for the nearby attractions such as the pukarás and the oasis of Catarpe. A group of French travellers was very enthusiastic about Orlando Mamani's good horses and well-informed tour of his native land. La Herradura, on Tocopilla, is slightly cheaper, and provides overnight options. Prices are reasonable, but bring plenty of water.

Nativa, on Caracoles, rents out mountain bikes.

Places to Stay

Local accommodation is hard to find around holiday periods like Chile's mid-September independence days. Prices are fairly uniform, but you may want to bargain them down.

Camping Puri, at the western end of O'Higgins, charges US$4 per person. *Camping Takha Takha*, south of town on Tocopilla, charges about US$5.

Residencial Andacollo, Tocopilla 11, with very comfortable beds, charges US$8 per person. *Residencial El Pukará* is similar in price and quality, although you can bargain with them. Highly recommended is the newly restored *Residencial Rayco* on Antofagasta, where the owners have respected the traditional design of their paternal home and kept some of the antique furniture. They have several toilets and showers with hot water, and a few rooms with private bath. A single with shared bath costs US$9.

The new owners of the *Residencial Juanita*, by the plaza, offer a few large and pleasant rooms at US$9 a single, distributed around a central patio that serves as a dining room. Another comfortable and clean place is *Residencial Corvatsch* on Antofagasta, with rooms at the same price.

Places to Eat

Restaurant Juanita, where the señora provides delicious and abundant dinners for about US$7 per person, is highly recommended. The excellent but pricier *Tambo Cañaveral* doubles as San Pedro's hottest nightspot. The restaurant at *Residencial La Florida* on Tocopilla has a reasonable set

CHILE

menu for dinner. For breakfast or healthy snacks and fresh fruit juices, try *Banana Chávez*. There is a great bakery on Toconao where you can get fresh cakes, bread and hot cheese empanadas.

Things to Buy

For handicrafts, including cardón carvings and llama and alpaca ponchos, try the craft market at the east end of Licancábur, by the museum.

Getting There & Away

Géminis has buses from Calama on Sunday. Morales y Moralito has buses from Calama (US$3) thrice daily (at 10.30 am and 3 and 6.30 pm) and to Toconao twice a day (11 am and 6 pm). Yusmar has four buses daily from Calama (8 and 11 am, 4 and 6 pm) and four days a week to Toconao (11 am and 6 pm). Yusmar goes thrice daily to Calama (8 am and 2 and 6 pm).

AROUND SAN PEDRO DE ATACAMA
Swimming Holes

For year-round swimming check the enormous pools of mineral water at Pozo 3, only three km east of San Pedro on the road to Toconao, reached by foot or with a minivan that stops in front of Residencial La Florida. There are camp sites and a restaurant here.

Pukará de Quitor & Catarpe

Three km north-west of San Pedro, on a promontory above the Río San Pedro, are the ruins of this 12th-century fortress. Across the river, Catarpe was an Inca administrative centre. The best way to get here is to walk.

Valle de la Luna

This area of oddly eroded landforms, 15 km west of San Pedro, is a popular excursion destination. If driving, don't get stuck in the sand; if hiking, carry water and food, and smear yourself with sunblock.

Salar de Atacama

The salar affords great views of the Andes with its chain of active and dormant volcanoes, of which Licancábur is really impos-

ing, as well as the Cordillera Domeyko, a lower chain. At the salt lake there are three species of flamingos (James, Chilean and Andean) as well as smaller plovers, coots and ducks that nest in the area. On the way to the salar are abundant desert shrubs such as *tamarugos* and *algarrobos* and trees like *chañares*.

Termas de Puritama

Camping is possible at these volcanic hot springs, about 30 km north of San Pedro, toward El Tatio, but there's no fuel for a fire and it gets very cold.

El Tatio Geysers

At an altitude of 4300 metres, 95 km north of San Pedro, El Tatio is the world's highest geyser field. In the azure clarity of the altiplano, the sight of the steaming fumaroles at sunrise is unforgettable, and there are strikingly beautiful individual structures formed when the boiling water evaporates and leaves behind mineral deposits. Watch your step – people have suffered serious burns after falling through the thin crust into scalding water. Camping is possible but the nights are freezing.

About 6 am is the best time to see the geysers; most tours return by about 8.30 am. The tours from San Pedro have better access and are a bit cheaper (about US$20 with lunch and a stop at Puritama) than those from Calama. If driving, take a high-clearance vehicle and leave San Pedro by 3 am. The route is signposted, but in the dark it's easier to follow tour agencies' minibuses. If you rent a car in Calama, you can return via the villages of Caspana, Toconce, Ayquina and Chiu Chiu, rather than via San Pedro.

TOCONAO

Known for its finely hewn volcanic stone, Toconao is a fruit-growing oasis about 40 km south of San Pedro, which has the pace that San Pedro had 15 years ago. The **Iglesia de San Lucas**, with a separate bell tower, dates from the mid-18th century. A visit inside reveals an interesting altar and very thick walls.

The **Quebrada de Jeria**, with an intricate irrigation system, is a delightful place for a walk or even a swim. Affluent San Pedro families once despatched peons with mules here to fetch casks of drinking water.

Near the plaza are several inexpensive residenciales and restaurants. Buses from Calama and San Pedro arrive late at night. Hitching is possible, but leave San Pedro early and be prepared to return early or stay the night.

Norte Chico

A semiarid transition zone from the Atacama to the Valle Central, the Norte Chico (Little North) is also the 'region of 10,000 mines'.

Politically, the Norte Chico includes the Third Region of Atacama (capital Copiapó) and the Fourth Region of Coquimbo (capital La Serena), but its customary boundaries encompass a slightly greater area. The main attractions are a pleasant climate, fine beaches and the city of La Serena, but intriguing mountain villages lie off the beaten track. Near the Panamericana are the Pan de Azúcar and Fray Jorge national parks.

History

Decades before the Spaniards, the Incas subdued Diaguita farmers, but the area was always peripheral to the Central Andean civilisations. Europeans first arrived in 1535, when Diego de Almagro crossed the Andes from Salta.

A few years later, Pedro de Valdivia founded La Serena, but Copiapó lagged behind until an 18th-century gold boom. When gold failed, silver took its place and Copiapó really took off, tripling its population to 12,000 after a bonanza find at Chañarcillo in 1832.

When silver declined in the late 19th century, copper took its place in Potrerillos and, later, in El Salvador. Recently, La Serena and Bahía Inglesa have enjoyed tourist booms, but mining continues to be significant. The area is also important culturally – Nobel Prize-winning poet Gabriela Mistral was a native of Vicuña, in the Elqui valley. The Copiapó, Huasco and Elqui valleys have contributed to Chile's flourishing fruit exports in recent years.

COPIAPO

The discovery of silver at nearby Chañarcillo provided Copiapó with several firsts: South America's first railroad (completed in 1852 to the port of Caldera), Chile's first telegraph and telephone lines, and the first gas works. While not a major destination for travellers, its pleasant climate and interesting history

CHILE

make it a worthwhile stopover between La Serena and Antofagasta.

Orientation & Information

Copiapó (population 69,000) is 800 km north of Santiago and 565 km south of Antofagasta. Sernatur (☎ 21-2838) occupies a concrete bunker on Plaza Prat; once you find the entrance, the congenial staff have a helpful list of accommodation, an excellent free map and many brochures. The telephone code is 52.

Things to See

Founded in 1857, the **Museo Mineralógico**, on Colipí and Rodríguez, is a literally dazzling tribute to the raw materials to which the city owes its existence. The **Museo de Ferrocarriles**, on Juan Martínez, was originally the terminal for the Copiapó-Caldera line.

Notable buildings from the mining boom include the **Iglesia Catedral** and the **municipalidad**, on the Plaza de Armas. At the foot of Batallón Atacama, directly south of the station, the **Palacete Viña de Cristo** was the town's most elegant mansion. A few blocks west, at the **Universidad de Atacama** (the former Escuela de Minas), is the Norris Brothers locomotive, the first on the Caldera-Copiapó line.

Places to Stay & Eat

In summer, Copiapó has a *hostel* at Juan Antonio Ríos 371. *Residencial Chacabuco* (☎ 21-3428), Chacabuco 271, is the cheapest at US$9 per person (twice that with private bath). *Residencial Chañarcillo* (☎ 21-3281), Chañarcillo 741, has small but clean singles/doubles for US$9/18. *Anexo Residencial Chañarcillo* (☎ 21-2284), at O'Higgins 804, is run-down but friendly; it charges US$6/11, with hot water available from 7 to 11 am only.

El Pollo, Chacabuco 340, has a fine three-course lunch. For seafood, try *Restaurant Galería*, at Colipí 635. The *Club Social Libanés*, Los Carrera 350, has Middle Eastern food. *Hao Hwa*, Colipí 340, is one of the better Chinese restaurants in northern Chile.

Getting There & Away

Air Aeropuerto Chamonate (☎ 21-4360) is seven km west of town. LanChile has flights to Calama and Antofagasta four times weekly, and to Santiago three times weekly. ALTA (☎ 21-7523), Colipí 484, flies daily to La Serena.

Bus All companies have offices at the terminal (☎ 21-2577) at the foot of Chacabuco, three blocks south of Plaza Prat, but some have downtown offices. All north-south buses, and many to the interior destinations, stop here.

Pullman Bus (☎ 21-1039), Colipí 109, and Inca Bus cover southerly destinations off the Panamericana, including Illapel and Salamanca, and northern mining towns like Diego de Almagro, El Salvador and Potrerillos. Regional carriers run frequently to Caldera and Bahía Inglesa (US$1), and to the upper Copiapó valley.

Getting Around

LanChile (☎ 21-3512), O'Higgins 640, operates its own minibus to Aeropuerto Chamonate.

CALDERA & BAHIA INGLESA

Caldera, 75 km west of Copiapó, grew rapidly with the discovery of silver in the Andes and the arrival of the railway, which gave people in Copiapó easy access to the beach. Bahía Inglesa, a refuge for privateers in colonial times, has better beaches, but Caldera is livelier and much cheaper.

Things to See

Caldera's **Cementerio Laico** was Chile's first non-Catholic cemetery and has interesting ironwork. Between the plaza and the **Muelle Pesquero** (fishing jetty) are many distinctive 19th-century buildings, including the **Iglesia San Vicente**, with its Gothic tower, the **Municipalidad**, the **Aduana** (old customs house) and the **Estación de Ferrocarriles** (train station).

Activities
Besides swimming and sunbathing, windsurfing is a popular pastime at Bahía Inglesa; rental equipment is available.

Places to Stay & Eat
Camping Bahía Inglesa, on Playa Las Machas, has good facilities but costs nearly US$20 per site in the high season.

The cheapest rooms, about US$6 a single, are at *Residencial Molina* at Montt 346. *Hotel Los Andes* at Edwards 360 and *Residencial Fenicia*, Gallo 370, have singles/doubles with shared bath for US$10/18.

Seafood is about the only reasonable option – try *Il Pirón de Oro*, at Cousiño 218, or *Nuevo Miramar*, at the foot of Gana.

Getting There & Away
Frequent buses to Copiapó leave from near the plaza. To catch a north-south bus, wait at the turn-off at the east end of Avenida Diego de Almeyda.

Getting Around
Buses and taxi colectivos shuttle visitors from Caldera to Bahía Inglesa.

PARQUE NACIONAL PAN DE AZUCAR
Just 30 km north of the dilapidated mining port of Chañaral, Pan de Azúcar is 44,000 hectares of coastal desert and precordillera, with beautiful coves among stony headlands, white sandy beaches, abundant wildlife and unique flora. The rich Humboldt current feeds otters, sea lions and many birds; pelicans, cormorants and penguins nest on Isla Pan de Azúcar, but access is restricted – bring binoculars. At higher altitudes, the camanchaca nurtures unique cacti and succulents, while farther inland, guanacos and foxes are common.

Places to Stay
CONAF camp sites (US$3) have picnic tables at Cerro Soldado, Playa Piqueros and Caleta Pan de Azúcar, but bring your own water. The nearest supplies are at Chañaral, but try buying fish at Caleta Pan de Azúcar.

Getting There & Away
You can arrange a taxi from Chañaral for about US$20 – double that if you want to be picked up. On weekends, try hitching, but carrying provisions and water might be a problem. CONAF collects an admission charge of US$4 at the south entrance.

LA SERENA
Founded in 1544, La Serena (population 107,000) maintains a colonial façade, thanks to President Gabriel González Videla's 'Plan Serena' of the late 1940s. Silver and copper were its economic backbone, along with irrigated agriculture. Capital of the Fourth Region of Coquimbo and 470 km north of Santiago, it's a very agreeable place which may supplant Viña del Mar as Chile's premier beach resort.

Orientation
Centred on the Plaza de Armas, the city plan is a regular grid. Most areas of interest fall within a rectangular area marked by Avenida Bohón and Parque Pedro de Valdivia to the west, the Río Elqui to the north, Calle Benavente to the east and Avenida Aguirre to the south.

Information
Tourist Offices Sernatur (☎ 22-5199) is on the 1st floor of the post office complex, on the corner of Prat and Matta, opposite the plaza. The kiosco de turismo is much more helpful, at Prat and Balmaceda. In summer it's open Monday to Saturday from 10 am to 10 pm, and on Sunday from 10 am to 2 pm. There's also an office at the bus terminal.

Money Exchange money at Gira Tour, Prat 689, or at La Portada (☎ 21-1516) at Prat 515. During holidays or after business hours, phone ahead.

Post & Communications The post office is on the corner of Matta and Prat, opposite the plaza. CTC is at Cordovez 446 and O'Higgins 536. Entel is at Prat 571. La Serena's telephone code is 51.

CHILE

La Serena

To Vallenar & Copiapó

Río Elqui

Parque Pedro de Valdivia

To Beaches

To Santiago

To Ovalle

Stadium

To Airport, Vicuña & Cerro Tololo

To Juan de Dios Peni

Anfión Muñoz

Medical Services La Serena's hospital (☎ 22-5569) is at Balmaceda 916 (entrance at Anfión Muñoz and Larraín Alcalde).

Things to See

Many key features are on or near the nicely landscaped Plaza de Armas. On the east side is the **Iglesia Catedral** (1844), while at the south-west corner, facing a smaller plaza, is the colonial **Iglesia Santo Domingo**.

In an annexe of the colonial **Iglesia San Francisco**, at Balmaceda 640, the **Museo Colonial de Arte Religioso** features poly-

chrome sculptures from Cuzco and paintings from 17th-century Quito. At present the museum is closed for restoration.

La Serena's native son and Chile's president from 1946 to 1952, González Videla was a controversial figure who drove Pablo Neruda out of the senate and into exile. Exhibits on González Videla's life in the **Museo Histórico Gabriel González Videla**, Matta 495, omit such episodes, but the museum also includes material about regional history.

The **Museo Arqueológico** is on the corner of Cordovez and Cienfuegos. Add

PLACES TO STAY		12	Restaurant Mai Lan Fan	35	Museo Arqueológico
1	Pensión Matus			36	Teatro Municipal
2	Hotel Pucar	16	La Mia Pizza	39	Colectivos to
6	Residencial Brasilia	18	La Crisis		Vicuña, Andacollo & Ovalle
7	Residencial El Loa	51	Restaurant Croata	40	Buses Expreso Norte
9	Hostal Del Turismo				
10	Pensión López		OTHER	41	Buses Tal
11	Hotel Casablanca	5	Iglesia La Merced & Kiosco de Turismo	42	Iglesia San Francisco & Museo Colonial de Arte Religioso
24	Hotel Francisco de Aguirre	8	Mercado La Recova		
27	Hotel Pacífico	13	Iglesia San Agustín	43	Automóvil Club de Chile
29	Residencial Lido	14	Gira Tour		
30	Residencial Chile	15	LanChile	44	Línea Ruta 41(To Vicuña)
31	Hotel Berlín	17	Entel		
33	Residencial Petit	19	CTC	46	Tur-Bus
34	Hotel Mediterráneo	20	Municipalidad	47	Hertz Rent-a-Car
37	Residencial Limmat	21	Catedral	48	Bicycle Rental
38	Residencial Norte Verde	22	Plaza de Armas	49	Buses Tramaca
		23	Sernatur & Post Office	50	Buses Libac
45	Hotel Alameda			53	Cine Arte Universidad La Serena
52	Hotel Los Balcones de Alcalá	25	Museo Histórico Gabriel González Videla	54	Museo Mineralógico
				55	Hospital
PLACES TO EAT		26	Iglesia Santo Domingo	56	Buses Frontera Elqui
3	Café del Patio	28	CONAF	57	Terminal Rodoviario
4	Boccaccio	32	Buses Tas Choapa		

this collection of Diaguita artefacts to the González Videla and you'd have one fine museum instead of two mediocre ones. Admission, about US$1, is valid for both museums.

Check **Mercardo La Recova** for musical instruments, woollens and dried fruits, as well as artisanal jewellery.

Beaches On a two-week vacation, you can visit a different beach every day, but watch out for strong currents. Safest for swimming are Canto del Agua, Las Gaviotas, El Pescador, La Marina, La Barca, Playa Mansa, Los Fuertes, Playa Blanca, El Faro (Sur) and Peñuelas (Coquimbo).

Suitable only for sunbathing are Cuatro Esquinas, El Faro (Norte), Playa Changa (Coquimbo), Punta de Teatinos, Los Choros, Caleta Hornos, San Pedro and Chungungo.

There is no bus service along Avenida del Mar. From the city centre take bus Liserco (which runs between La Serena and Coquimbo) and get off at Peñuelas and Cuatro Esquinas, one block from the beach.

Places to Stay

Residencial Limmat (☎ 21-1373), Lautaro 914, charges US$10 for hostel accommodation with shared bath.

Many families house university students, and rent to tourists in summer only, but they may have a spare bed at other times. *Pensión López*, Cantournet 815, has spacious singles with comfortable beds and excellent hot showers for about US$8.

Residencial El Loa, O'Higgins 362, charges US$10 per person with shared bath, as does *Residencial Lido*, which is very good value, at Matta 547. Also recommended is *Residencial Chile*, very central at Matta 561, which charges US$13/23 for a single/ double with shared bath.

Several readers have recommended *Hotel Pacífico*, Eduardo de la Barra 252, with rooms for US$15/21 including breakfast. One reader raved about *Hotel Los Balcones de Alcalá*, Larraín Aguirre 781, where singles cost US$51.

Places to Eat

For seafood, any restaurant in the *Mercado*

CHILE

La Recova, on the corner of Cienfuegos and Cantournet, is a good option, but try the chupe de locos or the sopa marinera at *Local 219*, where they offer a complementary pisco sour. One reader praised *Domingo Domínguez*, on Avenida del Mar, sector Peñuelas.

Coffee, ice cream and desserts are outstanding at *Boccaccio*, corner of Prat and Balmaceda. *La Crisis*, Balmaceda 487, is another popular ice-cream parlour and snack bar. For coffee, snacks and sandwiches, try *Café do Brasil*, at Balmaceda 465; and for pizza, visit *La Mía Pizza*, O'Higgins 460. To meet locals and visitors, the best place is the intimate *Café del Patio*, Prat 470 (interior), where Rodrigo, the owner, goes out of his way to make everyone comfortable.

Getting There & Away

Air Aeropuerto La Florida is a short distance east of the city centre. Ladeco (☎ 22-5753), Cordovez 484, flies to Santiago daily, except Saturday; the Saturday flight from Santiago continues to Calama and Iquique. ALTA, Los Carrera 525, connects La Serena with cities to the north.

Bus – domestic The Terminal Rodoviario (☎ 22-4573), which also serves nearby Coquimbo, is on the outskirts of town, on the corner of Amunátegui and Avenida El Santo. Many companies also have offices in town.

Via Elqui and Frontera Elqui, on the corner of Juan de Dios Pení and Regimiento Coquimbo, serve upper Elqui valley destinations like Vicuña. Los Diamantes de Elqui goes to Vicuña and Ovalle, as does Expreso Norte, O'Higgins 675.

Tas Choapa, O'Higgins 599, Buses Tal, Balmaceda 594, and Buses Palacios, Amunátegui 251, also serve Ovalle. Postal Bus and Buses Carlos Araya, at Frontera Elqui offices, both go to Andacollo. Fares to these destinations range from US$1 to US$3.

Companies serving Santiago (seven hours) include Inca Bus; Tramaca at Aguirre 375; Buses Lit at Balmaceda 1302; Flota Barrios at Domeyko 550; Los Diamantes de Elqui; Tas-Choapa; Buses Palacios; Flecha Dorada at Aguirre 344; Expreso Norte; Libac at Aguirre 452; and Pullman Bus at O'Higgins 663. Los Corsarios, Inca Bus and Pullman Bus all serve Valparaíso and Viña del Mar.

For Copiapó and other northern destinations, try Inca Bus, Flecha Dorada, Flota Barrios, Libac, Pullman, Tramaca, Chile Bus, Carmelita or Fénix Pullman Norte.

Typical fares include Santiago or Viña/ Valparaíso US$10, Los Vilos US$7, Illapel/ Salamanca or Copiapó US$7, Chañaral US$10, Antofagasta US$30, Calama US$40, Iquique US$48 and Arica US$50.

Bus – international Covalle Bus (☎ 21-3127) at Infante 538, connects La Serena with Mendoza and San Juan, Argentina (US$40, 16 hours), via the Libertadores pass, twice weekly in summer. Services to San Juan over the shorter but higher Agua Negra pass have not yet commenced.

Taxi Colectivo Taxi colectivos serving many regional destinations run frequently. Anserco goes to Andacollo, Línea Ruta 41 to the upper Elqui, and Secovalle to Ovalle. All these companies share offices at Domeyko 524, near the corner of Cienfuegos and Aguirre. Sol del Elqui, on Esmeralda between Colo Colo and Peni, goes to Vicuña and Pisco Elqui.

AROUND LA SERENA

At 2200 metres above sea level, 88 km southeast of La Serena, the **Observatorio Cerro Tololo** is one of the southern hemisphere's most important observatories. You make tour reservations by calling the La Serena office (☎ 22-5415). It opens to the public on Saturday only, and they can only receive 90 visitors a day, so plan in advance. There is no public transport; hitching is possible from the junction on the highway to Vicuña, but allow plenty of time.

VICUÑA

Vicuña (population 7000) is a quiet village

of adobe houses in the upper Elqui valley, 62 km from La Serena, in an area which produces grapes, avocados, papayas and other fruit. Thanks to several groups convinced that UFOs frequent the area, the village and nearby countryside have acquired an oddball reputation. The tourist office is opposite the plaza in the eccentric Torre Bauer, which resembles a castle with wooden battlements.

Vicuña's **Museo Gabriela Mistral** is a tangible eulogy to the famous literary figure. Mistral was born Lucila Godoy Alcayaga in 1889, in the village of Montegrande, but her house was moved to Vicuña and is now on show at the entrance to the museum. Exhibits include a photo biography and modest personal possessions like a desk and bookcase. Her genealogy indicates Spanish, Indian and African ancestry.

Places to Stay & Eat

Residencial La Moderna (☎ 41-1790), on Mistral near Baquedano, charges US$6 per person. Next door is *Hostal Valle Hermoso* (☎ 41-1206) a well-kept place with good lunches. One reader strongly praised the hospitality and good food at *Residencial La Elquina*, O'Higgins 65, where a double with private bath and breakfast costs US$30. There are several modest restaurants, including *Yo y Soledad*, at Mistral 448, and the nearby *Restaurant Halley* – probably inspired by the local space cadets.

Getting There & Away

Frequent buses and taxi colectivos to La Serena leave from the Plaza de Armas.

OVALLE

Ovalle (population 75,000), half an hour off the Panamericana, is the tidy capital of the prosperous agricultural province of Limarí. The kiosco de turismo is opposite the plaza, on Victoria, between the Hotel Turismo and Banco de Chile.

The **Museo del Limarí**, Independencia 329, is a modest endeavour which stresses the trans-Andean links between the Diaguita people of coastal Chile and north-west Argentina. The **Feria Modelo**, a lively fruit and vegetable market with several restaurants, occupies the former railway workshops.

Places to Stay & Eat

Hotel Roxy (☎ 62-0080), Libertad 155 is great value at US$13 per person with bath, and is very friendly and clean, with a huge, attractive patio. *Hotel Francia* (☎ 62-0828), Libertad 261, is cheaper (US$7) but less appealing.

For a good fixed-price lunch, try the *Club Comercial*, at Aguirre 244. The *Club Social Arabe*, Arauco 255, offers Middle Eastern specialities.

Getting There & Away

North-south bus services resemble those leaving from La Serena, though some companies bypass Ovalle. Those with local offices include Incabus, at Ariztía Oriente 398, Pullman at Ariztía Poniente 159, Carmelita at Ariztía Poniente 351, and Tramaca.

AROUND OVALLE

The **Monumento Arqueológico Valle del Encanto**, 19 km from Ovalle, is a rocky tributary canyon of the Río Limarí, with pre-Columbian petroglyphs, pictographs and mortars. Any westbound bus will drop you at the highway marker. It's an easy five-km walk on a clearly marked road to the canyon.

PARQUE NACIONAL FRAY JORGE

Moistened by the camanchaca, Fray Jorge is an ecological island of Valdivian cloud forest in a semiarid region, 110 km south of La Serena. Of its 10,000 hectares, only 400 contain this truly unique vegetation – still enough to make it a UNESCO International Biosphere Reserve. Some believe this area is evidence of dramatic climate change, but others argue that such forests were more extensive before their destruction by humans.

Fray Jorge is open to the public in summer (January to mid-March) from Thursday to Sunday, plus holidays, from 8.30 am to 6 pm;

CHILE

during other seasons, it's open on weekends only. Admission is US$2 for Chileans and US$4 for foreigners. A visitor centre is still in preparation.

Places to Stay

El Arrayancito has 13 *camp sites* (US$10) with fireplaces, picnic tables, water and toilets.

Getting There & Away

Fray Jorge is reached by a westward lateral off the Panamericana, about 20 km north of the Ovalle junction. Several agencies offer tours from La Serena and Ovalle; it may be possible to leave the tour, stay overnight in the park and then return to La Serena or Ovalle the next day. North-south buses can drop you at the clearly marked turn-off, 22 km from the gate; walking is not easy, but try hitching.

La Araucanía & the Lake District

Beyond the Biobío, glaciated volcanoes tower above deep blue lakes, ancient forests and verdant farmland, while waterfalls spill into limpid pools. Temuco, capital of the Ninth Region (La Araucanía), is the staging point for visits to Parque Nacional Conguillío, the upper Biobío, and lakeside resorts like Villarrica and Pucón. Farther south, near Osorno, there is an easy land crossing to Argentina via Lago Puyehue, and a more scenic bus-boat combination.

Puerto Montt, on the Seno de Reloncaví, is the capital of the 10th Region (Los Lagos) and gateway to Isla Chiloé and Chilean Patagonia. Hikers should acquire Lonely Planet's *Trekking in the Patagonian Andes*, by Clem Lindenmayer, which also covers southern Argentina.

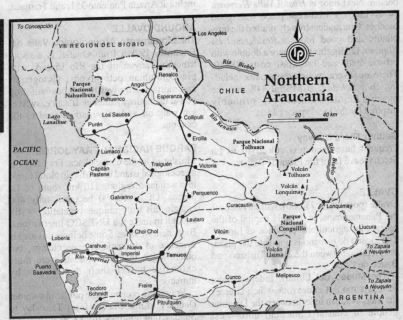

History

South of Concepción, the Spaniards found small gold mines, good farmland and a large potential workforce, but constantly suffered Mapuche attacks or natural disasters. By the mid-17th century, they had abandoned most settlements, except for the heavily fortified Valdivia. Early 19th-century travellers still referred to 'Arauco' as a separate country, not safe for European settlers until the 1880s.

Today, several hundred thousand Mapuche still live in La Frontera, the area between the Biobío and the Río Toltén, earning a precarious livelihood from farming and crafts. Nineteenth-century German immigrants started industries and left a palpable architectural heritage, while Chilean-Germans have left their mark on the region's food and the agricultural landscape.

TEMUCO

Fast-growing Temuco (population 220,000), 675 km south of Santiago, is the service centre for a large hinterland and supports a range of industries, including steel, textiles, food processing and wood products. The gateway to the Lake District, it's also a market town for Mapuche produce and crafts.

Information

Tourist Offices Sernatur (☎ 21-1969), Bulnes 586, has city maps and the very useful brochure *Datos Utiles Temuco*. It's open Monday to Saturday and Sunday mornings in summer; weekdays only the rest of the year.

Money Change cash and travellers' cheques at Cambio Global (Bulnes 655, Local 1), Turcamb (Claro Solar 733) or Christopher Money Exchange (Prat 696, Oficina 419). Banks around the Plaza de Armas have Redbanc ATMs.

Post & Communications The post office is on the corner of Diego Portales and Arturo Prat. There are CTC offices at Prat 565, Manuel Bulnes 368, and on the corner of

Caupolicán and Manuel Montt. Temuco's telephone code is 45.

Medical Services Temuco's hospital (☎ 21-2525) is at Manuel Montt 115.

Things to See

The memorial park **Monumento Natural Cerro Ñielol** is where Mapuche leaders ceded land for Temuco in 1881. It is popular for picnics and has a small lagoon, trails and an environment information centre.

The **Mercado Municipal**, three blocks north of the plaza, has food, clothing, restaurants and crafts. It's open Monday to Saturday from 8 am to 7 pm, and on Sunday from 8.30 am to 2 pm.

Open daily from 9 am until 2 pm or whenever the last Mapuche vendors pack up, the **Feria Libre** (produce market) fills several blocks along Barros Arana near the train station.

At Alemania 084, reached by bus No 9 from downtown, the **Museo Regional de la Araucanía** chronicles Mapuche history since pre-Columbian times. It also has materials on European colonisation, historical maps, a gallery of regional art and a library. It's open Tuesday to Saturday from 9 am to 1 pm, and on Sunday and holidays from 10 am to 1 pm and 3 to 6 pm.

Places to Stay

Hostel accommodation at the delightful *Residencial Temuco* (☎ 23-3721), Rodríguez 1341, 2nd floor, offers warm, clean and comfortable family ambience for US$9 with breakfast. Señora María Eugenia and her assistant Magali go out of their way to make your stay enjoyable.

In summer, many families rent out rooms for about US$9 a single: ask at the tourist office or try side streets near the plaza. *Hospedaje Espejo*, Aldunate 124, has singles for US$8; nearby is the very attractive and friendly *Hospedaje Aldunate*, Aldunate 187, with rooms for US$10. The nameless *hospedaje* at General Mackenna 496, 2nd floor, is a very fine place. At the rambling,

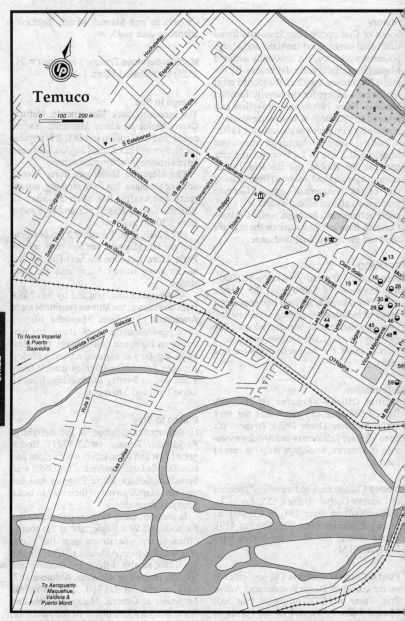

Temuco

0   100   200 m

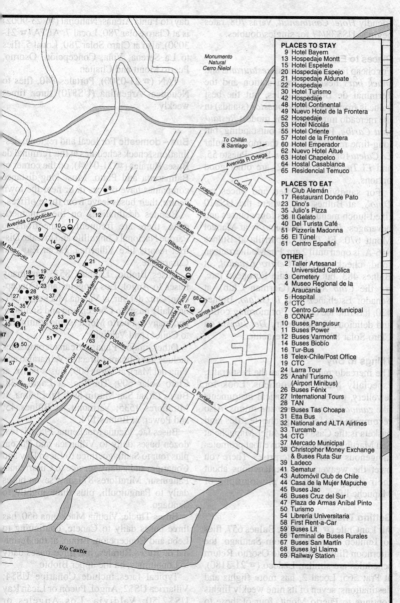

To Chillán
& Santiago

Monumento
Natural
Cerro Ñielol

To Chillán
& Santiago

To Chillán
& Santiago

Río Cautín

PLACES TO STAY
9 Hotel Bayern
13 Hospedaje Montt
15 Hotel Espelete
20 Hospedaje Espejo
21 Hospedaje Aldunate
22 Hospedaje
30 Hotel Turismo
42 Hospedaje
48 Hotel Continental
49 Nuevo Hotel de la Frontera
52 Hospedaje
53 Hotel Nicolás
55 Hotel Oriente
57 Hotel de la Frontera
60 Hotel Emperador
62 Nuevo Hotel Aitué
63 Hotel Chapelco
64 Hostal Casablanca
65 Residencial Temuco

PLACES TO EAT
1 Club Alemán
17 Restaurant Donde Pato
23 Dino's
35 Julio's Pizza
36 Il Gelato
40 Del Turista Café
51 Pizzería Madonna
56 El Túnel
61 Centro Español

OTHER
2 Taller Artesanal
  Universidad Católica
3 Cemetery
4 Museo Regional de la
  Araucanía
5 Hospital
6 CTC
7 Centro Cultural Municipal
8 CONAF
10 Buses Panguisur
11 Buses Power
12 Buses Varmontt
14 Buses Biobío
16 Tur-Bus
18 Telex-Chile/Post Office
19 CTC
24 Larra Tour
25 Anahí Turismo
   (Airport Minibus)
26 Buses Fénix
27 International Tours
28 TAN
29 Buses Tas Choapa
31 Etta Bus
32 National and ALTA Airlines
33 Turcamb
34 CTC
37 Mercado Municipal
38 Christopher Money Exchange
   & Buses Ruta Sur
39 Ladeco
41 Sematur
43 Automóvil Club de Chile
44 Casa de la Mujer Mapuche
45 Buses Jac
46 Buses Cruz del Sur
47 Plaza de Armas Aníbal Pinto
50 Turismo
54 Librería Universitaria
59 First Rent-a-Car
59 Buses Lit
66 Terminal de Buses Rurales
67 Buses San Martín
68 Buses Igi Llaima
69 Railway Station

CHILE

friendly *Hotel Continental*, Varas 708, rates begin at US$38/47 for singles/doubles.

Places to Eat

For cheap food, try the small *restaurants* and *snack bars* near the train station and the Terminal de Buses Rurales, but the best value is from the seafood *puestos* (stands) in the mercado municipal. The modest *Restaurant Caribe*, Puesto 45, is outstanding, but long-time residents praise the more popular *La Caleta* for a splurge. *Don Yeyo*, Puesto 55, and *El Turista*, Puesto 32, are other good options.

For sandwiches, coffee and onces try *Dino's*, at Bulnes 360, where the US$10 fixed-lunch menu includes four courses and beverages. *Pizzería Madonna* is at Manuel Montt 670. *El Túnel*, a parrilla at Bulnes 846-A, is open until 2 am. For Mediterranean food, check out the *Centro Español*, at Bulnes 483, but for middle European fare, try the *Club Alemán* (German Club), at Senador Estebáñez 772. *Il Gelato*, Bulnes 420, has fine ice cream. For morning coffee and delicious chocolates try *Del Turista* on Claro Solar 839, next to Sernatur.

Things to Buy

The mercado municipal has the best crafts, especially Mapuche woollens. Look for jewellery, pottery, and musical instruments like *zampoñas* (pan pipes) and drums. Also recommended for Mapuche textiles and baskets is the Casa de la Mujer Mapuche at San Martín 433, a cooperative that promotes indigenous women's enterprises. There you meet the weavers, get explanations about their designs, and see photographs of Mapuche life.

Getting There & Away

Air LanChile (☎ 21-1339), Bulnes 657, flies to Temuco twice daily from Santiago; the afternoon flight continues to Osorno. Return schedules are similar. Ladeco (☎ 21-3180), at Prat 565, Local 2, has more flights and destinations; seven of its nine weekly flights continue to Puerto Montt, four of those to Balmaceda/Coyhaique, and one (Wednes-

day) to Punta Arenas. National (☎ 23-9002) is at Claro Solar 780, Local 7. ALTA (☎ 21-3090), also at Claro Solar 780, Local 5, flies to La Serena, Viña, Concepción, Osorno, Puerto Montt and Chaitén.

TAN (☎ 21-0500), Portales 840, flies to Neuquén, Argentina (US$70) three times weekly.

Bus – domestic For local and regional destinations, check schedules at the Terminal de Buses Rurales (☎ 21-0494), on the corner of Balmaceda and Pinto. Most long-distance companies have offices in or near the town centre; their buses leave from these offices.

Besides destinations on the Panamericana, there are frequent connections to Parque Nacional Conguillío and to Lake District resorts like Villarrica, Licán Ray and Curarrehue.

Buses Biobío, Lautaro 853, has many buses to Angol, Los Angeles and Concepción. Cruz del Sur, at Vicuña Mackenna 671, has daily buses to Concepción and Santiago, and many to Puerto Montt (some continuing to Chiloé) and Valdivia.

Other major Panamericana companies include Tas Choapa (direct to Valparaíso and Viña del Mar), at Varas 609; Buses Fénix, at Claro Solar 609; Tur-Bus, at Lagos 538; Buses Lit, at San Martín 894; Igi Llaima, at Miraflores 1535; Varmontt, at Bulnes 45; and Power, at Bulnes 174.

Buses Jac, Vicuña Mackenna 798, has two dozen buses daily to Villarrica and Pucón, plus four to Santiago, three to Licán Ray and Coñaripe, and a daily service to Curarrehue. Panguisur, Miraflores 871, has seven buses daily to Panguipulli, plus three nightly to Santiago.

Buses Thiele, Vicuña Mackenna 650, has three buses daily to Cañete, continuing to Lebú and Concepción. Erbuc, at the Terminal de Buses Rurales, has three buses daily to Lonquimay, on the upper Biobío.

Typical fares include Coñaripe US$4; Villarrica US$2; Angol, Pucón or Licán Ray US$2.50; Valdivia, Los Angeles or Lonquimay US$4; Chillán or Currarehue

US$6; Concepción or Osorno US$5; Puerto Montt US$9; and Santiago US$16.

Bus – international Buses Fénix goes to Buenos Aires (US$75) via Santiago on Monday and Wednesday. Both Fénix and Tas Choapa have nightly buses to Mendoza (US$40) via Santiago.

Jac, Igi Llaima and San Martín (at Balmaceda 1598) connect Temuco with Junín de los Andes, San Martín de los Andes and Neuquén, usually via Paso Mamuil Malal, east of Pucón. Ruta Sur, Claro Solar 692, and Igi Llaima both go to Neuquén via Zapala. Typical fares are Junín or San Martín US$15, Zapala US$23 and Neuquén US$29.

Tas Choapa and Cruz del Sur have a daily service to Bariloche (US$27) via Osorno.

Train Trains go north to Santiago (all year) and south to Puerto Montt (summer only). Buy tickets at the railway station (☎ 23-3416), eight blocks west of the plaza on Barros Arana, or in the town centre (☎ 23-3522) at Bulnes 582.

Getting Around

To/From the Airport Aeropuerto Maquehue is six km south of town. Agencia de Viajes Anahi (☎ 21-1155), Aldunate 235, runs airport minibuses (US$2.50).

To/From the Bus Terminal & Train Station These are some distance from the city centre, but taxi colectivos are quick. Bus No 1 goes to the train station from the centre of town.

Car Consider renting a car for easy access to national parks and Indian villages. Agencies include the Automóvil Club (☎ 24-8901), at San Martín 0278; Hertz (☎ 23-5385), at Las Heras 999; Avis (☎ 23-7575), at Aldunate 656; First (☎ 23-3890), at Varas 1036; and Budget (☎ 21-4911), at Lynch 471.

ANGOL

Destroyed half a dozen times by the Mapuche, Angol managed to survive after the Indian resistance abated in 1862. Some distance off the Panamericana, it offers the best access to Parque Nacional Nahuelbuta, which preserves the largest remaining stands of coastal araucarias (monkey puzzle trees).

Angol's hard-working, well-informed tourist office is near the bridge, on the east side of the Río Vergara. CONAF, on the corner of Prat and Chorrillos, may offer transport to Nahuelbuta.

The **Escuela Agrícola El Vergel**, created in the 19th century as a plant nursery and gardens, has a national reputation for training gardeners and farmers. Its **Museo Bullock** has local natural history specimens and archaeological artefacts. Five km east of Angol, reached by taxi colectivo No 2 from the plaza, it's open from 9 am to 8 pm daily.

Places to Stay & Eat

Accommodation at the *Casa del Huésped*, Dieciocho 465, is US$9 per person; *Pensión Chorrillos*, Chorrillos 724, is slightly dearer but serves good, cheap lunches. *Residencial Olimpia*, Caupolicán 625, charges US$10/20 a single/double, while *Hostería Las Araucarias*, Prat 499, has singles with breakfast for US$11.

Café Stop, Lautaro 176, offers sandwiches and parrillada, while *Pizzería Sparlatto*, at Lautaro 418, has the obvious. For wider selections, try *Las Totoras*, at Ilabaca and Covadonga, or the *Club Social*, Caupolicán 498.

Things to Buy

Angol is known for its ceramics from two small factories: Cerámica Serra, at Bunster 153, and Cerámica Lablé, at Purén 864.

Getting There & Away

The Terminal Rodoviario, at Caupolicán 200, north of the plaza, has buses to Santiago, Temuco and Concepción. The Terminal Rural, on the corner of Ilabaca and Lautaro, runs buses along the Costa del Carbón to Concepción. Buses JB has 14 buses daily to Los Ángeles (US$1.50).

Buses Angol goes to Vegas Blancas (US$1.75), seven km from the entrance to Parque Nacional Nahuelbuta, on Monday, Wednesday and Friday at 7 am and 4 pm.

PARQUE NACIONAL NAHUELBUTA

Araucarias up to 50 metres in height and two metres in diameter cover the slopes of Nahuelbuta, one of the monkey puzzle's last non-Andean refuges. About 35 km west of Angol, most of the park is a slightly undulating plain, 950 metres above sea level, but permanent streams have cut deep canyons, and jagged granitic peaks reach to 1565 metres. Summers are warm and dry but snow touches the summits in winter.

Things to See & Do

Rangers offer audiovisual presentations at CONAF's Pehuenco visitor centre. Nahuelbuta has 30 km of roads and 15 km of footpaths, so car-touring, camping and hiking are all possible. Admission is US$2.

Piedra del Aguila, a four-km hike from Pehuenco, is a 1400-metre overlook with views to the Andes and the Pacific. **Cerro Anay** (1450 metres) is similar.

Places to Stay

Camping grounds at Pehuenco and at Coimallín charge US$7 per site.

Getting There & Away

Besides regular services to Vegas Blancas, Buses Angol offers Sunday tours for US$10, leaving the Terminal Rural at 7 am.

PARQUE NACIONAL CONGUILLIO

Towering above 60,000 hectares of alpine lakes, canyons and forests, the 3125-metre Volcán Llaima recorded violent eruptions as recently as 1957. Conguillío's Los Paraguas sector protects the monkey puzzle tree (in Spanish *paragua*, meaning 'umbrella', because of its unusual shape; *pehuén* to the Mapuche, who gather its edible nuts). Southern beeches blanket lower elevations. Three metres of snow can accumulate in winter.

Things to See & Do

From November to March, CONAF's Lago Conguillío visitor centre offers slide shows, ecology talks, guided hikes and boat trips, but independent travellers can undertake many of the same activities.

Experienced climbers can tackle Llaima from Los Paraguas. For ski information contact the newly opened Centro de Ski Las Araucarias (☎ (09) 443-4246) in Temuco.

Places to Stay

From mid-December to early March, *Cabañas y Camping Conguillío* (☎ 22-0254 in Temuco) rents rustic but comfortable six-bed cabañas for US$50 per night. Camp sites are not cheap at US$17 (for up to five people) – the best alternative is the back country.

At Los Paraguas, the *Refugio Escuela Ski* has 40 beds and a restaurant.

Getting There & Away

For Los Paraguas, take Erbuc or Nar Bus from Temuco's Terminal de Buses Rurales to Cherquenco (US$2), then walk or hitch the 17 km to the ski lodge.

For the northern entrance to the Conguillío sector, take a bus to Curacautín, 42 km from park headquarters, via Victoria (US$1.75) or Lautaro (US$2). From Curacautín, it is necessary to hitch. A southern approach passes through Cunco and Melipeuco (US$2), where buses leave Hostería Hue-Telén for the headquarters. With a rental car, you can make a loop from Temuco.

PUCON

Until Volcán Villarica's next major eruption obliterates it, the up-market resort of Pucón will offer fine accommodation and superb food. Villarrica is cheaper (and less vulnerable to lava flows), but a visit to Pucón is worthwhile.

Information

Tourist Offices In summer, the tourist office, at O'Higgins 640, is open Monday to Saturday from 8 am to 10 pm, and Sunday from 10 am to 1 pm and 6 to 9 pm. Winter hours are shorter. There is also a very helpful private tourist office at Brasil 115. Pucón's telephone code is 45.

Money Turcamb, O'Higgins 472, will change cash and travellers' cheques. The main market, Supermercado Eltit, O'Higgins 336, also changes money.

Travel Agencies Pucón is Chile's mecca for adventure travel, with climbing, rafting, mountain biking, horse riding, fishing and other activities. Most agencies are on or near O'Higgins, but prices do not vary greatly – tours to Volcán Villarrica, a day climb if the weather holds, cost about US$50 per person. It is obligatory to have a local guide for the climb to the summit. For fishing trips contact Rodolfo Aliante (☎ 44-1721) at Residencial Lucía, who provides transportation, equipment and guides between November and May.

National Parks CONAF, on Camino Internacional (the 1400 block on the extension of O'Higgins), may help with transport to Villarrica and Huerquehue national parks.

Places to Stay

Camping Mapu-Rayen (☎ 44-1378), Colo Colo 475, is very clean and friendly.

In summer, several hospedajes charge around US$9 (some with breakfast or kitchen privileges), including *Hospedaje Sonia* (comfortable, with a very outgoing owner and a good place to meet people), at Lincoyán and Brasil. Hospitable *Hospedaje Lucía*, Lincoyán 565, has nice rooms and camp sites; Lucía herself is experienced in tourist information. *Hospedaje Juan Torres*, Lincoyán 443, is another possibility. The tourist office keeps a list of private houses that provide lodging.

Clean, pleasant *Ecole* (☎ 44-1081), at General Urrutia and Arauco, is open all year and charges US$11 for singles. *Residencial Lincoyán*, Lincoyán 323, and *Hostería Millarrahue* (with a restaurant that received a warm endorsement from an LP reader), O'Higgins 460, are similar in price and quality.

Places to Eat

Besides hotel restaurants, there are scores of other eateries. For empanadas, visit *Los Hornitos de Pucón*, Caupolicán 710. Nearby

Marmonch, Ecuador 175, has a different lunch daily, also takeaway food. *El Fogón*, O'Higgins 480, is a parrilla, while *La Terraza*, O'Higgins 323, has pizza, pancakes, meat and seafood.

Club 77, O'Higgins 635, offers traditional specialities like pastel de choclo, baked empanadas and smoked trout. For exquisite German goodies, try *Holzapfel Bäckerei*, Clemente Holzapfel 524. For tea or coffee, *Hostería Suiza*, O'Higgins 116, offers delicious baked goods.

Getting There & Away

The bus terminal is on Palguín between Urrutia and O'Higgins. Buses Jac has many departures to Villarrica (US$0.75). Tur-Bus, Fénix and Power have services to Santiago. In summer Tur-Bus goes to Puerto Montt daily.

Buses Cordillera goes to Paillaco, on Lago Caburgua (Parque Nacional Huerquehue). Buses Regional Villarrica has several buses to Currarehue and Puesco, the last stop before Junín de los Andes, Argentina.

VILLARRICA

Founded in 1552, colonial Villarrica withered under repeated Mapuche attacks until treaties were signed in 1883. The present resort, 86 km south-west of Temuco, on Lago Villarrica, also shares its name with a smouldering, snowcapped volcano.

Information

Tourist Offices The tourist office (☎ 41-1162), Pedro de Valdivia 1070, has the very useful publication *Datos Utiles Villarrica* and an updated list of accommodation and prices. In summer, it stays open from 8.30 am to 11 pm; during other seasons, hours are 8.30 am to 1 pm and 1.30 to 6.30 pm.

Money To change US and Argentine cash, and US travellers' cheques, go to Turismo Christopher, Pedro de Valdivia 1061. Banks on Pedro de Valdivia have ATMs.

Post & Communications The post office is on General Urrutia near Anfión Muñoz. CTC

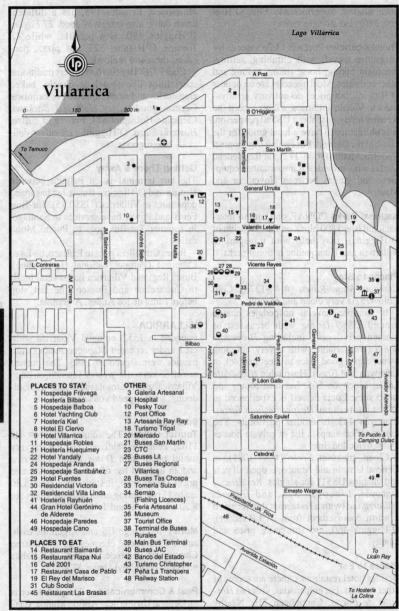

Villarrica

Lago Villarrica

A Prat

B O'Higgins

Camilo Henríquez

San Martín

General Urrutia

Valentín Letelier

Vicente Reyes

Pedro de Valdivia

Bilbao

Anfión Muñoz

Aldereta

Pedro Montt

General Körner

Julio Zegers

Aviador Acevedo

P Léon Gallo

Saturnino Epulef

Catedral

Ernesto Wagner

Presidente JA Ríos

Avenida Estación

To Temuco

JM Balmaceda

JM Carrera

L Contreras

Andrés Bello

MA Matta

To Pucón & Camping Dulac

To Licán Ray

To Hostería La Colina

PLACES TO STAY
1 Hospedaje Frávega
2 Hostería Bilbao
5 Hospedaje Balboa
6 Hotel Yachting Club
8 Hostería Kiel
8 Hotel El Ciervo
9 Hotel Villarrica
11 Hospedaje Robles
18 Hostería Huequimey
22 Hotel Yandaly
24 Hospedaje Aranda
25 Hospedaje Santibáñez
29 Hotel Fuentes
30 Residencial Victoria
32 Residencial Villa Linda
41 Hostería Rayhuén
44 Gran Hotel Gerónimo de Alderete
46 Hospedaje Paredes
49 Hospedaje Cano

PLACES TO EAT
14 Restaurant Baimarán
15 Restaurant Rapa Nui
16 Café 2001
17 Restaurant Casa de Pablo
19 El Rey del Marisco
31 Club Social
45 Restaurant Las Brasas

OTHER
3 Galería Artesanal
4 Hospital
10 Pesky Tour
12 Post Office
17 Artesanía Ray Ray
18 Turismo Trigal
20 Mercado
21 Buses San Martín
23 CTC
26 Buses Lit
27 Buses Regional Villarrica
28 Buses Tas Choapa
33 Tornería Suiza
34 Sernap (Fishing Licences)
35 Feria Artesanal
36 Museum
37 Tourist Office
38 Terminal de Buses Rurales
39 Main Bus Terminal
40 Buses JAC
42 Banco del Estado
43 Turismo Christopher
47 Peña La Tranquera
48 Railway Station

is at Henríquez 430. Villarrica's telephone code is 45.

Medical Services Villarrica's hospital (☎ 41-1169) is at San Martín 460.

Things to See

Next to the tourist office, a skeletal **museum** displays Mapuche jewellery, musical instruments and roughly hewn wooden masks. Nearby is an oblong Mapuche **ruca**, with thatched walls and roof.

Behind the tourist office, the **Feria Artesanal** has a selection of crafts and traditional Mapuche food.

Places to Stay

The most convenient and economical place to stay is *Camping Dulac*, two km east of town. It can be crowded, but the shady sites (US$7) provide reasonable privacy.

Some hotels operate in summer only. One reader enjoyed *Hospedaje Balboa*, San Martín 734, with singles for US$10. Check the tourist office for additional listings.

One of the cheapest permanent places, charging about US$7 per person, is *Hotel Fuentes*, Vicente Reyes 665. Rooms are basic, but pleasant and comfortable, while the downstairs bar and restaurant are cosy in winter.

Residencial Victoria, Anfión Muñoz 530, also charges US$7 per person, while *Residencial Villa Linda*, Pedro de Valdivia 678, has singles/doubles with shared bath for US$8/13. *Hostería Rayhuén*, Pedro Montt 668, is a charming place with well-heated rooms and a very fine restaurant. Rooms here cost US$25/35 with breakfast.

Places to Eat

The popular *Club Social*, Valdivia 640, serves German dishes and Chilean seafood, while *Cale*, Valentín Letelier 726, has Mexican and Spanish food. *La Carreta*, Alderete 768, is a parrilla. *El Rey del Marisco*, Valentín Letelier 1030, specialises in fish and shellfish.

Café 2001, Henríquez 379, is a typical tourist café, with good sandwiches and kuchen; *Café Amadeus*, at Henríquez 552, is similar. *Baimarán*, Henríquez 331, serves Brazilian food.

Getting There & Away

Buses are frequent to Santiago, Puerto Montt and many Lake District destinations, and even to Argentina; fares resemble those from Temuco. The main terminal is on Pedro de Valdivia at Anfión Muñoz, but offices are scattered around the centre. The Terminal de Buses Rurales is at Muñoz 657.

Buses Jac, corner of Anfión Muñoz and Bilbao, goes to Temuco and Pucón every half-hour, and to Licán Ray and Coñaripe. Buses Regional Villarrica, near Hotel Fuentes, has buses to Pucón and Curarrehue.

AROUND VILLARRICA

The hot-springs resorts **Termas de Huife** and **Termas de Palguín**, both within 30 km of Pucón, are up-market but not prohibitively expensive for day use. Buses Cordillera (☎ 44-1903) go to Huife at 12.30 and 5 pm weekdays, but transport to Palguín is hard to arrange, except for taxis or tours.

PARQUE NACIONAL HUERQUEHUE

Mountainous Huerquehue, 35 km from Pucón on Lago Caburgua's eastern shore, is a 12,500-hectare reserve. Rushing streams have cut deep canyons, whose walls reach 2000 metres. Bird life is abundant.

From park headquarters at Lago Tinquilco, the seven-km **Lago Verde Trail** climbs through dense beech forests and past waterfalls, with great views of Volcán Villarrica. At upper elevations there are solid stands of pehuén trees.

CONAF's Lago Tinquilco camping ground charges US$7 per site. Buses Cordillera has two buses daily from Pucón to Paillaco, at the south end of Lago Caburgua, but Tinquilco is eight km farther on a dusty, mostly uphill road; start walking and hope for a lift. Park admission is US$2.

PARQUE NACIONAL VILLARRICA

Parque Nacional Villarrica's centrepiece is its very active, 2850-metre namesake

CHILE

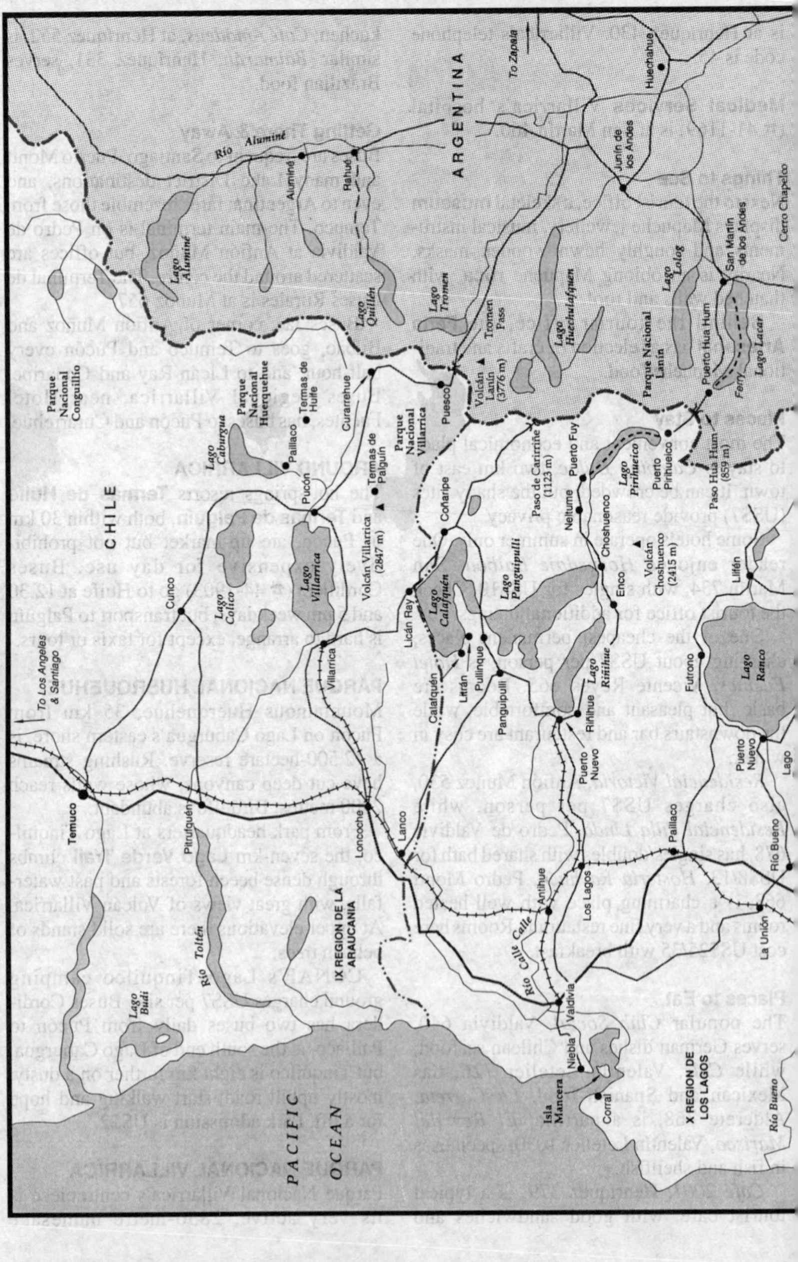
ARGENTINA
CHILE
PACIFIC OCEAN
To Los Angeles & Santiago
Temuco
Pitrufquén
Loncoche
Villarrica
Cunco
Lago Colico
Lago Villarrica
Volcán Villarrica (2847 m)
Pucón
Lago Caburgua
Paillaco
Termas de Huife
Parque Nacional Huerquehue
Parque Nacional Conguillio
Curarrehue
Termas de Palguín
Parque Nacional Villarrica
Puesco
Volcán Lanín (3776 m)
Tromen Pass
Lago Tromen
Lago Quillén
Lago Aluminé
Río Aluminé
Aluminé
Rahué
To Zapala
Huechahue
Junín de los Andes
Lago Huechulafquen
Parque Nacional Lanín
Lago Lolog
San Martín de los Andes
Cerro Chapelco
Lago Lacar
Ferry
Puerto Hua Hum
Paso Hua Hum (859 m)
Puerto Pirihueico
Lago Pirihueico
Puerto Fuy
Paso de Carirriñe (1123 m)
Coñaripe
Neltume
Choshuenco
Volcán Choshuenco (2415 m)
Enco
Lago Panguipulli
Lago Calafquén
Licán Ray
Calafquén
Litrán
Pullinque
Panguipulli
Lago Riñihue
Riñihue
Puerto Nuevo
Lanco
Lago Budi
Río Toltén
IX REGION DE LA ARAUCANIA
Río Calle Calle
Antilhue
Los Lagos
Valdivia
Niebla
Isla Mancera
Corral
X REGION DE LOS LAGOS
Río Bueno
Paillaco
La Unión
Río Bueno
Puerto Nuevo
Lago
Lago Ranco
Futrono
Llifén

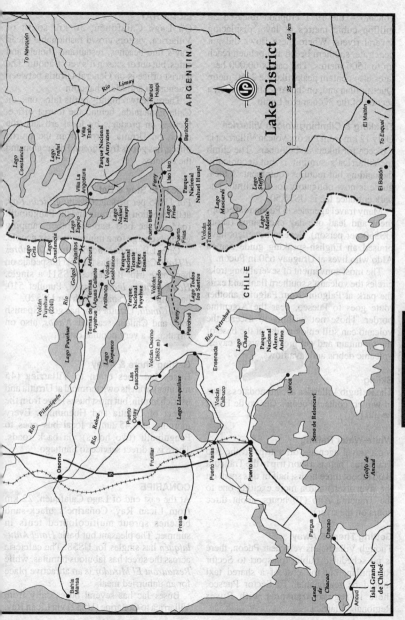

volcano – the 1971 eruption released 30 million cubic metres of lava, displacing several rivers. Where these flows did not penetrate, southern beech and pehuén reach up to 1500 metres. The park's 60,000 hectares also contain peaks like the 2360-metre Quetrupillán and, on the Argentine border, a section of the 3746-metre Lanín.

Trekking & Climbing Volcán Villarrica

Only 12 km from Pucón, Volcán Villarrica is a mecca for hikers and climbers. The climb to Villarrica's summit is not technically demanding but requires equipment. A local guide is now obligatory for the climb. The park entrance fee is US$6.50.

Many travel agencies in Pucón rent equipment and lead one-day excursions (about US$50 per person). Several travellers have praised an English-speaking guide named Aldo who lives at Uruguay 650 in Pucón.

The most convenient of several long treks circles the volcano's southern flank and exits the park at Palguín; from Palguín, another route goes to Puesco, near the Argentine border. Those not wishing to ascend the volcano can still enjoy a hike at the base of the mountain and get great views of caves, volcanic debris and lava flows.

Skiing

The Refugio Villarrica accommodates skiers in winter; contact Pucón's Centro de Esquí (☎ 44-1901).

White-Water Rafting

Most travel agencies offer trips to the Río Trancura. There is a short trip to the Trancura Bajo (about three hours, half of this spent on the river itself) and a more exciting one to the Trancura Alto (10 hours, about three hours on the river).

Getting There & Away

Though Villarrica is very near Pucón, there is no scheduled public transport to Sector Rucapillán, but the cost of a shared taxi should be reasonable. To Sector Puesco, there is regular transport with Buses Regional Villarrica.

LICAN RAY

On Lago Calafquén, 30 km south of Villarrica, visitors crowd fashionable Licán Ray's fine beaches, restaurants, hotels and cafés, but out of season it's very tranquil. The tourist office is on General Urrutia between Huenumán and Marichanquín.

There are two nightly crafts fairs: one, on Calle Esmeralda, behind the tourist office, focuses on products by local artisans; the other, on Urrutia, across from the tourist office, has goods from around the region and the country.

Places to Stay & Eat

For US$5 per person, *Camping Licán Ray*, at the junction of Urrutia and the Panguipulli road, is the best bargain; other camping grounds charge for a minimum of six people.

One LP reader nominated *Chambres d'Hote*, Catriñi 140, as the best hospedaje in her entire trip; it charges US$11 a single. *Hotel Refugio Inaltulafquén*, Punulef 510, has singles with shared bath for US$20.

El Candil, Urrutia 845, has good Spanish food and Chilean seafood. *Ñaños*, also on Urrutia, is a very popular eatery.

Getting There & Away

Buses Jac goes often to Villarrica (45 minutes) from its own terminal at Urrutia and Marichanquín, but most buses leave from the corner of Urrutia and Huenumán. Every morning at 7.45 am, a local bus goes to Panguipulli (two hours) via back roads. There is a direct service to Santiago.

COÑARIPE

At the east end of Lago Calafquén, 22 km from Licán Ray, Coñaripe's black-sand beaches sprout multicoloured tents in summer. The pleasant but basic *Hotel Antulafquén* has singles for US$8. The cafeteria across the street has fabulous humitas, while *Restaurant El Mirador* is an attractive place for an unhurried meal.

Buses Jac has several buses daily from Villarrica to Coñaripe (US$2) via Licán Ray.

PANGUIPULLI

Quieter and slower paced than other resorts, Panguipulli is 115 km east of Valdivia by paved highway via Lanco. It has sensational views across Lago Panguipulli to Volcán Choshuenco. In summer the tourist office, on the plaza, is open daily from 10 am to 8.30 pm.

One reader has praised *Hospedaje Berrocal*, at Carrera 834, but a nameless *hospedaje* on Pedro de Valdivia, directly opposite the bus terminal, charges only US$9 per person. The *family house* of Nicolás Pozas on Calle Pedro de Valdivia, opposite the bus terminal, charges US$11. *Hostal España*, on the corner of O'Higgins and Rodríguez, has singles for US$23 with breakfast.

Erwin Bittner, a German, rents *rooms* and *camping space* 18 km from Panguipulli but will offer free housing and meals in return for work on his organic farm. Contact him through Restaurant Girasol (which also has accommodation), on Calle Martínez de Rozas.

Try *Restaurant Chapulín*, at Rozas 639, for meat and seafood, or *Girasol*, on Rozas near Matta, which is recommended. The most intriguing option is *Restaurant Didáctico El Gourmet*, a highly regarded cooking school, at Freire 0394.

Getting There & Away

Panguipulli's main bus terminal, on 11 de Septiembre, has regional and long-distance services, plus buses to Choshuenco, Neltume and Puerto Fuy (Lago Pirehueico). Several companies have daily buses to Valdivia (2½ hours); Tur-Bus has a separate terminal, at Valdivia and Rozas.

For the latest information on the ferry from Puerto Fuy to Puerto Pirehueico and the Argentine border, ask at Hostería Quetropillán (☎ 31-1348), Etchegaray 381.

Ruta Andes uses a smaller terminal, on Freire near Etchegaray, for its daily service to Coñaripe (US$1.50), Licán Ray and Villarrica.

CHOSHUENCO

Tiny Choshuenco, at the south-east end of Lago Panguipulli, survives from farming, a sawmill and visitors who enjoy its attractive black-sand beach. *Hotel Rucapillán*, near the beach, is very clean, with heated rooms, a good restaurant, hot showers and friendly staff; it charges about US$11 per person. The basic but agreeable *Claris Hotel* charges US$9.

Getting There & Away

Buses from Panguipulli to Puerto Fuy pass through Choshuenco. From Puerto Fuy, there are daily ferries to Puerto Pirehueico, but times vary.

VALDIVIA

Pedro de Valdivia himself founded Santa María La Blanca de Valdivia. After Mapuche raids, it became a military camp, but its architecture, local surnames and regional cuisine show the influence of 19th-century German immigrants. Valdivia (population 110,000), also known as the City of the Rivers, is 160 km south-west of Temuco, 45 km off the Panamericana. Across the Río Calle Calle is Isla Teja, a leafy suburb.

Information

Tourist Offices Sernatur (☎ 21-3596), on the riverfront at Avenida Prat 555, is open on weekdays from 9 am to 8.30 pm, Saturday from 10 am to 4 pm, and Sunday from 10 am to 2 pm. The information booth at the bus terminal is also very helpful.

Money Try the Turismo Money Exchange, at Arauco 331, Local 23, or Money Exchange El Libertador, at Carampangue 325.

Post & Communications The post office is at O'Higgins 575. Telefónica del Sur has offices at San Carlos 107, O'Higgins 386 and Picarte 461, Local 2. Valdivia's telephone code is 63.

Medical Services The Hospital Regional (☎ 21-4066) is at Bueras 1003, near Aníbal Pinto.

CHILE

CHILE

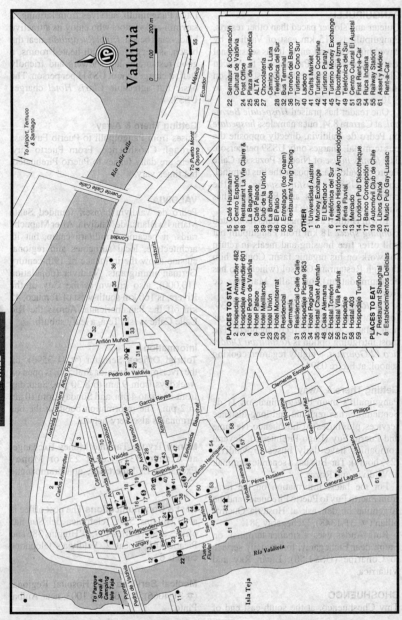

Valdivia

0   100   200 m

PLACES TO STAY
2 Hospedaje Anwandter 482
3 Hospedaje Anwandter 601
4 Hotel Regional
9 Hotel Palace
10 Hotel Melillanca
23 Hotel Unión
29 Hotel Montserrat
30 Residencial Germania
31 Residencial Calle Calle
33 Hospedaje Picarte 953
34 Hotel Regional
35 Hotel Chalet Alemán
48 Casa Alemana
52 Hotel Torreón
56 Hostal Villa Paulina
57 Hospedaje
58 Hostal 403
59 Hospedaje Turismos

PLACES TO EAT
7 Restaurant Shanghai
8 Establecimientos Delicias
15 Café Hausmann
16 Centro Español
18 Restaurant La Vie Claire &
   La Baguette
38 Café Palace
39 Club de la Unión
43 La Bomba
46 El Patio
50 Entrelagos (Ice Cream)
60 Restaurant Yang Cheng

OTHER
1 Universidad Austral
5 Money Exchange
6 Telefónica del Sur
11 Museo Histórico y Arqueológico
12 Feria Fluvial
13 Mercado
14 London Pub Discotheque
17 Banco Concepción
19 Automóvil Club de Chile
20 Libros Chiloé
21 Music Pub Gay-Lussac
22 Sernatur & Corporación
   Cultural de Valdivia
24 Post Office
25 Plaza de la República
26 Altel
27 Chocolatería
28 Camino de Luna
   Telefónica del Sur
32 Bus Terminal
36 Torreón del Barco
37 Turismo Cono Sur
40 Ladeco
41 Crafts Market
42 Turismo Cochrane
44 Turismo Paraty
45 Turismo Money Exchange
47 Discotheque Izma
49 Telefónica del Sur
51 Centro Cultural El Austral
53 First Rent-a-Car
54 Railway Station
55 Asset y Médez
   Rent-a-Car
61 Music Pub Gay-Lussac

Things to See

On Sunday, people jam the **Feria Fluvial**, a riverside market north of the tourist office, to buy fish and fruit for the week. On Isla Teja, shady **Parque Saval** has a riverside beach and a pleasant trail to lily-covered **Laguna de los Lotos**. Nearby, the **Universidad Austral** operates a first-rate dairy outlet, with ice cream, yoghurt and cheese at bargain prices.

In a riverfront mansion on Isla Teja, the **Museo Histórico y Arqueológico** has a well-labelled collection containing fine displays of Mapuche artefacts and household items from early German colonists. You can get there in a rowing boat which leaves from the tourist office. Well-organised tours (Spanish only) are a bit rushed but the guides respond well to questions. Admission is about US$1.

Places to Stay

Camping For US$8 per site, *Camping Isla Teja* (☎ 21-3584), at the end of Calle Los Robles, has a pleasant orchard setting, good facilities and a riverside beach. Cheaper but less comfortable sites at Parque Saval cost about US$4.

Hostels Valdivia has two Hostelling International affiliates. *Residencial Germania* (☎ 21-2405), Picarte 873, which is owned by friendly German-speakers, charges US$15 with breakfast, hot showers and clean rooms. At the beautiful *Hostal Torreón* (☎ 21-2622), where the friendly host is constantly improving the service, singles are US$18 with breakfast.

Hotels & Hospedajes Sernatur provides a thorough list of seasonal accommodation, much of which is on Avenidas Ramón Picarte and Carlos Anwandter.

Hotel Regional, Picarte 1005, is plain but clean, with hot water, friendly staff and a small restaurant; it charges US$10. Highly regarded *Hostal 403*, Yerbas Buenas 403, charges US$13 with breakfast and has a good restaurant. *Hospedaje Picarte 953*, Picarte 953, near the bus terminal, is very

clean and attractive; it charges US$15 per person with breakfast. *Casa Alemana* (☎ 21-2015) at García Reyes 658 (interior) has a hospitable German-speaking owner who charges US$13/25 for a single/double. Another popular place is *Hotel Montserrat*, a few doors from the Germania, at Picarte 849, charging US$15/30 with breakfast. Also recommended is the *hospedaje* at Philippi 804 (☎ 22-4221), where a clean double with breakfast costs US$20.

Places to Eat

Stroll along Arauco between Caupolicán and Pérez Rosales for eateries like *El Patio*, Arauco 343, 2nd floor. *Hostal 403* has a different dinner special nightly.

Club de la Unión, Camilo Henríquez 540, offers well-prepared three-course meals for about US$4. Try also the *Centro Español*, at Henríquez 436, or *La Bomba*, Caupolicán 594.

For coffee and snacks, check out *Café Palace*, Pérez Rosales 580. For fine pastries and desserts, try *Establecimientos Delicias*, at Henríquez 372, or *Café Hausmann*, at O'Higgins 394. For very fine kuchen, visit *La Baguette*, at Caupolicán 435-B; for ice cream, try *Entrelagos*, Pérez Rosales 630.

Things to Buy

For chocolate specialities, go to Chocolatería Entrelagos, at Pérez Rosales 622; Confitería Sur, at Henríquez 374; or Chocolatería Camino de Luna, at Picarte 417. There's an interesting, informal evening crafts market on the north-east corner of Maipú and Henríquez.

Getting There & Away

Air Aeródromo Las Marías is north of the city via the Puente Calle Calle. Ladeco (☎ 21-3392), Caupolicán 579, flies to Santiago four times weekly. ALTA (☎ 22-8150) is at Caupolicán 535.

Bus From the Terminal de Buses (☎ 21-2212), Anfión Muñoz 360, there are frequent buses to destinations on or near the Carretera

Panamericana between Puerto Montt and Santiago. Typical fares are Temuco US$3.50, Puerto Montt US$6, Concepción US$10 and Santiago US$18.

Tas Choapa, Cruz del Sur, Andesmar and Buses Norte all serve Bariloche, Argentina (US$23).

Línea Verde, Pirehueico, Valdivia and Chile Nuevo go to Panguipulli (US$3), and Línea Verde goes to Futrono. Buses Jac has a regular service to Villarrica and Temuco.

Getting Around

To Valdivia airport, Transfer (☎ 22-5533) offers a minibus service. Phone to make a reservation and they will pick you up at your hotel or at the Ladeco office. From the bus terminal, any bus marked 'Plaza' goes to the central Plaza de la República. Buses from the plaza to the terminal go down Arauco before turning onto Picarte.

AROUND VALDIVIA

At Corral, Niebla and Isla Mancera, at the mouth of the Río Valdivia, is a series of 17th-century Spanish forts. Largest and most intact is the **Fuerte de Corral** (1645), site of

a key naval encounter between Chilean patriots and Spanish loyalists in 1820.

Corral and nearby Armagos are most easily reached by boat, but buses from the municipal market in Valdivia go directly to Niebla (US$1.50) where launches across the river cost US$0.75. The best option is a morning cruise from Valdivia's Puerto Fluvial, returning by afternoon bus.

OSORNO

In the late 16th century, huge encomiendas supported over 1000 Spaniards and mestizos in San Mateo de Osorno, but rebellion in 1599 forced them to flee to Chiloé. Only in 1796 was resettlement successful, and well after independence the Mapuche still made overland travel difficult and dangerous.

German immigrants have left their mark on Osorno, particularly in dairy farming and manufacturing. Tourism is increasing because Osorno (910 km south of Santiago; population 110,000) is a key road junction for lakes Puyehue and Rupanco, Parque Nacional Puyehue, and the Argentine border.

Information

Tourist Offices Sernatur's (☎ 23-4104)

PLACES TO STAY		PLACES TO EAT			
2	Hospedaje	7	Deutscher Verein	17	Terminal de Buses
5	Hospedaje Amunátegui	8	Dino's Restaurant	19	Disco Mario's
12	Hotel Interlagos	28	Pastelería Rhenania	20	Railway Station
13	Residencial	38	Casa del Altillo	21	CONAF
	Schulz	39	Pizzería Los	24	Post Office
14	Residencial Aitu		Platos	25	Sernatur
18	Hospedaje de la			26	Plaza de Armas
	Fuente	**OTHER**		27	Galería Cated-
22	Hotel Tirol	1	Automóvil Club de		ral/Turismo Frontera
23	Gran Hotel Osorno		Chile	29	Telefónica del Sur
31	Hotel García Hurtado	3	ALTA	30	Cambiotur (Money
	de Mendoza	4	German		Exchange)
33	Residencial Ortega		Cemetery	32	Los Detalles
34	Hotel Rayantú	6	Cine Lido		(Crafts)
41	Residencial La	9	Centro Cultural	35	Banco de Chile
	Posada	10	Ñiltur Rent-a-Car	36	First Rent-a-Car
45	Residencial Hein	11	Galería Rombocol &	37	German Consulate
46	Hotel Waeger		Osorno Tour	40	Alta Artesanía
47	Residencial Bilbao	15	Mercado Municipal &	42	Hertz Rent-a-Car
48	Residencial Stop		Terminal de Buses	43	Museo Histórico
49	Hotel Villa Eduvijes		Rurales		Municipal
50	Residencial Riga	16	Orlandina Regalos	44	LanChile & Budget
					Rent-a-Car

CHILE

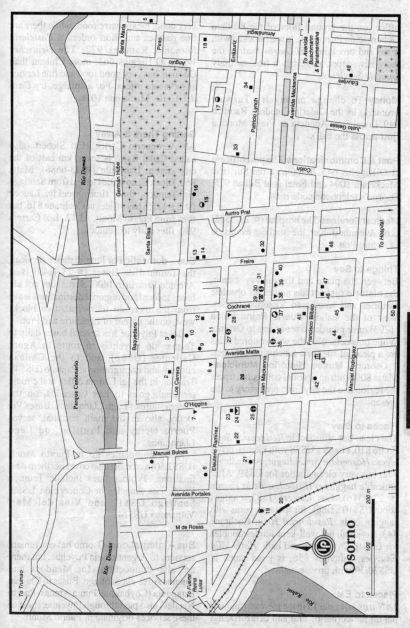

Osorno

To Trumao

To Tumao

Río Damas

To Fuerte
Reina Luisa

Río Rahue

Río Damas

Río Damas

Parque Centenario

Santa María

Pinto

Angulo

Germán Hübe

Santa Elisa

Baquedano

Los Carrera

Amunátegui

Errázuriz

To Avenida
Buschmann &
Panamericana

Patricio Lynch

Avenida Mackenna

Justo Geisse

Colón

Aurtro Prat

Freire

Cochrane

Avenida Matta

O'Higgins

Manuel Bulnes

Eleuterio Ramírez

Avenida Portales

M de Rosas

Francisco Bilbao

Juan Mackenna

Manuel Rodríguez

To Hospital

To Avenida
Buschmann &
Panamericana

Eduviges

CHILE

0   100   200 m

office, on the ground floor of the Edificio Gobernación Provincial, is well stocked with maps and brochures. *El Diario Austral*, the daily newspaper, publishes a free, monthly *Guía de Servicios*.

Money To change money try Turismo Frontera, in the Galería Catedral, Ramírez 949, Local 5, or Agencia de Viajes Mundial (just across the hall).

Post & Communications The post office is at O'Higgins 645. Telefónica del Sur is at Mackenna 1004 and Entel is at Bilbao 975. Osorno's telephone code is 64.

Medical Services The hospital (☎ 23-5572) is on Avenida Bühler, the southern extension of Arturo Prat.

Things to See

Between the plaza and the railway station, the **historic district** has numerous obsolete factories and weathered Victorian houses. West of the station, **Fuerte Reina Luisa** (1793) once guarded river access to Osorno. While unspectacular, the well-restored ruins are a pleasant site for a lunch-time breather.

Osorno's **Museo Histórico Municipal**, Matta 809, with an unusual collection, traces the region and the city from prehistory to the present.

Places to Stay

The clean but ramshackle *Residencial Stop*, Freire 810, charges US$8 with kitchen privileges. *Hospedaje Amunátegui*, Amunátegui 372, has very clean singles for US$9. After amicable haggling, *Hospedaje de la Fuente* (☎ 23-9516), Los Carrera 1587, charges about US$10 a single for spotless rooms with sagging beds. *Residencial Hein*, Cochrane 843, has small but well-kept singles/doubles for US$16/26 with shared bath. *Hotel Villa Eduvijes*, Eduvijes 856, is good value at US$20/39 with private bath.

Places to Eat

La Naranja, Local 13 in the mercado municipal on the corner of Prat and Errázuriz, has very good, inexpensive food, while there are fine pastries and short orders at *Pastelería Rhenania*, Ramírez 977. The *Deutscher Verein*, O'Higgins 563, more Chilean than German, has very good food and fine service at moderate prices. For a splurge, try *Casa del Altillo*, Mackenna 1011.

Getting There & Away

Air Aeropuerto Carlos Hott Siebert (also called Cañal Bajo) is seven km east of the city centre. LanChile (☎ 23-6688), Matta 862, Block C, now flies to and from Santiago via Temuco, three times weekly. Ladeco (☎ 23-4355) has offices at Cochrane 816, but flies from Puerto Montt. ALTA, Los Carrera 930, flies daily to Temuco.

Bus – domestic For long-distance services, the Terminal de Buses (☎ 23-4149) is at Avenida Errázuriz 1400. Some, but not all, buses to local and regional destinations leave from the mercado municipal, two blocks west, on the corner of Errázuriz and Prat.

Buses Puyehue has several buses daily to Termas de Puyehue en route to Aguas Calientes (US$2), and to the Chilean customs and immigration at Pajarito (US$4). Transur, in the Igi Llaima office at the main terminal, goes to Las Cascadas, on the eastern shore of Lago Llanquihue. Buses Via Octay, also in the main terminal, serves Puerto Octay and Frutillar, on Lago Llanquihue.

Many companies go to Puerto Montt (US$2.50) and most also cover northern destinations. Typical fares include Temuco US$5, Los Ángeles or Concepción US$8, Santiago US$12 and Viña del Mar/Valparaíso US$14.

Bus – international Osorno has convenient services to Argentina via Puyehue, but there are also connections for Mendoza and Buenos Aires via Santiago. Buses to Chilean Patagonia (Coyhaique, Punta Arenas, Puerto Natales) also pass through Puyehue; most of these services originate in Puerto Montt.

Fares to Bariloche are about US$20, and to Mendoza US$35.

Train The train station (☎ 23-2992) is at the west end of Mackenna, on the corner of Portales. In summer, trains go to Temuco and Santiago.

AROUND OSORNO

One of Chile's most famous hot-springs resorts, **Termas de Puyehue** is a very expensive place to stay, but worth a visit for its old-world elegance. It's 76 km east of Osorno, where paved Ruta 215 forks; the north fork goes to Anticura and the Argentine border, while its southern lateral goes to Aguas Calientes and Antillanca, in Parque Nacional Puyehue.

PARQUE NACIONAL PUYEHUE

Puyehue's 107,000 hectares of verdant montane forest and starkly awesome volcanic scenery are about 75 km east of Osorno. In its lower Valdivian forest, the dominant tree is the multitrunked *ulmo*. The dense understorey includes the delicate, rust-barked *arrayán* (a myrtle), *quilla* (a solid bamboo which makes some areas impenetrable) and wild fuchsia. At higher altitudes, southern beeches dominate.

Birds are the most visible fauna. On the peaks, you may spot the Andean condor, and look for the Chilean torrent duck in river rapids.

Altitudes range from 250 metres on the Río Golgol to 2236 metres on Volcán Puyehue. January and February are best for the high country, but winter skiing is also popular. Despite the moist climate, many areas north of Ruta 215 have been barren since 1960, when there was a major eruption of Volcán Puyehue. On the western slopes are many extinct fumaroles and still active hot springs.

Aguas Calientes

At Aguas Calientes, CONAF's visitor centre is open daily from 9 am to 1 pm and 2.30 to

8.30 pm. It has a simple but effective display on natural history and geomorphology, with slide shows daily at 5 pm.

Nearby **Sendero El Pionero** is a steep 1800-metre nature trail with splendid views of Lago Puyehue, the valley of the Golgol, and Volcán Puyehue. Watch for the *nalca*, resembling an enormous rhubarb with edible stalks and leaves the size of umbrellas, and the ulmo, which grows to 45 metres. For a longer excursion, take the 11-km trail to **Lago Bertín**.

CONAF rangers lead overnight trips to Lago Paraíso, Volcán Puyehue, Lago Constancia and Pampa Frutilla. For schedules and to reserve a spot (free of charge), contact CONAF here or in Osorno (☎ 23-4393), at Mackenna 674. Bring your own tent, food and rain gear.

Skiing

For some of the finest views of Puyehue and its surroundings, visit the Antillanca ski lodge, at the foot of Volcán Casablanca. The season runs from early June to late October.

Anticura

Anticura is the best base for exploring Puyehue's wildest areas. The highway follows the Río Golgol, but the finest scenery is the desolate plateau at the base of Volcán Puyehue, reached by an overnight hike from El Caulle, two km west of Anticura.

On Puyehue's western slope, a steep morning's walk from El Caulle, CONAF's well-kept refugio is a good place to lodge or camp. From the refugio, it's another four hours over a moonscape of lava flows and fumaroles to a spring with rustic thermal baths, and a fine and private camp site.

Places to Stay & Eat

CONAF charges US$5 for camp sites at Catrue, near Anticura, which has fresh water, picnic tables, firepits and basic toilets. At Aguas Calientes, concessionaires operate *Camping Chanleufú* (US$20 per site) and *Camping Los Derrumbes* (US$16). Fees are for up to eight people and include use of the

CHILE

thermal baths, but these sites are crowded and noisy in summer.

Getting There & Away

From Osorno, Buses Puyehue has several buses daily to Termas de Puyehue and Aguas Calientes (US$2), and to Chilean immigration at Pajaritos (US$4). In winter, the Club Andino de Osorno (☎ 23-2297) offers direct services to Antillanca.

PUERTO OCTAY

In the early days of German settlement, Puerto Octay was an important port on Lago Llanquihue between Puerto Montt and Osorno. Its municipal tourist office is on Pedro Montt. The **Museo El Colono**, on Independencia near Esperanza, displays antique farm machinery and other turn-of-the-century artefacts.

Many readers have praised the clean, comfortable and friendly *hospedaje* (☎ 31-1260) upstairs at Wulf 712 (US$11 per person with breakfast). The same folks run *Restaurant Cabaña*, across the road. *Café Kali*, opposite the Plaza de Armas, is good for breakfast, drinks and desserts. For empanadas, try *La Naranja*, at Independencia and Pedro Montt.

Via Octay buses go to and from Osorno's main bus terminal several times daily. On weekdays, one late-afternoon bus goes to Las Cascadas.

LAS CASCADAS

Las Cascadas, a village on the eastern shore of Lago Llanquihue, has an attractive black-sand beach. The highly recommended *Hostería Irma*, one km south of town on the Ensenada road, charges about US$18 per person. Diagonally opposite, along the lake, is a peaceful and free *camp site* with almost no facilities. *Camping Las Cañitas*, three km down the road, charges US$5 per site for basic services, including cold showers.

The bus from Puerto Octay arrives in the early evening, but there is no service on the poor 20-km road to Ensenada, the entry point to Parque Nacional Vicente Pérez Rosales – either walk or hitch, or return to the Pan-americana and take the bus from Puerto Varas.

FRUTILLAR

From Frutillar, 70 km south of Osorno, snowcapped Volcán Osorno seems to float on the horizon across Lago Llanquihue. Noted for its Germanic architecture, Frutillar consists of Frutillar Bajo, beside the lake, and Frutillar Alto, two km west, near the Panamericana.

Frutillar Bajo's helpful kiosco de turismo, at the jetty on Avenida Philippi, is open from 9 am to 9 pm in January and February; the rest of the year, it's open from 10 am to 6 pm. The telephone code is 65.

Museo de la Colonización Alemana

The Museum of German Colonisation displays immaculate 19th-century farm implements and household artefacts. There are perfectly reconstructed buildings, including a water mill, a functioning blacksmith's building and a typical mansion (as typical as mansions can be) among manicured gardens.

A short walk up from the lakeshore, it's open from 10 am to 2 pm and 5 to 9 pm in summer; from 10 am to 6 pm in other seasons. Admission is US$1.

Places to Stay

Camping Los Ciruelillos, at the far south end of Frutillar Bajo, has shady sites with beach access for US$11. There are hot showers, and fresh home-made bread is available in the morning.

Residencial Winkler (☎ 42-1388), Philippi 1155, has hostel accommodation for US$10 as well as regular rooms in the mid-range category.

Residencial Bruni, at Las Piedras 60, on the escarpment above the lake, charges just US$9 per person, but is open in summer only. *Hostería Trayén*, Philippi 963, is open all year, with rooms with private bath for US$18 and a highly regarded restaurant. With a hearty breakfast, *Hospedaje Kaiserseehaus*, Philippi 1333, charging $US20 per person, is highly recommended.

Places to Eat

For kuchen and fruit preserves, try the mobile *Cinco Robles* stand on Avenida Philippi. The *Club Alemán*, on San Martín above Philippi, has fixed-price lunches for US$11. *Café del Sur*, Pérez Rosales 580, serves reasonable home-cooked lunches. For unforgettable onces, try *Hotel Klein Salzburg* on Philippi, where for about US$6 you get two large portions of cake, warm bread rolls, butter, jam, ham, cheese and salami and all the tea, chocolate or coffee that you can drink.

Things to Buy

Local specialities include fresh raspberries, jams and kuchen, and miniature woodcarvings of the buildings at the museum.

Getting There & Away

Buses Varmontt and Cruz del Sur, on Alessandri in Frutillar Alto, have buses to Puerto Montt and Osorno every half-hour most of the day. Trains and buses stop at Frutillar Alto, not Frutillar Bajo.

Getting Around

Taxi colectivos shuttle between Frutillar Alto and Frutillar Bajo.

PUERTO VARAS

Puerto Varas, a 19th-century lake port 20 km north of Puerto Montt, is the gateway to Lago Todos los Santos and the popular boat-bus crossing to Bariloche, Argentina.

Information

Tourist Offices The municipal tourist office (☎ 23-2437), Del Salvador 328, has free maps and brochures about the entire area. It's open daily from 10 am to noon and 4 to 7 pm. The man in charge speaks English and is extremely helpful.

Money You can change cash and travellers' cheques at Turismo Los Lagos, Del Salvador 257, Local 11.

Post & Communications The post office is at San José 324. Telefónica del Sur, on the corner of Santa Rosa and Del Salvador, is open from 8 am to 11 pm in summer. The telephone code is 65.

Medical Services Clínica Alemana (☎ 23-2336) is at Dr Bader 810.

Activities

Several agencies on Avenida Costanera organise adventure travel activities like trekking, climbing, bird-watching and rafting. The lake and its hinterland provide opportunities for swimming, windsurfing and cycling. In summer you can rent mountain bikes at the feria artesanal (about US$14 per day); check the travel agencies for rental equipment for other sports.

Places to Stay

Hospedaje Hernández, Del Salvador 1025, charges US$13, but most others are in the US$15-plus range. *Hospedaje Ceronni* (☎ 23-2016), Estación 262, is recommended.

The rooms at *Residencial Hellwig* (☎ 23-2472), San Pedro 210, are reasonably spacious and cost at US$11 per person. *Residencial Las Rosas* (☎ 23-2770), Santa Rosa 560, is pleasant with comfortable beds for US$15/28 a single/double. A good deal is the spotless *Residencial Alemana* (☎ 23-2419), San Bernardo 416, where singles are US$15 with a good breakfast.

Places to Eat

Café Real, upstairs at Del Salvador 257, has cheap lunches but *Café Mamusia*, San José 316, has better food. *El Gordito* and *El Mercado*, both in the mercado municipal, at Del Salvador 582, have very fine seafood. The *Club Alemán*, San José 415, is another good option, as is *Il Gato Renzo*, Del Salvador 314. *Merlin Restaurant*, Walker Martínez 584, has appealing if rather expensive meals.

Getting There & Away

Bus Many northbound buses from Puerto Montt pick up passengers here. Puerto Varas has no central bus terminal, but most companies have offices near the centre.

Varmontt, San Francisco 666, has daily buses to Santiago and many to Puerto Montt. Cruz del Sur, Del Salvador 257, has frequent buses daily to Osorno, Valdivia, Temuco and Chiloé. Other nearby companies include Lit, at Walker Martínez 230; Igi Llaima, at Del Salvador 100; Tas Choapa, at Walker Martínez 230; and Buses Norte (both at San Francisco 447). All go to Santiago and to Argentina.

At 12.30 pm daily in summer (except Sunday), Buses Esmeralda, at San Pedro 210, goes to Ensenada (US$1.50) and Petrohué (US$2). The rest of the year, these run only on Tuesday, Thursday and Saturday.

From September to March, Andina del Sud, Del Salvador 243, has daily buses to Ensenada and Petrohué, connecting with its own bus-boat crossing to Bariloche. These leave Puerto Montt at 8.30 am and return at 5 pm; the rest of the year, they run Wednesday to Sunday, leaving Puerto Montt at 10 am and returning at 5 pm. From November to mid-March, Varastur, San Francisco 242, runs buses to Petrohué from Wednesday to Sunday at 10 am, returning at 5 pm.

For fares, see the Puerto Montt section.

Train The station is up the hill on Klenner, across from the casino.

ENSENADA

Ensenada, on the road to Petrohué and Lago Todos los Santos, is on the eastern shore of Lago Llanquihue, at the base of Volcán Osorno. To the south is the jagged crater of Calbuco, which blew its top during the Pleistocene.

For US$13/25 a single/double, *Hostería Ruedas Viejas* has cosy cabins with double bed, private bath and small wood stove. Meals are cheap and helpings bountiful. The hostería also has very limited hostel accommodation (US$10). For excellent meals try any of the restaurants along Ruta 225 where you can get meat, fish and German desserts.

Buses Bohle has four buses daily from

Puerto Montt; for other services, see the Puerto Varas section.

PARQUE NACIONAL VICENTE PEREZ ROSALES

Beneath Volcán Osorno's flawless cone, the scoured glacial basin of Lago Todos los Santos offers dramatic views and a scenic boat-bus route to Argentina. Volcán Puntiagudo's needle point lurks to the north, while Volcán Tronador marks the Argentine border.

Chile's first national park (established in 1926), the 251,000-hectare Vicente Pérez Rosales, is 50 km east of Puerto Varas via paved Ruta 225. Its forests and climate (more than 200 rainy days yearly) resemble those of Puyehue, but January and February are fairly dry.

Volcán Osorno

Many companies in Puerto Varas and Puerto Montt organise guided ascents of Osorno, which requires snow and ice gear, but experienced climbers can handle it solo. Centro de Esquí La Burbuja, 1250 metres above sea level, is not operating for the moment. For information, contact Hotel Vicente Pérez Rosales (☎ 25-2571), Antonio Varas 447 in Puerto Montt.

The *Teski Ski Club* has a refugio just below the snow line, a nine-km uphill hike from the signpost on the Ensenada-Puerto Octay road. Beds are available all year.

Petrohué

In the shadow of Volcán Osorno, Petrohué is the departure point for the ferry to Peulla, which leaves early in the morning and returns after lunch.

CONAF's visitor centre has several interesting displays. From Hotel Petrohué, a dirt track leads to **Playa Larga**, a long black-sand beach. The **Sendero Rincón del Osorno** is a five-km trail on the western shore of Lago Todos los Santos.

Peulla

Approaching the tiny village of Peulla,

which bustles in summer with tourists en route to Argentina, Lago Todos los Santos' deep blue becomes an emerald green. **Cascada de los Novios** is a waterfall just a few minutes walk from Hotel Peulla along an easy footpath. For a longer excursion, take the eight-km **Sendero Laguna Margarita**, a rewarding climb.

Across the river at the Küscher house (reached by rowboat), you can camp or rent a room for US$7.50 a single. The army now occupies the lakeside camping ground, which may have sites available in a pinch. Bring food from Puerto Varas.

One km from the dock, *Hotel Peulla* (☎ 25-8041) charges US$86/126 with half-pension and has a buffet in summer. The modest *Residencial Palomita* has rooms for US$13 per person with half-board. There's a *camp site* opposite CONAF, or you can stay with *Elmo & Ana Hernández*, on the right side as you leave the jetty, for US$9. The officer at the *registro civil* (civil register) also offers lodging.

Getting There & Away
Bus For bus services, see Getting There & Away for Puerto Varas. Some buses from Varas arrive after the ferry, so plan to stay overnight at Petrohué.

Boat Andina del Sud's ferry (☎ 23-2511) departs Petrohué early for the three-hour voyage to Peulla, the first leg of the journey to Bariloche. Get tickets (US$25) at the kiosk near the jetty, or from Andina del Sud in Puerto Varas or Puerto Montt.

PUERTO MONTT
Puerto Montt (population 90,000), capital of the 10th Region (Los Lagos), on the Seno de Reloncaví, resembles Seattle or Vancouver in site, but its older architecture is middle European. It has excellent transport connections to Chiloé, Aisén and Patagonia.

Information
Tourist Offices Sernatur (☎ 25-3551) on the Plaza de Armas, is open daily from 9 am to 7 pm in summer.

The English-run travel agency Travellers (☎ & fax 25-8555), Avenida Angelmó 2456, near the ferry terminal, is also an information centre for overseas travellers.

Money Cambios include Turismo Los Lagos (at Varas 595, Local 3), El Libertador (at Urmeneta 529, Local 3) and La Moneda de Oro (at the bus terminal). Several banks have Redbanc ATMs.

Post & Communications The post office is at Rancagua 126. Telefónica del Sur has offices at Pedro Montt 114, Chillán 98, and at the bus terminal. The telephone code is 65.

Consulates The Argentine Consulate (☎ 25-3996), at Cauquenes 94, 2nd floor, is open weekdays from 9 am to 2 pm.

Medical Services Puerto Montt's hospital (☎ 25-3991) is on Seminario, behind the hilltop Intendencia Regional.

Things to See
About three km west of the city centre, the fishing port of **Angelmó** has an outstanding crafts market, with handmade boots, curios, copperware, ponchos, and woollen sweaters, hats and gloves. Don't leave Puerto Montt without trying a dish of curanto at one of the waterfront cafés. For a quieter perspective on the gulf, launches from the docks go to **Isla Tenglo**.

Places to Stay
Hostels *Residencial Urmeneta* (☎ 25-3262), at Urmeneta 290, has very comfortable hostel accommodation at US$10. It also has rooms with private bath for a bit more. Try the breakfast (US$2.50) of freshly baked bread, home-made jams and dairy products from the family farm. They look after luggage at no extra cost. In summer, accommodation (US$1.40) is available at Escuela No 1, on the corner of Lillo and Lota, opposite the bus terminal. Cold showers, an 11.30

Seminario

Germania

Egaña

Huasco

Copiapó

To Hospedaje Steffen

53

Serena

España

Illapel

San Felipe

Quillota

Avenida Solar Manfredini

To Pelluco

51

B O'Higgins

Rengifo

Ochagavía

Vial

Rancagua

San Martín

G Gallardo

Antonio Varas

Avenida Portales

Benavente

Pedro Montt

Umeneta

Talca

Cauquenes

Chillán

Concepción

Talcahuano

Valdivia

Varas

Andrés Bello

Ancud

Juan Mira

Lota

Pérez Rosales

Peloroca

Freire

Baquedano

Aníbal Pinto

Balmaceda

Ochagavía

Rengifo

Vial

Rodríguez

Umeneta

Lota

Costanera

To Santiago

To Hospedaje Uribe

To Angelmó & Isla Tenglo

Puerto Montt

0   100   200 m

1 2 3 4 5 7 9 10 11 12 13 14 15 16 17 18 19 20 21 22 23 24 25 26 27 28 29 30 31 32 33 34 35 36 37 38 39 40 41 42 43 44 45 46 47 48 49 50 51 52 53

PLACES TO STAY					
1	Hospedaje	49	Residencial Millantú	13	Terminal de Buses
4	Hotel Le Mirage	52	Hotel El Candil	16	Museo Juan Pablo II
5	Hospedaje	53	Hospedaje El Toqui	23	Avis Rent-a-Car
	Benavente			24	Telefónica del Sur
6	Hospedaje	**PLACES TO EAT**		25	Automóvil Club de
14	Escuela No 1	7	Tenten (Vegetarian)		Chile
17	Hospedaje La Nave	12	Centro Español	26	Argentine
19	Hospedaje Polz	15	Restaurant Embassy		Consulate
20	Residencial	18	El Jabalí	27	Colina Rent-a-Car
	Embassy	21	Restaurant El	28	Turismo Los Lagos
22	Hospedaje Raúl		Bodegón	31	Telefónica del Sur
	Arroyo	26	Pastelería Lisel	34	Banco de Chile
27	Hotel Colina	32	Dino's	37	Andina del Sud
29	Hotel Gamboa	33	Restaurant Amsel	38	Post Office
30	Hospedaje Pedro	35	Café Real	39	Plaza de Armas
	Montt	36	Café Central	40	Sernatur
33	Hotel Burg			41	ALTA
37	Hotel Vicente Pérez	**OTHER**		42	National Airlines
	Rosales	2	Budget Rent-a-Car	45	Transportes Aéreos
43	Residencial Urmeneta	3	CONAF		Don Carlos
44	Gran Hotel Don Luis	8	Hospital	47	Casa de Arte Diego
46	Hotel Montt	9	Turismo Odisea		Rivera
48	Residencial Sur	10	LanChile	50	Aerosur
		11	Ladeco	51	Railway Station

pm curfew and the need to supply your own sleeping bag may put off some travellers.

Hotels, Hospedajes & Residenciales The *hospedaje* at Aníbal Pinto 328 is warm, clean, friendly and good value. Also recommended is *Residencial La Nave* (☎ 25-3740) at Antonio Varas and Ancud, where rooms are comfortable and bathrooms spotless. They charge US$9 for a single and US$20 for a double with bath.

Another popular option is *Hospedaje Uribe* (☎ 26-2104), at Trigal 312 (from the bus terminal take colectivo No 5 'Crucero-Mirasol' to the corner of Pérez Rosales and Trigal); its amusing owner speaks English and French. In the same area one traveller highly praised the home-made bread at the *Hospedaje Familiar* (☎ 25-4493), Los Maquis 430, where the US$10 price includes breakfast.

Several readers have recommended *Hospedaje Steffen* (☎ 25-3823) at Serrano 286 (reached by colectivo No 3 from Egaña) and an unnamed *hospedaje* at Vial 754, near Balmaceda. *Residencial Costanera* (☎ 25-5242), at Angelmó 1528, offers nice views, breakfast, clean bathrooms with hot water

and an upbeat owner who speaks some English.

Places to Eat
For drinks, snacks and Streuselkuchen, try *Café Central*, Rancagua 117. There is a fine bakery, *Pastelería Lisel*, at Cauquenes 82. Another possibility is *Café Real*, at Rancagua 137. For vegetarian dishes and juices, try *Tenten* at Vial 467.

Dino's, at Varas 550, is recommended, as is the paila marina at *El Jabalí*, Andrés Bello 976. The paella at the *Centro Español*, O'Higgins 233, is definitely worth a try. Another fine option is *Restaurant Embassy*, Ancud 104.

Pelluco, east of the city centre via Avenida Juan Soler, is a good hunting ground for restaurants: try the parrillada at *El Fogón Criollo*. Don't leave without trying curanto or other seafood specialities at Angelmó's waterfront cafés, including *Marfino*, Angelmó 1856, and *Asturias*.

Getting There & Away
Air Ladeco (☎ 25-3002), Benavente 350, flies twice daily to Santiago every day except

CHILE

Saturday (one flight only); to Punta Arenas daily, except Saturday; and to Balmaceda/Coyhaique four times weekly.

LanChile (☎ 25-3141), San Martín 200, has 15 flights weekly to Santiago, eight to Punta Arenas and nine to Coyhaique.

Enquire about the new discount carrier National (☎ 25-8277) at Benavente 305. ALTA (☎ 26-8646), at Benavente 301, flies to Valdivia, Concepción, Temuco, Serena, Antofagasta, Iquique, Arica and Chaitén, and is planning future routes to Argentina.

TAN (☎ 25-0071), in the Todo Turismo travel agency, Edificio O'Higgins, 1st floor, flies to Argentine Patagonia. Transportes Aéreos Don Carlos (☎ 25-3219), Quillota 127, and Aerosur (☎ 25-2523), Urmeneta 149, fly air taxis to the Aisén region. ETM buses go to Aeropuerto El Tepual, 16 km west of town (US$1.50).

Bus – domestic The Terminal de Buses (☎ 25-3143) is on the waterfront, at Avenida Portales and Lota, and serves all Lake District destinations, Chiloé, Santiago, Coyhaique, Punta Arenas and Argentina.

Buses Fierro has daily buses (at 8 am and 3 pm) along the Camino Austral as far as Hornopirén. Transport information changes frequently, so check details in Puerto Montt.

Bus – regional Cruz del Sur and Trans Chiloé have frequent services to Ancud (US$4.50) and Castro (US$7). Varmontt, Igi Llaima and Lit go to Concepción (US$16) and Santiago (US$18). Other companies include Turibus, Bus Norte, Tas Choapa, Tur-Bus, Via Tur and Inter Sur. Lit and Tur-Bus have daily services to Valparaíso/Viña del Mar.

For Punta Arenas (US$57), via Argentina, contact Turibus, Bus Norte or Bus Sur. Turibus also goes to Coyhaique (US$33) via Argentina on Thursday and Saturday.

Bus – international Bus Norte and Río de La Plata have daily buses to Bariloche via Puyehue (US$20). Igi Llaima goes four times weekly to San Martín de los Andes (US$33) and Neuquén (US$45). Tas Choapa, Turismo Lanín and Cruz del Sur go less frequently.

Andina del Sud at Varas 437, and Varastur, Benavente and Aníbal Pinto, 3rd floor, offer one-day bus-boat combinations to Bariloche via Lago Todos los Santos (US$46). With an overnight stop at Peulla and including dinner, this costs about US$90.

Train The train station (☎ 25-2922) is at the east end of Avenida Portales. But trains now only run between Puerto Varas and Santiago. There are no passenger trains from Puerto Montt.

Boat The most appealing route south is by sea, but schedules change frequently and the information following should only be considered a general guide.

Ferry or bus-ferry combinations go to Chiloé and Chaitén, in the 10th Region; those to Chiloé leave from Pargua, on the Canal de Chacao, as do other southbound ferries on occasion. Some continue to Puerto Chacabuco (port of Coyhaique), in the 11th Region (Aisén), or go to Puerto Natales, in the 12th Region (Magallanes). Travellers prone to motion sickness may consider medication before the gut-wrenching crossing of the Golfo de Penas.

Navimag (☎ 25-3754), at the port of Angelmó, sails to Puerto Chacabuco twice weekly on the ferry *Evangelistas*, and once a week to Puerto Natales, a memorable four days and three nights.

Fares to Puerto Chacabuco start at US$50 without meals. These sailings continue to Laguna San Rafael; see the Aisén section for more details.

Fares to Puerto Natales range from US$175 to US$230. Try to book at Navimag's Santiago office (☎ 203-5030), Avenida El Bosque Norte 0440, 1st floor; otherwise, Travellers (see Information above) has a good record for arranging passages.

Transmarchilay (☎ 25-4654), Angelmó 2187, sails to Chaitén (10 hours, departures on Tuesday, Friday and Sunday) and to Puerto Chacabuco (26 hours, departures on Tuesday and Friday). Fares to Chaitén start at US$11 for deck space and US$20 for a reclining seat. Fares to Chacabuco are slightly less than double the fares to Chaitén.

Transmarchilay also runs car ferries from Pargua, 60 km south-west of Puerto Montt, to Chacao, on Isla Chiloé. Fares are about US$2 for walk-ons, US$11 per car (no matter how many passengers).

Getting Around

Car rental agencies include the Automóvil Club (☎ 25-4776) at Esmeralda 70, Budget (☎ 25-4888) at Gallardo 450, First (☎ 25-2036) at Antonio Varas 447, Hertz (☎ 25-9585) at Varas 126, and Avis (☎ 25-3307) at Urmeneta 1037.

PARQUE NACIONAL ALERCE ANDINO

Only 40 km south-east of Puerto Montt, this 40,000-hectare reserve of Andean peaks and glacial lakes shelters *Fitzroya cupressoides*, also known as alerce, a conifer similar to California's giant sequoia in appearance and longevity. A 3000-year-old specimen can reach 40 metres in height and four metres in diameter, but its attractive wood has exposed it to commercial overexploitation.

Exposed to Pacific storms, Alerce Andino receives up to 4500 mm of rain and snow annually, but hiking the back country is the best reason for a visit. Lonely Planet's *Trekking in the Patagonian Andes* describes a good trail, with several refugios, between Río Chamiza and Río Chaica sectors. CONAF has a 10-site camping ground at Río Chamiza, in the park's north, and a three-site facility at Lago Chaiquenes, at the head of the Río Chaica valley.

From Puerto Montt, Buses Fierro goes daily to the village of Correntoso, three km from the Río Chamiza entrance. Fierro also has buses to the crossroads at Lenca, on the Camino Austral, where a lateral up the valley of the Río Chaica gives better access to a number of lakes and peaks – probably a better choice for the non-trekker.

CHAITEN

Chaitén is a tiny, quiet port and military base towards the north end of the Camino Austral. The tourist office in the mercado municipal has a handful of leaflets and a list of hospedajes, but change money elsewhere – Banco del Estado gives very poor rates. The telephone code is 65.

Places to Stay & Eat

Look for handwritten signs on private houses, which may be open only from mid-December to late March. Most charge US$9 to US$13, including *Hospedaje Lo Watson* (☎ 73-1237) at Ercilla 580; *Hospedaje Mary*, at Piloto Pardo 593; *Hospedaje Sebastián*, at Todesco 188; and *Hospedaje Gabriel*, at Todesco 141. *Residencial Astoria* (☎ 73-1263), Corcovado 442, has singles for US$11.

For seafood restaurants, try the mercado municipal. Hotel El Triángulo's restaurant is also good.

Getting There & Away

Air Aerosur, on Corcovado, and Don Carlos, Todesco 42, have air taxis.

Bus Details change rapidly as the highway improves. Connections are best to the south: Transaustral (once weekly) and Artetur (twice weekly) go to Coyhaique (12 hours). Chaitur and Bus Yelcho go to Palena and Futaleufú on the Argentine border.

Boat Transmarchilay, Corcovado 266, has eight ferries monthly to Quellón, on Isla Chiloé, and another eight to Puerto Montt or Pargua. Confirm schedules at Transmarchilay; for fares, see the sections for Quellón, Chonchi and Puerto Montt.

FUTALEUFU

Futaleufú, at the confluence of the Río Espolón and the Río Futaleufú, is 155 km from Chaitén via an indirect route around Lago Yelcho. Only a few km from the border with Argentina's Chubut province, it is

CHILE

renowned for fishing and white-water rafting.

Accommodation costs about US$9 to US$13 at *Residencial Carahue* (☎ 72-1221) at O'Higgins 332; *Hospedaje El Campesino* at Prat 107; *Hospedaje Cañete* (☎ 72-1214) at Gabriela Mistral 374; and *Hotel Continental* (☎ 72-1222) at Balmaceda 595. Chaitur has buses to Chaitén (US$10), while Transporte Samuel Flores has minibuses to Argentina.

PARQUE NACIONAL QUEULAT

Along the Camino Austral between Chaitén and Coyhaique, 154,000-hectare Queulat is a zone of steep-sided fjords, rushing rivers, evergreen forests, creeping glaciers and high volcanic peaks. More accessible since completion of the highway, it's still an off-the-beaten-track destination. The Río Cisnes and the glacial fingers of Lago Rosselot, Lago Verde and Lago Risopatrón offer excellent fishing.

Queulat is popular with adventure travel agencies, but also attracts independent travellers – though heavy brush inhibits off-trail exploration. There is a good two-km trail to the **Ventisquero Colgante** (Hanging Glacier), 36 km south of Puyuhuapi, and another up the **Río Guillermo**. Consult the rangers at Pudú, Ventisquero, Puyuhuapi, El Pangue or La Junta.

Places to Stay

Camping El Pangue, on Lago Risopatrón five km north of Puyuhuapi, charges US$7 per site. *Camping Río Queulat*, 34 km south of Puyuhuapi, is free.

Puyuhuapi's *Hostería Ludwig* has singles for US$23. At the village of La Junta, at the north end of the park, near the turn-off to Lago Rosselot and Lago Verde, *Hostería Copihue* and *Hostería Valdera* both charge about US$12 a single.

Getting There & Away

Buses from Chaitén or Coyhaique will drop passengers at points along the park's western boundary. Renting a car in Coyhaique is more flexible, but expensive without several people to share the cost.

Chiloé

Isla Grande de Chiloé is a well-watered, forested island of undulating hills; it's 180 km long but just 50 km wide. Surrounded by smaller islands, it has a temperate maritime climate. Distinctive shingled houses line the streets and dot the verdant countryside. When the sun finally breaks through the rain and mist, it reveals majestic panoramas of snowcapped mainland volcanoes.

Huilliche Indians first raised potatoes and other crops in the fertile volcanic soil. Jesuits were among the earliest European settlers, but mainland refugees arrived after the Mapuche uprising of 1599. A Spanish royalist stronghold, Chiloé resisted *criollo* attacks on Ancud until 1826.

Chiloé is part of the 10th Region (Los Lagos), and Ancud and Castro are the island's only large towns. Castro and some villages have picturesque *palafitos*, rows of houses on stilts over estuaries. In rural areas, there are more than 150 distinctive wooden churches up to two centuries old.

Nearly all the 115,000 Chilotes live within sight of the sea. More than half make their living from farming, but many also depend on fishing for food and money. The eastern littoral contributes wheat, oats, vegetables and livestock to a precarious economy, but the nearly roadless western shores and interior preserve extensive forests.

Despite its natural beauty, Chiloé is one of Chile's poorest areas, and perpetual hardship has forced many Chilotes to leave. The island's rich tradition of folklore and legend has contributed to Chilean literature, but to some urban dwellers, 'Chilote' is synonymous with 'bumpkin'. In part, this reputation derives from insularity, but isolation has encouraged self-reliance, courtesy and a hospitality which has changed little since Darwin wrote, more than 150 years ago: '

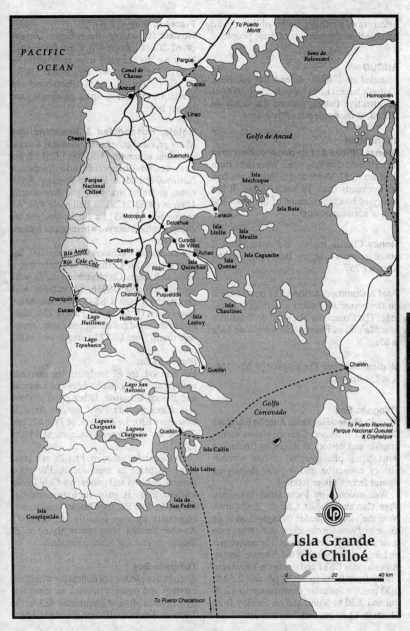

PACIFIC
OCEAN

To Puerto
Montt

Pargua

Seno de
Reloncaví

Canal de
Chacao

Chacao

Ancud

Homopirén

Linao

Chepu

Golfo de Ancud

Quemchi

Parque
Nacional
Chiloé

Isla
Mechuque

Isla Buta

Mocopulli

Tenaún

Dalcahue

Isla
Linlín

Castro

Curaco
de Vélez

Isla
Meulín

Río Anay

Nercón

Achao

Isla Caguache

Río Cole Cole

Rilán

Isla
Quinchao

Isla
Quenac

Vilupulli

Chanquín

Chonchi

Puqueldón

Cucao

Lago
Huillinco

Huillinco

Isla
Lemuy

Isla
Chaulínec

Lago
Tepuhueco

Queilén

Lago San
Antonio

Chaitén

CHILE

Golfo
Corcovado

Laguna
Chaiguata

Laguna
Chaiguaco

Quellón

To Puerto Ramírez,
Parque Nacional Queulat
& Coyhaique

Isla Cailín

Isla Laitec

Isla
Guapiquilán

Isla de
San Pedro

lp

Isla Grande
de Chiloé

0   20   40 km

To Puerto Chacabuco

never saw anything more obliging and humble than the manners of these people'.

ANCUD

Founded in 1767 to defend the coastline, Chiloé's largest town (population 17,000) is an attractive fishing port on the Bahía de Ancud, at the north end of the island.

Information

Tourist Offices At Libertad 665, the tourist office (☎ 62-2665) is open weekdays from 8.30 am to 12.30 pm and 2.30 to 8 pm, and on weekends from 10 am to 2 pm. It has plenty of brochures, maps of the town and lists of accommodation.

Money Change money in Puerto Montt if possible; otherwise, try Banco de Crédito, Ramírez 257.

Post & Communications The post office is on the corner of Pudeto and Blanco Encalada. The Compañía Nacional de Teléfonos is at Maipú and Pudeto. The telephone code is 65.

Medical Services The hospital (☎ 62-2356) is at Latorre 405.

Things to See

Ancud's **Museo Regional Aurelio Bórquez Canobra** (or Museo Chilote) shows ethnographic and historical materials (including outstanding photographs), a fine natural-history collection and a patio displaying figures from Chilote folklore.

Watercolours by local artist Francisco Vera Cárcamo depict Chilote landscapes. Note the varied *tejuelas* (shingles) on scale models of wooden churches, and a relief map indicating major settlements. The museum is on Libertad, just south of the Plaza de Armas. Admission is US$1 and it is open Tuesday to Friday from 9 am to 12.30 pm and 2.30 to 6.30 pm; on Saturday from 10 am to 12.30 pm and 2.30 to 6 pm; and on Sunday from 11 am to 12.30 pm and 2.30 to 5 pm.

Places to Stay

Hostels In summer, the *Albergue Juvenil* (☎ 62-2065), Latorre 478, offers floor space, but travellers can pitch tents in the patio for US$1. The *Casa del Apostolado* (☎ 62-3256), on the corner of Chacabuco and Errázuriz, offers floor space, mattresses and proper beds.

Hotels, Hospedajes & Residenciales

Many private houses offer seasonal accommodation for around US$10 to US$13, but year-round places include *Hospedaje Navarro*, at Pudeto 361; *Hospedaje Bellavista*, at Bellavista 449; and *Residencial Madryn* (☎ 62-2128), at Bellavista 491. All charge around US$15 a single (doubles are cheaper at the Madryn, where prices include breakfast).

Residencial Wechsler, Cochrane 480, has a reputation for Germanic austerity but is very well kept. Comfortable singles with shared bath cost US$16, while those with private bath cost US$25 with breakfast. *Hotel Lydia* (☎ 62-2879), Pudeto 256, has a highly regarded restaurant and clean, agreeable rooms from US$22 a single with bath.

Places to Eat

For seafood, try *El Sacho*, in the mercado municipal, on Dieciocho between Libertad and Blanco Encalada. Other good seafood restaurants include *Polo Sur*, at Avenida Costanera 630; *La Pincoya*, at Prat 61; and *Restaurant & Hospedaje Capri*, at Mocopulli 710.

La Cueva de la Suegra, Prat 28, is a good fast-food place to meet locals. For good dinners, desserts and coffee, try *Café Lydia*, Pudeto 256. Highly recommended is *Kurantón*, Prat 94, for Chilean cuisine, and especially curanto (mostly in summer). Another curanto place worth trying is *El Trauco* on Prat and Blanco Encalada.

Things to Buy

Ancud has a plethora of outlets for woollens, carvings and pottery. Besides the museum, try Artesanía Moai, at Baquedano 429, or the Taller de Artesanía, Blanco Encalada 730.

Getting There & Away

Cruz del Sur, Chacabuco 650, has a dozen buses a day to Puerto Montt (US$4.50), Osorno and points north. Another dozen go to Castro (US$2.50) and several more to Chonchi (US$4.50) and Quellón. Varmontt, at Errázuriz 330, has buses to Puerto Montt and southbound on Chiloé.

Trans Chiloé, Chacabuco 750, has several buses daily to Castro, Chonchi, Quellón and Puerto Montt. Turibus, on Dieciocho at Libertad, goes to Concepción and Santiago, Punta Arenas and Puerto Natales.

CASTRO

Founded in 1567, Castro is the capital of the Chiloé province, 90 km south of Ancud. In 1834, Darwin found it 'a most forlorn and deserted place', but its most conspicuous landmark – the bright, incongruously painted cathedral – dates from 1906. Waterfront palafitos, with their tejuelas, add vernacular architectural distinction.

Information

Tourist Offices There is a privately owned and aggressively commercial tourist information kiosk on the plaza that offers a map of Castro. It is open year round. The Transmarchilay office, Thompson 241, also provides information.

Money For cash, try Julio Barrientos (☎ 63-5079), Chacabuco 286, instead of banks. Bancos de Crédito and del Estado have ATMs.

Post & Communications The post office is at O'Higgins 388. CNT telephone services are at Latorre 289. The telephone code is 65.

Medical Services The hospital (☎ 63-2445) is at Freire 852.

Things to See

At the north end of the Plaza de Armas, Castro's **Iglesia San Francisco de Castro** assaults the vision with its dazzling exterior – salmon with violet trimmings. On Esmeralda, half a block south of the plaza, the **Museo Regional de Castro** houses an idiosyncratic collection of Huilliche Indian relics, farm implements and exhibits on Chilote urbanism.

The waterfront **Feria Artesanal** has a selection of woollens and basketry. Note the bundles of dried seaweed and nalca, both eaten by Chilotes, and the chunks of peat fuel.

Palafitos All around Castro, shingled houses on stilts stretch into the estuaries and lagoons. Look out for them along the Costanera Pedro Montt, at the northern end of town, at the Feria Artesanal (where some house restaurants), and at both ends of the bridge over the Río Gamboa.

Places to Stay

In summer, the *Albergue Juvenil*, in the Gimnasio Fiscal, at Freire 610, charges about US$4.

Hospedajes charge about US$10, but some are only seasonal – look for handwritten signs on the 600 to 800 blocks of San Martín and O'Higgins, near the bus terminal. One reader recommended the green house across the street from Hotel Castro on Chacabuco 205. It offers very clean rooms and breakfast for US$10.

Despite an unimpressive exterior, *Hotel La Bomba* (63-2300), at Esmeralda 270, has simple but bright and airy singles with private bath for US$13. *Hospedaje O'Higgins*, O'Higgins 831, charges US$11 with shared bath, or US$15 with private bath.

Places to Eat

Palafito restaurants at the waterfront market have the best food for the fewest pesos. *Brisas del Mar* and *Mariela* both have cheap fixed-price lunches as well as specialities. *Restaurant Octavio*, on Pedro Montt near the palafitos on the eastern sector, has three-course dinners. *Restaurant Maucari*, Lillo 93, has curanto.

Try *El Fogón Chilote*, at Luis Espinoza

309, for a varied menu stressing parrillada, or *Sacho*, at Thompson 213, for curanto. For tea or coffee, *La Brújula*, at the plaza on O'Higgins and Portales, serves exquisite raspberry kuchen.

Getting There & Away
Bus The Terminal de Buses Rurales is on San Martín near Sargento Aldea. Buses Arroyo has two to three buses a day to Huillinco and Cucao (US$3), gateway to the Parque Nacional Chiloé, while Ocean Bus has two per day.

Expreso Dalcahue, Ramírez 233, has buses every half-hour to Dalcahue on weekdays but fewer on weekends. There are also minibuses every half-hour to Dalcahue from the bus terminal. Buses Lemuy serves Chonchi and Isla Lemuy, including Puqueldón, while Buses Queilén (also a tour operator) has regular services to Queilén and intermediate destinations.

Most but not all long-distance companies have offices nearby. Cruz del Sur, on San Martín at Sotomayor, has a dozen buses daily to Ancud, Puerto Montt (US$7) and points north, as does Varmontt, Errázuriz 330. Cruz del Sur also has several to Chonchi and Quellón (US$4.50), as does Regional Sur, at the terminal. Trans Chiloé, at the terminal, has several north-south buses daily.

From Castro there is a direct service to Punta Arenas (US$55 in summer, 36 hours) and Puerto Natales via Argentina once weekly with Buses Queilén and Austral Bus and two to four times weekly with Bus Sur at the terminal.

DALCAHUE
Dalcahue, 20 km north-east of Castro, takes its name from the seagoing *dalcas* (canoes) of Chiloé. A tsunami in 1960 washed away the palafitos, but it still has a 19th-century church, gorgeous vernacular architecture and the island's best crafts market. Its tourist office, in the municipalidad, is open daily (except Monday) from 9.30 am to 1.30 pm and 3 to 7 pm.

Artisans from offshore islands travel to the Sunday **Feria Artesanal**, with a fine selection of woollens, wooden crafts and basketry, plus good cheap food. Sellers often drop their prices without even hearing a counteroffer.

Places to Stay & Eat
For about US$6 per person, try the very friendly *Pensión Montana*, at Rodríguez 009, or if it's full, the less amiable *Pensión La Feria*, next door. For excellent cheap food and waterfront atmosphere, try *Restaurant Brisas Marinas*, on palafitos above the Feria Artesanal.

Getting There & Away
Buses load and unload at the feria. Expreso Dalcahue has buses to Castro every half-hour on weekdays, with fewer on weekends. Taxi colectivos charge US$1 for the half-hour trip. There are launches to Isla Quinchao, with bus connections to Achao and its landmark 18th-century church.

CHONCHI
Jesuits founded Chonchi in 1767, but the **Iglesia San Carlos de Chonchi**, with its three-storey tower and multiple arches, dates from the 19th century. Connected by launch and ferry to Isla Lemuy, the town is 23 km south of Castro. The tourist office is at Sargento Candelaria and Centenario.

Hospedaje Mirador, Alvarez 198, is the most economical in town at US$9 per person, or US$11 with breakfast. *Hotel Huildín*, Centenario 102, has singles with breakfast and shared bath for US$10. For seafood dinners, try *El Trébol*, on the 2nd floor of the Mercado Municipal, or *La Sirena*, at Irarrázaval 52.

Getting There & Away
Cruz del Sur and Trans Chiloé have several buses daily from Castro. Taxi colectivos from the corner of Chacabuco and Esmeralda in Castro cost US$1; in Chonchi, they leave from Pedro Montt, opposite Iglesia San Carlos.

Transmarchilay is at the foot of the pier, but ferries to Chaitén and Puerto Chacabuco were not leaving from here at the time of writing.

There are launches to Ichuac, on Isla Lemuy, but the ferry leaves every two hours from 8 am to 8 pm from Puerto Huichas, five km south, with connections to Puqueldón.

PARQUE NACIONAL CHILOE

Nowhere in South America can a traveller follow Darwin's footsteps more closely than in Parque Nacional Chiloé. The great naturalist's vivid account of his passage to Cucao merits lengthy citation:

At Chonchi we struck across the island, following intricate winding paths, sometimes passing through magnificent forests, and sometimes through pretty cleared spots, abounding with corn and potato crops. This undulating woody country, partially cultivated, reminded me of the wilder parts of England, and therefore had to my eye a most fascinating aspect. At Vilinco (Huillinco), which is situated on the borders of the lake of Cucao, only a few fields were cleared...

The country on each side of the lake was one unbroken forest. In the same periagua (canoe) with us, a cow was embarked. To get so large an animal into a small boat appears at first a difficulty, but the Indians managed it in a minute. They brought the cow alongside the boat, which was heeled towards her; then placing two oars under her belly, with their ends resting on the gunwale, by the aid of these levers they fairly tumbled the poor beast, heels overhead into the bottom of the boat, and then lashed her down with ropes.

Chiloé's Pacific coast still harbours native coniferous and evergreen forests, plus an almost pristine coastline. The Chilote fox and pudu inhabit the shadowy forests of the contorted tepú tree, while the 110 bird species include the Magellanic penguin. About 30 km west of Chonchi and 54 km south-west of Castro, the park is open all year, but fair weather is likelier in summer.

Bruce Chatwin, the late gifted travel writer, left a superlative essay on Cucao in his *What Am I Doing Here?*. Huilliche communities resent CONAF's park management plan, which has restricted access to traditional subsistence while allowing some commercial exploitation. Ironically, Darwin, 150 years ago, also wrote of the 'harsh and authoritative manner' of government officials toward Chilotes.

Sector Chanquín

CONAF's visitor centre, across the suspension bridge from Cucao, is open daily from 9 am to 7.30 pm, with good displays on flora and fauna, the Huilliche people, the early mining industry and local folklore. The **Museo Artesanal** is a typical Chilote house, with farm and household implements, reed-insulated walls, and a recessed fireplace in the floor – a feature which caused many such houses to burn to the ground.

The **Sendero Interpretivo El Tepual** is a winding nature trail through gloomy forest where you might meet the Trauco, a troll-like creature from Chilote folklore. The **Sendero Dunas de Cucao** leads to a series of dunes behind a long, white-sand beach, but the sea is too cold for swimming.

Three km north on the coastal trail, at **Lago Huelde**, is a Huilliche community. At Río Cole Cole, 12 km north of Chanquín, and at Río Anay, eight km beyond, are rustic refugios, but a tent is advisable in this changeable climate. Wear water-resistant footwear and wool socks since, in Darwin's words, 'everywhere in the shade the ground soon becomes a perfect quagmire'.

Places to Stay & Eat

Camping Chanquín, 200 metres beyond the visitor centre, has secluded sites with running water, firewood and cold showers.

Within easy walking distance of the park entrance, *Hospedaje El Paraíso* and *Hospedaje Pacífico* have B&B for US$7 per person, while *Posada Cucao* is slightly dearer.

Getting There & Away

From Castro, Buses Arroyo has two or three buses a day to Cucao (US$3). Ocean Bus has two per day.

QUELLON

From Quellón, 92 km south of Castro, ferries sail to Chaitén and Puerto Chacabuco. *Anexo*

CHILE

Hotel Playa, at Pedro Montt 245, is a decent place with single rooms for US$7 with hot water. Comparably priced *Pensión Vera*, Gómez García 18, is OK despite a shabby exterior. Quellón has fine seafood restaurants near the jetty. Also recommended are *Las Quilas*, at La Paz 053, *Quilineja*, at Pedro Montt 201, and *Estrella del Mar*, at Gómez García 18.

Getting There & Away
Bus Cruz del Sur, at Aguírre Cerda 52, around the corner from the jetty, goes to Castro (US$3, 1½ hours).

Boat Transmarchilay is at the foot of the jetty. You can reach the Aisén Region from Quellón via Chaitén or go direct to Puerto Chacabuco (port of Coyhaique). Schedules change, so verify the following information. The car ferry *La Pincoya* sails to Puerto Chacabuco (18 hours) on Saturday and alternate Mondays at 6 pm.

Camarotes (sleepers) are expensive, *clase económica* (US$23) is an upright bench seat, while *pasaje general* (US$20) is an uncomfortable deck or corridor space.

La Pincoya and *El Colono* alternate sailings to Chaitén (six hours) on Monday and Thursday afternoons. The cheapest pasaje general is about US$20. The *butaca pullman* (US$30) is more spacious.

Aisén

The islands, fjords and glaciers of Aisén resemble Alaska's Inside Passage and New Zealand's South Island. Air and sea access, and overland routes from Argentina, are much better than the Camino Austral which supposedly links the area to Puerto Montt.

For millennia, Chonos and Alacalufes Indians fished and hunted the intricate canals and islands. Several expeditions visited the area in the late 18th and early 19th centuries, and Chilean naval officer Enrique Simpson's survey in the 1870s mapped areas as far south as the Península de Taitao.

Chile later promoted colonisation with grazing and timber leases, allowing a single company to control nearly a million hectares near Coyhaique. The bleached trunks of downed trees still litter hillsides where, encouraged by a land law which rewarded clearance, the company and colonists burned nearly three million hectares of lenga forest in the 1940s.

See the Southern Patagonia map later in this chapter for all destinations south of Coyhaique.

COYHAIQUE
Founded in 1929, Coyhaique (sometimes spelt Coihaique) has outgrown its pioneer origins to become a modest but tidy regional capital with a population of 40,000. Most visitors arrive by air from Puerto Montt or by ferry at Puerto Chacabuco, 80 km west.

Information
Tourist Office Sernatur (☎ 23-1752), Cochrane 320, is open on weekdays from 9 am to 1 pm and 3 to 7 pm.

Money You change cash or travellers' cheques at Cambio El Libertador, at Arturo Prat 340, Oficina 208, or at Turismo Prado, 21 de Mayo 417. Banco de Crédito has an ATM.

Post & Communications The post office is at Cochrane 202. The CTC telephone office is at Moraleda 495. The telephone code is 67.

Medical Services The hospital (☎ 23-1286) is on Calle Hospital, at the west end of Carrera.

National Parks For transport to parks and reserves which have no bus transport, enquire at CONAF (☎ 23-1065), Avenida Ogana 1060.

Things to See & Do
On most lakes and rivers, the fishing season

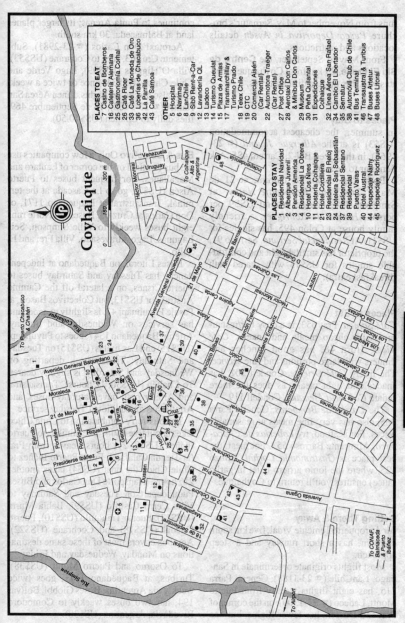

Coyhaique

0   150   300 m
0   1000 ft

PLACES TO EAT
7   Casino de Bomberos
16   Cafetería Alemana
25   Gastronomía Coñal
26   Café Ricer
33   Café La Moneda de Oro
36   Loberías de Chacabuco
42   La Parrilla
43   Café Samoa

OTHER
5   Hospital
6   Navimag
8   LanChile
9   Sibb Rent-a-Car
12   Lavandería QL
13   Ladeco
14   Turismo Queulat
15   Plaza de Armas
17   Transmarchillay &
     Turismo Prado
18   Telex Chile
19   CTC
20   Comercial Aisén
     (Car Rental)
22   Automotora Traeger
     (Car Rental)
27   Post Office
28   Aerotaxi Don Carlos
     & Minibus Don Carlos
29   Museum
30   Peña Quilantal
31   Expediciones
     Coihaique
32   Línea Aérea San Rafael
34   Cambio El Libertador
35   Sematur
38   Automóvil Club de Chile
41   Bus Terminal
46   Transaustral & Turibus
47   Buses Arteitur
48   Buses Litoral

PLACES TO STAY
1   Residencial Navidad
2   Albergue Juvenil
3   Pensión America
4   Residencial La Obrera
10   Hotel Los Ñires
11   Hostería Coihaique
21   Hotel Cordillera
23   Residencial El Reloj
24   Hotelera San Sebastián
37   Residencial Serrano
39   Residencial
40   Hotel Austral
44   Hospedaje Nathy
45   Hospedaje Rodríguez

runs from November to May. Sernatur's brochure *Pesca Deportiva in Aysén* details locations and restrictions.

From May to September, the **Centro de Ski El Fraile**, 29 km from Coyhaique, operates two lifts on five different runs.

Places to Stay

In summer, the cheapest accommodation (US$3) is at the *Albergue Juvenil* (☎ 23-1961), in the Liceo BN-2, Carrera 485. Ask Sernatur to be sure.

Both *Residencial La Obrera*, at 21 de Mayo 264, and *Hospedaje Nathy*, at Simpson 417, charge around US$9 per person. *Hospedaje Rodríguez*, a friendly family house at Colón 495, has singles for US$11. At *Residencial Serrano*, Serrano 91, the proprietor has small, bright and comfortable singles for US$13 with shared bath (breakfast extra).

Places to Eat

Café Samoa, Prat 653, is a cosy bar/restaurant with cheap meals and snacks. *Café Ricer*, Horn 48, has good lunches and dinners with large portions and fine service. The lively *Café Oriente*, Condell 201, has snacks and light meals, as does the more sedate *Cafetería Alemana*, Condell 119.

The *Casino de Bomberos*, General Parra 365, also has very fine meals at reasonable prices. For seafood, try *Loberías de Chacabuco*, Almirante Barroso 553. For meat, the best place is *Gastronomía Corhal*, Bilbao 125, where the lomo arriero (filet in garlic sauce) ensures you'll return to Coyhaique.

Getting There & Away

Air Aeropuerto Teniente Vidal, five km south of town, has a short runway and a steep approach.

Most flights originate or terminate in Santiago. LanChile (☎ 23-1188), General Parra 215, has eight flights weekly from Puerto Montt. Ladeco (☎ 23-1300), on the corner of Prat and Dussen, has fewer flights, but one continues to Punta Arenas; its larger planes land at Balmaceda, 30 km south.

Aerotaxi Don Carlos (☎ 23-2981), Subteniente Cruz 63, flies to Cochrane (US$53), Villa O'Higgins (US$99), Lago Verde and Chile Chico (US$34) once or twice a week. They also do charter flights. Línea Aérea San Rafael (☎ 23-3408), 18 de Septiembre 469, flies daily to Chaitén (US$40.50).

Bus & Colectivo Only a few companies use the bus terminal on the corner of Lautaro and Magallanes. For frequent buses to Puerto Aisén (US$2), go to La Cascada at the terminal, Transaustral at Baquedano 1171, or Don Carlos at Cruz 63. Buses del Norte runs eight buses weekly to Valle Simpson, Seis Lagunas, Lago Atravesado, Villa Frei and El Salto.

Buses Litoral, on Baquedano at Independencia, has Tuesday and Saturday buses to Puerto Cisnes, on a lateral off the Camino Austral, for US$13, but Colectivos Basoli, at Pasaje Puyuhuapi 47, is slightly cheaper and has services on Wednesday and Sunday. Artetur, Baquedano 1347, goes to Puyuhuapi (US$15) and Las Juntas (US$15) on Tuesday and Saturday; Transaustral, departing on Wednesday and Saturday, is slightly dearer. To Chaitén (US$30, 12 hours), Transaustral and Artetur both have Saturday buses, and Artetur has an additional Tuesday service.

The bus-ferry combination to Chile Chico takes about five hours. The minibus to Puerto Ibáñez (US$7, 2½ hours) leaves from Prat (at Tienda Calafate). From Puerto Ibáñez to Chile Chico the boat (US$4) takes another 2½ hours. Transporte Don Carlos and Buses Pudú depart on Tuesday and Saturday to Villa Cerro Castillo (US$9), Bahía Murta (US$12), Puerto Tranquilo (US$10), Puerto Guadal (US$18) and Cochrane (US$22). Aerobus covers most of these same destinations on Monday, Wednesday and Friday.

To Osorno and Puerto Montt (US$38), Turibus, at Baquedano 1171, goes twice weekly via Argentina. Buses Giobbi, Bolívar 194, has two buses weekly to Comodoro Rivadavia, Argentina (US$38).

Boat Ferries to Chiloé, Chaitén and Puerto Montt leave from Puerto Chacabuco, which is two hours from Coyhaique by bus.

Transmarchilay (☎ 22-1971), upstairs at 21 de Mayo 417, sails to Chaitén and Puerto Montt on Monday at noon, Wednesday at 8 pm, and Saturday at 4 pm; fares range from US$17 to US$43. To Quellón, it sails on Tuesday at 4 pm and Sunday at 6 pm; fares range from US$13 to US$35. Schedules are subject to change.

Navimag (☎ 22-3306), Presidente Ibáñez 347, Oficina 1, sails from Chacabuco to Puerto Montt on Tuesday, Thursday and Sunday at 4 pm (US$25).

Getting Around
To/From the Airport Shared cabs from the airport to the city centre cost only about US$7; informal colectivos to the airport (US$4) leave from the LanChile office.

Car Shoestring travellers might consider pooling resources to rent a car to explore the region. Shop around, since prices vary, but try Comercial Aisén, at Moraleda 420, or Sibb Rent-a-Car, at General Parra 95. The Automóvil Club, Bilbao 583, meets clients at the airport and picks up the car there as well. The going rate is about US$68 per day.

AROUND COYHAIQUE
Reserva Nacional Coyhaique
Despite its proximity to Coyhaique, this 2150-hectare reserve is wild country, with exhilarating panoramas of the town and the enormous basalt columns of Cerro Macay. A popular retreat for town residents, it's spacious and forested enough never to feel crowded.

On the slopes of Cerro Cinchao, about 1000 metres above sea level, the reserve is only five km south of town via the paved highway and a steep dirt lateral. With a tent, you can stay at CONAF's rustic camping grounds (US$3) at Laguna Verde and El Brujo. Without a car, it's a casual hike of about 1½ hours to the park entrance (admis-

sion US$1), plus another hour to Laguna Verde.

Reserva Nacional Río Simpson
Río Simpson is an accessible, scenic combination of river, canyon and valley, 37 km west of Coyhaique. CONAF's visitor centre consists of a small natural history museum and botanical garden. There's a beach for swimming, and many people fish in the river. It's a short walk to the **Cascada La Virgen**, a shimmering waterfall.

Camping Río Correntoso, 24 km west of Coyhaique, has spacious riverside sites for US$15. Buses from Coyhaique will drop you anywhere on the route.

PUERTO CHACABUCO
Connected to Coyhaique by an excellent paved highway, Chacabuco is the usual port of entry to the Aisén region. *Hotel Moraleda* (☎ 35-1155), on O'Higgins just outside the harbour compound, has singles/doubles for US$13/26 and is convenient for late arrivals.

Navimag and Transmarchilay sail to Quellón or Chonchi, on Isla Chiloé, and to Puerto Montt; for details, see the Coyhaique section. Buses to Coyhaique meet arriving ferries.

PARQUE NACIONAL LAGUNA SAN RAFAEL
Glaciers brush the sea at the edge of the massive Campo de Hielo Norte (the northern Patagonian ice sheet). Dense with floating icebergs from its namesake glacier, Laguna San Rafael is a memorable sight even beneath the sombre clouds that usually hang over the surrounding peaks.

Laguna San Rafael is 225 km south-west of Puerto Chacabuco via a series of channels between the Chonos archipelago and the Patagonian mainland. At higher elevations, snow nourishes the 19 major glaciers which form a 300,000-hectare icefield, but the San Rafael glacier is receding because of the relatively mild maritime climate.

CHILE

Things to See & Do

Sightseeing is the major attraction, but fishing, climbing and hiking are possible for well-equipped travellers in top physical condition. Darwin cautioned that:

The coast is so very rugged that to attempt to walk in that direction requires continued scrambling up and down over the sharp rocks of mica-slate; and as for the woods, our faces, hands and shin-bones all bore witness to the maltreatment we received, in attempting to penetrate their forbidding recesses.

Those who overcome these obstacles may see flightless steamer ducks, albatrosses and Magellanic penguins. Otters, sea lions and elephant seals also frequent the icy waters, while pudus, pumas and foxes inhabit the surrounding forests.

Places to Stay

Laguna San Rafael has no permanent accommodation. Most visitors stay on board the ship, but CONAF may provide basic lodging in the hotel which serves as park headquarters (US$6). There is an entrance fee of about US$5 per visitor.

Getting There & Away

Air Charter flights from Coyhaique land at the gravel airstrip. Contact Línea Aérea Hein (☎ 23-2772), at Baquedano 500, or Línea Aérea San Rafael (☎ 23-3408), at 18 de Septiembre 469.

Boat Compañía Naviera's (☎ 35-1106 in Chacabuco) *Calbuco* sails on Friday at 6 pm from Chacabuco and returns on Sunday at 7 am; reclining seats are US$147. Navimag's (☎ 23-3306, Presidente Ibáñez 347 in Coyhaique) *Evangelistas* sails three times monthly from Puerto Montt, taking five days and four nights (from US$149 return).

Transmarchilay (☎ 23-1971, 21 de Mayo 417 in Coyhaique), runs the ferry *El Colono*, with fares from US$212 to US$265.

PUERTO INGENIERO IBÁÑEZ

Puerto Ingeniero Ibáñez, on Lago General Carrera, has recovered quickly from the 1991 eruption of Volcán Hudson, which nearly buried it in ash. Local *huasos*, counterparts to the Argentine *gauchos*, drive cattle and sheep along the roads, and orchard crops do well in the lakeside microclimate; rows of poplars separate the fields. Ferries cross the lake to Chile Chico.

Residencial Ibáñez, Dickson 31, has unheated singles with plenty of extra blankets for about US$7 with breakfast; other meals are available.

Getting There & Away

For transport from Coyhaique, see the Coyhaique section.

Transporte Mar del Sur's car and passenger (US$1.50) ferry sails on Tuesday, Wednesday and Saturday mornings to Chile Chico. On alternate Tuesdays it calls at all the small ports along Lago Carrera.

RESERVA NACIONAL CERRO CASTILLO

This reserve, south of Coyhaique, consists of 180,000 hectares of southern beech forests. It is overshadowed by the 2700-metre basalt spires of Cerro Castillo and flanked by three major glaciers on its southern slopes. CONAF operates two modest camping grounds for US$3 per site, but camping is free and spectacular in the back country, after CONAF's US$1 admission fee.

There is an excellent four-day trek from Km 75, at the north end of the reserve, to Villa Cerro Castillo, at the south end, detailed in Lonely Planet's *Trekking in the Patagonian Andes*. At Villa Cerro Castillo, *Pension El Viajero* has rooms (US$6 a single), a bar and a cheap restaurant.

CHILE CHICO

On the south shore of Lago General Carrera, tiny Chile Chico derived its early prosperity from copper, but fruit cultivation in its unique microclimate has kept it alive – though not prosperous, since it's remote from markets. In summer only, there's a

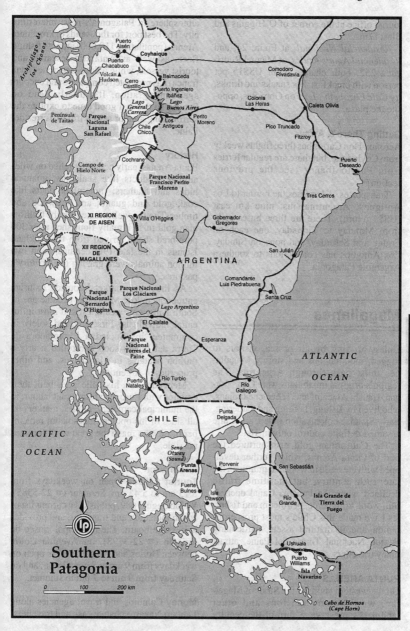

Southern
Patagonia

0   100   200 km

tourist office at the corner of O'Higgins and Blest Gana.

Residencial Nacional, at Freire 24, and *Residencial Aguas Azules*, at Manuel Rodríguez 252, both charge about US$15 per person with breakfast. For snacks and drinks, try *Café Elizabeth y Loly* on Gonzales, opposite the plaza.

Getting There & Away

Aerotaxi Don Carlos has three flights weekly from Coyhaique, but there are regular ferries from Puerto Ibáñez (see the previous section).

Transportes VH crosses the border to Los Antiguos, Argentina, just nine km east (US$4 return). There are three buses daily from Monday to Thursday, one each on Friday and Saturday, and none on Sunday. Los Antiguos has connections to southern Argentine Patagonia.

Magallanes

Unless arriving by air or sea, visitors to rugged, mountainous and stormy Magallanes must pass through Argentina. The region's original inhabitants were Ona, Yahgan, Haush, Alacaluf and Tehuelche Indians, who lived by fishing, hunting and gathering. Early Spanish colonisation failed, and Chile assumed definite control only in 1843.

The Californian gold rush nurtured the port of Punta Arenas, which further developed with the trade in wool and mutton in the late 19th century, but maritime traffic declined when the Panama Canal opened. Still wool, commerce, petroleum and fisheries have made this Chile's most prosperous region and its natural assets, particularly Parque Nacional Torres del Paine, attract many travellers.

PUNTA ARENAS

On the western shore of the Strait of Magellan, wool-boom mansions and other landmarks preserve a turn-of-the-century atmosphere in Patagonia's most interesting city. The best port for thousands of km, Punta Arenas (population 110,000) attracts fishing fleets as well as Antarctic research and tourist vessels, while a duty-free zone (zona franca) has promoted commerce and encouraged immigration. It's utterly dead on Sunday so this is a good time to explore the surrounding area or start a trip to Torres del Paine.

History

Punta Arenas' early economy relied on wild-animal products like sealskins, guanaco hides and feathers; mineral products like coal, gold and guano; and firewood and timber. Though well situated for the Californian gold rush, it really flourished after 300 pure-bred sheep arrived from the Falkland Islands in the late 19th century; soon two million animals were grazing the territory's pastures.

As the wool market boomed, Asturian entrepreneur José Menéndez became one of South America's wealthiest and most influential individuals. First engaged solely in commerce, his Sociedad Explotadora de Tierra del Fuego soon controlled nearly a million hectares in Magallanes, and other properties in Argentina.

Menéndez and his colleagues built their empires with European immigrant labour; in the municipal cemetery, modest markers on all sides of his opulent mausoleum remember those who made the great wool fortunes possible.

Information

Tourist Offices Open on weekdays from 8.15 am to 5.45 pm, Sernatur (☎ 22-5385), Waldo Seguel 689, publishes a current list of accommodation and transport, and provides a message board. The municipal kiosco de turismo (☎ 22-3798), on Avenida Colón between Bories and Magallanes, is open on weekdays from 9 am to 7 pm all year, and on Saturday from 9 am to 7 pm in summer.

Money Cambios and travel agencies along Lautaro Navarro change cash and travellers' cheques on weekdays and Saturday mornings. There are several ATMs around Plaza Muñoz Gamero.

Post & Communications The post office is at Bories 911. CTC has a long-distance office at Nogueira 1116, Chilesat is at Errázuriz 856, and Entel is at Lautaro Navarro 931. The telephone code is 61.

Consulate Argentina's consulate (☎ 26-1912), 21 de Mayo 1878, is open on weekdays from 10 am to 2 pm.

Walking Tour
Landscaped with exotic conifers, **Plaza Muñoz Gamero** is the setting for landmarks like **Club de la Unión** (the former Sara Braun mansion), the **Catedral** and the headquarters of the powerful **Sociedad Menéndez Behety** (now a branch of Citibank).

Half a block north, at Magallanes 949, the spectacular **Casa Braun-Menéndez** (the family's mansion) is now a cultural centre and regional history museum. Three blocks west of the plaza, the outlandish **stone castle** at Avenida España 959 belonged to Charly Milward, whose eccentric exploits inspired his distant relation Bruce Chatwin to write *In Patagonia*.

Four blocks south of the plaza, at the foot of Avenida Independencia, is the entrance to the port, a harbour for seafarers from Spain, Poland, Japan, France, the USA and many other countries, as well as local fishing boats, the Chilean navy and countless seabirds. On the corner of Colón and O'Higgins, four blocks north-west of the Plaza, is a very fine **mural** of Gabriela Mistral.

Six blocks north of the Plaza, on the corner of Bories and Sarmiento, is the **Museo Salesiano**. Another four blocks north, the **Cementerio Municipal** (municipal cemetery) is an open-air historical museum in its own right.

Places to Stay
Open November through March, the *Albergue Backpacker's Paradise* (☎ 22-2554), Ignacio Carrera Pinto 1022, charges

US$6.50 per person. At Bellavista 697, six blocks south of Plaza Muñoz Gamero, the *Colegio Pierre Fauré* (☎ 22-6256) operates as a hostel in January and February. Singles cost US$7 with breakfast, or US$6 without; campers can pitch a tent for US$4 per person.

Several LP readers have exuberantly praised the homey *Hospedaje Guisande* (☎ 24-3295), JM Carrera 1270, which charges US$8 with breakfast. Recommended *Hostal Calafate* (☎ 24-8415), Lautaro Navarro 850, charges US$13 per person including a substantial breakfast, while the aging but spacious *Hotel Montecarlo* (☎ 22-3438), Avenida Colón 605, charges US$16/26 for singles/doubles with shared bath, or US$26/39 with private bath. Popular *Hostal Koiuska* (☎ 22-8520), Waldo Seguel 480, charges US$20 per person.

Places to Eat
Fusión, Mejicana 654, offers a very good fixed-price lunch for US$4. *Quijote*, Lautaro Navarro 1087, also has reasonable lunches. A good choice for breakfast and onces is *Café Garogha*, at Bories 817.

Upstairs at Mejicana 617 (the ground-level entrance is inconspicuous), the moderately priced *El Mercado* prepares spicy ostiones al pil pil and a delicate but filling chupe de locos. The *Centro Español*, above the Teatro Cervantes on Plaza Muñoz Gamero, serves delicious congrio and ostiones. The *Golden Dragon*, Colón 529, serves very good Chinese food.

Highly regarded *Sotitos*, O'Higgins 1138, serves outstanding (though expensive) centolla, but also more reasonably priced items. Lamb is a speciality at *El Mesón del Calvo*, Jorge Montt 687.

Things to Buy
The zona franca (duty-free zone), open daily except Sunday, is good for cameras, film and other luxuries. Taxi colectivos to the shopping centre are numerous.

Getting There & Away
Air LanChile (☎ 24-1232), Lautaro Navarro

CHILE

CHILE

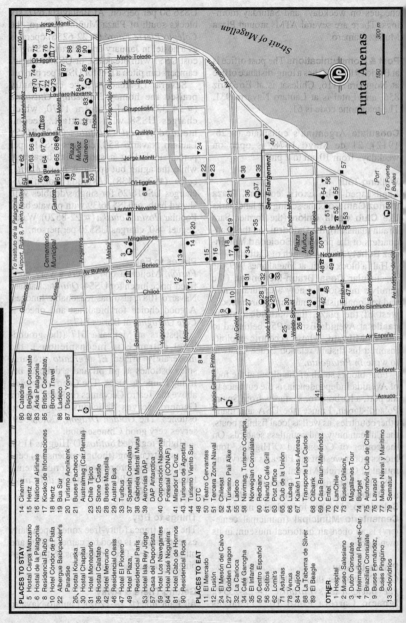

Punta Arenas

Strait of Magellan

PLACES TO STAY
5 Hostal Carpa Manzano
6 Hostal de la Patagonia
8 Residencial Rubio
10 Hotel Cóndor de Plata
22 Albergue Backpacker's Paradise
26 Hostal Koluska
30 Hostal Chapital
31 Hotel Montecarlo
36 Hostal Calafate
42 Hotel Mercurio
46 Residencial Oasis
47 Hotel El Pionero
49 Hotel Plaza,
    Residencial Paris
53 Hotel Isla Rey Jorge
57 Casa del Deportista
59 Hotel Los Navegantes
64 Hotel José Nogueira
81 Hotel Cabo de Hornos
90 Residencial Roca

PLACES TO EAT
11 El Mercado
12 Fusión
24 El Mesón del Calvo
27 Golden Dragon
32 La Carioca
34 Café Garogha
35 El Infante
50 Centro Español
62 Sottos
71 Asturias
78 Venus
84 Quijote
88 La Taberna de Silver
89 El Beagle

OTHER
1 Hospital
2 Museo Salesiano
3 Dutch Consulate
7 Internacional Rent-a-Car
9 Buses Fernández,
    Buses Pingüino
13 Solovidrios
14 Cinema
15 Hertz
16 National Airlines
17 Kiosko de Informaciones
18 Hertz
19 Bus Sur
20 Turismo Aonikenk
21 Buses Pacheco,
    Australmag (Car Rental)
23 Chile Típico
25 Stone Castle
28 Buses Mansilla
29 Austral Bus
33 Turibus
37 Spanish Consulate
38 Gabriela Mistral Mural
39 Aerovías DAP,
    DAP Antarctica
40 Corporación Nacional
    Forestal (CONAF)
41 Mirador La Cruz
43 Turismo de Agostini
44 Turismo Viento Sur
48 CTC
50 Teatro Cervantes
51 Tercera Zona Naval
54 Turismo Pali Aike
55 Ladeco
58 Navimag, Turismo Comapa,
    Norwegian Consulate
60 Redbanc
61 Nandú Café Grill
63 Post Office
65 Club de la Unión
66 Lubag
67 Kaikén Líneas Aéreas,
    Transporte Los Carlos
68 Casa Braun-Menéndez
69 Casa Braun-Menéndez
70 Entel
72 LanChile
73 Buses Ghisoni,
    Magallanes Tour
74 Budget
75 Automóvil Club de Chile
76 Lavasol
77 Museo Naval y Marítimo
79 Sematur
80 Catedral
82 Belgian Consulate
83 Arka Patagonia
85 British Consulate,
    Broom Travel
86 Ladeco
87 Disco Yordi

999, flies daily to Puerto Montt and Santiago, while Ladeco (☎ 22-6100), Lautaro Navarro 1155, flies daily to Puerto Montt and Santiago, and on Saturday and Sunday to Balmaceda/Coyhaique and Santiago. National Airlines (☎ 22-1636), at Bories and Ignacio Carrera Pinto, flies daily, except Thursday, to Santiago via either Puerto Montt or Concepción.

Aerovías DAP (☎ 22-3340, fax 22-1693), O'Higgins 891, flies to Porvenir (US$18) and back twice daily except Sunday (one flight only). On Monday, Wednesday and Friday it flies to and from Puerto Williams, on Isla Navarino (US$69 one way). It also has flights on Tuesday, Thursday and Sunday to Ushuaia, Argentina (US$60) and to Río Gallegos, Argentina (US$49). Its weekly flights to the Falkland Islands (US$237 one way), which originate in Santiago, leave on Thursday.

Kaikén Líneas Aéreas (☎ 24-1321), Magallanes 974, flies nine times weekly to Ushuaia, Argentina (US$80), with discounts for return tickets.

Bus Buses Fernández (☎ 24-2313), Armando Sanhueza 745, has five buses daily to Puerto Natales (US$7). Bus Sur (☎ 24-4464), at Magallanes and Colón, also goes frequently to Natales.

Austral Bus (☎ 24-1708), José Menéndez 565, goes nightly at 7.30 pm to Puerto Natales, and on Tuesday to Puerto Montt (US$97). Buses Ghisoni (☎ 22-3205), Lautaro Navarro 971, departs sporadically to Puerto Montt (US$75). Turibus (☎ 24-1463), José Menéndez 647, goes Tuesday, Thursday and Saturday to Puerto Montt (US$80) and Santiago (US$100), and on Wednesday and Saturday to Concepción (US$97).

To Río Gallegos, Argentina (US$20, five hours), the most frequent service is Buses Pingüino (☎ 24-1684), Armando Sanhueza 745. Ghisoni, Buses Mansilla (☎ 22-1516), at José Menéndez 556, and Magallanes Tour (☎ 22-2078), at Lautaro Navarro 975, also have several departures.

Buses Pacheco (☎ 24-2174), Avenida Colón 900, departs on Tuesday, Thursday and Saturday at 7 am to Río Grande (US$27) in Argentine Tierra del Fuego, with connections to Ushuaia. On Tuesday and Saturday at 7 am, Transporte Los Carlos (☎ 24-1321), Magallanes 974, goes to Río Grande and Ushuaia (US$49).

Boat From the Tres Puentes ferry terminal (taxi colectivos going here leave from Casa Braun-Menéndez), Transbordador Austral Broom (☎ 21-8100) sails to Porvenir, Tierra del Fuego (US$6, 2½ hours). Boats depart daily, except Monday and Thursday, at 9 am and return at 2 pm, except on Sunday and holidays (5 pm). Arrange vehicle reservations at Avenida Bulnes 05075.

Navimag (☎ 24-4448), which offers a car and passenger-ferry service from Puerto Natales to Puerto Montt, is at Avenida Independencia 830. For details, see the Puerto Natales entry.

Getting Around

To/From the Airport Aerovías DAP runs its own bus to the airport, 20 km north of town; LanChile and Ladeco use local companies (US$1.25).

Bus & Colectivo Taxi colectivos are quicker, more comfortable and only slightly dearer than buses at about US$0.30, or a bit more late at night and on Sunday.

Car Hertz (☎ 24-8742) is at Avenida Colón 798 and Ignacio Carrera Pinto 700, while Budget (☎ 24-1696) and the Automóvil Club de Chile (☎ 24-3675) are at O'Higgins 964 and O'Higgins 931, respectively.

AROUND PUNTA ARENAS
North-west of Punta Arenas is a substantial colony of Magellanic penguins (also gulls, cormorants and sea lions) at **Seno Otway** (Otway Sound). *Spheniscus magellanicus*, also known as the jackass penguin for its characteristic braying, comes ashore in the spring to nest in burrows or under shrubs. Naturally curious, jackasses will back into

their burrows or toboggan into the water if approached too quickly. Their bills can inflict serious cuts – *never* stick your hand or face into a burrow, but sit nearby and wait for them to emerge.

About 55 km south of Punta Arenas, is the military outpost of **Fuerte Bulnes**; this was abandoned soon after its founding in 1843, because of its poor soil and pasture, lack of potable water and exposed site. Across the Strait are **Isla Dawson** (a 19th-century Salesian mission to the Yahgans and then a notorious prison camp after the 1973 coup) and the Cordillera Darwin.

Several agencies organise tours of the Otway penguin colony, Fuerte Bulnes and Torres del Paine. These include Turismo Pali Aike (☎ 22-3301) at Lautaro Navarro 1129, Arka Patagonia (☎ 22-6370) at Roca 886, Local 7, Turismo Aonikenk (☎ 22-8332) at Magallanes 619, and Turismo Viento Sur (☎ 22-5167) at Fagnano 565. Most companies can now do both Otway and Fuerte Bulnes in the same day for about US$12 per person.

Porvenir

Populated by Yugoslav immigrants in the 1880s, Chilean Tierra del Fuego's largest settlement (population 5143) is a cluster of corroding, metal-clad Victorian buildings belying its optimistic name (the future). For most travellers, it's a brief stopover en route to Ushuaia, Argentina, but it makes a good Sunday ferry excursion from Punta Arenas.

The cheapest rooms are at *Hotel España* (☎ 58-0160), Yugoslavia 698, which has singles for US$10 with shared bath, or US$13 with private bath. The mid-range *Hotel Rosas* has a fine seafood restaurant. *Club Croata* – formerly the *Club Yugoslavo* – also serves meals.

Transporte Senkovic, Bories 295, goes to Río Grande, Argentina (US$11) on Tuesday and Saturday. See the Punta Arenas entry for air and ferry services.

PUERTO NATALES

On the shores of Seno Ultima Esperanza (Last Hope Sound), 250 km north-west of Punta Arenas, Puerto Natales (population 18,000) is the southern terminus of the spectacular ferry trip through the Chilean fjords. Once dependent on wool, mutton and fishing, it's now a burgeoning destination for visitors to Parque Nacional Torres del Paine, the Balmaceda Glacier and the famous Cueva del Milodón.

Information

Sernatur (☎ 41-2125) occupies a chalet on the Costanera Pedro Montt at the junction with the Philippi diagonal. It's open from 8.30 am to 1 pm and 2.30 to 6.30 pm on weekdays all year, and from 9 am to 1 pm on weekends from December to March only.

Stop Cambios, Baquedano 380, changes cash and travellers' cheques. There are no ATMs, but Banco O'Higgins, Bulnes 637, issues cash advances on MasterCard.

The post office is at Eberhard 423. CTC, Blanco Encalada 298, offers long-distance services from 8 am to 10 pm daily. Puerto Natales' telephone code is 061, the same as Punta Arenas.

Places to Stay

Puerto Natales is popular, but competition keeps prices reasonable. Rates start at around US$5 per person at the popular *Hospedaje Elsa* (☎ 41-1807), O'Higgins 657, including breakfast and hot showers. Convenient to the ferry, *Hospedaje Tierra del Fuego*, Avenida Bulnes 29, charges US$8 with shared bath. Comparably priced *Hospedaje Tequendama*, Ladrilleros 141, is very obliging but rooms are basic and some are very dark.

For US$8, Swiss-run *Hospedaje Cecilia* (☎ 41-1797), Tomás Rogers 64, includes delicious breakfasts with fresh bread and muesli, though some rooms are small. Comparably priced *Hospedaje Teresa*, Esmeralda 463, has enthusiastic adherents. Also recommended, *Residencial Almirante Nieto* (☎ 41-2249), Bories 206, charges US$9 per person.

A traditional mid-range favourite is Eduardo Scott's *Hotel Austral* (☎ 41-1593),

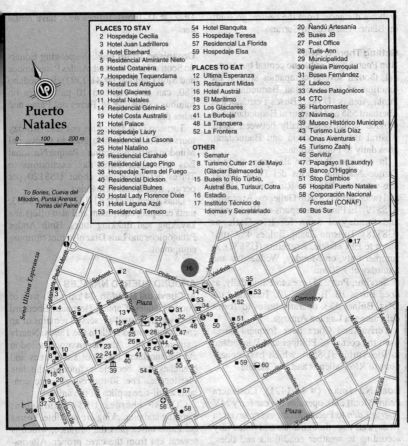

Puerto Natales

0   100   200 m

To Bories, Cueva del
Milodón, Punta Arenas,
Torres del Paine

PLACES TO STAY
2 Hospedaje Cecilia
3 Hotel Juan Ladrilleros
4 Hotel Eberhard
5 Residencial Almirante Nieto
6 Hostal Costanera
7 Hospedaje Tequendama
9 Hostal Los Antiguos
10 Hotel Glaciares
11 Hostal Natales
14 Residencial Géminis
19 Hotel Costa Australis
21 Hotel Palace
22 Hospedaje Laury
24 Residencial La Casona
25 Residencial Natalino
26 Residencial Carahué
35 Residencial Lago Pingo
38 Hospedaje Tierra del Fuego
40 Residencial Dickson
42 Residencial Bulnes
50 Hostal Lady Florence Dixie
51 Hotel Laguna Azul
53 Residencial Temuco
54 Hotel Blanquita
55 Hospedaje Teresa
57 Residencial La Florida
59 Hospedaje Elsa

PLACES TO EAT
12 Ultima Esperanza
13 Restaurant Midas
16 Hotel Austral
18 El Marítimo
23 Los Glaciares
41 La Burbuja
48 La Tranquera
52 La Frontera

OTHER
1 Sernatur
8 Turismo Cutter 21 de Mayo (Glaciar Balmaceda)
15 Buses to Río Turbio, Austral Bus, Turisur, Cotra
16 Estadio
17 Instituto Técnico de Idiomas y Secretariado
20 Ñandú Artesanía
26 Buses JB
27 Post Office
28 Turis-Ann
29 Municipalidad
30 Iglesia Parroquial
31 Buses Fernández
32 Ladeco
33 Andes Patagónicos
34 CTC
36 Harbormaster
37 Navimag
39 Museo Histórico Municipal
43 Turismo Luis Díaz
44 Onas Aventuras
45 Turismo Zaahj
46 Servitur
47 Papagayo II (Laundry)
49 Banco O'Higgins
51 Stop Cambios
56 Hospital Puerto Natales
58 Corporación Nacional Forestal (CONAF)
60 Bus Sur

CHILE

Valdivia 955; singles/doubles with shared bath cost US$13/21, while those with private bath are US$19/27.

Places to Eat
Highly recommended, *La Frontera*, on Bulnes between Baquedano and Ramírez, has superb home-cooked meals for only US$4, but the service could be better. *El Marítimo*, a moderately priced seafood restaurant at Costanera Pedro Montt 214, is deservedly doing excellent business.

Popular *La Tranquera*, Bulnes 579, has good food, friendly service, reasonable

prices and one of the continent's most hilarious English-language menus (try 'poor eel' or 'chicken in a gas cooker'). Other good options include *La Burbuja* at Bulnes 371, *Ultima Esperanza* at Eberhard 354, and *Los Glaciares* on Eberhard between Barros Arana and Magallanes.

Hotel Austral has a good restaurant (serving a steady diet of salmon), while the huge dining room at the unpretentious *La Bahía*, Serrano 434, accommodates large groups for a superb curanto if given sufficient notice. It's less central than its competitors, but still within reasonable walking distance; from the centre, go south on Blanco Encalada to Serrano.

Getting There & Away

Bus Puerto Natales has no central bus terminal, though several companies stop at the junction of Valdivia and Baquedano. To Punta Arenas (US$7), Buses Fernández at Eberhard 555 and Bus Sur at Baquedano 534 provide seven buses daily between them. Austral Bus, at Valdivia and Baquedano, goes daily to Punta Arenas.

In summer, Bus Sur also goes daily to Parque Nacional Torres del Paine (US$7 one-way), weekdays to Río Turbio (US$3) and twice weekly to Río Gallegos, Argentina (US$19). El Pingüino departs on Wednesday and Sunday at noon for Río Gallegos (US$18). Turismo Zaahj, Bulnes 459, runs buses to El Calafate, Argentina (US$32), in summer only, on Monday, Wednesday and Saturday at 7.30 am.

Servitur, Prat 353, goes to Paine daily, as does Buses JB, Bulnes 370. Turismo Luis Díaz, Bulnes 433, operates buses to Torres del Paine via Laguna Amarga.

Turisur and Cotra have frequent buses from the corner of Philippi and Baquedano to Río Turbio (US$3), which has connections to Río Gallegos and El Calafate.

Boat Navimag (☎ 41-1421), Costanera Pedro Montt 380, operates the car ferry MV *Puerto Edén* to Puerto Montt every seven to 10 days all year, though dates and times vary according to weather conditions and tides. The four-day, three-night voyage is heavily booked in summer, so try to reserve as far ahead as possible.

Fares start around US$110 in the low season (May to October) and are slightly more in the high season. Accommodation in all categories is very comfortable and includes breakfast, lunch and dinner, but incidentals like drinks and snacks are extra. There are many activities on board.

Getting Around

Car Both Andes Patagónicos (☎ 41-1594), Blanco Encalada 226, and Turismo Luis Díaz (☎ 41-1050), Bulnes 433, have rental cars.

Organised Tours

English-speaking Eduardo Scott at Hotel Austral, Andes Patagónicos and Stop Cambios (☎ 41-1393), Baquedano 380, can take eight to 10 passengers on minibus excursions to Torres del Paine and other destinations.

Turismo Luis Díaz runs one and two-day tours to Paine, and also goes to Cueva del Milodón and to Argentina's Parque Nacional Los Glaciares. Three-day excursions to Torres del Paine cost about US$120 per person with Buses Fernández.

Onas Aventuras (☎ 41-1321), Bulnes 453, rents camping equipment and also offers sea kayaking and trekking tours. Both Andes Patagónicos and Luis Díaz also rent camping equipment.

AROUND PUERTO NATALES

At **Cueva del Milodón**, 24 km north-west of Puerto Natales, Captain Hermann Eberhard discovered the well-preserved remains of an enormous ground sloth in the 1890s. Nearly four metres high, the herbivorous milodon ate the succulent leaves of small trees and branches, but became extinct in the late Pleistocene. The 30-metre-high cave contains a full-size replica of the animal.

CONAF charges US$4 admission; camping and picnicking are possible. Torres del Paine buses pass the entrance, which is several km from the cave proper. Alternatively, take a taxi or hitch.

PARQUE NACIONAL TORRES DEL PAINE

The Torres del Paine, granite pillars soaring almost vertically above the Patagonian steppe, are only one feature of this miniature Alaska of shimmering turquoise lakes, roaring creeks and rivers, cascading waterfalls, sprawling glaciers, dense forests and abundant wildlife. A UNESCO Biosphere Reserve, the 180,000-hectare park has a well-developed trail network and hut system

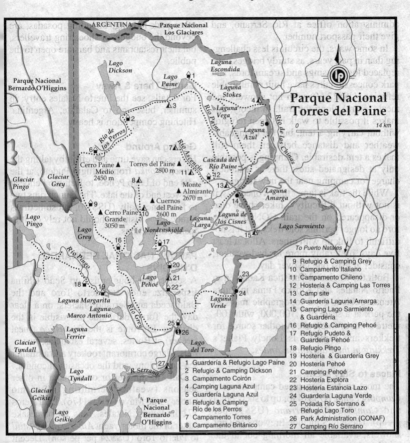

Parque Nacional
Torres del Paine

0   7   14 km

To Puerto Natales

1   Guardería & Refugio Lago Paine
2   Refugio & Camping Dickson
3   Campamento Coirón
4   Camping Laguna Azul
5   Guardería Laguna Azul
6   Refugio & Camping
    Río de los Perros
7   Campamento Torres
8   Campamento Británico
9   Refugio & Camping Grey
10 Campamento Italiano
11 Campamento Chileno
12 Hostería & Camping Las Torres
13 Camp site
14 Guardería Laguna Amarga
15 Camping Lago Sarmiento
    & Guardería
16 Refugio & Camping Pehoé
17 Refugio Pudeto &
    Guardería Pehoé
18 Refugio Pingo
19 Hostería & Guardería Grey
20 Hostería Pehoé
21 Camping Pehoé
22 Hostería Explora
23 Hostería Estancia Lazo
24 Guardería Laguna Verde
25 Posada Río Serrano &
    Refugio Lago Toro
26 Park Administration (CONAF)
27 Camping Río Serrano

CHILE

for trekkers, who can also camp at designated camp sites (bring a warm sleeping bag, waterproof gear and a tent). Weather is changeable, but long summer days permit outdoor activities late into the evening.

Paine's major conservation success has been the guanaco *(Lama guanicoe)*, which grazes the open steppes. The elusive huemul, or Chilean deer, is more difficult to spot.

Information

Entrance to the park is via the guarderías at Laguna Azul, Laguna Amarga, Lago Sarmiento and Laguna Verde. CONAF charges

an entry fee of US$12 per person at Guardería Lago Sarmiento, where maps and information brochures are available, or at Guardería Laguna Amarga (where most inbound buses stop), Guardería Laguna Verde, or Guardería Laguna Azul. There are special, expensive fees for climbers.

Trekking

Most trekkers start the inordinately popular Paine circuit, now approaching gridlock, at Guardería Laguna Amarga. Trekkers must register with rangers or at the CONAF administration office at Río Serrano, and give their passport number.

In some ways, the circuit is less challenging than in past years, as sturdy bridges have replaced log crossings and stream fords, and park concessionaires have built comfortable refugios (US$12.50) with hot showers and meals (extra) along the trail. In theory, this makes it possible to walk between refugios without carrying a tent, but the changeable weather and distance between them still makes a tent desirable. Camping is possible only at designated sites; there is a modest charge for camping near the new refugios.

While the trek is tamer than it once was, it is not without difficulty – hikers have died or disappeared on the trail. CONAF therefore no longer permits solo treks, but it is not difficult to link up with others. Allot at least five days, preferably more for bad weather; consider at least one layover day.

Both the Sociedad Turística Kaonikén in Puerto Natales and Kiosko Puma in Punta Arenas publish good topographic maps of the park at a scale of 1:100,000, with 100-metre contour intervals. Another source for trekkers and campers is Lonely Planet's *Trekking in the Patagonian Andes*.

Places to Stay & Eat

The most central, organised camp sites are *Camping Pehoé* (US$14 for up to six people) and *Camping Río Serrano* (US$11 per group). These fees include firewood and hot showers, available all morning but in the evenings by request only.

Camping Las Torres, on the grounds of Estancia Cerro Paine, charges US$4 per person and is popular with hikers taking the short trek up the Río Ascencio before doing the circuit. At the more remote, recently privatised *Camping Laguna Azul*, charges are US$14 per group per night.

A short distance from the CONAF administration office, *Refugio Lago Toro* has bunks for US$5 (US$2 for hot showers), but your own sleeping bag is essential. Other refugios, such as *Pudeto* on Lago Pehoé are free but *very* rustic.

The lakeside *Hostería Pehoé* and most

other park lodging, including posadas, are beyond the budgets of shoestring travellers, but their restaurants and bars are open to the public.

Getting There & Away

For details, see the Puerto Natales entry; in summer, buses go to Calafate, Argentina. Hitching competition is heavy.

Getting Around

Hikers can save time and effort by taking the launch *Tzonka* from Refugio Pudeto, at the east end of Lago Pehoé, to Refugio Pehoé at the west end of the lake. The launch runs two to four times daily (US$10), but sometimes erratically – visitors should not rely on it to make connections.

PARQUE NACIONAL BERNARDO O'HIGGINS

A scenic four-hour cruise up Seno Ultima Esperanza ends at Puerto Toro and the Balmaceda and Serrano glaciers; on a clear day, the Torres del Paine are visible in the distance. En route is the *frigorífico* (meat freezer) at Bories, several estancias, waterfalls, a large cormorant rookery and a smaller sea-lion colony, and the occasional condor.

Daily in summer or on demand in other seasons (weather permitting), Turismo Cutter 21 de Mayo (☎ 41-1176), Ladrilleros 171 in Puerto Natales, runs its namesake cutter or the motor yacht *Alberto de Agostini* to Puerto Toro (US$24 per person). Decent meals are available on board for about US$6, along with hot and cold drinks.

Juan Fernández Islands

In 1966, a tourist-motivated government renamed Isla Masatierra to Isla Robinson Crusoe, after literature's most renowned castaway. Scot Alexander Selkirk, who spent more than four years in complete isolation on Masatierra, was the real-life model for Daniel Defoe's fictional character.

Juan Fernández Islands

Tropic of Capricorn

0 400 800 km

CHILE

ARGENTINA

Isla Alejandro Selkirk

Isla Robinson Crusoe

Valparaíso

SANTIAGO

Archipiélago Juan Fernández

PACIFIC

Isla Grande de Chiloé

OCEAN

The tranquil Juan Fernández archipelago is also a national park and UNESCO World Biosphere Reserve.

History

In 1574, Juan Fernández discovered the islands which still bear his name. For over two centuries, the islands sheltered pirates and sealers, but were most renowned for Selkirk's exile on Masatierra after going ashore, at his own request, in 1704. Most castaways soon starved or shot themselves, but the adaptable Selkirk survived on feral goats (a Spanish introduction).

In 1708, Commander Woodes Rogers, of the privateers *Duke* and *Duchess*, rescued Selkirk. On returning to Scotland, Selkirk became a celebrity and Defoe's fictionalised account, set in the Caribbean, became a classic.

After Selkirk's departure, the presence of privateers and sealers compelled Spain to found the village of San Juan Bautista in

1750, but there was no really permanent presence until 1877. During WW I the British navy sank a German cruiser at Cumberland Bay.

Since then, the islands have played a less conspicuous but more significant role. In 1935, Chile declared them a national park for the sake of their unique flora and fauna, then undertook a programme to remove the feral goats. Mainland demand for the tasty local lobster provides substantial income for some Islanders.

Geography & Climate

Separated from Valparaíso by 670 km of open Pacific, Juan Fernández consists of Isla Robinson Crusoe, Isla Alejandro Selkirk (ex-Masafuera) and Isla Santa Clara. The islands are really emergent peaks from a submarine mountain range. Robinson Crusoe's area is only 93 sq km, its length a maximum of 22 km and its width a maximum of 7.3 km. Cerro El Yunque (the Anvil) reaches an altitude of 915 metres. The climate is Mediterranean, but rainfall varies greatly because of irregular topography.

Getting There & Away

Air Two companies fly air taxis almost daily in summer, less often in other seasons, from Santiago's Los Cerrillos airport. Travellers should allow for an extra two or three days' stay when poor weather makes landings risky at Robinson Crusoe's dirt airstrip.

LASSA (☎ 273-4309), in the Aeródromo Tobalaba, at Avenida Larraín 7941 in the eastern Santiago suburb of La Reina, flies six-passenger taxis, as does Transportes Aéreos Robinson Crusoe (☎ 531-4343), at Monumento 2570 in the suburb of Maipú. Fares are about US$404 return, but check for discount packages with accommodation and all meals.

From the airstrip, it is about 1½ hours by a combination of 4WD (to the jetty at Bahía del Padre) and subsequent motor launch (sailing along the island's awesome volcanic escarpments) to San Juan. Both flight and voyage can be rough. The round trip from the airstrip to San Juan Bautista costs US$15.

Boat Sailing to Juan Fernández is not easy, but quarterly naval supply ships carry passengers very cheaply. Since even the most innocuous naval movements are top secret, it's hard to learn departure dates, but try calling the Comando de Transporte (☎ 25-8457) at the Primera Zona Naval, opposite Plaza Sotomayor in Valparaíso.

Irregularly scheduled fishing boats carry passengers for about US$85 from Valparaíso. Contact Empresa Pesquera Chris (☎ 681-1543) at Cueto 622 in Santiago, or in Valparaíso (☎ 21-6800) at Cochrane 445.

Getting Around

Getting around sometimes requires hiring a fishing boat (rates are fixed by the municipalidad) or accompanying lobster-catchers on their rounds. To arrange a launch, contact Polo González at LASSA's office on the plaza. CONAF rangers visiting outlying sites may take along passengers.

PARQUE NACIONAL JUAN FERNANDEZ

Juan Fernández is a storehouse of rare plants and animals which evolved in isolation and adapted to specific ecological niches. Its native flora has suffered from the introduction of non-native species, but much remains in areas where even the agile goat could not penetrate or dominate.

Local flora have evolved into something very distinct from their continental origins. Of the 87 plant genera, 16 are endemic, found nowhere else on earth; of 140 plant species, 101 are endemic.

The most notable animal species is the only native mammal, the Juan Fernández fur seal. It was nearly extinct a century ago, but about 2500 individuals now breed here. Of 11 endemic bird species, the bright-red male Juan Fernández hummingbird is the most eye-catching; the female is a more subdued green, with a white tail. About 250 of these birds survive, feeding off the endemic

cabbage which grows in many parts of San Juan Bautista, but the species does best in native forest. Introduced rodents and feral cats have endangered nesting marine birds like Cook's petrel, by preying on their eggs and young.

Books

Defoe's classic is an obvious choice, but Rogers' *A Cruising Voyage Round the World* is available as a Dover Publications facsimile. The most thorough history is Ralph Lee Woodward's *Robinson Crusoe's Island*.

Things to See & Do

Yielding great views, the **Mirador Alejandro Selkirk**, Selkirk's lookout, is at the end of a steep three-km walk from San Juan Bautista. Hikers can continue to the airstrip for the flight back to the mainland, but should confirm their reservations in San Juan.

Plazoleta El Yunque, half an hour from San Juan, is a tranquil forest clearing with picnic and camping areas. Only 15 minutes from San Juan by launch, **Puerto Inglés** has a reconstruction of Selkirk's shelter, ruins of a cowherd's shed and adequate water for camping, but no firewood. The boat is expensive without a group, but there is a steep trail from San Juan which takes about two hours.

Robinson Crusoe's only breeding colony of fur seals is **Lobería Tierras Blancas**, a short distance from the airstrip. The trail to the airstrip from San Juan passes near the colony, which lacks drinking water. If you can't visit Tierras Blancas, you can still see fur seals at Bahía del Padre on arrival, or just north of San Juan's cemetery.

SAN JUAN BAUTISTA

San Juan Bautista (population 600) is one of the most tranquil places in Chile. Most visitors stay here or at nearby Pangal, and camping is possible.

The economy depends on fishing, mostly for lobsters, which are flown to Santiago by air taxi, but many Islanders never visit the continent.

The municipalidad, near the plaza, has Sernatur leaflets with decent maps and information. Bring money from the mainland, preferably in small bills. Hotels accept US dollars for accommodation. The CONAF offices are at the top of Vicente González, about 500 metres above the Costanera.

Things to See
Near the lighthouse, the polyglot European surnames on the headstones in San Juan's **cementerio** provide a unique perspective on local history – the Germans were survivors of the WW I battleship *Dresden*.

Over 40 participants in Chile's independence movement spent years in the **Cuevas de Los Patriotas** after defeat at Rancagua in 1814. Directly above the caves is **Fuerte Santa Bárbara**, built by the Spaniards in 1749 to discourage pirate incursions.

Places to Stay & Eat
Camping is permitted just about anywhere except the *zona intangible*, an off-limits area, but in some areas water is scarce. At El Palillo, at the south end of San Juan, CONAF has a quiet, pleasant and free camping ground, with running water and a pit latrine. The nearest shower (cold water only) is a 15-minute walk away at the jetty. There is another site at Plazoleta El Yunque.

Hotel accommodation starts at about US$30 per person with breakfast, US$45 with half-board, or US$60 with full board (including lobster every day) in triple rooms. If not staying at a hotel, give restaurants several hours' notice for lunch or dinner.

Despite its modest appearance, *Restaurant La Bahía* is outstanding value; owner Jorge Angulo prepares an extraordinary ceviche (cholera warnings do not apply to Juan Fernández , so raw seafood should be fine) and succulent lobster for about US$15 per person, with a two-person minimum so the other half of the lobster doesn't go to waste. The tasty vidriola (a type of fish) is much cheaper at about US$7.

Hostería Daniel Defoe is dearer and no better, but will prepare lobster for one person. *Restaurant Remo*, on the plaza, serves sandwiches and drinks.

Easter Island

How the Polynesians arrived at the earth's most remote inhabited island is an enigma as great as its hundreds of colossal moai, sculpted from volcanic stone, transported from quarry to coast, and raised on stone *ahu* (platforms). Polynesians named the tiny volcanic land mass Rapa Nui, but Dutchman Jacob Roggeveen renamed it Easter Island, a legacy which survived among Europeans.

History
Easter Island raises issues disproportionate to its size (117 sq km) and population (about 2800). The nearest populated landmass, 1900 km west, is the even tinier Pitcairn. The South American coast is 3700 km east. Orthodox opinion favours an Asiatic origin for the Polynesians who apparently built the Rapa Nui monuments. Legends describe two different peoples – the Long Ears of the east and the Short Ears of the west.

The Legend of Hotu Matua Oral tradition divides local history into three periods. King Hotu Matua brought the original settlers, followed by a period of rivalry between Long Ear and Short Ear groups which ended in the extermination of the latter. More recent warfare, between peoples of the Tuu and Hotu-iti regions, resulted in destruction of the moai.

Some have speculated that the Long Ears arrived with Hotu Matua from Polynesia, followed by Short Ears under Tuu-ko-ihu from the west. At some time, though, conflict resulted in the near extermination of the Long Ears; one estimate placed a single survivor in the late 17th century. Reasons for warfare appear to have been demographic and ecological.

CHILE

Early Europeans In 1722, the expedition led by Roggeveen brought the first Europeans to Rapa Nui. The Islanders, living from intensively cultivated gardens, were friendly, but the great moai baffled the Dutch, despite obvious religious significance. The absence of goods and metal implements suggested no contact with the outside world, but gardens of sugar cane, sweet potatoes, taro and yams provided a healthy subsistence.

In 1774, the famous Englishman James Cook, familiar with the Pacific, concluded that Rapa Nui's inhabitants resembled those of the Society Islands, Tonga and New Zealand. Topknots had fallen from some moai, their ahu had been damaged, and Cook found the Islanders poor, small, lean, timid and miserable.

It seems probable, then, that war had impoverished the people and destroyed some moai, but the Frenchman La Perouse, visiting in 1786, found them prosperous and calm, suggesting a quick recovery. In 1804, a Russian visitor reported more than 20 standing moai, but ensuing accounts suggest further disruption.

Alfred Metraux estimated an early 19th-century population of up to 4000, while another anthropologist, Katherine Routledge, speculated on a maximum of about 7000, but some informed guesses range up to 20,000.

Colonialism The Rapa Nui people may have inflicted havoc on themselves, but outsiders nearly annihilated them. A Peruvian slave raid in 1862 led directly or indirectly to many deaths. This was followed by the transportation of many Islanders to foreign mines and plantations, the arrival of previously unknown diseases, and forced emigration at the hands of missionaries.

Spain had always ignored Rapa Nui, but Chile annexed it in 1888 during a period of expansion. By 1897, the island had come under the control of a Valparaíso businessman who had bought or leased nearly all the land for wool, but it soon fell into the hands of Williamson, Balfour & Company, a British-Chilean enterprise which managed the island through its Compañía Explotadora de la Isla de Pascua (CEDIP). CEDIP was the de facto government until the 1950s.

The Islanders' welfare under CEDIP is a controversial topic, but there were several uprisings against the company. In 1953, the government revoked CEDIP's lease and the navy took charge of the island, continuing imperial rule.

Rapa Nui was under military rule until the mid-1960s, when the Chilean presence became more benevolent, with advances in water supply, medical care, education and electrification. After 1967, external contacts increased after the establishment of a regular commercial air link between Santiago and Tahiti, with Easter Island as a refuelling stop. The coup of 1973 once again brought direct military control, but there is now local self-government. Cattle and sheep still graze on parts of the island, but nearly everyone now makes a living, directly or indirectly, from the tourist trade.

In 1990, Islanders protested fare increases by LanChile (the only air carrier) by occupying Mataveri airport, even preventing the landing of a jetload of carabineros by blocking the runway with cars and rubble. The global impulse toward self-determination has clearly reached Rapa Nui as some Islanders argue for return of native lands and speak of independence or at least autonomy.

Geography & Climate

Just south of the Tropic of Capricorn, lava flows from three separate volcanic cones coalesced to form Rapa Nui's single triangular landmass. The coastal terrain is mostly gentle and grass-covered, except where wave erosion has created nearly vertical cliffs. Rugged lava fields cover much of the interior, but several areas have cultivable soil. Vulcanism left many caves, some of which served as permanent shelters, wartime refuges, or storage or burial sites.

Rapa Nui rests on a submarine platform which drops precipitously just off the coast. There are no reefs and no natural sheltered

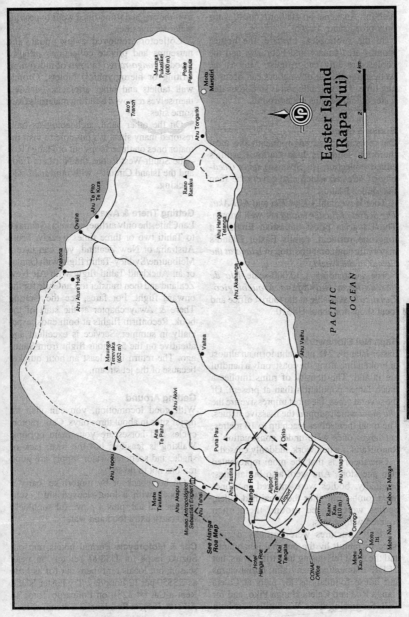

Easter Island (Rapa Nui)

PACIFIC OCEAN

Poike Peninsula

Maunga Pukatikei (400 m)

Motu Marotiri

Iko's Trench

Ahu Tongariki

Ahu Te Pito Te Kura

Ovahe

Rano Raraku

Anakena

Ahu Ature Huki

Ahu Hanga Tetenga

Ahu Akahanga

Maunga Terevaka (652 m)

Ahu Akivi

Ahu Vaihu

Vaitea

Ahu Tepeu

Ana Te Pahu

Motu Tautara

Puna Pau

Orito

Ahu Anakai

Museo Antropológico Sebastián Englert

Ahu Tahai

Ahu Tautira

Ahu Vinapu

Hanga Roa

Airport Terminal

See Hanga Roa Map

Hotel Hanga Roa

Ana Kai Tangata

Airport

Rano (410 m)

Orongo

CONAF Office

Cabo Te Manga

Motu Kao Kao

Motu Iti

Motu Nui

0   2   4 km

CHILE

harbour. Anakena, on the north coast, is the only broad sandy beach.

In the subtropical climate, the hottest months are January and February, and the coolest are July and August. May is the wettest month, but downpours can occur at any time. The volcanic soil is so porous that water quickly drains underground.

Books & Maps

On geography and environment, the most thorough source is Juan Carlos Castilla's edited collection (in Spanish) *Islas Oceánicas Chilenas*, which also covers the Juan Fernández Islands.

Thor Heyerdahl's *Kon-Tiki* and *Aku-Aku: The Secret of Easter Island* are well known. The Bavarian priest Sebastian Englert, a longtime resident, retells Easter Island's history through oral tradition in *Island at the Center of the World*.

The outstanding 1:30,000-scale *Isla de Pascua-Rapa Nui: Mapa Arqueológico-Turístico* is available at the tourist office and local shops for about US$10.

Rapa Nui Stonework

Easter Island's 245 or so ahu form an almost unbroken line along the coast; only a handful are inland. The density of ruins implies a much larger population than at present. Of the several types, the most impressive are the *ahu moai* which support the massive statues. The moai themselves reach up to 10 metres, but larger ones were under construction at Rano Raraku when work suddenly ceased.

One theory is that the moai represented clan ancestors. Ahu were also burial sites: originally, bodies were interred in stone-lined tombs, but after the moai had fallen, bodies were placed around them, then covered with stones.

Many structures were partially demolished or rebuilt by the original inhabitants, and the moai fell during intertribal wars, but CEDIP dismantled many ahu, burial cairns and house foundations for piers at Caleta Hanga Roa and Caleta Hanga Piko, and for walls for grazing areas. Windmills were built over the original stone-lined wells to provide water for livestock.

Collectors removed a few moai, and museums and private collections pillaged wooden *rongo-rongo* (a form of indigenous writing or hieroglyphics) tablets, Orongo wall tablets and other artefacts. Islanders themselves removed building materials from some sites.

On the other hand, archaeologists have restored many sites. It's possible to visit the major ones on three loops out of Hanga Roa – the South-West Route, the Northern Loop and the Island Circuit – with minimal backtracking.

Getting There & Away

LanChile, the only airline, connects Santiago to Tahiti two or three times weekly. From Australia or New Zealand, you can take a Melbourne/Sydney-Tahiti flight with Qantas or an Auckland-Tahiti flight with Air New Zealand and then transfer to LanChile for the onward flight. For fares, see the Getting There & Away chapter at the start of the book. Reconfirm flights at both ends, especially in summer. Service is excellent and attentive on the 5½ hour flight from Santiago. The return is at least an hour quicker because of the jet stream.

Getting Around

With good locomotion, you can visit all major sites in about three days. Cars, motorcycles and horses are your main options. Walking is feasible, but the heat, lack of shade, and scattered water supply are good reasons not to do so.

On horseback or by motorbike, carry a day-pack with a long-sleeved shirt, sunglasses and hat, plus a powerful sunblock. Also carry extra food and water.

Car & Motorcycle Formal hotels rent out Suzuki jeeps for US$90 per day in peak season, but locals rent them out for as little as US$50 per 12-hour day. Try Easter Island Rent-a-Car (☎ 328), on Policarpo Toro; Te Aiki (☎ 366), at Residencial Tekena; or look for signs in windows. Outside the high season, prices are negotiable.

Motorbikes are rented for about US$30 to US$35 a day. Given occasional tropical downpours, a jeep is more convenient, and even more economical for two or more people.

Horse For sites near Hanga Roa, horses can be hired for about US$15 per day. Horse gear is very basic and potentially hazardous for inexperienced riders, but Hotel Hotu Matua or Hotel Hanga Roa may organise riding excursions and locate proper stirrups and reins.

HANGA ROA

Nearly all Islanders live in Hanga Roa, a sprawling village with an irregular street plan. Nearly everyone depends on the tourist trade, but there is some fishing, plus livestock (mostly cattle) and kitchen gardens. Government and small shops are the only other employers.

Information

Tourist Offices Sernatur (☎ 105-255) is on the corner of Tuu Maheere and Apina, near Caleta Hanga Roa. The staff speak Rapa Nui, Spanish, English and French. An airport office is open for arriving flights.

Money Banco del Estado, next to Sernatur, changes US dollars, but pays the disadvantageous official rate and charges high commissions on travellers' cheques, so bring Chilean currency from the mainland.

Post & Communications The post office is on Te Pito o Te Henua, half a block above Caleta Hanga Roa. Entel, with its conspicuous satellite dish, is in a cul-de-sac opposite Sernatur.

Medical Services The hospital is one long block from the church.

Museo Antropológico Sebastián Englert

Researchers and visitors often neglect the Rapa Nui people and their experience, but this museum partly redresses that shortcoming. It clearly shows, for instance, that they are a Polynesian people whose subsistence depended on crops like kumara (sweet potato), a staple which Islanders still prefer to wheat.

Historical photographs depict the encounter with European culture since the mid-19th century. The museum also displays obsidian spearheads, *moai kavakava* (the strange statues of ribs) and replicas of rongo-rongo tablets.

The museum (admission US$1) is midway between Ahu Tahai and Ahu Akapu – consult the map for directions. As of late 1995 it was closed for remodelling.

Places to Stay

The least expensive rooms are about US$20/40 for a single/double, with breakfast. Other meals may cost up to US$15 each, but Hanga Roa has several reasonable restaurants. Neither streets nor residenciales are well signposted, and buildings rarely have numbers, so locate places by referring to the map.

Reservations are not essential, except in summer. Hosts often meet incoming flights with a discount offer, including transport to town; most charge around US$45/75 with full board, but this is inconvenient if you're visiting remote archaeological sites and can't return to Hanga Roa for lunch.

Camping Some residenciales offer garden camp sites, but CONAF allows camping only at Anakena (ask about the water supply).

Hostel The *Residencial Kona Tau* (☎ 321-286) on Avaripua has hostel accommodation at US$20 per person. The owners are a delightful family.

Residenciales Residenciales start at around US$25/50 for a single/double with breakfast, and include the popular, friendly *Residencial El Tauke* (☎ 105-253), *Residencial Tekena* (☎ 105-289), *Residencial Vai A Repa* (☎ 105-331), *Residencial Tiare Anani*

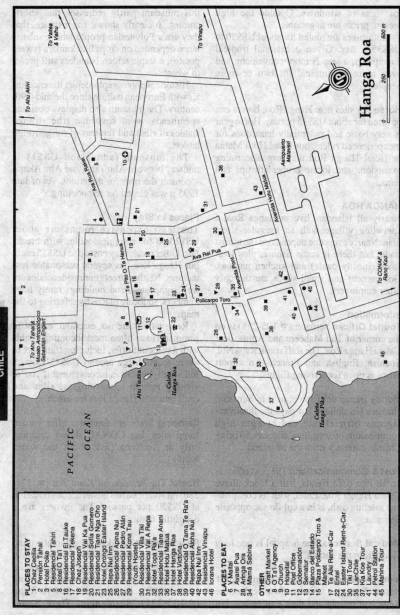

Hanga Roa

To Vaitea & Vaihu

To Vinapu

To Ahu Akivi

Aeropuerto Mataveri

Avenida Hotu Matua

To CONAF & Rano Kao

Avenida Pont.

Avenida Vinapu

Ava Rei Pua

Te Pito O Te Henua

Ava Pua Raket

Policarpo Toro

Caleta Hanga Roa

Caleta Hanga Piko

To Ahu Tahai & Museo Antropológico Sebastián Englert

PACIFIC OCEAN

0   250   500 m

(☎ 105-249) and *Residencial Tiare Nga Oho* (☎ 105-259). Two readers have endorsed *Hereveri Guest House* (☎ 105-593), 100 metres behind the church, whose friendly owners Martín and Anita offer singles/doubles with bath for US$20/30 and camping sites for US$7.

María Hey runs the *Residencial Tahai* (☎ 105-395), which charges US$25/40 for a single/double with breakfast in a clean bungalow with a large, quiet and relaxing garden; it's on the Ahu Tahai road. Another good place is the *Rapa Nui Inn* (☎ 22-3228), on the corner of Policarpo Toro and Avenida Hotu Motua. Rates are US$30/45 with breakfast for a large, clean room with double bed and private bath. In the same range, *Residencial Vinapu* (☎ 22-3393) is also recommended. The cheapest place is *Residencial Ma'Ori* (☎ 22-3497), on Te Pito o Te Henua, with singles/doubles at US$15/25.

Places to Eat

Restaurants offer fine seafood at reasonable prices (except for lobster, which is expensive). Try *V Maitai*, at Caleta Hanga Roa; *Avarei Pua*, across the street; *Mamá Sabina* (with very well-prepared and appetising food), across from LanChile; or *Aringa Ora*.

If camping or cooking your own food, get provisions at general stores and bakeries on the main street. The open-air market on Policarpo Toro, across from the gobernación, has fresh fish and vegetables.

Things to Buy

For crafts, the best selection and prices (open to haggling) are at the market across from the church. Look for stone or wooden replicas of standard moai, as well as moai kavakava, replica rongo-rongo tablets, and obsidian fragments from Orito (sometimes made into earrings).

PARQUE NACIONAL RAPA NUI

Since 1935, Easter Island's monuments have been part of this open-air museum administered by CONAF. Non-Chileans pay admission fees of about US$10 to Orongo

ceremonial village and Ahu Tahai. These are valid for the length of your stay.

In cooperation with foreign and Chilean archaeologists as well as locals, the government has successfully restored monuments and attracted visitors, but some Islanders view the park as a land grab. A native rights organisation, the Consejo de Ancianos (Council of Elders) wants the park (a third of the island's surface) returned to its aboriginal owners, who control almost no land outside the town of Hanga Roa. However, many Islanders also work for CONAF and other government agencies.

The South-West Route

From Hanga Roa, take the road to the top of Rano Kau crater and Orongo ceremonial village. After backtracking to Hanga Roa, take the road north of the airport to the old obsidian quarries at Orito, then south to Ahu Vinapu.

Orongo Ceremonial Village Perched 400 metres above the reedy crater lake of Rano Kau, Orongo is one of the island's most dramatic sites, a much later construction than the great moai and ahu.

Overlooking several small *motu* (islets), Orongo was the centre of an island-wide bird cult in the 18th and 19th centuries. The climax of its rituals was a competition for the first egg of the sooty tern *(Sterna fuscata)*, which bred on the motu just off Cabo Te Manga; whoever found the first egg won the god Makemake's favour and great status.

Built into the slope, Orongo's semisubterranean houses had walls of horizontally overlapping stone slabs, with an earthcovered arched roof. Since the walls were thick to support the roof's weight, the doorway is a low, narrow tunnel. At the crater's edge is a cluster of boulders with birdman petroglyphs.

Orito Having overthrown the Long Ears, Short Ear tribes enjoyed peace until resource-centred conflicts resulted in bloody warfare, leading to the toppling of the moai.

Their weapons were made from hard black obsidian, quarried at Orito.

Ahu Vinapu Follow the Mataveri road to the end of the runway, then head south between the airstrip and some large oil tanks to an opening in a stone wall, where a sign points to Ahu Vinapu.

Vinapu's tight-fitting stonework so resembles that of the Inca Cuzco and pre-Inca Tiahuanaco that some researchers have concluded it has South American origins. Others argue for independent invention.

The Northern Loop

Take the route from Hanga Roa to Puna Pau crater, the source of the reddish volcanic scoria used for moai topknots, and continue inland to Ahu Akivi, where the seven moai have been re-erected. From Ahu Akivi, follow the track to Ahu Tepeu, on the coast, then south to Hanga Roa past several restored ahu with their moai re-erected.

Puna Pau Quarried from soft, easily worked stone from Puna Pau, the reddish cylindrical topknots on some moai reflect a once common hairstyle worn by Rapa Nui males. Most *pukao* had a partly hollow underside which allowed them to be slotted onto the heads of the moai.

Ahu Akivi Unlike most moai, the seven on this restored inland ahu look out to sea.

Ana Te Pahu Follow the faint, rough, but passable track to Ahu Tepeu, on the west coast, stopping at Ana Te Pahu, a former cave dwelling where the entry way is a garden planted with sweet potatoes, taro and bananas.

Ahu Tepeu This large ahu is on the northwest coast between Ahu Akapu and Cabo Norte. Maunga Terevaka, to the north-east, is the island's highest point; to the south, a large grassy plain covers a jagged lava sheet. To the west, the Pacific breaks against rugged cliffs.

Several moai here have fallen. Nearby is an extensive village site with foundations of several *hare paenga* (elliptical houses) and the walls of several round houses. South of here the road is very rough, but it is always passable.

Ahu Akapu Ahu Akapu, with its solitary moai, stands on the coast between Ahu Tepeu and Ahu Tahai.

Ahu Tahai A short hike north of Hanga Roa, this site contains three restored ahu: Ahu Tahai proper is in the middle, supporting a large, solitary moai with no topknot. To one side is Ahu Ko Te Riku, which has a large, solitary moai with its topknot in place. On the other side is Ahu Vai Uri, supporting five moai of varying sizes.

Ahu Tautira Ahu Tautira overlooks Caleta Hanga Roa, the fishing port at the foot of Calle Te Pito o Te Henua. Torsos of two broken moai have been re-erected.

The Island Circuit

From Hanga Roa, follow the south coast to Vaihu and Akahanga, then continue west and detour inland to Rano Raraku, a quarry for the moai. Leaving Rano Raraku, follow the road west to Ahu Tongariki, where a 1960 tsunami hurled moai and masonry far inland.

From Tongariki, follow the north coast to Ahu Te Pito Te Kura, with the largest moai ever erected on an ahu, then continue east to the beach at Ovahe and to Anakena, the island's main beach and site of two more restored ahu. Return to Hanga Roa via Vaitea.

Ahu Vaihu This ahu's eight large moai now lie face down, their topknots scattered nearby.

Ahu Akahanga This large ahu has many large fallen moai, while a second ahu across the estuary has several more. On the slopes opposite are the remains of several elliptical and round houses.

Ahu Hanga Tetenga Almost completely ruined, this coastal ahu's two large moai are both in fragments. Just beyond Hanga Tetenga, a faint track off the main road branches inland toward Rano Raraku crater.

Rano Raraku Rano Raraku was the source for the hard volcanic stone from which the moai were cut. Moai in all stages of progress litter its southern slopes and the crater, which contains a small lake. Most are upright but partly buried, so that only their heads gaze across the grassy slopes. A trail leads straight up the slope to a 21-metre giant – the largest moai ever built – but most moai range from 5.5 to seven metres.

The total number of moai from Rano Raraku exceeds 600. Most were carved face up, horizontal or slightly reclined. Leaving each attached only along its back, workers excavated a channel large enough for carvers. Nearly all the carving with basalt *tokis*, including fine detail, occurred at this stage, after which the moai was detached and transported downslope for further details on the back. Rano Raraku's most unusual statue is the kneeling Moai Tukuturi, slightly less than four metres high, which now sits on the south-eastern slope of the mountain.

Transporting the moai must have been difficult and dangerous, but despite this, Islanders placed 300 moai on distant ahu or left them along the old roads.

Ahu Tongariki In 1960, a tsunami demolished several moai and scattered topknots far inland from the largest ahu ever built, which supported 15 massive moai; a recent Japanese expedition has restored the site. Nearby petroglyphs show a variety of designs.

Poike Peninsula Rapa Nui's eastern end is a high plateau called the Poike Peninsula, crowned by the extinct volcano Maunga Pukatikei.

Legend says that the Long Ears built the trench to defend themselves, filling it with branches and tree trunks to be fired should the Short Ears try to storm across. The ditch was once thought natural, but carbon dating

of ash and charcoal suggested that a great fire occurred perhaps 350 years ago, while genealogical research has placed the onset of conflict at around 1680.

Ahu Te Pito Te Kura Overlooking a fishing cove at La Perouse Bay is the largest moai ever moved from Rano Raraku and erected on an ahu. Nearly 10 metres high, in proportion and general appearance it resembles the moai still partly buried at Rano Raraku and, thus, was probably the last ever erected on an ahu.

Ovahe Between La Perouse and Anakena, this is an attractive beach with interesting caves. Beware of sharks.

Anakena Anakena is the legendary landing place of Hotu Matua. One of several caves may have sheltered him as he waited for completion of his boat-shaped house.

Popular for swimming and sunbathing, the sheltered, white-sand beach is a pleasant place to spend the afternoon. You can stay overnight at CONAF's camping ground, but bring food and water from Hanga Roa.

Ahu Ature Huki On the hillside above Anakena stands Ahu Ature Huki and its lone moai. Heyerdahl and a dozen Islanders took nine days to raise the moai on its ahu with wooden poles, supporting the giant with stones, and levering the logs with ropes when the men could no longer reach them.

Legend says that priests moved the moai by the power of *mana*, an ability to make it walk a short distance each day. After suggestions that Islanders could have moved the moai with a forked sledge, pulled with ropes made from tree bark, Heyerdahl organised 180 Islanders to pull a four-metre moai across the field at Anakena, and speculated that they could have moved a larger one with wooden runners and more labour. US archaeologist William Mulloy proposed a different method, which involved fitting a sledge to the moai and dragging it forward with ropes on a bipod. His complex theory,

CHILE

requiring large amounts of timber, may partly explain the island's deforestation.

Ahu Nau Nau In 1979, excavation and restoration of Ahu Nau Nau, in Anakena, revealed that the moai were not 'blind' but had inlaid coral and rock eyes – 'eyes that look to the sky', in a Rapa Nui phrase.

Fundo Vaitea Midway between Anakena and Hanga Roa, Vaitea was the centre of food and livestock production under Williamson, Balfour & Company; the large building on the east side of the road is the former shearing shed. The property on the west side belongs to the state-controlled development corporation CORFO, which raises fruit and vegetables.

Colombia

For most travellers, Colombia is unknown territory – a land of myths, cocaine, emeralds and the mysterious El Dorado. It is the realm of Gabriel García Márquez and his famous novel *One Hundred Years of Solitude* – a tale as magical as the country itself. And it is the nation which bears the name of Columbus, discoverer of the Americas, but where people have changed the order of the letters to make Locombia, the mad country.

Colombia's geography is among the most varied in South America, as are its flora and fauna. The inhabitants form a palette of ethnic blends uncommon elsewhere on the continent and include a few dozen Indian groups, some of which still have traditional lifestyles. In effect, it's a country of amazing natural and cultural diversity and contrast, where climate, topography, wildlife, crafts, music and architecture change within hours of overland travel – it's as if Colombia were several countries rolled into one.

Through its turbulent history, Colombia has been soaked with blood in innumerable civil wars, and has endured the largest and longest guerrilla insurgency on the continent. The country is also the world's major producer of cocaine. With such a background, it's no wonder that violence occurs here more frequently than in neighbouring countries, and that Colombia is not as safe.

However, don't be put off. If you take the necessary precautions (see Dangers & Annoyances under Facts for the Visitor), Colombia is worth the challenge. It is exotic, sensual, wild, complex and fascinating. And it's hard to find such hospitable, spirited and stimulating people as those in Colombia.

Country Name República de Colombia
Area 1,141,748 sq km
Population approx 37.5 million (1995)
Population Density 33 per sq km
Capital Santa Fe de Bogotá
Head of State President Ernesto Samper
Official Language Spanish
Other Languages About 200 Indian languages
Currency Peso
Exchange Rate US$1 = 1076 pesos
Per Capita GNP US$1400 (1993)
Inflation Rate 19% (1995)

Facts about the Country

HISTORY
The Pre-Columbian Period
Colombia lies at the north-western gateway to South America, and must have been on the route for the first inhabitants, who migrated from North and Central America. Some tribes headed farther south, while others formed permanent settlements in what is now Colombia and, in time, reached a remarkably high level of development. However, these civilisations are little known internationally, partly because few left spectacular, enduring monuments. There are only three important archaeological sites in Colombia: San Agustín, Tierradentro and

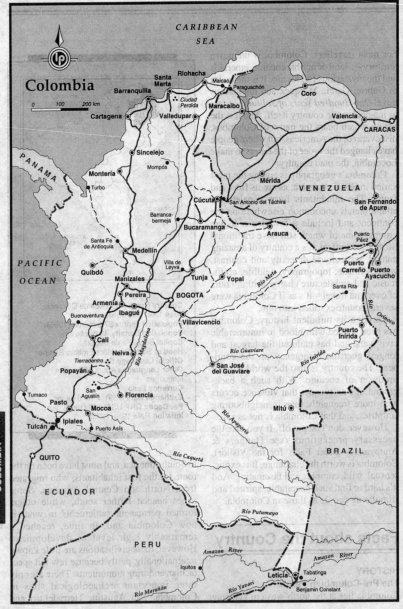

Colombia

0   100   200 km

CARIBBEAN
SEA

PANAMA

PACIFIC
OCEAN

VENEZUELA

BRAZIL

PERU

ECUADOR

Barranquilla
Santa Marta
Riohacha
Maicao
Paraguachón
Ciudad Perdida
Cartagena
Valledupar
Maracaibo
Coro
Valencia
CARACAS
Sincelejo
Mompós
Montería
Mérida
San Fernando de Apure
Turbo
Cúcuta
San Antonio del Táchira
Santa Fe de Antioquia
Barranca-bermeja
Bucaramanga
Arauca
Puerto Páez
Medellín
Villa de Leyva
Tunja
Yopal
Puerto Carreño
Puerto Ayacucho
Quibdó
Manizales
Río Meta
Santa Rita
Pereira
BOGOTA
Armenia
Ibagué
Villavicencio
Buenaventura
Río Guaviare
Puerto Inírida
Cali
Río Inírida
Neiva
Río Magdalena
Tierradentro
San José del Guaviare
Río Orinoco
Popayán
San Agustín
Florencia
Mitú
Tumaco
Pasto
Mocoa
Río Apaporis
Ipiales
Tulcán
Puerto Asís
Río Caquetá
QUITO
Río Guaviare
Río Putumayo
Amazon River
Amazon River
Iquitos
Leticia
Tabatinga
Benjamin Constant
Río Marañón
Río Yavarí

Ciudad Perdida. Other cultures left behind little more than artefacts, mainly gold and pottery, which are now held in museums across the country. Yet their art reveals a high degree of skill, and their goldwork is the best in the continent, both for the techniques used and for its artistic design.

In contrast to the Aztecs or Incas, who dominated vast regions, several independent Colombian groups occupied relatively small areas scattered throughout the Andean region and along the Pacific and Atlantic (Caribbean) coasts. Despite trading and cultural contacts, these cultures developed independently. Among the most outstanding were the Tayrona, Sinú, Muisca, Quimbaya, Tolima, Calima, Tierradentro, San Agustín, Nariño and Tumaco. Tierradentro and San Agustín flourished before the Spanish conquest, while the other cultures are believed to have been at the height of their cultural and social development when the Spaniards arrived.

San Agustín, one of the most extraordinary ceremonial centres in South America, is noted for hundreds of monolithic statues and tombs scattered over a wide area. Another culture with developed funeral rites flourished in Tierradentro, an area separated by a mountain range from San Agustín. There, the Indians built a number of underground burial chambers, where they kept the remains of tribal elders. The chambers were laboriously dug out of the soft rock, and the walls and vaults were decorated with paintings. These funeral chambers are unique in South America.

The Muisca culture became widely known for its part in the famous myth of El Dorado, created by the Spaniards. The Muiscas (also confusedly called the Chibchas because they formed the largest part of the Chibcha linguistic family) were known far and wide for their wealth, and had a flourishing civilisation which occupied what are now the departments of Cundinamarca and Boyacá. From around the 3rd century BC, they took good advantage of fertile soils, and rich salt and emerald mines, creating extensive trading links with other cultures.

In the mountainous jungles along the Caribbean coast, *guaqueros* (grave robbers who search for pre-Columbian treasures) discovered Ciudad Perdida (Lost City) in 1975. The find has shed new light on the Tayrona (or Tairona) culture, which developed from about the 5th century AD in the Sierra Nevada de Santa Marta. The Tayrona had long been considered one of the most advanced early Indian civilisations, yet it was only after the discovery of the Lost City that their greatness as architects and builders was confirmed. Ciudad Perdida, thought to be their capital, is one of the largest ancient cities ever found in the Americas; resplendent with several hundred stone terraces linked by a network of stairs, it is spectacularly sited in the heart of a tropical rainforest.

The Spanish Conquest

In 1499, Alonso de Ojeda was the first conquistador to set foot on Colombian soil and to see indigenous people using gold objects. Attracted by the presumed riches of the Indians, the shores of present-day Colombia became the target of numerous coastal expeditions by the Spaniards. Several short-lived settlements were founded, but it was not until 1525 that Rodrigo de Bastidas laid the first stones of Santa Marta, the earliest surviving town. In 1533, Pedro de Heredia founded Cartagena, which soon became the principal centre of trade.

In 1536, a general advance towards the interior began independently from three different directions, under Jiménez de Quesada, Sebastián de Benalcázar (known in Colombia as Belalcázar) and Nikolaus Federmann.

Quesada set off from Santa Marta, pushed up the Magdalena valley, then climbed the Cordillera Oriental, arriving in Muisca territory early in 1537. After conquering the Muiscas, he founded Santa Fe de Bogotá in 1538. Quesada didn't actually find gold, despite the elaborate rituals of the Indians, who threw gold offerings into the waters of their sacred lake, the Laguna de Guatavita, and thus gave birth to the mysterious legend of El Dorado.

Belalcázar deserted from Francisco

Pizarro's army, which was conquering the Inca empire, and mounted an expedition from Ecuador. He subdued the southern part of Colombia, founding Popayán and Cali along the way, and reached Bogotá in 1539.

Federmann started from the Venezuelan coast and, after successfully crossing Los Llanos, arrived in Bogotá shortly after Belalcázar.

The three groups fought tooth and nail for supremacy, and it was not until 1550 that King Charles V of Spain, in an effort to establish law and order, created the Real Audiencia del Nuevo Reino de Granada, a tribunal based in Bogotá. Administratively, the new colony was subject to the Viceroyalty of Peru.

The Colonial Period

With the growth of the Spanish empire in the New World, a new territorial division was created in 1717, and Bogotá became the capital of its own viceroyalty, the Virreinato de la Nueva Granada. It comprised the territories of what are today Colombia, Panama, Venezuela and Ecuador.

Towards the end of the 18th century, the general disillusionment with Spanish domination gave rise to open protests and rebellions. This, together with events such as the North American and French revolutions and, most importantly, the invasion of Spain by Napoleon Bonaparte, slowly paved the way to independence.

When, in 1808, Napoleon placed his own brother on the Spanish throne, the colonies refused to recognise the new monarch. One by one, Colombian towns declared their independence.

In 1812, Simón Bolívar, who was to become the hero of the independence struggle, arrived in Cartagena to take the offensive against the Spanish armies. In a brilliant campaign to seize Venezuela, he won six battles but was unable to hold Caracas, and had to withdraw to Cartagena. By then, Napoleon had been defeated at Waterloo, and Spain set about reconquering its colonies. Colonial rule was re-established in 1817.

Bolívar took up arms again. After assembling an army of horsemen from the Venezuelan Llanos, strengthened by a British legion, he marched over the Andes into Colombia. The last and most decisive battle took place at Boyacá on 7 August 1819. Colombia's independence was won.

After Independence

A revolutionary congress was held in Angostura (modern-day Ciudad Bolívar, in Venezuela) in 1819. Still euphoric with victory, the delegates proclaimed the Gran Colombia, a new state uniting Venezuela, Colombia and Ecuador. The congress was followed by another, held in Villa del Rosario, near Cúcuta, in 1821. It was there that the two opposing tendencies, centralist and federalist, came to the fore. Bolívar supported a centralised unified republic, while Francisco de Paula Santander favoured a federal republic of sovereign states. Bolívar succeeded in imposing his will, and the Gran Colombia came into being. Bolívar was elected president and Santander became vice president.

From its inception, the state started to disintegrate. It soon became apparent that a central regime was incapable of governing such a vast and diverse territory. The Gran Colombia had split into three separate countries by 1830, the year of Bolívar's death.

The two political currents, centralist and federalist, were formalised in 1849 when two political parties were established: the Conservatives (with centralist tendencies) and the Liberals (with federalist leanings). Colombia became the scene of fierce rivalries between the two forces, resulting in complete chaos. During the 19th century, the country experienced no less than eight civil wars. Between 1863 and 1885, there were more than 50 antigovernment insurrections.

In 1899, a Liberal revolt turned into a full-blown civil war, the so-called War of a Thousand Days. That carnage resulted in a Conservative victory and left 100,000 dead. In 1903, the USA took advantage of the country's internal strife and fomented a secessionist movement in Panama (at that time a Colombian province). By creating a new republic, the USA was able to build a canal across the Central American isthmus under its control. It wasn't until 1921 that Colombia finally recognised the sovereignty of Panama and settled its dispute with the USA.

La Violencia

After a period of relative peace, the struggle between Liberals and Conservatives broke out again in 1948 with La Violencia, the most destructive of Colombia's many civil wars, which left a death toll of some 300,000. The first urban riots broke out on 9 April 1948 in Bogotá with the assassination of Jorge Eliécer Gaitán, a charismatic populist Liberal leader. Liberals soon took up arms throughout the country.

To comprehend the brutality of this period, one must understand that for a century Colombians were born either Liberal or Conservative and reared with a mistrust of the other party. In the 1940s and 1950s, these 'hereditary hatreds' were the cause of countless atrocities, rapes and murders, particularly in rural areas. Hundreds of thousands of people took to the hills and shot each other for nothing more than the name of their party.

By 1953, some groups of the Liberal guerrillas had begun to demonstrate a dangerous degree of independence, in some cases making alliances with the small bands of communist guerrillas that also operated during this period. As it became evident that the partisan conflict was taking on revolutionary overtones, the leaders of both the Liberal and Conservative parties decided to support a military coup as the best means to retain power and pacify the countryside. The 1953 coup of General Gustavo Rojas Pinilla was the only military intervention the country has experienced this century.

The dictatorship of General Rojas was not to last. In 1957, the leaders of the two parties signed a pact to share power for the next 16 years. The agreement, later approved by a plebiscite (in which women were, for the first time, allowed to vote), became known as the Frente Nacional (National Front). During the life of the accord, the two parties alternated in the presidency every four years.

The Frente Nacional repressed all political activity that remained outside the scope of the two parties, thus sowing the seeds for the appearance of guerrilla groups.

Guerrillas & Paramilitaries

Guerrillas are, unfortunately, quite an important part of Colombian political life, and a headache for the government. With roots that extend back to La Violencia, they are the oldest insurgent forces in Latin America. They continue to engage in armed struggle and are more active than ever.

Colombia saw the birth of perhaps a dozen different guerrilla groups, each with its own ideology and its own political and military strategies. The movements which have had the biggest impact on local politics (and left the largest number of dead) include the FARC (Fuerzas Armadas Revolucionarias de Colombia), the ELN (Ejército de Liberación Nacional) and the M-19 (Movimiento 19 de Abril).

Until 1982, the guerrillas were treated as a problem of public order and severely persecuted by the military forces. President Belisario Betancur (1982-86) was the first to open direct negotiations with the guerrillas in a bid to reincorporate them into the nation's political life. Yet the talks ended in failure. The rupture was poignantly symbolised by the takeover of Bogotá's Palacio de Justicia by the M-19 guerrillas in November 1985.

Following the failure of Betancur's peace process, the Liberal government of Virgilio Barco (1986-90), after long and complicated negotiations with the M-19, signed an agreement under which this group handed over its arms, ceased insurgent activity and transformed itself into a political party. However, the FARC and the ELN remain under arms and are more violent than ever. Having lost support from Moscow and Havana, they now rely on extortion, robbery and kidnapping to finance their struggle. They are also increasingly involved in the drug business.

COLOMBIA

Since the state has been unable to control some areas of the country, private armies – the so-called *paramilitares* or *autodefensas* – have mushroomed, with the army turning a blind eye or even supporting them. These armies operate in several regions, including Urabá, Cesar, Córdoba and Magdalena Medio, and have committed some horrendous massacres. They are another nightmare for the government.

Drug Cartels

The cocaine industry has also affected Colombia's politics and economy. Colombia is the world's biggest producer of cocaine, controlling some 80% of the world market. The mafia started in a small way in the early 1970s but, within a short time, developed the trade into a powerful industry, with their own plantations, laboratories, transport services and protection.

The boom years began in the early 1980s. The Medellín Cartel, led by Pablo Escobar, became the principal mafia, and its bosses lived in freedom and luxury. They even founded their own political party and two newspapers, and in 1982 Escobar was elected to the Congress. In 1983 the government launched a campaign against the drug trade, which gradually turned into an all-out war. The cartel responded violently and managed to liquidate many of its adversaries.

The war became even bloodier in August 1989, when Luis Carlos Galán, the leading Liberal contender for the 1990 presidential election, was assassinated. The government responded with the confiscation of nearly 1000 mafia-owned properties, and announced new laws on extradition – a nightmare for the drug barons.

The cartel resorted, for the first time in Colombia, to the use of terrorist tactics, principally car bombs. For its part, the army succeeded in killing one of the top bosses of the cartel, Gonzalo Rodríguez Gacha.

The election of the Liberal César Gaviria 1990-94) brought a brief period of hope. Following lengthy negotiations, which included a constitutional amendment to ban extradition of Colombians to the USA,

Escobar and the remaining cartel bosses surrendered and the narco-terrorism subsided. However, Escobar escaped from his palace-like prison following the government's bumbling attempts to move him to a more secure site. An elite 1500-man special unit sought Escobar for 499 days, until it tracked him down and killed him in December 1993.

Despite this, the drug trade continued unaffected. While the military concentrated on hunting one man and persecuting one cartel, the other cartels were quick to take advantage of the opportune circumstances. The Cali Cartel, led by the Rodríguez Orejuela brothers, swiftly moved into the shattered Medellín Cartel's markets, and became Colombia's largest cocaine trafficker. It also diversified into opium poppies and heroin. Although most of the cartel's top bosses were captured in 1995 and are now behind bars, the drug trade continues to flourish.

Recent Developments

The 1994 elections put the Liberal Ernesto Samper into the presidency. Even before he took office, his major opponent, Andrés Pastrana, released tapes (called 'narco-cassettes') of wire-tapped telephone conversations, in which Cali Cartel bosses discussed making donations of some US$4 million to Samper's presidential campaign. The issue was discreetly manoeuvred out, but resurfaced in August 1995, when Santiago Medina, Samper's campaign treasurer, testified that the party had received large amounts of money from the cartel. A further blow came from Fernando Botero, the campaign manager, who in a televised interview confirmed that Samper knowingly took the cartel's money.

Both Medina and Botero, plus several members of parliament, former ministers and a former general attorney, were linked to an amazing web of corruption (referred to as the Proceso 8000) and went to jail. Meanwhile, the president maintained he was unaware that drug money had gone to his campaign fund.

Throughout early 1996 the 'Colombian

Watergate' occupied the top of the political agenda, pushing all other issues into the shade. The economy began to plunge, guerrilla activity intensified dramatically and the government lost much of its credibility.

An increasing number of local groups, including the economic barons, the Church and even sections of Samper's own Liberal party, demanded the president's resignation. As this book went to press, Samper was still desperately defending his position, and the investigation set up to determine whether he had acted illegally was widely considered a farce. Most analysts agreed, however, that his days were numbered. By the time you come to Colombia, you may find Samper's vice president, Humberto de la Calle, occupying the top office.

GEOGRAPHY

Colombia covers 1,141,748 sq km, roughly equal to the area of France, Spain and Portugal combined. It is the fourth-largest country in South America, after Brazil, Argentina and Peru. Colombia occupies the north-western part of the continent and is the only country in South America with coasts on both the Pacific (1350 km long) and the Caribbean (over 1600 km). Colombia is bordered by Panama, Venezuela, Brazil, Peru and Ecuador.

The country is very varied in its geography. The western part, about 45% of the total territory, is mountainous, with three Andean chains – the Cordillera Occidental, Cordillera Central and Cordillera Oriental – running roughly parallel north-south across most of the country.

The Sierra Nevada de Santa Marta, an independent and relatively small formation, rises from the Caribbean coastline to permanent snows. It is the highest coastal mountain range in the world, and its twin peaks of Simón Bolívar (5775 metres) and Cristóbal Colón (5775 metres) are the highest in Colombia.

Over 50% of the territory east of the Andes is a vast lowland, which can be generally divided into two regions: Los Llanos in the north and the Amazon in the south.

Colombia has several small islands. The major ones are the archipelago of San Andrés and Providencia (in the Caribbean Sea, and closer to Nicaragua than to mainland Colombia), the Islas del Rosario and San Bernardo (along the Caribbean coast), and Gorgona and Malpelo (in the Pacific Ocean).

CLIMATE

Its proximity to the equator means Colombia's temperature varies little throughout the year. However, the temperature does change with altitude, creating various climatic zones, from hot lowlands to permanent snows, and you can experience completely different climates within a couple of hours of travel.

Colombia has two seasons: dry and wet. The dry season is called *verano* (literally, summer) and the rainy months are known as *invierno* (winter).

The pattern of seasons varies in different parts of the country. In the Andean regions, there are two dry and two rainy seasons per year. The main dry season falls between December and March, with a shorter and less dry period between July and August. This general pattern has wide variations throughout the Andean zone, with the seasons being wetter or drier, shorter or longer and occurring at different times. In southern Colombia particularly, there are considerable differences between neighbouring regions.

The weather in Los Llanos has a more definite pattern: there is one dry season, between December and March, and the rest of the year is wet. The Amazon doesn't have a uniform climate but, in general, is quite wet year round.

FLORA & FAUNA

Colombia claims to have more plant and animal species per unit area than any other country in the world. Its variety of flora and fauna is second only to Brazil's, even though Colombia is seven times smaller than its neighbour. This abundance reflects Colombia's numerous climatic zones and microclimates, which have created plenty of different habitats and biological islands in which wildlife has evolved independently.

Colombia is home to the jaguar, ocelot, peccary, tapir, deer, armadillo, spectacled bear and numerous species of monkey, to mention just a few of the 300-odd species of mammals. There are more than 1550 recorded species of birds, ranging from the huge Andean condor to the tiny hummingbird. There is also abundant marine life in Colombia's extensive river systems and along its two coastlines.

Colombia's flora is equally impressive and includes some 3000 species of orchid alone. The national herbariums have classified over 130,000 plants, including many endemic species. This richness is still not the whole picture, because large areas of the country, such as inaccessible parts of the Amazon, have never been investigated by botanists.

NATIONAL PARKS

Colombia has 34 national parks and a dozen other state-run nature reserves. Their combined area constitutes 7.9% of the country's territory. This figure may sound impressive but, unfortunately, there have never been sufficient funds or personnel to properly guard the parks. In many areas, simply decreeing a national park has not eliminated colonisation, logging, ranching, hunting or fishing.

Only a dozen parks provide accommodation choices and food facilities; several more offer only camping. The remaining parks have no tourist amenities at all and some, especially those in remote regions, are virtually inaccessible.

There are also about 100 private nature reserves, administered by individual proprietors, rural communities, foundations and other nongovernment organisations. They are usually small, but often contain an interesting sample of habitat. See Useful Organisations in the Facts for the Visitor section for more information.

GOVERNMENT

A new constitution came into effect in July 1991. The president is directly elected for a four-year term and cannot be re-elected. The Congress consists of two houses, the 102-seat Senate and the 165-seat Chamber of Representatives. The members are also elected in a direct vote for a four-year term. The cabinet is appointed by the president.

Administratively, the country is divided into 32 departments, plus Bogotá's Special District.

ECONOMY

Colombia has long had one of the steadiest economies on the continent. Despite its social and political problems, the economy has grown consistently for the past two decades, and the growth rate now stands at an admirable 5% annually. Colombia managed to avoid the debt crises and bouts of hyper-inflation which plagued most of its neighbours in the 1980s.

Colombia is the world's second-largest coffee producer, after Brazil. Other main agricultural products are sugar (with production concentrated in the Cali region), cotton and bananas. Thanks to the diverse climate, there is a variety of other crops, such as rice, maize, potatoes, tobacco, barley, beans and cocoa.

Mineral resources are plentiful but underexploited, and the extent of deposits has still not been thoroughly explored. Coal mining has become one of the most dynamic sectors of the economy, as the country possesses the largest deposits of coal in Latin America.

With the discovery of new oilfields in Casanare in the early 1990s (thought to be the biggest new fields found in the world in the last 10 years), Colombia has joined the ranks of the world's oil-exporting nations, a fact which may have significant repercussions on the overall economy. The country also has deposits of gold, silver, platinum, nickel, copper and iron, to list just a few. It produces half of the world's emeralds, and Colombian stones are considered to be the best.

Industry has grown notably in recent decades, mainly in the fields of petrochemicals, metallurgy, car assembly (Renault,

Chevrolet, Mazda), textiles, domestic electrical appliances, and food and agriculture.

And then, behind the official economic statistics, there are the illegal exports of drugs, principally cocaine, which account for a significant portion of the GNP. Cocaine alone earns an estimated US$5 billion annually, US$3 billion of which is thought to be re-invested in Colombia. The country is also the world's third-largest producer of marijuana. The new illegal export is heroin, which is quickly making inroads into northern markets, pushing out the traditional Asian suppliers.

POPULATION & PEOPLE

By 1995, the population had reached 37.5 million, making Colombia the second-most populous country in South America, after Brazil. Population growth is about 2%, which is among the highest rates in Latin America.

Population density varies a great deal across the country. The western half, consisting of the Andean region and the coast, is home to over 90% of the total population.

About 75% of people are of mixed blood, comprising 50 to 55% *mestizos* (of European-Indian blood) and 15 to 20% *mulatos* (of European-African blood). There are also some *zambos* (of African-Indian blood).

Whites, mainly descendants of the Spaniards, constitute about 20% of the population and live almost entirely in the urban centres. Blacks represent about 4% of the population and are most numerous on the Caribbean and Pacific coasts.

Indians number between 300,000 and 400,000, representing roughly 1% of the population. This number comprises over 50 Indian groups belonging to several linguistic families.

ARTS
Architecture

The most outstanding example of pre-Columbian urban planning is the Ciudad Perdida (Lost City) of the Tayrona Indians in the Sierra Nevada de Santa Marta. Although the dwellings haven't survived, the stone structures, including a complex network of terraces, paths and stairways, remain in remarkably good shape.

After the arrival of the Spaniards, bricks and tiles became the main construction materials. The colonial towns followed rigid standards laid down by the Spanish Crown. They were constructed on a grid plan, centred around the Plaza Mayor (main square). This pattern was applied both during and after the colonial period, and is the dominant feature of Colombia's cities, towns and villages.

Spain's strong Catholic tradition led to the construction of numerous churches and convents in the colony – the central areas of Cartagena, Tunja, Bogotá, Popayán and Pasto are good examples. Unlike in Mexico or Peru, colonial churches in Colombia have rather sober exteriors, but their interiors are often richly decorated.

In the 19th century, despite independence, the architecture continued to be predominantly Spanish in style. Modern architectural trends only began to appear in Colombia after WW II. This process accelerated during the 1960s when city skyscrapers appeared.

Visual Arts

The colonial period was dominated by Spanish religious art, and although the paintings and sculptures of this era were generally executed by local artists, they reflected the Spanish trends of the day. With the arrival of independence, visual arts departed from strictly religious themes, but it was not until the revolution in European painting in the early 20th century that Colombian artists began to experiment and produce original art.

Among the most distinguished modern painters and sculptors are Pedro Nel Gómez, known mainly for his murals but also for his watercolours, oils and sculptures; Luis Alberto Acuña, a painter and sculptor who used motifs from pre-Columbian art; Alejandro Obregón, a painter tending to abstract forms; Edgar Negret, an abstract sculptor; Rodrigo Arenas Betancur, Colombia's most famous monument-maker; and Fernando

Botero, the most internationally renowned Colombian artist, whose somewhat ironic style in painting and sculpture is easily recognisable by the characteristic fatness of the figures.

Literature

During the independence period and up to WW II, Colombia produced few internationally acclaimed writers other than José Asunción Silva (1865-96), perhaps the country's best poet, considered the precursor of modernism in Latin America.

A postwar literary boom thrust at least a dozen great Latin American authors into the international sphere, including the Colombian Gabriel García Márquez (born 1928). His novel *One Hundred Years of Solitude*, published in 1967, immediately became a worldwide best seller. It mixed myths, dreams and reality, and amazed readers with a new form of expression which critics called *realismo mágico* (magic realism). In 1982, García Márquez won the Nobel Prize for literature.

In his most recent work, *Noticia de un Secuestro*, which appeared in May 1996, García Márquez returned to journalism, where his career began. This book relates a series of kidnappings ordered by Medellín Cartel boss, Pablo Escobar. The combination of the author's literary talents and Colombia's action-movie-like modern history makes the book a fascinating if terrifying read.

Music

In very broad terms, Colombia can be divided into four musical zones: the two coasts, the Andean region and Los Llanos. All the rhythms described below have corresponding dance forms.

The Caribbean coast vibrates with hot African-related rhythms, such as the *cumbia*, *mapalé* and *porro*, which have many similarities with other Caribbean musical forms. The music of the Pacific coast, such as the *currulao*, is more purely African, with strong use of drums, but tinged with Spanish influences.

Colombian Andean music has been strongly influenced by Spanish rhythms and instruments, and differs notably from the Indian music of the Peruvian and Bolivian highlands. Among the typical forms are the *bambuco*, *pasillo* and *torbellino*, all of which are instrumental and use predominantly string instruments.

The music of Los Llanos, *música llanera*, is sung and usually accompanied by a harp, *cuatro* (a sort of four-string guitar) and maracas. It has much in common with the music of the Venezuelan Llanos.

Apart from these traditional forms, two newer musical styles have conquered large parts of the country. They are the *salsa*, which spread throughout the Caribbean in the 1960s, and the *vallenato*, which emanated from La Guajira and Cesar. The latter is based on the European accordion.

RELIGION

The great majority of Colombians are Roman Catholic. Other creeds are officially permitted but their numbers are small. However, over the past decade there has been a proliferation of various Protestant congregations, which have succeeded in capturing some three million former Catholics.

Many Indian groups adopted the Catholic faith, sometimes incorporating some of their traditional beliefs. Only a few indigenous communities, particularly those living in isolation, still practise their ancient native religions.

On the islands of San Andrés and Providencia, the Protestant faith is still practised – a sign of their English colonial past.

LANGUAGE

The official language is Spanish, and apart from some remote Indian groups, all inhabitants speak it. On San Andrés and Providencia, English is still widely used.

The Spanish spoken in Colombia is generally clear and easy to understand, though there are regional variations which Colombians easily recognise. For the visitor, these differences won't be so noticeable, except for the *costeños*, the inhabitants of the Caribbean coast, who speak quickly and are more difficult to understand.

Facts for the Visitor

VISAS & EMBASSIES

Only nationals of China, the Dominican Republic, Haiti, India, Iran, Iraq, Nicaragua and Taiwan need a visa to enter Colombia. Others will simply get an entry stamp in their passport from DAS (the security police who are also responsible for immigration) upon arrival at any international airport or land border crossing. DAS will note on the stamp the period you can stay in the country. The maximum allowed is 90 days, but you may receive only 60 or 30 days. If you want to stay for up to three months, politely request this *before* anything is written in your passport. Otherwise you will have to apply for an extension, which costs money.

Officially, an onward ticket is required, but this is no longer enforced. Keep in mind the golden rule: the better your appearance, the less hassle you are likely to get.

If you receive a 90-day stay at the border, you are entitled to one 30-day extension. If you receive less, you're allowed two or three 30-day extensions, up to a total of 120 days (including your original stay). Extensions can be obtained from DAS in any departmental capital, and cost US$25 each. Apply shortly before the expiry of your allowed stay, as the extension runs from the day it is stamped in your passport.

Colombian Embassies Abroad

Colombia has embassies or consulates in all neighbouring countries, and also in:

Australia
101 Northbourne Ave, Turner, ACT 2601 (☎ (06) 257- 2027)
5th floor, 220 Pacific Hwy, Crows Nest, NSW 2065 (☎ (02) 9955 0311, 9922 5597)
Canada
1010 Sherbrooke West, Suite 420, Montreal, Quebec H3A 2R7 (☎ (514) 849-4852, 849-2929)
1 Dundas St West, Suite 2108, Toronto, Ontario M5G 1Z3 (☎ (416) 977-0098, 977-0475)
France
12 Rue de Berri, Paris 75008 (☎ 01 42 89 15 94)

Germany
Friedrich-Wilhelm Strasse 35, 5300 Bonn 1 (☎ (0228) 23 42 91)
Clara Zetkin Strasse 89, 10117 Berlin (☎ (030) 2 29 26 69)
UK
Suite 10, 140 Park Lane, London W1Y 3DF (☎ (0171) 495-4233)
USA
2118 Leroy Place, Washington, DC (☎ (202) 387-8338)
280 Aragon Ave, Coral Gables, Miami, FL 33134 (☎ (305) 444-5084, 441-1235)
10 East 46th St, New York, NY 10017 (☎ (212) 949-9898)

Foreign Embassies in Colombia

For foreign diplomatic representatives in Colombia, see the Bogotá section. If yours is not listed, ask at the tourist office in Bogotá or consult the telephone directory.

CUSTOMS

On arrival, the duty-free allowance is 200 cigarettes or 50 cigars or 500 grams of tobacco, and two bottles of wine or spirits. You are also allowed to bring in still, cine and video cameras plus accessories, a personal computer, a portable radio/cassette recorder, camping equipment, sporting accessories etc – in effect, one item of each class.

Customs procedures are usually a formality, both on entering and on leaving the country, and your luggage is likely to pass through with only a cursory glance. However, thorough checks occasionally occur, more often at the airports than at the land borders, and they can be very exhaustive, with a body search included. They aren't looking for your extra Walkman, but for drugs. Trying to smuggle dope through the border is the best way to see what the inside of a Colombian jail looks like, for quite a few years!

On departure, you may be asked for receipts for any emeralds, antiques, and articles of gold and platinum purchased in Colombia.

MONEY

There is no black market in Colombia, and

you will probably not get a better exchange rate than that offered by the bank. Given this, and the country's hazards, it's better to carry travellers' cheques (American Express cheques are by far the most popular and easy to change) than cash, though some US dollars in small notes may be useful if you get stuck without pesos somewhere off the road. A Visa card, however, is the most useful way to carry money.

Currency

The official currency is the *peso* ($). There are 10, 20, 50, 100, 200 and 500-peso coins, and paper notes of 500, 1000, 2000, 5000 and 10,000 pesos. Two kinds of 5000 and 10,000-peso bill are in circulation – both valid – but the old kind is being gradually withdrawn from the market. Forged notes do exist, so watch exactly what you get; forgeries are generally of poor quality and easy to recognise.

Exchange Rates

Approximate official exchange rates at July 1996 were as follows:

Australia	A$1	=	845 pesos
Canada	C$1	=	790 pesos
France	FF1	=	208 pesos
Germany	DM1	=	704 pesos
Japan	¥100	=	992 pesos
New Zealand	NZ$1	=	732 pesos
United Kingdom	UK£1	=	1660 pesos
USA	US$1	=	1079 pesos

Banks change travellers' cheques at rates some 2 to 5% lower than the official rate, and usually pay about a further 1 to 3% less for cash. Exchange rates vary from bank to bank, so shop around. Some banks charge a commission for changing cheques.

The depreciation of the peso against the US dollar is roughly 20% per year.

Currency Exchange

Some banks change cash and/or travellers' cheques, but others don't. Some branches of a bank will change your money while other branches of the same bank will refuse. This seems to vary constantly from bank to bank, city to city, day to day, and can be further complicated by a myriad of local factors, eg the bank may have reached its daily limit of foreign exchange.

All banks in Colombia (except for those in Bogotá – see that section for details) are open Monday to Thursday from 8 to 11.30 am and 2 to 4 pm, and on Friday from 8 to 11.30 am and 2 to 4.30 pm. However, they usually offer foreign exchange services within limited hours, which may mean only one or two hours daily; your best chances are in the morning.

Your passport is needed in any banking operation. Some banks will also request a photocopy of your passport (two pages are required, the one with your photo and personal details and the one with the entry stamp), while other banks won't change your travellers' cheques before sighting the purchase receipt for the cheques. Finally, as the banks are often crowded and there's much paperwork involved in changing money, the process may be time-consuming – set aside up to an hour.

The banks which are most likely to exchange your cash and/or travellers' cheques include Banco Anglo Colombiano, Banco Unión Colombiano, Banco Industrial Colombiano, Banco Sudameris Colombia, Banco Popular and Banco Comercial Antioqueño.

You can also change cash (but rarely travellers' cheques) in *casas de cambio* (authorised money exchange offices) which are found in most major cities and the border towns. These are open weekdays till 5 or 6 pm, and usually till noon on Saturday. They deal mainly with US dollars and offer rates comparable to, or slightly lower than, the banks. The whole operation takes seconds.

You can change cash dollars on the street, but it's not recommended. The only street money markets worth considering are those at the borders, where there may be simply no alternative. There are moneychangers at every land border crossing.

The Tierra Mar Aire (TMA) travel agency, which has offices in major cities, represents

American Express. It doesn't change travellers' cheques, but is the place to go if your cheques are lost or stolen.

Credit Cards

You can use your credit card for car rental, air tickets, and in most top-class hotels and restaurants. Plastic money is also becoming popular for purchasing goods and payment for services in many other commercial establishments. More importantly, getting an advance on credit cards at the bank is much faster than changing travellers' cheques, and the banks will usually do it during their full opening hours. Furthermore, you get more money on cards because these transactions are calculated on the basis of the official exchange rate.

Visa is by far the best card for Colombia, and most banks will give advance payments on it. MasterCard is the next best, but it's only useful for advances at Banco Industrial Colombiano and Banco de Occidente. Other cards are of limited use.

There are an increasing number of *cajeros automáticos* (automatic teller machines) which accept Visa and MasterCard, and will pay you pesos.

WHEN TO GO

The most pleasant time to visit Colombia is in the dry season, but there are no major obstacles to general sightseeing in the wet period. Most Colombians take their holidays between late December and mid-January, so transport is more crowded and hotels tend to fill up faster at this time.

TOURIST OFFICES

The national tourist information board, the Corporación Nacional de Turismo (CNT), has only a few outlets around the country. Municipal tourist information bureaus fill the vacuum, with varying degrees of success. In some cities they are helpful and knowledgeable, in others less so. By and large, the staff are friendly but few of them speak English.

USEFUL ORGANISATIONS
National Parks

National parks are administered by the Unidad Administrativa Especial del Sistema de Parques Nacionales, a department of the Ministry of the Environment. The central office is in Bogotá, and there are five regional offices: in Bucaramanga, Cali, Medellín, Popayán and Santa Marta. If you plan on visiting the parks, you must (in theory, at least) first visit an office of the Unidad to pay the entrance fee and for accommodation (if the park offers this facility). The Bogotá office handles all parks, whereas subsidiary offices only service the parks in their regions.

Park entrance fees are different for Colombians and foreigners, and are quite stiff for budget travellers. The fee to most parks is US$10 (US$4 for Colombians), accommodation costs roughly US$15 per bed and camping is US$20 to US$35 per tent per night. The staff of some parks have been known to let foreigners in without prior payment, and charge them the lower fees Colombians pay. Check for news with other travellers.

Private Nature Reserves

Growing ecological awareness has led to the creation of an increasing number of privately run nature reserves; as of early 1996 they numbered about 100. They are scattered countrywide, although most are in the Andean region. Some reserves offer tourist facilities, including accommodation, food and guides, and may be an interesting (and cheaper) alternative to national parks. The reserves are affiliated to the Red de Reservas Naturales de la Sociedad Civil, an association based in Cali (see that section for further details).

HOLIDAYS

The following days are observed as public holidays in Colombia:

1 January
 La Circuncisión (Circumcision)
6 January*
 Los Reyes Magos (Epiphany)

COLOMBIA

19 March*
    San José (St Joseph)
March/April (Easter, dates vary)
    Jueves Santo (Maundy Thursday)
    Viernes Santo (Good Friday)
1 May
    Día del Trabajo (Labour Day)
May (date varies)*
    La Ascensión del Señor (Ascension)
May/June (date varies)*
    Corpus Cristi (Corpus Christi)
June (date varies)*
    Sagrado Corazón de Jesús (Sacred Heart)
29 June*
    San Pedro y San Pablo (St Peter & St Paul)
20 July
    Día de la Independencia (Independence Day)
7 August
    Batalla de Boyacá (Battle of Boyacá)
15 August*
    La Asunción de Nuestra Señora (Assumption)
12 October*
    Diá de la Raza (Discovery of America)
1 November*
    Todos los Santos (All Saints' Day)
11 November*
    Independencia de Cartagena (Independence of
    Cartagena)
8 December
    Inmaculada Concepción (Immaculate Concep-
    tion)
25 December
    Navidad (Christmas Day)

When the dates marked with an asterisk do
not fall on a Monday, the holiday is moved
to the following Monday to make a three-day
long weekend, referred to as the *puente*.

SPECIAL EVENTS

Colombians love fiestas. A tourist guide of
events lists over 200 of them, ranging from
small, local affairs to international festivals
lasting several days. Most of the celebrations
are regional, and the most interesting ones
are listed in the sections on individual places.

POST & COMMUNICATIONS
Post

The Colombian postal service is operated by
two companies, Avianca and Adpostal. Both
cover national and international post, but
Avianca only deals with air mail, so if you
want to ship a parcel overseas, you need
Adpostal.

Both operators seem to be efficient and
reliable and have similar air-mail rates for
letters, postcards and packages. The domestic rates are reasonably cheap but
international air mail is fairly expensive. The
Adpostal surface-mail rates are far cheaper.

The poste restante system is operated by
Avianca. You can receive poste restante
letters in any city where Avianca has a post
office, but not all provincial offices do a good
job. The most reliable office is in Bogotá.
The service costs US$0.40 per letter.

Telephone

The telephone system is controlled by
Telecom, which has offices even in the most
remote villages. In major cities, offices are
open late; in rural areas, they tend to close
earlier. The system is largely automated for
both domestic and international calls.

Public telephones dot the streets of the
larger cities, but many are out of order. Most
take coins, although newly installed telephones accept phonecards *(tarjeta
telefónica)*. Phonecards can be used for international, intercity and local calls, so it's
worth buying one (from a Telecom office) if
you are using telephones frequently.

You can call direct to just about anywhere
in Colombia. Area codes for the major cities
and some other places detailed in this chapter
are listed in individual city sections.

The international service is expensive.
Reverse-charge (collect) calls *(llamadas de
pago revertido)* are possible to most major
countries. The country code for Colombia is
57. If you are dialling a telephone number in
Colombia from abroad, drop the initial '9' in
the area code.

TIME

All of Colombia lies within the same time
zone, five hours behind GMT/UTC. There's
no daylight-saving time.

ELECTRICITY

Electricity is 110V, 60 Hz AC throughout the
country. Plugs are of the flat two-pin American type.

COLOMBIA

WEIGHTS & MEASURES
The metric system is commonly used, except for petrol which is measured in US gallons.

BOOKS
For more detailed travel information, there is Lonely Planet's *Colombia – a travel survival kit*, 2nd edition.

John Hemming's *The Search for El Dorado* provides a captivating insight into the Spanish conquest of Venezuela and Colombia. The well-balanced *Colombia: Portrait of Unity and Diversity* by Harvey F Kline is a general overview of Colombian history.

Titles covering Colombia's modern history include *The Politics of Colombia* by Robert H Dix, *Colombia: Inside the Labyrinth* by Jenny Pearce, *The Politics of Coalition Rule in Colombia* by Jonathan Hartlyn and *The Making of Modern Colombia: A Nation in Spite of Itself* by David Bushnell.

For an insight into the drug cartels, read *Kings of Cocaine* by Guy Gugliotta & Jeff Leen. This book reads like a thriller.

The Fruit Palace by Charles Nicholl is an excellent introduction to Colombia's crazy reality. It's a journalist's account of what was intended to be an investigation into cocaine trafficking in Colombia. The author did not get to the heart of the cartels, but he provides a vivid picture of the country.

Finally, you shouldn't set off for Colombia before reading Gabriel García Márquez's *One Hundred Years of Solitude*. Although generally considered a highly imaginative work, the novel is solidly based on acute observation and helps enormously to understand Colombian culture, mentality and philosophy of life.

MAPS
Folded national road maps are produced by several publishers and distributed through bookshops. *Mapa vial de Colombia* (scale 1:2,000,000), published by Rodríguez in Bogotá, is probably the best.

The widest selection of maps of Colombia is produced and sold by the Instituto Geográfico Agustín Codazzi (IGAC). This is the government mapping body, and has its head office in Bogotá (see that section).

MEDIA
All major cities have a daily newspaper. Bogotá's leading newspapers, *El Tiempo* and *El Espectador*, have nationwide distribution. Both have relatively good sections on national and international news, culture, sport and economics. *Semana* is the biggest national weekly magazine. It covers local and international affairs, and has an extensive section on culture.

Over 500 FM and AM radio stations operate in Colombia. They mainly broadcast music programmes. There are three nationwide and four regional TV channels. Satellite TV has boomed in Bogotá and, to a lesser extent, in other major cities.

HEALTH
A yellow fever vaccination certificate is required if you arrive from an infected area; no other vaccinations are necessary, though some are recommended. In particular, guard against malaria and hepatitis.

The pharmacy network is extensive, and there are *droguerías* or *farmacias* even in small towns. In the cities, they are usually well stocked. Many drugs are available without prescription, but always check the expiry date.

In most of the larger cities, the water can be safely drunk from the tap, though it is best to avoid it if possible. Outside these areas, drink boiled or bottled water.

Travel in Colombia is almost always up and down, from humid tropical lowlands to cold, windy highlands. When travelling by bus, you can experience dramatic climate changes within a few hours, so have appropriate clothes handy to avoid being frozen solid.

DANGERS & ANNOYANCES
It is not pleasant news, but Colombia definitely isn't the safest of countries, and you should be careful at all times. The biggest

COLOMBIA

potential dangers are being ripped off or robbed. The problem is more serious in the major cities, Bogotá, Medellín and Cali being the worst.

Keep your passport and money next to your skin and your camera inside your bag, and don't wear jewellery or expensive watches. If you can, leave your money and valuables somewhere safe before walking around the city streets. Always carry your passport with you, as document checks on the streets are not uncommon. If stopped by a plain-clothes man who claims to be from the secret police, check his documents first. If still in doubt, call any uniformed police officer.

Robbery can be very dangerous. Armed hold-ups become more common every year, mainly in slum *barrios* of the large cities. Avoid dubious-looking areas, especially if you are alone and particularly at night. If you are accosted by robbers, it is best to give them what they are after.

Be exceptionally careful about drugs – never carry them. The police and army can be extremely thorough in searching travellers, often looking for a nice fat bribe. Don't buy dope on the street; the vendors may well be setting you up for the police. There have been reports of drugs being planted on travellers, so keep your eyes open.

Burundanga is more bad news. It is a drug obtained from a species of tree widespread in Colombia. Burundanga is used by thieves to render a victim unconscious. It can be put into sweets, cigarettes, chewing gum, spirits, beer – virtually any kind of food or drink – and it doesn't have any particular taste or smell. The main effects are loss of will and memory, and sleepiness which can last from a few hours to several days. An overdose can be fatal. Think twice before accepting a cigarette from a stranger or a drink from a new 'friend'.

Finally, keep an eye on guerrilla movements, so as not to get caught in the crossfire. The local press is your best source of information. Unfortunately, certain regions of Colombia (parts of the Amazon Basin, Los Llanos, Urabá and the Sierra Nevada de Santa Marta) are becoming off limits for secure travel.

ACTIVITIES

With its amazing geographical diversity, Colombia offers fascinating and adventurous opportunities for hiking, though certain regions are infiltrated by guerrillas and should be avoided. Some national parks and private reserves have trails and these are among the best for hiking and wildlife watching.

Colombia's coral reefs have prompted swift development of the scuba-diving market. The main centres are San Andrés, Providencia, Santa Marta and Cartagena, each of which has several diving schools offering courses (NAUI and PADI), dives, equipment for sale and rental etc.

Other possible activities include mountaineering, rock climbing, windsurfing, canoeing, fishing, caving and even bathing in mud volcanoes (see the Around Cartagena section).

HIGHLIGHTS

These include Ciudad Perdida, San Agustín and Tierradentro (archaeological sites); Cartagena and Popayán (colonial cities); Mompós, Barichara and Villa de Leyva (small colonial towns); and the Museo del Oro in Bogotá (arguably the world's best gold museum).

ACCOMMODATION

There is a constellation of places to stay in Colombia, from large cities to the smallest villages. Accommodation appears under a variety of names including *hotel, residencias, hospedaje, pensión, hostería, hospedería, estadero, apartamentos, amoblados* and *posada*. Residencias and hospedaje are the most common names for budget places. A hotel generally suggests a place of a higher standard, or at least a higher price, though the distinction is often academic.

On the whole, residencias and hospedajes are unremarkable places without any style or atmosphere. This is particularly true in the cities, where the budget places are often poor or overpriced, or both. Hardboard partitions instead of walls are not unusual, making noise and security a problem.

Some budget hotel rooms have a toilet and shower attached. Note that cheap hotel plumbing can't cope with toilet paper, so throw it in the box or basket which is usually provided.

In hot places (ie the lowland areas), a ceiling fan or table fan is often provided. Always check the fan before you take a room. On the other hand, above 2500 metres, where the nights can be chilly, look to see how many blankets you have, and check the hot water if they claim to have it.

By and large, residencias (even the cheapest) provide a sheet and some sort of cover (another sheet or blankets, depending on the temperature). Most also give you a towel, a small piece of soap and a roll of toilet paper. The cheapies cost around US$3 to US$6 for a single room, US$5 to US$10 for a double.

Many hospedajes have *matrimonios*, rooms with a double bed intended for couples. A matrimonio is often cheaper than a double, and only slightly more expensive than a single (or even the same price). Travelling as a couple considerably reduces the cost of accommodation.

Some residencias offer a deposit facility, which usually means that they can put your gear into their own room, as there are no other safe places. Better hotels usually have the reception desk open round the clock, with proper facilities to safeguard your things. Remember that a hotel (no matter what hotel it is) is almost always safer than the street of a big city at night.

There are almost no gringo hotels in Colombia. Except for a handful of places which have gained popularity among travellers, the rest are straight Colombian hotels where you are unlikely to meet foreigners.

Brothels are not uncommon in Colombia, so check before booking – these places are usually easy to recognise by the hordes of *putas* (prostitutes) at the entrance or on the closest street corner.

Another kind of accommodation, very common in Colombia, are love hotels. These places are designed for couples and rent rooms by the hour or for a full night. Many cheap residencias double as love hotels. Intentionally or not, you are likely to find yourself in such a place from time to time. This is actually not a problem, as love hotels are usually clean, as safe as any other and do not allow prostitutes.

Colombia has just two genuine youth hostels, in Bogotá and Cali (see those sections for details).

Camping is not popular in Colombia, and there are only a handful of camp sites in the country. Camping wild is theoretically possible outside the urban centres but you should be extremely careful. Try to pitch your tent under someone's protection (next to a *campesino* house or in the grounds of a holiday centre), after getting permission from the owners, guards or management. Only far away from human settlement is camping relatively safe, such as in the mountains. Even there, you should never leave your tent or gear unattended.

FOOD

Colombian cuisine is varied and regional. Among the most typical regional dishes are:

Ajiaco – a soup with chicken and three varieties of potato, served with corn and capers; a *bogotano* speciality

Bandeja paisa – a typical Antioquian dish consisting of ground beef, a sausage *(chorizo)*, red beans *(fríjoles)*, rice, fried green banana *(plátano)*, a fried egg, a piece of fried salt pork *(chicharrón)* and avocado; it can be found almost everywhere

Chocolate santafereño – a cup of hot chocolate accompanied by a piece of cheese and bread (traditionally, you put the cheese into the chocolate); another bogotano speciality

Cuy – grilled guinea pig, typical of Nariño

Hormiga culona – large fried ants; probably the most exotic Colombian speciality, unique to Santander

Lechona – a pig carcass, stuffed with its own meat, rice and dried peas and then baked in an oven; a speciality of Tolima

Tamales – chopped pork with rice and vegetables folded in a maize dough, wrapped in banana leaves and steamed; there are plenty of regional varieties

Variety does not, unfortunately, apply to the basic set meal, the *comida corriente*, which is the principal diet of the majority of Colombians eating out. It is a two-course meal consisting of *sopa* (soup) and *bandeja* or *seco* (main course), and usually includes a *sobremesa* (a bottled fizzy drink or a juice). At lunch time (from midday to 2 pm), it is called *almuerzo*. At dinner time (after 6 pm), it becomes *comida*, but it is in fact identical to lunch. Despite some local additions, it's almost exactly the same across the length and breadth of the country.

The almuerzos and comidas are the staple, sometimes the only, offering of the countless budget restaurants. Some serve them continuously from noon until they close at night, but most only serve them during lunch time and, less often, at dinner time. The comida corriente is the cheapest way to fill yourself up, costing between US$1 and US$2.50 – roughly half the price of any à-la-carte main course.

The barbecued chicken restaurants (there are plenty of them) are a good alternative to the comida. Half a chicken with potatoes will cost around US$3 to US$4. Another budget option, particularly in smaller towns and villages, is the market, where the food is usually fresh, tasty and cooked on the spot.

Western food is readily available, either in fast-food outlets (including McDonald's and Pizza Hut) or in the up-market restaurants. Over the last decade there has been a noticeable trend towards vegetarian food, and most major cities have a choice of budget vegetarian restaurants.

Colombia has an amazing variety of fruits, some of which are to be found only in particular regions of the country. You should try *guanábana*, *lulo*, *curuba*, *zapote*, *mamoncillo*, *uchuva*, *feijoa*, *granadilla*, *maracuyá*, *tomate de árbol*, *borojó*, *mamey* and *tamarindo*, to list just a few.

DRINKS

Coffee is undoubtedly the number one drink and almost a ritual. *Tinto* (a small cup of black coffee) is served everywhere. Other coffee drinks are *perico* or *pintado*, a small

milk coffee, and *café con leche*, which is larger and uses more milk.

Tea is of poor quality and not very popular. On the other hand, the *aromáticas* – herb teas made with various plants like *cidrón* (citrus leaves), *yerbabuena* (mint) and *manzanilla* (camomile) – are very cheap and good. *Agua de panela* (unrefined sugar melted in hot water) is very tasty with lemon.

Beer is popular, cheap and generally not bad. This can't be said about Colombian wine, which is best avoided.

Aguardiente is the local alcoholic spirit, flavoured with anise and produced by several companies throughout the country under their own brand names. *Ron* (rum) is another popular local spirit, particularly on the Caribbean coast.

In some regions, mostly in rural areas, you will find *guarapo* and *chicha*, which are low (or not so low) in alcohol. They are homemade by the fermentation of fruit or maize in sugar or panela water.

Getting There & Away

Sitting on the north-western edge of the continent, Colombia is a convenient gateway to South America from the USA and Central America, and even from Europe.

Colombia still, technically, has an onward ticket requirement, which means that you are formally not allowed into the country if you don't have a ticket out. This is practically never enforced by immigration officials, either at international airports or at land border crossings.

AIR

Colombia is not a good place to buy international air tickets. Airfares to Europe and Australia are expensive and there are hardly any attractive discounted tickets available. Flights to the USA are cheaper, but discounts are still few and far between. Furthermore, if you buy an international air ticket in Colombia, you pay 21% tax (10.5% on a return ticket) on top of the fare. The airfares given in this chapter don't include this tax.

The airport tax on international flights out of Colombia is US$20 if you have stayed in the country up to 60 days, and US$40 if you've stayed longer.

To/From Europe

The cheapest flights are from London – tickets to Bogotá start at around £220 one way, £420 to £500 return.

To/From North America

Avianca offers discount return flights from New York and Miami to Colombia. Other options to check include the New York/ Miami-San José-Barranquilla flight with Lacsa, and the New York/Miami-Caracas-Bogotá flight with Avensa.

Zuliana de Aviación, a little-known Venezuelan carrier, flies from Miami to Medellín or Bogotá for US$255 (US$447 one-year return).

To/From Central America

Colombia has regular flight connections with most Central American capitals. It usually works out cheaper to go via the Colombian island of San Andrés and then fly to the Colombian mainland by a domestic flight. See the San Andrés section later in this chapter for details.

Several carriers, including Copa, Avianca/ Sam and Aces, operate direct flights between Panama and Colombia. One-way fares out of Panama City are: Medellín US$123, Cartagena US$123, Bogotá US$156 and Cali US$169. Discount fares are available on return flights.

To/From Ecuador

There are over a dozen regular flights a week between Quito and Bogotá, operated by Avianca, Ecuatoriana, Viasa and Servivensa (US$161 one way, US$258 30-day return). Cheaper connections between the two countries include the Esmeraldas-Cali and Tulcán-Cali flights, both serviced twice weekly by Intercontinental/Saeta (both US$77).

To/From Venezuela

There are several flights daily between Caracas and Bogotá, with Viasa, Avianca, Servivensa and a few other carriers. The regular one-way fare is US$204; a discount return ticket, valid for 30 days, originating from either end, costs US$263.

Other connections between Venezuela and Colombia include Caracas-Cartagena with Viasa (US$180, US$238 30-day return), Caracas-Barranquilla with Lacsa (US$172, US$213 30-day return), Maracaibo-Bogotá or Medellín with Zuliana de Aviación (US$100, US$150 one-year return), Santo Domingo-Bogotá with Servivensa (US$50, US$100 one-year return) and San Antonio del Táchira-Medellín with Servivensa (US$50, US$100 one-year return).

LAND

To/From Central America

The Darién Gap very effectively separates Colombia from Panama. There are no roads through, and it will be a while before one is built to fill the missing part of the Carretera Panamericana (Pan-American Highway). There are basically two ways to pass the Darién Gap: along the northern coast or through the jungle. See the introductory Getting There & Away chapter for details.

To/From Ecuador

Almost all travellers use the Carretera Panamericana border point passing through Tulcán and Ipiales. See the Ipiales section in this chapter and the Tulcán section in the Ecuador chapter for more information.

Another, rather adventurous way to get to Colombia passes the fringe of the Amazon, through Lago Agrio and San Miguel. From Lago Agrio, buses regularly run to La Punta, on the Ecuador border (US$1, one hour). From there, take a canoe to San Miguel in Colombia (US$3, half an hour). There are about 10 buses or *chivas* daily from San Miguel to Puerto Asís (US$5, five hours). The region around Puerto Asís is partly controlled by guerrillas and is so unsafe that the DAS office was closed down and moved to Mocoa, where you get the entry stamp in your passport (check to see whether the Puerto Asís office has reopened). From Puerto Asís, there are several buses daily to Mocoa (US$5, four hours), continuing to Pasto by the rough, dangerous, but extremely spectacular mountain roads across the Cordillera de los Andes.

One more way to get to Colombia is by boat along the Pacific coast from San Lorenzo or Limones (both in Ecuador) to Tumaco (Colombia).

To/From Venezuela

There are four border crossings between Colombia and Venezuela. By far the most popular with travellers is the route via San Antonio del Táchira and Cúcuta, on the main Caracas-Bogotá road. See the Cúcuta section in this chapter and the San Antonio del Táchira section in the Venezuela chapter for details.

Another entry point to Colombia is Paraguachón, on the Maracaibo-Maicao road. This may be your route if you plan on heading directly to the Colombian Caribbean coast. There are buses and shared taxis between Maracaibo and Maicao. Your passport is stamped by both Venezuelan and Colombian officials in Paraguachón, on the border. You'll find further details on transport in the Maracaibo section of the Venezuela chapter.

The third possible route leads through the Orinoquia, from either Puerto Páez or Puerto Ayacucho (both in Venezuela) to Puerto Carreño (in Colombia). See the Puerto Ayacucho section of the Venezuela chapter for details.

Finally, you can reach Colombia via Los Llanos, from El Amparo de Apure (Venezuela) to Arauca (Colombia), then continue overland or by air farther into Colombia. Note that the Arauca region has serious guerrilla problems. This route is rarely used by travellers.

RIVER

There is an official border crossing between Colombia and Peru/Brazil at Leticia, in the far south-eastern corner of the Colombian Amazon. Leticia is reached by boat along the Amazon River from Iquitos (Peru) and Manaus (Brazil). For details, see the Leticia section in this chapter.

SEA

There's a good ferry service between Colón (Panama) and Cartagena. See the Cartagena section for details.

Getting Around

AIR

Colombia has a well-developed airline system and a dense network of domestic flights. Main passenger airlines include Avianca, Sam, Aces, Aires, Intercontinental de Aviación, AeroRepública and Satena, most of which also have international flights. There are also a number of small airlines, which operate over limited areas, as well as several cargo carriers.

Airfares differ between the carriers. Avianca and Sam (which operate jointly) keep their regular fares high, but offer a limited number of discounted fares called *tarifas supereconómicas*. AeroRepública and Intercontinental are possibly the cheapest, and they too have some discounted fares. The difference in fares over the same route may be up to 40%, or even more. The fares listed in this chapter are regular fares of the more expensive carriers, so it's likely that you'll find something cheaper if you shop around.

There's a US$4 airport tax on domestic flights, which you usually pay when buying the ticket. This tax is included in the airfares listed in this chapter. Be sure to reconfirm your reservation at least 72 hours before departure.

Avianca offers a 21-day domestic air pass called Descubra Colombia. The pass allows for five stopovers of your choice serviced by Avianca/Sam, but you cannot visit the same place twice. The pass can only be bought outside the country. If you fly into Colombia with Avianca, the pass costs US$280 (including San Andrés and Leticia as two of the five stopovers) or US$190 (excluding these two destinations). If you fly with any other carrier, the pass costs US$529 or US$409, respectively.

BUS

Buses are the main means of getting around the country. The bus system is well developed and extensive, reaching even the smallest villages, if there is a road. There are three principal classes of bus: ordinary (called *corriente*), 1st class (or *pullman*) and air-con *(climatizado)*.

The corriente buses are of rather older technology and mostly service side roads. The pullmans are more modern, reliable and comfortable. They ply both side and main routes. Climatizados are the best, with plenty of leg room, reclining seats and large luggage compartments, and some have toilets. They are predominantly long-distance buses covering the main routes, and many travel at night. The climatizado category is dramatically expanding these days, becoming a dominant means of intercity transport.

There is one more kind of bus – the *chiva*. This trolley-type vehicle was the principal means of transport several decades ago. Its body is made almost entirely of wood, covered with colourful decorative patterns, with a main painting on the back. Today, the chivas have disappeared from the main roads, but they still play an important role on outback roads between small villages.

Colectivos are quite widespread. These shared taxis (sometimes jeeps or minibuses) cover fixed routes, mainly on short and medium distances. They leave when full, not according to a schedule, and are a good option if there is a long wait for the next bus or if you want more speed.

On the main roads, buses run every hour, or more frequently, so there is little point in booking a seat in advance. In some places off the main routes, where there are only a few buses daily, it's better to buy a ticket some time before departure. The only time you need to book is during the Christmas and

Easter periods, when hordes of Colombians are on holiday.

All major cities have a central bus terminal, often well outside of the centre but linked by urban transport. In smaller localities, where there is no terminal, bus company offices tend to be concentrated along one or two adjacent streets.

Bus travel is not that cheap in Colombia. As a rule of thumb, the corriente bus costs about US$3 for every 100 km, pullmans cost about 20% more than corrientes and climatizados 20% more than pullmans.

TRAIN

There are no railway lines of any importance operating passenger services.

BOAT

With some 3000 km of Pacific and Atlantic coastline, there is a considerable amount of shipping, consisting mostly of irregular cargo boats. These may also take passengers, which may interest you if you plan on exploring the Pacific coast. The main port on this coast is Buenaventura.

Rivers are also important transport routes, particularly in the Chocó and the Amazon, where there is no other way of getting around. Very few river boats run on any regular schedule, and as most are primarily cargo boats, they are far from fast. Conditions are primitive and food (when provided) is poor. The fares are a matter of discussion with the captain, but will not be cheap.

Bogotá

The capital of the country, Bogotá is the quintessence of all things Colombian. It's a city of futuristic architecture, of universities, intellectuals, artists, splendid colonial churches and brilliant museums, offering a vibrant and diverse cultural life. Yet it is also a city of vast shantytowns, street urchins, beggars, thieves, drug dealers, street vendors, wild traffic and graffiti.

It is not a particularly pleasant or peaceful

place, and the bizarre mixture of everything from oppressive poverty to sparkling prosperity gives newcomers an impression of disarray – perhaps more so than most other large capital cities on the continent. Bogotá is amazing but awful, fascinating but dangerous. You may love it or hate it, but it won't leave you indifferent.

The city was founded in 1538 and baptised Santa Fe de Bogotá, but after independence the name was shortened to Bogotá. Though it always played an important political role as the capital, its rapid progress only came in the 1940s, with industrialisation and the consequent migrations from the countryside. Over the past 50 years, Bogotá has grown 20-fold to its present population of between six and seven million. Recently, the city's official name was changed back to Santa Fe de Bogotá.

Bogotá lies at an altitude of about 2600 metres, and the temperature averages 14°C year round, with cold nights and warm days. The dry season is from December to March, and there is also a semidry period (with only light rainfall), from July to August.

Bogotá is not a safe place. Parts of the city centre become quite dangerous after dark and are notorious for robbery. Keep nighttime strolls to a minimum and don't carry money or valuables. In practice, it's good to have a bundle of small notes, the equivalent of, say, US$5 to US$10, to hand over in case of an assault; if you really don't have a peso, robbers can become frustrated and, as a consequence, unpredictable.

Orientation

Set in the Sabana de Bogotá, the city has grown along its north-south axis and is bordered to the east by a mountain range with the two remarkable peaks of Monserrate and Guadalupe. Having expanded up the mountain slopes as far as possible, Bogotá is now rapidly developing to the west and north.

The central city area divides the metropolis into two very different parts. The northern sector consists mainly of up-market residential districts, while the southern part is a vast spread of undistinguished suburbs populated by lower-income dwellers. The western part, away from the mountains, is the most heterogeneous and is more industrial. This is where the airport and the bus terminal are located.

Information

Tourist Offices The Instituto Distrital de Cultura y Turismo (☎ 334 8749, 286 6554) is the city tourist office which focuses on Bogotá. It's at the western corner of Plaza de Bolívar and is open weekdays from 7 am to 4 pm.

The CNT (national tourist board) office (☎ 281 4341) is at Calle 28 No 13A-15, on the ground floor. It's open weekdays from 8.30 am to 12.45 pm and 2 to 5 pm. There is an outlet of CNT on the 1st floor of the airport (departure hall).

The Corporación de Turismo de Cundinamarca (☎ 284 8452), Calle 16 No 7-76, deals with Cundinamarca department, the region surrounding Bogotá. The office is open weekdays from 7 am to 4 pm.

Money Bogotá's banks have different working hours to banks elsewhere in the country – they work without a lunch break, from 9 am to 3 pm Monday to Thursday, and from 9 am to 3.30 pm on Friday. However, they usually handle foreign exchange operations only until 1 or 2 pm.

The Banco Anglo Colombiano, Carrera 8 No 15-60, changes travellers' cheques at probably the best rate in town. The Banco Unión Colombiano, Carrera 8 No 14-45, is possibly the next best for cheques.

These banks also change cash, but check the casas de cambio beforehand, which may pay the same amount and do it within seconds. Novatours, Carrera 6 No 14-64, and Exprinter, next door, both handle money exchange, though they don't always pay the best rate; the casas de cambio in the nearby buildings may offer more attractive rates. Several casas de cambio can be found in the large edifice at Carrera 7 No 17-01. Another four are at Carrera 7 No 26-62.

All banks shown on the Central Bogotá map give cash advances on either Visa or MasterCard. The Credibanco of Banco de

COLOMBIA

Bogotá, Calle 14 No 7-73, handles Visa in its extended business hours: weekdays from 9 am to 5 pm, and Saturday from 10 am to 4 pm.

Tierra Mar Aire travel agency (☎ 283 2955), which represents American Express, has its office in the Centro Internacional, Carrera 10 No 27-91.

Post & Communications The Avianca main post office, Carrera 7 No 16-36, is open weekdays from 7.30 am to 7 pm, and Saturday from 8 am to 6 pm. They have poste restante here. Adpostal has its main office in Edificio Murillo Toro, Carrera 7, between Calles 12A and 13.

The main office of Telecom is at Calle 23 No 13-49, but you can make long-distance calls and send faxes and telegrams from the branch Telecom offices scattered throughout the city. Bogotá's telephone code is 91.

Foreign Embassies & Consulates There are no Australian or New Zealand embassies in Colombia – nationals of these countries should try the UK embassy. Foreign diplomatic representatives include:

Brazil
    Calle 93 No 14-20, piso 8 (☎ 218 0800)
Canada
    Calle 76 No 11-52 (☎ 313 1355)
Costa Rica
    Carrera 15 No 102-25 (☎ 610 4070)
Ecuador
    Calle 100 No 14-63, oficina 601 (☎ 257 9947)
France
    Carrera 11 No 93-12 (☎ 618 0511)
Germany
    Carrera 4 No 72-35, piso 6 (☎ 212 0511)
Guatemala
    Transversal 29A No 139A-41 (☎ 259 1496)
Honduras
    Carrera 16 No 85-15, oficina 302 (☎ 236 0357)
Israel
    Calle 35 No 7-25, piso 14 (☎ 232 0764)
Panama
    Calle 92 No 7-70 (☎ 257 5067)
Peru
    Calle 90 No 14-26, oficina 417 (☎ 257 3147)
UK
    Calle 98 No 9-03, piso 4 (☎ 218 5111)
USA
    Calle 22D Bis No 47-51 (☎ 315 0811)

Venezuela
    Avenida 13 No 103-16 (☎ 256 3015)

Visa Extensions A 30-day extension can be obtained from the DAS office (☎ 610 7315), Calle 100 No 11B-29. Only your passport is required (no photos, no onward ticket). The office is open weekdays from 7.30 am to 3.30 pm, but be there early, as you have to pay the US$25 fee at the bank. You get the extension on the spot.

National Parks The Unidad Administrativa Especial del Sistema de Parques Nacionales (☎ 283 0964) is at Carrera 10 No 20-30, oficina 802. The office issues permits and provides information for the parks all around the country. The permits are usually issued the same day. For more details see Useful Organisations under Facts for the Visitor.

Tour Operators There are loads of travel agencies organising tours. Viajes Chapinero (☎ 612 7716, fax 215 9099), Avenida 7 No 124-15, is one of the biggest operators and has a wide number of tours, including out-of-the-way tours for tourists interested in environmental issues.

Eco-Guías (☎ 212 6049, fax 212 7450), Carrera 8 No 63-27, is a small, alternative agency focusing on ecotourism. It organises individualised trips at reasonable prices to various regions, including many national parks.

Sal Si Puedes (☎ 283 3765, 341 5854), Carrera 7 No 17-01, oficina 640, is an association of hiking enthusiasts who organise weekend walks to the countryside. These are mostly one-day excursions around Cundinamarca, but longer hikes to other regions are also arranged. Other organisations of this type include Clorofila Urbana (☎ 615 6888), Calle 128 No 38A-26, Interior 3, oficina 502, and Vagabundos del Cosmos (☎ 222 1079, 342 0169).

Maps The best Bogotá city map, *Plano de Bogotá* (scale 1:25,000), is produced by Rodríguez and distributed through some of

COLOMBIA

Central Bogotá

PLACES TO STAY
15 Hotel Tequendama
52 Platypus
54 Hotel El Dorado
55 Residencias Aragón
56 Hotel Dann Colonial
57 Hotel Turístico de Santafé
89 Hostería La Candelaria
97 Alcom Youth Hostel

PLACES TO EAT
6 Restaurante El Patio
17 Restaurante Casa Vieja
29 Restaurante Vegetariano Govinda's
30 Pastelería Florida
32 Restaurante Vegetariano Nuevos Horizontes
47 Restaurante Vegetariano El Champiñón
49 Restaurante La Pola
53 Restaurante Casa Vieja
58 Restaurante Vegetariano Loto Azul
88 Restaurante Los Ultimos Virreyes
95 Restaurante Claustro de San Agustín

OTHER
1 CNT Tourist Office
2 Intercontinental de Aviación
3 Museo Nacional
4 Tierra Mar Aire
5 Sam
6 Crucero Express
7 Banco de Occidente
8 Banco de Occidente
9 Satena, AeroRepública & Zuliana de Aviación
10 Adpostal
11 Banco Popular
12 Telecom
13 Aces
14 Viasa
16 Avianca Airline Office
18 Iglesia de San Diego
19 Casas de Cambio
20 Crafts Market
21 Plaza de Toros de Santamaría
22 Planetario Distrital & Museo de Historia Natural

Parque de la Independencia

CENTRO INTER-NACIONAL

To Airport

Central Cemetery

COLOMBIA

Avenida Caracas

0   125   250 m

Carrera 30
Calle 30
Calle 29
Carrera 5
Carrera 4A
Carrera 44
Carrera 27
Calle 28
Calle 27
Calle 26
Carrera 7
Carrera 28
Carrera 13
Carrera 13
Calle 13
Calle 10
Carrera 10
Carrera 9
Carrera 8
Carrera 7
Carrera 5
Carrera 23
Calle 24
Calle 23
Calle 22
Calle 21
Calle 20
Carrera 12
Carrera 13
Carrera 13A
Calle 22
Calle 21
Calle 20
Calle 19 (Avenida 19)
Carrera 15
Calle 18
Calle 17
Calle 16
Calle 24
Calle 23A
Calle 23
Calle 22A
Calle 18

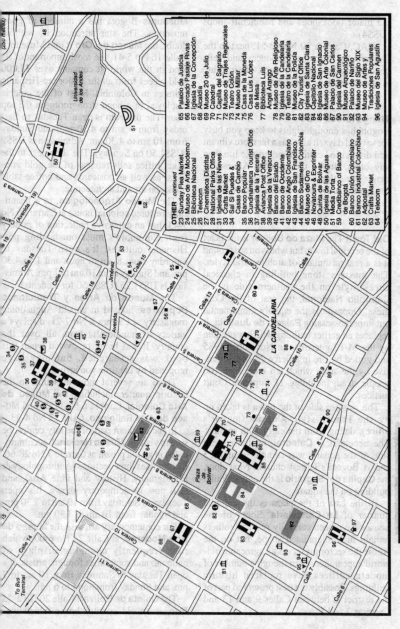

Universidad
de los Andes

(250 metres)

LA CANDELARIA

Plaza
de Bolívar

To Bus
Terminal

Carrera 3 (9)
Avenida 19
Carrera 1
Jiménez
Carrera 4
Carrera 5
Carrera 6
Carrera 7
Carrera 8
Carrera 9
Carrera 10
Carrera 11

Calle 18
Calle 17
Calle 16
Calle 15
Calle 14
Calle 13
Calle 12
Calle 11
Calle 10
Calle 9
Calle 8
Calle 7
Calle 6

OTHER continued
23 Sunday Flea Market
24 Museo de Arte Moderno
25 Biblioteca Nacional
26 Telecom
27 Cinemateca Distrital
28 National Parks Office
31 Iglesia de las Nieves
33 Crafts Market
34 Sal Si Puedes &
   Casas de Cambio
35 Banco Popular
36 Cundinamarca Tourist Office
37 Iglesia de la Tercera
38 Iglesia de la Veracruz
39 Iglesia de Occidente
41 Banco de Occidente
42 Banco Anglo Colombiano
43 Iglesia de San Francisco
44 Banco Sudameris Colombia
46 Novatours & Exprinter
48 Quinta de Bolívar
50 Iglesia de las Aguas
51 Media Torta
59 Credibanco of Banco
   de Bogotá
60 Banco Unión Colombiano
61 Banco Industrial Colombiano
62 Adpostal
63 Crafts Market
64 Telecom

65 Palacio de Justicia
66 Mercado Pasaje Rivas
67 Iglesia de la Concepción
68 Alcaldía
69 Museo 20 de Julio
70 Catedral
71 Capilla del Sagrario
72 Museo de Trajes Regionales
73 Teatro Colón
74 Iglesia de Santa Clara
75 Casa de la Moneda
76 Casa Luis López
   de Mesa
77 Biblioteca Luis
   Ángel Arango
78 Museo de Arte Religioso
79 Iglesia de la Candelaria
80 Teatro de la Candelaria
81 Museo de la Policía
82 City Tourist Office
83 Iglesia de Santa Clara
84 Capitolio Nacional
85 Iglesia de San Ignacio
86 Museo de Arte Colonial
87 Palacio de San Carlos
90 Iglesia del Carmen
91 Museo Arqueológico
92 Palacio de Nariño
93 Museo del Siglo XIX
94 Museo de Artes y
   Tradiciones Populares
96 Iglesia de San Agustín

COLOMBIA

the major bookshops and handicraft shops (US$4).

IGAC, Carrera 30 No 48-51, next to the Universidad Nacional, produces and sells general, regional and city maps. The institute is open weekdays from 8 am to 3.30 pm.

Things to See & Do

Bogotá has enough sights to keep you busy for several days. It also has a far more vibrant and diversified cultural and artistic life than any other city in the country. Almost all major attractions are conveniently sited in the central city area, within easy walking distance of each other.

Old Town The **Plaza de Bolívar** is the heart of the original town, but what you see around it is a real mishmash of architectural styles. The massive stone building in classical Greek style on the southern side is the **Capitolio Nacional**, the seat of the Congress. Opposite is the equally monumental but unprepossessing **Palacio de Justicia**. It replaces an earlier building which was taken by the M-19 guerrillas in November 1985 and gutted by fire in a fierce 28-hour offensive by the army which left more than 100 people dead, including 11 Supreme Court justices.

The western side of the plaza is taken up by the French-style **Alcaldía** (mayor's office), dating from the early 20th century. The neoclassical **Catedral**, on the eastern side of the square, was completed in 1823 and is Bogotá's largest church. Next door, the **Capilla del Sagrario** is the only colonial building on the square.

To the east of the plaza is the colonial quarter of **La Candelaria**. Some of the houses have been carefully restored, others remain in a dilapidated shape, but on the whole the sector preserves an agreeable old-world appearance, even though a number of modern edifices have replaced historic buildings. Possibly the best preserved part of the district is between Calles 9 and 13 and Carreras 2 and 5.

Museums Bogotá has a number of good museums. The star attraction is, without doubt, the **Museo del Oro** (Gold Museum), Calle 16 No 5-41, the most important of its kind in the world. It contains over 33,000 gold pieces from all the major pre-Hispanic cultures in Colombia. Most of the gold is displayed in a huge strongroom on the top floor. The museum is open Tuesday to Saturday from 9 am to 4.30 pm, and Sunday from 10 am to 4.30 pm. Admission is US$2 (US$1.50 on Sunday). The shop next to the ticket office sells replicas of the gold artefacts, as well as postcards and coffee-table books on art and architecture.

The **Museo Arqueológico**, in a beautifully restored colonial house at Carrera 6 No 7-43, has an extensive collection of pottery from Colombia's most outstanding pre-Hispanic cultures. It's open Tuesday to Saturday from 8 am to noon and 1 to 4.30 pm, and Sunday from 10 am to 1 pm. Admission is US$1.25 (US$0.50 for students).

The **Museo de Artes y Tradiciones Populares**, housed in an old Augustinian monastery at Carrera 8 No 7-21, displays a variety of handicrafts from all over the country. It was being renovated when this book was researched, but may have reopened by the time you arrive.

There are several more museums in the historic quarter, including the **Museo de Arte Colonial**, Carrera 6 No 9-77, and **Museo de Arte Religioso**, Calle 12 No 4-33.

In the northern part of the city centre, be sure to visit the **Museo Nacional**, accommodated in an old prison at Carrera 7 No 28-66. It comprises three sections (Anthropology & Ethnography, History and Fine Arts), and also puts on temporary shows. It's open Tuesday to Saturday from 10 am to 5.30 pm, and Sunday from 10 am to 3.30 pm.

For contemporary art, visit the **Museo de Arte Moderno**, at Calle 24 No 6-00, which runs frequently changing displays of national, and sometimes foreign, artists. It's open Tuesday to Saturday from 10 am to 7 pm, and Sunday from noon to 6 pm.

The **Quinta de Bolívar**, Calle 20 No 2-23 Este, is an old country house which was donated to Simón Bolívar in gratitude for his services. Today, it's a museum displaying Bolívar's possessions, documents, maps, weapons, uniforms etc. It's open Tuesday to Sunday from 10 am to 5 pm.

Churches Having been the capital since the early days of Spanish rule and a centre of evangelism in the vast province, Bogotá boasts many colonial churches, most dating from the 17th and 18th centuries. They are usually austere on the outside, but internal decoration is often very elaborate.

One of the most remarkable is **Santa Clara**, open as a museum Tuesday to Friday from 9 am to 1 pm and 2 to 5 pm, and weekends from 10 am to 4 pm.

Other churches worth a look include: **San Francisco**, for the extraordinary decoration of its chancel; **La Concepción**, with probably Bogotá's most beautiful Mudejar vault; **San Ignacio**, distinguished by both its size and its valuable works of art; **La Tercera**, with its walnut and cedar carvings; and **San Diego**, a charming country church (it was well outside the town when built) now surrounded by a forest of high-rise buildings.

Cerro de Monserrate For a spectacular view of the city, go to the top of the Cerro de Monserrate, the mountain overlooking the city centre from the east. There is a church on the summit, with a statue of the Señor Caído (Fallen Christ), to which many miracles have been attributed.

There are three ways to get to the top: by cable car (*teleférico*), funicular railway or along the footpath.

The cable car operates Monday to Saturday from 10 am to midnight (US$4 return), and Sunday from 5.30 am to 6 pm (US$2.50 return). The funicular only runs on Sunday, from 5.30 am to 6 pm (US$2.50 return). If you want to do the trip on foot (one hour uphill), do it only on Sunday, when crowds of pilgrims go; on weekdays, take it for granted that you will be robbed along the way. The lower stations of both the cable car and the funicular are close to the city centre, but the access road leads through a shabby

barrio, so take the bus marked 'Funicular', from Avenida Jiménez, or a taxi.

Other Sights The city has interesting botanical gardens, the **Jardín Botánico José Celestino Mutis**, at Calle 57 No 61-13, with a variety of national flora from different climatic zones. On Sunday, don't miss the **Mercado de las Pulgas**, a colourful flea market which is held at the car park on Carrera 7 between Calles 24 and 26.

Places to Stay

The most popular budget place among backpackers is the *Platypus* (☎ 341 2874, 341 3104), Calle 16 No 2-43 (no sign on the door, just a picture of the platypus). It has three dorms (US$6 per person) and several singles (US$8) and doubles (US$13). Although conditions are quite simple and only a few rooms have private baths, the place is safe, clean and pleasant and has hot water in the communal baths. The hotel offers book exchange, laundry and kitchen facilities, and there's a cosy dining room where you can eat, read and have a tinto, which is provided free of charge. The friendly owner, Germán, a longtime traveller himself, speaks several languages and is an excellent source of practical information. He also offers a poste restante service (your name, AA 3902, Bogotá, Colombia).

There are several cheap places nearby. You can try the *Residencias Aragón* (☎ 284 8325, 342 5239), Carrera 3 No 14-13, which has fairly large rooms with shared bath and hot water for US$6 per person. Alternatively, check the *Hotel El Dorado* (☎ 334 3988), Carrera 4 No 15-00, which has smaller rooms, some with own bath (US$7 per person).

Better and cheaper than either of the above is the *Alcom* youth hostel (☎ 280 3202, 280 3318), Carrera 7 No 6-10, four blocks south of Plaza de Bolívar. It's not ideally located but often has foreign travellers. Clean six and eight-bed dorms with shared bath (hot water in the morning only) cost US$5 per person (US$4 with an HI membership card). The hostel has a cheap restaurant.

For somewhere plusher, go to the *Hotel Turístico de Santafé* (☎ 342 0560), Calle 14 No 4-48, which has large rooms with bath and TV for US$16/24/32 a single/double/triple. You can eat in the hotel restaurant, which is cheap and has acceptable food. Better still is the *Hotel Dann Colonial* (☎ 341 1680), opposite at Calle 14 No 4-21, but it's far more costly (US$48/64/75 with breakfast). Don't be confused by the name: the hotel is modern, not colonial.

The *Hostería La Candelaria* (☎ 286 1479, 342 1727), Calle 9 No 3-11, offers colonial style and atmosphere. Singles/doubles with bath cost US$32/44, and there are a few more spacious suites. The hotel has its own restaurant, Café de Rosita, which serves satisfying food.

All the hotels listed above are in or just off La Candelaria, the most popular area to stay among budget travellers. While it's not a particularly safe area at night, neither is the rest of the city centre. There are also hotels in the northern part of the centre, but you won't find many cheapies there.

Places to Eat

Innumerable places have set meals for US$1.50 to US$2 – just drop into the first one, see what people are eating, and stay or move on to the next one. For cheap vegetarian food try *El Champiñón*, Avenida Jiménez No 5-32; *Loto Azul*, Carrera 5 No 14-00; *Nuevos Horizontes*, Calle 20 No 6-37; or *Govinda's*, Carrera 8 No 20-55. Some only open for lunch.

Pastelería Florida, Carrera 7 No 20-82, is a cheap bakery serving good chocolate santafereño (hot chocolate with cheese, accompanied by pan de yuca or almojábanas). Some of the best typical soups can be found at *Las 7 Sopas*, Calle 30 No 6-70. For about US$3, you get a large clay bowl of hearty ajiaco, mondongo or sancocho, a filling meal in itself.

Bogotá has a number of barbecued-chicken restaurants, where a half-chicken with potatoes or chips makes a filling meal for US$3. For pizza, there's a row of pizzerias on Calle 19, between Carreras 3 and 7.

The *Claustro de San Agustín* (open weekdays till 5 pm), in the Museo de Artes y Tradiciones Populares, has delicious local food (served until 3 pm only). *Los Ultimos Virreyes*, Calle 10 No 3-16, is one of the better restaurants in La Candelaria, serving international and local cuisine.

La Pola, Calle 19 No 1-85, has a list of fine regional dishes at middle-bracket prices. *Casa Vieja* is also acclaimed for its local specialities, but it's not cheap. It has two outlets in the centre: at Avenida Jiménez No 3-73 and at Carrera 10 No 26-50 (Iglesia de San Diego). *El Patio*, a cosy place with only a few tables, at Carrera 4A No 27-86, is becoming one of the trendiest places for lunch or dinner. It serves excellent, if not cheap, Italian food.

Entertainment

Bogotá has lots of cinemas offering the usual commercial fare, mainly from the USA. For something more thought-provoking, check the programmes of the *cinematecas* (art cinemas). The two most popular places of this kind are the *Cinemateca Distrital* at Carrera 7 No 22-79 and the *Museo de Arte Moderno*, which has its own cinema hall (entrance from Calle 26).

Leading theatres include the *Teatro de la Candelaria*, Calle 12 No 2-59; the *Teatro Libre de Bogotá*, Calle 62 No 10-65; and the *Teatro Nacional*, in its two locations at Calle 71 No 10-25 and Calle 95 No 30-13.

For classical music, check the programme of the *Biblioteca Luis Ángel Arango*, which runs concerts in its own concert hall.

Soccer fans may like to attend some matches; it's Colombia's national sport. The principal venue is the *Estadio El Campín*, on the corner of Carrera 30 and Calle 55. Bullfighting is also very popular, with fights held at the *Plaza de Toros de Santamaría*, Carrera 6, on most Sundays of January and February.

The main focus of night entertainment is the Zona Rosa, in the northern sector of the city, between Carreras 11 and 15, and Calles 81 and 84. There's a maze of music spots, bars, restaurants, cafés and snack bars in the area, which become particularly vibrant on weekend nights. The better known *salsotecas* (discos which play mostly salsa) include *Salomé* at Carrera 14A No 82-16, *Galería Café Libro* at Calle 81 No 11-92 and *Quiebra Canto* at Carrera 15 No 79-28, but there are plenty of other places playing reggae, rock, heavy metal etc.

Getting There & Away

Air El Dorado airport, which handles all domestic and international flights, is 13 km north-west of the city centre. It has two terminals. The main one, El Dorado, houses the CNT tourist office (on the 1st floor) and moneychanging facilities. Aerocambios, on the ground floor (open daily from 7 am to 11 pm), changes cash. The Banco Popular, at the next window (the same opening hours), changes both cash and travellers' cheques. The Banco Comercial Antioqueño, on the 1st floor (open Monday to Friday from 9 am to 3 pm and 5 to 9 pm, Saturday and Sunday from 9 am to 4 pm), gives advances on Visa.

The other terminal, Puente Aéreo, is about one km before El Dorado. It handles Avianca's international flights to the USA, and domestic flights to Cali, Medellín and a few other destinations. Make sure to check which terminal your flight departs from.

There are plenty of domestic flights to destinations all over the country, including Medellín (US$74), Cali (US$82), Cartagena (US$129), San Andrés (US$180) and Leticia (US$172). You can usually find discounted fares on these routes, sometimes just 60% of the listed figures. Aerosucre has cargo flights to Leticia (see the Leticia section later in this chapter).

There are also a lot of international flights, including Quito (US$161), Panama City (US$156), San José (US$246) and Guatemala City (US$290). The cheapest way of getting to Venezuela is with Servivensa to Santo Domingo, near San Cristóbal (US$50). The next cheapest is with Zuliana de Aviación to Maracaibo (US$81). Add the 21% Colombian tax to all international fares listed here.

Bus The bus terminal is large, functional and well organised. It has restaurants, cafeterias, showers and left-luggage rooms, plus a number of well-dressed thieves who will wait for a moment's inattention to grab your stuff and disappear: watch your bags closely.

The terminal handles buses to just about every corner of the country. On the main roads, buses run frequently round the clock: to Cali (US$23, 12 hours), Medellín (US$19, nine hours) and Bucaramanga (US$19, 10 hours). There are direct buses to Cartagena (US$47), Santa Marta (US$40), Cúcuta (US$28), San Agustín (US$17), Popayán (US$27) and Ipiales (US$42). All prices (except for San Agustín) are for climatizados, the dominant class of bus on these routes.

Getting Around

To/From the Airport Both El Dorado and Puente Aéreo terminals are accessible from the centre by *busetas* (small buses) and colectivos marked 'Aeropuerto'; catch them on Calle 19 or Carrera 10. Alternatively, go by taxi (US$6).

To/From the Bus Terminal The terminal is a long way west of the city centre. To get there from the centre, take the bus or colectivo marked 'Terminal' from Avenida Jiménez. Taxis between the terminal and the city centre shouldn't cost more than US$3.

Local Bus & Buseta Buses and busetas run the length and breadth of the city. On most streets you just wave the vehicle down, but on Carrera 7, Avenida Caracas and some other routes there are now bus stops. The flat fare (US$0.20 to US$0.50) is always posted by the door or on the windscreen. Colectivos operate on the major routes and cost about US$0.40.

Taxi Bogotá's taxis all have meters and most drivers use them; insist, or take another taxi. A 10-km ride (eg from Plaza de Bolívar to Avenida 100 in northern Bogotá) shouldn't cost more than US$4.

COLOMBIA

AROUND BOGOTA

Zipaquirá

Zipaquirá, 50 km north of Bogotá, is noted for its salt mines. Although the mines date back to the Muisca period and have been intensively exploited, they still contain vast reserves; they tap into virtually a huge mountain of rock salt. In the heart of the mountain, an underground **salt cathedral** has been carved out of the solid salt and was opened to the public in 1954. It was closed in 1992 for safety reasons, but a new cathedral was scooped out 60 metres below the old one and opened for visitors in December 1995. It is 75 metres long and 18 metres high, and is capable of accommodating 8400 people.

The cathedral is open Tuesday to Sunday from 10 am to 4 pm. The entrance fee is US$8 (half-price Wednesday). Tours are guided and take one hour. Guides with basic English are available at no extra charge.

Buses to Zipaquirá run from Bogotá every 10 minutes; they depart from the corner of Calle 19 and Carrera 20 (US$1, 1½ hours). The mines are a 15-minute walk uphill from the town centre.

Guatavita

Also called Guatavita Nueva, this town was built from scratch in the late 1960s when the old colonial Guatavita was flooded by the waters of a hydroelectric reservoir. The town is an architectural blend of old and new, and has become a weekend destination for bogotanos.

About 15 km from the town is the famous **Laguna de Guatavita**, the ritual centre and sacred lake of the Muisca Indians, and a cradle of the myth of El Dorado. The lagoon was an object of worship, where gold pieces, emeralds and food were offered by Indians. The myth of incalculable treasures at the bottom gave rise to numerous attempts to salvage the riches. Despite enormous efforts by the Spanish and later the Colombians, very little has actually been found. Legend claims that the lake retains its treasures.

Buses to Guatavita Nueva depart from Carrera 15 No 14-59 in Bogotá's centre (US$2, two hours). They run every hour on weekdays and every half-hour on Sunday. For the lake, get off 11 km before the town (drivers will let you off at the right place) and walk seven km uphill along a dirt track. At weekends, when tourists come, it's possible to hitch a lift.

Boyacá, Santander & Norte de Santander

The three departments of Boyacá, Santander and Norte de Santander cover the northern part of the Cordillera Oriental to the north of Bogotá. The region offers a variety of landscapes, from green fertile valleys, such as the Valle de Tenza (southern Boyacá), to the arid Cañón del Chicamocha (Santander) and the snowy peaks of the Sierra Nevada del Cocuy (northern Boyacá).

Once the territory of the Muiscas (Boyacá) and the Guane Indians (central Santander), the region was one of the first to be explored and settled by the Spaniards. Many towns founded by them have been preserved in remarkably good shape. Villa de Leyva, Barichara and Girón are among the best examples.

Of the three departments, Boyacá is perhaps the safest, easiest and most pleasant in which to travel. It is also the most traditional province, widely known for its handicrafts, particularly pottery, basketwork and weaving.

TUNJA

Tunja, the capital of Boyacá, was founded in 1539 on the site of Hunza, the ancient Muisca seat. Though almost nothing is left of the Indian period, much colonial architecture remains. The central sector was carefully restored for the town's 450-year anniversary, and many historic public buildings have recovered their original splendour. Tunja is a city of churches: several imposing examples from the 16th century are almost untouched by time.

COLOMBIA

The city sits at an altitude of about 2800 metres and has a cool climate; you'll need warm clothing, especially at night.

Information

Tourist Office The municipal tourist office (☎ 423272) is in the Casa del Fundador, on Plaza de Bolívar. It's open Monday to Saturday from 8 am to noon and 2 to 6 pm, and Sunday from 9 am to 1 pm and 2 to 5 pm.

Money Probably no bank in Tunja will change cash. Try the Joyería Francesa or the Agencia de Viajes Roka, which usually buy US dollars; the latter may pay better. Only the Banco de Bogotá exchanges travellers' cheques (morning only). All banks marked on the map give cash advances on Visa or MasterCard.

Telephone Tunja's telephone code is 987.

Things to See

The **Casa del Fundador Suárez Rendón** (the house of the founder of Tunja) and the **Casa de Don Juan de Vargas** have both been converted into museums containing colonial artworks. The ceilings in both houses are covered with intriguing paintings featuring human figures, animals and plants, coats of arms and other motifs, and constitute a somewhat astonishing decoration. A similar ceiling can be seen in the **Casa de Don Juan de Castellanos**, now the public library.

Among the churches, **Santo Domingo** and **Santa Clara La Real** are the most beautiful and richly decorated. The latter is open as a museum. Also worth a visit are **Santa Bárbara**, **San Francisco** and the **Catedral**. Tunja's churches are noted for their Mudejar art, an Islamic-influenced style which developed in Christian Spain between the 12th and 16th centuries. It is particularly visible in the ornamented, coffered vaults.

The tourist office will point you to other sights of interest, as well as inform you about the opening hours of the museums and churches.

Places to Stay

Nights in Tunja are cold and not all cheap hotels provide enough blankets. Ask for more if you think you might get frozen solid. Another problem of local cheapies (and even some of the mid-price hotels) is that they have erratic hot water supply, and usually only for a few hours in the morning.

There are several budget hotels on Carrera 7, close to the bus terminal, but they are basic and not worth a look. It's much more pleasant to stay in the heart of the city, around Plaza de Bolívar. The cheapest there is the *Hotel Lord* (☎ 423556), Calle 19 No 10-64, which has singles/doubles/triples without bath for US$5/9/11 and rooms with bath for US$12/12/15. The *Hotel Savoy* (☎ 423492) and the *Hotel Dux* (☎ 425736), on either side of the Lord, offer much the same but are slightly more expensive.

Other reasonably priced options in the central area include the very simple *Hotel Don Camilo* (☎ 426574), on Plaza de Bolívar (US$7/11/13 without bath); the *Hotel San Francisco* (☎ 426645), Carrera 9 No 18-90 (US$12/20/24 with bath); and the *Hostal El Cid* (☎ 423458), Carrera 10 No 20-78 (US$13/20/25 with bath and TV).

If money is not a big problem, try the recently revamped *Hotel El Conquistador* (☎ 438624), Calle 20 No 8-92 (US$26/36 a single/double), or the *Hostería Pila del Mono* (☎ 403380), Carrera 8 No 19-81 (US$30/42).

Places to Eat

Plenty of undistinguished restaurants serve inexpensive set meals. There are also a number of outlets serving snacks, fast food, chicken etc. The *Pila del Mono*, Calle 20 No 8-19, is one of the better restaurants in the central area.

Getting There & Away

The bus terminal is on Avenida Oriental, within a short walking distance from the Plaza de Bolívar, the city's heart.

There are frequent buses to Bogotá (US$5, 2½ to three hours) and Bucaramanga (US$14, seven hours). Buses to Villa de

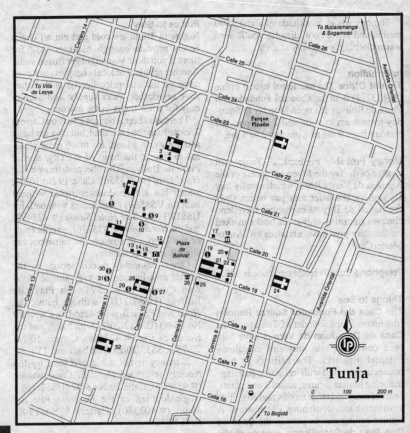

Leyva leave every two to three hours (US$1.50, one hour). For marginally more, you can get there faster by colectivo; they also depart from the terminal and are more frequent than buses.

VILLA DE LEYVA

This small colonial town, founded in 1572, remains largely unspoilt, and is one of the finest architectural gems in the country. As it lies relatively close to the capital, it has become a trendy weekend spot for bogotanos. This has made the town somewhat artificial, with a noticeably split personality – on weekdays, it is a sleepy, old-style

village, but on weekends and holidays it comes alive, crammed with tourists and their cars. It's up to you to choose which of the town's faces you prefer, but don't miss it.

Information

Tourist Office The tourist office (☎ 320232, ext 22), on the eastern corner of the main square, is open Tuesday to Saturday from 8 am to 1 pm and 2 to 5 pm, and Sunday from 9 am to 1 pm and 2 to 4 pm.

Money Probably the only place you can change cash (at a very poor rate) is the Miscelánea, the shop a few doors from the up to US$50 for a double, check the Hostería La Coralejo (☎ 32034). The Hospedería parish church. Travellers' cheques are useless in Villa de Leyva. The Banco Popular, on the main square, is likely to give advances on your Visa card.

Telephone The telephone code is 987.

Things to See & Do

The **Plaza Mayor** is an impressive central square paved with massive cobblestones and lined with whitewashed colonial houses. Drop in to the **parish church**, on the square, and the **Iglesia del Carmen**, a block north;

both have interesting interiors. Next to the latter is a good museum of religious art, the **Museo del Carmen**, open weekends only, from 10 am to 1 pm and 2 to 5 pm.

Some of the town's historic mansions have been converted into museums. The **Museo de Luis Alberto Acuña**, on the main square, contains various works of the painter, sculptor, writer and historian. Other places worth visiting include the **Casa de Antonio Nariño**, in the house where the forefather of independence lived; the **Casa de Antonio Ricaurte**, the home of another national hero; and the **Museo Paleontológico**, one km out of town on the road to Arcabuco, displaying fossils dating from the period when the area was a sea bed (100 to 150 million years ago). Most museums are open Wednesday to Sunday from 10 am to 1 pm and 3 to 5 pm.

Give yourself a couple of hours to wander about the charming cobbled streets and to climb the hill behind the Hospedería Duruelo for a marvellous bird's-eye view of the town. Inspect handicrafts shops noted for fine basketry and good-quality woven items, such as sweaters and *ruanas* (ponchos). The **market** on Saturday, on Carrera 6, is very colourful and is best early in the morning.

Places to Stay

The town has over two dozen places to stay, and most hotels, particularly the up-market ones, are stylish and pleasant. Keep in mind that accommodation becomes limited on weekends, and can fill up completely on puentes and during Easter week, despite the fact that the prices tend to rise, sometimes significantly, at these times.

The cheapest place in town is the basic *Hospedería La Villa*, on the western corner of the main square. It has rooms of varying quality, so have a look before paying. The price is US$5 per person, but it's negotiable, especially if you come in a larger party on weekdays.

The recently revamped *Hospedería Colonial*, a few steps from La Villa on Calle 12, offers better standards, but charges US$10 per person in rooms with bath; bargaining is possible.

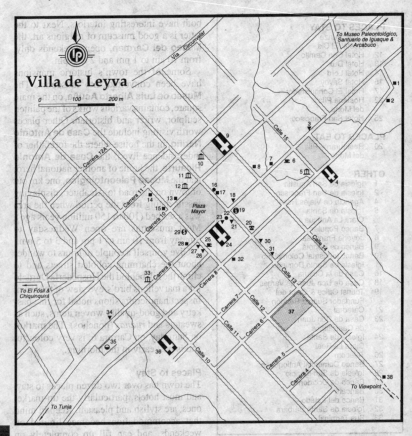

Villa de Leyva

The *Hostería La Roca*, on the main square, has a nice patio but is otherwise not significantly better than the Colonial, and it charges US$25 per double with bath.

Better standards are to be found at the *Hospedaje El Sol de la Villa* (☎ 320224), Carrera 8 No 12-28. Neat rooms with bath and TV cost US$10 per person (US$15 on weekends).

More up-market, there is a range of charming hotels, most of which are set in colonial mansions with flower-filled patios. One of the cheapest is the *Hospedería El Marqués de San Jorge* (☎ 320240), costing US$18 per person. If you are willing to pay

up to US$50 for a double, check the *Hostería La Candelaria* (☎ 320534), the *Hospedería El Mesón de la Plaza Mayor* (☎ 320425), the *Hospedería El Mesón de los Virreyes* (☎ 320252) or the *Hostería El Zaguán de los Héroes* (☎ 320476).

At the top of the range are the *Hostería del Molino La Mesopotamia* (☎ 320235), in an amazing 400-year-old flour mill, and the beautifully maintained hacienda-style *Hospedería Duruelo* (☎ 320222).

Places to Eat

A rash of restaurants has appeared in Villa de Leyva over recent years, yet many don't open on weekdays. The cheapest set meals (US$2) are probably to be found in the *Nueva Granada*. The *Casa Blanca*, just down the street, has better almuerzos and comidas (US$3). *Los Kioskos de los Caciques*, diagonally opposite the bus terminal, is another good choice for a tasty and filling set meal (including breakfast). The *Tienda Naturalista* is planning to serve vegetarian meals.

Other reasonably priced restaurants include *El Tenedor* and *El Estar de la Villa*. *La Dicha Buena* is somewhat more expensive but has an inventive menu, including some vegetarian dishes. The *Rincón de Bachué* is a good and pleasant place for the comida típica.

Among the hotel restaurants, those deserving a special mention are *La Candelaria* (Spanish cuisine), *La Mesopotamia* and *El Duruelo*. All are rather expensive.

The *Panadería Pancho Coco*, next to the parish church, has good pasteles and other pastries. *Pizzería Dino's*, next door, serves tasty but expensive pizzas and spaghetti. The best coffee is at the *Café... y qué Café* and the *Café Real Galería*.

Getting There & Away

There are several direct buses daily to Bogotá (US$7, four hours). There are few buses to Tunja but colectivos ply this route every half an hour or so (US$2, 45 minutes). The bus terminal is on the Tunja road.

AROUND VILLA DE LEYVA

Villa de Leyva is a good jumping-off place for short excursions; the surrounding region is noted for a variety of attractions and is a great place for fossil hunting.

You can move around the area on foot, and use some local buses. The Villa Tour agency, on the main square in Villa de Leyva, operates chiva tours, providing an easy way of visiting some of the sights. The tours depart on Saturday and Sunday, and on request on weekdays if there are at least six people.

El Fósil

This is a reasonably complete fossil of a kronosaurus, a prehistoric marine reptile vaguely resembling a crocodile and about 110 million years old. It is off the road to Chiquinquirá, six km from Villa de Leyva. You can walk there by a path in one hour, or the Chiquinquirá bus will drop you one km from El Fósil.

El Infiernito

About two km from El Fósil, this recently uncovered Muisca astronomic observatory was also a ritual site, notable for a number of large, phallic stone monoliths.

COLOMBIA

Convento del Santo Ecce Homo

This convent, founded in 1620, is a large stone and adobe construction with a lovely courtyard. A nun will show you around, pointing out the most important treasures. The convent is 13 km from Villa de Leyva. The colectivo to Santa Sofía will drop you within a 15-minute walk of the convent.

Ráquira

A small village 25 km from Villa de Leyva, Ráquira is known for its **pottery**, which is some of the best in Colombia and ranges from excellent kitchen utensils to fine copies of indigenous pots. There are a number of small workshops in the village where you can watch the production process. Most of the houses have recently been painted in bright colours, which gives the village much life and charm. There are two hotels on the main square (neither is very cheap) and a couple of restaurants.

Two buses run daily from Villa de Leyva to Ráquira (US$2, 30 minutes). The 8.30 am bus returns to Villa de Leyva at noon, giving you three hours to look around Ráquira. A return taxi trip from Villa de Leyva can be arranged for around US$15 per taxi (up to five people), including a couple of hours in Ráquira.

La Candelaria

This tiny hamlet, seven km beyond Ráquira, is noted for the **Monasterio de la Candelaria**, founded in 1597 by the Augustinians. Part of it is open to the public; the monks will show you around. The *Parador La Candelaria*, close to the monastery, is a nice (if not that cheap) place to stay and eat. Only two buses a day call at La Candelaria. Otherwise, walk by a short cut from Ráquira (one hour).

Santuario de Iguaque

About 15 km north-east of Villa de Leyva, at an altitude of some 3600 metres, is a group of eight small lakes, including the Laguna de Iguaque, which was a sacred lake of the Muiscas. The area is now a nature reserve. The *visitor centre*, a couple of km off the Villa de Leyva-Arcabuco road, offers accommodation for about US$13 per person (for foreigners), and will also charge the hefty US$10 entrance fee to the reserve. From the centre, it's a leisurely three-hour walk uphill to Laguna de Iguaque.

SAN GIL

This 300-year-old town, on the main Bogotá-Bucaramanga road, is worth a stop to see **El Gallineral**, a riverside park where the trees are covered with *barbas de viejo*, long silvery fronds of tillandsia that form spectacular transparent curtains of foliage. San Gil also has a pleasant main square with huge old ceibas and an 18th-century cathedral.

If you stop here, be sure to make the short trip to Barichara, a beautiful small colonial town (see below).

Places to Stay & Eat

There are several cheap residencias, including the *Villas del Oriente*, Calle 10 No 10-47, and *San Gil*, Carrera 11 No 11-25, where you shouldn't pay more than US$4 per person. If you need something better, the *Hostal Isla Señoral*, Calle 10 No 8-14, has comfortable singles/doubles/triples with bath and TV for US$15/22/28.

Plenty of budget restaurants around the residencias serve basic meals. If you visit El Gallineral, there's an agreeable restaurant in the park, with typical food at reasonable prices.

Getting There & Away

The bus terminal is two km west of the town centre. Frequent buses run north and south along the main road. There are buses to Bucaramanga (US$4, 2½ hours) and Bogotá (US$15, 7½ hours). Cotrasangil operates half-hourly minibuses to/from Bucaramanga (US$5, two hours). Buses to Barichara leave every hour or two from Carrera 10 No 14-82 in the town centre.

BARICHARA

Barichara is a small 250-year-old town founded on Guane Indian territory. It's remarkably well preserved and maintained. The streets are paved with massive stone slabs and lined with fine whitewashed single-storey houses. Although there are no outstanding individual sights, the town's charm lies in its beauty as a whole, and its lazy old-world atmosphere.

From Barichara, you might want to visit the tiny village of **Guane**, 10 km away. It has a fine rural church, and a museum with a collection of locally found fossils and Guane Indian artefacts. There's no reliable transport except for a morning *lechero* (milk truck), so you may have to walk by road (a good two hours) or by the path (half an hour less).

Places to Stay & Eat

There are several hotels in Barichara, including the *Coratá*, Carrera 7 No 4-02, the *Bahía Chalá*, Calle 7 No 7-61, and the *Posada Real*, Carrera 6 No 4-69. All cost about US$9 per person, and have their own restaurants. There are a couple of other cheap restaurants around the square.

More comfortable accommodation is in the *Hostal Misión Santa Bárbara*, Calle 5 No 9-12. It's in a tastefully refurbished colonial house, and meals are available for guests.

Getting There & Away

There are several buses daily between Barichara and San Gil (US$1, 45 minutes).

BUCARAMANGA

Bucaramanga, the capital of Santander, is a fairly modern, busy commercial and industrial centre with an agreeable climate. It is noted for its cigars and the *hormiga culona*, a large ant which is fried and eaten.

There is not much to do here, but it may be a stopover on the long route from Bogotá to the coast or Cúcuta. If so, take a side trip to Girón, 10 km away (see the section below).

Information

Tourist Office The tourist office is in the Hotel Bucarica, on the corner of Carrera 19 and Calle 35.

Money Banks which might deal with your cash, travellers' cheques and credit cards

(Visa or MasterCard) are marked on the map; they are packed within a small central area.

Things to See & Do

You can visit the **Casa de Bolívar**, which contains ethnographic and historic collections (open Tuesday to Friday from 8 am to noon and 2 to 6 pm, and on Saturday from 9 am to 1 pm), and have a walk in the **Jardín Botánico Eloy Valenzuela**, in the suburb of Bucarica (open daily from 8 to 11 am and 2 to 5 pm). To get there, take the Bucarica bus from Carrera 15 in the city centre.

Places to Stay

Budget accommodation is centred near the Parque Centenario, particularly on Calle 31 between Carreras 19 and 21, where you'll be able to find a single/double for below US$5/7. They are mostly basic, but some have private baths. One of the best cheapies is the clean and friendly *Hotel Elena* (☎ 428845), Carrera 21 No 30-55 (US$4 for a single without bath, US$8 for a double with bath).

If the Elena is full (as often happens), try the *Residencias ABC* (☎ 337352), Calle 31 No 21-44, or the *Residencias Amparo* (☎ 304098), Calle 31 No 20-29, both just around the corner and costing much the same. Similar prices and value are offered by the *Hotel Tamaná* (☎ 304726), Carrera 18 No 30-31, though the area is less pleasant.

If you want something flashier, go to the *Hotel Balmoral* (☎ 426232), Carrera 21 No 34-85, which is pleasant and friendly. Singles/doubles/triples with private bath and hot water are US$12/16/20.

Even better, stay in the *Hotel Morgan No 2* (☎ 424732), Calle 35 No 18-83, just off the Parque Santander. Clean, ample rooms cost US$15/20/25; choose one with a window facing the street. Don't confuse this hotel with the *Hotel Morgan No 1*, a few paces down Calle 35, which is marginally cheaper but not as good.

If you want somewhere up-market, choose between the *Hotel Bucarica* (☎ 301-592), in the Parque Santander, and the *Hotel*

COLOMBIA

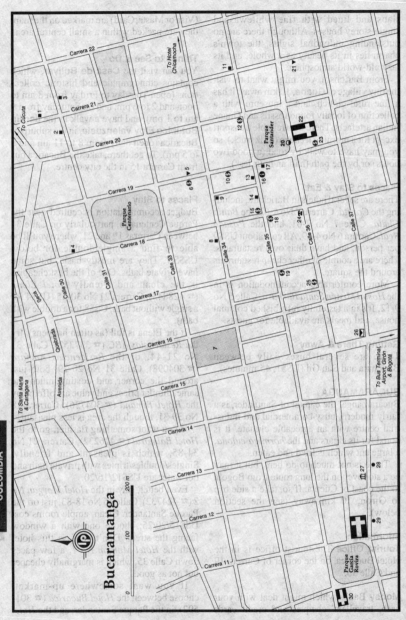

Bucaramanga

PLACES TO STAY

1 Hotel Elena
2 Residencias Amparo
3 Residencias ABC
4 Hotel Tamaná
8 Hotel Farallones
9 Hotel Andino
11 Hotel Balmoral
13 Hotel Morgan No 2
14 Hotel Morgan No 1
17 Hotel Bucarica

PLACES TO EAT

5 Restaurante El Consulado Antioqueño
21 Restaurante El Paisa

OTHER

6 Banco Sudameris Colombia
7 Market
10 Banco Unión Colombiano
12 Banco Popular
15 Banco Industrial Colombiano
16 Tourist Office
18 Banco de Colombia
19 Banco de Bogotá
20 Colectivos to Airport
22 Catedral
23 Banco Anglo Colombiano
24 Telecom
25 Banco de Occidente
26 Avianca Airline & Post Offices
27 Casa de Bolívar
28 Casa de la Cultura
29 Casa de Perú de la Croix
30 Capilla de los Dolores

Chicamocha (☎ 343000), at Calle 34 No 31-24, in the more easy-going residential district, one km to the east.

Places to Eat

There are plenty of cheap restaurants around, or attached to, the budget hotels, where you can grab a set meal for US$2 or less. There are few really good restaurants in the city centre, save perhaps the expensive one in the Hotel Bucarica. At more affordable prices are *El Paisa*, Carrera 21 No 36-28, and *El Consulado Antioqueño*, Carrera 19 No 33-81, both serving local and Antioquian food.

A better area for dining is the eastern sector of the city, particularly on and around Carreras 27 and 33, where you'll find some of the best of the city eateries. Try, for example, *La Pampa*, Carrera 27 No 42-27,

serving Argentine food, or the *Casona de Chiflas*, Carrera 33/Calle 36, for its parrillada and other meat dishes.

On weekend evenings, stroll around the Hotel Chicamocha, where a string of live music bars and discos attract young local people.

Getting There & Away

Air The Palonegro airport is on a meseta high above and overlooking the city, off the Barrancabermeja road. The landing here is breathtaking. The airport and the city centre are linked by very infrequent (every hour or two) local buses marked 'Aeropuerto'. You catch them on Carrera 15. It's much faster to go by taxi colectivo (US$2). In the centre, you will find them in the Parque Santander, opposite the cathedral.

There are flights to most major Colombian cities, including Bogotá (US$89), Medellín (US$95) and Cartagena (US$113).

Bus Bucaramanga has a new, well-organised bus terminal. It's quite a distance from the centre, off the road to Girón, but you can move easily between the two using the frequent city buses marked 'Terminal'. In the centre, wave one down on Carrera 15.

There are plenty of buses to Bogotá (US$19, 10 hours), Santa Marta (US$21, nine hours), Cartagena (US$28, 13 hours) and Cúcuta (US$10, six hours). All prices are for climatizado, which is the dominant type of bus on these routes.

GIRON

Girón is a pretty town 10 km from Bucaramanga. It was founded in 1631 and has preserved much of its colonial character. It's a nice place to stroll around looking at the fine houses, charming patios and a few small bridges. The Plazuela Peralta and Plazuela de las Nieves are among its most enchanting spots.

Girón has become a trendy place, and is home to some intellectuals and artists. Due to its proximity to the city, the town fills up with *bumangueses* at weekends.

COLOMBIA

Places to Stay & Eat

Girón is just a day trip from Bucaramanga, but if you wish to stay longer, there is the good if expensive *Hotel Las Nieves* (☎ 468968), on the main square. A cheaper alternative is the *Hotel Río de Oro*, also on the plaza.

Antón García, Calle 29 No 24-47, and *El Carajo*, Carrera 25 No 28-08, are two places for cheap food. More up-market are *La Casona*, Calle 28 No 27-47, and *Mansión del Fraile*, on the main square, both pleasant and serving good, typical food. On weekends, stalls open at the riverside and offer a choice of regional snacks and dishes.

Getting There & Away

There are frequent city buses from Carrera 15 in Bucaramanga, which will deposit you on the main square of Girón in half an hour.

CUCUTA

Cúcuta is a hot, uninspiring city of around half a million people. It's the capital of Norte de Santander and a busy commercial centre, fuelled by its proximity to Venezuela, just 12 km away. The city doesn't have significant tourist attractions, so unless you're travelling to or from Venezuela, there's little reason to come here.

Information

Tourist Office The tourist office (☎ 713395) is at Calle 10 No 0-30.

Money At the time of writing, no banks in Cúcuta were interested in changing cash dollars, and only the Banco del Estado and Banco Industrial Colombiano changed travellers' cheques. Other banks marked on the map give advances on Visa or Master-Card.

Plenty of casas de cambio, at the bus terminal and in the city centre, change dollars, pesos and bolívares. There's also a rash of casas de cambio in San Antonio (on the Venezuela side of the border), paying much the same as in Cúcuta.

Venezuelan Consulate The consulate is on the corner of Calle 8 and Avenida 0. It is open weekdays from 8 am to 3 pm but closes for almuerzo. At the time of writing, this was one of the very few Venezuelan consulates in Colombia which issued visas for non-Colombians. Regardless of your nationality, you do need a visa for an overland crossing to Venezuela.

You need your passport and one photo, and you have to fill in a form. The visa costs US$30. You may be lucky enough to get it the same afternoon – start queuing early, because you pay the fee at the bank (not at the consulate), and this can only be done before 11 am.

Immigration The DAS check post (where you get an exit/entry stamp in your passport) is just before the frontier on the Río Táchira, on the left side of the road going towards Venezuela. The office is open daily from 7.30 am to noon and 2 to 6.30 pm. You can also have your passport stamped in the DAS main office in Cúcuta, at Avenida 1 No 28-57, in the San Rafael district, but it's less convenient.

Things to See & Do

If you have a couple of hours to spare, visit the **Museo de Arte e Historia de Cúcuta**, Calle 14 No 1-03, which has a private collection of objects relating to the town's history. It's open Tuesday to Saturday from 8 am to noon and 2 to 6 pm.

Outside the city, about 10 km from Cúcuta on the road to the border, is **Villa del Rosario**. It was here that the constitution of Gran Colombia was drawn up and passed in 1821. The central park, on the main road, contains several historic buildings, including the Casa de Santander and the Templo del Congreso. The Casa de la Bagatela, across the road, houses a modest archaeological collection.

Places to Stay

There are plenty of residencias around the bus terminal, particularly along Avenida 7, but they range from basic to ultra-basic and most double as love hotels or brothels. The

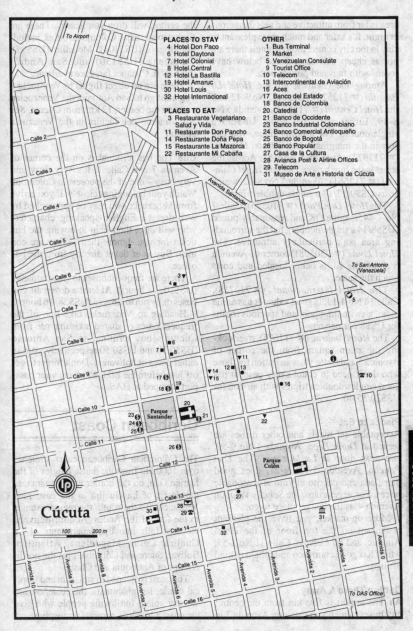

PLACES TO STAY
4 Hotel Don Paco
6 Hotel Daytona
7 Hotel Colonial
8 Hotel Central
12 Hotel La Bastilla
19 Hotel Amaruc
30 Hotel Louis
32 Hotel Internacional

PLACES TO EAT
3 Restaurante Vegetariano Salud y Vida
11 Restaurante Don Pancho
14 Restaurante Doña Pepa
15 Restaurante La Mazorca
22 Restaurante Mi Cabaña

OTHER
1 Bus Terminal
2 Market
5 Venezuelan Consulate
9 Tourist Office
10 Telecom
13 Intercontinental de Aviación
16 Aces
17 Banco del Estado
18 Banco de Colombia
20 Catedral
21 Banco de Occidente
23 Banco Industrial Colombiano
24 Banco Comercial Antioqueño
25 Banco de Bogotá
26 Banco Popular
27 Casa de la Cultura
28 Avianca Post & Airline Offices
29 Telecom
31 Museo de Arte e Historia de Cúcuta

Cúcuta

0 100 200 m

To Airport
Calle 2
Calle 3
Avenida Santander
Calle 4
Calle 5
Calle 6
Calle 7
Calle 8
Calle 9
Calle 10
Calle 11
Calle 12
Calle 13
Calle 14
Calle 15
Calle 16

To San Antonio (Venezuela)

Parque Santander
Parque Colón

To DAS Office

Avenida 0
Avenida 1
Avenida 2
Avenida 3
Avenida 4
Avenida 5
Avenida 6
Avenida 7
Avenida 8
Avenida 9
Avenida 10

COLOMBIA

area is far from attractive and gets dangerous at night. It's safer and much more pleasant to stay in the city centre, though hotels there are not as cheap. All those listed below have rooms with fans and private bath.

Among the cheapest are the *Hotel La Bastilla* (☎ 712576), Avenida 3 No 9-42, and the *Hotel Central* (☎ 713673), Avenida 5 No 8-89. Either will cost about US$6/9 a single/double. For a dollar more, you can stay in the marginally better *Hotel Daytona* (☎ 717927), Avenida 5 No 8-57. Across the street is the much more pleasant *Hotel Colonial* (☎ 712661), Avenida 5 No 8-62, which costs US$9/12/17 a single/double/triple.

The *Hotel Don Paco* (☎ 710575), Calle 7 No 4-44, is quite OK and reasonably priced (US$8/14 a single/double), but the surrounding area isn't particularly attractive. The *Hotel Louis* (☎ 730598), corner of Avenida 6 and Calle 13, is better located and costs much the same.

The *Hotel Internacional* (☎ 712718), Calle 14 No 4-13, is good value. It has a fine patio, a swimming pool and spacious rooms for US$8 per person.

The *Hotel Amaruc* (☎ 717625), overlooking the main square from the corner of Avenida 5 and Calle 10, is an option for those who don't need to count every peso. It has good singles/doubles/triples with air-con for US$30/35/40.

Places to Eat

Acceptable set meals and other dishes are served at *Doña Pepa*, Avenida 4 No 9-59, and next door at *La Mazorca*. The *Don Pancho*, Avenida 3 No 9-21, does good parrillada and cabrito al vino at reasonable prices. For vegetarians, the *Salud y Vida*, on Avenida 4, is the budget place to go.

More up-market, you have the pleasant restaurant on the top floor of the Hotel Amaruc, and *Mi Cabaña*, Calle 11 No 2-53, which has good churrasco and róbalo (a kind of fish).

Getting There & Away

Air The airport is five km from the centre; city buses, which you catch on Avenida 3 in the centre, will drop you nearby. There are flights to all major Colombian cities, including Bogotá (US$104), Medellín (US$95), Cartagena (US$130) and San Andrés (US$180). Cheaper fares are available.

There are no direct flights to Venezuela – you must go to San Antonio, the Venezuelan town on the border, 12 km from Cúcuta. See San Antonio del Táchira in the Venezuela chapter.

Bus The bus terminal is on the corner of Avenida 7 and Calle 1. It's very dirty and very busy – one of the poorest in Colombia. Watch your belongings closely. If you arrive from Venezuela, you may be approached by well-dressed English-speaking characters who will offer their help in buying the bus ticket for you. Ignore them – they are con men. Buy your ticket directly from the bus office.

There are frequent buses to Bucaramanga (US$10, six hours). At least a dozen air-con buses daily run to Bogotá (US$28, 16 hours).

Heading to Venezuela, take one of the frequent buses or shared taxis that run from Cúcuta's bus terminal to San Antonio (US$0.30 and US$0.50 respectively, paid in either pesos or bolívares). Don't forget to get off just before the bridge to have your passport stamped at DAS.

Caribbean Coast

The Colombian Caribbean coast stretches over 1600 km from the dense jungles of the Darién Gap, on the border with Panama, to the desert of La Guajira in the east, near Venezuela. To the south, the region extends to the foot of the Andes. Administratively, the area falls into the departments of La Guajira, Cesar, Magdalena, Atlántico, Bolívar, Sucre and Córdoba, plus the northern tips of Antioquia and Chocó.

The coast is steeped in sun, rum and tropical music. Its inhabitants, the costeños, are an easy-going, fun-loving people who give the coast a touch of carnival atmosphere.

Special attractions include Cartagena, one of the most beautiful colonial cities in Latin America, and the town of Mompós, a small architectural gem. You can take it easy on the beach – some of the best are in the Parque Nacional Tayrona – or go snorkelling or scuba diving amidst the magnificent coral reefs of the Islas del Rosario. There's also Ciudad Perdida, the ancient lost city of the Tayrona Indians, hidden deep in the lush tropical forest on the slopes of the Sierra Nevada de Santa Marta.

SANTA MARTA

Founded in 1525, Santa Marta is the oldest surviving town in Colombia, though its colonial character has virtually disappeared. The climate is hot, but the sea breeze, especially in the evening, cools the city and makes it pleasant to wander about, or to sit over a beer in any of the numerous open-air waterfront cafés. Santa Marta has become a popular tourist centre, not for the city itself but for its surroundings. Nearby El Rodadero is one of Colombia's most fashionable beach resorts, though its beach and water are being dangerously polluted by the Santa Marta port.

Don't miss out on trips to Taganga and the Parque Nacional Tayrona. Santa Marta is also the place to arrange a tour to Ciudad Perdida.

Information

Tourist Office The CNT tourist office (☎ 211833, 211873), Calle 17 No 3-120, is open weekdays from 8 am to noon and 2 to 6 pm.

Money The Banco Comercial Antioqueño and the Banco Industrial Colombiano change travellers' cheques. The Banco del Estado, Banco Popular and Banco Industrial Colombiano will change cash, but check the casas de cambio first, which may give comparable rates and save long waits in banks. There are plenty of casas de cambio in the bank area, especially on Calle 14 between Carreras 3 and 4. A particularly useful one is

the 24-hour La Posada, Calle 11 No 1C-51, which usually pays well for US dollars. All banks marked on the map give advances on Visa or MasterCard.

Telephone The telephone code is 954.

Tour Operators Santa Marta's tour market revolves principally around Ciudad Perdida and the Parque Nacional Tayrona (see those sections). Tours to Ciudad Perdida are monopolised by Turcol (☎ 212256), Carrera 1C No 22-79. You can book and pay for a tour through some hotels (eg the Hotel Miramar or Casa Familiar), which will then transfer your application and payment to Turcol.

Tours to the Parque Nacional Tayrona are run by several operators, of which the Hotel Miramar is the cheapest.

Things to See

The **Museo Arqueológico Tayrona** in the Casa de la Aduana on the corner of Calle 14 and Carrera 2 is open weekdays from 8.15 to 11.45 am and 2 to 5.45 pm. It has a good collection of Tayrona objects, mainly in pottery and gold. Don't miss the model of Ciudad Perdida, especially if you plan on visiting the place.

The **Quinta de San Pedro Alejandrino** is in the far suburb of Mamatoco (take the Mamatoco bus from the waterfront to get there). This is the hacienda where Simón Bolívar spent his last days and died, and is today a national monument. The **Museo Bolivariano**, built on the grounds, features contemporary art donated by artists from Colombia, Venezuela, Panama, Ecuador, Peru and Bolivia, the countries liberated by Bolívar. The Quinta is open daily from 9.30 am to 4.30 pm (it may be closed on Tuesday in the off season); entry is US$2.50.

The **Catedral**, a large whitewashed building on the corner of Carrera 4 and Calle 17, is supposedly the oldest church in Colombia, but work was not actually completed until the end of the 18th century. It holds the ashes

COLOMBIA

Santa Marta

0   100   200 m

CARIBBEAN
SEA

To El Rodadero, Airport
& Barranquilla

PLACES TO STAY
1 Hotel Miramar
2 Casa Familiar
4 Hotel Tayrona
5 Hotel Yuldama
23 Hotel Panamerican
24 Park Hotel
25 Sol Hotel Inn

PLACES TO EAT
22 Restaurante
Panamerican

OTHER
3 Casa de Cambio
La Posada
6 Iglesia de
San Francisco
7 Telecom
8 Banco Industrial
Colombiano
9 Banco de Bogotá
10 Museo Arqueológico
Tayrona
11 Monumento a Rodrigo
de Bastidas
12 Banco Comercial
Antioqueño
13 Banco de Colombia
14 Banco Popular
15 Tierra Mar Aire
16 Banco de Occidente
17 Bancafé
18 Banco del Estado
19 Catedral
20 CNT Tourist Office
21 Avianca Post &
Airline Offices
26 Turcol

COLOMBIA

of its founder, Rodrigo de Bastidas (just to
the left as you enter the church).

Places to Stay

The *Hotel Miramar* (☎ 214756), Calle 10C
No 1C-59, offers the cheapest accommodation in town (US$3/5 a single/double without
bath, US$4/6 with bath), or you can string up
your hammock for US$1. The hotel has a
café serving meals, snacks, soft drinks and
beer. The manager runs tours to the Parque
Nacional Tayrona in his own chivas, and will
store your gear free of charge. The place has
long been the archetypal gringo hotel, with

a hippie-type atmosphere, but if you find it
too noisy or freak-filled, go to the *Casa
Familiar* (☎ 211697), a few steps away at
Calle 10C No 2-14. It's quieter, costs
US$6/10 a single/double with bath, and
serves meals. The place is also popular with
gringos and the staff are friendly.

If you need more comfort (but less atmosphere), there are several modern hotels on
the waterfront (Carrera 1C). In ascending
order of price (and possibly value) they are:
the *Sol Hotel Inn* (☎ 211131), Carrera 1C No
20-23 (US$16/19/23 a single/double/triple);
the *Park Hotel* (☎ 211215), Carrera 1C No

18-67 (US$18/22/27); and the *Hotel Panamerican* (☎ 214751), Carrera 1C No 18-23 (US$20/26/32). The latter also offers air-con rooms (US$27/35/44).

For somewhere with a more individual style, go to the *Hotel Tayrona* (☎ 212408), Carrera 1C No 11-41, in an old house with a fine wooden interior and beautiful tiling. It costs US$9 per person in rooms with bath. The *Hotel Yuldama* (☎ 210063), Carrera 1C No 12-19, is the top-end option (US$40/50/60 for an air-con single/double/triple).

Places to Eat

There are a lot of cheap restaurants around the Hotel Miramar, particularly on Calles 11 and 12 near the waterfront, where you can get an unsophisticated set meal for about US$1.75.

The waterfront is packed with cafés and restaurants offering almost anything from snacks and pizzas to local cuisine and seafood. The *Restaurante Panamerican*, on the corner of Calle 18, is one of the best.

Several thatched restaurants between Calles 26 and 28, south of the town centre and close to the beach, are noted for good fish. Choose between the *Terraza Marina* and *El Gran Manuel*.

Getting There & Away

Air The airport is 16 km out of the city on the road to Barranquilla. City buses marked 'El Rodadero Aeropuerto' will take you there from Carrera 1C (45 minutes).

Avianca has flights to Bogotá (US$129), Medellín (US$110) and Cúcuta (US$113); as elsewhere, it's advisable to shop around for cheaper fares – check AeroRepública and Intercontinental first.

Bus The terminal is on the south-eastern outskirts of the city. Frequent minibuses go there from Carrera 1C in the centre.

Half a dozen air-con buses run daily to Bogotá (US$40, 18 hours). Plenty of buses go to Barranquilla (US$3 corriente, US$4 climatizado; two hours). Some climatizados

(but no corrientes) go direct to Cartagena (US$9, four hours). Frequent buses depart for Riohacha; take any of these for Cañaveral in the Parque Nacional Tayrona.

AROUND SANTA MARTA
Taganga

Taganga is a small fishing village set in a beautiful bay, five km north of Santa Marta. The waterfront is packed with boats, and open-air cafés blasting out music at full volume. Boat excursions along the coast are offered by locals, or you can walk around the surrounding hills, which provide splendid views.

Go to the **Playa Grande**, a magnificent bay north-west of the village. Either walk there (20 minutes) or take a boat from Taganga (US$1). The beach is lined with palm-thatched restaurants serving good fish. You can walk farther along the coast on a path which winds along the slopes of the hilly coast up to the Playa Granate.

Taganga is a popular scuba-diving centre; there are half a dozen dive shops/schools (most packed on the waterfront) which offer courses and dives. They are slightly cheaper than those in Cartagena and San Andrés.

There's a choice of accommodation in Taganga, though it's not cheap. One of the cheapest is the *Hotel El Delfín* (US$8 per person). The *Hotel Playa Brava* offers more comfort (US$20 a double with fan, US$25 air-con). The *Hotel La Ballena Azul* focuses on more affluent tourists (US$45 a double with fan, US$55 air-con) and has a good (though not cheap) restaurant. All three hotels are on the waterfront. Some locals rent rooms, which may be cheaper than staying in a hotel.

Frequent minibuses run between Santa Marta and Taganga; catch them on Carrera 1C in Santa Marta.

Parque Nacional Tayrona

This is one of the most popular national parks in the country. It is set on the jungle-covered coast to the east of Santa Marta. The beaches in the park, set in deep bays and shaded with coconut palms, are among the loveliest in

Colombia. Some are bordered by coral reefs, and snorkelling is good, but be careful of the treacherous offshore currents.

The region was once the territory of the Tayrona Indians, and some remains have been found in the park, the most important being the ruins of the ancient town of Pueblito.

The main entrance to the park is in **El Zaíno** (where you pay the US$4.50 entrance fee), 35 km from Santa Marta on the coastal road to Riohacha. From El Zaíno, walk four km on a paved road to **Cañaveral**, on the shore. Here you'll find the administrative centre of the park, which runs *cabañas* (currently being restored) and an outrageously overpriced camping ground (US$30 per tent!). There is also a restaurant. Most travellers walk for 50 minutes along a well-marked trail to **Arrecifes**, where the beaches are more spectacular and locals run cabañas, a camp site (US$3) and restaurants, and also hire hammocks (US$2).

From Arrecifes, you can walk to Pueblito in two hours along a path with splendid tropical forest scenery. There have been some cases of robbery on this route, so don't walk alone.

The Hotel Miramar in Santa Marta runs a chiva to Cañaveral (US$11 return trip, including the entry fee to the park) and is the cheapest operator. The chiva shuttles daily, and you can return any day you want.

Other popular sites in the park include Bahía Concha (US$1 entry fee) and Naguange (US$4), but they are difficult to get to on one's own, as there is no public transport. Several travel agents in Santa Marta organise tours to both these places. The Hotel Miramar plans to operate another chiva on one of these routes.

CIUDAD PERDIDA

Ciudad Perdida (literally, the Lost City) is one of the largest pre-Columbian towns discovered in the Americas. It was built by the Tayrona Indians between the 11th and 14th centuries, on the north-western slopes of the Sierra Nevada de Santa Marta, and was most probably their biggest urban centre. During their conquest of South America, the Spaniards wiped out the Tayronas, and their settlements disappeared without trace under the lush tropical vegetation. So did Ciudad Perdida, until its discovery in 1975 by guaqueros (grave robbers).

Ciudad Perdida lies on the relatively steep slopes of the Buritaca valley, at an altitude of between 1000 and 1300 metres. The central part of the city is set on a ridge, from which various stone paths lead down to other sectors on the slopes. There are about 150 stone terraces – some in remarkably good shape – which once served as foundations for the houses. Originally, the urban centre was completely cleared of trees, before being reclaimed by the jungle. Today, the city is quite overgrown, which gives it a somewhat mysterious air.

Getting There & Away

There are two ways of getting to Ciudad Perdida: a helicopter tour or a trek. Both begin from Santa Marta. The former takes less than three hours; the other takes six days.

Helicopter The Aviatur travel agency has irregular helicopter tours during the peak holiday seasons (Christmas and Easter). It is a 20-minute flight from Santa Marta airport to Ciudad Perdida, followed by a two-hour guided visit and the return journey. In all, it takes about two hours and 40 minutes and costs US$350 per person. If you are captivated by this whirlwind speed, and are not deterred by the price, contact an Aviatur office in any of the major cities.

Trekking There are two trails leading to the Lost City: through La Tagua and Alto de Mira; and through El Mamey and up along the Río Buritaca. The former trail was abandoned a few years ago, and now all visitors take the Buritaca trail, which is shorter and easier but perhaps less spectacular. The section between Santa Marta and El Mamey is done by vehicle.

Access to Ciudad Perdida is by tour only, organised by Turcol in Santa Marta (☎ 212-

256). You cannot do the trip on your own, or hire an independent guide. The price is US$200 per person for the all-inclusive tour, and is not negotiable. This includes transport, food, accommodation (in hammocks), porters, guides and all necessary permits. You carry your own personal belongings. Take a torch, water container and insect repellent.

Tours are in groups of between four and 10 people, and depart all year round as soon as the group has been collected. In the high season, expect a tour to set off every few days. In the off season, there may be just one tour a week.

The trip takes three days uphill to Ciudad Perdida, one day at the site and two days back down. The hike is not very difficult in technical terms, though it may be tiring due to the heat, and if it's wet (as it is most of the year) the paths are pretty muddy. The only fairly dry period is from late December to February or early March.

CARTAGENA

Cartagena de Indias is legendary, for both its history and its beauty. It is Colombia's most fascinating city, and shouldn't be missed. Don't be in a hurry either, as the city's charm will keep you here for at least several days.

Dating from 1533, Cartagena was one of the first cities founded by the Spaniards in South America. Within a short time, the town blossomed into the main Spanish port on the Caribbean coast and the gateway to the north of the continent. It was the place where treasure plundered from the Indians was stored until the galleons could ship it to Spain. As such, it became a tempting target for pirates and, in the 16th century alone, suffered five dreadful sieges, the best known of which was that led by Francis Drake in 1586.

In response to pirate attacks the Spaniards decided to make Cartagena an impregnable port, and constructed elaborate walls encircling the town and a chain of outer forts. These fortifications helped save Cartagena from subsequent sieges, particularly the fiercest attack of all, led by Edward Vernon in 1741.

In spite of these attacks, Cartagena continued to flourish. During the colonial period, the city was the key outpost of the Spanish empire, and influenced much of Colombia's history.

Today, Cartagena has expanded dramatically and is surrounded by vast suburbs. It is now Colombia's second port and an important industrial centre. Nevertheless, the old walled town has changed very little. It is a living museum of 16th and 17th-century Spanish architecture, with narrow winding streets, palaces, churches, monasteries, plazas and large mansions with overhanging balconies, shady patios and formal gardens.

Over the past couple of decades, Cartagena has become a fashionable seaside resort, though its beaches are actually not very good. An expensive modern tourist district has sprung up on Bocagrande and El Laguito, an L-shaped peninsula which fronts the Caribbean. This sector, packed with top-class hotels and expensive restaurants, has become the main destination point for moneyed Colombians and international charter tours.

The climate is hot, but a fresh breeze blows in the evening, making this a pleasant time to stroll around the city. The driest period is from December to April. October and November are the wettest months.

Information

Tourist Offices The CNT office (☎ 664 7015), in the Casa del Marqués de Valdehoyos, is open weekdays from 8 am to noon and 2 to 6 pm.

The city tourist office, the Promotora de Turismo de Cartagena, has three offices: at the airport; at the Muelle de los Pegasos (☎ 665 1843), outside the walls of the inner town; and in Bocagrande (☎ 665 4987), on the corner of Carrera 1 and Calle 4. All three are open weekdays from 8 am to 6 pm, and weekends from 8 am to noon.

Money Banks which change travellers' cheques and cash, and tend to give good

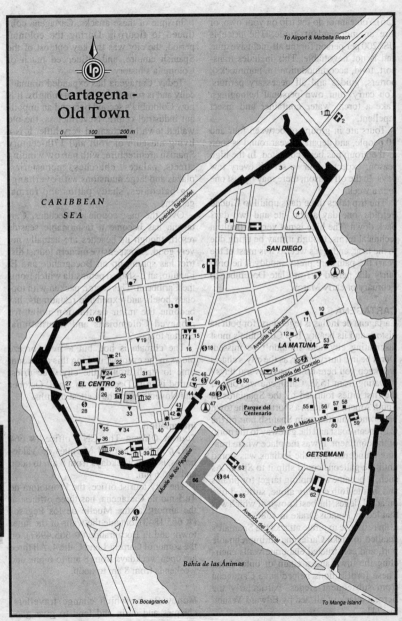

Cartagena - Old Town

0   100   200 m

CARIBBEAN
SEA

To Airport & Marbella Beach

SAN DIEGO

EL CENTRO

LA MATUNA

Parque del
Centenario

GETSEMANI

Calle de la Media Luna

Muelle de los Pegasos

Avenida Santander

Avenida Venezuela

Avenida del Concejo

Avenida del Arsenal

Bahía de las Ánimas

To Bocagrande   To Manga Island

COLOMBIA

PLACES TO STAY
5	Hotel Santa Clara
10	Hotel del Lago
12	Hotel Montecarlo
14	Hotel Veracruz
15	Hostal Arthur
17	Hotel Bucarica
26	Hostal Santo Domingo
54	Hotel San Felipe
55	Hotel Viena
56	Hostal Valle
57	Hotel Holiday
58	Hostal Baluarte
60	Hotel Doral
61	Hotel Familiar

PLACES TO EAT
9	Restaurante Nautilus
16	Restaurante San Agustín
19	Restaurante Vegetariano Natural
21	Café de la Plaza
22	Café Santo Domingo
24	La Sartén por el Mango & Paco's
25	El Burlador de Sevilla
27	Restaurante La Vitrola
33	La Crêperie
34	El Bodegón de la Candelaria
35	Restaurante Classic de Andrei

36	La Escollera de la Marina
43	El Café del Portal de los Dulces
45	Restaurante Vegetariano Govinda's

OTHER
1	Casa de Rafael Núñez
2	Ermita del Cabrero
3	Las Bóvedas
4	Plaza de Toros de la Serrezuela
6	Iglesia de Santo Toribio de Mangrovejo
7	Teatro Heredia
8	Monumento a la India Catalina
11	Aces Office
13	Universidad de Cartagena
18	Banco Comercial Antioqueño
20	CNT Tourist Office & Casa del Marqués de Valdehoyos
23	Iglesia de Santo Domingo
28	Banco Anglo Colombiano
29	Palacio de la Inquisición
30	Plaza de Bolívar
31	Catedral

32	Museo del Oro y Arqueología
37	Museo Naval del Caribe
38	Iglesia y Convento de San Pedro Claver
39	Museo de Arte Moderno
40	Plaza de la Aduana
41	Avianca Office
42	Tu Candela
44	Plaza de los Coches & Puerta del Reloj
46	Banco Unión Colombiano
47	Monumento a Pedro de Heredia
48	Banco Popular
49	Banco Industrial Colombiano
50	Banco de Colombia
51	Adpostal
52	Banco del Estado
53	Telecom
59	Iglesia de San Roque
62	Iglesia de la Santísima Trinidad
63	Iglesia de la Santa Orden
64	Banco Sudameris Colombia
65	Mister Babilla
66	Centro de Convenciones
67	City Tourist Office

rates, include: the Banco Anglo Colombiano, Banco Unión Colombiano, Banco Comercial Antioqueño, Banco Sudameris Colombia and Banco Industrial Colombiano. Most major banks will accept Visa card, while MasterCard is recognised only by Banco Industrial Colombiano and Banco de Occidente.

There are plenty of casas de cambio, particularly around Plaza de los Coches. They are open till 6 pm, and change cash (at marginally lower rates than the banks) but usually not travellers' cheques (those few which change them give very low rates).

Cartagena is probably the only Colombian city where you will receive plenty of offers to change money in the street, at a very attractive rate. Give the street changers a big miss – they are all con men.

The Tierra Mar Aire office (☎ 665 1062) is in Bocagrande, Carrera 4 No 7-196.

Telephone The telephone code is 95.

Consulates The Venezuelan consulate (☎ 665 0382, 665 0353) is at Avenida Piñango (Calle 5A) No 10-106 in Castillo Grande. This is one of the very few consulates that issues tourist visas (US$32) for an overland crossing, as long as you have an onward ticket out of Venezuela. The paperwork takes one day.

The Panamanian consulate is on the corner of Carrera 5 and Calle 67 in Crespo, near the airport. The visa is usually issued within 10 minutes and costs US$10 to US$15, depending on your nationality.

Things to See & Do

The **old town** is the principal attraction, particularly the inner walled town, consisting of the historical districts of El Centro and San Diego. Almost every street is worth strolling down. Getsemaní, the outer walled town, is less impressive and not so well preserved, but it is also worth exploring. Be careful – this part of the city may not be safe, especially after dark.

The old town is surrounded by **Las Murallas**, the thick walls built to protect it. Construction was begun towards the end of the 16th century, after the attack by Francis Drake; until that time, Cartagena was almost completely unprotected. The project took two centuries to complete, due to repeated damage from storms and pirate attacks.

The main gateway to the inner town was what is now the **Puerta del Reloj** (the clock tower was added in the 19th century). Just behind it is the **Plaza de los Coches**, a square once used as a slave market. Note the fine old houses with colonial arches and balconies.

A few steps south-west is the **Plaza de la Aduana**, the largest and oldest square in the old town. It was used as a parade ground, and all administrative buildings were gathered around it. In the centre stands a statue of Christopher Columbus.

Close by, to the west, is the **Iglesia y Convento de San Pedro Claver**, built by the Jesuits, originally under the name of San Ignacio de Loyola. The name was changed in honour of the Spanish-born monk Pedro Claver, who lived and died in the convent. He spent his life ministering to the slaves brought from Africa. The convent, built in the first half of the 17th century, is a monumental three-storey building surrounding a tree-filled courtyard, and part of it is open to visitors, including the cell where Claver lived and died. You can also climb a narrow staircase to the choir of the church and, at times, get on to the roof. The convent is open daily from 8 am to 6 pm. The church alongside was built long after, and has an imposing stone façade. The remains of San Pedro Claver are kept in a glass coffin in the high altar.

Nearby, on Calle de las Damas, is a beautiful mansion, the **Casa de la Candelaria**, housing an excellent though expensive restaurant. You can visit the house without eating; go up to the bar in the tower for views of the town.

The **Plaza de Bolívar** is in a particularly beautiful area of the old town. On one side of the square stands the **Palacio de la Inquisición**, completed in 1776 and a fine example of late colonial architecture, with its overhanging balconies and magnificent Baroque stone gateway. It is now a museum displaying instruments of torture used by the Inquisitors, pre-Columbian pottery, and works of art from the colonial and independence periods. It's open weekdays from 8 am to 5.30 pm and weekends from 10 am to 5.30 pm.

Directly opposite, across the plaza, the **Museo del Oro y Arqueología** has a good collection of gold and pottery of the Sinú culture. It's open weekdays from 8 am to noon and 2 to 6 pm. On the corner of the plaza is the **Catedral**, which was begun in 1575 but was partially destroyed by Drake's cannons in 1586, and not completed until 1612. The dome on the tower was built early this century. Apart from this, the church basically retains its original form; it is a massive structure with a fort-like exterior and a simply decorated interior.

One block west of the plaza is Calle Santo Domingo, a street which has hardly changed since the 16th century. On it stands the **Iglesia de Santo Domingo**, the oldest church in the city. It is a large, heavy construction, and buttresses had to be added to the walls to support the naves of the church. The convent is right alongside, and you can see its fine courtyard.

Farther north on the same street is the **Casa del Marqués de Valdehoyos**, a magnificent colonial mansion dating from the 18th century, now open as a museum (daily from 8 am to noon and 2 to 6 pm).

At the northern tip of the old city are **Las Bóvedas**, 23 dungeons built in the city walls at the end of the 18th century. This was the last construction done in colonial times, and was destined for military purposes. Today, the dungeons are tourist shops.

While you're wandering around, call at the **Muelle de los Pegasos**, a lovely old port in the south of the old town full of fishing, cargo and tourist boats.

Several forts were built at key points outside the wall to protect the city from pirates. The greatest fortress is undoubtedly the **Castillo de San Felipe de Barajas**. This huge stone structure was begun in 1639 but not completed until some 150 years later. It is open daily from 8 am to 5 pm; the entrance fee for foreigners is US$4 (US$2 for students). Don't miss an impressive walk through the complex system of tunnels, built to facilitate the supply and evacuation of the fortress.

The **Convento de la Popa**, perched on top of a 150-metre hill beyond the San Felipe fortress, was founded by the Augustinians in 1607. It has a nice chapel and a lovely flower-filled patio, and offers panoramic views over the city. There have been some cases of armed robbery on the zigzagging access road to the top – go by taxi (no public transport).

Places to Stay

Despite its tourist status, Cartagena has reasonable budget accommodation; the prices of the residencias are much the same as in other cities. The tourist peak is from late December to late January but, even then, it's relatively easy to find a room.

If you need something cheap, walk directly to the Getsemaní area. There are plenty of cheapies here, mostly on Calle de la Media Luna. Many are dives that double as love hotels or brothels, but there are several 'clean' and safe options.

The *Hotel Doral* (☎ 664 1706), on Calle de la Media Luna, has a reputation as a travellers' lodge. It has spacious rooms surrounding a large, pleasant courtyard with umbrella-shaded tables, where travellers

gather. Rooms without/with bath cost US$5/6 per person.

Right across the street from the Doral, the new *Hotel Holiday* (☎ 664 0948) has swiftly become even more popular with backpackers. It offers higher standards for the same prices as the Doral. The staff are friendly and the place is well kept.

The *Hotel Viena* (☎ 664 6242, fax 629 5700) is owned by a helpful, multilingual Belgian, Patrick. The hotel is unusual in that it allocates most of its profits to a programme to assist street children. Rooms without/with bath cost US$5/6 per person, and there are cooking and laundry facilities.

Other budget places in the same area include the *Hotel Familiar* (☎ 664 8374) and the *Hostal Valle* (☎ 664 2533). The former has a nice patio and charges US$5/6 per person in rooms without/with bath; the latter is more basic and slightly cheaper.

The hotels in El Centro, the heart of the old town, are more expensive. One of the few acceptable budget places is the *Hotel Bucarica* (☎ 664 1263), which costs US$9/16/21 a single/double/triple with private bath.

If you don't mind staying outside the old town, try *Hotel Bellavista* (☎ 664 6411), at Marbella Beach, on Avenida Santander, a 10-minute walk from the walled city. It is a good place, and some foreign travellers stay there. Clean rooms with bath and fan cost US$9 per person.

There are several mid-price hotels scattered throughout the old town area. They are nothing particularly special, but do have air-conditioning. Try the *Hostal Arthur* (☎ 664 2633) in El Centro (US$26/32/40 a single/double/triple); the diagonally opposite *Hotel Veracruz* (☎ 664 1521), with rooms at US$29/36/42; the modern *Hotel Montecarlo* (☎ 664 5835) in La Matuna (US$32/42/48); the nearby *Hotel del Lago* (☎ 664 0526), with rooms at US$27/40/54; and the *Hotel San Felipe* (☎ 664 5439) in Getsemaní (US$28/38/48). All of them also offer slightly cheaper rooms with fan.

The small *Hostal Santo Domingo* (☎ 664 2268) is quite simple and rather overpriced (US$35 a double with bath and fan), but it's

COLOMBIA

quiet and ideally located in an attractive area of El Centro.

Most of the city's mid-price and top-end hotels are in Bocagrande. In the old town, there's one extraordinary place, the *Hotel Santa Clara* (☎ 664 6070). Even if you're not up to staying there (US$230 a double), go and see it.

Places to Eat

Cartagena is a good place to eat, particularly for up-market places, but cheap places are also plentiful. Dozens of simple restaurants in the walled town serve set almuerzos for less than US$2, and many also offer set comidas. Some better restaurants also do set lunches, eg the *Restaurante San Agustín*. The *Restaurante Vegetariano Govinda's* and the *Restaurante Vegetariano Natural* provide cheap vegetarian meals.

Plenty of cafés all over the old town serve arepas de huevo, dedos de queso, empanadas, buñuelos and a large variety of other snacks. A dozen stalls on the Muelle de los Pegasos operate round the clock and have an unbelievable choice of fruit juices.

Cartagena has some local specialities. Huevos de iguana (iguana eggs), cooked and threaded together like rosaries, are still sold by street vendors (January to April only) despite an official ban on the eggs introduced for ecological reasons. Butifarras are a kind of small smoked meatball, sold only on the street by butifarreros, who walk along and strike big pots with a knife to get your attention. Peto is a milk soup made of maize, sweetened with panela and served hot. It, too, is only sold by street vendors.

If you are not after such exotic curiosities, there are enough places offering some familiar Western fare. *La Crêperie* on Plaza de Bolívar does appetising crêpes and tortillas, while *El Café del Portal de los Dulces* has good sandwiches and pasta. Two new open-air cafés facing Santo Domingo Church, the *Café de la Plaza* and *Café Santo Domingo*, serve some short-order dishes, although their food is not that cheap.

There are a number of expensive restaurants in the old town, most of which are set in historic interiors. Recommended places are: *El Bodegón de la Candelaria* (ask for their lobster); *Classic de Andrei*, just a few steps from La Candelaria; *Nautilus*, facing the India Catalina monument (good seafood); *El Burlador de Sevilla* (Spanish cuisine); and *La Sartén por el Mango*. The posh *Hotel Santa Clara* has good Italian and French restaurants. There are many other up-market establishments in Bocagrande.

Entertainment

A number of tabernas, discos and other venues stay open late at night. Several of them are to be found on Avenida del Arsenal in Getsemaní, close to the Centro de Convenciones; *Mister Babilla* is the most popular disco in this area. *Tu Candela*, an informal bar on Plaza de los Coches, serves beer and taped music till late.

There are several up-market restaurants in El Centro, which have bands playing Caribbean/Cuban music, usually Wednesday or Thursday to Saturday. Try *La Vitrola*, *La Sartén por el Mango* or *La Escollera de la Marina*.

In Bocagrande the place to go is *La Escollera* (corner of Carrera 1 and Calle 5), a disco in a large thatched open hut, which goes nightly till 4 am. On the beach beside La Escollera, plenty of vallenato groups play music till dawn.

Getting There & Away

Air The airport is in the suburb of Crespo, three km north-east of the old city, and is serviced by frequent local buses from the centre. Avianca/Sam, Aces, AeroRepública and Intercontinental operate flights to/from Cartagena. There are flights to Bogotá (US$129), Medellín (US$110), Cali (US$143), Cúcuta (US$130), San Andrés (US$128) and other major cities. Note that these are regular fares; discount fares (sometimes as much as 60% less) are often possible, so shop around. For example, AeroRepública and Intercontinental fly passengers to Bogotá for US$71, which can be a tempting alternative to full-day bus travel.

A small local carrier, Aerocorales, flies

every Wednesday and Friday morning to Mompós (US$53 one way). Return flights are on the same days.

Avianca flies to Miami and New York, while Copa, the Panamanian airline, has daily flights to Panama City (US$133 plus 21% tax). Viasa, the Venezuelan carrier, flies five times a week to Caracas (US$180 plus 21% tax).

Bus The bus terminal is on the eastern outskirts of the city, a long way from the centre. Air-con urban buses shuttle between the two every 10 minutes (US$0.50, 30 minutes).

There are a dozen buses daily to Bogotá (US$47 climatizado, 22 hours) and about the same number of buses to Medellín (US$30 climatizado, 13 hours). Buses to Barranquilla run every 15 minutes or so (US$4 corriente, US$5.50 climatizado; two hours). Unitransco has one corriente bus to Mompós, at 6.30 am (US$10, eight hours); see the Mompós section for more details.

Boat Cargo ships depart for San Andrés from the Muelle de los Pegasos but they don't take passengers. Irregular cargo boats go to Turbo (about US$15, one to two days), and it's relatively easy to get a ride. Take a hammock.

For a year or so, the Colombian ferry *Crucero Express* offered travellers the opportunity to travel between Cartagena and Colón, in Panama. Unfortunately, this ferry is no longer in operation, as the service was cancelled in late 1996. The alternative at present is to take one of the cargo boats that operate between Colón and Barranquilla (north-east of Cartagena), some of which will also take motorcycles and cars. Not surprisingly, though, these services are irregular and infrequent. The price is negotiable but by and large expect to pay around US$70 per person, US$100 for a motorcycle and up to US$400 for a car. Remember that Panama requires a visa or tourist card, onward ticket, and sufficient funds, and has been known to turn back those who don't meet the requirements.

You may be approached by men offering you fabulous trips around the Caribbean in 'their boats' for a little help on board; if you seem interested, they will ask you to pay some money for a boarding permit or the like. Don't pay a cent – you'll see neither the man, nor your money, again.

AROUND CARTAGENA
Islas del Rosario
This archipelago of small coral islands is about 35 km south-west of Cartagena. There are about 25 islands, including tiny islets only big enough for a single house. The archipelago is surrounded by coral reefs, where the colour of the sea ranges from turquoise to purple. The whole area has been declared a national park.

Cruises through the islands are a well-established business. Tours operate daily all year round from the Muelle de los Pegasos in Cartagena. Boats leave between 7 and 9 am and return about 4 or 5 pm. The tour costs roughly US$15 per person, which includes lunch but not the US$2 entrance fee to the aquarium on one of the islands, the usual stop en route.

Fuerte de San Fernando
This is an old fortress on the southern tip of Isla de Tierrabomba, about 10 km south of Cartagena's centre. It can only be reached by water. Boats leave from the Muelle de los Pegasos between 8 and 10 am and return in the afternoon. The tour costs US$9, including lunch and entrance to the fort, or US$6 for the journey only.

La Boquilla
This is a small fishing village, populated by blacks, seven km north of Cartagena on a peninsula between the sea and the Ciénaga de Tesca. The locals fish at the *ciénaga* (lagoon) in the afternoon with their famous *atarrayas*, a kind of net. Plenty of palm-thatched shack restaurants on the beach attract people from Cartagena on weekends; most of them are closed at other times. The fish is good but not that cheap. Frequent city buses run to La Boquilla from India Catalina in Cartagena, taking half an hour.

Jardín Botánico Guillermo Piñeres

A pleasant half-day escape from the city rush, these botanical gardens are on the outskirts of the town of Turbaco, about 15 km south-east of Cartagena. Take the Turbaco bus departing every 10 minutes from the place known as Chambacú near India Catalina and ask the driver to drop you at the turn-off to the gardens (US$0.50, 45 minutes). From there it's a comfortable 20-minute stroll down the largely unpaved side road.

The 20-acre gardens (open daily except Monday from 9 am to 4.30 pm) contain plants typical of the coast, including two varieties of coca plant. While buying your entry ticket (US$2) you get a leaflet which lists 250 plants identified in the gardens.

Volcán de Lodo El Totumo

About 50 km north-east of Cartagena, on the bank of the shallow Ciénaga del Totumo, one can find an intriguing 15-metre-high mound, looking like a miniature volcano. It's indeed a volcano but instead of lava and ashes, it eructs mud, a phenomenon due to the pressure of gases emitted by decaying organic matter underground.

El Totumo is the highest mud volcano in Colombia. Lukewarm mud with the consistency of cream fills its crater. You can climb to the top by specially built stairs, then go down into the crater and have a refreshing mud bath (US$2). It's a unique experience – surely volcano-dipping is something you haven't yet tried! The mud contains minerals acclaimed for their therapeutic properties. You can wash the mud off in the ciénaga. There are several restaurants around the volcano.

To get to the volcano from Cartagena, take a bus from the old town to Mercado Bazurto, from where hourly buses depart in the morning to Galerazamba. Get off at Loma Arena (US$1.50, 1¾ hours) and walk along the main road for 20 minutes, then to the right to the volcano for another 10 minutes. The last direct bus from Loma Arena back to Cartagena departs at 3 pm.

MOMPOS

Mompós, some 200 km south-east of Cartagena, is an exceptional town. It was founded in 1537 on the eastern branch of the Río Magdalena, which in this region has two arms: Brazo Mompós and Brazo de Loba. The town soon became an important port, through which all merchandise from Cartagena passed to the interior of the country. Several imposing churches and many luxurious mansions were built.

Towards the end of the 19th century, shipping was diverted to the other branch of the Magdalena, bringing the town's prosperity to an end. Mompós has been left in isolation, and its colonial character is almost intact.

Mompós has a long tradition in hand-worked filigree gold jewellery, of outstanding quality. Nowadays the gold is slowly being replaced by silver. Another speciality of the town is its furniture, particularly rocking chairs.

On 26 February 1998 there will be a total eclipse of the sun and the centreline (longest duration) will pass near Turbo, Mompós and a bit south of Valledupar.

Information

Chipi Tours (☎ 855593), next door to the Hostal Doña Manuela, can provide information about the town. The agency organises reasonably priced city tours and boat trips. Boys hang around to guide tourists through the town and into some private colonial homes.

The Fundación Neotrópicos (☎ 855240) operates El Garcero, the 600-hectare nature reserve about 40 km upriver from Mompós.

Bring enough pesos with you, as money may be difficult to change, or only for a poor rate.

The telephone code for Mompós is 952.

Things to See & Do

Most of the central streets are lined with rows of fine whitewashed colonial houses with characteristic metal-grille windows, imposing doorways and lovely hidden patios. Six colonial churches complete the scenery; all

COLOMBIA

To Bodega, Airport & Cartagena

Calle 20
Calle 19
Calle 18
Calle 17
Calle 16
Calle 15
Calle 14
Calle 13

Carrera 4
Carrera 3
Carrera 2

Río Magdalena (Brazo Mompós)

Mompós

0   100   200 m

To El Banco & Bogotá

PLACES TO STAY
4	Residencias La Valerosa
5	Residencias La Isleña
6	Residencias San Andrés
7	Residencias La Casona
8	Residencias Solmar
21	Hostal Doña Manuela
23	La Posada del Virrey
30	Residencias Aurora
31	Residencias Villa de Mompox

PLACES TO EAT
10	Restaurante Tebe's
11	Restaurante Robin Hood
12	Restaurante Frío Carlis
18	Restaurante Milena Paola
24	La Pizzería
27	Asadero Pollo Rico
28	Piequeteadero Lo Sabroso
29	Estadero Los Cobos

OTHER
1	Iglesia de San Francisco
2	Iglesia de San Juan de Dios
3	Market
9	Aces Airlines
13	Colegio Pinillos
14	Iglesia de Santo Domingo
15	Boats to El Banco & Magangué
16	Plaza Real de la Concepción, Buses to Bosconia & Jeeps to Bodega & El Banco
17	Iglesia de la Concepción
19	Cemetery
20	Chipi Tours
22	Museo Cultural
25	Casa de la Cultura
26	Iglesia de San Agustín
32	Fundación Neotrópicos
33	Iglesia de Santa Bárbara
34	Unitransco Office (Buses to Cartagena)

re interesting, though rarely open. In particular, don't miss the **Iglesia de Santa Bárbara**, with its Moorish-style tower, unique in Colombian religious architecture.

The **Casa de la Cultura**, a fine old *casona*, houses memorabilia relating to the own's history, and the **Museo Cultural**, nstalled in the house where Simón Bolívar once stayed, displays some religious art. There's a small **Jardín Botánico**, with lots of hummingbirds and butterflies, on Calle 14 three blocks west of Iglesia de Santa Bárara. Knock to be let in.

There are a couple of workshops near the

museum where you can see and buy local jewellery. The management of the Hostal Doña Manuela can give you the addresses of artisans who work at home.

It's fun to wander aimlessly about this clean and tranquil town, absorbing its old-time atmosphere. In the evening, people rest in front of their homes, sitting in – of course – the Mompós-made rocking chairs.

Special Events
Holy Week celebrations are very elaborate in Mompós. The solemn processions circle the

streets for several hours on Maundy Thursday and Good Friday nights.

Places to Stay

Except for Holy Week, you won't have problems finding somewhere to stay. There are a dozen hotels in town, most of them pleasant and friendly.

The cheapest is the *Residencias Solmar* (US$4/6 a single/double), but it's the most basic place. Somewhat better is the *Residencias La Valerosa* or, better still, the *Residencias La Isleña* (☎ 855245), both of which cost US$5 per person. There are several reasonably priced and good places to stay, including *Residencias Villa de Mompox* (☎ 855208), *Residencias Aurora*, *La Posada del Virrey* (☎ 855630) and *Residencias San Andrés*. All cost about US$8 per person in rooms with bath.

The newer *Residencias La Casona* (☎ 855307) is friendly and agreeable, and costs US$10/16 per person in rooms with fan/air-con.

At the top of the range, there's the *Hostal Doña Manuela* (☎ 855620), in a restored colonial mansion with two ample courtyards, a swimming pool and a restaurant. Singles/doubles with bath and fan cost US$35/44 (US$42/55 with air-con). The pool can be used by nonguests (US$3).

Places to Eat

Food stalls at the market along the riverfront provide cheap meals. There are several budget restaurants around the small square behind Iglesia de la Concepción, near the corner of Carrera 2 and Calle 18. They all serve set meals for about US$2.

The *Piqueteadero Lo Sabroso* has inexpensive typical food (good mondongo). For chicken, try the *Asadero Pollo Rico*, while for pizza, check *La Pizzería*, though neither is anything special.

The *Hostal Doña Manuela* has possibly the best restaurant in town, and it's not that expensive. It also has a bar, or you can have your evening drink (and a dance if you wish) in the *Estadero Los Cobos*, open till late.

They also serve tasty food and have good taped music.

Getting There & Away

Air Aerocorales has flights to/from Cartagena (US$53) on Wednesday and Friday. The Aces office in town takes bookings and sells tickets.

Bus & Boat Mompós is well off the main routes but can be reached relatively easily by dirt road and river. Most probably, you will come here from Cartagena. There is one direct bus daily, with Unitransco, leaving Cartagena at 6.30 am (US$10, eight hours). Otherwise, take a bus to Magangué (US$8, four hours, at least a dozen per day with Unitransco or Brasilia), continue by boat to Bodega (US$1.75, 20 minutes, frequent departures till about 3 pm) and take a jeep to Mompós (US$2, one hour); the jeeps wait for the boats. There are also direct boats from Magangué to Mompós, but they're not so frequent.

If you head for Mompós from Bucaramanga, take a bus to El Banco (US$12, seven hours) and continue to Mompós by jeep or boat (either costs US$5 and takes two hours); jeep is a bit faster but the trip is less comfortable and can be pretty dusty.

From Santa Marta, there are two options. Either take a bus to El Banco (US$10, six hours) and continue as above, or catch any of the frequent buses to Bosconia (US$5, three hours), from where the morning Valledupar bus goes to Mompós on the back road, via La Gloria and Santa Ana (US$7, five hours).

TURBO

Turbo is the main port on the Gulf of Urabá from where bananas, cultivated in the region are shipped overseas. It's a ramshackle, dirty and noisy town, and best avoided. The streets look unsafe, especially after dark, and the surrounding region is infiltrated by guerrillas and paramilitary squads, and is notorious for problems of public order.

However, the region does have a couple of places of great natural beauty, namely the

Parque Nacional Los Katíos, and the Capurganá area with its beautiful coast. It's virtually impossible to avoid passing through Turbo if you plan on visiting these places. Turbo is also an obligatory stopover to get an entry or exit stamp in your passport if you are coming from or heading to Panama via the Darién Gap. See the introductory Getting There & Away chapter for details on Darién routes.

Information

Money No banks in Turbo will change cash or travellers' cheques. Some shops and other establishments will change US dollars but at a poor rate.

Try Banco de Bogotá or Banco Ganadero, both on Calle 101, for a peso advance on your Visa card.

Panamanian Consulate The nearest consulate is in Capurganá, but it's unreliable. It is recommended you get a visa beforehand, eg in Medellín or Cartagena (see those sections for consulate addresses).

Immigration The DAS office (where you need to have your passport stamped when coming from or going to Panama) is at the Apostadero Naval in the Naval Base, on the bank of the Golfo de Urabá, three km west of the town's centre on the road to the airport. Jeep-colectivos from Carrera 13 between Calles 101 and 102 will take you there. The office is open daily from 8 am to noon and 1 to 5 pm.

Places to Stay & Eat

The friendly *Residencias Marcela*, at Carrera 14B No 100-54, is the best bet among the cheapies. Rooms don't have private baths but they do have fans, are clean and cost US$4 per person. If it's full, try the *Residencias Turbo* next door, or the *Residencias El Viajero*, just round the corner at Calle 101 No 14-48. Neither has private baths but both have fans.

If you want a private bath, go to the *Hotel Saussa* (☎ 682020), at Carrera 13 No 99A-

28, which costs US$7/11 for a single/double. Its restaurant serves filling set meals.

The best place in town is the *Hotel Castilla de Oro* (☎ 682466), at Calle 100 No 14-07. It has air-con singles/doubles with TV, private bath and hot water for US$26/38, and a restaurant. There are more eateries around the central streets, but nothing great.

Getting There & Away

Air Aces has three flights a day to Medellín (US$58). Its office is at Calle 101 No 14-10.

Bus Six buses daily run to Medellín (US$15, 13 hours). If you are heading for Cartagena, take a jeep to Montería (from the market), and make a connection there.

Boat To Parque Nacional Los Katíos, take a boat up the Río Atrato to Riosucio, and get off at Sautatá (US$12, 1½ hours). The boats leave early in the morning.

If you are heading for Panama along the north coast, take a boat to Capurganá (US$14, 2½ hours), then walk 1½ hours to Sapzurro (the last village on the Colombian side), cross the border and keep walking for a couple of hours to Puerto Obaldía (Panama). There are also unscheduled boats between Capurganá, Sapzurro and Puerto Obaldía.

PARQUE NACIONAL LOS KATIOS

This is one of the most beautiful parks in Colombia. Set on the border with Panama, the park covers an extensive stretch of hilly land covered by thick tropical rainforest, and a marshy plain with a chain of lakes and mangroves. Several footpaths through the woods allow you to enjoy the rich vegetation and animal life, mainly birds and butterflies. The major attractions are the waterfalls, the most spectacular, the Salto de Tilupo, being some 100 metres high.

There are tourist facilities in the administrative centre, including accommodation in a house (US$10 per person), camping and food. The friendly rangers will give you information or even take you around. Bring a strong insect repellent, swimming costume, biodegradable soap (you are not allowed to use other soaps) and candles.

A permit for the park can be obtained in Bogotá or Medellín. Guerrillas operate in the region, so check the situation at the office. See the Turbo section for information on how to get to the park. From the Sautatá wharf, it's a 20-minute walk to the administrative centre.

The best time to visit is from December to March, which is the only relatively dry period; August may be OK. Even at these times the paths can be muddy. Bring suitable shoes and be prepared to get them wet frequently during walks.

San Andrés & Providencia

This archipelago of small coral islands in the Caribbean lies about 700 km north-west of the Colombian mainland and only 230 km east of Nicaragua. The archipelago is Colombian territory and is made up of a southern group (with San Andrés the largest and main island) and a northern group (with Providencia the main island).

For a long time, the islands were a British colony and, although Colombia took possession after independence, the English influence on language, religion and architecture remained virtually intact until modern times. In the 1950s, when a regular domestic air service was established with the Colombian mainland and San Andrés was declared a duty-free zone, the situation started to change. A significant migration of Colombians to the islands, a boom in tourism and commerce, and government policies have meant that some of the original character of San Andrés has been lost. Providencia will probably go the same way in the near future.

Nonetheless, the islands, especially Providencia, still provide a good opportunity to experience the ambience of the Caribbean. The turquoise sea, extensive coral reefs and rich underwater life are a paradise for snorkellers and scuba divers. The easy-going life, friendly natives (descendants of Jamaican slaves), adequate (if not cheap) tourist facilities and general safety are other traits welcoming visitors to the islands.

San Andrés lies on a convenient and cheap route between Central America and Colombia, and is quite popular among travellers. All visitors to San Andrés staying more than one day are charged US$15 on arrival and handed the so-called Tarjeta de Turista. This is a local government levy designed to improve the island's budget; in practical terms, it's the entry ticket to the islands.

The dry season on the archipelago is from January to May, with another not-so-dry period from August to September.

SAN ANDRES

San Andrés is about 13 km long and three km wide. It is relatively flat and largely covered by coconut palms. A 30-km scenic paved road circles the island, and several roads cross inland.

The urban centre and capital of the whole archipelago is the town of San Andrés (known locally as El Centro), in the extreme north of the island. It has more than two-thirds of the island's 57,000 inhabitants, and is the principal tourist and commercial area, packed with hotels, restaurants and stores.

Information
Tourist Offices The municipal tourist office, the Secretaría de Turismo (☎ 24343), is on the ground floor of the airport. The CNT office (☎ 24230) is on Avenida Colombia, near the airport.

Money Travellers' cheques and cash can be changed at the Banco Popular, Banco Industrial Colombiano and, occasionally, at the Banco del Estado. All the banks marked on the map will pay cash advances on either MasterCard (Banco Industrial Colombiano and Banco de Occidente) or Visa (the remaining ones).

There are several casas de cambio scattered throughout the central area (eg Boulevard Los Reyes in the Centro Comer-

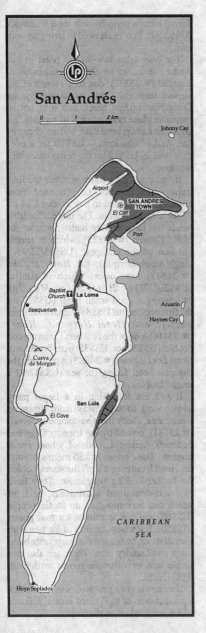

San Andrés

0   1   2 km

Johnny Cay

Airport

SAN ANDRÉS TOWN

El Cliff

Port

Baptist Church   La Loma

Seaquarium

Acuario

Haynes Cay

Cueva de Morgan

San Luis

El Cove

CARIBBEAN SEA

Hoyo Soplador

cial New Point, Local 229), which change cash at rates comparable to those of the banks. Some also change travellers' cheques but the rates are poorer. You can probably get more for your dollars from the money-changers who gather near the Banco Industrial Colombiano.

Plenty of shops and some hotels accept payments in cash dollars, and can change them for pesos (but usually at a lower rate than the banks).

Telephone The telephone code is 9811.

Consulates Costa Rica, Guatemala, Honduras and Panama have consulates in San Andrés town (see the map). The Honduran Consulate is in the Hotel Tiuna, while the others are in shops. It's a good idea to get visas on the mainland, as consuls do not always stay on the island and you may be stuck for a while waiting for one to return.

Things to See & Do
You will probably stay in El Centro, but you may want to take some time to look around the island. **El Cliff** is a 50-metre-high rocky hill, 20 minutes walk from the airport. It offers good views over the town and the surrounding coral reefs.

The small village of **La Loma**, in the central hilly part, is perhaps the most traditional place on the island and is noted for its Baptist church, the first to be established on San Andrés.

The recently opened, overpriced **Sea-quarium** contains marine species including sharks and turtles, and dolphins perform shows for visitors. The kiosk near the CNT tourist office in El Centro sells tickets and takes tourists in a minibus to the place (US$10 entry fee plus return transport).

The **Cueva de Morgan** is an unprepossessing underwater cave where the Welsh pirate Henry Morgan is said to have buried some of his treasure. The **Hoyo Soplador**, at the southernmost tip of the island, is a sort of small geyser where the sea water spouts into the air through a natural hole in the coral

COLOMBIA

rock. This phenomenon can be observed only when the winds and tide are right.

Buses run along the circular coastal road, as well as on the inner road to La Loma and El Cove, and can drop you near any of the sights. Otherwise, hire a bicycle in town (US$1.50 per hour or US$8 for a full day). Motorbikes, scooters, minimokes and cars can also be hired at various locations throughout the centre. Shop around, as prices and conditions vary.

Another way of visiting the island is the Tren Blanco, a sort of road train pulled by a tractor dressed up like a locomotive. It leaves daily at 9.30 am from the corner of Avenida Colombia and Avenida 20 de Julio to circle the island, stopping at sites of interest (US$5, three to four hours). The same route can be done by taxi for US$15 (up to five people fit). Taxi drivers will be happy to show you around other sights, for extra fare, of course.

There are several small **cays** off the coast, and the most popular trip is to Johnny Cay, opposite the main town beach (US$3 return). You can go by one boat and return by another, but make sure there will be a boat to take you back. Haynes Cay and Acuario, off the eastern coast of the island, are good for snorkelling (US$4 return).

The main town beach is good but it may be crowded. There are no beaches along the western shore, and those along the east coast are nothing special, except for the good beach in San Luis.

Places to Stay

Accommodation in San Andrés is expensive. The cheapest place to stay is the *Hotel Restrepo* (☎ 26744), on the opposite side of the runway from the airport terminal. It has become a mecca for foreign backpackers; Colombians are rare guests here. It is basic but friendly, and costs US$6 per person, regardless of what room you get – some have their own bath, others don't, but all rooms have fans. There is a dining room, where you can get breakfast, lunch and dinner (US$2 per meal). If the rooms are full, and you don't mind mosquitoes (they are only a problem

during certain periods), ask for a hammock (US$2.50). You're allowed to string up your own.

The only other low-budget hotel in San Andrés seems to be the *Apartamentos El Español* (☎ 23337), one block south of the airport terminal. This is essentially the Colombian budget hotel, and it is not an attractive place to stay, nor is its vicinity. Yet all rooms have private bath, and are cheap by San Andrés standards – US$10 for a poor dark double, US$12 for the better one with a window.

If you can't get a room at either the Restrepo or El Español, or you need more comfort, be prepared to pay at least US$15/25 for a single/double. The more affordable hotels (all have private baths) include: the *Hotel Coliseo* (☎ 23335), which is simple but one of the cheapest (US$15/25/35 a single/double/triple); the *Hotel Malibú* (☎ 24342) next door, which is similar (US$20/27/34); *Hotel Mary May Inn* (☎ 25669), a good small hotel (US$25 for the first person plus US$8 for each additional guest); and *Hotel Hernando Henry* (☎ 23416), one of the best bets for an air-con double (US$30, or US$35 with breakfast). *Hotel Los Delfines* (☎ 24083) is probably the cheapest hotel facing the sea (US$42/52 a single/double).

If you are travelling in a larger party and/or want to stay away from the main tourist area, check the *Apartamentos Sumeli* (☎ 25781), owned by the friendly Olga and Federico Archbold, both of whom speak English. Their house is 250 metres beyond the Hotel Restrepo; it's off the street, behind the bunker-looking warehouse. They have two self-contained apartments, each of which can accommodate up to six people (US$60) and one apartment for four guests (US$50). Each unit consists of kitchen with a small stove, fridge and dishes, private bathroom and laundry area. There are also two single and two double rooms with bath (US$15/25).

If money is not a problem, San Andrés has a good choice of top-priced hotels, some of which are marked on the map.

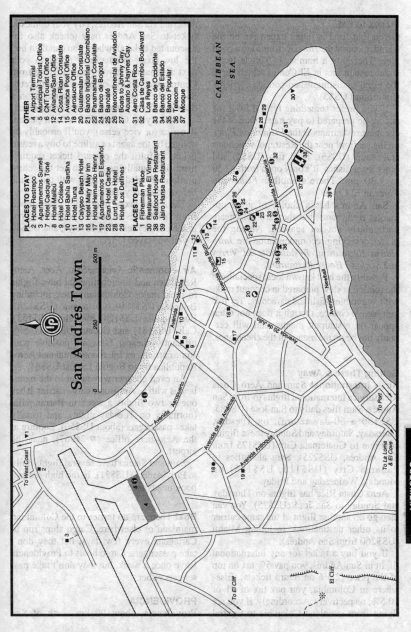

San Andrés Town

PLACES TO STAY
2 Hotel Restrepo
3 Apartamentos Sumeli
5 Hotel Cacique Toné
7 Hotel Malibú
8 Hotel Coliseo
10 Hotel Bahía Sardina
11 Hotel Tiuna
13 Calypso Beach Hotel
16 Hotel Mary May Inn
17 Hotel Hernando Henry
19 Apartamentos El Español
23 Gran Hotel Caribe
28 Lord Pierre Hotel
29 Hotel Los Delfines

PLACES TO EAT
1 Fisherman Place
30 Restaurante El Virrey
38 Seafood House Restaurant
39 Jairo Hansa Restaurant

OTHER
4 Airport Terminal
5 Municipal Tourist Office
6 CNT Tourist Office
12 Avianca/Sam Office
14 Costa Rican Consulate
15 Avianca Post Office
18 Aerosucre Office
20 Guatemalan Consulate
21 Banco Industrial Colombiano
22 Panamanian Consulate
24 Banco de Bogotá
25 Bancafé
26 Intercontinental de Aviación
27 Boats to Johnny Cay,
   Acuario & Haynes Cay
31 Aero Costa Rica
32 Casa de Cambio Boulevard
   Los Reyes
33 Banco de Occidente
34 Banco del Estado
35 Banco Popular
36 Telecom
37 Mosque

COLOMBIA

Places to Eat

Given that food is rather expensive on the island, meals at the *Hotel Restrepo* are a good idea. There are a number of simple back-street restaurants in El Centro which serve the usual undistinguished comida corriente (for around US$3).

If you prefer something typical from the island, be prepared to pay more. One of the cheapest restaurants is the *Fisherman Place* on the seafront near the Restrepo, which has crab soup (US$5), fried fish (US$4) and other local dishes. It's only open from 12.30 to 4.30 pm. There's another *Fisherman Place* in El Cove.

San Andrés has a choice of good up-market restaurants, but they are not cheap, particularly not for seafood. Among the places deserving recommendation are *Jairo Hansa Restaurant*, *Restaurante El Virrey* and *Seafood House Restaurant*.

Possibly the best known local speciality is the rondón, a stew prepared in coconut milk, with vegetables, fish and caracoles. Try it if you have a chance, though it does not often appear on restaurant menus, and will certainly not be on the menus of the cheap ones.

Getting There & Away

Air – international Sam and Aero Costa Rica service international flights to/from San Andrés. Sam flies daily to San José (US$85, US$150 a 60-day return); on Tuesday, Thursday, Saturday and Sunday these flights continue to Guatemala City (US$125 from San Andrés, US$225). Sam also flies to Panama City (US$115, US$185) on Monday, Wednesday and Friday.

Aero Costa Rica has flights on Thursday and Sunday to San José (US$75). You can then go on another flight of the same carrier to its other destinations, including Miami (US$260 from San Andrés).

If you buy a ticket for any international flight in San Andrés, you pay 5% tax on top of the price (2.5% on return tickets). Elsewhere in Colombia, you pay tax of 21 or 10.5%, respectively. Accordingly, if you are flying from mainland Colombia to Central America via San Andrés, buy your domestic ticket to San Andrés only (check also for discounted tickets), where you can then buy the low-taxed international ticket to your next destination. If you plan on flying from Central America to Colombia, buy a ticket to San Andrés only, then another ticket on a domestic flight to the Colombian mainland.

While flying to San Andrés from Central America (or vice versa), you'll probably be obliged by the agent or airline to buy a return ticket, to fulfil the onward ticket requirement. It's usually possible to get the return portion refunded, but check with the airline before you buy your ticket.

The airport tax on international departures from San Andrés is US$20 if you have stayed in the country less than 60 days, and US$40 if you've stayed longer.

Air – domestic Avianca/Sam, Aces, Aero-República and Intercontinental have flights to most major Colombian cities, including Bogotá (US$180), Cartagena (US$128), Barranquilla (US$128), Medellín (US$153), Cali (US$181) and Cúcuta (US$141). Significantly cheaper fares are possible with some carriers, eg Intercontinental and Aero-República fly to Bogotá for just US$84.

An even cheaper way to get to the mainland is with an Aerosucre cargo carrier. It has one or two flights a week to Barranquilla (normally on Tuesday night), and usually takes passengers (about US$50). Enquire at the Aerosucre office (☎ 24967), near the airport.

Sam and Satena have several flights daily to Providencia (US$31). In the high season, book in advance.

Boat There are no ferries to the Colombian mainland or elsewhere. Cargo ships run to Cartagena every few days, but they don't take passengers. Cargo boats to Providencia leave once a week, but they don't take passengers either.

PROVIDENCIA

Providencia, about 90 km north of San

Andrés, is the second-largest island of the archipelago, at seven km long and four km wide. It is a mountainous island of volcanic origin, much older than San Andrés. The highest peak is El Pico, at 320 metres.

An 18-km road skirts the island, and virtually the entire population of 5000 lives along it, in scattered houses or in one of the several hamlets. Santa Isabel, a village at the northern tip of the island, is the administrative seat. Santa Catalina, a smaller island just to the north, is separated from Providencia by the shallow Canal Aury, spanned by a pedestrian bridge.

Providencia is much less affected by tourism than San Andrés. English is widely spoken, and there's still much Caribbean English-style architecture to be seen. The locals are even friendlier than those on San Andrés, and the duty-free business fever is unknown. However, the island is quite rapidly becoming a fashionable spot for Colombian tourists. Aguadulce, on the western coast, has already been converted into a tourist centre, with hotels and restaurants, and boat, motorbike and snorkelling gear for hire. So far, the rest of the island is largely unspoilt, though this situation is changing.

The coral reefs around Providencia are more extensive than those around San Andrés, and snorkelling and scuba diving are even better. The interior of the island provides for pleasant walks, with El Pico being the major goal. The trail to the peak begins from Casabaja, at the southern side of the island. It's a steady hour's walk to the top.

Getting around the island is pretty straightforward. Two chivas and several pick-ups run the circular road, charging US$0.50 for any distance. Providencia is an expensive island for food and accommodation, even more so than San Andrés.

Information

There's a tourist office at the airport, theoretically open from 8 am to noon and 2 to 6 pm. The Banco Central Hipotecario in Santa Isabel may change cash (but not cheques),

but at a very poor rate. Bring enough pesos with you from San Andrés.

Places to Stay

The only really cheap place to stay is the *Residencias Sofía* (☎ 48109), in Pueblo Viejo, two km south of Santa Isabel. Get off by the SENA centre and take the rough track that branches off the main road (next to a two-storey, green-painted shop) and leads towards the seaside; the residencias is only a couple of hundred metres away, on the shore. This very rustic place costs US$5 per person, and Miss Sofía can cook meals for you (around US$3 each).

The next-cheapest, and far better place, is the *Cabañas Santa Catalina* (☎ 48037), on the island of Santa Catalina (just opposite Santa Isabel) by the pedestrian bridge. It's a pleasant place with a family atmosphere, and costs US$12 per person in rooms with private bath.

The overwhelming majority of places to stay are in Aguadulce, which is apparently an exclusively tourist village. A dozen cabañas line the main road, charging US$15 to US$20 per person. One of the cheapest of these is the small *Cabañas Marcelo* (☎ 48190), at the southern end of the village.

Places to Eat

Food is expensive, though usually good, particularly the seafood. Most restaurants are in Aguadulce. One of the best for comida isleña (the local food), and reasonably priced, is the *Miss Elma*. In Santa Isabel, there are three restaurants, of which the *Junto al Mar* is the cheapest. Set meals go for around US$3.50, fried fish for a dollar more. You can buy good, fresh coconut bread in some shops.

Getting There & Away

Sam and Satena fly between San Andrés and Providencia several times per day (US$31). Buy your ticket in advance, and be sure to reconfirm return tickets at the Satena office at the airport, or the Sam office in Santa Isabel.

COLOMBIA

The North-West

In broad terms, the north-west is made up of two large regions, quite different in their geography, climate, people and culture. The first, the Chocó department, along the Pacific coast, is essentially an extensive stretch of tropical forest with an average rainfall largely surpassing that of the Amazon. The region is sparsely populated, mainly by blacks. As the roads are few and poor, transport is either by water or air.

The other part of the north-west, the departments of Antioquia, Caldas, Risaralda and Quindío, cover the hilly portions of the Cordillera Occidental and the Cordillera Central. This is picturesque mountainous country, crisscrossed by an array of roads and sprinkled with little towns noted for their distinctive architecture. There is a larger proportion of whites than elsewhere. Medellín, the capital of Antioquia, is the main city of the north-west.

MEDELLIN

Medellín was founded in 1616, but only at the beginning of the 20th century did it begin to expand rapidly, first as a result of the coffee boom and then as the centre of the textile industry. Today, it is a dynamic industrial and commercial city with a population of nearly two million, the country's largest urban centre after Bogotá. The city is spectacularly set in the Aburrá valley, with the modern centre in the middle and vast slum barrios all over the surrounding slopes.

Medellín is not a top travellers' destination, yet it's a vibrant and friendly city with a pleasant climate, and it does have some museums, and developed tourist facilities. Although no longer the world capital of the cocaine business, Medellín may not be very safe, so keep your night-time strolls to a minimum.

Information

Tourist Offices The Oficina de Turismo y Fomento (☎ 254 0800), Calle 57 No 45-129,

is open weekdays from 7.30 am to 12.30 pm and 2 to 6 pm. You can also try Turantioquia (☎ 291 1111), Carrera 48 No 58-11, especially if you are interested in tours.

Money The banks which change travellers' cheques at good rates include the Banco Sudameris Colombia, Banco Comercial Antioqueño and Banco Anglo Colombiano. All these banks will also change cash, but you'll probably get a similar or even better rate (and will save time) in some of the casas de cambio. There are several in the Edificio La Ceiba at Calle 52 No 47-28; before changing at the Intercambio 1A on the ground floor, check the three casas on the 3rd floor (room Nos 410, 412 and 416), which are likely to pay better. All are open weekdays from 8 am to noon and 2 to 5 pm. Cash advances on credit cards are easily available at most banks.

Tierra Mar Aire (☎ 242 0820) is at Calle 52 No 43-124.

Telephone Medellín's telephone code is 94.

Consulates The Panamanian consulate (☎ 268 1157) is at Calle 10 No 42-45, oficina 233. The Venezuelan consulate (☎ 235 1020) is at Calle 32B No 69-59.

National Parks The regional office of national parks (☎ 234 3661) is at Carrera 76 No 49-92.

Things to See & Do

Apart from a couple of old churches, the city's colonial architecture has virtually disappeared. Perhaps the most interesting of the churches is the **Basílica de la Candelaria**, in Parque Berrío. You also might like to visit the **Basílica Metropolitana**, in the Parque de Bolívar, completed early this century and thought to be the largest brick church on the continent (1,200,000 bricks were used).

The **Museo de Antioquia**, Carrera 52A No 51A-29, features a collection of paintings and sculptures by Fernando Botero, the most internationally known Colombian contemporary artist. It's open weekdays from 10 am to 5.30 pm, and Saturday from 9 am to 2 pm. The city has a fine botanical garden, the **Jardín Botánico Joaquín Antonio Uribe**, open daily from 9 am to 5 pm. Each April and May there is an orchid exposition in the garden's Orquideorama.

For panoramic views of the city, go to the **Cerro Nutibara**, a hill quite close to the centre. The **Pueblito Paisa**, a replica of a typical Antioquian village, has been built on the summit and is home to several handicrafts shops. A cheaper place for handicrafts, however, is the **Mercado de San Alejo**, held in the Parque de Bolívar on the first Saturday of every month.

Special Events

On the last Friday of every month, the Tangovía springs to life, on Carrera 45 in the Manrique district. This is tango night, when you can hear and dance to the nostalgic rhythms. Medellín is Colombia's capital of tango; it was here that Carlos Gardel, the legendary tango singer, died in an aeroplane crash in 1935.

If you come in early August, you have a chance to see the biggest event in Antioquia, the Feria de las Flores. The highlight of this festival is the Desfile de Silleteros, on 7 August, when hundreds of campesinos come down from the mountains and parade along the streets carrying *silletas* full of flowers on their backs.

Places to Stay

Some of the cheapest hotels are located around the street market, between Carreras 52 and 54 and Calles 47 and 50, but the area is dirty, noisy and unpleasant. The best budget bet in this sector is the *Hotel Comercial* (☎ 513 0006), Calle 48 No 53-102. This well-run hotel has singles/doubles/triples without bath for US$7/9/12 (US$9/12/16 with bath).

It's more pleasant, and perhaps safer, to stay in the Parque de Bolívar area. Possibly the cheapest acceptable place here is the *Hotel Plaza* (☎ 231 8984), Calle 54 No 49-23 (US$8 for a double with bath). The *Hotel*

Americano, next door, is a love dive and won't accept you for the whole night until after about 7 pm (never on weekends).

The *Hotel Camino Real* (☎ 512 4400), Calle 54 No 50-48, is better than the Plaza and costs US$8/10 for singles/doubles with bath. Other budget places include the *Hotel Residencias Gómez Córdoba* (☎ 513 1676), Carrera 46 No 50-29, and the *Residencias Doris* (☎ 251 2245), Carrera 45 No 46-23. Both have rooms with bath and cost much the same as the Camino Real.

If you can afford to pay more, the *Aparta Hotel El Cristal* (☎ 512 0911), Carrera 49 No 57-12, is one of the best value-for-money options and is therefore often full. This clean and pleasant place costs US$23/28/33 for a single/double/triple. All rooms have bath (with hot water), telephone, fan, colour TV and fridge. Some rooms are even equipped with a stove.

The *Aparta Hotel Santelmo* (☎ 231 2728), Calle 53 No 50A-08, and the *Hotel La Bella Villa* (☎ 511 0144), Calle 53 No 50-28, are two central places, and airport minibuses will deposit you a few steps from either. Both have comfortable rooms with bath. The latter is slightly cheaper (US$27/33/39). In the same price bracket is the *Hotel El Capitolio* (☎ 512 0003), Carrera 49 No 57-24.

Places to Eat

The *Restaurante La Estancia*, Carrera 49 No 54-15, in the Parque de Bolívar, is the cheapest place to eat. It's not very clean or pleasant but does have filling set meals for just US$1.

Vegetarians have several budget options, including *Govinda's* at Calle 51 No 52-17, the *Palased* at Carrera 50 No 52-35 and the somewhat more expensive *Paracelso* at Calle 52 No 45-06.

There are many moderately priced restaurants and cafés on and around the pedestrian walkway Pasaje Junín (Carrera 49), between the Parque de Bolívar and Calle 52. *Salón Versalles*, Pasaje Junín No 53-39, has a tasty menú económico, good cakes, fruit juices and tinto. The area on the 1st floor is more pleasant.

COLOMBIA

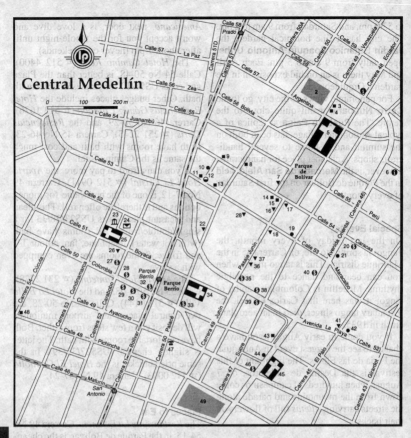

Central Medellín

0   100   200 m

Several restaurants on Pasaje Junín are set on the 1st floor overlooking the street and are pleasant places for lunch or dinner, or for watching the world go by while sipping a beer. To name just a few: the *Aleros del Parque*, *El Café del Parque* and *Hacienda Real*. If you just want to grab something quickly, try the *Boulevard de Junín*, where several self-service joints serve pizza, chicken, pasteles, salpicón and ice cream.

Hato Viejo, on the 1st floor of the Centro Comercial Los Cámbulos on the corner of Pasaje Junín and Calle 53, is one of the best places in the area. It serves regional dishes at affordable prices.

Getting There & Away

Air The José María Córdoba airport, 30 km south-east of the city, takes all international and most domestic flights, except for some regional flights on light planes (which still use the old Olaya Herrera airport right inside the city). The terminal houses the tourist office (on the lower level by the exit of the domestic arrival hall) and the Banco Comercial Antioqueño (on the upper level, at the departure hall), which exchanges travellers' cheques and gives advances on Visa. Cash can be changed at the Charcutería Johnny Carl, a snack outlet in the opposite end of the departure hall from the bank.

PLACES TO STAY		26	Restaurante	25	Ermita de la Veracruz
3	Hotel El Capitolio		Vegetariano	27	Banco Sudameris
4	Aparta Hotel		Govinda's		Colombia
	El Cristal	36	Hacienda Real	28	Banco Industrial
8	Hotel Veracruz	37	Boulevard de		Colombiano
9	Hotel Camino Real		Junín	29	Banco Comercial
11	Aparta Hotel	41	Restaurante		Antioqueño
	Santelmo		Paracelso	30	Banco de Bogotá
13	Hotel La Bella			31	Banco de Colombia
	Villa	**OTHER**		32	Banco Anglo
14	Hotel Plaza	1	Turantioquia		Colombiano
15	Hotel Americano	2	Centro Comercial	33	Banco Popular
43	Hotel Residencias		Villanueva & Copa	34	Basílica de la
	Gómez Córdoba		Office		Candelaria
48	Hotel Comercial	5	Basílica Metropolitana	35	Banco Industrial
		6	Tourist Office		Colombiano
PLACES TO EAT		10	Intercontinental de	38	Edificio La Ceiba
7	Restaurante La		Aviación	39	Banco de Occidente
	Estancia	12	Minibuses to José	40	Banco Industrial
16	Salón Versalles		María Córdoba		Colombiano
17	Restaurante Aleros		Airport	42	Tierra Mar Aire
	del Parque & El	19	AeroRepública	44	Aces Office
	Café del Parque		Office	45	Iglesia de San
18	Restaurante Hato	20	Banco de Occidente		José
	Viejo	21	Sam Office	46	Banco Unión
22	Restaurante	23	Museo de Antioquia		Colombiano
	Vegetariano	24	Avianca Post &	47	Telecom
	Palased		Airline Offices	49	Almacén Exito

Frequent minibuses shuttle between the city centre and the airport from the corner of Carrera 50A and Calle 53 (US$2, one hour). A taxi will cost US$15.

There are plenty of flights throughout the country – to Bogotá (US$74), Cali (US$87), Cartagena (US$110), Cúcuta (US$95) and San Andrés (US$153). Cheaper fares are available on some routes with some carriers.

Sam and Copa fly daily to Panama City (US$123). Zuliana de Aviación (a Venezuelan carrier) has four flights a week to Maracaibo (US$81), Caracas (US$122) and Miami (US$236). Servivensa flies to San Antonio del Táchira in Venezuela (US$50).

Bus Medellín has two bus terminals. The Terminal del Norte, three km north of the city centre, handles buses to the north, east and south-east (Turbo, Cartagena, Barranquilla, Bucaramanga, Bogotá). It's easily reached from the city centre by metro (six minutes). The brand-new Terminal del Sur, four km south-west of the centre, handles all traffic to the west and south (Quibdó, Manizales,

Cali, Popayán). It's accessible by the Guayabal bus (Ruta No 160), which you catch on Avenida Oriental near the Almacén Exito in the centre.

Frequent buses depart to Bogotá (US$19, nine hours), Cartagena (US$30, 13 hours) and Cali (US$19, nine hours); all prices are for climatizados. Six buses daily travel the rough road to Turbo (US$15 corriente, about 13 hours).

Getting Around

Medellín is Colombia's first (and for a long time will be the only) city to have the Metro, or fast metropolitan train (opened in November 1995). It consists of the 23-km north-south line and a six-km western leg. The train operates on the ground level except in the central area where it goes on viaducts above the streets.

AROUND MEDELLÍN

The rugged region surrounding Medellín is picturesque, and the temperate climate provides a variety of plants and flowers, including orchids. The region is sprinkled with haciendas and *pueblos paisas*, lovely little towns noted for their style of architecture.

If you have a couple of days to spare, it is a good idea to do a trip around Medellín to see what Antioquia is really like. Among the most interesting places are the towns of **La Ceja**, **El Retiro** and **Marinilla** (all good examples of the regional architecture), **Carmen de Viboral** (well known for its hand-painted ceramics) and the spectacular, 200-metre-high granite rock of **El Peñón**.

There is accommodation in all of these places, as well as an array of restaurants. The buses are frequent.

SANTA FE DE ANTIOQUIA

Founded in 1541, this is the oldest town in the region. It was an important and prosperous centre during the Spanish days, and the capital of Antioquia until 1826. It still retains its colonial character and atmosphere. The town is about 80 km north-west of Medellín, on the way to Turbo.

Things to See & Do

Give yourself a couple of hours to wander through the streets to see the decorated doorways of the houses, the windows with their carved wooden guards, and the patios with flowers in bloom. Of the town's four churches, the nicest is the **Iglesia de Santa Bárbara**. The **Museo Juan del Corral** displays historic objects collected in the region, and is open Tuesday to Saturday from 9.30 am to noon and 2 to 6 pm, and Sunday from 10 am to 5 pm. The **Museo de Arte Religioso** features sacral art and is open weekends only, from 10 am to 5 pm.

There is a curious 291-metre-long bridge, the **Puente de Occidente**, over the Río Cauca, six km east of town. When built in 1886, it was one of the first suspension bridges in the Americas. Walk there, or negotiate with taxi drivers in Santa Fe.

Places to Stay & Eat

The *Residencias Colonial*, Calle 11 No 11-72, set in an old mansion, is quiet and friendly. Rooms on the upper floor are more pleasant and have a balcony. Doubles cost US$10. The hotel serves cheap set meals.

El Mesón de la Abuela, Carrera 11 No 9-31, is in the same price range. It's quite simple, but clean and with a friendly atmosphere. It has a restaurant, which offers good breakfast, lunch and dinner but is more expensive than the restaurant in the Colonial. There are several cheaper residencias in town, including the *Franco*, Carrera 10 No 8-67, and *Dally*, Calle 10 No 8-50.

Top of the range is the *Hotel Mariscal Robledo*, Carrera 12 No 9-70, which costs US$20/35 a single/double. It has a swimming pool and a restaurant.

The cheapest place to eat is at the market on the main square, where you can get a tasty bandeja for a little over US$1. Apart from the hotel restaurants, there are at least half a dozen other places to eat.

Don't miss trying pulpa de tamarindo, a local sweet made from tamarind, sold on the main square.

Getting There & Away

There are several buses daily to/from Medellín's northern terminal (US$3, three hours), and also hourly minibuses until 7 pm (US$4, 2½ hours).

There are six buses a day to Turbo (US$12, 11 hours). They all come from Medellín, and might be full by the time they reach Santa Fe.

The South-West

The south-west covers the departments of Cauca, Valle del Cauca, Huila and Nariño. The region is widely diverse, both culturally and geographically. The biggest tourist attractions are the two outstanding archaeological sites of San Agustín and Tierradentro, and the colonial city of Popayán. Cali is the region's largest urban centre.

CALI

Cali is a prosperous and lively city with a fairly hot climate. Although founded in 1536, its growth came only in this century, primarily with the development of the sugar industry, followed by dynamic progress in other sectors. Today, Cali is Colombia's third-largest city, with a population of about 1.5 million.

The city, apart from a few fine churches and museums, does not have many tourist attractions. Its appeal lies rather in its atmosphere and its inhabitants, who are, in general, easy-going and friendly. Be careful of thieves and muggers, however.

The women of Cali, *las caleñas*, are considered to be among the most beautiful in the nation. Cali is also noted for its salsa music. These hot rhythms originated in Cuba in the 1940s, matured in New York and spread like wildfire throughout the Caribbean, reaching Colombia in the 1960s. The Cali region and the Caribbean coast traditionally remain the major centres of salsa music.

Finally, Cali has been known as the home of the Cali drug cartel and as the world capital of cocaine trafficking. Since most of the mafiosos were captured and put behind bars in 1995, this is no longer true, though the lower-rank bosses still run the business quite efficiently.

Orientation

The city centre is split in two by the Río Cali. To the south is the historic heart, laid out on a grid plan and centred around the Plaza de Caycedo. This is the area of tourist attractions, including old churches and museums.

To the north of the river is the newer centre, whose main axis is Avenida Sexta (Avenida 6N). This sector is essentially modern, with trendy shops and good restaurants, and it comes alive in the evening when a refreshing breeze cools down the city heat. This is the area to come and dine after a day of sightseeing on the opposite side of the river.

Information

Tourist Office The departmental tourist office, Cortuvalle (☎ 660 5000), Avenida 4N

No 4N-10, is open weekdays from 7.30 am to 12.30 pm and 2.30 to 6 pm. There's also a Cortuvalle outlet at the airport.

Money Most of the major banks are grouped around Plaza de Caycedo. At the time of writing, only the Banco Industrial Colombiano and the Banco Popular changed travellers' cheques and cash, and both wanted photocopies of your passport. Check the Casa de Cambio Titan Intercontinental on the 2nd floor of the Edificio Ulpiano Lloreda on Plaza de Caycedo, which is far more efficient and may give comparable rates for both cash and cheques. All banks marked on the map will pay peso advances on credit cards.

The Tierra Mar Aire office (☎ 667 6767) is at Calle 22N No 5BN-53.

Telephone Cali's telephone code is 92.

National Parks & Private Reserves The office dealing with national parks in the region is at Avenida 4N No 37AN-37 (☎ 664 9334).

The Red de Reservas Naturales de la Sociedad Civil (☎ 661 2581), Calle 23N No 6AN-43, piso 3, has a full list of nature reserves operated by nongovernment organisations, complete with their locations, features, tourist facilities, and names and phone numbers of people who can provide further details.

Things to See & Do

There is a beautiful colonial church, the **Iglesia de la Merced**, on the corner of Carrera 4 and Calle 7. It is Cali's oldest church. The monastery adjoining the church houses two good museums: the **Museo de Arte Colonial**, with mostly religious objects from the colonial period, is open weekdays from 8.30 am to noon and 2 to 4.30 pm, and Saturday from 8.30 am to noon; and the **Museo Arqueológico**, with pre-Columbian pottery of several cultures from southern Colombia, is open Monday to Saturday from 9 am to 12.30 pm and 1.30 to 5.30 pm.

The **Museo del Oro**, one block away, has

COLOMBIA

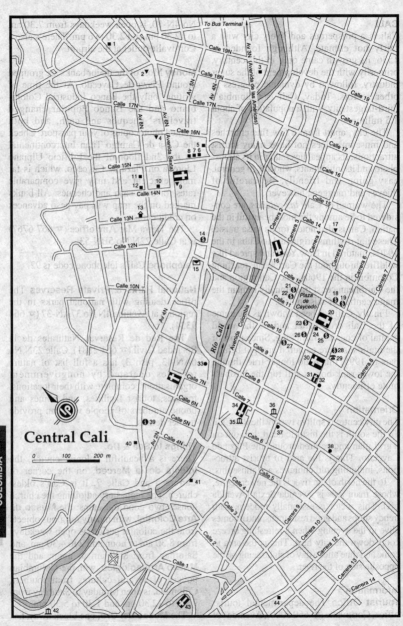

Central Cali

0   100   200 m

PLACES TO STAY		17	Restaurante	29	Telecom
1	Hostal Santor		Vegetariano Hare	30	Iglesia de San
3	Hotel La Torre de Cali		Krishna		Francisco
5	Residencial Chalet			31	Capilla de la
6	Hotel Granada	**OTHER**			Inmaculada
7	Hotel Posada del	14	Banco de Occidente	32	Torre Mudéjar
	Monarca	15	Avianca Post Office	33	Avianca Airline
8	Casa del Viajero	16	Iglesia de la Ermita		Office
10	Hotel La Familia	18	Banco de Occidente	34	Iglesia de la Merced
11	Residencial JJ	19	Banco Comercial	35	Museo de Arte
12	Residencial 86		Antioqueño		Colonial & Museo
13	Youth Hostel	20	Catedral		Arqueológico
24	Hotel Astoria	21	Banco de Bogotá	36	Museo del Oro
40	Pensión Stein	22	Casa de	37	Teatro Municipal
41	Hotel Intercontinental		Cambio Titan	38	Teatro Experimental
44	Casa Turística Sharon		Intercontinental		de Cali (TEC)
		23	Banco Anglo	39	Cortuvalle Tourist
PLACES TO EAT			Colombiano		Office
2	Restaurante	25	Banco de Colombia	42	Museo de Arte
	Vegetariano Raíces	26	Banco de Bogotá		Moderno La
4	Restaurante El	27	Banco Popular		Tertulia
	Caballo Loco	28	Banco Industrial	43	Iglesia de San
9	Restaurante Balocco		Colombiano		Antonio

a collection of gold from the Calima culture. It is open weekdays from 8 to 11.30 am and 2 to 5.30 pm. Another interesting museum, the **Museo de Arte Moderno La Tertulia**, Avenida Colombia No 5 Oeste-105, presents temporary exhibitions of contemporary painting, sculpture, photography etc.

For a view of the city centre, go to the **Iglesia de San Antonio**, set on top of a hill only a short walk from the centre. The church itself is worth seeing. Alternatively, go to **La Torre de Cali**, the highest building in the city, on the corner of Avenida 3N and Calle 19N. It's an expensive hotel, but ask at reception on the ground floor for permission to go up to a viewpoint on the 43rd floor, or have a meal at their top-floor restaurant.

Special Events
The main city event is the Feria de Cali, which begins annually on 25 December and goes till the end of the year, with parades, concerts of salsa bands, bullfights and a beauty contest.

Places to Stay
There is a selection of budget accommodation right in the heart of the northern city centre, which is a relatively secure and pleas-

ant area. The dark side is that the residencias are pretty poor, and some double as love hotels.

Three basic hotels side by side on Calle 15N are used by budget travellers: *Hotel Granada* (☎ 661 2477), No 4N-44, *Hotel Posada del Monarca* (☎ 661 2483), No 4N-52, and *Casa del Viajero* (☎ 661 0986), No 4N-60. All have rooms with private bath and charge about US$6/10 for a single/double. The Casa del Viajero has some primitive cage-like rooms without bath for US$4. Just around the corner, at Avenida 4N No 15N-43, is the *Residencial Chalet* (☎ 661 2709), offering much the same.

There are also three budget hotels near the corner of Calle 14N and Avenida 8N: the *Residencial 86* (☎ 661 2054), Avenida 8N No 14N-01; the *Hotel La Familia* (☎ 661 2925), Calle 14N No 6N-42; and the *Residencial JJ* (☎ 661 3134), Avenida 8N No 14-47. They are nothing special either. The JJ has some better but overpriced rooms; La Familia is the most basic.

The *youth hostel* (☎ 661 4249), Calle 13N No 8N-14 in the same area, is probably a more pleasant place to stay, though it only has large dorms. Friendly, neat and well run, it would be a popular haunt with travellers,

COLOMBIA

if not for its inflated prices: US$11 per bed (US$9 with membership card). If you decide to try it, be sure to bargain.

One of the better yet affordable places in the area is the *Hostal Santor* (☎ 668 6482), Avenida 8N No 20N-50, which has rooms with bath for around US$18/24. There are also several cheaper rooms without bath, but they are rather poor.

On the southern side of the Río Cali there's not much budget accommodation, except for the maze of seedy hospedajes east of Calle 15 (don't walk there – this is one of the most dangerous areas of central Cali), and the warmly recommended *Casa Turística Sharon* (☎ 884 4885), Carrera 12 No 2-54 (no sign on the door), near Iglesia de San Antonio. This tasteful and friendly family house offers 12 neat rooms (US$12/17 a single/double). There are cooking and laundry facilities.

There's quite a choice of mid-price hotels within a couple of blocks of the Plaza de Caycedo, a convenient area to stay. Perhaps the best value for money is the *Hotel Astoria* (☎ 883 0140), on the corner of the plaza at Calle 11 No 5-16. Airy, comfortable singles/doubles/triples with TV and private bath cost US$30/38/45. Ask for a room on one of the top floors, for less noise and better views.

If you want something with more character and are prepared to pay more, the *Pensión Stein* (☎ 661 4927), in a large, beautiful house at Avenida 4N No 3N-33, is probably the choice. Run by a Swiss couple, the hotel offers spotlessly clean rooms with bath and also has a restaurant. Singles/doubles cost US$50/80, breakfast included.

Places to Eat

The best eating sector is on and around Avenida 6N, where there are loads of restaurants and cafés selling everything from simple snacks, burgers and pizzas to regional Colombian cuisine and Chinese, Arab and German specialities. There are some cheap restaurants in the area, which serve set meals for around US$2.50 (eg the *Restaurante Balocco*, Avenida 6N No 14N-06).

For vegetarian food, probably the best budget place is the attractive *Restaurante Vegetariano Raíces*, Calle 18N No 6N-25, but it only serves meals between 11.30 am and 2.30 pm. Not as pleasant, but open from 6 am to 8 pm, is the *Restaurante Vegetariano Hare Krishna*, at Calle 14 No 4-49.

For a satisfying dinner, try *El Caballo Loco*, Calle 16N No 6N-31 (international cuisine), or *Los Girasoles* (fish) and *Las Dos Parrillas* (steaks), both on the corner of Avenida 6N and Calle 35N. There are plenty of other, equally good restaurants on and around Avenida 6N.

Entertainment

Colombia's national theatre started with the foundation of the *Teatro Experimental de Cali* (TEC). If you understand Spanish well enough, go to the TEC theatre, at Calle 7 No 8-63, and see one of their plays.

There are several *salsotecas* (discos with salsa music) along Avenida 6N and another collection on Calle 5, but the best known place for nightlife is Juanchito, a popular suburb on the Río Cauca. Go on a Friday or Saturday night but don't take anything of value; better still, find some local company to take you.

Night tours in chivas depart from the Hotel Intercontinental, Avenida Colombia No 2-72, on Friday and Saturday at 8 pm. The five-hour tour covers a few nightspots and costs about US$20, including half a bottle of aguardiente and a snack.

Getting There & Away

Air The Palmaseca airport is 16 km north-east the city. Minibuses between the airport and the bus terminal run every 10 minutes till about 8 pm (US$1, 30 minutes).

There are plenty of flights to all major Colombian cities, including Bogotá (US$82), Medellín (US$87), Cartagena (US$143), Pasto (US$80) and San Andrés (US$181); cheaper fares are available.

Avianca, Intercontinental and Copa fly to Panama City (US$169), while Intercontinental and Saeta have flights to Tulcán and Esmeraldas, both in Ecuador (US$77 to either). Add the 21% tax.

Bus The bus terminal is a 20-minute walk from the city centre, or less than 10 minutes by one of the frequent city buses. Buses to Bogotá run at least every half-hour (US$23 climatizado, 12 hours). Air-con buses go regularly to Medellín (US$19, nine hours) and Pasto (US$16, nine hours). The Pasto buses will drop you off in Popayán (US$4.50, three hours). There are also a number of cheaper pullman buses to both Popayán and Pasto.

AROUND CALI
Parque Nacional Farallones de Cali
This fine mountain national park, to the south-west of the city, covers 150 sq km of rugged terrain of the Cordillera Occidental. It's noted for its lush vegetation and diverse wildlife.

If you just want to do a day trip to the park, take a bus from Cali's bus terminal to **Pance**, a weekend holiday resort, popular with the *caleños*, on the border of the park; from there, footpaths lead into the park. There are hotels and restaurants in the Pance area.

If you want to hike deeper into the park, contact the Fundación Farallones in Cali (☎ 556 8335), Carrera 24B No 2A-99, which operates the Reserva Natural Hato Viejo in the park, eight km uphill from Pance. The reserve offers accommodation, food and guides.

Old Haciendas
There are plenty of old haciendas in the region of Cali, most of which date from the 18th and 19th centuries, with some engaged in the cultivation and processing of sugar cane. The closest to Cali, the **Hacienda Cañasgordas**, is on the southern outskirts of the city, beyond the Universidad del Valle. It's currently closed for renovation, but may be open by the time you read this.

The two best known are the **Hacienda El Paraíso** and **Hacienda Piedechinche**, both about 40 km north-east of Cali and open as museums. There are tours from Cali, or you can visit them on your own using public transport, though the latter option is a bit time-consuming as both places are off the

main roads. The tourist office in Cali will give you information.

POPAYAN
Popayán is one of the most beautiful colonial cities in Colombia. Founded in 1537 by Sebastián de Belalcázar, the town quickly became an important political, cultural and religious centre, and was an obligatory stop-over on the route between Cartagena and Quito. Its mild climate attracted the wealthier Spanish families from the tropical sugar states of the Cali region, and they built mansions and founded schools. Several imposing churches and monasteries were built in the 17th and 18th centuries.

During the 20th century, while many other Colombian cities were caught up in the race to modernise and industrialise, Popayán somehow managed to retain its colonial character. In March 1983, a violent earthquake seriously damaged a lot of the historic buildings and most of the churches. The difficult restoration work continued for a decade, and the result is admirable: little damage can be seen and the city looks better than it did before the disaster. Apart from its beauty, Popayán is a very inviting, tranquil and clean city, and truly worth a visit. Furthermore, it has a good tourist office and a range of places to stay and eat, and is not expensive by Colombian standards.

Information
Tourist Office The helpful Caucatur tourist office (☎ 242251), Calle 3 No 4-70, has good information about the city and the region. It's open weekdays from 8 am to noon and 2 to 6.30 pm, and weekends from 10 am to 5 pm.

Money No bank in Popayán will change cash or travellers' cheques, so come prepared. If you happen to run out of money, the best place to go is the Almacén Salvador Duque, a store on the main square, Calle 5 No 6-25. The owner changes both cash and cheques and consistently pays about the best rate in town, though it's less than you could get in banks in Cali or Pasto, the two nearest places with useful banks to change money. Note also that San Agustín and Tierradentro, two popular tourist destinations from Popayán, don't have banks.

MasterCard will get you an advance at Banco de Occidente, while all the remaining banks marked on the map pay advances on Visa card.

Telephone The telephone code is 928.

Things to See & Do

All the colonial churches have been carefully restored but most are only open for mass, usually early in the morning and late in the afternoon, so plan your sightseeing accordingly. Don't miss the **Iglesia de San Francisco**, the city's best church (only reopened in 1996), which has exquisite side altars. Other churches noted for their rich original furnishings include the **Iglesia de Santo Domingo** and the **Iglesia de San Agustín**.

Iglesia La Ermita is Popayán's oldest church (from 1546), worth seeing for its fine high altar, and for the fragments of old frescoes, which were only discovered after the earthquake of 1983. The **Catedral** dates from the second half of the 19th century. It was almost completely destroyed by the earthquake (as was its internal decoration) and rebuilt virtually from the ground up.

All of Popayán's renowned museums have reopened, usually Tuesday to Sunday from 9 am to noon and 2 to 5 pm (some don't open on weekend afternoons). The **Casa Museo Mosquera** contains a collection of colonial art, including some religious objects. More sacred art is to be found in the **Museo de Arte Religioso**. The **Casa Museo Negret** features abstract sculpture by Edgar Negret and works of art by some Latin American contemporary artists, while the **Museo Guillermo Valencia** is dedicated to the poet who once lived here.

The **Museo de Historia Natural** is noted for its extensive collections of insects, butterflies and stuffed birds. Part of the top floor is taken up by an archaeological display of pre-Columbian pottery from southern Colombia.

Churches and museums are only a part of what Popayán has to offer. The best approach is to take a leisurely walk along the streets lined with whitewashed colonial mansions, savour the architectural details and drop inside to see the marvellous patios (most are open to the public). Have a look at the **Palacio Nacional**, the **Puente del Humilladero**, the **Casa de la Cultura** and the **Casa de Julio Arboleda**.

The **Capilla de Belén** offers good views over the town, but it's better not to walk there: there have been some armed attacks on travellers on the access alley.

Special Events

If you are in the area during Holy Week, you'll have the chance to see the famous night-time processions on Maundy Thursday and Good Friday. Popayán's Easter celebrations are the most elaborate in the country. The Festival of Religious Music is held concurrently. Note that hotels are full around that time, so get there early or book in advance.

Places to Stay

Popayán has a good array of accommodation to suit every pocket. Many hotels are in old colonial houses, and have a style and atmosphere rare in Colombia.

The two most popular places among backpackers are the *Casa Familiar Turística No 1* (☎ 240019), Carrera 5 No 2-41, and the *Casa Familiar Turística No 2* (☎ 242100), Carrera 8 No 3-25. Both are clean and have a family atmosphere. Each has just five rooms with shared facilities, charging US$5 per person. You can have a filling breakfast for US$2, and leave your gear free of charge if you go for a trip around the region. Neither Casa displays its name on the door – ring the door bell.

If both these places are full, go to the *Hotel Diana* (☎ 241203), Carrera 6 No 8-58, which has two lovely spacious patios and costs US$4.50/5.50 per person in rooms without/with bath. Alternatively, try the

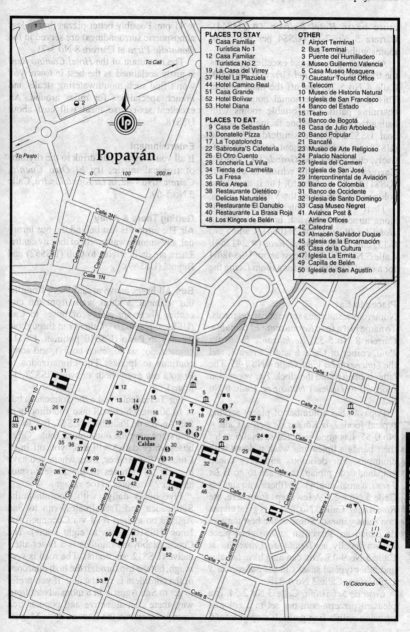

Popayán

0   100   200 m

PLACES TO STAY
6   Casa Familiar
    Turística No 1
12 Casa Familiar
    Turística No 2
19 La Casa del Virrey
37 Hotel La Plazuela
44 Hotel Camino Real
51 Casa Grande
52 Hotel Bolívar
53 Hotel Diana

PLACES TO EAT
9   Casa de Sebastián
13 Donatello Pizza
17 La Topatolondra
22 Sabrosura'S Cafetería
26 El Otro Cuento
28 Lonchería La Viña
34 Tienda de Carmelita
35 La Fresa
36 Rica Arepa
38 Restaurante Dietético
    Delicias Naturales
39 Restaurante El Danubio
40 Restaurante La Brasa Roja
48 Los Kingos de Belén

OTHER
1   Airport Terminal
2   Bus Terminal
3   Puente del Humilladero
4   Museo Guillermo Valencia
5   Casa Museo Mosquera
7   Caucatur Tourist Office
8   Telecom
10 Museo de Historia Natural
11 Iglesia de San Francisco
14 Banco del Estado
15 Teatro
16 Banco de Bogotá
18 Casa de Julio Arboleda
20 Banco Popular
21 Bancafé
23 Museo de Arte Religioso
24 Palacio Nacional
25 Iglesia del Carmen
27 Iglesia de San José
29 Intercontinental de Aviación
30 Banco de Colombia
31 Banco de Occidente
32 Iglesia de Santo Domingo
33 Casa Museo Negret
41 Avianca Post &
    Airline Offices
42 Catedral
43 Almacén Salvador Duque
45 Iglesia de la Encarnación
46 Casa de la Cultura
47 Iglesia La Ermita
49 Capilla de Belén
50 Iglesia de San Agustín

To Cali

To Pasto

To Cali

Calle 3N

Carrera 11

Carrera 104

Carrera 10

Carrera 9

Calle 1N

Calle 1

Calle 2

Calle 3

Calle 4

Calle 5

Calle 6

Calle 7

Calle 8

Carrera 10

Carrera 9

Carrera 8

Carrera 7

Carrera 6

Carrera 5

Carrera 4

Carrera 3

Carrera 1

Parque
Caldas

To Coconuco

COLOMBIA

more basic *Hotel Bolívar* (☎ 244844), Carrera 5 No 7-11 (US$4 per person in rooms without bath).

A more expensive, but excellent, place is the friendly *La Casa del Virrey* (☎ 240836), Calle 4 No 5-78, just off the main square. This is a beautiful colonial house with a charming patio. Comfortable rooms with bath attached (choose one facing the street) cost US$20/32/40 a single/double/triple (US$8 per person without bath). Alternatively, check the *Casa Grande* (☎ 240908), Carrera 6 No 7-11, which is cheaper (US$11/20/28 with bath), but it hasn't the colonial atmosphere of the Virrey.

There's a choice of splendid historic mansions turned into stylish hotels, including *Hotel La Plazuela* (☎ 241084), Calle 5 No 8-13, and *Hotel Camino Real* (☎ 241254), Calle 5 No 5-59. Both cost about US$48/64 for a single/double; ask for a room facing the street.

Places to Eat

Numerous restaurants serve cheap set meals. To name just a few: *Restaurante El Danubio*, Carrera 8 No 5-53; *Restaurante La Brasa Roja*, corner of Calle 6 and Carrera 8; and the *Lonchería La Viña*, Calle 4 No 7-85. The latter is open round the clock. For vegetarian food, go to *Delicias Naturales*, Calle 6 No 8-21.

Popayán has a number of places serving typical food. *Los Kingos de Belén*, Calle 4 No 0-55, has good regional specialities; try their bandeja típica and wash it down with champús. For delicious and very cheap empanadas de pipián, the place to go is *La Fresa*, a small cubbyhole (there's no sign) at Calle 5 No 8-83. A few steps from here, the *Rica Arepa*, Calle 5 No 8-71, has great arepas con maíz y queso. Some of the best tamales de pipián are served in an unsigned place known locally as *Tienda de Carmelita* at Calle 5 No 9-45. You can also have tamales and other typical snacks in the *Sabrosura'S Cafetería* at Calle 3 No 4-31.

Casa de Sebastián, Calle 3 No 2-54, is a pleasant pizzeria-cum-bar set in a colonial mansion with a fine patio. It's open from 5 to 11 pm. Possibly better pizzas (but in less atmospheric surroundings) are served in the *Donatello Pizza* at Carrera 8 No 3-71.

The restaurant of the *Hotel Camino Real* is justly acclaimed as the best in town: you won't find such mouthwatering steaks and French specialities for miles around. An excellent six-course meal will cost about US$18.

Entertainment

If all you want is a late drink to the rhythms of tropical music, try *El Otro Cuento*, Carrera 9 No 4-42, or *La Topatolondra*, Calle 3 No 5-69.

Getting There & Away

Air The airport is just behind the bus terminal, a 15-minute walk north of the city centre. There are daily flights to Cali (US$52) and Bogotá (US$69).

Bus All buses arrive at and leave from the bus terminal, a short walk from the city centre. There are plenty of buses to Cali (US$4, three hours). Others run throughout the day to Pasto (US$10 pullman, US$12 climatizado; six to seven hours), and some continue to Ipiales. The climatizados to Bogotá run every hour or two (US$27, 14 hours).

For Tierradentro, take the Sotracauca bus at 10.30 am, which will take you directly to San Andrés de Pisimbalá (US$7, five to six hours), passing the museum en route. Other buses (three daily) will drop you off in El Cruce de San Andrés, from where you have to walk 25 minutes to the museum plus another 25 minutes to the village.

Five buses daily (with Cootranshuila, Sotracauca and Transipiales) run to San Agustín on a short road via Coconuco and Isnos (US$10, seven to eight hours). The Cootranslaboyana minibus is a faster alternative (US$12, six hours). The road is very rough, but the trip through the lush rainforest of the cordillera is spectacular. If you prefer to get to San Agustín in a more adventurous way, there's an attractive and popular trek from Valencia via the Laguna de la Magdalena (see the San Agustín section). Caucatur tourist office will give you the necessary information.

AROUND POPAYAN

Silvia

A small town 60 km north-east of Popayán, Silvia is the centre of the Guambianos, one of the most traditional Indian communities in Colombia. Though the Indians no longer live in the town, they come to Silvia on Tuesday (market day) to sell fruit, vegetables and handicrafts. That's the best day to visit Silvia, as a pleasant day trip from Popayán, when there are plenty of Indians in town in their traditional dress, the women in hand-woven garments and beaded necklaces, busily spinning wool.

Bring a sweater with you – it can be pretty cold if the weather is cloudy. If you decide to stay longer in Silvia, there are at least half a dozen cheap residencias, and also some up-market options.

To get to Silvia from Popayán, take the Coomotoristas bus (US$2, 1½ hours) or the Belalcázar minibus (US$2.50, 1¼ hours). You can also take any of the frequent buses to Cali, get off in Piendamó (US$1, 40 minutes), then take a colectivo to Silvia (US$1, another 40 minutes). On Tuesday, there are also direct colectivos between Popayán and Silvia.

Parque Nacional Puracé

The park, about 60 km east of Popayán, is one of the most picturesque in Colombia, offering a wide variety of landscapes and sights, from volcanoes and mountain lakes to waterfalls and hot springs. Among the highlights are the **Termales de San Juan**, spectacular hot sulphur springs set in beautiful surroundings. The hot waters meeting the ice-cold mountain creeks create multicoloured moss, algae and lichens.

The springs are in the northern part of the park and can be easily reached by the Popayán-La Plata buses which pass nearby. There are two fine waterfalls and a lake walking distance from the springs.

About 10 km west of the spring is

Pilimbalá, which has the only accommodation in the park, with three cabins, a restaurant and thermal pools. The cabin with attached bath and hot water costs US$36 and can sleep up to seven people.

If you feel fit enough, hike to the top of the **Volcán Puracé** (4780 metres). It is about a four-hour steady ascent from Pilimbalá. You can do it easily in a day, but start early. The weather is precarious all year round, so take good rain gear. Generally, only the early mornings are sunny; later on, the volcano is covered with clouds.

In the southern part of the park, you can hike from Valencia to San Agustín (or vice versa) – see the San Agustín section for details.

SAN AGUSTIN

This is one of the most important archaeological sites on the continent. The region was inhabited more than a thousand years ago by a mysterious civilisation which left behind several hundred freestanding monumental statues carved in stone, as well as a number of tombs.

Little is known about the culture which created the statues. Most probably, it flourished between the 6th and 14th centuries AD, though its initial stages are thought to have been perhaps a millennium earlier. The best statuary was made only in the last phase of the civilisation and the culture had presumably vanished before the Spaniards came. Perhaps, like many other civilisations of the Andean region, it fell victim to the Incas – this area of Colombia was the northernmost point of the Inca empire.

What is certain is that the statues were not discovered until the middle of the 18th century. So far, some 500 statues have been found and excavated. A great number are anthropomorphic figures – some of them realistic, others very stylised, resembling masked monsters. Others are zoomorphic, depicting sacred animals such as the eagle, the jaguar and the frog. The statues vary both in size, from 20 cm to seven metres, and in their degree of detail.

The site was a ceremonial centre where the

people of San Agustín buried their dead, placing the statues next to the tombs. Pottery and gold objects were left in more important tombs.

The statues and tombs are scattered in groups over a wide area on both sides of the gorge formed by the upper Río Magdalena. The main town of the region is San Agustín, where you'll find most of the accommodation and restaurants. From there, you can explore the region; count on three days for leisurely visits to the most interesting places.

The weather is variable, with the driest period from December to February and the wettest from April to June.

Information

Tourist Office The very helpful and knowledgeable CNT tourist office (☎ 373019) is at Calle 5 No 14-75. Sadly, it is likely to have closed down by the time you read this. A municipal tourist office may open instead, but if not, travel agents will become the major source of information. There are already several of these, of which the Viajes Lanky Balonky (☎ 373246), Carrera 13 No 2-38, is probably the major operator.

Money As yet, no banks or casas de cambio in San Agustín will change cash or travellers' cheques. The closest bank which handles these transactions is the Banco Industrial Colombiano in Neiva. Some shops and travel agents in San Agustín may change US dollars and, occasionally, cheques but at a ridiculously poor rate.

The Caja Agraria, corner of Carrera 13 and Calle 4, usually gives peso advances on Visa. MasterCard is useless; the closest place which will accept it is the Concasa in Pitalito.

Telephone The telephone code is 988.

Things to See & Do

The most important place is the **Parque Arqueológico**, 2½ km west of the town, where you can see about 130 statues, including some of the best examples of San Agustín statuary. The park covers several archaeological sites, with statues, tombs and burial mounds. It also has a museum displaying smaller statues and pottery, and the Bosque de las Estatuas, where 35 statues of different origins are placed along a footpath that snakes through the forest.

The park is open daily from 8 am to 6 pm, but most sites and the museum close at 5 pm. The ticket office closes at 4 pm. The ticket (US$2.50) bought here also covers entry to the Alto de los Ídolos, but it's only valid for two days.

The **Alto de los Ídolos** is another archaeological park, noted for burial mounds and large stone tombs. The largest statue, seven metres high, is to be found here. The park is a few km south-west of San José de Isnos, on the other side of the Río Magdalena from San Agustín town.

There are some 15 other archaeological sites scattered over the area. The region is also noted for its natural beauty, with two lovely **waterfalls**, Salto de Bordones and Salto del Mortiño. **El Estrecho**, where the Río Magdalena passes through a two-metre narrows, is also an attractive sight. See Getting Around later in this section for possible ways of visiting the area.

The **Laguna de la Magdalena**, where the Río Magdalena has its source, has become yet another popular destination. It's a five-day return trip from San Agustín, or a three-day trip from Quinchana. It can be done on foot or on horseback. Instead of coming back, you can continue to Valencia and then take the bus to Popayán. There are some simple accommodation and food facilities on the way, so no camping gear is necessary.

Some travellers do this trip in the opposite direction, from Popayán to San Agustín. Accommodation, food and horse rental are available in Valencia. There's one bus daily in each direction, between Popayán and Valencia (US$8, seven hours).

Places to Stay

On the whole, the accommodation in San Agustín is good and cheap. There are a dozen budget residencias in and around town, most

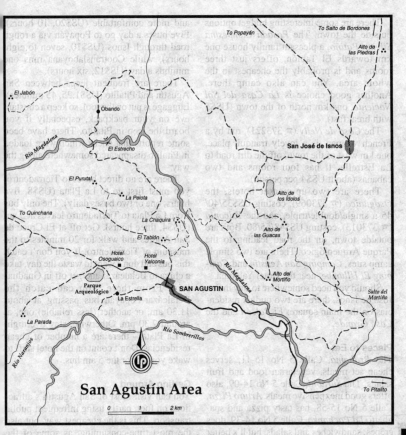

San Agustín Area

To Popayán
To Salto de Bordones
Alto de las Piedras
El Jabón
Obando
San José de Isnos
Río Magdalena
El Estrecho
El Purutal
Alto de los Idolos
La Pelota
To Quinchana
La Chaquira
Alto de las Guacas
El Tablón
Hotel Osoguaico
Hotel Yalconia
Alto del Mortiño
Parque Arqueológico
SAN AGUSTÍN
Río Magdalena
La Estrella
Salto del Mortiño
La Parada
Río Sombrerillos
To Pitalito

0   1   2 km

COLOMBIA

of which are clean and friendly and have hot water.

The best area in which to look for a budget room is the vicinity of the tourist office. The first option might be the new *Residencias Menezú* (☎ 373693), Carrera 15 No 4-74, with its very clean rooms with shared baths and hot water, and super-friendly proprietors. *Mi Terruño*, Calle 4 No 15-85, has some rooms with private bath and a pleasant long balcony overlooking the garden. Just a few steps away are two slightly simpler (but cheaper) residencias: *Luis Tello* (☎ 373037), Calle 4 No 15-33, and *Eduardo Motta*

(☎ 373031), Calle 4 No 15-71. Neither displays its name on the door. Two blocks away, at Carrera 13 No 3-42, is yet another budget place, *El Imperio* (☎ 373055), which does have private baths. Any of the above will cost about US$3 to US$4 per person in rooms without bath, and a dollar more in rooms with private bath.

There are a few hotels right by the bus offices, including the *Colonial* (☎ 373159), Calle 3 No 11-25, and the *Central* (☎ 373-027), Calle 3 No 10-32. Both cost US$5/10 per person in rooms without/with bath (cold water only), which is rather poor value.

There are some interesting budget options outside the town. The *Posada Campesina Silvina Patiño*, a pleasant family house one km towards El Tablón, offers just three rooms and is probably the cheapest in the whole area. You can also camp there. Another good choice is *La Casa del Sol Naciente*, one km north of the town (US$5 with breakfast).

The *Casa de Nelly* (☎ 373221), run by a French woman, is a lovely tranquil place, one km west of the town, off the dirt road to La Estrella. It has four rooms and two cabañas (about US$4 per person).

There are two up-market hotels, the *Osoguaico* (☎ 373069), costing US$35/40/45 a single/double/triple, and the *Yalconia* (☎ 373013), costing US$48/65/80. Both are outside town, on the road leading to the Parque Arqueológico. There are two simple camp sites, *Camping San Agustín* and *Camping El Ullumbe*, near the Hotel Yalconia.

Should you need somewhere to stay in San José de Isnos, there are two budget residencias on the main square: *El Balcón* and the *Casa Grande*.

Places to Eat

The *Brahama*, Calle 5 No 15-11, serves cheap set meals, vegetarian food and fruit salads. The *Surabhi*, Calle 5 No 14-09, also offers good inexpensive meals. *Arturo Pizza*, Calle 5 No 15-58, has tasty pizza and spaghetti. *La Pachanka*, Calle 5 No 14-39, does crêpes, sandwiches and salads, but it's better known as a place for an evening drink.

There are half a dozen eating outlets near the Hotel Yalconia, of which *La Brasa* (grilled meat) and *Para y Coma* (typical food) are probably the best.

If you're staying at the Casa de Nelly, you can eat in the two friendly places just a stone's throw away: the *Tea Rooms* (all-day breakfast, home-made soups, pies and real, strong tea) and the *Casa de Clara* (vegetarian meals). Both are run by English women.

Getting There & Away

Coomotor has two buses daily to Bogotá (US$17, 12 hours), but Taxi Verde is faster and more comfortable (US$20, 10 hours). Five buses a day go to Popayán via a rough road through Isnos (US$10, seven to eight hours), while Cootranslaboyana runs one minibus a day (US$12, six hours).

There are frequent jeeps between San Agustín and Pitalito (US$1.25, 45 minutes). Luggage is put on the roof, so keep a constant eye on your backpack, especially if you board the jeep in Pitalito. There have been some reports that packs which were loaded in Pitalito disappeared somewhere along the way.

There are no direct buses to Tierradentro; you must first go to La Plata (US$8, five hours, one or two buses daily). The only bus from La Plata to Tierradentro leaves at 5 am (US$4, three hours). Get off at El Cruce de San Andrés and walk for 20 minutes to the museum of Tierradentro. If you don't catch this bus and don't want to waste the day, take a chiva to Belalcázar and get off in Guadalejo. From there, you can catch the Belalcázar-Popayán bus passing at about 11.30 am, or another (less reliable) one, at around 2.30 pm. Otherwise, stay overnight in La Plata – there are a number of cheap residencias. Don't count on the hotel staff to wake you up for the 5 am bus.

Getting Around

You can visit most of San Agustín's attractions on foot, partly using infrequent public transport. This is the cheapest way, but also the most time-consuming, as some of the sites are pretty distant and will involve long hikes. If you are not up to that, plenty of operators in San Agustín offer excursions, by jeep or on horseback.

Jeep tours can be arranged at Asotranstur (☎ 373340) at Calle 5 No 14-50, or at Viajes Lanky Balonky (☎ 373246). The standard jeep tour includes El Estrecho, Alto de los Ídolos, Alto de las Piedras, Salto de Bordones and Salto de Mortiño. The trip takes seven to eight hours and costs US$15 per person.

Horse rental is operated by the Asociación de Alquiladores y Baquianos, corner of Calle 5 and Carrera 17. Horses are hired out for a specific route, or by the hour (US$2.50) or the day (US$10).

TIERRADENTRO

Tierradentro is an archaeological zone where a number of underground burial chambers have been found. They are circular tombs scooped out of the soft rock and ranging from two to seven metres in diameter. The dome-like vaults of the larger tombs are supported by massive columns. The chambers were painted in geometric patterns, and the decoration in some of them has been remarkably well preserved.

About a hundred tombs have been discovered to date. These funeral temples contained the cremated remains of tribal elders. The ashes were kept in ceramic urns, which are now displayed in the museum of Tierradentro. A number of stone statues similar to those of San Agustín have also been found in the region.

Not much is known about the people who built the tombs and the statues. Most likely, they were of different cultures, and the people who scooped out the tombs preceded those who carved the statues. Today, the region is inhabited by the Páez Indians, who have lived here since before the Spanish conquest, but it is doubtful whether they are the descendants of the sculptors.

Information

There are no tourist office or money changing facilities. The owner of Los Lagos de Tierradentro (see Places to Stay) is a good source of information about the area.

Things to See

There are four sites with tombs and one with statues, as well as a museum and the village of San Andrés de Pisimbalá. Except for El Aguacate, all the sites are quite close to each other.

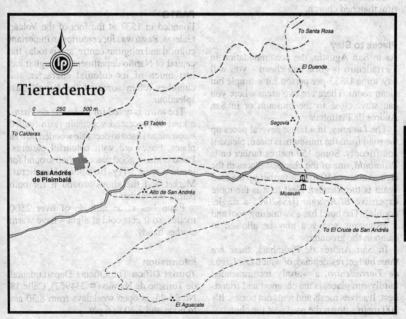

You begin your visit from the museum, where you buy one combined ticket (US$2.50), valid for two consecutive days to all archaeological sights and the museum itself, which actually consists of two sections across the road from one another. The **Museo Arqueológico** contains pottery urns which have been found in the tombs, while the **Museo Etnográfico** has utensils and artefacts of the Páez Indians. Both museums are open daily from 8 am to 5 pm.

A 10-minute walk up the hill from the museum will take you to **Segovia**, the most important burial site. There are 28 tombs here, some with well-preserved decoration. Seven of the tombs are lit; for the others, you need a torch – don't forget to bring one.

Other burial sites include **El Duende** (four tombs without preserved decoration) and the more interesting **Alto de San Andrés** (five tombs, two of which have their original paintings). Statues can be seen at **El Tablón**.

The village of **Pisimbalá**, a 25-minute walk from the museum, is noted for its beautiful thatched church.

Places to Stay

As in San Agustín, the accommodation in Tierradentro is good and cheap – you will pay some US$3 per person for a simple but clean room. There are two areas where you can stay: close to the museum or in San Andrés de Pisimbalá.

The *Lucerna*, in a house several paces up the road from the museum, is clean, pleasant and friendly. Some 150 metres farther on is *Pisimbalá*, one of the cheapest places in the area. Another 150 metres farther up the road again is the *Ricabet*. Next to it is the more expensive *El Refugio* (US$20/25 a single/double). The hotel has a swimming pool and a restaurant, and you may be allowed to camp in the grounds.

In San Andrés de Pisimbalá, there are three budget residencias, of which *Los Lagos de Tierradentro*, a warmly recommended family-run place, is the cheapest and friendliest. It serves meals and rents out horses. It's 100 metres down the road past the church.

Places to Eat

In the museum area, the *Pisimbalá* (see Places to Stay) is the cheapest place to eat, serving set meals for about US$2. Slightly more expensive, but better, is the *Restaurante 86*, just across the road. Possibly the best in the area is the pricier restaurant of *El Refugio*. In San Andrés de Pisimbalá, the obvious choice is *Los Lagos*.

Getting There & Away

Only sporadic buses call at San Andrés de Pisimbalá. Most buses ply the Popayán-Belalcázar road, passing El Cruce de San Andrés, so you must walk to El Cruce (20 minutes from the museum). In theory, there are three buses daily to Popayán, at about 7.30 am, 12.30 and 3 pm (US$7, five hours). It's a bumpy but very spectacular trip on a winding mountain road. Also theoretically, there are three buses to La Plata which pass by El Cruce at around 6 am, noon and 3 pm.

PASTO

Founded in 1537 at the foot of the Volcán Galeras, Pasto was for centuries an important cultural and religious centre, and is today the capital of Nariño department. Though it has lost much of its colonial character, the churches retain some of the town's past splendour.

The town is noted for its *barniz de Pasto*, a kind of processed vegetable resin (called *mopa mopa*) used to decorate wooden bowls, plates, boxes etc with colourful patterns. Pasto is also a good place to shop around for leather ware. Try Bomboná Handicraft Market and the shops around it for both barniz and leather.

Pasto lies at an altitude of over 2500 metres, so it gets cold at night – have warm clothes handy.

Information

Tourist Office The Oficina Departamental de Turismo de Nariño (☎ 234962), Calle 18 No 25-25, is open weekdays from 8.30 am to noon and 2.30 to 6 pm.

Money Most major banks are located around the main square, Plaza de Nariño. The Banco Industrial Colombiano, Banco Anglo Colombiano and Banco Industrial Antioqueño change cash. They also change travellers' cheques, as does Banco de Bogotá. Other banks marked on the map only handle credit-card operations.

Optica San Francisco, on the main square, changes cash till 7 pm on weekdays and is the best private moneychanger, though it pays less than the banks.

Telephone Pasto's telephone code is 927.

Things to See

There are more than half a dozen colonial churches in town, most of which are large constructions with richly decorated interiors. The **Iglesia de Cristo Rey**, with its fine stained-glass windows, is arguably the most beautiful. Also have a look at the elaborately decorated **Iglesia de San Juan Bautista**, the oldest city church.

There is a small but good **Museo del Oro** in the building of the Banco de la República, Calle 19 No 21-27, containing gold and pottery of the pre-Columbian cultures of Nariño. It's open weekdays from 8 am to noon and 2 to 6 pm.

Another interesting museum, the **Casona de Taminango**, is at Calle 13 No 27-67. Accommodated in a meticulously reconstructed 17th-century house, the museum displays artefacts and other historic objects from the region. It's open weekdays from 9 am to noon and 2 to 6 pm, and Saturday from 9 am to 1 pm.

The **Museo Maridíaz** and **Museo María Goretti** both have missionary collections and, as such, resemble antique shops crammed with anything from images of the saints to cannonballs.

Special Events

The city's major event is the Carnaval de Blancos y Negros, held from 3 to 6 January. Its origins go back to the time of Spanish rule, when slaves were allowed to celebrate on 5 January and their masters showed approval by painting their faces black. The following day, the slaves painted their faces white. On these two days the city goes wild, with everybody painting one another with anything available. It's a serious affair – wear the worst clothes you have.

Places to Stay

The most popular place with backpackers is without doubt the *Koala Inn* (☎ 221101) at Calle 18 No 22-37. Set in a fine old building, the hotel offers spotlessly clean, spacious rooms without/with bath for US$4/5, laundry and kitchen facilities, a book exchange, and cable TV in the patio. The friendly manager, Oscar, speaks several languages and is a good source of information.

Alternatively, try the *Hotel Manhattan* (☎ 215675), at Calle 18 No 21B-14. It is also a lovely historic building, with large rooms costing much the same as the Koala.

There are plenty of hotels throughout the central area which can provide some better comfort, but they generally lack style and atmosphere. In ascending order of price (and possibly standard), you can check the *Hotel Isa* (☎ 235343), Calle 18 No 22-33 (US$11/18/22 a single/double/triple); the *Hotel Zorocán* (☎ 233243), Calle 18 No 23-39 (US$15/22/30); the *Hotel San Diego* (☎ 235050), Calle 16A No 23-27 (US$18/24/32); and the *Hotel El Dorado* (☎ 233-260), Calle 16A No 23-42 (US$26/35 a single/double).

Places to Eat

There are loads of cheap restaurants and cafés all over the city centre, where you can get a set meal for less than US$2. For vegetarian food, go to *Govinda's*, Carrera 24 No 13-91 (lunch time only). The self-service *Punto Rojo*, on the main square, is a good place to put together a reasonably priced meal. It's clean, and open 24 hours.

The *Picantería Ipiales*, Calle 19 No 23-37, has great llapingachos (fried mashed-potato-and-cheese pancakes). The *Salón Guadalquivir*, on the main square, does hearty tamales. In the *Don Pancho*, Calle 18 No 26-93, you'll get a filling plate of comida

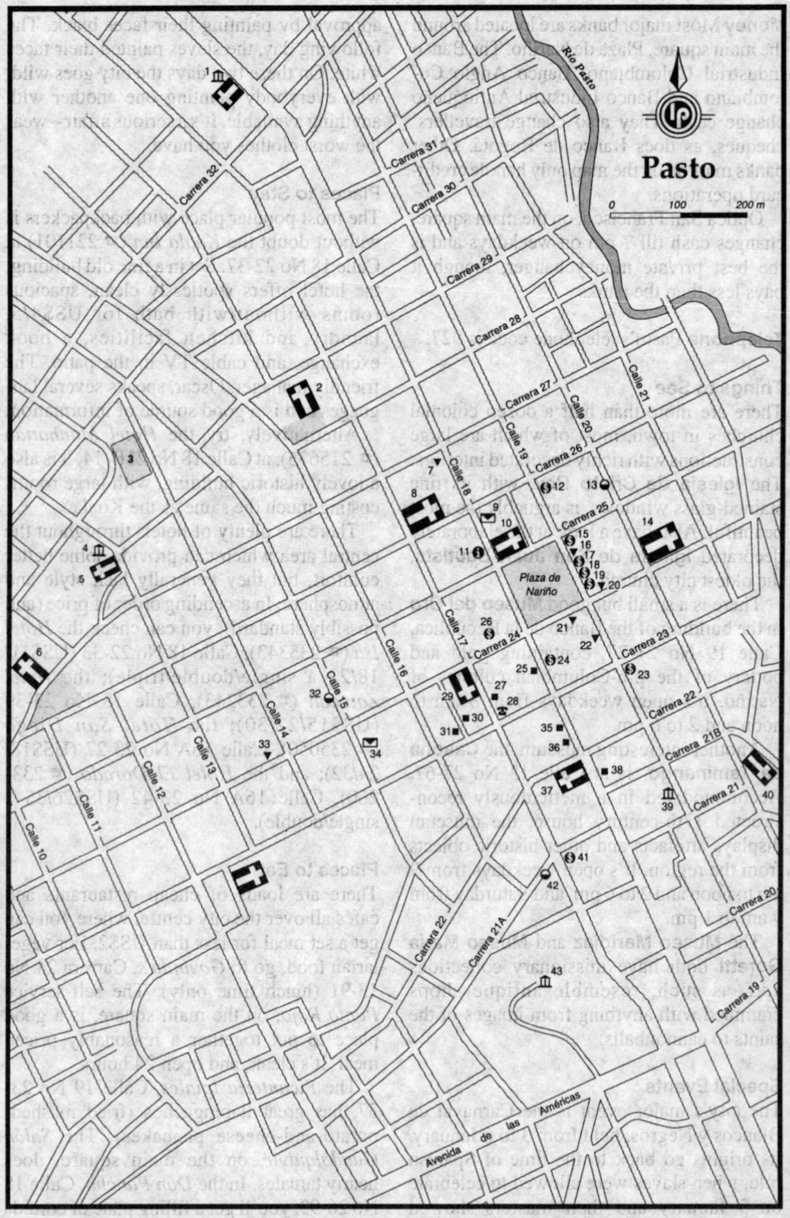

Pasto

0   100   200 m

Río Pasto

Carrera 32

Carrera 31

Carrera 30

Carrera 23

Carrera 28

Carrera 27

Carrera 26

Calle 20

Calle 19

Calle 21

Carrera 25

Carrera 23

Carrera 22

Calle 18

Calle 17

Calle 16

Calle 15

Calle 14

Calle 13

Calle 12

Calle 11

Calle 10

Plaza de Nariño

Carrera 24

Carrera 21B

Carrera 21

Carrera 20

Carrera 19

Carrera 22

Carrera 21A

Avenida de las Américas

criolla (such as sobrebarriga, chuleta or arroz con pollo) for US$3. The restaurant in the *Casona de Taminango* (see Things to See) was closed at the time of writing, but planned to reopen and serve regional dishes.

The best known local speciality is the cuy, or whole roasted guinea pig, yet hardly any central restaurant serves it. Some of the best cuys in town can be had in the *Gualcacuy* at Carrera 40A No 19-66 (US$10).

Los Portales del Plaza, in the Edificio Pasto Plaza, off the main square, is one of the best central restaurants. It offers Mediterranean cuisine at affordable if not bargain prices. If you prefer some Middle-Eastern specialities, the restaurant at the up-market *Hotel Don Saúl*, Calle 17 No 23-52, can be considered. Its menu also includes other international and local dishes.

Getting There & Away
Air The airport is 35 km north of the city on the road to Cali. Colectivos go there from the corner of Calle 18 and Carrera 25 (US$2.50). Pay the day before your flight at the airline office or at a travel agency, and the colectivo will pick you up from your hotel. Avianca has daily flights to Cali (US$80) and Bogotá (US$117); Intercontinental is cheaper.

Bus The bus terminal is two km south of the city centre. Urban buses go there from different points of the central area (see the map for locations).

Frequent buses, minibuses and colectivos go to Ipiales (US$2.50 to US$4, 1½ to two hours); sit on the left for better views. Plenty of buses ply the very spectacular road to Cali (US$13 pullman, US$16 climatizado; nine hours). These buses will drop you off in Popayán in six hours. There are a dozen direct buses to Bogotá (US$38 climatizado, 22 hours).

AROUND PASTO
Laguna de la Cocha
This is one of the biggest and most beautiful lakes in Colombia, about 25 km east of Pasto. Its small island, **La Corota**, is covered by dense forest and was declared a nature reserve, due to its highly diverse flora. It is accessible by boat from the lake shore.

La Corota apart, there are two dozen small reserves, collectively known as the **Reservas Naturales de la Cocha**, established by the local people on their farms scattered around the lake. They will show you around, and some provide accommodation and food. They can also arrange boat excursions – the main departure point is Puerto El Encano on

COLOMBIA

the northern side of the lake. For more information about the reserves, enquire at the Asociación para el Desarrollo Campesino (☎ 231022) in Pasto, Calle 10 No 36-28.

Jeeps for the lake (US$1, 40 minutes) depart from the back of the Hospital Departamental in Pasto, on the corner of Calle 22 and Carrera 7. Frequent city buses will take you to the hospital.

Volcán Galeras

A hike or ride to the top of this volcano (4267 metres) was once a popular trip from Pasto. However, the volcano's activity rose dangerously in mid-1989, putting the city and the surrounding region in a state of emergency. Since that time, the volcano has had several eruptions and is still smoking. The access is currently closed; check for news with the tourist office.

Volcán Azufral

This volcano (4070 metres) lies 10 km west of the town of Túquerres, about 80 km southwest of Pasto. It's extinct, and its crater contains a lovely emerald-coloured lake, the **Laguna Verde**.

Buses and colectivos run regularly from Pasto to Túquerres, from where it's a four-hour walk uphill to the volcano (three hours back down) along a road also capable of taking jeeps. Túquerres has a choice of accommodation and restaurants.

Reservas La Planada & Río Ñambi

These two nature reserves are roughly midway between Pasto and Tumaco. Both are largely covered with lush tropical forest, home to rich and diverse wildlife. There is accommodation and food for visitors (about US$35 for bed and three meals). Pasto's tourist office has information about the reserves, or try the manager of the Koala Inn.

IPIALES

Ipiales, a couple of km from the Ecuador border, is an uninteresting commercial town driven by contraband trade across the frontier. There is little to see, except for the big,

colourful Saturday market, where the campesinos from surrounding villages come to sell and buy goods. A short side trip to Las Lajas is a must (see below).

Information

Money No bank in Ipiales changes cash or travellers' cheques. The banks marked on the map are likely to give advances on Visa card (Banco de Occidente on MasterCard). Plenty of moneychangers on the Plaza La Pola (the main square) and at the border will change US dollars, Colombian pesos and Ecuadorian sucres. There are also a number of casas de cambio in the town's centre.

Ecuadorian Consulate The consulate on the border is your last chance to get a visa, if you need one. There's no Ecuadorian consulate in Ipiales or in Pasto; the nearest is in Cali.

Immigration All passport formalities are done at the border, not in Ipiales or Tulcán. On the Colombian side of the frontier, there's a brick building which houses the DAS office, the Ecuadorian consulate and the Telecom office. The DAS office claims to be open from 6 am till 10 pm, but the Ecuadorian post, just across the river, closes at 8 pm and also for lunch from noon to 2 pm.

Places to Stay

The hotels tend to fill up early (particularly on Saturday), and you may have to look around a bit if you arrive late. The nights are quite chilly, so check the number of blankets before you book a room in a cheapie.

One of the cheapest is the *Residencias Nueva York*, on the corner of Carrera 4 and Calle 13, which has acceptable rooms but without bath or hot water. They cost US$3 per person. Next door is the *Hotel Bahamas* (☎ 2884), which has hot water in shared baths and costs US$3.50 per head.

The *Hotel San Fernando No 1* has rooms with private bath and hot water (US$4/6 for a single/double). The *Hotel San Fernando*

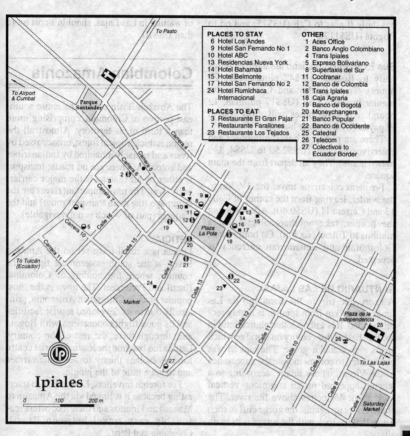

PLACES TO STAY
6 Hotel Los Andes
9 Hotel San Fernando No 1
10 Hotel ABC
13 Residencias Nueva York
14 Hotel Bahamas
15 Hotel Belmonte
17 Hotel San Fernando No 2
24 Hotel Rumichaca Internacional

PLACES TO EAT
3 Restaurante El Gran Pajar
7 Restaurante Farallones
23 Restaurante Los Tejados

OTHER
1 Aces Office
2 Banco Anglo Colombiano
4 Trans Ipiales
5 Expreso Bolivariano
8 Supertaxis del Sur
11 Cootranar
12 Banco de Colombia
16 Trans Ipiales
18 Caja Agraria
19 Banco de Bogotá
20 Moneychangers
21 Banco Popular
22 Banco de Occidente
25 Catedral
26 Telecom
27 Colectivos to Ecuador Border

Ipiales

0   100   200 m

No 2 has similar standards but shared baths only, for the same price.

The *Hotel Belmonte* (☎ 2771), Carrera 4 No 12-111, is a small, friendly, family-run place, possibly the most popular with backpackers. It has no private baths but does have hot water. It costs US$4 per person.

The *Hotel ABC* (☎ 2311), Carrera 5 No 14-43, offers good value for money. Singles/doubles/triples with bath and hot water cost US$5/9/12. For something appreciably better, check the *Hotel Rumichaca Internacional* (☎ 2692), Calle 14 No 7-114 (about US$12/20/25), or the *Hotel Los Andes*

(☎ 4338), Carrera 5 No 14-44 (US$22/34/45).

Places to Eat

Several cheap restaurants on the main square serve set meals, and many more are scattered around the town. Better eating places include *El Gran Pajar*, *Los Tejados* and *Farallones*.

Getting There & Away

Air The airport is seven km north-west of Ipiales, on the road to Guachucal, accessible by colectivo (US$0.50) or taxi (US$4). Aces has daily flights to Cali (US$75) and on to Bogotá (US$117).

Bus Expreso Bolivariano has a dozen buses daily to Bogotá (US$42 climatizado, 24 hours). Trans Ipiales and Cootranar run regular buses to Cali (US$17 pullman, 12 hours). All these buses will drop you in Popayán (US$13, nine hours).

There are plenty of buses, minibuses and colectivos to Pasto (US$2.50 to US$4, 1½ to two hours). They all depart from the main square.

Frequent colectivos travel the 2½ km to the border, leaving from the corner of Calle 13 and Carrera 11 (US$0.40). After crossing the border, take another colectivo or a minibus to Tulcán (six km). On both routes, Colombian and Ecuadorian currency is accepted.

SANTUARIO DE LAS LAJAS

A short side trip to the Santuario de Las Lajas, seven km from Ipiales, is highly recommended. It is a neo-Gothic church built in the first half of this century on a bridge which spans a spectacular gorge. The church was constructed to commemorate the appearance of the Virgin, whose image, according to a legend, appeared on an enormous vertical rock about 45 metres above the river. The church is set up against the gorge cliff in such a way that the rock with the image is its main altar.

Pilgrims from all over Colombia and from abroad come here year-round. Many have left thanksgiving plaques along the alley leading to the church. Note the number of miracles which are said to have occurred.

You can stay in Las Lajas in the *Casa Pastoral*, which overlooks the gorge. Double rooms with bath attached cost US$3.50 per person.

Getting to Las Lajas is very easy. Frequent colectivos run from Ipiales, leaving from the corner of Carrera 6 and Calle 4 (US$0.50, 15 minutes). A taxi from Ipiales' main square to Las Lajas will cost about US$3.50. A return taxi trip for four people, including one hour

of waiting in Las Lajas, shouldn't cost more than US$10.

Colombian Amazonia

The Amazon Basin covers the entire southeast portion of Colombia, comprising more than a third of its territory. Almost all the region is thick tropical forest, crisscrossed by rivers and sparsely inhabited by Indian tribes and colonists. There are no roads; transport is either by air (Satena is the major carrier) or by river. The most important rivers are the Putumayo (the main transport route) and the Caquetá (part of which is not navigable).

LETICIA

Leticia is a small town set on the Amazon River, at the south-easternmost tip of the country, where the borders of Colombia, Brazil and Peru meet. The town is the most popular place in Colombian Amazonia, principally due to its developed tourist facilities and its good flight connections with Bogotá and, through there, the rest of the country. Leticia has become the leading tourist centre for Colombians thirsty to see Indian tribes and to get a taste of the jungle.

For foreign travellers, Leticia is also interesting because it is linked via the Amazon to Manaus and Iquitos and therefore offers reasonably easy travel between Brazil, Colombia and Peru.

July and August are the only relatively dry months. The wettest period is from March to May. The Amazon River's highest level is in June, while the lowest is from August to October. The difference between low and high water can be as great as 15 metres.

Orientation

Leticia lies right on the Colombia-Brazil border. Just across the frontier sits Tabatinga, the first Brazilian settlement, smaller and poorer than Leticia, but with its own airport. Leticia and Tabatinga are virtually merging together, and there are no border checkpoints between the two. Frequent colectivos link the two towns, or you can just walk. Traffic of both locals and foreigners is allowed without visas, but if you plan on heading farther into either country, you must get exit/entry stamps in your passport from DAS, in Leticia, and Policía Federal, in Tabatinga (not on the actual border).

On the island in the Amazon opposite Leticia/Tabatinga is Santa Rosa, a Peruvian village. Boats go there from Tabatinga wharf, not from Leticia.

On the opposite side of the Amazon from Leticia, and about 20 km away, is the Brazilian town of Benjamin Constant, the main port for boats downstream to Manaus. Tabatinga and Benjamin Constant are connected by two boats daily in each direction.

Of the four border towns, Leticia has the best-developed tourist facilities, and is the most pleasant. It's therefore a good idea to stay there, regardless of which way you are headed.

Information

Tourist Office The municipal tourist office (☎ 27505), Carrera 11 No 11-35, is open weekdays from 7 am to noon and 2 to 5 pm.

Money The Banco de Bogotá, on the corner of Carrera 10 and Calle 7, is the only bank which changes travellers' cheques for pesos, and it's an experience. The bank will need photocopies of your passport, cheques and the purchase receipts. It will then call its office in Bogotá to check the exchange rate, and take your picture and fingerprints (!) before dealing with lengthy paperwork. The whole operation may take up to three hours. The only other place which is likely to change your cheques is the Cambios El Opita, Calle 7 No 10-43. It's more efficient but pays about 7% less.

The Banco de Bogotá and Banco Ganadero give peso advances on Visa card, and this is usually faster than changing cheques. MasterCard is useless for cash advances.

No bank in Leticia will touch your cash dollars, but there are plenty of casas de cambio on Calle 8, from Carrera 11 down towards the river. They change US dollars,

Colombian pesos, Brazilian *reais* and Peruvian *nuevos soles*. They are open weekdays till 5 or 6 pm and Saturday till around 2 pm. Shop around, as the rates vary.

There are also some moneychanging facilities in Tabatinga and Benjamin Constant, but they are fewer and usually pay less than in Leticia. The Banco do Brasil in Tabatinga pays cash advances in reales on Visa (from 8 to 9 am only).

Telephone Leticia's telephone code is 9819.

Consulates The Peruvian consulate in Leticia, Carrera 11 No 7-20, next to the Hotel Anaconda, is open weekdays from 8 am to 3 pm. If you need a visa, it will usually be issued on the spot (around US$14).

The Brazilian consulate, Calle 13 No 10-51, is open weekdays from 8 am to 2 pm. Check if you need a visa – citizens of some countries do need one (USA, Australia, New Zealand, Canada, Japan, Israel and France among others), while other nationals do not (most of western Europe) and the price varies greatly from country to country. Visas normally take 24 hours to be issued (sometimes available on the spot) and are valid for a stay of 90 days. You need to present an onward ticket out of Brazil, but any ticket out of South America (eg Caracas-Amsterdam, Buenos Aires-Sydney, Bogotá-Miami) will usually do.

Immigration The DAS office in Leticia, on Calle 9, is open daily from 8 am to noon and 2 to 6 pm. This is where you get your passport stamped when leaving or entering Colombia.

Entry/exit stamps for Brazil must be obtained at the Policía Federal, on Avenida da Amizade (the main road) in Tabatinga, near the hospital. The office is open daily from 8 am to noon and 2 to 6 pm. A yellow fever vaccination certificate may be required by officials when you enter Brazil.

If heading for or coming from Iquitos (Peru) by boat, you get your entry/exit stamp in Santa Rosa.

Things to See & Do

In the town itself, you can visit the **Jardín Botánico Zoológico**, near the airport, which has almost nothing in the way of flora but does have some animals typical of the region, including anacondas, manatees, anteaters, capybaras, monkeys and crocodiles. It's open daily from 7 am to 6 pm; admission is US$1.

The modern building on Carrera 11 houses the small **Museo del Hombre Amazónico**, featuring artefacts and household implements of Indian tribes living in the region, and open weekdays from 8 am to noon and 2 to 5 pm.

Have a look around the market near the river and stroll along the waterfront, crammed with boats and with stalls selling freshly caught fish. Make sure you're at the Parque Santander before sunset for an impressive spectacle when hundreds of small parrots (locally called *pericos)* arrive for their nightly rest on the palms in the park.

Leticia has become a tourist spot not for what the town itself offers but for the surrounding region, which is populated by several indigenous groups, among which the Ticuna and Yagua are the dominant communities. This is also a place to explore the jungle and its exuberant flora and fauna. However, as all transport is by river and there are almost no regular passenger boats, it's difficult to get around cheaply on your own. All trips are monopolised by tourist agents and by locals with their own boats. One of the few easily accessible sites is the Parque Nacional Amacayacu.

Parque Nacional Amacayacu This national park takes in 2930 sq km of jungle on the northern side of the Amazon, 75 km upstream from Leticia. A spacious visitor centre with food and accommodation facilities has been built on the bank of the Amazon. Accommodation in bed/hammock costs US$15/12 per person, and three meals (breakfast, lunch and dinner) will run to about US$10. The entry fee is US$10. Theoretically, you have to book and pay at the national parks office in Bogotá, but practice

indicates you can do this in the park. Contact the office of Corpoamazonía in Leticia (☎ 27124), Carrera 11 No 12-45, which can give some information about the park and, if necessary, call the visitor centre.

From the centre, you can explore the park, either by marked paths or by water. The rangers will point out places to visit, and local guides can take you around. In the high-water period (May to June), much of the land turns into swamps and lagoons, greatly reducing walking options, but canoes can be rented.

Two small boat companies, Tres Fronteras and Expreso Amazonas (both with offices near the waterfront in Leticia), operate fast passenger boats to Puerto Nariño, daily around noon. They will drop you off at the visitor centre (US$8, 1½ hours).

Jungle Trips

There are a dozen travel agencies in Leticia focusing on jungle trips. Some agencies offer standard one-day tours, which go up the Amazon to Puerto Nariño and include a visit to an Indian village on the way, plus a lunch. These excursions are usually well organised, comfortable and trouble-free but can hardly give you a real picture of the jungle or the Indians. They are probably not worth the time and money, unless you have just a day to spend in the region.

The real wilderness begins well off the Amazon proper, on its small tributaries. The farther you go, the more chance you have to observe wildlife in relatively undamaged habitat and visit Indian settlements. This will obviously involve more time and money, but the experience will be much more rewarding. A tour of some three to five days is usually a good length of time.

Amazon Jungle Trips (☎ 27377), Avenida Internacional No 6-25, in Leticia near the border, is an experienced agency specialising in adventurous trips. Its manager, Antonio Cruz Pérez (who speaks English), has good guides and boatmen/cooks who will take you deep into wild areas of the region in Brazil, Peru and Colombia (no visas necessary). The agency operates a

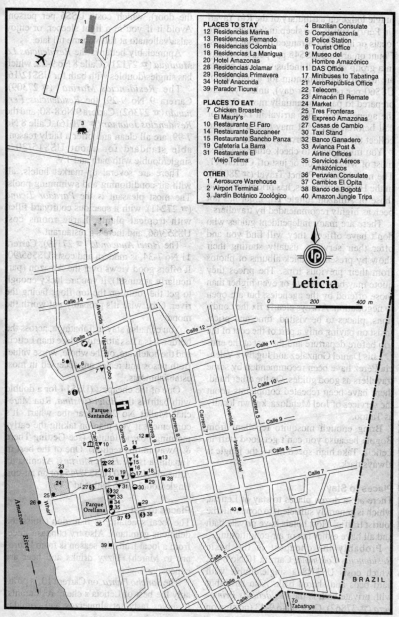

PLACES TO STAY
12 Residencias Marina
13 Residencias Fernando
16 Residencias Colombia
18 Residencias La Manigua
20 Hotel Amazonas
28 Residencias Jolamar
29 Residencias Primavera
34 Hotel Anaconda
39 Parador Ticuna

PLACES TO EAT
7 Chicken Broaster
   El Maury's
10 Restaurante El Faro
14 Restaurante Buccaneer
15 Restaurante Sancho Panza
19 Cafetería La Barra
31 Restaurante El
   Viejo Tolima

OTHER
1 Aerosucre Warehouse
2 Airport Terminal
3 Jardín Botánico Zoológico

4 Brazilian Consulate
5 Corpoamazonía
6 Police Station
8 Tourist Office
9 Museo del
   Hombre Amazónico
11 DAS Office
17 Minibuses to Tabatinga
21 AeroRepública Office
22 Telecom
23 Almacén El Remate
24 Market
25 Tres Fronteras
26 Expreso Amazonas
27 Casas de Cambio
30 Taxi Stand
32 Banco Ganadero
33 Avianca Post &
   Airline Offices
35 Servicios Aéreos
   Amazónicos
36 Peruvian Consulate
37 Cambios El Opita
38 Banco de Bogotá
40 Amazon Jungle Trips

Leticia

0   200   400 m

Calle 14
Calle 13
Calle 12
Calle 11
Calle 10
Calle 9
Calle 8
Calle 7

Avenida Vázquez Cobo
Carrera 11
Carrera 9
Carrera 8
Carrera 7
Avenida Internacional
Avenida 5

Parque Santander
Parque Orellana

Amazon River
Wharf

BRAZIL

To Tabatinga

COLOMBIA

jungle lodge on a tributary of the Río Yavarí (in Peru). You'll also sleep in the huts of the locals or in camps arranged by your guides. Count on around US$45 per person per day in a group of six, all inclusive. Four people are usually the minimum for a trip (about US$60 per person per day), unless you are prepared to pay substantially more. Contact the agency soon after arrival in Leticia (or call beforehand), as it may take a while to collect the party and arrange the trip.

You might want to check other agencies, most of which are on or just off Carrera 11. The new Mowgli Planet Travel (☎ 28027), in the Hotel Amazonas, has prices similar to those of Amazon Jungle Trips, but has not been as highly recommended by travellers.

There are many independent guides who don't have offices; they will find you and offer their services, usually starting their show by presenting thick albums of photos from their previous trips. The prices they quote may be similar to or even higher than those offered by the agencies, but are open to negotiation. Always clearly fix the conditions, places to be visited, time and price. Insist on paying only a part of the cost of the trip before departure and the rest at the end.

Luis Daniel González and Jugalviz Valencia Pérez have been recommended by some travellers as good guides. On the other hand, there have been repeated complaints about the services of Joel Mendoza, known locally as Tattoo.

Bring enough mosquito repellent from Bogotá because you can't get good stuff in Leticia. Take high-speed film – the jungle is always dark.

Places to Stay
There are a dozen places to stay in Leticia, which is generally sufficient to cope with the tourist traffic. Most hotels have private bath and all have either fan or air-conditioning.

Probably the cheapest is the basic *Residencias Colombia*, Carrera 10 No 8-56, which costs US$7/8 a single/double with hard beds and shared bath. Also basic but with private bath is the *Residencias Primavera* (☎ 27862), Calle 8 No 9-43 (no sign on the door), which costs US$6 per person. Avoid it if you're a light sleeper, or enjoy salsa/vallenato at full volume till late.

Appreciably better is the *Residencias La Manigua* (☎ 27121), Calle 8 No 9-22, which has singles/doubles with bath for US$12/16.

The *Residencias Marina* (☎ 27309), Carrera 9 No 9-29; the *Residencias Fernando* (☎ 27362), Carrera 9 No 8-80; and the *Residencias Jolamar* (☎ 27016), Calle 8 No 7-99, are all clean and offer a fairly reasonable standard for about US$15/20 a single/double with bath and TV.

There are several up-market hotels, all with air-conditioning and swimming pools. The most pleasant is the *Parador Ticuna* (☎ 27241), with a spacious courtyard filled with tropical plants. Large rooms cost US$53/66, and there's a restaurant.

The *Hotel Anaconda* (☎ 27119), Carrera 11 No 7-34, is modern and costs US$65/90. It offers good views over the Amazon (particularly at sunset), if you are lucky enough to get the room on the top floor facing the river. Otherwise it's probably not worth the money.

You can also stay in Tabatinga, across the border. It is a less attractive place than Leticia and the hotels are, on the whole, worse value. Both pesos and reales are accepted in most establishments.

One of the cheapest (US$14 for a double with bath) is the *Hotel Cristina*, Rua Marechal Mallet No 248, near the wharf. It's convenient if you plan on taking the early-morning boat to Iquitos (see Getting There & Away in this section). One of the best in Tabatinga is the *Hotel Martins*, Avenida da Amizade No 1440 (US$32/45 for an air-con single/double with bath and TV).

Places to Eat
The local speciality is fish: don't miss the delicious gamitana. Also try cupuasú juice, from a local fruit (the season is from February to March). Fizzy drinks and beer are expensive.

The *Sancho Panza*, on Carrera 10, is probably the best of Leticia's cheap restaurants. It serves tasty set almuerzos and comidas

(US$2) and reasonably priced dishes à la carte. You can have much the same for marginally more at *El Viejo Tolima*, on Calle 8, one block away. The *Buccaneer* and *El Faro* are not bad either, though they are a bit more expensive. More up-market restaurants are at the *Hotel Anaconda* and the *Parador Ticuna*.

Cafetería La Barra, opposite El Viejo Tolima, is popular with locals for a good tinto and cheap fruit juices. The *Chicken Broaster El Maury's* is possibly the best place for chicken.

The best restaurant in Tabatinga is the *Tres Fronteras del Amazonas* on Rua Rui Barbosa.

Getting There & Away – air
Domestic Avianca flies to/from Bogotá on Monday, Wednesday and Friday (US$172). AeroRepública flies to/from Bogotá on Tuesday, Friday and Sunday (US$162). Both carriers usually offer discounted fares of around US$100.

Before you book on a commercial flight, check the cargo flights. Aerosucre shuttles between Leticia and Bogotá almost daily and usually takes passengers for about US$75. You must hunt for the plane at the airport, as there is no fixed schedule. The Aerosucre *bodega* (warehouse) is just behind the passenger terminal. In Bogotá, the Aerosucre departure point for the planes is the cargo building (Edificio de Carga No 1) just before the El Dorado passenger terminal, on your right going towards the airport from the city centre.

To/From Brazil There are no flights into Brazil from Leticia, but from Tabatinga, Varig has flights to Manaus on Monday, Wednesday and Friday (US$180). The airline's office is on Avenida da Amizade, 500 metres past the frontier. The airport is some two km from Tabatinga; colectivos from Leticia will drop you off nearby. Remember to get your exit/entry stamps in your passport.

To/From Peru Varig no longer flies to Iquitos. A small Peruvian carrier, Servicios Aéreos Amazónicos, has flights from Leticia to Iquitos on Monday, Wednesday and Friday in light Fokker planes (US$80). The company's office is at Carrera 11 No 7-28, next door to the Hotel Anaconda.

Getting There & Away – boat
Sitting on the border between Brazil, Colombia and Peru, Leticia is an attractive transit point for travellers looking for a somewhat adventurous, backwater route between these three countries. Although boat fares have risen considerably over the past few years, they are still worthwhile for the adventure they provide.

To/From Brazil Boats down the Amazon to Manaus leave from Benjamin Constant but usually come up to Tabatinga to unload/load. They anchor in Porto de Tabatinga, one km south of the town's wharf near the market.

Theoretically, there are two boats per week, leaving Tabatinga on Wednesday and Saturday around noon and Benjamin Constant the same evenings. The trip to Manaus takes three days and three nights and costs US$80 in your own hammock, or US$300 for a double cabin. Food is included but is poor and monotonous. It's a good idea to buy some snacks as a supplement, and bottled water, easily available in Leticia. The cheapest places to buy an ordinary cloth hammock (US$10 to US$12) are the Lojas Esplanada Tecidos shop, on Rua Marechal Mallet, near the Hotel Cristina in Tabatinga; and the Almacén El Remate, at Calle 8A No 11-136 in Leticia.

The boats come to Tabatinga one or two days before their scheduled departure back down the river. You can string up your hammock or occupy the cabin as soon as you've paid the fare, saving on hotels. Food, however, is only served after departure. Beware of theft on board. If the boat doesn't come up to Tabatinga but only to Benjamin Constant, you must go there by a passenger boat, which departs twice daily from Tabatinga's wharf (US$3, 1½ hours).

COLOMBIA

Upstream from Manaus to Benjamin Constant, the trip takes six to seven days.

To/From Peru Expreso Loreto, Rua Marechal Mallet No 248 in Tabatinga, near the wharf, runs a *rápido*, a high-powered passenger boat, between Tabatinga and Iquitos. The boats are supposed to depart Tabatinga's wharf on Wednesday and Sunday at 5 am, to arrive 10 to 12 hours later. From Iquitos to Tabatinga, the boats depart on Tuesday and Friday and the trip is about two hours shorter. The boats call at Santa Rosa's immigration

posts. The journey costs US$50 in either direction, including lunch.

There are irregular cargo boats to Iquitos once or twice a week, departing from Santa Rosa. The journey takes three days and costs US$25 to US$30, after some negotiations. Downstream from Iquitos to Santa Rosa, it takes around 36 hours.

Note that there are no roads out of Iquitos into Peru. You have to fly or continue by river to Pucallpa (another four to seven days), from where you can go overland to Lima and elsewhere.

Ecuador

Facts about the Country

HISTORY

Ecuadorian stone-age tools have been dated to 9000 BC, and the oldest signs of a more developed culture have been dated back to 3400 BC. These are mainly ceramics of the Valdivia period, found in the central coastal area of Ecuador.

Early Peoples

Pre-Inca Ecuador is less well known than areas farther south in Peru, but the existence of numerous raised field earthworks (*camellones*) for cultivation suggests a large population in the Guayas lowlands in very early times. In the 11th century AD, there were two dominant cultures: the expansionist Caras in the coastal areas and the peaceful Quitus in the highlands. These peoples merged to form the Shyri nation. In about 1300, the Puruhás of the southern highlands became powerful, and the marriage of a Shyri princess to Duchicela, a Puruhá prince, gave rise to a successful alliance. Duchicela's descendants ruled more or less peacefully for about 150 years.

The Inca Conquest

By the mid-1400s, Duchicela's descendants dominated the north, and the south was in the hands of the Cañari people, who defended themselves fiercely against the Inca invaders. It was some years before the Inca Tupac-Yupanqui was able to subdue them and turn his attention to the north. During this time, a Cañari princess bore him a son, Huayna Capac.

The subjugation of the north took many years and Huayna Capac grew up in Ecuador. He succeeded his father on the Inca throne and spent years travelling all over his empire, from Bolivia to Ecuador, constantly putting

down uprisings. Wherever possible, he strengthened his position by marriage; his union with Paccha, the daughter of the defeated Cacha Duchicela, produced a son, Atahualpa.

Huayna Capac died in 1526 and left his empire not to one son, as was traditional, but to two, thus dividing the Inca Empire for the first time. In the same year the first Spaniards, led by Bartolomé Ruiz de Andrade, landed near Esmeraldas in northern Ecuador,

Country Name República del Ecuador
Area 272,045 sq km
Population 11,700,000 (1996 estimate)
Population Density 43 per sq km
Capital Quito
Head of State President Abdalá Bucaram
Official Language Spanish
Other Languages Quechua, Quichua, other indigenous languages
Currency Sucre (S/)
Exchange Rate US$1 = S/2910
Per Capita GNP US$1170 (1993)
Inflation Rate 45% (1993); under 20% (1995 estimate)

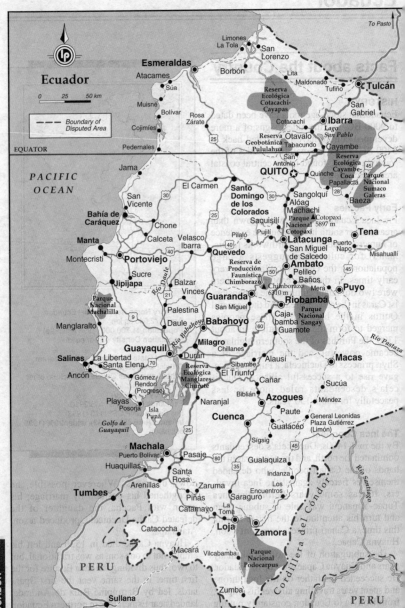

Ecuador

0   25   50 km

Boundary of Disputed Area

EQUATOR

PACIFIC OCEAN

To Pasto

Limones
La Tola
San Lorenzo
Borbón
Lita
Maldonado
Tufiño
Tulcán

Atacames
Súa
Muisne
Bolívar
Rosa Zárate
Cojimíes
Pedernales

Esmeraldas

Reserva Ecológica Cotacachi-Cayapas
Cotacachi
Ibarra
San Gabriel
Lago San Pablo
Otavalo
Reserva Geobotánica Pululahua
Tabacundo
Cayambe

Jama

El Carmen
Santo Domingo de los Colorados
San Antonio
QUITO
Quinche
Reserva Ecológica Cayambe-Coca
Papallacta
Parque Nacional Sumaco Galeras
Baeza

San Vicente
Bahía de Caráquez
Chone
Calceta
Velasco Ibarra
Quevedo
Saquisilí
Pujilí
Pilaló
Sangolquí
Alóag
Machachi
Parque Nacional Cotopaxi
▲Cotopaxi 5897 m

Manta
Montecristi
Portoviejo
Sucre
Balzar
Vinces
Latacunga
San Miguel de Salcedo
Tena
Puerto Napo
Misahuallí

Jipijapa
Reserva de Producción Faunística Chimborazo
Ambato
Pelileo
Baños
Mera
Puyo

Parque Nacional Machalilla
Río Daule
Guaranda
San Miguel
▲Chimborazo 6310 m
Riobamba

Manglaralto
Palestina
Daule
Babahoyo
Caja-bamba
Guamote
Parque Nacional Sangay

Río Babahoyo
Milagro
Chillanes
Alausí
Macas

Salinas
La Libertad
Santa Elena
Guayaquil
Durán
Reserva Ecológica Manglares-Churute
El Triunfo
Sibambe
Cañar
Sucúa
Méndez

Ancón
Gómez Rendón (Progreso)
Naranjal
Biblián
Azogues
Paute
General Leonidas Plaza Gutiérrez (Limón)

Playas
Posorja
Isla Puná
Cuenca
Gualaceo

Golfo de Guayaquil
Sigsig
Gualaquiza

Machala
Puerto Bolívar
Pasaje
Santa Rosa
Paute

Huaquillas
Zaruma
Indanza
Los Encuentros
Río Santiago

Tumbes
Arenillas
Piñas
Saraguro

Catamayo
La Toma
Zamora
Catacocha
Loja
Parque Nacional Podocarpus

Macará
Vilcabamba

PERU
Zumba
Cordillera del Cóndor

Sullana

PERU

Río Pastaza

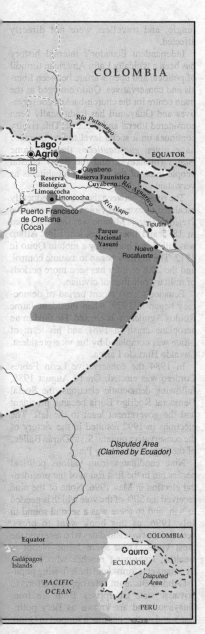

Disputed Area
(Claimed by Ecuador)

COLOMBIA

Lago Agrio

EQUATOR

Cuyabeno
Reserva Faunística
Cuyabeno

Reserva Biológica Limoncocha

Limoncocha

Puerto Francisco de Orellana (Coca)

Río Putumayo

Río Aguarico

Río Napo

Tiputini

Parque Nacional Yasuní

Nuevo Rocafuerte

Equator

Galápagos Islands

PACIFIC OCEAN

COLOMBIA

QUITO

ECUADOR

Disputed Area

PERU

ECUADOR

a portent of the invasion that subjugated the empire a few years later.

Meanwhile, the rivalry between the Incas, led by Huáscar of Cuzco and Atahualpa of Quito, flared into civil war. After years of fighting, Atahualpa defeated Huáscar in a battle near Ambato in central Ecuador. Atahualpa thus ruled a weakened and still divided Inca Empire when Pizarro landed in Peru in 1532.

The Colonial Era

Francisco Pizarro appointed his brother Gonzalo as governor of Quito in 1540. Gonzalo, hoping to find more gold, sent his lieutenant Francisco de Orellana to explore the Amazon. Orellana and his force ended up floating all the way to the Atlantic – the first men to descend the Amazon and cross the continent. This feat, which took a year, is still commemorated in Ecuador. It constitutes part of a historical claim by Ecuador to a greater part of the Amazon Basin than it actually possesses.

Lima was the seat of the political administration of Ecuador during the first centuries of colonial rule. Ecuador was at first a *gobernación* (province), but in 1563 it became the Audiencia de Quito, a more important political division. In 1739, the audiencia was transferred from the Viceroyalty of Peru to the Viceroyalty of Colombia (then known as Nueva Grenada).

Ecuador remained a peaceful colony during these centuries, and agriculture and the arts flourished. Cattle, bananas and other agricultural products were introduced by Europeans. There was prolific construction of churches and monasteries; these were decorated with unique carvings and paintings resulting from the blend of Spanish and Indian artistic influences.

Life was comfortable for the ruling Spaniards, but Indians and mestizos were treated abysmally. Systems of forced labour and tribute were not only tolerated but encouraged, and it is no surprise that, by the 18th century, there were several uprisings of Indians against their Spanish rulers.

One of the best remembered heroes of the early revolutionary period was Eugenio Espejo, born in Quito in 1747 of an Indian father and a mulatto mother. A brilliant man who obtained his doctorate by the age of 20, Espejo became a major literary voice for independence. He wrote political satire, founded a liberal newspaper and spoke out strongly against colonialism. He was imprisoned several times and died in jail in 1795.

Independence

The first serious attempt at independence was made by a partisan group led by Juan Pío Montúfar, on 10 August 1809. The group managed to take Quito and install a government, but this lasted for only 24 days before royalist troops were able to regain control.

Independence was finally achieved when Simón Bolívar, the Venezuelan liberator, freed Colombia in his march southward from Caracas in 1819. Bolívar then supported the people of Guayaquil when they claimed independence on 9 October 1820. It was almost two years before Ecuador was entirely liberated from Spanish rule. The decisive battle was fought on 24 May 1822, when Field Marshal Sucre, one of Bolívar's best generals, defeated the royalists at Pichincha and took Quito.

Bolívar's idealistic dream was to form a United South America. He began by amalgamating Venezuela, Colombia and Ecuador into the independent state of Gran Colombia, which lasted eight years. Ecuador became fully independent in 1830. In the same year, a treaty was signed with Peru, drawing up a boundary between the two nations. This boundary is marked on Ecuadorian maps today but, after a war with Peru, the border was redrawn by a conference of foreign government ministers in the 1942 Protocol of Rio de Janeiro, and it is this border that is found on all non-Ecuadorian maps. The border is still contested with minor skirmishes between Ecuador and Peru, the most serious of which was the recent short war in early 1995 when several dozen soldiers on both sides were killed. Hostilities were confined to remote border areas in the jungle, and travellers were not directly affected.

Independent Ecuador's internal history has been a typically Latin American turmoil of political and open warfare between liberals and conservatives. Quito emerged as the main centre for the church-backed conservatives and Guayaquil has traditionally been considered liberal and socialist. This rivalry continues on a social level today: *quiteños* have given *guayaquileños* the nickname *monos* (monkeys), and the lively coastal people think of the highland inhabitants as very staid and dull.

The rivalry between the groups frequently escalated to extreme violence: conservative President García Moreno was shot and killed in 1875 and liberal President Eloy Alfaro was killed and burned by a mob in Quito in 1912. The military began to assume control, and the 20th century has seen more periods of military rule than of civilian.

Ecuador's most recent period of democracy began in 1979, when President Jaime Roldos Aguilera was elected. He died in an aeroplane crash in 1981 and his term of office was completed by his vice president, Osvaldo Hurtado Larrea.

In 1984 the conservative León Febres Cordero was elected. On 10 August 1988, following democratic elections, the Social Democrat Rodrigo Borja became president and the government leant to the left. The elections in 1992 resulted in the victory of the conservative quiteño Sixto Durán Ballén, of the Republican Unity Party.

Nine candidates from various political parties ran in the first round of the presidential election in May 1996. None of the nine received the 50% of the vote which is needed to win, and so there was a second round in July 1996, as this book went to press, between the two candidates who received the most votes. These were Jaime Nebot, a wealthy, right-wing rancher who favours free-market reforms, and the left-wing populist Abdalá Bucaram, who opposes efforts to privatise state enterprises. Both are from Guayaquil and are known as fiery politicians, and neither has much support in Quito.

Bucaram emerged the winner after the second round.

GEOGRAPHY

Ecuador straddles the equator on the Pacific coast of South America and is bordered by only two countries: Colombia to the north and Peru to the south. Despite its small size, Ecuador has some of the world's most varied geography.

The country is divided into three regions. The backbone of Ecuador is the Andean range, within which lies the capital, Quito. At 2850 metres above sea level, it is the second-highest capital in the world (after La Paz, Bolivia). The mountains split the country into the western coastal lowlands and the eastern jungles of the upper Amazon Basin, known in Ecuador as the Oriente. In only 200 km as the condor flies, you can climb from the coast to snowcaps at over six km above sea level, then descend back down to the steaming rainforest on the eastern side. The Galápagos Islands (Islas Galápagos) lie on the equator, 1000 km west of Ecuador's coast, and constitute one of the country's 21 provinces.

CLIMATE

Instead of the four seasons, Ecuador has wet and dry seasons. The local weather patterns vary greatly, depending on which geographical region you are in.

The Galápagos and coastal areas have a hot and rainy season from January to April. It doesn't rain all the time but you can expect torrential downpours, which often disrupt communications. Daytime temperatures average about 31°C but are often much higher, and it is generally unpleasant to travel in the coastal regions during this time. From May to December, temperatures are a little lower and it rains infrequently.

In the Oriente it's usually almost as hot as on the coast, and it rains during most months. September to December are the driest, and June to August the wettest, with regional variations.

The dry season in the highlands is from

June to September, and a short dry season also occurs during the month around Christmas. It doesn't rain daily in the wet season: April, the wettest month, averages one rainy day in two. Daytime temperatures in Quito average a high of 20°C to 22°C and a low of 7°C to 8°C all year round. Remember, however, that the most predictable aspect of Ecuador's weather is its unpredictability.

FLORA & FAUNA

Ecuador, despite its small size, has many more plant and animal species than do much larger countries. Acre for acre, Ecuador is one of the most species-rich countries on the globe. Scientists have long realised that the tropics harbour many more species than do more temperate countries, but the reasons for this are still a matter of debate and research. The most commonly held belief is that the tropics acted as a refuge for plants and animals during the many ice ages affecting more temperate regions; the much longer and relatively stable climatic history of the tropics has enabled speciation to occur.

Another reason for Ecuador's biodiversity is simply that there are a great number of different habitats within the borders of this small country. Obviously, the Andes will support very different species from the low tropical rainforests, and when intermediate habitats are included and the coastal areas added, the result is a wealth of habitats, ecosystems and wildlife. Ecologists consider Ecuador to be one of the world's 'mega-diversity hot spots'. This has attracted increasing numbers of nature lovers from all over the world.

Plants

There are over 20,000 species of plants in Ecuador and new species are being discovered every year. In comparison, there are only 17,000 species in the entire North American continent.

Birds

Bird-watchers come to Ecuador because of the great number of species recorded here –

some 1500, or about twice the number found in any one of the continents of North America, Europe or Australia. New species are often added to the list.

Mammals

These are well represented, with some 300 species recorded. These vary from monkeys in the Amazonian lowlands to the rare Andean spectacled bear in the highlands. The most diverse mammals are the bats: there are well over 100 species in Ecuador alone.

Conservation

Ecotourism has become important in the economy of Ecuador and other nations with similar natural resources. People are more likely to visit Ecuador to see monkeys in the forest than to see cows at pasture. Those visitors then spend money on hotels, transport, food etc. Many people who spend time in the tropics gain a better understanding of the problems facing the forests and of the importance of preserving them. As a result, visitors return home and become goodwill ambassadors for tropical forests. Be aware, however, that some 'ecotourism' companies are more interested in short-term profit than long-term protection.

Other innovative projects for sustainable development of tropical forests are being researched and implemented. For example, the nut of the tagua palm, which is as hard as ivory, can be used to carve ornaments (as souvenirs). Under programmes such as the 'debt for nature' swaps, local groups received Ecuadorian funds for preserving crucial habitats, and parts of Ecuador's national debt were paid off in return.

Local conservation groups have blossomed in the late 1980s and early 1990s. Some have been quite successful in providing legal protection for forests. Others have concentrated on improving environmental data collection and on training members in the disciplines needed to create a strong information base for national conservation research. Perhaps most important are the small local groups that protect specific

natural areas. These groups involve nearby communities through environmental education, agroforestry and community development projects. Such grass-roots community involvement is essential for viable conservation in Ecuador.

NATIONAL PARKS

Ecuador's first national park was the Islas Galápagos, formed in 1959. The first mainland park was Cotopaxi, established in 1975, followed by Machalilla, Yasuní and Sangay in 1979, Podocarpus in 1982, and Sumaco-Galeras in 1994. As well as these six national parks, there are various reserves and protected areas, most created in 1979. These include Manglares-Churute, Cotacachi-Cayapas, Cuyabeno and Cajas. Additionally, local conservation organisations have set aside private nature reserves. All of Ecuador's major ecosystems are partly protected in one (or more) of these areas.

These parks lack the tourist infrastructure found in many other parts of the world. There are few camping grounds, ranger stations, museums, scenic lookouts or information centres. Some of the parks and reserves are remote, difficult to get to, lack all facilities and are inhabited by indigenous peoples who had been living in the area for generations before the area achieved park or reserve status.

All of these areas are susceptible to interests incompatible with full protection – oil drilling, logging, mining, ranching, fishing and colonisation. Despite this, the national parks do preserve large tracts of pristine habitat and many travellers visit at least one park or reserve during their stay in Ecuador.

The national park system is administered, but perhaps not protected, by the Instituto Ecuatoriano Forestal de Areas Naturales y Vida Silvestre (INEFAN), a branch of the Ministerio de Agricultura y Ganadería (MAG), or Ministry of Agriculture and Ranching.

Entrance fees are US$10 or US$20 on the mainland (a little less if paid in *sucres*) and US$80 in the Galápagos. Private reserves are often free to guests staying at the pricey but worthwhile lodges within them.

GOVERNMENT

Ecuador is a republic with a democratic government headed by a president. The first constitution was written in 1830, but it has had several changes since then, the most recent in 1978. Democratically elected governments have regularly been toppled by coups, often led by the military. Since 1979, however, all Ecuador's governments have been freely elected. All literate citizens over 18 have the vote, and the president must receive over 50% of the vote to be elected. With at least 13 different political parties, 50% of the vote is rarely achieved, in which case there is a second round between the top two contenders. A president governs for a maximum of four years and cannot be re-elected. The president is also the head of the armed forces and appoints the 12 cabinet ministers who form the executive branch of the government.

The legislative branch of government consists of a single Chamber of Representatives (or Congress), which has 77 members. The Congress appoints the justices of the Supreme Court.

There are 21 provinces *(provincias)*, each with a governor appointed by the president and democratically elected prefects. The provinces are subdivided into smaller political units called *cantones*; each cantón has a democratically elected *alcalde*, or mayor.

ECONOMY

Bananas were the most important export until the early 1970s. This changed with the discovery of oil. Petroleum exports rose to first place in 1973, and by the 1980s accounted for about half of the total export earnings. Ecuador's current output of about 300,000 barrels per day does not provide as much income as it did in the early to mid-1980s. In 1992 exports were worth US$3007 million. Crude oil accounted for 41.6% of these, and new reserves discovered in 1993 mean that current rates of production can continue at least until 2030. However, most oil reserves are in the Amazon region and oil extraction is posing serious threats to the rainforest.

Ecuador's main trading partner is the USA. Bananas remain important, comprising about 22% of the nation's exports, followed by shrimp (17.5%). These are cultivated on farms, which are having devastating effects on coastal habitats.

Tourism is a significant part of the economy.

Despite the new-found wealth produced by oil exportation, Ecuador remains a poor country. Distribution of wealth has been patchy, and much of the rural population continues to live at the same standards it did in the 1970s. However, education and medical services have improved. In 1993 the foreign debt was about $14,110 million.

POPULATION & PEOPLE

Ecuador has the highest population density of any South American country. The birth rate is 26.5 per 1000 inhabitants, which means the population will double by about 2028.

About 40% of the population are Indians and an equal number are mestizos. Whites account for 15%, blacks for 5% and other races account for less than 1%.

Most of the Indians are Quechua or Quichua-speaking and live in the highlands. A few other small groups live in the lowlands. About 48% of the population live on the coast (and the Galápagos) and about 46% in the highlands. The remainder live in the jungle region of the Oriente, where colonisation is slowly increasing. The urban population is 55%. In recent years, the indigenous peoples have become more involved in national politics and have mobilised to protect their special interests.

EDUCATION

Six years of elementary education are compulsory, but many children drop out. In the highlands, the school year is from October to July. On the coast, the school year is from May to January. There are about 20 universities and technical colleges. Adult literacy

ECUADOR

in 1990 was 90.5% for males and 86.2% for females.

ARTS
Visual Arts

The Spanish conquistadors trained local indigenous artists to produce the colonial religious art that is now seen in many churches and art museums. Thus arose the *escuela quiteña* (Quito school) of art – Spanish religious concepts portrayed by Indian artists, who incorporated their own beliefs. The Quito school died out with the coming of independence.

The 19th century is referred to as the Republican period, and its art is characterised by formalism. Favourite subjects included heroes of the revolution, important members of the new republic's high society, and florid landscapes.

The 20th century saw the rise of the indigenist school, whose unifying theme is the oppression and the burdens of Ecuador's indigenous inhabitants. Important artists include Eduardo Kingman, Endara Crow, Camilo Egas and Oswaldo Guayasamín. These and other artists have works in modern galleries and museums in Quito; Egas (1889-1962) and Guayasamín (born 1919) have museums in their homes.

Architecture

Many of Quito's churches were built during the colonial period, and the architects were influenced by the Quito school. In addition, churches often had Moorish (Arab) influences. The overall appearance of the architecture of colonial churches is overpoweringly ornamental, and almost cloyingly rich – in short, Baroque.

Many colonial houses had two storeys, with the upper floors bearing ornate balconies. The walls were whitewashed and the roofs were of red tile. Quito's colonial architecture has been well preserved and led to UNESCO declaring the old part of Quito Patrimonio de la Humanidad (World Cultural Heritage) in 1978. Several other towns, notably Cuenca, have attractive colonial architecture.

Music

Traditional Andean music has a distinctive and haunting sound which has been popularised in Western culture by songs like Paul Simon's version of *El Condor Pasa* and the score of the excellent TV natural history series 'The Flight of the Condor'.

Two main reasons contribute to the otherworldly quality of traditional music. The first is the scale: it is pentatonic, or made up of five notes, rather than the eight-note octaves Westerners are used to. The second is the fact that string and brass instruments were imported by the Spanish; pre-Columbian instruments consisted of wind and percussion, which effectively portrayed the windswept quality of *páramo* (highland) life.

Most traditional music is a blend of pre-Columbian and Spanish influences. It is best heard in a *peña*, or folk music club. Traditional music can also be heard on the streets during fiestas, but increasingly often, fiesta ensembles are cacophonous brass bands.

Literature

Ecuadorian literature is not well known outside Latin America, but indigenous novelist Jorge Icaza's *Huasipungo*, a naturalistic tale of the miserable conditions on Andean haciendas in the early 20th century, is available in English translation as *The Villagers*.

RELIGION

The predominant religion is Roman Catholicism, though a small minority of other churches are found. The indigenous peoples tend to blend Catholicism with their own traditional beliefs.

LANGUAGE

Spanish is the main language. Most Indians are bilingual, either Quechua or Quichua being their mother tongue and Spanish their second language. Also, some small lowland groups speak their own languages. English is understood in the best hotels, airline offices and tourist agencies.

ECUADOR

Facts for the Visitor

VISAS & EMBASSIES

Most tourists entering Ecuador require a passport (valid for six months or more) and a T-3 tourist card, which is obtainable on arrival in Ecuador. The T-3 is free, but don't lose it, as you will need it for stay extensions, passport checks and leaving the country. Lost cards can be replaced at the immigration office in Quito or Guayaquil, or at the exit point from the country.

On arrival, you get identical stamps on both your passport and T-3, indicating how long you can stay. The maximum is 90 days but less is often given. You can get an extension in Quito at the immigration office, Avenida Amazonas 2639.

Tourists can stay for 90 days in any 12-month period. (If you leave with only some of your 90 days used, you receive the balance upon re-entry.) UK citizens may stay longer. People with business, work, student or residence visas (difficult to get in Ecuador) may also stay longer. To stay longer than 90 days, leaving the country and returning doesn't usually work because the border officials check for entry and exit dates (though they aren't always thorough). If you leave the country and return with a new passport, the story is different. With no Ecuadorian stamps in your passport, you have no problem.

Officially, a ticket out of Ecuador and sufficient funds for your stay (US$20 per day) are required, but they are rarely asked for. If you're flying in, it's safest to buy an onward ticket. It can be refunded if you don't use it. In Ecuador, this can take a couple of weeks, but they'll give you the money in US dollars.

Always carry your passport and T-3 card for occasional document checks on public transport. You can be arrested if you have no ID and deported if you don't have a visa or T-3.

Ecuadorian Embassies Abroad

Ecuador has embassies in the neighbouring countries of Colombia and Peru, and also in the following countries:

Australia
388 George St, Suite 1702A, American Express Tower, Sydney, NSW 2000 (☎ (02) 9223-3266, 9223-0041)

Canada
50 O'Connor St, Suite 1311, Ottawa K1P 6L2 (☎ (613) 563-8206, fax 235-5776)

France
34 Avenue de Messine, 75008 Paris (☎ 01 45 61 10 21)

Germany
Koblenzer Strasse 37, 5300 Bonn 2 (☎ (0228) 35 25 44)

New Zealand
Ferry Building, Quay St, Auckland (☎ (09) 309 0229, fax (09) 303-2931)

UK
3 Hans Crescent, Knightsbridge, London SW1X 0L5 (☎ (0171) 584-1367)

USA
2535 15th St NW, Washington, DC 2009 (☎ (202) 234-7200)

Foreign Embassies in Ecuador

Most don't work all day so call ahead for hours. Also check the address: the addresses of consular offices may change every year or two but the same phone number is often retained.

Australia
Calle San Roque and Avenida Francisco de Orellana, Ciudadela Kennedy, Guayaquil (☎ (04) 298 823, fax 288 822)

Canada
6 de Diciembre 2816 and J Orton, Quito (☎ (02) 543 214)
Córdova 810 and VM Rendón, 21st floor, Guayaquil (☎ (04) 563 580, 566 747, fax 314 562)

Colombia
Atahualpa 955 and República, 3rd floor, Quito (☎ (02) 458 012, fax 460 054)
Córdova 812 and VM Rendón, 2nd floor, Guayaquil (☎ (04) 563 308, fax 563 854)

France
Leonidas Plaza 107 and Patria, Quito (☎ (02) 560 789, fax 566 424)

Germany
Edificio Banco Consolidado, Patria and 9 de Octubre, 6th floor, Quito (☎ (02) 225 660, fax 563 697)

Ireland
Montes 577 and Las Casas, Quito (☎ (02) 503 674, fax 501 444)

Peru

    Edificio España, Amazonas 1429 and Colón, 2nd floor, Quito (☎ (02) 527 678, 549 255)

    9 de Octubre 411 and Chile, 6th floor, Guayaquil (☎ (04) 322 738, fax 325 679)

UK

    González Suárez 111 and 12 de Octubre, Quito (☎ (02) 560 670, fax 560 730)

    Córdova 623 and Padre Solano, Guayaquil (☎ (04) 560 400, fax 562 641)

USA

    Patria and 12 de Octubre, Quito (☎ (02) 562 890, fax 502 052)

    9 de Octubre and García Moreno, Guayaquil (☎ (04) 323 570, fax 325 286)

DOCUMENTS

International vaccination certificates are not required by law, but some vaccinations, particularly against yellow fever, are advisable. Student cards are sometimes useful, especially in the Galápagos. Cards should bear your photograph and be issued by your own college or university. International student cards are treated with suspicion because fake ones are available.

CUSTOMS

One litre of alcohol and 300 cigarettes are allowed duty free. It is illegal to export pre-Columbian artefacts and illegal to bring them into most countries. Taking endangered animal products home is also illegal.

MONEY

The currency in Ecuador is the *sucre* (S/). There are bills of 10,000, 5000, 1000, 500, 100, 50, 20, 10 and five sucres – though bills smaller than S/100 are rarely seen. There are coins of 50, 20, 10, five and one sucres.

Changing Money

The sucre is regularly devalued, so it is impossible to give accurate exchange rates. The US dollar is the easiest currency to exchange, and all prices in this chapter are given in US dollars. Other hard currencies can be exchanged in Quito, Guayaquil and Cuenca, but carry sucres or US dollars. Exchange rates are lower in smaller towns. In some places, notably the Oriente, it is difficult to exchange money. Exchange houses,

or *casas de cambio*, are normally the best places to change money; banks also will, but tend to be slower. Usually, exchange rates are within 2% of one another in any given city. There is little difference between exchange rates for cash and travellers' cheques.

There is a black market on the streets of the major towns, near the big casas de cambio. Rates are about the same, but street changing is illegal, and forged currency and cheating have been reported.

Credit cards are useful, particularly when buying dollars from a bank. Visa and MasterCard are the most widely accepted. ATMs are appearing in Quito.

You can receive money from home by finding an Ecuadorian bank that will cooperate with your bank at home (eg Bank of America, Bank of London & South America) and telexing someone to deposit the money in your name at the bank of your choice. Allow at least three days. You can also have money sent to Western Union in Quito; this is fast but expensive (US$75 to receive US$1000). Ecuador allows you to receive the money in the currency of your choice. Ecuador is one of the best Latin American countries to have money sent to.

Banks are open for business Monday to Friday from 9 am to 1.30 pm. In some cities, banks may stay open later or open on Saturday, especially if Saturday is market day. Casas de cambio are usually open Monday to Friday from 9 am to 6 pm, and on Saturday until noon. A lunch hour is common.

You can buy back dollars at international airports when leaving the country. You can also change money at the major land borders.

Costs

Costs in Ecuador are low. If you're on a very tight budget and attempting to be really economical, you could survive on US$5 to US$7 per day by staying in the cheapest pensiones and eating the meal of the day in restaurants. (Quito and the main tourist centres are more expensive.) For a little more, a simple room with private hot shower, and table and chair, can be had for about

US$6 a double. Simple à-la-carte meals start at about US$2.50.

A taxi isn't expensive, particularly when you're in a group, and it usually costs about US$1 for short rides. It helps if you are fluent in Spanish. Buses cost roughly US$1 per hour of travel. Trains have a dual pricing system with foreigners paying several times more than locals. The same is true of some air fares. National park fees are US$10 to US$20 per person for foreigners. There is a recent trend to charge 'rich' foreigners more. Most budget hotels and restaurants will charge locals and foreigners the same, especially if you speak Spanish and act as if you know what you are doing.

The biggest problem for budget travellers is reaching the Galápagos archipelago. Getting there is very expensive and staying there isn't particularly cheap; see the Galápagos Islands section in this chapter for more information.

Tipping

Better restaurants add 10% tax and 10% service charge to the bill. Cheaper restaurants don't include tax or service charge and tipping is not necessarily expected. If you want to tip your waiter, do so directly – don't just leave the money on the table.

Tip porters at the airport US$0.25 per bag (US$0.50 minimum). Taxi drivers do not receive a tip, though you can leave small change from a metered ride. Hairdressers get US$0.50 to US$1. On a guided tour, a tip is expected. About US$2 to US$3 per passenger per day is average, or rather more in the Galápagos.

WHEN TO GO

There's no perfect time for a general tour of Ecuador. The coast is hot and wet from January to May (tropical rainstorms may make poorer roads impassable), overcast and humid from June to September, and drier and cooler the rest of the year. The dry season in the highlands is late May to September, which coincides with the wettest months in the Oriente, where roads may be closed.

The high seasons are June to August and December and January.

WHAT TO BRING

Clothes are relatively cheap in Ecuador if you need them, though shoes bigger than size 43 Ecuadorian (size 10 American, size nine British) are hard to find.

The highlands are often cold, so bring a windproof jacket and a warm layer to wear underneath, or plan on buying a thick sweater. Cheap highland hotels often lack heating; they may provide extra blankets on request, but a sleeping bag is useful.

Don't expect many toilets to have toilet paper.

Tampons are expensive and available in regular sizes only in major cities; sanitary pads are cheaper and more common. Stock up before travelling away from the cities.

Condoms are widely sold, but spermicidal jelly for diaphragms is hard to find. The choice of oral contraceptives is limited, so bring your preferred brand from home.

Good insect repellent and sunscreen are expensive and hard to find.

Use Quito as a base for storing unneeded luggage as you take short trips around the country.

TOURIST OFFICES

The government tourist information agency, CETUR, has offices in the major cities. CETUR seems geared mostly towards helping affluent tourists and it is rarely of much help with information about budget hotels etc. English is rarely spoken.

USEFUL ORGANISATIONS
South American Explorers Club

For general information about the SAEC, see Useful Organisations in the Facts for the Visitor chapter. See Useful Organisations in Quito for details of the Quito office.

Other Organisations

For indigenous issues, see Quito, Information. For homestays, see Quito, Places to Stay.

ECUADOR

BUSINESS HOURS

Most stores, businesses, casas de cambio and government offices are open Monday to Friday from about 9 am to 5.30 pm; usually an hour of this time is taken for lunch. In smaller towns lunch breaks of two or more hours are common. On Saturday, many stores and businesses are open from 9 am to noon.

Restaurants tend to remain open late in the big cities, where 10 pm is not an unusual time to eat the evening meal. In smaller towns, restaurants often close by 9 pm (much earlier in villages). Restaurants are often closed on Sunday.

HOLIDAYS & SPECIAL EVENTS

Many of the major festivals are oriented to the Roman Catholic liturgical calendar. They are often celebrated with great pageantry, especially in highland Indian villages, where a Catholic feast day is often the excuse for a traditional Indian fiesta with drinking, dancing, rituals and processions. Other holidays are of historical or political interest. On major holidays, banks, offices and other services are closed and public transport is often very crowded; book ahead if possible.

The following list describes the major holidays and festivals; they may well be celebrated for several days around the actual date.

1 January
    New Year's Day
6 January
    Epiphany
March/April
    Carnaval – the last few days before Lent, celebrated with water fights; Ambato has its fruit and flower festival
March/April (dates vary)
    Easter – Palm Sunday, Holy Thursday, Good Friday, Holy Saturday and Easter Sunday, celebrated with religious processions
1 May
    Labour Day – workers' parades
24 May
    Battle of Pichincha – national holiday commemorating the decisive battle in the struggle for independence from the Spanish in 1822
June
    Corpus Christi – religious feast day combined with the traditional harvest fiesta in many high-

land towns; includes processions and street dancing
24 June
    St John the Baptist – fiestas in Otavalo area
29 June
    St Peter & St Paul – fiestas in Otavalo area and other northern highland towns
24 July
    Simón Bolívar's Birthday – national holiday
25 July
    Founding of Guayaquil – major festival for Guayaquil
10 August
    Quito's Independence Day
1-15 September
    Fiesta del Yamor – held in Otavalo
9 October
    Guayaquil's Independence Day
12 October
    Columbus Day (locally called *Día de la Raza*) – national holiday
1-2 November
    All Saints' Day
    All Souls' Day – celebrated by flower-laying ceremonies in the cemeteries; especially colourful in rural areas, where entire Indian families show up at the cemeteries to eat, drink, and leave offerings in memory of their departed relatives
3 November
    Cuenca's Independence Day
6 December
    Founding of Quito – celebrated throughout the first week of December with bullfights, parades and street dancing
24-25 December
    Christmas Eve/Christmas Day
28-31 December
    End-of-year Celebrations – parades and dances culminate in the burning of life-sized effigies in the streets on New Year's Eve

POST & COMMUNICATIONS

Most letters sent from Ecuador arrive at their destinations, sometimes in as little as a week to the USA or Europe. Incoming mail is another matter. Some letters take as long as two months to arrive, and a few never do.

Sending Mail

Aerograms and postcards are available at the post office, and because they contain no enclosure, they're more likely to arrive safely. Rates are about $US0.30 to the Americas and US$0.40 elsewhere. For a few cents extra, you can send them *certificado* (certified). Sending parcels of two to 20 kg is best done from the post office on Calle Ulloa near Calle Dávalos, in Quito. A 20-kg air-mail parcel will cost almost US$100 to the Americas and well over US$200 elsewhere. Combination surface/air rates are about US$50 to the Americas and US$75 elsewhere.

Receiving Mail

Mail sent to the post office is filed alphabetically, so make sure that your last name is clear, eg John PAYSON, Lista de Correos, Correo Central, Quito (or town and province of your choice), Ecuador. American Express will hold mail for its clients (c/- American Express, Apartado 2605, Quito, Ecuador; the street address is Avenida Amazonas 339). The SAEC holds mail for members. You have to recover your mail from customs (and pay high duty) if it weighs over two kg.

Telephone

EMETEL provides long-distance national and international telephone, fax and telegram services. EMETEL offices are open on a daily basis from 6 am to 10 pm (except in small, remote towns or in hotels and airports, where they keep shorter hours). Service is expensive and inadequate.

Even the most remote villages can often communicate with Quito and connect you into an international call. These cost about US$9 for three minutes to the USA, and about US$12 to Europe. Rates are cheaper on Sunday. Waiting time to make a connection can vary from 10 minutes to over an hour. Reverse-charge (collect) phone calls are possible to the USA, Brazil, Colombia, Argentina, Spain and the UK only. Direct dialling to a North American or European operator is technically possible, but EMETEL and hotels don't like to deal with these calls because they don't make any money on them!

Local numbers are made up of six digits. Area codes are divided by province, as shown on the map. Dial 09 for mobile phones. If calling from abroad, drop the 0 from all codes. Ecuador's country code is 593.

To call locally, you can use coins, phonecards, or tokens, depending on the telephone. In Quito's international airport, there are no coin-operated phones and no-one sells tokens or cards except the EMETEL office, which is supposedly open from 7 am to 8 pm. At other times, you can't make a call unless you can bum a token from someone. It's pathetic.

Fax services are available from EMETEL, private companies and hotels in the larger cities. Rates for sending are about US$9 per page; it costs a small amount, which varies between agencies, to receive.

TIME

The mainland is five hours behind GMT/UTC and the Galápagos are six hours behind. There is no daylight-saving time.

ELECTRICITY

Ecuador uses 110V, 60 Hz AC.

BOOKS & MAPS

For more detailed travel information, there is Lonely Planet's *Ecuador & the Galápagos Islands – travel survival kit*, 4th edition, by Rob Rachowiecki. *Ecuador – a fragile*

ECUADOR

democracy by David Corkill & David Cubitt is a recent look at the history and trends of Ecuadorian politics. Tom Miller's *The Panama Hat Trail* is a good travel book on Ecuador that focuses on the hat industry. The best general book on the Galápagos is Michael Jackson's *Galápagos: A Natural History Guide*. *Climbing & Hiking in Ecuador* by Rob Rachowiecki & Betsy Wagenhauser is a detailed guide to climbing Ecuador's mountains, and also describes many beautiful hikes, some of which are simple day hikes suitable for the beginner. *The Ecotourist's Guide to the Ecuadorian Amazon* by Rolf Wesche et al is available in Quito and covers in detail the Baeza, Tena, Misahuallí and Coca area. Other books are listed in the Facts for the Visitor chapter.

Ecuadorian bookshops have a limited selection of Ecuadorian maps. The best selection is available from the Instituto Geográfico Militar (IGM) or the SAEC; both are in Quito. *The Pocket Guide to Ecuador*, published in Quito, has maps of the entire country plus major city maps.

MEDIA

The best newspapers – *El Comercio* and *Hoy*, published in Quito, and *El Telégrafo* and *El Universo*, published in Guayaquil – cost about US$0.40. Two English-language newspapers, *Q.* and *Inside Ecuador*, are published at erratic intervals and have interesting articles. The *Explorer* is a free monthly booklet in English and Spanish listing what's on in Quito.

Foreign newspapers and magazines are sold at good bookshops and at the international airports. Latin American editions of *Time* and *Newsweek* (in English) are available for about US$2.

There are 10 television channels, though not all can be picked up throughout the country. Some remote towns receive only one or two. A cable network offers US satellite stations such as CNN, ABC, NBC and CBS. There are about 300 radio stations.

FILM & PHOTOGRAPHY

Camera gear is very expensive in Ecuador

and film choice is limited. Always check expiry dates. Kodachrome slide film is hard to find, and slide developing tends to be shoddy. Print film is cheaper and better developing is available. Try the El Globo stores in major cities for film, and Ecuacolor, at Amazonas 848 in Quito, for same-day printing. Fotomania, at 6 de Diciembre and Patria in Quito, is quite good for printing.

HEALTH

See the Health section in the Facts for the Visitor chapter.

DANGERS & ANNOYANCES

Although Ecuador is safer than Peru and Colombia, you should still be careful. Pickpocketing is definitely on the increase and is common in crowded places. Armed robbery is still unusual in most of Ecuador although parts of Guayaquil, some coastal areas, and the stairs up the Panecillo in Quito have a reputation for being very dangerous.

Every year or so, a couple of long-distance night buses are held up and robbed in the Guayaquil area. Avoid taking night buses through Guayas province unless you have to.

Take the normal precautions as outlined in Dangers & Annoyances in the Facts for the Visitor chapter. If you are robbed, get a police report *(denuncia)* within 48 hours – they won't process a report after that. In Quito, go to the police station at the intersection of Cuenca and Mideros, in the old town, between 9 am and noon. In other towns, go to the main police headquarters.

Talk to other travellers and to the folk at the SAEC in Quito for advice and up-to-date information.

WORK

Officially you need a work visa to be allowed to work in Ecuador. You might, however, get a job teaching English in language schools, usually in Quito. Pay is low but enough to live on if you're broke. Schools, such as the American School in Quito, will often hire teachers with bona fide teaching credentials in mathematics, biology and other subjects, and may help you get a work visa if you want to stay on. They also pay much better than the language schools.

Another way of making money is by selling good-quality equipment such as camping or camera items. The SAEC in Quito can help you post notices about the equipment you wish to sell.

ACTIVITIES

Climbing and hiking adventures around Cotopaxi, the Baños area, Las Cajas (near Cuenca) and on Chimborazo (Ecuador's highest mountain) are all worthwhile. Gear can be rented in Quito and some other towns.

The Islas Galápagos, the Amazon, and birds throughout the country are all big attractions for nature lovers. The Galápagos may be too expensive for budget travellers (though a great number get there anyway), but the Amazon can be visited easily and relatively cheaply. Diving is offered in the Galápagos.

Spanish language courses are taught in Quito, Cuenca and a few smaller towns.

HIGHLIGHTS

These include visiting the markets (Otavalo is the first choice for shopping, and Saquisilí for watching the locals shop), taking a railway trip, visiting the Amazon and, if you can afford it, the Galápagos.

ACCOMMODATION

There is no shortage of places to stay in Ecuador, but during major fiestas or the night before market day, accommodation can be rather tight, so as many hotels as possible are shown on the town maps. If you are going to a town specifically for a market or fiesta, try to arrive a day early, or at least by early afternoon of the day before the market is due to commence.

Single rooms may be hard to find, and you might get a room with two or three beds. Often, you are only charged for one bed and won't have to share, unless the hotel is full. Check that you won't be asked to share with a stranger or to pay for all the beds – there is usually no problem. Youth hostels have recently become popular, and staying with

families is another option. The SAEC can provide information about homestays.

FOOD

For breakfast, eggs and bread rolls or toast are available. A good local change from eggs are sweet corn tamales called *humitas*, which are often served for breakfast with coffee.

Lunch is the main meal of the day for many Ecuadorians. A cheap restaurant will serve a decent *almuerzo* (lunch of the day) for as little as US$1. An almuerzo consists of a *sopa* (soup) and a *segundo* (second dish), which is usually a stew with plenty of rice. Sometimes, the segundo is *pescado* (fish) or a kind of lentil or pea stew (*lenteja, arveja*). Some places serve a salad (often cooked), juice and *postre* (dessert) as well as the two main courses.

The evening meal of the day is usually similar to lunch. Ask for the *merienda*. If you don't want the almuerzo or merienda, you can choose from the menu, but this is always more expensive.

A *churrasco* is a hearty dish of a slice of fried beef, one or two fried eggs, vegetables (usually boiled beet slices, carrots and beans), fried potatoes, a slice of avocado and tomato, and the inevitable rice. *Arroz con pollo* is a mountain of rice with little bits of chicken mixed in. *Pollo a la brasa* restaurants serve roast chicken, often with French fries. *Gallina* is usually boiled chicken, as in soups, and *pollo* is more often spit-roasted or fried. Pollo tends to be underdone, but you can return it and ask for it to be cooked a bit more.

Parrilladas are mixed grills. Steaks, pork chops, chicken breasts, blood sausages, liver and tripe are all served on a table-top grill – a lot of food! If you don't want the whole thing, choose just a chop or a steak. Although parrilladas aren't cheap, they are reasonably priced and good value.

Seafood is good, even in the highlands, as it is brought fresh from the coast and iced. The most common types of fish are *corvina* (white sea bass) and *trucha* (trout). *Ceviche* is popular throughout Ecuador; this is seafood marinated in lemon and served with popcorn and sliced onions, and it's delicious. Ceviche can be *de pescado* (fish), *de camarones* (shrimp), *de concha* (shellfish, such as clams, mussels or oysters) or *mixto*. Unfortunately, improperly prepared ceviche is a source of cholera, so avoid it if in any doubt.

Chifas (Chinese restaurants) are generally inexpensive and good value. Apart from rice dishes, they serve *tallarines*, or noodles mixed with your choice of pork, chicken, beef, or vegetables *(legumbres, verduras)*. Portions tend to be filling. Vegetarians will find that chifas offer the best choice for nonmeat dishes. Vegetarian restaurants are rare in Ecuador.

Restaurants usually have a wide range of dishes, including the following:

Caldo – Soups and stews are very popular and are often served in markets for breakfasts. Soups are known as *caldos, sopas,* or *locros*. Chicken soup, or *caldo de gallina*, is the most popular. *Caldo de patas* is soup made by boiling cattle hooves and, to the author's taste, is as bad as it sounds.

Cuy – Whole roasted guinea pig is a traditional food dating back to Inca times. It tastes rather like a cross between rabbit and chicken. The sight of the little paws and teeth sticking out and tightly closed eyes is a little unnerving, but cuy is supposed to be a delicacy and some people love it.

Lechón – Suckling pig is often roasted whole and is a common sight at Ecuadorian food markets. Pork is also called *chancho*.

Llapingachos – fried mashed-potato-and-cheese pancakes often served with *fritada* – scraps of fried or roast pork

Seco – Literally 'dry' (as opposed to a 'wet') soup, this is stew, usually meat served with rice. It may be *seco de gallina* (chicken stew), *de res* (beef), *de chivo* (goat) or *de cordero* (lamb).

Tortillas de maíz – tasty fried corn pancakes

Yaguarlocro – potato soup with chunks of barely congealed blood sausage floating in it. Many people prefer straight *locro*, which usually has potatoes, corn and an avocado or cheese topping.

DRINKS

Water

Purify all tap water or buy bottled water. Bottled mineral water, *agua mineral*, is carbonated. *Agua sin gas* is not carbonated. *Güitig* (pronounced *weetig*) is the most popular brand.

Soft Drinks

Bottled drinks are cheap, but the deposit on the bottle is usually worth more than the drink.

All the usual soft drinks are available, and some local ones have endearing names such as Bimbo or Lulu. Ask for your drink *helada* if you want it out of the refrigerator, *al clima* if you don't. Remember to say *sin hielo* (without ice) unless you really trust the water supply.

Fruit Juices

Juices *(jugos)* are available everywhere. Make sure you get *jugo puro* (pure) and not *con agua* (with water). The most common kinds are *mora* (blackberry), *naranja* (orange), *toronja* (grapefruit), *piña* (pineapple), *maracuyá* (passion fruit), *sandía* (watermelon), *naranjilla* (a local fruit tasting like bitter orange) and *papaya*.

Coffee & Tea

Coffee is available almost everywhere but is often disappointing. It is usually served as a liquid concentrate in cruets and diluted with milk or water. It doesn't taste that great and it looks like soy sauce, so always check before pouring it into your milk (or over your rice)! Espresso coffee is available in the better restaurants.

Tea, or *té*, is served black with lemon and sugar. *Té de hierbas* (herb tea) and hot chocolate are also popular.

Alcohol

Local beers *(cerveza)* are good and inexpensive. Pilsener is available in 650-ml bottles and Club comes in 330-ml bottles.

Local wines are terrible but imported wines are expensive.

Rum *(ron)* is cheap and good. The local firewater, *aguardiente* (sugar-cane alcohol), is an acquired taste but is also good. It's very cheap. Imported spirits are expensive.

THINGS TO BUY

Souvenirs are good, varied and cheap. If you have time for only one big shopping expedition, the Saturday market at Otavalo is both convenient and full of variety. In markets and smaller stores, bargaining is expected, though don't expect to reduce the price by more than about 20%. In 'tourist stores' in Quito, prices are usually fixed. Some of the best shops are quite expensive; on the other hand, the quality of their products is often superior.

Woollen goods are popular and are often made of a pleasantly coarse homespun wool. The price of a thick sweater will begin at under US$10, depending on size and quality. Wool is also spun into a much tighter textile used for making ponchos. *Otavaleño* Indian ponchos are among the best in Latin America. Hand-embroidered clothes are also attractive, but it's worth getting them from a reputable shop, otherwise they may shrink or the colours may run.

Panama hats are worth buying. A really good panama is so finely made that it can be rolled up and passed through a man's ring. They are made from a palmlike bush that grows abundantly in the coastal province of Manabí; Montecristi is a major centre.

Weavings are found all over the country; there's a good selection in Otavalo. Two small weavings are often stitched together to make a shoulder bag. Agave fibre is used to make macramé bags or tough woven bags called *shigras*. Cotacachi and Ambato are centres for leatherwork. San Antonio de Ibarra, between Otavalo and Ibarra, is the major woodworking centre of Ecuador. Balsa-wood models, especially of brightly coloured birds, are popular; these are made in the jungles of the Oriente and sold in many of Quito's gift shops. Painted and varnished ornaments made of bread dough are unique to Ecuador and are best obtained in Calderón, north of Quito.

Getting There & Away

AIR
The main international airports are in Guayaquil and Quito.

To/From Latin America
Direct flights go to Bogotá (Colombia), Buenos Aires (Argentina), Caracas (Venezuela), Curaçao, Guatemala City, Havana (Cuba), Lima (Peru), Mexico City, Panama City, Rio de Janeiro (Brazil), San José (Costa Rica), Santiago (Chile) and São Paulo (Brazil). There are connecting flights to Asunción (Paraguay) and La Paz (Bolivia) via Lima. In addition, Esmeraldas and Tulcán airports each have a couple of flights a week to Cali (Colombia).

To/From North America
There are direct flights to Miami, Houston, Los Angeles and New York, and connecting flights to other cities.

To/From Europe
You can get direct flights to Amsterdam, Barcelona, Madrid and Paris, with connections to other European cities.

To/From Other Continents
Flights to Sydney, Auckland and Johannesburg all have connecting flights to Buenos Aires. Flights to Tokyo go via Miami or Lima. Flights to Tel Aviv go via Madrid.

LAND
International bus tickets sold in Quito require a bus change at the border. It is cheaper and no less convenient to buy a ticket to the border and then another ticket in the next country.

To/From Colombia
Buses go from Colombia to Ecuador via Tulcán. See Tulcán in this chapter for further details.

To/From Peru
Buses go from Peru to Ecuador via either Huaquillas or Macará (both in Ecuador). Huaquillas is the main route. See Huaquillas and Macará in this chapter for further details.

LEAVING ECUADOR
A US$25 departure tax (payable in cash

dollars or sucres) is levied for international flights, unless you are in transit.

Getting Around

You can usually get anywhere quickly and easily. The bus is the most common form of transport; buses can take you from the Colombian to the Peruvian border in 18 hours. Aeroplanes and boats (especially in the Oriente) are also used frequently, but trains less so.

Whichever form of transport you use, remember to have your passport with you, as you may need to show it to board planes and boats. People without documents may be arrested. Buses go through a transit police checkpoint upon entering some towns, and passports may be requested. If your passport is in order, these procedures are cursory. If you're travelling anywhere near the borders or in the Oriente, you can expect more frequent passport checks.

AIR

With the exception of flying to the Galápagos, most internal flights are fairly cheap. Many flights originate or terminate in Quito or Guayaquil. In late 1995, flights between Quito and Coca, Lago Agrio or Macas all had a surcharge for foreigners, and cost US$50 each way (about twice what locals pay). This surcharge may spread to other mainland flights, which otherwise are all cheaper. Flights from Guayaquil to the Galápagos cost US$333 return for foreigners (US$377 from Quito). Students can get a 25% discount with SAN-Saeta to the Galápagos, but TAME are reluctant to give this discount.

Ecuador's major domestic airline is TAME, which flies between Quito and Guayaquil, Cuenca, Loja, Macas, Coca, Lago Agrio, Tulcán, Esmeraldas, Manta, Portoviejo, Bahía de Caráquez and Baltra in the Galápagos. TAME may also fly to Tarapoa, east of Lago Agrio. From Guayaquil TAME flies to and from Quito, Cuenca, Loja, Machala and Baltra. There are seasonal TAME flights to Salinas. SAN-Saeta has flights between Quito, Guayaquil and Cuenca, and flights to San Cristóbal in the Galápagos. The prices of TAME and SAN-Saeta flights are the same. Other small, local airlines have light aircraft that fly mainly along the coast.

Ten to 12 flights a day connect Quito and Guayaquil. There are one to three flights a day between Quito and Cuenca, daily flights to Baltra, and several flights a week to other towns. There are no Sunday flights to the Oriente.

Domestic flights have neither seat reservations nor separate sections for smokers and nonsmokers. Flights are subject to frequent delays, changes and cancellations. Some flights give good views of the snow-capped Andes. When flying from Quito to Guayaquil, the mountain views are on the left-hand side.

If you can't get a ticket for a particular flight (especially out of small towns), go to the airport early and get on the waiting list in the hope of a cancellation. If you have a reservation, confirm it and reconfirm it or you may be bumped.

BUS
Long-Distance Bus

Most towns have a central bus terminal (*terminal terrestre*). In some towns buses leave from other places (where possible, these are indicated on the map). Timetables change frequently and are not always adhered to.

Busetas are fast, small buses that carry 22 passengers in rather cramped seats. Service is direct and sometimes frighteningly speedy. Larger coaches allow standing passengers, can get crowded, and are generally slower than the busetas, but they can be more interesting, with passengers getting on and off, perhaps accompanied by chickens or 50-kg bags of potatoes.

Buy tickets in advance from the terminal to get your choice of seat: avoid the cramped seats over the wheels, and the back seats, which are the bumpiest. Some companies have frequent departures and don't sell advance tickets. During holiday weekends buses can be booked up for several days in advance. For immediate travel, go to the terminal and listen for your destination to be yelled out. Make sure your bus goes direct to your destination if you don't want to change.

If you're travelling light, keep your luggage with you inside the bus. If your luggage won't fit under the seat, it will go on top or in a luggage compartment. Watch your stuff: it can get soaked on top, stained with grease in a luggage compartment, and stolen anywhere.

At many bus stops on the main routes, vendors selling fruit, rolls, ice cream or drinks suddenly appear. Long-distance buses usually stop for 20-minute meal breaks at the appropriate times. The food in the terminal restaurants is basic. Most buses lack toilets, but there are rest stops every few hours.

Local Bus

These are usually slow and crowded but cheap. You can get around most towns for about US$0.10. Local buses often go out to nearby villages, and this is a good way to see an area.

TRUCK

In remote areas, *camiones* (trucks) often double as buses. If the weather is OK, you get fabulous views; if not, you have to crouch underneath a dark tarpaulin. Truck drivers charge standard fares, depending on distance, which are almost as much as bus fares.

TRAIN

Trains run from Quito to Durán (Guayaquil) via Riobamba and Alausí. In the north, trains run from Ibarra to San Lorenzo, on the coast, and between Otavalo and Ibarra. *Autoferros*, which are buses mounted on railway chassis, are used on the latter two routes. Foreigners are charged much more than locals on the scenic and exciting Alausí-Durán and Ibarra-San Lorenzo sections.

BOAT

Motorised dugout canoes, which carry up to three dozen passengers, are the only way to get around many roadless areas. Regularly scheduled boats are quite affordable, though not as cheap as a bus for a similar distance. Hiring your own boat and boatman is possible but expensive. You are most likely to travel in dugouts in the Misahuallí and Coca regions of the Oriente, and on the north-west coast.

Seating is on hard, low wooden benches: bring something padded to sit on. Luggage is stashed under a tarpaulin, so hang onto hand baggage containing essentials for the journey. Pelting rain and glaring sun are major hazards and an umbrella is excellent defence against both. Use a good sunscreen lotion, or wear long sleeves, long pants and a sun hat. A light jacket is worth having against chilling rain, and insect repellent is useful during stops along the river. A water bottle and food will complete your hand baggage. Keep your spare clothes in plastic bags or they'll get soaked by rain or spray.

TAXI

Taxis are cheap. Bargain the fare beforehand, or you're likely to be overcharged. A long ride in a large city (Quito or Guayaquil) shouldn't go over US$4 and short hops can cost under US$1. Meters are obligatory in Quito but rarely seen elsewhere. At weekends and at night, fares are always about 25% to 50% higher.

A full-day taxi hire might cost about US$50. If you hire a taxi to take you to another town, expect to pay about US$1 for every 10 km. Remember to include the km for the return trip. Pick-ups can be hired to remote places such as climbers' refuges.

CAR

Car rental in Quito, Guayaquil and Cuenca is not cheap. A small car is about US$200 a week and includes only 1200 'free' km.

HITCHING

Private cars are not very common and trucks are used as public transport in remote areas, so trying to hitch a free ride is not easy. If the driver is stopping to drop off and pick up other passengers, then you can assume that payment will be expected. If you are the only

ECUADOR

passenger, the driver may have picked you up just to talk to a foreigner, and may waive payment.

Quito

At 2850 metres above sea level and only 22 km south of the equator, Quito has a wonderful spring-like climate. It is in a valley flanked by mountains and on a clear day several snowcapped volcanoes are visible from the capital.

Quito was a major Inca city that was destroyed by Atahualpa's general, Rumiñahui, shortly before the arrival of the Spanish conquistadors; there are no Inca remains. The present capital was founded on top of the Inca ruins by Sebastián de Benalcázar on 6 December 1534, and many colonial buildings survive in the old town. In 1978, UNESCO declared Quito one of the world's cultural heritage sites, and building and development in Quito's old town is now strictly controlled. There are few modern buildings next to centuries-old architecture, and no flashing neon signs to disrupt the ambience of the past.

Orientation

With a population of about 1.2 million, Quito is Ecuador's second-largest city. It can be divided into three segments. The centre is the site of the old town, which has whitewashed and red-tiled houses and colonial churches. The north is modern Quito, with major businesses, airline offices, embassies, shopping centres and banks. This area also contains the airport and middle and upper-class residential areas. Avenida Amazonas is the best known street, though Avenida 10 de Agosto and Avenida 6 de Diciembre are the most important thoroughfares. The south consists mainly of working-class housing areas.

Information

Tourist Offices The main CETUR tourist information office is at Eloy Alfaro 1214 (☎ 225 101). There is also one at the airport's domestic terminal and one at Venezuela 914 (☎ 514 044) in the old town. Hours are Monday to Friday from 9 am to 5 pm.

Money Many banks are on Amazonas; hours are from 9 am to 1.30 pm. Casa de cambio hours are weekdays from 9 am to 6 pm, and Saturday morning. Casas de cambio are the usual places to exchange money. Casa Paz is the best known casa de cambio, and has an old town office (☎ 511 364) at Sucre and Venezuela, and a new town office at Amazonas 370. The office at the airport is open on Sunday, and the one at the Hotel Colón is open on Sunday and often until 7 pm on weekdays. There are several other good casas de cambio. Western Union (☎ 565 059) is at Avenida República 396.

You can receive cash with your credit card at the following places, all in the new town; commissions vary. MasterCard and Visa are currently the most acceptable.

American Express
   Amazonas 339 and Jorge Washington, 5th floor (☎ 560 488)
Diners Club
   Avenida República 710 and Eloy Alfaro (☎ 221 372)
MasterCard
   Naciones Unidas 825 and Los Shyris (☎ 462 770)
Visa
   Banco de Guayaquil, Avenida Colón and Reina Victoria (☎ 566 824)
   Filanbanco, Amazonas 530 and Roca

Post & Communications The central post office is in the old town, at Espejo 935 and Guayaquil. This is where you pick up lista de correos mail, but ask about a possible move to the new town. The main branch office in the new town is at Colón and Reina Victoria. Hours are Monday to Friday from 7.30 am to 7.30 pm, and Saturday from 8 am to 2 pm. To mail a package of over two kg, use the office in the new town at Calle Ulloa 273, near Ramírez Dávalos (☎ 521 730).

The main EMETEL office for international calls is at 10 de Agosto and Colón; it's open daily from 6 am to 9.30 pm. There are smaller EMETEL offices at the Terminal

Terrestre Cumandá, at the airport and at Benalcázar and Mejía, in the old town.

Tourist Card Extensions For tourist card extensions, go to Migraciones (☎ 454 122, 454 099), Avenida Amazonas 2639 (also numbered 3149) and Avenida de la República, open Monday to Friday from 8 am to noon and 3 to 6 pm. It takes anywhere from 10 minutes to two hours to get a tourist card extension. Onward tickets out of Ecuador and 'sufficient funds' are rarely asked for. Bring airline tickets or travellers' cheques if you have them, just in case.

South American Explorers Club The clubrooms of the SAEC (☎ & fax 225 228, e-mail explorer@saec.org.ec) moved in 1996 to Jorge Washington 311 and Leonidas Plaza Gutiérrez, Mariscal Sucre. Hours are Monday to Friday from 9.30 am to 5 pm. Mail should still be sent to Apartado 17-21-431, Eloy Alfaro, Quito, Ecuador. See Useful Organisations in the introductory Facts for the Visitor chapter for a full description of the club and its services.

Tour Agencies Tours are usually cheaper if they are booked in the town closest to where you want to go rather than in Quito. However, if you prefer to start in Quito, the following operators are reliable. Safari (☎ 552 505, fax 220 426), Calamá 380 and JL Mera, Apartado 17-11-6060, arranges just about any kind of adventure tour from bird-watching to volcano climbing. Emerald Forest (☎ 526 403), Amazonas 1023 and Pinto, specialises in jungle tours to the Coca area, and Native Life (☎ 550 836), Pinto 446 and Amazonas, specialises in Cuyabeno Reserve jungle trips. Sierra Nevada (☎ 553 658) at JL Mera 741 and Veintimilla, and Pamir Adventure (☎ 542 605, fax 547 576), JL Mera 721, have experienced climbing guides. Sierra Nevada offers river rafting and mountain biking as well. Flying Dutchman (☎ 542 806, fax 449 568), Foch 714 and Mera, offers recommended bike tours.

Fundación Golondrinas (☎ 226 602), Isabel La Católica 1559 is a conservation project with volunteer opportunities. It arranges four-day walking tours in the páramo and forests west of Tulcán. Costs are US$50 per day.

Indigenous Issues Fundación Pueblo Indio (☎ 529 361), Ruiz de Castilla 216 and Sosaya, and CONAIE (☎ 248 930), Los Granados 2553 and 6 de Diciembre, provide information.

Bookshops Libri Mundi (☎ 234 791), JL Mera 851, has a good selection of books in English, German and French. Another recommended bookshop is Libro Express, at Amazonas 816.

Maps The Instituto Geográfico Militar (IGM), on top of steep Calle Paz y Miño, is open Monday to Friday from 8 am to 3 pm. Mornings are recommended. Bring your passport.

Laundry At Lava Hotel Self Service (☎ 506 129), Almagro 818 and Colón, they wash, dry and fold your clothes in 24 to 48 hours. Opera de Jabón/Soap Opera (☎ 543 995), Pinto 325 and Reina Victoria, will wash your clothes the same day, or you can do it yourself if you ask and there is a machine available.

Emergency The Hospital Voz Andes (☎ 241 540), at Juan Villalengua 267 (near América and 10 de Agosto) is an American-run hospital with outpatient and emergency rooms. Fees are low. Good, but pricier, is the Metropolitano (☎ 431 457, 431 520), Avenida Mariana de Jesús and Occidental. A private clinic specialising in women's health is Clínica de la Mujer (☎ 458 000), Amazonas 4826 and Gaspar de Villarroel.

Recommended dental clinics include the Clínica de Especialidades Odontológicas (☎ 521 383, 237 562), Orellana 1782 and 10 de Agosto, Clínica Dental Arias Salazar (☎ 524 582), Amazonas 239 and 18 de Septiembre, and Clínica Dental Dr Pedro Herrera (☎ 554 316), Amazonas 353 and Jorge Washington.

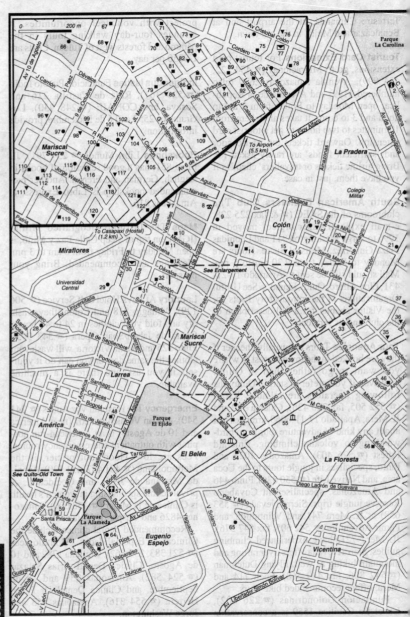

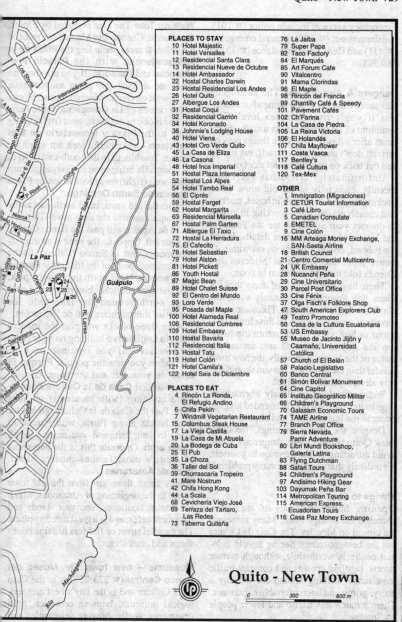

PLACES TO STAY
10 Hotel Majestic
11 Hotel Versalles
12 Residencial Santa Clara
13 Residencial Nueve de Octubre
14 Hotel Ambassador
22 Hostal Charles Darwin
23 Hostal Residencial Los Andes
26 Hotel Quito
27 Albergue Los Andes
31 Hostal Coqui
32 Residencial Carrión
34 Hotel Koronado
38 Johnnie's Lodging House
40 Hotel Viena
43 Hotel Oro Verde Quito
45 La Casa de Eliza
46 La Casona
48 Hotel Inca Imperial
51 Hostal Plaza Internacional
52 Hostal Los Alpes
54 Hotel Tambo Real
56 El Ciprés
59 Hostal Farget
62 Hostal Margarita
63 Residencial Marsella
67 Hostal Palm Garten
71 Albergue El Taxo
72 Hostal La Herradura
75 El Cafecito
78 Hotel Sebastian
79 Hotel Alston
81 Hotel Pickett
86 Youth Hostal
87 Magic Bean
89 Hotel Chalet Suisse
92 El Centro del Mundo
93 Loro Verde
95 Posada del Maple
100 Hotel Alameda Real
108 Residencial Cumbres
109 Hotel Embassy
110 Hostal Bavaria
112 Residencial Italia
113 Hostal Tatu
119 Hotel Colón
121 Hotel Camila's
122 Hotel Seis de Diciembre

PLACES TO EAT
4 Rincón La Ronda,
 El Refugio Andino
6 Chifa Pekin
7 Windmill Vegetarian Restaurant
15 Columbus Steak House
17 La Vieja Castilla
19 La Casa de Mi Abuela
20 La Bodega de Cuba
25 El Pub
35 La Choza
36 Taller del Sol
39 Churrascaría Tropeiro
41 Mare Nostrum
42 Chifa Hong Kong
44 La Scala
68 Cevichería Viejo José
69 Terraza del Tartaro,
 Las Redes
73 Taberna Quiteña

76 La Jaiba
79 Super Papa
82 Taco Factory
84 El Marqués
85 Art Forum Cafe
90 Vitalcentro
91 Mama Clorindas
96 El Maple
98 Rincón del Francia
99 Chantilly Café & Speedy
101 Pavement Cafés
102 Ch'Farina
104 La Casa de Piedra
105 La Reina Victoria
106 El Holandés
107 Chifa Mayflower
111 Costa Vasca
117 Bentley's
118 Café Cultura
120 Tex-Mex

OTHER
1 Immigration (Migraciones)
2 CETUR Tourist Information
3 Café Libro
5 Canadian Consulate
8 EMETEL
9 Cine Colón
16 MM Arteaga Money Exchange,
 SAN-Saeta Airline
18 British Council
21 Centro Comercial Multicentro
24 UK Embassy
28 Ñucanchi Peña
29 Cine Universitario
30 Parcel Post Office
33 Cine Fénix
47 Olga Fisch's Folklore Shop
47 South American Explorers Club
49 Teatro Promoteo
50 Casa de la Cultura Ecuatoriana
53 US Embassy
55 Museo de Jacinto Jijón y
 Caamaño, Universidad
 Católica
57 Church of El Belén
58 Palacio Legislativo
60 Banco Central
61 Simón Bolívar Monument
64 Cine Capitol
65 Instituto Geográfico Militar
66 Children's Playground
70 Galasam Economic Tours
74 TAME Airline
77 Branch Post Office
80 Sierra Nevada,
 Pamir Adventure
80 Libri Mundi Bookshop,
 Galería Latina
83 Flying Dutchman
88 Safari Tours
94 Children's Playground
97 Andisimo Hiking Gear
103 Dayumak Peña Bar
114 Metropolitan Touring
115 American Express,
 Ecuadorian Tours
116 Casa Paz Money Exchange

Quito – New Town

0   300   600 m

ECUADOR

Emergency services include police (☎ 101), fire department (☎ 102), general emergency (☎ 111) and Red Cross/ambulance (☎ 131 or 580 598).

Dangers & Annoyances The 2850-metre elevation will make you somewhat breathless if you arrive from sea level. This symptom of altitude sickness usually disappears after a day or two. Take things easy on arrival: don't overexert yourself, eat lightly and cut back on cigarettes and alcohol.

Unfortunately, crime has increased recently, especially in the old town. Pickpockets work crowded public buses, markets and church plazas, often working in groups to distract your attention; see the Facts for the Visitor chapter for more details. If you are robbed, obtain a police report within 48 hours from the station at Mideros and Cuenca (old town) from 9 am to noon.

There have been reports of many thefts at Plaza San Francisco. Definitely avoid the climb up El Panecillo hill. There are many reports of armed muggers on this climb. Take a tour or hire a taxi for the return trip to the top and stay in the paved area around the statue of the Virgin. Generally, the new town is safer than the old town, but you should still stay alert, especially at night.

Watch your luggage closely when travelling: snatch thefts of poorly attended luggage occur at the bus terminal and airport.

Despite the above warnings, we don't think Quito is particularly dangerous. If you avoid attracting undue attention to yourself, it's unlikely that you'll have many problems.

Things to See

Opening hours and fees of museums, churches etc change often. Many museums are closed on Monday. The Casa de Cultura has the best museums. Seeing the old colonial centre is worthwhile, although narrow streets, bustling crowds and constant traffic jams make walking around the old city a noisy, grimy and uncomfortable experience. There's much less traffic and fewer people on Sunday.

Walking Tour The area bounded by Flores, Rocafuerte, Cuenca and Manabí has most of the colonial areas, including the **Plaza de la Independencia**, with the **Palacio Presidencial** and **Catedral**. If you are short on time, see at least this plaza and continue south-west on García Moreno for two blocks to the church of **La Compañía**. From here, it's one block to the north-west (right) along Sucre to the **Plaza y Monasterio de San Francisco** – a wonderful area, but watch for thieves. Two blocks to the south-east (left) of La Compañía brings you to Guayaquil; turn south-west (right) for a block to see the **Plaza y Iglesia de Santo Domingo**.

From the old town, head north-east along Guayaquil towards the new town. Turn left on 10 de Agosto and pass the Banco Central on your left. Opposite the bank is an impressive **monument** to Simón Bolívar; it's the southernmost point of the triangular **Parque La Alameda**. Head north through the park, pass the astronomical observatory and continue north around the lake onto the important thoroughfare of 6 de Diciembre.

After three blocks you pass the modern **Palacio Legislativo** building on your right, on Montalvo. If you continue on 6 de Diciembre you pass the popular **Parque El Ejido** on your left and the huge, circular, mirror-walled **Casa de la Cultura Ecuatoriana** building (with museums) on your right. Past the Casa de la Cultura, go left for three blocks along Patria, with Parque El Ejido to your left, and you reach a small **stone arch**. Opposite this is the beginning of Quito's most famous modern street, **Avenida Amazonas**.

It is about three km from the old town centre to the beginning of Amazonas, which has banks, boutiques, souvenir stands and pavement cafés, and is a great meeting place. The parallel street of JL Mera has fine bookshops and craft shops.

Museums – new town The **Museo del Banco Central** (☎ 223 259) is in the Casa de la Cultura and is the city's best archaeological museum, housing ceramics, gold ornaments, skulls showing deformities and early surgical methods (trepanning), a mummy, and much else of interest. There is also a display of colonial furniture and religious art and carving. Hours are Tuesday to Friday from 9 am to 5 pm, and weekends 10 am to 3 pm. Entry is US$2, or US$1.25 for students.

The **Casa de la Cultura Ecuatoriana** (☎ 565 808, 522 410) houses several other collections. There is a 19th-century and contemporary art collection, a fascinating display of traditional musical instruments, and examples of traditional Ecuadorian regional dress. Hours are Tuesday to Friday from 10 am to 6 pm, and weekends 10 am to 2 pm. Entry is US$2, or US$1 for students.

The **Museo de Jacinto Jijón y Caamaño** (☎ 521 834, 529 240), an interesting private archaeology museum, is on the 3rd floor of the library in the Catholic University, on 12 de Octubre. Hours are Monday to Friday from 9 am to 4 pm; entry is US$0.40.

The **Museo Guayasamín** (☎ 242 779, 244 373), José Bosmediano 543, is the home of Oswaldo Guayasamín, the renowned Ecuadorian Indian painter. It's an uphill walk or you can take a bus along 6 de Diciembre to Eloy Alfaro, then a Bellavista bus up the hill. Hours are Monday to Friday from 9.30 am to 1 pm and 3 to 6 pm, and Saturday morning; entry is US$1.

The **Museo Amazónico** (☎ 562 633), 12 de Octubre 1436, has a small collection of jungle Indian artefacts collected by the Salesians and sells Indian cultural publications (in Spanish). Hours are Monday to Friday from 11.30 am to 12.30 pm and 1 to 5 pm, and Saturday from 11.30 am to 12.30 pm. Entry is US$0.50.

The **Instituto Geográfico Militar** (☎ 522 066) at the end of the steep Calle Paz y Miño, south-east of the Parque El Ejido, has a geographical museum and planetarium and sells topographical maps. Museum hours are Tuesday to Friday from 8 am to noon and 2 to 4 pm. There are several half-hour shows daily in the planetarium; admission is US$0.35. You must leave your passport at the gate.

The **Museo de Ciencias Naturales** (☎ 449 824) houses a natural history collection. It is at Parque La Carolina, on the Los Shyris side, opposite República de El Salvador. Hours are Monday to Friday from 8.30 am to 1 pm and 1.30 pm to 4.30 pm, and Saturday from 9 am to 1 pm. Entry is US$1, or US$0.80 for students.

The **Vivarium** (☎ 452 280, 230 988), Reina Victoria 1576 and Santa María, has live animals such as the highly poisonous fer-de-lance snake, boa constrictors, turtles and tortoises, lizards and iguanas. Hours are Tuesday to Sunday from 9 am to 1 pm and 2.30 to 6 pm. Entry is US$2.

Museums – old town The **Museo de Arte y Historia** (☎ 214 018, 210 863), Espejo 1147, contains a wealth of 16th and 17th-century colonial art. Hours are Tuesday to Friday from 9 am to 4.45 pm, and Saturday from 9 am to 1 pm; entry is free. At the time of writing the museum was closed.

The **Casa de Sucre** (☎ 512 860), Venezuela 573, is where the hero of the revolution lived. The restored house contains period (1820s) furniture and a small museum. Hours are Tuesday to Friday from 8 am to noon and 1.30 to 4 pm, and Monday and Saturday from 8 am to 1 pm. Entry is US$1.25.

Dating from 1534, the **Casa de Benalcázar** (☎ 218 102), Olmedo 968, was restored in 1967. There are sometimes classical piano recitals here; entry is free during business hours.

The **Museo de Arte Colonial** (☎ 212 297), on Cuenca near Mejía, houses what many consider to be Quito's best collection of colonial art. Hours are Tuesday to Friday from 10 am to 6 pm, and weekends from 10 am to 2 pm. Entry is US$2, or US$1 for students.

The **Museo Camilo Egas** (☎ 514 511), Venezuela 1302, contains works by Ecuadorian painter Camilo Egas and others. Hours are Monday to Friday from 9 am to 1 pm and 3 to 5 pm. Entry is US$0.35.

Churches The most interesting colonial churches are in the old town. Photography is

Quito – Old Town

San Juan

See Quito
New Town Map

El Tejar

Santa Prisca

Quito –
Old Town

0   250   500 m

Gonzalez
Suarez

Barahona

To Monastery
of San Diego

El Panecillo

Manosalvas

La Tola

ECUADOR

not usually permitted because camera flashes damage the pigment in the many valuable religious paintings.

The **Monasterio de San Francisco** is on the plaza of the same name. Construction began a few days after the founding of Quito in 1534, but it was not finished until 70 years later. It is the largest and oldest colonial structure in Quito. Much of the church has been rebuilt because of earthquake damage, but some of it is original. The chapel of Señor Jesús de Gran Poder, to the right of the main altar, has original tilework. The main altar itself is a spectacular example of Baroque carving, and the roof and walls are also wonderfully carved and richly covered in gold leaf. Much of the roof shows Moorish influence. It is open daily from 7 to 11 am and Monday to Thursday from 3 to 6 pm. To the right of the main entrance is the **Museo Franciscano** (☎ 211 124) with some of the monastery's finest paintings, sculptures and furniture dating from the 16th century. Hours are Monday to Saturday from 9 to 11 am and 3 to 6 pm, and entry is US$0.50.

It is claimed that seven tonnes of gold were used to decorate **La Compañía**, Ecuador's most ornate church. Moorish influence can be seen in the intricate designs carved on the red and gold columns and ceilings. There is a beautiful cupola over the main altar. The remains of the quiteña saint Mariana de Jesús, who died in 1645, lie here. The church is on García Moreno near Sucre, and is open daily from 9.30 to 11 am and 4 to 6 pm.

The **Catedral**, the oldest colonial church in South America (1562), though much remodelled, is a stark structure overlooking the Plaza de la Independencia. Plaques on the outside walls commemorate Quito's founders. General Sucre, the leading figure of Quito's independence struggle, is buried inside. To the left of the main altar is a statue of Juan José Flores, Ecuador's first president. Behind the main altar, a plaque marks the spot where President Gabriel García Moreno died on 6 August 1875; he was shot outside the presidential palace and was carried, dying, to the cathedral. Hours are Monday to Saturday from 8 to 10 am and 2

to 4 pm; entry is free. Next door, the church of **El Sagrario** is being renovated, and it is interesting to see how the restoration work is carried out.

Two blocks from the Plaza de la Independencia is the monastery of San **Agustín**, the site of the signing of Ecuador's declaration of independence on 10 August 1809. The church is another fine example of 17th-century architecture. A museum (☎ 515 525, 580 263), with independence mementos and colonial art, is in the convent to the right of the church. Hours are 9 am to 1 pm and 3 to 6 pm.

In the evening when the domes of the church of **Santo Domingo** are floodlit, the church is especially attractive. It, too, dates back to early Quito. In the busy Plaza Santo Domingo, in front of the church, is a statue of General Sucre. He is pointing in the direction of Pichincha, where he won the decisive battle for independence in 1822.

Begun in 1700 and completed in 1742, **La Merced**, on Cuenca near Chile, is one of colonial Quito's most recent churches. Its tower is the highest (47 metres) in the old town and contains the largest bell of Quito's churches. The church has a wealth of fascinating art. Paintings depict volcanoes glowing and erupting over the church roofs of Quito, the capital covered with ashes, General Sucre going into battle, and many other scenes. The stained-glass windows also show scenes of colonial life, such as priests and conquistadors among the Indians of the Oriente. Hours are Monday to Saturday from 3 to 8 pm.

The 17th-century monastery, museum and cemetery of **San Diego** are east of the Panecillo, between Calicuchima and Farfán. The monastery's colonial art includes a pulpit by the noted Indian woodcarver Juan Bautista Menacho; it is one of the country's finest pulpits. The cemetery, with its numerous tombs, mausoleums and other memorials, is also worth a visit. Hours are 9 am to 1 pm and 3 to 6 pm.

High on a hill, on Venezuela, is the unfinished church of **La Basílica**. Construction commenced in 1926, so the tradition of

ECUADOR

taking decades to construct a church is obviously still alive. At the north end of Parque La Alameda is the small church of **El Belén**, built where the first Catholic mass was held in Quito.

The **Santuario of Guápulo**, in a precipitous valley on the east side of town, was built between 1644 and 1688. Good views of this delightful colonial church can be seen from behind the Hotel Quito, at the end of 12 de Octubre. A steep footpath leads down to Guápulo. It's a pleasant walk, though strenuous coming back. The No 21 Santo Domingo-Guápulo bus goes there. Hours are Monday to Saturday from 8 to 11 am and 3 to 6 pm.

Other Sights The historic alley of **La Ronda** (also called Juan de Dios Morales) is just off 24 de Mayo, between García Moreno and Venezuela, and on to Maldonado. This street is perhaps the best preserved in colonial Quito and is full of old, balconied houses. Just walk along the street (in daylight) and you'll see some open to visitors; they usually sell handicrafts.

The **Palacio Presidencial** is the low, white building on the north-western side of the Plaza de la Independencia. The entrance is flanked by a pair of handsomely uniformed presidential guards. Sightseeing is limited to the entrance area.

Language Courses

Quito is one of the better places in South America for learning Spanish. All levels are available, private or group, live-in with family or not – talk to several schools to see what is best for you. Most schools charge about US$4 to US$5 per hour, though cheaper and rather more expensive places exist. The SAEC and other travellers are good sources for current recommendations.

Places to Stay

The cheapest hotels are in the old town. However, a big increase in theft in the old town and an increase of cheap hotels in the new town have resulted in more budget travellers staying in the new town than before.

Old Town Many cheap hotels are at the south end, on the streets heading towards the bus terminal. You'll find a score or more cheap hotels within a few blocks of one another. Many budget travellers stay in this area, but watch your belongings on the streets and ensure your room is always locked. Some travellers (particularly single women) do not feel comfortable staying in this area.

The *Hotel Grand* (☎ 210 192, 519 411), Rocafuerte 1001, is popular with international budget travellers and has been recommended. Basic but clean rooms are US$4.50/8 for singles/doubles or US$6/10 with private bath. The hotel is family-run and friendly, with hot water and a laundry service, and a restaurant. A block away, *La Posada Colonial* (☎ 212 859), at Paredes 188, is also a popular choice, with similar facilities at US$3.50 per person or US$4.50 with private bath. Another popular and recommended place for travellers is the *Hotel Belmont* (☎ 516 235), on Antepara, between the old and new towns. This clean, safe, family-run hotel charges US$4 per person.

The legendary *Hotel Gran Casino* (☎ 516 368), García Moreno 330, used to be a classic backpackers' dive in a poor area of town. It's still there but is poor value, even at the US$2.40 price. Opposite is the newer and much nicer *Gran Casino Colonial* (☎ 211 914) with a pleasant colonial courtyard, restaurant, and doubles with bath at US$6. Two blocks away is the *Gran Casino Internacional* (☎ 211 214), at 24 de Mayo and Bahía de Caráquez. It has decent rooms with private hot bath for about US$3.50 per person (mostly doubles and triples). It has a travel agency for the cheapest Galápagos tours.

On the Plaza Santo Domingo is the *Hotel Santo Domingo* (☎ 512 810, 211 958), Rocafuerte 1345, charging US$3 per person or US$3.50 with private hot bath. It's noisy but OK. Next door, the similarly priced *San Fernando* is grimy. The pleasant, friendly but noisy *Hotel Juana del Arco* (☎ 214 175, 511 417), Rocafuerte 1311, has hot water and charges US$4 each or US$6/10 with bath. Some rooms have plaza views. Just off the plaza, *Hotel Félix* (☎ 514 645), Guayaquil 431, has pretty flowers on the balconies. There is only one hot shower for about 30 basic rooms but the place is clean and secure; ring the bell to get in. It's a good deal for US$2 per person. The nearby *Hotel Venecia* (☎ 211 403), Rocafuerte 1514, is basic but clean; the electric showers deliver lukewarm water. Rates are US$3/4.50 with shared bath or US$6 for a double with bath.

There are several cheap and basic hotels on La Ronda. The best is *Residencial Los Shyris* (☎ 515 536), La Ronda 691, at US$3 each or US$9 for a double with bath. There are cheaper but worse places on this street, which can be unsafe after dark.

There are many hotels on Maldonado in the vicinity of the terminal terrestre. Some are shown on the map. These are convenient to the terminal, but the street attracts pickpockets. The following are OK and have hot water. The basic but secure and reasonably clean *Hotel Ingatur* (☎ 216 461) is only US$2.25/3.50 for singles/doubles or US$3.50/5 with bath. The similar *Hotel Guayaquil* (☎ 211 520) has varied rooms, some quite big, for US$4 for a double or US$5/6 for singles/doubles with bath. Also basic but decent is the *Hotel Capitalino* (☎ 513 433) at US$2.50/4. The *Hotel Indo-americano* (☎ 515 094) is the best of a cluster of very basic dives by the terminal. It charges US$4/7.50 or US$6/10 with bath. The *Hotel Colonial* (☎ 510 338), down an alley from Maldonado 3035, is quiet and has hot water in the morning. Basic but clean rooms are US$5/8. The *Hotel Interamericano* (☎ 214 320) charges US$5 to US$9 for a single and US$9 to US$15 for a double, depending on whether or not you have a bathroom, telephone, or TV in your room.

Going from Plaza Santo Domingo along Calle Flores, there's the friendly *Huasi Continental* (☎ 517 327), Flores 332, with spartan but clean rooms for US$4/6.50 or US$6/10 with private hot bath. The nearby *Hotel Montúfar* (☎ 211 419), Sucre 160, is recommended for those on a tight budget. It's basic but quiet and clean, has warm water and is only US$2 per person or US$5 for a

double with bath. Farther along Flores is the better *Hotel San Agustín* (☎ 216 051, 212 847), at No 626, costs US$6/8 or US$8/12 with private bath, and the *Hotel Los Canarios* (☎ 519 103), at No 856, which is US$5/8 with bath.

The *Hotel Hogar* (☎ 218 183), Montúfar 208, is US$9 for a clean double with bath and hot water in the mornings. The clean *Hostal Rumiñahui* (☎ 211 407), Montúfar 449, is US$8 for a double with bath. Nearby the friendly *Hotel Italia* (☎ 518 643), Junín 765, has clean but basic rooms for US$3.50 per person.

Other budget hotels in the old town include the *Hotel Sucre* (☎ 514 025), on Calle Cuenca at the corner of Plaza San Francisco. The hotel is attractive from the outside but has only basic rooms, though some have excellent views worth the US$2 per person rate. Showers are cold. Also on this plaza is the *Hotel Benalcázar* (☎ 518 302), Benalcázar 388, which is OK at US$3 per person or US$3.50 with private bath.

The *Hotel Plaza del Teatro* (☎ 216 195, 514 293, 519 462), Guayaquil 1317, in a nice old house by the theatre plaza, charges about US$10/14 in good rooms with private bath. Nearby, the pleasant old *Hostal La Casona* (☎ 514 764), Manabí 255, has clean rooms for US$11/16, including breakfast.

Casa Patty (☎ 510 407), Iquique 233 and Manosalvas (in La Tola, six blocks east from Plaza Marin on Chile to Iquique, then three blocks south – a steep walk), is run by the same family that has Pensión Patty in Baños. The large house has double rooms for US$5. Kitchen facilities are available and the management is friendly. Call ahead to see if there's room.

The *Hotel Viena Internacional* (☎ 213 605, 211 329), Flores 600, is popular with travellers wanting comfort in the old town. Large, carpeted rooms, some with balconies and all with telephones, bathrooms and hot water, are US$10 per person. There's a book exchange and restaurant.

New Town A popular (and often full) budget hotel at the edge of the new town is the

Residencial Marsella (☎ 515 884), Los Ríos 2035. The hotel is clean, with hot water and a roof with a view, is family-run and is well recommended. Rates are about US$3 to US$6 per person; rooms vary quite widely in quality, from comfortable doubles with bath to a few airless singles with shared bath. If this is full, try the newer *Hostal Margarita* (☎ 512 599, 510 441), around the corner at Elizalde 410 and Los Ríos, with clean rooms at US$3 each, or more with bath.

The small, family-run *Residencial Italia* (☎ 224 332), 9 de Octubre 237, has plenty of kids running around. Basic rooms are US$4 per person or US$5 with bath; this place is often full.

Several small, family-run hostales cater to backpackers, budget travellers and students, and have been well received. Hot showers, kitchen and laundry facilities, luggage storage, a living room, a notice board and information are available in a friendly and relaxed environment. They normally have a few double and triple rooms and a larger dormitory-style room. Single rooms are less common. Showers are usually shared. It is best to phone ahead for availability and price. The following are all in the small hostal category.

Casapaxi (☎ 542 663, 551 401), Pasaje Navarro 364, near Avenida La Gasca, is about one km north and uphill from Avenida América; the No 19 bus passes by. It is friendly, clean and helpful and costs about US$5 for one night, with long-stay discounts given (as is true for most hostales). *Hostal Tatu* (☎ 544 414), 9 de Octubre 275, is recommended and charges US$4.50 per person in dorms or US$12 for a double. *La Casona* (☎ 230 129, 544 036), Andalucía 213, is US$6.50 per person, and is in a lovely house. *La Casa de Eliza* (☎ 226 602), Isabel La Católica 1559, is US$6.50 per person. Eliza and Piet (the owners) arrange excellent treks through northern Ecuador in association with the Cerro Golondrinas Cloudforest Conservation Project. If La Casa Eliza is full, Eliza can send you to her sister's house a few blocks away.

El Centro del Mundo (☎ 229 050), Lizardo García 569, is a newly opened backpackers hostal with dorm rooms at US$4 and US$5 per person and doubles/triples at US$12/15. There's plenty of hot water in the showers, laundry and kitchen facilities, TV room, sundeck, friendly owners and many young international budget travellers hanging out. Other good ones at US$6 or US$7 per person are *Johnnie's Lodging House*, Caamaño 145; *El Cafecito* (☎ 234 862), Cordero 1124, over the restaurant of the same name; *El Ciprés* (☎ & fax 225 412), Lérida 381 and Toledo, a block south-west of Madrid and Toledo; and the *Albergue Los Andes* (☎ 521 944, fax 508 639), at Santa Rosa 163 and Avenida Universitaria, which has dorm beds at US$5 and doubles for US$14. *Hostal La Herradura* (☎ 226 340), Pinto 570, has individual rooms at US$6/10 or US$12 with bath.

The *Magic Bean* (☎ 566 181), Foch 681, above the popular restaurant of that name, is a great meeting place. It's US$7 in dorm rooms, US$20 for a double or US$24 for a double with bath. *Hostal Eva Luna* (☎ 220 426), Roca Pasaje 405 and Amazonas, is down a little alley off Roca and Amazonas. It is a hostal for women, opened by Safari Tours in late 1995. Rates are US$8 each. *Albergue El Taxo* (☎ 225 593), Foch 909, charges US$9 per person. It is run by artists who are a good source of local information. The Hostelling International *Youth Hostal* (☎ 543 995, fax 226 271), Pinto 325, is spotless and has rooms with three or four beds at US$9.50 per bed (private bath) or US$8.50 (shared bath). Youth hostel members pay about US$8/7.

The clean *Hotel Viena* (☎ 235 418), Tamayo 879, has good hot private showers. It's good value for US$7/11. The similarly priced *Hotel Koronado* (☎ 565 643), Cordero 779, is another reasonable choice. The clean and friendly *Hostal Coqui* (☎ 223 148, ☎ & fax 565 972), Versalles 1075, is good at US$10/13 for rooms with bath or US$6/10 without. There is a cafeteria. The *Hotel Versalles* (☎ 547 321), Versalles 1442, is OK for US$10/15 with bath. The nearby *Residencial Santa Clara* (☎ 541 472),

Darquea Teran 1578, is clean and OK for US$8/16 with bath. The *Loro Verde* (☎ 226 173), Rodríguez 241, has a great central location and spacious rooms with bath for US$12/18. Nearby, the *Posada del Maple* (☎ 544 507), Rodríguez 148, is a pleasant and friendly little hotel charging US$15/20 with bath, a little less with shared bath, and US$8 per bed in a dorm. The new and clean *Hostal Farget* (☎ 570 066), Farget 109 and Santa Prisca, has nice rooms for US$14/18.

Homestays The SAEC (see Useful Organisations under Quito) has a list of a dozen families that offer homestays for US$5 to US$12 per person. Some include meals.

Places to Eat

If economising, stick to the standard almuerzos or meriendas.

Old Town Many simple, inexpensive restaurants serve Ecuadorian food in the old town, but most are unremarkable. Some recommended ones include the cheap restaurants on the 1400 block of Rocafuerte, near the Plaza Santa Domingo. One is the *Restaurant Los Olivos* (☎ 514 150), at Rocafuerte 1421; there are equally good places within a block. Others are the *Restaurant Oasis*, Espejo 812, the *Pizza Hut* (☎ 583 764) opposite, with pizzas under US$4, and the more expensive *El Criollo* (☎ 219 828), at Flores 825. The *Chifa El Chino*, on Bolívar near Guayaquil, is a decent Chinese place. For desserts, snacks and coffee, a good choice is *Café Plazuela Teatro Pastelería* on the Plaza del Teatro Sucre – a lovely place for rest and refreshment during a busy sightseeing visit to the old town.

New Town There is an international range of eateries here, as behoves a capital city. Even the most expensive fancy restaurants are reasonable by gringo standards. Budget travellers tend to stick with either the simple Ecuadorian places, or the European/US-style restaurants that cater to travellers. These are a little pricier, but it's worth it to meet other travellers.

Cevichería Don José (☎ 540 187), Veintimilla 1254, has friendly service and good, cheap seafood. *El Marqués*, Calamá 443, has good vegetarian food, including US$2 set lunches that are popular with Ecuadorians. *Vitalcentro*, Lizardo García 630, is another decent vegetarian place. *Mamá Clorindas* (☎ 544 362), Reina Victoria 1144, is a good place to try local food, particularly at lunch time; meals are under US$2. For fast food, the block of Carrión east of Amazonas has been nicknamed 'Hamburger Alley' with a dozen places serving burgers and their usual accompaniments. It's popular with students. Other inexpensive places can be found by wandering around and seeing where the local office workers eat.

Avenida Amazonas is a good place to watch the world go by. The *pavement cafés* on Amazonas near Roca are a popular meeting-place and are not exorbitant. They serve a decent cup of coffee and don't hassle you if you sit there for hours.

El Holandés (☎ 522 167), Reina Victoria 600 and Carrión, serves excellent international vegetarian meals for under US$3. (It's also the contact for mountain bike tours.) Other good vegetarian places are *El Maple* (☎ 520 994), Páez 485, where you can eat the salad, and the *Windmill* (☎ 222 575), Colón 2245. In the US$3 to US$5 range, the *Taco Factory* (☎ 543 956), at Foch and JL Mera, has good Mexican food; *Ch'Farina* (☎ 434 481), Carrión 619, serves Italian; *La Bodega de Cuba* (☎ 542 476), Reina Victoria 1721, is great for Cuban food and ambience.

Travellers congregate in the following places. The *Magic Bean* (☎ 566 181), Foch 681, is great for slightly pricey breakfasts and good coffee (that's the magic bean!); it goes all day with appetising snacks and meals, and occasional live music nights. It has both indoor and outdoor dining and sporadic surprises: for instance, bottled Guinness at not much above the price in a London pub. The *Cafe Cultura*, Robles 513, has great breakfasts and English afternoon teas – again, good but not cheap by Ecuadorian standards. *El Cafecito*, Luis Cordero 1124, has a warming fireplace and a variety of light meals. *Super Papa*, JL Mera 741, serves yummy baked potatoes with about a dozen different fillings. Its notice board is full of useful information. There are dozens of other places, but this will get you started.

Entertainment

Entertainment reaches its height during the fiestas, such as the founding of Quito (first week of December), when there are bull-fights at the Plaza de Toros. There is also street dancing on the night of 5 December. On New Year's Eve, life-sized puppets (often of politicians) are burnt in the streets at midnight. Carnaval is celebrated with intense water fights – no-one is spared. Colourful religious processions are held during Easter week.

There are some 20 cinemas; a few show good English-language films with Spanish subtitles. These include the *Cine Colón*, at the intersection of Avenida Colón and 10 de Agosto, and the *Cine Universitario*, at the Indoamerican Plaza, on Avenida América across from Pérez Guerrero. Entry is less than US$2. English and French movies are shown at the *British Council* (☎ 540 225, 508 282), Amazonas 1646, and *Alliance Française*, Eloy Alfaro 1900.

Dances, concerts and plays in Spanish are presented at various venues. The *Teatro Sucre*, on Guayaquil in the old town, is the most elegant but it is being renovated. *Jacchigua*, an Ecuadorian folk ballet, used to be presented here but it has moved to *Teatro San Gabriel* (☎ 506 650, 464 780), on América at Mariana de Jesús, with shows on Friday, and Monday or Wednesday, at 7 pm. Entry is US$8 to US$16. The National Symphony plays at *Teatro Politécnico* in the Escuela Politécnica on Andalucía (two blocks east of the Universidad Católica). Concerts are mainly on Friday night (except mid-August to mid-September) and costs range from free to US$4. The *Casa de la Cultura* and, behind it, the *Teatro Prometeo*, on 6 de Diciembre, both have a variety of performances. There are several other venues. *El Comercio* newspaper has the best entertainment listings.

There are several bars and 'pubs', which are not cheap by Ecuadorian standards, but they're popular with travellers and expats. Popular bars, usually with loud music and dancing, include the *Arribar*, JL Mera 1238 and García, *No Bar* (☎ 546 955), Calamá 442 and Amazonas, *Blues Bar*, La Granja 112 and Amazonas, *Reggae Bar* (☎ 540 906), Amazonas 1691 and Orellana (popular late at night), and *Seseribó* in the Edificio El Girón at Veintimilla and 12 de Octubre – a great place to salsa. *Hopp y Ex* (☎ 522 779), Reina Victoria 854 and Baquedano, is gay-friendly. *Café Libro* (☎ 526 827), Diego de Almagro 1500 and Pradera, has jazz, poetry readings, drama and peñas. *Ñucanchi Peña* (☎ 540 967), Universitaria 496 and Armero, has good peñas with a US$4 cover. Quieter places include *La Reina Victoria* (☎ 233 369), Reina Victoria 530, run by a friendly US-British couple, with a fireplace, dart board, bumper pool and excellent pub ambience. See also Places to Eat.

Getting There & Away

Air The airport (☎ 430 555), 10 km north of the centre, has a domestic and international terminal. Services include tourist information, money exchange, post office, cafeteria/bar, EMETEL international telephone office and gift shops.

Flight schedules and prices change frequently. TAME and SAN-Saeta have flights to Guayaquil (US$31) from eight to 14 times a day, most frequently on weekdays. Flights to Cuenca (US$31) leave one to three times a day. Other cities served (several times a week and sometimes daily) are: Tulcán, Esmeraldas, Portoviejo, Manta, Bahía de Caráquez, Macas, Coca, Lago Agrio, Loja, Machala and the Galápagos. See the earlier Getting Around section for more detail.

In the old town, TAME is at Manabí 635 (☎ 512 988); in the new town, TAME has an office at Avenida Colón 1001 (☎ 554 905). SAN-Saeta shares an office at Guayaquil 1228 in the old town (☎ 211 431) and Santa María and Amazonas (☎ 502 706, 564 969) in the new town. There are other offices and most travel agents sell plane tickets for the same price as do the airlines.

Bus The Terminal Terrestre de Cumandá (☎ 570 529 for information) is in the old town on Maldonado, a few hundred metres south of the Plaza Santo Domingo. The terminal is reached along Maldonado on foot or by bus, or from the back by taxi.

Dozens of bus companies serve most destinations and there is an information booth. Book in advance to travel during holiday periods and on Friday evening. Watch your luggage carefully in the terminal.

Several buses a day go to most destinations, and there are several departures an hour to some places, such as Ambato or Otavalo. Approximate costs and journey times are shown in the following table. More expensive luxury services are available on long trips.

To	Cost (US$)	Hours
Ambato	2.00	2½
Bahía de Caráquez	5.50	8
Baños	2.50	3½
Coca	10.00	13
Cuenca	6.00	8
Guaranda	3.00	5
Guayaquil	6.00	8
Ibarra	2.00	3
Lago Agrio	8.50	10
Latacunga	1.20	1½
Loja	10.00	14
Machala	7.25	11
Manta	5.50	8
Otavalo	1.60	2¼
Portoviejo	5.50	8
Puyo	4.00	8
Riobamba	3.00	4
Santo Domingo	2.20	2½
Tena	4.00	6
Tulcán	4.00	5½

Panamericana has opened a terminal in the new town at Colón and Reina Victoria with comfortable (and more expensive) long-haul buses to Guayaquil, Huaquillas, Manta, Loja, Esmeraldas and Cuenca.

Companies will sell international tickets to Peru or Colombia. These involve bus changes at the border and are expensive.

Train There is a Saturday 8 am train to Riobamba (US$10, five hours) and a train tour to Cotopaxi on Sunday (US$20 return). Tickets are sold at Bolívar 443 and Benalcázar (☎ 513 422) in the old town and, on Friday, at the train station (☎ 656 142), on Sincholagua near Maldonado, two km south of the old town.

Getting Around

To/From the Airport Many of the northbound buses on Amazonas and 10 de Agosto go to the airport. Some have 'Aeropuerto' placards and others say 'Quito Norte'. A taxi from the new town should be under US$4, or US$5 from the old town. From the airport, taxi drivers try to overcharge: bargain hard.

Bus The crowded local buses have a flat fare of US$0.10, which you pay as you board. There are also *ejecutivo* and *selectivo* buses; these don't allow standing, and charge about US$0.25. Generally speaking, buses run north-south and have a fixed route. The ejecutivo and selectivo buses particularly are found on 10 de Agosto and 6 de Diciembre. Buses have destination placards in their windows and drivers usually will tell you which bus to take if they are not going to your destination. Traffic in the old town is very heavy, and you may find it faster to walk than to take a bus, especially during the rush hours.

Trolleybus Quito's long-awaited trolleybus service began operation in mid-1996. The line runs between the Estación Trolebús Sur, on Avenida Maldonado south of Villaflora, and the Estación Trolebús Norte, on 10 de Agosto just north of Avenida de La Prensa. Trolleybuses run along Maldonado and 10 de Agosto about every 10 minutes from 6 am to 12.30 am and stop every couple of blocks. The fare is US$0.25. As a result of this new service, fewer buses now use the major thoroughfare of 10 de Agosto. The government has restricted the number of buses on

ECUADOR

city routes, and this is expected to result in an improvement in air quality, especially in the old town.

Taxi Cabs are yellow and have red 'TAXI' stickers in the window. Quito cabs have meters and drivers should use them. Sometimes a fare is arranged beforehand so the driver can take a roundabout route to avoid traffic, thus saving time. Short journeys cost US$1 to US$2; up to US$5 for a long trip. Cabs can be rented by the hour or day – about US$50 for the day.

AROUND QUITO

The most famous excursion is to the equator at **La Mitad del Mundo**, 22 km north of Quito. Here, a large monument houses a viewing platform and an excellent ethnographical museum. Hours are Tuesday to Sunday from 10 am to 4 pm; admission is US$0.80. A planetarium, a wonderful scale model of Quito's old town and other attractions cost extra. **Rumicucho** is a small pre-Inca site under excavation about 3.5 km north of Mitad del Mundo. About five km north of Mitad del Mundo, on the way to the village of Calacalí, is the ancient volcanic crater of **Pululahua**, which can be descended into on foot – an interesting walk.

From Quito, the Mitad del Mundo bus (US$0.25, one hour) leaves frequently from the short street of J López, between Hermano Miguel and Mejía, near the Ipiales street market in the old town. It's not an obvious bus stop, so ask.

Several companies offer tours for US$20 or you can take a return-trip taxi for the same price (including waiting time).

The **Reserva Forestal de Pasochoa** is operated by the Fundación Natura (☎ 447 341/2/3/4), Avenida América 5663. The reserve is 30 km south-east of Quito and has one of the last stands of undisturbed humid Andean forest left in the central Ecuadorian valley. Over 100 species of bird and many rare plants have been recorded; it is recommended to naturalists and bird-watchers. Trails range from easy to long and strenuous.

The daily fee for foreign visitors is US$7.

Overnight camping in designated areas is US$12 per person (including the daily fee); it may be full at weekends. There are latrines, picnic areas and water. Check with the Fundación Natura to obtain directions, maps, information and permits.

Quito's closest volcano is **Pichincha**, looming over the western side of the city. There are two summits, the closer Rucu Pichincha (about 4700 metres) and the higher Guagua Pichincha (4794 metres). Both can be climbed from Quito in a very long day, but the hiking routes are plagued with thieves, rapists and rabid dogs. Go in a large group and get the latest information. The SAEC is an excellent source of up-to-date information.

North of Quito

The Andean highlands north of Quito are one of the most popular destinations in Ecuador. Few travellers spend any time in the country without visiting the famous Indian market at the small town of Otavalo, where you can buy a wide variety of weavings, clothing and handicrafts.

The dramatic mountain scenery of the region is dotted with shining white churches set in tiny villages, and includes views of Cayambe, the third-highest peak in the country, as well as a beautiful lake district. Several small towns are noted for speciality handicrafts such as woodcarving or leatherwork.

Ibarra is a small, charmingly somnolent colonial city that is linked to San Lorenzo on the coast by railway. If you are travelling overland to or from Colombia, it's almost impossible to avoid this region.

OTAVALO

This town of 22,000 inhabitants, 95 km from Quito, is justly famous for its friendly people and their Saturday market. The market dates from pre-Inca times, when jungle products were brought up from the eastern lowlands and traded for highland goods.

The most evident feature of the otavaleños' culture is their traditional dress. The men wear long single pigtails, calf-length white pants, rope sandals, reversible grey or blue ponchos and dark felt hats. The women are very striking, with beautifully embroidered blouses, long black skirts and shawls, and interesting folded head cloths. They also wear bright jewellery: many strings of gold-coloured blown-glass beads around their necks, and bracelets made of long strands of red beads.

The inhabitants of Otavalo are mainly whites or mestizos. There are about 40,000 Indians, most of whom live in the many nearby villages and come into Otavalo for market day. However, quite a few Indians own craft shops in Otavalo.

Information

Zulaytour (☎ 921 176), on the eastern corner of Sucre and Colón, 2nd floor, is the longest standing and best known information and guide service. It's run by the knowledgeable Rodrigo Mora, who speaks English. A variety of guided tours enable you to visit local Indian homes, learn about the entire weaving process, buy products off the loom and take photographs. An emphasis on anthropological and sociological background information makes these tours very worthwhile. The most popular tour visits several local villages and takes all day. Transport is included and the tour costs about US$10 per person. Other companies nearby run similar tours. Horse riding can be arranged.

Money Casas de cambio (see map) give good rates and the Banco de la Previsora gives cash advances on credit cards.

Things to See & Do

The main market day is Saturday. There are three main plazas, with the overflow filling the streets linking them. **Poncho Plaza** is for crafts (a 'market' happens most days, especially Wednesday). Bargaining is expected. The Saturday market gets under way soon after dawn and continues until about noon. It gets crowded mid-morning, when the big tour groups arrive. Thieves and bag-slashers are reported in the markets. There is an **animal market** from 6 to 8 am on the outskirts of town.

The **Instituto Otavaleño de Antropología** has a museum.

The **Fiesta del Yamor** in the first two weeks of September features processions, music and dancing, as well as firework displays, cockfights and the election of the Queen of the Fiesta.

The Quito-based **Instituto Superior** has Spanish language classes at Sucre 11-10 and Morales.

Places to Stay

Otavalo is crowded on Friday, so arrive on Thursday for the best choice. Cheaper rates can be negotiated for long stays. There have been reports of theft from hotel rooms in Otavalo. Keep doors locked, even if just leaving for the bathroom.

Currently, the most popular budget choice is the clean and helpful *Hostal Valle del Amanecer* (☎ 920 990, fax 920 286), Roca and Quiroga. It charges about US$4 per person or US$6 with bath, has hot water and a café, and rents mountain bikes at US$7 a day. Also good and recommended is the very clean and friendly *Residencial El Rocío* (☎ 920 584), Morales 11-70, which charges US$3.25 per person and has a couple of rooms with private bath for US$8.50 a double. There is hot water and a nice view from the roof. The clean *Hotel Riviera-Sucre* (☎ 920 241), G Moreno 3-14, is in an old house with a courtyard, has hot water and is popular with budget travellers. Rates are about US$4 per person. The similarly priced *Residencial La Sonrisa*, Colón 6-10, has a games room and a decent, inexpensive café. Other OK places at US$4 per person with hot water in shared baths include the *Residencial Santa Fe* (☎ 920 161), Colón 5-07 and the *Residencial Inti Ñan* (☎ 921 373), Montalvo 602.

The cheapest is the very basic but friendly *Pensión Los Andes* at about US$2 per person. It has cold water and a private

ECUADOR

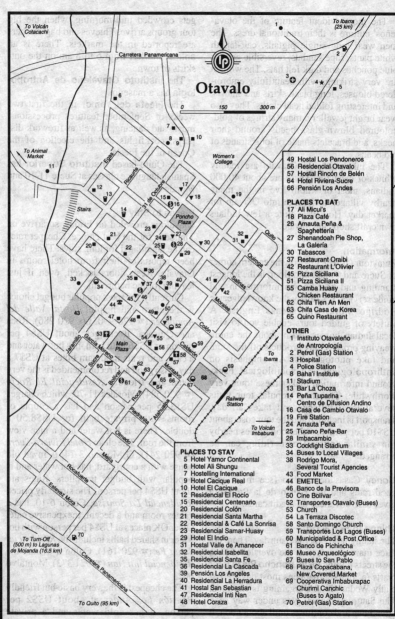

Otavalo

0   150   300 m

To Volcán Cotacachi

To Ibarra (25 km)

Carretera Panamericana

To Animal Market

Women's College

Epos

Ricaurte

31 de Octubre

Stairs

Poncho Plaza

Quito

Quiroga

Selinas

Morales

Colón

To Ibarra

Railway Station

To Volcán Imbabura

Jaramillo

García Moreno

Sucre

Main Plaza

Bolívar

Roca

Montalvo

Calderón

Piedrahita

Atahualpa

Olmedo

Mejía

Rocafuerte

Estevez Mora

To Turn-Off (500 m) to Lagunas de Mojanda (16.5 km)

Carretera Panamericana

To Quito (95 km)

49 Hostal Los Pendoneros
56 Residencial Otavalo
57 Hostal Rincón de Belén
64 Hotel Riviera-Sucre
66 Pensión Los Andes

PLACES TO EAT

17 Ali Micui's
18 Plaza Café
26 Amauta Peña & Spaghettería
27 Shenandoah Pie Shop, La Galería
30 Tabascos
37 Restaurant Oraibi
42 Restaurant L'Olivier
45 Pizza Siciliana
51 Pizza Siciliana II
55 Camba Huasy Chicken Restaurant
62 Chifa Tien An Men
63 Chifa Casa de Korea
65 Quino Restaurant

OTHER

1 Instituto Otavaleño de Antropología
2 Petrol (Gas) Station
3 Hospital
4 Police Station
8 Baha'i Institute
11 Stadium
13 Bar La Choza
14 Peña Tuparina - Centro de Difusion Andino
16 Casa de Cambio Otavalo
19 Fire Station
24 Amauta Peña
25 Tucano Peña-Bar
28 Imbacambio
33 Cockfight Stadium
34 Buses to Local Villages
38 Rodrigo Mora, Several Tourist Agencies
43 Food Market
44 EMETEL
46 Banco de la Previsora
52 Transportes Otavalo (Buses)
54 La Terraza Discotec
59 Transportes Los Lagos (Buses)
60 Municipalidad & Post Office
61 Banco de Pichincha
66 Museo Arqueológico
67 Buses to San Pablo
68 Plaza Copacabana, New Covered Market
69 Cooperativa Imbaburapac Churimi Canchic (Buses to Agato)
70 Petrol (Gas) Station

PLACES TO STAY

5 Hotel Yamor Continental
6 Hotel Ali Shungu
7 Hostelling International
9 Hotel Cacique Real
10 Hotel El Cacique
12 Residencial El Rocío
15 Residencial Centenario
20 Residencial Colón
21 Residencial Santa Martha
22 Residencial & Café La Sonrisa
23 Residencial Samar-Huasy
31 Hotel El Indio
31 Hostal Valle de Amanecer
32 Residencial Isabelita
35 Residencial Santa Fe
36 Residencial La Cascada
39 Pensión Los Angeles
40 Residencial La Herradura
41 Hostal San Sebastian
47 Residencial Inti Ñan
48 Hotel Coraza

ECUADOR

archaeology museum! For about US$3 per person the *Residencial Samar-Huasy*, Jaramillo 6-11, has clean, small rooms. Hot showers are available at times. Other OK places at US$3 include the *Residencial Otavalo* (☎ 920 739), Montalvo 4-44, the *Residencial Santa Martha* (☎ 920 568), Colón 7-04, (though I've received reports of theft here), the friendly *Residencial La Herradura*, on Bolívar near Morales, the *Residencial La Cascada*, on Colón near Sucre, and the *Residencial Isabelita*, Roca 11-07. Other cheapies include the *Pensión Los Angeles* and *Residencial Colón*.

The *Residencial Centenario* (☎ 920 467) on Quiroga is clean and looks good for US$5 per person or US$6 with private bath. The *Hostal San Sebastian* (☎ 920 208), Roca 9-05, is friendly and has large but overpriced rooms at US$6.50/9.50 for singles/doubles or US$8/12 with private bath. The *Hostal Los Pendoneros* (☎ 921-258), Calderón 5-10, is good and clean. Doubles with hot bath are US$12, singles are US$6 with shared bath. The restaurant downstairs is popular. The *Hoteles El Cacique* and *Cacique Real* (☎ 922 303, 922 438, 921 740), opposite one another on the northern end of 31 de Octubre, have nice, carpeted rooms with TV for US$15 a double. The *Hotel El Indio* (☎ 920 601), Sucre 12-14, is clean and has hot water and a local restaurant. There are only 10 rooms at US$16 a double with bath; some have a balcony.

Places to Eat

There are many restaurants aimed at the ever-present gringo visitor to Ecuador's most famous market. On the Poncho Plaza *La Galería* is a good café that has vegetarian dishes and serves decent espresso. The nearby *Shenandoah* pie shop is also popular, although quality seems to have gone downhill recently. For more up-market meals, try the *Plaza Café*, open from 8 am to 10 pm, with delicious and innovative dinners for about US$5. *Ali Micui's*, on the Poncho Plaza, serves both vegetarian and non-vegetarian food at inexpensive prices.

Off the plaza, *Tabascos* has pricey Mexican food, decent breakfasts, and a rack of magazines in English. For good breakfasts and cheap pizzas, the German-run *Café La Sonrisa* has been recommended. The *Pizza Siciliana* is said to have the best pizzas. The *Quino Restaurant* is popular and has good seafood. The *Restaurant Oraibi* has cheap vegetarian food. The *Restaurant L'Olivier* has medium-priced French food. *SISA*, next to the Hotel Coraza, is mid-priced and serves a good variety of food.

The best chifas are the *Tien An Men* and the *Casa de Korea*, on the same block. If you're after fried chicken, try the *Camba Huasy*. All these are reasonably priced. The *Hotel El Indio* does good local food, particularly fritada (not always available). For a splurge, try the excellent *Ali Shungu*, in the hotel of the same name, the best in town, on Quito near Quiroga.

Entertainment

Otavalo is quiet during the week but lively on the weekend. The popular *Amauta Peña* (☎ 920 967), Jaramillo 6-14, has spawned another one around the corner; it serves spaghetti dinners. Music gets under way after 10 pm and there is a US$1 cover charge. The music and ambience can vary but are usually pretty good. The newer *Peña Tuparina*, on Morales near 31 de Octubre, is similar and popular; the cover charge here is about US$0.50. The *Tucano Peña-Bar*, at Morales 5-10, has both folkloric and salsa music and may open midweek. The place can get rather wild. *The Hard Rock Café* on the east corner of the Poncho Plaza is a popular hang-out (we hear it's been renamed as a result of legal hassles). These places have all been around for a while, and you'll probably find newer ones.

Getting There & Away

Bus Transportes Otavalo has frequent buses to Ibarra, where you change for buses farther north. Transportes Otavalo and Transportes Los Lagos have many Quito-bound buses (under US$2), which take you into Otavalo. Many other companies go from Quito past

Otavalo heading north (and vice versa), and will drop you off on the Panamericana.

Buses from Plaza Copacabana go to the villages around Lago San Pablo. A few blocks away, at Calderón and 31 de Octubre, are decrepit old buses that go to other local villages.

Train The train service to Ibarra runs irregularly. It wasn't operating in 1995, but in 1996 there were several autoferros a day (under US$1) and passengers could ask to get off wherever they wanted, including the Aya Huma in Peguche (see the next section), near the track.

AROUND OTAVALO
Many of the Indians live and work in the nearby villages of **Peguche**, **Ilumán** and **Agato**. These are loosely strung together on the north-eastern side of the Panamericana, a few km away from Otavalo. There are many other otavaleño villages in the area, and a visit to Otavalo tour agencies will yield more information. You can walk or take local buses to these villages. The *Aya Huma* (☎ 922 663) in Peguche, three km north-east of Otavalo, has clean beds for US$5 per person (US$8 with private bath), serves good, cheap home-made meals, and often has live music in the evenings. There's a pretty waterfall two km south of Peguche. Sunday is not a good day to visit the villages: many people prefer to get blind drunk than to deal with gringos.

Lago San Pablo can be reached on foot from Otavalo by heading roughly south-east on any of the paths heading over the hill behind the railway station. When you get to the lake, you'll find that a paved road goes all the way around it, with beautiful views of both the lake and Volcán Imbabura behind it. There have been isolated reports of robberies: plan your walks to return before nightfall, and go with a friend.

COTACACHI
This small village, some 15 km north of Otavalo, is famous for its leatherwork, which is sold in stores all along the main street.

From Otavalo, there are buses every hour. There are a couple of pricey hotels.

LAGUNA CUICOCHA
About 18 km east of Cotacachi is an extinct, eroded volcano, famous for the deep lake in its crater. The lake is part of the Reserva Ecológica Cotacachi-Cayapas, established to protect a large area of western Andean forest that extends from Volcán Cotacachi (4939 metres) to the Río Cayapas in the coastal lowlands; there is no entrance fee at the time of writing.

There are half-hour boat rides around the islands on the lake (US$0.50). These are popular with locals on sunny weekends, but may not operate midweek. A walk around the lake takes about six hours. Don't eat the blue berries: they are poisonous. Trucks, taxis and occasional buses go from Cotacachi.

IBARRA
About 22 km north of Otavalo and 135 km north of Quito is the attractive colonial town of Ibarra, the provincial capital of Imbabura. One of the main reasons for coming here is to take the train from Ibarra to San Lorenzo, on the coast.

Horse-drawn carts still clatter along cobbled streets flanked by 19th-century buildings, dark-suited old gentlemen sit in the shady parks discussing the day's events, and most people are in bed by 10 pm. It's a fairly quiet town, and some travellers prefer to stay here when visiting the Otavalo area.

Information
CETUR is at Colón 7-43. Change US dollar travellers' cheques at the Banco Continental, Olmedo near Colón. Quito has better rates.

Places to Stay
Ibarra has some of the cheapest hotels in Ecuador and it's a good base for budget travellers wanting to visit Otavalo and northern Ecuador. Nightlife is poor, however.

Hotels charging just under US$2 per person include the *Residencial San Lorenzo*, Olmedo 10-56, and *Residencial Paraíso*,

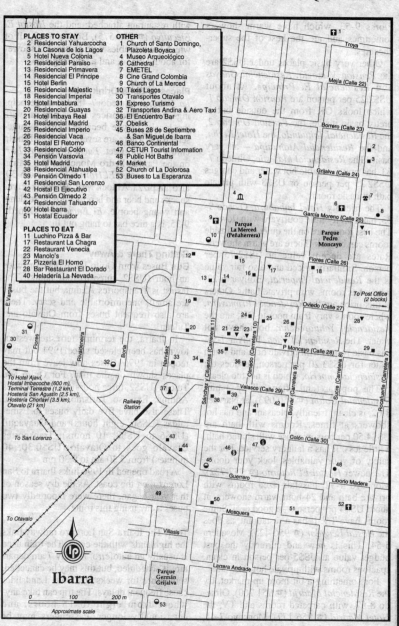

PLACES TO STAY
2 Residencial Yahuarcocha
3 La Casona de los Lagos
5 Hotel Nueva Colonia
12 Residencial Paraíso
13 Residencial Primavera
14 Residencial El Príncipe
15 Hotel Berlín
16 Residencial Majestic
18 Residencial Imperial
19 Hotel Imbabura
20 Residencial Guayas
21 Hotel Imbaya Real
24 Residencial Madrid
25 Residencial Imperio
26 Residencial Vaca
29 Hostal El Retorno
33 Residencial Colón
34 Pensión Varsovia
35 Hotel Madrid
38 Residencial Atahualpa
39 Pensión Olmedo 1
41 Residencial San Lorenzo
42 Hostal El Ejecutivo
43 Pensión Olmedo 2
44 Residencial Tahuando
50 Hotel Ibarra
51 Hostal Ecuador

PLACES TO EAT
11 Luchino Pizza & Bar
17 Restaurant La Chagra
22 Restaurant Venecia
23 Manolo's
27 Pizzería El Horno
28 Bar Restaurant El Dorado
40 Heladería La Nevada

OTHER
1 Church of Santo Domingo,
    Plazoleta Boyaca
4 Museo Arqueológico
6 Cathedral
7 EMETEL
8 Cine Grand Colombia
9 Church of La Merced
10 Taxis Lagos
30 Transportes Otavalo
31 Expreso Turismo
32 Transportes Andina & Aero Taxi
36 El Encuentro Bar
37 Obelisk
45 Buses 28 de Septiembre
    & San Miguel de Ibarra
46 Banco Continental
47 CETUR Tourist Information
48 Public Hot Baths
49 Market
52 Church of La Dolorosa
53 Buses to La Esperanza

Parque
La Merced
(Peñaherrera)

Parque
Pedro
Moncayo

To Post Office
(2 blocks)

Troya

Mejía (Calle 22)

Borrero (Calle 23)

Grijalva (Calle 24)

García Moreno (Calle 25)

Flores (Calle 26)

Oviedo (Calle 27)

P Moncayo (Calle 28)

Velasco (Calle 29)

Colón (Calle 30)

Mosquera

E Vargas

Flores

Rivadeneira

Boria

Narváez

Sánchez y Cifuentes (Carrera 11)

Olmedo (Carrera 10)

Bolívar (Carrera 9)

Sucre (Carrera 8)

Rocafuerte (Carrera 7)

Railway
Station

To Hotel Ajaví,
Hostal Imbacocha (600 m),
Terminal Terrestre (1.2 km),
Hostería San Agustín (2.5 km),
Hostería Chorlaví (3.5 km),
Otavalo (21 km)

To San Lorenzo

To Otavalo

Villalis

Larrera Andrade

Guerrero

Liborio Madera

Parque
Germán
Grijalva

Ibarra

0   100   200 m

Approximate scale

ECUADOR

Flores 9-53, which have warm showers sometimes and are the best of the super-cheapies.

Other very basic places under US$2 are the *Pensión Varsovia*, *Residencial Guayas* and *Residencial El Príncipe*. At about US$2.25 per person are *Pensión Olmedo 1*, which looks OK from the outside but is pretty basic inside, the *Pensión Olmedo 2*, the *Residencial Tahuando*, the *Hotel Berlin*, and the *Residencial Atahualpa* – all very basic. The *Residencial Majestic*, Olmedo 7-63, has pretty reliable hot water and charges US$2.25 per person or US$3 with private bath in basic rooms.

The friendly *Hotel Imbabura*, Oviedo 9-33, has a pretty little courtyard with flowers. The best rooms are on the quiet street; inside rooms can be dark. There are warm showers. Rates are decent value at US$2.75 per person. Similarly priced and also fair value is the *Residencial Imperial*, Bolívar 6-22, which has rooms with private baths. Others at this price are the *Residencial Primavera*, where rooms vary from poor to OK, and the *Residencial Yahuarcocha*; both have hot water. The *Residencial Vaca*, Bolívar 7-53, has basic rooms with private bath and warm water for US$3.20 per person, as does the *Residencial Imperio*, which is not too clean.

The popular (and often full by 3 pm) *Residencial Colón* (☎ 950 093), at Narváez 8-62, is clean, friendly, pleasant and has hot showers at times. Rooms with bath are US$4.50 per person; those with shared bath, a little less. It has a laundry service. For the safety of your valuables, lock your doors. The newer *Hostal El Retorno* (☎ 957 722), Moncayo 4-32, has fair-sized rooms with private bath and 24-hour warm showers, at about US$4 per person – a good deal. Some rooms have TV. It has a restaurant, as does the *Hostal Ecuador* (☎ 956-425), Mosquera 5-54. This is new and currently the best budget value at US$5 per person in clean, spacious rooms with private hot shower.

For something a bit more up-market, try the *Residencial Madrid* (☎ 951 760), Olmedo 8-57, with carpeted rooms and TV; the *Hotel Madrid* (☎ 956 177), Moncayo 7-41, with restaurant attached; and the *Hostal El Ejecutivo* (☎ 956 575), Bolívar 9-69, all of which have doubles with private hot shower for about US$14, and a few singles.

Places to Eat & Drink

La Chagra, Olmedo 7-48, has large help-ings, reasonable prices and is popular with the locals, maybe because it has a large-screen TV. There are several good and cheap chifas on this street. *Luchino Pizza & Bar*, on the Parque Pedro Moncayo, has Italian food and snacks; *El Horno*, Moncayo 6-30, also has pizza. A block west, *Manolo's* serves snacks and beer and is popular with students and young people. *El Encuentro*, Olmedo 9-35, is a nice bar to hang out in.

Getting There & Away

Bus Buses from Quito leave once or twice an hour (US$2, three to four hours). The fastest is Transportes Andina but the buses are small, uncomfortable and scary. There are also frequent buses from Otavalo and Tulcán.

In Ibarra, the terminal terrestre west of town has been closed since 1994 but may reopen in 1996. Buses now leave from the places shown on the map. For Quito and Tulcán (US$2, three hours) use Transportes Andina, Expreso Turismo or Aero Taxi. These also have five daily buses to Esme-raldas (US$6, eight hours) and Guayaquil (US$6 to US$8, 10 hours). Transportes Otavalo goes to Otavalo (US$0.30, 40 minutes) from 5.30 am to 9.30 pm.

A road opened in 1996 links Ibarra to San Lorenzo, on the coast. As the dry season of that year began, there were reportedly two buses a day using this route.

Train The Ibarra-San Lorenzo railway links the highlands with the coast. The train used is usually an autoferro. A daily 7 am depar-ture is scheduled, but this may be cancelled, sometimes for weeks at a time. Landslides cause frequent delays. The trip can take any-where from eight to 15 hours, and occasionally longer. Passengers may be bussed part of the way. Sometimes the train leaves every other day. Watch luggage very closely in the station. Supposedly, you have to buy tickets on the day of departure (very crowded shoving at the ticket window) but you can often buy a ticket the day before. (If you are told 'No reservations', try slipping the clerk 2000 sucres or so.) There is a dual pricing system; foreigners pay US$15 and locals pay about US$2.50 – there's not much you can do about that.

The spectacular journey from Ibarra, at 2225 metres above sea level, to San Lorenzo, at sea level and 193 km away, gives a good cross-sectional view of Ecuador. You may be able to ride on the roof; beware of overhanging branches. At several stops, food is sold, but take a water bottle and some emergency food.

The train between Ibarra and Otavalo was running several times a day in 1996, and dropped passengers off at intermediate destinations on request.

SAN ANTONIO DE IBARRA

This village, almost a suburb of Ibarra, is famous for its woodcarving. It has a pleasant main square, around which are a number of shops selling carvings.

The *Hostería Los Nogales* has rooms for US$3.

Buses leave frequently for San Antonio from Guerrero and Sánchez y Cifuentes in Ibarra, or walk five km south on the Panamericana (the western extension of Velasco).

LA ESPERANZA

This pretty little village, seven km south of Ibarra, is the place to stay if you're looking for peace and quiet. There's nothing to do except talk to the locals and take walks in the surrounding countryside.

The basic but friendly *Casa Aida* costs US$2.50 per person. It serves good, cheap meals, including vegetarian dishes. The *Restaurant María* also rents basic rooms.

Buses from Parque Germán Grijalva in Ibarra serve the village frequently, but can be very crowded at weekends.

TULCAN

This small city of 40,000 is the provincial capital of Carchi, the northernmost province of the Ecuadorian highlands and an important market town. It is popular with Colombian shoppers. For travellers, it is the gateway to Colombia, only seven km away.

Information

The CETUR office is at Pichincha and Bolívar. The Colombian consul is on Bolívar at García Moreno, though quicker service is reported in Quito if you need a visa. Exchange rates in Tulcán and at the border are usually lower than in Quito. The bus between Tulcán and the border accepts Colombian or Ecuadorian currency. Filanbanco, casas de cambio and street moneychangers on Ayacucho between Bolívar and Sucre are the best exchange choices, but few of them accept travellers' cheques. If leaving Ecuador, change sucres to US dollars, and then dollars to pesos. If arriving, cash dollars are the strongest currency.

Things to See

The big tourist attraction is the **topiary garden** in the cemetery. Behind the cemetery, the locals play *pelota de guante* at weekends. It's a strange game, played with a small, soft ball and large, spiked paddles. Thursday and Sunday **market days** are crowded with Colombian bargain hunters (few tourist goods).

West of Tulcán is the **Páramo de El Angel** dropping down into the **Cerro Golondrinas** cloud forests. A recommended trek through remote villages of this area is organised by the Casa de Eliza (see Quito, Places to Stay).

Places to Stay

Hotels are busy, mainly with Colombian visitors. The closest alternative town is San Gabriel, 40 minutes away, which has a couple of basic hotels.

All hotels claim to have hot water. The basic but reasonably clean *Residencial Quito* (☎ 980 541), at Ayacucho 450, is US$2 per person. The *Pensión Avenida*, opposite the

ECUADOR

bus terminal, has adequate but dark rooms and not-too-clean showers at US$2 per person. The *Hotel Sucre* is US$2.50 per person but bathrooms are poor and some lack hot water. The *Residencial Florida* has rooms from US$2 to US$4 per person – only the US$4 ones have hot water. Next door, the *Hotel Carchi* has clean rooms with shared bath at US$4 per person. The *Hotel Atahualpa* has basic rooms at US$3 per person.

Two decent places near the bus station, at US$4.50/7.50 for singles/doubles with private bath and TV, are the *Hotel Acacias* (some rooms have a balcony) and *Hotel Los Alpes* (with a restaurant). The *Hotel Granada* is OK for US$3.50 per person with shared bath, and the *Residencial Oasis* (☎ 980 342) is also OK at US$4 per person with private bath. The *Hotel Imperial* (☎ 981 094) has nice, light rooms with shared showers at US$4 per person and the *Hotel San Francisco* (☎ 980 760) seems OK at the same price and has private showers.

Nice places for about US$12 a double (with bath, of course) include the *Hotel Unicornio* (☎ 980 638), which has TV or balconies in some rooms, the *Hotel Quillasinga* (☎ 981 892), which has TV, a restaurant and a weekend disco, the *Hotel Alejandra* (☎ 981 784), and the *Hotel San Andrés*, which also has a few singles with shared bath for US$4.

Places to Eat

The *El Patio*, Bolívar 13-91, has large serves and good breakfasts, and is one of Tulcán's best restaurants. *Café Tulcán* has ice cream, pastries and decent breakfasts. *Max Pan* has also been recommended for breakfasts. The *Chifa Pack Choy* is the best chifa, according to most travellers. For more Ecuadorian-style food, the cheap *Restaurant Danubio* is OK but has a limited menu. The *Restaurant La Mulata* has much better but pricey Ecuadorian food. *Andersson Fried Chicken* and *El Marinero* are OK for chicken and ceviche, respectively. There is a basic café in the bus terminal, and the *Asadero Pollo Piko* chicken restaurant is across the street.

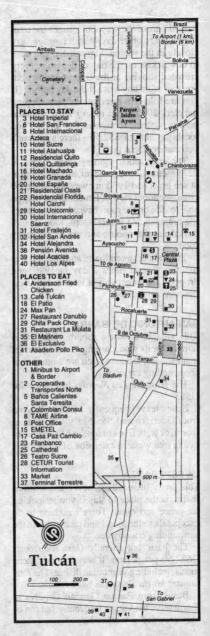

PLACES TO STAY
3 Hotel Imperial
6 Hotel San Francisco
8 Hotel Internacional Azteca
10 Hotel Sucre
11 Hotel Atahualpa
12 Residencial Quito
14 Hotel Quillasinga
16 Hotel Machado
19 Hotel Granada
20 Hotel España
21 Residencial Oasis
22 Residencial Florida, Hotel Carchi
29 Hotel Unicornio
30 Hotel Internacional Saenz
31 Hotel Fraílejón
32 Hotel San Andrés
34 Hotel Alejandra
38 Pensión Avenida
39 Hotel Acacias
40 Hotel Los Alpes

PLACES TO EAT
4 Andersson Fried Chicken
13 Café Tulcán
18 El Patio
24 Max Pan
27 Restaurant Danubio
29 Chifa Pack Choy
31 Restaurant La Mulata
35 El Marinero
36 El Exclusivo
41 Asadero Pollo Piko

OTHER
1 Minibus to Airport & Border
2 Cooperativa Transportes Norte
5 Baños Calientes Santa Teresita
7 Colombian Consul
8 TAME Airline
9 Post Office
15 EMETEL
17 Casa Paz Cambio
23 Filanbanco
25 Cathedral
26 Teatro Sucre
28 CETUR Tourist Information
33 Market
37 Terminal Terrestre

Tulcán

0   100   200 m

To San Gabriel

ECUADOR

Getting There & Around

Air TAME (☎ 980 675), Bolívar 16-47 and at the airport (☎ 982 850), has flights from Quito (US$19) Monday to Friday at noon, returning at 1 pm or, on Tuesday and Thursday, at 4.50 pm. These are usually full. There are flights to Cali, Colombia (US$87, plus US$25 international departure tax) on Tuesday and Thursday afternoons. The airport is two km north-east of the town centre en route to the border.

Bus Buses to and from Ibarra (US$2, three hours) and Quito (US$4, 5½ hours) leave and arrive from the terminal terrestre, 2.5 km uphill to the south-west from the town centre. Buses to Guayaquil are also available. Buses to Otavalo usually drop you on the Panamericana in the outskirts – ask.

City buses (US$0.10) run along Avenida Bolívar between the terminal and the centre.

To/From Colombia Formalities are taken care of at the border, 6.5 km north of Tulcán. Minibuses (US$0.35) and taxis (US$3) leave all day from Parque Isidro Ayora. The border is open daily from 6 am to 8 pm (closed for lunch from noon to 1 or 2 pm). Entrance formalities for Ecuador are usually no problem.

Entering Ecuador, you get a stamp in your passport and on a separate tourist card. Leaving Ecuador, you get an exit stamp in your passport and hand in your tourist card. If you lose it, they should give you another one free – but it's best not to lose it. (See Visas & Embassies and Documents in the Facts for the Visitor section of this chapter.)

South of Quito

The Panamericana heads almost directly south from Quito along a long valley flanked by two parallel ranges of mountains, many of which are volcanoes. This central valley contains almost half of Ecuador's population. The relatively rich volcanic soils are suitable for agriculture and the valley makes a good communication route between north and south. A string of towns stretches south from the capital to Ecuador's third-largest city, Cuenca, some 300 km away. In between is some of Ecuador's wildest scenery, with nine of the country's 10 highest peaks, and scores of tiny villages of Andean Indians whose lives have changed little in centuries.

LATACUNGA

Latacunga (population 40,000) is the capital of Cotopaxi province and a good base for several excellent excursions. The drive from Quito is magnificent. Cotopaxi, at 5897 metres the second-highest Ecuadorian peak, is the cone-shaped mountain looming to the east of the Panamericana. The two Ilinizas (Sur and Norte), also snowcapped and over 5000 metres, are on your right, and several other peaks are visible during the 90-km drive.

Information

There is no tourist office, but Coltur, on Salcedo, provides tours, guides and information. Changing money is a hassle.

Special Events

The major annual fiesta honours La Virgen de las Mercedes, and is held from 23 to 24 September. This is more popularly known as the Fiesta de la Mama Negra, and there are processions, costumes and fireworks, as well as street dancing and Andean music. This is one of those festivals that, although superficially Christian, has much Indian influence, and is worth seeing.

Places to Stay

The best (but not cheapest) budget hotel is the *Hotel Estambul* (☎ 800 354), at US$4 per person or US$12 for a double with bath in very clean, well-maintained rooms. A recent recommendation (not on the map) at this price is the *Residencial Santiago* (☎ 800 899, 802 164), 2 de Mayo and Guayaquil, with large rooms (shared bath) or smaller, darker rooms with private bath. Both places have hot water, and are helpful and secure.

ECUADOR

PLACES TO STAY
1 Residencial Los Andes
2 Hostal Quilotoa
6 Hostal Residencial Jackeline
7 Residencial El Salto
10 Residencial La Estación
13 Residencial Los Rieles
15 Hotel Costa Azul
16 Hotel Los Nevados,
   Hotel Turismo
23 Hotel Tulipan
24 Hotel Estambul
26 Hotel Rodelu
27 Hotel Cotopaxi
28 Hotel Central

PLACES TO EAT
8 Restaurantes El Mashca
   & La Borgoña
15 Restaurant Costa Azul
20 Gran Pan Bakery
21 Restaurant Candilejas
22 Pingüino Ice Cream
26 Pizzería Rodelu
31 Parrilladas Los Copihues

OTHER
3 Buses (Passing) to Ambato,
   Baños, Riobamba
4 Petrol Station
5 Buses to Saquisilí
9 La Merced Market
11 Transportes Cotopaxi Buses
   to Zumbagua & Quevedo
12 Buses (passing) to Quito
14 Buses to Pujilí
17 Buses to Ambato
18 Market
19 Church
25 Coltur
29 Molinos de Monserrat Museum
30 EMETEL & Post Office
32 Cathedral
33 Town Hall
34 Old Hospital
35 General Hospital

Latacunga

0   100   200 m

For US$2.50 per person, the basic but friendly *Hostal Residencial Jackeline* (☎ 801 033) and *Residencial El Salto* both have warm showers. The *Hotel Costa Azul* and *Hotel Turismo* both are friendly, have good cheap restaurants and very basic rooms with shared cold showers at US$2 per person. A more basic cold-water cheapie is the *Residencial La Estación*.

The *Residencial Los Rieles* (☎ 801 254) has simple rooms at US$3.50/4.50 for singles/doubles or US$7/8 with private bath; there is hot water. The *Hostal Quilotoa* (☎ 801 866) has good, clean, carpeted double rooms with bath and hot water for US$12.

Hotels fill fast on Wednesday afternoon for the Thursday morning Indian market at Saquisilí.

Places to Eat

Parrilladas Los Copihues (steaks and meat dishes), *Restaurant Candilejas* ('international' food) and *Pizzería Rodelu* are supposedly the best places and they aren't terribly expensive. *Restaurantes La Borgoña* and *Costa Azul* (simple Ecuadorian food) and *El Mashca* (for chicken) are cheaper and quite good. *Pingüino* is a good place for ice cream and *Gran Pan* bakery is good for bread for picnics.

Most restaurants close by 8 pm. *Pollos Gus*, near the Hoastal Quilotoa on the Panamericana, serves fast-food-style hamburgers and roast chicken and is open late. It's hard to find a place for early breakfasts.

Getting There & Away

Buses drop and pick up passengers on the Panamericana, at the corner of Avenida 5 de Junio. Some go direct to and from Latacunga's Plaza Chile (also known as El Salto); these may be slower but a seat is usually guaranteed. Buses go to Quito (US$1.20, two hours), Ambato (one hour), Riobamba (2¼ hours) and Baños (1¾ hours).

The bus stop west for Pujilí (US$0.25) and beyond is near the Panamericana. Beyond Pujilí the road goes past Zumbagua (US$1.50, two hours), and down the western Andes to Quevedo (US$3, four hours). This rough but spectacular ride from the highlands to the western lowlands leaves about seven times a day.

Buses for Saquisilí (US$0.25, 30 minutes) and nearby villages (Sigchos, Chugchilán and Mulaló) leave from Plaza Chile, near the market. Departures are every few minutes on market-day mornings, but less frequently otherwise.

SAQUISILI

Saquisilí's Thursday morning market is for the inhabitants of remote Indian villages, most of whom are recognised by their little felt 'pork pie' hats and red ponchos. Ecuadorian economists consider this to be the most important Indian village market in the country and many travellers rate it as the most interesting in Ecuador. Be alert for pickpockets.

Buses leave from Quito's terminal terrestre on Thursday morning and go directly to Saquisilí. Many buses also leave from Latacunga.

WEST OF LATACUNGA

Pujilí, 10 km west of Latacunga, has a

Sunday market and interesting Corpus Christi and All Soul's day celebrations.

The tiny village of **Zumbagua** (3500 metres, 67 km west of Latacunga) has a small but fascinating Saturday market, but the two small residenciales fill up fast on Friday, so get there early. The better of the two is the *Hostal Quiroga* below the square. Accommodation and food are basic. From Zumbagua, a 14-km unpaved road leads north to the beautiful volcanic **Laguna Quilotoa**. Carry water – the lake is alkaline; camping near the lake is possible. The basic but friendly *Cabaña Quilotoa* near the lake provides US$2 beds, typical meals, horses and local guides.

About 14 km north of the lake is the little village of **Chugchilán**, where you can stay at the *Black Sheep Inn* for US$4 per night. Meals are available, the staff speak English, and this is a good base for hiking and mountain biking. A farther 23 km north is the village of **Sigchos**, which has a couple of basic pensiones. From here, it's about 52 km east to Saquisilí.

Getting There & Away

Buses leave several times a day to either Zumbagua or Sigchos, but there are few between these towns. A daily 11 am bus from Latacunga goes to Chugchilán via Sigchos. Buses from Sigchos past Chugchilán and on to Zumbagua leave well before dawn on Wednesday, Friday and Saturday. Buses from Zumbagua to Sigchos leave on Thursday and Saturday mornings. There are occasional trucks, or you can walk.

PARQUE NACIONAL COTOPAXI

This is mainland Ecuador's most frequently visited national park, but it is almost deserted during the middle of the week. There is a small museum, a llama herd, a climbers' refuge *(refugio)*, and camping and picnicking areas. The entrance fee (for foreigners) is US$10 and the gate is open from 8 am to 6 pm (longer at weekends). Camping is about US$1 per person. A bunk in the climbers' refuge costs US$10. Cooking facilities are available, but you should definitely bring a warm sleeping bag. (See *Climbing & Hiking in Ecuador*, 3rd edition, by Rob Rachowiecki & Betsy Wagenhauser.)

Getting There & Around

There are two entrances on the Panamericana, about 20 and 26 km north of Latacunga. Buses will drop you at these entrances – you can then follow the signposted dirt roads to the administration building and museum, about 15 km from either entrance. You can walk or hitchhike into the park, but there is very little traffic, except on weekends. Pick-ups from Latacunga cost about US$20 to US$30, but bargain. The owner of the Hotel Estambul provides a truck service to the park; clarify how far in you want to go.

The Limpiopungo lake area for camping (very cold) and picnicking is about four km beyond the museum, and the climbers' refuge is about 12 km farther on. You can drive up a very rough road to a car park about one km before the refuge. The lake is at 3800 metres and the refuge is 1000 metres higher; it is very hard work walking at this altitude if you are not used to it. Altitude sickness is a very real danger, so acclimatise for several days in Quito before attempting to walk in.

Continuing beyond the climbers' refuge requires snow and ice-climbing gear and expertise. Guides and gear are available in Quito and Ambato. Ask at the SAEC in Quito for advice.

AMBATO

Ambato (population 125,000), the Tungurahua province capital, is 40 km south of Latacunga. Badly damaged in a 1949 earthquake, it is now a modern and growing city, famous for its flower festival in the second half of February when hotels tend to be full. The Monday market is huge. Most travellers just pass through Ambato on their way to Baños, but the museum in the Colegio Bolívar on the Parque Cevallos, open weekdays (US$2) is worth a visit.

Information

CETUR (☎ 821 800) is on Guayaquil by the Hotel Ambato. Several banks, and Cambiato (☎ 821 008), at Bolívar 686, change dollars at fair rates. Surtrek (☎ 844 448, fax 844 512), L Cordero 2-10 and Los Shyris, rents climbing equipment and has guides.

Places to Stay

The area around the Parque 12 de Noviembre and the nearby Mercado Central has many cheap and basic hotels including the *Residencial América* (☎ 821 092), JB Vela 737, which has tepid electric showers and is one of the better cheapies. Rooms are about US$2.50 per person. Next door is the similarly priced *Residencial Europa*, which claims to have hot water but often doesn't. For US$3 the *Residencial Laurita* (☎ 821 377), JL Mera 333, is basic but friendly, and has hot water in one bathroom; so too does the similar *Hotel Guayaquil* (☎ 821 194, 823 886), at JL Mera 311. The *Residencial 9 de Octubre* (☎ 820 018), at JL Mera 325, is also US$3, but has only cold water. There are several other very basic, grungy-looking hotels in this area (which we enjoyed researching – ha!). The *Hotel Nacional* (☎ 823 820), on Vela near Lalama, charges US$2.75 and has hot water – sometimes.

The noisy *Hotel Carrillo* (☎ 827 200), above the bus terminal, has hot showers and charges US$3.50 per person. A walk of several minutes brings you to the friendly *Residencial Pichincha*, at 12 de Noviembre 2323. Clean singles/doubles are US$3/5 but the showers are cold.

The *Hotel San Francisco* (☎ 821 739), M Egüez 837, is quite clean and friendly (though one critic calls it 'seedy') at US$5 per person or US$7 with private hot bath. More up-market are the new *Hostal Señorial* (☎ 825 124), on Cevallos at Quito, with carpeted rooms with bath at US$10 per person, and the *Hotel Pirámide Inn* (☎ 825 252), on Cevallos at Egüez, which is US$12/18 (one bed) in carpeted rooms with bath and TV.

Places to Eat

Chifa Jao Fua (☎ 829 306), on Cevallos near JL Mera, has good meals for under US$2. Cheaper and almost as good is the *Chifa Nueva Hong Kong*, at Bolívar 768. For breakfast pastries and coffee, try *Panadería Enripan* on JL Mera. *Oasis Heladería*, Sucre near M Egüez, is a popular café. *Mama Miche Restaurant* (☎ 822 913), on 13 de Abril, behind the Centro Comercial Ambato, is quite good value and open 24 hours.

For good, medium-priced steak, try *Parrilladas El Gaucho* (☎ 828 969), on Bolívar near Quito, or *Parrilladas Favid* on Bolívar near JL Mera. The *Pizzería La Cigarra* (☎ 828 411), at Bolívar 373, cooks a reasonable pizza.

Entertainment

The *Peña Tungurahua Bar*, on Martínez near the Centro Comercial Ambato, has a peña at weekends; the *La Cascada Discoteca* is on the same block. The *Restaurant Coyote Disco Club* on Bolívar near Quito, is a popular restaurant for young people with dancing in the evenings. There are a few cinemas.

Getting There & Away

Bus The terminal terrestre, two km from the centre, has many buses to Baños ($US0.60, 45 minutes), Riobamba (one hour), Quito (US$2, three hours) and Guayaquil (six hours). Less frequent are buses to Guaranda (US$1.60, 2 hours), Cuenca (seven hours) and Tena (six hours).

Local buses marked 'Terminal' leave from Parque Cevallos in the centre. Outside the terminal, buses marked 'Centro' go to Parque Cevallos for US$0.10. There are also other local buses.

BAÑOS

This small town, famous for its hot springs, is popular with Ecuadorian and foreign tourists alike. Baños' elevation of 1800 metres gives it an agreeable climate. The surroundings are green and attractive and offer good walking and climbing opportunities. Baños is also the gateway to the jungle via Puyo and Misahuallí. East of Baños, the road descends, and spectacular views of the upper Amazon Basin stretch away before you. The annual fiesta is held on 16 December and preceding days.

Information

There is no CETUR office, but the town hall may have some information. The Banco del Pacífico changes US dollars and travellers' cheques at Quito rates.

Things to See

The **Santuario de Nuestra Señora de Agua Santa** and museum within the basilica are worth seeing. Hours are 7.30 am to 4 pm; entry is US$0.30. An annual October celebration in the Virgin's honour sees Indian musicians flock to the streets. The **zoo**, three km west of town, has local animals in small but clean cages. Entry is US$0.50.

Activities

Clarify with operators of all excursions whether you will be entering a park and, if so, who will pay the entrance fees.

Hot Baths There are two baths in Baños and a third out of town. All have changing rooms and bathing costume rental. The best known bath is Piscina de La Virgen, by the waterfall. Hours are 4.30 am to 4.30 pm; entrance is US$0.80. It's busy by 7 am and crowded at weekends. The Piscina El Salado, two km west of town, is similar but has more pools of different temperatures. The water is natural but the pools are concrete – better for soaking than swimming. Catch the bus outside Residencial La Delicia 1.

Hiking & Climbing From the bus terminal there is a short trail to the San Francisco bridge across the Río Pastaza. Continue up the other side as far as you want. South on Maldonado is a footpath to Bellavista (the white cross high over Baños) and then to the settlement of **Runtun**, two hours away. South on JL Mera, a footpath leads to the Mirador de La Virgen del Agua Santa and on to Runtun. There are good views from both these steep paths.

Climbers with crampons can climb **Tungurahua** (5016 metres) in two days (an easy ascent for experts). The volcano is part of Parque Nacional Sangay, with a US$10

ECUADOR

entrance fee and US$5 to overnight in the climbers' refuge. A road goes halfway up from Baños; a ride in a truck will cost US$2.50. Ask at Pensión Patty about their 8 am truck departures and guides, Carlos and José. Expediciones Amazónicas (☎ 740 506), on Oriente at Halflants, has rental equipment and guides. Willie Navarrete (contact at Café Higuerón) is a recommended guide. US$50 per person is the going rate for the two-day climb with a group. Beware of cheap but inexperienced guides.

The jagged, extinct volcano **El Altar** (5319 metres) is hard to climb but the wild páramo surrounding it is a target for adventurous backpackers with gear; don't leave anything unattended or it will disappear. Get there by bus to Penipe, halfway between Baños and Riobamba. Continue on occasional trucks to Candelaria, 15 km away. From here, it is two km to the **Parque Nacional Sangay**, where US$10 is charged. It is a full-day hike to the crater. Guides and mules can be hired in Candelaria.

Warning There have been isolated robberies on some trails and at the climbers' refuge. Seek local updates and go with a group.

Mountain Biking Several companies rent bikes from about US$4 per day. Check equipment carefully. A popular ride is the dramatic descent (mainly) to Puyo, about 70 km. Parts of the road are unpaved. There is a passport control at Shell. From Puyo take a bus to Baños with the bike on the roof.

Horse Riding Angel Aldáz (☎ 740 175), Montalvo and JL Mera, rents horses for about US$10 per half-day, more with a guide. Christian, at Hostal Isla del Baños, has guided half and multi-day horse trips. Both are recommended. There are other places.

Rafting Geoturs (☎ 740 703), on Maldonado half a block south of the bus terminal, has half-day raft trips on the Río Patate, north-west of Baños (US$20), and full days on the Río Pastaza (US$40).

Jungle Trips Many are advertised from Baños but not all guides are experienced or recommended. Guides should have a Patente de Operación Turística licence issued by INEFAN. The bottom left box shows the areas in which they are authorised to work. They should also have a CETUR card, which ranks them as Naturalista 1 (lowest ranking), Naturalista 2 or Nacional (highest ranking), and states the languages in which they guide.

Rainforestur (☎ 740 423, ☎ & fax 740 743), on Ambato near Maldonado, has been recommended by several readers for Cuyabeno Reserve tours and other areas. Tsantsa Tours (☎ 740 957, fax 740 717), on Oriente near Eloy Alfaro, has been recommended also, particularly Sebastian Moya. Guides are Shuar Indians who are sensitive of the local people and environment. Dayuma Tours has a Baños office but it is better to book at the Misahuallí office. Vasco Tours (☎ 740 017), on Eloy Alfaro and Martínez, run by the Vasco brothers, has reportedly moved here recently from Misahuallí. Its guide, Juan Medina, has been recommended.

Three to seven-day jungle tours are about US$30 to US$45 per person depending on destination (three or four person minimum). Some focus more on Indian culture and plants; others more on wildlife. Don't expect to see many animals in the rainforest; you need patience and luck. June to September is the busy season.

Language Courses
Spanish School for Foreigners (☎ 740 612), on 16 de Diciembre and Espejo, Elizabeth Barrionuevo (☎ 740 314, 740 632), at T Halflants 656, and Pepe Eras (☎ 740 232), at Montalvo 526, are recommended for private lessons at US$3 per hour.

Places to Stay
Because of Baños' huge popularity, most popular places are full for the weekend by mid-Friday (or earlier). Hotels prefer guests to stay for a few days. Ask for long-stay discounts. Most hotels are under US$5 per person – a good town for budget travellers.

One of the cheapest is the basic but clean

Baños

To Agoyan (18 km), Puyo (61 km)

To Piscina El Salado, Zoo (3 km), Ambato, Riobamba

To Piscina El Salado (1.5 km)

Santa Clara

12 de Noviembre

Parque de la Basílica

16 de Diciembre

Eloy Alfaro

T Halflants

Parque Central

Maldonado

OF Reyes

Pastaza

Rocafuerte

Martínez

JL Mera

Montalvo

Main Road

E Espejo

Oriente

Ambato

Plaza

To Bellavista

To La Virgen del Agua Santa, Casa Amarilla (1 km), Runtun (2 km)

Río Pastaza

Puente San Francisco

Waterfall

PLACES TO STAY
5 Hostal Residencial
6 María Isabel
8 Residencial Julia
11 Monik's Hostal
12 Residencial El Rey
14 Residencial Charvic
16 Residencial La Delicia 1
17 Resión Benoño
 Rincón Angelly
19 Pensión Angelly
21 Pensión Patty
22 Hostal Magdalena
23 Residencial Baños,
 Hostal Bolívar
 & others
28 Residencial La Delicia 2
35 Residencial Cordillera
 & others
37 Residencial Lucy
38 Hotel Alborada,
 Hotel Achupallas
39 Residencial Olguita,
 Residencial Los Piños
41 Residencial Las Orquideas
42 Hotel Danubio
44 Hostal Anita
46 Hostal Agoyán,
 Hostal Vikingo
47 Hotel Americano
48 Residencial Teresita
49 Residencial Timara
53 Residencial Rosita
54 La Petite Auberge
59 Hospedaje Santa Cruz
62 Hostal El Castillo
66 Hotel Sangay
67 Hotel Isla del Baños
72 Hostería Monte Selva
74 Villa Gertrudis
 Las Esteras
77 Casa Real
 Hotel Palace
78 Residencial Villa
 Santa Clara

PLACES TO EAT
3 Cafetería Chushi
9 Restaurant Monica
10 La Closerie de Lilas
18 Chifa Central
24 Donde Marcelo
31 Mamá Inés
36 Regine Café Alemán II,
 Rincón de Suecia
44 El Jardín
51 Le Petit Restaurant
52 Café Hood
56 Restaurant El Artesano
60 Regine Café Alemán
61 Café Higuerón
64 Café Cultura
65 La Casa Mia
69 Venus Y Bacchus
76 Restaurant y Peña
 El Marqués

OTHER
1 Sugar-Cane Stalls
2 Terminal Terrestre
7 Peña Ananitay
13 Tsantsa Tours
20 Rain Forestur
25 Hard Rock Café
26 Basílica & Museum
27 Baños Cultural Centre
29 La Burbuja Disco
30 Dayuma Tours
32 Post Office
34 Town Hall & Clock Tower
40 Bus Stop for Agoyán
45 Market
50 Illusions Peña Bar
55 EMETEL
58 Horse Rental
63 Bamboo Bar
 Banco del Pacífico
 Galería de Arte
67 Piscina de La Virgen
68 Hospital
73 Piscina (Hot Baths)
 Children's Playground
79 Santa Clara
 Swimming Pool

ECUADOR

Residencial Rincón Baneño (☎ 740 316), Oriente 662 (enter from Halflants), with hot water and doubles for under US$4. The family-run *Pensión Patty* (☎ 740 202), Eloy Alfaro 556, has basic rooms for US$2 per person and is very popular with gringos. Rooms vary in quality. There is one hot and several cold showers, and a communal kitchen. Opposite is the *Pensión Angelly*, which is similarly priced and OK. Other basic places for about US$2 per person include the *Residencial Olguita* (☎ 740 271) with hot water, and front rooms overlooking the Parque Central, *Residencial Julia* with cold water, by the bus station, the nearby *Residencial El Rey*, where three rooms share a hot shower, and the small *Las Esteros*.

The friendly *Residencial Timara* (☎ 740 599), Maldonado near Martínez, is about US$2.80 per person and has hot water and kitchen facilities. The *Residencial Villa Santa Clara* (☎ 740 349), 12 de Noviembre near Ibarra, is popular and has kitchen facilities, hot showers and a garden. Rooms in the old house are US$2 per person and new cabins are US$5/8 for singles/doubles with hot shower. The friendly *Residencial Lucy* (☎ 740 466) is US$3.50 per person in rooms with private bath and hot water, or US$2.50 with shared bath.

Other very basic hotels for about US$3 or less per person include the following. The friendly *Hotel Americano* (☎ 740 352), 12 de Noviembre near Martínez, has a simple restaurant and large rooms. The *Residencial Teresita* (☎ 740 471), 12 de Noviembre near Rocafuerte, has some rooms overlooking the Parque de la Basílica. Both have hot water and kitchen facilities on request. Others nearby are the *Hostal Agoyán* and *Residencial Vikingo*. The *Residencial Los Piños* (☎ 740 252) has some rooms with Parque Central views. So do the *Residencial La Delicia 1* (☎ 740 477) and *Residencial La Delicia 2* (☎ 740 537), though both these are grubby, as is the *Hotel Danubio*.

The very popular *Hostal Plantas y Blanco* (☎ & fax 740 044), Martínez and 12 de Noviembre, is attractively decorated with plants and has a pleasant rooftop terrace (for breakfast) and a steam bath. Clean rooms are US$5 per person with private bath or US$4 with shared bath. There is a laundry and bike rental, and service is helpful. Next door, the *Hostal Cordillera* is clean and friendly but may lack hot water. Rooms are US$3 per person or US$4 with bath. Around the corner, the *Hospedaje Santa Cruz* (☎ 740 648), is clean and good value at US$4 per person with bath and hot water; opposite is the similar *Rosita Residencial*. The good *Hostal Las Orquideas* (☎ 740 911) on the corner of the Parque Central has light, clean rooms, some with balconies, for US$4 per person with private hot shower. The pleasant *Hostal El Castillo* (☎ 740 285), Martínez 255, is also good at US$4 per person in rooms with hot showers most of the time. It offers guests three meals for US$2.50.

Others for about US$4 per person include the hotels on the busy pedestrian block of Ambato, such as the *Residencial Baños* (☎ 740 284), *Residencial Cordillera* (☎ 740 536) and the *Hostal Bolívar* (☎ 740 497). Also in this price range are the modern *Hotel Alborada* (☎ 740 814) and *Hotel Achupallas* (☎ 740 422, 740 389), both on the Parque de la Basílica, the friendly but quite basic *Residencial Anita* (☎ 740 319), the *Hostal Los Andes, Monik's Hostal, Hostal Grace, Hotel Residencial María Isabel* and *Le Petite Auberge.*

Places to Eat

Donde Marcelo, on Ambato near 16 de Diciembre, has adequate Ecuadorian food with a very popular bar upstairs. On the same block, the cheaper *Restaurant Latino* and *Restaurant Los Alpes* are good. The *Chifa Central* is good for Chinese and local food. Almost next door, *Mi Abuela* is a recommended little café. *Mamá Inés* has Mexican and other meals and is very popular. There are several other cheap restaurants and bakeries on Ambato and around the market. *El Jardín* is good for a variety of food and snacks, which can be enjoyed in the outdoor area.

Several international restaurants are slightly pricey but popular with travellers.

ECUADOR

Café Hood features international vegetarian food and has a book exchange and music. It's open daily except Tuesday from 8 to 11 am and 1.30 to 9 pm. *Café Higuerón* (☎ 740 910) has a good variety of meat and meatless dishes, teas and desserts, and is open daily except Wednesday from 8 am to 10 pm. *La Closerie de Lilas* has good meals showing a French influence at very reasonable prices. *Le Petit Restaurant* also has food with a French twist but it's pricier. Several places serve good-value Italian food; our favourite is the friendly *La Bella Italia* (☎ 740 072). Others prefer *Paolo's Pizzería* (☎ 740 944) next to Café Hood (one critic calls this 'one of the hemisphere's best restaurants') or *Scaligeri* at Eloy Alfaro and Ambato. *Regine Café Alemán*, on Montalvo near 16 de Diciembre, is good for breakfast (from 8 am), light meals and drinks – it's German in style. A second one serves more solid meals. The British-run *Café Cultura* (☎ 740 419), on Montalvo near Santa Clara, features home-made breads, quiches, fruit pies, fresh fish etc.

Entertainment

The *Hard Rock Café* plays old rock classics and is popular, as is the somewhat pricier bar above *Donde Marcelo*, which plays rock music and has a dance floor. The friendly and hip *Bamboo Bar* has Latin music and dancing. The *Peña Ananitay* has live folklórico music late on weekend nights. *El Marqués* has weekend peñas with varied music. *Illusions Peña Bar* offers a variety of entertainment. *La Burbuja* disco has dancing on weekends (US$2 cover). *Baños Cultural Center* screens classic movies nightly at 8 pm (US$1.25) and has a book exchange.

Getting There & Away

From many towns, it may be quicker to change buses in Ambato, where there are frequent buses to Baños (US$0.60, one hour).

From the Baños terminal terrestre, many buses leave for Quito (US$2.40, 3½ hours) and Riobamba (US$0.75, one hour), and less

often to Puyo (US$1.50, two hours) and Tena (US$3.50, five hours).

Tunnel construction on the road to Puyo has closed the route to through traffic every day except Monday. Buses go as far as the construction area, then passengers disembark, carry their luggage through the construction area, and continue by another bus on the other side. People riding bicycles can get through. The project should be finished by late 1997.

GUARANDA

This small, quiet provincial capital is worth a visit for the spectacular views of Chimborazo on the wild, unpaved road from Riobamba or the paved road from Ambato. Saturday is market day.

Places to Stay & Eat

Basic cold-water cheapies include the *Pensión San José* on Sucre near Rocafuerte, with large clean rooms at US$1.75 per person. Others, not as good, are the *Pensión Rosita Elvira* (opposite the San José), and the *Residencial La Posada*, on Arregon near 10 de Agosto. The clean *Residencial Acapulco* (☎ 981 953), on 10 de Agosto near 9 de Abril, has hot showers and is US$4 per person or US$6 with private bath. The similarly priced *Residencial Santa Fé* has an overly amorous manager and the *Pensión Tequendama*, on Rocafuerte near José García, is used by short-stay couples. The *Hotel Matiaví* (☎ 980 295), at the bus terminal, has hot water and charges US$4 per person. The pleasant *Hotel Bolívar* (☎ 980 547), Sucre 7-04 near Olmedo, has clean rooms and hot showers. Rooms with private bath are US$8 per person, or US$6 with shared bath, US$10 with TV and phone. The 'best' is the *Hotel Cochabamba* (☎ 981 958, fax 982 125), on García Moreno near 7 de Mayo, charging US$8/12 for singles/doubles or US$16/20 with private bath, TV and phone. Rooms vary widely in quality.

Most restaurants close by 7.30 pm. The *Restaurante Rumipamba*, on the Parque Bolívar, is nothing great, but is one of the better ones. Nearby, the *Chifa Hong Kong* has cheap almuerzos and meriendas, as well as inexpensive à-la-carte choices.

Getting There & Away

The bus terminal is half a km east of town. Buses leave for Ambato (US$1.60, two hours), Quito (US$3, five hours), Babahoyo (US$2.25, four hours), Guayaquil (US$3, five hours) and Riobamba (US$2, three hours), and also go to remote towns and villages.

RIOBAMBA

Riobamba is the heart of an extensive and scenic road network. Plan your journey for daylight hours to enjoy the great views. The town is a traditional and old-fashioned city, which both bores and delights travellers.

Information

The helpful CETUR office is on 10 de Agosto, half a block south-west of the Parque Sucre, and is open Tuesday to Saturday from 8 am to noon and 2.30 to 5 pm. Next door, Casa de Cambio Chimborazo is a good place to change money.

Things to See

Saturday is market day and there's much street activity, especially around 5 de Junio and Argentinos.

The famous **Museo de Arte Religioso** (☎ 952 212), in the restored church of La Concepción, has many paintings, sculptures and religious artefacts. The major piece is a huge, gem-encrusted, gold monstrance. The museum is open Tuesday to Saturday from 9 am to noon and 3 to 7 pm; on Sunday and holidays, it may open in the morning. Entrance is US$2.

The observation platform in the **Parque 21 de Abril** gives good views and has tilework showing the history of Ecuador.

Places to Stay

Near the bus terminal, nearly two km west of the town centre, are a handful of hotels charging about US$3 per person. These include the *Residencial San Carlos*, *Hotel*

Monterrey (☎ 962 421) and *Hotel Las Retamas* (☎ 965 005). All have hot water.

In the town centre, the cheapest hotels are near the railway station. *Residencial Ñuca Huasi* (☎ 966 669), 10 de Agosto 10-24, is a basic place popular with backpackers. The owner has climbing information and arranges transport to the mountains. Rooms are a bit grimy but the sheets are clean. Rates are US$2.50 per person or US$4 with private bath and hot water between 7 and 9 am or pm. Also popular is the clean and friendly but noisy *Hotel Imperial* (☎ 960 429), Rocafuerte 22-15. Rooms are US$4 per person or US$5 with bath and hot water. The manager will arrange trips to Chimborazo.

Other basic hotels in the US$2 to US$3 per person range include the *Residencial Colonial* and the *Hotel Bolívar* (☎ 968 294) near the train station, and the *Residencial Venecia*, Dávalos 22-21. These have hot water and seem OK. If they are full you can try the basic *Hotel Americano* and *Puruha, María Ester, Los Andes* and *Chimborazo* residenciales.

The *Hotel Metro* (☎ 961 714), León Borja and J Lavalle, and the *Hotel Segovia* (☎ 961 269), Primera Constituyente 22-26, charge US$4.50 per person in rooms with bath and hot water and are just OK. Better at this price is the quiet and clean *Residencial Rocío*, Brazil 21-68.

For US$6 per person, the friendly and recommended *Hotel Los Shyris* (☎ 960 323), Rocafuerte and 10 de Agosto, has good, clean rooms with hot showers. The similarly priced *Hotel Manabí* (☎ 967 967), Colón 19-58, also seems quite good. After that, hotel prices jump to over US$10 per person. The friendly *Hotel Humboldt* (☎ 961 788), León Borja 35-48, is quite good at US$11 per person and the *Hotel Whymper* (☎ 964 575), Angel León 23-10, is just adequate at this price.

Places to Eat

A favourite place for both locals and tourists is the lively and popular *Pizzería San Valentín*; order your pizza at the counter. *Charlie's Pizzería* is more sedate but very

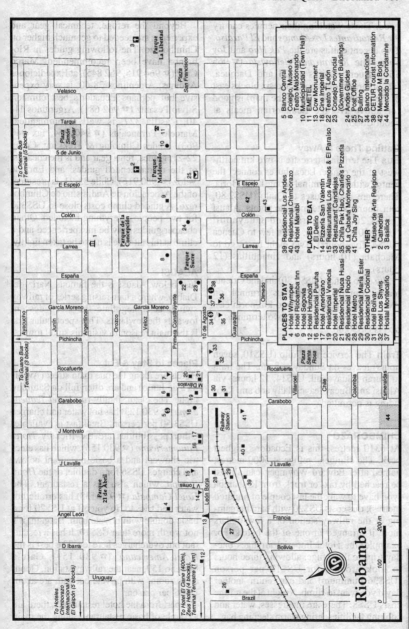

Riobamba

PLACES TO STAY
4 Hotel Whymper
6 Hotel Riobamba Inn
9 Hotel Segovia
12 Hotel Humboldt
16 Residencial Puruha
17 Residencial Americano
19 Hotel Ñañan Velencia
20 Hotel Imperial
21 Residencial Nuca Huasi
26 Residencial Rocío
28 Hotel Metro
29 Residencial María Ester
30 Residencial Colonial
31 Hotel Bolívar
32 Hotel Los Shyris
37 Hostal Montecarlo

39 Residencial Los Andes
40 Residencial Chimborazo
43 Hotel Manabí

PLACES TO EAT
7 El Delirio
14 Pizzería San Valentín
15 Restaurantes Los Álamos & El Paraíso
23 Restaurant Candilejas
35 Chifa Pak Hao, Charlie's Pizzería
36 La Cabaña Montecarlo
41 Chifa Joy Sing

OTHER
1 Museo de Arte Religioso
2 Cathedral
3 Basílica

5 Banco Central
8 Colegio, Museo &
  Teatro Maldonando
10 Municipalidad (Town Hall)
11 EMETEL
13 Cow Monument
18 Teatro T León
22 Consejo Provincial
  (Government Buildings)
24 Andes Guides
25 Post Office
27 Bullring
34 Banco Internacional
38 CETUR Tourist Information
42 Mercado M Borja
44 Mercado la Condamine

good. Those watching their pennies can try the *Restaurantes Los Alamos* and *El Paraíso*. Two decent chifas are the *Pak Hao* and *Joy Sing*. The *Restaurante Bellavista* (☎ 965 861), Buenos Aires 12-34 and Darquea, (about three blocks north and six blocks east of the north-east corner of the map) is good for above-average Ecuadorian meals at about US$3.

Getting There & Away

Bus The terminal terrestre is two km north-west of the centre. Local buses connect the centre with the terminal along León Borja. There are many buses to Quito (US$2.80, four hours) and intermediate points, Alausí (US$1.20, 1½ hours) and Guayaquil (US$3.50, five hours), and a few to Cuenca (US$4, five hours). Two night buses go to Machala (10 hours) and Huaquillas (12 hours).

Buses to Baños (US$0.80) and the Oriente leave from the Oriente bus terminal, on Avenida E Espejo some two km north-east of town. No buses link the two terminals. A taxi is US$0.80.

Train The service for Quito (US$10, seven hours) leaves on Sunday at 8 am. The train to Durán (Guayaquil, US$14, 12 hours) via Alausí and Bucay leaves daily at 6 am. Roof riding is permitted.

CHIMBORAZO

At 6310 metres, this is Ecuador's highest peak. The climbers' refuge at 5000 metres, named after Edward Whymper, can almost be reached by taxi or truck from Riobamba (you have to walk the last couple of hundred metres); this costs US$20 with hard bargaining at the railway station or a few dollars more if arranged in one of the hotels. For example, the Hotel Imperial arranges one-day trips to the refuge, allowing three hours to look around, for US$12 per person (US$36 minimum) and can return another day if you want to climb. A night at the refuge costs US$8. There are mattresses, water and cooking facilities; bring warm sleeping bags.

Beyond the refuge, technical gear and experience are needed to get much higher on Chimborazo. The following guides in Riobamba have been recommended: Marco Cruz (☎ 964 915, 962 845), at Expediciones Andinas, Argentinos 38-60, is very expensive but perhaps Ecuador's best climber; Silvio Pesantz (☎ 962 681), Argentinos 11-40, Casilla 327, is well recommended; Marcelo Puruncajas (☎ 940 964, fax 940 963), Andes Climbing & Trekking, Colón 22-21, guides, rents gear and is the cheapest of the recommended guides; and Enrique Veloz (☎ 960 916), Chile 33-21, is president of the Asociación de Andinismo de Chimborazo. A guided climb costs close to US$300 for two people, everything included. Other, cheaper guides may be inexperienced and a climb at this altitude is not to be taken lightly.

ALAUSI

Just below Alausí is the famous Nariz del Diablo, where a hair-raising series of railway switchbacks negotiate the steep descent towards the lowlands. This spectacular ride is the main reason to visit this small town.

Places to Stay & Eat

Hotels are along the one main street (Avenida 5 de Junio) and are often full on Saturday night. The clean, family-run *Hotel Tequendama* (☎ 930 123) has hot water and charges US$3.50 per person. Breakfast is available. Other possibilities are the friendly *Hotel Panamericano* (☎ 930 156), which has electric showers and a basic restaurant below, and charges US$6 for a double, or the *Hotel Europa*, which also has a restaurant. The *Hotel Gampala* (☎ 930 138) has erratic hot water and tries to rip you off at US$20 for a basic double with private bath. Bargain: it's not worth more than US$10. It has a restaurant but overcharges here too. The best is the *Hotel Americano* (☎ 930 159), García Moreno 159, near the railway station. Good, clean rooms with private hot bath are about US$6 per person.

Apart from the hotel restaurants, there are a couple of basic restaurants along the main street – little choice. *Danielito's* opposite the Tequendama is simple but friendly.

Getting There & Away

Bus There are hourly buses to and from Riobamba and several a day to Cuenca. Riobamba-Cuenca buses leave passengers on the Panamericana – a one-km walk into town. Pick-up trucks act as buses to various local destinations.

Train The train for the coast leaves Alausí daily at 9 am and costs US$12 for foreigners, wherever you get off. Tickets go on sale at 7.30 am. It is three to four hours to Bucay and about eight hours to Durán. Passengers may ride on the roof; wear old clothes because of steam, soot and cinders (though a non-steam train has been operating recently).

The train from Durán passes through late in the afternoon and goes to Riobamba.

BUCAY

The most spectacular part of the train ride to Durán is between Alausí and Bucay (General Elizalde on most maps). Many people get off the train here and continue by bus. It is two hours to Guayaquil. There are also buses to Riobamba. Buses go to El Triunfo (25 minutes) where there are frequent buses to Cuenca (four hours). You can take the train from Riobamba or Alausí to Bucay and get to Cuenca by about nightfall. There are a couple of basic pensiones.

Cuenca & the Southern Highlands

CUENCA

Founded by the Spanish in 1557, Cuenca is Ecuador's third-largest city and its prettiest. The old centre has churches dating from the 16th and 17th centuries, and many other old buildings and cobblestone streets. Nearby is the Inca fortress of Ingapirca, Ecuador's best preserved precolonial ruin.

Information

CETUR (☎ 822 058) is at Hermano Miguel 6-86. INEFAN is at Simón Bolívar 5-33. Cambistral, on Mariscal Sucre near Borrero, changes various currencies at good rates. Of several hospitals and clinics, Clínica Santa Inés (☎ 817 888), on D Córdova two blocks west of Fray Vicente Solano, has been recommended. The immigration office is in the Municipio on Parque Calderón. The Asociación Hotelera de Azuay (☎ 836 925, 821 659), at Presidente Córdova and Padre Aguirre, has local hotel information.

Warning A known local man asks female travellers to write letters for him in English for 'friends' abroad. He may claim to be a businessman. He is a known rapist, but is friendly with the police. He has been active for years, and continued to be so in 1995.

Things to See & Do

The **Río Tomebamba** is attractively lined with colonial buildings, and people doing their washing place their clothes to dry on its grassy banks. There is a pleasant walk along Avenida 3 de Noviembre, following the northern bank of the river.

The **Museo del Banco Central** (no sign) on Larga at Huayna Capac, has old B&W photographs of Cuenca, ancient musical instruments and temporary exhibitions. Hours are Monday to Friday from 9 am to 5 pm, and Saturday from 9 am to 1 pm; entry is free. The new **Museo de las Culturas Aborígenes** (☎ 811 706), 10 de Agosto 4-70, has 5000 archaeological pieces representative of about 20 pre-Columbian cultures of Ecuador. Hours are Monday to Saturday from 9 am to noon and 3 to 6 pm; entry is US$2. Call ahead for tours in English.

There are **Inca ruins** near the river. Most of the stonework was destroyed to build colonial buildings but there are some fine

ECUADOR

niches and walls (though don't expect to compare them with those you'll see in Peru). There is a small site museum.

The **Museo de Artes Populares** (☎ 828 878), Hermano Miguel 3-23, has a small but good exhibit of traditional instruments, clothing and crafts. Hours are Monday to Friday from 9.30 am to 1 pm and 2.30 to 5 pm and Saturday from 10 am to 1 pm; entry is free. The **Museo de las Conceptas** (☎ 830 625), Hermano Miguel 6-33, has a fine display of religious art and artefacts housed in a 17th-century convent. Hours are Tuesday to Friday from 9 am to 4 pm, and

Saturday from 9 am to noon. Entry is US$2. The **Museo Remigio Crespo Toral**, Calle Larga 7-07, has been undergoing restoration for some years; check with CETUR for current conditions.

The **Parque Calderón** (main plaza) is dominated by the rather stark new **cathedral**, with its huge blue domes. Opposite is the squat **old cathedral** (El Sagrario). At the south-western corner is the **Casa de la Cultura**, with a local art gallery.

The **Plazoleta del Carmen**, at the corner of Sucre and Padre Aguirre, has a colonial church and a colourful flower market.

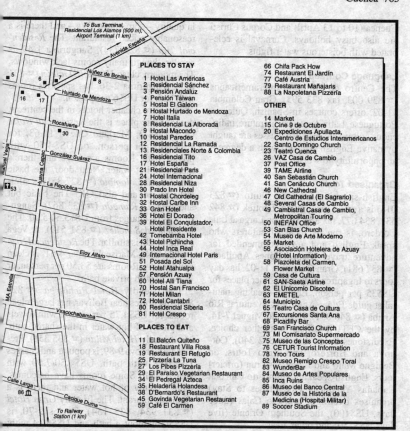

PLACES TO STAY

1 Hotel Las Américas
2 Residencial Sánchez
3 Pensión Andaluz
4 Pensión Taiwan
5 Hostal El Galeon
6 Hostal Hurtado de Mendoza
7 Hotel Italia
8 Residencial La Alboreda
9 Hostal Macondo
10 Hostal Paredes
12 Residencial La Ramada
13 Residenciales Norte & Colombia
16 Residencial Tito
17 Hotel España
21 Residencial Paris
24 Hotel Internacional
28 Residencial Niza
30 Prado Inn Hotel
31 Hostal Chordeleg
32 Hostal Caribe Inn
33 Gran Hotel
36 Hotel El Dorado
39 Hotel El Conquistador,
   Hotel Presidente
42 Tomebamba Hotel
43 Hotel Pichincha
44 Hotel Inca Real
49 Internacional Hotel Paris
51 Posada del Sol
52 Hotel Atahualpa
57 Pensión Azuay
60 Hotel Alli Tiana
70 Hostal San Francisco
71 Hotel Milan
72 Hotel Cantabri
80 Residencial Siberia
81 Hotel Crespo

PLACES TO EAT

11 El Balcón Quiteño
18 Restaurant Villa Rosa
19 Restaurant El Refugio
25 Pizzería La Tuna
27 Los Pibes Pizzería
29 El Paraíso Vegetarian Restaurant
34 El Pedregal Azteca
35 Heladería Holandesa
38 D'Bernardo's Restaurant
40 Govinda Vegetarian Restaurant
59 Café El Carmen

66 Chifa Pack How
74 Restaurant El Jardín
77 Café Austria
79 Restaurant Mañajaris
88 La Napoletana Pizzería

OTHER

14 Market
15 Cine 9 de Octubre
20 Expediciones Apullacta,
   Centro de Estudios Interamericanos
22 Santo Domingo Church
23 Teatro Cuenca
26 VAZ Casa de Cambio
37 Post Office
39 TAME Airline
40 San Sebastián Church
41 San Cenáculo Church
   New Cathedral
47 Old Cathedral (El Sagrario)
48 Several Casas de Cambio
49 Cambistral Casa de Cambio,
   Metropolitan Touring
50 INEFAN Office
53 San Blas Church
54 Museo de Arte Moderno
55 Market
56 Asociación Hotelera de Azuay
   (Hotel Information)
58 Plazoleta del Carmen,
   Flower Market
59 Casa de Cultura
61 SAN-Saeta Airline
62 El Unicornio Discotec
63 EMETEL
64 Municipio
65 Teatro Casa de Cultura
67 Excursiones Santa Ana
68 Picadilly Bar
69 San Francisco Church
73 Mi Comisariato Supermercado
75 Museo de las Conceptas
76 CETUR Tourist Information
78 Yroo Tours
82 Museo Remigio Crespo Toral
83 WunderBar
84 Museo de Artes Populares
85 Inca Ruins
86 Museo del Banco Central
87 Museo de la Historia de la
   Medicina (Hospital Militar)
89 Soccer Stadium

Plaza de San Sebastián is quiet and pleasant with the interesting old church of San Sebastián at the north end. The park has a mural of infant art, a couple of art galleries, and the **Museo de Arte Moderno** (☎ 830 499) at the southern end. Hours are Monday to Friday from 9 am to 1 pm and 3 to 6 pm; entry is free.

Markets Market day is Thursday, with a smaller market on Saturday. The main market areas are around the Church of San Francisco and at the plaza by the corner of Avenidas Mariscal Lamar and Hermano

Miguel. The colourful market is aimed more at locals than tourists. Watch out for pickpockets.

Mountain Biking Bikes can be rented for US$15 a day (helmet included) from Explorbike (☎ 833 362), J Jaramillo 5-100 at Hermano Miguel. For an extra US$10 you can hire a guide.

Special Events

Cuenca's independence is celebrated on 3 November – a major fiesta. Christmas Eve parades are very colourful. The founding of

ECUADOR

Cuenca (10 to 13 April) and Corpus Christi are also busy holidays. Carnaval is celebrated with boisterous water fights.

Language Courses

The Centro de Estudios Interamericanos (☎ 839 003, fax 833 593), Gran Colombia 11-02, offers courses in Spanish, Quichua, Portuguese, Latin American literature, indigenous culture etc. English classes are taught by native English speakers with a degree – an opportunity to work.

Organised Tours

English-speaking Eduardo Quito (☎ 823 018) is a good local guide. Ecotrek (☎ 842 531, 834 677, fax 835 387), on Larga at Luis Cordero, is run by local adventurers who speak English and are recommended for adventure travel. Expediciones Apullacta (☎ 837 681), Gran Colombia 11-02, has day tours to Ingapirca, Cajas and other places for US$35 per person. English-speaking naturalist guide Edgar Aguirre at Aventuras Río Arriba (☎ 840 031), Hermano Miguel 7-14, by the CETUR office, is another choice. Excursiones Santa Ana (☎ 832 340), Córdova and Borrero, and Yroo Tours, on Benigno Malo and Larga, also run (pricier) tours. English-speaking Humberto Chico at Cabañas Yanuncay (see Places to Stay) organises overnight tours to Cajas (three days, US$100), the Southern Oriente (five days US$250) and other areas.

Places to Stay

Hotels are often full (and prices rise) for the celebrations mentioned above, so arrive early. At other times, try bargaining.

Opposite the bus terminal, 1.5 km from the city centre, is the *Residencial Los Alamos* (☎ 825 644), with a simple restaurant. Clean rooms with shared/private baths are US$3.50/5 per person. A few minutes walk away is *Residencial La Alborada* (☎ 831 062), Olmedo 13-82, at US$3/5 for singles/doubles with shared hot baths. Nearby, the friendly *Hotel España* (☎ 824 723), Sangurima 1-19, is US$4 per person, or US$7/12 with private bath. Rooms vary

in quality – some have TVs – and there is a reasonably priced restaurant. The *Residencial Tito* (☎ 829 734), Sangurima 1-49, is similar, though many rooms lack windows. The modern, clean *Hostal El Galeón* (☎ 831 827), Sangurima 2-36, has spacious rooms with bath for US$6 per person.

There are cheaper hotels in the centre. A decent basic place is the *Residencial Norte* (☎ 827 881), Mariano Cueva 11-63, for US$3.50 per person, or US$4.50 with private bath. Rooms are large and there's plenty of hot water. Next door, the basic *Residencial Colombia* (☎ 827 851) is similarly priced and also OK. The basic but adequate *La Ramada* (☎ 833 862), Sangurima 5-51, charges from US$3.50/5.50. The *Residencial Sánchez* (☎ 831 519), A Vega Muñoz 4-28, is similar. The *Residencial Niza* (☎ 823 284), Mariscal Lamar 4-51, is clean and friendly. Rooms are $3.50 per person, or US$4.50 with private bath.

The friendly *Hotel Pichincha* (☎ 823 868), on Torres near Bolívar, has large, clean rooms for US$4.75 per person with towels and plenty of hot water in the shared bath. The friendly *Hotel Milan* (☎ 835 351), Presidente Córdova 9-89, is popular and charges US$7/12 with bath, US$4.50/7.50 with shared bath. Some rooms have balconies, there's plenty of hot water and there's a simple restaurant. The friendly *Gran Hotel* (☎ 831 934, 835 154), Torres 9-70, is US$5/8 without a bath and US$8/14 with; some rooms have TVs. There is a restaurant and an attractive courtyard (which can get noisy). The clean *Residencial Paris* (☎ 842 656, 827 257), Torres 10-48, has a helpful English-speaking manager. Rooms are US$6 per person with bath, including breakfast.

Other basic places that are not as good but are cheap and OK include the *Pensión Azuay* (☎ 824 119), Padre Aguirre 7-61, *Pensión Taiwan*, and *Pensión Andaluz*, all with doubles for about US$4 or US$5. Equally cheap but worse are the *Hostal San Francisco* and the run-down *Hotel Cantabri*.

Two hotels are affiliated with Hostelling International. The *Hostal Macondo* (☎ 831 198, fax 833 593), Tarqui 11-64, is quiet and friendly, with kitchen privileges and a nice courtyard. Good-sized rooms are US$8/12 (shared bath) and a few have private bath for US$12/16. Reservations are recommended in the high season. The *Posada del Sol* (☎ 838 695, fax 838 995), Bolívar 5-03, is a small hotel in an attractive 18th-century house. Comfortable rooms with telephone and plenty of hot water are US$18/24 and there is a restaurant.

About three km south-west of the centre is the well-recommended *Cabañas Yanuncay* (☎ 810 265, ☎ & fax 819 681), Calle Canton Gualaceo 2-149. Take a taxi or bus out on Avenida Loja and take the first right after 'Arco de la Luz', 200 metres along the river. Rooms are in a private house or in two cabins in the garden. Rates are US$8/12 per person with shared/private bath and breakfast, and US$4 more for a delicious dinner made with organic products from the owners' farm. One of the owners is a recommended local guide, and the place is family-run and friendly; English is spoken.

Places to Eat

Those on a tight budget will find set lunches at the hotels with restaurants (see Places to Stay) to be a good deal. One of the best is at the *Hostal Chordeleg* with a set lunch under US$2. *Restaurant El Refugio*, Gran Colombia 11-24, looks quite elegant and is good value for lunch. Also inexpensive are the vegetarian restaurants, such as the Hare Krishna-run *Govinda*, Aguirre 8-15, the homely little *Restaurant El Paraíso*, Tomás Ordóñez 10-19, and *Mañajaris*, Borrero 5-33, which has Hindu specials. A bit pricier are the locally popular *El Balcón Quiteño* (☎ 824 281), Gaspar Sangurima 6-49, and *Chifa Pak How*, Córdova 5-46.

The *Heladería Holandesa*, Benigno Malo 9-45, a popular hang-out for international travellers, has excellent ice cream, cakes, coffee, yoghurt and fruit salad. Also good is *Café Austria*, Benigno Malo 5-45, with delicious Austrian-style cakes and coffee. *Café El Carmen*, on the south-west corner of the Parque Calderón, has good snacks and inex-pensive local dishes, many of which are not on the menu; ask.

Two pizzerías on Gran Colombia, on either side of Luis Cordero, are the *Los Pibes* and *La Tuna*. Both have been recommended. The best Italian place is said to be *La Napoletana Pizzería*, Fray Vicente Solano 3-04. *El Pedregal Azteca* (☎ 823 652), Gran Colombia 10-33, is in an attractive old building, serves Mexican food and is popular with travellers, but it's pricey.

On Gran Colombia, about one km west off the map, is an area of restaurants and bars that are popular with young locals. Recommended places include *Doña Charito*, Gran Colombia 20-33, with good Ecuadorian and international food, *El Tequila*, Gran Colombia 20-59, with good *cuencano* dishes and *The Stone Bar*, Gran Colombia 21-130. Prices are mid to high.

Entertainment

Apart from the area on Gran Colombia (see Places to Eat), popular bars for young people include the *WunderBar* on Hermano Miguel and the *Cine Café Marilyn Monroe*, Gran Colombia 10-29, which shows music videos. There are good peñas at *La Morada del Cantor*, on Ordóñez Lazo (the western extension of Gran Colombia). *La Bulería*, Larga 8-49, has a pool table, and *Bar Años 60*, Bolívar 5-69, has a disco. There are several cinemas.

Getting There & Away

Air The airport, two km from the centre on España, has two or three daily flights to Quito (US$31), but the last one gets cancelled quite often. Guayaquil (US$31) is served every weekday. The TAME and SAN-Saeta offices in the city centre are shown on the map.

Bus The terminal is also on España, 1.5 km from the centre. The terminal has an information desk and a 24-hour cafeteria.

Many buses go to Guayaquil (US$4, five hours). There are hourly buses to Quito (US$6 to US$10, eight to 11 hours) and many buses go to Machala (US$3.50, four hours) – a few continue to Huaquillas. Hourly buses go to Azogues (US$0.50, 45 minutes), many continuing to Cañar (US$1, 1½ hours) and Alausí. Several buses a day leave for Saraguro and Loja (US$4, six hours). There are a few buses each day to Macas (US$6, 12 hours) and other Oriente towns. Buses for Gualaceo (1½ hours) leave from the corner of the terminal. Buses for El Tambo leave every 30 minutes; at 9 am and 1 pm on weekdays they continue to Ingapirca (US$1.25).

Train The station south-east of town used to have trains to Sibambe, connecting to Guayaquil and Alausí, but these have not run for some years. Enquire locally.

Getting Around
To/From the Airport Local buses (US$0.10) to the airport pass the flower market on Aguirre. A taxi to the airport is about US$2.

AROUND CUENCA
Ingapirca
The Inca site of Ingapirca, 50 km north of Cuenca, was built with the same mortarless, polished-stone technique as those in Peru, but the site is less impressive than Peruvian ones. Excavation and reconstruction work is still going on. Admission to the ruins and museum is US$4. The museum is open Monday to Saturday from 9 am to 5 pm. Guides (both the human and the written varieties) are available.

Ingapirca village has a craft shop, simple restaurants and a basic pensión. A shelter by the ruins may be available for overnighting. Friday is market day.

Direct buses go from Cuenca on weekdays or there's a bus to El Tambo (seven km beyond Cañar) from where it's an eight-km walk. Trucks (US$0.50) and taxis are available in El Tambo; beware of overcharging. El Tambo has a basic hotel and Cañar has two.

Area Nacional de Recreación Cajas
This high páramo 30 km west of Cuenca is famous for its many lakes (good fishing) and

rugged camping and hiking. Buses (two hours) leave Cuenca at 6.30 am (except Thursday) from San Sebastián church and return in the afternoon. Entry is US$10. You may be able to sleep in a refuge and camping is allowed. The INEFAN office in Cuenca has information and basic maps.

GUALACEO, CHORDELEG & SIGSIG
These villages are famous for their Sunday markets. If you start early from Cuenca, you can visit all three and be back in the afternoon. Gualaceo has the biggest market, with fruit and vegetables, animals and various household goods. Chordeleg's market, five km away, is smaller and more touristy but sells textiles and jewellery. Sígsig market is 25 km from Gualaceo and less visited by tourists.

There are a few cheap hotels in Gualaceo and a basic one in Sígsig. Chordeleg has a small but interesting museum, on the Plaza.

Getting There & Away
Buses from Cuenca to Gualaceo leave about every hour (more often on Sunday). Walk or take a local bus to Chordeleg. A 40-minute local bus ride will take you to Sígsig, from where there are buses to Cuenca.

LOJA
Loja is an attractive provincial city with beautiful surrounding countryside. It makes a convenient stopover on the route to Peru via Macará. The village of Vilcabamba and the Parque Nacional Podocarpus are delightful attractions not far from Loja.

Information
CETUR (☎ 572 964) is at B Valdivieso 08-22. INEFAN (☎ 571 534) is at Miguel Riofrío 13-54. Banks on the Parque Central give poor exchange rates. It's better to change in Cuenca or Macará. The Peruvian Consul (☎ 571 668) is at Sucre 10-56.

The main market day is Sunday. The annual fiesta of the Virgen del Cisne is on 8 September; it's celebrated with huge parades and a produce fair.

Hidaltur (☎ 571 031), Bolívar 10-33, sells

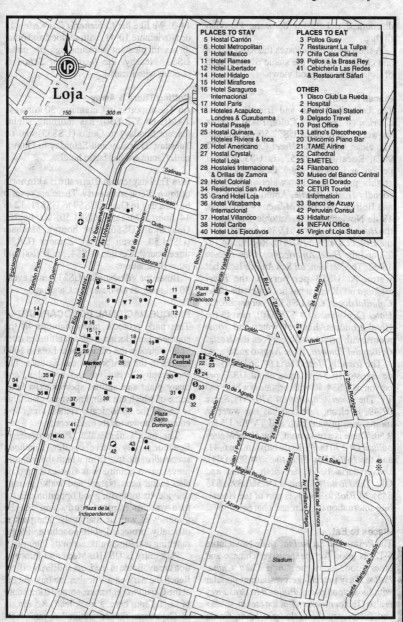

Loja

0   150   300 m

PLACES TO STAY
5 Hostal Carrión
6 Hotel Metropolitan
8 Hotel Mexico
11 Hotel Ramses
12 Hotel Libertador
14 Hotel Hidalgo
15 Hotel Miraflores
16 Hotel Saraguros
   Internacional
17 Hotel Paris
18 Hoteles Acapulco,
   Londres & Cuxubamba
19 Hostal Pasaje
25 Hostal Quinara,
   Hoteles Riviera & Inca
26 Hotel Americano
27 Hostal Crystal,
   Hotel Loja
28 Hostales Internacional
   & Orillas de Zamora
29 Hotel Colonial
34 Residencial San Andres
35 Grand Hotel Loja
36 Hotel Vilcabamba
   Internacional
37 Hostal Villanoco
38 Hotel Caribe
40 Hotel Los Ejecutivos

PLACES TO EAT
3 Pollos Gusy
7 Restaurant La Tullpa
17 Chifa Casa China
39 Pollos a la Brasa Rey
41 Cebichería Las Redes
   & Restaurant Safari

OTHER
1 Disco Club La Rueda
2 Hospital
4 Petrol (Gas) Station
9 Delgado Travel
10 Post Office
13 Latino's Discotheque
20 Unicornio Piano Bar
21 TAME Airline
22 Cathedral
23 EMETEL
24 Filanbanco
30 Museo del Banco Central
31 Cine El Dorado
32 CETUR Tourist
   Information
33 Banco de Azuay
42 Peruvian Consul
43 Hidaltur
44 INEFAN Office
45 Virgin of Loja Statue

ECUADOR

discounted tickets for domestic Peruvian flights.

A short walk east crosses the Río Zamora and climbs a hill to the statue of the Virgin of Loja; there are good views.

Places to Stay

The basic but clean and friendly *Hostal Carrión* (☎ 561 127), Colón 16-30, has hot showers and charges US$2.50 per person. The clean and decent *Hotel Caribe* (☎ 572 902), Rocafuerte 15-52, is US$2.25 per person, and has hot water. Other OK places at this price with hot water include the friendly *Hostal Pasaje*, Antonio Eguiguren and Bolívar, the *Hotel México* (☎ 570 581), 18 de Noviembre and Antonio Eguiguren, the *Hotel Londres* (☎ 561 936), Sucre 07-41, the *Hotel Loja* (☎ 570 241), Rocafuerte 15-27, and the *Hotel Americano*, 10 de Agosto 16-62. The *Residencial San Andrés* lacks hot water. At US$3 per person, the *Hotel Hidalgo* is OK and it has hot water; the *Hotel Colonial* doesn't. At US$3.50 per person, the *Hotel Cuxubamba* (☎ 578 570), next to the Hotel Londres, has hot water and some rooms with private bath, as does the *Hostal Orillas del Zamora*, 10 de Agosto and Sucre.

The friendly *Hotel Paris* (☎ 561 639), 10 de Agosto 16-37, charges about US$3 per person or US$4.50 with private hot bath and TV. The *Hotel Acapulco* (☎ 570 651), Sucre 07-49, is clean, safe and has hot water in rooms with private bath and TV for US$6/9.50. There is a restaurant. The *Hotel Metropolitan* (☎ 570 007), 18 de Noviembre 6-41, and the *Hotel Los Ejecutivos* (☎ 960 004), Universitaria 10-96, are both similar and OK. The *Hostal Villanoco* (☎ 560 895, 575 845), M Riofrío 16-61, is part of the Hostelling International chain and charges US$7.

Places to Eat

The *Restaurant La Tullpa*, 18 de Noviembre 5-12, is good for inexpensive Chinese and other food, as is the *Chifa Casa China*. *Pollos Gusy* is a chicken restaurant popular with local youngsters. *Pollos a la Brasa Rey* is also OK for chicken. For ice cream, snacks and coffee, try the *Heladería Sinai*, Colón

14-3. We like the *Cebichería Las Redes*, 18 de Noviembre 10-41, with seafood and other dishes in pleasant surroundings for under US$3. Nearby, the *Restaurant Safari* is popular with locals.

Getting There & Away

Air The airport is in Catamayo, 30 km west. TAME (☎ 573 030) has morning flights (except Sunday) to Quito (US$35) and on Tuesday, Thursday and Saturday to Guayaquil. Catamayo has basic hotels.

Bus The busy terminal terrestre is a km north of town. Book seats early. There are several buses a day to Quito (US$9 to US$11, 12 to 14 hours), Macará (US$4.50, six hours), Guayaquil (US$6, nine hours), Machala (US$4.50, seven hours), Zamora (US$2, three hours), Cuenca (US$4, six hours) and other destinations.

Buses for Vilcabamba (US$1) leave every 30 minutes, as do buses for Catamayo.

PARQUE NACIONAL PODOCARPUS

This park protects many habitats in the southern Ecuadorian Andes at altitudes from 3600 metres in the páramo near Loja to 1000 metres in the rainforests near Zamora. The topography is rugged and complex, and many plant and animal species exist here, some of which are found nowhere else. This is one of the biologically richest areas in a country known for its biodiversity.

The park's namesake, *Podocarpus*, is Ecuador's only native conifer. *Cinchona succirubra*, the tree from which the malarial preventative quinine was first extracted, is also found here. Nature and walking trails provide visitors with good opportunities for bird-watching, plant study and maybe glimpses of various mammals. The park is officially protected, but poaching, illegal ranching and logging threaten its integrity.

Park entry is US$10. Maps and information are available at the Loja INEFAN office. Reach the park on a Vilcabamba bus; get off at the Cajanuma entrance, some 10 km south of Loja. From here, a track leads 8.5 km up to Cajanuma ranger station. A taxi costs about US$10 from Loja. Camping is allowed, but carry everything you need. Access from Vilcabamba is possible.

VILCABAMBA

This village, 45 km south of Loja, is in the 'valley of longevity', where people supposedly live to be over 100. Scientists find no basis for this claim, but the area is attractive and travellers enjoy relaxing here for a few days. Tourism is booming and both locals and gringos sometimes complain that it's a bit of a scene. Travel sensitively and responsibly here.

Information

A local tourist office is on the plaza. Money exchange is poor so think ahead. The telephone service is unreliable.

Activities

Orlando Falco, a trained, English-speaking naturalist guide, can be contacted in his craft shop, Primavera, on the plaza. He leads recommended tours to the Parque Nacional Podocarpus and other areas for about US$15 per person, plus US$10 park fee. The folks at the Cabañas Río Yambala have a private reserve, camping gear, horse rental and plenty of hiking/riding opportunities with or without guides. Gavilan (ask at tourist information) rents horses for three-day treks at US$75 per person. Several other people rent horses, and hotels will arrange this as well. Massages are advertised – nice after riding or hiking. Spanish lessons are available.

Places to Stay & Eat

The basic, cold-water *Hotel Valle Sagrado* (☎ 673 179), on the plaza, is US$2.25 per person and often full with budget travellers. It has a popular vegetarian restaurant. The similarly priced *Hostal Mandango* behind the bus station also has some rooms with private bath for US$3.25 per person. Warm showers are available and there's a cheap restaurant. For a family stay, call *Señora Lydia Toledo* (☎ 673 130), a block from the plaza. She charges US$3 per person with shared hot bath and kitchen privileges. The

clean *Posada Real*, behind the hospital, charges US$5/7 for singles/doubles with bath. *Orlando Falco* at the Primavera shop rents out an inexpensive house.

Almost a km from the square is the *Parador Turístico Vilcabamba* (☎ 673 122), with a restaurant, where rooms with private bath are US$10/17 (ask for low-season discount). Farther out on this road is the more expensive *Hostería Vilcabamba* (☎ 673 131), with a good restaurant, pool, massage, jacuzzi and Spanish lessons all available to the general public.

The *Hostal Madre Tierra* (☎ 673 123), two km north of town (reservations to PO Box 354, Loja), is a rustic, laid-back hostal run by an Ecuadorian-Canadian couple. Rooms are in damp cabins spread over a steep hillside, sometimes reached by long, slippery paths (torch needed). Lodging is US$10 to US$15 (depending on the room) per person including breakfast and dinner. Showers are shared. Local hiking and riding information, a book exchange, a steam bath, a video room and table games are available. It's popular and often full, but it's not to everyone's taste.

About four km south-east of town, the rustic *Cabañas Río Yambala* is run by friendly Charlie and Sarah. You can walk there or hire a taxi or pick-up for US$4. Miguel Carpio, half a block from the plaza, is their recommended driver. They have rooms and cabins, some with private baths, from US$3 to US$8 per person. A vegetarian restaurant and kitchen privileges are available and the owners arrange camping, hiking, and horse riding. This place may be full in the high season but reservations can be left at Commercial Karmita (☎ 637 186), a shop on the plaza.

Getting There & Away

Buses to Loja leave hourly.

MACARA

The small border town of Macará offers a more scenic and less travelled route to Peru than the conventional border crossing at

Huaquillas. The Peruvian Consul (☎ 694 030), is at Bolívar 127.

Places to Stay & Eat

In the town centre are a few cheap, basic, cold-water hotels charging about US$3 to US$6 per person. The *Hotel Paraíso*, Veintimilla 553, the *Hotel Amazonas*, M Rengel 418, and *Hotel Espiga de Oro* are among the better ones and may have private baths. There are a few basic restaurants near the corner of Bolívar and M Rengel, open only at meal times.

Getting There & Away

Transportes Loja has six buses a day (last one at 3 pm) to Loja (US$4.50, six hours), and a morning bus to Guayaquil and Quito (20 hours). Transportes Cariamanga has two morning buses to Loja.

To/From Peru Pick-up trucks leave the market often for the border, less than three km away. Bargain hard or walk. Border hours are daily from 8 am to 6 pm. Formalities are OK if your papers are in order. Peru doesn't have much accommodation until Sullana, 150 km away. Cross in the morning for bus connections.

Moneychangers are found in the market and at the border. Banks don't change money. Arrive with minimal Ecuadorian or Peruvian money and change into US dollars before crossing.

The Oriente

The Oriente is that part of Ecuador east of the Andes in the lowlands of the Amazon Basin. A 1942 treaty ceded a large portion of the Oriente to Peru. This treaty is internationally recognised, but Ecuador continues to claim the land as far as Iquitos and the Amazon. The dispute means that foreign travellers are unable to cross the border into the Peruvian jungle.

More travellers visit the northern Oriente; the region south of the Río Pastaza has a real sense of remoteness. Buses from Cuenca go through Limón (officially General Plaza Gutiérrez) to Macas. Buses from Loja go via Zamora to Limón and on to Macas. From Macas, there is now a road to Puyo and the northern Oriente. Buses from Quito frequently go to the northern Oriente towns of Puyo, Tena, Coca and Lago Agrio.

The Oriente section is described from south to north in the following section.

ZAMORA

Three hours from Loja by bus, this town on the edge of the jungle has boomed since the recent discovery of gold in Nambija, a few km to the north. Food prices are relatively high. There are military checkpoints near the town. Zamora has a few cheap hotels, and there's an entrance to the Parque Nacional Podocarpus, described earlier.

Continuing by bus into the southern Oriente, you will find basic hotels in the small towns of Gualaquiza, Limón, Méndez and Sucúa.

MACAS

This small, old and friendly town is the capital of the province of Morona-Santiago and it's the biggest in the southern Oriente. A couple of tour companies are beginning to offer excursions into the area.

The best hotel is the *Peñón del Oriente* (☎ 700 124), near the bus terminal. It's US$10 per person with private hot bath or US$4 with cold bath. The second-best is the *Hotel Orquideas* (☎ 700 970) for US$6 per person with hot water or US$5 with cold. The *Residencial Upano* (☎ 700 057) is the best of the cheapest at US$3 per person. The best restaurants are considered to be the *Pagoda*, next to the Hotel Peñón del Oriente, and the *El Jardín*.

TAME (☎ 700 162) has Monday, Wednesday and Friday flights to Quito (US$45). TAO (☎ 700 174) flies light aircraft to jungle destinations. The bus terminal has several daily departures for Cuenca and Gualaquiza. Several buses a day leave for the Río Pastaza, which you cross by a footbridge. On the other side, buses wait to continue to Puyo.

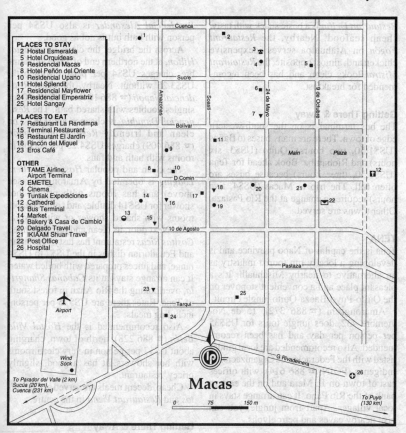

PLACES TO STAY
2 Hostal Esmeralda
5 Hotel Orquídeas
6 Residencial Macas
8 Hotel Peñón del Oriente
10 Residencial Upano
11 Hotel Splendit
17 Residencial Mayflower
24 Residencial Emperatriz
25 Hotel Sangay

PLACES TO EAT
7 Restaurant La Randimpa
15 Terminal Restaurant
16 Restaurant El Jardín
18 Rincón del Miguel
23 Eros Café

OTHER
1 TAME Airline,
  Airport Terminal
3 EMETEL
4 Cinema
9 Tuntiak Expediciones
12 Cathedral
13 Bus Terminal
14 Market
19 Bakery & Casa de Cambio
20 Delgado Travel
21 IKIAAM Shuar Travel
22 Post Office
26 Hospital

Macas

0   75   150 m

To Parador del Valle (2 km)
Sucúa (20 km),
Cuenca (231 km)

To Puyo
(130 km)

PUYO

North of the Río Pastaza are the provinces of
Pastaza, Napo and Sucumbios, which make
up the northern Oriente. Two good roads,
with impressive views, go from Quito into
the northern Oriente.

Puyo, on the edge of the jungle, is an
important town used as a stopover for travellers. There may be good views of the
volcanoes to the west. There's a passport
check near the Shell-Mera airstrip, a few km
north of town (bus drivers will stop).

Places to Stay

Hotel Granada, by the market, charges

US$2 per person or US$3.50 with bath, and
is just OK. *Hotel Chasi* (☎ 883 059), on 9 de
Octubre, north of the market, is quite good
for US$2.50 per person or US$4.50 with
bath. There are several other cheapies near
the market. The clean *Hotel Barandua*
(☎ 885 604), Villami at Atahualpa, charges
US$5 per person with bath. The good *Hotel
Araucano* (☎ 883 834), C Marin 575, has
rooms from US$4 to US$11 per person.
Better rooms have TV, fan, fridge and bath.

Places to Eat

The *Chifa Oriental* next to the Hotel Araucano is OK. Farther west on C Marin, the

Restaurant Delfín is a basic shack with tasty, cheap seafood. Nearby, the *Restaurant Fogón* on Atahualpa serves inexpensive chicken and, almost opposite, the *Restaurant Mistral* looks clean and has been recommended for breakfast.

Getting There & Away

The bus terminal is on the south-western edge of town. There are many buses to Baños (US$1.50, two hours), Quito (US$3, six hours) and Riobamba. Book ahead for Tena (US$1.50, three hours) because buses are often full. The trip to Macas (US$4, five hours) requires a change at the Río Pastaza. Other towns are served.

TENA

Tena is the capital of Napo province and is developing a locally run tourist industry as an alternative to nearby Misahuallí. It's a pleasant place and a convenient stopover on the Quito-Puyo-Baeza-Quito jungle circuit.

Amarongachi (☎ 886 372), 15 de Noviembre 432, does jungle tours for US$35 per person per day and has been recommended. Also recommended are local guides listed with the Federación de Organizaciones Indígenas (FOIN; ☎ 886 614), with offices east of town on JL Mera and on the eastern bank of the Río Pano. It can arrange stays in local villages. Apart from jungle, you can visit nearby caves and petroglyphs.

Places to Stay & Eat

The cheapest hotels suffer from water shortages. The basic *Hotel Amazonas*, on the corner of the plaza, is just over US$2 per person and is OK if you can get an outside room. The *Residencial Jumandy*, a block north of the main plaza, and the *Hotel Baños* near the bus terminal are similarly priced and just acceptable. By the bus terminal, the *Hostal Camba Huasi* (☎ 887 429) charges US$4/7 with cold bath in clean, bare rooms.

The friendly *Residencial Enmita*, on Bolívar, is about US$4 per person in rooms with cold bath (less without). The *Enmita Restaurant* is simple but good. Nearby, the

Residencial Alexander is also US$4 per person with bath but is not as good.

Across the bridge, the clean *Residencial Hilton*, at the northern end of 15 de Noviembre, charges US$4 per person with bath, US$3.25 without. Nearby, the clean *Residencial Napoli* (☎ 886 194) is US$4/6.50 for singles/doubles with shared bath. The *Residencial Danubio* is cheaper and OK. The clean and friendly *Residencial Alemán* (☎ 886 409) charges US$4.25 per person in rooms with bath and fans.

The clean and popular *Hostal Travellers Lodging* is operated by Amarongachi (see above) and has rooms with private hot shower for US$14 double, and some cheaper rooms with shared shower or with several beds. Next door, its clean and recommended *Cositas Ricas* restaurant has tasty vegetarian and Ecuadorian dishes in the US$2 to US$4 range, and juices prepared with boiled water. It can arrange stays at its *Cabañas Shangrila*, overlooking the Río Anzu in forest south of Tena. Rates there are US$25 per person, including meals.

Also recommended is the *Hostal Villa Belén* (☎ 886 228), north of town, charging about US$7 per person in very clean rooms with hot showers. It has a good, slightly pricey, restaurant.

Cheap, decent meals are served at *Chuquitos* and *Restaurant Viena* in the centre.

Getting There & Away

The bus terminal is 1.5 km south of town. There are several buses a day for Quito via Baeza (US$4, six hours), Lago Agrio (US$7, 10 hours), Coca (US$5.50, seven hours), Baeza (US$2), Baños (US$3.50, five hours) and other places.

Military planes fly to Shell and Coca; ask at the airstrip. Seats are hard to get.

MISAHUALLI

This village is popular for jungle tours. However, little is virgin jungle: the area has been colonised and most animals have gone. What you can see is many jungle birds, tropical flowers, army ants and dazzling

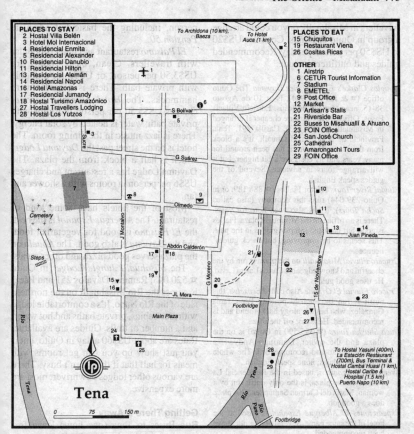

PLACES TO STAY
2 Hostal Villa Belén
3 Hotel Mol Internacional
4 Residencial Enmita
5 Residencial Alexander
10 Residencial Danubio
11 Residencial Hilton
13 Residencial Alemán
14 Residencial Napoli
16 Hotel Amazonas
17 Residencial Jumandy
18 Hostal Turismo Amazónico
27 Hostal Travellers Lodging
28 Hostal Los Yutzos

PLACES TO EAT
15 Chuquitos
19 Restaurant Viena
26 Cositas Ricas

OTHER
1 Airstrip
6 CETUR Tourist Information
7 Stadium
8 EMETEL
9 Post Office
12 Market
20 Artisan's Stalls
21 Riverside Bar
22 Buses to Misahuallí & Ahuano
23 FOIN Office
24 San José Church
25 Cathedral
27 Amarongachi Tours
29 FOIN Office

To Archidona (10 km), Baeza
To Hotel Auca (1 km)

S Bolívar
Sucre
G Suárez
Olmedo
J Montalvo
Amazonas
Abdón Calderón
G Moreno
JL Mera
15 de Noviembre
Juan Pineda
Cemetery
Steps
Footbridge
Main Plaza

Tena

0   75   150 m

To Hostal Yasuni (400m),
La Estación Restaurant
(700m), Bus Terminal &
Hostal Camba Huasi (1 km),
Hostal Caribe &
Hospital (1.5 km),
Puerto Napo (10 km)

Río Tena
Río Pano
Footbridge

butterflies. You can arrange an excursion deeper into the jungle. This requires patience and money but is still less expensive than most jungle expeditions.

Moneychanging facilities are limited, so bring sucres.

Jungle Tours

Guided tours of up to 18 days are available, but few guides speak English. Longer tours are recommended if you hope to see wildlife. Some tours visit Huaorani villages. Most are degrading for the Indians and not recommended. A small number of guides have good relationships with the Huaorani; they are mostly in Coca.

Plan details carefully to avoid disappointment. Costs, food, equipment, itinerary and group numbers must be agreed upon before the tour. A good guide is essential and you may have to wait for a specific one. Some outfitters switch guides at the last moment; this is not to your advantage. The SAEC makes good recommendations, or talk to other travellers. Guides should have a licence. Tours usually require a minimum of four people and are cheaper per person with larger groups. It's easy to meet up with other travellers in Misahuallí, or you could arrange a group in Quito or Baños. Costs are US$20 to US$50 per person per day. Recommended guides and outfitters include:

Douglas Clarke's Expediciones Dayuma The Quito office (☎ & fax 564 924), is at 10 de Agosto 38-15, near Mariana de Jesús, Edificio Villacís Pasos, Office 301. Tours are cheaper if arranged in Misahuallí (☎ 571 513), Casilla 291, Tena, Provincia de Napo. In Misahuallí, it's a block from the Plaza. This outfit has been around for many years and its costs are a bit higher, but it will arrange tours in advance. Several of the guides speak English.

Fluvial River Tours Héctor Fiallos (☎ 886 189, or in Quito 239 044) runs this company (also called *Sacha Tours*); it has also been here for years. There is an office on the Misahuallí plaza. Fiallos is good but has used inferior guides in the past. This seems to be improving, but check guides' licences.

Crucero Fluvial Misahuallí on the plaza is run by the cheerful and knowledgeable Carlos Lastra Lasso. He uses good guides.

Crucero Fluvial El Oriente Also called *Ecoselva*, this outfit is run by English-speaking Pepe Tapia González, who has a biology background and is recommended. He is just off the plaza.

Ñuca Shasha Tours (☎ 355 590 in Quito) is on the plaza and the owner, Domingo Andy, is a Quichua Indian and recommended. The whole staff are Quichuas; none speak English.

Aventuras Amazónicas, based in the Residencial La Posada on the plaza, is the only outfit run by a woman, María del Carmen Santander. This place does a good job.

Expediciones El Albergue Español is based at the hotel of the same name. Several of its guides have been recommended.

Other Guides They should produce a licence on request. Recommended are Sócrates Nevárez, Alfredo Andrade, Luis Duarte, Billy Clarke (a woman), Marcos Estrada and Elías Arteaga. There are others; they have signs on the plaza.

Places to Stay & Eat

Water and electricity failures are frequent. Water may stop after about 7 pm. *Residencial El Balcón de Napo*, on the plaza, has small rooms; ask for one with a window. It's clean, though the showers are a bit grungy. At under US$2 per person, it's the cheapest. The rambling old *Residencial La Posada*, nearby, charges a little more. There are others on the plaza for about US$2.50 per person, including the basic but adequate *Pensión 50*.

El Paisano restaurant and hotel is popular with travellers. Clean, basic rooms are US$3.50 per person, or US$9 for a double with private bath. There is a garden with hammocks. The *Hotel Albergue Español* charges US$5.50 per person in rooms with private bath; water is heated by solar energy. There is jazz music in the dining room. The hotel is on the street past the *Dayuma Lodge*, which is half a block from the plaza. The Dayuma Lodge has a restaurant and charges US$6 per person in rooms with a shower and fan.

Most of the hotels have some kind of restaurant. The *Albergue Español* is the best, the *El Paisano* is good for vegetarian food, and the *Dayuma* is also good. The *Abuela* on the plaza serves good pizza and other meals.

The *Misahuallí Jungle Lodge* (in Quito ☎ 520 043; Ramírez Dávalos 251 and Páez) is across the Río Misahuallí on the northern side of the Río Napo. It's a comfortable lodge with nice cabins, private baths and hot water, and a number of trails. Guides are available. Rates are about US$60 a day in Quito, but if you just show up you can get rooms with meals for half that if they aren't busy. There are various other lodges downriver; most are more expensive.

Getting There & Away

Bus Buses to Tena (one hour) leave frequently from the plaza.

Boat Motorised dugout canoes take all day to reach Coca; they leave every few days. Tickets are US$20. If there is a group of eight or so, you can go any day. You must register your passport with the Capitanía (port captain). Be prepared for strong sun: bring sunscreen and a hat.

Daily canoes go to various villages along the river, and as far up as halfway to Coca.

AROUND MISAHUALLI
Jatun Sacha

Jatun Sacha, a rainforest conservation and research foundation, operates the highly recommended *Cabañas Aliñahui* (in Quito ☎ 253 267, fax 253 266; Río Coca 1734 and Isla Fernandina). The lodge is on the southern bank of the Río Napo, about seven km east of Misahuallí, and can be reached by canoe or by road (backtrack 17 km west to Puerto Napo, then 26 km east to the lodge). The Jatun Sacha research facility is three km away. Information is also available from co-owners Health and Habitat (☎ (415) 383-6130, fax 381-9214), 76 Lee St, Mill Valley, CA 94941, USA.

There are 22 rooms in 10 cabins, and each cabin has a bathhouse with solar-heated showers. The lodge is near primary rainforest and guided hikes to both the forest and the research facility are offered. Professional scientists and volunteers can work and stay at Jatun Sacha. Profits from Aliñahui go towards research, conservation, education and training programmes. Rates are US$61 per day, including good meals, or US$72 a day including guided tours. Children under 12 get a 40% discount. This place is well recommended.

The research facility has dormitory accommodation for US$20 per person, including meals.

COCA

This sprawling oil town, at the junction of the Coca and Napo rivers, is officially named Puerto Francisco de Orellana. River travellers must report to the Capitanía by the landing dock. Moneychanging and telephone facilities are available, but poor.

Tours

There is a burgeoning tourist industry; see the Misahuallí section for more background. Coca is closer to large tracts of virgin jungle, but tourism is not yet as advanced as in Misahuallí. Trips down the Río Tiputini and into the **Parque Nacional Yasuní** are possible. This is the largest Ecuadorian national park, and it contains a variety of rainforest habitats, wildlife and a few Huaorani communities. Unfortunately, there is no money for staffing and protection so poaching and,

increasingly, oil exploration are damaging the park.

Some guides offer tours to visit Huaorani villages. The Huaorani remain ambivalent about tourism; some villages have arrangements with particular guides whereas others prefer no tourism. A good source of information about this is Randy Smith (☎ 880 606, 880 451) who works with Amazon Jungle Adventures in Coca. This company employs Huaorani staff with the support of the tribe. Safari Tour in Quito can put you in contact with this outfit or you can ask at Pappa Dan's restaurant in Coca.

Other guides who have positive relationships with the Huaorani are Ernesto Juanka at Pankitour Alternativo (☎ 880 405), 6 de Diciembre and García Moreno in Coca; Julio Jarrín (☎ 880 251) opposite the Hotel Oasis; and Juan Enomenga – ask for him on the waterfront. They don't speak English.

Places to Stay & Eat

Water shortages are frequent. The *Hotel El Auca* (☎ 880 127) is popular (often full before nightfall) and isn't bad for US$10 a double, or in cabins for US$10/18 for singles/doubles with bath. It has the nicest garden in Coca and an acceptable restaurant. Three very basic residenciales a block from the Auca charge US$2.50 to US$3.50 per person, are popular with oil workers, and are not recommended for women alone. The similarly poor *Pensión Rosita* is by the port. Other cheapies are the *Residencial Macará*, *Hotel Cofan* and *Residencial Las Brisas*. A better place is the *Residencial Cotopaxi* at US$4.50 per person with bath. The *Hotel Oasis* (☎ 880 174), is OK for US$10 a double with bath and fan. The *Hotel Florida* (☎ 880 177) and the *Hotel Delfín Azul* are similarly priced and OK. The *Hostería La Misión* (☎ 880 260) is the best hotel at US$16/20 with fan, or US$25/30 with air-con. It has a good, pricey restaurant.

Locals recommend the *Cevichería Amazonas* and *Ocaso Restaurant* as the best outside the hotels. The *Safari* and *La Costeñita* are cheaper and quite good too. The *Restaurant El Cóndor* is a basic chicken

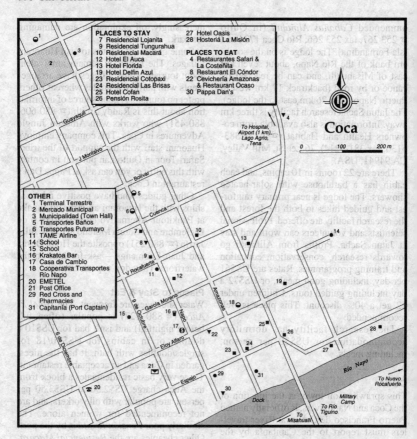

PLACES TO STAY
7 Residencial Lojanita
9 Residencial Tungurahua
10 Residencial Macará
12 Hotel El Auca
13 Hotel Florida
19 Hotel Delfin Azul
23 Residencial Cotopaxi
24 Residencial Las Brisas
25 Hotel Cofan
26 Pensión Rosita
27 Hotel Oasis
28 Hostería La Misión

PLACES TO EAT
4 Restaurantes Safari & La Costeñita
8 Restaurant El Cóndor
22 Cevichería Amazonas & Restaurant Ocaso
30 Pappa Dan's

OTHER
1 Terminal Terrestre
2 Mercado Municipal
3 Municipalidad (Town Hall)
5 Transportes Baños
6 Transportes Putumayo
11 TAME Airline
14 School
15 School
16 Krakatoa Bar
17 Casa de Cambio
18 Cooperativa Transportes Río Napo
20 EMETEL
21 Post Office
29 Red Cross and Pharmacies
31 Capitanía (Port Captain)

Coca

To Hospital, Airport (1 km), Lago Agrio, Tena

0   100   200 m

Río Napo

To Nuevo Rocafuerte

To Misahuallí

To Río Tiguino

Dock

Military Camp

place. *Pappa Dan's* opens at 4 pm and is a recommended bar with burgers and similar food.

Getting There & Around
Air TAME flies to Quito (US$51) daily except Sunday. Book well ahead. The airport is two km north of town.

Bus There are bus offices in town and at the terminal terrestre, north of town. Make sure you know where your bus will leave from. Several buses a day go to Quito (US$10, nine hours via Loreto, 14 hours via Lago Agrio),

Tena (US$6, six hours), Lago Agrio (US$2, three hours), and other jungle towns. There are night buses to Ambato.

Boat Boats to Misahuallí (US$20, up to 14 hours against the current) leave every few days. Boats to Nuevo Rocafuerte (US$25, nine to 12 hours), on the Peruvian border, require a military permit. Boats leave on Monday and return Friday. Passenger boats to intermediate destinations leave most days. Ask at the dock. Hiring your own boat is pricey but you can often get rides for a few dollars on various boats heading downriver.

ECUADOR

DOWN THE RIO NAPO

Several villages and lodges east of Coca can be reached down the Río Napo. Ask at the Coca docks for boats. *Hacienda Primavera* (in Quito ☎ 565 999, José Trevinio 114 and 12 de Octubre), is about one hour from Coca. It costs about US$20 a day to stay here, including meals, or more if you arrange your stay in Quito. Guided excursions are available at extra cost.

Two hours east of Coca is the mission of **Pompeya**. From here an eight-km road goes north to **Limoncocha** village, where there is a basic place to stay (US$2.50 per person) and eat. Nearby is the locally run Limoncocha Biological Reserve, with a beautiful lake recommended for bird-watching at dawn and dusk. A visit costs US$16 per person. Limoncocha can also be reached by several buses a day from the oil base of **Shushufindi** (which is a two or three-hour bus trip from either Coca or Lago Agrio).

About an hour east of Pompeya, are the well-recommended but expensive *Sacha* and *La Selva* lodges (over US$100 per night). **Pañacocha** village, five hours east of Coca, has several simple places to stay for about US$2.50 a person. Food and local guides are available. About five more hours brings you to the border at **Nuevo Rocafuerte**, where a basic *pensión* (US$3.50) and local guides are available. Tours up the Río Yasuní into the **Parque Nacional Yasuní** can be arranged.

LAGO AGRIO

Built in virgin jungle after oil was discovered in the 1970s, Lago is Ecuador's largest new oil town. A tourism industry is developing to visit the nearby **Reserva Faunística Cuyabeno**. This protects the rainforest home of Siona and Secoya Indians and conserves the Cuyabeno river and lake system, but there have been numerous oil spills. Nevertheless, parts of the reserve are still pristine and well worth a visit (US$20 entry). Most visitors make arrangements in Quito, Tena, Misahuallí or Coca. An outfitter in Lago Agrio is Harpía Eagles Tours (☎ 830 438), Río Amazonas 117.

A Sunday morning market is visited by the local Cofan Indians. They may take you to their village of Dureno, from which further explorations are possible with Cofan guides.

Places to Stay & Eat

Mosquito nets or fans are worth having in your room. Water shortages are common. The cheapest places are about US$3.50 per person but they are very basic and run-down. These include the *Chimborazo, Río Amazonas, Putumayo* and *Lago Agrio*. Better places at US$4.50 per person are the *Residencial Secoya*, *Hotel Willigram* (you'll need a padlock for the doors) and the *Hotel Oro Negro*. The clean *Hotel San Carlos* has some simple rooms at US$4.50 per person, and singles/doubles with air-con and bath for US$12/16. The *Residencial Ecuador* is US$4.50 per person or US$7 with bath. The *Hotel D'Marios* is US$7 per person with bath and is clean and good. The *Hostal Machala 2* (☎ 830 073) is quite good at US$9 per person with bath and TV. The *Hotel Sayonara* (☎ 830 562) is US$6 per person with bath and fan, US$8 with air-con and US$10 with TV. Others at this price are the *Hotels Paris, Los Guacamayos* and *La Cabaña*.

Of several restaurants, the one under the *Hotel D'Marios* is the best, with a choice of dishes for about US$3.

Getting There & Away

Air The airport is five km east of town (taxi, US$2). TAME has Monday to Saturday flights to Quito (US$51); book in advance.

Bus Transportes Baños has eight buses daily to Quito (US$8.50, eight hours), and there are several other companies. For Tena, take a bus to Baeza and wait. Open-sided *rancheros* go from the market area to Coca and other jungle towns.

To/From Colombia Get your exit stamp at Migración, Quito 111, near the Colombian Consulate. Rancheros from the market go 21 km north to La Punta, on the Río San Miguel. Canoes cross here to Puerto Colón or go downriver one hour to San Miguel, both in

Lago Agrio

0   100   200 m

To Airport
(5 km)

PLACES TO STAY
2 Hotel San Carlos
5 Hotel Paris
7 Hostal El Cofan
9 Residencial Chimborazo
10 Residencial Secoya
11 Hotel Oro Negro
12 Residencial Ecuador
14 Hotel Sayonara
17 Hostal Machala 2
18 Hotel Imperial Lago

20 Residencial Lago Agrio
21 Hotel La Cabaña
22 Residencial Putumayo,
     Hotel Willigram
24 Hoteles D'Marios &
     Río Amazonas
25 Hotel Los Guacamayos

OTHER
1 TAME Airline
3 EMETEL

4 Cine Oriente
6 Banco Internacional
8 Cinema
10 Transportes Baños,
     Other Bus Companies
13 Colombian Consulate
15 Casa de Cambio
16 Post Office
19 Market
23 Transportes Occidentales
     (Buses)

Colombia. San Miguel has a basic hotel and Colombian immigration. From Puerto Colón or San Miguel, buses continue into Colombia via the towns of Puerto Asís (about five hours) and Mocoa (about nine hours), both with hotels. Mocoa has an immigration office.

The Western Lowlands

West of the Andes is a large coastal plain with banana and palm plantations. The descent from the mountains is dramatic, particularly if you take the route from Quito to Santo Domingo.

SANTO DOMINGO DE LOS COLORADOS

This city is an important road hub and a convenient place to break the journey to the coast. The descent from the highlands is spectacular, and best done in the morning to avoid afternoon fog.

The area was famous for the Colorado (Tsachila) Indians, who painted their faces with black stripes and dyed their hair a bril-

To Esmeraldas (85 km)

To Post Office (500 m)

To Lions Traffic Circle (500m), Hotel Toachi (1 km), Hotel Zaracay & Hotel Tropical Inn (1.3 km), Río Toachi (4.5 km), Quito (130 km)

To Terminal Terrestre (2 km)

PLACES TO STAY
2 Hotel Turistas 2
3 Hotel Ejecutivo
4 Hotel Genova
5 Hotel El Colorado
7 Hotel Ejecutivo
9 Residencial Madrid
10 Hotel Amanbay, Residencial Viajero
12 Residencial San José
13 Hostal Jennefer
14 Hotel Caleta
15 Hotel Turistas 3
16 Pensión Guayaquil

18 Residencial San Martín
20 Residencial Ontaneda
24 Hostal Santo Domingo
25 Pensión San José, Hotel Turistas 1
26 Hostal Galápagos
30 Pensión El Oro
31 Hostal Las Brisas

PLACES TO EAT
12 Pollos Gus Chicken Restaurant
17 Chifa Happy

21 Chicken Restaurant
22 Chicken Restaurant
28 Elite Restaurant

OTHER
1 Market
6 Local Buses
8 Market
11 Police
19 Banco del Pichincha
23 EMETEL
27 Teatro Amazonas
29 Filanbanco

Santo Domingo de los Colorados

0   100   200 m

liant red. Their traditions are now almost lost and they prefer to be left alone. Taxis go to **Chihuilpe**, seven km south of Santo Domingo, where there is a small cultural museum.

Sunday is the main market day, so the town closes down on Monday. There's little of interest in this large town.

Places to Stay

The basic but clean and helpful *Residencial San Martín* (☎ 750 813), on 29 de Mayo, is US$2.50 per person. The basic *Hotel Turistas 1, 2,* and *3* (at three locations) claim to have hot water and charge US$2.25 per person. They seem OK. The *Hostal Santo Domingo* is also OK at US$2.50 per person or US$4.50 with bath. The *Pensión Guayaquil* is acceptable at US$3 per person. Other basic cheapies for under US$3 per person are the *San José, Ontaneda, Viajero, El Oro* and *Madrid*. The best budget choice is the *Hostal Jennefer* (☎ 750 577), 29 de Mayo and Latacunga, at US$3.50 per person with warm electric shower.

Also OK are the *Hotel Ejecutivo* (☎ 751 943), 29 de Mayo and Ambato, the *Hostal Las Brisas* (☎ 750 560), on Quito near Iturralde, and the *Hostal Galápagos*, all at US$4.50 per person with bath. For something more up-market, the *Hotel Genova* (☎ 759 694), 29 de Mayo and Ibarra, is clean and friendly and costs US$9/13 for singles/ doubles with hot bath. For US$1 less, the *Hotel Caleta* (☎ 750 277), Ibarra and 29 de Mayo, and *Hotel El Colorado* (☎ 750 226), 29 de Mayo and Esmeraldas, are OK.

Places to Eat

Pollos Gus, a clean fried-chicken restaurant, and the *Elite Restaurant* are both on the main plaza and recommended. The *Hotel Caleta Cebichería* has tables on the street and serves good snacks and meals, but it's pricey.

Getting There & Away

Bus The terminal terrestre is two km west of the centre. There are frequent buses to most major towns.

ECUADOR

QUEVEDO

This is another convenient stopover between the highlands and the coast, particularly on the wild descent from Latacunga. The town is important commercially and is known for its Chinese community and chifas, but it has no special attractions.

Places to Stay & Eat

The hotels are poor. Basic hotels around US$3 per person include the *Hotel Turistas* (which also has rooms for US$6 per person with bath and TV). This is the best of the cheapest. Others at this price are the *Guayaquil* and *Charito*. The best budget choice is the *Hotel Imperial*, by the river, at Séptima. Safe, clean rooms with cold showers are US$4.50 per person. The similarly priced *Hotel Condado*, on Quinta near the river, is OK and friendly, and the *Hotel Hilton* (☎ 751 359), Novena 429, has TV in some of the rooms. Its 2nd floor is better. The cheapest place with air-con is the basic *Hotel Continental* (☎ 750 080), 7 de Octubre and Octava, at US$5.50 per person. The *Hotel Ejecutivo Internacional* (☎ 750 596), 7 de Octubre and Quarta, has frayed air-con singles/doubles with bath and TV for US$9/15.

Most cheap restaurants are along 7 de Octubre.

Getting There & Away

Many bus companies are at the west end of 7 de Octubre. There are many buses to Guayaquil (US$2, three hours) but only two to Quito. Buses go to Santo Domingo, Babahoyo, Portoviejo and other towns. Transportes Cotopaxi, by the market, has Latacunga buses.

Travelling around the area is interesting because of the banana and other tropical fruit plantations. In the dry season, rice is spread out on huge concrete slabs to dry in the sun.

The Coast

The mainland has a 2800-km coastline with warm currents so swimming is pleasant year round. The north coast is wet from December to June and the south coast (the provinces of Guayas and El Oro) is drier and more barren, with a January to April wet season. These months are hot, humid and uncomfortable, and people flock to the beaches for relief during the weekends. There are mosquitoes in the wet months, so bring repellent and consider using antimalarial medication, especially in the north.

The north coast is less developed and has some tropical rainforest. Farther south, remnants of tropical dry forest are found in the Parque Nacional Machalilla. Guayas and El Oro provinces use irrigation to produce bananas, rice, coffee, cacao and African palm. Shrimping is a fast-growing industry fraught with environmental problems.

Fishing villages and popular beach resorts are scattered along the coast, but none are outstanding. As a general rule, theft is a major problem on beaches: never leave anything unattended.

The coast is described from north to south.

SAN LORENZO

Travellers arrive by train or bus from Ibarra and continue south by boat. San Lorenzo is not attractive but it's the best stopover between Ibarra and farther south. Marimba music might be heard in town; ask around. A new road from Ibarra reached San Lorenzo during 1996.

Orientation & Information

The centre is a 15-minute walk from the station and a few minutes from the port. Moneychanging is poor. Excursiones El Refugio (☎ & fax 780 134), 30 metres from the EMETEL office, has local beach, mangrove and cultural excursions from US$10 per day.

Places to Stay & Eat

Hotels are basic. Mosquito nets and fans are recommended. Water shortages are frequent. Friendly but persistent kids badger travellers for tips to show them to a hotel.

The best place is the *Gran Hotel San Carlos* (☎ 780 267, 780 284), Imbabura and Garces (near the train station), with clean rooms for US$4.50 per person or US$7 with tepid shower. Most rooms have TV, fan and mosquito net. Also decent are the *Hotel Imperial* (☎ 780 242, 780 221), on the right on Calle Imbabura as you walk in from the station, and the *Hotel Continental* (☎ 780 125) on the left. They charge US$4.50 per person in rooms with private bath. The owners of the Imperial also have the OK *Hotel San Lorenzo* at US$2.50 per person. In town the basic but adequate *Hotel Ecuador* (☎ 780 137) is US$2 per person or US$3.50 with bath. The friendly *Hotel Carondolet* (☎ 780 202) has clean rooms with nets and baths for US$4.50 per person and some cheaper ones. The *Yeaniny* is new and similarly priced.

Meals are not cheap. The *Hotel Ecuador* has a decent restaurant. The set meals are the cheapest. The nearby *El Fogón* is considered the 'best' but is more expensive.

Getting There & Away

Bus Two buses a day reportedly use the new road between San Lorenzo and Ibarra – in the dry season, at least.

Train The autoferro for Ibarra (US$15) leaves daily at 7 am (supposedly). See Ibarra for details.

Boat The Capitanía on the waterfront has boat information. Motorised dugouts are used; prepare for sun, wind and spray. Locals pay less than foreigners. Two companies between them have hourly departures for **La Tola** (US$4.50, 2½ hours), from 5.30 am to 2.30 pm. The ride through coastal mangroves, with pelicans and frigatebirds flying around, is interesting. Some boats connect with a bus to Esmeraldas (US$7 from San Lorenzo), and you can reach Atacames or Quito in one day from San Lorenzo. La Tola has a very basic pensión. Boats for Borbón (US$6, 3½ hours) leave twice a day. Boats for other destinations can be arranged.

BORBON

This small port with a predominantly black population of 5000 is on the Río Cayapas. There are buses to Esmeraldas and boats up the Cayapas and San Miguel rivers to the **Reserva Ecológica Cotacachi-Cayapas** – an interesting trip to a remote area.

Places to Stay & Eat

Angel Cerón, the school principal, runs the *Pampa de Oro Hotel* (US$3.50 per person) and is a good source of information. There are a couple of other basic, cheap hotels. There are several simple restaurants, most closing by 7.30 pm.

Getting There & Away

Bus Buses to Esmeraldas (US$2.50, four hours) leave frequently.

Boat Boats to San Lorenzo leave at 7 and 11 am. A daily boat leaves at 11 am for San Miguel (US$8, five hours), passing the Catholic mission of **Santa María** and the Protestant mission of **Zapallo Grande** (both have basic accommodation).

SAN MIGUEL

This community of black people is the access for the **Reserva Ecológica Cotacachi-Cayapas** (US$20 fee). A shop sells a few supplies, and basic meals are available for US$5. Cayapas Indians live across the river and can be visited.

The ranger station has four beds (US$3, no running water or mosquito nets), or you may camp outside. Beware of ferocious chiggers; put repellent on ankles and legs upon arrival. Rangers will guide you into the reserve by dugout and on foot for about US$10 per guide a day plus food (two guides are needed on some trips). Camping is possible. There are waterfalls, rainforest trails, great bird-watching, and there's a chance you'll see monkeys and other wildlife. September to December is recommended.

The boat back to Borbón leaves before dawn. Arrange in advance which day you want to return.

ESMERALDAS

This has been a major port for centuries and an oil refinery is a major source of income and employment. The beaches are dirty and

ECUADOR

Esmeraldas

PLACES TO STAY
1 Hostal Residencial Sandri
2 Hotel Chaberrin Internacional
4 Hotel Turismo
14 Hostal Miraflores
15 Hotel Asia
17 Nuevo Hotel
23 Hotel Galeón
24 Hotel Roma
25 Residencial Zulema
26 Hostal Americano
28 Hotel Diana

PLACES TO EAT
13 Fuente de Soda Estrecho de Bering, Las Redes Restaurant
18 Restaurant Bo Derek
27 Restaurant Budapest
31 Chifa Asiática
33 Fuente de Soda Porteñito

OTHER
3 Market
5 Post Office, EMETEL
6 Banco Central
7 CITA (Buses)
8 Aero Taxi (Buses)
9 Transportes Esmeraldas (Buses)
10 Cinema
11 Transportes La Costeñita
12 Church
15 Reina del Camino (Buses)
16 Transportes Occidentales (Buses)
19 TAME Airline
20 CETUR Tourist Office
21 Cine Bolívar
22 Banco del Pichincha
29 Filanbanco
30 Transportes del Pacífico (Buses)
32 Police
34 Fish & Vegetable Market

the city has theft and drug problems. Avoid ill-lit areas and the southern end of the Malecón. Most travellers pass through quickly. Filanbanco and Banco del Pichincha change travellers' cheques.

Places to Stay

The cheapest hotels are in poor condition. Many places turn on water on request only. For about US$3 per person, try *Hostal Miraflores* or *Hotel Turismo* (☎ 712 700), which are just OK. The *Nuevo Hotel* (☎ 711 327) is US$3.50 per person or US$5.50 with a poor private bath. The *Residencial Zulema* (☎ 711 789), Olmedo near Cañizares, isn't

bad for US$9 for a double with bath. The clean *Hotel Asia* (☎ 714 594), 9 de Octubre 116, is OK for US$4 to US$6 per person, (some rooms with bath).

For US$6 per person with bath and fan, the friendly *Hotel Diana* (☎ 710 333), Cañizares 224, and the clean *Hostal Residencial Sandri* (☎ 713 547), Libertad and J Montalvo, are both recommended. The *Hostal Americano* (☎ 713 978), Sucre 709, is also OK for US$6 per person or US$8 with air-con. The *Hotel Roma* (☎ 710 136), Olmedo 718, has rather run-down rooms with bath and TV at US$8 per person or US$10 with air-con. The *Hostal El Galeón* (☎ 713 116),

Olmedo near Piedrahita, is well kept and costs a couple of dollars more.

Three km north in the quieter suburb of Las Palmas are the basic *Residencial Chimborazo* and the family-run *Residencial Mechita* at US$3.50 per person. Nearby, the good *Hotel Ambato* (☎ 710 344), Kennedy and A Guerra, is US$6 with bath and TV.

Places to Eat

Las Redes Restaurant on the plaza is good for seafood, and the nearby *Fuente de Soda Estrecho de Bering* is good for ice cream and people-watching. The *Chifa Asiática*, Cañizares near Sucre, has good Chinese food. The *Fuente de Soda Porteñito*, Sucre and Mejía, is locally popular and good.

Getting There & Away

Air The airport is 25 km away (taxi US$5). TAME (712 633), on Bolívar by the plaza, has late morning flights to Quito (US$23) on weekdays and an evening flight on Sunday.

Bus Aero Taxi is frighteningly fast to Quito (US$6, five hours); Transportes Occidentales, Esmeraldas and Panamericana (with luxury buses) are slower. Occidentales and Esmeraldas have many buses to Guayaquil (US$5.50 to US$7, eight hours), as well as Ambato, Machala and other cities. CITA has buses to Ambato. Reina del Camino has buses to Manta and Bahía de Caráquez.

For provincial buses, use Transportes La Costeñita or del Pacífico. There are frequent buses for Atacames and Súa (US$0.60) and Muisne (US$1.40, 2½ hours). Several buses go to La Tola and the US$7 fare includes the boat to San Lorenzo. Several buses daily go to Borbón (US$2.75, four hours). La Tola and Borbón buses pass near the airport.

ATACAMES

This small town, 30 km west of Esmeraldas, is popular among young travellers wanting a beach vacation. It's often busy with visitors from Quito, Colombia and all over the world. The nightlife is often loud and boisterous, and the beaches littered.

Warnings

A powerful undertow causes drownings every year, so keep within your limits. Bring insect repellent, especially in the wet season. The cheapest hotels may have rats, and water shortages are frequent. The fresh water in bathrooms is often brackish.

I have received many reports of assaults on late-night beach walkers and on single people or couples in quiet areas during the day. Stay in brightly lit and well-travelled areas, and go with friends. Don't leave anything unattended on the beach.

Places to Stay

Hotels are full on weekends and holidays, so arrive early. April to October is the high season and prices rise to what the market will bear. Bargain, especially if you're staying a few days.

Many hotels are near the beach, which is reached by a footbridge. Rooms are geared to families and have several beds so, go in a group to economise. Cheap singles are hard to find. Always check your room or cabin for security before renting it.

The cheapest is *Hotel Doña Pichu* (☎ 731 441), on the main street in the village, not on the beach. Basic rooms are US$2.50 per person and bathrooms are primitive. There are other basic places in the village. On the beach, US$10 for a double is cheap. *Cabañas Rincón del Mar* (☎ 731 064), to the left after crossing the footbridge, is clean and secure but small. It charges US$10 for a double with bath, more at weekends. *La Casa del Manglar*, by the footbridge, is clean and friendly and charges US$8 to US$16 for a double with bath. More hotels are right of the bridge. The *Cabañas Los Bohios* (☎ 731 089) has decent double cabins with bath at US$10, and has singles midweek. The *Rincón Sage* (☎ 731 246) has decent rooms with bath for US$8/12. The *Hostal Jennifer* (☎ 710 482, 731 055) has some singles and charges about US$8 per person with bath, less without. The popular *Hotel Galerias Atacames* (☎ 731 149) has English-speaking owners, and rooms for US$16 a double with bath at weekends. Others to try with doubles in this price range include the *Hotel Rodelu* (☎ 731 033), the *Hotel Chavalito* (☎ 731 113), the *Hotel El Tiburón* and the *Hostería Cayapas*. There are several others, usually more expensive.

Places to Eat

Comedores near the beach all serve the same thing – that morning's catch. Ask the price before ordering or you may be overcharged. Many places double as bars or discos in the evening, and their popularity changes with the seasons. *Marco's* and *Paco Foco* are currently popular restaurants.

Getting There & Away

Buses stop on the road near the footbridge to the beach. There are many from Esmeraldas to Súa and back. Buses to Muisne may be full; ride on the roof or return to Esmeraldas for a seat.

SUA

This friendly fishing village is six km west of Atacames. Follow the beach at low tide – but join a large group to avoid robbery.

Places to Stay & Eat

There are fewer places than in Atacames but they are quieter and often better value if you aren't looking for nightlife. Prices don't rise as much at weekends. The *Hotel Chagra Ramos* (☎ 731 006) has a little beach and nice views, and charges US$5 or US$6 per person in decent rooms with bath. It has a good, inexpensive restaurant. *Hotel El Peñón de Súa* (☎ 731 013) is 300 metres away from the beach but has nice rooms with bath at US$4 per person. Other OK places in the US$4 to US$6 per person range are the *Hostal Mar y Sol* (☎ 731 293) and *Hotel Las Buganvillas* (☎ 731 008). The *Hotel Súa* (☎ 731 004) is US$16 a double with hot shower and has a good restaurant.

MUISNE

Muisne is on an island, 1½ hours from Atacames by bus. Boats are US$0.20 to Muisne. From the dock, the main road heads into the 'centre' and becomes a track to the beach 1.5

km away. The beach is quieter than Atacames, but the usual precautions apply.

In the centre, Fundación de Defensa Ecológica (☎ 480 167) arranges boat trips (US$20 per person) to local mangroves.

Places to Stay & Eat

There's a residencial on the mainland side of the river, and a few more in the centre. All are cheap and basic. The *Residencial Sarita* and *La Isla* are OK. Halfway to the beach, the *Hotel Galápagos* (☎ 480 158) charges US$6 per person with bath; this is the best hotel. On the beach are several cheap cabins; check that the rooms have locks, as thefts have occurred. *Hotel Calade* (☎ 480 279) is quite good for US$4 each and the *Cabañas Ipanema* are US$5 for basic doubles.

There are basic *comedores* on the beach and in the centre.

Getting There & Away

Bus La Costeñita has hourly buses to Esmeraldas (US$1.30, 2½ hours) via Atacames. Transportes Occidentales has night buses to Quito (US$5.75, seven hours) and Guayaquil (US$6.25).

Boat Two boats a day go to Cojimíes (US$6, two hours).

SOUTH OF MUISNE

It's possible to walk along the beach at low tide to **Bolívar**, crossing rivers by canoes. It takes all day. Bolívar (no hotels) can also be reached by bus. Boats go to **Cojimíes** for US$2 per person, but it is more easily reached by direct boat from Muisne. Cojimíes has a few cheap and very basic hotels.

From Cojimíes, buses go via **Pedernales** (cheap and basic hotels) and **Jama** (a basic pensión) to San Vicente (US$5.50, five hours). Buses depend on low tides and services are disrupted in the wet season. Pedernales has buses to Santo Domingo (US$3).

SAN VICENTE

This resort village is a short ferry ride across

the Río Chone from Bahía de Caráquez. It has nice beaches and an airport.

Places to Stay & Eat
The basic *Hostal San Vicente* is US$2 each. There are several fancier hotels with decent restaurants.

Getting There & Away
Air The airstrip is behind the market, 10 minutes walk from the pier (turn right). TAME has flights to Quito (US$29) on Friday and Sunday. AECA and NICA (☎ 690 377) offer occasional flights from Guayaquil to San Vicente and Esmeraldas via Pedernales in small aircraft. Flights may go to Cojimíes and other places on demand. Travel light, as there are baggage restrictions.

Boat Launches to Bahía de Caráquez (US$0.20) leave often but charge more after 9 pm. A car ferry takes passengers for free.

Bus Costa del Norte, near the pier, has hourly departures to Pedernales, one or two a day to Cojimíes, and two inland to Chone.

BAHIA DE CARAQUEZ
This small port and resort across the river from San Vicente has decent beaches. The best are half a km north on Avenida Montúfar. The mouth of the Río Chone is quite busy, and you can watch the boats go by from a riverside café. It's a quiet and pleasant town, known to locals as 'Bahía'.

Information
The CETUR office is near the river. Guacamayo Adventures (☎ 691 412) is a good source of local information and arranges tours to islands with seabird colonies, tours to coastal forests, cultural tours and mountain bike rentals, among other things. Recommended. The Banco Comercial changes travellers' cheques.

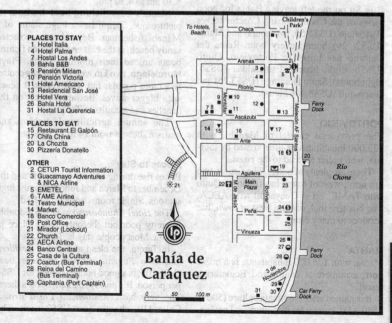

PLACES TO STAY
1 Hotel Italia
4 Hotel Palma
7 Hostal Los Andes
8 Bahía B&B
9 Pensión Miriam
10 Pensión Victoria
11 Hotel Americano
13 Residencial San José
16 Hotel Vera
26 Bahía Hotel
31 Hostal La Querencia

PLACES TO EAT
15 Restaurant El Galpón
17 Chifa China
20 La Chozita
30 Pizzería Donatello

OTHER
2 CETUR Tourist Information
3 Guacamayo Adventures & NICA Airline
5 EMETEL
7 TAME Airline
12 Teatro Municipal
14 Market
18 Banco Comercial
19 Post Office
21 Mirador (Lookout)
22 Church
23 AECA Airline
24 Banco Central
25 Casa de la Cultura
27 Coactur (Bus Terminal)
28 Reina del Camino (Bus Terminal)
29 Capitanía (Port Captain)

Bahía de Caráquez

0   50   100 m

ECUADOR

Places to Stay & Eat

The cheapest places have water supply problems. The very basic *Pensión Victoria* is US$2 per person. The *Pensión Miriam* is a bit cleaner at US$2.50. Other cheapies are the *Residencial San José* at US$3.50 each and the better *Hotel Vera*, which has some rooms with bath. The OK *Hotel Palma* (☎ 690 467) is US$4 each or US$6 with bath, but many rooms lack windows. The *Hostal Los Andes* (☎ 690 587), is basic but clean at US$6 each. The *Hostal La Querencia* (☎ 690 009) is good value for Bahía at US$8 and the *Hotel Bahía* is US$10 and pleasant. The *Bahía B&B* is also US$10, clean but basic, and includes breakfast.

The *Chifa China* is simple but serves decent Chinese food. The *Restaurant El Galpón* is cheap and good. *La Chozita* is a good place to watch the river happenings.

Getting There & Away

Air & Boat See San Vicente, above.

Bus Sit on the left leaving Bahía for good views of the Chone estuary. Coactur serves Portoviejo (US$1.50, two hours) and Manta (US$2, 2½ hours) every hour. Reina del Camino has buses to Portoviejo, Quito (US$6, eight hours), Esmeraldas (US$6, eight hours), Santo Domingo (US$3.75) and Guayaquil (US$5, six hours).

PORTOVIEJO

The provincial capital of Manabí, with 133,000 inhabitants, is little visited by tourists, who prefer to head to the coast.

There are plenty of hotels. The airport, two km north-west of town, has flights to Quito with TAME and to Guayaquil with AECA. The bus terminal, one km west of town, has services to many cities.

MANTA

Manta, with 126,000 inhabitants, is a major port, commercial centre and Ecuadorian resort.

It is named after the Manta culture (500 to 1550 AD), known for its pottery and naviga-

tional skills. The Mantas sailed to Central America and Peru and, possibly, the Galápagos. In 1526 the Spanish captured a Mànta balsa sailing raft with a crew of 20. Similar, smaller balsa rafts are still seen along the coast.

Information

An inlet divides the town into Manta (west side) and Tarqui (east side). They are joined by a road bridge. Manta has the main offices, shopping areas and bus terminal. Tarqui has more hotels and beaches. Streets numbered 100 and up are in Tarqui.

CETUR (☎ 622 944) is on the pedestrian-only block of Avenida 3. The Banco del Pacífico, Banco del Pichincha and casas de cambio change travellers' cheques.

Things to See

The **Museo del Banco Central** (☎ 622 878) has a small but good exhibit on the Manta culture. Hours are Monday to Friday from 8.30 am to 4.30 pm.

Manta's busy **fishing-boat harbour** is picturesque. Tarqui has a huge statue of a Manabí fisherman. Beyond is a protected sandy beach, at the east end of which fishing boats unload their morning catch. **Playa Murciélago**, two km west of Manta's centre, is a more popular but less protected beach with bigger waves. Beware of theft on the beaches and assaults in Tarqui.

The annual agricultural, fishing and tourism show is from 14 to 18 October.

Places to Stay

Prices rise during holiday weekends and the December to March and June to August high seasons. Single rooms are hard to find.

The *Hotel Chimborazo* at US$6 a double is pretty poor but the only cheap place in Manta. Most people stay in Tarqui.

In Tarqui, the clean and secure *Residencial Villa Eugenia*, on the Malecón near Calle 105, is a good budget choice for US$4 per person. It's poorly marked, but it's there. The very basic *Residencial Playa Brava*, Calle 110, charges just US$2 each. The

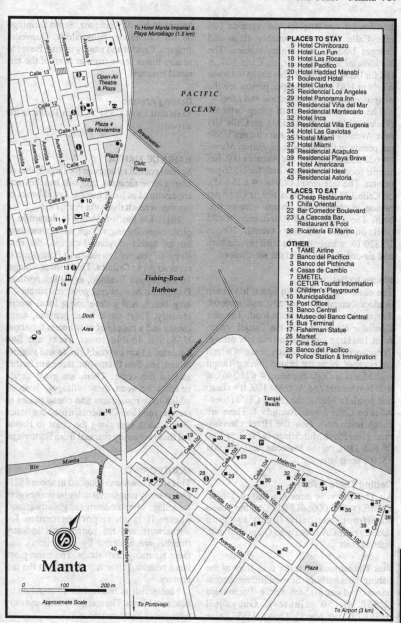

Manta

0   100   200 m

Approximate Scale

To Portoviejo

To Airport (3 km)

PLACES TO STAY
5 Hotel Chimborazo
16 Hotel Lun Fun
18 Hotel Las Rocas
19 Hotel Pacifico
20 Hotel Haddad Manabí
21 Boulevard Hotel
24 Hotel Clarke
25 Residencial Los Angeles
29 Hotel Panorama Inn
30 Residencial Viña del Mar
31 Residencial Montecarlo
32 Hotel Inca
33 Residencial Villa Eugenia
34 Hotel Las Gaviotas
35 Hostal Miami
37 Hotel Miami
38 Residencial Acapulco
39 Residencial Playa Brava
41 Hotel Americana
42 Residencial Ideal
43 Residencial Astoria

PLACES TO EAT
6 Cheap Restaurants
11 Chifa Oriental
22 Bar Comedor Boulevard
23 La Cascada Bar, Restaurant & Pool
36 Picantería El Marino

OTHER
1 TAME Airline
2 Banco del Pacífico
3 Banco del Pichincha
4 Casas de Cambio
7 EMETEL
8 CETUR Tourist Information
9 Children's Playground
10 Municipalidad
12 Post Office
13 Banco Central
14 Museo del Banco Central
15 Bus Terminal
17 Fisherman Statue
26 Market
27 Cine Sucre
28 Banco del Pacífico
40 Police Station & Immigration

PACIFIC OCEAN

Fishing-Boat Harbour

Tarqui Beach

ECUADOR

Residencial Los Angeles, on Avenida 108 near Calle 102, is reasonably clean and charges US$4/6 for singles/doubles. The *Residencial Viña del Mar*, on Calle 104, is OK for US$8 a double. Other cheap but basic hotels at US$3 or US$4 per person are the *Acapulco*, *Montecarlo*, *Astoria* and *Ideal*.

The student and youth-group-oriented *Boulevard Hotel* (☎ 625 333), on Calle 103 near Avenida 105, is OK and charges US$6 per person in the high season. *Hostal Miami* (☎ 622 055), Calle 107 and Avenida 102, has simple rooms with private bath for US$6 per person. The safe *Hotel Clarke* (☎ 625 835), on Calle 102 near Avenida 109, is US$6 per person in clean, basic rooms with private bath. The clean *Hotel Americana* (☎ 623 069), on Calle 105 near Avenida 106, is US$20 for a basic double with private bath and air-con; rooms with fans are cheaper.

Places to Eat

The eastern end of Tarqui beach has cheap outdoor comedores serving fresh seafood. The market also has cheap food. The *Bar Comedor Boulevard*, on the Tarqui waterfront, has large servings and outdoor dining. There are other places nearby, some of which are cheaper. Near the bridge joining Tarqui with Manta is *Chifa Popular* (☎ 621 346), at 4 de Noviembre and Avenida 109. It's cheap and good. In Manta, the cheap *Chifa Oriental* is on Calle 8 near Avenida 4. There are cheap restaurants near the Hotel Chimborazo. Near Playa Murciélago is *Pizzería Topi* (☎ 621 180), on the Malecón near Avenida 15. It's open late.

Getting There & Away

Air The airport is three km east of Tarqui. TAME (☎ 622 006, 613 210), on the Manta waterfront, has daily flights to Quito (US$29). AECA may fly to Guayaquil with light aircraft.

Bus The terminal terrestre is in front of the fishing-boat harbour. Several different companies between them serve Portoviejo (US$0.60, 50 minutes), Guayaquil (US$3.75, 3½ hours), Quito (US$7, nine

hours), Bahía de Caráquez, Santo Domingo de los Colorados, Esmeraldas, Quevedo, Jipijapa, Crucita and nearby towns. Buses to nearby towns leave from in front of the terminal terrestre.

Getting Around

Taxis cost about US$1.25 from Tarqui to the airport.

BAHIA DE MANTA

Several coastal villages on the large Bahía de Manta have pleasant, unspoilt beaches and are favoured as local resorts. Local buses or rancheros reach them via Portoviejo.

Eight km east of Manta is **Jaramijó**, a picturesque fishing village with comedores but no hotels. Beyond Jaramijó, the road stops, so you need to return to Portoviejo in order to get to **Crucita**. This fishing village, 16 km beyond Jaramijó, or 30 km north of Portoviejo, has several good restaurants, a long beach, and a developing local tourist industry. There are a basic pensión, some cabins and a couple of new hotels for about US$16 a double room. Next are **San Jacinto**, 13 km beyond Crucita and slightly inland, and **San Clemente**, three km farther and on the coast. There are good sandy beaches between these villages, both of which have restaurants and cheap places to stay. Beyond San Clemente, a road continues 20 km north-east along the coast to Bahía. All these are easily reached from Portoviejo.

MONTECRISTI

This small town was founded in about 1628, and its many unrestored colonial houses give the village a tumbledown and ghostly atmosphere. It is an important centre for wickerwork and the panama hat industry (tourists are besieged by hat sellers), and there are many craft shops. The main plaza has a beautiful church built early in the last century.

Montecristi is reached in 15 minutes by bus from Manta. There are no hotels and only a couple of basic comedores.

JIPIJAPA

Pronounced *hipihapa*, this is the main town on the Manta-Guayaquil road. Parque Nacional Machalilla is a short distance to the south-west. There are a couple of basic pensiones and comedores. CITM and CITMS buses go through Machalilla.

PARQUE NACIONAL MACHALILLA

Ecuador's only coastal national park preserves beaches, unusual tropical dry forest, coastal cloud forest, several archaeological sites, and 20,000 hectares of ocean containing Ecuador's only mainland coral formations and two offshore islands.

The tropical dry forest is characterised by weirdly bottle-shaped trees whose heavy spines protect them against herbivores. There are various figs, cacti and the giant kapok tree. Parrots, parrotlets and parakeets are some of the forest's many inhabitants. Along the coastal edges, frigatebirds, pelicans and boobies are seen, some of which nest in colonies on the offshore islands. The tropical dry forest used to stretch along much of the Pacific coast of Central and South America but it has almost disappeared entirely. Machalilla is, therefore, a unique park.

The park headquarters and museum are in Puerto López (see below). It is open daily from 8 am to 4 pm and visitor information is available. Entrance to the park is US$20 (less if paid in sucres). Get a receipt or ticket (valid for a week) so you can enter both the mainland and island sections. The park entrance is six km north of Puerto López and, from here, a dirt road goes five km to **Agua Blanca**, a little village with an archaeological museum (8 am to 6 pm, US$1.25) and a nearby Manta archaeological site. There are hiking and horse trails, and guides are available. You cannot visit the archaeological site and many parts of the park without a local guide (from US$8 a tour). Camping is permitted, or you can stay in people's houses.

The **Isla de la Plata**, 40 km north-west of Puerto López, is a favourite part of the national park. There are nesting sea-bird colonies and you may see whales or dolphins, particularly from mid-June to mid-October. Boat tours, some with snorkelling to see tropical fish and coral reefs, can be arranged in Puerto López or at Alandaluz, 11 km south of Puerto López. The park office may know of other boats. Some boats lack life jackets. It takes two to three hours to reach the island, where there are hiking trails. Camping is not permitted.

PUERTO LOPEZ

This coastal fishing village houses the national park headquarters. Moneychanging facilities are poor. Pacarina Travel (☎ 604 173) uses small boats that will take up to eight passengers to Isla de la Plata for US$160, including snorkelling. Pacarina Travel is also a general travel agency. Salangome (☎ 604 120) has guided tours in larger boats for US$34 per person. The park entry fee is extra. Salangome will also arrange tours to the mainland part of the park and other areas.

Places to Stay & Eat

There are a few very basic but friendly pensiones charging US$3 to US$4 per person. *Carmita's*, on the shorefront, is a good, cheap restaurant that also has a few simple rooms with bath for US$6 per person. Next door, the *Mayflower* is a locally popular restaurant. The *Hotel Pacífico* (☎ 604 133) is the most comfortable place; it has good singles/doubles with hot bath and air-con at US$16/24 and cabins with shared bath for US$9/14.

Getting There & Away

Buses between La Libertad (2½ hours) and Jipijapa (US$1.60, 1½ hours) stop in Puerto López every 45 minutes. They can drop you at the national park entrance, and at other points along the coast. Buses stop running in the late afternoon.

SOUTH OF PUERTO LOPEZ

Salango, five km south of Puerto López, has a decent archaeological museum (US$0.80) and *El Delfín*, a good seafood restaurant.

ECUADOR

The **Alandaluz Ecocultural Hostal** is six km south of Salango. This unusual hotel, run by Ecuadorians, built from fast-growing (and easily replaced) local bamboos and palm leaves and designed as a minimum impact project, is a popular pastoral getaway for travellers. An undisturbed beach is nearby, horses can be rented, there is volleyball, and the atmosphere is very relaxed. Some people love it; others find it hard to deal with. Rustic rooms are US$12 to US$14 per person, most with shared solar showers outside. Toilets are latrines, designed to conserve water and fertilise the orchard. You can sleep in a hammock or camp (US$4). Meals are US$3 for breakfast, and US$6 for lunch or dinner. Food is quite good but you have to eat what is available (rice, vegetables and seafood usually). Reservations can be made in Quito (☎ & fax 543 042), Baquedano 330 and Reina Victoria, 2nd floor. Otherwise, show up early in the day, especially in summer, when it's often full. The hostel works in conjunction with Pacarina Travel (see Puerto López) to arrange tours.

About 12 km south of Alandaluz is the coastal village of **Olón**, where there is a nice beach. There is a cheap pensión and a pricey hotel. A few km farther south is the village of **Montañita**, with good surfing (some say the best in Ecuador). Beach bums and travellers like the basic but friendly *El Rincón del Amigo* (☎ in Quito 223 720, fax 225 907), where beds are about US$2 or US$3 per person. Robberies have been reported from the cabin farthest away from the entrance. Mountain bike and surfboard rental and are reportedly available and there's a relaxed beach restaurant and bar. Nearby, *Vitos Cabañas* at US$6.50 a double have been recommended, as have the cheap local restaurants *Pelicano, Las Olas* and *Blancas*. A new, up-market hotel has reportedly opened and the tourism industry is developing.

Four km south is **Manglaralto**, with a few basic pensiones and comedores, as well as a regional hospital. Good waves are found around here too. Ten km farther on is **Valdivia**, where Ecuador's oldest archaeo-logical site is. The best artefacts are in museums in Quito and Guayaquil, but there is a small museum at the site. (Artefacts offered for sale are fakes.)

LA LIBERTAD

This fishing port, with 50,000 inhabitants, is the largest town and bustling hub of Península de Santa Elena. Although lively, it is not an attractive place.

Places to Stay

If you must stay, try the basic and ugly *Residencial Libertad* at US$2 per person or US$4/6 for a single/double with bath. The *Residencial Collins* on 9 de Octubre is no better at US$2 per person or US$8 for a double with bath. Nearby, the *Turis Palm* is slightly better at US$4 each or US$8 with private bath. The basic *Residencial Seven Seas* on the Malecón is US$3 per person or US$5 with bath. *Hotel Viña del Mar* (☎ 785 979), Avenida 3 and Guayaquil, is US$12/20 with bath; it's the only decent cheap hotel.

Getting There & Away

Buses for Guayaquil (US$2, three hours) leave from several places along 9 de Octubre. Buses going north along the coast leave from the market on Guayaquil. Various local destinations are also served.

SALINAS

Salinas, the so-called 'best' resort in Ecuador, has high-rise condominiums and expensive deep-sea fishing trips, making it the haunt of affluent Ecuadorians from January to April. The beaches are OK but nothing special. Budget hotels are about US$6 per person in the low season and US$10 in the high season. Try *Hotel Florida* (☎ 772 780), *Hotel Albita* (☎ 773 211), *Residencial Rachel* (☎ 772 501), or *Hostal Las Rocas* (☎ 774 219).

PLAYAS

This, the nearest beach resort to Guayaquil, is busy during the January to April season (when prices rise) but almost deserted at other times. Playas is a fishing village, and you can still see a few traditional small balsa rafts with one sail, though most boats are motorised nowadays.

Places to Stay & Eat

The cheapest places have brackish running water and are pretty basic. Get a room with mosquito netting or a fan. The cheapest are the basic *Hotel Turismo* at US$3 per person and the similar *Hotel Caracol*, which also has rooms with bath at US$6 per person. The best of the cheapies is the *Hostal Brisas Marina* (☎ 760 324) at US$14 for a double with bath, fan and mosquito nets. Also decent is the *Hotel Marianela* (☎ 760 058), at US$4 per person or US$6 with mosquito nets and private bath. The *Hotel Acapulco* (☎ 760 343) has a cheap restaurant and is just OK at US$4 per person, and the basic but clean and safe *Hostería Costa Verde* (☎ 760 645) is US$4 per person or US$6 with bath and nets. The *Hotel San Andrés* (☎ 761 209) is OK at US$6 per person, with bath. The similarly priced *Hotel Reina del Mar* (☎ 760 882) can get loud at weekends with the attached disco and restaurant. The *Residencial El Galeón* (☎ 760 270), with a good cheap restaurant, is clean and friendly at US$5 per person or US$6 with bath and nets.

The *Hotel Playas* (☎ 760 121) is near the beach and quite good for US$8/12 for singles/doubles. It has a restaurant. The *Hostería La Gaviota* (☎ 760 133) is friendly and has a decent restaurant, though the rooms are very basic at US$7 per person with bath. The *Hotel Rey David* (☎ 760 024) is on the beach and has characterless rooms at US$12/16. The *Hostería El Delfín* (☎ 760 125) is a km east of the centre and has decent rooms, some of which have sea views, for US$20 a double with bath. It has a restaurant and bar. Nearby is the good *Hostería Estrella del Mar* (☎ 760 430) charging US$16 for a double with hot water. It also has a restaurant.

Apart from the hotel restaurants, you'll find several inexpensive comedores on the beach with fresh seafood.

Getting There & Away

Buses to Guayaquil (US$1.75, 1¾ hours) leave every half hour with Transportes Villamil.

GUAYAQUIL
Information
Tourist Office CETUR (☎ 328 312), Aguirre 104 near the Malecón, is open Monday to Friday from 8.30 am to 5 pm.

Money Casas de cambio are on the first few blocks of 9 de Octubre and the first blocks of Pichincha. Few are open on Saturday. The one at the airport is open at weekends for incoming international flights. The Banco del Pacífico is also good.

Consulates The Peruvian Consulate (☎ 322 738), 9 de Octubre 411, 6th floor, is open on weekdays from 8.30 am to 1.30 pm. Many countries have consulates in Guayaquil; see Visas & Embassies in the Facts for the Visitor section of this chapter, or consult the phone book.

Tourist Card Extensions T-3 tourist card extensions are available from Migraciones (☎ 322 539, 290 502), in the Palacio de Gobierno.

Bookshops The best shop for books in English is the Librería Científica (☎ 328 569), Luque 223.

Medical Services The best hospital is the Clínica Kennedy (☎ 286 963, 289 666), in the Nueva Kennedy suburb.

Dangers & Annoyances Guayaquil has a reputation for thefts and muggings. Be alert everywhere and at all times.

Things to See

The **Museo Municipal** (☎ 516 391), P Carbo at Sucre, is small but varied: there are rooms devoted to archaeology, colonial art, modern art and ethnography. The last houses the famous *tsantsas*, or shrunken heads. Hours are Monday to Friday from 9 am to noon and

ECUADOR

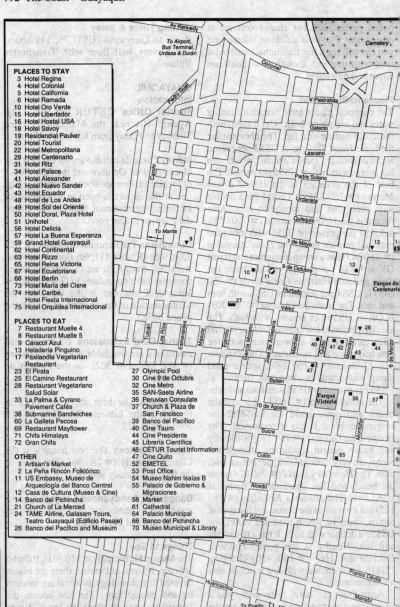

PLACES TO STAY

3 Hotel Regina
4 Hotel Colonial
5 Hotel California
6 Hotel Ramada
10 Hotel Oro Verde
15 Hotel Libertador
16 Hotel Hostal USA
18 Hotel Savoy
19 Residencial Pauker
20 Hotel Tourist
22 Hotel Metropolitana
29 Hotel Centenario
31 Hotel Ritz
34 Hotel Palace
41 Hotel Alexander
42 Hotel Nuevo Sander
43 Hotel Ecuador
48 Hotel de Los Andes
49 Hotel Sol del Oriente
50 Hotel Doral, Plaza Hotel
51 Unihotel
56 Hotel Delicia
57 Hotel La Buena Esperanza
59 Grand Hotel Guayaquil
62 Hotel Continental
63 Hotel Rizzo
65 Hotel Reina Victoria
67 Hotel Ecuatoriana
68 Hotel Berlin
73 Hotel María del Cisne
74 Hotel Caribe,
   Hotel Fiesta Internacional
75 Hotel Orquidea Internacional

PLACES TO EAT

7 Restaurant Muelle 4
8 Restaurant Muelle 5
9 Caracol Azul
14 Heladería Pinguino
17 Paxilandia Vegetarian
   Restaurant
23 El Pirata
25 El Camino Restaurant
28 Restaurant Vegetariano
   Salud Solar
33 La Palma & Cyrano
   Pavement Cafés
38 Submarine Sandwiches
60 La Galleta Pecosa
69 Restaurant Mayflower
71 Chifa Himalaya
72 Gran Chifa

OTHER

1 Artisan's Market
2 La Peña Rincón Folklórico
11 US Embassy, Museo de
   Arqueología del Banco Central
12 Casa de Cultura (Museo & Cine)
13 Banco del Pichincha
21 Church of La Merced
24 TAME Airline, Galasam Tours,
   Teatro Guayaquil (Edificio Pasaje)
26 Banco del Pacífico and Museum

27 Olympic Pool
30 Cine 9 de Octubre
32 Cine Metro
35 SAN-Saeta Airline
36 Peruvian Consulate
37 Church & Plaza de
   San Francisco
39 Banco del Pacífico
40 Cine Tauro
44 Cine Presidente
45 Librería Científica
46 CETUR Tourist Information
47 Cine Quito
52 EMETEL
53 Post Office
54 Museo Nahim Isaías B
55 Palacio de Gobierno &
   Migraciones
58 Market
61 Cathedral
64 Palacio Municipal
66 Banco del Pichincha
70 Museo Municipal & Library

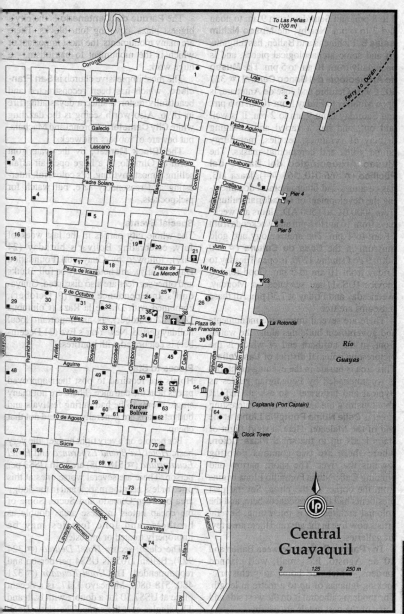

To Las Peñas
(100 m)

Coronel

Loja

V Piedrahita

J Montalvo

Galeclo

Padre Aguirre

Lascano

Martínez

Imbabura

Mendiburo

Padre Solano

Orellana

Panamá

Pier 4

Roca

Pier 5

Junín

VM Rendón

Plaza de
La Merced

Paula de Icaza

9 de Octubre

Vélez

Plaza de
San Francisco

Luque

Aguirre

Ballén

Parque
Bolívar

10 de Agosto

Sucre

Colón

La Rotonde

Río
Guayas

Capitanía (Port Captain)

Clock Tower

Chiriboga

Luzarraga

Olmedo

ECUADOR

Central
Guayaquil

0   125   250 m

3 to 8 pm, and Saturday from 9 am to noon and 3 to 6 pm. Nearby, the **Museo Nahim Isaías B**, Pichincha and Ballén, has religious art and some archaeological pieces, and is open daily from 10 am to 5 pm. The **Museo de Arqueología del Banco Central** (☎ 327 402), 9 de Octubre and José de Antepara, is open Monday to Friday from 10 am to 6 pm, and Saturday from 9 am to 2 pm. It is well laid out, and has a varied and changing display of ceramics, textiles, metallurgy (some gold) and ceremonial masks. The **Museo Arqueológico del Banco del Pacífico** (☎ 566 010, 563 744), Icaza 113, has ceramics and other artefacts documenting the development of Ecuadorian cultures from 3000 BC to 1500 AD. Hours are weekdays from 10 am to 6 pm and weekends from 11 am to 1 pm. The archaeology and gold museum in the **Casa de Cultura** (☎ 300 500), 9 de Octubre 1200, is open Tuesday to Friday from 10 am to 5 pm. Good foreign movies (US$1) are screened on Monday, Wednesday and Friday at 7.30 pm. All these museums are free.

There are several impressive monuments and government buildings along the waterfront, at the northern end of which is the picturesque colonial district of **Las Peñas**. This area is unsafe in the evening/night, but is recommended by Ecuadorian guides as 'typical and historical', so ask at CETUR about visiting the area. The most interesting street is **Calle Numa Pompillo Llona**, at the end of the Malecón. Here, a short flight of stairs leads up to the small **Plaza Colón**, where there are two cannons pointing towards the river. The short, narrow and winding Calle Numa Pompillo Llona begins from the corner of the plaza. Several past presidents had their residences here, and the colonial architecture is interesting. Several artists now live in the area and there are a few art galleries.

The **Parque Bolívar**, between Ballén and 10 de Agosto, has small, well-planned gardens, which are home to prehistoric-looking iguanas of up to a metre in length. The modern cathedral is on the west side and some of the best hotels are nearby.

The **Parque del Centenario** is the city's biggest plaza, covering four blocks. There are many monuments, the most important of which is the monument to patriotism – a huge work.

The most impressive church is **San Francisco**, which has been reconstructed and beautifully restored since a devastating fire in 1896. Also worth seeing is the dazzling white **City Cemetery**, Coronel and Machala, but beware of robbers midweek.

The **'Black Market'**, by the waterfront north of Olmedo, is a huge open-air affair selling almost anything. It's colourful, interesting and reasonably safe, but watch for pickpockets.

Special Events

The whole city parties in the last week of July, celebrating Bolívar's birthday (24 July), followed by Guayaquil Foundation Day (25 July), and hotels may be full. Banks and other services are also disrupted. Guayaquil's Independence Day (9 October), combined with Día de la Raza (Columbus Day, 12 October), is an important local holiday period. New Year's Eve (31 December) is celebrated with bonfires.

Places to Stay

Hotels are required to post their approved prices near the entrance. There are not many single rooms to be had during festivals and budget hotels are generally poor and not that cheap.

For people on a very tight budget, the very basic *Hotel La Buena Esperanza* and *Hotel Ecuatoriana* (☎ 518 105) are both US$3 per person. There are several worse ones at this price or less near the market and in the dodgy area between Olmedo and Sucre. Some of the cheap hotels in these areas double as brothels, and lone females may be improperly treated or molested.

The clean, secure *Hotel Delicia* (☎ 324 925), Ballén 1105, is US$4 per person and recommended. The *Hotel Ecuador* (☎ 321 460, 518 680), Moncayo 1117, is a decent place at US$7.50 for a double with bath and TV; singles cost the same. The clean *Hotel*

Berlin at Rumichaca and Sucre is quite good at US$3.75 per person. The similarly priced *Hotel Reina Victoria* (☎ 322 188) is basic but OK. Other acceptable places for about US$4 per person are the *Hotel Savoy* (☎ 308 296) and the *Residencial Pauker* (☎ 565 385).

The *Hotel Hostal USA* (☎ 307 804), Quisquis 305, has small, windowless rooms with fans for US$4/6 for singles/doubles and better rooms with bath and TV for US$5/8. The *Hotel Caribe* (☎ 526 162), Olmedo 250, is OK for US$8 for a double with bath and fan or US$10 with TV and air-con. Next door, the OK *Hotel Fiesta Internacional* (☎ 329 813) is US$2 more. The *Hotel Libertador* (☎ 304 637) isn't bad for US$5 per person. The *Hotel Colonial*, Rumichaca at Urdaneta, is safe, clean and friendly at US$8/10 with bath, TV and air-con.

The *Hotel Alexander* (☎ 532 000), Luque 1107, is good value at US$11/14 for singles/doubles with bath, hot water, air-con, telephone, and a decent restaurant. The similarly priced *Hotel Metropolitana* (☎ 565 250, 565 251), VM Rendón 120, safely up on the 4th floor, also has air-con and hot water and is a good deal. The reasonable *Hotel Nuevo Sander* (☎ 320 030), Luque 1101, has air-con and cold-water private baths at US$11 for one or two people. The decent *Hotel Regina* (☎ 312 893), Garaycoa 423, is US$13 (one or two people) with air-con, hot water and TV. The *Hotel Centenario* (☎ 524 467), Vélez 726, is about US$14 for one or two people. Rooms vary: some have fans, others air-con. Some have TVs. All have cold baths and some are nicer than others.

Hostal Ecuahogar (☎ 248 357, 240 388), is near the airport on Isidro Ayora in front of the Banco Ecuatoriana de Vivienda. It is part of the Hostelling International chain and charges US$10/18 or US$8 in dorms. There is a discount for hostel members. There are private hot baths, kitchen facilities and a café; information and airport or bus pick-up service are available. The No 22 city bus goes past here from the terminal terrestre.

Places to Eat

For breakfast (and all day) we like *La Palma*, which serves coffee and croissants at pavement tables on Escobedo near Vélez. Next door, *El Cyrano* is a locally popular pavement hang-out for lunch, dinner and beers. For good coffee and breakfast in elegant surroundings at surprisingly low prices, try the fancy hotels.

La Galleta Pecosa, on 10 de Agosto near Boyacá, sells good home-made cookies. *Heladería Pingüino* on the Parque del Centenario is good for ice creams.

The *Gran Chifa* (☎ 512 488), P Carbo 1016, is elegant but reasonably priced. The cheaper *Chifa Himalaya* (☎ 329 593), Sucre 308, is good and popular. Also popular is the *Restaurant Mayflower*, on Colón near Chimborazo.

Paxilandia, VM Rendón 751, is a good, cheap vegetarian restaurant open for lunch. The *Restaurant Vegetariano Salud Solar*, on Luque near Moncayo, serves good, simple and cheap lunches. *El Camino*, on Icaza near Córdova, serves inexpensive lunches, including a few meatless ones.

There are several piers along the Malecón where restaurant boats are moored; these are OK for lunch, when you can watch the river traffic go by; they get pricier at dinner time. One is *El Pirata*, another is the pricier *Muelle 5*. Modern cafeterias, restaurants and fast-food places line Avenida 9 de Octubre, but they are not very cheap.

The suburb of Urdesa, six km north-west of the centre, has good and popular restaurants, some reasonably priced but none dirt cheap. There is some nightlife – this is a good area to hang out in. The main drag is VE Estrada, and most of the restaurants, bars and clubs are found along this street. *La Parrillada del Ñato* (☎ 387 098), on VE Estrada near Laurales, serves good Ecuadorian-style steaks, grills and barbecues, as well as pizza. *Pizzería Ch'Enano*, VE Estrada 1320, also serves good pizzas. *La Tablita* (☎ 388 162), Ebanos 126 near VE Estrada, has good Ecuadorian-style grills and steaks. For Mexican dinners, try *Paco's* (☎ 442 112), at Acacias 725 near Guayacanes. Mariachi bands play here sometimes. *El Caribe* on VE Estrada has Caribbean specialities.

ECUADOR

Entertainment

El Telégrafo and *El Universo* publicise entertainment. There are some 18 cinemas; English-language movies with Spanish subtitles are often shown. Friday newspapers advertise weekend peñas, which are rarely cheap and always start late. A good one is *La Peña Rincón Folklórico*, at Malecón 208. It opens at 10 pm for food and drinks, the show starts about midnight and continues until the early hours; the cover charge is US$3 and drinks aren't cheap. *Los Checitos*, PP Gómez and Garaycoa, has live salsa bands and dancing from Wednesday to Sunday. A US$6 cover charge includes five beers! It's a lively spot.

Along VE Estrada in Urdesa, there are plenty of clubs, bars and discos. *Tequilala* dance club is currently popular.

Getting There & Away

Air The main airport is on Avenida de las Américas, five km north of the centre. The international/domestic terminals are side by side. A casa de cambio is open for all incoming international flights. International flights (to Latin America, USA and Europe) out of Guayaquil are subject to a US$25 departure tax.

There are many daily flights to Quito (US$31) with TAME or SAN-Saeta. One or two flights a day go to Cuenca (US$27), three a week to Loja (US$22), and one every weekday to Machala (US$20).

Flights to the Galápagos (US$333 return) go to Baltra with TAME, or to San Cristóbal with SAN-Saeta (most days).

One km south of the main airport is the *avioneta* (light aircraft) terminal, with flights to many coastal destinations. The baggage limit is 10 kg and passenger weight limit is 100 kg.

AECA
    Avioneta Terminal (☎ 294 711)
AvioPacífico
    Avioneta Terminal (☎ 283 304, 283 305)
CEDTA
    Avioneta Terminal
    Escobedo 924 and VM Rendón (☎ 561 954, 301 165)

SAN-Saeta
    Vélez 226 and Chile (☎ 329 855, 326 466)
TAME
    9 de Octubre 424, Gran Pasaje (☎ 561 751, 563 993, 565 806)

Bus The terminal terrestre is two km beyond the airport. There are dozens of bus offices, stores, restaurants, tourist information, a bank, hairdresser and so on. You can get buses to most towns; ask at the passenger information desk. For fares and hours, see under the town you wish to go to.

Train Daily trains for Alausí (US$12) and on to Riobamba (US$14) leave from the Durán railway station at 6.25 am; see under Alausí for more information. Durán is a suburb on the opposite side of the Río Guayas; a taxi will cost about US$5. Passengers arriving from Alausí will find the ferry just west of the station but may arrive too late to catch it. (Getting off at Bucay avoids this problem.) Durán has basic hotels, including the *Hotel Paris* at US$6 a double, perhaps the least offensive. The train ride is spectacular.

Boat The daily Durán ferry across the Río Guayas (US$0.10, 15 minutes) leaves a few times an hour from 7 am to 6.30 pm. This is a good sightseeing trip for the impecunious! The dock is on the Malecón near Montalvo.

Getting Around

A taxi from the centre to the airport or terminal terrestre is about US$2.50, but from the airport, higher fares are charged. For cheaper taxis, cross Avenida de las Américas in front of the airport and bargain. From this street, there are buses to the town centre or bus terminal.

From the centre, buses run along the Malecón and pass the airport (US$0.25, 30 minutes); allow plenty of time if catching a flight. Buses to the terminal terrestre leave from Parque Victoria, near 10 de Agosto and Moncayo.

MACHALA

This is the capital of El Oro province and the centre of a major banana-growing area. With 150,000 inhabitants, it's Ecuador's fourth-largest city. Most travellers to and from Peru pass through here, but few stay more than a night. Puerto Bolívar, the international port, seven km away, is worth visiting.

Information

CETUR (☎ 932 106) is upstairs at 9 de Mayo and Pichincha.

Banco del Pacífico, on Rocafuerte at Junín, and Delgado Travel, on 9 de Mayo near the plaza, change travellers' cheques.

The Peruvian Consulate (☎ 930 680), on Bolívar near Colón, is open Monday to Friday from 9 am to 1.30 pm.

The No 1 bus to Puerto Bolívar (US$0.20) plies 9 de Octubre from the central plaza. Boats can be hired to visit the mangroves. Several boats a day go to **Jambelí** (US$1, 30 minutes), with a beach and basic hotels.

Places to Stay

Most hotels have only cold water. The cheapest are the very basic *Residencial Machala* at US$2 per person, and the *Almache* and *Pichincha* residenciales at US$2.50 per person. Somewhat better are the *Hotel Molina* (☎ 938 365) at US$4/6 for singles/doubles, the acceptable *Residencial Pesantez* and *Hotel La Delicia*, both at US$3.50 per person, and the friendly *Residencial La Internacional* at US$4 per person. The *Hostal La Bahía* (☎ 920 518) is a good cheap place at US$4.50 for a double or US$4.50 per person with bath.

One of the best cheap hotels, often full by lunch time, is the clean *Hostal Mercy* (☎ 920 116) at US$4.50 per person with bath or US$6 with air-con. The friendly *Residencial La Cueva de los Tayos* (☎ 935 600), is clean at US$4.50 per person or US$5.50 with bath and fan. The *Hotel Ecuatoriano* (☎ 930 197) is rather noisy but convenient if you are arriving late at the adjoining bus terminal. Reasonably clean but shabby rooms, some with air-con, are US$5 per person.

The *Hotel Suites Guayaquil* (922 570) is OK for US$6.50 per person with bath, air-con and, in some rooms, TV and telephone. The *Hotel Mosquera Internacional* (☎ 931 752) is US$8/13 in small clean rooms with a fan and US$10/18 with air-con. All have private hot showers and most have a TV and telephone. Also with hot showers are the decent *Hotel Inés* (☎ 932 301) at US$10/15 with air-con and TV and the *Hotel Internacional San Francisco* (☎ 922 395) at US$9/16 with a fan and US$12/20 with air-con. Both have good restaurants.

Places to Eat

Restaurant Chifa Central, on Tarqui near 9 de Octubre, is good and reasonably priced, especially the filling chaulafan (fried rice with pork, chicken, egg etc). Many locals eat lunch here. Other cheap places are along 9 de Octubre, including *La Fogata* for grilled chicken. *Bar Restaurant El Bosque* (☎ 924 344), on 9 de Mayo near Bolívar, has an outdoor dining area and simple but decent meals for US$2. *Café América* is quite good and open till midnight. The better hotel restaurants are good.

Puerto Bolívar has seafood restaurants.

Getting There & Away

Air The airport is one km south-west of town along Montalvo (taxi US$1). At the airport, CEDTA and LANSA have light aircraft for Guayaquil. TAME (☎ 930 139), on Montalvo near Pichincha, has weekday flights to Guayaquil (US$20).

Bus To the Peruvian border at Huaquillas (US$1.20, two hours), use CIFA, which operates frequent buses from the corner of Bolívar and Guayas. Be prepared for passport checks en route. You must leave the bus to register, but the driver will wait.

CIFA buses also go to Guayaquil (US$3, 3½ hours) from 9 de Octubre near Tarqui. Rutas Orenses and Ecuatoriana Pullman also serve Guayaquil, the latter in air-conditioned coaches.

Panamericana has several coaches a day to Quito (US$7.50, 10 to 12 hours). Ciudad de Piñas has several buses a day to Piñas, and

Machala

PLACES TO STAY
2 Hotel Mosquera Internacional
4 Hotel Montecarlo
5 Residencial Pesantez
6 Hotel Ines
8 Residencial Machala
9 Residencial La Internacional
10 Hotel Ejecutivo
12 Hotel Molina
13 Hotel Mercia
15 Residencial Pichincha
16 Residencial Almache
17 Hotel Oro
19 Hotel Suites Guayaquil
20 Hotel Perla del Pacifico
21 Hostal La Bahia
22 Hostal Mercy
24 Hotel Internacional San Francisco
32 Residencial La Cueva de los Tayos
34 Rizzo Hotel
45 Hotel Ecuatoriano

PLACES TO EAT
3 Café América
7 La Fogata
31 Restaurant Chifa Central
35 Bar Restaurant El Bosque

OTHER
1 EMETEL
11 Market
14 Church
18 Cine Tauro
23 Transportes Pullman Sucre (Buses)
25 Cooperativa Pullman Azuay (Buses)
26 CIFA Buses to Huaquillas
27 Travel Agencies
28 Delgado Travel
29 Casa de Cambio Illauri
30 Puffo Crespo (Buses)
33 Ecuatoriana Pullman (Buses)
36 CETUR Tourist Information
37 CEDTA-LANSA (Local Airlines)
38 TAME Airline
39 Post Office
40 Banco del Pacifico
41 Transportes El Oro
42 CIFA Buses to Guayaquil
43 TranSportes Cooperativa Loja (Buses)
44 Ciudad de Piñas (Buses)
46 Peruvian Consulate
47 Transportes TAC (Buses)
48 Transportes Union Yantzaza (Buses)
49 Panamericana (Buses)

the 6 am bus continues to Loja. It also has one or two buses to Cuenca (US$3.50, 4½ hours). Transportes Cooperativa Loja also goes to Loja (US$2.20, eight hours). Pullman Azuay has eight buses daily to Cuenca.

HUAQUILLAS

Huaquillas, 80 km from Machala, is the main border town with Peru. It is called Aguas Verdes on the Peruvian side. There is a busy street market on the Ecuadorian side of the border, which is full of Peruvians shopping on day passes. Almost everything happens on the long main street.

Information

Banks don't change money, but there are street moneychangers. They offer poor rates, are pushy, and may used 'fixed' calculators or offer outdated bills. Check with travellers going the opposite way for up-to-date exchange rates and information. It is best to use US dollars for exchange, so arrive with as few sucres (or Peruvian *nuevos soles*) as possible. Beware of thieves in the street market on the border.

Places to Stay & Eat

Several cheap but poor hotels (under US$3 per person) are near the immigration office. *Residencial Huaquillas* is the best of these. There are cheap and basic restaurants nearby.

For about US$9 a double with bath, the *Hotel Rodey*, Teniente Cordovez and 10 de Agosto, is clean and reasonable. Also good is the *Parador Turístico Huaquillas* (☎ 907 374), 1.5 km from the border on the main road out of town, with the town's best restaurant and simple clean doubles with bath for US$14. The *Hotel Vanessa*, 1 de Mayo 323, has clean air-conditioned doubles with bath for US$18.

Getting There & Away

CIFA buses run frequently to Machala (US$1.20, two hours) from the main street, two blocks beyond the immigration office when heading away from Peru. Panamericana has four daily buses to Quito (US$8, 13 hours). Ecuatoriana Pullman has buses to

Guayaquil (US$4, 5½ hours). A few buses go to Loja and Cuenca.

To/From Peru The Ecuadorian immigration office is 200 metres from the international bridge and has the yellow, blue and red striped Ecuadorian flag. Entrance and exit formalities are carried out here. The Ecuadorian office is open daily from 8 am to noon and 2 to 5 pm.

Those entering Ecuador need an exit stamp in their passport from the Peruvian authorities. Entrance formalities are usually straightforward. Travellers need a T-3 tourist card, which is available free at the immigration office. Usually only 30 days are given, but it is easy to obtain a renewal in Quito or Guayaquil. Show of funds or onward tickets are very rarely asked for.

Those leaving Ecuador need an exit stamp from the Ecuadorian immigration office before entering Peru. If you have lost your T-3 card, you should be able to get a free replacement at the border, as long as the stamp in your passport has not expired.

After showing your passport to the international bridge guard, take a shared mototaxi (US$0.50) to the Peruvian immigration building, about two km beyond the border. Officially, an onward ticket is required to enter Peru, but this is not often asked for and, if it is, you can (politely) talk your way out of it. Border officials may be looking for a bribe; don't give in. From here, shared colectivos go to Tumbes (US$1). Beware of overcharging by drivers: every one is out to make a fast buck!

The Galápagos Islands

The Galápagos archipelago is famous for its fearless and unique wildlife. Here, you can swim with sea lions, float eye-to-eye with a penguin, stand next to a blue-footed booby feeding its young, watch a giant 200-kg tortoise lumbering through a cactus forest, and try to avoid stepping on iguanas scurrying over the lava. The scenery is barren and volcanic and has its own haunting beauty, though some people find it bare and ugly. Visiting the islands is very expensive, however, so this is for the wilderness and wildlife enthusiast, not the average sun-seeker.

The islands were uninhabited when they were first discovered by the Spanish in 1535. They lie on the equator, about 1000 km west of Ecuador, and consist of 13 major islands and many small ones. Five islands are inhabited. The archipelago's most famous visitor was Charles Darwin, who came here in 1835. The Galápagos as a whole are one of Ecuador's 21 provinces.

Orientation

The most important island is Isla Santa Cruz in the middle of the archipelago. On the southern side of the island is Puerto Ayora, the largest town in the Galápagos and the place in which most tours are based. There are many hotels and restaurants. North of Santa Cruz, separated by a narrow strait, is Isla Baltra, with the islands' major airport. A public bus and a ferry connect the Baltra airport with Puerto Ayora.

Isla San Cristóbal, the most easterly island, has the provincial capital, Puerto Baquerizo Moreno. There are hotels and an airport, but more travellers fly into Baltra.

The other inhabited islands are Isla Isabela, with the small port of Puerto Villamil, and Isla Santa María (Floreana), with Puerto Velasco Ibarra; both have places to stay. Inter-island transport is by infrequent public ferries or private boat.

Information

The islands are a national park. All foreign visitors must pay US$80 upon arrival (US$40 for children under 12; students under 26 with ID from their home college or uni may also pay US$40, but this is subject to change). In addition there's a city tax of US$30 per person at Puerto Baquerizo Moreno and US$10 at Puerto Ayora (the latter may soon rise to US$30). The high seasons are from December to January, around Easter, and from June to August;

during these periods, budget tours may be more difficult to arrange. Note that most of the islands have two or even three names. Galápagos time is one hour behind mainland Ecuador.

Tourist Office CETUR has a Puerto Ayora office. Self-styled tourist information agencies mainly provide information about their own boat trips and charters. Adatur is one dealing with budget boats. The SAEC in Quito has recent travel information.

Money Banco del Pacífico in Puerto Ayora changes money at reasonable rates. Most tours can be paid for in US dollars.

Post & Communications Mail is slow. Have stamps franked to avoid them being removed. EMETEL occasionally doesn't work.

Electricity This is cut off at 11 pm or earlier in some places.

Books Lonely Planet's *Ecuador & the Galápagos Islands – a travel survival kit*, 4th edition, by Rob Rachowiecki has plenty of Galápagos information, plus a wildlife guide for the nonspecialist. The best general wildlife guide, with background information on history and geology, is Michael H Jackson's *Galápagos: A Natural History Guide*. Birdwatchers consult *A Field Guide to the Birds of the Galápagos* by Michael Harris. Amateur botanists use the pocket-sized *Plants of the Galápagos Islands* by Eileen K Schofield. There is also *A Field Guide to the Fishes of Galapagos* by Godfrey Merlen. Most are available at major bookshops in Quito and Guayaquil or from the SAEC.

What to Bring Many things are expensive or unavailable in the Galápagos. Stock up on sunscreen, insect repellent, film, batteries, toiletries and medication on the mainland.

Getting There & Away

Flying to the Galápagos is recommended. If you go by boat, you will probably waste a lot of time in the port of Guayaquil getting one of the infrequent passages. With the extra food and accommodation costs, you are unlikely to save much money.

Air Most visitors fly to Isla Baltra, from where public buses and a ferry go to Puerto Ayora, on Isla Santa Cruz. (Tour groups are sometimes picked up directly from Baltra by their boats.) There are flights to Puerto Baquerizo Moreno, on Isla San Cristóbal, but there are more facilities in Puerto Ayora, and travellers wanting to arrange tours in the islands should go there.

TAME flies Monday to Saturday (daily in the high season) from both Quito (US$377 return) and Guayaquil (US$333 return, 1½ hours) to Baltra. Flights are 25% less in the low season. Ecuadorians or foreigners on residence visas pay about half price. Students with ID from their home college or uni can get discounts (15% or more) at the Quito TAME office.

SAN-Saeta flights to Puerto Baquerizo Moreno are similarly priced with departures daily except Thursday and Sunday. TAME and SAN-Saeta do not honour one another's tickets. You can buy one-way tickets to one island and leave from the other. It's possible to buy tickets with open return dates. Always reconfirm flights.

If you are signed up with a tour, make sure that you are flying to the right island! People occasionally end up in the wrong place and miss their tour.

If you fly Miami-Ecuador-Galápagos with SAETA, the Galápagos portion is about US$100 cheaper.

Military *logístico* (supply) flights leave on Wednesday and Saturday from Quito to Baltra (US$140 one way) but getting on is difficult. Go to the military airport (☎ 445 043) just north of the civil airport to make reservations. If successful, you have to pay for the ticket in exact US dollars.

Some tour agencies give discounts on air fares if you take their tours, especially in the off season (February to May, September to November). Agencies may sell a discounted

ticket at the last moment if they can't sell the reserved tour space.

If flights are full, try going to the airport. Agencies book blocks of seats for their tours and release unsold seats on the day of the flight (these are full-price tickets). During the high season, large cruise ships pick up passengers at Baltra on Monday, Wednesday, Thursday and Sunday – the busiest days. Tuesday is the quietest day to fly.

Boat Cargo ships leave irregularly and charge about US$150 to US$200. It takes 3½ days to get to the islands. Conditions are tolerable but basic. These ships normally do round trips and are for cargo purposes, not for wildlife viewing. If you stay aboard while the boat spends about a week making deliveries around the islands you are charged about US$50 a day, or you can get off and return later. The most reliable boat is the *Piquero*, which leaves Guayaquil around the 25th of every month. The agent for the *Piquero* is Acotramar (☎ 401 004, 401 711, 402 371), at General Gómez 522 and Coronel, Guayaquil. Naval vessels may take passengers. Try at Transnave (☎ 561 453), 9 de Octubre 416 and Chile, Guayaquil. Also ask at the Capitanía in Guayaquil, or at the boats, which anchor near dock No 4. Be prepared to wait weeks for a boat – though you might get lucky.

Getting Around

Arriving air passengers in Baltra are met by a crew member (if on a prearranged tour) or take a bus-ferry-bus combination to Puerto Ayora (US$4, two hours). Buy tickets in the airport.

From Puerto Ayora, buses leave at 7.30 am from the park for the return trip to Baltra. Buy tickets at the supermarket.

Air passengers arriving in Puerto Baquerizo Moreno can walk into town in a few minutes.

Inter-island transport is with INGALA (☎ 526 151 in Puerto Ayora) open Monday to Friday from 7.30 am to 12.30 pm and 1.30 to 4 pm. Recently, boat schedules were as follows:

Departure	From	To
Tues 10 am	Puerto Ayora	Puerto Baquerizo Moreno
Wed 10 am	Puerto Baquerizo Moreno	Puerto Ayora
Thurs 8 am	Puerto Ayora	Puerto Velasco Ibarra (Isla Santa María) and on to Puerto Villamil (Isla Isabela)
Fri 10 am	Puerto Villamil	Puerto Ayora
Sat 8 am	Puerto Ayora	Puerto Baquerizo Moreno
Mon 10 am	Puerto Baquerizo Moreno	Puerto Ayora

In 1995 a new, larger vessel was introduced, which alleviates some of the previous problems with obtaining tickets. Fares are US$36 on any passage (US$24 for locals) and subject to change. If you can't get on an INGALA boat, ask around for private trips, which are more expensive.

PUERTO AYORA

This is the main population centre of the archipelago and the centre of the tourist industry. See Orientation above.

Things to See & Do

See the following Around Puerto Ayora section for places to visit.

You can rent bicycles (see map) for about US$12 a day.

Galápagos Sub-Aqua (☎ 526 350) provides everything you'll need for **scuba diving**. It has been well recommended and its rates are very competitive. A one-week certification course for beginners, including all gear, boat, instructor and certificate costs from US$350. Diving only, including gear, boat and guide, is from US$75 a day (two dives). Divemaster Fernando Zambrano speaks English and is very experienced.

Places to Stay

The *Residencial Los Amigos* is a popular budget hotel with clean rooms for US$3 per person. Also popular is *La Peregrina B&B* which is US$4 per person including a good breakfast. It is run by Jehovah's Witnesses but they don't try and convert you! The *Residencial Flamingo* is OK for US$3/5 for singles/doubles with bath. The *Hotel Sir Francis Drake* has a decent restaurant and is quite good at about US$3.50 per person. Other cheap places include the *Hotel Santa Cruz* and *Residencial España*.

The *Hotel Darwin* charges US$5/8 with private bath and has a restaurant. The *Hotel Lobo del Mar* is popular with Ecuadorian tour groups and tends to be noisy. Rooms are basic but reasonably clean at US$8/10 for singles/doubles with bath. There are some triples and quadruples which are not much more expensive. For about US$5 extra per person three meals a day are included. The hotel organises day trips to various islands for about US$40 per passenger. The *Hotel Sol y Mar* is similarly priced.

The *Hotel Las Palmeras* is quite good but often full. Prices are about US$10/15 for clean singles/doubles with private bath. Similarly priced and also clean and modern-looking are the *Hotel Salinas* and *Hotel Lirio del Mar*, nearby.

Places to Eat, Drink & Dance

Restaurants and bars in Puerto Ayora are where to meet people. Service is leisurely. Places change owners and names quite often, as places frequented by seasonal influxes of people tend to do. Most of the following have been around for a few years.

Restaurant Salvavidas, by the dock, is a good place for a beer, snack or meal while waiting for your *panga* (the small dinghy that every boat carries for shore trips). *Las Cuatro Linternas* has a variety of Italian and other food and *Pizzería Media Luna* is also good. *Parrillada Don Guillo* has meaty dishes. *La Panga* has a restaurant, bar and disco, all of which are popular. *La Terraza* is a long-standing nightspot which varies from dead to packed with dancers. On that block are a changing variety of places to eat. More places to eat are out along Avenida Padre Julio Herrera. Some of these are inexpensive; look for places where locals are eating, especially at lunch. The *Five Fingers* is a popular drinking and dancing spot.

ECUADOR

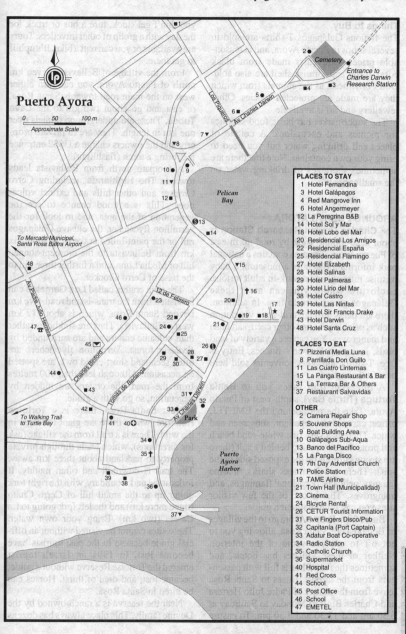

Puerto Ayora

0   50   100 m
Approximate Scale

Pelican Bay

To Mercado Municipal,
Santa Rosa Baltra Airport

12 de Febrero

Charles Binford

Tomás de Berlanga

To Walking Trail
to Turtle Bay

Av Charles Darwin

Park

Av Charles Darwin

Los Piqueros

Av Padre Julio Herrera

Pelican Bay

Entrance to
Charles Darwin
Research Station

Cemetery

*Puerto
Ayora
Harbor*

ECUADOR

Things to Buy

The famous Galápagos T-shirts are sold in several shops in Puerto Ayora, and at reasonable prices. Souvenirs made from black coral, turtle and tortoise shell are also sold. Don't buy these, as the animals from which they are made are protected species. Other jewellery and art is available.

The supermarket has basic food supplies for picnics and excursions. A couple of places sell drinking water but you need to bring your own container. Note that there are sometimes shortages of drinking water on the smaller boats.

AROUND PUERTO AYORA

The **Charles Darwin Research Station** is about a 20-minute walk by road north-east of Puerto Ayora. The area contains a national park information centre, a museum, a baby tortoise nursery, and a walk-in adult tortoise enclosure where you can meet these Galápagos giants face to face. In addition, there are paths through arid-zone vegetation such as prickly pear and other cacti, salt bush and mangroves. You can see a variety of land birds, including Darwin's finches. Entry is free. T-shirts and other souvenirs sold here benefit the station.

A three-km trail takes you to **Bahía Tortuga (Turtle Bay)**, south-west of Puerto Ayora. Take the path behind the EMETEL office; carry insect repellent, sunscreen and water. There is a very fine white-sand beach and protected swimming behind a spit (there are strong currents on the exposed side of the spit). There are harmless sharks, marine iguanas, pelicans, occasional flamingos, and mangroves. This is one of the few visitor sites you can go to without a guide.

Buses from Puerto Ayora go to the villages of Bellavista or Santa Rosa, allowing you to get off to explore some of the interior. Neither of these villages has hotels, and sometimes the return bus is full with passengers from the airport. Buses to Santa Rosa leave from the corner of Padre Julio Herrera and Charles Binford Monday to Saturday at 6.30 am and 12.30 and 4.30 pm. To ensure you don't get stuck, hire a bus or truck for the day with a group of other travellers. Tours are available or you can rent a bike. It's uphill to get there.

From the village of Bellavista, seven km north of Puerto Ayora, you can turn either west on the main road towards Santa Rosa, or east and go about two km to the **Lava Tubes**. These are underground tunnels over one km in length. They are in private property and the owners charge a US$2 entrance fee; bring a torch (flashlight).

A footpath north from Bellavista leads towards **The Highlands**, including Cerro Crocker and other hills and extinct volcanoes. This is a good chance to see the vegetation of the area, and to look for the vermilion flycatcher, the elusive Galápagos rail or the paint-billed crake. It is about six km from Bellavista to the crescent-shaped hill of Media Luna, and a further three km to the base of Cerro Crocker.

The twin craters called **Los Gemelos** can be visited from the trans-island road, five km beyond Santa Rosa, which is about 12 km west of Bellavista. They are sinkholes rather than volcanic craters and are surrounded by *Scalesia* forest. Vermilion flycatchers are often seen, and short-eared owls are spotted on occasion. Although less than 100 metres from the road, the craters are hidden by vegetation, so go with a guide.

Near Santa Rosa, there is a **Tortoise Reserve**, where there are giant tortoises in the wild. There is a trail from the village (ask for directions), which leads through private property to parkland about three km away. The trail is downhill and often muddy. It forks at the park boundary, with the right fork going up to the small hill of Cerro Chato (three more km) and the left fork going to La Caseta (two km). Bring your own water. These sites cannot be visited without an official guide because in the past tourists have become lost. In 1991 an Israeli tourist entered the Tortoise Reserve without a guide, became lost, and died of thirst. Horses can be hired in Santa Rosa.

Near the reserve is a ranch owned by the Devine family. This place always has dozens of giant tortoises and you can wander around at will and take photos for a US$2 fee. Remember to close the gates as you go through. The café sells cold drinks and hot tea, which is welcome if the highland *garúa* (mist) has soaked you.

PUERTO BAQUERIZO MORENO
Places to Stay & Eat

With the recent increase in tourism, more hotels are being opened and there are now about a dozen. The cheapest hotels include the *Pensión San Francisco* (☎ 520 104), which is clean and good value (US$8 a double with bath), the *Residencial Northia*, the *Cabañas Don Jorge* (☎ 520 208) and several others, some more expensive.

Rositas Restaurant serves tasty bacalao (a local fish) and is one of the best cheap restaurants in town. The *Casa Blanca* is pricier but good, and there are several other restaurants, cafés and bars.

AROUND PUERTO BAQUERIZO MORENO

Frigatebird Hill (locally called Cerro de las Tijeretas) is about 1.5 km east of Puerto Baquerizo Moreno and can be reached on a foot trail without a guide. There is a national park information office en route. From the hill, there is a beautiful view of a bay below and the town behind. Frigatebirds nest here and you might see lava lizards.

There are a few buses a day from Baquerizo Moreno to the farming centre of El Progreso, about eight km to the east, and lying at the base of the Cerro San Joaquín (896 metres), the highest point on San Cristóbal. From here, there are occasional buses, or you can hire a jeep or walk 10 km to the visitor site of **El Junco Lagoon**, a freshwater lake at about 700 metres above sea level. The road continues beyond the lagoon, but it's in poor shape. It may reach the northern end of the island, at the **Los Galápagos** visitor site, where giant tortoises can be seen in the wild. Enquire in town.

About an hour north of Puerto Baquerizo Moreno by boat is the tiny, rocky **Isla Lobos**, which is the main sea-lion and blue-footed booby colony open to visitors to San Cristóbal. There is a 300-metre trail, and you can see lava lizards here.

ISLA ISABELA

Most hotels are in Puerto Villamil, from which an 18-km road leads up to the tiny village of Santo Tomás.

There are about six places to stay, all fairly inexpensive (about US$10 a double or less). One of the cheapest is *Posada San Vicente* in Puerto Villamil, which has rooms with private bath. The owner, Antonio Gil, is a local guide and can take you up the volcano on horseback. The *Hotel Ballena Azul* is one of the most popular places, and you can contact the staff in Puerto Ayora by asking around. It arranges tours and is one of the more expensive (though still quite cheap). Others include the *Hotel Alexandra* and *El Refugio del Capitán*, both by the beach, the *Tero Real* and the *Hotel Loja*, on the road up to the highlands.

The *Hotel Loja* has a good restaurant. Most hotels can arrange meals. There are some cheap *comedores* in the port, but you need to ask them in advance to cook a meal for you – that gives you an idea of how few visitors there are.

ISLA SANTA MARIA

This island has less than 100 inhabitants. They are centred around Puerto Velasco Ibarra. There is a small hotel and restaurant, run by the famous Margaret Wittmer and her family, as well as a small gift shop and post office. You can write for reservations (Señora Wittmer, Puerto Velasco Ibarra, Santa María, Galápagos; allow a couple of months) or just show up. The place is rarely full.

VISITOR SITES

To protect the islands, the national park authorities allow access to about 50 visitor sites, in addition to the towns and public areas. Other areas are off limits. The visitor sites are where the most interesting wildlife and geology are seen. Apart from the ones mentioned above (near Puerto Ayora and Baquerizo Moreno), most are reached by boat.

Normally, landings are made in a panga. Landings are 'wet' (where you have to hop overboard and wade ashore in knee-deep water) or 'dry' (where you get off onto a pier or rocky outcrop.) Take care with these landings; cameras should be wrapped in a plastic bag. People occasionally fall in the surf of a wet landing or slip on the algae-covered rocks of a dry one. Boat captains will not land groups in places other than designated visitor sites. In addition, there are many designated marine sites for snorkelling or diving.

On a cruise of under a week, try to visit the following islands. South Plaza has land iguana, sea-lion and swallow-tailed gull colonies, an *Opuntia* cactus forest and good snorkelling. Seymour has nesting colonies of both blue-footed boobies and magnificent frigatebirds. Caleta Tortuga Negra (Black Turtle Cove), on the north shore of Santa Cruz, has marine turtles and white-tipped sharks.

Isla Bartolomé has a volcanic cone that is easy to climb and gives one of the best views of the islands. There are also penguins, sea lions and good snorkelling on Isla Bartolomé. On San Salvador, you can walk on a lava flow by Sullivan Bay, and see marine iguanas, sea lions, fur seals, Galápagos hawks and many kinds of sea birds near Puerto Egas. Rábida has a flamingo colony, as well as a colony of irascible bachelor sea lions. You'll see other species almost everywhere. Masked and blue-footed boobies, pelicans, mockingbirds, finches, Galápagos doves, frigatebirds, lava lizards and red sally lightfoot crabs are common.

If you have a full week or more, visit some outlying islands. The red-footed booby is found on Genovesa and the small islets surrounding Santa María. The waved albatross breeds only on Española, and the flightless Galápagos cormorant is found on the western islands of Isabela and Fernandina.

ACTIVITIES
Snorkelling
If you don a mask and snorkel, a new world unfolds for you. Baby sea lions stare at you, various species of ray come slowly undulating by, and penguins dart past in a stream of bubbles. The hundreds of species of fish are spectacularly colourful, and you can watch flapping sea turtles as they circle you. This won't, of course, happen immediately you enter the water, but you have a good chance of seeing most of these things if you spend, say, half an hour a day in the water during a week of cruising.

A mask and snorkel also allow you to observe more sedentary forms of marine life. Sea urchins, starfish, sea anemones, algae and crustaceans combine colourfully in an exotic underwater display. Bring a snorkel and mask. The ones on the boats aren't very good. You may be able to buy a snorkel and mask in sporting goods shops in Quito or Guayaquil. Consider bringing them from home to ensure a good fit.

The water temperature is about 21°C from January to April, and 19°C at other times. You may want a wet-suit top with you.

Scuba Diving
See under Puerto Ayora for a good dive operator. A few boats will run diving tours, but it's cheaper to book in Puerto Ayora.

ORGANISED TOURS
There are three kinds of tour: day trips, returning to the same hotel each night; hotel-based trips, where you stay on different islands; and boat-based trips, with nights spent aboard. These can be arranged in advance from home, or in Quito or Guayaquil, or they can be arranged when you get to the islands. Note that tips are not included. On a cheap one-week tour, the crew and guide are tipped at least US$20 per passenger (about half to the guide). On more expensive tours, the tip can go over US$50.

Day Trips
Most are based in Puerto Ayora, and a few in

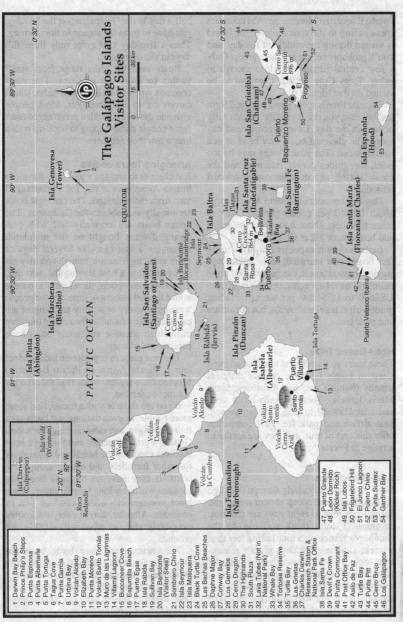

The Galápagos Islands Visitor Sites

0°30' N

89°30' W

0°30' S

1° S

EQUATOR

PACIFIC OCEAN

0   15   30 km

Isla Pinta (Abingdon)

Isla Marchena (Bindloe)

Isla Genovesa (Tower)

Isla Wolf (Wenman)

Isla Darwin (Culpepper)

Roca Redonda

1°20' N 91°30' W 92° W

91° W

90°30' W

90° W

Volcán Wolf

Volcán Darwin

Volcán Alcedo

Isla Fernandina (Narborough)

Volcán la Cumbre

Volcán Cerro Azul

Volcán Santo Tomás

Isla Isabela (Albemarle)

Puerto Villamil

Santo Tomás

Isla San Salvador (Santiago or James)

Cerro Cowan 905 m

Isla Rábida (Jervis)

Isla Pinzón (Duncan)

Isla Bartolomé
Rocas Bainbridge

Isla Seymour

Isla Tortuga

Islas Plazas

Isla Baltra

Cerro Crocker 864 m

Santa Rosa

Bellavista

Puerto Ayora

Academy Bay

Isla Santa Cruz (Indefatigable)

Isla Santa Fe (Barrington)

Isla San Cristóbal (Chatham)

Cerro San Joaquín 896 m

El Progreso

Puerto Baquerizo Moreno

Isla Santa María (Floreana or Charles)

Isla Española (Hood)

Puerto Velasco Ibarra

1 Darwin Bay Beach
2 Prince Philip's Steps
3 Punta Espinosa
4 Punta Albemarle
5 Tagus Cove
6 Punta Garcia
7 Punta Moreno
8 Urbina Bay
9 Volcán Alcedo
10 Elizabeth Bay
11 Punta Moreno
12 Volcán Santo Tomás
13 Muro de las Lágrimas
14 Villamil Lagoon
15 Buccaneer Cove
16 Espumilla Beach
17 Puerto Egas
18 Isla Rábida
19 Sullivan Bay
20 Isla Bartolomé (Visitor Sites)
21 Sombrero Chino
22 Isla Seymour
23 Isla Mosquera
24 Black Turtle Cove
25 Las Bachas Beaches
26 Daphne Major
27 Conway Bay
28 Los Gemelos
29 Cerro Dragón
30 The Highlands
31 South Plaza
32 Lava Tubes (Not in National Park)
33 Whale Bay
34 Tortoise Reserve
35 Turtle Bay
36 Las Gretas
37 Charles Darwin Research Station & National Park Office
38 Isla Santa Fe
39 Devil's Crown
40 Punta Cormorant
41 Post Office Bay
42 Asilo de Paz
43 Turtle Bay
44 Punta Pitt
45 Cerro Brujo
46 Los Galápagos
47 Puerto Grande
48 León Dormido (Kicker Rock)
49 Isla Lobos
50 Frigatebird Hill
51 El Junco Lagoon
52 Puerto Chino
53 Punta Suárez
54 Gardner Bay

ECUADOR

Puerto Baquerizo Moreno. Several hours are spent sailing to the visitor site(s), the island is visited during the middle of the day, and you'll probably be part of a large group. Only a few central islands are close enough to either Santa Cruz or San Cristóbal to be visited on day trips.

Because time is spent going back and forth and because you don't visit the islands early or late in the day, I don't recommend day tours. The cheapest boats may be slow and overcrowded. The island visits may be too brief, the guides poorly informed and the crew lacking an adequate conservationist attitude.

Day-trip operators in Puerto Ayora charge about US$40 per person per day. Talk to other travellers about how good the guide and boat are, or ask at CETUR.

Better and more expensive day trips, using fast boats with knowledgeable guides and staying in good hotels, can be arranged at the mainland travel agencies. Prices range from US$600 to US$1000 per week, including guided trips, hotel and meals, but not airfare and park fee.

Hotel-Based Trips

These tours go from island to island and you sleep in hotels on three or four different islands (Santa Cruz, San Cristóbal, Santa María, Isabela). Tours typically last a week and cost US$600 to US$1000 per person, plus airfare and park fee. Few companies offer this sort of tour, and they are harder to arrange in Puerto Ayora.

Boat-Based Trips

Most visitors (particularly foreign ones) go on boat tours, and sleep aboard overnight. Tours from four to eight days are the most common. I don't think you can do the Galápagos justice on a tour lasting less than a week, although five days gives a reasonable look. To visit the outlying islands of Isabela and Fernandina, a two-week cruise is recommended. On the first day of a prearranged tour, you arrive from the mainland by air at about lunch time, and so this is only

half a day in the Galápagos; on the last day, you have to be in the airport in the morning. Thus a five-day tour gives only three full days in the islands.

Boats used for tours range from small yachts to large cruise ships. The most common type of boat is a motor sailer, which carries six to 16 passengers. Most people arrive in the islands with a prearranged tour; some people come hoping to hook up with a tour when they get there.

Arranging Tours on Site

It is cheaper to arrange a tour for yourself in Puerto Ayora than to pay for a prearranged tour from the mainland. The cheapest boats are usually available in the Galápagos. The better boats are normally full with prearranged tours bought on the mainland. Arranging a tour can take several days or more in the high season, though you may get lucky and find a boat leaving the next day. This is not an option, therefore, for people with a limited amount of time, nor for people wanting a luxury boat. July and August are especially busy months when cheap tours are difficult to organise and many boats have prearranged charters.

The best place to organise an independent tour is Puerto Ayora. In Puerto Baquerizo Moreno there are few boats available and it's not recommended.

If you are alone or with a friend, find some more people, as even the smallest boats take four passengers and most take eight or more. Getting a group together and finding a boat involves checking the hotels and restaurants for other travellers and asking around for boats. If they have no business lined up, captains will be looking for passengers. Your hotel manager can often introduce you to someone. After all, almost everyone knows everybody else, so word will quickly get around.

The cheapest and most basic boats are available for about US$50 per day per person, and this should include everything (except park fees and tips). The cheaper the boat, the more simple the food, and the more crowded the accommodation.

Boats won't sail until all passenger berths are taken; empty spots add to group space and comfort, but they must be paid for. Bargaining over the price is acceptable and sometimes necessary.

The most important thing is to find a boat whose crew you get along with and which has a good and enthusiastic naturalist guide who will be able to point out and explain the wildlife and other items of interest. It is worth paying a little more for a good guide. The cheapest boats may have Spanish-speaking Naturalista II guides whose function is to fulfil the legal obligation that every boat has a certified guide aboard. Some of these Naturalista II guides know little about the wildlife and simply act as rangers, making sure that groups stay together on the trails and don't molest the wildlife. (You cannot land without a guide and you must always walk around more or less in a group.) Naturalista III guides, on the other hand, are trained, multilingual guides with degrees in biology. Note that all guides are required to carry a guiding card.

Owners, captains, guides and crews change frequently and, in addition, many boats make changes and improvements from year to year. Generally speaking, a boat is only as good as its crew. You should be able to meet the naturalist guide and captain and inspect the boat before you leave, and you should have an itinerary agreed upon with the boat owner or captain. You can deal with a crew member or boat representative during your search, but don't hand over any money until you have an agreed itinerary, and then pay only the captain.

Get the itinerary in writing to avoid disagreements between you and other passengers and the crew during the cruise. Even with a written agreement, the itinerary may sometimes be changed, but at least it does give you some measure of bargaining power. The SAEC in Quito has a Galápagos information packet, which is updated every year and includes a detailed contract in Spanish/English.

Conditions can be cramped and primitive. Washing facilities vary from a bucket of sea water on the very cheapest boats to fresh-water deck hoses or showers on the better boats. However, many of the cheapest boats have improved their facilities recently and it is possible to find a cheap boat with adequate freshwater showers. If you don't want to stay salty for a week, ask about washing facilities. Also inquire about drinking water. I'd recommend treating the water on most of the cheaper boats or, alternatively, bringing your own large containers of fresh water. Bottled drinks are carried but cost extra; agree on the price before you leave port, and make sure that enough of your favourite refreshments are loaded aboard if you don't want to run out.

Because a boat is only as good as the crew running it, it is difficult to make foolproof recommendations. However, although I have received a number of complaints about boats, none of them consistently complained about the same vessel. Adatur, on the waterfront in Puerto Ayora, is a co-operative of economic boat owners and it can assist with tour arrangements.

Although this is the cheapest option, even in the low season total costs (with flight) will be US$750 minimum for a week-long tour. Budget travellers will find that mainland operators (and other guidebooks) discourage them from attempting to make arrangements on the islands, citing the difficulty of finding appropriate boats. As long as you avoid the high season and are flexible with your schedule, you shouldn't have major problems.

Arranging Tours in Advance

If you don't have the time or patience to arrange tours once you're in the Galápagos, you can arrange tours from your home country (expensive but efficient) or from Quito or Guayaquil (cheaper but you sometimes have to wait several days or weeks during the high season).

You might get a substantial discount by checking various agencies and seeing if they have any spaces to fill on boats leaving in the next day or two. This applies to the cheaper tours and some of the more expensive ones.

Particularly out of the high season, agencies may let you travel cheaply at the last minute rather than leave berths unfilled. This depends on luck and your skill at bargaining.

The cheapest prearranged tours that we know of are sold by César Gavela, at the Gran Casino Hotel in Quito. Departures are on limited dates and getting something suitable is largely a matter of luck; don't expect any luxury. The boats used are similar to those run by Galasam.

A little more expensive and with more frequent departure dates are the economy tours run by Galasam (Economic Galápagos Tours) in Quito (☎ 550 094), at Pinto 523, and in Guayaquil (☎ 306 289), at 9 de Octubre 424. Galasam has three levels of tour: economy, tourist and luxury.

Seven-day economy tours are aboard small boats with six to 12 bunks in double, triple and quadruple cabins. All bedding is provided and the accommodation is clean but spartan, with little privacy. Plenty of simple but fresh food and juice is served at all meals and a Naturalista II guide accompanies the boat (few guides on the economy tours speak English).

There are toilets, and fresh water is available for washing of faces and drinking. Bathing facilities may be saltwater deck hoses or freshwater showers on some boats. There are pre-set itineraries, which allow you to visit most of the central islands and give enough time to see the wildlife.

I have received some letters criticising both the Gran Casino trips and the economy-class Galasam tours. Things go wrong occasionally, and when they do, a refund is extremely difficult to obtain. Problems have included last-minute changes of boat (which the contractual small print allows), poor crew, lack of bottled drinks, not sticking to the agreed itinerary, mechanical breakdowns and overbooking. Passengers have to share cabins and are not guaranteed that their cabin mates will be of the same gender; if you are uncomfortable with sharing a cabin with a stranger of the opposite sex, make sure you are guaranteed in writing that you won't have

to do this. Generally speaking, the cheaper the tour the less comfortable the boat and the less knowledgeable the guide. On the other hand, for every letter I get saying a tour was poor, I get another letter saying that they had a great trip that was good value.

One-week (eight-day) economy tours start at about US$500 to US$600 per person. The US$80 park fee, city tax, airfare and bottled drinks are not included. There are weekly departures. Typically, you'll leave Quito on a specific morning, say Monday, and begin the boat tour on Monday afternoon or evening. The tour may finish on Sunday night or, possibly, Monday morning at the airport for your flight back. Shorter and cheaper tours are available. Sometimes, a one-week tour is a combination of two shorter tours, for example a Monday to Thursday tour combined with a Thursday to Monday tour. People on the full week spend most of Thursday dropping off and picking up passengers. Try and avoid one-week trips like this.

If you add up the cost of the cheapest one-week tour plus airfare and park fees, you get almost no change out of US$1000. Sorry, budget travellers, that's the way it is. My feeling is that if you're going to spend that much, the Galápagos are probably an important destination for you and you want to get as much out of it as possible. The economy-class boats are usually OK, but if something is going to go wrong, it's more likely to happen on the cheaper boats. If this is all you can afford and you really want to see the Galápagos, go! It'll probably be the adventure of a lifetime. But you might consider spending an extra few hundred dollars and go on a more comfortable, reliable boat and get a decent guide (though more expensive boats have their problems too).

Safari Tours in Quito runs a booking service for a number of Galápagos boats and agencies and charges a straight US$25 fee on top of the tour cost. The advantage of using this service is that it has a wide variety of contacts and can help you make the best choice, saving yourself a lot of legwork and uncertainty. It can tell you which boats are more comfortable or have better satisfaction records.

The most luxurious tours cost US$1000 to US$2000 (or more) per person per week, plus the usual extras. The most expensive boats are quite comfortable, with superb food and excellent crews and guides. Occasionally, you can get onto them at a discount of several hundred dollars if they need some last-minute passengers. Keep your eyes open for ads in tourist cafés and bars in Quito and ask at Safari Tours if they know of any hot deals.

Tours can also be booked on large cruise boats, if you like that sort of thing. Large, by Galápagos standards, is a boat with 48 double cabins, and supporting amenities.

Falkland Islands (Islas Malvinas)

In the South Atlantic Ocean, 300 miles (500 km) east of Argentine Patagonia, the controversial Falklands consist of two large islands and many smaller ones.

Facts about the Islands

HISTORY

Despite possible early Indian presence, the Islands were unpeopled when 17th-century European sailors began to frequent the area. Their Spanish name, Malvinas, derives from French navigators of St Malo.

In 1764, French colonists settled at Port Louis, East Falkland, but soon withdrew under Spanish pressure. Spain forcibly expelled a British outpost from Port Egmont, West Falkland, in 1767, but restored it under threat of war; the British later abandoned Port Egmont in ambiguous circumstances.

Spain placed a penal colony at Port Louis, then abandoned it to whalers and sealers. In the early 1820s, after the United Provinces of the River Plate claimed successor rights to Spain, Buenos Aires entrepreneur Louis Vernet attempted a livestock and sealing project, but Vernet's seizure of American sealers triggered reprisals which damaged Port Louis beyond recovery. Buenos Aires then maintained a token force, expelled by the British navy in 1833.

The Falklands languished until wool became an important commodity in the mid-19th century. The Falkland Islands Company (FIC) became the Islands' largest landholder, but the population of stranded mariners and holdover gauchos grew with the arrival of English and Scottish immigrants, some of whom occupied remaining pasture lands in large holdings. Half the population resided in the port capital of Stanley, founded in 1844, while the rest worked on sheep stations. Most original landowners lived and worked locally, but their descendants often

Country Name Falkland Islands
Area 7564 sq km
Population 2050
Population Density 0.27 per sq km
Capital Stanley
Head of State Queen Elizabeth II (Governor Richard Ralph)
Official Language English
Currency Falkland Islands Pound/Pound Sterling (£)
Exchange Rate US$1 = FI£0.65; UK£1 = FI£1
Per Capita GNP US$25,000 (1996 estimate)

returned to Britain and ran their businesses as absentees.

From the late 1970s, local government encouraged subdivision of large landholdings to benefit family farmers. Change became even more rapid with the 1982 Falklands war, subsequent expansion of deep-sea fishing, and preliminary offshore petroleum exploration.

The Falklands War

Although Argentina had persistently

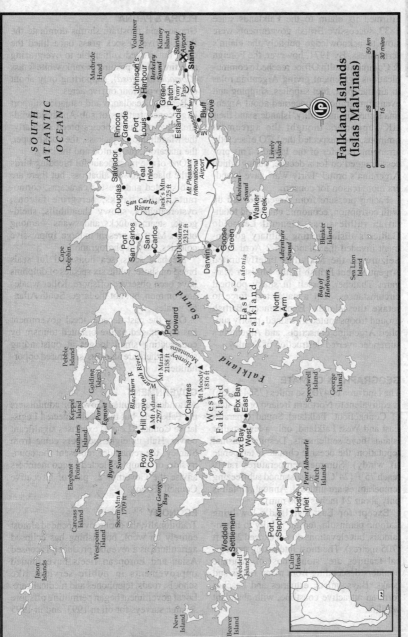

SOUTH ATLANTIC OCEAN

Macbride Head

Volunteer Point

Kidney Island

Johnson's Harbour

Berkeley Sound

Stanley Airport

Rincon Grande

Green Patch

Stanley

Port Louis

Pony's Pass

Bluff Cove

Estancia

Pleasant Hwy

Douglas

Salvador

Teal Inlet

Jack's Mtn 2125 ft

Mt Pleasant International Airport

Lively Island

Cape Dolphin

San Carlos River

Port San Carlos

San Carlos

Mt Usborne 2312 ft

Choiseul Sound

Walker Creek

Darwin

Goose Green

EAST FALKLAND

Lafonia

North Arm

Adventure Sound

Bay of Harbours

Bleaker Island

Sea Lion Island

Pebble Island

Port Howard

Falkland Sound

Golding Island

Keppel Island

Port Egmont

Saunders Island

Blackburn R.

Warrah River

Mt Maria 2158 ft

Hornby Mountains

Mt Adam 2297 ft

Mt Moody 1816 ft

WEST FALKLAND

Chartres

Fox Bay East

Fox Bay West

Hill Cove

Roy Cove

Elephant Point

Byron Sound

Carcass Island

Storm Mtn 1709 ft

Westpoint Island

King George Bay

Port Albemarle

Arch Islands

Jason Islands

New Island

Beaver Island

Weddell Settlement

Port Stephens

Hoste Inlet

Speedwell Island

George Island

Weddell Island

Calm Head

Falkland Islands (Islas Malvinas)

50 km

30 miles

25

15

0

N

affirmed its claim to the Falklands since 1833, successive British governments were slow to acknowledge publicly the claim's seriousness. By 1971, however, the Foreign & Commonwealth Office reached a communications agreement giving Argentina roles in air transport, fuel supplies, shipping and even immigration. Concerned about Argentina's chronic instability, Islanders and their UK supporters thought the agreement ominous, and suspected the FCO of secretly arranging transfer of the Islands. This process dragged on for a decade, during which Argentina's brutal 'Dirty War' gave Islanders more reason for concern.

Facing pressure from Argentines fed up with corruption, economic chaos and totalitarian ruthlessness, General Leopoldo Galtieri's disintegrating military government invaded the Islands on 2 April 1982. Seizure of the Malvinas briefly united Argentina, but British Prime Minister Margaret Thatcher, herself in shaky political circumstances, sent a naval task force to retake the Islands. Experienced British ground troops routed ill-trained, poorly supplied Argentine conscripts, and Argentina's surrender averted destruction of Stanley.

GEOGRAPHY & CLIMATE

The land area of 4700 sq miles (7564 sq km) is equivalent to Northern Ireland or the state of Connecticut. Falkland Sound separates East and West Falkland; only a few smaller islands have settlements. Despite a dismal reputation, the oceanic climate is temperate (if windy). Summer temperatures rarely reach 75°F (24°C), but sustained subfreezing temperatures are unusual. Annual rainfall is only about 24 inches (600 mm).

Except for East Falkland's low-lying Lafonia peninsula, terrain is hilly to mountainous, but elevations do not exceed 2300 ft (705 metres). The most interesting geological features are 'stone runs' of quartzite boulders descending from many ridges and peaks. Bays, inlets, estuaries and beaches form an attractive coastline, with abundant wildlife.

FLORA & FAUNA

Grasses and prostrate shrubs dominate the flora. Native tussock grass once lined the coast but proved vulnerable to overgrazing and fire. Most pasture is rank white grass (*Cortaderia pilosa*), supporting only about one sheep per four or five acres.

Beaches, headlands and estuaries support large concentrations of sub-Antarctic wildlife. Five penguin species breed regularly: the Magellanic or jackass, the rockhopper, the macaroni, the gentoo and the king.

One of the most beautiful breeding birds is the black-browed albatross, but there are also striated and crested caracaras, cormorants, gulls, hawks, peregrine falcons, oystercatchers, snowy sheathbills, sheldgeese, steamer ducks and swans – among others. Most are present in large, impressive colonies, easy to photograph.

Elephant seals, sea lions and fur seals breed on shore, while six species of dolphins have been observed offshore. Killer whales are common, but not the larger South Atlantic whales.

Over the past decade, local government has encouraged nature-oriented tourism by constructing small lodges at outstanding sites, but there are also less-structured opportunities.

GOVERNMENT

A London-appointed Governor administers the Falklands, but the locally elected Legislative Council (Legco) exercises significant power. Half its eight members come from Stanley; the remainder represent the countryside, or 'camp'. Selected Legco members advise the Governor as part of Executive Council (Exco).

ECONOMY

Traditionally, the economy depended almost entirely on wool, but fishing has eclipsed agriculture as a revenue-producer. Licensed Asian and European fleets have funded improvements in public services like schools, roads, telephones and medical care. Local government began permitting offshore seismic surveys for oil in 1993, and in 1995 began to issue exploration licenses, a matter about which Islanders feel great ambivalence because of the potential environmental impact.

Most Stanley residents work for local government (FIG) or FIC. While FIC has sold all its pastoral property, it continues to provide shipping and other commercial services. In camp, nearly everyone is involved in wool on relatively small, widely dispersed family-owned units. Tourism is economically limited, but facilities are always adequate and often excellent.

POPULATION & PEOPLE

By the 1991 census, the population is 2050; three-quarters live in Stanley, the rest in camp. Over 60% are native-born, some tracing their ancestry back seven generations, while most of the others are immigrants or temporary residents from the UK. Islanders' surnames indicate varied European backgrounds, but all speak English.

Because of their isolation and small numbers, Falklanders are versatile and adaptable. They are also hospitable, often welcoming strangers for 'smoko', the traditional mid-morning tea or coffee break, or for a drink. This is especially true in camp, where visitors can be infrequent, but it is customary to bring a small gift – rum is a special favourite.

About 2000 British military personnel ('squaddies') reside at Mt Pleasant Airport, about 35 miles (60 km) south-west of Stanley, and at a few other scattered sites.

Facts for the Visitor

In many ways the Falklands are a small country, with their own immigration and customs regulations, currency and other unique features.

VISAS & CUSTOMS

All nationalities, including Britons, need valid passports and may need a return ticket or to prove sufficient funds. For non-Britons, visa requirements are usually the same as for visitors to the UK. For details, consult Falkland House (☎ (0171) 222-2542, fax 222-2375), 14 Broadway, Westminster, London SW1H 0BH. In Punta Arenas, Chile, contact Aerovías DAP (☎ 22-3340, fax 22-1693) at O'Higgins 891, which operates flights to the Islands, or British consul John Rees (☎ 22-8312) at Roca 924.

Customs regulations are few except for limits on alcohol and tobacco, which are heavily taxed.

MONEY

The Falkland Islands pound (£), divided into 100 pence (p), is at par with sterling. There are banknotes for £5, £10, £20 and £50, and coins for 1p, 2p, 5p, 10p, 20p, 50p and £1. Sterling circulates alongside local currency, which is not valid in the UK.

Credit cards are not widely used, but travellers' cheques are readily accepted. Britons with guarantee cards can cash personal cheques up to £50 at the Standard Chartered Bank.

Costs

Recent development has encouraged short-stay accommodation at prices up to £50 per day (meals included), but B&B in Stanley starts around £20. Cheaper, self-catering cabins are available in camp, as are opportunities for trekking and camping at little or no cost; some isolated families still welcome visitors without charge.

Air travel within the Falklands costs approximately £1 per minute. See the Getting Around section for some sample fares.

Food prices are roughly equivalent to the UK, but fresh meat (chiefly mutton) is cheap. Stanley restaurants are fairly expensive, except for short orders and snacks.

WHEN TO GO & WHAT TO BRING

From October to March, migratory birds and mammals return to beaches and headlands. Very long daylight hours permit outdoor activities even if poor weather spoils part of the day.

Visitors should bring good waterproof clothing; a pair of Wellingtons is useful. Summer never gets truly hot and high winds can lower the ambient temperature, but the climate does not justify Antarctic preparations. Trekkers should bring a sturdy tent with a rainfly, and a warm sleeping bag.

TOURIST OFFICES
Besides their Stanley office and Falkland House (see Visas & Customs, above), the Islands have tourist representation in Europe and the Americas.

Chile
> Broom Travel, Roca 924, Punta Arenas (☎ (61) 22-8312)

Germany
> HS Travel & Consulting, PO Box 1447, 64529 Moerfelden (☎ & fax (61) 05-1304)

USA
> Leo Le Bon & Associates, 190 Montrose Ave, Berkeley, CA 94707 (☎ & fax (510) 525-8846)

USEFUL ORGANISATIONS
Based in both the UK and Stanley, Falklands Conservation is a nonprofit organisation promoting wildlife conservation research as well as the preservation of wrecks and historic sites in the Islands. Membership, costing £15 per year and including its annual newsletter, is available from Falklands Conservation (☎ (0181) 346-5011), 1 Princes Rd, Finchley, London N3 2DA, England. The Stanley representative (☎ 22247, fax 22288) is at the Beauchene Complex on John St between Philomel and Dean Sts.

The Falkland Islands Association (☎ (0171) 222-0028), 2 Greycoat Place, Westminster, London SW1P 1SD, is a political lobbying group that publishes a quarterly newsletter.

BUSINESS HOURS & HOLIDAYS
Government offices are open on weekdays from 8 am to noon and 1.15 to 4.30 pm. Most larger businesses in Stanley stay open until 7 or 8 pm, but smaller shops may open for only a few hours daily. Weekend business hours are reduced. In camp, shops keep limited schedules but often open on request.

The following holidays are observed:

1 January
> New Year's Day

Late February (dates vary)
> Camp Sports

March/April (date varies)
> Good Friday

21 April
> Queen's Birthday

14 June
> Liberation Day

14 August
> Falklands Day

8 December
> Battle of the Falklands (1914)

25 December
> Christmas Day

26/27 December
> Boxing Day/Stanley Sports

SPECIAL EVENTS
In a land where most people lived in physical and social isolation, the annual sports meetings provided a regular opportunity to share news, meet new people and participate in friendly competitions like horse racing, bull riding and sheep-dog trials.

The rotating camp sports meeting on West Falkland maintains this tradition best, hosting 'two-nighters' at which Islanders party till they drop, sleep a few hours, and get up and start all over again. Independent visitors are welcome, but you should arrange accommodation (usually floor space for your sleeping bag) in advance.

POST & COMMUNICATIONS
Postal services are good. There are one or two airmails weekly to the UK, but parcels heavier than one pound (0.45 kg) go by sea four or five times yearly. The Falkland Islands Government Air Service (FIGAS) delivers to outer settlements and islands. Correspondents should address letters to 'Post Office, Stanley, Falkland Islands, via London, England'.

Cable and Wireless PLC operates both local and long-distance telephones; local numbers have five digits. The international country code is 500, and is valid for numbers in Stanley and in camp.

Local calls cost 5p per minute, calls to the UK 15p for six seconds, and calls to the rest of the world 18p per six seconds. Operator-assisted calls cost the same, but with a three-minute minimum. Reverse-charge (collect) calls are possible only locally and to the UK.

TIME
The Falklands are four hours behind GMT/ UTC. In summer, Stanley observes daylight-saving time, but camp remains on standard time.

ELECTRICITY
Electric current operates on 220/240V, 50 Hz. Plugs are identical to those in the UK.

WEIGHTS & MEASURES
The metric system is official, but most people use imperial measures. There is a conversion table at the back of this book.

BOOKS
The most readily available general account is Ian Strange's *The Falkland Islands*, 3rd edition. For a summary of the Falklands controversy, see Robert Fox's *Antarctica and the South Atlantic: Discovery, Development and Dispute*. On the war, try Max Hastings & Simon Jenkins' *Battle for the Falklands*.

Robin Woods' *Guide to Birds of the Falkland Islands* is a detailed account of the Islands' bird life. Strange's *Field Guide to the Wildlife of the Falkland Islands and South Georgia* is also worth a look. Trekkers should acquire Julian Fisher's *Walks and Climbs in the Falkland Islands*.

MAPS
Excellent DOS topographic maps are available from the Secretariat in Stanley for about £2 each. The two-sheet, 1:250,000 map of the Islands is suitable for most uses, but 1:50,000 sheets have more detail.

MEDIA
The Falkland Islands Broadcasting Service (FIBS) produces local programmes and carries BBC news programmes from the British Forces Broadcasting Service (BFBS). The nightly public announcements, to which people listen religiously, are worth hearing.

Television, with programmes taped and flown in from the UK, is available through BFBS. The only print media are the *Teaberry Express* and the weekly *Penguin News*.

FILM & PHOTOGRAPHY
Colour and B&W print film are readily available at reasonable prices. Colour slide film is less dependably available.

HEALTH
No special precautions are necessary, but carry adequate insurance. Flights from Britain may be diverted to yellow fever zones in Africa, so authorities recommend vaccination.

Wind and sun can combine to burn unsuspecting visitors severely. Wind can contribute to the danger of hypothermia in inclement weather. Stanley's King Edward VII Memorial Hospital has excellent medical and dental facilities.

DANGERS & ANNOYANCES
Near Stanley and in a few camp locations on both East and West Falkland, there remain unexploded plastic land mines, but mine-fields are clearly marked and no civilian has ever been injured. *Never* enter a minefield: mines bear the weight of a penguin or even a sheep, but not of a human. Report suspicious objects to the Explosive Ordnance Disposal office (☎ 22229), near Town Hall, which has free minefield maps.

Despite its firm appearance, 'soft camp', covered by white grass, is very boggy though not dangerous.

ACTIVITIES
Wildlife is the major attraction. Penguins, other birds and marine mammals are tame and easily approached, even at developed sites like Sea Lion Island, but there are other

equally interesting, undeveloped areas. Keep a respectful distance.

Fishing can be excellent; early March to late April is the best season for hooking sea trout, which requires a licence (£10) from the Stanley post office. Trekking and camping are possible, though many landowners and the tourist board discourage camping because of fire danger and disturbance to stock and wildlife. It is possible to visit the 1982 battlefields.

ACCOMMODATION

Stanley has several B&Bs and hotels, while some farms have converted surplus buildings into comfortable lodges. Others have self-catering cottages, caravans or Portakabin shelters.

In areas not frequented by tourists, Islanders often welcome house guests; many farms have 'outside houses' or shanties which visitors may use with permission. Camping is possible only with permission.

FOOD & DRINKS

Mutton, the dietary staple, is very cheap. Islanders usually consume their own produce, but a hydroponic market garden now produces aubergines (eggplant), tomatoes, lettuce and other salad greens.

Stanley snack bars offer fish and chips, mutton-burgers (not that bad), pizza, sausage rolls and pasties, while the hotels have decent restaurants. At pubs, beer and hard liquor (whisky, rum) are the favourites.

Getting There & Away

AIR

From RAF Brize Norton, Oxfordshire, there are regular flights to Mt Pleasant International Airport (16 hours, plus an hour's layover on Ascension Island). Southbound flights leave Brize Norton on Monday and Thursday; northbound flights leave Mt Pleasant on Wednesday and Saturday.

The return fare is £2180, but reduced Apex

fares cost £1340 with 30-day advance purchase. Groups of six or more pay £1130 each. Travellers continuing to Chile can purchase one-way tickets for half the return fare. For reservations in London, contact Carol Stewart at Falkland House (☎ (171) 222-2542), 14 Broadway, Westminster SW1H 0BH. In Stanley, contact the Falkland Islands Company (☎ 27633), on Crozier Place.

Aerovías DAP (☎ 334-9672, fax 334-5843), Luis Thayer Ojeda 0180, Oficina 1304 in Santiago, has weekly flights between Santiago and Stanley via Punta Arenas, which connect with British Airways flights between London and Santiago. Flights leave Santiago on Thursday at 2 pm, and leave Mt Pleasant on the return leg on Thursday at 8 pm.

The one-way Y-class fare between Punta Arenas and Mt Pleasant is £158, while Santiago-Mt Pleasant costs £396. Hence it is cheaper to fly to Punta Arenas with another airline, such as LanChile, Ladeco or National, then continue to the Falklands with Aerovías DAP (though scheduling may be awkward).

In Punta Arenas, DAP is at O'Higgins 891 (☎ 22-3340, fax 22-1693).

Getting Around

Outside the Stanley-Mt Pleasant area the only regular flights are provided, on demand, by FIGAS. Sample return fares from Stanley include Salvador (£50), Darwin (£76), San Carlos (£78), Port Howard (£94), Sea Lion Island (£95), Pebble Island (£106), Fox Bay East or West (£121) and Carcass Island (£145). Some grass airstrips only accept a limited payload, so baggage is limited to 30 pounds (14 kg) per person.

Rental vehicles are available in Stanley, and visitors may use their own state or national driving licences in the Falklands for up to 12 months. Some lodges provide 4WDs with drivers/guides for their guests.

Stanley

Stanley's metal-clad houses, brightly painted corrugated metal roofs and large kitchen gardens are a striking contrast to the surrounding moorland. Founded in 1845, the new capital was a supply and repair port, but Cape Horn shipping began to avoid it when boats were scuttled under questionable circumstances. In the late 19th century, Stanley grew more rapidly as the transshipment point for wool between camp and the UK.

As the wool trade grew, so did the influence of the Falkland Islands Company, Stanley's largest employer. Although its political and economic dominance were uncontested, its relatively high wages and good housing offered a paternalistic security. 'Tied houses', however, were available only while the employee remained with FIC.

Stanley remains the service centre for the wool industry, but has also become a significant port for Asian and European fishing fleets.

Orientation
On a steep north-facing hillside, Stanley has sprawled east and west along Stanley Harbour. Ross Rd, the main street, runs the length of the harbour, but most government offices, businesses and houses are within a few blocks of each other.

Information
Tourist Offices The Falkland Islands Tourist Board (☎ 22215, 22281) at the Public Jetty distributes an excellent guide to Stanley and other useful brochures. Hours are weekdays, 8 am to noon and 1.15 to 4.30 pm.

The Mt Pleasant Travel Office (☎ (7) 6691) is at 12 Facility Main Reception, at Mt Pleasant International Airport.

Money Standard Chartered Bank, on Ross Rd between Barrack and Villiers Sts, changes foreign currency and travellers' cheques, and cashes personal cheques drawn on several UK banks with the appropriate guarantee card. Hours are weekdays, 8.30 am to noon and 1.15 to 3 pm.

Post & Communications The Post Office is in Town Hall, on Ross Rd at Barrack St. Cable and Wireless PLC, on Ross Rd West near Government House, operates phone, telegram, telex and fax services. Magnetic cards are cheaper than operator-assisted overseas calls. Counter hours are 8.30 am to 5 pm, but public booths are open 24 hours.

Emergency King Edward VII Memorial Hospital (☎ 27328 for appointments, ☎ 27410 for emergencies), at the west end of St Mary's Walk, has superb facilities.

Things to See
Distinguished **Christ Church Cathedral** (1892), is a massive brick and stone construction with attractive stained-glass windows. On the small nearby plaza, the restored **Whalebone Arch** commemorates the 1933 centenary of British rule.

Since the mid-19th century, London-appointed governors have inhabited rambling **Government House**, on Ross Rd. Just beyond it, the **Battle of the Falklands Memorial** commemorates a WW I naval engagement, while **Falkland Islands Museum** is a recent project, with changing exhibits. Curator John Smith is especially conversant with maritime history.

Just opposite the Secretariat, on Ross Rd, is the **1982 War Memorial**, designed by a Falklander living overseas, paid for by public subscription and built with volunteer labour. At the east end of Ross Road, both the Islands' tiny elite and working class rest at **Stanley Cemetery**, where surnames like Felton and Biggs are as common as Smith and Jones are in the UK.

Activities
Stanley's new swimming pool, on Reservoir Rd, has become very popular. There are also now sites for squash, badminton, basketball and the like.

Fishing for sea trout, mullet and smelt is popular on the Murrell River, which is walking distance from Stanley, but there are many other suitable places, some easily accessible from Mt Pleasant highway.

Special Events

The Stanley Sports, held after Christmas, feature horse racing (and betting), bull riding and other events. In March, the competitive Horticultural Show displays the produce of kitchen gardens in Stanley and camp, plus a variety of baked goods, and includes a spirited auction. The July Crafts Fair presents the work of local weavers, leatherworkers, photographers and artists (there are many talented illustrators and painters).

Places to Stay

Accommodation is good, but limited and not cheap; reservations are advisable. Breakfast is always included; enquire about full board. The most economical is *Kay McCallum's B&B* (☎ 21071), 14 Drury St, charging £15 per person, while *Sue Binnie's B&B* (☎ 21051), 3 Brandon Rd, charges £25. *Warrah Guest House* (☎ 22649), a renovated 19th-century stone house at 46 John St, charges £25, while popular *Emma's Guest House* (☎ 21056), 36 Ross Rd, costs £30.50/55 for a single/double.

At *Malvina House Hotel* (☎ 21355), 3 Ross Rd, rates start at £37.50 per person; it has beautiful grounds and a conservatory restaurant. The venerable *Upland Goose Hotel* (☎ 21455), a mid-19th century building at 20/22 Ross Rd, starts at £39.50.

Places to Eat

Most Stanley eateries are modest snack bars with limited hours. Two bakeries serve bread, snacks and light meals: *Clayton's Bakery* on Dean St and *Stanley Bakery Café*, Waverley House, Philomel St. The *Boathouse Café* (☎ 21145), on Ross Rd near the Cathedral, is open for lunch on weekdays only. *Woodbine Café* (☎ 21002), 29 Fitzroy Rd, serves fish and chips, pizza, sausage rolls and similar items. *Leif's Deli* (☎ 22721), 23 John St, has speciality foods and snacks.

Most Stanley hotels have better restau-rants, but meals should be booked in advance.

Entertainment

Of Stanley's several pubs, the most popular is the *Globe Hotel* on Crozier Place, but try also the *Rose Hotel* on Brisbane Rd and the *Victory Bar* on Philomel St. The *Upland Goose Hotel* has a public bar, and Monty's Restaurant, on John St, also has a bar, *Deano's*.

In winter, the pubs sponsor a darts league, with tournaments in Town Hall, where there are also many dances, with live music, throughout the year. There are no cinemas, but hotels and guesthouses have video lounges.

Things to Buy

For locally spun and knitted woollens, visit the Home Industries Cooperative on Fitzroy Rd. Kiddcrafts, 2-A Philomel St, makes stuffed penguins and other soft toys with great appeal for children.

The Pink Shop, 33 Fitzroy Rd, sells gifts and souvenirs, Falklands and general interest books (including selected LP guides), and excellent wildlife prints by owner Tony Chater.

Postage stamps, available from the Post Office and from the Philatelic Bureau, are popular with collectors. The Bureau also sells stamps from South Georgia and British Antarctic Territory. The Treasury, in the Secretariat behind the Liberation Monument, sells commemorative coins.

Getting There & Away

Air For international flight information, see the Getting There & Away section earlier in this chapter.

From Stanley, FIGAS (☎ 27219) serves outlying destinations in nine-passenger aircraft, arranging itineraries by demand; contact FIGAS when you know where and when you wish to go, and listen to FIBS at 6.30 pm the night before departure to learn your departure time. Occasionally, usually around holidays, flights are heavily booked and seats may not be available.

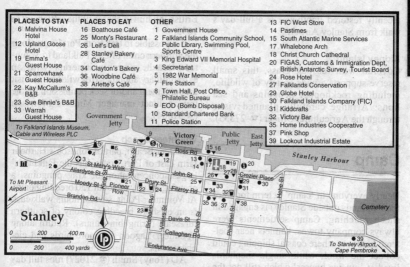

PLACES TO STAY	PLACES TO EAT	OTHER	
6 Malvina House Hotel	16 Boathouse Café	1 Government House	13 FIC West Store
12 Upland Goose Hotel	25 Monty's Restaurant	2 Falkland Islands Community School, Public Library, Swimming Pool, Sports Centre	14 Pastimes
19 Emma's Guest House	26 Leif's Deli		15 South Atlantic Marine Services
21 Sparrowhawk Guest House	28 Stanley Bakery Café	3 King Edward VII Memorial Hospital	17 Whalebone Arch
22 Kay McCallum's B&B	34 Clayton's Bakery	4 Secretariat	18 Christ Church Cathedral
23 Sue Binnie's B&B	36 Woodbine Café	5 1982 War Memorial	20 FIGAS, Customs & Immigration Dept, British Antarctic Survey, Tourist Board
33 Warrah Guest House	38 Arlette's Café	7 Fire Station	24 Rose Hotel
		8 Town Hall, Post Office, Philatelic Bureau	27 Falklands Conservation
		9 EOD (Bomb Disposal)	29 Globe Hotel
		10 Standard Chartered Bank	30 Falkland Islands Company (FIC)
		11 Police Station	31 Kiddcrafts
			32 Victory Bar
			35 Home Industries Cooperative
			37 Pink Shop
			39 Lookout Industrial Estate

Passages may also be arranged through the Tourist Board on the Public Jetty.

Bus Few places are accessible by road, but C&M Travel (☎ 21468) serves Stanley and Mt Pleasant airports, and will also make day trips to Darwin/Goose Green and elsewhere in summer.

Getting Around

To/From the Airport Mt Pleasant International Airport is 35 miles south-west of Stanley by road, while Stanley Airport is about three miles east of town.

C&M Travel (☎ 21468) takes passengers to Mt Pleasant for £13 single; call for reservations the day before. They also take groups to Stanley Airport or meet them there. For cabs, contact Ben's Taxi Service (☎ 21191) or Lowe's Taxis (☎ 21381).

AROUND STANLEY
Stanley Harbour Maritime History Trail

See the Tourist Board for a brochure on wrecks and condemned ships. There are informational panels near vessels like the *Jhelum* (a sinking East Indiaman deserted by her crew in 1871), the *Charles Cooper* (an

American packet still used for storage) and the *Lady Elizabeth* (a three-masted freighter which struck a rock in 1913).

Penguin Walk & Gypsy Cove

The Falklands' most convenient penguin colonies are about 1½ hours walk from Stanley; from the east end of Ross Rd, continue beyond the cemetery and cross the bridge over the inlet known as The Canache, past the *Lady Elizabeth* and Stanley Airport to Yorke Bay.

Gentoo penguins crowd the sandy beach where, unfortunately, the Argentines buried plastic mines; get your view of the penguins by walking along the minefield fence. Further on, at Gypsy Cove, are Magellanic penguins (avoid stepping on burrows) and other shore birds.

Battlefields

Mr AD (Tony) Smith (☎ 21027) offers tours of 1982 battlefield sites near Stanley.

Cape Pembroke Lighthouse

Built in 1855 and rebuilt in 1906, this

recently restored lighthouse is a full day's walk from Stanley Airport.

Kidney Island

Covered with tussock grass, this small reserve supports a wide variety of wildlife, including rockhopper penguins and sea lions. Arrange carefully planned visits through the Agricultural Officer (☎ 27355).

Camp

Nearly everyone in 'camp' (a term for all of the Falklands outside Stanley) is engaged in sheep ranching. Camp settlements were always company towns, hamlets near sheltered harbours where coastal shipping could collect the wool, while single shepherds lived at 'outside houses' which still dot the countryside.

Many wildlife sites are on smaller offshore islands like Sea Lion Island and Pebble Island, whose comfortable tourist lodges are costly, but budget alternatives also exist.

EAST FALKLAND

East Falkland's road network consists of a good highway to Mt Pleasant International Airport and Goose Green. From Pony's Pass on the highway, a good track heads north to the Estancia, a farm west of Stanley, to Port Louis, and also towards Port San Carlos, but most other tracks are usable for 4WDs only. FIGAS is still the most reliable means of transport to most destinations.

Port Louis

Dating from the French foundation of the colony in 1764, Port Louis is the Falklands' oldest settlement. One of the colony's oldest buildings is the ivy-covered 19th-century farmhouse, still occupied by farm employees, but there are also ruins of the French governor's house and fortress and Louis Vernet's settlement scattered nearby. Visit the grave of Matthew Brisbane, Vernet's lieutenant, murdered by gauchos after the British left him in charge of the settlement in 1833.

It is possible to trek from Port Louis along the northern coast of East Falkland to Volunteer Beach, a scenic itinerary with an extraordinary abundance of wildlife. To visit the settlement and/or seek permission for the trek, contact manager Michael Morrison (☎ 31004).

Volunteer Beach

Volunteer Beach, part of Johnson's Harbour farm east of Port Louis, has the Falklands' largest concentration of king penguins, a growing colony of about 150 breeding pairs. At Volunteer Point, several hours walk east, is an offshore breeding colony of southern fur seals (bring binoculars). Return along Volunteer Lagoon for more birds and elephant seals.

AD (Tony) Smith (☎ 21027) runs full day excursions to Volunteer Beach from Stanley, as does Mel Lloyd's Falcon Tours (☎ 32220). Mike Rendell at Stanley's Malvina House Hotel (☎ 21084) arranges overnight excursions for a maximum of five people. If attempting the trip on your own, contact owner George Smith of Johnson's Harbour (☎ 31399) for permission.

San Carlos

In 1982, British forces came ashore at San Carlos, on Falkland Sound; in 1983, the sheep station was subdivided and sold to half a dozen local families. There is fishing on the San Carlos River, north of the settlement. Comfortable *Blue Beach Lodge* (☎ 32205) charges £49 for full board. Self-catering accommodation is available at *Waimea Fishing Lodge* (☎ 32220) for £15 per person.

Across San Carlos Water, but four hours away by foot, is the **Ajax Bay Refrigeration Plant**, a 1950s CDC (Colonial Development Corporation) boondoggle. Gentoo penguins wander through its ruins, which served as a field hospital in 1982. Take a torch if you plan to explore.

Darwin & Goose Green

At the narrow isthmus which separates

Lafonia from northern East Falkland, Darwin was the site of an early *saladero*, where gauchos slaughtered feral cattle and tanned their hides; it later became the centre of FIC's camp operations and, with nearby Goose Green, the largest settlement outside Stanley. The heaviest ground fighting of the Falklands War took place at Goose Green.

Sea Lion Island
Off East Falkland's south coast, tiny Sea Lion is less than a mile across, but teems with wildlife, including five species of penguins, enormous cormorant colonies, giant petrels, and the charmingly tame predator known as the 'Johnny Rook' (striated caracara). Hundreds of elephant seals crowd its sandy beaches, while sea lions dot the narrow gravel beaches below its southern bluffs or lurk in the towering tussock.

Much of the credit for Sea Lion's wildlife has to go to Terry and Doreen Clifton, who farmed it from the mid-1970s until they sold it recently. The Cliftons developed their 2300-acre (930-hectare) ranch with the idea that wildlife, habitat and livestock were compatible uses, and Sea Lion is one of few working farms with any substantial cover of native tussock grass. Through improved fencing and other conscientious practices, the Cliftons made it a successful sheep station and a popular tourist site, mostly for day trips from Stanley and Mt Pleasant.

Sea Lion Lodge (☎ 32004) offers twin-bed rooms with full board for £51 per person. At least two full days would be desirable for seeing the island in its entirety.

WEST FALKLAND
Pioneers settled West Falkland only in the late 1860s, but within a decade new sheep stations covered the entire island and others offshore. One of the most interesting experiments was the Keppel Island mission for Indians from Tierra del Fuego.

West Falkland (nearly as large as East Falkland) and adjacent islands have fine wildlife sites. The only proper road runs from Port Howard on Falkland Sound to Chartres on King George Bay, but a system of rough tracks is also suitable for Land Rovers and motorcycles, and there is good trekking in the mountainous interior. Only a few places have formal tourist facilities.

Port Howard
Scenic Port Howard, at the foot of 2158-ft (658-metre) Mt Maria, remains intact after its sale to its local managers in 1987. About 50 people live on the station, which has its own dairy, grocery, abattoir, social club and other amenities. It will be the West Falkland port for the anticipated ferry across Falkland Sound.

The immediate surroundings offer hiking, riding and fishing; wildlife sites are more remote. Visitors can view shearing and other camp activities, and there is a small war museum. Accommodation at *Port Howard Lodge* (☎ 42150), the former manager's house, costs £48 per person with full board, but make arrangements in advance to lodge at the cookhouse for a fraction of the cost.

It is possible to hike up the valley of the Warrah River, a good trout stream, and past Turkey Rocks to the Blackburn River and Hill Cove, another pioneer farm. Ask permission to cross property boundaries, and remember to close gates; where the track is faint, look for old telephone lines. There are longer hikes south toward Chartres, Fox Bay and Port Stephens.

Pebble Island
Off the north coast of West Falkland, elongated Pebble has varied topography, extensive wetlands, and a good sample of wildlife. *Pebble Island Hotel* (☎ 41093) charges £48 per person with full board, but ask for self-catering cottages at the settlement and *Marble Mountain Shanty* at the west end of the island, for £15 per night.

Keppel Island
In 1853, the South American Missionary Society established itself on Keppel to catechise Indians from Tierra del Fuego and teach them to grow potatoes. The settlement was controversial, because the government

suspected that the Yahgans had been brought against their will, but still lasted until 1898.

Interesting ruins include the chapel, the bailiff's house, and the stone walls of Indian dwellings. Keppel is also a good place for wildlife, but visits are difficult to arrange because it has no permanent residents. If interested in visiting, contact Mr LR Fell (☎ 41001).

Saunders Island

Saunders was the site of the first British garrison (1765). In 1767, Spanish forces dislodged the British from Port Egmont and nearly precipitated a general war. After the British left in 1774, Spain razed the settlement, but extensive ruins still remain.

Saunders has a fine sample of wildlife and good trekking to 'The Neck', whose sandspit beach links it to Elephant Point peninsula, about four hours from the settlement. Near The Neck is a large colony of black-browed albatrosses and rockhopper penguins, along with a few king penguins, while farther on are thousands of Magellanic penguins, kelp gulls, skuas and a colony of elephant seals.

David and Suzan Pole-Evans on Saunders (☎ 41298) rent a comfortable self-catering cottage in the settlement for £10 per person per night, as well as a six-bunk Portakabin (bedding supplied), with a gas stove and outside chemical toilet, at The Neck. Fresh milk and eggs are usually available in the settlement, but otherwise visitors should bring their own food. Depending on the farm workload, transportation to The Neck is available for £10 per person.

Port Stephens

Port Stephens' rugged headlands, near the settlement's sheltered harbour, host thousands of rockhoppers and other sea birds, while Calm Head, about two hours walk, has excellent views of the jagged shoreline and the powerful South Atlantic. One longer trek

goes to the abandoned sealing station at Albemarle and huge colonies of gentoo penguins. The Arch Islands, inaccessible except by boat, take their name from the huge gap which the ocean has eroded in the largest of the group.

If interested in visiting Port Stephens and trekking in the vicinity, contact Peter or Anne Robertson (☎ 42307) at the settlement or Leon and Pam Berntsen (☎ 42309) at Albemarle Station.

Weddell Island

Scottish pioneer John Hamilton acquired this western offshore island and others to experiment with tussock grass restoration and forest plantations, importation of Highland cattle and Shetland ponies, and exotic wildlife like guanacos, Patagonian foxes and otters. The abundant local wildlife includes gentoo and Magellanic penguins, great skuas, night herons, giant petrels and striated caracaras.

Farm owners John and Steph Ferguson (☎ 42398) welcome guests at *Seaview Cottage* or *Hamilton Cottage* for £15 per person (self-catering) or £30 with full board.

New Island

The Falklands' most westerly inhabited island was a refuge for whalers from Britain and North America from the late 18th century well into the 19th. There remain ruins of a shore-based, turn-of-the-century Norwegian whaling factory that failed because there simply were not enough whales.

On the precipitous western coast are gigantic colonies of rockhopper penguins and black-browed albatrosses and a large rookery of southern fur seals. Potential visitors should contact Tony or Annie Chater (☎ 21399), or Ian or María Strange (☎ 21185) in Stanley.

Guyana, Suriname & French Guiana

On the north coast of South America, British, Dutch and French colonisation left a curious political geography comprising the independent republics of Guyana and Suriname, and the territory of French Guiana (Guyane Française). Collectively referred to as the Guianas, these territories are culturally more Caribbean than South American, and make a fascinating contrast with the rest of the continent. The interior regions, never dominated by Europeans, retain some of the world's best preserved tropical forests.

History

The muddy Guyanese coastline, covered by mangroves, and sparsely populated with warlike Carib Indians, did not attract early European settlement. Spaniards first saw the coast in 1499, but there was no prospect of gold or cheap labour, though they made occasional slave raids. Interior forest peoples like the Macushi and Tirió survived in relative isolation. Several 16th-century explorers, including Sir Walter Raleigh, placed the mythical city of El Dorado in the region, but Spain's European rivals displayed no sustained interest until the mid-17th century.

The Netherlands made the first move, placing a settlement on the lower Essequibo River in 1615. After forming the Dutch West India Company in 1621, they traded with Indian peoples of the interior, but also established riverside plantations of sugar, cocoa and other tropical commodities. The indigenous peoples were almost wiped out by introduced diseases, so the Dutch imported West African slaves to construct dykes and polders, and work the plantation economies. From the mid-18th century, escaped slaves formed Maroon (Bush Negro) settlements in the interior, and retained many African customs.

England established sugar and tobacco plantations on the west bank of the Suriname River around 1650, followed by the founding of what is now Paramaribo. After the second Anglo-Dutch War, under the Treaty of Breda (1667), the Dutch retained Suriname and their colonies on the Guyanese coast (in exchange for New York), but ceded the area east of the Maroni (Marowijne) River to the French. For the next 150 years sovereignty of the region shifted between the three powers, in response to the fortunes of their navies in the Caribbean, and various wars and alliances in Europe. By 1800, Britain had become the dominant power, though Suriname remained under Dutch control, and France retained a precarious hold on Cayenne.

At the end of the Napoleonic Wars, the Treaty of Paris reaffirmed the sovereignty of the Dutch in Suriname and of the French east of the Maroni (Marowijne), while Britain formally purchased the Dutch colonies in what became British Guyana. By 1834, slavery was abolished in all British colonies, and the Royal Navy suppressed the slave

Guyana, Suriname & French Guiana

trade in the Caribbean. This created a need for more plantation labour, and the subsequent immigration of indentured labour from other colonies created a unique ethnic mix in each of the Guianas.

Colonial rule left an unfortunate legacy of border disputes. Venezuela claims 130,000 sq km of Guyanese territory west of the Essequibo, while Suriname claims another 13,000 km along its border with Guyana and Brazil. Suriname also claims the area between the upper Maroni (Marowijne) River and the Litani River, which is currently under French control.

Flora & Fauna

An extensive and largely pristine tropical rainforest covers the interior of the Guianas, and is the habitat of many plant and animal species. Among the more conspicuous plants are water lilies (including the giant *Victoria regis*), orchids, giant bromeliaeds, heliconia and markoesa.

The jaguar is the most spectacular wild animal, but other wildlife includes the puma, ocelot, sloth, armadillo, capybara (the world's largest rodent), deer, wild pig and howler monkey. There are also small but colourful creatures like the golden frog, the blue arrow frog and numerous butterflies. In the many rivers there are giant river otter, alligator, cayman, tortoise, piranha and arapaima (the world's largest freshwater fish). Along the coasts are seasonal nesting sites for hawksbill, green, leatherback and olive ridley turtles.

Increasing numbers of birders come to spot some of the hundreds of Guianese bird species, including scarlet macaw, toucan, Harpy eagle, hoatzin, cock-of-the-rock, jabiru, stork, scarlet ibis, heron, egret, anhinga, flamingo, waarus and hummingbird.

Getting Around the Guianas

It's possible, almost, to travel overland across all three Guianas. From the west, you can get into Guyana from Boa Vista in northern Brazil, but the road connection to Georgetown is dodgy, and you may have to take a flight. From Georgetown, roads follow the coast eastward, with a river crossing into Suriname and another into French Guiana, and several others along the way. There's no road yet from Cayenne to the Brazilian border, but you could fly to St

Georges, cross the Oiapoque River to Brazil, and continue by road to Macapá, at the mouth of the Amazon.

There is a lot of illegal immigration (called 'backtracking') across all these borders, and papers are scrutinised carefully. French Guiana requires an onward ticket, so currently it's best to do the trip from west to east, and fly out from Cayenne to Macapá or Belém in Brazil. Some of the river crossings are done in quite small boats, so you can't do this trip with your own car, or even a motorbike, but it's feasible with a bicycle. Ideally, you should speak English, French, Dutch and Portuguese, but a smattering of each will suffice.

Guyana

Country Name Co-operative Republic of Guyana
Area 214,970 sq km
Population 729,425 (1994 estimate)
Population Density 3.39 per sq km
Capital Georgetown
Head of State President Cheddi Jagan
Official Language English
Other Languages Amerindian languages; creole dialects
Currency Guyanese Dollar ($)
Exchange Rate US$1 = G$139
Per Capita GNP US$1900 (1993)
Inflation Rate 7% (1992)

FACTS ABOUT THE COUNTRY
History
In 1831, the three colonial settlements of Essequibo, Demerara and Berbice merged to become British Guyana. After the abolition of slavery, Africans refused to work on the plantations for wages, and many established their own villages in the bush. Plantations closed or consolidated because of the shortage of labour. A British company, Bookers, resurrected the sugar industry by importing indentured labour from India. From 1846 to 1917 nearly 250,000 labourers entered Guyana, drastically transforming its demography and laying the basis of fractious racial politics.

British Guyana was run very much as a colony until 1953 when a new constitution provided for home rule and an elected government. In 1966 the country became an independent member of the British Commonwealth with the name of Guyana, and in 1970 it became a republic with an elected president. Guyana hit world news in 1979 with the mass suicide/murder of nearly 1000 cultists in the expatriate religious community Jonestown. It's alleged that the president was bribed to permit the settlement.

A new constitution was proclaimed in 1980, by socialist president Forbes Burnham. The state controls the two main export industries, sugar and bauxite, but the recent trend is to reduce government involvement in the economy, and both these industries may be privatised.

Geography
Though Caribbean in culture, Guyana actually fronts the Atlantic Ocean. Roughly the size of the UK or the US state of Idaho, the country takes its name from an Amerindian word meaning 'land of many waters', after the many north-flowing rivers, the most important being the Demerara, Berbice and Essequibo. The narrow strip of coastal lowland, from 16 km to 60 km wide, comprises 4% of the total land area, but is home to 90% of the population. Much of the marshy coastal land was reclaimed by the Dutch, using a system of drainage canals, sea walls and groynes. These polders support most of Guyana's agriculture. There are very few beaches.

Dense tropical rainforest covers most of the interior, though south-western Guyana features an extensive savanna between the Rupununi River and the border with Brazil. The most prominent geological feature is the Guiana Shield, an extensive, weathered crystalline upland. Once part of the larger Brazilian Shield to the south, it became separated in Tertiary times when the rising Andes

GUIANAS

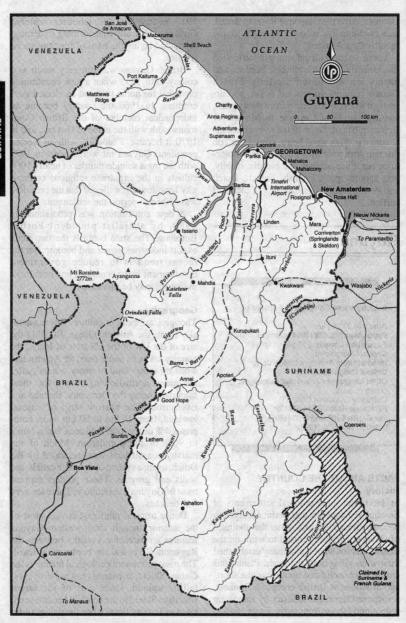

ATLANTIC
OCEAN

Guyana

0   50   100 km

Claimed by
Suriname &
French Guiana

reversed the course of west-flowing rivers and created the Amazon Basin. The Shield falls away in steps from 2772-metre Mt Roraima, on the Brazilian border, down to sea level.

Climate

The equatorial climate has high temperatures with little seasonal variation, though coastal breezes moderate the heat. Guyana has two distinct rainy seasons: May to mid-August and mid-November to late January. Precipitation declines toward the interior, where temperatures are more variable.

Government

Guyana's 1980 constitution established an executive branch with an elected president and a prime minister appointed by the president; the 65-member National Assembly is also elected, mostly by proportional representation. The High Court is the supreme judicial authority.

The main political parties are the People's National Congress (PNC) and the Marxist-oriented People's Progressive Party (PPP). The PPP is supported principally by the East Indian community, while the PNC is supported by Afro-Guyanese. In October 1992, in an election marred by violence, PPP candidate Cheddi Jagan easily defeated the incumbent PNC president, Desmond Hoyte. Since independence, most of the important posts in the Guyanese Defence Force, the police and the civil service have been occupied by Afro-Guyanese, but with the change of government more East Indians have been appointed to influential positions. The next election is due in 1997.

Economy

Guyana's economy relies on exports of primary commodities, especially bauxite, but also gold, sugar, rice, timber and shrimp. East Indians control most of the small business, while the Afro-Guyanese dominate the government sector. Guyana is a member of the Caribbean economic group, Caricom.

Guyana Sugar Company (Guysuco), the state-controlled sugar enterprise, employs more Guyanese than any other industry and produces 28% of Guyana's export earnings. The company has a 300-year history, and the Demerara River has given its name to a type of raw cane sugar.

Multinational corporations, including US-based Reynolds Metals and Canada's Alcan, are major investors in the mineral sector. There are substantial gold-mining ventures – one gold extraction plant spilt a huge quantity of cyanide in the Essequibo River during 1995. Petroleum reserves have been found in the Rupununi savanna's Takutu Basin, but no agreement for their exploitation has been reached. A Malaysian company has been granted a concession for selective logging which covers around 7% of Guyana's total land area.

Though the PPP used to express scepticism about multinationals, the new government has permitted, and even encouraged, foreign investment. Economic reforms have led to a resumption of foreign aid, but despite some debt cancellations and rescheduling, the country still has a large foreign debt. The infrastructure, once very run-down, is improving, with more reliable phones and fewer electricity blackouts.

Population & People

There are about 800,000 Guyanese, but many of them, perhaps 70,000, live abroad, mostly in the UK, USA, Canada, or in other Caribbean countries. About 51% are East Indian (ie from the Indian subcontinent), 43% are Afro-Guyanese, and 2% are of Chinese or European extraction. Amerindians, in scattered interior settlements, comprise about 4% of the population; the main groups are Arawak, Carib, Wapishana and Warao.

Public education is free of charge to university level, but physical facilities have deteriorated, books and supplies are limited, and qualified teachers are few. The literacy rate is about 95%, but many educated Guyanese live overseas.

Arts

Georgetown has a vibrant music scene, with

a wide variety of Western, Caribbean and East Indian sounds. You'll hear rock, reggae, dub, calypso, soka and some fascinating fusions, like chutney music, a mixture of East Indian and calypso styles.

Probably the best known work of literature by a Guyanese is ER Braithwaite's novel *To Sir With Love*, which is actually set in London and became a popular film. To see contemporary Guyanese painting and sculpture, look for special exhibitions at the Georgetown Museum.

Religion

Most Afro-Guyanese are Christian, usually Anglican, but a handful are black Muslim. The East Indian population is mostly Hindu, with a sizeable Muslim minority, but Hindu-Muslim friction is uncommon.

Language

English is the official national language, but most Guyanese speak a creole which can be incomprehensible to outsiders. Some East Indians speak Hindi or Urdu. Amerindian languages include Arawak, Akawaio, Carib, Macushi, Patamona, Wapishana, Wai Wai and Warao. Along the Brazilian border, many Guyanese are bilingual in Portuguese.

FACTS FOR THE VISITOR
Visas & Embassies

All visitors require a passport, but those from the USA, Canada, EU countries, Australia, New Zealand and the British Commonwealth do not need a visa. A 30-day stay is granted on arrival. If you need a visa make your application at least six weeks before you leave home.

Guyanese Embassies Abroad Guyana's overseas diplomatic representation is limited:

Belgium
  12 Avenue de Brasil, Brussels (☎ (02) 675 62 16)
Canada
  151 Slater St, Suite 309, Ottawa (☎ (613) 235-7249)
  505 Consumers Rd, Suite 900, Willowdale, Toronto (☎ (416) 494-6040)

UK
  3 Palace Court, Bayswater Rd, London (☎ (0171) 229-7684, fax 727-9809)
USA
  2490 Tracy Place, Washington, DC (☎ (202) 265-6900)
  866 United Nations Plaza, New York, NY (☎ (212) 527-3215)

Documents

As well as a passport, carry an international yellow-fever vaccination certificate, and keep other immunisations up to date.

Money

The currency is the Guyanese dollar (G$). There are no coins, only notes, in denominations of G$5, G$20, G$100, G$500 and G$1000. The currency is more or less stable, but declining in line with domestic inflation. The official exchange rate is about the same as the parallel rate offered by *cambios* (exchange houses). Rates as of July 1996 included the following:

Australia	A$1	=	G$109
Canada	C$1	=	G$102
France	FF1	=	G$27
Germany	DM1	=	G$91
Japan	¥100	=	G$129
New Zealand	NZ$1	=	G$95
United Kingdom	UK£1	=	G$215
USA	US$1	=	G$139

Cash and travellers' cheques can be exchanged in banks and cambios. Banks are more bureaucratic and are generally open only on weekday mornings, while cambios keep longer hours. Sometimes you can change cash unofficially, at hotels for example, for the same rates that banks offer – there is no real black market. Rates are almost the same for travellers' cheques and cash. British pounds are widely accepted. Credit cards are accepted at Georgetown's better hotels and restaurants.

When to Go

The best time to visit Guyana may be at the end of either rainy season, in late January or late August, when the discharge of water over Kaieteur Falls is greatest. Some locals recommend mid-October to mid-May, which may be wet, but not as hot. If you want to travel overland to the interior, come during the dry seasons.

What to Bring

Dress is informal; coats and ties are exceptional, even among businessmen and state officials, though Guyanese men seldom wear shorts. Downpours can occur even in the 'dry' seasons, so an umbrella is worthwhile.

Tourist Offices

The government has no official tourist representative overseas. The private Tourism Association of Guyana (☎ 50807, fax 50817), PO Box 101147, Georgetown, is more active in promoting the country, and publishes *Guyana Tourist Guide*, a useful brochure. Try its US and UK contacts for the most current information.

UK
  c/- Guyanese High Commission, 3 Palace Court, Bayswater Rd, London (☎ (0171) 229-7684, fax 727-9809)
USA
  Ms Mary Lou Callahan, Unique Destinations, 307 Peaceable St, Ridgefield, CT (☎ (203) 431-1571)

Business Hours & Holidays

Many businesses close at 2.30 or 3.30 pm. There are numerous national holidays, on which government offices and businesses are closed. The Muslim holidays occur on a different date each year.

1 January
  New Year's Day
Early January
  Youman Nabi
23 February
  Republic Day (Slave Rebellion of 1763)
March (date varies)
  Phagwah (Hindu New Year)
March/April
  Good Friday/Easter Sunday
1 May
  Labour Day
3 July
  Caricom Day

First Monday in August
  Emancipation Day
November
  Divali
25 & 26 December
  Christmas Day/Boxing Day

Special Events

Republic Day celebrations in February are the most important national cultural event of the year, though Hindu and Muslim religious festivals are important to those communities.

Post & Communications

Postal services are generally unreliable; use registered mail for essential correspondence. UPS (☎ 71853), 265 Thomas St, Georgetown, may be a better alternative.

Atlantic Tele-Network Company operates the new Guyana Telecommunications Corporation, a joint venture with the government, and has made major improvements in the telephone service. The country code for Guyana is 592.

At blue public telephones, scattered around Georgetown, you can make home-country direct and reverse-charge (collect) overseas calls, but credit-card calls have been suspended because of frequent fraud. For a USA Direct (AT&T) line, dial ☎ 165; to Canada, dial ☎ 161; and to the UK, dial ☎ 169. For the international operator, dial ☎ 002. Yellow public telephones are for local calls, and are free. Hotels and restaurants generally allow free use of their phones for local calls.

Time

Guyanese time is four hours behind GMT/UTC and one hour behind Suriname.

Electricity

The electricity supply (when it's working!) is 110V in Georgetown, and 220V in most other places.

Weights & Measures

The metric system is official but imperial measures are still more commonly used.

GUIANAS

There is a conversion table at the back of this book.

Books & Maps

Covering all the Guianas, David Lowenthal's *West Indian Societies* is deep in history and geography. VS Naipaul's *The Middle Passage* is a more literary and philosophical travelogue, originally published in 1962 but still a valuable introduction to the region. Evelyn Waugh described a rugged trip through the interior in *Ninety-Two Days* (out of print).

VS Naipaul's late brother Shiva wrote movingly of the Jonestown massacre at the People's Temple colony in *Journey to Nowhere: a New World Tragedy*. In the UK, its title was *Black and White*.

Media

Georgetown has two daily newspapers, *Stabroek News* and the *Guyana Chronicle*, plus the influential weekly *Catholic Standard*. Local television programming is limited, but international cable services are widely available.

Health

Adequate medical care is available in Georgetown, at least at private hospitals, but elsewhere, facilities are few. Chloroquine-resistant malaria is endemic, and dengue fever is also a danger, particularly in the interior – protect yourself against mosquitoes and take malaria prophylaxis. Typhoid inoculation is recommended. Guyana is regarded as a yellow-fever infected area, and your next destination may require a vaccination certificate, as does Guyana if you arrive from another infected area. Tap water is suspect, even in Georgetown.

Cholera outbreaks have occurred in areas with very unsanitary conditions, but precautions are recommended everywhere.

Dangers & Annoyances

Guyana in general, and Georgetown in particular, are notorious for street crime and physical violence. Avoid potentially hazardous situations, and be aware of others on the street. For further information see the Georgetown Dangers & Annoyances section.

Try not to arrive at Georgetown's Timehri international airport at night, to avoid drunken cab drivers and 'choke and rob' assaults along the highway. It is better to fly into Port of Spain (Trinidad) or to Curaçao (Netherlands Antilles), spend the night there and continue to Georgetown the next morning.

All baggage should be locked and, ideally, enclosed in a duffel or other secure covering. Backpacks are particularly vulnerable.

Activities

Guyana has few facilities for recreational activities. The coast is generally unsuitable for water sports, but the interior offers possibilities for river rafting and trekking. You'd have to arrange it with a local tour operator, or do an awful lot of organisation yourself.

Highlights

The Kaieteur Falls are Guyana's most spectacular single attraction, usually seen on a sightseeing flight. The rainforested interior, rich in bird life, is an attraction for eco-tourists, though it can be expensive to visit. The music scene in Georgetown, with its mix of Indian, Caribbean and Western sounds, is a real highlight, as is the variety of ethnic foods. The country as a whole is such an anomaly, with so few tourists, that just being there is an experience.

Accommodation

In Georgetown there are modest hotels which are clean, secure and comfortable, for US$15 to US$25. Better accommodation, with air-con, costs from US$40, while the growing number of rainforest lodges also have up-market prices. Outside the capital, accommodation is generally pretty basic, but considerably cheaper.

Food & Drinks

Guyanese food is distinctive, especially the seafood. Creole dishes include pepperpot (a spicy stew), cook-up rice, cow-heel soup and salt fish. Edible local fauna includes iguana and watrash, a small arboreal beastie. The East Indian element has added dishes like curry and roti to the everyday diet. Chinese food is also common.

Local rum is a favourite drink – Eldorado 5 Star is a good one to try. Banks beer, brewed at Thirst Park, South Georgetown, is very drinkable. Also try fruit punch, at any of Georgetown's better restaurants.

Entertainment
There's hot nightlife in Georgetown, where quite a few places have live reggae and rock until the early hours. Before visiting a place, enquire as to its suitability for foreigners.

Spectator Sport
In racially polarised Guyana, sport is one of the few unifying factors, and sport mainly means cricket. Internationally, Guyanese play with the West Indies; Clive Lloyd is the best known local cricketer.

Things to Buy
Woodcarvings are the most distinctive and appealing local product. Paintings, gold and silver jewellery, and Amerindian pottery are also worth a look. If you enjoy the local music, take home some cassettes.

GETTING THERE & AWAY
Air
To/From Europe There are no direct flights to Guyana from Europe. The most direct route is from the UK to Barbados, from where there are several flights weekly to Georgetown. BWIA (British West Indian Airways) also has regular flights from Germany via Trinidad.

To/From North America BWIA has the most extensive schedule, with direct flights daily from New York and Miami. ALM and Guyana Airways also have flights, from New York, Miami and Toronto. Most stop over in Trinidad. Both ALM and BWIA include overnight hotel accommodation at Trinidad or Curaçao on flights from Miami. Guyana Airways charges US$302 one way from

Miami; US$506 for a 30-day excursion (return) fare.

To/From Brazil There are currently no direct flights to Guyana from any Brazilian city.

To/From Suriname SLM (Surinam Airways) flies between Georgetown and Paramaribo five times weekly (US$113).

To/From Venezuela There are no direct flights to Venezuela. The most convenient connection is via Trinidad.

Land
To/From Brazil From Bonfim (Brazil) you can cross the river to Lethem, in Guyana's south-western Rupununi savanna. Bonfim has a good road connection to the larger Brazilian city of Boa Vista, but the road from Lethem to Georgetown is rough, and may be impassable in wet weather. See the Lethem section for details.

To/From Suriname A ferry from Corriverton (Springlands) crosses the Corentyne River to the Surinamese border town of Nieuw Nickerie. It doesn't carry vehicles.

To/From Venezuela There are no road connections west to Venezuela, and no legal border crossing points. The only overland route is through Brazil via Boa Vista and Bonfim.

Leaving Guyana
Travellers from Timehri international airport pay a departure tax of US$13.

GETTING AROUND
Air
Guyana Airways has reasonably cheap scheduled flights to Lethem and a few other interior destinations, and there are also more expensive charter services.

Bus
Minibuses link Georgetown with secondary towns, including Parika, Linden, New Amsterdam and Corriverton. These have no

fixed schedules, and leave when full from stops around Stabroek Market.

Taxi
In Georgetown, taxis are imperative for foreign travellers for safety reasons, especially at night.

Car & Motorcycle
Rental cars are available in Georgetown. They're quite expensive and you'll need an International Driving Permit. Traffic drives on the left. Paved two-lane roads run from Georgetown eastward along the coast, and inland to Linden, but other roads are few and generally poor.

Bicycle
Guyana's modest road network also limits cycling, but truly dedicated mountain bikers might be able to follow the road to Lethem and Bonfim (Brazil). Beware of bandits on this road.

Hitching
Hitching is not advisable because of security problems.

Boat
Ferries cross most major rivers. There is regular service on the Essequibo between Charity and Bartica, stopping at Parika (reached by paved highway from Georgetown). More frequent, but relatively expensive, speedboats (river taxis) carry passengers from Parika to Bartica.

Ferry docks are known as *stellings*, a term adapted from Dutch.

Organised Tours
Recently, Guyanese companies have begun to promote 'adventure tourism' in rainforest and riverside lodges. Costs are US$110 to US$150 per person per night. For details, contact the Tourism Association of Guyana, PO Box 101147, Georgetown, or one of the following operators, all based in Georgetown.

Malcolm and Margaret Chan-A-Sue, at Torong Guyana (☎ 65298), 56 Coralita

Avenue, Bel Air Park East, arrange tours into the interior. While many of their trips are not cheap, they will advise budget travellers on alternatives, and their service on flights to Kaieteur Falls and Orinduik Falls (US$175) is excellent.

Discover Tours (☎ 72011), in the Hotel Tower, also runs trips to Kaieteur and Orinduik (US$175), Santa Mission (US$50) and around Georgetown (US$25). Tropical Adventures (☎ 52853), PO Box 101147, in the Pegasus Hotel, runs seven to 14-day tours starting at US$750. Other operators worth checking include Wilderness Explorers (☎ 62085), also at the Pegasus; Wonderland Tours (☎ 59795), 65 Main St, Georgetown; Greenheart Tours (☎ 71399), 36 Craig St, Campbellville; and Cattleya Rainforest Tours (☎ 76590), 228 South Rd, Lacytown.

GEORGETOWN
Originally designed by the Dutch on a regular grid pattern, Georgetown (population 200,000) is Guyana's capital and only large city. It retains some 19th-century colonial architecture, though many buildings are in poor condition.

Orientation
Low-lying Georgetown sits on the east bank of the Demerara River, where it empties into the Atlantic. A long sea wall prevents flooding, while the Dutch canal system drains the town. Tree-lined pedestrian paths pass between the traffic lanes of the town's broad avenues, and there are many open spaces, but the canals can be smelly.

Street numbering is discontinuous in Georgetown's various boroughs – the same number may appear twice on the same street, say in Cummingsburg and Lacytown. Some streets change names west of Main St and Avenue of the Republic.

Information
Tourist Offices The Ministry of Trade, Tourism & Industry (☎ 62505), 229 South Rd, Lacytown, is supposedly open weekdays from 8 am to 4.30 pm. Much more helpful is

the private Tourism Association of Guyana (☎ 50807), nearby at 228 South Rd, Lacytown, open from 8 am to 5 pm weekdays. It publishes the useful *Guyana Tourist Guide*.

Money Cambios offer better rates and less red tape than banks; a reliable one is the Trust Company (Guyana) Ltd, upstairs at Joe Chin's Travel Agency, 69 Main St. Another is Globe Trust & Investment, at 92 Middle St next to Rima Guest House.

Post & Communications The main post office, the GPO, is on North Rd, just west of Avenue of the Republic. Guyana Telephone & Telegraph (GT&T), in the Bank of Guyana Building (entrance on North Rd, near Avenue of the Republic), is open daily from 7 am to 10 pm. The area code for Georgetown is 02.

Foreign Embassies & Consulates Most foreign legations are in central Georgetown.

Brazil
    Embassy: 308-309 Church St (☎ 57970)
Canada
    High Commission: cnr High and Young Sts (☎ 72081)
Colombia
    Embassy: 306 Church St (☎ 71410)
France
    Consular Agent: 7 Sheriff St, Subryanville (☎ 75435); if you need a visa for French Guiana, get it at the French Embassy in Suriname.
Suriname
    Embassy: 304 Church St (☎ 67844); tourist visas are usually issued in two working days (sometimes straight away) and cost US$42 for Canadians, US$30 for other nationalities.
UK
    High Commission: 44 Main St (☎ 65881)
USA
    Embassy: 100 Young St (☎ 54900)
Venezuela
    Embassy: Thomas St, between Quamina and Church Sts (☎ 60841)

Visa Extensions The Immigration Office (☎ 51744, 63011) is on Camp Rd, just north of Cowan St. It's open weekdays from 8 am to 11.30 am and 1 to 3 pm.

Cultural Centres The National Cultural Centre (☎ 63845), on Mandela Avenue in D'Urban Park, frequently puts on plays and concerts.

Bookshops For a good selection of paperback novels, mostly by Caribbean writers, visit the National Book Store on Church St.

Medical Services Georgetown Public Hospital (☎ 56900), on New Market St, has inadequate and run-down facilities. Travellers may prefer private clinics and hospitals like St Joseph's Mercy Hospital (☎ 72070), 130-132 Parade St (behind the US Embassy).

Dangers & Annoyances Street crime, often violent, is common in Georgetown. Electricity blackouts are quite frequent, and street lighting is poor at the best of times. Avoid walking anywhere after dark, be alert even in daylight, and *never* enter the Tiger Bay area (north of Church St and west of Main St), or the Albouystown area (south of Bent St) under any circumstances. Hotels, restaurants and other businesses gladly ring cabs for visitors. It may seem extreme to hail a taxi to go a block or two, but defer to the judgment of local people.

Georgetown has many beggars, and persuasive street people who follow foreign tourists in hopes of extracting meal money (or more). Most are harmless, but they can be tiresome.

Things to See
The best 19th-century buildings are along Main St and, especially, Avenue of the Republic, just east of the Demerara River.

On an oval on the corner of Church and Carmichael Sts is the Gothic-style **St George's Cathedral**. Built mostly with local materials, most notably the Guyanese hardwood 'greenheart', it's said to be the world's tallest wooden building. The nearby **Non-Aligned Monument**, at Company Path Garden, is a reminder of the outspoken Third World activism of the late Guyanese President Forbes Burnham. It contains busts of

Georgetown

ATLANTIC OCEAN

0 200 400 m

National Park

See Enlargement

Cummingsburg

Lacytown

Demerara River

Botanic Gardens

D'Urban Park

---

former presidents Nasser of Egypt, Nkrumah of Ghana and Tito of Yugoslavia, and Prime Minister Nehru of India.

Farther south on Avenue of the Republic is the distinctive neo-Gothic **Town Hall** (1889), and just beyond are the **Victoria Law Courts** (1887). At the south end is the well-kept **Parliament Building** (1833), while to its west is the landmark **Stabroek Market**, on Water St, a striking cast-iron building with a corrugated-iron clock tower. Don't go in unless accompanied by Guyanese friends.

At Avenue of the Republic and Church St, is the **National Library**. Three blocks farther

north, at Main and New Market Sts, is the **State House** (1852), now the president's residence. The fenced **Promenade Gardens**, at Middle and Carmichael Sts, are a welcome relief from midday heat but are dark and dangerous at night.

Near the Pegasus Hotel, the conical **Umana Yana** is an Amerindian *benab* (communal dwelling) erected by the Wai Wai people of the interior for the 1972 Non-Aligned Foreign Ministers' Conference. Beyond the Pegasus is Georgetown's **sea wall**, a popular site for late-afternoon walks.

Opposite the GPO, on North Rd, is the

PLACES TO STAY
1   Pegasus Hotel
12 Woodbine
    International Hotel
13 Park Hotel
16 Rima Guest
    House
23 Hotel Ariantze
25 Hotel Tropicana
26 Alpha Hotel
28 Water Chris Hotel
30 Florentene's Hotel
33 German's Hotel
34 Friends Hotel
36 Trio La Chalet Guest
    House
37 Campala
    International Hotel
44 Hotel Tower

PLACES TO EAT
10 Orient
18 Caribbean Rose
24 Del Casa
32 Salt & Pepper
    Restaurant
54 Rice Bowl
55 Coal Pot
56 Country Pride
59 Hack's Halaal
65 Idiho Food Service

OTHER
2   Umana Yana
3   Canadian High
    Commission
4   US Embassy
5   St Joseph's Mercy
    Hospital
6   Cuban Consulate
7   Immigration Office
8   British High
    Commission
9   Prime Minister's
    Residence
11 Public Hospital
14 State House;
    President's
    Residence
15 Roth Museum of
    Anthropology
17 Promenade Gardens
19 Library Club & Disco
20 Guyana Airways
21 Joe Chin's Travel
    Agency (Money
    Exchange)
22 Independence Square
27 Blue Note Disco
29 Venezuelan Embassy
31 N&R Car Rental
35 Roman Catholic
    Cathedral

38 Xanadu Disco
39 Surinamese Embassy
40 Colombian Embassy
41 Brazilian Embassy
42 Zoo
43 National Cultural
    Centre
45 National Bookstore
46 National Library
47 Wieting & Richter
    Travel Agency
48 Museum of Guyana
49 Telephone Office &
    LIAT Airline
50 Non-Aligned
    Monument
51 St George's Cathedral
52 GPO
53 BWIA Airlines
57 Houseproud
58 Town Hall
60 Victoria Law Courts
61 Tourism Association
    of Guyana
62 Minibuses to Rosignol
63 Stabroek Market
64 Minibuses to Airport
66 Ferry Stelling
67 Parliament Building
68 Brickdam Police
    Station

Museum of Guyana, a curious institution with some very old-fashioned exhibits. Occasional special exhibitions of Guyanese painting and sculpture are imaginative and first-rate. It's open weekdays from 9 am to 5 pm, and Saturdays from 9 am to noon. Admission is free.

At the east end of Regent Rd, Georgetown's **Botanical Gardens** are attractive and well-maintained. Within the gardens is the **zoo**, which focuses on animals found in Guyana. It has a very fine selection of birds (notably the rare hyacinth macaw and the harpy eagle), a good aquarium, and large ponds where visitors can feed fresh grass to manatees. Admission is a token US$0.28, but US$7 with a video camera.

Places to Stay

One of Georgetown's cheapest lodgings is *Hotel Tropicana* (☎ 62108), 177 Waterloo St, with singles for US$4.50/6.50 with shared/private bathroom. It's very basic, but

it has character and a good location. *German's Hotel* (☎ 53972), 53 Robb St, is similarly priced. *Trio La Chalet Guest House* (☎ 56628), 5 Camp St, is OK and slightly dearer, as is *Alpha Hotel* (☎ 54324), 203 Camp St, at US$10. The *Water Chris Hotel* (☎ 71980), 184 Waterloo St, has a variety of rooms from US$10.50 for a basic single up to US$31 for a twin room with air-con and private bath. At *Friends Hotel* (☎ 72383), 82 Robb St, Lacytown, rates start around US$23 for a nice clean single with private bath and fan.

Highly recommended is *Florentene's Hotel* (☎ 62283), 3 North Rd, where a very clean room with bath and fan costs US$14 for a single. For a friendly family place, try the central and secure *Rima Guest House* (☎ 57401), 92 Middle St, at US$18 a single with shared bath.

Hotel Ariantze (☎ 65363), 176 Middle St, is a mid-range option with pleasant rooms from US$45. The rambling *Park Hotel*

(☎ 54911), 37 Main St, is a pleasantly old-style place, with fan-cooled rooms from just US$32/38, and air-con rooms at US$60/70 a single/double. The *Campala International* (☎ 52951), 10 Camp St, Werk-en-Rust, seems overpriced at US$61, while the modern *Woodbine International* (☎ 59430), 41 New Market St, asks US$45/60 and up.

For up-market comfort, *Hotel Tower* (☎ 72011), 74-75 Main St, has a pool and rooms from US$85, but may give a good discount. Most expensive is the *Pegasus Hotel* (☎ 52856), on Seawall Rd, at US$110 plus, and probably not worth it.

Places to Eat

Some of Georgetown's better restaurants don't like faded jeans or sneakers – check first. Many of the cheaper places open only for lunch.

The *Coal Pot*, 17 Hincks St, has a diverse lunch menu; it is often crowded, but its seafood is much cheaper than elsewhere in town; meals start at around US$2 to US$3. For East Indian food try *Hack's Halaal*, on Commerce St near Avenue of the Republic. The *Rice Bowl*, 34 Robb St, is also worth a try, as is *Country Pride*, across the road at 64 Robb St. Two places for cheap, authentic local food are *German's*, in German's Hotel, and *Salt & Pepper*; they're both on Robb St. *Idiho Food Service*, is a snack place near Stabroek Market.

Palm Court, 35 Main St, is lively and popular, with good seafood. *Caribbean Rose*, 175 Middle St, is a superb rooftop restaurant, though it's not cheap. *Del Casa*, 232 Middle St, is fairly expensive and formal, with a dress code and surprisingly indifferent service, but it has good meat and seafood. The *Orient*, on Lamaha St, is a fine Chinese place with good service. In the Hotel Tower, *Main Street Cafe* is good for breakfast, while the *Cazabon* is also highly regarded. The Pegasus has two good restaurants, including the *Jade Garden*.

Entertainment

Georgetown's popular discos stay open very late. The best nightlife is along Sheriff St,

east of the town centre, where *The Sheriff*, *C&S* and *Tennessee*, are all popular spots, and Chinese restaurants open till all hours. The *Library Club & Disco*, 226 Camp St, is jammed with Guyanese and foreign gold miners. Other possibilities include *Xanadu* (at Vliessengen Rd and Duncan St), and the *Blue Note*, on Camp St. Most places have a cover charge of a few dollars, which is worth it for the live music. The Tower and the Pegasus hotels also have discos.

Things to Buy

For pottery, paintings and woodcarvings, try Houseproud at 6 Avenue of the Republic, Creation Craft at 7A Water St, or The Basket Shop at 72 Sixth St.

Getting There & Away

Air Timehri international airport is 41 km south of Georgetown. Regional airlines link the capital to Caribbean islands and to Suriname but not directly to Venezuela or Brazil.

Airline offices in Georgetown include:

BWIA
    4 Robb St (☎ 58900, 71250)
Guyana Airways
    32 Main St (☎ 57337, 64011)
LIAT
    Bank of Guyana Building, cnr Church St and
    Avenue of the Republic (☎ 61260)
SLM
    230 Camp St (☎ 54894, 53473)

SLM has flights every weekday to Paramaribo (US$98) and Cayenne (US$113). Barbados-based LIAT (☎ 64011) has daily flights with connections to other Caribbean islands, including Antigua, Dominica, Grenada, Martinique, Port of Spain, St Lucia and St Vincent.

Bus Minibuses to Parika (No 32, for ferries to Bartica and Charity), to Rosignol (No 44, for the ferry to New Amsterdam, connecting to Corriverton) and to Linden leave from Stabroek Market. If you're interested in overland travel to Lethem, ask around at Stabroek about trucks going that way –

safety not guaranteed. Negotiate the price, around US$25 to US$30.

Getting Around

To/From the Airport Minibuses connect Timehri with Georgetown for about US$1; they are safe enough in the daytime, but at night, a taxi is a better choice, despite the US$18 price tag (taxis may be shared). For early morning flights from Timehri, make taxi arrangements the day before.

Bus Minibuses within the city limits cost about US$0.15.

Taxi Taxis within central Georgetown cost about US$1 per ride or US$5 per hour. Try Tower Taxi Service (☎ 72011), in front of Hotel Tower, or City (☎ 56222).

AROUND GEORGETOWN
Linden

Linden, 107 km upriver from Georgetown by excellent paved road, is a mining centre of 60,000, with a lively riverside market on Sunday mornings. It is the headquarters of Guymine, the state bauxite enterprise. To arrange a visit, contact the public relations office (☎ (04) 2839).

Modest accommodation is available at the friendly *Centurion Guest House* (☎ (04) 3666), 47 Republic Ave, which has big, clean rooms with air-conditioning from US$10.

Getting There & Away Minibuses from Stabroek Market in Georgetown charge about US$2.20.

THE COASTAL PLAIN
New Amsterdam

New Amsterdam is a sugar port on the east bank of the Berbice River, about 100 km east of Georgetown. It has no special attractions, but you may have to stop here to wait for a ferry. Don't wander around at night, and avoid areas east of Main St.

Places to Stay & Eat Closest to the ferry stelling is the *Aster Hotel*, with basic singles from US$7.50. *Hotel Penguin*, just north of

the market, has rooms from US$10.50. Better places are the *Church View Hotel* (☎ (03) 2880), opposite the mosque at Main and King Sts, with fan-cooled rooms from US$16 and air-con rooms for US$50. Nearby, at 4 Main St, *Parkway Hotel* (☎ (03) 3928) is pretty good with rooms for US$29 to US$42.

There are several eating places between the market and the Hotel Penguin. The *Brown Derby Restaurant*, at Church and Main Sts, has a nice upstairs verandah and serves Chinese and East Indian dishes.

Getting There & Away Minibuses (No 44) from Stabroek Market in Georgetown charge US$2.15 to the stelling at Rosignol, where there are 10 ferries daily, from 4.50 am to 8.20 pm, across the Berbice to New Amsterdam (US$0.15 for passengers). Launches (US$0.30) also cross the river, from the sugar docks about one km north; minibuses will drop you there if no ferry is due to leave soon.

To continue to Corriverton, take another minibus (US$1.50) from the New Amsterdam stelling or market.

Corriverton

Together known as Corriverton, the towns of Springlands and Skeldon, on the west bank of the Corentyne River, are at the eastern end of the coastal road from Georgetown. From Springlands, an old passenger ferry crosses the river to Suriname. A new ferry terminal is under construction a short distance upriver, and the proposed new ferry service should be much quicker and will probably carry vehicles.

The town's Main St is a long strip with mosques, churches, a Hindu temple, cheap hotels, eateries and bars. Brahmin (zebu) cattle roam round the market like the sacred cows of India. At the north end of town, the Skeldon Estate of Guysuco is quite a large complex, and the biggest local employer.

Places to Stay & Eat *Hotel Par Park*, on Main St south of the stelling, is clean, cheap and secure. It charges US$8.50 to US$10 for

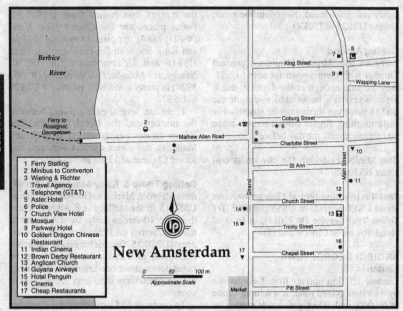

Berbice River

Ferry to Rossignol, Georgetown

New Amsterdam

King Street
Wapping Lane
Coburg Street
Mathew Allen Road
Charlotte Street
St Ann
Church Street
Trinity Street
Chapel Street
Pitt Street
Market
Strand
Main Street

0   50   100 m
Approximate Scale

1 Ferry Stelling
2 Minibus to Corriverton
3 Wieting & Richter Travel Agency
4 Telephone (GT&T)
5 Aster Hotel
6 Police
7 Church View Hotel
8 Mosque
9 Parkway Hotel
10 Golden Dragon Chinese Restaurant
11 Indian Cinema
12 Brown Derby Restaurant
13 Anglican Church
14 Guyana Airways
15 Hotel Penguin
16 Cinema
17 Cheap Restaurants

a single with private bath – check the room first. *Mahogany Hotel* (☎ 03-2289), farther south on Main St, is a nice old place with rooms from US$10.50 to US$21, some with good views over the river. The *Arawak Hotel* is dirt cheap, but should be avoided.

The restaurant at the Mahogany Hotel serves some really good food, which you can enjoy at a table on the verandah overlooking Main St. *Station View*, on Main St, is a good place for lunch. There are a couple of 'Snackettes' and Chinese restaurants, but avoid the one next to the Par Park.

Getting There & Away For travellers heading to Suriname, a ferry sails to Nieuw Nickerie daily except Sundays and holidays (check Suriname as well as Guyana holidays). Catching the ferry is a major hassle and the crossing takes almost a whole day. The booking office near the stelling opens at around 8 am, but people start queuing as early as 7 am. There's a US$0.20 booking fee

(payable in Guyanese dollars), and they check your passport. Around 10 am you go out onto the stelling, and queue up for Guyanese emigration formalities – after giving you an exit stamp, they hold your passport till you board the boat. Some time after 11.30 am the boat arrives, docks and unloads; it may be loaded again and ready to make the return trip some time between noon and 1.30 pm. The fare is US$2.50 (payable on board in Surinamese guilders only), and they may charge extra for luggage. It takes around two hours to cross the river to Nieuw Nickerie, where more bureaucracy awaits you.

There is lots of smuggling and backtracking here – frequent small, fast boats cross the river in about 15 minutes. Travellers may be tempted to take one of these boats to save the hassle of the ferry, but this is inadvisable: you may be robbed on these boats, and at best you'll wind up in Suriname without the proper stamps in your passport.

Moneychangers on the stelling sell Suriname guilders and buy excess Guyanese currency at fair rates. Although it is reasonably safe to change money with them you should still be careful. You'll need enough guilders to pay for the ferry and for your first night in Suriname.

THE NORTH-WEST COAST

The west bank of the Essequibo River can be reached by boat from Parika to Supenaam. A coastal road will take you, via Adventure, as far as Charity, about 50 km away. From there, you will need a boat to get any farther. There are several expensive jungle lodges in the western part of the country, mainly reached by air. **Shell Beach** extends for about 140 km along the coast near the Venezuelan border, and is a nesting site for turtles, including olive ridleys, leatherbacks and hawksbills.

THE INTERIOR

Bartica

Bartica is a friendly mining town at the junction of the Essequibo and Mazaruni rivers, upstream from Parika. The best accommodation is the *Hotel Modern*, at the ferry stelling, which has comfortable singles for about US$8. The hotel has a good restaurant and bar (request meals in advance).

Getting There & Away From Stabroek Market in Georgetown, take minibus No 32 to Parika (US$1, 45 minutes), then catch a river taxi to Bartica (about US$5.50, one hour); these 15-passenger speedboats leave when full and carry only one or two life jackets. There is a cheaper, slower ferry (US$1.50, five hours) on Monday, Thursday and Saturday at 9.30 am.

From Bartica, it is possible to travel to Kaieteur Falls by mining truck and on foot, but expect to return the same way – planes to and from Kaieteur rarely have an empty seat.

Around Bartica

Fort Island In the Essequibo River, Fort Island was an early Dutch outpost; the ferry from Parika to Bartica makes a brief stop here, but it is also possible to arrange a speedboat from Parika or Bartica. There is a 17th-century graveyard.

Kyk-Over-Al This ruined Dutch fortress, at the junction of the Mazaruni and Cuyuni rivers, dates from 1616. Nearby Marshall Falls is a good place for riverine wildlife. Again, you can arrange boats from Bartica.

Kaieteur Falls

Guyana's best known attraction, majestic Kaieteur Falls, is the most impressive of a series of three falls on the upper Potaro River, a tributary of the Essequibo. An Amerindian legend tells that a Patamona chieftain sacrificed himself by canoeing over the falls, to save his people from destruction by an evil spirit.

In its own way, Kaieteur is no less impressive than the better-known Iguazú Falls of Argentina and Brazil. Its waters drop precipitously 822 feet (250 metres) from a sandstone tableland, much higher than Iguazú. Depending on the season, the falls range in width from 250 feet (76 metres) to 400 feet (122 metres). Swifts nest under the overhang of the falls and dart in and out of the waters.

There is currently no accommodation, but camping is possible nearby.

Getting There & Away Several operators offer day trips in small planes for about US$175 per person; make early enquiries, since the flights go only when a full load of eight passengers can be arranged. For details, see Organised Tours in the Getting Around section earlier in this chapter.

Overland travel from Bartica (via the village of Mahdia) is possible, but it's rugged and very time-consuming, usually requiring a guide and several days walking. It is difficult to catch a plane back to Georgetown, even if you have money – miners are often lined up waiting on the airstrip.

Orinduik Falls

Orinduik Falls, a miniature Niagara on the Ireng River, on the Guyana-Brazil border, is a secondary destination for most day trips to Kaieteur Falls. Patamona Indians live nearby. There is a minor border crossing, from which it is possible to get a bus to the Brazilian settlement of Bonfim and on to the cities of Boa Vista and Manaus.

Lethem

In the Rupununi savanna along the Brazilian border, Lethem itself has little of interest, but its scenic surroundings have some wildlife, and fishing possibilities. Ranches round here are home to Guyana's cowboys – there's a rodeo at Easter.

The Guyanese are suspicious about drug smuggling in this area, so seek permission before visiting, especially if you want to spend some time here – ask Colonel Fabian Liverpool of Home Affairs (☎ 62444), in Brickdam, Georgetown. Communications to Lethem are very limited – there are only a few radio telephones.

Don & Shirley's shop, at the airstrip, is the best place to get information about the area. Ask about local transport and guide services. There are a couple of guesthouses in Lethem, which usually serve meals. The *Takatu Guest House* charges about US$5 for an OK room, and serves breakfast (US$1.50), lunch (US$3) and supper (US$3.50).

Getting There & Away Guyana Airways flies between Lethem and Georgetown on Tuesday, Wednesday, Friday and Saturday, at 7 am, for about US$50 one way. It's a small plane (18 seats) and it can be difficult to get on it – offering to pay the check-in clerk a 'special booking fee' of about US$20 may help. Try to reconfirm your flight by 9 am the day before to avoid getting bumped. If you're coming in overland, try booking a ticket by phone from Brazil, through Weiting & Richter Travel Agency in Georgetown (from Brazil ☎ (592-2) 65121), and paying with a credit card.

In the dry season, overland truck transport is feasible between Lethem and Linden (via Kurupukari), but this is only for travellers with both time and stamina – it takes from two days to two weeks. The Hinterland road to Lethem is even more difficult.

To/From Brazil From Brazil, take an early bus from Boa Vista to Bonfim, get off at the last stop (after the bus station) and walk about 2.5 km to the Brazilian customs post. Get your exit stamp, and take one of the small boats across the Takatu River to Guyana. Officially, the border crossing closes at 6 pm. Go immediately to the police station in Lethem (about 1.5 km from the crossing point) to have your passport stamped. There's also an immigration office at the airport, open most mornings.

Going to Brazil is the same in reverse – do it early to ensure you are in time for a bus to Boa Vista. Make sure your papers are in order, as illegal immigration and smuggling are rife here, and checks can be thorough.

Suriname

> **Country Name** Republiek Suriname
> **Area** 163,270 sq km
> **Population** 404,000 (1992 estimate)
> **Population Density** 2.47 per sq km
> **Capital** Paramaribo
> **Head of State** President Ronald Venetiaan
> **Official Language** Dutch
> **Other Languages** Amerindian & creole dialects
> **Currency** Suriname Guilder (Sf)
> **Exchange Rate** US$1 = Sf411
> **Per Capita GNP** US$2800 (1993)
> **Inflation Rate** 367% (1994 – probably lower now)

Suriname is an unusual cultural enclave whose extraordinary ethnic variety derives from British and Dutch colonisation, the early importation of African slaves and, later, indentured labourers from India and Indonesia. Paramaribo, the capital, retains some fine Dutch colonial architecture, but for many the greatest attraction is Suriname's

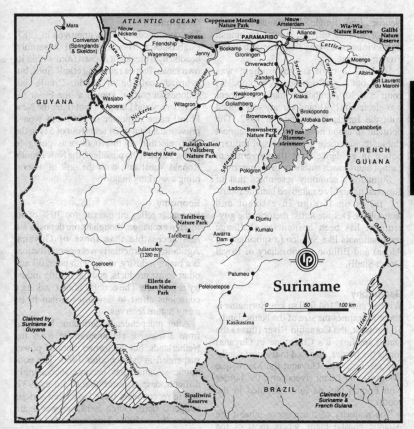

Suriname

0   50   100 km

well-managed system of nature parks and reserves.

FACTS ABOUT THE COUNTRY
History

Suriname was the last outpost of a once substantial Dutch presence in South America – the Netherlands controlled large parts of Brazil and most of the Guianas, until territorial conflicts with Britain and France left them only Dutch Guiana and a few Caribbean islands.

Suriname's 19th-century influx of Hindustanis and Indonesians resulted in less overt racial tension than in Guyana, though ma-nipulative Creole politicians limited the representation of immigrants in the colonial Staten (parliament). Despite limited autonomy, Suriname remained a colony until 1954, when it became a self-governing state; another 20 years passed before it became independent.

Since independence, political developments have been discouraging. A coup in 1980, led by Sergeant (later Lieutenant Colonel) Desi Bouterse, brought a repressive military regime to power. The regime brutally executed more than a dozen prominent opponents, and carried out a vicious campaign to suppress a 1986 rebellion of Bush

Negroes (the 'Jungle Commando'), whose interior villages suffered systematic human rights violations. Many fled to neighbouring French Guiana.

In 1987 a civilian government was elected, but it was deposed by a bloodless coup in 1990. Another civilian government was elected in 1991, and a treaty was signed with the Jungle Commando in 1992. The political situation now appears to be almost stable, though there are still lots of military police in evidence, and the government cannot exert much authority in the interior.

Suriname's economy resembles that of Guyana. Its highly capitalised bauxite industry relies on foreign investment and technology. Despite leftist rhetoric, the government has been hesitant to challenge multinationals like Suralco (a subsidiary of Alcoa) and Billiton (a subsidiary of Royal Dutch Shell).

Geography

With an area of 164,000 sq km, Suriname is about four times the size of the Netherlands. To the west, the Corantijn River (this is the Dutch spelling; it's Corentyne in Guyana) forms the border, disputed in its most southerly reaches, with Guyana; the Marowijne (Maroni) and Litani rivers form the border with French Guiana (also disputed in the south).

The majority of Surinamese inhabit the Atlantic coastal plain, where most of the country's few roads are located. The major links to the interior are by air or north-south rivers, though there is a road to Brokopondo. The nearby Afobaka Dam created one of the world's largest reservoirs (1550 sq km), the WJ van Blommesteinmeer, on the upper Suriname River. Rapids limit the navigability of most rivers. Interior mountain ranges are not so high as Guyana's; 1280-metre Julianatop is the highest point in the country.

Climate

Temperatures and humidity are high. The major rainy season is from April to July, with a shorter one in December and January.

Government

The current constitution, approved in 1987, establishes a 51-seat National Assembly, headed by a president chosen from within its own ranks. Parties run along ethnic lines, but a broad coalition of Hindu, Creole and Indonesian parties, known as the Front for Democracy and Development (later the New Front) came to power in 1991 and won a provisional total of 24 seats (out of 51) in the 1996 election as this book was going to press. This left the president, the New Front's Ronald Venetiaan, with the task of assembling a working majority.

Economy

Suriname relies on bauxite for 70% of its foreign exchange, though its ore deposits are less accessible than those of Guyana. Agriculture, particularly wet rice cultivation, is a major industry, along with palm oil and other forest products, and the fishing industry is growing. The country is also making a conscious effort to develop tourism in its many nature reserves.

After independence, Suriname benefited from a massive aid programme from the Netherlands, but the former colonial power suspended assistance after 1980. The economic situation has become increasingly difficult, despite restoration of aid in 1987, and in recent years there have been serious budget deficits. Dutch assistance was again suspended in 1991. This, and a fall in the world price of alumina, led to an economic crisis in Suriname.

A structural adjustment package included the reduction of the official rate of exchange to realistic (ie parallel market) levels, but inflation increased, and key imported commodities were rationed to contain the trade deficit. Shortages have eased, and the exchange rate is holding, but the country still has serious long-term economic problems. Limited Dutch aid has resumed.

Population & People

Of Suriname's 400,000-plus citizens, about 35% are East Indian (both Hindu and Muslim), 32% are Afro-Surinamese, 15%

are Indonesian and about 10% are Bush Negroes (descendants of escaped slaves who now inhabit the upland forests), with much smaller numbers of Amerindians, Chinese and Europeans. Many Surinamese live, or have lived, in the Netherlands, partly because of greater economic opportunities there and partly to escape military repression.

Education

A fragmented linguistic heritage has made literacy a major problem, though innovative programmes in recent years have raised the level to over 90%. Paramaribo's Anton de Kom University offers degrees in medicine, law, social sciences, physical sciences and engineering.

Arts

Because the language of literacy is Dutch, Surinamese literature is not easily accessible to English-speaking visitors. There are a number of fine painters, many of whom have trained in the Netherlands or Belgium. Some cultural forms derive from the immigrant populations, such as Indonesian *gamelan* music, which can be heard at some special events. The country's Amerindian and Bush Negro populations produce interesting wooden sculptures.

Religion

About 40% of the population is nominally Christian, mostly Roman Catholic (22% of the total) and Moravian Brethren, but some adherents of these and other Christian groups also practise traditional African beliefs like *obeah* and *winti*. Hindus comprise 26% of the population (most of the East Indian community), while 19% are Muslim (ethnic Indonesians plus a minority of the East Indians). There are also small numbers of Buddhists, Jews and followers of Amerindian beliefs.

Language

Dutch is the official national language, and standard English is widely understood. The common, vernacular language is Sranan Tongo, an English-based creole, also called Surinaams or Taki-Taki. Other languages are Hindi, Javanese, Chinese, Djuka and Saramaccan (the last two also English-based creoles). Amerindian languages include Arawak, Carib, Tirió, Warao and Waiana.

FACTS FOR THE VISITOR
Visas & Embassies

Suriname is becoming more liberal with its entry requirements, and in late 1995 visas were not required by nationals of Denmark, Finland, Guyana, Israel, Norway, Sweden, Switzerland and the UK. Visas are still needed by Australian, Canadian, Dutch, German, New Zealand and US nationals. For a visitor visa, you need to supply an application in duplicate, with two passport photos, and pay a fee. Suriname's overseas representation is very limited, so you can contact the nearest embassy for an application form, but allow four weeks for a postal application. Consulates in Georgetown (Guyana) or Cayenne (French Guiana) charge US$30 for a visitor visa and US$175 for a one-year multiple-entry visa, and issue them within a couple of days.

The visitor visa is usually good for two months, but on arrival you will be given only a one-week entry stamp. If you want to stay longer, you could try giving some good reasons to the military police at the point of entry, but you will probably finish up having to get an extension from the immigration office in Paramaribo. There may also be a requirement to change a certain amount of foreign currency – see the Money section.

Surinamese Embassies Abroad There are representatives in Guyana, French Guiana, Brazil and Venezuela (for addresses, see the capital city entries under each of those countries), and also in:

Germany
    Adolf-Kolping-Strasse 16, Munich (☎ (089) 55 33 63)
Netherlands
    Alexander Gogelweg 2, The Hague (☎ (070) 65 08 44)
    De Cuserstraat 11, Amsterdam (☎ (020) 42 61 37)

USA

4301 Connecticut Ave NW, Suite 108, Washington, DC (☎ (202) 244-7488)

7235 NW 19th St, Miami, FL (☎ (305) 593-2163)

Foreign Embassies in Suriname Several countries have representatives in Paramaribo. See the Paramaribo Foreign Embassies & Consulates section for addresses.

Documents

Passports are obligatory, and those who don't need a visa will be given a tourist card. In theory, all visitors staying over a week must register with the police and obtain an exit visa at the police station in Paramaribo (see the Paramaribo Visas section for more details). It may also be wise to keep a record of any official bank currency exchanges (see the Money section below).

Customs

Surinamese regulations permit the importation of two cartons of cigarettes, 100 cigars or 200 cigarillos, or one-half kilo of tobacco; two litres of spirits or four litres of wine may also be imported. In theory, there is a limit of eight rolls of unexposed film, 60 metres of cine film and 100 metres of recording tape, and officials may demand an 'export licence' for souvenirs, but these rules are rarely enforced.

Money

US dollars are the most common foreign currency in Suriname, but Dutch guilders and other major currencies are accepted at banks. Banks are open weekdays from 7 am to 2 pm. Changing money can involve time-consuming paperwork. Black market rates are almost the same as bank rates, but the black market is quicker and can be useful outside banking hours. This is technically illegal and not without risk – short-changing is the most frequent problem. In practice, many businesses will accept US dollars at the usual rate, and many quote their prices in dollars.

There is a requirement that foreign visitors

change US$180, at the official rate, at a bank or authorised dealer. This may be enforced if you arrive during banking hours at the international airport, and possibly at land borders as well. The authorities have been known to hold a traveller's passport until proof of a bank currency exchange is shown, but this is unusual. Usually the immigration officer gives the traveller a form on which banks record foreign exchange transactions, and this is supposed to be submitted on departure – in practice they usually don't ask for it. You'll probably need more than US$180 for your stay, and the black market rate is not significantly better, so it's no great problem to comply with this rule. The requirement may be scrapped soon anyway, as the black market becomes obsolete.

Currency The Surinamese guilder (Sf) is divided into 100 cents. There are coins for 25 and 50 cents and one guilder, and banknotes for five, 10, 25, 50, 100 and 500 guilders. In July 1996, exchange rates included the following:

Australia	A$1	=	Sf323
Canada	C$1	=	Sf302
France	FF1	=	Sf79
Germany	DM1	=	Sf269
Japan	¥100	=	Sf379
New Zealand	NZ$1	=	Sf280
United Kingdom	UK£1	=	Sf635
USA	US$1	=	Sf411

Costs Suriname is moderately expensive. The cheapest accommodation is very basic and costs US$6 per night, while a good room is at least US$25. A reasonable restaurant meal is at least US$5. Budget travellers can get by on around US$25 per day.

Credit Cards Credit cards are accepted at major hotels and at travel agencies. American Express is more common than either MasterCard or Visa.

When to Go

Suriname's dry seasons, from early February to late April and from mid-August to early

December, are the best times for a visit. From March to July, several species of sea turtles come ashore to nest at Wia Wia and Galibi reserves.

Tourist Offices

There's a Tourist Department office (☎ 471163, fax 420425) in Paramaribo; its postal address is PO Box 656. Intending visitors should contact a Surinamese embassy if possible – the one in Washington provides a superb collection of tourist information, including a very fine publication on biological conservation, to correspondents who send a self-addressed envelope (22 by 28 centimetres) with US$2.50 postage. Other embassies and Surinam Airways offices may also give tourist information.

Business Hours & Holidays

Most businesses and government offices open weekdays by 7 am and close by mid-afternoon, slightly earlier on Fridays. Banks are open weekdays from 7 am to 2 pm. Shops mostly open from 8 am to 4 pm weekdays but close by 1 pm on Saturdays. Government offices and businesses are closed on national holidays.

1 January
    New Year's Day
25 February
    Day of the Revolution
Early March (date varies)
    Phagwah (Hindu New Year)
March/April
    Good Friday/Easter Monday
1 May
    Labour Day
1 July
    National Union Day
25 November
    Independence Day
25 & 26 December
    Christmas Day/Boxing Day

Special Events

The Hindu New Year festival, Holi Phagwah, is held in March or April, while the Muslim holiday Idul Fitr (Lebaran or Bodo in Indonesian) celebrates the end of fasting at Ramadan.

Post & Communications

Postal services from Paramaribo are reliable, but may be less so from other places.

TeleSur (Telecommunicatiebedrijf Suriname) is the national telephone company. Overseas calls can be made from blue public phones. You can pay with *fiches* (coin-like tokens) purchased from a TeleSur office, call reverse charges, or use a home-country direct service (☎ 156 to the USA; ☎ 157 to the Netherlands).

Time

Suriname is three hours behind GMT/UTC.

Electricity

Electricity supply is 127V and quite reliable. Sockets take a European-style plug with two round pins.

Weights & Measures

Suriname uses the metric system.

Books & Maps

A good introduction is Henk E Chin's and Hans Buddingh's *Surinam: Politics, Economics & Society*, complemented by Betty Sedoc-Dahlberg's edited collection *The Dutch Caribbean: Prospects for Democracy. Reizen In Suriname* by Roy Tijn is a useful little guidebook if you can read Dutch.

William F Leitch's *South America's National Parks* is one of the few easily available sources for readers interested in nature parks and reserves.

The locally published and printed *A Portrait of the Republic of Suriname* is a large-format book with some useful text and many colour photographs of varying quality, but it is very expensive. It's available in Paramaribo at Vaco Bookshop in Domineestraat, and the shop at the Royal Torarica Hotel.

Media

There are two daily newspapers, *De Ware Tijd* and *De West*. The *Suriname Weekly*, in both English and Dutch, is a bit skeletal.

The Surinaams Nieuws Agentschaap (Suriname News Agency, or SNA) prints a daily bulletin in readable if imperfect English. Copies are at the front desk of the Royal Torarica Hotel.

There are two TV stations and seven commercial radio stations. TV broadcasts are in Dutch, but radio transmissions are also in Hindustani, Javanese and Sranan (Surinaams).

Health
A yellow-fever vaccination certificate is required for travellers arriving from infected areas. Typhoid and chloroquine-resistant malaria are present in the interior. Tap water outside Paramaribo is generally unsafe to drink.

Dangers & Annoyances
The civil war has ended, but there are still armed bandits, or guerillas, in the countryside. The main coastal highway is usually safe, despite occasional incidents on the section between Moengo and Albina, but it is best to avoid interior roads at night, especially the one between Zanderij (site of the international airport) and Brokopondo. Paramaribo is mostly safe, but avoid walking around at night.

Activities
There are few facilities for outdoor recreational activities. The coast is not suitable for water sports, though trekking and river rafting may be possible in the interior. Outdoor activities need to be arranged with a local tour operator.

Highlights
The nature reserves of the interior offer unspoilt rainforest, and lots of birds and wildlife – a major attraction for ecotourists. The quaint Dutch colonial buildings of Paramaribo will intrigue anyone with a sense of architecture and history.

Accommodation
The cheapest hotels and guesthouses cost around US$5, though many are pretty uninviting. Some very ordinary places ask over

US$15 for a room, while modern hotels want at least US$35.

Food & Drinks
Suriname's food reflects its ethnic diversity and can be superb. The cheapest eateries are *warungs* (Javanese food stalls) serving *bami goreng* (fried noodles) and *nasi goreng* (fried rice), but some of the best up-market restaurants are also Javanese. Creole food uses tubers such as manioc (cassava), and sweet potatoes, plantains, chicken and fish (including shrimp, which is particularly choice). Chinese and Hindustani dishes are also common.

Parbo, the local beer, is acceptable and cheaper than imported Heineken. Rum is the most common hard liquor.

Spectator Sport
Sport is important to the Surinamese, and it was a source of great pride when swimmer Anthony Nesty won a gold medal in the 100-metre butterfly at the 1988 Olympic Games. There are national organisations promoting basketball, boxing, tennis, volleyball, cycling, weightlifting and many other sporting activities.

Things to Buy
Bush Negro handicrafts, especially folding chairs and stools carved from single pieces of cedar, are very appealing, and cheaper than in Guyana or French Guiana. Amerindian and Javanese crafts are also attractive. The requirement for an export licence for items costing over Sf50 doesn't appear to be in force any longer.

GETTING THERE & AWAY
Air
To/From Europe The most direct connection is with KLM, which flies from Amsterdam to Paramaribo twice weekly. Surinam Airways (SLM) does the route twice weekly also – a two-month, low-season return costs US$1050. It may be cheaper to fly Air France from Paris to Cayenne (French Guiana) and then go overland to Paramaribo.

To/From North America SLM flies to Paramaribo from Miami and New York several times per week, mostly via the Netherlands Antilles. A 30-day Apex fare is US$560.

To/From the Caribbean From Paramaribo there are connections to the islands of Curaçao, Bonaire and Aruba, in the Netherlands Antilles, and also to Barbados, Martinique and Trinidad.

To/From Brazil SLM flies between Paramaribo and Belém, in the Brazilian state of Pará, for US$251 one way; US$255 for a 30-day return.

To/From French Guiana Air France, SLM and Varig connect Paramaribo with Cayenne, for US$110 one way, US$155 return.

To/From Guyana SLM flies to Georgetown five times weekly, for US$103 one way.

Land
To/From French Guiana From Albina, a passenger ferry and more frequent canoes cross the Marowijne (Maroni) River to St Laurent de Maroni, from where there's a good road to Cayenne.

To/From Guyana A passenger ferry crosses the Corantijn (Corentyne) River between Corriverton (Springlands), Guyana, and Nieuw Nickerie, Suriname, daily except Sundays and holidays.

Leaving Suriname
International departure tax is US$5.

GETTING AROUND
Air
Gum Air and Gonini operate services to the interior, usually on a charter basis.

Bus
Medium-sized buses on the coastal highway are frequent and cheap. Government buses cost less than private buses, but may be more crowded. Off the main routes there are very few buses.

Taxi
Shared taxis cover routes along the coast, from Paramaribo to Nieuw Nickerie in the west and to Albina in the east. Fares are negotiable, but generally reasonable. Though several times more expensive than buses, they are notably faster.

Car
Rental cars are available but expensive. The road from Paramaribo to Albina still has some damage from the civil war. Other back-country roads may be unsafe, especially at night. When passing through villages, slow for *drempels*, the huge speed bumps on the highway.

Bicycle
Bicycles are a popular means of transport, but good roads are relatively few, so a mountain bike would be the best choice.

Boat
To visit the interior, river transport is the only option. Some coastal areas, such as the Galibi marine turtle reserve near Albina, are also accessible only by boat. There are few scheduled services, and prices are negotiable. Ferries and launches cross some major rivers, like the Suriname and the Coppename, and are very cheap.

Local Transport
Bus There are a few local bus and minibus services in Paramaribo. They are crowded, irregular and cheap.

Taxi Taxis are reasonably priced but unmetered, so set a price before getting in; within town a fare is around US$2 to US$3. Most Paramaribo taxi drivers speak English.

Organised Tours
Visitors interested in Suriname's exemplary system of national parks and reserves should contact Stinasu (Stichting Natuur Behoud

GUIANAS

Suriname; the Foundation for Nature Preservation in Suriname), which coordinates research and tourism in these areas. Stinasu (☎ 475845) has an office in Paramaribo (write to PO Box 436) and runs some inexpensive guided trips. They seem to be limited to only a few destinations at the moment, basically to the montane rainforest of Natuurpark Brownsberg, only two hours from Paramaribo. Ask about trips to Raleighvallen/Voltzberg National Park (on the upper Coppename River), Galibi Nature Reserve (at the mouth of the Marowijne River) and the Coppename Monding Nature Park.

METS (☎ 477088), 2 Nassylaan, Paramaribo, arranges ecotours in conjunction with Surinam Airways. They have three resorts in the interior and conduct a wide range of trips, from a three-hour tour of Paramaribo (US$15) to an eight-day expedition to Mt Kasikasima (US$575). Most popular is a five-day river tour of Kumalu and the Awarra Dam region (US$375). Tours include all meals, accommodation, transport and guides. There is usually a minimum and maximum number for each trip, so it is a good idea to make arrangements in advance. Most trips are offered during the main tourist season in August and September.

Other operators based in Paramaribo include Suriname Safari Tours (☎ 424025), Waterkant 54 bv, PO Box 2982, with two, three and four-day trips into the interior; Amar's Tour Service (☎ 400372), Estalbrielstraat 16, which does shorter and cheaper trips; Independent Tours (☎ 474770), Rooseveltkade 20; Toucan Travel & Tours (☎ 465692), Kwattaweg 589; and Cardy Adventures (☎ 476676), Heerenstraat 19.

PARAMARIBO

Suriname's capital city, Paramaribo (often abbreviated to 'Parbo' in speech and print), is a curious hybrid of northern Europe, Asia and tropical America. Imposing buildings overlook grassy squares, wooden houses crowd narrow streets, mosques and synagogues sit side by side, and mangroves still hug the riverside. The vigorous street life

includes Javanese vendors peddling bami and satay and Dutch-speaking Creoles guzzling Parbo beer at pavement cafés. However, things shut down fairly early.

Orientation

Sprawling Parbo sits on the west bank of the meandering Suriname River. Its core is a compact triangular area whose boundaries are Gravenstraat on the north, Zwartenhovenbrugstraat on the west, and the river to the south-east. Regular ferries cross the river to Meerzorg, on the east bank. The letters 'bv' in an address mean 'boven' – 'above', or upstairs.

Information

Tourist Office The Suriname Tourist Department office (☎ 471163) is at Cornelius Jongbawstraat 2, a short distance north-east of Royal Torarica Hotel. It's open Monday to Thursday from 7 am to 3 pm, but sometimes closes earlier, especially on Fridays. The staff speak English and German and have an excellent city map (sometimes out of stock), some brochures and a map of the country.

Money The Centrale Bank van Suriname is at Waterkant 20, while the ABN Amro Bank is at Kerkplein 1. They change travellers' cheques and stamp foreign-exchange transaction forms. Changing money near Waterkant Market is quicker, but exercise caution – don't pull out your wallet, carry only a modest amount of cash, and count your money carefully, twice. Shopkeepers and hotels may also change money, at about the same rate as the banks.

Post & Communications The main post office is at the corner of Korte Kerkstraat and Wagenwegstraat. To send urgent or important packages call DHL (☎ 474007). TeleSur's long-distance telephone office is a block south of the post office.

Foreign Embassies & Consulates Most

delegations, except Brazil's, are in central Paramaribo:

Brazil
    Embassy: Maratakastraat 2, Zorg-en-Hoop (☎ 491011)
Canada
    Honorary Consulate: Waterkant 92-94 (☎ 471222)
France
    Embassy: Gravenstraat 5-7 (☎ 476455)
Germany
    Consulate: Maagdenstraat 46 bv (☎ 410382)
Guyana
    Embassy: Gravenstraat 82 (☎ 477895)
Netherlands
    Embassy: Dr JC Mirandastraat 10 (☎ 477211)
UK
    Embassy: VSH United Bldg, Van't Hogerhuys-straat (☎ 472870)
USA
    Embassy: Dr Sophie Redmondstraat 129 (☎ 477881)
Venezuela
    Embassy: Gravenstraat 23-25 (☎ 475401)

Visas In theory visitors spending more than a week in Suriname require an exit visa (blue card) from the Vreemdelingendienst (Immigration) office (☎ 473101), in Nieuwe Haven. Getting an exit visa involves completing a rather long form and submitting two passport photographs, then crossing town to the District Commissaris Paramaribo (☎ 471131), on Wilhelminastraat, to pay a Sf10 (US$0.20) fee, and returning to Nieuwe Haven for the stamp. This irritating requirement is rarely enforced, and some foreign visitors ignore the whole procedure.

Stinasu The Foundation for Nature Preservation in Suriname (☎ 475845) is at Cornelius Jongbawstraat 14, a bit farther out than the tourist office.

Bookshops Vaco, Domineestraat 26, has a good selection of books in Dutch and a handful in English, as does Kersten's, a department store at Domineestraat and Steenbakkerijstraat.

Emergency Paramaribo's hospital is on Gravenstraat, but St Vincentius Katholic Hospital (☎ 471212), Koninginnestraat 4, may be better for emergency treatment.

Things to See

Central Paramaribo's focus is the **Onafhan-kelijksplein** (Unity Square), fronting the **Presidential Palace**, on Gravenstraat. Immediately behind the palace is the **Palmentuin**, an attractive park with tall palms, picnic tables and benches, and a good sample of tropical birds. The finance building, on the west side of the square, looks like it's straight from Amsterdam.

To the east is **Fort Zeelandia**, a pentagonal 17th-century fort which overlooks the river. It has been well restored, and is being developed as a venue for small exhibitions – it's well worth a look. Going south-west along Waterkant, you pass some of the city's most impressive colonial buildings, mostly merchants' houses built after the fires of 1832. The streets inland from here, particularly **Lim-a-Po Straat**, have many old wooden buildings, some restored, others in picturesque decay.

Another block inland, on Gravenstraat, is the Roman Catholic **Kathedraal** (1885), which is closed until its sagging wooden superstructure can be repaired. A few blocks to the south-east are some other religious buildings – the main **Mosque** and the **Dutch Israeli Synagogue** – side by side on Keizerstraat.

Paramaribo's commercial centre is around **Domineestraat** and nearby streets. **Waterkant Market** is at the foot of Jodenbreestraat; ferries to Meerzorg leave from nearby.

Out in the suburbs, the **Surinaams Museum**, at Commewijnstraat 18, Zorg-en-Hoop, has a small collection of Amerindian artefacts and worthwhile special exhibits. It's open weekdays from 7.30 am to 2 pm, and Friday, Saturday and Sunday from 5 to 8 pm. Admission is cheap, but a cab from the city centre will cost about US$2. The museum has a modest selection of souvenirs and books, including some in English.

North of town, Paramaribo's zoo, **Culturtuin**, is a pretty grim place, with some interesting animals in small enclosures. The

GUIANAS

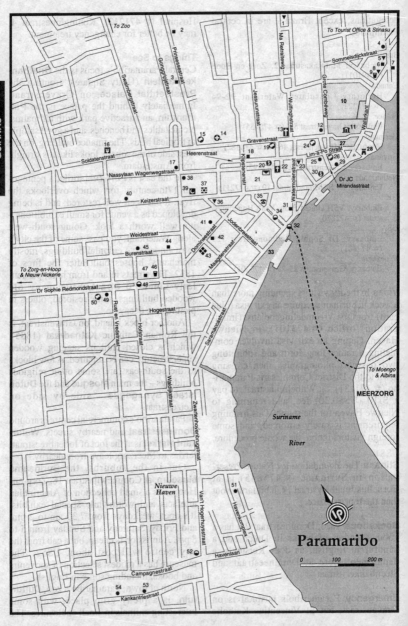

GUIANAS

To Zoo

To Tourist Office & Stinasu

Sommelsdijckstraat

To Moengo
& Albina

MEERZORG

Suriname

River

Paramaribo

0   100   200 m

To Zorg-en-Hoop
& Nieuw Nickerie

surrounding parkland (out along Swalmbergstraat) is woodsy, and many locals go jogging in the area.

Places to Stay

Paramaribo's best budget accommodation is the friendly *YWCA Guest House* (☎ 476-981), Heerenstraat 14-16, which has clean, simple singles/doubles for US$12/14. Commonly referred to as 'wyka', it often fills up, so make a reservation if you can. *Flair Guesthouse*, on Kleine Waterstraat, is new, clean and recommended, and costs about US$14 for a room.

Friendly, funky and cheap, *La Brise Hotel* (☎ 410346), at the south end of Watermolenstraat, is in a rough-looking area, but it's OK for US$6/7.50. *Fanna Guest House* (☎ 476-789), Prinsessestraat 31, is cheap but unattractive with ramshackle rooms for about US$6. Farther up Prinsessestraat is the *Blue Moon Hotel* (☎ 473062), where small, basic rooms with shared bath cost about US$10. *Lisa's Guest House* (☎ 476927), Burenstraat 6, is quite a bit better, but overpriced at US$16/20 for singles/doubles with shared bath.

Hotel Ambassador (☎ 477555), Dr Sophie Redmondstraat 66, has supposedly been renovated, but is not good value at US$37/50. The *Hotel Krasnapolsky* (☎ 475-050), Domineestraat 39, is one of Paramaribo's more expensive places, at US$50/60 a single/double. The best place is *Royal Torarica Hotel* (☎ 471500), Mr LJ Rietbergplein 1, with rooms from US$82/88.

Places to Eat

For a cheap breakfast or lunch, try the *Chalet Swiss* on Lim-a-Po Straat, which is more like a Dutch broodjeswinkel (sandwich shop) than a Swiss chalet, but has good sandwiches for under US$0.50. *Algeria*, on Keizerstraat, is an inexpensive fast food place with burgers, chicken, chips etc. Most of the cheaper places are closed in the evening, but the *Javanese food stalls* along Waterkant will provide a tasty budget supper. *Natasha*, opposite Royal Torarica Hotel, has good, cheap Indian food and stays open late.

Some of the best places for dinner are the numerous Asian restaurants, but many are quite expensive and some are away from the centre, so you'll need to spend a few dollars on taxis. *Bali* (☎ 422325), Ma Retraiteweg 3, serves very good Indonesian dishes for around US$8, including a rijstaffel for US$11. Despite the name, *La Bastille* (☎ 473991), Kleine Waterstraat 3, has mainly Indonesian and Chinese food, from around US$7. *Iwan's*, at Grote Hofstraat 6 off Watermolenstraat, is one of the best and most expensive Chinese places. Verlengde Gemenelandsweg is a long way out of town, but has some excellent restaurants, like *Sarinah* or *Jawa* for Indonesian food, the *New China* and the *New Korean*.

Royal Torarica Hotel has an excellent but expensive restaurant, as does the *Hotel Krasnapolsky*. For Creole food, try *Sunshine*, Wilhelminastraat 23.

Entertainment

Paramaribo is pretty quiet at night. On weekends, people gather around *'K Vat*, at the south end of Klein Waterstraat, where there are outdoor tables and sometimes live music. You could also try *Touché* disco, near the Hotel Ambassador on Dr Sophie Redmondstraat. Around 7.30 am on Sunday, there is a birdsong competition in Onafhankelijksplein.

Things to Buy

Several shops along Domineestraat sell attractive souvenirs, most notably woodcarvings, batik and basketwork. You could also look in Redi Tex, on Jodenbreestraat, and Elegancia Arts & Crafts, Zwartenhovenbrugstraat 120.

Getting There & Away

Air Paramaribo has two airports, nearby Zorg-en-Hoop (for domestic flights and some flights to Georgetown, Guyana) and the larger Zanderij (for all other international flights). Note that SLM's Paramaribo office will not reconfirm a reservation made at another travel agency.

Airlines with offices in Paramaribo include:

Air France
    Waterkant 12 (☎ 473838)
ALM
    Burenstraat 34 (☎ 476066)
Gonini Air Service
    Dookhieweg Oost 1 (☎ 499098)
Gum Air
    Kwattaweg 254 (☎ 498888)
KLM
    Mirandastraat, near Lim-a-Po Straat (☎ 472421)
SLM
    Nassylaan 2 (☎ 465700)

Bus Minibuses to Nieuw Nickerie (US$3.60 for a private bus) and other western destinations leave from the corner of Dr Sophie Redmondstraat and Hofstraat. Buses to Moengo, Albina (US$2) and other eastern destinations leave from the ferry terminal at the foot of Heiligenweg.

Taxi Taxis leave from the same areas as the minibuses (see above under Bus). Going east, it might be better to catch a taxi on the Meerzorg side of the river rather than from the ferry terminal.

Car Rental agencies include Torarica (☎ 479977), Kankantriestraat 44-48, and Para (☎ 450447). Rental cars are expensive and may not be in perfect condition.

Getting Around

To/From the Airport Johan Adolf Pengel airport, also known as Zanderij, is 45 km south of Paramaribo. A taxi will cost about US$30, but De Paarl Airport Service (☎ 479-600), Kankantriestraat 42, is cheaper. The much cheaper POZ minibus goes to Zanderij from the corner of Campagnestraat and Van't Hogerhuysstraat, near Nieuwe Haven, in daytime hours only.

A taxi to Zorg-en-Hoop airfield from central Paramaribo is about US$8.

Bus The tourist office has photocopied routes of Paramaribo's extensive bus system; most buses leave from Heiligenweg, just above the Meerzorg ferry terminal.

Taxi Taxis are reasonably priced but unmetered, so agree on the fare in advance; most drivers speak passable English. A short trip will cost around Sf1000 (less than US$1).

AROUND PARAMARIBO
Nieuw Amsterdam

At the confluence of the Commewijne and Suriname rivers, Nieuw Amsterdam is a ruined Dutch colonial fort, but the 18th-century armoury is in good repair and the jail, used into this century, is being restored. There is no admission charge to the open-air museum, but the attendant will want a tip.

Take Bus No 4 from central Parbo to the end of the line, at Leonsberg, then catch a launch across the river. For a few guilders more, the boat will take you to the fort's jetty; otherwise, walk north along the river road about one km to the entrance.

Natuurpark Brownsberg

Brownsberg Nature Park is an area of montane tropical rainforest overlooking WJ van Blommesteinmeer (reservoir), about 1½ hours south of the capital via a good highway. Stinasu operates occasional day trips, with a short walk on the Mazaroni plateau, with fine views of the reservoir, and a longer hike down into a canyon with pretty waterfalls (about US$30, including lunch and transport). It is possible to arrange an overnight stay, but transport is problematic except on weekends. Put some insect repellent around your ankles to discourage chiggers (mites), whose irritating but otherwise harmless bites may not become apparent for some days.

Colakreek

A recreation area 50 km south of Paramaribo, Colakreek gets its name from the dark colour of the water. Nevertheless, it's a good place to swim and relax. Some operators, like METS, do tours to the area. To get there independently take a bus to the international airport, and then a taxi.

NIEUW NICKERIE

Near the mouth of the Nickerie River, Nieuw

Nickerie is Suriname's second port, exporting rice and bananas. It has a daily passenger ferry to Corriverton, Guyana.

Places to Stay & Eat

The best budget place to stay is the *Hotel Luxor* (☎ 231365), at St Jozefstraat 22. It's an old-fashioned place where a clean room with bath, toilet and fan will cost about US$5. Nearby, the *Hotel De President* is slightly more expensive and much less pleasant. The *Hotel Tropical*, Gouverneurstraat 114, has rooms for around US$6, and is not bad if the bar downstairs isn't too noisy. *Hotel de Vesting*, Balatastraat 6, is a motel-style place, with air-con doubles for around US$18. The most comfortable place is *Hotel Ameerali* (☎ 231265), Maynardstraat 32, with clean but smallish air-con singles/doubles for US$20/30.

Moksie Patoe, Gouverneurstraat 115, is a friendly and interesting bar/restaurant, with a varied menu and good food. You can rent a comfortable apartment there for US$10 per night. Other places to eat include the *New Kowloon* Chinese restaurant and *Pak Hap*, with creole food.

Getting There & Away

Air SLM (☎ 031359), Gouverneurstraat 96, has daily flights to Paramaribo.

Bus Government buses to Paramaribo (US$1.85, four hours) leave from the market on Maynardstraat at 6 am and 1 pm. A private bus leaves at 4 pm and costs around US$3.60.

Taxi Taxis to Paramaribo also leave from the market. With five passengers to share the cost the charge is around US$12.50 per person. They're slightly faster than the buses.

To/From Guyana There is a ferry to Corriverton every morning, returning to Nieuw Nickerie in the afternoon. It leaves at 7.30

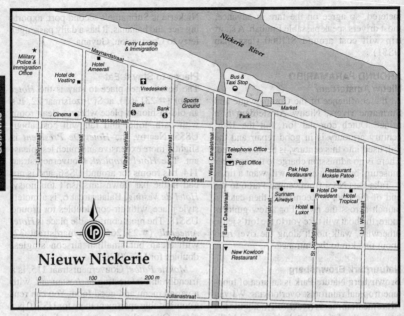

Nieuw Nickerie

0   100   200 m

am, and you need to book the day before. You have to pay Sf1000 in Surinamese currency (about US$2.50). Expect a thorough customs check and tedious formalities on each side; see the entry on Corriverton in the Guyana section.

MOENGO

Moengo, a centre for bauxite mining and shipping on the Cottica River, is 160 km east of Paramaribo. There is a reasonably priced *YWCA Guesthouse* at Lijneweg 18.

ALBINA

Albina is a small village which was destroyed in the civil war and has not yet recovered. It's on the Marowijne River, which is the border with French Guiana. With permission from Carib Indians (and a hired canoe), it is possible to visit the nearby **Galibi Nature Reserve**, where ridley, green and leatherback turtles nest in June and July.

Albina is not an inviting place and has no accommodation. Arrive early in the day so you can continue to Paramaribo or cross to French Guiana without having to stop here.

Getting There & Away

Minibuses and taxis to Paramaribo leave from just outside the customs and immigration office.

To/From French Guiana The French ferry crosses to St Laurent du Maroni two or four times daily. The last boat departs at 5 pm on Monday, Thursday, Friday and Sunday; 9.30 am on Saturday; and 10 am on Tuesday and Wednesday. There is no charge. At other times, you can hire a dugout (about US$5) for the short crossing. Arriving by bus or taxi you will be surrounded by people eager to take you across in a dugout; not all of them are reliable. Go to Surinamese immigration first, get your passport stamped, and ask the official to recommend a boatman.

French Guiana

> **Name** Guyane Française (département d'outre-mer de France)
> **Area** 91,250 sq km
> **Population** 134,000 (1994 estimate)
> **Population Density** 1.47 per sq km
> **Capital** Cayenne
> **Head of State** President Jacques Chirac
> **Official Language** French
> **Other Languages** Amerindian dialects creole
> **Currency** French Franc (FF)
> **Exchange Rate** US$1 = FF5.17 (but exchange rates are lower in French Guyana)
> **Per Capita GNP** US$6000 (1993 estimate)
> **Inflation Rate** 2.5% (1992)

Smallest of the Guianas, French Guiana is a former colony, now administered as an overseas department of France. Officially, it is a part of France, and therefore a member of the EU. The urban areas of Cayenne and Kourou have excellent facilities and an infrastructure comparable to rural France, but the hinterland is sparsely populated and little developed. Historically, Guiana is best known as the penal colony where Captain Alfred Dreyfus (a French army officer wrongly convicted of treason in 1894) and Papillon (see Books & Maps in Facts for the Visitor) were imprisoned, but today it's famous as the home of the Centre Spatial Guyanais, launch site for the Ariane rockets of the European Space Agency.

FACTS ABOUT FRENCH GUIANA
History

The earliest French settlement was in Cayenne in 1643, but development of plantations was very limited because of tropical diseases and the hostility of the local Indians. After various conflicts with the Dutch and British, and an eight-year occupation by Brazil and Portugal, the French resumed control in 1817. Slavery was abolished in 1848 and the few plantations almost col-

lapsed. A small gold rush in the 1850s saw more labourers desert the plantations, and precipitated border disputes with Suriname and Brazil.

At about the same time, it was decided that penal settlements in Guiana would reduce the cost of prisons in France and contribute to the development of the colony. Convicts who survived their initial sentence had to remain in Guiana as exiles for an equal period of time, but 90% of them died of malaria or yellow fever so this policy did little for population growth. French Guiana became notorious for the brutality and corruption of its penal system, and was associated with some celebrated cases. The last penal settlement closed in 1953.

Guiana became an overseas department of France in 1946, and receives substantial economic support from the metropole. In 1964, work was started on the European space centre, which has brought an influx of engineers, technicians and service people from Europe, and turned Kourou into a sizeable town with every modern amenity.

Geography

French Guiana is roughly the size of Portugal, or the US state of Indiana. It borders Brazil in the east and south, while to the west, the Maroni (Marowijne) and Litani rivers form the border with Suriname (the southern part is disputed).

The majority of Guianais live in the Atlantic coastal zone, which contains most of the country's limited road network. Most of the coast is mangrove swamp, but there are a few sandy beaches.

The densely forested interior, whose terrain rises gradually toward the Tumac-Humac Mountains on the Brazilian frontier, is very thinly populated. The highest peaks barely exceed 900 metres.

Climate

French Guiana's rainy season runs from January to June, with the heaviest rains in May.

GUIANAS

GUIANAS

French Guiana

0   50   100 km

ATLANTIC OCEAN

To Paramaribo

Moengo

Awala
Mana

Organabo
Iracoubo

Albina
St Laurent
du Maroni

Portal

Mana

Sinnamary

Centre
Spatial

Îles du Salut

Kourou

Apatou

Tonate

CAYENNE
Rémire

Camp
Voltaire

Kokioko

St Elie

Montsinéry

Matoury
Roura

Maroni
(Marowijne)

Sinnamary

Comté

Kaw

Baie de
Oiapoque

Grand
Santi

Abounami

Kourcibo

Orena

Régina

Ouanary

Maripasoula

Sinnamary

Aratai

Approuague

Matarani

St Georges
de l'Oiapoque

Oiapoque

To Macapá

SURINAME

Montagne
Machoulou
(782 m)

Saül

Inini

Waki

Pic Coudreau
(711 m)

Camopi

Camopi

Tampok

Camopi

BRAZIL

Litani

Maroni

Mont
Saint-Marcel
(635 m)

Yalaupi

Claimed by
Suriname &
French Guiana

SERRA   TUMUCUMAQUE

Government

French Guiana elects one representative to the French Senate and one to the National Assembly. It also elects a member to the European Parliament. Locally, there are two elected legislative houses, a 19-member general council and a 34-member regional council. Executive authority resides with the commissioner of the republic, usually a career civil servant, appointed for a term of two to three years.

Conservatives have traditionally ruled French Guiana, but the Parti Socialiste Guyanaise has done well since the early 1980s. Many Guianais favour greater autonomy from France, but very few support complete independence – not surprising given the high level of French economic assistance.

Economy

French Guiana's economy is traditionally dependent on metropolitan France and, to some degree, benefits from its membership in the EU. Successive French governments have provided state employment and billions of francs in subsidies, resulting in a near-European standard of living in the urban areas. The rural villages are much poorer, and in the hinterland many Amerindians and Marrons still lead a subsistence lifestyle.

Historically, the main export product has been rainforest timber. There is virtually no manufacturing, and agriculture is very poorly developed, except for a few plantations and Hmong market gardens – the vast majority of food and consumer goods are imported. The space centre employs nearly 1000 people and comprises about 15% of economic activity.

The main industries now are fishing (fresh and processed shrimp constitute nearly three-quarters of total exports by value), forest products and mining. There are large reserves of bauxite yet to be developed. The tourist industry is embryonic.

Population & People

French Guiana has only about 110,000 permanent inhabitants, with temporary and migrant workers from Haiti and elsewhere making up the balance. Estimates of the ethnic mix vary, but probably around 70% are Creole (of African or Afro-European descent, including Maronsa and Haitians), 10% European, 8% Asian, 8% Brazilian and 4% Amerindian.

Education is compulsory to the age of 16, and school attendance is fairly high, but literacy is only about 80%.

Arts

Music and dance are the liveliest art forms – Caribbean rhythms with a French accent. Some of the African traditions are seen in artwork with brightly coloured circular geometric designs.

Religion

French Guiana is predominantly Catholic, but Bush Negroes and Amerindians follow their own religious traditions.

Language

French is the official language, but French Guianese is a creole spoken by nearly everyone but expatriates. Amerindians speak Arawak, Carib, Emerillon, Oyapi, Palicur and Wayana.

FACTS FOR THE VISITOR
Visas & Embassies

Most visitors, except EU nationals, need a visa: apply at a French embassy, with two passport photos, and be prepared to show an onward or return ticket, to pay a fee of about US$25, and to wait for two or three days. It might take a lot longer at a consulate if they have to refer the application to an embassy. Officially all visitors, even French citizens, should have an onward or return ticket, though it may not be checked at land borders.

French Embassies Abroad France has embassies and consulates in neighbouring countries (for addresses, see the city entries under each of those countries) and also in:

Australia
6 Perth Ave, Yarralumla, ACT 2600 (☎ (06) 216-0100)

Canada
42 Sussex Drive, Ottawa, Ontario K1M 2C9, (☎ (613) 789-1795)

Ireland
36 Ailesbury Rd, Dublin 4 (☎ (01) 260 1666)

New Zealand
1-3 Willeston St, Wellington (☎ (04) 472-0200)

South Africa
2 Dean St, Gardens, Cape Town (☎ (021) 23 1575)

UK
6A Cromwell Place, London SW7 (☎ (0171) 823-9555)

USA
Belmont Rd NW, Washington, DC (☎ (202) 328-2600)

Foreign Embassies in French Guiana

Several countries have representatives in Cayenne (see the Cayenne section for details). The nearest US representative is in Martinique, at 14 Rue Blenac, Fort-de-France (☎ 71-9493).

Documents

Passports are obligatory for all visitors, except those from France. A yellow-fever vaccination certificate should also be carried.

Money

The French *franc* (FF) is the official currency, divided into 100 *centimes*. There are copper-coloured five, 10 and 20-centime coins, silver-coloured 50-centime, one-franc, two-franc and five-franc coins, and banknotes for 20, 50, 100 and 500 francs.

It is easy to change US dollars cash or travellers' cheques in Cayenne, but the rates are about 5% lower than official published rates – bring some francs with you. Credit cards are widely accepted, and it is easy to get Visa or MasterCard cash advances at an ATM *(guichet automatique)*. Eurocard and Carte Bleue are also widely accepted, and the ATMs at post offices are on the Plus and Cirrus networks. Credit card charges are billed at a better rate of exchange.

In July 1996, official rates of exchange included the following:

Australia	A$1	=	FF4.06
Canada	C$1	=	FF3.79
Germany	DM1	=	FF3.38
Japan	¥100	=	FF4.77
New Zealand	NZ$1	=	FF3.52
United Kingdom	UK£1	=	FF7.98
USA	US$1	=	FF5.17

Costs French Guiana is quite expensive, with prices comparable to metropolitan France. It is difficult to find accommodation for less than FF160, but meals are better value, from about FF35. Public transport is limited, and far dearer than in neighbouring countries. Tourist services to the interior are very expensive. Even parsimonious travellers should budget at least FF250 per day.

When to Go

The dry season, from July to December, may be more comfortable, but Carnaval, usually in February, is a great attraction.

Tourist Offices

French tourist offices can supply basic information about French Guiana.

Business Hours & Holidays

Many businesses close for lunch, from about noon to 3 pm. Public holidays include:

January 1
 New Year's Day
February
 Ash Wednesday – end of Carnaval
March/April
 Good Friday/Easter Monday
May 1
 Labour Day
June 10
 Abolition of Slavery
July 14
 Bastille Day
August 15
 Assumption
November 1
 All Saints Day
November 2
 All Souls Day
November 11
 Veterans Day
December 25
 Christmas Day

Special Events

Carnaval is a big and colourful occasion, with festivities every weekend from Epiphany and for four days solid before Ash Wednesday.

Post & Communications

The postal service is reliable. There are no central telephone offices, but you can make an international call from any pay phone – dial 19, then the country code, then the area code, then the local number. For an operator, dial 19, then 594. You need a telephone card to use public telephones – they should be available at post offices, newsstands, tobacconists etc, but they are often in short supply. The country code for French Guiana is 594.

Time

French Guiana is three hours behind GMT/UTC.

Books & Maps

The best known book on French Guiana as a penal colony is Henri Charrière's novel *Papillon*, made into a Hollywood film. A factual but very readable account is Alexander Miles' *Devil's Island: Colony of the Damned*.

Thurston Clarke's seriously hilarious *Equator* devotes a chapter to his experiences in French Guiana.

France's Institut Géographique National publishes a superb 1:500,000 map of French Guiana, with fine city maps of Cayenne and Kourou (FF59 in Cayenne), as well as more detailed maps of the populated coastal areas.

Media

France Guyane is Cayenne's daily newspaper, with good local and international coverage. French newspapers and magazines are readily available. The *International Herald Tribune* arrives regularly at local newsstands. *Petites Annonces*, a free paper with advertisements and entertainment listings, comes out on Thursdays.

Cayenne has two TV channels and several FM radio stations.

Health

Chloroquine-resistant malaria is present, particularly in the interior, and French Guiana is regarded as a yellow-fever infected area. Typhoid prophylaxis is recommended. Good medical care is available, but few doctors speak English.

Dangers & Annoyances

Generally French Guiana is very safe, but parts of Cayenne are definitely not, especially at night. Even a small town like St Laurent seems to have some disaffected and hostile people.

Work

High wages draw workers from neighbouring countries, especially in construction, but illegal workers are deported when demand slackens. Despite official disapproval, travellers sometimes find work, with payment in cash. An EU passport simplifies matters. Kourou is the best place to look for construction employment, legal or otherwise.

Activities

Surfing, windsurfing and sailing are possible on quite nice beaches near Cayenne and Kourou, but there are few public facilities, so befriend a local. Some operators offer expensive sea and river fishing trips.

Highlights

French Guiana does exhibit French style, especially in its architecture and its cuisine. The old colonial buildings are cute and colourful, and some of the traditional design features are attractively incorporated in the modern buildings of Cayenne and Kourou. Splurging on some good restaurant meals could be a highlight, but even on a budget you can enjoy French bread and pastries, great coffee, crêpes from street vendors, and some of the tastiest Asian food outside Asia.

The forested interior has great potential for ecotourism, though trips are expensive here. The Îles du Salut are very scenic, but to really enjoy the remains of the penal settlements you'll need imagination and morbid tastes. Carnaval in Cayenne is a highlight for anyone.

Accommodation

Accommodation is quite good, but expensive – cheap hotels start at around FF160 for a single. There are also *gîtes* (rooms or apartments in private houses), which cost from FF120 to FF200 per day, but are cheaper by the week or month. In rural areas, it is possible to hang a hammock in some camp areas from about FF30.

Food & Drinks

Excellent food is available, though the better restaurants are very expensive, rarely less than FF50 and frequently more than twice that. Cheaper cafés and delis have meals for around FF35 which are still very tasty. Asian restaurants and food stalls serve truly delicious Chinese, Vietnamese and Indonesian dishes for as little as FF20.

Imported alcoholic drinks, and even soft drinks, are particularly expensive in bars and restaurants, but can be bought from groceries at more reasonable prices.

Entertainment

Bars and restaurants in Cayenne often have excellent live music, but cover charges and drinks can be ruinous – try listening from the sidewalk.

Things to Buy

Most handicrafts resemble those of Guyana and Suriname, but are more expensive here. Elaborate Hmong tapestries are not found elsewhere, and can be good value though they're not cheap. They are produced by the Hmong community that immigrated to Suriname in the 1970s.

GETTING THERE & AWAY
Air

There are direct flights to Caracas, Quito and the French Caribbean, as well as the following destinations.

To/From Europe The most direct route is from Paris to Cayenne with Air France or AOM. The cheapest published fares are about FF3800 return. There are also connections via the islands of Guadeloupe and Martinique.

To/From North America There are regular flights with Air France from Miami and other US cities to Guadeloupe and Martinique, with connections to Cayenne.

To/From Brazil TABA flies three times per week from Cayenne to Macapá and Belém. SLM flies to/from Belém (FF1322).

To/From Suriname SLM connects Cayenne with Paramaribo six times weekly (FF792); four flights continue to Georgetown.

Land

To/From Brazil From St Georges, on the Oiapoque River, there are launches to the Brazilian town of Oiapoque, but you'll have to fly to St Georges.

To/From Suriname From St Laurent de Maroni there is a passenger ferry to Albina, Suriname, with road connections to Paramaribo.

Leaving French Guiana

To Suriname, Brazil and other international destinations, the tax is FF117. Flights from Cayenne to Paris are regarded as domestic, and there's no departure tax.

GETTING AROUND
Air

Air Guyane has scheduled flights to St Georges, Régina, Saül and Maripasoula.

Bus

There is daily service from Cayenne to St Laurent du Maroni via Kourou, Sinnamary and Iracoubo.

Taxi

Taxis collectifs (actually minibuses) are faster, much more comfortable and only very slightly more expensive than the bus from

Cayenne to St Laurent. They also run frequently from Cayenne to Kourou.

Car & Motorcycle
Both car and motorbike rentals are available in Cayenne, Kourou and St Laurent.

Hitching
Because private cars are numerous and roads are fairly good, hitching is a realistic alternative for budget travellers, but competition is considerable in certain areas, such as on the outskirts of Cayenne on the highway to Kourou.

Boat
River transport into the interior is possible but requires patience and good timing, unless you are taking an expensive tour.

Local Transport
In Cayenne, the local SNTC bus services the beach areas of Rémire-Montjoly, but in general, public transport is limited, so you may need a taxi.

Organised Tours
Because public transport is so limited, especially in the interior, tours are a good way to see the country, but they are not cheap. For example, a five-day trip up the Maroni (Marowijne), with transport from Cayenne, costs about FF2790 per person, all-inclusive. Tours of the space centre are free.

CAYENNE
Dating from 1664, French Guiana's capital (population 40,000) has only a handful of early colonial buildings – many were destroyed in a fire in 1888. Nevertheless, there are still lots of buildings with great character, and the ethnic diversity and the atmosphere of 'France in the tropics' make Cayenne an interesting place.

Orientation
Cayenne is at the west end of a small, somewhat hilly peninsula between the Cayenne and Mahury rivers. The liveliest area is the Place des Palmistes, in the north-west corner

of town, where there are many cafés and outdoor food stalls. To its west, the Place Grenoble (also known as Place Léopold Héder) is one of the oldest parts of Cayenne. The area south of the market, called the Village Chinois, has many black residents and some of the best music and nightlife, but it's not safe unless you're with a local, especially not at night. It's nicknamed 'Chicago'.

Information
Tourist Office The Agence Régionale de Développement du Tourisme et des Loisirs de la Guyane (☎ 30-0900), at 12 Rue Lalouette, is open weekdays from 8 am to noon and 3 to 6 pm (closing at 5 pm on Friday), and Saturday from 8 am to noon. It has good maps of Cayenne, many brochures, and some of the staff speak English.

Money The Bureau de Change Caraïbes, 64 Avenue du Général de Gaulle, is open daily (except Sunday) from 8 am to 1 pm, and from 3 to 6.30 pm weekdays. Guyane Change, almost opposite at 63 Avenue du Général de Gaulle, has similar rates.

Post & Communications The most convenient Bureau de Poste (post office) is on the south side of the Place Grenoble. Poste restante goes to another office outside the centre. There is no central telephone office, but there are quite a few pay phones, especially on and near Place des Palmistes.

Consulates You can obtain visas for neighbouring countries. The Surinamese Consulate may charge up to FF150 for the privilege.

Brazil
    23 Chemin Saint Antoine (☎ 30-0467)
Suriname
    38 Rue Christophe Colomb (☎ 30-0461); visas take one or two days, cost FF150, and require a photo and a ticket out of South America.
UK
    16 Avenue du Président Monerville (☎ 31-1034)

Tour & Travel Agencies Takari Tour (☎ 30-3888) is in the Hôtel Novotel, a distance

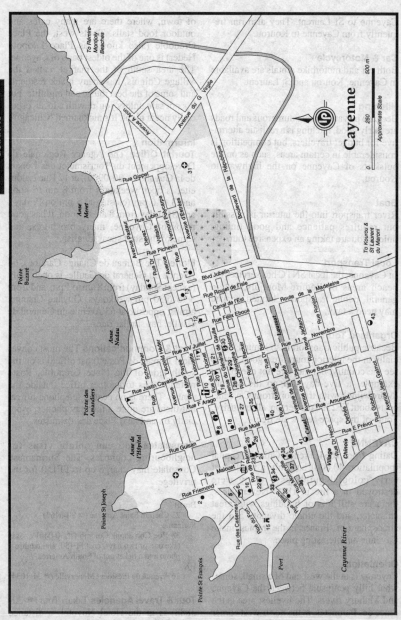

Cayenne

GUIANAS

PLACES TO STAY
12 Hôtel Neptima
27 Hôtel Amazonia
28 Chez Matilde
40 Central Hotel

PLACES TO EAT
1 Restaurant Les Amandiers
11 La Victoire
19 Pakhap
20 Le Fourville de Jimmy
21 Deli France
24 Les Pyramides
26 La Caravelle
29 Mille Pâtes Pizzeria
38 Ha Hay Yan

OTHER
2 Préfecture
3 Hôpital Jean Martial
4 JAL Voyages
5 Place Grenoble
6 Post Office
7 Place des Palmistes
8 Air France
9 Tourist Office
10 Cathedral
13 Avis (Car Rental)
14 AJC Bookshop
15 Fort Cépérou
16 Mairie (Town Hall)
17 Musée Départemental
18 Cinema
22 Sainte Claire Voyages
23 Bar Les Palmistes
25 Maison de la Presse
30 Bureau de Change Caraïbes
31 Hôpital St Denis
32 Atlas Voyages; SLM Airlines
33 Place Victor Schoelcher
34 Banque Nationale de Paris
35 Surinamese Consulate
36 Market
37 Place du Coq
39 Havas Voyages
41 Gare Routière & Taxis
   Collectifs
42 Takari Tour
43 Buses Ruffinel

from the centre on the road to Montabo. The Cayenne agent for Guyane-Excursions (☎ 32-0541) is Havas Voyages (☎ 31-2726), 2 Place du Marché (its main office is in the Centre Comercial Simarouba, in Kourou). JAL Voyages (☎ 31-6820), at Boulevard Jubelin and Avenue Pasteur, runs one and two-day trips to the Kaw marshes for FF500 and FF1100. Sainte Claire Voyages (☎ 30-

0038), 8 Rue de Rémire, is a helpful travel agency.

Bookshops Maison de la Presse, on the Place des Palmistes, carries French, Brazilian and English-language newspapers and magazines, as well as Institut Géographique National topographic maps. AJC, 31 Blvd Jubelin, has the biggest selection of books.

Emergency The Hôpital Jean Martial is on the north side of the Place des Palmistes. For emergencies call Hôpital la Madelaine (☎ 39-5253).

Things to See
Little remains of 17th-century **Fort Cépérou**, up a narrow alleyway off the Place Grenoble, but there are good views of the town, the port and the river. Around the **Place Grenoble** are the main public buildings, including the **Mairie** (Town Hall), the **post office** and the **Préfecture**. Across the **Place des Palmistes**, Avenue du Général de Gaulle is the main commercial street.

South across Rue de Rémire, the **Place Victor Schoelcher** commemorates the man most responsible for ending slavery in French Guiana. Farther south is **Place du Coq**, with Cayenne's main vegetable market nearby.

The centrally located **Musée Départemental** has preserved natural-history specimens, OK displays on archaeology, indigenous peoples and early colonial times, and excellent material on the penal colonies, including oil paintings by Francis Lagrange (Flag), a skilled counterfeiter. Some of the exhibits are really creepy. It's on Rue Rémire, just west of the Place des Palmistes, and is open Monday and Wednesday from 9 am to 1.30 pm, Tuesday and Friday from 9 am to 1.30 pm and 4.30 to 6.30 pm, Thursday from 10.30 am to 1.30 pm, and Saturday from 9 am to noon. Admission is FF10.

Special Events
Carnaval is the annual highlight and it gets bigger and wilder every year.

Places to Stay

Chez Matilde (☎ 30-2513), 42 Avenue du Général de Gaulle, is pretty basic but one of the cheapest, with rooms from FF130. *Hôtel Ajoupa* (☎ 30-3308) is two km out of town, on Route de Cabassou, but it's comfortable, with a pool and rooms from FF160 to FF270. Friendly, comfortable *Hôtel Neptima* (☎ 30-1115), 21 Rue Félix Eboué, has singles with private bath and air-conditioning from FF160, but most rooms are more expensive. Other places are much dearer, like *Central Hotel* (☎ 31-3000), on the corner of Molé and Becker, with singles/doubles from FF250/280, and *Hôtel Amazonia* (☎ 31-0000), 26 Avenue du Général de Gaulle, which goes even higher. A few top-end places, like the *Hôtel Novotel* (☎ 30-3888), start at around FF550. The tourist office has a full list of gîtes, which might be worth considering if you're staying for a week or more, but are no cheaper for a short stay.

Places to Eat

Best quality for the lowest prices are the mobile food stalls around the Place des Palmistes in the evening, where delicious crêpes, Indonesian fried noodles or tasty hamburgers will cost from FF10 to FF15.

Deli France, on the corner of Rue Justin Cayatée and Avenue du Général de Gaulle, has great coffee, sandwiches and yummy pastries. Nearby, *La Fourville de Jimmy*, 42 Rue Justin Cayatée, is another good place for a budget breakfast or a snack. *La Victoire*, 40 Rue 14 Juillet, serves very tasty Chinese and Creole dishes at outdoor tables, and is an economical and friendly place to eat. *Mille Pâtes Pizzeria* (☎ 31-9019), 52 Rue Justin Cayatée, is a little more expensive, but they make a mean pizza for FF30 to FF40. *Pakhap*, 29 Rue Arago, is a cheap Chinese place, and not bad at all.

There are other interesting eateries in the streets south of Place des Palmistes. *Les Pyramides*, on the corner of Rue Christophe Colomb and Rue Malouet, is a Middle Eastern restaurant with couscous for FF55 and grills for FF45. Going east on Christophe Colomb you come to *La Caravelle*, one of the cheaper French restaurants, serving main courses from FF50 to FF90; there's a wild-west style saloon next door. A couple of blocks away on Rue Monerville, *Ha Hay Yan* serves delicious Chinese and Vietnamese dishes at budget prices, to eat in or take away.

Perhaps the best restaurant is *Les Amandiers* (☎ 31-3875), facing the pleasant park at Pointe des Amandiers – starters cost FF55 to FF65, fish from FF70 to FF90, and main courses around FF100. This is pricey, but good value compared with Parisian prices, and the set menus, at FF65, FF70 and FF120 for three courses, are almost a bargain. The better hotels, like the Amazon and Novotel, also have good but expensive restaurants.

Entertainment

Bar Les Palmistes, an indoor/outdoor café/bar on Avenue du Général de Gaulle, at the south-west corner of Place des Palmistes, is an expensive place to drink but sometimes has good live music. *Le Cric Crac*, at Motel Beauregard in Rémire-Montjoly, has a dance band on Saturday nights. Some of the best reggae music is in small clubs in Village Chinois, but you'd be ill advised to go there at night without a local friend. Cinemas on the east side of Place des Palmistes show European and American films, mostly in French but sometimes in English with French subtitles.

Things to Buy

There are several souvenir shops along Avenue du Général de Gaulle. Handicrafts are similar to those in Suriname, but prices are much higher.

Getting There & Away

Air Rochambeau airport (☎ 35-9350), which is about 15 km south-west of Cayenne, has flights to local, regional and international destinations.

Note that SLM offices in Cayenne will not reconfirm Saturday flights from Paramaribo to Georgetown, because those flights leave from Zorg-en-Hoop rather than Zanderij.

Airlines with offices in Cayenne include:

Air France
    13 Place Léon Gontrand Damas (☎ 30-2740)
Air Guyane
    2 Rue Lalouette (☎ 35-6555)
AOM
    (☎ 35-7746)
SLM
    915 Rue Louis Blanc (☎ 31-7298)
TABA
    5 Route de Baduel (☎ 31-2147)

Bus Buses Ruffinel (☎ 31-2666), 8 Ave Jean Galmot, has a scheduled service to St Laurent du Maroni (FF140, five hours) and intermediate destinations like Kourou (FF50) at 5.30 am daily, except Sunday.

Taxi Taxis collectifs to Kourou and St Laurent du Maroni leave when full from the Gare Routière on Avenue de la Liberté. Only FF10 dearer than the bus to St Laurent, they are much faster and more comfortable, but you may have to wait before they fill with passengers.

Car Because of limited public transport, car rental is worth considering, even though it's expensive. Eurofranc (☎ 31-9042) is one of the cheapest, with cars from FF85 per day, plus FF95 for insurance and FF1.20 per km. Avis (☎ 30-2522), at 77 Rue du Lt Goinet, and at the airport, may give you a good deal if you book the car in advance through an Avis agency at home. Other companies include Aria (☎ 30-4050), ACL (☎ 30-4756), Jasmin (☎ 30-8490), Hertz (☎ 35-1171) and Europcar (☎ 35-1827). Most have an office at the airport, but it's easier to shop around by phone.

Hitching Hitching to Kourou and St Laurent is feasible, but competition is considerable at the junction of the Kourou and Régina highways. On Sunday it may be the only option.

Getting Around
To/From the Airport Taxis to Rochambeau cost about FF100, but they can be shared. It is far cheaper to take a taxi collectif to Matoury, but that still leaves a five-km hitch or walk to Rochambeau.

Bus SNTC runs several local bus routes. A useful one is Ligne No 6, which goes from the bus station to the beach area of Rémire-Montjoly. Buses don't run on Sundays.

Taxi Taxis have meters and charge a hiring fee of FF10.60 plus FF5.30 per km. The per-km charge is FF7.42 at night, and on Sundays and holidays.

AROUND CAYENNE
Rémire-Montjoly
Montjoly has Cayenne's best beach, reached by SNTC bus or by taxi. It also features historical ruins at **Fort Diamant**, a hiking trail to the top of **Montagne du Mahury** and an early colonial sugar mill at **Vidal de Lingendes**. Often referred to jointly, Montjoly and adjacent Rémire are prime residential areas.

Roura
In a scenic area on the highway to Kaw, this village on the east bank of the Mahury River has an interesting 19th-century church. It is the beginning of a series of hills, the Montagne de Kaw, covered by well-preserved tropical rainforest (despite occasional slash-and-burn clearing and commercial timber operations). An unsurfaced highway follows the ridge to the Kaw marshes.

Near Roura is the Laotian village of **Dacca**; canoe trips are possible on Gabrielle Creek, and there is a side road to Fourgassier Falls. *Le Relais de Patawa* (☎ 31-9395), on the Kaw highway, has hammock space (FF20), rents hammocks (FF40) and offers beds (FF60). Meals cost FF70 to FF90.

Kaw
Reached by paved and dirt highway to the Kaw River, then by launch across the river, this is one of French Guiana's most accessible wildlife areas. There are many birds, and the marshes are also home to caymans. Basic lodging is available. JAL and other agencies run trips from Cayenne. It is also possible to catch a launch downstream from Régina.

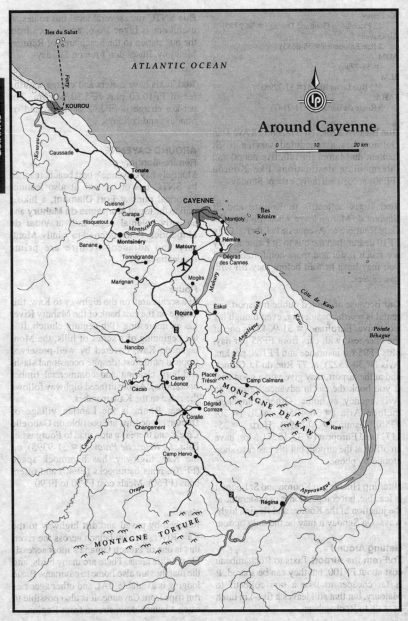

GUIANAS

ATLANTIC OCEAN

Îles du Salut

KOUROU

Around Cayenne

0   10   20 km

CAYENNE

Îles
Rémire

Montsinéry

On the Montsinéry River, some 45 km west of Cayenne, this town has a zoo, open daily from 9 am to 7 pm. Its big attraction is the feeding of the caymans at 5 pm.

Cacao

Cacao is about 75 km from Cayenne by a side road off the Régina highway. This village of Hmong refugees was transplanted from the Asian to the South American tropics in the 1970s. Hmong embroidery and weaving are interesting (see them at the Sunday market) and authentic Asian food is available quite cheaply.

From Cayenne there are Monday morning and Friday afternoon minibuses to Cacao with Transport Collectif Bruno Le Vessier (☎ 30-5132), making it possible to spend the weekend. For lodging, try *Restaurant Lau Faineng* (☎ 30-2830).

Régina

On the Approuague River, about 100 km from Cayenne, Régina is at the end of Route Nationale 2. There are plans to continue the highway to St Georges. Once a gold-mining area, Régina is a small village, and somewhat run-down.

KOUROU

Until recently, Kourou was a moribund ex-penal settlement on the west bank of the Kourou River, 65 km west of Cayenne. Establishment of the European space centre here has led to a modern new town, overwhelming Kourou's colonial core. Boats from here go to the ruins of penal settlements on the Îles du Salut, now a favourite weekend destination.

Centre Spatial Guyanais

In 1964, the French government chose this site (900 sq km along 50 km of coastline) because it's close to the equator, has a large ocean frontage away from tropical storm tracks and earthquake zones, and has a low population density.

Currently, three separate organisations operate here – the Agence Spatiale Euro-péenne (European Space Agency), the Centre National d'Études Spatiales (French Space Agency) and Arianespace (a private commercial enterprise developing the Ariane rocket). Between them, they employ about 1100 people and conduct eight or nine launches per year.

Free tours (☎ 33-4200) take place at 7.45 am and 1.45 pm Monday to Thursday. Phone ahead for reservations, though sometimes you can join on a tour on the spot (bring identification). Tour guides sometimes speak English or German – ask when you book. At the end of the tour, you can see the **Spacexpo** exhibition.

Places to Stay & Eat

Accommodation and food are very expensive. You might try *Kourou Accueil* (☎ 32-2540), in the old part of town, but most budget travellers will stay in Cayenne. Camping on Île Royale is another cheap option (see the Île du Salut section below).

AROUND KOUROU

Beyond Kourou, Route Nationale 1 detours around the space centre to Sinnamary, then parallels the coast, passing through several picturesque villages, before turning inland at Organabo. A side road goes to the village of Mana, while the main highway continues to St Laurent du Maroni.

Îles du Salut

Best known for the notorious prison at Devil's Island, the Îles du Salut (Salvation Islands) are 15 km north of Kourou over choppy, shark-infested waters. For 18th-century colonists the islands were an escape from mainland fever and malaria because the sea breezes kept mosquitoes away. The prisons came later, with as many as 2000 convicts.

Île Royale, the largest of the three islands, was the administrative headquarters of the penal settlement, while the smaller Île St Joseph, close by, was reserved for solitary confinement. Île du Diable, a tiny islet now covered with coconut palms, was home to political prisoners, including Dreyfus.

Nearly inaccessible because of hazardous currents, it was linked to Île Royale by a 225-metre supply cable.

The space centre has some installations on Île Royale, but the atmospheric ruins are the main attraction. The surprisingly abundant wildlife includes macaws, agoutis and sea turtles.

Places to Stay & Eat L'Auberge des Îles du Salut (☎ 32-1100) offers hammock space (FF50), dormitory accommodation (FF70) and single/double accommodation (from FF200/250). Their midday prix fixe meal is good, but expensive at FF130. Free camping is possible, but bring food unless you can subsist on coconuts and fallen mangos; the water is not potable, but mineral water is available at the auberge.

Getting There & Away From the jetty at Kourou's Marché de Poisson (Fish Market), a very comfortable launch crosses to Île Royale daily at 8 am (FF180 return, one hour). Make reservations with Carbet des Îles (☎ 32-0995), or Takari Tours (☎ 31-1969) in Cayenne, though usually it is possible to show up and buy a ticket on the spot. The problem is getting from Cayenne in time – the Ruffinel bus is the best bet, but doesn't run on Sunday. Taxis colectifs don't leave until they're full, and even the first ones may not make it. On the return trip, ask drivers in the parking lot for a lift back to Cayenne.

Sinnamary
Sinnamary, a village of 3500 people, is 50 km north-west of Kourou. It has a substantial Indonesian community, producing excellent handicrafts including woodwork and jewellery. The cheapest accommodation is the Sinnarive Motel (☎ 34-5646), with rooms at FF260.

Iracoubo
Iracoubo, 30 km west of Sinnamary, is best known for its parish church, with an interior elaborately painted by a convict who remained in the area after his release. Ask the driver of your bus or taxi colectif to stop so you can see it. Accommodation at the Hôtel Au Fil de L'eau (☎ 34-6351) costs FF200. Nearby is the Amerindian village of Belle-vue, with attractive Galibi pottery.

ST LAURENT DU MARONI
Once a reception camp for newly arrived convicts, St Laurent retains some picturesque colonial buildings and a certain backwater charm. It is on the east bank of the Maroni (Marowijne) River, which forms the border with Suriname. You can arrange boat trips up the river, which has many Maron and Amerindian settlements.

Information
Tourist Office St Laurent's helpful Office de Tourisme (☎ 34-2398), near the jetty at the north end of town, is open daily from 8 am to 1 pm and 3 to 6 pm (Sunday 9 am to 1 pm). Some staff speak English, and the office has maps and brochures.

Money The Banque Nationale de Paris is on the corner of Avenue Félix Eboué and Rue Montravel. The bureau de change on Rue Montravel is quicker, and open longer hours. There's an ATM at the post office.

Post The post office is at the north end of Avenue du Général de Gaulle.

Travel Agencies For river excursions contact Youkaliba Expeditions (☎ 34-1645), 3 Rue Simon. A five-day trip up the Maroni (Marowijne) River to Maripasoula costs around FF3200 per person, but there are cheaper trips over shorter distances and of shorter duration.

Medical Services The Hôpital André Bouron (☎ 34-1037) is on Avenue du Général de Gaulle.

Camp de la Transportation
At the Camp de la Transportation (1857), prisoners arrived for processing and transfer to the various prison camps throughout the territory. You can walk through the same

St Laurent du Maroni

0	100	200 m

PLACES TO STAY
7 Hôtel La Tentiaire
13 Hôtel Le Toucan
27 Hôtel Star

PLACES TO EAT
9 Le Saramacca
14 Calamity Jane
18 Chez Felicia
20 Loon Fa
20 Kowloon Restaurant
21 Restaurant Vietnam
22 Tai Loong
25 Wen Ki Snack
26 La Grande Muraille
   Chinese Restaurant

OTHER
1 Swimming Pool
2 Tourist Office
3 Post Office
4 Office Nationale
   de Forêts
5 Mairie (Town Hall)
6 Church
8 Gendarmerie (Police)
10 Banque Nationale
   de Paris
11 Bureau de Change
12 Avis (Car Rental)
15 Libramar Bookshop
16 Market
17 Hôpital André Bouron
23 Youkaliba Expeditions
28 Customs & Immigration
29 Taxis Collectifs
   to Cayenne

Place de la République

Malouet

Avenue

Avenue

Avenue de la Gare

Franklin

Roosevelt

Rue du Lt Colonel Chandon

Camp de la Transportation

La Roche Bleue

Rue Schoelcher

Rue Montravel

Rue V Hugo

Rue Felix Eboué

Avenue Felix Eboué

Avenue du Général de Gaulle

Rue Rousseau

Rue Marceau

Allée des Bambous

To Kourou & Cayenne

Rue Thiers

Rue Simon

Rue du Lieutenant Colonel Tourtet

Sports Ground

Rue Guymener

Marne

Rue Justin Cayateé

Rue R Barral

Rue René Jadfard

Rue René Marran

Avenue August Boudinot

Village Chinois

Rue Nouvelle No 7

Rue Nouvelle No 9

Rue Nouvelle No 8

Maroni (Marrowijne) River

Ferry to Albina (Suriname)

To Aérodrome & St Maurice

To St Jean

gates as Dreyfus and Papillon – but you can leave more easily than they did.

Many of the buildings have deteriorated, and exuberant tropical vegetation has softened some of the grim history, but you can still see the long common cell blocks, with shackles and open toilets, and the solitary confinement cells with their tiny windows. Several buildings have been restored, and free guided tours (mostly in French) leave from the tourist office seven times daily. The camp is open daily from 8.30 am to 12.30 pm and 2.30 to 6.30 pm.

Places to Stay & Eat

At *Hôtel Le Toucan* (☎ 34-1259), on Avenue du Général de Gaulle at the corner of Rue Schoelcher, they charge from FF150/190 for singles/doubles with no windows, peeling linoleum, private bath and fan. *Hôtel Star* (☎ 34-1084), at 109 Rue Thiers, has a pool and is much better value, with its cheapest rooms at FF160 and others at FF180 to FF300. *Hôtel La Tentiaire* (☎ 34-2600), 12 Avenue Franklin Roosevelt, is the best in town, with very nice rooms from FF240/420.

St Laurent has many good but mostly expensive restaurants; the cheapest alternative is the Javanese food stalls along Avenue Felix Eboué, which offer a good and filling bami goreng with a side order of satay for about FF20. Other Asian eateries include the reasonably priced *Restaurant Vietnam*, 19 Avenue Félix Eboué, and the nearby *Tai Loong*. For Creole cuisine, try *Chez Felicia*, on Avenue du Général de Gaulle, or for North African, *Casablanca*, on Rue Guynemer. The snack bar at *Le Toucan* is much better than the accommodation there.

Getting There & Away

Bus Service de Transport Ruffinel leaves Hôtel Star for Cayenne daily, at 5 am (FF140).

Taxi Taxis collectifs leave from the pier when full, or nearly so. They are faster, more comfortable and more convenient than a bus, and only slightly dearer (FF150 to Cayenne).

To/From Suriname The free ferry crosses to Albina two or four times daily; the last boat is at 4 pm most days, but it would be much wiser to get a morning boat, at 7 or 9 am daily, except Sunday, to make sure you can get through to Paramaribo before dark. You don't want to stay in Albina. At other times, you can hire a motorised dugout pirogue (about US$5) for the short crossing.

Getting Around

Avis (☎ 34-2456) has an office at 20 Rue Montravel, but there are often no rental vehicles available. Taxis around town cost FF25.

AROUND ST LAURENT DU MARONI
Mana

About 50 km north-east of St Laurent by a good road is the rustic village of Mana. There are Indian settlements at Awala, 20 km west. At nearby **Plage Les Hattes**, leatherback turtles come ashore to nest from April to July; their eggs hatch between July and September. Off the St Laurent-Mana road is **Acarouany**, a Hmong refugee village. It has a popular Sunday market, and accommodation at the *Relais de l'Acarouany* (☎ 34-1720), once a leprosarium.

Maripasoula

Maripasoula is a popular destination for upstream travellers from St Laurent du Maroni, because it has an airfield with connections to Cayenne. Going beyond Maripasoula to the Amerindian villages in the area requires permission from the Préfecture in St Laurent or Maripasoula.

ST GEORGES DE L'OIAPOQUE

This town on the Brazilian border is not accessible by road, though a track has been cut to Régina and a road is planned. Air Guyane has two flights daily from Cayenne (FF299 one way). Take your chances on food and accommodation at *Chez Modestine* (☎ 37-0013).

From St Georges, you can take a launch (FF20) across the river to the Brazilian town of Oiapoque, where a scheduled daily bus ostensibly departs for Macapá at noon (in fact, it leaves when it's full).

There is much illegal immigration from Oiapoque to Cayenne, by precarious, ocean-going dugout canoes. People have died on these voyages, and travellers bound for French Guiana should avoid them. Unscheduled coastal freight boats might take a passenger to Cayenne or Macapá.

Paraguay

Once a notorious police state, Paraguay now welcomes adventurous visitors to the riverside capital of Asunción, the Jesuit missions of the upper Río Paraná, and the vast, arid Chaco.

Facts about the Country

HISTORY
Pre-Colonial Paraguay
Early Guaraní cultivators occupied most of what is now eastern Paraguay, but several hunter-gatherer groups, known collectively as Guaycurú, inhabited the Chaco, west of the Río Paraguay. Other hunter-gatherers lived in forest enclaves near the modern Brazilian border. Though usually peaceful, the Guaraní sometimes ventured into Guaycurú territory and even raided the Andean foothills.

Arrival of the Spaniards
In 1524, Alejo García walked across southern Brazil, Paraguay and the Chaco with Guaraní guides; his discoveries of silver led to the Río de Solís being renamed the Río de la Plata (River of Silver). Sebastián Cabot sailed up the Paraguay in 1527, but founded no permanent settlements.

Pedro de Mendoza's expedition, fleeing Buenos Aires, settled at Asunción, where Spanish-Indian relations took an unusual course: the Guaraní absorbed the Spaniards into their social system by providing them with women, and therefore food, since women were the farmers in Guaraní society. As heads of household, an informal arrangement ratified by the *encomienda*, the Spaniards adopted Guaraní food, language and other customs, but there emerged a hybrid, Spanish-Guaraní society in which Spaniards dominated politically and *mestizo*

Country Name República del Paraguay
Area 406,752 sq km
Population 5.4 million
Population Density 13.2 per sq km
Capital Asunción
Head of State President Juan Carlos Wasmosy
Official Languages Spanish, Guaraní
Other Languages German, Lengua, Nivaclé, Aché, other Indian languages
Currency Guaraní (G/)
Exchange Rate US$1 = G/2064
Per Capita GNP US$2950
Inflation Rate 18%

children adopted many Spanish cultural values.

The Jesuit Missions
Colonial 'Paraguay' encompassed parts of modern Brazil and Argentina, where Jesuit missionaries created highly organised settlements in which the Guaraní learned many aspects of European high culture, as well as new crafts, crops and methods of cultivation. Until their expulsion in 1767, the Jesuits

deterred Portuguese intervention and protected Spanish interests. For more information on Jesuit missions, see the entry on Argentine Mesopotamia.

The Jesuits were less successful among the Guaycurú, for whom, wrote one Austrian father, the Chaco was a refuge 'which the Spanish soldiers look upon as a theatre of misery, and the savages as their Palestine and Elysium'. There they had 'mountains for observatories, trackless woods for fortifications, rivers and marshes for ditches, and plantations of fruit trees for storehouses...' After secular Spaniards realised that the

Chaco lacked precious metals, they ignored the area.

Independence & the Reign of 'El Supremo'

Within a few year's of Paraguay's uncontested independence in 1811, José Gaspar Rodríguez de Francia emerged as the strongest member of a governing junta. Until his death in 1840, the xenophobic 'El Supremo' sealed the country's borders to promote national self-sufficiency – subsistence on a large scale. He expropriated the properties of landholders, merchants and even the Church, controlled the small agricultural surplus – mostly *yerba mate* and tobacco – and ruled by fear, imprisoning opponents in what one visiting Englishman called 'state dungeons'.

Francia himself succumbed to the climate of terror. After escaping an attack in 1820, El Supremo so feared assassination that he had his food and drink checked for poison, no one could approach him closer than six paces, streets were cleared for his carriage and he slept in a different place every night. Perhaps thanks to these precautions, he died a natural death; in 1870, opponents who knew how to hold a grudge threw his disinterred remains into the river.

The López Dynasty & the War of the Triple Alliance
By the early 1860s, Francia's successor Carlos Antonio López ended Paraguay's isolation, building railways, telegraph, an iron foundry, a shipyard – and a standing army of 28,000, with another 40,000 reserves (Argentina had only 6000 men in uniform). His megalomaniacal son, Francisco Solano López, led the country into a catastrophic war against the triple alliance of Argentina, Uruguay and Brazil. Paraguay lost 150,000 sq km of territory, and perhaps 20% of its population through combat, famine and disease; it was said that only women, children and burros remained.

Reconstruction & the Chaco War
After 1870, a trickle of European and Argentine immigrants resuscitated the agricultural sector, but political life did not stabilise for decades. At the turn of the century, tension arose with Bolivia over the ill-defined borders of the Chaco, but full-scale hostilities did not erupt until 1932. A 1935 cease-fire left no clear victor, but a treaty awarded Paraguay three-quarters of the disputed territory. Petroleum speculation fuelled the hostilities, but none was ever found.

Modern Developments
After the Chaco War, Paraguay endured a decade of disorder before a brief civil war brought the Colorado party to power in 1949. A 1954 coup installed General Alfredo Stroessner, who ruled harshly for 35 years until his overthrow in 1989. Since then the political environment has improved, but Stroessner supporters still dominate a faction of the Colorado party. For more information on the regime and its successors, see the Government section below.

GEOGRAPHY & CLIMATE
Paraguay appears small on the map, but at 407,000 sq km it is larger than Germany and almost exactly the size of California. About 40% of its territory is east of the Río Paraguay, where a well-watered plateau of rolling grasslands, with patches of subtropical forest, extends all the way to the Río Paraná, which forms much of Paraguay's borders with Brazil and Argentina.

Evenly distributed throughout the year, annual rainfall averages 2000 mm near the Brazilian border, declining to about 1500 mm near Asunción. Summer highs average 35°C; winter temperatures average a pleasant 22°C in July, the coldest month. Spring and autumn cold fronts can cause temperatures to drop 20°C within a few hours.

West of the Río Paraguay, the Gran Chaco is an extensive plain whose principal economic activity is cattle ranching. Hotter than eastern Paraguay, its erratic rainfall and high evaporation make rain-fed agriculture undependable, but Mennonite immigrants have raised cotton and other commercial crops successfully.

FLORA & FAUNA
Like rainfall, vegetation diminishes from east to west. Humid subtropical forests are dense in eastern Paraguay's valleys and sparse on thinner upland soils. Toward the Río Paraguay, the dominant vegetation is savanna grass, with occasional gallery forests, while to its west, palm savanna gives way to scrub and thorn forest.

Wildlife is diverse, but the dense rural population has put great pressure on eastern Paraguay's fauna. A notable international conservation success has been the survival of the Chacoan peccary, once thought extinct. Bird life is abundant, especially in the Chaco, where the most conspicuous species are jabirú and wood storks. Many reptiles, including caiman, anaconda and boa constrictor, inhabit the riverine lowlands.

Paraguay has several national parks and other reserves protecting a variety of habitats. The three largest are in the Chaco, with smaller but more biologically diverse units in eastern Paraguay. Because of corruption, economic pressure and traditionally weak political commitment, some have experienced serious disruption.

For detailed information on Paraguayan parks and reserves, contact the Dirección de Parques Nacionales y Vida Silvestre (☎ 445-214), on the 12th floor of the Edificio Garantía, 25 de Mayo 640, Asunción.

GOVERNMENT

Paraguay's 1992 constitution establishes a strong president, popularly elected for a five-year term, who in turn appoints a seven-member cabinet. Congress consists of a lower Cámara de Diputados (Chamber of Deputies) and an upper Senado (Senate), elected concurrently with the president. The Corte Suprema (Supreme Court) is the highest judicial authority.

From 1947 to 1989, under Stroessner and his military-dominated Colorado party, the country experienced one of the continent's most corrupt, odious and durable dictatorships. In 1989 General Andrés Rodríguez (also a Colorado) deposed Stroessner and then won the presidency, unopposed, in a 1991 election in which opposition congressional parties were more successful than ever before. In May 1993 Juan Carlos Wasmosy, a civilian engineer from Stroessner's Colorado faction, won presidential elections which, despite an atmosphere of intimidation, were probably the fairest in Paraguayan history.

Whether these promising developments will result in enduring democracy is still uncertain, given Paraguay's authoritarian tradition and the entrenched Colorado elite. Nominated by the Colorados as a figurehead, Wasmosy has come into conflict with the still powerful military, most notably coup-monger General Lino Oviedo, who was forced out of the military in 1996 and plans to run for the presidency in 1998. At the same time, military prestige and authority have come under scrutiny as groups like the Movimiento de Objeción de la Conciencia publicise problems such as the abuse of conscripts, and Wasmosy has faced allegations of shady business dealings.

ECONOMY

Historically, the economy depends on exports of beef, maize, sugar cane, soybeans, lumber and cotton, but many rural people cultivate subsistence crops on smallholdings. Paraguay's major industry remains contraband, including electronics and agricultural produce, but Mercosur tariff reductions may decrease smuggling by making imported goods cheaper in the neighbouring member countries of Argentina, Brazil and Uruguay. Stolen cars and illegal drugs, including cocaine, are other unfortunate goods which pass into or through Paraguay.

Paraguay lacks mineral energy resources, but enormous multinational dam projects have developed its hydroelectric potential over the past 15 years. A construction slowdown due to completion of Itaipú and continuing problems with Yacyretá have nearly eliminated the economic growth of the 1970s. The growth rate for 1994 was a modest 3.6%, while inflation has been running at roughly 45%. The official minimum wage is US$200 per month, but lax enforcement means that probably 70% of Paraguayan workers fall below this level.

POPULATION & PEOPLE

Paraguay's population is about 5.4 million, while Asunción (population 500,000) is the largest city; many exiles have returned since the fall of Stroessner, but others remain outside the country for economic reasons. Fewer than half live in urban areas, compared with more than 80% in Argentina and Uruguay. More than 95% live in eastern Paraguay. Infant mortality is relatively high at about 2.4%, but life expectancy has risen to about 74 years.

More than 75% of Paraguayans are mestizos, speaking Guaraní by preference, though almost all speak Spanish as well. Another 20% are descendants of European immigrants, including German Mennonite farmers in the central Chaco. Japanese immigrants have settled parts of eastern Paraguay, along with Brazilian colonists who have moved across the border in recent years. Asunción has seen a substantial influx of Koreans, mostly involved in commerce.

Most of Paraguay's Indians, about 3% of the population, live in the Chaco. The largest groups are the Nivaclé and the Lengua, each numbering around 10,000. Isolated peoples like the Ayoreo have lived almost untouched by European civilisation, but many Indians have become dependent labour for immigrant farmers.

ARTS

Paraguay's major literary figures are poet-novelist Augusto Roa Bastos, winner of the 1990 Cervantes Prize, and poet-critic Josefina Pla. Despite many years in exile, Roa Bastos has focused on Paraguayan themes and history in the context of politics and dictatorship. Little Paraguayan literature is available to English-speaking readers; for suggestions, see the Books & Maps entry in the Facts for the Visitor section.

Theatre is popular, with occasional offerings in Guaraní as well as Spanish. Numerous art galleries emphasise modern, sometimes very unconventional works. Venues in Asunción offer classical and folk music.

SOCIETY & CONDUCT

English-speaking visitors may find Paraguay exotic because of its unique racial and cultural mix, but Paraguayans are eager to meet and speak with foreigners. An invitation to drink *mate*, often in the form of ice-cold *tereré*, can be a good introduction.

An ability to speak German may dissolve barriers in the culturally insular Mennonite communities, but it is more difficult to meet the region's indigenous people, and undiplomatic to probe too quickly into relations between the two. Some Chaco Indians speak German (rather than Spanish) as a second language.

Paraguayans in general are sports-minded; the most popular soccer team, Olimpia, has beaten the best Argentine sides. Tennis and basketball have become popular spectator sports.

RELIGION

Roman Catholicism is official, but folk variants are important, and the Church is less influential than in other Latin American countries. Native peoples have retained their religious beliefs, or modified them only slightly, despite nominal allegiance to Catholicism or evangelical Protestantism. Protestant sects have made fewer inroads than in other countries, although Mennonites have proselytised among Chaco Indians since the 1930s.

LANGUAGE

Spanish is the language of government and commerce, but Paraguay is officially bilingual. Spanish has influenced the Guaraní language, but Guaraní has also modified Spanish in vocabulary and speech patterns. During the Chaco War against Bolivia, Guaraní enjoyed resurgent popularity when, for security reasons, field commanders prohibited Spanish on the battlefield.

Several other Indian languages, including Lengua, Nivaclé and Aché, are spoken in the Chaco and isolated parts of eastern Paraguay.

Facts for the Visitor

VISAS & EMBASSIES

All foreigners need visas, except those from bordering countries (who need national identification cards), most Western European countries and the USA. Canadian, Australian and New Zealand applicants need a clean police record, a bank statement and a US$10 fee. Canadians should apply through the New York consulate.

Paraguayan Embassies Abroad

Paraguay has no diplomatic representation in Australia or New Zealand, but has representatives in neighbouring countries, and in:

UK
    Braemar Lodge, Cornwall Gardens, London SW7 4AQ (☎ (0171) 937-1253)
USA
    2400 Massachusetts Ave NW, Washington, DC (☎ (202) 483-6960)
    7205 NW 19th St, Miami, FL (☎ (305) 477-4002)
    Suite 1947, 1 World Trade Center, New York, NY (☎ (212) 432-0733)
    18377 Beach Blvd, Suite 212, Huntington Beach, CA (☎ (714) 848-3168)

Foreign Embassies in Paraguay

South American countries, the USA and most Western European countries have representatives in Asunción. For Argentine and Brazilian consulates in border towns, see the relevant city or town section for addresses.

CUSTOMS

Paraguayan customs admits 'reasonable quantities' of personal effects, alcohol and tobacco.

MONEY

The unit of currency is the *guaraní* (plural *guaraníes*), indicated by the symbol 'G/'. Banknote values are 100, 500, 1000, 5000 and 10,000 guaraníes; there are coins for one, five, 10, 20, 50 and 100 guaraníes. At the time of writing, Paraguay was cheaper for the traveller than Argentina or Uruguay but more expensive than Bolivia.

Cambios in Asunción and at border towns change both cash and travellers' cheques (with small commissions); try banks in the interior. Some travellers have reported that cambios will not cash travellers' cheques without the bill of sale. Street changers give slightly lower rates, and for cash only, but can be helpful on weekends or evenings.

Better hotels, restaurants and shops in Asunción accept credit cards, but their use is less common outside the capital. Paraguayan ATMs generally do not recognise foreign credit cards.

Exchange Rates

Prices in this chapter are given in US dollars. No black market exists.

Australia	A$1	=	G/1620
Canada	C$1	=	G/1514
France	FF1	=	G/399
Germany	DM1	=	G/1349
Japan	¥100	=	G/1902
New Zealand	NZ$1	=	G/1404
United Kingdom	UK£1	=	G/3183
USA	US$1	=	G/2064

TOURIST OFFICES

There are tourist offices in Asunción, Encarnación and Ciudad del Este.

Overseas Representatives

The larger Paraguayan consulates (see the list above), usually have a tourist representative in their delegation. North American offices of Líneas Aéreas Paraguayas (Lapsa; ☎ (800) 795-2772 toll free) also serve as de facto tourist representatives.

Líneas Aéreas Paraguayas
    Suite 375, 6033 W Century Blvd, Los Angeles, CA 90045 (☎ (310) 670-0807)
    Suite 402, 7200 NW 19th St, Miami, FL 33126 (☎ (305) 477-2104)
    Suite 2050, 500 5th Ave, New York, NY 10110 (☎ (212) 302-0004)

USEFUL ORGANISATIONS

The Fundación Moisés Bertoni (☎ 440-238), Rodríguez de Francia 770 in Asunción, sponsors projects which encourage biological diversity and restoration of degraded ecosystems, cooperates with the state in strengthening national parks, promotes environmental education and research, and tries to involve local citizens and private enterprise in conservation.

BUSINESS HOURS & HOLIDAYS

Most shops are open on weekdays and on

Saturday from 7 am to noon, then close until midafternoon and stay open until 7 or 8 pm. Banking hours are usually 7.30 to 11 am on weekdays, but exchange houses keep longer hours. In summer, from mid-November to mid-March, government offices open as early as 6.30 am and usually close before noon.

1 January
  Año Nuevo (New Year's Day)
3 February
  Día de San Blas (Patron Saint of Paraguay)
February (date varies)
  Carnaval
1 March
  Cerro Corá (Death of Mariscal Francisco Solano López)
March/April (dates vary)
  Viernes Santo/Pascua (Good Friday/Easter)
1 May
  Día de los Trabajadores (Labor Day)
15 May
  Independencia Patria (Independence Day)
12 June
  Paz del Chaco (End of Chaco War)
15 August
  Fundación de Asunción (Founding of Asunción)
29 September
  Victoria de Boquerón (Battle of Boquerón)
8 December
  Día de la Virgen (Immaculate Conception)
25 December
  Navidad (Christmas Day)

SPECIAL EVENTS

Paraguay's celebration of Carnaval is liveliest in Asunción, Encarnación, Ciudad del Este, Caacupé and Villarrica. The religious centre of Caacupé is the most important site for the Roman Catholic Día de la Virgen (Immaculate Conception).

POST & COMMUNICATIONS

Essential mail should go registered. Antelco, the state telephone monopoly, has central long-distance offices; it may soon undergo privatisation. Offices in Asunción have fibreoptic lines with direct connections to the USA and Japan. Credit-card or reverse-charge (collect) calls to the USA and other overseas destinations are cheaper than

paying locally. Public phone boxes (which take *fichas* rather than coins) are few.

Paraguay's international telephone code is 595. For an international operator, dial 0010; for Discado Directo Internacional (DDI), dial 002.

TIME

Paraguay is three hours behind GMT/UTC except in winter (1 April to 30 September), when daylight-saving time adds an hour.

ELECTRICITY

Electric current operates on 220V, 50 Hz.

WEIGHTS & MEASURES

The metric system is official.

BOOKS & MAPS

Roa Bastos' novel *Son of Man*, originally published in 1961, links several episodes in Paraguayan history, including the Francia dictatorship and the Chaco War. *I the Supreme* is a historical novel about the paranoid dictator Francia.

History

Elman and Helen Service's *Tobatí: Paraguayan Town* is a standard account of rural Paraguay, in historical context. Harris Gaylord Warren's *Rebirth of the Paraguayan Republic* analyses Paraguay's incomplete recovery from the War of the Triple Alliance.

The Stroessner Period

Rule by Fear: Paraguay After Thirty Years Under Stroessner is an account of human rights abuses. Carlos Miranda's *The Stroessner Era* is a thoughtful, nonpolemical analysis with a short political obituary.

Maps

The new *Guía Shell*, despite limited and conventional tourist information, contains the most useful road map of the country, plus a good general country map at a scale of 1:2,000,000, and a very fine map of Asunción, with a street index, at 1:25,000. The guide and maps cost about US$7.50, but the Touring y Automóvil Club offers it to members of its international affiliates for a slight discount.

MEDIA

Asunción's daily *ABC Color* made its reputation opposing the Stroessner dictatorship; independent Radio Ñandutí also criticised the regime. The editorially bold newspaper *Ultima Hora* is very independent, breaking stories like the deaths of army conscripts – usually termed 'suicides' – under suspicious circumstances; it also has an excellent cultural section. Stroessner cronies control *Hoy* and *Patria* (the official Colorado newspaper). *El Pueblo* is an independent with a small circulation. Asunción's German community publishes the twice-monthly *Neues für Alle*.

HEALTH

Malaria is not a major threat, though Itaipú dam appears to have created mosquito vector habitat. Causes for concern, but not hysteria, are tuberculosis, typhoid, hepatitis, and hookworm (*susto*) – avoid going barefoot. Cutaneous leishmaniasis (*ura*), transmitted by biting sandflies and resulting in open sores, is unpleasant and dangerous if untreated.

DANGERS & ANNOYANCES

In Asunción and elsewhere, carjackings of conspicuously valuable vehicles have been a problem, but personal safety concerns are generally less serious than in Brazil. Since the ousting of Stroessner, police and the military operate with less impunity, but try not to aggravate them and always carry your passport.

Poisonous snakes are common in the Chaco, but mosquitos are a likelier nuisance.

ACTIVITIES

Conventional beach and river activities such as swimming and fishing are common options, but Paraguay's biological diversity is making it a notable destination for nature-oriented visitors like birders.

HIGHLIGHTS

Southern Paraguay's Jesuit mission ruins are no less appealing than those of Argentina, while the riverside capital of Asunción is a livelier city since the overdue return of democracy. The Chaco, with its abundant bird life, is still one of South America's last frontiers.

ACCOMMODATION

Hotels and residenciales are similar to those in Argentina, but generally less expensive. Facilities for camping are less common, but in remote areas you could probably camp just about anywhere.

FOOD & DRINKS

Parrillada is popular, but meat consumption is lower than in Argentina or Uruguay. Tropical and subtropical foodstuffs, nourishing the rural poor, play a greater role in the Paraguayan diet.

Grains, particularly maize, and tubers like manioc (cassava) are part of almost every meal. *Locro*, a maize stew, resembles its Argentine namesake, while *mazamorra* is a corn mush. *Sopa paraguaya* is corn bread with cheese and onion; *chipa guazú* is a variant. *Mbaipy so-ó* is a hot maize pudding with meat chunks, while *bori-bori* is a chicken soup with corn meal balls. *Sooyo sopy* is a thick soup of ground meat, accompanied by rice or noodles, while *mbaipy he-é* is a dessert of corn, milk and molasses.

In *chipa de almidón*, manioc flour replaces the corn meal of chipa guazú. *Mbeyú*, or *torta de almidón*, is a grilled manioc pancake resembling the Mexican tortilla. During Holy Week, the addition of eggs, cheese and spices transforms ordinary food into a holiday treat.

Paraguayans consume quantities of *mate*, most commonly as ice-cold *tereré*. Roadside stands offer *mosto* (sugar-cane juice), while *caña* (cane alcohol) is a popular alcoholic beverage.

PARAGUAY

Getting There & Away

Asunción is a convenient hub for Southern Cone air transport, but overland travellers may find Paraguay a bit out of the way.

AIR

To/From South American Countries

Lapsa flies to Buenos Aires daily; to São Paulo several times weekly; to Santa Cruz (Bolivia) on Saturday, continuing to Quito; and to Lima and Guayaquil. Lloyd Aéreo Boliviano (LAB) also flies to Santa Cruz on Tuesday, Friday and Sunday, with onward connections. AeroPerú also flies to Santa Cruz and Lima.

Aerolíneas Argentinas flies at least daily to Asunción from Ezeiza, while Lufthansa, Varig, Alitalia, Canadian Airlines International and American Airlines fly to and from São Paulo.

Lapsa and Pluna fly to Montevideo; some Pluna flights continue to Punta del Este. Lapsa flies to Santiago, Chile, five times weekly, while Ladeco does so seven times weekly, sometimes via Iquique. National Airlines also flies between Asunción and Santiago, and to Iquique.

LAND

To/From Argentina

Asunción to Clorinda There is frequent bus service from Asunción to Clorinda, in Formosa province.

Encarnación to Posadas Buses use the Puente Internacional Beato Roque González to Argentina, and passenger launches still cross the Río Paraná.

Ciudad del Este to Puerto Iguazú Frequent buses link Ciudad del Este to the Brazilian city of Foz do Iguaçu, with easy connections to Puerto Iguazú, Argentina. Alternatively, cross directly to Puerto Iguazú by unscheduled launch from Puerto Presidente Franco, a few km south of Ciudad del Este, without passing through Brazil.

To/From Bolivia

Recently Stel Turismo and Yacyretá have begun an experimental bus service from Asunción to Boyuibe and Santa Cruz de la Sierra. Beyond Filadelfia, the dirt road is subject to long delays in the event of heavy,

if infrequent, rains. In the absence of a bus, there are countless military checkpoints where you can wait for days in hope of a truck across the border.

To/From Brazil

Ciudad del Este to Foz do Iguaçu Vehicles and pedestrians move freely across the Puente de la Amistad (Friendship Bridge) over the Río Paraná. If spending more than a day in either country, complete immigration formalities.

Pedro Juan Caballero to Ponta Porã Reached by road from Asunción, Pedro Juan Caballero is a small town on the Brazilian border. Ponta Porã is its Brazilian counterpart.

RIVER

From Asunción, Cruceros SRL offers improved upriver services to the Brazilian city of Corumbá, and crossing to Formosa province, Argentina, is also possible. See Getting There & Away under Asunción for details.

LEAVING PARAGUAY

The departure tax for international flights from Asunción's Aeropuerto Silvio Pettirossi is US$15. Travellers who have spent less than 24 hours in Paraguay are exempt.

Getting Around

AIR

The new private carriers Ladesa and Arpa serve Pedro Juan Caballero, Ciudad del Este and Encarnación. Líneas Aéreas de Transporte Nacional (LATN) and Transporte Aéreo Militar (TAM), the air force passenger service, fly to isolated parts of the Chaco. Commercial domestic fares are expensive; the return trip from Asunción to Pedro Juan Caballero costs around US$180, for example.

BUS

Bus quality varies. *Servicio removido* makes flag stops, while *servicio directo* adds passengers only at fixed locations. Larger towns have central terminals, but elsewhere companies are within easy walking distance of each other. Fares are reasonable: for example, Asunción to Filadelfia, a distance of about 450 km, costs only about US$10 removido or US$13 directo.

TRAIN

Paraguay's antique, wood-burning trains are more entertaining than practical. Asunción visitors should enjoy the short hop to Areguá, on Lago Ypacaraí, but it's basically a day excursion.

CAR & MOTORCYCLE

Paraguay officially requires the International Driving Permit. The Touring y Automóvil Club Paraguayo provides information, road services, and excellent maps and guidebooks for its own members and those of overseas affiliates. Its Asunción office (☎ 210-550/53) is on Calle Brasil between Cerro Corá and 25 de Mayo.

Operating a vehicle is relatively economical because the price of super-grade petrol, at about US$0.45 per litre, is about half that in Argentina.

Car theft is common, so be certain your vehicle is secure. Conspicuously valuable vehicles have been targeted by carjackers. High-wheeled wooden ox-carts and livestock are road hazards, making night driving inadvisable.

LOCAL TRANSPORT
Bus

Asunción and other sizeable towns have extensive public transport systems, but late-night buses are infrequent. The usual fare is about US$0.30.

Taxi

Cabs operate on the basis of direct meter readings. Fares are slightly lower than Argentina's, but drivers may levy surcharges after midnight and for luggage.

ORGANISED TOURS

Intertours/Natur (☎ 27804, fax 211-870), Perú 436 in Asunción, arranges trips of greater or lesser duration to the Chaco, Parque Nacional Ybycuí, Lago Ypacaraí and other destinations. Per person rates range from US$35 for day trips to easily accessible destinations like Ypacaraí and the more accessible parts of the Chaco to US$230 for four-day, three-night excursions. All trips include an English-speaking guide.

Asunción

From its central location, Asunción is the pivot of Paraguay's political, economic and cultural life. Only about 15% of Paraguayans live in the capital, but most of the rest live within 150 km.

History

Early Spaniards found Asunción more attractive than Buenos Aires because of Guaraní food and hospitality, but the city lost favour when the arid Chaco, with its hostile Indians, proved an unsuitable route to Perú.

When the López dynasty opened the country to foreign influence, they nearly obliterated the city's colonial remains in the process of erecting major public buildings, which a British journalist called 'extravagant luxuries' among modest surroundings. Well into the 20th century, much of central Asunción was unpaved, but the city's appearance gradually improved.

The Chaco War retarded progress, but the sprawling capital has encompassed ever more distant suburbs. Despite a recent construction boom, the centre retains a 19th-century feeling, with low buildings lining narrow streets.

Orientation

Its riverside location and some modern developments have created irregularities in Asunción's conventional grid, centred on Plaza de los Héroes. Names of east-west streets change at Independencia Nacional. Nearby Plaza Uruguaya offers shade from the midday heat, but prostitutes frequent the area at night.

North, along the riverfront, Plaza Constitución contains the Palacio Legislativo.

Below the bluff, subject to flooding, lie *viviendas temporarias*, Asunción's shanty-towns. The diagonal El Paraguayo Independiente leads north-west to the Palacio de Gobierno (Presidential Palace).

Information

Tourist Office The Dirección de Turismo (☎ 441-530, 441-620), Palma 468, is friendly but not especially knowledgeable or helpful; it supplies a good city centre map/brochure and has several loose-leaf notebooks full of information. It's open on weekdays from 7 am to 7 pm, and on Saturday from 8 am to noon. There's a satellite office at the bus terminal.

The Spanish-English monthly *Amerindia* and the weekly *Fin de Semana*, a calendar of entertainment and cultural events, are both widely distributed throughout the city.

Money Cambios along Palma and side streets post exchange rates prominently; street changers hang out at the corner of Palma and Chile. The only ATM that seems to function with a foreign credit card is at Banco Unión (Cirrus system), at the corner of Alberdi and Estrella.

Post & Communications The main post office is at Alberdi and El Paraguayo Independiente. Antelco, at Alberdi and General Díaz, has direct fibreoptic connections to operators in the USA (ATT, MCI, Sprint), Britain, Australia, Germany, Argentina, Uruguay, Brazil and Japan for reverse-charge (collect) or credit-card calls. There's another office at the bus terminal. Asunción's telephone code is 021.

Foreign Embassies The nearest Australian and New Zealand embassies are in Buenos Aires. Representatives in Asunción include:

Argentina
    cnr Avenidas España and Perú (☎ 212-320/1)
Bolivia
    Eligio Ayala 2002 (☎ 210-676)
Brazil
    3rd floor, General Díaz 521 (☎ 448-084)

Canada
    Edificio Colón, El Paraguayo Independiente and Colón, Entrepiso (☎ 449-505)
France
    Avenida España 676 (☎ 212-439)
Germany
    Avenida Venezuela 241 (☎ 214-009)
UK
    4th floor, Presidente Franco 706 (☎ 496-067)
USA
    Avenida Mariscal López 1776 (☎ 213-715)

Cultural Centres Asunción's several inter-national cultural centres offer films at little or no cost, plus artistic and photographic exhibitions. These include the Casa de la Cultura Paraguaya, 15 de Agosto and El Paraguayo Independiente, the Centro Juan de Salazar (☎ 449-221) at Herrera 834, and the weirdly neoclassical Centro Paraguayo Japonés at Julio Correa and Portillo (take bus No 16), whose modern gymnasium is open to the public.

Bookshops Librería Comuneros, Cerro Corá 289, offers historical and contemporary books on Paraguay. Another good shop is Librería Internacional, Caballero 270. Plaza Uruguay has open-air bookstalls.

Medical Services Asunción's Hospital de Clínicas (☎ 80982) is at the corner of Avenida Dr J Montero and Lagerenza, about one km west of the city centre.

Things to See

It is now safe to approach and photograph the **Palacio de Gobierno**, on El Paraguayo Independiente near Ayolas. This is a notable improvement over the situation under both Stroessner and Francia: by one 19th-century account, El Supremo ordered that 'every person observed gazing at the front of his palace should be shot in the act'.

The restored colonial **Casa Viola** (1750), at Ayolas and El Paraguayo Independiente, is now a museum. Two blocks east, at 14 de Mayo, is the **Casa de la Cultura Paraguaya** (ex-Colegio Militar). On Plaza Constitución, at the foot of Alberdi, sits the **Palacio Legislativo** (1857).

At the east end of Plaza Constitución are the 19th-century **Catedral** and its museum. At Chile and Presidente Franco is the **Teatro Municipal** (1893), while a block west, at Franco and 14 de Mayo, Asunción's oldest building is the **Casa de la Independencia** (1772), where Paraguayans declared independence in 1811.

Panteón de los Héroes On the Plaza de los Héroes, at Chile and Palma, a military guard protects the remains of Carlos Antonio López, Francisco Solano López, Bernardino Caballero, Marshal José Félix Estigarribia and other key figures of Paraguay's catastrophic wars.

Museo Etnográfico Andrés Barbero This anthropological and archaeological museum at España 217 displays indigenous tools, ceramics and weavings, plus superb photographs, and good maps showing where each item comes from. One of Asunción's best, the museum is open on weekdays from 8 to 11 am.

Museo de Historia Natural Inside the Jardín Botánico (the former López estate), this museum houses an impressive collection of poorly labelled and displayed specimens, but is worth seeing for the spectacular insects – one butterfly has a wingspan of 274 mm. It's open Monday to Saturday from 7.30 to 11.30 am and 1 to 5 pm, and on Sunday and holidays from 8 am to 1 pm.

Admission to the park, which includes a pathetic zoo and the municipal camping ground, is cheap. Take the No 44 bus (Artigas) from the corner of Oliva and 15 de Agosto, directly to the gates. Alternatively, take a No 23 or No 35 bus.

Museo del Barro Asunción's foremost modern art museum displays some very unconventional work, and has other interesting exhibits from colonial times to the present, including political caricatures. To get there, take any No 30 bus out Avenida Aviadores del Chaco and ask the driver to drop you at Avenida Molas López in newly developed Isla de Francia, where the Museo occupies a new facility at Callejón Cañada and Calle 1. It's open daily except Sunday from 4 to 8.30 pm.

Places to Stay

Camping Five km from the centre of town, in the shady Jardín Botánico, the quiet, secure *Camping Municipal* has friendly staff, lukewarm showers, adequate toilets and ferocious ants. Bring mosquito repellent. Fees are negligible; when returning at night, tell the attendant at the Artigas entrance that you are camping. From the centre, take bus No 44 (Artigas), 23 or 35.

Hostel Affiliated with Hostelling International, the *Albergue Juvenil* (☎ 450-470) is at 15 de Agosto 155, between Avenida República and El Paraguayo Independiente. Rates are US$6 per person. Another hostel is due to open on Presidente Franco between 14 de Mayo and 15 de Agosto.

Residenciales & Hotels *Residencial Ambassador* (☎ 445-901), Montevideo 110, is basic and a bit musty, but it's friendly, has ceiling fans and charges only US$5 for a single. Charging US$5/7 with shared bath or US$7/10 with private bath, *Hotel Hispania* (☎ 444-108), Cerro Corá 265, has long been a popular budget alternative, but there are recent complaints of declining cleanliness, and noise from a nearby pub has disturbed some travellers. *Hotel Itapúa* (☎ 445-121), Moreno 943, costs about US$7/12, as does *Residencial Siria* (☎ 447-258), Herrera 166.

Hotel Azara (☎ 44-9754), Azara 850, has rooms with private bath, fridge and air-con for US$13/17. Korean-run *Hotel Amigo* (☎ 491-987), Caballero 521, charges US$10/14 for rooms with private bath and air-con. *Hotel Stella d'Italia* (☎ 448-731) at Cerro Corá 933, popular with US Peace Corps volunteers, has singles/doubles with shared bath for US$11/15 with breakfast, plus a quiet upstairs lounge with international cable TV.

At *Hotel Miami* (☎ 444-950), México 449, rates are US$13/20 for rooms with

PARAGUAY

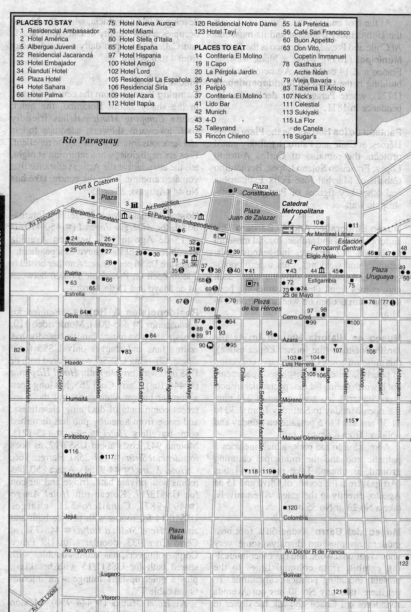

PLACES TO STAY	
1 Residencial Ambassador	75 Hotel Nueva Aurora
2 Hotel América	76 Hotel Miami
5 Albergue Juvenil	80 Hotel Stella d'Italia
22 Residencial Jacarandá	85 Hotel España
33 Hotel Embajador	97 Hotel Hispania
34 Ñandutí Hotel	100 Hotel Amigo
46 Plaza Hotel	102 Hotel Lord
64 Hotel Sahara	105 Residencial La Española
66 Hotel Palma	106 Residencial Siria
	109 Hotel Azara
	112 Hotel Itapúa

120 Residencial Notre Dame	55 La Preferida
123 Hotel Tayí	56 Café San Francisco
	60 Buon Appetito
PLACES TO EAT	63 Don Vito,
14 Confitería El Molino	Copetín Immanuel
19 Il Capo	78 Gasthaus
20 La Pérgola Jardín	Arche Noah
26 Anahi	79 Vieja Bavaria
31 Periplo	83 Taberna El Antojo
37 Confitería El Molino	107 Nick's
41 Lido Bar	111 Celestial
42 Munich	113 Sukiyaki
43 4-D	115 La Flor
52 Talleyrand	de Canela
53 Rincón Chileno	118 Sugar's

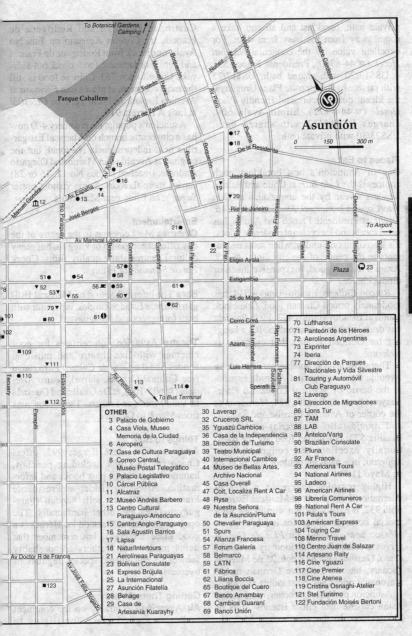

Asunción

To Botanical Gardens, Camping

Parque Caballero

Parque Caballero

To Airport

To Bus Terminal

Plaza

OTHER

3 Palacio de Gobierno
4 Casa Viola, Museo Memoria de la Ciudad
6 Aeroperú
7 Casa de Cultura Paraguaya
8 Correo Central, Museo Postal Telegráfico
9 Palacio Legislativo
10 Cárcel Pública
11 Alcatraz
12 Museo Andrés Barbero
13 Centro Cultural Paraguayo-Americano
15 Centro Anglo-Paraguayo
16 Sala Agustín Barrios
17 Lapsa
18 Natur/Intertours
21 Aerolíneas Paraguayas
23 Bolivian Consulate
24 Expreso Brújula
25 La Internacional
27 Asunción Filatelía
28 Behage
29 Casa de Artesanía Kuarayhy

30 Laverap
32 Cruceros SRL
35 Yguazú Cambios
36 Casa de la Independencia
38 Dirección de Turismo
39 Teatro Municipal
40 Internacional Cambios
44 Museo de Bellas Artes, Archivo Nacional
45 Casa Overall
47 Coit, Localiza Rent A Car
48 Rysa
49 Nuestra Señora de la Asunción/Pluma
50 Chevalier Paraguaya
51 Spurs
54 Alianza Francesa
57 Forum Galería
58 Belmarco
59 LATN
61 Fábrica
62 Liliana Boccia
65 Boutique del Cuero
67 Banco Amambay
68 Cambios Guaraní
69 Banco Unión

70 Lufthansa
71 Panteón de los Héroes
72 Aerolíneas Argentinas
73 Exprinter
74 Iberia
77 Dirección de Parques Nacionales y Vida Silvestre
81 Touring y Automóvil Club Paraguayo
82 Laverap
84 Dirección de Migraciones
86 Lions Tur
87 TAM
88 LAB
89 Antelco/Varig
90 Brazilian Consulate
91 Pluna
92 Air France
93 Americana Tours
94 National Airlines
95 Ladeco
96 American Airlines
98 Librería Comuneros
99 National Rent A Car
101 Paula's Tours
103 American Express
104 Touring Club
108 Menno Travel
110 Centro Juan de Salazar
114 Artesano Raity
116 Cine Yguazú
117 Cine Premier
118 Cine Atenea
119 Cristina Osnaghi-Atelier
121 Stel Turismo
122 Fundación Moisés Bertoni

PARAGUAY

private bath, breakfast and air-con; take a room away from the busy front door. For excellent value try the congenial *Ñandutí Hotel*, (☎ 44-6780), Presidente Franco 551 – US$13/20 with shared bath, US$17/25 with private bath. Opposite Plaza Uruguaya, the clean, quiet, secure and friendly *Plaza Hotel* (☎ 444-772), Eligio Ayala 609, charges US$15/22 with shared bath, US$23/30 with private bath.

Places to Eat

One of Asunción's best breakfast/lunch choices is the *Lido Bar*, at Chile and Palma. Readers swear by the empanadas at *Don Vito/Copetín Immanuel*, Avenida Colón 346. *Anahi*, at Presidente Franco and Ayolas, has good meals and ice cream at moderate prices; it's also open on Sunday, when most restaurants in the centre of the city close. *Nick's*, Azara 348, is a good, inexpensive lunch or dinner choice.

Rincón Chileno, Estados Unidos 314, has moderately priced Chilean food. One block south, at Estados Unidos 422, *Vieja Bavaria* has draft lager and short orders. It's a hangout for German visitors, but everyone is welcome.

There are several notable parrillas along Avenida Brasilia, north of Avenida España, in the barrio of Mariscal López: *La Paraguaya* at Avenida Brasilia 624, *Maracaná* at the corner of Avenida Brasilia and Salazar, and *Anrejó* (also a pizzería) at Avenida Brasilia 572. For Italian food, try the traditionally excellent and congenial *Buon Appetito*, in a pleasant outdoor setting at 25 de Mayo 1199.

Highly regarded *Talleyrand*, a French/international restaurant at Mariscal Estigarribia 932, is expensive, but worthwhile for a special occasion. Open for lunch only, on México near Moreno, *La Flor de Canela* serves excellent Peruvian food: try the surubí al ajo. *Gasthaus Arche Noah*, 25 de Mayo at Tacuary, has an extensive German menu, reasonable prices and outstanding service.

Asunción probably has better, more varied Asian cuisine than either Buenos Aires or Montevideo. In the area around Mercado

Cuatro, at Pettirossi and Rodríguez de Francia, try *Copetín Koreano* on Eusebio Ayala, one block from Rodríguez de Francia and Perú. For Japanese food, check out *Sukiyaki*, Constitución 763. Chinese food is still the most common, at places like *Formosa* at Avenida España 780 near Perú, or *Celestial* at Luis A Herrera 919.

Asunción's popular ice creamery *4-D* now has a city centre branch on Mariscal Estigarribia near Independencia Nacional, but the original at Avenida San Martín and Olegario Andrade, (reached by bus No 12, 16 or 28) carries more flavours. Some visitors prefer *Sugar's*, on Chile near Manduvirá.

Entertainment

Cinemas Most cinemas in the centre of the city offer cheap porno or kung fu, but many cultural centres show quality films. Check *Fin de Semana* for listings.

Bars The informal *Spurs*, on Mariscal Estigarribia near Estados Unidos, is popular with both foreigners and Paraguayans.

Theatre Asunción compensates for poor cinemas with live theatre and music at venues like the *Casa de Cultura Paraguaya* (see Cultural Centres, above), *Teatro Arlequín* (☎ 605-107), at De Gaulle and Quesada in Villa Morra, and others. The season runs from March to October.

Things to Buy

Artesanía Viva, José Berges 993, offers Chaco Indian crafts, including ponchos, hammocks and bags, plus books and information. Artesanía Hilda, at Presidente Franco and O'Leary, sells ñandutí (Paraguayan lace) and other handicrafts. The open-air market on Plaza de los Héroes is a good place for crafts, but remember that items made with feathers are probably subject to endangered-species regulations overseas.

Getting There & Away

Air Asunción's centrality on the continent makes it a good place for flights to neighbouring countries, Europe and the USA, but domestic services are limited.

Aerolíneas Argentinas
  Independencia Nacional 365 (☎ 491-012)
Aerolíneas Paraguayas (Arpa)
  San José 136 (☎ 206-634)
AeroPerú
  Benjamín Constant 536 (☎ 493-122)
Air France
  Oliva 393 (☎ 498-768)
American Airlines
  Independencia Nacional 557 (☎ 443-331)
Iberia
  25 de Mayo 161 (☎ 493-351)
Líneas Aéreas del Cobre (Ladeco)
  General Díaz 347 (☎ 447-028)
Lapsa (Líneas Aéreas Paraguayas)
  Perú 456 (☎ 491-040, fax 496-484)
Ladesa (Líneas Aéreas del Este)
  Mariscal López 4531 (☎ 600-948)
LATN
  Brasil & Mariscal Estigarribia (☎ 212-277)
Lloyd Aéreo Boliviano (LAB)
  14 de Mayo 563 (☎ 441-586)
Lufthansa
  3rd floor, Estrella 345 (☎ 447-964)
National Airlines
  Oliva 381 (☎ 440-831)
Pluna
  Alberdi 513 (☎ 490-128)
TAM
  Oliva 471 (☎ 445-843)
Varig
  General Díaz & 14 de Mayo (☎ 497-351)

Bus Asunción's Terminal de Omnibus (☎ 551-728/740) is at Avenida Fernando de la Mora and República Argentina in the Barrio Terminal, reached from the city centre by bus No 8, 10, 25, 31 or 38 from Oliva. Some companies maintain convenient offices on Plaza Uruguaya.

From the corner of Presidente Franco and Avenida Colón, hourly buses leave for Falcón, on the Argentine border. Direct buses leave the terminal for Clorinda (US$1.50), and there is frequent service to Posadas (US$11, five hours) and Buenos Aires (US$50, 20 hours). Fewer buses run to Córdoba (18 hours).

Stel Turismo and Yacyretá (☎ 551-617) now operate two to three services weekly to the Bolivian destinations of Boyuibe (US$56, 24 hours) and Santa Cruz (US$67,

30 hours). There are daily buses to Montevideo, Uruguay (US$64), and less frequent ones to Santiago, Chile (30 hours). Brazilian destinations include Foz do Iguaçu (five hours), Curitiba (14 hours), São Paulo (18 hours) and Rio (US$42, 22 hours).

Countless domestic buses link Asunción with other Paraguayan cities, including Ciudad del Este (US$8.50, 4½ hours) and Encarnación (US$10, five hours). Services to north-eastern destinations like Pedro Juan Caballero and Concepción are less frequent, but those to Filadelfia (US$11, eight hours) and other Chaco destinations are dependable. Towns near Asunción, like San Bernardino and Caacupé, have very frequent services.

Train Departing on Sunday only at 8.30 am from the Estación Ferrocarril Central (☎ 447-316) on Plaza Uruguaya, the antique steam train tours the back yards of Asunción's shantytowns en route to Areguá, on Lago Ypacaraí (US$0.75 return); it returns at 5 pm.

River An alternative crossing to Argentina is the launch from Puerto Itá Enramada, west of the city centre, to Puerto Pilcomayo, Formosa. These leave on weekdays every half-hour between 7 am and 5 pm, and on Saturday irregularly from 7 to 10 am.

For scheduled long-distance boat services up the Río Paraguay, visit Cruceros SRL (☎ & fax 445-098), 25 de Mayo 150, which offers monthly excursions as well as straightforward transportation upriver to Concepción (310 km, 26 hours), continuing to Corumbá, Brazil (another 830 km, 72 hours more) if river conditions permit. Fares for the 10-day round trip to the Brazilian Pantanal and back, including meals and excursions, start at US$372 per person in quadruple rooms, but transportation alone starts as low as US$41 for 3rd-class deck space for hammocks. Up to a dozen naval supply boats per week also carry passengers as far as Concepción; enquire at the port at the end of Calle Montevideo. These go to Isla Margarita on

PARAGUAY

the Brazilian border, then cross to Porto Murtinho, Brazil, with buses to Corumbá.

Getting Around
City buses go almost everywhere for around US$0.30, but there are few after about 10 or 11 pm.

To/From the Airport From the centre of Asunción, bus No 30A takes 50 to 60 minutes to Aeropuerto Silvio Pettirossi and costs US$0.30.

To/From the Bus Terminal Bus No 8 runs from Cerro Corá to the bus terminal, as does No 25 from Plaza Uruguaya.

Taxi Cabs are metered and reasonable, but may tack on a surcharge late at night. A cab to the bus terminal costs about US$5, to the airport about US$10.

AROUND ASUNCION
Museo Boggiani
At the turn of the century, Italian ethnographer Guido Boggiani assembled an impressive collection of Chamacoco Indian feather art. It is on display in this expanding museum, at Coronel Bogado 888 in the suburb of San Lorenzo. Open Tuesday to Saturday from 10 am to noon and 3 to 6 pm, it's well worth the 45-minute bus ride out Avenida Mariscal López on Línea 27.

Villa Hayes
Across the river from Asunción, Villa Hayes honours one of the USA's most undistinguished presidents, Rutherford B Hayes (1877-81). Nearly forgotten even in his home town of Delaware, Ohio, he is here commemorated by a club and local soccer team, a school and a monument.

Why this homage to a man who never set foot in Paraguay? After the War of the Triple Alliance, Argentina claimed the entire Chaco, but the two countries eventually submitted claims over a smaller area to arbitration; in 1878, Argentine and Paraguayan diplomats presented their cases to Hayes in Washington. After he decided in Paraguay's favour, the Paraguayan Congress immortalised him by renaming Villa Occidental, the territory's largest town.

To reach Villa Hayes, take bus No 46 from downtown Asunción. It leaves every half-hour from 5.30 am to noon, then every 45 minutes from noon to 9 pm.

Eastern Paraguay

East of the Río Paraguay is the nucleus of historical Paraguay. About 90% of Paraguayans live within 100 km of Asunción, but the border towns of Encarnación (opposite Posadas, Argentina) and Ciudad del Este (opposite Foz do Iguaçu, Brazil) have grown rapidly because of multinational hydroelectric projects, corruption and contraband.

Attractions convenient to Asunción include the weaving centre of Itauguá, the lakeside resorts of San Bernardino and Areguá, the shrine of Caacupé, colonial villages like Piribebuy and Yaguarón and Parque Nacional Ybycuí.

Jesuit ruins near Encarnación match or surpass those of Argentina. In the boom zone of north-eastern Paraguay, Brazilian colonists are moving across the border, deforesting the countryside for coffee and cotton, squeezing out Paraguayan peasants and the few remaining Aché Indians.

CIRCUITO CENTRAL
This 200-km round trip from Asunción is suitable for day trips, weekend excursions or longer outings.

Areguá
Higher and cooler than Asunción, this resort on Lago Ypacaraí is 28 km from the capital. *Hospedaje Ozli* has rooms with fan for US$6 per person, with pleasant gardens and good food.

Most visitors arrive and return by bus (Línea 11 from Avenida Perú in Asunción, about every half-hour), but there's a Sunday excursion steam train. Launches cross from

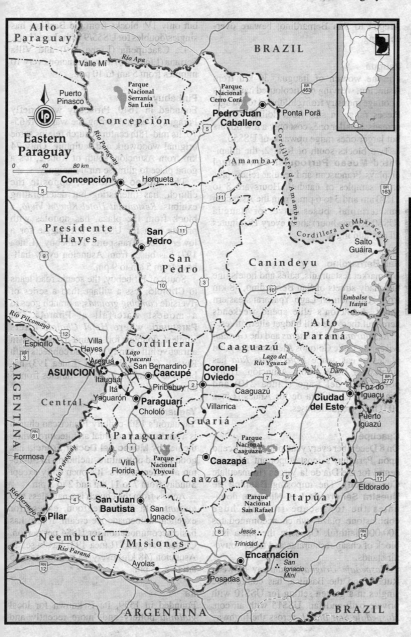

Areguá to San Bernardino; beware over-charging.

Itauguá

For the women of Itauguá, 30 km from Asunción, weaving multicoloured ñandutí is a cottage industry from childhood to old age. Pieces range in size from doilies to bed-spreads; smaller ones cost only a few dollars but larger ones range upwards of US$50.

Two blocks south of Ruta 2, the dilapi-dated **Museo Parroquial San Rafael** displays Franciscan and secular relics, plus early samples of ñandutí. Hours are 8 to 11.30 am and 3 to 6 pm. From the Asunción bus terminal, buses leave for Itauguá (US$0.50, one hour) about every 15 minutes all day and night.

San Bernardino

Up-market restaurants, cafés and hotels line the shady streets of San Bernardino, 48 km from Asunción on Lago Ypacaraí's eastern shore. Asunción's elite spend weekends here, but there are still budget alternatives.

Restaurant Las Palmeras and the *German bakery* on Calle Colonos Alemanes are good places to eat, while *Hotel Santa Rita* has singles for US$9. From Asunción, Trans-porte Villa del Lago (Línea 210) and Transporte Cordillera de los Andes (Línea 103) have frequent buses.

Caacupé

On 8 December every year, pilgrims descend upon Paraguay's most important religious centre for the Día de la Virgen (Immaculate Conception). The imposing **Basílica de Nuestra Señora de Los Milagros** domi-nates the townscape from its huge cobblestone plaza, which accommodates 300,000 faithful. Opposite the plaza is a block of cheap restaurants and tacky souve-nir stands.

Hospedaje Uruguayo, midway between Ruta 2 and the Basílica, has comfortable singles in a garden setting for US$10 with private bath and fan, US$15 with air-con. *Hospedaje San Blas I*, across the highway but only 1½ blocks from the Basílica, has singles/doubles for US$5/9 with shared bath.

La Caacupeña (Línea 119) and Villa Serrana (Línea 110) leave Asunción every 10 minutes from 5 am to 10 pm.

Piribebuy

Founded in 1640, Piribebuy was briefly Paraguay's capital during the war of 1865-70; its mid-18th century church retains some original woodwork and sculpture. Only 74 km from Asunción, south of Ruta 2, it's a good place to glimpse rural Paraguay.

The **Museo Histórico**, opposite the church, has interesting but deteriorating exhibits. *Restaurant Hotel Rincón Viejo*, a block from the plaza, has doubles with private bath for US$20, but haggle for a lower price. Transporte Piribebuy (Línea 197) has buses from Asunción every half-hour from 5 am to 9 pm.

South of Piribebuy, the scenic road leads to **Chololó**, less a village than a series of riverside *camping grounds*; a branch goes to a modest waterfall at **Piraretá**. At **Paraguarí**, where *Hotel Chololó* offers singles/ doubles for around US$26/36 in attractive hill country, the road connects with Ruta 1. Ciudad Paraguarí (Línea 193) has buses to Asunción every 15 minutes from 5 am to 8 pm.

Yaguarón

Yaguarón's 18th-century Franciscan church is a landmark of colonial architecture, while the nearby **Museo del Doctor Francia** has good period portraiture, including El Supre-mo at different ages. It's open daily except Sunday from 7 to 11 am and 2 to 5 pm.

Across from the church is a nameless *res-taurant* with mediocre food, except for excellent homemade ice cream. It also has basic accommodation for US$4 per person. Ciudad Paraguarí (Línea 193) has buses to Asunción (48 km) every 15 minutes from 5 am to 8.15 pm.

Itá

Founded in 1539, Itá is known for local *gallinita* pottery and, more recently and notoriously, for the apparent discovery of Nazi war criminal Martin Bormann's burial site. There are very frequent buses to Asunción (37 km) with 3 de Febrero (Línea 159) and Cotrisa (Línea 159).

PARQUE NACIONAL YBYCUI

Parque Nacional Ybycuí preserves one of eastern Paraguay's last stands of Brazilian rainforest. Its steep hills, dissected by creeks with attractive waterfalls and pools, reach 400 metres. The dense forest makes it difficult to see animals, which hide rather than run.

Things to See & Do

Ybycuí is tranquil and undeveloped, though weekenders can disrupt its peacefulness; in this event, take refuge on the extensive hiking trails. Rangers at the new visitor centre distribute a brochure for a self-guided nature trail.

The **Salto Guaraní** waterfall is near the camping ground. Below it, a bridge leads to a pleasant creekside trail with a wealth of butterflies, including the metallic blue morpho, but watch for poisonous snakes. The trail continues to **La Rosada**, an iron foundry destroyed by Brazilian forces in the War of the Triple Alliance. Ybycuí's forest has recovered in the century since the foundry operated on charcoal. Note the water wheel; engineers dammed Arroyo Mina to provide water and power for the bellows, while ox carts brought ore from 25 km away.

At La Rosada is a **museum** with irregular hours, at the park entrance two km west of the camping ground.

Places to Stay

The only option is *camping* at Arroyo Mina, which has adequate toilets, cold showers and a confitería serving weekend meals. Level sites are few and insects are a nuisance.

Getting There & Away

Parque Nacional Ybycuí is 151 km from Asunción. Ruta 1, to Encarnación, leads 84 km south to Carapeguá, where a turn-off continues another 67 km via the villages of Acahay and Ybycuí. Transporte Emilio Cabrera has eight buses daily to Acahay for local connections to Ybycuí village. A bus leaves daily at noon for the park entrance, returning to the village every day at 2 pm.

ENCARNACION

Gateway to the nearby Jesuit mission ruins at Trinidad and Jesús, Encarnación is in limbo as the reservoir created by Yacyretá dam slowly inundates the city's riverfront. As established businesses move onto higher ground, the area has become a tawdry bazaar of imported trinkets – digital watches, Walkmans and the like – and decaying public buildings and housing.

Orientation

Encarnación sits on the north bank of the Río Paraná, directly opposite Posadas, Argentina. The new Puente Internacional Beato Roque González links the two cities. From the riverside, Avenida Mariscal JF Estigarribia leads from the old commercial centre to the new one around Plaza Artigas.

Information

Tourist Office The Sección de Cultura at the Municipalidad, at Estigarribia and Kreusser, is helpful but lacks printed matter. It's open on weekdays from 7 am to 12.30 pm.

Money Cambios Guaraní is at Estigarribia 307 in the old city. On higher ground, try Banco Continental, Estigarribia 1418. Moneychangers jam the bus terminal on weekends.

Post & Communications The post office remains at Capellán Molas 337, in the old city. Antelco is at PJ Caballero and López; Encarnación's telephone code is 071.

Foreign Consulates The Argentine Consulate (☎ 3446), Mallorquín 788, is open on weekdays from 7.30 am to 1.30 pm. The Brazilian Vice-Consulate (☎ 3950), Memmel 452, is open on weekdays from 8 am to noon.

PARAGUAY

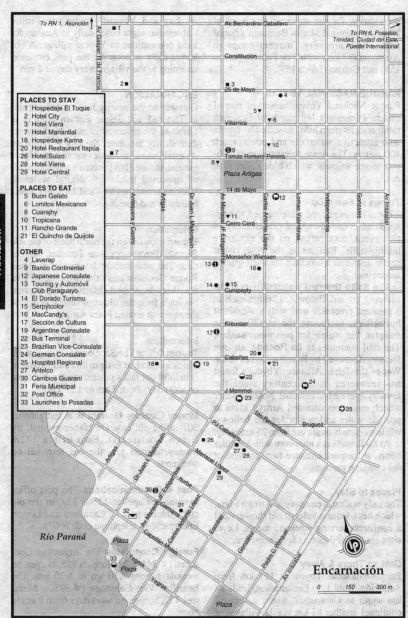

To RN 1, Asunción

Av Gaspar R de Francia

Av Bernardino Caballero

To RN 6, Posadas,
Trinidad, Ciudad del Este,
Puente Internacional

Constitución

25 de Mayo

3 de Mayo

Villarrica

Tomás Romero Pereira

Plaza Artigas

14 de Mayo

Antequera y Castro

Artigas

Dr Juan L Mallorquín

Av Mariscal JF Estigarribia

Carlos Antonio López

Lomas Valentinas

Independencia

Gonzales

Av Irrazábal

Cerro Corá

Monseñor Wiessen

Curupayty

Kreusser

Cabañas

J Memmel

Bruguez

Sta Reverchón

PJ Caballero

Mariscal López

Iturbe

Gamarra

Carlos Antonio López

Capellán Molas

Escobar

González

Padre C Vinqueli

Av Irrazábal

Dr Juan L Mallorquín

Av Mariscal JF Estigarribia

Artigas

Río Paraná

Plaza

Yegros

Yegros

Plaza

Plaza

Encarnación

0   150   300 m

PLACES TO STAY
1 Hospedaje El Toque
2 Hotel City
3 Hotel Viera
7 Hotel Manantial
18 Hospedaje Karina
20 Hotel Restaurant Itapúa
26 Hotel Suizo
28 Hotel Viena
29 Hotel Central

PLACES TO EAT
5 Buon Gelato
6 Lomitos Mexicanos
8 Cuarajhy
10 Tropicana
11 Rancho Grande
21 El Quincho de Quijote

OTHER
4 Laverap
9 Banco Continental
12 Japanese Consulate
13 Touring y Automóvil
   Club Paraguayo
14 El Dorado Turismo
15 Serpylcolor
16 MacCandy's
17 Sección de Cultura
19 Argentine Consulate
22 Bus Terminal
23 Brazilian Vice-Consulate
24 German Consulate
25 Hospital Regional
27 Antelco
30 Cambios Guaraní
31 Feria Municipal
32 Post Office
33 Launches to Posadas

Feria Municipal

At the corner of López and Gamarra, petty merchants are milking every last peso out of visiting Argentines before the flood. The market's liveliness transcends its baubles and gadgets, and it's also a good, inexpensive place to eat.

Places to Stay

The windowless singles at *Hospedaje Karina*, at Cabañas and General Artigas, cost only US$4; the shared toilets are clean. *Hospedaje El Toque*, on Avenida Caballero between Francia and Antequera, has clean but small singles for US$5 with shared bath, US$7.50 with private bath, but the hot water is erratic and the rooster next door starts early.

Convenience is the major attraction of *Hotel Itapúa* (☎ 3346), directly across from the bus terminal at Cabañas and Carlos Antonio López, which costs US$6/9 with shared bath, US$8/13 with private bath. Rooms at clean, quiet *Hotel Viena* (☎ 3486), PJ Caballero 568, are excellent value for US$10/17 with private bath.

Places to Eat

Packed with locals and Argentines, *Cuarajhy*, on Plaza Artigas, is a good, moderately priced parrilla. *Rancho Grande*, at the corner of Estigarribia and Cerro Corá, is a large, pleasant parrilla under a thatched roof, also popular with locals; at night, Paraguayan folk musicians perform.

El Quincho de Quijote, opposite the bus terminal at Carlos Antonio López and Cabañas, offers decent food and excellent service at very moderate prices. *Tropicana*, on Carlos Antonio López between Villarrica and Tomás Romero Pereira, is a reasonably priced parrilla with US$3 lunch specials. *Lomitos Mexicanos*, on the corner of Villarrica and Carlos Antonio López, is the only place in Paraguay to get a taco.

Getting There & Away

Air Arpa now flies daily except Sunday to Asunción; consult travel agencies for details. Posadas, across the river in Argentina, has air connections with Buenos Aires and Puerto Iguazú.

Bus There are very frequent buses to Asunción (US$10, five hours) and Ciudad del Este (US$8, four to five hours). From 6 am to 11 pm, local buses cross to Posadas (US$1 regular, US$2 servicio diferencial).

Boat Launches (US$1) still cross the Paraná to Posadas frequently.

TRINIDAD & JESUS

Trinidad, Paraguay's best preserved Jesuit *reducción*, occupies an imposing hilltop site 28 km from Encarnación. Though its church is smaller and its grounds are less extensive than those at San Ignacio Miní, Trinidad is in many ways its equal. From its bell tower the mission at Jesús de Tavarangue, 10 km north, is easily visible. Jesús is strictly speaking not ruins but rather an incomplete construction project, interrupted by the Jesuits' expulsion in 1767.

Trinidad's grounds and museum are open Monday through Saturday from 7.30 to 11.30 am and 1.30 to 5.30 pm; Sunday and holiday hours are 8 am to 5 pm. Admission costs US$1 for adults, US$0.50 for children above the age of 12. Camping is possible outside the ruins.

Jesús, 11 km north of Trinidad by a generally good dirt road off Ruta 6, keeps similar hours and collects identical fees. From Encarnación, Empresa Ciudad de Encarnación goes to Trinidad nine times daily between 6 am and 7 pm, and has two buses daily to Jesús, at 8 and 11.30 am.

SAN IGNACIO GUAZU

About 100 km north of Encarnación, San Ignacio has few ruins, but its **Museo Jesuítico** holds valuable Guaraní carvings. Open daily from 8 to 11.30 am and 2 to 5 pm, it charges US$1 admission.

Budget accommodation is available at *Hotel del Puerto*, on the main highway at the plaza, for US$4/6 a single/double with shared bath. There are many buses to

Asunción (3½ hours), Encarnación and the village of Santa María.

SANTA MARIA

Twelve km east of San Ignacio, the former reducción of Santa María has a **Museo Jesuítico** with a superb collection of Jesuit statuary, open daily from 8.30 to 11.30 am and 1.30 to 5 pm. Admission is US$1.

Basic *Pensión San José* charges US$3 for a single. There are five buses daily from San Ignacio.

CIUDAD DEL ESTE

Ciudad del Este is an important border crossing where Brazilian and Argentine shoppers jam the streets in search of cheap electronic goods. On the west bank of the Paraná, across from Foz do Iguaçu, it has an irregular plan, but the centre is compact and easily managed on foot. Avenida San Blas, the westward extension of the bridge from Foz, becomes Ruta 2 to Asunción.

Information

Tourist Office The Dirección de Turismo (☎ 62417, 66051) at the border is friendly but not particularly well informed. Try instead the Municipalidad on Avenida Alejo García, which opens very early but closes before noon. Many shops distribute a small brochure with a basic map.

Money Ubiquitous street changers give poorer rates than the numerous cambios.

Post & Communications The post office is at Alejo García and Ortellado, across from the bus station. Antelco is on the corner of Alejo García and Paí Pérez, directly alongside the Municipalidad. The telephone code is 061.

Foreign Consulate The Brazilian Consulate (☎ 62308), Pampliega 337, is open on weekdays from 7 am to noon.

Places to Stay

The most reasonably priced place is *Hotel Paraná* (☎ 62568), Camilo Recalde 128, where singles/doubles cost US$12/16. Cosy, friendly *Hotel Mi Abuela* (☎ 62373), with an attractive garden courtyard at Alejo García and Adrián Jara, has singles/doubles with private bath, ceiling fans and breakfast for US$12/18; for air-con, add US$3 per person.

Also good value is the German-run *Hotel Munich* (☎ 62371), at the corner of Emilio R Fernández and Capitán Miranda, where singles/doubles with private bath, good breakfast and air-con cost US$12/17. Down the block, at Emiliano Fernández 165, is the comparably priced, enthusiastically recommended *Hotel Austria* (☎ 68614).

Places to Eat

Restaurant Oriental, on Adrián Jara near Avenida Boquerón, has very good Japanese/Chinese food, especially *agropicante* (hot-and-sour) soup. Alongside it, *Osaka* has an equally appealing menu but keeps shorter hours. *New Tokio*, on Pampliega between Adrián Jara and Paí Pérez, comes highly recommended.

Mi Ranchito, a sidewalk parrilla at the corner of Curupayty and Avenida Adrián Jara, offers a good, complete meal for around US$4. *Cavi*, at Monseñor Rodríguez and Nanawa, is a popular Paraguayan restaurant.

Getting There & Away

Air Ciudad del Este's new Aeropuerto Internacional Guaraní is 30 km west of town on Ruta 2, but flights are as yet very limited. The military airline TAM (☎ 68352), in the Edificio SABA just off Monseñor Rodríguez, offers occasional flights to Asunción, as does Aerolíneas Paraguayas (Arpa, ☎ 62995), on Nanawa near Adrián Jara.

Bus Buses to Foz do Iguaçu leave from near the bridge every 10 minutes on weekdays and Saturday, less frequently on Sunday and holidays. On the other side, disembark for Brazilian immigration (unless just crossing for the day); if you hold on to your ticket, any following bus will take you to Foz.

To Asunción (US$8.50, five hours), there are 34 buses daily; nearly as many go to Encarnación (US$8, four to five hours).

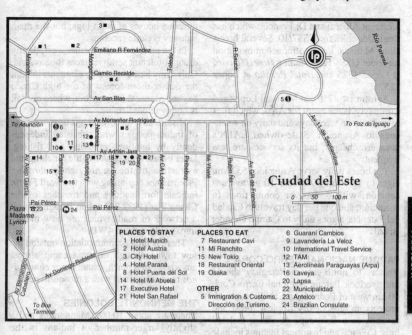

PLACES TO STAY
1 Hotel Munich
2 Hotel Austria
3 City Hotel
4 Hotel Paraná
8 Hotel Puerta del Sol
14 Hotel Mi Abuela
17 Executive Hotel
21 Hotel San Rafael

PLACES TO EAT
7 Restaurant Cavi
11 Mi Ranchito
15 New Tokio
18 Restaurant Oriental
19 Osaka

OTHER
5 Immigration & Customs,
  Dirección de Turismo

6 Guaraní Cambios
9 Lavandería La Veloz
10 International Travel Service
12 TAM
13 Aerolíneas Paraguayas (Arpa)
16 Laveya
20 Lapsa
22 Municipalidad
23 Antelco
24 Brazilian Consulate

PARAGUAY

Boat Travellers preferring to bypass Brazil should try to locate one of the (infrequent) launches from Puerto Presidente Franco to Puerto Iguazú, Argentina.

ITAIPÚ DAM

Itaipú, the world's largest hydroelectric project, has benefited Paraguay because of the construction activity, and Brazil's purchase of surplus power. However, should the price of competing sources of electricity drop, reduced Brazilian demand could saddle Paraguay with unexpected costs.

Project propaganda omits the US$25 billion price tag and ignores environmental concerns. The 1350 sq km reservoir, 220 metres deep, drowned Sete Quedas, a more impressive set of waterfalls than Iguazú, and stagnant water has provided new habitat for anopheles mosquitoes, a malaria vector.

Well-rehearsed guides lead tours from the Centro de Recepción de Visitas, north of

Ciudad del Este near the town of Hernandarias, Monday to Saturday at 8.30, 9.30 and 10.30 am; passports are required. There is a documentary film, also available in English-language video format, half an hour before the tour departs.

From Ciudad del Este, take any Hernandarias Transtur or Tacurú Pucú bus from the roundabout at the intersection of Avenidas San Blas and Alejo García. These leave every 10 to 15 minutes throughout the day.

PEDRO JUAN CABALLERO

Capital of Amambay department, Pedro Juan Caballero is adjacent to Ponta Porã, Brazil. Locals cross the border at will, but to continue any distance into either country, visit immigration at Calle General Bruguez 1247. There are reports of contraband drugs, so beware of unsavoury characters.

Exchange houses are numerous. The Brazilian Consulate (open on weekdays from 8 am to noon and 2 to 6 pm) is in *Hotel La*

Siesta, at Alberdi and Dr Francia, which has singles/doubles for US$7/10. Several hotels along Mariscal López offer accommodation for about US$8/12, including *Hotel Guavirá* at López 1325 and *Hotel Peralta* at López 1257.

Agrotur (☎ 2710), at Mariscal López and Curupayty, is the agent for Arpa, which flies twice daily on weekdays and daily on weekends to Asunción. State-owned LATN's fares are cheaper, but its services are less frequent.

Ten buses daily serve Asunción (532 km, eight to 12 hours). Another 10 go to Concepción, with downriver connections to Asunción, and one per day travels to Ciudad del Este. Nasa goes daily to Campo Grande, Brazil.

PARQUE NACIONAL CERRO CORÁ

Visitors to north-eastern Paraguay should not overlook Parque Nacional Cerro Corá, 40 km west of Pedro Juan Caballero, which protects an area of dry tropical forest and savanna in a landscape of steep, isolated hills. Cultural and historical features include pre-Columbian caves, petroglyphs and the site of Francisco Solano López's death at the end of the War of the Triple Alliance.

The park has nature trails, a camping area, and a few basic cabañas. There are rangers, but no formal visitor centre.

The Chaco

In Paraguay's Chaco frontier, great distances separate tiny settlements. Its only paved highway, the Ruta Trans-Chaco, leads 450 km to Filadelfia, colonised by Mennonites since the late 1920s. Here the pavement ends, but the highway continues 300 km to the Bolivian border.

The Chaco is an almost featureless plain of three distinct zones. Across the Río Paraguay, the low Chaco is a soothing palm savanna whose ponds and marshes shelter colourful birds; peasant cultivators build picturesque houses of palm logs, but the main industry is cattle ranching.

In the middle Chaco, farther west, thorny drought-tolerant scrub replaces the savanna. Only army bases and cattle *estancias* inhabit the denser thorn forests of the high Chaco beyond Mariscal Estigarribia, where rainfall is highly unpredictable.

Historically, the Chaco has been a refuge of Indian peoples who subsisted independently by hunting, gathering and fishing. Later industries included cattle ranching and extraction of the tannin-rich *quebracho*. Place names beginning with the word *Fortín* indicate fortifications and trenches of the Chaco War (1932-35), when Paraguay built a network of roads which are now mostly impassable without 4WD.

There is little accommodation outside the few towns, though one can camp almost anywhere. In a pinch, estancias or *campesinos* may offer a bed with a mosquito net.

THE MENNONITE COLONIES

There are about 10,000 Mennonites and a slightly larger number of Indians in the Chaco. Mennonites believe in adult baptism, separation of church and state, and pacifist opposition to military service. They speak *Plattdeutsch* (Low German), and also *Hochdeutsch* (High German), the language of school instruction. Most adults now speak Spanish and some speak passable English. Indians are as likely to speak German as Spanish.

The first Mennonites to arrive, in 1927, were *Sommerfelder* (Summerfield) Mennonites, from the Canadian prairies, who left after Canadian authorities reneged on guarantees against conscription. The Sommerfelder formed Menno Colony, centred around the town of Loma Plata. A few years later, refugees from the Soviet Union established Fernheim (Distant Home), with its capital at Filadelfia. Ukrainian Germans, many of whom served unwillingly in WW II, founded Neuland (New Land) in 1947. Its largest settlement is Neu-Halbstadt.

As more Paraguayans settle in the Chaco, Mennonites worry that the government may eliminate their privileges; some have begun to participate in national politics. Others are disgruntled with developments in Filadelfia, whose material prosperity has spawned a generation more interested in motorbikes and videos than traditional values. Alcohol and tobacco, once absolutely *verboten*, are now sold openly.

Filadelfia

Filadelfia is the administrative and service centre of Fernheim, whose main products are dairy foods and cotton. Still a religious community, Filadelfia shuts down on Sunday, but on weekday mornings, farmers cruise the streets in search of Indians for day labour, returning them in the afternoon. At midday, the town is exceptionally quiet, as Mennonites have adopted the custom of the tropical siesta.

Orientation & Information Filadelfia is 480 km from Asunción via the Trans-Chaco and a 20-km side road to its north. Its dusty streets form an orderly grid whose *Hauptstrasse* (main street) is north-south Hindenburg. Perpendicular Calle Trébol leads east to Loma Plata (Menno Colony) and west to the Trans-Chaco and Fortín Toledo.

Filadelfia's de facto tourist office is the Reisebüro (travel agency) on Hindenburg between Trébol and Unruh. Hotel Florida shows a video cassette on the Mennonite colonies.

To change cash, try the Reisebüro or the Cooperativa Mennonita supermarket, at Unruh and Hindenburg. The post office and Antelco are both at the corner of Hindenburg and Unruh; Filadelfia's telephone code is 091. The modern hospital is at the corner of Hindenburg and Trébol.

Unger Museum On Hindenburg opposite Hotel Florida, this museum chronicles Fernheim from 1930 to the present, and also displays materials on Chaco Indians. Hartmut Wohlgemuth, manager of the Florida, provides guided tours in Spanish or German when his schedule permits. Admission is about US$1.

Places to Stay & Eat Camping is possible free of charge in shady Parque Trébol, five km east of Filadelfia, but there is no water and only a single pit toilet. Filadelfia's most established accommodation is *Hotel Florida* (☎ 258), whose budget annex is an excellent bargain at US$7 per person with comfortable beds, shared bath with cold showers (not a bad idea here), and fans.

Besides the restaurant at Hotel Florida, try the parrillada at *La Estrella*, around the corner on Unruh, which has a shady outdoor dining area. *Girasol*, across the street, also serves a good asado. The modern Cooperativa Mennonita supermarket has excellent dairy products and other groceries.

Getting There & Away Several bus companies have offices along and near Hindenburg, with daily service to Asunción. Buses are less frequent to Mariscal Estigarribia and Colonia La Patria, farther west on the Trans-Chaco, and Santa Cruz, Bolivia.

Expreso CV connects Filadelfia with Loma Plata (25 km) daily at 8 am, returning at 9 am. Buses to Asunción also stop at Loma Plata and most continue to Neu-Halbstadt.

Around Filadelfia

Fortín Toledo About 40 km west of Filadelfia, Fortín Toledo hosts the **Proyecto Taguá**, a small reserve nurturing a population of Wagner's peccary *(Catagonus wagneri)*, thought extinct for nearly half a century until its rediscovery in 1975. The current project manager, Christopher Jahncke, is a Chicago doctoral student doing research on three-banded armadillos and welcomes visits if his schedule permits.

To get to Fortín Toledo, hitch or take a bus out along Calle Trébol to the Trans-Chaco. Cross the highway and continue three km to an enormous tyre with the painted words 'pasar prohibido'; continue another seven km on the main road, passing several buildings occupied by squatters, before taking a sharp right leading to a sign reading 'Proyecto Taguá'. Hitching may be possible along this segment.

Loma Plata The administrative centre of Menno Colony is the oldest and most traditional of the Mennonite settlements. Its excellent museum has an outdoor exhibit of early farming equipment, a typical pioneer house and an outstanding photographic history of the colony. Ask for keys at the nearby Secretariat. *Hotel Loma Plata* has singles for about US$7 with shared bath.

Neu-Halbstadt Founded in 1947, Neu-Halbstadt is the centre of Neuland Colony, south of Filadelfia. *Hotel Boquerón* has singles/doubles for US$15/22, and a good restaurant. Nearby Fortín Boquerón preserves a sample of Chaco War trenches.

South of Neuland are Indian reserves, where many Lengua and Nivaclé have become settled farmers. Neu-Halbstadt is a good place for Indian handicrafts like bags, hammocks and woven goods. For information and a great selection, contact Walter and Verena Regehr, who sell goods on a non-profit basis here and at Artesanía Viva in Asunción.

Several buses from Asunción to Filadelfia continue to Neu-Halbstadt, while others come directly from Asunción.

PARQUE NACIONAL DEFENSORES DEL CHACO

Once the province of nomadic Ayoreo foragers, Defensores del Chaco is a wooded alluvial plain about 100 metres in elevation; isolated 500-metre Cerro León is its greatest landmark. The dense thorn forest harbours large cats like jaguar, puma, ocelot and Geoffroy's cat, despite the pressures of illicit hunting.

Defensores del Chaco is 830 km from

Asunción over roads impassable to ordinary vehicles. There is no regular public transportation, but the **Dirección de Parques Nacionales** in Asunción, which may be able to put you in contact with rangers who must occasionally travel to Asunción and sometimes, if space is available, take passengers on the return trip.

MARISCAL ESTIGARRIBIA

According to LP reader Jerry Azevedo, the last sizeable settlement on the Trans-Chaco before the Bolivian border has '300 soldiers, half that many civilians, and an equal number of roosters'.

Mariscal Estigarribia is 540 km from Asunción; motorists should be sure to fill up and carry extra petrol, food and water.

Lodging is available at *Hotel Alemán* for US$16 a double; food, at *Restaurant Achucarro* (which also has simple accommodation). The petrol station is a good place to try to catch a lift onward to Bolivia. It's conceivable to board buses to Santa Cruz (Bolivia) here, but advisable to purchase your ticket in Asunción.

Every Friday at 8 am, a Nasa bus goes to Colonia La Patria (three hours), the last Trans-Chaco outpost accessible by public transport. Buses to Asunción (US$12.50, 10 hours) leave daily, twice on Sunday.

COLONIA LA PATRIA

Only 85 km from the Bolivian border, Colonia La Patria is becoming a service centre for High Chaco estancias. Every Friday at 2 pm, eastbound buses go to Mariscal Estigarribia (three hours), Filadelfia (five hours), and Asunción (14 hours). Petrol may be available here.

Peru

Facts about the Country

ARCHAEOLOGY & HISTORY

Peru is unequalled in South America for its archaeological wealth, thanks to excellent preservation conditions on the arid coast and in highland caves. For many travellers, visiting centuries-old ruins is one of the highlights of their journey, and even people with little interest in archaeology will enjoy visiting a few major sites. Peru's rich pre-Columbian history is the subject of debate and disagreement amongst scholars, so the outline given here may not be consistent with all other sources.

The famous Inca civilisation is merely the tip of the archaeological iceberg. Peru had many pre-Columbian cultures preceding the Incas, but none of them had a written language so knowledge of them is based almost entirely on archaeological research. The Spanish, however, left written records which give us an insight into the Incas.

One of the main sources of information for archaeologists has been the realistic decoration on the ceramics, textiles and other artefacts of Peru's pre-Columbian inhabitants. These relics often depict everyday life in some detail, so it is worth inspecting them in Peru's museums.

Country Name República del Perú
Area 1,285,216 sq km
Population 24,000,000 (1996 estimate)
Population Density 18.7 per sq km
Capital Lima
Head of State President Alberto Fujimori
Official Languages Spanish, Quechua, Aymara
Currency Nuevo Sol (S/)
Exchange Rate US$1 = S/2.44
Per Capita GNP US$1490
Inflation Rate From 10,000% (early 1990s) to 10% (1995 estimate)

Preceramic Period

The first inhabitants of Peru were nomadic hunter-gatherers who lived in caves or along the coast and roamed the country in loose-knit bands. Pikimachay cave, near Ayacucho, is the oldest site in central Peru, dating from 12,000 BC or earlier.

Early cultural development included the improvement of stone implements for hunting. Hunting scenes recorded in cave paintings have been found near Huánuco at Lauricocha (which may date from 8000 BC), and at Toquepala near Tacna. People knew how to make fires, wore animal skins and made simple tools and weapons from stone and bone. Domestication of the llama and guinea pig began between 7000 and 5000 BC.

By about 4000 BC (some sources claim earlier), people began planting seeds and improving crops by simple methods such as weeding. In those days, the coastal strip was wetter than today, and a number of small settlements were established. Crops included cotton, chilli peppers, beans,

PERU

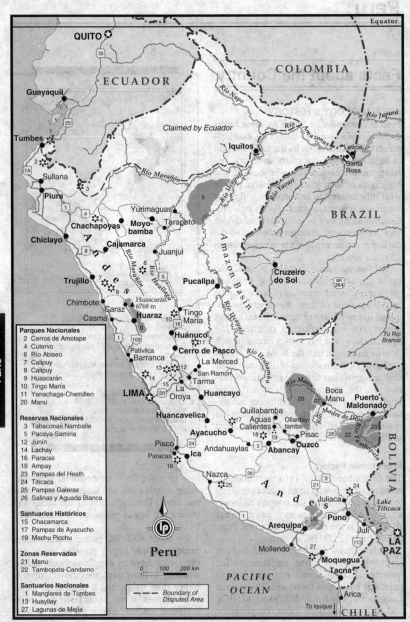

Equator

QUITO

ECUADOR

COLOMBIA

Guayaquil

Río Napo

Claimed by Ecuador

Río Japurá

Tumbes

Sullana

Iquitos

Leticia

Río Marañón

Santa Rosa

Piura

BRAZIL

Yurimaguas

Moyo-bamba

Tarapoto

Chachapoyas

Chiclayo

Cajamarca

Juanjui

Amazon Basin

Cruzeiro do Sol

Trujillo

Pucallpa

Chimbote

Caraz

Casma

Huascarán 6768 m

Huaraz

Tingo María

Huánuco

Parques Nacionales
2 Cerros de Amotape
4 Cutervo
6 Río Abiseo
7 Calipuy
8 Calipuy
9 Huascarán
10 Tingo María
20 Manu

Pativilca

Barranca

Cerro de Pasco

La Merced

San Ramón

Tarma

Boca Manu

Puerto Maldonado

Reservas Nacionales
3 Tabaconas Namballe
5 Pacaya-Samiria
12 Junín
14 Lachay
16 Paracas
18 Ampay
23 Pampas del Heath
24 Titicaca
25 Pampas Galeras
26 Salinas y Aguada Blanca

LIMA

La Oroya

Huancayo

Huancavelica

Quillabamba

Aguas Calientes

Ollantay-tambo

Pisac

Cuzco

BOLIVIA

Santuarios Históricos
15 Chacamarca
17 Pampas de Ayacucho
19 Machu Picchu

Pisco

Paracas

Ayacucho

Andahuaylas

Abancay

Ica

Zonas Reservadas
21 Manu
22 Tambopata-Candamo

Nazca

Juliaca

Lake Titicaca

Puno

Santuarios Nacionales
1 Manglares de Tumbes
13 Huayllay
27 Lagunas de Mejía

Peru

0   100   200 km

Boundary of Disputed Area

PACIFIC OCEAN

Arequipa

Mollendo

Juli

LA PAZ

Moquegua

Tacna

Arica

To Iquique

CHILE

squash and, later, corn. Cassava was important in the Amazonian region. The cotton was used to make clothing by the simple techniques of twining and, later, weaving. Cotton was also used for fishing nets. The people lived in one-room stone-lined pit dwellings, or in branch or reed huts. Jewellery of bone, shell etc was used, but metalwork and ceramics were unknown, which is why archaeologists call this the preceramic period.

Initial Period

Our knowledge of this period (about 2000 to 1000 BC) derives from remains in the Virú valley and Guañape area (near Trujillo) and other coastal sites. Ceramics developed from undecorated pots to sculptured, incised and simply coloured pots of high quality. Weaving, fishing and horticulture also improved, and simple funerary offerings have been found. Large ceremonial temples from this period have recently been found.

Early Horizon

Lasting very roughly from 1000 to 300 BC, this period has also been called the Chavín Horizon, after the site of Chavín de Huantar, 40 km east of Huaraz. Termed a 'horizon' because its artistic and religious influences are seen in several contemporary cultures, indicating some kind of interchange of ideas and increasing cultural complexity. The salient feature of the Chavín is the repeated representation of a stylised jaguar, with clearly religious overtones. Most importantly, this period represents great cultural developments – weaving, pottery, agriculture, religion and architecture.

Early Intermediate Period

Around 300 BC the Chavín style inexplicably disappeared, but over the next 500 years several cultures became locally important. Well known are the Salinar culture of the Chicama valley near Trujillo, and the Paracas Necropolis south of Lima. The Salinar ceramics show advanced firing techniques, whilst the Paracas textiles are considered the finest pre-Columbian textiles in the Americas.

Between about 100 AD and 700 AD, pottery, metalwork and textiles reached a pinnacle of technological development throughout Peru. The Moche (north coast) and the Nazca (south coast) depicted their ways of life on their ceramics, providing archaeologists with invaluable information. The Moche built massive pyramids, such as the temples of the Sun and Moon near Trujillo and at Sipán near Chiclayo, where wonderful graves were discovered in 1987. The Nazca made their enigmatic giant lines and designs in the coastal desert.

Middle Horizon

Wari (Huari) was the capital and the name of the first expansionist empire known in the Andes. Unlike the earlier Chavín, its expansion was not limited to the diffusion of artistic and religious influence. The Wari were vigorous military conquerors who built and maintained important outposts throughout much of Peru, including Pikillacta (near Cuzco), Cajamarquilla (near Lima) and Wilcahuaín (near Huaraz). The Wari imposed their own cultural values on the peoples they subdued, and from about 600 to 1000 AD, Wari influence is apparent in the art, technology and architecture of most of Peru.

Late Intermediate Period

During the next four centuries several separate regional states thrived. The best known is the Chimu, whose capital was the huge adobe city of Chan Chan near Trujillo. Roughly contemporary with the Chimu was the Chachapoyas culture which left the infrequently visited highland ruin of Kuélap. Other contemporaries were the Chancay people, just north of Lima (their artefacts can be seen in Lima's Museo Amano), and the Ica-Chincha culture, further south, whose artefacts can be seen in Ica's Museo Regional.

Several small altiplano tribes lived near Lake Titicaca and frequently warred with one another. They left impressive, circular funerary towers dotting the bleak landscape;

PERU

the best are to be seen at Sillustani. There were also the Chanka (of the Ayacucho-Apurímac area) and the Kingdom of Cuzco, predecessor of the Inca empire.

The Inca Empire

For all its greatness, the Inca empire existed for barely a century. Prior to 1430, the Incas ruled over only the valley of Cuzco, but victory over the Chankas in the 1430s marked the beginning of a rapid military expansion. The Incas conquered and incorporated most of the area from southern Colombia to central Chile. Around 1525, a civil war broke out between followers of the Inca Huáscar, in Cuzco, and followers of his half-brother Atahualpa, in Quito. When the Spaniards arrived, they took advantage of the civil war to divide and conquer the Inca empire.

The Spanish Conquest

In November 1526, Francisco Pizarro headed south from Panama, and by 1528 had explored as far as Peru's Río Santa. He noted coastal Inca settlements, became aware of the richness of the Inca empire, and returned to Spain to raise money and recruit men for the conquest. On his next expedition he left Panama in late 1530, landed on the Ecuadorian coast and began to march overland towards Peru. In September 1532, Pizarro founded the first Spanish town in Peru – San Miguel de Piura. Then he marched into the heart of the Inca empire, reached Cajamarca in November 1532, captured the Inca Atahualpa, and put an end to Inca rule.

Colonial Peru

In 1535, Pizarro founded the coastal city of Lima, which became the capital of the Viceroyalty of Peru. The next 30 years were a period of turmoil, with the Incas resisting their conquerors, who were fighting among themselves for control of the rich colony. Pizarro was assassinated in 1541. Manco Inca nearly regained control of the highlands in 1536, but then retreated to his rainforest hide-out of Vilcabamba, where he was killed in 1544. Inca Tupac Amaru attempted to overthrow the Spaniards in 1572, but was defeated and executed.

The next 200 years were relatively peaceful. Lima became the major political, social and commercial centre of the Andean nations, while Cuzco became a backwater whose main colonial legacy was the *escuela cuzqueña* (Cuzco school) of art, the result of a unique blend of Spanish and highland Indian influences. The Indians were exploited as expendable labourers under the *encomienda* system. This led to the 1780 uprising under the self-styled Inca Tupac Amaru II. The uprising was quelled and its leaders cruelly executed.

Independence

By the early 1800s the colonists were dissatisfied with the lack of freedom and high taxation imposed by Spain, and were ready for revolt and independence. For Peru, the change came from two directions. José de San Martín liberated Argentina and Chile, and in 1821 entered Lima. Meanwhile, Simón Bolívar had freed Venezuela and Colombia. In 1822 San Martín left Latin America to live in France and Bolívar continued with the liberation of Peru. The two decisive battles for independence were at Junín on 6 August 1824 and Ayacucho on 9 December 1824.

Peru won a brief war with Spain in 1866, and lost a longer war with Chile (1879-83) over the nitrate-rich areas of the northern Atacama Desert. Chile annexed much of coastal southern Peru but the area around Tacna was returned in 1929. Peru went to war with Ecuador over a border dispute in 1941. The 1942 treaty of Rio de Janeiro gave Peru the area north of the Río Marañón, but Ecuador disputes this border and armed skirmishes occur every few years, the most recent of which was in 1995.

Modern Times

Government in the 20th century has been by military dictatorship and coups, with periods of civilian rule. The most recent of these began in 1980. In the late 1980s, after some years of relative stability, the country began experiencing some of its worst economic and guerrilla problems in decades.

The Maoist Sendero Luminoso (Shining Path) waged a guerrilla war for over a decade, resulting in many thousands of lives lost. Sendero leaders were captured and imprisoned in 1993, thus ameliorating guerrilla problems.

The elections of June 1990 saw Alberto Fujimori, the 52-year-old son of Japanese immigrants, elected president. Strong, semi-dictatorial actions led to unprecedented improvements in the economy and also the capture of terrorist leaders. This resulted in popular support which propelled Fujimori to a second term in 1995 (although he had to change the constitution before he was able to run for a second term).

GEOGRAPHY

Peru is the third-largest country in South America and lies entirely within the tropics.

Geographically, Peru has three major regions – a narrow coastal belt, the wide Andean mountains and the Amazon rainforest. The coastal strip is mainly desert, but contains Peru's major cities and its best highway, the Carretera Panamericana. Rivers running down the western slopes of the Andes form about 40 oases, which are agricultural centres.

The Andes rise rapidly from the coast; heights of 6000 metres are reached just 100 km inland. Huascarán (6768 metres) is Peru's highest mountain. Most of Peru's Andes lie between 3000 and 4000 metres, with jagged ranges separated by deep, vertiginous canyons. Although the roads are often in terrible condition, the traveller is rewarded by spectacular scenery.

The eastern Andes receive much more rainfall than do the dry western slopes and so are covered in green cloud forest. As elevation is lost, the cloud forest becomes the rainforest of the Amazon Basin, a region of few roads. The traveller wishing to penetrate the Amazon Basin must do so by river or air.

CLIMATE

Peru's climate can be divided into wet and dry seasons, though this varies depending on the geographical region.

The coast and western Andean slopes are generally dry. During the coastal summer (late December to early April), the sky is often clear and the weather tends to be hot and sticky. This is when Peruvians go to the beach. During the rest of the year, the *garúa* (coastal fog) moves in, and the sun is rarely seen on the central and south coasts. Inland, above the coastal garúa, it is hot and sunny for most of the year.

In the Andes proper, the dry season is from May to September. The mountains can be cold at night, with occasional freezing temperatures in Cuzco (3326 metres), but the dry weather means beautiful sunshine during the day. The wet season in the mountains is from October to May, but it doesn't get really wet until late January.

On the eastern Andean slopes, the drier months are similar to the highlands, but the wet season is more pronounced. The wettest months are January to April, when roads are often closed by landslides or flooding. The Amazon lowlands have a similar weather pattern.

FLORA & FAUNA

Peru's varied geography, with long coastal deserts, glaciated mountain ranges, vast tropical rainforests and almost every imaginable habitat in between, means that the country is host to one of the world's richest assemblages of plants and animals.

The desert coast has few plants but marine and bird life is abundant. Travellers visit the Islas Ballestas and Península de Paracas to view sea-lion colonies and vast numbers of sea birds and shore birds such as the Humboldt penguin, guanay cormorant, Peruvian and brown booby, Chilean flamingo, seaside cinclodes, Peruvian pelican and the exquisitely pretty Inca tern.

The Andean condor is seen along the coast on occasion, but this, among the largest of flying birds, is normally an Andean inhabitant. Other interesting highland birds are puna ibis, Andean geese and a variety of hummingbirds, which eke out a precarious

PERU

existence in the forbidding elevations. The highlands, too, are the home of all four members of the South American camelids: the llama, alpaca, guanaco and vicuña. In the high country are bleak páramo and puna habitats with hardy and unique plants adapted to withstand the rigours of high altitude: blazing tropical sun alternating with freezing winds and rains. Small, colourful patches of *Polylepis* woodland are found – this shrubby tree grows at the highest elevation of any tree in the world.

The Amazon Basin begins in Peru – the most distant tributary rises in the southern mountains of the country. The eastern slopes of the Andes, as they tumble to the Amazon Basin, are among the least accessible and least known areas of the planet. These are the haunts of jaguars, Andean spectacled bears and tapirs – spectacular large mammals only rarely seen in the wild. Peru's Amazon is home to most of the country's approximately 1700 bird species. Peru is considered the world's second-most diverse country for birds, as well as having the third-greatest mammal diversity and the fifth-greatest plant diversity. Areas such as the Zona Reservada Tambopata (5500 hectares) have had over 540 bird and 1100 butterfly species recorded; Parque Nacional Manu (1.8 million hectares) has about 1000 bird species (compare with about 700 for the USA) and 13 different species of monkey.

This vast wealth of wildlife is being protected in a system of national parks and reserves with almost 30 areas covering about 7% of the country. For the most part, this national park system includes remote and inaccessible places which are rarely visited – but they are there, nonetheless. Protecting these areas is vitally important but difficult because of the lack of finance. Groups like the Worldwide Fund for Nature and The Nature Conservancy are all active in Peruvian conservation and you can donate money to these organisations and specifically request that the funds be used in Peru. The Fundación Peruana para la Conservación de la Naturaleza (FPCN) is a local organisation which can help with information: Apartado 18-1393, Lima, Peru (fax 446-9178). It accepts donations. US citizens can make tax-deductible donations to the FPCN at The Nature Conservancy, Latin American Program, 1815 North Lynn St, Arlington, VA 22209, USA.

GOVERNMENT

Peru is a constitutional republic. The president has two vice-presidents and 12 cabinet members. A unicameral congress has 120 members. Voting is compulsory for citizens aged 18 to 70.

President Fujimori was elected in 1990 and re-elected for a second five-year term in 1995.

ECONOMY

Peru's disastrous economy of recent years (with inflation at over 10,000% per year) has been brought under control by the current Fujimori administration and inflation has dropped to under 20%. In 1992, exports were worth US$3484 million. Major exports are copper (23.1%), fishmeal (12.6%), zinc (9.6%), gold (5.6%), and petroleum products (5.6%). However, unreported revenue from coca (exported for cocaine production) is, according to some sources, roughly comparable in value to all legal exports combined.

Peru's major economic partner is the USA.

POPULATION & PEOPLE

Over half of Peru's 24 million inhabitants are concentrated in the narrow coastal desert. Lima has a population approaching eight million, and the second and third-largest cities, Arequipa and Trujillo (also in the coastal region) have populations of nearly a million.

Almost half of the population lives in the highlands, and these people are mainly *campesinos* – rural people who practise subsistence agriculture. There are few large cities in the highlands. The standard of living there is poor, and many campesinos have migrated to the coast, where population growth is a problem.

Over 60% of Peru is in the Amazon Basin,

but only 5% of the population lives there. The region is slowly becoming colonised.

Over half the population is Indian and one-third is mestizo. About 12% are white and 2% are black or of Asian or other descent.

ARTS

The heritage of the Andean Indians is best seen in the many folk art forms which are still common today and which serve as much to preserve an ancient culture as to entertain. For the visitor, the most obvious of these art forms will be music, dance, and crafts. Pre-Columbian and colonial architecture are also of great interest to the visitor.

Music & Dance

Andean Pre-Columbian Andean music was based on a pentatonic scale and used wind and percussion instruments. Some of those found in archaeological museums are as old as 5000 BC. The stringed instruments used today are based on instruments introduced by the Spanish. Traditional Andean music is popularly called *música folklórica* and is frequently heard at fiestas as well as being performed in bars and restaurants. Bars which specifically cater to musical entertainment are called *peñas*.

There are many different forms of wind instruments, which vary according to the region. The most representative are the *quena* and the *zampoña*. The quena (or *kena*) is a flute, usually made of bamboo and of varying lengths depending on the pitch desired. A variation is the *mohseno*, a large bamboo flute producing the deepest bass notes. The zampoña, or *siku* in Quechua, is a set of panpipes with two rows of bamboo canes, seven in one row and six in the other. Zampoñas come in sizes ranging from the tiny, high-pitched *chuli* to the metre-long, bass *toyo*. Also seen and heard are the *ocarina*, a small, oval clay instrument with up to 12 holes, and, occasionally, horns made of animal horn or sea shells.

Percussion instruments include the inevitable drum, called a *bombo*, usually made from a hollowed-out segment of a cedar,

walnut or other tree, and using stretched goatskin for the pounding surface. Rattles, called *shajshas*, are made of polished goat hooves tied together.

Almost all of today's *música folklórica* groups also use stringed instruments. The guitar is sometimes seen, but the most typical is the *charango*, which was based on a Spanish instrument but can now be considered an Andean instrument in its own right. It is a tiny, five-stringed guitar with a resonance box traditionally made of an armadillo shell, though most are wooden these days. It has five pairs of strings, usually tuned to E-A-E-C-G.

More recent additions to the instruments used in the Andes include harps, violins, and a variety of brass instruments including saxophones. These are most often seen in large outdoor bands strolling around towns and villages during fiesta days, producing a cacophony of sound and surrounded by masked and elaborately costumed dancers.

Of the many regionally based forms of música folklórica, the most representative is the *huayno*, which is associated with a dance of the same name. Hundreds of other dances are known and performed in the highlands. Many have a religious and ceremonial as well as a social background. Although dance performances can be seen in theatres and restaurants in the highlands, nowhere are they as colourful and authentic as those performed communally during the many fiestas.

Música folklórica bands have toured North America, Europe and Australasia, and their music is becoming familiar outside the Andes. It varies from melancholy and soulful to upbeat and festive. Perhaps the most widely known Andean melody is *El Cóndor Pasa*, adapted by Paul Simon.

Coastal On the coast, music and associated dance are quite different. The coastal *música criolla* has its roots in Spain and Africa. Its main instruments are guitars and a *cajón*, a wooden box on which the player sits and pounds out a rhythm with his hands. The cajón is attributed to black slaves which the Spanish bought with them. The most popular of the coastal dances is the *marinera*, a graceful, romantic dance employing much waving of handkerchiefs. This is a performance to be watched rather than a dance with audience participation. Marinera dance competitions are frequently held in coastal Peru with the most important being in Trujillo, on the north coast.

In the last few decades Afro-Peruvian music has enjoyed a comeback, especially in the Chincha area on the south coast. This music and the dancing that accompanies it are becoming increasingly popular on TV and as a performance art, though Peruvians will go to clubs and dance to it as well. A popular performance dance is the *alcatraz*, during which one partner carrying a candle attempts to light a paper flag tucked into the back of the other's waist.

Just as in the highlands, coastal music can be heard at peñas in the main towns.

Modern Although there is a national symphony orchestra and ballet company, and touring companies from other countries often visit, classical music is enjoyed by relatively few people.

Modern popular music includes rock, pop, reggae, punk, blues etc, which is usually imported though there are a few Peruvian bands. Chilean-style protest songs and jazz also enjoy a limited popularity. Much more popular are other forms of Latin American music such as the omnipresent salsa, and *cumbia* and *chicha*, both from Colombia. This is music to dance to, and *salsatecas* can be found which cram in hundreds of Peruvians for all-night dance-fests.

Crafts
Handicrafts made in the Andes are based on pre-Columbian necessities such as weaving (for clothes), pottery and metallurgy. Today, woven cloth is still seen in the traditional ponchos, belts and other clothes worn by Andean Indians. As well, weaving has extended to cover a variety of rugs and tapestries, which are popular souvenirs. The traditionally worked alpaca wool is also in great demand for sweaters and other items.

Pottery, very important and well developed among many pre-Columbian cultures in Peru, is still important today as a source of souvenirs. The best are often based on ancient designs, shapes and motifs. Jewellery, especially the gold and silver pieces which are a direct link back to ancient rituals and heritage, is also in demand as a craft.

Architecture
The Inca architecture of Machu Picchu is, perhaps, the single greatest attraction in Peru. But there is much more in the way of Inca architecture, especially in (but not limited to) the Cuzco area. Various other pre-Columbian cultures have left us with magnificent examples of their architecture. See Activities & Highlights later in this chapter for some examples.

Colonial architecture is most importantly represented by the many imposing cathedrals, churches, monasteries and convents built during the 16th, 17th and 18th centuries. These are extremely ornate, both outside and inside. Altars are often covered in gold leaf. Many of the religious statues and paintings found inside churches were carved or painted by early Indian artists with strong Spanish influence. These gave rise to the *escuela cuzqueña* (Cuzco school) of art – colonial art blending Andean and Spanish ideas.

Literature
Peru's most famous novelist is the internationally recognised Mario Vargas Llosa (born 1936), who ran second in the Peruvian presidential election of 1990. Most of his books have been translated into various languages including English. In common with many Peruvian authors, his novels often delve deeply into Peruvian society, politics, and culture. His first novel, *The Time of the Hero*, was publicly burned because of its detailed exposé of life in a Peruvian military academy. Vargas Llosa's work is very complex, with multiple plots and changing time sequences or flashbacks.

Two Peruvian writers are particularly noted for their portrayals of the difficulties facing Peru's Indian communities. José María Arguedas (1911-69) wrote *Deep Rivers* and *Yawar Fiesta* among others. Ciro Alegría (1909-67) was the author of *The Golden Serpent* about life in a jungle village on the Río Marañón, and *Broad and Alien is the World* about repression among Andean Indians. These are all in English translations. Other writers who are considered important but await translation include Julio Ramón Ribeyro (born 1929) and Alfredo Bryce Echeñique (born 1939).

César Vallejo (1892-1938) wrote *Trilce*, a book of 77 avant-garde poems which some critics say is one of the best books of poetry ever written in Spanish. Vallejo is considered Peru's greatest poet. Anthologised modern Peruvian poetry is available in English in *Peru: The New Poetry* (London Magazine Editions, 1970; Red Dust, NY, 1977), and *The Newest Peruvian Poetry in Translation* (Studia Hispanica Editions, 1979).

LANGUAGE

Spanish is the main language. Most Andean Indians are bilingual, with Quechua being their mother tongue (Aymara around Lake Titicaca) and Spanish their second language. One to two million inhabitants of remote areas speak no Spanish. English is understood in the best hotels, airline offices etc.

Facts for the Visitor

VISAS & EMBASSIES

Most travellers do not need visas to enter Peru. This includes Australians, New Zealanders, Spaniards and South Africans, who until recently were exceptions. Your passport should be valid for six months or more. A free tourist card is given to everybody on arrival. Don't lose this, as it's needed for stay extensions and passport checks and on leaving the country. Replacements are obtainable at Migraciones in Lima. Although you officially need a ticket out of the country to get in, it's rare to be asked for one unless you are travelling on a visa.

On arrival, you can usually get a 90-day stay if you ask for it, though sometimes only 30 days are given. Extensions cost US$20 for 30 days at Migraciones in major cities; it's best to go first thing in the morning for best service. After 180 days, you must leave the country, but you are allowed to return the next day and begin again.

You should carry your passport and tourist card at all times, as there are occasional document checks on public transport; you can be arrested if you don't have identification. If you're just walking around town, carry a photocopy and leave the original passport in a safe place, but don't travel without it.

Peruvian Embassies Abroad

Peruvian embassies are found in all neighbouring countries, and addresses are listed in those chapters. There are also Peruvian representatives in:

Australia
 43 Culgoa Circuit, O'Malley, ACT 2606 (☎ (06) 290-0922, fax 257-5198)
 Postal address: PO Box 106, Red Hill, ACT 2603
Canada
 170 Laurier Ave West, Suite 1007, Ottawa K1P 5V5 (☎ (613) 238-1777, fax 232-3062)
France
 50 Ave Kléber, 75007 Paris (☎ 01 47 04 34 53, fax 01 47 55 98 30)
Germany
 53175 Bonn, Godesberger Allee 127 (☎ (0228) 37 30 45, fax 37 94 75)
Israel
 52 Rehov Pinkas, Apt 31, 8th floor, Tel Aviv 62261 (☎ (03) 544-2081, fax 546-5532)
New Zealand
 Level 8, Cigna House, 40 Mercer St, POB 2566, Wellington (☎ (04) 499-8087, fax 499-8057)
Spain
 Príncipe de Vergara 36, 5D, 28001 Madrid (☎ (01) 431 4242, fax 577 6861)
UK
 52 Sloane St, London SW1X 9SP (☎ (0171) 235-1917, fax 235-4463)
USA
 1700 Massachusetts Ave, NW, Washington, DC 20036 (☎ (202) 833-9860, fax 659-8124)

Foreign Embassies in Peru

Almost 50 nations are represented. Some

important ones follow. Australian travellers should go to the Canadian Embassy in the event of a lost passport or other emergency; there is Australian representation in Santiago, Chile, and Guayaquil, Ecuador.

Bolivia
Los Castaños 235, San Isidro (☎ 422-8231)

Brazil
José Pardo 850, Miraflores (☎ 446-2635, ext 131, 132)

Canada
Frederico Gerdes 130, Miraflores (☎ 444-4015)

Chile
Javier Prado Oeste 790, San Isidro (☎ 440-7965, 440-3280)

Colombia
Natalio Sánchez 125, 4th floor, Lima (☎ 433-8922, 433-8923)

Ecuador
Las Palmeras 356, San Isidro (☎ 442-4184), 9 am to 1 pm

Germany
Arequipa 4210, Miraflores (☎ 445-7033)

Israel
Natalio Sánchez 125, 6th floor, Lima (☎ 433-4431)

New Zealand
Natalio Sánchez 125, 11th floor, Lima (☎ 433-4738, 433-5032)

South Africa
Natalio Sánchez 125, Lima (new embassy, ☎ not available)

Spain
Jorge Basadre 498, San Isidro (☎ 470-5600, 470-5678)

UK
Natalio Sánchez 125, 11th floor, Lima (☎ 433-4738, 433-5032)

USA
Grimaldo del Solar 346, Miraflores (☎ 444-3621, 434-3000)

DOCUMENTS
International vaccination certificates are not required by law, though vaccinations are advisable (see Health in the Facts for the Visitor chapter). Student cards save you money at some archaeological sites, museums etc.

CUSTOMS
If bringing a valuable item for personal use (eg a bicycle or a laptop computer) you may be asked to pay a (supposedly) refundable bond of 25% of its value. It can be hard to get a refund in the few hours that you are at the airport leaving the country. Insist that the item is for personal use and you will not be selling it in Peru. If you have to pay, undervalue the item as much as you dare to minimise potential loss, and check with customs a day or two before you leave.

It is illegal to export pre-Columbian artefacts and illegal to bring them into most countries. Bringing endangered animal products home is also illegal. Coca leaves are legal in Peru but can't be brought into most other countries.

MONEY
The currency, introduced in 1991, is the *nuevo sol* (S/), divided into 100 *céntimos*. The following bills are in circulation: S/10, S/20, S/50, S/100. Old 5,000,000-*inti* bills (worth S/5) are still being used but will be phased out (check locally). Coins of S/0.05, S/0.10, S/0.20, S/0.50, S/1, S/2 and S/5 are in use.

Changing Money
Currencies other than US dollars can be exchanged only in major cities and at a high commission, so you are advised to obtain US dollars before your trip. The exchange rate in mid-1996 was US$1 to S/2.44. Money can be changed in banks and *casas de cambio* or with moneychangers. All cities or towns of any size can change US dollars. Dollar bills which are slightly torn or damaged are never accepted by anybody, although torn Peruvian currency is OK.

Banking hours are erratic. In the summer (January to March), banks in Lima may open only from 8.30 to 11.30 am. During the rest of the year, hours extend well into the afternoon, but don't count on it. Expect long queues in banks and go early in the morning. Casas de cambio open from 9 am to 6 pm, or later in tourist areas, and are much faster. Moneychangers are useful for exchange outside banking hours, or at borders where there are no banks. Street rates are equivalent to bank rates, but you may be cheated, so beware. Calculators are often 'fixed' and short-changing is common; count the money carefully before handing over the dollars.

The exchange rates for cash dollars are better than for travellers' cheques which were recently being changed at a 1% to 5% commission (and worse in the past). Change travellers' cheques into nuevos soles rather than US dollars to get the best rates. Banks charge the lowest commissions, but you can spend over an hour in them. Casas de cambio are much quicker, but not all will change travellers' cheques and those that do often charge a higher commission. Money-changers only take cash. Torn bills are not accepted. Rates for cash dollars vary by no more than 1% or 2% between different places. Recommended banks are Banco de Crédito, Interbanc and Banco Mercantil. The best accepted travellers' cheques are American Express and Thomas Cook.

Bank transfers from home are possible, but take at least three days even if you use telex. Check with the bank to ensure that you can receive your money in US dollars. Only some banks will provide this service (for a small commission); the Banco de Crédito has been recommended. Bills paid by credit cards are usually increased by 8% so it's best to pay with cash. Visa is the most easily accepted card, and cash withdrawals can be made at banks.

You can buy back US dollars, at a slight loss, when leaving the country. There are moneychangers working on the land borders, and Lima airport has banks open for international departures. Don't get left with a lot of excess cash, because occasional strikes or currency freezes mean banks won't buy back soles.

The currency exchange rules can change at any time, so consult a traveller who has been in the country for a while.

Costs

Prices can triple (in dollar terms) within months and can fall equally rapidly. Costs in Peru increased threefold during the early 1990s but are stable now. On a tight budget, you can get by on US$10 to US$15 per day by staying in the most basic hotels and trav-

elling slowly. Big cities are more expensive than small towns. Most budget travellers spend over US$20 per day because of the large distances that have to be covered.

Tipping & Bargaining

Fancy restaurants add 31% in tips and tax to your bill, but cheap restaurants don't: ask before you order if in doubt. You don't have to tip the server in the cheapest restaurants, but they don't make much money, so leaving some change isn't a bad idea. Don't leave it on the table; give it to the server.

Taxi drivers are not tipped; bargain a fare beforehand and stick to it. Tip bellboys US$0.50 per bag. Tip a local guide US$3 to US$5 per client for each full day's work if they are good, professional, multilingual guides – less if they aren't. On treks it is customary also to tip the cook and porters. Tip them at least as much as the guide and split it between them.

Bargaining is expected in markets when buying crafts and occasionally in other situations. If not sure, try asking for a discount or *descuento*. These are often given in hotels, tour agencies, souvenir shops, and other places where tourists spend money.

WHEN TO GO

June to August is the highland dry season, and the most popular time to travel in Peru. Hotels are more likely to be full and charge full prices. In other months (except for major holidays) expect lower prices and try bargaining. January to March are the 'summer' months on the coast, and many Peruvians visit the coastal areas then.

WHAT TO BRING

Shoes larger than size 43 Peruvian (or US10½) are not sold in Peru. Tampons are available only in major cities and in regular sizes. Condoms are sold in cities but the choice is limited. A sleeping bag or warm (down) jacket is useful if you plan on travelling in the highlands, where temperatures can drop below freezing at night (cheap highland hotel rooms and overnight buses

PERU

often lack heat). Good insect repellent and sunscreen are hard to find.

USEFUL ORGANISATIONS

The South American Explorers Club (SAEC) has a Lima office. See Information in the Lima section for details.

BUSINESS HOURS

Shops open at 9 or 10 am and close about 8 pm. A two or three-hour lunch break is common. There are 24-hour supermarkets in Lima, and shops may stay open through lunch in big cities. Most shops close on Sunday. Banks and offices have very variable hours.

HOLIDAYS

Asterisked dates are legal holidays when banks close.

1 January*
  Año Nuevo (New Year's Day)
2 February
  La Virgen de la Candelaria (Candlemas) – a colourful highland fiesta, particularly in the Puno area
February-March
  Carnaval – many water fights
March-April*
  Semana Santa (Holy Week) – spectacular religious processions almost daily
1 May*
  Labour Day
June
  Corpus Christi – Cuzco processions are especially dramatic
24 June*
  Inti Raymi – winter solstice, the greatest Inca festival, which brings thousands of visitors to Cuzco
29 June*
  San Pedro y San Pablo (St Peter & St Paul)
16 July
  La Virgen del Carmen – especially celebrated in Paucartambo and Pisac near Cuzco and Pucara near Lake Titicaca
28-29 July*
  Fiestas Patrias (Peru's Independence) – the biggest national holiday; buses and hotels are booked long in advance and hotel prices can triple
30 August*
  Santa Rosa de Lima – patron saint of Lima and of the Americas; major processions in Lima

8 October*
  Battle of Angamos
18 October
  El Señor de los Milagros (Lord of the Miracles) – huge religious processions in Lima; people wear purple
1 November*
  Todos Santos (All Saint's Day)
2 November
  Día de los Muertos (All Soul's Day) – food, drink and flowers are taken to family graves; especially colourful in the sierra
5 November
  Puno Day – spectacular costumes and street dancing in Puno commemorate the legendary emergence of the first Inca, Manco Capac, from Lake Titicaca; celebrated for several days
8 December*
  Fiesta de la Purísima Concepción (Feast of the Immaculate Conception)
25 December*
  Navidad (Christmas Day)

POST & COMMUNICATIONS

Post

Postal services have improved recently but are expensive: airmail postcards or letters are US$1 to most countries. Letters from major Peruvian cities to other countries take from one to three weeks. Parcel post is not recommended because there is no surface rate and airmail is prohibitively expensive. Regulations change from year to year.

Travellers receive mail at either the post office (addressed to Lista de Correos, Correos Central, City, Peru) or American Express (Lima Tours, Casilla 4340, Belén 1040, Lima). The SAEC will hold mail for members, and return or forward it, according to your instructions.

Telephone & Fax

Telefónica del Perú provides national and international telephone and fax services. Lima also has La Compañía Peruana de Teléfonos. The system is being modernised and changes can be expected during the late 1990s. Main offices are marked on city maps, and sub-offices and phone booths are becoming widespread. Calls are expensive. Direct-dial payphones accept coins or telephone cards bought at Telefónica offices. A card for S/30 (about US$13) lasts 4½

PERU

minutes to the USA, or less to Europe. These are the cheapest calls. In smaller towns you go through a Telefónica operator until new equipment is installed. Rates are cheaper on Sunday and in the evening after 9 pm. Telefónica offices are usually open from 8 am to 10 pm, or sometimes later in the major cities.

Telephone numbers have seven digits in Lima and six digits elsewhere. Area telephone codes begin with 0 (01 in Lima, 0 plus two digits elsewhere; these are given under each city in the text). To call long distance within Peru, include the 0 in the code.

Peru's country code is 51. To call from overseas, dial your international access code, then 51, the area telephone code *without* the 0, and the six or seven-digit number.

Fax services are available at most Telefónica del Perú offices for US$3 to US$7 per page (higher rates outside Lima). Telefónica offices will hold faxes clearly marked 'ATENCION (your name)', and charge under US$1.

TIME
Peru is five hours behind GMT/UTC and currently has no daylight-saving time.

ELECTRICITY
Peru uses 220V, 60 Hz, except Arequipa, which is on 50 Hz. Plugs are of the flat, two-pronged type found in the USA.

BOOKS & MAPS
Books in English are expensive in Peru. Many useful books, including Lonely Planet's *Peru – travel survival kit*, 3rd edition, by Rob Rachowiecki, are listed in the Facts for the Visitor chapter. Some other suggestions follow.

Cut Stones and Crossroads by Ronald Wright is a fine travel book by a writer very well informed on archaeology and contemporary Peru. *Exploring Cuzco* by Peter Frost is recommended for anyone planning to spend some time in the Cuzco area.

Readers seriously interested in Peruvian archaeology should read the recent *The Incas and Their Ancestors: The Archaeology of*

Peru by Michael E Moseley, and Richard L Burger's *Chavín and the Origins of Andean Civilizations*.

Topographical maps are sold at the Instituto Geográfico Nacional in Lima. The SAEC (see Information in the Lima section for details) has hiking maps.

MEDIA
The best newspapers are the dry, conservative *El Comercio*, good for what's going on in Lima, the conservative *Expreso* and the moderately left-wing *La República*, all published in Lima. A shorter *El Comercio* (lacking the Lima cultural section) is sold in other cities. There are many trashy tabloids. The *Lima Times* is a monthly magazine in English.

Peru has seven TV channels plus cable, but the local programming is poor, though evening news broadcasts are OK for local news. Radio stations broadcast in Quechua and Spanish. BBC World Service and Voice of America can be picked up on short-wave radio.

HEALTH
Definitely avoid salads and fruit you cannot peel, and don't drink tap water. There are good medical services in the major cities; the best are in Lima, where you should go if seriously ill. See Health in the Facts for the Visitor chapter.

DANGERS & ANNOYANCES
Many travellers report thefts: there are pickpockets, bag-snatchers, razor-blade slashers (slashing your pack or pocket), con artists and crooked police. Take taxis when first arriving in a new city until you get the feel of the place. One scam involves locals spending days befriending you and then, when they have your trust, offering you a joint. You get busted two drags later. Be aware and take precautions but don't be paranoid: violent crime is uncommon. See the Dangers & Annoyances section in the Facts for the Visitor chapter.

PERU

Terrorism

The leaders of Peru's major guerrilla groups, the Sendero Luminoso and MRTA, were imprisoned in 1992. Since then, travel has become reasonably safe over most of Peru. Areas to avoid are the Río Huallaga valley between Tingo María and Tarapoto (these towns are safe but the area between is prime drug country) and the Nazca-Puquio-Abancay route, which has been held up by bandits.

ACTIVITIES & HIGHLIGHTS

Visiting archaeological sites, especially Machu Picchu, is high on everyone's list. Other important sites are Chan Chan (the huge adobe capital of the Chimu) near Trujillo, the 2500-year-old Chavín ruins near Huaraz, the newly-discovered site of El Señor del Sipán near Chiclayo, the funerary towers at Sillustani, near Puno, and Kuélap near Chachapoyas.

Trekking, backpacking, and mountaineering are popular during the May to September dry season. See the Cuzco section for details on the Inca Trail, and the Huaraz section for the Cordillera Blanca.

River running is possible year round, with higher water levels in the rainy season. See the Cuzco, Huaraz and Cañete sections.

Surfing is enjoyed by a few middle and upper class young people. The water is cold and locals wear wet suits. The surfing is OK but facilities and equipment are basic. Swimming is locally popular from January to March, but the beaches are very contaminated near cities and there are many dangerous currents. The beaches are unattractive and we wouldn't come to Peru to swim!

Wildlife enthusiasts should visit the Islas Ballestas near Pisco for huge sea-lion and sea-bird colonies. Seeing the rainforest is also exciting, but expensive.

Finally, try to spend a night with a family on one of the islands in Lake Titicaca.

ACCOMMODATION

Accommodation can be tight during major fiestas, or the night before market day.

Therefore as many hotels as possible are shown on town maps. If you are going to a town for a fiesta, arrive a day or two early.

Single rooms may be hard to find, so you may get a room with two or three beds. Check that you won't have to pay for all the beds – usually no problem, unless the hotel is full. Many hotels have triple and quad rooms, which is cheaper for people in a group. Hotels offering hot water usually have it for a few hours a day; ask when. Young local couples use some cheap hotels for short stays.

Villages off the beaten track may lack a basic *pensión*. If you have a sleeping bag, find somewhere to sleep by asking around; the store owner should know who rents rooms or floor space. People in remote areas are generally hospitable.

FOOD

Those with a tight budget and a strong stomach can eat from street and market stalls provided the food looks hot and freshly cooked. *Chifas* (Chinese restaurants) are often good value. Most will offer *tallarines* (noodles) with chopped chicken, beef, pork or shrimp for US$2. Many restaurants offer a *menú* (inexpensive set lunch), which consists of a soup and a second course, and costs from US$1.25 to US$3, depending on location. Lunch is the main meal of the day; dinner is usually served late (from 8 pm). Better restaurants add 18% to 31% tax: ask before you eat.

Some typical dishes are:

Ceviche de corvina – white sea bass marinated in lemon, chilli and onions, served cold with a boiled potato or yam. It's delicious. *Ceviche de camarones* is the same made with shrimps. These dishes are appetisers rather than full meals.
Lomo saltado – chopped steak fried with onions, tomatoes, potatoes and served with rice
Palta a la jardinera – avocado stuffed with cold vegetables and mayonnaise; *a la reina* is stuffed with chicken salad.
Sopa a la criolla – lightly spiced noodle soup with beef, egg, milk and vegetables; hearty and filling

The term 'a la criolla' describes spicy foods.

The highlands have their own distinctive cuisine; see the Cuzco section for details.

DRINKS
Nonalcoholic Drinks
Agua mineral (mineral water) is sold *con gas* (carbonated) or *sin gas* (noncarbonated) and costs up to US$2 for a two litre plastic, non-returnable bottle.

The usual soft drinks are available, as well as local ones such as Inca Cola, which is appropriately gold-coloured and tastes like fizzy bubble gum. Soft drinks are collectively called *gaseosas*, and the local brands are very sweet. Ask for *helada* if you want a refrigerated drink, *al clima* if you don't. Remember *sin hielo* (without ice) unless you really trust the water supply.

Jugos (fruit juices) are available everywhere. Make sure you get *jugo puro* and not *con agua*. The most common kinds are *mora* (blackberry), *naranja* (orange), *toronja* (grapefruit), *piña* (pineapple), *maracuyá* (passion fruit), *sandía* (watermelon), *naranjilla* (a local fruit tasting like bitter orange) or papaya.

Coffee is available almost everywhere but is often disappointing. It doesn't taste that great and it looks very much like soy sauce! Instant coffee is also served. Good espresso and cappuccino are available in the bigger towns. *Café con leche* is milk with coffee, and *café con agua* is black coffee. *Té* (tea) is served black with lemon and sugar. Hot chocolate is also popular. *Mate* or *té de hierbas* are herb teas. *Mate de coca* is made from coca leaves and served in highland restaurants. It supposedly helps the newly arrived visitor to acclimatise.

Alcoholic Drinks
There are about a dozen kinds of beer, and they are quite palatable and inexpensive. Both light, lager-type beers and sweet, dark beers are available. Dark beer is *malta* or *cerveza negra*. Cuzco and Arequipa are known for their beers: Cuzqueña and Arequipeña, respectively, both available in lager and dark. Cuzqueña is Peru's best beer, according to many drinkers. Arequipeña

tastes slightly sweet. Beer is sold in bottles of 355 ml and 620 ml in restaurants and litre bottles in shops.

The traditional highland *chicha* (corn beer) is stored in earthenware pots and served in huge glasses in small Andean villages and markets, but is not commercially available elsewhere. It is home-made, and definitely an acquired taste.

Peruvian wines are acceptable but not as good as those from Chile and Argentina. The best labels are Tacama and Ocucaje, and begin at US$5 a bottle (more in restaurants).

Spirits are expensive if imported and not very good if made locally, with some exceptions. *Ron* (rum) is cheap and quite good. A white grape brandy called *pisco* is the national drink, most frequently served in a pisco sour, a tasty cocktail made from pisco, egg white, lemon juice, syrup, crushed ice and bitters. *Guinda* is a sweet cherry brandy. The local *aguardiente*, sugar-cane alcohol, is an acquired taste but is good and very cheap.

THINGS TO BUY
Souvenirs from Peru are good, varied and cheap. You won't necessarily save much money by shopping in villages and markets rather than in shops. In markets and smaller stores, bargaining is expected.

You can buy everything in Lima, be it a blowpipe from the jungle or a woven poncho from the highlands. Although Lima is usually a little more expensive, the choice is varied and the quality is high. Cuzco also has a great selection of craft shops, but the quality is rarely as high as in Lima. Old and new weavings, ceramics, paintings, woollen clothing and jewellery are all found here.

The Puno-Juliaca area is good for knitted alpaca sweaters, and knick-knacks made from the *totora* reed which grows on Lake Titicaca. The Huancayo area is the place for carved gourds, and excellent weavings and clothing are available in the cooperative market. The Ayacucho area is famous for modern weavings and stylised ceramic churches. San Pedro de Cajas is known for its peculiar weavings, which are made of rolls of yarn stuffed with wool. The Shipibo pottery sold in Yarinacocha (near Pucallpa) is the best of the jungle craft available. Superb reproductions of Moche and Mochica pottery are available in Trujillo.

Warning

Objects made from skins, feathers, turtle shells etc should not be bought: their purchase contributes to the degradation of the wildlife and their importation into most countries is illegal.

Getting There & Away

AIR

Lima's Aeropuerto Internacional Jorge Chávez is the main hub for flights to the Andean countries from Europe and North America. There are also some international flights to Iquitos, in Peru's Amazon region. June to September is the high season; discounted fares may be available in other months.

There is a US$25 departure tax (payable in cash dollars or nuevos soles) for travellers leaving Peru on an international flight. Peru charges 18% tax on all tickets bought here.

To/From Bolivia

Lloyd Aéreo Boliviano (LAB) and AeroPerú have daily flights between La Paz (Bolivia) and Lima and between La Paz and Cuzco, which can be heavily booked. There are several flights a week from Santa Cruz (Bolivia) to Lima.

To/From Brazil

There are several flights a week between either Rio (Brazil) or São Paulo (Brazil) and Lima with AeroPerú and Varig.

To/From Chile

AeroPerú and LanChile have daily flights between Santiago (Chile) and Lima.

To/From Colombia

There are daily flights from Bogotá (Colombia) to Lima with AeroPerú, Avianca, and other airlines.

To/From Ecuador

AeroPerú, Ecuatoriana and American Airlines fly to Lima from the Ecuadorian cities of Quito and Guayaquil.

LAND

To/From Bolivia

The overland routes between Peru and Bolivia are around Lake Titicaca. For details, see the Puno section (in this chapter).

To/From Chile

The main border crossing is from Arica in northern Chile to Tacna (Peru). For details, see Tacna (in this chapter) and Arica (in the Chile chapter).

To/From Ecuador

This is a straightforward crossing. For details, see Tumbes (in this chapter) or Huaquillas (in the Ecuador chapter).

RIVER

To/From Brazil & Colombia

River boats ply the Amazon from Tabatinga (Brazil), at the Brazil-Colombia-Peru border, to Iquitos (Peru), take two to three days and cost US$20. Express boats from Leticia (Colombia) take 12 hours and cost US$50. Tabatinga and Leticia are adjacent to one another.

Getting Around

When travelling, have your passport with you, not packed in your luggage or left in the hotel safe. Buses may go through police checkpoints. If your passport is in order, these are cursory procedures.

AIR

AeroPerú, Faucett, Americana, Aero-Continente, Imperial Air and Expreso Aéreo are the main domestic carriers. Their prices are usually similar, though Imperial Air is often cheaper but has less extensive air services. Expreso Aéreo serves some of the remoter towns, as does AeroCóndor. The military airline, Grupo Ocho, occasionally provides flights but has infrequent service. Americana has air passes available from travel agents specialising in Peru or agents in neighbouring countries. These allow from one internal flight for US$55 to five flights for US$215 – a good deal if you can plan ahead. Faucett and AeroPerú fly to Peru from the USA and other Latin American countries and often have deals available for domestic flights if you fly internationally with them. Regulations and schedules change often.

The following towns are served by one or more domestic airlines: Andahuaylas, Arequipa, Ayacucho, Cajamarca, Chachapoyas, Chiclayo, Chimbote, Cuzco, Huánuco, Iquitos, Juliaca, Piura, Pucallpa, Puerto Maldonado, Rioja (for Moyobamba), Tacna, Talara, Tarapoto, Tingo María, Trujillo, Tumbes and Yurimaguas. Some of the smaller towns have only one or two flights per week. Inquire locally about smaller airlines in other towns.

Flights are often late. Morning flights are more likely to be on time, but by afternoon things fall an hour or more behind schedule. Show up at least an hour early for all domestic flights, as baggage handling and check-in procedures are chaotic. It is not unknown for flights to leave *before* their official departure time if bad weather has been predicted. Flights are overbooked during holiday periods so make reservations well in advance and confirm, reconfirm and reconfirm again. The airlines are notorious for bumping you off your flight if you don't reconfirm. There are no nonsmoking sections on internal flights. Many flights have good views of the Andes, so get a window seat.

One-way flights are half the cost of return flights. An 18% tax is charged on domestic fares. The same flights are sold in Arica, Chile with a 2% tax. A US$4 departure tax is charged on local flights out of most airports. On internal flights, 20 kg of checked luggage is allowed (though you can get away with more). Lost luggage is depressingly frequent. It often turns up on the next day's flight, but carry valuables and essentials (a warm coat or medications) in your hand luggage. Lock your checked luggage and label it clearly.

BUS

Peru's buses are cheap and go just about everywhere, except for the deep jungle and Machu Picchu.

Few cities have central bus terminals. Usually, different bus companies have their offices clustered around a few city blocks. It's best to buy your ticket in advance. There may be a separate 'express' window for tickets for another day. Schedules and fares change frequently and vary from company to company. Discounted fares are offered in the low season. Buses occasionally don't leave from by the ticket office – ask.

Long-distance buses stop for meals. The driver announces how long the stop will be, but it's your responsibility to be on the bus when it leaves. Many companies have their own restaurants in the middle of nowhere, so you have to eat there. The food is generally inexpensive but unexciting but you can bring your own food. Also carry a roll of toilet paper.

During long holiday weekends or special fiestas, buses are booked up for several days in advance. Book early. Bus fares often double around Christmas and 28 July (Independence). Always be prepared for delays and don't plan on making important connections after a bus journey.

A torch (flashlight) is useful on an overnight bus. It can get freezing cold on night buses in the highlands, so bring a blanket.

Armed robberies on night buses are occasionally reported. Considering the number of buses, the chance of being held up is remote; nevertheless, travel by day when possible. Some routes (eg Puno-Cuzco), however, are served only by night buses. Do not take the bus between Abancay and Nazca or between Tingo María and Tarapoto.

In remote areas, trucks or pick-ups may carry passengers. Most ride in the back, (though seats in the cab are available at higher cost). Because the trucks double as buses, they usually charge almost as much.

PERU

TRAIN

There are two unconnected railway networks; both go from the coast to the highlands. The Central Railroad runs from Lima to Huancayo through Galera station, which, at 4781 metres, is the world's highest standard-gauge railway station. This line has carried only freight trains since 1991, but there are plans to reopen passenger services by 1997.

The Southern Railroad runs passenger trains from Arequipa to Puno and Cuzco. Trains from Arequipa to Puno run four nights a week (less often than in the past). Change at Juliaca, 40 km before Puno, for trains to Cuzco. The Arequipa-Juliaca (or Puno) service takes all night; the Puno-Cuzco service takes a day.

There are two classes. Second class is cheap but very crowded and uncomfortable. First class is about 25% more expensive, but is much more comfortable, and cheaper, than a bus journey of comparable length. In addition, there are buffet and Pullman cars, for which you pay a surcharge. There is also a more expensive tourist train from Cuzco to Machu Picchu.

Thieves haunt the trains, particularly second class in the night train from Arequipa to Puno, where a dozing traveller is almost certain to get robbed. Dark stations also have many thieves. Travel with a group or in 1st class. The buffet or Pullman classes have a surcharge and are the safest because only ticket holders are allowed aboard.

Buy tickets in advance (the day before is usually best) so you don't have to worry about looking after your luggage whilst lining up to buy a ticket.

TAXI

There are no meters so ask the fare in advance. Haggle over a taxi fare: drivers often double or triple the standard rate for an unsuspecting foreigner. For a short run in Lima, the fare is about US$1.50; it's a little less in other cities. Taxis are recognisable by the small red 'TAXI' sticker on the windshield. More expensive radio taxis (called by telephone) are available.

CAR & MOTORCYCLE

Road conditions are poor, distances great, rental cars in poor condition – we don't recommend renting cars. Motorbikes can be rented in major Peruvian towns.

HITCHING

Hitching is not very practical in Peru because there are few private cars. Many drivers of *any* vehicle will pick you up but will also expect payment. Women are advised against hitching alone.

BOAT

Small motor boats that take about 20 passengers sail from Puno to visit islands on Lake Titicaca. There are departures every day, and the costs are low.

In Peru's eastern lowlands, dugout canoes, usually powered by an outboard engine, act as water buses on the smaller rivers. Where the rivers widen, larger cargo boats are normally available. You can travel from Pucallpa or Yurimaguas to Iquitos, where you change boats to the Brazilian border, and on to the mouth of the Amazon. The boats are small but have two or more decks. The lower deck is for cargo, the upper for passengers and crew. Bring a hammock. Food is provided, but is basic and not always very hygienic. You may want to bring some of your own. To get a passage, go down to the docks and ask for a boat going to your destination. Arrange a passage with the captain (nobody else). Departure time depends, more often than not, on filling up the hold. Sometimes you can sleep on the boat while waiting for departure, thus saving on hotel bills.

Boats to Iquitos from upriver towns like Yurimaguas or Pucallpa leave every few days and are smaller and slower. Beyond Iquitos, services are more frequent and comfortable. Things are generally more organised, too: there are blackboards at the docks with ship's names, destinations and departure times displayed reasonably clearly and accurately.

Lima

Lima, Peru's capital, was founded by Francisco Pizarro on 6 January 1535, the Catholic feast of Epiphany, or the Day of the Kings. Hence the city was first named the City of the Kings. Many of the old colonial buildings can still be seen. Unfortunately, much of Lima's colonial charm has been overwhelmed by an uncontrolled population explosion which began in the 1920s. About one-third of the nation's 24 million inhabitants now live in Lima, and most of the city is overcrowded, polluted and noisy.

Much of the growth has been due to the influx of very poor people from other areas of Peru who come searching for a better life. But jobs are scarce, and most end up living in the *pueblos jóvenes* (literally, young towns). These shantytowns surround the capital, lacking electricity, water and adequate sanitation.

Lima has a dismal climate. From April to December, the city suffers from garúa, which blots out the sun and blankets the buildings in a fine grey mist. During the short Lima summer (January to March), the situation is hardly better. Although the sun does come out, the smog makes walking the streets unpleasant, and the city beaches are overcrowded cesspools. The waste products of seven million inhabitants have to go somewhere, and mostly end up in the Pacific; the newspapers publish health warnings about beaches during the summer months.

Despite all this, there are reasons for visiting the city. The inhabitants are generally friendly and hospitable, there are plenty of opportunities for dining, nightlife and other entertainment, and there is a great selection of museums. Besides, it is virtually impossible to avoid Lima.

Orientation

The heart of the city is the Plaza de Armas, flanked by the Government Palace, the Catedral, the Archbishop's Palace and other important buildings. The Plaza de Armas is linked to the Plaza San Martín by the crowded pedestrian street of Jirón (de la) Unión, which is lined with shops. The area around these plazas is historically interesting, and it is here that the majority of budget hotels are found.

South of Plaza San Martín, Jirón Unión continues as Belén and runs to the Paseo de la República. (Many streets in Lima change their names every few blocks, which is confusing to the first-time visitor.) Paseo de la República is graced by the huge Palacio de Justicia, the Sheraton Hotel and many interesting monuments. At the south end of the Paseo is the Plaza Grau, from which the Vía Expresa (locally called 'El Zanjón' – the ditch) is an important expressway to the southern suburbs. Parallel and to the west of the Vía Expresa is Avenida Garcilaso de la Vega, which runs south into Avenida Arequipa and is the main street for bus transport to the southern suburbs of San Isidro, Miraflores and Barranco.

Continuing along Avenida Arequipa for several km to Miraflores leads you to Avenida Larco, which leads in turn to the Pacific Ocean. Half a century ago, Avenida Arequipa traversed ranches and countryside between Lima and the coast; today, every inch of land has been built upon.

The old heart of Lima is the most dangerous area from the point of view of pickpockets and poverty: keep alert. The southern suburbs are not as dangerous. This is where the better-off *limeños* live, and where the more exclusive shops and restaurants are found. Several important museums are also here.

Information

Tourist Offices Infotur (☎ 424-5131, 431-0117), Jirón Unión 1066, is open Monday to Friday from 9.30 am to 6 pm, and on Saturday from 10 am to 2 pm. It has general Peru information. The Municipalidad (☎ 427-6080), Jirón Unión 300, open Monday to Friday from 8.30 am to 1.30 pm, has Lima information. In Miraflores a municipal tourist information booth in Parque Kennedy is open daily from 9 am to 8 pm.

South American Explorers Club (☎ & fax 425-0142) The SAEC's Lima office is at República de Portugal 146 in the Breña district. Hours are Monday to Friday, 9.30 am to 5 pm. The postal address is Casilla 3714, Lima 100, Peru. For more information see Useful Organisations in the Facts for the Visitor chapter.

Money Interbanc, at Jirón Unión 600 or at Larco 690, Miraflores (and other branches), changes travellers' cheques with low commissions. Hours on weekdays are 9.45 am to 3 pm, and on Saturday 9.45 am to 12.45 pm. The American Express office will not cash its own cheques. Good rates for American Express cheques are given at the Banco Mercantil, at Carabaya and Ucayali or at Larco 467, Miraflores. Hours are weekdays 9 am to 5 pm and Saturday 10 am to noon. Banco de Crédito, Lampa 499, also changes American Express cheques and gives cash advances on Visa cards. Citibank, Dean Valdivia 423, San Isidro, cashes Citicorp cheques at no commission. It is better to cash travellers' cheques into nuevos soles rather than into US dollars to get the best rates.

From January to March, some banks open only in the mornings. During other months hours vary from bank to bank. Expect long queues, especially on Monday morning.

Casas de cambio usually give the same rate as banks for cash, tend to be quicker and are open longer, but don't always change travellers' cheques. There are casas de cambio in the centre of Lima at the intersection of Ocoña and Camaná, and along Larco in Miraflores.

Moneychangers often hang around the casas de cambio – the corner of Plaza San Martín and Ocoña is a favourite spot – and they match the rates in banks or casas de cambio.

Banks at the airport are open late and the one in the international arrivals area is open 24 hours.

If you need money from home, the Banco de Crédito has been recommended.

Report lost American Express travellers' cheques to the company's office at Lima Tours (☎ 427-6624), Belén 1040. Report lost Citicorp cheques to Citibank, and Visa cheques to Banco de Crédito (see above). The Thomas Cook representative is Viajes Laser, Comandante Espinar 331, but Viajes Laser doesn't replace stolen cheques. Other cheques are less easy to negotiate.

Visa cards can be used in Unicard ATMs and at Banco de Crédito, Interbanc and Banco Mercantil. MasterCard can be used at Banco Wiese, at Cuzco 245 and at Diagonal 176, Miraflores. The Banco Mercantil also gives cash advances on MasterCard. American Express cards can be used at Interbanc.

Post & Communications The central post office is in the block on the north-west corner of the Plaza de Armas. It is open Monday to Saturday from 8 am to 8 pm, and on Sunday from 8 am to 2 pm.

Mail held by American Express can be picked up from Lima Tours, Belén 1040, on weekdays from 9 am to noon and 3 to 5 pm.

There are many Telefónica del Perú offices, most of which can send and receive faxes. The office at Bolivia 347 is open from 7 am to 11 pm (later than most others). The telephone code for Lima is 01.

Visa Extensions Since late 1995, Migraciones has been at España and Huaraz, four blocks west of Alfonso Ugarte.

Cultural Centres These present a variety of cultural programmes (plays, film screenings, art shows, lectures etc) at irregular intervals.

Alliance Française
    Arequipa 4598, Miraflores (☎ 446-8511)
British Council
    Alberto Lynch 110, San Isidro (☎ 470-4350)
Goethe Institut
    Jirón Nazca 722, Jesús María (☎ 433-3180)
Instituto Cultural Peruano-Norteamericano
    Arequipa 4798, Miraflores (☎ 446-0381)
    Cuzco 446, Lima (☎ 428 3530)
Peruvian British Cultural Association
    Arequipa 3495, San Isidro (☎ 470-5577)

Bookshops The best selection of English-language guidebooks is at the SAEC. The

ABC bookshop (☎ 444-0372) and the Librería El Pacífico, both near Cine El Pacífico at the Ovalo in Miraflores, have good but expensive selections of English, German and French newspapers, magazines, and books.

The SAEC has hiking maps, road maps and maps of Lima. For topographical maps, the Instituto Geográfico Nacional (☎ 475-9960), Aramburu 1198, Surquillo, is open on weekdays from 9 am to 3 pm; you need your passport to get in.

Emergency The best and most expensive general clinic is the Clínica Anglo-American (☎ 221-3656), on the 3rd block of Salazar, San Isidro. A consultation costs up to US$45 and a gamma globulin shot costs US$35. In San Borja, try the Clínica San Borja (☎ 441-3141), Avenida del Aire 333. In central Lima, there's the Clínica Internacional (☎ 428-8060), Washington 1475. All these have 24-hour service and some English-speaking staff. The Clínica Adventista (☎ 445-9040), Malecón Balta 956, Miraflores, is cheaper – about US$23 for a consultation.

For the cheapest yellow fever, tetanus, and typhoid shots, try the Hospital de Niños (☎ 424-6045), Brasil 600. For tropical diseases, try Instituto de Medicina Tropical (☎ 482-3903, 482-3910), at the Universidad Particular Cayetano Heredia, Avenida Honorio Delgado, San Martín de Porres.

If you are bitten by a dog or other animal and need a rabies shot, call the Centro Antirrábico (☎ 431-4047).

A recommended English-speaking doctor is Dr Alejandro Bussalle Rivera (☎ 471-2238), León Velarde 221, Lince. For dental work, see Dr Gerardo Aste and son (☎ 441-7502), Antero Aspillaga 415, Office 101, San Isidro.

There are several opticians along Cailloma, in the centre, and around Schell and Larco in Miraflores. Having a new pair of glasses made is not expensive.

For emergencies ranging from robbery to rabies contact the Policía de Turismo (☎ 437-8171, 435-1342), Museo de la Nación, Javier Prado Este 2465, San Borja,

open from 8 am to 8 pm. They are helpful and some speak English.

Other emergency numbers are for the police (☎ 105) and fire service (☎ 116).

A 24-hour hot line (☎ 471-2994, 471-2809, fax 471-1617) is available to answer questions and give advice in case of emergencies and for visitors who feel they have been cheated or overcharged by hotels, tour operators etc. Both English and Spanish-speaking operators are available.

Museums

Opening hours change frequently, and are often shortened drastically from January to March, when it is best to go in the morning. Photography is usually not allowed.

The **Museo de la Nación** (☎ 437-7797), Javier Prado Este 2465, San Borja, is a new state-run museum with the best overview of Peru's archaeology and other exhibits. There is a theatre, and lectures are given. Hours are Tuesday to Friday from 9 am to 7 pm, and Saturday and Sunday from 10 am to 7 pm. Adults/students pay US$1.50/0.75. This is the best value of Lima's museums and is a must-see.

The **Museo de Oro del Perú** (☎ 435-0791, 435-2917), Alonso de Molina 100, Monterrico, has two museums in the same building. The gold museum is in a huge basement vault. There are literally thousands of gold pieces, ranging from ear plugs to ponchos embroidered with hundreds of solid gold plates. There are also many artefacts of silver and precious stones. Unfortunately, there are few signs. The top half of the building houses a **Museo de Armas**, reputedly one of the best arms museums in the world. Hours are noon to 7 pm daily. Entry (to both museums) is US$5.

The **Museo Rafael Larco Herrera** (☎ 461-1312), Bolívar 1515, Pueblo Libre, contains one of the most impressive collections of ceramics to be found anywhere. There are said to be about 55,000 pots here, as well as exhibits of mummies, a gold room, a small cactus garden, textiles made from feathers, and a Paracas weaving which contains 398 threads to a linear inch – a world

Central Lima

0   150   300 m

4
Hualgayoc

Otero Castañeda

Amauta de los Desagües

Julian Piñeyro

Marañon

Tumpayode

Chiclayo

Amauta Prida

Cajamarca

Trujillo

Chira

Ayacucho

Ica

3

16   17

15   13

14   12

Ancash

Junin

La Catedral

Plaza
de Armas

Estación
Desamparados

Amazonas

22   21   20   19   18   34

24   23

Plaza
Bolivar

51

Huallaga

49

48   47

46   45

43
42   41   40

33

31   32

30

29   28

27   26   25

Av de los Proceres

Francisco Pizarro

Héctor García Ribeyro

Emilio Bujanda

Julio Becerra

Santa Cruz Pachacci

Polo de Ortiguera

Fray Andrés Díaz

Río Rímac

Sancho de Rivera

Conde de Superunda

Callao

Ramón Espinoza

Puente Santa Rosa

Jesús de Asin

Puente Ricardo Palma

Huancavelica

Emancipación

Moquegua

Ferreñafe

Cuzco

Ucayali

Nicolás de Piérola (Colmena)

Ocoña

Zepita

39

38

37

36

35

Plaza
Castilla

Alfonso Ugarte

Plaza
2 de
Mayo

Huarochin

Argentina

G. Dansey

R. Benavides

Borda

Sánchez Pinillos

Zepita

Huaraz

Augustín de Zárate

PERU

PERU

PLACES TO STAY
- 6 Pensión Ibarra
- 9 Hotel Residencial Roma
- 10 Gran Hotel Savoy
- 18 Hostal Lima
- 21 Hotel Europa
- 23 Hostal España
- 25 Wilson Hotel
- 28 Hotel Claridge
- 33 Pensión Unión
- 34 Hostal Wiracocha
- 36 Hostal Residencial Los Virreyes
- 38 Hotel Crillón
- 39 Hostal del Sol
- 40 Hotel La Casona
- 41 Hostal Samaniego
- 46 Hostal Damascus
- 47 Gran Hotel Maury
- 56 Familia Rodríguez
- 58 Hostal San Martín & Hotel El Plaza
- 60 Gran Hotel Bolívar
- 65 Hotel Richmond
- 72 Hotel Eiffel
- 73 Hostal Kori Wasi II
- 76 Hostal Belén
- 77 Hostal La Estrella de Belén
- 79 Hostal Universo
- 81 Gran Hotel
- 88 Hostal Iquique
- 91 Lima Sheraton
- 96 Hotel Grand Castle
- 104 Hostal de las Artes

PLACES TO EAT
- 2 Govinda
- 11 Manhattan Restaurant
- 12 Tic Tac Chifa
- 19 El Cordano
- 20 Restaurant Machu Picchu
- 24 Las Trece Monedas
- 30 La Casera
- 32 El Pan Nuestro
- 44 Raimondi
- 55 Pastelería Kudani
- 57 Casa Vasca
- 58 Parrilladas San Martín
- 63 Natur
- 68 L'Eau Vive
- 80 Heydi
- 82 El Capricho
- 87 Chifa La Paisana
- 89 La Choza Náutica

OTHER
- 1 Santuario de Santa Rosa de Lima
- 3 Hatuchay
- 4 Plaza de Acho & Museo Taurino
- 5 Church of Las Nazarenas
- 7 Cine Central
- 8 Teatro Municipal
- 13 Municipalidad
- 14 Church of Santo Domingo
- 15 Monumento de Francisco Pizarro
- 16 Correos Central & Museo Filatélico
- 17 Palacio de Gobierno
- 22 Church of San Francisco & Catacombs
- 26 Cine Tacna
- 27 Cine Lido
- 29 Teatro Segura
- 31 Church of San Agustín
- 35 Museo de la Cultura Peruana
- 37 Cine Portofino
- 42 Interbanc
- 43 Church of La Merced
- 45 Banco Mercantil
- 48 Museo del Banco Central de Reserva
- 49 Banco de Crédito
- 50 Museo de la Inquisición
- 51 Congreso
- 52 Turismo Chimbote
- 53 Cruz del Sur
- 54 Faucett Airline
- 59 P&P Casa de Cambio
- 61 McDollar & Other Casas de Cambio
- 62 Cine Plaza
- 64 Cine Excelsior
- 66 Cine Adán y Eva
- 67 Banco Wiese
- 69 Palacio Torre Tagle
- 70 Church of San Pedro
- 71 Mercado Central
- 74 Infotur
- 75 Lima Tours & American Express
- 78 CPT International Telephone Office & Cine Metro
- 83 Telefónica del Perú 24-Hour Fax Location
- 84 Cine República
- 85 Olano
- 86 South American Explorers Club
- 90 Cine Conquistador
- 92 Museo de Arte Italiano
- 93 Palacio de Justicia
- 94 TEPSA
- 95 Transportes Rodríguez
- 97 Ormeño & Subsidiaries
- 98 Transportes Vista Alegre
- 99 Movil Tours, Paradise Tours
- 100 Buses to Chosica
- 101 Empresa Huaraz
- 102 Buses to Pachacámac & Pucusana
- 103 Santa Catalina Convent
- 105 Colectivos to Chosica; Cruz del Sur Ticket Office, Civa Cial; Mariscal Cáceres, Soyuz
- 106 Buses to Cañete, Chincha, Ica
- 107 Expreso Sudamericano
- 108 Transfysa
- 109 Comité 12 to Huancayo
- 110 Olano
- 111 Las Brisas del Lago Titicaca
- 112 Museo de Arte, Filmoteca
- 113 Transportes León de Huánuco & Transmar

record. In a separate building is the famous collection of pre-Columbian erotic pots, depicting the sexual practices of several Peruvian cultures. Hours are 9 am to 6 pm daily, except Sunday, when it closes at 1 pm. Adults/students pay US$5/2.50.

Housed in a handsome building, Lima's **Museo de Arte** (☎ 423-4732), Paseo de Colón 125, has a collection which ranges from colonial furniture to pre-Columbian artefacts, and includes canvases from four centuries of Peruvian art. Hours are Tuesday to Sunday, 10 am to 1 pm and 2 to 5 pm. Entry is about US$1. Nearby in a park on the 2nd block of Paseo de la República is the neoclassical building housing the **Museo de Arte Italiano** (☎ 423-9932). Italian and other European paintings, sculptures and prints, mainly from the early 20th century, are exhibited. Hours are Monday to Friday from 8.30 am to 2 pm. Adults/students pay US$0.50/0.25.

The **Museo Amano** (☎ 441-2909), Retiro 160, off the 11th block of Angamos in Miraflores, houses a fine private collection of ceramics, arranged chronologically to show the development of pottery through Peru's various pre-Columbian cultures. The museum specialises in the Chancay culture. Entry is in small groups and by telephone appointment only. All groups are met by a guide, who will show you around in exactly an hour; it is best if you understand Spanish. Tours are free, and are available on weekdays at 2, 3, 4 and 5 pm, very punctually.

Another private collection is the **Museo Pedro de Osma** (☎ 467-0915, 467-0019), Pedro de Osma 421, Barranco, with a fine selection of colonial art, furniture, sculpture, metalwork etc from all over Peru. Entry is limited to 10 persons and is by appointment only. Call the day before. Guided tours (US$3) last 90 minutes and leave on weekdays at 11 am or 4 pm.

The **Museo Nacional de Antropología y Arqueología** (☎ 463-5070), Plaza Bolívar, Pueblo Libre, used to be Lima's best, but many pieces are now in the Museo de la Nación. It's still worth a visit. Hours are Tuesday to Saturday from 9 am to 6 pm, and Sunday from 9 am to 5 pm. Entry is US$1.50. Next door, the **Museo Nacional de la República** (☎ 463-2009), has similar hours and admission. It is mainly of interest to students of the Peruvian revolution.

The **Museo del Banco Central de Reserva** (☎ 427-6250), in the Banco Central de Reserva at the corner of Ucayali and Lampa, specialises in ceramics from the Vicus culture, among other exhibits. It offers welcome relief from the hustle and bustle of the city centre. Hours are Tuesday to Friday

from 10 am to 4 pm, and on weekends from 10 am to 1 pm. Entry is by showing your passport.

The **Museo de la Inquisición** (☎ 428-7980), Junín 548, is in the building used by the Spanish Inquisition from 1570 to 1820 and now a university library. Visitors can visit the basement where prisoners were tortured. Student guides give tours (Spanish) of ghoulish waxworks of life-sized unfortunates on the rack or having their feet roasted. There's a remarkable wooden ceiling in the library upstairs. Hours are 9 am to 1 pm and 2.30 to 5 pm on weekdays. Entry is free.

The **Museo de la Cultura Peruana** (☎ 423-5892), Alfonso Ugarte 650, is a small museum concentrating on popular art and handicrafts. Ceramics, carved gourds, recent and traditional folk art, and regional costumes are exhibited. Hours are Tuesday to Saturday, 10 am to 2 pm. Adults/students pay US$0.50/0.25.

The **Museo de Historia Natural** (☎ 471-0117), Arenales 1256, has a modest collection of stuffed animals if you want to familiarise yourself with Peru's fauna. Hours are weekdays from 9 am to 6 pm, and Saturday from 9 am to 1 pm. Adults/students pay US$1/0.50.

The **Museo Numismático del Banco Wiese** (☎ 427-5060, ext 553), Cuzco 245, exhibits Peruvian coins, bills and medals from colonial days to today. Hours are 9.15 am to 12.45 pm weekdays and entry is free. The **Museo Filatélico** (☎ 428-7931) in Lima's main post office, has an incomplete collection of Peruvian stamps and has stamps for sale. Hours are weekdays from 9 am to 2 pm, and weekends from 10 am to noon. Entry is free.

The **Museo Taurino** (☎ 482-3360), Hualgayoc 332, Rimac, is next to Lima's bullring. Exhibits include a holed and bloodstained costume worn by a matador who was gored and killed in the bullring some years ago. Hours are Monday to Saturday, 8 am to 4 pm. Adults/students pay US$0.50/0.25.

Religious Buildings

There are many churches, monasteries and

convents in Lima, and they are a quiet break. Hours are very erratic; those given below are subject to change.

The original **Catedral** was built on the south-eastern side of the Plaza de Armas in 1555, but has been destroyed by earthquakes and reconstructed several times, most recently in 1746. The present reconstruction is based on early plans. The coffin and remains of Francisco Pizarro are in the mosaic-covered chapel to the right of the main door. Also of interest are the carved choir and the small religious museum at the back of the Cathedral. Hours are 10 am to 1 pm and 2 to 5 pm on weekdays and 10 am to 3.30 pm on Saturday. Adults/students pay US$1.50/0.75.

The **San Francisco** monastery is famous for its catacombs, estimated to contain the remains of 70,000 people. Less famous is the remarkable library, with thousands of antique texts, some dating back to the Spanish conquest. The church, on the corner of Lampa and Ancash, is one of the best preserved of Lima's early colonial churches and much of the church has been restored in its original baroque style with Moorish (Arab) influence. Guided tours (English and Spanish) are worth joining to see the catacombs, library and cloister, and a museum of religious art, which nonguided visitors don't see. Hours are 9.30 am to 5.30 pm. Entry is US$2 (tour included). English tours leave at least every hour; Spanish tours, more often.

The infrequently visited **Convento de los Descalzos** is at the end of the Alameda de los Descalzos, an attractive if somewhat forgotten avenue in the Rimac district. The visitor can see the refectory, the infirmary, typical Franciscan cells, old wine-making equipment in the 17th-century kitchen, and 300 colonial paintings. Spanish-speaking guides give tours lasting 40 minutes. Entry is US$0.50 and hours are 9.30 am to 1 pm and 3 to 5.45 pm daily.

At the **Santuario de Santa Rosa de Lima** is a peaceful garden and chapel on the site where Santa Rosa (the western hemisphere's first saint) was born. The sanctuary itself is a small adobe hut built by Santa Rosa in the early 1600s for prayer and meditation. Hours are 9.30 am to 1 pm and 3 to 6 pm daily. Entry is free.

The church of **Santo Domingo**, on the first block of Camaná, was built on the land that Francisco Pizarro granted in 1535 to his Dominican friar Vicente Valverde. Construction began in 1540 and finished in 1599, but much of the interior was modernised in the late 1700s. The tombs of Santa Rosa and San Martín de Porras (the Americas' first black saint) are in the church. There is an alabaster statue of Santa Rosa, presented to the church by Pope Clement in 1669, and fine tilework showing the life of St Dominic. The cloisters are pleasantly quiet. Hours are from 7 am to 1 pm and 4 to 8 pm daily. The monastery and tombs are open Monday to Saturday from 9 am to 12.30 pm and 3 to 6 pm, and on Sunday and holy days from 9 am to 1 pm. Entry is US$1.

The church of **La Merced** was built on the site of the first mass said in Lima (in 1534). Inside are an ornately carved chancel and attractively decorated cloister. It is on Jirón Unión, near the corner with Miró Quesada. Hours are 8 am to 12.30 pm and 4 to 8 pm daily. The cloister is open on weekdays from 9 am to noon and 3 to 5 pm. A museum is planned.

The small baroque church of **San Pedro**, on the corner of Azangaro and Ucayali, is one of the finest examples of early colonial architecture in Lima. Consecrated by the Jesuits in 1638, it has changed little since. The interior is sumptuously decorated with gilded altars and an abundance of beautiful glazed tilework. Hours are 7 am to 12.30 pm and 4.45 to 8 pm daily.

Markets

Lima's main market is north-west of the corner of Ayacucho and Ucayali. Although it occupies the whole city block, this is not nearly enough space, and stalls and vendors completely congest the streets for several blocks around. You can buy almost anything, but be prepared for crowds and pickpockets. Don't bring valuables.

The streets behind the Central Post Office

are the focus of the **Polvos Azules** black market. It's as crowded as the main market and has a remarkable variety of consumer goods. This is the place if you're looking for smuggled luxuries such as ghetto blasters or perfume.

The **Indian artisans' market** is along the northern side of Avenida de la Marina, on the 600 to 1000 blocks. There is a great selection of handicrafts here, but the quality and prices vary a good deal, so shop carefully.

Plazas

The oldest part of the **Plaza de Armas** is the impressive bronze fountain, which was erected in the centre in 1650. The exquisitely balconied Archbishop's palace, to the left of the Cathedral, is a relatively modern building dating from 1924. The Palacio de Gobierno, on the north-eastern side of the plaza, dates from the same period. The handsomely uniformed presidential guard is on duty all day, and the ceremonial changing of the guard takes place at 11.45 am. The other buildings around the plaza are also modern. the Municipalidad (town hall) built in 1945, the Unión Club and various shops and cafés. There is an impressive statue of Francisco Pizarro on horseback, on the corner of the plaza opposite the Catedral.

The major **Plaza San Martín** dates from the early 1900s. The bronze statue of the liberator, General José de San Martín, was erected in 1921. Five blocks of the pedestrian street **Jirón Unión** connect Plaza San Martín with the Plaza de Armas. Along it are jewellery stores, bookshops and cinemas, and the church of La Merced. It is always very crowded with shoppers, sightseers, vendors and pickpockets.

Zoo

This is in Parque Las Leyendas, between Lima and Callao. Most of the animals are from Peru, and there are three sections, representing the coast, the sierra and the Amazon Basin. Entry is US$1. Hours are 9 am to 5 pm daily, except Monday.

Suburbs

The suburb most frequently visited is **Miraflores**, on the beachfront. Many of the capital's best restaurants and nightspots are found here, and the pavement cafés are places to hang out, to see and be seen. The prices and quality of everything from a sweater to a steak will be higher in Miraflores than in other parts of the city.

The suburb of **Barranco** is popular with artists and students and has excellent nightlife. There are several good restaurants, craft shops and *peñas* (live music venues) in the area.

Activities

Swimming and surfing are popular with limeños from January to March, though surfers are seen year round. The water is heavily polluted and newspapers warn of serious health hazards. Thieves on the beach mean you can't leave anything unattended for a second. Despite this, beaches are crowded at weekends in season; hanging out on the beach is free and very popular, despite the dirty water. It's best to go in a sizeable group and avoid bringing valuables. Cleaner beaches south of Lima often have dangerous currents, and drownings are frequent. I (Rob) don't like any of them.

Organised Tours

Tours bought in Lima which visit other parts of Peru are much more expensive than tours bought in the nearest major town to the area you wish to visit.

For various guided tours of Lima, Lima Tours (☎ 427-6624), Belén 1040, is one of the best. Its tours start at US$15 to US$20 per person. Comfortable transport and English-speaking guides are provided.

For specialised tours for individuals or small groups, the SAEC recommends Tino Guzmán (☎ 429-5779). Rates start at US$6 per hour plus expenses.

The Río Cañete, three or four hours drive south of Lima, has river-running opportunities. Organised trips start at US$20. The following run trips there:

PERU

Apumayo Expediciones, Emilio Cavencia 160, Oficina 201, San Isidro (☎ & fax 442-3886)

Aventura Perú (☎ 440-5584)

CanoAndes, San Martín 455, Barranco (☎ 477-0188)

Cascada Expediciones, San Lorenzo 219, Miraflores (☎ 446-6022)

Peruvian River & Mountain (☎ 448-2168)

TrekAndes, Benavides 212, Miraflores (☎ 445-8078)

Places to Stay

Hotels are more expensive in Lima than in other cities. Most of the cheapest are in the centre, which is less safe (though not really dangerous) than the more expensive suburb of Miraflores.

Central Lima *Hostal España* (☎ 428-5546), Azangaro 105, (no sign), is a favourite of gringo budget travellers. Accommodation is basic, clean, safe and friendly and costs US$3 each in shared rooms and US$6/9 for singles/doubles. There are hot showers, laundry facilities, a small café and a roof-top terrace (where animals are kept in too-small cages). Nearby is the equally cheap but shabbier and less pleasant *Hotel Europa* (☎ 427-3351), Ancash 376. The communal showers sometimes have hot water. The dingy old *Hostal Lima* (☎ 428-5782), Carabaya 145, charges US$8 for a double or US$5 for a couple (one bed), and claims to have hot water. The friendly *Pensión Unión* (☎ 428-4136), Unión 442, 3rd floor, charges US$4 per person (US$3 for students) and, sometimes, has hot water in the evenings.

The old but clean *Hostal Belén* (☎ 427-8995), Jirón Belén 1049, has hot water and is popular with young Europeans. Rooms cost US$7/10. The basic but safe *Hostal Universo* (☎ 428-0619), Azangaro 754, is near several bus terminals. Rooms with private tepid showers are US$7/10, less with communal baths.

The friendly *Familia Rodríguez* (☎ 423-6465), Nicolás de Piérola 730, 2nd floor, is popular, helpful and recommended. Dormitory-style rooms are US$5 per person including breakfast. The *Hostal Samaniego*, Emancipación 184, Apartment 801, is also friendly with dorm rooms for US$5 per person.

The recommended *Pensión Ibarra*, Tacna 359, 16th floor, is run by women who keep this place safe, comfortable, and clean. Kitchen facilities are available. Rates are $7 per person including breakfast.

The *Hostal Damascus* (☎ 427-6029), Ucayali 199, is fairly clean and friendly although the rooms are musty. A double is US$10 with hot shower, less with shared bath. The *Hotel Claridge* (☎ 428-3680), Cailloma 437, has adequate rooms for US$7.50/10 with hot showers. The friendly *Hostal Wiracocha* (☎ 427-1178), Junín 270, has rooms with hot water for US$10/12; less without hot showers. The *Hotel La Casona* (☎ 427-6273/6275), Moquegua 289, has a plant-filled lobby which hints at an elegant past. The carpeted rooms are shabby but OK and the hot water is reliable. Rooms with bath cost US$10/12.50. The *Wilson Hotel* (☎ 424-8924), Chancay 633, has doubles with hot showers for US$12.

The *Hostal Iquique* (☎ 433-4724), Iquique 758, is clean, friendly and has hot water. Rooms are US$7.50/11 or US$11/12.50 with bath. *Hostal Kori Wasi II* (☎ 433-8127), Washington 1139, is clean and has rooms with bath, mini-fridge and TV for $13 a double (one bed). The friendly *Hotel Residencial Roma* (☎ 427-7576, fax 427-7572), Ica 326, is clean, central and attractive, and charges US$15/20 with hot shower and US$10/15 with shared bath. An inexpensive travel agency is attached.

Miraflores The *Youth Hostel* (☎ 446-5488), Casimiro Ulloa 328, charges US$8 or US$10 per person. There are laundry facilities, travel information, and minimal kitchen facilities. The similarly priced *Pensión José Luis* (☎ 444-1015), F Paula Ugarriza 727, (no sign) is clean and quiet. Reservations are needed at this popular pensión, which has rooms of various sizes, some with kitchenettes. The *Pensión San Antonio* (☎ 447-5830), Paseo de la República 5809, is friendly and often full. It costs $10 per person or $12.50 with private hot shower.

The following have *rooms in private houses*. M Luisa Chávez (☎ 447-3996),

Género Castro Iglesias 273, charges US$8/15 for singles/doubles or US$10/17 with breakfast. Señora Jordan (☎ 445-9840), Porta 724, is friendly and charges US$12 per person, including breakfast. Rosa Alonso (☎ 423-7463), Larraboren 231, Jesús María, charges US$10 per person.

Pensión Yolanda, run by the friendly English-speaking Yolanda Escobar (☎ 445-7565), Domingo Elías 230, charges US$12/20 for singles/doubles including breakfast and kitchen privileges.

Places to Eat

Taxes and service charges on meals can be an exorbitant 31%; check first if you're on a tight budget. Cheaper restaurants don't add taxes.

Central Lima Here, a menú (set lunch) is under US$2 in some places. The unnamed *chifa* at Ancash 306 has large, inexpensive portions of tallarines (noodle dinners). Nearby, *Restaurant Machu Picchu*, Ancash 312, is popular with gringos while *El Capricho*, Bolivia 328, is popular with locals. Both are good and cheap. The *Tic Tac Chifa*, Callao 184, is cheap and clean with set lunches for US$1.25. *Chifa La Paisana*, 13th block of Alfonso Ugarte, has cheap, large portions of good food.

The friendly, family-run *Natur*, Moquegua 132, has inexpensive vegetarian meals. *Govinda*, Callao 480, is cheaper but worse than the one in Miraflores. *Heydi*, Puno 367, is a popular lunch-time cevichería. *La Casera*, Huancavelica 244, has a good range of typical Peruvian food at reasonable prices. The *Manhattan Restaurant*, Cailloma 225, has a pleasant atmosphere and good set lunch menu for US$2. *El Pan Nuestro*, Ica 129, has a US$2.50 set lunch in very nice surroundings. The *Pastelería Kudani*, Nicolás de Piérola 716, serves good cakes and pastries.

On Quilca, between the Plaza San Martín and Avenida Garcilaso de la Vega, there are several inexpensive restaurants. There are plenty of others all over Lima.

Our favourite seafood restaurant is *La Choza Náutica* (☎ 424-1766), Breña 204.

Great ceviches and other dishes are about US$6. The *Raimondi*, Miró Quesada 110, is a good lunch-time restaurant popular with Lima's businesspeople. There's no sign and the exterior gives no indication of the spacious comfort within. A set lunch is US$3.50 and there are many more expensive options.

Another favourite is *L'Eau Vive* (☎ 427-5712), Ucayali 370, which features dishes from all over the world, prepared and served by a French order of nuns. It's in a quiet colonial-style house and offers welcome relief from the Lima madhouse. Set lunches are US$6 and evening dinners close to US$20, but profits go to charity. The nuns sing an Ave María at the end of dinner (9 pm).

Miraflores Here, restaurants are more expensive. The vegetarian places are among the cheapest, including *Govinda*, Schell 630, run by the Hare Krishnas, and the *Bircher Berner* (☎ 444-4250), Schell 598, with good food but very slow service. The lunch menu here is US$3. *Restaurant Vegetariano*, Manuel Bonilla 178, also has breads and products to take away.

Burger King, Larco 235, and *Whatta Burger*, Grau 120, are cheap and popular. Inexpensive Peruvian-style fast food is available 24 hours a day at *Tomas*, above the MASS supermarket, Benavides 486. The trendy *La Huerta del Sol* (☎ 444-2900), La Paz 522, in the pricey El Alamo shopping plaza, has a US$3 set lunch and other plates for about US$5. Many meals are vegetarian. *Super Rueda II*, Porta 133, is good for tacos and sandwiches.

Cebichería Don Beta (☎ 446-9465), José Gálvez 667, is a good seafood restaurant and there are several others nearby. They are locally popular for lunch but quiet in the evenings. Ceviches start around US$7. *Las Tejas* (☎ 444-4360), Diez Canseco 340, has good Peruvian fare around US$10. *El Trapiche*, Larco 1031, is a locally popular place serving good seafood and meat in the US$15 to US$20 range.

Lovers of Italian food will find several pizzerías by the Parque Kennedy in Miraflores which are a bit pricey, but are popular

PERU

Parque
Blume

Parque
Villena

Parque
Palacios

Parque
Tahuantinsuyo
Huaca Juliana

José Antonio Sarrio Montero

Tarapacá Domingo Elías
2 ■ ■ 3

1 ▼
Av Angamos Oeste Av Angamos Este

Av Angamos

Sucre

Av Mariscal la Mar

Av Santa Cruz

Córdova

Chiclayo

El Rosario

Piura

Plaza
Manuel
Solan

Chiclayo

Piura

Ricardo Flores
▼ 4

Av Petit Thouars

Grau-Suárez

Paseo de la República (Vía Expresa)

5 ●

Aguero

Gonzales

Enrique Palacios

Pershing

Parque
Miranda

27 de Noviembre

Gestelio Chiacallaria

Juan Bardelli (antes Varela)

Av José Pardo

Av Espinar

Julio Iglesias

Elías Aguirre

Iglesias

Borgoño

Independencia

Inclán

Dos de Mayo

Alfahuina

Narciso de la Colina

Gonzales Prada

▼ 8
12 ■

13 ■ 14 ■

16 ● ■ 17

Av Arequipa

24 ▼

Plaza
Centro
América

CR-Morales

Túpac Amaru

Figueredo

Gálvez

Ramón Zavala

Martín Nádalga

Plaza
Morales
Barros

7 ●

Roma

Berlín

José Gálvez

Francia

25 ▼

Madrid

Bolognesi

9 ●

Av Grau

Av José Pardo

10 ●

11 ●

Federico Recavarren

Gerdes

Bellavista

▼ 15

18 ▼

Óvalo

Av Ricardo Palma

20 21 ■ 23
▼ ▼ S

Manuel Bonilla

19 ▼ 22
Esperanza

Parque
Central

26 ▼

32 ●
31 ▼ 30
29 ●
28

33

Cantuarias

34

37 38 ■ 39

Ernesto Díez Canseco

35 36

■ 40

27 ▼

Schell

41 ●

42 ●

43 ▼ 44
▼ 45

Diagonal

Tarata

Schell

50 ● 53 ▼ ■ 54

51 52 55 ▼ 56

46 S

47 ▼
48 ▼
49 ●

■ 57

Alfredo Benavides

65 ▼

Av de la Paz

69 ▼

70 ▼

67 ▼

Bolívar

66 ▼

68 ▼

San Martín

64 ▼

Grimaldo del Solar

61 ●

62 ■

63 ■

Porta

Ocharán

Colón

2a de Julio

Av Larco

Manco Cápac

73 ▼ 74
▼

José Gonzales

Diez Canseco

72 ■

Juan Fanning

75 ▼

Diego Ferré

76 ■

Aristides Alfovin

Las Dalias

Alcanfores

Santa Isabel

San Fernando

71 ▼

PACIFIC
OCEAN

Playa Costa Verde

77 ▼

Parque
Salazar

Av Armendáriz

Parque
Melitón
Porras

Vasco Núñez de Balboa

Carolinga

Ignacio de Loyola

Las Acacias

cliff

Málecon Cisneros

Parque
Raimondi

Parque
del Amor

Málecon Balta

Málecon 2a de Julio

Málecon de la Reserva

Italia

Trípoli

Venecia

P. Asunción

Plaza
Bolognesi

Miraflores

0   200   400 m

PLACES TO STAY	
2	Hostal Residencial Alemana
3	Pensión Yolanda
6	Hostal Torreblanca
12	Residencial Huaychulo
14	Hotel El Doral
14	El Pardo
37	Hostal El Patio
39	Miraflores César
40	Hostal Esperanza
47	Hotel Las Américas
49	El Condado
50	Hotel María Angola
54	Hostal Inca Palace
55	La Castellana
58	Pensión San Antonio
59	Youth Hostel
60	Hostal San Antonio Abad
61	Grand Hotel Miraflores
62	Hostal El Ejecutivo
63	Hotel José Antonio
67	La Hacienda
70	Hostal Ariosto
72	Señora Jordan
74	Hostal Señorial
76	Hostal Lucerna

PLACES TO EAT	
1	Quattro D
8	Pizza Hut
15	La Tranquera
19	Burger King
20	La Tiendecita Blanca (Café Suisse)
21	Liverpool & Vivaldis
22	La Trattoria
25	Cebichería Don Beta
26	La Pizzería & other Italian restaurants
35	Las Tejas
36	La Huerta del Sol
44	Super Rueda II
45	Nonno Rossi and others
48	Tomas
51	Carlin
52	El Mono Verde, La Creperie
53	Bircher Berner
56	Govinda
64	La Sueca
65	Fragola & Pasta Subito
71	La Rosa Náutica
73	El Trapiche
75	New York Pizza Company
77	El Rincón Gaucho

OTHER	
4	Post Office
5	Handicraft Market
7	LAB, LanChile, Viasa, American Airlines
9	Santa Isabel Supermarket
10	AeroContinente Airline
11	AeroPerú Airline
16	Lavavelos
17	Brenchley Arms
18	Cine Pacífico, ABC Bookstore
23	Banco Financiero
24	Casa de Ricardo Palma
27	Handicraft Market
28	Bizarro
29	Centro Cultural de Miraflores
30	Municipalidad
31	Church (La Virgen Milagrosa)
32	Tourist Information Booth, Artists' Market
33	Alpamayo Store
34	Banco Mercantil
36	El Alamo Shopping Arcade
38	Telefónica del Perú
41	Faucett
42	Cine Romeo & Cine Julieta
43	Bowling Alley
46	Interbanc
48	MASS Supermarket (24 hours)
51	El Suche Shopping Arcade
57	Taller de Fotografía Profesional
66	Centro de Información y Promoción Turístico
68	El Sargento Pimienta
69	LavaQuick

Parque
Tradiciones

Parque
Reducto

PERU

gathering spots. *New York Pizza Company*, Larco 1145, has good vegetarian pizza. *La Trattoria* (☎ 446-7002), Bonilla 106, has tasty, home-made pasta (which you can watch being made). Meals are about US$8 to US$15. Cheaper but still good is *Nonno Rossi*, Porta 185a. Also cheap is *Pasta Subito*, serving Italian fast food almost next door to *Fragola*, Benavides 468, which has good Italian ice cream. *Quattro D* (☎ 447-1523), Angamos Oeste 408, has great ice cream, desserts and coffee.

Miraflores has many outdoor cafés which are pricey but great for people-watching. The *Haití* (☎ 445-0539), on the traffic circle next to the El Pacífico cinema, and, opposite, *La Tiendecita Blanca* (☎ 445-9797), Larco 111, are among the best known. Others are found on the 200 block of Ricardo Palma and along Larco.

The *Brenchley Arms* (☎ 445-9680), Atahualpa 174, is a British pub run by Englishman Mike Ella and his Peruvian wife, Martha. Prices are steep for budget travellers, but it's worth it if you're homesick for a pub. There is a dart board and you can read the British newspapers. Hours are 6 pm till late; pub meals are served till 10 pm daily, except Sunday.

Barranco Budget travellers should try the *anticucho stands* by El Puente de los Suspiros. Or grab a you-know-what at *Sandwiches Monstruos*, on Piérola near Grau, or a reasonably priced pizza around the corner at *Tío Dan. La Canta Rana* (☎ 445-0498), Génova 101, has good ceviches starting around US$5 and other seafood is also available; it's open for lunch only. *Abdala*, Grau 340, is good for felafel and Arabic food. *D'Puccio*, San Pedro de Osma at Lavalle, has a cosy atmosphere, and seafood and meat dishes around US$8.

Entertainment

El Comercio lists cinemas, theatres, art galleries and music shows. The English monthly magazine *Lima Times* has an abbreviated listing of what's going on.

There are dozens of cinemas. Foreign

films are normally screened with their original sound track and Spanish subtitles. Entry is US$2 to US$4 and may be half-price on Tuesday. Cinema clubs show better films. The *Filmoteca* at Lima's Museo de Arte is good and charges only US$1. The *Cinematógrafo* (☎ 477-1961), Pérez Roca 196, Barranco, screens excellent films for about US$3.50.

The *Teatro Municipal* (☎ 428-2303), Ica 300, has the symphony, opera, plays and ballet. The best seats are relatively expensive, and cheap tickets cost several dollars. Another good venue is the *Teatro Segura* (☎ 427-7437), Huancavelica 261. For plays in English, see the local theatre group *The Good Companions* (☎ 447-9760), run by the British Council. They are always looking for help, so call if interested.

A good peña folklórica which is popular with limeños is *Las Brisas del Lago Titicaca* (☎ 423-7405), Wakulski 168. The peña *Hatuchay* (☎ 427-2827), Trujillo 228, Rimac, just across the bridge behind the Government Palace, is mainly folklórica, with plenty of audience participation and dancing (during the second half). This popular place is one of the less expensive ones. The doors open about 9 pm and the music gets under way about 10 pm. Get there early for a good seat. A taxi is not a bad idea.

In Miraflores, *Sachun Peña* (☎ 441-0123, 441-4465), Avenida del Ejército 657, has a variety of acts which get under way around midnight. The cover charge is about US$10.

Barranco is currently the most happening place with many bars, peñas and revellers on Friday and Saturday night. *La Estación* (☎ 467-8804), Pedro de Osma 112, and *Los Balcones* (☎ 495-1149), Grau 294, are among the best criolla peñas, but cover charge can be as high as US$15. There are several others.

Barranco's bars include *Juanito*, Grau 274, a leftist peña of the 1960s which retains its early simple decor and is a popular hangout now for expats. The party crowd are often in *La Noche* (☎ 477-4154), Bolognesi 317, which nestles snugly at the end of a street crammed with trendy bars. *Ludwig Bar*

Beethoven, Grau 687, has classical music, often live. *El Ekeko Café Bar* (☎ 467-1729), Grau 266, is another popular choice.

Getting There & Away

Air Lima's Aeropuerto Internacional Jorge Chávez is in Callao, 12 km from the centre or 16 km from Miraflores. There is a post office (open during the day), a long-distance telephone office (open until late at night) and a 24-hour luggage storage room, which charges about US$2 per piece per day. Banks are open during all flight times. A 24-hour restaurant is open upstairs.

About 30 international airlines have offices in Lima. Check the yellow pages under 'Aviación' for telephone numbers, and call before you go, as offices change address frequently.

Airlines offering domestic flights include:

AeroCóndor
> Juan de Arona 781, San Isidro (☎ 442-5215, 442-5663, fax 442-9487)
> Airport (☎ 452-3254)

AeroContinente
> Francisco Masías 544, San Isidro (☎ 442-6458, 442-7829)
> Reservations (☎ 451-8280, 442-8770)
> Central Switchboard (☎ 221-3069, 221-3099, fax 221-0835)
> Miami, USA (☎ (1-800) 249-4733, fax (1-305) 346-0430)

AeroPerú
> Garcilaso de la Vega 870 (☎ 433-1341)
> José Pardo 601, Miraflores (☎ 447-8900, 447-8255)
> 24-hour reservations (☎ 447-8333)

Americana
> Larco 345, Miraflores (☎ 447-1902)
> Benavides 439, Miraflores (☎ 444-1246, 444-0027, fax 444-3950)
> 24-hour reservations (☎ 447-1919)
> Airport (☎ & fax 452-5408)

Expreso Aéreo
> Edificio Caracol, Larco 101, 3rd floor (☎ 447-4631, 241-2547)

Faucett
> Garcilaso de la Vega 865 (☎ 433-6364, fax 433-7137)
> Diagonal 592, Miraflores (☎ 446-3444, fax 445-7649)
> Reservations (☎ 464-3322, 452-6641, 451-9711, fax 464-3510)

PERU

Imperial Air
   Avenida Javier Prado Este 1372, San Isidro (☎ 476-0775, 476-4305, 476-4542, fax 476-7799)
   Airport (☎ & fax 464-9460)
Transportes Aéreos Andahuaylas (TAA)
   Camaná 828, Office 102, Lima (☎ 427-0986, fax 427-2975)

Flight schedules and ticket prices change frequently. Recent one-way fares from Lima were US$50 to US$95 to most towns.

Remote towns require connecting flights, and smaller towns are not served every day. Getting flight information, buying tickets and reconfirming flights are best done at the airline offices (or a reputable travel agent) rather than at the airport counters, where things can be chaotic. You can buy tickets at the airport on a space-available basis, however, if you want to leave for somewhere in a hurry.

Grupo Ocho (the military airline) has weekly flights to Cuzco, Puerto Maldonado, Pucallpa and some small jungle towns. Go to their airport counter early on the day of the flight, get your name on the waiting list and be prepared for a long wait. Grupo Ocho flies to Cuzco on Thursday morning; get your name on the list by 6 am and hope. Flights are half the price of commercial airlines but are subject to overbooking and cancellation, and priority is given to Peruvians so few gringos get on.

Overbooking is the norm on domestic flights, so be there at least an hour early. For all flights, domestic and international, reconfirm several times.

Bus The most important road is the Carretera Panamericana, which runs north-west and south-east from Lima roughly parallel to the coast. Long-distance north and southbound buses leave Lima every few minutes; it takes approximately 24 hours to drive to either the Ecuadorian or the Chilean border. Other buses ply the much rougher roads inland into the Andes and across into the eastern jungles.

There is no central bus terminal; each bus company runs its own office and terminal.

Lima's bus stations are notorious for theft, and it makes sense to find the station and buy your tickets in advance, unencumbered by luggage.

The biggest bus company in Lima is Ormeño (☎ 427-5679, 428-8453), Carlos Zavala Loayza 177. There are various subsidiaries at the same address. Among them, they have frequent departures for Ica, Arequipa, Tacna, Cuzco, Puno, Trujillo, Chiclayo, Tumbes, Huaraz, Caraz and various intermediate points. Cruz del Sur (☎ 424-1005, 427-1311, 423-1570), Quilca 531, serves the entire coast plus Huaraz, Huancayo, Arequipa, Puno and Cuzco. Cruz del Sur also has a ticket office at the corner of Zavala and Montevideo, where there are several other companies. Both companies have normal services and more expensive buses which are more comfortable and stop less often.

Expreso Sudamericano (☎ 427-6540, 427-1077), Montevideo 618, also has buses to most of these destinations as does TEPSA (☎ 473-1233, 427-6077), Paseo de la República 129.

Olano, (☎ 428-2370, 427-3519), Grau 617, also has buses to the north and south coast, as well as inland to Chachapoyas and Moyobamba. Coastal routes have 'buscamas' – buses with seats which recline completely for sleeping.

For Huaraz, several companies compete, including Civa Cial (☎ 428-5649, 432-4926), Zavala and Montevideo, and Transportes Rodríguez (☎ 428-0506), Roosevelt 354. Problems have been reported with this company's luggage storage. Also try Empresa Huaraz, (☎ 427-5260), Leticia 655, or Movil Tours (☎ 428-1414) and Paradise Tours (☎ 427-5369, 428-0740), both at Abancay 947. If going to Chiquian, the best bet is Transfysa (☎ 428-0412), Montevideo 724, with departures at 8 am every other day, or TUBSA (☎ 428-4510), Leticia 633. Civa Cial also goes to Chachapoyas, Cajamarca and Cuzco.

For Huancayo, there's Cruz del Sur or the recommended Mariscal Cáceres, (☎ 427-2844, 474-7850), with offices at the corner

PERU

of Zavala and Montevideo and at 28 de Julio 2195, La Victoria. For Tarma/Chanchamayo, there's Transportes Chanchamayo (☎ 432-4517), Luna Pizarro 453, La Victoria. This is a poor neighbourhood: use a taxi if laden with luggage.

Transportes León de Huánuco (☎ 432-9088), 15th block of 28 de Julio, La Victoria, go to Pucallpa (via Huánuco and Tingo María), and to La Merced. Transmar (☎ 433-7440), on the same block, goes to Pucallpa and Ayacucho (via Pisco).

Transportes Vista Alegre (☎ 427-6110, 427-4155), Abancay 900, has decent buses to Trujillo, Chimbote, and Casma. Turismo Chimbote (☎ 424-0501), Huarochiri 785, has buses to Chimbote. Soyuz, in the terminal at Zavala and Montevideo, goes to Cañete, Chincha and Ica. Buses for these towns also leave from further down the block on Montevideo.

For approximate fares and journey times, see the respective city sections.

Train The train from Lima goes inland to Huancayo but has carried only freight since 1991. In 1995, the World Bank reportedly invested US$35 million into getting the Lima-Huancayo passenger train running again, so ask locally.

Meanwhile, on Sunday at 8 am, a train does an excursion to San Bartolomé, 1600 metres above sea level and about 70 km inland. The train returns at 4 pm and the fare is US$3.50.

Lima's train station, Desamparados, is on Avenida Ancash, behind the Presidential Palace.

Getting Around
To/From the Airport The cheapest way to the airport is by city bus No 35 or 11, going from Plaza 2 de Mayo along Alfonso Ugarte to the airport (not recommended if you have a pile of luggage).

Taxi colectivos taking six passengers (US$1 each) leave from Colmena near Tacna. There is an extra charge for luggage.

An ordinary taxi will take you from the centre to the airport for about US$5, if you bargain. Taxis are charged US$1.50 to enter the airport but you can get off outside and walk 200 metres in. A radio taxi called by telephone will charge US$15.

Leaving the airport, you'll find plenty of airport taxis, charging anywhere from US$12 to US$15. You can bargain these down with some insistence. If you don't have much luggage, turn left outside the terminal and walk 100 metres to a gate, turn right and walk another 100 metres to the road, where you can get a cab for US$3.50 to US$7 to Lima, depending on bargaining and what time of day (or night) it is.

An airport hotel bus charges US$5 per passenger to your hotel and leaves about every hour.

Recent road construction has led to lengthy delays. Allow at least an hour to the airport, more during rush hours.

Bus Taking the local buses around Lima is rather a challenge. They are slow and crowded, but very cheap (fares are generally US$0.30). Bus lines are identifiable by their destination cards, numbers and colour schemes. At last count, there were nearly 200 bus lines. The last transport map available is now out of date and out of print (though look for an update).

A few colectivo lines operate minibuses which drive up and down the same streets all day long. The most useful goes from Lima to Miraflores along Avenidas Tacna, Garcilaso de la Vega and Arequipa. You can flag them down or get off anywhere. The fare is about US$0.50.

Taxi Taxis usually have a red-and-white taxi sticker on the windshield. Taxis can be any make or colour. Most are unlicensed. Licensed cabs are usually blue and yellow, often park outside the best hotels and restaurants, and charge twice as much as other cabs. Unlicensed cabs charge US$3 to US$4 for a Miraflores-Lima run; bargaining is expected.

AROUND LIMA

The closest major archaeological site to Lima is **Pachacamac**, 31 km south of the city. Pachacamac's origin predates the Incas by roughly 1000 years. Most of the buildings are now little more than walls of piled rubble, except for the main temples, which are huge pyramids. These have been excavated, and look like huge mounds with rough steps cut into them. One of the most recent of the complexes, the Mamacuña (House of the Chosen Women), was built by the Incas and has been excavated and reconstructed.

The site is extensive, and a thorough visit takes some hours. Near the entrance is a visitor centre with a small museum and a cafeteria. From there, a dirt road leads around the site. You can walk around it in an hour at a leisurely pace, if you don't stop for long at any of the sections. Although the pyramids are badly preserved, their size is impressive, and you can climb the stairs to the top of some of them, from where you can get excellent views of the coast on a clear day.

Guided tours to Pachacamac are offered by Lima Tours daily except Monday for US$21 per person (six people needed), including return transportation and English-speaking guide.

From Lima, minibuses to Pachacamac leave from near the corner of Colmena and Andahuaylas, by the Santa Catalina convent. The buses are line No 120, light blue in colour with orange trim, and they leave about every 30 minutes, as soon as they have a load. The fare is US$0.50. Tell the driver to let you off near the *ruinas*; otherwise, you will end up at Pachacamac village, about a km beyond the entrance. Alternatively, use the colectivo to Lurín, which leaves from the 900 block of Montevideo.

The ruins are open Tuesday to Sunday from 9 am to 5 pm. Entry costs US$3.50, and a bilingual booklet describing the ruins is available for US$1. When you are ready to leave, flag down any bus outside the gate. It's advisable to leave before late afternoon to avoid getting stuck in the dark with no bus.

The South Coast

The Panamericana goes through many places of interest south of Lima and is the route to Lake Titicaca and Cuzco. Thus, the south coast gets more visitors than the north.

CAÑETE & LUNAHUANA

The small town of Cañete, 144 km south of Lima, is the turn-off from the Panamericana up the Río Cañete to the village of Lunahuaná, 40 km away. River runners begin trips down the Cañete from here during the December-April season. February is the best month, with Class 3 rapids. (See Lima for agency addresses). Lunahuaná has vineyards, with a harvest festival in March. There are small ruins in the Cañete valley.

Places to Stay

A couple of basic but clean hotels on Cañete's Plaza de Armas charge US$8 to US$12 for a double with bath and cold water.

Lunahuaná has the *Hostals Candela* and *Lunahuana* with doubles for roughly US$10. There are more expensive places here, too.

Getting There & Away

Ormeño subsidiary, Expreso Chinchano, has several daily buses from Lima to Cañete (US$3, 2½ hours). Minibuses go to Lunahuaná from near the Plaza de Armas in Cañete.

CHINCHA

This small town, 190 km south of Lima, has a large black population and is known for Afro-Peruvian music. The best place to hear and dance to this is El Carmen, a 30 minute minibus ride from the Plaza de Armas in Chincha. The best times to go are during Fiestas Patrias in late July, Verano Negro at the end of February, Christmas, and a local fiesta in late October. During these times, minibuses run from Chincha to El Carmen all night long and the peña is full of limeños and local blacks dancing all night long –

PERU

quite a scene. The cover charge is about US$5.

Places to Stay

During the festivals, hotels double or triple their prices and are completely full. Some people avoid this problem by dancing all night and then taking an early morning bus back to Lima! At other times, a few cheap places are easy to find.

PISCO

Pisco, a fishing port 235 km south of Lima, shares its name with the white grape brandy made in the region. This is a base to see the wildlife of the Islas Ballestas and Península de Paracas, and the area is also of archaeological interest. The telephone code is 034.

Archaeology

In 1925, the Peruvian archaeologist JC Tello discovered burial sites of the Paracas culture, which existed in the area from approximately 1300 BC until 200 AD. The people of ancient Paracas produced the finest textiles in pre-Columbian America.

The main Paracas culture is divided into two periods, named Paracas Cavernas and Paracas Necropolis after the two main burial sites discovered. Cavernas is the earlier (500 BC to 300 BC) and is characterised by communal bottle-shaped tombs dug into the ground at the bottom of vertical shafts six metres deep.

Paracas Necropolis (300 BC to 100 AD) yielded the treasure trove of exquisite textiles for which the culture is known today. The necropolis contained over 400 funerary bundles, each of which consisted of a mummy (probably a nobleman or priest) wrapped in layers of weavings. It is best to visit the Lima museums for a look at the Paracas mummies, textiles and other artefacts. In the Pisco region, visit the JC Tello museum (on Península de Paracas) and the Museo Regional de Ica.

Places to Stay

Pisco is occasionally and unpredictably full of people from the fishing boats; hotels are booked up then, and prices rise. It's also full and pricey during national holidays, especially Fiestas Patrias (28-29 July).

The *Hostal Pisco*, on the plaza, charges US$4 per person in rooms with shared and not very clean hot baths. Doubles with private bath are US$10. This place is popular with budget travellers, but mixed reports have been received and prices fluctuate. The *Hotel Colonial*, on the Plaza Belén, charges US$9/13 for doubles/triples with clean shared hot showers (no singles).

Several basic, cold-water hotels charge US$3 or US$4 per person. These include, in roughly descending order of attraction, the *Hostales San Jorge, Angamos, Josesito Moreno, Perú, Callao, Grau* and *Mi Casa*.

The clean *Hotel Embassy* (☎ 53-2809) is US$10/16 for singles/doubles with private bath and warm water. It may be noisy with tour departees in the mornings. Next door, the *Hotel Comercio* charges US$7/11 with private tepid showers, but is not very clean. The *Gran Hotel Belén* (☎ 53-3046) is around the corner and similar to the Embassy. *Hostal El César* (☎ 53-2512) costs US$8 for a double, US$15 for a double with private hot shower. It's OK and open to bargaining if things are quiet.

Places to Eat

A few cafés on the Plaza de Armas are open early enough for breakfast before a Ballestas tour, and stay open all day. The *Restaurant Candie* is a reasonably priced restaurant on the plaza, and there is a *chifa* next door. There are cheap places within a block of the plaza: *El Norteño* is popular but serves no beer, *Roberto's* and *La Cabaña* are cheap local places where a set lunch menu will be under US$2. *El Muelle* is a cheap local restaurant which has large portions. *Restaurant Don Manuel* is one of the best, charging US$2 to US$7 for meals. San Andrés, on the coast five km south of Pisco, has several good, reasonably priced seafood restaurants.

Turtles (endangered and protected) wind up on the menu. Don't encourage the catching of turtles by ordering dishes made with turtle meat.

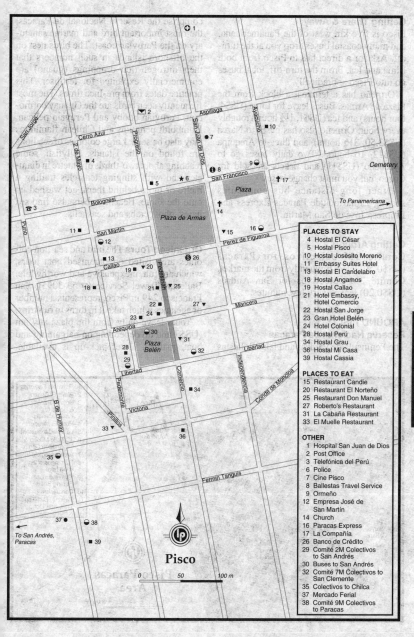

PLACES TO STAY
4 Hostal El César
5 Hostal Pisco
10 Hostal Josésito Moreno
11 Embassy Suites Hotel
13 Hostal El Candelabro
18 Hostal Angamos
19 Hostal Callao
21 Hotel Embassy,
   Hotel Comercio
22 Hostal San Jorge
23 Gran Hotel Belén
24 Hostal Colonial
28 Hostal Perú
34 Hostal Grau
36 Hostal Mi Casa
39 Hostal Cassia

PLACES TO EAT
15 Restaurant Candie
20 Restaurant El Norteño
25 Restaurant Don Manuel
27 Roberto's Restaurant
31 La Cabaña Restaurant
33 El Muelle Restaurant

OTHER
1 Hospital San Juan de Dios
2 Post Office
3 Telefónica del Perú
6 Police
7 Cine Pisco
8 Ballestas Travel Service
9 Ormeño
12 Empresa José de
   San Martín
14 Church
16 Paracas Express
17 La Compañía
26 Banco de Crédito
29 Comité 2M Colectivos
   to San Andrés
30 Buses to San Andrés
32 Comité 7M Colectivos to
   San Clemente
35 Colectivos to Chilca
37 Mercado Ferial
38 Comité 9M Colectivos
   to Paracas

Plaza

To Panamericana

Cemetery

Plaza de Armas

Plaza Belén

To San Andrés,
Paracas

Pisco

0   50   100 m

PERU

Getting There & Away

Pisco is five km west of the Panamericana, and many coastal buses drop you at the turn-off. Ask for a direct bus to Pisco from both Lima and Ica. From the turn-off, local buses go into Pisco sporadically.

Ormeño has a terminal a block from the Plaza de Armas. Buses leave for Lima (US$4, four hours) and Ica (US$1, 1½ hours) roughly every hour. Ormeño also has buses to Nazca (US$3.50, 3½ hours), and three to Arequipa (US$12, 16 hours). Two daily buses go to Ayacucho (US$11) and tickets are sold for Cuzco, but you must change buses.

Other long-distance bus companies serving Lima include Paracas Express and Empresa José de San Martín.

Getting Around

Comité 9M colectivos for Paracas (US$0.50) leave frequently from the market. Comité 2M colectivos for San Andrés (US$0.20) leave every few minutes.

AROUND PISCO
Reserva Nacional de Paracas

The Península de Paracas and Islas Ballestas comprise the Reserva Nacional de Paracas, the most important bird and marine sanctuary on the Peruvian coast. The birds nest on the offshore islands in such numbers that their nitrogen-rich droppings (guano) are commercially exploited for fertiliser. This practice dates from pre-Inca times. The most frequently seen birds are the Guanay cormorant, Peruvian booby and Peruvian pelican. Humboldt penguins and Chilean flamingos may also be seen. Large colonies of sea lions are found on the islands. Jellyfish, some reaching about two-thirds of a metre in diameter and with stinging tentacles trailing a metre or more behind them, get washed up onto the shore. Beachcombers also find sea hares, ghost crabs and seashells.

Organised Tours The bird and sea-lion colonies are visited on organised boat tours, which are fun, inexpensive and worthwhile. Ballestas Travel Service (☎ 53-3095), San Francisco 249 in Pisco, represents a number of agencies which take it in turns to run trips.

Tours leave daily from the plaza at 7 am (US$7 and up depending on bargaining and boat quality). Hotel pick-up is available.

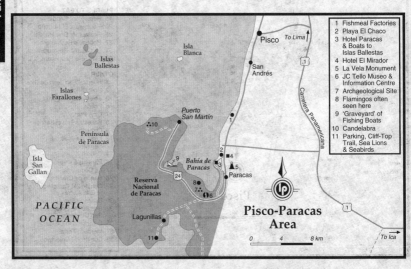

1	Fishmeal Factories
2	Playa El Chaco
3	Hotel Paracas & Boats to Islas Ballestas
4	Hotel El Mirador
5	La Vela Monument
6	JC Tello Museo & Information Centre
7	Archaeological Site
8	Flamingos often seen here
9	'Graveyard' of Fishing Boats
10	Candelabra
11	Parking, Cliff-Top Trail, Sea Lions & Seabirds

Pisco-Paracas Area

PACIFIC OCEAN

0   4   8 km

To Ica

Minibuses go to Paracas, where slow motor boats are boarded for the excursion; there's no cabin, so dress for wind and spray and bring sun protection. The outward boat journey takes about 1½ hours, and en route you see the Candelabra, a giant figure etched into the coastal hills, like the Nazca Lines.

About an hour is spent cruising around the islands. You'll see plenty of sea lions on the rocks and swimming around your boat. Wear a hat: there are a lot of birds in the air, and it's not unusual for someone to receive a direct hit!

Once you return to the mainland, a minibus will take you back to Pisco in time for lunch. Alternatively, you can join the afternoon Reserva de Paracas tour (also US$7). If there are several of you wishing to do both tours in one day, bargain for a reduced combined rate. The Paracas tour requires an extra US$1 reserve entrance fee and a US$1 museum entrance fee. Coastal sea-lion and flamingo colonies are visited and geological formations are observed. There is usually time for a swim from a secluded beach. It is also possible to drive or walk around the reserve yourself.

ICA
Ica, capital of its department, is a pleasant colonial town of 150,000 inhabitants, 305 km south of Lima. The Panamericana heads inland from Pisco, climbing gently to 420 metres at Ica. The town is high enough to be free of the garúa, and the climate is dry and sunny. The desert surrounding Ica is noted for its huge sand dunes. Water from the Río Ica supports vineyards and thriving wine and pisco-producing industries. The distilleries and wineries can be visited. Ica has a fine museum and several annual fiestas.

Information
A tourist office, Grau 148, is open Monday to Friday from 8 am to 2.30 pm. The Banco de Crédito changes cash and travellers' cheques and street moneychangers are found nearby. The telephone code is 034.

Things to See
Museo Regional de Ica This is in the south-western suburbs, 1.5 km from the centre. Take a No 17 bus from the plaza, or it's a pleasant walk. Hours are weekdays 8 am to 6 pm, Saturday 9 am to 6 pm, and Sunday 9 am to 1 pm. Adults/students pay US$1.20/0.50, with an extra US$1.50 camera fee. It is one of the best small regional museums in Peru, and concentrates on the Paracas, Nazca and Inca cultures.

Museo Cabrera There is no sign to mark this museum, on the Plaza de Armas, at Bolívar 170. It has a collection of 11,000 carved stones and boulders showing pre-Columbian surgical techniques and day-to-day living. The owner, Dr J Cabreras, claims that these stones are centuries old, but most authorities don't believe him. You can see some of the stones in the museum entrance, but a proper look along with a guided tour costs US$5. Hours are 9 am to 1 pm and 4 to 8 pm.

Vineyards *Bodegas* are best visited during the grape harvest, from late February until early April. Tacama and Ocucaje wineries produce the best wine but are isolated and hard to get to. The Vista Alegre winery makes reasonable wine and is the easiest of the large commercial wineries to visit. To get there, walk across the Grau bridge and take the second left. It's about three km; all the locals know it. This walk goes through a rough neighbourhood; you can hire a taxi or take city bus No 8 or 13, both of which pass the plaza and go near the winery. The Vista Alegre entrance is a yellow-brick arch and hours are 9 am to 5 pm on weekdays; morning is the best time to visit.

Huacachina
This tiny resort village is nestled in huge sand dunes about five km west of Ica (buses from Lambayeque at Municipalidad in Ica). A small, murky-looking lagoon supposedly has curative properties. The surroundings are pretty: graceful palm trees, colourful flowers, attractive buildings in pastel shades and the backdrop of giant sand dunes which invite hiking and playing. Sandboards are

PERU

rented for US$1.50 an hour. There are several inexpensive restaurants and food vendors by the lagoon, or bring a picnic lunch.

Special Events

Ica's famous Festival Internacional de Vendimia (Wine Harvest Festival) is held during the 10 days beginning the first Friday in March. There are processions and beauty contests, cockfights and horse shows, arts and crafts fairs, music and dancing, and, of course, the pisco and wine flow freely.

In October, the pilgrimage of El Señor de Luren culminates in an all-night procession on the third Monday of the month. This festival is repeated in March, and sometimes coincides with Holy Week celebrations.

The Carnaval de Yunza is in February. Participants dress in beautiful costumes and there is public dancing. There is also water-throwing typical of Latin American carnavales.

The founding of the city, on 17 June 1563, is celebrated during Ica week. The more important Ica tourist festival takes place in the latter half of September.

Places to Stay

The cheapest hotels may double (or more) their prices during the festivals, especially the March harvest festival, when hotels are often fully booked. The prices below are for nonfestival times.

The area around Independencia and Castrovirreyna has cheap hotels. The *Hostal Europa*, Independencia 258, is US$4/6 for basic but clean singles/doubles with a wash-basin. Similarly priced cold-water cheapies include the clean *Hostal Díaz* (☎ 23-1601), Independencia 167, which has some rooms with private bath for US$2 more. Others on the same block are *Hostal Royal* (OK), *Hostal Aries* (friendly but charges a little more), *Hostal Jaimito* (looks run-down) and *Hostal Aleph* (☎ 22-1332; US$4.50 a person). The nearby *Hostal Toño* is OK for US$5/6.50. The *Hostal Callao* (☎ 23-5976), has rooms for US$5/7, or US$7/9 with private hot showers. The *Hostal Lima*, Lima 262, and *Hostal LM*, Salaverry and Loreto,

are other reasonable cold-water cheapies at US$5/8. The *Hostal Inti* (☎ 23-3141), Amazonas 235, charges US$5/9 in basic rooms with private cold showers. There are also the cheap and very basic *Hostales San Martín, Titos and Libertad*.

The popular *Hostal La Viña* (☎ 22-1043), San Martín and Huánuco, charges US$5/7, or US$7/9 with private hot shower (although we hear it's been renovated and improved, and doubled in price). The *Hotel Presidente* (☎ 22-5977), Amazonas 223, is good and clean at US$7/9 with private hot shower. The *Hostal Sol de Oro* (☎ 23-3735), La Mar 371, is very clean and friendly and charges US$8/10 with private hot shower. The *Hotel Confort* (☎ 23-3072), La Mar 257, is clean and good at US$9/13 with tepid shower. Others are *Hostal Palace* and *Hostal Tumi*.

Places to Eat

The *Restaurant Venezia*, on Lima just off the Plaza de Armas, serves good pizza, pasta, desserts and coffee at reasonable prices and is recommended. Calle Lima has several *chifas* and other inexpensive restaurants. The cheap *Mogambo* just north of the plaza and the *Plaza 125* on the plaza serve inexpensive chicken. *El Velasco*, on the plaza, serves good snacks and cakes. *El Otro Peñoncito*, Bolívar 255, is clean and serves good sandwiches and meals at medium prices.

Getting There & Away

Most of the bus companies are clustered around a little park at the western end of Salaverry. Several companies run frequent buses up and down the Panamericana. Ormeño has the most departures but others may be cheaper. There are many departures for Lima (US$4.50, five hours), Pisco (US$1, one hour), Nazca (US$2.50, three hours) and Arequipa (US$12 to US$16, 15 hours). Some continue to Tacna or Cuzco. Taxi colectivos for Lima (five passengers) and Nazca (seven passengers) leave from opposite Ormeño as soon as they are full. Fares are US$12 to Lima (3½ hours) and US$3 to Nazca (2½ hours).

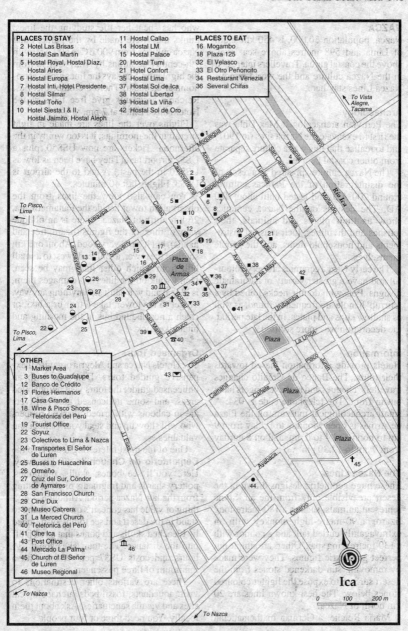

PLACES TO STAY
2 Hotel Las Brisas
4 Hostal San Martín
5 Hostal Royal, Hostal Díaz,
   Hostal Aries
6 Hostal Europa
7 Hostal Inti, Hotel Presidente
8 Hostal Silmar
9 Hostal Toño
10 Hotel Siesta I & II,
   Hostal Jaimito, Hostal Aleph

11 Hostal Callao
14 Hostal LM
15 Hostal Palace
20 Hostal Tumi
21 Hotel Confort
35 Hostal Lima
37 Hostal Sol de Ica
38 Hostal Libertad
39 Hostal La Viña
42 Hostal Sol de Oro

PLACES TO EAT
16 Mogambo
18 Plaza 125
32 El Velasco
33 El Otro Peñoncito
34 Restaurant Venezia
36 Several Chifas

OTHER
1 Market Area
3 Buses to Guadalupe
12 Banco de Crédito
13 Flores Hermanos
17 Casa Grande
18 Wine & Pisco Shops;
   Telefónica del Perú
19 Tourist Office
22 Soyuz
23 Colectivos to Lima & Nazca
24 Transportes El Señor
   de Luren
25 Buses to Huacachina
26 Ormeño
27 Cruz del Sur, Cóndor
   de Aymares
28 San Francisco Church
29 Cine Dux
30 Museo Cabrera
31 La Merced Church
40 Telefónica del Perú
41 Cine Ica
43 Post Office
44 Mercado La Palma
45 Church of El Señor
   de Luren
46 Museo Regional

To Vista
Alegre,
Tacama

To Pisco,
Lima

To Pisco,
Lima

Plaza de
Armas

Plaza

Plaza

Plaza

To Nazca

To Nazca

Ica

0   100   200 m

PERU

NAZCA

Nazca, population 30,000, is 450 km south of Lima and 598 metres above sea level, above the coastal garúa. Travellers interested in the Nazca culture and the world-famous Nazca Lines stay here.

Archaeology

The Peruvian archaeologist Max Uhle was the first to excavate the Nazca sites (in 1901) and to realise that this was a culture separate from other coastal peoples.

The Nazca culture appeared as a result of the disintegration of the Paracas culture, around 200 AD, and lasted until about 800 AD. The designs on the Nazca ceramics show us their plants and animals, their fetishes and divinities, their musical instruments and household items, and the people themselves.

The early Nazca ceramics are very colourful and have a greater variety of naturalistic designs. Pots with double necks joined by a 'stirrup' handle are frequently found, as well as shallow cups and plates. In the late period, the decoration was more stylised.

Information

Hotels provide information biased towards their tours. The Banco de Crédito changes travellers' cheques and moneychangers hang out in front. The telephone code is 034. A small archaeological museum on the Plaza de Armas is open Monday to Friday from 9 am to noon and 4 to 6 pm, and on Saturday from 9 am to 12.30 pm.

The Nazca Lines

These huge geometric designs drawn in the desert are visible only from the air. Some represent animals, such as a 180-metre-long lizard, a 90-metre-high monkey with an extravagantly curled tail, and a condor with a 130-metre wing span. Others are simple but perfect geometric figures. They were made by removing sun-darkened stones from the desert surface to expose the lighter coloured stones below. The best-known lines are 20 km north of Nazca.

María Reiche, a German mathematician who has spent her life studying the lines, thinks they were made by the Paracas and Nazca cultures from 900 BC to 600 AD, with 7th-century additions by Wari settlers from the highlands. She says the lines are an astronomical calendar. There are other theories. Reiche's assistants give free talks at the Hotel Nazca Lines at 7 pm.

Flights over the lines are made in light aircraft in the mornings; it is too windy in the afternoon. Tickets are now US$50, plus a US$2 airport tax. (They have been as low as US$20 in the past.) A taxi to the airport is US$3. Flights last 40 minutes.

You can also view the lines from the observation tower beside the Panamericana, 26 km north of Nazca. There is an oblique view of three of the figures (lizard, tree and hands), but it's not very good. About one km south of the tower, a trail leads west to a small hill, from which other lines may be seen. Don't walk on the lines – it damages them, is illegal and you can't see anything anyway. To get to the tower, take a tour or a taxi, or catch a northbound bus in the morning and hitchhike back.

Organised Tours

The Hotels Nazca and Alegría organise inexpensive guided tours. Don't go with an unlicensed guide: the tours visit uninhabited areas, and some unlicensed guides/drivers are in cahoots with armed, masked robbers who will show up and steal your camera and valuables.

One of the most interesting tours is to the **Cementerio de Chauchilla**, 30 km away. Here you'll see bones, skulls, mummies, pottery shards and fragments of cloth dating from the late Nazca period. Although everything of value has gone, it's quite amazing to stand in the desert and see tombs surrounded by bleached skulls and bones that stretch off into the distance. The tour takes about 2½ hours and costs US$7 per person, with a minimum of three passengers.

There are various other destinations to visit: aqueducts, fossil beds, archaeological sites and vicuña sanctuaries. Ask about them locally. You need three or four people.

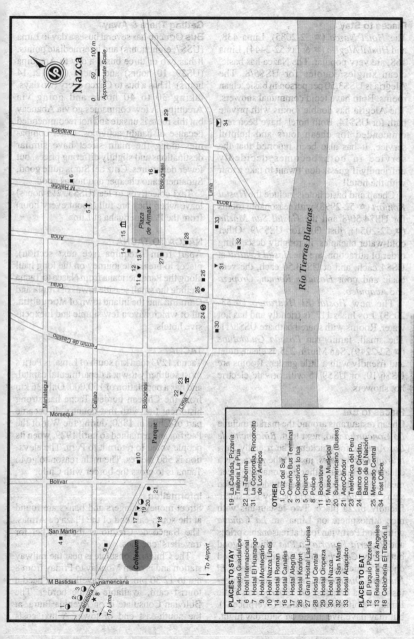

Nazca

0   50   100 m

Approximate Scale

Plaza de Armas

Parque

Coliseum

Río Tierras Blancas

To Lima

Carretera Panamericana

To Airport

To Lima

Tarabaca

M Helcre

Bolognesi

Lima

Tacna

Anca

Grau

Callao

Bolognesi

Lima

Camino de Castillo

Morsequi

Bolivar

San Martín

M Bastidas

Marialegui

PLACES TO STAY

4   Posada Guadalupe
6   Hotel Internacional
7   Hostal El Huarango
9   Hotel Montecarlo
10 Hotel Nazca Lines
14 Hostal Roman
16 Hostal Canales
17 Hostal Alegria
26 Hostal Konfort
27 Gran Hostal Las Lineas
28 Hostal Central
29 Hostal Oropeza
30 Hotel Nazca
32 Hostal San Martin
33 Hostal Las Lineas

PLACES TO EAT

12 El Purquio Pizzeria
13 Restaurant Los Angeles
18 Cebicheria El Tiburón II,

19 La Cañada, Pizzeria
    Tratoria La Pua
22 La Taberna
31 La Concordia, Rinconcito
    de Los Amigos

OTHER

1   Cruz del Sur
2   Ormeño Bus Terminal
3   Colectivos to Ica
5   Church
8   Police
11 Bookstore
15 Museo Municipal
20 Sudamericano (Buses)
21 AeroCóndor
23 Telefónica del Perú
24 Banco de Crédito,
    Banco de la Nación
25 Mercado Central
34 Post Office

PERU

Places to Stay

The *Hotel Nazca* (☎ 52-2085), Lima 438, and *Hostal Alegría* (☎ & fax 52-2444), Lima 168, are very popular. The Nazca has basic, clean singles/doubles for US$5/8. The Alegría is US$3.50 per person in basic, clean rooms. Both have tepid communal showers. The Alegría has double rooms with private bath for US$14. Both hotels have been recommended for cheap tours and helpful service. It has also been reported that the service in both becomes decidedly unfriendly if guests don't want to take a tour with the hotel!

Cheap and basic hotels include the *Hostal Konfort* (☎ 52-2998) with reasonable rooms for US$4.50/8 and the *Hostal San Martín* (☎ 52-2054), just OK for US$5/9. Other cold-water cheapies, in roughly descending order of attraction, are the *Hostal Central* at US$4 each, and at US$3.50 each, the very basic and poor *Hostales Roman, Oropeza* and *Acapulco*.

The new *Hostal El Huarango* (☎ 55-2053), Los Incas 117, is friendly and has hot water. Rooms with shared bath are US$8/11. The small, family-run *Posada Guadalupe* (☎ 52-2249), San Martín 225, is clean, quiet and friendly with a little garden. Rooms are US$6/10, or US$9/15 with private electric hot showers.

Places to Eat

Cheap restaurants around the market include *La Concordia* and, next to it, *Rinconcito de Los Amigos* for chicken. The friendly *Restaurant Los Angeles*, just off the plaza, has a cheap set lunch, other reasonably priced meals, nice chocolate cake, and decent pisco sours. *El Puquío Pizzería* nearby is a small, friendly pizza place. Two restaurants with nice atmosphere on Lima are *La Cañada* with good Peruvian food at reasonable prices and *Pizzería Tratoria La Pua* which is good but pricey. *Cebichería El Tiburón II* has good cheap ceviches. At night it becomes *El Huakero Discotec* with music and strange-tasting piña coladas. *La Taberna*, on Calle Lima, is a bit more up-market (overpriced?), but may have live music on Saturday night.

Getting There & Away

Bus Ormeño has several buses a day to Lima (US$7, eight hours) and intermediate points. It has two or three buses a day to Arequipa (US$9, 10 hours) and Tacna (US$12, 14 hours). It has a bus to Cuzco every two days, taking 30 to 40 hours and going via Arequipa. A few companies go via Abancay but this route is unsafe and not recommended because of bandit activities. Other companies along the main street have similar destinations and slightly differing prices, but fewer departures. Cruz del Sur is quite good, Sudamericano cheaper and not as good.

Taxi colectivos to Ica (US$3, 2½ hours) leave when they are full (about every hour) from the Panamericana at Lima.

NAZCA TO TACNA

Apart from Arequipa (see next section), places to break the journey on the long haul along the Panamericana from Nazca to Tacna include the small seaside towns of **Chala** and **Camaná** and the inland town of **Moquegua**, all of which have a few simple and inexpensive hotels.

TACNA

Tacna, 1293 road km south of Lima, is Peru's most southerly town, a departmental capital, and has a population of 150,000. Only 36 km from the Chilean border, Tacna has strong historical ties with that country. It became part of Chile in 1880, during the War of the Pacific, and remained so until 1929, when its people voted to return it to Peru. The elevation is 560 metres. The main reason to go to Tacna is to cross the border with Chile.

Information

Street moneychangers and banks are found at the south-east end of the Plaza de Armas. The Banco de Crédito is the best bet for travellers' cheques.

The Chilean Consulate is near the railway station and is open Monday to Friday from 8 am to 12.30 pm. Most travellers just need a tourist card, available at the border. The Bolivian Consulate is on Avenida Piura, at the south-east end of town. A taxi costs

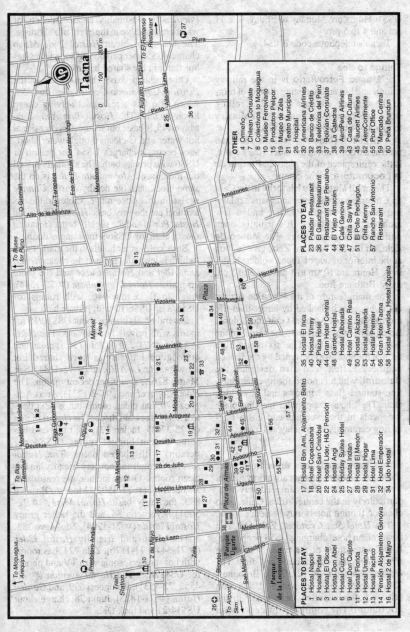

Tacna

0   100   200 m

To El Remanso
Restaurant

PERU

PLACES TO STAY
1 Hostal Napoli
2 Hostal Portal
3 Hostal El Oscar
5 Hostal Don Abel
6 Hostal Cuzco
11 Hotel Don Quijote
12 Hostal Florida
13 Hostal Unanue
14 Hostal Pacifico
16 Hostal 2 de Mayo
17 Hostal Bon Ami, Alojamiento Betito
18 Hotel Copacabana
20 Hotel San Cristobal
22 Hostal Lider, H&C Pensión
24 Hostal Angi
25 Holiday Suites Hotel
27 Hostal Inclan
28 Hostal El Mesón
29 Hostal Hogar
31 Hostal Lima
32 Hotel Emperador
34 Lido Hostal
35 Hostal El Inca
40 Hostal Virrey
42 Plaza Hotel
44 Gran Hotel Central
48 Garden Hostal,
     Hostal Alborada
49 Hotel Camino Real
50 Hostal Alcázar
53 Hostal Alameda
54 Hostal Premier
56 Gran Hotel Tacna
58 Hostal Avenida, Hostal Zapata

PLACES TO EAT
23 Paladar Restaurant
36 El Gaucho Restaurant
41 Restaurant Sur Peruano
44 El Viejo Almacén
46 Café Genova
47 Chifa Say Wa
51 El Pollo Pechugón,
     Chifa Kenny
57 Rancho San Antonio
     Restaurant

OTHER
4 Ormeño
7 Chilean Consulate
8 Colectivos to Moquegua
10 Museo Ferroviario
15 Productos Pelipor
19 Museo de Zela
21 Teatro Municipal
26 Hospital
30 Americana Airlines
32 Banco de Crédito
33 Telefónica del Perú
37 Bolivian Consulate
38 La Catedral
39 AeroPerú Airlines
43 Casa de Cultura
45 Faucet Airlines
52 AeroContinente
55 Post Office
59 Mercado Central
60 Peña Brundun

Piura

To El Remanso
Restaurant

To Moquegua,
Arequipa

To Bus
Terminal

To Buses
for Piura

To Moquegua.
Arequipa

To Airport
5km

Train
Station

Parque
de la Locomotora

Parque
Ugarte

Parque
2 de Mayo

Plaza de Armas

Market
Area

Plaza

US$1. Hours are Monday to Friday, 9 to 11 am and 4 to 5 pm.

Tacna's telephone code is 054.

Things to See

The **Museo Ferroviario** is in the railway station and has an interesting display of turn-of-the-century engines and other rolling stock. It is open from 9 am to 3 pm Monday to Friday. Admission is US$0.10.

A British locomotive, built in 1859 and used as a troop train in the War of the Pacific, is the centrepiece of the pleasant **Parque de la Locomotora**, in the centre.

The small **Museo de Historia**, in the Casa de Cultura, has paintings and maps explaining the War of the Pacific, and a few archaeological pieces. It's usually open during weekday mornings. The **Museo de Zela**, on the 500 block of Zela, gives a look at the interior of one of Tacna's oldest buildings. Hours are 10 am to 1 pm and 3 to 5 pm daily. Both are free.

The main feature of the **Plaza de Armas** is the huge arch flanked by larger-than-life bronze statues of Admiral Grau and Colonel Bolognesi – a monument to the heroes of the War of the Pacific. The six-metre-high bronze fountain was designed by the French engineer Eiffel, who also designed the **Catedral**, which is noted for its clean lines, fine stained-glass windows and onyx high altar. The plaza is a popular meeting place for locals in the evenings and has a flag-raising ceremony on Sunday at 10 am.

Places to Stay

Cheap Tacna hotels may suffer from water shortages. Showers are not always available. Despite this, hotel prices are relatively high, particularly in the centre. Arica, Chile, is no cheaper, though hotels may be better.

The *Hotel San Cristóbal*, Zela 660, is a basic, clean hotel charging US$4 per person. It has water most of the time. Nearby, the *Hostal Unión* is cheap, basic and dirty. The *Hostal Alameda* (☎ 72-3071), Bolognesi 780, charges US$4 per person, US$5 with private bath, but often lacks water in the afternoon. The similarly priced *Hostal Pacífico* is reasonably clean. Buckets of water are available in the event of a shortage. The basic but clean *Hostal 2 de Mayo* charges US$5 per person and sometimes has hot water in the shared bathrooms.

Other cheap, basic hotels include the *Pensión Alojamiento Genova*, Deustua 559, which also has a restaurant serving cheap lunch menús. The *Hostal Bon Ami*, 2 de Mayo 445, is basic but secure, has occasional hot water and is clean, though water shortages occur. It charges US$4 per person or US$6 with private bath. The similarly priced but more basic *Alojamiento Betito* is on the same block, and the nearby *Hostal Unanue* is also in this price range. Closer to the bus terminal are the very basic *Hostal Napoli* and *Hostal Portal* and the slightly better *Hostal El Oscar*, charging US$6/9 for a single/ double.

Basic cold-water hotels in the market area (which is less safe) include the cheap *Hostal Don Abel* and *Hostal Cuzco* and the more up-market *Hotel Don Quijote* (☎ 72-1514), Augusto B Leguía 940, with rooms for US$5/8 or US$6/10 with private bath.

Several hotels charge about US$10/15 for rooms with private hot showers. The *H&C Pensión* (☎ 71-2391), Zela 734, is clean and quite good but singles have shared hot showers. The *Lido Hostal* (☎ 72-1184), San Martín 876A, is another decent option. The *Hotel Copacabana* (☎ 72-1721), Arias Araguez 370, has clean rooms but is next door to a noisy weekend disco. The *Hostal Inclan* (☎ 72-3701), Inclan 171, isn't bad and has some decent budget rooms (US$4 per person) with shared baths. The *Hostal Alcázar* is small and not very friendly but has clean rooms. Others include the reasonable *Hostal Angi* (☎ 71-3502), Modesto Basadre 893, the fairly basic *Hostal Virrey* (☎ 72-3061), Ayacucho 88, and the rather grimy *Hostal Florida* (☎ 71-1204), 2 de Mayo 382.

The clean and friendly *Hostal Lider* (☎ 71-5441, 71-1176), Zela 724, has rooms with hot showers, some with TV and phone, for US$12/20. The *Hostal Avenida* (☎ 72-4582, 72-4531), Bolognesi 699, and *Garden Hostal* (☎ 71-1825), Junín 78, charge about US$14/21 and look OK.

Places to Eat

Restaurant Sur Peruano, Ayacucho 80, is inexpensive and locally popular for lunch. Another local favourite is the clean *Paladar*, Meléndez 228, with menús under US$2. The best chicken is at *El Pollo Pechugón*, Bolognesi 378, where half a grilled chicken with fries is US$3.50. Next door, *Chifa Kenny* has good lunch menús starting at US$1.50. Good Chinese food is served at *Chifa Say Wa*. Other budget restaurants line Bolognesi between the post office and Junín. *Helados Piamonte* has good ice cream. *El Viejo Almacén*, San Martín 577, has good steaks, pasta, ice cream, coffee, local wine and desserts. Meals are US$3 to US$6. Nearby is the cheaper *Café Genova* with outdoor tables and good coffee.

The lively *Cevichería El Corsario* (☎ 72-4506), Avenida Arica and San José, near the Ciudad Universitaria (take a taxi), has great ceviches (US$5 and up) and seafood. Nearby, the *Silvia* (☎ 72-4345), Miraflores 702, is another recommended seafood restaurant. The *Rancho San Antonio* (☎ 72-4471), Coronel Bustios 298, serves good Peruvian and international food in a garden setting and has peñas on weekend nights. *El Remanso* (☎ 71-2034, 72-1722) also has international food and entertainment including rock music.

Pocollay, five km north-east of Tacna, has rural restaurants that are popular for weekend lunches.

Getting There & Away

Air There are several daily flights to Arequipa and Lima. Same-day connections are made via Arequipa to Juliaca, Cuzco and Puerto Maldonado, and via Lima to major northern Peruvian cities. AeroContinente, AeroPerú, Americana, Imperial Air and Faucett all serve Tacna. Fares are US$94 to Lima and US$22 to Arequipa.

Peruvian airlines have offices in Arica, Chile, where fares are cheaper (2% tax versus Peru's 18%). Ask in Arica about discounts and air passes (see the Getting There & Away chapter at the start of the book).

If you fly Lima-Tacna, cross to Arica by land, then fly Arica-Santiago, you'll save US$100 over the Lima-Santiago fare bought in Peru.

Bus The Terminal Terrestre is on Unanue, at the north-east end of town. Passengers pay a US$0.45 departure tax. The terminal can get disorganised with large groups of Peruvians going home after shopping sprees. Flores Hermanos (☎ 72-6691) is the biggest local company, with 14 daily buses to Arequipa, seven to Moquegua, 10 to Ilo, and a daily 3.45 pm bus (more on weekends) to Toquepala. Several companies serve Lima (US$17 to US$35, 21 to 28 hours). Some are luxury services and most leave in the evening. Arequipa (US$4 to US$7, seven hours) is frequently served, as are south coast destinations. Cruz del Sur has buses to Cuzco in the evening.

Ormeño (☎ 72-4401), with buses to Arequipa and Lima, is at Arias Araguez 700. Buses to Puno (US$8, 12 hours) leave, usually in the evenings, from the jumble of bus companies on Avenida Circunvalación, north of the city and east of the main terminal. They may move to the terminal in future.

Buses (US$2) and taxi colectivos (US$4) to Arica, Chile, leave frequently from the terminal. Drivers help with border formalities (if your papers are in order). A new terminal for buses or taxis to Arica is planned on the Panamericana, two km south of town, and may open by 1997.

Northbound buses are frequently stopped and searched by immigration and/or customs officials not far north of Tacna. Have your passport handy and don't hold packages for strangers.

Train Trains go from Tacna to Arica and back, supposedly daily, but are subject to cancellation. Check locally. They are slower but cheaper than buses.

To/From Chile Formalities at the Peru-Chile border are relatively straightforward in both directions. The border closes at 10 pm. Chile is one hour ahead of Peru (two hours with daylight saving).

PERU

Getting Around
There is no airport bus, so you have to take a taxi (US$4) or walk (about five km).

Arequipa

Arequipa, 2325 metres above sea level, is capital of its department and, with almost a million inhabitants, is Peru's second-largest city. It is a beautiful city, surrounded by spectacular mountains, including the volcano El Misti. Many of the buildings are made of a light-coloured volcanic rock called *sillar*, hence Arequipa's nickname – 'the white city'.

The founding of Arequipa, on 15 August 1540, is commemorated with a week-long fair. The fireworks show in the Plaza de Armas on 14 August is particularly spectacular. Unfortunately, the city is built in an earthquake-prone area, and none of the original buildings remains. However, several 17th and 18th-century buildings survive, and are frequently visited. The most interesting of these is the Santa Catalina monastery.

Information
Tourist Office The tourist office (☎ 21-1021) is on the Plaza de Armas, opposite the Catedral. Hours are Monday to Friday from 8 am to 5 pm. The helpful Policía de Turismo (☎ 23-9888), Jerusalén 317, also provide tourist information.

Money The Banco de Crédito changes travellers' cheques, and moneychangers outside give as good a rate as anywhere for cash.

Post & Communications The post office (☎ 21-5245) is at Moral 118. The main telephone office (☎ 21-1111) is at Alvarez Thomas 201. The telephone code is 054.

Visa Extensions Migraciones (☎ 21-2552) is at Palacio Viejo 216.

Emergency The tourist police are helpful and open 24 hours. The best hospital is Clínica Arequipa (☎ 25-3408, 25-3424), at Avenida Bolognesi and Puente Grau.

Dangers & Annoyances Pickpockets abound on the busy street of San Juan de Dios, so watch your belongings carefully here – and everywhere else in town. There have been reports of belongings being stolen from restaurants: keep your stuff in sight.

Religious Buildings
The tourist office can give opening hours, but these change often.

The **Monasterio de Santa Catalina** is Peru's most fascinating colonial religious building. It was built in 1580 and enlarged in the 17th century. Surrounded by imposing high walls, it's almost a city within a city. At one time, 450 nuns and lay servants led a completely secluded life within. In 1970 it was opened to the public, and the few remaining nuns now live in the northern corner of the complex. Visitors are free to wander around other areas. Entry is US$3.50, multilingual guide services are available (tip expected) and hours are 9 am to 4 pm daily.

The imposing **Catedral** stands on the Plaza de Armas. The original structure, dating from 1656, was destroyed by fire in 1844, and the second building was toppled by the 1868 earthquake, so most of what you see has been rebuilt. The outside is impressive; the interior is luminous, spacious and airy, with high vaults which are much less cluttered than those of churches in other parts of Peru.

One of the oldest churches in Arequipa, **La Compañía**, on the south-eastern corner of the Plaza de Armas, is noted for its ornate main façade. This Jesuit church was so solidly built that it withstood the earthquakes. Inside, many of the original murals were covered with plaster and white paint by 19th-century restorers, but the polychrome cupola of the San Ignacio chapel survived and is worth seeing. Entry is US$0.45 to the San Ignacio chapel, free otherwise.

The 16th-century church of **San Francisco** has been damaged by earthquakes:

you can see a large crack in the cupola. There is an impressive silver altar.

La Recoleta, a Franciscan monastery, was built on the western side of the Río Chili in 1648, but has been completely rebuilt. There is a huge and fascinating library of over 20,000 books, many of which are centuries old. They have several *incunables*, or books printed before 1500. There is a museum of Amazonian objects collected by the missionaries, an extensive collection of preconquest artefacts, and religious artworks of the Cuzco school. You can visit the cloisters and monks' cells. Hours are Monday to Saturday from 9 am to noon and 3 to 5 pm. Entry is US$2. A Spanish-speaking guide is available (tip expected).

Museums
The **Museo Histórico Municipal** has a few paintings, documents, photographs, maps and other historical items. Hours are Monday to Friday from 8 am to 6 pm and entry is US$0.50. An archaeological collection at the Universidad de San Agustín, on Avenida Ayacucho, about one km east of the centre, is closed for maintenance.

Colonial Houses
Many old homes are now being used as art galleries, banks or offices, and can be visited. One of the best is the Casa Ricketts, built in 1738, which was first a seminary, then passed through several hands before being sold to the Banco Central. It now houses a small art gallery and museum, and bank offices. Entry is free. Hours are Monday to Friday from 8 am to noon and 3 to 6 pm. Also worth a look are the Casa de Moral, now owned by the Banco Industrial; the Casona Iriberry, housing the Complejo Cultural Chaves de la Rosa; and the Palacio Goyeneche.

Suburbs
The suburb of **Yanahuara**, north-west of the centre of town, makes a good excursion. Go west on Avenida Grau, cross the bridge, and continue on Avenida Ejército for six or seven blocks. Turn right on Avenida Lima and walk five blocks to a small plaza with the church of Yanahuara, dating from 1750. There's a viewing platform at the end of the plaza, with fine views of Arequipa and El Misti.

Head back along Avenida Jerusalén (in Yanahuara), which is the next street parallel to Avenida Lima; just before Avenida Ejército you'll see the well-known Picantería Sol de Mayo restaurant. The green Yanahuara city bus leaves Arequipa along Puente Grau and returns from Yanahuara Plaza to the city every few minutes.

Beyond Yanahuara is **Cayma**, another suburb with an often-visited church. Continue along Avenida Ejército about three blocks beyond Avenida Jerusalén, then turn right on Avenida Cayma and climb this road for about one km. The church of San Miguel Arcángel is open from 9 am to 4 pm, and the church warden will take you up the small tower, for a tip. Buses marked 'Cayma' go there from Arequipa, along Avenida Grau.

The suburb of **Paucarpata** is seven km south-east of town and has a nice church and great local restaurant. Two km away is the Sabandía mill, which was built in 1621, restored in 1973, and is now working again. Entry is US$1. Gray buses to Paucarpata leave Arequipa along Socabaya.

Places to Stay
The *Hotel Crillon Serrano* (☎ 21-2392), Perú 109, is cheap and basic but clean and friendly, and has warm water in the morning. It charges US$3 per person or US$4 with private bath. The clean and friendly *Pensión Tito* (☎ 23-4424), Perú 105B, is just a little more. The *Hotel Regis* (☎ 22-3612), Ugarte 202, is clean, safe and friendly, has hot water and a rooftop terrace, and charges US$4.50 per person. The *Hostal Colca Tours* (☎ 21-1679), Victor Lira 105, is also clean, safe and friendly, though in a poor area. It's US$5.50/ 10 for a single/double with private warm shower.

Cheaper but poorer hotels which may be dirty and lack hot water include the *Hostal Comercio* (☎ 21-2186), the *Gran Hotel* (☎ 21-2001), A Thomas 451, the *Hostal Granada*, on Perú near the market, and the *Hostal América* (☎ 24-3141), Peral 202, all

PERU

PERU

To Sol de Mayo,
Mirador, Iglesia de
Yanahuara, Airport

Ejército

Recoleta

Av Bolognesi

Puente Grau

C Llosa

Río Chili

Via Circunvalación

Moral

Ugarte

Villalva

Bolívar

Santa Catalina

San Francisco

San Agustín

Puente Bolognesi

Ayacucho

Melgar

Jerusalén

Santa Marta

Rivero

San José

Portal

Colón

Palacio Viejo

Consuelo

Cruz Verde

Sucre

La Merced

Plaza de
Armas

Mercaderes

Santo Domingo

Valdivia

Alvarez Thomas

San Camilo

Muñoz

Peral

Luna

San Martín

28 de Julio

Salaverry

Parra

Sepúlveda

Garci Carbajal

N de Piérola

San Juan de Dios

Alto de la Luna

Market

Peru

Pizarro

Calle Nueva

Cortaderas

Victor Lira

Garci Carbajal

Romaña

Leticia

Olimpica

Av Jorge Chavez

Estadio

Tacna y Arica

Quiroz

Huascar y Argamosa

To Terminal
Terrestre

Railway
Station

To Paucarpata

Av Independencia

Arequipa

0   100   200 m

PLACES TO STAY

2	La Posada del Puente Grau
5	Hostal Wilson
6	Hostal Santa Catalina
7	Hotel Jerusalén
8	La Casa de Mi Abuela
9	Hostal Latino
10	Hostal Núñez
16	La Boveda Inn
19	Residencial Rivero
27	La Casa de Melgar
29	Hotel Regis
33	Hotel Crismar
35	Hotel La Fontana
36	Hostal América
37	Hostal Tumi de Oro
49	Hostal Mercaderes
50	Hotel Conquistador
53	Hotel Maison Plaza
55	Hostal Nikos
56	Hostal Mirador
57	Hotel El Portal
60	Hotel Crillon Serrano, Pensión Tito
65	Hostal V Lira
66	Hostal Hugo, Jorge's
68	Hostal Imperial
69	Hotel La Condesa
71	Hotel Viza
72	Hostal Lider Inn
76	Hostal Royal
78	Hotel San Francisco
79	Hostal Granada
82	Hostal Comercio
83	Hostal Colca Tours
84	Hostal Americano
85	Gran Hotel
86	Hostal San Juan
89	Hotel San Gregory
90	Hostal Virrey
94	Hostal Florida
95	Hostal Europa, Hostal Paris
97	Hostal Grace
98	Hostal Premier
99	Hostal Colonia
100	Hostal Extra

PLACES TO EAT

2	La Posada del Puente Grau
11	Govinda Vegetarian Restaurant, Other Budget Places
15	Pizzería Los Leños
16	Lakshimivan Vegetarian Restaurant
28	Lluvia de Oro
31	Café Peña Anuschka
34	Pizzería San Antonio
41	Central Garden Restaurant
47	Restaurant Bonanza
52	Restaurant Cuzco, Balcony Restaurant, Others
59	La Rueda Parrilladas
67	Monzas
74	Cevichería 45
75	Restaurant América
77	Restaurant Dalmacia, Puerto Rico

OTHER

1	Clínica Arequipa
3	Monasterio de La Recoleta, Museo
4	National Car Rental
12	Museo Municipal, Crafts Shops
13	San Francisco
14	Conresa Tours
17	Continental Tours
18	Instituto Cultural Peruano-NorteAmericano
20	Santa Teresa
21	Monasterio de Santa Catalina
22	Las Quenas
23	Romie's Peña
24	Blues Bar
25	Instituto Cultural Peruano-Alemán
26	Tourist Police, Information
30	Alianza Francesa
32	Coltur
35	Peña Picantería
38	Casa de Moral
39	Complejo Cultural Chaves de la Rosa, Casona Iriberry
40	Lima Tours
42	La Catedral
43	Casa Ricketts
44	Correos Central
45	Map Shop
46	Carnaby Disco
48	Cine Municipal
51	San Agustín
54	AeroPerú, Faucett, Americana, AeroContinente (Airlines)
57	Cine Portal, Imperial Air
58	Banco de Crédito
61	Casablanca Disco
62	Tourist Office
63	La Compañía
64	Cine Fenix
70	Santo Domingo
73	Telefónica del Perú
80	La Merced
81	Cine Ateneo
84	Cine Variedades
87	Bus Companies to Colca
88	Many Bus Companies
91	Cruz del Sur, Sur Peruano
92	Cruz del Sur
93	Ormeño
96	Expreso Sudamericano

PERU

under US$3 per person. The *Hostal Lider Inn* (☎ 23-8210), Consuelo 429, is US$5.50 for fairly clean doubles with hot showers and is popular with young local couples. The *Hostal Europa* (☎ 23-9787) and *Hostal Paris* (☎ 23-6250) are basic but have hot water in the morning. The Europa is US$3 per person and the Paris is US$4/5, or US$6/8 in rooms with bath. The grubby *Hotel San Francisco* (☎ 23-4006), San Juan de Dios 314A, has hot water in the morning. Rooms are US$3 per person or US$8 for a double with bath.

The noisy *Hostal San Juan* (☎ 24-3861), San Juan de Dios 521, is US$4/7 or US$8 for doubles with hot showers. The *Hostal Mercaderes* (☎ 21-4830), Peral 117, is basic but OK for US$4/6 or US$6 per person with private warm showers. The *Hostal Mirador* charges a little more and receives mixed reports but a few rooms have great plaza views. *La Boveda Inn*, Jerusalén 402, has doubles for US$8 and a popular vegetarian restaurant. The basic *Hostal V Lira* (☎ 21-3161), charges US$5/8, has hot water and is secure. The equally basic *Hostal Virrey* (☎ 23-5191) may have hot water at US$4/6, or US$6/9 with bath.

The reasonably clean and friendly *Hostal Royal* (☎ 21-2071), San Juan de Dios 300A, has hot water at US$4.50 per person, or US$10 for a double with bath. The basic *Hostal Santa Catalina* (☎ 22-2722), Santa Catalina 500, has hot water and is fairly clean and popular. It's US$6/8 or US$7.50/10 with bath. The similarly priced *Residencial Rivero* (☎ 22-9266), Rivero 420, has tepid water and is just OK. The basic but clean and adequate *Hostal Grace* (☎ 23-5924), Quiroz 121, is US$7/9 with shared warm showers. The *Hostal Imperial* (☎ 21-2125), San Juan de Dios 210, is similar but the *Hostal Nikos* (☎ 21-7713), Mercaderes 142, is reportedly dirty and poorly maintained.

The secure and friendly *Hostal Núñez* (☎ 21-8648, 22-0111), Jerusalén 528, is US$5 per person or US$9/15 with bath. There is hot water, a terrace, and it's popular with gringos. The *Hostal Tumi de Oro*, San Agustín 311A, is clean and friendly and has hot water. It's US$5 per person or US$7.50/12.50 with bath. The basic but clean *Hostal Americano* (☎ 21-1752), A Thomas 435, has rooms for US$10 (one or two people) with shared hot showers. In this price range are the friendly *La Casa de Melgar* (☎ 22-2459), Melgar 108A, in a nice building with OK rooms; the basic *Hostal Colonia* (☎ 24-2766), Cáceres 109, which has large rooms; the friendly *Hostal Extra* (☎ 22-1217), which has a garden; and the decent *Hotel San Gregory* (☎ 24-5036), A Thomas 535, which has clean rooms with bath.

Hostal Hugo/Jorge's (☎ 21-3988), Santo Domingo 110, has basic rooms for US$6/10 and rooms with hot bath for US$11/15. The nice *Hostal Wilson* (☎ 23-8781), Grau 306, is US$6 per person or US$7.50 with bath. The *Hostal Florida* (☎ 23-8467, 22-8710), San Juan de Dios 664B, is reasonable at US$7.50/12.50 or US$11/16 with bath. The clean *Hostal Premier* (☎ 24-1091), Quiroz 100, is US$9/14 or US$12/16 with bath.

The very respectable and secure *La Casa de Mi Abuela* (☎ 22-3194), Jerusalén 606, is a good up-market choice. Rooms are US$16/23 with bath or half this price with shared bath. There's an attractive garden full of singing birds where you can enjoy breakfast. The similarly priced *Hostal Latino* (☎ 24-4770), Carlos Llosa 135, has large, comfortable rooms with bath, and a café.

Places to Eat

For cheap vegetarian food try *Govinda*, Jerusalén 505, run by Hare Krishnas, or the popular *Lakshimivan*, Jerusalén 402. There are more cheap restaurants on these blocks, including *Lluvia de Oro*, Jerusalén 308. Good Italian food is served at *Pizzería San Antonio* (☎ 21-3950), at Jerusalén and Santa Marta, and *Pizzería Los Leños*, Jerusalén 407. Both are popular with young locals. The *Bonanza*, Jerusalén 114, serves a variety of dishes at US$3 to US$7 and is also locally popular.

The *Balcony Restaurant* and *Restaurant Cuzco*, on the north-west side of the plaza, 2nd floor, have fine plaza views; the food is OK and cheap but service is very slow. Below the Balcony are other cheap to mid-priced restaurants. Three good, reasonably priced restaurants in the 300 block of San Juan de Dios are the *Puerto Rico* (☎ 21-7512), the *Dalmacia* and the *América* – this last has good ice creams and snacks. Several places on this street serve half a grilled chicken for US$2.50. There are restaurants with set lunch menús for US$1.50 along La Merced.

Two up-market cafés on the first block of San Francisco have good espresso, cappuccino and snacks. The best but most expensive coffee is at *Monzas*, on Santo Domingo, a block east of the plaza. The best ceviche (and nothing else) can be had at the *Cevichería 45* (☎ 24-2400), A Thomas 221, from 9 am to 3 pm. The friendly *Café Peña Anuschka*, Santa Catalina 204, has home-made pastries, German specialities and tropical cocktails.

An excellent place for arequipeño food is the locally popular *Tradición Arequipeña* (☎ 24-2385), Avenida Dolores 111, Paucarpata, with meals in the US$3 to US$6 range. Most taxi drivers know it (under US$2 from the centre). Also good for local dishes is the *Sol de Mayo*, Jerusalén 207, Yanahuara. Both places open only for lunch.

Entertainment

Pizzería Los Leños has rock music interspersed with live Peruvian folklórico musicians wandering in during the evening. *Las Quenas* (☎ 21-5468), Santa Catalina 302, has live music nightly from 9 pm. The music varies though folklórico predominates. There is a US$2.50 cover charge and they serve food.

The *El Sillar* is a good weekend peña which gets under way around 11 pm and where dancing continues through the wee hours. The cover charge is US$2.50 but the address has changed recently so ask locals. Locals recommend *El Búho* (folklórico) and *La Pirámide* (criollo) peñas in Yanahuara. Occasionally, there is entertainment at the *Peña Picantería*, Jerusalén 204.

The *Blues Bar*, on the last block of San Francisco, has good drinks and music and is the current gathering point of young arequipeños. The best disco is the locally popular *Casablanca*, in a basement on Sucre near Bolognesi, with a US$4 cover charge. Or try *Carnaby*, on Jerusalén. There are several cinemas.

Getting There & Away

Air The airport is nine km north-west of the city centre. AeroPerú (☎ 21-2835, 21-6820), AeroContinente (☎ 21-9721, 21-7314), Americana (☎ 21-2892) and Faucett (☎ 21-2322, 21-2352) have offices on the plaza. On most days, there are seven flights to Lima (US$89), and four each to Tacna (US$22), Cuzco (US$46) and Juliaca (US$42).

Bus Most buses leave from the modern Terminal Terrestre, three km south of the centre. There is a US$0.50 departure tax. Many bus offices are near the 600 block of San Juan de Dios, where tickets are sold.

Lima (16 to 21 hours) is served by Ormeño, Cruz del Sur, CIVA, Flores Hermanos, Sudamericano and others, most with buses leaving in the afternoon. Fares range from US$12 for regular service to US$25 for luxury service. Many buses stop in Nazca (US$7 and up, nine to 12 hours) as well as in Camaná, Chala and Ica. There are also many buses a day via Moquegua to Tacna (US$4 to US$7, seven hours).

Ormeño has two night buses to Puno, Cruz del Sur has two day buses to Puno, and Transportes Jacantay has an afternoon bus to Juliaca, Puno, Desaguadero and La Paz, Bolivia. Other companies also go to Lake Titicaca and beyond. It's about US$8 and 13 hours to Puno, US$18 to La Paz. The road to Juliaca is in terrible shape and many travellers prefer the train. There have been cases of night buses to Juliaca being held up. These and other companies also have buses to Cuzco (US$10 to US$12, around 18 hours) on a poor road. The journeys to Juliaca and Cuzco can take much longer in wet weather. This is a cold night trip: dress warmly.

Ormeño has three international buses a week to Santiago, Chile (US$80) and Buenos Aires, Argentina (US$130).

Transportes Transandino, Turismo Expreso Cóndor, Transportes Prado, Transportes Colca and Transportes Cristo Rey have departures at 4 am, 1 pm, and 1.30 pm for Chivay (US$2.50, three hours) continuing through Yanque, Achoma and Maca to Cabanaconde (US$4, seven hours) on the upper Cañón del Colca. Empresa Jacantay has a 6.30 am departure for Cabanaconde via Huambo.

For buses to Corire (US$2.50, three hours) to visit the Toro Muerto petroglyphs, go with Flores Hermanos, El Chasqui or Transportes del Carpio. There are departures almost every hour from about 5.30 am. El Chasqui also goes to Valle de Majes (US$2) for river running as do Transportes Berrios and Mendoza. Transportes Mendoza has buses to the Valle de Los Volcanes.

Train The journey to Juliaca is much more comfortable by train than by bus. The train leaves Arequipa at 8 pm on Tuesday, Wednesday, Friday and Sunday and arrives at Juliaca at 6 am the following day. You can continue to Puno, an hour away, or connect

PERU

with the 9 am Juliaca-Cuzco train, arriving at 6 pm. If going to Puno, it is quicker to buy a ticket to Juliaca and then catch one of the many minibuses to Puno waiting for the train.

Many people have been robbed on the night train, especially in crowded 2nd class. You are safest buying a Pullman ticket instead of just a 1st-class ticket. The Pullman car has comfortable reclining seats so you can sleep, and is heated. The doors are locked and only ticket holders are admitted into the carriages.

Fares from Arequipa change frequently and drastically. Recent fares to Puno are US$15/12/9.50 for Pullman/1st/2nd class, to Juliaca they are US$15/10/8 and to Cuzco they are US$33/21.50/17.

Buy your tickets in advance rather than while guarding your luggage. Ticket office hours change constantly, and there are usually long lines with several hours wait. Travel agencies (eg Conresa Tours and Continental Tours, on the 400 block of Jerusalén) will sell tickets, for a 25% commission, and provide transport from your hotel to the station. Shop around for the best deal.

Getting Around

To/From the Airport Buses marked 'Río Seco', 'Cono-Norte' or 'Zamacola' go along Puente Grau and Ejército and pass within a km of the airport; ask the driver where to get off. A taxi from the city centre costs about US$5. From the airport, shared taxi colectivos charge US$2.50 per person and take you to your hotel.

To/From the Bus Terminal Buses go south along Bolívar and Sucre bound for the Terminal Terrestre. A taxi will cost about US$2.

AROUND AREQUIPA
Cañón del Colca

The most popular excursion from Arequipa is to the Cañón del Colca (Colca Canyon), which can be visited by public transport or with a guided tour. Controversy rages about whether or not this is the world's deepest canyon. The sections which you can see from the road are very impressive but are not the deepest sections. To see these, you have to hike in on an overnight trip.

Guided tours are US$20 to US$25 for a day or US$10 more for two days. The one-day trip is rushed and we recommend a two-day trip which includes lodging with breakfast in Chivay. Day tours leave before dawn and go through the **Reserva Nacional Salinas y Aguada Blanca**, where vicuñas are often sighted. A breakfast stop is often made at Vizcachani (4150 metres). The road continues through bleak altiplano to about 4800 metres, from where the snowcaps of Ampato (6288 metres) are seen. Then the road drops spectacularly to Chivay, about 160 km from Arequipa. The road continues west, following the south side of the Cañón del Colca. The landscape has Inca terracing and several villages whose inhabitants still use the terraces. The end point of the tour is at the Cruz del Cóndor lookout, about 60 km beyond Chivay and an hour before you get to the village of Cabanaconde. Andean condors may be seen here and the view is impressive, with the river flowing 1200 metres below. Overnight tours stop in Chivay, where there are hot springs, continuing to Cruz del Cóndor early the next day.

Several tour companies do the trip; some aren't very good, so check locally before you part with your money. Guides should be able to produce a Tourist Guide card. Operators will often pool their clients. Conresa (☎ 21-1847, 21-5820), Jerusalén 409, or Continental, Jerusalén 402, often provide the vehicle and the lowest prices. Unfortunately, the minibuses used don't have adequate leg room for tall people, so it may be better to go in a smaller group with a car. Guides don't always speak English. A car taking a maximum of five people can be hired for US$70/110 for one/two days; the hotel is extra.

By public transport, you can get off at Cruz del Cóndor and camp. It is a two-hour walk from the lookout to Cabanaconde, where there are hotels. You could also take the 4 am Arequipa bus from Cabanaconde, get off at the lookout for dawn and condor

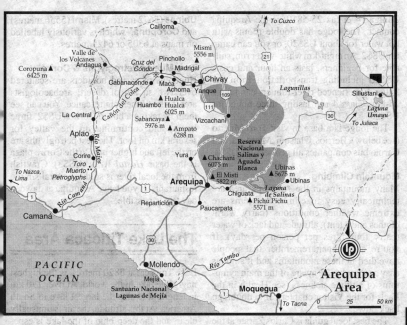

Arequipa Area

viewing, then return to Cabanaconde for a second night. The best condor viewing is from 7 to 9 am, but it's not bad in the late afternoon. You can also get directions at Cabanaconde for overnight camping trips into the canyon; bring everything you'll need. The best trips to Colca are unrushed ones!

Places to Stay Chivay, at an altitude of about 3700 metres, has four basic but friendly cold-water hotels around the plaza for US$2 per person. The *Hostal Colca* and *Hostal Posada del Inca* are two or three blocks west of the plaza. Both have restaurants and hot water and charge US$7.50 per person with private bath. The Colca has rooms with shared bath for US$4.50 per person. There are hot springs four km northeast of Chivay by road. There is a clean swimming pool (with changing rooms), a basic cafeteria and a US$0.25 fee.

Cabanaconde has three basic *pensiones*, charging US$2.50 per person. Walk 10 minutes west of the plaza to a hill with good views and occasional condors in the early morning. Ask for directions to hike into the canyon. It takes about six hours one way, so you should be prepared to camp. Longer overnight trips are also done. The SAEC in Lima has details.

Getting There & Away If you don't want a guided tour, see the Arequipa section for details of bus companies which have daily dawn departures to Chivay. Most continue to Cabanaconde and return from there to Arequipa at 4 am daily. The section of road between Cabanaconde and Huambo veers away from the canyon. It is also the roughest part, and there is little transport.

Rafting

Running the Colca is a difficult undertaking, and is for experienced people only. The Río Majes is much easier. The best base is the *Majes River Lodge* (☎ 21-0256), 190 km by road west of Arequipa. River guide Carlos

PERU

Zúñiga (☎ & fax 25-5819) is the Arequipa contact. The lodge has double rooms with hot water for about US$20, or you can camp for US$2. An eight-km white-water run, suitable for beginners, lasts an hour and costs US$10 including transportation from the lodge. Experienced river runners can take a 25-km, Class 4 run lasting three hours for US$25.

The lodge is a base to visit Toro Muerto (see below). Berrios, Chasqui, Mendoza, and Carpio bus companies all go there for US$2.

Mountain Climbing

Many mountains in the Arequipa area are technically easy to climb. Problems are extreme weather conditions (carry warm clothes and a tent), altitude and lack of water (carry four litres per person per day). If you're a beginner, remember that people have died in these mountains and it's not as easy as it looks. Be aware of the main symptoms of altitude sickness (see Health in the Facts for the Visitor chapter). If in doubt, go back down.

The best local guide is Carlos Zárate at the Alianza Francesa (☎ 21-5579), Santa Catalina 208. His wife, Olivia Mazuelos, works there and can tell you where he is. He provides information, gear rental, and guide referral.

The 5822-metre-high volcano **El Misti** is the most popular local climb. There are several routes. One is to take a bus to Chiguata (US$0.75, one hour) at 6 am from Avenida Sepulveda in the Miraflores district. From Chiguata to the base camp is an eight-hour hard uphill slog on rough trails. From there to the summit and back takes eight more hours and there's no water. The summit is marked by a 10-metre-high metal cross. The return from the base camp to Chiguata takes three hours or less. A bus returns from Chiguata to Arequipa at 4 pm.

Chachani (6075 metres) is one of the easiest 6000-metre peaks in the world. You need crampons, an ice axe and good equipment. Other nearby peaks of interest include **Sabancaya** (5976 metres), **Hualca Hualca** (6025 metres), **Ampato** (6288 metres),

Ubinas (5672 metres), **Mismi** (5556 metres) and **Coropuna**, which is variously labelled on maps at 6305 or 6425 metres.

Toro Muerto Petroglyphs & Corire

Hundreds of carved boulders are scattered over two sq km of desert; archaeologists aren't sure of their significance. You can see them by taking a bus to Corire (US$2, three hours) and continuing up the valley for several km on foot. The best petroglyphs are on the left and higher up. On the Corire plaza is the basic *Hostal Willy* (US$3). Crayfish from the local river is sold in several simple restaurants. If you leave Arequipa at dawn, a day trip is possible.

The Lake Titicaca Area

Lake Titicaca, at 3820 metres, is the highest navigable lake in the world. At over 170 km in length, it is also the largest lake in South America. At this altitude, the air is unusually clear, and the deep blue of the lake is especially pretty. If you arrive from the coast, take it easy: the altitude can make you sick.

The lake straddles the Peru-Bolivia border. The most common route into Bolivia is via Yunguyo, crossing the border to Copacabana, then by bus and boat to La Paz; see the To/From Bolivia section. The Lake Titicaca section of the Bolivia chapter has more information about that side of the border, and a map of the area.

Interesting boat trips can be made from Puno, Peru's major port on Lake Titicaca. Several colonial churches and archaeological monuments are worth visiting. The Department of Puno is famous for its folk dances, which are the wildest and most colourful in the Peruvian highlands. There are huge herds of alpacas and llamas. It is a fascinating area.

JULIACA
With 100,000 inhabitants, Juliaca is the largest town in the Department of Puno, has the only commercial airport and is a major

railway junction, with connections to Arequipa, Puno and Cuzco. It is of comparatively little interest, however, and most people prefer nearby Puno, which has better hotels and views of Lake Titicaca.

Information

The Banco de Crédito, M Núñez 138, changes travellers' cheques. Other moneychangers are on the block north of this bank. The telephone code is 054. Juliaca's Clínica Adventista is the best hospital in the Puno department.

Places to Stay

Cheap hotels have an unreliable water supply. The following are very basic but cheap. *Hotel Don Pedro* and *Hostal Loreto* charge US$2.50/4 for a single/double and are opposite the train station. Nearby, the *Hotel Ferrocarril* is US$1.50 per person, *Hotel del Sur* is US$2 per person and the unfriendly *Gran Hotel Juliaca* is US$3.50 per person. The *Hotel Centro* (☎ 32-1636), Núñez 350, and the *Hostal Rosedal* by the post office are just OK for US$4/5.

Better cheapies include the *Hostal San Antonio* (☎ 32-1701), San Martín 347, at US$3.50/5. Rooms have toilets but showers are shared. Hot water is US$1.20 extra and there's a sauna. The *Hostal Sakura* (☎ 32-1194), Unión 133, is OK for US$3 per person or US$5/8 with bath and occasional hot water. Also decent is the friendly *Hostal Aparicio* (☎ 32-1625), Loreto 270, at US$3.50 per person, with occasional hot water.

The clean, friendly and often full *Hotel Yasur* (☎ 32-1501), Nuñez 414, is US$4.50/6.50 or US$5.50/8 with private bath. There is hot water morning and evening. The clean, comfortable and recommended *Hostal Perú* (☎ 32-1510), opposite the train station, is US$5.50/8.50, or US$7/11 with bath, and has hot water in the evening.

Getting There & Away

Air The airport serves Juliaca and Puno. There are about eight daily flights to/from Lima (US$94), many via Arequipa (US$42) and a few via Cuzco (US$42), with Aero-Continente, AeroPerú (☎ 32-2001), Americana (☎ 32-1844) or Faucett (☎ 32-2993, 32-1966). Americana has evening flights to Tacna.

Bus San Cristóbal (☎ 32-1181), Cruz del Sur (☎ 32-2011) and others have the same destinations as from Puno. Empresa de Transportes San Martín has night buses to Moquegua, Tacna and Ilo. Transportes 3 de Mayo goes to Huancané (US$1.25, 2½ hours). Minibuses to Puno (US$0.50) pass the railway station looking for passengers.

Train See the Puno section for details about trains, times and fares. Fares from Juliaca are a few cents cheaper than from Puno and trains leave one to two hours after the Puno departure time. Passengers from Arequipa continuing to Cuzco have time between trains to wander around. Alpaca sweaters, ponchos etc are sold, and you can shop through the carriage window. Bargain hard. Passengers to Puno can take a minibus from Juliaca and beat the train. The ill-lit Juliaca station has a reputation for luggage snatching and pickpocketing. Read the warnings in the Arequipa Train section and watch your belongings.

PUNO

Puno was founded on 4 November 1668, but few colonial buildings remain except the Catedral. The town itself is drab and uninteresting, but there's a good hotel selection and plenty to see nearby.

Information

The tourist office (☎ 35-1449, 35-3804) is on the north-east corner of the plaza; hours are Monday to Saturday, 8 am to 1 pm and 2 to 6 pm. The Policía de Turismo is at Deustua 588.

Money The Banco de Crédito changes travellers' cheques. Moneychangers hang out on Calle Lima. Buy or sell Bolivian pesos at the border for the best exchange rates.

PERU

Telephone Puno's telephone code is 054.

Bolivian Consulate This is at Puno 350. For visa requirements, see Facts for the Visitor in the Bolivia chapter.

Travel Agencies Feiser Tours (☎ 35-3112), Valcárcel 155, Panamericano Travel Service, Tacna 245, Kontiki Tours (☎ 35-2771), Melgar 188, and Inca Tours (☎ 35-1062), Ugarte 145, have been recommended. There are many others. It pays to shop around.

Things to See

The **Museo Carlos Dreyer**, Conde de Lemos 289, is open on weekdays from 8.30 am to 1.30 pm. Entry is US$1.

The **Parque Huajsapata**, a little hill about 10 minutes south-west of town, features a statue of the first Inca, Manco Capac, looking out at Lake Titicaca. The view of the town and the lake is excellent. The **Arco Deustua**, an arch on Calle Independencia, also has good views.

Special Events

The Department of Puno has a wealth of traditional dances and music. The costumes, often worth more than an entire family's clothes, are ornate and imaginative. Check the tourist office for local fiesta information. Apart from the major Peruvian festivals, the following are important in the Lake Titicaca region:

6 January
   Día de los Reyes (Epiphany)
2-14 February
   Virgen de la Candelaria (Candlemas)
7-8 March
   Día de San Juan (St John)
2-4 May
   Alacitas (Puno miniature handicrafts fair)
   Día de Santa Cruz (Holy Cross; Huancané, Taquile, Puno)
25 July
   Día de Santiago (St James; Taquile)
24 September
   La Virgen de La Merced (Our Lady of Mercy)
1-7 November
   Semana Cívica de Puno (Puno Week)

Places to Stay

Hotels fill quickly after the evening train arrives. Prices may double during festivals, and sometimes do so in the evening. Many hotels have triple and quadruple rooms. Water and power shortages are a problem, but there are public hot showers (US$1) on Avenida El Sol. Lock your luggage; thefts from hotel rooms have been reported.

The following are US$3/5 for very basic singles/doubles: *Hostal Torino* and *Hostal Venecia* are both bad; *Hostal Extra* (☎ 35-1123), Moquegua 124, sometimes has hot water and is the best of the super-cheapies; *Hotel Centenario*, Deza 211; and the *Hostal Rosario* (☎ 35-2272), Moquegua 325. The *Hostal Los Incas*, Los Incas 105, has no singles, plenty of triples and quads, and hot showers (US$1), and *Hostal Roma* (☎ 35-1501), Libertad 115, has dorm rooms for US$2 per person.

The *Hostal Europa* (☎ 35-3023), Ugarte 112, is popular with gringos. Doubles are US$8. It's OK, with left-luggage facilities and hot water in the evening if the showers work. The *Hotel Arequipa* (☎ 35-2071), Arequipa 153, is similar. Probably the best cheap hotel is the quiet *Hostal Los Uros* (☎ 35-2141), Valcarcel 135. It has a cafeteria, open for simple breakfasts, and hot water in the evening. There are a few singles but plenty of triples and even quads. Rates are US$5.50/8.50 for a single/double, or US$7/11 with private bath.

The clean *Hostal San Carlos* (☎ 35-1862), Ugarte 161, has telephones in the rooms and claims to have hot water all day. Rates are US$8/11 or US$13/18 with private bath. There is a restaurant for breakfast. The *Hostal Nesther* (☎ 35-1631), Deustua 268, has hot water from 6 to 8 am only, is clean and is quite good for US$8/13 with bath. The *Hotel Tumi* (☎ 35-3270), Cajamarca 253, is another OK choice at US$10/14 with bath. They are open to bargaining.

Places to Eat

The *Comedor Vegetariano Delta*, Libertad 215, is dingy but cheap and recommended for early breakfasts and vegetarian food. The

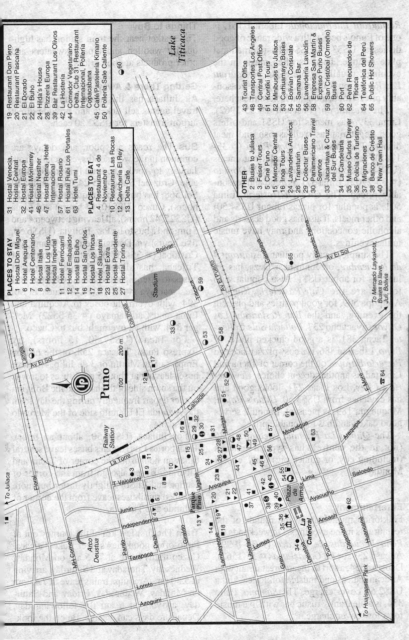

PLACES TO STAY

1 Hostal Don Miguel
6 Hostal Arequipa
7 Hotel Centenario
8 Hostal Italia
9 Hostal Los Uros,
   Hostal Internacional
11 Hotel Ferrocarril
12 Hotel Embajador
14 Hostal El Buho
16 Hostal San Carlos
17 Hostal Los Incas
18 Hotel Sillustani
23 Hostal Extra
25 Hostal Presidente
27 Hostal Torino
31 Hostal Venecia,
   Hostal Central
32 Hostal Europa
41 Hostal Monterrey
46 Hostal Nesther
47 Hostal Roma, Hotel
   Internacional
57 Hostal Rosario
61 Hostal Rubi Los Portales
63 Hotel Turni

PLACES TO EAT

4 Restaurant 4 de
   Noviembre
10 Restaurant Las Rocas
12 Cevichería El Rey
13 Delta Cafe
19 Restaurant Don Piero
20 Restaurant Pascana
21 El Dorado
22 El Buho
24 Hilda's House
28 Pizzeria Europa
39 Bar Restaurant Los Olivos
42 La Hostería
44 Comedor Vegetariano
   Delta, Club 31, Restaurant
   Internacional, Polleria
   Copacabana
45 Café/Pastelería Kimano
50 Polleria Sale Caliente

OTHER

2 Buses to Juliaca
3 Feiser Tours
5 Ciné Puno
15 Mercado Central
16 Inca Tours
24 Lavandería América
26 Transturin
29 Colectur Buses
30 Panamericano Travel
   Service
33 Jacantaya & Cruz
   del Sur Buses
34 La Candelaria
35 Museo Carlos Dreyer
36 Policia de Turismo
37 Migraciones
38 Banco de Crédito
40 New Town Hall
43 Tourist Office
48 Transportes Los Angeles
49 Central Post Office
51 Kontiki Tours
52 Minibuses to Juliaca
53 Carhuamayo Buses
54 Bolivian Consulate
55 Samana Bar
56 Lavandería Lavaclin
58 Empresa San Martín &
   Expreso Puno Buses
59 San Cristóbal (Ormeño)
   Buses
60 Port
62 Peña Recuerdos de
   Titicaca
64 Telefónica del Perú
65 Public Hot Showers

Restaurant Internacional, Libertad 161, is one of Puno's best, with a wide range of good dishes at US$3 or US$4. Its international plate is huge. There is often music in the evenings, usually before 8 pm. *Restaurant Las Rocas*, on Valcárcel, has good, reasonably priced food, though it lacks atmosphere.

The *Restaurant Pascana* (☎ 35-1962), Lima 339, has menús for US$1 and offers good vegetarian as well as fish and meat dishes. The *Restaurant Don Piero* (☎ 35-1788), Lima 354, has local trout meals (US$4) and other cheaper dishes. *El Dorado* (☎ 35-2702), Lima 371, is good and reasonably priced. The cosy *La Hostería*, Lima 501, is popular for pizzas (about US$4.50) and other meals. It also has good desserts and alcoholic concoctions and may have music in the evenings.

The simple, locally popular *Restaurant 4 de Noviembre*, on Junín near Deza, has set lunches for about US$1. Also popular with locals are the *Café/Pastelería Kimano*, Arequipa 509, for good pastries and pizza in the evening, and the *Bar Restaurant Los Olivos*, Ayacucho 237. *Pollería Sale Caliente*, Tacna 381, is a good chicken place. *El Búho*, Libertad 386, is a cosy pizza place and *Pizzería Europa*, on the corner of Tacna and Libertad, is another decent choice. *Cevichería El Rey*, Los Incas 271, looks good and has ceviches from US$3.50. *Hilda's House*, Moquegua 189, is pleasant, tranquil, serves good cakes and has reasonable prices.

The *Quinta La Kantuta*, Arequipa 1086 (not in the centre), has typical lunches (including cuy, or guinea pig) daily, except Monday.

Entertainment

Folklórico musicians do the rounds of the restaurants in the evenings. On weekends try *Peña Recuerdos de Titicaca* (☎ 35-1999), Ancash 239, or *La Candelaria* (☎ 35-1562), Deustua 654, a sort of theatre-restaurant with Andean dances and música folklórica, and a US$2.50 cover charge. The *Samana*, Puno 334, is a pleasantly rustic bar with live music for a low cover charge.

Things to Buy

The market near the train station has high-quality woollen and alpaca sweaters and other products at good prices.

Getting There & Away

Air Juliaca has the nearest airport. Puno travel agents sell tickets and provide direct airport transfers for US$2.50 each.

Bus The roads are poor, and delays are common in the wet months, especially from January to April. The train is more comfortable. Cruz del Sur (☎ 35-2451), Avenida El Sol 568, has buses to Arequipa (US$10, 12 hours), Cuzco (US$10, 14 hours) and Lima (US$25, 42 hours), all leaving between 4 and 5 pm, and a bus to La Paz, Bolivia, (US$6.50, five hours) via Desaguadero, at 10 am. San Cristóbal (☎ 35-2321), on the 300 block of Titicaca, has slightly cheaper overnight buses to Arequipa and Lima. Cheaper still are Jacantaya (☎ 35-1931), Avenida El Sol 594, with overnight buses to Arequipa and Lima, and Carhuamayo (☎ 35-3522), Melgar 334, with an overnight bus to Cuzco.

For Tacna (US$7.50, 15 hours), try Expreso Puno, Titicaca 258, or the nearby Empresa San Martín or 3 de Julio. All have buses leaving at about 5 pm. Buses to towns on the south side of the lake and the Bolivian border depart frequently during the day from the Avenida El Ejército side of the Mercado Laykakota.

For Juliaca (US$0.50, about an hour), Transportes Los Angeles buses leave several times an hour from the corner of Tacna and Libertad. Buses also go from the corner of Lampa and El Sol. Slightly faster but more cramped minibuses leave from the corner of Cahuide and Titicaca.

Train The first few km of the journey out of Puno offer good views over Lake Titicaca. Cuzco trains leave at 7.25 am on Monday, Wednesday, Thursday and Saturday, arriving at 5.30 pm. Arequipa trains leave at 7.45 pm on Monday, Wednesday, Friday and Saturday, arriving at 6 am the following day. Departure days can change. Be on the look-

PERU

out for thieves at the station and on the trains, especially to Arequipa (see the Arequipa section for details).

Cuzco fares are US$18/13.50/10.50 in Pullman/1st/2nd class, and Arequipa fares are US$15/12/9.50. Fares have varied greatly in past years. There have been complaints of 1st-class tickets being sold for Pullman prices, so check carefully. Pullman class is safest, but 1st class is reasonably safe on the Cuzco day train and 2nd class is OK if you are in a group or have no valuables.

You should buy your Cuzco ticket the day before, but sometimes the numbered 1st-class/Pullman seats get sold out. Lines are always long. We've heard that seats sell out fast because travel agencies buy them for resale at a commission of US$2 to US$4. This is OK if you don't want to stand in line for hours but a pain if you are on a budget. The ticket office opens at 8 am; arrive early. Arequipa tickets are sold on the day of travel. It is quicker and cheaper to take the bus to Juliaca and continue by train from there.

Boat Hydrofoil and catamaran services, combined with bus, link Puno to La Paz but cost about US$150.

Boats from the Puno dock leave for various islands in the lake (see Around Puno). Tickets bought directly from the boats are always cheaper than those from agencies in town. A new dock a few km north of town reportedly opened in late 1995.

Getting Around
Tricycle taxis are a popular way of getting around Puno and are a little cheaper than ordinary taxis.

AROUND PUNO
Sillustani
The southern 'quarter' of the Inca empire was Collasuyo, named after the Collas, who became part of the empire. Colla nobles were buried in *chullpas* (funerary towers) at Sillustani, a small hill-top site on a peninsula in Lake Umayo. The chullpas are up to 12 metres high and look impressive against the bleak landscape.

Getting There & Away Tours leave at 2.30 pm from near Panamericano Travel on Tacna. Tours start at US$7.50 and include entry to the ruins (US$2.50). Not all guides speak English. The round trip is 3½ hours with 1½ hours at the ruins. There is a small on-site museum. For more time at the site, a taxi is US$15.

The Floating Islands
The excursion to the floating islands of the Uros people has become somewhat over-commercialised. Despite this, it remains popular because there is nothing quite like it anywhere else.

The Uros have intermarried with Aymara-speaking Indians, and no pure-blooded Uros remain. Always a small tribe, they began their unusual floating existence to isolate themselves from the Collas and the Incas. About 300 people live on the islands.

The Uros' lives are totally interwoven with the *totora* reed which grows abundantly in the shallows of Lake Titicaca. They harvest these reeds and use them to make everything from the islands themselves to little model boats to sell to tourists. The islands are constructed from many layers of reeds, which rot away from the bottom and are replaced at the top. The 'ground' is soft and springy, so step carefully.

The Uros build canoe-shaped boats from tightly bundled reeds. A well-constructed boat carries a whole family and lasts six months. You can pay the Uros to give you a ride on a boat. Begging and selling is common here, and be prepared to tip for taking photographs. One island has a seven-metre-high rickety platform from which you can view the islands for US$0.50.

Getting There & Away Boats leave the Puno dock every hour from about 7 am until early afternoon. The standard trip (about four hours) takes in the main island and perhaps one other. The boats leave as soon as there are 15 to 20 passengers and charge about US$3.50 each. Tour companies charge US$7 or more.

PERU

Isla Taquile

Taquile is a fascinating island. The people wear colourful traditional clothes, which they make themselves and sell in the island's cooperative store. They speak Quechua and have maintained a strong group identity. The island does not have roads, and electricity was introduced in the 1990s; there are no vehicles and almost no dogs. The island is about six or seven km long, and has several hills with pre-Inca terracing and small ruins. Visitors can wander around, exploring these ruins and enjoying the peaceful scenery.

Special Events St James' Day (25 July) is a big fiesta, and dancing, music and carousing go on from mid-July till the beginning of August, when the Indians traditionally make offerings to Paccha Mama (Mother Earth). New Year's Day is also festive and rowdy.

Many islanders go to Puno for La Virgen de la Candelaria and Puno week, and Taquile is liable to be somewhat deserted then.

Places to Stay & Eat From the dock, a steep stairway leads to the island centre. The climb takes at least 20 minutes (not recommended unless you're acclimatised). In the centre, individuals or small groups are assigned to families who will put you up in their houses. These are rustic, but there are no hotels. The charge is US$2 per person and gifts of fresh food are appreciated. You are given blankets, but bring a sleeping bag, as it gets very cold. Facilities are minimal. Bring a torch.

A few simple restaurants in the island centre sell whatever is available: fresh lake trout, boiled potatoes or eggs. Bottled drinks are available, but are pricey and have been known to run out. Beware of overcharging in restaurants. Boiled tea is usually safe to drink, but it's a good idea to bring purified water. Also bring extra food, unless you want to take pot luck on what's available in the restaurants. Bring small bills (change is limited), and extra money for the unique clothes on sale.

Getting There & Away Boats for Taquile leave from the Puno dock daily, at about 8 or 9 am; show up by 7.30 am. The 24-km passage takes four hours (sometimes including a brief stop at the Floating Islands) and costs US$5 one way. You get about two hours on Taquile, and the return trip leaves at 2.30 pm, arriving in Puno around nightfall. Bring sunscreen for this long trip.

Isla Amantaní

This island a few km north of Taquile is less visited and has fewer facilities. Basic room and board is available for US$4 per day, or pay US$2 to sleep and eat in one of the few 'restaurants'. Boats leave from Puno's dock between 7.30 and 8.30 am on most days. The trip costs US$5.

You can make a round trip from Puno to the floating islands, Amantaní and Taquile. Most boats to Amantaní stop at the floating islands, and you stay overnight on Amantaní. There is a boat from Amantaní to Taquile on most days. Puno tour agencies offer two-day trips, staying overnight in Amantaní and also visiting the floating islands and Taquile, for US$20 (bargain for a low fare). Two-night tours are also available.

The South Shore Towns

An interesting bus excursion can be made to Chimu, Chucuito, Ilave, Juli, Pomata and Zepita, on Titicaca's south shore. If you start early, you can visit all of them in one day and be back in Puno for the night, or continue to Bolivia.

The road east of Puno follows the edge of the lake. After eight km, you reach the village of **Chimu**, famous for its totora-reed industry. Bundles of reeds are seen piled up to dry, and there are often reed boats in various stages of construction.

Juli, 80 km south-east of Puno, is famous for its four colonial churches, which are being slowly restored. San Juan Bautista, the oldest, dates from the late 1500s, and has richly framed colonial paintings. This church is now a museum, usually open in the morning. Market day is Thursday. There is a basic alojamiento.

Pomata, 106 km from Puno, is dominated by the Dominican church atop a small hill.

The church, which is being restored, has many Baroque carvings, and windows made of translucent alabaster; hours are erratic. There is a basic place to stay.

Just beyond Pomata, the road forks. The main road continues south-east through **Zepita** (where there is another colonial church) to the Bolivian border at Desaguadero, while a side road hugs the shore of Lake Titicaca and goes to the other border crossing, at Yunguyo.

Getting There & Away Buses to these places leave frequently from Puno's Mercado Laykakota, on the Avenida Ejército side.

TO/FROM BOLIVIA

Bolivian time is one hour ahead of Peru.

There are two routes to Bolivia: via Yunguyo and via Desaguadero. The Yunguyo route is more attractive and has the added interest of a boat crossing at the Strait of Tiquina. It is longer and a little more complicated than the Desaguadero route, so some travellers prefer to go via Desaguadero.

Via Yunguyo

Buses from Puno to Yunguyo leave from the Mercado Laykakota, take 2½ hours and cost US$2.50 (watch for thieves). There are moneychangers in the Yunguyo plaza and by the border, which is about two km away. Count your money carefully. The border is open from 8 am to 6 pm. Bolivian immigration is a km beyond the border. Taxis are available. Copacabana is the first town in Bolivia, about 10 km away. Sunday is market day in Yunguyo, and there is more frequent transport on that day. Copacabana is a much more pleasant place than Yunguyo to break the journey, and has several hotels.

Several buses a day leave Copacabana for La Paz (US$4, five hours, including a boat crossing of the Strait of Tiquina). If you leave Puno early, you can reach La Paz in one day. It is more convenient to buy a Puno-La Paz ticket with a company such as Colectur, for a few extra dollars. They will drive you to Yunguyo, stop at the money exchange, show you exactly where to go for exit and entrance

formalities, and meet a Bolivian bus which will take you to La Paz. This through service costs about US$10.

Via Desaguadero

Buses from Puno's Mercado Laykakota leave every hour or two for Desaguadero (US$2, two hours). At Desaguadero, there are basic hotels. Border hours are 8 am to 5 pm daily. There are moneychangers at the border and a casa de cambio around the corner.

Several buses a day go from Desaguadero to La Paz (US$2, 4½ hours), passing the ruins of Tiahuanaco.

Crossing the Border

Usually, there's little hassle entering Bolivia at either border crossing, and you can get 90-day permits without difficulty. Beware of immigration officials trying to charge a small 'entry tax': this is not legal. You can either pay or brazen it out.

Cuzco

Cuzco was the capital of the Inca empire, and most of Cuzco's central streets are lined with Inca-built stone walls, which now form the foundations of colonial or modern buildings. The streets are often stepped and narrow, and throng with Quechua-speaking descendants of the Incas. Cuzco is the archaeological capital of the Americas and the oldest continuously inhabited city on the continent. Today, it is the capital of its department and has 300,000 inhabitants. It is the hub of the South American travel network. The elevation is 3326 metres.

History

Several poorly known cultures lived here before the Incas arrived in the 12th century. Around 1438, the ninth Inca, Pachacutec, defeated the Chancas who were attempting to take over Cuzco, and during the next 25 years he conquered most of the central Peruvian Andes. Pachacutec was a great urban developer. He devised the famous puma shape of Cuzco and diverted the Sapphi and Tullumayo rivers into channels which crossed the city, providing water and keeping the city clean. He built agricultural terraces and many buildings, including the famous Coricancha temple, and his palace on what is now the western corner of the Plaza de Armas.

By 1532 Atahualpa had defeated his half-brother Huáscar in the Inca civil war. The conquistador Pizarro exploited this situation, marching into Cuzco after taking Atahualpa prisoner, and later having him killed. Pizarro was permitted into the heart of the empire by a people whose sympathy lay more with the defeated Huáscar than with Atahualpa. After Atahualpa was killed, Manco Inca was appointed by Pizarro as a puppet ruler of the Inca. (See History in the Facts about South America chapter.)

Once Cuzco had been captured, looted and settled, its importance declined. In 1535, Pizarro founded his capital at Lima. By 1600, Cuzco was a quiet colonial town, with all the gold and silver gone and many of the Inca buildings pulled down to make room for churches and colonial houses. Despite this, enough remains of the Inca foundations to make a walk around the heart of Cuzco a veritable journey back through time.

Orientation

Cuzco's heart is the Plaza de Armas and Avenida Sol is the main business street. Streets to the north or east of the plaza have changed little in centuries; many are for pedestrians only. A new pedestrian street between the Plaza del Tricentenario and Huaynapata gives great views over the Plaza de Armas. Recently, the city has had a resurgence of Quechua pride and the official names of many streets have changed from Spanish to Quechua spellings. Cuzco has become Qosco, Cuichipunco has become K'uychipunko etc. Many people (and maps) still use the old names.

Information

The tourist office on the Plaza de Armas, shown on many maps, is closed but may reopen. Information is provided next to the Banco de la Nación on Avenida Sol. Cuzco visitor tickets are sold here and at Avenida Sol 106. They cost US$10 (US$5 for students with ID), are good for 10 days, and give admittance to 14 sites in the Cuzco area. Get one.

Money Travellers' cheques are accepted by a few casas de cambio (on the plaza or along Avenida Sol) or at the Banco de Crédito, which has lower commission. Street money-changers are at the plaza end of Avenida Sol. Rates for cash vary little; street changers and casas de cambio are quicker than banks, but count money carefully before handing over your dollars on the street.

American Express at Lima Tours, on the Plaza de Armas, doesn't refund lost travellers' cheques (go to Lima).

Post & Communications The post office, open Monday to Saturday from 8 am to 8 pm, holds mail for three months addressed to you c/- Lista de Correos, Correo Central, Cuzco, Peru. The telephone code is 084. Telefónica del Perú on Avenida Sol holds incoming faxes for you at 24-1111. Hours are from 7 am to 11.30 pm.

Visa Extensions Tourist cards are renewed at Migraciones, on Avenida Sol, next to the post office. Hours are Monday to Friday from 7.45 am to 2 pm. An extension costs US$20 for 30 days.

Travel Agencies There are dozens of travel and tour agencies. The best are expensive. The cheaper ones change addresses often and have been criticised for being unreliable. Shop around.

Emergency The best clinic is the Hospital Regional (☎ 23-1131), on Avenida de la Cultura. The Policía de Turismo are helpful. They have moved often in recent years; their most recent location is in the basement of Torre de Pachacutec, south-east of the city centre.

Dangers & Annoyances Many tourists attract many thieves. Avoid displays of wealth (expensive jewellery, wristwatches, wallets) and leave most of your money in a hotel safe (carry what you need in inside pockets and money belts). Avoid walking alone around town late at night: revellers returning from bars etc late at night have been mugged. Take special care going to and from the Machu Picchu railway station and the nearby market: these are prime areas for pickpockets and bag-slashers. I (Rob) have to mention that in scores of visits to Cuzco since 1982, I have never been robbed on the street (though I had a camera taken from my hotel room once – I shouldn't have left it out in plain view).

Things to See

Buy a Cuzco visitor ticket (see Information), which gives entry to the Catedral, Santo Domingo and Coricancha, San Blas, Santa Catalina, the Museo de Historia Regional and the Museo de Arte Religioso. Outside Cuzco it is valid for Sacsayhuamán, Qenko, Puca Pucara, Tambo Machay, Pisac, Chinchero, Ollantaytambo and Piquillacta. Each site can be visited once. Other places in and around Cuzco can be visited for free, or by paying a modest admission fee. Opening hours change frequently.

Plaza de Armas Two flags fly over the plaza: the red-and-white Peruvian flag, and the rainbow flag of Tahuantinsuyo – the four quarters of the Inca empire. The plaza has colonial arcades on all sides. The Catedral is to the north-east and the ornate church of La Compañía to the south-east. Some Inca walls remain, notably from Pachacutec's palace on the western corner. The pedestrian alleyway of Loreto is a quiet and historical way to enter or leave the plaza. Both sides of Loreto have Inca walls.

Churches Begun in 1559, the **Catedral** is one of the city's greatest repositories of colonial art. It is joined with two other churches: to the left is the **Iglesia Jesus María**, dating from 1733, and to the right is the **Iglesia El Triunfo**, which is the tourist entrance to the three-church complex. El Triunfo is the oldest church in Cuzco and dates from 1536.

Near the entrance of El Triunfo is a vault with the remains of the Inca historian Garcilaso de la Vega, born in Cuzco in 1539. In the north-eastern corner of the cathedral is a huge painting of the *Last Supper*, by Marcos Zapata, an example of the Cuzco school. The supper includes the Inca delicacy, *cuy* (guinea pig). At the back of the Catedral is the original wooden altar, behind the new silver altar. Opposite the silver altar is the magnificently carved choir, dating from the 17th century. There are many splendid side chapels. Some contain the elaborate silver trolleys used to cart religious statues around during processions. Others have intricate altars. Hours are 2 to 5.30 pm. Admission is with the Cuzco visitor ticket. The huge main doors are open for worship from 6 to 10 am (no ticket required).

La Compañía is also on the plaza and is often lit up at night. It has an incredibly Baroque façade and is one of Cuzco's most ornate churches. Its foundations contain stones from the palace of the Inca Huayna Capac. The interior has fine paintings and richly carved altars. Two large canvases near the main door show early marriages in Cuzco and are noteworthy for their wealth of period detail. The 1986 earthquake damaged the church badly and hours are erratic. Repairs are continuing.

La Merced dates from 1654; an earlier church was destroyed in the 1650 earthquake. Hours of worship are 7 to 9 am and 5 to 7.30 pm. Left of the church is the monastery and museum, open Monday to Saturday from 8 am to noon and 2 to 5 pm. Entry is US$1.50. The museum contains conquistador/friar Vicente de Valverde's vestments, religious art and a priceless gold monstrance, 1.3 metres high and covered with 1500 diamonds and 1600 pearls.

The 16th and 17th-century church and monastery of **San Francisco** has a well-carved cedar-wood choir and a large collection of colonial religious paintings, one of which shows the family tree of St Francis of Assisi and is supposedly the largest in South

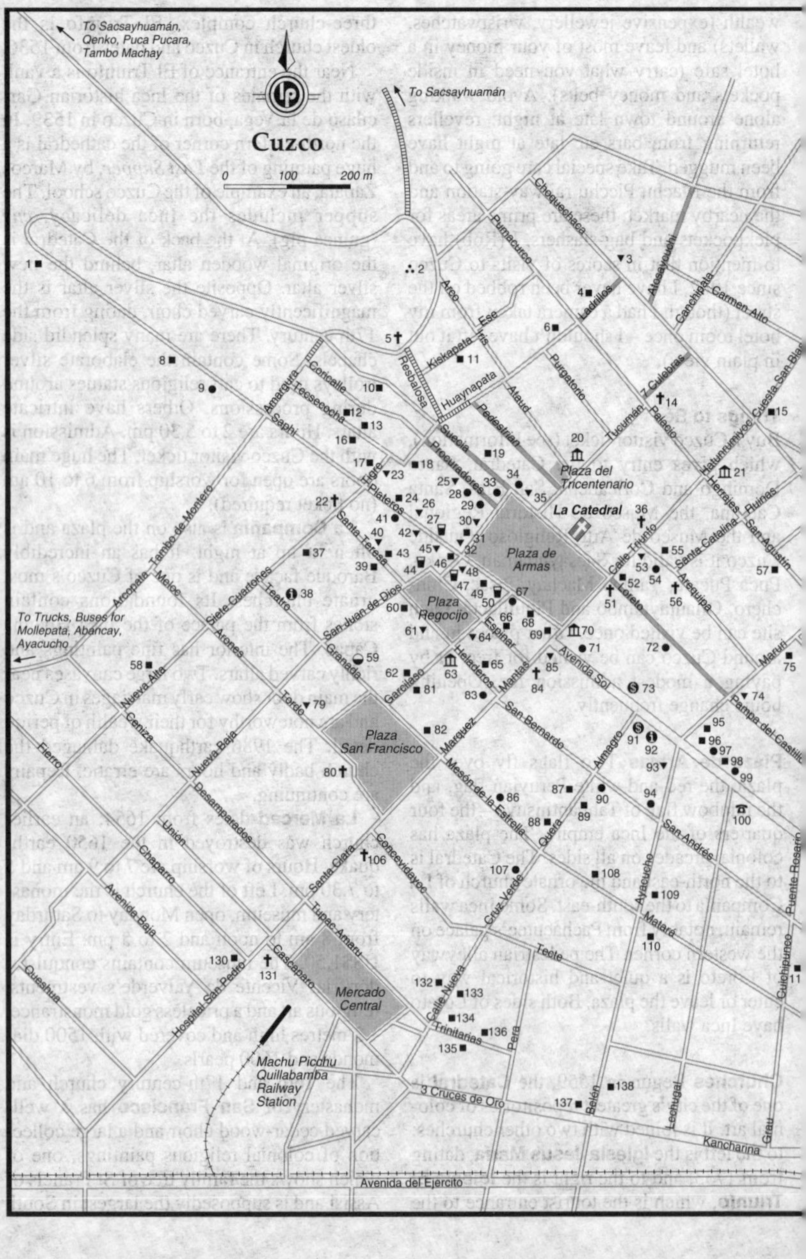

To Sacsayhuamán, Qenko, Puca Pucara, Tambo Machay
To Sacsayhuamán
Cuzco
0 100 200 m
To Trucks, Buses for Mollepata, Abancay, Ayacucho
Machu Picchu Quillabamba Railway Station
Plaza del Tricentenario
La Catedral
Plaza de Armas
Plaza Regocijo
Plaza San Francisco
Mercado Central
Chequechaca
Pumacurco
Atoqsaycuchi
Canchipata
Carmen Alto
Ladrillos
Arco
Ese
Iris
Kiskapata
Resbalosa
Huaynapata
Purgatorio
Ataud
Pedestrian
7 Culebras
Tucumán
Palacio
Hatunrumiyoc
Cuesta San Blas
Herrajes
Ruinas
San Agustín
Santa Catalina
Suecia
Procuradores
Amargura
Coricalle
Tecsecocha
Saphi
Tigre
Plateros
Santa Teresa
Arcopata
Tambo de Montero
Meloc
Siete Cuartones
Teatro
San Juan de Dios
Arones
Granada
Nueva Alta
Ceniza
Fierro
Nueva Baja
Tordo
Garcilaso
Heladeros
Espinar
Mantas
Avenida Sol
Marquez
San Bernardo
Calle Triunfo
Loreto
Arequipa
Maruri
Pampa del Castillo
Almagro
Mesón de la Estrella
Desamparados
Unión
Chaparro
Avenida Baja
Santa Clara
Concevidayoc
Tupac Amaru
Cascaparo
Hospital San Pedro
Queshua
Quera
Cruz Verde
Calle Nueva
Trinitarias
Pera
San Andrés
Ayacucho
Matará
Tecte
Puente Rosario
Cuichipunco
3 Cruces de Oro
Belén
Lechugal
Grau
Kancharina
Avenida del Ejercito
1 2 3 4 5 6 8 9 10 11 12 13 14 15 16 17 18 19 20 21 22 23 24 25 26 27 28 29 30 31 32 33 34 35 36 37 38 39 40 41 42 43 44 45 46 47 48 49 50 51 52 53 54 55 56 57 58 59 60 61 62 63 64 65 66 67 68 69 70 71 72 73 74 75 79 80 81 82 83 84 85 86 87 88 89 90 91 92 93 94 95 96 97 98 99 100 106 107 108 109 110 130 131 132 133 134 135 136 137 138

PERU

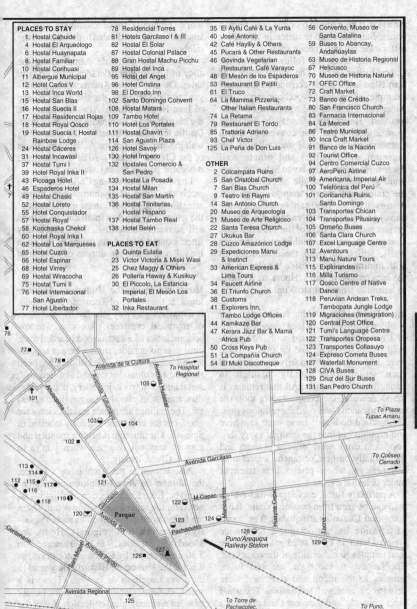

PLACES TO STAY

1. Hostal Cahuide
4. Hostal El Arqueólogo
6. Hostal Huaynapata
8. Hostal Familiar
10. Hostal Corihuasi
11. Albergue Municipal
12. Hotel Carlos V
13. Hostal Inca World
15. Hostal San Blas
16. Hostal Suecia II
17. Hostal Residencial Rojas
18. Hostal Royal Qosco
19. Hostal Suecia I, Hostal Rainbow Lodge
24. Hostal Cáceres
31. Hostal Incawasi
37. Hostal Tumi I
39. Hotel Royal Inka II
43. Picoaga Hotel
46. Espaderos Hotel
49. Hostal Chaski
52. Hostal Loreto
55. Hotel Conquistador
57. Hostal Royal
58. Korichaska Chekol
60. Hotel Royal Inka I
62. Hostal Los Marqueses
65. Hotel Cuzco
66. Hotel Espinar
68. Hotel Virrey
69. Hostal Wiracocha
75. Hostal Tumi II
76. Hotel Internacional San Agustín
77. Hotel Libertador
78. Residencial Torres
81. Hotels Garcilaso I & III
82. Hostal El Solar
87. Hostal Colonial Palace
88. Gran Hostal Machu Picchu
89. Hostal del Inca
95. Hotel del Angel
96. Hotel Cristina
98. El Dorado Inn
102. Santo Domingo Convent
108. Hostal Matará
109. Tambo Hotel
110. Hostal Los Portales
111. Hostal Chavín
114. San Agustín Plaza
126. Hotel Savoy
130. Hotel Imperio
132. Hostales Comercio & San Pedro
133. Hostal La Posada
134. Hostal Milan
135. Hostal San Martín
136. Hostal Trinitarias, Hostal Hispano
137. Hostal Tambo Real
138. Hotel Belén

PLACES TO EAT

3. Quinta Eulalia
23. Victor Victoria & Miski Wasi
25. Chez Maggy & Others
26. Pollería Haway & Kusikuy
30. El Piccolo, La Estancia Imperial, El Mesón Los Portales
32. Inka Restaurant
35. El Ayllu Café & La Yunta
40. José Antonio
42. Café Hayllly & Others
45. Pucará & Other Restaurants
46. Govinda Vegetarian Restaurant, Café Varayoc
48. El Mesón de los Espaderos
53. Restaurant El Paititi
61. El Truco
64. La Mamma Pizzería, Other Italian Restaurants
74. La Retama
79. Restaurant El Tordo
85. Trattoria Adriano
93. Chef Victor
125. La Peña de Don Luis

OTHER

2. Colcampata Ruins
5. San Cristóbal Church
7. San Blas Church
9. Teatro Inti Raymi
14. San Antonio Church
20. Museo de Arqueología
21. Museo de Arte Religioso
22. Santa Teresa Church
27. Ukukus Bar
28. Cuzco Amazónico Lodge
29. Expediciones Manu & Instinct
33. American Express & Lima Tours
34. Faucett Airline
36. El Triunfo Church
38. Customs
41. Explorers Inn, Tambo Lodge Offices
44. Kamikaze Bar
47. Kerara Jazz Bar & Mama Africa Pub
50. Cross Keys Pub
51. La Compañía Church
54. El Muki Discoteque
56. Convento, Museo de Santa Catalina
59. Buses to Abancay, Andahuaylas
63. Museo de Historia Regional
67. Helicusco
70. Museo de Historia Natural
71. OFEC Office
72. Craft Market
73. Banco de Crédito
80. San Francisco Church
83. Farmacia Internacional
84. La Merced
86. Teatro Municipal
90. Inca Craft Market
91. Banco de la Nación
92. Tourist Office
94. Centro Comercial Cuzco
97. AeroPerú Airline
99. Americana, Imperial Air
100. Telefónica del Perú
101. Coricancha Ruins, Santo Domingo
103. Transportes Chican
104. Transportes Pitusiray
105. Ormeño Buses
106. Santa Clara Church
107. Excel Language Centre
112. Aventours
113. Manu Nature Tours
115. Explorandes
116. Milla Turismo
117. Qosco Centre of Native Dance
118. Peruvian Andean Treks, Tambopata Jungle Lodge
119. Migraciones (Immigration)
120. Central Post Office
121. Tumi's Language Centre
122. Transportes Oropesa
123. Transportes Collasuyo
124. Expreso Cometa Buses
127. Waterfall Monument
128. CIVA Buses
129. Cruz del Sur Buses
131. San Pedro Church

PERU

America. There are two crypts with human bones. San Francisco is currently closed for restoration but will reopen soon.

You can enter the following with the Cuzco visitor ticket. The adobe church of **San Blas** has a pulpit considered the finest example of colonial wood-carving in the Americas. The gold-leaf main altar has been restored. Hours are Monday to Saturday from 2 to 5.30 pm. The convent of **Santa Catalina** has a colonial and religious art museum, with statues and ornate wall friezes. Hours are Monday to Saturday from 9 am to 6 pm. On the site of Coricancha is the church of **Santo Domingo**, which was destroyed by the 1650 earthquake and badly damaged by the 1950 earthquake. Photographs show the extent of the 1950 damage. Compare the colonial building with the Inca walls, which survived these earthquakes with minimal effects. Inside the cloister are the Inca temple remains. Hours are Monday to Saturday from 8 am to 5 pm.

Inca Ruins Coricancha is Quechua for 'Golden Courtyard'. In Inca times, the walls of Coricancha were lined with 700 solid-gold sheets weighing two kg apiece. There were life-size gold and silver replicas of corn, which were ritually 'planted' in agricultural ceremonies. All that remains is the stonework; the conquistadors took the rest. Coricancha was used for religious rites. Mummified bodies of Incas were kept here and brought out into the sunlight every day. Food and drink were offered to them and then ritually burnt. Coricancha was also an observatory, where priests kept track of major celestial events.

A perfectly fitted, curved, six-metre-high wall can be seen from outside the site. It has withstood Cuzco's earthquakes. The courtyard inside has an octagonal font, once covered with 55 kg of solid gold. There are Inca temples to either side of the courtyard. The largest, to the right, are said to be temples to the moon and stars, and were perhaps covered with solid silver. The walls taper upwards, and the niches and doorways are fine examples of Inca trapezoidal stone-

work. Opposite these chambers are the smaller temples, dedicated to thunder and the rainbow.

Leaving the Plaza de Armas along the alley of Loreto, you have Inca walls on both sides. On the right is Amarucancha (Courtyard of the Serpents), the site of the palace of Inca Huayna Capac. After the conquest, the church of La Compañía was built here. On the left side of Loreto is the oldest Inca wall in Cuzco, part of the Acllahuasi (House of the Chosen Women). After the conquest, it became part of Santa Catalina.

Leaving the plaza along Calle Triunfo you reach the street of Hatunrumiyoc, named after the great 12-sided stone on the right of the second city block; a small knot of Indians sell souvenirs next to it. This excellently fitted stone is part of the palace of the sixth Inca, Roca. There are dozens of other Inca walls to see.

Museums Inside the **Museo de Arqueología**, at the corner of Tucumán and Ataúd, is a massive stairway guarded by sculptures of mythical creatures. A corner window column looks like a statue of a bearded man, until you go outside, from where it appears to be a naked woman. The building has been restored in colonial style and is filled with metal and gold work, jewellery, pottery, textiles, mummies, wooden *queros* (Inca vases) etc. The ceilings are ornate and the views are good, but the collection is poorly labelled in Spanish. The museum is being expanded and may or may not be open when you're in Cuzco. Check locally.

Also known as the Archbishop's Palace, the **Museo de Arte Religioso**, on Hatunrumiyoc, has a fine collection of religious art noted for the accuracy of period detail. There are fine stained-glass windows and colonial-style tilework (not original). Hours are Monday to Saturday, 9 to 11.30 am and 3 to 5.30 pm. Entry is by Cuzco visitor ticket, as it is for the **Museo de Historia Regional** in the Casa Garcilaso de la Vega. There is a small, chronologically arranged but poorly labelled archaeological collection. Art of the Cuzco school as well as more recent mestizo art is displayed and there are changing local art shows. Hours are Monday to Saturday from 9 am to 6 pm.

Markets The best area to buy local craftwork and see it made is the Plaza San Blas and the streets leading up to it from the Plaza de Armas. The Mercado Central is a colourful affair in front of the church of San Pedro. This is not a crafts market and if you want to go there don't bring much money or a camera, because the thieves are extremely persistent and professional. There are craft markets on the corner of Quera and San Bernardo, and every night under the arches around the Plaza de Armas and Regocijo.

Language Courses

The Excel language centre (☎ 23-5298), Cruz Verde 336, charges US$3.50 per hour for private lessons and is recommended. Excel arranges homestays with local families. Tumi's, Ahuacpinta 732, offers lessons for US$3 an hour and can also arrange homestays.

Work

The language centres above hire native English-speakers to teach English.

Organised Tours

Standard tours include a half-day city tour, a half-day tour of the nearby ruins (Sacsayhuamán, Qenko, Puca Pucara and Tambo Machay), a half-day trip to the Sunday markets at Pisac or Chinchero, a full-day tour to the Sacred Valley (Pisac and Ollantaytambo and perhaps Chinchero) and a full-day tour to Machu Picchu. There are many tour companies, and most of them do a good job. The cheaper tours are crowded, multilingual affairs. You can visit all the places mentioned using public transport.

Many agencies run adventure trips. Rafting the Urubamba for one or two days is popular (US$25 a day). The Inca Trail is also popular; you can hire porters, cooks and guides (the cheapest tours are US$60) or just rent equipment (about US$2 per item per day) and carry it yourself. There are several

cheap agencies on Procuradores and around the Plaza de Armas. You can also go on mountaineering, horse-riding, mountain-biking and jungle trips.

Special Events

Inti Raymi, the sun festival, is on 24 June and is Cuzco's most important festival. It attracts tourists from all over the world, and the entire city celebrates in the streets. The festival culminates in a re-enactment of the Inca winter solstice festival at Sacsayhuamán. Reserved tourist tickets in the bleachers are about US$20, or you can sit for free with the locals on the stone ruins.

Held on the Monday before Easter, the procession of El Señor de los Temblores (Lord of the Earthquakes) dates from the 1650 earthquake. The feast of Corpus Christi occurs in early June (usually the ninth Thursday after Easter), with fantastic religious processions and celebrations in the Catedral.

Places to Stay

Accommodation is tight from June to August, especially during the 10 days before Inti Raymi and around the Fiestas Patrias (28 July) when prices rise. During other times, try bargaining for better rates: many hotels are half-empty. Budget travellers find the best cheap hotels are in poor areas, and taking cabs or going in groups is advised after dark. Most hotels store luggage for a few days so you can hike the Inca Trail or whatever. Lock and label your luggage, don't leave valuables, and ask for a receipt. Haphazard water supplies are the norm and hot water is on for a few hours each day. Ask when.

Hostal Royal Qosco (☎ 22-6221), Tecsecocha 2, is popular with budget travellers. Basic rooms are US$4 per person and there's hot water. The *Santo Domingo Convent*, Ahuacpinta 600, is clean, safe and friendly, and has hot water, but has a 10.30 pm curfew. Rates are US$6 per person. The basic, clean and friendly *Korichaska Chekol* (☎ 22-8974), Nueva Alta 458, is US$4 per person or US$5 with private bath and hot water. The *Hostal Tumi I*, Siete Cuartones 245, and *Hostal Tumi II* (☎ 22-8361), 312 Maruri, are

PERU

friendly budget places with hot water at US$5 per person. The *Hostal Suecia I* (☎ 23-3282), Suecia 332, is popular with budget travellers, though thefts have been reported. There is hot water, and rooms are US$5 per person. Nearby, the clean, friendly *Hostal Rainbow Lodge*, Suecia 310, is a little cheaper and has hot water. The *Hostal Residencial Rojas* (☎ 22-8184), Tigre 129, is basic but OK for US$5/7.50 a single/double or US$10 for a double with bath and hot water. The *Hostal Cáceres* (☎ 22-8012), Plateros 368, has hot water and is reasonably clean but security is lax. Rates are US$5 per person. The basic *Hostal Chaski* (23-6093), Portal Confitería 257 on the plaza, charges US$7/10 or US$9/12 with bath. The *Espaderos Hotel* (☎ 23-8894), Espaderos 136, has tepid water but dirty bathrooms. Rooms are US$5/7.50. Basic, cheap hotels with erratic or nonexistent hot water include the *Hostal Matará* (☎ 22-4432), Matará 501, the *Hostal Royal* (☎ 23-3859), San Agustín 256, and the *Residencial Torres* (☎ 22-6697), Limacpampa Chico 485.

There are good hotels near the Mercado Central but in an unsafe area. The *Hotel Imperio* (☎ 22-8981), Chaparro 121, is clean, very friendly and helpful, and has hot water. Rates are US$3 per person with private bath or less without. In the same area are the similarly priced *Hostales San Pedro* and *La Posada* and then, in increasing order of price (up to about US$15 a double with bath), are the *San Martín, Comercio, Belén, Trinitarias, Tambo Real, Milan* and *Hispano*. All are OK and have hot water. The friendly and helpful *Hostal Tambo Real* (☎ 22-1621), Belén 588, is US$10/15 with bath and hot showers.

Another area for rock-bottom prices is around the Puno train station, which is unsafe at night. Over a dozen hotels here are US$3/5 and may have hot water. Look along Tacna, Huayna Capac, Manco Capac, Manco Inca, Huáscar, Pachacutec, Tullumayo and Ahuacpinta to find these basic places, which aren't marked on the map.

The *Hostal Chavín* (☎ 22-8857), Cuichipunco 299, charges US$5/6. The *Albergue Juvenil* (☎ 22-3320), on Huayruropata in the suburb of Huanchac, is good, clean and safe at US$7.50 per person with breakfast, but is far from the centre. Take a taxi. The *Albergue Municipal* (☎ 25-2506), Kiskapata 240, has a balcony with fine city views, helpful owners, hot water, common room, small café and laundry facilities. Clean rooms have four to eight bunk beds at US$7 each but the area is not safe at night: take a cab. In this area is the good, friendly *Hostal Huaynapata* (☎ 22-8034), Huaynapata 369, at US$16/22 for clean rooms with bath or half that with shared bath. Nearby, the *Hostal El Arqueólogo* (☎ 23-2569), Ladrillos 425, is clean and has hot water, kitchen privileges, and a nice garden. It's popular with French tourists. Rates are US$12/16 with bath, less without. Another option is the *Hostal Corihuasi* (☎ & fax 23-2233), Suecia 561, at US$18 a double with bath, some with great views. There's a café.

The clean *Gran Hostal Machu Picchu* (☎ 23-1111), Quera 282, has OK rooms (US$7.50 per person) around two pleasant patios. The *Hostal Familiar* (☎ 23-9353), Saphi 661, has doubles for US$7.50 or US$12 with bath. It is clean, popular and often full, but we found it unfriendly. The *Hostal Incawasi* (☎ 23-8245), Portal de Panes 143, has a good location on the plaza and is US$12/18. The friendly *Hostal San Blas* (☎ 22-5781), Cuesta San Blas 526, is US$12/18.

Places to Eat

Breakfast & Snacks The simple and reasonably priced *El Ayllu* café, next to the Catedral, is popular. It plays classical music and has good juices, coffee, tea, yoghurt, cakes, sandwiches and other snacks. Next door, the equally popular *La Yunta* also serves juices, cakes and coffee, and light meals. The *Café Haylliy*, on the first block of Plateros, is also popular for cheap breakfasts and lunches. The *Café Varayoc*, on Espaderos, is another good choice.

Vegetarian Food *Govinda* vegetarian restaurant on Espaderos is cheap and adequate, though with slow service. Their home-made bread lasts for days – good for the Inca Trail. The clean *Restaurant El Tordo*, Tordo 238, has good cheap vegetarian food. Vegetables used for salads are washed in iodised water.

Peruvian Food A few restaurants serve typical Peruvian food, have outside patios and are open for lunch or afternoon snacks only. Most are closed on Monday. Cuy may need to be ordered a day in advance. Also try anticucho de corazón (beef-heart shish kebab), rocoto relleno (spicy bell peppers stuffed with ground beef and vegetables), adobo (spicy pork stew), chicharrones (deep-fried meat chunks), choclo con queso (corn on the cob with cheese), tamales (boiled corn dumplings filled with cheese or meat and wrapped in a banana leaf), cancha (toasted corn) and various locros (hearty soups and stews). The meal is washed down with chicha – either a fruit drink or a fermented, mildly alcoholic corn beer.

Quinta Eulalia (☎ 22-4951), Choquechaca 384 (no sign), has a colourful courtyard. Further afield is the *Quinta Zárate*, in a garden on Calle Tortera Paccha – not easy to find, so hire a taxi. *La Peña de Don Luis*, on Avenida Regional, is popular with Peruvians for lunch. There are local hole-in-the-wall places along Pampa del Castillo serving chicharrones hot from the grill, which is often placed in the door of the restaurant. One of these is *Oh Que Rico* at No 445.

Other local restaurants serve fish, chicken and meat, with a small selection of the more traditional dishes. Just off the plaza, along the first block of Calle Plateros, there are several good local restaurants. These include the *Café Haylliy* (for good snacks), *El Tronquito* and *Los Candiles* (good, cheap set meals), the *Pollería Haway* (for chicken), the *Kusikuy* (with the best selection of traditional dishes) and the *Pucará* (☎ 22-2027), which, with dishes in the US$4 to US$10 range, is the most expensive on this block but also has by far the best food.

Around the corner on Calle Tigre are the recommended budget restaurants, the *Victor Victoria* and *Miski Wasi*. Other recommended budget restaurants are *Chef Victor*, Ayacucho 217, and the chicken restaurant next to the Hostal del Inca on Quera.

On the Plaza de Armas, the *Inka Restaurant* and *El Paititi* (☎ 22-6992) both have Inca walls. El Paititi is pricey but good. The cheaper Inka Restaurant may have a peña at night, for which there is a cover charge. *El Mesón de los Espaderos* (☎ 23-5307), Espaderos 105, (upstairs) serves parrillada (mixed grill), steak, cuy and chicken. Get there early to sit in the attractively carved balcony overlooking the plaza.

Other Food Procuradores has several popular cheap restaurants including *Chez Maggy Pizzería*, *Mia Pizza* and *Los Cuates* Mexican restaurant. There's another *Chez Maggy* on Plateros, as well as the *Pizzería América*. These often have live music (a hat is passed round for tips). There are other Italian places on Plaza Regocijo.

Entertainment
The *Ukukus Bar*, Plateros 316, has both live and recorded music, plenty of dancing, and is popular with travellers. There's a happy hour from 8 to 9.30 pm, and a US$1.50 cover charge after 9.30 pm. The older *Kamikaze*, at the north-western corner of Plaza Regocijo, has lively taped music and live performers (usually from 10.30 pm). Happy hour is 8.30 to 9.30 pm and the cover charge varies.

The *Cross Keys Pub*, Portal Confituría 233, identified on the plaza by the huge keys hanging outside, is an English pub run by British ornithologist Barry Walker. He knows the area well and is a good contact for the Manu area. There is a dart board and pool and it's a great meeting place where you can talk without having to scream over the music. It's pricier than other places, though there are 6 to 7 pm and 9 to 9.30 pm happy hours (beer not included). *Tumi's Video Bar*, Saphi 456-478, shows films on a 52-inch screen and has a friendly bar. It has pool and darts, is open for lunch, and has an 8 to 9 pm happy hour.

A new and up-market place is the *Kerara Jazz Bar* (☎ 23-5706), on Espaderos. This

PERU

place has seven different bars with various attractions. In the same building is the *Mama Africa Pub*, which has good live music.

Getting There & Away

Air LAB and AeroPerú have flights to La Paz (US$110) almost daily during the high season.

There are about seven flights a day to and from Lima (US$89) with Faucett, AeroPerú, Americana, AeroContinente and Imperial Air. Many get cancelled or lumped together with another flight during low periods. The earliest flights are less likely to be cancelled. There are one to three flights a day to Arequipa (US$46), Juliaca (US$42), Puerto Maldonado (US$38) and Ayacucho (US$42) with one or more of these airlines. Transportes Aéreos Andahuaylas (TAA) flies to Andahuaylas on Tuesday and Friday. Same-day connections to Tacna via Arequipa and to most northern cities via Lima can be arranged. Flights may be overbooked in the high season, so confirm and reconfirm your flights.

Airline offices in Cuzco are along Avenida Sol or on the Plaza de Armas (see map). The military airline, Grupo Ocho, sells tickets at the airport for its flights (usually on Thursday) to Lima and Puerto Maldonado but these are hard to get on to.

Bus & Truck Buses to Pisac, Calca and Urubamba leave frequently with Transportes Pitusiray from Avenida Tullumayo from 5.30 am until dusk. Transportes Chican, nearby, has buses to Chinchero, some continuing to Urubamba and Ollantaytambo, all day. (These stations change locations every year or two.) It takes 2½ hours to Urubamba, one hour to Pisac. Buses are crowded.

Buses to Oropesa, Urcos, Sicuani and Ocongate leave from the Coliseo Cerrado on Manco Capac, five blocks east of Tacna. Urcos buses also leave from Avenida de la Cultura between the university and the Hospital Regional. Take these buses to visit the ruins of Tipón, Pikillacta, Rumicolca and Raqchi.

Trucks for Limatambo, Mollepata, Aban-

cay and other destinations leave from Arcopata, or you can take a bus to Abancay from the same street. Two or three companies on Granada have buses to Abancay (US$6, eight hours) and Andahuaylas (US$9, 14 hours) leaving at 6 am, 10 am and 1 pm. To continue to Ayacucho, change at Andahuaylas. Empresa Andahuaylas on Arcopata has buses to Ayacucho (US$18) at 6 am, with an overnight stay in Andahuaylas. This road is atrocious and very cold at night. Cramped minibuses are often used.

There are no buses to the south-eastern jungles except for those to Quillabamba (US$6, 10 hours) every night with Empresa Carhuamayo at the Plaza Tupac Amaru. Trucks to Puerto Maldonado (2½ days in the dry season) leave from two blocks east of Tacna along Avenida Garcilaso, or get a bus to Urcos or Ocongate and wait for a truck there. Transportes Sol Andino has buses to Paucartambo (US$3, six hours) at 10 am on Monday, Wednesday and Friday morning from the Coliseo Cerrado. Get there by 7 am for a seat or book with the Andino office on Avenida Huáscar. Trucks also do the journey (same days) from the Coliseo Cerrado: ask around. From Paucartambo to Manu there are passing trucks or expedition buses. From Cuzco, trucks from the Coliseo Cerrado go to Shintuyo (20 hours) for Manu. Expediciones Manu is a source of information about these, or try Explorers Transport, which advertises in the popular gringo cafes and bars in Cuzco and has an expedition vehicle going to Manu at irregular intervals.

Cruz del Sur, on Pachacutec, has day buses to Sicuani and night buses to Juliaca and Puno (US$10, 14 hours). The road is bad and the train is more comfortable. The same company has a nightly service to Arequipa via Imata (16 hours, US$12) – also a rough journey. This continues to Lima (US$24, 40 hours). Expect delays in the rainy season. The route to Lima through Abancay and Puquio is not recommended because of banditry. Other companies on Pachacutec have buses to southern Peruvian towns. Try CIVA, Expreso Cometa, Transportes Collasuyo and others for different prices. Ormeño, on

Avenida Huáscar, also has buses to these destinations.

Train Cuzco has two unlinked train stations. Estación Huancho (☎ 23-3592, 22-1992) near the end of Avenida Sol serves Urcos, Sicuani, Juliaca, Puno and Arequipa. Estación San Pedro (☎ 22-1291, 23-8722 for reservations, 23-1207 for information) next to the Mercado Central serves Machu Picchu and Quillabamba.

The Puno train (10½ hours) leaves at 8 am on Monday, Wednesday, Friday and Saturday, reaching Juliaca at 5 pm for connections to the night train to Arequipa. See the Puno and Arequipa sections for details of classes and fares.

For Machu Picchu there are cheap local trains and expensive tourist trains. The local train *(tren local)* is the cheapest and stops everywhere. It has a reputation for robbery, so travel in 1st class. The train leaves Cuzco daily at 6.20 am and Monday to Saturday at 1.15 pm, and takes four hours to Machu Picchu and seven hours to Quillabamba. First class is US$4.50 to Machu Picchu and US$5.50 to Quillabamba. Second class is 20% cheaper. There may be a more expensive Pullman class available. The train barely stops at some stations: descend quickly, particularly at Km 88.

The tourist train stops only at Ollantaytambo and Puente Ruinas (for the Machu Picchu ruins). Many people visit Machu Picchu on a tiring day trip using this train. It's better to stay overnight at Aguas Calientes near the ruins. The tourist train leaves Cuzco at 6.30 am (another departure on demand). Passengers may be taken part of the way by bus. The trip to Puente Ruinas takes three hours and costs about US$50 return. Travel agents sell the trip for about US$90, including the bus from the Puente Ruinas station to the ruins, entry to the ruins, and a guide.

Getting Around
To/From the Airport A taxi from the airport to the centre of Cuzco costs about US$2 to US$3; the local bus costs about US$0.25.

Around Cuzco

NEARBY RUINS
These are the four ruins closest to Cuzco: Sacsayhuamán, Qenko, Puca Pucara and Tambo Machay. Admission is with the Cuzco visitor ticket. A cheap and easy way to visit them is to take a Cuzco-Pisac bus and get off at Tambo Machay, the ruin furthest from Cuzco (and, at 3700 metres, the highest). From here, walk eight km back to Cuzco, visiting all four ruins along the way. Colourfully dressed locals with llamas hang around the sites, hoping to be photographed. A tip of about US$0.30 per photograph is expected. This is a popular and rewarding walk, but it's best to go in a group and return before nightfall, to avoid potential robbery.

Tambo Machay
This small ruin about 300 metres from the main road is a beautifully wrought ceremonial stone bath, popularly called El Baño del Inca. Opposite it is a small signalling tower, from where Puca Pucara can be seen.

Puca Pucara
The small ruin of Puca Pucara looks red in some lights; the name means 'red fort'.

Qenko
The name of this small, fascinating ruin means 'zigzag'. It is a large limestone rock covered with carvings, including zigzagging channels. These may have been for the ceremonial usage of chicha. Tunnels are carved below the boulder, and there's a curious cave with altars carved into the rock. Qenko is on the left side of the road as you descend from Tambo Machay, four km before Cuzco.

Sacsayhuamán
This huge ruin is the most impressive in the immediate Cuzco area. You can reach it from Cuzco by climbing the steep street of Resbalosa, turning right at the top and continuing until you come to a hairpin bend in the road. Here, take the old Inca road linking

PERU

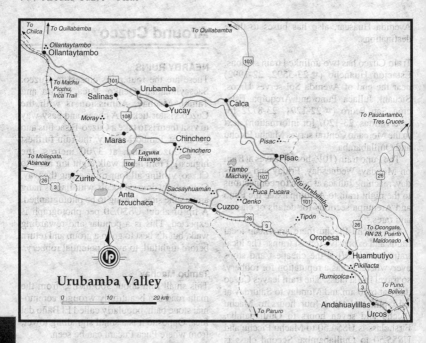

Urubamba Valley

To Chilca / To Quillabamba

To Quillabamba

103

To Quillabamba

Ollantaytambo
Ollantaytambo

101

To Machu
Picchu,
Inca Trail

Salinas

Urubamba

108

Yucay

Calca

Moray

To Paucartambo,
Tres Cruces

Maras

Chinchero

Laguna
Huaypo

Chinchero

Pisac

To Mollepata,
Abancay

108

Pisac

26

Zurite

Sacsayhuamán

Tambo
Machay

107

26

Anta
Izcuchaca

Qenko

Puca Pucara

Poroy

Cuzco

101

26

Tipón

3

26

To Ocongate,
RN 28, Puerto
Maldonado

Oropesa

Huambutiyo

Pikillacta

Rumicolca

To Puno,
Bolivia

To Paruro

Andahuaylillas

3

Urcos

LP

0   10   20 km

PERU

Cuzco with Sacsayhuamán. It takes less than an hour from Cuzco.

Sacsayhuamán (which means 'satisfied falcon') is huge, but only about 20% of the original structure remains. The Spaniards used the blocks to build their own houses in Cuzco, but they left the most impressive of the original rocks, one of which weighs more than 300 tonnes. Most of the rocks form the main battlements.

The Incas envisioned Cuzco as having a puma shape. Sacsayhuamán was the head. The site is essentially three different areas, the most obvious being the three-tiered zigzag walls of the main fortifications. These 22 zigzags form the puma's teeth. Opposite is Rodadero hill, with retaining walls, polished rocks and a finely carved series of stone benches, known as the 'throne of the Incas'. In between the zigzag ramparts and Rodadero hill lies a large, flat parade ground, which today is used for the colourful tourist spectacle of Inti Raymi, held every 24 June.

The magnificent zigzag walls are the major attraction even though much has been destroyed. Three towers stood above these walls, but only the foundations remain. It is thought the site had important religious and military significance. This was the site of one of the most bitter battles of the conquest, between the Spanish and the rebellious Manco Inca. Manco lost narrowly and retreated to Vilcabamba, but most of his forces were killed. The dead attracted flocks of Andean condors, which is why there are eight condors on Cuzco's coat of arms.

Robberies have been reported. Avoid going early in the morning or in the evening, and don't go alone.

PISAC

Pisac is 32 km north-east of Cuzco by paved road and is the most convenient starting point for visits to the villages and ruins of the Valle Sagrado (Sacred Valley), as the Río Urubamba valley is locally called. Pisac consists of a colonial and modern village alongside the river, and an Inca site on a mountain spur 600 metres above the river. Colonial Pisac is a quiet Andean village which comes alive on Sunday morning, when the famous weekly market takes place.

Ruins

The ruins above the village are reached by a 10-km paved road up the Chongo valley, or by a shorter but steep footpath from the plaza. There is little traffic along the road. The five-km footpath to the ruins leaves town from the left-hand side of the church. Allow roughly two hours for the climb, which is spectacular and worthwhile. Admission to the ruins is with the Cuzco visitor ticket and it's worth spending a day.

Pisac is known for the agricultural terracing around the south and east flanks of the mountain. Above the terraces are some cliff-hanging footpaths, well defended by massive stone doorways, steep stairs and, at one point, a tunnel carved out of the rock. At the top of the terraces is the religious centre, with very well constructed rooms and temples. At the back (northern end) of the ruins a series of ceremonial baths have been rebuilt. A cliff behind the site is honeycombed with hundreds of Inca tombs which were plundered by grave robbers.

Markets

The weekly Sunday morning market attracts both tourists and traditionally dressed locals. Selling and bartering of produce goes on alongside the stalls full of weavings, sweaters and souvenirs. The plaza throngs with people, and it becomes even more crowded after the Quechua mass, when the congregation leaves the church in a colourful procession led by the mayor holding his silver staff of office. There is a smaller market on Thursday and some kind of selling activity every day of the week.

Places to Stay & Eat

The *Parador Pisaq* has two clean rooms with eight beds at US$5 each. It may have food available. The *Residencial Beho* is cheaper and has cold showers. Some families rent rooms; ask around. The *Hostal & Café Pisaq* is US$6 per person for clean beds and hot showers. The food is OK. The *Samana Wasi* is one of the better cafés, though a bit overpriced. There are basic eateries near the bridge. Stop by the bakery near the plaza for oven-fresh flat bread rolls typical of the area.

Getting There & Away

Frequent minibuses leave from Cuzco. To return to Cuzco or continue to Urubamba, wait for a bus by the bridge. Note that buses to Cuzco start in Urubamba and are often full or have standing room only – prime territory for pickpockets.

URUBAMBA

Urubamba is 40 km beyond Pisac, at the junction of the valley and Chinchero roads. The village of Tarabamba is about six km further down the valley. Here, cross the river

Pisac
Not to Scale

Residencial Beho — Path to Pisac Ruins
Church — To Bakery, Road to Ruins
Plaza de Armas
Parador Pisac
Samana Wasi
Hostal & Café Pisaq
Bolognesi
Small Restaurants — Telefónica del Perú
To Urubamba, Ollantaytambo
Police Post, Buses
To Royal Inka, Road to Ruins
Río Urubamba
To Cuzco

PERU

by footbridge and continue on a footpath, climbing roughly southwards up a valley for a further three km to the salt pans of Salinas, which have been exploited since Inca times – a fascinating sight. Admission is US$1.

Places to Stay & Eat

The friendly *Hotel Urubamba*, on Bolognesi near the plaza (10 minutes from the main road), is US$6 for a double. Showers are cold. There is another cheap and basic place in the centre and the *Hostal Vera* on the main road, as well as several pricey hotels. There are simple restaurants on the plaza and along the road leading from the main valley road into the town centre.

The *Quinta Los Geranios* restaurant, on the main valley road, near the petrol station, is good for local lunches.

Getting There & Away

Buses leave Cuzco frequently from the bus stop on Avenida Tullumayo. Buses back to Cuzco or on to Ollantaytambo stop at the petrol station on the main road.

OLLANTAYTAMBO

This is the end of the road: travellers continue by rail or on foot, though there are a few drivable dirt tracks into the countryside. Ollantaytambo is a major Inca site and admission is with the Cuzco visitor ticket (or US$2). The site is one of the few places where the Spaniards lost a major battle during the conquest. Below the ruins is the village of Ollantaytambo, built on traditional Inca foundations; it is the best surviving example of Inca city planning.

The Incas considered Ollantaytambo a temple rather than a fortress, but the Spanish, after their defeat, called it a fortress, and it has been referred to as such ever since. The temple area is at the top of the terracing. The stone used for these buildings was quarried

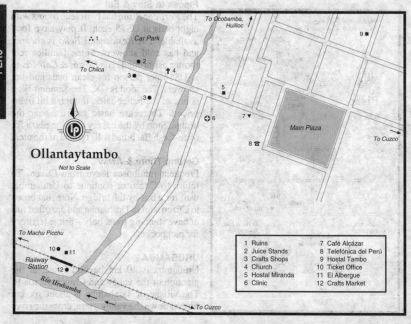

Ollantaytambo
Not to Scale

To Ocobamba, Huilloc

Car Park

To Chilca

To Machu Picchu

Railway Station

Río Urubamba

To Cuzco

Main Plaza

To Cuzco

1 Ruins	7 Café Alcázar
2 Juice Stands	8 Telefónica del Perú
3 Crafts Shops	9 Hostal Tambo
4 Church	10 Ticket Office
5 Hostal Miranda	11 El Albergue
6 Clinic	12 Crafts Market

PERU

from the mountainside six km away and high above the opposite bank of the Río Urubamba. Transporting the blocks from the quarry to the site was a stupendous feat, involving the labour of thousands of Indians.

Places to Stay & Eat

Basic places for US$3 per person include the *Hostal Miranda* (☎ 20-4009), *Café Alcázar* and the pleasanter *Hostal Tambo* (☎ 20-4003). They claim to have warm showers on request. The *Hostal Orquideas* has been recommended. *El Albergue Ollantaytambo* (☎ & fax 20-4014), in the train station, is US$15 per person, is very tranquil, has a sauna, hot showers and garden, and provides meals on request. The cheaper *Albergue Kapuly* has recently opened next door. You'll find simple, cheap restaurants around the plaza.

Getting There & Away

Bus Minibuses leave from Urubamba's petrol station several times a day, but services peter out in mid-afternoon. Buses from Cuzco are infrequent, and many people change in Urubamba. Buses return to Cuzco from the plaza; several go via Chinchero.

Train All trains stop here, 1½ to two hours after leaving Cuzco. The local train is overcrowded by the time it reaches Ollantaytambo, and standing room only is the rule, though there may be a few seats in 1st class. The tourist train costs the same from Ollantaytambo to Machu Picchu as it does from Cuzco. The local train is much cheaper.

CHINCHERO

This site (entry with the Cuzco visitor ticket) combines Inca ruins with an Andean Indian village, a colonial country church, mountain views and a colourful Sunday market. There is a smaller Thursday market. The main square of the village has a massive Inca wall with 10 huge trapezoidal niches. Just above the square is the colonial church, which is built on Inca foundations.

Buses leave Cuzco from Avenida Tullumayo a few times each day, some con-

tinuing to Urubamba or even Ollantaytambo. Buses also go from the plazas in Urubamba and Ollantaytambo to Chinchero.

THE INCA TRAIL

This, the most famous hike in South America, is walked by thousands of people every year. The views of snowcapped mountains and high cloud forest are stupendous, weather permitting. Walking from one ruin to the next is a mystical and unforgettable experience.

Conservation

Enjoy the hike, but please don't spoil it for others. Please don't defecate in the ruins, don't leave garbage anywhere, don't damage the stonework by building fires against the walls (it blackens and, worse still, cracks the rocks), use a stove for cooking (the trail has been badly deforested over the past decade) and don't pick the orchids and other plants in this national park. The SAEC organised an Inca Trail clean-up in 1980 and collected about 400 kg of unburnable garbage. Other clean-up campaigns since then record similar figures. Please carry out your trash.

Preparations

Bring a stove, sleeping pad, warm sleeping bag and a tent. (Everything can be rented in Cuzco, but check gear carefully. Many rented tents leak.) Also bring insect repellent, sunscreen, water purification tablets and basic first-aid supplies. The trek takes three full days, overnight temperatures can drop below freezing and it rains even in the dry season. There is nowhere to buy food. The ruins are roofless and don't provide shelter. Caves marked on some maps are usually wet, dirty overhangs. The total distance is only 33 km, but there are three high passes to be crossed and the trail is often steep. One reader called it 'the Inca Trial'.

You can obtain maps and information in Lima at the SAEC, and from trekking agencies or the tourist office in Cuzco. The map in this book is perfectly adequate. Robberies have been reported so you shouldn't hike alone. The most popular period is the dry

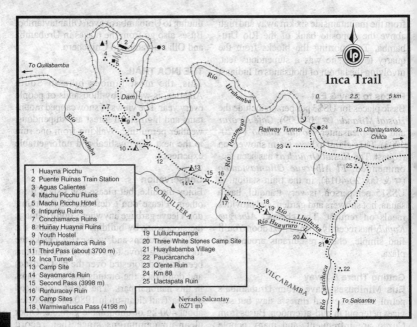

Inca Trail

0   2.5   5 km

1 Huayna Picchu
2 Puente Ruinas Train Station
3 Aguas Calientes
4 Machu Picchu Ruins
5 Machu Picchu Hotel
6 Intipunku Ruins
7 Conchamarca Ruins
8 Huiñay Huayna Ruins
9 Youth Hostel
10 Phuyupatamarca Ruins
11 Third Pass (about 3700 m)
12 Inca Tunnel
13 Camp Site
14 Sayacmarca Ruin
15 Second Pass (3998 m)
16 Runturacay Ruin
17 Camp Sites
18 Warmiwañusca Pass (4198 m)
19 Llulluchupampa
20 Three White Stones Camp Site
21 Huayllabamba Village
22 Paucarcancha
23 Q'ente Ruin
24 Km 88
25 Llactapata Ruin

Nevado Salcantay
▲ (6271 m)

season, from June to September. The trail is fairly empty during the rest of the year but is wet: the mud can be 30 cm deep. Nevertheless, the hike is possible all year round.

Organised Tours

Guided tours are sold by outfitters in Cuzco for about US$60 and up per person. This includes the local train to the beginning of the trail at Km 88, a tent, food, a porter, a cook and entrance to the ruins. While this may seem like a good deal, consider the following. The low costs mean that the porters are not provided with camping equipment and food, and so have to fend for themselves. This leads to them cooking and warming themselves with scarce wood from the already badly damaged woodlands. The cheap guided tours generally have no idea of ecologically sensitive camping, and the result is garbage left everywhere. No attempt is made to carry out garbage, bury shit or safeguard the delicate Andean woodlands. It has been over a decade since we first hiked

the trail, and the degradation of the route and the ruins is clear. Do whatever you can to preserve this hike.

There are no easy solutions. You can rent gear in Cuzco (or use your own), avoid outfitters, and camp as cleanly as possible. You could even pack out garbage that you encounter. You can go on an expensive guided trip with a local tour operator used by international adventure travel companies. At least these folks make some effort to camp cleanly and provide adequate facilities for porters. They also contribute to Inca Trail clean-up campaigns. Or you can use the cheap outfitters and insist on clean camping by setting an example and ensuring that there is enough fuel and tentage for the porters.

It is normal to tip guides, cooks and porters. Don't forget the porters: they are woefully underpaid and work the hardest of all. Tip them as well as you are able.

Trail Fee

It costs US$17 per person to hike the Inca

Trail, which includes a one-day entrance fee to Machu Picchu. If taking a guided trek, check to see if this fee is included.

The Hike

After crossing the Río Urubamba at Km 88, turn left and begin the Inca Trail as it climbs gently through a eucalyptus grove for one km. You will pass the minor ruin of Llactapata to your right; cross the Río Cusichaca on a footbridge and head south along the east bank of the river. It's six km along the river to Huayllabamba, climbing gently all the way and recrossing the river after four km.

Huayllabamba is a village a few minutes above the fork of the Llullucha and Cusichaca rivers, at an elevation of 2750 metres. The Llullucha is crossed by a log bridge. You can camp in the plaza in front of the school, but beware of thieves slitting your tent at night. (You can continue south along the Cusichaca to the ruins of Paucarcancha, three km away, if you want to get away from the crowds. Camping is possible at the ruins, but carry water up from the river.)

The Inca Trail climbs steeply along the southern bank of the Río Llullucha. After an hour, the river forks. Continue up the left fork for 500 metres and then cross the river on a log bridge. There are camp sites on both sides of the bridge. The area is called *tres piedras blancas* (three white stones) and is the first camp for many people.

The Inca Trail beyond this camp turns right after the log bridge and then sweeps back to the Llullucha. It is a long, steep climb to the 4198-metre high point of the trek, the Warmiwañusca (Dead Woman's) Pass. The trail passes through cloud forest for 1½ hours before emerging on the high, bare mountain. At some points, the trail and the stream bed become one. Llulluchupampa is a flat area above the forest, where water is available and camping is good, though it is cold at night. From here, follow the left-hand side of the valley and climb for two to three hours to the pass.

At Warmiwañusca, you'll see the Río Pacamayo far below and Runturacay ruin halfway up the hill above the river. The trail

heads down to the river, where there are good camp sites.

The trail crosses the river (via a foot bridge) below a small waterfall. Climb up to the right towards Runturacay, which is an oval-shaped ruin with superb views, an hour's walk from the river. Above Runturacay, the trail climbs to a false summit, then continues past two small lakes to the top of the second pass at 3998 metres (about one hour). The clear trail descends past another lake to the ruin of Sayacmarca, which is visible from the trail a km before you get there. The site is most impressive: a tightly constructed town on a small mountain spur with superb views. The trail continues downwards and crosses the headwaters of the Río Aobamba, where there is a small camp site.

The gentle climb to the third pass then begins. There is a causeway across a dried-out swampy lake and later on, a tunnel, both Inca constructions. The trail goes through beautiful cloud forest, but the high point of the pass, at almost 3700 metres, isn't very obvious. There are great views of the Urubamba valley, and soon you reach the beautiful ruin of Phuyupatamarca, at 3650 metres, three hours beyond Sayacmarca.

Phuyupatamarca has been well restored and contains a beautiful series of ceremonial baths, which have water running through them. A ridge above the ruin offers camp sites with spectacular views. There are camp guards here sometimes.

From Phuyupatamarca, the more recently opened (1985) section of the Inca Trail is a dizzying drop into the cloud forest below, down hundreds of Inca steps. This rejoins the old trail near the electric power pylons which go down the hill to the dam on the Río Urubamba. Follow the pylons down to a red-roofed, white building – a youth hostel (US$5 per bed, less if you sleep on the floor). There are hot showers (US$1.25), and meals and bottled drinks are available. Camping is possible nearby. A 500-metre trail behind the hostel leads to the beautiful Inca site of Huiñay Huayna, which cannot be seen from the hostel.

About a km above the hotel is the recently

discovered terraced ruin of Conchamarca, excavated in 1993. It can now be visited.

Huiñay Huayna is a small but exquisite place – don't miss it. Climb down to the lowest part of the town, where it tapers off into a tiny exposed ledge overlooking the Río Urubamba far below. This ruin is a three-hour descent from Phuyupatamarca. The very difficult climb down to the Río Urubamba is prohibited.

From Huiñay Huayna, the trail continues through the cliff-hanging cloud forest, and is very thin in places, so watch your step. It takes two hours to reach the penultimate site on the trail, Intipunku (Sun Gate). You can see Machu Picchu from here. There is room for a couple of tents, but no water. This is the last place to camp on the Inca Trail.

From Intipunku, Machu Picchu is an hour's descent. Backpacks aren't allowed into the ruins; on arrival, check your pack at the lower entrance gate and have your trail permit stamped. It is valid only for the day it is stamped, so arrive in the morning.

Getting There & Away

Take the local train from Cuzco to Km 88. Watch your pack like a hawk. The station at Km 88 is very small and badly marked, so ask where to get off. Cross the river by footbridge and buy a trail permit. Doing the hike in reverse is not officially permitted.

MACHU PICCHU

This is the best known and most spectacular archaeological site on the continent. From June to September, hundreds of people come daily to visit the 'Lost City of the Incas'. Despite this great tourist influx, the site manages to retain its air of grandeur and mystery, and is a must for all visitors to Peru.

Archaeology

Apart from a few locals, nobody knew of Machu Picchu's existence until American historian Hiram Bingham stumbled upon it on 24 July 1911. The buildings were thickly overgrown with vegetation, and his team had to be content with roughly mapping the site. Bingham returned in 1912 and 1915 to clear the thick forest from the ruins. Further studies and clearings were carried out by Peruvian archaeologist Luis E Valcárcel in 1934 and by a Peruvian-American expedition under Paul Fejos in 1940-41. Despite these and more recent studies, our knowledge of Machu Picchu remains sketchy. One thing is obvious: the quality of the stonework and the abundance of ornamental sites indicate that Machu Picchu must have been an important ceremonial centre.

Budget Travellers

Visiting Machu Picchu cheaply is possible, once you have budgeted for the US$10 admission fee to the ruins.

The cheapest way to go is via the local train (1st class recommended) to Aguas Calientes. Spend the night there, a full day at Machu Picchu ruins and another night at Aguas Calientes, then return via the local train. This avoids the tourist train completely and maximises your time at the ruins. The ruins are most heavily visited from June to August, especially on Friday, Saturday and Monday, between about 11 am and 2.30 pm.

The ruins deserve a full day: hike Huayna Picchu or Intipunku or beyond. Going back for a second day is also worth the money.

The Ruins

To the left of the central plaza (with the entrance behind you) lie the most significant buildings. A long staircase leads up to the Hut of the Caretaker of the Funerary Rock, from where some of the best views are to be had. Further on, a small hill is topped by the Intihuatana, which is the major shrine of Machu Picchu. The carved rock at the summit is called a sun dial, but it was used by the high priests to tell the seasons rather than the time of day. This is the only such Intihuatana that has survived; others were destroyed by the Spaniards.

Machu Picchu is open from 7.30 am to 5 pm. Foreigners pay US$10 entry, or US$15 for two days. A *boleto nocturno* (US$10) allows you in at night. This is popular around full moon. You aren't allowed to bring large packs or food into the ruins; packs are checked in at the gate. The guards check the ruins at closing time, so you can't spend the night.

Short Hikes

Behind the ruins is the steep-sided mountain of Huayna Picchu; it takes an hour to climb and has great views. The entrance to the trail is to the right, at the back of the ruins, and is closed at 1 pm. From the base of Huayna Picchu, a recently cleared trail leads steeply down and up to the Temple of the Moon, from where you can climb to Huayna Picchu – a circuitous route taking two hours. Other short hikes in the area include walking back to Intipunku along the Inca Trail, or walking an interesting trail from the Hut of the Caretaker of the Funerary Rock to the Inca Bridge (Puente), which takes 20 minutes from the hut and gives good views of cloud-forest vegetation; this trail closes at 1 pm.

Places to Stay & Eat

At the ruins the *Hotel de Turistas* (US$75/105 for singles/doubles) has an expensive cafeteria and snack bar. The nearest cheap place to stay is in Aguas Calientes. It's illegal to bring food into the ruins.

Getting There & Away

Machu Picchu is 700 metres above the Puente Ruinas train station. Buses take visitors up the six-km zigzag road to the ruins. Tickets cost US$3 each way and are sold at the railway station. Buses are frequent when the tourist train arrives, but there may be an hour or more to wait at other times. Usually, there is a bus for the arrival of the local train. Otherwise, you can walk. Rather than walk up the road, hike up the shorter and steeper footpath. Cross the bridge behind the station and turn right. Arrows mark the path, which crosses the road at several points on the ascent. Drivers don't stop for passengers at intermediate points unless there are seats, which is unusual. The climb takes 1½ hours from the station, but the descent takes only 40 minutes.

Tourist and local trains leave in the afternoon for the return trip. Departure times vary depending on the season, but the tourist train normally goes first. Buses start descending from the ruins two hours before departure time, and bus lines can get very long during the busy season.

AGUAS CALIENTES

This is the closest village to Machu Picchu and is not a bad spot to hang out in. There are basic hotels, restaurants, and hot springs. (Destroyed in a 1995 landslide, the springs have reopened with rudimentary facilities.)

Places to Stay

The basic but clean *Hostal Los Caminantes* (☎ 21-1007) is US$6/9 for a single/double with shared bath or US$11 for a double with bath. Showers are cold. Other cheap and basic cold-water places include *Hostal La Cabaña* and *Hostal Ima Sumac*, both at US$5 per person. The popular *Hostal Qoñi* (☎ 21-1046), also called *Gringo Bill's*, has 24-hour hot water. Rates are US$6.50 per person in dorm rooms or US$20 for a double. Some rooms have private bath. The *Hostal Machu Picchu* (☎ 21-1034) is simple but clean at US$10/15 with shared hot showers.

The *Hotel Machu Picchu Inn* (reservations in Cuzco ☎ 21-1056, 22-3339, fax 21-1011) has clean rooms but mediocre bathrooms with hot water. It's US$11 per person in dorm rooms, US$15/25 with shared bath and US$24/31 with private bath. Breakfast is included. The very clean *Hostal El Inka* (☎ 21-1034) is helpful, friendly and often full. Rooms are US$22/35 with private bath and hot water.

Places to Eat

Some reasonably good and clean places near the tracks include the *Aiko, El Refugio, Samana Wasi* and *Chez Maggy*, the last of which is currently quite popular. Away from the tracks are the *Govinda Vegetarian Restaurant* and the *Restaurant Huayna Picchu*. All are fairly cheap and there are several others to choose from. The better hotels have restaurants too.

PERU

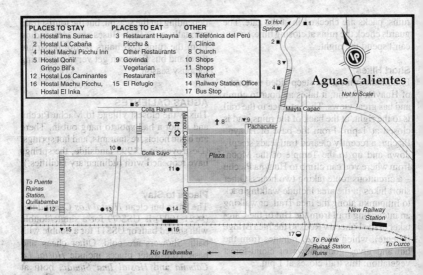

PLACES TO STAY
1 Hostal Ima Sumac
2 Hostal La Cabaña
4 Hotel Machu Picchu Inn
5 Hostal Qoñi/
   Gringo Bill's
12 Hostal Los Caminantes
16 Hostal Machu Picchu,
   Hostal El Inka

PLACES TO EAT
3 Restaurant Huayna
   Picchu &
   Other Restaurants
9 Govinda
   Vegetarian
   Restaurant
15 El Refugio

OTHER
6 Telefónica del Perú
7 Clínica
8 Church
10 Shops
11 Shops
13 Market
14 Railway Station Office
17 Bus Stop

Aguas Calientes

Not to Scale

To Hot Springs

Colla Raymi
Mayta Capac
Pachacutec
Plaza
Colla Suyo

To Puente
Ruinas
Station,
Quillabamba

New Railway
Station

To Puente
Ruinas Station,
Ruins

To Cuzco

Río Urubamba

Getting There & Away

Aguas Calientes is two km before the Puente Ruinas station (for Machu Picchu). A road has recently been built, and buses go to Machu Picchu (US$3.50). Alternatively, walk two km to Puente Ruinas and take more frequent buses from there, or walk the entire eight km uphill to the ruins.

The tourist train doesn't stop here, but the local train does.

QUILLABAMBA

Quillabamba is on the Río Urubamba, at the end of the train line from Cuzco to Machu Picchu. Peru's only jungle town accessible by railway, it is quiet and pleasant, and can be used as a base for trips further into the jungle.

Places to Stay

The *Hotel Borranecha*, on Espinar three blocks north of the Plaza de Armas, is US$2.50/4 for a single/double. Other cheap and basic places are the *Hostal Progreso* (no singles) and *Hostal San Martín* (dirty), on San Martín; *Hostal San Antonio* (dormitory accommodation), on Pio Concha just south of the plaza; and *Hostal Thomas* and *Hostal*

Urusayhua, near the market. All have cold-water communal bathrooms only.

Clean and recommended, the *Hostal Alto Urubamba* (☎ 21-6131), on 2 de Mayo one block north of the plaza, is US$4/6 or US$5/7.50 with private bath. The similarly priced and pleasant *Hostal Cuzco*, near the market, has an erratic water supply. Rooms have private cold showers. The nearby *Hostal Quillabamba* (☎ 21-6369) has clean rooms with hot showers, roof-top restaurant, pool and a pleasant garden. Rates are US$10/14. The similarly priced *Hostal Lira* (☎ 21-6324) is also good. The best is *Hostal Don Carlos* (☎ 21-6371), on Libertad just west of the plaza, at US$14/17 with hot bath.

Places to Eat

The *Hostal Quillabamba* restaurant has good views and adequate meals, but slow service. The *Hostal Lira* has a reasonable restaurant. *La Trucha* and *Don Felix*, both just south of the plaza, are among the best restaurants in town. A few *heladerías* on the plaza serve ice creams and light snacks.

Getting There & Away

Bus & Truck Trucks and buses for the spectacular drive to Cuzco (US$6, 11 hours) leave from Avenida Lima south of the market on an irregular basis. Ask around. Pick-up trucks leave every morning from the market area for the village of Kiteni (six to 12 hours) further into the jungle (one cheap hotel). A reader suggests asking around the plaza for trucks to Huancacalle (a long, bumpy ride), from where you can proceed to Vilcabamba.

Train For information on getting to Quillabamba, see the Cuzco section. Tickets for the return can be bought a day in advance. Trains leave at 4 am and 1.40 pm to Cuzco, via Aguas Calientes.

SOUTH-EAST FROM CUZCO
Tipón
This little-known Inca site is noted for its irrigation system. Take an Urcos bus from Cuzco to the Tipón turn-off, 23 km away. A steep dirt road from the turn-off climbs four km to the ruins.

Pikillacta & Rumicolca
Pikillacta is the only major pre-Inca ruin near Cuzco and was built around 1100 AD by the Wari culture. Entry is with the Cuzco visitor ticket. The site is 32 km from Cuzco. It is a large city of crumbling two-storey buildings, all with entrances strategically located on the upper floor. A defensive wall surrounds the city. The stonework here is much cruder than that of the Incas. There are local guides available, particularly on weekdays.

About a km away is the huge Inca gate of Rumicolca, built on Wari foundations. Here, too, the cruder Wari stonework contrasts with the Inca blocks. Get here on the Urcos bus from Cuzco.

Andahuaylillas
Andahuaylillas is 40 km from Cuzco and seven km before Urcos. It is famous for its beautiful 17th-century church, comparable to the best in Cuzco, and attractive colonial houses.

Raqchi
These are the ruins of the Temple of Viracocha, which once supported the largest known Inca roof. They are visible from the road and the railway at San Pedro, a few km before Sicuani, and look like a huge aqueduct. This was one of the holiest shrines of the Inca empire but was destroyed by the Spanish. Entry is US$2.50. There is a colourful, traditional fiesta in mid-June. Both buses and trains from Cuzco go to **Sicuani** (three hours), which has basic hotels but can be visited in a day trip from Cuzco.

FROM CUZCO TO THE JUNGLE
Two poor roads, in addition to the Quillabamba railway, leave Cuzco for the jungle. One road heads to Paucartambo, Tres Cruces and Shintuya for Parque Nacional Manu, while the other goes through Ocongate and Quince Mil to Puerto Maldonado. Travel on these in the dry months (June to September), as they are muddy and slow in the wet months, especially from January to April.

Paucartambo
This village is 115 km east of Cuzco on a very narrow dirt road. There are fine views of the Andes dropping away to the high Amazon Basin beyond. The road is one-way: traffic goes from Cuzco to Paucartambo on Monday, Wednesday and Friday, and in the other direction on Tuesday, Thursday and Saturday. Trucks for Paucartambo leave Cuzco early in the morning from near the Urcos bus stop. The journey takes six hours.

Paucartambo is famous for its authentic and colourful annual Fiesta de la Virgen del Carmen, held on and around 16 July. Camp, rent a room in one of the two extremely basic small hotels, or find a local to give you floor space. Tourist agencies in Cuzco run buses specifically for the fiesta.

Tres Cruces
Tres Cruces, with its locally famous jungle views, is 45 km beyond Paucartambo. From May to July, sunrise here tends to be optically distorted, so double images, halos and unusual colours may be seen. During these months, adventure tour agencies run sunrise-watching trips to Tres Cruces.

PERU

Shintuya & Parque Nacional Manu

Shintuya is the end of the road, reached by truck from Cuzco (US$15, 20 hours). From here, hire a boat and boatman for the voyage down the Río Madre de Dios to Manu (about US$100 to US$120 per day, plus fuel and food); a minimum of a week is recommended. It is also recommended that you hire a guide with training in ecology and biology; otherwise, your trip will be a meaningless cruise through the rainforest. A good guide is US$30 to US$50 per day, plus food. It is illegal to enter the park without some kind of a guide. You should bring everything you need from Cuzco. Obviously, this is not a budget trip, but if you get a group together, it's not too expensive.

Further information can be obtained from the SAEC in Lima or from Expediciones Manu (☎ 22-6671, 23-9974, fax 23-6706), Procuradores 50, Cuzco. Because of the expense and hassle of getting a group together, we think it's worth taking a tour. Expediciones Manu has fixed guided departures to Manu leaving every month from May to December. Its nine-day camping tour costs about US$850 per person, with a minimum of seven passengers; smaller groups can band together to make up the numbers. Expert bilingual naturalist guides and all equipment, food and transportation are provided. Staff are very helpful in tailoring itineraries to fit your needs, and the tours are good value. Also recommended is Pantiacolla Tours (☎ 23-8323, fax 23-3727), Plateros 360, which charges about US$500 for an eight-day trip. Cheaper agencies exist, but we haven't heard much in the way of positive reports about them.

The park is closed in January and open only to people staying in the expensive Manu Lodge from February to April. Both Expediciones Manu and Pantiacolla Tours can arrange for you to stay in lodges outside the park, but still in good wildlife areas, for US$40 a day plus transportation.

To Ocongate & Puerto Maldonado

The trip to Puerto Maldonado (see the Amazon Basin section later in this chapter) is a spectacular but difficult journey on poor roads, which takes three days in the dry season (a week in the wet) and costs US$15. The journey can be broken at Ocongate or Quincemil (both with basic hotels). Trucks leave from the little plaza just east of Tacna and Pachacutec (in Cuzco) a few times a week. It may be better to wait in Urcos: all trucks to Puerto Maldonado go via Urcos. This trip involves a degree of hardiness, self-sufficiency and good luck.

From Ocongate, trucks take an hour to reach the village of **Tinqui**, which is the start of the five to seven-day trek encircling the 6384-metre-high **Ausangate**, southern Peru's highest peak. Tinqui has a very basic hotel and mules can be rented for the trek.

WEST OF CUZCO

Going west through Abancay and Andahuaylas to Ayacucho (in the Central Highlands) is a tough ride on a rough road, but is safe. The road is high and night travel is very cold; be prepared. The trip south from Abancay to Nazca through Puquio (the old route to Lima) is not recommended because of banditry near Puquio.

Abancay

This remote town, capital of the Department of Apurímac and 2377 metres above sea level, is a seven-hour drive west of Cuzco (in the dry season). It's a place to break the Cuzco-Ayacucho trip. The Banco de Crédito changes money. The telephone code is 084. Abancay's carnaval is an especially colourful one.

Places to Stay & Eat The grim *Hotel Gran* and *Hostal El Misti* charge US$2.25 per person. Slightly cleaner, but still a very basic cold-water place, the *Gran Hotel* charges US$3.50/5.50 for a single/double with private bath, or less with shared bath. The *Hostal Leonidas* (☎ 32-1199) is better and has clean rooms for US$4.50/7 or US$5.50/8 with private cold shower. The *Leonidas 2* is similar. The best is the *Hotel de Turistas* (☎ 22-3339 in Cuzco), in an old-fashioned country mansion. Rooms are US$6.50/8.50, or US$11/15 with private hot shower, and the restaurant has meals for US$3. There are cheap cafés near the bus stations.

Getting There & Away Buses leave from Arenas near Núñez for Cuzco or Andahuaylas (six hours) at 6 am and 1 pm in both directions. Fares are US$5 to either town and journeys take longer in the wet season. For Ayacucho, change in Andahuaylas. Uncomfortable minibuses are used.

Andahuaylas

Andahuaylas is halfway between Cuzco and Ayacucho and a convenient place to stay overnight. Most inhabitants speak Quechua. This is a very rural and poor part of Peru, and only parts of the town centre have electricity. The elevation here is 2980 metres.

Places to Stay & Eat The *Hostal Cusco* is clean, has hot water and is good value at US$3/5 for a single/double, or US$4.50/6.50 with private bath. There are a couple of cheaper cold-water places. The *Hostal Los Libertadores Wari* (☎ 72-1434) is clean, safe and has hot water but closes its doors at 11 pm. Rates are US$4.50/7 or US$6/8 with private baths. The *Hostal Las Américas* is similar, but open later. The best hotel, in a poor neighbourhood, is the modern *Hotel de Turistas* (☎ 72-1229, in Cuzco 22-3339), at US$18/25 with breakfast.

The simple *Ají Seco*, on Ramón Castilla, serves good, inexpensive, highland Peruvian food. There are equally good places on this street.

Getting There & Away For Lima (US$50), Imperial Air flies daily and Expreso Aéreo flies three times a week. Transportes Aéreos Andahuaylas (TAA; ☎ 72-1891) flies to Lima daily and to Cuzco on Tuesday and Friday. Taxi colectivos charge US$1 into town.

Señor de Huanca has uncomfortable minibuses to Abancay (US$5, six hours) at 6 am and 1 pm. The 6 am departure continues to Cuzco (US$9, 14 hours). Transportes Molina and Transportes Faro have a large

bus to Ayacucho (US$9, 17 hours in the dry season) at 1 pm. Both continue to Lima (US$18, 30 hours).

The Central Highlands

The central Peruvian Andes are one of the least visited areas of Peru. The mountainous terrain makes overland transport difficult and the region has poor air services. Most of the people of the Central Andes are subsistence farmers.

It was in this environment of isolation and poverty that the Sendero Luminoso, Peru's major terrorist organisation, emerged in the 1960s and grew in the 1970s. The violent activities of the Sendero escalated dramatically in the 1980s, and headlines all over the world proclaimed Peru's internal unrest. Tourism declined, and during most of the 1980s, the departments of Ayacucho, Huancavelica and Apurímac were almost completely avoided by travellers.

Since the 1992 arrest and imprisonment of many guerrilla leaders, including Abimael Guzmán, founder and head of the Sendero Luminoso, the power of the guerrilla organisations has been broken and the main routes and towns of the region are safe to visit.

TARMA

This pleasant town, 250 km east of Lima, at 3050 metres, is nicknamed 'the pearl of the Andes'. There are many little-known ruins in the surrounding hills.

Information

Servicios Turísticos Maeedick (☎ 32-2530), 2 de Mayo 547, has tours and information. The telephone code is 064.

Things to See

Trips are made to the village of Acobamba, 10 km away, to see the famous religious sanctuary of **El Señor de Muruhuay**. From the village of Palcamayo, 28 km north-west of Tarma, it's four km to the **Gruta de Guagapo**, a huge limestone cave officially protected as a 'national speleological area'. A guide lives opposite the entrance; caving gear is required for a full exploration.

Special Events
The Semana Santa processions, including several candlelit ones after dark, are the big attraction. The Easter Sunday procession to the Catedral follows a route carpeted with flower petals, as does the procession on the annual fiesta of El Señor de Los Milagros, in late October. Other fiestas include Semana de Tarma in late July, and San Sebastián, on 20 January.

Places to Stay
Cheap and basic cold-water hotels near the Mercado Modelo that charge US$3.50/5.50 for a single/double include: the OK *Hostal Ritz*, the dirty *Hostal Anchoraico*, the dingy *Hostal Tarma* and the *Hostal Córdova*. *Baños del Sol*, near the market, has public hot showers.

The following places have occasional hot water. The adequate *Hostal Central* (☎ 32-2466) is US$4/5.50, or US$5.50/7.50 with private bath. The *Hotel Tuchu* is good value at US$5/7.50 with bath. The *Hotel Vargas* has good beds at US$5 per person with private bath, less without. The *Hotel El Dorado* (☎ 32-2598), is OK at US$6.50/8.50 with bath. The clean, popular *Hotel Galaxia* on the plaza is US$9.50/13 with bath. The good *Hostal Internacional* (☎ 32-2830) is US$7.50/12 or US$10/14 with bath.

Places to Eat
Cheap restaurants line Avenida Lima. The *Restaurant Chavín* on the plaza is good and the *Restaurant Don Lucho* is acceptable and cheap. The best restaurant in town is the *El Rosal*.

Getting There & Away
Empresa de Transportes San Juan has frequent buses to Chanchamayo (US$2), some continuing to Villa Rica or Oxapampa. Comité 20 taxi colectivos leave from the market at US$3.25 to go to Chanchamayo.

San Juan also has many buses to

Huancayo (US$2.25). Los Canarios goes to Huancayo and Lima (US$4). Others for Lima are Transportes DASA, Transportes Chanchamayo and Hidalgo.

HUANCAYO
This modern city, at 3260 metres, lies in the broad and fertile Río Mantaro valley, in the Central Andes, and is famous for its Sunday market. Huancayo is the capital of the Department of Junín and the main commercial centre for the area. The road from Lima has improved recently, and the bus (or train) trip is spectacular as you rise from the coast to about 4700 metres before dropping into the Mantaro valley.

Information
The tourist office is on the corner of Calle Real at Breña. Hours are Monday to Friday from 8 am to 1.30 pm and 4 to 6 pm. It has good information. Lucho Hurtado and Beverly Stuart, who run La Cabaña Pizzería and Incas del Perú tour agency, Giráldez 652, are a recommended source of information and help.

Casas de cambio and banks are on the 400 and 500 blocks of Calle Real. Banco de Crédito and Banco Wiese have the best rates for travellers' cheques.

The telephone code is 064.

Things to See
The Mercado Mayorista (daily produce market) overflows onto the railway tracks from the covered market off Ica east of the tracks. The meat section sells various Andean delicacies, including fresh and dried frogs, and guinea pigs.

The Sunday crafts market along Calle Huancavelica has weavings, sweaters and other textile goods, embroidered items, ceramics, woodcarvings and the carved gourds which are a specialty of the area. Watch your wallet!

Walk (or bus) two km north-east on Giráldez to the Cerro de la Libertad, which has good city views. Continue two km to see the eroded sandstone towers at Torre Torre.

Activities

Incas del Perú (☎ 22-3303, fax 22-2395), Giráldez 652, has day hikes, local tours, bicycle rental and Spanish lessons.

Places to Stay

The clean and good *La Casa de la Abuela*, Giráldez 1081, is US$5 per person with breakfast and hot showers. The popular *Residencial Baldeón*, Amazonas 543, in a friendly family house, is US$5 per person with hot water, breakfast and kitchen privileges. The basic but popular *Residencial Huancayo* (☎ 23-3541), Giráldez 356, is US$6/7 for a single/double and has hot water. It is basic but popular with budget travellers.

Basic cold-water hotels include the *Hostal Universal*, Pichis 100, the *Hostal Roma*, Loreto 447, the *Hostal Tivoli*, Puno 488, and the *Hotel Centro*, Loreto 452, at US$4/6. The Centro also has US$6/8 rooms with cold bath as does the *Hotel Prince*, Calixto 578, and the clean *Hostal Villa Rica*, Calle Real 1291. *Duchas Tina* and *Sauna Blub* have hot showers.

The basic *Hostal Will Roy*, Calixto 452, is US$6/8. The clean *Hotel Torre Torre*, Calle Real 873, is US$5.50/7.50 or US$2 more with bath. The *Hostal Los Angeles*, Calle Real 245, is the same price. The clean *Percy's Hotel*, Calle Real 1339, is US$7.50/10 with bath. The clean, safe and friendly *Hostal Pussy* (☎ 23-1565), 300 block of Giráldez, is US$9/12.50 with bath. The following are clean and have similar rates and private baths: the *Hotel Roger* (☎ 23-3488), Ancash 460; the *Hotel Palace* (☎ 23-8501), Ancash 1127; the *Hotel Plaza*, Ancash 171, is good value. The *Hotel El Dorado* (☎ 22-3947), Piura 428, is clean and friendly at US$11/15. All these have hot water.

Places to Eat

The local specialty is papa a la huancaína, a boiled potato topped with a tasty white sauce of cheese, milk, hot pepper and butter, served with an olive and eaten as a cold potato salad.

Restaurants serving good cheap set meals include *El Pino*, Calle Real 539, and *Pinky's*, Giráldez 147. The *Chifa Central* has good Chinese food and *El Parque* is a good chicken place. The up-market *Restaurant Olímpico* has good menús for US$2 and Peruvian à-la-carte plates from US$5. Other good, similarly priced places are the *Restaurant El Inca*, Puno 530, and *Lalo's Restaurant*, Giráldez 363. The popular *La Cabaña* (☎ 22-3303), Giráldez 652, has good pizzas, sandwiches and anticuchos, and live music from Thursday to Saturday nights.

Entertainment

La Cabaña restaurant has the liveliest action at night and live folklórico and rock from Thursday to Saturday. The *Taj Mahal*, Huancavelica 1052, is a popular club with video karaoke and dancing. There's also dancing at *Coconut*, at Huancavelica 430, near Puno.

Getting There & Away

Bus Mariscal Cáceres (☎ 23-1232), Huánuco 350, has nine daily buses to Lima for US$7 or US$9 for nonstop 'presidential service'. Others for Lima are ETUCSA (☎ 23-2638), Puno 220, and Cruz del Sur (☎ 23-4251), Puno 250, both with regular and nonstop buses, and (with cheaper buses) Empresa Molina, Angaraes 334, Transportes Costa Sierra, Antezana, and Hidalgo. Comité 12 (☎ 23-3281), Loreto 421, and Comité 22 (☎ 23-5841), Loreto 345, have cars to Lima (US$13, five to six hours).

Empresa Molina and Empresa Hidalgo buses to Huancavelica (US$3 or US$4, seven hours). Empresa Molina and Empresa Ayacucho have buses to Ayacucho (US$8, 12 to 14 hours) as do the less comfortable Hidalgo and Antezana. Expect delays in the rainy season.

Empresa de Transportes San Juan, Quito 136, has hourly minibuses to Tarma (US$2.50). Some continue to Chanchamayo. San Juan also has buses to Satipo, in the jungle. You can also find buses north to Cerro de Pasco, Huánuco, and Tingo María.

Local buses to most of the nearby villages leave from the street intersections shown on the Huancayo map.

PERU

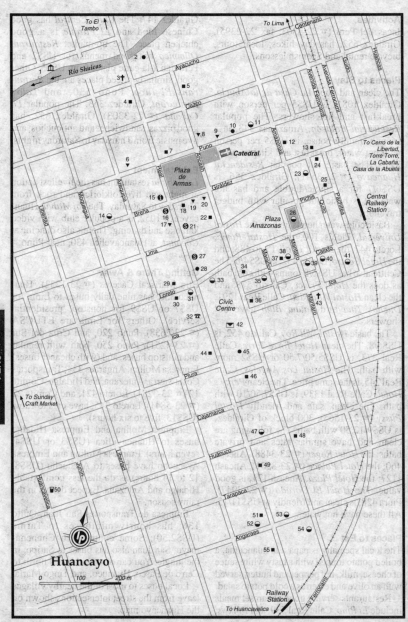

PERU

Huancayo

To El Tambo

To Lima

Río Shulcas

Centenario

Ayacucho

Cuzco

Puno

Catedral

Plaza de Armas

Giráldez

Breña

Lima

Civic Centre

To Sunday Craft Market

Cajamarca

Huánuco

Tarapacá

Angaraes

To Cerro de la Libertad, Torre Torre, La Cabaña, Casa de la Abuela

Central Railway Station

Plaza Amazonas

Railway Station

To Huancavelica

0   100   200 m

PLACES TO STAY
4 Hostal Los Angeles
5 Hotel Plaza
7 Hostal Tivoli
12 Residencial Baldeón
13 Residencial Huancayo
18 Hotel Kiya
19 Hotel Santa Felicita
22 Hotel Roger
24 Hostal Pussy
25 Hostal Universal
29 Hotel Centro
30 Hostal Roma
34 Hotel Prince
36 Turismo Hotel
37 Hostal Will Roy
44 Hotel Torre Torre
46 Hotel El Dorado
48 Hotel Palace
49 Hotel Presidente
51 Hostal Villa Rica
55 Percy's Hotel

PLACES TO EAT
6 Restaurant El Inca
8 El Parque
9 Chifa Central

17 El Pino
19 Pinky's Restaurant
20 Restaurant Olímpico
24 Lalo's Restaurant

OTHER
1 Museo Salesiano
2 Sauna Blub
3 Iglesia La Merced
10 Duchas Tina
11 ETUCSA & Cruz del Sur Buses
14 Transportes Costa Sierra
15 Tourist Office
16 Banco de Crédito
17 Banco de la Nación
21 Casa de Cambio
23 Empresa de Transportes San Juan
26 Buses to Chupaca & Pilcomayo
27 Casa de Cambio
28 Cine Pacifico
31 Comité 12 Colectivos to Lima

32 Telefónica del Perú
33 Comité 22 Colectivos to Lima
35 Buses to San Jerónimo & Concepción
38 Expreso Huaytapalana
39 Buses to San Jerónimo, Concepción & Jauja
40 Buses to La Oroya
41 Buses to Hualhuas, Cajas & Huamancaca
42 Central Post Office
43 Iglesia La Inmaculada
45 Municipalidad
47 Mariscal Cnceres
50 Taj Mahal
52 Empresa Molina
53 Empresa Hidalgo, Antezana, many small bus companies
54 Empresa Ayacucho

Train There are two unconnected train stations. The central station serves Lima. This train has not run since 1991 but may reopen in 1996 or 1997. The Huancavelica train station serves Huancavelica by *expreso* (US$2.50, 4½ hours) at 6.30 am, except Sunday, when it leaves at 2 pm. The *tren extra* (US$2 in 1st class, 6½ hours) leaves at 12.30 pm, Monday to Saturday. Advance tickets are recommended.

AROUND HUANCAYO
The Mantaro Valley
The twin villages of Cochas Grande and Cochas Chico, 11 km from Huancayo, are centres for production of the incised gourds for which the area is famous. San Agustín de Cajas is known for the manufacture of broad-brimmed wool hats, though it seems to be a dying industry now. Hualhuas is famous for wool products. San Jerónimo de Tunán is known for its filigreed silverware, and its 17th-century church with fine wooden altars.

North of Huancayo is the village of Concepción (with basic accommodation),

from which the famous 18th-century **Convento de Santa Rosa de Ocopa** can be visited. This beautiful building with an interesting museum and library is open daily, except Tuesday, from 9 am to noon and 3 to 6 pm. Admission is US$0.50.

HUANCAVELICA
This city is 147 km south of Huancayo, in a high and remote area. It's a pleasant small colonial town with seven 16th- and 17th-century churches with silver-plated altars. Hours are irregular.

Information
The Ministerio de Turismo, Nicolás de Piérola 180, and the Instituto Nacional de Cultura, on Plaza San Juan de Dios, have local information. Travellers' cheques may be hard to change. The telephone code is 064. Market day is Sunday.

Places to Stay
Hostal Savoy, M Muñoz 290, has no water, and the *Hostal Santo Domingo*, Barranca

366, has cold water. Very basic rooms are US$1.50 per person. *Mi Hotel*, Carabaya 481, is a few cents more but has hot water and is better. *Hotel Tahuantinsuyo*, at Carabaya and M Muñoz, has hot water and charges US$3/4.50 for singles/doubles with private bath. The *Mercurio*, Torre Tagle 455, is similar but charges twice as much.

Places to Eat

Cheap restaurants along M Muñoz serve decent set menús for US$1.50. *La Estrellita*, S Barranca 255, has excellent trout. *El Misti, La Amistad* and others are on the same block. Also try the *Ganso de Oro*, V Toledo 283, the *Restaurant Joy*, V Toledo 230, *Césars*, M Muñoz 390, and *Las Magnolias*, just off the Plaza de Armas. All are reasonable.

Getting There & Away

Bus Most buses leave from Avenida M Muñoz. Various companies have buses for Huancayo (US$3.50, six hours) and Lima (US$9, 14 hours). There are no direct services to Ayacucho.

Train The tren extra leaves Huancavelica at 6.30 am and the expreso leaves at 12.30 pm, except on Sunday, when it leaves at 7 am. You should buy tickets in advance.

AYACUCHO

Ayacucho is where the Sendero Luminoso arose in the 1960s. Since the capture of the Sendero's founder and leader in 1992, this area, once unsafe to visit, is again open to overland travel. This fascinating Andean colonial town is well worth a visit, particularly during the famous Semana Santa celebrations.

Information

La Dirección General de Industria y Turismo, Asamblea 481, is good for information. The travel agencies are also helpful. The Banco de Crédito cashes travellers' cheques. The telephone code is 064.

Things to See

The centre has two museums, a 17th-century Catedral, many churches from the 16th, 17th and 18th centuries, and several old mansions around the plaza.

The ruins of **Wari** (Huari), capital of the Wari empire, which predated the Incas by 500 years, are worth seeing. Beyond is the village of Quinua, where a huge monument and small museum mark the site of the Battle of Ayacucho (1824). There is a Sunday market. Wari is 20 km and Quinua about 40 km north-east of Ayacucho. Agencies on the plaza have tours there, or you can use public transport.

Places to Stay

Hotel prices double during Semana Santa. The very basic and grubby *Hostal Ayacucho* (☎ 91-2759), Lima 165, is US$3.50/5 for a single/double. Other basic cold-water cheapies include the *Hostal Sixtina* (☎ 91-1018), Callao 336, at US$5/7 and the *Hostal Central* (☎ 91-2144), Arequipa 180, at US$5/9.

The following have hot water at times. The basic *Hotel Santiago* (☎ 91-2132), Nazarena 177, is US$4/6.50 or US$10 for a double with bath. The slightly better *Hotel Crillonesa* (☎ 91-2350), Nazarena 165, is US$4.50/8. The clean *Hostal Magdalena* (☎ 91-2910), Centenario 277, is US$5/9 or US$15 for a double with bath. The *Hostal Huamanga* (☎ 91-3527), Bellido 535, is not as good for US$5.50 per person or US$7.50 per person in rooms with bath. The simple but clean *Hostal Samary* (☎ 91-2442), Callao 329, has rooftop views and is US$7.50/9.50, or US$9/11 with private bath. The recommended (often full) *La Colmena Hotel* (☎ 91-2146), Cuzco 140, has a nice courtyard and is US$8/12 or US$12/15 with bath. There are pricier hotels.

Places to Eat

The *Alamo Restaurant* opens at 7 am for varied breakfasts and good cheap food all day. Beer is not sold. Marginally more expensive, *La Casona* is popular and recommended. *La Tradición* is also good and the nearby *Restaurant Camara Comercio* has cheap set menús. *Los Portales* on the plaza is a popular local place. *San Agustín Café* has decent desserts; for Chinese food try the *Chifa El Dorado*.

Getting There & Away

Air Between them, AeroContinente, Faucett and Americana have two or three flights a day to and from Lima (US$47). Aero-Continente continues to Cuzco (US$42). The airport is three km from the town centre; taxis and buses are available.

Bus & Truck For Lima (US$10 to US$12), Transportes Molina, Los Libertadores, Transmar and Fano all have mid-afternoon buses. Hidalgo, Transportes Antezana and Transportes Molina have night buses to Huancayo (US$7 to US$8, 12 to 14 hours); Molina also has one Huancayo departure at 6.30 am. Transportes Molina and Transportes Fano have dawn departures to Andahuaylas (US$9, about 15 hours).The cheapest way to Cuzco is to wait at Grifo Chakchi (petrol station) for a truck and ride in the back with the locals. This is slow and uncomfortable but the views are great and you will experience the Andes from a very different perspective.

Pick-up trucks and occasional buses go to many local villages, including Quinua, and to the Wari ruins, departing from beyond the statue at the east end of Avenida Centenario.

NORTH OF LA OROYA

A road from Lima to Pucallpa (in the jungle) goes through the central Andes north of La Oroya, via Cerro de Pasco, Huánuco and Tingo María. This route is again safe, but there are several police controls on the Tingo María-Pucallpa section.

Cerro de Pasco

This is a cold, dirty mining town 4333 metres above sea level – the highest city of its size (pop 30,000) in the world. There are a few basic hotels, but it's not worth staying unless you must.

Huánuco

This town, elevation 1894 metres, is capital of its department and the nicest place between Lima and Pucallpa. There is a decent museum at General Prado 495, and a pleasant Plaza de Armas.

Information A tourism office is on the plaza at General Prado 714. The Banco de Crédito changes money. The telephone code is 064.

Places to Stay & Eat Hotels fill quickly. The cheapest are US$3/5 for a single/double. Several are near the market, such as *Hotel La Victoria*, which is just OK. The best cheapie is the clean *Hotel Imperial*, Huánuco 581, at US$5/7 or US$7/10 with private bath and cold water. Opposite are the similarly priced hotels *Marino* and *Caribe*. There are more at this price near the market. The *Hostal Santo Domingo* is US$6/8 or US$7/10 with bath, and has cold water, but seems OK. For US$6/8 for rooms with bath and, perhaps, hot water, try the *Hotel Paraíso* (☎ 51-1953), on the Plaza de Armas. Also on the plaza are the *Hotel Lima* (☎ 51-3020) at US$7/10 with bath, and *Hostal Las Vegas* (☎ 51-2315) at US$8/12 with bath. Both have occasional hot water and a café. The *Hotel Kotosh* is US$7/10 with cold bath and the similar *Hotel Tours* is US$8/11.

The pleasant *Hostal Huánuco* (☎ 51-2050), Huánuco 777, has good hot water and is often full. Rates are US$11/14 with bath. The clean, well-run *Hostal Garu* (☎ 51-3096, fax 51-3097), P Puelles 459, is US$17/25 with hot showers.

There's a good choice of restaurants on or near the plaza.

Getting There & Away Expreso Aéreo and AeroContinente serve Lima daily (US$65). Both continue to Tingo María, and Expreso Aéreo has a milk run to Tingo María, Tocache, Juanjui, Saposoa, Tarapoto and Trujillo, with connecting flights to other northern cities. AeroCóndor also flies here and onwards. The airport is eight km from town. Schedules change often.

For Lima (US$9, nine hours), León de Huánuco has 8 am and 8 pm buses. Others are Transportes Rey and ETNASA, which also has night buses to Pucallpa (US$11.50, 15 hours). Transportes Oriental has day and night buses to Pucallpa. On the other side of the Río Huallaga, 10 minutes walk from the centre, shared taxis or minibuses go to Tingo María. You can flag down buses to Pucallpa. Transportes Oriental has day and night buses to Huancayo (US$6, eight hours). Rucay Hermanos and Expreso Huallaga have several buses a day to Cerro de Pasco and Huancayo. Turismo Central also goes to Huancayo daily. For remote Andean towns like La Unión and Tantamayo, look around the market.

Tingo María

Just 650 metres above sea level, Tingo María is surrounded by Andean foothills, but is almost a jungle town. North is the dangerous drug-growing Río Huallaga valley; east is Pucallpa. Tingo María is a busy market town and a safe enough stop.

Places to Stay & Eat Hotels fill quickly and all have cold showers. The basic *Hostal Cuzco* (☎ 56-2095), Raimondi 671, is US$3.50/5.50 for a single/double. Across the road, the *Hostal La Cabaña* is reasonably clean at US$5/8. The *Hostal Diana*, on Benavides, has poor rooms with bath at US$6/9. The similarly priced *Hostal Belén* is a block closer to the plaza and has nicer rooms with shared showers. Other basic cheapies include the secure *Hostal Raimondi* (☎ 56-2095), Raimondi 344, the *Hotel Royal*, on Benavides, and the *Hostal Progreso*, on Callao.

The clean *Hostal Viena* (☎ 56-2194), Lamas 254, is US$6/9 or US$8/11 with bath. The *Hotel Coloso* (☎ 56-2027), Benavides 440, is also US$8/11 with bath. The *Hotel Palacio* (☎ 56-2319), Raimondi 158, looks OK at US$7.50/10.50, or US$9/13 with private bath. The best cheap hotel is the *Hotel Nueva York* (☎ 56-2406), Alameda Perú 553, at US$12/17 with tepid showers.

There are several inexpensive restaurants along Raimondi.

Getting There & Away The airfare to Lima is US$60. See Huánuco for carriers.

Bus departures change frequently: ask around. Transtel has dawn buses to Pucallpa (US$9, 12 hours). Empresa La Marginal and others go to Pucallpa. Empresa Transmar and Transportes Rey have night buses to Lima (US$12, 12 hours). León de Huánuco has day buses. Turismo Central has a night bus to Huancayo (US$8, 12 hours). Taxi colectivos and minibuses leave for Huánuco from Raimondi at Callao.

The North Coast

The coast road north of Lima passes huge, rolling sand dunes, dizzying cliffs, oases of farmland, busy fishing villages, archaeological sites and some large and historic cities.

BARRANCA & PARAMONGA

The small town of Barranca, 190 km north of Lima, is four km before the Huaraz turn-off. Four km north of the turn-off is the Chimú pyramid of Paramonga, a huge structure which is worth a visit. Admission is US$2.50. There is a small site museum.

There are a few cheap hotels and restaurants in Barranca. No buses go to the ruins, though local buses going to the port at Paramonga will drop you three km away.

CASMA

The small town of Casma is 370 km north of Lima, and the archaeological site of Sechín is five km away.

Sechín

This site dates from 1600 BC and is one of the more important and well-preserved coastal ruins. There is a small museum. The outside walls of the main temple are covered with gruesome bas-relief carvings of warriors and of captives being eviscerated. To get there, go three km south of Casma on the Panamericana, then left on the paved road to Huaraz for two more km. Hours are 9 am to

5 pm; entry is US$1.80. Bring your own food.

Places to Stay
The basic, unattractive *Hostal Central* charges US$4 each. The clean and friendly *Hostal Gregori* (☎ 71-1073 or 1173), L Ormeño 579, is US$5/7.50 for a single/ double with shared cold showers. The clean *Hostal Indoamericano* (☎ 71-1235) is US$6/11 or US$8/14 with private cold bath. The best is the *Hostal El Farol* (☎ & fax 71-1064) at US$12.50/17.50 with private warm shower and breakfast.

Getting There & Away
Bus offices and stops are clustered together on the main road, near the junction with the Panamericana. There are buses to Lima, Tru- jillo and Huaraz, but most are just passing through so few seats are available. Alterna- tively, take a colectivo 50 km north to Chimbote (US$1, 1¼ hours), which has better connections.

CHIMBOTE
This is Peru's biggest fishing port and is smelly! Stop here to take the day bus through the spectacular Cañon del Pato to Huaraz. There are about 15 hotels. Empresa Moreno, Gálvez 1178 (a poor area, take a taxi at night), has an 8 am bus to Huaraz (US$6.50, 10 hours) via the Cañon del Pato.

TRUJILLO
Trujillo, 560 km north of Lima, is northern Peru's main city (750,000 inhabitants). It is an attractive town, founded in 1536 by Pizarro and retaining much of its colonial flavour. Nearby are the 1500-year-old Moche Pyramids of the Sun and Moon (Las Huacas del Sol y de la Luna), and the ancient Chimú capital of Chan Chan, which pre- ceded the Incas. There are some pleasant beaches.

Information
The tourist office (☎ 24-6941), Pizarro 402, run by friendly tourist police, is open from 8 am to 7.30 pm. A recommended guide is

Clara Luz Bravo D (☎ 24-3347), Huayna Capac 542, Santa María district. She speaks English and will provide transport or accom- pany you on public buses. Guía Tours, Independencia 519, has daily tours for US$15. Several banks change travellers' cheques at varying rates. The telephone code is 044. The best hospital is the Americano- Peruano (☎ 23-1261), Mansiche 702.

Warning Trujillo is conservative and women are not expected to be out alone in the eve- nings. Single women are more likely to be hassled by men in Trujillo bars than in other parts of Peru.

Things to See
The spacious and attractive **Plaza de Armas**, with its impressive statue of the heroes of Peruvian independence, is fronted by the **Catedral**, which was begun in 1647, destroyed in 1759 and rebuilt soon after- wards. It has a famous basilica and is often open in the evenings around 6 pm. On Sunday at 10 am, there is a flag-raising cer- emony and parade on the Plaza de Armas. Sometimes there are dance or *caballos de paso* (pacing horses) demonstrations.

There are several elegant **colonial man- sions** in the centre. Their wrought-iron grillwork and pastel shades are typical of Trujillo. The **colonial churches** are worth a look, though hours are erratic. La Merced, El Carmen and San Agustín are three of the best.

The **Museo Cassinelli** has an excellent archaeological collection in the basement of a petrol station! It's open Monday to Satur- day from 8.30 to 11.30 am and 3.30 to 5.30 pm, and entry is US$1.50. The university- run **Museo de Arqueología**, Pizarro 349, has an interesting collection of art and pottery, and a reproduction of the murals in the Moche Pyramid of the Moon. Entry is US$1.50. The university also has a poor **Museo de Zoología**, at San Martín 368. Both open in the mornings.

The Catedral and El Carmen church have **art museums** featuring religious and colo- nial art. **Casona Orbegoso**, on the 5th block

PERU

To Airport

To Chiclayo

Trujillo

0   150   300 m

Approximate Scale

To Airport

1

2

3

4

5

6

De la Torre

Chávez

7   8

Carrión

Mansiche Stadium

9

10

Zepita

13

14

11   12

San Martín

22

16

15

17

18

Miraflores

20

21

Independencia

23   24   25

26   27

Ejército

19

Corne

30

31

32

Pizarro

35

Catedral

33

34

36

37

Plazuela
El Recreo

38

39

28   29

Larco

40

41 42

43

44

45

46

47   49

48   50

51 53 54

52

55

56

57

58

59

Bolívar

61

63

Ayacucho

60

62

64

65

66

67

68

69

70

71

72

Peru

La Unión

82

Plaza
de
Toros

83

To Hostal JR
& Hotel España

73

75

74

76

77

78

79

80

81

Gráu

87

24 de Diciembre

85

84   86

Nicaragua

88

89

92

91   93

90

Los Incas

94

Sinchi Roca

Mercado
Mayorista

PERU

P Muñiz

Salaverry

Mansiche

Industria

España

Orbegoso

Gamarra

Junín

Colón

Estete

Almagro

Bolognesi

Ugarte

Larco

España

Moche

Huayna Capac

Atahualpa

Prada

Juárez

Suárez

Equren

Piérola (Transamericana)

of Calle Orbegoso, is a beautiful 18th-century mansion with a period art exhibit. Several colonial buildings contain **art galleries** with changing shows. Admission is normally free or nominal. The Santo Domingo gallery, by the church, and Casa de los Leones, on Independencia (the Ganoza Chopitea residence), are worth a look. Hours are changeable.

Special Events

The marinera dance is the highlight of many of Trujillo's festivals. Caballos de paso are another highlight. The Fiesta de la Marinera, at the end of January, is the biggest in Peru. The Fiesta de la Primavera, held in late September, has Peru's most famous parade, and much dancing and entertainment. Hotels are fully booked at those times.

Places to Stay

Many cheap hotels, especially in the poor area east of Gamarra and Bolívar, are used for short stays by young local couples, but aren't very dangerous. The cheapest is the very basic and poor-looking *Hostal Perú* at about US$3/5 for a single/double. Opposite is the slightly better *Hotel Paris* (☎ 24-2701). The basic *Hostal Lima* (☎ 24-4751), Ayacucho 718, is quite popular with gringos. It looks like a jail but is secure and friendly at US$7.50 for a double. The *Hostal Central* (☎ 24-6236), next door, is similarly priced and OK. All have cold water and aren't too clean. The *Hostal Acapulco* (☎ 24-3524), Gamarra 681, is US$5/6 with private cold bath and reportedly has warm showers for US$2 more. These places are friendly and have been recommended as good value among the basic hotels. The *Hostal Colón* (☎ 23-4545) charges US$5/7.50, or US$10 for a double with warm shower. The cold-water *Hotel Oscar* (☎ 24-2523), looks OK for US$5/7.50. The similar *Hotel España* is near the Empresa Antisuyo bus terminal, and the *Hostal JR*, a block away, has rooms with bath for US$6/8.

The perennially popular *Hotel Americano* (☎ 24-1361), Pizarro 792, is in a rambling and dilapidated old mansion with lots of

PERU

character. The rooms are basic but fairly clean (US$8/11 with bath or a bit less without). We've found the showers to be cold, but readers have reported hot ones. The *Hostal Roma*, on Nicaragua, is clean and secure (US$9 for a double with cold bath). The *Hotel La Querencia* is clean but noisy at US$6/9 with bath and warm water. To stay with a local family (about US$5 to US$7 per person), call Clara Luz Bravo D (☎ 24-3347).

The following hotels have rooms with private bath and hot shower. The clean *Hostal Rosell* (☎ 25-3583), España 250, (look for the small hostel sign) charges US$8/13 and gives discounts to youth hostel members. The *Hotel Chan Chan* (☎ 24-2964) is basic but OK at US$8/12. The *Hotel Primavera*, Piérola 872, is out of the centre but is clean, modern and good value (US$10/15). The clean and friendly *Hotel Sudamericano* (☎ 24-3751), Grau 515, is OK for US$8/13, but check the water: some showers are cold. The *Hotel San Martín* (☎ 23-4011), 745 San Martín, has over 100 rooms and so is rarely full. It's fair value, at US$11/17. The *Hostel Recreo* (☎ 24-6991), Estete 647, has rooms with telephone, TV and (usually) hot water at US$12/18. Other reasonable choices with doubles in the teens are the *Hotel Rosalia* (☎ 25-6411), Grau 611, *Hostal Palacios* (☎ 25-8194), Grau 709, and the *Residencial Los Escudos* (☎ 25-5691), Orbegoso 676.

Places to Eat

The market on Ayacucho has the cheapest places to eat in Trujillo. A block away on Gamarra, the *Chifa Oriental* and *Chifa Ak Chan* are decent Chinese places. Nearby, the *Restaurant 24 Horas* is inexpensive and always open. Next door, the *Restaurant Oasis* is good for local food like fritadas. Simple restaurants on the 700 block of Pizarro include the *Café Romano* for strong espresso coffee and *Marco's Café* for ice cream and home-made desserts. Both have lunch menús under US$2. *ABC* chicken restaurant serves a grilled quarter-chicken for US$2.25. Also good for menús, meat and

chicken are *Las Tradiciones* and *El Maizal*, whilst *Restaurant Vegetariano El Sol* is cheap and recommended for vegetarians. *Restaurant Big Ben* is good for ceviches and local food.

Entertainment

The *Peña Catana* at Colón and Miraflores has live music on the weekend, as does *El Maizal* restaurant. There are other peñas away from the centre.

Getting There & Away

Air The airport is 10 km north-west of town. Faucett, AeroPerú and Americana have offices in central Trujillo and AeroContinente will do soon. They all fly to Lima (US$54) on most days. Faucett has daily flights to Chiclayo. AeroContinente has two flights a week to Tarapoto (US$58) and Rioja. AeroPerú has flights most days to Piura and twice a week to Iquitos (US$65). Americana has a daily flight to Piura (US$30). Expreso Aéreo flies from Lima daily stopping at about five towns. TAA flies from Lima and on to Chachapoyas on Thursday. Schedules and destinations vary often.

Bus Buses are often full, so book as far in advance as you can for the best choice of departure times. Companies are spread out all over town (see map).

Many companies have services to Lima and towns along the north Panamericana. Fares vary depending on the company (some have luxury buses with video, toilet etc), so shop around. Lima is US$7 to US$15 (eight to 10 hours), Piura is US$5 to US$9 (seven to nine hours) and Chiclayo is about US$3 (three hours). The best services to Lima are said to be Ormeño (Continental) and Trujillo Express. Las Dunas, España 1445, has overnight luxury buses to Lima. EMTRAFESA (☎ 24-3981), on Miraflores near España, has Chiclayo buses leaving every half-hour during the day, as well as Lima and Piura buses. Vulcano also has frequent Chiclayo buses as well as service to Cajamarca. El Dorado has good buses north to Piura and Tumbes, and Expreso Sudamericano has cheaper, slower buses there. Both also go to Cajamarca. ETHMOPESA also goes north and Cruz del Sur and ITTSA go north and south. Empresa El Aguila has frequent buses to Chimbote. Olano goes to Chachapoyas and Guadalupe goes to Tarapoto. Chinchaysuyo and Cruz del Sur go to Huaraz (or change in Chimbote).

Getting Around

To/From the Airport The bus to Huanchaco passes within one km or so of the airport. A taxi from the centre is about US$5.

Bus White-yellow-and-orange 'B' colectivos pass the corner of España and Industrial (and other places; see map) for Huaca Esmeralda, Chan Chan and Huanchaco every few minutes. Red-blue-and-white minibuses or green-and-white buses for Esperanza go north-east along Mansiche and can drop you at La Huaca Arco Iris. Minibuses leave every half-hour from Calle Suárez for Las Huacas del Sol y de la Luna. Note that these buses are worked by professional thieves looking for cameras and money; ask the tourist police for updates. A taxi or tour group may be worthwhile.

AROUND TRUJILLO

The Moche and the Chimú are the two cultures which have left the greatest mark on the Trujillo area. There are four major archaeological sites.

Warning

Single travellers have been mugged, robbed or raped whilst visiting archaeological sites. Stay on main footpaths, don't visit the ruins late in the day and go with friends or hire a guide. Beware of pickpockets in all the ruins.

Archaeology

The Moche (Mochica) culture flourished from 0 to 700 AD and is known especially for its ceramics. The pots are decorated with realistic figures and scenes, and most of what we know about the Moche is from this pottery: there was no written language. They lived around massive ceremonial pyramids

such as the nearby Huacas del Sol y de la Luna.

The Chimú period was from about 1000 to 1470 AD. The Chimú capital, at Chan Chan, was the largest pre-Columbian city in Peru, covering 28 sq km and housing about 60,000 people.

Chan Chan

The city was built around 1300 AD and contained about 10,000 dwellings. There were storage bins for food and other products, huge walk-in wells, canals, workshops and temples. The royal dead were buried in mounds containing a wealth of funerary offerings. The whole city was decorated with designs moulded into the mud walls, and the more important areas were layered with precious metals. The Chimú were conquered by the Incas around 1460, but the city was not looted until the Spanish arrived.

The Chimú capital consisted of nine subcities, called the Royal Compounds. Each contained a royal burial mound with a rich array of funerary offerings. Visitors today see only a huge area of crumbling mud walls, some decorated with marvellous friezes. The treasures are gone, though a few can be seen in museums. The Tschudi compound has been partially restored and is open to visitors. Chan Chan is five km west of Trujillo. Tschudi is to the left of the main road, about 1.5 km along a dirt road. You'll see the crumbling ruins of the other compounds all around you. Stick to the road and don't try to visit the ruins on either side, which are muggers' haunts.

The entrance booth is at the Tschudi complex. There is a snack/souvenir stand, guides are available and tourist police are on duty. Hours are 9 am to 4 pm; entry is US$2.50. The ticket admits you to the Huaca Esmeralda and Huaca Arco Iris ruins and is valid for two days. Guides here charge about US$5 per hour.

La Huaca Esmeralda

This temple was built by the Chimú at about the time of Chan Chan. Hours and fees are as for Chan Chan. Huaca Esmeralda is at

PERU

Mansiche, halfway between Trujillo and Chan Chan, and it is possible to walk there (check with the tourist police). If returning from Chan Chan to Trujillo, the huaca is to the right of the main road, about four blocks behind the Mansiche church. The site is eroded, but you can make out the characteristic designs of fish, seabirds, waves and fishing nets. The temple consists of two stepped platforms, and an on-site guard will take you around (for a tip).

La Huaca Arco Iris

This Chimú site (also called La Huaca del Dragón) is left of the Panamericana, in La Esperanza, four km north-west of Trujillo. Hours and fees are as for Chan Chan.

This is one of the best preserved Chimú temples, because it was covered by sand until excavation began in 1963. The site has a defensive wall enclosing 3000 sq metres. There is one entrance. Inside is a single large structure, the temple itself. This is about 800 sq metres, and has two levels with a combined height of about 7.5 metres. The walls are covered with repeated rainbow designs, most of which have been restored. Ramps lead to the very top of the temple, from where there are good views.

Las Huacas del Sol y de la Luna

These Moche temples predate Chan Chan by 700 years and are 10 km south-east of Trujillo. Hours are 8 am to 1 pm due to afternoon wind storms. Entry is US$1. The Huaca del Sol is Peru's largest pre-Columbian structure; 140 million adobe bricks were used to build it. Originally, the pyramid had several levels, connected by steep stairs, huge ramps and walls sloping at 77° to the horizon. Now it resembles a giant sand pile, but the brickwork remains impressive from some angles. The smaller Huaca de la Luna, 500 metres away, has rooms with friezes which may be open.

La Huaca El Brujo

This newly excavated ruin is 60 km from Trujillo on the coast and hard to reach

without a guide. It has burial sites and some of the best friezes in the area.

Huanchaco

This fishing village is a 15-km bus ride north-west of Trujillo and has the best beach in the area, though faecal contamination has been reported. The water is too cold for locals most of the year, except from January to March. Totora-reed boats, like those depicted on Moche ceramics, are locally constructed and used. Fishermen often arrive around 9 or 10 am, and some boats are usually seen stacked up at the northern end of the beach.

Warning Robberies and rape have occurred on the beach walk from Huanchaco to Trujillo. Use the bus.

Places to Stay & Eat Several families rent rooms; ask around. Heidi, a Swiss woman at Los Pinos 451, charges about US$3.50 per person. Señora Lola, Manco Capac 136, has cheap rooms.

The clean *Hostal Huanchaco* (☎ 23-0813), Larco 287, is US$6 per person (communal cold showers) or US$8 (private hot bath). There is a small pool and pleasant courtyard. The run-down *Hostal Caballito de Totora* (☎ 22-3389) is US$10/16 for a single/double with bath. The similarly priced *Hostal Esteros* (☎ 23-0810) is a little better. Best is the *Hostal Bracamonte* (☎ 23-0808), Los Olivos 503, with a pool and nice gardens. Rooms with private hot showers are US$12/18. Bargain for reduced rates in the off season.

There are simple seafood restaurants at the northern end of the beach, near where the totora-reed boats are stacked. On the plaza, the *Colonial Club* is the best, but pricey.

Getting There & Away Buses leave from Industrial and España in Trujillo at frequent intervals during daylight hours.

CHICLAYO

The next major coastal city is Chiclayo, 200 km north of Trujillo. With over 400,000

Chiclayo

0   100   200 m
Approximate Scale

PERU

PLACES TO STAY

9   Hotels Santa Rosa, América
11 Hostal Chimú
12 Hostal Cruz de Chalpón
13 Hostal Americano
14 Hostal Adriático
15 Hostals Balta,
    Nueva Estrella
16 Hostal Venezuela
18 Hostal Señor de los Milagros
19 Hostal Tumi de Oro
23 Gran Hotel Chiclayo
24 Hotel El Sol
29 Hostal Ronald
30 Hotel Royal
35 Hotel Real
38 Inca Hotel
39 Hostal Lido
40 Hotel Europa
47 Hotel Aristi
49 Hostal Sol Radiante
55 Sipán Hotel
62 Garza Hotel

PLACES TO EAT

17 La Nueva Barcarola
28 Kafé D'Kaly
45 Las Americas,
    Elio's Snack Bar
46 Restaurant Marítimo
    Italian Restaurants
51 Chifa Pollería San Pablo
52 Restaurant Imperial
53 Restaurant Romana
54 Restaurant Le Paris
55 Oasis

OTHER

1   Mini Buses to Sipán
2   Sports Stadium
3   Buses to Monsefú
4   Buses to Puerto Etén
5   Buses to Túcume
6   Buses to Motupe
7   Buses to Monsefú,
    Nearby Towns
8   Empresa D Olano
10 Buses to Pimentel
20 Buses to Chongoyape
21 Peña Hermanos Balcázar
22 Peña El Brujo
25 Empresa Chiclayo
26 Transportes San Pablo
27 AeroContinente
31 Cine Colonial
32 Telefónica del Perú
33 Post Office
34 Hospital Las Mercedes
36 Clínica Santa Cecilia
39 Americana Airline
41 AeroPerú Airline
42 Cine Tropical
43 Banco de Crédito,
    other banks
44 Faucett (Airline)
48 Cine Oro
56 TEPSA Buses
57 Atahualpa Buses
58 Expreso
    Sudamericano
59 Vulcano, El Águila
60 EMTRAFESA Buses
61 Cruz de Chalpón
63 CIVA, LTTSA, Cruz
    del Sur, Roggero
64 Peru Express
65 Transportes Piura
66 Expreso Continental
67 Empresa D Olano
68 Chiclayo Express
69 Transportes
    El Cumbe
70 Empresa Díaz

inhabitants, it's the capital of Lambayeque department, a major commercial centre and one of Peru's fastest growing cities. Important archaeology sites are nearby.

Information
The tourist office has closed (but may reopen). The Banco de Crédito changes travellers' cheques. Street moneychangers hang out on the 600 block of Balta. The telephone code is 074.

Things to See
Wander around the Mercado Modelo and see the herbalist and *brujo* (witch-doctor) stalls, with their healing charms. Also look for the heavy woven saddlebags, called *alforjas*, which are typical of the area. Watch your belongings.

Places to Stay
The cheapest hotels on Balta north of the plaza are very basic. Few have hot water. The *Hotel Royal* (☎ 23-3421) on the plaza is old and run-down but OK for US$5/7 a single/double, or US$6/8 with bath. At this price the *Hostal Cruz de Chalpón* (☎ 23-3004) is also OK. The *Hostal Adriático* is acceptable at US$4 per person or US$8.50/10 with private, dank bath. Cheaper, worse places include the *Balta, Nueva Estrella, Chimu* and *Ronald*. The *Hostal Americano* and *Hotel Real* cost more but are no better.

Better budget hotels include the friendly *Hostal Lido* (☎ 24-4050), E Aguirre 412, at US$5/8, or US$7.50/10 with cold bath, and the quiet and reasonably clean *Hostal Venezuela* (☎ 23-2665), Lora y Cordero 954, at US$8/12 with bath. Others at this price are the clean *Hostal Tumi de Oro* (☎ 22-7108), L Prado 1145, with private hot bath (less without), the *Hotel Santa Rosa* (☎ 22-4411), L Gonzales 927, which is one of the cleanest, and the nearby *Hotel América* (☎ 22-9305). The *Hostal Señor de los Milagros* looks OK for US$9/13. The *Hostal Sol Radiante* (☎ 23-7858), Izaga 392, is a quiet, family-run place at US$10/14 with hot bath. The *Hotel Europa* (☎ 23-7919), E Aguirre 466, looks nice and charges US$14/17/21 for one

to three people with private hot bath or less with communal showers.

Places to Eat
There are plenty of cheap restaurants on Avenida Balta; *Restaurant Romana*, Balta 512, is a good, locally popular one. Also recommended are *La Nueva Barcarola*, Vicente de la Vega 961, for cheap but tasty meals, the clean *Kafé D'Kaly* on the plaza, and the nearby *Las Américas* and *Restaurant Marítimo*.

Getting There & Away
Air The airport is two km south-east of town (US$1 taxi). AeroPerú, Faucett, Americana and AeroContinente have offices in central Chiclayo. There are four or five flights a day to Lima (US$65), one or two a day to Piura, Tumbes (US$40) and Trujillo, and two a week to Iquitos, Rioja and Tarapoto.

Bus Many companies are near the corner of Sáenz Peña and Bolognesi. Look here for long-distance buses to Lima, Tumbes, Trujillo, Cajamarca, Chachapoyas and elsewhere. See the map for bus stops for buses going to the sites around Chiclayo.

Getting Around
Tours Indiana Tours (☎ 24-2287, fax 24-0833), Colón 556, has good English-language tours to Sipán or Túcume for US$35 (one person), US$17 (five or more people). Other sites can be toured.

AROUND CHICLAYO
Lambayeque
This small town 11 km north of Chiclayo has the excellent and recommended **Bruning Museum**, with a good collection of artefacts from several cultures. A new exhibit features finds from Sipán. Labels are in Spanish. Entry is US$1.50 and a guide is US$2.50. Hours are Monday to Friday from 8 am to 6.30 pm, and weekends and holidays 9 am to 6 pm. Buses from Chiclayo drop you a block from the museum.

Sipán

Hundreds of dazzling and priceless artefacts have been recovered from Sipán, where a royal Moche burial site was discovered in 1987. Excavation continues. One tomb has a replica of one of the several burials, and there is a good on-site museum, but the most spectacular finds are on display in Lambayeque's Bruning Museum. Sipán is 30 km south-east of Chiclayo. Buses (see map; US$0.50) leave often in the morning, less so in the afternoon. Sipán entry is US$1.

Túcume

This vast and little-known site can be seen from a spectacular cliff-top viewpoint about 30 km north of Lambayeque on the Panamericana. It's worth the climb to see over 200 hectares of crumbing walls, plazas and pyramids. There is an on-site museum. Túcume is currently being investigated by a team led by Thor Heyerdahl (of *Kon Tiki* fame). Entry is US$1, hours are weekdays 8.30 am to 4.30 pm, weekends to 6 pm. Guides may be available, or hire one in Chiclayo or at the Bruning Museum. Buses go from Chiclayo or from the museum; it's about a km walk from where the bus drops you in Túcume.

Coastal Villages

Buses from Chiclayo go to the coastal villages of **Pimentel**, **Santa Rosa** and **Puerto Etén**. Pimentel has a decent beach and the many km of coast stretching north-west are good for surfing, though there are no public transport or facilities. There are no hotels but simple rooms can be rented. Both Pimentel and Santa Rosa are active fishing villages and totora-reed boats can be seen in action. Puerto Etén is another fishing town. All three have simple but good seafood restaurants and can be easily visited using frequent minibuses from Chiclayo.

PIURA

Founded by Pizarro in 1532, Piura is Peru's oldest colonial city. The Catedral dates from 1588. The centre has some colonial buildings, though many were destroyed in a 1912 earthquake. The city's focal point is the large, shady and pleasant Plaza de Armas. Irrigation of the desert has made Piura a major agricultural centre; rice is the main crop. Piura is capital of its department and has over 300,000 inhabitants.

Information

There is no tourist office. The Banco de Crédito changes travellers' cheques. The telephone code is 074.

Things to See

The small **Museo de la Cultura**, Huánuco and Sullana, houses archaeology and art exhibits. Hours are Tuesday to Saturday, 9 am to 1 pm and 4 to 8 pm; admission is free. **Casa Grau**, the house on Tacna (near Ayacucho) where Almirante Miguel Grau was born, on 27 July 1834, is now the naval museum. Grau was a hero of the War of the Pacific against Chile (1879-80). Hours vary and admission is free.

Places to Stay

Water shortages are reported and few hotels have hot water. The cheapest and most basic are the *Hotel Edén*, on Arequipa near Huancavelica, the *Hotel Hispano* (☎ 32-5901), Ica 650, which claims hot water (!?), and *Hostal Ica* (☎ 32-6411), Ica 760. None is very clean. The friendly *Hostal California* (☎ 32-8789), Junín 835, is cleaner, has occasional warm water, and charges US$4.50 per person. Opposite, the *Hostal Lalo* (☎ 32-5798), Junín 838, looks basic but is reasonably clean. The friendly *Hostal Continental* (☎ 33-4531), Junín 924, has clean doubles for US$9. The *Hostal Oriental* (☎ 32-8891), Callao 446, is very clean at US$5/8 a single/double, or US$6/11 with private cold bath. The clean *Hostal Amauta* (☎ 32-2976), Apurímac 580, is US$7.50/9 or US$15 for a double with bath. The *Hostal Terraza* (☎ 32-5043), Loreto 530, charges US$6/10 with bath, a little less with communal bath. It's dark and worn, but clean enough. Next door is the unsigned *Hotel Dallas*, at US$8/13 with bath. The *Hotel Tambo* (☎ 32-5379), Callao 546, is good,

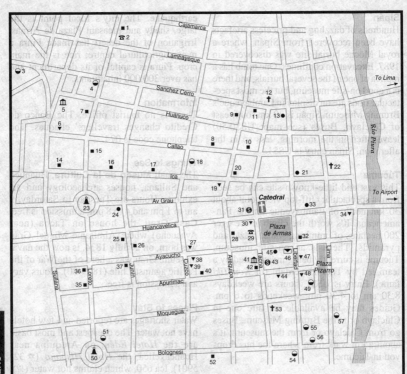

Cajamarca

Lambayeque

Sanchez Cerro

Huánuco

Callao

Ica

Av Grau

Huancavelica

Ayacucho

Apurímac

Moquegua

Bolognesi

Catedral

Plaza de Armas

Plaza Pizarro

To Lima

To Airport

Río Piura

Piura

0   100   200 m

PLACES TO STAY	PLACES TO EAT	13 Local Ceramics Shop
1 Hotel Esmeralda	6 Chifa Tay Loy	18 Transportes Piura
7 Hostal Terraza,	19 Restaurant Las	(Bus Tickets)
Hotel Dallas	Tres Estrellas	21 Americana Airline
8 Hotel Tambo	27 Pizzería La Cabaña,	22 San Francisco Church
9 Hotel Perú	Snack Bar Romano	23 Grau Monument
10 Hostal Oriental	30 Heladería Chalan	24 Cine Variedades
11 Hostal El Sol	35 Ferny's	31 Banco de Crédito, AeroPerú,
14 Hostal El Almirante	38 Las Tradiciones	AeroContinente
15 Hostal Cristina	39 La Posada Vasca	33 Faucett Airline
16 Hostal Ica	44 Las Redes Bar,	41 Casa Grau (Naval Museum)
17 Hotel Hispano	Italian Restaurant	43 Banco de la Nación
20 Hostal Tangara	47 El Arrero	45 Municipalidad
25 Hostal Lalo	48 Heladería Venecia	49 Colectivos to Catacaos
26 Hostal California		50 Bolognesi Monument
28 Hotel Eden	OTHER	52 TEPSA
32 Los Portales	2 Telefónica del Perú	53 San Sebastian Church
35 Hostal San Jorge	3 EPPO (Buses to	54 ITTSA
36 Residencial Piura	Tumbes & Chiclayo)	55 Chinchaysuyo
37 Hostal Continental	4 Comité 2 Colectivos	56 Cruz del Sur
40 Hostal Amauta	to Sullana	57 Expreso Sudamericano
42 Hotel Plaza Suite	5 Museo de la Cultura	
52 Residencial Bolognesi	12 El Carmen	

clean and friendly but noisy at US$8/12 with bath. If hot showers are important, try the good and very clean *Hostal San Jorge* (☎ 32-7514), Loreto 960, at US$11/15, or the *Hostal El Sol* (☎ 32-4461), Sánchez Cerro 455, with TV and phone in the rooms, at US$16/20.

Places to Eat

Restaurants generally seem a bit pricey. Some cheap ones are on the 700 block of Junín. Good mid-range choices are *Las Tradiciones, Bar Romano* and others at Ayacucho and Cuzco. *Ferny's*, at the Hostal San Jorge, is clean and good. There are a couple of snack bars on the Plaza de Armas.

Getting There & Away

Air The airport is two km south-east of the centre. AeroPerú, Faucett, Americana and AeroContinente have offices in the centre. They all have daily flights to Lima (US$77), and daily flights to Chiclayo, Trujillo and Talara are also available.

Bus & Truck Buses, cars and trucks for various local destinations leave from the fifth block of Avenida Sullana Norte. Buses for Tumbes (six hours), Chiclayo (three hours) and Trujillo leave from Sánchez Cerro a couple of blocks north-west of Sullana with Empresa Chiclayo and Trans El Dorado. Here, EPPO has buses to Sullana. Expreso Sudamericano, Chinchaysuyo, Cruz del Sur and ITTSA are at the river end of Bolognesi, and TEPSA is at Bolognesi and Loreto, by the monument. These companies are best for Lima (prices vary, 18 hours). Chinchaysuyo goes to Huaraz. CIVA, across the river on Huancavelica, has buses to Huancabamba and other small towns in the Andes east of Piura.

The standard route to Ecuador is via Tumbes, but the route via La Tina is possible. Take an early morning bus to Sullana (US$0.50, one hour) and continue from Sullana to La Tina by truck (the bus driver will show you where). Sullana has poor, basic hotels; Piura is a better place to stay.

December to April is the rainy season and

El Niño climatic events occur every few years. The 1992 El Niño washed out roads and bridges; going to Tumbes required wading through rivers and the La Tina road was closed. They have now all reopened.

LA TINA

This border post has no hotels, but Macará in Ecuador has a few. La Tina is connected by poor road with Sullana (US$3 to US$6, four to six hours). The last bus to Sullana leaves at 2 pm. There are several passport checks. There is a basic hotel in El Suyo, 15 km away, then no hotels until Sullana.

To/From Ecuador

The border is open from 8 am to 6 pm daily, with irregular lunch hours. Formalities are fairly relaxed, though guards try to get bribes. There are no banks, but money-changers in Macará will change cash.

TUMBES

Although half an hour from the Ecuadorian border, Tumbes is where transportation and accommodation for border-crossers is found. It is the departmental capital, but there's little of interest.

Information

There is no tourist office. The Banco de Crédito changes travellers' cheques, though rates are a little better away from the border. Street moneychangers here and at the border give good rates if you know what the best rate is and bargain. Otherwise, you'll get poor rates. Beware of 'fixed' calculators. The telephone code is 074.

Places to Stay

During holidays and trade fairs, hotels are often full by noon. At other times, hotels are full by late afternoon. Single rooms are difficult to find. Most hotels have only cold water but are pricey. There are frequent water and electricity outages.

The cheapest basic hotels start at around US$6 for a single and US$8 or US$9 for a double. The following are the best – friendly and reasonably clean: the *Hostal Estoril*, which has hot showers; the *Hostal Elica* (☎ 52-3870), the *Hostal Tumbes*, the *Hostal Amazonas* (☎ 52-3495) and the *Hostal Italia* (☎ 52-2925), the last of which has private baths. The *Hotel Bolívar* is also cheap and basic but reasonably clean. The *Hostal Franco* (☎ 52-5295) also looks OK. Others include the *Hostal Los Once* (☎ 52-3717), which has private baths, is fairly clean and handy to the buses (but noisy), and the basic but friendly *Hostal Premier* (☎ 52-3077), which lacks singles. Also in this price range are the poorer hostales *Kiko's, Toloa II* and *Chicho*, which have private baths, and the

poorer still *Residencial Gandolfo, Hotel Rodrich, Hostal Jugdem* and a few other places around the market.

The *Hostal Florian* (☎ 52-2464) charges US$10/14 with private hot bath and is recommended. Also decent at this price are the *Hostal Toloa* (☎ 52-3771) and *Hostal César* (☎ 52-2883).

Places to Eat

Bars and *restaurants* on the Plaza de Armas have shaded tables and chairs outside. The best (and most expensive) are on the western

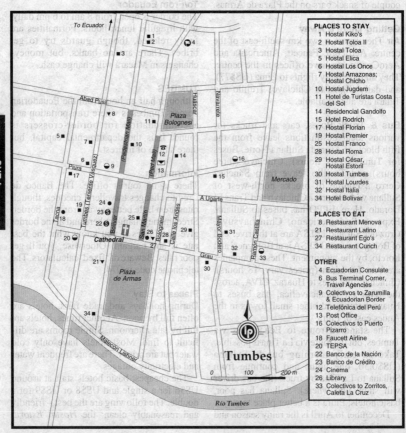

PLACES TO STAY
1 Hostal Kiko's
2 Hostal Toloa II
3 Hostal Toloa
5 Hostal Elica
6 Hostal Los Once
7 Hostal Amazonas;
   Hostal Chicho
10 Hostal Jugdem
11 Hotel de Turistas Costa
    del Sol
14 Residencial Gandolfo
15 Hotel Rodrich
17 Hostal Florian
19 Hostal Premier
25 Hostal Franco
28 Hostal Roma
29 Hostal César,
    Hostal Estoril
30 Hostal Tumbes
31 Hostal Lourdes
32 Hostal Italia
34 Hotel Bolívar

PLACES TO EAT
8 Restaurant Menova
21 Restaurant Latino
27 Restaurant Ego's
34 Restaurant Curich

OTHER
4 Ecuadorian Consulate
6 Bus Terminal Corner,
   Travel Agencies
9 Colectivos to Zarumilla
   & Ecuadorian Border
12 Telefónica del Perú
13 Post Office
16 Colectivos to Puerto
    Pizarro
18 Faucett Airline
20 TEPSA
22 Banco de la Nación
23 Banco de Crédito
24 Cinema
26 Library
33 Colectivos to Zorritos,
    Caleta La Cruz

To Ecuador

Plaza Bolognesi

Mercado

Cathedral

Plaza de Armas

Tumbes

0   100   200 m

Río Tumbes

side. North of the plaza, the pedestrian street of Bolívar has inexpensive *chicken restaurants, ice-cream parlours* etc and is a popular hang-out for young and old alike. The *Restaurant Menova* has good set meals for about US$2. Several simple restaurants near the bus terminals serve good, cheap food.

Getting There & Away
Air Faucett (☎ 52-2655) has daily afternoon flights to Lima (US$98) via Talara on Friday and Saturday and via Chiclayo (US$41) on other days. Americana has a daily late-morning flight to Lima via Chiclayo. If coming from Ecuador, look into discounted multicity Americana tickets available outside Peru. Flights are often full; reconfirm.

Bus Most bus companies are on Avenida Tumbes (formerly Teniente Vásquez), near the intersection with Avenida Piura. Fares to Lima (22 to 24 hours) are US$16 to US$30. Some companies offer 'luxury service', with air-con, toilets and video. There are several buses a day; most stop at Piura (six hours), Chiclayo (12 hours), Trujillo (15 hours) and other intermediate cities. If you arrive in Tumbes early in the morning, you'll probably get out the same day; otherwise, be prepared to stay overnight.

Getting Around
A taxi to the airport is US$2, to the border about US$4. Colectivos for Aguas Verdes, on the border, leave from the corner of Bolívar and Piura (US$1, 26 km).

TO/FROM ECUADOR
Aguas Verdes is linked, by an international bridge across the Río Zarumilla, with the Ecuadorian border town of Huaquillas (see the Huaquillas section in the Ecuador chapter for more border-crossing details.)

Exit formalities as you cross from Peru to Ecuador are fairly quick. Immigration is open daily from 8 am to noon and 2 to 6 pm. The Peruvian border post is two km from the border; *mototaxis* take you to the border for US$0.50. In Aguas Verdes, there are a few simple restaurants, a bank and no hotels.

Border guards, taxi drivers and money-changers all try to rip you off. There are no entry fees into either country so be polite but insistent with border guards, bargain hard with drivers, and find out exchange rates ahead of time before changing money. Moneychangers' calculators are sometimes rigged to read low! Buy and sell Peruvian currency in Peru and Ecuadorian in Ecuador for the best rates.

The Huaraz Area

Huaraz is the climbing, trekking and backpacking centre of Peru. The nearby Cordillera Blanca is exceptionally beautiful, and many travellers come to Peru just to visit this region, which is in the **Parque Nacional Huascarán**. You can enjoy great views on bus trips in the Huaraz area: Huascarán, at 6768 metres the highest mountain in Peru, lies only 14 km from the main road. A full range of hiking and climbing equipment can be hired in Huaraz. Trail maps and guidebooks can be bought and mule drivers and guides are available. The best time for hiking is the dry season, from June to August. May and September are usually quite good.

HUARAZ
Most of Huaraz was destroyed by the 1970 earthquake which killed 70,000 people in central Peru. Huaraz has been rebuilt and is the capital of the Department of Ancash, with 80,000 inhabitants. Huaraz lies in the valley called El Callejón de Huaylas.

Information
The tourist office on the Plaza de Armas is open erratically. The Parque Nacional Huascarán office is in the Ministerio de Agricultura at the east end of Avenida Raymondi. Hours are Monday to Friday from 7 am to 2.15 pm. The Casa de Guías (☎ 72-1811), on Plaza Ginebra one block north-east of the Plaza de Armas, has a list of registered guides and is a good source of

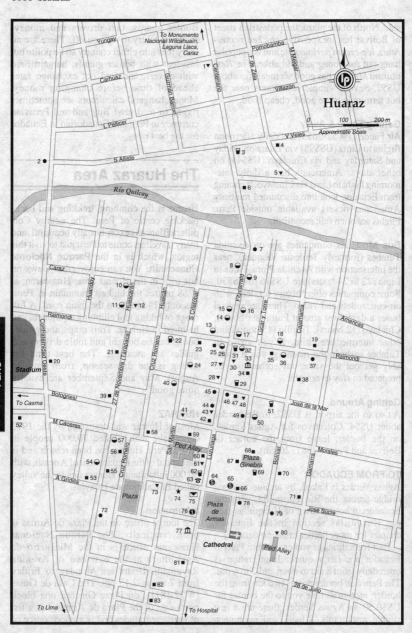

To Monumento
Nacional Wilcahuain,
Laguna Llaca,
Caraz

Yungay

Pomobamba

M Melgar

Carhuaz

Centenario

F de Zela

Villazón

Guzmán Barrón

Huaraz

0   100   200 m
Approximate Scale

L Pellicer

V Veles

S Alliste

Río Quilcay

Caraz

Huandoy

Fitzcarrald

Raimondi

Huascarán

S Cristóbal

Lucar y Torre

Cajamarca

Americas

Raimondi

Confraternidad Oeste

Cruz Romero

27 de Noviembre (Tarapaca)

Stadium

To Casma

Bolognesi

M Cáceres

José de la Mar

San Martín

Luzuriaga

Ped Alley

Morales

Bolívar

Gamarra

A Gridilla

Cruz Romero

Plaza

Plaza
Ginebra

Plaza de
Armas

José Sucre

Cathedral

Ped Alley

To Lima

28 de Julio

To Hospital

PLACES TO STAY		27	Creperíe Patrick,	24	Transportes
4	Hostal Colombo		Chifa Min Hua		Huascarán &
6	Hostal Yanett	28	Monte Rosa		TROME (Buses)
19	Hostal Los Portales	30	Restaurant Familiar	26	Transportes Rodríguez
20	Hostal Alpamayo	41	Las Puyas	27	Imantata Bar
21	Hotel Casablanca	43	Chez Pepe	29	El Pub
23	Hotel Barcelona	48	Restaurant Samuels	31	Campo Base
25	Hostal Cataluña	61	Montrek	32	Movil Tours
34	Alojamiento Tany	66	Café Pizzería Piccolo	33	Museo de Miniaturas
35	Hostal Raimondi	68	Casa de Guías	36	Transportes Moreno
38	Hostal Monte Rosa	73	Miski Huasi	37	Duchas Raimondi
39	Hotel Los Andes	80	Rinconcito	40	Civa Cial
42	Hostal Huaraz		Huaracino	44	Pyramid Adventures,
47	Hostal Oscar	81	Café Central		Milla Tours
52	Edward's Inn, Señora			45	Chavín Tours
	López	**OTHER**		46	Pablo Tours
53	Casa de Jaime	2	ElectroPerú	49	Mountain Bike
55	Pensión Maguina	3	Paccha'k Pub		Adventures
56	Pensión Galaxia	7	Lavandería	50	Cruz del Sur
58	Alojamiento		Fitzcarrald	51	El Tambo Bar
	Quintana	8	Empresa 14	54	Transportes Rodríguez
59	Hostal Estoico	9	Empresa Huandoy	57	Chavín Express
60	Hostal El Pacífico		(Buses to Monterrey,	61	Montrek
66	Hotel Landauro		Carhuaz,	62	La Cueva del Oso
67	Hostal Montañero		Yungay & Caraz)		Peña
68	Casa de Guías	10	Virgen del Carmen	63	Telefónica del Perú
70	Hostal Copa	11	El Rnpido	64	Banco de Crédito
71	Hotel Santa Victoria	13	Empresa Norpacífico	65	Interbanc
81	Hostal Continental	14	Expreso	69	Taberna Amadeus
82	Hostal Tumi I		Sudamericano	72	Ames River Runners
83	Hostal Tumi II	15	Turismo Chimbote	74	Police Station
		16	Paradise Tours	75	Post Office
PLACES TO EAT		17	Taxis 1 & 2 (Local & to	76	Tourist Office
1	Pío Pío		Caraz)	77	Museo Regional de
5	Recreo La Unión	18	Expreso Ancash		Ancash
12	Huaraz Querido	22	Petrol Station	78	Cine Radio
				79	Lavandería Liz

PERU

hiking and climbing information. Guide services and equipment rental can be found along Avenida Luzuriaga. During the dry season, Huaraz swarms with hikers and climbers. They have the best information.

Banks are on the north side of the Plaza de Armas and on the 600 block of Luzuriaga. Moneychangers are found on the streets outside. The Banco de Crédito changes travellers' cheques. The telephone code is 044.

Things to See
The **Museo Regional**, on the Plaza de Armas, has a small, interesting archaeology exhibit. Hours are Tuesday to Saturday from 9 am to 6 pm, Sunday and Monday 9 am to 2 pm. Admission is US$1.50, which includes entry to the small Wari **Ruinas Wilcahuaín**, about eight km north of Huaraz. There is no

regular transport, but you can walk or hire a taxi for a few dollars. Head north on Avenida Centenario to a dirt road to your right a few hundred metres past the Hotel de Turistas. The dirt road climbs six km (passing through the communities of Jinua and Paria) to the ruins and continues another 20 km to Laguna Llaca, where there are excellent mountain views. The site is open daily.

Activities & Organised Tours
Visiting the national park (entry US$1) is the main activity. Several outfitters rent climbing and hiking gear and provide information and guides. Casa de Guías and Montrek, Luzuriaga 646, have good selections. Maps are sold in Huaraz. Bradt's *Backpacking and Trekking in Peru and Bolivia* is a good guide for independent hikers. Mountain Bike Adventures (☎ 72-1203, 72-4259), Lúcar y

Torre 538, rents bikes. You can raft the Río Santa (better in the rainy season). Montrek has been recommended, or try Ames River Runners (☎ 72-3375), 27 de Noviembre 773.

Bus day tours are another choice. One visits the ruins at Chavín de Huantar, another goes through Yungay to the beautiful Lagunas Llanganuco, where there are spectacular views of Huascarán and other mountains, and a third goes to see the giant *Puya raimondi* plant and ice caves at Nevado Pastoruri. Prices are about US$7 to US$12 each, including a guide who doesn't necessarily speak English. A US$1 national park fee is levied. There are daily departures in the high season. Recommended agencies are Pablo Tours, Chavín Tours and Milla Tours.

Places to Stay

Dry-season prices can be double the off-season rates. The period around Fiestas Patrias (28 July) is especially busy. Most places have warm or hot showers some of the time: ask. Otherwise, you can have a hot shower at Duchas Raimondi, Raimondi 904.

The basic, friendly *Casa de Jaime*, A Gridilla 267, has cooking and laundry facilities and hot water at US$2.50 per person. *Pensión NG*, Pasaje Valenzuela 837 (parallel to and a few blocks south of 28 de Julio), has hot water and is US$5 each with breakfast and dinner. The clean *Edward's Inn* (☎ 72-2692), Bolognesi 121, is friendly and has plenty of local info. It has hot water, laundry facilities and a café, and is popular at US$5 each in dorms or US$13 for a double, some with baths. *Señora López* behind Edward's Inn is another budget place. The *Casa de Guías* (☎ 72-1811), Plaza de Ginebra, charges US$6 each in dorms and has laundry facilities, hot water and a popular restaurant.

Small, family-run places with occasional hot water include the basic but clean, friendly and popular *Alojamiento Quintana*, Cruz Romero 593, at US$5 each, and *Pensión Galaxia* (☎ 72-2230), Romero 638, at US$8 a double. Others at US$4 or US$5 per person include the just OK *Pensión Maguiña* (☎ 72-2320), Tarapacá 643, and the *Hotel Barcelona*, Raimondi 612, (good views, cold water) which also has very basic space for under US$3 per person on the top floor. The friendly, helpful *Hotel Los Andes* (☎ 72-1346), Tarapacá 316, charges US$5 each. The *Hostal Estoico* (☎ 72-2371), San Martín 635, and the *Alojamiento Tany* (☎ 72-2534), Lúcar y Torre 468-A, are both basic but clean and friendly at US$4 per person.

The *Hostal Oscar* (☎ 72-1314), José de la Mar 624, is US$6/10 for a single/double and has hot water. The *Hostal Raimondi* (☎ 72-1082), Raimondi 820, has a pleasant courtyard and is US$10 for a double. Also in this price range are the *Hostal Copa*, Bolívar 615, which has been popular but has had recent reports of theft, and the *Hostal Monte Rosa*, Bolívar 419, which is frequently full. The clean, pleasant and safe *Hostal Yanett* (☎ 72-1466), Centenario 106, is recommended. Rooms with hot bath are US$8 per person. The *Hostal Continental* (☎ 72-1557), 28 de Julio 586, is about US$7 per person and is clean with private baths and hot water. The *Hostal El Pacífico* (☎ 72-1683), Luzuriaga 630, is US$10 per person in rooms with hot bath.

Places to Eat

The following are cheap but good. The *Restaurant Familiar* has a wide variety; the *Pío Pío* is simple; *Recreo La Unión* serves typical local lunches; *Restaurant Samuels* serves big helpings and is popular with locals and gringos; *Las Puyas* has large meals and is popular with budget travellers; *Miski Huasi* is friendly and can prepare vegetarian dishes with a few hours notice. For breakfasts, *Café Central* is cheap. *Casa de Guías* is very popular and has granola, yogurt and fruit as well as the more usual fare. *Rinconcito Huaracino* serves typical Peruvian food and ceviche. *Huaraz Querido* is also good for ceviche.

There are several good pizzerías and international restaurants, which are pricier than the Peruvian places. Some add a 31% tax. The best pizzerías are *Chez Pepe* (also has other good meals), *Montrek* (with a climbing wall!) and the cheaper *Monte Rosa*. The *Café Pizzería Piccolo* is one of the cheapest.

Creperie Patrick is recommended for crêpes, ice creams, and continental dinners. *Chifa Min Hua* is quite good.

Entertainment

The friendly *El Pub* is currently the most popular hang-out for climbers and trekkers. *El Tambo Bar* has crowded dancing to live and recorded music from about 10 pm; budget travellers can save a night's lodging by dancing till 4 am and staggering onto the first bus out of town! There are other places.

Getting There & Away

Air Expreso Aéreo and AeroCóndor have had irregular flights from Lima to Anta (23 km north of Huaraz).

Bus There are many buses to Lima (US$5 to US$9, eight hours) so shop around. Cruz del Sur (☎ 72-2491) has nightly Imperial non-stop service (the most expensive). Others include Civa Cial (☎ 72-1947), Móvil Tours (☎ 72-2555), Paradise Tours (☎ 72-2207, 72-1834), Transportes Rodríguez (☎ 72-1353), Expreso Ancash (the Ormeño subsidiary, ☎ 72-1102), Empresa 14 (☎ 72-1282), Expreso Sudamericano (☎ 72-1576) and TROME (☎ 72-1542). Most have day and night buses. Buses to Chimbote (US$7 or US$8, eight hours) go north through the spectacular Cañón del Pato, or west over the 4225-metre-high Punta Callán. Both are worth seeing in daylight. Transportes Moreno (☎ 72-1344), Transportes Rodríguez, Comité 14 and Turismo Chimbote (☎ 72-1984) go to Chimbote, some continuing to Trujillo.

Frequent daytime buses north to Yungay and Caraz (US$1.25, 1½ hours) leave from Fitzcarrald north of Raimondi with Empresa Huandoy, which also has a few buses a week across the Cordillera Blanca to Chacas and Chavín. Faster minibuses to Caraz leave from the same block. Chavín Express goes to Chavín de Huantar (US$3.50, five hours) continuing on to Huari (seven hours) daily at 12.20 pm. Transportes Huascarán (at the TROME office) also has buses to Chavín and Huari. For Chiquián (and the Cordillera Huayhuash), El Rápido (☎ 72-2610) and Virgen del Carmen have daily buses. Other destinations are served by occasional buses and trucks.

NORTH OF HUARAZ

The road through the Callejón de Huaylas follows the Río Santa and is paved to Caraz. Five km north is **Monterrey**, where there are hot springs. **Carhuaz** is 31 km north of Huaraz and has a few basic hotels. It is near the entrance to the Ulta valley, where there is beautiful trekking. Between Carhuaz and Yungay, there are excellent views of Huascarán.

Yungay

The town and its 18,000 inhabitants were buried by a catastrophic avalanche during the 1970 earthquake. The site is marked by a white statue of Christ on a knoll overlooking old Yungay. The avalanche path is visible from the road. The tomb of 18,000 people is marked by flower gardens in the **Campo Santo** (US$0.50 admission) culminating in old Yungay's plaza, where parts of the church spire are all that remain. New Yungay has been rebuilt just beyond the avalanche path, about 59 km north of Huaraz.

Llanganuco From Yungay begins the trip to Lagunas Llanganuco, one of the most beautiful and popular excursions in the Cordillera Blanca. To get there, take a tour from Huaraz or buses or taxis from Yungay. From June to August, minibuses (US$5) leave from the plaza in Yungay, allowing two hours near the lakes. (Trips in other months depend on passenger demand.) National park entry is US$1. Llanganuco is the start of the popular and spectacular four or five-day Llanganuco to Santa Cruz hiking loop.

Places to Stay & Eat The very friendly *Hostal Gledel*, near the plaza, is US$5/7.50 with hot water and meals available. A few other cheap hotels may close in the low season. The *Restaurant Turístico Alpamayo* serves typical food; there are others.

PERU

Caraz

This pleasant little town (elevation 2270 metres) is 67 km north of Huaraz; it is the end point of the Llanganuco to Santa Cruz trek. Caraz has survived earthquakes and landslides. The Plaza de Armas is attractive, there are several cheap hotels, and you can take pleasant walks in the surrounding hills. Pequeña Pony (☎ 72-0221), Daniel Villar 416, is a source for local information, equipment rental, guides etc.

Places to Stay The basic, clean and friendly *Señor Caballero* has hot showers and is owned by the Pequeña Pony folks. The friendly *Hostal Morovi* is US$3/4 for singles/doubles with bath. The *Albergue Los Pinos* in Parque San Martín – ask how to get there – is US$4/5 and has hot water and breakfast. The *Hostal La Casona* (☎ 72-2335) is clean, has hot water, and is US$4/7 or US$7/10 with bath. The *Hostal Suizo Peruano* (☎ 72-2166), San Martín 1133, charges US$1 more but is no better. Next door, the *Hostal Chavín* (☎ 72-2171) is friendly and charges US$8/12 in clean rooms with hot showers. There are other cheapies.

SOUTH-EAST OF HUARAZ
Chavín de Huantar

This small village is by the interesting ruins of Chavín. The Chavín culture (1300 to 400 BC) is Peru's oldest major culture. The principal Chavín deity was feline; there were also lesser condor, snake and human deities. Highly stylised carvings of these deities are found at the site. The most interesting parts of Chavín were built underground (it's lit, but bring a torch in case of power failure). It's worth hiring a local guide. In the heart of the underground complex is an exquisitely carved, four-metre-high dagger-like rock, the Lanzón de Chavín.

The site is open daily; admission is US$2.

Places to Stay & Eat Hotels are very basic and cheap. The 'best' is the *Inca* at US$4/6, or try the *Montecarlo* or *Gantu*. Restaurants close soon after sunset, so eat early.

Getting There & Away Tour buses make day trips from Huaraz (US$11). See Huaraz for daily public buses (US$3.50, five hours).

Chiquián

This village (3400 metres) is the gateway to the spectacular Cordillera Huayhuash. Few supplies are available but *burros* and *arrieros* (mules and their handlers, respectively) can be hired here.

Places to Stay & Eat The basic but clean *Hostal San Miguel*, Comercio 233, (no sign) is US$4 per person. There are a couple of even more basic places and a few simple restaurants.

Getting There & Away TUBSA and Transfysa go to Lima (US$7.50, 10 hours) every other day. Turismo Cavassa has a night bus to Lima. Transportes Virgen del Carmen and Transportes Huandoy have buses to Huaraz.

Across the Northern Highlands

CAJAMARCA

Cajamarca (2650 metres) is the capital of its department and five hours east of the coast by paved road. It is a traditional and tranquil colonial city with a friendly population of 70,000. The surrounding countryside is green and attractive.

Cajamarca has impressive colonial architecture, interesting people and customs, and excellent Andean food. It was in Cajamarca that Pizarro deceived, captured and finally assassinated the Inca Atahualpa (see History in the Facts about South America chapter). Relatively few foreigners visit Cajamarca.

Information

A tourist office at the Complejo de Belén is open Monday to Friday from 7.30 am to 1.30 pm and 3.30 to 5.30 pm. The Banco de Crédito and Interbanc change travellers' cheques. Street moneychangers are near the Plaza de Armas. The telephone code is 044.

Cumbe Mayo Tours (☎ 92-2938), Puga 635, and Cajamarca Tours (☎ 92-2813), 2 de Mayo 323, are recommended for local tours.

Things to See

The only remaining Inca building in Cajamarca is **El Cuarto del Rescate** (the ransom chamber), just off the plaza. It is where Atahualpa was imprisoned, not where the ransom was stored. It's open daily, except Tuesday, from 9 am to noon and 3 to 5 pm. Entry is US$1.50, and includes the following sites, which have similar hours.

Construction of the **Complejo de Belén** began in the 17th century. Inside what once was the Women's Hospital there is a small archaeology museum. In the kitchen and dispensary of the hospital there is an art museum. Next door is the **church**, with a fine cupola and a carved and painted pulpit. Woodcarvings include a tired-looking Christ sitting cross-legged on his throne, looking as if he could do with a pisco sour after a hard day's miracle-working. Close by, the small **Museo de Etnografía** displays local costumes and clothing, domestic and agricultural implements, musical instruments and other examples of Cajamarcan culture.

The university-run **Museo Arqueológico** is open daily, except Tuesday, from 8 am to 1.30 pm; knock on the door to get in. Hours change often; entry is US$0.50. The **Iglesia San Francisco** has a religious art museum, open on weekdays from 2 to 5 pm. Entry is US$0.50.

The **Cerro Santa Apolonia** hill overlooks the city from the south-west. Climb the stairs at the end of 2 de Mayo. There are pre-Columbian carvings and pretty gardens. Entry is US$0.50.

Special Events

Water-throwing during Carnaval is without respite. Corpus Christi is very colourful and Fiestas Patrias events include a bullfight.

Places to Stay

Prices rise around fiestas and during the dry months. Cheap hotels with hot water have it only a few hours a day: ask when.

The very basic *Hostal Chota* (☎ 92-2610), La Mar 637, is US$3 or US$4 per person and has cold showers. Similar are the *Hostal Bolívar* (☎ 92-2969), Apurímac 670, and the *Hostal Amalia Puga* (☎ 92-2117), Puga 1118. The basic *Hostal Sucre* (☎ 92-2596), Puga 811, is US$5 per person with private cold shower. The cleaner *Hotel San Francisco* (☎ 92-3070), Belén 790, is also US$5 per person with private cold shower. The similar *Hotel Becerra* (☎ 92-3490), Arequipa 195, charges US$7/12 for a single/double. The similarly priced *Hostal Perú*, Puga 605, has private cold showers and is OK.

The clean *Hostal Prado* (☎ 92-3288), La Mar 582, has hot water. Rates are US$5/9 or US$10/15 with bath. The *Hotel Plaza* (☎ 92-2058), Puga 669, is in a colourful old building on the plaza. It has hot water and a few rooms with balconies and plaza views. A double with bath and view is US$14; cheaper rooms (no views and with dirty communal showers) are available. The *Hostal Dos de Mayo* (☎ 92-2527), 2 de Mayo 585, has hot communal showers and is US$6/10 in rooms with washbasin and toilet. The *Hotel Delfort* (☎ 92-3375), Apurímac 851, looks OK at US$8/13 with private hot shower. The bare-looking *Hostal Turismo* (☎ 92-3101), 2 de Mayo 817, has clean, carpeted rooms with comfortable beds and private hot showers at US$9/15. The *Hostal Atahualpa* (☎ 92-2157), on Lima near Atahualpa, looks quite good for US$10/18 with warm showers. A few rooms with shared showers are cheaper. The *Hotel Amazonas* (☎ 92-2620, 92-3496), Amazonas 528, has doubles with hot showers for US$20.

Places to Eat

The *Salas*, on the plaza, is a locally popular barn of a place serving various reasonably priced local dishes. Similar, but a little cheaper, is the *Chifa El Zarco*, around the corner. *El Real Plaza*, 2 de Mayo 569, has a pleasant courtyard and serves local dishes. For a typical local lunch (including cuy), try the rustic *La Namorina*, 1.5 km from the

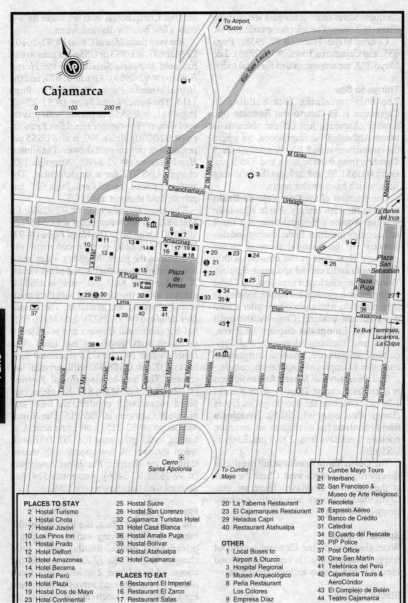

Cajamarca

0   100   200 m

To Airport, Otuzco

To Baños del Inca

To Bus Terminals, Llacanora, La Colpa

To Cumbe Mayo

Cerro Santa Apolonia

Plaza de Armas

Plaza San Sebastián

Plaza A Puga

Mercado

Río San Lucas

PLACES TO STAY
2 Hostal Turismo
4 Hostal Chota
7 Hostal Jusovi
10 Los Pinos Inn
11 Hostal Prado
12 Hotel Delfort
13 Hotel Amazonas
14 Hotel Becerra
17 Hostal Perú
18 Hotel Plaza
19 Hostal Dos de Mayo
23 Hotel Continental
24 Hotel San Francisco

25 Hostal Sucre
26 Hostal San Lorenzo
32 Cajamarca Turistas Hotel
33 Hotel Casa Blanca
36 Hostal Amalia Puga
39 Hostal Bolívar
40 Hostal Atahualpa
42 Hotel Cajamarca

PLACES TO EAT
6 Restaurant El Imperial
16 Restaurant El Zarco
17 Restaurant Salas
19 Restaurant El Real Plaza

20 La Taberna Restaurant
23 El Cajamarques Restaurant
29 Helados Capri
40 Restaurant Atahualpa

OTHER
1 Local Buses to
   Airport & Otuzco
3 Hospital Regional
5 Museo Arqueológico
8 Peña Restaurant
   Los Colores
9 Empresa Díaz
15 Laundry

17 Cumbe Mayo Tours
21 Interbanc
22 San Francisco &
   Museo de Arte Religioso
27 Recoleta
28 Expreso Aéreo
30 Banco de Crédito
31 Catedral
34 El Cuarto del Rescate
35 PIP Police
37 Post Office
38 Cine San Martín
41 Telefónica del Perú
42 Cajamarca Tours &
   AeroCóndor
43 El Complejo de Belén
44 Teatro Cajamarca
45 Museo de Etnografía

PERU

centre on the road to the Baños del Inca, or *Sabor Cajabambino*, on La Paz near the bus stations. The *Atahualpa*, next to the hotel, and *El Imperial*, on the 600 block of Amazonas, have good, cheap fixed menús and other meals. *La Taberna*, on the plaza, serves good international food at prices a little higher than other places. The up-market (but not expensive) *Hotel Cajamarca* restaurant has a nice ambience and decent food, and often has musicians in the evenings.

Getting There & Away

Air Expreso Aéreo (☎ 92-3480, 92-5113) and AeroCóndor (☎ 92-2813) have flights to Lima (US$90) and Chachapoyas (US$45). AeroContinente also has flights. Other towns are sometimes served and cancellations or delays are common. Local buses for Otuzco pass by the airport.

Bus Most bus terminals are on the third block of Atahualpa (not the Atahualpa in the town centre, but another street of the same name), 1.5 km south-east of town on the road to the Baños del Inca. Cumbe Mayo Tours and Cajamarca Tours sell some bus tickets, or you can buy them at the terminals.

Many companies have buses to Trujillo (US$6 to US$8, eight to nine hours), Chiclayo (US$5.50 to US$7.50, seven hours) and Lima (US$10 to US$15, 15 to 17 hours). Lima buses go overnight. CIVA (☎ 92-1460), Independencia 386, is the most expensive and comfortable. Empresa Atahualpa (☎ 92-3075), also has good buses. Cheaper Lima buses are with Tepsa (☎ 92-3306), Sudamericano (☎ 92-3270), Cruz del Sur, Nor Perú (☎ 92-4550), and Palacios (☎ 92-2600). For Trujillo, buses leave in the afternoon and arrive late at night. The earliest is with Vulkano (☎ 92-1090) or Empresa Díaz (☎ 92-5630), Ayacucho 753, near the centre. The Lima-bound companies also stop in Trujillo. For Chiclayo, El Cumbe (☎ 92-3088), Independencia 236, has three or four daily buses and goes during the day. Jarcer Express, (☎ 92-3337), Sudamericano and Vulkano also go to Chiclayo. Transportes Atahualpa, Nor Perú and Palacios go to Cajabamba (US$5, seven hours). Empresa Díaz and Nor Perú go to Chota (US$6, nine hours through wild scenery). Empresa Atahualpa, Palacios, and Empresa Díaz go to Celendín (US$5, five hours).

AROUND CAJAMARCA

Baños del Inca These natural hot springs are six km east of Cajamarca. The water is channelled into private cubicles (US$1 per hour), some large enough to hold six people, and a cheaper public pool. Taxi colectivos (US$0.50) and cheaper buses leave from the Cajamarca Plaza de Armas.

Cumbe Mayo Pre-Inca channels run for several km across the bleak mountain tops, about 23 km south-west of Cajamarca by road. Nearby are caves with petroglyphs. The countryside is high, windswept and slightly eerie. The site can be reached on foot from Cerro Santa Apolonia via a signposted road. The walk takes about four hours, if you take the obvious short cuts and ask passers-by for directions. Tours (US$8) are sold in Cajamarca.

Ventanillas de Otuzco This pre-Inca graveyard has hundreds of funerary niches built into the hillside. The site is in beautiful countryside, and you can walk here from Cajamarca or the Baños del Inca. There are local buses and tours from Cajamarca.

Llacanora & Hacienda La Colpa Llacanora, a picturesque village where the traditional *clarín* (a three-metre-long bamboo trumpet) is still played, is 13 km south-east of Cajamarca. A few km beyond, the Hacienda La Colpa cattle ranch is often visited on tours to Llacanora.

CELENDIN

This small, pleasant town is a possible stopover between Cajamarca (five hours) and Chachapoyas (a rough but spectacular 12-hour trip). Buses may be delayed in the wet season (December to April). There are several cheap, basic hotels.

PERU

CHACHAPOYAS

This quiet, pleasant little town is at about 2000 metres on the eastern slopes of the Andes. Nearby are many little-known archaeological sites. One of the most accessible is the magnificent ruin of Kuélap. Chachapoyas has a small museum, at Merced 800.

Information

The Banco de Crédito changes travellers' cheques. The telephone code is 074. Martín Antonio Olivo Chumbe (☎ 75-7212), Piura 909, or at the radio station above Expreso Aéreo, is a good local guide.

Places to Stay

The following charge US$6 per person in rooms with bath and hot water: the *Hostal Johumaji* (☎ 75-7138), Ayacucho 711; *Hotel El Dorado* (☎ 75-7147), Ayacucho 1062; and *Hostal Kuélap* (☎ 75-7136), Amazonas 1057, which also has cheaper rooms with shared bath or cold water. The *Hotel Amazonas* is cheaper and you'll find a couple of more basic pensions if you ask around.

Places to Eat

The *Chacha* on the plaza is popular with locals. Opposite, *Mass Burger* has baked goods and fruit salads as well as burgers. Nearby, the Restaurants *Vegas*, *Kuélap*, *Oh Qué Bueno* and *Chifa El Turista* serve OK cheap Peruvian food.

Getting There & Away

Air Expreso Aéreo has flights on Sunday and Thursday from Lima (US$90) via Chimbote and Cajamarca.

Bus Olano, ETOSA and CIVA have buses to Chiclayo (US$9.50, 12 hours) and Lima (US$23, 30 hours).

Minibuses and pick-ups leave from near the market for various destinations. Several

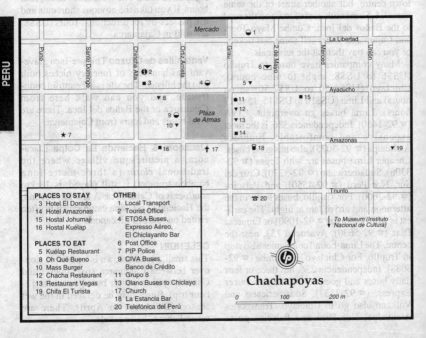

PLACES TO STAY	OTHER
3 Hotel El Dorado	1 Local Transport
14 Hotel Amazonas	2 Tourist Office
15 Hostal Johumaji	4 ETOSA Buses,
16 Hostal Kuélap	Expresso Aéreo,
	El Chiclayanito Bar
PLACES TO EAT	6 Post Office
5 Kuélap Restaurant	7 PIP Police
8 Oh Qué Bueno	9 CIVA Buses,
10 Mass Burger	Banco de Crédito
12 Chacha Restaurant	11 Grupo 8
13 Restaurant Vegas	13 Olano Buses to Chiclayo
19 Chifa El Turista	17 Church
	18 La Estancia Bar
	20 Telefónica del Perú

Chachapoyas

0   100   200 m

To Museum (Instituto Nacional de Cultura)

a day go to Tingo (US$2, two hours) and on to Leimebamba (from where pick-ups continue to Celendín daily in the dry season). Minibuses go to Pedro Ruiz (US$2, two hours), from where you continue east to the Amazon.

KUELAP

This immense, oval-shaped pre-Inca city is at 3100 metres on a ridge above the Río Utcubamba, south-east of Chachapoyas. It's a major site with very little tourism. Entry is US$4.

A small, cheap and very basic *hostel* has a few beds and floor space, or you can camp. You'll need to purify your water. Very simple meals are available. The friendly *guardian* will show you where to stay, and give a tour – a small tip is appreciated.

To get there, take a minibus from Chachapoyas to **Tingo**. This village was badly damaged by floods in 1993 but a couple of basic hotels have reopened. A signposted trail leads from the southern end of Tingo to the ruins, 1200 metres higher. Allow five hours for the climb and carry water. Mules can be hired.

EAST OF CHACHAPOYAS

First go north to Pedro Ruiz (see Chachapoyas Getting There & Away information), where there are a couple of basic hotels. From here a rough road goes east to Yurimaguas (definitely off the gringo trail). Money is changed at the Banco de Crédito and other places in the towns below.

Rioja

About 11 hours east of Pedro Ruiz, Rioja has the regional airport (with flights from Lima) and a few basic hotels.

Moyobamba

At 860 metres, this is the capital of the department of San Martín, but the Rioja airport has most flights. It's under an hour from Rioja by minibus. The town was almost demolished by earthquakes in 1990 and 1991 but is recovering. The telephone code is 094. There are half a dozen fairly cheap hotels.

Tarapoto

About 3½ hours beyond Moyobamba, Tarapoto, at 356 metres, is the largest and most important town in the area. It has plenty of hotels but is pricier than most of Peru. Travel from Moyobamba and on to Yurimaguas (see the Amazon Basin section) is safe but the route south along the Río Huallaga valley to Tingo María goes through Peru's major coca-growing region and is not recommended. The telephone code is 094.

Places to Stay Some hotels don't have water all day; none has hot water. The friendly *Hostal Juan Alfonso* (☎ 52-2179), Ursua and Raimondi, at US$3.50/5.50 a single/double, or US$5/7.50 with private bath, is one of the better cheap hotels. Other basic cheapies nearby are the *Hostal Meléndez*, *Hostal Pasquelandia* (☎ 52-2290), *Hostal El Dorado* and *Hostal Viluz*. Within three blocks north-west of the plaza are the cheapish *Hostal Las Palmeras*, *Hostal Misti* (☎ 52-2439) and *Hostal Central* (☎ 52-2234). The recommended *Hostal San Antonio*, just off the plaza, has clean rooms with shower, fan and cable TV (US channels) for US$10/12.50. There are about 10 more expensive places.

Places to Eat *El Mesón* and *La Terraza* on the plaza have decent set lunches. The market has the cheapest places.

Getting There & Away The airport is 2.5 km from town (US$1.50 by mototaxi). Aero-Continente, Faucett, Imperial Air and Expreso Aéreo have many flights to Lima (US$77). Several flights a week go to Yurimaguas (US$24), Pucallpa (US$47), Iquitos (US$54), Trujillo (US$58), Chiclayo (US$58) and various jungle towns.

Buses, taxi colectivos and pick-ups leave from the eighth block of Ramón Castillo for Moyobamba (this departure point may move further out of town). Pick-ups for Yurimaguas (US$8, five hours) leave from the south-eastern end of Ursua. Buses to Chiclayo (US$20, 36 hours) and on to Lima leave daily.

PERU

The Amazon Basin

Half of Peru lies in the Amazon Basin, but access from the rest of Peru is limited. Pucallpa and Yurimaguas are reached by long road trips. Both have boats to Iquitos, which has no road connections. Puerto Maldonado can be reached by truck from Cuzco – a very long and difficult trip. All these towns have commercial airports and all have Bancos de Crédito for changing travellers' cheques.

PUCALLPA

Pucallpa is an unlovely, fast-growing jungle town linked directly to Lima by road. The main reasons to visit are to go to the nearby lake of Yarinacocha or to take a boat to Iquitos. It is the capital of Ucayali department. The telephone code is 064.

Places to Stay

The *Hostal Europa, Hostal Excelsior* and *Hospedaje Mori* are under US$4 each – but are dirty and not recommended. The *Hostal Sun* (☎ 57-4260), Ucayali 380, is better at

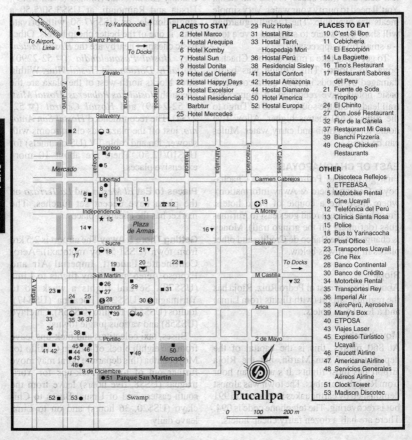

PLACES TO STAY		PLACES TO EAT
2 Hotel Marco	29 Ruíz Hotel	10 C'est Si Bon
4 Hostal Arequipa	31 Hostal Ritz	11 Cebichería
6 Hotel Komby	33 Hostal Tariri,	El Escorpión
7 Hostal Sun	Hospedaje Mori	14 La Baguette
9 Hostal Donita	36 Hostal Perú	16 Tino's Restaurant
19 Hotel del Oriente	38 Residencial Sisley	17 Restaurant Sabores
22 Hostal Happy Days	41 Hostal Confort	del Peru
23 Hostal Excelsior	42 Hostal Amazonia	21 Fuente de Soda
24 Hostal Residencial	44 Hostal Diamante	Tropitop
Barbtur	50 Hotel America	24 El Chinito
25 Hotel Mercedes	52 Hostal Europa	27 Don José Restaurant
		32 Flor de la Canela
		37 Restaurant Mi Casa
		39 Bianchi Pizzería
		49 Cheap Chicken
		Restaurants

OTHER
1 Discoteca Reflejos
3 ETFEBASA
5 Motorbike Rental
8 Cine Ucayali
12 Telefónica del Perú
13 Clínica Santa Rosa
15 Police
18 Bus to Yarinacocha
20 Post Office
23 Transportes Ucayali
26 Cine Rex
28 Banco Continental
30 Banco de Crédito
34 Motorbike Rental
35 Transportes Rey
36 Imperial Air
38 AeroPerú, Aeroselva
39 Many's Box
40 ETPOSA
43 Viajes Laser
45 Expreso Turístico
Ucayali
46 Faucett Airline
47 Americana Airline
48 Servicios Generales
Aéreos Airline
51 Clock Tower
53 Madison Discotec

Pucallpa

0   100   200 m

US$5/7.50 for a single/double, or US$7.50/ 11 with private cold showers. Also decent are the *Hostal Confort* (☎ 57-5815) and *Hostal Amazonia* (☎ 57-1080) at US$7/9 with bath. The small, friendly and popular *Hostal Residencial Barbtur* (☎ 57-2532), Raimondi 670, is US$6/9 or US$9/14 with cold bath and fan. The similarly priced *Hostal Perú* (☎ 57-5128) is also OK. Other cheap and basic places are the *Hostal Diamante* at US$6/10, the *Residencial Sisley* (☎ 57-5137) at US$8/10 and the *Hotel Marco* (☎ 57-1048) at US$9/12, all with bath and fan. The *Hostal Donita* (☎ 57-1480) is OK at US$6 each, or US$9 with bath. The *Hotel Komby* (☎ 57-1184) is US$15/22 for clean rooms and has a swimming pool. The *Hotel Arequipa* (☎ 57-1348, 57-3171, 57-3112) is US$15/22, or US$28/35 with air-con.

Places to Eat

For cheap local breakfasts, the pavement cafés on Portillo near 7 de Junio are OK. *La Baguette* is squeaky clean and sells bread, snacks and pastries. For ceviches and other meals in the US$3 to US$6 range, *Cebichería El Escorpión* is good. Near the intersection of Raimondi and Ucayali are several popular places with outdoor tables, such as *El Chinito* with set lunches for US$1.50, *Restaurant Mi Casa* and the *Bianchi Pizzería and Bar*, the latter a popular hang-out for young people. *Restaurant Sabores del Perú* is a local place with pizza, chicken, meat and fish. A couple of cheap, popular chicken restaurants are on Tacna by the Parque San Martín.

Getting There & Away

Air The airport is five km north-west of town. AeroContinente, AeroPerú, Americana and Faucett have daily flights to and from Lima (US$65). Imperial Air has three a week. Aero-Continente and Americana have daily flights to Iquitos (US$46) whilst AeroPerú and Faucett have flights two or three times a week. Services to other towns are provided but schedules change frequently.

Bus Several companies leave at 6 or 7 am for Lima (US$12 to US$15, 24 hours –

longer in the wet season). There are several police checks (because of drugs) between Pucallpa and Tingo María. Faster minibuses to Tingo María leave from 7 de Junio.

River La Hoyada, Pucallpa's port, is 2.5 km north-east of the town. During the drier months (June to October) boats leave from El Mangual, a further three km away. Minibuses go there from the centre (US$0.50). Boats along the Río Ucayali from Pucallpa to Iquitos (US$25) take three to five days, US$25). There are more boats when the river is high. Hammocks are not provided, but you can buy one in Pucallpa.

Getting Around

Mototaxis are US$1 to the airport and US$2 to Yarinacocha: bargain. Car taxis charge twice that. Buses (US$0.30) and colectivos (US$0.50) to Yarinacocha leave from the corner of Ucayali and Sucre.

YARINACOCHA

This lovely oxbow lake is 10 km north-east of Pucallpa. You can take canoe rides, observe wildlife, visit Indian communities and purchase handicrafts in the village of Puerto Callao. On the plaza, the Shipibo have a cooperative craft shop (Maroti Shobo) with thousands of handmade ceramics to choose from. You can visit the Shipibo in some of their villages, especially San Francisco.

Organised Tours

Peki-peki boats and drivers are about US$7 per hour (four passengers). Overnight trips start at US$30 per person per day. Recommended guides include Gilber Reategui Sangama (with the boat *La Normita*), his uncle, Nemecio Sangama (with *El Rayito*), Marly Alemán Arévalo (with *Julito*), Roy Riaño and Jorge Morales.

Places to Stay & Eat

In Puerto Callao, the basic *Hotel El Pescador* is US$4/6 for a single/double. The *Hostal El Delfín* (☎ & fax 57-1129) is better; it has old rooms with bath at US$5/7.50 and new rooms with bath and TV at US$8/11. A

PERU

couple of more expensive lodges are across the lake. Several inexpensive restaurants and lively bars line the waterfront.

YURIMAGUAS

This quiet, pleasant little town is the major port on the Río Huallaga and has boats to Iquitos. Reaching Yurimaguas involves a hard road trip of several days or a simple flight from Lima. The US Drug Enforcement Agency (DEA) has a high profile but there are no real problems for overland travellers. The telephone code is 094.

Places to Stay & Eat

Hotels don't have hot water. The very basic *Quinta Ruthcita*, is US$2.50 per person. The *Quinta Lucy* has private baths at US$3/5 for a single/double. The *Hostal Jauregui* has dark and dingy rooms with bath for US$3.50/5. At US$4/6, the *Hostal Baneo* has shared baths and the *Hostal El Cisne* and *Hostal La Estrella* have private baths. The best basic cheapie is the clean and quiet *Hostal César Gustavo* at US$5/7 with bath and fan. The *Hostal Florindez* has air-con and baths in otherwise basic rooms for US$7/9.50. The new *Hostal de Paz* (☎ 35-2123) has clean rooms with bath, fan and TV for US$8.50/11. Also good are the quiet *Hostal Residencial Cajamarca* at US$11/14 and *Hostal El Naranjo* (☎ 35-2650, 35-0554) at US$14/16, both with bath, fan and TV. *Leo's Palace* (☎ 35-2213, 35-2544) is US$12/16 and has some rooms with balconies and plaza views.

El Naranjo Restaurant and *Cheraton* (in El Naranjo and Leo's Palace hotels) are among the best, though nothing special. Also OK is the *Copacabana* for general food, the *Pollería La Posada* for chicken and *La Prosperidad* for tropical juices and sandwiches.

Getting There & Away

Air Carriers and schedules change frequently. Recently, AeroContinente and Faucett were flying from Lima (US$78), Tarapoto (US$24) and Iquitos (US$54) a few times a week.

Truck Pick-ups leave from J Riera several times a day for Tarapoto (US$7 to US$9, five hours). Expect delays in the rainy season.

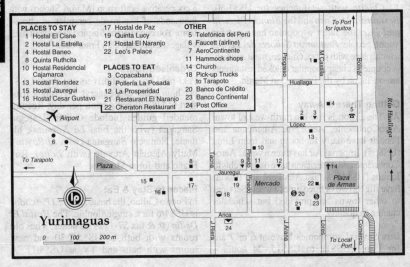

PLACES TO STAY
1 Hostal El Cisne
2 Hostal La Estrella
4 Hostal Baneo
8 Quinta Ruthcita
10 Hostal Residencial Cajamarca
13 Hostal Florindez
15 Hostal Jauregui
16 Hostal Cesar Gustavo
17 Hostal de Paz
19 Quinta Lucy
21 Hostal El Naranjo
22 Leo's Palace

PLACES TO EAT
3 Copacabana
9 Pollería La Posada
12 La Prosperidad
21 Restaurant El Naranjo
22 Cheraton Restaurant

OTHER
5 Telefónica del Perú
6 Faucett (airline)
7 AeroContinente
11 Hammock shops
14 Church
18 Pick-up Trucks to Tarapoto
20 Banco de Crédito
23 Banco Continental
24 Post Office

Yurimaguas

Boat Cargo boats leave a few times a week to Iquitos (US$20, about three days). They stop in Lagunas.

Getting Around
Mototaxis charge about US$0.60 to the port, or walk 13 blocks north.

LAGUNAS & RESERVA NACIONAL PACAYA-SAMIRIA
Lagunas is a small, remote village with no moneychanging facilities and limited and expensive food. Guides are available to visit Pacaya-Samiria and they charge less than guides in Iquitos. They speak only Spanish. Some guides hunt and fish but we discourage hunting because, after all, this is a reserve! If you ask guides not to hunt, they'll listen. The going rate is US$8 to US$10 per person per day (four people) for a guide and boat; food is extra. Good guides are Job and Luis Gongora (nephew and uncle) who can be contacted at the Hostal La Sombra. They recently charged US$150 plus food for a six-day trip for two tourists. Also recommended are Edinson Saldaña Gutiérrez and Juan Huaycama, both well known locally. Ask anyone.

Places to Stay & Eat
The friendly *Hostal La Sombra* (also known as Hostal Piñedo) has hot, stuffy rooms at US$2 per person. Shared showers and food are available. The smaller *Hotel Montalbán* is another possibility. You can stay in a *hostal* above the farmacia, but it doesn't have showers (buckets of water are provided). *Doña Dina* in a blue-fronted building just off the plaza serves good cheap meals.

Getting There & Away
Boats from Yurimaguas take about 12 hours and leave most days.

IQUITOS
With 400,000 inhabitants, Iquitos is Peru's largest jungle city, and the capital of the huge Department of Loreto. Iquitos is linked with the outside world by air and river; it is the largest city in the Amazon Basin without road links.

Iquitos was founded in the 1750s as a Jesuit mission. In the late 19th century, it was a rubber boom town, and signs of the opulence of those days remain in some of the mansions and tiled walls. Today, both the oil and tourist industries play an important part in the economy of the area.

Being so isolated, Iquitos seems to have been bypassed by the problems of terrorism and thievery – but watch your possessions nevertheless! The people are friendly and easy-going.

Information
The tourist office is unsigned at Napo 176. Hours are weekdays from 7.30 am to 1 pm. The Brazilian Consulate (☎ 23-2081) is at Sargento Lores 363 and the Colombian Consulate (☎ 23-1461) is at Putumayo 247. Migraciones (☎ 23-1021, 23-1072) is at Malecón Tarapacá 368. Several banks cash travellers' cheques and there are street moneychangers on Lores between Próspero and Arica. Changing Brazilian or Colombian currency is best done at the border. The telephone code is 094.

Things to See
The **Casa de Hierro** (Iron House) designed by Eiffel (of Tower fame) is on the northeastern corner of Putumayo and Raymondi and looks like a bunch of scrap-metal sheets bolted together.

The floating shantytown of **Belén** has a certain charm; it has scores of huts built on rafts, which rise and fall with the river. Thousands of people live here, and canoes float from hut to hut selling and trading. Boatmen will paddle you around. This is a very poor area but seems safe enough in daylight. The **market**, in the blocks in front of Belén, has strange stuff like piles of dried frogs and fish, armadillo shells, piranha teeth and a great variety of tropical fruits. Watch your wallet.

Laguna Quistacocha (entry US$1.50) is 15 km south of Iquitos and makes a pleasant day trip. Minibuses leave frequently from Plaza 28 de Julio (US$1.20). There is a small

PERU

zoo of local fauna, and a fish hatchery with two-metre *paiche* fish swimming around.

Places to Stay

All these hotels have private cold baths and fans unless stated otherwise. Erratic water supply is the norm in Iquitos. The following are OK budget places. The clean, friendly and popular *Hostal Alfert* (☎ 23-4105), G Sáenz 001, is US$7 (one or two people) and there's a view of the Amazon. It has water problems, but buckets of water are available. The *Hostal Tacna* (☎ 23-2839, Tacna 516, is basic and noisy but clean at US$4.50/6.50 for a single/double. The *Hostal Monterico* (☎ & fax 23-5395), Arica 633, is US$7/8. Also decent is the *Hostal Fortes* (☎ 23-5221), Próspero 665, at US$7/9. The *Hostal La Pascana* (☎ 23-1418), Pevas 133, is good, safe, popular with travellers and often full. Rooms are US$10/13. The quiet and clean *Hostal Lima* (☎ 23-5152), Próspero 549, is US$9/12.

The following are cheap and very basic. *Hostal San Antonio* (☎ 23-5221), Próspero 655, is US$4.50/5.50 and lacks fans. The similarly priced *Hostal Anita*, Hurtado 742, is friendly. The *Hostal Lozano* (☎ 23-2486), Hurtado 772, is US$6/9. The *Hostal Iquitos* (☎ 23-9015), Hurtado 955, is US$7/10. The *Hostal Perú* (☎ 23-4961), Próspero 318, and the *Hostal Loreto*, Próspero 311, are reasonably clean for US$7/9. Other cheapies are the friendly *Hostal Karina* (☎ 23-5367), Putumayo 467, and the *Hostal Maynas* (☎ 23-5861), Próspero 388,

The *Hostal Libertad* (☎ 23-5763), Arica 361, has simple rooms with air-con for US$10/15. Others at about this price are the *Hostal Bon Bini* (☎ 23-8422), Pevas 386, which is clean and quiet, the *Hostal Baltasar* (☎ 23-2240), Condamine 265, which is clean and acceptable, the *Hostal José In*, which is overpriced, the *Hostal Isabel* (☎ 23-4901), Brasil 164, with rooms ranging from poor to quite good, and *Roland's Amazon River Lodge*, which is dirty. The *Hostal Florentina* (☎ 23-3591), Huallaga 212, has clean, pleasant rooms at US$12/16. The clean *Hostal Dos Mundos* (☎ 23-2635),

Tacna 631, is US$17/23, but often offers discounts.

Jungle Lodges & Camps There are about a dozen jungle lodges in the Iquitos area – none for budget travellers. Prices range from about US$40 to over US$100 per day depending on services. Lodge offices are found in central Iquitos. The further away from Iquitos you are, and the further off the Amazon itself, the better your chances of seeing wildlife.

Explorama Tours is one of the longest established and best known companies; it has three lodges. Its Explornapo camp, 160 km from Iquitos on the Río Napo, is the most interesting and boasts the new Canopy Walkway System developed by scientists from the Amazon Center for Environmental Education & Research (ACEER). The walkway, several hundred metres long and 30 metres above the forest floor, gives the visitor a unique look at the rainforest canopy; unfortunately for budget travellers, it's also one of the most expensive options. More information can be obtained from Explorama Tours, Apartado 446, Iquitos (☎ 23-5471, fax 23-4968), Avenida La Marina 340; or ACEER, 10 Environs Park, Helena, AL 35080, USA (☎ (800) 255 8206).

Ecological Jungle Trips (☎ 23-7154), Soledad 1321, has very rustic cabins at various points 75 to 180 km from Iquitos. These may be worth checking out, particularly for travellers on a budget. Rates are about US$40 a night.

Adventure Tours Amazonia, Lores 267, has recently been recommended. They reportedly start with the 'official' price of US$80 per day, but come down to under US$30 per person a day if there's a group of you. Another recent recommendation is *Arturo Díaz Ruiz*, Soledad 1226, who charged US$60 per person for a three-night expedition, meeting local people, building shelters to sleep in, fishing and canoeing. There are many others.

Places to Eat

Inexpensive chifas are near the Plaza 28 de

PLACES TO STAY
3 Hostal José In
4 Hostal Baltasar
5 Hostal Bon Bini
6 Hotel Ambassador
12 Hostal La Pascana
14 Roland's Amazon
   River Lodge
16 Hotel El Dorado
18 Hotel Safari
21 Hostal Florentina
23 Hostal Amazonas
28 Grand Hotel Iquitos
30 Hostal Jhuliana
32 Hostal Karina
33 Hostal Acosta I
47 Hostal Libertad
48 Hostal Perú
49 Hostal Maynas
51 Hostal Loreto
58 Hotel Europa
59 Hostal Fortes
60 Hostal Isabel
61 Hostal Tacna
63 Hotel Acosta II
65 Hostal Caravel
66 Hostal Lima
68 Hostal Dos Mundos
72 Hostal Monterico
73 Hostal María Antonia
75 Hostal San Antonio
80 Hostal Anita,
   Hostal Lozano
82 Hostal Internacional
85 Hostal Alfert
86 Hostal Iquitos
88 Hostal Económico

PLACES TO EAT
15 La Barca
19 El Mesón
22 La Terracita
24 Ari's Burger
29 La Maloka
31 Olla de Oro
42 Don Giovanni
43 El Tuquito
44 Casa de Jaime
69 Chifa Wai Ming
71 Several Chifas
79 Pollería El Pollo
   Suave
81 La Pascana

OTHER
1 Museo Regional
2 Extasis Discoteca
7 Anaconda Lara Lodge
   (office)
8 Rápido Expresso
   Boat Office
9 Francesco Pub
10 Motorcycle Rental
11 El Amauta Café Bar
13 Dreams Discotheque
17 Municipalidad
20 Marandú Bar
25 Tourist Office
26 Craft shops, galleries
27 Iron House
34 Church
35 Colombian Consulate
36 Banco de Crédito
37 Telefónica del Perú
38 Servicios Aéreos
   Amazónicos
39 Banco Wiese
40 AeroPerú,
   Three Roses Travel
41 Americana (airline)
45 Brazilian Consulate
46 Adventure Tours
   Amazonia
50 Aero Continente
52 Banco Continental
53 TANS Airline
54 Bambolea Discoteca
55 Migraciones
57 Police
57 Post Office
62 Moisés Torres Viena
64 Interbanc
67 Motorcycle Rental
70 Cine Bolognesi
74 Faucett Airline,
   Paucar Tours
76 Motorcycle Rental
77 Dirección Regional
   de Turismo
78 Local Buses to Laguna
   Quistacocha & Airport
83 Colectivos to Laguna
   Moronacocha
84 Cine Iquitos
87 Boats for Hire to
   Belén Area

PERU

Río Amazonus

Iquitos

0   100   200 m

BELÉN

Julio. The best (and priciest) is *Wai Ming*. *El Pollo Suave* on this plaza is a good cheap chicken place, and other cheap restaurants are on Tacna and Huallaga north of this plaza. *La Barca*, Fitzcarrald 137, and *La Terracita* nearby are clean, cheap and have OK food.

Slightly pricier but good eateries include *La Pascana* (☎ 23-9021), R Hurtado 735, a simple place with good ceviches and fine Amazon river views. *La Olla de Oro* (☎ 23-4350), Araujo 579, has a good selection of Peruvian food. *Ari's Burger* (☎ 23-1470), on the Plaza de Armas, is a clean, brightly lit joint dubbed 'gringolandia'. It is rarely closed, changes US dollars, is generally helpful and popular with foreign travellers. *El Tuquito* (☎ 23-6770), Putumayo 157, has good seafood.

Don Giovanni on the Plaza de Armas has medium-priced Italian food. *El Mesón* (☎ 23-1197), Napo 116, is a little pricey and serves local specialities. *La Casa de Jaime* (☎ 23-9456) on the Malecón has good local food, steaks and fish.

Entertainment

For a cold beer and recorded and live music, look in the blocks between the Plaza de Armas and the waterfront. The *Marandú Bar* and *Francesco Pub* on the Malecón have both been recommended. *El Amauta Café Bar* (☎ 23-3109), Nauta 250, has live Peruvian music on most nights. *La Pergola*, Napo 735, is a nice bar in a tropical garden and has live music some nights.

For dancing, the *Agricobank* on Condamine a couple of blocks north of the map is a huge outdoor place where hundreds of locals gather to drink, dance and socialise.

Getting There & Away

Air Iquitos has a small airport about eight km from town with flights to Miami and Colombia, as well as local flights. Paucar Tours (next to the Faucett office) and Three Roses Agency, Próspero 246, are recommended travel agents.

Faucett flies Miami-Iquitos-Lima and reverse on Saturday. Faucett has an Iquitos-Cuzco flight on Sunday morning (supposedly direct but usually stopping in Lima) for US$107.

AeroPerú, Faucett, AeroContinente and Americana have offices in town. About six flights a day go to Lima (US$82), two or three a day to Pucallpa (US$46), and almost daily flights go to Tarapoto (US$54). Several flights a week go to Trujillo or Chiclayo (US$65), Yurimaguas (US$53) and other towns.

TANS (☎ 23-4632), Lores 127, flies to Caballococha (US$40) near the Colombian border on Saturday. (**Caballococha** has two simple hotels and daily boats to Leticia, Colombia.) Servicios Aéreos Amazónicos (☎ 23-5776), Arica 273, flies to Caballococha (US$45) and Leticia, Colombia (US$60) on Tuesday, Thursday and Saturday. Flights are often full and subject to delay. Schedules, destinations and fares change frequently so check locally.

Boat Boats leave from Puerto Masusa, on Avenida La Marina, two or three km north of the centre. Boats have blackboards saying when they are leaving and for where. Boats to Pucallpa (six to eight days) or Yurimaguas (four to six days) cost about US$20 to US$30 per person. Boats leave about once a week to Pucallpa, more often to Yurimaguas, less often if the river is low.

Boats to the border with Brazil and Colombia leave every few days, take two to three days and cost under US$20, but gringos have to bargain hard. Expreso Loreto (☎ 23-8652), Loreto 171, has fast launches to the border (US$50, 12 hours) at 6 am on Tuesday, Thursday and Sunday.

Passengers can sleep aboard the boat while waiting for departure. Boats often leave hours or days late!

Getting Around

Buses and trucks for nearby destinations, including the airport, leave from the Plaza 28 de Julio. Taxis to the airport cost US$5 or US$6. Motorcycle taxis *(motocarros)* are cheaper. Motorcycles can be hired (see places on map).

TO/FROM COLOMBIA & BRAZIL

Brazil, Colombia and Peru share a three-way border. The biggest town is Leticia (Colombia), which is linked with Tabatinga (Brazil) by road (it's a short walk). You can freely go from one to the other without border hassles unless you are travelling farther into Brazil or Colombia. Leticia has the best choice of hotels, restaurants and moneychanging facilities, and a hospital. On the south bank of the Amazon, opposite Leticia/Tabatinga, is Santa Rosa (Peru). This is marked on most maps as Ramón Castilla, which is the old port. Because of changes in the flow of the river, Ramón Castilla is no longer on the main Amazon; Santa Rosa is used as the port instead, though there is nowhere to stay here.

Exit formalities when leaving Peru are strict, and Peruvian border officials may send you back to Iquitos if your entry stamp has expired. Riverboats stop at the Peruvian guard post in Santa Rosa for passport formalities, but make sure the captain knows that you need to do this. Check with the immigration office in Iquitos about exit formalities. The Peruvian immigration office moves quite often because of changes in the river.

To enter or leave Colombia, get your passport stamped in Leticia. To enter or leave Brazil, formalities are normally carried out in Tabatinga, although the town of Benjamin Constant, an hour downriver, also has an immigration office. You don't need to get stamps for all three countries – just the one you are leaving and the one you are continuing to. Regulations change, but the boat captains know where to go. Don't try to enter a country without getting the required exit stamp first. You can easily travel between the three countries without having the correct stamps, as long as you stay in the tri-border area. As soon as you leave the border ports, however, your documents must be in order.

Boats to Iquitos leave from Leticia or Tabatinga every few days (about US$20, 2½ days). Alternatively, take the thrice-weekly Rápido Expreso from Leticia (US$50, 14 hours).

Boats to Manaus (Brazil) leave from Tabatinga, then spend a night in Benjamin Constant before continuing. The fare is about US$100 in a shared cabin (less for hanging your own hammock) for the three to six-day trip, including very basic meals; as always, bring your own if you have a sensitive stomach. Bottled soft drinks and beer are usually available. Hammocks are airier, and many travellers prefer them to the stuffy cabins.

Leticia and Tabatinga have airports, with flights into the interiors of Colombia and Brazil, respectively.

PUERTO MALDONADO

Founded at the turn of the century, Puerto Maldonado has been a rubber boom town, a logging centre and, recently, a gold and oil centre. It is an unlovely, fast-growing town with a frontier feel, and is the capital and most important port of the Department of Madre de Dios. The jungle around Puerto Maldonado has been almost totally cleared. The most fun activity is to take the five-minute ferry ride across the Río Madre de Dios.

Information

Migraciones is down by the river. There are no Brazilian or Bolivian consulates. The telephone code is 084.

Places to Stay

Hotels fill up quickly. Foreigners may be overcharged. The following basic, cold-water places are US$2.50 or US$3 each. The clean and friendly *Hostal Moderno* looks run-down and is noisy. It has a café attached, as does the *Hostal Español*. The *Hotel Oriental* is unfriendly. The *Hostal Chávez* is the cheapest and looks it. Also try the *Hotels Tambo de Oro, Central, El Astro* and *Cross*, which are OK and have some rooms with private bath for about US$5/8. The clean and recommended *Hotel Wilson* (☎ 57-1296), G Prada 355, charges US$3.50 each, or US$6/ 10 for a single/double with bath. It has a basic cafeteria. The *Hotel Rey Port* is similarly priced and is just adequate. The *Hostal Royal Inn* has large, clean rooms with bath for US$6/10. Others in this price range are

Río Madre de Dios

Puerto Maldonado

0   100   200 m

PLACES TO STAY
4 Hostal Moderno
6 Hotel Oriental
13 Hostal Cabaña Quinta
14 Hostal Chávez
16 Hotel Rey Port
17 Hostal Español
19 Hostal Royal Inn
22 Hotel Tambo de Oro
24 Hotel del Solar
28 Hotel Wilson
30 Hotel Central,
   Hotel El Astro
33 Hostal Gamboa
34 Hotel Cross

PLACES TO EAT
3 El Mirador
8 El Califa
10 Heladería Trópico
15 El Tenedor
18 Chifa Wa-Seng
21 Huasoroco
32 La Cusqueñita

OTHER
1 River Boat Hire
2 Migraciones
5 AeroPerú Airline
7 Imperial Air
9 Banco de la Nación
11 Banco de Crédito
12 Explorer's Inn Office
20 Americana Airline
23 AeroSul
25 Telefónica del Perú
26 De Los Angeles Agency
27 Casa de Cambio
29 Motorcycle Hire
31 Post Office
35 Trucks to Cuzco,
   buses to Laberinto

the *Hostal Gamboa* and *Hotel del Solar*. The *Hostal Cabaña Quinta* (☎ 57-1863, 57-1864), Cuzco 535, is the best in the centre and has a decent restaurant and friendly staff. Rooms are US$6/10, or US$10/16 with private cold shower.

Places to Eat
Huasoroco serves typical Peruvian food. *El Mirador* has a screened-in dining area overlooking the Río Madre de Dios and has a Friday night peña. *La Cusqueñita* is clean and has a good variety of dishes. *El Tenedor* and *Chifa Wa-Seng* are also satisfactory

cheap places and there are many others that offer a set meal for as low as US$1. *Heladería Trópico* has a helpful staff and serves juices, tropical ice creams, burgers and vegetarian food. It supports local conservation work.

Getting There & Away
Air The airport is seven km out of town. Colectivos from the airport are US$1, mototaxis are US$4. Daily morning flights to Lima (US$94) via Cuzco (US$38) are with AeroPerú, Americana or Imperial Air, but these may get cancelled because of rain.

Grupo Ocho has a Thursday flight to Iberia and flies to Iñapari occasionally. Light aircraft fly wherever you hire them to go to.

Truck Trucks to Cuzco during the dry season leave from the Mercado Modelo. The rough 500-km trip takes three days, depending on road and weather conditions, and costs about US$15.

Boat Boats at the Madre de Dios ferry dock make local excursions and go down to the Bolivian border (US$80 per boat). Upriver boats to Manu are hard to find and expensive.

AROUND PUERTO MALDONADO

The closest lodge to Puerto Maldonado is the *Albergue Tambo Lodge*, 10 km away on the Río Madre de Dios. It has three-day, two-night visits for US$100 per person; extra days are US$35. There's not much virgin jungle but there are tours to Lago Sandoval or to gold-panning areas. Reservations can be made in Cuzco (☎ 23-6159), Plateros 351.

About 15 km away, the more comfortable *Cuzco Amazónico Lodge* has local tours and perhaps a better look at the jungle. Rooms have private cold showers and porch with hammock at US$143 per person for three days and two nights; ask for low-season discounts. There are 18 km of trails in a reserve around the lodge. Reservations for this lodge can be made at Procuradores 48, Cuzco (☎ 23-2161, 23-3769). There are other, pricier, places – none luxurious.

A pleasant jungle lake, **Lago Sandoval**, is two hours from Puerto Maldonado down the Madre de Dios. Half the trip is by boat and half on foot. Bring food and water. A boat will drop you at the beginning of the trail and pick you up later for about US$25 to US$30

(several people can go for this price). The boatman will guide you to the lake if you wish. A cheap lodge recently opened here; ask in Puerto Maldonado. You can arrange various other trips to local lakes, beaches and islands; boats start at about US$30 per day, plus fuel.

TO BRAZIL

A track to Iñapari, on the Brazilian border, is open but the last part is in bad shape. Wet season travel is reportedly not possible but, during the drier months, pick-up trucks leave daily from the north side of the Madre de Dios (US$10, one day). Iberia, 170 km north of Puerto Maldonado, has a couple of basic hotels and weekly air service from Cuzco with Grupo Ocho. Iñapari, 70 km beyond Iberia, has occasional Grupo Ocho flights but most people come by road. There is a basic hotel. From Iñapari, wade across the Río Acre to Assis, Brazil, which has a better hotel and a dry-season road to Brasiléia and Río Branco. Peruvian exit/entry formalities are in Puerto Maldonado.

TO BOLIVIA

Boats can be hired to the Bolivian border at Puerto Pardo (about US$80, half a day). Cheaper passages are available on infrequent cargo boats. From Puerto Heath, on the Bolivian side, it takes several days (even weeks) to arrange a boat (expensive) to Riberalto, where road and air connections are available. Travel in a group to share costs, and avoid the months when the water is too low. Get exit stamps at the Migraciones office in Puerto Maldonado before leaving. Reportedly, Bolivian border officials are unfriendly and demand bribes. Few foreigners go by this route.

PERU

Uruguay

Across the Río de la Plata from Buenos Aires, Uruguay draws many Argentines to the charming town of Colonia, the capital city of Montevideo, and Atlantic beach resorts, but towns along the Río Uruguay are also pleasant. Uruguay's hilly interior is gaucho country.

The República Oriental del Uruguay (Eastern Republic of Uruguay) was long called the Banda Oriental (Eastern Shore) of the Río de la Plata.

Facts about the Country

HISTORY

The aboriginal Charrúa Indians, a hunter-gatherer people who also fished, deterred European settlement – in part because the Spaniards, as William Henry Hudson wrote, 'loved gold and adventure above everything, and finding neither in the Banda, they little esteemed it'. As on the Argentine Pampas, gauchos subsisted on wild cattle until *estancias* pushed them back into the interior.

European Colonisation

Jesuit missionaries settled near Soriano, on the Río Uruguay, but in 1680 Portugal established Nova Colônia do Sacramento on the Río de la Plata. This challenge forced Spain to build its own citadel at Montevideo.

National hero José Artigas fought against Spain, but could not prevent a Brazilian takeover of the Banda. Exiled to Paraguay, he inspired the '33 Orientales' who, with Argentine support, liberated the area in 1828, establishing Uruguay as an independent buffer between the emerging continental powers.

Independence & Development

Uruguay's neighbours threatened its fragile political independence, while Britain menaced its economic autonomy. The

Country Name República Oriental del Uruguay
Area 176,215 sq km
Population 3.2 million
Population Density 18.1 per sq km
Capital Montevideo
Head of State President Julio María Sanguinetti
Official Languages Spanish
Other Languages Portuguese, Fronterizo
Currency Peso ($)
Exchange Rate US$1 = Ur$7.93
Per Capita GNP US$7200
Inflation Rate 35%

Argentine dictator Rosas besieged Montevideo from 1838 to 1851; Uruguay's major political parties, the Blancos and Colorados, originated as armed gaucho sympathisers of Federalist and Unitarist causes. As Hudson wrote, 'Endless struggles for mastery ensued, in which the Argentines and Brazilians, forgetting their solemn compact, were for ever taking sides'.

The Liebig Meat Extract Company of London started operations at Fray Bentos in

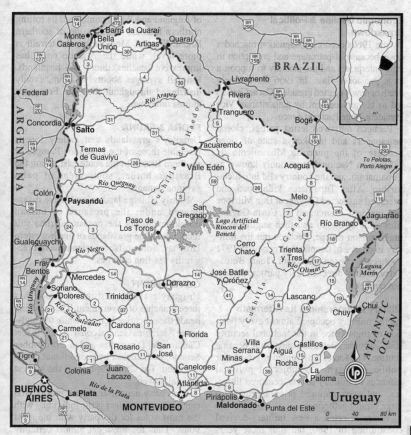

1864 and merino wool brought further opportunities. In 1868 a British railway connected Montevideo with the countryside, where Hereford and shorthorn cattle replaced rangy criollo stock. At the turn of the century, Fray Bentos' massive Anglo plant was the country's first *frigorífico*. Commercialisation of livestock meant the demise of the gaucho and the rise of the *latifundios* or large landholdings.

Batlle & the Modernisation of Uruguay

In the early 20th century, the visionary President José Batlle y Ordóñez achieved such innovations as pensions, farm credits, unemployment compensation and eight-hour working days. State intervention led to the nationalisation of many industries, the creation of others, and general prosperity. Taxing the livestock sector financed Batlle's reforms, but when this sector faltered the welfare state crumbled.

Conservatives blamed the state for 'killing the goose that laid the golden egg', but even earlier, landowners squandered their wealth in conspicuous consumption rather than reinvest it to increase productivity. Redistributive policies worked only as long as there was something to redistribute.

Economic Decline & Political Breakdown

By the 1960s economic stagnation reached a crisis because of patronage and corruption in state enterprises and the inability to support a large pensioner class. In 1966 the untimely death of newly elected President Oscar Gestido led to his replacement by authoritarian Vice President Jorge Pacheco Areco.

Pacheco outlawed leftist parties, closed newspapers and invoked a state of siege because of the guerrilla Movimiento de Liberación Nacional (commonly known as Tupamaros), and the country slid into dictatorship. After Tupamaros kidnapped and executed suspected CIA agent Dan Mitrione (an incident dramatised in Costa-Gavras' film *State of Siege*) and then engineered a major prison escape, Pacheco put the military in charge of counterinsurgency. In 1971 Pacheco's chosen successor, Juan Bordaberry, invited direct military participation in government.

Military Dictatorship & Its Aftermath

As the military occupied almost every position of importance in the 'national security state', arbitrary detention and torture became routine. The forces determined eligibility for public employment, subjected political offences to military courts, censored libraries, and even required prior approval for large family gatherings.

Voters rejected a new military-devised constitution in 1980, but four more years passed before Colorado candidate Julio María Sanguinetti became President under the previous constitution. His presidency implied a return to democratic traditions, but he also supported a controversial amnesty, approved by voters in 1989, for military human rights abuses.

Later in 1989, the Blancos' Luis Lacalle succeeded Sanguinetti in a peaceful transition of power, while Sanguinetti returned to office at the head of a coalition government in November 1994.

GEOGRAPHY & CLIMATE

Uruguay's 176,000 sq km are about the size of England and Wales combined. Its rolling northern hills are an extension of southern Brazil. West of Montevideo, the terrain is more level, while the Atlantic coast has impressive beaches, dunes and headlands. Rainfall averages about 1000 mm, evenly distributed throughout the year. Frosts are almost unknown.

FLORA & FAUNA

Uruguay's grasslands and gallery forests resemble those of the Argentine Pampas or southern Brazil. In the south-east, along the Brazilian border, some areas of palm savanna remain.

Nearly all large land animals have disappeared under the pressure of human development, but the occasional rhea still races across the grasslands of north-western Uruguay. Some offshore islands have noteworthy sea-lion colonies.

GOVERNMENT

Uruguay's 1967 constitution establishes three branches of government. The president heads the executive branch, while the legislative Asamblea General consists of a 99-seat Cámara de Diputados and a 30-member Senado, both chosen by proportional representation. The Corte Suprema is the highest judicial power.

Each party may offer several presidential candidates; the winner is the individual with the most votes for the party with the most votes. Thus the president almost certainly lacks a majority and may not be the candidate with the most overall votes. In eight elections from 1946 to 1984, no candidate won over 31%.

The major political parties are the Colorados (heirs of Batlle) and the generally more conservative Blancos, who have alternated in the presidency since the end of the dictatorship and now form a coalition government at the national level. The leftist coalition Frente Amplio, now the official opposition, also controls the mayoralty of Montevideo.

ECONOMY

Low prices for wool, the primary export,

have caused problems in recent years. Only the south-west littoral has intensive agriculture, but this cropland makes a major economic contribution. Many inefficient industries produce inferior products at high cost, surviving only because of protective tariffs. Tourism is increasingly important, as beaches east of Montevideo attract many Argentines.

In many ways, Uruguay is an economic satellite of both Brazil and Argentina. With those two countries and Paraguay, it now forms the new Mercosur common market. Conceivably, by encouraging investment and creating jobs, Mercosur could reduce emigration of youthful talent, but it will also destroy subsidised industries. Pensions consume 60% of public expenditure. Inflation remains high by European standards, and Uruguay has one of the region's largest per capita debt burdens.

POPULATION & PEOPLE

About 85% of Uruguay's 3.2 million people reside in cities, almost half of them in Montevideo. Most Uruguayans are of Spanish and Italian origin, but there are 60,000 Afro-Uruguayans who are descended from slaves.

Infant mortality is low and the life expectancy of 75 years is comparable to that of many Western European countries, but economic hardship has forced half a million Uruguayans to leave the country, mostly for Brazil and Argentina.

ARTS

For a small country, Uruguay has an impressive literary and artistic tradition; for details on literature, see Books in the Facts for the Visitor section. Theatre is also a popular medium and playwrights like Mauricio Rosencof are prominent.

Uruguay's most renowned artist was the late painter Joaquín Torres García. Punta Ballena, near Punta del Este, is a well-known artists' colony.

RELIGION

Uruguayans are almost exclusively Roman Catholic, but the Church lacks official status.

A Jewish minority, about 25,000, live almost exclusively in Montevideo. Evangelical Protestantism has made some inroads.

LANGUAGE

Spanish is official, but along the Brazilian border many people also speak Portuguese or the hybrid *fronterizo*.

Facts for the Visitor

VISAS & EMBASSIES

All foreigners need visas, except those from bordering countries (who need only national ID cards) and nationals of Western Europe, Israel, Japan and the USA. All visitors need a tourist card, valid for 90 days and renewable for 90 more. For extensions, visit the Dirección Nacional de Migración (☎ 96-0471), Misiones 1513 in Montevideo.

Uruguayan Embassies Abroad

Uruguay's network of diplomatic representatives is less extensive than Argentina's. It has representatives in neighbouring countries and in:

Australia
    1st floor, MLC Tower, Keltie St (GPO Box 318), Woden, ACT 2606 (☎ (06) 282-4800)
Canada
    Suite 1905, 130 Albert St, Ottawa, Ontario (☎ (613) 234-2937)
France
    15 rue Le Sueur, Paris (☎ 01 45 00 81 37)
Germany
    Gotenstrasse 1-3, Bonn 2 (☎ (0228) 35 65 70)
UK
    140 Brompton Rd, 2nd floor, London SW3 1HY (☎ (0171) 584-8192, Consulate: 589-8735)
USA
    1918 F St NW, Washington, DC (☎ (202) 331-4219)

Foreign Embassies in Uruguay

South American countries, the USA and most Western European countries have representatives in Montevideo, but Australians and New Zealanders must rely on their embassies in Buenos Aires.

URUGUAY

For Argentine and Brazilian consulates in border towns, see the appropriate town sections. For other countries, see the Montevideo section.

CUSTOMS

Customs regulations permit the entry of used personal effects and other articles in 'reasonable quantities'.

MONEY

The unit of currency is the *peso* ($), which replaced the *peso nuevo* (N$) of a few years back. Older banknotes of N$5000 and N$10,000 are still in circulation; deduct three zeros to get current values. There are coins of five, 10, 20 and 50 *centésimos*, and one, two and five pesos. Older coins of N$100, N$200 and N$500 still in circulation are worth 10, 20 and 50 centésimos.

Cambios in Montevideo, Colonia and Atlantic beach resorts change US dollars cash and travellers' cheques (the latter at slightly lower rates or modest commissions). Banks are the rule in the interior. Better hotels, restaurants and shops accept credit cards, but Uruguayan ATMs reject North American or European credit cards. There is no black market.

Annual inflation is about 45%, but steady devaluations keep prices from rising rapidly in dollar terms. Costs are slightly lower than in Argentina, especially with respect to accommodation and transportation.

Exchange Rates

Rates in July 1996 included the following:

Australia	A$1	=	Ur$6.22
Canada	Can$1	=	Ur$5.81
France	FF1	=	Ur$1.53
Germany	DM1	=	Ur$5.18
Japan	¥100	=	Ur$7.30
New Zealand	NZ$1	=	Ur$5.39
United Kingdom	UK£1	=	Ur$12.22
USA	US$1	=	Ur$7.93

WHEN TO GO

Uruguay's main attraction is its beaches, so most visitors come in summer. Along the littoral, summer temperatures are smotheringly hot, but the hilly interior is cooler, especially at night.

TOURIST OFFICES

Almost every municipality has a tourist office, usually on the plaza or at the bus terminal. Maps are mediocre, but many brochures have excellent historical information.

Foreign Representatives

Foreign residents can direct enquiries to the following addresses:

Australia
　　Direct tourist inquiries to the Uruguayan Consulate-General, GPO Box 717, Sydney, NSW 2001 (☎ (02) 9251-5544)
Canada
　　Suite 1905, 130 Albert St, Ottawa, Ontario (☎ (613) 234-2937)
UK
　　Tourist information can be obtained from the Uruguayan Embassy, 140 Brompton Rd, 2nd floor, London SW3 1HY (☎ (0171) 584-8192)
USA
　　541 Lexington Ave, New York, NY (☎ (212) 755-1200, ext 346)
　　1918 F St NW, Washington, DC (☎ (202) 331-1313)

USEFUL ORGANISATIONS

Uruguay's limited youth-hostel network can be an alternative to standard accommodation. Contact the Asociación de Alberguistas del Uruguay (☎ 40-4245), Pablo de María 1583, Montevideo.

BUSINESS HOURS & HOLIDAYS

Most shops open on weekdays and on Saturday from 8.30 am to 12.30 or 1 pm, then close until mid-afternoon and reopen until 7 or 8 pm. Food shops also open on Sunday mornings.

Government offices vary: from mid-November to mid-March, they open from 7.30 am to 1.30 pm; the rest of the year, it's noon to 7 pm. Banks are open on weekday afternoons in Montevideo; elsewhere, mornings are the rule.

Public Holidays

1 January
Año Nuevo (New Year's Day)
6 January
Epifanía (Epiphany)
March/April (dates vary)
Viernes Santo/Pascua (Good Friday/Easter)
19 April
Desembarco de los 33 (Return of the 33 Exiles)
1 May
Día del Trabajador (Labour Day)
18 May
Batalla de Las Piedras (Battle of Las Piedras)
19 June
Natalicio de Artigas (Artigas' Birthday)
18 July
Jura de la Constitución (Constitution Day)
25 August
Día de la Independencia (Independence Day)
12 October
Día de la Raza (Columbus Day)
2 November
Día de los Muertos (All Souls' Day)
25 December
Navidad (Christmas Day)

SPECIAL EVENTS

Uruguay's Carnaval, the Monday and Tuesday before Ash Wednesday, is livelier than in Argentina but more sedate than in Brazil. The Afro-Uruguayan population of Montevideo's Barrio Sur celebrates traditional *candomblé* ceremonies. Holy Week (Easter) is also La Semana Criolla, with gaucho *asados* (barbecues) and folk music.

POST & COMMUNICATIONS

Postal rates are reasonable but service is poor. Send important items registered. For poste restante, address mail to the main post office in Montevideo.

Antel, the state telephone monopoly, has central long-distance offices in every town. As in Argentina, public telephones take *fichas* (tokens), each good for about three minutes. More convenient magnetic cards are also available.

International discount rates are in effect between 10 pm and 7 am on weekdays, from midnight to 7 am and 1 pm to midnight on Saturday, and all day Sunday.

Credit-card or reverse-charge (collect) calls to overseas destinations are cheaper than paying locally; the list below gives the numbers of foreign direct operators for them:

Canada	☎ 000419
France	☎ 000433
Italy	☎ 000439
Spain	☎ 000434
United Kingdom	☎ 000444
USA – AT&T	☎ 000410
USA – MCI	☎ 000412
USA – Sprint	☎ 000417

TIME

Like Argentina, Uruguay is three hours behind GMT/UTC.

ELECTRICITY

Electric current operates on 220V, 50 Hz.

WEIGHTS & MEASURES

The metric system is official.

BOOKS

Uruguay's major contemporary writers are Juan Carlos Onetti, whose novels *No Man's Land*, *The Shipyard* and *A Brief Life* are available in English, and poet, essayist and novelist Mario Benedetti. Journalist Eduardo Galeano *(Open Veins of Latin America)* is also Uruguayan.

History

For a discussion of Uruguay's welfare system, see George Pendle's *Uruguay; South America's First Welfare State* or Milton Vanger's *The Model Country: Jose Batlle y Ordóñez of Uruguay, 1907-1915*.

William Henry Hudson's *The Purple Land* is a 19th-century classic.

Contemporary Government & Politics

A good starting point is Martin Weinstein's *Uruguay, Democracy at the Crossroads*. For an account of Uruguay's own Dirty War, see Lawrence Weschler's *A Miracle, A Universe: Settling Accounts with Torturers*.

MAPS

See the Automóvil Club Uruguayo, Shell and Ancap for the best available road maps. For more detail, try Montevideo's Instituto

URUGUAY

Geográfico Militar (☎ 81-6868), at 12 de Octubre and Abreu.

MEDIA

Montevideo dailies include the morning *El Día*, *La República*, *La Mañana* and *El País*. *Gaceta Comercial* is the voice of the business community. Afternoon papers are *El Diario*, *Mundocolor* and *Ultimas Noticias*, the latter operated by followers of Sun Myung Moon. Most are identified with political parties, but the weekly *Búsqueda* takes a more independent stance.

There are 20 TV stations (four in Montevideo) and 100 radio stations (about 40 in the capital).

ACTIVITIES

Conventional beach activities like swimming and fishing are the major options for visitors to Uruguay, but surfing is possible on the outer Atlantic beaches.

HIGHLIGHTS

The narrow streets and port zone of Montevideo's Ciudad Vieja (Old City), currently being redeveloped, have immense colonial charm. Besides sophisticated resorts and broad sandy beaches, the Atlantic coast also has scenic headlands. Up the estuary of the Río de la Plata, the colonial contraband port of Colonia is one of the continent's least known treasures.

ACCOMMODATION

Accommodation options, hotels and residenciales, are essentially the same as those in Argentina. Uruguay has a substantial network of youth hostels, and many camping grounds, especially along the coast.

FOOD & DRINKS

Parrillas, *confiterías*, *pizzerías* and restaurants resemble their Argentine namesakes. Montevideo, Punta del Este and other beach resorts have good international restaurants. Seafood is usually a good choice.

The standard short order is *chivito*, a steak sandwich with cheese, lettuce, tomato, bacon and condiments. *Chivito al plato* is a larger steak topped with a fried egg, plus potato salad, green salad and chips. Other typical items are *olímpicos* (club sandwiches), *húngaros* (spicy sausages) and blander *panchos* (hot dogs).

Uruguayans consume even more *mate* than Argentines and Paraguayans. *Clericó* is a mixture of white wine and fruit juice, while *medio y medio* is a mixture of sparkling wine and white wine. Beer is also good.

Getting There & Away

AIR
To/From the USA

From Miami, Lapsa has three flights weekly with a long stopover and change of planes in Asunción. Lloyd Aéreo Boliviano has slightly better connections, twice weekly, via Santa Cruz de la Sierra. All other flights pass through Buenos Aires.

To/From Europe

Pluna, the privatised national carrier, has Thursday and Sunday flights from Madrid via Rio de Janeiro. KLM flies from Amsterdam via Rio and São Paulo on Wednesday and Sunday, but all other carriers stop in Buenos Aires.

To/From Neighbouring Countries

There are frequent flights from Montevideo's Aeropuerto Internacional Carrasco to Buenos Aires' Aeroparque Jorge Newbery, as well as from Punta del Este and Colonia to Aeroparque.

Pluna flies to Brazilian destinations, including Porto Alegre, Florianópolis, Rio de Janeiro and São Paulo. Varig has similar routes, some flights continuing to Bahia and Recife.

To/From Other South American Countries

Pluna flies to Asunción, Paraguay (twice weekly) and to Santiago, Chile (three times). Lapsa flies to Asunción three times weekly, while Lloyd Aéreo Boliviano flies on

Sunday to Santa Cruz de la Sierra, and on Sunday and Wednesday to Asunción and Santa Cruz de la Sierra.

LAND

Uruguay shares borders with Argentina's Entre Ríos province and the Brazilian state of Rio Grande do Sul.

To/From Argentina

Buses to Buenos Aires via Gualeguaychú are slower and less convenient than crossing the Río de la Plata by boat. For other crossings of the Río Uruguay see the Getting There & Away section in the Argentina chapter.

To/From Brazil

Chuy to Chuí & Pelotas Only a median strip separates the twin cities of Chuy and Chuí, on the main highway from Montevideo.

Río Branco to Jaguarão This alternative route goes via Treinta y Tres or Melo. There are buses from Jaguarão to Pelotas.

Rivera to Livramento This route from Paysandú goes via Tacuarembó. Buses continue from Livramento to Porto Alegre.

Artigas to Quaraí This route crosses the Río Quareim, but the main highway goes south-east to Livramento.

Bella Unión to Barra do Quaraí This north-western crossing leads to Uruguaiana, Brazil, opposite Paso de los Libres in Argentina's Corrientes province.

RIVER

Several crossings link Uruguay to Argentina:

Montevideo to Buenos Aires High-speed ferries connect the two capitals in about 2½ hours (US$37 one way).

Colonia to Buenos Aires Morning and evening ferries between Colonia and Buenos Aires (2½ hours) cost US$11. Faster hydrofoils (45 minutes) are dearer.

Carmelo & Nueva Palmira to Tigre There are launches across the Plata estuary to the Buenos Aires suburb of Tigre.

LEAVING URUGUAY

Air

International passengers pay a departure tax of US$2.50 to Argentina, US$6 to other South American countries, and US$7 to other destinations.

River

Montevideo passengers pay a US$5 port terminal and departure tax, while those from Colonia pay US$3.

Getting Around

AIR

Pluna flies to Punta del Este, while Aviasur and the inexpensive military airline Tamu serve the interior cities of Artigas, Salto, Rivera, Paysandú, Melo and Tacuarembó.

BUS

Most cities lack central terminals, but companies are usually within walking distance of the plaza. Buses are so frequent that reservations are rarely necessary. Fares are reasonable: Montevideo to Fray Bentos (300 km) costs only about US$8.

CAR

Uruguayan drivers are less ruthless than Argentines, but there are many Argentines on the road. Uruguay ostensibly requires the Inter-American Driving Permit rather than the International Driving Permit. Arbitrary stops and searches are less common than in Argentina, but police do solicit bribes for traffic violations.

Car rental costs about the same as in Argentina. The Automóvil Club del Uruguay (☎ 91-1251), at Colonia and Yí in Montevideo, has good maps and information.

LOCAL TRANSPORT

Bus

To make sense of Montevideo's extensive public transport, consult routes and schedules in the yellow pages of the telephone directory. Retain your ticket for inspection. The standard fare is about US$0.45.

Taxi

Drivers correlate meter readings with a photocopied fare chart. Fares are higher from midnight to 6 am. There is a small additional

URUGUAY

luggage charge, and passengers generally round off the fare.

Montevideo

Founded in 1726 as a response to Colonia, Montevideo soon became an important port. In the 19th century, it endured a long siege by the Argentine dictator Rosas, but normal commerce resumed after his fall in 1851. Montevideo absorbed many immigrants from Spain and Italy in the early 20th century.

Many refugees from rural poverty live in *conventillos*, large, older houses converted into multifamily slum dwellings, in the colonial Ciudad Vieja. Urban redevelopment is displacing people from this picturesque and valuable central area.

Orientation

Montevideo lies on the east bank of the Río de La Plata. Its functional centre is Plaza Independencia, east of the Ciudad Vieja. Avenida 18 de Julio is its most important commercial and entertainment area. At the north-east end of 18 de Julio, Parque José Batlle y Ordóñez contains a 75,000-seat stadium, the Estadio Centenario. Perpendicular to its terminus is the major artery of Bulevar Artigas.

Across the harbour, the 132-metre Cerro de Montevideo was a landmark for early navigators. To the east, the riverfront Rambla leads past residential suburbs and sandy beaches frequented by *montevideños* in summer and on weekends.

Information

Tourist Office The Ministerio de Turismo (☎ 90-4148) maintains a cubbyhole office on the ground floor at Avenida Lavalleja 1409. Its Oficina de Informes (☎ 41-8998) at Terminal Tres Cruces, the new bus station at Bulevar Artigas and Avenida Italia, is open daily from 7 am to 11 pm and is better prepared to deal with inquiries. The useful *Guía del Ocio*, listing cultural events,

cinemas, theatres and restaurants, comes with the Friday edition of *El País*.

Money There are many cambios on Avenida 18 de Julio.

Post & Communications The Correo Central (main post office) is at Buenos Aires 451. Antel has offices at San José 1108 (open 24 hours) and Rincón 501.

Foreign Embassies Countries with diplomatic representation in Montevideo include:

Argentina
  WF Aldunate 1281 (☎ 90-0897)
Brazil
  Convención 1343, 6th floor (☎ 98-1713)
Canada
  Tagle 2828 (☎ 95-8583)
France
  Avenida Uruguay 853 (☎ 92-0077/8)
Germany
  La Cumparsita 1435 (☎ 91-3970)
United Kingdom
  Marco Bruto 1073 (☎ 62-3630)
USA
  Lauro Muller 1776 (☎ 23-6061)

Bookshops Linardi y Risso, Juan Carlos Gómez 1435, has many out-of-print items in history and literature. The Librería Inglesa-Británica, Sarandí 580, has a selection in English.

Medical Services The Hospital Maciel (☎ 95-6810) is at 25 de Mayo and Maciel, in the Ciudad Vieja.

Walking Tour

On **Plaza Independencia**, a huge statue of the country's greatest hero tops the **Mausoleo de Artigas**. The 18th-century **Palacio Estévez** served as the Casa de Gobierno until 1985, while the 26-storey **Palacio Salvo**, on the east side, was once South America's tallest building. Just off the plaza, the **Teatro Solís** is Montevideo's leading theatre.

Beyond the remnant colonial **Puerta de la Ciudadela**, Calle Sarandí leads to **Plaza Constitución**, where the **Iglesia Matriz**

(Cathedral), at Sarandí and Ituzaingó, is the city's oldest public building (1799). Continue to **Casa Rivera**, corner of Rincón and Misiones, the **Museo Romántico**, 25 de Mayo 428, and **Casa Lavalleja**, corner of Zabala and 25 de Mayo, all part of the Museo Histórico Nacional. Half a block west is **Casa Garibaldi**, where the Italian hero once lived. From nearby **Plaza Zabala**, continue along Washington to Colón and then to Piedras and the **Mercado del Puerto** (see below).

Museo del Gaucho y de la Moneda
In the Banco de la República, Avenida 18 de Julio 998, this museum displays artefacts of Uruguay's gaucho past. It's open Tuesday to Friday from 9.30 am to 12.30 pm, and Tuesday to Sunday from 3.30 to 7.30 pm.

Museo Torres García
This museum in the Ciudad Vieja, on the *peatonal* (pedestrian mall) at Sarandí 683, displays the works of Joaquín Torres García, who spent much of his career in France producing abstract and even cubist work like that of Picasso, as well as unusual portraits of historical figures such as Columbus, Mozart, and Beethoven. It's open on weekdays from 3 to 7 pm and on Saturday from 11 am to 1 pm; admission is free.

Mercado del Puerto
At the foot of Calle Pérez Castellano, the wrought-iron superstructure of this port market (1868) shelters a gaggle of modest parrillas and finer seafood restaurants. On Saturdays, it's a lively place frequented by artists and musicians.

Special Events
Montevideo's Carnaval takes place the first Monday and Tuesday after Ash Wednesday.

Places to Stay
Hostel The official *Albergue Juvenil* (☎ 98-1324), Canelones 935, costs US$8 with hostel card. It has kitchen facilities, a lounge and an 11 pm curfew.

Hospedajes & Hotels The simple but friendly *Hospedaje Solís* (☎ 95-0437), Bartolomé Mitre 1314, charges only US$8 for spacious singles with shared bath; those with private bath cost US$20.

The centrally located *Hotel Nuevo Ideal* (☎ 98-2913), Soriano 1073, has mildewy singles/doubles with private bath for US$13/18. For US$10/13 with shared bath, slightly more with private bath, *Hospedaje del Centro* (☎ 90-1419), Soriano 1126, is clean but declining. *Hotel Ideal* (☎ 91-6389), Colonia 914, is clean and friendly with good baths; singles/doubles with shared bath cost US$15/20, with private bath US$18/25.

Not the value it once was, *Hotel Palacio* (☎ 96-3612), Bartolomé Mitre 1364, may be living on reputation after unwarranted price increases. Singles cost US$17 with shared bath, but the 6th-floor rooms, with huge balconies, are worth a look. Across the street, the friendly *Hospedaje Nuevo Savoy* has bright doubles with shared bath for US$10, with private bath for US$12, but some rooms are windowless and it can be noisy at times.

Probably the best mid-range value is *Hotel Mediterráneo* (☎ 90-5090), Paraguay 1486, charging US$30/40 with breakfast for well-kept rooms with excellent service. The pleasant, comparably priced *Hotel Aramaya* (☎ 98-6192) is at Avenida 18 de Julio 1103.

Places to Eat
Reasonably priced, worthwhile restaurants in the city centre include *Morini*, Ciudadela 1229; *Mesón Viejo Sancho*, San José 1229; and *Del Ferrocarril* at Río Negro 1746.

Central parrillas include *El Fogón* at San José 1080, *Las Brasas* at San José 909, and the many stalls at the Mercado del Puerto. The recommended *Shorthorn Grill*, Avenida Uruguay 1923, has moderate prices and excellent service. For vegetarian alternatives, try *La Vegetariana* at Yí 1334 and San José 1056, *Natura* at Rincón 414, or *Vida Natural* at San José 1184.

La Genovesa, San José 1262, has good seafood with abundant portions. *La Posada del Puerto* has two stalls in the Mercado del

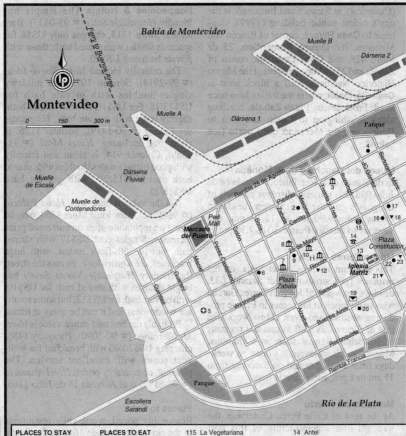

PLACES TO STAY	PLACES TO EAT	115 La Vegetariana	14 Antel
20 Hotel City	12 Natura	116 La Genovesa	15 Banco La Caja Obrera
28 Hotel Arapey	18 Olivier	118 Mesón del Club Español	16 Linardi y Risso (Bookshop)
31 Hotel Mediterráneo	21 Confitería de la Corte	122 El Horreo	17 Barreiro y Ramos
32 Residencial Acevedo	23 Confitería La Pasiva		19 Correo Central
42 Hotel Ideal	24 Club Alemán	OTHER	(Main Post Office)
54 Hotel Aramaya	25 Club Libanés	1 Ferry Port	22 Librería Inglesa-Británica
57 Hotel Ateneo	30 La Camargue	2 Dirección Nacional	26 French Consulate
60 Hospedaje El Aguila,	38 Oro del Rhin	de Migración	27 Autocar
Pensión Catalunya	59 Pizza Bros	3 Museo Municipal de la	29 Budget Rent A Car
63 Hospedaje Nuevo Savoy	73 Mercado Central,	Construcción Tomás Toribio	33 Kodak Uruguaya
64 Hotel Palacio	Restaurant Morini	4 Casa Mario	34 National Rent A Car
70 Hospedaje Solís	77 Oriente	5 Hospital Maciel	35 Hertz Rent A Car
80 Hotel Español	78 Las Brasas	6 Casa Garibaldi	36 Chilean Consulate
81 Hotel Cervantes	82 La Suiza	7 Palacio Taranco,	37 Aerolíneas Argentinas
83 Albergue Juvenil	94 El Fogón	Museo de Arte Decorativo	39 Peletería Holandesa
87 Hotel Casablanca	95 La Vegetariana	8 Casa Lavalleja	40 Dollar Rent A Car
96 Hotel Nuevo Ideal	106 Ruffino	9 Teatro El Picadero	41 Intendencia Municipal de Rocha
103 Hotel Royal	107 Vida Natural	10 Museo Romántico	43 Barreiro y Ramos
112 Hotel Windsor	108 Taberna Vasca	11 Casa Rivera	44 Turisport (American Express)
114 Hotel Libertad	110 Mesón Viejo Sancho	13 Cabildo, Museo y Archivo	45 Tamu, Iberia
		Histórico Municipal	

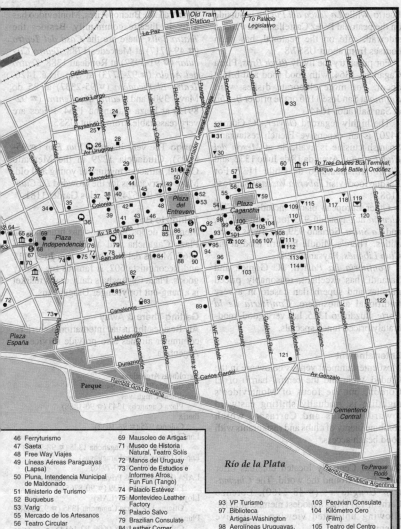

46 Ferryturismo	69 Mausoleo de Artigas
47 Saeta	71 Museo de Historia
48 Free Way Viajes	Natural, Teatro Solís
49 Líneas Aéreas Paraguayas	72 Manos del Uruguay
(Lapsa)	73 Centro de Estudios e
50 Pluna, Intendencia Municipal	Informes Afros,
de Maldonado	Fun Fun (Tango)
51 Ministerio de Turismo	75 Montevideo Leather
52 Buquebus	Factory
53 Varig	76 Palacio Salvo
55 Mercado de los Artesanos	79 Brazilian Consulate
56 Teatro Circular	84 Leather Corner
58 Museo Pedagógico	85 Museo del Gaucho y de
José Pedro Varela	la Moneda, Centro Cultural
61 Automóvil Club del Uruguay,	Uruguayo-Brasileiro
Museo del Automóvil	86 Peletería Holandesa
62 Mercado de los Artesanos	88 Carlos Andersen (Jeweler)
65 Museo Torres García	89 Centro Artesanal
66 American Airlines	90 Argentine Consulate
67 Exprinter (Cambio,	91 Cambio Gales
Travel Agency)	92 Bolivian Consulate
68 Puerta de la Ciudadela	

93 VP Turismo	103 Peruvian Consulate
97 Biblioteca	104 Kilómetro Cero
Artigas-Washington	(Film)
98 Aerolíneas Uruguayas,	105 Teatro del Centro
Líneas Aéreas Privadas	109 Technifilm
Argentinas (LAPA),	(Camera Repair)
Lloyd Aéreo Boliviano	111 Lobezón
(LAB)	113 Alianza Francesa
99 LanChile	117 Multicar
100 Indamex, Viajes COT,	119 Post Office
Balmoral Plaza Hotel	120 Palacio Municipal
101 Manos del Uruguay	121 La Cumparsita
102 Antel	(Tango Nightclub)

Río de la Plata

To Parque
Rodó

Puerto, while *La Tasca del Puerto* is outside on the peatonal Pérez Castellano. *La Proa*, a sidewalk café on the peatonal, has main courses from about US$7/8.

For pizza, try the lively *Pizza Bros*, Plaza Cagancha 1364, with good food and bright decor. For more elaborate dishes, visit *Ruffino* at San José 1166 or the pricier *Bellini* at San Salvador 1644.

The highly regarded *Olivier*, JC Gómez 1420, is an expensive French restaurant. Spanish cuisine is available at *Mesón del Club Español*, Avenida 18 de Julio 1332, and *El Horreo*, Santiago de Chile 1137. For Basque food, visit *Taberna Vasca* at San José 1168.

Other European places include the *Club Alemán* at Paysandú 935 for German food, and *La Suiza*, Soriano 939, for Swiss specialities. There's Middle Eastern food at the *Club Libanés*, Paysandú 898.

Confitería La Pasiva, JC Gómez and Sarandí, has excellent, reasonably priced minutas and superb flan casero in a very traditional atmosphere. *Confitería de la Corte*, Ituzaingó 1325, has very good, moderately priced lunch specials.

Entertainment

Most entertainment venues below are in the Ciudad Vieja and the central barrio of El Cordón, but the focus of Montevideo's nightlife is gradually shifting eastward toward Pocitos and Carrasco, which combine plenty of clubs and restaurants with good beach access.

Cinemas Centrally located cinemas offer films from around the world. The *Cinemateca Uruguaya* (☎ 48-2460), Lorenzo Carnelli 1311, has a modest membership fee allowing unlimited viewing at its five cinemas.

Music *Tin-Pan-Alley* (☎ 48-4736), Jackson 872, is an informal place for live blues and rock'n'roll. *Lobezón* (☎ 91-1334), Zelmar Michelini 1264, is a popular pub hang-out which also serves meals.

Theatre Like Buenos Aires, Montevideo has a lively theatre community. Besides the *Teatro Solís*, there are the *Casa del Teatro* (☎ 49-0717) at Mercedes 1788, *Teatro Circular* (☎ 91-5952) at Rondeau 1388, *Teatro del Anglo* (☎ 92-3773) at San José 1426, *Teatro El Picadero* (☎ 95-2337) at 25 de Mayo 390, and *Teatro del Centro* (☎ 92-8915) at Plaza Cagancha 1164. Prices are very reasonable, from about US$5.

Tango The very informal *Fun Fun* (☎ 95-8005), Ciudadela 1229 in the Mercado Central, attracts a mixture of young and old. Make reservations for the crowded *La Cumparsita* (☎ 91-6245), Carlos Gardel 1181.

Things to Buy

Mercado de los Artesanos has branches on Plaza Cagancha and at Bartolomé Mitre 1367. Manos del Uruguay, at San José 1111 and Reconquista 602, is famous for quality goods. Plaza Cagancha's daily crafts market is a hang-out for younger Uruguayans.

Getting There & Away

Air Besides the usual international carriers, commuter airlines also provide services to Argentina.

Aerolíneas Argentinas
    Colonia 851 (☎ 91-9466)
Aerolíneas Uruguayas
    Plaza Cagancha 1343 (☎ 90-1868)
Iberia
    Colonia 975 (☎ 98-1032)
LanChile
    11th floor, Plaza Cagancha 1335 (☎ 98-2727)
Lapsa (Líneas Aéreas Paraguayas)
    Colonia 1001 (☎ 90-7946)
LAPA (Líneas Aéreas Privadas Argentinas)
    Plaza Cagancha 1339 (☎ 90-8765)
Lloyd Aéreo Boliviano (LAB)
    Oficina 119, Plaza Cagancha 1335 (☎ 92-2656)
Pluna
    Colonia 1021 (☎ 98-0606, 92-1414)
Saeta
    Colonia 981 (☎ 91-3570)
Varig
    Río Negro 1362 (☎ 98-2321)

LAPA (☎ 90-8765), Plaza Cagancha 1339, runs a bus-and-plane combination to Colonia and Buenos Aires' Aeroparque (US$30.50). Aerolíneas Regionales Uruguayas (☎ 93-1608), Yí 1435, flies to Colonia and Aeroparque.

Aviasur (☎ 61-4618), at Carrasco only, and the inexpensive military airline Tamu (☎ 90-0904; 60-8383 at Carrasco), Colonia 959, fly several times weekly to interior destinations which include Salto and Paysandú.

Bus Montevideo's new Terminal Tres Cruces (☎ 41-8998), at Bulevar Artigas and Avenida Italia, has superseded the individual bus terminals that once cluttered and congested Plaza Cagancha and nearby side streets, but most companies have kept offices in the centre of town. Tres Cruces has decent restaurants, clean toilets, a left-luggage counter, public telephones, a cambio and other services. .

Domestic COT (☎ 49-4949) has over 20 buses daily to Piriápolis (US$4), Maldonado and Punta del Este (US$6, 2½ hours); Copsa (☎ 48-1521) also goes to Maldonado. COT also runs nine buses daily to Colonia (US$7, 2½ hours) and goes to Rocha (US$8) and La Paloma (US$9).

Agencia Central (☎ 1717) goes to littoral destinations like Mercedes, Paysandú (US$17, five hours), and Salto (US$20, six hours). Chadre (☎ 1717), Sabelín (☎ 1717), Copay (☎ 40-9926) and Intertur (☎ 49-7098) all serve littoral destinations, including Colonia and Carmelo. CUT (☎ 42-5054) and Corporación (☎ 42-1920) go to Mercedes (US$10) and Fray Bentos (US$11).

Rutas del Sol (☎ 42-5451) serves Rocha and La Paloma eight times daily. Cita (☎ 42-5425) goes to Chuy, as do COT, Cynsa (☎ 48-6670) and Rutas del Sol. Several companies go to Minas (US$5) and other interior destinations, including Rutas del Plata (☎ 42-5159), Núñez (☎ 48-6670), Cita, Corporación, Cota (☎ 42-1307), Cromín (☎ 42-5451), Emdal (☎ 49-7098), and Expreso Minuano (☎ 42-5075).

International COT/Bus de la Carrera (☎ 42-1313) has three direct buses daily to Buenos Aires (US$22, eight hours), and one to Porto Alegre, Brazil (US$30, 12 hours). Cita and Cacciola also serve Buenos Aires.

Several companies go elsewhere in Argentina, including EGA (☎ 92-5335) to Rosario (US$43) and Mendoza (US$61, 21 hours), continuing to Santiago de Chile US$95, 28 hours); EGA also serves Brazilian destinations. Expreso Encon (☎ 48-6670) goes to Rosario, Paraná, Santa Fe and Córdoba, while Cora (☎ 49-8799) goes to Córdoba four times weekly. Núñez has one daily to Santa Fe (US$40, 10 hours), Rosario (US$43, 10 hours), and Córdoba (US$56, 13 hours).

El Rápido Internacional (☎ 41-4764) and Tas Choapa (☎ 49-8598) go to Rosario, Mendoza and Chile. Brújula (☎ 1717) goes to Asunción on Tuesday, Friday and Sunday (US$64), while Coit (☎ 41-5628) goes on Monday, Wednesday and Saturday.

Cauvi (☎ 41-9196) goes to the Brazilian cities of Porto Alegre, Curitiba (US$55, 23 hours) and São Paulo (US$62, 27 hours). Other companies serving Brazil are Cynsa and TTL (☎ 41-1410).

River To Buenos Aires (US$37, 2½ hours), Buquebus (☎ 92-0670), Río Negro 1400, operates the so-called 'Aviones de Buquebus', high-speed ferries from the port at the foot of Pérez Castellano. Cacciola (☎ 91-0755), Plaza Cagancha 1326, runs a bus-and-launch service to the Buenos Aires suburb of Tigre via Carmelo twice daily.

Aliscafos Belt (☎ 90-4608) is at Plaza Cagancha 1325, while Ferryturismo (☎ 90-6617), at Río Branco 1368, runs a bus-and-hydrofoil combination to Buenos Aires (US$35 on peak weekends, US$25 on weekdays, four hours) via Colonia three times daily except Sunday, when it runs only twice. Deltanave (☎ 91-5143), which runs launches from Nueva Palmira to Tigre, is at Plaza Cagancha 1340.

Most companies that cross the Río de la Plata also have offices at Tres Cruces, including Aliscafos Belt (☎ 48-8146), Delta-nave (☎ 49-8598), Ferryturismo (☎ 49-8198) and Buquebus (☎ 48-8146).

Getting Around

To/From the Airport Consult the schedule posted at Pluna's city centre offices for buses to Aeropuerto Carrasco (US$4). Tamu passengers get free bus rides. COT buses to Punta del Este and the D-1 Expreso from the Ciudad Vieja also stop at Carrasco.

Bus Montevideo's improving fleet of buses goes everywhere for about US$0.45.

Taxi Drivers correlate meter readings with a photocopied fare chart.

The Uruguayan Littoral

West of Montevideo, the littoral's wheatfields and gardens feed the capital. Its major attraction is the 17th-century Portuguese contraband port and fortress of Colonia, but overland travellers from Argentina may find towns along the Río Uruguay pleasant enough for a stopover.

COLONIA

Only an hour from Buenos Aires, Colonia del Sacramento attracts only a handful of the foreigners who visit the Argentine capital. Founded in 1680, it occupied a strategic position across the river from Buenos Aires, as its contraband undercut Spain's mercantile trade policy. Spain captured the city in 1762, holding it until 1777, when Spanish reforms finally permitted foreign goods to proceed directly to Buenos Aires.

Orientation

On the east bank of the Río de la Plata, Colonia (population 20,000) is 50 km from Buenos Aires by ferry or hydrofoil. Its Barrio Histórico, a jumble of cobblestone streets shaded by sycamores on a small peninsula, is a must-see. The commercial centre, near

Plaza 25 de Agosto, and the river port are a few blocks east, while the Rambla Costanera leads north to Real de San Carlos, another area of interest.

Information

Tourist Office The municipal Oficina de Información Turística (☎ 2182), General Flores 499, is open on weekdays from 7 am to 8 pm, and on weekends from 10 am to 7 pm. The Ministerio de Turismo (☎ 4897) at the ferry port is more efficient.

Money Cambio Viaggio, General Flores 350, is open on Sunday. Cambio Libertad and Banco República operate exchange facilities at the port.

Post & Communications The post office is at Lavalleja 226. Antel, Rivadavia 420, has direct fibreoptic lines overseas. Colonia's telephone code is 0522.

Foreign Consulate The Argentine Consulate (☎ 2091), General Flores 350, is open on weekdays from 8 am to 1 pm.

Walking Tour

Also known as La Colonia Portuguesa, the Barrio Histórico begins at the restored **Puerta de Campo** (1745), on Calle Manoel Lobo, where a thick fortified wall runs to the river. A short distance west, off Plaza Mayor 25 de Mayo, tile-and-stucco colonial houses line narrow, cobbled **Calle de los Suspiros**; just beyond is the **Museo Portugués**. Colonia's museums generally open from 11.30 am to 6 pm.

At the south-west corner of the Plaza Mayor are the **Casa de Lavalleja**, once General Lavalleja's residence, ruins of the 17th-century **Convento de San Francisco**, and the restored 19th-century **Faro** (lighthouse). At the west end, on Calle del Comercio, are the **Museo Municipal** and the so-called **Casa del Virrey** (no viceroy ever lived here).

At the west end of Misiones de los Tapes, the **Museo de los Azulejos** is a 17th-century

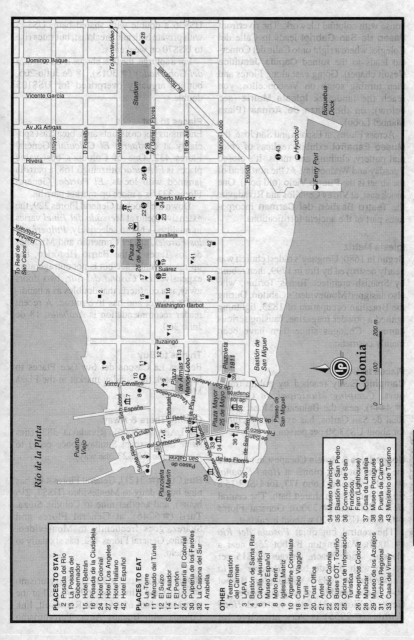

Colonia

Río de la Plata

Puerto Viejo

PLACES TO STAY
2 Posada del Río
13 La Posada del Gobernador
15 Hotel Beltrán
16 Posada de la Ciudadela
24 Hotel Colonial
27 Hotel Los Angeles
40 Hotel Italiano
42 Hotel Español

PLACES TO EAT
5 La Torre
11 Mercado del Túnel
12 El Suizo
14 El Asador
17 El Portón
24 Confitería El Colonial
30 Pulpería de los Faroles
32 La Casona del Sur
41 Arabella

OTHER
1 Teatro Bastión del Carmen
3 LAPA
4 Bastión de Santa Rita
7 Museo Español
8 Moto Rent
9 Iglesia Matriz
10 Argentine Consulate
18 Cambio Viaggio
19 Turil
20 Post Office
21 Antel
22 Cambio Colonia
23 Buses COT, Tourño
25 Oficina de Información Turística
26 Receptivos Colonia
28 Multicar
29 Museo de los Azulejos
31 Archivo Regional
33 Casa del Virrey
34 Museo Municipal
35 Bastión de San Pedro
36 Convento de San Francisco, Faro (Lighthouse)
37 Casa de Lavalleja
38 Museo Portugués
39 Puerta de Campo
43 Ministerio de Turismo

house with colonial tilework. The riverfront **Paseo de San Gabriel** leads to Calle del Colegio, where a right onto Calle del Comercio leads to the ruined **Capilla Jesuítica** (Jesuit chapel). Going east along Flores and then turning south on Vasconcellos, you reach the landmark **Iglesia Matriz** (see below), on the **Plaza de Armas** (Plaza Manoel Lobo).

Across Flores, at España and San José, the **Museo Español** exhibits replicas of colonial pottery, clothing and maps. It's closed Tuesday and Wednesday. At the north end of the street is the **Puerto Viejo** (old port). One block east, at Virrey Cevallos and Rivadavia, the **Teatro Bastión del Carmen** incorporates part of the ancient fortifications.

Iglesia Matriz
Begun in 1680, Uruguay's oldest church was nearly destroyed by fire in 1799, then rebuilt by Spanish architect Tomás Toribio, who also designed Montevideo's Cabildo. During the Brazilian occupation of 1823, lightning ignited a powder magazine, causing serious damage. Changes since then have been mainly cosmetic.

Places to Stay
Camping Easily reached by public transport, *Camping Municipal de Colonia* (☎ 4444), near the Balneario Municipal at Real de San Carlos, has excellent facilities for about US$3.50 per person.

Hospedajes & Hotels Cheapest in town are the large but dark rooms at *Hotel Español* (☎ 2314), Manoel Lobo 377, for US$8/15 a single/double with shared bath. The central *Hotel Colonial* (☎ 2906), General Flores 440, costs US$13/20 without breakfast.

The central but quiet *Posada del Río* (☎ 3002), Washington Barbot 258, near a pleasant sandy beach, charges US$15 per person with private bath. *Posada de la Ciudadela* (☎ 2683), Washington Barbot 164, is comparable but slightly dearer. At General Flores 311, the restored *Hotel Beltrán* (☎ 2955) is very attractive for

US$36 a double with shared bath, US$45 with private bath and breakfast, but rates rise to US$70 on weekends.

For a splurge, the best choice is *La Posada del Gobernador* (☎ 3018), 18 de Julio 205, but it's arguably overpriced for US$105 double.

Places to Eat
Enormous hot croissants are a breakfast speciality at *Confitería El Colonial*, General Flores 432. One of Colonia's best-value places is *El Asador*, Ituzaingó 168, a parrilla jammed with locals. *El Portón*, General Flores 333, is a more up-market parrilla.

Down the block at General Flores 229, the extensive menu at *Mercado del Túnel* varies in quality – choose selectively. *Pulpería de los Faroles*, at Del Comercio and Misiones de los Tapes in the Barrio Histórico, has up-market ambience but is not outrageously expensive. *La Casona del Sur*, two doors away, is a confitería that doubles as a handicrafts market and has live music. A recent reader recommendation is *Arabella*, 18 de Julio 360.

Things to Buy
Besides La Casona del Sur (see Places to Eat), check the Sunday market in the Plaza Mayor.

Getting There & Away
Air LAPA (☎ 2006), Rivadavia 383, flies twice daily except Sunday (once only) to Aeroparque (US$23 one way).

Bus COT (☎ 3121), General Flores 440, has nine buses daily to Montevideo (US$7, 2½ hours), and another nine to Colonia Suiza. Turil (☎ 5246), at General Flores and Suárez, goes frequently to Montevideo. Touriño, General Flores 432, has six daily to Carmelo.

River Buquebus (☎ 2975), Ferryturismo (☎ 2919) and Aliscafos (☎ 3664), all at the port at the foot of Avenida Roosevelt, link Colonia with Buenos Aires. Ferryturismo and Buquebus ferries (2½ hours) charge US$10 for adults, US$7 for children. Aliscafos and Ferryturismo hydrofoils (45 minutes) charge US$21, but impose a luggage limitation. There is a US$3 departure tax from the ferry terminal.

Getting Around

The city bus company Cotuc goes to the Camping Municipal and Real de San Carlos.

AROUND COLONIA
Real de San Carlos

At the turn of the century, Argentine entrepreneur Nicolás Mihanovich invested US$1.5 million in a huge tourist complex at Real de San Carlos, five km west of Colonia. Among the attractions were a 10,000-seat bullring, a 3000-seat jai alai *frontón*, a racecourse, and a hotel-casino with its own power plant. Only the racecourse functions today, but the ruins make an interesting excursion.

COLONIA SUIZA

Settled by Swiss immigrants in 1862, Colonia Suiza soon provided wheat for Montevideo, 120 km away. A quiet destination with a demonstrably European ambience, it produces dairy goods known throughout the country.

On the central Plaza de los Fundadores, the impressive sculpture **El Surco** commemorates Swiss pioneers. Interesting buildings include ruins of the first flour mill, the **Molino Quemado**, and the **Hotel del Prado** (1884), which also functions as a youth hostel.

Places to Stay & Eat

The most reasonable accommodation is friendly but inconspicuous *Hotel Comercio*, 18 de Julio 1209, for about US$10. On the outskirts of town, the 80-room *Hotel del Prado* is a magnificent but declining building with huge balconies. Rooms cost US$25 per person, but it's also the official hostel, offering beds for US$8.

For dining, try *La Góndola*, Luis Dreyer and 25 de Agosto, *L'Arbalete* on Avenida

Batlle y Ordóñez, or *Don José*, 18 de Julio 1214.

Getting There & Away

COT (☎ 5231), next to Bar Meny at 18 de Julio and Treinta y Tres, has services to Montevideo, Colonia, Fray Bentos (three daily) and Paysandú (one daily).

CARMELO

Carmelo, 75 km north-west of Colonia, is a centre for exploring the Paraná delta by boat. From Plaza Independencia, Avenida 19 de Abril leads to Arroyo de las Vacas, where a large park offers camping, swimming and a monstrous casino.

The municipal Oficina de Turismo (☎ 2001) is at 19 de Abril 250, four blocks from the Arroyo. West Tour, 19 de Abril 267, is also a good source of information, and there are two exchange houses near the plaza. The Argentine Consulate (☎ 2266) is at Roosevelt 442. Carmelo's telephone code is 0542.

Places to Stay & Eat

Camping Náutico Las Higueritas (☎ 2058), on the south side of Arroyo de las Vacas, charges US$3 per person. Rates are similar at *Camping Don Mauro*, at Ignacio Barros and Arroyo de las Vacas, six blocks from the centre.

Very basic, run-down *Hotel Carmelo*, 19 de Abril 561, rents rooms with shared bath for US$5 per person. Singles with shared bath at *Hotel La Unión* (☎ 2028), Uruguay 368, are better value for US$9; singles/doubles with private bath cost US$12/20. Friendly *Hotel San Fernando* (☎ 2503), 19 de Abril 161, has clean rooms with private bath for US$15/20.

El Vesubio, 19 de Abril 451, serves a huge, tasty chivito al plato. Other restaurants include *Perrini*, at 19 de Abril 440, and the *Yacht Club*, *Morales* and *El Refugio*, all across the bridge, in the park.

Getting There & Away

Bus Sabelín and Chadre (☎ 2987), both at Uruguay and 18 de Julio, go to Montevideo

(US$9, four hours) and north to Fray Bentos, Paysandú and Salto. Turil goes to Colonia (US$2), as do Klüver (☎ 3411) and Intertur, both at 18 de Julio and Uruguay.

River Movilán/Deltanave, Constituyentes 263, sails twice daily to Tigre, at 4 am and 10.30 am. Cacciola, Constituyentes 219, goes at 4.30 and 11.30 am except on Monday, when departures are 11.30 am and 6.30 pm. Fares are US$11 for adults, US$7.50 for children.

FRAY BENTOS

In 1864 Uruguay's first meat extract plant opened here, 300 km west of Montevideo, across the Río Uruguay from Gualeguaychú (Argentina). In 1902 British interests built the country's first frigorífico, the enormous Anglo plant, now a museum.

Barren Plaza Constitución has only a few palms and a Victorian bandshell, but the helpful Oficina de Turismo (☎ 3261), at 25 de Mayo and 18 de Julio, is open on weekdays from 8 am to noon and 5 to 9 pm. Cambio Fagalde is at 18 de Julio 1163.

The Argentine Consulate (☎ 2638), Sarandí 3193, is open on weekdays from 8 am to 1 pm. The telephone code is 0535.

Things to See

The landmark 400-seat **Teatro Young**, bearing the name of the Anglo-Uruguayan *estanciero* who sponsored its construction from 1909 to 1912, hosts cultural events throughout the year. It's a block from Plaza Constitución, at the corner of 25 de Mayo and Zorrilla.

In 1865, the Liebig Extract of Meat Company located its pioneer South American plant in the **Barrio Histórico del Anglo**, south-west of the town centre. Most of the defunct Frigorífico Anglo del Uruguay, still the dominant landmark in a neighbourhood with an active street life, has become the **Museo de la Revolución Industrial** (☎ 2918). Note the manager's residence and the former British Consulate.

Places to Stay & Eat

The *Club Atlético Anglo* (☎ 2787) maintains a camping ground, with hot showers and beach access, 10 blocks from Plaza Constitución. Eight km south of town, sprawling *Balneario Las Cañas* (☎ 1611), charges US$3 per person and US$2 per tent, plus US$3 per vehicle.

Ask the tourist office about accommodation in private houses. Clean, friendly *Nuevo Hotel Colonial* (☎ 2260), 25 de Mayo 3293, charges US$18 per double with shared bath, US$22 with private bath. *Hotel 25 de Mayo* (☎ 2586), at 25 de Mayo and Lavalleja, is a modernised 19th-century building with singles/doubles for US$12/18 with shared bath, US$15/20 with private bath.

La Enramada, on España between 25 de Mayo and 25 de Agosto, offers cheap minutas. The best dining may be at the *Club de Remeros*, where the yacht crowd hangs out, near Parque Roosevelt.

Getting There & Away

ETA, at the Plaza Hotel, has three buses daily to Gualeguaychú (US$4), as does CUT, which has four daily to Mercedes (US$1.50) and four to Montevideo (US$11, five hours). Chadre, on Plaza Constitución, has two daily in each direction between Bella Unión and Montevideo, stopping at intermediate destinations. Agencia Central (☎ 3470) and Sabelín, in the same offices, and Corporación also go to Montevideo.

MERCEDES

The livestock centre of Mercedes is also a minor resort on the Río Negro, a tributary of the Uruguay, popular for boating, fishing and swimming. Mercedes has better bus connections than Fray Bentos, 30 km away.

Plaza Independencia is the city centre. The municipal Oficina de Turismo (☎ 2733), Artigas 215, has friendly, enthusiastic staff and a good city map. It's open on weekdays only, from 7.30 am to 1.30 pm and 3.30 to 9.30 pm. Cambio Fagalde, on Plaza Independencia, or Cambio España, Colón 262, will change cash but not travellers' cheques. The post office is at Rodó 650, while Antel is on 18 de Julio between Roosevelt and Castro y Careaga. Mercedes' telephone code is 0532.

Plaza Lavalleja has a Sunday flea market and crafts fair.

Places to Stay & Eat

Eight blocks from Plaza Independencia, linked to the mainland by a bridge, Mercedes' *Camping del Hum* has excellent swimming, fishing and sanitary facilities. Fees are only US$0.75 per person plus US$1 per tent. There is a youth hostel at the *Club Remeros Mercedes* (☎ 2534), De la Rivera 949.

Hotel San Martín, Artigas 305, has singles for US$6 with shared bath, US$8 with private bath. Quiet, friendly *Hotel Marín* (☎ 2987), Rodó 668, has singles for US$10; its annex, at Roosevelt 627, has more character but is slightly dearer.

La Churrasquera, Castro y Careaga 790, is a parrilla serving large portions. On the Isla del Puerto, near the camping ground, the *Comedor Municipal* and the *Club Surubí* both have good fish and outdoor seating.

Getting There & Away

For Chadre, Artigas 176, Mercedes is a stop-over between Bella Unión and Montevideo. Agencia Central (☎ 2982) and Sabelín, both at Sánchez 782, connect Paysandú and Montevideo via Mercedes.

CUT and ETA, with services to Gualeguaychú (Argentina), share offices at Artigas 233. ETA also goes to interior destinations like Paso de los Toros and Tacuarembó. CUT has four buses daily to Montevideo (US$10, 4½ hours).

PAYSANDU

Uruguay's second-largest city (population 100,000) started as an 18th-century estancia for the Jesuit mission at Yapeyú, Corrientes. Processing beer, sugar, textiles and leather, it is the only significant industrial centre outside Montevideo.

Across the Uruguay from Colón, Argentina, Paysandú is 110 km north of Fray

Bentos. Avenida 18 de Julio, the main commercial street, runs along the south side of Plaza Constitución. The flood-prone riverfront is mostly parkland.

Opposite the plaza, at 18 de Julio 1226, the Oficina de Turismo (☎ 6677) has a superb city map and a good selection of brochures. Cambio Fagalde is at 18 de Julio 1004, while the Argentine Consulate (☎ 2253) is at Leandro Gómez 1034. Paysandu's telephone code is 0722.

Worthwhile museums include the **Museo de la Tradición**, at the Balneario Municipal north of the city centre, the **Museo Salesiano**, at 18 de Julio and Montecaseros, and the **Museo Histórico**, at Zorrilla and Sarandí.

Places to Stay & Eat

Paysandú has basic, free camping grounds at the riverside *Balneario Municipal Parque Guyunusa*, two km north of downtown, and at *Parque Sacra*.

The cheapest (and friendliest) lodging is *Hotel Victoria* (☎ 4320), 18 de Julio 979, at US$7 per person with shared bath, US$10 with private bath. *Hotel Artigas* (☎ 4343), Baltasar Brum 943, costs US$10 per person with shared bath, US$12 with private bath.

Don Diego, 19 de Abril 917, has reasonable parrillada, pizza and minutas. Other good eateries include the *Sociedad Española*, Leandro Gómez 1192, and the highly recommended *Artemisio*, 18 de Julio 1248.

Getting There & Away

Air Pluna (☎ 3071), Florida 1249, sells tickets for Tamu flights to Montevideo (US$20). Aviasur, in the same office, flies to Montevideo and Salto.

Bus Paysandú's new Terminal de Omnibus is at Montecaseros and Artigas, south of Plaza Constitución. Chadre stops here en route between Bella Unión and Montevideo. Agencia Central goes to interior destinations. Copay, Núñez and Sabelín also serve Montevideo (US$17, six hours).

URUGUAY

SALTO

Directly across the Uruguay from Concordia, Entre Ríos, 520 km from Montevideo, the most northerly border crossing into Argentina is the site of the enormous Salto Grande hydroelectric project. The area's main attraction are hot springs resorts at nearby Daymán and Arapey. To visit the dam, make arrangements at the municipal Oficina de Turismo (☎ 34096), Uruguay 1052. Salto's telephone code is 0732.

Places to Stay & Eat

The *Club Remeros de Salto* (☎ 33418), at Rambla César Mayo Gutiérrez (Costanera Norte) and Belén, runs an official hostel. Otherwise, try the very modest *Pensión 33*, Treinta y Tres 269, or inexpensive accommodation like *Hotel Plaza* (☎ 33744) at Uruguay 465, both in the US$10 to US$12 range per person.

Restaurant Cheff, Uruguay 639, is a good dinner choice. The many pizzerías include *Firenze* at Uruguay 945 and *Las Mil y Una* at Uruguay 906.

Getting There & Away

Air Aviasur (☎ 32724), Uruguay 657, flies four or five times weekly to Montevideo.

Bus The Terminal Municipal de Omnibus is at Larrañaga and Andrés Latorre. Chadre (☎ 32603) goes to Concordia twice daily except Sunday, as does Flecha Bus (☎ 32150). Chadre has international service to Uruguaiana, Brazil.

Domestic carriers to Montevideo include Chadre/Agencia Central, Núñez (☎ 35581), and El Norteño (☎ 32150).

River From the port at the foot of Brasil, San Cristóbal launches cross the river to Concordia (US$3) five times daily during the week, four times daily on weekends and holidays.

TACUAREMBO

In the rolling hills of the Cuchilla de Haedo, 390 km north of Montevideo, Tacuarembó's sycamore-lined streets make it one of Uruguay's most agreeable interior towns. Authorities have kept sculptors busy providing monuments honouring the usual military heroes but also writers, clergy and educators. The late-March **Fiesta de la Patria Gaucha** (gaucho festival) merits a visit for travellers in the area.

Tacuarembó is a major highway junction, as roads lead west to Argentina, north to Brazil, east to Brazil and the Uruguayan coast, and south to Montevideo. Its centre is Plaza 19 de Abril. The municipal Oficina de Turismo (☎ 4671), 18 de Julio 164, offers a simple map and brochures. Antel is at Sarandí 242. The telephone code is 0632. The **Museo del Indio y del Gaucho**, at Flores and Artigas, pays romantic tribute to Uruguay's Indians and gauchos.

Places to Stay & Eat

The *Balneario Municipal Iporá*, seven km north of town, has both free and paying camp sites (US$1.50) near an artificial lake. Free sites have clean toilets but lack showers. Buses leave from near Plaza 19 de Abril.

Friendly *Pensión Paysandú* (☎ 2453), 18 de Julio 154, offers good accommodation for US$8 in a shared room, US$10/14 a single/double for a private room with shared bath. *Hotel Central* (☎ 2341), Flores 300, charges US$13 per person with private bath.

Hotel Tacuarembó, 18 de Julio 133, has a good restaurant serving parrillada and other dishes; other parrillas are *La Rueda*, Beltrán and Flores, and *La Cabaña*, 25 de Mayo 217. *Rotisería del Centro*, on 18 de Julio near Plaza Colón, sells an enormous, tasty chivito which is a meal in itself.

Getting There & Away

Air Tamu (☎ 2341), Flores 300, flies on Monday and Friday to Montevideo (US$20).

Bus To Montevideo (US$14, 5½ hours), try Buses Chadre/Agencia Central (☎ 3455), 25 de Mayo 169, or Turil (☎ 3305), at 25 de Mayo and 25 de Agosto. Chadre/Agencia Central also serves interior destinations and connects Tacuarembó with the littoral.

The Uruguayan Riviera

East of Montevideo, countless resorts dot a scenic coastline whose sandy beaches, vast dunes and dramatic headlands extend to the Brazilian border. In summer the area attracts hordes of tourists, but by early March prices drop, the weather is still ideal and the pace is much more leisurely.

PIRIAPOLIS

In the 1930s entrepreneur Francisco Piria built the landmark Hotel Argentino and an eccentric residence known as 'Piria's castle', and ferried tourists directly from Argentina. Almost everything in Piriápolis, about 100 km from Montevideo, is within walking distance of the waterfront Rambla de los Argentinos and defined by proximity to Hotel Argentino. The nearby countryside offers features like Cerro Pan de Azúcar (one of Uruguay's highest points) and the hill resort of Minas.

The private Asociación de Fomento y Turismo (☎ 22560), Rambla de los Argentinos 1348, is open daily from 9.30 am to 1 pm and 3.30 to 9 pm, and has maps, a few brochures, and current hotel listings. Change cash, but not travellers' cheques, at Hotel Argentino.

Places to Stay

Many hotels open only from December to April; nearly all raise prices from mid-December to March. The best bargains come after 1 March, when the weather is delightful but crowds are gone.

Open from mid-December to late April, *Camping Piriápolis FC* (☎ 23275) is at Misiones and Niza, 350 metres behind Hotel Argentino. Sites cost US$7 for two persons, while a few rooms with shared bath cost US$7 per person.

Close behind Hotel Argentino, *Albergue Piriápolis 1* (☎ 20394) at Simón del Pino 1106 and *Albergue Antón Grassi* (☎ 22157) at Simón del Pino 1136 both charge around US$7 per person with hostel card and are

open all year. Reservations are essential in January and February.

The friendly *Petite Pensión* (☎ 22471) is a tiny (seven-room), family-run hotel at Sanabria 1084, two blocks from the beach. Rates are US$18 off-season, US$22 in summer. Winter rates are comparable at *Hotel Centro* (☎ 22516), Sanabria 931, but summer rates are US$36 per person.

Even if you can't stay at *Hotel Argentino* (☎ 22791), you should visit this elegant, 350-room European-style spa on the Rambla. Rates are US$86 per person with half board, US$107 with full board, plus IVA. The hotel has thermal baths, a casino, a classic dining room and other luxuries.

La Langosta, Rambla 1215, has good seafood and parrillada at moderate prices. Other appealing restaurants along the Rambla include *Viejo Martín*, at the corner of Trapani, and *Restaurant Delta*, at the corner of Atanasio Sierra.

Things to Buy

The Paseo de la Pasiva, an attractive colonnade along the Rambla, is a good place for handicrafts.

Getting There & Away

Bus companies have offices along the Rambla. In high season, COT (☎ 22259) runs up to 27 buses daily to Punta del Este and Montevideo (US$2.50), while Díaz has 14 daily to Pan de Azúcar and Minas.

AROUND PIRIAPOLIS
Pan de Azúcar

Ten km north of town, there's a foot trail to the top of 493-metre **Cerro Pan de Azúcar**, Uruguay's third-highest point, and a small but well-kept zoo at the nearby **Parque Municipal**. Across the highway, the **Castillo de Piria** was Piria's outlandish residence.

Minas

Sixty km north of Piriápolis, this amiable hill town draws its name from nearby quarries. The municipal Oficina de Turismo (☎ 4118) is at Lavalleja 572. For cheap but adequate lodgings, try *Residencial Minas*, 25 de Mayo 502. Inexpensive camping is possible at *Parque Arequita*, nine km north on the road to Polanco (public transport available), where two-bed cabañas cost US$5 per person with shared bath.

Every 19 April, up to 70,000 pilgrims visit the **Cerro y Virgen del Verdún**, six km west of Minas. **Parque Salus**, source of Uruguay's best-known mineral water and the site of a brewery, is 10 km west of town (accommodation available at *El Parador Salus*). In **Villa Serrana**, 23 km beyond Minas, *Chalet Las Chafas* has hostel accommodation with kitchen facilities, a pool and a lake; make reservations at the Asociación de Alberguistas del Uruguay (☎ 40-4245), Pablo de María 1583, Montevideo. Buses go no closer than three km, so you'll need to walk or hitch the rest of the way.

MALDONADO

In 1755, Spanish authorities established Maldonado at the mouth of the Río de la Plata as an outpost to provision ships. Its centre retains a colonial feeling, but the town has sprawled because of tourist development in exclusive Punta del Este. It remains a more economical alternative to Punta for food and accommodation.

Orientation

Maldonado is 30 km from Piriápolis. The original grid centres on Plaza San Fernando, but streets are highly irregular between Maldonado and Punta. West, along the Río de la Plata, Rambla Claudio Williman is the main thoroughfare, while to the east, Rambla Lorenzo Batlle Pacheco follows the Atlantic coast. Locations along these routes are usually identified by numbered *paradas* (bus stops). Both routes have fine beaches, but the ocean beaches have rougher surf.

Information

Tourist Office In the Intendencia Municipal, on Sarandí between Juan A Ledesma and Enrique Burnett, the Dirección de Turismo

(☎ 21920) is open on weekdays from 12.30 to 6.30 pm.

Money Several exchange houses are clustered around Plaza San Fernando.

Post & Communications The post office is at Ituzaingó and San Carlos. Antel is at the corner of Artigas and Florida; Maldonado's telephone code is 042.

Things to See

On Plaza San Fernando is the **Catedral de Maldonado** (1895). At Gorriti and Pérez del Puerto, the colonial watchtower at the **Plaza de la Torre del Vigía** was built with peepholes for viewing the approach of hostile forces.

Built between 1771 and 1797, the **Cuartel de Dragones y de Blandengues** is a block of military fortifications along 18 de Julio and Pérez del Puerto. Its **Museo Didáctico Artiguista** (☎ 25378), honouring Uruguay's independence hero, is open daily from 8 to 11 pm.

Currently undergoing restoration as a cultural centre, the **Museo San Fernando de Maldonado** (☎ 25929) is a fine arts museum at Sarandí and Pérez del Puerto, open Monday to Saturday from 12.30 to 8 pm, and on Sunday from 4.30 to 8 pm. Maldonado's oddest sight is the eclectic **Museo Mazzoni** (1782) at Ituzaingó 789, open Tuesday to Saturday from 10 am to 12.30 pm and 5 to 9.30 pm, and on Sunday from 5 to 9.30 pm.

Activities

Sport fishing is a popular pastime along the coast, at sea and on offshore islands; see the tourist office for a map of recommended spots. Cassarino Hermanos (☎ 23735), Sarandí 1253, arranges boat trips. Surfing, wind-surfing and diving are also possible.

Places to Stay

Peak season accommodation can be costly, but prices decline at summer's end. Much depends on economic conditions in Argen-

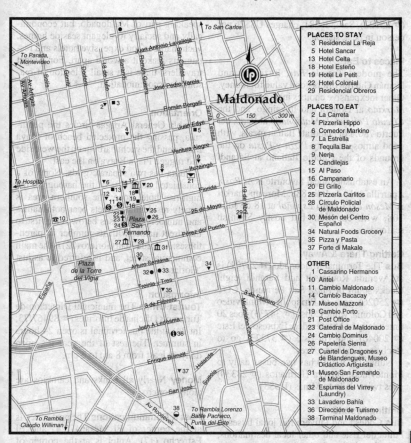

Maldonado

0   150   300 m

PLACES TO STAY
3 Residencial La Reja
5 Hotel Sancar
13 Hotel Celta
18 Hotel Esteño
19 Hotel Le Petit
22 Hotel Colonial
29 Residencial Obreros

PLACES TO EAT
2 La Carreta
4 Pizzería Hippo
6 Comedor Markino
7 La Estrella
8 Tequila Bar
9 Nerja
12 Candilejas
15 Al Paso
16 Campanario
20 El Grillo
25 Pizzería Carlitos
28 Círculo Policial
    de Maldonado
30 Mesón del Centro
    Español
34 Natural Foods Grocery
35 Pizza y Pasta
37 Forte di Makale

OTHER
1 Cassarino Hermanos
10 Antel
11 Cambio Maldonado
14 Cambio Bacacay
17 Museo Mazzoni
19 Cambio Porto
21 Post Office
23 Catedral de Maldonado
24 Cambio Dominus
26 Papelería Sienra
27 Cuartel de Dragones y
    de Blandengues, Museo
    Didáctico Artiguista
31 Museo San Fernando
    de Maldonado
32 Espumas del Virrey
    (Laundry)
33 Lavadero Bahía
36 Dirección de Turismo
38 Terminal Maldonado

tina: if Argentina's economy or currency is weak, prices drop here.

Camping *Camping San Rafael* (☎ 86715), on the outskirts of town beyond Aeropuerto El Jagüel, has fine facilities on leafy grounds. Sites cost US$11 for two in January and February, US$10 the rest of the year. Take bus No 5 from the city centre.

Hostel The recently opened *Albergue Puebla Nueva* (☎ 71427) is across from the Club de Pesca in Manantiales, about 15 km

east of Maldonado. Reached by Codesa bus, it's open November through March.

Residenciales & Hotels In Maldonado proper, check out *Residencial La Reja* (☎ 23712), 18 de Julio 1092, where singles/doubles with shared bath cost US$18/20.

The Irish-owned *Hotel Celta* (☎ 30139), Ituzaingó 839, is a popular choice for foreign travellers. Standard rates are US$20 per person, but cheaper budget rooms are available, especially outside peak season. Rates are similar or a little higher at *Hotel Sancar* (☎ 23563), Juan Edye 597. *Hotel Esteño*

URUGUAY

(☎ 25222), Sarandí 881, charges US$26 per person in peak season.

Places to Eat

The modest *Tequila Bar*, Ituzaingó and Román Guerra, offers good value for money. Other inexpensive choices include *Comedor Markino* at Dodera and Ituzaingó, and the *Círculo Policial de Maldonado* at Pérez del Puerto 780. For elaborate Italian meals, with good atmosphere, try *Pizza y Pasta* on the grounds of the Circolo Italiano at Sarandí 642.

An established local favourite is *Al Paso*, a parrilla at 18 de Julio 888. More up-market is *Mesón del Centro Español* at 18 de Julio 708, with excellent but costly Spanish seafood.

Getting There & Away

Bus The Terminal Maldonado (☎ 25701) is at Avenida Roosevelt and Sarandí, eight blocks south of Plaza San Fernando. COT (☎ 25026) goes to Piriápolis, Montevideo and Colonia, while Copsa (☎ 34733) goes 20 times daily to Montevideo. Expreso del Este (☎ 20040) and Tur-Este (☎ 37323) go to Rocha and Treinta y Tres.

Núñez (☎ 30170) has two buses daily to Montevideo. Olivera Hermanos (☎ 28330) goes twice daily to Minas (US$3).

Getting Around

Bus Codesa and Olivera run local buses to Punta del Este and other local destinations, including the beach circuit.

AROUND MALDONADO
Casapueblo

At scenic Punta Ballena, 10 km west of Maldonado, Carlos Páez Vilaró built this unconventional Mediterranean villa/art gallery (admission US$3) without right angles. Visitors can tour the gallery, view a slide presentation, and dine or drink at the bar/cafeteria.

PUNTA DEL ESTE

Swarming with upper-class Argentines, the tiny peninsula of Punta del Este is strictly speaking part of Maldonado, but economically and socially its elegant seaside homes, yacht harbour and expensive hotels and restaurants make it a world apart. For budget travellers, there is a small selection of reasonable accommodation.

Orientation

Rambla General Artigas circles the peninsula, passing the protected beach of Playa Mansa and the yacht harbour on the west side and rugged Playa Brava on the east.

Punta has two separate grids. North of a constricted neck east of the harbour is the high-rise hotel zone; the southern area is largely residential. Streets bear both names and numbers: addresses below refer first to the street name, with its number in parentheses. Avenida Juan Gorlero (22) is the main commercial street, and is referred to as just 'Gorlero'.

Information

Tourist Office The municipal Dirección de Turismo's Oficina de Informes (☎ 89467/73, Int 24) at the bus terminal is open 24 hours in summer. The rest of the year it's open daily, at least from 8 am to 6 pm.

Money Nearly all banks and cambios are along Gorlero.

Post & Communications The post office is at the corner of El Mesana (24) and El Estrecho (17). Antel is at the corner of Arrecifes (25) and El Mesana (24). The telephone code is 042, identical to Maldonado's.

Foreign Consulates Argentina operates a high-season consulate (☎ 43530) in the Edificio Padua, Las Focas (30) 619.

Beaches

Rambla Artigas snakes along the riverside Playa Mansa on the west side of Punta del Este, then circles around the peninsula to the wilder Playa Brava, on the Atlantic. In the other direction from Playa Mansa, along Rambla Williman, the main beach areas are

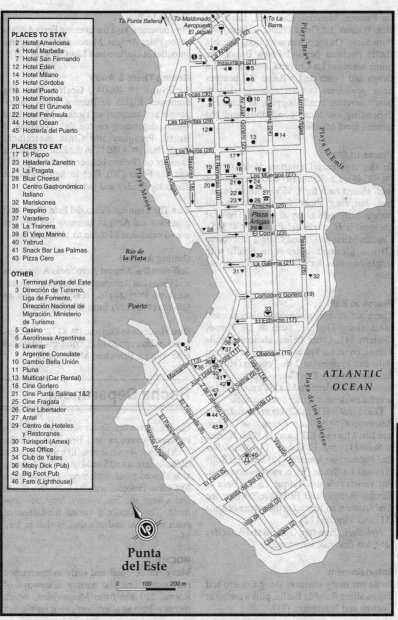

PLACES TO STAY
2   Hotel Americana
4   Hotel Marbella
7   Hotel San Fernando
12 Hotel Edén
14 Hotel Milano
15 Hotel Córdoba
16 Hotel Puerto
19 Hotel Florida
20 Hotel El Grumete
22 Hotel Península
44 Hotel Ocean
45 Hostería del Puerto

PLACES TO EAT
17 Di Pappo
23 Heladería Zanettin
24 La Fragata
28 Blue Cheese
31 Centro Gastronómico Italiano
32 Mariskonea
37 Peppino
37 Varadero
38 La Trainera
39 El Viejo Marino
40 Yabrud
41 Snack Bar Las Palmas
43 Pizza Cero

OTHER
1   Terminal Punta del Este
3   Dirección de Turismo, Liga de Fomento, Dirección Nacional de Migración, Ministerio de Turismo
5   Casino
6   Aerolíneas Argentinas
8   Laverap
9   Argentine Consulate
10 Cambio Bella Unión
11 Pluna
12 Multicar (Car Rental)
18 Cine Gorlero
21 Cine Punta Salinas 1&2
25 Cine Fragata
26 Cine Libertador
27 Antel
29 Centro de Hoteles y Restoranes
30 Turisport (Amex)
32 Post Office
34 Club de Yates
36 Moby Dick (Pub)
42 Big Foot Pub
46 Faro (Lighthouse)

To Punta Ballena
To Maldonado, Aeropuerto El Jaguel
To La Barra

Playa Brava
Playa El Emir
Playa Mansa
Río de la Plata
Puerto
ATLANTIC OCEAN
Playa de los Ingleses

Punta del Este

0   100   200 m

URUGUAY

La Pastora, Marconi, Cantegril, Las Delicias, Pinares, La Gruta (Punta Ballena) and Portezuelo. On the ocean side, along Rambla Batlle Pacheco beyond Playa Brava, the prime areas are La Chiverta, San Rafael, La Draga and Punta de La Barra. All beaches have *paradores* (small restaurants) with beach service; beach-hopping is common, depending on local conditions and the general level of action.

Places to Stay

In the residential quarter, *Hotel Ocean* (☎ 43248), La Salina (9) 636, has doubles with shared bath for US$30 without breakfast, but ring ahead for reservations (it occasionally gets noisy at night). The next cheapest is *Hostería del Puerto* (☎ 45345), Capitán Miranda (7) and Calle 2 de Febrero (10), a pleasant older-style hotel, with singles/doubles for US$25/35 with private bath.

Places to Eat

There are several reasonable pizzerías and cafés along Gorlero, such as *Di Pappo*, Gorlero 841. Other Italian choices include *Pizza Cero* at La Salina (9) and 2 de Febrero (10), and *Peppino* at 2 de Febrero (10) and Rambla Artigas. The *Centro Gastronómico Italiano* at Gorlero and La Galerna (21) has several moderately priced restaurants.

Good seafood is available at *Mariskonea*, Resalsero (26) 650, *La Fragata* at Gorlero and Los Muergos (27), and *El Viejo Marino* at Solís (11) and El Foque (14). *Snack Bar Las Palmas*, on Virazón (12) between Solís (11) and La Salina (9), is more economical. For variety, try the Basque *La Trainera* at Rambla Artigas and El Foque (14), or the Arab/Armenian *Yabrud* at the corner of Solís (11) and Virazón (12).

Heladería Zanettin, Gorlero and Arrecifes (25), has first-rate ice cream.

Entertainment

Punta has many cinemas along Gorlero and discos along Rambla Batlle, plus a casino at Gorlero and Inzaurraga (31).

Things to Buy

For souvenirs, visit the evening Feria Artesanal on Plaza Artigas. Manos del Uruguay has an outlet at Gorlero and Las Gaviotas (29).

Getting There & Away

Air Pluna (☎ 40004), Gorlero 940, has numerous flights to Buenos Aires' Aeroparque and summer services to Montevideo which, depending on the day, continue to Brazil, Paraguay and Chile. Aerolíneas Argentinas (☎ 43801), in the Edificio Santos Dumont on Gorlero between Inzaurraga (31) and Las Focas (30), flies to Aeroparque on Thursday, Friday and twice on Sunday.

Bus The Terminal Punta del Este (☎ 89467) is at Riso and Artigas. Intercity bus services are an extension of those to Maldonado.

Getting Around

To/From the Airport Aerolíneas Argentinas and Pluna use Aeropuerto Laguna del Sauce, west of Portezuelo, reached by Buses Olivera (☎ 24039) from Maldonado.

Bus Maldonado Turismo (☎ 81725), at Gorlero and Inzaurraga (31), connects Punta del Este with La Barra and Manantiales.

Rocha Department

Conflicts between Spain and Portugal, then between Argentina and Brazil, left Rocha with historical monuments like the fortresses of Santa Teresa and San Miguel. The fighting also slowed rural settlement, sparing areas like Cabo Polonio, with its extensive dunes and a large sea-lion colony, from development. The interior's varied landscape of palm savannas and marshes is rich in bird life.

ROCHA

Many late colonial and early independence era houses line the narrow alleyways of Rocha, 220 km from Montevideo, which merits at least an afternoon's visit for visitors to La Paloma (see below). The municipal Oficina de Turismo (☎ 2995) is at Artigas 176. Rocha's telephone code is 0472.

The tidy *Hotel Municipal Rocha* (☎ 2404), a block off Plaza Independencia on 19 de Abril between Ramírez and Presbítero Aquiles, which charges US$17/24 for a single/double. The modest *Hotel Centro* (☎ 2349), Ramírez 152, is slightly dearer. *Confitería La Candela*, on Plaza Independencia, has tasty and visually appealing sweets and pastries.

Rutas del Sol runs eight buses daily to Montevideo and five to Chuy via La Paloma, plus six daily to Barra Valizas (US$3.50). Cynsa has 10 daily to La Paloma and nine from La Paloma back to Rocha, where you can catch its service to Chuy. COT also serves Rocha.

LA PALOMA

Placid La Paloma (population 5000), 28 km south of Rocha, is less developed, cheaper and much less crowded than Punta del Este, but lacks Punta's hyperactive nightlife. Beaches to the east are less protected from ocean swells. Streets are named, but hotels and restaurants lack numbers and are more easily located by their relationship to prominent intersections and landmarks.

The Oficina de Turismo (☎ 6107) is on the traffic circle at the east end of Avenida Nicolás Solari. In summer, it's open from 8 am to 11 pm, but the rest of the year only from 9 am to 9 pm.

Places to Stay & Eat

Camping Parque Andresito (☎ 6107), at the northern entrance to town, has excellent beach access and amenities like hot showers, a supermarket, restaurant and electricity. Rates are US$10 for two people; inexpensive cabañas are also available.

The best budget accommodation is the *Albergue Altena 5000* (☎ 6396), in Parque Andresito. It's open November through March; make reservations at the Asociación de Alberguistas del Uruguay (☎ 40-4245),

Pablo de María 1583, Montevideo. At US$45 for a double, *Residencial Canopus* (☎ 6068) on Avenida Nicolás Solari near Sirio, is now one of the better value places in town.

La Marea, on Avenida del Parque, has good, fresh, reasonably priced seafood, but the service is slow. Pizzerías include *La Currica*, on Solari, and *Ponte Vecchio*, on La Aguada beach. Try also the hotel restaurants.

Getting There & Away

Buses Cynsa, on Avenida del Parque next to Restaurant La Marea, goes to Rocha (US$1) and Montevideo (US$10), along with COT and Rutas del Sol.

PARQUE NACIONAL SANTA TERESA

More a historical than a natural attraction, this coastal park 35 km south of Chuy contains the hilltop **Fortaleza de Santa Teresa**, begun by the Portuguese but captured and finished by the Spaniards. By international standards, Santa Teresa is a humble place, but it attracts many Uruguayan and Brazilian visitors because of uncrowded beaches and decentralised forest camping (US$10 per site for basic facilities).

The park gets very crowded during Carnaval, but most of the time it absorbs visitors without difficulty. Services at headquarters include telephones and post offices, a supermarket, bakery, butchery and restaurant.

CHUY

Pedestrians and vehicles cross freely between Uruguay and Brazil at Chuy, the grubby but energetic border town at the terminus of Ruta 9, 340 km from Montevideo. There are several exchange houses along Avenida Brasil.

Hotel Plaza (☎ 2309), at Artigas and Arachanes, has singles for US$22, but accommodation is usually cheaper at *Hotel Rivero* or *Hotel San Francisco* on the Brazilian side. Ten km south of Chuy, a coastal side road heads to *Camping Chuy* (☎ 2425), which charges US$10 per site, and *Camping*

URUGUAY

de la Barra (☎ 1611), which costs US$4 per person, with all facilities. Local buses from Chuy go directly to both.

If proceeding into Brazil, complete Uruguayan emigration formalities on Ruta 9, 2.5 km south of town. Travellers needing visas will find the Brazilian Consulate at Fernández 147. Several bus companies connect Chuy with Montevideo (US$12, five hours),

including Rutas del Sol, Cynsa, Cita and COT, all on or near Avenida Brasil. Brazilian buses have a central terminal three blocks north of the border.

Seven km west of Chuy, do not miss restored **Fuerte San Miguel**, a pink-granite fortress built in 1734 during hostilities between Spain and Portugal and protected by a moat. It's closed on Monday.

Venezuela

Venezuela's modern history has been strongly influenced by oil money, which has turned the country into one of the wealthiest nations on the continent. As a result, Venezuela today has some of the best road networks in South America, spectacular 21st-century architecture and a Western-standard tourism infrastructure. Yet deep in the countryside, people live their traditional way of life as if the 20th century got lost somewhere down the road. There are a number of Indian groups still unconquered by encroaching civilisation, the most mysterious being the Yanomami, a stone-age culture lost in time along the Venezuela-Brazil border.

The variety of Venezuela's landscapes won't disappoint even the most demanding visitor. The country boasts the northern tip of the Andes topped with snowcapped peaks, and the vast Orinoco delta (equal in area to Belgium), crisscrossed by a maze of natural channels. The southern part of the country is taken up by the legendary wilderness of the Amazon, while the north is bordered for some 3000 km by the Caribbean and lined with countless beaches.

Venezuela's most unusual natural formations are the *tepuis*, the flat-topped mountains with vertical flanks which loom over 1000 metres above rolling savannas. Their tops are noted for their moon-like landscape and their peculiar endemic flora. There are about 100 tepuis scattered throughout the south-east of the country. From one spills Angel Falls, the world's highest waterfall (979 metres) and Venezuela's most famous tourist sight.

In practical terms, Venezuela is a relatively safe and friendly country in which to travel, with fairly inexpensive accommodation, food and domestic transport. Venezuela has South America's cheapest air links with both Europe and the USA, and is thus a convenient gateway to the continent. Don't treat it, however, just as a bridge; give yourself some time to discover this land – it's worth it.

Country Name República de Venezuela
Area 916,445 sq km
Population 21 million (1995)
Population Density 23 per sq km
Capital Caracas
Head of State President Rafael Caldera (1994-99)
Official Language Spanish
Other Languages More than 25 Indian languages
Currency Bolívar (Bs)
Exchange Rate US$1 = 470 Bs
Per Capita GNP US$2840 (1993)
Inflation Rate 57% (1995)

Facts about the Country

HISTORY
The Pre-Columbian Period
It's estimated that by the time of the Spanish conquest, about half a million Indians lived

NETHERLANDS ANTILLES

CARIBBEAN SEA

Aruba

Curaçao

Bonaire

Islas Las Aves

Islas Los Roques

Isla Orchila

Isla Blanquilla

Península de La Guajira

Península de Paraguaná

Pueblo Nuevo

Los Taques

Punto Fijo

Riohacha

Maicao

San Rafael

Coro

San Luis

Churuguara

San Juan

Isla Tortuga

Tucacas

Puerto Cabello

Maiquetía

Los Teques

CARACAS

Puerto La Cruz

Maracaibo

Santa Rita

Cabimas

Carora

Quíbor

Barquisimeto

Valencia

Maracay

Barcelona

Machiques

Lago Maracaibo

Araure

San Carlos

San Juan

Aragua

Anaco

To Santa Marta

Acarigua

El Sombrero

Valle de la Pascua

Zaraza

Cantaura

Trujillo

Guanare

Calabozo

El Vigía

Mérida

Barinas

Pico Bolívar 5007m

Libertad

La Fría

Bruzual

Río Apure

San Fernando de Apure

Cúcuta

San Cristóbal

San Antonio del Táchira

Apurito

Río Orinoco

Caicara de Orinoco

Guasdualito

Mantecal

To Bogotá

Elorza

Arauca

Puerto Páez

Río Meta

Puerto Carreño

El Burro

Puerto Ayacucho

To Bogotá

Puerto Gaitán

COLOMBIA

Samariapo

San Fernando de Atabapo

Río Orinoco

Río Guainía

San Carlos de Río Negro

Río Casiquiare

Venezuela

0   100   200 km

Río Negro

in the region which is now Venezuela. They were isolated tribes of various ethnic backgrounds, belonging to three main linguistic families: Carib, Arawak and Chibcha.

The warlike Carib tribes inhabited the central and eastern coast, living by fishing and shifting agriculture. Various Arawak groups were scattered over a large area of western Llanos and north up to the coast. They lived by hunting and food-gathering, and only occasionally practised farming.

The Timote-Cuica, of the Chibcha linguistic family, were the most advanced of Venezuela's pre-Columbian societies. They founded settlements in the Andes linked by a network of trails. They had a fairly well developed agriculture, including the use of irrigation and terraces where the topography required it.

The Spanish Conquest

Columbus was the first European to set foot on Venezuelan soil – indeed, it was the only South American mainland country Columbus landed on. On his third trip to the New World, in 1498, he anchored at the eastern tip of the Península de Paria, opposite Trinidad. He at first thought he had discovered yet another island, but continuing along the coast, he found the voluminous mouth of the Río Orinoco – sufficient proof that the place was much more than an island. Astonished by his discovery, he wrote in his diary: 'Never have I read or heard of so much sweet water within a salt ocean.'

A year later another explorer, Alonso de Ojeda, accompanied by the Italian Amerigo Vespucci, sailed up to the Península de la Guajira, at the western extremity of present-day Venezuela. On entering Lago Maracaibo the Spaniards saw the local Indians living in rustic thatched huts on stilts above the water. They called the land Venezuela (literally, 'Little Venice'), though the place was far from the opulence of the Italian city they knew.

The first Spanish settlement on Venezuelan soil, Nueva Cádiz, was established in around 1500 on the small island of Cubagua, just south of Isla de Margarita. Living by harvesting pearls, the town swiftly developed into a busy port, but it was completely destroyed by an earthquake and tidal wave in 1541. The earliest Venezuelan town still in existence, Cumaná, dates from 1521.

Officially, Venezuela was ruled by Spain from Santo Domingo, or Hispaniola (today the Dominican Republic), until 1717, when it fell under the administration of the newly created Viceroyalty of Nueva Granada with its capital in Bogotá, to remain so until independence. In practice, however, the region was allowed a large degree of autonomy. It was such an unimportant backwater, with an uninviting steamy climate, that the Spaniards gave it low priority. In many ways, Venezuela remained a backwater until the oil boom of the 1920s.

Independence Wars

Apart from three brief rebellions between 1749 and 1797, colonial Venezuela had a relatively uneventful history. All this changed at the beginning of the 19th century, when Venezuela gave Latin America its greatest hero, Simón Bolívar. 'El Libertador', as he is commonly known, together with his most able lieutenant, Antonio José de Sucre, were to be largely responsible for ending colonial rule all the way to the borders of Argentina.

The revolutionary flame was lit by Francisco de Miranda in 1806, but his efforts to set up an independent administration in Caracas ended when he was handed over to the Spanish by his fellow conspirators. He was shipped to Spain and died shortly afterwards in a Cádiz jail.

Leadership of the revolution was taken over by Bolívar. After unsuccessful attempts to defeat the Spaniards at home, he withdrew to Colombia, then to Jamaica, until the opportune moment came in 1817.

At the time, the Napoleonic Wars had ended and Bolívar's agent in London was able to raise money and arms and to recruit over 5000 British veterans of the Peninsular War. With this force, and an army of horsemen from Los Llanos, Bolívar marched over the Andes and defeated the Spanish at the battles of Pantano de Vargas and Boyacá, thus bringing independence to Colombia in August 1819.

Four months later in Angostura (present-day Ciudad Bolívar), the Angostura Congress proclaimed Gran Colombia, a new state unifying Colombia, Venezuela and Ecuador (though the last two were still under Spanish rule).

The liberation of Venezuela was completed with Bolívar's victory over Spanish forces at Carabobo in 1821, though the royalists put up a desultory rearguard fight from Puerto Cabello for another two years. Bolívar and Sucre went on to liberate Ecuador, Peru and Bolivia by the end of 1824.

Although both economically and demographically Venezuela was the least important of the areas which made up Gran Colombia, it bore the brunt of the fighting. Not only did Venezuelan patriots fight on their own territory, they also fought in the armies which Bolívar led into Colombia and down the Pacific coast. It is estimated that over a quarter of the Venezuelan population died in these wars.

Gran Colombia existed for only a decade before splitting into three separate countries. Bolívar's dream of a unified republic fell apart even before his death, in 1830.

After Independence

Venezuela's independence period was marked by serious governmental problems which continued for over a century. For the most part, these were times of despotism and anarchy, with the country being ruled by a series of military dictators known as *caudillos*. It wasn't until 1947 that the first democratic government was elected.

The first of the caudillos, General José Antonio Páez, represented the conservative oligarchy, and controlled the country for 18 years (1830-48), though not as president for all that time. Despite his tough rule, he established a certain political stability and put the weak economy on its feet.

The period which followed was an almost uninterrupted chain of civil wars and political strife, only stopped by another long-term dictator, General Guzmán Blanco. He came to power in 1870 and kept it, with a few breaks, until 1888. A conservative with liberal leanings, he launched a broad programme of reform, including a new constitution, compulsory primary education, religious freedom and regulations designed to improve the economy. No doubt he tackled some of the crucial domestic issues and assured temporary stability, but his despotic rule triggered wide popular opposition, and when he stepped down, the country plunged again into civil war.

Things were not much better on the international front. In the 1840s Venezuela raised the question of its eastern border with British Guiana (today Guyana). Based on vague pre-independence territorial divisions, the Venezuelan government laid claim to as much as two-thirds of Guiana, up to the Río Essequibo. The issue, which led to severe strains in international relations in the 1890s, was finally settled in 1899 by an arbitration tribunal, which gave rights over the questioned territory to Great Britain. Despite this, Venezuela continues to claim it to this day. All Venezuelan-produced maps have this chunk of Guyana within Venezuelan boundaries, labelled 'Zona en Reclamación'.

Another conflict during this time was Venezuela's failure to meet payments to Great Britain, Italy and Germany, on loans accumulated during the irresponsible government of yet another caudillo, General Cipriano Castro. In response, in 1902, the three countries sent their navies to blockade Venezuelan seaports.

Modern Times

The first half of the 20th century was dominated by five successive military rulers from the Andean state of Táchira, the first of whom was the incompetent Cipriano Castro. The longest lasting and most despotic was General Juan Vicente Gómez, who seized power in 1908 and didn't relinquish it until his death in 1935. Gómez phased out the parliament, squelched the opposition and

thus monopolised power, supported by a strong army, extensive police force and well-developed spy network. Thanks to the discovery of oil in the 1910s, the Gómez regime was able to stabilise the country. By the late 1920s, Venezuela became the world's largest exporter of oil. This not only contributed notably to economic recovery but also enabled the government to pay off the country's entire foreign debt.

Little of the oil-related wealth filtered down to people on the street. The vast majority continued to live in poverty, with little or no educational or health facilities, let alone reasonable housing. Oil money also resulted in the neglect of agriculture. Food had to be imported in increasing amounts, and prices rose rapidly. When Gómez died in 1935, the people of Caracas went on a rampage, burning down the houses of his relatives and supporters and even threatening to set fire to the oil installations on Lago Maracaibo.

Gómez was succeeded by his own war minister, Eleázar López Contreras, and six years later by yet another Táchiran general, Isaías Medina Angarita. Meanwhile, popular tensions rose dangerously, exploding in 1945 when Rómulo Betancourt (founder and leader of the left-wing Acción Democrática party), with the support of the majority of the people and some junior army officers, took control of the government. A new constitution was adopted in 1947, and a noted novelist, Rómulo Gallegos, became president in Venezuela's first democratic election.

The pace of reform was too fast, however, given the strength of old military forces greedy for power. The inevitable coup took place only eight months later, with Colonel Marcos Pérez Jiménez emerging as leader. Once in control, Jiménez began ruthlessly crushing his opposition, at the same time ploughing the oil money back into public works, into industries which would help diversify the economy and, particularly, into modernising Caracas.

Spectacular buildings mushrooming in the capital were a poor substitute for a better standard of living and access to political power. Opposition to Jiménez's rule grew, and in 1958 he was overthrown by a coalition of civilians and navy and air force officers.

The country returned to democratic rule and an election was held, in which Betancourt was elected president. He put an end to the former dictator's solicitous policy towards foreign big business, but was careful this time not to act too impetuously.

Betancourt enjoyed widespread popular support and succeeded in completing the constitutional five-year term in office, the first democratically elected Venezuelan president to do so. He voluntarily stepped down in 1963. Since then, all changes of president have been by constitutional means.

Presidents Raúl Leoni (1964-69) and Rafael Caldera (1969-74) had relatively easy and quiet terms, since the steady stream of oil money that flowed into the country kept the economy healthy. President Carlos Andrés Pérez (1974-79) witnessed the oil bonanza. Not only did production of oil rise but, following the Arab-Israeli war, the price quadrupled overnight. Pérez nationalised the iron ore and oil industries and went on a spending spree. Imported luxury goods crammed shops and the nation got the impression that El Dorado had materialised. Not for long, though.

In the late 1970s, the growing international recession and oil glut began to shake Venezuela's economic stability. Oil revenues started to decline, pushing up unemployment and inflation, and consequently popular discontent increased. Presidents Luis Herrera Campins (1979-84) and Jaime Lusinchi (1984-89) witnessed a gradual slowing down of the economy.

The 1988 drop in world oil prices cut the country's revenue in half, putting into serious doubt Venezuela's ability to pay off its foreign debt. Austerity measures introduced in February 1989 by President Pérez (elected for the second time) triggered a wave of protests, culminating in three days of bloody riots known as the *caracazo* and costing over 300 lives. All further measures (which basically consisted of price increases) immediately spurred protests and not infrequently escalated into riots. Strikes

and street demonstrations came to be part of everyday life, as they continue to be today. Meanwhile, the economy was slipping downward and this increasingly affected political stability.

To make matters worse, there were two attempted coups d'état in 1992. The first, launched in February by a faction of mid-rank military officers led by Hugo Chávez Frías, was a shock to most Venezuelans. There was shooting throughout Caracas, claiming over 20 lives, but the government retained control.

Another attempt, in November, was led by junior air force officers. The air battle over Caracas, with warplanes flying between the skyscrapers, gave the coup a cinematographic, if not apocalyptic, dimension. The Palacio de Miraflores (the presidential palace) was bombed and partially destroyed. The army was again called to defend the president, which it dutifully did. This time, over 100 people lost their lives.

Although both coups failed, the army is increasingly divided, and disillusioned with the economic stalemate which is cutting its income. The two coup attempts have left a clear message: despite 35 years of democracy, the army is ready to take centre stage at any time.

Things became even more complicated when Pérez was accused of involvement in corruption. The Supreme Court examined the issue and, in May 1993, declared there was enough evidence to charge the president. Pérez was automatically suspended from his duties and Ramón Velásquez was appointed to serve as interim president for the last eight months of the statutory Pérez term.

Recent Politics

Amidst the corruption scandals and a general political stalemate, the December 1993 elections put Rafael Caldera back into the presidency, with voters probably hoping he would repeat his success of the early 1970s. However, 25 years on, the economic situation was quite different, as was the man himself, now 77 years of age.

Caldera's problems began on the eve of taking office. In February 1994, Venezuela's second-largest bank, Banco Latino, collapsed and had to be rescued by a government takeover at an estimated cost of US$2 billion. The domino-like failure of a dozen other banks throughout 1994 cost the government another US$6 billion to pay off depositors. Several further banks failed in 1995, probably the largest financial collapse experienced by any country in recent history.

Unlike previous free-market-oriented governments, Caldera's opted for a state-controlled economy. By suspending economic rights by decree, the government gave itself the power to intervene in any area of economic activity, including price controls. It fixed the exchange rate and introduced restrictions on the export of foreign currencies.

The economic situation, however, continued to worsen. In December 1995 the government devalued the currency by more than 70%, yet it fell even farther on the parallel free market. Facing a catastrophic economic decline on the one hand, and subject to the requirements of the International Monetary Fund on the other, in April 1996 the government introduced drastic rescue measures. These included increasing petrol prices by about 500% and freeing the exchange rate.

Economic problems apart, the government is in an uneasy situation as it tries to keep cautious relations with the military. Hugo Chávez Frías, pardoned by Caldera and now free, doesn't miss any opportunity to discredit the president and hasn't ruled out the possibility of another coup d'état.

The country is in its deepest crisis since the 1950s. Its economic and political prospects are uncertain and are likely to remain so for a while.

GEOGRAPHY

With an area of 916,445 sq km, Venezuela is South America's sixth-largest country. It occupies the northernmost extremity of the continent, including much of the Caribbean coast within its frontiers. The country has borders with Colombia to the west, Brazil to the south and Guyana to the east.

Venezuela is very varied geographically. Just south of the Caribbean coast looms a chain of mountain ranges, the Cordillera de la Costa, with a number of peaks exceeding 2000 metres. The mountains roll southward into a vast area of plains known as Los Llanos, which stretches down to the Orinoco and Meta rivers and occupies one-third of the country's territory.

The land south of the Río Orinoco (nearly half the country) can be broadly divided into two regions. To the south-west is a chunk of the Amazon Basin, a dense tropical forest of which large areas are hardly accessible. To the north-east lies an extensive plateau of open savannas, the Guiana Highlands. It's here that the majority of tepuis are located. These gigantic table mountains, with vertical walls and flat tops, are all that's left of the upper layer of a plateau which has gradually eroded over millions of years.

North-western Venezuela is another area of geographical contrasts. Here lies the Sierra Nevada de Mérida, the northern end of the Andean chain and Venezuela's highest mountain range, culminating at 5007 metres on snowcapped Pico Bolívar. North of the cordillera extends the marshy lowland basin around Lago Maracaibo. Some 160 km long and 120 km wide, it's the largest lake in South America, linked to the Caribbean Sea by a narrow strait, and is Venezuela's main oil-producing area. Farther north-east along the coast, near the town of Coro, is the country's sole desert, the Médanos de Coro.

The 2150-km Río Orinoco is Venezuela's main river, its entire course lying within the national boundaries. The Orinoco delta consists of over 50 major distributive channels along nearly 400 km of the Atlantic coast, covering an area of some 25,000 sq km.

Venezuela possesses a number of islands scattered along the Caribbean coast, the largest being Isla de Margarita. Other islands and archipelagos of importance include Las Aves, Los Roques, La Orchila, La Tortuga and Blanquilla.

VENEZUELA

CLIMATE

Given Venezuela's latitude, the temperature is fairly constant throughout the year. Temperature does, however, vary with altitude, dropping about 6°C with every 1000-metre increase. Since over 90% of Venezuela lies below 1000 metres, you'll experience average temperatures of at least 23°C in most parts of the country. The Andean and coastal mountain ranges are colder, and if you plan on climbing peaks of the Sierra, expect temperatures below freezing point at night.

Rainfall varies seasonally. Broadly speaking, the dry season is from December to April, while the wet period lasts for the rest of the year. There are many regional variations in the amount of precipitation and the length of the seasons. For example, the mountains receive more rainfall than the coast and can be relatively wet for most of the year. The Amazon has no distinct dry season, with the annual rainfall exceeding 2000 mm and distributed relatively evenly throughout the year.

FLORA & FAUNA

As a tropical country with a diverse geography, Venezuela has varied and abundant flora and fauna. Distinctive biohabitats have evolved in different regions, each with its own peculiar wildlife.

There are some 1250 species of bird, including the macaw *(guacamayo)*, parrot *(loro)*, toucan *(tucán)*, heron *(garza)*, pelican *(pelícano)*, flamingo *(flamenco)*, hummingbird *(colibrí)*, condor *(cóndor)* and oilbird *(guácharo)*.

Numbering some 250 species, mammals are also well represented and include the jaguar *(tigre)*, capybara *(chigüire)*, armadillo *(armadillo)*, anteater *(oso hormiguero)*, tapir *(danta)*, puma *(puma)*, ocelot *(ocelote)* and peccary *(báquiro)*, to name just a few.

There are numerous species of reptile, including the iguana, five species of cayman (American crocodile) and a variety of snakes.

Possibly the most unusual flora is on the tops of the tepuis. Isolated from the savanna below and from other tepuis for millions of years, the plant life on each of these plateaux developed independently. In effect, these biological islands have a totally distinctive flora, half of which is considered endemic and typical of only one or a group of tepuis.

Tropical forest – which still covers a quarter of the country's total area – features a maze of plant species uncommon in forests of moderate climates.

National Parks

Venezuela has 42 national parks and 20 other nature reserves called *monumentos naturales*. The latter are usually smaller than the parks and are intended to protect a particular natural feature such as a lake, mountain peak or cave. The whole system of parks and reserves covers about 15% of the country.

The Instituto Nacional de Parques, commonly referred to as Inparques, is the governmental body created to run and take care of national parks and reserves. Only a handful of parks have any Inparques-built tourist facilities. Most other parks are either wilderness or have been swiftly taken over by private operators, who have built their own tourist facilities and charge what they wish.

You need a permit to visit the national parks and you can get one from the central or regional Inparques offices. However, except at a few parks, you'll probably never be asked for the permit.

GOVERNMENT

Venezuela is a federal republic. The president, who is head of state and of the armed forces, is elected by a direct vote for a five-year term and cannot be elected for two consecutive terms. The national congress has a 47-seat senate and a 199-seat chamber of deputies, both elected for five-year terms. Voting is compulsory for citizens from the age of 18. The supreme court is the highest judicial body, with judges elected by the congress.

There are numerous political parties, of which the two major traditional movements are Acción Democrática (AD) and Partido Social Cristiano (Copei).

ECONOMY

Oil is Venezuela's main natural resource and the heart of the economy. Since its discovery in 1914, it has turned Venezuela – then a poor debtor nation – into one of South America's richest countries. Until 1970, Venezuela was the world's largest exporter of oil, and though it was later overtaken by the Arab countries, its oil income expanded year after year. As co-founder of OPEC, Venezuela influenced the fourfold rise of oil prices introduced by this organisation in 1973-74, which quadrupled its revenue. Oil export earnings peaked in 1982, at US$19.3 billion, representing about 96% of the country's exports. However, the global recession and the decline in world oil prices in the early 1980s were severe setbacks. Export earnings from oil fell drastically, to a low of US$7.2 billion in 1986.

The main oil deposits are in the basin of Lago Maracaibo, but other important reserves have been discovered and exploited in the Orinoco delta and on the eastern extremities of Los Llanos.

Predictably, oil has overshadowed other sectors of the economy. Agriculture has been largely neglected, and only a small portion of the country is under cultivation. Major crops include bananas, sugar cane, maize, coffee, cacao, cotton and tobacco.

Iron ore is the most important mineral after oil, with huge deposits found south of Ciudad Bolívar. The iron ore industry is centred around the city of Ciudad Guayana. Among other major subsoil riches are bauxite, gold and diamonds (all in Guayana), and coal (near the border with Colombia, north of Maracaibo).

Manufacturing industries have progressed as an effect of the government's policy to diversify the economy. The motor vehicle assembly, textile, footwear, paper and food industries are now well established.

Venezuela's hydroelectric potential is considerable; the Guri dam, south of Ciudad Guayana, is the second-largest hydroelectric plant in the world, with a potential of 10 million kW.

POPULATION & PEOPLE

As of 1995, the population was estimated at 21 million, of which about one-fifth lived in Caracas. The rate of population growth, around 2.4%, is one of the highest in Latin America. Venezuela is a young nation, with over half its inhabitants below 18 years of age. Yet, at nearly 70 years, life expectancy is remarkably high.

Population density, averaging about 23 per sq km, is low, though it varies a great deal throughout the country. The central coastal region, including the cities of Valencia, Maracay and Caracas, is the most densely populated, while the Amazon, Los Llanos and Guayana are sparsely populated. About three-quarters of Venezuelans live in towns and cities.

Venezuela is a country of mixed blood. About 70% of the population have a blend of European, Indian and African ancestry, or any two of the three. The rest are white (about 20%), black (8%) or Indian (2%). Indians don't belong to a single ethnic or linguistic family, but form different, independent groups scattered throughout the country. Major Indian communities include the Guajiro (north of Maracaibo), the Piaroa, Guajibo, Yekuana and Yanomami (in the Amazon), the Warao (in the Orinoco delta) and the Pemón (in south-eastern Guayana). There are over 40 Indian languages used in the country.

ARTS

Architecture

As the Province of Venezuela was a backwater of the Spanish Crown, local architecture never reached the grandeur that marked its wealthier neighbours Colombia, Ecuador and Peru. Churches were rather unpretentious and houses followed the modest Andalusian style. Only in the last half-century of the colonial era, when there was noticeable economic growth, did a class of wealthier merchants emerge who built residences reflecting their new social position.

VENEZUELA

Nonetheless, these were few and far between, and only a handful of remarkable examples survive.

The first 50 years of independence didn't affect Venezuelan architecture much, until a thorough modernisation programme for Caracas was launched in the 1870s by the dictator Guzmán Blanco, which resulted in a number of monumental public buildings.

The second rush towards modernity came with oil money and culminated in the 1970s. This period was characterised by an indiscriminate demolition of the old urban fabric and its replacement by modern architecture. Many colonial buildings, dilapidated by time and use, fell prey to progressive urban planners. Accordingly, Venezuela's colonial legacy can be disappointing when compared to that of other Andean countries. On the other hand, Venezuela has some of the best ultramodern architecture on the continent. Carlos Raúl Villanueva, who began work in the 1930s, is the most outstanding Venezuelan architect and has left behind a large number of projects in Caracas and other cities.

Visual Arts

Some of the best of pre-Columbian creativity is reflected in the petroglyphs, predominantly carvings on rock, which have been found at about 200 locations throughout the country. The majority of the petroglyphs are in the central coastal region between Barquisimeto and Caracas, and along the Orinoco and Caroní rivers. A number of cave paintings have also been discovered, almost all of them in Bolívar and Amazonas states.

The painting and sculpture of the colonial period had an almost exclusively religious character, and the style followed the Spanish art of the day. Consisting mainly of paintings of saints, carved wooden statues and retables, it can be seen in old churches and museums.

With independence, painting turned to historical themes; the outstanding figures of the genre include Martín Tovar y Tovar (1827-1902), particularly remembered for his monumental works in Caracas' Capitolio Nacional, and Tito Salas (1888-1974), who dedicated himself to commemorating Bolívar's life and achievements.

Modern painting began with Armando Reverón (1889-1954), while Francisco Narváez (1905-82) is commonly acclaimed as Venezuela's first modern sculptor. The most remarkable contemporary artists include Héctor Poleo (1918-89), Alejandro Otero (1921-90), Marisol Escobar (born 1930) and Jacobo Borges (born 1931).

The most internationally renowned Venezuelan artist of the last decades is Jesús Soto (born 1923), the leading representative of kinetic art. Carlos Cruz Díez (born 1923), somewhat overshadowed by Soto's fame, is also noted for his kinetic art.

Literature

Simón Bolívar (1783-1830) has left an extensive heritage, including letters, proclamations, discourses and dissertations, and also some more literary achievements such as *Mi Delirio sobre El Chimborazo*. Bolívar was influenced by his close friend Andrés Bello (1781-1865), the first important Venezuelan poet.

Andrés Eloy Blanco (1896-1955) is commonly considered the best poet Venezuela has produced, while Rómulo Gallegos (1884-1969) is perhaps the Venezuelan writer best known internationally. *Doña Bárbara*, his most famous novel, was first published in Spain in 1929 and since then has been translated into a dozen languages.

Today, Arturo Uslar Pietri (born 1906) stands out as an authority in the field of literature. A novelist, essayist, historian, literary critic and journalist, he has also been a prominent figure in politics.

Music

The most characteristic Venezuelan rhythm is the *joropo*, which developed in Los Llanos and gradually conquered the country. The joropo is usually sung and accompanied on harp, *cuatro* (a small, four-stringed guitar) and maracas. There's a dance form of joropo as well.

There are also plenty of regional beats. In

the eastern part of the country you'll hear, depending on the region, the *estribillo*, *polo margariteño*, *malagueñas*, *fulías*, and *jotas*. In the west, the *gaita zuliana* is typical for Maracaibo while the *bambuco* is one of the popular rhythms of the Andes. The central coast echoes with African drumbeats, an audible mark of the sizeable black population. Caracas has absorbed all the influences, both local and international, and blasts as much with joropo and *merengue* as with salsa and Western rock.

RELIGION
Most Venezuelans are Roman Catholic. Many Indian tribes adopted Catholicism, and only a few, primarily those living in isolation, still practise their ancient beliefs. There are various Protestant churches in Venezuela, and lately they have been gaining in importance, taking adherents away from the Roman Catholic Church. There are small populations of Jews and Muslims.

LANGUAGE
Spanish is Venezuela's official language and, except for some remote Indian tribes, all the inhabitants speak it. Venezuelan Spanish is not the clearest or easiest to understand. Most Venezuelans (except for people from the Andes) speak rapidly and tend to drop some endings, especially plurals. Many people, mostly in large urban centres, speak some English, but it's certainly not a commonly understood or spoken language.

Facts for the Visitor

VISAS & EMBASSIES
Nationals of the USA, Canada, Australia, New Zealand, Japan, the UK and most of Western and Scandinavian Europe don't need visas if they fly into Venezuela; a tourist card *(tarjeta de ingreso)* is issued by the airline at no cost. The tourist card is normally valid for 90 days (unless the immigration officers note on the card a shorter period) and can be extended for another 60 days.

All foreign nationals who enter Venezuela by land from Brazil, Colombia or Guyana do need a visa. However, Venezuelan consulates in South American countries may prove difficult places to get visas. In Colombia, for example, possibly only the consulates in Cúcuta and Cartagena will give visas to non-Colombians. Even the consulate in Bogotá is likely to refuse you a visa. The same may happen in the consulate in Boa Vista, Brazil.

The only viable alternative in this situation is to fly into Venezuela, in which case you will be automatically granted the tourist card. There are cheap flights from Colombia, but not so from Brazil (see the Getting There & Away section in this chapter).

If you plan on travelling overland, it's best to get the visa in your country of residence. Venezuela has introduced multiple-entry tourist visas which are valid for one year from the date of issue. Consulates in most major Western countries, including the USA, the UK and Australia, now issue this type of visa. The official requirements are: your passport (valid for at least one year), a bank letter stating your funds, an employer's letter stating your wages, an onward ticket and one photo. The visa may take several days to be issued, and its cost varies depending on the country from which you apply (up to US$30).

On entering Venezuela your passport and the tourist card will be stamped (make sure this happens) by Dirección de Identificación y Extranjería (DIEX) border officials. You may be asked for an onward ticket, though it's no longer a rule; it varies from one border crossing to another and from one official to another.

Visa extensions are handled by the Caracas office of DIEX (see the Caracas section for details).

Venezuelan Embassies Abroad
Venezuela has representatives in neighbouring countries and in:

Australia
   MLC Tower, Phillip, ACT 2606 (☎ (06) 282-4828)

Canada
    32 Range Rd, Ottawa, Ontario K1N 8J4 (☎ (613) 235-5151)
France
    11 Rue Copernie, 75116 Paris (☎ 01 45 53 29 98)
Germany
    Im Rheingarten 7, 5300 Bonn 3 (☎ (0228) 40 09 20)
UK
    1 Cromwell Rd, London SW7 2HW (☎ (0171) 581-2776, 581-2777)
USA
    1099 30th St NW, Washington, DC 20007 (☎ (202) 342-2214)

Foreign Embassies in Venezuela

See the Caracas section for some foreign representations. If yours is not listed, consult the phone directory.

CUSTOMS

Customs regulations don't differ much from other countries on the continent. You are allowed to bring in personal belongings and presents you intend to give to Venezuelan residents. You can bring with you cameras (still, video and movie), a tape recorder, a radio, camping equipment, sports accessories, a personal computer and the like without any problems.

According to Venezuelan law, the possession, trafficking and consumption of drugs is a serious offence and subject to heavy penalties. You would be crazy to try smuggling them across the border. If you're coming overland from Colombia your baggage is likely to be searched at the border and/or at *alcabalas* (police road checkpoints). This is because of the considerable drug traffic that passes this way.

MONEY
Currency

The unit of currency is – not surprisingly – the *bolívar* (abbreviated to Bs), which is divided into 100 *céntimos*. There are one-half, one, two and five-bolívar coins and five, 10, 20, 50, 100, 500, 1000, 2000 and 5000-bolívar notes.

Exchange Rates

During the period of the state-imposed, fixed exchange rates of the bolívar against foreign currencies (June 1994 to April 1996), there was a thriving black market in Venezuela, where you could get up to 70% more bolívares for your dollars on the street than in the bank. Since the bolívar was freed, it seems the situation has returned to normal. This means that there's no longer a black market and you'll again have to change money in the bank or other authorised money-exchange office. Given the precarious state of the economy, however, some other unexpected measures may be introduced. Check for news with other travellers on the road. As of July 1996, approximate exchange rates included:

Australia	A$1	=	369 Bs
Canada	C$1	=	345 Bs
France	FF1	=	91 Bs
Germany	DM1	=	307 Bs
Japan	¥100	=	433 Bs
New Zealand	NZ$1	=	320 Bs
United Kingdom	UK£1	=	725 Bs
USA	US$1	=	470 Bs

Changing Money

US dollars and American Express travellers' cheques are by far the most popular in Venezuela, so stick to them. Among credit cards, Visa and MasterCard are the most useful to get cash advances from banks and are accepted as a means of payment in a variety of (mostly up-market) establishments, including hotels, restaurants, airlines and shops. Curiously, many regional tour operators may refuse payments by credit card, or charge 10% more if you pay with plastic money.

You can change money at a bank or at a *casa de cambio* (an authorised money-exchange office). Banks change cash and travellers' cheques and give cash advances to credit-card holders. Casas de cambio change cash but seldom change travellers' cheques.

Banks are plentiful in Venezuela but only a handful of them handle foreign exchange. Furthermore, the availability of this service seems to differ from bank to bank, branch to branch and city to city, and changes from day to day. As a general rule, the banks to look for are:

Banco Consolidado (which almost always changes American Express travellers' cheques and sometimes cash)
Banco Unión (which gives advances on Visa and sometimes on MasterCard, and usually changes cash but rarely travellers' cheques)
Banco de Venezuela (which irregularly changes cash and travellers' cheques and accepts credit cards)
Banco Mercantil (which pays advances on MasterCard)

Banco Latino, Banco Construcción, Banco Provincial, Banco Italo Venezolano and some regional banks may, sometimes, also be useful.

The opening hours of banks are the same throughout the country: Monday to Friday from 8.30 to 11.30 am and 2 to 4.30 pm. Banks are usually crowded, inefficient and often handle exchange operations during limited hours (mostly in the morning). Casas de cambio are much faster; the whole operation takes a minute or two.

The place to report the loss or theft of American Express travellers' cheques and apply for a replacement or refund is Turisol. Its head office is in Caracas and it has branches in Barquisimeto, Maracay, Valencia, Maracaibo, Mérida, Puerto La Cruz and Porlamar.

Costs
Venezuela was a very cheap country to travel in during the period of the fixed exchange rates, provided you came with cash US dollars and changed them on the black market. Since the bolívar was freed, there has been a massive increase in prices of goods and services. Given the complex and volatile financial situation, treat the prices listed in this chapter as orientation figures only.

WHEN TO GO
The tourist season in Venezuela runs year round so, theoretically, any time you visit is OK. However, the dry season is certainly more pleasant for travelling, though some

sights – such as waterfalls, including the famous Angel Falls – are certainly more impressive in the wet season.

Also keep in mind the periods when Venezuelans take their holidays. They are mad about travelling to visit friends and family over Christmas, Carnaval (several days prior to Ash Wednesday) and Holy Week (the week before Easter Sunday). In these three periods, you'll have to plan ahead and do a little more legwork before you find a place to stay. On the other hand, these periods are colourful and alive with a host of festivities.

TOURIST OFFICES
The Corporación de Turismo, or Corpoturismo, is the government agency which promotes tourism and provides tourist information. Its head office is in Caracas. Outside the capital, the provision of tourist information has been taken over by regional tourist bodies which have their offices in the respective state capitals and in some other cities. Some are better than others, but on the whole they lack city maps and brochures and the staff rarely speak English.

BUSINESS HOURS & HOLIDAYS
The office working day is theoretically eight hours long, from 8 am to noon and 2 to 6 pm, Monday to Friday. All banks in Venezuela have the same business hours (see under Money earlier in this chapter). Almost all firms and offices, including most tourist offices, are closed on Saturday and Sunday.

The usual shopping hours are from 9 am to 6 or 7 pm, Monday to Friday, and a half-day on Saturday. Many shops close for lunch but some work the *horario corrido*, ie without a lunch-time break. Many restaurants don't open at all on Sunday. Most museums are closed on Monday but are open Sunday.

Official public holidays include 1 January (New Year's Day), Monday and Tuesday before Ash Wednesday (Carnaval), Maundy Thursday and Good Friday (Easter), 19 April (Declaration of Independence), 1 May (Labour Day), 24 June (Battle of Carabobo), 5 July (Independence Day), 24 July

(Bolívar's Birthday), 12 October (Discovery of America) and 25 December (Christmas Day).

SPECIAL EVENTS

Given the strong Catholic character of Venezuela, a good number of the feasts and celebrations follow the Church calendar. Possibly the biggest event celebrated throughout the country is Carnaval, which takes place on the Monday and Tuesday prior to Ash Wednesday, although feasting breaks out by the end of the preceding week.

Venezuela's most colourful event is perhaps Los Diablos Danzantes, or the Devil Dancers. It's held on Corpus Christi in San Francisco de Yare, about 60 km south of Caracas. The ceremony consists of a spectacular parade and the dance of devils, performed by dancers disguised in elaborate masks and costumes.

Cultural events such as festivals of theatre, film or classical music are almost exclusively confined to Caracas.

POST & COMMUNICATIONS
Post

The postal service is run by Ipostel which has post offices throughout the country. The service is slow, inefficient and unreliable. Air mail to the USA or Europe can take up to a month to arrive; that's assuming it arrives at all. Internal mail is also painfully slow.

Telephone

The telephone system is largely automated for both domestic and international connections. Public telephones exist in the larger cities but are often out of order. Coins are sometimes used for local calls, although most of the telephones now only operate on phonecards (tarjeta CANTV, also known as tarjeta inteligente). It's worth buying one if you think you might be using public phones from time to time. You can buy cards to the value of 500, 1000 or 2000 Bs (a standard local call costs approximately 5 Bs for three minutes). They are convenient for local and intercity calls. You can also use the tarjeta for short international calls, or go to the nearest

CANTV office and make the call through an operator. For city and town area codes, see specific town entries.

The international telephone service is expensive. Reverse-charge (collect) phone calls (llamadas de cobro revertido) are possible to most countries. The country code for Venezuela is 58. To call a number in Venezuela from abroad, dial the international access code of the country you're calling from, the country code (58), the area code (drop the initial '0') and the local phone number.

TIME

All of Venezuela lies within the same time zone, four hours behind GMT/UTC, and there's no daylight saving.

ELECTRICITY

Electricity is 110V, 60 Hz AC all over the country. US-type flat two-pin plugs are used.

WEIGHTS & MEASURES

Venezuela uses the metric system.

BOOKS

For more detailed travel information, get a copy of Lonely Planet's Venezuela – a travel survival kit. Among other guidebooks, Venezuela by Hilary Dunsterville Branch focuses on outdoor activities, predominantly hiking in national parks. Hiking in the Venezuelan Andes by Forest Leighty is a useful guide for those planning walks in the Andes. Insight Guides – Venezuela provides interesting reading and fascinating photography, but sparse practical information.

Janice Bauman & Leni Young's Guide to Venezuela, edited by Ernesto Armitano, is a 925-page book covering virtually every sight and town together with background information. It includes practical information, though not much of it is for the budget traveller. Unfortunately, the book hasn't been updated since 1987 and is almost impossible to obtain outside Venezuela.

A captivating overview of the period of Spanish colonisation is provided by John Hemming's The Search for El Dorado. Ven-

ezuela: the Search for Order, the Dream of Progress by John V Lombardi provides good general reading on history, politics, geography and people.

For a comprehensive 20th-century history, try *Venezuela, a Century of Change* by Judith Ewell or *Venezuela* by David Eugene Blank. *Paper Tigers and Minotaurs* by Moisés Naim provides information on economic policies over the past decade.

Travellers with a serious interest in Venezuelan wildlife may want to check *Neotropical Rainforest Mammals – A Field Guide* by Louise H Emmons, *A Guide to the Birds of South America, Where to Watch Birds in South America* by Nigel Wheatley and *A Guide to the Birds of Venezuela* by Rodolphe Meyer de Schauensee & William H Phelps.

MAPS

The best general map of Venezuela (scale 1:1,750,000) is published by International Travel Maps (Canada). Within Venezuela, folded road maps of the country are produced by Lagoven, Corpoven and several other publishers. Dirección de Cartografía Nacional is the government mapping body which produces and sells a variety of maps; see the Caracas section for details.

MEDIA

All the main cities have their own daily newspapers. The two leading Caracas papers, *El Universal* and *El Nacional*, have countrywide distribution. Both have reasonable coverage of national and international affairs, sport, economics and culture. *The Daily Journal* is the main English-language newspaper published in Venezuela. It's available at major newsstands and at selected bookshops in Caracas. Elsewhere, it can be difficult to come by.

Most of the numerous radio stations are dominated by musical programmes, principally imported pop, rock, disco and the like. Jazz and classical music are less popular but some stations do grant them airtime.

One government and three private TV stations operate out of Caracas and reach most of the country. They all offer the usual TV fare, including news, music, feature films, sport and culture. Prime time is dominated by *telenovelas*, or soap operas, Venezuelans' favourite TV entertainment. Almost all programming is in Spanish, including foreign films, which are dubbed.

Apart from the above-mentioned stations, there's Omnivisión, a pay-TV station, which offers a mixed Spanish/English package of feature films, sport, music, soap operas and CNN news. Satellite TV has boomed in Caracas and, to a lesser extent, in the other major cities.

HEALTH

Venezuela has quite a well-developed health service, with an array of well-stocked *farmacias* (pharmacies), private clinics and hospitals. Tap water is safe to drink in Caracas and several larger cities, but if you prefer to avoid it, a choice of mineral waters and other drinks is readily available in supermarkets and shops.

Sanitary conditions are probably a bit above average South American standards but are declining – yet another effect of economic crisis. No vaccinations are required on entering Venezuela, unless you come from an affected area. However, a vaccination or jab of gamma globulin against hepatitis is not a bad idea. Mosquitoes infest many low-lying areas, particularly the Amazon and Los Llanos, so use the usual prophylactics.

DANGERS & ANNOYANCES

Venezuela is a relatively safe country in which to travel, though robbery is becoming a problem. Common crime is increasing in the large cities. Caracas is by far the most dangerous place in the country, and you should take care while strolling about the streets, particularly at night. Keep your passport and money next to the skin, and your camera, if you are carrying one, hidden in a pack or bag. Venturing into poor shantytowns is asking for trouble.

Avoid police if you can, and if they stop you, be polite but not overly friendly. Don't get nervous or angry – this only works against you.

Never show disrespect for Bolívar – he is a saint to Venezuelans. For instance, sitting on a bench in Plaza Bolívar with your feet on the bench, or crossing the plaza carrying bulky parcels (or even a backpack) may be considered disrespectful, and police may hassle you for it.

When travelling around the country, there are plenty of alcabalas, though not all are actually operating. They sometimes check the identity documents of passengers, and only seldom the luggage as well. In the cities, police checks are uncommon, but they do occur, so always have your passport with you. If you don't, you may end up at the police station.

ACTIVITIES

Venezuela's 42 national parks provide a good choice of walks ranging from easy, well signposted trails to jungle paths where a machete might be a useful tool. Sierra Nevada de Mérida is the best region in Venezuela for high-mountain trekking and, if you're up to it, you can try mountaineering and rock climbing there. Mérida state is also the best area for mountain biking and paragliding.

Some national parks, including Morrocoy, Henri Pittier and Yacambú, are excellent for wildlife-watchers, and particularly for bird-watchers. Parts of Venezuela's coast are lined with coral reefs, providing good conditions for snorkelling and scuba diving. Other possible activities include sailing, fishing, rafting and caving, to name just a few.

HIGHLIGHTS

Angel Falls are Venezuela's promotional landmark, and few tourists want to miss an air view of this one-km-high waterfall. For some more adventurous travellers, a trek to the top of Roraima is without doubt a fascinating and unforgettable experience. Cueva del Guácharo is one of the most amazing caves on the continent. Other natural highlights include Andean tops around Mérida, the coral reefs of the Morrocoy national park, the waterfalls of La Gran Sabana and the wildlife of Los Llanos.

ACCOMMODATION

Venezuela has hotels for every budget, and it's usually easy to find a room. With some exceptions, low-budget hotels are uninteresting, styleless places – just bare walls, a bed and perhaps a few other bits of furniture. However, most cheapies have private baths. As most of the country lies in the lowland tropics, rooms usually have a fan, sometimes even air-conditioning, but there's no hot water. Always have a look at the room and check the fan or air-con before you book in and pay.

The price of cheap hotels is pretty similar throughout the country and doesn't seem to depend much on whether you're in a big city or a small town, or whether the place is touristy or not. Count on roughly US$4 to US$8 a single and US$5 to US$10 a double. Many budget hotels have *matrimoniales*, rooms with one wide bed intended for couples, which often cost only marginally more than singles.

Mid-range hotels provide more facilities but often lack character. They are usually reasonably priced for what they offer, and you can often stay in quite a good place for, say, US$20 to US$25 per double room. Only Caracas and Isla de Margarita have a choice of hotels with three-digit prices, and a few other cities such as Puerto La Cruz and Maracaibo have one or two such places. Hotels often charge foreigners a 10% tax on top of the room price, though not all budget places do so.

Brothels are not uncommon in Venezuela. More numerous, though, are love hotels (places which rent rooms by the hour). Many cheap hotels double as love hotels, and it's often impossible to avoid staying in one from time to time.

Venezuela has no youth hostels. Camping grounds, as the term is understood in the West, are few and far between; you can camp rough outside urban centres. Camping on the beach is popular, but be cautious and don't leave your tent unattended.

FOOD

Venezuela is a good place to eat. On the whole, food is good and relatively inexpensive. Apart from a variety of typical local dishes, there are plenty of Western cuisines available, including a dense array of gringo fast-food outlets. Spanish and Italian restaurants are particularly well represented, thanks to a sizeable migration from these two countries. There are also some good Chinese and Arab restaurants, mostly in the main cities.

In virtually every dining or drinking establishment a 10% service charge will automatically be added to the bill. In budget eateries, tipping is uncommon, but in up-market restaurants, a small tip is customary.

Gourmets should stay in Caracas, which offers the widest range of international delicacies (at a price, of course). On the other hand, undemanding rock-bottom travellers should look for restaurants which serve the so-called *menú del día*, a set meal consisting of soup and a main course, cheaper than any à-la-carte dish. As in most of South America, the market is a good, cheap option, offering local food, usually tasty and fresh.

The following list includes some typical Venezuelan snacks and dishes:

Arepa – this small toasted or fried maize pancake, which is itself plain, is often included as an accompaniment to some dishes. More popularly, it's served stuffed with cheese, meat, seafood etc. There are plenty of snack bars, commonly called *areperas*, which serve arepas with a choice of fillings, including octopus, shrimps, sausage, vegetable salad and avocado. It's a good snack for about US$1.
Cachapa – a large, round pancake made of fresh corn, often served with cheese and/or ham
Cachito – a sort of croissant filled with chopped ham and served hot
Hallaca – chopped pork, beef or/and chicken with vegetables and olives, all folded in a maize dough, wrapped in banana leaves and steamed; particularly popular during Christmas
Mondongo – a seasoned tripe cooked in bouillon with maize, potatoes and other vegetables
Muchacho – roast loin of beef served in sauce
Pabellón – main course consisting of shredded beef, rice, beans and fried plantain; it's Venezuela's national dish

Parrillada – a barbecue of different kinds of meat; originally an Argentine speciality but now widespread in Venezuela
Sancocho – a vegetable stew with fish, meat or chicken

DRINKS

Espresso coffee is strong and excellent in Venezuela. It's served in *panaderías* (coffee shops-cum-bakeries), which are plentiful. Ask for *café negro* if you want it black, *café marrón* if you prefer half coffee, half milk, and *café con leche* if you like very milky coffee.

Fruit juices are readily available in restaurants, *fuentes de soda*, *fruterías*, *refresquerías* and other eating outlets. Given the variety of fruit in the country, you have quite a choice. Juices come pure or watered down (*batidos*), or as milk shakes (*merengadas*).

The number one alcoholic drink is beer (*cerveza*), particularly Polar beer, which is the dominant brand. It's sold everywhere either in cans or small bottles. Among spirits, rum (*ron*) heads the list and comes in numerous varieties and qualities.

Getting There & Away

AIR

The official Venezuelan entry requirement is an onward ticket, so it is possible that no airline will sell you a one-way ticket unless you show them an onward ticket. The cheapest fares out of Venezuela are Servivensa's San Antonio del Táchira-Medellín flight (US$45) and its Santo Domingo-Bogotá flight (US$50).

To/From Europe & North America

Set at the northern edge of South America, Venezuela is the cheapest gateway to the continent from both Europe and North America. There are cheap tickets available from many European cities. In many cases, London will be the best budget jumping-off point, but there are special deals here and there, so you may also find agents in Paris,

Amsterdam, Madrid or Lisbon offering attractive fares.

From North America, the major gateway city is Miami. Several airlines fly from there to Caracas and a few other Venezuelan cities. Major carriers tend to have relatively high prices, but there are usually some minor South or Central American airlines which are cheaper. Servivensa may have Miami-Caracas discounted fares for as little as US$120 one way. At the time of writing, Zuliana de Aviación, a little known Venezuelan carrier based at Maracaibo, offered a Miami-Maracaibo fare of US$155 (US$285 60-day return). Check the offers of these and other regional airlines, which may include some good deals.

Before making a final decision, check Avensa's air pass (detailed in the Getting Around section), which may be a more attractive option than any combination of individual tickets.

To/From Brazil

Flights from Brazil to Venezuela are offered by several airlines, including Viasa and Varig, but are painfully expensive. For example, a flight to Caracas from the Brazilian cities of São Paulo or Rio de Janeiro will cost about US$750 (US$850 return). Possibly the cheapest air link between these two countries is the Manaus-Caracas flight serviced by Lloyd Aéreo Boliviano, but it's still pricey (US$450 one way).

To/From Colombia

There are plenty of flights between Bogotá and Caracas with several carriers, including Avianca, AeroPerú, Saeta, Servivensa and Viasa (US$204 one way, US$263 30-day return).

Other possible links between Colombia and Venezuela include Cartagena-Caracas with Viasa (US$180, US$238 30-day return), Barranquilla-Caracas with Lacsa (US$172, US$213 30-day return), Bogotá or Medellín to Maracaibo with Zuliana de Aviación (US$81, US$162 one-year return), Bogotá-Santo Domingo with Servivensa (US$50) and Medellín-San Antonio del Táchira with Servivensa (US$45). The two last-listed flights have become popular with travellers as a cheap and convenient way to enter Venezuela without visa problems. See the San Cristóbal and San Antonio del Táchira sections for details.

Note that when buying any international ticket in Colombia, you pay a 21% tax (10.5% on return flights) on top of the listed fares.

To/From the Netherlands Antilles

There are flights from Aruba to Caracas (US$100), Las Piedras (US$59), Maracaibo (US$100) and Valencia (US$100); from Curaçao to Caracas (US$85), Las Piedras (US$80) and Maracaibo (US$105); and from Bonaire to Caracas (US$91). All these flights are serviced by Servivensa and discount return fares are available. There are also flights on light planes (operated by regional carriers) from Aruba and Curaçao to Coro. See the Coro section for information.

To/From Trinidad

Flights between Port of Spain and Caracas are operated by United Airlines and ALM (US$114 one way). There are no longer any flights between Port of Spain and Maturín.

To/From Guyana & Suriname

There are no direct flights between these countries and Venezuela; you have to use Port of Spain as a bridge. Flights from Georgetown or Paramaribo to Caracas will cost around US$300.

LAND

To/From Brazil

Only one road runs between Brazil and Venezuela. It leads through Boa Vista to Santa Elena de Uairén and continues via El Dorado to Ciudad Guayana. See the Santa Elena de Uairén section for details.

To/From Colombia

You can enter Venezuela from Colombia at four border crossings. In the north-west there's a coastal smuggling route between Maicao and Maracaibo (see the Maracaibo section for details). Farther south is the most popular border crossing, between Cúcuta and San Antonio del Táchira (see the San Antonio section in this chapter and the Cúcuta section in the Colombia chapter). Next comes an unpopular, dangerous and inconvenient crossing from Arauca to El Amparo de Apure. Finally, there's an uncommon but interesting outback route from Puerto Carreño in Colombia to either Puerto Páez or Puerto Ayacucho in Venezuela (see the Puerto Ayacucho section).

To/From Guyana

There are no land border crossings between Guyana and Venezuela; you must go via Brazil.

SEA
To/From the Netherlands Antilles

There's no longer a ferry service between Curaçao and La Vela de Coro (the port of Coro), nor between Aruba and Punto Fijo; they may or may not reopen in the future.

To/From Trinidad

A ferry service operates between Port of Spain and Güiria and Isla de Margarita (see those sections for information).

ORGANISED TOURS

Venezuela is quite a popular destination with overseas tour operators, particularly those in the USA, UK and Germany. However, these tours are expensive; you are likely to save a lot of money arranging one in Venezuela. Information about local tour operators is included in the relevant sections.

LEAVING VENEZUELA

The airport tax for tourists leaving Venezuela is US$10, payable in either US dollars or bolívares.

Getting Around

AIR

Venezuela has a well-developed airline system. Viasa is the main international carrier, flying to Europe, the USA and most South American capitals, but it doesn't service domestic routes. Avensa and its young offspring, Servivensa, are the major domestic airlines, landing at two dozen airports throughout the country, and they too operate international flights. Aeropostal was another important domestic carrier before it became bankrupt a few years ago, but there are plans to reopen it. There are also a dozen minor passenger carriers which cover mostly regional routes, although a few of them (such as Zuliana de Aviación) also fly abroad.

Flying in Venezuela is still relatively cheap compared to countries such as Colombia or Brazil, but no longer the bargain it was several years ago. Though fuel remains cheap, airfares have doubled or even tripled over the past few years. Details on routes and fares are included in the relevant sections.

Be sure to reconfirm your flight at least 72 hours before departure, and arm yourself with patience, as not all flights depart at the scheduled time.

Avensa Air Pass

Avensa offers an air pass which allows you to fly within 45 days with Avensa and Servivensa on all the routes they service in the Americas. Travel can begin and end in any city on the network. One-way, return and open-jaw trips are permitted, but you cannot fly more than once on the same route. The pass includes a number of flight coupons (minimum of four, maximum unlimited) of your choice, each of which has a determined price. Coupons for any of the domestic routes cost US$40 each; those for international routes range from US$55 to US$200. For example, the New York-Caracas and Lima-Caracas coupons cost US$180 each, while Miami-Caracas and Bogotá-Caracas coupons are US$80. Contact Avensa's representatives in Europe or the USA (there are none in Australia) for details.

BUS

As there are no railways of any importance in Venezuela, most travelling is done by bus. Buses are generally fast and efficient, especially on the main roads, which are all surfaced. There's regular transport between most major population centres.

All intercity buses depart from and arrive at the *terminal de pasajeros*, or bus terminal. Every city has such a terminal, usually outside the city centre but always linked to it by local transport. Caracas is the most important transport hub, handling buses to just about every corner of the country.

There are dozens of bus companies, each owning a plethora of buses ranging from archaic junk to more recent models. The junk plies the regional secondary roads, while the newer buses serve the main long-distance routes. If various companies operate on the same route, fares are much the same with all of them. The standard of service, however, may differ from one company to another, and you'll soon become familiar with which are better than others.

Many major companies have introduced the so-called *servicio ejecutivo*, in modern, air-conditioned buses, which provide better standards and shorter travelling time, and cost about 20% to 40% more than the ordinary service. Note that the air-conditioning can be *very* efficient, so have warm clothing at hand to avoid being frozen solid.

In general, there's no need to buy tickets in advance for major routes, where there are plenty of buses. This rule, however, doesn't apply around Christmas, Carnaval and Easter, when plenty of Venezuelans rush to travel.

Many short regional routes are serviced by the so-called *por puesto* (literally, 'by the seat'). It's a cross between a bus and a taxi – the same kind of service as a *colectivo* in Colombia or Peru. Por puestos are usually taxis (less often, minibuses) which ply fixed routes and depart when all seats are filled. They cost about 30% to 50% more than ordinary buses, and are faster and usually more comfortable. On some routes, they are the dominant or even the exclusive means of transport.

TAXI

Taxis are fairly inexpensive and are worth considering, particularly for transport between the bus terminal and city centre, when you are carrying all your bags. Except for some major cities, taxis rarely have meters, so always fix the fare with the driver *before* boarding the cab. It's a good idea to find out the correct fare beforehand from an independent source, eg from terminal officials or a hotel reception desk.

CAR

Travelling by car is a comfortable and attractive way of getting around Venezuela. The country is sufficiently safe, the network of roads is extensive and usually in acceptable shape, and driving manners seem to be a bit better than in neighbouring countries. Petrol stations are numerous and fuel is cheap: US$0.15 to US$0.30 per litre, depending on the octane level.

There are a number of international and local car rental companies, including Hertz, Avis, Budget and National, with offices at major airports throughout the country and in the centres of the main cities. The addresses are not included in the text, but tourist offices, travel agencies or top-class hotels will give you the information.

Car rental is expensive: as a rough guide, a small car will cost around US$80 per day, while the discount rate for a full week is about US$400. A 4WD vehicle is considerably more expensive, and harder to obtain.

BOAT

Venezuela has a number of offshore territories, the main one being Isla de Margarita. See the Puerto La Cruz, Cumaná and Isla de Margarita sections for details about ferries going to/from the island. There's no regular boat service to Venezuela's other islands.

The Río Orinoco is the country's major waterway, navigable from its mouth up to Puerto Ayacucho. However, there's no passenger service on any stretch of the river.

ORGANISED TOURS

Tours are a popular way to visit some parts of Venezuela, largely because vast areas of the country are virtually inaccessible by public transport (eg the Amazon Basin) or because a visit on one's own to scattered sights over a large territory (eg in La Gran Sabana) may be considerably more time-consuming and, eventually, more expensive than a tour.

It's cheapest to arrange the tour from the regional centre closest to the area you are going to visit. Accordingly, for hikes in the Andes, the place to look for a guide is Mérida; for excursions around La Gran Sabana, the cheapest organised trips are to be found in Santa Elena de Uairén; for the Amazon, the obvious point for talking to agents is Puerto Ayacucho; and for tours to Angel Falls, Ciudad Bolívar is the place to shop around. You'll find details in the respective sections. Note that not many regional tour agents will want to accept credit cards or else will charge you 10% more if you pay with one.

Caracas

Founded by Diego de Losada in 1567, Santiago de León de Caracas was for three centuries a small and unhurried place, its inhabitants living their provincial way of life. The first to launch an extensive programme of modernisation was General Guzmán Blanco, who in the 1870s commissioned a number of monumental edifices, among them the Capitolio Nacional and the Panteón Nacional. However, the town grew at a relatively slow pace until well into the 20th century.

Then came the oil boom, and all began to change at the speed of light. During the last 50 years, the city's population has increased from about 350,000 to over four million. Oil money has been pumped into modernisation, successfully transforming the somewhat bucolic colonial town into a vast urban sprawl of concrete. In the name of progress, the colonial architecture, save for a handful of buildings, was effectively eradicated and replaced by spanking-new commercial centres and futuristic steel-and-glass towers. In the 1980s the metro was opened, the last important achievement of urban planning.

It cannot be denied that Caracas today has some of the best modern architecture on the continent. It also has a web of motorways unseen in other South American capitals. Yet unbalanced expansion has created vast areas of *barrios*, slum suburbs which sprawl up the hills all around the city centre. These are the result of huge postwar migration, spurred on by an illusory dream of wealth. Caracas' spectacular setting in a valley amidst rolling hills only highlights the contrast between wealth and poverty.

Its size and capital status make Caracas the unquestioned centre of Venezuela's political, scientific, cultural and educational life. Whether you are interested in good food, plush hotels, theatre, museums or shopping, nowhere else in Venezuela will you find as much to choose from.

Set at an altitude of about 900 metres, Caracas enjoys an agreeable, relatively dry and sunny climate with a mean temperature of about 22°C. The rainy season is from June to October.

On a less enticing note, Caracas is the least secure of all Venezuelan cities. Petty crime in general, and robbery and armed assaults in particular, are increasing, especially at night. The historic centre is unsafe for strolling after 8 pm or so, as is the area around the Nuevo Circo bus terminal.

Orientation

Nestled in a long, east-west valley, the city is at least 20 km from end to end. To the north looms the steep, green wall of Parque Nacional El Avila, beautifully free of human dwellings. To the south, by contrast, the city is expanding up the hillsides, with modern *urbanizaciones* and shabby *ranchitos* invading and occupying every acceptably flat piece of land.

The valley itself is a dense urban fabric with forests of skyscrapers sticking out of a mass of low-rise architecture. The area from El Silencio to Chacao can be considered the greater centre, packed with banks, offices,

VENEZUELA

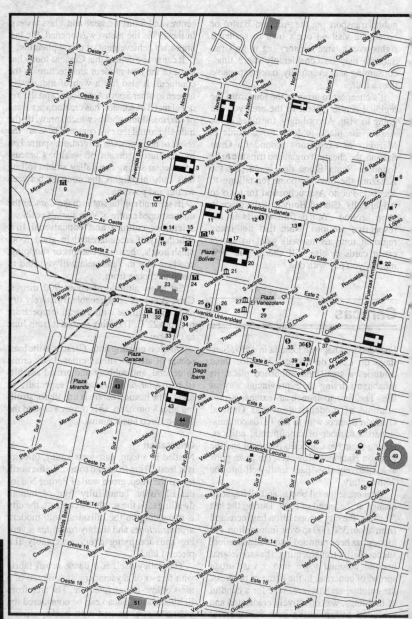

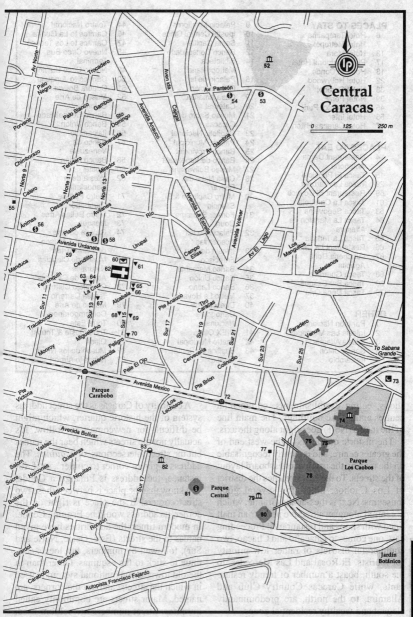

Central Caracas

PLACES TO STAY		9	Palacio Miraflores	44	Teatro Nacional
6	Hotel Terepaima	10	Ipostel Central Office	46	Carritos to La Guaira
7	Hotel Metropol	11	Santa Capilla	47	Carritos to Los Teques
13	Hotel Mara	12	Banco Consolidado	48	Nuevo Circo Bus
17	Plaza Catedral Hotel	14	Biblioteca		Terminal
18	Hotel El Conde		Metropolitana	49	Nuevo Circo Bullring
22	Hotel Hollywood	16	Palacio de la	50	Carritos to Junquito
38	Hotel Caracol		Gobernación	51	Cuadra Bolívar
39	Hotel Peral	19	Casa Amarilla	52	Museo de Arte
45	Hotel Center Park	20	Catedral		Colonial
55	Hotel Inter	21	Museo Sacro de	53	Banco Consolidado
77	Hotel Caracas Hilton		Caracas	54	Banco Unión
		23	Capitolio Nacional	56	Italcambio
		24	Palacio Municipal	57	Banco de
PLACES TO EAT		25	Banco Provincial		Venezuela
4	Restaurant Dama	26	Banco de Venezuela	58	Banco Unión
	Antañona	27	Museo Bolivariano	60	Ipostel
15	Tasca El Principal	28	Casa Natal de	62	Iglesia de la
29	Tasca La Atarraya		Bolívar		Candelaria
59	Restaurant El Coyuco	30	Metro Capitolio & El	71	Metro Parque
61	Tasca La Carabela		Silencio		Carabobo
63	Tasca Segoviana	31	Former Supreme	72	Metro Bellas Artes
64	Tasca La Mansión de		Court	73	Mosque
	Altamira	32	Palacio de las	74	Galería de Arte
65	Tasca La Tertulia		Academias		Nacional & Museo
66	Restaurant La Cita	33	Iglesia de San		de Bellas Artes
67	Lunchería Doña		Francisco	75	Museo de Ciencias
	Agapita	34	Banco Mercantil		Naturales
68	Tasca Guernica	35	Banco Unión	76	Ateneo de Caracas
69	Tasca Bar Basque	36	Banco Latino	78	Complejo Cultural
70	Tasca Dena Ona	37	Metro La Hoyada		Teresa Carreño
		40	Dirección de	79	Museo de Arte
OTHER			Cartografía		Contemporáneo
1	Panteón Nacional		Nacional	80	Torre Este
2	Iglesia Las Mercedes	41	DIEX Office	81	Torre Oeste & Tourist
3	Iglesia Altagracia	42	Teatro Municipal		Office
5	Banco Unión	43	Basílica de Santa	82	Museo de los Niños
8	Italcambio		Teresa	83	Buses to Airport

shops, eating establishments, commercial centres and public buildings. The main line of the metro (No 1) goes right along the axis.

The historic quarter is at the west end of the greater centre, and is clearly recognisable on the map by the original chessboard layout of the streets. To the east stretches the district of Los Caobos, noted for several good museums. Next is the Sabana Grande, which is centred along an attractive pedestrian mall lined with shops and restaurants. Proceeding east, one comes to Chacaíto and Chacao, two commercial districts of rather low priority for tourists. El Rosal and Las Mercedes, to the south, boast a number of trendy restaurants, while Caracas Country Club and Altamira, to the north, are predominantly elegant and wealthy residential zones.

A curiosity of Caracas is the street address system of the historic quarter, which might be difficult for newcomers to follow. It's actually not the streets which bear the names but the street intersections, or *esquinas*. The address is given 'corner to corner', so if, for instance, the address is Piñango a Conde, you know that the place is between these two street corners. If the place is right on the corner, its address would be Esquina Conde. In modern times, the authorities have given names to the streets (Este, Oeste, Norte and Sur), followed by numbers, but locals continue to stick to the esquinas. Other than in the old town, a conventional system is used in which the streets, and not the corners, are named. Major streets are commonly called *avenidas*. Street numbers are seldom used, and you rarely find one on façades or entrance doors.

Information

Tourist Office The Corpoturismo tourist office (☎ 5078600, 5078607) is on the 35th floor of the Torre Oeste (West Tower), Parque Central (metro: Bellas Artes). The office is open weekdays from 8.30 am to 12.30 pm and 2 to 5 pm. There's a Corpoturismo outlet in the international terminal of Maiquetía airport.

Money Caracas has plenty of banks, but few of them will change cash or travellers' cheques. Those that do include the Banco Consolidado (which deals with American Express cheques) and Banco Unión (which changes cash, though not at all branches). It's easier to come across a bank that gives cash advances to holders of a MasterCard or Visa card. The Banco de Venezuela, Banco Mercantil, Banco Unión and Banco Provincial, among others, tend to handle this operation.

There are plenty of casas de cambio, including Italcambio, which has several offices throughout the city. They are open weekdays from 8 am to 12.30 pm and 1.30 to 5 pm, and on Saturday from 8.30 am to noon. They change cash and travellers' cheques, paying about 0.5% less than the banks. There's also an Italcambio office at the Maiquetía airport (international terminal), open 24 hours.

The refund assistance point for the holders of American Express travellers' cheques is Turisol (☎ 9596091, 9598147, 9599417) in the Centro Ciudad Comercial Tamanaco (CCCT), Nivel Planta Baja. The American Express 24-hour information number is ☎ 2060222.

Post & Communications The central post office is on Avenida Urdaneta, Esquina Carmelitas, close to Plaza Bolívar. Have a look at the building itself – it was one of the most sumptuous palatial residences in 18th-century Caracas.

The telephone code for Caracas is 02. The code for Maiquetía is 031.

Foreign Embassies See the phone directory for a full list of foreign embassies in Caracas. This includes the following:

Australia
    Quinta Yolanda, Avenida Luis Roche entre Transversales 6 y 7, Altamira (☎ 2634033)
Brazil
    Centro Gerencial Mohedano, Calle Los Chaguaramos con Avenida Mohedano, La Castellana (☎ 2617553)
Canada
    Torre Europa, Avenida Francisco de Miranda, Campo Alegre (☎ 9516174)
Colombia
    Embassy: Torre Credival, Segunda Avenida de Campo Alegre con Avenida Francisco de Miranda, Campo Alegre (☎ 2618358)
    Consulate: Edificio Consulado de Colombia, Calle Guaicaipuro, Chacaíto (☎ 9513631)
France
    Edificio Embajada de Francia, Calle Madrid con Avenida Trinidad, Las Mercedes (☎ 9936666)
Germany
    Edificio Panaven, Avenida San Juan Bosco con Transversal 3, Altamira (☎ 2611205, 2610181)
Guyana
    Quinta Roraima, Avenida El Paseo, Prados del Este (☎ 9771158, 9782781)
Suriname
    Quinta Los Milagros, Avenida 4 entre Transversales 7 y 8, Altamira (☎ 2612724, 2631545)
Trinidad & Tobago
    Quinta Serrana, Avenida 4 entre Transversales 7 y 8, Altamira Norte (☎ 2614772, 2613748)
UK
    Edificio Torre Las Mercedes, Avenida La Estancia, Chuao (☎ 9934111)
USA
    Calle F con Avenida Suapure, Colinas de Valle Arriba (☎ 9772011, 9770553)

Visa Extensions Visa extensions for one month (US$12.50), or the maximum period of two months (US$25), are issued by the DIEX office on Avenida Baralt, facing Plaza Miranda. Your passport, one photo, a photocopy of your onward ticket and a letter explaining the purpose of the extension, written on the so-called *papel sellado*, are required, plus the form which they'll give you to fill in. All that has to be delivered between 8 and 11 am on a weekday, and the procedure takes up to eight working days.

VENEZUELA

Inparques The Dirección General de Parques Nacionales, commonly called Inparques (☎ 2854106, 2854360, 2854859), is just east of the Parque del Este metro station and is open weekdays from 8.30 am to 12.30 pm and 1.30 to 5 pm. This is the place to get permits to the national parks, which cost a mere US$0.20 for each park and are issued on the spot. Get permits to all the parks you plan to visit. Specify 'camping' if you plan on doing this and the park has such facilities.

Maps Some bookshops have a folded city map of Caracas which has a map of Venezuela on its reverse. The best Caracas map has been published by Lagoven Oil Company. It's sold at Lagoven petrol stations but stocks seem to be running out. There is a reasonable Caracas city map at the back of the local phone directory.

For large-scale maps of various regions of the country, go to the Dirección de Cartografía Nacional (☎ 4081614, 4081637), Calle Este 6, Colón a Dr Díaz, near Plaza Diego Ibarra. The office is open weekdays from 8.30 to 11.30 am and 2 to 4 pm.

Things to See

Despite the city's size, most tourist sights are grouped in a few areas. The excellent metro system helps enormously in moving from one district to another.

Old Caracas The historic sector has lost much of its identity. In a rush towards modernisation, many colonial houses were replaced with 20th-century architecture, which ranges from nondescript eclectic buildings to modern dyed-glass cubes.

The nucleus of the old quarter of the city is **Plaza Bolívar**, with the inevitable monument to the hero in the middle. The equestrian statue was cast in Europe, shipped in pieces, assembled and unveiled in 1874.

The **Catedral**, on the eastern side of the plaza, was built between 1665 and 1713 after an earthquake destroyed the previous church in 1641. A wide, five-nave interior supported on 32 columns was largely remodelled in the late 19th century. The Bolívar family chapel is in the middle of the right-hand aisle and is easily recognised by a modern sculpture of El Libertador mourning his parents and wife. Next to the cathedral is the **Museo Sacro de Caracas** (open Tuesday to Sunday from 10 am to 5 pm) featuring a collection of religious art.

The **Palacio Municipal**, on the southern side of the square, houses the **Museo Criollo**, which features exhibits related to the town's history, including dioramas depicting the life of turn-of-the-century Caracas. It's open Tuesday to Friday from 9 to 11.30 am and 2.30 to 4.30 pm, and on weekends from 10.30 am to 4 pm. The western side of the palace accommodates the **Capilla de Santa Rosa de Lima**, where on 5 July 1811 the Congress declared Venezuela's independence (though it was another 10 years before this became fact).

The entire block south-west of Plaza Bolívar is taken up by the neoclassical **Capitolio Nacional**, a complex of two buildings commissioned in the 1870s by Guzmán Blanco. In the northern building is the **Salón Elíptico**, an oval hall boasting a large mural on its domed ceiling. The painting, depicting the battle of Carabobo, was executed in 1888 by perhaps the most notable Venezuelan artist of the day, Martín Tovar y Tovar. The hall is open to visitors daily from 9 am to 12.30 pm and 3 to 5 pm.

Just south of the Capitolio is the **Iglesia de San Francisco**, with a number of richly gilded altarpieces embellishing its interior. It was in this church in 1813 that Bolívar was proclaimed El Libertador, and also here that his much-celebrated funeral was held in 1842, when his remains were brought from Colombia 12 years after his death.

Two blocks east is the **Casa Natal de Bolívar**, the house where he was born on 24 July 1783. Its reconstructed interior has been decorated with paintings by Tito Salas depicting Bolívar's battles and other scenes from his life. A few paces north, in another colonial house, the **Museo Bolivariano** displays independence memorabilia, documents, period weapons and banners, plus a number of portraits of Bolívar. Both museums are open weekdays from 9 am to noon and 2 to 5 pm, and weekends from 10 am to 1 pm and 2 to 5 pm.

Seven blocks south is yet another place associated with El Libertador, the **Cuadra Bolívar**. It's a summer house where Bolívar spent much of his childhood and youth. Restored to its original appearance and stuffed with period furnishing, the house is today a museum, open weekdays from 9 am to noon and 2 to 5 pm, and weekends from 10 am to 1 pm and 2 to 4 pm.

The **Panteón Nacional** is on the opposite, northern edge of the old quarter, five blocks north of Plaza Bolívar. Erected by Guzmán Blanco on the site of a church wrecked by the 1812 earthquake, the pantheon is the last resting place for eminent Venezuelans. The whole central nave is dedicated to Bolívar – his bronze sarcophagus put in the presbytery in place of the high altar – while 163 tombs of other distinguished figures (including three women) were pushed out to the aisles. Two tombs are empty and open, awaiting the remains of Francisco de Miranda, who died in a Spanish jail in 1816 and was buried in a mass grave, and Antonio José de Sucre, whose ashes are in the Quito Cathedral. The vault of the pantheon is covered by paintings depicting scenes from Bolívar's life, all done by Tito Salas in the 1930s. The pantheon is open weekdays from 9 am to noon and 2.30 to 5 pm, and on weekends from 10 am to noon and 3 to 5 pm.

About 1.5 km east of the pantheon is the **Museo de Arte Colonial**, housed in a fine colonial country mansion known as the Quinta de Anauco. You'll be guided around meticulously restored interiors filled with carefully selected works of art, furniture and household implements. The museum is open Tuesday to Friday from 9 to 11.30 am and 2 to 4.30 pm, and on weekends from 10 am to 5 pm.

New Caracas A good place to go for a taste of modern Caracas is **Parque Central**, 1.5 km south-east of Plaza Bolívar. The parque

is not, as you might expect, a green area, but a concrete complex consisting of several high-rise residential slabs of rather apocalyptic appearance, plus two 53-storey octagonal towers, the tallest in the country. Even if you are not impressed by the architecture, there are some important sights in the area, especially if you are interested in art, music and theatre.

The **Museo de Arte Contemporáneo**, at the eastern end of the complex, is by far the best in the country and one of the best on the continent. In 16 halls on five levels you'll find works by many prominent national artists, including Jesús Soto, and works by international figures such as Miró, Chagall, Leger and Picasso. The museum's pride is the collection of about 100 engravings by Picasso, created by the artist from 1931-34. Part of the exhibition space is given to changing displays. The museum is open Tuesday to Sunday from 10 am to 6 pm. You can take photographs (without flash) of the exhibits.

In the opposite, western end of Parque Central is the **Museo de los Niños** (Children's Museum), open Wednesday to Sunday from 9 am to noon and 2 to 5 pm. It's a good museum where adults have as much fun as the kids. Avoid weekends, when the museum is besieged by visitors.

Just to the east of Parque Central is the **Complejo Cultural Teresa Carreño**, a modern performing-arts centre inaugurated in 1983, which hosts concerts, ballet, theatre, recitals etc in its 2500-seat main hall. Hour-long guided tours are run several times a day for US$1.50. At the back of the building is a small museum dedicated to Teresa Carreño (1853-1917), the best pianist Venezuela has produced.

On the north side of this complex is another cultural centre, the **Ateneo de Caracas**, which houses a concert hall, theatre, cinema, art gallery, bookshop and café. Behind the Ateneo is the **Museo de Ciencias Naturales**, open weekdays from 9 am to 4.45 pm, and on weekends from 10 am to 4.45 pm.

Opposite, the **Galería de Arte Nacional** has a permanent collection of some 4000 works of art embracing four centuries of Venezuelan artistic expression, plus some pre-Hispanic art. Adjoining the gallery is the modern six-storey building of the **Museo de Bellas Artes**, which features mainly temporary exhibitions. Go to the rooftop terrace for views over the city, including a mosque to the north. Both art museums are open Tuesday to Friday from 9 am to 5 pm, and on weekends from 10 am to 5 pm.

Other Sights The **Jardín Botánico**, open daily from 8 am to 5 pm, is a place to rest after tramping around museums. The entrance is from Avenida Interna UCV, south of Plaza Venezuela. South of the gardens is the **Universidad Central de Venezuela**, Caracas' largest university. There's an excellent concert hall, Aula Magna, on the grounds, with a fairly regular and interesting programme – check what's going on.

Don't miss strolling along the **Boulevard de Sabana Grande**, a fashionable city mall, vibrant till late. It stretches between the metro stations of Plaza Venezuela and Chacaíto.

In the far eastern part of the city is the **Parque del Este** (get off at the metro station of the same name), the city's largest park. It's good for leisurely walks, and you can visit the snake house, aviary and cactus garden, and (on weekend afternoons only) enjoy a show in the Planetario Humboldt. The park is open daily, except Monday, from 5 am to 5 pm.

The famous **Teleférico**, a cable car to the top of El Avila which provided breathtaking views over the city, was closed down in the late 1980s. There have been some murmurings about giving it into private hands, which might speed up its reopening, but so far, its future is unclear.

Places to Stay

There are loads of hotels scattered throughout the city, with several areas where they are particularly numerous. On the whole, low-budget accommodation is poor and located in unprepossessing, often unsafe areas.

Many of the bottom-end hotels double as love hotels, and some as brothels; business becomes particularly active on Friday and Saturday. Consequently, some hotels may turn you down on weekends.

Note that staying in a distant district of the city is not a problem, as long as you are close to the metro line.

The Bus Terminal Area The vicinity of the Nuevo Circo bus terminal is the cheapest area in which to stay, yet it's very unattractive and not safe at night, and even in the daytime you should be on your guard.

At the rock-bottom end, there are several basic hotels on Avenida Lecuna, just south of the terminal, and on Calle Sur 9, farther south again. One of the few places worth considering in the area is the *Hotel Center Park* (☎ 5418619), on Avenida Lecuna, Velásquez a Miseria, two blocks west of the terminal. It's clean and has gained some popularity with travellers. It costs US$7/9/12 a single/matrimonial/double with bath.

If you decide to stay near the bus terminal, it's more convenient and probably safer to be north of Avenida Bolívar. There are two hotels on Esquina Peinero, near La Hoyada metro station: the *Hotel Caracol* (☎ 545-1228) and the poorer *Hotel Peral* (☎ 545-3111), both charging around US$10/12 for a single/matrimonial with air-con and private bath.

The Centre Some of the budget hotels in the centre are grouped on or near Avenida Fuerzas Armadas, within easy walking distance of the bus terminal. One of the cheapest is the *Hotel Hollywood* (☎ 5614989), on Avenida Fuerzas Armadas, Esquina Romualda, which has matrimoniales with bath and fan/air-con for US$9/10. Another budget option is the *Hotel Mara* (☎ 5615622), on Avenida Urdaneta, Esquina Pelota. Spacious doubles with fan, bath and hot water cost US$11. Choose a room on one of the top floors to avoid street noise.

The *Hotel Metropol* (☎ 5628666), Plaza López a Socorro, and *Hotel Terepaima* (☎ 5625184), Socorro a San Ramón, are both OK if a bit noisy. The Metropol charges

US$12/17/20 for air-con matrimoniales/doubles/triples; the Terepaima is slightly worse but cheaper: US$10/12/15. One block east, on Esquina Calero, is the quieter *Hotel Inter* (☎ 5640251), which costs much the same as the Metropol. It's clean and popular with business people.

Perhaps the best value for money in the centre is the *Plaza Catedral Hotel* (☎ 564-2111), perfectly located on the corner of Plaza Bolívar. It costs US$22/25/28 for comfortable singles/doubles/triples with all facilities. There's a pleasant restaurant on the top floor.

Sabana Grande There are plenty of hotels throughout Sabana Grande, many of which are concentrated on Prolongación Sur Avenida Las Acacias and the neighbouring streets. There are perhaps 30 hotels here, packed in a small area just a few minutes walk south of Plaza Venezuela metro station. Some of the cheapest hotels are on Calles El Colegio and San Antonio, but several of these double as love hotels. If you don't mind this, try, for example, the *Hotel Capri Casanova* (7627270), on Calle San Antonio near the corner of Avenida Casanova, which has matrimoniales/doubles with bath and fan for about US$7/9.

There are some better places among the many hotels on Prolongación Sur Avenida Las Acacias. Going from north to south, you could try the *Tanausú* (☎ 7937691) for US$11/13 a double/triple; the *Odeón* (☎ 7931345) for US$14/16; the *Bruno* (☎ 7818324) for US$12/14; and *La Mirage* (☎ 7932733) for US$15/18. All offer rooms with bath, TV and air-con.

The *Hotel Cristal* (☎ 7619131) is not very classy but is perfectly located right on Boulevard de Sabana Grande (corner of Pasaje Asunción). It costs US$14/17 a matrimonial/double with bath and air-con. For something better near the Boulevard, try the tranquil *Royal Hotel* (☎ 7625494), on Calle San Antonio, which has neat singles/doubles/triples for US$20/24/28.

There's quite a choice of plusher accommodation in Sabana Grande, including the

Hotel El Cóndor (☎ 7629911), Avenida Las Delicias; the *Hotel Coliseo* (☎ 7627916), Avenida Casanova; the *Hotel Tampa* (☎ 7623771), Avenida Francisco Solano; and the *Lincoln Suites* (☎ 7628575), Avenida Francisco Solano.

Places to Eat

Caracas has an enormous choice of places to eat, and you could easily stay in town a full year and eat out three times a day without visiting the same restaurant twice. This unfortunately makes any objective and comprehensive selection difficult. However, the food is generally good, even in the cheap eateries, so you can safely explore the culinary market by yourself. Many restaurants place their menus outside, so you can get an idea what's on offer and how much it costs.

There's a range of budget eateries in the centre and beyond, which have menú del día for about US$2 to US$4. An alternative can be chicken, and the places which serve it are also in good supply. Don't forget about arepas – a perfect between-meals snack – sold in numerous areperas. For breakfast, try any of the ubiquitous panaderías, which will invariably have a choice of croissants, pasteles and cachitos, and fresh bread. Wash it all down with a batido or café negro, perhaps the world's most caffeinated coffee. For the evening, countless Spanish *tascas* (bar/restaurants) dot many central corners, particularly near Iglesia de la Candelaria; some of these are marked on the map.

Some of the best inexpensive cachapas in the centre can be got at the *Lunchería Doña Agapita*, off Plaza La Candelaria. The *Restaurant El Coyuco*, on Avenida Urdaneta, is one of the better budget places for chicken and parrillas. The *Dama Antañona*, Jesuitas a Maturín, serves good regional food at reasonable prices.

Another good area for dining is Sabana Grande. Avenida Francisco Solano is flooded with Italian pasta houses (eg the relatively inexpensive *Al Vecchio Mulino*) and Spanish tasca bars (eg *El Caserío*). Here also is the *Chez Wong*, a Chinese restaurant that does Szechuan and Hunan food. Next

Caracas – Sabana Grande

door is the inexpensive *Restaurant Sorrento* which serves typical food. *Restaurant Las Cancelas* has arguably the best paella in town (US$12 for two people).

Vegetarians can get cheap set meals at the *Tasca Tolo*, on Pasaje Asunción, just south of the Boulevard (Monday to Friday at lunch time only), or at *The Stacion's* (their spelling, not mine), on the Boulevard off Plaza Chacaíto (until around 8 pm). Better vegetarian food (but more expensive) is to be found at the *Delicatesses Indú*, on Calle Villa Flor.

El Rosal and Las Mercedes are fashion-

able dining districts and come alive late in the evening. The restaurants there mostly focus on a more affluent clientele, but there are also some which do cheap food. A good example is the *Real Past*, one of the cheapest pasta houses in town, on Avenida Río de Janeiro in Las Mercedes. The *Jardín des Crêpes*, Calle Madrid, is an enjoyable restaurant offering a variety of crêpes, as well as fish and meat dishes. *La Castañuela*, corner of Calle París and Avenida La Trinidad, is among the best for seafood.

Another area dotted with well-appointed restaurants is Altamira and its environs. *Café*

L'Attico, an attractive bar/restaurant on Avenida Luis Roche, is one of the trendiest places, thanks to a good atmosphere and food (including some North American specialities) at affordable prices. It's hard to get a table in the evening. The new, open-air *Tonino's Café & Sandwichs*, Avenida Andrés Bello, serves exquisite sandwiches with chips and salad – a filling meal in itself. *El Hostal de la Castellana*, at Plaza La Castellana, is an atmospheric Spanish restaurant with three separate dining rooms, each with its own ambience. Other remarkable restaurants in the area include *El Barquero*, Avenida Luis Roche (seafood); *Casa Juancho*, Avenida San Juan Bosco (Spanish cuisine); *Lasserre*, Tercera Avenida (French cuisine); and *El Alazán de Altamira*, Avenida Luis Roche (steaks).

Entertainment

The Friday edition of *El Universal* carries a what's-on addition called *La Brújula*, which covers museums, art galleries, music, theatre, art cinemas and other cultural events. The *Urbe*, a magazine published every other Thursday, covers mostly lighter entertainment, including commercial cinema, pop music, night spots etc.

For thought-provoking films, check the two leading *cinematecas* (art cinemas), in the *Galería de Arte Nacional* and the *Ateneo de Caracas*. The Ateneo often has something interesting in its theatre. Next door, the *Cómplejo Cultural Teresa Carreño* may present a good concert or ballet. *Aula Magna*, in the Universidad Central de Venezuela, has concerts, usually on Sunday morning. The university also has many other cultural activities.

Las Mercedes, El Rosal and La Castellana are the scene of most night-time activity. The *Gran Pizzería El León*, at Plaza La Castellana, has a spacious terrace which has become a popular youth haunt for an evening beer. There are a few discos around. *Weekends*, on Avenida San Juan Bosco, one long block north of the Altamira metro station, is an American-style short-order restaurant open till late, with live music, bingo and other performances.

Juan Sebastián Bar, on Avenida Venezuela in El Rosal (metro: Chacaíto), is a bar/restaurant, and one of the few real jazz spots in the city. Live jazz goes from early afternoon till 2 am. *El Maní es Así*, Avenida El Cristo, Sabana Grande, has taped and live salsa music.

Getting There & Away

Air Simón Bolívar international airport is in Maiquetía near the port of La Guaira on the Caribbean coast, about 25 km from Caracas. It's linked to the city by a freeway which cuts through the coastal mountain range with three tunnels, the main one being two km long. The airport has separate terminals for international and domestic flights, 400 metres from each other.

The international terminal has a range of facilities, including a tourist office (☎ 551-060), car rental desks, three casas de cambio (including Italcambio, which is open 24 hours), post and telephone offices, a restaurant, two cafeterias and several travel agencies, but no left-luggage office. The domestic terminal doesn't have much apart from airline offices.

There are plenty of international flights. TAP (Air Portugal; ☎ 9510511, 9515508) offers some of the cheapest tickets to Europe (US$800 one way to Lisbon). Also check Ive Tours (☎ 9933930), which may have attractive student fares to Madrid with Iberia (US$430 one way). For other international connections, see the Getting There & Away section earlier in this chapter.

Avensa and Servivensa are the main domestic carriers and cover all major routes, including Barcelona (US$41), Ciudad Bolívar (US$52), Ciudad Guayana (US$56), Coro (US$40), Maracaibo (US$56), Mérida (US$58), Porlamar (US$42), Puerto Ayacucho (US$56), San Antonio del Táchira (US$63), Santa Elena de Uairén (US$83) and Santo Domingo (US$61). Servivensa also flies to Canaima, the base for Angel Falls (US$77), but they probably won't sell the tickets unless you buy their Campamento

Canaima package. If this is the case, they will apply a discount return airfare of US$85.

Two new airlines, Aserca and Laser, service some major routes (including Porlamar) and can be cheaper than Avensa/Servivensa. Rutaca, AeroEjecutivos and Aereotuy have flights to the Archipiélago de Los Roques (US$105 return).

Bus Caracas has two bus terminals. The older Nuevo Circo terminal, right in the city centre, is poor, chaotic, noisy, dirty and unsafe. It handles all intercity runs to the west and south-west of the country, including Coro (US$7, seven hours), Maracaibo (US$11, 11 hours), Maracay (US$2, two hours), Mérida (US$11, 11 hours), San Antonio del Táchira (US$14, 14 hours) and San Cristóbal (US$13, 13 hours). *Carritos* (small buses) to La Guaira, Macuto, Los Teques and El Junquito park around the bus terminal.

. The new terminal is on the eastern outskirts of Caracas, on the freeway to Barcelona, five km beyond the suburb of Petare. It's modern and functional, and handles all traffic to the east and south-east, including Barcelona (US$5.50, 4½ hours), Carúpano (US$9, 8½ hours), Ciudad Bolívar (US$9.50, nine hours), Ciudad Guayana (US$11, 10 hours), Cumaná (US$7, 6½ hours), Güiria (US$12, 11 hours), Puerto La Cruz (US$6, five hours) and Santa Elena de Uairén (US$21, 17 hours). All the fares given here are for ordinary bus service.

The two terminals are linked by frequent local carritos; a taxi on this route will cost about US$7.

Getting Around

To/From the Airport There's half-hourly bus service from 6 am to 11 pm between the airport and the city centre (though taxi drivers at the airport will swear blind that there are no buses). In the city, buses depart from Calle Sur 17, directly underneath Avenida Bolívar, next to Parque Central. There are no stairs connecting the two levels; get down to the buses by Calle Sur 17 from Avenida Mexico. At the airport, the buses stop in front of both the domestic and international terminals. The trip costs US$1.75 and generally takes about 50 minutes, but traffic jams, particularly on weekends and holidays, can double that time. If you are going from the airport to the city, it may be faster to get off at Gato Negro metro station and take the metro to your final destination.

A taxi to/from the airport will cost about US$11; ask at the taxi desk in the international terminal for the official fare, thus avoiding overcharging.

If you have just an overnight stop in Maiquetía, there may be no point in going to Caracas. Instead, you can stay the night on the coast, eg in Macuto (see El Litoral in the Around Caracas section). For a carrito to Macuto (US$0.40) cross the car park outside the international terminal to the main road and wave one down. A taxi to Macuto should cost US$6.

Bus The bus network is extensive and covers all suburbs within the metropolitan area as well as all the major neighbouring localities. The main type of vehicle operating city routes is a small bus, commonly called a carrito. Carritos run frequently but move only as fast as the traffic allows, which means they are often trapped in traffic jams. Use them only if you are going to destinations inaccessible by metro.

Metro The metro is probably all you'll use to get around Caracas. It's fast, well organised, clean and cheap. The only thing its designers seem to have forgotten are public toilets at the stations.

The underground system has three lines and 39 stations. The longest line, No 1, goes east-west all the way along the city axis, and you will probably use it most frequently. Line No 2 leads from the centre south-west to the distant suburb of Caricuao and the zoo. The newest and shortest line, No 3, goes from Plaza Venezuela south-west to El Valle. The metro also includes several bus routes, known as Metrobus, which link some of the southern suburbs to metro stations.

The metro operates daily from 5.30 am to 11 pm. Tickets cost US$0.23 a ride for up to three stations, US$0.25 for four to seven stations, and US$0.27 for any longer route. The transfer ticket (*boleto integrado*) for the combined metro-plus-bus route costs US$0.27. It's worth buying the *multiabono*, a multiple ticket costing US$2.30, which is valid for 10 rides of any distance. Not only do you save money, but you also avoid queuing each time at the ticket counters. Bulky packages which might obstruct other passengers are not allowed on the metro.

Taxi Taxis, identifiable by a sign that reads either 'Taxi' or 'Libre', are fairly inexpensive and are useful for places not reached by the metro.

AROUND CARACAS
El Hatillo
A small, old town 15 km south-east of the city centre, El Hatillo is today a distant suburb within Caracas' administrative boundaries. Centred around Plaza Bolívar, with the statue of the hero looking as though he's on his way home from a heavy drinking session, the town retains some colonial architecture. The parish church on the plaza has preserved its original external shape pretty well, but the interior has been radically modernised.

The town has become a trendy spot for *caraqueños* (the inhabitants of Caracas) and becomes packed with cars and people, particularly on weekends. Every second house is either an eating establishment or a handicrafts shop.

Frequent carritos run to El Hatillo from Avenida Humboldt, just off Boulevard de Sabana Grande, near the Chacaíto metro station.

Parque Nacional El Avila
El Avila National Park looms steeply just north of Caracas. The park encompasses about 90 km of the coastal mountain range running west-east along the coast and separating the city from the sea. The highest peak is Pico Naiguatá (2765 metres).

The southern slope, overlooking Caracas, is uninhabited, while the northern side, running down into the sea, is dotted with several hamlets, the major one being San José de Galipán. A few jeepable tracks cross the park from south to north, as well as the inoperative cable car, which went from Caracas up to Pico El Avila (2150 metres) before dropping to the coast at Macuto.

El Avila has the best tourist facilities of all Venezuela's parks. There are about 200 km of walking trails, most of them well signposted. Half a dozen camping grounds are equipped with sanitary facilities, and there are many more good places for camping, though without facilities.

A dozen entrances lead into the park from Caracas; all originate from Avenida Boyacá, commonly known as Cota Mil, as it runs at an altitude of 1000 metres. Any route you choose will require quite a steep ascent, and you will soon come across a guard post, where you pay a nominal entrance fee. The *guardaparques* (rangers) may have a trail map of the park, though it seems to be out of print; in any case, they can inform you about the routes.

There are plenty of possibilities for half or full-day hikes. You can, for example, go up to Pico El Avila; at least four routes lead there. If you are prepared to camp, possibly the most scenic walk is the two-day hike to Pico Naiguatá. Take good rain gear and warm clothes. Water is scarce, so bring some along. The dry season is from December to April and often goes into May.

El Litoral
Parque El Avila slopes steeply almost into the sea, leaving only a narrow flat belt, commonly referred to as El Litoral, between the mountains and the shore. Yet the area is quite well developed, with as many as 400,000 people living in a chain of towns lining the waterfront. From west to east, the most populous urban centres of El Litoral are Catia La Mar, Maiquetía, La Guaira, Macuto, Caraballeda and Naiguatá. The first

two towns sit at opposite ends of the airport and have little charm. La Guaira is an important and busy port, while the three remaining places have developed into popular seaside resorts for caraqueños. Farther east, the holiday centres thin out, though the paved road continues for another 20 km to Los Caracas.

This part of the coast is dramatic and spectacular (especially the stretch from Naiguatá to Los Caracas) but not particularly good for bathing. The shore is mostly rocky all the way from Catia La Mar to Los Caracas, and there are only short stretches of beach (good wild beaches begin east of Los Caracas). The straight coastline is exposed to open-sea surf, and strong currents can make swimming dangerous. Most of the holidaying activity is confined to *balnearios*, sections of the beaches that have been walled in and dotted with facilities, and to private beach clubs. Macuto, Caraballeda and Naiguatá all have balnearios, and there are a few more, such as Camurí Chico, between Macuto and Caraballeda.

Things to See The sea apart, you can visit the **Museo Reverón** in Macuto, accommodated in the former home and studio of a renowned painter, Armando Reverón (1889-1954).

La Guaira has a partly preserved and restored old town, noted for its narrow streets lined by houses with grilled windows. The most imposing building in town is the **Casa Guipuzcoana** (1734), on the waterfront. Behind it is the **Museo Boulton**, featuring some of the town's history. Enveloped in *ranchos* (shantytowns), La Guaira doesn't seem to be the safest place on earth, so be on your guard while visiting.

Places to Stay & Eat If you want to be close to the airport, you can stay in the *Hotel Ovetense* in Maiquetía, close to Centro Comercial Litoral, or in the *Hotel Aeropuerto* in Catia La Mar.

In Macuto, there are a number of hotels near the waterfront, including *El Coral*, *Santiago*, *Alamo*, *Riviera*, *Mar Azul*, *Tijuana* and *Diana*. The Diana is one of the cheapest in the area, costing around US$10 a double. El Coral and Santiago have pleasant open-air restaurants overlooking the sea.

Caraballeda, five km east of Macuto, also has a choice of accommodation and restaurants. The two best hotels on the central coast, the *Macuto Sheraton* (☎ 944300) and *Meliá Caribe* (☎ 945555), are located here. For somewhere cheaper, try either the *Litoral Palacios* or *Costa Azul*.

Getting There & Away There are frequent carritos from Caracas (catch them one block west of Nuevo Circo bus station) to Macuto, and many go all the way to Caraballeda or even Naiguatá.

Colonia Tovar

Lost amidst the rolling cloud forests of the coastal cordillera, about 60 km west of Caracas, sits the unusual mountain town of Colonia Tovar. It was founded in 1843 by 376 German settlers from Schwarzwald, following Venezuela's opening to immigration in the search for new people to cultivate the land devastated by independence wars.

Effectively isolated by lack of roads and by internal rules prohibiting marriage outside the colony, the village followed the mother culture, language and architecture for a century. Only in the 1940s was Spanish introduced as the official language and the ban on marrying outside the community abandoned. It was not until 1963 that a serviceable road was opened linking Colonia to Caracas. This marked a turning point in the history of the town, which even then had only 1300 inhabitants.

Today, Colonia Tovar has perhaps five times as many inhabitants and is a classic example of a tourist town. On weekends, the central streets are lined with countless stalls selling crafts, fruits and vegetables. You can still see some of the original architecture, enjoy a genuine German lunch or dinner, and buy bread or sausage made according to an old German recipe. Taking advantage of the temperate climate (the town lies at an altitude of about 1800 metres), the locals turned to fruit-growing, and you can buy delicious strawberries, apples, peaches and blackberries.

Colonia Tovar's telephone code is 033.

Things to See Call at the **Museo de Historia y Artesanía** (open on weekends only, from 9 am to 6 pm) for a taste of the town's history, and don't miss the local **church**, a curious L-shaped building with two perpendicular naves (one for women, the other for men) and the high altar placed in the angle where the naves join.

Places to Stay & Eat There are perhaps a dozen hotels and *cabañas* (cabins), most of which have their own restaurants. Accommodation is expensive; bottom-end prices run at about US$15 a double. Some places offer a lodging-plus-meals plan.

Hotel Selva Negra (☎ 51415) is the oldest and best known lodge in town. Built in the 1930s, it now has about 40 cabañas of different sizes, for two to six people (US$40 for two people, plus US$8 for each additional person). The atmospheric restaurant is in the original house.

Cheaper options include *Hotel Edelweiss* (☎ 51260), *Hotel Drei Tannen* (☎ 51246) and *Hotel Bergland* (☎ 51229), the last being noted for its good food.

Getting There & Away The trip from Caracas to Colonia Tovar includes a change in El Junquito. Carritos to El Junquito (US$0.50) depart from the corner just south of Nuevo Circo bus terminal. From El Junquito, vans take you the remaining half of the journey (US$0.60). The whole trip takes about two hours.

If you don't want to return directly to Caracas, you can take an exciting ride south down to La Victoria. Over a distance of only 34 km, the road descends about 1250 metres. Por puestos depart from Colonia Tovar several times a day; the ride takes one hour and costs US$0.70. There's regular bus transport from La Victoria to both Caracas and Maracay.

Archipiélago de Los Roques

Los Roques is an archipelago of small coral islands some 150 km due north of El Litoral. Stretching about 36 km from east to west and 27 km from north to south, the atoll consists of some 40 islands big enough to deserve a name and perhaps 250 other islets, rocks and cays. The soft white-sand beaches are clean and lovely, although shadeless, and the coral reefs even better – a paradise for snorkelling and scuba diving. The whole archipelago (2211 sq km) is a national park.

The island of El Gran Roque, on the northern edge of the archipelago, has a small fishing village of about 800 souls and an airstrip. There is also a wharf from which locals can take you in their fishing boats to other islands of the atoll. Bring along snorkelling gear and good sun protection – there's almost no shade on the islands.

Places to Stay & Eat There are a dozen *posadas* in Gran Roque, most of them being small and simple places which offer both lodging and dining. Food is expensive and limited, as everything except fish has to be shipped in from the mainland. Possibly the cheapest place to stay is the house of Señora Carmen on Plaza Bolívar. Expect to pay around US$15 per person for a bed plus breakfast and dinner, half this price for a bed only. Prices vary from weekdays to weekends, depending on demand.

Getting There & Away Several small airlines, including Rutaca, AeroEjecutivos and Aereotuy, operate flights between Maiquetía and Los Roques (about US$105 return). They also offer tours which include the return flight, a boat excursion around the nearby islands, lunch, soft drinks and snorkelling (equipment provided). A one-day tour will cost around US$150. Two-day tours (which include accommodation) are available for about US$275.

There's no regular boat service to Los Roques. To get there, either talk to the fishermen in La Guaira port, or ask around the marinas in Caraballeda and Naiguatá.

The North-West

The north-west is a region of contrasts, with coral islands and beaches, the unique desert near Coro, and South America's largest lake, Lago Maracaibo. The region combines the traditional with the contemporary, from living Indian cultures (such as that of the Guajiros) and colonial heritage (the best is found in Coro) to the modern city of Maracaibo. Favourite travel spots in the region are the national parks of Henri Pittier and Morrocoy. Administratively, the north-west encompasses the states of Aragua, Carabobo, Yaracuy, Lara, Falcón and Zulia.

MARACAY

The capital of Aragua state, Maracay is a thriving city of some 450,000 inhabitants. The town was founded in 1701, but its rapid growth only came with the rule of Juan Vicente Gómez, the most enduring (1908-35) and probably the most ruthless of Venezuela's caudillos. He made Maracay his home and commissioned a number of constructions, including the government house, a bullring, an aviation school, an opera house, a zoo, a splendid hotel and ... his own mausoleum. Maracay has a number of parks and leafy plazas, including the largest Plaza Bolívar in the country. The city is a gateway to the Parque Nacional Henri Pittier (see the section below).

Information

The tourist office is in Edificio Fundaragua, in La Soledad district, north of the city centre. Most of the useful banks are within a few blocks of Plaza Girardot – see the map for locations. The telephone code for Maracay is 043.

Things to See

The historic heart of Maracay, the **Plaza Girardot**, has no colonial buildings left except for the fair-sized **Catedral**, which was completed in 1743. The southern side of the plaza is occupied by an arcaded building,

erected by Gómez as the seat of government. Today, the building houses the **Museo de Historia** and the **Museo de Arqueología**, both open Tuesday to Friday from 8 am to noon and 2 to 6 pm, and on weekends from 9 am to 1 pm.

One block east of the plaza is the **Santuario de Madre María de San José**, probably the most revered and visited city sight. Madre María (1875-1967) was venerated in 1992 by a papal decree, and solemnly beatified in 1995. Her remains were exhumed and, to everybody's surprise, the corpse was intact. You can see it in a crystal sarcophagus in the Santuario (though the face is covered with a mask). The Santuario is open Tuesday to Sunday from 8.30 to 11.30 am and 2.30 to 5 pm.

A few paces to the north is the large Spanish-Moorish **Plaza de Toros Maestranza**. The bullring was modelled on the one in Seville and built in 1928; it's possibly the most stylish and beautiful bullring in the country.

A few blocks to the east is the **Museo Aeronáutico** with 30-odd aircraft displayed, dating from the 1910s to the 1950s. The collection's gem is a French plane from 1918, reputedly in perfect working order. The museum also has a replica of the famous Jimmie Angel's plane; the engine is original. It's open on weekends from 9 am to 4 pm. A hundred metres north is the **Museo de Arte**, which stages temporary exhibitions of modern art and is open Tuesday to Sunday from 9 am to 4.30 pm.

At the far northern city limits is the **Jardín Zoológico**, which features many animals typical of Venezuela. It's open Tuesday to Sunday from 9 am to 5 pm. Take the Castaño/Zoológico carrito from the city centre to get there.

Places to Stay

There are several budget hotels right in the city centre. The cheapest are the *Hotel Central* (☎ 452834) and *Hotel María Isabel*, next to each other on Calle Santos Michelena. Both have rooms with private bath and fan, and cost US$6 for a single or matrimonial and US$7 for a double.

Maracay

Scale: 0 100 200 m

To Tourist Office,
Zoo & Choroni

To Ocumare
de la Costa

To Ocumare
de la Costa

To Valencia

To Caracas

To Mausoleo
de Gómez

PLACES TO STAY
1 Hotel Caroní
11 Hotel Central
12 Hotel María Isabel
15 Hotel Mar del Plata
19 Hotel Bolívar
21 Hotel Wladimir
23 Hotel Canaima

PLACES TO EAT
4 La Trattoria
6 Pollo en Brassas Friulana
8 Cervecería Restaurant
    La Maracayera
22 Restaurant Arena Caney
    Tropical

OTHER
2 Banco Metropolitano
3 Banco Italo Venezolano
5 Banco Latino
7 Mercado Principal
9 Casa de Dolores Amelia
10 Ipostel
13 Teatro Ateneo de Maracay
14 Plaza de Toros Maestranza
16 Casa de la Cultura
17 Museo de Arte
18 Museo Aeronáutico
20 Santuario de Madre María
    de San José
24 Banco Mercantil
25 CANTV
26 Catedral
27 Banco del Caribe &
    Banco de Venezuela
28 Museo de Historia
29 Museo de Arqueología
30 Banco Consolidado
31 Banco Consolidado
32 Banco Unión
33 Teatro de la Opera
34 Palacio de Gobierno
35 Bus Terminal

The *Hotel Mar del Plata*, Calle Santos Michelena Este No 23, is one of the cheapest places for those who need air-conditioning. A matrimonial/double with private bath will cost US$7/10. Alternatively, try the *Hotel Canaima* (☎ 338278), Avenida Bolívar Este No 53, which offers and costs much the same. Marginally better and more expensive is the *Hotel Bolívar* (☎ 450253), Avenida Bolívar Este No 9, opposite the cathedral.

One of the better central options is the *Hotel Wladimir* (☎ 461115), Avenida Bolívar Este No 27. Air-con singles/doubles/triples with TV, bath and hot water are US$14/19/24. The *Hotel Caroní* (☎ 541817, 547855), Avenida Ayacucho Norte No 19, offers similar standards for US$10/14/17.

Places to Eat

Some of the cheapest meals are to be got in the *Mercado Principal*, which has half a dozen restaurants (the *Felipe* is arguably the best). There are plenty of reasonably priced places to eat scattered throughout the centre. To name a few: *La Maracayera* serves inexpensive set meals; *Caney Tropical* is good for arepas; *La Trattoria* has cheap pizzas and Italian-influenced local food; and *Pollo en Brasas Friulana* is the place for chicken. All these, as well as some other places, are marked on the map.

Getting There & Away

The bus terminal is on the south-eastern outskirts of the city centre. It's vast and handles frequent transport to most major cities. Buses to Caracas depart every 10 or 15 minutes (US$2, two hours), as do buses to Valencia (US$0.60, one hour).

PARQUE NACIONAL HENRI PITTIER

This is Venezuela's oldest national park, created in 1937. It stretches from the Caribbean coast in the north, almost as far south as the Valencia-Caracas freeway and Maracay. The park covers part of the Cordillera de la Costa, the coastal mountain range which exceeds 2000 metres in some areas. From its ridge, the cordillera rolls dramatically down to the seashore to the north, and south to Maracay.

There's a variety of plant life within the park, including semidry deciduous woods, evergreen tropical forest, lush cloud forest, arid coastal scrub, mangroves and coconut groves, and accordingly, a diverse animal world. The park is particularly famous for its birds; about 520 species have been identified here, which represents some 42% of the bird species found in Venezuela.

Two roads, both paved, cross the park from north to south. The western road leads from Maracay to Ocumare de la Costa and continues on to Cata; it ascends to 1128 metres at Paso Portachuelo. The eastern road heads from Maracay due north to Choroní and reaches the seashore two km farther on at Puerto Colombia. It's narrower, poorer and more twisting, but it climbs up to 1830 metres and is more spectacular. Both roads are about 55 km long. There's no road connection between the coastal ends of these roads; a rented boat is the only way to get from one end to the other.

The coast consists of rocky cliffs in some parts, interspersed with bays filled with coconut groves and bordered by beaches. A few seaside resorts have already sprung up, the main ones being Cata and Puerto Colombia. Both offer a choice of hotels and restaurants, and boat-hire facilities.

Things to See & Do

The park has something for nearly everyone, including beachgoers, bird-watchers, hikers, architecture buffs and fiesta lovers. Unless you are specifically after bird-watching, it's better to take the eastern road, which provides access to a number of attractions and, passing through cloud forest, is fascinating in itself.

Stop in **Choroní**, probably the finest colonial town in the park. Most of its narrow streets are lined with old, pastel-coloured houses. In one of them Madre María de San José was born. The well-shaded Plaza Bolívar boasts a lovely parish church, featuring a finely decorated ceiling; the wall over the high altar is painted to look like a carved retable.

Walk two km north to **Puerto Colombia**, the main tourist destination in the area. Its major magnet is **Playa Grande**, a fine beach shaded by coconuts, a five-minute walk east of town. Sadly, it suffers from litter when Venezuelans come en masse during weekends and holidays.

Boats from the town can take you to isolated beaches farther down the coast, such as **Playa Aroa** (US$25 return per boat), **Playa Chuao** (US$25) or **Playa Cepe** (US$30).

From Playa Chuao, you can walk up a rough five-km track to the isolated village of **Chuao**, surrounded by cacao plantations. Chuao has a very simple colonial church and is widely known for its Diablos Danzantes celebrations.

There's a significant black population in Chuao and Puerto Colombia, so drumbeats are an integral part of life, and can be heard all year round – particularly on weekend nights. The music immediately sparks dancing and the atmosphere is great.

Chuao is a starting point for an adventurous hike along a trail which traverses the cordillera to Turmero, 14 km east of Maracay. It's unmarked, unclear in parts and its upper reaches may be very wet and muddy in the rainy season. You need two to three days to complete the hike. Camping gear is necessary. The trek can also be done in reverse, from Turmero to Chuao.

The western road will also bring you to fine beaches, of which **Playa Cata** is the most popular and well developed. Boats from Cata take tourists to the smaller but quieter **Playa Catita**, on the eastern side of the same bay. Farther east is the unspoilt and usually deserted **Playa Cuyagua**. It's accessible by a 2.5-km sand track from the town of Cuyagua, or by boat from Cata (US$25 return).

The highlight of the western road is the **Paso Portachuelo**, a fabulous area for birdwatching. The pass is the lowest point on the ridge, so it has become a natural corridor for migratory birds and insects flying both inland and out to sea between such distant places as Argentina and Canada.

Close to the pass is the **Estación Biológica Rancho Grande**, a biological station run by the Escuela de Agronomía (School of Agronomy) of the Universidad Central de Venezuela. There are several paths leading from the station into the forest, which provide excellent opportunities for birdwatching. The best conditions are to be found early in the morning. September and October are the best months for viewing migratory birds. You may also see agoutis, peccaries, snakes (wear good, calf-length boots) and butterflies.

The station lies just off the Maracay-Ocumare road, 28 km from Maracay. Any Ocumare bus will set you down near the entrance.

Places to Stay & Eat
The park offers a variety of accommodation options, some of which are listed below. You can camp free on the beaches, but never leave your tent unattended.

Puerto Colombia There are a dozen hotels here, and locals also rent out their rooms if there's the demand. The prices usually rise on weekends. Restaurants, too, are in good supply, so starving is improbable; fried fish is the local staple.

One of the cheapest places to stay is the family-run *Habitaciones La Abuela*, near the bus terminus. Rooms have fan but no private bath, and cost US$5/7/10 for a single/matrimonial/triple. *Hotel Bahía*, 20 metres from the pedestrian bridge leading to Playa Grande, offers doubles with bath and fan for US$11. Other budget options include the *Hotel Don Miguel* (☎ 911081), next to the alcabala at the entrance to the town, and the *Hostal Colonial* (☎ 911087) next door (US$12 a double for either). Among the best in town are the *Hospedaje La Montañita* (☎ 832560) and the *Hotel Club Cotoperix* (which has four outlets). A double room in either will cost about US$30, breakfast included.

Budget eating is provided by several simple restaurants gathered near the bridge, of which the *Araguaney* is arguably the favourite among tourists. Restaurants at Playa Grande are also good (probably even better) for inexpensive meals, mostly fried fish.

Choroní Choroní has a few hotels, of which the undistinguished *Hospedaje del Pueblo* is the cheapest (US$12 a double). The four-room *Posada Colonial Choroní* is the most charming (US$24 per person, including breakfast and dinner). It can be booked in Caracas (☎ 9771234).

Choroní's sole restaurant, *Santa Clara*, on Plaza Bolívar, opens on weekends only.

Playa Cata Accommodation here is expensive compared to elsewhere, but many people camp on the beach, either in tents or swinging in hammocks from the palms. There are toilets and showers, and stalls on the beach sell cooked meals and drinks.

Rancho Grande The biological station grants permission to stay on the premises to those who are seriously interested, but you have to arrange this beforehand. Contact the director of the Escuela de Agronomía, Professor Alberto Fernández Badillo (☎ 450-153). Alternatively, call the Sociedad de Amigos Parque Nacional Henri Pittier (☎ 544454), and talk to its director, Ernesto Fernández Badillo, Alberto's brother.

Conditions in the station are simple; they include beds and kitchen facilities, but no food is provided. Bring a sleeping bag, some warm clothing, reliable rain gear and your own food. Camping is also possible if you have your own tent.

Getting There & Away

The departure point for the park is the Maracay bus terminal. Buses to Ocumare de la Costa depart every hour, from 7 am to 5 pm (US$1, two hours). In Ocumare, you catch a carrito to Cata beach (US$0.60, 15 minutes). To Puerto Colombia, buses leave every two hours (US$1, 2¼ hours). The last bus from both Ocumare and Puerto Colombia back to Maracay departs at 5 pm (later on weekends), but is not reliable.

PARQUE NACIONAL MORROCOY

This is one of the most popular parks among travellers looking for beaches and snorkelling. Located at the eastern edge of Falcón state, it comprises a strip of the coast and the offshore area dotted with islands, islets and cays. Many of the islands are skirted with white-sand beaches and surrounded by coral reefs. Morrocoy is also noted for its variety of water birds, including ibis, herons, cormorants, ducks, pelicans and flamingos. The park lies between the towns of Tucacas and Chichiriviche, which are its main gateways.

Tucacas is a hot town on the Valencia-Coro road, with nothing to keep you for long. Yet, with the park just a stone's throw away, the town is steadily developing into a holiday centre, and has an array of hotels and other facilities. The nearest island that is part of the park is over the bridge from the town's waterfront. If you want to go farther into the park, go to the *embarcadero* (wharf) close to the bridge, from where boats can take you for a trip along *caños* (channels) through mangroves, or put you down on one of the many islands. The most popular of these is **Cayo Sombrero**, which has fine coral reefs and beaches. Boats take up to seven people and charge the same for one as for seven. The return fare to Cayo Sombrero is around US$25. On weekdays during the off season, you can usually beat the price down.

Another popular gateway to the park is **Chichiriviche**, which provides access to half a dozen neighbouring cays. Boats depart from the wharf, which is at the end of Avenida Zamora, the main street. As in Tucacas, the boat takes a maximum of seven passengers and the fare is per boat, regardless of the number of people aboard. The return fare to the closest cays, such as Cayo Muerto, Cayo Sal or Cayo Pelón, is about US$10, whereas the return fare to the farthest cays, such as Cayo Borracho, Cayo Sombrero or Cayo Pescadores, is about US$25. For about US$4 more, you can arrange with the boatman to pick you up from the island in the afternoon or at a later date. Haggling over the price is also possible here. Only pay after they have returned you to the mainland.

Information

Tourist information is available from some tour operators, eg Varadero Tours, in the Hotel Otidalimar in Tucacas (☎ 831478), and on Avenida Zamora in Chichiriviche (☎ 86919).

There are no useful banks in Chichiriviche, and the only helpful bank in Tucacas is Banco Unión, on Avenida Principal. Some travel agencies and other establishments will change your dollars.

Recommended scuba-diving operators are Submatur (☎ 84082), on Calle Ayacucho in Tucacas, and Agua-Fun Diving (☎ 86-265), on Calle El Sol in Chichiriviche.

Snorkelling gear can be rented from many tour and boat operators and hotel managers (about US$6 per day). Some hotels have their own boats and offer excursions (beaches, snorkelling, bird-watching).

The telephone code for both Tucacas and Chichiriviche is 042.

Places to Stay & Eat

If you have a tent or a hammock, you can stay on the islands; if not, you'll be limited to one-day trips out of Tucacas or Chichiriviche. When camping on the islands, take food, water, snorkelling gear, sun protection and a good insect repellent. Some of the islands, including Sal, Muerto and Sombrero, have eating facilities, but none has a hotel.

Tucacas The most popular place to stay among travellers is *Posada de Carlos* (☎ 831493), Avenida Principal No 5. There's no name on the door; the place is recognisable by the 'si hay habitación' inscription. Run by its friendly owner, Carlos Lissir, the hotel offers matrimoniales/triples/quads with bath for US$9/12/15, and you can use the kitchen and fridge at no additional cost.

Across the road is *La Esperanza* (☎ 84950), a complex of a restaurant, a tasca and a hotel, where double rooms cost US$10. A few steps from here, Carlos' brother runs *Hotel Otidalimar*, with rooms costing much the same as in the Posada.

Possibly the cheapest place to stay is the undistinguished *Hotel La Suerte*, next to the Posada, which offers doubles for US$7. Just around the corner is yet another budget place, the *Posada Johnatan* (☎ 84239), with prices similar to those of Carlos.

There's quite a choice of mid-price and top-end accommodation, including the centrally located *Hotel Gaeta* (☎ 84414), Avenida Principal No 34. Air-con doubles/triples with bath and TV cost US$25/30.

Budget restaurants include *Nuevo Tito*, on Calle Sucre close to the Johnatan, and *El Timón*, diagonally opposite Banco Unión. For somewhere better, try *Fruti Mar*, opposite La Suerte, or *Venemar*, close to the bridge.

Chichiriviche Some of the cheapest accommodation is to be found at *Hotel El Centro*, near the waterfront. The entrance is from the back of the Panadería El Centro on Avenida Zamora. Matrimoniales without/with bath cost US$8/12, and the price seems to be negotiable. Next door is the unsigned *Habitaciones Rigoberto*, which offers matrimoniales with bath for US$9.

Far more pleasant are two friendly family-run places – *Villa Gregoria* (☎ 86359) and *Residencias Delia* (☎ 86089) – next to each other on Calle Mariño, one block north of Avenida Zamora. Either will cost about US$6 per person.

The *Hotel Capri* (☎ 86026), opposite the Panadería El Centro, is a good air-con option. Comfortable singles/doubles/triples with bath and hot water are US$14/17/20.

In the southern part of the town are the German-run *Posada Alemania* (☎ 86979), set in a coconut-palm garden (US$6 per person), and the more expensive, waterfront *Hotel Náutico* (☎ 86024). There are a dozen more hotels in town, and some locals rent out rooms in their homes.

For budget meals try *El Juncal* and *Marvilla*, both on Avenida Zamora. Among the best places in town are *Txalupa*, on the waterfront, and *Il Ristorante*, at the Hotel Capri.

Getting There & Away

Bus Tucacas lies on the main Valencia-Coro road and there are frequent buses between these cities. Chichiriviche is about 22 km off the main road, and is serviced by half-hourly *busetas* (small buses) from Valencia (US$2, 2½ hours); there are no direct buses from Caracas or Coro. To get there from Caracas, take any of the frequent buses to Valencia (US$2.50, 2½ hours) and change there. From Coro, take any bus to Valencia, get off in Sanare, the turn-off for Chichiriviche (US$3, 3½ hours), and catch the Valencia-Chichiriviche buseta.

The last 12-km stretch of the road to Chichiriviche runs along a causeway through mangrove swamps. This is a favourite feeding ground for flamingos, which mostly gather here between November and February but can occasionally be spotted at other times of the year as well.

CORO

Set at the base of the curiously shaped Península de Paraguaná, Coro is a pleasant, peaceful town of some 130,000 people. It has some of the best colonial architecture in the country and a few good museums.

Founded in 1527, it was one of the earliest towns on the continent and the first capital

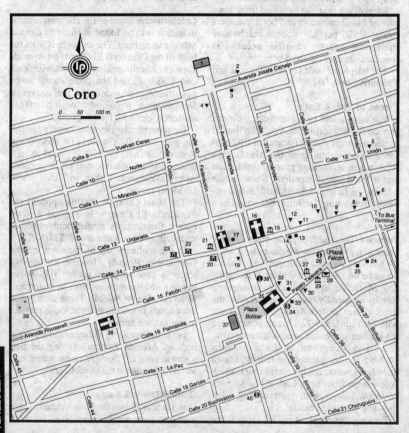

Coro

0   50   100 m.

Avenida Josefa Camejo

Vuelvan Caras

Calle 9

Calle 10

Calle 11

Norte

Miranda

Calle 13   Urdaneta

Calle 14   Zamora

Calle 15 Falcón

Avenida Roosevelt   Calle 16 Palmasola

Calle 17 La Paz

Calle 18 Garces

Calle 20 Buchivacoa   Calle 21 Churuguara

Avenida Manaure

Calle 12   Unión

To Bus Terminal

Plaza Falcón

Paseo Talavera

Plaza Bolívar

of the Province of Venezuela. Four years later, the Episcopal See, the first in the New World, was established in Coro. Despite its early and promising start, the town was almost deserted a century later, and only revived thanks to trade with Curaçao and Bonaire at the end of the 18th century. Most of its historic heritage dates from that time.

Information

Tourist Office The tourist office (☎ 511132) is on the pedestrian mall, just north of Plaza Bolívar. It's open weekdays from 8 am to noon and 1 to 4 pm.

Money Some of the useful banks are marked on the map. Camel Tours may also change money.

Telephone Coro's telephone code is 068.

Tour Operators Camel Tours (☎ 526217), on Paseo Talavera, organises tours around the region, including Península de Paraguaná, sand dunes and caves, charging about US$20 for a full-day tour. Agencia Kuriana (☎ 513035), Calle Zamora, may also have some tours on offer.

Things to See

The oldest building in town is the **Catedral**. This massive, fortress-like structure was begun in the 1580s and completed half a century later, making it perhaps the oldest church in Venezuela.

One block east, the **Museo de Arte Coro**, in a beautiful colonial house, is a branch of the Museo de Arte Contemporáneo in Caracas and, like its parent, focuses on modern art. It is open Tuesday to Saturday from 9 am to 12.30 pm and 3 to 7.30 pm, and Sunday from 9 am to 4 pm.

For an insight into Coro's colonial past, go to the **Museo de Coro Lucas Guillermo Castillo**, accommodated in an old convent. The museum has an extensive collection of both religious and secular art from the region and beyond. It's one of the best museums of its kind in the country. It's open Tuesday to Saturday from 9 am to noon and 3 to 6 pm, and Sunday from 9 am to 2 pm; all visits are guided (in Spanish only) and the tour takes about an hour. Adjacent to the museum is the **Iglesia de San Francisco**, recently thoroughly restored.

Across the street, in a grilled pavilion on a small plaza, stands the **Cruz de San Clemente**, said to be the cross used in the first

PLACES TO STAY		11	Restaurant Casavieja	21	Casa de los Arcaya &
3	Hotel Miranda	12	Restaurant Naturalista		Museo de
	Cumberland		Hipócrates		Cerámica Histórica
7	Hotel Intercaribe	19	Fonda Turística Sabor		y Loza Popular
13	Hotel Capri		Coriano	22	Casa de las Ventanas
24	Hotel Roma	30	Pub 1527		de Hierro
25	Hotel Martín	32	La Tasca	23	Casa del Tesoro
33	Hotel Colonial		Española	26	Banco Federal
				27	Museo de Arte Coro
				28	Ipostel
PLACES TO EAT		OTHER		29	Museo de Arte de la
2	Il Restorante Da	1	Airport Terminal		UNEFM Alberto
	Vicenzo Pastas	14	Agencia		Henríquez
4	Restaurant Don		Kuriana	31	Camel Tours
	Camilo	15	Museo de Coro Lucas	34	Banco de
5	Pizzería La Barra del		Guillermo Castillo		Venezuela
	Jacal	16	Iglesia de San	35	Catedral
6	Panadería Costa		Francisco	36	Tourist Office
	Nova	17	Cruz de San	37	Ateneo de Coro
8	Fuente de Soda Mi		Clemente	38	Iglesia de San Nicolás
	Casona	18	Iglesia de San		de Bari
9	Comedor Popular		Clemente	39	Cementerio Judío
10	Pizzería Mersi	20	Casa del Sol	40	Banco Consolidado

VENEZUELA

mass celebrated right after the foundation of the town. The 18th-century **Iglesia de San Clemente**, on the western side of the plaza, was laid out on the Latin-cross plan, one of the few examples of its kind in the country.

West across the street stands the **Casa de los Arcaya**, noted for its long, tile-roofed balconies. The mansion houses the **Museo de Cerámica Histórica y Loza Popular**, a small but interesting museum of pottery and ceramics, open the same hours as the Museo de Coro Lucas Guillermo Castillo. One block west are two carefully restored colonial houses: the **Casa de las Ventanas de Hierro** and the **Casa del Tesoro**.

The **Cementerio Judío**, three blocks west along Calle Zamora, was established in the 1830s and is the oldest Jewish cemetery still in use on the continent. If it's locked (as it usually is), go to the house diagonally opposite and ask the occupants to open it.

North-east of the town spreads the **Médanos de Coro**, a unique mini-Sahara with sandy dunes rising to some 40 metres and now a national park. To get there from the city centre, take the city bus marked 'Carabobo' and get off past the huge Monumento a la Federación. Then walk 10 minutes north along a wide avenida to another public sculpture, Monumento a la Madre. A few paces north, there is nothing but sand. Some cases of robbery have been reported, so don't go alone and keep yourself on guard.

About 4.5 km west of the Monumento a la Federación, on the road to La Vela de Coro, is the **Jardín Xerófilo**, open daily, except Monday, from 8.30 to 11.30 am and 2 to 3.30 pm. Beautiful and well kept, this xerophytic botanical garden is worth a trip. To get there, take the La Vela bus from Calle Falcón, anywhere east of Avenida Manaure.

Places to Stay

There are four budget hotels in the historic sector of the city. The *Hotel Capri* is the cheapest acceptable place, offering simple doubles with fan and bath for US$7. The *Hotel Colonial* has air-con singles/doubles/triples for US$7/9/11. The two remaining hotels, *Martín* and *Roma*, are basic and double as love hotels.

If you need more comfort and facilities, go to the *Hotel Intercaribe* (☎ 511844), Avenida Manaure, which costs US$14/20/23 in singles/doubles/triples. The top central option is the *Hotel Miranda Cumberland* (☎ 523022), opposite the airport (US$40 a double).

Places to Eat

Some of the cheapest meals can be had (at lunch time only) in the *Comedor Popular*. Vegetarians can eat in the budget *Restaurant Naturalista Hipócrates*. The *Restaurant Casavieja* serves reasonably priced food on its pleasant patio. The open-air *Pizzería La Barra del Jacal* is also enjoyable, and offers more than just pizzas. There are a few fast-food joints on the Paseo Talavera, plus the *Pub 1527*, which is open till late. You'll find more eating options marked on the map.

Getting There & Away

Air The airport is just a five-minute walk north of the city centre. There are daily flights to Caracas (US$40) via Barquisimeto (US$29); for other domestic destinations, you have to change in either Caracas or Barquisimeto. You can also use the busier Las Piedras airport (near Punto Fijo, on the Península de Paraguaná), but it's about 90 km from Coro. From Las Piedras, Avensa has daily flights to Aruba (US$59) and Curaçao (US$80).

From Coro airport, two small carriers, Aeropar and Aero Falcón, fly light planes to Aruba (US$80) and Curaçao (US$70) on weekdays provided they collect a minimum of three passengers.

Bus The bus terminal is on Avenida Los Médanos, about two km east of the city centre, and is easily accessible by frequent city transport. Half a dozen buses daily run to Caracas (US$7, seven hours), and even more buses go to Maracaibo (US$4, four hours). There are two direct buses a day to Mérida (US$11, 12 hours) and one to San Cristóbal (US$12, 13 hours); all these buses go via Maracaibo. Buses to Punto Fijo run every hour (US$1.50, 1¼ hours).

MARACAIBO

Although the region around Maracaibo was explored as early as 1499 and Maracaibo itself was founded in 1574, the town only really began to grow in the 18th century as a result of trade with the Dutch Antilles (now the Netherlands Antilles). The republicans' naval victory over the Spanish fleet, fought on Lago Maracaibo on 24 July 1823, brought the town some political importance. In the 1920s the oil boom took off and the city developed into Venezuela's oil capital, with nearly three-quarters of the nation's output coming from beneath the lake.

With a population of about 1.3 million, Maracaibo is the country's largest urban centre after Caracas, and a predominantly modern, prosperous city. Its climate is damp and hot, with an average temperature of about 29°C.

Maracaibo doesn't rank high among tourist attractions, and there's not much to see. However, you may need to stop here on the way to/from the Colombian coast. If you have more time, you can explore the region, which offers striking contrasts of new and old, from forests of oil derricks on Lago Maracaibo to a community living in houses on stilts on Laguna de Sinamaica.

Information

Tourist Office The Corpozulia tourist office (☎ 921811, 921840) is on Avenida Bella Vista between Calles 83 and 84, about two km north of the city centre; the Bella Vista por puestos from Plaza Bolívar will take you there. The office is open weekdays from 8.30 am to 4.30 pm.

Money Most banks are just south of Plaza Bolívar – see the map for their locations.

Telephone The telephone code is 061.

Things to See

If you are in Maracaibo in transit, you probably won't go far beyond the downtown area, the oldest part of the city. The axis of this sector is the **Paseo de las Ciencias**, a wide green belt seven blocks long that was created by demolishing old buildings and establishing a park on the site.

Off the west end of the Paseo stands the **Basílica de Chiquinquirá**, with its opulent, somewhat hotchpotch interior. On the high altar is the venerated image of the Virgin of Chiquinquirá, to whom numerous miracles are attributed. Pilgrims flock here all year round, but the major celebrations are held for a full week in November, culminating in a procession on 18 November.

The east end of the Paseo borders **Plaza Bolívar**, which has the usual Bolívar statue in the middle and the 19th-century **Catedral** on the eastern side. To the north is the **Casa de la Capitulación**, also known as Casa Morales, where on 3 August 1823 the act of capitulation was signed by the Spanish defeated in the naval battle of Lago Maracaibo, thus sealing the independence of Gran Colombia. The house can be visited.

One block north are the **Museo Arquidiocesano** and the **Templo Bautismal Rafael Urdaneta**, both of which are open daily from 9 am to 6 pm. A short walk north-west will take you to the **Museo Urdaneta**. Born in Maracaibo in 1788, General Rafael Urdaneta is the city's greatest hero; he distinguished himself in numerous battles in the War of Independence.

Calle 94 has been restored in parts to its former state, and is worth a stroll. The best section is between Avenidas 7 and 8.

The sector south of the Paseo is busy, chaotic and dirty. Many streets are crowded with vendors and their stalls, which makes the area feel like a market. The most striking sight is the old market building overlooking the docks, restored and reopened as the **Centro de Arte de Maracaibo**.

The most popular tourist sight around Maracaibo is the **Laguna de Sinamaica**, 60 km north of the city, noted for several lakeside hamlets whose inhabitants live in *palafitos*, houses built on piles on or off the shore. Perhaps it was here that in 1499 the Spaniards first saw Indians in similar houses

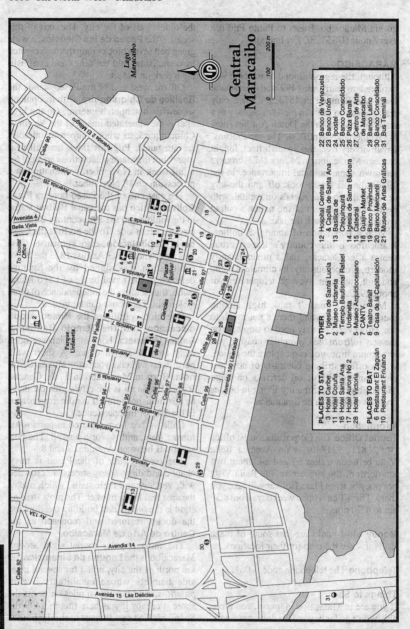

Central Maracaibo

Lago Maracaibo

0   100   200 m

Avenida 2 El Milagro
Avenida 2A
Avenida 2B
Avenida 4 Bella Vista
Avenida 3
Avenida 4
Avenida 5
Avenida 93 Padilla
Avenida 6
Avenida 7
Avenida 8
Avenida 9
Avenida 10
Avenida 11
Avenida 12
Avenida 100 Libertador
Av 13A
Avenida 14
Avenida 15 Las Delicias
Calle 90
Calle 91
Calle 92
Calle 94
Calle 95
Calle 96
Calle 97
Calle 98
Calle 99
Calle 97
Calle 98
Calle 98A
Calle 99

Parque Urdaneta
Plaza Bolívar
Ciencias
Paseo de las Ciencias

To Tourist Office

PLACES TO STAY
3 Hotel Caribe
11 Hotel Coruña
16 Hotel Santa Ana
17 Hotel Aurora No 2
28 Hotel Victoria

PLACES TO EAT
6 Restaurant El Zaguán
10 Restaurant Friulano

OTHER
1 Iglesia de Santa Lucía
2 Museo Urdaneta
4 Templo Bautismal Rafael Urdaneta
5 Museo Arquidiocesano
7 CANTV
8 Casa de la Capitulación
9 Teatro Baralt
12 Hospital Central & Capilla de Santa Ana
13 Basílica de Chiquinquirá
14 Iglesia de Santa Bárbara
15 Catedral
18 Guajiro Market
19 Banco Provincial
21 Museo de Artes Gráficas
22 Banco de Venezuela
23 Banco Unión
24 Ipostel
25 Banco Consolidado
26 Plaza Baralt
27 Centro de Arte de Maracaibo
29 Banco Latino
30 Banco Mercantil
31 Bus Terminal

VENEZUELA

and gave Venezuela its name. Excursion boats take tourists for a trip around the lagoon (US$15 per boat for up to six people).

Places to Stay

The cheapest accommodation can be found behind the cathedral, but these hotels tend to rent rooms by the hour. If you don't mind that, try the *Santa Ana*, *Coruña* or *Aurora No 2*, all of which are basic but have some rooms with private baths. Expect to pay about US$6 for a matrimonial with bath and fan. Somewhat better is *Hotel Caribe*, on Avenida 7, which costs US$10/12/14 for a single/double/triple with air-con and bath.

The old-style *Hotel Victoria* (☎ 229697), overlooking Plaza Baralt and the old market building, is the best option in the city centre. It has clean, spacious rooms with bath and air-con for US$10/11/13 a single/double/triple. Make sure to choose a room with a balcony and a good view over the plaza before booking in.

Places to Eat

There are a lot of cheap, greasy places in the centre, but most of them serve meals only during the lunch hours. One of the few which keeps going till 9 pm is *Restaurant Friulano*. If you need somewhere better, try *Restaurant El Zaguán*.

Getting There & Away

Air The airport is about 12 km south-west of the city centre. Avensa and Servivensa handle flights to the main cities in the country, including Caracas (US$56). They also have daily flights to Miami (US$100).

Zuliana de Aviación operates daily flights to Miami (US$155), Medellín (US$100) and Bogotá (US$100), and domestic flights to Caracas (US$48) and Porlamar (US$59).

Bus The bus terminal is about one km southwest of the city centre, linked by frequent local transport. Buses run regularly to Coro (US$4, four hours) and Caracas (US$11, 11 hours). There are several night buses to Mérida (US$8, nine hours) and San Cristóbal (US$8, eight hours).

For Laguna de Sinamaica, take a bus to Guane or Los Filuos, get off in the town of Sinamaica (US$0.80, two hours) and take a por puesto to Puerto Cuervito (US$0.20, 10 minutes) where pleasure boats anchor.

To Maicao in Colombia, buses (US$4, four to five hours) and shared taxis (US$7, three hours) operate regularly from about 5 am to 3 pm. All passport formalities are done in Paraguachón, on the border. If you come this way from Colombia, expect a search of your luggage by Venezuelan officials.

Maicao is widely and justifiably known as a lawless town, and is far from safe – stay there as briefly as possible. Buses from Maicao to Santa Marta are operated by several companies and depart frequently until about 5 pm (US$9, four hours).

The Andes

The Venezuelan Andes extend for some 400 km from the Táchira depression on the Colombian border north-eastward to the vicinity of Barquisimeto. The range is about 50 to 100 km wide. Administratively, the mountains are covered by three states: Táchira, Mérida and Trujillo.

The state of Mérida is the heart of Venezuela's Andes. The mountains here are not a single ridge, but two roughly parallel chains separated by a verdant mountain valley. The southern chain culminates with the Sierra Nevada de Mérida, crowned with a series of snowcapped peaks. The country's highest summits are here, including Pico Bolívar (5007 metres), Pico Humboldt (4942 metres) and Pico Bompland (4883 metres). All this area has been declared the Parque Nacional Sierra Nevada. The northern chain, the Sierra de la Culata, reaches 4730 metres and is also a national park. In the deep valley between the two sierras sits the city of Mérida, the region's major urban centre and the country's mountain capital.

The Andes are popular hiking territory, offering everything from lush rainforest to permanent snow. Particularly interesting are the *páramos*, open highland moors which start at about 3300 metres and reach almost to the snow line. Their most common plant is the *frailejón* (espeletia), typical only of highland areas of Venezuela, Colombia and Ecuador. Frailejones are especially amazing when in bloom, between November and December.

The Andean dry season lasts from December to April. It's followed by a mixed dry/wet period from May to July, noted for changeable weather with much sunshine but also frequent rains (or snow at high altitudes). August to October are the wettest months; hiking can be miserable and you probably won't see many panoramic views. The snowy period (June to October) can be dangerous for mountaineering.

MERIDA

Mérida is arguably Venezuela's most popular destination among foreign backpackers. It has an unhurried, friendly atmosphere, plenty of tourist facilities, the famous teleférico (recently reopened) and beautiful mountains all around, with the country's rooftop, Pico Bolívar, just 12 km to the east as the crow flies.

Home to the large Universidad de los Andes (the second-oldest university in the country), the city has a sizeable academic community, which gives it a cultured and bohemian air. Mérida enjoys a pleasant mild climate, with an average temperature of 19°C. Furthermore, it's inexpensive and relatively safe by Venezuelan standards.

Mérida was founded in 1558 but its transition from a town into a city really only took place over the last few decades. It sits on a flat meseta, a terrace stretching for a dozen km between two parallel rivers, its edges dropping abruptly to the riverbanks. Having filled the meseta as densely as possible, Mérida is now expanding beyond it, and is approaching some 220,000 inhabitants.

Information

Tourist Office The Cormetur tourist office (☎ 524359, 529566) is at the junction of Avenidas 1 and 2, five minutes north of Plaza

Sucre. The office is open weekdays from 8 am to noon and 2 to 6 pm, and you'll probably find city maps and good information here. Cormetur also operates several outlets throughout the city, including one at the airport and another at the bus terminal.

Money Banks which may handle foreign-exchange transactions are marked on the map.

Telephone Mérida's telephone code is 074.

Inparques The Inparques office (☎ 633-689), at Calle 19 No 5-44 (same opening hours as the tourist office), issues permits for trekking. There's an Inparques outlet at the (inoperable) cable-car station.

Tour Operators There are plenty of tour operators in Mérida and prices are generally reasonable. Probably the most responsible, knowledgeable, stable and competitive operators include:

Bum Bum Tours
    In the new Posada Las Heroínas, Calle 24 No 8-301 (☎ 524160)
Guamanchi Expeditions
    Calle 24 No 8-39 (☎ 522080)
Italia Tours
    In Hotel Italia, Calle 19 No 2-55 (☎ 525737)
Mucuaventura
    Calle 25, corner of Pasaje Ayacucho (☎ 523580)
Natoura
    Avenida 4, between Calles 18 and 19 (☎ 524075)

Other operators that you might consider include Yana Pacha Tours (☎ 526910), Calle 24 No 8-97 (which has recently been criticised by some travellers, but might have got over its problems), Ozono Paragliding School (☎ 523927), Calle 24 No 6-52 (which specialises in paragliding but also offers other services), and Beryl Tours (☎ 525516), Avenida 2 No 15-48.

Bum Bum is among the cheapest operators. It's also the best place to buy maps of the region, country and continent, plus other travel publications including, occasionally, Lonely Planet guidebooks. Bum Bum and

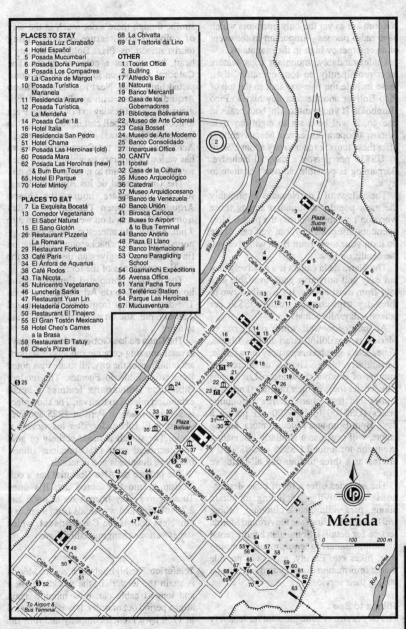

PLACES TO STAY
3 Posada Luz Caraballo
4 Hotel Español
5 Posada Mucumbarí
6 Posada Doña Pumpa
8 Posada Los Compadres
9 La Casona de Margot
10 Posada Turística
   Marianela
11 Residencia Araure
12 Posada Turística
   La Merideña
14 Posada Calle 18
16 Hotel Italia
28 Residencia San Pedro
51 Hotel Chama
57 Posada Las Heroínas (old)
60 Posada Mara
62 Posada Las Heroínas (new)
   & Bum Bum Tours
65 Hotel El Parque
70 Hotel Mintoy

PLACES TO EAT
7 La Exquisita Bocatá
13 Comedor Vegetariano
   El Sabor Natural
15 El Sano Glotón
26 Restaurant Pizzería
   La Romana
29 Restaurant Fortune
33 Café París
34 El Ánfora de Aquarius
38 Café Rodos
45 Tía Nicota
46 Nutricentro Vegetariano
47 Lunchería Sarkis
47 Restaurant Yuan Lin
49 Heladería Coromoto
50 Restaurant El Tinajero
55 El Gran Tostón Mexicano
58 Hotel Cheo's Carnes
   a la Brasa
59 Restaurant El Tatuy
66 Cheo's Pizzería

68 La Chivatta
69 La Trattoria da Lino

OTHER
1 Tourist Office
2 Bullring
17 Alfredo's Bar
18 Natoura
19 Banco Mercantil
20 Casa de los
   Gobernadores
21 Biblioteca Bolivariana
22 Museo de Arte Colonial
23 Casa Bosset
24 Museo de Arte Moderno
25 Banco Consolidado
27 Inparques Office
30 CANTV
31 Ipostel
32 Casa de la Cultura
35 Museo Arqueológico
36 Catedral
37 Museo Arquidiocesano
39 Banco de Venezuela
40 Banco Unión
41 Birosca Carioca
42 Buses to Airport
   & to Bus Terminal
44 Banco Andino
48 Plaza El Llano
52 Banco Internacional
53 Ozono Paragliding
   School
54 Guamanchi Expéditions
56 Avensa Office
61 Yana Pacha Tours
63 Teleférico Station
64 Parque Las Heroínas
67 Mucuaventura

Mérida

0   100   200 m

VENEZUELA

Natoura are as yet the only operators which have radio phones – important in the event of an emergency high in the mountains.

Understandably, mountain trips feature most prominently on tour operators' lists; these include the five-day trek to the top of Pico Bolívar and the four-day hike to Pico Humboldt. If you want to 'do' both peaks in one go, it will be a six to eight-day trek. Almost all operators (except Mucuaventura) offer these tours; expect to pay about US$30 to US$35 per person a day, all-inclusive. Bargaining is possible, so don't hesitate to try it.

The village of Los Nevados is probably the most popular destination among those who don't attempt to climb the peaks. Most operators offer this trip, but you can easily do it on your own; Bum Bum will give you the details on how.

The Sierra de la Culata is a relatively new but easy and attractive goal, available as a tour from most agents. It's usually a two to three-day trip, costing around US$30 per person a day, all-inclusive.

An excursion well worth doing out of Mérida is a wildlife safari in Los Llanos, Venezuela's greatest repository of wildlife, particularly birds. There's an increasing number of ecotourist camps in Los Llanos which offer tours in their ranches (known as *hatos*), but they charge rather astronomic prices (US$100 to US$200 per person a day). Bum Bum and Mucuaventura, among others, will organise a similarly fascinating excursion for around US$35 to US$50. It's offered as a three to four-day all-inclusive trip.

The agencies offer a lot of other destinations, and activities including mountain biking, paragliding, rock climbing, fishing and horseback riding (see the Around Mérida section for details). Some also handle rental of mountaineering equipment, camping gear, bikes etc. Finally, most will provide tourist information even if you don't plan on buying their services.

Things to See

The city centre is quite pleasant for leisurely strolls, though there's not much in the way of colonial architecture or outstanding tourist attractions. Plaza Bolívar is the city's heart, but it's not a colonial square. The **Catedral** was begun in 1800 but not completed until 1958. Next to it is the **Museo Arquidiocesano**, with a collection of religious art, open Tuesday to Friday from 9 am to noon. Note the bell cast in 909, thought to be the world's second-oldest surviving bell. Across the square, the **Casa de la Cultura** has various temporary exhibitions. It's open weekdays from 8 am to noon and 2 to 6 pm.

The Universidad de los Andes building, just off the square, houses the **Museo Arqueológico**, open Tuesday to Friday from 3 to 6 pm, and on weekends from 3 to 7 pm. A small but interesting collection supported by extensive background information (in Spanish only) gives an insight into the pre-Hispanic times of the region.

The recently completed Centro Cultural houses the **Museo de Arte Moderno**, open Tuesday to Friday from 9 am to noon and 2.30 to 6 pm, and on weekends from 10 am to 6 pm.

The **Casa de los Gobernadores** displays several amazing ceramic models of important buildings of the city, all made by a noted local artist, Eduardo Fuentes. The modern **Biblioteca Bolivariana** features a small exhibition related to Bolívar. The showpiece is a sword made in Peru in 1825 and presented to El Libertador after his victory at Junín. The sheath is made entirely of gold and encrusted with 1380 precious stones, including diamonds and emeralds.

The **Museo de Arte Colonial** has a collection of mostly sacred art. It's open Tuesday to Friday from 8 am to noon and 2.30 to 6 pm, and weekends from 9 am to 4 pm. Next door is the **Casa Bosset**, which stages various changing exhibitions.

Teleférico The highlight of a visit to Mérida is again the teleférico, the world's highest and longest cable car, now running again after a period out of order. It was constructed in 1958 by a French company and runs the

12.6 km from Mérida to the top of Pico Espejo (4765 metres), covering the 3188-metre climb in four stages. There are five stations: Barinitas (1577 metres), Montaña (2436 metres), Aguada (3452 metres), Loma Redonda (4045 metres) and Pico Espejo.

Apart from splendid views during the trip itself, the cable car provides easy access to convenient starting points for hiking and mountaineering. Four of the eight cars are back in service, and it is expected that full capacity will be restored by March 1997.

Places to Stay

Mérida has heaps of hotels and most of them offer good value for money. There's an array of places called posadas, which are small, family-run guesthouses, often with a friendly atmosphere. Many provide kitchen and laundry facilities.

The cheapest place in the city centre is *Hotel Italia* (☎ 525737), Calle 19 No 2-55. It has small, simple singles/doubles/triples without bath for US$3/6/7 and rooms with bath for US$6/7/8. It's popular with travellers but faces increasing competition from the more enjoyable posadas.

The most popular backpacker haunt is the *Posada Las Heroínas* (☎ 522665), Calle 24 No 8-95, in Parque Las Heroínas, run by a polyglot Swiss, Tom, and his wife Raquel. You pay US$4 per person in rooms without bath, and can use their kitchen and laundry. The place is often full.

The owners have just moved to a new place nearby, at Calle 24 No 8-301, and are turning it into another posada and a restaurant, which may be operating by the time you read this. Bum Bum Tours is based here.

Other good, cheap posada-style places include: *Residencia San Pedro* (☎ 522735), Calle 19 No 6-36; *Posada Mucumbarí* (☎ 526015), Avenida 3 No 14-73; and *Residencia Araure* (☎ 525103), Calle 16 No 3-34. All are clean and pleasant and cost US$4 per head in doubles or triples without bath.

The *Posada Turística Marianela* (☎ 526-907), Calle 16 No 4-33, is yet another agreeable budget place, run by a friendly English-speaking woman. It costs US$5 per person in rooms without bath, breakfast included. Equally friendly is the small *Posada Calle 18* (☎ 522986), Calle 18 No 3-51, which has doubles/triples with shared facilities for US$10/12. One of the cheapest posadas offering rooms with private bath (US$5 per person) is the *Posada Mara* (☎ 525507), Calle 24 No 8-215.

Places costing a little more (all with private bath) include: the *Hotel Español* (☎ 529235), Avenida 2 No 15-48 (spotlessly clean doubles for US$11); *Posada Luz Caraballo* (☎ 525441), Avenida 2 No 13-80 (US$13/18 a double/triple); *Posada Los Compadres* (☎ 522841), Avenida 4 No 15-05 (US$10/14/17 a matrimonial/double/triple); *La Casona de Margot* (☎ 523312), Avenida 4 No 15-17 (US$14 a matrimonial); *Posada Turística La Merideña* (☎ 525738), Avenida 3 No 16-39 (US$14/20 a double/triple); and *Posada Doña Pumpa* (☎ 527-286), Calle 14 No 5-11.

There are plenty of up-market hotels, including the *Hotel Chama* (☎ 524851), Calle 29 near Avenida 4, and *Hotel Mintoy* (☎ 520340), Calle 25 No 8-130, just off Parque Las Heroínas. Both have comfortable doubles for around US$25.

Places to Eat

If you are used to unpretentious, low-budget dining, Mérida is for you: it's one of the cheapest places to eat in Venezuela. Plenty of restaurants serve set meals for around US$1 to US$2 – just take your pick.

Cheap vegetarian set meals are served (at lunch time only) in *El Sano Glotón*, Avenida 4 No 17-76; *El Sabor Natural*, Avenida 3 No 16-80; *El Tinajero*, Calle 29 near Avenida 4; *Nutricentro Vegetariano*, Avenida 5 No 25-46; and *El Anfora de Aquarius*, Avenida 2 No 23-18.

The reasonably priced *Restaurant El Tatuy*, at Parque Las Heroínas, has a long menu including typical food. Also affordable is *Hotel Cheo's Carnes a la Brasa*, which serves good steaks and trout. *Cheo's Pizzería*, in Hotel El Parque, does some of the better pizzas in town. Another good (and cheaper) place for pizzas is *Restaurant Pizzería La Romana*, Calle 19 No 5-13.

El Gran Tostón Mexicano, Calle 24 No 8-32, offers some inexpensive Mexican snacks, while *Lunchería Sarkis*, corner of Calle 26 and Avenida 5, has cheap Middle-Eastern fast food. *La Exquisita Bocatá*, Avenida 4 No 15-24, does delicious bocatás (a sort of sandwich with a meat filling). For Chinese food, choose between *Yuan Lin*, Calle 26 No 4-50, and *Fortune*, Calle 21 No 4-59.

La Trattoria da Lino, Pasaje Ayacucho No 25-30, serves excellent Italian food at reasonable prices, whereas *La Chivatta*, next door, is the place to go for chicken.

Café París, on Calle 23 off Plaza Bolívar, has tables outside and is a pleasant meeting place frequented by both locals and foreigners. *Café Rodos*, on the corner of Plaza Bolívar, has good espresso, juices, pastries and the like. Great cakes are served in the cosy *Tía Nicota*, in the Centro Comercial Galerías 1890, Avenida 3 No 25-42.

You shouldn't miss *Heladería Coromoto*, Avenida 3 No 28-75, which is about the most famous ice-cream parlour on the continent, appearing in the Guinness Book of Records. The place offers about 620 flavours, though not all are available on an average day. Among the more unusual varieties, you can try Polar beer, shrimp, trout, chicken with spaghetti or 'el vegetariano'. You can even ask for the Lonely Planet flavour (by its Spanish name, Planeta Solitario). The place is open 2 to 10 pm (closed Monday).

Entertainment
For an evening beer with music in a 'student' atmosphere, go to *Birosca Carioca*, Calle 24 No 2-04, which is one of the most popular nightspots in the city centre. Or try the noisy *Alfredo's Bar*, corner of Calle 19 and Avenida 4.

Getting There & Away
Air The airport is on the meseta, right inside the city, two km south-west of Plaza Bolívar. Frequent urban busetas pass by the airport. The runway is short, and the proximity of

high mountains doesn't make landing an easy task, especially in bad weather. Consequently, particularly in the rainy season, flights are often diverted elsewhere, usually to El Vigía (102 km from Mérida, but a new, shorter road via a tunnel is expected to open soon). If this is the case, the airline should provide free transport to/from Mérida – be sure to insist. The only flights from Mérida are to Caracas (US$59). For other destinations, change in Caracas or use the busier El Vigía airport.

Bus The bus terminal is three km south-west of the city centre; it's linked by frequent public transport, or you can take a taxi (US$1). Half a dozen buses a day run to Caracas (US$11, 11 hours) and to Maracaibo (US$8, nine hours). Busetas to San Cristóbal depart every two hours (US$4, 5½ hours). Por puestos service many regional routes, such as Apartaderos and Jají.

AROUND MÉRIDA
The region surrounding Mérida offers plenty of attractions, and you can easily spend a week or two here, walking in the mountains or exploring old villages and other sights by road.

Things to See
The region is sprinkled with old mountain villages, the best known of which is **Jají**, 38 km west of Mérida, accessible by por puestos from the bus terminal. Jají was extensively reconstructed in the late 1960s to become a manicured typical *pueblo andino* (Andean town), and is pretty touristy. There are two pleasant posadas in the village.

For something more authentic, try **Mucuchíes**, a 400-year-old town 48 km east of Mérida. Several km farther down the road is **San Rafael**, noted for an amazing small stone chapel built by a local artist, Juan Félix Sánchez. This is his second chapel; the first, equally beautiful, was constructed two decades ago in the remote hamlet of **El Tisure**, a five to seven-hour walk from San Rafael (there is no access road).

North of San Rafael, at an altitude of 3600

metres, is the **Centro de Investigaciones de Astronomía**, an astronomical observatory which can be visited on some days and evenings (their main telescope has recently broken down, so check for news in Mérida before you go). The place is off the main road and accessible only by a rough track, and there is no public transport.

There are three theme parks in the vicinity of Mérida. **Los Aleros**, on the road to Mucuchíes, is a re-creation of a typical Andean village from the 1930s, brought to life with period events, crafts and food, plus a few extra surprises. Por puestos from the corner of Calle 19 and Avenida 4 in Mérida will take you there. **La Venezuela de Antier**, on the Jají road, is a sort of Venezuela in a capsule, encompassing its landmarks, costumes and traditions. The Jají bus will drop you off next to the park. The third, most recent park, **Xamu – Pueblo Indígena**, is based on an Indian theme. Admission to each park is US$5.

Activities

Hiking Climbing Venezuela's highest peaks, **Pico Bolívar** (with a bust of the hero on the summit) and **Pico Humboldt**, shouldn't be attempted without a guide unless you have climbing experience. Trips to both are offered by a number of tour operators in Mérida (see the Mérida section).

What you can do on your own are the hikes along the trails leading up to both peaks. The trail to Pico Bolívar originates in Mérida and roughly follows the cable-car line. The starting point for the trek up to Pico Humboldt is La Mucuy, accessible by road from Mérida.

An easier and more popular destination is **Los Nevados**, a charming mountain pueblo at an altitude of about 2700 metres (accommodation and food available). Since the teleférico has been out of order, the usual way of getting to the village is by jeep along a breathtaking mountain track hugging the cliffside (US$30 per jeep for up to five people, four to five hours). You stay the night in Los Nevados, from where you walk, or ride on muleback to Loma Redonda cable-car station, then walk downhill to the beautiful Valle Los Calderones for another night, and return to Mérida on the third day.

The **Sierra de la Culata** also offers some amazing hiking territory, and is particularly noted for its desert-like highland landscapes. Take a por puesto to La Culata, from where you can hike uphill amidst a frailejón-filled páramo. Return before 4 pm, the time the last por puesto tends to depart back to Mérida. If you have camping gear, you can continue farther on to the top of **Pico Pan de Azúcar** (4600 metres), then go down south through a deserted, moonscape-like terrain to a chain of mountain lakes and on to the hot springs. Trails are faint here, so don't wander too far from them unless you're an experienced trekker.

Another interesting area for hiking is farther east, near **Pico El Aguila** (4118 metres). Take a morning bus to Valera and get off at Venezuela's highest road pass (4007 metres), at the foot of the peak, about 60 km from Mérida. There's a roadside restaurant where you can have a hot chocolate before you set off. Locals with mules wait by the road to take you to **Laguna Mucubají**, five km due south, but it's better to walk there, so as to get a closer look at the splendid páramo. From Laguna Mucubají, it's well worth walking one hour up the reforested pine slope to **Laguna Negra**, a small but beautiful mountain lake with amazingly dark water.

Some of Mérida's tour operators, including Bum Bum and Guamanchi, will provide information about these and other do-it-yourself tours; Bum Bum has trekking maps of the area.

Mountain Biking This is becoming increasingly popular in the region. Guamanchi is the leading specialist and has the best bikes. They organise bike tours (the most popular is a trip to remote mountain villages south of Mérida, known as Pueblos del Sur), and handle bike rental (US$2 an hour, US$12 a day). Ask them for recommended bike tours to do on your own.

Paragliding Paragliding is the newest craze in the region. Most tour operators offer tandem flights with a skilled pilot, so no previous experience is necessary. The usual starting point for flights is Las Gonzales, an hour's jeep ride from Mérida, from where you fly for about half an hour over a 1000-metre altitude difference. The cost of the flight is much the same with all agencies (US$50), jeep transport included.

SAN CRISTOBAL

Set 40 km from the Colombian border, San Cristóbal is the capital of Táchira state and a busy city of about 300,000 people. Spread over a mountain slope 800 metres above sea level, the city has an attractive location and an agreeable climate, with an average temperature of 21°C. Apart from this, San Cristóbal has little to offer tourists and is really just a place to pass through. Yet it is an almost unavoidable transit point between Venezuela and Colombia, whether you go overland via Cúcuta or fly via Santo Domingo. If you arrive here late, you may need to stay overnight.

Information

The tourist office is in the Complejo Ferial (Fair Complex) in the northern district of Pueblo Nuevo, on the opposite side of the city from the bus terminal. Major banks are close to Plaza Bolívar in the centre.

San Cristóbal's telephone code is 076.

Places to Stay & Eat

There are perhaps a dozen budget hotels in the city centre, but some double as love hotels. *Hotel Andorra*, Carrera 4 No 4-67, near the Catedral, is one of the cheapest options (US$5/7 a matrimonial/double). Set in an old house with a fine patio, it has some charm, but fairly basic rooms. In the same area, at Calle 6 No 3-25, the *Hotel Ejecutivo* (☎ 446298) offers marginally better standards in matrimoniales with bath for US$6.

Better is the *Hotel Parador del Hidalgo* (☎ 432839), Calle 7 No 9-35. It's simple and lacks style, but has clean rooms with private bath and hot water (US$9/12 a double/triple). The hotel has its own restaurant, serving unpretentious cheap meals. More prepossessing is *Hotel Rossio* (☎ 432330), Carrera 9 No 10-98, which has doubles with bath and fan for US$9. Another nearby option is *Hotel Prados del Torbes* (☎ 439-055), Carrera 9, corner of Calle 11 (US$10/14 a double/triple).

For something considerably better, go to *Hotel Bella Vista* (☎ 437866), corner of Carrera 9 and Calle 9. Comfortable singles/doubles/triples with bath go for US$14/20/24.

There are plenty of restaurants all over the centre, including numerous greasy places serving set meals for about US$1.50. Vegetarians can get budget lunches at *El Encanto*, Calle 6 No 3-57, and *El Oasis*, Avenida 5, corner of Calle 13.

Getting There & Away

Air San Cristóbal's airport is in Santo Domingo, about 35 km south-east of the city. It appears in all airline schedules as Santo Domingo, not San Cristóbal. There's no public transport all the way to the airport, but frequent El Piñal busetas from San Cristóbal's bus terminal will drop you off at the turn-off to the airport (US$0.70, one hour), from where it's a 25-minute walk (two km) to the terminal. By the same token, if you are arriving at Santo Domingo, walk two km to the main road and wave down any of the frequent busetas. A taxi between the city and the airport costs about US$10.

Avensa/Servivensa operates two flights a day to/from Caracas (US$61) and two to/from Bogotá (US$50). The latter is a cheap and convenient way of entering Venezuela without visa hassles.

There are no moneychanging facilities at the terminal but some people may be interested in selling bolívares for US dollars or Colombian *pesos* – ask around. Better still, bring some bolívares from Bogotá. You pay a departure tax of about US$4 when leaving Venezuela via Santo Domingo.

Bus The bus terminal is about two km south of the city centre, linked by frequent city bus services. There are about 10 buses daily to Caracas (US$13 ordinary, US$17 deluxe, 13 hours). Most depart in the late afternoon/early evening for an overnight trip via El Llano highway. Busetas go to Mérida every two hours until 6 pm (US$4, 5½ hours). Por puestos to San Antonio del Táchira, on the border, run every 10 or 15 minutes (US$1, 1¼ hours).

SAN PEDRO DEL RIO

San Pedro del Río is a tiny town about 40 km north of San Cristóbal. It's clean, well cared for, lethargic and colonial-looking. There are perhaps four calles and four carreras altogether, all cobblestoned and lined with restored whitewashed single-storey houses. There are no great sights here, but the town as a whole makes for a fine architectural piece and an oasis of peace.

Places to Stay & Eat

The only regular hotel, the *Posada Turística La Vieja Escuela* (☎ 93664), Calle Real No 3-61, is a pleasant old-time place with neat doubles/triples/quads for US$11/15/18. There are four or five restaurants; the best is probably *El Balcón*, near the Posada.

Getting There & Away

San Pedro del Río lies five km off the San Cristóbal-La Fría road. From San Cristóbal, take the half-hourly bus to San Juan de Colón (US$0.80, one hour) and change for the bus to San Pedro (US$0.20, 15 minutes); it departs every half-hour from just off the main square.

SAN ANTONIO DEL TACHIRA

San Antonio is a Venezuelan border town of some 50,000 people, living off trade with neighbouring Colombia. You will pass through it if taking this route between the two countries; otherwise there's no point in coming here as the town has no significant tourist sights. Move your watch one hour forward when crossing from Colombia to Venezuela, one hour backward if you enter Colombia from Venezuela.

Information

Tourist Office There's no tourist office in town, but any of several travel agencies (most of which are on Carrera 4) should solve any transport problems.

Money There are more than half a dozen banks in San Antonio, none of which changes cash. Probably only Banco Consolidado will change American Express travellers' cheques, and Banco Unión may service Visa card-holders.

There are plenty of casas de cambio in the centre, particularly on Carrera 4 and around the DIEX office. They all change dollars, bolívares and pesos, at rates similar to those in Cúcuta across the border. None of the casas changes travellers' cheques.

Telephone The telephone code is 076.

Immigration The DIEX office is on Carrera 9, between Calles 6 and 7, and is theoretically open daily from 6 am to 8 pm, though it may close earlier. You must get an exit or entry stamp in your passport here. There's a departure tax of some US$4 (it seems to change frequently), paid in bolívares, required from all tourists leaving Venezuela via this border crossing.

Nationals of most countries don't need a visa for Colombia, but all travellers must get an entry stamp from DAS (see the Cúcuta section in the Colombia chapter for further information).

Places to Stay & Eat

Hotel Frontera (☎ 715245), Calle 2 No 8-70, is possibly the cheapest in town (US$4/6 a double without/with bath), but basic. *Hotel Villa de San Antonio* (☎ 711023), Carrera 6 No 1-61, is also on the basic side but is more expensive.

Probably the best budget bet is *Hotel Colonial* (☎ 712679), Carrera 11 No 2-51, which has clean matrimoniales/doubles with fan and private bath for US$7/9. It has its own inexpensive restaurant. Quite similar is the *Hotel Terepaima* (☎ 711763), Carrera 8

No 1-37, which costs US$10 a double. It also has a cheap restaurant.

The best accommodation in town is to be found in *Hotel Don Jorge* (☎ 711932), Calle 5 No 9-20, and *Hotel Adriático* (☎ 715757), Calle 6, corner of Carrera 6. Either costs US$18/25/32 a single/double/triple, and both have their own restaurants.

Getting There & Away

Air The airport is a couple of km north-east of town, reached by local transport. Avensa/Servivensa has four flights daily to Caracas (US$63), and one to Maracaibo (US$45) and to several other domestic destinations. Servivensa flies five times a week (except Tuesday and Saturday) to Medellín in Colombia (US$45). Note that this is the cheapest onward ticket out of Venezuela.

Bus San Antonio has a new bus terminal, halfway to the airport. Four bus companies – Expresos Mérida, Expresos Los Llanos, Expresos Alianza and Expresos San Cristóbal – operate buses to Caracas, with a total of seven buses daily. All depart between

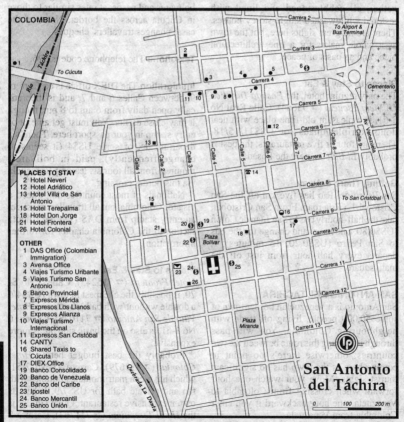

COLOMBIA

To Cúcuta

To Airport & Bus Terminal

Río Táchira

Cementerio

To San Cristóbal

Plaza Bolívar

Plaza Miranda

PLACES TO STAY
2 Hotel Neverí
12 Hotel Adriático
13 Hotel Villa de San Antonio
15 Hotel Terepaima
18 Hotel Don Jorge
21 Hotel Frontera
26 Hotel Colonial

OTHER
1 DAS Office (Colombian Immigration)
3 Avensa Office
4 Viajes Turismo Uribante
5 Viajes Turismo San Antonio
6 Banco Provincial
7 Expresos Mérida
8 Expresos Los Llanos
9 Expresos Alianza
10 Viajes Turismo Internacional
11 Expresos San Cristóbal
14 CANTV
16 Shared Taxis to Cúcuta
17 DIEX Office
19 Banco Consolidado
20 Banco de Venezuela
22 Banco del Caribe
23 Ipostel
24 Banco Mercantil
25 Banco Unión

San Antonio del Táchira

0   100   200 m

VENEZUELA

4 and 7 pm and use the El Llano route (US$14 ordinary, US$17 deluxe, about 14 hours). Bus companies still maintain their offices in the town centre, close to each other on Carrera 4, where they also sell tickets.

There are no direct buses to Mérida; go to San Cristóbal and change. Por puestos to San Cristóbal leave frequently from the bus terminal (US$1, 1¼ hours).

Buses and shared taxis run frequently to Cúcuta in Colombia, about 12 km from San Antonio. Catch buses (US$0.30) on Calle 6 or Carrera 4, and shared taxis (US$0.50) on Calle 6 near the corner of Carrera 9. Both will deposit you at Cúcuta bus terminal, passing through the centre. You can pay in bolívares or pesos.

The North-East

Venezuela's north-east is essentially for outdoor activities; it's the region for sailing, walking, snorkelling and sunbathing. Perhaps the most amazing section of the coast is in the Parque Nacional Mochima. Totally different is the Delta del Orinoco, a vast marshy green carpet crisscrossed by a maze of water channels. Another of the region's star attractions is the Cueva del Guácharo (Guácharo Cave).

Although it was here that the Spaniards first arrived and settled, there's not much of the colonial legacy left, except for the partly preserved old towns of Barcelona and Cumaná and some old churches and forts scattered over the region.

Administratively, the north-east covers the states of Anzoátegui, Sucre, Monagas and Delta Amacuro. The Isla de Margarita, which geographically belongs to the region, is detailed separately later in this chapter.

BARCELONA
Barcelona was founded in 1671 by Catalans and named after their mother town in Spain. Today, it's a city of about 280,000 people and the capital of Anzoátegui state. It's gradually merging into a single urban sprawl with its dynamic young neighbour, Puerto La Cruz.

Barcelona has several central plazas and some colonial architecture. The historic quarter has been partly restored and whitewashed throughout, and this gives it a pleasant general impression, even though the urban fabric is a mishmash of houses dating from different periods. The city hasn't rushed into modernity, and the air of lethargic yesterdays is still noticeable in the old sector.

Information
The Dirección de Cultura y Turismo, just off Plaza Boyacá, is open on weekdays from 8 am to noon and 2 to 5.30 pm.

There are only a few banks in central Barcelona, and you'd better have sufficient bolívares before coming here.

The telephone code for Barcelona is 081.

Things to See
The historic nucleus of the city is **Plaza Boyacá**, with a statue of General José Antonio Anzoátegui, the Barcelona-born hero of the War of Independence, in its centre. On the western side of this tree-shaded square stands the **Catedral**, built a century after the town's foundation.

On the southern side of the plaza is the **Museo de Anzoátegui**. Accommodated in the carefully restored, oldest surviving building in town, the museum features a variety of objects related to Barcelona's history. It is open Tuesday to Sunday from 8 am to noon and 2 to 5 pm.

An extension of the museum is housed in the **Ateneo de Barcelona**, two blocks east. On the 1st floor of this building is a small collection of paintings (most dating from the 1940s and 1950s) by modern Venezuelan artists. The Ateneo also presents temporary exhibitions on the ground floor, and conducts various cultural activities. The museum here is open weekdays from 8 am to noon and 2 to 5 pm, and on weekends from 9 am to noon and 2 to 5 pm.

The **Plaza Rolando** is lined by more recent buildings, including the Iglesia del

Barcelona

0   100   200 m

To Puerto La Cruz

To Airport

To Bus Terminal

Avenida 5 de Julio

Plaza Miranda

Avenida Miranda

Carrera 18 Liberal

Parque El Indio

Carrera 17 Ayacucho

Avenida Caracas

Plaza Bolívar

Carrera 16 Buroz

Carrera 15 Carabobo

Carrera 14 Freites

Carrera 13 Bolívar

Avenida 5 de Julio

Carrera 12 Juncal

Carrera 11 Anzoátegui

Carrera 10 Unión

Carrera 9 Páez

Plaza Rolando

Plaza Boyacá

Río Neverí

Avenida Fuerzas Armadas

Avenida Cajigal

El Progreso

Carmen and the Teatro Cajigal, both dating from the 1890s. There are a few more plazas to the north-west, including Plaza Miranda and **Plaza Bolívar**, just one block from each other. The western side of the latter is occupied by the **Casa Fuerte**, once a Franciscan hospice, destroyed by the royalists in a heavy attack in 1817. Over 1500 people lost their lives in the massacre which followed the takeover. The surviving parts of the walls have been left in ruins as a memorial.

Places to Stay
The *Hotel Plaza* (☎ 772843), on Plaza

Boyacá, is one of the most pleasant budget places in town. It's in a fine colonial house with a patio, and has rooms of different standards and prices. Matrimoniales don't have private bath (US$8), but they are spacious and overlook the plaza and the Catedral. There are also some less attractive air-con doubles for around US$10.

Another good inexpensive option is the *Hotel Canarias* (☎ 771034), on Carrera Bolívar. Singles/matrimoniales with fan are US$6/8, while matrimoniales/triples with air-con cost US$10/12. All rooms have private bath. There are some other budget

VENEZUELA

PLACES TO STAY
2   Hotel Neverí
6   Hotel Nacional
8   Hotel Cultura
11 Hotel Barcelona
19 Hotel Canarias
20 Hotel Madrid
21 Hotel Plaza

PLACES TO EAT
15 Lunchería Doña Arepa
17 Restaurant Boyacá

OTHER
1   Edificio de la Gobernación
3   Banco Mercantil
4   Casa Fuerte
5   Teatro Cajigal
7   Iglesia del Carmen
9   Gunda Arte Popular
10 Banco de Venezuela
12 Ipostel
13 CANTV
14 Ateneo de Barcelona
16 Tourist Office
18 Catedral
22 Museo de Anzoátegui
23 Galería de Arte
24 Banco Unión

places in the centre, including *Hotel Nacional*, *Hotel Madrid* and *Hotel Cultura*, but they are nothing special.

The large *Hotel Barcelona* (☎ 771087) has good air-con doubles/triples for around US$17/20. Similar standards for slightly less are to be found at *Hotel Neverí* (☎ 772373), Avenida Miranda.

Places to Eat
Central Barcelona is not a place to go for a culinary treat. There's a choice of eating outlets but nothing extraordinary. Avenida 5 de Julio is the main area for eating, with several restaurants, snack bars and food vendors. In the old town, budget eateries include the *Restaurant Boyacá*, on Plaza Boyacá, and *Lunchería Doña Arepa*, on Carrera Bolívar.

Getting There & Away
Air The airport is two km south of the city centre, accessible by urban transport. Avensa/Servivensa has four flights a day to Caracas (US$41) and one to Porlamar (US$27).

Bus The bus terminal is about one km south of the city centre, next to the market; take a buseta going south along Avenida 5 de Julio, or walk 15 minutes. The terminal handles mostly regional routes; relatively few long-distance buses call here. The terminal in Puerto La Cruz is far busier.

To Puerto La Cruz, catch a city bus going north on Avenida 5 de Julio (US$0.20). They use two routes, 'Vía Intercomunal' and 'Vía Alterna'. Either will set you down in the centre of Puerto La Cruz.

PUERTO LA CRUZ
Puerto La Cruz is a young, dynamic and expanding city. Until the 1930s it was no more than an obscure village, but it boomed after rich oil deposits were discovered in the region to the south. The port of Guanta was built east of town to serve as an oil terminal and to ship oil piped from the wells overseas.

The city has become a popular destination among Venezuelan holiday-makers, and is very touristy, with prices to match. It has a lively 10-block-long waterfront boulevard, Paseo Colón, which skirts a polluted beach and is packed with hotels, tour agencies, bars and restaurants. This apart, the city has little to show tourists: a block or two back from the beach and it's just an ordinary place. Some travellers may be disappointed.

Puerto La Cruz is the major gateway to Isla de Margarita. It's also a jumping-off point to the beautiful Parque Nacional Mochima, which stretches just north and east of the city.

Information
Tourist Office The Coranztur tourist office (☎ 688170) is midway along Paseo Colón and is open daily from 8 am to 8 pm. City maps can bought at Kiosko El Universal.

Money Most banks are within a few blocks south of Plaza Colón (see the map for locations). The most useful banks include the Banco Unión and the Banco de Venezuela

Puerto La Cruz

0   100   200 m

CARIBBEAN SEA

To Cumaná

To Barcelona

Parque Andrés Eloy Blanco

PLACES TO STAY

1   Hotel Meliá
6   Hotel Riviera
10   Hotel Senador
14   Hotel Gaeta
18   Hotel Comercio
22   Hotel Diana
26   Hotel Cristal Park
27   Hotel Guayana
28   Hotel Europa
29   Hotel Neptuno
30   Hotel Margelina
31   Hotel Margarita
33   Hotel Rasil

PLACES TO EAT

2   Restaurant El
     Rancho del Tío
3   Il Ristorante Porto Vecchio
4   Restaurant Tío Pepe
5   Pizza Hut
11   Trattoria d'Franca
21   Le Stop
24   Parrilla y Pollo en
     Brasas Las Islas
25   Tasca Restaurant
     Punta de Piedras
32   Restaurant El Rincón
     del Bucanero

OTHER

7   Banco Provincial
8   Banco del Orinoco
9   Banco Mercantil
12   CANTV
13   Ipostel
14   Banco de Venezuela
15   Banco Unión
16   Kiosko El Universal
19   Excursion Boats
20   Tourist Office
23   Banco Consolidado &
     Turisol
34   Bus Terminal
35   Conferry Terminal

(cash, Visa, MasterCard) and the Banco Consolidado (American Express travellers' cheques).

Telephone The city's telephone code is 081.

Places to Stay

Puerto La Cruz is an expensive place to stay, and hotels fill up fast in the tourist season. It's difficult to find anything reasonable for below US$10 a double. Many hotels have gathered on Paseo Colón and the adjoining streets. All the hotels listed below have rooms with private bath and either fan or air-con.

The small *Hotel Guayana* (☎ 652175), on Plaza Bolívar, is one of the cheapest acceptable places. It has doubles/triples with fan for US$8/10 (air-con US$12/14).

The cheapest options on Paseo Colón include the *Hotel Montecarlo* (☎ 687677), *Hotel Neptuno* (☎ 653261), *Hotel Diana* (☎ 650017) and *Hotel Margelina* (☎ 687-545). All have rooms with air-con, but are otherwise nothing special. Check a few of them and inspect rooms before deciding. Expect a double to cost US$12 to US$14.

One block back from the Paseo is the slightly better *Hotel Europa* (☎ 650034), which costs US$14/17/21 a single/double/triple. Yet another reasonable place, the *Hotel Comercio* (☎ 651429), on Calle Maneiro, has doubles for US$15.

More comfortable yet still affordable options include the *Hotel Gaeta* (☎ 650411) and *Hotel Senador* (☎ 673522). A double with a sea view in either will cost around US$30. The just-opened *Hotel Cristal Park*, Calle Buenos Aires, is good value at US$30 for a suite, with breakfast included.

Places to Eat

The waterfront is essentially the up-market area, but there are also some cheaper places, including *Le Stop*, the restaurant of the *Hotel Neptuno*, and several outlets serving Middle Eastern fast food. For more budget eating, comb the streets back from the beach. Try, for example, *Parrilla y Pollo en Brasas Las Islas* (good chicken and grilled beef), *Tasca*

Restaurant Punta de Piedras (fish and meat dishes) or *Trattoria d'Franca* (pizzas and pasta).

The cream of the city's restaurants and trendy bars are in the area of Plaza Colón and along the beach; some of these places have been included on the map.

Getting There & Away

Air The airport is in Barcelona (see that section for details).

Bus The bus terminal is conveniently sited in the middle of the city, just three blocks from Plaza Bolívar. Frequent buses run to Caracas (US$5, five hours) and to Cumaná (US$1.25, 1½ hours); some continue east from Cumaná to Carúpano (US$3.50, 3½ hours) or even to Güiria (US$5.50, 5½ hours). There are half a dozen buses daily to Ciudad Guayana (US$6, six hours), and all go via Ciudad Bolívar (US$4.50, 4½ hours).

To Barcelona, take a city bus from Avenida 5 de Julio.

Boat Puerto La Cruz is the major departure point for Isla de Margarita. Conferry operates ferries to the island, with six departures a day (there may be fewer in the off season). The passenger fare is US$6/4 in 1st/tourist class and the trip takes 4½ hours. The Conferry terminal is accessible by por puestos from the centre. Do this trip in the daytime – it's a spectacular journey between the islands of Parque Nacional Mochima.

PARQUE NACIONAL MOCHIMA

Mochima National Park covers the offshore belt of the Caribbean coast between Puerto La Cruz and Cumaná, including a wealth of islands and islets, plus a strip of the hilly coast noted for deep bays and white-sand beaches.

The main groups of islands include, from west to east, Las Borrachas, Las Chimanas and Las Caracas. There are also a number of islands closer to the mainland, including Isla de Plata and Isla de Monos. Most of the islands are barren, rocky in parts and quite spectacular. Some islands are surrounded by coral reefs and offer good snorkelling. The waters are warm and usually calm, and abound in marine life. The weather is fine for most of the year, with moderate rainfall mainly between July and October.

The **Isla de Plata** is one of the most popular islands among Venezuelan tourists, and it has food and drink facilities. It's about 10 km east of Puerto La Cruz and is accessible by boat from the pier near Pamatacualito, the eastern suburb of the port of Guanta (serviced by por puestos from Puerto La Cruz). It can also be reached by excursion boats directly from Puerto La Cruz, but this is more expensive (US$5 return per person).

Other standard boat excursions offered from Puerto La Cruz include a trip to Playa Puinare, Playa El Saco and El Faro (US$3 per person), a La Piscina tour with an hour's snorkelling (US$14 per person, equipment provided), and a trip to the distant Playa Blanca in the north-eastern part of the park (US$17 per person). Boats depart in the morning from the city waterfront near the tourist office and return in the afternoon.

Parts of the Puerto La Cruz-Cumaná road skirt the seafront, so you'll have some spectacular glimpses of the park. There are several beaches off the road, possibly the best being Playa Arapito, some 23 km from Puerto La Cruz, and Playa Colorada, four km farther east. On weekends, popular beaches swarm with holiday-makers, some of whom seem to come just to drink beer and listen to loud music. On the other hand, some deserted beaches can be unsafe, particularly at night – use common sense.

About 20 km farther along the Puerto La Cruz-Cumaná road, a side road branches off to the north and goes several km to the village of **Mochima**. Mochima sits in the deep Bahía Mochima, and is a good jumping-off point for exploring the surrounding area. From the village's wharf, boats can take you to the offshore islands or put you down on one of several mainland beaches, such as Playa Blanca or Playa Cautaro, that are inaccessible by road. Accommodation and food are available in the village.

For a sweeping view of the park, complete with its islands, bays and beaches, go to **Los Altos de Santa Fe**, a village some 25 km east of Puerto La Cruz. It sits at an altitude of about 900 metres and is only three km from the seashore, making it a fabulous lookout. The village is surrounded by verdant highlands, sprinkled with coffee and cacao haciendas. Jeeps to Los Altos depart from Puerto La Cruz bus terminal, regularly in the morning but not so in the afternoon (US$0.80, 45 minutes). There are some accommodation facilities in the area.

CUMANÁ

The capital of Sucre state, Cumaná is a city of some 250,000 inhabitants and an important port for sardine fishing and canning. Founded by the Spaniards in 1521, it takes pride in being the oldest existing town on South America's mainland. There's not much colonial architecture, however; three destructive earthquakes, in 1684, 1765 and 1929, reduced the town each time to little more than a pile of rubble, and its historic character largely disappeared in subsequent reconstructions.

Cumaná is noted more for its environs than for the city itself. There are beaches nearby, the closest being Playa San Luis, on the south-western outskirts of the city. The Parque Nacional Mochima begins a little farther down the coast. To the north is the intriguing Península de Araya, while to the south-east is the Cueva del Guácharo. Cumaná is also a gateway to Isla de Margarita.

Information

Tourist Office The Dirección de Turismo (☎ 316051) is on Calle Sucre, close to Iglesia de Santa Inés. The office is open weekdays from 8 am to noon and 2.30 to 5.30 pm.

Money Most major banks are on Avenida Mariño and Avenida Bermúdez; see the map for locations. The Banco Consolidado is farther west on Avenida Bermúdez, seven blocks beyond the Banco Mercantil.

Telephone Cumaná's telephone code is 093.

Cumaná

0   50   100 m

To Bus Terminal

Plaza Bolívar

Plaza Blanco

Plaza Miranda

Parque Ayacucho

Río Manzanares

Avenida Humboldt

Parque Gualquerí

To Airport

To Ferry Terminal

Carabobo

Avenida Bermúdez

Rojas

Junín

Rendón

Sarmiento

García

Gutiérrez

Avenida Mariño

Avenida Arismendi

Bolívar

Sucre

Boyacá

Montes

Ayacucho

Nigüitao

Comuna

Cantaura

América

Ichál

PLACES TO STAY	
11	Hotel Dos Mil
12	Hotel Master
16	Hotel Mariño
20	Hotel Turismo Gualquerí
21	Hotel Regina
24	Hotel Italia
25	Hotel América
27	Hotel Cumaná
28	Hotel Vesuvio
29	Hotel Astoria
31	Hospedaje Lucila
34	Hospedaje La Gloria

PLACES TO EAT	
3	Panadería Super Kaity
5	Restaurant El Colmao
6	Arepera 19 de Abril
7	Restaurant Bar Jardín Sport
9	Arepera El Punto Criollo
22	Restaurant París

OTHER	
1	CANTV
2	Museo Gran Mariscal del Ayacucho
4	Catedral
8	Ipostel
10	Por Puestos to Ferry Terminal
13	Banco Construcción
14	Banco Unión
15	Banco de Venezuela
17	Banco del Caribe
18	Banco Mercantil
19	Banco Internacional
23	Casa Natal de Andrés Eloy Blanco
26	Arepera El Consulado
30	Tourist Office
32	Castillo de San Antonio de la Eminencia
33	Iglesia de Santa Inés

VENEZUELA

Things to See

Some streets around **Iglesia de Santa Inés** retain some of their former appearance. The church itself is a 1929 construction, and has few objects of an earlier date inside, apart from the 16th-century statue of the patron saint over the high altar. The **Catedral**, on Plaza Blanco, is also relatively young, and has a hotchpotch of altarpieces in its largely timbered interior.

Perhaps the best restored colonial structure in town is the **Castillo de San Antonio de la Eminencia**, on a hill just south-east of the centre. Originally constructed in 1659 on a four-pointed star plan, it suffered from pirate attacks and earthquakes, but the coral walls have survived in pretty good shape. The fort commands good views over the city and the bay; go there at sunset.

The city has three museums. The **Casa Natal de Andrés Eloy Blanco** is the house where the poet, considered one of Venezuela's most outstanding literary talents, was born in 1896. The **Museo Gran Mariscal de Ayacucho** is dedicated to the Cumaná-born hero of the War of Independence, General Antonio José de Sucre. The **Museo del Mar** is at the old airport, a couple of km west of the city centre. None of these museums is particularly inspiring.

Places to Stay

There's quite a choice of budget accommodation conveniently located in the city centre. All hotels listed here have rooms with private bath and either fan or air-con.

One of the cheapest in town (US$5 a matrimonial) is the unprepossessing *Hospedaje La Gloria* (☎ 661284), on Calle Sucre. More pleasant is the *Hospedaje Lucila*, on Calle Bolívar. It's clean and quiet, and has matrimoniales with fan/air-con for US$6/9. Other inexpensive options in the area include *Hotel Astoria* (☎ 662708), *Hotel Vesuvio* (☎ 314077), *Hotel Cumaná* and *Hotel Italia* (☎ 663678), all on Calle Sucre, and *Hotel América* (☎ 321955), on Calle América. None should cost more than about US$10 a double. The Astoria and Italia have rooms with air-con.

There are also some budget hotels just west across the river, including *Hotel Dos Mil* and *Hotel Master* (☎ 663884). If you want somewhere appreciably better, try *Hotel Regina* (☎ 321168), which has good air-con singles/doubles/triples for US$14/19/22. The *Hotel Turismo Guaiquerí* (☎ 310821) and *Hotel Mariño* (☎ 322311) provide comparable facilities but are more expensive (US$17/22/25 at either).

Places to Eat

About the cheapest central place for a soup and a main course is the basic *Restaurant París*, on Plaza Miranda, but the food is nothing special. The restaurant of the *Hotel Italia* is better and not much more expensive. The open-air *Restaurant Bar Jardín Sport*, at Plaza Bolívar, also serves cheap food (steaks, spaghetti, hamburgers etc), but most guests come here for a beer (or 10). The place is popular with both locals and foreigners and is open till late. The old jukebox playing typical music adds to the atmosphere.

Other inexpensive eating options include three areperas, *19 de Abril*, *El Consulado* and *El Punto Criollo*. *El Colmao* is one of the better restaurants in the centre.

Getting There & Away

Air The new airport is a couple of km south-east of the city. Avensa/Servivensa has flights to Caracas (US$43) and Porlamar (US$26).

Bus The bus terminal is 1.5 km north-west of the city centre, and it's linked by frequent urban buses. There is regular bus service to Caracas (US$7, 6½ hours); all buses go through Puerto La Cruz (US$1.25, 1½ hours). Half a dozen buses daily depart for Ciudad Bolívar (US$6, six hours) and continue to Ciudad Guayana (US$7.50, 7½ hours). For Cueva del Guácharo, take the Caripe bus (US$2.50, 3½ hours); there are two departures daily, at 7.15 am and 12.30 pm.

Boat Conferry operates two ferries a day to Isla de Margarita (US$3.50, 3½ hours).

Boats to Araya run every hour or two until about 4 pm (US$0.75, one hour). All ferries and boats depart from the ferry docks next to the mouth of Río Manzanares, two km west of the centre; por puestos go there from the door of Hotel Dos Mil (US$0.20).

PENINSULA DE ARAYA

This 70-km-long arid peninsula stretches from east to west along the mainland coast, with its western end lying due north of Cumaná. The population is thinly scattered in a handful of coastal villages, of which Araya, on the tip, is the largest. This is the place to go to see the peninsula's two major attractions, the *salinas* (saltpans) and the *castillo* (fort).

Salinas

The salinas were discovered by the Spaniards in 1499 and have been exploited almost uninterruptedly up to the present day. They were, and still are, Venezuela's largest salt deposits. The salt mining is operated by ENSAL, a government company, which has built installations on the seafront and produces half a million tonnes of salt per year. The salt works can be visited and they're an unusual sight.

Go to the company's main office, at the northern end of the town, to get a free permit and a guide, who will show you around the complex. There are three areas to visit: the *salinas naturales*, the *salinas artificiales* and the buildings where the salt is sorted, packed and stored. The tour takes somewhere between two and three hours. Start early and be prepared for baking heat: a hat or other head protection is a must. It's wise to carry a large bottle of water or other drink.

Castillo

The fort was built in the first half of the 17th century to protect the salinas from plunder. It was the most costly Spanish project in the New World up to that time. In 1726 a hurricane produced a tide which broke over the salt lagoon, flooding it and turning it into a gulf. Salt could no longer be exploited, and the Spanish decided to abandon the fortress.

Before leaving, they tried to blow it up, but although they used all the available gunpowder, the structure largely resisted their efforts to destroy it. The mighty bulwarks still proudly crown the waterfront cliff. The fort is a 10-minute walk along the beach from the wharf. You can wander freely around the place, as there's no gate.

Getting There & Away

Boats go from Cumaná every two hours or so until 4 or 5 pm (US$0.75, one hour). Upon arrival at Araya, check the schedule of the boats back to Cumaná and keep in mind that the last boat may depart earlier than scheduled, or sometimes not at all. There are several simple posadas and restaurants in Araya.

CARIPE

Set in a mountain valley 55 km back from the coast, Caripe is a pleasant, easy-going small town renowned for its agreeable climate, its attractive environs, its coffee and orange plantations and its proximity to the spectacular Cueva del Guácharo. Little more than two parallel streets, around which most activities and services are centred, the town is quite touristy.

Information

Caripe has a few banks, including Banco Unión and Banco de Venezuela, but it may be wise to bring bolívares with you.

The telephone code for Caripe is 092.

Things to See & Do

There's nothing special to see in town, but the rugged surroundings are beautiful and pleasant for walks. The number one sight is obviously the **Cueva del Guácharo** (see the following section). Among other attractions, there are two nice waterfalls: **Salto La Payla**, near the cave, and the 80-metre **Salto El Chorrerón**, an hour's walk from the village of Sabana de Piedra.

El Mirador (1100 metres), to the north of the town, commands sweeping views over the Valle del Caripe. It's a 45-minute walk from town, or you can get there by road.

VENEZUELA

Numerous longer trips are possible, including the hike to the highest peak in the region, **Cerro Negro** (2600 metres).

Places to Stay & Eat

There are a score of places to stay in and around the town. Hotel prices tend to rise on weekends.

The cheapest place in town (US$8 a double with bath) is the *Hotel San Francisco* (☎ 51018), opposite the church. Marginally better are the *Hotel Berlín* (☎ 51246) and *Posadas Oriente* (☎ 51257), opposite one another on the main street, but they cost US$13 a double. For a little more, you can stay in the *Hotel Venezia* or the *Mini Hotel Familiar Nicola*.

If you are in a large party, it may work out cheaper to take a cabaña; there are several on the road between Caripe and the village of El Guácharo. There's also the pleasant *Hacienda Campo Claro* (☎ 551013) in Teresén, five km east of Caripe.

Most hotels and cabañas have their own restaurant. One of the cheapest places for a meal is the restaurant of the *Hotel San Francisco*, whereas the restaurant of the *Hotel Venezia* is among the best.

Getting There & Away

There's no bus terminal; buses and por puestos depart from the town centre. There's an evening bus direct to Caracas via Maturín (US$11, 11 hours), and buses every two hours to Maturín (US$2, three hours). Por puestos also service this latter route (US$3, two hours).

Two buses a day, at 6 am and noon, go to Cumaná (US$2.50, 3½ hours). They pass the Cueva del Guácharo on the way. There are also infrequent por puestos to Cumaná, mostly in the morning.

CUEVA DEL GUACHARO

The Guácharo Cave, 10 km from Caripe on the road towards the coast, is Venezuela's longest, largest and most magnificent cave. It had been known to the local Indians long before Columbus crossed the Atlantic, and was later explored by Europeans. The eminent explorer Alexander von Humboldt penetrated 472 metres into the cave in September 1799, and it was he who first classified its unusual inhabitant, the guácharo, or oilbird *(Steatornis caripensis)*.

The guácharo is a nocturnal, fruit-eating bird, the only one of its kind in the world. It inhabits caves in various tropical parts of the Americas, living in total darkness and leaving the cave only at night for food, principally the fruit of some species of palms. The guácharo has a sort of radar-like location system similar to that of bats, which enables it to get around. The adult bird is about 60 cm long, with a wingspan of a metre.

In Venezuela, the guácharo has been seen in over 40 caves; the biggest colony, estimated at about 18,000 birds, is here, in the Guácharo Cave. They inhabit only the first chamber of the cave, the 760-metre-long Salón de Humboldt. The cave also boasts a variety of other wildlife, and amazing natural formations including a maze of stalactites and stalagmites.

The cave is open daily from 8 am to 4 pm, and all visits are in guided groups of up to 10 people; the tour takes about 1½ hours. A 1200-metre-long portion of the total 10.2-km length of the cave is visited, though occasionally in August the water can rise, limiting sightseeing to half a km. You have to leave backpacks and bags by the ticket office, but cameras with flash are permitted beyond the area where the guácharos live. The ticket costs US$1.25 (no student discounts). Don't miss visiting the small museum related to the cave.

You can camp near the entrance to the cave (but only after closing time; US$5 per tent); if you do so, watch the hundreds of birds pouring out of the cave mouth at around 7 pm and returning about 4 am. There's a 35-metre waterfall, Salto La Payla, 25 minutes walk from the cave.

GÜIRIA

Güiria is the easternmost point on Venezuela's coast that you can reach by road, a 275-km ride from Cumaná. Home to some 20,000 people, it's the largest town of

Península de Paria and an important fishing port. The town itself is rather an ordinary place with no tourist attractions.

Güiria is probably not worth a trip unless you plan on continuing to Trinidad or exploring the rugged Parque Nacional Península de Paria, which stretches along the northern coast. Near the eastern tip of the peninsula, about 40 km east of Güiria, is the small town of Macuro (accessible only by water), the only place on South America's mainland where Columbus set foot, in August 1498, having come from Trinidad.

Information

Banco de Venezuela (Calle Concepción, off Plaza Bolívar) and Banco del Orinoco (corner of Calles Valdez and Trinchera) may change cash and travellers' cheques. Banco de Venezuela and Banco Unión (Calle Bolívar off Plaza Bolívar), may give advances on Visa and MasterCard.

Acosta Asociados (☎ 81679, 81112), Calle Bolívar 31, offers tours and other travel services. They sell tickets for the Windward Lines ferry to Trinidad and arrange all the necessary formalities.

The telephone code for Güiria is 094.

Places to Stay & Eat

At the low-budget end, a popular place to stay is the *Hotel Plaza*, on the corner of Plaza Bolívar. It costs US$8 a double with bath and fan, and its restaurant is probably the best inexpensive eatery in town.

For a similar price, you can have a double in *Hotel Fortuna*, on Calle Bolívar near the plaza, or in *Hotel Miramar*, on Calle Turpial, a little bit farther toward the port.

The *Residencia Gran Puerto* (☎ 81085), on Calle Vigirima close to the plaza, has good singles/doubles with bath and fan for US$10/12, and also a few air-con doubles for US$15. Its sibling, the *Hotel Gran Puerto* (☎ 81343), Calle Pegallos near Calle Bideau, offers marginally better standards for US$12/15. The best in town is *La Posada de Chuchú* (☎ 81266), Calle Bideau 35, which has doubles/triples for US$20/25 and its own restaurant.

Getting There & Away

Air The airport is a 15-minute walk west of the town centre. Light planes fly a few times a week to Porlamar (US$32).

Bus Several bus companies have offices around the triangular Plaza Sucre, two blocks from Plaza Bolívar. There are three or four buses to Caracas (US$11, 11 to 12 hours). They all go via Cumaná and Puerto La Cruz. From the same square, frequent por puestos run to Carúpano (US$3, two hours).

Boat Windward Lines operates a ferry on the Güiria-Trinidad-St Vincent-Barbados-St Lucia route. The ferry is supposed to arrive at Güiria from Trinidad every second Tuesday night and return to Trinidad on Wednesday night. On alternate weeks it goes to Pampatar on Isla de Margarita. The Güiria-Port of Spain deck fare is US$78 (US$105 return) and the trip takes seven hours. Optional air-con cabins are available for US$20 a double. The ferry docks are at the southern end of the port, a 15-minute walk from the town centre.

Boats to Port of Spain can be arranged; expect to pay about US$50 per person, provided they collect eight passengers, the boat's full capacity. The trip takes about four hours. DIEX is near the port – get an exit stamp here. In Port of Spain, immigration formalities are done in the port.

Peñeros (open fishing boats) to Macuro leave every morning without a fixed schedule, from the northern end of the Güiria port (US$2.50, 1½ to two hours). There are a few simple posadas in Macuro, which can also provide meals. There's a path from Macuro to Uquire, on the northern coast (a six-hour walk); you can hire a boat to take you there, but it's expensive.

Irregular fishing and cargo boats (one or two per week) go to Pedernales, at the northern mouth of the Orinoco delta. The trip takes four to five hours and the fare is largely negotiable; you shouldn't pay more than US$8 per person. From Pedernales, there are infrequent boats south to Tucupita.

TUCUPITA

Set at the base of the vast Delta del Orinoco, Tucupita is a hot river town of about 60,000 people and the capital of Delta Amacuro state. The town was born in the 1920s as one of a chain of Capuchin missions that were founded in the delta to convert the local Indians. For travellers, Tucupita is essentially a jumping-off point for exploring the delta rather than an attraction in itself.

The Delta del Orinoco covers an area of about 25,000 sq km, thus being the second-largest delta on the continent (after the Amazon). The Río Orinoco splits into 40-odd major *caños* (channels) which carry the waters down into the Atlantic. Their *bocas* (mouths) are distributed along 360 km of the coast. The southernmost channel, Río Grande, is the main one and is used by ocean-going vessels sailing upriver to Ciudad Guayana.

The climate of the delta is hot and humid, with an average annual temperature around 26°C. The driest period is from January to March; the remaining part of the year is wet or very wet. The water reaches its highest level from August to September, when parts of the delta become marshy or flooded.

The delta is inhabited by the Warao Indians, who are the second-largest indigenous group in Venezuela (after the Guajiro), numbering about 24,000. They live along the caños, constructing palafitos on the riverbanks and living mostly by fishing. Many of the Waraos still use their native language.

Information

Tourist Office The Diturda municipal tourist office is on Calle Bolívar, Edificio San Juan (2nd floor).

Money Only Banco de Venezuela is likely to change your cash and travellers' cheques, while Banco Unión might possibly give advances on Visa card. Most of the tour agencies will accept payments in dollars, but not by credit card.

Telephone Tucupita's area code is 087.

Tour Operators There are half a dozen tour operators in town and all focus on trips into the delta. Tours are usually all-inclusive two to four-day trips (there are hardly any one-day tours) and the going rate is about US$50 to US$80 per person a day, depending on the number of people in the group. Most agencies can provide a guide who speaks English or German, though their knowledge of the language may leave a bit to be desired.

Most agents offer tours to the northern part of the delta, towards Pedernales. Of these, Aventura Turística Delta (☎ 210835), Calle Centurión No 62, receives possibly the best comments from travellers. Other agencies operating northern routes include Wakeriana Tours (☎ 210224), Calle Pativilca; Tucupita Expeditions (☎ 212986), Calle Mánamo; and Bujana Tours (☎ 212776), Calle Dalla Costa.

Delta Surs (☎ 213877), Calle Mariño, is perhaps the only operator which offers tours to the far eastern area of the delta, which is arguably more interesting both for its more diverse wildlife and for its more numerous Indian population. These tours are more expensive.

Mánamo Tours (☎ 210179), on Plaza Bolívar, doesn't run tours, but sells air tickets and may provide tourist information.

There are also independent guides who descend like vultures as soon as you arrive in town. Their tours may be cheaper, though you never actually know what you'll get for your money; we have received very mixed (even totally contradictory) comments about their services. If you decide on one these guides, clarify the duration of the tour, the places to be visited and details of food and lodging, and have a look at the boat and its engine before you commit yourself. After you and your guide agree on a price, pay only the money necessary for pre-departure expenses (gasoline, food). Insist on paying the substantial part only on your return.

Places to Stay

Accommodation is scarce in Tucupita. There are only three or four hotels in the town

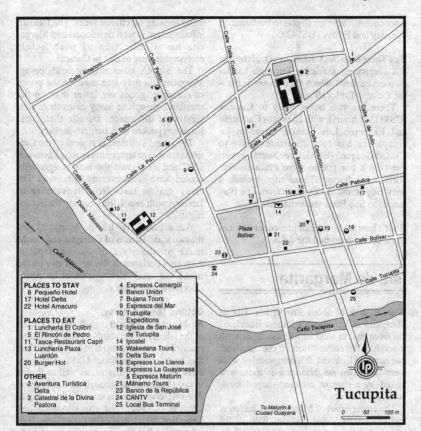

PLACES TO STAY
8 Pequeño Hotel
17 Hotel Delta
22 Hotel Amacuro

PLACES TO EAT
1 Lunchería El Colibrí
5 El Rincón de Pedro
11 Tasca-Restaurant Capri
13 Lunchería Plaza
  Luantón
20 Burger Hot

OTHER
2 Aventura Turística
  Delta
3 Catedral de la Divina
  Pastora

4 Expresos Camargüí
6 Banco Unión
7 Bujana Tours
9 Expresos del Mar
10 Tucupita
  Expeditions
12 Iglesia de San José
  de Tucupita
14 Ipostel
15 Wakeriana Tours
16 Delta Surs
18 Expresos Los Llanos
19 Expresos La Guayanesa
  & Expresos Maturín
21 Mánamo Tours
23 Banco de la República
24 CANTV
25 Local Bus Terminal

Tucupita

To Maturín &
Ciudad Guayana

0   50   100 m

centre, and two or three more outside the central area. All the hotels listed have rooms with private bath.

The cheapest, *Pequeño Hotel* (☎ 210523), Calle La Paz, has doubles with fan/noisy air-con for US$7/9. The *Hotel Delta* (☎ 212467), Calle Pativilca, has marginally better doubles with fan/slightly quieter air-con for US$8/10. The third of the central options, the *Hotel Amacuro* (☎ 210404), Calle Bolívar, is the best of the lot. Air-con singles/doubles/triples are US$10/12/14.

Places to Eat

There's a range of simple places to eat in

town. The *Burger Hot*, Calle Mariño, provides some of the cheapest meals and is open till 10 pm. *El Rincón de Pedro*, Calle Petión, has good chicken among other dishes, while the *Lunchería El Colibrí* serves typical food. *Tasca-Restaurant Capri*, on Calle Mánamo, is better but more expensive. For a good coffee, go to the *Lunchería Plaza Luantón*, on Plaza Bolívar, which also serves a choice of snacks.

Getting There & Away

Air The airport is several km north of town; the San Rafael carrito goes there from the town centre. There are flights to Porlamar on Tuesday and Friday (US$42).

Bus There is no bus terminal; each of the five bus companies servicing Tucupita has its own office from which their buses leave – see the map for locations.

There are two buses daily to Caracas (US$11, 11 hours), with Expresos Camargüí and Expresos Los Llanos. Expresos La Guayanesa has two departures daily to Ciudad Guayana (US$3, three hours), or you can take a por puesto from Plaza Bolívar (US$4, 2½ hours). These trips include a ferry ride across the Orinoco from Los Barrancos to San Félix (no extra charge).

Boat There are no regular passenger services from Tucupita around the delta.

Isla de Margarita

With an area of about 920 sq km, Isla de Margarita is Venezuela's largest island, 67 km from east to west and 32 km from north to south. It lies some 40 km off the mainland, due north of Cumaná. It's composed of what were once two neighbouring islands, now linked by a narrow, crescent-shaped sandbank, La Restinga.

The eastern part of Margarita is the larger and more fertile, and contains 95% of the island's total population of 320,000. All the major towns are here, connected by quite a well-developed array of roads. The western part, known as the Península de Macanao, is arid and sparsely populated, with its 16,000 people living in a dozen villages located mostly along the coast. Both sections of the island are mountainous, their highest peaks approaching 1000 metres.

Generally speaking, two reasons draw people to the island. The first is the beaches which skirt its coast. Margarita has become the number one destination for Venezuelan holiday-makers seeking white sand, surfing, snorkelling and scuba diving. It's also popular with international visitors, mostly those arriving on charter tours. The tourism infrastructure is well developed and Margarita has a collection of posh hotels comparable only to that in Caracas.

The island's other magnet is shopping. Margarita is a duty-free zone, so the prices of consumer goods are lower than on the mainland, though in many cases there's no significant difference. Despite that, local shops are packed with bargain-seekers.

The island's climate is typical of the Caribbean: average temperatures range between 25°C and 28°C, and the heat is agreeably cooled down in the evening by breezes. The rainy season lasts from November to January, with rain falling mostly during the night.

Administratively, Isla de Margarita and the two small islands of Cubagua and Coche make up the state of Nueva Esparta. Although Porlamar is the largest city on the island, the small, sleepy town of La Asunción is the state capital.

Getting There & Away

Air Margarita's airport is in the southern part of the island, 20 km south-west of Porlamar, reached by por puestos (US$0.50). A taxi on this route will cost about US$8. There are some international flights, as well as flights to most major cities throughout the country. Avensa/Servivensa has seven flights a day to Caracas (US$42), but check Aserca and Laser first, which may offer better fares. Half a dozen small airlines operate flights (mostly on a charter basis) on light planes around the region and beyond (Cumaná, Barcelona, Los Roques, Canaima, Güiria, Tucupita).

Boat Isla de Margarita has ferry links with Cumaná (two departures a day, US$3.50, 3½ hours) and Puerto La Cruz (six departures, US$6 1st class, US$4 tourist class, 4½ hours). In the off season, there may be fewer boats than listed. Tickets can be bought at the Conferry office in Porlamar (☎ 619235) or at the ferry terminal (☎ 98-148) in Punta de Piedras, 29 km west of Porlamar. There are frequent *micros* and por puestos (US$0.75 for either) between Punta

Isla de Margarita

0 5 10 km

CARIBBEAN SEA

Playa El Humo
Playa El Agua
Playa Parguito
Playa El Tirano
Playa El Cardón
Playa Guacuco

Pampatar

PORLAMAR

Paraguachi
El Salado
El Cardón
La Fuente

Los Robles

La Asunción

Manzanillo
Playa Manzanillo
Playa Guayacán
Playa Puerto Cruz

Pedro González
Santa Ana
Tacarigua

El Cercado
El Copey

Parque Nacional Cerro El Copey

El Valle del Espíritu Santo

El Tirano

Juangriego

Playa Caribe
Playa La Galera
Playa Juangriego

San Juan Bautista

Villa Rosa

La Isleta

El Yaque

San Pedro de Coche

Isla de Coche

El Bichar
El Amparo
El Guamache

Playa La Guardia

La Guardia

Los Algodones

Playa La Restinga

Punta de Piedras

Parque Nacional Laguna de la Restinga

Boca de Río
Guayacancito

Playa La Auyama
Playa El Tunal
Playa La Carmela

El Tunal
La Carmela
La Carmela
Robledal

San Francisco
Boca Chica
Boca de Pozo

Barrancas

Mangrillo

El Saco

Península de Macanao

Punta Arenas
Playa Punta Arenas

Isla de Cubagua

Ruins of Nueva Cádiz

To Cumaná

To Puerto La Cruz

VENEZUELA

de Piedras and Porlamar, or go by taxi (US$10).

Windward Lines operates a ferry from Pampatar to Port of Spain, Trinidad, which is supposed to depart every other Wednesday (US$85, US$115 return). The ferry then continues to St Vincent, Barbados and St Lucia. For information and reservations contact Acosta Asociados (☎ 623527) in Porlamar.

PORLAMAR

Porlamar is the largest urban centre on the island and will probably be your first stop when coming from the mainland. It's a modern, bustling city of 80,000 inhabitants, replete with shopping centres, hotels and restaurants. Tree-shaded Plaza Bolívar is the historic centre of the city, but Porlamar is progressively expanding eastward, where new hotels and other tourist facilities have been built.

Porlamar is not a place for sightseeing, other than wandering around trendy shops packed with imported goods. The most elegant and expensive shopping areas are on and around Avenidas Santiago Mariño and 4 de Mayo.

Information

Tourist Offices The private corporation Cámara de Turismo (☎ 635644, 635922), on Avenida Santiago Mariño, is open weekdays from 8 am to noon and 2 to 6 pm. It also has a stand at the airport. The government-run Dirección de Turismo is based in the Centro Artesanal Los Robles, in Los Robles, midway between Porlamar and Pampatar.

Pick up a copy of *Margarita La Guía*, a useful guide in Spanish, English and German that's published quarterly. Also get hold of *Mira!*, an English-language monthly paper which features practical details and background information about the island and beyond. Both are distributed free through tourist offices, selected up-market hotels and some other tourist establishments.

Money Many of Porlamar's banks handle some foreign-exchange operations (see the map for locations). There are several casas

de cambio, mostly in the area of Avenida Santiago Mariño. Many stores will also exchange cash.

Telephone Porlamar's area code is 095.

Things to See

One of the few real tourist sights is the **Museo de Arte Contemporáneo Francisco Narváez**, in a large, modern building on the corner of Calles Igualdad and Díaz. On the ground floor is a collection of sculptures and paintings by this Margarita-born artist (1905-82), while the salons on the upper floor are used for temporary exhibitions. The museum is open Tuesday to Friday from 9 am to 5 pm, and on weekends from 10 am to 4 pm.

A small but colourful **market** is held in the morning on the waterfront at the outlet of Boulevard Gómez. As might be expected, there are plenty of fish, including some sharks.

Places to Stay

Porlamar has loads of hotels for every pocket. As a general rule, the price and standard rise from west to east. Accordingly, cheapies are plentiful west of Plaza Bolívar, but looking for a budget room around Avenida Santiago Mariño is a waste of time.

There are a score of budget hotels within the few blocks south-west of Plaza Bolívar. One of the most popular with travellers is the *Hotel España* (☎ 612479), Calle Mariño No 6-35, near the waterfront. It has a variety of rooms. Expect to pay about US$8/10 for a double/triple with bath, a dollar less without bath.

Other budget options in the area include the *Hotel Plaza* (☎ 630395) on Calle Velázquez, and *Hotel OM-21* (☎ 632367) on Calle San Nicolás. Both have doubles with bath and fan/air-con for US$7/10. There are some cheaper hotels around, including the *Hotel San Miguel* (☎ 633021) and the basic *Residencia El Paraíso*, which has doubles with bath for US$5.

The *Hotel Central* (☎ 614757) is conveniently located on Boulevard Gómez and has

Porlamar

CARIBBEAN
SEA

Market

0   100   200 m

air-con doubles/triples for US$10/14. Much the same cost, but better, is *Hotel Torino* (☎ 610734), Calle Mariño.

There are several reasonable hotels a couple of blocks east of Plaza Bolívar, including *Hotel Porlamar* (☎ 630271) for US$13/15 a double/triple, and *Hotel Canadá* (☎ 615920) for US$15/18. Still better is the *Hotel Internacional* (☎ 618912), on Avenida 4 de Mayo, which has spacious triples for US$18.

The *Hotel Gran Avenida* (☎ 617457), on Calle Cedeño, is one of the cheaper options around the trendy Avenida Santiago Mariño. Air-con doubles with TV cost US$25.

Places to Eat
Some of the cheapest meals are served in the *Restaurant España*, in the hotel of the same name. The *Restaurant Punto Criollo*, Calle Igualdad, is popular with locals and visitors for its good food and reasonable prices. *Pizzas Pastas* offers what it says and is good value; take away or eat in.

Most of the finer restaurants are in the eastern sector of the city. On Calle Cedeño alone, just east of Avenida Santiago Mariño, there are half a dozen good restaurants, including *El Chipi*, *Flor de Margarita*, *Il Castello Romano*, *Max's* and *El Faro de Julio*. Just round the corner is the *Public Place*, which offers some French and Italian cuisine.

The *Paris Croissant* café has tables outside and serves breakfast, ice cream, pastries etc. The *Gran Café Corleone* is open 24 hours.

Getting Around
There's frequent transport to most of the island, including Pampatar, La Asunción and Juangriego, operated by small buses locally called micros. They leave from different points in the city centre; the departure points for some of the main tourist destinations are indicated on the map.

PAMPATAR
Pampatar, 10 km north-east of Porlamar, is today a town of some 10,000 people.

Founded in the 1530s, it was perhaps the first settlement on Margarita and still has some colonial buildings.

Things to See
Pampatar's fort, the **Castillo de San Carlos Borromeo**, built in the 1660s on the site of the previous stronghold (which was destroyed by pirates), is the best preserved and restored construction of its type on the island. The fort is right in the centre of town, on the waterfront. It can be visited daily from 9 am to noon and 2 to 5 pm.

Opposite the fort is the **parish church**, dating from the mid-18th century. A hundred metres east of the church is the neoclassical **Casa de la Aduana**, dating from 1864, which has temporary exhibitions on the ground floor.

The beach, which extends for a km east of the fort, has some old-world charm, with rustic boats anchored in the bay or on the shore, and fishers repairing nets on the beach. The cape at the far eastern end of the bay is topped with another fort, the ruined **Fortín de la Caranta**, which commands better views than the Castillo.

Places to Stay & Eat
Few travellers stay in Pampatar, but if you want, there are some places just back from the beach. Most of them are the so-called *aparthoteles*, offering mini-apartments including a kitchen complete with pots and pans. There are many open-air eateries along the beach.

LA ASUNCION
La Asunción, set in a fertile valley in the inland portion of the island, is the capital of the Nueva Esparta state, though it's far smaller than Porlamar. It's distinguished for its tranquillity and its verdant environs. There's virtually no duty-free commerce here, and hotels and restaurants are scarce.

Things to See
Built in the second half of the 16th century, the **catedral** on the tree-shaded Plaza Bolívar is just about the oldest colonial

church in the country. It's noted for its austere, simple form, with a delicate Renaissance portal on the façade and two more doorways on the side walls.

On the northern side of the plaza is the **Museo Nueva Cádiz**, named after the first Spanish town in South America, founded around 1500 on Isla Cubagua, south of Margarita. The town was completely destroyed by an earthquake in 1541, and the traces disappeared until an excavation in 1950 uncovered the town foundations, some architectural details and various period objects. The museum displays photos of the excavation work, plus a small, rather haphazard collection of exhibits, including two huge anchors recovered from shipwrecks.

Just outside town, a 10-minute walk southward up the hill, is the **Castillo de Santa Rosa**, one of numerous forts built on the island to protect it from pirate attacks. Apart from the view of the town, there is some old armour on display.

JUANGRIEGO

Set on the edge of a fine bay in the northern part of Margarita, Juangriego is a swiftly growing town of 10,000 people, and is popular with tourists. Most of them hang around the beach along the bay, with the rustic fishing boats and visiting yachts. Far away on the horizon, the peaks of Macanao are visible, and are particularly spectacular when the sun sets behind them.

The **Fortín de la Galera**, the fort crowning the hill just north of town, is today nothing more than stone walls with a terrace and a refreshment stand on the top. It provides a good view of the sunset, at which time it is packed with tourists, though a similarly attractive vista can be had from the beach.

Places to Stay & Eat

In the middle of Juangriego beach is the overpriced *Hotel Nuevo Juangriego*. Choose a room facing the bay (double with bath for US$16) for a perfect snap of the sunset from your window. Downstairs is the restaurant, with some umbrella-shaded tables outside on a terrace.

Hotel El Fortín, a few hundred metres north along the beach, is slightly cheaper and has equally excellent sunset views if you choose the right room. Its restaurant, and *El Búho*, next door, are more pleasant places to eat than the Nuevo Juangriego. *El Viejo Muelle*, a few paces away, is yet another place for a meal or beer at sunset, though again, the food prices seem to be inflated. There are several other accommodation and food options in the same area and farther back from the beach.

PARQUE NACIONAL LAGUNA DE LA RESTINGA

Laguna de la Restinga is one of two national parks on the island (the other is Cerro El Copey, near La Asunción). The park covers the lagoon and a mangrove area at its western end. This is a favourite habitat for a variety of birds including pelicans, cormorants and scarlet ibis.

Micros from the waterfront in Porlamar go regularly to La Restinga (US$0.80) and will deposit you at the entrance to the wharf. From there, five-seat motorboats will take you for a return trip (US$9 per boat) along the caños that cut through the mangroves. The excursion includes a stop on a fine shell beach, where you can grab a fried fish in one of the open-air restaurants before returning.

BEACHES

Isla de Margarita has 167 km of shoreline endowed with some 50 beaches big enough to deserve a name, not to mention smaller bits of sandy coast. Many beaches have been developed, with a range of services such as restaurants, bars, and deckchairs and sunshades for hire. Though the island is no longer a virgin paradise, you can still find a relatively deserted strip of sand. On the whole, Margarita's beaches have little shade, and some are virtually barren.

The trendy Playa El Agua is the most heavily promoted and developed beach. Other popular destinations include Playa Guacuco and Playa Manzanillo. Perhaps

Margarita's finest beach is Playa Puerto Cruz, which arguably has the widest, whitest stretch of sand and still isn't overdeveloped. If you want to escape from people, head for the northern coast of Macanao, which is the wildest part of the island.

You can camp on the beaches, but use common sense and be cautious. Don't leave your tent unattended.

Guayana

Guayana occupies the whole of Venezuela's south-east, to the south of the Río Orinoco, and it's one of the most amazing and unusual regions of the country. Here are the famous Angel Falls, the world's highest, and the unique Gran Sabana, a mysterious rolling savanna dotted with dozens of tepuis, the massive table mountains. One of them, Roraima, can be climbed, and this trip is a fascinating adventure.

The only two important cities in the region are Ciudad Bolívar and Ciudad Guayana, both on the bank of the Orinoco; these apart, the region is very sparsely populated, without any significant urban centres. Much of the southern part of the region (30,000 sq km) has been declared the Parque Nacional Canaima, which includes La Gran Sabana, Roraima and Angel Falls. The Ciudad Guayana-Santa Elena de Uairén highway, which cuts across the region, provides access to this fascinating land.

CIUDAD BOLIVAR
Ciudad Bolívar is a hot city set on the southern bank of the Orinoco, about 420 km upstream from the Atlantic. Founded in 1764 on a rocky elevation at the river's narrowest point, the town was appropriately named Angostura (literally, 'narrows'), and grew slowly as a sleepy river port hundreds of miles from any important centres of population. Then, suddenly and unexpectedly, Angostura became the place where much of the country's (and the continent's) history was forged.

It was here that Bolívar came in 1817, soon after the town had been liberated from Spanish control, and set up a base for military operations against the Spaniards. The town was made the provisional capital of the country, which had yet to be liberated. It was in Angostura that the British Legionnaires joined Bolívar before they all set off for the battle of Boyacá which secured Colombia's independence. Finally, it was here that the Angostura Congress convened in 1819 and gave birth to Gran Colombia. In honour of El Libertador, in 1846 the town was renamed Ciudad Bolívar.

Today, Ciudad Bolívar is the capital of Venezuela's largest state, Bolívar, and a city of nearly 300,000 inhabitants. It has retained the flavour of an old river town, and still conserves some of the architecture dating from its 50-year colonial era. It's a popular stop on the travellers' route, partly for the city itself, and partly as a jumping-off point for Angel Falls.

Information
Tourist Office The tourist office (☎ 26491), in a pavilion close to the airport terminal, is open weekdays from 8.30 am to noon and 2 to 5.30 pm.

Money There are a few useful banks on or near Paseo Orinoco, including Banco de Venezuela and Banco Unión. Money-changers hang around the entrance of Hotel Colonial. The Banco Consolidado is on the corner of Avenidas Jesús Soto and Andrés Bello, 100 metres east of the airport terminal.

Telephone The area code for Ciudad Bolívar is 085.

Inparques The Inparques office is in the Edificio de la CVG, on Avenida Germania (corner of Avenida Andrés Bello). You can get a permit here for Parque Nacional Canaima if you want to camp in Canaima.

Tour Operators Ciudad Bolívar is the main gateway to Angel Falls, and trips to the falls are the staple of most tour operators in the city. The most popular tour is a one-day return trip which includes a flight over Angel Falls, lunch in Canaima and a boat excursion to Salto El Sapo. Many agents offer Kavac as an alternative to Canaima, in which case the tour will include, apart from the Angel Falls overflight, an excursion to the Cueva de Kavac. Either tour will cost around US$130. A Canaima-Kavac two-day tour which combines all the attractions of the two one-day trips is also popular and is available from most agencies for about US$170. Three-days tours are also offered; in the rainy season they will usually include a boat trip to the foot of Angel Falls.

There are plenty of tour operators in the city, most of which are grouped in two areas: around Paseo Orinoco and around the airport. In the former area, start shopping around at Neckar Tour (☎ 24402) in the Hotel Colonial. In the airport area, Turi Express (☎ 28910), in the airport terminal, is one of the better agencies.

All the operators use the air services of small local airlines, which can be found at the airport. Possibly the most reliable are Aero Servicios Caicara and Rutaca, and both have their offices at the terminal. They can fly you to Canaima (US$50 either way) and to Kavac (US$55), and can also include a flight over Angel Falls for US$35 extra. These are mostly charter flights, with three people being a minimum to take off. See the Angel Falls section for more tour options.

Other tours out of Ciudad Bolívar include trips to La Gran Sabana and Río Caura. The former is offered by most agents, usually as a four-day jeep trip (about US$170 per person, all-inclusive), but can be organised more cheaply from Santa Elena de Uairén. The latter is best done in Ciudad Bolívar with Soana Travel (☎ 22536), Calle Bolívar (US$250 per person for a five-day trip, all-inclusive). A minimum of four people is necessary for these tours.

Things to See

Midway along the lively waterfront boulevard, **Paseo Orinoco**, is the **Mirador Angostura**, a rocky headland that juts into the river at its narrowest point. The lookout commands good views up and down the Orinoco. Five km upriver you'll see a suspension bridge, **Puente de Angostura**, which was constructed in 1967; it's the only bridge across the Orinoco along its entire course.

Across the Paseo from the lookout, the **Instituto de Cultura del Orinoco** (open daily, except Monday, from 9.30 am to 5.30 pm) houses an ethnographic exhibition featuring the crafts of Indian groups from Venezuela's south. Two blocks west along the Paseo is the **Museo de Ciudad Bolívar**, accommodated in the Casa del Correo del Orinoco. It was here that the republic's first newspaper was printed in 1818, and you can see the original press on which it was done, along with other objects related to the town's history. The museum is open Tuesday to Saturday from 9 am to noon and 2 to 5 pm, and Sunday from 9 am to noon.

Walk south up the hill to the historic heart of the city, **Plaza Bolívar**. There are five allegorical statues on the square which personify the five countries Bolívar liberated. To the east looms the massive **Catedral**, begun right after the town's foundation and completed 80 years later. Half of the western side of the plaza is taken by the **Casa del Congreso de Angostura**, built in the 1770s. It was the seat of the lengthy debates of the 1819 Angostura Congress. You can have a look around the interior.

Three blocks south of Plaza Bolívar is the pleasantly shaded **Plaza Miranda**. A sizeable building on its eastern side is the **Centro de las Artes**, (open daily, except Monday, from 9.30 am to 5.30 pm), which stages temporary exhibitions. Go upstairs to the mirador on the roof for a view of the **Fortín El Zamuro**, crowning the top of the highest hill in the city, half a km south-west of the Centro. The fort is open for visitors and provides views over the old town.

Beyond the fort, on Avenida Táchira, is the **Museo Casa San Isidro**, installed in a fine colonial house surrounded by a garden. The house interior is maintained in its original

18th-century style. It can be visited Tuesday to Sunday from 9.30 am to 5 pm.

Proceed one km south on Avenida Táchira and take the perpendicular Avenida Briceño Irragorry to the left, which will lead you to the **Museo de Arte Moderno Jesús Soto**. The museum has an amazing collection of works by this kinetic artist (born in Ciudad Bolívar in 1923) as well as works by other modern artists. It's open Tuesday to Friday from 9.30 am to 5 pm, and weekends from 10 am to 5 pm.

In front of the airport terminal stands the legendary **aeroplane of Jimmie Angel** (see the Angel Falls section). This is the original plane, which was removed from the top of Auyantepui.

Places to Stay

The most pleasant area to stay is the bustling Paseo Orinoco, and there's a choice of budget hotels in this area. All hotels listed have rooms with private bath and fan (or air-con where indicated).

The most popular travellers' haunts are the *Hotel Caracas* (☎ 26089), Paseo Orinoco No 82, and *Hotel Italia* (☎ 20015), Paseo Orinoco No 131. The Caracas is quite simple

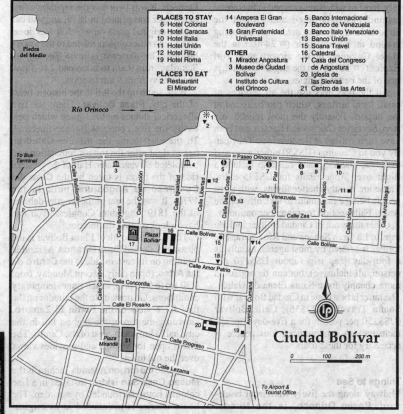

PLACES TO STAY
6 Hotel Colonial
9 Hotel Caracas
10 Hotel Italia
11 Hotel Unión
12 Hotel Ritz
19 Hotel Roma

PLACES TO EAT
2 Restaurant El Mirador

14 Arepera El Gran Boulevard
18 Gran Fraternidad Universal

OTHER
1 Mirador Angostura
3 Museo de Ciudad Bolívar
4 Instituto de Cultura del Orinoco

5 Banco Internacional
7 Banco de Venezuela
8 Banco Italo Venezolano
13 Banco Unión
15 Soana Travel
16 Catedral
17 Casa del Congreso de Angostura
20 Iglesia de las Siervas
21 Centro de las Artes

Piedra del Medio

Río Orinoco

To Bus Terminal

Paseo Orinoco

Ciudad Bolívar

0   100   200 m

To Airport & Tourist Office

but cheap (US$7/8 a matrimonial/double) and has a large terrace overlooking the Paseo, where you can sit over a bottle of beer, watch the world go by and enjoy the evening breeze. The Italia is better and has a budget restaurant, but there have recently been some critical comments about cleanness and security. It costs US$8/9 a matrimonial/double with fan, US$11/12 with air-con.

The *Hotel Unión* (☎ 23374), Calle Urica No 11, is clean if styleless, and has rooms with fan and air-con for slightly less than those in the Italia. The *Hotel Ritz* (☎ 23886), Calle Libertad No 3, offers air-con doubles for US$10, and has some doubles without bath for US$5 – possibly the cheapest acceptable accommodation near the riverfront. For the cheapest rooms with bath (US$4/6 a matrimonial/double), go to *Hotel Roma*, on Avenida Cumaná five blocks south of the river. The rooms are dark but otherwise OK.

The best place to stay on the Paseo is the old-style *Hotel Colonial* (☎ 24402), where spacious air-con singles/doubles/triples cost US$18/21/24.

Places to Eat

Perhaps the best inexpensive choice in the area of Paseo Orinoco is the restaurant of the *Hotel Italia*. Alternatively, try the *Restaurant El Mirador*, which is even cheaper but closes early. *El Gran Boulevard* is the best central arepera, where you can get arepas with a score of fillings. The *Gran Fraternidad Universal*, on Calle Amor Patrio, has good, cheap vegetarian meals, at weekday lunch time only. The two restaurants in *Hotel Colonial* have some Italian dishes at affordable prices.

Getting There & Away

Air The airport is two km south-east of the riverfront, and is linked to the city centre by local transport. There are two flights daily to Caracas with Avensa/Servivensa (US$52). For information about flights to Angel Falls, see Tour Operators in that section.

Bus The bus terminal is at the junction of Avenidas República and Sucre, about two km south of the centre. To get there, take the westbound buseta marked 'Terminal' from Paseo Orinoco.

Buses to Caracas run regularly throughout the day (US$9.50, nine hours). There are at least a dozen departures a day to Puerto Ayacucho (US$13, 10 hours). Turgar, Línea Orinoco and Travircan service the route to Santa Elena de Uairén, with a total of eight departures daily (US$13, nine to 11 hours). To Ciudad Guayana, buses depart every 15 minutes or so (US$1.50, 1½ hours).

CIUDAD GUAYANA

Set on the southern bank of the Orinoco at its confluence with the Río Caroní, Ciudad Guayana is a somewhat strange city. It was officially founded in 1961 to serve as an industrial centre for the region, and took into its metropolitan boundaries two quite different urban components: the old town of San Félix, on the eastern side of the Caroní, and the newborn Puerto Ordaz on the opposite bank. At the time of its foundation the total population of the area was about 40,000. Thirty years later, the two parts have virtually merged together into a 20-km-long urban sprawl populated by some 600,000 people – it's Venezuela's fastest growing city. Despite its unified name, people persistently refer to San Félix and Puerto Ordaz.

San Félix was founded in the 16th century, but there's nothing historic or attractive about the town. It's essentially the workers' suburb, and can be unsafe. Puerto Ordaz is quite a different story: it's modern and well planned, with a good infrastructure of roads, supermarkets and services. Yet it lacks the soul of those cities that have evolved in a natural way. Save for two beautiful waterfalls, there's not much to see or do.

Information

The tourist office is at the airport, six km west of Puerto Ordaz's centre.

As elsewhere, changing money is a bit of a trial-and-error affair and may involve some tramping around. Most central banks are marked on the map.

The area code for Ciudad Guayana is 086.

Things to See

The city's number one attraction is the **Parque Cachamay**, a pleasant riverside park, a 15-minute walk south-east from the centre of Puerto Ordaz. It's here that the Río Caroní speeds its flow, turning into a series of rapids and eventually into a spectacular 200-metre-wide line of waterfalls. Adjoining the park from the south-west is the **Parque Loefling**, where there's a small zoo with some animals in cages and others wandering freely around. Both parks are open Tuesday to Sunday from 5.30 am to 6.30 pm.

Another park noted for its falls, **Parque La Llovizna**, is on the island in the Río Caroní. The access is from San Félix, but there's no public transport all the way to the park. If this doesn't deter you, take the urban bus marked 'Buen Retiro' south from the bus terminal along Avenida Gumilla (towards El Pao). Get off when the bus turns left, continue walking two km south on the avenida and take the right turn-off marked 'Salto La Llovizna' for another two km, to the visitor centre. It's better and safer to go by taxi. From the visitor centre, a free bus shuttles to the park every hour or so from 9 am to 3 pm, Tuesday to Sunday. Several vantage points within the park will let you see the falls from various angles.

Places to Stay

Both San Félix and Puerto Ordaz have a range of hotels, but it's advisable to stay in the latter, for better value, convenience, nicer surroundings and security. All hotels listed below have private bath (unless indicated otherwise) and either fan or air-con. Only the top-end hotels have hot water, but it's hardly necessary in this steamy climate.

The main budget hotel area in Puerto Ordaz is around the Avenida Principal de Castillito. One of the cheapest is the *Hotel Roma* (☎ 223780), which has matrimoniales with fan/air-con for US$5/10, and some cheaper rooms with shared facilities. At first

sight, you might think the hotel has been demolished, but it hasn't. Look out for the steps and go downstairs (watch your head). Alternatively, try the *Residencias Santa Cruz*, in the same area, which offers much the same for similar prices.

The recently revamped *Hotel Teixeira*, next door to the Roma, provides more comfort for marginally more money and is good value. The *Hotel Jardín II* (☎ 225645) is not bad either, though it's a little pricier (US$9/12 a matrimonial/triple with air-con).

It's more pleasant to stay farther to the west and south of Avenida Principal de Castillito. The cheapest places in this area include the *Hotel Saint Georges* (☎ 220088), *Hotel Habana Cuba* (☎ 224904) and *Hotel La Guayana* (☎ 227375); none of them should cost more than about US$15/18 for an air-con double/triple. Some other, better options have also been included on the map.

Places to Eat

The bottom end of the gastronomic scene is represented by the street stalls along Avenida Principal de Castillito and Calle Los Llanos, in the cheap hotel area. As for restaurants, budget places include the restaurant of the *Hotel La Guayana*, *Lunchería El Araguaney* and *Restaurant Géminis*. The *Restaurant Marcelo* is better and not much more expensive. *El Arepazo Guayanés* serves arepas filled with everything from cheese to seafood (US$1 each). *La Cuisine Express* and *La Casa del Croissant*, next door to each other, are two enjoyable cafés. You will find several more up-market restaurants marked on the map.

Getting There & Away

Air The airport is at the western end of Puerto Ordaz, on the road to Ciudad Bolívar. Avensa/Servivensa flies direct to Caracas (US$56), Valencia (US$71) and Porlamar (US$40), and has connections to other destinations. Check the Aserca flights, which may be cheaper.

Servivensa has daily flights on DC-3s to Canaima (US$52). These flights continue (except Tuesday and Saturday) to Santa

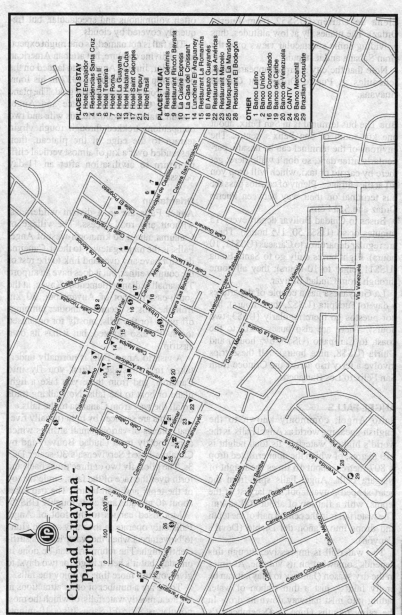

Ciudad Guayana – Puerto Ordaz

PLACES TO STAY
3 Hotel Embajador
4 Residencias Santa Cruz
5 Hotel Jardín II
6 Hotel Texeira
7 Hotel Roma
12 Hotel La Guayana
13 Hotel Habana Cuba
21 Hotel Saint Georges
27 Hotel Tepuy
27 Hotel Rasil

PLACES TO EAT
8 Restaurant Géminis
9 Restaurant Rincón Bavaria
10 La Cuisine Express
11 La Casa del Croissant
14 Lunchería El Araguaney
15 Restaurant La Romanina
18 El Arepazo Guayanés
22 Restaurant Las Américas
23 Restaurant Marcelo
25 Marisquería La Mansión
28 Restaurant El Bodegón

OTHER
1 Banco Latino
2 Banco Unión
16 Banco Consolidado
19 Banco del Caribe
20 Banco de Venezuela
24 CANTV
26 Banco Mercantil
29 Brazilian Consulate

Elena de Uairén (US$52 from Puerto Ordaz). The planes fly at low altitudes, thus providing some spectacular views over the Gran Sabana and its tepuis.

Note that the city's airport appears in all schedules as Puerto Ordaz, not Ciudad Guayana.

Bus The bus terminal is in San Félix, about one km south of San Félix's centre. The environs of the terminal can be unsafe, particularly after dark, so don't walk there; get there by carrito or taxi, which will drop you off at the entrance. Plenty of carritos pass the bus terminal on their way between Puerto Ordaz and San Félix.

Buses to Ciudad Bolívar depart every 15 minutes or so (US$1.50, 1½ hours). There are regular departures to Caracas (US$11, 10 hours). Eight buses daily go to Santa Elena (US$11, eight to 10 hours); they all come through from Ciudad Bolívar.

La Guayanesa has a couple of departures a day to Tucupita (US$2, three hours), but por puestos go there regularly (US$3, two hours). There are also buses north to the coast, to Carúpano (US$6, 6½ hours) and Güiria (US$8, nine hours). All these trips involve a ferry trip across the Orinoco from San Félix to Los Barrancos.

ANGEL FALLS

Salto Angel, commonly known to the English-speaking world as Angel Falls, is the world's highest waterfall. Its total height is 979 metres, of which the uninterrupted drop is 807 metres, about 16 times the height of Niagara Falls. Angel Falls spill from the heart-shaped Auyantepui, the largest of the tepuis, with a flat top of about 700 sq km. The waterfall is in the central part of the tepui and drops into Cañón del Diablo (Devil's Canyon).

The waterfall is impressive, though this depends somewhat on its volume. At times in the dry season (January to May), it can be pretty faint – just a thin ribbon of water fading into mist halfway down its drop. In the rainy months (June to December) it's often voluminous and spectacular, but frequently covered by clouds.

The fall is not named, as one might expect, after a divine creature, but after an American bush pilot, Jimmie Angel, who landed on the boggy top of the tepui in 1937 in his four-seater aeroplane, in search of gold. The plane stuck in the marshy surface and Angel couldn't take off again. He, his wife and two companions trekked through rough virgin terrain to the edge of the plateau, then descended over a km of almost vertical cliff, to return to civilisation after an 11-day odyssey.

Orientation

Angel Falls are in a distant wilderness, without any road access. The village of Canaima, about 50 km north-west of Angel Falls, is the major gateway to them. Canaima doesn't have any overland link to the rest of the country either, but it does have an airport. The small Indian settlement of Kavac, at the south-eastern foot of Auyantepui, 20 km from the falls, is becoming another jumping-off point for the falls, mostly for organised tours. It's also isolated, but it has its own airstrip.

A visit to Angel Falls is normally undertaken in two stages. First you fly into Canaima, and from there you take a light plane or boat to the falls. No walking trails go all the way from Canaima to the falls.

Flights are serviced by light (usually five-seat) planes of various small airlines which come mostly from Ciudad Bolívar, and by Canaima-based Servivensa's 30-seater DC-3s. The pilots fly two or three times back and forth over the face of the falls, circle the top of the tepui and then return. The trip takes about 40 minutes and costs roughly US$35.

Motorised canoes to the foot of Angel Falls only operate in the rainy season (June to November) when the water level is sufficiently high. The return trip can be done in one day, but it's better to go for two days, to give yourself more time to enjoy the falls.

There are a number of other attractions in the area, mostly waterfalls, of which the most popular is Salto El Sapo. It's a 10-minute boat trip from Canaima plus a short walk. Salto El Sapo is beautiful and unusual in that you can walk under it. You'll probably get drenched by the waterfall, so take a swimsuit. A few minutes walk from El Sapo is Salto El Sapito, another attractive waterfall which is normally included in the same excursion.

Canaima

Once a small Pemón Indian settlement, Canaima is now a tourist base for Angel Falls. It is spectacularly set on a peaceful, wide stretch of the Río Carrao, known as Laguna Canaima, just below the point where the river turns into several magnificent falls, Saltos Hacha.

The centrepoint of the village is the Campamento Canaima, a tourist camp built right on the bank of the lake. The airport is just a few minutes walk to the west.

Money Campamento Canaima changes cash US dollars (but not travellers' cheques), as do some other establishments including the souvenir shop near the airport. Tomás of Bernal Tours may change your cheques. The rate is lower then in the cities, so it's best to come with a sufficient amount of bolívares. Some tour operators may accept payment in US dollars.

Tour Operators Hoturvensa (Hoteles y Turismo Avensa), which runs Campamento Canaima, is the oldest operator and caters to the well-off tourists. It offers packages which include accommodation and full board in its camp, a flight over Angel Falls in a DC-3 (weather permitting) and a short boat trip around the lake (but don't include the flight into and out of Canaima). Two kinds of package are available: a two-day/one-night stay for US$330, and a three-day/two-night stay for US$570. The packages can be bought from any Avensa office in Venezuela and from most travel agencies. Hoturvensa doesn't offer any tours other than these two packages.

There are half a dozen other tour operators in Canaima, including Canaima Tours, Tiuna Tours, Excursiones Canaima, Kamaracoto Tours, Yenkarum and Bernal Tours. They all wait for incoming flights at the airport, and this is the place and the time to shop around for a tour.

Bernal Tours, run by Tomás Bernal, is the most expensive agency, but his tours are of good quality. His three-day tour, which includes a one-day boat trip to Angel Falls, costs US$260, though the price seems to be largely negotiable. Tomás lives on the island on Laguna Canaima, opposite the Campamento Canaima. Tour participants stay in his house and sleep in hammocks. Facilities are quite simple, but there's much charm about the place, plus a fantastic pink beach in front of Saltos Hacha with an excellent view over the falls.

Canaima Tours is the agent of Hoturvensa and has its office in Campamento Canaima. The remaining operators are slightly cheaper and their advertised prices can be negotiated to some extent. Most operators won't accept credit cards, or will charge 5% to 10% more if you pay with a credit card.

There are plenty of tours on offer. The most popular short trip is Salto El Sapo (US$15, two hours). Of the longer excursions, the boat trip to Angel Falls heads the list (in the rainy season only), and is normally offered as an all-inclusive one/two/three-day tour for about US$100/130/160 per person. Some operators provide boat transport only (you take your own food and camping gear), which may be considerably cheaper. Agents can also arrange flights to Angel Falls (US$35).

See Tour Operators in the earlier Ciudad Bolívar section for tours organised from that city, which may work out cheaper and more convenient.

Places to Stay & Eat The main lodging/eating venue is Hoturvensa's *Campamento Canaima*. The camp consists of a few dozen palm-thatched cabañas (with rooms with bath and hot water), its own restaurant, bar and fuente de soda. Accommodation is only available as part of a package, but the camp's restaurant, bar and fuente de soda are open to all. The restaurant is expensive (breakfast US$6, lunch US$8, dinner US$8), but the food is good and you can eat as much as you want.

There are now half a dozen other campamentos in Canaima, some of which also serve meals. They mostly service organised tours, but usually have vacancies which they rent out to individual tourists. Expect to pay US$5 to US$10 for a hammock, and US$12 to US$25 for a bed. Some campamentos will let you string up your own hammock under their roof (and use their facilities) for US$3 to US$5. Tour agents at the airport will direct you to the campamentos.

If you have your own tent, you can camp free in Canaima, but get a permit (US$0.40 per person a day) from the Inparques officer at the airport (if you didn't get one in Caracas or Ciudad Bolívar). The usual place to camp is on the beach next to the helpful Guardia Nacional post, just off Campamento Canaima. You may be able to arrange with the Guardia to leave your stuff at the post while you are away.

There are a few shops in Canaima which sell basic supplies such as bread, canned fish, biscuits etc, but the prices are rather high. If you plan on self-catering, it's best to bring your own food with you to Canaima.

Getting There & Away Servivensa has one flight a day on jets from Caracas to Canaima, via Porlamar. If you buy either of their packages, they will sell you a discount ticket (US$85 return from either Caracas or Porlamar). Otherwise they will charge their normal fare (US$77 one way, US$154 return), but they may not want to sell tickets in advance, hoping to fill up their flights with the package passengers. Even if you succeed in buying one, there may still be difficulties at the airport. Some travellers have reported they had to insist before they were let on the plane. Servivensa also has daily flights on DC-3s from Puerto Ordaz (US$52) and (except Tuesday and Saturday) from Santa Elena de Uairén (US$42). Tickets for these flights can apparently be bought with less hassle.

Several small regional carriers fly from Ciudad Bolívar to Canaima on a semi-regular or charter basis (US$50). See Tour Operators in the Ciudad Bolívar section for details.

All visitors coming to Canaima pay the US$7 entrance fee to Parque Nacional Canaima, which is collected upon arrival at the airport (if you haven't paid it when buying your ticket).

LA GRAN SABANA

A rolling grassy highland in Venezuela's far south-eastern corner, La Gran Sabana is vast, wild, beautiful, empty and silent. The only town in the region is Santa Elena de Uairén, near the Brazil frontier. The rest of the sparse population, mostly Pemón Indians, who were the traditional inhabitants of this land, live in scattered villages.

Until recently, La Gran Sabana was virtually inaccessible by land. Only in 1973 was an unsurfaced road between El Dorado and Santa Elena completed, and it was not until 1990 that the last stretch of this road was paved. Today it's one of the best highways in the country, and one of the most spectacular. The road is signposted with km signs from the El Dorado fork (Km 0) southwards to Santa Elena (Km 316) – a great help in orientation.

Undoubtedly the most striking natural feature of La Gran Sabana are the tepuis, gigantic sandstone mesas that dominate the skyline. Tepui (also spelled tepuy) is the Pemón Indian word for 'mountain', and it has been adopted as the term to identify this specific type of mesa. Over 100 such mesas dot the vast region from the Colombian border in the west up into Guyana and Brazil in the east. Their major concentration is in La Gran Sabana. The best known of all tepuis is Roraima, one of the few that can be climbed (see the section below).

There are many other sights in the Sabana, some conveniently close to the main road. Particularly amazing are the waterfalls, and there are a maze of them. One of the best examples easily accessible from the road is **Salto Kamá** (Km 202), 50-metre-high twin waterfalls. Don't miss going down to the foot of the falls for the best view.

Salto Yuruaní (Km 247) is a wonderful mini-Niagara, about seven metres high and 100 metres wide. **Quebrada de Jaspe** (Km 273) is a small cascade made particularly beautiful by the red jasper rock of the creekbed.

The star attraction is probably the 105-metre-high **Salto Aponguao**, also known by its Indian name of Chinak Merú. This one is harder to get to, as it's about 40 km off the highway, near the small Indian hamlet of Iboribó, which is accessible by a rough road.

Places to Stay & Eat

Simple accommodation and meals are available in a number of places throughout La Gran Sabana, including Kavanayén, Chivatón, Iboribó, Rápidos de Kamoirán (Km 172), Salto Kamá (Km 202), Quebrada Pacheco (Km 237) and San Francisco de Yuruaní (Km 250). You can camp virtually anywhere you wish.

Getting Around

Getting around the Sabana is not all that easy, as public transport only operates on the

VENEZUELA

highway and is infrequent. Given time, you can visit the sights on the main road using a combination of hitching and buses. Heading towards Kavanayén, however, may prove difficult, as there are no buses on this road and traffic is sporadic. A comfortable solution is a tour from Santa Elena de Uairén (see that section for details).

Make sure you bring plenty of good insect repellent. The Sabana is infested by a kind of small gnat known as *jején*, commonly called *la plaga*. They are particularly voracious in the morning and late afternoon, and the bites itch for days.

RORAIMA

Roraima, on the tripartite border of Venezuela, Guyana and Brazil, is one of the largest and highest tepuis: its plateau is at some 2700 metres and the highest peak at 2810 metres. It was the first of the tepuis on which a climb was recorded (in 1884) and has been much explored by botanists. It's the easiest mesa to ascend, and is increasingly popular among travellers. Perhaps 200 people trek to the top every month in the dry season. You need a minimum of five days to do this trip.

San Francisco de Yuruaní

The starting point for the trip is the small village of San Francisco de Yuruaní, 69 km north of Santa Elena on the main road.

There are two tour operators, Roraima Tours and Arapena Tours, which offer expensive all-inclusive tours and arrange guides. Guides charge US$25 a day per group. Porters, should you need one, charge US$30 per day and can carry about 17 kg. Some travellers have recommended Kendal Mitchel as a good English-speaking guide, even though he charges a little more. Both guides and porters can also be hired in the village of Paraitepui, your next stop on the way to Roraima.

Accommodation options include the roadside *Hospedaje Minina*, 100 metres north of the bus stop (US$10 a triple), and an unmarked house just next to the stop (US$4 per person). A few basic eateries, including *Restaurant Roraima*, at the central junction,

will keep you going. The restaurant also provides accommodation in hammocks (US$2).

Paraitepui

Paraitepui is about 25 km east of San Francisco. To get there, hire a jeep from the tour operators in San Francisco (US$50, regardless of the number of passengers, up to about eight) or walk. The road to Paraitepui branches off the highway one km south of San Francisco. The unpaved but acceptable road becomes a dusty jeepable track halfway along. It's a hot, steady seven-hour walk, mostly uphill, to Paraitepui (back to San Francisco, it's six hours). You may be lucky enough to hitch a jeep ride on this road, but traffic is sporadic and the drivers will probably charge you for the lift (a more reasonable fare than the jeep rental in San Francisco).

Paraitepui is a nondescript Indian village of about 270 people, whose identity has been largely shattered by tourists and their money. Heaps of empty beer cans will tell you how the money is spent.

Upon arrival, you will invariably be greeted by one of the village headmen, who will show you the list of guides (apparently every adult male in the village is a guide) and inform you about prices. They are much the same as in San Francisco. Although you don't really need a guide to follow the track up to the tepui, the village headmen won't let you pass through without one.

There are no hotels in the village, but you can camp on the square near the school, in one of the two shelters (US$2 per person). Overpriced hot meals are available in the house behind the school. A few shops in the village sell basic food (canned fish, biscuits, packet soups) at exorbitant prices.

Climbing Roraima

Once you have your guide, you can set off for Roraima. The trip to the top takes two days (the total walking time is about 12 hours up and 10 hours down). There are several good places to camp (with water) on the way. The most popular camp sites are on the Río

Tek (four hours from Paraitepui), on the Río Kukenán (30 minutes farther on) and the so-called *campamento base* (base camp) at the foot of Roraima (three hours uphill from the Río Kukenán). The steep and tough four-hour ascent from the base camp to the top is the most spectacular part of the hike.

Once you reach the top, you walk for some 15 minutes to the place known as El Hotel, one of the few sites good for camping. It's actually a patch of sand large enough for about four small tents, partly protected by an overhanging rock. There are several other, smaller 'hotels' in the area.

The scenery all around is a moonscape, evocative of a science-fiction movie: impressive blackened rocks of every imaginable shape, gorges, creeks, pink beaches, and gardens filled with unique flowering plants. Frequent and constantly changing mists and fogs add to the mysterious air.

It's here that the guide finally becomes handy, as it's very easy to get lost in this labyrinth. Your guide will take you to some of the attractions around the plateau, including El Foso, a curious round pool in a deep rocky hole. It's about a three-hour walk from El Hotel. On the way, you'll pass the amazingly lush Valle Arabopo. Beyond the pool is the Valle de los Cristales and the Laberinto, both well worth a trip. Plan on staying at least one full day on the top; it's better to allow two or three days.

When to Go

The dry season is from December to April, but the tops of the tepuis receive rain off the Atlantic all year round. The weather changes in a matter of minutes, with bright sunshine or heavy rain possible at any time.

What to Bring

A good tent, preferably with a fly sheet, is a must. It gets bitterly cold at night on the top, so bring a good sleeping bag and warm clothes. You also need reliable rain gear, sturdy shoes, a cooking stove and the usual hiking equipment. Bring enough food to last you one or two days more than planned: you may not be able to resist the temptation of

staying longer on the top. There's no plaga atop Roraima, but you'll have plenty of these nasty biting gnats on the way, so take an effective insect repellent. Don't forget a good supply of film. A macro lens is a great help in photographing the unique small plants. Make sure to bring along plastic bags, to take *all* your garbage back down to civilisation.

Getting There & Away

San Francisco de Yuruaní is on the Ciudad Guayana-Santa Elena highway, and several buses a day run in either direction. There are also por puestos between Santa Elena and San Francisco. Buy all food at either starting point; don't count on shopping in San Francisco, let alone in Paraitepui.

SANTA ELENA DE UAIREN

Founded in 1922, Santa Elena began to grow when diamonds were discovered in the 1930s in the region of Icabarú, some 100 km to the west. However, isolated from the centre of the country by the lack of roads, it remained a small village. The second development push came with the opening of the highway from El Dorado.

Today, Santa Elena is a pleasant, easygoing border town of 10,000 people, with an agreeable if damp climate and a Brazilian air thanks to the significant number of residents from over the frontier.

Information

Tourist Office Santa Elena has no tourist office. Travel agencies are the place to go for information about the region.

Money Banco del Orinoco is the only bank which may change your money. Banco Guayana is as yet useless. Various establishments, including shops, travel agencies and hotels, may change cash and occasionally travellers' cheques. There are also money-changers.

If you are heading north into Venezuela, keep in mind that the next place you may be able to change money is El Dorado, 320 km away, though it's better to count on the banks in either Ciudad Guayana or Ciudad Bolívar.

Telephone Santa Elena's area code is 088.

Foreign Consulate The Brazilian consulate is at the north-eastern end of town and is open on weekdays from 8 am till noon.

Immigration The DIEX office, behind the large new building of the Prefectura, is open Monday to Saturday from 8 am to noon and 2 to 5 pm, and Sunday from 8 to 9 am. Be sure to have your passport stamped here before leaving, or upon arrival in Venezuela. Brazilian passport formalities are done at the border itself.

Tour Operators There are half a dozen tour agencies in Santa Elena (see the map for locations). Their staple is a two or three-day jeep tour around La Gran Sabana, with visits to the most interesting sights. They can bring you back to Santa Elena, or drop you on the road at the northernmost point of the tour if you plan to continue northwards. Count on roughly US$25 to US$30 per day per person in a group of three or four, and about US$5 less than this in a larger party.

Some operators can take you to Paraitepui, the starting point for the Roraima trek, for around US$80 per jeep for up to six or seven people (plus another US$80 if you want them to pick you up on a prearranged date and take you back). It works out cheaper to go by bus or por puesto to San Francisco, and hire a jeep there (US$50) or walk.

Alfonso Tours (☎ 951171), Calle Urdaneta No 187 (in the Posada Alfonso), is possibly the most popular tour operator among travellers. Apart from the standard Gran Sabana trip, it offers tours to the gold and diamond mines and also some longer and more adventurous trips. Another recommended agency is Adventure Tour's Khazen (☎ 951371), Avenida Perimetral, run by Frank Khazen. It has a range of tours and rents out camping equipment for those using its services.

Places to Stay

There's no shortage of accommodation in Santa Elena, and it's easy to find a room, except perhaps in mid-August, when the town celebrates the feast of its patron saint. The town has a problematical water supply, so check whether your hotel has water tanks. All hotels listed have rooms with fan and private bath.

The favourite travellers' lodge is the *Posada Alfonso*, run by a friendly couple, Alfonso and Gladys. Neat doubles/triples are US$7/10, and you can use their kitchen and fridge. Good coffee is served free all day.

When this book was being researched, Frank (of Adventure Tour's Khazen) was busily finishing work on a posada and camp site, which may become another hang-out among backpackers.

Other budget places (costing much the same as the Alfonso) include the *Hotel Las Tres Naciones* (no sign outside), *Hospedaje Turístico Uairén*, *Hotel Panayma* and *Hotel Luz*. Next door to the latter is the more basic *Hotel Yarima*, but it doubles as a love hotel.

For a little more, you have several options, including *Hotel Panzarelli* and *Hotel Los Castaños*. Some other places in this price bracket have also been included on the map. One of the best in town is the *Hotel Frontera*, which has doubles with TV and fan/air-con for US$18/20.

Places to Eat

The *Parador Turístico Venezuela Primero* has good inexpensive food. The *Pizzería* next door is not bad either, but it only opens in the evening. *La Dorada* is the place for cheap chicken.

Other reasonably priced places serving tasty meals include *Mi Sitio*, *Don Carleone*, *Tasca de Carlitos* and *Tropicalia*.

Panadería Santa Elena opens at 6 am and is a good place for an early breakfast, while *Panadería Trigo Pan* has tables outside to sit over a cup of coffee and watch the unhurried world go by.

Getting There & Away

Air The airport is about five km from town,

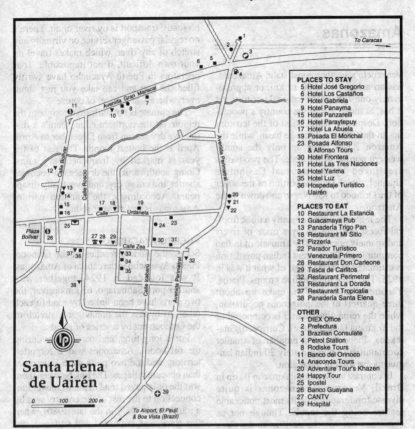

To Caracas

PLACES TO STAY
5 Hotel José Gregorio
6 Hotel Los Castaños
7 Hotel Gabriela
9 Hotel Panayma
15 Hotel Panzarelli
16 Hotel Paraytepuy
17 Hotel La Abuela
19 Posada El Morichal
23 Posada Alfonso
 & Alfonso Tours
30 Hotel Frontera
31 Hotel Las Tres Naciones
34 Hotel Yarima
35 Hotel Luz
36 Hospedaje Turístico
 Uairén

PLACES TO EAT
10 Restaurant La Estancia
12 Guacamaya Pub
13 Panadería Trigo Pan
18 Restaurant Mi Sitio
21 Pizzería
22 Parador Turístico
 Venezuela Primero
28 Restaurant Don Carleone
29 Tasca de Carlitos
32 Restaurant Perimetral
33 Restaurant La Dorada
37 Restaurant Tropicalia
38 Panadería Santa Elena

OTHER
1 DIEX Office
2 Prefectura
3 Brazilian Consulate
4 Petrol Station
8 Rodiske Tours
11 Banco del Orinoco
14 Anaconda Tours
20 Adventure Tour's Khazen
24 Happy Tour
25 Ipostel
26 Banco Guayana
CANTV
39 Hospital

Santa Elena de Uairén

0   100   200 m

To Airport, El Paulí
& Boa Vista (Brazil)

off the road to the frontier. There's no public transport; a taxi will cost around US$3. Servivensa has flights (daily except Tuesday and Saturday) to Puerto Ordaz (US$52), with a stopover in Canaima (US$42). These flights are serviced by DC-3s, which probably remember WWII. It's a good opportunity for picture shooting since the plane flies at only about 1000 metres and close to the tepuis. Anaconda Tours and some other agencies will book and sell tickets.

Bus The new bus terminal is on the Ciudad Guayana highway, about 2.5 km east of town. There are eight buses daily to Ciudad Bolívar (US$13, nine to 11 hours) and one air-con bus directly to Porlamar (US$20, 19 hours). Por puestos to San Francisco de Yuruaní run infrequently, mostly in the morning.

There are four buses a day to Boa Vista, Brazil (US$12, 3½ to four hours). The road is now paved all the way. Remember to get an exit stamp in your passport from DIEX beforehand. The border, locally known as La Línea, is about 15 km south of Santa Elena. The bus calls at the Brazilian border immigration post for passport formalities.

Amazonas

Venezuela's southernmost state, Amazonas, has an area of 175,000 sq km, or approximately one-fifth of the national territory, yet it has, at most, 1% of the country's population. Despite its name, most of the territory lies in the Orinoco drainage basin, while the Amazon Basin takes up only the southwestern portion of the state. The two basins are linked by the unusual Casiquiare channel, which sends a portion of the water of the Orinoco to Río Negro and down to the Amazon.

The region is predominantly a thick tropical forest crisscrossed by a maze of rivers and sparsely populated by a mosaic of Indian communities. The current Indian population is estimated at 40,000, half of what it was in 1925. The three main Indian groups, Piaroa, Yanomami and Guajibo, make up about three-quarters of the indigenous population, while the remaining quarter is composed of the Yekuana (Maquiritare), Curripaco, Guarekena, Piapoco and a number of smaller communities. Approximately 20 Indian languages are used in the region.

In contrast to the central Amazon Basin in Brazil, Venezuelan Amazonas is quite diverse topographically, its most noticeable feature being the tepuis. Though not as numerous nor as 'classical' as in La Gran Sabana, they do give the green carpet a distinctive and spectacular appearance.

The best known of the Amazonas tepuis is Cerro Autana, about 80 km south of Puerto Ayacucho. It is the sacred mountain of the Piaroa Indians, who consider it the birthplace of the universe. The tepui is reminiscent of a gigantic tree trunk which looms about 700 metres above the surrounding plains.

Puerto Ayacucho, at the north-western tip of Amazonas, is the only town of significance, and is the main gateway and supply centre for the entire state. It's also the chief transport hub, from where a couple of small regional airlines fly in light planes to the major settlements of the region. As there are no roads, transport is by river or air. There's no regular passenger service on virtually any stretch of any river, which makes travel on your own difficult, if not impossible. Tour operators in Puerto Ayacucho have swiftly filled the gap and can take you just about everywhere – at a price, of course.

The climate is not uniform throughout the region. At the northern edge, there's a distinctive dry season from December to April. April is the hottest month. The rest of the year is marked by frequent heavy rains. Going southwards, the dry season becomes shorter and not so dry, and eventually disappears. Accordingly, the southern part of Amazonas is wet all year round.

PUERTO AYACUCHO

Set on the middle reaches of the Orinoco, Puerto Ayacucho is the capital of Amazonas. It was founded in 1924, together with another port, Samariapo, 63 km upriver; the two ports have been linked by road to each other, to bypass the unnavigable stretch of the Orinoco cut by a series of rapids.

For a long time, and particularly during the oil boom, Amazonas was a forgotten territory and the two ports were little more than obscure villages. The link between them was the only paved road in the whole region; connection to the rest of the country was by a rough track. Only in the late 1980s, when this track was improved and surfaced, did Puerto Ayacucho start to grow dramatically, to become a town of some 60,000 inhabitants. Paradoxically, the port, which was responsible for the town's birth and initial growth, has lost its importance as most cargo is now trucked by road.

Puerto Ayacucho is the main gateway to Venezuelan Amazonia and is swiftly becoming a tourist centre. There's a range of hotels and restaurants, and travel agents can take you up the Orinoco and its tributaries, deep into the jungle. Puerto Ayacucho is also a transit point on the way to Colombia.

Information

Tourist Office The tourist office is in the

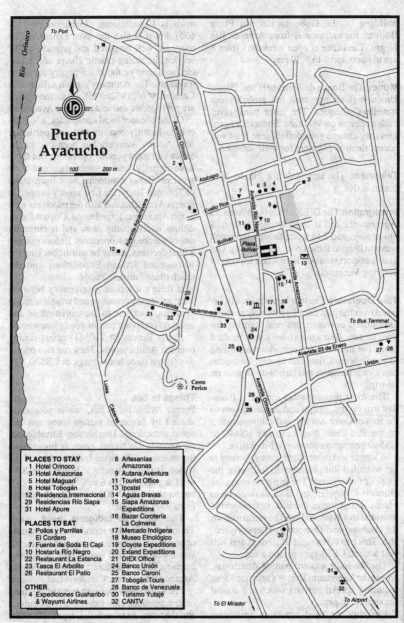

Puerto Ayacucho

0   100   200 m

PLACES TO STAY
1 Hotel Orinoco
3 Hotel Amazonas
5 Hotel Maguarí
8 Hotel Tobogán
12 Residencia Internacional
29 Residencias Río Siapa
31 Hotel Apure

PLACES TO EAT
2 Pollos y Parrillas
   El Cordero
7 Fuente de Soda El Capi
10 Hostaría Río Negro
22 Restaurant La Estancia
23 Tasca El Arbolito
26 Restaurant El Patio

OTHER
4 Expediciones Guaharibo
   & Wayumi Airlines

6 Artesanías
   Amazonas
9 Autana Aventura
11 Tourist Office
13 Ipostel
14 Aguas Bravas
15 Siapa Amazonas
   Expeditions
16 Bazar Corotería
   La Colmena
17 Mercado Indígena
18 Museo Etnológico
19 Coyote Expeditions
20 Exland Expeditions
21 DIEX Office
24 Banco Unión
25 Banco Caroní
27 Tobogán Tours
28 Banco de Venezuela
30 Turismo Yutajé
32 CANTV

Río Orinoco
To Port
Avenida Orinoco
Atabapo
Evelio Roa
Avenida Aguerrevere
Bolívar
Avenida Río Negro
Plaza Bolívar
Avenida Amazonas
Avenida Aguerrevere
Avenida 23 de Enero
Unión
To Bus Terminal
Luisa
Cáceres
Cerro Perico
To El Mirador
To Airport

VENEZUELA

building of the Gobernación, on Plaza Bolívar; the entrance is from Avenida Río Negro. The office is open weekdays from 8 am to noon and 2 to 5.30 pm.

Money The Banco de Venezuela and Banco Unión may change cash but probably not travellers' cheques. The latter bank gives cash advances on Visa card. Some tour agencies may change your dollars or at least will accept them as payment for their services.

Telephone The area code for Puerto Ayacucho is 048.

Immigration The DIEX office is on Avenida Aguerrevere and is open weekdays from 8 am to noon and 2 to 6 pm, though it doesn't seem to keep to these hours very strictly. Get your passport stamped here when leaving or entering Venezuela.

Tour Operators The tour business has flourished over the past decade; probably as many as a dozen operators are now hunting for your money. Tour agents have some standard tours, but most can arrange a tour according to your interests, time and money. Be sure to carry your passport and tarjeta de ingreso on all trips.

The most popular tours include a three-day trip up the Sipapo and Autana rivers to the foot of Cerro Autana, and a three-day trip up the Río Cuao. Expect to pay US$40 to US$60 per person per day, all-inclusive.

A longer and more adventurous journey is the so-called Ruta Humboldt, following the route of the explorer. The trip goes along the Orinoco, Casiquiare and Guainía rivers up to Maroa. From there, the boat is transported overland to Yavita, and you then return down the Atabapo and Orinoco to Puerto Ayacucho. This trip takes eight to 10 days and will cost around US$80 per person a day.

The far south-eastern part of Amazonas, where the Yanomami live, is a restricted area requiring special permits which are almost impossible to get.

Probably the most reputable agency in town is Expediciones Guaharibo (☎ 210-635), but it is also the most expensive. Its tours are well prepared and provide a VIP service, including plastic chairs and table-cloths: it may be too much luxury for some travellers. The company's main office is in Caracas (☎ (02) 9526996), where most tours are put together and sent to Puerto Ayacucho.

Of the cheaper local companies, it's difficult to heartily recommend any particular one. Autana Aventura has been one of the major and most popular operators, but there have recently been complaints about their services. Better comments have been made of Tobogán Tours, the first agency to open in Puerto Ayacucho, and also the relatively new Siapa Amazonas Expeditions. Coyote Expeditions is also pretty new, and is currently one of the cheapest operators. Before making a final decision, it may be worth checking the just-opened Exland Expeditions and the much older Turismo Yutajé.

If there's a serious discrepancy between what an agency promises and what it actually provides, complain to the tourist office and insist on receiving part of your money back.

Aguas Bravas (☎ 210541) offers rafting over the Atures rapids. They run two trips a day (about three hours long), at US$30.

Things to See

Puerto Ayacucho is hot, but is pleasantly shaded by luxuriant mango trees and has some attractions. The **Museo Etnológico**, on Avenida Río Negro, gives an insight into the culture of the main Indian tribes of the region. It's open Tuesday to Friday from 8.30 to 11 am and 2.30 to 6 pm, Saturday from 9 am to noon and 3.30 to 7 pm, and Sunday from 9 am to 1 pm.

The **Mercado Indígena**, held every Thursday to Sunday morning on the square opposite the museum, sells Indian crafts, but you'll probably find some more interesting artefacts in the handicraft shops, Artesanías Amazonas and Bazar Corotería La Colmena.

The **Cerro Perico**, south-west of the town centre, provides views over the Río Orinoco and the town. Another hill, Cerro El Zamuro, commonly known as **El Mirador**, is 1.5 km south of the centre and overlooks the Raudales Atures, the spectacular rapids that block river navigation. They are more impressive in the wet season, when the water is high.

There are some attractions around Puerto Ayacucho. The **Parque Tobogán de la Selva** is a large, steep, smooth rock with water running over it – a sort of natural slide. It's 30 km south of town along the Samariapo road, then six km off to the east. There's no transport directly to the park. You can either take a por puesto to Samariapo, get off at the turn-off and walk the remaining distance, or negotiate a taxi in Puerto Ayacucho. The rock is a favourite weekend place among the townspeople, who, unfortunately, leave it pretty littered. There's a less well known natural waterslide farther upriver.

The **Cerro Pintado** is a large rock with pre-Columbian petroglyphs carved high above the ground in a virtually inaccessible place. It's 17 km south of town and a few km off the main road to the left. The best time to see the carvings is early in the morning or late in the afternoon.

Places to Stay

The most popular choice with backpackers is the *Residencia Internacional* (☎ 210242), at Avenida Aguerrevere 18. It's simple, but clean, safe and friendly, and costs US$6/7/9 a single/matrimonial/double with own bath. For a similar price, you can stay in the more central but less pleasant *Hotel Maguarí* (☎ 213189), Calle Evelio Roa 35.

The *Residencias Río Siapa* (☎ 210138) is a good place with friendly management. Air-con matrimoniales/doubles/triples with bath cost US$10/12/14. There's no sign at the entrance.

The *Hotel Amazonas* (☎ 210155) was perhaps the best hotel in town when built, but its good days have gone. It costs much the same as the Río Siapa. Better options include the *Hotel Orinoco* (☎ 210285), on the north-western fringes of town, and the *Hotel Apure* (☎ 210516), at the southern end. Both have

comfortable air-con doubles for around US$25.

Places to Eat

There's quite a choice of eating outlets in town, but most are closed on Sunday. *Fuente de Soda El Capi*, Calle Evelio Roa, has savoury food, including vegetable salads, at very moderate prices. For tasty chicken and parrillas, try the cheap *Pollos y Parrillas El Cordero*, in the market area on Avenida Orinoco.

La Estancia, Avenida Aguerrevere, has good food and prices. Alternatively, try *Hostaría Río Negro*, Avenida Río Negro. Yet another good choice is *El Patio*, Avenida 23 de Enero, which specialises in Middle Eastern cuisine. *Tasca El Arbolito*, Avenida Aguerrevere, is one of the few places for a beer and music on weekend nights.

Getting There & Away

Air The airport is six km south-east of the town centre; taxis cost US$4. Avensa has two flights daily to San Fernando de Apure (US$38), one of which continues to Caracas (US$56 from Puerto Ayacucho).

A small local carrier, Wayumi, operates flights within Amazonas. It has daily flights (except Sunday) to San Fernando de Atabapo (US$50) and San Juan de Manapiare (US$50), and one flight a week (usually on Friday) to San Carlos de Río Negro (US$80). Other, smaller localities are serviced irregularly on a charter basis.

Bus The bus terminal is six km east of the centre, on the outskirts of town. To get there, take the city bus from Avenida 23 de Enero, or a taxi (US$1). Buses to Ciudad Bolívar depart regularly throughout the day (US$13, 10 hours). There are half a dozen departures a day to San Fernando de Apure (US$9, seven hours), from where you get buses to Caracas, Maracay, Valencia, Barinas and San Cristóbal. There are also direct buses from Puerto Ayacucho to Caracas, Maracay and

VENEZUELA

Valencia, but they go via a longer route through Caicara.

Boat There is no passenger boat service down the Río Orinoco, and cargo boats are infrequent.

To/From Colombia The nearest Colombian town, Puerto Carreño, is at the confluence of the Meta and Orinoco rivers and is accessible from Puerto Ayacucho in two ways. Remember to get an exit stamp in your passport at DIEX before setting off.

The first way leads via Casuarito, a Colombian hamlet right across the Orinoco from Puerto Ayacucho. A boat between Puerto Ayacucho's wharf (at the northeastern end of town) and Casuarito shuttles regularly throughout the day (US$1). From Casuarito, the *voladora* (high-speed boat) departs in the afternoon to Puerto Carreño (US$5, one hour); in the opposite direction, the voladora leaves Puerto Carreño at 6 am. In the dry season (December to April), there

may also be some occasional jeeps from Casuarito to Puerto Carreño.

The other way goes via Puerto Páez, a Venezuelan village about 80 km north of Puerto Ayacucho. Get there by San Fernando bus (US$2.50 two hours); the trip includes a ferry crossing of the Orinoco from El Burro to Puerto Páez. The bus will drop you off in the centre of the village. Go to the wharf and take a boat across the Río Meta to Puerto Carreño (US$1); they run regularly between 6 am and 6 pm.

Puerto Carreño is a long, one-street town with an airport, six or so hotels (*El Vorágine*, near the Venezuelan consulate, is perhaps the best budget bet) and a number of places to eat. Go to the DAS office, one block west of the main square, for an entry stamp. A number of shops will change bolívares to pesos. There are two flights per week to Bogotá (US$90). Buses go only in the dry season, approximately from mid-December to mid-March. They depart once a week for the two-day journey by rough road to Villavicencio (US$55), which is four hours by bus from Bogotá.

Glossary

Unless otherwise indicated, the terms below refer to Spanish-speaking South America in general, but regional variations in meaning are common. The list adopts English, not Spanish, alphabetical order.

abra – in the Andes, a mountain pass

aerosilla – (Arg) chair lift (see also *telesilla*)

aguardente – (Bra) any strong drink, but usually *cachaça*

aguardiente – cane alcohol or similar drink

alameda – street lined with trees, usually poplars

albergue – lodging house; youth hostel

alcaldía – town hall, virtually synonymous with *municipalidad*

alcabala – (Ven) roadside police checkpoint

álcool – (Bra) fuel made from sugar cane; about half of Brazil's cars, including all new ones, run on álcool

aldeia – (Bra) originally a Jesuit mission village; now any small village

alerce – large coniferous tree, once common in parts of the southern Argentine and Chilean Andes; it has declined greatly due to overexploitation for timber

almuerzo – lunch; often an inexpensive fixed-price meal

altiplano – Andean high plain of Peru, Bolivia, Chile and Argentina

andar – the verb 'to walk'; (Bra) denotes floor number in a multistorey building

apartado – post office box

apartamento – apartment or flat; (Bra) hotel room with private bath

api – in Andean countries, a syrupy *chicha* made of maize, lemon, cinnamon and sugar

apunamiento – altitude sickness

arepera – (Ven) snack bar

arrayán – reddish-barked tree of the myrtle family; common in forests of southern Argentina and Chile

arriero – mule driver

artesanía – handicrafts; crafts shop

asado – roasted; (Arg) barbecue, often a family outing in summer

asunceño/a – native or resident of Asunción

audiencia – colonial administrative subdivision, under a president who held civil power in areas where no viceroy was resident

autopista – freeway or motorway

Aymara – indigenous people of highland Bolivia, Peru, Chile and Argentina (also called *Kollas*); also their language

azulejos – ceramic tiles, mostly blue, of Portuguese origin

balneario – bathing resort or beach

bandeirantes – (Bra) colonial slavers and gold prospectors from São Paulo who explored the interior

barraca – (Bra) any stall or hut, including food and drink stands at beach, park etc

barrio – neighbourhood, district or borough; (Ven) shantytown

bencina – petrol

bencina blanca – white gas (Shellite) for camping stoves, usually available only in hardware stores or chemical supply shops

bicho de pé – (Bra) literally, foot bug; burrowing parasite found near beaches and in some rainforest areas

bilheteria – (Bra) ticket office

blocos – (Bra) groups of musicians and dancers who perform in street parades during Brazil's Carnavals

bodega – a winery or a storage area for wine; (Bol) boxcar, sometimes used for train travel by 2nd-class passengers

bofedal – in the Andean altiplano, a swampy alluvial pasture

boleadoras – heavily weighted thongs, once used for hunting guanaco and rhea; also called *bolas*

boletería – ticket office

bomba – among many meanings, a petrol (gasoline) station

burro – donkey, mule

burundanga – (Col) drug obtained from a plant commonly known as *borrachero* or *cacao sabanero*; used to intoxicate unsuspecting tourists in order to rob them

cabaña – cabin

cabildo – colonial town council

cachaça – (Bra) sugar-cane rum, also called *pinga* or *aguardente*, produced by hundreds of small distilleries throughout the country; the national drink

cachaco/a – (Col) resident of Bogotá

cachoeira – (Bra) waterfall

cacique – Indian chieftain; among Araucanian Indians, a *toqui*

callampas – literally, mushrooms; (Chi) shantytowns on the outskirts of Santiago

calle – street

cama matrimonial – double bed

camanchaca – (Chi) dense convective fog on the coastal hills of the Atacama desert; equivalent to Peru's *garúa*

câmara – (Bra) colonial town council

cambista – street moneychanger

camellones – (Ecu) pre-Columbian raised-field earthworks in the Guayas Basin; evidence of large early populations

camino – road, path, way

camión – open-bed truck; a popular form of local transport in the Andean countries

camioneta – pick-up or other small truck; a form of local transport in the Andean countries

campesino/a – rural dweller who practises subsistence agriculture; a peasant

campo – the countryside; a field or paddock

Candomblé – (Bra) Afro-Brazilian religion of Bahia

capoeira – (Bra) martial art/dance performed to rhythms of an instrument called the *berimbau*; developed by Bahian slaves

caraqueño/a – native or resident of Caracas

carioca – native or resident of Rio de Janeiro

Carnaval – all over Latin America, pre-Lenten celebration

casa de cambio – foreign currency exchange house

casa de familia – modest family accommodation, usually in tourist centres in Southern Cone countries

casilla de correos – post office box

casona – large house, usually a mansion; term often applied to colonial architecture in particular

catarata – waterfall

caudillo – in 19th-century South American politics, a provincial strongman whose power rested more on personal loyalty than political ideals or party organisation

ceiba – a common tropical tree; can reach a huge size

cena – dinner; often an inexpensive set menu

cerro – hill; a term used to refer to even very high Andean peaks

ceviche – marinated raw seafood (be cautious about eating ceviche as it can be a source of cholera; see Health in the Facts for the Visitor chapter)

chachacoma – *Senecio graveolens*; a native Andean plant, which yields a tea that helps combat mild symptoms of altitude sickness

chacra – garden; small, independent farm

charango – Andean stringed instrument, traditionally made with an armadillo shell as a soundbox

chicha – in Andean countries, a popular beverage (often alcoholic) made from ingredients like yuca, sweet potato or maize

chifa – Chinese restaurant (term most commonly used in Peru and northern Chile)

Chilote – (Chi) a person from the island of Chiloé

chiva – (Col) a basic rural bus with wooden bench seats; until the 1960s, the main means of transport throughout the country

cholo/a – Quechua or Aymara-speaking person who has migrated to the city but continues to wear peasant dress

chullo – Andean knitted hat, often with ear-flaps

churrascaria – (Bra) restaurant featuring barbecued meat

coa – (Chi) lower-class slang of Santiago

coima – in the Andean countries and the Southern Cone, a bribe

colectivo – depending on the country, either a bus, a minibus or a shared taxi

comedor – basic cafeteria or dining room in a hotel

confitería – (Arg) café which serves coffee, tea, desserts and simple food orders

congregación – in colonial Latin America, the concentration of native populations in central settlements, usually to aid political control or religious instruction; also known as a *reducción*

Cono Sur – Southern Cone; a collective term for Argentina, Chile, Uruguay and parts of Brazil and Paraguay

conuco – in the Andean and Caribbean countries, a small cultivated plot of land

cordillera – mountain range

corregidor – in colonial Spanish America, governor of a provincial city and its surrounding area; the corregidor was usually associated with the *cabildo*

corrida – bullfight

cospel – token used in public telephones; also known as a *ficha*

costanera – in the Southern Cone, a seaside, riverside or lakeside road

criollo/a – a Spaniard born in colonial South America; in modern times, a South American of European descent

curanto – Chilean seafood stew

cuy – guinea pig, a traditional Andean food

DEA – US Drug Enforcement Agency

dendê – (Bra) palm-tree oil, a main ingredient in the cuisine of Bahia

denuncia – affidavit or statement, usually in connection with theft or robbery

desayuno – breakfast

dique – sea wall, jetty or dock; also a reservoir used for recreational purposes

edificio – building

empanada – baked or fried turnover filled with vegetables, egg, olive, meat or cheese

encomienda – colonial labour system under which Indian communities had to provide labour and tribute to a Spanish *encomendero* (land-holder) in exchange for religious and language instruction; usually the system benefited the Spaniards far more than the Indians

esquina – corner (abbreviated to 'esq')

estancia – extensive grazing establishment, either for cattle or sheep, with dominating owner or manager and dependent resident labour force

estanciero – owner of an estancia

farinha – (Bra) manioc flour, the staple food of Indians before colonisation, and of many Brazilians today, especially in the Nordeste and the Amazon

favela – (Bra) slum or shantytown

fazenda – (Bra) large ranch or farm, roughly equivalent to Spanish American *hacienda*; also cloth or fabric

ferrobus – bus on railway wheels

ferroviária – (Bra) railway station

ficha – token used for public telephone, subway etc, in lieu of coins

flota – fleet; often a long-distance bus line

frigorífico – meat-freezing factory

fundo – *hacienda* or farm

gamines – street children of Colombia

gamonal – local ruler or leader; (Per) rural landowner, equivalent to *hacendado*

garúa – (Per) a convective coastal fog

gaseosa – carbonated soft drink

gas-oil – in the Southern Cone, diesel fuel; generally much cheaper than petrol

gasolero – vehicle which uses diesel fuel

gaúcho – (Bra) counterpart of Argentine gaucho; pronounced *gaooshoo*

golpe de estado – coup d'état

gringo/a – throughout Latin America, a foreigner or person with light hair and complexion; not necessarily a derogatory term; (Arg) a person of Italian descent

guanaco – undomesticated relative of the llama; (Chi) a water cannon

guaquero – robber of pre-Columbian tombs

guaraná – Amazonian shrub whose berry is believed to have magical and medicinal powers; also a popular soft drink in Brazil

guardaparque – park ranger

hacendado – owner of a hacienda; usually lived in a city and left day-to-day management of his estate to underlings

hacienda – large rural landholding with a dependent resident labour force under a dominant owner; (Chi) the term *fundo* is more common; (Arg) a much less common form of *latifundio* than the *estancia*

hospedaje – budget accommodation with shared bathroom; usually a large family home with an extra room or two for guests

ichu – bunch grass of the Andean *altiplano*

iglesia – in Brazil, *igreja*; church

Inca – the dominant indigenous civilisation of the Central Andes at the time of the Spanish conquest; refers both to the people and, individually, to their leader

indígena – native American (Indian)

indigenismo – movement in Latin American art and literature which extols aboriginal traditions, often in a romantic or patronising manner

inquilino – tenant or tenant farmer

invierno – literally, winter; the rainy season in the South American tropics

invierno boliviano – (Chi) 'Bolivian winter'; the summer rainy season in the altiplano

IVA – *impuesto de valor agregado*, a value-added tax (VAT)

Kolla – another name for the Aymara

Kollasuyo – 'Land of the Kolla'; early indigenous name for the area now known as Bolivia

ladrón – in Brazil, *ladrão*; a thief

lago – lake

laguna – lagoon; shallow lake

lanchonete – (Bra) stand-up snack bar

latifundio – large landholding, such as an *hacienda* or cattle *estancia*

legía – alkaloid (usually made of potato and quinoa ash) chewed with coca leaves to activate their mild narcotic properties

leito – (Bra) luxury overnight express bus

limeño/a – of Lima; an inhabitant of that city

llanos – plains

llareta – *Laretia compacta*, a dense, compact *altiplano* shrub, used for fuel

loma – mound or hill; a coastal hill in the Atacama Desert

lunfardo – street slang of Buenos Aires

machismo – the exaggerated masculine pride of the Latin American male

manta – a shawl or bedspread

mate – see *yerba mate*

menú del día – inexpensive set meal

mercado – market

mercado negro – black market

mercado paralelo – euphemism for black market

meseta – interior steppe of eastern Patagonia

mestizo/a – a person of mixed Indian and Spanish descent

micro – small bus or minibus

mineiro – (Bra) a miner; person from Minas Gerais state

minifundio – small landholding, such as a peasant farm

minga – reciprocal labour system, common throughout the Andean region and other parts of South America

minuta – (Arg) a short-order snack

mirador – viewpoint or lookout, usually on a hill but often in a building

monte – scrub forest; any densely vegetated area

morro – a hill or headland; (Bra) person or culture of the *favelas*

mulato/a – person of mixed African and European ancestry

municipalidad – city or town hall

museo – in Brazil, *museu*; museum

nafta – (Arg) gasoline or petrol; *nafta blanca* is white gas (Shellite)

ñandú – large, flightless bird, resembling the ostrich

ñapa – a little extra over the specified amount; ask for it in markets etc

nevado – snow-covered peak

novela – novel; especially in Brazil, a TV soap opera

NS – (Bra) Nosso Senhor (Our Father), or Nossa Senhora (Our Lady); often used in the name of a church

oca – edible Andean tuber resembling a potato

oferta – promotional fare, often seasonal, for plane or bus travel

onces – 'elevenses'; morning or afternoon tea

orixás – (Bra) gods of Afro-Brazilian religions

paceño/a – of La Paz; an inhabitant of that city

pampero – South Atlantic cold front which brings dramatic temperature changes to

Uruguay, Paraguay and the interior of northern Argentina

parada or **paradero** – bus stop

páramo – humid, high-altitude grassland of the northern Andean countries

parque nacional – national park

parrillada – barbecued or grilled meat

pasarela – footbridge

paseo – an outing, such as a walk in the park or downtown

pau brasil – brazil-wood tree which produces a red dye that was the colony's first commodity; the tree is now scarce

paulistano – (Bra) native of São Paulo city

peatonal – pedestrian mall

pehuén – *Araucaria auracana*, the monkey-puzzle tree of southern South America

peña – club which hosts informal folk music gatherings; a performance at such a club

peninsulares – in colonial South America, Spaniards born in Europe (as opposed to *criollos*, who were born in the colonies)

pensión – short-term budget accommodation in a family home, which may also house permanent lodgers

pingüinera – penguin colony

piropo – a sexist remark, ranging from relatively innocuous to very offensive

Planalto – enormous plateau that covers much of southern Brazil

pongaje – (Bol) non-feudal system of peonage, abolished in 1952

por puesto – (Ven) shared taxi

porteño/a – (Arg) inhabitant of Buenos Aires; (Chi) a native or resident of Valparaíso

posta – (Chi) first-aid station in a smaller town which lacks a proper hospital

pousada – (Bra) hotel

prato feito, prato do dia – (Bra) literally, made plate or plate of the day; typically an enormous and very cheap meal

precordillera – foothills of the Andes

preservativo – condom

propina – a tip, eg in a restaurant or cinema

pucará – an indigenous Andean fortification

pueblos jóvenes – literally, young towns; (Per) shantytowns surrounding Lima

puna – Andean highlands, usually above 3000 metres

puxar – (Bra) pull, rather than push

quarto – (Bra) hotel room with shared bath

quebracho – 'axe-breaker' tree (*Quebra-chua lorentzii*) of the Chaco, a natural source of tannin

quebrada – ravine, normally dry

Quechua – indigenous language of the Andean highlands, spread by Inca rule and widely spoken today

quena – simple reed flute

quilombo – (Bra) a community of runaway slaves; (Arg) a slang term for a brothel or a mess

quinoa – native Andean grain, the dietary equivalent of rice in the pre-Columbian era

quinto real – the 'royal fifth', a Spanish tax on all precious metals mined in colonial America

quipu – coloured, knotted cord used for record-keeping by the Incas

quiteño/a – of Quito; an inhabitant of that city

rancho – rural house; (Ven) shantytown

recargo – surcharge; added by many businesses to credit-card transactions

reducción – see *congregación*

refugio – a usually rustic shelter in a national park or remote area

residencial – budget accommodation, sometimes only seasonal; in general, *residenciales* are in buildings designed expressly for short-stay lodging

río – in Brazil, *rio*; river

rodeo – annual roundup of cattle on an *estancia* or *hacienda*

rodoferroviária – (Bra) combined bus and train station

rodoviária – (Bra) bus station

ruana – (Col) traditional woollen poncho

ruta – route or highway

salar – salt lake or salt pan, usually in the high Andes or Argentine Patagonia

salteña – meat and vegetable pastie, generally a spicier version of an *empanada*

santiaguino/a – native or resident of Santiago, Chile

selva – natural tropical rainforest

Semana Santa – all over South America, Holy Week, the week before Easter

siesta – lengthy afternoon break for lunch and, occasionally, a nap

s/n – *sin número*; indicating a street address without a number

sobremesa – after-dinner conversation; (Col) carbonated drink served with a meal

soroche – altitude sickness

Southern Cone – see *Cono Sur*

stelling – (Gui) a ferry dock or pier

suco – (Bra) fruit juice; a fruit juice bar

taguá – Wagner's peccary; a species of wild pig thought extinct but recently rediscovered in the Paraguayan Chaco

Tahuantinsuyo – Hispanicised name of the Inca Empire; in Quechua, Tawantinsuyu

tambo – in Andean countries, a wayside market and meeting place; an inn

tapir – large hoofed mammal; a distant relative of the horse

taxista – taxi driver

teleférico – cable-car

telenovela – TV soap opera

telesilla – chair lift (see also *aerosilla*)

tenedor libre – 'all-you-can-eat' restaurant

tepui – (Ven) elevated, sandstone-capped mesa; these are home to unique flora

termas – hot springs

terra firme – (Bra) Amazonian uplands of limited fertility

tinto – red wine; (Col) a small cup of black coffee

todo terreno – mountain bike

toqui – Mapuche Indian chieftain (see also *cacique*)

totora – type of reed, used as a building material

tranca – (Bol) police post

tugurios – (Col) shantytowns

Tupi – (Bra) major coastal people at the time of European contact; also their language

turismo aventura – 'adventure tourism' activities such as trekking and river rafting

tuteo – use of the pronoun *tú* (you, singular)

and its corresponding verb forms (see also *voseo*)

Umbanda – (Bra) Rio's version of the principal Afro-Brazilian religion

vaquero – in Brazil, *vaqueiro*; cowboy

várzea – (Bra) Amazonian floodplain

verano – literally, summer; also the dry season in the South American tropics

vicuña – wild relative of the domestic llama and alpaca, found only at high altitudes in the south-central Andes

villas miserias – (Arg) shantytowns on the outskirts of Buenos Aires and other cities

vinchuca – reduviid bug; a biting insect found in thatched dwellings with dirt floors, which transmits Chagas' disease

viviendas temporarias – literally, temporary dwellings; (Par) riverfront shantytowns of Asunción

vizcacha – also written as *viscacha*; wild relative of the domestic chinchilla

voladora – (Col, Ven) river speedboat

voseo – use of the pronoun *vos* (you, singular) and its corresponding verb forms in preference to *tú*; standard usage in Argentina, Uruguay and Paraguay (see also *tuteo*)

yacaré – South American alligator, found in tropical and subtropical river systems

yapa – variant spelling of *ñapa*

yareta – variant spelling of *llareta*

yatire – Andean healer or witch doctor

yerba mate – 'Paraguayan tea' *(Ilex paraguariensis)*; *mate* is consumed regularly in Argentina, Paraguay, Uruguay and Brazil

yuca – manioc tuber; in Portuguese, *mandioca* is the most common term

zambo/a – a person of mixed African and Amerindian ancestry

zampoña – pan flute featured in traditional Andean music

zona franca – duty-free zone

zonda – (Arg) in the central Andes, a powerful, dry north wind

Index

ABBREVIATIONS

MAPS

TEXT

Map references are in **bold** type.

LONELY PLANET PHRASEBOOKS

Nepali phrasebook

Ethiopian Amharic phrasebook

Latin American Spanish phrasebook

Ukrainian phrasebook

Greek phrasebook

Vietnamese phrasebook

Building bridges,
Breaking barriers,
Beyond babble-on

Listen for the gems

Speak your own words

Ask your own questions

Master of your own image

- handy pocket-sized books
- easy to understand Pronunciation chapter
- clear and comprehensive Grammar chapter
- romanisation alongside script to allow ease of pronunciation
- script throughout so users can point to phrases
- extensive vocabulary sections, words and phrases for every situation
- full of cultural information and tips for the traveller

'...vital for a real DIY spirit and attitude in language learning' – Backpacker

'the phrasebooks have good cultural backgrounders and offer solid advice for challenging situations in remote locations' – San Francisco Examiner

'...they are unbeatable for their coverage of the world's more obscure languages' – The Geographical Magazine

---

Arabic (Egyptian)
Arabic (Moroccan)
Australia
  Australian English, Aboriginal and Torres Strait languages
Baltic States
  Estonian, Latvian, Lithuanian
Bengali
Brazilian
Burmese
Cantonese
Central Asia
Central Europe
  Czech, French, German, Hungarian, Italian and Slovak
Eastern Europe
  Bulgarian, Czech, Hungarian, Polish, Romanian and Slovak
Ethiopian (Amharic)
Fijian
French
German
Greek

Hindi/Urdu
Indonesian
Italian
Japanese
Korean
Lao
Latin American Spanish
Malay
Mandarin
Mediterranean Europe
  Albanian, Croatian, Greek, Italian, Macedonian, Maltese, Serbian and Slovene
Mongolian
Nepali
Papua New Guinea
Pilipino (Tagalog)
Quechua
Russian
Scandinavian Europe
  Danish, Finnish, Icelandic, Norwegian and Swedish

South-East Asia
  Burmese, Indonesian, Khmer, Lao, Malay, Tagalog (Pilipino), Thai and Vietnamese
Spanish (Castilian)
  Basque, Catalan and Galician
Sri Lanka
Swahili
Thai
Thai Hill Tribes
Tibetan
Turkish
Ukrainian
USA
  US English, Vernacular, Native American languages and Hawaiian
Vietnamese
Western Europe
  Basque, Catalan, Dutch, French, German, Irish, Italian, Portuguese, Scottish Gaelic, Spanish (Castilian) and Welsh

LONELY PLANET JOURNEYS

JOURNEYS is a unique collection of travel writing – published by the company that understands travel better than anyone else. It is a series for anyone who has ever experienced – or dreamed of – the magical moment when they encountered a strange culture or saw a place for the first time. They are tales to read while you're planning a trip, while you're on the road or while you're in an armchair, in front of a fire.

JOURNEYS books catch the spirit of a place, illuminate a culture, recount a crazy adventure, or introduce a fascinating way of life. They always entertain, and always enrich the experience of travel.

'Idiosyncratic, entertainingly diverse and unexpected . . . from an international writership'
– The Australian

'Books which offer a closer look at the people and culture of a destination, and enrich travel experiences'
– American Bookseller

FULL CIRCLE
A South American Journey
Luis Sepúlveda
Translated by Chris Andrews

Full Circle invites us to accompany Chilean writer Luis Sepúlveda on 'a journey without a fixed itinerary'. Whatever his subject – brutalities suffered under Pinochet's dictatorship, sleepy tropical towns visited in exile, or the landscapes of legendary Patagonia – Sepúlveda is an unflinchingly honest yet lyrical storyteller. Extravagant characters and extraordinary situations are memorably evoked: gauchos organising a tournament of lies, a scheming heiress on the lookout for a husband, a pilot with a corpse on board his plane . . . Part autobiography, part travel memoir, *Full Circle* brings us the distinctive voice of one of South America's most compelling writers.

Luis Sepúlveda was born in Chile in 1949. Imprisoned by the Pinochet dictatorship for his socialist beliefs, he was for many years a political exile. He has written novels, short stories, plays and essays. His work has attracted many awards and has been translated into numerous languages.

'Detachment, humour and vibrant prose' – El País

'an absolute cracker' – The Bookseller

This project has been assisted by the Commonwealth Government through the Australia Council, its arts funding and advisory body.

LONELY PLANET TRAVEL ATLASES

Lonely Planet has long been famous for the number and quality of its guidebook maps. Now we've gone one step further and produced a handy companion series: Lonely Planet travel atlases – maps of a country produced in book form.

Unlike other maps, which look good but lead travellers astray, our travel atlases have been researched on the road by Lonely Planet's experienced team of writers. All details are carefully checked to ensure the atlas corresponds with the equivalent Lonely Planet guidebook.

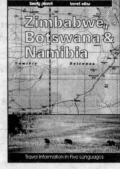

The handy atlas format means no holes, wrinkles, torn sections or constant folding and unfolding. These atlases can survive long periods on the road, unlike cumbersome fold-out maps. The comprehensive index ensures easy reference.

- full-colour throughout
- maps researched and checked by Lonely Planet authors
- place names correspond with Lonely Planet guidebooks
  – no confusing spelling differences
- legend and travelling information in English, French, German, Japanese and Spanish
- size: 230 x 160 mm

Available now:
Chile & Easter Island • Egypt • India & Bangladesh • Israel & the Palestinian Territories •Jordan, Syria & Lebanon • Kenya • Laos • Portugal • South Africa, Lesotho & Swaziland • Thailand • Turkey • Vietnam • Zimbabwe, Botswana & Namibia

---

LONELY PLANET TV SERIES & VIDEOS

Lonely Planet travel guides have been brought to life on television screens around the world. Like our guides, the programmes are based on the joy of independent travel, and look honestly at some of the most exciting, picturesque and frustrating places in the world. Each show is presented by one of three travellers from Australia, England or the USA and combines an innovative mixture of video, Super-8 film, atmospheric soundscapes and original music.

Videos of each episode – containing additional footage not shown on television – are available from good book and video shops, but the availability of individual videos varies with regional screening schedules.

Video destinations include: Alaska • American Rockies • Australia – The South-East • Baja California & the Copper Canyon • Brazil • Central Asia • Chile & Easter Island • Corsica, Sicily & Sardinia – The Mediterranean Islands • East Africa (Tanzania & Zanzibar) • Ecuador & the Galapagos Islands • Greenland & Iceland • Indonesia • Israel & the Sinai Desert • Jamaica • Japan • La Ruta Maya • Morocco • New York • North India • Pacific Islands (Fiji, Solomon Islands & Vanuatu) • South India • South West China • Turkey • Vietnam • West Africa • Zimbabwe, Botswana & Namibia

The Lonely Planet TV series is produced by:
Pilot Productions
The Old Studio
18 Middle Row
London W10 5AT UK

For video availability and ordering information contact your nearest Lonely Planet office.

Music from the TV series is available on CD & cassette.

PLANET TALK

Lonely Planet's FREE quarterly newsletter

We love hearing from you and think you'd like to hear from us.

*When...*is the right time to see reindeer in Finland?
*Where...*can you hear the best palm-wine music in Ghana?
*How...*do you get from Asunción to Areguá by steam train?
*What...*is the best way to see India?

For the answer to these and many other questions read PLANET TALK.

Every issue is packed with up-to-date travel news and advice including:

- a letter from Lonely Planet co-founders Tony and Maureen Wheeler
- go behind the scenes on the road with a Lonely Planet author
- feature article on an important and topical travel issue
- a selection of recent letters from travellers
- details on forthcoming Lonely Planet promotions
- complete list of Lonely Planet products

To join our mailing list contact any Lonely Planet office.

Also available: Lonely Planet T-shirts. 100% heavyweight cotton.

LONELY PLANET ONLINE

Get the latest travel information before you leave or while you're on the road

Whether you've just begun planning your next trip, or you're chasing down specific info on currency regulations or visa requirements, check out Lonely Planet Online for up-to-the minute travel information.

As well as travel profiles of your favourite destinations (including maps and photos), you'll find current reports from our researchers and other travellers, updates on health and visas, travel advisories, and discussion of the ecological and political issues you need to be aware of as you travel.

There's also an online travellers' forum where you can share your experience of life on the road, meet travel companions and ask other travellers for their recommendations and advice. We also have plenty of links to other online sites useful to independent travellers.

And of course we have a complete and up-to-date list of all Lonely Planet travel products including guides, phrasebooks, atlases, Journeys and videos and a simple online ordering facility if you can't find the book you want elsewhere.

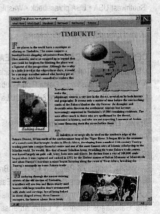

www.lonelyplanet.com
or
AOL keyword: lp

LONELY PLANET PRODUCTS

Lonely Planet is known worldwide for publishing practical, reliable and no-nonsense travel information in our guides and on our web site. The Lonely Planet list covers just about every accessible part of the world. Currently there are nine series: *travel guides, shoestring guides, walking guides, city guides, phrasebooks, audio packs, travel atlases, Journeys – a unique collection of travel writing and Pisces Books - diving and snorkeling guides.*

EUROPE

Amsterdam • Andalucia • Austria • Baltic States phrasebook • Berlin • Britain • Canary Islands • Central Europe on a shoestring • Central Europe phrasebook • Czech & Slovak Republics • Denmark • Dublin • Eastern Europe on a shoestring • Eastern Europe phrasebook • Estonia, Latvia & Lithuania • Europe • Finland • France • French phrasebook • Germany • German phrasebook • Greece • Greek phrasebook • Hungary • Iceland, Greenland & the Faroe Islands • Ireland • Italian phrasebook • Italy • Lisbon • London • Mediterranean Europe on a shoestring • Mediterranean Europe phrasebook • Paris • Poland • Portugal • Portugal travel atlas • Prague • Romania & Moldova • Russia, Ukraine & Belarus • Russian phrasebook • Scandinavian & Baltic Europe on a shoestring • Scandinavian Europe phrasebook • Slovenia • Spain • Spanish phrasebook • St Petersburg • Switzerland • Trekking in Spain • Ukrainian phrasebook • Vienna • Walking in Britain • Walking in Italy • Walking in Switzerland • Western Europe on a shoestring • Western Europe phrasebook
Travel Literature: The Olive Grove: Travels in Greece

NORTH AMERICA

Alaska • Backpacking in Alaska • Baja California • California & Nevada • Canada • Chicago • Deep South • Florida • Hawaii • Honolulu • Los Angeles • Mexico • Mexico City • Miami • New England • New Orleans • New York City • New York, New Jersey & Pennsylvania • Pacific Northwest USA • Rocky Mountain States • San Francisco • Seattle • Southwest USA • USA phrasebook • Washington, DC & the Capital Region
Travel Literature: Drive thru America

CENTRAL AMERICA & THE CARIBBEAN

• Bahamas and Turks & Caicos • Bermuda • Central America on a shoestring • Costa Rica • Cuba • Eastern Caribbean • Guatemala, Belize & Yucatán: La Ruta Maya • Jamaica • Panama
Travel Literature Green Dreams: Travels in Central America

SOUTH AMERICA

Argentina, Uruguay & Paraguay • Bolivia • Brazil • Brazilian phrasebook • Buenos Aires • Chile & Easter Island • Chile & Easter Island travel atlas • Colombia Ecuador & the Galápagos Islands • Latin American Spanish phrasebook • Peru • Quechua phrasebook • Rio de Janeiro • South America on a shoestring • Trekking in the Patagonian Andes • Venezuela
Travel Literature: Full Circle: A South American Journey

ISLANDS OF THE INDIAN OCEAN

Madagascar & Comoros • Maldives • Mauritius, Réunion & Seychelles

AFRICA

Africa - the South • Africa on a shoestring • Arabic (Moroccan) phrasebook • Cairo • Cape Town • Central Africa • East Africa • Egypt • Egypt travel atlas • Ethiopian (Amharic) phrasebook • The Gambia & Senegal • Kenya • Kenya travel atlas • Malawi, Mozambique & Zambia • Morocco • North Africa • South Africa, Lesotho & Swaziland • South Africa, Lesotho & Swaziland travel atlas • Swahili phrasebook • Tunisia • Trekking in East Africa • West Africa • Zimbabwe, Botswana & Namibia • Zimbabwe, Botswana & Namibia travel atlas
Travel Literature: Mali Blues • The Rainbird: A Central African Journey • Songs to an African Sunset: A Zimbabwean Story

MAIL ORDER

Lonely Planet products are distributed worldwide. They are also available by mail order from Lonely Planet, so if you have difficulty finding a title please write to us. North American and South American residents should write to 150 Linden St, Oakland CA 94607, USA; European and African residents should write to 10a Spring Place, London NW5 3BH; and residents of other countries to PO Box 617, Hawthorn, Victoria 3122, Australia.

NORTH-EAST ASIA

Beijing • Bhutan • Cantonese phrasebook • China • Hong Kong • Hong Kong, Macau & Guangzhou • Japan • Japanese phrasebook • Japanese audio pack • Korea • Korean phrasebook • Kyoto • Mandarin phrasebook • Mongolia • Mongolian phrasebook • North-East Asia on a shoestring • Seoul • South-West China • Taiwan • Tibet • Tibet phrasebook • Tokyo

Travel Literature: Lost Japan

MIDDLE EAST & CENTRAL ASIA

Arab Gulf States • Arabic (Egyptian) phrasebook • Central Asia • Central Asia phrasebook • Iran • Israel & the Palestinian Territories • Israel & the Palestinian Territories travel atlas • Istanbul • Jerusalem • Jordan & Syria • Jordan, Syria & Lebanon travel atlas • Lebanon • Middle East • Turkey • Turkish phrasebook • Turkey travel atlas • Yemen

Travel Literature: The Gates of Damascus • Kingdom of the Film Stars: Journey into Jordan

ALSO AVAILABLE:

Brief Encounters • Travel with Children • Traveller's Tales • Not the Only Planet

INDIAN SUBCONTINENT

Bangladesh • Bengali phrasebook • Bhutan • Delhi • Goa • Hindi/Urdu phrasebook • India • India & Bangladesh travel atlas • Indian Himalaya • Karakoram Highway • Nepal • Nepali phrasebook • Pakistan • Rajasthan • South India • Sri Lanka • Sri Lanka phrasebook • Trekking in the Indian Himalaya • Trekking in the Karakoram & Hindukush • Trekking in the Nepal Himalaya

Travel Literature: In Rajasthan • Shopping for Buddhas

SOUTH-EAST ASIA

Bali & Lombok • Bangkok • Burmese phrasebook • Cambodia • Ho Chi Minh City • Indonesia • Indonesian phrasebook • Indonesian audio pack • Indonesia's Eastern Islands • Jakarta • Java • Laos • Lao phrasebook • Laos travel atlas • Malay phrasebook • Malaysia, Singapore & Brunei • Myanmar (Burma) • Philippines • Pilipino phrasebook • Singapore • South-East Asia on a shoestring • South-East Asia phrasebook • South-West China • Thailand • Thailand's Islands & Beaches • Thailand travel atlas • Thai phrasebook • Thai audio pack • Thai Hill Tribes phrasebook • Vietnam • Vietnamese phrasebook • Vietnam travel atlas

AUSTRALIA & THE PACIFIC

Australia • Australian phrasebook • Bushwalking in Australia • Bushwalking in Papua New Guinea • Fiji • Fijian phrasebook • Islands of Australia's Great Barrier Reef • Melbourne • Micronesia • New Caledonia • New South Wales • New Zealand • Northern Territory • Outback Australia • Papua New Guinea • Papua New Guinea phrasebook • Queensland • Rarotonga & the Cook Islands • Samoa • Solomon Islands • South Australia • Sydney • Tahiti & French Polynesia • Tasmania • Tonga • Tramping in New Zealand • Vanuatu • Victoria • Western Australia

Travel Literature: Islands in the Clouds • Sean & David's Long Drive

ANTARCTICA

Antarctica

THE LONELY PLANET STORY

Lonely Planet published its first book in 1973 in response to the numerous 'How did you do it?' questions Maureen and Tony Wheeler were asked after driving, busing, hitching, sailing and railing their way from England to Australia.

Written at a kitchen table and hand collated, trimmed and stapled, *Across Asia on the Cheap* became an instant local bestseller, inspiring thoughts of another book.

Eighteen months in South-East Asia resulted in their second guide, *South-East Asia on a shoestring*, which they put together in a backstreet Chinese hotel in Singapore in 1975. The 'yellow bible', as it quickly became known to backpackers around the world, soon became *the* guide to the region. It has sold well over half a million copies and is now in its 9th edition, still retaining its familiar yellow cover.

Today there are over 350 titles, including travel guides, walking guides, language kits & phrasebooks, travel atlases and travel literature. The company is the largest independent travel publisher in the world. Although Lonely Planet initially specialised in guides to Asia, today there are few corners of the globe that have not been covered.

The emphasis continues to be on travel for independent travellers. Tony and Maureen still travel for several months of each year and play an active part in the writing, updating and quality control of Lonely Planet's guides.

They have been joined by over 80 authors and 200 staff at our offices in Melbourne (Australia), Oakland (USA), London (UK) and Paris (France). Travellers themselves also make a valuable contribution to the guides through the feedback we receive in thousands of letters each year and on our web site.

The people at Lonely Planet strongly believe that travellers can make a positive contribution to the countries they visit, both through their appreciation of the countries' culture, wildlife and natural features, and through the money they spend. In addition, the company makes a direct contribution to the countries and regions it covers. Since 1986 a percentage of the income from each book has been donated to ventures such as famine relief in Africa; aid projects in India; agricultural projects in Central America; Greenpeace's efforts to halt French nuclear testing in the Pacific; and Amnesty International.

'I hope we send people out with the right attitude about travel. You realise when you travel that there are so many different perspectives about the world, so we hope these books will make people more interested in what they see. Guidebooks can't really guide people. All you can do is point them in the right direction.'

– Tony Wheeler

LONELY PLANET PUBLICATIONS

Australia
PO Box 617, Hawthorn 3122, Victoria
tel: (03) 9819 1877 fax: (03) 9819 6459
e-mail: talk2us@lonelyplanet.com.au

USA
150 Linden St
Oakland, CA 94607
tel: (510) 893 8555 TOLL FREE: 800 275-8555
fax: (510) 893 8572
e-mail: info@lonelyplanet.com

UK
10a Spring Place,
London NW5 3BH
tel: (0171) 428 4800 fax: (0171) 428 4828
e-mail: go@lonelyplanet.co.uk

France:
1 rue du Dahomey, 75011 Paris
tel: 01 55 25 33 00 fax: 01 55 25 33 01
e-mail: bip@lonelyplanet.fr

World Wide Web: http://www.lonelyplanet.com
or *AOL keyword: lp*